P9-BYD-579

Finance &
Investment
Handbook

Fourth Edition

Finance & Investment Handbook

Fourth Edition

John Downes
Editor, *Beating the Dow*
Former Vice President; AVCO Financial Services, Inc.
Office for Economic Development, City of New York

Jordan Elliot Goodman
Wall Street Correspondent
Money Magazine, Time-Warner Incorporated
Commentator
NBC News, Mutual Broadcasting System
Co-Author, *Everyone's Money Book*

© Copyright 1995, 1990, 1987, 1986 by Barron's Educational Series, Inc.

All rights reserved.

No part of this book may be reproduced in any form, by
photostat, microfilm, xerography, or any other means,
or incorporated into any information retrieval system,
electronic or mechanical, without the written permission
of the copyright owner.

All inquiries should be addressed to:
Barron's Educational Series, Inc.
250 Wireless Boulevard
Hauppauge, New York 11788

Library of Congress Catalog Card No.: 95-10864

International Standard Book No.: 0-8120-6465-8

Library of Congress Cataloging-in-Publication Data
Downes, John, 1936–
    Barron's finance & investment handbook / John Downes, Jordan Elliot
Goodman. — 4th ed.
        p.   cm.
    Includes index.
    ISBN 0-8120-6465-8
    1. Finance—Handbooks, manuals, etc.   2. Investments—Handbooks,
manuals, etc.   3. Finance—Dictionaries.   4. Investments—Dictionaries.
I. Goodman, Jordan Elliot.   II. Title.   III. Title: Finance & investment
handbook.
HG173.D66   1995
332.6'78—dc20   95-10864
                                                                 CIP

PRINTED IN THE UNITED STATES OF AMERICA

678   8800   9876543

CONTENTS

PART II   HOW TO READ AN ANNUAL REPORT

PART III   HOW TO READ THE FINANCIAL PAGES

PART IV   DICTIONARY OF FINANCE AND INVESTMENT

PART V   FINANCE AND INVESTMENT READY REFERENCE

APPENDIX

ACKNOWLEDGMENTS

A project as massive as this *Handbook* is clearly the work of more than two people, and to thank all adequately would add considerably to its bulk. There are several individuals and organizations, however, without whose help the project in its present form would not have been feasible at all.

Following is the list of individuals, companies, and organizations whose help in preparation of this book was invaluable.

American Association of Individual Investors
American Bankers Association
American Council of Life Insurance
American Express Co.
American Institute of Certified Public Accountants
American Resort Development Association
American Society of CLU & ChFC (Chartered Life Underwriters)
American Stock Exchange
Associated Credit Bureaus
Bankers Trust Company
The Bond Buyer
Boston Stock Exchange
Bureau of the Public Debt
Chase Manhattan Bank NA
Chicago Board Options Exchange
Coffee, Sugar, & Cocoa Exchange
Commodity Futures Trading Commission
DD&W Ltd.
Dow Jones Information Services
Employee Benefit Research Institute
European Union Delegation of the European Commission
Fannie Mae
Federal Energy Regulatory Commission
Federal Reserve Bank of New York
Federal Trade Commission
FINEX
Frank Russell Company
Futures Industry Association
Goldman, Sachs & Co.
Health Insurance Institute of America
Hulbert Financial Digest
IBC/Donoghue Inc.
I/B/E/S Inc.
Institute of Certified Financial Planners

Insurance Information Institute
Intermarket Management Inc.
Internal Revenue Service
International Petroleum Exchange
International Swaps and Derivatives Association
Investment Company Institute
Investment Management Consultants Association
Investment Program Association
J. P. Morgan
Richard J. Kittrell, Esq./Kittrell & Kittrell P.C.
Liquidity Financial Corp.
London International Financial Futures and Options Exchange
Mercer and Company
Merrill Lynch
Montreal Exchange
Morgan Stanley
Morningstar
Mortgage Bankers Association
Municipal Bond Investors Assurance Corp.
National Association of Investors Corp.
National Association of Real Estate Investment Trusts
National Association of Realtors
National Association of Variable Annuities
National Credit Union Administration
National Foundation for Consumer Credit
New York Cotton Exchange
New York Mercantile Exchange
New York Life Insurance Co.
New York Stock Exchange
Office of Thrift Supervision
Options Clearing Corp.
Options Institute
Pension Benefit Guaranty Corp.
Prudential Securities
Public Securities Association
Salomon Brothers, Inc.
Securities and Exchange Commission
Securities Industry Association
Standard & Poor's
Toronto Stock Exchange
Trimedia, Inc.
U.S. Department of Commerce
U.S. Department of Labor
Value Line
Vancouver Stock Exchange
Visa International
The Weiser Walek Group
Wheat First Butcher Singer Inc.
Wilshire Associates
Winnipeg Commodity Exchange
World Gold Council
Wrap Industry Association
Zacks Investment Research

Other people made contributions for which the word acknowledgement doesn't do. Thomas F. Hirsch, Barron's editor for the first two editions, was a full partner in the original project and we value his professional guidance and ongoing friendship. Mary Falcon of Barron's handled an unbelievable amount of editorial work with skill and patience and guided this Fourth Edition to print. Roberta Yafie's contributions in fact-checking and research were immeasurable and went well beyond the call of duty. Austin Lynas and Janet Lowe spent more than a year tirelessly and meticulously updating and cataloguing the ready-reference sections. We are immensely grateful to them all.

Suzanne and Jason Goodman, Katie and Annie Downes, and Nancy Weinberg all sacrificed at various stages of the project and are in our debt.

John Downes
Jordan Elliot Goodman

PREFACE TO THE FOURTH EDITION

People retiring in the early years of the 21st century, the so-called baby boom generation, face a finance and investment environment that went through a revolution during
their working years. Deregulation and the mass marketing of investments starting in the
1970s, the merger-mania, scandals and general excesses of the "Roaring 1980s," and
the downsizing and return to frugality marking the 1990s, all occurred as the mega-
trends of computerization and globalization gained momentum.

Deregulation in the banking, securities, and savings and loan industries trans-
formed the financial marketplace and made a vast range of innovative financial and
investment products and services available to people at all economic levels. It also led
to the most expensive financial rescue and restructuring project in history, in which
the government was forced to bail out the depositors in hundreds of savings and loan
associations that failed because their managers abused the freedom from regulation.

Amid merger-mania, many of America's best-known corporations figured in
hostile takeovers or leveraged buyouts financed by junk bonds—or resorted to
defensive tactics known by such colorful names as the "poison pill," the "Pac-Man
strategy," or the "white knight." Insider-trading scandals were one result, but another
was the creation of imaginative investment techniques designed to capitalize on the
profit opportunities created by corporate takeovers.

Accelerated by the fall of the Iron Curtain, the world economy, now more free
of trade and economic barriers, has become ever more interdependent. This has
given birth to a wide range of new investment instruments, including foreign stock
index options, denominated in both dollars and foreign currencies created by governments and firms competing for debt and equity capital in worldwide markets.

The computer and advanced communications systems have created both greater
simplicity and greater complexity in the universe of finance and investment. By linking
markets and processing massive information, these systems have given rise to investment vehicles, transactions, and methods of managing risk not previously imaginable.
In some cases, sophisticated "derivatives" were misused by corporations, municipalities and large banks, causing substantial losses and leading to new regulation.

The children of the baby boomers must now do their financial planning in an economy, although no longer dominated by fears of communism and runaway inflation,
offering less assurance of their future financial security. The restructurings and down-
sizings of the 1990s made corporations more efficient but took their human toll just as
the demographics that earlier created surpluses in the Social Security system became
less favorable for recipients of the future. The enormous growth of 401K and individual retirement plan accounts addresses this problem but also points up its seriousness.

This thoroughly revised *Finance and Investment Handbook, Fourth Edition*, begins
with a discussion of 30 key investment alternatives—with their many variations—as
they have emerged from this period of historic change. Some are new, others are
modernized versions of traditional investment vehicles. Each is presented with an
introductory overview followed by questions and answers offering concise information
on such crucial matters as costs; minimum purchase amounts; risks; liquidity; tax

implications; and suitability for tax-deferred retirement plans. The section's purpose is not to offer specific recommendations, but rather to set forth in an easy-to-read format the vital features distinguishing the various investments so you will be able to make better-informed investment decisions.

Corporate annual reports and other communications of publicly held corporations, as an ironic result of stricter disclosure requirements, have become increasingly elaborate and difficult to understand, leaving many investors more befuddled than enlightened. The second section of the *Handbook* explains what corporate reports contain, what to focus on, and how to analyze and interpret the data provided.

You must know how to read and understand financial information in newspapers in order to make intelligent investment choices and then to follow their progress. Not surprisingly, the proliferation of investment products and the broadening of public participation in the securities markets has fattened the financial sections of daily newspapers with information aimed at individual and institutional investors. Also, with the growth of cable television, many investors are getting their financial news from channels displaying a running ticker tape throughout the business day. The third part of the *Handbook* explains how to read the financial pages and the ticker tape.

Essential to decision-making in any field is understanding the language in which information is communicated. In a technical, dynamic field like finance and investment, keeping up with changing terminology would be a challenge in any event, but developments of the last decade have added a whole new lexicon of finance and investment terms and largely redefined the traditional vocabulary. The argot of the field has been spiced by a wave of new Wall Street buzzwords, like "chastity bonds," "goodbye kiss," and "Lady Macbeth strategy." These and approximately 5000 other key terms are defined clearly and comprehensively, with examples and illustrations, in the *Handbook's* fourth major section, the Dictionary of Finance and Investment.

The fifth section of the *Handbook* presents wide-ranging reference material. The information, arranged in an easily accessible manner, is designed to be *used* by investors—beginners and professionals alike—to locate specific data as well as to gain a broader understanding of finance and investment.

The finance and investment marketplace has not only grown in size but has changed character as a result of diversification, mergers, and the introduction of new firms that exist either to market new investment products or to provide information on them. The regulatory establishment, which consists of federal and state government agencies as well as self-regulatory organizations, and relevant trade association and consumer protection groups have expanded and adapted to an industry and has become more consumer-oriented. The most important of these government and nongovernment organizations—including those of Canada—are listed in the opening portions of the *Handbook's* reference listings.

The growing importance of the individual consumer in the investment community has been a catalyst for the burgeoning financial information industry. The *Handbook* lists the major finance and investment publications from national magazines to specialized newsletters, providing addresses and telephone numbers so they can be contacted easily. The industry also has an important electronic dimension in the form of computer databases and software, and the major sources of these products are presented.

"You can't tell the players without a scorecard" goes an old baseball adage, which certainly applies to today's major leagues of financial services. Despite diversification, financial institutions continue to be discussed mainly in terms of their principal and traditional activities—that is, as commercial banks, thrifts, brokerage firms, and life insurance companies. The *Handbook* lists the 100 largest in each of these categories. Also listed are the Federal Reserve and Federal Home Loan banks and branches, the primary government securities dealers, major limited partnership sponsors, the 25 largest accounting firms, and the world's major security and commodity exchanges.

Highly useful information, including name, address, phone number, and investment objective of both open-end and closed-end mutual funds and fund families is provided for those who would rather leave portfolio decisions to a professional manager.

Increasingly, U.S. and Canadian exchanges, in response to growing investor interest, are listing options and futures on financial instruments, stock indexes, and foreign currencies, as well as traditional stock options and futures on agricultural and other commodities. The *Handbook* provides a complete and detailed summary of contracts of all types on all U.S. and Canadian exchanges.

No handbook would be complete if it didn't supply the historical framework of the investment markets and the overall economy. This *Handbook* includes easy to understand but telling historical graphs together with background information and related statistical data on the principal stock and bond market indexes, as well as key economic indicators.

To facilitate ordering through brokers, particularly discount brokers, and to help you take advantage of an increasing willingness on the part of corporations to communicate directly with shareholders or potential shareholders, the *Handbook* provides a list—not readily available elsewhere—of the name, stock symbol, address, phone number, and line of business of approximately 6000 public companies in which you can buy shares or American Depositary Receipts on the New York Stock Exchange, the American Stock Exchange, the Toronto Stock Exchange, and over the counter on the NASDAQ National Market System. In addition, we indicate stocks on which listed options are traded and those offering dividend reinvestment plans. A limited number of companies offer free merchandise or other items or services of value as part of their shareholder relations efforts. You'll find a list of companies providing such "freebies."

The Appendix is an important part of the *Handbook*. In it you will find an annotated bibliography of selected key works on finance and investment. There is also a listing of the currencies of independent countries, which will be helpful in tracking international developments. At the conclusion of the *Handbook* is one of its important assets—the index—which will make is easier to find all the information on a particular topic in the book.

As in the previous edition, this revision recognizes the growing global context in which finance and investment decisions will be made as the 1990s lead into the new millennium.

HOW TO USE THIS *HANDBOOK* EFFECTIVELY

Each section of this *Handbook* is a self-contained entity. At the same time, however, the relevance of the various sections to each other is clear, since the objective of the *Handbook* is to join in one volume the different elements that together make up today's world of finance and investment. Tempting though it was from an editorial standpoint, cross-referencing has been kept to a minimum in the belief that readers would prefer not to be distracted by such editorial devices. At certain points, however, where reliance on the fuller explanation of a term in the *Handbook's* Dictionary of Finance and Investment seemed preferable to a discussion, cross-references to the dictionary are indicated by small capitals (for instance, ABC AGREEMENT). In any case, the dictionary is a source of comprehensive information on terms and concepts used throughout the *Handbook* and should be consulted whenever an aspect of finance and investment is not clear to you. The Table of Contents and especially the Index will also help you locate related information in different part of the *Handbook* and should be consulted regularly.

* * *

Although the *Handbook* was a collaborative effort in every sense of the word, primary responsibility was divided as follows: The sections on investment alternatives and reading financial reports were written by John Downes. The section on reading the financial pages was written by Charles Koshetz and edited by John Downes and Jordan Elliot Goodman. The Dictionary of Finance and Investment was authored coequally by John Downes and Jordan Elliot Goodman. The reference lists and the accompanying explanatory material were compiled, edited, and written by Jordan Elliot Goodman.

John Downes
Jordan Elliot Goodman

PART I

How to Invest Your Money: 30 Key Personal Investment Opportunities

INTRODUCTION

Perhaps the most important benefit of deregulation and other recent landmark changes in the securities and banking industries has been the availability to the average individual of investment alternatives that were formerly reserved for the wealthy. But welcome though this development is, it has brought with it choices that are bewildering both in range and complexity. Traditional investment vehicles have been modernized, new ones have been introduced, and, as the marketing departments of financial services conglomerates have sought to give their products mass appeal, the distinctions between different investment alternatives have become blurred.

This section presents 30 basic investment alternatives as they have emerged from the revolutionary events of the 1970s, 80s, and 90s. It is divided into 30 *basic* alternatives; each discussion, however, includes important variations, which, if counted separately, would more than double the number of alternatives.

The purpose of the section is not to provide advice. Investment decisions must always be made in subjective terms, taking into account one's financial position, risk comfort level, and goals. Rather, the section is designed to set forth in current terms the vital features distinguishing different investments, so you can talk knowledgeably with your investment counselor or, if you are a finance or investment professional, so you can be a better source of advice.

Preceding the discussions of investments is a table showing important characteristics of each investment. The chart is a quick way to learn pertinent facts, but should be used in conjunction with the discussions themselves to make sure you are aware of nuances and exceptions associated with a particular type of investment.

The discussions of investment alternatives begin with short overviews designed to describe the essential features of the investment and, where helpful, provide some historical perspective. These overviews are followed by sections in question-and answer format designed to present concisely and informatively the basic data needed to evaluate investment alternatives. Let's look at the questions and what they mean. (Remember, if you don't understand a finance or investment term, consult the extensive dictionary in this *Handbook*.)

Buying, Selling, and Holding

How do I buy and sell it? A few years ago, things were simpler: you bought your stocks and bonds from a broker, your life insurance from an insurance agent, and went to a bank with your savings or your loan request. The trend today is toward FULL-SERVICE BROKERS and FINANCIAL SUPERMARKETS that offer all these services and more. We have tried to be as helpful as possible, but there is no universality as to what full-service means from one firm to the next. One thing can be said for certain, though: you won't sound foolish these days if you ask a bank or broker if a given investment—no matter how specialized—can be bought or sold through his or her firm. DISCOUNT BROKERS are a special breed. They handle a variety of securities, but as a rule function strictly as brokers; some provide research, but do not look to them for investment guidance.

Is there a minimum purchase amount, and what is the price range? This question is aimed at giving you an idea of what it costs to get in the game, which is often more than just the minimum DENOMINATION or UNIT in which an investment is issued. The question cannot always be answered in absolute terms, since broker policies vary in terms of minimum orders and there may be SUITABILITY RULES requiring that you prove a certain financial capacity to take the risks associated with a particular investment. Certain securities trade in ROUND LOTS (for instance, 100 shares of common stock), though it is usually possible to buy ODD LOT quantities (for instance, 35 shares) at a higher commission per unit. In any event, call the broker and ask; many large firms have special programs that combine small orders from different investors and thereby make it possible to buy and sell modest amounts at modest commissions.

What fees and charges are involved? Again, we have been specific wherever possible, but with some investments, notably common stocks, commissions are sometimes negotiated, based on the size and nature of the transaction. DISCOUNT BROKERS, which as a rule do not give investment advice but execute trades at rates that are roughly half those of most full-service brokers, also have different rates for different transactions. See the entries for SHARE BROKER and VALUE BROKER in this *Handbook's* dictionary for discussions of different categories of discount broker. You will also frequently see references to DEALER spreads. This term refers to the MARKDOWNS and markups that are deducted from your selling price or added to your buying price when a broker-dealer is operating as a DEALER rather than simply as a BROKER.

Does it mature, expire, or otherwise terminate? Some investments are issued with a fixed MATURITY DATE, others are not. But even those with a fixed maturity date may be CALLABLE—that is, bought back at the pleasure of the issuer, or as part of a SINKING FUND provision. Others may have PUT OPTIONS, permitting REDEMPTION by the investor before maturity.

Can I sell it quickly? This question has to do with LIQUIDITY, the ability to convert an investment into cash without significant loss of value. Investments normally enjoying high liquidity are those with an active SECONDARY MARKET, in which they are actively traded among other investors subsequent to their original issue. Shares of LISTED SECURITIES have high liquidity. Liquidity can also be provided in other ways: for example, the SPONSOR of a unit investment trust might offer to MAKE A MARKET— to find a buyer to match you as a seller, should the need arise for you to sell.

How is market value determined and how do I keep track of it? MARKET VALUE is the price your investment would fetch in the open market, assuming that it is traded in a SECONDARY MARKET. In these discussions you will often encounter the word, VOLATILE, referring to the extent to which the market price of an investment fluctuates. Professionals use the term SYSTEMATIC RISK or its synonym market risk when discussing an investment's tendency to rise or fall in price as a result of market forces.

Investment Objectives

Should I buy this if my objective is capital appreciation? The purpose here is to identify investments likely to gain in value—to produce CAPITAL GAINS. Although APPRECIATION does not refer to capital growth due to factors such as reinvested dividends or compound interest, such factors are noted as a matter of relevance where they exist to a substantial degree. In the same category is appreciation due to ORIGINAL ISSUE DISCOUNT on fixed-income securities, which is considered interest. Other fixed-income investments bought in the market at a DISCOUNT from PAR because rising rates (or other factors) caused lower prices, create appreciation in the sense of capital gains either at REDEMPTION or when resold in the market at a higher price. Prices can also be at a PREMIUM, meaning higher than par value, when speaking of fixed-income investments.

Should I buy this if my objective is income? Here the purpose is to identify investments whose primary feature is providing regular income, as distinguished from alternatives primarily featuring capital gains or other potential values.

To what extent does it protect against inflation? If the value of an investment usually rises at the same rate or a higher rate than the rate of INFLATION erodes the value of the dollar, the investment is inflation-sensitive. Investments vary in the degree of protection they provide—some provide no protection. Although it is probably safe to assume that inflation will continue at a controlled rate for the foreseeable future, some economists, for the first time in many years, acknowledge a possibility of deflation in an era in which budget balancing, deficit-reduction, and downsizing have become watchwords. Assets that rise in value during inflation would decline in value during deflation.

Is it suitable for tax-deferred retirement accounts? Such accounts include INDI-VIDUAL RETIREMENT ACCOUNTS (IRAs), KEOGH PLANS, 401(K) PLANS, and other pension plans that are TAX-DEFERRED. The question addresses both the legality and, in some cases, the practicality of using a particular investment in such an account. Investments that might be ruled out for an IRA because of the $2000 annual maximum per person, might be appropriate for an IRA ROLLOVER.

Can I borrow against it? This question considers the general value of an investment as COLLATERAL at a bank or other lending institution, and also the eligibility of an investment for trading in MARGIN ACCOUNTS with brokers under Federal Reserve Board MARGIN REQUIREMENTS. A key consideration is the concept of LEVERAGE, the ability to control a given amount of value with a smaller amount of cash. Borrowing can also be a way of raising cash when an investment is ILLIQUID.

Risk Considerations

How assured can I be of getting my full investment back? Here the discussion concerns safety of PRINCIPAL, which has mainly to do with two types of risk: (1) market or SYSTEMATIC RISK and (2) financial or CREDIT RISK (risk that an issuer will DEFAULT on a contractual obligation or that an EQUITY investment will lose value because of financial difficulty or BANKRUPTCY of an issuer). Insurance considerations and HEDGING, protecting against loss of value through an offsetting position, are also discussed where appropriate.

How assured is my income? Assuming an investment produces income, this question deals with market risk as it may (or may not) affect income, with an issuer's legal obligation to pay income, and with priority of claim in LIQUIDATION.

Are there any other risks unique to this investment? This question intends only to highlight risks peculiar to a particular investment. It is not meant to imply that any risks not included do not exist.

Is it commercially rated? Commercial RATING agencies, such as MOODY'S INVESTORS SERVICE and STANDARD & POOR'S CORPORATION, analyze and rate certain securities and their issuers on a continuous basis. Most ratings are designed to indicate a company's financial strength and thus guide investors as to the degree of CREDIT RISK a security represents, though sometimes other factors are rated. Rating changes usually affect market values.

Tax Considerations

What tax advantages (or disadvantages) does it offer? This discussion is designed to present the tax considerations associated with an investment. Obviously, each individual's tax situation is unique and each investor should obtain professional advice to determine whether an investment with certain tax features represents an advantage or disadvantage in his or her particular case. Many tax advantages formerly enjoyed by investors disappeared with the landmark Tax Reform Act of 1986 and subsequent tax acts. Instances where investment values have changed are noted.

Economic Considerations

What economic factors most affect buy, hold, and sell decisions? Here again, only the most general economic considerations are covered and what applies in general might not apply to you.

PERSONAL INVESTMENTS AT A GLANCE

The following chart applies nine key investment criteria to the 30 personal investment alternatives discussed in this section. It is designed simply to answer the question: Is this alternative one I might want to learn more about in view of my own investment objectives? A bullet (●) means that a given characteristic is usually associated, to one degree or another, with a particular alternative. A blank means it is not. A V means that variation within the investment category exists to such an extent that even broad classification would be misleading.

Exceptions abound, and in every case there is a question of degree. In the modern universe of investment alternatives, just about nothing is pure; that fact is indeed what this section of the Handbook is all about. So with cognizance of its limitations, use this chart for quick and handy reference and refer to the overviews and questionnaires for more complete understanding.

Investment	Regular Current Income	Capital Appreciation	Tax Benefits	Safety of Principal	Liquidity	Inflation Protection	Leverage*	Future Income or Security	Suitability for IRAs and other Tax-Deferred Accounts
Annuity		●	●	●		V		●	
Bond, Corporate	●	●		●	●				●
Closed-End Fund	●	●		V	●	V			●
Collectible		●				●			
Common Stock	●	●		V	●	●	●		●
Convertible Security	●	●		●	●	●	●		●
Foreign Stocks and Bonds	●	●		V	V	●			●
Futures Contract on a Commodity		●			●		●		
Futures Contract on an Interest Rate		●			●		●		
Futures Contract on a Stock Index		●			●		●		
Government Agency Security	●	●	●	●	●				●
Life Insurance (Cash Value)		●	●	●		V		●	
Limited Partnership	●	●	●	V		V			●

Investment								
Money Market Fund	●		●	●	●			●
Mortgage-Backed (Pass-Through) Security	●	●	●	●				●
Municipal Security	●●	●	●	●				
Mutual Fund (Open-End)	●	●	● V	● V	V			●
Option Contract (Put or Call)	●		●	●		●		
Option Contract on a Futures Contract (Futures Option)			●			●		
Option Contract on an Interest Rate (Debt Option)	●		●	●		●		
Option Contract on a Stock Index	●		●	●		●		
Option Contract or Futures Contract on a Currency	●		●	●		●		
Precious Metals	●		● V	●	V			●
Preferred Stock (Nonconvertible)	●		●	●	●			●
Real Estate Investment Trust (REIT and FREIT)	●	●	● V	●	●			●
Real Estate, Physical	V	● V	●	●	●	●		
Savings Alternatives	●	V	●	●	●			V
Treasury Securities	●	● V	● V	●	●			●
Unit Investment Trust	●	V	V	●	V			●
Zero-Coupon Security			●	●	●		●	●

* Refers to margin securities and investments wherein large amounts of value can be controlled with small amounts of cash. The general value of investments as loan collateral is covered in the discussions of each of the investment alternatives.

HOW TO INVEST YOUR MONEY: 30 KEY PERSONAL INVESTMENT OPPORTUNITIES

ANNUITY

After a period of modernization, tax rulings, and the shock of a big insurance company bankruptcy, the time-honored annuity is again gaining popularity as an investment alternative. It comes in several varieties, with two basic attractions: (1) tax-deferred capital growth and (2) the option of income for life or a guaranteed period. Among the drawbacks are high penalties (by insurers and the Internal Revenue Service) on premature withdrawal and lower investment returns than could usually be realized directly.

Traditionally, annuities provided fixed income payments for an individual's remaining lifetime in exchange for a lump-sum cash payment. But inflation's negative impact on fixed-income annuities combined with increased life expectancy gave rise, in the late 1950s, to the variable annuity, invested in assets, like stocks, that rise with inflation, thus preserving some purchasing power, although at the price of some market risk.

In the late 1960s and early 70s came the wraparound annuity, which enabled investors to wrap their own mutual funds, savings accounts, or other investments in the annuity vehicle, thus sheltering them from taxes. In the early 1980s, the IRS blew the whistle, ruling that to qualify for tax deferral, annuity investments had to be managed by insurance companies and be available only to annuity contract holders. The annuity once again became a vehicle largely limited to retirement goals, but it has gained appeal with the modern features acquired along the way.

Annuities are available in two basic types:

Fixed annuities are "fixed" in two ways: (1) The amount you invest earns interest (tax-deferred) at a guaranteed rate (1% to 2% under long-term U.S. government bonds, typically) while your principal is guaranteed not to lose value. (2) When you withdraw or opt to "annuitize" (begin taking monthly income) you receive a guaranteed amount based on your age, sex, and selection of payment options. Inflation protection is, of course, minimal.

Variable annuities, in contrast, are "variable" in two ways: (1) The amount you put in is invested in your choice of a stock, fixed-income bond or money market account, the value and/or earnings of which vary with market conditions. (2) Market value determines the amount available for withdrawals, or (with actuarial factors) the amount the annuitant is paid from one month to the next. Variable annuities thus offer inflation protection in exchange for market risk (minimized somewhat when switching among funds is permitted).

The bankruptcy in the early 1980s of the Baldwin-United Corporation, the biggest name in deferred annuities, shook the confidence of an investor community that had learned to take the financial strength of insurance companies for granted. As it turned out, arrangements were made for investors to regain most of their money, and confidence in the industry, which is heavily regulated and high on any scale of safety, was restored.

In general, annuities, with a variety of optional features for both accumulation and payout, are for long-term investors willing to trade liquidity and some degree of return for safety and tax-deferred capital growth, and whose objective is to defer taxability until later (lower tax-rate) years and/or to guarantee retirement income.

* * *

What Is an Annuity?

An annuity is a contract between an insurance company and an annuitant whereby the company, in exchange for a single or flexible premium guarantees a fixed or variable payment to the annuitant at a future time. *Immediate annuities* begin paying out as soon as the premium is paid; *deferred annuities,* which may be paid for in a lump sum or in installments, start paying out at a specified date in the future.

Buying, Selling, and Holding

How do I buy and sell it? Insurance brokers, insurance company sales agents, savings institutions, full-service brokers, commercial banks, and other financial service organizations sell annuities.

Is there a minimum purchase amount, and what is the price range? It varies with the plan, but deferred annuities typically have minimums ranging from $1000 to $5000.

What fees and charges are involved? Fees and charges may include front-end load sales charges ranging from 1% to 10% (although there is a trend toward no initial commissions), premium taxes (imposed on the insurance company by some states and passed on to contract holders), annual fees (typically $15 to $30 per year up to a maximum of $1^1/2\%$ of account value), surrender charges or early withdrawal penalties (typically starting at 6% and decreasing to zero over a seven-year period), and other charges. (See Tax Considerations, below, for tax penalties).

Does it mature, expire, or otherwise terminate? Yes; both the accumulation period and the payout period are specified in the contract.

Can I sell it quickly? Accumulated cash value (principal payments plus investment earnings) can always be withdrawn, but there may be substantial withdrawal penalties as well as tax penalties.

How is market value determined and how do I keep track of it? Annuities do not have secondary market value, but information concerning account balances is supplied by the insurance company.

Investment Objectives

Should I buy an annuity if my objective is capital appreciation? Not in the sense that you would buy an investment at one price and hope to sell it at a higher price. But deferred annuities accumulate value through (tax-deferred) compounding, and variable annuities may be invested in stocks or other securities having capital gains potential.

Should I buy this if my objective is income? Annuities are designed to provide income for future guaranteed periods, so you would not buy a deferred annuity for current income needs.

To what extent does it protect against inflation? Fixed annuities provide no inflation protection. Variable annuities provide protection when their portfolios are invested in inflation-sensitive securities.

Is it suitable for tax-deferred retirement accounts? Yes, but since annuities have tax-deferred status themselves, it may be wiser to use them as supplements to IRAs, Keoghs, and other tax-deferred programs.

Can I borrow against it? Yes.

Risk Considerations

How assured can I be of getting back my full investment in an annuity? Insurance companies are heavily regulated and required to maintain reserves, so with established companies there is low risk of loss due to corporate failure. Most annuities permit early withdrawal of principal, but penalties may apply. Once annuitized (i.e., when payments by the insurance company begin) it becomes a question of how long you live. The insurance company (with the odds in its favor) bets you will die before the annuity is fully paid out.

How assured is my income? While variable annuity income can fluctuate, the risk of default is low. (See previous question.)

Are there any other risks unique to this investment? Although heavily regulated, insurance companies are potentially subject to mismanagement and fraud, and policyholders are not themselves covered by federal protection as bank depositors, for example, are covered by the Federal Deposit Insurance Corporation (FDIC).

Is it commercially rated? Yes. Insurance companies are rated by Best's Rating Service.

Tax Considerations

What tax advantages (or disadvantages) does an annuity offer? Earnings on money invested in deferred annuities, including all interest, dividends, and capital gains, accumulate and compound tax-deferred. Portions of payments to annuitants are returns of investor's principal and thus are not subject to income taxes. Withdrawals of accumulated earnings prior to age 59$^1/_2$ or within 5 years of the purchase date (whichever comes first) are subject to a 10% tax penalty. (An exception is made for life annuities, payable for the lifetimes. or life expectancies, of one or more annuitants.)

Economic Considerations

What economic factors most affect buy, hold, and sell decisions? Although factors such as inflationary expectations and anticipated interest rate movements may guide choices among types of annuities, the decision to buy and hold is based on insurance rather than economic considerations. Annuities are appropriate for people without dependents or heirs, who seek assured income for their remaining lives.

BOND, CORPORATE (INTEREST-BEARING)

The traditional attractions of a corporate bond have been (1) higher yield compared to government bonds and (2) relative safety. Whether secured (usually a mortgage bond) or unsecured (called a debenture), it has a higher claim on earnings than equity investments. If the firm goes out of business, bonds also have a higher claim on the assets of the issuer, whose financial well-being is safeguarded by provisions in bond indentures and is closely monitored by the major bond rating services. Interest on corporates is fully taxable.

Much publicized in the 1980s because of their widespread use in financing corporate takeovers were so-called junk bonds, corporate bonds with lower than investment-grade ratings that pay high yields to compensate for high risk. Although issuers could point to the fact that high-yield bonds in general have had a low default record historically, fears that a prolonged recession would put the more heavily leveraged issuers in trouble have caused depressed prices and poor liquidity in the junk bond market at times when the economic outlook was gloomy.

Bonds are contracts between borrowers and lenders in which the issuer (borrower) promises the bondholder (lender) a specified rate of interest and repayment of principal at maturity.

The face, or par, value of a corporate bond is almost always $1000 (the exceptions being baby bonds with pars of $500 or less), but bonds do not necessarily sell at par value. Particularly in the secondary market, bonds are traded at discounts or premiums relative to par in order to bring their stated (coupon) rates in line with market rates. This inverse relationship between bond prices and interest rate movements causes market risk as the term applies to bonds; when interest rates rise, there is a decline in the price of a bond with a lower fixed interest rate.

Bond prices also vary with the time remaining to maturity. This is because of the time value of money and because time involves risk and risk means higher yield. Bond yields thus normally decrease (and prices increase) as the bond approaches maturity. The concept of yield-to-maturity is basic to bond pricing, and it takes into account the price paid for the bond and all cash inflows and their timing.

The safety and value of corporate bonds are also related to credit risk, quite simply the borrower's ability to pay interest and principal when due. The relative financial strength of the issuer, as reflected in the regularly updated rating assigned to its bonds by the major services, influences yield, which is adjusted by changes in the market price.

Concern that hostile takeovers and recapitalizations would weaken the value of existing holdings has inspired protective provisions in bond indenture agreements. Standard & Poor's publishes "Event Risk Covenant Rankings," a system's supplementing its credit ratings, that evaluates such protection. A common provision is the "poison put," which gives bondholders the right to redeem at par if certain designated events occur, such as a hostile takeover, the purchase of a big block of stock, or an excessive dividend payout.

Other considerations influencing corporate bond prices include the existence of call features, which empower the issuer to redeem prior to maturity, often to the disadvantage of the bondholder; call protection periods, which benefit holders; sinking funds, which require the issuer to set aside funds for the retirement of the bonds at maturity; put options giving the investor the right to redeem at specified times prior to maturity; subordinations, which give issues precedence over other issues in liquidation; and guarantees or insurance.

Variable-rate issues, usually called floating-rate notes even though some issues have terms of 30 years, adjust interest rates periodically in line with market rates. These issues generally have lower yields to compensate for the benefit to the holder, but they enjoy greater price stability to the extent the rate adjustments are responsive to market rate movements.

See also the discussions of Convertible Securities and Zero-Coupon Securities.

* * *

What Is a Corporate Bond?

A corporate bond is a debt security of a corporation requiring the issuer to pay the holder the par value at a specified maturity and to make agreed scheduled interest payments.

Buying, Selling, and Holding

How do I buy and sell a corporate bond? Through a securities broker-dealer.

Is there a minimum purchase amount, and what is the price range? Bonds are normally issued with $1000 par values, with baby bonds in smaller denominations. Issuers often have 5-bond minimums and broker-dealers trade in round lots of 10 or 100 units. Odd lots may be available at higher brokerage commissions or dealer spreads.

What fees and charges are involved? A per-bond commission of $2.50 to $20, depending on the broker and negotiations with the customer. However, a minimum charge of $30 is common. New issues involve no charges to the investor.

Does it mature, expire, or otherwise terminate? All bonds have maturity dates, but may be callable prior to maturity.

Can I sell it quickly? Usually yes. Most major issues are actively traded, but in large amounts. Small lots can be harder to trade and may involve some price sacrifice and higher transaction costs. Some high-yield junk bonds have been hard to sell because of the fear of default.

How is market value determined and how do I keep track of it? The market value of a fixed-income bond is a function of its yield to maturity and prevailing market interest rates. Prices thus decline when interest rates rise and rise when interest rates decline to result in an appropriate competitive yield. A change in the issuer's rating can also cause a change in price as higher (or lower) risk is reflected in the price/yield relationship. Even without a formal rating change, reduced demand can cause lower bond prices; this has been seen in junk bond prices reflecting fears that a recession will cause defaults. Bond prices are quoted in daily newspapers and electronic databases.

Investment Objectives

Should I buy a corporate bond if my objective is capital appreciation? Usually not, although capital appreciation is possible when bonds can be bought at a discount to their par value, bought prior to a drop in market interest rates, or bought at a favorable price because of a decline in the issuer's credit rating.

Should I buy this if my objective is income? Yes; bonds pay interest, usually semiannually. Yields on top-rated bonds are lower than on bonds of less than investment grade, called junk bonds, which pay more and have higher credit risk.

To what extent does it protect against inflation? Although normal inflationary expectations are built into interest rates, fixed-rate bonds offer no protection against high inflation. Variable-rate issues offer some protection.

Is it suitable for tax-deferred retirement accounts? Yes.

Can I borrow against it? Yes, subject to Federal Reserve margin rules (convertible bonds only) and brokerage-firm and lending-institution policies.

Risk Considerations

How assured can I be of getting my full investment back? If you hold to maturity, it will depend on the issuer's credit, which is evaluated regularly by the major investor's rating services and reflected in ratings from AAA down to D. If you plan to sell in the secondary market before maturity, you are subject also to market risk, the risk that bond prices will be down as a result of higher interest rates. Sophisticated investors sometimes protect against loss of value due to market risk by hedging, using options and futures available on long-term Treasury securities which are similarly affected by interest rate changes.

How assured is my income? Uninterrupted payment of interest depends on the issuer's financial strength and stability of earnings, factors reflected in its bond rating. Inflation can erode the dollar value of fixed-interest payments.

Are there any other risks unique to this investment? A callable bond can be redeemed by the issuer after a certain period has elapsed. Issuers normally force redemption when interest rates have declined and financing can be obtained more cheaply. Under just those circumstances, however, the investor finds the holding most attractive; the market price is up and the coupon interest rate is higher than the prevailing market interest rate. Look for bonds with call protection (typically 10 years). Event risk, the risk of a deterioration in credit quality owing to takeover-related changes in capitalization, is another consideration. Although issuers considering themselves vulnerable may have indenture provisions to protect bondholders (rated by Standard & Poor's Event Risk Covenant Rankings), such measures can result in early redemption and deprive the holder of a long-term investment.

Is it commercially rated ? Yes. Duff & Phelps/MCM, Fitch Investors Service, Moody's Investors Service, and Standard & Poor's Corporation are the major rating services.

Tax Considerations

What tax advantages (or disadvantages) does a corporate bond offer? None. Bond interest is taxed as ordinary income and realized gains are subject to capital gains tax, except that appreciation resulting from original issue discounts is taxed (as earned) at ordinary income rates.

Economic Considerations

What economic factors most affect buy, hold, or sell decisions? It is best to buy a corporate bond when interest rates are high and the best yields can be obtained. Holding is most attractive when rates are declining, causing an upward move in the market values of fixed-income securities. High inflation erodes the dollar value of fixed interest payments. Poor business conditions over a prolonged period can cause financial weakness and jeopardize a firm's ability to pay.

CLOSED-END FUND

Closed-end funds, so-called because, unlike open-end mutual funds, their sponsoring investment companies do not stand ready to issue and redeem shares on a continuous basis, have a fixed capitalization represented by publicly traded shares that are often listed on the major stock exchanges. Because the net asset value of a closed-end fund varies independently of its own share price, the investment has been compared to a water bed on a boat.

Closed-end funds tend to have specialized portfolios of stocks, bonds, convertibles, or combinations thereof, and may be oriented toward income, capital gains, or a combination of those objectives. Examples are the Korea Fund, which specializes in the stock of Korean firms and is an example of a "single country fund," and ASA Ltd., which invests in South African gold mining stocks. Both are traded on the New York Stock Exchange.

The attraction of a closed-end fund is twofold: (1) Because management is not concerned with continuous buying and selling to accommodate new investors and redemptions, a responsibility of open-end funds that frequently conflicts with ideal market timing, a well-managed closed-end fund can often buy and sell on more favorable terms. (2) Because the popular investor perception is just the opposite—that closed-end funds have less flexibility than open-end funds—shares of closed-end funds can usually be obtained at a discount from net asset value. As a result of these combined factors, annual earnings of closed-end funds sometimes exceed earnings of open-end funds with comparable portfolios.

A special form of closed-end fund is the *dual-purpose fund.* These hybrids have two classes of stock. Preferred shareholders receive all the income from the portfolio—dividends and interest—while common shareholders receive all capital gains realized on the sale of securities in the fund's portfolio. Dual-purpose funds are set up with a specific expiration date, when preferred shares are redeemed at a predetermined price and common shareholders claim the remaining assets, voting either to liquidate or continue the fund on an open-end basis.

Closed-end funds, of which more than 400 are publicly and actively traded, are regulated by the Securities and Exchange Commission.

See also the discussion of Mutual Funds.

$$* \quad * \quad *$$

What Is a Closed-End Fund?

A closed-end fund is a type of mutual fund that invests in diversified holdings and has a fixed number of shares that are publicly traded.

Buying, Selling, and Holding

How do I buy and sell a closed-end fund? Through a securities broker-dealer.

Is there a minimum purchase amount, and what is the price range? Round-lot 100 share purchases save commissions. Prices vary but many funds sell for $25 or less per share.

What fees and charges are involved? Standard brokerage commissions plus an annual management fee averaging 1/2% to 1% of the investment.

Does it mature, expire, or otherwise terminate? Funds can be liquidated or converted to open-end funds or operating companies if a majority of shareholders approve. Dual-purpose funds expire, typically in ten years.

Can I sell it quickly? Usually yes. Most funds offer good liquidity.

How is market value determined and how do I keep track of it? By supply and demand factors affecting shares in the market. Whether shares trade at a premium (rare) or at more or less of a discount (the rule) relative to the net asset value of the fund, can depend on the portfolio, yield, the general market, and factors like year-end tax selling. Some funds have stock buyback programs designed to reduce outstanding shares and increase earnings per share. New issues tend initially to sell at premiums, then to slack off when brokers turn their aggressive sales efforts to other products. *The Wall Street Journal* and *The New York Times* on Monday and the weekly *Barron's,* report the net asset value, price, and discount or premium for the previous week on actively traded funds.

Investment Objectives

Should I buy a closed-end fund if my objective is capital appreciation? Although fund shares rise and fall in the marketplace, influenced, among other factors, by the value of the fund's portfolio, investors seeking to participate in capital gains would select a fund having appreciation as its primary objective—an aggressive stock fund, for example, as opposed to a bond fund, though gains and losses are possible in both. Dual-purpose funds offer two classes of stock, common shareholders benefiting from all the capital gains, preferred shareholders getting all the interest and dividend income. Funds bought at a discount offer the prospect of additional appreciation through increases in fund share prices.

Should I buy this if my objective is income? Yes, especially funds whose objective is income. (See the preceding question.) Some funds offer guaranteed payouts, but it should be recognized that unless the fund generates income equal to the guaranteed payment, it may come out of funds contributed by investors.

To what extent does it protect against inflation? Some portfolios are more sensitive (less vulnerable) to inflation than others, stocks being better than bonds, for example. Of course, increases in the portfolio benefit investors only when passed on in capital gains distributions or reflected in higher fund share values.

Is it suitable for tax-deferred retirement accounts? Yes.

Can I borrow against it? Yes, subject to Federal Reserve margin requirements and individual lender policies.

Risk Considerations

How assured can I be of getting my full investment back? Fund shares can be just as volatile as common stock. Professionals use various techniques to hedge funds selling at discounts or premiums or converting to open-end funds. These techniques include purchasing options and selling short other funds, treasury securities and futures, and stocks in the same fund's portfolio. Some funds have "open-ending" provisions, whereby they guarantee that investors can choose to collect the full net asset value of fund shares on a specified future debt; it is important to note, however, that although the net asset value may be higher than the market price, it can be lower than your original investment.

How assured is my income? It depends on the quality of the portfolio and the risk characteristics of the investments comprising it. Funds offering guaranteed payouts may have to liquidate capital to make good.

Are there any other risks unique to this investment? The risk unique to closed-end funds is that the value of fund shares can move independently of the value of the securities comprising the fund's portfolio. If this causes shares to trade at a discount to net asset values, it is bad for holders, although it can be viewed as a buying opportunity.

Is it commercially rated? Funds are not usually rated, but information helpful to investors is provided by Standard & Poor's Stock Record Sheets, Moody's Finance Manuals, and other sources.

Tax Considerations

What tax advantages (or disadvantages) does a closed-end fund offer? The tax treatment of closed-end fund shares is the same as for common stock except that capital gains distributions enjoy preferential long-term capital gains treatment regardless of how long the fund has been held.

Economic Considerations

What economic factors most affect buy, hold or sell decisions? Most experts say to buy when shares can be obtained at a good discount and the stock market seems poised for a rise. Otherwise, decisions should consider the effects of different economic and market scenarios on various types of portfolios, such as bonds, stocks, or convertibles. It is probably wise to view closed-end funds as long-term investments and to sell when significant appreciation has occurred.

COLLECTIBLE

Collectibles, the name for a diverse range of physical possessions presumed to gain value with time, enjoyed a wave of popularity as a haven for investment money during the inflation-ravaged 1970s. Then the 1981–82 recession revealed how fickle the marketplace can be and how vulnerable collectibles are to adverse economic conditions. When that period was followed by one in which inflation was brought under control and financial investments became attractive again, enthusiasm for collectibles as an investment alternative, exclusive of their utility or personal enjoyment value, waned considerably. Some collectibles continued to perform well in the 1980s and 1990s, although the frenzied interest of the 1970s never returned.

There is no universal definition of a collectible. Some experts apply the criteria of rarity, quality, uniqueness, and age, while others put commodities with utilitarian value (like gemstones) or intrinsic value (like coins with gold or silver content) in addition to collector's value in separate categories.

In the broadest definition, however, collectibles are physical assets (not financial or real, in the sense of real estate), that have psychic or utilitarian value for their owners, are unique or in limited supply, and can be expected to increase in value with time and demand. The category thus includes stamps, coins, antiques, gemstones, fine art, photographs, and an almost endless list of other groups and subdivisions ranging from folk art and crafts to baseball cards, comic books, antique automobiles, and miscellaneous collectible junk.

While books have been written on the major categories of collectibles, certain common denominators exist to varying degrees from an investment perspective: often high costs to trade and own; high price volatility; no current income; and undependable or poor liquidity.

These factors plus the opportunity cost of an unproductive investment lead to one conclusion: Collectibles, especially when the relevant group of collectors is solidly in place and in good communication, will probably gain value and outstrip inflation over the long term, but the costs and risks of holding collectibles for investment purposes can be justified only when the assets also provide their owners pleasure or utility.

* * *

What Is a Collectible?

A collectible is a physical asset of a non-real estate and nonfinancial nature that exists in limited supply, usually provides enjoyment or utility to its owner, and is expected to increase in value because of inflation or supply and demand factors such as popularity and rarity.

Buying, Selling, and Holding

How do I buy and sell a collectible? Through dealers, galleries, auctions, private owners, flea markets, and catalogs and other collector publications.

Is there a minimum purchase amount, and what is the price range? Minimums and price ranges vary with the collectible and run a gamut from a few pennies to millions of dollars.

What fees and charges are involved? This depends on the collectible, where it is traded, and many other factors, but fees are an important consideration. Costs may include dealer profits (markups), sales taxes, appraisal fees, storage and safe keeping, maintenance, insurance, as well as opportunity cost—the return you would get if your money were invested more productively.

Does it mature, expire, or otherwise terminate? No.

Can I sell it quickly? A collectible varies in liquidity, from one, like a painting or an antique, bought through established dealers standing ready to repurchase at an agreed-on price, to another salable only through consignment to dealers or auction houses.

How is market value determined and how do I keep track of it? Market value is determined by supply and demand. Some collectibles are more vulnerable to fads than others, and the marketplace can be more efficient in one type of collectible than another because it has more dealers and better communication among dealers and collectors. Some major newspapers, like *The New York Times*, carry advertisements for collectibles of various types; most of the main categories of collectibles are served by specialized periodicals or newsletters; and a number of national magazines contain classified sections and even articles aimed at collectors within their fields of interest. Dealers and appraisers are a source of information about market value, but it is important to satisy oneself as to their objectivity.

Investment Objectives

Should I buy a collectible if my objective is capital appreciation? Yes, but short-term profits depend on a combination of expertise and luck, and long-term appreciation can be affected by fads as well as economic developments.

Should I buy this if my objective is income? No.

To what extent does it protect against inflation? Although there are many risks that can undermine the value of a collectible, if the condition of the collectible remains good and supply and demand factors stay favorable, values will increase with inflation.

Is it suitable for tax-deferred retirement accounts? Collectibles are not legal investments in such accounts unless they are part of portfolios directed by trustees.

Can I borrow against it? Yes; many lenders will accept marketable collectibles as collateral.

Risk Considerations

How assured can I be of getting my full investment back? With most collectibles, this has mainly to do with your level of expertise and the amount of time you hold the asset. In the short term, it is likely that costs and commissions will offset whatever small gain might be realized. In the long run, collectibles become more limited in supply and (assuming good quality and condition) more valuable, but only if the demand has continued strong and economic conditions have not eroded purchasing power. Many collectibles are vulnerable to fads, though some bought from well-established and reputable dealers may be sold back at agreed upon prices.

How assured is my income? Collectibles normally provide no income, and are in fact a drain on cash that might otherwise be invested for income.

Are there any other risks unique to this investment? Collectibles are subject to a wide range of unique risks—forgery and other frauds; physical risk, such as deterioration, fire, and theft; "warehouse finds," where a large supply of a previously limited item is suddenly discovered and becomes a drug on the market; the reverse situation, where a large chunk of a given collectible's supply goes "in collection," leaving so little in circulation that diminished interest reduces demand.

Each category has its own special risks and prospective collectors are advised to research them.

Is it commercially rated ? No.

Tax Considerations

What tax advantages (or disadvantages) does it offer? Realized capital gains and capital losses are subject to standard rates for capital assets. Other tax advantages may pertain, depending on whether the collecting is done as a hobby or as a for-profit investment activity. Tax advice should be obtained.

Economic Considerations

What economic factors most affect buy, hold, and sell decisions? Collectibles have traditionally been favored by investors in times of inflation, though the value of this investment category as an inflation hedge is tempered by the many risks. The marketability of collectibles is more dependent on good economic conditions than most other investments.

COMMON STOCK

For total return over the long term, no publicly traded investment alternative offers more potential under normal conditions than common stock.

A share of common stock is the basic unit of equity ownership in a corporation. The shareholder is usually entitled to vote in the election of directors and on other important matters and to share in the wealth created by corporate activities, both through the appreciation of share values and the payment of dividends out of the earnings remaining after debt obligations and holders of preferred stock are satisfied. In the event of liquidation of assets, common shareholders divide the assets remaining after creditors and preferred shareholders have been repaid.

In public corporations, shares have market values primarily based on investor expectations of future earnings and dividends. The relationship of this market price to the actual or expected earnings, called the price-earnings ratio or "multiple," is a measure of these expectations. Stock values are also affected by forecasts of business activity in general and by whatever "investor psychology" is produced by the immediate business and economic environment.

Stocks of young, fast-growing companies, particularly those in industries that are cyclical or high technology-oriented, tend to be volatile, to have high price-earnings ratios, and generally to carry a high degree of risk. Called *growth stocks,* they seldom pay dividends, since earnings are reinvested to finance growth. These stocks are often traded in the over-the-counter market or on the American Stock Exchange.

At the other end of the spectrum, stocks of old, established firms in mature industries and with histories of regular earnings and dividends tend to be characterized by relative price stability and low multiples. These stocks are usually found listed on the New York Stock Exchange (although there are exceptions) and the cream of the crop are known as blue chips. As a general category, these regular dividend payers are called *income stocks.*

Spanning the growth income continuum is a wide range of common stock investment choices that can be made only in terms of one's personal objectives and risk comfort level. To help in the process is a professional establishment comprised of brokers, investment advisers, and financial planners supported by practitioners of various securities analysis approaches—those trained in fundamental analysis, technical analysis, chartists, and others.

Investors with limited means can gain the advantages of common stock ownership together with the benefits of professional management and portfolio diversification through mutual funds, which are discussed elsewhere in this section.

* * *

What Is Common Stock?

A common stock represents ownership in a corporation, usually carries voting rights, and often earns dividends (paid out at the discretion of the corporation's board of directors).

Buying, Selling, and Holding

How do I buy and sell common stock? Through a securities broker-dealer.

Is there a minimum purchase amount, and what is the price range? There is no minimum, but buying in round lots (usually 100 shares) saves extra odd-lot (under 100 shares) charges. Some brokers offer programs allowing odd-lot purchases at regular rates. Stock prices range widely, with the majority under $50.

What fees and charges are involved? The brokerage commission, the principal charge, varies by the value and/or size of transaction. Discount brokers charge less than full-service brokers. A nominal transfer tax is imposed on sellers by the federal government and several state governments. Interest and other charges may be incurred in margin accounts, in which qualifying stocks can be traded on credit within requirements of the Federal Reserve Board and individual brokerage firms.

Does it mature, expire, or otherwise terminate? No, although tender offers by issuing companies and outside acquirers often give shareholders the opportunity to sell within a set period at a premium over prevailing stock market prices.

Can I sell it quickly? Usually, yes. Shares of publicly held and actively traded companies are highly liquid.

How is market value determined and how do I keep track of it? Market value is basically determined by investor expectations of future earnings and dividend payments, although the value of assets is also important. Prices may also be affected temporarily by large transactions creating bid-offer imbalances, by rumors of various sorts, and by public tender offers. Newspapers and electronic databases show daily prices on stocks traded on exchanges and over the counter.

Investment Objectives

Should I buy common stock if my objective is capital appreciation? Yes, especially growth stocks of younger firms, which tend to reinvest earnings rather than pay dividends as older, established firms do.

Should I buy this if my objective is income? Yes, especially if your objectives also include some capital appreciation and inflation protection. Established companies are more likely to pay dividends regularly than are fast-growing firms that tend to reinvest earnings.

To what extent does it protect against inflation? Over the long run, stocks rise in value and increase dividends with inflation, though they do not protect against hyperinflation.

Is it suitable for tax-deferred retirement accounts? Yes. Stocks are suitable for IRAs, Keoghs, 401(K) plans, and other tax-deferred plans.

Can I borrow against it? Yes, subject to Federal Reserve margin rules and lender policies concerning marketable securities collateral.

Risk Considerations

How assured can I be of getting my full investment back? There is no concrete assurance. There is always the risk that market prices will decline in value, though some stocks are more volatile than others. When a company goes out of business and liquidates its assets, common shareholders are paid last—after preferred stock-holders and creditors.

How assured is my income? Dividends come out of earnings and are declared at the discretion of the board of directors. They can be suspended if profits are off, or if the directors decide reinvestment is preferable. Older, established, blue chip companies are the most dependable dividend payers; young, growth-oriented firms tend to reinvest earnings and thus pay no (or low) dividends.

Are there any other risks unique to this investment? Anything that can affect the fortunes of a company can affect its stock value and dividend payments.

Is it commercially rated? Yes, Moody's, Standard & Poor's, Value Line Investment Survey, and others rate many publicly traded issues.

Tax Considerations

What tax advantages (or disadvantages) does common stock offer? Dividends to individuals are fully taxable in the year they are paid, at the shareholder's tax rate. Gains on the sale of stock held more than one year receive a preferential long-term capital gains rate of 28%. After-tax corporate earnings not paid out as dividends accumulate without being taxed. Corporations can exclude 70% of dividends received from other domestic corporations.

Economic Considerations

What economic factors most affect buy, hold, or sell decisions? Stocks are most attractive as holdings when inflation is moderate, interest rates are low, and business conditions are generally favorable to growth and bigger profits.

CONVERTIBLE SECURITY

Convertible securities—bonds (debentures) or preferred stock convertible into common stock (usually of the issuer but, in rare cases. of the issuer's subsidiary or affiliate)—offer both fixed income and appreciation potential but are not quite the best of both worlds. The yield on the convertible bond or preferred is normally less than that of a "straight" bond or preferred, and the potential for capital gain is less than with a common stock investment.

On the other hand, convertibles (sometimes called CVs and identified that way in the newspaper bond tables, but not the stock tables) do offer less credit risk and market risk than common shares while providing an opportunity to share in the future wealth of the corporation for whose shares the convertible can be exchanged.

In terms of priority of claim on earnings and assets, convertible bonds and convertible preferred stock have the same status as regular bonds and preferred. Bonds, whether convertible or straight, receive payments before preferred stock, whatever its type, and both bonds and preferred have precedence over common stock.

From the investor's standpoint, convertibles must be understood in terms of what is called their *investment value* and their *conversion value.* Investment value is the market value the convertible would have if it were not convertible—its value as a straight bond or straight preferred. Conversion value is the market price of the common stock times the number of shares into which the bond or preferred is convertible (called the conversion rate or ratio).

Since convertible owners hope to capitalize on rises in common shares through conversion and therefore value the conversion privilege, CVs begin trading at a premium over conversion value. As the common rises and the CV is viewed more and more as a common stock investment, the CV tends to sell for its common stock equivalent. Conversion is not advisable until the common dividend has more value than the income on the CV and it is normal for the common price to rise beyond the CV price until that equation is reached.

Of course, common-share prices cannot be guaranteed to rise, and in a down market convertible holders look at their investment in terms of its value as a bond or preferred stock. This investment value represents downside risk protection in the sense that the convertible will never be worth less than this value. Investment value is, however, subject to market risk; it can be pushed down by a general rise in interest rates. But should that happen, investors have downside protection in that the CV will never drop significantly below its conversion value.

Conventional wisdom holds that investors should not buy convertibles unless attracted by the soundness of the underlying common stock. They should be wary also of issues selling at high premiums over the value of the common stock or the prices at which they are callable.

See also the discussion of Zero-coupon Securities.

*   *   *

What Is a Convertible Security?

A convertible security is a preferred stock or debenture (unsecured bond) paying a fixed dividend or rate of interest and convertible into common stock, usually of the issuer, at a specified price or conversion ratio.

Buying, Selling, and Holding

How do I buy and sell a convertible security? Through a securities broker-dealer.

Is there a minimum purchase amount and what is the price range? Convertible preferred stock typically trades in 10-share round lots and has par values ranging from $100 down to $10. Bonds sell in $1000 units but exceptions, called baby bonds, can have lower par values, usually $500 down to $25. Brokers often have minimum orders of 10 bonds or, frequently, 100 bonds. Odd lots involve higher commissions or dealer spreads.

What fees and charges are involved ? Standard brokerage commissions or dealer spreads. Bonds usually involve a per-bond commission of $2.50 to $20, depending on the broker and the size of the order. However, a minimum of $30 is common.

Does it mature, expire, or otherwise terminate? Bonds mature; preferred stocks do not. Both may be callable, however, and the regular redemption and retirement of both shares and bonds may be provided for by sinking fund agreements. Of course, once converted to common stock, there are no maturities or calls.

Can I sell it quickly? Most can be readily sold, but trading volume is not ordinarily heavy and prices can fluctuate significantly.

How is market value determined and how do I keep track of it? Market value is influenced both by the market price of the underlying common stock and the investment value of the convertible security—that is, its value as a bond or preferred stock exclusive of the conversion feature. When the conversion premium—the amount by which the price of the convertible security exceeds the price of the underlying common stock—is high, the convertible trades like a bond or preferred stock. When trading like a fixed-income investment, its value fluctuates in inverse relation to interest rates, though it will not decline below its investment value. Once parity has been reached—that is, the price of the convertible and its value assuming conversion are the same—the convertible will rise along with the underlying common stock. Prices of convertibles are reported in the stock or bond tables of daily newspapers and in electronic databases.

Investment Objectives

Should I buy a convertible security if my objective is capital appreciation? Yes; convertibles offer the opportunity to capitalize on growth in common share values while enjoying the greater yield and safety of bonds or preferred.

Should I buy this if my objective is income? Yes; but since growth is a feature, the yield is less than on a straight bond or preferred.

To what extent does it protect against inflation? Convertible prices tend to rise with common share prices, which tend to rise with inflation.

Is it suitable for tax-deferred retirement accounts? Yes, CVs qualify for IRAs, Keoghs, 401(K) plans, and other tax-deferred plans.

Can I borrow against it? Yes, subject to margin rules. CVs are acceptable general collateral, with bonds having more loan value than stock.

Risk Considerations

How assured can I be of getting my full investment back? CVs have downside protection in that their value will not sink below the market value the same investment would have as a straight (nonconvertible) bond or preferred. That "investment value" varies inversely with rates, however, so when rates go up the "floor" goes down. The price of a CV is determined, on the other hand, by the value of its conversion feature, so as long as the common holds up, the CV should not decline to its investment value. Of course, once converted, your investment becomes subject to all the risks of common stock. In liquidation, convertible bonds are paid before convertible preferred stock, and both have precedence over the corporation's common stock.

How assured is my income? The interest on convertible bonds, as a legal obligation of the issuer, has a higher claim on earnings than dividends on convertible preferred stock, which can be omitted if the issuer gets tight for cash. Preferred dividends must be paid before common dividends, however. Assuming the issuer is strong financially and has dependable earnings, there is little to worry about.

Are there any other risks unique to this investment? Dilution—a decrease in the value of common shares into which the CV converts—can happen for many reasons. Provision for such obvious corporate actions as stock splits, new issues, or spinoffs of stock or other properties, is normally made in the bond indenture or preferred stock agreement, but subtle developments, such as small quarterly stock dividends or unplanned events, can be a risk.

Is it commercially rated? Yes, by Moody's, Standard & Poor's, Value Line, and other services.

Tax Considerations

What tax advantages (or disadvarltagex) does it offer? None, except that gains resulting from conversion to the issuer's common stock are not treated as gains for tax purposes, provided the stock you receive is that of the same corporation that issued the convertible. Corporations can exclude from taxes 70% of preferred dividends.

Economic Considerations

What economic factors most affect buy, hold, or sell decisions? Assuming economic conditions are not threatening the issuer's financial health, convertibles offer holders protection from adverse factors affecting both common stock and fixed-income securities. The CV is thus a security for all seasons, though the price of having it both ways is less appreciation potential than common stock and less yield than straight bonds or preferred stock. It follows that CVs are popular in times of economic and market uncertainty. The ideal time to buy is when rates are high and stocks are low and the best time to hold is in a rising stock market. Stagflation is the worst scenario because stocks are hurt by the stagnation and fixed-income securities are hurt by the inflation; both the conversion and investment values of CVs thus suffer.

FOREIGN STOCKS AND BONDS

Foreign stocks and bonds—those of foreign issuers denominated in foreign currencies—offer opportunities (1) to invest where economies or industry sectors may be faster growing than those at home and (2) to augment total returns through profits on currency movements.

Foreign securities have acquired luster in recent years, as ways to shift money from sluggish United States markets into more vibrant overseas economies (while gaining an edge on domestic inflation) and as "dollar plays," ways of capitalizing on expected declines in the value of the U.S. dollar vis-a-vis foreign currencies. Generally, foreign investment activity has picked up with deregulation of foreign markets, improved communications, and increased internationalization of businesses, banks, and broker-dealers.

Problems that remain, depending on the issue and the market, include inadequate financial information and regulation; high minimum purchase requirements; additional transaction costs and risks; taxes; possible illiquidity; political risk; and the possibility of currency losses. Unless you are wealthy, able to take big risks, and sophisticated in the ways of international interest rates and foreign exchange, you are better advised to achieve international diversification through open-end and closed-end funds or other investment pools specializing in foreign securities.

An exception for some investors might be American Depositary Receipts (ADRs). Many foreign stocks can be owned by way of these negotiable receipts, which are issued by United States banks and represent actual shares held in their foreign branches. ADRs are actively traded on the major stock exchanges and in the over-the-counter market. Although currency risks and foreign withholding taxes remain, the depositary pays dividends and capital gains in U.S. dollars and handles rights offerings, splits, stock dividends, and other corporate actions. ADRs eliminate trading inconveniences and custodial problems that otherwise exist with foreign stocks.

Eurobonds—bonds issued by governments and their agencies, banks, international institutions, and corporations (U.S. and foreign) and sold outside their countries through international syndicates for purchase by international investors—also warrant a special word. They may be denominated in foreign currencies, Eurodollars, or composite currency units, such as Special Drawing Rights (SDRs) or European Units of Account (EUAs) whose certificates representing the combined value of two or more currencies are designed to minimize the effects of currency fluctuations. Most are fixed-income obligations, but some Eurodollar issues have floating rates tied to the London Interbank Offered Rate (LIBOR). Eurobonds, which are issued in bearer form, attract upscale personal investors because they are available in a wide range of maturities, are not subject to a withholding tax, and offer good liquidity.

New issues of Eurobonds may not be sold legally to United States investors until a 90-day seasoning period has expired. Actually, most United States broker-dealers extend this rule to include all new issues in foreign currencies; foreign banks and broker-dealers are generally more solicitous of United States investors in selling new issues. Except for Yankee bonds, obligations of foreign borrowers issued in the United States and denominated in dollars, foreign bonds are not subject to Securities and Exchange Commission regulation.

* * *

What Are Foreign Stocks and Bonds?

Foreign stocks and bonds are stock of foreign companies listed on foreign exchanges; stock of foreign companies listed on United States exchanges or represented by listed American Depositary Receipts (ADRs); bonds of foreign government entities and corporations, including Eurobonds and nondollar-denominated bonds issued by local syndicates.

Buying, Selling, and Holding

How do I buy and sell foreign stocks and bonds? Through securities broker-dealers with foreign offices or with expertise in foreign markets, and through foreign banks and their American offices. (ADRs and shares traded on U.S. exchanges can be bought and sold through any broker.)

Is there a minimum purchase amount, and what is the price range? ADRs and U.S. exchange-listed foreign stocks trade just like domestic common stock. Minimums on other stocks and bonds vary widely by issue and dealer, but are often high. With the extra risks, diversification is important, which raises the cost even higher. Unless you are wealthy, you should probably opt for one of the mutual funds or other investment vehicles pooling foreign securities.

What fees and charges are involved? Transaction costs can be a significant consideration. They vary depending on many factors, but may include custodial fees, local turnover or transfer taxes, and currency conversion fees, in addition to broker commissions or dealer spreads. Transaction and custodial costs are minimized with ADRs.

Do foreign stocks and bonds mature, expire, or otherwise terminate? Bonds mature, stocks do not. However remote, the risk exists that a sovereign government will confiscate or devalue assets of foreign investors.

Can I sell them quickly? U.S. exchange-listed foreign stocks and ADRs normally enjoy high liquidity. With other foreign securities, illiquidity is often a problem. Even widely held issues are often kept as permanent investments by governments, banks, and other companies and may not trade actively. Canada, England, and Japan have high average turnover on their stock exchanges.

How is market value determined and how do I keep track of it? Economic, market, and monetary (interest-rate) factors affect foreign stock and bond values the same way they do domestic equity and debt securities, though conditions and growth rates differ among countries. Traditionally, foreign stocks, on average, have been less volatile than domestic issues, because issuers tended to be older firms whose stock was held largely by long-term investors. Today, foreign exchanges list a growing number of young, dynamic companies whose shares are actively traded and often quite volatile. *The Wall Street Journal,* the *Financial Times* (London), and other leading newspapers report on major foreign exchanges, as well as ADRs and foreign stocks and bonds traded in domestic markets.

Investment Objectives

Should I buy foreign stocks and bonds if my objective is capital appreciation? Especially in growing economies, stocks offer potential for both capital and currency appreciation. Unless bought at a discount or in a period of declining interest rates, bonds do not appreciate, although gains due to currency movements are possible.

Should I buy them if my objective is income? Yes, but most foreign stocks have lower dividend yields than domestic stocks, and exchange-rate fluctuations are a factor in the expected returns of both stocks and bonds.

To what extent do they protect against inflation? Foreign stocks can hedge inflation to the extent local economies and industry sectors offer better growth prospects than exist in the United States. But gains from dividends and appreciation can be eroded by foreign-exchange losses.

Are they suitable for tax-deferred retirement accounts? Yes.

Can I borrow against them? Yes; quality securities are acceptable collateral at most banks, and banks headquartered in the country of the issuer will often lend higher percentages of value. Foreign stocks listed on American exchanges are subject to Federal Reserve margin requirements.

Risk Considerations

How assured can I be of getting my full investment back? Although more young, growing firms appear every day on foreign exchanges, most shares represent solid issuers and volatility has traditionally been low, so foreign equities, on average, may actually be safer than many domestic issues, assuming no adverse currency fluctuations. Bondholders, who lack regulatory protection and full credit information, have more credit risk than owners of domestic issues, in addition to having political, interest rate, and currency risks. (Foreign exchange risk can be hedged using currency futures and options.)

How assured is my income? Since issuers tend to be established, reputable firms or governments, there have historically been few defaults on payments of interest or instances of omitted dividends. On the other hand, a lack of full financial disclosure and regulatory supervision makes it difficult to anticipate adverse financial developments. Also, many newer companies, whose securities are riskier than those of traditional foreign issuers, are likewise listed on foreign exchanges. Foreign-exchange risk can also affect income.

Are there any other risks unique to this investment? Political or sovereign risk—the risk, for example, that foreign assets might be expropriated or devalued or that local tax policies might adversely affect debt or equity holders; the risk of transactional losses caused by settlement delays or fraud; with stock not registered with the Securities and Exchange Commission, there are legal difficulties for Americans in subscribing to rights offerings, a fact which can also affect the salability of rights (rights problems do not exist with ADRs or U.S. exchange-listed foreign shares).

Are they commercially rated? Some foreign debt issues are rated. Information can be found in a publication called *Credit Week International,* available at some larger brokerage firms.

Tax Considerations

What tax advantages (or disadvantages) do they offer? Some countries impose a withholding tax, typically from 15% to 20%, on dividends and interest (except Eurobonds). U.S. tax treaties can result in partial reclamation of withholdings in some countries, and the tax can be offset to some extent against federal income taxes. There is usually no capital gains tax imposed by foreign governments, though such gains are taxed by the U.S. government. Special rules apply to 10% or more ownership of a foreign corporation.

Economic Considerations

What economic factors most affect buy, hold, or sell decisions? Foreign securities are best bought when the U.S. dollar is strong against the currency of denomination. To profit from currency movements (or, conversely, to avoid losses) it is best to hold when the dollar is declining against the local currency. Foreign equities are attractive relative to American investments when the foreign economy or industrial sector has a better outlook than its domestic counterpart. Foreign bonds rise and fall in inverse relation to market interest rates.

FUTURES CONTRACT ON A COMMODITY

A futures contract is a commitment to buy or sell a specified quantity of a commodity or financial instrument at a specified price during a particular delivery month. Once restricted largely to agricultural commodities and metals, futures contracts have in recent years been extended to include what are broadly termed financial futures—contracts on debt instruments, such as Treasury bonds and Government National Mortgage Association ("Ginnie Mae") certificates and on foreign currencies—and, even more recently, contracts on stock indexes. Contract prices are determined through open outcry—a system of verbal communication between sellers and buyers on the floors of regulated commodities exchanges.

The futures markets are broadly divided into two categories of participants: (1) Hedgers have a position in (i.e., own) the underlying commodity or instrument (such as a farmer in the case of an agricultural commodity or an investor in the case of a financial or index future). Hedgers use futures to create countervailing positions, thus protecting against loss due to price (or rate) changes. (2) Speculators do not own the underlying asset for commercial or investment purposes, but instead aim to capitalize on the ups and downs (the volatility) of the contracts themselves. It is the speculators who provide the liquidity essential to the efficient operation of the futures markets.

As with option contracts, which are also discussed in this section, the great majority of futures contracts are closed out before their expiration—or delivery—date. This is done by buying or selling an offsetting contract. It is vital to note that with futures, in contrast to options (which simply expire), the alternative to an offset is a delivery, though this is done with title documentation or, in the case of index futures, cash, not by the legendary dumping of pork bellies on the front steps of absentminded contract holders. When the future is a contract to buy value, delivery of the future is avoided by buying an offsetting future to sell.

The attraction of futures for speculators, again like options, is the enormous leverage they provide. Although brokers normally require investors to meet substantial net worth and income requirements, it is possible to trade contracts with outlays of cash (or sometimes U.S. Treasury securities) equal to 5% to 10% of contract values. Such "margins" (actually good-faith deposits, more in the nature of performance bonds and required of both buyers and sellers) are set by the exchanges, although brokers normally have their own maintenance requirements. Margin calls are normally made when deposits drop to one half the original percentage value.

The commodity exchanges, with oversight by the Commodities Futures Trading Commission (CFTC), each day set limits, based on the previous day's closing price, to the extent a given contract's trading price may vary. While these trading limits help preclude exaggerated short-term volatility and thus make it possible for margin requirements to be kept low, they can also lock a trader into a losing position, where he must meet a margin call but is prevented from trading out of the position because the contract is either up limit or down limit (as high or as low as the daily limit permits it to be traded).

Speculators in futures contracts fall into three groups: (1) the exchange floor traders (scalpers), who make markets in contracts and turn small profits usually within the trading day; (2) spread traders, who hope to profit from offsetting positions in contracts having different maturities but the same underlying commodity or instrument, similar maturities but different (although usually closely related) underlying commodities, or similar contracts in different markets; and (3) position traders, who have the expertise and financial ability to analyze longer-term factors and ride out shorter term fluctuations in the expectation of ultimate gains.

While speculation in futures contracts is not recommended for the average investor, individuals with the money and risk tolerance may participate by choosing among the following alternatives: trading for one's own account, which involves time and expertise; trading through a managed account or a discretionary account with a commodities broker, which utilizes a professional's time and expertise for a fee or sometimes involves a participation in profits; or mutual funds, which offer both professional management and diversification and are regulated by both the CFTC and the Securities and Exchange Commission.

*　*　*

What Is a Commodity Futures Contract?

A commodity futures contract is an agreement to buy or sell a specific amount of a commodity at a particular price in a stipulated future month.

Buying, Selling, and Holding

How do I buy and sell it? Through a full-service broker or firm specializing in commodities transactions.

Is there a minimum purchase amount, and what is the price range? Contract sizes and unit prices vary widely from commodity to commodity, but the exchanges have liberal margin rules making it possible to trade with as little as 5% to 10% down. In some commodities, that can be $100, but brokers often have minimum deposits of $1000 to $2500. (They may also have strict personal income and net worth rules for investors.) One national exchange, the Mid-America Commodity Exchange, offers minicontracts in a number of commodities, currencies, and instruments; they range from one fifth to one half the size of regular contracts.

What fees and charges are involved? Broker commissions, which vary by contract but average $25 to $50 for a round-turn (buy and sell) trade with lower rates for intraday and spread (e.g., buy soybeans, sell soybean oil) transactions. Managed accounts involve management fees and, sometimes, participation in profits.

Does a commodity futures contract mature, expire, or otherwise terminate? Yes. All contracts have a stipulated expiration date.

Can I sell it quickly? Most established contracts are liquid, though daily price limits can create illiquidity when a commodity is down limit or up limit (as high or as low as the daily trading limit permits).

How is market value determined and how do I keep track of it? By supply and demand, which is affected by natural causes as well as general economic developments. Futures prices are quoted daily in the financial pages of newspapers and electronic databases.

Investment Objectives

Should I buy a commodity futures contract if my objective is capital appreciation? Only if you are expert, wealthy, and have a high tolerance for risk. Then, with the high leverage possible, capital gains (and losses) can be huge.

Should I buy this if my objective is income? No. Contracts pay no income.

To what extent does it protect against inflation ? Forward commodity prices reflect inflation expectations, but since contracts are short-term oriented, inflation protection is a secondary consideraton.

Is it suitable for tax-deferred retirement accounts? Although not prohibited by the Internal Revenue Service, most brokerage firms rule out futures contracts as too risky for retirement accounts. They may have a limited role in managed accounts, primarily as a hedging tool. Certain pooled investment vehicles trading in futures may be appropriate in selected situations for people with high risk tolerance.

Can I borrow against it? Futures are not acceptable collateral with most lenders. Of course, they provide leverage inherently because of the relatively small deposits required to control contracts.

Risk Considerations

How assured can I be of getting my full investment back? Commodity futures are inherently speculative and it is actually possible to lose more than your investment (though margin calls would usually limit losses to the amount deposited if the account was sold out—that is, liquidated by the broker to meet the margin call).

How assured is my income? Futures provide no income.

Are there any other risks unique to this investments? The possibility of losses in excess of investment and the risk of illiquidity when a contract is down or up limit (thus making it impossible to trade out of a position) are risks unique to commodity futures trading. Of course, there is the risk (nightmare?) of actual delivery of a commodity if you fail to close out a position prior to expiration of a contract.

Is it commercially rated? No.

Tax Considerations

What tax advantages (or disadvantages) does a commodity futures contract offer? Speculators' open positions are marked to market at year end and paper profits and losses taxed as though realized. Sixty percent of profits are taxed as long-term capital gains and 40% at short-term (ordinary income) rates. Other tax treatments apply to nonspeculative and hedging uses and tax advice is recommended.

Economic Considerations

What economic factors most affect buy, hold, and sell decisions? Anything that affects supply and demand for a commodity makes contract values move up and down.

FUTURES CONTRACT ON AN INTEREST RATE

For a general discussion of a futures contract, see Futures Contract on a Commodity.

* * *

What Is a Futures Contract on an Interest Rate?

A futures contract on an interest rate is an agreement to buy or sell a given amount of a fixed-income security, such as a Treasury bill, bond, or note or Government National Mortgage Association security at a particular price in a stipulated future month.

Buying, Selling, and Holding

How do I buy and sell it? Through a full-service broker or firm specializing in commodities transactions.

Is there a minimum purchase amount, and what is the price range? Contract sizes vary with the underlying security and the exchange, but range from $20,000 to $1 million; since exchange margin rules allow trading with as little as 5% deposited, the actual cost of investing can be relatively low.

What fees and charges are involved? Broker commissions averaging $25 to $50 per contract transaction.

Does it mature, expire, or otherwise terminate? Yes; futures contracts have specific expiration dates.

Can I sell it quickly? Yes, except that liquidity may become a problem if the contract reaches the maximum price movement allowable in one day, in effect locking you into a position.

How is market value determined and how do I keep track of it? By market interest rate movements, essentially. When rates go up, the prices of fixed-income securities (and futures related to them) go down, and vice versa. Prices are reported daily in newspapers and electronic databases.

Investment Objectives

Should I buy a futures contract on an interest rate if my objective is capital appreciation? Speculators use the leverage available with futures to capitalize on expected interest rate movements, standing to gain (or lose) substantially more than the amount invested.

Should I buy this if my objective is income? No, though you might use futures to hedge the value of securities bought for income or to lock in the yield on a security to be bought at a later date.

To what extent does it protect against inflation? To the extent inflation expectations are a factor in the volatility of fixed-income investments, futures can offer some protection against loss.

Is it suitable for tax-deferred retirement accounts? Although not prohibited by the Internal Revenue Service, most brokerage firms rule out futures contracts as too risky for retirement accounts. They may have a limited role in managed accounts, primarily as a hedging tool. Certain pooled investment vehicles trading in futures may be appropriate in selected situations for people with high risk tolerance.

Can I borrow against it? No; futures contracts are not acceptable collateral at most lenders. Of course, there is considerable leverage inherent in the small deposit required to control contracts.

Risk Considerations

How assured can I be of getting my full investment back? Just as interest rate movements cannot be predicted with certainty, interest rate futures can result in losses as well as gains; it is in fact possible to lose more than your investment (called open-ended risk) but margin calls would normally limit losses to the amount invested, assuming the account was sold out (liquidated) to meet the call.

How assured is my income? Futures do not provide income.

Are there any other risks unique to this investment? Open-ended risk and the risk of illiquidity when a contract is down limit or up limit, making it impossible to trade out of a position, are risks unique to futures contracts.

Is it commercially rated? No.

Tax Considerations

What tax advantages (or disadvantages) does it offer? Speculators' open positions are marked to market at year end and paper profits and losses taxed as though realized. Sixty percent of profits are taxed as long-term capital gains and 40% at short-term (ordinary income) rates. Other tax treatments apply to nonspeculative and hedging uses and tax advice is recommended.

Economic Considerations

What economic factors most affect buy, hold, and sell decisions? Economic and monetary factors affecting interest rates govern choices having to do with interest rate futures.

FUTURES CONTRACT ON A STOCK INDEX

For a general discussion of a futures contract, see Futures Contract on a Commodity.

* * *

What Is a Futures Contract on a Stock Index?

A futures contract on a stock index is an agreement to buy or sell a stock index at a price based on the index value in a stipulated future month with settlement in cash.

Buying, Selling, and Holding

How do I buy and sell it? Through a full-service broker or firm specializing in commodities transactions.

Is there a minimum purchase amount, and what is the price range? Contracts are priced according to formulas based on index values, and vary in terms both of formulas and index values. For example, the contracts on the New York Stock Exchange Composite Index, the Standard & Poor's 500 Stock Index, and The Value Line Stock Index are priced by multiplying $500 times the index value, which ranges roughly between 100 and 300; if one of those indexes had a value of

200, a contract would cost $100,000, which might require a deposit of 10% or $10,000. To play, though, you would probably have to meet an income and liquid net worth test requiring substantial means.

What fees and charges are involved? Broker commissions.

Does it mature, expire, or otherwise terminate? Yes, all contracts have specific expirations.

Can I sell it quickly? Yes, except that liquidity may become a problem if the contract reaches the maximum price movement allowable in one day (i.e., becomes down limit or up limit).

How is market value determined and how do I keep track of it? By the market performance of the stocks comprising the index as they affect the index value. Index futures are reported with other futures prices in the financial pages of daily newspapers and electronic databases.

Investment Objectives

Should I buy a futures contract on a stock index if my objective is capital appreciation? Speculators use the leverage available with futures to capitalize on expected market movements, standing to gain (or lose) substantially more than the amount invested.

Should I buy this if my objective is income? No, but they are used, mainly by professionals, to hedge the value of income-producing stocks.

To what extent does it protect against inflation? This is not an investment you would hold as an inflation hedge.

Is it suitable for tax-deferred retirement accounts? Although not prohibited by the Internal Revenue Service, most brokerage firms rule out futures contracts as too risky for retirement accounts. They may have a limited role in managed accounts, primarily as a hedging tool. Certain pooled investment vehicles trading in futures may be appropriate in selected situations for people with high risk tolerance.

Can I borrow against it? No; futures are not acceptable collateral at most lenders. Of course, there is considerable leverage inherent in the relatively small deposit required to control contracts.

Risk Considerations

How assured can I be of getting my full investment back? Just as market movements cannot be predicted with certainty, index futures can result in losses as well as gains; in fact, it is quite possible to lose more than your investment (called open-ended risk), although margin calls are a safeguard against losses in excess of investment if an account is sold out (liquidated) to meet the call.

How assured is my income? Index futures do not provide income.

Are there any other risks unique to this investment? Index futures and the individual stocks comprising the index may not move exactly together, so it is not a perfect hedging tool.

Is it commercially rated? No.

Tax Considerations

What tax advantages (or disadvantages) does it offer? Speculators' open positions are marked to market at year end and paper profits and losses taxed as though realized. Sixty percent of profits are taxed as long-term capital gains and 40% at short-term (ordinary income) rates. Other tax treatments apply to nonspeculative and hedging uses and tax advice is recommended.

Economic Considerations

What economic factors most affect buy, hold, and sell decisions? The myriad factors affecting the market outlook affect choices having to do with stock index futures, whether they are used to speculate or as a hedging tool.

GOVERNMENT AGENCY SECURITY

Government agency securities, popularly called agencies, are indirect obligations of the United States government, issued by federal agencies and government-sponsored corporations under authority from the United States Congress, but, with a few exceptions, not backed, as U.S. Treasury securities are, by the full faith and credit of the government.

While it is highly unlikely—even unthinkable—that they could ever be allowed to default on principal or interest, these agency securities cannot be considered absolutely risk-free, and therein lies their attraction—because of the slight difference in safety, they generally yield as much as a half percentage point more than direct obligations.

Agencies are also, like Treasuries, exempt from state and local taxes, although there are exceptions—for example, securities guaranteed by the Government National Mortgage Association (GNMA), and issues of the Federal National Mortgage Association (FNMA) and the Federal Home Loan Mortgage Corporation (FHLMC), including both mortgage-backed pass-throughs and bonds and notes issued to finance their operations.

Unlike Treasuries, agencies are not sold by auction but rather are marketed at the best yield possible by the Federal Reserve Bank of New York, as fiscal agent, through its network of primary dealers. Information can be obtained from the Federal Reserve Bank of New York, Treasury and Agency Issues Division, from the issuing agencies, or from dealer commercial banks and securities brokers.

Agencies that have issued or guaranteed securities include:

Asian Development Bank

College Construction Loan Insurance Corporation (Connie Lee)

District of Columbia Armory Board (D.C. Stadium)

Export-Import Bank of the United States

Farm Credit Financial Assistance Corporation

Farmers Home Administration

Federal Agricultural Mortgage Corporation (Farmer Mac)

Federal Farm Credit Consolidated System-Wide Securities

Federal Home Loan Bank

Federal Home Loan Mortgage Corporation

Federal Housing Administration (FHA)

Federal National Mortgage Association (FNMA)

Financing Corp. (FICO)

Government National Mortgage Association (GNMA)

Interamerican Development Bank

International Bank for Reconstruction and Development (World Bank)

Maritime Administration

Resolution Funding Corporation (Refcorp.)

Resolution Trust Corporation (RTC)

Small Business Administration (SBA)

Student Loan Marketing Association (SLMA)

Tennessee Valley Authority (TVA)

United States Postal Service

Washington Metropolitan Area Transit Authority

* * *

What Is a Government Agency Security?

A government agency security is a negotiable debt obligation of an agency of the United States government, which may be backed by the full faith and credit of the federal government but is more often guaranteed by the sponsoring agency with the implied backing of Congress.

Buying, Selling, and Holding

How do I buy and sell it? Through a securities broker-dealer or at many commercial banks.

Is there a minimum purchase amount, and what is the price range? Denominations and minimums vary widely from $1000 to $25,000 and up, depending on the issue, the issuing agency, and the dealer.

What fees and charges are involved? None in the case of new issues bought from a member of the underwriting group; otherwise a commission or dealer markup.

Does it mature, expire, or otherwise terminate? Yes, maturities range from 30 days to 25 years.

Can I sell it quickly? Yes, but bid and asked spreads tend to be wider than with direct Treasury obligations, which raises the cost of trading in the secondary market.

How is market value determined and how do I keep track of it? Market values vary inversely with market interest rate movements. Daily newspapers, brokers, and large banks provide price information.

Investment Objectives

Should I buy a government agency security if my objective is capital appreciation? No, though appreciation is possible when fixed-rate securities are bought prior to a drop in market interest rates.

Should I buy this if my objective is income? Yes. Yields are a bit higher than those of direct government obligations, but lower than those of corporate obligations.

To what extent does it protect against inflation? As fixed-income securities, agencies offer no protection, though shorter-term issues offer less exposure to inflation risk.

Is it suitable for tax-deferred retirement accounts? Yes.

Can I borrow against it? Yes; lenders will often lend 90% of value.

Risk Considerations

How assured can I be of getting my full investment back? Agencies are second only to Treasury securities as good credit risks. Market prices fall as interest rates rise, however, so you may not get a full return of principal if you sell in the secondary market prior to maturity. Some sophisticated investors hedge market risk using options, futures, and futures options that are available on certain Treasury securities and Government National Mortgage Association securities.

How assured is my income? Very assured. It is highly unlikely the U.S. Treasury, Congress, or a regulatory body like the Federal Reserve Board would allow a government agency to default on interest.

Are there any other risks unique to a government agency security? No, but mortgage-backed pass-through securities issued by government-sponsored entities have different characteristics and are covered separately in this section.

Is it commercially rated? Some issues are rated by major services.

Tax Considerations

What tax advantages (or disadvantages) does it offer? Agencies are fully taxable at the federal level but are exempt from state and local taxes with certain exceptions, such as issues of the Federal National Mortgage Association and the Government National Mortgage Association.

Economic Considerations

What economic factors most affect buy, hold, or sell decisions? It is best to buy when interest rates are high and the best yields can be obtained. Holding is most attractive when rates are declining, causing an upward move in the market values of fixed-income securities, and high inflation is not present to erode the value of fixed returns.

LIFE INSURANCE (CASH VALUE)

For young families as yet without sufficient financial security to provide for expenses in the event of the premature death of the breadwinner or homemaker, life insurance provides essential protection. By far the cheapest and simplest way to obtain that protection is *term life insurance,* a no-frills deal whereby premiums buy insurance but do not create cash value. The alternatives—variously called cash value, straight, whole, permanent, or ordinary life insurance—combine protection with an investment program.

The traditional cash value policy requires a fixed premium for the life of the insured and promises a fixed sum of money on the death of the insured. A portion of the premium covers expenses and actual insurance, the rest earns interest in a tax-deferred savings program, gradually building up a cash value. The latter can be cashed in by canceling the policy (hence the term "cash surrender value"), can be used to buy more protection, or can be borrowed at a below-market or even zero interest rate with the loan balance deducted from the death benefit. On the death of the insured, the beneficiary receives only the death benefit.

Variations called single-premium or limited-payment life policies, have higher up-front premiums so that a policy becomes paid-up—the cash value becomes sufficient to cover the death benefit without further premiums. Later, if the insured is still living, the policy begins paying benefits that can supplement retirement income or be converted to an annuity, thus guaranteeing income for life.

The one serious drawback of cash value policies has been that the interest rate is not competitive with other investments. With soaring interest rates and inflation in the 1970s and in the excitement of new investment products spawned by deregulation in the 1980s, upwardly mobile young investors began questioning the value of insurance policies providing neither competitive investment returns nor the flexibility their dynamic personal financial circumstances required. Faced with cancellations and poor sales, insurers came forth with the following:

> *Universal Life,* which clearly separates the cash value and protection elements of the policy and invests the cash value in a tax-deferred savings program tied to a money market rate. The cost of the insurance is fixed, based on the insured's age and sex, so depending on what the cash value portion earns (it is guaranteed to earn a minimum rate, but can earn more if market rates rise), the premium can vary. The insured may also change the amount of protection at any time. Flexibility is the main feature of this type of policy.

> *Variable Life,* which has a fixed premium like straight life, but the cash value goes into a choice of stock, bond, or money market portfolios, which the investor can alternate. The insurer guarantees a minimum death benefit regardless of portfolio performance, although excess gains buy additional coverage. The attraction here is capital growth opportunity.

> *Universal Variable Life,* a mid-1980s innovation that combines the flexibility of universal life with the growth potential of variable life.

Even with modern policies, however, the question persists: Why sacrifice a portion of income to an insurance company when pure protection can be more cheaply obtained through term insurance and returns as good or better can be obtained by investing directly? The answer depends on an individual's expertise, self-confidence, and willingness to spend time managing investments.

*   *   *

What Is Cash Value Life Insurance?

Cash value life insurance is a contract combining payment to beneficiaries, in the event of the insured's premature death, with investment programs.

Buying, Selling, and Holding

How do I buy and sell it? Through insurance brokers, insurance company sales agents, savings institutions, full-service brokers, commercial banks, financial planners, and other financial services organizations.

Is there a minimum purchase amount, and what is the price range? Annual premiums vary widely with the type of policy and such factors as the age and sex of the insured.

What fees and charges are involved? Cost of coverage, sales commissions, and insurance company operating costs are built into premiums. Some policies have penalties for cancellation before specified dates.

Does it mature, expire, or otherwise terminate? Policies mature in 10 years to life, depending on the program.

Can I sell it quickly? Yes. Policies can be canceled and cash values claimed anytime (although actual payment may require several weeks of processing time).

How is market value determined and how do I keep track of it? Policies are not traded in a secondary market. Cash values are determined by accumulated premiums plus investment income and performance.

Investment Objectives

Should I buy cash value life insurance if my objective is capital appreciation? Assuming death benefits are your primary objective, you might buy a variable life insurance policy or a universal variable life insurance policy with investments in a stock fund to gain capital appreciation.

Should I buy this if my objective is income? No, although policies combining annuities provide for income payments on annuitization.

To what extent does it protect against inflation? Universal, variable, and universal variable policies can offer some inflation protection through adjustable death benefits and the investment of cash values in inflation-sensitive securities.

Is it suitable for tax deferred retirement accounts? No; life insurance is not an eligible investment.

Can I borrow against it? Yes. Insurance companies will normally loan cash value at lower-than-market rates and reduce the death benefit by the amount of the loan.

Risk Considerations

How assured can I be of getting my full investment back? Insurance companies are highly regulated and there is little risk they will not meet commitments. However, policies that provide for market returns on cash value investments also carry market risk: e.g., a variable life policy invested in a bond fund would lose cash value if interest rates rose, while one invested in stocks would lose in a down market.

How assured is my income? That depends on how cash values are invested. Policies that invest cash value in money market instruments, for example, are subject to fluctuating income.

Are there any other risks unique to cash value life insurance? Although heavily regulated, insurance companies are potentially subject to mismanagement and fraud and are not themselves covered by federal protection in the sense that banks, for example, are covered by the Federal Deposit Insurance Corporation.

Is it commercially rated? Yes. Insurance companies are rated by Best's Rating Service.

Tax Considerations

What tax advantages (or disadvantages) does it offer? Income earned on cash value accumulates and compounds tax-deferred. Though subject to federal estate taxes (after a $600,000 exclusion) and local inheritance taxes, life insurance proceeds paid to a named beneficiary avoid probate. Proceeds to beneficiaries are normally not subject to federal income taxes. Single-premium life insurance, which offers tax-free cash value accumulation and tax-free access to funds in the form of policy loans, was one of the few tax shelters to survive the Tax Reform Act of 1986. In 1987, however, tax legislation made tax-free borrowings possible only when a test is met requiring substantial insurance coverage relative to premiums over a lengthy time period.

Economic Considerations

What economic factors most affect buy, hold, and sell decisions? Inflation and volatility of interest rates gave rise to life insurance policies whose cash values vary with market conditions. Investors concerned about such factors can choose among such "new breed" alternatives, rather than buying traditional fixed-rate policies, and make their choices based on their expectations. Thus an investor anticipating high inflation and high interest rates would not choose a variable life policy invested in fixed-income bonds but might choose one with a stock fund or one that is money market-oriented. Variable and universal variable life insurance permit switching between bond, stock, and money market funds to afford maximum market flexibility.

LIMITED PARTNERSHIP (LP)

The unique feature of a limited partnership is that financial and tax events flow directly through to individual investors. Until 1987 this meant that limited partners in real estate ventures, oil and gas projects, and other activities could use liberal tax benefits such as depreciation, depletion, intangible drilling costs, and tax credits, as well as operating losses, as deductions against taxable income from wages and investment income. With aggressive marketing by brokers and financial planners, LPs attracted some $100 billion of funds from 12 million investors in the 1980s.

The Tax Reform Act of 1986 severely curtailed the use of LPs as tax shelters by ruling that losses from "passive" sources, like LPs, could be used only against passive income. And while some "economic programs"—those LPs emphasizing income, appreciation, and safety—have continued to provide attractive returns, their ability to shelter cash flow has been lessened by reduced benefits, notably the elimination of accelerated depreciation of real property and the repeal of the investment credit. In the 1990s, partnerships were offered, but in much lower volumes since the partnership form of ownership had been largely discredited.

A limited partnership is an organization comprising a general partner with unlimited liability, who is both sponsor and manager, and limited partners, who provide most of the capital, have limited liability, and have no active management role. Most LPs aim to sell or refinance their assets within seven to ten years and distribute proceeds to shareholders.

Limited partnerships may be private, which are restricted to small numbers of wealthy investors and not required to register with the Securities and Exchange Commission, or public, which market shares in typical amounts of $1000 to $5000 to as many limited partners as the sponsor desires. Public LPs must register with the SEC and provide investors with a prospectus and other disclosures.

Limited partnerships are also distinguished in terms of their use of leverage to finance assets. *Leveraged programs,* whose assets are financed 50% or more with borrowed money, offer greater tax benefits because (1) with a larger asset base they generate more deductions, such as depreciation, and because (2) the interest is deductible. *Unleveraged programs* are favored by investors seeking maximum income and less risk.

From the investor's standpoint, one drawback of limited partnerships traditionally has been lack of liquidity. Although a growing number of independent investment firms buy and sell partnership shares, they represent more of a distress market than a formal secondary market for shares. While some sponsors offer market-making services to investors under some circumstances, the selling of shares during the life of the partnership is generally discouraged.

Inspired by investor reservations about the future of tax-advantaged partnerships after tax reform, some sponsors in the mid-1980s began marketing programs featuring depositary receipts, which represent unit interests and can be traded in the open marketplace. Liquidity provided this way is a feature of *master limited partnerships,* a mid-1980s innovation in which corporate assets or private partnerships are reorganized as public limited partnerships combining various objectives. Master limited partnerships, however, were deemed taxable as corporations starting in 1998 and most converted to corporate form in advance of that deadline.

* * *

What Is a Limited Partnership?

A limited partnership is a form of business organization, having any of a variety of activities and investment objectives, which is made up of a general partner who organizes and manages the partnership and its operations, and limited partners who contribute capital, have limited liability, and assume no active role in day-to-day business affairs.

Buying, Selling, and Holding

How do I buy and sell it? Unit shares are bought through a securities broker-dealer or financial planner. There is no official secondary market, although some sponsors agree to make markets under certain circumstances and a number of firms trade in partnership shares at distress prices.

Is there a minimum purchase amount, and what is the price range? Public limited partnerships usually have a $1000 to $5000 minimum, with a $2000 minimum for IRAs. Private limited partnerships require at least $20,000. Offerings frequently involve suitability rules, requiring that individuals meet minimum net worth, income, and tax bracket criteria.

What fees and charges are involved? Brokerage commissions and other front-end costs, often totaling 20% or more of the amount invested. There may be additional management fees during the partnership's operating phase.

Does it mature, expire, or otherwise terminate? Most partnerships intend to dispose of their holdings within a specified period (7 to 10 years typically) and distribute the proceeds as capital gains to investors.

Can I sell it quickly? Usually not. There is no secondary market for partnership shares, although some sponsors offer to try to make a market to accommodate investors under certain circumstances. Certain private firms buy LP shares from holders, but the price for this kind of marketability can be high. Some partnerships offer liquidity through depositary receipts, which represent shares and are traded in secondary markets.

How is market value determined and how do I keep track of it? There is no active secondary market for limited partnerships shares and independent firms that buy shares pay widely varying and deeply discounted prices.

The 1986 Tax Act required that sponsors provide annual valuation reports for LPs held in IRAs, and some sponsors provide valuations to all shareholders. Valuation standards are not uniform, however. Industry guidelines recommend that interests be valued at cost for the first three years (even if a high percentage of cost is sales charges unrelated to asset values) and at asset values thereafter; asset appraisals however, may be independent or "direct," meaning estimates are made by the sponsor.

In any event, share values to be ultimately realized as capital gains are affected by various factors, depending on the activities of the partnership and assets it holds.

Investment Objectives

Should I buy a share in a limited partnership if my objective is capital appreciation? Certain types of partnerships emphasize capital gains potential; others do not. Those offering the greatest potential are the riskiest.

Should I buy this if my objective is income? Yes, though not all partnerships have income as a primary objective and some emphasize the tax sheltering of income from other passive sources.

To what extent does it protect against inflation? Some, like all-cash equity programs with investments in inflation-sensitive real estate, offer high protection. Others, such as programs specializing in fixed-rate mortgages, suffer.

Is it suitable for tax-deferred retirement accounts? Yes.

Can I borrow against it? Because of their low liquidity, partnership shares may not be acceptable as marketable securities with many lenders.

Risk Considerations

How assured can I be of getting my full investment back? Safety of principal depends on the type of partnership and the quality of its holdings. Insured mortgage programs held for the life of the partnership offer high safety, but no appreciation, while leveraged programs aimed at high capital gains involve commensurate risk.

How assured is my income? Only insured mortgage programs offer any real assurance of income. Other income partnerships vary with the type and quality of their portfolios.

Are there any other risks unique to this investment? Yes, because limited partners have no active role in management, everything depends on the integrity and management ability of the general partner. In fact, some partnerships (such as those in real estate) are sold as blind pools—that is, the general partner has not even made property selections at the time that investment is made. Programs set up primarily as tax shelters run the risk of being declared abusive, subjecting the investor to heavy penalties and interest as well as back taxes. A sponsor may postpone liquidation to "ride out" a soft market, thus delaying the payout to holders. LPs bought in the secondary market may have hidden tax liabilities stemming from deductions taken by previous shareholders.

Is it commercially rated? Yes. Standard & Poor's Corporation rates limited partnerships, and several firms, such as Robert A. Stanger & Co., analyze limited partnerships and rate such factors as offering terms.

Tax Considerations

What tax advantages (or disadvantages) does it offer? Tax benefits flow through to limited partners. Losses thus generated through 1986 may be used to offset tax-able income from any source. Since 1986, however, such "passive" losses have been usable only to offset income from other passive sources and not earned or investment income. The provision phased in over five years, so that 35% of passive losses were disallowed in 1987, 60% in 1988, 80% in 1989, 90% in 1990, and 100% in 1991. Net losses are tax preference items. Unused losses may be carried forward, and after offsetting any gain from the disposition of the passive invest-ment, may be used against any other passive investment. Any excess losses then remaining can be generally applied. At risk rules now include real estate. Master limited partnerships were made taxable as corporations after 1998.

Economic Considerations

What economic factors most affect buy, hold, and sell decisions? Because limited partnership investments are generally held for the life of the partnership, hold and sell decisions have limited applicability. Buy decisions should be guided by the outlook for the type of activity in which the partnership specializes and such factors as the expected life of the program and whether it is leveraged or unleveraged.

MONEY MARKET FUND

This special breed of mutual fund gives personal investors the opportunity to own money market instruments that would otherwise be available only to large institu-tional investors. The attraction is higher yields than individuals could obtain on their own or from most bank money market deposit accounts, plus a high degree of safety and excellent liquidity, complete with checkwriting.

Money market funds are sponsored by mutual fund organizations (investment companies), brokerage firms, and institutions, like insurance companies, which sell and redeem shares without any sales charges or commissions. The company charges only an annual management fee, usually under 1%, although extra services may entail additional charges. Income earned from interest-bearing investments is credited and reinvested (in effect compounded) for shareholders on a daily basis.

The disadvantage of money market funds over other short-term investment alternatives is that income (although normally paid out monthly) fluctuates daily as investments in the fund's portfolio mature and are replaced with new investments bearing current interest rates. In a declining rate market, this can be a disadvantage as compared, say, to a certificate of deposit, which would continue to pay an above-market rate until maturity. As a general rule, fund dividend rates lag behind money market rate changes by a month or so, depending on the average length of their ponfolios, which is controlled to an extent by the manager's expectations as to where rates will go. Major sponsors permit switching among different funds in their families.

The market value of a money market fund investment is normally maintained at a constant figure, usually $1 a share. This means capital gains (and the favorable tax treatment they receive) are not a feature of money market funds, though investors may achieve some growth through compounding by opting to reinvest monthly payments.

Funds may differ in terms of the type of securities comprising their portfolios, some specializing only in U.S. Treasury bills or in tax-exempt municipal securities. A general portfolio, however, would typically be comprised of bank and industrial commercial paper, certificates of deposit, acceptances, repurchase agreements, direct and indirect U.S. government obligations, Eurodollar CDs, and other safe and liquid investments. Bonds and foreign debt securities are sometimes included to lift yields.

Money market funds are not covered by federal insurance the way bank deposits are, although funds sponsored by brokerage firms are insured by the Securities Investor Protection Corporation (SIPC) against losses caused by a failure of the firm. Some funds may also be covered by private insurance.

For longer-term investment purposes, alternative investments offer better yield with comparable safety while also providing growth opportunity, tax advantages, and similar inflation protection. The convenience and income of money market funds, although increasingly challenged by bank deposit products, remain attractive for providing for emergencies and for parking temporarily idle cash.

* * *

What Is a Money Market Fund?

A money market fund is a type of mutual fund in which a pool of money is invested in various money market securities (short-term debt instruments) and which compounds interest daily and pays out (or reinvests) dividends to shareholders monthly.

Buying, Selling, and Holding

How do I buy and sell it? Through sponsoring brokerage firms and mutual fund organizations. Accounts are also offered by insurance companies and other financial institutions as a parking place for temporarily idle funds.

Is there a minimum purchase amount, and what is the price range? The minimum investment usually ranges from $500 to $5000. For funds offered through brokers, $1000 is typical; $2500 is a typical minimum investment for funds offered directly by fund sponsors. Additional investment is usually allowed in increments as small as $100.

What fees and charges are involved? Most are no-load (without sales fee), charging only an annual management fee, which is usually less than 1% of the investment. There may be extra fees for special services, such as money transfers.

Does it mature, expire, or otherwise terminate? No.

Can I sell it quickly? Yes. Shares are redeemable anytime and most funds offer checkwriting privileges, though $500 minimums for checks are common.

How is market value determined and how do I keep track of it? Market values of shares are kept constant. Yields change in response to money market conditions as investments turn over and are calculated on a daily basis. Seven and 30-day average yields are reported weekly in the financial pages of newspapers and current information can be obtained directly by calling the sponsoring organizations.

Investment Objectives

Should I buy this if my objective is capital appreciation? No.

Should I buy this if my objective is income? Yes. The attraction of money market funds is that the individuals can earn the same high yields that would otherwise be available only to institutional investors. Of course, income fluctuates and there is little protection against a decline in market rates.

To what extent does it protect against inflation? Because interest rates on newly offered debt instruments rise with inflation, money market funds, being composed of constantly rotating short-term investments, have performed well in inflation and paid dividends that kept pace with rising price levels.

Is it suitable for tax-deferred retirement accounts? Yes.

Can I borrow against it? Yes, banks and brokers will lend a high percentage (often 90%) of the value of your shares.

Risk Considerations

How assured can I be of getting my full investment back? Your investment in a money market fund is quite safe, since portfolios comprise securities of banks, governments, and top corporations. Investors seeking maximum safety can choose funds investing exclusively in U.S. government direct obligations, though at some sacrifice of yield; while this does not mean the fund is guaranteed by Uncle Sam, the fact that its investments are so guaranteed actually does provide a high degree of security. Some funds are privately insured against default.

How assured is my income? While the risk of default is very small, there is no way of preventing fluctuations in money market interest rates. Dividend rates could therefore decline, although the reaction to market rate changes may be more or less delayed, depending on the average maturity of a portfolio. Most fund sponsors permit shifting into other investment vehicles within their families when adverse developments can be foreseen or when better opportunities exist.

Are there any other risks unique to this investment? A fund that invested relatively long-term just prior to a drastic rise in rates could be forced to sell investments at a loss to meet redemptions. Well-managed and established funds are aware of this obvious risk and take measures to avoid it. Overall, the industry, which is regulated by the Securities and Exchange Commission, has enjoyed an excellent safety record.

Is it commercially rated? A number of organizations record past performance and a few predict future yields, but money market funds arc not rated in the sense that bonds and stocks are.

Tax Considerations

What tax advantages (or disadvantages) does it offer? Where portfolios are comprised of tax-exempt securities, investors are exempt from federal taxes and, depending on state laws, possibly state and local taxes. (States may treat tax-exempt funds differently from tax-exempt direct investments.) Otherwise, dividends are fully taxable. Some states that do not tax interest earned on direct investments will tax dividends from funds, even though the fund's income is from interest earned.

Economic Considerations

What economic factors most affect buy, hold and sell decisions? Money market funds are most attractive when short-term interest rates are high and alternative investments are beset with uncertainty. As a rule, investors use money market funds to park cash temporarily, choosing other investments for longer-term purposes.

MORTGAGE-BACKED (PASS-THROUGH) SECURITY

A mortgage-backed (pass-through) security offers one of the best risk/return deals available to investors, plus excellent liquidity. Two drawbacks, though, are that monthly income payments fluctuate and the term of the investment cannot be predicted with certainty.

Pass-through securities represent shares in pools of home mortgages having approximately the same terms and interest rates. They were introduced in the 1960s to make lenders liquid and stimulate home buying.

The process begins when prospective homeowners apply for mortgages to banks, savings and loan associations, and mortgage bankers. The loan paper is sold to intermediaries, such as Freddie Mac or private organizations who repackage it in units represented by certificates, which are marketed to investors. Interest and principal, including prepayments, pass from the homeowner through the intermediary to the investor. When the mortgages mature or are prepaid, the investment expires.

Pass-throughs also enjoy an active secondary market, where securities trade either at discounts or premiums depending on prevailing interest rates. Interestingly, pass-throughs representing pools of low-rate mortgages, when they can be bought favorably to result in attractive yields, are the most desirable holdings because the prepayment risk is low.

The following are principal mortgage-backed securities:

> *Government National Mortgage Association (GNMA):* Ginnie Maes are the most widely held pass-throughs and are backed by Federal Housing Administration (FHA)-insured and Veterans Administration (VA) guaranteed mortgages plus the general guarantee of GNMA, which (by virtue of rulings of the Treasury and Justice departments) brings the full faith and credit of the U.S. government behind these securities. They are as safe as Treasury bonds but typically yield 1% to 2% higher.

> *Federal Home Loan Mortgage Corporation (FHLMC):* Freddie Mac PCs (Participation Certificates) are backed by both FHA and VA

mortgages and privately insured conventional mortgages plus the general guarantee of FHLMC, a privately managed public institution owned by the Federal Home Loan Bank Board System members. With less safety, PCs yield 15–40 basis points more than GNMAs.

Federal National Mortgage Association (FNMA): Fannie Mae MBSs (Mortgage-Backed Securities) are issued and guaranteed by FNMA, a government-sponsored, publicly held (NYSE-traded) company, and backed by both conventional and FHA and VA mortgages. They are essentially similar to Freddie Macs and tend to have similar yields.

Private mortgage participation certificates issued by lending institutions or conduit firms have varying characteristics and different ratings, depending on such factors as private mortgage insurance, cash-fund backing, and over-collateralization (the extent to which the market values of underlying properties exceed the mortgages). These include jumbo pools of mortgages trom different lenders.

Collateralized mortgage obligations (CMOs), a variation, are instruments, technically mortgage-backed bonds, that break up mortgage pools into separate maturity classes, called tranches. This is accomplished by applying mortgage income first to the bonds with the shortest maturity. Tranches pay different rates of interest and typically mature in 2, 5, 10, and 20 years. Issued by Freddie Mac and private issuers, CMOs are usually backed by government-guaranteed or other top-grade mortgages and most have AAA bond ratings. For a slight sacrifice of yield, CMOs lessen anxiety about the uncertain term of pass-through investments.

Variations exist on CMOs that are really too sophisticated for most individual investors to risk owning. These include Z tranches having characteristics of zero-coupon bonds, multiple Z tranches, Y tranches with sinking fund features, and even equity CMOs representing residual cash flows.

Real estate mortgage investment conduits (REMICs), still another variation, created by the Tax Reform Act of 1986. REMICs offer issuers, who may be government or private entities, more flexibility than CMOs and protection from double taxation, which CMOs have avoided with legal technicalities. They are thus able to separate mortgage pools not only into maturity classes but also into classes of risk. The practical effect of this has been that whereas CMOs have financed top-quality mortgages in order to obtain AAA ratings, REMICs have been used to finance mortgages of lesser quality, even some that are financially distressed. More often than not, a REMIC obligation in the late 1980s was a high-yield, junk mortgage bond.

More exceptions are being created all the time. Fannie Mae routinely issues REMIC-backed Ginnie Mae pass-throughs. They are divided into many parts with many average lives and a wide range of yields.

Strips: Mortgage-backed securities are also stripped and sold as zero-coupon securities. See the section on zero coupon securities for a discussion of this alternative.

* * *

What Is a Mortgage-Backed (Pass-Through) Security?

A mortgage-backed security is a share in an organized pool of residential mortgages, the principal and interest payments on which are passed through to shareholders, usually monthly. The category includes collateralized mortgage obligations (CMOs), technically mortgage-backed bonds, which provide for different maturities, and real estate mortgage investment conduits (REMICs), which provide for both separate maturity and separate risk classes. It does not include mortgage-backed securities that are corporate bonds or government agency securities and are covered in those sections.

Buying, Selling, and Holding

Where do I buy and sell it? At a securities broker-dealer.

Is there a minimum purchase amount, and what is the price range? Most new pass-throughs are sold in minimum amounts of $25,000, although some older issues can be bought with less and some private issues and CMOs and REMICs can be bought for as little as $1000. Shares of funds, limited partnerships, and unit investment trusts that buy such securities range from $1000–$5000.

What fees and charges are involved? This varies among vehicles and brokers, but can be either a flat fee or a dealer spread. Sponsors deduct modest fees from passed-through income.

Does it mature, expire, or otherwise terminate? Yes, the life of a pool, and its related securities, ends when the mortgages mature or are prepaid. CMOs and REMICs offer investors a choice of earlier or later payouts.

Can I sell it quickly? Yes, liquidity is very good.

How is market value determined and how do I keep track of it? Market value, to the extent mortgage pools have fixed-rate obligations, goes up when market interest rates go down, and vice versa. On the other hand, prepayments rise when rates decline, shrinking the pool and lowering share values. Daily price and yield information is published in the financial pages of newspapers and in electronic databases.

Investment Objectives

Should I buy this if my objective is capital appreciation? Although most investors plan to hold for the life of the issue, capital appreciation is possible as the result of declining market interest rates.

Should I buy this if my objective is income? Yes; mortgage pass-throughs generally offer good yields. The most conservative, Ginnie Maes, normally yield at least 1% more than U.S. Treasury bonds and have the same safety from default. CMOs and REMICs pay slightly lower yields than straight pass-throughs with comparable risk characteristics.

To what extent does it protect against inflation? Because they are based largely on fixed-income mortgages, pass-throughs suffer in high inflation.

Is it suitable for tax-deferred retirement accounts? Yes; except for rollovers, however, the minimum investments exceed IRA limits.

Can I borrow against it? Yes.

Risk Considerations

How assured can I be of getting my full investment back? Although some issues are safer than others (Ginnie Maes are U.S. government-guaranteed against default on underlying mortgages, for example) most pass-throughs are either government-sponsored or otherwise insured in addition to being over-collateralized (i.e., the market value of the real estate behind the mortgages exceeds the face value of the mortgages). They thus offer a high degree of credit safety, although loss of value due to rising interest rates is a risk if sold in the secondary market. REMICs tend to have riskier backing and should be analyzed.

How assured is my income? Income is safe from the credit standpoint (see the previous question) but can vary from month to month as the result of prepayments and other factors.

Are there any other risks unique to this investment? Prepayments may shorten the life of the investment, although the cash they create is of course passed through to investors.

Is it commercially rated? Yes, Standard & Poor's and other services rate mortgage-backed securities.

Tax Considerations

What tax advantages (or disadvantages) does it offer? None. Interest is taxed as ordinary income and profits or losses from the sale of pass-through securities in the secondary market are taxed as capital gains or losses. But the monthly payment received by an investor in a pass-through is only partly interest. Because payments to the investor are simply pass-throughs of payments by homeowners on their mortgages, and those payments are part interest and part principal, the investor pays taxes only on the portion of his payment representing interest; the rest, as principal, is treated as a nontaxable return of capital. Since home mortgage payments have a higher ratio of interest to principal in the earlier years of the mortgage, it follows that income payments on pass-through securities normally have a higher proportion of taxable interest in the earlier years of the life of the pool.

Economic Considerations

What economic factors most affect buy, hold, and sell decisions? Mortgage-backed pass-throughs are most attractive to hold when general interest rates are low relative to the yield on the mortgage pool. However, this scenario can also cause a high rate of prepayments just when the investment is most attractive. The best holding is a pool of low-rate mortgages whose shares are bought at a good discount; that results in an attractive yield for investors, but since the homeowners are also happy with their low-rate mortgages, the risk of prepayment is much less. Of course, inflation erodes the value of fixed payments, which are the basis of income from pass-throughs.

MUNICIPAL SECURITY

A municipal security, or muni, is a debt obligation of a U.S. state, territory, or political subdivision, such as a county, city, town, village, or authority.

What has historically made munis special has been their exemption from federal income taxes and, frequently, from state and local income taxes as well. Because of this tax-exempt status, munis have traditionally paid lower rates of interest than taxable securities, making their after-tax return more attractive as an individual's income moved into higher brackets.

The Tax Reform Act of 1986 changed the municipal bond investment environment in fundamental ways primarily by dividing obligations into two basic groups:

Public purpose bonds, also called traditional government purpose bonds or essential purpose bonds, continue to be tax-exempt and to be issued without limit.

Private purpose bonds, vaguely defined as a bond involving more than a 10% benefit to private parties, are taxable unless specifically exempted. Such exempted *permitted private purpose bonds* are subject, with exceptions, to caps.

Whether tax-exempt or not, munis are either (1) general obligations, notes or bonds backed by the full faith and credit (including the taxing power) of the issuing entity and used to finance capital expenditures or improvements; or (2) *revenue obligations,* which are used to finance specific projects and are repaid from the revenues of the facilities they finance.

Although munis vary in the degree of credit strength backing them, and although there have been some famous defaults, such as the Washington Public Power Supply System (WHOOPS) in the 1980s and Orange County in 1994, their safety record has generally been excellent, earning them a place between Treasuries and high-grade corporate bonds in terms of investor confidence.

In addition to taxable bonds, recent innovations in the municipal securities field have included *tax-exempt commercial paper,* short-term discounted notes usually backed by bank lines of credit; *bonds with put options* typically exercisable after one to five years, which carry a somewhat lower yield in exchange for the put privilege; *floating (or variable) rate* issues tied to the Treasury bill or another market rate: and *enhanced security issues,* in which the credit of the municipal entity is supplemented by bank lines of credit or other outside resources.

For smaller investors, open and closed-end funds, unit investment trusts, and other pooled vehicles with portfolios of municipal obligations offer diversification and professional management with lower minimums.

Munis are also available as zero-coupon securities and are covered in the section dealing with that investment alternative.

∗   ∗   ∗

What Is a Municipal Security?

A municipal security is a negotiable bond or note issued by a U.S. state or subdivision. A muni may be a general obligation backed by the full faith and credit (i.e., the borrowing and taxing power) of a government; a revenue obligation paid out of the cash flow from an income-producing project; or a special assessment obligation paid out of taxes specially levied to finance specific public works. Some municipal bonds, such as those to finance low-income housing, may be backed by a federal government agency.

Buying, Selling, and Holding

How do I buy and sell it? Most securities broker-dealers handle municipal securities.

Is there a minimum purchase amount, and what is the price range? Although munis are issued in units of $5000 or $1000 par value as a rule, with exceptions as low as $100, broker-dealers usually require minimum orders of at least $5000 and often want $10,000, $25,000, or up to $100,000. Odd lots are sometimes available from broker-dealers at extra commissions or spreads. Smaller investments can be made through mutual funds, closed-end funds, unit investment trusts and other pooled vehicles with tax-exempt portfolios.

What fees and charges are involved? Sometimes a commission, but usually a spread (rarely exceeding 5%) between the dealer's buying and selling prices.

Does it mature, expire, or otherwise terminate? Yes. Maturities range from one month (notes) to 30 years (bonds). Serial bonds mature in scheduled stages. Munis may also be callable or have put features.

Can I sell it quickly? Some munis have good liquidity, although issues of obscure municipalities and authorities can have inactive markets and be hard to sell.

How is market value determined and how do I keep track of it? Most munis are fixed-income securities and thus rise and fall in opposite relationship to market interest rates. Variable-rate issues, whose rates are periodically adjusted to reflect changes in U.S. Treasury bill yields or other money market rates, tend to sell at or close to their par values. Muni quotes are not normally published in daily newspapers, but prices published in *The Daily Bond Buyer* (mainly new muni issues) and the *Blue List of Current Municipal Offerings* (a Standard and Poor's publication reporting details of secondary market offerings and their size) are available through brokers or directly by subscription.

Investment Objectives

Should I buy a municipal security if my objective is capital appreciation? No, although appreciation is possible when munis sell at discounts because rates have risen or credit questions arise.

Should I buy this if my objective is income? Yes, but only if the after-tax yield in your tax bracket compares favorably to the yield on a taxable investment of comparable safety.

To what extent does it protect against inflation? Fixed-income munis offer no inflation protection. Variable-rate munis would offer some, if interest rates rose.

Is it suitable for tax-deferred accounts? Tax-exempt issues bearing a lower interest rate than a taxable security are not suitable. Taxable munis are suitable.

Can I borrow against it? You can, but the interest you pay is not tax-deductible if the proceeds are used to buy municipals. With the lower rate you earn on most munis, it would hardly pay. While munis are acceptable collateral for other loans, care must be taken to avoid the appearance of a violation of the rule against deducting interest.

Risk Considerations

How assured can I be of getting my full investment back? In most cases, you can be quite sure of getting your investment back at maturity. Munis generally rank between U.S. government securities and corporate bonds in credit safety. But the risk of default varies with the credit of the issuer and the type of obligation (mainly general obligation or revenue obligations). Some munis are covered for default by private insurers. Of course, prices of all fixed-income securities decline when interest rates go up.

How assured is my income? Munis are relatively safe (see the preceding question) but defaults are possible due to such factors as limited ability to impose taxes, disappointing revenues from the use of facilities, or mismanagement of municipal finances. Issues may also be callable, enabling the issuer to force redemption after specified times.

Are there any other risks unique to this investment? Munis are not subject to Securities and Exchange Commission regulation, so the legality of the issue must be established. Make sure a legal opinion accompanies the issue.

Is it commercially rated? Moody's Investors Service, Standard & Poor's, and others rate credit. White's Tax-Exempt Bond Rating Service rates market risk.

Tax Considerations

What tax advantages (or disadvantages) does it offer? Interest may be exempt from federal income taxes and frequently from state and local income taxes (36 states tax exempt munis of other states but not their own: 5 states tax their own exempt munis and those of other states; 9 states plus the District of Columbia do not tax any exempt munis). Munis issued by Puerto Rico, Guam, and the Virgin Islands (U.S. territories) are tax-exempt in all states. Capital gains are taxable. Permitted private purpose bond interest may be a tax preference item in computing the Alternative Minimum Tax. Up to 85% of Social Security benefits can be taxed if municipal bond interest income plus adjusted gross income plus half the Social Security payments exceeds $32,000 for couples or $25,000 for single taxpayers.

Economic Considerations

What economic factors most affect buy, hold, or sell decisions? Personal tax considerations, of course, then interest rate levels and the inflation rate. Buy when rates are high to get good yields; hold as rates decline to see market values rise. Because tax-exempt munis pay a relatively low interest rate, inflation is especially devastating if the rate is fixed. Prolonged economic downturns can increase the risk of municipal defaults. Special supply and demand factors owing to the uncertain status of tax-exempt issues under tax reform legislation then pending, caused abnormally high municipal yields in the mid-1980s.

MUTUAL FUNDS (OPEN END)

An open-end mutual fund is so named because its sponsoring organization, called an investment company or a management company, stands ready at any time to issue new shares or to redeem existing shares at their daily-computed net asset value. An open-end fund offers investors with moderate means the diversification, professional management (for a fee), economy of scale, and, where it might not otherwise exist, the liquidity available only to large investors.

Mutual funds are available with portfolio compositions designed for an almost infinite variety of investment objectives and risk levels. The following is a partial list of types of funds, with their basic portfolio or mode of operation:

Income Fund (stocks paying dividends, preferred stocks, corporate bonds)

Growth Fund (growth stocks)

Aggressive Growth Fund (smaller, riskier growth stocks)

Balanced Fund (stocks and bonds)

Performance Fund (high-risk stocks, venture capital investments, etc.)

Conservative Balanced Fund (high-grade income and growth securities)

United States Government Bond Fund (U.S. Treasury or agency bonds)

International Fund (foreign stocks or bonds)

Global Fund (foreign and U.S. stocks or bonds)

Domestic Taxable Bond Fund (corporate bonds with investment-grade ratings)

Corporate High-Yield Bond Fund (corporate bonds with ratings below investment grade)

Municipal Bond Fund (tax-exempt municipal securities)

Special Situations Fund (venture capital, debt/equity securities)

Stock Index Fund (replicating or representative of the major stock indexes)

Market Sector Fund or *Specialized Fund* (securities of high-growth industries or specialized industries like gold-mining)

Tax-managed Fund (utility stocks whose dividends are reinvested for long-term capital gains)

Speculative Fund (engages in selling short and leverage)

Commodities Fund (commodity futures contracts)

Option Fund (sells puts and calls for extra income, sometimes speculating by taking positions without owning underlying securities or instruments)

Socially-conscious Fund (excludes investments offensive on moral or ethical grounds)

Fund of Funds (invests in other funds with top performance)

Money Market Fund (short-term, interest-bearing debt instruments)

Tax-exempt Money Market Fund (trades long-term and short-term municipals for best yields and capital gains)

Ginnie-Mae Fund (mortgage-backed pass-through securities guaranteed by Government National Mortgage Association)

Major sponsors allow switching of investments from shares of one fund to another within their fund families. Other services commonly available to investors include term life insurance; automatic reinvestment plans; regular income checks; open account plans allowing fractional share purchases with Social Security or pension checks or other relatively small amounts of cash; loan programs; and toll-free information services.

* * *

What Is an Open-End Mutual Fund?

An open-end mutual fund is an investment company that pools shareholder funds and invests in a diversified securities portfolio having a specified objective. It provides professional management and stands ready to sell new shares and redeem outstanding shares on a continuous (open-end) basis.

Buying, Selling, and Holding

Where do I buy and sell it? Load funds, in which a sales charge is deducted from the amount invested, are bought from securities brokers and financial planners. No-load funds are bought directly from the sponsor. Shares are not sold in the sense that shares of stock are transferred to other owners; rather they are redeemed (by phone, mail, or checkwriting privilege) by the fund at net asset value.

Is there a minimum purchase amount, and what is the price range? Some funds have minimum deposits of $1000–$2500. Others have no minimum. Share prices vary, but a majority are under $20. Many funds offer convenient share accumulation plans for investors of modest means.

What fees and charges are involved? Load funds charge a sales commission, typically 8¹/2% of the amount invested, though with larger purchases the load can go as low as 1¹/2%. No-load funds have no sales commissions. A hybrid, low-load funds, charge commissions of 3% or less. Both load and no-load funds charge annual management fees of from ¹/2% to 1% of the value of the investment. There is usually no redemption charge (back-end load, or exit fee), with load funds; no-loads may or may not have a 1% to 2% redemption fee to discourage short-term trading. Various share accumulation plans may involve extra service charges. Some funds discourage frequent switching by imposing extra charges. 12B-1 mutual funds, a type of fund that covers all or part of its sales and marketing expenses by charging fees to shareholders, may charge ¹/4% or less of assets in the case of no-load funds, ranging to 8¹/2% for load funds.

Does it mature, expire, or otherwise terminate? No.

Can I sell it quickly? Funds stand ready to redeem shares daily. Some managing companies allow switching among different funds they sponsor at either no charge (no-load fund families) or a small transaction fee.

How is market value determined and how do I keep track of it? Market value, called net asset value, depends on the way various economic and market forces affect the type of investments composing a particular fund's portfolio; a given economic or interest-rate scenario will have a different effect on bond fund values than stock fund values. Mutual fund quotations are reported daily in newspapers and a fund management company reports, usually quarterly, on the composition of portfolios and transactions during the reporting period.

Investment Objectives

Should I buy an open-end mutual fund if my objective is capital appreciation? Yes, but you would buy a fund with capital gains as a primary objective, such as a growth stock or special situations fund.

Should I buy this if my objective is income? Yes, but you would buy a fund with income as its primary objective, such as a bond or money market fund or a stock fund investing in high-yield stocks.

To what extent does it protect against inflation? That depends on the type of fund. Equity-oriented funds or money market funds offer more protection than fixed income bond portfolios, which provide little or no protection.

Is it suitable for tax-deferred retirement accounts? Yes, except when the fund is invested in tax-exempt securities, such as municipal bonds.

Can I borrow against it? Yes, subject to Federal Reserve margin rules. Collateral value varies with the type of fund. A lender that might loan 90% of the value of money market fund shares might find a high-risk fund unacceptable as collateral.

Risk Considerations

How assured can I be of getting my full investment back? It depends on the type of fund, the quality of the portfolio, and the adroitness of management in avoiding adverse developments. A money market fund has high safety of principal, whereas a bond fund is vulnerable to interest rate movements and a stock fund is subject to market risk, for example.

How assured is my income? Again, it depends on the type of portfolio, its quality, and the skill of the manager. A fund with AAA bonds will be a safer source of income than one comprised of higher-yielding but riskier junk bonds. Other funds stress capital growth at the expense of income. Money market funds offer assured income at a conservative rate, which goes up and down with market conditions.

Are there any other risks unique to this investment? Except for the fact that funds provide automatic diversification, the same risk considerations apply as affect individual investments.

Is it commercially rated? No, but some funds invest exclusively in securities with given commercial ratings, and a number of organizations rate mutual funds in terms of historical performance.

Tax Considerations

What tax advantages (or disadvantages) does it offer? Income is subject to the same federal income taxes as the investments from which it derives. Thus, a shareholder pays taxes just as if he owned the portfolio directly, except that all capital gains distributions are considered long-term, regardless of the time the fund has been held. Funds invested in tax-exempt municipal securities (some are triple—federal, state, and local—tax-exempt) provide tax-free income, at least at the federal level. States vary in their tax treatment of income from municipal securities (see the discussion of tax considerations in the section on Municipal Securities) and the same rules usually apply to fund income. Some states that would not tax interest will tax dividends from funds, however, even though the fund's income is from interest earned. In such states, dividends from a tax-exempt fund would be taxable.

Economic Considerations

What economic factors most affect buy, hold, or sell decisions? The same economic and market forces that affect individual investments affect funds made up of those investments, so choices should be made in the same terms.

OPTION CONTRACT (PUT OR CALL)

Put and call options are contracts that give holders the right, for a price, called a premium, to sell or buy an underlying stock or financial instrument at a specified price, called the exercise or strike price, before a specified expiration date. Option sellers are called writers—covered writers if they own the underlying security or financial instrument, naked writers if they don't—and buyers of options are called option buyers. A put is an option to sell and a call is an option to buy.

Listed options are options traded (since 1973) on national stock and commodity exchanges and thus have both visibility and liquidity, as opposed to conventional over-the-counter options, which are individually negotiated, more expensive, and less liquid. Listed options are available on stocks, stock indexes, debt instruments, foreign currencies, and futures of different types. The issuance and settlement—all the mechanics of options clearing—are handled by the options clearing corporation (OCC), which is owned by the exchanges.

Options make it possible to control a large amount of value with a much smaller amount of money. Because a small percentage change in the value of a financial instrument can result in a much larger percentage change in the value of an option, large gains (and losses) are possible with the leverage that options provide. Although sometimes options are bought with the idea of holding the underlying security as an investment after the exercise of the option, options are usually bought and sold without ever being exercised and settled. They have a life of their own.

The value of options—that is, the amount of their premiums—is mainly determined by the relationship between the exercise price and the market price of the underlying instrument, by the volatility of the underlying instrument, and by the time remaining before expiration.

When the relationship between an option's strike price (exercise price) and the underlying market price is such that the holder would profit (transaction costs aside) by exercising it, an option has intrinsic value and is said to be in the money. In contrast, there is no intrinsic value in an out-of-the-money option—such as a put whose strike price is below the market price or a call whose strike price is above the market price. A premium will normally trade for at least its intrinsic value, if any. An out-of-the-money option, on the other hand, has obviously more risk and a lower premium than an option that is more likely to become profitable. Options on highly volatile securities and instruments command higher premiums because they are more likely to produce profits when and if they move.

Time value influences premiums because the longer the time remaining, the greater the chance of a favorable movement and the higher the present value of the underlying instrument if exercised. This time value, also called net premium, decreases as the option approaches its expiration. (For this reason, options are called wasting assets.) The value of an out-of-the-money option is all time value; that of an in-the-money option is a combination of time value and intrinsic value. In general, the greater the potential for gain, the greater the risk of not achieving it. The farther from expiration and the greater the volatility, the higher the premium an option will have.

Professional traders have multioption strategies, some quite complex, designed to limit risk while capitalizing on premium movements. Called straddles, combinations, and spreads (which have many varieties), they involve close monitoring, expertise, and sometimes onerous commissions. Options trading is not for the average investor.

Options do have a conservative role, however, for personal as well as institutional investors. Options can be used very much like term life insurance policies to protect investors against losses in investments already owned. Option selling (writing) can be a source of added returns.

The use of options as insurance involves the purchase of a put to limit losses or lock in the profit on a position already owned, or the purchase of a call to limit losses or lock in the profit on a short sale. For example, an individual with 100 shares of XYZ at a market value of $60 who expects the price to rise to $70 might buy, at a premium of $125, a put at $55 expiring in three months. If the stock rises, the insurance would have cost $125 and that amount would have to be subtracted from the capital gain. If the stock dropped, however, the put could be exercised and the stock sold for no lower than $55; that would limit the investor's loss to $625—$60 less $55 (times 100 shares) plus the premium of $125. The investor who thought the stock would drop could have sold it short and bought a call to assure the ability to buy the shares to cover at the call price.

Covered option writing—writing calls on stock or other instruments that are owned—is a safe way to increase the income return on an investment, provided the investor is prepared to sell the underlying holding at the exercise price if the price moves that way. Potential gains are limited to the amount of the premium (a significant drawback if the underlying holding rises in value and the option is exercised).

Calls can be written at, in, deep in, out of, or deep out of the money. The farther out of the money it is, the less the chance of exercise and the lower the premium it will command. The main problem with writing covered calls is that to warrant a premium high enough to offset the commissions, the underlying asset has to be volatile, and the option close to the money; the more volatile it is and the closer the option is to the money, the greater the chance it will be exercised. If it's exercised the writer's profit is limited to the premium, when a greater profit could have been made by holding the investment.

Mutual funds that make their income by writing and trading options are an alternative for small investors.

What are LEAPS? LEAPS are among the most notable innovations of the 1990s. An acronym for Long-Term Equity Anticipation Securities, LEAPS were introduced by the Chicaco Board Options Exchange (CBOE) in October 1990. LEAPS are long-term put and call options that by the mid-nineties were being traded (on the NYSE, Amex, Philadelphia, and options exchanges) on about 150 stocks and several stock indexes. LEAPS are presently available with expirations of 1 to 3 years and applications for 5-year LEAPS are pending as this is written. Generally speaking, everything that is said in the following pages about regular puts and calls applies to LEAPS, except, of course, that being longer in term, LEAPS have higher premiums.

* * *

What Is an Option Contract (Put or Call)?

An option contract is a contract that grants the right, in exchange for a price or premium to buy (call) or sell (put) an underlying security at a specified price within a specified period of time.

Buying, Selling, and Holding

Where do I buy and sell it? At a full-service or discount broker.

Is there a minimum purchase amount, and what is the price range? The minimum is one option contract covering 100 shares. Contracts typically cost a few hundred dollars (usually less than $500).

What fees and charges are involved? In addition to the premium, brokerage commissions are charged for buying, selling, and exercising options. The maximum charge is $25 for a transaction covering one option; the average for multiple-contract transactions is about $14.

Does it mature, expire, or otherwise terminate? Yes; options have a specified expiration date, usually within nine months.

Can I sell it quickly? Yes; most options enjoy good liquidity.

How is market value determined and how do I keep track of it? The market value of an option is its premium value, which is determined by a combination of its intrinsic value (the difference between its exercise price and the market value of the underlying stock) and its time value (the value investors place on the amount of time until the expiration of the option). A small change in a stock price can cause a larger percentage change in an option premium; premium changes are reported daily in the financial sections of newspapers.

Investment Objectives

Should I buy an option contract if my objective is capital appreciation? Because a small change in a stock price causes a higher percentage change in a related option premium, speculators gain leverage using options. Of course, if the underlying stock fails to move in the right direction, the speculator is out the cost of the premium. Options are also used as hedging tools to protect the value of shares held for capital gains.

Should I buy this if my objective is income? Although sellers (writers) of options receive income from premiums and thereby augment the income return on the underlying holding, they may be forced to buy or sell the underlying holding if its price moves adversely. Options are not themselves income-producing investments, although speculators and some mutual funds create income through option writing and various spread strategies.

To what extent does it protect against inflation? Puts and calls, as short-term options, are not designed to capitalize on longer-term movements in common stock prices as might be caused by inflationary factors. Of course, LEAPS subscription warrants and employee stock options, which are related to put and call options, could be viewed as inflation protection.

Is it suitable for tax-deferred retirement accounts? Although not prohibited by the Internal Revenue Service, most brokerage firms rule out options contracts as too risky for retirement accounts. They may have a limited role in managed accounts, primarily as a hedging tool. Mutual funds or other pooled investments that generate income by writing and speculating in options may be appropriate investments in selected situations for people with high risk tolerance.

Can I borrow against it? No. Although Federal Reserve margin rules allow options transactions in margin accounts, options cannot be used as part of the borrowing base. Of course, options are themselves a source of considerable leverage.

Risk Considerations

How assured can I be of getting my full investment back? Your investment is the premium plus commissions. It is recovered only if the underlying stock or instrument moves favorably to such an extent that the profit gained from selling or exercising the option exceeds the investment; whether it does or not is pure speculation.

How assured is my income? The only income that options provide is from premiums earned in selling them. That is assured income, but it can be more than offset if the underlying stock moves adversely and the option is exercised by its holder.

Are there any other risks unique to this investment? The risk in options ranges from the simple loss of a premium if the option proves valueless to the risk of a magnified loss in the case of uncovered or naked positions—that is, where a put or call is sold without owning the underlying security or instrument. Upon exercise, the security or instrument must be bought or sold at a market price that may be in wide variance from the exercise price.

Is it commercially rated? No.

Tax Considerations

What tax advantages (or disadvantages) does it offer? Options on stocks are subject to the same capital gains taxation as the stocks themselves. Some traditional uses of options to defer income from one year to another have been curtailed by recent tax legislation and advice should be sought. See also the entry for Tax Straddle in Part IV.

Economic Considerations

What economic factors most affect buy, hold, and sell decisions? The same economic factors that affect stock investments in the short term apply essentially to decisions involving put and call options used in speculation and hedging.

OPTION CONTRACT ON A FUTURES CONTRACT (FUTURES OPTION)

For a general discussion of an option, see Option Contract (Put or Call).

* * *

What Is an Option Contract on a Futures Contract?

A futures option is a contract that grants the right, in exchange for a price (premium) to buy (call) or sell (put) a specified futures contract within a specified period of time.

Buying, Selling, and Holding

How do I buy and sell it? At a full-service or discount broker.

Is there a minimum purchase amount, and what is the price range? The minimum purchase is one option on one futures contract. It can cost several hundred to several thousand dollars, depending on the underlying future.

What fees and charges are involved? In addition to the premium, brokerage commissions are charged for buying, selling, and exercising an option. Generally, the maximum charge is $25, and the average charge for multiple option transactions is around $14, with lower rates for high-volume transactions.

Does it mature, expire, or otherwise terminate? Yes; options have a specified expiration date, usually within one year.

Can I sell it quickly? Yes; most futures options have good liquidity and they are not subject to daily trading limits that can affect the liquidity of futures themselves.

How is market value determined and how do I keep track of it? The same factors that affect the market value of futures affect the premium values of futures options. (See the sections Futures Contract on a Commodity and Futures Contract on an Interest Rate.) Prices are reported daily in newspapers and electronic databases.

Investment Objectives

Should I buy a futures option if my objective is capital appreciation? Only if you are a speculator attracted to the high degree of leverage offered by options, although options on futures are used by investors to hedge the value of other investments held for capital gains.

Should I buy this if my objective is income? Although selling options is a source of income, options are not themselves an income-producing investment. Some mutual funds trade in options for the purpose of generating income, however.

To what extent does it protect against inflation? Only to the limited extent that futures offer the opportunity to capitalize on inflation expectations and their effects on interest rates and commodity prices.

Is it suitable for tax-deferred retirement accounts? Although not prohibited by the Internal Revenue Service, most brokerage firms rule out options contracts as too risky for retirement accounts. They may have a limited role in managed accounts, primarily as a hedging tool. Mutual funds or other pooled investments that generate income by writing and speculating in options may be appropriate investments in selected situations for people with high risk tolerance.

Can I borrow against it? No. Although Federal Reserve margin rules allow options transactions in margin accounts, options cannot be used as part of the borrowing base. Of course, options are themselves a source of significant leverage.

Risk Considerations

How assured can I be of getting my full investment back? Your investment is the premium plus commissions. It is recovered only if the underlying futures contract moves favorably to such an extent that the proceeds realized from selling or exercising the option exceed the amount expended; whether it does or not is pure speculation.

How assured is my income? The only income that options provide is from premiums earned in selling them. That is assured income, but it can be more than offset if the underlying future moves adversely and the option is exercised by the holder.

Are there any other risks unique to this investment? Essentially the same risks apply as are involved with regular options and futures on the same underlying assets. A special positive feature, however, is that futures options, particularly on debt instruments, have better liquidity than either straight options or straight futures; that is because of less restrictive trading limits on futures options than on futures, and because the open interest on futures options tends to be much higher than on regular interest-rate (debt) options.

Is it commercially rated? No.

Tax Considerations

What tax advantages (or disadvantges) does it offer? Options on futures are subject to the same tax treatment as futures are. See the section on a Futures Contract on a Commodity.

Economic Considerations

What economic factors most affect buy, hold, and sell decisions? The same economic forces that affect interest rate and commodity futures affect the options available on those contracts.

OPTION CONTRACT ON AN INTEREST RATE (DEBT OPTION)

For a general discussion of an option, see Option Contract (Put or Call).

* * *

What Is an Option Contract on an Interest Rate?

An interest-rate option is a contract that grants the right, in exchange for a price (premium), to buy (call option) or sell (put option) a certain debt security at a specified price within a specified period of time, thereby producing a particular yield.

Buying, Selling, and Holding

How do I buy and sell it? Through a full-service or discount broker.

Is there a minimum purchase amount, and what is the price range? The minimum purchase is one contract. Premiums, where the underlying security is interest-bearing, are determined as a percentage (in 32nds for Treasury bonds and notes) of par value. Thus a contract on a $100,000 par value U.S. Treasury bond with a premium of 2.50 (2 and $16/32$) would cost $2500, while a $20.000 minicontract with a premium of 1.24 (1 and $24/32$ or $13/4$) would cost $350. Where the underlying security is discounted rather than interest-bearing, as with the 13-week Treasury bill, premiums are quoted with reference to basis point (100ths of one percent) differences between prices, expressed as complements of annualized discount rates. For example, with a 9% yield, a 13-week Treasury bill (par value $1 million) would have a price basis of 91 and might have an option trading at 92.20. With a premium thus quoted at 1.20

(120 basis points), it would cost $3000, calculated: $.012 \times {}^{13}/_{52} \times \$1$ million. (A quick way of approximating dollar premiums is to multiply basis points times $25.)

What fees and charges are involved? Brokerage commissions are charged for buying, selling, or exercising options. The maximum charge is $25 for a transaction covering one contract, with reduced rates for larger trades. Margin accounts may entail interest and other added charges. There may also be income and net worth rules to qualify investors.

Does it mature, expire, or otherwise terminate? Yes. All options have expiration dates, usually within nine months.

Can I sell it quickly? Interest rate options have generally good liquidity. Those with the most contracts outstanding (represented by open interest figures in newspapers) are usually easiest to trade.

How is market value determined and how do I keep track of it? Market value, which is premium value, is determined by a combination of intrinsic value (exercise value less market value of the underlying security) and time value (the diminishing value investors place on the time remaining to expiration). Intrinsic value changes with interest rate movements, which are influenced by Federal Reserve Board monetary policy and other economic factors. Option prices are reported daily in newspapers and electronic databases.

Investment Objectives

Should I buy an interest-rate option if my objective is capital appreciation? Speculators use the high leverage possible with options to capitalize on the price volatility resulting from interest rate movements.

Should I buy this if my objective is income? Option writers earn income in addition to the interest they receive on the underlying security, while taking the risk that the option will be exercised if rates move adversely. Investors also use interest rate options to hedge the value of other income-producing investments.

To what extent does it protect against inflation? As short-term instruments, interest-rate options are not designed for dealing with the longer-term effects of inflation on debt securities. However, inflation expectations are a factor in the term structure of interest rates, and it is possible, using options, to capitalize on short-term movements.

Is it suitable for tax-deferred retirement accounts? Although not prohibited by the Internal Revenue Service, most brokerage firms rule out options contracts as too risky for retirement accounts. They may have a limited role in managed accounts, primarily as a hedging tool. Mutual funds or other pooled investments that generate income by writing and speculating in options may be appropriate investments in selected situations for people with high risk tolerance.

Can I borrow against it? No. Although Federal Reserve margin rules allow options transactions in margin accounts, options cannot be used as part of the borrowing base. Of course, options are themselves a source of considerable leverage.

Risk Considerations

How assured can I be of getting my full investment back? Your investment is recovered only if interest rates move favorably to the extent that the proceeds of the sale of the option exceed the premium plus commissions already expended; that is a matter of pure speculation.

How assured is my income? The only income is from premiums earned in selling options and even that can be negated by losses resulting from exercise by the holder.

Are there any other risks unique to this investment? The marketplace of interest-rate options is dominated on one hand by large institutional investors and their portfolio managers and on the other by dealers who handle the large volumes of high-denomination securities that underlie the options. This puts the smaller investor at a disadvantage in terms both of information and transaction cost. Other special risks have to do with the Option Clearing Corporation's power to remedy shortages of underlying securities by permitting substitutions and adjusting strike prices, and with trading hour differences between options and underlying debt instruments. Sellers of options on discount instruments settled in current instruments take a risk to the extent that they cannot hedge perfectly against exercise.

Is it commercially rated? No.

Tax Considerations

What tax advantages (or disadvantages) does it offer? Unlike regular put and call options, traders in interest-rate options are subject to tax rules covering futures trading; this means open positions are marked to market at year-end with paper gains or losses treated as if realized and taxed as net capital gains (see page 31). Tax advice should be sought.

Economic Considerations

What economic factors most affect buy, hold, and sell decisions? Economic and monetary factors affecting interest rates govern choices having to do with interest-rate options.

OPTION CONTRACT ON A STOCK INDEX

For a general discussion of an option, see Option Contract (Put or Call).

* * *

What Is an Option Contract on a Stock Index?

A stock-index option is a contract that grants the right, in exchange for a price (premium), to buy (call option) or sell (put option) the value of an underlying stock index or subindex at a specified price within a specified period of time with settlement in cash.

Buying, Selling, and Holding

How do I buy and sell it? Through a full-service or discount broker.

Is there a minimum purchase amount, and what is the price range? The minimum purchase is one contract. The premium is the difference in index values times $100. A contract based on a 5-point difference between the current (base) value and the exercise value would thus cost $500. Because contracts are settled in cash, margin security in the form of cash or securities is required by brokers, who may also have suitability requirements calling for substantial net worth and income.

What fees and charges are involved? In addition to the premium, brokerage commissions are charged for buying, selling, and exercising options. The maximum charge is $25 for a transaction covering one contract, with reduced rates for large trades. Margin accounts may entail interest and other additional charges.

Does it mature, expire, or otherwise terminate? Yes; options have a specified expiration date.

Can I sell it quickly? Most stock-index options have good liquidity, though newly introduced contracts may have less active markets than contracts that are better established and more popular. Those with many contracts outstanding (represented by large open interest figures in the newspapers) are generally the easiest to trade.

How is market value determined and how do I keep track of it? Premium value is determined by a combination of intrinsic value (exercise price less the index value) and time value (the value investors place on the amount of time remaining to expiration). The intrinsic value is subject to all the forces that make the stock market go up and down; a small movement in the market, as represented by the index, will result in a much larger percentage change in premium value. Indexes are revalued constantly during the trading day and closing prices are published in daily newspapers and electronic databases along with the option values based on them.

Investment Objectives

Should I buy a stock-index option if my objective is capital appreciation? You might if you were a speculator expecting a move in the stock market and were attracted to the high leverage provided by options. You might also use index options to hedge against possible losses in other securities being held for capital gains.

Should I buy this if my objective is income? Although sellers of options receive premium income and thereby increase the income return on their portfolios, options are not themselves income securities.

To what extent does it protect against inflation? Index options are short-term investments and not designed to capitalize on longer-term market movements as might be caused by inflation.

Is it suitable for tax-deferred retirement accounts? Although not prohibited by the Internal Revenue Service, most brokerage firms rule out options contracts as too risky for retirement accounts. They may have a limited role in managed accounts, primarily as a hedging tool. Mutual funds or other pooled investments that generate income by writing and speculating in options may be appropriate investments in selected situations for people with high risk tolerance.

Can I borrow against it? No. Although Federal Reserve margin rules allow options transactions in margin accounts, options cannot be used as part of the borrowing base. Of course, options are themselves a source of significant leverage.

Risk Considerations

How assured can I be of getting my full investment back? Your investment is recovered only if the underlying index value moves favorably to such an extent that the proceeds gained from selling or exercising the option exceed the cost plus commissions; whether it does is pure speculation.

How assured is my income? The only income that options provide is from premiums earned in selling the options. Even that, however, can be negated if the underlying index moves adversely and the option is exercised by the holder.

Are there any other risks unique to this investment? Index options share the same risks as regular puts and calls, but have a few that are unique. These have basically to do with (1) the limitations of index options as a hedging tool (it is impractical to compose a portfolio that duplicates an index exactly and even then there is rarely dollar-for-dollar variation) and with (2) the fact that settlement is made in cash; the settlement figure is the difference between the strike price and the closing value of the index on the day of exercise, and since the seller is not informed of the assignment until the next business day or even later, his hedge position may have lost value. This timing risk must be considered in all multioption strategies using index options. Other risks have to do with trading halts affecting underlying shares (but not the indexes) and causing index values to be based on noncurrent prices, or trading halts in the index options themselves, with the risk that the index value will move adversely before a position can be closed out.

Is it commercially rated? No.

Tax Considerations

What tax advantages (or disadvantages) does it offer? Unlike regular put and call options, index options are subject to tax rules covering futures trading. This means open positions are marked to market at year-end; paper profits or losses are treated as if realized and taxcd as net capital gains (see page 31). Tax advice should be sought.

Economic Considerations

What economic factors most affect buy, hold, and sell decisions? Index options are used to make market bets or to protect other holdings against market risk. Any and all economic factors affecting the market become relevant to decisions involving stock options.

OPTION CONTRACT OR FUTURES CONTRACT ON A CURRENCY

For a general discussion of an option, see Option Contract (Put or Call); for a general discussion of a futures contract, see Futures Contract on a Commodity.

* * *

What Is a Futures Contract or an Option Contract on a Currency?

They are contracts to buy or sell (futures) or that represent rights (options) to buy or sell a foreign currency at a particular price within a specified period of time.

Buying, Selling, and Holding

How do I buy and sell them? Through a full-service broker or commodities dealer.

Is there a minimum purchase amount, and what is the price range? Contract sizes vary with different currencies and different markets. The minimum purchase is one contract, which, for an option, typically costs a few hundred dollars. Futures contracts tend to be sizable (standard-size contracts are 12.5 million yen and 125,000 Swiss francs, for example, which on one day in the mid-1980s both equalled about $62,500) but they can be bought with small (1.5% to 4.2%) margins. Also, minicontracts are traded in several currencies on the Mid-America Commodity Exchange—6.25 million yen and 62,500 Swiss francs, for example.

What fees and charges are involved? Broker's commissions, typically $25 or less per contract for options; $50 to $80 for a round-trip futures contract transaction (purchase and sale). In the event of actual delivery, other fees, charges, or taxes may be required.

Do they mature, expire, or otherwise terminate? Yes; all contracts have specified expiration dates.

Can I sell them quickly? Yes; option and futures contracts enjoy good liquidity, although daily price limits on futures can create illiquidity when contracts are down limit or up limit and it is impossible to trade out of a position, because maximum allowable price movement has occurred during the trading day.

How is market value determined and how do I keep track of it? Premiums and contract values change as the exchange rate between the dollar and the foreign currency changes. The exchange rate is determined by the relative value of two currencies, which can change as events affect either or both of the underlying currencies. Daily prices are published in newspapers and electronic databases.

Investment Objectives

Should I buy them if my objective is capital appreciation? Speculators use the high leverage afforded by options and futures contracts to seek gains on relative currency values.

Should I buy them if my objective is income? Except for premium income earned from selling (writing) options, contracts do not provide income. Contracts are frequently used in hedging strategies to protect other income-producing securities from losses due to currency values.

To what extent do they protect against inflation? Because they are short-term contracts, currency options and futures are not affected directly by inflation.

Are they suitable for tax-deferred retirement accounts? Although not prohibited by the Internal Revenue Service, most brokerage firms rule out options and futures contracts as too risky for retirement accounts. They may have a limited role in managed accounts, primarily as a hedging tool. Mutual funds or other pooled investments that generate income through options and futures may be appropriate investments in selected situations for people with high risk tolerance.

Can I borrow against them? Options can be traded in margin accounts but cannot be used as collateral. Moreover, since foreign currency does not have borrowing value either for margin purposes, purchases as the result of exercise may require extra cash or securities. Futures cannot be used as collateral, but provide leverage because they can be held with small margins, actually good faith deposits.

Risk Considerations

How assured can I be of getting my full investment back? With options, the only investment is the premium plus commissions and it is recovered only when the underlying rate of exchange moves favorably to such an extent that the proceeds gained from sale or exercise exceed the amount expended. Futures are inherently speculative and it is possible to lose more than your investment, although margin calls would normally limit losses to the amount invested, assuming the account was closed out (liquidated) to meet the call.

How assured is my income? Other than premium income from option writing (selling), options and futures provide no income.

Are there any other risks unique to these investments? Since two currencies are involved, developments in either country can affect the values of options and futures. Risks include general economic factors as well as government actions affecting currency valuation and the movements of currencies from one country to another. The quantities of currency underlying option contracts represent odd lots in a market dominated by transactions between banks; this can mean extra transaction costs upon exercise. The fact that options markets may be closed while round-the-clock interbank currency markets are open can create problems due to price and rate discrepancies. With futures, there is always the risk of actual delivery if a position is not closed out prior to expiration of the contract.

Are they commercially rated? No, neither options nor futures are rated.

Tax Considerations

What tax advantages (or disadvantages) do they offer? Options are subject to the same capital gains rules as the underlying assets. Futures are subject to special rules requiring that open positions be marked to market at year-end and be taxed as realized capital gains (see page 31). Net trading losses can be applied against capital gains on other investments and unused portions carried forward. Other tax treatments may apply where contracts are used for hedging purposes. Tax advice should be sought.

Economic Considerations

What economic factors most affect buy, hold, and sell decisions? All factors that affect either currency affect the values of options and futures contracts.

PRECIOUS METALS

Precious metals—gold, silver, platinum, and palladium—are bought by investors primarily to hedge against inflation, economic uncertainty, and foreign exchange risk, in the belief that these metals are repositories of absolute value, whereas paper currencies and securities denominated in such currencies have relative value and are vulnerable to loss.

The economics of precious metals have less to do with the production process, industrial demand, or their greatly diminished monetary role than with the psychology of the financial marketplace. There, precious metals—gold especially—are perceived to be the best store of value available when anxiety causes the value of other assets to go into a tailspin. Historically, in such scenarios gold and other precious metals have risen.

The most famous example was in January 1980 when high international inflation due to rising oil prices, the American-hostage crisis in Iran, and civil disorder in Saudi Arabia combined to cause abnormally heavy buying of precious metals, which drove gold to a record price of $887.50 per ounce and led silver and platinum to peak levels as well. When calmer times returned, however, prices soon fell and stabilized at lower levels. It was a memorable lesson in how volatile this store of value can be.

Physical ownership is one way of owning precious metals, available in bullion form in units ranging from 400-Troy-ounce gold bars to 1-ounce platinum ingots. These are sold by dealers at markups or premiums that fall as weights and dollar values rise. Gold can also be held in coins, such as the South African Krugerrand, the Canadian Maple Leaf, and the U.S. Eagle series, introduced in 1986. Generally, the more popular the coin, the greater its liquidity and the higher its premium. Silver can be bought in bags containing U.S. coins of $1000 total face value, priced at a discount to the silver value to cover melting and refining costs. The drawbacks of physical ownership are mainly the high premiums, safekeeping and insurance costs, and sales taxes.

Certificates—actually warehouse receipts issued by some banks, dealers, and full-service brokers—represent gold, silver, platinum, or palladium held in safekeeping. Typically, for a fee of 3% or higher, the bank or dealer will buy metals in $1000 units and, for a small annual charge, provide insurance and storage. It will also, for 1% or so, sell the bullion or deliver it without a sales tax. The attraction is the convenience and lower transaction costs compared to physical ownership.

Other alternatives include *securities* of companies engaged in mining or processing, including some exchange-traded South African companies (many represented by American Depositary Receipts) as well as highly speculative penny stocks, traded over-the-counter or on regional or Canadian exchanges. There are also *mutual funds* and *closed-end funds* that specialize in both debt and equity issues of precious metals firms.

Finally, *commodity futures, options,* and *options on futures* are traded on precious metals. They provide leverage and hedging opportunities for well-capitalized investors with high expertise and risk tolerance. Scc separate discussions of these investment vehicles.

* * *

What Are Investments in Precious Metals?

Investments in precious metals involve gold, silver, platinum, and palladium as commodities (i.e.. not as money), owned by investors, in physical form or through securities, because of their presumed value as stores of wealth and as hedges against inflation and economic uncertainty. Precious metals are traded by speculators who hope to profit from volatility in the financial marketplace.

Buying, Selling, and Holding

How do I buy and sell them? Through various dealers and brokers, depending on the form of ownership. Coins and certificates are bought and sold through major banks.

Is there a minmum purchase amount and what is the price range? Precious metals can be bought with almost any amount of money, depending on the form of investment. Ccrtificates generally have $1000 minimums.

What fees and charges are involved? Bullion involves a dealer markup, varying with quantity. Certificates cost 3% and up, with storage and insurance another 1% or more and sales fees of 1% or higher. Domestic and foreign securities and other forms of investment, like mutual funds, are subject to standard fees and commissions. Depending on the form of ownership, other costs may include sales or transfer taxes, shipping and handling, assay fees, insurance, storage, and safekeeping. Physical ownership involves an opportunity cost as well, since the money tied up could otherwise be invested in assets producing income.

Do they mature, expire, or otherwise terminate? Certain investment vehicles, such as options and futures, have specified expirations.

Can I sell them quickly? Usually yes, though platinum and palladium are less liquid than gold and silver. Larger ingots and less popular gold coins can have uncertain liquidity.

How is market value determined and how do I keep track of it? Market value is a complex affair. While investor demand is highest when inflation and economic uncertainty loom largest, industrial demand depends on economic health and certainty. Other factors, such as interest rates and foreign exchange rates, play a key role, and speculators are active. Different forms of investment may be affected in different ways at different times. Dealers are a source of information concerning physical assets; securities and commodities information is reported in the financial pages of daily newspapers.

Investment Objectives

Should I invest in precious metals if my objective is capital appreciation? Yes, but myriad forces affect market value, and a high degree of expertise is required to achieve short-term gains.

Should I buy them if my objective is income? Some forms of ownership, like stocks and mutual funds, may provide income, while others, like physical ownership, provide none and may involve negative returns. In general, precious metals are not purchased for income.

To what extent do they protect against inflation? Although used by investors primarily to hedge political and economic uncertainty, precious metals over the long term have risen in value with inflation. Investors buying precious metals for inflation protection should be mindful, however, that many factors can cause volatility in the shorter term.

Are they suitable for tax-deferred retirement accounts? Except for American gold and silver coins, physical investment is not permitted. Common stocks and mutual fund shares involving precious metals may be suitable for some accounts.

Can I borrow against them? Yes; depending on the form of investment, there are various ways to leverage investments and use them as loan collateral.

Risk Considerations

How assured can I be of getting my full investment back? Precious metals tend to be volatile and offer no assurance that values will be retained.

How assured is my income? Where such investments provide income at all, such as mining stocks paying dividends, the risk is often great.

Are there any other risks unique to these investments? Many investors in precious metals have lost money doing business with unscrupulous dealer-brokers. Political risks in countries where mining is done and related developments, such as the sentiment in the mid-1980s for divestiture of shares of firms doing business in South Africa, can jeopardize investment values. Inaccurate or misleading estimates of reserves of mining companies is another risk.

Are they commercially rated? Some common stocks are rated by Standard & Poor's and other major services.

Tax Considerations

What tax advantages (or disadvantages) do they offer? Assuming you are not engaged in mining or processing or using gold in a business or profession, dividend income and capital gains and losses are subject to the usual tax treatment. In addition, you may have to pay state sales taxes on physical purchases.

Economic Considerations

What economic factors most affect buy, hold, and sell decisions? Investors favor precious metals to hedge anticipated high inflation; however, many other economic factors can affect the value of precious metals and related investment alternatives, often in different ways.

PREFERRED STOCK (NONCONVERTIBLE)

Preferred stock is a hybrid security that combines features of both common stock and bonds. It is equity, not debt, however, and is thus riskier than bonds. It rarely carries voting rights.

Preferred dividends, like bond interest, are usually a fixed percentage of par value, so share prices, like bond prices, go up when interest rates move down and vice versa. But whereas bond interest is a contractual expense of the issuer, preferred dividends, although payable before common dividends, can be skipped if earnings are low. If the issuer goes out of business, preferred shareholders do not share in assets until bondholders are paid in full, though preferred shareholders rank ahead of common stockholders. Like bonds, preferreds may have sinking funds, be callable, or be redeemable by their holders.

Because preferred issues are designed for insurance companies and other institutional investors which, as corporations, enjoy a 70% tax exclusion on dividends earned, fully taxable yields for individuals are not much better than those on comparable bonds offering more safety. Moreover, trading is often inactive or in big blocks, meaning less liquidity and higher transaction costs for small investors.

Still, personal investors do hold preferred stock. A broker can usually find good buys as investor perceptions of risk in different industrial sectors create yield differences in stocks that are otherwise comparable. Capital appreciation can result from shares bought at a discount from the prices at which a sinking fund will purchase them, or from discounted shares of turnaround firms with dividend arrearages.

Different types of preferred stock include:

Convertible preferred, convertible into common shares and thus offering growth potential plus fixed income; tends to behave differently in the marketplace than straight preferred (see Convertible Security).

Noncumulative preferred is a hangover from the heyday of the railroads and is rare today. Dividends, if unpaid, do not accumulate.

Cumulative preferred is the most common type. Dividends, if skipped, accrue, and common dividends cannot be paid while arrearages exist.

Participating preferred is unusual and typically issued by firms desperate for capital. Holders share in profits with common holders by way of extra dividends declared after regular dividends are paid. This type may have voting rights.

Adjustable (floating or variable) rate preferred adjusts the dividend rate quarterly (usually based on the 3-month U.S. Treasury bill) to reflect money market rates. It is aimed at corporate investors seeking after-tax yields combined with secondary market price stability. Individuals, looking at modest, fully taxable dividends that can go down as well as up, might prefer the safety of a money market fund.

Prior preferred stock (or preference shares) has priority of claim on assets and earnings over other preferred shares.

PIK Preferred Stock—PIK is an acronym for payment in kind—refers to an oddity spawned in the wave of leveraged buyouts in the 1980s. PIK preferred pays its dividend in the form of additional preferred stock. It is highly speculative almost by definition, since it implies a dearth of cash and raises a question about the adequacy of the issuer's working capital.

* * *

What Is Nonconvertible Preferred Stock?

Nonconvertible preferred is a form of owner's equity, usually nonvoting, paying dividends at a specified rate and having prior claim over common stock on earnings and assets in liquidation.

Buying, Selling, and Holding

How do I buy and sell it? Through a securities broker-dealer.

Is there a minimum purchase amount, and what is the price range? Buying round lots (usually 10 shares) saves commissions. Shares have par (face) values normally ranging from $100 down to $10, and market prices may be higher or lower than par values to bring yields in line with prevailing interest rate levels.

What fees and charges are involved? Standard commissions, with added transaction charges on inactively traded shares.

Does it mature, expire, or otherwise terminate? Preferred stock may be outstanding indefinitely, but many issues have call features or sinking fund provisions, whereby the issuer, usually for a small premium over par value, can require holders to redeem shares. Preferred issues may also have put features, which allow holders to redeem shares.

Can I sell it quickly? In most cases, yes. As a rule, preferreds are less liquid than common stocks and more liquid than bonds. Because large corporate investors dominate, smaller lots can sometimes be difficult for brokers to transact quickly.

How is market value determined and how do I keep track of it? Assuming good financial condition, fixed-income preferreds vary inversely with market interest rates. Adjustable-rate preferreds tend to be less volatile because dividends are adjusted quarterly to reflect money market conditions. Preferred prices are reported daily in the stock tables of newspapers and in databases, identified by the abbreviation "PF" in newspapers and "PR" in most electronic media.

Investment Objectives

Should I buy nonconvertible preferred stock if my objective is capital appreciation? No, although appreciation is possible in shares bought at a discount from par or redemption value or bought prior to a decline in interest rates. Substantial appreciation is possible in turnaround situations where cumulative preferred issues of troubled companies are selling at big discounts and there is a sizable accumulated dividend obligation.

Should I buy this if my objective is income? Yes, but unless you're a corporation or you buy at a discount, your yield won't be much better than that on a comparable corporate bond, and bonds are less risky in terms of both income and principal.

To what extent does it protect against inflation? Fixed-rate preferred offers no protection against inflation. Adjustable-rate preferred offers some.

Is it suitable for tax-deferred retirement accounts? Yes.

Can I borrow against it? Yes, subject to lender policies and Federal Reserve margin requirements.

Risk Considerations

How assured can I be of getting my full investment back? The market value of fixed-rate preferred stock declines as interest rates rise. (Adjustable-rate preferred has greater price stability.) In liquidation, holders of preferred stock are paid after bondholders but before common stockholders.

How assured is my income? Dividends, unlike interest, are not legal obligations and are paid from earnings, so income is as reliable as the issuer's earnings are stable. Established companies, such as utilities, with predictable cash flows are better bets than young firms or firms in cyclical industries, such as housing. Preferred dividends must be paid before common distributions, however; that means common dividends wait until all unpaid preferred dividends of cumulative issues are satisfied.

Are there any other risks unique to this investment? Call features, when present, allow the issuer to force holders to redeem shares, usually at par value plus a small premium. Firms normally call issues when market rates have declined and they can obtain financing more cheaply. But it is exactly under such circumstances that shares are enjoying higher market values and paying higher than market yields to holders who bought before rates declined. So call features represent a risk to investors; indeed the very presence of a call feature can limit upside price potential. Another risk of preferred stock is that should a dividend be omitted, the market may perceive financial weakness and drive down the share values

Is it commercially rated? Yes. Major issues are rated by Moody's, Standard & Poor's, Value Line Investment Survey, and other services.

Tax Considerations

What tax advantages (or disadvantages) does it offer? None for personal investors. Corporations enjoy a 70% exemption from federal income taxes on dividends from other domestic corporations, effectively raising returns.

Economic Considerations

What economic factors most affect buy, hold, or sell decisions? Since most preferred stock pays a fixed dividend, it is best to buy when market rates are high and the issuer is forced to offer a competitive yield. Prices vary inversely with interest rates, so values increase as interest rates decline. Fixed-rate preferred stock loses value in inflation. Poor business conditions may affect profits and threaten dividends.

REAL ESTATE INVESTMENT TRUST (REIT AND FREIT)

If 1986 Tax Reform spoiled the party for "tax-advantaged" real estate limited partnerships, it made real estate investment trusts, or REITs, which are all about income, more popular than ever. The reasons are two:

First, by extending depreciation from 19 to 27.5 years, tax reform removed one the sweetest tax deductions benefiting limited partners, but REITs had always used a mandatory 35-year schedule, and thus were unaffected. Second, the use of writeoffs against salary and other investment income, a major benefit to limited partners before Tax Reform limited passive loss deductions to passive income, was never a benefit of REITs; REITs generate portfolio income, which is now worth relatively more.

The market environment for REITs has also become more favorable. Overbuilding before Tax Reform, then slow construction when tax benefits dried up, caused both depressed prices and a *projected* dearth of supply in the commercial market. Since this should mean rising rents and values for existing properties, many analysts foresee higher dividends and higher share prices for selected REITs in the 1990s.

REITs were authorized by Congress in the early 1960s to provide small investors with an opportunity to invest in large-scale real estate. After a tumultuous period in the mid-1970s, when rising interest rates and tight money pressured builders, causing loan defaults and forcing many REITs into financial difficulty, the industry, wiser for the experience, enjoyed a resurgence.

Like shares of stock, REITs trade publicly, and like mutual funds their money is invested in a diverse array of assets, from shopping malls and office buildings to health care facilities, apartment complexes and hotels, usually with geographical diversification as well.

Some REITs, called *equity REITs*, take ownership positions in real estate; shareholders receive income from the rents received from the properties and receive capital gains as properties are sold at a profit. Because both rents and property values rise with inflation, inflation protection is an important benefit of equityoriented real estate investments. Other REITs specialize in lending money to real estate developers. Called *mortgage REITs*, they pass interest income on to shareholders. *Hybrid* or *balanced REITs* feature a mix of equity and debt investments.

By law, REITs must derive 75% of income from rents, dividends, interest, and gains from the sale of real estate properties, and must pay out 95% to shareholders. Companies meeting those requirements are exempt from federal taxation at the corporate level, although dividends are taxable to shareholders. REITs thus allow investors to share, with limited liability, the financial and tax benefits of real estate while avoiding the double taxation of corporate ownership. REITs also offer liquidity, since you can sell your shares on the market any time you wish.

On the negative side, REIT shares can be just as volatile as shares of stock. When conditions are unfavorable, such as when interest rates are high, materials are short, and the real-estate market is overbuilt, share values suffer.

FREITS: A variation of the REIT is the *finite life real estate investment trust,* or FREIT. FREITs, like limited partnerships, are self-liquidating—that is, they aim to sell or finance their holdings by a given date and distribute the proceeds to investors, thereby enabling them to realize capital gains. Investors thus have the choice of (1) selling their FREIT shares in the market (share values tend to more closely reflect market values of property holding than with REITs) or of (2) waiting to receive the full value of their shares when the portfolio is sold and the cash is distributed. Of course, the disadvantages of REITs apply to FREITs as well—the risk of a soft market at the time of sale or liquidation, and the inability to share in tax-deductible losses.

CMO REITs: A recent and popular innovation has been the CMO REIT, a complex and risky investment created when the issuer of a collateralized mortgage obligation—see section on mortgage-backed (pass-through) securities—sells the CMO's residual cash flows (the spread between the rate paid by mortgage holders and the lower, shorter-term rate paid to CMO investors) to the CMO REIT. REIT shareholders benefit when the spread widens and and get lower returns as the spread narrows.

The main variable affecting the spread is the prepayment rate on the mortgages underlying the CMO. Prepayments fall and spreads widen when market interest rates increase; the reverse happens when rates decrease. Because returns rise and fall with interest rates, CMO REIT investors theoretically enjoy an investment that is countercyclical to other equity investments in real estate, which react adversely to rate increases.

CMO REITs may be vulnerable to more than prepayment risk, however. Depending on how they are structured, an increase in short-term versus long-term interest rates can create a rate squeeze. Moreover, spreads tend to narrow as a function of time as normal prepayments are made and as faster-pay, lower-rate CMO components are paid off, leaving the REIT with more costly longer-term bonds.

CMO REITs, which have been marketed aggressively, can seem appealing because of high initial yields and AAA ratings of the underlying CMOs. But at least one CMO REIT has gone bankrupt, and only investors who understand this sophisticated vehicle and can afford high risk should get involved.

* * *

What Is a Real Estate Investment Trust (REIT)?

A REIT is a trust that invests in real estate-related assets, such as properties or mortgages, with funds obtained by selling shares, usually publicly traded, to investors.

Buying, Selling, and Holding

How do I buy and sell it? Through a securities broker-dealer.

Is there a minimum purchase amount, and what is the price range? Like common stocks, shares trade in round lots of 100 shares, with odd-lot transactions involving higher commissions. Prices vary, but most shares trade under $50.

What fees and charges are involved? Standard brokerage commissions.

Does it mature, expire, or otherwise terminate? Not normally. A recent development, called the finite life real estate investment trust or FREIT, is self-liquidating—that is, the management has an expressed intention to sell all its properties and distribute the proceeds within a specified time frame.

Can I sell it quickly? Yes, good liquidity is a major attraction.

How is market value determined and how do I keep track of it? Shares of equity REITs reflect property values, rent trends, and market sentiment about real estate. Mortgage REITs fluctuate as market interest rates affect profits. Balanced REITs—part equity, part mortgage—tend to have greater price stability. CMO REITs tend to rise in value as interest rates increase, and vice versa. FREITs, because shareholders will sooner or later realize capital gains income, tend to have share values somewhat more reflective of underlying property values. Share prices are reported in the stock tables of daily newspapers and in electronic databases.

Investment Objectives

Should I buy this if my objective is capital appreciation? Yes, but the potential for share value increases is greater with equity REITs than mortgage REITs. Also, automatic reinvestment of dividends increases capital gains potential. FREITs aim to pay out realized capital gains within a targeted period.

Should I buy this if my objective is income? Yes, especially since yields are not reduced by taxation at the corporate level. Mortgage REITs and CMO REITs are more income-oriented than equity REITs.

To what extent does it protect against inflation? Since income from rents and capital gains increases with inflation, equity REITs provide excellent inflation protection. Mortgage REITs provide less.

Is it suitable for tax-deferred retirement accounts? Yes.

Can I borrow against it? Yes, subject to Federal Reserve margin rules and individual lender policies.

Risk Considerations

How assured can I be of getting my full investment back? REITs shares have the same market risks as common stocks plus the risk of a decline in property values. Mortgage REIT shares suffer when rising interest rates squeeze profits, and unless insured, can involve the risk of default on mortgages. CMO REITs are subject to special risks (see overview discussion). You should not buy REITs if safety of principal is a paramount concern.

How assured is my income? Assuming REITs are well managed, income, which derives from rents or mortgage interest primarily, should be relatively secure. Still, real estate is sensitive to economic adversity, and there are many safer ways to invest for income. CMO REITs are subject to special risks (see overview discussion).

Are there any other risks unique to this investment? Much depends on expert management in terms of selecting, diversifying, and managing portfolios.

Valuation of real estate is anything but an exact science. Certain types of REIT portfolios are riskier than others, those whose portfolios comprise short-term construction loan paper being the riskiest.

Is it commercially rated? Yes, by Standard & Poor's, Moody's, and others.

Tax Considerations

What tax advantages (or disadvantages) does it offer? REITs are not taxed at the corporate level, so dividends are higher. But shareholders personally are taxed. Unlike real estate limited partnerships, REITs cannot offer flow-through tax benefits, but some trustees pass on tax-sheltered cash flow (in excess of income) as a nontaxable return of capital. When shares are sold, however, the cost basis must be adjusted by such returns of capital in calculating capital gains taxes. To meet Internal Revenue Service tax-exemption requirements, 75% of a REIT's income must be real-estate related and 95% of it must be paid out to shareholders.

Economic Considerations

What economic factors most affect buy, hold, or sell decisions? REITs are most attractive to buy and hold when interest rates are low and supply and demand factors in the real estate industry favor growth in property values. Shares tend to be inflation-sensitive as values increase and dividends rise with higher rentals. Real estate is a cyclical industry and the risk-return relationship is maximized when investments are made over the long term. CMO REITs tend to be countercyclical.

REAL ESTATE, PHYSICAL

No investment alternative has been more ballyhooed as a way to get rich quick than real estate. With inflation a fact of life for half a century, this inflation-sensitive investment, with its high potential for leverage through mortgage financing and its abundant tax benefits, has indeed made many millionaires and provided millions of average home owners with nest eggs in the form of home equity.

Although the most liberal tax benefits of investment property were casualties of Tax Reform in 1986 and the baby boom that kept residential property values ascending for 30 years gave way in the 1990s to the baby bust, physical real estate, as long as the country continues to grow, holds the potential for substantial gain for those who know how to locate the best values and have the patience to endure the inevitable cycles, both regional and national.

Real estate has many drawbacks and risks, however, whether owned as an individual; in one of the several forms of joint ownership, which are distinguished mainly in terms of how an interest can be terminated and what happens to it in death or divorce; or through a corporation, which has the advantage of limited liability and the disadvantage of double taxation.

Among the problems of real estate ownership are high carrying costs in the form of property taxes, insurance, maintenance, and repairs; the risk of illiquidity; the risk of loss of value as the result of deflation or of demographic factors, declining neighborhoods, local economic changes, or government policies (such as a rise in property taxes or the imposition of rent controls); competition from professional and institutional investors affecting local supply and demand factors; changes in federal tax provisions; high costs of selling; and a host of special risks associated with specific types of holdings.

Physical real estate can be categorized as (1) residential, where, because the owner lives there, the utility of shelter or recreational use is an important part of the value but depreciation and maintenance are not allowable tax deductions; (2) rental, where income and tax benefits are primary goals, and appreciation secondary; (3) speculative, where income and utilitarian values are traded off for capital gains potential and losses can result from carrying costs (an example is investment in raw land); and (4) multipurpose, such as a multifamily residence used partly to live in and partly to rent, or a vacation property combining recreational use and rental income (tax implications where the status is not clearly established can be serious).

Properties can also be held in forms of shared ownership, which bring tax advantages and other benefits of home ownership to apartments and town houses. Cooperatives, where owners hold shares in total projects, and condominiums, where apartment units are owned along with a share of commonly shared facilities and amenities, often require a tradeoff of certain lifestyle prerogatives (e.g., a ban on pets) and have eligibility criteria advertising restrictions, or even prohibitions against renting that can severely limit liquidity. Condominium time-shares, where each of two or more owners has exclusive right of occupancy for a defined period, make condominium units much more affordable. The occupancy rights of some time-shared property even trade in a secondary market, not unlike securities.

The inflation protection, tax breaks, and total returns of real estate are also available through limited partnerships and real estate investment trusts (REITs). Such syndications offer diversification (by type of holding and geography), professional management, economies of scale, and limited liability for small investments, along with some risks and costs of their own.

* * *

What Is Physical Real Estate?

Physical real estate includes personal residences and investment properties in the form of developed and undeveloped land, established commercial or residential properties, condominiums, and cooperatives.

Buying, Selling, and Holding

How do I buy and sell it? Through a real estate broker or direct negotiation.

Is there a minimum purchase amount, and what is the price range? There is no minimum purchase amount; the price range is limitless. Properties can generally be financed with a down payment of 5% to 50% of value.

What fees and charges are involved? Real estate involves broker commissions and carrying costs in the form of debt interest, real estate taxes, and maintenance costs. Though there are many tax benefits associated with such costs, they can nonetheless be highly burdensome, especially if a property is not producing income.

Does it mature, expire, or otherwise terminate? Not in a financial sense, although related debt instruments have fixed maturities. Physical real estate is, of course, subject to destructive acts of nature, vandalism, and deterioration from use and time.

Can I sell it quickly? Liquidity varies with the type of property and market conditions; as a general rule, real estate is not a liquid investment.

How is market value determined and how do I keep track of it? Although general economic conditions and such factors as money supply and mortgage interest rates have an important effect, real estate is often characterized by independent markets. One segment of the industry (such as residential homes) can be booming, while another (such as office buildings) is depressed, and market conditions can vary widely from one community or geographical area to another. There is no formalized source of information about real estate prices. Trade associations can be a source of national and regional statistics and real estate brokers keep abreast of local values.

Investment Objectives

Should I buy this if my objective is capital appreciation? Yes.

Should I buy this if my objective is income? Yes, but only rental properties provide regular income.

To what extent does it protect against inflation? Real estate is inflation-sensitive, that is, both property values and rental income increase with inflation.

Is it suitable for tax-deferred retirement accounts? Personal residences are not legal investments. Real estate securities, such as real estate investment trusts (REITs) or income-oriented limited partnerships, can be appropriate investments, however.

Can I borrow against it? Yes; first, second, even third mortgages are common ways of borrowing against real estate. Home equity loans, a popular product of banks and other financial services institutions, are a convenient form of borrowing for home owners. On a professional scale, substantial fortunes have been made and lost using the financial leverage provided by real estate.

Risk Considerations

How assured can I be of getting my full investment back? Real estate offers no guarantees that values will not decline.

How assured is my income? A lease assures income for its term, to the extent the tenant is dependable and creditworthy.

Are there any other risks unique to this investment? Yes, many—including some not invented yet. Common risks include shifting population centers, changing local economies (including tax policies and rent control legislation), zoning changes, acts of nature, crimes like vandalism and arson, and physical deterioration.

Is it commercially rated? No.

Tax Considerations

What tax advantages (or disadvantages) does it offer? The main tax benefits are deductibility from federal income taxes of mortgage interest and property taxes, and on investment property, depreciation (which reduces taxable income without affecting cash flow) and deductible maintenance costs. All rental income is passive, but $25,000 of passive activity losses can be offset against nonpassive income (phased out for high-income taxpayers). Owners of personal residences can defer capital gains taxes by reinvesting the proceeds in another residence of equal or greater value within two years and are entitled to a one-time exemption from capital gains taxes up to certain limits after age 55. Unlike other consumer interest, which became nondeductible at the end of 1991, interest on loans secured by home equity is deductible up to $100,000. The tax code on this has changed several times, however, and you should get up-to-date advice.

Economic Considerations

What economic factors most affect buy, hold, and sell decisions? Real estate values parallel general economic cycles but are also subject to supply and demand conditions in local markets and in segments of the industry (such as commercial, industrial, residential). The most successful real estate investors have diversified portfolios (in terms of geography and type of holding) and stay in an investment until it becomes profitable. These opportunities, together with professional management and economies of scale, are available to individuals through real estate investment trusts (REITs) and limited partnerships.

SAVINGS ALTERNATIVES

For emergencies and for the sake of prudence, every investor should keep a certain amount of money in cash and in risk-free financial assets. Depending on one's need for liquidity, this often means choosing among the deposit accounts and certificates of deposit offered by banks and thrift institutions and U.S. Savings Bonds.

The following are brief descriptions of major savings alternatives:

Deposit accounts Depositors in subscribing banks, savings and loans, and credit unions are insured up to $100,000, respectively, by the Bank Insurance Fund (BIF), the Savings Association Insurance Fund (SAIF), and the National Credit Union Administration (NCUA). (BIF and SAIF are units of the Federal Deposit Insurance Corporation (FDIC) that were created in 1989 as pan of the regulatory reform accompanying the federal bailout of failing savings and loan associations). Different accounts have different features, however.

With full deregulation in March 1986, institutions became legally free to pay any rate of interest. Because banks and thrift institutions must keep costly reserves, however, and because their federal insurance gives them a marketing advantage, their best rates tend generally to be a hair below money market mutual funds. The exceptions are the more aggressive money center banks and institutions with riskier (thus higher-yielding) loan portfolios or skimpier services.

Certificates of Deposit CDs are issued by banks, savings and loan associations (S&Ls), and credit unions, in various denominations and maturities (some institutions offer designer CDs, with maturities to suit the customer) are also federally insured at member institutions. CDs, which can have similar maturities and vary a couple of points between issuers, are issued both in discount and interest-bearing form and sometimes with variable rates. Other variations include split-rate CDs, where a higher rate is paid early in the CD's term than in its later life; convertible-term CDs, which convert from fixed-rate to variable-rate instruments; and expandable CDs, which allow adding to the investment at the original rate. CDs can also be bought from some brokers, who make bulk purchases of high-yielding CDs from issuing institutions around the country and then resell them; since the brokers make markets in such CDs, buyers have liquidity they would not enjoy as direct investors.

Savings Bonds Savings bonds come with flexible yields (Series EEs, issued on a zero-coupon basis, pay 85% of the average yield on 5-year Treasury notes during the preceding six months with a minimum of 4% if held for 5 years), plus deferred federal taxability and exemption from state and local taxes. Previously issued Series E bonds can be rolled into EEs or HHs and Es and EEs can be rolled into HHs. HHs are interest-bearing and pay 4% over 10 years. Individuals meeting income qualifications can buy EE bonds to save for a child's higher education and enjoy total or partial federal tax exemption (see Tax Considerations below).

* * *

What Are Savings Alternatives?

Savings alternatives include interest-bearing deposit accounts at banks, savings and loans, and credit unions; bank certificates of deposit (CDs); and Series EE and HH U.S. Savings Bonds.

Buying, Selling, and Holding

How do I buy and sell them? Deposit accounts, CDs, and savings bonds may be transacted at banks or other savings and financial services institutions. Series EE bonds may also be available through employer-sponsored payroll savings programs. Series HH bonds can be acquired by exchanging Series E, EE, and freedom share bonds at Federal Reserve banks and branches or the Bureau of Public Debt (Parkersburg, West Virginia 26106). The Federal Reserve or BPD will also redeem HH bonds after six months from issue.

Is there a minimum purchase amount, and what is the price range? Deposit accounts are available with no minimum deposits, but interest may vary with balances and some banks impose charges (negative interest) when low balances become an administrative burden. CDs are usually issued for $500 and up, although some $100 CDs are available. Jumbo CDs are issued for $100,000 and up. Series EE bonds sell for $25 ($50 face value) to $5000 ($10,000 face value). Series HH bonds are issued in $500 to $10,000 denominations.

What fees and charges are involved? Fees and charges on deposit accounts vary with the institution and its product. As a general rule, the higher the balance, the longer the commitment, and the less service, the less the cost to the depositor. Such factors usually are reflected both in rates and in fees and charges. Although CDs involve no fees or charges to buy or to redeem at maturity, the Federal Reserve Board voted in March 1986 to impose a penalty of seven days' interest on amounts withdrawn within the first week from personal CDs. (Institutional CDs were made subject to other penalties for early withdrawal.) Savings bonds involve no fees or charges.

Do they mature, expire, or otherwise terminate? CDs have maturities ranging from 32 days to 10 years. Series EE bonds have adjustable maturities. Series HH bonds mature in 10 years.

Can I sell them quickly? Certain deposit accounts may require notice of withdrawal. CDs may be subject to early withdrawal penalties or the issuer may refuse withdrawal prior to maturity, except in cases of hardship. (Of course, it is usually possible to borrow against such collateral and interest is tax-deductible.) NOW and other savings accounts offer instant liquidity through checkwriting. CDs bought through brokers can be sold in the secondary market. Savings bonds may be redeemed after 6 months, but there may be interest penalties.

How is market value determined and how do I keep track of it? Large CDs traded by dealers and institutional investors and smaller CDs marketed by brokers have secondary market values that rise and fall in inverse relation to prevailing interest rates. There is no secondary market for consumer-size CDs bought directly from banks and other issuing institutions or for savings bonds and deposit accounts.

Investment Objectives

Should I buy these if my objective is capital appreciation? Other than interest compounding, there is no capital gains opportunity except in CDs traded in the secondary market.

Should I buy these if my objective is income? Deposit accounts provide income, although they vary in terms of how rates are determined, how interest is compounded and credited, and how effective annual yields compare competitively. CDs are used for income, but those due in less than one year and zero-coupon CDs are issued on a discount basis—that is, they are sold at less than face value and redeemed at face value. Series EE bonds do not pay interest until maturity and must be held 5 years to receive the full rate on redemption. Series HH bonds issued after March 1, 1993, pay a fixed rate of 4%.

To what extent do they protect against inflation? To the extent rates move with inflation, deposit accounts offer some protection. Fixed-rate CDs provide none, but short maturities limit risk. Variable-rate CDs provide some protection. Series EE bonds offer some protection because the rate is adjustable. Series HH bonds have a fixed rate and offer none.

Are they suitable for tax-deferred retirement accounts? Deposit accounts are legally eligible, but CDs are a better choice due to their higher yields. Because savings bonds already offer tax deferral, there would be no advantage in putting them in such accounts.

Can I borrow against them? Yes.

Risk Considerations

How assured can I be of getting my full investment back? Most deposits and CDs are insured to $100,000 per depositor by the Bank Insurance Fund (BIF) and the Savings Association Insurance Fund (SAIF)—both are units of the Federal Deposit Insurance Corporation (FDIC)—and by the National Credit Union Administration (NCUA). The FDIC and NCUA are federally sponsored agencies. (Nonmembers are insured by state-backed or private insurers, but check the exact conditions.) Savings bond are direct obligations of the federal government and are risk-free.

How assured is my income? Although rates may in some cases fluctuate, income is very safe because the agencies that insure principal oversee the financial affairs of the institutions.

Are there any other risks unique to these investments? No.

Are they commercially rated? Moody's and other services rate CDs.

Tax Considerations

What tax advantages (or disadvantages) do they offer? Savings bonds are exempt from state and local taxes. Interest on Series EE bonds is tax-deferred until cashed-in or redeemed at maturity; when exchanged for Series HH bonds, interest is tax-deferred until the HH bonds are redeemed (although interest on the HH bonds, paid semiannually, is taxed in the year received). EE bonds used to finance a child's higher education (tuition and fees, but not room and board) are exempt from federal taxes as follows: couples with modified adjusted gross income, adjusted annually for inflation (income including such items as Social Security and other retirement income) of $68,250 ($45,500 for single taxpayers) *at the time of redemption* may exempt 100% of interest; for higher incomes, the exemption graduates downward and is eliminated entirely at the level of $98,250 for couples ($60,500 for singles). Interest on deposit accounts and CDs is fully taxable.

Economic Considerations

What economic factors most affect buy, hold, and sell decisions? Safety and growth of principal through interest compounding are the main objectives with savings vehicles, although expectations concerning interest rate movements and inflation may guide decisions.

TREASURY SECURITIES (BILLS, BONDS, AND NOTES)

United States Treasury securities, called Treasuries for short. are backed by the full faith and credit of the U.S. government and are issued to finance activities ranging from daily cash management to the refinancing of long-term bonded debt.

Investors seeking income thus have a wide choice of maturities, yields, and denominations along with the utmost safety. The government would have to become insolvent before default could occur, and as long as it has the power to create money, that is not a real possibility.

Treasuries also offer excellent liquidity and exemption from taxation at the state and local (but not federal) levels, an advantage that can add significantly to yield in high-tax states and localities.

Being fixed-income securities, however, Treasuries are not immune to the ravages of high inflation, nor are they safe from market risk. When general interest rates move up, the prices of Treasuries, like all fixed-rate investments, move down—unluckily for investors forced to sell prior to maturity in the secondary market. On the other hand, Treasuries, unlike many other fixed-income investments, are not usually callable. With the exception of a recent 20-year issue with a 5-year call provision and some 30-year bonds callable 5 years before maturity, the government cannot force redemption when rates move down.

The major categories of Treasury securities are:

Treasury bills   Called T-bills for short, they are issued weekly with 13-week and 26-week maturities and monthly with a 52-week maturity, on a discount basis and in denominations beginning at $10,000 with multiples of $5000 thereafter. They are issued through the Federal Reserve System, and investors may submit tenders either on a competitive basis, specifying terms and risking rejection, or on a noncompetitive basis, in which case the average rate established in the regular auction applies and purchase is assured. T-bills can also be bought for a fee through banks and other dealers.

Treasury bonds and notes   These are interest-bearing, paying semiannually in most cases, and, like T-bills, sold through Federal Reserve banks and branches on a competitive or noncompetitive basis. Maturities of bonds range from 10 to 30 years, those of notes from 2 to 10 years. Bonds and notes can be bought in denominations as low as $1000. Except for 2-year notes, which are usually sold monthly, bonds and notes are offered as the need arises. Of course, outstanding issues with almost any maturity can be bought in the secondary market.

Other Treasury securities, covered elsewhere, include Series EE and HH Savings Bonds and zero-coupon products created by separating the principal and interest coupons from Treasury bonds. A special class, known as flower bonds, is discussed under Tax Considerations below.

Investors may also buy shares of mutual funds or unit investment trusts that invest in portfolios of Treasury securities.

* * *

What Is a Treasury Security?

A Treasury security is a negotiable debt obligation of the United States government, backed by its full faith and credit, and issued with various maturities.

Buying, Selling, and Holding

How do I buy and sell it? New issues of bills, bonds, and notes may be purchased through competitive or noncompetitive auction at Federal Reserve banks and branches. They can also be bought and sold at commercial banks, securities broker-dealers, and other financial services companies.

Is there a minimum purchase amount, and what is the price range? Treasury bills are issued in minimum denominations of $10,000 and multiples of $5000 thereafter. Notes and bonds are issued in denominations of $1000, $5000, $10,000, $100,000, and $1 million. Notes due in less than 4 years are usually issued in $5000 denominations.

What fees and charges are involved? Treasury securities bought and redeemed through Federal Reserve banks and branches are without fees. Purchases and sales through banks or broker-dealers involve modest fees (about $25) and/or markups.

Does it mature, expire, or otherwise terminate? Yes. Maturities range from 23 days (cash management bills) to 30 years (bonds).

Can I sell it quickly? Yes; bills, bonds, and notes enjoy an active secondary market and are highly liquid.

How is market value determined and how do I keep track of it? As fixed-income securities, Treasuries rise and fall in price in inverse relation to market interest rates. Because they are risk-free investments, money flows into Treasuries when investors are worried about the credit safety of other debt securities, causing lower yields and higher prices. The financial sections of daily newspapers report new offerings and secondary market yields. The Bureau of Public Debt (Washington, DC 20226) or the Federal Reserve bank or branch in your district will respond to inquiries concerning upcoming offerings.

Investment Objectives

Should I buy this if my objective is capital appreciation? No, but appreciation is possible if market rates decline.

Should I buy this if my objective is income? Yes, particularly Treasuries with longer maturities, but you are sacrificing yield in return for safety. After-tax yields get a boost in high-tax states and localities because interest is not taxed at the state and local levels.

To what extent does it protect against inflation? There is no protection, though short maturities offer less exposure to the risk of inflation.

Is it suitable for tax-deferred retirement accounts? Yes.

Can I borrow against it? Yes, to 90% at most banks and brokers.

Risk Considerations

How assured can I be of getting my full investment back? From the credit standpoint, Treasuries offer the highest degree of safety available. You can be assured of getting your money back at maturity. Should you wish to sell earlier in the secondary market, you may find market prices have declined because of rising market interest rates. (Experts sometimes hedge this risk using interest-rate options, futures, and futures options.) Inflation, of course, erodes dollar values.

How assured is my income? There is virtually no risk the government will default on interest. Some bonds may be callable, terminating interest prematurely. Inflation, of course, can erode the value of fixed-interest payments, and low-yielding securities, like Treasuries, are especially vulnerable in hyperinflation, where the inflation rate can exceed the interest rate.

Are there any other risks unique to this investment? No.

Is it commercially rated? No, since Treasuries are risk-free, there is no need for commercial credit ratings.

Tax Considerations

What tax advantages (or disadvantages) does it offer? Treasuries are fully taxable at the federal level but are exempt from state and local taxes. A special class, called estate tax anticipation bonds or flower bonds, can be used, regardless of cost, at par value in payment of estate taxes, if legally held by the decedent at time of death. Savings bonds, discussed in the section dealing with savings alternatives, are exempt from federal taxes in a specific instance.

Economic Considerations

What economic factors most affect buy, hold, or sell decisions? As with any fixed-income investment, it is best to buy when market rates are high and issues carry a competitive yield. Since prices vary inversely with market interest rates, the holding becomes more attractive as market rates decline. As low-yielding, fixed income securities, treasuries fare poorly in inflation. Because they are virtually default-proof, they are highly desirable holdings when poor business conditions make other investments vulnerable to default, though yields of Treasuries may decline as a result.

UNIT INVESTMENT TRUST

Like a mutual fund, a unit investment trust (UIT) offers to small investors the advantages of a large, professionally selected and diversified portfolio. Unlike a mutual fund, however, its portfolio is fixed; once structured, it is not actively managed, except for some limited surveillance. It is also self-liquidating, distributing principal as debt securities mature or are redeemed, and paying out the proceeds from equities as they are sold in accordance with predetermined timetables. A one-time sales charge of less than 5% is the only significant cost, and considering this buys you a share in a "millionaire's portfolio," it is one of the attractions. Increasingly, equity UITs holding as few as five stocks, maturing annually, and following a formula investing approach, are being sold on their economic merits; it simply costs you less to buy shares of the UIT than to trade the same stocks yourself at the commission rates a full-service broker would charge.

While sponsors commonly offer instant liquidity as a feature of UITs, liquidity is provided specifically through agreements to make markets in shares or to redeem them; there is not an active secondary market in the public sense, and investors should read the prospectus to determine whether and by what means liquidity provisions exist.

The most common form of UIT is made up of tax-exempt municipal bonds, put together by an investment firm with special expertise in the municipals field. The bonds are deposited with a trustee, usually a bank, which distributes interest and the proceeds from redemptions, calls, and maturities and provides unitholders with audited annual reports. Since unitholders pay taxes as though they were direct investors, portions of income payments representing interest are not taxable, nor are portions representing principal, which are tax-free returns of capital. Capital gains, however, are taxable, technically at the time the trust realizes them, although unit-holders commonly recognize them only after their investment in the trust has been recovered from distributions of principal or at the time they sell their shares. It is important to get tax advice on this.

Unit investment trusts are also available with portfolios of money market securities; corporate bonds of different grades; mortgage-backed securities; U.S. government securities; adjustable and fixed-rate preferred stocks; utility common stocks; foreign bonds; replications of stock indexes; and other investments. New varieties of UITs are being created all the time.

Some sponsors offer additional conveniences to investors, including checkwriting, reinvestment options, and exchanging or swapping, for modest fees, among other unit investment trusts under their sponsorship.

*   *   *

What Is a Unit Investment Trust?

A unit investment trust (UIT) is a trust that invests in a fixed portfolio of income-producing securities and sells shares to investors.

Buying, Selling, and Holding

How do I buy and sell it? UITs are bought from sponsoring broker-dealers, who usually stand ready to redeem shares.

Is there a minimum purchase amount, and what is the price range? Shares (units) costing $1000 are typical.

What fees and charges are involved? A sales charge (load) ranging from less than 1% to 5% of your investment (4% is typical, with discounts for volume). An annual fee, usually 0.15%, is factored into the yield. Additional fees (0.30% typically) may apply when the portfolio is insured. Some equity trusts, such as the popular Select Ten Portfolios that hold high-yielding Dow Jones Industrial stocks for one year, offer reduced fees for annual "renewals."

Does it mature, expire, or otherwise terminate? Trusts are self-liquidating. Proceeds are distributed as securities mature or are sold. The life of most municipal UITs is 25 to 30 years. but 10-year trusts are common and some are as short as six months.

Can I sell it quickly? Liquidity is not guaranteed, but it usually exists to some extent because of most sponsors' intentions, once shares are sold, to make markets as an accommodation to holders wishing to sell. Trustees may also redeem shares, but such provisions should be investigated before buying shares. Sponsors may also allow switching into their other investment products at little or no cost.

How is market value determined and how do I keep track of it? Since shares represent units in an investment pool, values are determined by the forces affecting the securities in the pool. Thus trusts composed of fixed-income bonds will increase in value as interest rates decline and vice versa. A trust made up of stocks will be affected by market movements and earnings forecasts for individual stocks, among other factors. Details of a particular trust and its portfolio are set forth in the prospectus that, by law, is provided to investors.

Investment Objectives

Should I buy this if my objective is capital appreciation? UITs usually are set up to provide income (but even with a fixed portfolio, capital gains and losses can result from interest rate movements and other factors). Stock index trusts and other equity products have capital gains or total returns as a primary goal.

Should I buy this if my objective is income? Yes.

To what extent does it protect against inflation? Bond trusts offer no protection; equity trusts and floating-rate trusts offer some.

Is it suitable for tax-deferred retirement accounts? Yes, except those with portfolios of securities that are already tax-exempt.

Can I borrow against it? Yes, subject to Federal Reserve margin rules. The lack of an active secondary market raises a question about ready marketability and the attractiveness of shares as collateral.

Risk Considerations

How assured can I be of getting my full investment back? This varies with the safety of the investments in the trust, government bonds and common equities being at opposite ends of the spectrum. Interest rates may decrease the value of bonds, and therefore of shares, unless held for the life of the trust; market risk is always a question with equities. A growing number of trusts purchase insurance against credit risk.

How assured is my income? Portfolios are well diversified, making income relatively secure.

Are there any other risks unique to this investment? The lack of active management, once the portfolio is established and the shares sold, limits responsive corrective action in the face of adverse portfolio developments. Diversification provides some protection, however.

Is it commercially rated? Yes.

Tax Considerations

What tax advantages (or disadvantages) does it offer? None. UITs are subject to the same taxes (or exemptions) as the investments comprising them. But trusts composed of municipal bonds, some specializing in triple-tax-exempt portfolios for qualified residents, are common, and many taxable UITs are designed for tax-deferred retirement programs.

Economic Considerations

What economic factors most affect buy, hold, or sell decisions? Unit investment trusts are bought with the intention of holding until they self-liquidate. The same considerations that would guide an investor in choosing debt, equity, or money market securities would guide the choice of a particular UIT.

ZERO-COUPON SECURITY

Zero-coupon securities don't pay out their fixed rate of interest like other debt securities; they are issued at deep discounts and accumulate and compound the interest, then pay the full face value at maturity. The attractions for the investor are mainly twofold: (1) They can be bought at very low prices because of the deep discount and (2) Their yield to maturity is locked in, which takes the guesswork out of interest reinvestment.

The mathematical effects of a zero-coupon security, unless one is used to thinking in terms of compound interest over long periods, can seem astonishing: $1000 invested today in a 7%, 30-year zero-coupon bond will bring $7878 at maturity!

The disadvantages of zeros are that income taxes (unless they are tax-exempt) are payable as interest accrues (and out of cash raised from another source); they are highly volatile; and their value at maturity can erode with inflation. (Of course, the opposites are also true: Higher volatility means advantageously higher capital gains when rates are declining, and in a deflationary environment, value at maturity would be greater.) Credit risk, especially with corporate zeros, can be greater than with a regular bond; if the issuer defaults after a certain amount of time has passed, the investor has more to lose, since nothing has been received along the way.

Not surprisingly, a popular use of taxable zeros. with their low purchase prices and automatic compounding, is tax-deferred retirement accounts, where they are sheltered from taxability on imputed interest.

The following are principal types of zeros:

Corporate zero-coupon securities   These are not usually recommended for individual investors because of credit risk and because the yield tends not to be competitive in relation to the risk. One explanation is that these issues are marketed to investors who do not have to pay taxes on imputed interest such as foreign investors.

Strips and STRIPS   Strips are U.S. Treasury or municipal securities that brokerage firms have separated into principal and interest which, represented by certificates (the actual securities are held in escrow), are marketed as zero-coupon securities under proprietary acronyms like Salomon Brothers' CATS (Certificates of Accrual on Treasury Securities) and M-CATS (Certificates of Accrual on Tax-exempt Securities). Although the obligor is actually the broker, the escrow arrangement assures a high degree of security. Free of risk altogether are STRIPS, Separate Trading of Registered Interest and Principal of Securities, the Treasury's acronym for its own zero-coupon securities. STRIPS are Treasury bonds issued in the traditional way but separated into interest and principal components at the discretion of bondholders using book entry accounts at Federal Reserve banks.

Strips of mortgage-backed securities placed privately or by government agencies are also available. To enter the Federal Reserve's book-entry system, however, federal agency strips must satisfy a technicality requiring a minimum of 1% of the principal of the underlying loans; in other words, they can't be 100% interest.

Municipal zero-coupon securities   These securities are issued by state and local governments and are usually exempt from federal taxes and from state taxes in the state of issue. They provide a convenient way of providing for the future goals of high-bracket investors who get an after-tax benefit from their lower interest rates. One caveat, however: some are issued with call features, which can defeat the purpose of a zero from the investor's standpoint, so avoid those.

Zero-coupon convertibles   Introduced in the mid-1980s, these convertibles come in two varieties: one, issued with a put option, converts into common stock, thus providing growth potential; the other, usually a municipal bond, converts into an interest-paying bond, thus enabling the investor to lock in a rate, then, 15 years later, to begin collecting interest.

* * *

What Is a Zero-Coupon Security?

A zero-coupon security is a debt security or instrument that does not pay periodic interest but is issued at a deep discount and redeemed at face value.

Buying, Selling, and Holding

How do I buy and sell it? Through a securities broker-dealer and many banks. Some products are proprietary, available only at the dealers marketing them.◆

Is there a minimum purchase amount, and what is the price range? Because of their deep discount, zero-coupon securities can be bought quite cheaply; a $1000 20-year bond yielding 12% would cost about $97, for example. Broker-dealer minimums of 10 bonds or more are common.

What fees and charges are involved? A broker commission or a dealer spread.

Does it mature, expire or otherwise terminate? Yes; zero-coupon securities have a specified maturity, although some may have put options or be convertible into common stock or interest-bearing bonds. Some zeros have been issued with call features.

Can I sell it quickly? Investors generally buy zeros intending to hold them until maturity. Should you need to sell, the broker-dealer you bought it from can probably make a market, although you would certainly pay a higher transaction cost. Zeros based on treasury securities are somewhat more liquid than corporate or municipal zeros.

How is market value determined and how do I keep track of it? Zeros, being essentially fixed-rate investments, rise and fall in inverse relation to interest rates and are especially volatile. Zeros are listed along with regular bonds in daily newspapers.

Investment Objectives

Should I buy zeros if my objective is capital appreciation? Investing one sum of money and getting back a larger sum is what zeros are all about, so the answer is really yes. Strictly speaking, however, the appreciation is not a capital gain, but is rather compounded interest. Capital gains are possible from secondary market sales after interest rates have declined, but zeros are not usually traded for capital gain.

Should I buy this if my objective is income? No. Zeros pay no periodic income.

To what extent does it protect against inflation? As fixed-rate investments, zeros generally offer no inflation protection. Zeros convertible into common stock offer some.

Is it suitable for tax-deferred retirement accounts? Because zeros are taxed as though annual interest were being paid, they are considered ideal candidates for tax-deferred plans. An exception, of course, would be municipal zeros, which are tax-exempt anyway.

Can I borrow against it? Yes, subject to Federal Reserve margin rules and lender policies.

Risk Considerations

How assured can I be of getting my full investment back? Corporate and municipal issues, unless insured, vary with the credit of the issuer, so credit ratings are important. Treasury issues that are stripped (split into two parts—principal and interest) by brokerage houses and marketed separately as zero-coupon securities represented by receipts or certificates, are highly safe as long as the broker holds the underlying Treasury security in escrow, as is the practice. Some municipal strips issued by brokers (e.g., M-CATS) have indirect U.S. government backing, since they represent prerefundings invested in Treasury securities. Direct Treasury zeros (STRIPS) are risk-free. Zeros sold in the secondary market are susceptible to interest rate risk and a wide dealer spread. Of course, full investment, when talking zeros, means face value, not the small amount originally invested, since money is assumed to have a time value

How assured is my income? Zeros do not pay income; the income return is built into the redemption value.

Are there any other risks unique to this investment? Other than the small risk of an issuing firm going bankrupt in the case of receipts and certificates issued by brokerages, the unique risk of zeros has to do with the degree of exposure; should a zero default, there is more to lose compared with an interest-bearing security, where some portion of interest would have been paid out and presumably been reinvested. Some municipal issues may be callable, which largely defeats the purpose for which most investors hold zeros. Mortgage-backed strips respond to the prepayment experience of the underlying loans. If rates fall, prepayments increase. This shortens the life of strips and decreases the amount of interest earned.

Is it commercially rated? Municipal and corporate issues are rated.

Tax Considerations

What tax advantages (or disadvantages) does it offer? Interest is taxable as it accrues each year, just as if it were paid out. An exception, of course, are tax-exempt municipal zeros, which may also be exempt from taxes in the state of issue. U.S. government zeros are taxable at the federal level but exempt from state and local taxes. Savings bonds, a form of U.S. Government zero-coupon bond are another exception. Series EE holders may elect to defer paying taxes until the bonds mature and can then exchange them for Series HH bonds and continue deferring taxation until the HH bonds come due. (See Savings Alternatives, page 74).

Economic Considerations

What economic factors most affect buy, hold, and sell decisions? Zeros are purchased based on competitive yield considerations and are normally held until maturity, their appeal being a locked-in interest rate as opposed to a yield that varies with the reinvestment value of periodic interest payments in changing markets. Should it be necessary to sell in the secondary market, lower rates mean higher prices. Considerations governing convertible zeros are complex and vary with the provisions of the issue.

PART II

How to Read an
Annual Report

How to Read a Quarterly Report

HOW TO READ AN ANNUAL REPORT

Weekend sailors know an axiom that if you can understand a dinghy you can sail a yacht. It's all in grasping the fundamentals. Annual reports are the yachts of corporate communications, and in full regalia they can be as formidable as they are majestic. Fashioned by accountants and lawyers as well as marketers and executives, and costing major companies as much as $250,000 to $750,000 to publish, the reports are aimed at a variety of audiences—stockholders, potential stockholders, securities analysts, lenders. customers, and even employees. Essentially, however, they are financial statements, and if you can understand the basics, you will find that the rest is elaboration, much of which is legally required and very helpful. Of course, there are other parts that are simply embellishment. and those you take with a grain of salt. First, let's look at a "dinghy."

Basically, a financial statement comprises a *balance sheet* and an *income statement*. Exhibit I illustrates a statement reduced to "bare timbers."

EXHIBIT 1
BALANCE SHEET
December 31, 19XX

Cash/near cash	**5**	Accounts and notes payable	15	
Accounts receivable	**20**	Accrued liabilities	5	
Inventory	35	Current portion, long-term debt	5	
CURRENT ASSETS	**60**	**CURRENT LIABILITIES**	**25**	
		Long-term liabilities	25	
		TOTAL LIABILITIES	**50**	
Net fixed assets	35			
Other assets	5	Capital stock	10	
		Retained earnings	40	
		NET WORTH	**50**	
TOTAL ASSETS	**$100**	**TOTAL LIABILITIES AND NET WORTH**	**$100**	

THE BASIC BALANCE SHEET

A balance sheet (also called a statement of financial position or a statement of condition) is simply the status of a company's accounts at one moment in time, usually the last business day of a quarter or year. It is often compared to a snapshot, in contrast to a motion picture. On one side, it lists what the company owns—its assets. On the other side it lists what the company owes—its liabilities—and its net worth, or owners' equity, which is what investors have put into the firm plus earnings that have been retained in the business rather than paid out in dividends. The two sides are always equal. Even if a firm were insolvent—that is, owed more than it had in assets—the sides would be equalized by showing a negative (or deficit) net worth.

(A minor technical point: Balance sheets can be presented with opposing sides, as just described, which is known as the account form, or with the assets above the liabilities and owners' equity, which is called the report form.)

EXHIBIT 1

INCOME STATEMENT
for the year ended December 31, 19XX

SALES		**$110**
Cost of goods sold	80	
Depreciation	5	
Selling, general, and administrative expenses	15	
	100	
NET OPERATING PROFIT		**10**
Other income or expense	1	
Interest expense	2	
Income taxes	2	
NET INCOME	5	**5**

THE BASIC INCOME STATEMENT

The income statement, which goes by such other names as statement of profit and loss, operating statement, and earnings statement, reports the results of operations over a specified period of time—12 months in the case of an annual report. As customers are billed, and as the costs and expenses of producing goods, running the business. and creating sales are incurred and recorded, the information summarized in the income statement is accumulated.

The income statement will be discussed below in more detail; it is enough for now to understand that its highlights are sales (or revenues), net operating profit (or operating income), and net income. It is this last amount—popularly called the bottom line because it comes after interest expense, unusual income and charges, and income taxes—that is available to pay dividends to shareholders or to be kept in the business as retained earnings.

A word about one expense item, called depreciation, which is important to understand because it is a major factor in cash flow, the net amount of cash taken into the business during a given period and the cash paid out during that period. Depreciation, which is sometimes combined in the figure for cost of goods sold, is merely a bookkeeping entry that reduces income without reducing cash. In other words, depreciation is a noncash expense, and it is added back to net income to determine a company's cash earnings. Net income plus depreciation equals cash flow from operations. More about depreciation and cash flow later.

BASIC RATIO TESTS

With the foregoing information on balance sheets and income statements, it is possible to look at a firm's year-to-year financial statements and make some tentative judgments about the firm's basic financial health and operating trends, particularly if you can compare the figures with those of other firms in a comparable industry. An in-depth look at important financial ratios is at the end of the discussion of the annual report, but much can be learned at a glance by applying the following basic ratio tests.

Current Ratio   The current ratio is current assets divided by current liabilities. Current assets are assets expected to be converted to cash within a normal business cycle (usually one year), and current liabilities are obligations that must be paid during the same short-term period. For a manufacturing company (standards vary from industry to industry), a ratio of between 1.5 to 1 and 2 to 1—$1.50 to $2.00 of current assets for each $1.00 of current liabilities—is generally considered an indication that the firm is sufficiently liquid. In other words, there is enough net working capital (the difference between the two figures) to ensure that the firm can meet its current obligations and operate comfortably.

It is important that a company have this cushion because the liquidity of current assets, with the exception of cash and its equivalents, cannot be taken for granted; receivables can become slow or uncollectible (although a reserve for expected write-offs is normally provided) and inventory can lose value or become unsalable. Such things happen in recessions, and can result from poor credit, purchasing, or marketing decisions. Liabilities, unfortunately, remain constant. Of course, a company can have too much liquidity, suggesting inefficient use of cash resources, shrinking operations, or even vulnerability to a takeover attempt by an outside party. Well-run companies are lean, not fat.

Quick Ratio The quick ratio, which is also known as the acid-test ratio, is the current ratio, with inventory, its least liquid and riskiest component, excluded. It is calculated by adding cash, near-cash (for instance, marketable securities), and accounts receivable (sometimes collectively termed monetary assets), and dividing by current liabilities. Assuming no negative trends are revealed in year-to-year comparisons, a ratio of between .50 to 1 and 1 to 1 generally signifies good health, depending on the quality of the accounts receivable.

Average Collection Period A quick way of testing accounts receivable quality is to divide annual sales by 360 and divide the result into the accounts receivable. That tells you the average number of days it takes to collect an account. Since terms of sale in most industries are 30 days, a figure of 30 to 60 would indicate normal collections and basically sound receivables—at least up to the date of the statement. It may be helpful to compare a company's figure with that of other firms in the same industry.

Inventory Turnover Inventory turnover ratio tells the approximate number of times inventory is sold and replaced over a 12 month period and can be a tipoff, when compared with prior years' figures or comparative industry data, to unhealthy accumulations. Inventory should be kept adequate but trim, because it ties up costly working capital and carries market risks. To calculate turnover, divide the balance sheet inventory into sales. (*Note:* Industry comparative data published by Dun & Bradstreet and other firms providing finaneial data on companies compute this ratio using sales, not cost of goods sold. While cost of goods sold, because it does not include profit, produces a purer result, it is necessary to use sales for the sake of comparability.) As a general rule, high inventory turnover reflects efficient inventory management, but there are exceptions. A firm may be stockpiling raw materials in anticipation of shortages, for instance, or preparing to meet firm orders not yet reflected as sales. If inventory turnover is falling compared to prior years or is out of line with industry data, you should investigate the reasons. Year-to-year comparisons of inventory turnover are of particular significance in high volume–low profit margin industries such as garment manufacturing and retailing.

Debt-to-Equity Ratio   The debt-to-equity ratio can be figured in several ways, but for our purposes it is total liabilities divided by net worth. It measures reliance on creditors to finance operations and is one of several capitalization ratios summarized below. Although financial leverage—using other people's money to increase earnings per share—is desirable to a point, too much debt can be a danger sign. Debt involves contractual payments that must be made regardless of earnings levels; it must usually be refinanced when it matures at prevailing (perhaps much higher) money costs; and it has a prior claim on assets in the event of liquidation. Moreover, debt can limit a company's ability to finance additional growth and can adversely affect a firm's credit rating, with implications for the market value of shares. What is considered a proper debt-to-equity ratio varies with the type of company. Those with highly stable earnings, such as many utilities, are able to afford higher ratios than companies with volatile or cyclical earnings. For a typical industrial company, a debt-to-equity ratio significantly higher than 1 to 1 should be looked at carefully.

Operating Profit Margin   This figure, obtained by dividing a firm's net operating profit by sales, is a measure of operating efficiency. (Analysts sometimes add depreciation back into net operating profit since it is not a cash expense.) Year-to-year comparisons can be a reflection on cost control or on purchasing and pricing policies. Comparisons with other firms in the same industry provide insight into a company's ability to compete.

Return on Equity   This is the bottom line as a percentage of net worth (net worth is divided into net income), and it tells how much the company is earning on shareholder investment. Compared with the figures of prior years and similar companies, it is a measure of overall efficiency—a reflection on financial as well as operational management. But it can also be affected by factors beyond the control of management, such as general economic conditions or higher tax rates. And be suspicious of a firm with abnormally high returns; it could be in for competition from firms willing to sacrifice returns to gain a larger market share. As a rule of thumb, return on equity should be between 10% and 20%.

By applying the foregoing ratio tests to a company's basic balance sheet and income statement, particularly with the help of data on the company's prior years and on other companies in the same industry, you get a sense of whether the company's financial structure and operational trends are essentially sound. There is, however, a great deal you still don't know, such as:

- How reliable are the numbers?
- Are results affected by changes in accounting methods?
- Have there been changes in the company's top management?
- From what product lines did sales and profits largely derive?
- Did any special events affect last year's results?
- What new products are on the horizon?
- Are there any lawsuits or other contingent liabilities that could affect future results or asset values?
- To what extent are the company's operations multinational, and what is its exposure to foreign exchange fluctuations and/or political risk?
- If the company is labor-intensive, what is the status of its union contracts?
- What is the status of the company's debt? Is any financing or refinancing planned that could affect share values?

- How sensitive is the company to changes in interest rates?
- What were the sources and applications of cash?
- Are any major capital expenditures (for instance, real estate, machinery, equipment) being planned? How are existing fixed assets depreciated?
- How much is allocated to research and development?
- What other operational or financial changes has management planned?
- Does the company have a broad base of customers, or a few major customers?
- To what extent is the company dependent on government contracts?
- What is the company's pension liability, and what are its pension assets? Has it adequately provided for other postretirement employee obligations?
- Does the company have significant financial assets (such as leases or "derivatives") that may represent "off-balance sheet" risk, deferral of losses, or premature recognition of gains?
- If the company has been "downsizing" (a 90s trend), is it clear what impact discontinued operations have had and what the future of continuing operations is likely to be?

WHAT THE ANNUAL REPORT INCLUDES

The majority of annual reports of major public companies include a table of contents on the inside front cover. The following is typical:

> **Contents**
> Highlights
> Letter to Shareholders
> Review of Operations
> Financial Statements
>   Report of Independent Accountants
>   Consolidated Financial Statements
>   Statement of Consolidated Cash Flows
>   Notes to Financial Statements
>   Supplementary Tables
>   Management's Discussion and Analysis
> Investor's Information
> Directors and Officers

Highlights

The highlights greet you at the start of an annual report. Often including charts and other graphics, they present basic information in a clear, comparative way that requires little explanation. At the very least, you should expect to find the company's total sales for the past two years and its net income, expressed both as a total and on a per-share basis. Needless to say, upward trends (usually, but with exceptions) are positive and downward trends negative. But what is most important to understand is that the company and its public relations advisors can include here whatever other information they feel will create the desired impression on the shareholder. That usually means you can expect to find highlights that add up to a positive impression, although it has become lately a matter both of fashion and good business to include a downward trend or two for the sake of credibility. Basically, though, what you can expect to find highlighted, aside from the unavoidable, are the statistics of which the company is most proud. If dividends were up, they will probably be highlighted; if they were down, the same space might be devoted to an increase in research and development (R&D) expenditures, with the implicit promise of a future payoff for shareholders.

Occasionally, you will see information about common shares presented on a primary basis and on a basis assuming full dilution. Dilution occurs when an increased number of shares compete for the same amount of earnings, and it is a potential development when a company has convertible bonds, convertible preferred stock, warrants, or other securities outstanding that, if converted or exercised, would result in the issuance of additional shares. When dilution would significantly affect shareholders, companies are required to report earnings per share on both bases: before dilution (primary) and assuming conversion or exercise of all dilutive securities.

Should you encounter any other unfamiliar figures in the highlights, consult the Ratio Analysis Summary at the end of this discussion of an annual report.

Letter to Shareholders

In the many spoofs that have been written about corporate annual reports and their reputation for obfuscation, the least mercy has been reserved for the letter to shareholders. This review of the year just passed and look at the year ahead leads off the textual part of the report. It is usually signed by the chairperson and president and is often accompanied by a picture of the two together, suggesting amity not always characteristic of their day-to-day relationship.

While it is certainly true that the letter to shareholders is worded to put the best face on the past year's results and to soothe any anxieties that might be aroused by the financial figures to follow, it is nonetheless a statement of management's intentions and, when compared to prior years' messages, a test of management's credibility. Although it is not an audited, formal part of the report, it purports to be a serious comment on the year's results and their financial impact, a report that puts into perspective the major developments affecting shareholders, a statement of management's position on relevant social issues, and an expression of management's plans for the company's future. An impressive letter is one that compares past predictions with actual results and explains in a candid way the disappointments as well as the successes. Be wary of euphemisms (a "challenging" year was probably a bad one) and wording that is vague or qualified, a product area "positioned for growth" may sound promising, but it's not growing yet. If it were, the letter would say so. Much of the meaning of the letter to shareholders is between the lines.

Review of Operations

This review section consists of pictures and prose and often occupies the bulk of the pages of an annual report. Frequently slick, public relations-oriented, and designed to impress a corporation's various publics, the review can nonetheless be a valuable source of information about the company's products, services, facilities, and future direction. Unfortunately, it is also sometimes designed to divert the reader's attention from unpleasant realities. Be suspicious of reviews that stress the future and give the present short shrift or that are built around themes, such as the loyalty of employees or the company's role in building a stronger America. Also, what is not discussed can be more significant that what is discussed. Lack of reference to an aspect of operations described in the preceding year's annual report as an area of rapid growth and expansion may indicate that the company's expectations were not fulfilled and a write-off may be on the horizon. By and large, though, companies are responding to pressures for greater straightforwardness in the way they present themselves. In addition, companies these days are required to provide detailed financial information about the various segments contributing to their sales and profits. Although that information appears later in the supplementary financial data, it allows you to relate the activities being "promoted" to actual results and thus to evaluate the financial significance of different product areas. The Securities and Exchange Commission (SEC) has imposed stricter disclosure requirements in recent years, and these requirements have had a generally positive effect in terms of making annual reports more credible documents.

Financial Statements

Financial statements are, of course, the basic purpose of annual reports, and as the result both of expanded SEC disclosure regulation and companies' own interest in satisfying the information requirements of securities and credit analysts, financial statements have evolved over the years into presentations that elaborate substantially on the basic balance sheet and income statements. Reporting has also become more complex due to the complexity of the companies themselves, which have become diversified in terms both of product lines and geography, with a trend toward multinational operations involving political and currency risks.

Report of Independent Accountants: This report, also known as the auditor's opinion, is sometimes found at the beginning of the financial statement section and sometimes at the end, but it should be the first thing you read. Numbers are only numbers, and the opinion of an independent accounting firm, which is legally required of public companies, certifies that the financial statements were examined and validated. A "clean" or unqualified opinion—we'll get to what a qualified opinion means in a minute—typically reads as shown in Exhibit 2.

EXHIBIT 2

Report of Independent Accountants

To the Shareholders of XYZ Corporation:

We have audited the accompanying consolidated balance sheets of XYZ Corporation and subsidiaries as of December 31, 19X9 and 19X8 and the related consolidated statements of earnings, shareholders' equity, and cash flows for each of the three years in the period ended December 31, 19X9. These financial statements are the responsibility of the Company's management. Our responsibility is to express an opinion on these financial statements based on our audits.

We conducted our audits in accordance with generally accepted auditing standards. Those standards require that we plan and perform the audit to obtain reasonable assurance about whether the financial statements are free of material misstatement. An audit includes examining, on a test basis, evidence supporting the amounts and disclosures in the financial statements. An audit also includes assessing the accounting principles used and significant estimates made by management, as well as evaluating the overall financial statement presentation. We believe that our audits provide a reasonable basis for our opinion.

In our opinion, the financial statements referred to above present fairly, in all material respects, the consolidated financial position of XYZ Corporation and subsidiaries as of 19X9 and 19X8, and the consolidated results of their operations and their cash flows for each of the three years in the period ended December 31, 19X9, in conformity with generally accepted accounting principles.

The above format was adopted by the American Institute of Certified Public Accountants (AIPCA) in 1988 and departs significantly from traditional form.

Until 1988, the words "subject to" in the opinion paragraph were a widely recognized red flag. Such a "qualified opinion" meant the auditors had a reservation about the fairness of the presentation. Typical reasons for qualifying might be a pending lawsuit that, if lost, would materially affect the firm's finances; an indeterminable tax liability relating to an unusual transaction; or an inability to confirm a portion of inventory because of an inaccessible location. Although a qualified opinion was not necessarily negative, it was clear warning that warranted investigation and often led to negative comments by securities analysts with implications for the stock price.

The new format uses explanation rather than qualification where exceptions to "present fairly" are not clear-cut. It is thus possible to have an opinion that is clean but followed by explanations of potential problems.

Advocates of the new form say such disclosure is preferable to a qualified opinion, which implies trouble when it may not materialize. Proponents of the traditional form feel that the reader has inherited the burden of evaluating the seriousness of a potential development and been deprived of the auditor's more competent judgment. In any event, "modified opinions" challenge the reader to understand the issues raised. Explanations are usually found in footnotes to the financial statements and/or the management's discussion and analysis section.

Qualified opinions since 1988 include a statement that "except for" specified problems or departures from generally accepted accounting principles, the report would present fairly the company's financial position. In contrast to traditional qualified opinions, which were fairly common, such language is rare, since it means the Securities and Exchange Commission will require the company to resolve the problem or make the accounting treatment acceptable.

Even rarer are two other types of auditor's opinion, the disclaimer of opinion and the adverse opinion. A disclaimer of opinion states that an opinion is not possible because of a material restriction on the scope of the audit (for example, an inability to verify inventory quantities) or a material uncertainty about the accounts (for example, doubt about the company's continued existence as a going concern). An adverse opinion states that the company's financial statements do not present fairly the financial position or results of operations in accordance with generally accepted accounting principles. Either type of opinion is cause for concern, but you are unlikely to run into these types of opinions since the company will normally take the auditor's advice and make the necessary corrections.

You should be wary of a company's figures if the company regularly replaces the independent auditors. Such conduct could indicate that the company is opinion shopping— looking for auditors whose approach would produce the most favorable sales and earnings figures for the company and thereby perhaps hide problem areas or potential problem areas.

Report by Management: Usually accompanying the Report of Independent Accountants is a similar Report by Management certifying responsibility for the information examined by the accounting firm. This section attests to the objectivity and integrity of the data, estimates, and judgments on which the financial statements were based. It alludes to the company's internal controls and oversight responsibility of the board of directors for the financial statements as carried out through an audit committee composed of directors who are not employees. It is sometimes signed by the chief financial officer of the company and/or the chief executive officer.

Consolidated Financial Statements—Part 1: The Balance Sheet: In the following pages, we will discuss the financial statement of our hypothetical company, XYZ Corporation. As required, the statement presents comparative balance sheets as of the company's two most recent fiscal year ends and income statements for the past three years. Many variations exist on the accounts discussed below, and there are as many unique items as there are companies. But if you grasp the following, you will understand the basis of the vast majority of balance sheets and income statements.

First, an item-by-item explanation of XYZ's balance sheet (see Exhibit 3).

CURRENT ASSETS

Cash and Cash Equivalents   Cash requires little explanation; it is cash in the bank, on its way to the bank, or in the till. Cash equivalents, sometimes listed separately under cash and called marketable securities, represent idle funds invested in highly safe, highly liquid securities with a maturity, when acquired, of less than 3 months. Examples would be U.S. Treasury bills, certificates of deposit, and commercial paper. They are carried at the lower of their cost or market value. If they are shown at cost, their market value is indicated parenthetically or in a footnote.

Accounts and Notes Receivable   These are customer balances owing. When a company makes a sale, a customer is required either to pay in cash (cash sales) or, as in the majority of cases, within credit terms (credit sales), which tend to be standardized within industries but are typically 30 days and rarely more than 90 days.

Accounts receivable—sometimes called just receivables—are credit accounts that are not yet received. Often there is a reference to a footnote containing an aging schedule, a breakdown of accounts in terms of where they stand in relation to their due dates. This reveals delinquency and trends and is a valuable tool for analysts. Of course, a company expects a certain percentage of uncollectible accounts and, based on its historical experience and current policies (it might, for example decide to liberalize credit policy to boost sales), it sets up a reserve (or allowance) for bad debts, which is deducted from gross receivables to arrive at the balance sheet value. This is either noted on the balance sheet or explained in a footnote. Special attention should be paid to accounts receivable if a company does a significant percentage of its business with a few key customers. If any of these key customers were to have financial problems, the worth of the receivables carried on the company's books would quickly be in jeopardy.

Notes receivable normally account for a small portion of the total and usually represent cases in which special terms were granted and obligations were documented with promissory notes. If a short-term note receivable arose out of a loan or the sale of property or some other nontrade transaction, it would, if material, normally be shown separately or footnoted.

Inventories   This figure, when a company is engaged in manufacturing, is a combination of finished goods, work in process, and raw materials. Conservative accounting practice requires that inventories be carried at the lower of cost or market value, but there are different methods of inventory valuation, principally First In, First Out (FIFO) and Last In, First Out (LIFO).

Under the FIFO method, inventory is assumed to be sold in the chronological order in which it was purchased. Under the LIFO method, the reverse is true: The goods sold in a period are assumed to be those most recently bought. When prices are rising or falling, the difference is reflected in the balance sheet value of inventory. A company using the LIFO method during a period of inflation, because its cost of goods sold reflects the most recent—and higher—prices, will show lower profits on its income statement and a lower balance sheet inventory, since its ending inventory remains valued at older (lower) prices. Because LIFO produces lower taxable income in times of inflation, it is the method adopted by a majority of companies in recent years. Thus, the balance sheet inventories of these companies are undervalued—in other words, they have a "LIFO cushion." It is important to remember that *de*flation would produce the opposite result. An explanation of inventory valuation methods (or, significantly, any change in methods) is provided in the footnotes to the statements, which will also explain adjustments required by the tax law changes.

A company's inventory figure cannot be analyzed in a vacuum. To determine if a company is maintaining adequate inventory control, relate the inventory figure to the growth in sales. Inventory growth should keep pace with sales growth, not exceed it. A buildup of inventory relative to sales should be viewed with skepticism.

Prepaid Expenses   This account represents expenses paid in advance, such as rent, insurance, subscriptions, or utilities, that are capitalized—that is, recognized as asset values, and gradually written off as expenses, as their benefit is realized during the current accounting period. If the amount is important, this account is usually deducted from current assets in computing the current ratio. However, it usually represents an insignificant percentage of current assets and is thus ignored for analytical purposes.

NET FIXED ASSETS

Property, Plant and Equipment   This section of the balance sheet lists the company's fixed assets, sometimes called capital assets or long-term assets. These assets include land, buildings, machinery and equipment, furniture and fixtures, and leasehold improvements—relatively permanent assets that are used in the production of income. The word tangible is sometimes used in describing these assets, to distinguish them from intangible assets (described below), which similarly produce economic benefits for more than a year but which lack physical substance.

Fixed assets are carried—that is, recorded on the books of the company and therefore reported on its balance sheet—at original cost (the cost the company incurred to acquire them) less accumulated depreciation—the cumulative amount of that original cost that the company has written off through annual depreciation expenses charged to income. Land, however, because it is assumed to have unlimited useful life, is not depreciated. (Companies engaged in mining and other extractive industries, whose capital assets represent natural resources, enjoy depletion allowances, a concept similar to depreciation write-offs.) As a result of depreciation writedowns and inflation, it is not unusual for the book value of a company's fixed assets to be considerably lower than their market value. On the other hand, market value is an indication of what it will cost to keep fixed assets up to date and maintain sufficient capacity to support sales growth. The relationship between sales levels and capital expenditures is therefore an important factor in evaluating a firm's viability. However, businesses vary in terms of how capital-intensive they are; manufacturers rely more on fixed assets to produce sales than wholesalers, for example.

The existence of fully depreciated assets on a company's balance sheet may signal that the company is a likely candidate for a takeover attempt or a leveraged buyout. The company's plant, for instance, has most likely appreciated in market value over the years and the depreciated basis on which it is carried on the balance sheet may have no relationship to reality. Thus, new owners could in part finance the purchase of the company by selling some assets at their higher market value.

OTHER ASSETS

This category can include any number of items such as cash surrender value of life insurance policies taken out to insure the lives of key executives; notes receivable after one year; long-term advance payments; small properties not used in daily business operations; and minority stock ownership in other companies or in subsidiaries that for some reason are not consolidated. Additional types of assets, if significant, would be discussed in the footnotes.

Another category of other assets, which is sometimes broken out separately (as in our example), is generally called intangible assets. These are nonphysical rights or resources presumed to represent an advantage to the firm in the marketplace. The most common intangibles are (1) goodwill and (2) a grouping typically labeled patents, trademarks, and copyrights.

Goodwill refers to a company's worth as an operating entity, or going concern—the prestige and visibility of its name, the morale of its employees, the loyalty of its customers, and other going-concern values. These are values beyond the book value of the firm's assets. Thus, when a company is purchased at a price exceeding its book value, the difference—the value of its goodwill—represents a real cost to the acquiring company. Goodwill, though intangible and abstract, *can* be valued. Because it has no liquidation value, however, it is classified as an intangible asset and must be amortized (written off) over time, in accordance with generally accepted accounting principles. As with fixed assets and depreciation, this is done by annual noncash charges to income. Unlike the case of depreciation deductions, however, there has traditionally been no tax benefit to the company when intangibles are written off. However, under the Revenue Reconciliation Act of 1993 (the

EXHIBIT 3

XYZ CORPORATION
Balance Sheet
As of December 31
(Dollars in Millions)

	19X9	19X8
ASSETS		
Cash and cash equivalents	**7.6**	7.0
Accounts and notes receivable	**10.2**	9.5
Inventories	**23.0**	20.9
Prepaid expenses	**.3**	.2
Total Current Assets	**41.1**	37.6
Property, plant and equipment	**83.3**	79.4
Less: Accumulated Depreciation	**23.5**	21.3
Net Fixed Assets	**59.8**	58.1
Other assets	**3.8**	3.0
Intangible assets	**.9**	.9
TOTAL ASSETS	**105.6**	99.6
LIABILITIES AND SHAREHOLDERS' EQUITY		
Accounts payable	**4.2**	4.3
Notes payable	**.8**	—
Accrued liabilities	**3.2**	2.7
Federal income taxes payable	**8.2**	7.1
Current portion (maturity) of long-term debt	**.7**	.8
Dividends payable	**1.4**	.9
Total Current Liabilities	**18.5**	15.8
Other liabilities	**2.0**	1.4
Long-term debt	**16.2**	17.0
Deferred federal income taxes	**.9**	.7
TOTAL LIABILITIES	**37.6**	34.9
6% cumulative preferred stock ($100 par value; authorized and outstanding: 50,000 shares)	**5.0**	5.0
Common stock ($10 par value; authorized 2,500,000 shares; outstanding 1,555,000 shares)	**15.6**	15.6
Capital surplus	**8.2**	8.2
Retained earnings	**39.2**	35.9
TOTAL STOCKHOLDERS' EQUITY	**68.0**	64.7
TOTAL LIABILITIES AND STOCKHOLDERS' EQUITY	**105.6**	99.6

Clinton tax bill), goodwill and related intangible assets can be deducted ratably over a 15-year period on a straight line basis.

Patents, trademarks and copyrights, the other most common intangible assets, have economic value in the sense that they translate into profits, but their carrying value is based on their cost. Being intangibles, they are written off over what accounting practice deems to be their useful lives.

Other intangible assets might include capitalized advertising costs, organization costs, licenses, permits of various sorts, brand names, and franchises.

Because intangible assets are assumed not to have value in liquidation, they are excluded from most ratios used in analyzing values. The term tangible net worth is used to mean shareholder equity less intangible assets.

CURRENT LIABILITIES

Accounts Payable   This account represents amounts owed to suppliers for raw materials and other goods, supplies, and services purchased on credit for use in the normal operating cycle of the business. In other words, one company's account payable is another company's account receivable. As with receivables, conventional credit terms vary from industry to industry, but 30 days is standard and anything over 90 days is the exception (except in highly seasonal industries, such as garment manufacturing, where longer-term dating is commonplace and liquidity is provided by cashing accounts receivable with finance companies known as factors). The level of accounts payable should vary with sales levels, or, more specifically, with the amount of annual purchases—a part of the cost of goods sold. Any bulging of accounts payable in relation to purchases could mean a firm is relying to an unhealthy extent on trade suppliers as a source of working capital.

Notes Payable   These are usually amounts due banks or financial institutions on short-term loans, often under lines of credit. A line of credit is an arrangement by which a company may borrow working capital up to a limit, and details are usually covered in the footnotes. Notes payable may also be due suppliers under special credit arrangements.

Accrued Liabilities   Accrued liabilities arise when an expense is recognized as an obligation but the cash has not yet actually been paid out. Expenses commonly reflected in this account include payroll, commissions, rent, interest, taxes, and other routine expenses.

Federal Income Taxes Payable This account is similar to accrued liabilities, but is usually broken out in recognition of its importance. (It is to be distinguished from the account called deferred federal income taxes, a noncurrent liability discussed below.)

Current Portion (Maturity) of Long-Term Debt When a company has a long-term debt obligation that requires regular payments, the amount due in the next 12 months is recorded here as a current liability.

Dividends Payable These represent dividends that have been declared by the board of directors but have not been paid. Dividends become an obligation when they are declared, and are normally paid quarterly. They include both preferred and common dividends.

LONG-TERM LIABILITIES

These are debt obligations due after one year. Included are term loans from financial institutions, mortgages, and debentures (unsecured bonds), as well as capital lease obligations, pension liabilities, and estimated liabilities under long-term warranties. Details are provided in footnotes.

Depending on a company's accounting practices, long-term liabilities may also include an item called deferred federal income taxes. This is often due to the fact that companies may use different rules for tax purposes and reporting purposes, and this creates timing differences. For example, a company using accelerated depreciation for tax purposes would get large depreciation write-offs in the early years of an asset's life, thus saving taxes, but would have higher taxable income in the later years. For reporting purposes, however, the company might wish to use the straight line method of depreciation, which each year produces equal (and lower) charges, thus resulting in higher reported earnings. The amount of taxes deferred are shown on the statement used for reporting purposes (the annual report) as deferred federal income taxes.

SHAREHOLDERS' EQUITY

This section of the balance sheet represents the owner's interest—the value of assets after creditors, who have a prior legal claim, have all been paid. It includes accounts for preferred stock, common stock, capital surplus, and retained earnings.

Preferred Stock   Not all companies issue preferred stock, and it exists in several varieties. Several general characteristics are particularly notable: It usually pays a fixed dividend that must be paid before common dividends can be paid; it has precedence over common stock in the distribution of assets in liquidation; and if it is cumulative, unpaid dividends accumulate and must be paid in full before common dividends can be declared.

In recent years companies have used preferred stock as part of antitakeover programs. Referred to as poison-pill preferreds, these shares are created when a hostile takeover attempt is imminent. The new class of preferred stock is designed to raise the cost of the acquisition to a point where it may be abandoned by the company attempting the takeover. You should check whether a company has issued preferred specifically to fend off a takeover attempt and, if so, try to determine the implications such preferred may have for common shareholders.

Common Stock   Shares of common stock are the basic units of ownership in a corporation. Common shareholders follow behind creditors and preferred shareholders in claims on assets and therefore take all the risks inherent in the business. But, with rare exceptions, they vote in elections of directors and on all important matters, and while they may or may not receive dividends, depending on earnings and whether the directors vote to declare dividends, the book value of their shares stands to grow as net worth (shareholders' equity) expands through earnings retained in the business. Common shareholders in publicly traded companies also stand to profit from increases in market prices of shares, which normally reflect expectations of future earnings. But on the balance sheet, common shares are listed either at a par or stated value, an accounting/legal value signifying nothing other than the lowest price at which shares can be initially sold. Sometimes different classes of stock exist and are listed separately, with the privileges or limitations of each indicated parenthetically or in referenced notes.

Capital Surplus   Sometimes seen as additional paid-in capital (as preferred stock and common stock are sometimes called paid-in capital), this account reflects proceeds from issuances of stock that were in excess of the par or stated value of shares. For example, XYZ common has a par value of $10 per share; when 100,000 shares were issued at $12 a share, $1,000,000 was added to common stock and $200,000 was added to capital surplus.

Retained Earnings   This account is made up of corporate earnings not paid out in dividends and instead retained in the business. Retained earnings are not put in a special bank account or stuffed into a figurative mattress—they are simply absorbed as working capital or to finance fixed assets in order to generate more earnings.

Consolidated Financial Statements—Part 2: The Income Statement: The income statement shows the results of operations over a period of 12 months. Results of the two years prior to the year reported on are included for comparative purposes (see Exhibit 4).

NET SALES

Most income statements (or, more formally, Statements of Income), lead off with Net Sales—the total of cash sales (negligible for most industrial companies) and credit sales for the accounting period (12 months for annual reports). Net simply means after returns of merchandise shipped; freight-out; and allowances for shortages, breakage, and other adjustments having to do with day-to-day commerce. (Note that some service companies, including utilities, and financial organizations use the term revenues instead of sales.) Needless to say, the trend of sales as revealed in the three years' worth of figures is a key indicator of how a company is faring in the marketplace. The figures should of course be adjusted for inflation to give an accurate reading of year-to-year changes.

Changes in the components of a company's sales can be more significant than changes in sales figures. If, for example, a chemical company can shift from marketing bulk chemicals (which have a relatively small profit margin) to marketing specialty chemicals (which have a relatively large profit margin) it will ultimately earn more even without an increase in sales. Changes in sales components can be determined by reviewing the business segment information in the annual report (discussed below.)

COST OF GOODS SOLD

This is the cost of producing inventory and includes raw materials, direct labor, and other overhead that can be directly related to production. It is directly affected by the company's choice of the FIFO or LIFO inventory valuation methods (see Inventories, above). The reason becomes clear when you look at the formula by which cost of goods sold is determined:

Beginning inventory + Purchases during the period – Ending inventory
= Cost of goods sold

When the ending inventory (the balance sheet inventory) is the oldest stock, which is the case when the LIFO method is used, the cost of goods sold, assuming prices are rising with inflation. becomes a higher number than would be the case using FIFO. Of course, the higher the cost of goods sold, the lower will be taxable income, as we will see.

DEPRECIATION

This noncash expense was alluded to at the start of the discussion of an annual report and again under Deferred Federal Income Taxes Payable in the discussion of balance sheet liabilities. To encourage firms to keep facilities modern and thus spur the economy, the U.S. government provides businesses a way to pay less tax and thereby conserve cash. This is accomplished by allowing firms to take an annual percentage (called a depreciation write-off) of what they spent for certain types of fixed assets, such as buildings, machinery, and equipment, and to treat the amount as though it were an actual expense thus reducing taxable income without requiring an outlay of cash.

Depreciation is a highly complex tax accounting concept, and for purposes of reading annual reports it is not necessary to understand it completely. It is enough to know that tax rules make it possible for companies to recover the cost of certain fixed asset investments on an accelerated basis and thus to get the benefit of tax savings sooner than they would using the straight-line method (now required for

EXHIBIT 4

XYZ CORPORATION
Income Statement
Fiscal Year Ended December 31
(Dollars in Millions)

	19X9	**19X8**	**19X7**
Net Sales	98.4	93.5	88.8
Cost of goods sold	64.9	62.2	59.7
Depreciation and amortization	2.2	3.0	2.0
Selling, general, and administrative expenses	12.1	11.1	10.3
	79.2	76.3	72.0
Net Operating Profit	19.2	17.2	16.8
Other Income or (Expenses)			
Income from dividends and interest	.2		
Interest expense	(1.0)	(.9)	(1.0)
Earnings before income taxes	18.4	16.3	15.8
Provision for income taxes	8.3	7.5	7.3
Net Income	10.1	8.8	8.5

Common shares outstanding: 1,555,000
Net earnings per share (after preferred dividend
requirements in 19X9 and 19X8: 19X9: $6.30; 19X8: $5.47;
19X7: $5.47.

Statement of Retained Earnings

Retained Earnings Beginning of Year	35.9	33.6	31.3
Net Income for Year	10.1	8.8	8.5
Less: Dividends Paid on:			
Preferred stock ($6 per share)	.3	.3	
Common stock (per share): 19X9: $4.20; 19X8: $4.00;	6.5	6.2	6.2
19X7: $4.00)			
Retained Earnings End of Year	39.2	35.9	33.6

newly purchased real property). At the same time. companies are allowed, for purposes of annual reports, to reflect depreciation charges based on the straight line method, whereby the estimated useful life of the asset is divided into its cost to get a uniform annual depreciation charge, which is generally much lower than the figure used for tax purposes. Annual reports thus show higher earnings, while the stockholder has the satisfaction of knowing that the company's tax liability has been minimized. It is all spelled out in the footnotes.

What is more important to know is that depreciation charges have a relationship to the age of the assets and vary with the amount of investment in fixed assets. An increase in depreciation usually reflects increases in depreciable assets—fixed assets like plant and equipment. Decreases usually mean fixed assets have been disposed of or have become fully depreciated. Particularly since straight line depreciation is used by most companies for reporting purposes, lower depreciation charges can signal a need for fixed asset expenditures meaning long-term financing, which has implications for shareholders in the form either of dilution of share values or higher interest costs. Of course, increased or modernized plant capacity should also translate eventually into higher sales, greater operating efficiency and higher earnings per share.

Selling, General, and Administrative (SG&A) Expenses

These are all the expenses associated with the normal operations of the business that were not included in cost of goods sold, which represented direct costs of production. Salaries, rent, utilities, advertising, travel and entertainment, commissions, office payroll, office expenses, and other such items are representative of this category, which varies from industry to industry in terms of its composition and the relative importance of selling expenses versus administrative expenses.

A good test of the quality of a company's management is its ability to control selling, general, and administrative expenses. Many companies have fallen into bankruptcy simply because management was unable or unwilling to control expenses and keep them in line with the growth of sales.

Net Operating Profit

The net operating profit is what is left over after costs of goods sold, depreciation, and SG&A expenses are deducted from sales, and it tells you the company's profit on a normal operating basis—that is, without taking into account unusual items of income or expense or nonoperating expenses such as interest and taxes. As stated above, it is a measure of operating efficiency, and significant variations from year to year or from industry standards should be investigated by looking more closely at the figures behind the totals. many of which are supplied in footnotes or published in the company's form 10-K (see Investor's Information, below). Lower than expected profit due to a rise in SG&A expenses as a percentage of sales might be traceable to a single factor, such as a rise in officers' salaries, for example.

Other Income or Expenses

This category picks up any unusual or nonoperating income or expense items. Examples might include income, gains, or losses from other investments; gains or losses on the sale of fixed assets; or special payments to employees. Nonrecurring items are usually explained in detail in footnotes. In this category is *interest expense,* which, unlike dividends, is a pretax expense. For companies with bonds or other debt outstanding, however, interest expense is a recurring item. Because interest on funded debt is a contractual, fixed expense that, if unpaid, becomes an event of default, analysts follow closely a company's fixed-charge coverage—how many times such fixed charges are covered by pretax annual earnings.

EARNINGS BEFORE INCOME TAXES

This figure nets out all pretax income and expense items, but it would not be accurate to say it is the figure on which federal income taxes are based. That is because tax returns of corporations, as we have seen, use difficult methods of depreciation for tax purposes than they use for reporting to shareholders and because other factors, such as tax-loss carrybacks and carryforwards, which are not visible on the current year's statement, may affect the company's tax liability.

PROVISION FOR INCOME TAXES

After taking advantage of all available benefits, this is the company's tax liability for the year in question. Note that it is termed a *provision*. Payments based on estimated taxes have been made during the year, and net payments on this liability are payable according to a timetable determined by the Internal Revenue Service. A portion of the liability will be reflected as an accrued liability, as described above.

A company's effective tax rate should be compared with other companies in the same or similar industries. Although many tax loopholes have been ended by recent tax legislation, it may be a mark of smart and aggressive management if a company has a lower effective rate than other companies similarly engaged.

NET INCOME

This is the bottom line, the "after everything except dividends" figure. Dividends, by law, must be paid out of earnings, though not necessarily out of current earnings Below the bottom line, figures for common shares outstanding and earnings per common share are given. Securities analysts usually focus on earnings per share in assessing a company's status. As a rule, earnings per share are expected to grow from year to year, and it may be a sign of trouble if they do not grow according to predictions or if they do not grow at all.

Consolidated Financial Statements—Part 3: The Statement of Retained Earnings (Shareholders' Equity): What typically follows the Income Statement is an analysis showing retained earnings at the beginning of the period; how net income increased retained earnings; dividends paid on preferred stock and common stock during the period; and the retained earnings account at the end of the fiscal year being reported (see Exhibit 4). The last figure will, of course, be the same as the retained earnings figure in the stockholders' equity section of the balance sheet.

A Statement of Retained Earnings may reflect stock dividends—new shares issued to existing shareholders. Stock dividends are accounted for by decreasing retained earnings and increasing common stock in equal amounts (using par or stated value if the stock dividend represents more than 20 to 25 percent of outstanding shares, and market value if it represents less). Many investors are attracted to companies that regularly declare stock dividends. It should be borne in mind, however, that stock dividends in no way enhance the actual assets of a company.

Statement of Consolidated Cash Flows: The Statement of Consolidated Cash Flows (Exhibit 5) replaced the traditional Sources and Uses (or Application) of Funds statement in financial statements issued from 1988 on. "Funds" had previously meant either cash or net working capital (the difference between current assets and current liabilities), and the vast majority of companies used a format focusing on working capital.

By requiring an analysis of changes affecting cash, the Financial Accounting Standards Board (FASB) was recognizing that the viability of a company hinges ultimately on liquidity and that increases in working capital do not necessarily translate into increased cash. For example, a company that relaxed its credit standards to generate increased sales might show higher profits and working capital from one year to another, but it would not be able to meet its obligations unless and until its accounts receivable were collected in cash. Cash means cash and equivalents, defined by FASB as all highly liquid securities with a known market value and a maturity, when acquired, of less than 3 months.

The statement of cash flows puts operating results on a cash basis while showing balance sheet changes as they affect the cash account. (In order to provide a complete "bridge" between two balance sheets, the statement of cash flows will also show major balance sheet changes not affecting cash, such as an exchange of bonds for stock or the purchase of a fixed asset that is 100% financed by long-term debt.)

The FASB requires that cash flows be analyzed in three separate categories: cash flows from operating activities, cash flows from investing activities, and cash flows from financing activities. The most commonly used format is XYZ Corporation's, illustrated in Exhibit 5.

The operating analysis begins with the net income figure (from the income statement) and follows with the adjustments necessary to convert that figure to a cash basis.

Depreciation and amortization, as earlier discussed, are bookkeeping transactions that reduced the net income figure without any expenditure of cash; this item (found on the income statement) is thus added back to net income. The increase in the (balance sheet liability) account called deferred federal income taxes represents the portion of income tax expense not actually paid in cash and is similarly added back to net income.

Next are adjustments to assets and liabilities that changed because of operating activities and provided or used cash. The increase in the accounts and notes receivable is subtracted because it represents sales revenue included in net income but not collected in cash. The increase in inventories is also subtracted because it represents cash spent for inventory purchases in excess of the expense recognized through cost of goods sold. The increase in prepaid expenses is deducted because it represents cash spent but not charged against income. The decrease in XYZ's accounts payable between 19X9 and 19X8 is subtracted because the cash paid to vendors in 19X9 was greater than the amount of expense recorded. (Cash was paid for some 19X8 accounts.) Increases in accrued liabilities and federal income taxes payable were charged to income but not (yet) paid in cash and are thus added back. Other assets and liabilities were either net users (19X9) or providers of cash.

(Note: Adjustments to particular asset and liability accounts will not always equal changes in balance sheet figures as they do in the case of XYZ Corporation. In the case of companies with foreign operations, operating assets and liabilities translated from other currencies have been purified of the effects of currency exchange and a separate line is provided to show the effect of exchange rate changes on cash and cash equivalents. Also, the effects of acquisitions, when accounted for by the PURCHASE ACQUISITION method, and divestitures have been excluded from the operating cash flow adjustments although they are reflected in the balance sheet accounts.)

Cash flows from investing activities include changes in the company's investments in property, plant, and equipment; investments in other companies; and loans made and collected. An increase in investment reduces cash and a decrease (sale) increases cash. It is notable that dividends and interest received are typically treated as operating cash flow, although changes in the same investments are analyzed here. In the case of XYZ, the only changes were those affecting fixed assets. XYZ's only other investments are in the securities comprising cash equivalents; since the whole cash flow statement focuses on cash and cash equivalents, it would be redundant to show those changes here. The small amount of income XYZ received on its cash equivalents is reflected in the net income figure above.

Cash flows from financing activities include all changes in cash resulting from financing, such as short- and long-term borrowings, the issuance or repurchase of common and preferred stock, dividends paid, and changes in dividends payable.

To interpret the cash flow statement it is helpful to remember a basic rule of thumb: In a conservatively operated company, *permanent* capital requirements—fixed assets and the portion of working capital that is not seasonal—should be financed through a combination of retained earnings and either long-term debt or equity. *Short-term* requirements should be financed with short-term liabilities in a cycle that begins when accounts payable are created to purchase inventory, which in turn is sold to create accounts receivable, which are collected to produce cash, and so on.

Once that is understood, the statement can be a valuable analytical tool that reveals healthy or unhealthy trends; a company's capacity for future investment; its future cash requirements; its cash position compared to similar companies; and its actual cash flows versus those anticipated.

A look at Exhibit 5 tells us XYZ Corporation has been generating operating cash flows that generally support its steadily increasing sales. Cash flow from operations has been sufficient to finance annual additions and improvements to its plant and equipment and still pay dividends without impairing its working capital. The statement reveals that in 19X8 the company, despite profitable operations, would have had a negative cash flow (more cash flowing out than in), after meeting $6.5 million of long-term debt repayments, had management not properly planned for the requirement by issuing $5 million of preferred stock.

Discontinued Operations: One final observation: Discontinued operations, although not a factor in XYZ's case, show up frequently as a separate section of the income statements of large companies. Readers are thus able to distinguish between operating results that can be expected to continue in the future and those that have only historical significance. Discontinued operations are those that have been sold, abandoned, or otherwise disposed of. Any gain or loss from the disposal of a segment must be shown along with the operating results of the discontinued segment.

In their statement of cash flows, however, companies are permitted but not required to separately disclose the flows from discontinued operations and extraordinary items. When companies voluntarily make the separation, they indicate clearly that the analysis of net income and adjustments relates to continuing operations and includes a separate line for net cash provided (or used) by discontinued operations. But when discontinued operations that show up in the income statement are not broken out in the statement of cash flows, it is up to the reader to ascertain if a significant portion of the flows relate to operations that are not ongoing.

Notes to Financial Statements: Footnotes to financial statements, sometimes just called notes, are unfortunately named if there's any implication that they represent superfluous detail. Indeed, the balance sheet, the income statement, and the statement of cash flows contain the sentence: "The Notes to Financial Statements are an integral part of this statement." Footnotes set forth the accounting policies of the business—and provide additional disclosure. They contain information having profound significance for the financial values presented elsewhere in the financial statements.

It would be impossible to list here all the types of information one might find in the notes to financial statements. Here is a sampling, though, and if it succeeds in impressing you with the importance of reading this section of a financial report, it will have accomplished its purpose.

Accounting procedure changes A change in the method of valuing inventory or a change in the company's method of depreciating fixed assets can have significant effects on reported earnings and asset values. You should investigate further if a company frequently changes accounting procedures. The company may, for instance, be trying to hide weak aspects of its operations.

EXHIBIT 5

XYZ CORPORATION
Statement of Consolidated Cash Flow
Fiscal Year Ended Decemher 31
(Dollars in Millions)

	19X9	19X8	19X7
CASH FLOWS FROM OPERATING ACTIVITIES			
Net Income	10.1	8.8	8.5
Adjustments to reconcile net income to net cash provided by operating activities:			
Depreciation and amortization	2.2	3.0	2.0
Deferred income taxes	.2	.3	.2
Accounts receivable	(.7)	(.6)	(.8)
Inventories	(2.1)	(1.9)	(1.2)
Prepaid expenses	(.1)	—	(.1)
Accounts payable	(.1)	1.2	.7
Accrued liabilities	.5	.3	.3
Federal income taxes payable	1.1	.8	.6
Other assets and liabilities, net	(.2)	.5	.5
Net cash from operating activities	**10.9**	**12.4**	**10.7**
CASH FLOWS FROM INVESTING ACTIVITIES			
Additions: property, plant, equipment	(3.9)	(4.2)	(2.8)
Net cash used for investing activities	**(3.9)**	**(4.2)**	**(2.8)**
CASH FLOWS FROM FINANCING ACTIVITIES			
Net change in short-term debt	.7	—	—
Repayments of long-term debt	(.8)	(6.5)	(1.0)
Proceeds from sale of preferred stock		5.0	
Payments of dividends	(6.8)	(6.5)	(6.2)
Increase in dividends payable	.5	.3	—
Net cash used for financing activities	**(6.4)**	**(7.7)**	**(7.2)**
NET INCREASE IN CASH AND EQUIVALENTS	.6	.5	.7
Cash and equivalents, beginning of year	7.0	6.5	5.8
Cash and equivalents at end of year	7.6	7.0	6.5

Pension and postretirement benefits   In rising securities markets, some companies have used overfunded pension plans to generate cash windfalls, but the reverse also occurs: Some are underfunded, so that the company may be faced with the prospect of cash burdens later on. Pension funding is, at best, an inexact science. Estimates based on a variety of actuarial, personnel, and financial assumptions determine the amount of annual expense required to cover future benefits earned by each year's additional service. Not only are these estimates subject to error, but management has used its discretion over the rate at which pension liabilities are funded to smooth out reported earnings by underfunding in poor years and overfunding in good years. Patterns of underfunding or overfunding can portend future deficiency or surplus, even when estimates are accurate. A liability account termed Unfunded Projected Benefit Obligation is another red flag, in this case meaning that the current return on pension fund investments is inadequate to cover projected future benefit payments.

Closely related are Postemployment Benefits Other than Pensions, consisting mainly of health care benefits payable to employees after retirement and before their eligibility for government benefits such as Medicare and Medicaid. The Financial Accounting Standards Board (FASB) now requires that if funding is elected, companies fund the present value of estimated future benefits earned by employees. The practice throughout the 1980s was to expense the costs of such benefits as incurred, leaving a question as to whether benefits actually paid were indicative of future liability. For example, a young company with a young work force would have small current expense, but unless some provision for future liability was made, it would be in for a clobbering when the work force reached retirement age. Funding, which remains optional, forces an estimate of future liability. It should be noted, however, that whereas with pensions, an additional liability has to be recognized if the accumulated benefit obligation is greater than the fair value of the plan assets, no such additional liability is required for postretirement benefits other than pensions.

Long-term debt   Detail on debt maturities makes it possible to anticipate refinancing needs, which have implications for investors in terms of the effect of interest costs on profits or potential dilution of common share values. A company's ability to manage its debt structure so as to obtain money at the lowest rate for the longest maturity is viewed by analysts as demonstrating that the company has a capable management team.

Look here (and also in footnotes concerning preferred stock) for information about antitakeover provisions, or "poison pills." The recent wave of hostile takeovers, usually taking the form of leveraged buyouts, has caused many companies to adopt provisions in their indentures or preferred stock agreements designed to make takeovers prohibitively expensive for acquirers or to protect existing holders from the adverse effects of additional debt or liquidation of assets. A common variety is the "poison put," a provision giving bondholders the right to redeem their bonds at par value in the event of a hostile takeover, thus creating an onerous cash requirement for the acquirer. Although generally designed to protect existing investors from unfavorable events, poison pill provisions can have major implications for a company's finances, and it is important to understand them.

Treasury stock By buying their own shares in the market, companies decrease shares outstanding and thus increase earnings per share for existing stockholders. The existence of an active stock purchase program can be viewed as a two-edged sword. On the one hand, such a program provides in effect a support price for the company's shares as well as a buyer with deep pockets—the company itself. On the other hand, a stock purchase program is frequently used as a defense against a hostile takeover attempt and raises the question whether repurchase of stock is the best way to use assets of the company.

Taxes The prospect of an assessment for a prior year's taxes may be disclosed in the footnotes. Of particular significance is any footnote disclosing that a company's tax returns are being audited or that any of the assumptions utilized by the company in determining the taxable basis of its assets are being questioned by the Internal Revenue Service.

Leases One of the most significant of the off-balance sheet liabilities is the long-term noncapital lease. A footnote dealing with a long-term lease should be reviewed carefully.

Financial Assets With computerization and internationalization have come sophisticated derivative instruments—contracts whose value is related to the value of underlying financial assets, including various financial instruments and securities. They come in different forms, including exotica such as interest rate swaps and caps, collateralized mortgage obligations, and financial futures and forward contracts. Some, having the effect of financial guarantees or loan commitments, may be, like the operating leases discussed above, off-balance sheet. Companies use financial assets for a variety of purposes, including financing, hedging, and investment.

The analytical challenge they present is that they are always complex and sometimes speculative, raising questions about unjustifiable deferral of losses, premature recognition of gains, and inadequate disclosure about risks.

SFAS (Statement of Financial Accounting Standard) No. 105 requires that financial statements provide significant information relating to all financial instruments with or without off-balance sheet risk. SFAS No. 107 requires disclosure about fair value of all financial instruments, assets and liabilities both on and off the balance sheet.

Supplementary Tables: The principal supplementary tables are the following.

Segment Reporting

The Financial Accounting Standards Board (FASB) requires companies meeting certain criteria having to do with product and geographical diversification to present certain information in segment form—that is, by product or industry category or markets serviced and by geographical territory. Although this can be done in the body of the financial statement, with supporting footnotes, or in the footnotes section itself, most companies do it in a separate schedule that is an integral part of the financial statements. The information required, which covers the same three-year period as the income statement, includes sales or revenues; operating profit or loss; the book value of identifiable assets; aggregate depreciation, depletion, or amortization; and capital expenditures.

These breakdowns enable shareholders to evaluate a company's exposure to the vagaries of various geographical markets, including political and other risks to a company that has foreign operations. For industry or product-line segments, a stockholder is able to evaluate the company's activities in particular areas in terms of the amount of its investment and the return it is realizing on the investment, as well as the year-to-year trends.

FINANCIAL REPORTING AND CHANGING PRICES

Another ruling of the FASB is aimed at accounting for the effect of inflation or deflation on the inventory, fixed assets, and the income statement values for cost of goods sold and depreciation as they are related to those assets. Thus, companies are encouraged to present the historical figures showing the effects of declines in the purchasing power of the dollar in contrast to the primary values as shown in the financial statements, based on historical cost.

FIVE-YEAR SUMMARY OF OPERATIONS

This required schedule essentially extends the three-year income statement to five years, including preferred and common stock dividend history. It is a useful supplement in terms of permitting analysis of operating trends, and a number of corporations have taken it upon themselves to provide summaries of the last ten years of operations.

TWO-YEAR QUARTERLY DATA

This schedule provides a quarterly breakdown of sales, net income, the high and low stock price, and the common dividend. The operating data is most valuable when a company's operations are subject to seasonal factors, as, for example, a retailer is subject to heavy demand during the Christmas season. The market price and dividend data reveal stock price volatility and the regularity with which the company has made dividend payments.

Management's Discussion and Analysis: The general credibility and informational value of annual reports was significantly advanced in the mid-1980s when the Securities and Exchange Commission began requiring and monitoring the section Management's Discussion and Analysis of the Financial Condition and Results of Operations. This is a narrative presentation designed to present management's candid comments on three key areas of a company's business: results of operations, capital resources, and liquidity. Companies are required to address all material developments affecting these three key areas, favorable or unfavorable, including the effects of inflation. In discussing results of operations, companies are required not only to detail operating and unusual events that affected results for the period under discussion, but also any trends or uncertainties that might affect results in the future. The capital resources part involves questions of fixed asset expenditures and considerations of whether it benefits shareholders more to finance such outlays with stock, bonds, or through lease arrangements. Addressing liquidity means discussing anything that affects net working capital, such as the convertibility into cash of accounts receivable or inventory and the availability of bank lines of credit.

When it made this section a requirement, the SEC sought to elicit, in a company's own words, an interpretation of the significance of past and future financial developments. Its intentions were clearly revealed following enactment of the Tax Reform Act of 1986, when it voted to direct companies to use this section of their 1986 reports to shareholders to quantify certain effects of the new law, such as a reduction in current liabilities for future taxes. Whether it will prove to be a satisfactory substitute for one's own analysis remains to be seen.

Investor's Information

This section of the annual report lists the name of the transfer agent, registrar, and trustees; the exchanges on which the company's securities are traded; the date, time, and place of the annual meeting; and a notice as to when proxy materials will be made available to shareholders of record. If the company has an automatic dividend reinvestment plan, the terms and procedures for participating are stated here.

The number of common shareholders (and preferred, if any) as of the fiscal year-end is also usually indicated in this section.

This section may also invite requests for Form 10-K, the annual Securities and Exchange Commission filing corporations are required to make available to shareholders. The 10-K is filed within 90 days of a company's fiscal year-end. It is a thick, drab report containing a mass of detail. Much of what it contains is in the annual report to shareholders or is incorporated by reference to the public annual report, but other information is unique to the 10-K. Such unique information includes historical background; names of principal security holders; security holdings of management; more detailed financial schedules; information about products or services, properties, markets, distribution systems, backlogs, and competitive factors; detail about patents, licenses, or franchises; number of employees; environmental and other regulatory compliances; information concerning amounts paid directors and their share holdings; and background, including employment history, of executives and their relationships to the firm.

Form 10-Q is a shorter, unaudited, update of the 10-K. It must be filed within 45 days of the end of a company's first, second, and third fiscal quarters. It is mainly useful as a source of information about changes in the status of securities outstanding, compliance with debt agreements, and information on matters to be voted on by shareholders, such as the election of directors.

Directors and Officers

The names of members of the board of directors and their affiliations are listed here as are the names and titles of senior executives. Also usually indicated is the membership of board members on various committees, such as the executive committee, the finance committee, the compensation committee, the committee on corporate responsibility, the research and development committee, and the audit committee. Corporations vary in terms of the use to which they put the backgrounds of their directors—in some cases the role of directors is ceremonial, in others directors are used to advantage—and this section can sometimes provide meaningful insight. The absence of directors unaffiliated with management may indicate a company dominated by senior officers and not responsive to the concerns of outside shareholders. Senior management can also become more entrenched in companies that stagger the terms of directors to help prevent a hostile takeover.

* * *

RATIO ANALYSIS SUMMARY

Ratios are the principal tools of financial statement analysis. By definition, however, ratios indicate relationships, and by excluding considerations such as dollar amounts and the overall size of a company, their meaning in and of themselves can be limited if not misleading. Ratios have their greatest significance when used to make year-to-year comparisons for the purpose of determining trends or when used in comparison with industry data. Composite ratios for different industries are published by Standard & Poor's Corporation, Dun & Bradstreet, Robert Morris Associates, and the Federal Trade Commission. The following is a summary of key ratios and what they signify. Each ratio is computed for XYZ Corporation, whose hypothetical financial statements are shown in the discussion above of the annual report.

Ratios That Measure Liquidity

Ratio	Calculation	XYZ Computation
Current ratio	$\dfrac{\text{Current assets}}{\text{Current liabilities}}$	$\dfrac{41.1}{18.5} = 2.22$

The current ratio measures the extent to which the claims of a firm's short-term creditors are covered by assets expected to be convened to cash within the same short-term period. In XYZ's industry, the standard is 1.9, so its 2.2 ratio indicates comfortable liquidity, although down slightly from last year's ratio of 2.4. In a recession, extra liquidity protection could make a vital difference; slack consumer demand would mean that XYZ's wholesale customers would have lower sales. That would mean less sales and lower inventory turnover for XYZ. As XYZ's customers became tighter for cash and slower paying, or went out of business, XYZ's accounts receivable would become less collectible. Ultimately that could mean insolvency. Hence the importance of this key measure of short-term solvency. Of course, in other types of companies, the current ratio would have less significance. A company whose sales were largely under United States government contracts would have less receivables and inventory risk, for example, and could thus afford a lower current ratio.

Quick ratio	$\dfrac{\text{Current assets-inventory}}{\text{Current liabilities}}$	$\dfrac{41.1 - 23.0}{18.5} = .97$

A refinement of the current ratio, the quick or acid-test ratio answers the question: If sales stopped, could the company meet its current obligations with the readily convertible assets on hand? XYZ has a quick ratio of .97, almost a dollar of quick assets for each dollar of current liabilities, and virtually in line with the industry standard of 1.0. Last year it was slightly better, 1.04 times, but that small a year-to-year difference is probably not enough to signify a negative trend.

Ratios That Measure Activity

Ratio	Calculation	XYZ Computation
Inventory turnover	$\dfrac{\text{Net Sales}}{\text{Inventory}}$	$\dfrac{98.4}{23.0} = 4.3 \text{ times}$

This tells us the number of times inventory is sold in the course of the year. As a general rule, high turnover means efficient inventory management and more marketable inventory with a lower risk of illiquidity. But it could also be a reflection on pricing policies or could reflect shortages and an inability to meet new orders. XYZ's turnover ratio is 4.3 times, down slightly from the prior year's 4.5 times, and the industry standard is 6.7 times. This should be looked into.

Average collection period	$\dfrac{\text{Accounts receivable}}{\text{Annual credit sales/360 days}}$	$\dfrac{10.2}{.270} = 37 \text{ days}$

Assuming a company's terms of sale are standard for its industry, the average collection period—which tells if customers are paying bills on time—can be a reflection on credit policy (a liberal policy, involving relaxed credit standards to generate higher sales volume, will usually result in a longer average collection period); on the diligence of a firm's collection effort; on the attractiveness of discounts offered for prompt payment; or on general economic conditions as they affect the finances of the firm's customers. XYZ's collection period was 38 days this year and 37 days last year compared with an industry average of 37 days. It thus enjoys typical collections, apparently reflecting a sound and competitive credit policy. Of course, there could be potential problems not revealed by this test; for example, a concentration of accounts receivable in one industry or with a few customers, which, if affected by adversity, would have a disproportionate effect on the total receivables portfolio. Footnotes to the financial statements will often contain information concerning the composition of accounts receivable and their age relative to the invoice date.

Fixed assets turnover $\quad \dfrac{\text{Net sales}}{\text{Net fixed assets}} \quad \dfrac{98.4}{59.8} = 1.6 \text{ times}$

Measured over time and against competitors, this ratio indicates how efficiently a firm is using its property, plant and equipment—its "plant capacity." Increases in fixed assets should produce increases in sales, although the investment will normally lag the sales effect. If, given time, sales fail to increase in relation to plant capacity, it usually reflects poor marketing strategy. XYZ's ratio is low by industry standards. It has recently added to its capacity and has plans to pursue a more aggressive policy aimed at higher sales and increased market share.

Total assets turnover $\quad \dfrac{\text{Net sales}}{\text{Total assets}} \quad \dfrac{98.4}{105.6} = .93 \text{ times}$

This ratio measures the amount of sales volume the company is generating on its investment in assets and is thus an indication of the efficiency with which assets are utilized. The relationship between sales and assets is sometimes called operating leverage, since any sales increases that can be generated from the same amount of assets increase profits and return on equity and vice versa. XYZ's turnover of .93, virtually unchanged from the prior year, is considerably under the industry standard of 2.1 meaning XYZ had better increase sales or dispose of some assets. As we observed above, however, it has plans to increase sales and recently added fixed assets in preparation.

Ratios That Measure Profitability

Ratio	Calculation	XYZ Computation
Operating profit margin	$\dfrac{\text{Net operating profit}}{\text{Net sales}}$	$\dfrac{19.2}{98.4} = 19.5\%$

This ratio is the key to measuring a firm's operating efficiency. It is a reflection on management's purchasing and pricing policies and its success in controlling costs and expenses directly associated with the running of the business and the creation of sales, excluding other income and expenses, interest, and taxes. (Some analysts exclude depreciation from this ratio, but we include it here for the sake of comparability.) XYZ's operating profit margin has been quite consistent over the past three years and is somewhat higher than industry averages. That could mean it is in for some competition or that it is exceptionally good at controlling costs. To zero in on the reasons for XYZ's better-than-average performance, relate cost of goods sold to sales and selling, general, and administrative expenses to sales. The explanation may lie in pricing policy or somewhere in the area of selling, general, and administrative expenses.

Net profit margin $\quad \dfrac{\text{Net income}}{\text{Net sales}} \quad \dfrac{10.1}{98.4} = 10.3\%$

This measures management's overall efficiency—its success not only in managing operations but in terms of borrowing money at a favorable rate, investing idle cash to produce extra income, and taking advantage of tax benefits. XYZ's ratio of 10.3% compares favorably with industry standards. A company in a field where the emphasis was on high volume—a supermarket, for instance—might show a net profit margin of much less—2 % for example.

Return on equity $$\frac{\text{Net income}}{\text{Total stockholders' equity}} = \frac{10.1}{68.0} = 15\%$$

This ratio measures the overall return on stockholders' equity. It is the bottom line measured against the money shareholders have invested. XYZ's 15% return is above average for the industry, which is good for shareholders as long as it doesn't invite competition.

Ratios That Measure Capitalization (Leverage)

Ratio	Calculation	XYZ Computation
Debt to total assets	$\dfrac{\text{Total liabilities}}{\text{Total assets}}$	$\dfrac{37.6}{105.6} = 36\%$

This measures the proportion of assets financed with debt as opposed to equity. Creditors, such as bankers, prefer that this ratio be low, since it means a greater cushion in the event of liquidation. Owners, on the other hand, may seek higher leverage in order to magnify earnings or may prefer to finance the company's activities through debt rather than yield control. XYZ's ratio is about average for its industry.

Ratio	Calculation	XYZ Computation
Long-term debt to total capitalization	$\dfrac{\text{Long-term debt}}{\text{Long-term debt} + \text{stockholders' equity}}$	$\dfrac{16.2}{68.0} = 24\%$

This ratio tells us the proportion of permanent financing that is represented by long-term debt versus equity. XYZ's ratio of 24% (24% of its permanent capital is debt) is low by industry standards, suggesting it might consider increasing its leverage—that is, financing its future growth through bonds rather than stock.

Debt to equity (debt ratio) $$\frac{\text{Total liabilities}}{\text{Total stockholders' equity}} = \frac{37.6}{68.0} = 55\%$$

This is the basic ratio. It measures the reliance on creditors—short and long term—to finance total assets and becomes critical in the event of liquidation, when the proceeds from the sale of assets go to creditors before owners. Since assets tend to shrink in liquidation, the lower this ratio the more secure owners can feel. Also, a high debt ratio makes it more difficult to borrow should the need arise. XYZ's debt ratio of 55% is very conservative, and is another indication that its shareholders could safely benefit from greater leverage.

Times interest earned $$\frac{\text{Earnings before taxes and interest charges}}{\text{Interest charges}} = \frac{19.4}{1.0} = 19 \text{ times}$$

This ratio measures the number of times fixed interest charges are covered by earnings. Since failure to meet interest payments would be an event of default under the terms of most debenture agreements, this coverage ratio indicates a margin of safety. Put another way, it indicates the extent to which earnings could shrink—in a recession, for example—before the firm became unable to meet its contractual interest charges. XYZ earns 19 times its annual interest payments, which is substantially more than is normally considered conservative. It is another indication that XYZ should consider increasing its leverage.

$$\text{Fixed charge coverage} \quad \frac{\text{Earnings before taxes and interest charges}}{\text{Interest charges + lease payments}} \quad \frac{19.4}{1.0} = 19 \text{ times}$$

This is the times interest earned ratio expanded to include other fixed charges, notably annual lease payments. XYZ has no lease obligations, so the ratio is the same. It is important to note, however, that the extent of this coverage should be sufficient to ensure that a company can meet its fixed contractual obligations in bad times as well as good times.

Ratios That Measure Stock Values

Ratio	Calculation	XYZ Computation
Price-earnings ratio	$\dfrac{\text{Market price of common share}}{\text{Earnings per common share}}$	$\dfrac{63.00}{6.30} = 10 \text{ times}$

This ratio reflects the value the marketplace puts on a company's earnings and the prospect of future earnings. It is important to shareholders because it represents the value of their holdings, and it is also important from the corporate standpoint in that it is an indication of the firm's cost of capital—the price it could expect to receive if it were to issue new shares. XYZs multiple of ten times earnings is about average for an established company.

Ratio	Calculation	XYZ Computation
Market-to-book ratio	$\dfrac{\text{Market price of common share}}{\text{Book value per share (total assets – intangible assets – total liabilities and preferred stock common shares outstanding)}}$	$\dfrac{63.00}{40.00} = 1.58 \text{ times}$

This indicates the value the market places on a firm's expected earnings—its value as a going concern—in relation to the value of its shares if the company were to be liquidated and the proceeds from the sale of assets, after creditor claims were satisfied, were paid to shareholders. XYZ's common shares have a market value that is half again as much as their value in liquidation, assuming its assets could be liquidated at book value.

Dividend payout ratio	$\dfrac{\text{Dividends per common share}}{\text{Earnings per common share}}$	$\dfrac{4.20}{6.30} = 67\%$

This ratio indicates the percentage of common share earnings that are paid out in dividends. As a general rule, young, growing companies tend to reinvest their earnings to finance expansion and thus have low dividend payout ratios or ratios of zero. XYZ's ratio of 67% is higher than most established companies show.

HOW TO READ A QUARTERLY REPORT

In addition to annual reports, publicly held companies issue interim reports usually on a quarterly basis. which update shareholders about sales and earnings and report any material changes in the company's affairs. Companies are also required to file quarterly information with the Securities and Exchange Commission on Form 10-Q within 45 days of the end of the first, second, and third fiscal quarters. These reports, which contain unaudited financial information and news of changes in securities outstanding, compliance with debt agreements, and matters to be voted on by shareholders, may be available from companies directly; at SEC libraries in Atlanta, Boston, Chicago. Denver, Fort Worth, Los Angeles, New York, Seattle, and the District of Columbia; or through firms that provide all SEC filings (and which advertise in the financial sections of newspapers).

Quarterly shareholder reports vary in comprehensiveness. Some reports provide complete, though usually unaudited, financial statements, but most simply contain summarized updates of the operating highlights of the annual report. Accounting regulations require that companies give at least the following information.

- Sales (or revenues)
- Net income (before and after potential dilution, if pertinent)
- Provision for federal income taxes
- Nonrecurring items of income or expense, with tax implications
- Significant acquisitions or disposals of business segments
- Material contingencies, such as pending lawsuits
- Accounting changes
- Significant changes in financial position, including working capital and capital structure

Accounting regulations require that figures be presented either for the quarter in question or cumulatively for the year-to-date, but prior year data must be included on a comparative basis. That requirement is designed to deal with seasonal factors. For example. the quarterly results of a department store, to cite an industry with marked seasonality (sales bulge at Christmastime), would be meaningless unless compared with the same quarter of the prior year.

The main thing to remember about quarterly reports is that they are designed to update existing shareholders, not to provide prospective shareholders with an overall perspective on the company. They should be read in conjunction with the annual report.

PART III

How to Read the
Financial Pages

How to Read Ticker Tapes

HOW TO READ THE
FINANCIAL PAGES

Financial news is a swift-running stream that can be harnessed to power your investment decision-making—or drown you in a flood of statistics. Its volume expanded greatly from the 1970s through the 1990s, following deregulation of the financial markets and other developments that increased public participation in a growing investment marketplace, prompting many of us to become our own money managers.

As a result, the financial press has staffed up and daily financial sections have been expanded and redesigned, often along the lines of *The New York Times* free-standing section (whose Sunday edition, in the mid-1990s, was renamed "Money and Business" from just "Business"). *The Wall Street Journal* added a second section and then a third. A relative newcomer, *Investor's Daily,* creates graphs from its computerized data base to show price movements of individual securities. *USA Today* uses innovative graphics to include as much financial information as possible in its pages.

The Financial Times of London responded to the growing appetite for foreign financial news by increasing its international distribution. as did *The Japan Economic Journal* with its weekly English-language edition. *Barron's National Business and Financial Weekly,* long an important weekly source of information for professionals, became more consumer-oriented and added many useful tables and features not found elsewhere.

These and other financial publications have three major goals: (1) To pack as much news as possible into a given space; (2) to attract as many readers as possible; and (3) to allow busy readers to obtain a quick overview and/or easily find whatever specific information they are seeking. These aims are accomplished through packaging the news, and as readers, we must understand how this is done so we can unpackage it to suit ourselves.

THE FIRST PAGE

The outside of the news package—the first page of the financial section of a major daily general-interest newspaper or daily financial newspaper—is aimed at the broadest audience: the consumer, the investor, the civic minded, the curious—all of us, in one way or another. As you move to the inside pages, the information becomes more specific: reports on individual people, companies, markets. The tabular material is the most specific of all, and is included for readers who seek detail—a stock price, currency exchange rates, bond yield, corporate earnings report, or information on a new securities offering, for example. The outside of the package may contain, depending on news developments, one or more of the following elements.

The Digest

The digest presents major stories of the preceding day in summary form, along with summaries of the more important analytical feature stories from that day's newspaper. A good digest also gives you an idea of why an event was important, and what it could lead to. It will also tell you what page to turn to for the full story.

The Economics Story

The fact that a general economics story often appears on the front page of the package is a tribute to the sophistication and interest of the readership. It also reflects the fact that government economic data is scheduled for release well in advance, giving editors and reporters time to reserve space, pull out charts for updating, and line up experts to offer commentary. A monthly cycle of major statistics often starts with the release of data on construction spending and the employment situation (the latter generally is released on the first Friday of the month) and continues with statistics on chain-store sales, crop production, consumer installment credit, industrial production, capacity utilization, housing starts and building permits, producer (wholesale) prices, personal income and outlays, consumer prices, average hourly wages, savings flows, and other matters. The month often ends with a report on the indexes of leading, coincident, and lagging economic indicators. Most of the statistics refer to the previous month, some to two months before. Motor-vehicle manufacturers report on sales every ten days.

Important statistics are also released on a quarterly basis. These statistics include information on U.S. import and export prices, corporate profits, and of particular significance—the gross domestic product (GDP). The GDP (especially its inflation-adjusted version, constant dollar or real GDP) is a measure of the total value of goods and services produced by the United States economy. Of key interest is how the seasonally adjusted annual growth rate of the GDP in a particular quarter compares to the previous quarter and to the same quarter in the previous year. Trends in the GDP are our primary measures of whether the U.S. economy is strong or weak, growing or in recession.

For investment purposes, watch for basic themes in overall stories on the economy. Favorable economic signals bode well for corporate profits, and therefore usually for stock prices, and unfavorable signals can have the opposite effect. A weakening economy can lift bond prices, however, because economic slackness means weaker demand for credit and thus lower rates for new loans, which translates into higher prices for existing bonds and notes. But one monthly figure doesn't make a trend, and other factors, including speculation about Federal Reserve Board monetary policy, also affect securities prices. In any event, between the time economic data is released and its appearance in newspapers, there has been ample opportunity for financial markets to react—to "discount the news," as they say on Wall Street. Most stock markets remained open until 4 P.M. EST the day before (the Pacific Stock Exchange closes 30 minutes later) while the bond market, which is mainly located in brokerage house trading rooms, has no official closing. Thus, the opportunity to react effectively to an economic event may have passed by the time you read of it in the newspaper.

The Interest Rate/Bond Market Story

As market interest rates move up or down, the prices of fixed income securities move in the opposite direction to adjust yields to market levels. Yield determines price, and vice versa. Thus, the daily bond market story is essentially an interest rate story. Major daily newspapers always reserve inside space for this story and move it to the outside of the financial package when warranted by major developments. The event could be a big move in bond values, a new prediction by a widely followed interest-rate forecaster, Congressional testimony or other action by the Federal Reserve Board (especially its chairman), or policy changes by foreign central banks. The bigger the development, the more attention will be focused on its significance to consumers—the prospect of higher or lower mortgage and personal borrowing costs, for instance. A complete story will also explain the significance of such news to investors and include comments by analysts and economists. The Federal Reserve's weekly report on the money supply (usually released on Thursday) provides much of the grist for late-week interest rate stories. If the money supply grows faster than the Federal Reserve had planned, the Fed may be tempted to adopt a restrictive monetary policy. That is, the Federal Reserve may reduce the amount of money in the economy to prevent a rise in inflation. Tighter money means higher interest rates, at least on short-term loans and securities, which usually exerts downward pressure on stock and bond prices. If the Fed thinks the money supply is growing too slowly, especially during an economic slowdown, the Fed could be expected to try to ease monetary policy and stimulate money growth. This often leads to lower interest rates and higher prices for fixed income securities, as well as to optimism and higher prices in the stock markets.

The Commodities Story

The roller coaster action in the prices of oil, gold, and silver in recent years helped make activity in the commodities markets a more frequent front-of-the-package story. When the commodities story gets front-page treatment, the consumer implications—for example, the effects on retail prices of gasoline or orange juice—will usually receive most attention. But there will also be economic and market forecasts and comments by professional analysts and traders, designed to inform investors about commodities futures or futures options contracts. Typical questions answered include: How fast has the price of the commodity futures contract reversed direction in the past? Are there new sources of supply that could affect prices—for example, soybeans from Brazil to replace those from Kansas, or beef from Argentina to replace meat from Texas? Is anything happening that could limit supply? What is the outlook for a political development causing activity in precious metals contracts?

The Takeover or Merger Story

Major takeover bids (called public tender offers) or merger announcements make big news partly because they have important implications for the securities prices of the companies involved. In a takeover or merger story look for (1) the price, total and per share, that's being offered for the target company. Also look at the form of payment cash, securities, or a combination—and how it's being raised. A leveraged buyout, for instance, can sometimes leave the acquired company laden with debt. (2) The reasons for the merger—to combine businesses for greater financial or marketing strength; to avoid an unfriendly takeover; to bail out a troubled corporation, for example. An unfriendly or hostile tender offer could trigger a bidding war which would drive up the price of the target company's stock or prompt legal action. Also, a large-scale takeover or merger runs the risk of antitrust action by the federal government in addition to other impediments. When takeover plans are set back or collapse, the price of the target's stock will most likely drop. (3) Comments by analysts on the acquirer's motives and management skills. A bid substantially above market could mean shares are undervalued or that the acquirer has exciting plans; particularly with reduced float, it might be wiser to hold than tender.

A complete takeover or merger story will also uncover what the risk arbitragers—professional traders who speculate in merger situations—are doing. Heavy buying of the stock of the takeover target combined with short selling of the shares of the acquirer, usually means the professionals think the takeover will succeed.

The Stock Market Story

This daily feature shifts to the front of the financial package when stock indexes undergo an especially big move. Although broader-based and more scientifically weighted indexes exist, the Dow Jones Industrial Average, which tracks 30 blue chip stocks, continues to be the most widely watched barometer and almost invariably is featured in the stock market story. A good roundup should give you the widest possible exploration of factors—the effect of other markets (bonds, commodities, currencies, and to an increased extent, stock options and financial futures), corporate earnings, takeover bids and merger rumors, economic developments, and changing market forecasts. The article should differentiate between different groups of stocks and different markets. The New York Stock Exchange activity often reflects buying and selling by institutional investors while the American Stock Exchange and over the counter (NASDAQ) markets reflect a higher proportion of activity by individual investors interested in less well-known growth stocks. In recent years, market volatility has been intensified by program trading, the computer-driven buying and selling by institutional traders and arbitrage specialists of all stocks in a "basket" or index. Some forms of program trading, particularly index arbitrage, also involve index options, index futures, and stock options, all of which expire together on the third Fridays of March, June, September, and December. Although measures have been instituted to process this extra activity with minimum disruption, expiration dates still cause a surge of trading, and the market closing on those Fridays is known on Wall Street as "the triple witching hour." A complete stock market story will usually include predictions by analysts who engage either in fundamental analysis, which focuses on business conditions and the financial strength of companies, or technical analysis, which concentrates on the conditions of the stock market, such as the supply and demand for shares and the emotional cycles of investors. Technical analysts, including those called chartists, who analyze historical market patterns, are usually more willing than fundamentalists to predict near-term market movements for newspaper stories.

The Company Story

Sometimes company stories are the result of breaking news—a profit report, a takeover attempt, a new product—and sometimes they are features that have been planned, and even written, well in advance of publication. Newspapers often carry a company stock story as part of their regular stock market coverage or because it is an important company to the newpaper's readership (it has a plant in town, for instance). Because stories on publicly owned companies can influence market values, there are laws to prevent capitalizing on advance knowledge of their content.

Among the things that you, as an investor or potential investor in a company, want to learn are: (1) The nature of the company's business, and whether or not it's diversified or a one-product operation; the size of its customer base; whether it does business mainly with the government or with private firms; whether it relies heavily on exports and is therefore sensitive to fluctuations in the dollar's value; whether its sources of supply are secure; and whether it can easily pass costs on to consumers. (2) The amount of debt of the company relative to its overall capital and whether it plans to borrow funds, issue more shares, or pay back loans. Among other things, this financial information will tell you whether the value of shares you may already own will undergo dilution, which could reduce earnings per share and thus reduce the market value of shares. (3) The nature of the company's ownership. Is a substantial proportion of stock held by the company's founders or by its current management? Closely held companies cannot be taken over by unwelcome acquirers as easily as widely held companies, but that can also deprive shareholders of profits they might otherwise gain through public tender offers at premiums to market value. You should also be told if financial institutions own large blocks of shares;

big institutional positions are an indication of how professional investors regard the company. In the case of companies with relatively few shares, however, that can also cause substantial price swings should institutions gobble up or dump large amounts of shares. Trends in insider or institutional ownership can be solid signals as to the prospects of a company—if top management is accumulating shares, they may know before the public about events that might cause the stock to rise. (4) Trends in the company's earnings history. How steady have profits been? Have they been increasing on a per-share basis? Is the company emerging from a period of weakness? Are earnings mainly the result of ongoing operations or of one-time extraordinary items, such as the sale of company property? (5) Trends in dividend payments.

The Industry Story

You'll find many of the same elements of a company story in an industry story, and you will in addition have the opportunity to look at one company in relation to others. These stories are often accompanied by charts comparing companies in an industrial sector (computer chip makers, retailers, or utilities, for instance) according to sales, per-share earnings, stock price range, recent stock price, price-earnings ratio, and other important data.

Advertisements

Throughout the financial pages of most newspapers—even on the front page—you will find advertisements for bank deposit instruments, mutual funds, and other investments. Early in the year many advertisements for individual retirement accounts appear. Some ads include order forms and encourage you to send a check—sometimes for a hefty amount—right away. Mutual funds and sponsors of other publicly offered securities, however, can't accept an investment from you without first sending you a prospectus. A mutual fund sometimes will print the prospectus as part of the advertisement. Never react impulsively to an attractive rate or yield or special deal. It is difficult to compare rates, yields, and terms because each situation is unique and different institutions use various methods to compute yields. Some have withdrawal penalties and other restrictions that might not be obvious in the ad.

You will also find advertisements for financial publications, advisory newsletters, and computer databases and software, among other products. Often these products can be very helpful, but it is usually best to request a sample or a demonstration to make sure the product suits your needs.

SCANNING THE INSIDE FINANCIAL PAGES

You can get a quick picture of current financial events and trends by scanning the financial pages. The news digest, already discussed, is a good starting point. The inside pages are peppered with daily, weekly, or monthly charts and graphs to give you a snapshot of aspects of business and economics. *The Wall Street Journal,* in addition to its news digest, brings such highlights together in its Markets Diary on the front page (C1) of the Money and Investing section. The Markets Diary, which is illustrated below, shows the prior day's change in key prices and rates in the context of the past week and the past 18 months, giving a quick reading of the status quo and trends. The *Journal's* compact summary provides an excellent overview of the financial markets and is an appropriate introduction to the inside financial pages of any newspaper. Let's look at each of its sections in turn:

MARKETS DIARY 6/1/95

STOCKS Dow Jones Industrial Average

4472.75 +7.61

INDEX	CLOSE	NET CHNG	PCT CHNG	12-MO HIGH	12-MO LOW	12-MO CHNG	PCT	FROM 12/31	PCT
DJIA	4472.75 +	7.61 +	0.17	4472.75	3624.96 +	713.76 +	18.99 +	638.31 +	16.65
DJ Equity	503.43 +	0.43 +	0.09	503.43	418.67 +	69.75 +	16.08 +	70.36 +	16.25
S&P 500	533.49 +	0.09 +	0.02	533.49	442.80 +	75.84 +	16.57 +	74.22 +	16.16
Nasdaq Comp.	868.82 +	4.24 +	0.49	879.64	693.79 +	129.32 +	17.49 +	116.86 +	15.54
DJ World Index	123.09 +	0.53 +	0.43	124.28	109.40 +	8.02 +	6.97 +	9.15 +	8.03
London (FT 100)	3340.6 +	21.2 +	0.64	3340.6	2876.6 +	359.8 +	12.07 +	275.1 +	8.97
Tokyo (Nikkei 225)	15594.57 +	157.78 +	1.02	21552.81	15381.29 −	5414.43 −	25.77 −	4128.49 −	20.93

BONDS Lehman Brothers T-Bond Index

6012.53 +22.76

INDEX	THUR	THUR YIELD	WED	WED YIELD	YR AGO	12-MO HIGH	12-MO LOW
Lehman Brothers Long T-Bond	6012.53	6.67%	5989.77	6.71%	5135.21	6012.53	4897.46
DJ 20 Bond (Price Return)	101.31	7.42	101.19	7.44	97.65	101.31	93.56
Salomon mortgage-backed	799.11	7.26	797.29	7.30	731.11	799.11	713.65
Bond Buyer municipal	94-7	6.02	94-2	6.04	91-29	95-25	80-26
Merrill Lynch corporate	760.97	7.11	757.07	7.21	670.96	760.97	661.57

INTEREST Fed Funds (NY Fed, Prebon Yamane)

6.05% −0.13

ISSUE	CLOSE	WED	YEAR AGO	12-MO HIGH	12-MO LOW
3-month T-bill	5.50%	5.63%	4.11%	5.90%	4.09%
3-month CD (new)	5.37	5.36	3.95	5.64	3.91
Dealer Comm. Paper (90 days)	6.02	6.02	4.59	6.32	4.50
3-month Eurodollar deposit	6.06	6.06	4.63	6.50	4.56

U.S. DOLLAR J. P. Morgan Index vs. 19 Currencies

90.2 +0.3

CURRENCY	LATE NY	LATE WED	DAY'S HIGH	DAY'S LOW	12-MO HIGH — LATE NY —	12-MO LOW
British pound (in U.S. dollars)	1.5970	1.5880	1.6000	1.5805	1.6383	1.5060
Canadian dollar (in U.S. dollars)	0.7282	0.7296	0.7297	0.7265	0.7456	0.7020
Swiss franc (per U.S. dollar)	1.1630	1.1670	1.1620	1.1890	1.1165	1.4190
Japanese yen (per U.S. dollar)	84.80	84.55	84.44	85.86	80.63	105.35
German mark (per U.S. dollar)	1.4083	1.4165	1.4050	1.4380	1.3530	1.6703

COMMODITIES KR-CRB Index (1967=100)

234.60 +1.88

COMMODITY	CLOSE	CHANGE	WED	YR AGO	12-MO HIGH — AT CLOSE —	12-MO LOW
Gold (Comex spot), troy oz.	$386.00	$+ 0.90	$385.10	$384.20	$398.00	$371.20
Oil (W. Tex. int. crude), bbl.	18.88	unch	18.88	18.25	20.75	16.70
Wheat (#2 hard KC), bu.	4.41	+ 0.06	4.35	3.52	4.47	3.32
Steers (Tex.-Okla. choice), 100 lb.	63.00	unch	63.00	Closed	75.00	60.50

NOTE: Monthly charts based on Friday close, except for Federal Funds, which are weekly average rates.

Stocks

Stock prices are measured by seven major U.S. and foreign indexes and are represented graphically by the Dow Jones Industrial Average. Although by far the most widely watched stock average in the world, the blue-chip DJIA has its limitations: Being "price-weighted," it can be unduly influenced by major moves in higher-priced components, and since it comprises only the stocks of 30 large corporations, primarily industrial issues, it is not as representative of the overall market as a broader-based index. Nonetheless, the question "How is the market doing?" is almost universally answered by quoting the Dow, which gives it unique status not only as a measure of market performance but as an influential force in market psychology.

Other indexes in the summary include the Dow Jones Equity Index, a relative newcomer made up of 700 stocks. which measures broader market performance; the Standard & Poor's Index of 500 Stocks. also a broad-based index and the most widely followed index after the DJIA; the NASDAQ (National Association of Securities Dealers Automated Quotations) Composite Index, which measures a large group of mostly smaller companies traded over-the-counter; and the Dow Jones World Index, a 90s innovation that brings together some 25 American, European, and Asian/Pacific Dow Jones equity indexes that tend to be broad-based.

The other two indexes track the two most important foreign exchanges: the ISE, or London Stock Exchange, which is the dominant European market, and the Tokyo Stock Exchange, which is the world's second largest exchange after the New York Stock Exchange. Both the London FT 100 index of 100 stocks (or "Footsie," as it is popularly called) and the Nikkei Stock Average of 225 stocks are, like the Dow Jones Industrial Average, made up of blue-chip companies. These indexes are widely watched not only because many people own stocks measured by them, but because of the growing interdependence of financial markets internationally. In reading the tables, keep in mind that Tokyo's trading day precedes London's, which precedes New York's, and that each market is affected by the others.

In the columns from left to right, the table shows the closing value of each index; the net change over the preceding close expressed in points and then as a percentage; the highest and lowest levels reached in the preceding 12-month period; the change both in points and as a percentage within the preceding 12-month period and for the calendar year to date.

What we can learn from the June 1, 1995, Markets Diary illustrated is that blue chip, broader-based, and smaller capitalization stocks were all up both domestically and abroad from the previous day. The year-to-date comparisons would indicate that for most of the year the same was true—that larger stocks, represented exclusively in the DJIA but influencing the DJ Equity and S&P indexes, slightly outperformed the smaller stocks dominating the NASDAQ.

The significance of this is that larger stocks tend to outshine smaller stocks in strong economies and vice versa. In slow economies the greater growth potential of small firms overshadows lower profit margins; thus, their stock prices rise (helped also by the fact that lower-priced stocks tend to register greater percentage changes than higher-priced shares in any market). In contrast, mature companies fare worse in weak economies because their sales and earnings per share tend to go down, taking share prices down with them.

Normally, the 12-month columns would help us detect the trend of stock prices. If, for example, the DJIA outperformed the NASDAQ by a greater amount over a 12-month period than over the shorter period represented by the year-to-date comparisons, one could conclude that smaller stocks were gaining on larger stocks. At the time of the table illustrated, the U.S. economy was thought to be headed for a "soft-landing," in other words, economic growth would be controlled with risk of neither significant inflation nor recession. That perception lent continued buoyancy to a long-running bull market benefiting domestic stocks in all categories while economic recovery around the world was benefiting foreign stocks.

Bonds

As was observed earlier, bond prices move in the opposite direction of interest rate so this is the market's way of bringing yields in line with prevailing rates. Of course, bond prices and yields are strongly influenced also by risk factors, by inflation expectations, and by supply and demand. Different types of bonds reflect these characteristics to different degrees.

The bond section is highlighted by graphs showing prices of a composite of Treasury bonds. Because T-bonds have the "full faith and credit" of the U.S. Government behind them and, with limited exceptions, are not callable, they are free of risks other than those associated with fluctuating interest rates and inflation. And because they are long-term (10 to 30 years) and not, like short-term Treasury bills, a direct instrument of Federal Reserve monetary policy, T-bond prices and yields reflect more purely than other investments the market's expectations with respect to interest rates and inflation. The T-bond rate is thus the benchmark for all other rates.

The DJ (Dow Jones) 20 Bond index is an arithmetic average of New York Exchange closing prices of 10 industrial and 10 utility bonds with investment-grade ratings from best to intermediate. (The words "price return" in parentheses tell us that changes in the index are the result purely of market activity as it affects prices and yields; in contrast, the other indexes in the group are based on "total return," meaning they reflect, in addition, changes in value resulting from the assumption that interest is reinvested. Under normal conditions this distinction does not materially affect the value of the indexes as indicators of the fixed-income market's direction.)

The Salomon mortgage-backed index tracks prices and yields of pass-through securities backed by home mortgages and issued or guaranteed by U.S. Government agencies such as Ginnie Mae, Freddie Mac, and Fannie Mae. Government-backed mortgage securities yield somewhat more than other government-backed bonds because they are subject to the risk that homeowners will prepay their mortgages, thus shortening the life of the investment. The prepayment risk is greatest when market interest rates decline, affording homeowners an opportunity to refinance at lower rates. Rising rates have the reverse effect and increase the demand for mortgage-backed securities.

The Bond Buyer municipal index, compiled by the *Bond Buyer* daily newspaper, tracks the prices and yields of newly issued AA- and A-rated tax-exempt bonds of states and localities. The Tax Reform Act of 1986 imposed certain restrictions on issuers of municipal securities, thus affecting both demand and supply in the tax-exempt market. The result has been that, on an equivalent taxable yield basis, municipals often yield more than taxable bonds of comparable quality and maturity.

The Merrill Lynch corporate index measures prices and yields of nearly 4,000 investment-grade (AAA to BBB) corporate issues. This index provides essentially the same information as the Dow Jones bond index, but differs in its broader base and its total-return method of computation.

Bond information is presented in seven columns. The first four (from left to right) compare the previous day's index value (based on price) and yield with the corresponding figures of the day before. The fifth column shows the index value a year ago, and the last two columns indicate the range of prices over the past 12 months.

It is important to understand that all the bonds covered in the foregoing tables are "straight" (not convertible), interest-bearing (not zero-coupon), and fixed-rate (not floating-rate). Such variations would behave differently in the marketplace and not be indicative of fixed-income securities. Also excluded were so-called "junk bonds," whose lower ratings and higher yields reflect their perceived greater risk of default.

The table illustrates that June 1 was a dull day in the bond market, little changed from the previous day. We do see that prices are substantially higher than a year ago and close to a 12-month high. This, of course, is a reflection of lower rates, and a glimpse at the 18-month graph indicates that higher prices and lower yields were clearly a trend as 1995 was approaching mid-year.

Interest

Bond prices and yields give an indication of how the market views the future, what existing fixed-income investments might be worth, and what rate of return we could expect from long-term fixed-income investments. Short-term rates, which are highlighted in this section. give an indication as to what the Federal Reserve is doing to regulate the money supply and thereby stimulate or slow down the economy. The Fed's actions, in turn, affect other rates and even the prices of stocks, which generally benefit from low rates. Short-term rate levels also have meaning to us directly, since many of the rates we pay—on credit cards, auto loans, adjustable-rate mortgages, and home-equity loans, for example—are "pegged" to the yields on these key money market instruments. And while high minimum purchase requirements exclude most individuals from participating in the short-term money market directly, these instruments are bought and sold by money market funds and affect the yields we get on those widely popular investments.

The charts here plot the federal funds rate, which is the rate banks with excess reserves charge other banks that need reserves for overnight money. Borrowings are heaviest, and the rate highest, when the Federal Reserve, through its monetary policy, is draining reserves from banks so they will have less money to lend and thus provide less stimulus to the economy. The fed funds rate is the most sensitive of rates—so sensitive, in fact, that daily fluctuations could be misleading. For that reason the graph does not plot daily changes but rather a weekly average. A trend in this rate often signals a change in the Fed's discount rate, and that, in turn, is usually followed by a change in the bank prime rate, the maximum rate banks charge their most creditworthy corporate customers. Other rates generally follow the prime.

Other short-term rates shown in the table increase with different degrees of risk and liquidity. The 3 month Treasury bill yield is established weekly at auction, and the bills are traded actively in the secondary market. Buying (and selling) T-bills, thus putting cash into (or taking cash out of) the economy and increasing (or decreasing) bank reserves, is the Fed's primary instrument of monetary policy, so T-bill yields are widely watched as an indicator of rate trends generally. The 90-day bill is also the benchmark for most floating-rate credit.

New 3-month bank certificates of deposit (CDs) tell us what banks are willing to pay for 3-month money. The rate they offer reflects their consensus that, for 3 months, rates are probably not going to drop significantly lower.

Dealer commercial paper (90 days) represents the IOUs of corporate borrowers. (Dealer means this "paper" is bought and sold through brokerage firms rather than issued and redeemed directly.) Commercial paper is unsecured and marketable only by the most creditworthy organizations, which use this method of borrowing as an alternative to more expensive prime rate bank loans. Commercial paper, which lacks secondary market liquidity, competes with risk-free T-bills for investors' cash and naturally commands a higher rate of interest.

The 3-month Eurodollar deposit rate is the rate paid by borrowers of U.S. dollar deposits held in banks, including U.S. bank subsidiaries, outside the United States, primarily, but not exclusively, in Europe. Whereas domestic short-term rates are directly or indirectly controlled by the monetary policies of central banks (such as the Federal Reserve in the United States and the Bank of England in the United Kingdom), the Eurodollar rate is a pure market rate, free to find its own level through supply and demand. This situation has attracted speculators, who are able to buy futures contracts on Eurodollar time deposit rates. Since overseas banks are relatively free of regulation and can operate on narrower spreads, they are able to compete easily with U.S. instruments for investor's money, although arbitrage keeps Eurodollar rates appropriately in line with rates paid by U.S. banks for deposits of similar maturity.

Eurodollar deposit rates and rates on other Eurodollar transactions and securities are based on the London Interbank Offer Rate (LIBOR), the offer side of quotes among major banks in London that trade deposits with each other in the same fashion that U.S. banks trade federal funds. The rate on 3-month Eurodollar deposits is also watched as a harbinger of changes in the U.S. prime rate, which is listed elsewhere in the financial pages. American banks like to maintain a spread of at least 1.5 percentage points between the prime rate and the Eurodollar rate; thus, whenever the spread is wider than that, conditions may be ripe for a drop in the prime.

The rate tables are straightforward and need little explanation. The previous day's closing rates are compared with those of the prior day, followed by columns showing the year-ago closings and the 12-month highs and lows. In the illustrated example, the tables bear out trends evident in the federal funds graph. Interest rates in general had been declining from their fall 1994 highs, and many observers believed a lowering of the Federal Reserve discount rate was overdue.

U.S. Dollar

The globalization of consumer, commercial, and financial markets in recent years has made us appreciate more keenly the effect of varying currency exchange rates. When the dollar becomes stronger—that is, when it buys more pounds, marks, yen, or other units of currency—it becomes cheaper in dollar terms for Americans to travel and shop abroad, to import foreign goods, and to buy foreign stocks and bonds. On the other hand, U.S. companies (and their shares) may suffer under such conditions because cheaper imported goods can hurt the sale of those produced domestically. When the dollar becomes weaker—that is, when it buys fewer units of foreign currencies—the cost of foreign travel and imports rise while U.S. exports become more competitive in world markets. Since the prices of foreign securities and the value of their interest and dividends increase as the dollar weakens, investing in foreign stock markets often means tracking the dollar.

The rates at which one currency can be converted to another are established by bid and offer. not unlike stocks, in a world-wide "over-the-counter" market that uses telephones and computers to link the major financial institutions, exchange brokers, and government agencies that dominate the foreign exchange marketplace. The demand for foreign exchange derives from trade, investment, travel and tourism, government needs of various sorts, and from speculators.

Since the exchange market operates 24 hours a day—when it's midnight in New York it's 2:00 P.M. in Tokyo—there are no closing quotes, although rates are reported at regular times late in the business day, making day-to-day comparisons meaningful. Currency rates are, however, highly sensitive to economic, financial, and political news and subject to rapid and pronounced shifts, which governments, except in extreme instances, are reluctant to counteract through market intervention. The exchange rates reported in newspapers can thus vary considerably from the rates prevailing at the time you read them.

The charts in this section show the J. P. Morgan Index of the dollar's value, one of two major U.S. dollar indexes (the other being the Federal Reserve Index, reported in *The New York Times*), compared with an average, weighted by volume of trade, of 15 foreign currencies. It shows a generally weakening dollar gaining strength between Novemeber 1994 and January 1995 before descending to a low in May 1995.

The tables compare the dollar to five selected major currencies. The British pound and Canadian dollar rates are expressed in U.S. dollars. For example, late on the trading day in New York on Thursday, June 1, it would have cost $1.60 to purchase one British pound and about 73 cents to purchase a Canadian dollar. The other currencies are expressed in units "per U.S. dollar." In other words, on that Thursday the dollar was worth 1.1630 Swiss francs, 84.80 yen, and 1.4083 West German marks. (The difference in the methods has to do simply with custom and practicality, and all rates apply to transactions of at least $1 million.)

The data illustrated show very little change between Thursday's exchange rates and the prior Wednesday's. The dollar weakened slightly against the pound, was slightly stronger against the Canadian dollar, weaker against the Swiss franc, stronger against the yen, and weaker against the mark.

Given the volatility of exchange rates, the two columns showing the high-low range for the trading day can often be more meaningful than the late New York rate by itself. In reading the intraday highs and lows and the 12-month highs and lows, remember that the higher the U.S. dollar figures for the British pound and Canadian dollar, the weaker the dollar, whereas the higher the figure shown for the other currencies, the stronger the dollar.

Thus, consistent with trends revealed by the chart, the dollar on June 1, 1995, was weaker against all the currencies listed in comparison with their 12-month highs but stronger compared to their 12-month lows.

Commodities

The commodities section of the Markets Diary highlights key prices and trends in the raw materials and provisions used by commerce and industry to meet our daily wants and needs.

In these Chicago-dominated markets, commodities are bought and sold on either (1) a "spot" basis, meaning the "actual"—the physical commodities (or warehouse receipts)—are ready for immediate delivery and traded at a "cash price" (for grains) or "spot price" (for other commodities), or (2) a futures basis, meaning a "futures contract" is entered into that provides for delivery and payment in a specified future month at a specified price.

Participants in the market fall into two categories: On one side are businesses buying the commodities for commercial use or using futures contracts to hedge against the risk of loss due to a change in prices. On the other side are traders and speculators who aim to profit from short-term and longer-term price movements.

The average investor may participate in the commodities market through professionally managed pooled investments, or may just be interested in watching commodity price trends for what they reveal about inflationary expectations and the prices of things we eat, drink, wear, or otherwise use in our daily lives.

The Commodity Research Bureau's (CRB) Futures Index tracks futures prices on 21 commodities, including a diverse range of agricultural contracts, oil, lumber, copper, and precious metals. (This index does not include financial futures traded at commodities exchanges, such as those on interest rates and foreign currencies.) Because commodity prices are direct factors in the cost of living, the CRB Index is a highly sensitive barometer of inflation expectations. Increased inflation, of course, usually means higher interest rates and yields and lower bond prices. The diversity of the CRB Index is important to its value as an indicator of the direction of prices in general, since individual commodity prices are subject not only to supply and demand, but also to all manner of other influences including weather conditions, crop failures, trading cycles, political developments, and government actions.

The tables show spot activity in four of the most economically significant and actively traded commodities. Gold, which receives more daily attention in the press than any other single commodity, is shown in U.S. dollars per troy ounce at the closing price on the Commodity Exchange (Comex) in New York. (The Comex close is actually a settlement price determined shortly after trading ends, and represents the futures contract set to expire soonest, the so-called nearest-month contract. Other reports use the morning and afternoon London gold fixings.) The reasons gold is so widely followed, in addition to its industrial and commercial uses, are primarily three: (1) Gold has historically tended to rise in value when the inflation rate increases, so it is viewed as a measure of inflation expectations. (2) Gold is considered a safe haven when political turmoil threatens the value of financial investments, so the price of gold bullion and bullion futures contracts is a measure of international tensions. (3) Gold is used internationally as an alternative to the U.S. dollar, rising as the dollar weakens and vice versa, thus it is seen as a measure of confidence in the dollar.

The other commodities listed reflect changes in the cash or spot prices of the units in which they are traded. Thus, crude oil is quoted in dollars and cents per barrel, wheat in dollars and cents per bushel, and steers in dollars and cents per hundred pounds.

The data illustrated reflect a generally uneventful day in the commodities markets. The *Journal's* commodities story led with the comment that grain prices, including wheat, had climbed amid conflicting forecasts for weather across flooded parts of the Farm Belt.

Earnings Reports

Quarterly profit reports for corporations are carried in major newspapers like *The New York Times* or *Wall Street Journal* as well as in many other newspapers. In most cases, the abbreviated reports appear in one place, and include the latest sales, net income, net income per share, and shares outstanding, compared with the year-earlier figures. Using year-earlier comparisons rather than comparisons with the previous quarter excludes purely seasonal fluctuations. Department stores, for example, as a rule report the most sales in the fourth quarter, owing to the Christmas season. Comparing the fourth and third quarters, therefore, might give an inaccurate impression of the health of a department-store chain. It is very important also to look at earnings on a per-share basis. Per-share earnings, more than total earnings, are a major determinant of stock prices.

By the time you read the brief earnings reports, the stock market usually has had time to react, since the reports are usually released during trading hours. Occasionally, a company releases earnings after the close of trading, and you may see the price of the stock market react to the news when trading resumes. (Some companies release disappointing earnings late Friday in the hope they will be overlooked or their impact lessened because of the two-day break in trading.)

XYZ PRODUCTS (N)

Qtr to March 31	19X6	19X5
Revenue	$5,600,000	$4,980,000
Net income	463,000	452,000
Share earns	.22	.22
Shares outstanding	2,100,000	2,050,000

Dividend Reports

Lists of quarterly dividends, organized alphabetically by corporation, appear in greater number during the third through fifth weeks of each calendar quarter when earnings reports are most numerous. The dividend reports are generally divided into categories: Irregular, Increased, Reduced, and Regular. The organization of columns looks like this:

DIVIDEND REPORTS

| | Regular | | | |
	Period	Rate	Stk of Record	Pay- able
XYZ Corp.	Q	.30	4–10	4–30

The table tells you that the regular dividend for the hypothetical XYZ Corporation is paid quarterly, that the dividend is 30 cents per share (which would result in $1.20 per share annually if the rate held steady), that the dividend will be paid to shareowners of record April 10, and that the actual payment will be made on April 30. It's important to remember that stocks go ex-dividend during the interval between the dividend announcement and the actual payment. This means that the dividend isn't payable to investors who buy the stock during that interval. (On the other hand, if you sell the stock during the ex-dividend period, you still collect the dividend.) Shares listed on the NYSE generally go ex-dividend four days before the stockholder of record date. Stocks normally decline by the amount of the dividend when they enter an ex-dividend trading period.

Securities Offerings

Announcements of newly issued or about-to-be issued stocks and bonds come in two forms. Large newspapers include calendars and digests of expected and newly announced securities issues to be distributed by underwriting groups or syndicates. These groups of investment banking houses also place paid advertisements, known as tombstones in the language of Wall Street, which give a very basic summary of the offerings. (Tombstone ads are also used for other purposes, such as announcing major personnel changes or a firm's important role in an acquisition or merger.)

The newspaper listings come under such headings as Finance Briefs (*The New York Times*) or Financing Business (*The Wall Street Journal*). Because a high proportion of the offerings are bonds, these listings can usually be found near the bond tables and the interest rate/bond market news story.

One advantage of buying new issues (which are often reserved for favored customers) over buying existing securities, is that the buyer pays no commission. The broker-dealer is paid out of the underwriting spread, the difference between the price at which the securities are sold to the public and the lower price paid to the issuer by the underwriters. Even if you're not interested in purchasing securities, these notices give you an idea of the prevailing interest rates (in the case of bonds) and the types of companies that are able to attract capital by issuing shares.

In the accompanying illustration of a typical tombstone ad, the boilerplate (standard legal language) advises you to read the prospectus before you buy. Many investors, of course, simply rely on the word of their brokers anyway, but the prospectus is a legally required summary of the facts and risks concerning the issue, and investors are well-advised to read it. The tombstone lists the names of the firms comprising the underwriting group and, by alphabetically organized groups, the relative importance of their participation. The par value of the stock, if any, is usually listed, but has no meaning in terms of market value. The offering price, of course, is included; however, this announcement doesn't tell you anything more, for example, how the proceeds of the sale are to be used.

Tender Offer Announcements

In both friendly and unfriendly takeover situations, the advertisements placed by corporations soliciting your shares may offer the greatest source of practical information regarding what you should or could do with your shares. Among other things,

---

This announcement is neither an offer to sell nor a solicitation of an offer to buy these Securities. The offer is made only by the Prospectus.

New Issue   October 2, 19--

750,000 Shares

ABXY Corporation

Common Stock
($.10 par value)

Price $30 per Share

Copies of the Prospectus may be obtained in any State in which this annoucement is circulated only from such of the undersigned as may legally offer these securities in such state.

First XYZ Inc.

                       MNO Inc.

                                     TUV Securities

    ABC Inc.   CDE & Co.   Monopoly Inc.

    Ajax Inc.   Dustby Inc.   ZXZ Inc.

                        HIJ Securities

---

these comprehensive tombstone type notices identify the company seeking to acquire another company; state the price being offered for your shares and whether payment will be in cash or securities or a combination of the two; inform you of various deadlines to send in your shares or to withdraw your offer; and announce various other conditions, such as the minimum number of shares the acquiring company requires for the deal to be completed. These notices also include the names of companies that act as soliciting and information agents, such as D.F. King & Co., Georgeson & Co., or the Carter Organization, along with their addresses and phone numbers. Such companies have been paid to provide you with information and prospectuses. Of course, these ads can also be biased and are often followed in a few days with ads placed by the target company, citing reasons to reject the bid.

Redemption Notices

Callable bonds and preferred stock can be redeemed by the issuer prior to maturity, and the likelihood of this happening is greatest when the issuer can replace them with new securities providing lower interest rate or dividends. When redemption takes place, issuers often place paid notices in a local newspaper and/or a major publication, such as *The Wall Street Journal*. These notices provide the serial numbers and denominations of the securities being redeemed and the call price of the securities.

Short Interest

Around the twentieth of each month, the New York and American stock exchanges and NASDAQ release data on short interest—shares sold when they are not actually owned by the seller (usually they are borrowed). The exchanges break down the statistics by individual stocks and also give a total number of shorted shares of their listed companies compared to the total the month before.

Short interest figures generally signify that professional investors anticipate a decline in share prices. However, the figures are somewhat inflated by the inclusion of the short positions of exchange floor specialists; they sell short as part of their stabilizing function as well as for investment purposes. Market analysts also view large short interest positions as potential buying pressure since short positions must ultimately be covered by purchasing shares.

Other Economic and Financial Indicators

Among the more common weekly graphic features relating to business activity, securities prices, and returns on your savings are the following:

Treasury Bill Bar Chart: This appears in many newspapers, usually on Tuesday, following the Treasury bill auction of the preceding day. This table of 3-month Treasury bill yields shows how discount rates have changed on a weekly basis over the past three months, and gives the year-earlier yield as well. This chart gives you an idea of the direction in which rates on adjustable rate mortgages are heading, and whether you'll earn more or less income from a money market fund or an adjustable rate CD.

Money Supply Chart: This type of chart appears on Friday, following the weekly report on the nation's money supply released by the Federal Reserve Board at 4:30 P.M. EST on Thursday. The chart contains a "cone," made up of diverging lines that indicate the upper and lower targets of money supply growth laid down by the Federal Reserve Board. If the line representing M-1 money supply growth moves above the cone, watch out for jittery speculation about tighter monetary policy—speculation that could hurt bond prices. If the M-1 line is below the cone, be prepared for speculation that the Federal Reserve Board intends to loosen monetary policy and push rates lower—speculation that often supports bond prices. M-1, however, fluctuates week to week because it's narrowly based. Broader measures of the money supply, M-2 and M-3, are reported monthly, and articles often include similar charts for these figures.

THE STOCK MARKETS: DAILY SUMMARIES

Key Stock Market Indexes and Charts

It's possible for all but the busiest person to get a quick overview of stock market activity—and even some sense of future market movement—by reviewing the key market indexes and charts clustered at the beginning of the daily stock tables. At first, the mass of figures may overwhelm you. But you can train your eyes and brain to march through such displays, dividing them into mentally digestible components. The principal display of *The Wall Street Journal* appears on the inside front page of the *Money and Investing* (C) section and is headed Stock Market Data Bank. The Market Indicators package of *The New York Times*, shown here, appears at the beginning of its New York Stock Exchange listings. It can be broken down as follows:

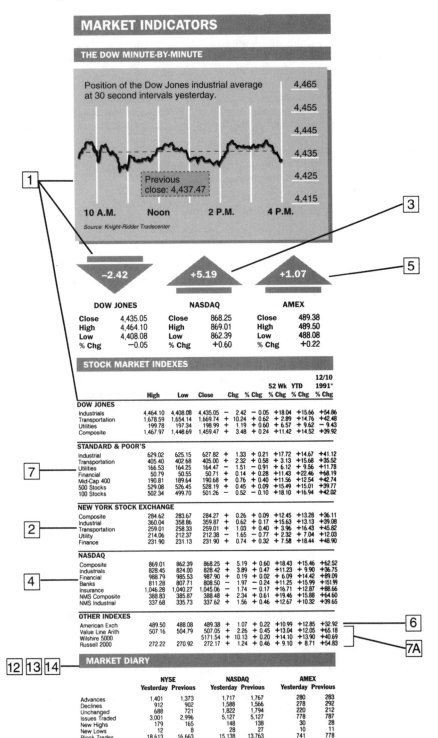

MARKET INDICATORS

THE DOW MINUTE-BY-MINUTE

Position of the Dow Jones industrial average at 30 second intervals yesterday.

4,465
4,455
4,445
4,435
4,425
4,415

Previous close: 4,437.47

10 A.M.   Noon   2 P.M.   4 P.M.

Source: Knight-Ridder Tradecenter

1

3

5

−2.42   +5.19   +1.07

	DOW JONES		NASDAQ		AMEX
Close	4,435.05	Close	868.25	Close	489.38
High	4,464.10	High	869.01	High	489.50
Low	4,408.08	Low	862.39	Low	488.08
% Chg	−0.05	% Chg	+0.60	% Chg	+0.22

STOCK MARKET INDEXES

	High	Low	Close	Chg	% Chg	52 Wk % Chg	YTD % Chg	12/10 1991* % Chg
DOW JONES								
Industrials	4,464.10	4,408.08	4,435.05	− 2.42	− 0.05	+18.04	+15.66	+54.86
Transportation	1,678.59	1,654.14	1,669.74	+ 10.24	+ 0.62	+ 2.89	+14.76	+42.48
Utilities	199.78	197.34	198.99	+ 1.19	+ 0.60	+ 6.57	+ 9.62	− 9.43
Composite	1,467.97	1,448.69	1,459.47	+ 3.48	+ 0.24	+11.42	+14.52	+39.92
STANDARD & POOR'S								
Industrial	629.02	625.15	627.82	+ 1.33	+ 0.21	+17.72	+14.67	+41.12
Transportation	405.40	402.68	405.00	+ 2.32	+ 0.58	+ 3.13	+15.68	+35.52
Utilities	166.53	164.25	164.47	− 1.51	− 0.91	+ 6.12	+ 9.56	+11.78
Financial	50.79	50.55	50.71	+ 0.14	+ 0.28	+11.43	+22.46	+68.19
Mid-Cap 400	190.81	189.64	190.68	+ 0.76	+ 0.40	+11.56	+12.54	+42.74
500 Stocks	529.08	526.45	528.19	+ 0.45	+ 0.09	+15.49	+15.01	+39.77
100 Stocks	502.34	499.70	501.26	− 0.52	− 0.10	+18.10	+16.94	+42.02
NEW YORK STOCK EXCHANGE								
Composite	284.62	283.67	284.27	+ 0.26	+ 0.09	+12.45	+13.28	+36.11
Industrial	360.04	358.86	359.87	+ 0.62	+ 0.17	+15.63	+13.13	+39.08
Transportation	259.01	258.33	259.01	+ 1.03	+ 0.40	+ 3.96	+16.43	+45.82
Utility	214.06	212.37	212.38	− 1.65	− 0.77	+ 2.32	+ 7.04	+12.03
Finance	231.90	231.13	231.90	+ 0.74	+ 0.32	+ 7.58	+18.44	+48.90
NASDAQ								
Composite	869.01	862.39	868.25	+ 5.19	+ 0.60	+18.43	+15.46	+62.52
Industrials	828.45	824.00	828.42	+ 3.89	+ 0.47	+11.23	+ 9.90	+36.75
Financial	988.79	985.53	987.90	+ 0.19	+ 0.02	+ 6.09	+14.42	+89.09
Banks	811.28	807.71	808.50	− 1.97	− 0.24	+11.25	+15.99	+151.99
Insurance	1,046.28	1,040.27	1,045.06	− 1.74	− 0.17	+16.71	+12.87	+88.66
NMS Composite	388.83	385.87	388.48	+ 2.34	+ 0.61	+19.46	+15.88	+64.60
NMS Industrial	337.68	335.73	337.62	+ 1.56	+ 0.46	+12.67	+10.32	+39.65
OTHER INDEXES								
American Exch	489.50	488.08	489.38	+ 1.07	+ 0.22	+10.99	+12.85	+32.92
Value Line Arith	507.16	504.79	507.05	+ 2.26	+ 0.45	+13.04	+12.05	+65.18
Wilshire 5000			5171.54	+ 10.13	+ 0.20	+14.10	+13.90	+40.69
Russell 2000	272.22	270.92	272.17	+ 1.24	+ 0.46	+ 9.10	+ 8.71	+54.83

7

2

4

6

7A

MARKET DIARY

12 **13** **14**

	NYSE Yesterday	Previous	NASDAQ Yesterday	Previous	AMEX Yesterday	Previous
Advances	1,401	1,373	1,717	1,767	280	283
Declines	912	902	1,588	1,566	278	292
Unchanged	688	721	1,822	1,794	220	212
Issues Traded	3,001	2,996	5,127	5,127	778	787
New Highs	179	165	148	138	30	28
New Lows	12	8	28	27	10	11
Block Trades	18,613	16,663	15,138	13,763	741	778

Block Trades are transaction of 5,000 or more shares.

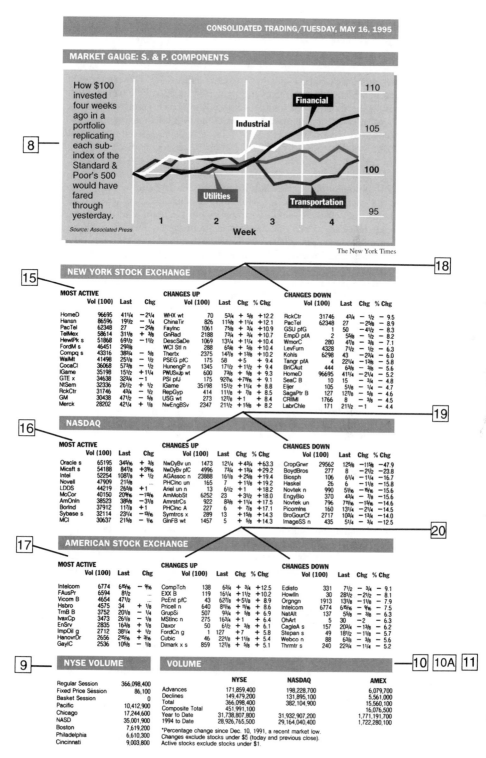

CONSOLIDATED TRADING/TUESDAY, MAY 16, 1995

MARKET GAUGE: S. & P. COMPONENTS

How $100 invested four weeks ago in a portfolio replicating each sub-index of the Standard & Poor's 500 would have fared through yesterday.

Source: Associated Press

Financial — Industrial — Utilities — Transportation

Week 1 2 3 4 — 110 / 105 / 100 / 95

The New York Times

NEW YORK STOCK EXCHANGE

MOST ACTIVE	Vol (100)	Last	Chg	CHANGES UP	Vol (100)	Last	Chg	% Chg	CHANGES DOWN	Vol (100)	Last	Chg	% Chg
HomeD	96695	41 1/4	−2 1/4	WHX wt	70	5 3/4	+ 5/8	+12.2	RckCtr	31746	43 1/4	− 1/2	− 9.5
Hansn	86596	19 1/2	− 1/4	ChinaTir	826	11 5/8	+1 1/4	+12.1	PacTel	62348	27	−2 5/8	− 8.9
PacTel	62348	27	−2 5/8	FayInc	1061	7 5/8	+ 3/4	+10.9	GSU pfG	1	50	−4 1/2	− 8.3
TelMex	58614	31 1/8	+ 3/8	GnRad	2188	7 3/4	+ 3/4	+10.7	EmpD pfA	2	55 5/8	− 1/2	− 8.2
HewlPk s	51868	69 1/2	−1 1/2	DescSaDe	1069	13 1/4	+1 1/4	+10.4	WmorC	280	47 1/8	− 3/8	− 7.1
FordM s	46451	29 3/8		WCI Stl n	288	6 5/8	+ 5/8	+10.4	LevFurn	4328	7 1/2	− 1/2	− 6.3
Compq s	43316	38 3/4	− 1/2	Thertx	2375	14 7/8	+1 3/8	+10.2	Kohls	6298	43	−2 3/4	− 6.0
WalMt	41498	25 1/8	− 1/2	PSEG pfC	175	58	+5	+ 9.4	Tangr pfA	4	22 1/4	−1 3/8	− 5.8
CocaCl	36068	57 3/8	− 1/2	HunengP n	1345	17 1/2	+1 1/2	+ 9.4	BriCAut	444	6 3/8	− 3/8	− 5.6
iGame	35198	15 1/2	+1 1/4	PWUSvJp wt	600	7 3/8	+ 5/8	+ 9.3	HomeD	96695	41 1/4	−2 1/4	− 5.2
GTE x	34638	32 3/4	−1	PSI pfJ	175	92 7/8	+7 7/8	+ 9.1	SeaC B	10	15	− 3/4	− 4.8
NtSem	32336	26 1/2	+ 1/2	iGame	35198	15 1/2	+1 1/4	+ 8.8	Eljer	105	5 1/8	− 1/4	− 4.7
RckCtr	31746	43 1/4	− 1/2	RepGyp	414	11 1/8	+ 7/8	+ 8.5	SagaPtr B	127	12 7/8	− 5/8	− 4.6
GM	30438	47 1/2	+ 1/8	USG wt	273	12 7/8	+1	+ 8.4	CRIIMI	1766	8	− 3/8	− 4.5
Merck	28202	42 1/4	+ 1/8	NwEngBSv	2347	21 1/2	+1 5/8	+ 8.2	LabrChle	171	21 1/2	−1	− 4.4

NASDAQ

MOST ACTIVE	Vol (100)	Last	Chg	CHANGES UP	Vol (100)	Last	Chg	% Chg	CHANGES DOWN	Vol (100)	Last	Chg	% Chg
Oracle s	65195	34 5/16	+ 3/8	NwDyBv un	1473	12 1/4	+4 3/4	+63.3	CropGrwr	29562	12 5/8	−11 5/8	−47.9
Micsft s	54188	84 7/8	+3 9/16	NwDyBv pfC	4996	73 1/4	+1 3/4	+29.2	BoydBros	277	8	−2 1/2	−23.8
Intel	52254	108 7/8	+ 1/2	AGAssoc n	23888	16 1/8	+2 5/8	+19.4	Biosph	106	6 1/4	−1 1/4	−16.7
Novell	47909	21 5/8	...	PHCInc un	165	7	+1 1/8	+19.2	Haskel	26	6	−1 1/8	−15.8
LDDS	44219	26 5/8	+1	Ariel un n	13	6 1/2	+1	+18.2	Novtek n	990	5 1/8	− 15/16	−15.6
McCor	40150	20 9/16	−1 9/16	AmMobSt	6252	23	+3 1/2	+18.0	EngyBio	370	4 3/4	− 7/8	−15.6
AmOnln	38523	38 5/8	−3 1/8	AmrstrCs	922	8 3/8	+1 1/4	+17.5	Novtek un	796	7 11/16	−1 5/16	−14.6
Borlnd	37912	11 7/8	+1	PHCInc A	227	6	+ 7/8	+17.1	Picomins	160	13 1/4	−2 1/4	−14.5
Sybase s	32114	23 1/4	−1 9/16	Symtrcs x	289	13	+1 5/8	+14.3	BroGourCf	2717	10 3/4	−1 3/4	−14.0
MCI	30637	21 5/8	− 1/16	GinFB wt	1457	5	+ 5/8	+14.3	ImageSS n	435	5 1/4	− 3/4	−12.5

AMERICAN STOCK EXCHANGE

MOST ACTIVE	Vol (100)	Last	Chg	CHANGES UP	Vol (100)	Last	Chg	% Chg	CHANGES DOWN	Vol (100)	Last	Chg	% Chg
Intelcom	6774	6 15/16	− 9/16	CompTch	138	6 3/4	+ 3/4	+12.5	Edisto	331	7 1/2	− 3/4	− 9.1
FAusPr	6594	8 1/2	...	EXX B	119	16 1/4	+1 1/2	+10.2	Howlln	30	28 1/2	−2 1/2	− 8.1
Vicom B	4654	47 1/2	...	PcEnt pfC	43	62 7/8	+5 1/8	+ 8.9	Orgngn	1913	13 1/8	−1 1/8	− 7.9
Hsbro	4575	34	+ 1/8	Pricell n	640	8 11/16	+ 11/16	+ 8.6	Intelcom	6774	6 15/16	− 9/16	− 7.5
TrnB B	3752	20 1/8	− 1/4	GrupSi	507	9 3/4	+ 5/8	+ 6.9	NatAlt	137	5 5/8	− 3/8	− 6.3
IvaxCp	3473	26 1/16	− 1/8	MStinc n	275	16 3/4	+1	+ 6.4	OhArt	5	30	−2	− 6.3
EnSrv	2835	16 3/8	+ 1/8	Daxor	50	6 1/2	+ 3/8	+ 6.1	CagleA s	157	20 3/4	−1 3/8	− 6.2
ImpOil g	2712	38 1/4	+ 1/2	FordCn g	1	127	+7	+ 5.8	Stepan s	49	18 1/2	−1 1/8	− 5.7
HanovrDr	2656	2 15/16	+ 3/8	Cubic	46	22 1/4	+1 1/8	+ 5.4	Webco n	88	6 3/8	− 3/8	− 5.6
GaylC	2536	10 5/8	− 1/8	Dimark x s	859	12 7/8	+ 5/8	+ 5.1	Thrmtr s	240	22 3/4	−1 1/4	− 5.2

NYSE VOLUME

Regular Session	366,098,400
Fixed Price Session	86,100
Basket Session	0
Pacific	10,412,900
Chicago	17,244,600
NASD	35,001,900
Boston	7,619,200
Philadelphia	6,610,300
Cincinnati	9,003,800

VOLUME

	NYSE	NASDAQ	AMEX
Advances	171,859,400	198,228,700	6,079,700
Declines	149,479,200	131,895,100	5,561,000
Total	366,098,400	382,104,900	15,560,100
Composite Total	451,991,100		16,076,500
Year to Date	31,738,807,800	31,932,907,200	1,771,191,700
1994 to Date	28,926,765,500	29,164,040,400	1,722,280,100

*Percentage change since Dec. 10, 1991, in recent market low.
Changes exclude stocks under $5 (today and previous close).
Active stocks exclude stocks under $1.

Charts 1 to 7A   These sets of graphs and tables represent price averages and indexes showing changes in issues listed on the NYSE (1 and 2), NASDAQ (3 and 4), Amex (5 and 6), Standard & Poor's (7), and the (equally weighted) Value Line index, Wilshire 5000 index (the broadest), and Russell 2000 (small companies) index (7A). They simply tell you in which direction the overall group of stocks each covers moved during the most recent trading session. The NYSE receives the most attention, with its list tracked by two families of indexes: the Dow Jones, and the exchange's own NYSE composite. Another important set of indexes, those of Standard & Poor's, are reported separately in *The New York Times* and will be discussed shortly. A composite index includes all the stocks traded on a particular market. A narrower index, such as those that appear here for utilities or transportation shares, tracks relatively few stocks. Utility and financial stocks are sensitive to interest rate changes—and by extension—to the bond market because these industries depend on huge amounts of credit. Therefore, pluses for these indexes immediately indicate the likelihood that the rate situation is stable or improving. Scanning the pluses and minuses in the various markets tells you if the previous day's movements were broadly based or varied from one market to another. The *Times* makes this easy by showing the highlights of the three major indexes in arrow-shaped boxes pointing in the direction the index moved the previous day. Declines for the Amex and NASDAQ next to rising indexes for the NYSE may indicate that institutional investors are more optimistic than individual investors. In the example illustrated, the three indexes all moved in the same direction—down.

Chart 8   This graph varies from day to day and illuminates a relevant aspect of market activity. (*The Wall Street Journal's* counterpart, called *Investment Insight,* appears regularly just below its Markets Diary.) The illustrated example shows how the four subindexes comprising the Standard & Poor's 500 stock index performed relative to each other over a 4-week period. (Current quarterly activity in the S&P 500 is depicted every day in a point-and-figure chart that appears at the beginning of the stock price tables just above another chart showing NYSE volume over the same period.) The S&P 500 is composed mostly of NYSE-listed stocks with some Amex and over-the-counter issues. Although numbers and proportions vary somewhat, its breaks down approximately into 400 industrials, 60 transportation and utility companies, and 40 financial issues. Although broader indexes exist (the Wilshire covers 5,000 stocks and the Value Line about 1,700), the S&P 500 is the most widely followed index of broader market activity and often behaves quite differently than the DJIA index of blue chip stocks. The S&P 100 stock index, which is reported in the table accompanying the graph, has a composition similar to the 500, but it is made up exclusively of stocks for which options are traded.

Charts 9, 10, 10A, and 11   Volume can help you determine in which direction the stock market will continue to move. If stock prices rise amid heavy volume, the indication is that many investors chose to invest heavily in stocks, and they intend to hold out for further price rises. Similarly, a market drop on heavy volume is considered a more serious setback than a drop on light volume. A market rise on light volume will cause the market rise to be questioned. The trick, of course, is to have an idea of what normal volume is for any given exchange during any particular season. Bar charts in *The New York Times* and *The Wall Street Journal* indicate daily volume for the NYSE for the past three months and six months, respectively.

Chart 9   This chart shows how the previous day's volume was distributed among the NYSE and the various regional and electronic exchanges on which NYSE-listed stocks are traded.

Charts 10, 10A, and 11   These tables compare NYSE, NASDAQ, and Amex volume figures. The up and down share volume helps you gauge the daily strength and weakness of the three major markets. The Advanced column presents the number of shares in each market that were rising when they changed hands, while the Declined column indicates the number of shares sold below the price of the previous sale. Shares sold at the same price are not included. These figures can signal an underlying weakness or strength often masked by the indexes. If stocks rose according to the indexes, but were sold on "weakness" (that is, when the shares were dropping) rather than on strength" (that is, on rising prices), this could mean that investors were using an overall price rise to take their profits and get out.

Charts 12, 13, and 14   Called Market Diary here, these figures, like the volume numbers, help you confirm or doubt the validity of changes in the price index. If, for example, the indexes have risen sharply in one of the markets, but the number of issues that advanced are fairly evenly matched with the number of issues that declined, it's possible that the movement of a few stocks was responsible for the rising indexes. Thus, the market isn't as strong as it first appeared. Similarly, the number of stocks that hit 52-week highs during the session indicates how strong the market really was. Major financial sections and publications carry lists of stocks that hit 52-week highs and lows. Obviously, you want to know if any of your stocks are included on these lists. Block trades, defined for this table as 5000 share trades or more, although a significant element in overall trading volume, are less significant as indicators of investor sentiment than aggregate figures for smaller trades. Block activity provides an indication of the portion of total volume transacted by institutional investors. These figures are particularly significant when we know what percentage of block trades was executed above the previous trade (uptick) and below (downtick). When upticks exceed downticks, it is considered a bullish sign and vice versa. This information is provided on Saturdays in *The New York Times* in a section called Tracking the Markets."

Charts 15, 16, and 17   The most active issues—stocks with the heaviest trading volume—are given in the descending order of shares traded for each issue—15 for each market. Sometimes stocks appear on the most active list because of a news item or a rumor regarding profits, mergers, or new products. Some stocks. however, constantly appear because they are actively traded by financial institutions, which often are restricted to buying stocks with large market capitalizations (the number of outstanding shares times the market price).

Charts 18, 19, and 20   Because up and down price changes are expressed in percentage terms, you can get a quick idea of the importance of your gain or loss if your stock appears on one of these lists. Cheaper stocks are more apt to be included on these lists, since small point changes translate into bigger percentage changes for cheaper stocks than for expensive ones. These lists may also help you find (or avoid) volatile stocks.

New York Stock Exchange and American Stock Exchange Consolidated Tables

You have to reach into stock tables to find specific information. Stock tables remain the heart of daily financial publications and sections, although the commodity, options, and bond tables are becoming increasingly more important as readers become more familiar with other types of investments. The tables for the two major U.S. stock exchanges, the New York and American stock exchanges, and the NASDAQ national market follow the same format. The information encompasses consolidated trading, which also includes trading on regional exchanges and on the over-the-counter market. Starting with the name of each stock, which we'll call Column I, the tables offer:

1. Name   It's not always easy to locate a particular stock, because the names are usually radically abbreviated. The abbreviation systems used by the Associated Press and United Press International, which supply most of the tables you see, are different (and not to be confused with stock ticker symbols used on the exchanges); thus, the alphabetical order will differ from one system to the other. Stocks like IBM and AT&T are easy to find; few investors, however, would know immediately that WTPTP is West Point Pepperell. Unless otherwise identified, these are names of common stock. A "pf" identifies preferred stocks that are convertible to common shares are identified as preferred stock, but the convertability feature is not indicated in the stock tables as it is in the corporate bond tables. A "v" indicates that trading was suspended in the primary market. Stock tables are usually accompanied by explanatory notes defining any letters that may appear. An "A," "B," or other capital letter differentiates between one class of stock and another. A "wt" identifies the security as a warrant. A "vj" indicates that the company is in bankruptcy proceedings, and "wi" means when issued, signifying that the shares have not yet been issued. If the issuance is canceled, the trades will also be canceled. Also included but not identified are exchange-listed American Depositary Receipts (ADRs), which are negotiable receipts representing shares of foreign issuers.

2. Annual dividend   Dividends are listed by dollars and cents per share. Don't confuse this figure with the amount you'll receive in the mail each quarter. The annual dividend is an estimate, based on the most recent quarterly dividend multiplied by four. If a company has a history of steadily rising dividends, consider this a conservative estimate. An "e" in this column indicates that dividends have been irregular, and that the figure represents the amount paid over the past year, rather than an estimate of future dividends. A "g" means dividends are paid in Canadian currency, although the other stock market data is given in terms of U.S. dollars.

3. Yield   This is the current dividend divided by the lastest closing price, rounded off to the nearest tenth of a percent. A low- or no-yield stock may be a growth stock. which means that profits are reinvested rather than paid out in dividends. Investors purchase growth stocks for capital gains, not for dividends; they hope that stock prices will

NEW YORK STOCK EXCHANGE

⑨		①	②	③	④	⑤	⑥		⑦	⑧
52-Week				Yid	PE	Sales				
High	Low	Stock	Div	%	Ratio	100s	High	Low	Last	Chg.
25	18	XYZ Corp.	.92	2.0	7	623	17³/₈	17¹/₈	17³/₈	+¹/₈

increase as profits do. Some investors, however, purchase stocks for dividends, or income. This yield figure allows you to compare the dividend income with the income from other types of investments. Remember, however, that while the yield on a stock represents the potential income, the yield on bonds is a combination of both the annual interest income and the lump-sum capital gain or loss that occurs when the bond is redeemed. In a way, therefore, comparing stock and bond yields is similar to comparing apples and oranges.

4. PE ratio The price earnings ratio is the latest price divided by the last 12 months' earnings per share, rounded to the nearest whole number. Be sure not to confuse PEs with dividends. PEs are used to compare the perceived value of stocks in the marketplace. PEs indicate how investors view the value of a company's profits. Stocks representing solid, uninflated profits that are expected to grow usually have higher PEs than stocks with questionable profits and profit-growth potential. Growth companies may have PEs of 20 or more. On the other hand, a high PE could be the result of a recent drop in earnings, and the prelude to a drop in the stock's price that will drop the PE to its former, lower level. A start-up or turnaround company could be attractive, but could have no earnings—and therefore no PE. PEs give you a way to calculate per share earnings roughly: divide the stock price by the PE.

5. Sales This column gives you the trading volume, in hundreds of shares. A "5," in most cases, means 500 shares changed hands; a "1067" means 106,700 shares were traded. A "z," however, indicates that the full figure is being given. Volume measures how liquid a stock is. Stocks that consistently show large volume and small price changes are liquid; it takes a large imbalance between buy and sell orders to move the price much. Stocks with consistently low trading volume may be subject to wide price swings when large orders are finally placed. Sudden surges in volume, accompanied by rising prices, may indicate that an individual or an organization is building up a stake. (If five percent or more of a company's stock is acquired, however, SEC rule 13(d) requires that information, including a statement of intentions, be filed with its offices, with the company, and with the relevant stock exchange.) Volume surges often trigger takeover rumors, which in turn result in even greater volume and price movements. Financial analysts and journalists often ask company executives about the reasons for unusually heavy volume. A response of "no known reason" may cool speculation, while a "no comment" may fuel the guessing game.

An "x" in the volume column means the stock is ex-dividend. During this time buyers do not receive the most recently declared dividend. Stock prices decline by the amount of the dividend when the shares go ex-dividend, and then usually recover gradually.

6. High/Low   These twin columns give the highest and lowest prices during the trading session. A "u" indicates a 52-week high; a "d" indicates a 52-week low.

7. Last sale   The last sale is the closing price. Prices are usually expressed in "eighths"; an eighth equals 12.5 cents. Increments of sixteenths (6.25 cents) and thirty-seconds (3.125 cents) are used for cheaper stocks. You'll see these increments most often with over-the-counter stocks. Tables provided by Associated Press don't indicate the location of the last sale. United Press International does include the location, using "p" for Pacific Stock Exchange, "x" for Philadelphia Stock Exchange, "u" for Midwest Stock Exchange, and "g" for over-the-counter.

8. Change   This figure represents the change in closing price from the previous day.

9. 52-week High-Low   The high-low column gives you the annual trading range, the highest and lowest prices of the previous 52 weeks plus the current trading week, up to, but not through, the last session. A broad range indicates that a stock has demonstrated the potential to make—and lose—money for shareholders. Sometimes, a stock that has traded up and down within a range will meet resistance when it approaches its previous high point, because some investors will use this high point as a benchmark to sell. Similarly, the low point could serve as a buffer against further price drops. At the low point, buyers, hoping history will repeat itself and the stock rise, may purchase shares and thus provide support for the stock's price.

Other Over-the-Counter Stocks Tables

The quantity of information available for over-the-counter stocks has grown dramatically over the years. It's still often necessary, however, to call your broker for a price because many of the lesser-known, less expensive stocks aren't included in the daily tables. Your broker will use the pink sheets published by the National Quotations Bureau, which list bid and asked prices, to give you a price. *Barron's* provides extensive over-the-counter tables on a weekly basis. The *National OTC Stock Journal,* another weekly, carries information about penny stocks, which usually sell for less than $1.00. The daily tables included in large newspapers have expanded, in part because of the efforts of the National Association of Securities Dealers, the umbrella group for over-the-counter dealers. Since the early 1970s, the NASD Automated Quotations, or NASDAQ Stock Market, has allowed dealers using desktop terminals to view each other's bid quotations (the highest prices they're willing to pay), and asked quotations (the lowest prices they'd accept). NASDAQ also passes this and other information on to wire services for use in daily stock tables. Since the early 1980s, the system has been upgraded to allow dealers to enter transaction prices and sizes of trades. As a result, the tables for the more expensive or more heavily traded NASDAQ stocks are identical to the NYSE and Amex tables. Stocks that are subject to this full-line reporting system are included in tables carrying such headings as NASDAQ National Market or NASDAQ National Market Issues.

However, not all the companies meeting NASD criteria to have their shares listed as part of the National Market System are included there. Instead, more limited market information for the shares of these and other NASDAQ-listed companies is included under the headings of NASDAQ National List or NASDAQ Bid and

Asked Quotations. In these tables, you'll mainly find volume figures and closing bid and asked quotations along with the daily change in the bid price from the previous day's closing bid.

The NASDAQ Bid and Asked Quotations table presents the following elements:

1. Name of the stock and its annual dividend, if any.

2. Sales, in hundreds of shares.

3. Last bid of the session, that is, the most a dealer will pay you for a share. You'll note that the spread between bid and asked prices often is considerable.

4. Last asked quotation of the day, that is, the lowest a dealer will accept for a share.

5. Change in the bid from the end of the previous trading day.

NASDAQ NATIONAL LIST

①	②	③	④	⑤
Stock & Div	**Sales 100s**	**Bid**	**Asked**	**Net Chg.**
ABZ Sys	90	$3/8$	$7/8$	$-1/4$
Quiljax	2	6	$6^3/4$	...
Zextap Inc .08	14	$15^1/2$	16	$-1/2$

Many over-the-counter stocks appear on neither the National Market nor the National List. Some of the larger financial publications and sections include as many of these stocks as they see fit, usually in an abbreviated form that includes only the name, bid, and asked, but no volume or daily change. These stocks are listed under various headings, including Additional OTC Quotes and NASDAQ Supplemental OTC.

Regional and Foreign Stock Market Tables

A relatively small number of stocks are listed only on regional exchanges, such as the Midwest, Pacific, Philadelphia, and Boston stock exchanges. These shares usually aren't very actively traded and attract mainly a regional following. Regional stock trading information in newspapers usually provides daily data on volume; high, low, and closing prices; and change in price. Readers must calculate dividends, yield, the PE ratio, and seek out 52-week high and low prices.

Of increasing importance are stocks traded on foreign markets. Information about the more important stocks are carried in such major newspapers as *The New York Times* and *The Wall Street Journal.* The stocks are organized by the exchange on which they're traded. The information carried for the Toronto and Montreal markets in Canada is the same as the information carried for the U.S. regional exchange-listed stocks. The data carried for other foreign stocks is more limited: often only the name and the closing price, given in local currency, such as Japanese yen, British pence, French francs, Swiss francs, West German marks, and so on. It's up to the reader to track the daily change, and, if necessary, make use of the foreign exchange tables to translate the price into U.S. dollars and cents. Other tables show foreign securities traded over the counter. The majority of these issues are American Depositary Receipts, representing ownership of securities physically deposited abroad. Where they are not ADRs, the indication "n" is used. Quotes are in U.S. dollars and these tables typically have four columns: sales, bid price, asked price, and net change.

STOCK OPTIONS TABLES

Stock options give you both a conservative way to increase the income on your holdings or insure your portfolio against losses, as well as relatively inexpensive and highly speculative ways to invest in stocks. In any case, don't assume you understand these investment vehicles until you at least understand the stock option tables. Although unheard of a generation ago, these tables now comprise a major portion of the inside of financial news packages. The longest tables are generated by the principal options exchanges, the Chicago Board Options Exchange, the American Stock Exchange, and the Philadelphia Stock Exchange. Shorter tables are included for small options trading operations found on other exchanges.

A 1990s innovation that has rapidly been gaining popularity is LEAPS, a term now used generically but that started as a proprietary acronym of the Chicago Board Options Exchange meaning Long-Term Equity AnticiPation Securities. LEAPS are long-term options expiring in 1 to 3 years (with applications for 5-year expirations pending). Currently being traded on some 150 stocks and several stock indexes, LEAPS are listed separately in the financial pages. Although the following explanations apply to traditional conventional options expiring typically in 9 months or less, LEAPS are essentially no different except that in having longer terms, they logically trade at higher premiums.

Daily Stock Options Tables

Options tables give you the prices of wasting assets. These contracts, which as a rule last no longer than nine months, give the holder the right, but not the obligation, to buy (call) or sell (put) shares of stock at a specified strike price by a specified expiration date. The daily table format, and what it includes, by columns, is as follows.

STOCK OPTIONS

	①	②	③			④		
	Option & NY Close	Strike Price	Calls—Last			Puts—Last		
			May	Aug	Nov	May	Aug	Nov
Ⓐ	XYZ	35	7	6^{1}/$_{2}$	6^{3}/$_{4}$	^{3}/$_{4}$	^{1}/$_{4}$	r
Ⓑ	40	40	2	1^{1}/$_{2}$	r	1	1^{1}/$_{2}$	r
Ⓒ	40	45	^{3}/$_{4}$	^{1}/$_{4}$	r	7	6^{1}/$_{2}$	r

1. Name of the underlying stock and under it, the closing price of the underlying stock, repeated for each row of strike prices. (Since New York Stock Exchange tables now generally include sales of NYSE stocks on other exchanges, the NY Close may differ from the NYSE table, which reports later sales on the Pacific Stock Exchange and elsewhere.) In this example, XYZ Corporation stock closed at 40 on the principal stock exchange on which it's traded, most likely the New York Stock Exchange. Because the stock is worth $40 per share, each 100-share options contract has an exercise value of $4000.

2. The strike price is given in this column. This is the price per share at which the option holder is entitled to buy or sell the stock. The accompanying table includes options series for three strike prices— $35, $40, and $45 per share. Therefore, the values of the 100-share contracts are $3500, $4000, and $4500, respectively.

3. and 4. These figures represent the closing prices, or premiums, that were paid for the various puts and calls. The prices are expressed on a per share basis, meaning that you must multiply by 100 shares to determine the cost of the contract. These prices are given for the different months of expiration, usually spaced three months apart. Each contract has a specific month of expiration, with expiration set at 11:59 A.M. EST on the third Saturday of that month. Whether you gain or lose in options trading usually depends on movements in the premium price. That is because options positions are generally closed out with an offsetting purchase or sale or are allowed to expire. Having to exercise the option, that is, actually buying the stock in the case of calls or coming up with the shares to sell in the case of puts, involves more cash than many options holders want to commit.

Notice how the strike prices of the options series straddle the current market value of the stock. This gives investors a choice of intrinsically worthless—but cheap—options as well as options that have considerable value, but which are expensive to buy. Options exchanges constantly create series with new strike prices to maintain this situation as the price of the underlying stock changes. For stocks selling at $25 to $50 per share, the strike prices are usually set in increments of $5; the increments are $10 on contracts for stocks priced $50 to $200 per share. For options on stocks worth $200 or more per share, strike prices are set $20 apart, and for options on stocks worth less than $25 per share, the increments are $2.50.

Using the Associated Press system of symbols, "r" in the premium column means options for that particular strike price and month of expiration did not trade. An "s" indicates that the Options Clearing Corporation, which guarantees your cash or shares when options are exercised or traded, isn't offering that particular contract. United Press International uses "nt" if an option did not trade, and "no" if the OCC isn't offering an option. Associated Press expresses sixteenths as "$^1/_{16}$" while United Press uses "1s" to represent that fraction.

The cheapest options are those on which you would lose money (even before considering commission costs) if you exercised them. These are referred to as out-of-the-money options. For example, an XYZ May45 call, giving you the right to pay $45 per share or $4500 per contract for 100 shares of XYZ, costs only $^3/_4$—75 cents per share or $75 per contract. (See Line C, Column 3.) In other words, someone is willing to pay these prices for the right to later pay out $4500 for a stock currently worth $4000. Of course, the hope is that XYZ stock will rise. For example, if the stock rises to $43 per share (which would still mean that the option is intrinsically worthless and out of the money) another investor may be willing to pay more for that option—perhaps $1^1/_2$ or $1.50 a share. The second investor hopes that the stock will rise to the point at which the option would produce a profit if exercised. In any case, the first buyer, who paid $75 for the contract, could get $150 for the contract—doubling his or her money before subtracting commission costs.

Options with intrinsic value, such as the XYZ May35 calls (which give you the right to pay $3500 for something already worth $4000) are naturally more expensive than those with no intrinsic value. In this table, these options finished the previous section at $7 per share (Line C, Column 4), or $700 per contract. The percentage gains or losses on such options are less than the volatile out-of-the-money options, but there is also less chance that these options will have to be allowed to expire worthless.

These tables also indicate how much money you can make by selling options and thus increase the income from your stock portfolio. For example, if you own 100 shares of XYZ, you may decide to sell calls; that is, you may give another person the right to buy your shares. In return, you receive the premium. Assuming the price of options held steady from the previous day's closing levels, you could expect to receive $150 for selling an XYZ Aug40 call (Line B, Column 3). Of course, if the stock price should rise, the call holder could exercise the option, and you would lose the capital gain. Ideally, you would hope that XYZ stock would hold at around 40 until the option you sold expired. In that case, after brokerage commissions were factored into the equation, it would not be worthwhile for another investor to exercise the option you sold.

If you are worried that your XYZ stock might drop, you can lock in a value of $35 a share through most of August by buying an Aug35 put (which gives you the right to get $35 a share) for $25 a contract (Line A, Column 4).

In addition to options on individual stocks, options are traded on debt instruments (interest rate options), foreign currencies, stock indexes, and certain futures contracts. What applies to puts and calls on stocks also applies to options on other instruments, with one major exception—index options. Because they are settled in cash and have other distinct features, they deserve special attention.

Daily Index Options Tables

Index options, which give you the right to buy and sell the dollar value of an index (rather than 100 shares of stock, as with stock options) are relatively few; sometimes, however, they are extremely popular. They often dominate the most-active lists that appear at the head of daily option tables. Index options tables run under their exchange headings: Chicago Board Options Exchange (often referred to in the tables as Chicago Board or just Chicago), the American, Philadelphia, Pacific, and New York stock exchanges, and NASD.

Index options are popular because they allow investors to play the whole market, in the case of broad-based indexes, or segments of the market, in the case of indexes that track technology stocks or gold stocks, among others. An index is assigned a value of a certain number of dollars per point—$100, for example. Standard & Poor's has allowed its indexes to be used for such purposes, as have the New York Stock Exchange and Value Line. Sometimes indexes are created specifically for trading options on them. Using the usual format, a hypothetical XYZ index option, which for example, tracks hundreds of stocks, would appear like the accompanying example.

INDEX OPTIONS

		①	②			③		
XYZ Index								
	Strike Price	**Calls—Last**			**Puts—Last**			
		Feb	**Mar**	**Apr**	**Feb**	**Mar**	**Apr**	
Ⓐ	290	$12^7/8$	$14^1/4$	$14^1/8$	$3/16$	2	$4^1/4$	
Ⓑ	295	$7^5/8$	$10^1/4$	$11^3/8$	$11/16$	$3^1/4$	$6^3/4$	
Ⓒ	300	$3^3/4$	$7^3/4$	$8^1/8$	$1^7/8$	$5^3/8$	$9^1/8$	
Ⓓ	305	$1^3/16$	$4^7/8$	$6^1/2$	$4^3/8$	$10^1/2$	12	
Ⓔ	310	$3/8$	$2^7/8$	$4^1/2$	⋯	14	⋯	
Ⓕ	Total call volume 27,435 Total call open int. 78,121							
Ⓖ	Total put volume 17,477 Total call open int. 75,940							
Ⓗ	The index: High 302.55; Low 296.90;							
	Close 302.51. + 4.32							

Index option tables have the following components:

1. The strike price is the price you would pay (if you owned a call) or would receive (if you owned a put) if the option were exercised. To compute the dollar value, multiply by $100 per point, because the XYZ Index has an assigned value of $100 per point. The 290 strike price, for example, would require the payment of $29,000.

2. Calls-last are the closing prices, or premiums, for calls. Unlike the much longer time periods available for stock options, index options expire in about three months at most. As you can see, investors were paying 12⅞, or $1287.50 per contract, for the expensive, deep-in-the-money Feb290 calls (Line A, Column 2). That's because the index closed at 302.51—the index's closing level is given on Line H—making its monetary value $30,251. The holder of a call with a strike price of 290, or $29,000, has an option with an intrinsic value of $1251 and hopes the value will rise even higher so the option can be sold or exercised at a profit after commissions.

Meanwhile, the 310 strike price call options have no intrinsic value; they are out of the money and thus, cheap. A Feb310 cost only ⅜, or $37.50 per contract (Line E, Column 2), because it gives the buyer the right to pay $31,000 for an investment that's currently worth only $30,251.

3. Premiums on puts move in the opposite direction of calls. The March puts with a 310 strike price (Line E, Column 3) are expensive, ($1400 per contract) because they are deep in the money; they give the holder the right to demand $31,000 for an index that's worth only $30,152.

F. This line indicates the number of call contracts that were traded during the session and the number of contracts still open (open interest). To some extent, these figures measure investor optimism, because calls are bets that the market index will rise.

G. This line presents the same type of information given in line F. except that line G deals with puts. These figures reflect investor pessimism, because puts are bets that the market will drop, at least insofar as the group of stocks being tracked by the index is concerned.

H. This line indicates how the index performed during the session, in terms of its highest, lowest, and closing values, and change from its previous close. The gain shown in this example, 4.32 points, signifies that the value of the XYZ index rose $432.

Weekly Options Tables

Weekly options tables, such as those found in *Barron's* or the Sunday *New York Times,* follow a format different from the daily tables. Calls and puts are stacked rather than placed next to each other. More information is included in these tables. Index options are still run separately.

In the accompanying example of a typical stock-option table, the columns include the following information:

1. Name of the option, as identified by the underlying stock, the expiration month, and the strike price. The closest expiration months and lowest strike prices appear first. A "p" identifies puts; the other options are calls.

WEEKLY OPTIONS TABLE

①	②	③	④	⑤		⑥	⑦
Option	Sales	Open Int.	High	Low	Last	Net Chg.	Stock close
ABZ Mar35	1437	10921	$6^{1}/8$	$3^{3}/4$	4	$-1^{1}/8$	39
ABZ Mar35 p	99	5089	$1/16$	$1/16$	$1/16$	$-1/16$	39
ABZ Mar40	5981	7332	$1^{15}/16$	$1/2$	$9/16$	$-1/16$	39
ABZ Mar40 p	237	402	2	1	$1^{3}/4$	$+^{3}/8$	39

2. Sales for the week, in terms of the number of contracts that changed hands.

3. Open interest—the number of contracts in investor and dealer hands that haven't been exercised or closed out yet. Comparing the number of outstanding calls to puts helps you assess the direction speculators expect the price of the stock to take.

4. The highest and lowest premiums, per share, paid for a particular contract during the past week.

5. The closing premium, or price, per share, at the end of the week.

6. Net Change—how much premiums per share rose or fell from the previous weekly close. The $1^{1}/8$ ($1.125 per share) loss for ABZ Mar35 calls indicates that the contracts lost $112.50 each.

7. The closing price of the underlying shares, which, when multiplied by 100, equals the exercise value of the contracts, $3900.

FUTURES TABLES

Futures tables are grouped by broad categories—agricultural (grains, edible oils, livestock, coffee, sugar, cocoa, orange juice), metals (gold, silver, platinum, palladium, copper), industrials (lumber, cotton, crude oil, heating oil, gasoline), and financial (U.S. Treasury bonds, notes, and bills, foreign currencies, certificates of deposit, stock index futures). About 50 contracts are listed in various futures markets and included in newspaper tables. Commodity contracts are agreements to deliver or take delivery of a commodity in the future. Hence, the "Futures Prices" label for these tables. Most investors in commodities futures contracts are speculators who hope to make big profits by predicting correctly the change in commodity prices. The contracts are identified by their delivery months. A typical table, in this case for cattle. is presented here. The type of contract and the exchange (CME, or Chicago Mercantile Exchange) as well as the size (44,000 pounds) and the units of trade (pennies per pound) are shown in lines B and C.

Other information is presented as follows:

1. The highest and lowest prices paid for a particular delivery month contract since the contract was listed. This indicates the price swings of the contract. The April futures (*Line D*) ranged between 67.07 cents and 55.30 cents per pound, or $29,510 and $24,332 per 44,000-pound contract—a difference of $5178. An investor smart enough or lucky enough to invest $2433 (10% margin when the contract reached its $24,332 low point) and sell when prices peaked

CATTLE FUTURES

	①	②	③	④	⑤	⑥
	...Season...					Open
Ⓐ	**High**	**Low**	**High**	**Low**	**Close**	**Chg.**	**Int.**
Ⓑ	CATTLE, LIVE BEEF (CME)						
Ⓒ	44,000 lb.; ¢ per lb.						
Ⓓ	67.07	55.30 Apr	61.75	60.32	60.40	–.30	29,042
Ⓔ	66.60	56.25 Jun	60.52	59.35	59.47	–.28	17.547
Ⓕ	61.75	55.20 Aug	58.40	57.45	57.47	–.25	5,939
Ⓖ	60.60	55.70 Oct	57.20	56.37	56.50	–.15	2,705
Ⓗ	61.75	57.55 Dec	58.80	58.10	58.35	–.02	612
Ⓘ	60.20	58.00 Feb	58.90	58.77	58.77	+.07	56
Ⓙ	Est. sales 21,859. Wed's sales 21.607.						
Ⓚ	Wed.'s open Int 55,901, up 63.						

would have more than doubled his or her money. On the other hand, someone who invested at the high point could easily have lost all of his or her money. When the loss of a contract's value equals the amount of money that's been invested, brokers will usually demand more margin. If they don't get it, they will sell the contract.

2. The delivery months differentiate one contract from another. The spacing between delivery months and the length of the longest contract varies from one commodity to the next. Most contracts last no longer than one year.

3. The daily high and low prices.

4. The closing price. At 60.40 cents, the close in the April future made that contract worth $26,576.

5. The change in price—the difference from one close to the next. The .3 cent loss for April cattle signifies a $132 loss for the contract.

6. The open interest—the number of contracts that have not been closed through delivery or offsetting transactions. This indicates which contracts will experience the heaviest trading in the future, as most contracts will be closed out through either a sale or a purchase of an offsetting contract, rather than by the delivery of the commodity.

J. This line estimates the number of contracts that changed hands during the last session, as well as the volume of the previous session.

K. This line presents the total open interest of the two previous days, and the change in the number of open contracts.

A great deal of information is omitted from these tables, including delivery days, delivery specifications (the locations to which the commodities would be sent and how they would arrive), and the daily limits in price changes that exchanges impose on most futures contracts. The contract specifications are available from the exchange on which the commodity is traded. Commodities don't possess the uniform qualities of options contracts; the sequence of delivery months and the maximum length of contracts varies from one commodity to another.

Comprehensive commodities tables also include a listing of cash prices, gathered from various sources each day—exchanges, warehouses, fabricators—which give you the immediate value of many of the commodities for which futures contracts are

traded as well as other materials, such as wool and cloth and mercury, which have
no formal futures market. In the case of futures-related commodities, remember
that the current cash price, while often determining the direction of futures contract
prices, is usually different. A glut in grain during the harvest could cause an immediate plunge in prices, while prices in the futures market, which anticipate conditions further down the road, could rise.

CORPORATE BOND TABLES

Although corporate bond tables give you valuable insight into a key financial
market, they present only part of the picture. While several thousand corporate
bonds are traded on the New York and American stock exchanges, many more that
are traded through broker/dealers do not appear in the tables of exchange-listed
bonds. In addition, exchange-listed bonds traded in lots of 10 or more are also handled off the exchange. According to the Nine Bond Rule, only lots of nine or fewer
must be sent to the exchange floor.

Nevertheless, these tables are important because they (1) give you specific information about bonds you may own or are considering buying and (2) indicate the
prevailing yields, which can help you estimate the value of similar bonds that you
may have in your portfolio or are considering buying.

The table listings look like this:

CORPORATE BONDS

	① Bonds	② Current Yield	③ Sales in $1,000	④ Last	⑤ Net Chg.
ABZ	9³/₈s01	11.6	42	81¹/₄	+¹/₄
MXY	8.15x00	9.5	285	85¹/₂	−1
KLO	10s09f	18	113	55¹/₂	+¹/₈
STU	zr98	...	17	69	+¹/₂
WVX	9¹/₂ 05	cv	101	141	−1

The accompanying typical bond table presents information as follows:

1. The company abbreviations may vary from the abbreviations used
in the stock tables. Also included in this column is the annual interest
each bond pays, expressed as a percentage of the par or face value.
Most corporate bonds are available in $1000 denominations (though
prices are quoted in $100 units), which would mean that ABZ's 9³/₈
payout would total $93.75 annually. Where a rate cannot be expressed
as a fraction, decimals are used, for example, 8.15 for MXY. The
annual interest rate is also referred to as the coupon. Noninterest-pay-
ing zero coupon securities are identified by a "zr," as with STU here.
The last two numbers in the name cluster represent the year in which
the bonds will mature—01 for 2001, 98 for 1998. Among the quali-
fiers that may also appear after the name is "f," meaning that the bond
is trading flat or without accrued interest, and that an interest payment
has been missed. The "s" often seen after the bond name is a stylistic
embellishment that reflects the verbal description of bonds; for example, "ABZ nine and three eighths of 2001."

2. The current yield represents the annual interest payment as a percentage of the last closing price. It provides a comparison with yields for other types of investments. In the case of convertible bonds, or convertibles, where prices, and therefore yields, are governed by movements in the underlying shares, no yield is given. Instead, "cv" is inserted in the yield column to indicate that this is a convertible issue. Of course, no yield is given with zero coupon bonds either.

3. This is volume on the exchange, expressed in sales of $1000 bonds, which is the normal corporate bond denomination. Events— mergers, earnings news, and so on—can cause volume surges, especially in the case of the convertibles. The amount of volume will tell you how liquid the bonds are.

4. The last sale, in terms of $100 units. Multiply by 10 to get the price per $1000 bond. Prices are quoted as a percentage of par value, as though the face value was $100, not $1000. For example, a $1000 face value bond sold at 81¼ actually sold at $812.50.

5. The net change indicates the gain or loss since the previous close, expressed as a percentage of par. Therefore, the + ¼ gain for ABZ translates into 25 cents per $100 face value, or $2.50 per $1000 bond. The −1 for WVX indicates a $10 loss for $1000 bond. Price changes reflect changes in interest rates. If bond prices have dropped it means interest rates probably rose, and vice versa.

You should also be familiar with the following information, which is not included in the corporate bond tables:

Ratings   These indicate the risk of default by the issuer on payments of interest or principal. The major bond rating agencies are Fitch Investor's Service, Moody's Investors Service and Standard & Poor's Corporation.

Denominations   Not all bonds are available in denominations of $1000. Some, called baby bonds, are denominated in amounts of $500 or less.

Yield to maturity   This represents the return, including both the annual interest payments and the gain or loss realized when the bonds are redeemed, taking into account the timing of payments and the time value of money. Yield to maturity will vary depending on whether you bought the bonds at a discount or a premium in relation to their face value, and with the time remaining to maturity. This type of yield calculation allows you to more easily compare bonds with other types of fixed income investments.

Payment dates   Interest payments on corporate bonds are usually, but not always, made semiannually. In any case, the payment cycles vary.

Callability   If a bond can be redeemed prior to maturity by the issuer, it will most likely be called when rates decline and conditions are favorable to the issuer. For this reason, another yield calculation, yield to call, can have more significance than yield to maturity.

GOVERNMENT SECURITIES TABLES

There's no uniform method of quoting the prices of government securities. In addition, the methods of presenting the values of these bills, notes, and bonds are sometimes as obscure as these markets once were to general investors. Because of the numbers of investors who are now familiar with these markets, however, it's worthwhile for you to know how to extract information from these tables.

Treasury Bills

These obligations—or IOUs—of the U.S. Treasury, are backed by the full faith and credit of the U.S. government. They always mature within one year (3 months, 6 months, 9 months and one year), and are included in many major daily newspapers in the form used in the accompanying table. Information is provided as follows.

TREASURY BILLS

①	②	③	④	⑤
Date	Bid	Asked	Chg	Yield
Mar 13	5.61	5.55	+0.09	5.63

1. This is the date on which the bills mature. The maturity date distinguishes one bill from another.

2. The bid is the price dealers were willing to pay late (there is never an official end) in the last trading session. A bid is presented in a way you may find confusing. It's the discount from the face value demanded by dealers, expressed as an annual percentage. The reason for this is that Treasury bills do not pay interest in the usual sense. Instead, you pay less than the face value of the bills, but you receive the full value when the bills mature. The difference equals the interest you would receive. Thus, if you pay $9000 for a one-year $10,000 bill ($10,000 is the minimum size for a Treasury bill), you're paying 10% less than par, or buying the bill at a 10% discount. A bid of 10 would appear in the table. The higher the discount, the lower the price.

3. The asked price is the price the dealer is willing to accept, again expressed as an annualized percentage discount rate. In these tables, the percentages are carried out to the nearest hundredth, or basis point. Note that the dealer demands a smaller discount—a higher price—when he resells the bonds.

4. The change indicates how much the bid discount rate rose or fell during the session. A plus change actually represents a drop in prices, because it indicates an increased discount from par. Just as a larger discount on merchandise in a store window signifies lower prices, so the .09%, or 9 basis point, indicates an increase in the discount. A minus change means that Treasury bill prices have risen and that the discount rate—and often other types of yields and rates—has dropped.

5. The yield represents a yield to maturity, based on the price you would actually pay for the Treasury bill, rather than its face value. The 10% discount rate tells you that you would pay 10% less than $10,000—or $9000 for a one year Treasury bill, for a difference—

representing interest—of $1000. The actual yield, however, is better expressed in terms of the amount you would really pay for this investment—$9000. In addition, a return of $1000 on a $9000 investment is greater than the 10% discount rate; it's an 11.11% yield. Note that the yield shown in the sample table, 5.63, is higher than the 5.61 discount rate bid shown in column 2.

Treasury Notes and Bonds

Treasury note and bond prices are included in the same tables. The only difference is that the notes, designated by an "n" or a "p," mature in from one to ten years after they are issued, while bonds mature in ten years or longer. These tables present the securities in the order of their maturity dates, with the closest maturity date at the top and the furthest (always the much-quoted government long bond) at the bottom. Notice the increase in yields as the period of maturity increases; this reflects the fact that lenders demand a greater return for locking up their money for longer time periods. As with other government bonds, prices are given as dealer bid and asked quotes, not in terms of last sales. The reason for this is that there is no way for the extensive network of government bond dealers to report transaction prices and amounts in order to register them onto a last-sale "tape." Extra care must be taken in reading the bid and asked quotes because the two digits following the decimal points are 32nds rather than hundredths, reflecting the traditional language of the government bond market.

The information on a typical daily table is as follows:

TREASURY BONDS

①	②	③	④	⑤	⑥
Date	Rate	Bid	Asked	Chg.	Yield
Apr 86 n	$11^{3/4}$	100.19	100.23	+ .4	6.13
Feb 93	$6^{3/4}$	95.18	96.18	+1.2	7.39
Nov 02–07	$7^{7/8}$	97.19	98.3	+1.2	8.06
Nov 15 k	$9^{3/8}$	118.1	118.5	+2.2	8.23

1. The date identifies the note or bond by its month and year of maturity; thus an "89" means 1989, a "16" means 2016. In addition, an "n" signifies a note (a "p" signifies notes not subject to withholding tax for foreign owners) while no notation (or a "k" if no withholding tax for foreign owners is required) appears for bonds. When the maturity figure consists of two years, such as the 02–07 in this table, the second year (2007 here) represents the maturity, while the first year (2002 here) indicates that the bonds could be repaid early, beginning in 2002. Such capability is rare with Treasury securities; it is found only in the final five years of certain 30-year bond issues.

2. The rate is the coupon rate, or the annual interest rate, expressed as a percentage of the face value ($1000 minimum denominations for bonds and $1000 or $5000 for notes).

3. The bid is the price dealers were offering to pay late in the session. It's presented as a percentage of face value. Note, however, that the two digits following the decimal point are 32nds, not tenths or hundredths. The 113.13 bid for the Oct 89 notes equals 113 13/32%. Because 1/32% of $1000 is 31¼ cents, 13/32 equals $4.06¼; the total bid, per $1000 of notes, equals $1134.06¼.

4. The asked, the price at which dealers are offering to sell the securities, is calculated similarly to the bid.

5. The daily change from two previous sessions to yesterday's session is based on the rise or fall of the bid price.

6. This figure represents yield to maturity, which combines your current yield (the percentage return in interest based on the price you actually pay) and the difference between the price you paid and the face value at redemption.

Government Agency Bonds

Securities of U.S. agencies such as the Federal Home Loan Bank and Government National Mortgage Association that appear in *The Wall Street Journal* and *The New York Times* use the same type of bid and asked quotes, expressed in 32nds of a percent, as appear in the Treasury note and bond tables.

Municipal Bonds

You probably won't find municipal bond prices in the financial pages. Even major financial publications include only a sampling of revenue bonds—those repaid from the income of a particular project rather than from general tax dollars. Such tables, typically headed Tax-exempt Authority Bonds, include the issuer's name, maturity date, the bid, the asked, and the daily change in the bid. Information on general obligation bonds is even harder to find. One way of approximating the value of your holdings, though, is to look at yields on newly issued bonds as revealed in tombstone ads placed by underwriters or in the short lists of new issues some papers provide. If the yields on new issues are lower than those your municipals are earning, your bonds are probably selling above face value and vice-versa, assuming the bonds are comparable in terms of quality and type of issuer.

The Tax Reform Act of 1986 profoundly altered the municipal bond landscape, and there are now taxable as well as tax-exempt general obligation and revenue issues. There will undoubtedly be a period of sorting out before reporting practices become conventionally adopted.

MUTUAL FUNDS TABLES

Mutual fund prices are listed several ways in newspapers. Prices of a fund offered by an open-end management company that invests in long-term securities either stocks or bonds—change with changes in market segments or the market as a whole. These funds sell and redeem their own shares. Large newspapers generally list these prices under the heading Mutual Funds.

MUTUAL FUNDS

①	②	③	④
	NAV	Buy	Chg.
ABZ Grp:			
Genrl Fd	14.38	NL	+ .03
AB Growth	10.50	11.03	+ .01
ABZ Incm	5.22	NL	+ .02
Tax Ex	8.21	NL	− .01

These tables contain the following information, by column:

1. The names of mutual funds are clustered by family of funds—funds sponsored by a particular management company. The names often reflect the type of investments that comprise each fund; for example, a general stock fund, growth stock fund, income fund, or tax-exempt bond fund.

Some fund names are followed by lowercase letters such as "a" (meaning a stock dividend was paid in the past 12 months), "d" (new 52-week low), "f" (quotation refers to previous day), "r" (redemption charge may apply), "u" (new 52-week high), and "x" (fund is trading ex-dividend).

2. NAV stands for net asset value, the per-share value of the fund's assets, minus management costs. This is the amount you would receive, per share, if you redeemed your shares. The numbers indicate dollars and cents per share. Sometimes the column carries the heading Sell, meaning that you would receive this amount per share if you were the seller.

3. The Buy column may also be headed Offer Price. It tells you, in dollars and cents per share, the price per share, the price you would pay to buy the shares. Funds that carry a sales charge, or front end load, cost more per share than their net asset value. Funds with back end loads discourage withdrawals by charging a fee to redeem your shares. Many funds, however, carry no sales charge; these are no-load funds whose buy-in costs are the same as their net asset values. These funds carry an "NL" or just "n" in the Buy column.

4. Change refers to the daily change in net asset value, determined at the close of each trading day.

Share prices of a fund offered by a closed-end management company, which issues a fixed number of shares that are then traded among investors, are often included in the daily stock tables. Some newspapers also provide weekly tables listing the prices and values of the shares as of the previous day's close-of-the-market.

CLOSED-END FUNDS

①	②	③	④
	N.A. Value	Stk Price	% Diff
Diversified funds			
ABZ Fund	17.55	21½	+ 3.1
WXY Fund	10.81	11⅜	− 1.8
ZBF Fund	24.74	20½	− 5.0
Specialized Equity and Convertible Funds			
ABZ Gold	33.10	33½	+ 2.2
XYZ Conv	15.77	16	+ 1.6
XYZ Tech	9.97	10⅛	− 4.4

1. Fund names are grouped alphabetically by fund type.

2. Net Asset Values, as of the last close (unless otherwise indicated) are listed in terms of dollars and cents per share.

3. Stock prices are the last close.

4. Percent difference represents the weekly rise or fall of the net asset value of the shares.

Listings of shares of dual purpose funds can be found in stock exchange tables. These closed-end funds have two classes of shares. One class entitles shareholders to capital gains based on the market value of the assets. The other class entitles holders to dividend and interest income from the fund. Some major newspapers also carry weekly tables of the pershare prices of the capital shares, the net asset value of the capital shares, and the weekly percentage or loss of price of those shares. These tables are useful because the daily stock tables don't include net asset values.

Tables for money market funds appear weekly, usually Thursday, after the release of data by Donoghue's money fund average or the National Association of Securities Dealers. Some newspapers print the tables again on Sunday. If you need information on a money market fund before Thursday, you can call the fund organizations. Many fund groups have toll-free 800 phone numbers for shareholders. Most investors need no more than weekly updates because per share values should remain constant at $1.00. These funds, which invest in short-term debt instruments, often are bought because they are liquid (most allow checkwriting) and the yield fluctuates with short-term interest rates. Market movements and the accompanying capital gains and losses don't play a major role in the decision to buy or sell shares. The yield is the main information included in such tables.

MONEY MARKET FUNDS

① Fund	② Assets ($ million)	③ Average maturity (days)	④ 7-day average yield (%)	⑤ Effective 7-day average yield (%)
ABzz Safety Fst	344.7	20	5.61	5.90
Blxx Liquid Secs	1,343.9	26	5.57	5.73
Xymo Govt. Fund	299.0	22	4.11	4.46

The accompanying table includes the following information, by column:

1. Name of the money-market fund.

2. Assets are stated in millions of dollars, to the nearest $100,000. These figures indicate the size of the fund. Investors constantly debate the advantages and disadvantages of size.

3. The average maturity figure represents how long, on average, it takes for the securities in a money fund's portfolio to mature. Shorter average maturities mean that the fund's yield will react more quickly to general interest-rate changes in the fixed-income securities market. This is beneficial when rates are rising, but disadvantageous when rates are dropping. In the latter case, you would want your fund to hold onto higher-yielding securities as long as possible. The move in the average maturity figure is considered by some to be a good predictor of short-term interest rate direction. If a fund's average maturity increases by several days for several weeks, this is an indication that portfolio managers expect short-term rates to drop. If the average maturity decreases, the managers probably expect short-term rates to rise.

4. The 7-day average yield indicates the average daily total return for that period, and is determined largely by subtracting the fund's costs from the investment income. The result is expressed as a percentage of the average share price:

5. The effective 7-day average yield is the 7-day average yield computed after assuming that the rate continues for a year and that dividends are reinvested. This permits comparison with other instruments whose yields are expressed on the same basis, such as bank certificates of deposit.

OTHER TABLES

Interest and currency rates

The key rates highlighted in the Markets Diary discussed earlier are followed up with more detailed summaries throughout the inside pages.

A complete rate and yield table, for example, would additionally list, with comparisons to the previous day and year ago, the (Federal Reserve) discount rate and the prime rate, whose significance we have already discussed. It might also list yields on 7-year Treasury notes, an important benchmark for intermediate-term corporate and other non-Treasury fixed-income obligations; yields on 30-year Treasury bonds, the ultimate indicator of the entire bond market and often of the stock market, where prices normally move inversely to "long bond" yields; and "telephone" bonds, top-rated obligations of phone companies or other public utilities whose yield is a direct benchmark tor other corporate bonds that are riskier to varying degrees. Major newspapers also carry additional lists of rates that are mainly of interest to professional traders. Some, like Eurodollar time deposits, the London Interbank Offer Rate (LIBOR), and commercial paper, were discussed above. Others include banker's acceptances, which are time drafts created in commerce, accepted (guaranteed, in effect) by major banks, and traded as money market instruments; and the broker loan rate (or call loan rate), which is the rate banks charge brokers for overnight loans to cover securities positions of customers. This rate, which usually hovers just above the rate on (also overnight) federal funds, has meaning to individual investors because it determines what brokers charge on margin loans.

Many financial newspapers and other media now carry weekly listings of the banks currently offering the highest interest rates on deposit accounts and certificates of deposit.

The meaning and importance of currency exchange rates was discussed earlier. In addition to highlighting major currency changes, most major financial papers carry full exchange tables, listed alphabetically by country, which provide the exchange rates from the previous two days in four columns—two in terms of dollars per unit of foreign currency, two in terms of units of foreign currency per dollar. Major currencies also list 30-, 90-, and 180-day forward rates. These represent guaranteed future delivery rates offered by banks for customers who must plan ahead and are willing to pay a premium to eliminate the risk of exchange rates moving adversely in the interim.

Some papers, including *The Wall Street Journal,* contain a table showing key currency cross rates. This table lists currencies in terms of each other's value. Complete currency sections also cover futures, options, and futures options on leading currencies.

HOW TO READ TICKER TAPES

With the growth of cable television, an increasing number of investors pick up financial news from cablecasters that cover the securities and commodities markets continuously throughout the business day. Like daily newspapers, the purveyors of electronic financial news aim for a broad audience. Through the creative use of graphics and commentary, they manage generally to communicate complex information in a way nonprofessionals can understand.

But unless you work for an investment firm or spend your leisure time sitting around a board room of a brokerage, the figures and symbols that pass constantly— sometimes with maddening rapidity—across the lower portion of the TV screen may require explanation. What you see there is the stock ticker tape, the same report of trading activity displayed on the floors of the major stock exchanges. The only difference is that to give stock exchange members an advantage, it is transmitted with a 15-minute delay.

The most frequently seen display is the consolidated tape, a combination of two networks (not to be confused with television networks): Network A reports all New York Stock Exchange issues traded on the NYSE or other identified markets, which include five regional exchanges, the over-the-counter market, and other markets, such as Instinet, a computerized market in which large institutional blocks are traded. Network B reports all American Stock Exchange issues traded on the Amex or other identified markets. National Association of Securities Dealers (NASDAQ) over-the-counter quotes are presented separately in the lower band.

Elements of the consolidated tape; which reports actual transactions (the term quotes is loosely used to mean trades in ticker tape jargon, although its proper financial meaning refers to bid and asked quotations) are explained as follows:

Stock Symbol The first letters are the stock ticker symbol—XON for Exxon, CCI for Citicorp, IBM for IBM, for example. (There is one exception to this, which is that the prefix Q is used when a company is in receivership or bankruptcy.) The ticker symbol may be followed by an abbreviation designating a type of issue, such as Pr to signify preferred stock, which may, in turn, be followed by a letter indicating a class of preferred. Thus XYZPrE means XYZ Corporation's preferred stock series E. If XYZ's preferred stock series E was convertible, the abbreviation .CV would be added to read XYZPrE.CV. Common stock classes, if any, are indicated by a period plus a letter following the ticker symbol. Thus XYZ's class B common would be designated XYZ.B. (A list of ticker symbols is included at the end of Part V of this book.)

Other abbreviations placed after the ticker symbol as necessary are rt for rights; wi for when issued; .WD for when distributed; .WS for warrants (the abbreviation may be preceded by another period and letter to identify the particular issue of warrant); and .XD for ex-dividend.

Market Identifiers When the information about the stock is followed by an ampersand (&) and a letter, the transaction took place in a market other than the New York Stock Exchange, if you are looking at Network A, or the American Stock Exchange, if you are looking at Network B. The letter identifies the market as follows:

A	American Stock Exchange
B	Boston Stock Exchange
C	Cincinnati Stock Exchange
M	Midwest Stock Exchange
N	New York Stock Exchange
O	Other Markets (mainly Instinet)
P	Pacific Stock Exchange
T	Third market (mainly NASDAQ)
X	Philadelphia Stock Exchange

Volume   The next portion of the transaction information provided on a ticker tape may appear below or to the right of the above stock symbol and market designation. It reports the number of shares traded. However, if the trade is in a round lot of 100 shares, which it usually is, no volume is indicated and the tape simply shows the issue and the price. Thus XYZ 26^1/$_2$ simply means that 100 shares of XYZ were traded at 26.50 a share. Where larger round lot transactions take place, the number of round lots is indicated followed by the letter "s" followed by the price. Thus, XYZ 4 s 26^1/$_2$ means 400 shares were traded at $26.50 a share. Similarly, 1700 shares would be XYZ 17 s 26^1/$_2$ and so on, except that when the volume is 10,000 shares or more the full number is given—XYZ 16,400 s 26^1/$_2$, for example.

Odd lots quantities other than multiples of 100 or whatever other unit represents the round lot—are not printed on the ticker tape unless approved by an exchange official. If approval is given, odd lots of 50 shares and 150 shares of XYZ would be displayed respectively: XYZ 50 SHRS 26^1/$_2$ and XYZ 150 SHRS 26^1/$_2$.

A limited number of issues—mainly inactive stocks or higher priced preferred issues—trade in round lots of less than 100 shares. On the New York Stock Exchange such round lots are always 10 shares, but on the Amex these round lots can be 10, 25, or 50 shares. Transactions in these special round lots are designated by a number indicating how many lots were traded followed by the symbols. Thus, on the New York Stock Exchange, XYZ Pr 3 ^s_s 55 means 3 10-share lots (30 shares) of XYZ preferred stock were traded at $55 a share. If XYZ were listed on the Amex, you would not know by looking at the tape whether the lot involved was 10, 25, or 50 shares. For that information, you would have to consult a stock guide.

Active Market Procedures   When trading becomes sufficiently heavy to cause the tape to run more than a minute behind, shortcuts are implemented. The most frequently taken measure to keep up with heavy trading is signified by the tape print-out DIGITS AND VOLUME DELETED. This means only the unit price digit and fraction will be printed (for example, 9^1/$_2$ instead of 19^1/$_2$) except when the price ends in zero or is an opening transaction. In addition, volume information will be deleted except when trades are 5000 shares or more (the threshold can be raised if required). Another common procedure is to announce REPEAT PRICES OMITTED, meaning that successive transactions at the same price will not be repeated. A third measure is MINIMUM PRICE CHANGES OMITTED, meaning trades will not be displayed unless the price difference exceeds ^{1}/$_8$ of a point. The second and third measures do not apply to opening transactions or to trades of 5000 shares or more. When activity slackens to a more normal level, the tape will read DIGITS AND VOLUME RESUMED with similar indications for the other measures.

Other Abbreviations   When a transaction is being reported out of its proper order, the letters .SLD will follow the symbol as in XYZ .SLD 3s 26^1/$_2$. SLR followed by a number signifies seller's option and number of days until settlement. This indication is found after the price. CORR indicates that a correction of information follows. ERR or CXL indicates a print is to be ignored. OPD signifies an opening transaction that was delayed or one whose price is significantly changed from the previous day's close.

PART IV

Dictionary of Finance and Investment

HOW TO USE THIS DICTIONARY EFFECTIVELY

Alphabetization: All entries are alphabetized by letter rather than by word so that multiple-word terms are treated as single words. For example, **NET ASSET VALUE** follows **NET ASSETS** as though it were spelled **NETASSETVALUE,** without spacing. Similarly, **ACCOUNT EXECUTIVE** follows **ACCOUN-TANT'S OPINION.** In unusual cases, abbreviations or acronyms appear as entries in the main text, in addition to appearing in the back of the book in the separate listing of Abbreviations and Acronyms. This is when the short form, rather than the formal name, predominates in common business usage. For example, NASDAQ is more commonly used in speaking of the National Association of Securities Dealers Automated Quotations system than the name itself, so the entry is at **NASDAQ.** Numbers in entry titles are alphabetized as if they were spelled out.

Where a term has several meanings, alphabetical sequence is used for subheads, except in special instances where clarity dictates a different order (for example, under **LEVERAGE** the subhead **Operating leverage** precedes **Financial leverage**). In some entries, the various meanings of the term are presented with simple numerical headings. Securities and Exchange Commission rules are presented in the official numerical order.

Abbreviations and Acronyms: A separate list of abbreviations and acronyms follows the Dictionary. It contains shortened versions of terms defined in the book, plus several hundred related business terms.

Cross references: In order to gain a fuller understanding of a term, it will sometimes help to refer to the definition of another term. In these cases the additional term is printed in SMALL CAPITALS. Such cross references appear in the body of the definition or at the end of the entry (or subentry). Cross references at the end of an entry (or subentry) may refer to related or contrasting concepts rather than give more information about the concept under discussion. As a rule, a term is printed in small capitals only the first time it appears in an entry. Where an entry is fully defined at another entry, a reference rather than a definition is provided; for example, **EITHER-OR ORDER** *see* ALTERNATIVE ORDER.

Italics: Italic type is generally used to indicate that another term has a meaning identical or very closely related to that of the entry. Occasionally, italic type is also used to highlight the fact that a word used is a business term and not just a descriptive phrase. Italics are also used for the titles of publications.

Parentheses: Parentheses are used in entry titles for two reasons. The first is to indicate that an entry's opposite is such an integral part of the concept that only one discussion is necessary; for example, **REALIZED PROFIT (OR LOSS).** The second and more common reason is to indicate that an abbreviation is used with about the same frequency as the term itself; for example, **OVER THE COUNTER (OTC).**

Examples, Illustrations, and Tables: The numerous examples in this Dictionary are designed to help readers gain understanding and to help them relate abstract concepts to the real world of finance and investment. Line drawings are provided in addition to text to clarify concepts best understood visually; for example, technical chart patterns used by securities analysts and graphic concepts used in financial analysis. Tables supplement definitions where essential detail is more effectively condensed and expressed in tabular form; for example, components of the U.S. money supply.

Special Definitions: Some entries are given expanded treatment to enhance their reference value. Examples are **ECONOMIC RECOVERY TAX ACT OF 1981, SECURITIES AND COMMODITIES EXCHANGES, SECURITIES AND EXCHANGE COMMISSION RULES, STOCK INDEXES AND AVERAGES,** and **TAX REFORM ACT OF 1986.**

DICTIONARY OF FINANCE
AND INVESTMENT

a

ABANDONMENT voluntarily giving up all rights, title, or claims to property that rightfully belongs to the owner. An example of abandoned property would be stocks, bonds, or mutual funds held in a brokerage account for which the firm is unable to locate the listed owner over a specified period of time, usually a few years. If ruled to be abandoned, the property may revert to the state under the laws of ESCHEAT. In addition to financial assets, other kinds of property that are subject to abandonment include patents, inventions, leases, trademarks, contracts, and copyrights.

ABC AGREEMENT agreement between a brokerage firm and one of its employees spelling out the firm's rights when it purchases a New York Stock Exchange membership for the employee. Only individuals can be members of the NYSE, and it is common practice for a firm to finance the purchase of a membership, or SEAT, by one of its employees. The NYSE-approved ABC Agreement contains the following provisions regarding the future disposition of the seat: (1) The employee may retain the membership and buy another seat for an individual designated by the firm. (2) The employee may sell the seat and give the proceeds to the firm. (3) The employee may transfer the seat to another employee of the firm.

ABILITY TO PAY

Finance: borrower's ability to meet principal and interest payments on long-term obligations out of earnings. Also called *ability to service*. *See also* FIXED CHARGE COVERAGE.

Industrial relations: ability of an employer, especially a financial organization to meet a union's financial demands from operating income.

Municipal bonds: issuer's present and future ability to generate enough tax revenue to meet its contractual obligations, taking into account all factors concerned with municipal income and property values.

Taxation: the concept that tax rates should vary with levels of wealth or income; for example, the progressive income tax.

ABOVE PAR *see* PAR VALUE.

ABS *see* AUTOMATED BOND SYSTEM.

ABSOLUTE PRIORITY RULE *see* BANKRUPTCY.

ABSORBED

Business: a cost that is treated as an expense rather than passed on to a customer. Also, a firm merged into an acquiring company.

Cost accounting: indirect manufacturing costs (such as property taxes and insurance) are called absorbed costs. They are differentiated from variable costs (such as direct labor and materials). *See also* DIRECT OVERHEAD.

Finance: an account that has been combined with related accounts in preparing a financial statement and has lost its separate identity. Also called *absorption account* or *adjunct account.*

Securities: issue that an underwriter has completely sold to the public.

Also, in market trading, securities are absorbed as long as there are corresponding orders to buy and sell. The market has reached the *absorption point* when further assimilation is impossible without an adjustment in price. *See also* UNDIGESTED SECURITIES.

ABUSIVE TAX SHELTER LIMITED PARTNERSHIP the Internal Revenue Service deems to be claiming illegal tax deductions—typically, one that inflates the value of acquired property beyond its fair market value. If these writeoffs are denied by the IRS, investors must pay severe penalties and interest charges, on top of back taxes.

ACCELERATED COST RECOVERY SYSTEM (ACRS) provision instituted by the ECONOMIC RECOVERY TAX ACT OF 1981 (ERTA) and modified by the TAX REFORM ACT OF 1986, which established rules for the DEPRECIATION (the recovery of cost through tax deductions) of qualifying assets within a shorter period than the asset's expected useful (economic) life. With certain exceptions, ACRS rules provided for greater acceleration over longer periods of time than ERTA rules, and were effective for property placed in service between 1980 and 1987.

See also MODIFIED ACCELERATED COST RECOVERY SYSTEM.

ACCELERATED DEPRECIATION Internal Revenue Service-approved methods used in the DEPRECIATION of fixed assets placed in service prior to 1980 when the ACCELERATED COST RECOVERY SYSTEM (ACRS) became mandatory. Such methods provided for faster recovery of cost and earlier tax advantages than traditional STRAIGHT LINE DEPRECIATION and included such methods as DOUBLE-DECLINING BALANCE METHOD (now used in some ACRS classes) and SUM-OF-THE-YEARS' DIGITS METHOD.

ACCELERATION CLAUSE provision, normally present in an INDENTURE agreement, mortgage, or other contract, that the unpaid balance is to become due and payable if specified events of default should occur. Such events include failure to meet interest, principal, or sinking fund payments; insolvency; and nonpayment of taxes on mortgaged property.

ACCEPTANCE

In general: agreement created when the drawee of a TIME DRAFT (bill of exchange) writes the word "accepted" above the signature and designates a date of payment. The drawee becomes the acceptor, responsible for payment at maturity.

Also, paper issued and sold by sales finance companies, such as General Motors Acceptance Corporation.

Banker's acceptance: time draft drawn on and accepted by a bank, the customary means of effecting payment for merchandise sold in import-export transactions and a source of financing used extensively in international trade. With the credit strength of a bank behind it, the banker's acceptance usually qualifies as a MONEY MARKET instrument. The liability assumed by the bank is called its acceptance liability. *See also* LETTER OF CREDIT.

Trade acceptance: time draft drawn by the seller of goods on the buyer, who becomes the acceptor, and which is therefore only as good as the buyer's credit.

ACCOMMODATIVE MONETARY POLICY Federal Reserve policy to increase the amount of money available for lending by banks. When the Fed implements an accommodative policy, it is known as easing the money supply. During a period of easing, interest rates fall, making it more attractive for borrowers to borrow, thereby stimulating the economy. The Fed will initiate an accommodative policy when interest rates are high, the economy is weak, and there is little fear of an outbreak of inflation. Once interest rates have been lowered enough to stimulate the economy, the Fed may become concerned about inflation again and switch to a TIGHT MONEY policy. *See also* MONETARY POLICY.

ACCOUNT

In general: contractual relationship between a buyer and seller under which payment is made at a later time. The term *open account* or *charge account* is used, depending on whether the relationship is commercial or personal.

Also, the historical record of transactions under the contract, as periodically shown on the *statement of account*.

Banking: relationship under a particular name, usually evidenced by a deposit against which withdrawals can be made. Among them are demand, time, custodial, joint, trustee, corporate, special, and regular accounts. Administrative responsibility is handled by an *account officer.*

Bookkeeping: assets, liabilities, income, and expenses as represented by individual ledger pages to which debit and credit entries are chronologically posted to record changes in value. Examples are cash, accounts receivable, accrued interest, sales, and officers' salaries. The system of recording, verifying, and reporting such information is called accounting. Practitioners of accounting are called *accountants*.

Investment banking: financial and contractual relationship between parties to an underwriting syndicate, or the status of securities owned and sold.

Securities: relationship between a broker-dealer firm and its client wherein the firm, through its registered representatives, acts as agent in buying and selling securities and sees to related administrative matters. *See also* ACCOUNT EXECUTIVE; ACCOUNT STATEMENT.

ACCOUNTANT'S OPINION statement signed by an independent public accountant describing the scope of the examination of an organization's books and records. Because financial reporting involves considerable discretion, the accountant's opinion is an important assurance to a lender or investor. Depending on the scope of an audit and the auditor's confidence in the veracity of the information, the opinion can be unqualified or, to some degree, qualified. Qualified opinions, though not necessarily negative, warrant investigation. Also called *auditor's certificate.*

ACCOUNT BALANCE net of debits and credits at the end of a reporting period. Term applies to a variety of account relationships, such as with banks, credit card companies, brokerage firms, and stores, and to classifications of transactions in a bookkeeping system. The same account may be an asset account balance or a liability account balance, depending on which side of the transaction you are on. For example, your bank balance is an asset account to you and a liability account to the bank. Your credit card (debit) balance is a liability account to you and an asset account (account receivable) to the credit card company.

ACCOUNT EXECUTIVE brokerage firm employee who advises and handles orders for clients and has the legal powers of an AGENT. Every account executive must pass certain tests and be registered with the NATIONAL ASSOCIATION OF SECURITIES DEALERS (NASD) before soliciting orders from customers. Also called *registered representative. See also* BROKER.

ACCOUNTING PRINCIPLES BOARD (APB) board of the American Institute of Certified Public Accountants (AICPA) that issued (1959–73) a series of ACCOUNTANT'S OPINIONS constituting much of what is known as GENERALLY ACCEPTED ACCOUNTING PRINCIPLES. *See also* FINANCIAL ACCOUNTING STANDARDS BOARD (FASB).

ACCOUNT RECONCILIATION the process of adjusting the balance in your checkbook to match your bank statement. Your checkbook balance, plus outstanding checks, less bank charges, plus interest (if any), should equal the balance shown on your bank statement.

ACCOUNTS PAYABLE amounts owing on open account to creditors for goods and services. Analysts look at the relationship of accounts payable to purchases for indications of sound day-to-day financial management. *See also* TRADE CREDIT.

ACCOUNTS RECEIVABLE money owed to a business for merchandise or services sold on open account, a key factor in analyzing a company's LIQUIDITY—its ability to meet current obligations without additional revenues. *See also* ACCOUNTS RECEIVABLE TURNOVER; AGING SCHEDULE; COLLECTION RATIO.

ACCOUNTS RECEIVABLE FINANCING short-term financing whereby accounts receivable serve as collateral for working capital advances. *See also* FACTORING.

ACCOUNTS RECEIVABLE TURNOVER ratio obtained by dividing total credit sales by accounts receivable. The ratio indicates how many times the receivables portfolio has been collected during the accounting period. *See also* ACCOUNTS RECEIVABLE; AGING SCHEDULE; COLLECTION RATIO.

ACCOUNT STATEMENT
In general: any record of transactions and their effect on charge or open-account balances during a specified period.
Banking: summary of all checks paid, deposits recorded, and resulting balances during a defined period. Also called a *bank statement.*
Securities: statement summarizing all transactions and showing the status of an account with a broker-dealer firm, including long and short positions. Such statements must be issued quarterly, but are generally provided monthly when accounts are active. Also, the OPTION AGREEMENT required when an option account is opened.

ACCREDITED INVESTOR under Securities and Exchange Commission Regulation D, a wealthy investor who does not count as one of the maximum of 35 people allowed to put money into a PRIVATE LIMITED PARTNERSHIP. To be accredited, such an investor must have a net worth of at least $1 million or an annual income of at least $200,000, or must put at least $150,000 into the deal, and the investment must not account for more than 20% of the investor's worth. Private limited partnerships use accredited investors to raise a larger amount of capital than would be possible if only 35 less-wealthy people could contribute.

ACCRETION
1. asset growth through internal expansion, acquisition, or such causes as aging of whisky or growth of timber.
2. adjustment of the difference between the price of a bond bought at an original discount and the par value of the bond.

ACCRUAL BASIS accounting method whereby income and expense items are recognized as they are earned or incurred, even though they may not have been received or actually paid in cash. The alternative is CASH BASIS accounting.

ACCRUAL BONDS bonds that do not make periodic interest payments, but instead accrue interest until the bond matures. Also known as *zero-coupon bonds. See also* ZERO-COUPON SECURITIES.

ACCRUED BENEFITS pension benefits that an employee has earned based on his or her years of service at a company. *See also* VESTING.

ACCRUED INTEREST interest that has accumulated between the most recent payment and the sale of a bond or other fixed-income security. At the time of sale, the buyer pays the seller the bond's price plus accrued interest, calculated by multiplying the coupon rate by the number of days that have elapsed since the last payment.

Accrued interest is also used in a real estate LIMITED PARTNERSHIP when the seller of a building takes a lump sum in cash at the time of sale and gives a second mortgage for the remainder. If the rental income from the building does not cover the mortgage payments, the seller agrees to let the interest accrue until the building is sold to someone else. Accrued interest deals were curtailed by the 1984 tax act.

ACCRUED MARKET DISCOUNT increase in market value of a DISCOUNT BOND that occurs because of its approaching MATURITY DATE (when it is redeemable at PAR) and not because of declining market interest rates.

ACCUMULATED DIVIDEND dividend due, usually to holders of cumulative preferred stock, but not paid. It is carried on the books as a liability until paid. *See also* CUMULATIVE PREFERRED.

ACCUMULATED PROFITS TAX surtax on earnings retained in a business to avoid the higher personal income taxes they would be subject to if paid out as dividends to the owners.

Accumulations above the specified limit, which is set fairly high to benefit small firms, must be justified by the reasonable needs of the business or be subject to the surtax. Because determining the reasonable needs of a business involves considerable judgment, companies have been known to pay excessive dividends or even to make merger decisions out of fear of the accumulated profits tax. Also called *accumulated earnings tax.*

ACCUMULATION
Corporate finance: profits that are not paid out as dividends but are instead added to the company's capital base. *See also* ACCUMULATED PROFITS TAX.

Investments: purchase of a large number of shares in a controlled way so as to avoid driving the price up. An institution's accumulation program, for instance, may take weeks or months to complete.

Mutual funds: investment of a fixed dollar amount regularly and reinvestment of dividends and capital gains.

ACCUMULATION AREA price range within which buyers accumulate shares of a stock. Technical analysts spot accumulation areas when a stock does not drop below a particular price. Technicians who use the ON-BALANCE VOLUME method of analysis advise buying stocks that have hit their accumulation area, because the stocks can be expected to attract more buying interest. *See* chart on next page. *See also* DISTRIBUTION AREA.

ACCUMULATION AREA

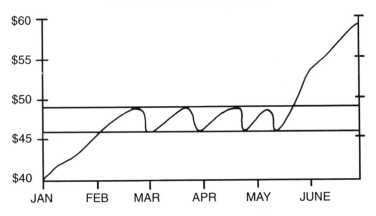

ACES acronym for *Advanced Computerized Execution System*, run by the NASDAQ stock market. ACES automates trades between order-entry and market-maker firms that have established trading relationships with each other, designating securities at specified quantities for automatic execution. Once trading parameters are set, ACES facilitates order entry, best-price order execution and limited-order maintenance, as well as a variety of inventory control capabilities. Trades are then automatically reported for public dissemination and sent for comparison and clearing.

ACID-TEST RATIO *See* QUICK RATIO.

ACKNOWLEDGMENT verification that a signature on a banking or brokerage document is legitimate and has been certified by an authorized person. Acknowledgment is needed when transferring an account from one broker to another, for instance. In banking, an acknowledgment verifies that an item has been received by the paying bank and is or is not available for immediate payment.

ACQUIRED SURPLUS uncapitalized portion of the net worth of a successor company in a POOLING OF INTERESTS combination. In other words, the part of the combined net worth not classified as CAPITAL STOCK.
In a more general sense, the surplus acquired when a company is purchased.

ACQUISITION one company taking over controlling interest in another company. Investors are always looking out for companies that are likely to be acquired, because those who want to acquire such companies are often willing to pay more than the market price for the shares they need to complete the acquisition. *See also* MERGER; POOLING OF INTERESTS; TAKEOVER.

ACQUISITION COST
Finance: price plus CLOSING COSTS to buy a company, real estate or other property.
Investments: SALES CHARGE incurred to buy a LOAD FUND or the original price, plus brokerage commissions, of a security. *See also* TAX BASIS.

ACROSS THE BOARD movement in the stock market that affects almost all stocks in the same direction. When the market moves up across the board, almost every stock gains in price.

An across-the-board pay increase in a company is a raise of a fixed percent or amount for all employees.

ACTING IN CONCERT two or more investors working together to achieve the same investment goal—for example, all buying stock in a company they want to take over. Such investors must inform the Securities and Exchange Commission if they intend to oust the company's top management or acquire control. It is illegal for those acting in concert to manipulate a stock's price for their own gain.

ACTIVE ACCOUNT account at a bank or brokerage firm in which there are many transactions. An active banking account may generate more fees for each check written or ATM transaction completed. An active brokerage account will generate more commission revenue for the brokerage firm than an inactive account. Banks usually impose minimum charges for maintaining a checking and savings account. Many brokerage firms levy a fee if an account does not generate a high enough level of activity. If there is no activity in an account for five years or more, the account may be subject to ESCHEAT procedures in which the account's assets revert to the state.

ACTIVE BOND CROWD members of the bond department of the New York Stock Exchange responsible for the heaviest volume of bond trading. The opposite of the active crowd is the CABINET CROWD, which deals in bonds that are infrequently traded. Investors who buy and sell bonds in the active crowd will tend to get better prices for their securities than in the inactive market, where spreads between bid and asked prices are wider.

ACTIVE BOX collateral available for securing brokers' loans or customers' margin positions in the place—or *box*—where securities are held in safekeeping for clients of a broker-dealer or for the broker-dealer itself. Securities used as collateral must be owned by the firm or hypothecated— that is, pledged or assigned— by the customer to the firm, then by the broker to the lending bank. For margin loans, securities must be hypothecated by the customer to the broker.

ACTIVE MARKET heavy volume of trading in a particular stock, bond, or commodity. The spread between bid and asked prices is usually narrower in an active market than when trading is quiet.

Also, a heavy volume of trading on the exchange as a whole. Institutional money managers prefer such a market because their trades of large blocks of stock tend to have less impact on the movement of prices when trading is generally active.

ACTUALS any physical commodity, such as gold, soybeans, or pork bellies. Trading in actuals ultimately results in delivery of the commodity to the buyer when the contract expires. This contrasts with trading in commodities of, for example, index options, where the contract is settled in cash, and no physical commodity is delivered upon expiration. However, even when trading is in actuals most futures and options contracts are closed out before the contract expires, and so these transactions do not end in delivery.

ACTUARY mathematician employed by an insurance company to calculate premiums, reserves, dividends, and insurance, pension, and annuity rates, using risk factors obtained from experience tables. These tables are based on both the company's history of insurance claims and other industry and general statistical data.

ADDITIONAL BONDS TEST test limiting the amount of new bonds that can be issued. Since bonds are secured by assets or revenues of a corporate or governmental entity, the underwriters of the bond must insure that the bond issuer can meet the debt service requirements of any additional bonds. The test usually sets specific financial benchmarks, such as what portion of an issuer's revenues or cash flow can be devoted to paying interest.

ADDITIONAL PAID-IN CAPITAL *see* PAID-IN CAPITAL.

ADDITIONAL VOLUNTARY CONTRIBUTIONS contributions made by an employee into a tax-deferred savings account, such as a 401(k) or 403(b), beyond the level at which an employer will match the investment. Depending on the level of contributions, these may be made on a pretax or aftertax basis. Tax law limits the total amount of money that can be contributed to such a tax-deferred account. In any case, all funds so contributed accumulate without taxation until withdrawn at retirement. The employee chooses the investment vehicles in which the money is invested.

ADEQUACY OF COVERAGE test of the extent to which the value of an asset, such as real property, securities, or a contract subject to currency exchange rates, is protected from potential loss either through INSURANCE or HEDGING.

ADJUSTABLE RATE MORTGAGE (ARM) mortgage agreement between a financial institution and a real estate buyer stipulating predetermined adjustments of the interest rate at specified intervals. Mortgage payments are tied to some index outside the control of the bank or savings and loan institution, such as the interest rates on U.S. Treasury bills or the average national mortgage rate. Adjustments are made regularly, usually at intervals of one, three, or five years. In return for making some of the risk of a rise in interest rates, borrowers get lower rates at the beginning of the ARM than they would if they took out a fixed rate mortgage covering the same term. A homeowner who is worried about sharply rising interest rates should probably choose a fixed rate mortgage, whereas one who thinks rates will rise modestly, stay stable, or fall should choose an adjustable rate mortgage. Critics of ARMs charge that these mortgages entice young homeowners to undertake potentially onerous commitments.

Also called a Variable Rate Mortgage (VRM), the ARM should not be confused with the GRADUATED PAYMENT MORTGAGE, which is issued at a fixed rate with monthly payments designed to increase as the borrower's income grows. *See also* CAP; COST OF FUNDS; GROWING EQUITY MORTGAGE; MORTGAGE INTEREST DEDUCTION; SELF-AMORTIZING MORTGAGE; SHARED APPRECIATION MORTGAGE; TEASER RATE.

ADJUSTABLE RATE PREFERRED STOCK (ARPS) PREFERRED STOCK, whose dividend instead of being fixed is adjusted, usually quarterly, based on changes in the Treasury bill rate or other money market rate. The prices of adjustable rate preferreds are less volatile than fixed rate preferreds. Also called *floating rate* or *variable rate* preferred. *See also* CAPS; DUTCH AUCTION PREFERRED STOCK; MANDATORY CONVERTIBLES.

ADJUSTED BALANCE METHOD formula for calculating finance charges based on ACCOUNT BALANCE remaining after adjusting for payments and credits posted during the billing period. Interest charges under this method are lower than those under the AVERAGE DAILY, PREVIOUS BALANCE, and PAST DUE BALANCE METHODS.

ADJUSTED BASIS base price from which to judge capital gains or losses upon sale of an asset like a stock or bond. The cost of commissions in effect is deducted at the time of sale when net proceeds are used for tax purposes. The price must be adjusted to account for any stock splits that have occurred since the initial purchase before arriving at the adjusted basis.

ADJUSTED DEBIT BALANCE (ADB) formula for determining the position of a margin account, as required under Regulation T of the Federal Reserve Board. The ADB is calculated by netting the balance owing the broker with any balance in the SPECIAL MISCELLANEOUS ACCOUNT (SMA), and any paper profits on short accounts. Although changes made in Regulation T in 1982 diminished the significance of ADBs, the formula is still useful in determining whether withdrawals of cash or securities are permissible based on SMA entries.

ADJUSTED EXERCISE PRICE term used in put and call options on Government National Mortgage Association (Ginnie Mae) contracts. To make sure that all contracts trade fairly, the final exercise price of the option is adjusted to take into account the coupon rates carried on all GNMA mortgages, If the standard GNMA mortgage carries an 8% yield, for instance, the price of GNMA pools with 12% mortgages in them are adjusted so that both instruments have the same yield to the investor.

ADJUSTED GROSS INCOME income on which an individual computes federal income tax. Adjusted gross income is determined by subtracting from gross income any unreimbursed business expenses and other allowable adjustments—for example INDIVIDUAL RETIREMENT ACCOUNT (with exceptions outlined in the TAX REFORM ACT OF 1986), SEP and Keogh payments, and alimony payments. Adjusted gross income is the individual's or couple's income before itemized deductions for such items as medical expenses, state and local income taxes, and real estate taxes.

ADJUSTMENT BOND bond issued in exchange for outstanding bonds when recapitalizing a corporation that faces bankruptcy. Authorization for the exchange comes from the bondholders, who consider adjustment bonds a lesser evil. These bonds promise to pay interest only to the extent earned by the corporation. This gives them one of the characteristics of income bonds, which trade flat—that is, without accrued interest.

ADMINISTRATOR court-appointed individual or bank charged with carrying out the court's decisions with respect to a decedent's estate until it is fully distributed to all claimants. Administrators are appointed when a person dies without having made a will or without having named an executor, or when the named executor cannot or will not serve. The term *administratrix* is sometimes used if the individual appointed is a woman.

In a general sense, an administrator is a person who carries out an organization's policies.

AD VALOREM Latin term meaning "according to value" and referring to a way of assessing duties or taxes on goods or property. As one example, ad valorem DUTY assessment is based on value of the imported item rather than on its weight or quantity. As another example, the city of Englewood, New Jersey, levies an ad valorem property tax based on the assessed value of property rather than its size.

ADVANCE

Employee benefits: cash given to an employee before it is needed or earned. A travel advance is supplied so that an employee has cash to use on an upcoming business trip. A salary advance is provided to help the employee cover emergency expenses.

Securities: increase in the price of stocks, bonds, commodities, or other assets. Often heard when referring to the movement of broad indexes, e.g., "The Dow Jones Industrials advanced 15 points today."

Trade: advance payment for goods or services that will be delivered in the near future. For example, home contractors require an advance from homeowners to pay for building materials.

ADVANCE-DECLINE (A-D) measurement of the number of stocks that have advanced and the number that have declined over a particular period. It is the ratio of one to the other and shows the general direction of the market. It is considered bullish if more stocks advance than decline on any trading day. It is bearish if declines outnumber advances. The steepness of the A-D line graphically shows whether a strong bull or bear market is underway.

ADVANCE-DECLINE LINE

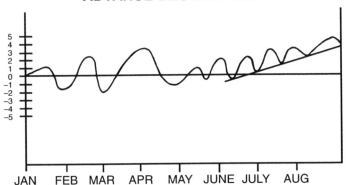

ADVANCED FUNDED PENSION PLAN pension plan under which assets are set aside in amounts and at times approximately coincident with the accruing of benefit rights. In this way, funds are set aside in advance of the date of retirement.

ADVANCE REFUNDING

Government securities: exchange of maturing government securities prior to their due date for issues with a later maturity. It is through advance refunding that the national debt is extended as an alternative to the economic disruptions that would result from eliminating the debt all at once.

Municipal bonds: sale of new bonds (the refunding issue) in advance, usually by some years, of the first call date of the old bonds (the issue to be refunded). The refunding issue would normally have a lower rate than the issue to be refunded, and the proceeds would be invested, usually in government securities, until the higher-rate bonds become callable. This practice, also called *prerefunding*, has been curtailed by several tax acts. *See also* REFUNDING ESCROW DEPOSITS (REDs).

ADVERSE OPINION opinion expressed by a company's independent auditors that the firm's financial statements do not accurately reflect the company's current financial position or operating results. An adverse opinion is a far more serious finding than a QUALIFIED OPINION, in which only some issues are of concern to the auditor. Investors should be extremely cautious about investing in any company with an adverse opinion from its auditors.

ADVERSE SELECTION tendency of people with significant potential to file claims wanting to obtain insurance coverage. For example, those with severe health problems want to buy health insurance, and people going to a dangerous place such as a war zone want to buy more life insurance. Companies employing workers in dangerous occupations want to buy more worker's compensation coverage. In order to combat the problem of adverse selection, insurance companies try to reduce their exposure to large claims by either raising premiums or limiting the availability of coverage to such applicants.

ADVISORY LETTER newsletter aiming to offer financial advice to subscribers. The letter may offer a broad economic and market outlook, or it may focus on a particular sector of the stock, bond, or commodity markets. Some advisory letters specialize in recommending only mutual funds. Some letters also advise their subscribers of new recommendations through a toll-free hotline, which can be updated much more quickly than a printed letter. If the advisory letter recommends specific securities, the author usually is registered with the Securities and Exchange Commission as a REGISTERED INVESTMENT ADVISOR. *See also* HULBERT RATING.

AFFIDAVIT written statement made under oath before an authorized person, such as a notary public.

AFFIDAVIT OF DOMICILE AFFIDAVIT made by the executor of an estate that certifies the decedent's place of residence at the time of death. Before securities can be transferred from an estate, it must be verified that no liens exist against them in the home state of the decedent.

AFFILIATE

In general: two companies are affiliated when one owns less than a majority of the voting stock of the other, or when both are subsidiaries of a third company. A SUBSIDIARY is a company of which more than 50% of the voting shares are owned by another corporation, termed the PARENT COMPANY. A subsidiary is always, by definition, an affiliate, but subsidiary is the preferred term when majority control exists. In everyday use, affiliate is the correct word for intercompany relationships, however indirect, where the parent-subsidiary relationship does not apply.

Banking Act of 1933: any organization that a bank owns or controls by stock holdings, or which the bank's shareholders own, or whose officers are also directors of the bank.

Internal Revenue Service: for purposes of consolidated tax returns an affiliated group is composed of companies whose parent or other inclusive corporation owns at least 80% of voting stock.

Interstate Commerce Commission, Account 706: 1. Controlled by the accounting company alone or with others under a joint agreement. **2.** Controlling the accounting company alone or with others under a joint agreement.

Investment Company Act: company in which there is any direct or indirect ownership of 5% or more of the outstanding voting securities.

AFFILIATED CORPORATION corporation that is an AFFILIATE.

AFFILIATED PERSON individual in a position to exert direct influence on the actions of a corporation. Among such persons are owners of 10% or more of the voting shares, directors, and senior elected officers and any persons in a position to exert influence through them—such as members of their immediate family and other close associates. Sometimes called a *control person.*

AFFORDABILITY INDEX standard established by the National Association of Realtors to gauge the financial ability of consumers to buy a home. A reading of 100 means that a family earning the national median income has exactly enough money to qualify for a mortgage on a median-priced home. Some economists maintain that every one-point increase in the home mortgage interest rate results in 300,000 fewer home sales.

AFTER ACQUIRED CLAUSE clause in a mortgage agreement providing that any additional mortgageable property acquired by the borrower after the mortgage is signed will be additional security for the obligation.

While such provisions can help give mortgage bonds a good rating and enable issuing corporations to borrow at favorable rates, by precluding additional first mortgages, they make it difficult to finance growth through new borrowings. This gives rise to various maneuvers to remove after acquired clauses, such as redemption or exchange of bonds or changes in indenture agreements.

AFTER-HOURS DEALING OR TRADING trading of stocks and bonds after regular trading hours on organized exchanges. This may occur when there is a major announcement about positive or negative earnings or a takeover at a particular company. The stock price may therefore soar or plummet from the level at which it closed during regular trading hours. Some brokerage firms specialize in making over-the-counter markets around the clock to accommodate after-hours dealing. *See* MAKE A MARKET.

AFTERMARKET *see* SECONDARY MARKET.

AFTERTAX BASIS basis for comparing the returns on a corporate taxable bond and a municipal tax-free bond. For example, a corporate bond paying 10% would have an aftertax return of 6.4% for someone in the 36% tax bracket. So any municipal bond paying higher than 6.4% would yield a higher aftertax return.

AFTERTAX REAL RATE OF RETURN amount of money, adjusted for inflation, that an investor can keep, out of the income and capital gains earned from investments. Every dollar loses value to inflation, so investors have to keep an eye on the aftertax real rate of return whenever they commit their capital. By and large, investors seek a rate of return that will match if not exceed the rate of inflation.

AGAINST THE BOX SHORT SALE by the holder of a LONG POSITION in the same stock. *Box* refers to the physical location of securities held in safekeeping. When a stock is sold against the box, it is sold short, but only in effect. A short sale is usually defined as one where the seller does not own the shares. Here the seller *does* own the shares (holds a long position) but does not wish to disclose ownership; or perhaps the long shares are too inaccessible to deliver in the time required; or he may be holding his existing position to get the benefit of long-term capital gains tax treatment. In any event, when the sale is made against the box, the shares needed to cover are borrowed, probably from a broker.

AGED FAIL contract between two broker-dealers that is still not settled 30 days after the settlement date. At that point the open balance no longer counts as an asset, and the receiving firm must adjust its capital accordingly.

AGENCY

In general: relationship between two parties, one a principal and the other an AGENT who represents the principal in transactions with a third party.

Finance: certain types of accounts in trust institutions where individuals, usually trust officers, act on behalf of customers. Agency services to corporations are related to stock purchases and sales. Banks also act as agents for individuals.

Government: securities issued by government-sponsored entities and federally related institutions. Agency securities are exempt from Securities and Exchange Commission (SEC) registration requirements. *See also* AGENCY SECURITIES.

Investment: act of buying or selling for the account and risk of a client. Generally, an agent, or broker, acts as intermediary between buyer and seller, taking no financial risk personally or as a firm, and charging a commission for the service.

AGENCY SECURITIES securities issued by U.S. government-sponsored entities (GSEs) and federally related institutions.

GSEs currently issuing securities comprise eight privately owned, publicly chartered entities created to reduce borrowing costs for certain sectors of the economy, such as farmers, homeowners, and students. They include the Federal Farm Credit Bank System, Farm Credit Financial Assistance Corporation, Federal Home Loan Bank, FEDERAL HOME LOAN MORTGAGE CORPORATION, FEDERAL NATIONAL MORTGAGE ASSOCIATION (FNMA), STUDENT LOAN MARKETING ASSOCIATION (SLMA), FINANCING CORPORATION (FICO), and RESOLUTION TRUST CORPORATION (RTC). GSEs issue discount notes (with maturities ranging from overnight to 360 days) and bonds. With the exception of the Farm Credit Financial Assistance Corporation, GSE securities are not backed by the full faith and credit of the U.S. government. Other GSEs that formerly issued directly now borrow from the FEDERAL FINANCING BANK.

Federally related institutions are arms of the U.S. government and generally have not issued securities directly into the marketplace since the Federal Financing Bank was established to meet their consolidated borrowing needs in 1973. They include the EXPORT-IMPORT BANK (EXIMBANK) of the United States, the Commodity Credit Corporation, the Farmers Housing Administration, the General Services Administration, the GOVERNMENT NATIONAL MORTGAGE ASSOCIATION (GNMA), the Maritime Administration, the Private Export Funding Corporation, the Rural Electrification Administration, the Rural Telephone Bank, the SMALL BUSINESS ADMINISTRATION (SBA), the Tennessee Valley Authority (TVA), and the Washington Metropolitan Area Transit Authority. Except for the Private Export Funding Corporation and the TVA, federally related institution obligations are backed by the full faith and credit of the U.S. government.

Agency securities are exempt from SEC registration and from state and local income taxes.

See also FEDERAL FARM CREDIT SYSTEM; FEDERAL HOME LOAN BANK SYSTEM.

AGENT individual authorized by another person, called the principal, to act in the latter's behalf in transactions involving a third party. Banks are frequently appointed by individuals to be their agents, and so authorize their employees to act on behalf of principals. Agents have three basic characteristics:
1. They act on behalf of and are subject to the control of the principal.
2. They do not have title to the principal's property.
3. They owe the duty of obedience to the principal's orders.
See also ACCOUNT EXECUTIVE; BROKER; TRANSFER AGENT.

AGGREGATE EXERCISE PRICE in stock options trading, the number of shares in a put or call CONTRACT (normally 100) multiplied by the EXERCISE PRICE. The price of the option, called the PREMIUM, is a separate figure not included in the aggregate exercise price. A July call option on 100 XYZ at 70 would, for example, have an aggregate exercise price of 100 (number of shares) times $70 (price per share), or $7,000, if exercised on or before the July expiration date.

In options traded on debt instruments, which include GOVERNMENT NATIONAL MORTGAGE ASSOCIATION (GNMA) pass-throughs, Treasury bills, Treasury notes, Treasury bonds, and certain municipal bonds, the aggregate exercise price is determined by multiplying the FACE VALUE of the underlying security by the exercise price. For example, the aggregate exercise price of put option Treasury bond December 90 would be $90,000 if exercised on or before its December expiration date, the calculation being 90% times the $100,000 face value of the underlying bond.

AGGREGATE SUPPLY in MACROECONOMICS, the total amount of goods and ser-vices supplied to the market at alternative price levels in a given period of time; also called *total output.* The central concept in SUPPLY-SIDE ECONOMICS, it corre-sponds with aggregate demand, defined as the total amount of goods and services demanded in the economy at alternative income levels in a given period, includ-ing both consumer and producers' goods; aggregate demand is also called *total spending.* The aggregate supply curve describes the relationship between price levels and the quantity of output that firms are willing to provide.

AGGRESSIVE GROWTH MUTUAL FUND mutual fund holding stocks of rapidly growing companies. While these companies may be large or small, they all share histories of and prospects for above-average profit growth. Aggressive growth funds are designed solely for capital appreciation, since they produce lit-tle or no income from dividends. This type of mutual fund is typically more volatile than the overall stock market, meaning its shares will rise far more than the average stock during bull markets and will fall much farther than the typical stock in a bear market. Investors in aggressive growth funds must realize that the value of their shares will fluctuate sharply over time. Aggressive growth funds are also called *maximum capital gains funds* or *capital appreciation funds.*

AGING SCHEDULE classification of trade ACCOUNTS RECEIVABLE by date of sale. Usually prepared by a company's auditor, the *aging,* as the schedule is called, is a vital tool in analyzing the quality of a company's receivables investment. It is frequently required by grantors of credit.

The schedule is most often seen as: (1) a list of the amount of receivables by the month in which they were created; (2) a list of receivables by maturity, clas-sified as current or as being in various stages of delinquency. The following is a typical aging schedule.

	dollars (in thousands)	
Current (under 30 days)	$14,065	61%
1–30 days past due	3,725	16
31–60 days past due	2,900	12
61–90 days past due	1,800	8
Over 90 days past due	750	3
	$23,240	100%

The aging schedule reveals patterns of delinquency and shows where col-lection efforts should be concentrated. It helps in evaluating the adequacy of the reserve for BAD DEBTS, because the longer accounts stretch out the more likely they are to become uncollectible. Using the schedule can help prevent the loss of future sales, since old customers who fall too far behind tend to seek out new sources of supply.

AGREEMENT AMONG UNDERWRITERS contract between participating members of an investment banking SYNDICATE; sometimes called *syndicate con-tract* or *purchase group agreement.* It is distinguished from the *underwriting agreement,* which is signed by the company issuing the securities and the SYNDI-CATE MANAGER, acting as agent for the underwriting group.

The agreement among underwriters, (1) appoints the originating investment banker as syndicate manager and agent; (2) appoints additional managers, if con-sidered advisable; (3) defines the members' proportionate liability (usually lim-ited to the amount of their participation) and agrees to pay each member's share on settlement date; (4) authorizes the manager to form and allocate units to a SELLING GROUP, and agrees to abide by the rules of the selling group agreement;

(5) states the life of the syndicate, usually running until 30 days after termination of the selling group, or ending earlier by mutual consent.

AIR POCKET STOCK stock that falls sharply, usually in the wake of such negative news as unexpected poor earnings. As shareholders rush to sell, and few buyers can be found, the price plunges dramatically, like an airplane hitting an air pocket.

AIRPORT REVENUE BOND tax-exempt bond issued by a city, county, state, or airport authority to support the expansion and operations of an airport. The repayment of principal and interest is backed by either the general revenues of airport authority or lease payments generated by one or more airlines using the facilities. In some cases, airport revenue bonds are backed directly by the financial strength of the major airline using the airport, which makes the bonds more risky, because airlines are particularly sensitive to economic cycles and could go out of business in a down cycle.

ALIEN CORPORATION company incorporated under the laws of a foreign country regardless of where it operates. "Alien corporation" can be used as a synonym for the term *foreign corporation.* However, "foreign corporation" also is used in U.S. state law to mean a corporation formed in a state other than that in which it does business.

ALIMONY PAYMENT money paid to a separated or divorced spouse as required by a divorce decree or a legal separation agreement. The IRS allows qualifying payments as DEDUCTIONS by the payor and they are taxable income to the payee.

ALLIED MEMBER general partner or voting stockholder of a member firm of the New York Stock Exchange who is not personally a member. Allied members cannot do business on the trading floor. A member firm need have no more than one partner or voting stockholder who owns a membership. So even the chairman of the board of a member firm may be no more than an allied member.

ALLIGATOR SPREAD spread in the options market that "eats the investor alive" with high commission costs. The term is used when a broker arranges a combination of puts and calls that generates so much commission the client is unlikely to turn a profit even if the markets move as anticipated.

ALL IN underwriting shorthand for *all included,* referring to an issuer's interest rate after giving effect to commissions and miscellaneous related expenses.

ALL OR NONE (AON)
Investment banking: an offering giving the issuer the right to cancel the whole issue if the underwriting is not fully subscribed.

Securities: buy or sell order marked to signify that no partial transaction is to be executed. The order will not automatically be canceled, however, if a complete transaction is not executed; to accomplish that, the order entry must be marked FOK, meaning FILL OR KILL.

ALL ORDINARIES INDEX the major index of Australian stocks, representing 280 of the most active listed companies, or the majority of the equity capitalization (excluding foreign companies) listed on the AUSTRALIA STOCK EXCHANGE (ASX).The index is made up of 23 sub-indices representing various industry categories, and it summarizes market price movements by following changes in the aggregate market values of the companies listed.

ALLOTMENT amount of securities assigned to each of the participants in an investment banking SYNDICATE formed to underwrite and distribute a new issue, called *subscribers* or *allottees*. The financial responsibilities of the subscribers are set forth in an allotment notice, which is prepared by the SYNDICATE MANAGER.

ALLOWANCE deduction from the value of an invoice, permitted by a seller of goods to cover damages or shortages. *See also* RESERVE.

ALL-SAVERS CERTIFICATE *see* ECONOMIC RECOVERY TAX ACT OF 1981 (ERTA).

ALPHA
1. coefficient measuring the portion of an investment's RETURN arising from specific (nonmarket) risk. In other words, alpha is a mathematical estimate of the amount of return expected from an investment's inherent values, such as the rate of growth in earnings per share. It is distinct from the amount of return caused by VOLATILITY, which is measured by the BETA coefficient. For example, an alpha of 1.25 indicates that a stock is projected to rise 25% in price in a year when the return on the market and the stock's beta are both zero. An investment whose price is low relative to its alpha is undervalued and considered a good selection.

   In the case of a MUTUAL FUND, alpha measures the relationship between the fund's performance and its beta over a three-year period.
2. on the London Stock Exchange, now called the International Stock Exchange of the United Kingdom and Republic of Ireland (ISE), the designation *alpha stocks* applied to the largest and most actively traded companies in a classification system that was adopted after the BIG BANG in October 1986 and was replaced in January 1991 with the NORMAL MARKET SIZE (NMS) classification system.

ALPHABET STOCK categories of General Motors' common stock associated with particular acquisitions, such as "E" stock issued to acquire Electronic Data Systems and "H" stock issued to acquire Hughes Aircraft. The significance of the categories is that they have different voting rights and pay dividends tied to the operating performance of the particular divisions. Alphabet stock differs from CLASSIFIED STOCK, which is typically designated Class A and Class B, in that classified stock implies a hierarchy of powers and privileges whereas alphabet stock simply separates differences.

ALTERNATIVE MINIMUM TAX (AMT) federal tax aimed at ensuring that wealthy individuals, trusts, estates, and corporations pay at least some income tax. For individuals, the AMT is computed by adding TAX PREFERENCE ITEMS such as PASSIVE losses from tax shelters, and tax-exempt interest on PRIVATE-PURPOSE BONDS issued after August 7, 1986, to adjusted gross income. From this amount, a $45,000 exemption must be subtracted for a married couple filing jointly, $33,750 for a single filer, and $22,500 for a married couple filing separately. The remaining amount, up to $175,000, is subject to a 26% tax rate. Any amount over $175,000 is subject to a 28% tax rate. The corporate AMT has the same exemptions but a tax rate of 20%. It is imposed on the amount of money in excess of the alternative minimum taxable income (AMTI) over the exemption amount. In determining the corporate AMT, an adjustment called the *adjusted current earnings* (ACE) must be made. The ACE adjustment increases a corporation's AMTI by 75% of the amount by which its ACE exceeds its AMTI. This adjustment is designed to eliminate some of the tax savings generated by corporations that have high income for accounting purposes but pay little or no tax as a result of tax benefits. Calculating the correct individual or corporate AMT can be extremely complex and is best left to a professional accountant.

ALTERNATIVE ORDER order giving a broker a choice between two courses of action; also called an *either-or order* or a *one cancels the other order.* Such orders are either to buy or to sell, never both. Execution of one course automatically makes the other course inoperative. An example is a combination buy limit/buy stop order, wherein the buy limit is below the current market and the buy stop is above.

AMBAC Indemnity Corporation *see* MUNICIPAL BOND INSURANCE.

AMENDED TAX RETURN Internal Revenue Service tax return filed on Form 1040X to correct mistakes made on the original return. Amended returns must be filed within three years of the original filing.

AMENDMENT addition to, or change, in a legal document. When properly signed, it has the full legal effect of the original document.

AMERICAN ASSOCIATION OF INDIVIDUAL INVESTORS nonprofit organization, based in Chicago, designed to educate individual investors about stocks, bonds, mutual funds, and other financial alternatives through seminars and publications. The AAII also evaluates investment-oriented software in a publication called *Computerized Investing.*

AMERICAN DEPOSITARY RECEIPT (ADR) receipt for the shares of a foreign-based corporation held in the vault of a U.S. bank and entitling the shareholder to all dividends and capital gains. Instead of buying shares of foreign-based companies in overseas markets, Americans can buy shares in the U.S. in the form of an ADR. ADRs are available for hundreds of stocks from numerous countries.

AMERICAN DEPOSITARY SHARE (ADS) share issued under a deposit agreement representing the underlying ordinary share which trades in the issuer's home market. The terms ADS and ADR tend to be used interchangeably. Technically, the ADS is the instrument that actually is traded, while the ADR is the certificate that represents a number of ADSs.

AMERICAN STOCK EXCHANGE (AMEX) stock exchange with the second biggest volume of trading in the United States. Located at 86 Trinity Place in downtown Manhattan, the Amex was known until 1921 as the *Curb Exchange,* and it is still occasionally referred to as the *Curb* today. For the most part, the stocks and bonds traded on the Amex are those of small to medium-size companies, as contrasted with the huge companies whose shares are traded on the New York Stock Exchange. A large number of oil and gas companies, in particular, are traded on the Amex. The Amex also houses the trading of options on many New York Stock Exchange stocks and some OVER THE COUNTER stocks and has expanded its listings of DERIVATIVES in recent years. More foreign shares are traded on the Amex than on any other U.S. exchange. Hours: 9:30 A.M.—4:00 P.M., Monday through Friday. *See also* EMERGING COMPANY MARKETPLACE (ECM); SPIDERS.

AMORTIZATION accounting procedure that gradually reduces the cost value of a limited life or intangible asset through periodic charges to income. For fixed assets the terms used is DEPRECIATION, and for wasting assets (natural resources) it is depletion, both terms meaning essentially the same thing as amortization. Most companies follow the conservative practice of writing off, through amortization, INTANGIBLE ASSETS such as goodwill. It is also common practice to amortize any premium over par value paid in the purchase of preferred stock or bond investments. The purpose of amortization is to reflect resale or redemption value.

Amortization also refers to the reduction of debt by regular payments of interest and principal sufficient to pay off a loan by maturity.

Discount and expense on funded debt are amortized by making applicable charges to income in accordance with a predetermined schedule. While this is normally done systematically, charges to profit and loss are permissible at any time in any amount of the remaining discount and expense. Such accounting is detailed in a company's annual report.

AMPS acronym for *Auction Market Preferred Stock,* Merrill Lynch's answer to Salomon Brothers' DARTS and First Boston's STARS. These and other proprietary products are types of DUTCH AUCTION PREFERRED STOCK. Since the auctions take place every 49 days, the shares meet the 46-day holding period required for the 70% dividend exclusion allowed corporations under the tax code.

AMSTERDAM STOCK EXCHANGE the stock exchange in the Netherlands, founded in 1602, is the oldest in the world. Most of the stocks traded on the exchange are Dutch-based, and energy firms represent the largest sector. The Central Bureau of Statistics (CBS) All Share Index and the Total Return Index include all ordinary shares of Dutch companies listed on the exchange. Trading hours are 9:30 A.M. to 4:30 P.M., Monday through Friday. Settlement is almost exclusively without physical delivery.

ANALYSIS *see* FUNDAMENTAL ANALYSIS; TECHNICAL ANALYSIS.

ANALYST person in a brokerage house, bank trust department, or mutual fund group who studies a number of companies and makes buy or sell recommendations on the securities of particular companies and industry groups. Most analysts specialize in a particular industry, but some investigate any company that interests them, regardless of its line of business. Some analysts have considerable influence, and can therefore affect the price of a company's stock when they issue a buy or sell recommendation. *See also* CREDIT ANALYST.

AND INTEREST phrase used in quoting bond prices to indicate that, in addition to the price quoted, the buyer will receive ACCRUED INTEREST.

ANGEL INVESTMENT GRADE bond, as distinguished from FALLEN ANGEL.

ANKLE BITER stock issue having a MARKET CAPITALIZATION of less than $500 million. Generally speaking, such small-capitalization stocks are more speculative than "high-cap" issues, but their greater growth potential gives them more RELATIVE STRENGTH in recessions. *See also* SMALL FIRM EFFECT.

ANNUAL BASIS statistical technique whereby figures covering a period of less than a year are extended to cover a 12-month period. The procedure, called *annualizing,* must take seasonal variations (if any) into account to be accurate.

ANNUAL EXCLUSION tax rule allowing a taxpayer to exclude certain kinds of income from taxation on a tax return. For example, interest earned from municipal bonds must be reported, even though it is not taxed by the federal government. Proceeds from life insurance policies paid by reason of the death of the insured are not taxable. Gifts received of $10,000 or less are also not taxable, and are therefore subject to the annual exclusion rule.

ANNUALIZE to convert to an annual basis. For example, if a mutual fund earns 1% in a month, it would earn 12% on an annualized basis, by multiplying the monthly return by 12. Many economists annualize a monthly number such as auto sales or housing starts to make it easier to compare to prior years.

ANNUAL MEETING once-a-year meeting when the managers of a company report to stockholders on the year's results, and the board of directors stands for election for the next year. The chief executive officer usually comments on the outlook for the coming year and, with other senior officers, answers questions from shareholders. Stockholders can also request that resolutions on corporate policy be voted on by all those owning stock in the company Stockholders unable to attend the annual meeting may vote for directors and pass on resolutions through the use of PROXY material, which must legally be mailed to all shareholders of record.

ANNUAL PERCENTAGE RATE (APR) cost of credit that consumers pay, expressed as a simple annual percentage. According to the federal Truth in Lending Act, every consumer loan agreement must disclose the APR in large bold type. *See also* CONSUMER CREDIT PROTECTION ACT OF 1968.

ANNUAL RENEWABLE TERM INSURANCE *See* TERM INSURANCE.

ANNUAL REPORT yearly record of a corporation's financial condition that must be distributed to shareholders under SECURITIES AND EXCHANGE COMMISSION regulations. Included in the report is a description of the company's operations as well as its balance sheet and income statement. The long version of the annual report with more detailed financial information—called the 10-K—is available upon request from the corporate secretary.

ANNUAL RETURN TOTAL RETURN per year from an investment, including dividends or interest and capital gains or losses but excluding commissions and other transactions costs and taxes. A *compound annual return* represents the annual rate at which money would have to compound to reach the cumulative figure resulting from annual total returns. It is a discount rate and different from *average annual return,* which is simply an arithmetic mean of annual returns.

ANNUITANT individual receiving benefits from an annuity. The annuity owner can choose to annuitize the policy, meaning that he or she begins to receive regular payments from the annuity.

ANNUITIZE to begin a series of payments from the capital that has built up in an ANNUITY. The payments may be a fixed amount, or for a fixed period of time, or for the lifetimes of one or two *annuitants,* thus guaranteeing income payments that cannot be outlived. *See also* DEFERRED PAYMENT ANNUITY; FIXED ANNUITY; IMMEDIATE PAYMENT ANNUITY; VARIABLE ANNUITY.

ANNUITY form of contract sold by life insurance companies that guarantees a fixed or variable payment to the annuitant at some future time, usually retirement. In a FIXED ANNUITY the amount will ultimately be paid out in regular installments varying only with the payout method elected. In a VARIABLE ANNUITY, the payout is based on a guaranteed number of units; unit values and payments depend on the value of the underlying investments. All capital in the annuity grows TAX-DEFERRED. Key considerations when buying an annuity are the financial soundness of the insurance company *(see* BEST'S RATING), the returns it has paid in the past, and the level of fees and commissions paid to salesmen.

ANNUITY CERTAIN annuity that pays a specified monthly level of income for a predetermined time period, frequently ten years. The annuitant is guaranteed by the insurance company to receive those payments for the agreed upon time period without exception or contingency. If the annuitant dies before the time period expires, the annuity payments are then made to the annuitant's designated beneficiaries. The level of payment in an annuity certain will be higher than for a LIFE ANNUITY because the insurance company knows exactly what its liability will be, whereas with a life annuity, payments depend on how long the annuitant lives.

ANNUITY STARTING DATE date on which an ANNUITANT begins receiving payments from an annuity. Generally, any distributions before age 59½ are subject to a 10% penalty from the IRS, so most annuities start paying after the annuitant has attained that age. The later an annuitant waits to start receiving payments, the higher his or her monthly payments will be under a life annuity, because the insurance company has had more time to invest the money, and the annuitant's remaining life expectancy is shorter.

ANTICIPATED HOLDING PERIOD time during which a limited partnership expects to hold onto an asset. In the prospectus for a real estate limited partnership, for instance, a sponsor will typically say that the anticipated holding period for a particular property is five to seven years. At the end of that time the property is sold, and, usually, the capital received is returned to the limited partners in one distribution.

ANTICIPATION

In general: paying an obligation before it falls due.

Finance: repayment of debt obligations before maturity, usually to save interest. If a formalized discount or rebate is involved, the term used is *anticipation rate.*

Mortgage instrument: when a provision allows prepayment without penalty, the mortgagee is said to have the *right of anticipation.*

Trade payments: bill that is paid before it is due, not discounted.

ANTITRUST LAWS federal legislation designed to prevent monopolies and restraint of trade. Landmark statutes include:
1. the Sherman Anti-Trust Act of 1890, which prohibited acts or contracts tending to create monopoly and initiated an era of trustbusting.
2. the Clayton Anti-Trust Act of 1914, which was passed as an amendment to the Sherman Act and dealt with local price discrimination as well as with the INTERLOCKING DIRECTORATES. It went further in the areas of the HOLDING COMPANY and restraint of trade.
3. the Federal Trade Commission Act of 1914, which created the Federal Trade Commission or FTC, with power to conduct investigations and issue orders preventing unfair practices in interstate commerce.

ANY-AND-ALL BID offer to pay an equal price for all shares tendered by a deadline; contrasts with TWO-TIER BID. *See also* TAKEOVER.

ANY-INTEREST-DATE CALL provision found in some municipal bond indentures that gives the issuer the right to redeem on any interest payment due date, with or without a premium (depending on the indenture).

APPRAISAL FEE fee charged by an expert to estimate, but not determine, the market value of property. An appraisal is an opinion of value, and is usually required when real property is sold, financed, condemned, taxed, insured, or partitioned. For example, the appraisal of a work of art done to establish value for the IRS when the art is to be donated to a charity may differ from the appraisal if the piece of art is about to be sold at auction. Similarly, the appraisal of a piece of real estate for insurance purposes may differ from an appraisal for determining property taxes. The appraisal fee is usually a set dollar amount, though in some cases may be calculated as a percentage of the value of the property appraised.

APPRECIATION increase in the value of an asset such as a stock, bond, commodity, or real estate.

APPROVED LIST list of investments that a mutual fund or other financial institution is authorized to make. The approved list may be statutory where a fiduciary responsibility exists. *See also* LEGAL LIST.

APS acronym for *Auction Preferred Stock,* Goldman Sach's DUTCH AUCTION PREFERRED STOCK product.

ARBITRAGE profiting from differences in price when the same security, currency, or commodity is traded on two or more markets. For example, an *arbitrageur* simultaneously buys one contract of gold in the New York market and sells one contract of gold in the Chicago market, locking in a profit because at that moment the price on the two markets is different. (The arbitrageur's selling price is higher than the buying price.) *Index arbitrage* exploits price differences between STOCK INDEX FUTURES and underlying stocks. By taking advantage of momentary disparities in prices between markets, arbitrageurs perform the economic function of making those markets trade more efficiently. *See also* RISK ARBITRAGE.

ARBITRAGE BONDS bonds issued by a municipality in order to gain an interest rate advantage by refunding higher-rate bonds in advance of their call date. Proceeds from the lower-rate refunding issue are invested in treasuries until the first call date of the higher-rate issue being refunded. Arbitrage bonds, which always raised a question of tax exemption, were further curtailed by the TAX REFORM ACT OF 1986.

ARBITRAGEUR person or firm engaged in ARBITRAGE. Arbitrageurs attempt to profit when the same security or commodity is trading at different prices in two or more markets. Those engaged in RISK ARBITRAGE attempt to profit from buying stocks of announced or potential TAKEOVER targets.

ARBITRATION alternative to suing in court to settle disputes between brokers and their clients and between brokerage firms. Traditionally, pre-dispute arbitration clauses in account agreements with brokers automatically assured that disputes would be arbitrated by objective third parties and precluded court cases. In 1989, the Securities and Exchange Commission (SEC) approved sweeping changes requiring brokers to disclose clearly when such clauses exist, prohibiting any restrictions on customers' rights to file arbitration claims, and imposing stricter qualifying standards for arbitrators. *See also* BOARD OF ARBITRATION.

ARITHMETIC MEAN simple average obtained by dividing the sum of two or more items by the number of items.

ARM'S INDEX better known as TRIN; technical indicator named for *Barron's* writer Richard Arms.

ARM'S LENGTH TRANSACTION transaction that is conducted as though the parties were unrelated, thus avoiding any semblance of conflict of interest. For example, under current law parents may rent real estate to their children and still claim business deductions such as depreciation as long as the parents charge their children what they would charge if someone who is not a relative were to rent the same property.

ARREARAGE

In general: amount of any past-due obligation.

Investments: amount by which interest on bonds or dividends on CUMULATIVE PREFERRED stock is due and unpaid. In the case of cumulative preferred stock, common dividends cannot be paid by a company as long as preferred dividends are in arrears.

ARTICLES OF INCORPORATION document filed with a U.S. state by the founders of a corporation. After approving the articles, the state issues a certificate of incorporation; the two documents together become the CHARTER that gives the corporation its legal existence. The charter embodies such information as the corporation's name, purpose, amount of authorized shares, and number and identity of directors. The corporation's powers thus derive from the laws of the state and from the provisions of the charter. Rules governing its internal management are set forth in the corporation's BYLAWS, which are drawn up by the founders.

ARTIFICIAL CURRENCY *currency substitute,* such as SPECIAL DRAWING RIGHTS (SDRs) and EUROPEAN CURRENCY UNITS (ECUs).

ASCENDING TOPS chart pattern tracing a security's price over a period of time and showing that each peak in a security's price is higher than the preceding peak. This upward movement is considered bullish, meaning that the upward trend is likely to continue. *See also* DESCENDING TOPS.

ASCENDING TOPS

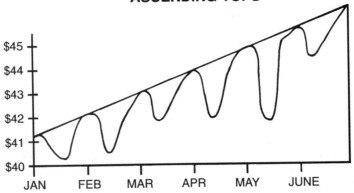

ASE INDEX *see* STOCK INDEXES AND AVERAGES.

ASKED PRICE

1. price at which a security or commodity is offered for sale on an exchange or in the over-the-counter market. Generally, it is the lowest round lot price at which a dealer will sell. Also called the *ask price, asking price, ask,* or OFFERING PRICE.
2. per-share price at which mutual fund shares are offered to the public, usually the NET ASSET VALUE per share plus a sales charge, if any.

ASPIRIN acronym for *Australian Stock Price Riskless Indexed Notes.* Zero-coupon, four-year bonds guaranteed by the Treasury of New South Wales repayable at face value plus the percentage increase by which the Australian Stock Index of All Ordinaries (common stocks) rises above 1372 points during the period. *See also* ALL ORDINARIES INDEX.

ASSAY test of a metal's purity to verify that it meets the standards for trading on a commodities exchange. For instance, a 100 troy-ounce bar of refined gold must be assayed at a fineness of not less than 995 before the Comex will allow it to be used in settlement of a gold contract.

ASSESSED VALUATION dollar value assigned to property by a municipality for purposes of assessing taxes, which are based on the number of mills per dollar of assessed valuation. If a house is assessed at $100,000 and the tax rate is 50 mills, the tax is $5000. Assessed valuation is important not only to homeowners but also to investors in municipal bonds that are backed by property taxes.

ASSET anything having commercial or exchange value that is owned by a business, institution, or individual. *See also* CAPITAL ASSET; CURRENT ASSETS; DEFERRED CHARGE; FIXED ASSET; INTANGIBLE ASSET; NONCURRENT ASSET.

ASSET ALLOCATION apportioning of investment funds among categories of assets, such as CASH EQUIVALENTS, STOCK, FIXED-INCOME INVESTMENTS, and such tangible assets as real estate, precious metals, and collectibles. Also applies to subcategories such as government, municipal, and corporate bonds, and industry groupings of common stocks. Asset allocation affects both risk and return and is a central concept in personal financial planning and investment management.

ASSET ALLOCATION MUTUAL FUND mutual fund that switches between stocks, bonds, and money market securities to maximize shareholders' returns while minimizing risk. Such funds, which have become extremely popular in recent years, relieve individual shareholders of the responsibility of timing their entry or exit into different markets, since the fund manager is making those decisions. Theoretically, asset allocation funds provide a built-in buffer against declining stock and bond prices because the manager can move all the fund's assets into safe money market instruments. On the other hand, the manager has flexibility to invest aggressively in international and domestic stocks and bonds if he or she sees bull markets ahead for those securities.

ASSET-BACKED SECURITIES bonds or notes backed by loan paper or accounts receivable originated by banks, credit card companies, or other providers of credit and often "enhanced" by a bank LETTER OF CREDIT or by insurance coverage provided by an institution other than the issuer. Typically, the originator of the loan or accounts receivable paper sells it to a specially created trust, which repackages it as securities with a minimum denomination of $1000 and a term of five years or less. The securities are then underwritten by brokerage firms who reoffer them to the public. Examples are CERTIFICATES FOR AUTOMOBILE RECEIVABLES (CARs) and so-called *plastic bonds,* backed by credit card receivables. Because the institution that originated the underlying loans or receivables is neither the obligor nor the guarantor, investors should evaluate the quality of the original paper, the worth of the guarantor or insurer, and the extent of the protection. *See also* PASS-THROUGH SECURITY.

ASSET COVERAGE extent to which a company's net assets cover a particular debt obligation, class of preferred stock, or equity position.
    Asset coverage is calculated as follows: from assets at their total book value or liquidation value, subtract intangible assets, current liabilities, and all obligations prior in claim to the issue in question. Divide the result by the dollar amount of the subject issue (or loan) to arrive at the asset coverage ratio. The same information can be expressed as a percentage or, by using units as the divisor, as a dollar figure of coverage per unit. The variation to determine preferred stock coverage treats all liabilities as paid; the variation to arrive at common stock coverage

considers both preferred stock and liabilities paid. The term most often used for the common stock calculation is *net book value per share of common stock.*

These calculations reveal *direct* asset coverage. *Overall* asset coverage is obtained by including the subject issue with the total of prior obligations and dividing the aggregate into total tangible assets at liquidating value.

Asset coverage is important as a cushion against losses in the event of liquidation.

ASSET DEPRECIATION RANGE SYSTEM (ADR) range of depreciable lives allowed by the Internal Revenue Service for particular classes of depreciable assets. The ADR system was replaced when the ECONOMIC RECOVERY TAX ACT OF 1981 (ERTA) introduced the ACCELERATED COST RECOVERY SYSTEM (ACRS) but was revived with modifications of ACRS under the TAX REFORM ACT OF 1986. The ADR system assigns an upper and lower limit to the estimated useful lives of asset classes. ACRS classes are based on the mid-points of these ranges. Under the alternative depreciation system, taxpayers may elect STRAIGHT LINE DEPRECI-ATION over the applicable ADR-class life.

ASSET FINANCING financing that seeks to convert particular assets into working cash in exchange for a security interest in those assets. The term is replacing *commercial financing* as major banks join commercial finance companies in addressing the financing needs of companies that do not fit the traditional seasonal borrower profile. Although the prevalent form of asset financing continues to be loans against accounts receivable, *inventory loans* are common and *second mortgage loans,* predicated as they usually are on market values containing a high inflation factor, seem to gain popularity by the day. *See also* ACCOUNTS RECEIVABLE FINANCING.

ASSET-LIABILITY MANAGEMENT matching an individual's level of debt and amount of assets. Someone who is planning to buy a new car, for instance, would have to decide whether to pay cash, thus lowering assets, or to take out a loan, thereby increasing debts (or liabilities). Such decisions should be based on interest rates, on earning power, and on the comfort level with debt. Financial institutions carry out asset-liability management when they match the maturity of their deposits with the length of their loan commitments to keep from being adversely affected by rapid changes in interest rates.

ASSET MANAGEMENT ACCOUNT account at a brokerage house, bank, or savings institution that combines banking services like check writing, credit cards, and debit cards; brokerage features like buying securities and making loans on margin; and the convenience of having all financial transactions listed on one monthly statement. Such accounts are also termed *central asset accounts* and are known by such proprietary names as the Cash Management Account (Merrill Lynch), and Active Assets Account (Dean Witter).

ASSET PLAY stock market term for a stock that is attractive because the current price does not reflect the value of the company's assets. For example, an analyst could recommend a hotel chain, not because its hotels are run well but because its real estate is worth far more than is recognized in the stock's current price. Asset play stocks are tempting targets for takeovers because they provide an inexpensive way to buy assets.

ASSET STRIPPER corporate raider who takes over a company planning to sell large assets in order to repay debt. The raider calculates that after selling the assets and paying off the debt, he or she will be left with valuable assets that are worth more than his or her purchase price.

ASSET VALUE net market value of a company's assets on a per-share basis as opposed to the market value of the shares. A company is undervalued by the stock market when asset value exceeds share value.

ASSIGN sign a document transferring ownership from one party to another. Ownership can be in a number of forms, including tangible property, rights (usually arising out of contracts), or the right to transfer ownership at some later time. The party who assigns is called the *assignor* and the party who receives the transfer of title—the assignment—is the *assignee.*

Stocks and registered bonds can be assigned by completing and signing a form printed on the back of the certificate—or, as is sometimes preferred for safety reasons, by executing a separate form, called an *assignment separate from certificate* or *stock/bond power.*

When the OPTIONS CLEARING CORPORATION learns of the exercise of an option, it prepares an assignment form notifying a broker-dealer that an option written by one of its clients has been exercised. The firm in turn assigns the exercise in accordance with its internal procedures.

An assignment for the benefit of creditors, sometimes called simply an *assignment,* is an alternative to bankruptcy, whereby the assets of a company are assigned to the creditors and liquidated for their benefit by a trustee.

ASSIMILATION absorption of a new issue of stock by the investing public after all shares have been sold by the issue's underwriters. *See also* ABSORBED.

ASSUMED INTEREST RATE rate of interest that an insurance company uses to determine the payout on an ANNUITY contract. The higher the assumed interest rate, the higher the monthly payout will be.

ASSUMPTION act of taking on responsibility for the liabilities of another party, usually documented by an *assumption agreement.* In the case of a MORTGAGE assumption, the seller remains secondarily liable unless released from the obligations by the lender.

ATP acronym for *arbitrage trading program,* better known as PROGRAM TRADING. Program traders simultaneously place orders for stock index futures and the underlying stocks in an attempt to exploit price variations. Their activity is often blamed for excessive VOLATILITY.

AT PAR at a price equal to the face, or nominal, value of a security. *See also* PAR VALUE.

AT RISK exposed to the danger of loss. Investors in a limited partnership can claim tax deductions only if they can prove that there's a chance of never realizing any profit and of losing their investment as well. Deductions will be disallowed if the limited partners are not exposed to economic risk—if, for example, the general partner guarantees to return all capital to limited partners even if the business venture should lose money.

ATHENS STOCK EXCHANGE principal stock exchange in Greece. There are no restrictions on foreign membership on the exchange. The ASE Composite Index is traded daily. The exchange uses an automated trading system, XTS, for all listed companies. Equities are traded on account or for cash. Settlement of nearly all transactions is within two days, along with the physical exchange of security certificates or depository receipt. Hours: 10:30 A.M.–1:30 P.M., Monday through Friday.

ATTAINED AGE age at which a person is eligible to receive certain benefits. For example, someone may be eligible to receive the proceeds from a trust when they reach age 21. Or someone who has attained the age of 65 may be eligible for certain pension or other retirement benefits. In some cases, the person may have to take some action when they reach the attained age, such as retire from a company.

AT THE CLOSE ORDER
Securities: market order that is to be executed in its entirety at the closing price on the exchange of the stock named in the order. If it is not so executed, the order is to be treated as canceled.

Futures/Options: in futures and options, a MARKET ON CLOSE ORDER, which is a contract to be executed on some exchanges during the closing period, during which there is a range of prices.

AT THE MARKET *see* MARKET ORDER.

AT THE MONEY at the current price, as an option with an exercise price equal to or near the current price of the stock or underlying futures contract. *See also* DEEP IN/OUT OF THE MONEY; IN THE MONEY; OUT OF THE MONEY.

AT THE OPENING ORDER
Securities: market or limited price order to be executed on the opening trade of the stock on the exchange. If the order, or any portion of it, is not executed in this manner, it is to be treated as canceled.

Futures/Options: in futures and options, a MARKET ON OPEN ORDER, during which there is a range of prices at the opening.

AUCTION MARKET system by which securities are bought and sold through brokers on the securities exchanges, as distinguished from the over-the-counter market, where trades are negotiated. Best exemplified by the NEW YORK STOCK EXCHANGE, it is a double auction system or TWO-SIDED MARKET. That is because, unlike the conventional auction with one auctioneer and many buyers, here we have many sellers and many buyers. As in any auction, a price is established by competitive bidding between brokers acting as agents for buyers and sellers. That the system functions in an orderly way is the result of several trading rules: (1) The first bid or offer at a given price has priority over any other bid or offer at the same price. (2) The high bid and low offer "have the floor." (3) A new auction begins whenever all the offers or bids at a given price are exhausted. (4) Secret transactions are prohibited. (5) Bids and offers must be made in an audible voice.

Also, the competitive bidding by which Treasury bills are sold. *See also* BILL; DUTCH AUCTION.

AUCTION-RATE PREFERRED STOCK *see* DUTCH AUCTION PREFERRED STOCK.

AUDIT professional examination and verification of a company's accounting documents and supporting data for the purpose of rendering an opinion as to their fairness, consistency, and conformity with GENERALLY ACCEPTED ACCOUNTING PRINCIPLES. *See also* ACCOUNTANT'S OPINION.

AUDITOR'S CERTIFICATE *see* ACCOUNTANT'S OPINION.

AUDITOR'S REPORT public accountant's declaration following the completion of an examination of corporate financial statements. Also called *accountant's opinion.*

AUDIT TRAIL step-by-step record by which accounting data can be traced to their source. Questions as to the validity or accuracy of an accounting figure can be resolved by reviewing the sequence of events from which the figure resulted.

AUNT MILLIE derogatory term for an unsophisticated investor. Wall Street professionals may say that "This investment will interest Aunt Millie," meaning that it is simple to understand. It may also imply that such small investors will not be able to appreciate the amount of risk posed by the investment relative to the opportunity for profit. Brokers and financial advisors, using the KNOW YOUR CUSTOMER rule, should not recommend complex and risky investments to Aunt Millie investors.

AUSTRALIAN OPTIONS MARKET (AOM) established in 1976 to trade put and call options in the securities of 38 leading Australian companies. Trading is by open outcry and is quote driven, with liquidity provided by market makers. The Options Automated Trading System, known as OATS, was started in October 1989.

AUSTRALIA STOCK EXCHANGE (ASX) six trading floors, formerly independent entities in Adelaide, Brisbane, Hobart (Tasmania), Melbourne, Perth, and Sydney, are linked through the Stock Exchange Automated Trading System (SEATS). Administrative headquarters is in Sydney. The most important Australian stocks are tracked by the ALL ORDINARIES INDEX. Settlement is five business days after a transaction, with less actively traded shares taking longer. In October 1993, the ASX launched Flexible Auxiliary Security Transfer (FAST), a computerized system. SEATS trading hours are 10 A.M.–4 P.M. (EST) Monday through Friday; dealings are permitted outside these hours according to the exchange's after-hours trading rules.

AUTEX SYSTEM electronic system for alerting brokers that other brokers want to buy or sell large blocks of stock. Once a match is made, the actual transaction takes place over the counter or on the floor of an exchange.

AUTHENTICATION identification of a bond certificate as having been issued under a specific indenture, thus validating the bond. Also, legal verification of the genuineness of a document, as by the certification and seal of an authorized public official.

AUTHORITY BOND bond issued by and payable from the revenue of a government agency or a corporation formed to administer a revenue producing public enterprise. One such corporation is the Port Authority of New York and New Jersey, which operates bridges and tunnels in the New York City area. Because an authority usually has no source of revenue other than charges for the facilities it operates, its bonds have the characteristics of revenue bonds. The difference is that bondholder protections may be incorporated in the authority bond contract as well as in the legislation that created the authority.

AUTHORIZED SHARES maximum number of shares of any class a company may legally create under the terms of its ARTICLES OF INCORPORATION. Normally, a corporation provides for future increases in authorized stock by vote of the stockholders. The corporation is not required to issue all the shares authorized and may initially keep issued shares at a minimum to hold down taxes and expenses. Also called *authorized stock.*

AUTOMATED BOND SYSTEM (ABS) New York Stock Exchange computerized system that records bids and offers for inactively traded bonds until they are cancelled or executed. Before the ABS, such limit orders were kept in steel cabinets, giving rise to the terms CABINET SECURITY and CABINET CROWD (traders in inactive bonds).

AUTOMATED ORDER ENTRY SYSTEM electronic system that expedites the execution of smaller orders by channeling them directly to the specialist on the exchange floor, bypassing the FLOOR BROKER. The New York Stock Exchange calls its system DOT (Designated Order Turnaround). Other systems include Auto Ex, OSS, PACE, SOES, and SOREX.

AUTOMATIC EXTENSION granting of more time for a taxpayer to file a tax return. By filing an IRS Form 4868 by the original due date of the tax return, a taxpayer can automatically extend his or her filing date by four months, though the tax payment (based on the taxpayer's best estimate) is still due on the original filing date.

AUTOMATIC FUNDS TRANSFER fast and accurate transfer of funds, often internationally, from one account or investment vehicle to another without direct management, using modern electronic and telecommunications technology. A broker's instant transfer of stock sale proceeds to a money market fund is one example.

AUTOMATIC INVESTMENT PROGRAM any program in which an investor can accumulate or withdraw funds automatically. Some of the most popular automatic investment programs include:
• mutual fund debit programs, in which a mutual fund will automatically debit a preset amount from a bank savings or checking account to buy fund shares on a weekly, monthly, quarterly, or annual basis.
• mutual fund reinvestment programs, in which all dividends and capital gains are automatically reinvested in more shares of the fund.
• stock dividend reinvestment plans, in which companies offer their shareholders the opportunity to reinvest their dividends in more shares of the company, and in some cases, buy additional shares at a discount with little or no brokerage commissions.
• defined contribution plans, offered by employers to their employees, which allow automatic investment in several funds through payroll deduction. Corporate plans are called 401(k), nonprofit and educational plans are called 403(b), and federal and municipal government plans are called 457s. To entice employees to participate in these plans, many employers match employee contributions.
• savings bond payroll savings plans, which allow employees to purchase savings bonds through payroll deduction.
    In addition to allowing automatic purchases of shares, automatic investment programs also permit participants to withdraw a set amount of money on a regular basis. These are known as AUTOMATIC WITHDRAWAL plans. For example, a retiree may request that a mutual fund automatically sell a fixed dollar amount of shares every month and send them a check.

AUTOMATIC REINVESTMENT see CONSTANT DOLLAR PLAN; DIVIDEND REINVESTMENT PLAN.

AUTOMATIC WITHDRAWAL mutual fund program that entitles shareholders to a fixed payment each month or each quarter. The payment comes from dividends, including realized capital gains and income on securities held by the fund.

AVERAGE appropriately weighted and adjusted ARITHMETIC MEAN of selected securities designed to represent market behavior generally or important segments of the market. Among the most familiar averages are the Dow Jones industrial and transportation averages.
    Because the evaluation of individual securities involves measuring price trends of securities in general or within an industry group, the various averages are important analytical tools.
    See also STOCK INDEXES AND AVERAGES.

AVERAGE COST

Investing: average cost of shares of stock or in a fund bought at different prices. *See also* AVERAGE DOWN; AVERAGE UP; CONSTANT DOLLAR PLAN.

Manufacturing: total of fixed and variable costs divided by units of production. Companies with relatively low average costs are better able to withstand price-cutting pressures from competition. Term also describes INVENTORY valuation method whereby the cost of goods available for sale is divided by the number of units available for sale.

AVERAGE DAILY BALANCE method for computing interest or finance charges on bank deposit accounts, credit cards, and charge accounts. Deposit accounts use the daily closing balance divided by the number of days in the period and apply the interest rate to that. Credit and charge cards divide the balances owed each day by the number of days and apply the finance charge. The average daily balance method, widely used by department stores, is less favorable to the consumer than the ADJUSTED BALANCE METHOD used for interest earned on bank deposit accounts but more favorable than the PREVIOUS BALANCE METHOD used by most credit cards.

AVERAGE DOWN strategy to lower the average price paid for a company's shares. An investor who wants to buy 1000 shares, for example, could buy 400 at the current market price and three blocks of 200 each as the price fell. The average cost would then be lower than it would have been if all 1000 shares had been bought at once. Investors also average down in order to realize tax losses. Say someone buys shares at $20, then watches them fall to $10. Instead of doing nothing, the investor can buy at $10, then sell the $20 shares at a capital loss, which can be used at tax time to offset other gains. However, the WASH SALE rule says that in order to claim the capital loss, the investor must not sell the $20 stock until at least 30 days after buying the stock at $10. *See also* CONSTANT DOLLAR PLAN.

AVERAGE EQUITY average daily balance in a trading account. Brokerage firms calculate customer equity daily as part of their procedure for keeping track of gains and losses on uncompleted transactions, called MARK TO THE MARKET. When transactions are completed, profits and losses are booked to each customer's account together with brokerage commissions. Even though daily fluctuations in equity are routine, average equity is a useful guide in making trading decisions and ensuring sufficient equity to meet MARGIN REQUIREMENTS.

AVERAGE LIFE average length of time before the principal of a debt issue is scheduled to be repaid through AMORTIZATION or SINKING FUND payments. *See also* HALF-LIFE.

AVERAGE UP buy on a rising market so as to lower the overall cost. Buying an equal number of shares at $50, $52, $54, and $58, for instance, will make the average cost $53.50. This is a mathematical reality, but it does not determine whether the stock is worth buying at any or all of these prices.

AVERAGING *see* CONSTANT DOLLAR PLAN.

AWAY FROM THE MARKET expression used when the bid on a LIMIT ORDER is lower or the offer price is higher than the current market price for the security. Away from the market limit orders are held by the specialist for later execution unless FILL OR KILL (FOK) is stipulated on the order entry.

b

BABY BELLS the seven regional telephone companies created when AT&T was broken up in 1984. The original consent decree creating the Baby Bells gave them a monopoly over local phone service but banned them from participating in the long-distance or equipment manufacturing business. AT&T was excluded from the local phone business in return. Over time these distinctions have been eroded. The seven Baby Bells are: NYNEX in the Northeast; Bell Atlantic in the Mid-Atlantic states; BELLSOUTH in the South; SBC (Southwestern Bell Corp.) in the Southwest; Ameritech in the Midwest; U.S. West in the Rocky Mountain States; and Pacific Telesis in the West.

BABY BOND convertible or straight debt bond having a par value of less than $1000, usually $500 to $25. Baby bonds bring the bond market within reach of small investors and, by the same token, open a source of funds to corporations that lack entree to the large institutional market. On the negative side, they entail higher administrative costs (relative to the total money raised) for distribution and processing and lack the large and active market that ensures the liquidity of conventional bonds.

BACKDATING
In general: dating any statement, document, check or other instrument earlier than the date drawn.
Mutual funds: feature permitting fundholders to use an earlier date on a promise to invest a specified sum over a specified period in exchange for a reduced sales charge. Backdating, which usually accompanies a large transaction, gives retroactive value to purchases from the earlier date in order to meet the requirements of the promise, or LETTER OF INTENT.

BACK-END LOAD redemption charge an investor pays when withdrawing money from an investment. Most common in mutual funds and annuities, the back-end load is designed to discourage withdrawals. Back-end loads typically decline for each year that a shareholder remains in a fund. For example, if the shareholder sells shares in the first year, a 5% sales charge is levied. The charge is 4% in the second year, 3% in the third year, 2% in the fourth year, 1% in the fifth year, and no fee is charged if shares are sold after the fifth year. Also called *contingent deferred sales load, deferred sales charge, exit fee, redemption charge.*

BACKING AWAY broker-dealer's failure, as market maker in a given security, to make good on a bid for the minimum quantity. This practice is considered unethical under the RULES OF FAIR PRACTICE of the NATIONAL ASSOCIATION OF SECURITIES DEALERS.

BACKLOG value of unfilled orders placed with a manufacturing company. Whether the firm's backlog is rising or falling is a clue to its future sales and earnings.

BACK MONTHS in futures and options trading, the months with the expiration dates furthest out in time. *See also* FURTHEST MONTH.

BACK OFFICE bank or brokerage house departments not directly involved in selling or trading. The back office sees to accounting records, compliance with government regulations, and communication between branches. When stock-market trading is particularly heavy, order processing can be slowed by massive volume; this is called a back office crunch.

BACK TAXES taxes that have not been paid when due. Taxpayers may owe back taxes if they underreported income or overstated deductions, either accidentally, or by design. The Internal Revenue Service and state and local taxing authorities have the right to audit past tax returns and demand payment of back taxes, plus interest and penalties.

BACK UP turn around; reverse a stock market trend. When prices are moving in one direction, traders would say of a sudden reversal that the market backed up.

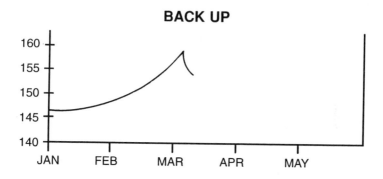

BACK UP

BACKUP LINE BANK LINE of credit in the name of an issuer of commercial paper, covering maturing notes in the event that new notes cannot be marketed to replace them. Ideally, the unused line should always equal the commercial paper outstanding. In practice, something less than total coverage is commonplace, particularly because the compensating balances normally required in support of the line are also available to meet maturing paper.

BACKUP WITHHOLDING system used by the Internal Revenue Service to ensure that taxpayers without Social Security numbers have taxes withheld on earnings. In an instance where a Form 1099 can not be filed by a payor, such as a bank or brokerage, 20% of the interest or dividends is withheld and remitted to the IRS. To avoid backup withholding, you must fill out a federal W-9 form for the financial institution, verifying that your Social Security number is correct.

BACKWARDATION
1. pricing structure in commodities or foreign-exchange trading in which deliveries in the near future have a higher price than those made later on. Backwardation occurs when demand is greater in the near future. *See also* CONTANGO.
2. London Stock Exchange term for the fees and interest due on short sales of stock with delayed delivery.

BAD DEBT open account balance or loan receivable that has proven uncollectible and is written off. Traditionally, companies and financial institutions have maintained a RESERVE for uncollectible accounts, charging the reserve for actual bad debts and making annual, tax deductible charges to income to replenish or increase the reserve. The TAX REFORM ACT OF 1986 required companies and large banks ($500 million or more in assets) to convert from the reserve method to a direct charge-off method for tax purposes beginning in 1987, although bad debt reserves will continue to appear on balance sheets for reporting purposes. Small banks and thrift institutions were allowed to continue using the reserve method for tax purposes, although with stricter limitations. The relationship of bad debt write-offs and recoveries to accounts receivable can reveal how liberal or conservative a firm's credit and charge-off policies are.

BAD DELIVERY opposite of GOOD DELIVERY.

BAD TITLE title to property that does not clearly confer ownership. Most frequently applied to real estate, a bad title may prevent a homeowner from selling the property. Title may be clouded by unpaid taxes or other unsatisfied liens, a faulty or incomplete certificate of occupancy, an incorrect survey, or uncorrected building violations, among other causes. Steps must be taken to rectify these problems before title to a property can be legally transferred. Also called *cloud on title.*

BAILING OUT selling a security or commodity quickly without regard to the price received. An investor bails out of a position if losses are mounting quickly and he or she is no longer able to sustain further losses. For example, someone who has sold a stock short may bail out by covering his or her position at a loss if the stock rises sharply.

The term is also used to describe the act of rescuing a person or corporate or government entity in financial distress. For example, the federal government bailed out the Federal Deposit Insurance Corporation with hundreds of billions of dollars when it had to pay for closing down hundreds of bankrupt savings and loans through the Resolution Trust Corporation. When the Chrysler Corporation was teetering near bankruptcy in the early 1980s, the federal government bailed it out by providing loan guarantees.

BAILOUT BOND BOND issued by RESOLUTION FUNDING CORPORATION (REFCORP) to finance the rescue or disposition of SAVINGS AND LOAN ASSOCIATIONS that were failing in the 1980s. The principal of REFCORP securities is backed by zero-coupon Treasury bonds and the U.S. Treasury guarantees interest payments. Because this is stronger backing than that enjoyed by other GOVERNMENT SECURITIES issued by agencies, bailout bonds yield only slightly more than TREASURIES of comparable maturity. *See also* OFFICE OF THRIFT SUPERVISION (OTS).

BALANCED BUDGET *see* BUDGET.

BALANCED MUTUAL FUND fund that buys common stock, preferred stock, and bonds in an effort to obtain the highest return consistent with a low-risk strategy. A balanced fund typically offers a higher yield than a pure stock fund and performs better than such a fund when stocks are falling. In a rising market, however, a balanced mutual fund usually will not keep pace with all-equity funds.

BALANCE OF PAYMENTS system of recording all of a country's economic transactions with the rest of the world during a particular time period. Double-entry bookkeeping is used, and there can be no surplus or deficit on the overall balance of payments. The balance of payments is typically divided into three accounts—current, capital, and gold—and these can show a surplus or deficit. The current account covers imports and exports of goods and services; the capital account covers movements of investments; and the gold account covers gold movements. The balance of payments helps a country evaluate its competitive strengths and weaknesses and forecast the strength of its currency. From the standpoint of a national economy, a surplus on a part of the balance of payments is not necessarily good, nor is a deficit necessarily bad; the state of the national economy and the manner of financing the deficit are important considerations. *See also* BALANCE OF TRADE.

BALANCE OF TRADE net difference over a period of time between the value of a country's imports and exports of merchandise. Movable goods such as automobiles, foodstuffs, and apparel are included in the balance of trade; payments abroad for services and for tourism are not. When a country exports more than it imports, it is said to have a favorable balance of trade; when imports predominate the balance is called unfavorable. The balance of trade should be viewed in the context of the country's entire international economic position, however. For example, a country may consistently have an unfavorable balance of trade that is offset by considerable exports of services; this country would be judged to have a good international economic position. *See also* BALANCE OF PAYMENTS.

BALANCE SHEET financial report, also called *statement of condition* or *statement of financial position,* showing the status of a company's assets, liabilities, and owners' equity on a given date, usually the close of a month. One way of looking at a business enterprise is as a mass of capital (ASSETS) arrayed against the sources of that capital (LIABILITIES and EQUITY). Assets are equal to liabilities and equity, and the balance sheet is a listing of the items making up the two sides of the equation. Unlike a PROFIT AND LOSS STATEMENT, which shows the results of operations over a period of time, a balance sheet shows the state of affairs at one point in time. It is a snapshot, not a motion picture, and must be analyzed with reference to comparative prior balance sheets and other operating statements.

BALLOON final payment on a debt that is substantially larger than the preceding payments. Loans or mortgages are structured with balloon payments when some projected event is expected to provide extra cash flow or when refinancing is anticipated. Balloon loans are sometimes called *partially amortized loans.*

BALLOON INTEREST in serial bond issues, the higher COUPON rate on bonds with later maturities.

BALLOON MATURITY bond issue or long-term loan with larger dollar amounts of bonds or payments falling due in the later years of the obligation.

BAN *see* BOND ANTICIPATION NOTE.

BANKER'S ACCEPTANCE *see* ACCEPTANCE.

BANK DISCOUNT BASIS *see* DISCOUNT YIELD.

BANK HOLDING COMPANY company that owns or controls two or more banks or other bank holding companies. As defined in the Bank Holding Company Act of 1956, such companies must register with the BOARD OF GOVERNORS of the FEDERAL RESERVE SYSTEM and hence are called registered bank holding companies. Amendments to the 1956 act set standards for acquisitions (1966) and ended the exemption enjoyed by one-bank holding companies (1970), thus restricting bank holding companies to activities related to banking.

BANK INSURANCE FUND (BIF) FEDERAL DEPOSIT INSURANCE CORPORATION (FDIC) unit providing deposit insurance for banks other than thrifts. BIF was formed as part of the 1989 savings and loan association bailout bill to keep separate the administration of the bank and thrift insurance programs. There are thus two distinct insurance entities under FDIC: BIF and SAVINGS ASSOCIATION INSURANCE FUND (SAIF). Deposit insurance coverage remains unaffected. *See also* OFFICE OF THRIFT SUPERVISION (OTS).

BANK INVESTMENT CONTRACT (BIC) bank-guaranteed interest in a portfolio providing a specified yield over a specified period. For insurance company equivalent, *see* GUARANTEED INVESTMENT CONTRACT (GIC).

BANK LINE bank's moral commitment, as opposed to its contractual commitment, to make loans to a particular borrower up to a specified maximum during a specified period, usually one year. Because a bank line—also called a *line of credit*—is not a legal commitment, it is not customary to charge a commitment fee. It is common, however, to require that compensating balances be kept on deposit—typically 10% of the line, with an additional 10% of any borrowings under the line. A line about which a customer is officially notified is called an *advised line* or *confirmed line*. A line that is an internal policy guide about which the customer is not informed is termed a *guidance line*.

BANKMAIL bank's agreement with a company involved in a TAKEOVER not to finance another acquirer's bid.

BANK QUALITY *see* INVESTMENT GRADE.

BANKRUPTCY state of insolvency of an individual or an organization— in other words, an inability to pay debts. There are two kinds of legal bankruptcy under U.S. law: involuntary, when one or more creditors petition to have a debtor judged insolvent by a court; and voluntary, when the debtor brings the petition. In both cases, the objective is an orderly and equitable settlement of obligations.

The 1978 Bankruptcy Reform Act removed some of the rigidities of the old law and permitted more flexibility in procedures. The Bankruptcy Reform Act of 1984 curtailed some of the more liberal provisions (mainly affecting consumer bankruptcy) of the 1978 act.

Chapter 7 of the 1978 act, dealing with LIQUIDATION, provides for a court-appointed interim trustee with broad powers and discretion to make management changes, arrange unsecured financing, and generally operate the debtor business in such a way as to prevent loss. Only by filing an appropriate bond is the debtor able to regain possession from the trustee.

Chapter 11, which deals with REORGANIZATION, provides that, unless the court rules otherwise, the debtor remains in possession of the business and in control of its operation. Debtor and creditors are allowed considerable flexibility in working together. The 1978 law relaxes the old *absolute priority rule,* which gave creditor claims categorical precedence over ownership claims. It also makes possible the negotiation of payment schedules, the restructuring of debt, and even the granting of loans by the creditors to the debtor.

BANK TRUST DEPARTMENT part of a bank engaged in settling estates, administering trusts and guardianships, and performing AGENCY services. As part of its personal trust and ESTATE PLANNING services, it manages investments for large accounts—typically those with at least $50,000 in assets. People who cannot or do not want to make investment decisions are commonly bank trust department clients. Known for their conservative investment philosophy, such departments have custody over billions of dollars, making them a major factor in the movement of stock and bond prices.

Among other things, the departments also act as trustee for corporate bonds, administer pension and profit-sharing plans, and function as TRANSFER AGENTS.

BANK WIRE computerized message system owned and administered by about 250 participating banks in about 75 U.S. cities. Like the FED WIRE, the bank wire transmits large dollar credit transfer information. It also provides information about loan participations, securities transactions, Federal Reserve System funds borrowings, credit history, the payment or nonpayment of "wire fate" items, and other essential matters requiring prompt communication.

BARBELL PORTFOLIO portfolio of bonds distributed like the shape of a barbell, with most of the portfolio in short-term and long-term bonds, but few bonds in intermediate maturities. This portfolio can be adjusted to emphasize short- or long-term bonds, depending on whether the investor thinks interest rates are rising or falling. A portfolio with a higher concentration in medium-term bonds than short- or long-term bonds is called a *bell-shaped curve portfolio.*

BAREFOOT PILGRIM unsophisticated investor who has lost his or her shirt and shoes in securities trading.

BAROMETER selective compilation of economic and market data designed to represent larger trends. Consumer spending, housing starts, and interest rates are barometers used in economic forecasting. The Dow Jones Industrial Average and the Standard & Poor's 500 Stock Index are prominent stock market barometers. The Dow Jones Utility Average is a barometer of market trends in the utility industry.

A *barometer stock* has a price movement pattern that reflects the market as a whole, thus serving as a market indicator. General Motors, for example, is considered a barometer stock.

BARRON'S CONFIDENCE INDEX weekly index of corporate bond yields published by *Barron's,* a Dow Jones financial newspaper. The index shows the ratio of Barron's average yield on 10 top-grade bonds to the Dow Jones average yield on 40 bonds. People who are worried about the economic outlook tend to seek high quality, whereas investors who feel secure about the economy are more likely to buy lower-rated bonds. The spread between high- and low-grade bonds thus reflects investor opinion about the economy.

BARTER trade of goods or services without use of money. When money is involved, whether in such forms as wampum, checks, or bills or coins, a transaction is called a SALE. Although barter is usually associated with undeveloped economies, it occurs in modern complex societies. In conditions of extreme inflation, it can be a preferred mode of commerce. Where a population lacks confidence in its currency or banking system, barter becomes commonplace. In international trade, barter can provide a way of doing business with countries whose soft currencies would otherwise make them unattractive trading partners.

BASE MARKET VALUE average market price of a group of securities at a given time. It is used as a basis of comparison in plotting dollar or percentage changes for purposes of market INDEXING.

BASE PERIOD particular time in the past used as a yardstick when measuring economic data. A base period is usually a year or an average of years; it can also be a month or other time period. The U.S. rate of inflation is determined by measuring current prices against those of a base period; for instance, the Consumer Price Index is determined by comparing current prices with prices in the base reference years of 1982–1984.

BASE RATE interest rate charged by banks to their best corporate customers in Great Britain. It is the British equivalent of the PRIME RATE in the United States. Many other consumer loan rates are pegged to the base rate in Britain.

BASIS

In general: original cost plus out-of-pocket expenses that must be reported to the Internal Revenue Service when an investment is sold and must be used in calculating capital gains or losses. If a stock was bought for $1000 two years ago and is sold today for $2000, the basis is $1000 and the profit is a capital gain.

Bonds: an investor's YIELD TO MATURITY at a given bond price. A 10% bond selling at 100 has a 10% basis.

Commodities: the difference between the cash price of a hedged money market instrument and a FUTURES CONTRACT.

BASIS POINT smallest measure used in quoting yields on bills, notes, and bonds. One basis point is .01%, or one one-hundredth of a percent of yield. Thus, 100 basis points equal 1%. A bond's yield that increased from 8.00% to 8.50% would be said to have risen 50 basis points.

BASIS PRICE
In general: price an investor uses to calculate capital gains when selling a stock or bond. *See also* BASIS.

Odd-lot trading: the price arbitrarily established by an exchange floor official at the end of a trading session for a buyer or seller of an odd lot when the market bid and asked prices are more than $2 apart, or if no round-lot transactions have occurred that day. The customer gets the basis price plus or minus the odd-lot differential, if any. This procedure for determining prices is rare, since most odd lots are transacted at the market bid (if a sale) or asked (if a buy) or at prices based on the next round-lot trade.

BASKET
1. unit of 15 or more stocks used in PROGRAM TRADING.
2. program trading vehicles offered by the New York Stock Exchange (called *Exchange Stock Portfolio* or *ESP)* and the Chicago Board Options Exchange (called *Market Basket)* to institutional investors and index arbitrageurs. Both baskets permit the purchase in one trade of all the stocks making up the STANDARD & POOR'S INDEX of 500 stocks. ESP's design requires a minimum trade of approximately $5 million, and Market Basket's, around $1.7 million. The baskets were introduced in late 1989 to solve problems revealed when institutions tried to negotiate large block trades on BLACK MONDAY and to head off an exodus of program trading business to overseas exchanges.
3. informal name for *index participations* (also called *cash index participations* or *CIPS)*, a controversial new financial instrument introduced and then withdrawn by the American and Philadelphia stock exchanges in 1989. The product allowed small investors to buy a portfolio position (in the Standard & Poor's Index of 500 stocks and in a 25-stock index that has historically correlated with the Dow Jones Industrial Average) without buying individual stocks. It retained advantages of stock ownership by having no expiration date (like a future or an option) and providing for quarterly dividend payments. Originally approved by the Securities and Exchange Commission as a security, the instrument was challenged by the Commodities Futures Trading Commission, which claimed it was a futures contract. When a federal court ruled against the SEC, the exchanges stopped trading the product.
See also SPIDERS.

BD FORM document that brokerage house must file and keep current with the Securities and Exchange Commission, detailing the firm's finances and officers.

BEACON acronym for the *Boston Exchange Automated Communication Order-routing Network.* This electronic system allows the automatic execution of trades based on the prevailing stock prices on the consolidated market, any of the seven U.S. securities exchanges.

BEAR person with a pessimistic market outlook. Contrast with BULL.

BEARER BOND *see* COUPON BOND.

BEARER FORM security not registered on the books of the issuing corporation and thus payable to the one possessing it. A bearer bond has coupons attached, which the bondholder sends in or presents on the interest date for payment, hence the alternative name COUPON BONDS. Bearer stock certificates are negotiable without endorsement and are transferred by delivery. Dividends are payable by presentation of dividend coupons, which are dated or numbered. Most securities issued today, with the exception of foreign stocks, are in registered form, including municipal bonds issued since 1983.

BEAR HUG TAKEOVER bid so attractive in terms of price and other features that TARGET COMPANY directors, who might be opposed for other reasons, must approve it or risk shareholder protest.

BEAR MARKET prolonged period of falling prices. A bear market in stocks is usually brought on by the anticipation of declining economic activity, and a bear market in bonds is caused by rising interest rates.

BEAR RAID attempt by investors to manipulate the price of a stock by selling large numbers of shares short. The manipulators pocket the difference between the initial price and the new, lower price after this maneuver. Bear raids are illegal under Securities and Exchange Commission rules, which stipulate that every SHORT SALE be executed on an UPTICK (the last price was higher than the price before it) or a ZERO PLUS TICK (the last price was unchanged but higher than the last preceding different price).

BEARS acronym for *Bonds Enabling Annual Retirement Savings* and the flip side of *CUBS*, acronym for *Calls Underwritten By Swanbrook*. Holders of BEARS receive the face value of bonds underlying call options but exercised by CUBS holders. If the calls are exercised, BEARS holders receive the aggregate of the exercise prices.

BEAR SPREAD strategy in the options market designed to take advantage of a fall in the price of a security or commodity. Someone executing a bear spread could buy a combination of calls and puts on the same security at different *strike prices* in order to profit as the security's price fell. Or the investor could buy a put of short maturity and a put of long maturity in order to profit from the difference between the two puts as prices fell. *See also* BULL SPREAD.

BEAR TRAP situation confronting short sellers when a bear market reverses itself and turns bullish. Anticipating further declines, the bears continue to sell, and then are forced to buy at higher prices to cover. *See also* SELLING SHORT.

BELL signal that opens and closes trading on major exchanges—sometimes actually a bell but sometimes a buzzer sound.

BELLWETHER security seen as an indicator of a market's direction. In stocks, 3M Company (MMM) is considered both an economic and a market bellwether because it sells to a diverse range of other producers and because so much of its stock is owned by institutional investors who have much control over supply and demand on the stock market. Institutional trading actions tend to influence smaller investors and therefore the market generally. In bonds, the 20-year U.S. Treasury bond is considered the bellwether, denoting the direction in which all other bonds are likely to move.

BELOW PAR *see* PAR VALUE.

BENEFICIAL OWNER person who enjoys the benefits of ownership even though title is in another name. When shares of a mutual fund are held by a custodian bank or when securities are held by a broker in STREET NAME, the real owner is the beneficial owner, even though, for safety or convenience, the bank or broker holds title.

BENEFICIARY
1. person to whom an inheritance passes as the result of being named in a will.
2. recipient of the proceeds of a life insurance policy.
3. party in whose favor a LETTER OF CREDIT is issued.
4. one to whom the amount of an ANNUITY is payable.
5. party for whose benefit a TRUST exists.

BEQUEST giving of assets, such as stocks, bonds, mutual funds, real estate, and personal property, to beneficiaries through the provisions of a will.

BEST EFFORT arrangement whereby investment bankers, acting as agents, agree to do their best to sell an issue to the public. Instead of buying the securities outright, these agents have an option to buy and an authority to sell the securities. Depending on the contract, the agents exercise their option and buy enough shares to cover their sales to clients, or they cancel the incompletely sold issue altogether and forgo the fee. Best efforts deals, which were common prior to 1900, entailed risks and delays from the issuer's standpoint. What is more, the broadening of the securities markets has made marketing new issues easier, and the practice of outright purchase by investment bankers, called FIRM COMMITMENT underwriting, has become commonplace. For the most part, the best efforts deals we occasionally see today are handled by firms specializing in the more speculative securities of new and unseasoned companies. *See also* BOUGHT DEAL.

BEST'S RATING rating of financial soundness given to insurance companies by Best's Rating Service. The top rating is A+. A Best's rating is important to buyers of insurance or annuities because it informs them whether a company is financially sound. Best's Ratings are also important to investors in insurance stocks.

BETA
1. coefficient measuring a stock's relative VOLATILITY. The beta is the covariance of a stock in relation to the rest of the stock market. The Standard & Poor's 500 Stock Index has a beta coefficient of 1. Any stock with a higher beta is more volatile than the market, and any with a lower beta can be expected to rise and fall more slowly than the market. A conservative investor whose main concern is preservation of capital should focus on stocks with low betas, whereas one willing to take high risks in an effort to earn high rewards should look for high-beta stocks. *See also* ALPHA.
2. on the London Stock Exchange, the designation *beta stocks* applies to the second tier in a four-level hierarchy introduced with BIG BANG in October 1986 and replaced in January, 1991 with the NORMAL MARKET SIZE (NMS) classification system. With ALPHA stocks representing the equivalent of American BLUE CHIP issues, beta stocks represented smaller issues that were less actively traded. *See also* DELTA (2); GAMMA STOCKS.

BID
1. price a prospective buyer is ready to pay. Term is used by traders who MAKE A MARKET (maintain firm bid and OFFER prices) in a given security by standing ready to buy or sell round lots at publicly quoted prices and by the SPECIALIST in a stock, who performs a similar function on an exchange.
2. TENDER OFFER in a TAKEOVER attempt.

3. any offer to buy at a specified price.
See also ANY-AND-ALL BID; COMPETITIVE BID; TREASURIES.

BID AND ASKED bid is the highest price a prospective buyer is prepared to pay at a particular time for a trading unit of a given security; asked is the lowest price acceptable to a prospective seller of the same security. Together, the two prices constitute a QUOTATION; the difference between the two prices is the SPREAD. Although the bid and asked dynamic is common to all securities trading, "bid and asked" usually refers to UNLISTED SECURITIES traded OVER THE COUNTER.

BID-ASKED SPREAD difference between BID and offer prices. The term *asked* is usually used in OVER-THE COUNTER trading; *offered* is used in exchange trading. The bid and asked (or offered) prices together comprise a QUOTATION (or *quote*).

BIDDER party that is ready to buy at a specified price in a TWO-SIDED MARKET or DUTCH AUCTION.

BIDDING UP practice whereby the price bid for a security is successively moved higher lest an upswing in prices leaves orders unexecuted. An example would be an investor wanting to purchase a sizable quantity of shares in a rising market, using buy limit orders (orders to buy at a specified price or lower) to ensure the most favorable price. Since offer prices are moving up with the market, the investor must move his limit buy price upward to continue accumulating shares. To some extent the buyer is contributing to the upward price pressure on the stock, but most of the price rise is out of his control.

BID-TO-COVER RATIO number of bids received in a Treasury security auction compared to the number of bids accepted. A high ratio (over 2.0) is an indication that bidding was aggressive and the auction successful. A low ratio, indicating the government had difficulty selling its securities, is usually accompanied by a long TAIL, a wide spread between the average and high yield (the average and lowest accepted bid).

BID WANTED (BW) announcement that a holder of securities wants to sell and will entertain bids. Because the final price is subject to negotiation, the bid submitted in response to a BW need not be specific. A BW is frequently seen on published market quotation sheets.

BIG BANG deregulation on October 27, 1986, of London-based securities markets, an event comparable to MAY DAY in the United States and marking a major step toward a single world financial market.

BIG BLUE popular name for International Business Machines Corporation (IBM), taken from the color of its logotype.

BIG BOARD popular term for the NEW YORK STOCK EXCHANGE.

BIG PRODUCER broker who is very successful, and thereby produces a large volume of commission dollars for the brokerage firm he or she represents. Big producers typically will bring in $1 million or more per year in commissions for their firms. In order to retain big producers, many brokerage firms try to tie them to the firm with GOLDEN HANDCUFFS.

BIG SIX largest U.S. accounting firms as measured by revenue. They do the accounting and auditing for most major corporations, signing the auditor's report that appears in every annual report. They also offer various consulting services. Over time, there have been several mergers among the top accounting firms, which formerly were called the Big Eight. In alphabetical order they are: Arthur Andersen & Co.; Coopers & Lybrand; Deloitte & Touche; Ernst & Young; KPMG Peat Marwick; and Price Waterhouse & Co.

BIG THREE the three large automobile companies in America, which are, alphabetically, Chrysler, Ford, and General Motors. Since the automobile business has such a major influence on the direction of the economy, the Big Three's fortunes are closely followed by investors, analysts, and economists. Because auto company profits rise and fall with the economy, they are considered to be CYCLICAL STOCKS.

In Switzerland, the term Big Three refers to the three most dominant banking institutions—Credit Suisse, Swiss Bank Corporation, and Union Bank of Switzerland.

BIG UGLIES stocks that are out of favor with the investing public. These usually are large industrial companies such as steel or chemical firms that are not in glamorous businesses. Because they are unpopular, Big Uglies typically sell at low price/earnings and price/book value ratios.

BILL

In general: (1) short for *bill of exchange,* an order by one person directing a second to pay a third. (2) document evidencing a debtor's obligation to a creditor, the kind of bill we are all familiar with. (3) paper currency, like the $5 bill. (4) *bill of sale,* a document used to transfer the title to certain goods from seller to buyer in the same way a deed to real property passes.

Investments: short for *due bill,* a statement of money owed. Commonly used to adjust a securities transaction when dividends, interest, and other distributions are reflected in a price but have not yet been disbursed. For example, when a stock is sold ex-dividend, but the dividend has not yet been paid, the buyer would sign a due bill stating that the amount of the dividend is payable to the seller.

A due bill may accompany delivered securities to give title to the buyer's broker in exchange for shares or money.

U.S. Treasury bill: commonly called bill or T-bill by money market people, a Treasury bill is a short-term (maturities up to a year), discounted government security sold through competitive bidding at weekly and monthly auctions in denominations from $10,000 to $1 million.

The auction at which bills are sold differs from the two-sided auction used by exchanges. Here, in what is sometimes termed a *Dutch auction,* the Treasury invites anyone interested to submit a bid, called a TENDER, then awards units to the highest bidders going down a list. Three-and six-month bills are auctioned weekly, nine-month and one-year bills monthly. Although the yield on bills may barely top the inflation rate, the high degree of safety together with the liquidity provided by an active SECONDARY MARKET make bills popular with corporate money managers as well as with banks and other government entities.

Individuals may also purchase bills directly, in amounts under $500,000, at no transaction charge, from a Federal Reserve bank, the Bureau of Federal Debt, or certain commercial banks. Bills bought on this basis are priced by noncompetitive bidding, with subscribers paying an average of the accepted bids.

Treasury bills are the most widely used of all government debt securities and are a primary instrument of Federal Reserve monetary policy. *See also* TAX ANTICIPATION BILL; TREASURY DIRECT.

BILLING CYCLE interval between periodic billings for goods sold or services rendered, normally one month, or a system whereby bills or statements are mailed at periodic intervals in the course of a month in order to distribute the clerical workload.

BILL OF EXCHANGE *see* DRAFT.

BINDER sum of money paid to evidence good faith until a transaction is finalized. In insurance, the binder is an agreement executed by an insurer (or sometimes an agent) that puts insurance coverage into force before the contract is signed and the premium paid. In real estate, the binder holds the sale until the closing and is refundable.

BI-WEEKLY MORTGAGE LOAN mortgage loan on which the borrower makes 26 half-month payments a year, resulting in earlier loan retirement and lower total interest costs than with a fully amortized loan with regular monthly payments. For example, a 30-year mortgage may be retired in 20 years if paid bi-weekly. Many bi-weekly plans offer automatic electronic debiting of the borrower's bank account.

BLACK FRIDAY sharp drop in a financial market. The original Black Friday was September 24, 1869, when a group of financiers tried to corner the gold market and precipitated a business panic followed by a depression. The panic of 1873 also began on Friday, and Black Friday has come to apply to any debacle affecting the financial markets.

BLACK MONDAY October 19, 1987, when the Dow Jones Industrial Average plunged a record 508 points following sharp drops the previous week, reflecting investor anxiety about inflated stock price levels, federal budget and trade deficits, and foreign market activity. Many blamed PROGRAM TRADING for the extreme VOLATILITY.

BLACK-SCHOLES OPTION PRICING MODEL model developed by Fischer Black and Myron Scholes to gauge whether options contracts are fairly valued. The model incorporates such factors as the volatility of a security's return, the level of interest rates, the relationship of the underlying stock's price to the *strike price* of the option, and the time remaining until the option expires. Current valuations using this model are developed by the Options Monitor Service and are available from Standard & Poor's Trading Systems, 11 Broadway, New York, NY 10004.

BLANK CHECK check drawn on a bank account and signed by the maker, but with the amount of the check to be supplied by the drawee. Term is used as a metaphor for any situation where inordinate trust is placed in another person.

BLANK CHECK OFFERING INITIAL PUBLIC OFFERING (IPO) by a company whose business activities have yet to be determined and which is therefore speculative. Similar to the BLIND POOL concept of limited partnerships.

BLANKET CERTIFICATION FORM *see* NASD FORM FR-1.

BLANKET FIDELITY BOND insurance coverage against losses due to employee dishonesty. Brokerage firms are required to carry such protection in proportion to their net capital as defined by the Securities and Exchange Commission. Contingencies covered include securities loss, forgery, and fraudulent trading. Also called *blanket bond.*

BLANKET RECOMMENDATION communication sent to all customers of a brokerage firm recommending that they buy or sell a particular stock or stocks in a particular industry regardless of investment objectives or portfolio size.

BLENDED RATE mortgage financing term used when a lender, to avoid assuming an old mortgage at an obsoletely low rate, offers the incentive to refinance at a rate somewhere between the old rate and the rate on a new loan.

BLIND POOL limited partnership that does not specify the properties the general partner plans to acquire. If, for example, a real estate partnership is offered in the form of a blind pool, investors can evaluate the project only by looking at the general partner's track record. In a *specified pool,* on the other hand, investors can look at the prices paid for property and the amount of rental income the buildings generate, then evaluate the partnership's potential. In general, blind pool partnerships do not perform better or worse than specified pool partnerships.

BLIND TRUST trust in which a fiduciary third party, such as a bank or money management firm, is given complete discretion to make investments on behalf of the trust beneficiaries. The trust is called blind because the beneficiary is not informed about the holdings of the trust. Blind trusts often are set up when there is a potential conflict of interest involving the beneficiary and the investments held in the trust. For example, a politician may be required to place his assets in a blind trust so that his votes are not influenced by his trust's portfolio holdings.

BLITZKREIG TENDER OFFER TAKEOVER jargon for a tender offer that is completed quickly, usually because it was priced attractively. *Blitzkreig* translates from the German as "lightning-like war" and was used to describe World War II bombing raids. Legislation passed in the 1960s was aimed at curtailing surprise takeovers, so the term is relative. *See also* SATURDAY NIGHT SPECIAL.

BLOCK large quantity of stock or large dollar amount of bonds held or traded. As a general guide, 10,000 shares or more of stock and $200,000 or more worth of bonds would be described as a block.

BLOCK POSITIONER dealer who, to accommodate the seller of a block of securities, will take a position in the securities, hoping to gain from a rise in the market price. Block positioners must register with the Securities and Exchange Commission and the New York Stock Exchange (if member firms). Typically they engage in ARBITRAGE, HEDGING, and SELLING SHORT to protect their risk and liquidate their position.

BLOCK TRADE *see* BLOCK.

BLOWOUT quick sale of all shares in a new offering of securities. Corporations like to sell securities in such environments, because they get a high price for their stock. Investors are likely to have a hard time getting the number of shares they want during a blowout. Also called *going away* or *hot issue.*

BLUE CHIP common stock of a nationally known company that has a long record of profit growth and dividend payment and a reputation for quality management, products, and services. Some examples of blue chip stocks: International Business Machines, General Electric, and Du Pont. Blue chip stocks typically are relatively high priced and have moderate dividend yields.

BLUE LIST daily financial publication listing bonds offered for sale by several hundred dealers and banks and representing billions of dollars in par value. The Blue List, published by a Standard & Poor's subsidiary, mainly contains data on municipal bonds. With its pertinent price, yield, and other data, the Blue List is the most comprehensive source of information on activity and volume in the SECONDARY MARKET for TAX-EXEMPT SECURITIES. Some corporate bonds offered by the same dealers are also included. Full name, *Blue List of Current Municipal Offerings.*

BLUE-SKY LAW law of a kind passed by various states to protect investors against securities fraud. These laws require sellers of new stock issues or mutual funds to register their offerings and provide financial details on each issue so that investors can base their judgments on relevant data. The term is said to have originated with a judge who asserted that a particular stock offering had as much value as a patch of blue sky.

BOARD BROKER employee of the CHICAGO BOARD OPTIONS EXCHANGE who handles AWAY FROM THE MARKET orders, which cannot immediately be executed. If board brokers act as agents in executing such orders, they notify the exchange members who entered the orders.

BOARD OF ARBITRATION group of three or fewer individuals selected to adjudicate cases between securities firms and claims brought by customers. Arbitration is the method approved by the NATIONAL ASSOCIATION OF SECURITIES DEALERS, the MUNICIPAL SECURITIES RULEMAKING BOARD, and the exchanges for resolving disputes, and it applies to both member and nonmember firms. Once the parties to a dispute agree to bring the matter before an arbitration board, the board's ruling is final and binding. Under rule changes approved by the Securities and Exchange Commission (SEC) in 1989, the qualifying standards for arbitrators were made stricter, while the number of arbitrators was lowered from five to three in cases involving claims of $500,000 or more. The ceiling for small claims, conducted with one arbitrator, was raised from $5000 to $10,000. *See also* ARBITRATION.

BOARD OF DIRECTORS group of individuals elected, usually at an annual meeting, by the shareholders of a corporation and empowered to carry out certain tasks as spelled out in the corporation's charter. Among such powers are appointing senior management, naming members of executive and finance committees (if any), issuing additional shares, and declaring dividends. Boards normally include the top corporate executives, termed *inside directors,* as well as OUTSIDE DIRECTORS chosen from business and from the community at large to advise on matters of broad policy. Directors meet several times a year and are paid for their services. They are considered control persons under the securities laws, meaning that their shares are restricted. As insiders, they cannot (1) buy and sell the company's stock within a 6-month period; (2) sell short in the company's stock, and if they sell owned shares must deliver in 20 days and/or place certificates in mail within 5 days; (3) effect any foreign or arbitrage transaction in the company's stock; (4) trade on material information not available to the public.

BOARD OF GOVERNORS OF THE FEDERAL RESERVE SYSTEM seven-member managing body of the FEDERAL RESERVE SYSTEM, commonly called the Federal Reserve Board. The board sets policy on issues relating to banking regulations as well as to the MONEY SUPPLY.

BOARD ROOM
Brokerage house: room where customers can watch an electronic board that displays stock prices and transactions.
Corporation: room where the board of directors holds its meetings.

BO DEREK STOCK perfect stock with an exemplary record of earnings growth, product quality, and stock price appreciation. These stocks are named after the movie "10" in which Bo Derek was depicted as the perfect woman.

BOGEY target for purchasing or selling a security or achieving some other objective. An investor's bogey may be a 10% rate of return from a particular stock. Or it may be locking in an 8% yield on a bond. A money manager's bogey may be to beat the Standard & Poor's 500 index.

BOILERPLATE standard legal language, often in fine print, used in most contracts, wills, indentures, prospectuses, and other legal documents. Although what the boilerplate says is important, it rarely is subject to change by the parties to the agreement, since it is the product of years of legal experience.

BOILER ROOM place where high-pressure salespeople use banks of telephones to call lists of potential investors (known in the trade as sucker lists) in order to peddle speculative, even fraudulent, securities. They are called boiler rooms because of the high-pressure selling. Boiler room methods, if not illegal, clearly violate the National Association of Securities Dealers' RULES OF FAIR PRACTICE, particularly those requiring that recommendations be suitable to a customer's account. *See also* BUCKET SHOP.

BOLSA Spanish term for *stock exchange*. There are Bolsas in Spain, Mexico, Chile, Argentina, and many other Spanish-speaking countries. In French, the term is BOURSE; in Italian, Borsa.

BOLSA DE VALORES DE SAO PAULO (BOVESPA) largest of Brazil's nine stock exchanges. Open outcry and computer assisted trading system (CATS) sessions are held simultaneously, in two sessions, from 9:30 A.M. to 1 P.M., and 3 P.M. to 4 P.M., Monday through Friday. Stock options of the 20 most actively traded companies are traded in the open outcry, while other stocks and options are traded only on the CATS system. Stock options and an option with a strike price quoted in points tied to the U.S. dollar are traded on the exchange as well. Physical settlement is on the first business day following the trade, and financial settlement is on the second business day.

BOMBAY STOCK EXCHANGE (BSE) largest of 22 stock exchanges in India. As such, it is the best indicator of economic and stock market activity in India. Settlement differs for "A" and "B" category stocks. The former, also known as the forward list, consists of the large capitalized companies, and involves a 14-day period, after which all transactions are settled on a net basis. The "B" group has a one-week settlement period. Trading Hours: 11:30 A.M.–2:30 P.M., Monday through Friday.

BOND any interest-bearing or discounted government or corporate security that obligates the issuer to pay the bondholder a specified sum of money, usually at specific intervals, and to repay the principal amount of the loan at maturity. Bondholders have an IOU from the issuer, but no corporate ownership privileges, as stockholders do.

An owner of *bearer bonds* presents the bond coupons and is paid interest, whereas the owner of *registered bonds* appears on the records of the bond issuer.

A SECURED BOND is backed by collateral which may be sold by the bondholder to satisfy a claim if the bond's issuer fails to pay interest and principal when they are due. An *unsecured bond* or DEBENTURE is backed by the full faith and credit of the issuer, but not by any specific collateral.

A CONVERTIBLE bond gives its owner the privilege of exchange for other securities of the issuing company at some future date and under prescribed conditions.

Also, a bond, in finance, is the obligation of one person to repay a debt taken on by someone else, should that other person default. A bond can also be money or securities deposited as a pledge of good faith.

A surety or PERFORMANCE BOND is an agreement whereby an insurance company becomes liable for the performance of work or services provided by a contractor by an agreed-upon date. If the contractor does not do what was promised, the surety company is financially responsible. *See also* INDENTURE; ZERO COUPON SECURITY.

BOND ANTICIPATION NOTE (BAN) short-term debt instrument issued by a state or municipality that will be paid off with the proceeds of an upcoming bond issue. To the investor, BANs offer a safe, tax-free yield that may be higher than other tax-exempt debt instruments of the same maturity.

BOND BROKER broker who executes bond trades on the floor of an exchange. Also, one who trades corporate, U.S. government, or municipal debt issues over the counter, mostly for large institutional accounts.

BOND BUYER, **THE** daily publication containing most of the key statistics and indexes used in the fixed-income markets. *See also* BOND BUYER'S INDEX; THIRTY-DAY VISIBLE SUPPLY.

BOND BUYER'S INDEX index published daily by the *BOND BUYER,* a newspaper covering the municipal bond market. The index provides the yardsticks against which municipal bond yields are measured. The index is composed of 40 actively traded general obligation and revenue issues rated A or better with a term portion of at least $50 million ($75 million for housing issues) and having at least 19 years remaining to maturity, a first call date between 7 and 16 years, and at least one call at par before redemption. The *Bond Buyer* also lists long-term government bonds and compares their after-tax yield with the yield from tax-free municipals. Investors use the publication's Bond Buyer Indexes to plot interest rate patterns.

BOND COUNSEL attorney or law firm that prepares the LEGAL OPINION for a municipal bond issue.

BOND CROWD exchange members who transact bond orders on the floor of the exchange. The work area in which they congregate is separate from the stock traders, hence the term bond crowd.

BOND DISCOUNT amount by which the MARKET PRICE of a bond is lower than its FACE VALUE. Outstanding bonds with fixed COUPONS go to discounts when market interest rates rise. Discounts are also caused when supply exceeds demand and when a bond's CREDIT RATING IS reduced. When opposite conditions exist and market price is higher than face value, the difference is termed a *bond premium.* Premiums also occur when a bond issue with a CALL FEATURE is redeemed prior to maturity and the bondholder is compensated for lost interest. *See also* ORIGINAL ISSUE DISCOUNT.

BOND EQUIVALENT YIELD restatement of a DISCOUNT YIELD as its interest-bearing equivalent.

BONDHOLDER owner of a bond. Bondholders may be individuals or institutions such as corporations, banks, insurance companies, or mutual funds. Bondholders are entitled to regular interest payments as due and return of principal when the bond matures. Bondholders may own corporate, government, or municipal issues. For corporate bonds, bondholders' claims on the assets of the issuing corporation take precedence over claims of stockholders in the event of liquidation. Unlike stockholders, however, straight bondholders do not own an equity interest in the issuing company. Some bonds, such as convertible bonds, do have some claim on the equity of the issuing corporation.

BOND MUTUAL FUND mutual fund holding bonds. Such funds may specialize in a particular kind of bond, such as government, corporate, convertible, high-yield, mortgage-backed, municipal, foreign, or zero-coupon bonds. Other bond mutual funds will buy some or all of these kinds of bonds. Most bond mutual funds are designed to produce current income for shareholders. Bond funds also produce capital gains when interest rates fall and capital losses when interest rates rise. Unlike the bonds in these funds, the funds themselves never mature. There are two types of bond mutual funds: open- and closed-end. *Open-end funds* continually create new shares to accommodate new money as it flows into the funds and they always trade at NET ASSET VALUE. *Closed-end funds* issue a limited number of shares and trade on stock exchanges. Closed-end funds trade at either higher than their net asset value (a premium) or lower than their net asset value (a discount), depending on investor demand for the fund.

BOND PREMIUM *see* BOND DISCOUNT.

BOND POWER form used in the transfer of registered bonds from one owner to another. Sometimes called *assignment separate from certificate*, it accomplishes the same thing as the assignment form on the back of the bond certificate, but has a safety advantage in being separate. Technically, the bond power appoints an attorney-in-fact with the power to make a transfer of ownership on the corporation's books.

BOND RATING method of evaluating the possibility of default by a bond issuer. Standard & Poor's, Moody's Investors Service, and Fitch's Investors Service analyze the financial strength of each bond's issuer, whether a corporation or a government body. Their ratings range from AAA (highly unlikely to default) to D (in default). Bonds rated BB or below are not INVESTMENT GRADE—in other words, institutions that invest other people's money may not under most state laws buy them. *See also* RATING.

BOND RATIO *leverage* ratio measuring the percentage of a company's capitalization represented by bonds. It is calculated by dividing the total bonds due after one year by the same figure plus all equity. A bond ratio over 33% indicates high leverage—except in utilities, where higher bond ratios are normal. *See also* DEBT-TO-EQUITY RATIO.

BOND SWAP simultaneous sale of one bond issue and purchase of another. The motives for bond swaps vary: *maturity swaps* aim to stretch out maturities but can also produce a profit because of the lower prices on longer bonds; *yield swaps* seek to improve return and *quality swaps* seek to upgrade safety; *tax swaps* create tax-deductible losses through the sale, while the purchase of a substitute bond effectively preserves the investment. *See also* SWAP, SWAP ORDER.

BON VOYAGE BONUS *see* GREENMAIL.

BOOK
1. in an underwriting of securities, (1) preliminary indications of interest rate on the part of prospective buyers of the issue ("What is the book on XYZ Company?") or (2) record of activity in the syndicate account ("Who is managing the book on XYZ?").
2. record maintained by a specialist of buy and sell orders in a given security. The term derives from the notebook that specialists traditionally used for this purpose. Also, the aggregate of sell orders left with the specialist, as in BUY THE BOOK.
3. as a verb, to book is to give accounting recognition to something. ("They booked a profit on the transaction.")
4. collectively, books are the journals, ledgers, and other accounting records of a business.
      See also BOOK VALUE.

BOOK-ENTRY SECURITIES securities that are not represented by a certificate. Purchases and sales of some municipal bonds, for instance, are merely recorded on customers' accounts; no certificates change hands. This is increasingly popular because it cuts down on paperwork for brokers and leaves investors free from worry about their certificates. *See also* CERTIFICATELESS MUNICIPALS.

BOOK PROFIT OR LOSS *see* UNREALIZED PROFIT OR LOSS.

BOOK VALUE

1. value at which an asset is carried on a balance sheet. For example, a piece of manufacturing equipment is put on the books at its cost when purchased. Its value is then reduced each year as depreciation is charged to income. Thus, its book value at any time is its cost minus accumulated depreciation. However, the primary purpose of accounting for depreciation is to enable a company to recover its cost, not replace the asset or reflect its declining usefulness. Book value may therefore vary significantly from other objectively determined values, most notably MARKET VALUE.

2. net asset value of a company's securities, calculated by using the following formula:

Total assets *minus* intangible assets (goodwill, patents, etc.) *minus* current liabilities *minus* any long-term liabilities and equity issues that have a prior claim (subtracting them here has the effect of treating them as paid) *equals* total net assets available for payment of the issue under consideration.

The total net asset figure, divided by the number of bonds, shares of preferred stock, or shares of common stock, gives the *net asset value*—or book value— per bond or per share of preferred or common stock.

Book value can be a guide in selecting underpriced stocks and is an indication of the ultimate value of securities in liquidation. *See also* ASSET COVERAGE.

BOOT STRAP to help a company start from scratch. Entrepreneurs founding a company with little capital are said to be boot strapping it in order to become established.

BORROWED RESERVES funds borrowed by member banks from a FEDERAL RESERVE BANK for the purpose of maintaining the required reserve ratios. Actually, the proper term is *net borrowed reserves,* since it refers to the difference between borrowed reserves and excess or free reserves. Such borrowings, usually in the form of advances secured by government securities or eligible paper, are kept on deposit at the Federal Reserve bank in the borrower's region. Net borrowed reserves are an indicator of heavy loan demand and potentially TIGHT MONEY.

BORROWING POWER OF SECURITIES amount of money that customers can invest in securities on MARGIN, as listed every month on their brokerage account statements. This margin limit usually equals 50% of the value of their stocks, 30% of the value of their bonds, and the full value of their CASH EQUIVALENT assets, such as MONEY MARKET account funds. The term also refers to securities pledged (hypothecated) to a bank or other lender as loan COLLATERAL. The loan value in this case depends on lender policy and type of security.

BOSTON STOCK EXCHANGE (BSE) established in 1834, the BSE is the first American exchange to open its membership to foreign brokers. It is the only U.S. exchange with a foreign linkage, with the Montreal Stock Exchange, established in 1984. In 1994, the exchange introduced competing specialists in an auction market environment. The BSE uses a three-day settlement. Trading hours are

Monday through Friday, 9:30 A.M.–4 P.M., with a limited crossing network at 5 P.M., matching the New York Stock Exchange's Session No. 1.

BOT
1. stockbroker shorthand for bought, the opposite of SL for sold.
2. in finance, abbreviation for balance of trade.
3. in the mutual savings bank industry, abbreviation for board of trustees.

BOTTOM
In general: support level for market prices of any type. When prices fall below that level and appear to be continuing downward without check, we say that the *bottom dropped out*. When prices begin to trend upward again, we say they have *bottomed out*.
Economics: lowest point in an economic cycle.
Securities: lowest market price of a security or commodity during a day, a season, a year, a cycle. Also, lowest level of prices for the market as a whole, as measured by any of the several indexes.

BOTTOM FISHER investor who is on the lookout for stocks that have fallen to their bottom prices before turning up. In extreme cases, bottom fishers buy stocks and bonds of bankrupt or near-bankrupt firms.

BOTTOM-UP APPROACH TO INVESTING search for outstanding performance of individual stocks before considering the impact of economic trends. The companies may be identified from research reports, stock screens, or personal knowledge of the products and services. This approach assumes that individual companies can do well, even in an industry that is not performing well. *See also* TOP-DOWN APPROACH TO INVESTING.

BOUGHT DEAL in securities underwriting, a FIRM COMMITMENT to purchase an entire issue outright from the issuing company. Differs from a STAND-BY COMMITMENT, wherein, with conditions, a SYNDICATE of investment bankers agrees to purchase part of an issue if it is not fully subscribed. Also differs from a BEST EFFORTS commitment, wherein the syndicate agrees to use its best efforts to sell the issue. Most issues in recent years have been bought deals. Typically, the syndicate puts up a portion of its own capital and borrows the rest from commercial banks. Then, perhaps through a selling group, the syndicate resells the issue to the public at slightly more than the purchase price.

BOUNCE return of a check by a bank because it is not payable, usually due to insufficient funds. In securities, the rejection and subsequent RECLAMATION of a security because of *bad delivery*. Term also refers to stock price's sudden decline and recovery.

BOURSE French term for *stock exchange*. See PARIS BOURSE.

BOUTIQUE small, specialized brokerage firm that deals with a limited clientele and offers a limited product line. A highly regarded securities analyst may form a research boutique, which clients use as a resource for buying and selling certain stocks. A boutique is the opposite of a FINANCIAL SUPERMARKET, which offers a wide variety of services to a wide variety of clients.

BOX physical location of securities or other documents held in safekeeping. The term derives from the large metal tin, or tray, in which brokerage firms and banks actually place such valuables. Depending on rules and regulations concerned with the safety and segregation of clients' securities, certificates held in safekeeping may qualify for stock loans or as bank loan collateral.

BRACKET CREEP edging into higher tax brackets as income rises to compensate for inflation.

BRADY BONDS public-issue, U.S. dollar-denominated bonds of developing countries, mainly in Latin America, that were exchanged, in a restructuring, for commercial bank loans in default. The securities, named for former Bush administration Treasury Secretary Nicholas Brady, are collateralized by U.S. Treasury zero-coupon bonds to ensure principal. In the mid-1990s prices of these bonds became depressed as a reflection of the risk that South American economies would be restructured a second time.

BRANCH OFFICE MANAGER person in charge of a branch of a securities brokerage firm or bank. Branch office managers who oversee the activities of three or more brokers must pass tests administered by various stock exchanges. A customer who is not able to resolve a conflict with a REGISTERED REPRESENTATIVE should bring it to the attention of the branch office manager, who is responsible for resolving such differences.

BREADTH OF THE MARKET percentage of stocks participating in a particular market move. Analysts say there was good breadth if two thirds of the stocks listed on an exchange rose during a trading session. A market trend with good breadth is more significant and probably more long-lasting than one with limited breadth, since more investors are participating. Breadth-of-the-market indexes are alternatively called ADVANCE/DECLINE indexes.

BREAK

Finance: in a pricing structure providing purchasing discounts at different levels of volume, a point at which the price changes—for example, a 10% discount for ten cases.

Investments: (1) sudden, marked drop in the price of a security or in market prices generally; (2) discrepancy in the accounts of brokerage firms; (3) stroke of good luck.

BREAKEVEN POINT

Finance: the point at which sales equal costs. The point is located by breakeven analysis, which determines the volume of sales at which fixed and variable costs will be covered. All sales over the breakeven point produce profits; any drop in sales below that point will produce losses.

Because costs and sales are so complex, breakeven analysis has limitations as a planning tool and is being supplanted by computer based financial planning systems. *See also* LEVERAGE (operating).

Securities: dollar price at which a transaction produces neither a gain nor a loss.
In options strategy the term has the following definitions:
1. long calls and short uncovered calls: strike price plus premium.
2. long puts and short uncovered puts: strike price minus premium.
3. short covered call: purchase price minus premium.
4. short put covered by short stock: short sale price of underlying stock plus premium.

BREAKING THE SYNDICATE terminating the investment banking group formed to underwrite a securities issue. More specifically, terminating the AGREEMENT AMONG UNDERWRITERS, thus leaving the members free to sell remaining holdings without price restrictions. The agreement among underwriters usually terminates the syndicate 30 days after the selling group, but the syndicate can be broken earlier by agreement of the participants.

BREAKOUT rise in a security's price above a resistance level (commonly its previous high price) or drop below a level of support (commonly the former lowest price). A breakout is taken to signify a continuing move in the same direction.

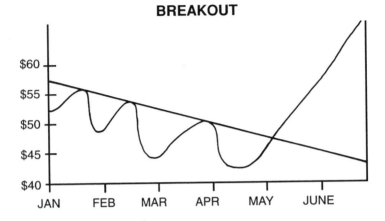

BREAKOUT

BREAKPOINT SALE in mutual funds, the dollar investment required to make the fundholder eligible for a lower sales charge. *See also* LETTER OF INTENT; RIGHT OF ACCUMULATION.

BREAKUP VALUE *see* PRIVATE MARKET VALUE.

BRETTON WOODS AGREEMENT OF 1944 *see* FIXED EXCHANGE RATE.

BRIDGE LOAN short-term loan, also called a *swing loan,* made in anticipation of intermediate-term or long-term financing.

BROAD TAPE enlargement of the Dow Jones news ticker tape, projected on a screen in the board room of a brokerage firm. It continually reports major news developments and financial information. The term can also refer to similar information provided by Associated Press, United Press International, Reuters, or Munifacts. The broad tape is not allowed on the exchange floor because it would give floor traders an unfair edge.

BROKER
Insurance: person who finds the best insurance deal for a client and then sells the policy to the client.
Real estate: person who represents the seller and gets a commission when the property is sold.
Securities: person who acts as an intermediary between a buyer and seller, usually charging a commission. A broker who specializes in stocks, bonds, commodities, or options acts as AGENT and must be registered with the exchange where the securities are traded. Hence the term *registered representative. See also* ACCOUNT EXECUTIVE; DEALER; DISCOUNT BROKER.

BROKER-DEALER *see* DEALER.

BROKERED CD CERTIFICATE OF DEPOSIT (CD) issued by a bank or thrift institution but bought in bulk by a brokerage firm and resold to brokerage customers. Brokered CDs pay as much as 1% more than those issued directly by major banks, carry federal deposit insurance up to $100,000, enjoy a liquid secondary market made by the broker, and do not require an investor to pay a commission.

BROKER LOAN RATE interest rate at which brokers borrow from banks to cover the securities positions of their clients. The broker loan rate usually hovers a percentage point or so above such short-term interest rates as the federal funds rate and the Treasury bill rate. Since brokers' loans and their customers' margin accounts are usually covered by the same collateral, the term REHYPOTHECATION is used synonymously with *broker loan borrowing*. Because broker loans are callable on 24-hour notice, the term *call loan rate* is also used, particularly in money rate tables published in newspapers.

BROUGHT OVER THE WALL when somebody in the research department of an investment bank is pressed into the service of the underwriting department in reference to a particular corporate client, the individual has been "brought over the ("Chinese") wall" that legally divides the two functions and, being thus privy to INSIDE INFORMATION, is precluded from providing opinions about the company involved. *See also* CHINESE WALL.

BRUSSELS STOCK EXCHANGE (BSE) largest and most active of the three stock exchanges in Belgium; other exchanges are in Antwerp and Liege. A Computerized Automated Trading System, called CATS, replaced open outcry for the forward market in 1989; the cash market was computerized in 1993. Cash market trading hours are 12:30 P.M.–2:30 P.M.; forward market, 10 A.M.–4 P.M. Both trade Monday through Friday.

BUCKET SHOP illegal brokerage firm, of a kind now almost extinct, which accepts customer orders but does not execute them right away as Securities and Exchange Commission regulations require. Bucket-shop brokers confirm the price the customer asked for, but in fact make the trade at a time advantageous to the broker, whose profit is the difference between the two prices. Sometimes bucket shops neglect to fill the customer's order and just pocket the money. *See also* BOILER ROOM.

BUDGET estimate of revenue and expenditure for a specified period. Of the many kinds of budgets, a CASH BUDGET shows cash flow, an expense budget shows projected expenditures, and a CAPITAL BUDGET shows anticipated capital outlays. The term refers to a preliminary financial plan. In a *balanced budget* revenues cover expenditures.

BUDGET DEFICIT excess of spending over income for a government, corporation, or individual over a particular period of time. The budget deficit accumulated by the federal government of the United States now runs into the trillions of dollars. It must be financed by the issuance of Treasury bonds. Corporate budget deficits must be reduced or eliminated by increasing sales and reducing expenditures, or the company will not survive in the long run. Similarly, individuals who consistently spend more than they earn will accumulate huge debts, which may ultimately force them to declare bankruptcy if the debt cannot be serviced.

BUDGET SURPLUS excess of income over spending for a government, corporation, or individual over a particular period of time. A government with a budget surplus may choose to start new programs or cut taxes. A corporation with a surplus may expand the business through investment or acquisition, or may choose to buy back its own stock. An individual with a budget surplus may choose to pay down debt or increase spending or investment.

BULGE quick, temporary price rise that applies to an entire commodities or stock market, or to an individual commodity or stock.

BULGE BRACKET the group of firms in an underwriting syndicate that share the largest participation. TOMBSTONE ads list the participants alphabetically within groupings organized by size of participation and presented in tiers. The first and lead grouping is the "bulge bracket." *See also* MEZZANINE BRACKET.

BULL person who thinks prices will rise. One can be bullish on the prospects for an individual stock, bond, or commodity, an industry segment, or the market as a whole. In a more general sense, bullish means optimistic, so a person can be bullish on the economy as a whole.

BULLION COINS coins composed of metal such as gold, silver, platinum, or palladium. Bullion coins provide the purest play on the "up or down" price moves of the underlying metal, and are the most actively traded. These coins trade at a slight premium over their metal content, unlike NUMISMATIC COINS, which trade on their rarity and artistic value. Some of the most popular bullion coins minted by major governments around the world include the American Eagle, the Canadian Maple Leaf, the South African Kruggerand, and the Australian Kangaroo. In addition to trading bullion in coin form, nearly pure precious metals also are available in bar form.

BULL MARKET prolonged rise in the prices of stocks, bonds, or commodities. Bull markets usually last at least a few months and are characterized by high trading volume.

BULL SPREAD option strategy, executed with puts or calls, that will be profitable if the underlying stock rises in value. The following are three varieties of bull spread:

Vertical spread: simultaneous purchase and sale of options of the same class at different strike prices, but with the same expiration date.

Calendar spread: simultaneous purchase and sale of options of the same class and the same price but at different expiration dates.

Diagonal spread: combination of vertical and calendar spreads wherein the investor buys and sells options of the same class at different strike prices and different expiration dates.

An investor who believes, for example, that XYZ stock will rise, perhaps only moderately, buys an XYZ 30 call for 1½ and sells an XYZ 35 call for ½; both options are OUT OF THE MONEY. The 30 and 35 are strike prices and the 1½ and ½ are premiums. The net cost of this spread, or the difference between the premiums, is $1. If the stock rises to 35 just prior to expiration, the 35 call becomes worthless and the 30 call is worth $5. Thus the spread provides a profit of $4 on an investment of $1. If on the other hand the price of the stock goes down, both options expire worthless and the investor loses the entire premium.

BUMP-UP CD certificate of deposit that gives its owner a one-time right to increase its yield for the remaining term of the CD if interest rates have risen from the date of issuance. The CD's yield will not be adjusted downward if rates fall, however. If rates remain stable or decline, the CD will pay its stated rate of interest until maturity.

BUNCHING

1. combining many round-lot orders for execution at the same time on the floor of an exchange. This technique can also be used with odd lot orders, when combining many small orders can save the odd-lot differential for each customer.

2. pattern on the ticker tape when a series of trades in the same security appear consecutively.

3. aggregating income items or deductions in a single year to minimize taxes in that year.

BURNOUT exhaustion of a tax shelter's benefits, when an investor starts to receive income from the investment. This income must be reported to the Internal Revenue Service, and taxes must be paid on it.

BURN RATE in venture capital financing, the rate at which a start-up company spends capital to finance overhead before generating a positive cash flow from operations.

BUSINESS COMBINATION *see* MERGER.

BUSINESS CYCLE recurrence of periods of expansion (RECOVERY) and contraction (RECESSION) in economic activity with effects on inflation, growth, and employment. One cycle extends from a GNP base line through one rise and one decline and back to the base line, a period averaging about 2½ years. A business cycle affects profitability and CASH FLOW, making it a key consideration in corporate dividend policy, and is a factor in the rise and fall of the inflation rate, which in turn affects return on investments.

BUSINESS DAY
In general: hours when most businesses are in operation. Although individual working hours may differ, and particular firms may choose staggered schedules, the conventional business day is 9 A.M. to 5 P.M.
Finance and investments: day when financial marketplaces are open for trading. In figuring the settlement date on a *regular way* securities transaction—which is the fifth business day after the trade date—Saturday, Sunday, and a legal holiday would not be counted, for example.

BUSINESS SEGMENT REPORTING reporting the results of the divisions, subsidiaries, or other segments of a business separately so that income, sales, and assets can be compared. When not a separate part of the business structure, a segment is generally defined as any grouping of products and services comprising a significant industry, which is one representing 10% or more of total revenues, assets, or income. Allocation of central corporate expenses is not required by the Financial Accounting Standards Board. Also called line of business reporting.

BUSTED CONVERTIBLES CONVERTIBLES that trade like fixed-income investments because the market price of the common stock they convert to has fallen so low as to render the conversion feature valueless.

BUST-UP TAKEOVER LEVERAGED BUYOUT in which TARGET COMPANY assets or activities are sold off to repay the debt that financed the TAKEOVER.

BUTTERFLY SPREAD complex option strategy that involves selling two calls and buying two calls on the same or different markets, with several maturity dates. One of the options has a higher exercise price and the other has a lower exercise price than the other two options. An investor in a butterfly spread will profit if the underlying security makes no dramatic movements because the premium income will be collected when the options are sold.

BUY acquire property in return for money. Buy can be used as a synonym for bargain.

BUY AND HOLD STRATEGY strategy that calls for accumulating shares in a company over the years. This allows the investor to pay favorable long-term capital gains tax on profits and requires far less attention than a more active trading strategy.

BUY AND WRITE STRATEGY conservative options strategy that entails buying stocks and then writing covered call options on them. Investors receive both the dividends from the stock and the premium income from the call options. However, the investor may have to sell the stock below the current market price if the call is exercised.

BUYBACK purchase of a long contract to cover a short position, usually arising out of the short sale of a commodity. Also, purchase of identical securities to cover a short sale. Synonym: *short covering*. See also STOCK BUYBACK.

Bond buyback: corporation's purchase of its own bonds at a discount in the open market. This is done in markets characterized by rapidly rising interest rates and commensurately declining bond prices.

BUY DOWN cash payment by a mortgage lender allowing the borrower to receive a lower rate of interest on a mortgage loan. For example, a home builder having trouble selling homes may offer a buy down with a local lender which will enable home buyers to qualify for mortgages that they would otherwise not qualify for. The buy down may lower the mortgage rate for the life of the loan, or sometimes just for the first few years of the loan.

BUYER'S MARKET market situation that is the opposite of a SELLER'S MARKET.

BUY HEDGE *see* LONG HEDGE.

BUY IN
Options trading: procedure whereby the responsibility to deliver or accept stock can be terminated. In a transaction called *buying-in* or CLOSING PURCHASE, the writer buys an identical option (only the premium or price is different). The second of these options offsets the first, and the profit or loss is the difference in premiums.

Securities: transaction between brokers wherein securities are not delivered on time by the broker on the sell side, forcing the buy side broker to obtain shares from other sources.

BUYING CLIMAX rapid rise in the price of a stock or commodity, setting the stage for a quick fall. Such a surge attracts most of the potential buyers of the stock, leaving them with no one to sell their stock to at higher prices. This is what causes the ensuing fall. Technical chartists see a buying climax as a dramatic runup, accompanied by increased trading volume in the stock.

BUYING ON MARGIN buying securities with credit available through a relationship with a broker, called a MARGIN ACCOUNT. Arrangements of this kind are closely regulated by the Federal Reserve Board. *See also* MARGIN.

BUYING POWER amount of money available to buy securities, determined by tabulating the cash held in brokerage accounts, and adding the amount that could be spent if securities were margined to the limit. The market cannot rise beyond the available buying power. *See also* PURCHASING POWER.

BUY MINUS order to buy a stock at a price lower than the current market price. Traders try to execute a buy minus order on a temporary dip in the stock's price.

BUY ON THE BAD NEWS strategy based on the belief that, soon after a company announces bad news, the price of its stock will plummet. Those who buy at this stage assume that the price is about as low as it can go, leaving plenty of room for a rise when the news improves. If the adverse development is indeed temporary, this technique can be quite profitable. *See also* BOTTOM FISHER.

BUY ORDER in securities trading, an order to a broker to purchase a specified quality of a security at the MARKET PRICE or at another stipulated price.

BUYOUT purchase of at least a controlling percentage of a company's stock to take over its assets and operations. A buyout can be accomplished through negotiation or through a tender offer. A LEVERAGED BUYOUT occurs when a small group borrows the money to finance the purchase of the shares. The loan is ultimately repaid out of cash generated from the acquired company's operations or from the sale of its assets. *See also* GOLDEN PARACHUTE.

BUY STOP ORDER BUY ORDER marked to be held until the market price rises to the STOP PRICE, then to be entered as a MARKET ORDER to buy at the best available price. Sometimes called a *suspended market order*, because it remains suspended until a market transaction elects, activates, or triggers the stop. Such an order is not permitted in the over-the-counter market. *See also* STOP ORDER.

BUY THE BOOK order to a broker to buy all the shares available from the specialist in a security and from other brokers and dealers at the current offer price. The book is the notebook in which specialists kept track of buy and sell orders before computers. The most likely source of such an order is a professional trader or a large institutional buyer.

BYLAWS rules governing the internal management of an organization which, in the case of business corporations, are drawn up at the time of incorporation. The charter is concerned with such broad matters as the number of directors and the number of authorized shares; the bylaws, which can usually be amended by the directors themselves, cover such points as the election of directors, the appointment of executive and finance committees, the duties of officers, and how share transfers may be made. Bylaws, which are also prevalent in not-for-profit organizations, cannot countermand laws of the government.

BYPASS TRUST agreement allowing parents to pass assets on to their children to reduce estate taxes. The trust must be made irrevocable, meaning that the terms can never be changed. Assets put in such a trust usually exceed the amount that children and other heirs can receive tax-free at a parent's death. Under the 1981 Tax Act, this amount reached $600,000 in 1987. Parents can arrange to receive income from the assets during their lifetimes and may even be able to touch the principal in case of dire need. One variation of a bypass trust is the qualified terminable interest property trust, or Q-TIP TRUST.

C

CABINET CROWD members of the New York Stock Exchange who trade in infrequently traded bonds. Also called *inactive bond crowd* or *book crowd*. Buy and sell LIMIT ORDERS for these bonds are kept in steel racks, called cabinets, at the side of the bond trading floor; hence the name cabinet crowd. *See also* AUTOMATED BOND SYSTEM (ABS).

CABINET SECURITY stock or bond listed on a major exchange but not actively traded. There are a considerable number of such bonds and a limited number of such stocks, mainly those trading in ten-share units. Cabinets are the metal storage racks that LIMIT ORDERS for such securities are filed in pending execution or cancellation. *See also* AUTOMATED BOND SYSTEM (ABS); CABINET CROWD.

CAC 40 INDEX broad-based index of common stocks on the Paris Bourse, based on 40 of the 100 largest companies listed on the forward segment of the official list (reglement menseul); it has a base of 100. It is comparable to the Dow Jones Industrial Average. There are index futures and index options contracts based on the CAC 40 index.

CAFETERIA EMPLOYEE BENEFIT PLAN plan offering employees numerous options among their employee benefits. Each employee is able to pick the benefits that are most valuable in his or her particular situation. For example, a young employee with children may want to receive more life and health insurance than a mid-career employee who is more concerned with building up retirement plan assets.

CAGE section of a brokerage firm's back office where funds are received and disbursed.
Also, the installation where a bank teller works.

CALENDAR list of securities about to be offered for sale. Separate calendars are kept for municipal bonds, corporate bonds, government bonds, and new stock offerings.

CALENDAR SPREAD options strategy that entails buying two options on the same security with different maturities. If the EXERCISE PRICE is the same (a June 50 call and a September 50 call) it is a HORIZONTAL SPREAD. If the exercise prices are different (a June 50 call and a September 45 call), it is a DIAGONAL SPREAD. Investors gain or lose as the difference in price narrows or widens.

CALL
Banking: demand to repay a secured loan usually made when the borrower has failed to meet such contractual obligations as timely payment of interest. When a banker calls a loan, the entire principal amount is due immediately. *See also* BROKER LOAN RATE.
Bonds: right to redeem outstanding bonds before their scheduled maturity. The first dates when an issuer may call bonds are specified in the prospectus of every issue that has a call provision in its indenture. *See also* CALLABLE; CALL PRICE.
Options: right to buy a specific number of shares at a specified price by a fixed date. *See also* CALL OPTION.

CALLABLE redeemable by the issuer before the scheduled maturity. The issuer must pay the holders a premium price if such a security is retired early. Bonds are usually called when interest rates fall so significantly that the issuer can save money by floating new bonds at lower rates. *See also* CALL PRICE; DEMAND LOAN.

CALL DATE date on which a bond may be redeemed before maturity. If called, the bond may be redeemed at PAR or at a slight premium to par. For example, a bond may be scheduled to mature in 20 years but may have a provision that it can be called in 10 years if it is advantageous for the issuer to refinance the issue. The date 10 years from the issue date is the call date. When buying a bond, it is important to know the bond's call date, because you cannot be assured that you will receive interest from that bond beyond the call date.

CALLED AWAY term for a bond redeemed before maturity, or a call or put option exercised against the stockholder, or a delivery required on a short sale.

CALL FEATURE part of the agreement a bond issuer makes with a buyer, called the indenture, describing the schedule and price of redemptions before maturity. Most corporate and municipal bonds have 10-year call features (termed CALL PROTECTION by holders); government securities usually have none. *See also* CALL PRICE.

CALL LOAN any loan repayable on demand, but used in newspaper money rate tables as a synonym for *broker loan* or *broker overnight loan. See* BROKER LOAN RATE.

CALL LOAN RATE *see* BROKER LOAN RATE.

CALL OPTION right to buy 100 shares of a particular stock or stock index at a predetermined price before a preset deadline, in exchange for a premium. For buyers who think a stock will go up dramatically, call options permit a profit from a smaller investment than it would take to buy the stock. These options can also produce extra income for the seller, who gives up ownership of the stock if the option is exercised.

CALL PREMIUM amount that the buyer of a call option has to pay to the seller for the right to purchase a stock or stock index at a specified price by a specified date.

In bonds, preferreds, and convertibles, the amount over par that an issuer has to pay to an investor for redeeming the security early.

CALL PRICE price at which a bond or preferred stock with a *call provision* or CALL FEATURE can be redeemed by the issuer; also known as *redemption price.* To compensate the holder for loss of income and ownership, the call price is usually higher than the par value of the security, the difference being the CALL PREMIUM. *See also* CALL PROTECTION.

CALL PROTECTION length of time during which a security cannot be redeemed by the issuer. U.S. government securities are generally not callable, although there is an exception in certain 30-year Treasury bonds, which become callable after 25 years. Corporate and municipal issuers generally provide 10 years of call protection. Investors who plan to live off the income from a bond should be sure they have call protection, because without it the bond could be CALLED AWAY at any time specified in the indenture.

CALL PROVISION clause in a bond's INDENTURE that allows the issuer to redeem the bond before maturity. The call provision will spell out the first CALL DATE and whether the bond will be called at PAR or at a slight premium to par. Some preferred stock issues also have call provisions spelling out the conditions of a redemption.

CALL RISK risk to a bondholder that a bond may be redeemed before scheduled maturity. Bondholders should read the CALL PROVISIONS in a bond's INDENTURE to understand the earliest potential CALL DATE for their bond. The main risk of having a bond called before maturity is that the investor will be unable to replace the bond's yield with another similar-quality bond paying the same yield. The reason the bond issuer will call the bond is that interest rates will have fallen from the time of issuance, and the bond can be refinanced at lower rates.

CAMPS acronym for *Cumulative Auction Market Preferred Stocks,* Oppenheimer & Company's DUTCH AUCTION PREFERRED STOCK product.

CANADIAN DEALING NETWORK, INC. (CDN) the organized over-the-counter stock market of Canada. The CDN became a subsidiary of the TORONTO

STOCK EXCHANGE in 1991. Previously, CDN was known as the Canadian Over-the-counter Automated Trading System (COATS).

CANCEL
In general: void a negotiable instrument by annulling or paying it; also, prematurely terminate a bond or other contract.

Securities trading: void an order to buy or sell. *See also* GOOD TILL CANCELED ORDER.

CAP
Bonds: highest level interest rate that can be paid on a floating-rate debt instrument. For example, a variable-rate note might have a cap of 8%, meaning that the yield cannot exceed 8% even if the general level of interest rates goes much higher than 8%.

Mortgages: highest interest rate level that an adjustable-rate mortgage (ARM) can rise to over a particular period of time. For example, an ARM contract may specify that the rate cannot jump more than two points in any year, or a total of six points during the life of the mortgage.

Stocks: short for CAPITALIZATION, or the total current value of a company's outstanding shares in dollars. A stock's capitalization is determined by multiplying the total number of shares outstanding by the stock's price. Analysts also refer to small-, medium- and large-cap stocks as a way of distinguishing the capitalizations of companies they are interested in. Many mutual funds restrict themselves to the small-, medium- or large-cap universes. *See also* COLLAR.

CAPACITY
Debt: ability to repay loans, as measured by credit grantors. Creditors judge an applicant's ability to repay a loan based on assets and income, and assign a certain capacity to service debt. If someone has many credit cards and credit lines outstanding, even if there are no outstanding balances, that is using up that person's debt capacity.

Economics: the amount of productive capacity in the economy is known as *industrial capacity*. This figure is released on a monthly basis by the Federal Reserve to show how much of the nation's factories, mines, and utilities are in use. If more than 85% of industrial capacity is in use, economists worry that production bottlenecks may form and create inflationary pressure. On the other hand, if less than 80% of capacity is in use, industrial production may be slack and inflationary pressures low.

CAPACITY UTILIZATION RATE percentage of production capacity in use by a particular company, an industry, or the entire economy. While in theory a business can operate at 100% of its productive capacity, in practice the maximum output is less than that, because machines need to be repaired, employees take vacations, etc. The operating rate is expressed as a percentage of the potential 100% production output. For example, a company may be producing at an 85% operating rate, meaning its output is 85% of the maximum that could be produced with its existing resources. *See also* CAPACITY.

CAPITAL ASSET long-term asset that is not bought or sold in the normal course of business. Generally speaking, the term includes FIXED ASSETS—land, buildings, equipment, furniture and fixtures, and so on. The Internal Revenue Service definition of capital assets includes security investments.

CAPITAL ASSET PRICING MODEL (CAPM) sophisticated model of the relationship between *expected risk* and *expected return*. The model is grounded in the theory that investors demand higher returns for higher risks. It says that the return on an asset or a security is equal to the risk-free return—such as the return on a short-term Treasury security— plus a risk premium.

CAPITAL BUDGET program for financing long-term outlays such as plant expansion, research and development, and advertising. Among methods used in arriving at a capital budget are NET PRESENT VALUE (NPV), INTERNAL RATE OF RETURN (IRR), and PAYBACK PERIOD.

CAPITAL BUILDER ACCOUNT (CBA) brokerage account offered by Merrill Lynch that allows investors to buy and sell securities. It may be a cash or credit account that allows an investor to access the loan value of his or her eligible securities. Unlike a regular brokerage account, with a CBA one can choose from a money market fund or an insured money market deposit account to have one's idle cash invested or deposited on a regular basis, without losing access to the money.

CAPITAL CONSUMPTION ALLOWANCE amount of depreciation included in the GROSS DOMESTIC PRODUCT (GDP), normally around 11%. This amount is subtracted from GDP, on the theory that it is needed to maintain the productive capacity of the economy, to get net national product (NNP). When adjusted further for indirect taxes, NNP equals national income. Economists use GDP rather than NNP in the analyses we read every day largely because capital consumption allowance figures are not always available or reliable. *See also* DEPRECIATION.

CAPITAL EXPENDITURE outlay of money to acquire or improve CAPITAL ASSETS such as buildings and machinery.

CAPITAL FLIGHT movement of large sums of money from one country to another to escape political or economic turmoil or to seek higher rates of return. For example, periods of high inflation or political revolution have brought about an exodus of capital from many Latin American countries to the United States, which is seen as a safe haven.

CAPITAL FORMATION creation or expansion, through savings, of capital or of *producer's goods*—buildings, machinery, equipment—that produce other goods and services, the result being economic expansion.

CAPITAL GAIN difference between an asset's purchase price and selling price, when the difference is positive. When the TAX REFORM ACT OF 1986 was passed, the profit on a CAPITAL ASSET held six months was considered a long-term gain taxable at a lower rate. The 1986 law eliminated the differential between long-term capital gain and ordinary income rates. In 1991, capital gains rates were limited to 28%.

CAPITAL GAINS DISTRIBUTION mutual fund's distribution to shareholders of the profits derived from the sale of stocks or bonds. Traditionally, mutual fund shareholders benefited from a lower long-term capital gains tax rate regardless of how long they held fund shares. The TAX REFORM ACT OF 1986 eliminated the rate differential and in 1991 capital gains rates were limited to 28%. The REVENUE RECONCILIATION ACT OF 1993 held the long-term capital gains limit at 28% but raised the maximum individual tax rate, applicable to short-term capital gains, to 39.6%.

CAPITAL GAINS TAX tax on profits from the sale of CAPITAL ASSETS. The tax law has traditionally specified a minimum HOLDING PERIOD after which a CAPITAL GAIN was taxed at a more favorable rate (recently a maximum of 20% for individuals) than ordinary income. The TAX REFORM ACT OF 1986 provided that all capital gains be taxed at ordinary income rates and in 1991 capital gains rates were limited to 28%. The REVENUE RECONCILIATION ACT OF 1993 held the long-term capital gains limit at 28% but raised the maximum individual tax rate, applicable to short-term capital gains, to 39.6%.

CAPITAL GOODS goods used in the production of other goods—industrial buildings, machinery, equipment—as well as highways, office buildings, government installations. In the aggregate such goods form a country's productive capacity.

CAPITAL-INTENSIVE requiring large investments in CAPITAL ASSETS, Motor-vehicle and steel production are capital-intensive industries. To provide an acceptable return on investment, such industries must have a high margin of profit or a low cost of borrowing. Sometimes used to mean a high proportion of fixed assets to labor.

CAPITAL INTERNATIONAL INDEXES indexes maintained by Morgan Stanley's Capital International division which track most major stock markets throughout the world. The Capital International World Index tracks prices of major stocks in all the major markets worldwide. There are also many indexes for European, North American, and Asian markets. Most mutual funds and other institutional investors measure their performance against Capital International indexes.

CAPITAL INVESTMENT *see* CAPITAL EXPENDITURE.

CAPITALISM economic system in which (1) private ownership of property exists; (2) aggregates of property or capital provide income for the individuals or firms that accumulated it and own it; (3) individuals and firms are relatively free to compete with others for their own economic gain; (4) the profit motive is basic to economic life.

Among the synonyms for capitalism are LAISSEZ-FAIRE economy, private enterprise system, and free-price system. In this context *economy* is interchangeable with *system*.

CAPITALIZATION *see* CAPITALIZE; CAPITAL STRUCTURE; MARKET CAPITALIZATION.

CAPITALIZATION RATE rate of interest used to convert a series of future payments into a single PRESENT VALUE.

CAPITALIZATION RATIO analysis of a company's capital structure showing what percentage of the total is debt, preferred stock, common stock, and other equity. The ratio is useful in evaluating the relative RISK and leverage that holders of the respective levels of security have. *See also* BOND RATIO.

CAPITALIZE
1. convert a schedule of income into a principal amount, called *capitalized value*, by dividing by a rate of interest.
2. issue securities to finance *capital outlays* (rare).
3. record capital outlays as additions to asset accounts, not as expenses. *See also* CAPITAL EXPENDITURE.
4. convert a lease obligation to an asset/liability form of expression called a *capital lease*, that is, to record a leased asset as an owned asset and the lease obligation as borrowed funds.
5. turn something to one's advantage economically—for example, sell umbrellas on a rainy day.

CAPITAL LEASE lease that under Statement 13 of the Financial Accounting Standards Board must be reflected on a company's balance sheet as an asset and corresponding liability. Generally, this applies to leases where the lessee acquires essentially all of the economic benefits and risks of the leased property.

CAPITAL LOSS amount by which the proceeds from the sale of a CAPITAL ASSET are less than the cost of acquiring it. Until the TAX REFORM ACT OF 1986, $2 of LONG-TERM LOSS could be used to offset $1 of LONG-TERM GAIN and (for noncorporate taxpayers) up to $3000 of ORDINARY INCOME, while short-term losses could be applied dollar-for-dollar against short-term gains and $3000 of ordinary income. Starting in 1987, capital losses were offsetable dollar-for-dollar against capital gains and $3000 of ordinary income. The short-term/long-term distinction ended starting 1988 but is operative under the REVENUE RECONCILIATION ACT OF 1993 except that short-term losses not offset by short-term gains must be applied to long-term gains before being applied to ordinary income (to a limit of $3000). *See also* TAX LOSS CARRYBACK, CARRY FORWARD.

CAPITAL MARKETS markets where capital funds—debt and equity—are traded. Included are private placement sources of debt and equity as well as organized markets and exchanges. *See also* PRIMARY MARKET.

CAPITAL OUTFLOW exodus of capital from a country. A combination of political and economic factors may encourage domestic and foreign owners of assets to sell their holdings and move their money to other countries that offer more political stability and economic growth potential. If a capital outflow becomes large enough, some countries may try to restrict investors' ability to remove money from the country with currency controls or other measures.

CAPITAL OUTLAY *see* CAPITAL EXPENDITURE.

CAPITAL REQUIREMENTS
1. permanent financing needed for the normal operation of a business; that is, the long-term and working capital.
2. appraised investment in fixed assets and normal working capital. Whether patents, rights, and contracts should be included is moot.

CAPITAL SHARES one of the two classes of shares in a dual-purpose investment company. The capital shares entitle the owner to all appreciation (or depreciation) in value in the underlying portfolio in addition to all gains realized by trading in the portfolio. The other class of shares in a dual-purpose investment company are INCOME SHARES, which receive all income generated by the portfolio. If the fund guarantees a minimum level of income payable to the income shareholders, it may be necessary to sell some securities in the portfolio if the existing securities do not provide a high enough level of dividends and interest. In this case, the value of the capital shares will fall.

CAPITAL STOCK stock authorized by a company's charter and having PAR VALUE, STATED VALUE, or NO PAR VALUE. The number and value of issued shares are normally shown, together with the number of shares authorized, in the capital accounts section of the balance sheet.

   Informally, a synonym for COMMON STOCK, though capital stock technically also encompasses PREFERRED STOCK.

CAPITAL STRUCTURE corporation's financial framework, including LONG-TERM DEBT, PREFERRED STOCK, and NET WORTH. It is distinguished from FINANCIAL STRUCTURE, which includes additional sources of capital such as short-term debt, accounts payable, and other liabilities. It is synonymous with *capitalization,* although there is some disagreement as to whether capitalization should include long-term loans and mortgages. Analysts look at capital structure in terms of its overall adequacy and its composition as well as in terms of the DEBT-TO-EQUITY RATIO, called *leverage. See also* CAPITALIZATION RATIO; PAR VALUE.

CAPITAL SURPLUS
1. EQUITY—or NET WORTH—not otherwise classifiable as CAPITAL STOCK or RETAINED EARNINGS. Here are five ways of creating surplus:
   a. from stock issued at a premium over par or stated value.
   b. from the proceeds of stock bought back and then sold again.
   c. from a reduction of par or stated value or a reclassification of capital stock.
   d. from donated stock.
   e. from the acquisition of companies that have capital surplus.
2. common umbrella term for more specific classifications such as ACQUIRED SURPLUS, ADDITIONAL PAID-IN CAPITAL, DONATED SURPLUS, and REEVALUATION SURPLUS (arising from appraisals). Most common synonyms: *paid-in surplus; surplus.*

CAPITAL TURNOVER annual sales divided by average stockholder equity (net worth). When compared over a period, it reveals the extent to which a company is able to grow without additional capital investment. Generally, companies with high profit margins have a low capital turnover and vice versa. Also called *equity turnover.*

CAPS acronym for *convertible adjustable preferred stock,* whose adjustable interest rate is pegged to Treasury security rates and which can be exchanged, during the period after the announcement of each dividend rate for the next period, for common stock (or, usually, cash) with a market value equal to the par value of the CAPS. CAPS solved a problem inherent with DUTCH AUCTION PREFERRED STOCK, which was that the investor could not be certain of the principal value of the preferred. *See also* MANDATORY CONVERTIBLES.

CAPTIVE AGENT insurance agent working exclusively for one company. Such an agent will tend to have more in-depth knowledge of that company's policies than an INDEPENDENT AGENT, who can sell policies from many companies. Captive agents are usually paid on a combination of salary and commissions earned from selling policies, in the first few years they sell policies. Later, they are usually paid exclusively on a commission basis.

CAPTIVE FINANCE COMPANY company, usually a wholly owned subsidiary, that exists primarily to finance consumer purchases from the parent company. Prominent examples are General Motors Acceptance Corporation and Ford Motor Credit Company. Although these subsidiaries stand on their own financially, parent companies frequently make SUBORDINATED LOANS to add to their equity positions. This supports the high leverage on which the subsidiaries operate and assures their active participation in the COMMERCIAL PAPER and bond markets.

CARDS acronym for *Certificates for Amortizing Revolving Debts,* a Salomon Brothers security collaterized by credit card accounts receivable. Also called *plastic bonds. See also* ASSET-BACKED SECURITIES.

CARROT EQUITY British slang for an equity investment with a KICKER in the form of an opportunity to buy more equity if the company meets specified financial goals.

CARRYBACK, CARRYFORWARD *see* TAX LOSS CARRYBACK, CARRYFORWARD.

CARRYING CHARGE
Commodities: charge for carrying the actual commodity, including interest, storage, and insurance costs.

Margin accounts: fee that a broker charges for carrying securities on credit.

Real estate: carrying cost, primarily interest and taxes, of owning land prior to its development and resale.

Retailing: seller's charge for installment credit, which is either added to the purchase price or to unpaid installments.

CARRYOVER *see* TAX LOSS CARRYBACK, CARRYFORWARD.

CARS *see* CERTIFICATE FOR AUTOMOBILE RECEIVABLES.

CARTE BLANCHE full authority to take action. For example, an employee may be given carte blanche to enter into contracts with suppliers. The term also refers to the ability to fill in any amount on a blank check. For example, a father may sign a blank check and give it to his son to fill in when the son makes a major purchase. Carte Blanche is also the brand name of a widely used travel and entertainment card which requires that all balances be paid in full every month.

CARTEL group of businesses or nations that agree to influence prices by regulating production and marketing of a product. The most famous contemporary cartel is the Organization of Petroleum Exporting Countries (OPEC), which, notably in the 1970s, restricted oil production and sales and raised prices. A cartel has less control over an industry than a MONOPOLY. A number of nations, including the United States, have laws prohibiting cartels. TRUST is sometimes used as a synonym for cartel.

CASH asset account on a balance sheet representing paper currency and coins, negotiable money orders and checks, and bank balances. Also, transactions handled in cash. In the financial statements of annual reports, cash is usually grouped with CASH EQUIVALENTS, defined as all highly liquid securities with a known market value and a maturity, when acquired, of less than three months.

To cash is to convert a negotiable instrument, usually into paper currency and coins. *See also* CASH EQUIVALENTS.

CASH ACCOUNT brokerage firm account whose transactions are settled on a cash basis. It is distinguished from a MARGIN ACCOUNT, for which the broker extends credit. Some brokerage customers have both cash and margin accounts. By law, a CUSTODIAL ACCOUNT for a minor must be a cash account.

CASH ADVANCE loan taken out against a line of credit or credit card. Normally, the bank begins to charge interest from the date of the loan. Many banks also levy a flat fee for each cash advance. The interest rate charged on the cash advance is usually different from the rate charged on purchases made with the same card. Frequently, the cash advance rate is higher. In many cases advance rates are variable, and are usually tied to a certain number of percentage points over the prime rate.

CASH ASSET RATIO balance sheet LIQUIDITY RATIO representing cash (and equivalents) and marketable securities divided by current liabilities. Stricter than the *quick ratio*.

CASH BASIS
Accounting: method that recognizes revenues when cash is received and recognizes expenses when cash is paid out. In contrast, the *accrual method* recognizes

revenues when goods or services are sold and recognizes expenses when obligations are incurred. A third method, called *modified cash basis,* uses accrual accounting for long-term assets and is the basis usually referred to when the term cash basis is used.

Series EE Savings Bonds: paying the entire tax on these bonds when they mature. The alternative is to prorate the tax each year until the bonds mature.

CASHBOOK accounting book that combines cash receipts and disbursements. Its balance ties to the cash account in the general ledger on which the balance sheet is based.

CASH BUDGET estimated cash receipts and disbursements for a future period. A comprehensive cash budget schedules daily, weekly, or monthly expenditures together with the anticipated CASH FLOW from collections and other operating sources. Cash flow budgets are essential in establishing credit and purchasing policies, as well as in planning credit line usage and short-term investments in COMMERCIAL PAPER and other securities.

CASH COMMODITY commodity that is owned as the result of a completed contract and must be accepted upon delivery. Contrasts with futures contracts, which are not completed until a specified future date. The cash commodity contract specifications are set by the commodity exchanges.

CASH CONVERSION CYCLE elapsed time, usually expressed in days, from the outlay of cash for raw materials to the receipt of cash after the finished goods have been sold. Because a profit is built into the sales, the term *earnings cycle* is also used. The shorter the cycle, the more WORKING CAPITAL a business generates and the less it has to borrow. This cycle is directly affected by production efficiency, credit policy, and other controllable factors.

CASH COW business that generates a continuing flow of cash. Such a business usually has well-established brand names whose familiarity stimulates repeated buying of the products. For example, a magazine company that has a high rate of subscription renewals would be considered a cash cow. Stocks that are cash cows have dependable dividends.

CASH DISCOUNT TRADE CREDIT feature providing for a deduction if payment is made early. For example: trade terms of "2% 10 days net 30 days" allow a 2% cash discount for payment in 10 days. Term also refers to the lower price some merchants charge customers who pay in cash rather than with credit cards, in which case the merchant is passing on all or part of the merchant fee it would otherwise pay to the credit card company.

CASH DIVIDEND cash payment to a corporation's shareholders, distributed from current earnings or accumulated profits and taxable as income. Cash dividends are distinguished from STOCK DIVIDENDS, which are payments in the form of stock. *See also* YIELD.

INVESTMENT COMPANY cash dividends are usually made up of dividends, interest income, and capital gains received on its investment portfolio.

CASH EARNINGS cash revenues less cash expenses—specifically excluding noncash expenses such as DEPRECIATION.

CASH EQUIVALENTS instruments or investments of such high liquidity and safety that they are virtually as good as cash. Examples are a MONEY MARKET FUND and a TREASURY BILL. The FINANCIAL ACCOUNTING STANDARDS BOARD (FASB) defines cash equivalents for financial reporting purposes as any highly liquid security with a known market value and a maturity, when acquired, of less than three months.

CASH FLOW

1. in a larger financial sense, an analysis of all the changes that affect the cash account during an accounting period. The STATEMENT OF CASH FLOWS included in annual reports analyzes all changes affecting cash in the categories of operations, investments, and financing. For example: net operating income is an increase; the purchase of a new building is a decrease; and the issuance of stock or bonds is an increase. When more cash comes in than goes out, we speak of a *positive cash flow;* the opposite is a *negative cash flow.* Companies with assets well in excess of liabilities may nevertheless go bankrupt because they cannot generate enough cash to meet current obligations.

2. in investments, NET INCOME plus DEPRECIATION and other noncash charges. In this sense, it is synonymous with CASH EARNINGS. Investors focus on cash flow from operations because of their concern with a firm's ability to pay dividends. *See also* CASH BUDGET.

CASHIERING DEPARTMENT *See* CAGE.

CASHIER'S CHECK check that draws directly on a customer's account; the bank becomes the primary obligor. Consumers requiring a cashier's check must pay the amount of the check to the bank. The bank will then issue a check to a third party named by the consumer. Many businesses require that bills be paid by cashier's check instead of personal check, because they are assured that the funds are available with a cashier's check.

CASH INDEX PARTICIPATIONS (CIPS) *see* BASKET.

CASH MANAGEMENT

Corporate finance: efficient mobilization of cash into income-producing applications, using computers, telecommunications technology, innovative investment vehicles, and LOCK BOX arrangements.

Investing: broker's efficient movement of cash to keep it working. Merrill Lynch pioneered its proprietary Cash Management Account to combine securities trading, checking account services, money market investment services, and a debit (Visa) card.

CASH MARKET transactions in the cash or spot markets that are completed; that is, ownership of the commodity is transferred from seller to buyer and payment is given on delivery of the commodity. The cash market contrasts with the futures market, in which contracts are completed at a specified time in the future.

CASH-ON-CASH RETURN method of yield computation used for investments lacking an active secondary market, such as LIMITED PARTNERSHIPS. It simply divides the annual dollar income by the total dollars invested; a $10,000 investment that pays $1000 annually thus has a 10% cash-on-cash return. Investments having a market value and a predictable income stream to a designated maturity or call date, such as bonds, are better measured by CURRENT YIELD or YIELD-TO-MATURITY (or to call).

CASH ON DELIVERY (COD)

Commerce: transaction requiring that goods be paid for in full by cash or certified check or the equivalent at the point of delivery. The term *collect on delivery* has the same abbreviation and same meaning. If the customer refuses delivery, the seller has round-trip shipping costs to absorb or other, perhaps riskier, arrangements to make.

Securities: a requirement that delivery of securities to institutional investors be in exchange for assets of equal value—which, as a practical matter, means cash. Alternatively called *delivery against cost* (DAC) or *delivery versus payment* (DVP). On the other side of the trade, the term is *receive versus payment.*

CASH OR DEFERRED ARRANGEMENT (CODA) *see* 401(K) PLAN.

CASH RATIO ratio of cash and marketable securities to current liabilities; a refinement of the QUICK RATIO. The cash ratio tells the extent to which liabilities could be liquidated immediately. Sometimes called *liquidity ratio.*

CASH SETTLEMENT in the United States, settlement in cash on the TRADE DATE rather than the SETTLEMENT DATE of a securities transaction. In Great Britain, delivery and settlement on the first business day after the trade date.

CASH SURRENDER VALUE in insurance, the amount the insurer will return to a policyholder on cancellation of the policy. Sometimes abbreviated *CSVLI* (cash surrender value of life insurance), it shows up as an asset on the balance sheet of a company that has life insurance on its principals, called *key man insurance.* Insurance companies make loans against the cash value of policies, often at a better-than-market rate.

CASH VALUE INSURANCE life insurance that combines a death benefit with a potential tax-deferred buildup of money (called cash value) in the policy. The three main kinds of cash value insurance are WHOLE LIFE INSURANCE, VARIABLE LIFE INSURANCE, and UNIVERSAL LIFE INSURANCE. In whole life, cash value is accumulated based on the return on the company's investments in stocks, bonds, real estate, and other ventures. In variable life, the policyholder chooses how to allocate the money among stock, bond, and money market options. In universal life, a policyholder's cash value is invested in investments such as money market securities and medium-term Treasury bonds to build cash value. All cash values inside an insurance policy remain untaxed until they are withdrawn from the policy. Unlike cash value insurance, TERM LIFE INSURANCE offers only a death benefit, and no cash value buildup.

CASUALTY-INSURANCE insurance that protects a business or homeowner against property loss, damage, and related liability.

CASUALTY LOSS financial loss caused by damage, destruction, or loss of property as the result of an identifiable event that is sudden, unexpected, or unusual. Casualty and theft losses are considered together for tax purposes; are covered by most *casualty insurance* policies; and are tax deductible provided the loss is (1) not covered by insurance or (2) if covered, a claim has been made and denied.

CATASTROPHE CALL premature redemption of a municipal revenue bond because a catastrophe destroyed the source of the revenue backing the bond. For example, a bond backed by toll revenues from a bridge might be called, meaning bondholders will receive their principal back, if a storm destroyed the bridge. Usually, the proceeds for the payment will come from a commercial insurance policy covering the revenue-producing asset such as the bridge. A bond's INDENTURE will spell out the conditions under which a catastrophe call can be implemented.

CATS *see* CERTIFICATE OF ACCRUAL ON TREASURY SECURITIES.

CATS AND DOGS speculative stocks that have short histories of sales, earnings, and dividend payments. In bull markets, analysts say disparagingly that even the cats and dogs are going up.

CAVEAT EMPTOR, CAVEAT SUBSCRIPTOR *buyer beware, seller beware.* A variation on the latter is *caveat venditor.* Good advice when markets are not adequately protected, which was true of the stock market before the watchdog SECURITIES AND EXCHANGE COMMISSION was established in the 1930s.

CBO *see* COLLATERALIZED BOND OBLIGATION (CBO).

CEILING highest level allowable in a financial transaction. For example, someone buying a stock may place a ceiling on the stock's price, meaning they are not willing to pay more than that amount for the shares. The issuer of a bond may place a ceiling on the interest rate it is willing to pay. If market interest rates rise beyond that ceiling, the underwriter must cancel the issue. *See also* CAP.

CENTRAL BANK country's bank that (1) issues currency; (2) administers monetary policy, including OPEN MARKET OPERATIONS; (3) holds deposits representing the reserves of other banks; and (4) engages in transactions designed to facilitate the conduct of business and protect the public interest. In the United States, central banking is a function of the FEDERAL RESERVE SYSTEM.

CERTIFICATE formal declaration that can be used to document a fact, such as a birth certificate.
    The following are certificates with particular relevance to finance and investments.
1. auditor's certificate, sometimes called certificate of accounts, or ACCOUNTANT'S OPINION.
2. bond certificate, certificate of indebtedness issued by a corporation containing the terms of the issuer's promise to repay principal and pay interest, and describing collateral, if any. Traditionally, bond certificates had coupons attached, which were exchanged for payment of interest. Now that most bonds are issued in registered form, coupons are less common. The amount of a certificate is the par value of the bond.
3. CERTIFICATE OF DEPOSIT.
4. certificate of INCORPORATION.
5. certificate of indebtedness, government debt obligation having a maturity shorter than a bond and longer than a treasury bill (such as a Treasury Note).
6. PARTNERSHIP certificate, showing the interest of all participants in a business partnership.
7. PROPRIETORSHIP certificate, showing who is legally responsible in an individually owned business.
8. STOCK CERTIFICATE, evidence of ownership of a corporation showing number of shares, name of issuer, amount of par or stated value represented or a declaration of no-par value, and rights of the shareholder. Preferred stock certificates also list the issuer's responsibilities with respect to dividends and voting rights, if any.

CERTIFICATE FOR AUTOMOBILE RECEIVABLES (CARS) PASS-THROUGH SECURITY backed by automobile loan paper of banks and other lenders. *See also* ASSET-BACKED SECURITIES.

CERTIFICATELESS MUNICIPALS MUNICIPAL BONDS that have no certificate of ownership for each bondholder. Instead, one certificate is valid for the entire issue. Certificateless municipals save paperwork for brokers and municipalities and allow investors to trade their bonds without having to transfer certificates. *See also* BOOK ENTRY SECURITIES.

CERTIFICATE OF ACCRUAL ON TREASURY SECURITIES (CATS) U.S. Treasury issues, sold at a deep discount from face value. A ZERO-COUPON security, they pay no interest during their lifetime, but return the full face value at maturity. They are appropriate for retirement or education planning. As TREASURY SECURITIES, CATS cannot be CALLED AWAY.

CERTIFICATE OF DEPOSIT (CD) debt instrument issued by a bank that usually pays interest. Institutional CDs are issued in denominations of $100,000 or more, and individual CDs start as low as $100. Maturities range from a few weeks to several years. Interest rates are set by competitive forces in the marketplace. *See also* BROKERED CD.

CERTIFIED CHECK check for which a bank guarantees payment. It legally becomes an obligation of the bank, and the funds to cover it are immediately withdrawn from the depositor's account.

CERTIFIED FINANCIAL PLANNER (CFP) person who has passed examinations accredited by the Denver-based Institute of Certified Financial Planners, testing the ability to coordinate a client's banking, estate, insurance, investment, and tax affairs. Financial planners usually specialize in one or more of these areas and consult outside experts as needed. Some planners charge only fees and make no money on the implementation of their plans. Others charge a commission on each product or service they sell. *See also* FINANCIAL PLANNER.

CERTIFIED FINANCIAL STATEMENTS financial statements accompanied by an ACCOUNTANT'S OPINION.

CERTIFIED PUBLIC ACCOUNTANT (CPA) accountant who has passed certain exams, achieved a certain amount of experience, reached a certain age, and met all other statutory and licensing requirements of the U.S. state where he or she works. In addition to accounting and auditing, CPAs prepare tax returns for corporations and individuals.

CHAIRMAN OF THE BOARD member of a corporation's board of directors who presides over its meetings and who is the highest ranking officer in the corporation. The chairman of the board may or may not have the most actual executive authority in a firm. The additional title of CHIEF EXECUTIVE OFFICER (CEO) is reserved for the principal executive, and depending on the particular firm, that title may be held by the chairman, the president, or even an executive vice president. In some corporations, the position of chairman is either a prestigious reward for a past president or an honorary position for a prominent person, a large stockholder, or a family member; it may carry little or no real power in terms of policy or operating decision making.

CHAPTER 7 *see* BANKRUPTCY.

CHAPTER 10 federal BANKRUPTCY law section providing for reorganization under a court-appointed independent manager (trustee in bankruptcy) rather than under existing management as in the case with Chapter 11.

CHAPTER 11 *see* BANKRUPTCY.

CHARGE OFF *see* BAD DEBT.

CHARITABLE LEAD TRUST *see* CHARITABLE REMAINDER TRUST.

CHARITABLE REMAINDER TRUST IRREVOCABLE TRUST that pays income to one or more individuals until the GRANTOR'S death, at which time the balance, which is tax free, passes to a designated charity. It is a popular tax-saving alternative for individuals who have no children or who are wealthy enough to benefit both children and charity.

The charitable remainder trust is the reverse of a *charitable lead trust,* whereby a charity receives income during the grantor's life and the remainder passes to designated family members upon the grantor's death. The latter trust reduces estate taxes while enabling the family to retain control of the assets.

CHARTER *see* ARTICLES OF INCORPORATION.

CHARTERED FINANCIAL ANALYST (CFA) designation awarded by the Institute of Chartered Financial Analysts (ICFA) to experienced financial analysts who pass examinations in economics, financial accounting, portfolio management, security analysis, and standards of conduct.

CHARTERED FINANCIAL CONSULTANT (ChFC) designation awarded by American College of Bryn Mawr, Pennsylvania, to a professional FINANCIAL PLANNER who completes a four-year program covering economics, insurance, taxation, real estate, and other areas related to finance and investing.

CHARTERED LIFE UNDERWRITER (CLU) designation granted by The American College, Bryn Mawr, PA, the insurance and financial service industry's oldest and largest fully accredited institution of higher learning in the United States. Designation requires completion of ten college-level courses, three years of qualifying experience, and adherence to a strict code of ethics. All CLUs may join the American Society of CLU and ChFC, a professional association also headquartered in Bryn Mawr, for continuing education opportunities and other member services. The American Society has chapters in all 50 states.

CHARTIST technical analyst who charts the patterns of stocks, bonds, and commodities to make buy and sell recommendations to clients. Chartists believe recurring patterns of trading can help them forecast future price movements. *See also* TECHNICAL ANALYSIS.

CHASING THE MARKET purchasing a security at a higher price than intended because prices have risen sharply, or selling it at a lower level when prices fall. For example, an investor may want to buy shares of a stock at $20 and place a limit order to do so. But when the shares rise above $25, and then $28, the customer decides to enter a market order and buy the stock before it goes even higher. Investors can also chase the market when selling a stock. For example, if an investor wants to sell a stock at $20 and it declines to $15 and then $12, he may decide to sell it at the market price before it declines even further.

CHASTITY BONDS bonds that become redeemable at par value in the event of a TAKEOVER.

CHECK bill of exchange, or draft on a bank drawn against deposited funds to pay a specified sum of money to a specified person on demand. A check is considered as cash and is NEGOTIABLE when endorsed.

CHECKING THE MARKET canvassing securities market-makers by telephone or other means in search of the best bid or offer price.

CHICAGO BOARD OF TRADE *see* SECURITIES AND COMMODITIES EXCHANGES.

CHICAGO BOARD OPTIONS EXCHANGE *see* SECURITIES AND COMMODITIES EXCHANGES.

CHICAGO MERCANTILE EXCHANGE *see* SECURITIES AND COMMODITIES EXCHANGES.

CHIEF EXECUTIVE OFFICER (CEO) officer of a firm principally responsible for the activities of a company. CEO is usually an additional title held by the CHAIRMAN OF THE BOARD, the president, or another senior officer such as a vice chairman or an executive vice president.

CHIEF FINANCIAL OFFICER (CFO) executive officer who is responsible for handling funds, signing checks, keeping financial records, and financial planning for a corporation. He or she typically has the title of vice president-finance or financial vice president in large corporations, that of treasurer or controller (also spelled comptroller) in smaller companies. Since many state laws require that a corporation have a treasurer, that title is often combined with one or more of the other financial titles.

The controllership function requires an experienced accountant to direct internal accounting programs, including cost accounting, systems and procedures, data processing, acquisitions analysis, and financial planning. The controller may also have internal audit responsibilities.

The treasury function is concerned with the receipt, custody, investment, and disbursement of corporate funds and for borrowings and the maintenance of a market for the company's securities.

CHIEF OPERATING OFFICER (COO) officer of a firm, usually the president or an executive vice president, responsible for day-to-day management. The chief operating officer reports to the CHIEF EXECUTIVE OFFICER and may or may not be on the board of directors (presidents typically serve as board members). *See also* CHAIRMAN OF THE BOARD.

CHINESE WALL imaginary barrier between the investment banking, corporate finance, and research departments of a brokerage house and the sales and trading departments. Since the investment banking side has sensitive knowledge of impending deals such as takeovers, new stock and bond issues, divestitures, spinoffs and the like, it would be unfair to the general investing public if the sales and trading side of the firm had advance knowledge of such transactions. So several SEC and stock exchange rules mandate that a Chinese Wall be erected to prevent premature leakage of this market-moving information. It became law with the passage of SEC Rule 10b-5 of the Securities Exchange Act of 1934. The investment banking department uses code names and logs of the people who have access to key information in an attempt to keep the identities of the parties secret until the deal is publicly announced.

CHUNNEL tunnel crossing the English Channel between Great Britain and France. The Chunnel project took years to build and cost billions of dollars, but was finally opened for passenger and freight traffic in 1994. The Chunnel was built and is operated by Euro-Tunnel PLC.

CHURNING excessive trading of a client's account. Churning increases the broker's commissions, but usually leaves the client worse off or no better off than before. Churning is illegal under SEC and exchange rules, but is difficult to prove.

CINCINNATI STOCK EXCHANGE (CSE) stock exchange established in 1887. The CSE became the first completely automated stock exchange, handling members' transactions without the benefit of a physical trading floor by using computers. The CSE has nominal jurisdiction over the National Securities Trading

System (NSTS), known popularly as the "Cincinnati experiment." Participating brokerage firms enter orders into the NSTS computer, which then matches orders and clears the orders back to the brokers. The NSTS contains some of the features envisioned for a national exchange market system.

CIRCLE underwriter's way of designating potential purchasers and amounts of a securities issue during the REGISTRATION period, before selling is permitted. Registered representatives canvass prospective buyers and report any interest to the underwriters, who then circle the names on their list.

CIRCUIT BREAKERS measures instituted by the major stock and commodities exchanges to halt trading temporarily in stocks and stock index futures when the market has fallen by a specified amount in a specified period. Circuit breakers were instituted after BLACK MONDAY in 1987 and modified following another sharp market drop in October 1989. They are subject to change from time to time, but may include trading halts, curtailment of automated trading systems, and/or price movement limits on index futures. Their purpose is to prevent a market free-fall by permitting a rebalancing of buy and sell orders. *See also* PROGRAM TRADING.

CITIZEN BONDS form of CERTIFICATELESS MUNICIPALS. Citizen bonds may be registered on stock exchanges, in which case their prices are listed in daily newspapers, unlike other municipal bonds. *See also* BOOK-ENTRY SECURITIES.

CITY CODE ON TAKEOVERS AND MERGERS *see* DAWN RAID.

CIVILIAN LABOR FORCE all members of the population aged 16 or over in the United States who are not in the military or institutions such as prisons or mental hospitals and who are either employed or are unemployed and actively seeking and available for work. Every month, the U.S. Department of Labor releases the unemployment rate, which is the percentage of the civilian labor force who are unemployed. The Labor Department also releases the percentage of the civilian non-institutional population who are employed.

CLASS
1. securities having similar features. Stocks and bonds are the two main classes; they are subdivided into various classes—for example, mortgage bonds and debentures, issues with different rates of interest, common and preferred stock, or Class A and Class B common. The different classes in a company's capitalization are itemized on its balance sheet.
2. options of the same type—put or call—with the same underlying security. A class of option having the same expiration date and EXERCISE PRICE is termed a SERIES.

CLASS A/CLASS B SHARES *see* CLASSIFIED STOCK.

CLASS ACTION legal complaint filed on behalf of a group of shareholders having an identical grievance. Shareholders in a class action are typically represented by one lawyer or group of attorneys, who like this kind of business because the awards tend to be proportionate to the number of parties in the class.

CLASSIFIED STOCK separation of equity into more than one CLASS of common, usually designated Class A and Class B. The distinguishing features, set forth in the corporation charter and bylaws, usually give an advantage to the Class A shares in terms of voting power, though dividend and liquidation privileges can also be involved. Classified stock is less prevalent today than in the 1920s, when it was used as a means of preserving minority control.

CLAYTON ANTI-TRUST ACT *see* ANTITRUST LAWS.

CLEAN
Finance: free of debt, as in a clean balance sheet. In banking, corporate borrowers have traditionally been required to *clean up* for at least 30 days each year to prove their borrowings were seasonal and not required as permanent working capital.

International trade: without documents, as in clean vs. documentary drafts.

Securities: block trade that matches buy or sell orders, sparing the block positioner any inventory risk. If the transaction appears on the exchange tape, it is said to be *clean on the tape*. Sometimes such a trade is called a *natural:* "We did a natural for 80,000 XYZ common."

CLEAR
Banking: COLLECTION of funds on which a check is drawn, and payment of those funds to the holder of the check. *See also* CLEARING HOUSE FUNDS.

Finance: asset not securing a loan and not otherwise encumbered. As a verb, to clear means to make a profit: "After all expenses, we *cleared* $1 million."

Securities: COMPARISON of the details of a transaction between brokers prior to settlement; final exchange of securities for cash on delivery.

CLEARING CORPORATIONS organizations, such as the NATIONAL SECURITIES CLEARING CORPORATION (NSCC), that are exchange-affiliated and facilitate the validation, delivery, and settlement of securities transactions.

CLEARING HOUSE FUNDS funds represented by checks or drafts that pass between banks through the FEDERAL RESERVE SYSTEM. Unlike FEDERAL FUNDS, which are drawn on reserve balances and are good the same day, clearing house funds require three days to clear. Also, funds used to settle transactions on which there is one day's FLOAT.

CLEAR TITLE title that is clear of all claims or disputed interests. It is necessary to have clear title to a piece of real estate before it can be sold by one party to another. In order to obtain a clear title, it is usually necessary to have a title search performed by a title company, which may find various clouds on the title such as an incomplete certificate of occupancy, outstanding building violations, claims by neighbors for pieces of the property, or an inaccurate survey. Once these objections have been resolved, the owner will have a clear and marketable title. *See also* BAD TITLE; CLOUD ON TITLE.

CLIFFORD TRUST trust set up for at least ten years and a day, which made it possible to turn over income-producing assets, then to reclaim the assets when the trust expired. Prior to the TAX REFORM ACT OF 1986, such trusts were popular ways of shifting income-producing assets from parents to children, whose income was taxed at lower rates. However, the 1986 Act made monies put into Clifford trusts after March 1, 1986, subject to taxation at the grantor's tax rate, thus defeating their purpose. For trusts established before that date, taxes are paid at the child's lower tax rate, but only if the child is under the age of 14. Since the Tax Act was implemented, few Clifford trusts are set up. *See also* INTER VIVOS TRUST.

CLONE FUND in a FAMILY OF FUNDS, new fund set up to emulate a successful existing fund.

CLOSE
1. the price of the final trade of a security at the end of a trading day.
2. the last half hour of a trading session on the exchanges.

3. in commodities trading, the period just before the end of the session when trades marked for execution AT THE CLOSE are completed.
4. to consummate a sale or agreement. In a REAL ESTATE closing, for example, rights of ownership are transferred in exchange for monetary and other considerations. At a *loan* closing, notes are signed and checks are exchanged. At the close of an *underwriting* deal, checks and securities are exchanged.
5. in accounting, the transfer of revenue and expense accounts at the end of the period—called *closing the books.*

CLOSE A POSITION to eliminate an investment from one's portfolio. The simplest example is the outright sale of a security and its delivery to the purchaser in exchange for payment. In commodities futures and options trading, traders commonly close out positions through offsetting transactions. Closing a position terminates involvement with the investment; HEDGING, though similar, requires further actions.

CLOSE MARKET market in which there is a narrow spread between BID and OFFER prices. Such a market is characterized by active trading and multiple competing market makers. In general, it is easier for investors to buy and sell securities and get good prices in a close market than in a wide market characterized by wide differences between bid and offer prices.

CLOSED CORPORATION corporation owned by a few people, usually management or family members. Shares have no public market. Also known as *private corporation* or *privately held corporation.*

CLOSED-END FUND type of fund that has a fixed number of shares usually listed on a major stock exchange. Unlike open-end mutual funds, closed end funds do not stand ready to issue and redeem shares on a continuous basis. They tend to have specialized portfolios of stocks, bonds, CONVERTIBLES, or combinations thereof, and may be oriented toward income, capital gains, or a combination of these objectives. Examples are the Korea Fund, which specializes in the stocks of Korean firms, and ASA Ltd., which specializes in South African gold mining stocks. Both are listed on the New York Stock Exchange. Because the managers of closed-end funds are perceived to be less responsive to profit opportunities than open-end fund managers, who must attract and retain shareholders, closed-end fund shares often sell at a discount from net asset value. *See also* DUAL-PURPOSE FUND.

CLOSED-END MANAGEMENT COMPANY INVESTMENT COMPANY that operates a mutual fund with a limited number of shares outstanding. Unlike an OPEN-END MANAGEMENT COMPANY, which creates new shares to meet investor demand, a closed-end fund has a set number of shares. These are often listed on an exchange. *See also* CLOSED-END FUND.

CLOSED-END MORTGAGE mortgage-bond issue with an indenture that prohibits repayment before maturity and the repledging of the same collateral without the permission of the bondholders; also called closed mortgage. It is distinguished from an OPEN-END MORTGAGE, which is reduced by amortization and can be increased to its original amount and secured by the original mortgage.

CLOSED FUND MUTUAL FUND that has become too large and is no longer issuing shares.

CLOSED OUT liquidated the position of a client unable to meet a margin call or cover a short sale. *See also* CLOSE A POSITION.

CLOSELY HELD corporation most of whose voting stock is held by a few share-holders; differs from a CLOSED CORPORATION because enough stock is publicly held to provide a basis for trading. Also, the shares held by the controlling group and not considered likely to be available for purchase.

CLOSING COSTS expenses involved in transferring real estate from a seller to a buyer, among them lawyer's fees, survey charges, title searches and insurance, and fees to file deeds and mortgages.

CLOSING PRICE price of the last transaction completed during a day's trading session on an organized securities exchange. *See also* CLOSING RANGE.

CLOSING PURCHASE option seller's purchase of another option having the same features as an earlier one. The two options cancel each other out and thus liquidate the seller's position.

CLOSING QUOTE last bid and offer prices recorded by a specialist or market maker at the close of a trading day.

CLOSING RANGE range of prices (in commodities trading) within which an order to buy or sell a commodity can be executed during one trading day.

CLOSING SALE sale of an option having the same features (i.e., of the same series) as an option previously purchased. The two have the effect of canceling each other out. Such a transaction demonstrates the intention to liquidate the holder's position in the underlying securities upon exercise of the buy.

CLOSING TICK gauge of stock market strength that nets the number of stocks whose New York Stock Exchange closing prices were higher than their previous trades, called an UPTICK or plus tick, against the number that closed on a DOWNTICK or minus tick. When the closing tick is positive, that is, when more stocks advanced than declined in the last trade, traders say the market closed on an uptick or was "buying at the close," a bullish sign. "Selling at the close," resulting in a minus closing tick or downtick, is bearish. *See also* TRIN.

CLOSING TRIN *see* TRIN.

CLOUD ON TITLE any document, claim, unreleased lien, or encumbrance that may superficially impair or injure the title to a property or make the title doubtful because of its apparent or possible validity. Clouds on title are usually uncovered in a TITLE SEARCH. These clouds range from a recorded mortgage paid in full, but with no satisfaction of mortgage recorded, to a property sold without a spouse's release of interest, to an heir of a prior owner with a questionable claim to the property. The property owner may initiate a quitclaim deed or a quiet title proceeding to remove the cloud on title from the record. Also called *bad title.*

CMO *see* COLLATERALIZED MORTGAGE OBLIGATION (CMO).

CMO REIT specialized type of REAL ESTATE INVESTMENT TRUST (REIT) that invests in the residual cash flows of COLLATERALIZED MORTGAGE OBLIGATIONS (CMOs). CMO cash flows represent the spread (difference) between the rates paid by holders of the underlying mortgage loans and the lower, shorter term rates paid to investors in the CMOs. Spreads are subject to risks associated with interest rate levels and are considered risky investments. Also called *equity CMOs.*

COATTAIL INVESTING following on the coattails of other successful investors, usually institutions, by trading the same stocks when their actions are made public. This risky strategy assumes the research that guided the investor wearing the coat is still relevant by the time the coattail investor reads about it.

CODE OF ARBITRATION *see* BOARD OF ARBITRATION.

CODE OF PROCEDURE NATIONAL ASSOCIATION OF SECURITIES DEALERS (NASD) guide for its District Business Conduct Committees in hearing and adjudicating complaints filed between or against NASD members under its Rules of Fair Practice.

CODICIL legal document that amends a will.

C.O.D. TRANSACTION *see* DELIVERY VERSUS PAYMENT.

COFFEE, SUGAR AND COCOA EXCHANGE (CSCE) New York-based commodity exchange trading futures and options on SOFTS, as typical commodities are called. The CSCE trades futures and options on coffee "C," No. 11 sugar, cocoa, nonfat dry milk, and cheddar cheese. Only futures contracts are traded on No. 14 sugar and white sugar. The exchange shares the trading floor at the COMMODITIES EXCHANGE CENTER with the NEW YORK MERCANTILE EXCHANGE and NEW YORK COTTON EXCHANGE. Contracts trade Monday through Friday, with trading hours falling between 9 A.M. and 3:15 P.M.

COINCIDENT INDICATORS economic indicators that coincide with the current pace of economic activity. The Index of Coincident Indicators is published monthly by the Commerce Department along with the Index of LEADING INDICATORS and the Index of LAGGING INDICATORS to give the public a reading on whether the economy is expanding or contracting and at what pace. The components of the Index of Coincident Indicators are: non-farm payroll workers, personal income less transfer payments, industrial production, manufacturing, and trade sales.

COINSURANCE sharing of an insurance risk, common when claims could be of such size that it would not be prudent for one company to underwrite the whole risk. Typically, the underwriter is liable up to a stated limit, and the coinsurer's liability is for amounts above that limit.

Policies on hazards such as fire or water damage often require coverage of at least a specified coinsurance percentage of the replacement cost. Such clauses induce the owners of property to carry full coverage or close to it.

COLA acronym for *cost-of-living adjustment,* which is an annual addition to wages or benefits to compensate employees or beneficiaries for the loss of purchasing power due to inflation. Many union contracts contain a COLA providing for salary increases at or above the change in the previous year's CONSUMER PRICE INDEX (CPI). Social Security recipients also have their monthly payments adjusted annually based on a COLA tied to the CPI.

COLD CALLING practice of making unsolicited calls to potential customers by brokers. Brokers hope to interest customers in stocks, bonds, mutual funds, financial planning, or other financial products and services in their cold calls. In some countries, such as Great Britain and parts of Canada, cold calling is severely restricted or even prohibited.

COLLAR in new issue underwriting, the lowest rate acceptable to a buyer of bonds or the lowest price acceptable to the issuer. Also used to mean the index level at which a CIRCUIT BREAKER is triggered.

COLLATERAL ASSET pledged to a lender until a loan is repaid. If the borrower defaults, the lender has the legal right to seize the collateral and sell it to pay off the loan.

COLLATERALIZE *see* ASSIGN; COLLATERAL; HYPOTHECATION.

COLLATERALIZED BOND OBLIGATION (CBO) INVESTMENT-GRADE bond backed by a pool of JUNK BONDS. CBOs are similar in concept to COLLATERALIZED MORTGAGE OBLIGATIONS (CMOs), but differ in that CBOs represent different degrees of credit quality rather than different maturities. Underwriters of CBOs package a large and diversified pool of high-risk, high-yield junk bonds, which is then separated into "tiers." Typically, a top tier represents the higher quality collateral and pays the lowest interest rate; a middle tier is hacked by riskier bonds and pays a higher rate; the bottom tier represents the lowest credit quality and instead of receiving a fixed interest rate receives the residual interest payments—money that is left over after the higher tiers have been paid. CBOs, like CMOs, are substantially overcollateralized and this, plus the diversification of the pool backing them, earns them investment-grade bond ratings. Holders of third-tier CBOs stand to earn high yields or less money depending on the rate of defaults in the collateral pool. CBOs provide a way for big holders of junk bonds to reduce their portfolios and for securities firms to tap a new source of buyers in the disenchanted junk bond market of the early 1990s.

COLLATERALIZED MORTGAGE OBLIGATION (CMO) mortgage-backed bond that separates mortgage pools into different maturity classes, called *tranches.* This is accomplished by applying income (payments and prepayments of principal and interest) from mortgages in the pool in the order that the CMOs pay out. Tranches pay different rates of interest and can mature in a few months, or as long as 20 years. Issued by the Federal Home Loan Mortgage Corporation (Freddie Mac) and private issuers, CMOs are usually backed by government-guaranteed or other top-grade mortgages and have AAA ratings. In return for a lower yield, CMOs provide investors with increased security about the life of their investment compared to purchasing a whole mortgage-backed security. Even so, if mortgage rates drop sharply, causing a flood of refinancings, prepayment rates will soar and CMO tranches will be repaid before their expected maturity. CMOs are broken into different classes, called COMPANION BONDS or PLANNED AMORTIZATION CLASS (PAC) bonds.

COLLATERAL TRUST BOND corporate debt security backed by other securities, usually held by a bank or other trustee. Such bonds are backed by collateral trust certificates and are usually issued by parent corporations that are borrowing against the securities of wholly owned subsidiaries.

COLLECTIBLE rare object collected by investors. Examples: stamps, coins, oriental rugs, antiques, baseball cards, photographs. Collectibles typically rise sharply in value during inflationary periods, when people are trying to move their assets from paper currency as an inflation hedge, then drop in value during low inflation. Collectible trading for profit can be quite difficult, because of the limited number of buyers and sellers.

COLLECTION
1. presentation of a negotiable instrument such as a draft or check to the place at which it is payable. The term refers not only to check clearing and payment, but to such special banking services as foreign collections, coupon collection, and collection of returned items (bad checks).
2. referral of a past due account to specialists in collecting loans or accounts receivable, either an internal department or a private collection agency.
3. in a general financial sense, conversion of accounts receivable into cash.

COLLECTION PERIOD *see* COLLECTION RATIO.

COLLECTION RATIO ratio of a company's accounts receivable to its average daily sales. Average daily sales are obtained by dividing sales for an accounting period by the number of days in the accounting period—annual sales divided by 365, if the accounting period is a year. That result, divided into accounts receivable (an average of beginning and ending accounts receivable is more accurate), is the collection ratio—the average number of days it takes the company to convert receivables into cash. It is also called *average collection period. See* ACCOUNTS RECEIVABLE TURNOVER for a discussion of its significance.

COLLECTIVE BARGAINING process by which members of the labor force, operating through authorized union representatives, negotiate with their employers concerning wages, hours, working conditions, and benefits.

COLLEGE CONSTRUCTION LOAN INSURANCE ASSOCIATION federal agency established in 1987 to guarantee loans for college building programs. Informally called *Connie Lee.*

COLTS acronym for *Continuously Offered Longer-term Securities,* 3-year to 30-year fixed rate, variable rate, or zero-coupon bonds offered on an ongoing basis by the INTERNATIONAL BANK FOR RECONSTRUCTION AND DEVELOPMENT (World Bank). Bonds finance general operations of the bank and the terms are determined by bank management at the time of each new offering.

COMBINATION
1. arrangement of options involving two long or two short positions with different expiration dates or strike (exercise) prices. A trader could order a combination with a long call and a long put or a short call and a short put.
2. joining of competing companies in an industry to alter the competitive balance in their favor is called a combination in restraint of trade.
3. joining two or more separate businesses into a single accounting entity; also called *business combination. See also* MERGER.

COMBINATION ANNUITY *see* HYBRID ANNUITY.

COMBINATION BOND bond backed by the full faith and credit of the governmental unit issuing it as well as by revenue from the toll road, bridge, or other project financed by the bond.

COMBINATION ORDER *see* ALTERNATIVE ORDER.

COMBINED FINANCIAL STATEMENT financial statement that brings together the assets, liabilities, net worth, and operating figures of two or more affiliated companies. In its most comprehensive form, called a combining statement, it includes columns showing each affiliate on an "alone" basis; a column "eliminating" offsetting intercompany transactions; and the resultant combined financial statement. A combined statement is distinguished from a CONSOLIDATED FINANCIAL STATEMENT of a company and subsidiaries, which must reconcile investment and capital accounts. Combined financial statements do not necessarily represent combined credit responsibility or investment strength.

COMEX division of NEW YORK MERCANTILE EXCHANGE, following its merger with the NYMEX. Formerly known as the Commodity Exchange, it is the the leading U.S. market for metals futures and options trading. Futures and futures options are traded on copper, the Eurotop 100, gold, and silver. *See also* NEW YORK MERCANTILE EXCHANGE; SECURITIES AND COMMODITIES EXCHANGES.

COMFORT LETTER

1. independent auditor's letter, required in securities underwriting agreements, to assure that information in the registration statement and prospectus is correctly prepared and that no material changes have occurred since its preparation. It is sometimes called *cold comfort letter*—cold because the accountants do not state positively that the information is correct, only that nothing has come to their attention to indicate it is not correct.

2. letter from one to another of the parties to a legal agreement stating that certain actions not clearly covered in the agreement will—or will not—be taken. Such declarations of intent usually deal with matters that are of importance only to the two parties and do not concern other signers of the agreement.

COMMERCIAL HEDGERS companies that take positions in commodities markets in order to lock in prices at which they buy raw materials or sell their products. For instance, Alcoa might hedge its holdings of aluminum with contracts in aluminum futures, or Eastman Kodak, which must buy great quantities of silver for making film, might hedge its holdings in the silver futures market.

COMMERCIAL LOAN short-term (typically 90-day) renewable loan to finance the seasonal WORKING CAPITAL needs of a business, such as purchase of inventory or production and distribution of goods. Commercial loans—shown on the balance sheet as notes payable—rank second only to TRADE CREDIT in importance as a source of short-term financing. Interest is based on the prime rate. *See also* CLEAN.

COMMERCIAL PAPER short-term obligations with maturities ranging from 2 to 270 days issued by banks, corporations, and other borrowers to investors with temporarily idle cash. Such instruments are unsecured and usually discounted, although some are interest-bearing. They can be issued directly—*direct issuers* do it that way—or through brokers equipped to handle the enormous clerical volume involved. Issuers like commercial paper because the maturities are flexible and because the rates are usually marginally lower than bank rates. Investors—actually lenders, since commercial paper is a form of debt—like the flexibility and safety of an instrument that is issued only by top-rated concerns and is nearly always backed by bank lines of credit. Both Moody's and Standard & Poor's assign ratings to commercial paper.

COMMERCIAL PROPERTY real estate that includes income-producing property, such as office buildings, restaurants, shopping centers, hotels, industrial parks, warehouses, and factories. Commercial property usually must be zoned for business purposes. It is possible to invest in commercial property directly, or through REAL ESTATE INVESTMENT TRUSTS or REAL ESTATE LIMITED PARTNERSHIPS. Investors receive income from rents and capital appreciation if the property is sold at a profit. Investing in commercial property also entails large risks, such as nonpayment of rent by tenants or a decline in property values because of overbuilding or low demand.

COMMERCIAL WELLS oil and gas drilling sites that are productive enough to be commercially viable. A limited partnership usually syndicates a share in a commercial well.

COMMINGLING

Securities: mixing customer-owned securities with those owned by a firm in its proprietary accounts. REHYPOTHECATION—the use of customers' collateral to secure brokers' loans—is permissible with customer consent, but certain securities and collateral must by law be kept separate.

Trust banking: pooling the investment funds of individual accounts, with each customer owning a share of the total fund. Similar to a MUTUAL FUND.

COMMISSION
Real estate: percentage of the selling price of the property, paid by the seller.
Securities: fee paid to a broker for executing a trade based on the number of shares traded or the dollar amount of the trade. Since 1975, when regulation ended, brokers have been free to charge whatever they like.

COMMISSION BROKER broker, usually a floor broker, who executes trades of stocks, bonds, or commodities for a commission.

COMMITMENT FEE lender's charge for contracting to hold credit available. Fee may be replaced by interest when money is borrowed or both fees and interest may be charged, as with a REVOLVING CREDIT.

COMMITTEE ON UNIFORM SECURITIES IDENTIFICATION PROCEDURES (CUSIP) committee that assigns identifying numbers and codes for all securities. These CUSIP numbers and symbols are used when recording all buy or sell orders. For International Business Machines the CUSIP symbol is IBM and the CUSIP number is 45920010.

COMMODITIES bulk goods such as grains, metals, and foods traded on a commodities exchange or on the SPOT MARKET. *See also* SECURITIES AND COMMODITIES EXCHANGES.

COMMODITIES EXCHANGE CENTER *see* SECURITIES AND COMMODITIES EXCHANGES.

COMMODITY-BACKED BOND bond tied to the price of an underlying commodity. An investor whose bond is tied to the price of silver or gold receives interest pegged to the metal's current price, rather than a fixed dollar amount. Such a bond is meant to be a hedge against inflation, which drives up the prices of most commodities.

COMMODITY FUTURES CONTRACT FUTURES CONTRACT tied to the movement of a particular commodity. This enables contract buyers to buy a specific amount of a commodity at a specified price on a particular date in the future. The price of the contract is determined using the OPEN OUTCRY system on the floor of a commodity exchange such as the Chicago Board of Trade or the Commodity Exchange in New York. There are commodity futures contracts based on meats such as cattle and pork bellies; grains such as corn, oats, soybeans and wheat; metals such as gold, silver, and platinum; and energy products such as heating oil, natural gas, and crude oil. For a complete listing of commodity futures contracts, *see* SECURITIES AND COMMODITIES EXCHANGES.

COMMODITY FUTURES TRADING COMMISSION (CFTC) independent agency created by Congress in 1974 responsible for regulating the U.S. commodity futures and options markets. The CFTC is responsible for insuring market integrity and protecting market participants against manipulation, abusive trade practices, and fraud.

COMMODITY INDICES indices that measure either the price or performance of physical commodities, or the price of commodities as represented by the price of futures contracts that are listed on commodity exchanges. The Journal of Commerce Index, Reuters Index and The Economist Index are three that measure industrial performance and raw commodities. Due to the complexities of holding physical commodities, however, investors tend to focus on futures indices that are liquid baskets of commodities. Institutional investors prohibited from investing directly in the futures market can include commodities in their portfolios through these indices.

Among the commodity indices that measure futures price performance are:

Bankers Trust Commodity Index (BTCI) is a weighted, composite measure of the values of a basket of five commodities. Energy prices are based on NEW YORK MERCANTILE EXCHANGE contracts. Aluminum is based on the LONDON METAL EXCHANGE contract, while gold and silver are based on London spot fixings. The base prices used are the average prices of each component commodity over the first quarter of 1984. The components are: crude oil—45/$30.191; gold—18/$384.18; aluminum—17/$1,543.67; heating oil—10/$0.8340; silver—10/$9.0043. The value of the index on any given day is calculated by multiplying the current price by the base weight and dividing this figure by the base price.

Energy and Metals Index (ENMET) is a geometrically weighted index based on the prices of futures contracts and developed by Merrill Lynch. ENMET is comprised of six commodities: crude oil (40%), natural gas (15%), gold (20%), silver (5%), copper (15%), aluminum (5%). The index is weighted to show optimal historic correlation with the CONSUMER PRICE INDEX and the PRODUCER PRICE INDEX. The index is computed daily.

Goldman Sachs Commodity Index (GSCI) consists of 22 commodities. All but the industrials, which trade on the LONDON METAL EXCHANGE, trade on U.S. futures markets. There are five component groups: energy—crude oil (15.89%), natural gas (15.73%), heating oil (9.94%), unleaded gasoline (9.70%); agriculture—wheat (8.87%), corn (6.34%), soybeans (2.99%), cotton (2.96%), sugar (2.84%), coffee (1.09%), cocoa (0.29%); livestock—live cattle (9.35%), live hogs (4.24%); industrials—aluminum (2.86%), copper (2.07%), zinc (0.77%), nickel (0.48%), lead (0.29%), tin (0.12%); precious metals—gold (2.53%), platinum (0.40%), silver (0.26%). Each commodity is weighted by quantity of world production as a means of measuring the impact of commodity performance on the global economy. The index includes a rolling yield, achievable by continually rolling forward the futures positions, and it is investable. Price movement reflects spot price changes in the underlying commodities. Commodity yield reflects roll yield and Treasury bill yield. Because delivery of the underlying commodity never occurs, the investor can keep his money invested in Treasury bills. Additionally, there are six sub-indices, representing each of the commodity component groups, calculated daily on real-time prices. Futures and options on the index are traded on the Chicago Mercantile Exchange. Other investment products based on the GSCI and the GSCI sub-indices include structured notes, swaps, customized over-the-counter options and principal-guaranteed annuity contracts.

Investable Commodity Index (ICI) is a broad-based index of 16 commodities based on exchange-traded commodity futures and developed by Intermarket Management, Inc. The index measures the reinvested total returns of an equally weighted, fully collateralized basket: grains (19%)—wheat, corn, soybeans; metals (19%)—gold, silver, copper; energy (25%)—crude oil, heating oil, gasoline, natural gas; livestock (12%)—live cattle, live hogs; food and fiber (25%)—cocoa, coffee, sugar, cotton. The ICI is a rolling index, and represents the compounded daily percentage change in the geometric mean of the 16 commodities' prices plus 100% of the daily compounded 13-week U.S. Treasury bill returns.

J. P. Morgan Commodity Index (JPMCI) uses a dollar-weighted arithmetic average of total returns by investment in 11 metals and energy commodities. The index is composed of base metals (22%)—aluminum (9%), copper (8%), nickel (2%), zinc (3%); energy (55%)—West Texas Intermediate crude oil (33%), heating oil (10%), natural gas (7%), unleaded gasoline (5%); and precious metals

(23%)—gold (15%), silver (5%), platinum (3%). As a total return index, returns are derived from changes in commodity futures prices, from rolling long futures positions through time along a sloping forward curve, and by full collateralization of the value of the index with Treasury bills. The index has a positive correlation with growth and inflation, and a negative correlation with bond and equity returns. The index is rebalanced monthly to maintain constant dollar weight.

Knight-Ridder Commodity Research Bureau Index (KR-CRB Index) is made up of 21 commodities whose futures trade on U.S. exchanges. The index is viewed widely as a broad measure of overall commodity price trends. There are six component groups: industrials (28.6%)—crude oil, heating oil, unleaded gasoline, copper, lumber, cotton; grains (23.8%)—corn, wheat, soybeans, soy meal, soy oil; metals (14.3%)—gold, silver, platinum; meats (14.3%)—cattle, hogs, pork bellies; imports (14.3%)—coffee, cocoa, sugar; miscellaneous (4.7%)—orange juice. Equal weighting is used for both arithmetic averaging of individual commodity months and for geometric averaging of the 21 commodity averages. As a result, no single month or commodity has undue impact on the index. Futures and options on the KR-CRB Index trade on the NEW YORK FUTURES EXCHANGE (NYFE). Futures are settled at contract maturity by cash payment. Values of the index are computed by Knight-Ridder Financial Publishing and disseminated by the NYFE every 15 seconds during the trading day.

COMMODITY PAPER inventory loans or advances secured by commodities. If the commodities are in transit, a bill of lading is executed by a common carrier. If they are in storage, a trust receipt acknowledges that they are held and that proceeds from their sale will be transmitted to the lender; a warehouse receipt lists the goods.

COMMON MARKET *see* EUROPEAN ECONOMIC COMMUNITY.

COMMON STOCK units of ownership of a public corporation. Owners typically are entitled to vote on the selection of directors and other important matters as well as to receive dividends on their holdings. In the event that a corporation is liquidated, the claims of secured and unsecured creditors and owners of bonds and preferred stock take precedence over the claims of those who own common stock. For the most part, however, common stock has more potential for appreciation. *See also* CAPITAL STOCK.

COMMON STOCK EQUIVALENT preferred stock or bond convertible into common stock, or warrant to purchase common stock at a specified price or discount from market price. Common stock equivalents represent potential dilution of existing common shareholder's equity, and their conversion or exercise is assumed in calculating fully diluted earnings per share. *See also* FULLY DILUTED EARNINGS PER SHARE.

COMMON STOCK FUND MUTUAL FUND that invests only in common stocks.

COMMON STOCK RATIO percentage of total capitalization represented by common stock. From a creditor's standpoint a high ratio represents a margin of safety in the event of LIQUIDATION. From an investor's standpoint, however, a high ratio can mean a lack of *leverage*. What the ratio should be depends largely on the stability of earnings. Electric utilities can operate with low ratios because their earnings are stable. As a general rule, when an industrial company's stock ratio is below 30%, analysts check on earnings stability and fixed charge coverage in bad times as well as good.

COMMUNITY PROPERTY property and income accumulated by a married couple and belonging to them jointly. The two have equal rights to the income from stocks, bonds, and real estate, as well as to the appreciated value of those assets.

COMPANION BONDS one class of a COLLATERALIZED MORTGAGE OBLIGATION (CMO) which is paid off first when the underlying mortgages are prepaid as interest rates fall. When interest rates rise and there are fewer prepayments, the principal on companion bonds will be prepaid more slowly. Companion bonds therefore absorb most of the prepayment risk inherent in a CMO, and are therefore more volatile. In return, they pay higher yields than the other class within a CMO, called PLANNED AMORTIZATION CLASS (PAC) bonds.

COMPANY organization engaged in business as a proprietorship, partnership, corporation, or other form of enterprise. Originally, a firm made up of a group of people as distinguished from a sole proprietorship. However, since few proprietorships owe their existence exclusively to one person, the term now applies to proprietorships as well.

COMPANY DOCTOR executive, usually recruited from the outside, specialized in corporate turnarounds.

COMPARATIVE STATEMENTS financial statements covering different dates but prepared consistently and therefore lending themselves to comparative analysis, as accounting convention requires. Comparative figures reveal trends in a company's financial development and permit insight into the dynamics behind static balance sheet figures.

COMPARISON
1. short for *comparison ticket*, a memorandum exchanged prior to settlement by two brokers in order to confirm the details of a transaction to which they were parties. Also called comparison sheet.
2. verification of collateral held against a loan, by exchange of information between two brokers or between a broker and a bank.

COMPENSATING BALANCE *or* **COMPENSATORY BALANCE** average balance required by a bank for holding credit available. The more or less standard requirement for a bank line of credit, for example, is 10% of the line plus an additional 10% of the borrowings. Compensating balances increase the effective rate of interest on borrowings.

COMPETITIVE BID sealed bid, containing price and terms, submitted by a prospective underwriter to an issuer, who awards the contract to the bidder with the best price and terms. Many municipalities and virtually all railroads and public utilities use this bid system. Industrial corporations generally prefer NEGOTIATED UNDERWRITING on stock issues but do sometimes resort to competitive bidding in selecting underwriters for bond issues.

COMPETITIVE TRADER *see* REGISTERED COMPETITIVE TRADER.

COMPLETE AUDIT usually the same as an unqualified audit, because it is so thoroughly executed that the auditor's only reservations have to do with unobtainable facts. A complete audit examines the system of internal control and the details of the books of account, including subsidiary records and supporting documents. This is done with an eye to locality, mathematical accuracy, accountability, and the application of accepted accounting principles.

COMPLETED CONTRACT METHOD accounting method whereby revenues and expenses (and therefore taxes) on long-term contracts, such as government defense contracts, are recognized in the year the contract is concluded, except that losses are recognized in the year they are forecast. This method differs from the *percentage-of-completion method,* where sales and costs are recognized each year based on the value of the work performed. Under the TAX REFORM ACT OF 1986, manufacturers with long-term contracts must elect either the latter method or the *percentage-of-completion capitalized cost method,* requiring that 40% of the contract be included under the percentage-of-completion method and 60% under the taxpayer's normal accounting method.

COMPLETION PROGRAM oil and gas limited partnership that takes over drilling when oil is known to exist in commercial quantities. A completion program is a conservative way to profit from oil and gas drilling, but without the capital gains potential of exploratory wildcat drilling programs.

COMPLIANCE DEPARTMENT department set up in all organized stock exchanges to oversee market activity and make sure that trading complies with Securities and Exchange Commission and exchange regulations. A company that does not adhere to the rules can be delisted, and a trader or brokerage firm that violates the rules can be barred from trading.

COMPOSITE TAPE *see* TAPE.

COMPOUND ANNUAL RETURN investment return, discounted retroactively from a cumulative figure, at which money, compounded annually, would reach the cumulative total. Also called INTERNAL RATE OF RETURN.

COMPOUND GROWTH RATE rate of growth of a number, compounded over several years. Securities analysts check a company's compound growth rate of profits for five years to see the long-term trend.

COMPOUND INTEREST interest earned on principal plus interest that was earned earlier. If $100 is deposited in a bank account at 10%, the depositor will be credited with $110 at the end of the first year and $121 at the end of the second year. That extra $1, which was earned on the $10 interest from the first year, is the compound interest. This example involves interest compounded annually: interest can also be compounded on a daily, quarterly, half-yearly, or other basis. *See also* COMPOUND ANNUAL RETURN.

COMPTROLLER OF THE CURRENCY federal official, appointed by the President and confirmed by the Senate, who is responsible for chartering, examining, supervising, and liquidating all national banks. In response to the *comptroller's call,* national banks are required to submit *call reports* of their financial activities at least four times a year and to publish them in local newspapers. National banks can be declared insolvent only by the Comptroller of the Currency.

COMPUTERIZED MARKET TIMING SYSTEM system of picking buy and sell signals that puts together voluminous trading data in search of patterns and trends. Often, changes in the direction of moving average lines form the basis for buy and sell recommendations. These systems, commonly used by commodity funds and by services that switch between mutual funds, tend to work well when markets are moving steadily up or down, but not in trendless markets.

CONCERT PARTY person ACTING IN CONCERT.

CONCESSION
1. selling group's per-share or per-bond compensation in a corporate underwriting.
2. right, usually granted by a government entity, to use property for a specified purpose, such as a service station on a highway.

CONDEMNATION legal seizure of private property by a public authority for public use. Using the powers and legal procedures of EMINENT DOMAIN, a state, city, or town may condemn a property owner's home to make way for a highway, school, park, hospital, public housing project, parking facility, or other public project. The homeowners must give up the property even if they do not want to, and in return they must be compensated at fair market value by the public authority.

CONDITIONAL CALL OPTIONS form of CALL PROTECTION available to holders of some HIGH-YIELD BONDS. In the event the bond is called, the issuing corporation is obligated to substitute a non-callable bond having the same life and terms as the bond that is called.

CONDOMINIUM form of real estate ownership in which individual residents hold a deed and title to their houses or apartments and pay a maintenance fee to a management company for the upkeep of common property such as grounds, lobbies, and elevators as well as for other amenities. Condominium owners pay real estate taxes on their units and can sublet or sell as they wish. Some real estate limited partnerships specialize in converting rental property into condominiums. *See also* COOPERATIVE.

CONDUIT THEORY theory regulating investment companies such as REAL ESTATE INVESTMENT TRUSTS and MUTUAL FUNDS holding that since such companies are pure conduits for all capital gains, dividends, and interest to be passed through to shareholders, the investment company should not be taxed at the corporate level. As long as the investment company adheres to certain regulations, shareholders are therefore taxed only once—at the individual level—on income and capital gains. In contrast, shareholders of corporations are taxed twice: once at the corporate level in the form of corporate income taxes and once at the individual level in the form of individual income taxes on all dividends paid by the corporation.

CONFIRMATION
1. formal memorandum from a broker to a client giving details of a securities transaction. When a broker acts as a dealer, the confirmation must disclose that fact to the customer.
2. document sent by a company's auditor to its customers and suppliers requesting verification of the book amounts of receivables and payables. *Positive confirmations* request that every balance be confirmed, whereas *negative confirmations* request a reply only if an error exists.

CONFORMED COPY copy of an original document with the essential legal features, such as the signature and seal, being typed or indicated in writing.

CONFORMING LOANS mortgage loans that meet the qualifications of FREDDIE MAC or FANNIE MAE, which buy them from lenders and then issue PASS-THROUGH SECURITIES.

CONGLOMERATE corporation composed of companies in a variety of businesses. Conglomerates were popular in the 1960s, when they were thought to provide better management and sounder financial backing, and therefore to generate more profit, than small independent companies. However, some conglomerates became so complex that they were difficult to manage. In the 1980s and

1990s, many conglomerates sold off divisions and concentrated on a few core businesses. Analysts generally consider stocks of conglomerates difficult to evaluate because they are involved in so many unrelated businesses.

CONNIE LEE nickname for COLLEGE CONSTRUCTION LOAN INSURANCE ASSOCIATION.

CONSERVATOR individual appointed by a court to manage the property of a person who lacks the capacity to manage his own property. A conservator may be charged with liquidating the assets of a business in bankruptcy, or may have to take control of the personal finances of an incompetent individual who needs to be protected by the court.

CONSIDERATION something of value that one party gives to another in exchange for a promise or act. In law, a requirement of valid contracts. A consideration can be in the form of money, commodities, or personal services; in many industries the forms have become standardized.

CONSOLIDATED FINANCIAL STATEMENT financial statement that brings together all assets, liabilities, and operating accounts of a parent company and its subsidiaries. *See also* COMBINED FINANCIAL STATEMENT.

CONSOLIDATED MORTGAGE BOND bond issue that covers several units of property and may refinance separate mortgages on these properties. The consolidated mortgage with a single coupon rate is a traditional form of financing for railroads because it is economical to combine many properties in one agreement.

CONSOLIDATED TAPE combined tapes of the New York Stock Exchange and the American Stock Exchange. It became operative in June 1975. Network A covers NYSE-listed securities and identifies the originating market. Network B does the same for Amex-listed securities and also reports on securities listed on regional exchanges.

CONSOLIDATED TAX RETURN return combining the reports of the companies in what the tax law defines as an affiliated group. A firm is part of an affiliated group if it is at least 80% owned by a parent or other inclusive corporation. "Owned" refers to voting stock. (Before the TAX REFORM ACT OF 1986 it also included nonvoting stock.)

CONSOLIDATION LOAN loan that combines and refinances other loans or debt. It is normally an installment loan designed to reduce the dollar amount of an individual's monthly payments.

CONSORTIUM group of companies formed to promote a common objective or engage in a project of benefit to all the members. The relationship normally entails cooperation and a sharing of resources, sometimes even common ownership.

CONSTANT DOLLAR PLAN method of accumulating assets by investing a fixed amount of dollars in securities at set intervals. The investor buys more shares when the price is low and fewer shares when the price is high; the overall cost is lower than it would be if a constant number of shares were bought at set intervals. Also called *dollar cost averaging.*

CONSTANT DOLLARS dollars of a base year, used as a gauge in adjusting the dollars of other years in order to ascertain actual purchasing power. Denoted as C$ by the FINANCIAL ACCOUNTING STANDARDS BOARD (FASB), which defines constant dollars as hypothetical units of general purchasing power.

CONSTANT RATIO PLAN type of FORMULA INVESTING whereby a predetermined ratio is maintained between stock and FIXED INCOME INVESTMENTS through periodic adjustments. For example, an investor with $200,000 and a 50-50 formula might start out with $100,000 in stock and $100,000 in bonds. If the stock increased in value to $150,000 and the bonds remained unchanged over a given adjustment period, the investor would restore the ratio at $125,000-$125,000 by selling $25,000 of stock and buying $25,000 of bonds.

CONSTANT YIELD METHOD method of allocating annual interest on a ZERO-COUPON SECURITY for income tax purposes. IRS Publication 1212 explains how to figure taxable interest on such ORIGINAL ISSUE DISCOUNT securities.

CONSTRUCTION LOAN short-term real estate loan to finance building costs. The funds are disbursed as needed or in accordance with a prearranged plan, and the money is repaid on completion of the project, usually from the proceeds of a mortgage loan. The rate is normally higher than prime, and there is usually an origination fee. The effective yield on these loans tends to be high, and the lender has a security interest in the real property.

CONSTRUCTION LOAN NOTE (CLN) note issued by a municipality to finance the construction of multi-family housing projects. The notes, which typically mature in three years or less, are normally repaid out of the proceeds of a long-term bond issue.

CONSTRUCTIVE RECEIPT term used by Internal Revenue Service for the date when a taxpayer received dividends or other income. IRS rules say that constructive receipt of income is established if the taxpayer has the right to claim it, whether or not the choice is exercised. For instance, if a bond pays interest on December 29, the taxpayer must report the income in that tax year and not in the following year.

CONSUMER CREDIT debt assumed by consumers for purposes other than home mortgages. Interest on consumer loans had been 100% deductible until the TAX REFORM ACT OF 1986 mandated that the deduction be phased out by 1991. Consumers can borrow through credit cards, lines of credit, loans against insurance policies, and many other methods. The Federal Reserve Board releases the amount of outstanding consumer credit on a monthly basis.

CONSUMER CREDIT PROTECTION ACT OF 1968 landmark federal legislation establishing rules of disclosure that lenders must observe in dealings with borrowers. The act stipulates that consumers be told annual percentage rates, potential total cost, and any special loan terms. The act, enforced by the Federal Reserve Bank, is also known as the *Truth in Lending Act.*

CONSUMER DEBENTURE investment note issued by a financial institution and marketed directly to the public. Consumer debentures were a popular means of raising lendable funds for banks during tight money periods prior to deregulation, since these instruments, unlike certificates of deposit, could compete freely with other money-market investments in a high-rate market.

CONSUMER DURABLES products bought by consumers that are expected to last three years or more. These include automobiles, appliances, boats, and furniture. Economists look at the trend in consumer expenditure on durables as an important indicator of the strength of the economy, since consumers need confidence to make such large and expensive purchases. Stock market analysts also classify companies that produce appliances, furniture, cars, and similar items as consumer durables manufacturers, contrasting them with consumer non-durables manufacturers, which make consumable items such as food or drugs.

CONSUMER FINANCE COMPANY *see* FINANCE COMPANY.

CONSUMER GOODS goods bought for personal or household use, as distinguished from CAPITAL GOODS or *producer's goods,* which are used to produce other goods. The general economic meaning of consumer goods encompasses consumer services. Thus the *market basket* on which the CONSUMER PRICE INDEX is based includes clothing, food, and other goods as well as utilities, entertainment, and other services.

CONSUMER INTEREST interest paid on consumer loans. Consumer interest is paid on credit cards, bank lines of credit, retail purchases, car and boat loans, and educational loans. Since the end of 1991, such interest is no longer deductible for tax purposes, based on provisions of the TAX REFORM ACT OF 1986. That tax law distinguished nondeductible consumer interest from other forms of interest which can be deductible, including business interest, investment interest, and mortgage-related interest.

CONSUMER PRICE INDEX (CPI) measures prices of a fixed basket of goods bought by a typical consumer, including food, transportation, shelter, utilities, clothing, medical care, entertainment, and other items. The CPI, published by the Bureau of Labor Statistics in the Department of Labor, is based at 100 in 1982 and is released monthly. It is widely used as a cost-of-living benchmark to adjust Social Security payments and other payment schedules, union contracts, and tax brackets. Also known as the *cost-of-living index.*

CONSUMPTION TAX *see* VALUE-ADDED TAX (VAT).

CONTANGO
1. pricing situation in which futures prices get progressively higher as maturities get progressively longer, creating negative spreads as contracts go farther out. The increases reflect carrying costs, including storage, financing, and insurance. The reverse condition, an inverted market, is termed BACKWARDATION.
2. in finance, the costs that must be taken into account in analyses involving forecasts.

CONTINGENT BENEFICIARY person named in an insurance policy to receive the policy benefits if the primary beneficiary dies before the benefits become payable.

CONTINGENT DEFERRED SALES LOAD sales charge levied by a mutual fund if a customer sells fund shares within a specified number of years. Instead of charging a traditional FRONT END LOAD of 5%, for example, a brokerage firm may offer the same fund with a contingent deferred sales load. Customers who sell the fund within the first year pay a 5% load. In the second year, the charge would be 4%. Each year the charge declines by one percentage point until there is no fee for selling fund shares after the fifth year. Also called *back-end load.*

CONTINGENT LIABILITIES
Banking: potential obligation of a guarantor or accommodation endorser; or the position of a customer who opens a letter of credit and whose account will be charged if a draft is presented. The bank's own ultimate responsibility for letters of credit and other commitments, individually and collectively, is its contingent liability.

Corporate reports: pending lawsuits, judgments under appeal, disputed claims, and the like, representing potential financial liability.

CONTINGENT ORDER securities order whose execution depends on the execution of another order; for example, a sell order and a buy order with prices stipulated. Where the purpose is to effect a swap, a price difference might be stipulated as a condition of the order's execution. Generally, brokers discourage these orders, favoring firm instructions.

CONTINUOUS NET SETTLEMENT (CNS) method of securities clearing and settlement that eliminates multiple fails in the same securities. This is accomplished by using a clearing house, such as the National Securities Clearing Corporation, and a depository, such as DEPOSITORY TRUST COMPANY, to match transactions to securities available in the firm's position, resulting in one net receive or deliver position at the end of the day. By including the previous day's fail position in the next day's selling trades, the firm's position is always up-to-date and money settlement or withdrawals can be made at any time with the clearing house. The alternative to CNS is window settlement, where the seller delivers securities to the buyer's cashier and receives payment.

CONTRA BROKER broker on the opposite side—the buy side of a sell order or the sell side of a buy order.

CONTRACT in general, agreement by which rights or acts are exchanged for lawful consideration. To be valid, it must be entered into by competent parties, must cover a legal and moral transaction, must possess mutuality, and must represent a meeting of minds. Countless transactions in finance and investments are covered by contracts.

CONTRACTUAL PLAN plan by which fixed dollar amounts of mutual fund shares are accumulated through periodic investments for 10 or 15 years. The legal vehicle for such investments is the *plan company* or *participating unit investment trust*, a selling organization operating on behalf of the fund's underwriter. The plan company must be registered with the Securities and Exchange Commission, as the underlying fund must be, so the investor receives two prospectuses. Investors in these plans commonly receive other benefits in exchange for their fixed periodic payments, such as decreasing term life insurance. *See also* FRONT END LOAD.

CONTRARIAN investor who does the opposite of what most investors are doing at any particular time. According to contrarian opinion, if everyone is certain that something is about to happen, it won't. This is because most people who say the market is going up are fully invested and have no additional purchasing power, which means the market is at its peak. When people predict decline they have already sold out, so the market can only go up. Some mutual funds follow a contrarian investment strategy, and some investment advisers suggest only out-of-favor securities, whose price/earnings ratio is lower than the rest of the market or industry.

CONTRIBUTED CAPITAL payments made in cash or property to a corporation by its stockholders either to buy capital stock, to pay an assessment on the capital stock, or as a gift. Also called *paid-in capital*. The contributed or paid-in capital of a corporation is made up of capital stock and capital (or contributed) surplus, which is contributed (or paid-in) capital in excess of PAR value or STATED VALUE. Donated capital and DONATED SURPLUS are freely given forms of contributed (paid-in) capital, but DONATED STOCK refers to fully paid (previously issued) capital stock that is given as a gift to the issuing corporation.

CONTROLLED COMMODITIES commodities regulated by the Commodities Exchange Act of 1936, which set up trading rules for futures in commodities markets in order to prevent fraud and manipulation.

CONTROLLED WILDCAT DRILLING drilling for oil and gas in an area adjacent to but outside the limits of a proven field. Also known as a *field extension.* Limited partnerships drilling in this area take greater risks than those drilling in areas of proven energy reserves, but the rewards can be considerable if oil is found.

CONTROLLER *or* COMPTROLLER chief accountant of a company. In small companies the controller may also serve as treasurer. In a brokerage firm, the controller prepares financial reports, supervises internal audits, and is responsible for compliance with Securities and Exchange Commission regulations.

CONTROLLING INTEREST ownership of more than 50% of a corporation's voting shares. A much smaller interest, owned individually or by a group in combination, can be controlling if the other shares are widely dispersed and not actively voted.

CONTROL PERSON *see* AFFILIATED PERSON.

CONTROL STOCK shares owned by holders who have a CONTROLLING INTEREST.

CONVENTIONAL MORTGAGE residential mortgage loan, usually from a bank or savings and loan association, with a fixed rate and term. It is repayable in fixed monthly payments over a period usually 30 years or less, secured by real property, and not insured by the FEDERAL HOUSING ADMINISTRATION or guaranteed by the Veterans Administration.

CONVENTIONAL OPTION put or call contract arranged off the trading floor of a listed exchange and not traded regularly. It was commonplace when options were banned on certain exchanges, but is now rare.

CONVERGENCE movement of the price of a futures contract toward the price of the underlying CASH COMMODITY. At the start of the contract price is higher because of the time value. But as the contract nears expiration the futures price and the cash price converge.

CONVERSION
1. exchange of a convertible security such as a bond into a fixed number of shares of the issuing corporation's common stock.
2. transfer of mutual-fund shares without charge from one fund to another fund in a single family; also known as fund switching.
3. in insurance, switch from short-term to permanent life insurance.

CONVERSION FEATURE right to convert a particular holding to another form of holding, such as the SWITCHING within a mutual fund family, the right to convert certain preferred stock or bonds to common stock, or the right to switch from one type of insurance policy to another. *See also* CONVERTIBLES.

CONVERSION PARITY common-stock price at which a convertible security can become exchangeable for common shares of equal value.

CONVERSION PREMIUM amount by which the price of a convertible tops the market price of the underlying stock. If a stock is trading at $50 and the bond convertible at $45 is trading at $50, the premium is $5. If the premium is high the bond trades like any fixed income bond. If the premium is low the bond trades like a stock.

CONVERSION PRICE the dollar value at which convertible bonds, debentures, or preferred stock can be converted into common stock, as announced when the convertible is issued.

CONVERSION RATIO relationship that determines how many shares of common stock will be received in exchange for each convertible bond or preferred share when the conversion takes place. It is determined at the time of issue and is expressed either as a ratio or as a conversion price from which the ratio can be figured by dividing the par value of the convertible by the conversion price. The indentures of most convertible securities contain an antidilution clause whereby the conversion ratio may be raised (or the conversion price lowered) by the percentage amount of any stock dividend or split, to protect the convertible holder against dilution.

CONVERSION VALUE

In general: value created by changing from one form to another. For example, converting rental property to condominiums adds to the value of the property.

Convertibles: the price at which the exchange can be made for common stock.

CONVERTIBLE ADJUSTABLE PREFERRED STOCK *see* CAPS.

CONVERTIBLES corporate securities (usually preferred shares or bonds) that are exchangeable for a set number of another form (usually common shares) at a prestated price. Convertibles are appropriate for investors who want higher income than is available from common stock, together with greater appreciation potential than regular bonds offer. From the issuer's standpoint, the convertible feature is usually designed as a sweetener, to enhance the marketability of the stock or preferred.

CONVEXITY mathematical concept that measures sensitivity of the market price of an interest-bearing bond to changes in interest rate levels. *See also* DURATION.

COOK THE BOOKS to falsify the financial statements of a company intentionally. A firm in financial trouble may want to cook the books to prevent investors from pushing down the company's stock price. Companies may also falsify their records to lower their tax liabilities. Whatever the reason, the practice is illegal under SEC, IRS, and stock exchange rules as well as the ethical code of the accounting profession.

COOLING-OFF PERIOD

1. interval (usually 20 days) between the filing of a preliminary prospectus with the Securities and Exchange Commission and the offer of the securities to the public. *See also* REGISTRATION.
2. period during which a union is prohibited from striking, or an employer from locking out employees. The period, typically 30 to 90 days, may be required by law or provided for in a labor agreement.

COOPERATIVE organization owned by its members.

In real estate, a property whose residents own shares in a cooperative giving them exclusive use of their apartments. Decisions about common areas—hallways, elevators, grounds—are made by a vote of members' shares. Members also approve sales of apartments.

Agriculture cooperatives help farmers sell their products more efficiently. Food cooperatives buy food for their members at wholesale prices, but usually require members to help run the organization.

COPENHAGEN STOCK EXCHANGE main securities market in Denmark. Both stocks and bonds are traded on the exchange using ELECTRA, the electronic trading system in which all Danish stock brokerage houses are connected. The market also offers futures and options based on Danish equities traded on the exchange and supervised by the Guarantee Fund for Danish Options and Futures. Stocks and bonds are settled three business days after the trading day. For stocks, the price is paid on delivery of share certificates. Bonds are settled through the Danish Securities Centre. Trading is conducted Monday through Friday, 9 A.M.–3:30 P.M.

CORE CAPITAL thrift institution's bedrock capital, which must be at least 2% of assets to meet proposed rules of the Federal Home Loan Bank. It comprises capital stock and surplus accounts, including perpetual preferred stock, plus minority interests in consolidated subsidiaries.

CORNERING THE MARKET purchasing a security or commodity in such volume that control over its price is achieved. A cornered market in a security would be unhappy news for a short seller, who would have to pay an inflated price to cover. Cornering has been illegal for some years.

CORPORATE BOND debt instrument issued by a private corporation, as distinct from one issued by a government agency or a municipality. Corporates typically have four distinguishing features: (1) they are taxable; (2) they have a par value of $1000; (3) they have a term maturity—which means they come due all at once—and are paid for out of a sinking fund accumulated for that purpose; (4) they are traded on major exchanges, with prices published in newspapers. *See also* BOND; MUNICIPAL BOND.

CORPORATE CHARTER *see* ARTICLES OF INCORPORATION.

CORPORATE EQUIVALENT YIELD comparison that dealers in government bonds include in their offering sheets to show the after-tax yield of government bonds selling at a discount and corporate bonds selling at par.

CORPORATE FINANCING COMMITTEE NATIONAL ASSOCIATION OF SECURITIES DEALERS standing committee that reviews documentation submitted by underwriters in compliance with Securities and Exchange Commission requirements to ensure that proposed markups are fair and in the public interest.

CORPORATE INCOME FUND (CIF) UNIT INVESTMENT TRUST with a fixed portfolio made up of high-grade securities and instruments, similar to a MONEY MARKET FUND. Most CIFs pay out investment income monthly.

CORPORATE INSIDER *see* INSIDER.

CORPORATION legal entity, chartered by a U.S. state or by the federal government, and separate and distinct from the persons who own it, giving rise to a jurist's remark that it has "neither a soul to damn nor a body to kick." Nonetheless, it is regarded by the courts as an artificial person; it may own property, incur debts, sue, or be sued. It has three chief distinguishing features:
1. limited liability; owners can lose only what they invest.
2. easy transfer of ownership through the sale of shares of stock.
3. continuity of existence.

Other factors helping to explain the popularity of the corporate form of organization are its ability to obtain capital through expanded ownership, and the shareholders' ability to profit from the growth of the business.

CORPUS Latin for *body.*
1. in trust banking, the property in a trust—real estate, securities and other personal property, cash in bank accounts, and any other items included by the donor.
2. body of an investment or note, representing the principal or capital as distinct from the interest or income.

CORRECTION reverse movement, usually downward, in the price of an individual stock, bond, commodity, or index. If prices have been rising on the market as a whole, then fall dramatically, this is known as a *correction within an upward trend.* Technical analysts note that markets do not move straight up or down and that corrections are to be expected during any long-term move.

CORRECTION

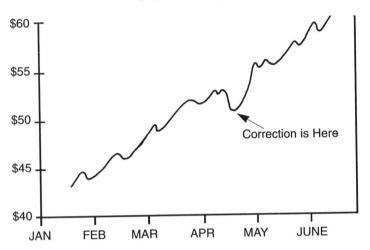

CORRELATION COEFFICIENT statistical measure of the degree to which the movements of two variables are related.

CORRESPONDENT financial organization that regularly performs services for another in a market inaccessible to the other. In banking there is usually a depository relationship that compensates for expenses and facilitates transactions.

COST ACCOUNTING branch of accounting concerned with providing the information that enables the management of a firm to evaluate production costs.

COST BASIS original price of an asset, used in determining capital gains. It usually is the purchase price, but in the case of an inheritance it is the appraised value of the asset at the time of the donor's death.

COST-BENEFIT ANALYSIS method of measuring the benefits expected from a decision, calculating the cost of the decision, then determining whether the benefits outweigh the costs. Corporations use this method in deciding whether to buy a piece of equipment, and the government uses it in determining whether federal programs are achieving their goals.

COST OF CAPITAL rate of return that a business could earn if it chose another investment with equivalent risk—in other words, the OPPORTUNITY COST of the funds employed as the result of an investment decision. Cost of capital is also calculated using a weighted average of a firm's costs of debt and classes of equity. This is also called the *composite cost of capital.*

COST OF CARRY out-of-pocket costs incurred while an investor has an investment position, among them interest on long positions in margin accounts, dividends lost on short margin positions, and incidental expenses.

COST OF FUNDS interest cost paid by a financial institution for the use of money. Brokerage firms' cost of funds are comprised of the total interest expense to carry an inventory of stocks and bonds. In the banking and savings and loan industry, the cost of funds is the amount of interest the bank must pay on money market accounts, passbooks, CDs, and other liabilities. Many adjustable rate mortgage loans are tied to a cost-of-funds index, which rises and falls in line with the banks' interest expenses.

COST-OF-FUNDS INDEX (COFI) index used by mortgage lenders on adjustable rate mortgage loans. Borrower's mortgage payments rise or fall based on the widely published COFI, which is based on what financial institutions are paying on money market accounts, passbooks, CDs, and other liabilities. The COFI tends to move far more slowly, both up and down, than other indexes for adjustable rate mortgages, such as one-year Treasuries or the prime rate.

COST OF GOODS SOLD figure representing the cost of buying raw materials and producing finished goods. Depreciation is considered a part of this cost but is usually listed separately. Included in the direct costs are clear-cut factors such as direct factory labor as well as others that are less clear-cut, such as overhead. *Cost of sales* may be used as a synonym or may mean selling expenses. See also DIRECT OVERHEAD; FIRST IN, FIRST OUT; LAST IN, FIRST OUT.

COST-OF-LIVING ADJUSTMENT (COLA) adjustment of wages designed to offset changes in the cost of living, usually as measured by the CONSUMER PRICE INDEX. COLAs are key bargaining issues in labor contracts and are politically sensitive elements of social security payments and federal pensions because they affect millions of people.

COST-OF-LIVING INDEX *see* CONSUMER PRICE INDEX.

COST OF SALES *see* COST OF GOODS SOLD.

COST-PLUS CONTRACT contract basing the selling price of a product on the total cost incurred in making it plus a stated percentage or a fixed fee—called a *cost-plus-fixed-fee contract.* Cost-plus contracts are common when there is no historical basis for estimating costs and the producer would run a risk of loss—defense contracts involving sophisticated technology, for example . The alternative is a FIXED PRICE contract.

COST-PUSH INFLATION inflation caused by rising prices, which follow on the heels of rising costs. This is the sequence: When the demand for raw materials exceeds the supply, prices go up. As manufacturers pay more for these raw materials they raise the prices they charge merchants for the finished products, and the merchants in turn raise the prices they charge consumers. *See also* DEMAND-PULL INFLATION; INFLATION.

COST RECORDS
1. investor records of the prices at which securities were purchased, which provide the basis for computing capital gains.
2. in finance, anything that can substantiate the costs incurred in producing goods, providing services, or supporting an activity designed to be productive. Ledgers, schedules, vouchers, and invoices are cost records.

COUNCIL OF ECONOMIC ADVISERS group of economists appointed by the President of the United States to provide counsel on economic policy. The council helps to prepare the President's budget message to Congress, and its chairman frequently speaks for the administration's economic policy.

COUNTERCYCLICAL STOCKS stocks that tend to rise in value when the economy is turning down or is in recession. Traditionally, companies in industries with stable demand, such as drugs, food, and tobacco, are considered countercyclical. Some firms actually do better when the economy or stock market is in turmoil. For example, firms offering money market mutual funds may enjoy an inflow of cash when stock prices fall. Temporary-help firms may benefit if companies are cutting costs by laying off full-time employees and replacing them with temps. Companies that can perform various functions for other companies more efficiently and at lower cost (called *outsourcing firms*) will tend to benefit during economic downturns. *See also* CYCLICAL STOCKS.

COUPON interest rate on a debt security the issuer promises to pay to the holder until maturity, expressed as an annual percentage of face value. For example, a bond with a 10% coupon will pay $10 per $100 of the face amount per year, usually in installments paid every six months. The term derives from the small detachable segment of a bond certificate which, when presented to the bond's issuer, entitles the holder to the interest due on that date. As the REGISTERED BOND becomes more widespread, coupons are gradually disappearing.

COUPON BOND bond issued with detachable coupons that must be presented to a paying agent or the issuer for semiannual interest payment. These are bearer bonds, so whoever presents the coupon is entitled to the interest. Once universal, the coupon bond has been gradually giving way to the REGISTERED BOND, some of which pay interest through electronic transfers. *See also* BOOK-ENTRY SECURITIES; CERTIFICATELESS MUNICIPALS; COUPON.

COUPON COLLECTION *see* COLLECTION.

COUPON-EQUIVALENT RATE same as EQUIVALENT BOND YIELD.

COUPON PASS canvassing by the DESK of the Federal Reserve's Open-Market Committee of PRIMARY DEALERS to determine the inventory and maturities of their Treasury securities. Desk then decides whether to buy or sell specific issues (coupons) to add or withdraw reserves.

COUPON YIELD (OR RATE) *see* COUPON.

COVARIANCE statistical term for the correlation between two variables multiplied by the standard deviation for each of the variables.

COVENANT promise in a trust indenture or other formal debt agreement that certain acts will be performed and others refrained from. Designed to protect the lender's interest, covenants cover such matters as working capital, debt-equity ratios, and dividend payments. Also called *restrictive covenant* or *protective covenant.*

COVER
1. to buy back contracts previously sold; said of an investor who has sold stock or commodities short.
2. in corporate finance, to meet fixed annual charges on bonds, leases, and other obligations, out of earnings.
3. amount of net-asset value underlying a bond or equity security. Coverage is an important aspect of a bond's safety rating.

COVERAGE *see* FIXED-CHARGE COVERAGE.

COVERED OPTION option contract backed by the shares underlying the option. For instance, someone who owns 300 shares of XYZ and sells three XYZ call options is in a covered option position. If the XYZ stock price goes up and the option is exercised, the investor has the stock to deliver to the buyer. Selling a call brings a premium from the buyer. *See also* NAKED OPTION.

COVERED WRITER seller of covered options—in other words, an owner of stock who sells options against it to collect premium income. For example, when writing a CALL OPTION, if a stock price stays stable or drops, the seller will be able to hold onto the stock. If the price rises sharply enough, it will have to be given up to the option buyer.

COVERING SHORT *see* COVER.

CPI *see* CONSUMER PRICE INDEX (CPI).

CRAM-DOWN DEAL merger or leveraged buyout slang for situation in which stockholders are forced, for lack of attractive alternatives, to accept undesirable terms, such as JUNK BONDS instead of cash or equity.

CRASH precipitate drop in stock prices and economic activity, as in the crash of 1929 or BLACK MONDAY in 1987. Crashes are usually brought on by a loss in investor confidence following periods of highly inflated stock prices.

CREDIT
In general: loans, bonds, charge-account obligations, and open-account balances with commercial firms. Also, available but unused bank letters of credit and other standby commitments as well as a variety of consumer credit facilities.
    On another level, discipline in which lending officers and industrial credit people are professionals. At its loftiest it is defined in Dun & Bradstreet's motto: "Credit—Man's Confidence in Man."
Accounting: entry—or the act of making an entry—that increases liabilities, owners' equity, revenue, and gains, and decreases assets and expenses. *See also* CREDIT BALANCE.
Customer's statement of account: adjustment in the customer's favor, or increase in equity.

CREDIT ANALYST person who (1) analyzes the record and financial affairs of an individual or a corporation to ascertain creditworthiness or (2) determines the credit ratings of corporate and municipal bonds by studying the financial condition and trends of the issuers.

CREDIT BALANCE
In general: account balance in the customer's favor. See *also* CREDIT.
Securities: in cash accounts with brokers, money deposited and remaining after purchases have been paid for, plus the uninvested proceeds from securities sold. In margin accounts, (1) proceeds from short sales, held in escrow for the securities borrowed for these sales; (2) free credit balances, or net balances, which can be withdrawn at will. SPECIAL MISCELLANEOUS ACCOUNT balances are not counted as free credit balances.

CREDIT BUREAU agency that gathers information about the credit history of consumers and relays it to credit grantors for a fee. Credit bureaus maintain files on millions of consumers detailing which lines of credit they have applied for and received, and whether they pay their bills in a timely fashion. Bureaus receive this information from credit grantors such as credit card issuers, retail stores, gasoline companies, and others. Credit grantors look at this information, which is constantly being updated, in making their decision as to whether or not to grant credit to a particular consumer, and if so, how much credit is appropriate. Consumers have rights under the FAIR CREDIT REPORTING ACT to see a copy of their credit report and to dispute any item they think is inaccurate. Credit data are maintained by 500 credit bureaus which operate off of three automated systems: Equifax, based in Georgia, Trans Union, based in Illinois, and TRW, based in California.

CREDIT CARD plastic card issued by a bank, savings and loan, retail store, oil company, or other credit grantor giving consumers the right to charge purchases and pay for them later. Most credit cards offer a grace period of about 25 days, during which interest charges do not accrue. After that, consumers pay nondeductible CONSUMER INTEREST on the remaining balance until it is paid off. Some credit cards start charging interest from the day the purchase is registered. Most credit cards also permit consumers to obtain cash on their card in the form of a CASH ADVANCE. *See also* CONSUMER CREDIT PROTECTION ACT OF 1968.

CREDIT ENHANCEMENT techniques used by debt issuers to raise the credit rating of their offering, and thereby lower their interest costs. A municipality may have their bond insured by one of the large insurance companies such as Municipal Bond Investor's Assurance (MBIA) or American Municipal Bond Assurance Corporation (AMBAC), thereby raising the bond's credit rating to AAA. A corporate bond issuer may arrange for a bank letter of credit to back its issue, raising its rating to AAA. While investors in such credit-enhanced issuers feel safer because an insurance company or bank stands ready to step in if there is a default by the underlying issuer, the yield received by the investor is lower than if the bond were uninsured.

CREDIT INSURANCE protection against *abnormal* losses from unpaid accounts receivable, often a requirement of banks lending against accounts receivable.

In consumer credit, life or accident coverage protecting the creditor against loss in the event of death or disability, usually stated as a percentage of the loan balance.

CREDIT LIMIT credit card term, meaning the maximum balance allowed for a particular customer.

CREDITOR party that extends credit, such as a trade supplier, a bank lender, or a bondholder.

CREDITOR'S COMMITTEE group representing firms that have claims on a company in financial difficulty or bankruptcy; sometimes used as an alternative to legal bankruptcy, especially by smaller firms.

CREDIT RATING formal evaluation of an individual's or company's credit history and capability of repaying obligations. Any number of firms investigate, analyze, and maintain records on the credit responsibility of individuals and businesses—TRW (individuals) and Dun & Bradstreet (commercial firms), for example. The bond ratings assigned by Standard & Poor's and Moody's are also a form of credit rating. Most large companies and lending institutions assign credit ratings to existing and potential customers.

CREDIT RISK financial and moral risk that an obligation will not be paid and a loss will result.

CREDIT SCORING objective methodology used by credit grantors to determine how much, if any, credit to grant to an applicant. Credit scoring is devised by three different methods: by a third-party firm, by the credit grantor, or by the credit bureau in cooperation with the credit grantor. Some of the most common factors in scoring are income, assets, length of employment, length of living in one place, and past record of using credit. Any negative events in the past, such as bankruptcies or tax delinquencies, will sharply reduce an applicant's credit score.

CREDIT SPREAD difference in the value of two options, when the value of the one sold exceeds the value of the one bought. The opposite of a DEBIT SPREAD.

CREDIT UNION not-for-profit financial institution typically formed by employees of a company, a labor union, or a religious group and operated as a cooperative. Credit unions may offer a full range of financial services and pay higher rates on deposits and charge lower rates on loans than commercial banks. Federally chartered credit unions are regulated and insured by the National Credit Union Administration.

CREDIT WATCH used by bond RATING agencies to indicate that a company's credit is under review and its rating subject to change. The implication is that if the rating is changed, it will be lowered, usually because of some event that affects the income statement or balance sheet adversely.

CREDITWORTHINESS general eligibility of a person or company to borrow money. *See* CREDIT RATING; CREDIT SCORING.

CREEPING TENDER OFFER strategy whereby individuals ACTING IN CONCERT circumvent WILLIAMS ACT provisions by gradually acquiring TARGET COMPANY shares from arbitrageurs and other sellers in the open market. *See also* TENDER OFFER.

CROSS securities transaction in which the same broker acts as agent in both sides of the trade. The practice—called crossing—is legal only if the broker first offers the securities publicly at a price higher than the bid.

CROSSED MARKET situation in which one broker's bid is higher than another broker's lowest offer, or vice versa. National Association of Securities Dealers (NASD) rules prohibit brokers from crossing the market deliberately.

CROSSED TRADE manipulative practice prohibited on major exchanges whereby buy and sell orders are offset without recording the trade on the exchange, thus perhaps depriving the investor of the chance to trade at a more favorable price. Also called *crossed sale.*

CROWD group of exchange members with a defined area of function tending to congregate around a trading post pending execution of orders. These are specialists, floor traders, odd-lot dealers, and other brokers as well as smaller groups with specialized functions—the INACTIVE BOND CROWD, for example.

CROWDING OUT heavy federal borrowing at a time when businesses and consumers also want to borrow money. Because the government can pay any interest rate it has to and individuals and businesses can't, the latter are crowded out of credit markets by high interest rates. Crowding out can thus cause economic activity to slow.

CROWN JEWELS the most desirable entities within a diversified corporation as measured by asset value, earning power and business prospects. The crown jewels usually figure prominently in takeover attempts; they typically are the main objective of the acquirer and may be sold by a takeover target to make the rest of the company less attractive.

CROWN LOAN demand loan by a high-income individual to a low-income relative, usually a child or elderly parent. This device was named for Chicago industrialist Harry Crown, who first used it. The money would be invested and the income would be taxable at the borrower's lower rates. For years, the crown loan provided a substantial tax benefit for all parties involved, since such loans could be made interest-free. In 1984 the U.S. Supreme Court ruled that such loans had to be made at the market rate of interest or be subject to gift taxes.

CUM DIVIDEND with dividend; said of a stock whose buyer is eligible to receive a declared dividend. Stocks are usually cum dividend for trades made on or before the fifth day preceding the RECORD DATE, when the register of eligible holders is closed for that dividend period. Trades after the fifth day go EX-DIVIDEND.

CUM RIGHTS with rights; said of stocks that entitle the purchaser to buy a specified amount of stock that is yet to be issued. The cut-off date when the stocks go from cum rights to EX-RIGHTS (without rights) is stipulated in the prospectus accompanying the rights distribution.

CUMULATIVE PREFERRED preferred stock whose dividends if omitted because of insufficient earnings or any other reason accumulate until paid out. They have precedence over common dividends, which cannot be paid as long as a cumulative preferred obligation exists. Most preferred stock issued today is cumulative.

CUMULATIVE VOTING voting method that improves minority shareholders' chances of naming representatives on the board of directors. In regular or statutory voting, stockholders must apportion their votes equally among candidates for director. Cumulative voting allows shareholders to cast all their votes for one candidate. Assuming one vote per share, 100 shares owned, and six directors to be elected, the regular method lets the shareholder cast 100 votes for each of six candidates for director, a total of 600 votes. The cumulative method lets the same 600 votes be cast for one candidate or split as the shareholder wishes. Cumulative voting is a popular cause among advocates of corporate democracy, but it remains the exception rather than the rule.

CURB see AMERICAN STOCK EXCHANGE.

CURRENCY FUTURES contracts in the futures markets that are for delivery in a major currency such as U.S. dollars, British pounds, French francs, German marks, Swiss francs, or Japanese yen. Corporations that sell products around the world can hedge their currency risk with these futures.

CURRENCY IN CIRCULATION paper money and coins circulating in the economy, counted as part of the total money in circulation, which includes DEMAND DEPOSITS in banks.

CURRENT ACCOUNT (1) an active TRADE CREDIT account; (2) an account with an extender of credit that is up to date; (3) See BALANCE OF PAYMENTS.

CURRENT ASSETS cash, accounts receivable, inventory, and other assets that are likely to be converted into cash, sold, exchanged, or expensed in the normal course of business, usually within a year.

CURRENT COUPON BOND corporate, federal, or municipal bond with a coupon within half a percentage point of current market rates. These bonds are less volatile than similarly rated bonds with lower coupons because the interest they pay is competitive with current market instruments.

CURRENT INCOME money that is received on an ongoing basis from investments in the form of dividends, interest, rents, or other income sources.

CURRENT LIABILITY debt or other obligation coming due within a year.

CURRENT MARKET VALUE present worth of a client's portfolio at today's market price, as listed in a brokerage statement every month— or more often if stocks are bought on margin or sold short. For listed stocks and bonds the current market value is determined by closing prices; for over-the-counter securities the bid price is used.

CURRENT MATURITY interval between the present time and the maturity date of a bond issue, as distinguished from original maturity, which is the time difference between the issue date and the maturity date. For example, in 1997 a bond issued in 1995 to mature in 2015 would have an original maturity of 20 years and a current maturity of 18 years.

CURRENT PRODUCTION RATE top interest rate allowed on current GOVERNMENT NATIONAL MORTGAGE ASSOCIATION mortgage-backed securities, usually half a percentage point below the current mortgage rate to defray administrative costs of the mortgage servicing company. For instance, when homeowners are paying 13½% on mortgages, an investor in a GNMA pool including those mortgages will get a current production rate of 13%.

CURRENT RATIO current assets divided by current liabilities. The ratio shows a company's ability to pay its current obligations from current assets. For the most part, a company that has a small inventory and readily collectible accounts receivable can operate safely with a lower current ratio than a company whose cash flow is less dependable. *See also* QUICK RATIO.

CURRENT YIELD annual interest on a bond divided by the market price. It is the actual income rate of return as opposed to the coupon rate (the two would be equal if the bond were bought at par) or the yield to maturity. For example, a 10% (coupon rate) bond with a face (or par) value of $1000 is bought at a market price of $800. The annual income from the bond is $100. But since only $800 was paid for the bond, the current yield is $100 divided by $800, or 12½%.

CUSHION
1. interval between the time a bond is issued and the time it can be called. Also termed CALL PROTECTION.
2. margin of safety for a corporation's financial ratios. For instance, if its DEBT-TO-EQUITY RATIO has a cushion of up to 40% debt, anything over that level might be cause for concern.
3. *see* LAST IN, FIRST OUT.

CUSHION BOND callable bond with a coupon above current market interest rates that is selling for a premium. Cushion bonds lose less of their value as rates rise and gain less in value as rates fall, making them suitable for conservative investors interested in high income.

CUSHION THEORY theory that a stock's price must rise if many investors are taking short positions in it, because those positions must be covered by purchases of the stock. Technical analysts consider it particularly bullish if the short positions in a stock are twice as high as the number of shares traded daily. This is because price rises force short sellers to cover their positions, making the stock rise even more.

CUSIP NUMBER number identifying all stocks and registered bonds, using the COMMITTEE ON UNIFORM SECURITIES IDENTIFICATION PROCEDURES (CUSIP). Brokers will use a security's CUSIP number to look it up on a computer terminal to get further information. The CUSIP number will also be listed on any trading confirmation tickets. The CUSIP number makes it easier to settle and clear trades. Foreign securities use a similar identification system called the CUSIP International Numbering System (CINS).

CUSTODIAL ACCOUNT account that is created for a minor, usually at a bank, brokerage firm, or mutual fund. Minors cannot make securities transactions without the approval of the custodian, who manages cash and other property gifted to minors under the UNIFORM GIFTS TO MINORS ACT or the Uniform Transfers to Minors Act. Any earnings or interest from the account up to $600 are tax-free if the child is under age 14. Earnings from $600 to $1200 are taxed at the child's tax rate. Any earnings over $1200 are taxed at the parents' rate. Once the child turns 14, the earnings are taxed at the child's tax rate. When the child reaches the age of majority, usually 18, they have full discretion over the account, unless the account is set up in a trust controlled by the parent. See also CLIFFORD TRUST; CROWN LOAN; UNIFORM GIFTS TO MINORS ACT.

CUSTODIAN bank or other financial institution that keeps custody of stock certificates and other assets of a mutual fund, individual, or corporate client. See also CUSTODIAL ACCOUNT.

CUSTODY legal responsibility for someone else's assets or for a child. Term implies management as well as safekeeping. The IRS does not require custodial parents or guardians to declare child support as income, nor is child support deductible by the noncustodial parent.

CUSTOMER'S LOAN CONSENT agreement signed by a margin customer permitting a broker to borrow margined securities to the limit of the customer's debit balance for the purpose of covering other customers' short positions and certain failures to complete delivery.

CUSTOMER'S MAN traditionally a synonym for *registered representative, account executive,* or *account representative.* Now used rarely, as more women work in brokerages.

CUSTOMERS' NET DEBIT BALANCE total credit extended by New York Stock Exchange member firms to finance customer purchases of securities.

CUTOFF POINT in capital budgeting, the minimum rate of return acceptable on investments.

CYCLE see BUSINESS CYCLE.

CYCLICAL STOCK stock that tends to rise quickly when the economy turns up and to fall quickly when the economy turns down. Examples are housing, automobiles, and paper. Stocks of noncyclical industries—such as foods, insurance, drugs—are not as directly affected by economic changes

d

DAILY TRADING LIMIT maximum that many commodities and options markets are allowed to rise or fall in one day. When a market reaches its limit early and stays there all day, it is said to be having an up-limit or down-limit day. Exchanges usually impose a daily trading limit on each contract. For example, the Chicago Board of Trade limit is two points ($2000 per contract) up or down on its treasury bond futures options contract.

DAISY CHAIN trading between market manipulators to create the appearance of active volume as a lure for legitimate investors. When these traders drive the price up, the manipulators unload their holdings, leaving the unwary investors without buyers to trade with in turn.

DATA BASE store of information that is sorted, indexed, and summarized and accessible to people with computers. Data bases containing market and stock histories are available from a number of commercial sources.

DATED DATE date from which accrued interest is calculated on new bonds and other debt instruments. The buyer pays the issuer an amount equal to the interest accrued from the dated date to the issue's settlement date. With the first interest payment on the bond, the buyer is reimbursed.

DATE OF ISSUE

Bonds: date on which a bond is issued and effective. Interest accrues to bondholders from this date.

Insurance: date on which a policy is issued. Normally, the policy is also declared effective on that date, though not in every case.

Stocks: date on which a new stock is publicly issued and begins trading.

DATE OF RECORD date on which a shareholder must officially own shares in order to be entitled to a dividend. For example, the board of directors of a corporation might declare a dividend on November 1 payable on December 1 to stockholders of record on November 15. After the date of record the stock is said to be EX-DIVIDEND. Also called *record date.*

DATING in commercial transactions, extension of credit beyond the supplier's customary terms—for example, 90 days instead of 30 days. In industries marked by high seasonality and long lead time, dating, combined with ACCOUNTS RECEIVABLE FINANCING, makes it possible for manufacturers with lean capital to continue producing goods. Also called *seasonal dating, special dating.*

DAWN RAID British term for a practice whereby a RAIDER instructs brokers to buy all the available shares of another company at the opening of the market, thus giving the acquirer a significant holding before the TARGET COMPANY gets wise to the undertaking. In London-based markets, the practice is restricted by the *City Code on Takeovers and Mergers. See also* SATURDAY NIGHT SPECIAL.

DAY LOAN loan from a bank to a broker for the purchase of securities pending delivery through the afternoon clearing. Once delivered the securities are pledged as collateral and the loan becomes a regular broker's call loan. Also called *morning loan.*

DAY OF DEPOSIT TO DAY OF WITHDRAWAL ACCOUNT bank account that pays interest based on the actual number of days that money is on deposit. Also called *actual balance method.*

DAY ORDER order to buy or sell securities that expires unless executed or canceled the day it is placed. All orders are day orders unless other-wise specified. The main exception is a GOOD-TILL-CANCELED ORDER, though even it can be executed the same day if conditions are right.

DAY TRADE purchase and sale of a position during the same day.

DEAD CAT BOUNCE sharp rise in stock prices after a severe decline. The saying refers to the fact that a dead cat dropped from a high place will bounce. Often, the bounce is the result of short-sellers covering their positions at a profit.

DEALER
1. individual or firm acting as a PRINCIPAL in a securities transaction. Principals trade for their own account and risk. When buying from a broker acting as a dealer, a customer receives securities from the firm's inventory; the confirmation must disclose this. When specialists trade for their own account, as they must as part of their responsibility for maintaining an orderly market, they act as dealers. Since most brokerage firms operate both as brokers and as principals, the term *broker-dealer* is commonly used.
2. one who purchases goods or services for resale to consumers. The element of inventory risk is what distinguishes a dealer from an agent or sales representative.

DEALER MARKET securities market in which transactions are between principals acting as DEALERS for their own accounts rather than between brokers acting as agents for buyers and sellers. Municipal and U.S. government securities are largely traded in dealer markets. *See also* AUCTION MARKET.

DEALER'S SPREAD *see* MARKDOWN; UNDERWRITING SPREAD.

DEAL FLOW rate of new deals being referred to the investment banking division of a brokerage firm. This might refer to proposals for new stock and bond issues, as well as mergers, acquisitions, and takeovers.

DEAL STOCK stock that may be rumored to be a TAKEOVER target or the party to some other major transaction such as a merger or leveraged buyout. The stock may be subject to a rumor of a prospective deal, or a deal may have been announced that attracts additional bidders and the company is said to be *in play*. Arbitrageurs and other speculators will attempt to buy deal stocks before the deal is finalized or profit when the stock price rises. Of course, if there is no deal, these speculators may lose money if the stock falls back to its pre-rumor price.

DEAR MONEY British equivalent of TIGHT MONEY.

DEATH-BACKED BONDS bonds backed by policyholder loans against life insurance policies. The loans will be repaid either by the policyholder while he or she is alive or from the proceeds of the insurance policy if the policyholder dies. Also called *policyholder loan bonds*.

DEATH BENEFIT amount of money to be paid to beneficiaries when a policyholder dies. The death benefit is the face value of the policy less any unpaid policy loans or other insurance company claims against the policy. Beneficiaries are not taxed on the death benefit when they receive it.

DEATH PLAY stock bought on the expectation that a key executive will die and the shares will gain value as a result. For example, there might be reason to believe that upon the imminent death of a CEO, a company will be broken up and that the shares will be worth more at their PRIVATE MARKET VALUE.

DEATH VALLEY CURVE venture capital term that describes a start-up company's rapid use of capital. When a company begins operations, it uses a great deal of its equity capital to set up its offices, hire personnel, and do research and development. It may be several months or even years before the company has products or services to sell, creating a stream of revenues. The Death Valley Curve is the time period before revenues begin, when it is difficult for the company to raise more equity or issue debt to help it through its cash-flow difficulties.

DEBENTURE general debt obligation backed only by the integrity of the borrower and documented by an agreement called an INDENTURE. An *unsecured bond* is a debenture.

DEBENTURE STOCK stock issued under a contract providing for fixed payments at scheduled intervals and more like preferred stock than a DEBENTURE, since their status in liquidation is equity and not debt.

Also, a type of bond issued by Canadian and British corporations, which refer to debt issues as stock.

DEBIT BALANCE
1. account balance representing money owed to the lender or seller.
2. money a margin customer owes a broker for loans to purchase securities.

DEBIT CARD card issued by a bank to allow customers access to their funds electronically. Debit cards could replace checks as a method of payment for goods and services, and are more convenient because they are more widely accepted than checks. Debit cards can also be used to withdraw cash from automatic teller machines. Unlike credit cards, however, consumers do not have the advantage of the FLOAT on their money since funds are withdrawn immediately.

DEBIT SPREAD difference in the value of two options, when the value of the one bought exceeds the value of the one sold. The opposite of a CREDIT SPREAD.

DEBT
1. money, goods, or services that one party is obligated to pay to another in accordance with an expressed or implied agreement. Debt may or may not be secured.
2. general name for bonds, notes, mortgages, and other forms of paper evidencing amounts owed and payable on specified dates or on demand.

DEBT BOMB situation in which a major financial institution defaults on its obligations, causing major disruption to the financial system of the institution's home country. If a major multinational bank were to run into such trouble, it could have a major negative impact on the global financial system.

DEBT CEILING *see* DEBT LIMIT.

DEBT INSTRUMENT written promise to repay a debt; for instance, a BILL, NOTE, BOND, banker's ACCEPTANCE, CERTIFICATE OF DEPOSIT, or COMMERCIAL PAPER.

DEBTOR any individual or company that owes money. If debt is in the form of a loan from a financial institution, you might use *borrower.* If indebtedness is in the form of securities, such as bonds, you would refer to the *issuer. See also* OBLIGOR.

DEBT LIMIT maximum amount of debt that a municipality can incur. If a municipality wants to issue bonds for an amount greater than its debt limit, it usually requires approval from the voters.

DEBT RETIREMENT repayment of debt. The most common method of retiring corporate debt is to set aside money each year in a SINKING FUND.

Most municipal bonds and some corporates are issued in serial form, meaning different portions of an issue—called series—are retired at different times, usually on an annual or semiannual schedule.

Sinking fund bonds and serial bonds are not classes of bonds, just methods of retiring them that are adaptable to debentures, convertibles, and so on. *See also* REFUNDING.

DEBT SECURITY security representing money borrowed that must be repaid and having a fixed amount, a specific maturity or maturities, and usually a specific rate of interest or an original purchase discount. For instance, a BILL, BOND, COMMERCIAL PAPER, or a NOTE.

DEBT SERVICE cash required in a given period, usually one year, for payments of interest and current maturities of principal on outstanding debt. In corporate bond issues, the annual interest plus annual sinking fund payments; in government bonds, the annual payments into the debt service fund. *See also* ABILITY TO PAY.

DEBT SERVICE COVERAGE
Corporate finance: amount, usually expressed as a ratio, of CASH FLOW available to meet annual interest and principal payments on debt, including SINKING FUND payments.
Government finance: export earnings required to cover annual principal and interest payments on a country's external debts.
Personal finance: ratio of monthly installment debt payments, excluding mortgage loans and rent, to monthly take-home pay.
See also FIXED-CHARGE COVERAGE.

DEBT SWAP exchange, between banks, of a loan, usually to a third-world country in local currency. *See also* SWAP.

DEBT-TO-EQUITY RATIO
1. total liabilities divided by total shareholders' equity. This shows to what extent owner's equity can cushion creditors' claims in the event of liquidation.
2. total long-term debt divided by total shareholders' equity. This is a measure of LEVERAGE—the use of borrowed money to enhance the return on owners' equity.
3. long-term debt and preferred stock divided by common stock equity. This relates securities with fixed charges to those without fixed charges.

DECLARATION DATE date on which a company announces the amount and date of its next dividend payment. There is normally an interim period of a few days between the declaration date and the EX-STOCK DIVIDEND date which allows people to buy shares and still qualify to receive the upcoming dividend.

DECLARE authorize the payment of a dividend on a specified date, an act of the board of directors of a corporation. Once declared, a dividend becomes an obligation of the issuing corporation.

DECREASING TERM LIFE INSURANCE form of life insurance coverage in which premiums remain constant for the life of the policy while the death benefit declines. Term insurance premiums usually increase every year as the policyholder ages, and the policy is renewed. If there is less need for coverage because, for example, children have become self-sufficient, it may be prudent to decrease the amount of outstanding coverage.

DEDUCTIBLE
Insurance: amount of money that the policyholders must pay out of their pockets before reimbursements from the insurance company begin. The deductible is usually set as a fixed dollar amount, though in some cases it can also be a

percentage of the premium paid or some other formula. Some group health insurance plans set the deductible at a set percentage of the employee's salary, for example. In general, the higher a deductible a policyholder will accept, the lower insurance premiums will be. The insurance company is willing to lower its premiums because the company is no longer liable for small claims.

Taxes: *see* TAX DEDUCTIBLE.

DEDUCTION

1. expense allowed by the Internal Revenue Service as a subtraction from adjusted gross income in arriving at a person's taxable income. Such deductions include some interest paid, state and local taxes, charitable contributions.
2. adjustment to an invoice allowed by a seller for a discrepancy, shortage, and so on.

DEED written instrument containing some transfer, bargain, or contract relating to property—most commonly, conveying the legal title to real estate from one party to another.

DEEP DISCOUNT BOND bond selling for a discount of more than about 20% from its face value. Unlike a CURRENT COUPON BOND, which has a higher interest rate, a deep discount bond will appreciate faster as interest rates fall and drop faster as rates rise. Unlike ORIGINAL ISSUE DISCOUNT bonds, deep discounts were issued at a par value of $1000.

DEEP IN/OUT OF THE MONEY CALL OPTION whose exercise price is well below the market price of the underlying stock (deep *in* the money) or well above the market price (deep *out of* the money). The situation would be exactly the opposite for a PUT OPTION. The premium for buying a deep-in-the-money option is high, since the holder has the right to purchase the stock at a striking price considerably below the current price of the stock. The premium for buying a deep-out-of-the-money option is very small, on the other hand, since the option may never be profitable.

DEFAULT failure of a debtor to make timely payments of interest and principal as they come due or to meet some other provision of a bond indenture. In the event of default, bondholders may make claims against the assets of the issuer in order to recoup their principal.

DEFAULT RISK risk that a debtholder will not receive interest and principal when due. One way to gauge default risk is the RATINGS issued by credit rating agencies such as Fitch Investors Service, Moody's, and Standard & Poor's. The higher the rating (AAA or Aaa is highest), the less risk of default. Some issues, such as Treasury bonds backed by the full faith and credit of the U.S. government, are considered free of default risk. Other bonds, such as JUNK BONDS, carry a much higher default risk. One investor defense against default, particularly for municipal bonds, is MUNICIPAL BOND INSURANCE.

DEFEASANCE

In general: provision found in some debt agreements whereby the contract is nullified if specified acts are performed.

Corporate finance: short for in-substance defeasance, a technique whereby a corporation discharges old, low-rate debt without repaying it prior to maturity. The corporation uses newly purchased securities with a lower face value but paying higher interest or having a higher market value. The objective is a cleaner (more debt free) balance sheet and increased earnings in the amount by which the face amount of the old debt exceeds the cost of the new securities. The use of defeasance in modern corporate finance began in 1982 when Exxon bought and put in an irrevocable trust $312 million of U.S. government securities yielding 14% to provide for the repayment of principal and interest on $515 million of old debt paying 5.8% to 6.7% and maturing in 2009. Exxon removed the defeased debt from its balance sheet and added $132 million—the after-tax difference between $515 million and $312 million— to its earnings that quarter.

In another type of defeasance, a company instructs a broker to buy, for a fee, the outstanding portion of an old bond issue of the company. The broker then exchanges the bond issue for a new issue of the company's stock with an equal market value. The broker subsequently sells the stock at a profit.

DEFENSIVE SECURITIES stocks and bonds that are more stable than average and provide a safe return on an investor's money. When the stock market is weak, defensive securities tend to decline less than the overall market.

DEFERRAL OF TAXES postponement of tax payments from this year to a later year. For instance, an INDIVIDUAL RETIREMENT ACCOUNT (IRA) defers taxes until the money is withdrawn.

DEFERRED ACCOUNT account that postpones taxes until a later date. Some examples: ANNUITY, INDIVIDUAL RETIREMENT ACCOUNT, KEOGH PLAN accounts, PROFIT-SHARING PLAN, SALARY REDUCTION PLAN, SIMPLIFIED EMPLOYEE PENSION (SEP) PLAN.

DEFERRED ANNUITY see DEFERRED PAYMENT ANNUITY.

DEFERRED CHARGE expenditure carried forward as an asset until it becomes relevant, such as an advance rent payment or insurance premium. The opposite is *deferred income,* such as advance rent received.

DEFERRED COMPENSATION currently earned compensation that, under the terms of a profit-sharing, pension, or stock option plan, is not actually paid until a later date and is therefore not taxable until that date.

DEFERRED INTEREST BOND bond that pays interest at a later date. A ZERO COUPON BOND, which pays interest and repays principal in one lump sum at maturity, is in this category. In effect, such bonds automatically reinvest the interest at a fixed rate. Prices are more volatile for a deferred interest bond than for a CURRENT COUPON BOND.

DEFERRED PAYMENT ANNUITY ANNUITY whose contract provides that payments to the annuitant be postponed until a number of periods have elapsed—for example, when the annuitant attains a certain age. Also called a *deferred annuity.*

DEFERRED SALES CHARGE see BACK-END LOAD.

DEFICIENCY LETTER written notice from the Securities and Exchange Commission to a prospective issuer of securities that the preliminary prospectus needs revision or expansion. Deficiency letters require prompt action; otherwise, the registration period may be prolonged.

DEFICIT
1. excess of liabilities and debts over income and assets. Deficits usually are corrected by borrowing or by selling assets.
2. in finance, an excess of expenditures over budget.

DEFICIT FINANCING borrowing by a government agency to make up for a revenue shortfall. Deficit financing stimulates the economy for a time but eventually can become a drag on the economy by pushing up interest rates. *See also* CROWD-ING OUT; KEYNESIAN ECONOMICS.

DEFICIT NET WORTH excess of liabilities over assets and capital stock, perhaps as a result of operating losses. Also called *negative net worth.*

DEFICIT SPENDING excess of government expenditures over government revenue, creating a shortfall that must be financed through borrowing. *See also* DEFICIT FINANCING.

DEFINED BENEFIT PENSION PLAN plan that promises to pay a specified amount to each person who retires after a set number of years of service. Such plans pay no taxes on their investments. Employees contribute to them in some cases; in others, all contributions are made by the employer.

DEFINED CONTRIBUTION PENSION PLAN pension plan in which the level of contributions is fixed at a certain level, while benefits vary depending on the return from the investments. In some cases, such as 401(k), 403(b), and 457 plans, employees make voluntary contributions into a tax-deferred account, which may or may not be matched by employers. The level of contribution may be selected by the employee within a range set by the employer, such as between 2% and 10% of annual salary. In other cases, contributions are made by an employer into a profit-sharing account based on each employee's salary level, years of service, age, and other factors. Defined contribution pension plans, unlike DEFINED BENEFIT PENSION PLANS, give the employee options of where to invest the account, usually among stock, bond and money market accounts. Defined contribution plans have become increasingly popular in recent years because they limit a company's pension outlay and shift the liability for investment performance from the company's pension plan to employees.

DEFLATION decline in the prices of goods and services. Deflation is the reverse of INFLATION; it should not be confused with DISINFLATION, which is a slowing down in the rate of price increases. Generally, the economic effects of deflation are the opposite of those produced by inflation, with two notable exceptions: (1) prices that increase with inflation do not necessarily decrease with deflation—union wage rates, for example; (2) while inflation may or may not stimulate output and employment, marked deflation has always affected both negatively.

DEFLATOR statistical factor used to convert current dollar activity into inflation-adjusted activity—in effect, a measure of prices. The change in the gross domestic product (GDP) deflator, for example, is a measure of economy-wide inflation.

DEFLECTION OF TAX LIABILITY legal shift of one person's tax burden to someone else through such methods as the CLIFFORD TRUST, CUSTODIAL ACCOUNTS, and SPOUSAL REMAINDER TRUSTS. Such devices were curtailed but not eliminated by the TAX REFORM ACT OF 1986.

DELAYED DELIVERY delivery of securities later than the scheduled date, which is ordinarily five business days after the trade date. A contract calling for delayed delivery, known as a SELLER'S OPTION, is usually agreed to by both parties to a trade. *See also* DELIVERY DATE.

DELAYED OPENING postponement of the start of trading in a stock until a gross imbalance in buy and sell orders is overcome. Such an imbalance is likely to follow on the heels of a significant event such as a takeover offer.

DELINQUENCY failure to make a payment on an obligation when due. In finance company parlance, the amount of past due balances, determined either on a contractual or recency-of-payment basis.

DELISTING removal of a company's security from an exchange because the firm did not abide by some regulation or the stock does not meet certain financial ratios or sales levels.

DELIVERABLE BILLS financial futures and options trading term meaning Treasury bills that meet all the criteria of the exchange on which they are traded. One such criterion is that the deliverable T-bill is the current bill for the week in which settlement takes place.

DELIVERY *see* DELIVERY DATE; GOOD DELIVERY.

DELIVERY DATE
1. first day of the month in which delivery is to be made under a futures contract. Since sales are on a SELLER'S OPTION basis, delivery can be on any day of the month, as long as proper notice is given.
2. third business day following a REGULAR WAY transaction of stocks or bonds. Seller's option delivery can be anywhere from 3 to 60 days, though there may be a purchase-price adjustment to compensate for DELAYED DELIVERY. The SETTLEMENT DATE was changed from 5 days to 3 days effective June 1, 1995, after approval by the SEC. New deadline is known as *T* (for trade)-*plus-three.*

DELIVERY NOTICE
1. notification from the seller to the buyer of a futures contract indicating the date when the actual commodity is to be delivered.
2. in general business transactions, a formal notice documenting that goods have been delivered or will be delivered on a certain date.

DELIVERY VERSUS PAYMENT securities industry procedure, common with institutional accounts, whereby delivery of securities sold is made to the buying customer's bank in exchange for payment, usually in the form of cash. (Institutions are required by law to require "assets of equal value" in exchange for delivery.) Also called CASH ON DELIVERY, delivery against payment, delivery against cash, or, from the sell side, RECEIVE VERSUS PAYMENT.

DELTA
1. measure of the relationship between an option price and the underlying futures contract or stock price. For a call option, a delta of 0.50 means a half-point rise in premium for every dollar that the stock goes up. For a put option contract, the premium rises as stock prices fall. As options near expiration, IN-THE-MONEY contracts approach a delta of 1.
2. on the London Stock Exchange, *delta stocks* were the smallest capitalization issues before the system was replaced with today's NORMAL MARKET SIZE.

DELTA HEDGING HEDGING method used in OPTION trading and based on the change in premium (option price) caused by a change in the price of the underlying instrument. The change in the premium for each one-point change in the underlying security is called DELTA and the relationship between the two price movements is called the *hedge ratio.* For example, if a call option has a hedge ratio of 40, the call should rise 40% of the change in the security move if the stock goes down. The delta of a put option, conversely, has a negative value. The value of the delta is usually good the first one-point move in the underlying security over a short time period. When an option has a high hedge ratio, it is usually more profitable to buy the option than to be a WRITER because the greater percentage movement vis a vis the underlying security's price and the relatively little time value erosion allow the purchaser greater leverage. The opposite is true for options with a low hedge ratio.

DEMAND DEPOSIT account balance which, without prior notice to the bank, can be drawn on by check, cash withdrawal from an automatic teller machine, or by transfer to other accounts using the telephone or home computers. Demand deposits are the largest component of the U.S. MONEY SUPPLY, and the principal medium through which the Federal Reserve implements monetary policy. *See also* COMPENSATING BALANCE.

DEMAND LOAN loan with no set maturity date that can be called for repayment when the lender chooses. Banks usually bill interest on these loans at fixed intervals.

DEMAND-PULL INFLATION price increases occurring when supply is not adequate to meet demand. *See also* COST-PUSH INFLATION.

DEMONETIZATION withdrawal from circulation of a specified form of currency. For example, the Jamaica Agreement between major INTERNATIONAL MONETARY FUND countries officially demonetized gold starting in 1978, ending its role as the major medium of international settlement.

DENKS acronym for *dual-employed, no kids,* referring to a family unit in which both husband and wife work, and there are no children. Without the expense and responsibility for children, DENKS have a larger disposable income that couples with children, making them a prime target for marketers of luxury goods and services, particularly various types of investments.

DENOMINATION face value of currency units, coins, and securities. *See also* PAR VALUE.

DEPLETION accounting treatment available to companies that extract oil and gas, coal, or other minerals, usually in the form of an allowance that reduces taxable income. Oil and gas limited partnerships pass the allowance on to their limited partners, who can use it to reduce other tax liabilities.

DEPOSIT
1. cash, checks, or drafts placed with a financial institution for credit to a customer's account. Banks broadly differentiate between demand deposits (checking accounts on which the customer may draw at any time) and time deposits, which usually pay interest and have a specified maturity or require 30 days' notice before withdrawal.
2. securities placed with a bank or other institution or with a person for a particular purpose.
3. sums lodged with utilities, landlords, and service companies as security.
4. money put down as evidence of an intention to complete a contract and to protect the other party in the event that the contract is not completed.

DEPOSITARY RECEIPT *see* AMERICAN DEPOSITARY RECEIPT.

DEPOSIT INSURANCE *see* CREDIT UNION; FEDERAL DEPOSIT INSURANCE CORPORATION.

DEPOSITORY INSTITUTIONS DEREGULATION AND MONETARY CONTROL ACT federal legislation of 1980 providing for deregulation of the banking system. The act established the Depository Institutions Deregulation Committee, composed of five voting members, the Secretary of the Treasury and the chair of the Federal Reserve Board, the Federal Home Loan Bank Board, the Federal Deposit Insurance Corporation, and the National Credit Union Administration, and one non-voting member, the Comptroller of the Currency. The committee was charged with phasing out regulation of interest rates of banks and savings institutions over a six-year period (passbook accounts were de-regulated effective April, 1986, under a different federal law). The act authorized interest-bearing NEGOTIABLE ORDER OF WITHDRAWAL (NOW) accounts to be offered anywhere in the country. The act also overruled state usury laws on home mortgages over $25,000 and otherwise modernized mortgages by eliminating dollar limits, permitting second mortgages, and ending territorial restrictions in mortgage lending. Another part of the law permitted stock brokerages to offer checking accounts. *See also* DEREGULATION.

DEPOSITORY TRUST COMPANY central securities repository where stock and bond certificates are exchanged. Most of these exchanges now take place electronically, and few paper certificates actually change hands. The DTC is a member of the Federal Reserve System and is owned by most of the brokerage houses on Wall Street and the New York Stock Exchange.

DEPRECIATED COST original cost of a fixed asset less accumulated DEPRECIATION; this is the *net book value* of the asset.

DEPRECIATION
Economics: consumption of capital during production—in other words, wearing out of plant and capital goods, such as machines and equipment.

Finance: amortization of fixed assets, such as plant and equipment, so as to allocate the cost over their depreciable life. Depreciation reduces taxable income but does not reduce cash.

Among the most commonly used methods are STRAIGHT-LINE DEPRECIATION; ACCELERATED DEPRECIATION; the ACCELERATED COST RECOVERY SYSTEM, and the MODIFIED ACCELERATED COST RECOVERY SYSTEM. Others include the annuity, appraisal, compound interest, production, replacement, retirement, and sinking fund methods.

Foreign Exchange: decline in the price of one currency relative to another.

DEPRESSED MARKET market characterized by more supply than demand and therefore weak (depressed) prices. *See also* SYSTEMATIC RISK.

DEPRESSED PRICE price of a product, service, or security that is weak because of a DEPRESSED MARKET. Also refers to the market price of a stock that is low relative to comparable stocks or to its own ASSET VALUE because of perceived or actual risk. Such stocks are identified by high dividend yield, abnormally low PRICE/EARNINGS RATIOS and other such yardsticks. *See also* FUNDAMENTAL ANALYSIS.

DEPRESSION economic condition characterized by falling prices, reduced purchasing power, an excess of supply over demand, rising unemployment, accumulating inventories, deflation, plant contraction, public fear and caution, and a general decrease in business activity. The Great Depression of the 1930s, centered in the United States and Europe, had worldwide repercussions.

DEREGULATION greatly reducing government regulation in order to allow freer markets to create a more efficient marketplace. After the stock-brokerage industry was deregulated in the mid-1970s, commissions were no longer fixed. After the banking industry was deregulated in the early 1980s, banks were given greater freedom in setting interest rates on deposits and loans. Industries such as communications and transportation have also been deregulated, with similar results:

increased competition, heightened innovation, and mergers among weaker competitors. Some government oversight usually remains after deregulation.

DERIVATIVE short for *derivative instrument,* a contract whose value is based on the performance of an underlying financial asset, index, or other investment. For example, an ordinary *option* is a derivative because its value changes in relation to the performance of an underlying stock. A more complex example would be an option on a FUTURES CONTRACT, where the option value varies with the value of the futures contract which, in turn, varies with the value of an underlying commodity or security. Derivatives are available based on the performance of assets, interest rates, currency exchange rates, and various domestic and foreign indexes. Derivatives afford leverage and, when used properly by knowledgeable investors, can enhance returns and be useful in HEDGING portfolios. They gained notoriety in the late '80s, however, because of problems involved in PROGRAM TRADING, and in the '90s, when a number of mutual funds, municipalities, corporations, and leading banks suffered large losses because unexpected movements in interest rates adversely affected the value of derivatives. *See also* BEARS, CERTIFICATES OF ACCRUAL ON TREASURY SECURITIES (CATS), COLLATERALIZED BOND OBLIGATION (CBO); COLLATERALIZED MORTGAGE OBLIGATION (CMO); CUBS; INDEX OPTIONS; OEX; SPIDERS; STRIP; SUBSCRIPTION RIGHT; SUBSCRIPTION WARRANT; SWAP; TIGER.

DERIVATIVE INSTRUMENT *see* DERIVATIVE.

DESCENDING TOPS chart pattern wherein each new high price for a security is lower than the preceding high. The trend is considered bearish.

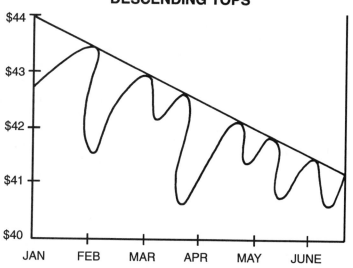

DESCENDING TOPS

DESIGNATED ORDER TURNAROUND (DOT) electronic system used by the New York Stock Exchange to expedite execution of small MARKET ORDERS by routing them directly from the member firm to the SPECIALIST, thus bypassing the FLOOR BROKER. A related system called *Super DOT* routes LIMIT ORDERS.

DESK trading desk, or Securities Department, at the New York FEDERAL RESERVE BANK, which is the operating arm of the FEDERAL OPEN MARKET COMMITTEE. The Desk executes all transactions undertaken by the FEDERAL RESERVE SYSTEM in the money market or the government securities market, serves as the Treasury Department's eyes and ears in these and related markets, and encompasses a foreign desk which conducts transactions in the FOREIGN EXCHANGE market.

DEUTSCHE BORSE AG operating company for the German cash and derivatives markets: the DEUTSCHE TERMINBORSE, the financial futures exchange, and the FRANKFURT STOCK EXCHANGE. Deutsche Borse provides the staff, facilities, premises, and financial resources for both operations. It also serves as the clearing house for DTB in a separate division.

DEUTSCHE TERMINBORSE (DTB) Germany's first fully computerized exchange, and the first German exchange for trading financial futures, opened in January 1990. In January 1994, DTB merged with DEUTSCHE BORSE AG. There is no open outcry system. Cooperative agreements have been undertaken for electronic linkages with the MATIF, the French derivatives exchange; MATIF members began trading DTB contracts in France in September 1994; DTB members also trade MATIF contracts via terminals in Germany. The exchange trades options on 16 German blue chip stocks, and three products linked to the DAX Index, the German stock index: DAX options, DAX futures, and options on DAX futures. The DTB trades four interest rate futures contracts with a full range of maturities: FIBOR futures (3 months), BOBL futures (3.3 to 5 years), BUND futures (8.5 to 10 years) and BUXL futures (15 to 30 years). Options are traded on BOBL and BUND futures.

DEVALUATION lowering of the value of a country's currency relative to gold and/or the currencies of other nations. Devaluation can also result from a rise in value of other currencies relative to the currency of a particular country.

DEVELOPMENTAL DRILLING PROGRAM drilling for oil and gas in an area with proven reserves to a depth known to have been productive in the past. Limited partners in such a program, which is considerably less risky than an EXPLORATORY DRILLING PROGRAM or WILDCAT DRILLING, have a good chance of steady income, but little chance of enormous profits.

DEWKS acronym for *dual-employed, with kids,* referring to a family unit in which both husband and wife work and there are children. Marketers selling products for children, including various investments, target DEWKS.

DIAGONAL SPREAD strategy based on a long and short position in the same class of option (two puts or two calls in the same stock) at different striking prices and different expiration dates. Example: a six-month call sold with a striking price of 40 and a three-month call sold with a striking price of 35. *See also* CALENDAR SPREAD; VERTICAL SPREAD.

DIALING AND SMILING expression for COLD CALLING by securities brokers and other salespeople. Brokers must not only make unsolicited telephone calls to potential customers, but also gain the customer's confidence with their upbeat tone of voice and sense of concern for the customer's financial well-being.

DIALING FOR DOLLARS expression for COLD CALLING in which brokers make unsolicited telephone calls to potential customers, hoping to find people with investable funds. The term has a derogatory implication, and is typically applied to salespeople working in BOILER ROOMS, selling speculative or fraudulent investments such as PENNY STOCKS.

DIAMOND INVESTMENT TRUST unit trust that invests in high-quality diamonds. Begun in the early 1980s by Thomson McKinnon, these trusts let shareholders invest in diamonds without buying and holding a particular stone. Shares in these trusts do not trade actively and are therefore difficult to sell if diamond prices fall, as they did soon after the first trust was set up.

DIFF short for *Euro-rate differential,* a futures contract traded on the Chicago Mercantile Exchange that is based on the interest rate spread between the U.S. dollar and the British pound, the German mark, or the Japanese yen.

DIFFERENTIAL small extra charge sometimes called the *odd-lot-differential—* usually ⅛ of a point—that dealers add to purchases and subtract from sales in quantities less than the standard trading unit or ROUND LOT. Also, the extent to which a dealer widens his round lot quote to compensate for lack of volume.

DIGITS DELETED designation on securities exchange tape meaning that because the tape has been delayed, some digits have been dropped. For example, 26½... 26⅝... 26⅛ becomes 6½... 6⅝... 6⅛.

DILUTION effect on earnings per share and book value per share if all convertible securities were converted or all warrants or stock options were exercised. *See* FULLY DILUTED EARNINGS PER (COMMON) SHARE.

DINKS acronym for *dual-income, no kids,* referring to a family unit in which there are two incomes and no children. The two incomes may result from both husband and wife working, or one spouse holding down two jobs. Since the couple do not have children, they typically have more disposable income than those with children, and therefore are the prime targets of marketers selling luxury products and services, including various investments. *See also* DENKS; DEWKS.

DIP slight drop in securities prices after a sustained uptrend. Analysts often advise investors to buy on dips, meaning buy when a price is momentarily weak.

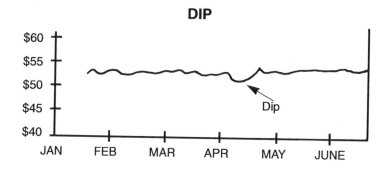

DIRECT INVESTMENT (1) purchase of a controlling interest in a foreign (international) business or subsidiary. (2) in domestic finance, the purchase of a controlling interest or a minority interest of such size and influence that active control is a feasible objective.

DIRECTOR *see* BOARD OF DIRECTORS.

DIRECT OVERHEAD portion of overhead costs—rent, lights, insurance—allocated to manufacturing, by the application of a standard factor termed a *burden rate.* This amount is absorbed as an INVENTORY cost and ultimately reflected as a COST OF GOODS SOLD.

DIRECT PARTICIPATION PROGRAM program letting investors participate directly in the cash flow and tax benefits of the underlying investments. Such programs are usually organized as LIMITED PARTNERSHIPS, although their uses as tax shelters have been severely curtailed by tax legislation affecting PASSIVE investments.

DIRECT PLACEMENT direct sale of securities to one or more professional investors. Such securities may or may not be registered with the SECURITIES AND EXCHANGE COMMISSION. They may be bonds, private issues of stock, limited partnership interests, mortgage-backed securities, venture capital investments, or other sophisticated instruments. These investments typically require large minimum purchases, often in the millions of dollars. Direct placements offer higher potential returns than many publicly offered securities, but also present more risk. Buyers of direct placements are large, sophisticated financial institutions including insurance companies, banks, mutual funds, foundations, and pension funds that are able to evaluate such offerings. Also called *private placement.*

DIRECT PURCHASE purchasing shares in a no-load or low-load OPEN-END MUTUAL FUND directly from the fund company. Investors making direct purchases deal directly with the fund company over the phone, in person at investor centers, or by mail. This contrasts with the method of purchasing shares in a LOAD FUND through a financial intermediary such as a broker or financial planner, who collects a commission for offering advice on which fund is appropriate for the client. Many companies also now allow shareholders to purchase stock directly from the company, thereby avoiding brokers and sales commissions.

DIRTY STOCK stock that fails to meet the requirements for GOOD DELIVERY.

DISABILITY INCOME INSURANCE insurance policy that pays benefits to a policyholder when that person becomes incapable of performing one or more occupational duties, either temporarily or on a long-term basis, or totally. The policy is designed to replace a portion of the income lost because of the insured's disability. Payments begin after a specified period, called the *elimination period,* of several weeks or months.

Some policies remain in force until the person is able to return to work, or to return to a similar occupation, or is eligible to receive benefits from another program such as Social Security disability. Disability insurance payments are normally tax-free to beneficiaries as long as they paid the policy premiums. Many employers offer disability income insurance to their employees, though people are able to buy coverage on an individual basis as well.

DISBURSEMENT paying out of money in the discharge of a debt or an expense, as distinguished from a distribution.

DISCHARGE OF BANKRUPTCY order terminating bankruptcy proceedings, ordinarily freeing the debtor of all legal responsibility for specified obligations.

DISCHARGE OF LIEN order removing a lien on property after the originating legal claim has been paid or otherwise satisfied.

DISCLAIMER OF OPINION auditor's statement, sometimes called an *adverse opinion,* that an ACCOUNTANT'S OPINION cannot be provided because of limitations on the examination or because some condition or situation exists, such as pending litigation, that could impair the financial strength or profitability of the client.

DISCLOSURE release by companies of all information, positive or negative, that might bear on an investment decision, as required by the Securities and Exchange

Commission and the stock exchanges. *See also* FINANCIAL PUBLIC RELATIONS; INSIDE INFORMATION; INSIDER.

DISCONTINUED OPERATIONS operations of a business that have been sold, abandoned, or otherwise disposed of. Accounting regulations require that continuing operations be reported separately in the income statement from discontinued operations, and that any gain or loss from the disposal of a segment (an entity whose activities represent a separate major line of business or class of customer) be reported along with the operating results of the discontinued segment.

DISCOUNT
1. difference between a bond's current market price and its face or redemption value.
2. manner of selling securities such as treasury bills, which are issued at less than face value and are redeemed at face value.
3. relationship between two currencies. The French franc may sell at a discount to the English pound, for example.
4. to apply all available news about a company in evaluating its current stock price. For instance, taking into account the introduction of an exciting new product.
5. method whereby interest on a bank loan or note is deducted in advance.
6. reduction in the selling price of merchandise or a percentage off the invoice price in exchange for quick payment.

DISCOUNT BOND bond selling below its redemption value. *See also* DEEP DISCOUNT BOND.

DISCOUNT BROKER brokerage house that executes orders to buy and sell securities at commission rates sharply lower than those charged by a FULL SERVICE BROKER.

DISCOUNT DIVIDEND REINVESTMENT PLAN *see* DIVIDEND REINVESTMENT PLAN.

DISCOUNTED CASH FLOW value of future expected cash receipts and expenditures at a common date, which is calculated using NET PRESENT VALUE or INTERNAL RATE OF RETURN and is a factor in analyses of both capital investments and securities investments. The net present value (NPV) method applies a rate of discount (interest rate) based on the marginal cost of capital to future cash flows to bring them back to the present. The internal rate of return (IRR) method finds the average return on investment earned through the life of the investment. It determines the discount rate that equates the present value of future cash flows to the cost of the investment.

DISCOUNTING THE NEWS bidding a firm's stock price up or down in anticipation of good or bad news about the company's prospects.

DISCOUNT POINTS *see* POINT.

DISCOUNT RATE
1. interest rate that the Federal Reserve charges member banks for loans, using government securities or ELIGIBLE PAPER as collateral. This provides a floor on interest rates, since banks set their loan rates a notch above the discount rate.
2. interest rate used in determining the PRESENT VALUE of future CASH FLOWS. *See also* CAPITALIZATION RATE.

DISCOUNT WINDOW place in the Federal Reserve where banks go to borrow money at the DISCOUNT RATE. Borrowing from the Fed is a privilege, not a right, and banks are discouraged from using the privilege except when they are short of reserves.

DISCOUNT YIELD yield on a security sold at a discount—U.S. treasury bills sold at $9750 and maturing at $10,000 in 90 days, for instance. Also called *bank discount basis*. To figure the annual yield, divide the discount ($250) by the face amount ($10,000) and multiply that number by the approximate number of days in the year (360) divided by the number of days to maturity (90). The calculation looks like this:

$$\frac{\$250}{\$10,000} \times \frac{360}{90} = .025 \times 4 = .10 = 10\%.$$

DISCRETIONARY ACCOUNT account empowering a broker or adviser to buy and sell without the client's prior knowledge or consent. Some clients set broad guidelines, such as limiting investments to blue chip stocks.

DISCRETIONARY INCOME amount of a consumer's income spent after essentials like food, housing, and utilities and prior commitments have been covered. The total amount of discretionary income can be a key economic indicator because spending this money can spur the economy.

DISCRETIONARY ORDER order to buy a particular stock, bond, or commodity that lets the broker decide when to execute the trade and at what price.

DISCRETIONARY TRUST
1. mutual fund or unit trust whose investments are not limited to a certain kind of security. The management decides on the best way to use the assets.
2. personal trust that lets the trustee decide how much income or principal to provide to the beneficiary. This can be used to prevent the beneficiary from dissipating funds.

DISHONOR to refuse to pay, as in the case of a check that is returned by a bank because of insufficient funds.

DISINFLATION slowing down of the rate at which prices increase— usually during a recession, when sales drop and retailers are not always able to pass on higher prices to consumers. Not to be confused with DEFLATION, when prices actually drop.

DISINTERMEDIATION movement of funds from low-yielding accounts at traditional banking institutions to higher-yielding investments in the general market—for example, withdrawal of funds from a passbook savings account paying 5½% to buy a Treasury bill paying 10%. As a counter move, banks may pay higher rates to depositors, then charge higher rates to borrowers, which leads to tight money and reduced economic activity. Since banking DEREGULATION, disintermediation is not the economic problem it once was.

DISINVESTMENT reduction in capital investment either by disposing of capital goods (such as plant and equipment) or by failing to maintain or replace capital assets that are being used up.

DISPOSABLE INCOME personal income remaining after personal taxes and noncommercial government fees have been paid. This money can be spent on essentials or nonessentials or it can be saved. See also DISCRETIONARY INCOME.

DISTRESS SALE sale of property under distress conditions. For example, stock, bond, mutual fund or futures positions may have to be sold in a portfolio if there is a MARGIN CALL. Real estate may have to be sold because a bank is in the process of FORECLOSURE on the property. A brokerage firm may be forced to sell securities from its inventory if it has fallen below various capital requirements imposed by stock exchanges and regulators. Because distress sellers are being forced to sell, they usually do not receive as favorable a price as if they were able to wait for ideal selling conditions.

DISTRIBUTING SYNDICATE group of brokerage firms or investment bankers that join forces in order to facilitate the DISTRIBUTION of a large block of securities. A distribution is usually handled over a period of time to avoid upsetting the market price. The term distributing syndicate can refer to a primary distribution or a secondary distribution, but the former is more commonly called simply a syndicate or an underwriting syndicate.

DISTRIBUTION
Corporate finance: allocation of income and expenses to the appropriate subsidiary accounts.

Economics: (1) movement of goods from manufacturers; (2) way in which wealth is shared in any particular economic system.

Estate law: parceling out of assets to the beneficiaries named in a will, as carried out by the executor under the guidance of a court.

Mutual funds and closed-end investment companies: payout of realized capital gains on securities in the portfolio of the fund or closed-end investment company.

Securities: sale of a large block of stock in such manner that the price is not adversely affected. Technical analysts look on a pattern of distribution as a tipoff that the stock will soon fall in price. The opposite of distribution, known as ACCUMULATION, may signal a rise in price.

DISTRIBUTION AREA price range in which a stock trades for a long time. Sellers who want to avoid pushing the price down will be careful not to sell below this range. ACCUMULATION of shares in the same range helps to account for the stock's price stability. Technical analysts consider distribution areas in predicting when stocks may break up or down from that price range. *See also* ACCUMULATION AREA.

DISTRIBUTION PERIOD period of time, usually a few days, between the date a company's board of directors declares a stock dividend, known as the DECLARATION DATE, and the DATE OF RECORD, by which the shareholder must officially own shares to be entitled to the dividend.

DISTRIBUTION PLAN plan adopted by a mutual fund to charge certain distribution costs, such as advertising, promotion and sales incentives, to shareholders. The plan will specify a certain percentage, usually .75% or less, which will be deducted from fund assets annually. *See also* 12b-1 MUTUAL FUND.

DISTRIBUTION STOCK stock part of a block sold over a period of time in order to avoid upsetting the market price. May be part of a primary (underwriting) distribution or a secondary distribution following SHELF REGISTRATION.

DISTRIBUTOR wholesaler of goods to dealers that sell to consumers.

DIVERSIFICATION
1. spreading of risk by putting assets in several categories of investments—stocks, bonds, money market instruments, and precious metals, for instance, or several industries, or a mutual fund, with its broad range of stocks in one portfolio.

2. at the corporate level, entering into different business areas, as a CONGLOMERATE does.

DIVERSIFIED INVESTMENT COMPANY mutual fund or unit trust that invests in a wide range of securities. Under the Investment Company Act of 1940, such a company may not have more than 5 percent of its assets in any one stock, bond, or commodity and may not own more than 10 percent of the voting shares of any one company.

DIVESTITURE disposition of an asset or investment by outright sale, employee purchase, liquidation, and so on.

Also, one corporation's orderly distribution of large blocks of another corporation's stock, which were held as an investment. Du Pont was ordered by the courts to divest itself of General Motors stock, for example.

DIVIDEND distribution of earnings to shareholders, prorated by class of security and paid in the form of money, stock, scrip, or, rarely, company products or property. The amount is decided by the board of directors and is usually paid quarterly. Dividends must be declared as income in the year they are received.

Mutual fund dividends are paid out of income, usually on a quarterly basis from the fund's investments. The tax on such dividends depends on whether the distributions resulted from capital gains, interest income, or dividends received by the fund. *See also* EQUALIZING DIVIDEND; EXTRA DIVIDEND.

DIVIDEND CAPTURE *See* DIVIDEND ROLLOVER PLAN.

DIVIDEND COVER British equivalent of the dividend PAYOUT RATIO.

DIVIDEND DISCOUNT MODEL mathematical model used to determine the price at which a stock should be selling based on the discounted value of projected future dividend payments. It is used to identify undervalued stocks representing capital gains potential.

DIVIDEND EXCLUSION pre-TAX REFORM ACT OF 1986 provision allowing for subtraction from dividends qualifying as taxable income under Internal Revenue Service rules—$100 for individuals and $200 for married couples filing jointly. The 1986 Tax Act eliminated this exclusion effective for the 1987 tax year.

Domestic corporations may exclude from taxable income 70% of dividends received from other domestic corporations. The exclusion was 85% prior to the 1986 Act, which reduced it to 80%.

DIVIDEND IN ARREARS ACCUMULATED DIVIDEND on CUMULATIVE PREFERRED stock, which is payable to the current holder. Preferred stock in a TURNAROUND situation can be an attractive buy when it is selling at a discount and has dividends in arrears.

DIVIDEND PAYOUT RATIO percentage of earnings paid to shareholders in cash. In general, the higher the payout ratio, the more mature the company. Electric and telephone utilities tend to have the highest payout ratios, whereas fast-growing companies usually reinvest all earnings and pay no dividends.

DIVIDEND RECORD publication of Standard & Poor's Corporation that provides information on corporate policies and payment histories.

DIVIDEND REINVESTMENT PLAN automatic reinvestment of shareholder dividends in more shares of the company's stock. Some companies absorb most or all of the applicable brokerage fees, and some also discount the stock price.

Dividend reinvestment plans allow shareholders to accumulate capital over the long term using DOLLAR COST AVERAGING. For corporations, dividend reinvestment plans are a means of raising capital funds without the FLOTATION COSTS of a NEW ISSUE.

DIVIDEND REQUIREMENT amount of annual earnings necessary to pay contracted dividends on preferred stock.

DIVIDEND ROLLOVER PLAN method of buying and selling stocks around their EX-DIVIDEND dates so as to collect the dividend and make a small profit on the trade. This entails buying shares about two weeks before a stock goes ex-dividend. After the ex-dividend date the price will drop by the amount of the dividend, then work its way back up to the earlier price. By selling slightly above the purchase price, the investor can cover brokerage costs, collect the dividend, and realize a small capital gain in three or four weeks. Also called *dividend capture*. See also TRADING DIVIDENDS.

DIVIDENDS PAYABLE dollar amount of dividends that are to be paid, as reported in financial statements. These dividends become an obligation once declared by the board of directors and are listed as liabilities in annual and quarterly reports.

DIVIDENDS-RECEIVED DEDUCTION tax deduction allowed to a corporation owning shares in another corporation for the dividends it receives. In most cases, the deduction is 70%, but in some cases it may be as high as 100% depending on the level of ownership the dividend-receiving company has in the dividend-paying entity.

DIVIDEND YIELD annual percentage of return earned by an investor on a common or preferred stock. The yield is determined by dividing the amount of the dividends per share by the current market price per share of the stock. For example, a stock paying a $1 dividend per year that sells for $10 a share has a 10% dividend yield. The dividend yields of stocks are listed in the stock tables of most daily newspapers.

DOCUMENTARY DRAFT *see* DRAFT.

DOLLAR BEARS traders who think the dollar will fall in value against other foreign currencies. Dollar bears may implement a number of investment strategies to capitalize on a falling dollar, such as buying Japanese yen, Deutsche marks, British pounds or other foreign currencies directly, or buying futures or options contracts on those currencies.

DOLLAR BOND
1. municipal revenue bond quoted and traded on a dollar price basis instead of yield to maturity.
2. bond denominated in U.S. dollars but issued outside the United States, principally in Europe.
3. bond denominated in U.S. dollars and issued in the United States by foreign companies.
   See also EUROBOND; EURODOLLAR BOND.

DOLLAR COST AVERAGING *see* CONSTANT DOLLAR PLAN.

DOLLAR DRAIN amount by which a foreign country's imports from the United States exceed its exports to the United States. As the country spends more dollars to finance the imports than it receives in payment for the exports, its dollar reserves drain away.

DOLLAR PRICE bond price expressed as a percentage of face value (normally $1000) rather than as a yield. Thus a bond quoted at 97½ has a dollar price of $975, which is 97½% of $1000.

DOLLAR SHORTAGE situation in which a country that imports from the United States can no longer pay for its purchases without U.S. gifts or loans to provide the necessary dollars. After World War II a world-wide dollar shortage was alleviated by massive infusions of American money through the European Recovery Program (Marshall Plan) and other grant and loan programs.

DOLLAR-WEIGHTED RETURN portfolio accounting method that measures changes in total dollar value, treating additions and withdrawals of capital as a part of the RETURN along with income and capital gains and losses. For example, a portfolio (or group of portfolios) worth $100 million at the beginning of a reporting period and $120 million at the end would show a return of 20%; this would be true even if the investments lost money, provided enough new money was infused. While dollar weighting enables investors to compare absolute dollars with financial goals, manager-to-manager comparisons are not possible unless performance is isolated from external cash flows; this is accomplished with the TIME-WEIGHTED RETURN method.

DOMESTIC ACCEPTANCE see ACCEPTANCE.

DOMESTIC CORPORATION corporation doing business in the U.S. state in which it was incorporated. In all other U.S. states its legal status is that of a FOREIGN CORPORATION.

DOMICILE place where a person has established permanent residence. It is important to establish a domicile for the purpose of filing state and local income taxes, and for filing estate taxes upon death. The domicile is created based on obtaining a driver's license, registering to vote, and having a permanent home to which one returns. Usually, one must be a resident in a state for at least six months of the year to establish a domicile.

DONATED STOCK fully paid capital stock of a corporation contributed without CONSIDERATION to the same issuing corporation. The gift is credited to the DONATED SURPLUS account at PAR VALUE.

DONATED SURPLUS shareholder's equity account that is credited when contributions of cash, property, or the firm's own stock are freely given to the company. Also termed *donated capital*. Not to be confused with contributed surplus or contributed capital, which is the balances in CAPITAL STOCK accounts plus capital contributed in excess of par or STATED VALUE accounts.

DONOGHUE'S MONEY FUND AVERAGE see IBC/DONOGHUE'S MONEY FUND AVERAGE

DO NOT INCREASE abbreviated *DNI*. Instruction on good-till-cancelled buy limit and sell stop orders that prevent the quantity from changing in the event of a stock SPLIT or stock dividend.

DO NOT REDUCE (DNR) instruction on a LIMIT ORDER to buy, or on a STOP ORDER to sell, or on a STOP-LIMIT ORDER to sell, not to reduce the order when the stock goes EX-DIVIDEND and its price is reduced by the amount of the dividend as usually happens. DNRs do not apply to rights or stock dividends.

DONOR individual who donates property to another through a TRUST. Also called a *grantor.* Donors also make tax-deductible charitable contributions of securities or physical property to nonprofit institutions such as schools, philanthropic groups, and religious organizations.

DON'T FIGHT THE TAPE don't trade against the market trend. If stocks are falling, as reported on the BROAD TAPE, some analysts say it would be foolish to buy aggressively. Similarly, it would be fighting the tape to sell short during a market rally.

DON'T KNOW Wall Street slang for a *questioned trade*. Brokers exchange comparison sheets to verify the details of transactions between them. Any discrepancy that turns up is called a don't know or a *QT*.

DOT (and SUPER-DOT) SYSTEM acronym for *Designated Order Turnaround*, New York Stock Exchange AUTOMATED ORDER ENTRY SYSTEMS for expediting small and moderate-sized orders. DOT handles market orders and Super DOT limited price orders. The systems bypass floor brokers and rout orders directly to the SPECIALIST, who executes through a CONTRA BROKER or against the SPECIALIST'S BOOK.

DOUBLE AUCTION SYSTEM *see* AUCTION MARKET.

DOUBLE-BARRELED municipal revenue bond whose principal and interest are guaranteed by a larger municipal entity. For example, a bridge authority might issue revenue bonds payable out of revenue from bridge tolls. If the city or state were to guarantee the bonds, they would be double-barreled, and the investor would be protected against default in the event that bridge usage is disappointing and revenue proves inadequate.

DOUBLE BOTTOM technical chart pattern showing a drop in price, then a rebound, then another drop to the same level. The pattern is usually interpreted to mean the security has much support at that price and should not drop further. However, if the price does fall through that level, it is considered likely to reach a new low. *See also* DOUBLE TOP.

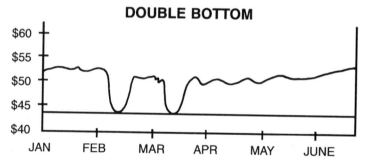

DOUBLE BOTTOM

DOUBLE-DECLINING-BALANCE DEPRECIATION METHOD (DDB) method of accelerated depreciation, approved by the Internal Revenue Service, permitting twice the rate of annual depreciation as the straight-line method. It is also called the 200 percent declining-balance method. The two methods are compared below, assuming an asset with a total cost of $1000, a useful life of four years, and no SALVAGE VALUE.

With STRAIGHT-LINE DEPRECIATION the useful life of the asset is divided into the total cost to arrive at the uniform annual charge of $250, or 25% a year. DDB permits twice the straight-line annual percentage rate—50% in this case—to be applied each year to the undepreciated value of the asset. Hence: 50% × $1000 = $500 the first year, 50% × $500 = $250 the second year, and so on.

YEAR	STRAIGHT LINE		DOUBLE DECLINING BALANCE	
	Expense	Cumulative	Expense	Cumulative
1	$250	$250	$500	$500
2	250	500	250	750
3	250	750	125	875
4	250	1000	63	938
	$1000		$938	

A variation of DDB, called *150 percent declining balance method,* uses 150% of the straight-line annual percentage rate.

A switch to straight-line from declining balance depreciation is permitted once in the asset's life—logically, at the third year in our example. When the switch is made, however, salvage value must be considered. *See also* MODIFIED ACCELERATED COST RECOVERY SYSTEM; DEPRECIATION.

DOUBLE TAXATION taxation of earnings at the corporate level, then again as stockholder dividends.

DOUBLE TOP technical chart pattern showing a rise to a high price, then a drop, then another rise to the same high price. This means the security is encountering resistance to a move higher. However, if the price does move through that level, the security is expected to go on to a new high. *See also* DOUBLE BOTTOM.

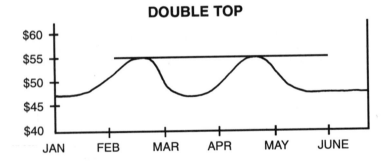

DOUBLE UP sophisticated stock buying (or selling short) strategy that reaffirms the original rationale by doubling the risk when the price goes (temporarily it is hoped) the wrong way. For example, an investor with confidence in XYZ buys 10,000 shares at $40. When the price drops to $35, the investor buys 10,000 additional shares, thus doubling up on a stock he feels will ultimately rise.

DOUBLE WITCHING DAY day when two related classes of options and futures expire. For example, index options and index futures on the same underlying index may expire on the same day, leading to various strategies by ARBITRAGEURS to close out positions. *See also* TRIPLE WITCHING HOUR.

DOW JONES AVERAGES *see* STOCK INDEXES AND AVERAGES.

DOW JONES INDUSTRIAL AVERAGE *see* STOCK INDEXES AND AVERAGES.

DOWNSIDE RISK estimate that a security will decline in value and the extent of the decline, taking into account the total range of factors affecting market price.

DOWNSIZING term for a corporate strategy popular in the 1990s whereby a company reduces its size and complexity, thereby presumably increasing its efficiency and profitability. Downsizing is typically accomplished through RESTRUCTURING, which means reducing the number of employees and, often, the SPIN-OFF of activities unrelated to the company's core business.

DOWNSTREAM flow of corporate activity from parent to subsidiary. Financially, it usually refers to loans, since dividends and interest generally flow upstream.

DOWNTICK sale of a security at a price below that of the preceding sale. If a stock has been trading at $15 a share, for instance, the next trade is a downtick if it is at 14⅞. Also known as MINUS TICK.

DOWNTURN shift of an economic or stock market cycle from rising to falling.

DOW THEORY theory that a major trend in the stock market must be confirmed by a similar movement in the Dow Jones Industrial Average and the Dow Jones Transportation Average. According to Dow Theory, a significant trend is not confirmed until both Dow Jones indexes reach the new highs or lows; if they don't, the market will fall back to its former trading range. Dow Theory proponents often disagree on when a true breakout has occurred and, in any case, miss a major portion of the up or down move while waiting for their signals.

DRAFT signed, written order by which one party (drawer) instructs another party (drawee) to pay a specified sum to a third party (payee). Payee and drawer are usually the same person. In foreign transactions, a draft is usually called a *bill of exchange*. When prepared without supporting papers, it is a *clean draft*. With papers or documents attached, it is a *documentary draft*. A *sight draft* is payable on demand. A *time draft* is payable either on a definite date or at a fixed time after sight or demand.

DRAINING RESERVES actions by the Federal Reserve System to decrease the money supply by curtailing the funds banks have available to lend. The Fed does this in three ways: (1) by raising reserve requirements, forcing banks to keep more funds on deposit with Federal Reserve banks; (2) by increasing the rate at which banks borrow to maintain reserves, thereby making it unattractive to deplete reserves by making loans; and (3) by selling bonds in the open market at such attractive rates that dealers reduce their bank balances to buy them. *See also* MULTIPLIER.

DRAWBACK rebate of taxes or duties paid on imported goods that have been reexported. It is in effect a government subsidy designed to encourage domestic manufacturers to compete overseas.

DRAWER *see* DRAFT.

DRESSING UP A PORTFOLIO practice of money managers to make their portfolio look good at the end of a reporting period. For example, a mutual fund or pension fund manager may sell certain stocks that performed badly during the quarter shortly before the end of that quarter to avoid having to report that holding to shareholders. Or they may buy stocks that have risen during the quarter to show shareholders that they owned winning stocks. Because these portfolio changes are largely cosmetic, they have little effect on portfolio performance except they increase transaction costs. In the final few days of a quarter, market analysts frequently comment that certain stocks rose or fell because of end-of-quarter WINDOW DRESSING.

DRILLING PROGRAM *see* BALANCED DRILLING PROGRAM; COMPLETION PROGRAM; DEVELOPMENTAL DRILLING PROGRAM; EXPLORATORY DRILLING PROGRAM; OIL AND GAS LIMITED PARTNERSHIP.

DRIP *see* DIVIDEND REINVESTMENT PLAN.

DRIP FEED supplying capital to a new company as its growth requires it, rather than in a lump sum at the beginning. *See also* EVERGREEN FUNDING.

DROP-DEAD DAY day on which a deadline, such as the expiration of the national debt limit, becomes absolutely final.

DROP-DEAD FEE British term meaning a fee paid to a lender only if a deal requiring financing from that lender falls through.

DROPLOCK SECURITY FLOATING RATE NOTE or bond that becomes a FIXED INCOME INVESTMENT when the rate to which it is pegged drops to a specified level.

DUAL BANKING U.S. system whereby banks are chartered by the state or federal government. This makes for differences in banking regulations, in lending limits, and in services available to customers.

DUAL LISTING listing of a security on more than one exchange, thus increasing the competition for bid and offer prices as well as the liquidity of the securities. Furthermore, being listed on an exchange in the East and another in the West would extend the number of hours when the stock can be traded. Securities may not be listed on both the New York and American stock exchanges.

DUAL PURPOSE FUND exchange-listed CLOSED-END FUND that has two classes of shares. Preferred shareholders receive all the income (dividends and interest) from the portfolio, while common shareholders receive all the capital gains. Such funds are set up with a specific expiration date when preferred shares are redeemed at a predetermined price and common shareholders claim the remaining assets, voting either to liquidate or to continue the fund on an open-end basis. Dual purpose funds are not closely followed on Wall Street, and there is little trading in them.

DUAL TRADING commodities traders' practice of dealing for their own and their clients' accounts at the same time. Reformers favor restricting dual trading to prevent FRONT RUNNING; advocates claim the practice is harmless in itself and economically vital to the industry.

DUE BILL *see* BILL.

DUE DATE date on which a debt-related obligation is required to be paid.

DUE DILIGENCE MEETING meeting conducted by the underwriter of a new offering at which brokers can ask representatives of the issuer questions about the issuer's background and financial reliability and the intended use of the proceeds. Brokers who recommend investment in new offerings without very careful due diligence work may face lawsuits if the investment should go sour later. Although, in itself, the legally required due diligence meeting typically is a perfunctory affair, most companies, recognizing the importance of due diligence, hold informational meetings, often in different regions of the country, at which top management representatives are available to answer questions of securities analysts and institutional investors.

DUE-ON-SALE CLAUSE clause in a mortgage contract requiring the borrower to pay off the full remaining principal outstanding on a mortgage when the mortgaged property is sold, transferred, or in any way encumbered. Due-on-sale clauses prevent the buyer of the property from assuming the mortgage loan.

DUMPING
International finance: selling goods abroad below cost in order to eliminate a surplus or to gain an edge on foreign competition. The U.S. Antidumping Act of 1974 was designed to prevent the sale of imported goods below cost in the United States.
Securities: offering large amounts of stock with little or no concern for price or market effect.

DUN & BRADSTREET (D & B) company that combines credit information obtained directly from commercial firms with data solicited from their creditors, then makes this available to subscribers in reports and a ratings directory. D & B also offers an accounts receivable collection service and publishes financial composite ratios and other financial information. A subsidiary, MOODY'S INVESTOR'S SERVICE, rates bonds and commercial paper.

DUN'S NUMBER short for Dun's Market Identifier. It is published as part of a list of firms giving information such as an identification number, address code, number of employees, corporate affiliations, and trade styles. Full name: Data Universal Numbering System.

DURABLE POWER OF ATTORNEY legal document by which a person with assets (the principal) appoints another person (the agent) to act on the principal's behalf, even if the principal becomes incompetent. If the power of attorney is not "durable," the agent's authority to act ends if the principal becomes incompetent. The agent's power to act for the principal may be broadly stated, allowing the agent to buy and sell securities, or narrowly stated to limit activity to selling a car.

DURATION concept first developed by Frederick Macaulay in 1938 that measures bond price VOLATILITY by measuring the "length" of a bond. It is a weighted-average term-to-maturity of the bond's cash flows, the weights being the present value of each cash flow as a percentage of the bond's full price. A Salomon Brothers' study compared it to a series of tin cans equally spaced on a seesaw. The size of each can represents the cash flow due, the contents of each can represent the present values of those cash flows, and the intervals between them represent the payment periods. Duration is the distance to the fulcrum that would balance the seesaw. The duration of a zero-coupon security would thus equal its maturity because all the cash flows—all the weights—are at the other end of the seesaw. The greater the duration of a bond, the greater its percentage volatility. In general, duration rises with maturity, falls with the frequency of coupon payments, and falls as the yield rises (the higher yield reduces the present values of the cash flows.) Duration (the term *modified duration* is used in the strict sense because of modifications to Macaulay's formulation) as a measure of percentage of volatility is valid only for small changes in yield. For working purposes, duration can be defined as the approximate percentage change in price for a 100-basis-point change in yield. A duration of 5, for example, means the price of the bond will change by approximately 5% for a 100-basis point change in yield.

For larger yield changes, volatility is measured by a concept called *convexity*. That term derives from the price-yield curve for a normal bond, which is convex. In other words, the price is always falling at a slower rate as the yield increases. The more convexity a bond has, the merrier, because it means the bond's price will fall more slowly and rise more quickly on a given movement in general interest rate levels. As with duration, convexity on straight bonds increases with lower coupon, lower yield, and longer maturity. Convexity measures the rate of change of duration, and for an option-free bond it is always positive because changes in yield do not affect cash flows. When a bond has a call option, however, cash flows are affected. In that case, duration gets smaller as yield decreases, resulting in *negative convexity.*

When the durations of the assets and the liabilities of a portfolio, say that of a pension fund, are the same, the portfolio is inherently protected against interest-rate changes and you have what is called *immunization.* The high volatility and interest rates in the early 1980s caused institutional investors to use duration and convexity as tools in immunizing their portfolios.

DUTCH AUCTION auction system in which the price of an item is gradually lowered until it meets a responsive bid and is sold. U.S. Treasury bills are sold under this system. Contrasting is the two-sided or DOUBLE AUCTION SYSTEM exemplified by the major stock exchanges. *See also* BILL.

DUTCH AUCTION PREFERRED STOCK type of adjustable-rate PREFERRED STOCK whose dividend is determined every seven weeks in a DUTCH AUCTION process by corporate bidders. Shares are bought and sold at FACE VALUES ranging from $100,000 to $500,000 per share. Also known as *auction rate preferred stock, Money Market Preferred Stock* (Shearson Lehman Brothers Inc.), and by such proprietary acronyms as DARTS (Salomon Brothers Inc.). *See also* AMPS; APS.

DUTY tax imposed on the importation, exportation, or consumption of goods. *See also* TARIFF.

DWARFS pools of mortgage-backed securities, with original maturity of 15 years, issued by the Federal National Mortgage Association (FANNIE MAE).

e

EACH WAY commission made by a broker involved on both the purchase and the sale side of a trade. *See also* CROSSED TRADE.

EAFE acronym for the *Europe and Australasia, Far East Equity* index, calculated by the Morgan Stanley Capital International (MSCI) group. EAFE is composed of stocks screened for liquidity, cross-ownership, and industry representation. Stocks are selected by MSCI's analysts in Geneva. The index acts as a benchmark for managers of international stock portfolios. There are financial futures and options contracts based on EAFE.

EARLY WITHDRAWAL PENALTY charge assessed against holders of fixed-term investments if they withdraw their money before maturity. Such a penalty would be assessed, for instance, if someone who has a six-month certificate of deposit withdrew the money after four months.

EARNED INCOME income (especially wages and salaries) generated by providing goods or services. Also, pension or annuity income.

EARNED INCOME CREDIT TAX CREDIT for qualifying taxpayers with at least one child in residence for more than half the year and incomes below a specified dollar level.

EARNED SURPLUS *see* RETAINED EARNINGS.

EARNEST MONEY good faith deposit given by a buyer to a seller prior to consummation of a transaction. Earnest money is usually forfeited in the event the buyer is unwilling or unable to complete the sale. In real estate, earnest money is the down payment, which is usually put in an escrow account until the closing.

EARNING ASSET income-producing asset. For example, a company's building would not be an earning asset normally, but a financial investment in other property would be if it provided rental income.

EARNINGS BEFORE TAXES corporate profits after interest has been paid to bondholders, but before taxes have been paid.

EARNINGS MOMENTUM pattern of increasing rate of growth in EARNINGS PER SHARE from one period to another, which usually causes a stock price to go up. For example, a company whose earnings per share are up 15% one year and 35% the next has earnings momentum and should see a gain in its stock price.

EARNINGS PER SHARE portion of a company's profit allocated to each outstanding share of common stock. For instance, a corporation that earned $10 million last year and has 10 million shares outstanding would report earnings of $1 per share. The figure is calculated after paying taxes and after paying preferred shareholders and bondholders.

EARNINGS-PRICE RATIO relationship of earnings per share to current stock price. Also known as *earnings yield,* it is used in comparing the relative attractiveness of stocks, bonds, and money market instruments. Inverse of PRICE-EARNINGS RATIO.

EARNINGS REPORT statement issued by a company to its shareholders and the public at large reporting its earnings for the latest period, which is either on a quarterly or annual basis. The report will show revenues, expenses, and net profit for the period. Earnings reports are released to the press and reported in newspapers and electronic media, and are also mailed to shareholders of record. Also called *profit and loss statement* (P&L) or *income statement.*

EARNINGS SURPRISE EARNINGS REPORT that reports a higher or lower profit than analysts have projected. If earnings are higher than expected, a company's stock price will usually rise sharply. If profits are below expectations, the company's stock will often plunge. Many analysts on Wall Street study earnings surprises very carefully on the theory that when a company reports a positive or negative surprise, it is typically followed by another surprise in the same direction. Two firms that follow general trends in earnings surprises are INSTITUTIONAL BROKER'S ESTIMATE SYSTEM (IBES) and ZACK'S ESTIMATE SYSTEM.

EARNINGS YIELD *see* EARNINGS-PRICE RATIO.

EARN-OUT in mergers and acquisitions, supplementary payments, not part of the original ACQUISITION COST, based on future earnings of the acquired company above a predetermined level.

EASY MONEY *see* TIGHT MONEY.

EATING SOMEONE'S LUNCH expression that an aggressive competitor is beating their rivals. For example, an analyst might say that one retailer is "eating the lunch" of a competitive retailer in the same town if it is gaining market share through an aggressive pricing strategy. The implication of the expression is that the winning competitor is taking food away from the losing company or individual.

EATING STOCK a block positioner or underwriter who can't find buyers may find himself eating stock, that is, buying it for his own account.

ECM *see* EMERGING COMPANY MARKETPLACE (ECM).

ECONOMETRICS use of computer analysis and modeling techniques to describe in mathematical terms the relationship between key economic forces such as labor, capital, interest rates, and government policies, then test the effects of changes in economic scenarios. For instance, an econometric model might show the relationship of housing starts and interest rates.

ECONOMIC GROWTH RATE rate of change in the GROSS NATIONAL PRODUCT, as expressed in an annual percentage. If adjusted for inflation, it is called the *real economic growth rate.* Two consecutive quarterly drops in the growth rate mean recession, and two consecutive advances in the growth rate reflect an expanding economy.

ECONOMIC INDICATORS key statistics showing the direction of the economy. Among them are the unemployment rate, inflation rate, factory utilization rate, and balance of trade. *See also* LEADING INDICATORS.

ECONOMIC RECOVERY TAX ACT OF 1981 (ERTA) tax-cutting legislation. Among the key provisions:
1. across-the-board tax cut, which took effect in three stages ending in 1983.
2. indexing of tax brackets to the inflation rate.
3. lowering of top tax rates on long-term capital gains from 28% to 20%. The top rate on dividends, interest, rents, and royalties income dropped from 70% to 50%.
4. lowering of MARRIAGE PENALTY tax, as families with two working spouses could deduct 10% from the salary of the lower-paid spouse, up to $3000.
5. expansion of INDIVIDUAL RETIREMENT ACCOUNTS to all working people, who can contribute up to $2000 a year, and $250 annually for nonworking spouses. Also, expansion of the amount self-employed people can contribute to KEOGH PLAN account contributions.
6. creation of the *all-savers certificate,* which allowed investors to exempt up to $1000 a year in earned interest. The authority to issue these certificates expired at the end of 1982.
7. deductions for reinvesting public utility dividends.
8. reductions in estate and gift taxes, phased in so that the first $600,000 of property can be given free of estate tax starting in 1987. Annual gifts that can be given free of gift tax were raised from $3000 to $10,000. Unlimited deduction for transfer of property to a spouse at death.
9. lowering of rates on the exercise of stock options.
10. change in rules on DEPRECIATION and INVESTMENT CREDIT.
    See also TAX REFORM ACT OF 1986.

ECONOMICS study of the economy. Classic economics concentrates on how the forces of supply and demand allocate scarce product and service resources. MACROECONOMICS studies a nation or the world's economy as a whole, using data about inflation, unemployment and industrial production to understand the past and predict the future. MICROECONOMICS studies the behavior of specific sectors of the economy, such as companies, industries, or households. Over the years, various schools of economic thought have gained prominence, including KEYNE-SIAN ECONOMICS, MONETARISM and SUPPLY-SIDE ECONOMICS.

ECONOMIES OF SCALE economic principle that as the volume of production increases, the cost of producing each unit decreases. Therefore, building a large factory will be more efficient than a small factory because the large factory will be able to produce more units at a lower cost per unit than the smaller factory.

The introduction of mass production techniques in the early twentieth century, such as the assembly line production of Ford Motor Company's Model T, put the theory of economies of scale into action.

ECU *see* EUROPEAN CURRENCY UNIT (ECU).

EDGE ACT banking legislation, passed in 1919, which allows national banks to conduct foreign lending operations through federal or state chartered subsidiaries, called Edge Act corporations. Such corporations can be chartered by other states and are allowed, unlike domestic banks, to own banks in foreign countries and to invest in foreign commercial and industrial firms. The act also permitted the FEDERAL RESERVE SYSTEM to set reserve requirements on foreign banks that do business in America. Edge Act corporations benefited further from the 1978 International Banking Act, which instructs the Fed to strike any regulations putting American banks at a disadvantage compared with U.S. operations of foreign banks.

EEC *see* EUROPEAN ECONOMIC COMMUNITY.

EFFECTIVE DATE
In general: date on which an agreement takes effect.
Securities: date when an offering registered with the Securities and Exchange Commission may commence, usually 20 days after filing the registration statement. *See also* SHELF REGISTRATION.
Banking and insurance: time when an insurance policy goes into effect. From that day forward, the insured party is covered by the contract.

EFFECTIVE DEBT total debt owed by a firm, including the capitalized value of lease payments.

EFFECTIVE NET WORTH net worth plus subordinated debt, as viewed by senior creditors. In small business banking, loans payable to principals are commonly subordinated to bank loans. The loans for principals thus can be regarded as effective net worth as long as a bank loan is outstanding and the subordination agreement is in effect.

EFFECTIVE RATE yield on a debt instrument as calculated from the purchase price. The effective rate on a bond is determined by the price, the coupon rate, the time between interest payments, and the time until maturity. Every bond's effective rate thus depends on when it was bought. The effective rate is a more meaningful yield figure than the coupon rate. *See also* RATE OF RETURN.

EFFECTIVE SALE price of a ROUND LOT that determines the price at which the next ODD LOT will be sold. If the last round-lot price was 15, for instance, the odd-lot price might be 15⅛. The added fraction is the *odd-lot differential.*

EFFECTIVE TAX RATE tax rate paid by a taxpayer. It is determined by dividing the tax paid by the taxable income in a particular year. For example, if a taxpayer with a taxable income of $100,000 owes $30,000 in a year, he has an effective tax rate of 30%. The effective tax rate is useful in tax planning, because it gives a taxpayer a realistic understanding of the amount of taxes he is paying after allowing for all deductions, credits, and other factors affecting tax liability.

EFFICIENT MARKET theory that market prices reflect the knowledge and expectations of all investors. Those who adhere to this theory consider it futile to seek undervalued stocks or to forecast market movements. Any new development is reflected in a firm's stock price, they say, making it impossible to beat the market.

This vociferously disputed hypothesis also holds that an investor who throws darts at a newspaper's stock listings has as good a chance to outperform the market as any professional investor.

EFFICIENT PORTFOLIO portfolio that has a maximum expected return for any level of risk or a minimum level of risk for any expected return. It is arrived at mathematically, taking into account the expected return and standard deviation of returns for each security, as well as the covariance of returns between different securities in the portfolio.

EITHER-OR ORDER *see* ALTERNATIVE ORDER.

ELASTICITY OF DEMAND AND SUPPLY
Elasticity of demand: responsiveness of buyers to changes in price. Demand for luxury items may slow dramatically if prices are raised, because these purchases are not essential, and can be postponed. On the other hand, demand for necessities such as food, telephone service, and emergency surgery is said to be inelastic. It remains about the same despite price changes because buyers cannot postpone their purchases without severe adverse consequences.
Elasticity of supply: responsiveness of output to changes in price. As prices move up, the supply normally increases. If it does not, it is said to be inelastic. Supply is said to be elastic if the rise in price means a rise in production.

ELECT
In general: choose a course of action. Someone who decides to incorporate a certain provision in a will elects to do so.
Securities trading: make a conditional order into a market order. If a customer has received a guaranteed buy or sell price from a specialist on the floor of an exchange, the transaction is considered elected when that price is reached. If the guarantee is that a stock will be sold when it reaches 20, and a stop order is put at that price, the sale will be elected at 20.

ELEPHANTS expression describing large institutional investors. The term implies that such investors, including mutual funds, pension funds, banks, and insurance companies, tend to move their billions of dollars in assets in a herd-like manner, driving stock and bond prices up and down in concert. CONTRARIAN investors specialize in doing the opposite of the elephants—buying when institutions are selling and selling when the elephants are buying. The opposite of elephants are SMALL INVESTORS, who buy and sell far smaller quantities of stocks and bonds.

ELEVEN BOND INDEX average yield on a particular day of 11 selected general obligation municipal bonds with an average AA rating, maturing in 20 years. It is comprised of 11 of the 20 bonds in the Twenty Bond Index, also referred to as the BOND BUYER INDEX, published by the *BOND BUYER* and used as a benchmark in tracking municipal bond yields.

ELIGIBLE PAPER commercial and agricultural paper, drafts, bills of exchange, banker's acceptances, and other negotiable instruments that were acquired by a bank at a discount and that the Federal Reserve Bank will accept for rediscount.

ELIGIBILITY REQUIREMENTS
Insurance: requirements by an insurance company to qualify for coverage. For example, a life insurance company may require that because of a person's health condition, a potential policyholder would need to pay a higher premium to obtain coverage. In this circumstance, the policyholder's ability to pay becomes a primary issue.

For employer group health insurance coverage, an employer may require a person be a full-time employee for coverage of the employee and the employee's dependents.

Pensions: conditions an employee must satisfy to become a participant in a pension plan, such as completing one year of service and reaching the age of 21. Federal pension laws allow plan participants to become VESTED after five years of service. Alternatively, some companies implement a graduated vesting schedule. Public pension plans sponsored by federal, state, and local governments have their own eligibility requirements.

ELVES ten technical analysts who predict the direction of stock prices over the next six months on the "Wall Street Week" television show on the Public Broadcasting System. If five or more analysts are bullish or bearish at one time, the Wall Street Week Elves Index is giving a signal to buy or sell.

EMANCIPATION freedom to assume certain legal responsibilities normally associated only with adults, said of a minor who is granted this freedom by a court. If both parents die in an accident, for instance, the 16-year-old eldest son may be emancipated by a judge to act as guardian for his younger brothers and sisters.

EMBARGO government prohibition against the shipment of certain goods to another country. An embargo is most common during wartime, but is sometimes applied for economic reasons as well. For instance, the Organization of Petroleum Exporting Countries placed an embargo on the shipment of oil to the West in the early 1970s to protest Israeli policies and to raise the price of petroleum.

EMERGENCY FUND cash reserve that is available to meet financial emergencies, such as large medical bills or unexpected auto or home repairs. Most financial planners advocate maintaining an emergency reserve of two to three months' salary in a liquid interest-bearing account such as a money market mutual fund or bank money market deposit account.

EMERGENCY HOME FINANCE ACT OF 1970 act creating the quasigovernmental Federal Home Loan Mortgage Corporation, also known as Freddie Mac, to stimulate the development of a secondary mortgage market. The act authorized Freddie Mac to package and sell Federal Housing Administration- and Veterans Administration-guaranteed mortgage loans. More than half the home mortgages were subsequently packaged and sold to investors in the secondary market in the form of pass-through securities.

EMERGING COMPANY MARKETPLACE (ECM) discontinued service of the AMERICAN STOCK EXCHANGE that focused on the needs of small, growth companies meeting special listing requirements. ECM provided matching of public orders, short sale protection, specialist oversight and support, and offered other services and programs designed to promote corporate visibility (through separate listings in newspaper stock tables, for example).

EMERGING MARKETS FREE (EMF) INDEX index developed by Morgan Stanley Capital International to follow stock markets in Mexico, Malaysia, Chile, Jordan, Thailand, the Philippines, and Argentina, countries selected because of their accessibility to foreign investors.

EMINENT DOMAIN right of a government entity to seize private property for the purpose of constructing a public facility. Federal, state, and local governments can seize people's homes under eminent domain laws as long as the homeowner is compensated at fair market value. Some public projects that may necessitate such CONDEMNATION include highways, hospitals, schools, parks, or government office buildings.

EMPLOYEE RETIREMENT INCOME SECURITY ACT (ERISA) 1974 law governing the operation of most private pension and benefit plans, The law eased pension eligibility rules, set up the PENSION BENEFIT GUARANTY CORPORATION, and established guidelines for the management of pension funds.

EMPLOYEE STOCK OWNERSHIP PLAN (ESOP) program encouraging employees to purchase stock in their company. Employees may participate in the management of the company and even take control to rescue the company or a particular plant that would otherwise go out of business. Employees may offer wage and work rule concessions in return for ownership privileges in an attempt to keep a marginal facility operating.

EMPTY HEAD AND PURE HEART TEST SEC Rule 14e-3, subparagraph (b), which, with strict exceptions, prohibits any party other than the bidder in a TENDER OFFER to trade in the stock while having INSIDE INFORMATION.

ENCUMBERED owned by one party but subject to another party's valid claim. A homeowner owns his mortgaged property, for example, but the bank has a security interest in it as long as the mortgage loan is outstanding.

ENDORSE transfer ownership of an asset by signing the back of a negotiable instrument. One can endorse a check to receive payment or endorse a stock or bond certificate to transfer ownership.
    See also QUALIFIED ENDORSEMENT.

ENDOWMENT permanent gift of money or property to a specified institution for a specified purpose. Endowments may finance physical assets or be invested to provide ongoing income to finance operations.

ENERGY MUTUAL FUND mutual fund that invests solely in energy stocks such as oil, oil service, gas, solar energy, and coal companies and makers of energy-saving devices.

ENTERPRISE a business firm. The term often is applied to a newly formed venture.

ENTREPRENEUR person who takes on the risks of starting a new business. Many entrepreneurs have technical knowledge with which to produce a saleable product or to design a needed new service. Often, VENTURE CAPITAL is used to finance the startup in return for a piece of the equity. Once an entrepreneur's business is established, shares may be sold to the public as an INITIAL PUBLIC OFFERING, assuming favorable market conditions.

ENVIRONMENTAL FUND MUTUAL FUND specializing in stocks of companies having a role in the bettering of the environment. Not to be confused with a SOCIAL CONSCIOUSNESS MUTUAL FUND, which aims in part to satisfy social values, an environmental fund is designed to capitalize on financial opportunities related to the environmental movement.

EOM DATING arrangement—common in the wholesale drug industry, for example—whereby all purchases made through the 25th of one month are payable within 30 days of the end of the following month; EOM means *end of month.* Assuming no prompt payment discount, purchases through the 25th of April, for example, will be payable by the end of June. If a discount exists for payment in ten days, payment would have to be made by June 10th to take advantage of it.

End of month dating with a 2% discount for prompt payment (10 days) would be expressed in the trade either as: *2%-10 days, EOM, 30,* or *2/10 prox. net 30,* where prox., or proximo, means "the next."

EPS *see* EARNINGS PER SHARE.

EQUAL CREDIT OPPORTUNITY ACT federal legislation passed in the mid-1970s prohibiting discrimination in granting credit, based on race, religion, sex, ethnic background, or whether a person is receiving public assistance or alimony. The Federal Trade Commission enforces the act.

EQUALIZING DIVIDEND special dividend paid to compensate investors for income lost because a change was made in the quarterly dividend payment schedule.

EQUILIBRIUM PRICE
1. price when the supply of goods in a particular market matches demand.
2. for a manufacturer, the price that maximizes a product's profitability.

EQUILIBRIUM PRICE

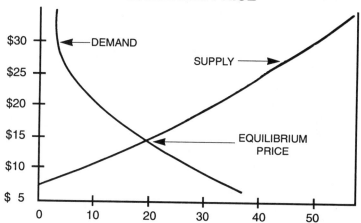

EQUIPMENT LEASING PARTNERSHIP limited partnership that buys equipment such as computers, railroad cars, and airplanes, then leases it to businesses. Limited partners receive income from the lease payments as well as tax benefits such as depreciation. Whether a partnership of this kind works out well depends on the GENERAL PARTNER's expertise. Failure to lease the equipment can be disastrous, as happened with railroad hopper cars in the mid-1970s.

EQUIPMENT TRUST CERTIFICATE bond, usually issued by a transportation company such as a railroad or shipping line, used to pay for new equipment. The certificate gives the bondholder the first right to the equipment in the event that interest and principal are not paid when due. Title to the equipment is held in the name of the trustee, usually a bank, until the bond is paid off.

EQUITABLE OWNER beneficiary of property held in trust.

EQUITY
In general: fairness. Law courts, for example, try to be equitable in their judgments when splitting up estates or settling divorce cases.

Banking: difference between the amount a property could be sold for and the claims held against it.

Brokerage account: excess of securities over debit balance in a margin account. For instance, equity would be $28,000 in a margin account with stocks and bonds worth $50,000 and a debit balance of $22,000.

Investments: ownership interest possessed by shareholders in a corporation—stock as opposed to bonds.

EQUITY CMO *see* CMO REIT.

EQUITY COMMITMENT NOTES *see* MANDATORY CONVERTIBLES.

EQUITY CONTRACT NOTES *see* MANDATORY CONVERTIBLES.

EQUITY FINANCING raising money by issuing shares of common or preferred stock. Usually done when prices are high and the most capital can be raised for the smallest number of shares.

EQUITY FUNDING type of investment combining a life insurance policy and a mutual fund. The fund shares are used as collateral for a loan to pay the insurance premiums, giving the investor the advantages of insurance protection and investment appreciation potential.

EQUITY KICKER offer of an ownership position in a deal that involves loans. For instance, a mortgage real estate limited partnership that lends to real estate developers might receive as an equity kicker a small ownership position in a building that can appreciate over time. When the building is sold, limited partners receive the appreciation payout. In return for that equity kicker, the lender is likely to charge a lower interest rate on the loan. Convertible features and warrants are offered as equity kickers to make securities attractive to investors.

EQUITY REIT REAL ESTATE INVESTMENT TRUST that takes an ownership position in the real estate it invests in. Stockholders in equity REITs earn dividends on rental income from the buildings and earn appreciation if properties are sold for a profit. The opposite is a MORTGAGE REIT.

EQUIVALENT BOND YIELD comparison of discount yields and yields on bonds with coupons. Also called *coupon-equivalent rate.* For instance, if a 10%, 90-day Treasury bill with a face value of $10,000 cost $9750, the equivalent bond yield would be:

$$\frac{\$250}{\$9750} \times \frac{360}{90} = 10.40\%.$$

EQUIVALENT TAXABLE YIELD comparison of the taxable yield on a corporate or government bond and the tax-free yield on a municipal bond. Depending on the tax bracket, an investor's aftertax return may be greater with a municipal bond than with a corporate or government bond offering a highest interest rate. For someone in a 31% federal tax bracket, for instance, a 7% municipal bond would have an equivalent taxable yield of 10.4%. An investor living in a state that levies state income tax should add in the state tax bracket to get a true measure of the equivalent taxable yield. *See* YIELD EQUIVALENCE for method of calculation.

ERISA *see* EMPLOYEE RETIREMENT INCOME SECURITY ACT.

ERM acronym for *exchange rate mechanism,* by which participating member countries agree to maintain the value of their own currencies through intervention.

ERTA *see* ECONOMIC RECOVERY TAX ACT OF 1981.

ESCALATOR CLAUSE provision in a contract allowing cost increases to be passed on. In an employment contract, an escalator clause might call for wage increases to keep employee earnings in line with inflation. In a lease, an escalator clause could obligate the tenant to pay for increases in fuel or other costs.

ESCHEAT return of property (for example, land, bank balances, insurance policies) to the state if abandoned or left by a person who died without making a will. If rightful owners or heirs later appear, they can claim the property.

ESCROW money, securities, or other property or instruments held by a third party until the conditions of a contract are met.

ESCROWED TO MATURITY (ETM) holding proceeds from a new bond issue in a separate escrow account to pay off an existing bond issue when it matures. Bond issuers will implement an ADVANCE REFUNDING when interest rates have fallen significantly, making it advantageous to pay off the existing issue before scheduled maturity at the first CALL DATE. The funds raised by the refunding are invested in government securities in the escrow account until the principal is used to prepay the original bond issue at the first call date. The escrowed funds may also pay some of the interest on the original issue up until the bonds are redeemed.

ESCROW RECEIPT in options trading, a document provided by a bank to guarantee that the UNDERLYING SECURITY is on deposit and available for potential delivery.

ESSENTIAL PURPOSE (or FUNCTION) BOND *see* PUBLIC PURPOSE BOND.

ESTATE all the assets a person possesses at the time of death—such as securities, real estate, interests in business, physical possessions, and cash. The estate is distributed to heirs according to the dictates of the person's will or, if there is no will, a court ruling.

ESTATE PLANNING planning for the orderly handling, disposition, and administration of an estate when the owner dies. Estate planning includes drawing up a will, setting up trusts, and minimizing estate taxes, perhaps by passing property to heirs before death or by setting up a BYPASS TRUST or a TESTAMENTARY TRUST.

ESTATE TAX tax imposed by a state or the federal government on assets left to heirs in a will. Under the Economic Recovery Tax Act of 1981, there is no estate tax on transfers of property between spouses. An exclusion which began at $250,000 in 1982 rose to $600,000 in 1987.

ESTIMATED TAX amount of estimated tax for the coming year, minus tax credits, based on the higher of regular or ALTERNATIVE MINIMUM TAX (AMT). Corporations, estates and trusts, self-employed persons, and persons for whom less than a fixed percentage of income is withheld by employers must compute estimated tax and make quarterly tax payments to the IRS and state tax authorities, if required. Generally, a taxpayer must pay at least 90% of his or her total tax liability for the year in withholding and/or quarterly estimated tax payments. Alternatively, taxpayers may base their current year's estimated tax on the prior year's income tax. For taxpayers with adjusted gross income (AGI) in the prior tax year of $150,000 or less, estimated taxes must equal 100% of the prior year's tax. For those reporting AGI of more than $150,000, the current year's estimated taxes must be based on 110% of the prior year's tax liability. Thus, for someone reporting an AGI of more than $150,000 who paid $50,000 in taxes in the prior year, estimated taxes of at least $55,000 will be due in the current tax year. Severe penalties are imposed by the IRS and state tax authorities for underpayment of estimated taxes.

ETHICAL FUND *see* SOCIAL CONSCIOUSNESS MUTUAL FUND.

EUROBOND bond denominated in U.S. dollars or other currencies and sold to investors outside the country whose currency is used. The bonds are usually issued by large underwriting groups composed of banks and issuing houses from many countries. An example of a Eurobond transaction might be a dollar-denominated debenture issued by a Belgian corporation through an underwriting group comprised of the overseas affiliate of a New York investment banking house, a bank in Holland, and a consortium of British merchant banks; a portion of the issue is sold to French investors through Swiss investment accounts. The Eurobond market is an important source of capital for multinational companies and foreign governments, including Third World governments.

EUROCURRENCY money deposited by corporations and national governments in banks away from their home countries, called *Eurobanks*. The terms Eurocurrency and Eurobanks do not necessarily mean the currencies or the banks are European, though more often than not, that is the case. For instance, dollars deposited in a British bank or Italian lire deposited in a Japanese bank are considered to be Eurocurrency. The Eurodollar is only one of the Eurocurrencies, though it is the most prevalent. Also known as *Euromoney.*

EURODOLLAR U.S. currency held in banks outside the United States, mainly in Europe, and commonly used for settling international transactions. Some securities are issued in Eurodollars—that is, with a promise to pay interest in dollars deposited in foreign bank accounts.

EURODOLLAR BOND bond that pays interest and principal in Eurodollars, U.S. dollars held in banks outside the United States, primarily in Europe. Such a bond is not registered with the Securities and Exchange Commission, and because there are fewer regulatory delays and costs in the Euromarket, Eurodollar bonds generally can be sold at lower than U.S. interest rates. *See also* EUROBOND.

EURODOLLAR CERTIFICATE OF DEPOSIT CDs issued by banks outside the United States, primarily in Europe, with interest and principal paid in dollars. Such CDs usually have minimum denominations of $100,000 and short-term maturities of less than two years. The interest rate on these CDs is usually pegged to the LONDON INTERBANK OFFERED RATE (LIBOR).

EUROPEAN COMMUNITY (EC) with ratification of the Maastricht Treaty on European Union in November 1993, the former name of European Economic Community was dropped. The EC is part of the EUROPEAN UNION. The EC is an economic and, increasingly, political alliance formed in 1957 by Germany, France, Belgium, Luxembourg, the Netherlands and Italy to foster trade and cooperation among its members and "an ever closer union among the peoples of Europe." Membership was subsequently extended to the UK, Ireland and Denmark (1973); Greece (1981); and Spain and Portugal (1986). Austria, Finland, and Sweden became members in 1995. Norway rejected membership in November 1994. Tariff barriers between the member states have been abolished, and import duties vis-a-vis non-EC countries have been standardized. Many former European dependencies in African, Caribbean, and Pacific countries have preferential trade terms with the EC through the Rome Convention. EC headquarters is in Brussels, administered by the European Commission, the executive arm of the European Union. By December 1992, most remaining non-tariff trade barriers between the member states had been eliminated, and common standards in many industries had been adopted. Also known as the *European Union*, of which it is a part and, anachronistically, the *Common Market.*

EUROPEAN CURRENCY UNIT (ECU) one of two international currency substitutes ("artificial currencies"), the other being the SPECIAL DRAWING RIGHTS (SDRs) of the INTERNATIONAL MONETARY FUND (IMF). Like the SDR, the ECU is a currency basket comprised of a predetermined amount of a number of different currencies. Whereas SDRs represent five currencies, ECUs include all the EUROPEAN ECONOMIC COMMUNITY (EEC) currencies except the Spanish peseta and the Portuguese escudo. Currency substitutes are less volatile than the currencies making them up and are expected to be used increasingly for commercial purposes as the European Community develops.

EUROPEAN OPTIONS EXCHANGE (EOE) the Dutch derivatives exchange, trading equity, index, bond, currency, and metal options. Futures and options are traded on its EOE Index, as well as the Eurotop 100 Index, the Dutch Top 5 Index and the U.S. dollar. Futures are traded on the notional bond. Options are traded on the OMX Index, XMI LEAPS, MMI Index (listed on the AMERICAN STOCK EXCHANGE), Jumbo dollar, gold and Guilder bond.

EUROPEAN-STYLE EXERCISE system of exercising options contracts in which the option buyer can exercise the contract only on the last business day prior to expiration (normally Friday). This system is widely used with index options traded on various U.S. exchanges.

EUROPEAN UNION (EU) umbrella term referring to a "three-pillar" construction comprising the EUROPEAN COMMUNITY (EC) and two new pillars: Common Foreign and Security Policy (including defense) and Justice and Home Affairs (notably cooperation between police and other authorities on crime, terrorism, and immigration issues). The EU is governed by a five-part institutional system, including the European Commission, the EU Council of Ministers, the European Parliament and the European Court of Justice, and the Court of Auditors, which monitors EU budget spending. Under the Maastricht Treaty on European Union of Nov. 1, 1993, the directly elected Parliament gained co-decision powers with the Council and Commission.

EUROYEN BOND EUROCURRENCY deposits in Japanese yen.

EVALUATOR independent expert who appraises the value of property for which there is limited trading—antiques in an estate, perhaps, or rarely traded stocks or bonds. The fee for this service is sometimes a flat amount, sometimes a percentage of the appraised value.

EVENT RISK risk that a bond will suddenly decline in credit quality and warrant a lower RATING because of a TAKEOVER-related development, such as additional debt or a RECAPITALIZATION. Corporations whose INDENTURES include protective COVENANTS, such as POISON PUT provisions, are assigned *Event Risk Covenant Rankings* by Standard & Poor's Corporation. Ratings range from E-1, the highest, to E-5 and supplement basic bond ratings.

EVERGREEN FUNDING similar to DRIP FEED, British term for the gradual infusion of capital into a new or recapitalized enterprise. In the United States, banks use the term *evergreen* to describe short-term loans that are continuously renewed rather than repaid.

EXACT INTEREST interest paid by a bank or other financial institution and calculated on a 365-days-per-year basis, as opposed to a 360-day basis, called ordinary interest. The difference—the ratio is 1.0139—can be material when calculating daily interest on large sums of money.

EX-ALL sale of a security without dividends, rights, warrants, or any other privileges associated with that security.

EXCESS MARGIN equity in a brokerage firm's customer account, expressed in dollars, above the legal minimum for a margin account or the maintenance requirement. For instance, with a margin requirement of $25,000, as set by REGULATION T and a maintenance requirement of $12,500 set by the stock exchange, the client whose equity is $100,000 would have excess margin of $75,000 and $87,500 in terms of the initial and maintenance requirements, respectively.

EXCESS PROFITS TAX extra federal taxes placed on the earnings of a business. Such taxes may be levied during a time of national emergency, such as in wartime, and are designed to increase national revenue. The excess profits tax differs from the WINDFALL PROFITS TAX, designed to prevent excessive corporate profits in special circumstances.

EXCESS RESERVES money a bank holds over and above the RESERVE REQUIREMENT. The money may be on deposit with the Federal Reserve System or with an approved depository bank, or it may be in the bank's possession. For instance, a bank with a reserve requirement of $5 million might have $4 million on deposit with the Fed and $1.5 million in its vaults and as till cash. The $500,000 in excess reserves is available for loans to other banks or customers or for other corporate uses.

EXCHANGE
Barter: to trade goods and services with another individual or company for other goods and services of equal value.
Corporate finance: offer by a corporation to exchange one security for another. For example, a company may want holders of its convertible bonds to exchange their holdings for common stock. Or a company in financial distress may want its bondholders to exchange their bonds for stock in order to reduce or eliminate its debt load. *See also* SWAP.
Currency: trading of one currency for another. Also known as *foreign exchange.*
Mutual funds: process of switching from one mutual fund to another, either within one fund family or between fund families, if executed through a brokerage firm offering funds from several companies. In many cases, fund companies will not charge an additional LOAD if the assets are kept within the same family. If one fund is sold to buy another, a taxable event has occurred, meaning that capital gains or losses have been realized, unless the trade was executed within a tax-deferred account, such as an IRA or Keogh account.
Trading: central location where securities or futures trading takes place. The New York and American Stock Exchanges are the largest centralized place to trade stocks in the United States, for example. Futures exchanges in Chicago, Kansas City, New York, and elsewhere facilitate the trading of futures contracts. *See also* SECURITIES AND COMMODITIES EXCHANGES.

EXCHANGEABLE DEBENTURE like CONVERTIBLES, with the exception that this type of debenture can be converted to the common stock of a SUBSIDIARY or AFFILIATE of the issuer.

EXCHANGE CONTROLS government regulation of foreign exchange (currency trading).

EXCHANGE DISTRIBUTION block trade carried out on the floor of an exchange between customers of a member firm. Someone who wants to sell a large block of stock in a single transaction can get a broker to solicit and bunch a large number of orders. The seller transmits the securities to the buyers all at once, and the trade is announced on the BROAD TAPE as an exchange distribution. The seller, not the buyers, pays a special commission to the broker who executes the trade.

EXCHANGE MEMBERS see MEMBER FIRM; SEAT.

EXCHANGE PRIVILEGE right of a shareholder to switch from one mutual fund to another within one fund family—often, at no additional charge. This enables investors to put their money in an aggressive growth-stock fund when they expect the market to turn up strongly, then switch to a money-market fund when they anticipate a downturn. Some discount brokers allow shareholders to switch between fund families in pursuit of the best performance.

EXCHANGE RATE price at which one country's currency can be converted into another's. The exchange rate between the U.S. dollar and the British pound is different from the rate between the dollar and the West German mark, for example. A wide range of factors influences exchange rates, which generally change slightly each trading day. Some rates are fixed by agreement; see FIXED EXCHANGE RATE.

EXCHANGE STOCK PORTFOLIO (ESP) see BASKET.

EXCISE TAX federal or state tax on the sale or manufacture of a commodity, usually a luxury item. Examples: federal and state taxes on alcohol and tobacco.

EXCLUSION
Contracts: item not covered by a contract. For example, an insurance policy may list certain hazards, such as acts of war, that are excluded from coverage.
Taxes: on a tax return, items that must be reported, but not taxed. For example, corporations are allowed to exclude 70% of dividends received from other domestic corporations. Gift tax rules allow DONORS to exclude up to $10,000 worth of gifts to donees annually.

EXCLUSIVE LISTING written listing agreement giving an agent the right to sell a specific property for a period of time with a definite termination date, frequently three months. There are two types of exclusive listings. With the exclusive agency, the owner reserves the right to sell the property himself without owing a commission; the exclusive agent is entitled to a commission if he or she personally sells the property, or if it is sold by anyone other than the seller. Under the exclusive right to sell, a broker is appointed as exclusive agent, entitled to a commission if the property is sold by the owner, the broker, or anyone else. "Right to sell" means the right to find a buyer. Sellers opt for exclusive listings because they think an agent will give their property more attention. An agent with an exclusive listing will not have to share the commission with any other agent as they would under a multiple-listing arrangement. If the property is not sold within the specified time, the seller may expand the selling group through an open, multiple listing.

EX-DIVIDEND interval between the announcement and the payment of the next dividend. An investor who buys shares during that interval is not entitled to the dividend. Typically, a stock's price moves up by the dollar amount of the dividend as the ex-dividend date approaches, then falls by the amount of the dividend after that date. A stock that has gone ex-dividend is marked with an *x* in newspaper listings.

EX-DIVIDEND DATE date on which a stock goes EX-DIVIDEND, typically about three weeks before the dividend is paid to shareholders of record. Shares listed on the New York Stock Exchange go ex-dividend four business days before the RECORD DATE. This NYSE rule is generally followed by the other exchanges.

EXECUTION
Law: the signing, sealing, and delivering of a contract or agreement making it valid.
Securities: carrying out a trade. A broker who buys or sells shares is said to have executed an order.

EXECUTOR/EXECUTRIX administrator of the estate who gathers the estate assets; files the estate tax returns and final personal income tax returns, and administers the estate; pays the debts of and charges against the estate; and distributes the balance in accordance with the terms of the will. The executor's responsibility is relatively short term, one to three years, ending when estate administration is completed. An executor (executrix if a female) may be a bank trust officer, a lawyer, or a family member or trusted friend.

EXEMPTION IRS-allowed direct reductions from gross income. Personal and dependency exemptions are allowed for: individual taxpayers; elderly and disabled taxpayers; dependent children and other dependents more than half of whose support is provided; total or partial blindness; and a taxpayer's spouse.

EXEMPT SECURITIES stocks and bonds exempt from certain Securities and Exchange Commission and Federal Reserve Board rules. For instance, government and municipal bonds are exempt from SEC registration requirements and from Federal Reserve Board margin rules.

EXERCISE make use of a right available in a contract. In options trading a buyer of a call contract may exercise the right to buy underlying shares at a particular price by informing the option seller. A put buyer's right is exercised when the underlying shares are sold at the agreed-upon price.

EXERCISE LIMIT limit on the number of option contracts of any one class that can be exercised in a span of five business days. For options on stocks, the exercise limit is usually 2000 contracts.

EXERCISE NOTICE notification by a broker that a client wants to exercise a right to buy the underlying stock in an option contract. Such notice is transmitted to the option seller through the Options Clearing Corporation, which ensures that stock is delivered as agreed upon.

EXERCISE PRICE price at which the stock or commodity underlying a call or put option can be purchased (call) or sold (put) over the specified period. For instance, a call contract may allow the buyer to purchase 100 shares of XYZ at any time in the next three months at an exercise or STRIKE PRICE of $63.

EXHAUST PRICE price at which broker must liquidate a client's holding in a stock that was bought on margin and has declined, but has not had additional funds put up to meet the MARGIN CALL.

EXIMBANK *see* EXPORT-IMPORT BANK.

EXIT FEE *see* BACK-END LOAD.

EX-LEGAL municipal bond that does not have the legal opinion of a bond law firm printed on it, as most municipal bonds do. When such bonds are traded, buyers must be warned that legal opinion is lacking.

EXPECTED RETURN *see* MEAN RETURN.

EXPENSE RATIO amount, expressed as a percentage of total investment, that shareholders pay annually for mutual fund operating expenses and management fees. These expenses include shareholder service, salaries for money managers and administrative staff, and investor centers, among many others. The expense ratio, which may be as low as 0.2% or as high as 2% of shareholder assets, is taken out of the fund's current income and is disclosed in the prospectus to shareholders.

EXPERIENCE RATING insurance company technique to determine the correct price of a policy premium. The company analyzes past loss experience for others in the insured group to project future claims. The premium is then set at a rate high enough to cover those potential claims and still earn a profit for the insurance company. For example, life insurance companies charge higher premiums to smokers than to non-smokers because smokers' experience rating is higher, meaning their chance of dying is much higher.

EXPIRATION

Banking: date on which a contract or agreement ceases to be effective.

Options trading: last day on which an option can be exercised. If it is not, traders say that the option *expired worthless.*

EXPIRATION CYCLE cycle of expiration dates used in short-term options trading. For example, contracts may be written for one of three cycles: January, April, July, October; February, May, August, November; March, June, September, December. Since options are traded in three-, six-, and nine-month contracts, only three of the four months in the set are traded at once. In our example, when the January contract expires, trading begins on the October contract. Commodities futures expiration cycles follow other schedules.

EX-PIT TRANSACTION purchase of commodities off the floor of the exchange where they are regularly traded and at specified terms.

EXPLORATORY DRILLING PROGRAM search for an undiscovered reservoir of oil or gas—a very risky undertaking. Exploratory wells are called *wildcat* (in an unproven area); *controlled wildcat* (in an area outside the proven limits of an existing field); or *deep test* (within a proven field but to unproven depths). Exploratory drilling programs are usually syndicated, and units are sold to limited partners.

EXPORT-IMPORT BANK (EXIMBANK) bank set up by Congress in 1934 to encourage U.S. trade with foreign countries. Eximbank is an independent entity that borrows from the U.S. Treasury to (1) finance exports and imports; (2) grant direct credit to non-U.S. borrowers; (3) provide export guarantees, insurance against commercial and political risk, and discount loans.

EX-RIGHTS without the RIGHT to buy a company's stock at a discount from the prevailing market price, which was distributed until a particular date. Typically, after that date the rights trade separately from the stock itself. *See also* EX-WARRANTS.

EX-STOCK DIVIDENDS interval between the announcement and payment of a stock dividend. An investor who buys shares during that interval is not entitled to the announced stock dividend; instead, it goes to the seller of the shares, who was the owner on the last recorded date before the books were closed and the stock went EX-DIVIDEND. Stocks cease to be ex-dividend after the payment date.

EXTENDED COVERAGE insurance protection that is extended beyond the original term of the contract. For example, consumers can buy extended warranties when they purchase cars or appliances, which will cover repairs beyond the original warranty period.

EXTENSION OF TIME FOR FILING TAXES time period beyond the original tax filing date. For example, taxpayers who file Form 4868 may get an automatic extension of four months to file their tax returns with the IRS. Though the return will then be due on August 15, the estimated tax is still due on the original filing date of April 15.

EXTERNAL FUNDS funds brought in from outside the corporation, perhaps in the form of a bank loan, or the proceeds from a bond offering, or an infusion of cash from venture capitalists. External funds supplement internally generated CASH FLOW and are used for expansion, as well as for seasonal WORKING CAPITAL needs.

EXTRA DIVIDEND dividend paid to shareholders in addition to the regular dividend. Such a payment is made after a particularly profitable year in order to reward shareholders and engender loyalty.

EXTRAORDINARY CALL early redemption of a revenue bond by the issuer due to elimination of the source of revenue to pay the stipulated interest. For example, a mortgage revenue municipal bond may be subject to an extraordinary call if the issuer is unable to originate mortgages to homeowners because mortgage rates have dropped sharply, making the issuer's normally below-market mortgage interest rate suddenly higher than market rates. In this case, the bond issuer is required to return the money raised from the bond issue to bondholders because the issuer will not be able to realize the expected interest payments from mortgages. Extraordinary calls may also be necessary if another revenue-producing project such as a road or bridge is not able to be built for some reason. Calls are usually made at PAR. Also called a *special call.*

EXTRAORDINARY ITEM nonrecurring occurrence that must be explained to shareholders in an annual or quarterly report. Some examples: writeoff of a division, acquisition of another company, sale of a large amount of real estate, or uncovering of employee fraud that negatively affects the company's financial condition. Earnings are usually reported before and after taking into account the effects of extraordinary items.

EX-WARRANTS stock sold with the buyer no longer entitled to the WARRANT attached to the stock. Warrants allow the holder to buy stock at some future date at a specified price. Someone buying a stock on June 3 that had gone ex-warrants on June 1 would not receive those warrants. They would be the property of the stockholder of record on June 1.

f

FACE-AMOUNT CERTIFICATE debt security issued by face-amount certificate companies, one of three categories of mutual funds defined by the INVESTMENT

COMPANY ACT OF 1940. The holder makes periodic payments to the issuer, and the issuer promises to pay the purchaser the face value at maturity or a surrender value if the certificate is presented prior to maturity.

FACE VALUE value of a bond, note, mortgage, or other security as given on the certificate or instrument. Corporate bonds are usually issued with $1000 face values, municipal bonds with $5000 face values, and federal government bonds with $10,000 face values. Although the bonds fluctuate in price from the time they are issued until redemption, they are redeemed at maturity at their face value, unless the issuer defaults. If the bonds are retired before maturity, bondholders normally receive a slight premium over face value. The face value is the amount on which interest payments are calculated. Thus, a 10% bond with a face value of $1000 pays bondholders $100 per year. Face value is also referred to as PAR VALUE or *nominal value.*

FACTORING type of financial service whereby a firm sells or transfers title to its accounts receivable to a factoring company, which then acts as principal, not as agent. The receivables are sold without recourse, meaning that the factor cannot turn to the seller in the event accounts prove uncollectible. Factoring can be done either on a *notification basis,* where the seller's customers remit directly to the factor, or on a *non-notification basis,* where the seller handles the collections and remits to the factor. There are two basic types of factoring:
1. **Discount factoring** arrangement whereby seller receives funds from the factor prior to the average maturity date, based on the invoice amount of the receivable, less cash discounts, less an allowance for estimated claims, returns, etc. Here the factor is compensated by an interest rate based on daily balances and typically 2% to 3% above the bank prime rate.
2. **Maturity factoring** arrangement whereby the factor, who performs the entire credit and collection function, remits to the seller for the receivables sold each month on the average due date of the factored receivables. The factor's commission on this kind of arrangement ranges from 0.75% to 2%, depending on the bad debt risk and the handling costs.

Factors also accommodate clients with "overadvances," loans in anticipation of sales, which permit inventory building prior to peak selling periods. Factoring has traditionally been most closely associated with the garment industry, but is used by companies in other industries as well.

FAIL POSITION securities undelivered due to the failure of selling clients to deliver the securities to their brokers so the latter can deliver them to the buying brokers. Since brokers are constantly buying and selling, receiving and delivering, the term usually refers to a net delivery position—that is, a given broker owes more securities to other brokers on sell transactions than other brokers owe to it on buy transactions. *See also* FAIL TO DELIVER; FAIL TO RECEIVE.

FAIL TO DELIVER situation where the broker-dealer on the sell side of a contract has not delivered securities to the broker-dealer on the buy side. A fail to deliver is usually the result of a broker not receiving delivery from its selling customer. As long as a fail to deliver exists. the seller will not receive payment. *See also* FAIL TO RECEIVE.

FAIL TO RECEIVE situation where the broker-dealer on the buy side of a contract has not received delivery of securities from the broker-dealer on the sell side. As long as a fail to receive exists, the buyer will not make payment for the securities. *See also* FAIL TO DELIVER.

FAIR CREDIT BILLING ACT federal law designed to facilitate the handling of credit complaints and eliminate abusive credit billing practices. For example, the law requires that bills be sent within a prescribed length of time and that consumers' complaints about credit bills be answered promptly.

FAIR CREDIT REPORTING ACT federal law enacted in 1971 giving persons the right to see their credit records at credit reporting bureaus. An individual may challenge and correct negative aspects of his or her record if it can be proven there is a mistake. One may also submit statements explaining why certain negative credit marks were accumulated. *See also* CREDIT RATING.

FAIR MARKET VALUE price at which an asset or service passes from a willing seller to a willing buyer. It is assumed that both buyer and seller are rational and have a reasonable knowledge of relevant facts. *See also* MARKET.

FAIRNESS OPINION professional judgment offered for a fee by an investment banker on the fairness of the price being offered in a merger, takeover, or leveraged buyout. For example, if management is trying to take over a company in a leveraged buyout, it will need a fairness opinion from an independent source to verify that the price being offered is adequate and in the best interests of shareholders. If shareholders sue on the grounds that the offer is not adequate, management will rely on the fairness opinion in court to prove its case. Fairness opinions are also obtained when a majority shareholder is trying to buy out the minority shareholders of a company.

FAIR RATE OF RETURN level of profit that a utility is allowed to earn as determined by federal and/or state regulators. Public utility commissions set the fair rate of return based on the utility's needs to maintain service to its customers, pay adequate dividends to shareholders and interest to bondholders, and maintain and expand plant and equipment.

FAIR TRADE ACTS state laws protecting manufacturers from price-cutting by permitting them to establish minimum retail prices for their goods. Fair trade pricing was effectively eliminated in 1975 when Congress repealed the federal laws upholding resale price maintenance.

FALLEN ANGELS bonds that were INVESTMENT GRADE at the time they were issued but have since declined in quality to below investment grade (BB or lower). Fallen angels are a type of JUNK BOND, but the latter term is usually reserved for bonds that are originally issued with ratings of BB or lower.

FALL OUT OF BED sharp drop in a stock's price, usually in response to negative corporate developments. For example, a stock may fall out of bed if a takeover deal falls apart or if profits in the latest period fall far short of expectations.

FAMILY OF FUNDS *see* FUND FAMILY.

FANNIE MAE (FEDERAL NATIONAL MORTGAGE ASSOCIATION) publicly owned, government-sponsored corporation established in 1938 to purchase both government-backed and conventional mortgages from lenders and securitize them. Its objective is to increase the affordability of home mortgage funds for low-, moderate- and middle-income home buyers. Fannie Mae is a congressionally chartered, shareholder-owned company, and the largest source of home mortgage funds in the United States Fannie Mae is a large issuer of debt securities which are used to finance its activities. Equity shares of Fannie Mae are traded on the New York Stock Exchange.

FARMER MAC see FEDERAL AGRICULTURAL MORTGAGE CORPORATION.

FARMER'S HOME ADMINISTRATION (FHA) federal agency under the Department of Agriculture that makes loans in low-income, rural areas of the United States for farms, homes, and community facilities.

FAR MONTH trading month that is farthest in the future in an options or futures contract. This may be a few months or up to a year or more. Under normal conditions, there is far less trading activity in the far month contracts than in the NEAREST MONTH or SPOT DELIVERY MONTH contracts. Also called *furthest month.*

FARTHER OUT; FARTHER IN relative length of option-contract maturities with reference to the present. For example, an options investor in January would call an option expiring in October farther out than an option expiring in July. The July option is farther in than the October option. *See also* DIAGONAL SPREAD.

FASB see FINANCIAL ACCOUNTING STANDARDS BOARD.

FAT CAT wealthy person who has become lazy living off the dividends and interest from investments. Fat cats also tend to be offered special treatment by brokers and other financial professionals because they have so much money and their accounts can therefore generate large fees and commissions.

FAVORABLE TRADE BALANCE situation that exists when the value of a nation's exports is in excess of the value of its imports. *See* BALANCE OF PAYMENTS; BALANCE OF TRADE.

FAVORITE FIFTY *See* NIFTY FIFTY.

FEDERAL AGENCY SECURITY debt instrument issued by an agency of the federal government such as the Federal National Mortgage Association, Federal Farm Credit Bank, and the Tennessee Valley Authority (TVA). Though not general obligations of the U.S. Treasury, such securities are sponsored by the government and therefore have high safety ratings.

FEDERAL AGRICULTURAL MORTGAGE CORPORATION federal agency established in 1988 to provide a secondary market for farm mortgage loans. Informally called *Farmer Mac.*

FEDERAL DEFICIT federal shortfall that results when the government spends more in a fiscal year than it receives in revenue. To cover the shortfall, the government usually borrows from the public by floating long- and short-term debt. Federal deficits, which started to rise in the 1970s, exploded to enormous proportions of hundreds of billions of dollars per year in the 1980s and 1990s. Some economists think that massive federal deficits can lead to high interest rates and inflation, since they compete with private borrowing by consumers and businesses, though this scenario did not come to pass in the '80s and '90s. Deficits also add to the demand for money from the Federal Reserve. *See also* CROWDING OUT; NATIONAL DEBT.

FEDERAL DEPOSIT INSURANCE CORPORATION (FDIC) federal agency established in 1933 that guarantees (within limits) funds on deposit in member banks and thrift institutions and performs other functions such as making loans to or buying assets from member institutions to facilitate mergers or prevent failures. In 1989, Congress passed savings and loan association bailout legislation that reorganized FDIC into two insurance units: the BANK INSURANCE FUND (BIF) continues the traditional FDIC functions with respect to banking institutions; the

SAVINGS ASSOCIATION INSURANCE FUND (SAIF) insures thrift institution deposits, replacing the FEDERAL SAVINGS AND LOAN INSURANCE CORPORATION (FSLIC), which ceased to exist. *See also* OFFICE OF THRIFT SUPERVISION (OTS).

FEDERAL FARM CREDIT BANK government-sponsored institution that consolidates the financing activities of the Federal Land Banks, the Federal Intermediate Credit Banks, and the Banks for Cooperatives. *See* FEDERAL FARM CREDIT SYSTEM.

FEDERAL FARM CREDIT SYSTEM system established by the Farm Credit Act of 1971 to provide credit services to farmers and farm-related enterprises through a network of 12 Farm Credit districts. Each district has a Federal Land Bank, a Federal Intermediate Credit Bank, and a Bank for Cooperatives to carry out policies of the system. The system sells short-term (5- to 270-day) notes in increments of $50,000 on a discounted basis through a national syndicate of securities dealers. Rates are set by the FEDERAL FARM CREDIT BANK, a unit established to consolidate the financing activities of the various banks. An active secondary market is maintained by several dealers. The system also issues Federal Farm Credit System Consolidated Systemwide Bonds on a monthly basis with 6- and 9-month maturities. The bonds are sold in increments of $5000 with rates set by the system. The bonds enjoy a secondary market even more active than that for the discounted notes. *See also* SECONDARY MARKET.

FEDERAL FINANCING BANK (FFB) U.S. government-owned bank that consolidates financing activities of government AGENCIES in order to reduce borrowing costs.

FEDERAL FUNDS
1. funds deposited by commercial banks at Federal Reserve Banks, including funds in excess of bank reserve requirements. Banks may lend federal funds to each other on an overnight basis at the federal funds rate. Member banks may also transfer funds among themselves or on behalf of customers on a same-day basis by debiting and crediting balances in the various reserve banks. *See* FED WIRE.
2. money used by the Federal Reserve to pay for its purchases of government securities.
3. funds used to settle transactions where there is no FLOAT.

FEDERAL FUNDS RATE interest rate charged by banks with excess reserves at a Federal Reserve district bank to banks needing overnight loans to meet reserve requirements. The federal funds rate is the most sensitive indicator of the direction of interest rates, since it is set daily by the market, unlike the PRIME RATE and the DISCOUNT RATE, which are periodically changed by banks and by the Federal Reserve Board, respectively.

FEDERAL GIFT TAX federal tax imposed on the transfer of securities, property or other assets. The DONOR must pay the tax based on the fair market value of the transferred assets. However, federal law allows donors to give up to $10,000 per year to any individual without incurring gift tax liability. So, a husband and wife may give $20,000 to their child in one year without tax if each parent gives $10,000.

FEDERAL HOME LOAN BANK SYSTEM system supplying credit reserves for SAVINGS AND LOANS, cooperative banks, and other mortgage lenders in a manner similar to the Federal Reserve's role with commercial banks. The Federal Home Loan Bank System is made up of 12 regional Federal Home Loan Banks. It raises money by issuing notes and bonds and lends money to savings and loans and other mortgage lenders based on the amount of collateral the institution can provide. The system was established in 1932 after a massive wave of bank failures. In 1989, Congress passed savings and loan bailout legislation revamping the regulatory structure of the industry. The Federal Home Loan Bank Board was dismantled and replaced with the FEDERAL HOUSING FINANCE BOARD, which now oversees the home loan bank system. *See also* OFFICE OF THRIFT SUPERVISION (OTS).

FEDERAL HOME LOAN MORTGAGE CORPORATION (FHLMC) publicly chartered agency that buys qualifying residential mortgages from lenders, packages them into new securities backed by those pooled mortgages, provides certain guarantees, and then resells the securities on the open market. The corporation's stock is owned by savings institutions across the U.S. and is held in trust by the Federal Home Loan Bank System. The corporation, nicknamed Freddie Mac, has created an enormous secondary market, which provides more funds for mortgage lending and allows investors to buy high-yielding securities backed by federal guarantees. Freddie Mac formerly packaged only mortgages backed by the Veteran's Administration or the Federal Housing Administration, but now it also resells nongovernmentally backed mortgages. The corporation was established in 1970. *See also* MORTGAGE BACKED CERTIFICATES.

FEDERAL HOUSING ADMINISTRATION (FHA) federally sponsored agency that insures lenders against loss on residential mortgages. It was founded in 1934 in response to the Great Depression to execute the provisions of the National Housing Act. The FHA was the forerunner of a group of government agencies responsible for the growing secondary market for mortgages, such as the Government National Mortgage Association (Ginnie Mae) and the Federal National Mortgage Association (Fannie Mae).

FEDERAL HOUSING FINANCE BOARD (FHFB) U.S. government agency created by Congress in 1989 to assume oversight of the FEDERAL HOME LOAN BANK SYSTEM from the dismantled Federal Home Loan Bank Board. *See also* OFFICE OF THRIFT SUPERVISION (OTS).

FEDERAL INCOME TAXES *see* INCOME TAXES.

FEDERAL INSURANCE CONTRIBUTIONS ACT (FICA) commonly known as Social Security, the federal law requiring employers to withhold wages and make payments to a government trust fund providing retirement and other benefits. *See also* SOCIAL SECURITY.

FEDERAL INTERMEDIATE CREDIT BANK one of 12 banks that make funds available to production credit associations, commercial banks, agricultural credit corporations, livestock loan companies, and other institutions extending credit to crop farmers and cattle raisers. Their stock is owned by farmers and ranchers, and the banks raise funds largely from the public sale of short-term debentures. *See also* FEDERAL FARM CREDIT BANK; FEDERAL FARM CREDIT SYSTEM.

FEDERAL LAND BANK one of 12 banks under the U.S. Farm Credit Administration that extends long-term mortgage credit to crop farmers and cattle raisers for buying land, refinancing debts, or other agricultural purposes. To obtain a loan, a farmer or rancher must purchase stock equal to 5% of the loan in any one of approximately 500 local land bank associations; these, in turn, purchase an equal amount of stock in the Federal Land Bank. The stock is retired when the loan is repaid. The banks raise funds by issuing Consolidated Systemwide Bonds to the public. *See also* FEDERAL FARM CREDIT BANK; FEDERAL FARM CREDIT SYSTEM.

FEDERAL NATIONAL MORTGAGE ASSOCIATION (FNMA) publicly owned, government-sponsored corporation chartered in 1938 to purchase mortgages from lenders and resell them to investors. The agency, known by the nickname Fannie Mae, mostly packages mortgages backed by the Federal Housing Administration, but also sells some nongovernmentally backed mortgages. Shares of FNMA itself, known as Fannie Maes, are traded on the New York Stock Exchange. The price usually soars when interest rates fall and plummets when interest rates rise, since the mortgage business is so dependent on the direction of interest rates.

FEDERAL OPEN-MARKET COMMITTEE (FOMC) committee that sets interest rate and credit policies for the Federal Reserve System, the United States' central bank. The FOMC has 12 members. Seven are the members of the Federal Reserve Board, appointed by the president of the United States. The other five are presidents of the 12 regional Federal Reserve banks. Of the five, four are picked on a rotating basis; the other is the president of the Federal Reserve Bank of New York, who is a permanent member. The Committee decides whether to increase or decrease interest rates through open-market operations of buying or selling government securities. The Committee's decisions are closely watched and interpreted by economists and stock and bond market analysts, who try to predict whether the Fed is seeking to tighten credit to reduce inflation or to loosen credit to stimulate the economy.

FEDERAL RESERVE BANK one of the 12 banks that, with their branches, make up the FEDERAL RESERVE SYSTEM. These banks are located in Boston, New York, Philadelphia, Cleveland, Richmond, Atlanta, Chicago, St. Louis, Minneapolis, Kansas City, Dallas, and San Francisco. The role of each Federal Reserve Bank is to monitor the commercial and savings banks in its region to ensure that they follow Federal Reserve Board regulations and to provide those banks with access to emergency funds from the DISCOUNT WINDOW. The reserve banks act as depositories for member banks in their regions, providing money transfer and other services. Each of the banks is owned by the member banks in its district.

FEDERAL RESERVE BOARD (FRB) governing board of the FEDERAL RESERVE SYSTEM. Its seven members are appointed by the President of the United States, subject to Senate confirmation, and serve 14-year terms. The Board establishes Federal Reserve System policies on such key matters as reserve requirements and other bank regulations, sets the discount rate, tightens or loosens the availability of credit in the economy, and regulates the purchase of securities on margin.

FEDERAL RESERVE OPEN MARKET COMMITTEE *see* FEDERAL OPEN MARKET COMMITTEE.

FEDERAL RESERVE SYSTEM system established by the Federal Reserve Act of 1913 to regulate the U.S. monetary and banking system. The Federal Reserve System (the Fed) is comprised of 12 regional Federal Reserve Banks, their 24 branches, and all national and state banks that are part of the system. National banks are stockholders of the FEDERAL RESERVE BANK in their region.

The Federal Reserve System's main functions are to regulate the national money supply, set reserve requirements for member banks, supervise the printing of currency at the mint, act as clearinghouse for the transfer of funds throughout the banking system, and examine member banks to make sure they meet various Federal Reserve regulations. Although the members of the system's governing board are appointed by the President of the United States and confirmed by the Senate, the Federal Reserve System is considered an independent entity, which is supposed to make its decisions free of political influence. Governors are appointed for terms of 14 years, which further assures their independence. *See also* FEDERAL OPEN MARKET COMMITTEE; FEDERAL RESERVE BOARD; OPEN MARKET OPERATIONS.

FEDERAL SAVINGS AND LOAN ASSOCIATION federally chartered institution with a primary responsibility to collect people's savings deposits and to provide mortgage loans for residential housing. Federal Savings and Loans may be owned either by stockholders, who can trade their shares on stock exchanges, or by depositors, in which case the associations are considered mutual organizations. Federal Savings and Loans are members of the Federal Home Loan Bank System. After deregulation, S&Ls expanded into nonhousing-related financial services such as discount stock brokerage, financial planning, credit cards, and consumer loans. *See also* FINANCIAL SUPERMARKET; MUTUAL ASSOCIATION; OFFICE OF THRIFT SUPERVISION (OTS); SAVINGS AND LOAN ASSOCIATION.

FEDERAL SAVINGS AND LOAN INSURANCE CORPORATION (FSLIC) federal agency established in 1934 to insure deposits in member savings institutions. In 1989, Congress passed savings and loan bailout legislation revamping the regulatory structure of the industry. FSLIC was disbanded and its insurance activities were assumed by a new agency, SAVINGS ASSOCIATION INSURANCE FUND (SAIF), a unit of the FEDERAL DEPOSIT INSURANCE CORPORATION (FDIC). Responsibility for insolvent institutions previously under FSLIC's jurisdiction was assumed by another newly created agency, RESOLUTION FUNDING CORPORATION (REFCORP). *See also* OFFICE OF THRIFT SUPERVISION (OTS).

FEDERAL TRADE COMMISSION (FTC) federal agency established in 1914 to foster free and fair business competition and prevent monopolies and activities in restraint of trade. It administers both antitrust and consumer protection legislation.

FEDERAL UNEMPLOYMENT TAX ACT (FUTA) legislation under which federal and state governments require employers (and in some states, such as New Jersey, employees) to contribute to a fund that pays unemployment insurance benefits.

FED PASS move by the Federal Reserve to add reserves to the banking system, thereby making credit more available. The Fed will initiate an open-market operation when it wants to add or subtract reserves in the banking system. It transacts these operations through a group of dealers called PRIMARY DEALERS, banks or security houses with which the Fed has agreed to do business. For example, the buying of securities by the Federal Reserve can be done in such a way that will make reserves more available, thus encouraging banks to lend and making credit easier to obtain by consumer and business borrowers.

FED WIRE high-speed, computerized communications network that connects all 12 Federal Reserve Banks, their 24 branches, the Federal Reserve Board office in Washington, D.C., U.S. Treasury offices in Washington, D.C., and Chicago, and the Washington, D.C. office of the Commodity Credit Corporation; also spelled FedWire and Fedwire. The Fed wire has been called the central nervous system of money transfer in the United States. It enables banks to transfer reserve balances from one to another for immediate available credit and to transfer balances for business customers. Using the Fed wire, Federal Reserve Banks can settle interdistrict transfers resulting from check collections, and the Treasury can shift balances from its accounts in different reserve banks quickly and without cost. It is also possible to transfer bearer short-term Government securities within an hour at no cost. This is done through a procedure called CPD (Commissioner of Public Debt of the Treasury) transfers, whereby one Federal Reserve Bank "retires" a seller's security, while another reserve bank makes delivery of a like amount of the same security from its unissued stock to the buyer.

FICA *see* FEDERAL INSURANCE CONTRIBUTIONS ACT.

FICO *see* FINANCING CORPORATION.

FICTITIOUS CREDIT the credit balance in a securities MARGIN ACCOUNT representing the proceeds from a short sale and the margin requirement under Federal Reserve Board REGULATION T (which regulates margin credit). Because the proceeds, which are held as security for the loan of securities made by the broker to effect the short sale, and the margin requirement are both there to protect the broker's position, the money is not available for withdrawal by the customer; hence the term "fictitious" credit. It is in contrast to a free credit balance, which can be withdrawn anytime.

FIDELITY BOND *see* BLANKET FIDELITY BOND.

FIDUCIARY person, company, or association holding assets in trust for a beneficiary. The fiduciary is charged with the responsibility of investing the money wisely for the beneficiary's benefit. Some examples of fiduciaries are executors of wills and estates, receivers in bankruptcy, trustees, and those who administer the assets of underage or incompetent beneficiaries. Most U.S. states have laws about what a fiduciary may or may not do with a beneficiary's assets. For instance, it is illegal for fiduciaries to invest or misappropriate the money for their personal gain. *See also* LEGAL LIST; PRUDENT MAN RULE.

FIFO *see* FIRST IN, FIRST OUT.

FILING STATUS category a taxpayer chooses in filing a tax return. It determines the filing requirements, standard deduction, eligibility to claim certain deductions and credits, and tax rates. Filing status is determined on the last day of the tax year. The four filing status categories are single, married filing jointly, married filing separately, and head of household. Depending upon the taxpayer's family situation and income, it is more advantageous to file using one category over others. Many accountants figure out a taxpayer's liability using two filing statuses—filing jointly or filing separately—to calculate which one results in the lower tax.

FILL execute a customer's order to buy or sell a stock, bond, or commodity. An order is filled when the amount of the security requested is supplied. When less than the full amount of the order is supplied, it is known as a *partial fill*.

FILL OR KILL (FOK) order to buy or sell a particular security which, if not executed immediately, is canceled. Often, fill or kill orders are placed when a client wants to buy a large quantity of shares of a particular stock at a particular price. If the order is not executed because it will significantly upset the market price for that stock, the order is withdrawn.

FINANCE CHARGE cost of credit, including interest, paid by a customer for a consumer loan. Under the Truth in Lending Act, the finance charge must be disclosed to the customer in advance. *See also* CONSUMER CREDIT PROTECTION ACT OF 1968; REGULATION Z.

FINANCE COMPANY company engaged in making loans to individuals or businesses. Unlike a bank, it does not receive deposits but rather obtains its financing from banks, institutions, and other money market sources. Generally, finance companies fall into three categories: (1) consumer finance companies, also known as *small loan* or *direct loan companies,* lend money to individuals under the small loan laws of the individual U.S. states; (2) sales finance companies, also called *acceptance companies,* purchase retail and wholesale paper from automobile and other consumer and capital goods dealers; (3) commercial finance companies, also called *commercial credit companies,* make loans to manufacturers and wholesalers; these loans are secured by accounts receivable, inventories, and equipment. Finance companies typically enjoy high credit ratings and are thus able to borrow at the lowest market rates, enabling them to make loans at rates not much higher than banks. Even though their customers usually do not qualify for bank credit, these companies have experienced a low rate of default. Finance companies in general tend to be interest rate-sensitive—increases and decreases in market interest rates affect their profits directly. For this reason, publicly held finance companies are sometimes referred to as money stocks. *See also* CAPTIVE FINANCE COMPANY.

FINANCIAL ACCOUNTING STANDARDS BOARD (FASB) independent board responsible for establishing and interpreting generally accepted accounting principles. It was formed in 1973 to succeed and continue the activities of the Accounting Principles Board (APB). *See* GENERALLY ACCEPTED ACCOUNTING PRINCIPLES.

FINANCIAL ADVISER professional adviser offering financial counsel. Some financial advisers charge a fee and earn commissions on the products they recommend to implement their advice. Other advisers only charge fees, and do not sell any products or accept commissions. Some financial advisers are generalists, while others specialize in specific areas such as investing, insurance, estate planning, taxes, or other areas.

FINANCIAL ANALYSIS analysis of the FINANCIAL STATEMENT of a company. *See also* FUNDAMENTAL ANALYSIS.

FINANCIAL ASSETS assets in the form of stocks, bonds, rights, certificates, bank balances, etc., as distinguished from tangible, physical assets. For example, real property is a physical asset, but shares in a REAL ESTATE INVESTMENT TRUST (REIT) or the stock or bonds of a company that held property as an investment would be financial assets.

FINANCIAL FUTURE FUTURES CONTRACT based on a financial instrument. Such contracts usually move under the influence of interest rates. As rates rise, contracts fall in value; as rates fall, contracts gain in value. Examples of instruments underlying financial futures contracts: Treasury bills, Treasury notes, Government National Mortgage Association (Ginnie Mae) pass-throughs, foreign currencies, and certificates of deposit. Trading in these contracts is governed by the federal Commodities Futures Trading Commission. Traders use these futures to speculate on the direction of interest rates. Financial institutions (banks, insurance companies, brokerage firms) use them to hedge financial portfolios against adverse fluctuations in interest rates.

FINANCIAL INSTITUTION institution that collects funds from the public to place in financial assets such as stocks, bonds, money market instruments, bank deposits, or loans. Depository institutions (banks, savings and loans, savings banks, credit unions) pay interest on deposits and invest the deposit money mostly in loans. Nondepository institutions (insurance companies, pension plans) collect money by selling insurance policies or receiving employer contributions and pay it out for legitimate claims or for retirement benefits. Increasingly, many institutions are performing both depository and nondepository functions. For instance, brokerage firms now place customers' money in certificates of deposit and money market funds and sell insurance. *See* FINANCIAL SUPERMARKET.

FINANCIAL INSTITUTIONS REFORM, RECOVERY AND ENFORCE-MENT ACT OF 1989 (FIRREA) legislation enacted into law on August 9, 1989, to resolve the crisis affecting U.S. savings and loan associations. Known as the *bailout bill*, it revamped the regulatory, insurance, and financing structures and established the OFFICE OF THRIFT SUPERVISION. The act created (1) the RESO-LUTION TRUST CORPORATION (RTC), which, operating under the management of the FEDERAL DEPOSIT INSURANCE CORPORATION (FDIC), was charged with closing or merging institutions that had become insolvent beginning in 1989; (2) the RES-OLUTION FUNDING CORPORATION (REFCORP), charged with borrowing from private capital markets to fund RTC activities and to manage the remaining assets and liabilities taken over by the FEDERAL SAVINGS AND LOAN INSURANCE CORPO-RATION (FSLIC) prior to 1989; (3) the SAVINGS ASSOCIATION INSURANCE FUND (SAIF) (pronounced "safe"), to replace FSLIC as insurer of thrift deposits and to be administered by the FDIC separately from its bank deposit insurance program, which became the BANK INSURANCE FUND (BIF); and (4) the FEDERAL HOUSING FINANCE BOARD (FHFB), charged with overseeing the FEDERAL HOME LOAN BANKS.

The RTC was authorized to accept additional insolvent institutions through June 1995; after that date, responsibilities for newly failed institutions shifted to the SAIF.

See also BAILOUT BOND.

FINANCIAL INTERMEDIARY commercial bank, savings and loan, mutual savings bank, credit union, or other "middleman" that smooths the flow of funds between "savings surplus units" and "savings deficit units." In an economy viewed as three sectors—households, businesses, and government—a *savings surplus unit* is one where income exceeds consumption; a *savings deficit unit* is one where current expenditures exceed current income and external sources must be called upon to make up the difference. As a whole, households are savings surplus units, whereas businesses and governments are savings deficit units. Financial intermediaries redistribute savings into productive uses and, in the process, serve two other important functions: By making savers infinitesimally small "shareholders" in huge pools of capital, which in turn are loaned out to a wide number and variety of borrowers, the intermediaries provide both diversification of risk and liquidity to the individual saver. *See also* DISINTERMEDIATION; FINDER'S FEE.

FINANCIAL LEASE lease in which the service provided by the lessor to the lessee is limited to financing equipment. All other responsibilities related to the possession of equipment, such as maintenance, insurance, and taxes, are borne by the lessee. A financial lease is usually noncancellable and is fully paid out *(amortized)* over its term.

FINANCIAL LEVERAGE *see* LEVER ',GE.

FINANCIAL MARKET market for the exchange of capital and credit in the economy. Money markets concentrate on short-term debt instruments; capital markets trade in long-term debt and equity instruments. Examples of financial markets: stock market, bond market, commodities market, and foreign exchange market.

FINANCIAL NEEDS APPROACH technique to assess the proper amount of life insurance for an individual. The person, either on his or her own or with the help of an insurance adviser, must estimate the financial needs of survivors in case the person dies unexpectedly. Projections for expenses, income, taxes, funeral costs, and other financial factors lead to an understanding of the amount of insurance proceeds that would be needed to allow the survivors to continue in their present lifestyle. Once the optimal amount of insurance protection is determined, various kinds of TERM and CASH VALUE INSURANCE programs can be designed to meet these needs.

FINANCIAL PLANNER professional who analyzes personal financial circumstances and prepares a program to meet financial needs and objectives. Financial planners, who may be accountants, bankers, lawyers, insurance agents, real estate or securities brokers, or independent practitioners, should have knowledge in the areas of wills and estate planning, retirement planning, taxes, insurance, family budgeting, debt management, and investments.

Fee-only planners charge on the basis of service and time and have nothing to sell. *Commission-only planners* offer their services for free but sell commission-producing products such as MUTUAL FUNDS, LIMITED PARTNERSHIPS, insurance products, stocks, and bonds. *Fee-plus-commission planners* charge an upfront fee for consultation and their written plan, then charge commissions on the financial products they sell. *Fee-offset planners* charge fees against which they apply credits when they sell commission-producing products.

The Certified Financial Planner Board of Standards, Inc., in Denver, Colorado, issues the CERTIFIED FINANCIAL PLANNER (CFP) license, and the Institute of Certified Financial Planners, also in Denver, maintains a referral list. The International Association for Financial Planning (IAFP) in Atlanta, Georgia, provides a list of financial planners with CFA, CFP, ChFC, or CPA designation; a law or financial planning degree; or those who have completed its Practical Knowledge Examination. The American Institute of Certified Public Accountants in Jersey City, New Jersey, provides a list of CPAs who offer financial planning services; The National Association of Personal Financial Advisors (NAPFA) in Buffalo Grove, Illinois, lists fee-only planners. The National Endowment for Financial Education, in Denver, offers a financial planning starter kit to consumers, on request.

FINANCIAL POSITION status of a firm's assets, liabilities, and equity accounts as of a certain time, as shown on its FINANCIAL STATEMENT. Also called *financial condition.*

FINANCIAL PUBLIC RELATIONS branch of public relations specializing in corporate disclosure responsibilities, stockholder relations, and relations with the professional investor community. Financial public relations is concerned not only with matters of corporate image and the cultivation of a favorable financial and investment environment but also with legal interpretation and adherence to Securities and Exchange Commission and other government regulations, as well as with the DISCLOSURE requirements of the securities exchanges. Its practitioners, therefore, include lawyers with expertise in such areas as tender offers and takeovers, public offerings, proxy solicitation, and insider trading. *See also* INVESTOR RELATIONS DEPARTMENT.

FINANCIAL PYRAMID
1. risk structure many investors aim for in spreading their investments between low-, medium-, and high-risk vehicles. In a financial pyramid, the largest part of the investor's assets is in safe, liquid investments that provide a decent return. Next, some money is invested in stocks and bonds that provide good income and the possibility for long-term growth of capital. Third, a smaller portion of one's capital is committed to speculative investments which may offer higher returns if they work out well. At the top of the financial pyramid,

where only a small amount of money is committed, are high-risk ventures that have a slight chance of success, but which will provide substantial rewards if they succeed.

2. acquisition of holding company assets through financial leverage. *See* PYRA-MIDING.

Financial pyramid is not to be confused with fraudulent selling schemes, also sometimes called *pyramiding.*

FINANCIAL PYRAMID

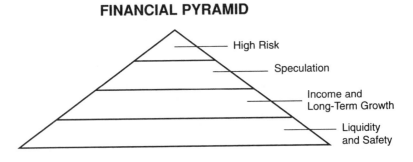

— High Risk

— Speculation

Income and
Long-Term Growth

Liquidity
and Safety

FINANCIAL STATEMENT written record of the financial status of an individual, association, or business organization. The financial statement includes a BALANCE SHEET and an INCOME STATEMENT (or operating statement or profit and loss statement) and may also include a STATEMENT OF CASH FLOWS, a statement of changes in retained earnings, and other analyses.

FINANCIAL STRUCTURE makeup of the right-hand side of a company's BALANCE SHEET, which includes all the ways its assets are financed, such as trade accounts payable and short-term borrowings as well as long-term debt and ownership equity. Financial structure is distinguished from CAPITAL STRUCTURE, which includes only long-term debt and equity. A company's financial structure is influenced by a number of factors, including the growth rate and stability of its sales, its competitive situation (i.e., the stability of its profits), its asset structure, and the attitudes of its management and its lenders. It is the basic frame of reference for analyses concerned with financial leveraging decisions.

FINANCIAL SUPERMARKET company that offers a wide range of financial services under one roof. For example, some large retail organizations offer stock, insurance, and real estate brokerage, as well as banking services. For customers, having all their assets with one institution can make financial transactions and planning more convenient and efficient, since money does not constantly have to be shifted from one institution to another. For institutions, such all-inclusive relationships are more profitable than dealing with just one aspect of a customer's financial needs. Institutions often become financial supermarkets in order to capture all the business of their customers.

FINANCIAL TABLES tables found in newspapers listing prices, dividends, yields, price/earnings ratios, trading volume, and other important data on stocks, bonds, mutual funds, and futures contracts. While local newspapers may carry limited tables, more extensive listings are available in *Barron's, Investor's Business Daily,* the *Wall Street Journal,* and other publications.

FINANCING CORPORATION (FICO) agency set up by Congress in 1987 to issue bonds and bail out the FEDERAL SAVINGS AND LOAN INSURANCE CORPORATION (FSLIC). *See also* BAILOUT BOND.

FINDER'S FEE fee charged by a person or company acting as a finder (intermediary) in a transaction.

FINEX financial futures and options division of the NEW YORK COTTON EXCHANGE, with a trading floor in Dublin, FINEX Europe, creating a 24-hour market in most FINEX contracts. FINEX/FINEX Europe trades U.S. dollar index (USDX) futures and options, and U.S. dollar-based currency futures, and cross-rate currency futures and options on those futures. Futures and options on Treasury auction five-year U.S. Treasury note futures and Treasury auction two-year U.S. Treasury note futures are traded only in New York.

FINITE LIFE REAL ESTATE INVESTMENT TRUST (FREIT) REAL ESTATE INVESTMENT TRUST (REIT) that promises to try to sell its holdings within a specified period to realize CAPITAL GAINS.

FIREWALL the legal separation of banking and broker/dealer operations within a financial institution. Under the GLASS-STEAGALL ACT OF 1933, banks are not allowed to own or control broker/dealers, though in recent years banks have offered many of the services traditionally provided by brokers. A firewall would prevent a bank from lending money to a securities affiliate, for example. To some extent, the separation is maintained to protect the FDIC insurance fund and insured bank deposits from the risks associated with the brokerage business.

FIRM
1. general term for a business, corporation, partnership, or proprietorship. Legally, a firm is not considered a corporation since it may not be incorporated and since the firm's principals are not recognized as separate from the identity of the firm itself. This might be true of a law or accounting firm, for instance.
2. solidity with which an agreement is made. For example, a firm order with a manufacturer or a firm bid for a stock at a particular price means that the order or bid is assured.

FIRM COMMITMENT
Lending: term used by lenders to refer to an agreement to make a loan to a specific borrower within a specific period of time and, if applicable, on a specific property. *See also* COMMITMENT FEE.
Securities underwriting: arrangement whereby investment bankers make outright purchases from the issuer of securities to be offered to the public; also called *firm commitment underwriting.* The underwriters, as the investment bankers are called in such an arrangement, make their profit on the difference between the purchase price—determined through either competitive bidding or negotiation—and the public offering price. Firm commitment underwriting is to be distinguished from conditional arrangements for distributing new securities, such as standby commitments and best efforts commitments. The word *underwriting* is frequently misused with respect to such conditional arrangements. It is used correctly only with respect to firm commitment underwritings or, as they are sometimes called, BOUGHT DEALS. *See also* BEST EFFORT; STANDBY COMMITMENT.

FIRM ORDER
Commercial transaction: written or verbal order that has been confirmed and is not subject to cancellation.
Securities: (1) order to buy or sell for the proprietary account of the broker-dealer firm; (2) buy or sell order not conditional upon the customer's confirmation.

FIRM QUOTE securities industry term referring to any round lot bid or offer price of a security stated by a market maker and not identified as a nominal (or subject) quote. Under National Association of Securities Dealers' (NASD) rules and practice, quotes requiring further negotiation or review must be identified as nominal quotes. *See also* NOMINAL QUOTATION.

FIRREA *see* FINANCIAL INSTITUTIONS REFORM AND RECOVERY ACT.

FIRST BOARD delivery dates for futures as established by the Chicago Board of Trade and other exchanges trading in futures.

FIRST CALL DATE first date specified in the indenture of a corporate or municipal bond contract on which part or all of the bond may be redeemed at a set price. An XYZ bond due in 2030, for instance, may have a first call date of May 1, 2013. This means that, if XYZ wishes, bondholders may be paid off starting on that date in 2013. Bond brokers typically quote yields on such bonds with both yield to maturity (in this case, 2030) and yield to call (in this case, 2013). *See also* DURATION; YIELD TO CALL; YIELD TO MATURITY.

FIRST IN, FIRST OUT (FIFO) method of accounting for inventory whereby, quite literally, the inventory is assumed to be sold in the chronological order in which it was purchased. For example, the following formula is used in computing the cost of goods sold:

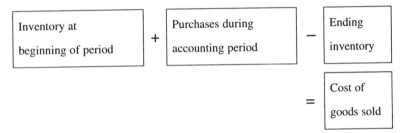

Under the FIFO method, inventory costs flow from the oldest purchases forward, with beginning inventory as the starting point and ending inventory representing the most recent purchases. The FIFO method contrasts with the LIFO or LAST IN, FIRST OUT method, which is FIFO in reverse. The significance of the difference becomes apparent when inflation or deflation affects inventory prices. In an inflationary period, the FIFO method produces a higher ending inventory, a lower cost of goods sold figure, and a higher gross profit. LIFO, on the other hand, produces a lower ending inventory, a higher cost of goods sold figure, and a lower reported profit.

    In accounting for the purchase and sale of securities for tax purposes, FIFO is assumed by the IRS unless it is advised of the use of an alternative method.

FIRST MORTGAGE real estate loan that gives the mortgagee (lender) a primary lien against a specified piece of property. A primary lien has precedence over all other mortgages in case of default. *See also* JUNIOR MORTGAGE; SECOND MORTGAGE.

FIRST PREFERRED STOCK preferred stock that has preferential claim on dividends and assets over other preferred issues and common stock.

FISCAL AGENT
    1. usually a bank or a trust company acting for a corporation under a corporate trust agreement. The fiscal agent handles such matters as disbursing funds for dividend payments, redeeming bonds and coupons, handling taxes related to the issue of bonds, and paying rents.

2. agent of the national government or its agencies or of a state or municipal government that performs functions relating to the issue and payment of bonds. For example, the Federal Reserve is the U.S. government's fiscal agent.

FISCAL POLICY federal taxation and spending policies designed to level out the business cycle and achieve full employment, price stability, and sustained growth in the economy. Fiscal policy basically follows the economic theory of the 20th-century English economist John Maynard Keynes that insufficient demand causes unemployment and excessive demand leads to inflation. It aims to stimulate demand and output in periods of business decline by increasing government purchases and cutting taxes, thereby releasing more disposable income into the spending stream, and to correct overexpansion by reversing the process. Working to balance these deliberate fiscal measures are the so-called built-in stabilizers, such as the progressive income tax and unemployment benefits, which automatically respond countercyclically. Fiscal policy is administered independently of MONETARY POLICY, by which the Federal Reserve Board attempts to regulate economic activity by controlling the money supply. The goals of fiscal and monetary policy are the same, but Keynesians and Monetarists disagree as to which of the two approaches works best. At the basis of their differences are questions dealing with the velocity (turnover) of money and the effect of changes in the money supply on the equilibrium rate of interest (the rate at which money demand equals money supply). *See also* KEYNESIAN ECONOMICS.

FISCAL YEAR (FY) accounting period covering 12 consecutive months, 52 consecutive weeks, 13 four-week periods, or 365 consecutive days, at the end of which the books are closed and profit or loss is determined. A company's fiscal year is often, but not necessarily, the same as the calendar year. A seasonal business will frequently select a fiscal rather than a calendar year, so that its year-end figures will show it in its most liquid condition, which also means having less inventory to verify physically. The FY of the U.S. government ends September 30.

FIT a situation where the features of a particular investment perfectly match the portfolio requirements of an investor.

FITCH INVESTORS SERVICE, INC. New York- and Denver-based RATING firm, which rates corporate and municipal bonds, preferred stock, commercial paper, and obligations of health-care and not-for-profit institutions.

FITCH SHEETS sheets indicating the successive trade prices of securities listed on the major exchanges. They are published by Francis Emory Fitch, Inc. in New York City.

FIVE HUNDRED DOLLAR RULE REGULATION T provision of the Federal Reserve that exempts deficiencies in margin requirements amounting to $500 or less from mandatory remedial action. Brokers are thus not forced to resort to the liquidation of an account to correct a trivial deficiency in a situation where, for example, a customer is temporarily out of town and cannot be reached. *See also* MARGIN CALL.

FIVE PERCENT RULE one of the Rules of Fair Practice of the National Association of Securities Dealers (NASD). It proposes an ethical guideline for spreads in dealer transactions and commissions in brokerage transactions, including PROCEEDS SALES and RISKLESS TRANSACTIONS.

FIXATION setting of a present or future price of a commodity, such as the twice-daily London GOLD FIXING. In other commodities, prices are fixed further into the future for the benefit of both buyers and sellers of that commodity.

FIXED ANNUITY investment contract sold by an insurance company that guarantees fixed payments, either for life or for a specified period, to an annuitant. In fixed annuities, the insurer takes both the investment and the mortality risks. A fixed annuity contrasts with a VARIABLE ANNUITY, where payments depend on an uncertain outcome, such as prices in the securities markets. See *also* ANNUITY.

FIXED ASSET tangible property used in the operations of a business, but not expected to be consumed or converted into cash in the ordinary course of events. Plant, machinery and equipment, furniture and fixtures, and leasehold improvements comprise the fixed assets of most companies. They are normally represented on the balance sheet at their net depreciated value.

FIXED BENEFITS payments to a BENEFICIARY that are fixed rather than variable.

FIXED-CHARGE COVERAGE ratio of profits before payment of interest and income taxes to interest on bonds and other contractual long-term debt. It indicates how many times interest charges have been earned by the corporation on a pretax basis. Since failure to meet interest payments would be a default under the terms of indenture agreements, the coverage ratio measures a margin of safety. The amount of safety desirable depends on the stability of a company's earnings. (Too much safety can be an indication of an undesirable lack of leverage.) In cyclical companies, the fixed-charge coverage in periods of recession is a telling ratio. Analysts also find it useful to calculate the number of times that a company's *cash flow*—i.e., *after*-tax earnings plus noncash expenses (for example, depreciation)—covers fixed charges. Also known as *times fixed charges.*

FIXED COST cost that remains constant regardless of sales volume. Fixed costs include salaries of executives, interest expense, rent, depreciation, and insurance expenses. They contrast with *variable costs* (direct labor, materials costs), which are distinguished from *semivariable costs.* Semivariable costs vary, but not necessarily in direct relation to sales. They may also remain fixed up to a level of sales, then increase when sales enter a higher range. For example, expenses associated with a delivery truck would be fixed up to the level of sales where a second truck was required. Obviously, no costs are purely fixed; the assumption, however, serves the purposes of cost accounting for limited planning periods. Cost accounting is also concerned with the allocation of portions of fixed costs to inventory costs, also called indirect costs, overhead, factory overhead, and supplemental overhead. *See also* DIRECT OVERHEAD; VARIABLE COST.

FIXED EXCHANGE RATE set rate of exchange between the currencies of countries. At the Bretton Woods international monetary conference in 1944, a system of fixed exchange rates was set up, which existed until the early 1970s, when a FLOATING EXCHANGE RATE system was adopted.

FIXED EXPENSES *see* FIXED COSTS.

FIXED-INCOME INVESTMENT security that pays a fixed rate of return. This usually refers to government, corporate, or municipal bonds, which pay a fixed rate of interest until the bonds mature, and to preferred stock, paying a fixed dividend. Such investments are advantageous in a time of low inflation, but do not protect holders against erosion of buying power in a time of rising inflation, since the bondholder or preferred shareholder gets the same amount of interest or dividends, even though consumer goods cost more.

FIXED PREMIUM equal installments payable to an insurance company for INSURANCE or an ANNUITY. *See also* SINGLE-PREMIUM DEFERRED ANNUITY (SPDA) and SINGLE-PREMIUM LIFE INSURANCE.

FIXED PRICE

Contracts: type of contract where the price is preset and invariable, regardless of the actual costs of production. *See also* COST-PLUS CONTRACT.

Investment: in a public offering of new securities, price at which investment bankers in the underwriting SYNDICATE agree to sell the issue to the public. The price remains fixed as long as the syndicate remains in effect. The proper term for this kind of system is *fixed price offering system.* In contrast, Eurobonds, which are also sold through underwriting syndicates, are offered on a basis that permits discrimination among customers; i.e., the underwriting spread may be adjusted to suit the particular buyer. *See also* EUROBOND.

FIXED RATE (LOAN) type of loan in which the interest rate does not fluctuate with general market conditions. There are fixed rate mortgage (also known as conventional mortgage) and consumer installment loans, as well as fixed rate business loans. Fixed rate loans tend to have higher original interest rates than flexible rate loans such as an ADJUSTABLE RATE MORTGAGE (ARM), because lenders are not protected against a rise in the cost of money when they make a fixed rate loan.

The term fixed rate may also refer to fixed currency exchange rates. *See* FIXED EXCHANGE RATE.

FIXED TERM REVERSE MORTGAGE mortgage granted by a bank or other lending institution providing payments to a homeowner for a fixed number of years. A retired couple who have paid off their traditional mortgage might be interested in such a plan if they do not want to move out of their house, but want to be able to tap the equity in their house for current cash income.

FIXED TRUST UNIT INVESTMENT TRUST that has a fixed portfolio of previously agreed upon securities; also called *fixed investment trust.* The securities are usually of one type, such as corporate, government, or municipal bonds, in order to afford a regular income to holders of units. A fixed trust is distinguished from a PARTICIPATING TRUST.

FIXTURE attachment to real property that is not intended to be moved and would create damage to the property if it were moved—for example, a plumbing fixture. Fixtures are classified as part of real estate when they share the same useful life. Otherwise, they are considered equipment.

FLAG technical chart pattern resembling a flag shaped like a parallelogram with masts on either side, showing a consolidation within a trend. It results from price fluctuations within a narrow range, both preceded and followed by sharp rises or declines. If the flag—the consolidation period—is preceded by a rise, it will usually be followed by a rise; a fall will follow a fall. *See* chart on next page.

FLASH tape display designation used when volume on an exchange is so heavy that the tape runs more than five minutes behind. The flash interrupts the display to report the current price—called the *flash price*— of a heavily traded security. Current prices of two groups of 50 stocks are flashed at five-minute intervals as long as the tape is seriously behind.

FLAT

1. in bond trading, without accrued interest. This means that accrued interest will be received by the buyer if and when paid but that no accrued interest is payable to the seller. Issues in default and INCOME BONDS are normally quoted and traded flat. The opposite of a flat bond is an AND INTEREST bond. *See also* LOANED FLAT.

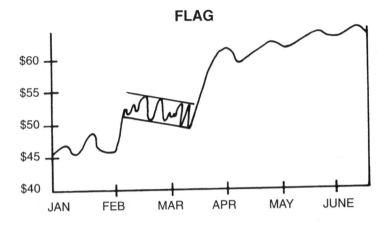

FLAG

2. inventory of a market maker with a net zero position—i.e., neither long nor short.
3. position of an underwriter whose account is completely sold.

FLAT MARKET market characterized by HORIZONTAL PRICE MOVEMENT. It is usually the result of low activity. However, STABILIZATION, consolidation, and DISTRIBUTION are situations marked by both horizontal price movement and active trading.

FLAT SCALE
Industry: labor term denoting a uniform rate of pay that makes no allowance for volume, frequency, or other factors.
Municipal bonds: bond trader's term describing a situation where shorter and longer term yields show little difference over the maturity range of a new serial bond issue.

FLAT TAX tax applied at the same rate to all levels of income. It is often discussed as an alternative to the PROGRESSIVE TAX. Proponents of a flat tax argue that people able to retain larger portions of higher income would have an added incentive to earn, thus stimulating the economy. Advocates also note its simplicity. Opponents argue it is a REGRESSIVE TAX in effect, comparing it to the sales tax, a uniform tax that puts a greater burden on households with lower incomes. The TAX REFORM ACT OF 1986 instituted a modified flat tax system—a progressive tax with fewer tax brackets and lower rates. However, the trend towards a flat tax was reversed with the REVENUE RECONCILIATION ACT OF 1993, which added another tax bracket and a tax surcharge to the income tax system.

FLEXIBLE BUDGET statement of projected revenue and expenditure based on various levels of production. It shows how costs vary with different rates of output or at different levels of sales volume.

FLEXIBLE EXCHANGE RATE *see* FLOATING EXCHANGE RATE.

FLEXIBLE EXPENSES in personal finance, expenses that can be adjusted or eliminated, such as those for luxuries, as opposed to fixed expenses, such as rent or car payments.

FLEXIBLE MUTUAL FUND fund that can invest in stocks, bonds, and cash in whatever proportion the fund manager thinks will maximize returns to shareholders at the lowest level of risk. Flexible funds, also called ASSET ALLO-CATION funds, can provide high returns if they are fully invested in stocks when stock prices soar, and they can also protect shareholders' assets by going largely to cash during a stock bear market. Flexible mutual funds are popular because the fund manager, not the shareholder, must make the difficult decisions on asset allocation and market timing. Some flexible funds allow managers to buy securities anywhere in the world in their quest to maximize shareholder returns.

FLIGHT OF CAPITAL *see* CAPITAL FLIGHT.

FLIGHT TO QUALITY moving capital to the safest possible investment to protect oneself from loss during an unsettling period in the market. For example, when a major bank fails, cautious money market investors may buy only government-backed money market securities instead of those issued by major banks. A flight to quality can be measured by the differing yields resulting from such a movement of capital. In the example just given, the yields on bank-issued money market paper will rise since there will be less demand for it, and the rates on government securities will fall, because there will be more demand for them.

FLIP-IN POISON PILL *see* POISON PILL.

FLIP-OVER POISON PILL *see* POISON PILL.

FLIPPING buying shares in an INITIAL PUBLIC OFFERING and selling them immediately for a profit. Brokerage firms underwriting new stock issues tend to discourage flipping, and will often try to allocate shares to investors who say they plan to hold on to the shares for some time. Still, the temptation to flip a new issue once it has risen in price sharply is too irresistible for many investors lucky enough to be allocated shares in a HOT ISSUE. An investor who flips stocks is called a *flipper.*

FLOAT

Banking: time between the deposit of a check in a bank and payment. Long floats are to the advantage of checkwriters, whose money may earn interest until a check clears. They are to the disadvantage of depositors, who must wait for a check to clear before they have access to the funds. As a rule, the further away the paying bank is from the deposit bank, the longer it will take for a check to clear. Some U.S. states limit the amount of float a bank can impose on the checks of its depositors. *See also* UNCOLLECTED FUNDS.

Investments: number of shares of a corporation that are outstanding and available for trading by the public. A small float means the stock will be more volatile, since a large order to buy or sell shares can influence the stock's price dramatically. A larger float means the stock will be less volatile.

FLOATER

Bonds: debt instrument with a variable interest rate tied to another interest rate, e.g., the rate paid by Treasury bills. A FLOATING RATE NOTE, for instance, provides a holder with additional interest if the applicable interest rate rises and less interest if the rate falls. It is generally best to buy floaters if it appears that interest rates will rise. If the outlook is for falling rates, investors typically favor fixed rate instruments. Floaters spread risk between issuers and debtholders.

Insurance: endorsement to a homeowner's or renter's insurance policy, a form of property insurance for items that are moved from location to location. Typically, a floater is bought to cover jewelry, furs, and other items whose full value is not covered in standard homeowner's or renter's policies. A standard homeowner's policy typically covers $1000 to $2000 for jewelry, furs, and watches. Also called a *rider.*

FLOATING AN ISSUE *see* NEW ISSUE; UNDERWRITE.

FLOATING DEBT continuously renewed or refinanced short-term debt of companies or governments used to finance ongoing operating needs.

FLOATING EXCHANGE RATE movement of a foreign currency exchange rate in response to changes in the market forces of supply and demand; also known as *flexible exchange rate.* Currencies strengthen or weaken based on a nation's reserves of hard currency and gold, its international trade balance, its rate of inflation and interest rates, and the general strength of its economy. Nations generally do not want their currency to be too strong, because this makes the country's goods too expensive for foreigners to buy. A weak currency, on the other hand, may signify economic instability if it has been caused by high inflation or a weak economy. The opposite of the floating exchange rate is the FIXED EXCHANGE RATE system. *See also* PAR VALUE OF CURRENCY.

FLOATING RATE NOTE debt instrument with a variable interest rate. Interest adjustments are made periodically, often every six months, and are tied to a money-market index such as Treasury bill rates. Floating rate notes usually have a maturity of about five years. They provide holders with protection against rises in interest rates, but pay lower yields than fixed rate notes of the same maturity. Also known as a FLOATER.

FLOATING SECURITIES
1. securities bought for the purpose of making a quick profit on resale and held in a broker's name.
2. outstanding stock of a corporation that is traded on an exchange.
3. unsold units of a newly issued security.

FLOATING SUPPLY
Bonds: total dollar amount of municipal bonds in the hands of speculators and dealers that is for sale at any particular time as offered in the BLUE LIST. Someone might say, for instance, "There is $10 billion in floating supply available now in the municipal bond market."
Stocks: number of shares of a stock available for purchase. A dealer might say, "The floating supply in this stock is about 200,000 shares." Sometimes called simply the *float.*

FLOOR in general, the lower limit of something. In securities, the part of a stock exchange where active trading takes place or the price at which a STOP LOSS order is activated. *See also* FLOOR BROKER.

FLOOR BROKER member of an exchange who is an employee of a member firm and executes orders, as agent, on the floor of the exchange for clients. The floor broker receives an order via teletype machine from his firm's trading department, then proceeds to the appropriate trading post on the exchange floor. There he joins other brokers and the specialist in the security being bought or sold, and executes the trade at the best competitive price available. On completion of the transaction, the customer is notified through his registered representative back at the firm, and the trade is printed on the consolidated ticker tape, which is displayed electronically around the country. A floor broker should not be confused with a FLOOR TRADER, who trades as a principal for his or her own account, rather than as a broker.

FLOOR OFFICIAL securities exchange employee, who is present on the floor of the exchange to settle disputes in the auction procedure, such as questions about priority or precedence in the settling of an auction. The floor official makes rulings on the spot and his or her judgment is usually accepted.

FLOOR TICKET summary of the information entered on the ORDER TICKET by the registered representative on receipt of a buy or sell order from a client. The floor ticket gives the floor broker the information needed to execute a securities transaction. The information required on floor tickets is specified by securities industry rules.

FLOOR TRADER member of a stock or commodities exchange who trades on the floor of that exchange for his or her own account. The floor trader must abide by trading rules similar to those of the exchange specialists who trade on behalf of others. The term should not be confused with FLOOR BROKER. See also REGISTERED COMPETITIVE TRADER.

FLOTATION (FLOATATION) COST cost of issuing new stocks or bonds. It varies with the amount of underwriting risk and the job of physical distribution. It comprises two elements: (1) the compensation earned by the investment bankers (the underwriters) in the form of the spread between the price paid to the issuer (the corporation or government agency) and the offering price to the public, and (2) the expenses of the issuer (legal, accounting, printing, and other out-of-pocket expenses). Securities and Exchange Commission studies reveal that flotation costs are higher for stocks than for bonds, reflecting the generally wider distribution and greater volatility of common stock as opposed to bonds, which are usually sold in large blocks to relatively few investors. The SEC also found that flotation costs as a percentage of gross proceeds are greater for smaller issues than for larger ones. This occurs because the issuer's legal and other expenses tend to be relatively large and fixed; also, smaller issues tend to originate with less established issuers, requiring more information development and marketing expense. An issue involving a RIGHTS OFFERING can involve negligible underwriting risk and selling effort and therefore minimal flotation cost, especially if the underpricing is substantial.

The UNDERWRITING SPREAD is the key variable in flotation cost, historically ranging from 23.7% of the size of a small issue of common stock to as low as 1.25% of the par value of high-grade bonds. Spreads are determined by both negotiation and competitive bidding.

FLOWER BOND type of U.S. government bond that, regardless of its cost price, is acceptable at par value in payment of estate taxes if the decedent was the legal holder at the time of death; also called *estate tax anticipation bond.* Flower bonds were issued as recently as 1971, and the last of them, with a 3½% coupon, will mature in 1998.

FLOW OF FUNDS

Economics: in referring to the national economy, the way funds are transferred from savings surplus units to savings deficit units through financial intermediaries. See also FINANCIAL INTERMEDIARY.

Municipal bonds: statement found in the bond resolutions of municipal revenue issues showing the priorities by which municipal revenue will be applied. Typically, the flow of funds in decreasing order of priority is operation and maintenance, bond debt service, expansion of the facility, and sinking fund for retirement of debt prior to maturity. The flow of funds statement varies in detail from issue to issue.

FLUCTUATION
1. change in prices or interest rates, either up or down. Fluctuation may refer to either slight or dramatic changes in the prices of stocks, bonds, or commodities. *See also* FLUCTUATION LIMIT.
2. the ups and downs in the economy.

FLUCTUATION LIMIT limits placed on the daily ups and downs of futures prices by the commodity exchanges. The limit protects traders from losing too much on a particular contract in one day. If a commodity reaches its limit, it may not trade any further that day. *See also* LIMIT UP, LIMIT DOWN.

FLURRY sudden increase in trading activity in a particular security. For example, there will be a flurry of trading in the stock of a company that was just the target of a surprise takeover bid. There are often trading flurries right after a company releases its quarterly earnings.

FNMA *see* FEDERAL NATIONAL MORTGAGE ASSOCIATION.

FOB *see* FREE ON BOARD.

FOCUS REPORT FOCUS is an acronym for the Financial and Operational Combined Uniform Single report, which broker-dealers are required to file monthly and quarterly with self-regulatory organizations (SROs). The SROs include exchanges, securities associations, and clearing organizations registered with the Securities and Exchange Commission and required by federal securities laws to be self-policing. The FOCUS report contains figures on capital, earnings, trade flow, and other required details.

FOOTSIE popular name for the *Financial Times'* FT-SE 100 Index (Financial Times-Stock Exchange 100 stock index), a market-value (capitalization)-weighted index of 100 blue chip stocks traded on the London Stock Exchange.

FORBES 500 annual listing by *Forbes* magazine of the largest U.S. publicly-owned corporations ranked four ways: by sales, assets, profits, and market value. *See also* FORTUNE 500.

FORCED CONVERSION when a CONVERTIBLE security is called in by its issuer. Convertible owners may find it to their financial advantage either to sell or to convert their holdings into common shares of the underlying company or to accept the call price. Such a conversion usually takes place when the convertible is selling above its CALL PRICE because the market value of the shares of the underlying stock has risen sharply. *See also* CONVERTIBLE.

FORECASTING projecting current trends using existing data.
  Stock market forecasters predict the direction of the stock market by relying on technical data of trading activity and fundamental statistics on the direction of the economy.
  Economic forecasters foretell the strength of the economy, often by utilizing complex econometric models as a tool to make specific predictions of future levels of inflation, interest rates, and employment. *See also* ECONOMETRICS.
  Forecasting can also refer to various PROJECTIONS used in business and financial planning.

FORECLOSURE process by which a homeowner who has not made timely payments of principal and interest on a mortgage loses title to the home. The holder of the mortgage, whether it be a bank, a savings and loan, or an individual, must go to court to seize the property, which may then be sold to satisfy the claims of the mortgage.

FOREIGN CORPORATION

1. corporation chartered under the laws of a state other than the one in which it conducts business. Because of inevitable confusion with the term ALIEN CORPORATION, *out-of-state corporation* is preferred.
2. corporation organized under the laws of a foreign country; the term ALIEN CORPORATION is usually preferred.

FOREIGN CORRUPT PRACTICES SECURITIES EXCHANGE ACT OF 1934 amendment passed in 1977 providing internal controls and penalties aimed at curtailing bribery by publicly held companies of foreign government officials and personnel.

FOREIGN CROWD New York Stock Exchange members who trade on the floor in foreign bonds.

FOREIGN CURRENCY FUTURES AND OPTIONS futures and options contracts based on foreign currencies, such as the Japanese yen, Deutsche mark, British pound, and French franc. The buyer of a foreign currency futures contract acquires the right to buy a particular amount of that currency by a specific date at a fixed rate of exchange, and the seller agrees to sell that currency at the same fixed price. *Call options* give call buyers the right, but not the obligation, to buy the underlying currency at a particular price by a particular date. Call options on foreign currency futures give call buyers the right to a long underlying futures contracts. Those buying *put options* have the right to sell the underlying currencies at a specific price by a specific date. Most buyers and sellers of foreign currency futures and options do not exercise their rights to buy or sell, but trade out of their contracts at a profit or loss before they expire. SPECULATORS hope to profit by buying or selling a foreign currency futures or options contract before a currency rises or falls in value. HEDGERS buy or sell such contracts to protect their cash market position from fluctuations in currency values. These contracts are traded on SECURITIES AND COMMODITIES EXCHANGES throughout the world, including the Chicago Mercantile Exchange, the Mid-America Commodity Exchange, and the Philadelphia Stock Exchange.

FOREIGN DIRECT INVESTMENT

1. investment in U.S. businesses by foreign citizens; usually involves majority stock ownership of the enterprise.
2. joint ventures between foreign and U.S. companies.

FOREIGN EXCHANGE instruments employed in making payments between countries—paper currency, notes, checks, bills of exchange, and electronic notifications of international debits and credits.

FOREIGN EXCHANGE RATE *see* EXCHANGE RATE. *See also* FOREIGN EXCHANGE.

FORFEITURE loss of rights or assets due to failure to fulfill a legal obligation or condition and as compensation for resulting losses or damages.

FORM 8-K Securities and Exchange Commission required form that a publicly-held company must file, reporting on any material event that might affect its financial situation or the value of its shares, ranging from merger activity to amendment of the corporate charter or bylaws. The SEC considers as material all matters about which an average, prudent investor ought reasonably to be informed before deciding whether to buy, sell, or hold a registered security. Form 8-K must be filed within a month of the occurrence of the material event. Timely disclosure rules may require a corporation to issue a press release immediately concerning an event subsequently reported on Form 8-K.

FORM 4 document, filed with the Securities and Exchange Commission and the pertinent stock exchange, which is used to report changes in the holdings of (1) those who own at least 10% of a corporation's outstanding stock and (2) directors and officers, even if they own no stock. When there has been a major change in ownership, Form 4 must be filed within ten days of the end of the month in which the change took place. Form 4 filings must be constantly updated during a takeover attempt of a company when the acquirer buys more than 10% of the outstanding shares.

FORM T National Association of Securities Dealers (NASD) form for reporting equity transaction executed after the market's normal hours.

FORM 10-K annual report required by the Securities and Exchange Commission of every issuer of a registered security, every exchange-listed company, and any company with 500 or more shareholders or $1 million or more in gross assets. The form provides for disclosure of total sales, revenue, and pretax operating income, as well as sales by separate classes of products for each of a company's separate lines of business for each of the past five years. A source and application of funds statement presented on a comparative basis for the last two fiscal years is also required. Form 10-K becomes public information when filed with the SEC.

FORM 10-Q quarterly report required by the Securities and Exchange Commission of companies with listed securities. Form 10-Q is less comprehensive than the FORM 10-K annual report and does not require that figures be audited. It may cover the specific quarter or it may be cumulative. It should include comparative figures for the same period of the previous year.

FORM 13D form used to comply with SCHEDULE 13D.

FORM 13G short form of SCHEDULE 13D for positions acquired in the ordinary course of business and not to assume control or influence.

FORM 3 form filed with the Securities and Exchange Commission and the pertinent stock exchange by all holders of 10% or more of the stock of a company registered with the SEC and by all directors and officers, even if no shares are owned. Form 3 details the number of shares owned as well as the number of warrants, rights, convertible bonds, and options to purchase common stock. Individuals required to file Form 3 are considered insiders, and they are required to update their information whenever changes occur. Such changes are reported on FORM 4.

FORMULA INVESTING investment technique based on a predetermined timing or asset allocation model that eliminates emotional decisions. One type of formula investing, called dollar cost averaging, involves putting the same amount of money into a stock or mutual fund at regular intervals, so that more shares will be bought when the price is low and less when the price is high. Another formula investing method calls for shifting funds from stocks to bonds or vice versa as the stock market reaches particular price levels. If stocks rise to a particular point, a certain amount of the stock portfolio is sold and put in bonds. On the other hand, if stocks fall to a particular low price, money is brought out of bonds into stocks. *See also* CONSTANT DOLLAR PLAN; CONSTANT RATIO PLAN.

FORTUNE 500 listings of the top 500 U.S. industrial corporations, and one of four Fortune 500 listings compiled by *Fortune* magazine. The companies are ranked by 12 indices, among them sales, profits, assets, stockholders' equity, earnings per share growth over a 10-year span, total return to investors in the year, and the 10-year annual rate of total return to investors. In separate listings, companies also are ranked by performance, within 26 industries, and within states. Headquarters city, phone number and the name of the chief executive officer are included. The Global 500 covers 27 industrial categories, from aerospace to metals to tobacco. The Service 500 of U.S. companies is divided into 8 categories: 100 diversified service companies, 100 commercial banks, 50 diversified financial companies, 50 savings institutions, 50 life insurance companies and 50 utilities. Its international companion is the Global Service 500.

FORWARD CONTRACT purchase or sale of a specific quantity of a commodity, government security, foreign currency, or other financial instrument at the current or SPOT PRICE, with delivery and settlement at a specified future date. Because it is a completed contract—as opposed to an options contract, where the owner has the choice of completing or not completing—a forward contract can be a COVER for the sale of a FUTURES CONTRACT. *See* HEDGE.

FORWARD EXCHANGE TRANSACTION purchase or sale of foreign currency at an exchange rate established now but with payment and delivery at a specified future time. Most forward exchange contracts have one-, three-, or six-month maturities, though contracts in major currencies can normally be arranged for delivery at any specified date up to a year, and sometimes up to three years.

FORWARD PRICING Securities and Exchange Commission requirement that open-end investment companies, whose share price is always determined by the NET ASSET VALUE of the outstanding shares, base all incoming buy and sell orders on the next net asset valuation of fund shares. *See also* INVESTMENT COMPANY.

FOR YOUR INFORMATION (FYI) prefix to a security price quote by a market maker that indicates the quote is "for your information" and is not a firm offer to trade at that price. FYI quotes are given as a courtesy for purposes of valuation. FVO (for valuation only) is sometimes used instead.

401(k) PLAN plan whereby employees may elect, as an alternative to receiving taxable cash in the form of compensation or a bonus, to contribute pretax dollars to a qualified tax-deferred retirement plan. Elective deferrals are limited to about $9000 a year (the amount is revised each year by the IRS based on inflation). Many companies, to encourage employee participation in the plan, match employee contributions anywhere from 10% to 100% annually. All employee contributions and employer matching funds can be invested in several options, usually including several stock mutual funds, bond mutual funds, a GUARANTEED INVESTMENT CONTRACT, a money market fund, and company stock. Employees control how the assets are allocated among the various choices, and can usually move the money at least once a year, and sometimes even daily. Withdrawals from 401(k) plans prior to age 59½ are subject to a 10% penalty tax except for death, disability, termination of employment, or qualifying hardship. Withdrawals after the age of 59½ are subject to taxation in the year the money is withdrawn. "Highly compensated" employees are subject to special limitations. 401(k) plans have become increasingly popular in recent years, in many cases supplanting traditional DEFINED BENEFIT PENSION PLANS. Employees favor them because they cut their tax bills in the year of contribution and their savings grow tax deferred until retirement. Companies favor these plans because they are less costly than traditional pension plans and also shift the responsibility for asset allocation to employees. Also called *cash or deferred arrangement* (CODA) or *salary reduction plan.*

403(b) PLAN type of INDIVIDUAL RETIREMENT ACCOUNT (IRA) covered in Section 403(b) of the Internal Revenue Code that permits employees of qualifying nonprofit organizations to set aside tax-deferred funds.

FOURTH MARKET direct trading of large blocks of securities between institutional investors to save brokerage commissions. The fourth market is aided by computers, notably by a computerized subscriber service called *INSTINET,* an acronym for Institutional Networks Corporation. INSTINET is registered with the Securities and Exchange Commission as a stock exchange and numbers among its subscribers a large number of mutual funds and other institutional investors linked to each other by computer terminals. The system permits subscribers to display tentative volume interest and bid-ask quotes to others in the system.

FRACTIONAL DISCRETION ORDER buy or sell order for securities that allows the broker discretion within a specified fraction of a point. For example, "Buy 1000 XYZ at 28, discretion ½ point" means that the broker may execute the trade at a maximum price of 28½.

FRACTIONAL SHARE unit of stock less than one full share. For instance, if a shareholder is in a dividend reinvestment program, and the dividends being reinvested are not adequate to buy a full share at the stock's current price, the shareholder will be credited with a fractional share until enough dividends accumulate to purchase a full share.

FRANCHISE
In general: (1) privilege given a dealer by a manufacturer or franchise service organization to sell the franchisor's products or services in a given area, with or without exclusivity. Such arrangements are sometimes formalized in *a franchise agreement,* which is a contract between the franchisor and franchisee wherein the former may offer consultation, promotional assistance, financing, and other benefits in exchange for a percentage of sales or profits. (2) The business owned by the franchisee, who usually must meet an initial cash investment requirement.

Government: legal right given to a company or individual by a government authority to perform some economic function. For example, an electrical utility might have the right, under the terms of a franchise, to use city property to provide electrical service to city residents.

FRANCHISED MONOPOLY monopoly granted by the government to a company. The firm will be protected from competition by government exclusive license, permit, patent, or other device. For example, an electric utility will be granted the exclusive right to generate and sell electricity in a particular locality in return for agreeing to be subject to governmental rate regulation.

FRANCHISE TAX state tax, usually regressive (that is, the rate decreases as the tax base increases), imposed on a state-chartered corporation for the right to do business under its corporate name. Franchise taxes are usually levied on a number of value bases, such as capital stock, capital stock plus surplus, capital, profits, or property in the state.

FRANKFURT STOCK EXCHANGE the German securities exchange, supported financially and administratively by the DEUTSCHE BORSE AG. The stock exchange, however, is responsible for rules of admission and trading, and supervision. There are three membership classes: banks that trade securities for their own accounts or on behalf of third parties; Kursmaklers, who act as intermediaries for trades in securities in the Official Market and at the same time determine their prices; and Free Maklers, who act as intermediaries in any securities. Branches of foreign brokerage firms, which under their national laws are not banks, are treated as banks. There are three markets, based on capitalization: the Official Market, Regular Market, Free Market. Trading is by open outcry and IBIS, a computer-assisted system launched in 1991.

FRAUD intentional misrepresentation, concealment, or omission of the truth for the purpose of deception or manipulation to the detriment of a person or an organization. Fraud is a legal concept and the application of the term in a specific instance should be determined by a legal expert.

FREDDIE MAC
1. nickname for FEDERAL HOME LOAN MORTGAGE CORPORATION (FHLMC).
2. mortgage-backed securities, issued in minimum denominations of $25,000, that are packaged, guaranteed, and sold by the FHLMC. Mortgage-backed securities are issues in which residential mortgages are packaged and sold to investors.

FREE AND OPEN MARKET market in which price is determined by the free, unregulated interchange of supply and demand. The opposite is a *controlled market*, where supply, demand, and price are artificially set, resulting in an *inefficient market*.

FREE BOX securities industry jargon for a secure storage place ("box") for fully paid ("free") customers' securities, such as a bank vault or the DEPOSITORY TRUST COMPANY.

FREED UP securities industry jargon meaning that the members of an underwriting syndicate are no longer bound by the price agreed upon and fixed in the AGREEMENT AMONG UNDERWRITERS. They are thus free to trade in the security on a market basis.

FREE ON BOARD (FOB) transportation term meaning that the invoice price includes delivery at the seller's expense to a specified point and no further. For example, "FOB our Newark warehouse" means that the buyer must pay all shipping and other charges associated with transporting the merchandise from the seller's warehouse in Newark to the buyer's receiving point. Title normally passes from seller to buyer at the FOB point by way of a bill of lading.

FREERIDING
1. practice, prohibited by the Securities and Exchange Commission and the National Association of Securities Dealers, whereby an underwriting SYNDICATE member withholds a portion of a new securities issue and later resells it at a price higher than the initial offering price.
2. practice whereby a brokerage client buys and sells a security in rapid order without putting up money for the purchase. The practice violates REGULATION T of the Federal Reserve Board concerning broker-dealer credit to customers. The penalty requires that the customer's account be frozen for 90 days. *See also* FROZEN ACCOUNT.

FREE RIGHT OF EXCHANGE ability to transfer securities from one name to another without paying the charge associated with a sales transaction. The free right applies, for example, where stock in STREET NAME (that is, registered in the name of a broker-dealer) is transferred to the customer's name in order to be eligible for a dividend reinvestment plan. *See also* REGISTERED SECURITY.

FREE STOCK (1) stock that is fully paid for and is not assigned as collateral. (2) stock held by an issuer following a PRIVATE PLACEMENT but that can be traded free of the restrictions bearing on a LETTER SECURITY.

FREEZE OUT put pressure on minority shareholders after a takeover to sell their shares to the acquirer.

FREIT *see* FINITE LIFE REAL ESTATE INVESTMENT TRUST.

FRICTIONAL COST in an INDEX FUND, the amount by which the fund's return is less than that of the index it replicates. The difference, assuming it is not otherwise adjusted, represents the fund's management fees and transaction costs.

FRIENDLY TAKEOVER merger supported by the management and board of directors of the target company. The board will recommend to shareholders that they approve the takeover offer, because it represents fair value for the company's shares. In many cases, the acquiring company will retain many of the existing managers of the acquired company to continue to run the business. A friendly takeover is in contrast to a HOSTILE TAKEOVER, in which management actively resists the acquisition attempt by another company or RAIDER.

FRINGE BENEFITS compensation to employees in addition to salary. Some examples of fringe benefits are paid holidays, retirement plans, life and health insurance plans, subsidized cafeterias, company cars, stock options, and expense accounts. In many cases, fringe benefits can add significantly to an employee's total compensation, and are a key ingredient in attracting and retaining employees. For the most part, fringe benefits are not taxable to the employee, though they are generally tax-deductible for the employer.

FRONT-END LOAD sales charge applied to an investment at the time of initial purchase. There may be a front-end load on a mutual fund, for instance, which is sold by a broker. Annuities, life insurance policies, and limited partnerships can also have front-end loads. From the investor's point of view, the earnings from the investment should make up for this up-front fee within a relatively short period of time. *See also* INVESTMENT COMPANY.

FRONT OFFICE sales personnel in a brokerage, insurance, or other financial services operation. Front office workers produce revenue, in contrast to BACK OFFICE workers, who perform administrative and other support functions for the front office.

FRONT RUNNING practice whereby a securities or commodities trader takes a POSITION to capitalize on advance knowledge of a large upcoming transaction expected to influence the market price. In the stock market, this might be done by buying an OPTION on stock expected to benefit from a large BLOCK transaction. In commodities, DUAL TRADING is common practice and provides opportunities to profit from front running.

FROZEN ACCOUNT
Banking: bank account from which funds may not be withdrawn until a lien is satisfied and a court order is received freeing the balance.
     A bank account may also be frozen by court order in a dispute over the ownership of property.
Investments: brokerage account under disciplinary action by the Federal Reserve Board for violation of REGULATION T. During the period an account is frozen (90 days), the customer may not sell securities until their purchase price has been fully paid and the certificates have been delivered. The penalty is invoked commonly in cases of FREERIDING.

FULL COUPON BOND bond with a coupon rate that is near or above current market interest rates. If interest rates are generally about 8%, for instance, a 7½% or 9% bond is considered a full coupon bond.

FULL DISCLOSURE
In general: requirement to disclose all material facts relevant to a transaction.

Securities industry: public information requirements established by the Securities Act of 1933, the Securities Exchange Act of 1934, and the major stock exchanges.

See also DISCLOSURE.

FULL FAITH AND CREDIT phrase meaning that the full taxing and borrowing power, *plus* revenue other than taxes, is pledged in payment of interest and repayment of principal of a bond issued by a government entity. U.S. government securities and general obligation bonds of states and local governments are backed by this pledge.

FULL REPLACEMENT COVERAGE *see* GUARANTEED REPLACEMENT COST COVERAGE INSURANCE.

FULL-SERVICE BROKER broker who provides a wide range of services to clients. Unlike a DISCOUNT BROKER, who just executes trades, a full-service broker offers advice on which stocks, bonds, commodities, and mutual funds to buy or sell. A full-service broker may also offer an ASSET MANAGEMENT ACCOUNT; advice on financial planning, tax shelters, and INCOME LIMITED PARTNERSHIPS; and new issues of stock. A full-service broker's commissions will be higher than those of a discount broker. The term *brokerage* is gradually being replaced by variations of the term *financial services* as the range of services offered by brokers expands.

FULL TRADING AUTHORIZATION freedom, even from broad guidelines, allowed a broker or adviser under a DISCRETIONARY ACCOUNT.

FULLY DEPRECIATED said of a fixed asset to which all the DEPRECIATION the tax law allows has been charged. Asset is carried on the books at its RESIDUAL VALUE, although its LIQUIDATING VALUE may be higher or lower.

FULLY DILUTED EARNINGS PER (COMMON) SHARE figure showing earnings per common share after assuming the exercise of warrants and stock options, and the conversion of convertible bonds and preferred stock (all potentially *dilutive* securities). Actually, it is more analytically correct to define the term as the smallest earnings per common share figure that can be obtained by computing earnings per share (EPS) for all possible combinations of assumed exercise or conversion (because antidilutive securities—securities whose conversion would add to EPS—may not be assumed to be exercised or converted). Fully diluted EPS must be reported on the profit and loss statement when the figure is 97% or less of earnings available to common shareholders divided by the average number of common shares outstanding during the period. *See also* DILUTION; PRIMARY EARNINGS PER (COMMON) SHARE.

FULLY DISTRIBUTED term describing a new securities issue that has been completely resold to the investing public (that is, to institutions and individuals and other investors rather than to dealers).

FULLY INVESTED said of an investor or a portfolio when funds in cash or CASH EQUIVALENTS are minimal and assets are totally committed to other investments, usually stock. To be fully invested is to have an optimistic view of the market.

FULLY VALUED said of a stock that has reached a price at which analysts think the underlying company's fundamental earnings power has been recognized by the market. If the stock goes up from that price, it is called OVERVALUED. If the stock goes down, it is termed UNDERVALUED.

FUND *see* FUND FAMILY; FUNDING; MUTUAL FUND.

FUNDAMENTAL ANALYSIS
Economics: research of such factors as interest rates, gross national product, inflation, unemployment, and inventories as tools to predict the direction of the economy. **Investment:** analysis of the balance sheet and income statements of companies in order to forecast their future stock price movements. Fundamental analysts consider past records of assets, earnings, sales, products, management, and markets in predicting future trends in these indicators of a company's success or failure. By appraising a firm's prospects, these analysts assess whether a particular stock or group of stocks is UNDERVALUED or OVERVALUED at the current market price. The other major school of stock market analysis is TECHNICAL ANALYSIS, which relies on price and volume movements of stocks and does not concern itself with financial statistics.

FUNDED DEBT
1. debt that is due after one year and is formalized by the issuing of bonds or long-term notes.
2. bond issue whose retirement is provided for by a SINKING FUND.
   See also FLOATING DEBT.

FUNDED PENSION PLAN pension plan in which all liabilities are fully funded. A pension plan's administrator knows the potential payments necessary to make to pensioners over the coming years. In order to be funded, the plan must have enough capital contributions from the plan sponsor, plus returns from investments, to pay those claims. Employees are notified annually of the financial strength of their pension plans, and whether or not the plans are fully funded. If the plans are not funded, the PENSION BENEFIT GUARANTY CORPORATION (PBGC), which guarantees pension plans, will act to try to get the plan sponsor to contribute more money to the plan. If a company fails with an underfunded pension plan, the PBGC will step in to make the promised payments to pensioners.

FUND FAMILY mutual fund company offering funds with many investment objectives. A fund family may offer several types of stock, bond, and money market funds and allow free switching among their funds. Large no-load fund families include Fidelity, Dreyfus, T. Rowe Price, Vanguard, Scudder, Strong, and Twentieth Century. Most major brokerage houses such as Merrill Lynch, Smith Barney and PaineWebber also sponsor fund families of their own. Many independent firms such as American Funds, Loomis-Sayles, Putnam, and Pioneer distribute their funds with a sales charge through brokerage firms and financial planners. Many investors find it convenient to place most of their assets with one or two fund families because of the convenience offered by such switching privileges. In recent years, several discount brokerage firms have offered the ability to shift assets from one fund family to another, making it less important than it had been to consolidate assets in one fund family. *See also* INVESTMENT COMPANY.

FUNDING
1. refinancing a debt on or before its maturity; also called REFUNDING and, in certain instances, PREREFUNDING.
2. putting money into investments or another type of reserve fund, to provide for future pension or welfare plans.
3. in corporate finance, the word *funding* is preferred to *financing* when referring to bonds in contrast to stock. A company is said to be funding its operations if it floats bonds.
4. to provide funds to finance a project, such as a research study.
   See also SINKING FUND.

FUND MANAGER manager of a pool of money such as a mutual fund, pension fund, insurance fund, or bank-pooled fund. Their job is to maximize the fund's returns at the least risk possible. Each fund manager tries his or her best to realize the fund's objectives, whether it be growth, income, or some combination of the two. Different fund managers use different styles to accomplish their objectives. For example, some stock fund managers use the value style of investing, while others concentrate on growth stocks. In picking a fund, it is important to know the fund manager's style, and how long he or she has been managing the fund. This information is generally available for publicly offered mutual funds from fund company literature or fund representatives.

FUND OF FUNDS mutual fund that invests in other mutual funds. The concept behind such funds is that they are able to move money between the best funds in the industry, and thereby increase shareholders' returns with more diversification than is offered by a single fund. The fund of funds has been criticized as adding another layer of management expenses on shareholders, however, because fees are paid to the fund's management company as well as to all the underlying fund management companies. The SEC limits the total amount of fees that shareholders can pay in such a fund. Funds of funds are usually organized in a fund family of their own, offering funds that will specialize in international stocks, aggressive growth, income, and other objectives. Funds of funds were extremely popular in the 1960s, but then faded in popularity in the 1970s because of a scandal involving Equity Funding, which was a fund of funds. They have enjoyed a modest comeback in recent years, however.

FUND SWITCHING moving money from one mutual fund to another, within the same FUND FAMILY. Purchases and sales of funds may be done to time the ups and downs of the stock and bond markets, or because investors' financial needs have changed. Several newsletters and fund managers specialize in advising clients on which funds to switch into and out of, based on market conditions. Switching among funds within a fund family is usually allowed without sales charges. Discount brokerages allow convenient switching of funds among fund families. Unless practiced inside a tax-deferred account such as an IRA or Keogh account, a fund switch creates a taxable event, since CAPITAL GAINS OR LOSSES are realized.

FUNGIBLES bearer instruments, securities, or goods that are equivalent, substitutable, and interchangeable. Commodities such as soybeans or wheat, common shares of the same company, and dollar bills are all familiar examples of fungibles.
Fungibility (interchangeability) of listed options, by virtue of their common expiration dates and strike prices, makes it possible for buyers and sellers to close out their positions by putting offsetting transactions through the OPTIONS CLEARING CORPORATION. *See also* OFFSET; STRIKE PRICE.

FUN MONEY money that is not necessary for everyday living expenses, and can therefore be risked in volatile, but potentially highly profitable, investments. If the investment pans out, the investor has had some fun speculating. If the investment turns sour, the investor's lifestyle has not been put at risk because he or she could afford to lose the money.

FURTHEST MONTH in commodities or options trading, the month that is furthest away from settlement of the contract. For example, Treasury bill futures may have outstanding contracts for three, six, or nine months. The six- and nine-month contracts would be the furthest months, and the three-month contract would be the NEAREST MONTH.

FUTA *see* FEDERAL UNEMPLOYMENT TAX ACT (FUTA).

FUTURES CONTRACT agreement to buy or sell a specific amount of a commodity or financial instrument at a particular price on a stipulated future date. The price is established between buyer and seller on the floor of a commodity exchange, using the OPEN OUTCRY system. A futures contract obligates the buyer to purchase the underlying commodity and the seller to sell it, unless the contract is sold to another before settlement date, which may happen if a trader waits to take a profit or cut a loss. This contrasts with options trading, in which the option buyer may choose whether or not to exercise the option by the exercise date. *See also* FORWARD CONTRACT; FUTURES MARKET.

FUTURES MARKET commodity exchange where FUTURES CONTRACTS are traded. Different exchanges specialize in particular kinds of contracts. The major exchanges are Amex Commodity Exchange, the Commodity Exchange Inc. (Comex), the New York Coffee, Sugar and Cocoa Exchange, the New York Cotton Exchange, the New York Mercantile Exchange, and the New York Futures Exchange, all in New York; the Chicago Board of Trade, the International Monetary Market, the Chicago Mercantile Exchange, the Chicago Rice and Cotton Exchange, and the MidAmerica Commodity Exchange, all in Chicago; the Kansas City Board of Trade, in Kansas City, MO; and the Minneapolis Grain Exchange, in Minneapolis. *See also* SPOT MARKET.

FUTURES OPTION OPTION on a FUTURES CONTRACT.

FUTURE VALUE reverse of PRESENT VALUE.

FVO (FOR VALUATION ONLY) *see* FOR YOUR INFORMATION.

g

GAAP *see* GENERALLY ACCEPTED ACCOUNTING PRINCIPLES (GAAP).

GAIJIN non-Japanese investor in Japan. The Japanese refer to foreign competitors, on both the individual and institutional levels, as gaijin. In particular, the large, prestigious American and European brokerage firms that compete with the major Japanese brokerage firms, such as Nomura and Nikko, are called gaijin.

GAIN profit on a securities transaction. A gain is realized when a stock, bond, mutual fund, futures contract, or other financial instrument is sold for more than its purchase price. If the instrument was held for more than a year, the gain is taxable at more favorable capital gains tax rates. If held for under a year, the gain is taxed at regular income tax rates.

GAMMA STOCKS obsolete classification of stocks traded on the London Stock Exchange. Ranking third behind ALPHA and BETA stocks in capitalization and activity, gamma stocks are less regulated, requiring just two market makers quoting indicative share prices. *See also* NORMAL MARKET SIZE (NMS).

GAP
Finance: amount of a financing need for which provision has yet to be made. For example, ABC company might need $1.5 million to purchase and equip a new plant facility. It arranges a mortgage loan of $700,000, secures equipment financing of $400,000, and obtains new equity of $150,000. That leaves a gap of $250,000 for which it seeks gap financing. Such financing may be available from state and local governments concerned with promoting economic development.

Securities: securities industry term used to describe the price movement of a stock or commodity when one day's trading range for the stock or commodity does not overlap the next day's, causing a range, or gap, in which no trade has occurred. This usually takes place because of some extraordinary positive or negative news about the company or commodity. *See also* PRICE GAP.

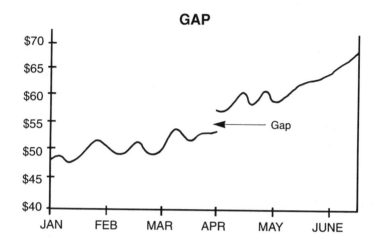

GARAGE annex floor on the north side of the main trading floor of the New York Stock Exchange.

GAP OPENING opening price for a stock that is significantly higher or lower than the previous day's closing price. For example, if XYZ Company was the subject of a $50 takeover bid after the market closed with its shares trading at $30, its share price might open the next morning at $45 a share. There would therefore be a gap between the closing price of $30 and the opening price of $45. The same phenomenon can occur on the downside if a company reports disappointing earnings or a takeover bid falls through, for example. Stocks trading on the New York or American Stock Exchange may experience a delayed opening when such an event occurs as the specialist deals with the rush of buy or sell orders to find the stock's appropriate price level.

GARAGE annex floor on the north side of the main trading floor of the New York Stock Exchange.

GARBATRAGE stock traders' term, combining garbage and ARBITRAGE, for activity in stocks swept upward by the psychology surrounding a major takeover. For example, when two leading entertainment stocks, Time, Inc., and Warner Communications, Inc., were IN PLAY in 1989, stocks with insignificant involvement in the entertainment sector became active. Garbatrage would not apply to activity in bona fide entertainment stocks moving on speculation that other mergers would follow in the wake of Time-Warner. *See also* RUMORTRAGE.

GARNISHMENT court order to an employer to withhold all or part of an employee's wages and send the money to the court or to a person who has won a lawsuit against the employee. An employee's wages will be *garnished* until the court-ordered debt is paid. Garnishing may be used in a divorce settlement or for repayment of creditors.

GATHER IN THE STOPS stock-trading tactic that involves selling a sufficient amount of stock to drive down the price to a point where stop orders (orders to buy or sell at a given price) are known to exist. The stop orders are then activated to become market orders (orders to buy or sell at the best available price), in turn creating movement which touches off other stop orders in a process called SNOW-BALLING. Because this can cause sharp trading swings, floor officials on the exchanges have the authority to suspend stop orders in individual securities if that seems advisable. *See also* STOP ORDER.

GDP IMPLICIT PRICE DEFLATOR ratio of current-dollar GROSS DOMESTIC PRODUCT (GDP) to constant-dollar GDP. Changes in the implicit price deflator reflect both changes in prices of all goods and services that make up GDP and changes in the composite of GDP. Over time, the implicit price deflator under-states inflation because people tend to shift consumption from goods that have high prices or rapidly increasing prices to goods that have less rapidly increasing prices. Therefore, theoretically, prices of all goods and service could increase and the implicit price deflator could decrease. *See also* PERSONAL INFLATION RATE.

GENERAL ACCOUNT Federal Reserve Board term for brokerage customer mar-gin accounts subject to REGULATION T, which covers extensions of credit by bro-kers for the purchase and short sale of securities. The Fed requires that all transactions in which the broker advances credit to the customer be made in this account. *See also* MARGIN ACCOUNT.

GENERAL AGREEMENT ON TARIFFS AND TRADE (GATT) United Nations-associated international treaty organization headquartered in Geneva that works to eliminate barriers to trade between nations. In December 1994 Congress approved a pact that reduced tariffs, enhanced international copyright protections, and generally liberalized trade.

GENERAL LEDGER formal ledger containing all the financial statement accounts of a business. It contains offsetting debit and credit accounts, the totals of which are proved by a trial balance. Certain accounts in the general ledger, termed *control accounts,* summarize the detail booked on separate subsidiary ledgers.

GENERAL LIEN LIEN against an individual that excludes real property. The lien carries the right to seize personal property to satisfy a debt. The property seized need not be the property that gave rise to the debt.

GENERAL LOAN AND COLLATERAL AGREEMENT continuous agreement under which a securities broker-dealer borrows from a bank against listed secu-rities to buy or carry inventory, finance the underwriting of new issues, or carry the margin accounts of clients. Synonymous with *broker's loan. See also* BROKER LOAN RATE; MARGIN ACCOUNT; UNDERWRITE.

GENERALLY ACCEPTED ACCOUNTING PRINCIPLES (GAAP) conven-tions, rules, and procedures that define accepted accounting practice, including broad guidelines as well as detailed procedures. The basic doctrine was set forth by the Accounting Principles Board of the American Institute of Certified Public Accountants, which was superseded in 1973 by the FINANCIAL ACCOUNTING STAN-DARDS BOARD (FASB), an independent self-regulatory organization.

GENERAL MORTGAGE mortgage covering all the mortgageable properties of a borrower and not restricted to any particular piece of property. Such a blanket mortgage can be lower in priority of claim in liquidation than one or more other mortgages on specific parcels.

GENERAL OBLIGATION BOND municipal bond backed by the FULL FAITH AND CREDIT (which includes the taxing and further borrowing power) of a municipality. A *GO bond,* as it is known, is repaid with general revenue and borrowings, in contrast to the revenue from a specific facility built with the borrowed funds, such as a tunnel or a sewer system. *See also* REVENUE BOND.

GENERAL PARTNER

1. one of two or more partners who are jointly and severally responsible for the debts of a partnership.
2. managing partner of a LIMITED PARTNERSHIP, who is responsible for the operations of the partnership and, ultimately, any debts taken on by the partnership. The general partner's liability is unlimited. In a real estate partnership, the general partner will pick the properties to be bought and will manage them. In an oil and gas partnership, the general partner will select drilling sites and oversee drilling activity. In return for these services, the general partner collects certain fees and often retains a percentage of ownership in the partnership.

GENERAL REVENUE when used in reference to state and local governments taken separately, the term refers to total revenue less revenue from utilities, sales of alcoholic beverages, and insurance trusts. When speaking of combined state and local total revenue, the term refers only to taxes, charges, and miscellaneous revenue, which avoids the distortion of overlapping intergovernmental revenue.

GENERAL REVENUE SHARING unrestricted funds (which can be used for any purpose) provided by the federal government until 1987 to the 50 states and to more than 38,000 cities, towns, counties, townships, Indian tribes, and Alaskan native villages under the State and Local Fiscal Assistance Act of 1972.

GENERATION-SKIPPING TRANSFER OR TRUST arrangement whereby your principal goes into a TRUST when you die, and transfers to your grandchildren when your children die, but which provides income to your children while they live. Once a major tax loophole for the wealthy because taxes were payable only at your death and your grandchildren's death, now only $1 million can be transferred tax-free to the grandchildren. Otherwise, a special generation-skipping tax—with rates equal to the maximum ESTATE TAX rate—applies to transfers to grandchildren, whether the gifts are direct or from a trust.

GHOSTING illegal manipulation of a company's stock price by two or more market makers. One firm will push a stock's price higher or lower, and the other firms will follow their lead in collusion to drive the stock's price up or down. The practice is called ghosting because the investing public is unaware of this coordinated activity among market makers who are supposed to be competing with each other.

GIC *see* GUARANTEED INVESTMENT CONTRACT.

GIFT INTER VIVOS gift of property from one living person to another, without consideration.

GIFT SPLITTING dividing a gift into $10,000 pieces to avoid GIFT TAX. For example, a husband and wife wanting to give $20,000 to their child will give $10,000 each instead of $20,000 from one parent, so that no gift tax is due.

GIFT TAX graduated tax, levied on the donor of a gift by the federal government and most state governments when assets are passed from one person to another. The more money that is given as a gift, the higher the tax rate. The Economic Recovery Tax Act of 1981 allowed a $10,000 federal gift tax exemption per recipient. This means that $10,000 a year can be given free of gift tax to one person ($20,000 to a married couple). The gift tax is computed on the dollar value of the asset being transferred above the $10,000 exemption level. Gifts between spouses are not subject to gift tax. Many states match the $10,000 gift tax exemption, but some allow a smaller amount to be gifted free of tax.

GILT-EDGED SECURITY stock or bond of a company that has demonstrated over a number of years that it is capable of earning sufficient profits to cover dividends on stocks and interest on bonds with great dependability. The term is used with corporate bonds more often than with stocks, where the term BLUE CHIP is more common.

GILTS bonds issued by the British government. Gilts are the equivalent of Treasury securities in the United States in that they are perceived to have no risk of default. Income earned from investing in gilts is therefore guaranteed. Gilt yields act as the benchmark against which all other British bond yields are measured. Gilt futures are traded on the LONDON INTERNATIONAL FINANCIAL FUTURES EXCHANGE. The name gilt is derived from the original British government certificates, which had gilded edges.

GINNIE MAE nickname for the GOVERNMENT NATIONAL MORTGAGE ASSOCIATION and the securities guaranteed by that agency. *See also* GINNIE MAE PASS-THROUGH.

GINNIE MAE PASS-THROUGH security, backed by a pool of mortgages and guaranteed by the GOVERNMENT NATIONAL MORTGAGE ASSOCIATION (Ginnie Mae), which passes through to investors the interest and principal payments of homeowners. Homeowners make their mortgage payments to the bank or savings and loan that originated their mortgage. After deducting a service charge (usually ½%), the bank forwards the mortgage payments to the pass-through buyers, who may be institutional investors or individuals. Ginnie Mae guarantees that investors will receive timely principal and interest payments even if homeowners do not make mortgage payments on time.
   The introduction of Ginnie Mae pass-throughs has benefited the home mortgage market, since more capital has become available for lending. Investors, who are able to receive high, government-guaranteed interest payments, have also benefited. For investors, however, the rate of principal repayment on a Ginnie Mae pass-through is uncertain. If interest rates fall, principal will be repaid faster, since homeowners will refinance their mortgages. If rates rise, principal will be repaid more slowly, since homeowners will hold onto the underlying mortgages. *See also* HALF-LIFE.

GIVE UP
1. term used in a securities transaction involving three brokers, as illustrated by the following scenario: Broker A, a FLOOR BROKER, executes a buy order for Broker B, another member firm broker who has too much business at the time to execute the order. The broker with whom Broker A completes the transaction (the sell side broker) is Broker C. Broker A "gives up" the name of Broker B, so that the record shows a transaction between Broker B and Broker C even though the trade was actually executed between Broker A and Broker C.
2. another application of the term: A customer of brokerage firm ABC Co. travels out of town and, finding no branch office of ABC, places an order with DEF Co., saying he is an account of ABC. After confirming the account relationship, DEF completes a trade with GHI Co., advising GHI that DEF is acting for ABC ("giving up" ABC's name). ABC will then handle the clearing details of the transaction with GHI. Alternatively, DEF may simply send the customer's order directly to ABC for execution. Whichever method is used, the customer pays only one commission.

GLAMOR STOCK stock with a wide public and institutional following. Glamor stocks achieve this following by producing steadily rising sales and earnings over a long period of time. In bull (rising) markets, glamor stocks tend to rise faster than market averages. Although a glamor stock is often in the category of a BLUE CHIP stock, the glamor is characterized by a higher earnings growth rate.

GLASS-STEAGALL ACT OF 1933 legislation passed by Congress authorizing deposit insurance and prohibiting commercial banks from owning full-service brokerage firms. Under Glass-Steagall, these banks were prohibited from investment banking activities, such as underwriting corporate securities or municipal revenue bonds. The law was designed to insulate bank depositors from the risk involved when a bank deals in securities and to prevent a bank collapse like the one that occurred during the Great Depression. The original separation of commercial and investment banking has been significantly eroded in recent years, however, since banks now own discount brokerage operations, sell mutual funds and can perform some corporate and municipal underwriting operations, and can provide other investment services.

GLOBAL DEPOSITARY RECEIPT receipt for shares in a foreign-based corporation traded in capital markets around the world. While AMERICAN DEPOSITARY RECEIPTS permit foreign corporations to offer shares to American citizens, Global Depositary Receipts (GDRs) allow companies in Europe, Asia, the United States and Latin America to offer shares in many markets around the world. The advantage to the issuing company is that they can raise capital in many markets, as opposed to just their home market. The advantage of GDRs to local investors is that they do not have to buy shares through the issuing company's home exchange, which may be difficult and expensive. In addition, the share price and all dividends are converted into the shareholder's home currency. Many GDRs are issued by companies in emerging markets such as China, India, Brazil, and South Korea and are traded on major stock exchanges, particularly the London SEAQ International Trading system. Because the companies issuing GDRs are not as well established and do not use the same accounting systems as traditional Western corporations, their stocks tend to be more volatile and less liquid.

GLOBAL MUTUAL FUND mutual fund that can invest in stocks and bonds throughout the world. Such funds typically have a portion of their assets in American markets as well as Europe, Asia, and developing countries. Global funds differ from INTERNATIONAL MUTUAL FUNDS, which invest only in non-U.S. securities. The advantage of global funds is that the fund managers can buy stocks or bonds anywhere they think has the best opportunities for high returns. Thus if one market is underperforming, they can shift assets to markets with better potential. Though some global funds invest in both stocks and bonds, most funds specialize in either stocks or bonds.

GNOMES OF ZÜRICH term coined by Labour ministers of Great Britain, during the sterling crisis of 1964, to describe the financiers and bankers in Zürich, Switzerland, who were engaged in foreign exchange speculation.

GNP see GROSS NATIONAL PRODUCT.

GOAL financial objective set by an individual or institution. For example, an individual investor might set a goal to accumulate enough capital to finance a child's college education. A pension fund's goal is to build up enough money to pay pensioners their promised benefits. Investors may also set specific price objectives when buying a security. For example, an investor buying a stock at $30 may set a price goal of $50, at which point he or she will sell shares, or at least reevaluate whether or not to continue holding the stock. Also called *target price*.

GO AROUND term used to describe the process whereby the trading desk at the New York Federal Reserve Bank ("the DESK"), acting on behalf of the FEDERAL OPEN MARKET COMMITTEE, contacts primary dealers for bid and offer prices. Primary dealers are those banks and investment houses approved for direct purchase and sale transactions with the Federal Reserve System in its OPEN MARKET OPERATIONS.

GODFATHER OFFER takeover offer that is so generous that management of the target company is unable to refuse it out of fear of shareholder lawsuits.

GO-GO FUND MUTUAL FUND that invests in highly risky but potentially rewarding stocks. During the 1960s many go-go funds shot up in value, only to fall dramatically later and, in some cases, to go out of business as their speculative investments fizzled.

GOING AHEAD unethical securities brokerage act whereby the broker trades first for his own account before filling his customers' orders. Brokers who go ahead violate the RULES OF FAIR PRACTICE of the National Association of Securities Dealers.

GOING AWAY bonds purchased by dealers for immediate resale to investors, as opposed to bonds purchased *for stock*—that is, to be held in inventory for resale at some future time. The significance of the difference is that bonds bought going away will not overhang the market and cause adverse pressure on prices.

The term is also used in new offerings of serial bonds to describe large purchases, usually by institutional investors, of the bonds in a particular maturity grouping (or series).

GOING-CONCERN VALUE value of a company as an operating business to another company or individual. The excess of going-concern value over asset value, or LIQUIDATING VALUE, is the value of the operating organization as distinct from the value of its assets. In acquisition accounting, going-concern value in excess of asset value is treated as an intangible asset, termed *goodwill*. Goodwill is generally understood to represent the value of a well-respected business name, good customer relations, high employee morale, and other such factors expected to translate into greater than normal earning power. However, because this intangible asset has no independent market or liquidation value, accepted accounting principles require that goodwill be written off over a period of time. The Revenue Reconciliation Act of 1993 provides that goodwill and related intangible assets can be deducted ratably over a 15-year (180-month) period on a straight-line method.

GOING LONG purchasing a stock, bond, or commodity for investment or speculation. Such a security purchase is known as a LONG POSITION. The opposite of going long is GOING SHORT, when an investor sells a security he does not own and thereby creates a SHORT POSITION.

GOING PRIVATE movement from public ownership to private ownership of a company's shares either by the company's repurchase of shares or through purchases by an outside private investor. A company usually goes private when the market price of its shares is substantially below their BOOK VALUE and the opportunity thus exists to buy the assets cheaply. Another motive for going private is to ensure the tenure of existing management by removing the company as a takeover prospect.

GOING PUBLIC securities industry phrase used when a private company first offers its shares to the public. The firm's ownership thus shifts from the hands of a few private stockowners to a base that includes public shareholders. At the moment of going public, the stock is called an INITIAL PUBLIC OFFERING. From that point on, or until the company goes private again, its shares have a MARKET VALUE. *See also* NEW ISSUE; GOING PRIVATE.

GOING SHORT selling a stock or commodity that the seller does not have. An investor who goes short borrows stock from his or her broker, hoping to purchase other shares of it at a lower price. The investor will then replace the borrowed stock with the lower priced stock and keep the difference as profit. *See also* SELL-ING SHORT; GOING LONG.

GOLD BARS bars made out of 99.5% to 99.99% pure gold which can be traded for investment purposes or held by central banks. Gold bars range in size from 400 troy ounces to as little as 1 ounce of gold; an individual can either hold on to these bars or store them in a safe deposit box. Central banks store gold bars weighing 400 troy ounces in vaults. In the United States, gold is stored at a few Federal Reserve banks and Fort Knox, for example. In the past, this gold directly backed the American currency, but now it serves more as a symbolic backing for dollars issued by the Federal Reserve.

GOLD BOND bond backed by gold. Such debt obligations are issued by gold-mining companies, who peg interest payments to the level of gold prices. Investors who buy these bonds therefore anticipate a rising gold price. Silver mining firms similarly issue silver-backed bonds.

GOLDBUG analyst enamored of gold as an investment. Goldbugs usually are wor-ried about possible disasters in the world economy, such as a depression or hyper-inflation, and recommend gold as a HEDGE.

GOLD BULLION gold in its purest form. The metal may be smelted into GOLD COINS or GOLD BARS of different sizes. The price of gold bullion is set by market forces of supply and demand. Twice a day, the latest gold price is fixed at the London GOLD FIXING. Gold bullion is traded in physical form, and also through futures and options contracts. Certain gold-oriented mutual funds also hold small amounts of gold bullion.

GOLD CERTIFICATE paper certificate providing evidence of ownership of gold bullion. An investor not wanting to hold the actual gold in his or her home because of lack of security, for example, may prefer to hold gold in certificate form; the physical gold backing the certificate is held in a secure bank vault. Certificate owners pay a small custodial charge each year to the custodian bank.

GOLD COIN coin minted in gold. Bullion coins are minted by governments and are traded mostly on the value of their gold content. Major gold bullion coins include the American Eagle, the Canadian Maple Leaf, the Mexican Peso, the Australian Kangaroo, and the South African Kruggerand. Other gold coins, called NUMISMATIC COINS, are minted in limited quantity and trade more on the basis of their aesthetic value and rarity, rather than on their gold content. Numismatic coins are sold at a hefty markup to their gold content, and are therefore not as pure a play on gold prices as bullion coins.

GOLDEN BOOT inducement, using maximum incentives and financial benefits, for an older worker to take "voluntary" early retirement, thus circumventing age discrimination laws.

GOLDEN HANDCUFFS contract that ties a broker to a brokerage firm. If the broker stays at the firm, he or she will earn lucrative commissions, bonuses, and other compensation. But if the broker leaves and tries to lure clients to another firm, the broker must promise to give back to the firm much of the compensation received while working there. Golden handcuffs are a response by the brokerage industry to the frequent movement of brokers from one firm to another.

GOLDEN HANDSHAKE generous payment by a company to a director, senior executive, or consultant who is let go before his or her contract expires because of a takeover or other development. See also GOLDEN PARACHUTE.

GOLDEN HELLO bonus paid by a securities firm, usually in England, to get a key employee away from a competing firm.

GOLDEN PARACHUTE lucrative contract given to a top executive to provide lavish benefits in case the company is taken over by another firm, resulting in the loss of the job. A golden parachute might include generous severance pay, stock options, or a bonus. The TAX REFORM ACT OF 1984 eliminated the deductibility of "excess compensation" and imposed an excise tax. The TAX REFORM ACT OF 1986 covered matters of clarification.

GOLD FIXING daily determination of the price of gold by selected gold specialists and bank officials in London, Paris, and Zürich. The price is fixed at 10:30 A.M. and 3:30 P.M. London time every business day, according to the prevailing market forces of supply and demand.

GOLD MUTUAL FUND mutual fund investing in gold mining shares. Some funds limit themselves to shares in North American mining companies, while others can buy shares anywhere in the world, including predominantly South Africa and Australia. Such mutual funds offer investors diversification among many gold mining companies, somewhat reducing risks. Still, such funds tend to be volatile, since the prices of gold mining shares tend to move up or down far more than the price of gold itself. Gold funds also tend to pay dividends, since many gold mining companies pay dividends based on gold sales.

GOLD STANDARD monetary system under which units of currency are convertible into fixed amounts of gold. Such a system is said to be anti-inflationary. The United States has been on the gold standard in the past but was taken off in 1971. See also HARD MONEY.

GOODBYE KISS see GREENMAIL.

GOOD DELIVERY securities industry designation meaning that a certificate has the necessary endorsements and meets all other requirements (signature guarantee, proper denomination, and other qualifications), so that title can be transferred by delivery to the buying broker, who is then obligated to accept it. Exceptions constitute *bad delivery.* See also DELIVERY DATE.

GOOD FAITH DEPOSIT
In general: token amount of money advanced to indicate intent to pursue a contract to completion.
Commodities: initial margin deposit required when buying or selling a futures contract. Such deposits generally range from 2% to 10% of the contract value.
Securities:
1. deposit, usually 25% of a transaction, required by securities firms of individuals who are not known to them but wish to enter orders with them.

2. deposit left with a municipal bond issuer by a firm competing for the under-writing business. The deposit typically equals 1% to 5% of the principal amount of the issue and is refundable to the unsuccessful bidders.

GOOD MONEY

Banking: federal funds, which are good the same day, in contrast to CLEARING HOUSE FUNDS. Clearing house funds are understood in two ways: (1) funds requir-ing three days to clear and (2) funds used to settle transactions on which there is a one-day FLOAT.

Gresham's Law: theory that money of superior intrinsic value, "good money," will eventually be driven out of circulation by money of lesser intrinsic value. *See also* GRESHAM'S LAW.

GOOD-THIS-MONTH ORDER (GTM) order to buy or sell securities (usually at a LIMIT PRICE or STOP PRICE set by the customer) that remains in effect until the end of the month. In the case of a limit price, the customer instructs the broker either to buy at the stipulated limit price or anything lower, or to sell at the limit price or anything higher. In the case of a stop price, the customer instructs the broker to enter a market order once a transaction in the security occurs at the stop price specified.

A variation on the GTM order is the *good-this-week-order* (GTW), which expires at the end of the week if it is not executed.

See also DAY ORDER; GOOD-TILL-CANCELED ORDER; LIMIT ORDER; OPEN ORDER; STOP ORDER.

GOOD THROUGH order to buy or sell securities or commodities at a stated price for a stated period of time, unless canceled, executed, or changed. It is a type of LIMIT ORDER and may be specified GTW (good this week), GTM (GOOD-THIS-MONTH ORDER), or for shorter or longer periods.

GOOD-TILL-CANCELED ORDER (GTC) brokerage customer's order to buy or sell a security, usually at a particular price, that remains in effect until executed or canceled. If the GTC order remains unfilled after a long period of time, a bro-ker will usually periodically confirm that the customer still wants the transaction to occur if the stock reaches the target price. *See also* DAY ORDER; GOOD-THIS-MONTH ORDER; OPEN ORDER; TARGET PRICE.

GOODWILL *see* GOING-CONCERN VALUE.

GOVERNMENT NATIONAL MORTGAGE ASSOCIATION (GNMA) gov-ernment-owned corporation, nicknamed Ginnie Mae, which is an agency of the U.S. Department of Housing and Urban Development. GNMA guarantees, with the full faith and credit of the U.S. Government, full and timely payment of all monthly principal and interest payments on the mortgage-backed PASS-THROUGH SECURITIES of registered holders. The securities, which are issued by private firms, such as MORTGAGE BANKERS and savings institutions, and typically mar-keted through security broker-dealers, represent pools of residential mortgages insured or guaranteed by the Federal Housing Administration (FHA), the Farmer's Home Administration (FmHA), or the Veterans Administration (VA). *See also* FEDERAL HOME LOAN MORTGAGE CORPORATION; FEDERAL NATIONAL MORT-GAGE ASSOCIATION; GINNIE MAE PASS-THROUGH.

GOVERNMENT OBLIGATIONS U.S. government debt instruments (Treasury bonds, bills, notes, savings bonds) the government has pledged to repay. *See* GOVERNMENTS.

GOVERNMENTS
1. securities issued by the U.S. government, such as Treasury bills, bonds, notes, and savings bonds. Governments are the most creditworthy of all debt instruments since they are backed by the FULL FAITH AND CREDIT of the U.S. government, which if necessary can print money to make payments. Also called TREASURIES.
2. debt issues of federal agencies, which are not directly backed by the U.S. government. *See also* GOVERNMENT SECURITIES.

GOVERNMENT SECURITIES securities issued by U.S. government agencies, such as the RESOLUTION FUNDING CORPORATION (REFCORP) or the Federal Land Bank; also called *agency securities*. Although these securities have high credit ratings, they are not considered to be GOVERNMENT OBLIGATIONS and therefore are not directly backed by the FULL FAITH AND CREDIT of the government as TREASURIES are. *See also* AGENCY SECURITIES.

GRACE PERIOD period of time provided in most loan contracts and insurance policies during which default or cancellation will not occur even though payment is due.
Credit cards: number of days between when a credit card bill is sent and when the payment is due without incurring interest charges. Most banks offer credit card holders a 25-day grace period, though some offer more and others fewer days.
Insurance: number of days, typically 30, during which insurance coverage is in force and premiums have not been paid.
Loans: provision in some long-term loans, particularly EUROCURRENCY syndication loans to foreign governments and multinational firms by groups of banks, whereby repayment of principal does not begin until some point well into the lifetime of the loan. The grace period, which can be as long as five years for international transactions for corporations, is an important point of negotiation between a borrower and a lender; borrowers sometimes will accept a higher interest rate to obtain a longer grace period.

GRADUATED CALL WRITING strategy of writing (selling) covered CALL OPTIONS at gradually higher EXERCISE PRICES so that as the price of the underlying stock rises and the options are exercised, the seller winds up with a higher average price than the original exercise price. The premiums naturally rise as the underlying stock rises, representing income to the seller that helps offset the loss if the stock should decline.

GRADUATED LEASE longer-term lease in which payments, instead of being fixed, are adjusted periodically based on appraisals or a benchmark rate, such as increases in the CONSUMER PRICE INDEX.

GRADUATED-PAYMENT MORTGAGE (GPM) mortgage featuring lower monthly payments at first, which steadily rise until they level off after a few years. GPMs, also known as "jeeps," are designed for young couples whose income is expected to grow as their careers advance. A graduated-payment mortgage allows such a family to buy a house that would be unaffordable if mortgage payments started out at a high level. Persons planning to take on such a mortgage must be confident that their income will be able to keep pace with the rising payments. *See also* ADJUSTABLE-RATE MORTGAGE; CONVENTIONAL MORTGAGE; REVERSE-ANNUITY MORTGAGE; VARIABLE-RATE MORTGAGE.

GRADUATED SECURITY security whose listing has been upgraded by moving from one exchange to another—for example, from the American Stock Exchange to the more prestigious New York Stock Exchange, or from a regional exchange to a national exchange. An advantage of such a transfer is to widen trading in the security.

GRAHAM AND DODD METHOD OF INVESTING investment approach outlined in Benjamin Graham and David Dodd's landmark book *Security Analysis,* published in the 1930s. Graham and Dodd founded the modern discipline of security analysis with their work. They believed that investors should buy stocks with undervalued assets and that eventually those assets would appreciate to their true value in the marketplace. Graham and Dodd advocated buying stocks in companies where current assets exceed current liabilities and all long-term debt, and where the stock is selling at a low PRICE/EARNINGS RATIO. They suggested that the stocks be sold after a profit objective of between 50% and 100% was reached, which they assumed would be three years or less from the time of purchase. Analysts today who call themselves Graham and Dodd investors hunt for stocks selling below their LIQUIDATING VALUE and do not necessarily concern themselves with the potential for earnings growth.

GRANDFATHER CLAUSE provision included in a new rule that exempts from the rule a person or business already engaged in the activity coming under regulation. For example, the Financial Accounting Standards Board might adopt a rule effective in 1998 relating, say, to depreciation that, under a grandfather clause, would exempt assets put in service before 1998.

GRANTOR

Investments: options trader who sells a CALL OPTION or a PUT OPTION and collects PREMIUM INCOME for doing so. The grantor sells the right to buy a security at a certain price in the case of a call, and the right to sell at a certain price in the case of a put.

Law: one who executes a deed conveying title to property or who creates a trust. Also called a *settlor.*

GRANTOR RETAINED INCOME TRUST (GRIT) type of TRUST designed to save estate taxes in the event the GRANTOR outlives the trust termination date. Under such a trust, which must be irrevocable and have a life of at least 15 years, the grantor transfers property immediately to the beneficiary but receives income until termination, at which time the beneficiary begins receiving it. At that point the grantor pays a GIFT TAX based on the original value of the gift. When the grantor dies, the gift is added back to the grantor's estate at the value as of the day of the gift, not its (presumably) higher current value.

GRAVEYARD MARKET bear market wherein investors who sell are faced with substantial losses, while potential investors prefer to stay liquid, that is, to keep their money in cash or cash equivalents until market conditions improve. Like a graveyard, those who are in can't get out and those who are out have no desire to get in.

GRAY KNIGHT acquiring company that, acting to advance its own interests, outbids a WHITE KNIGHT but that, not being unfriendly, is preferable to a hostile bidder.

GRAY MARKET

Consumer goods: sale of products by unauthorized dealers, frequently at discounted prices. Consumers who buy gray market goods may find that the manufacturer refuses to honor the product warranty. In some cases, gray market goods may be sold in a country they were not intended for, so, for example, instructions may be in another language than the home market language.

Securities: sale of securities that have not officially been issued yet by a firm that is not a member of the underwriting syndicate. Such trading in the when-issued, or gray, market can provide a good indication of the amount of demand for an upcoming new stock or bond issue.

GREATER FOOL THEORY theory that even though a stock or the market as a whole is FULLY VALUED, speculation is justified because there are enough fools to push prices further upward.

GREENMAIL payment of a premium to a raider trying to take over a company through a proxy contest or other means. Also known as BON VOYAGE BONUS, it is designed to thwart the takeover. By accepting the payment, the raider agrees not to buy any more shares or pursue the takeover any further for a specified number of years. *See also* GOODBYE KISS.

GREEN SHOE clause in an underwriting agreement saying that, in the event of exceptional public demand, the issuer will authorize additional shares for distribution by the syndicate.

GRESHAM'S LAW theory in economics that bad money drives out good money. Specifically, people faced with a choice of two currencies of the same nominal value, one of which is preferable to the other because of metal content or because it resists mutilation, will hoard the good money and spend the bad money, thereby driving the good money out of circulation. The observation is named for Sir Thomas Gresham, master of the mint in the reign of Queen Elizabeth I.

GRIT *see* GRANTOR RETAINED INCOME TRUST (GRIT).

GROSS DOMESTIC PRODUCT (GDP) market value of the goods and services produced by labor and property in the United States. GDP is made up of consumer and government purchases, private domestic investments, and net exports of goods and services. Figures for GDP are released by the Commerce Department on a quarterly basis. Growth of the U.S. economy is measured by the change in inflation-adjusted GDP, or real GDP. Formerly called *Gross National Product.*

GROSS EARNINGS personal taxable income before adjustments made to arrive at ADJUSTED GROSS INCOME.

GROSS ESTATE total value of a person's assets before liabilities such as debts and taxes are deducted. After someone dies, the executor of the will makes an assessment of the stocks, bonds, real estate, and personal possessions that comprise the gross estate. Debts and taxes are paid, as are funeral expenses and estate administration costs. Beneficiaries of the will then receive their portion of the remainder, which is called the *net estate.*

GROSS INCOME total personal income before exclusions and deductions.

GROSS LEASE property lease under which the lessor (landlord) agrees to pay all the expenses normally associated with ownership (insurance, taxes, utilities, repairs). An exception might be that the lessee (tenant) would be required to pay real estate taxes above a stipulated amount or to pay for certain special operating expenses (snow removal, grounds care in the case of a shopping center, or institutional advertising, for example). Gross leases are the most common type of lease contract and are typical arrangements for short-term tenancy. They normally contain no provision for periodic rent adjustments, nor are there preestablished renewal arrangements. *See also* NET LEASE.

GROSS NATIONAL PRODUCT (GNP) *see* GROSS DOMESTIC PRODUCT.

GROSS PER BROKER gross amount of commission revenues attributable to a particular REGISTERED REPRESENTATIVE during a given period. Brokers, who typically keep one third of the commissions they generate, are often expected by their firms to meet productivity quotas based on their gross.

GROSS PROFIT net sales less the COST OF GOODS SOLD. Also called *gross margin*. *See also* NET PROFIT.

GROSS SALES total sales at invoice values, not reduced by customer discounts, returns or allowances, or other adjustments. *See also* NET SALES.

GROSS SPREAD difference (spread) between the public offering price of a security and the price paid by an underwriter to the issuer. The spread breaks down into the manager's fee, the dealer's (or underwriter's) discount, and the selling concession (i.e., the discount offered to a selling group). *See also* CONCESSION; FLOTATION (FLOATATION) COST.

GROUND LEASE lease on the land. Typically, the land will be under a building, which will have its own leases with tenants.

GROUP INSURANCE insurance coverage bought for and provided to a group instead of an individual. For example, an employer may buy disability, health, and term life insurance for its employees at a far better rate than the employees could obtain on their own. Credit unions, trade associations, and other groups may also offer their members preferential group insurance rates. Group insurance is not only advantageous to employees or group members because it is cheaper than they could obtain on their own, but some people may be able to get coverage under the group umbrella when they would be denied coverage individually because of preexisting conditions or other factors.

GROUP OF TEN ten major industrialized countries that try to coordinate monetary and fiscal policies to create a more stable world economic system. The ten are Belgium, Canada, France, Germany, Italy, Japan, the Netherlands, Sweden, the United Kingdom, and the United States. Also known as the *Paris Club*.

GROUP ROTATION tendency of stocks in one industry to outperform and then underperform other industries. This may be due to the economic cycle or what industry is popular or unpopular with investors at any particular time. For example, CYCLICAL stocks in the auto, paper, or steel industry may be group leaders when the economy is showing robust growth, while stocks of stable-demand firms such as drug or food companies may be market leaders in a recession. Alternatively, investor demand for stocks in certain industries, such as biotechnology, computer software, or real estate investment trusts may rise and fall because of enthusiasm or disappointment with the group, creating rotation into or out of such stocks. Market analysts watch which industry group is coming into and going out of vogue in recommending stocks that might lead or lag in coming months.

GROUP SALES term used in securities underwriting that refers to block sales made to institutional investors. The securities come out of a syndicate "pot" with credit for the sale prorated among the syndicate members in proportion to their original allotments.

GROUP UNIVERSAL LIFE POLICY (GULP) UNIVERSAL LIFE INSURANCE offered on a group basis, and therefore more cheaply than one could obtain it personally, to employees and, sometimes, their family members.

GROWING EQUITY MORTGAGE (GEM) mortgage with a fixed interest rate and growing payments. This technique allows the homeowner to build equity in the underlying home faster than if they made the same mortgage payment for the life of the loan. Borrowers who take on GEM loans should be confident in their ability to make higher payments over time based on their prospects for rising income.

GROWTH AND INCOME FUND MUTUAL FUND that seeks earnings growth as well as income. These funds invest mainly in the common stock of companies with a history of capital gains but that also have a record of consistent dividend payments.

GROWTH FUND mutual fund that invests in growth stocks. The goal is to provide capital appreciation for the fund's shareholders over the long term. Growth funds are more volatile than more conservative income or money market funds. They tend to rise faster than conservative funds in bull (advancing) markets and to drop more sharply in bear (falling) markets. *See also* GROWTH STOCK.

GROWTH RATE percentage rate at which the economy, stocks, or earnings are growing. The economic growth rate is normally determined by the growth of the GROSS DOMESTIC PRODUCT. Individual companies try to establish a rate at which their earnings grow over time. Firms with long-term earnings growth rates of more than 15% are considered fast-growing companies. Analysts also apply the term *growth rate* to specific financial aspects of a company's operations, such as dividends, sales, assets, and market share. Analysts use growth rates to compare one company to another within the same industry.

GROWTH STOCK stock of a corporation that has exhibited faster-than-average gains in earnings over the last few years and is expected to continue to show high levels of profit growth. Over the long run, growth stocks tend to outperform slower-growing or stagnant stocks. Growth stocks are riskier investments than average stocks, however, since they usually sport higher price/earnings ratios and make little or no dividend payments to shareholders. *See also* PRICE/EARNINGS RATIO.

G-7 FINANCE MINISTERS the finance ministers of the seven largest industrial countries: Canada, France, Germany, Great Britain, Italy, Japan, and the United States. In recent years, the Russian finance minister has also been invited to participate in G-7 meetings. Such meetings take place at least once a year and are important in coordinating economic policy among the major industrial countries. The political leaders of the G-7 countries also meet once a year, usually in July, at the Economic Summit, which is held in one of the seven countries.

GUARANTEE to take responsibility for payment of a debt or performance of some obligation if the person primarily liable fails to perform. A guarantee is a CONTINGENT LIABILITY of the guarantor—that is, it is a potential liability not recognized in accounts until the outcome becomes probable in the opinion of the company's accountant.

GUARANTEED BOND bond on which the principal and interest are guaranteed by a firm other than the issuer. Such bonds are nearly always railroad bonds, arising out of situations where one road has leased the road of another and the security holders of the leased road require assurance of income in exchange for giving up control of the property. Guaranteed securities involved in such situations may also include preferred or common stocks when dividends are guaranteed. Both guaranteed stock and guaranteed bonds become, in effect, DEBENTURE (unsecured) bonds of the guarantor, although the status of the stock may be questionable in the event of LIQUIDATION. In any event, if the guarantor enjoys stronger credit than the railroad whose securities are being guaranteed, the securities have greater value.

Guaranteed bonds may also arise out of parent-subsidiary relationships where bonds are issued by the subsidiary with the parent's guarantee.

GUARANTEED INSURABILITY feature offered as an option in life and health insurance policies that enables the insured to add coverage at specified future times and at standard rates without evidence of insurability.

GUARANTEED INVESTMENT CONTRACT contract between an insurance company and a corporate profit-sharing or pension plan that guarantees a specific rate of return on the invested capital over the life of the contract. Many defined contribution plans, such as 401(k) and 403(b) plans, offer guaranteed investment contracts as investment options to employees. Although the insurance company takes all market, credit, and interest rate risks on the investment portfolio, it can profit if its return exceeds the guaranteed amount. Only the insurance company backs the guarantee, not any governmental agency, so if the insurer fails, it is possible that there could be a default on the contract. For pension and profit-sharing plans, guaranteed investment contracts, also known as GICs, are a conservative way of assuring beneficiaries that their money will achieve a certain rate of return. *See also* BANK INVESTMENT CONTRACT.

GUARANTEED RENEWABLE POLICY INSURANCE policy that requires the insurer to renew the policy for a period specified in the contract provided premiums are paid in a timely fashion. The insurer cannot make any changes in the provisions of the policy other than a change in the premium rate for all insureds in the same class.

GUARANTEED REPLACEMENT COST COVERAGE INSURANCE policy that pays for the full cost of replacing damaged property without a deduction for depreciation and without a dollar limit. This policy is different from an actual cash value policy, which takes into account depreciation for lost and damaged items, if the damage resulted from an insured peril.

GUARANTEED STOCK *see* GUARANTEED BOND.

GUARANTEE LETTER letter by a commercial bank that guarantees payment of the EXERCISE PRICE of a client's PUT OPTION (the right to sell a given security at a particular price within a specified period) if or when a notice indicating its exercise, called an assignment notice, is presented to the option seller (writer).

GUARANTEE OF SIGNATURE certificate issued by a bank or brokerage firm vouching for the authenticity of a person's signature. Such a document may be necessary when stocks, bonds, or other registered securities are transferred from a seller to a buyer. Banks also require guarantees of signature before they will process certain transactions.

GUARDIAN individual who has the legal right to care for another person as a parent or to act as an administrator of the assets of a person declared incompetent for mental or physical reasons. Guardians can be *testamentary,* meaning appointed in a parent's will; *general,* meaning having the general responsibility to care for another person and that person's estate; or *special,* meaning the guardian has limited authority, such as half the responsibility of a general guardian but not the other.

GULP *see* GROUP UNIVERSAL LIFE POLICY (GULP).

GUN JUMPING
1. trading securities on information before it becomes publicly disclosed.
2. illegally soliciting buy orders in an underwriting, before a Securities and Exchange Commission REGISTRATION is complete.

GUNSLINGER aggressive portfolio manager who buys speculative stocks, often on margin. In the great bull market of the 1960s, several hot fund managers gained reputations and had huge followings as gunslingers by producing enormous returns while taking great risks. However, the bear market of the early 1970s caused many of these gunslingers to lose huge amounts of money, and in most cases, their followings. The term is still used when referring to popular managers who take big risks in search of high returns.

h

HAIRCUT securities industry term referring to the formulas used in the valuation of securities for the purpose of calculating a broker-dealer's net capital. The haircut varies according to the class of a security, its market risk, and the time to maturity. For example, cash equivalent GOVERNMENTS could have a 0% haircut, equities could have an average 30% haircut, and fail positions (securities with past due delivery) with little prospect of settlement could have a 100% haircut. *See also* CASH EQUIVALENTS; FAIL POSITION.

HALF-LIFE point in time in which half the principal has been repaid in a mortgage-backed security guaranteed or issued by the GOVERNMENT NATIONAL MORTGAGE ASSOCIATION, the FEDERAL NATIONAL MORTGAGE ASSOCIATION, or the FEDERAL HOME LOAN MORTGAGE CORPORATION. Normally, it is assumed that such a security has a half-life of 12 years. But specific mortgage pools can have vastly longer or shorter half-lives, depending on interest rate trends. If interest rates fall, more homeowners will refinance their mortgages, meaning that principal will be paid off more quickly, and half-lives will drop. If interest rates rise, homeowners will hold onto their mortgages longer than anticipated, and half-lives will rise.

HALF-STOCK common or preferred stock with a $50 par value instead of the more conventional $100 par value.

HAMMERING THE MARKET intense selling of stocks by those who think prices are inflated. Speculators who think the market is about to drop, and therefore sell short, are said to be hammering the market. *See also* SELLING SHORT.

HANDS-OFF INVESTOR investor willing to take a passive role in the management of a corporation. An individual or corporation with a large stake in another company may decide to adopt a "hands-off" policy if it is satisfied with the current performance of management. However, if management falters, it may become more actively involved in corporate strategy.

HANDS-ON INVESTOR investor who takes an active role in the management of the company whose stock he or she has bought.

HANG SENG INDEX the major indicator of stock market performance in Hong Kong. The index is comprised of 33 companies, divided into four sub-indices: financial (4), property (9), utilities (6), commerce and industry (14). It is computed on an arithmetic basis, weighted by market capitalization, and strongly influenced by large capitalization stocks such as Hongkong Bank, Hang Seng Bank, Hongkong Land and Cheung Kong.

HARD DOLLARS actual payments made by a customer for services, including research, provided by a brokerage firm. For instance, if a broker puts together a financial plan for a client, the fee might be $1000 in hard dollars. This contrasts with SOFT DOLLARS, which refers to compensation by way of the commissions a broker would receive if he were to carry out any trades called for in that financial plan. Brokerage house research is sold for either hard or soft dollars.

HARD MONEY (HARD CURRENCY)
1. currency in which there is widespread confidence. It is the currency of an economically and politically stable country, such as the U.S. or Switzerland. Countries that have taken out loans in hard money generally must repay them in hard money.
2. gold or coins, as contrasted with paper currency, which is considered *soft money*. Some hard-money enthusiasts advocate a return to the GOLD STANDARD as a method of reducing inflation and promoting economic growth.

HEAD AND SHOULDERS patterns resembling the head and shoulders outline of a person, which is used to chart stock price trends. The pattern signals the reversal of a trend. As prices move down to the right shoulder, a head and shoulders top is formed, meaning that prices should be falling. A reverse head and shoulders pattern has the head at the bottom of the chart, meaning that prices should be rising.

HEAD AND SHOULDERS

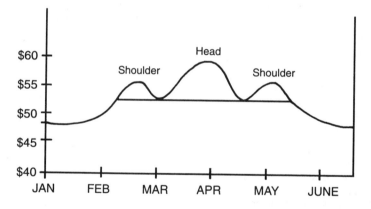

HEAD OF HOUSEHOLD tax filing status available in the tax code to individuals who provide more than half of the financial support to their household during the tax year. Heads of household can be married or single, as long as they support dependent children or grandchildren, parents, or other close relatives living at home. Those qualifying for head-of-household status pay the same tax rates as single and married couples filing jointly, but the rates apply at different levels of income. For example, a head of household pays a 28% tax rate on taxable income between $29,601 and $76,400, while a single pays the same tax rate on income between $22,101 and $53,500 and a married couple filing jointly pays 28% on $36,901 to $89,150.

HEALTH INSURANCE in popular usage, any insurance plan that covers medical expenses or health care services, including HMOs, insured plans, preferred provider organizations, etc. In insurance, protection against loss by sickness or bodily injury, in which sense it is synonymous with accident and health, accident and sickness, accident, or disability income insurance.

HEAVY MARKET stock, bond, or commodity market with falling prices resulting from a larger supply of offers to sell than bids to buy.

HEDGE/HEDGING strategy used to offset investment risk. A perfect hedge is one eliminating the possibility of future gain or loss.

A stockholder worried about declining stock prices, for instance, can hedge his or her holdings by buying a PUT OPTION on the stock or selling a CALL OPTION. Someone owning 100 shares of XYZ stock, selling at $70 per share, can hedge his position by buying a put option giving him the right to sell 100 shares at $70 at any time over the next few months. This investor must pay a certain amount of money, called a PREMIUM, for these rights. If XYZ stock falls during that time, the investor can exercise his option—that is, sell the stock at $70—thereby preserving the $70 value of the XYZ holdings. The same XYZ stockholder can also hedge his position by selling a call option. In such a transaction, he sells the right to buy XYZ stock at $70 per share for the next few months. In return, he receives a premium. If XYZ stock falls in price, that premium income will offset to some extent the drop in value of the stock.

SELLING SHORT is another widely used hedging technique.

Investors often try to hedge against inflation by purchasing assets that will rise in value faster than inflation, such as gold, real estate, or other tangible assets.

Large commercial firms that want to be assured of the price they will receive or pay for a commodity will hedge their position by buying and selling simultaneously in the FUTURES MARKET. For example, Hershey's, the chocolate company, will hedge its supplies of cocoa in the futures market to limit the risk of a rise in cocoa prices.

Managers of large pools of money such as pension and mutual funds frequently hedge their exposure to currency or interest rate risk by buying or selling futures or options contracts. For example, a GLOBAL MUTUAL FUND manager with a large position in Japanese stocks who thinks the Japanese yen is about to fall in value against the U.S. dollar may buy futures or options on the Japanese yen to offset the projected loss on the currency.

HEDGE CLAUSE disclaimer seen in market letters, security research reports, or other printed matter having to do with evaluating investments, which purports to absolve the writer from responsibility for the accuracy of information obtained from usually reliable sources. Despite such clauses, which may mitigate liability, writers may still be charged with negligence in their use of information. Typical language of a hedge clause: "The information furnished herein has been obtained from sources believed to be reliable, but its accuracy is not guaranteed."

HEDGED TENDER SELLING SHORT a portion of the shares being tendered to protect against a price drop in the event all shares tendered are not accepted. For example, ABC Company or another company wishing to acquire ABC Company announces a TENDER OFFER at $52 a share when ABC shares are selling at a market price of $40. The market price of ABC will now rise to near the tender price of $52. An investor wishing to sell all his or her 2000 shares at $52 will tender 2000 shares, but cannot be assured all shares will be accepted. To lock in the $52 price on the tendered shares the investor thinks might not be accepted—say half of them or 1000 shares—he or she will sell short that many shares. Assuming the investor has guessed correctly and only 1000 shares are accepted, when the tender offer expires and the market price of ABC begins to drop, the investor will still have sold all 2000 shares for $52 or close to it—half to the tenderer and the other half when the short sale is consummated.

HEDGE FUND private investment partnership (for U.S. investors) or an off-shore investment corporation (for non-U.S. or tax-exempt investors) in which the general partner has made a substantial personal investment, and whose offering memorandum allows for the fund to take both long and short positions, use leverage and derivatives, and invest in many markets. Hedge funds often take large risks on speculative strategies, including PROGRAM TRADING, SELLING SHORT, SWAPS, and ARBITRAGE. A fund need not employ all of these tools all of the time; it must merely have them at its disposal. Since hedge funds are not limited to buying securities, they can potentially profit in any market environment, including one with sharply declining prices. Because they move billions of dollars in and out of markets quickly, hedge funds can have a significant impact on the day-to-day trading developments in the stock, bond, and futures markets.

Hedge funds entitle the general partner to an additional incentive management fee based upon positive returns—the higher the returns, the higher their fee. Hedge funds require that 65% of all investors be of the *accredited* type, defined as an individual or couple who have a net worth of at least $1 million, or an individual who had income in the previous year of at least $200,000, or a couple with at least $300,000 of income in the previous year. In reality, though, an investor needs much more than that.

The funds also require substantial minimum investments that can make it hard even for accredited investors to ante up. Minimums typically range from about $250,000 to $10 million. An investor gives up liquidity in hedge funds. They typically have a one-year lock-up for first-time investors.

HEDGE WRAPPER options strategy where the holder of a long position in an underlying stock buys an OUT OF THE MONEY put and sells an out of the money call. It defines a range where the stock will be sold at expiration of the option, whatever way the stock moves. The maximum profit is made if the call is exercised at expiration, since the holder gets the strike price plus any dividends. The maximum loss occurs if the put option is exercised, and represents the cost of the hedge wrapper less the strike price plus dividends received. The cost of the hedge wrapper less dividends received is the breakeven point. The strategy produces a loss whenever the breakeven price is higher than the strike price of the call.

HEIR one who inherits some or all of the estate of a deceased person by virtue of being in the direct line (*heir of the body*), or being designated in a will or by a legal authority (*heir at law*).

HELSINKI STOCK EXCHANGE smallest of the Nordic exchanges. Electronic trading began in 1992 with the switch to computer registered book entries. The Helsinki Stock Exchange Automated Trading System permits all 19 members to receive a feed from terminals in their own offices. The HEX Index includes all shares quoted on the Helsinki Stock Exchange (HSE), and share price indices also are computed for industry groups. The rapidly expanding derivatives market is traded on two options exchanges, open to international investors. The Finnish Options Market (FOM) trades equity and currency derivatives, offering standardized options and forward contracts on the Finnish Options Index (FOX). Trading is conducted Monday through Friday, 8:30 A.M.–5:05 P.M.

HEMLINE THEORY whimsical idea that stock prices move in the same general direction as the hemlines of women's dresses. Short skirts in the 1920s and 1960s were considered bullish signs that stock prices would rise, whereas longer dresses in the 1930s and 1940s were considered bearish (falling) indicators. Despite its sometimes uncanny way of being prophetic, the hemline theory has remained more in the area of wishful thinking than serious market analysis.

HIBOR acronym for *Hong Kong Interbank Offer Rate,* the annualized offer rate paid by banks for Hong Kong dollar-denominated three-month deposits. It acts as a benchmark for many interest rates throughout the Far East.

HIDDEN LOAD sales charge which may not be immediately apparent to an investor. For example, a 12b-1 MUTUAL FUND assesses an annual asset base charge of up to 0.75% to cover marketing, distribution, and promotion expenses incurred by the fund. Even though it has been disclosed in the prospectus, many investors do not realize that they are paying this load. The sales charges levied on insurance policies are also hidden, because they are not explicitly disclosed to customers, and are instead subtracted from premiums paid by policyholders.

HIDDEN VALUES assets owned by a company but not yet reflected in its stock price. For example, a manufacturing firm may own valuable real estate that could be sold at a much higher price than it appears on the company's books, which is usually the price at which the real estate was purchased. Other undervalued assets that could have significant value include patents, trademarks, or exclusive contracts. Value-oriented money managers search for stocks with hidden values on their balance sheet in the hope that some day, those values will be realized through a higher stock price either by actions of the current management or by a takeover.

HIGH CREDIT
Banking: maximum amount of loans outstanding recorded for a particular customer.
Finance: the highest amount of TRADE CREDIT a particular company has received from a supplier at one time.

HIGH CURRENT INCOME MUTUAL FUND mutual fund with the objective of paying high income to shareholders. Such funds usually take higher risks than more conservative, but lower-yielding funds in order to provide an above-market rate of current yield. For example, JUNK BOND funds buy corporate bonds with below investment grade credit ratings in order to pay higher levels of income to shareholders than would be available from Treasury or high-quality corporate bonds. Another example of a high current income mutual fund is an international bond fund.

HIGH FLYER high-priced and highly speculative stock that moves up and down sharply over a short period. The stock of unproven high-technology companies might be high flyers, for instance.

HIGH-GRADE BOND bond rated triple-A or double-A by Standard & Poor's or Moody's rating services. *See also* RATING.

HIGHJACKING Japanese term for a TAKEOVER.

HIGHLY CONFIDENT LETTER letter from an investment banking firm that it is "highly confident" that it will be able to arrange financing for a securities deal. This letter might be used to finance a leveraged buyout or multibillion-dollar takeover offer, for example. The board of directors of the target firm might request a highly confident letter in evaluating whether a proposed takeover can be financed. After the letter has been issued and the deal approved, the investment bankers will attempt to line up financing from banks, private investors, stock and bond offerings, and other sources. Though the investment banker professes to be highly confident he can arrange financing, the letter is not an iron-clad guarantee of his ability to do so.

HIGHLY LEVERAGED TRANSACTION (HLT) loan, usually by a bank, to an already highly LEVERAGED COMPANY.

HIGH-PREMIUM CONVERTIBLE DEBENTURE bond with a long-term, high-premium, common stock conversion feature and also offering a fairly competitive interest rate. Premium refers in this case to the difference between the market value of the CONVERTIBLE security and the value at which it is convertible into common stock. Such bonds are designed for bond-oriented portfolios, with the "KICKER," the added feature of convertibility to stock, intended as an inflation hedge.

HIGHS stocks that have hit new high prices in daily trading for the current 52-week period. (They are listed as "highs" in daily newspapers.) Technical analysts consider the ratio between new highs and new LOWS in the stock market to be significant for pointing out stock market trends.

HIGH-TECH STOCK stock of companies involved in high-technology fields (computers, semiconductors, biotechnology, robotics, electronics). Successful high-tech stocks have above-average earnings growth and therefore typically very volatile stock prices.

HIGH-TICKET ITEMS items with a significant amount of value, such as jewelry and furs. Most standard homeowner's/renter's policies have limits on specific types of high-ticket items. Most policies have a limit of $1000–$2000 for all jewelry and furs. To provide appropriate coverage for these items, they should be scheduled separately in the form of a FLOATER or endorsement. Also called *valuables.*

HIGH-YIELD BOND bond that has RATING of BB or lower and that pays a higher yield to compensate for its greater risk. *See also* JUNK BOND.

HISTORICAL COST accounting principle requiring that all financial statement items be based on original cost or acquisition cost. The dollar is assumed to be stable for the period involved.

HISTORICAL TRADING RANGE price range within which a stock, bond, or commodity has traded since going public. A VOLATILE stock will have a wider trading range than a more conservative stock. Technical analysts see the top of a historical range as the RESISTANCE LEVEL and the bottom as the SUPPORT LEVEL. They consider it highly significant if a security breaks above the resistance level or below the support level. Usually such a move is interpreted to mean that the security will go onto new highs or new lows, thus expanding its historical trading range.

HISTORICAL YIELD yield provided by a mutual fund, typically a money market fund, over a particular period of time. For instance, a money market fund may advertise that its historical yield averaged 10% over the last year.

HISTORIC REHABILITATION LIMITED PARTNERSHIP partnership designed to take advantage of the historic rehabilitation tax credit available in the Internal Revenue Code. These partnerships rehabilitate structures to their original condition, and limited partners receive credits that reduce partners' taxes dollar for dollar. For example, $5000 in tax credits reduces the amount of taxes due by $5000. Tax credits of 20% are available if the partnership rehabilitates a historic structure built before 1936. Tax credits of 10% are available for the restoration of buildings built before 1936 that are not certified as historic by the Department of the Interior. Historic rehabilitation limited partnerships can be assembled by local builders and investors, or by professional general partners specializing in such projects.

HIT informally, a significant securities loss or a development having a major impact on corporate profits, such as a large WRITE-OFF. Term is also used in the opposite sense to describe an investing success, similar to a "hit" in show business.

HIT THE BID to accept the highest price offered for a stock. For instance, if a stock's ask price is $50¼ and the current bid price is $50, a seller will hit the bid if he or she accepts $50 a share.

HOLD
Banking: retaining an asset in an account until the item has been collected. For example, a hold can be put on a certain amount of funds in a checking account if a certified check has been issued for that amount.

Securities: maintaining ownership of a stock, bond, mutual fund, or other security for a long period of time. Proponents of the BUY AND HOLD STRATEGY try to buy high-quality securities which they hope will grow in value over many years. By holding for a long time, the investor can delay capital gains taxes until the position is sold many years in the future.

Securities analysts also issue a HOLD recommendation if they are not enthusiastic enough about a security to recommend purchasing it, yet are not pessimistic enough to recommend selling it. However, many analysts who downgrade a stock from a buy to a hold rating are in fact saying that investors should sell the stock, since there are better opportunities to invest elsewhere.

HOLDER OF RECORD owner of a company's securities as recorded on the books of the issuing company or its TRANSFER AGENT as of a particular date. Dividend declarations, for example, always specify payability to holders of record as of a specific date.

HOLDING COMPANY corporation that owns enough voting stock in another corporation to influence its board of directors and therefore to control its policies and management. A holding company need not own a majority of the shares of its subsidiaries or be engaged in similar activities. However, to gain the benefits of tax consolidation, which include tax-free dividends to the parent and the ability to share operating losses, the holding company must own 80% or more of the subsidiary's voting stock.

Among the advantages of a holding company over a MERGER as an approach to expansion are the ability to control sizeable operations with fractional ownership and commensurately small investment; the somewhat theoretical ability to take risks through subsidiaries with liability limited to the subsidiary corporation; and the ability to expand through unobtrusive purchases of stock, in contrast to having to obtain the approval of another company's shareholders.

Among the disadvantages of a holding company are partial multiple taxation when less than 80% of a subsidiary is owned, plus other special state and local taxes; the risk of forced DIVESTITURE (it is easier to force dissolution of a holding company than to separate merged operations); and the risks of negative leverage effects in excessive PYRAMIDING.

The following types of holding companies are defined in special ways and subject to particular legislation: public utility holding company (*see* PUBLIC UTILITY HOLDING COMPANY ACT), BANK HOLDING COMPANY, railroad holding company, and air transport holding company.

HOLDING PERIOD length of time an asset is held by its owner. Effective in 1994, capital assets held for 12 months or more qualify for special CAPITAL GAINS TAX treatment. See also ANTICIPATED HOLDING PERIOD; INVESTMENT LETTER.

HOLDING THE MARKET entering the market with sufficient buy orders to create price support for a security or commodity, for the purpose of stabilizing a downward trend. The Securities and Exchange Commission views "holding" as a form of illegal manipulation except in the case of stabilization of a new issue cleared with the SEC beforehand.

HOME BANKING service offered by banks allowing consumers and small businesses to perform many banking functions at home through computers, telephones, and cable television links to the bank, thereby providing them with a number of convenience services. Bank customers are able to shift money between accounts, apply for loans and make loan payments, pay bills, check balances, and buy and sell securities, among other services. As home banking becomes easier and more convenient to use, more and more consumers sign up for it. It offers the advantages of privacy, speed, accuracy and the ability to perform transactions at any time. Most banks charge an extra fee for access to home banking services. Home banking does not currently offer the ability to obtain cash, for which customers must still visit a bank teller or automatic teller machine.

HOMEOWNER'S EQUITY ACCOUNT credit line offered by banks, savings and loans, brokerage firms, and other mortgage lenders allowing a homeowner to tap the built-up equity in his or her home. Such an account is, in effect, a REVOLVING CREDIT second mortgage, which can be accessed with the convenience of a check. Most lenders will provide a line of credit up to 70% or 80% of the appraised value of a home, minus any outstanding first mortgage debt. When a homeowner receives the loan, a LIEN is automatically placed against the house; the lien is removed when the loan is repaid. A homeowner's equity account often carries a lower interest rate than a second mortgage; typically, the rate is tied to the PRIME RATE. Many banks charge one or two percentage points higher than the prime rate. Most such programs require an initial sign-up fee and payment of additional fees called POINTS when the credit line is tapped. Interest on such loans is tax deductible up to $100,000, though a tax specialist should be consulted for the latest information. See also SECOND MORTGAGE LENDING.

HOMEOWNER'S INSURANCE POLICY policy protecting a homeowner against property and casualty perils. A basic HO-3 policy (HO stands for homeowner's) is a standard policy and the most comprehensive. It will cover damage to the home from natural causes such as fire, lightning, windstorms, hail, rain, or volcanic eruption. In addition, man-made disasters such as riots, vandalism, damage from cars or airplanes, explosions, and theft will also be reimbursed. Damage caused by falling objects, the weight of ice, snow or sleet, freezing of plumbing, heating or air conditioning systems, electrical discharges, or the rupture of water heating or protective sprinkler systems also fall under the HO-3 policy. Flood, earthquake, war, and nuclear accident are not covered; flood and earthquake insurance can be purchased separately. Other types of homeowner's policies include HO-4 for renters (which also could include co-ops), HO-6 for condominium owners, and HO-8 for older homes. In general, homeowners should try to purchase coverage that will pay for the replacement of damaged or stolen items at current market prices, not at the prices for which those items may have been acquired years ago. There are dollar limits for high-ticket items such as jewelry. A FLOATER or an endorsement, purchased separately, can provide the additional coverage needed.

The average homeowner's or renter's policy provides approximately $100,000 of liability protection. A special policy is required for homeowner's business risk coverage. Home business owners need both property and liability insurance, since the homeowner's policy provides only limited coverage for business equipment, in most cases up to $2,500 for business equipment in the home and $250 away from the home.

Most mortgage lenders require homeowners to obtain adequate insurance coverage before they agree to provide a mortgage.

HOME RUN large gain by an investor in a short period of time. Someone who aims to hit an investment home run may be looking for a potential TAKEOVER target, for example, since takeover bids result in sudden price spurts. Such investing is inherently more risky than the strategy of holding for the long term.

HORIZON ANALYSIS method of measuring the discounted cash flow (time-adjusted return) from an investment, using time periods or series *(horizons)* that differ from the investment's contractual maturity. The horizon date might be the end of a BUSINESS CYCLE or some other date determined in the perspective of the investor's overall portfolio requirements. Horizon analysis calculations, which include reinvestment assumptions, permit comparison with alternative investments that is more realistic in terms of individual portfolio requirements than traditional YIELD-TO-MATURITY calculations.

HORIZONTAL MERGER *see* MERGER.

HORIZONTAL PRICE MOVEMENT movement within a narrow price range over an extended period of time. A stock would have a horizontal price movement if it traded between $47 and $51 for over six months, for instance. Also known as *sideways price movement. See also* FLAT MARKET.

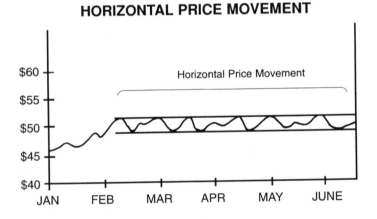

HORIZONTAL PRICE MOVEMENT

HORIZONTAL SPREAD options strategy that involves buying and selling the same number of options contracts with the same exercise price, but with different maturity dates; also called a CALENDAR SPREAD. For instance, an investor might buy ten XYZ call options with a striking price of $70 and a maturity date of October. At the same time, he would sell ten XYZ call options with the same striking price of $70 but a maturity date of July. The investor hopes to profit by moves in XYZ stock by this means.

HOSPITAL REVENUE BOND bond issued by a municipal or state agency to finance construction of a hospital or nursing home. The latter is then operated under lease by a not-for-profit organization or a for-profit corporation such as Hospital Corporation of America. A hospital revenue bond, which is a variation on the INDUSTRIAL DEVELOPMENT BOND, is tax exempt, but there may be limits to the exemption. *See also* REVENUE BOND.

HOSTILE TAKEOVER takeover of a company against the wishes of current management and the board of directors. This takeover may be attempted by another company or by a well-financed RAIDER. If the price offered is high enough, shareholders may vote to accept the offer even if management resists and claims that the company is actually worth even more. If the acquirer raises the price high enough, management may change its attitude, converting the hostile takeover into a friendly one. Management has many weapons at its disposal to fend off a hostile takeover, such as GREENMAIL, POISON PILLS, the SCORCHED EARTH POLICY, and SUICIDE PILLS, among others. Also called *unfriendly takeover. See also* TAKEOVER.

HOT ISSUE newly issued stock that is in great public demand. Hot issue stocks usually shoot up in price at their initial offering, since there is more demand than there are shares available. Special National Association of Securities Dealers rules apply to the distribution of hot issues by the selling investment banking syndicate. *See also* UNDERWRITE.

HOT MONEY investment funds capriciously seeking high, short-term yields. Borrowers attracting hot money, such as banks issuing high-yielding CERTIFICATES OF DEPOSIT, should be prepared to lose it as soon as another borrower offers a higher rate.

HOT STOCK
1. stock that has been stolen.
2. newly issued stock that rises quickly in price. *See* HOT ISSUE.

HOUSE
1. firm or individual engaged in business as a broker-dealer in securities and/or investment banking and related services.
2. nickname for the London Stock Exchange.

HOUSE ACCOUNT account handled at the main office of a brokerage firm or managed by an executive of the firm; in other words, an account distinguished from one that is normally handled by a salesperson in the territory. Ordinarily, a salesperson does not receive a commission on a house account, even though the account may actually be in his or her territory.

HOUSE CALL brokerage house notification that the customer's EQUITY in a MARGIN ACCOUNT is below the maintenance level. If the equity declines below that point, a broker must call the client, asking for more cash or securities. If the client fails to deliver the required margin, his or her position will be liquidated. House call limits are usually higher than limits mandated by the National Association of Securities Dealers (NASD), a self-regulatory group, and the major exchanges with jurisdiction over these rules. Such a margin MAINTENANCE REQUIREMENT is in addition to the initial margin requirements set by REGULATION T of the Federal Reserve Board. *See also* HOUSE MAINTENANCE REQUIREMENT; MARGIN CALL.

HOUSE MAINTENANCE REQUIREMENT internally set and enforced rules of individual broker-dealers in securities with respect to a customer's MARGIN ACCOUNT. House maintenance requirements set levels of EQUITY that must be maintained to avoid putting up additional equity or having collateral sold out.

These levels are normally higher than maintenance levels required by the NATIONAL ASSOCIATION OF SECURITIES DEALERS (NASD) and the stock exchange. *See also* HOUSE CALL; MINIMUM MAINTENANCE.

HOUSE OF ISSUE investment banking firm that underwrites a stock or bond issue and offers the securities to the public. *See also* UNDERWRITE.

HOUSE POOR short of cash because the bulk of your money is tied up in your house. Implication is that without the real estate investment and associated mortgage, you would be financially comfortable.

HOUSE RULES securities industry term for internal rules and policies of individual broker-dealer firms concerning the opening and handling of customers' accounts and the activities of the customers in such accounts. House rules are designed to assure that firms are in comfortable compliance with the requirements of outside regulatory authorities and in most cases are more stringent than the outside regulations. *See also* HOUSE CALL; HOUSE MAINTENANCE REQUIREMENT.

HOUSING AFFORDABILITY INDEX *see* AFFORDABILITY INDEX.

HOUSING AND URBAN DEVELOPMENT, DEPARTMENT OF (HUD) cabinet-level federal agency, founded in 1965, which is responsible for stimulating housing development in the United States. HUD has several programs to subsidize low- and moderate-income housing and urban renewal projects, often through loan guarantees. The GOVERNMENT NATIONAL MORTGAGE ASSOCIATION (Ginnie Mae), which fosters the growth of the secondary mortgage market, is within HUD.

HOUSING BOND short- or long-term bond issued by a local housing authority to finance short-term construction of (typically) low- or middle-income housing or long-term commitments for housing, plants, pollution control facilities, or similar projects. Such bonds are free from federal income taxes and from state and local taxes where applicable.

Shorter-term bonds sell in $5000 denominations and have maturities from 18 months to 4 years. They cannot be called (redeemed prior to maturity) and are paid at maturity with the proceeds from Federal Housing Administration-insured loans. Longer-term bonds are typically issued by local authorities under federal agency contracts, thus providing complete safety. Yields are competitive.

HOUSING STARTS category of residential construction monitored by the Department of Commerce. Housing starts represent the start of construction of a house or apartment building, which means the digging of the foundation. Other categories are housing permits, housing completions, and new home sales. In the aggregate, residential construction accounts for roughly 3% of GROSS DOMESTIC PRODUCT.

HULBERT RATING rating by *Hulbert Financial Digest* of Alexandria, Virginia, of how well the recommendations of various investment advisory newsletters have performed. The ratings cover performance as far back as 1980, if data are available. The *Digest* ranks over 150 investment advisory newsletters covering stocks, bonds, mutual funds, futures, and options by tabulating the profits and losses subscribers would have received had they followed the newsletter's advice exactly.

HUMAN CAPITAL skills acquired by a worker through formal education and experience that improve the worker's productivity and increase his or her income.

HUNG UP term used to describe the position of an investor whose stocks or bonds have dropped in value below their purchase price, presenting the problem of a substantial loss if the securities were sold.

HUNKERING DOWN trader's term for working to sell off a big position in a stock.

HURDLE RATE term used in the budgeting of capital expenditures, meaning the REQUIRED RATE OF RETURN in a DISCOUNTED CASH FLOW analysis. If the EXPECTED RATE OF RETURN on an investment is below the hurdle rate, the project is not undertaken. The hurdle rate should be equal to the INCREMENTAL COST OF CAPITAL.

HYBRID ANNUITY contract offered by an insurance company that allows an investor to mix the benefits of both fixed and variable annuities. Also called *combination annuity*. For instance, an annuity buyer may put a portion of his assets in a FIXED ANNUITY, which promises a certain rate of return, and the remainder in a stock or bond fund VARIABLE ANNUITY, which offers a chance for higher return but takes more risk.

HYBRID INVESTMENT OR SECURITY investment vehicle that combines two different kinds of underlying investments. For example, a structured note, which is a form of a bond, may have the interest rate it pays tied to the rise and fall of a commodity's price. Hybrid investments are also called *derivatives*.

HYPERINFLATION *see* INFLATION.

HYPOTHECATION
Banking: pledging property to secure a loan. Hypothecation does not transfer title, but it does transfer the right to sell the hypothecated property in the event of default.
Securities: pledging of securities to brokers as collateral for loans made to purchase securities or to cover short sales, called margin loans. When the same collateral is pledged by the broker to a bank to collateralize a broker's loan, the process is called *rehypothecation*.

i

IBC/DONOGHUE'S MONEY FUND REPORT AVERAGE average for all major money market mutual fund yields, published weekly for 7- and 30-day simple and compound (assumes reinvested dividends) yields. IBC/Donoghue also tracks the average maturity of securities in money fund portfolios. A short maturity of about 30 days reflects the conviction of fund managers that interest rates are going to rise, and a long maturity of 60 days or more reflects a sentiment that rates are going to fall. The IBC/Donoghue's Money Fund Report Average is published in major newspapers, including the *Wall Street Journal, The New York Times* and *Barron's*.

I/B/E/S INTERNATIONAL INC. provides the I/B/E/S data base, which comprises analysts' estimates of future earnings for thousands of publicly traded companies. These estimates are tabulated, and companies whose estimates have increased or decreased significantly are pinpointed. Reports also detail how many estimates are available on each company and the high, low, and average estimates for each. *See also* ZACK'S ESTIMATE SYSTEM.

IDENTIFIED SHARES shares of stock or a mutual fund that have been identified as having been bought at a particular price on a particular date. If a shareholder wishes to minimize his tax liability when selling shares, he must identify which shares were bought at what price in order to determine his cost basis. If he has acquired shares over a long period of time, for example through a CONSTANT DOLLAR PLAN or a DIVIDEND REINVESTMENT PLAN, he will have many shares at many different prices. By identifying the shares with the highest cost basis, he will generally be able to pay lower capital gains taxes than if he identified shares bought at a lower cost. If shares are being sold at a loss, the shareholder can pick how large or small a loss he wants to take based on which shares he identifies. In addition, if the identified shares were held for a year or more, the investor qualifies for long-term capital gains tax rates. If the identified shares were held for less than one year, he will have to pay regular income tax rates on the gain.

ILLEGAL DIVIDEND dividend declared by a corporation's board of directors in violation of its charter or of state laws. Most states, for example, stipulate that dividends be paid out of current income or RETAINED EARNINGS; they prohibit dividend payments that come out of CAPITAL SURPLUS or that would make the corporation insolvent. Directors who authorize illegal dividends may be sued by stockholders and creditors and may also face civil and criminal penalties. Stockholders who receive such dividends may be required to return them in order to meet the claims of creditors.

ILLIQUID.
Finance: firm that lacks sufficient CASH FLOW to meet current and maturing obligations.
Investments: not readily convertible into cash, such as a stock, bond, or commodity that is not traded actively and would be difficult to sell at once without taking a large loss. Other assets for which there is not a ready market, and which therefore may take some time to sell, include real estate and collectibles such as rare stamps, coins, or antique furniture.

IMBALANCE OF ORDERS too many orders of one kind—to buy or to sell—without matching orders of the opposite kind. An imbalance usually follows a dramatic event such as a takeover, the death of a key executive, or a government ruling that will significantly affect the company's business. If it occurs before the stock exchange opens, trading in the stock is delayed. If it occurs during the trading day, the specialist suspends trading until enough matching orders can be found to make for an orderly market.

IMF *see* INTERNATIONAL MONETARY FUND.

IMMEDIATE FAMILY parents, brothers, sisters, children, relatives supported financially, father-in-law, mother-in-law, sister-in-law, and brother-in-law. This definition is incorporated in the NATIONAL ASSOCIATION OF SECURITIES DEALERS RULES OF FAIR PRACTICE on abuses of *hot issues* through such practices as FREERIDING and WITHHOLDING. The ruling prohibits the sale of such securities to members of a broker-dealer's own family or to persons buying and selling for institutional accounts and their families.

IMMEDIATE OR CANCEL ORDER order requiring that all or part of the order be executed as soon as the broker enters a bid or offer; the portion not executed is automatically canceled. Such stipulations usually accompany large orders.

IMMEDIATE PAYMENT ANNUITY annuity contract bought with a single payment and with a specified payout plan that starts right away. Payments may be for a specified period or for the life of the annuitant and are usually on a monthly basis. *See also* ANNUITIZE.

IMMUNIZATION *see* DURATION.

IMPAIRED CAPITAL total capital that is less than the stated or par value of the company's CAPITAL STOCK. *See also* DEFICIT NET WORTH.

IMPAIRED CREDIT deterioration in the credit rating of a borrower, which may result in a reduction in the amount of credit made available by lenders. For example, a company may launch a product line that is a failure, and the resulting losses will seriously weaken the company's finances. Concerned lenders may reduce the firm's credit lines as a result. The same process can apply to an individual who has been late paying bills, or in an extreme case, has filed for bankruptcy protection. Also called *adverse credit.*

IMPORT DUTY *see* TARIFF.

IMPUTED INTEREST interest considered to have been paid in effect even though no interest was actually paid. For example, the Internal Revenue Service requires that annual interest be recognized on a ZERO-COUPON SECURITY.

IMPUTED VALUE logical or implicit value that is not recorded in any accounts. Examples: in projecting annual figures, values are imputed for months about which actual figures are not yet available; cash invested unproductively has an imputed value consisting of what it would have earned in a productive investment (OPPORTUNITY COST); in calculating national income, the U.S. Department of Commerce imputes a dollar value for wages and salaries paid in kind, such as food and lodging provided on ships at sea.

INACTIVE ASSET asset not continually used in a productive way, such as an auxiliary generator.

INACTIVE BOND CROWD *see* CABINET CROWD.

INACTIVE POST trading post on the New York Stock Exchange at which inactive stocks are traded in 10-share units rather than the regular 100-share lots. Known to traders as *Post 30. See also* ROUND LOT.

INACTIVE STOCK/BOND security traded relatively infrequently, either on an exchange or over the counter. The low volume makes the security ILLIQUID, and small investors tend to shy away from it.

IN-AND-OUT TRADER one who buys and sells the same security in one day, aiming to profit from sharp price moves. *See also* DAY TRADE.

INCENTIVE FEE compensation for producing above-average results. Incentive fees are common for commodities trading advisers who achieve or top a preset return, as well as for a GENERAL PARTNER in a real estate or oil and gas LIMITED PARTNERSHIP.

INCENTIVE STOCK OPTION plan created by the ECONOMIC RECOVERY TAX ACT OF 1981 (ERTA) under which qualifying options are free of tax at the date of grant and the date of exercise. Profits on shares sold after being held at least two years from the date of grant or one year from the date of transfer to the employee are subject to favorable CAPITAL GAINS TAX rates. *See also* QUALIFYING STOCK OPTION.

INCESTUOUS SHARE DEALING buying and selling of shares in each other's companies to create a tax or other financial advantage.

INCOME AVAILABLE FOR FIXED CHARGES *see* FIXED-CHARGE COVERAGE.

INCOME AVERAGING method of computing personal income tax whereby tax is figured on the average of the total of current year's income and that of the three preceding years. According to 1984 U.S. tax legislation, income averaging was used when a person's income for the current year exceeded 140% of the average taxable income in the preceding three years. The TAX REFORM ACT OF 1986 repealed income averaging.

INCOME BOND obligation on which the payment of interest is contingent on sufficient earnings from year to year. Such bonds are traded FLAT—that is, with no accrued interest—and are often an alternative to bankruptcy. *See also* ADJUSTMENT BOND.

INCOME DIVIDEND payout to shareholders of interest, dividends, or other income received by a mutual fund. By law, all such income must be distributed to shareholders, who may choose to take the money in cash or reinvest it in more shares of the fund. All income dividends are taxable to shareholders in the year they are received, unless the fund is held in a tax-deferred account such as an IRA or Keogh plan.

INCOME EXCLUSION RULE INCOME TAX rule excluding certain items from taxable income. Personal exclusions include interest on tax-exempt securities, returns of capital, life insurance death benefits, dividends on veterans' life insurance, child support, welfare payments, disability benefits paid by the Veterans Administration, and amounts received from an insurer because of the loss of use of a home. *See also* EXCLUSION.

INCOME INVESTMENT COMPANY management company that operates an income-oriented MUTUAL FUND for investors who value income over growth. These funds may invest in bonds or high-dividend stocks or may write covered call options on stocks. *See also* INVESTMENT COMPANY.

INCOME LIMITED PARTNERSHIP real estate, oil and gas, or equipment leasing LIMITED PARTNERSHIP whose aim is high income, much of which may be taxable. Such a partnership may be designed for tax-sheltered accounts like Individual Retirement Accounts, Keogh plan accounts, or pension plans.

INCOME MUTUAL FUND mutual fund designed to produce current income for shareholders. Some examples of income funds are government, mortgage-backed security, municipal, international, and junk bond funds. Several kinds of equity-oriented funds also can have income as their primary investment objective, such as utilities income funds and equity income funds. All distributions from income funds are taxable in the year received by the shareholder unless the fund is held in a tax-deferred account such as an IRA or Keogh or the distributions come from tax-exempt bonds, such as with a municipal bond fund.

INCOME PROPERTY real estate bought for the income it produces. The property may be placed in an INCOME LIMITED PARTNERSHIP, or it may be owned by individuals or corporations. Buyers also hope to achieve capital gains when they sell the property.

INCOME SHARES one of two kinds or classes of capital stock issued by a DUAL-PURPOSE FUND or split investment company, the other kind being *capital shares*. Holders of income shares receive dividends from both classes of shares, generated from income (dividends and interest) produced by the portfolio, whereas holders of capital shares receive capital gains payouts on both classes. Income shares normally have a minimum income guarantee, which is cumulative.

INCOME STATEMENT *see* PROFIT AND LOSS STATEMENT.

INCOME STOCK stock paying high and regular dividends to shareholders. Some industries known for income stocks include gas, electric, and telephone utilities; real estate investment trusts; banks; and insurance companies. High-quality income stocks have established a long history of paying dividends, and in many cases have a track record of regularly increasing dividends. All dividends paid to shareholders of income stocks are taxable in the year received unless the stock is held in a tax-deferred account such as an IRA or Keogh plan.

INCOME TAX annual tax on income levied by the federal government and by certain state and local governments. There are two basic types: the personal income tax, levied on incomes of households and unincorporated businesses, and the corporate (or corporation) income tax, levied on net earnings of corporations.

The U.S. income tax was instituted in 1913 by the Sixteenth Amendment to the Constitution. It has typically accounted for more than half the federal government's total annual revenue. Nearly all states tax individual and corporate incomes, as do many cities, though sales and property taxes are the main sources of state and local revenue. The personal income tax, and to a lesser extent the corporate income tax, were designed to be progressive—that is, to take a larger percentage of higher incomes than lower incomes. The ranges of incomes to which progressively higher rates apply are called TAX BRACKETS, which also determine the value of DEDUCTIONS, such as business costs and expenses, state and local income taxes, or charitable contributions.

In 1986, the individual income tax comprised 15 marginal tax brackets (including the ZERO BRACKET AMOUNT) ranging to a high of 50%. Corporations paid a base rate on the first $25,000 of income, a higher rate on the second $25,000, and a still higher rate on anything over $50,000. LONG-TERM CAPITAL GAINS received preferential tax treatment both for individuals and corporations. Because capital gains rates rewarded taxpayers in a position to take risks, and because LOOPHOLES and TAX SHELTERS enabled the wealthiest corporations and individuals to escape the higher tax brackets, the progressiveness of the tax system was often more theoretical than real.

The TAX REFORM ACT OF 1986 introduced a modified FLAT TAX system and contained the most sweeping changes in tax laws since 1913. Signed into law in the fall of 1986, it drastically reduced tax rates for both individuals and corporations, collapsed the marginal rate structure for individuals into two basic brackets, ended preferential capital gains tax treatment, curtailed loopholes and shelters, and imposed a stricter ALTERNATIVE MINIMUM TAX. In 1990 Congress upped the top rate and limited capital gains rates to 28%.

Although the capital gains limitation remained at 28%, the REVENUE RECONCILIATION ACT OF 1993 reintroduced higher tax rates and greater complexity.

INCONTESTABILITY CLAUSE provision in a life insurance contract stating that the insurer cannot revoke the policy after it has been in force for one or two years if the policyholder concealed important facts from the company during the application process. For example, a policyholder who stated that he had never had a heart attack, but in fact had experienced one, would still be covered by the policy if the insurance company had not discovered this discrepancy within one or two years. However, if a policyholder lies about his age on the application, the policy's death benefit can be adjusted higher retroactively to account for the insured's true age.

INCORPORATION process by which a company receives a state charter allowing it to operate as a corporation. The fact of incorporation must be acknowledged in the company's legal name, using the word *incorporated,* the abbreviation *inc.,* or other acceptable variations. *See also* ARTICLES OF INCORPORATION.

INCREMENTAL CASH FLOW net of cash outflows and inflows attributable to a corporate investment project.

INCREMENTAL COST OF CAPITAL weighted cost of the additional capital raised in a given period. Weighted cost of capital, also called *composite cost of capital,* is the weighted average of costs applicable to the issues of debt and classes of equity that compose the firm's capital structure. Also called *marginal cost of capital.*

INDEMNIFY agree to compensate for damage or loss. The word is used in insurance policies promising that, in the event of a loss, the insured will be restored to the financial position that existed prior to the loss.

INDENTURE formal agreement, also called a deed of trust, between an issuer of bonds and the bondholder covering such considerations as: (1) form of the bond; (2) amount of the issue; (3) property pledged (if not a debenture issue); (4) protective COVENANTS including any provision for a sinking fund; (5) WORKING CAPITAL and CURRENT RATIO; and (6) redemption rights or call privileges. The indenture also provides for the appointment of a trustee to act on behalf of the bondholders, in accordance with the TRUST INDENTURE ACT OF 1939.

INDEPENDENT AGENT agent representing several insurance companies. The agent is independent from all the companies he or she sells for, and can therefore in theory evaluate different insurance policies objectively. Independent agents pay all their own expenses and keep their own records and earn their income from commissions on the policies they sell. The opposite of an independent agent is a CAPTIVE AGENT, who works exclusively for one company.

INDEPENDENT AUDITOR certified public accountant (CPA) who provides the ACCOUNTANT'S OPINION.

INDEPENDENT BROKER New York Stock Exchange member who executes orders for other floor brokers who have more volume than they can handle, or for firms whose exchange members are not on the floor. Formerly called $2 brokers because of their commission for a round lot trade, independent brokers are compensated by commission brokers with fees that once were fixed but are now negotiable. *See also* GIVE UP.

INDEX statistical composite that measures changes in the economy or in financial markets, often expressed in percentage changes from a base period or from the previous month. For instance, the CONSUMER PRICE INDEX uses 1982–84 as the base period. That index, made up of key consumer goods and services, moves up and down as the rate of inflation changes. By the mid-1990s the index had climbed from 100 in '82–84 to 150 and higher, meaning that the basket of goods the index is based on had risen in price by more than 50%.

Indexes also measure the ups and downs of stock, bond, and commodities markets, reflecting market prices and the number of shares outstanding for the companies in the index. Some well-known indexes are the New York Stock Exchange Index, the American Stock Exchange Index, Standard & Poor's Index, and the Value Line Index. Subindexes for industry groups such as beverages, railroads, or computers are also tracked. Stock market indexes form the basis for trading in INDEX OPTIONS. *See also* STOCK INDEXES AND AVERAGES.

INDEX ARBITRAGE *see* ARBITRAGE.

INDEXATION *see* INDEXING, at meaning (2).

INDEX BOND bond whose cash flow is linked to the purchasing power of the dollar or a foreign currency. For example, a bond indexed to the CONSUMER PRICE INDEX (CPI) would ensure that the bondholder receives real value by making an upward adjustment in the interest rate to reflect higher prices.

INDEX FUND mutual fund that has a portfolio matching that of a broad-based portfolio. This may include the Standard & Poor's 500 Index, indexes of mid- and small-capitalization stocks, foreign stock indexes, and bond indexes, to name a few. Many institutional and individual investors, especially believers in the EFFICIENT MARKET theory, put money in index funds on the assumption that trying to beat the market averages over the long run is futile, and their investments in these funds will at least keep pace with the index being tracked. In addition, since the cost of managing an index fund is far cheaper than the cost of running an actively managed portfolio, index funds have a built-in cost advantage.

INDEXING
1. weighting one's portfolio to match a broad-based index such as Standard & Poor's so as to match its performance—or buying shares in an INDEX FUND.
2. tying wages, taxes, or other rates to an index. For example, a labor contract may call for indexing wages to the consumer price index to protect against loss of purchasing power in a time of rising inflation.

INDEX OF LEADING INDICATORS *see* LEADING INDICATORS.

INDEX OPTIONS calls and puts on indexes of stocks. These options are traded on the New York, American, and Chicago Board Options Exchanges, among others. Broad-based indexes cover a wide range of companies and industries, whereas narrow-based indexes consist of stocks in one industry or sector of the economy. Index options allow investors to trade in a particular market or industry group without having to buy all the stocks individually. For instance, someone who thought oil stocks were about to fall could buy a put on the oil index instead of selling short shares in half a dozen oil companies.

INDEX PARTICIPATION *see* BASKET.

INDICATED YIELD coupon or dividend rate as a percentage of the current market price. For fixed rate bonds it is the same as CURRENT YIELD. For common stocks, it is the market price divided into the annual dividend. For preferred stocks, it is the market price divided into the contractual dividend.

INDICATION approximation of what a security's TRADING RANGE (bid and offer prices) will be when trading resumes after a delayed opening or after being halted because of an IMBALANCE OF ORDERS or another reason. Also called *indicated market.*

INDICATION OF INTEREST securities underwriting term meaning a dealer's or investor's interest in purchasing securities that are still *in registration* (awaiting clearance by) the Securities and Exchange Commission. A broker who receives an indication of interest should send the client a preliminary prospectus on the securities. An indication of interest is not a commitment to buy, an important point because selling a security while it is in registration is illegal. *See also* CIRCLE.

INDICATOR technical measurement securities market analysts use to forecast the market's direction, such as investment advisory sentiment, volume of stock trading, direction of interest rates, and buying or selling by corporate insiders.

INDIRECT COST AND EXPENSE *see* DIRECT OVERHEAD; FIXED COST.

INDIRECT LABOR COSTS wages and related costs of factory employees, such as inspectors and maintenance crews, whose time is not charged to specific finished products.

INDIVIDUAL RETIREMENT ACCOUNT (IRA) personal, TAX-DEFERRED, retirement account that an employed person can set up with a deposit limited to $2000 per year ($4000 for a couple when both work, or $2250 for a couple when one works and the other's income is $250 or less). Under the TAX REFORM ACT OF 1986, rules effective in the tax year 1987 include: deductibility of IRA contributions regardless of income if neither the taxpayer nor the taxpayer's spouse is covered by a QUALIFIED PLAN OR TRUST; even if covered by a qualified plan, taxpayers may deduct IRA contributions if ADJUSTED GROSS INCOME is below $40,000 on a joint return or $25,000 on a single return; couples with incomes of $40,000 to $50,000 and single taxpayers with incomes of $25,000 to $35,000 are allowed partial deductions in amounts reduced proportionately over the $10,000 range with a minimum deduction of $200; taxpayers with incomes over $50,000 (joint) and $35,000 (single) are not allowed deductions, but may make the same contributions (treated as a nontaxable RETURN OF CAPITAL upon withdrawal) and thus gain the benefit of tax-deferral; taxpayers who cannot make deductible contributions because of participation in qualified retirement plans may make nondeductible contributions. Withdrawals from IRAs prior to age 59½ are generally subject to a 10% (of principal) penalty tax. *See also* SIMPLIFIED EMPLOYEE PENSION (SEP) PLAN.

INDIVIDUAL RETIREMENT ACCOUNT (IRA) ROLLOVER provision of the IRA law that enables persons receiving lump-sum payments from their company's pension or profit-sharing plan because of retirement or other termination of employment to ROLL OVER the amount into an IRA investment plan within 60 days. Also, current IRAs may themselves be transferred to other investment options within the 60-day period. Through an IRA rollover, the capital continues to accumulate tax-deferred until time of withdrawal.

INDIVIDUAL TAX RETURN tax return filed by an individual instead of a corporation. The 1040 tax form used by individuals comes in three varieties: the 1040EZ basic form, the 1040A short form, and the 1040 long form. Attached to the 1040 are several schedules, including Schedule A for itemized deductions, Schedule B for interest and dividend income, Schedule C for profits and losses from a business, Schedule D for reporting capital gains and losses, Schedule E for supplemental income and losses, and Schedule K-1 for a limited partner's share of gains, losses, and credits. The 1040T is a new tax form developed by the IRS to replace the 1040A form. It features bigger type, more space between lines, and a box for every numeral.

INDUSTRIAL in stock market vernacular, general, catch-all category including firms producing or distributing goods and services that are not classified as utility, transportation, or financial companies. *See also* STOCK INDEXES AND AVERAGES; FORTUNE 500.

INDUSTRIAL DEVELOPMENT BOND (IDB) type of MUNICIPAL REVENUE BOND issued to finance FIXED ASSETS that are then leased to private firms, whose payments AMORTIZE the debt. IDBs were traditionally tax-exempt to buyers, but under the TAX REFORM ACT OF 1986, large IDB issues ($1 million plus) became taxable effective August 15, 1986, while tax-exempt small issues for commercial and manufacturing purposes were prohibited after 1986 and 1989 respectively.

Also, effective August 7, 1986, banks lost their 80% interest deductibility on borrowings to buy IDBs.

INDUSTRIAL PRODUCTION monthly statistic released by the FEDERAL RESERVE BOARD on the total output of all U.S. factories and mines. These numbers are a key ECONOMIC INDICATOR.

INDUSTRIAL REVENUE BOND *see* INDUSTRIAL DEVELOPMENT BOND.

INEFFICIENCY IN THE MARKET failure of investors to recognize that a particular stock or bond has good prospects or may be headed for trouble. According to the EFFICIENT MARKET theory, current prices reflect all knowledge about securities. But some say that those who find out about securities first can profit by exploiting that information; stocks of small, little-known firms with a large growth potential most clearly reflect the market's inefficiency, they say.

INELASTIC DEMAND OR SUPPLY *see* ELASTICITY OF DEMAND OR SUPPLY.

IN ESCROW *see* ESCROW.

INFANT INDUSTRY ARGUMENT case made by developing sectors of the economy that their industries need protection against international competition while they establish themselves. In response to such pleas, the government may enact a TARIFF or import duty to stifle foreign competition. The infant industry argument is frequently made in developing nations that are trying to lessen their dependence on the industrialized world. In Brazil, for example, such infant industries as automobile production argue that they need protection until their technological capability and marketing prowess are sufficient to enable competition with well-established foreigners.

INFLATION rise in the prices of goods and services, as happens when spending increases relative to the supply of goods on the market—in other words, too much money chasing too few goods. Moderate inflation is a common result of economic growth. Hyperinflation, with prices rising at 100% a year or more, causes people to lose confidence in the currency and put their assets in hard assets like real estate or gold, which usually retain their value in inflationary times. *See also* COST-PUSH INFLATION; DEMAND-PULL INFLATION.

INFLATION ACCOUNTING showing the effects of inflation in financial statements. The Financial Accounting Standards Board (FASB) requires major companies to supplement their traditional financial reporting with information showing the effects of inflation. The ruling applies to public companies having inventories and fixed assets of more than $125 million or total assets of more than $1 billion.

INFLATION HEDGE investment designed to protect against the loss of purchasing power from inflation. Traditionally, gold and real estate have a reputation as good inflation hedges, though growth in stocks also can offset inflation in the long run. Money market funds, which pay higher yields as interest rates rise during inflationary times, can also be a good inflation hedge. In the case of hyperinflation, hard assets such as precious metals and real estate are normally viewed as inflation hedges, while the value of paper-based assets such as stocks, bonds, and currency erodes rapidly.

INFLATION RATE rate of change in prices. Two primary U.S. indicators of the inflation rate are the CONSUMER PRICE INDEX and the PRODUCER PRICE INDEX, which track changes in prices paid by consumers and by producers. The rate can be calculated on an annual, monthly, or other basis.

INFLATION RISK *see* RISK.

INFLEXIBLE EXPENSES *see* FLEXIBLE EXPENSES.

INFRASTRUCTURE a nation's basic system of transportation, communication, and other aspects of its physical plant. Building and maintaining road, bridge, sewage, and electrical systems provides millions of jobs nationwide. For developing countries, building an infrastructure is a first step in economic development.

INGOT bar of metal. The Federal Reserve System's gold reserves are stored in ingot form. Individual investors may take delivery of an ingot of a precious metal such as gold or silver or may buy a certificate entitling them to a share in an ingot.

INHERITANCE part of an estate acquired by an HEIR.

INHERITANCE TAX RETURN state counterpart to the federal ESTATE TAX return, required of the executor or administrator to determine the amount of state tax due on the inheritance.

INITIAL MARGIN amount of cash or eligible securities required to be deposited with a broker before engaging in margin transactions. A margin transaction is one in which the broker extends credit to the customer in a margin account. Under REGULATION T of the Federal Reserve Board, the initial margin is currently 50% of the purchase price when buying eligible stock or convertible bonds or 50% of the proceeds of a short sale. *See also* MAINTENANCE REQUIREMENT; MARGIN CALL; MARGIN REQUIREMENT; MARGIN SECURITY.

INITIAL PUBLIC OFFERING (IPO) corporation's first offering of stock to the public. IPO's are almost invariably an opportunity for the existing investors and participating venture capitalists to make big profits, since for the first time their shares will be given a market value reflecting expectations for the company's future growth. *See also* HOT ISSUE.

INJUNCTION court order instructing a defendant to refrain from doing something that would be injurious to the plaintiff, or face a penalty. The usual procedure is to issue a temporary restraining order, then hold hearings to determine whether a permanent injunction is warranted.

IN PLAY stock affected by TAKEOVER rumors or activities.

INSIDE INFORMATION corporate affairs that have not yet been made public. The officers of a firm would know in advance, for instance, if the company was about to be taken over, or if the latest earnings report was going to differ significantly from information released earlier. Under Securities and Exchange Commission rules, an INSIDER is not allowed to trade on the basis of such information.

INSIDE MARKET bid or asked quotes between dealers trading for their own inventories. Distinguished from the retail market, where quotes reflect the prices that customers pay to dealers. Also known as *inter-dealer market; wholesale market.*

INSIDER person with access to key information before it is announced to the public. Usually the term refers to directors, officers, and key employees, but the definition has been extended legally to include relatives and others in a position to capitalize on INSIDE INFORMATION. Insiders are prohibited from trading on their knowledge.

INSIDER TRADING practice of buying and selling shares in a company's stock by that company's management or board of directors, or by a holder of more than 10% of the company's shares. Managers may trade their company's stock as long as they disclose their activity within ten days of the close of the month within the time the transactions took place. However, it is illegal for insiders to trade based on their knowledge of material corporate developments that have not been announced publicly. Developments that would be considered *material* include news of an impending takeover, introduction of a new product line, a divestiture, a key executive appointment, or other news that could affect the company's stock positively or negatively. Insider trading laws have been extended to other people who have knowledge of these developments but who are not members of management, including investment bankers, lawyers, printers of financial disclosure documents, or relatives of managers and executives who learn of these material developments.

INSIDER TRADING SANCTIONS ACT OF 1984 amendment to the SECURITIES EXCHANGE ACT OF 1934 that outlined civil and criminal penalties for insider trading violations. Fines up to triple the amount of illegal gains can be levied. The amendment applies not only to people who buy or sell using material nonpublic information, but to anyone who gives them such information or aids and abets them.

INSOLVENCY inability to pay debts when due. *See also* BANKRUPTCY; CASH FLOW; SOLVENCY.

INSTALLMENT SALE
In general: sale made with the agreement that the purchased goods or services will be paid for in fractional amounts over a specified period of time.
Securities: transaction with a set contract price, paid in installments over a period of time. Gains or losses are generally taxable on a prorated basis.

INSTINET *see* FOURTH MARKET.

INSTITUTIONAL BROKER broker who buys and sells securities for banks, mutual funds, insurance companies, pension funds, or other institutional clients. Institutional brokers deal in large volumes of securities and generally charge their customers lower per-unit commission rates than individuals pay.

INSTITUTIONAL INVESTOR organization that trades large volumes of securities. Some examples are mutual funds, banks, insurance companies, pension funds, labor union funds, corporate profit-sharing plans, and college endowment funds. Typically, upwards of 70% of the daily trading on the New York Stock Exchange is on behalf of institutional investors.

INSTRUMENT legal document in which some contractual relationship is given formal expression or by which some right is granted—for example, notes, contracts, agreements. *See also* NEGOTIABLE INSTRUMENT.

INSTRUMENTALITY federal agency whose obligations, while not direct obligations of the U.S. Government, are sponsored or guaranteed by the government and backed by the FULL FAITH AND CREDIT of the government. Well over 100 series of notes, certificates, and bonds have been issued by such instrumentalities as Federal Home Loan Bank, and Student Loan Marketing Association.

INSURABILITY conditions under which an insurance company is willing to insure a risk. Each insurance company applies its own standards based on its own underwriting criteria. For example, some life insurance companies do not insure people with high-risk occupations such as stuntmen or firefighters, while other companies consider these people insurable, though the premiums they must pay are higher than for those in low-risk professions.

INSURABLE INTEREST relationship between an insured person or property and the potential beneficiary of the policy. For example, a wife has an insurable interest in her husband's life, because she would be financially harmed if he were to die. Therefore, she could receive the proceeds of the insurance policy if he were to die while the policy was in force. If there is no insurable interest, an insurance company will not issue a policy.

INSURANCE system whereby individuals and companies that are concerned about potential hazards pay premiums to an insurance company, which reimburses them in the event of loss. The insurer profits by investing the premiums it receives. Some common forms of insurance cover business risks, automobiles, homes, boats, worker's compensation, and health. Life insurance guarantees payment to the beneficiaries when the insured person dies. In a broad economic sense, insurance transfers risk from individuals to a larger group, which is better able to pay for losses.

INSURANCE AGENT representative of an insurance company who sells the firm's policies. CAPTIVE AGENTS sell the policies of only one company, while INDEPENDENT AGENTS sell the policies of many companies. Agents must be licensed to sell insurance in the states where they solicit customers.

INSURANCE BROKER independent broker who searches for the best insurance coverage at the lowest cost for the client. Insurance brokers do not work for insurance companies, but for the buyers of insurance products. They constantly are comparing the merits of competing insurance companies to find the best deal for their customers.

INSURANCE CLAIM request for payment from the insurance company by the insured. For example, a homeowner files a claim if he or she suffered damage because of a fire, theft, or other loss. In life insurance, survivors submit a claim when the insured dies. The insurance company investigates the claim and pays the appropriate amount if the claim is found to be legitimate, or denies the claim if it determines the loss was fraudulent or not covered by the policy.

INSURANCE DIVIDEND money paid to cash value life insurance policyholders with participating policies, usually once a year. Dividend rates are based on the insurance company's mortality experience, administrative expenses, and investment returns. Lower mortality experience (the number of policyholders dying) and expenses, combined with high investment returns, will increase dividends. Technically, dividends are considered a return of the policyholder's premiums, and are thus not considered taxable income by the IRS. Policyholders may choose to take these dividends in cash or may purchase additional life insurance.

INSURANCE POLICY insurance contract specifying what risks are insured and what premiums must be paid to keep the policy in force. Policies also spell out DEDUCTIBLES and other terms. Policies for life insurance specify whose life is insured and which beneficiaries will receive the insurance proceeds. HOME-OWNER'S INSURANCE POLICIES specify which property and casualty perils are covered. *Health insurance policies* detail which medical procedures, drugs, and devices are reimbursed. *Auto insurance policies* describe the conditions under which car owners will be covered in case of accidents, theft, or other damage to their cars. *Disability policies* specify the qualifying conditions of disability and how long payments will continue. *Business insurance policies* describe which liabilities are reimbursable. The policy is the written document that both insured and insurance company refer to when determining whether or not a claim is covered.

INSURANCE PREMIUM payment made by the insured in return for insurance protection. Premiums are set based on the probability of risk of loss and competitive pressures with other insurers. An insurance company's actuary will figure out the expected loss ratio on a particular class of customers, and then individual applicants will be evaluated based on whether they present higher or lower risks than the class as a whole. If a policyholder does not pay the premium, the insurance or policy may lapse. If the policy is a cash value policy, the policyowner can choose to take a paid-up insurance policy with a lower face value amount or an extended term policy.

INSURANCE SETTLEMENT payment of proceeds from an insurance policy to the insured under the terms of an insurance contract. Insurance settlements may be either in the form of one lump-sum payment or a series of payments.

INSURED individual, group, or property that is covered by an INSURANCE POLICY. The policy specifies exactly which perils the insured is indemnified against. The insured may be a particular individual, such as someone covered by a life insurance policy. It may be a group of people, such as those covered by a group life insurance policy purchased by a company on behalf of its employees. The insured may also refer to property, such as a house and its possessions which are covered by a HOMEOWNER'S INSURANCE POLICY.

INSURED ACCOUNT account at a bank, savings and loan association, credit union, or brokerage firm that belongs to a federal or private insurance organization. Bank accounts are insured by the BANK INSURANCE FUND (BIF), and savings and loan deposits are insured by the SAVINGS ASSOCIATION INSURANCE FUND (SAIF); both programs are administered by the FEDERAL DEPOSIT INSURANCE CORPORATION (FDIC). Credit union accounts are insured by the *National Credit Union Administration*. Brokerage accounts are insured by the SECURITIES INVESTOR PROTECTION CORPORATION. Such insurance protects depositors against loss in the event that the institution becomes insolvent. Federal insurance systems were set up in the 1930s, after bank failures threatened the banking system with collapse. Some money market funds are covered by private insurance companies.

INSURED BONDS municipal bonds that are insured against default by a MUNICIPAL BOND INSURANCE company. The company pledges to make all interest and principal payments when due if the issuer of the bonds defaults on its obligations. In return, the bond's issuer pays a premium to the insurance company. Insured bonds usually trade based on the credit rating of the insurer rather than the rating of the underlying issuer, since the insurance company is ultimately at risk for the repayment of principal and interest. Insured bonds will pay slightly lower yields, because of the cost of the insurance protection, than comparable noninsured bonds. Some of the major municipal bond insurance firms include MBIA and AMBAC Indemnity Corporation.

INTANGIBLE ASSET right or nonphysical resource that is presumed to represent an advantage to the firm's position in the marketplace. Such assets include copyrights, patents, TRADEMARKS, goodwill, computer programs, capitalized advertising costs, organization costs, licenses, LEASES, FRANCHISES, exploration permits, and import and export permits.

INTANGIBLE COST tax-deductible cost. Such costs are incurred in drilling, testing, completing, and reworking oil and gas wells—labor, core analysis, fracturing, drill stem testing, engineering, fuel, geologists' expenses; also abandonment losses, management fees, delay rentals, and similar expenses.

INTERBANK RATE see LONDON INTERBANK OFFERED RATE (LIBOR).

INTERCOMMODITY SPREAD spread consisting of a long position and a short position in different but related commodities—for example, a long position in gold futures and a short position in silver futures. The investor hopes to profit from the changing price relationship between the commodities.

INTERDELIVERY SPREAD futures or options trading technique that entails buying one month of a contract and selling another month in the same contract—for instance, buying a June wheat contract and simultaneously selling a September wheat contract. The investor hopes to profit as the price difference between the two contracts widens or narrows.

INTEREST
1. cost of using money, expressed as a rate per period of time, usually one year, in which case it is called an annual rate of interest.
2. share, right, or title in property.

INTEREST COVERAGE see FIXED-CHARGE COVERAGE.

INTEREST DEDUCTION DEDUCTION allowable for certain types of interest expense, such as for interest on a home mortgage or interest on a MARGIN ACCOUNT.

INTEREST EQUALIZATION TAX (IET) tax of 15% on interest received by foreign borrowers in U.S. capital markets, imposed in 1963 and removed in 1974.

INTEREST-ONLY LOAN form of loan where the only current obligation is interest and where repayment of principal is deferred.

INTEREST OPTION insurance policyholder's choice to reinvest dividends with the insurer to earn a guaranteed rate of interest. A beneficiary may also reinvest proceeds to earn interest.

INTEREST RATE rate of interest charged for the use of money, usually expressed at an annual rate. The rate is derived by dividing the amount of interest by the amount of principal borrowed. For example, if a bank charged $10 per year in interest to borrow $100, they would be charging a 10% interest rate. Interest rates are quoted on bills, notes, bonds, credit cards, and many kinds of consumer and business loans.

INTEREST-RATE FUTURES CONTRACT futures contract based on a debt security or inter-bank deposit. In theory, the buyer of a bond futures contract agrees to take delivery of the underlying bonds when the contract expires, and the contract seller agrees to deliver the debt instrument. However, most contracts are not settled by delivery, but instead are traded out before expiration. The value of the contract rises and falls inversely to changes in interest rates. For example, if Treasury bond yields rise, futures contracts on Treasury bonds will fall in price. Conversely, when yields fall, Treasury bond futures prices rise. There are many kinds of interest rate futures contracts, including those on Treasury bills, notes, and bonds; Government National Mortgage Association (GNMA) mortgage-backed securities; municipal bonds; and inter-bank deposits such as Eurodollars.

Speculators believing that interest rates are about to rise or fall trade these futures. Also, companies with exposure to fluctuations in interest rates, such as brokerage firms, banks, and insurance companies, may use these contracts to HEDGE their holdings of Treasury bonds and other debt instruments or their costs of future borrowings. For a list of interest rate futures contracts, *see* SECURITIES AND COMMODITIES EXCHANGES.

INTEREST-RATE OPTIONS CONTRACT options contract based on an underlying debt security. Options, unlike futures, give their buyers the right, but not the obligation, to buy the underlying bond at a fixed price before a specific date in the future. Option sellers promise to sell the bonds at a set price anytime until the contract expires. In return for granting this right, the option buyer pays a premium to the option seller. Yield-based calls become more valuable as yields rise, and puts become more valuable as yields decline. There are interest rate options on Treasury bills, notes, and bonds; GNMA mortgage-backed securities; certificates of deposit; municipal bonds; and other interest-sensitive instruments. For a complete list of these contracts, *see* SECURITIES AND COMMODITIES EXCHANGES.

INTEREST-RATE RISK RISK that changes in interest rates will adversely affect the value of an investor's securities portfolio. For example, an investor with large holdings in long-term bonds and utilities has assumed a significant interest-rate risk, because the value of those bonds and utility stocks will fall if interest rates rise. Investors can take various precautionary measures to HEDGE their interest-rate risk, such as buying INTEREST-RATE FUTURES or INTEREST-RATE OPTIONS CONTRACTS.

INTEREST-SENSITIVE INSURANCE POLICY cash value life insurance with dividend rates tied to the fluctuations in interest rates. For example, holders of UNIVERSAL LIFE INSURANCE policies will be credited with a greater increase in cash values when interest rates rise and a slower rate of increase in cash values when interest rates fall.

INTEREST-SENSITIVE STOCK stock of a firm whose earnings change when interest rates change, such as a bank or utility, and which therefore tends to go up or down on news of rate movements.

INTERIM DIVIDEND DIVIDEND declared and paid before annual earnings have been determined, generally quarterly. Most companies strive for consistency and plan quarterly dividends they are sure they can afford, reserving changes until fiscal year results are known.

INTERIM FINANCING temporary, short-term loan made conditional on a TAKE-OUT by intermediate or long-term financing. Also called *bridge loan* financing.

INTERIM LOAN *See* CONSTRUCTION LOAN.

INTERIM STATEMENT financial report covering only a portion of a fiscal year. Public corporations supplement the annual report with quarterly statements informing shareholders of changes in the balance sheet and income statement, as well as other newsworthy developments.

INTERLOCKING DIRECTORATE membership on more than one company's board of directors. This is legal so long as the companies are not competitors. Consumer activists often point to interlocking directorates as an element in corporate conspiracies. The most flagrant abuses were outlawed by the Clayton Anti-Trust Act of 1914.

INTERMARKET SPREAD *see* INTERDELIVERY SPREAD.

INTERMARKET SURVEILLANCE INFORMATION SYSTEM (ISIS) DATA-
BASE sharing information provided by the major stock exchanges in the United
States. It permits the identification of CONTRA BROKERS and aids in preventing
violations.

INTERMARKET TRADING SYSTEM (ITS) video-computer display system
that links the posts of specialists at the New York, American, Boston, Midwest,
Philadelphia, and Pacific Stock Exchanges and NASD market makers who are
trading the same securities. The quotes are displayed and are firm (good) for at
least 100 shares. A broker at one exchange may direct an order to another
exchange where the quote is better by sending the order through the electronic
workstation. A transaction that is accepted by the broker at the other exchange is
analogous to an electronic handshake and constitutes a contract.

INTERMEDIARY person or institution empowered to make investment decisions
for others. Some examples are banks, savings and loan institutions, insurance
companies, brokerage firms, mutual funds, and credit unions. These specialists
are knowledgeable about investment alternatives and can achieve a higher return
than the average investor can. Furthermore, they deal in large dollar volumes,
have lower transaction costs, and can diversify their assets easily. Also called
financial intermediary.

INTERMEDIATE TERM period between the short and long term, the length of
time depending on the context. Stock analysts, for instance, mean 6 to 12 months,
whereas bond analysts most often mean 3 to 10 years.

INTERMEDIATION placement of money with a financial INTERMEDIARY like a
broker or bank, which invests it in bonds, stocks, mortgages, or other loans,
money-market securities, or government obligations so as to achieve a targeted
return. More formally called *financial intermediation.* The opposite is DISINTER-
MEDIATION, the withdrawal of money from an intermediary.

INTERNAL AUDITOR employee of a company who examines records and procedures to ensure against fraud and to make certain board directives and management policies are being properly executed.

INTERNAL CONTROL method, procedure, or system designed to promote efficiency, assure the implementation of policy, and safeguard assets.

INTERNAL EXPANSION asset growth financed out of internally generated
cash—usually termed INTERNAL FINANCING—or through ACCRETION or APPRECIA-
TION. *See also* CASH EARNINGS.

INTERNAL FINANCING funds produced by the normal operations of a firm, as
distinguished from external financing, which includes borrowings and new
equity. *See also* INTERNAL EXPANSION.

INTERNAL RATE OF RETURN (IRR) discount rate at which the present value
of the future cash flows of an investment equal the cost of the investment. It is
found by a process of trial and error; when the net present values of cash outflows
(the cost of the investment) and cash inflows (returns on the investment) equal
zero, the rate of discount being used is the IRR. When IRR is greater than the
required return—called the hurdle rate in capital budgeting—the investment is
acceptable

INTERNAL REVENUE CODE blanket term for complexity of statutes comprising the federal TAX law.

INTERNAL REVENUE SERVICE (IRS) U.S. agency charged with collecting nearly all federal taxes, including personal and corporate income taxes, social security taxes, and excise and gift taxes. Major exceptions include taxes having to do with alcohol, tobacco, firearms, and explosives, and customs duties and tariffs. The IRS administers the rules and regulations that are the responsibility of the U.S. Department of the Treasury and investigates and prosecutes (through the U.S. Tax Court) tax illegalities.

INTERNATIONAL BANK FOR RECONSTRUCTION AND DEVELOP-MENT (IBRD) organization set up by the Bretton Woods Agreement of 1944 to help finance the reconstruction of Europe and Asia after World War II. That task accomplished, the *World Bank,* as IBRD is known, turned to financing commercial and infrastructure projects, mostly in developing nations. It does not compete with commercial banks, but it may participate in a loan set up by a commercial bank. World Bank loans must be backed by the government in the borrowing country.

INTERNATIONAL MARKET INDEX market-value weighted proprietary index of the American Stock Exchange which tracks the performance of 50 American Depositary Receipts traded on the American Stock Exchange, New York Stock Exchange and NASDAQ Market. Options are no longer traded on the index.

INTERNATIONAL MONETARY FUND (IMF) organization set up by the Bretton Woods Agreement in 1944. Unlike the World Bank, whose focus is on foreign exchange reserves and the balance of trade, the IMF focus is on lowering trade barriers and stabilizing currencies. While helping developing nations pay their debts, the IMF usually imposes tough guidelines aimed at lowering inflation, cutting imports, and raising exports. IMF funds come mostly from the treasuries of industrialized nations. *See also* INTERNATIONAL BANK FOR RECONSTRUCTION AND DEVELOPMENT.

INTERNATIONAL MONETARY MARKET (IMM) division of the Chicago Mercantile Exchange that trades futures in U.S. Treasury bills, foreign currency, certificates of deposit, and Eurodollar deposits.

INTERNATIONAL MUTUAL FUND mutual fund that invests in securities markets throughout the world so that if one market is in a slump, profits can still be earned in others. Fund managers must be alert to trends in foreign currencies as well as in world stock and bond markets. Otherwise, seemingly profitable investments in a rising market could lose money if the national currency is falling against the dollar. While international mutual funds tend to concentrate only on non-American securities, GLOBAL MUTUAL FUNDS buy both foreign and domestic stocks and bonds.

INTERNATIONAL PETROLEUM EXCHANGE (IPE) London-based energy futures and options exchange, trading Brent crude oil futures and options, gas oil futures and options, and unleaded gasoline futures. Brent crude futures are cash settled. There are three classes of IPE membership: floor members who are voting members, hold seats on the exchange and own a share of the exchange; trade associates, which are companies with direct interests in producing, refining, or trading oil and oil products; and local floor members, individuals who can trade on the exchange floor. Trading is carried out on the IPE floor through floor members; anyone can trade through them. Locals can trade for their own accounts or for floor members and other locals, but not for clients. The IPE trades Monday through Friday, from 9:15 A.M. to 8:15 P.M.

INTERNATIONAL STOCK EXCHANGE OF THE U.K. AND THE REPUBLIC OF IRELAND (ISE) organization formed after BIG BANG to replace the London Stock Exchange following its merger with the International Securities Regulatory Organization (ISRO). ISRO is a professional trade association of brokers and dealers in the United Kingdom that functions as a self-regulatory organization. The term *London Stock Exchange* persists in investment parlance despite the name change.

INTERPOLATION estimation of an unknown number intermediate between known numbers. Interpolation is a way of approximating price or yield using bond tables that do not give the net yield on every amount invested at every rate of interest and for every maturity. Interpolation is based on the assumption that a certain percentage change in yield will result in the same percentage change in price. The assumption is not altogether correct, but the variance is small enough to ignore.

INTERPOSITIONING placement of a second broker in a securities transaction between two principals or between a customer and a marketmaker. The practice is regulated by the Securities and Exchange Commission, and abuses such as interpositioning to create additional commission income are illegal.

INTERSTATE COMMERCE COMMISSION (ICC) federal agency created by the Interstate Commerce Act of 1887 to insure that the public receives fair and reasonable rates and services from carriers and transportation service firms involved in interstate commerce. Legislation enacted in the 1970s and 80s substantially curtailed the regulatory activities of the ICC, particularly in the rail, truck, and bus industries.

INTER VIVOS TRUST trust established between living persons—for instance, between father and child. In contrast, a TESTAMENTARY TRUST goes into effect when the person who establishes the trust dies. Also called *living trust.*

INTESTACY; INTESTATE a person who dies without a valid will is said to die *intestate* or *in intestacy.* State law determines who is entitled to inherit and who is entitled to manage the decedent's estate.

INTESTATE DISTRIBUTION distribution of assets to beneficiaries from the estate of a person who dies without a written will of instructions. This distribution is overseen by a PROBATE court and the appointed EXECUTOR of the estate. Each state has specific laws outlining how intestate distributions are to be made.

IN THE MONEY option contract on a stock whose current market price is above the striking price of a call option or below the striking price of a put option. A call option on XYZ at a striking price of 100 would be in the money if XYZ were selling for 102, for instance, and a put option with the same striking price would be in the money if XYZ were selling for 98. *See also* AT THE MONEY; OUT OF THE MONEY.

IN THE TANK slang expression meaning market prices are dropping rapidly. Stock market observers may say, "The market is in the tank" after a day in which stock prices fell.

INTRACOMMODITY SPREAD futures position in which a trader buys and sells contracts in the same commodity on the same exchange, but for different months. For instance, a trader would place an intracommodity spread if he bought a pork bellies contract expiring in December and at the same time sold a pork bellies contract expiring in April. His profit or loss would be determined by the price difference between the December and April contracts.

INTRADAY within the day; often used in connection with high and low prices of a stock, bond, or commodity. For instance, "The stock hit a new intraday high today" means that the stock reached an all-time high price during the day but fell back to a lower price by the end of the day. The listing of the high and low prices at which a stock is traded during a day is called the *intraday price range.*

INTRASTATE OFFERING securities offering limited to one state in the United States. *See also* BLUE-SKY LAW.

INTRINSIC VALUE

Financial analysis: valuation determined by applying data inputs to a valuation theory or model. The resulting value is comparable to the prevailing market price.

Options trading: difference between the EXERCISE PRICE or strike price of an option and the market value of the underlying security. For example, if the strike price is $53 on a call option to purchase a stock with a market price of $55, the option has an intrinsic value of $2. Or, in the case of a put option, if the strike price was $55 and the market price of the underlying stock was $53, the intrinsic value of the option would also be $2. Options AT THE MONEY or OUT OF THE MONEY have no intrinsic value.

INVENTORY

Corporate finance: value of a firm's raw materials, work in process, supplies used in operations, and finished goods. Since inventory value changes with price fluctuations, it is important to know the method of valuation. There are a number of inventory valuation methods; the most widely used are FIRST IN, FIRST OUT (FIFO) and LAST IN, FIRST OUT (LIFO). Financial statements normally indicate the basis of inventory valuation, generally the lower figure of either cost price or current market price, which precludes potentially overstated earnings and assets as the result of sharp increases in the price of raw materials.

Personal finance: list of all assets owned by an individual and the value of each, based on cost, market value, or both. Such inventories are usually required for property insurance purposes and are sometimes required with applications for credit.

Securities: net long or short position of a dealer or specialist. Also, securities bought and held by a dealer for later resale.

INVENTORY FINANCING

Factoring: sometimes used as a synonym for overadvances in FACTORING, where loans in excess of accounts receivable are made against inventory in anticipation of future sales.

Finance companies: financing by a bank or sales finance company of the inventory of a dealer in consumer or capital goods. Such loans, also called wholesale financing or *floorplanning*, are secured by the inventory and are usually made as part of a relationship in which retail installment paper generated by sales to the public is also financed by the lender. *See also* FINANCE COMPANY.

INVENTORY TURNOVER ratio of annual sales to inventory, which shows how many times the inventory of a firm is sold and replaced during an accounting period; sometimes called *inventory utilization ratio*. Compared with industry averages, a low turnover might indicate a company is carrying excess stocks of inventory, an unhealthy sign because excess inventory represents an investment with a low or zero rate of return and because it makes the company more vulnerable to falling prices. A steady drop in inventory turnover, in comparison with prior periods, can reveal lack of a sufficiently aggressive sales policy or ineffective buying.

Two points about the way inventory turnover may be calculated: (1) Because sales are recorded at market value and inventories are normally carried at cost, it is more realistic to obtain the turnover ratio by dividing inventory into cost of goods sold rather than into sales. However, it is conventional to use sales as the numerator because that is the practice of Dun & Bradstreet and other compilers of published financial ratios, and comparability is of overriding importance. (2) To minimize the seasonal factor affecting inventory levels, it is better to use an average inventory figure, obtained by adding yearly beginning and ending inventory figures and dividing by 2.

INVERSE FLOATER derivative instrument whose coupon rate is inversely related to some multiple of a specified market rate of interest. Typically a cap and floor are placed on the coupon. As interest rates go down, the amount of interest the inverse floater pays goes up. For example, if the inverse floater rate is 32% and the multiple is four times the London Interbank Offered Rate (LIBOR) of 7%, the coupon is valued at 4%. If the LIBOR goes to 6%, the new coupon is 8%. Many inverse floaters are based on pieces of mortgage-backed securities such as COLLATERALIZED MORTGAGE OBLIGATIONS which react inversely to movements in interest rates.

INVERTED SCALE serial bond offering where earlier maturities have higher yields than later maturities. *See also* SERIAL BOND.

INVERTED YIELD CURVE unusual situation where short-term interest rates are higher than long-term rates. Normally, lenders receive a higher yield when committing their money for a longer period of time; this situation is called a POSITIVE YIELD CURVE. An inverted YIELD CURVE occurs when a surge in demand for short-term credit drives up short-term rates on instruments like Treasury bills and money-market funds, while long-term rates move up more slowly, since borrowers are not willing to commit themselves to paying high interest rates for many years. This situation happened in the early 1980s, when short-term interest rates were around 20%, while long-term rates went up to only 16% or 17%. The existence of an inverted yield curve can be a sign of an unhealthy economy, marked by high inflation and low levels of confidence. Also called *negative yield curve.*

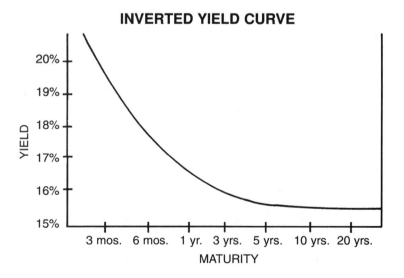

INVERTED YIELD CURVE

INVESTMENT use of capital to create more money, either through income-producing vehicles or through more risk-oriented ventures designed to result in capital gains. *Investment* can refer to a financial investment (where an investor puts money into a vehicle) or to an investment of effort and time on the part of an individual who wants to reap profits from the success of his labor. Investment connotes the idea that safety of principal is important. SPECULATION, on the other hand, is far riskier.

INVESTMENT ADVISERS ACT legislation passed by Congress in 1940 that requires all investment advisers to register with the Securities and Exchange Commission. The Act is designed to protect the public from fraud or misrepresentation by investment advisers. One requirement, for example, is that advisers must disclose all potential *conflicts of interest* with any recommendations they make to those they advise. A potential conflict of interest might exist where the adviser had a position in a security he was recommending. *See also* INVESTMENT ADVISORY SERVICE.

INVESTMENT ADVISORY SERVICE service providing investment advice for a fee. Investment advisers must register with the Securities and Exchange Commission and abide by the rules of the INVESTMENT ADVISERS ACT. Investment advisory services usually specialize in a particular kind of investment—for example, emerging growth stocks, international stocks, mutual funds, or commodities. Some services only offer advice through a newsletter; others will manage a client's money. The performance of many investment advisory services is ranked by the *Hulbert Financial Digest. See* HULBERT RATING.

INVESTMENT BANKER firm, acting as underwriter or agent, that serves as intermediary between an issuer of securities and the investing public. In what is termed FIRM COMMITMENT underwriting, the investment banker, either as manager or participating member of an investment banking syndicate, makes outright purchases of new securities from the issuer and distributes them to dealers and investors, profiting on the spread between the purchase price and the selling (public offering) price. Under a conditional arrangement called BEST EFFORT, the investment banker markets a new issue without underwriting it, acting as agent rather than principal and taking a commission for whatever amount of securities the banker succeeds in marketing. Under another conditional arrangement, called STANDBY COMMITMENT, the investment banker serves clients issuing new securities by agreeing to purchase for resale any securities not taken by existing holders of RIGHTS.

Where a client relationship exists, the investment banker's role begins with preunderwriting counseling and continues after the distribution of securities is completed, in the form of ongoing expert advice and guidance, often including a seat on the board of directors. The direct underwriting responsibilities include preparing the Securities and Exchange Commission registration statement; consulting on pricing of the securities; forming and managing the syndicate; establishing a selling group if desired; and PEGGING (stabilizing) the price of the issue during the offering and distribution period.

In addition to new securities offerings, investment bankers handle the distribution of blocks of previously issued securities, either through secondary offerings or through negotiations; maintain markets for securities already distributed; and act as finders in the private placement of securities.

Along with their investment banking functions, the majority of investment bankers also maintain broker-dealer operations, serving both wholesale and retail clients in brokerage and advisory capacities and offering a growing number of related financial services. *See also* FLOTATION COST; SECONDARY DISTRIBUTION; UNDERWRITE.

INVESTMENT CERTIFICATE certificate evidencing investment in a savings and loan association and showing the amount of money invested. Investment certificates do not have voting rights and do not involve stockholder responsibility. Also called *mutual capital certificate*. See also MUTUAL ASSOCIATION.

INVESTMENT CLIMATE economic, monetary, and other conditions affecting the performance of investments.

INVESTMENT CLUB group of people who pool their assets in order to make joint investment decisions. Each member of the club contributes a certain amount of capital, with additional money to be invested every month or quarter. Decisions on which stocks or bonds to buy are made by a vote of members. Besides helping each member become more knowledgeable about investing, these clubs allow people with small amounts of money to participate in larger investments, own part of a more diversified portfolio, and pay lower commission rates than would be possible for individual members on their own. The trade group for investment clubs is the National Association of Investors Corporation (NAIC) in Madison Heights, Michigan. The NAIC helps clubs get started and offers several programs, such as the Low-Cost Investment Plan allowing clubs to purchase an initial share of individual stocks at low commissions and reinvest dividends automatically at no charge.

INVESTMENT COMPANY firm that, for a management fee, invests the pooled funds of small investors in securities appropriate for its stated investment objectives. It offers participants more diversification, liquidity, and professional management service than would normally be available to them as individuals.

There are two basic types of investment companies: (1) *open-end,* better known as a MUTUAL FUND, which has a floating number of outstanding shares (hence the name *open-end*) and stands prepared to sell or redeem shares at their current NET ASSET VALUE; and (2) *closed-end,* also known as an *investment trust,* which, like a corporation, has a fixed number of outstanding shares that are traded like a stock, often on the New York and American Stock Exchanges.

Open-end management companies are basically divided into two categories, based on the way they distribute their funds to customers. The first category is *load funds,* which are sold in the over-the-counter market by broker-dealers, who do not receive a sales commission; instead a "loading charge" is added to the net asset value at time of purchase. For many years the charge was 8½%, but more recently it has been reduced to 4.5%–5%. Many load funds do not charge an upfront load, but instead impose a BACK-END LOAD which customers must pay if they sell fund shares within a certain number of years, usually five. The second category is *no-load funds,* which are bought directly from sponsoring fund companies. Such companies do not charge a loading fee, although some funds levy a redemption fee if shares are sold within a specified number of years.

Some funds, both load and no-load, are called 12b-1 MUTUAL FUNDS because they levy an annual 12b-1 charge of up to 0.75% of assets to pay for promotional and marketing expenses.

Dealers in closed-end investment companies obtain their revenue from regular brokerage commissions, just as they do in selling any individual stock.

Both open-end and closed-end investment companies charge annual management fees, typically ranging from 0.25% to 2% of the value of the assets in the fund.

Under the INVESTMENT COMPANY ACT OF 1940, the registration statement and prospectus of every investment company must state its specific investment objectives. Investment companies fall into many categories, including: diversified common stock funds (with growth of capital as the principal objective); balanced funds (mixing common and preferred stocks, bonds, and cash); bond and preferred stock funds (emphasizing current income); specialized funds (by industry, groups of industries, geography, or size of company); income funds buying high-yield stocks and bonds; dual-purpose funds (a form of closed-end investment company offering a choice of income shares or capital gains shares); and money market funds which invest in money market instruments.

INVESTMENT COMPANY ACT OF 1940 legislation passed by Congress requiring registration and regulation of investment companies by the Securities and Exchange Commission. The Act sets the standards by which mutual funds and other investment vehicles of investment companies operate, in such areas as promotion, reporting requirements, pricing of securities for sale to the public, and allocation of investments within a fund portfolio. *See also* INVESTMENT COMPANY.

INVESTMENT COUNSEL person with the responsibility for providing investment advice to clients and executing investment decisions. *See also* PORTFOLIO MANAGER.

INVESTMENT CREDIT reduction in income tax liability granted by the federal government over the years to firms making new investments in certain asset categories, primarily equipment; also called *investment tax credit.* The investment credit, designed to stimulate the economy by encouraging capital expenditure, has been a feature of tax legislation on and off, and in varying percentage amounts, since 1962; in 1985 it was 6% or 10% of the purchase price, depending on the life of the asset. As a credit, it has been deducted from the tax bill, not from pretax income, and it has been independent of DEPRECIATION. The TAX REFORM ACT OF 1986 generally repealed the investment credit retroactively for any property placed in service after January 1, 1986. The 1986 Act also provided for a 35% reduction of the value of credits carried over from previous years, which was later changed to 50%.

INVESTMENT GRADE bond with a RATING of AAA to BBB. *See also junk bond.*

INVESTMENT HISTORY body of prior experience establishing "normal investment practice" with respect to the account relationship between a member firm and its customer. For example, the Rules of Fair Practice of the National Association of Securities Dealers (NASD) prohibit the sale of a new issue to members of a distributing dealer's immediate family, but if there was sufficient precedent in the investment history of this particular dealer-customer relationship, the sale would not be a violation.

INVESTMENT INCOME income from securities and other nonbusiness investments; such as DIVIDENDS, INTEREST, OPTION PREMIUMS, and income from a ROYALTY or ANNUITY. Under the TAX REFORM ACT OF 1986, interest on MARGIN ACCOUNTS may be used to offset investment income without limitation. Investment income earned by passive activities must be treated separately from other PASSIVE income. The REVENUE RECONCILIATION ACT OF 1993 eliminated net gains from selling investment property from the definition of *investment income.* Expenses incurred to generate investment income can reduce investment income to the extent they exceed 2% of adjusted gross income. By excluding capital gains from the calculation, the 1993 Act, in effect, prevents a taxpayer from claiming an ordinary deduction for margin interest incurred to carry an investment that is taxable at the favorable capital gains rate. Also called UNEARNED INCOME and *portfolio income.*

INVESTMENT LETTER in the private placement of new securities, a letter of intent between the issuer of securities and the buyer establishing that the securities are being bought as an investment and are not for resale. This is necessary to avoid having to register the securities with the Securities and Exchange Commission. (Under provisions of SEC Rule 144, a purchaser of such securities may eventually resell them to the public if certain specific conditions are met, including a minimum holding period of at least two years.) Use of the investment letter gave rise to the terms *letter stock* and *letter bond* in referring to unregistered issues. *See also* LETTER SECURITY.

INVESTMENT MANAGEMENT in general, the activities of a portfolio manager. More specifically, it distinguishes between managed and unmanaged portfolios, examples of the latter being UNIT INVESTMENT TRUSTS and INDEX FUNDS, which are fixed portfolios not requiring ongoing decisions.

INVESTMENT OBJECTIVE financial objective that an investor uses to determine which kind of investment is appropriate. For example, if the investor's objective is growth of capital, he may opt for growth-oriented mutual funds or individual stocks. If he is more interested in income, he might purchase income-oriented mutual funds or individual bonds instead. Consideration of investment objectives, combined with the risk tolerance of investors, helps an investor narrow his search to an investment vehicle designed for his needs at a particular time.

INVESTMENT PHILOSOPHY style of investment practiced by an individual investor or money manager. For example, some investors follow the growth philosophy, concentrating on stocks with steadily rising earnings. Others are value investors, searching for stocks that have fallen out of favor, and are therefore cheap relative to the true value of their assets. Some managers favor small-capitalization stocks, while others stick with large blue-chip companies. Some managers have a philosophy of remaining fully invested at all times, while others believe in market timing, so that their portfolios can accumulate cash if the managers think stock or bond prices are about to fall.

INVESTMENT SOFTWARE software designed to aid investors' decision-making. Some software packages allow investors to perform TECHNICAL ANALYSIS, charting stock prices, volume, and other indicators. Other programs allow FUNDAMENTAL ANALYSIS, permitting investors to SCREEN STOCKS based on financial criteria such as earnings, price/earnings ratios, book value, and dividend yields. Some software offers recordkeeping, so that an investor can keep track of the value of his portfolio and the prices at which he bought or sold securities. Many software packages allow investors to tap into databases to update securities prices, scan news items, and execute trades. Specialty programs allow investors to value options, calculate yield analysis on bonds, and screen mutual funds.

INVESTMENT STRATEGY plan to allocate assets among such choices as stocks, bonds, CASH EQUIVALENTS, commodities, and real estate. An investment strategy should be formulated based on an investor's outlook on interest rates, inflation, and economic growth, among other factors, and also taking into account the investor's age, tolerance for risk, amount of capital available to invest, and future needs for capital, such as for financing childrens' college educations or buying a house. An investment adviser will help to devise such a strategy. *See also* INVESTMENT ADVISORY SERVICE.

INVESTMENT STRATEGY COMMITTEE committee in the research department of a brokerage firm that sets the overall investment strategy the firm recommends to clients. The director of research, the chief economist, and several top analysts typically sit on this committee. The group advises clients on the amount of money that should be placed into stocks, bonds, or CASH EQUIVALENTS, as well as the industry groups or individual stocks or bonds that look particularly attractive.

INVESTMENT TAX CREDIT *see* INVESTMENT CREDIT.

INVESTMENT TRUST *see* INVESTMENT COMPANY.

INVESTMENT VALUE OF A CONVERTIBLE SECURITY estimated price at which a CONVERTIBLE security (CV) would be valued by the marketplace if it had no stock conversion feature. The investment value for CVs of major companies is determined by investment advisory services and, theoretically, should never fall lower than the price of the related stock. It is arrived at by estimating the price at which a nonconvertible ("straight") bond or preferred share of the same issuing company would sell. The investment value reflects the interest rate; therefore, the market price of the security will go up when rates are down and vice versa. *See also* PREMIUM OVER BOND VALUE.

INVESTOR party who puts money at risk; may be an individual or an institutional investor.

INVESTOR RELATIONS DEPARTMENT in major listed companies, a staff position responsible for investor relations, reporting either to the chief financial officer or to the director of public relations. The actual duties will vary, depending on whether the company retains an outside financial public relations firm, but the general responsibilities are as follows:
- to see that the company is understood, in terms of its activities and objectives, and is favorably regarded in the financial and capital markets and the investment community; this means having input into the annual report and other published materials, coordinating senior management speeches and public statements with the FINANCIAL PUBLIC RELATIONS effort, and generally fostering a consistent and positive corporate image.
- to ensure full and timely public DISCLOSURE of material information, and to work with the legal staff in complying with the rules of the SEC, the securities exchanges, and other regulatory authorities.
- to respond to requests for reports and information from shareholders, professional investors, brokers, and the financial media.
- to maintain productive relations with the firm's investment bankers, the specialists in its stock, major broker-dealers, and institutional investors who follow the company or hold sizeable positions in its securities.
- to take direct measures, where necessary, to see that the company's shares are properly valued. This involves identifying the firm's particular investment audience and the professionals controlling its stock float, arranging analysts' meetings and other presentations, and generating appropriate publicity.

    The most successful investor relations professionals have been those who follow a policy of full and open dissemination of relevant information, favorable and unfavorable, on a consistent basis. The least successful, over the long run, have been the "touts"—those who emphasize promotion at the expense of credibility.

INVESTORS SERVICE BUREAU New York Stock Exchange public service that responds to written inquiries of all types concerning securities investments.

INVOICE bill prepared by a seller of goods or services and submitted to the purchaser. The invoice lists all the items bought, together with amounts.

INVOLUNTARY BANKRUPTCY *see* BANKRUPTCY.

IRA *see* INDIVIDUAL RETIREMENT ACCOUNT.

IRA ROLLOVER *see* INDIVIDUAL RETIREMENT ACCOUNT ROLLOVER.

IRREDEEMABLE BOND
1. bond without a CALL FEATURE (issuer's right to redeem the bond before maturity) or a REDEMPTION privilege (holder's right to sell the bond back to the issuer before maturity).
2. PERPETUAL BOND.

IRREVOCABLE something done that cannot legally be undone, such as an IRREVOCABLE TRUST.

IRREVOCABLE LIVING TRUST trust usually created to achieve some tax benefit, or to provide a vehicle for managing assets of a person the creator believes cannot or should not be managing his or her own property. This trust cannot be changed or reversed by the creator of the trust.

IRREVOCABLE TRUST trust that cannot be changed or terminated by the one who created it without the agreement of the BENEFICIARY.

IRS *see* INTERNAL REVENUE SERVICE.

IRS PRIVATE LETTER RULING *see* PRIVATE LETTER RULING.

ISIS *see* INTERMARKET SURVEILLANCE INFORMATION SYSTEM (ISIS).

INTERNATIONAL SECURITIES REGULATORY ORGANIZATION (ISRO) *see* INTERNATIONAL STOCK EXCHANGE OF THE UNITED KINGDOM AND THE REPUBLIC OF IRELAND (ISE).

ISSUE
1. stock or bonds sold by a corporation or a government entity at a particular time.
2. selling new securities by a corporation or government entity, either through an underwriter or by a private placement.
3. descendants, such as children and grandchildren. For instance, "This man's estate will be passed, at his death, to his issue."

ISSUED AND OUTSTANDING shares of a corporation, authorized in the corporate charter, which have been issued and are outstanding. These shares represent capital invested by the firm's shareholders and owners, and may be all or only a portion of the number of shares authorized. Shares that have been issued and subsequently repurchased by the company are called *treasury stock,* because they are held in the corporate treasury pending reissue or retirement. Treasury shares are legally issued but are not considered outstanding for purposes of voting, dividends, or earnings per share calculations. Shares authorized but not yet issued are called *unissued shares.* Most companies show the amount of authorized, issued and outstanding, and treasury shares in the capital section of their annual reports. *See also* TREASURY STOCK.

ISSUER legal entity that has the power to issue and distribute a security. Issuers include corporations, municipalities, foreign and domestic governments and their agencies, and investment trusts. Issuers of stock are responsible for reporting on corporate developments to shareholders and paying dividends once declared. Issuers of bonds are committed to making timely payments of interest and principal to bondholders.

ITEMIZED DEDUCTION item that allows a taxpayer to reduce adjusted gross income on his or her tax return. For example, mortgage interest, charitable contributions, state and local income and property taxes, unreimbursed business expenses, IRA contributions, and other miscellaneous items are considered deductible under certain conditions, and are listed as itemized deductions on Schedule A of an individual's tax return. However, at certain income levels, deductions are phased out. For example, in the 1994 tax year, itemized deductions were phased out by 3% of the excess of adjusted gross income over $111,800 (if married and filing separately, then $55,900) adjusted annually for inflation.

J

JANUARY BAROMETER market forecasting tool popularized by *The Stock Traders Almanac,* whose statistics show that with 88% consistency since 1950, the market has risen in years when the STANDARD & POOR'S INDEX of 500 stocks was up in January and dropped when the index for that month was down.

JANUARY EFFECT phenomenon that stocks (especially small stocks) have historically tended to rise markedly during the period starting on the last day of December and ending on the fourth trading day of January. The January Effect is owed to year-end selling to create tax losses, recognize capital gains, effect portfolio WINDOW DRESSING, or raise holiday cash; since such selling depresses the stocks but has nothing to do with their fundamental worth, bargain hunters quickly buy in, causing the January rally.

JEEP *see* GRADUATED PAYMENT MORTGAGE.

JOBBER
1. wholesaler, especially one who buys in small lots from manufacturers, importers, and/or other wholesalers and sells to retailers.
2. London Stock Exchange term for MARKET MAKER.

JOHANNESBURG STOCK EXCHANGE (JSE) only stock exchange in South Africa, established in 1886. Gold and mining shares dominate the shares listed, though there are also many other industrial and service stocks trading on the exchange. The mining-related sector accounts for nearly 41% of market capitalization of all quoted companies. Futures contracts are traded on the All Share, All Gold, and Industrial indices; options are traded on All Share and All Gold. Share options are traded on some of the top mining stocks, including DeBeers Consolidated Mines Ltd., Driefontein Consolidated Ltd., Rustenburg Platinum Holdings Ltd., Barlow Rand Ltd., and Gencor Ltd. Trading is by open outcry. The exchange uses a weekly computerized clearing system for settlement between brokers. Trades executed in one week are settled the following week. Hours: 9:30 A.M.–4 P.M., Monday through Friday.

JOINT ACCOUNT bank or brokerage account owned jointly by two or more people. Joint accounts may be set up in two ways: (1) either all parties to the account must sign checks and approve all withdrawals or brokerage transactions or (2) any one party can take such actions on his or her own. *See also* JOINT TENANTS WITH RIGHT OF SURVIVORSHIP.

JOINT ACCOUNT AGREEMENT form needed to open a JOINT ACCOUNT at a bank or brokerage. It must be signed by all parties to the account regardless of the provisions it may contain concerning signatures required to authorize transactions.

JOINT AND SURVIVOR ANNUITY annuity that makes payments for the lifetime of two or more beneficiaries, often a husband and wife. When one of the annuitants dies, payments continue to the survivor annuitant in the same amount or in a reduced amount as specified in the contract.

JOINT BOND bond that has more than one obligator or that is guaranteed by a party other than the issuer; also called *joint and several bond.* Joint bonds are common where a parent corporation wishes to guarantee the bonds of a subsidiary. *See* GUARANTEED BOND.

JOINT LIABILITY mutual legal responsibility by two or more parties for claims on the assets of a company or individual. *See also* LIABILITY.

JOINTLY AND SEVERALLY
In general: legal phrase used in definitions of liability meaning that an obligation may be enforced against all obligators jointly or against any one of them separately.
Securities: term used to refer to municipal bond underwritings where the account is undivided and syndicate members are responsible for unsold bonds in proportion to their participations. In other words, a participant with 5% of the account would still be responsible for 5% of the unsold bonds, even though that member might already have sold 10%. *See also* SEVERALLY BUT NOT JOINTLY.

JOINT OWNERSHIP equal ownership by two or more people, who have right of survivorship.

JOINT STOCK COMPANY form of business organization that combines features of a corporation and a partnership. Under U.S. law, joint stock companies are recognized as corporations with unlimited liability for their stockholders. As in a conventional corporation, investors in joint stock companies receive shares of stock they are free to sell at will without ending the corporation; they also elect directors. Unlike in a limited liability corporation, however, each shareholder in a joint stock company is legally liable for all debts of the company.

There are some advantages to this form of organization compared with limited-liability corporations: fewer taxes, greater ease of formation under the common law, more security for creditors, mobility, and freedom from regulation, for example. However, the disadvantages—such as the fact that the joint stock company usually cannot hold title to real estate and, particularly, the company's unlimited liability—tend to outweigh the advantages, with the result that it is not a popular form of organization.

JOINT TAX RETURN tax return filed by two people, usually a married couple. Both parties must sign the return and they are equally responsible for paying the taxes due. Thus if one party does not pay the taxes, the IRS can come after the other party to make the required payment. Because of the way the tax tables are designed, it is frequently more advantageous for a married couple to file a joint return than for them to file separate returns. *See also* FILING STATUS; HEAD OF HOUSEHOLD.

JOINT TENANCY *see* TENANCY IN COMMON. *See also* JOINT TENANTS WITH RIGHT OF SURVIVORSHIP.

JOINT TENANTS WITH RIGHT OF SURVIVORSHIP when two or more people maintain a JOINT ACCOUNT with a brokerage firm or a bank, it is normally agreed that, upon the death of one account holder, ownership of the account assets passes to the remaining account holders. This transfer of assets escapes probate, but estate taxes may be due, depending on the amount of assets transferred.

JOINT VENTURE agreement by two or more parties to work on a project together. Frequently, a joint venture will be formed when companies with complementary technology wish to create a product or service that takes advantage of the strengths of the participants. A joint venture, which is usually limited to one project, differs from a partnership, which forms the basis for cooperation on many projects.

JOINT WILL single document setting forth the testamentary instructions of a husband and wife. The use of joint wills is not common in the United States, and it may create tax and other problems.

JONESTOWN DEFENSE tactics taken by management to ward off a hostile TAKEOVER that are so extreme that they appear suicidal for the company. For example, the company may try to sell its CROWN JEWELS or take on a huge amount of debt to make the company undesirable to the potential acquirer. The term refers to the mass suicide led by Jim Jones in Jonestown, Guyana, in the early 1980s. *See also* SCORCHED EARTH POLICY.

JUDGMENT decision by a court of law ordering someone to pay a certain amount of money. For instance, a court may order someone who illegally profited by trading on INSIDE INFORMATION to pay a judgment amounting to all the profits from the trade, plus damages. The term also refers to condemnation awards by government entities in payment for private property taken for public use.

JUMBO CERTIFICATE OF DEPOSIT certificate with a minimum denomination of $100,000. Jumbo CDs are usually bought and sold by large institutions such as banks, pension funds, money market funds, and insurance companies.

JUMBO LOANS loans in amounts exceeding the national guidelines of FREDDIE MAC and FANNIE MAE.

JUNIOR ISSUE issue of debt or equity that is subordinate in claim to another issue in terms of dividends, interest, principal, or security in the event of liquidation. *See also* JUNIOR SECURITY; PREFERRED STOCK; PRIORITY; PRIOR LIEN BOND: PRIOR PREFERRED STOCK.

JUNIOR MORTGAGE mortgage that is subordinate to other mortgages—for example, a second or a third mortgage. If a debtor defaults, the first mortgage will have to be satisfied before the junior mortgage.

JUNIOR REFUNDING refinancing government debt that matures in one to five years by issuing new securities that mature in five years or more.

JUNIOR SECURITY security with lower priority claim on assets and income than a SENIOR SECURITY. For example, a PREFERRED STOCK is junior to a DEBENTURE, but a debenture, being an unsecured bond, is junior to a MORTGAGE BOND. COMMON STOCK is junior to all corporate securities. Some companies—finance companies, for example—have senior SUBORDINATED and junior subordinated issues, the former having priority over the latter, but both ranking lower than senior (unsubordinated) debt.

JUNK BOND bond with a credit rating of BB or lower by RATING agencies. Although commonly used, the term has a pejorative connotation, and issuers and holders prefer the securities be called *high-yield bonds*. Junk bonds are issued by companies without long track records of sales and earnings, or by those with questionable credit strength. They are a popular means of financing TAKEOVERS. Since they are more volatile and pay higher yields than INVESTMENT GRADE bonds, many risk-oriented investors specialize in trading them. Institutions with FIDUCIARY responsibilities are regulated (*see* PRUDENT-MAN RULE). *See also* FALLEN ANGELS.

JURISDICTION defined by the American Bankers Association as "the legal right, power or authority to hear and determine a cause; as in the jurisdiction of a court." The term frequently comes up in finance and investment discussions in connection with the jurisdictions of the various regulatory authorities bearing on the field. For example, the Federal Reserve Board, not the Securities and Exchange Commission (as might be supposed), has jurisdiction in a case involving a brokerage MARGIN ACCOUNT (*see also* REGULATION T).

The term also is important with respect to EUROCURRENCY loan agreements, where it is possible for a loan to be funded in one country but made in another by a group of international banks each from different countries, to a borrower in still another country. The determination of jurisdiction, not to mention the willingness of courts in different countries to accept that jurisdiction, is a matter of obvious urgency in such cases.

JURY OF EXECUTIVE OPINION forecasting method whereby a panel of experts—perhaps senior corporate financial executives—prepare individual forecasts based on information made available to all of them. Each expert then reviews the others' work and modifies his or her own forecasts accordingly. The resulting composite forecast is supposed to be more realistic than any individual effort could be. Also known as *Delphi forecast*.

JUSTIFIED PRICE fair market price an informed buyer will pay for an asset, whether it be a stock, a bond, a commodity, or real estate. *See also* FAIR MARKET VALUE.

JUST TITLE title to property that is supportable against all legal claims. Also called *clear title, good title, proper title*.

k

KAFFIRS term used in Great Britain that refers to South African gold mining shares. These shares are traded over the counter in the U.S. in the form of American Depositary Receipts, which are claims to share certificates deposited in a foreign bank. Under South African law, Kaffirs must pay out almost all their earnings to shareholders as dividends. These shares thus not only provide stockholders with a gold investment to hedge against inflation, but also afford substantial income in the form of high dividend payments. However, investors in Kaffirs must also consider the political risks of investing in South Africa, as well as the risk of fluctuations in the price of gold. *See also* AMERICAN DEPOSITARY RECEIPT.

KANGAROOS nickname for Australian stocks. The term normally refers to stocks in the ALL ORDINARIES INDEX, and refers to the animal most closely associated with Australia.

KANSAS CITY BOARD OF TRADE (KCBT) futures exchange trading No. 2 red wheat futures and options; Value Line Index futures; and Mini Value Line futures and options. Hours: 8:30 A.M.–3:15 P.M., Monday through Friday.

KEOGH PLAN tax-deferred pension account designated for employees of unincorporated businesses or for persons who are self-employed (either full-time or part-time). As of 1995, eligible people could contribute up to 25% of earned income, up to a maximum of $30,000. Like the INDIVIDUAL RETIREMENT ACCOUNT (IRA), the Keogh plan allows all investment earnings to grow tax deferred until capital is withdrawn, as early as age 59½ and starting no later than age 70½. Almost any investment except precious metals or collectibles can be used for a Keogh account. Typically, people place Keogh assets in stocks, bonds, money-market funds, certificates of deposit, mutual funds, or limited partnerships. The Keogh plan was established by Congress in 1962 and was expanded in 1976 and again in 1981 as part of the Economic Recovery Tax Act.

KEY INDUSTRY industry of primary importance to a nation's economy. For instance, the defense industry is called a key industry since it is crucial to maintaining a country's safety. The automobile industry is also considered key since so many jobs are directly or indirectly dependent on it.

KEY MAN (OR WOMAN) INSURANCE life insurance policy bought by a company, usually a small business, on the life of a key executive, with the company as beneficiary.

KEYNESIAN ECONOMICS body of economic thought originated by the British economist and government adviser, John Maynard Keynes (1883–1946), whose landmark work, *The General Theory of Employment, Interest and Money*, was published in 1935. Writing during the Great Depression, Keynes took issue with the classical economists, like Adam Smith, who believed that the economy worked best when left alone. Keynes believed that active government intervention in the marketplace was the only method of ensuring economic growth and stability. He held essentially that insufficient demand causes unemployment and that excessive demand results in inflation; government should therefore manipulate the level of aggregate demand by adjusting levels of government expenditure and taxation. For example, to avoid depression Keynes advocated increased government spending and EASY MONEY, resulting in more investment, higher employment, and increased consumer spending.

Keynesian economics has had great influence on the public economic policies of industrial nations, including the United States. In the 1980s, however, after repeated recessions, slow growth, and high rates of inflation in the U.S., a contrasting outlook, uniting monetarists and "supply siders," blamed excessive government intervention for troubles in the economy.

See also AGGREGATE SUPPLY; LAISSEZ-FAIRE; MACROECONOMICS; MONETARIST; SUPPLY-SIDE ECONOMICS.

KICKBACK

Finance: practice whereby sales finance companies reward dealers who discount installment purchase paper through them with cash payments.

Government and private contracts: payment made secretly by a seller to someone instrumental in awarding a contract or making a sale—an illegal payoff.

Labor relations: illegal practice whereby employers require the return of a portion of wages established by law or union contract, in exchange for employment.

KICKER added feature of a debt obligation, usually designed to enhance marketability by offering the prospect of equity participation. For instance, a bond may be convertible to stock if the shares reach a certain price. This makes the bond more attractive to investors, since the bondholder potentially gets the benefit of an equity security in addition to interest payments. Other examples of equity kickers are RIGHTS and WARRANTS. Some mortgage loans also include kickers in the form of ownership participation or in the form of a percentage of gross rental receipts. Kickers are also called *sweeteners.*

KIDDIE TAX tax filed by parents on Form 8615 for the investment income of children under age 14 exceeding $1200. Tax is at parent's top tax rate. In some cases, however, parents may elect to report such children's income on their own returns.

KILLER BEES those who aid a company in fending off a takeover bid. "Killer bees" are usually investment bankers who devise strategies to make the target less attractive or more difficult to acquire.

KITING
Commercial banking: (1) depositing and drawing checks between accounts at two or more banks and thereby taking advantage of the FLOAT—that is, the time it takes the bank of deposit to collect from the paying bank. (2) fraudently altering the figures on a check to increase its face value.

Securities: driving stock prices to high levels through manipulative trading methods, such as the creation of artificial trading activity by the buyer and the seller working together and using the same funds.

KNOCK-OUT OPTION form of derivative that gives the buyer the right, but not the obligation, to buy an underlying commodity, currency, or other position at a preset price. Unlike regular options, however, knock-out options expire worthless, or are "knocked out" if the underlying commodity or currency goes through a particular price level. For example, a knock-out option based on the value of the U.S. dollar against the German mark gets knocked out if the dollar falls below a specified exchange rate against the mark. Regular options can have unlimited moves up or down. Knock-out options are much cheaper to buy than regular options, allowing buyers to take larger positions with less money than regular options. Knock-out options are frequently used by hedge funds and other speculators.

KNOW YOUR CUSTOMER ethical concept in the securities industry either stated or implied by the rules of the exchanges and the other authorities regulating broker-dealer practices. Its meaning is expressed in the following paragraph from Article 3 of the NASD Rules of Fair Practice: "In recommending to a customer the purchase, sale or exchange of any security, a member shall have reasonable grounds for believing that the recommendation is suitable for such customer upon the basis of the facts, if any, disclosed by such customer as to his other security holdings and as to his financial situation and needs." Customers opening accounts at brokerage firms must supply financial information that satisfies the know your customer requirement for routine purposes.

KONDRATIEFF WAVE theory of the Soviet economist Nikolai Kondratieff in the 1920s that the economies of the Western capitalist world were prone to major up-and-down "supercycles" lasting 50 to 60 years. He claimed to have predicted the economic crash of 1929–30 based on the crash of 1870, 60 years earlier. The Kondratieff wave theory has adherents, but is controversial among economists. Also called *Kondratieff cycle.*

KRUGGERAND gold bullion coin minted by the Republic of South Africa which comes in one-ounce, half-ounce, quarter-ounce and one-tenth-ounce sizes. Kruggerands usually sell for slightly more than the current value of their gold content. Kruggerands, which had been the dominant gold coin in the world, were banned from being imported into the United States in 1985 because of the South African government's policy of apartheid. The ban was lifted on July 10, 1991.

Other GOLD COINS traded in addition to the Kruggerand include the United States Eagle, Canadian Maple Leaf, Mexican Peso, Austrian Philharmonic, and Australian Kangaroo.

KUALA LUMPUR COMMODITY EXCHANGE exchange trading futures in crude palm oil, crude palm kernel oil, cocoa, tin, and rubber. The exchange has formed a wholly owned subsidiary, Kuala Lumpur Futures Market Sdn Bhd (KLFM) to trade in financial futures. Hours: 11 A.M.–7 P.M., Monday through Friday.

KUALA LUMPUR STOCK EXCHANGE largest securities exchange in Malaysia, formerly affiliated with Singapore as the Stock Exchange of Malaysia. Trading must be carried out through one of the exchange's member firms at a fixed commission rate. Open outcry was phased out in November 1989 and SCORE, the System on Computerized Order Routing and Execution, was introduced. Settlement is through the Central Depository System (CDS), by book entry, with CDS accounts of buyers credited on the fifth day but held in lien until payment by the seventh market day, while sellers are debited on the fifth market day. The Kuala Lampur Composite Index is the benchmark index, with 11 other indices traded. Hours: 9:30 A.M.–12:30 P.M., and 2:30 P.M.–5 P.M., Monday through Friday.

L

LABOR-INTENSIVE requiring large pools of workers. Said of an industry in which labor costs are more important than capital costs. Deep-shaft coal mining, for instance, is labor-intensive.

LADY MACBETH STRATEGY TAKEOVER tactic whereby a third party poses as a white knight then turns coat and joins an unfriendly bidder.

LAFFER CURVE curve named for U.S. economics professor Arthur Laffer, postulating that economic output will grow if marginal tax rates are cut. The curve is used in explaining SUPPLY-SIDE ECONOMICS, a theory that noninflationary growth is spurred when tax policies encourage productivity and investment.

LAGGING INDICATORS economic indicators that lag behind the overall pace of economic activity. The Commerce Department publishes the Index of Lagging Indicators monthly along with the index of LEADING INDICATORS and the index of COINCIDENT INDICATORS. The six components of the lagging indicators are the unemployment rate, business spending, unit labor costs, bank loans outstanding, bank interest rates, and the book value of manufacturing and trade inventories.

LAISSEZ-FAIRE doctrine that interference of government in business and economic affairs should be minimal. Adam Smith's *The Wealth Of Nations* (1776) described laissez-faire economics in terms of an "invisible hand" that would provide for the maximum good for all, if businessmen were free to pursue profitable opportunities as they saw them. The growth of industry in England in the early 19th century and American industrial growth in the late 19th century both occurred in a laissez-faire capitalist environment. The laissez-faire period ended by the beginning of the 20th century, when large monopolies were broken up and government regulation of business became the norm. The Great Depression of the 1930s saw the birth of KEYNESIAN ECONOMICS, an influential approach advocating government intervention in economic affairs. The movement toward deregulation of business in the United States that began in the 1970s and 80s is to some extent a return to the laissez-faire philosophy. Laissez-faire is French for "allow to do."

LAND CONTRACT creative real estate financing method whereby a seller with a mortgage finances a buyer by taking a down payment and being paid installments but not yielding title until the mortgage is repaid. Also called *contract for deed* and *installment sales contract.*

LANDLORD owner of property who rents it to a TENANT.

LAPSE expiration of a right or privilege because one party did not live up to its obligations during the time allowed. For example, a life insurance policy will lapse if the policyholder does not make the required premium payments on time. This means that the policyholder is no longer protected by the policy.

LAPSED OPTION OPTION that reached its expiration date without being exercised and is thus without value.

LAST IN FIRST OUT (LIFO) method of accounting for INVENTORY that ties the cost of goods sold to the cost of the most recent purchases. The formula for cost of goods sold is:

beginning inventory + purchases – ending inventory = cost of goods sold

In contrast to the FIRST IN, FIRST OUT (FIFO) method, in a period of rising prices LIFO produces a higher cost of goods sold and a lower gross profit and taxable income. The artificially low balance sheet inventories resulting from the use of LIFO in periods of inflation give rise to the term *LIFO cushion.*

LAST SALE most recent trade in a particular security. Not to be confused with the final transaction in a trading session, called the CLOSING SALE. The last sale is the point of reference for two Securities and Exchange Commission rules: (1) On a national exchange, no SHORT SALE may be made below the price of the last regular sale. (2) No short sale may be made at the same price as the last sale unless the last sale was at a price higher than the preceding different price. PLUS TICK, MINUS TICK, ZERO MINUS TICK, and ZERO PLUS TICK, used in this connection, refer to the last sale.

LAST TRADING DAY final day during which a futures contract may be settled. If the contract is not OFFSET, either an agreement between the buying and selling parties must be arranged or the physical commodity must be delivered from the seller to the buyer.

LATE CHARGE fee charged by a grantor of credit when the borrower fails to make timely payment.

LATE TAPE delay in displaying price changes because trading on a stock exchange is particularly heavy. If the tape is more than five minutes late, the first digit of a price is deleted. For instance, a trade at 62¾ is reported as 2¾. *See also* DIGITS DELETED.

LAUNDER to make illegally acquired cash look as if it were acquired legally. The usual practice is to transfer the money through foreign banks, thereby concealing its purpose. SEC Rule 17a-8 prohibits using broker-dealers for this purpose.

LAW OF LARGE NUMBERS statistical concept holding that the greater the number of units in a projection, the less important each unit becomes. Group insurance, which gets cheaper as the group gets larger, is an example of the principle in application; actuarial abnormalities have less influence on total claims.

LAY OFF

Investment banking: reduce the risk in a standby commitment, under which the bankers agree to purchase and resell to the public any portion of a stock issue not subscribed to by shareowners who hold rights. The risk is that the market value will fall during the two to four weeks when shareholders are deciding whether to exercise or sell their rights. To minimize the risk, investment bankers (1) buy up the rights as they are offered and, at the same time, sell the shares represented by these rights; and (2) sell short an amount of shares proportionate to the rights that can be expected to go unexercised—to ½% of the issue, typically. Also called *laying off.*

Labor: temporarily or permanently remove an employee from a payroll because of an economic slowdown or a production cutback, not because of poor performance or an infraction of company rules.

LEADER
1. stock or group of stocks at the forefront of an upsurge or a downturn in a market. Typically, leaders are heavily bought and sold by institutions that want to demonstrate their own market leadership.
2. product that has a large market share.

LEADING INDICATORS components of indicators released monthly by the U.S. Commerce Department's Bureau of Economic Analysis, along with the Index of LAGGING INDICATORS and the Index of COINCIDENT INDICATORS. The 11 components are: the average workweek of production workers; average weekly claims for state unemployment insurance; manufacturers' new orders for consumer goods and materials; vendor performance (companies receiving slower deliveries from suppliers); contracts and orders for plant and equipment; building permits; change in manufacturers' unfilled orders for durable goods; changes in sensitive materials prices; stock prices; MONEY SUPPLY (M-2); and index of consumer expectations. The index of leading indicators, the components of which are adjusted for inflation, accurately forecasts the ups and downs of the business cycle.

LEAD REGULATOR leading self-regulatory organization (SRO) taking responsibility for investigation of a particular section of the law and all the cases that pertain to it. In the securities business, for example, the New York Stock Exchange may take the lead in investigating certain kinds of fraud or suspicious market activity, while the American Stock Exchange or NASDAQ may be the lead regulator in other areas. The lead regulator will report its findings to the other self-regulatory organizations, and ultimately to a government oversight agency, such as the Securities and Exchange Commission.

LEAPS acronym for Long-Term Equity AnticiPation Securities, LEAPS are long-term equity options traded on U.S. exchanges and over the counter. Instead of expiring in two near-term and two farther out months as most equity OPTIONS do, LEAPS expire in two or three years, giving the buyer a longer time for his strategy to come to fruition. LEAPS are traded on many individual stocks listed on the New York Stock Exchange, the American Stock Exchange, and NASDAQ.

LEARNING CURVE predictable improvements following the early part of the life of a production contract, when costly mistakes are made.

LEASE contract granting use of real estate, equipment, or other fixed assets for a specified time in exchange for payment, usually in the form of rent. The owner of the leased property is called the lessor, the user the lessee. *See also* CAPITAL LEASE; FINANCIAL LEASE; OPERATING LEASE; SALE AND LEASEBACK.

LEASE ACQUISITION COST price paid by a real estate LIMITED PARTNERSHIP, when acquiring a lease, including legal fees and related expenses. The charges are prorated to the limited partners.

LEASEBACK transaction in which one party sells property to another and agrees to lease the property back from the buyer for a fixed period of time. For example, a building owner wanting to get cash out of the building may decide to sell the building to a real estate or leasing company and sign a long-term lease to occupy the space. The original owner is thereby able to receive cash for the value of his property, which he can reinvest in his business, as well as remain in the property. The new owner is assured of the stability of a long-term tenant and a steady income. Leaseback deals (also called sale and leaseback deals) also are executed for business equipment such as computers, cars, trucks, and airplanes. Partial ownership interests in leasing deals are sold to investors in LIMITED PARTNERSHIP form, and are designed to produce a fixed level of income to limited partners for the lease term.

LEASEHOLD asset representing the right to use property under a LEASE.

LEASEHOLD IMPROVEMENT modification of leased property. The cost is added to fixed assets and then amortized.

LEASE-PURCHASE AGREEMENT agreement providing that portions of LEASE payments may be applied toward the purchase of the property under lease.

LEG
1. sustained trend in stock market prices. A prolonged bull or bear market may have first, second, and third legs.
2. one side of a spread transaction. For instance, a trader might buy a CALL OPTION that has a particular STRIKE PRICE and expiration date, then combine it with a PUT OPTION that has the same striking price and a different expiration date. The two options are called legs of the spread.
   Selling one of the options is termed LIFTING A LEG.

LEGACY gift under a WILL of cash or some other specific item of personal property, such as a stock certificate, a car, or a piece of jewelry. The legacy usually is conditioned, meaning the legatee is required to be employed by the TESTATOR— the person who makes the will—or related to the testator by marriage. In other cases, a legacy to a legatee who has not attained a particular age at the testator's death will be held in trust for the legatee, instead of being distributed outright.

LEGAL computerized data base maintained by the New York Stock Exchange to track enforcement actions against member firms, audits of member firms, and customer complaints. LEGAL is not an acronym, but is written in all capitals.

LEGAL AGE age at which a person can enter into binding contracts or agree to other legal acts without the consent of another adult. In most states, the legal age, also called the *age of majority,* is 18 years old.

LEGAL ENTITY person or organization that has the legal standing to enter into a contract and may be sued for failure to perform as agreed in the contract. A child under legal age is not a legal entity; a corporation is a legal entity since it is a person in the eyes of the law.

LEGAL INVESTMENT investment permissible for investors with FIDUCIARY responsibilities. INVESTMENT GRADE bonds, as rated by Standard & Poor's or Moody's, usually qualify as legal investments. Guidelines designed to protect investors are set by the state in which the fiduciary operates. *See also* LEGAL LIST.

LEGAL LIABILITY (1) monies owed, shown on a balance sheet. (2) individual's or company's obligation to act responsibly or face compensatory penalties. *See also* LIABILITY.

LEGAL LIST securities selected by a state agency, usually a banking department, as permissible holdings of mutual savings banks, pension funds, insurance companies, and other FIDUCIARY institutions. To protect the money that individuals place in such institutions, only high quality debt and equity securities are generally included. As an alternative to the legal list, some states apply the PRUDENT MAN RULE.

LEGAL MONOPOLY exclusive right to offer a particular service within a particular territory. In exchange, the company agrees to have its policies and rates regulated. Electric and water utilities are legal monopolies.

LEGAL OPINION
1. statement as to legality, written by an authorized official such as a city attorney or an attorney general.
2. statement as to the legality of a MUNICIPAL BOND issue, usually written by a law firm specializing in public borrowings. It is part of the *official statement,* the municipal equivalent of a PROSPECTUS. Unless the legality of an issue is established, an investor's contract is invalid at the time of issue and he cannot sue under it. The legal opinion is therefore required by a SYNDICATE MANAGER and customarily accompanies the transfer of municipal securities as long as they are outstanding.

LEGAL TRANSFER transaction that requires documentation other than the standard stock or bond power to validate the transfer of a stock certificate from a seller to a buyer—for example, securities registered to a corporation or to a deceased person. It is the selling broker's responsibility to supply proper documentation to the buying broker in a legal transfer.

LEGISLATIVE RISK risk that a change in legislation could have a major positive or negative effect on an investment. For instance, a company that is a large exporter may be a beneficiary of a trade agreement that lowers tariff barriers, and therefore may see its stock price rise. On the other hand, a company that is a major polluter may be harmed by laws that stiffen fines for polluting the air or water, thereby making its share price fall.

LEMON product or investment producing poor performance. A car that continually needs repairs is a lemon, and consumers are guaranteed a full refund in several states under so-called lemon laws. A promising stock that fails to live up to expectations is also called a lemon.

LENDER individual or firm that extends money to a borrower with the expectation of being repaid, usually with interest. Lenders create debt in the form of loans, and in the event of LIQUIDATION they are paid off before stockholders receive distributions. But the investor deals in both debt (bonds) and equity (stocks). It is useful to remember that investors in commercial paper, bonds, and other debt instruments are in fact lenders with the same rights and powers enjoyed by banks.

LENDER OF LAST RESORT

1. characterization of a central bank's role in bolstering a bank that faces large withdrawals of funds. The U.S. lender of last resort is the FEDERAL RESERVE BANK. Member banks may borrow from the DISCOUNT WINDOW to maintain reserve requirements or to meet large withdrawals. The Fed thereby maintains the stability of the banking system, which would be threatened if major banks were to fail.

2. government small business financing programs and municipal economic development organizations whose precondition to making loans to private enterprises is an inability to obtain financing elsewhere.

LENDING AGREEMENT contract between a lender and a borrower. *See also* INDENTURE; REVOLVING CREDIT; TERM LOAN.

LENDING AT A PREMIUM term used when one broker lends securities to another broker to cover customer's short position and imposes a charge for the loan. Such charges, which are passed on to the customer, are the exception rather than the rule, since securities are normally LOANED FLAT between brokers, that is, without interest. Lending at a premium might occur when the securities needed are in very heavy demand and are therefore difficult to borrow. The premium is in addition to any payments the customer might have to make to the lending broker to MARK TO THE MARKET or to cover dividends or interest payable on the borrowed securities.

LENDING AT A RATE paying interest to a customer on the credit balance created from the proceeds of a SHORT SALE. Such proceeds are held in ESCROW to secure the loan of securities, usually made by another broker, to cover the customer's short position. Lending at a rate is the exception rather than the rule.

LENDING SECURITIES securities borrowed from a broker's inventory, other MARGIN ACCOUNTS, or from other brokers, when a customer makes a SHORT SALE and the securities must be delivered to the buying customer's broker. As collateral, the borrowing broker deposits with the lending broker an amount of money equal to the market value of the securities. No interest or premium is ordinarily involved in the transaction. The Securities and Exchange Commission requires that brokerage customers give permission to have their securities used in loan transactions, and the point is routinely covered in the standard agreement signed by customers when they open general accounts.

LESS DEVELOPED COUNTRIES (LDC) countries that are not fully industrialized or do not have sophisticated financial or legal systems. These countries, also called members of the *Third World,* typically have low levels of per-capita income, high inflation and debt, and large trade deficits. The World Bank may be helping them by providing loan assistance. Loans to such countries are commonly called *LDC debt.*

LESSEE *see* LEASE.

LESSOR *see* LEASE.

LETTER BOND *see* LETTER SECURITY.

LETTER OF CREDIT (L/C) instrument or document issued by a bank guaranteeing the payment of a customer's drafts up to a stated amount for a specified period. It substitutes the bank's credit for the buyer's and eliminates the seller's risk. It is used extensively in international trade. A *commercial letter of credit* is normally drawn in favor of a third party, called the beneficiary. A *confirmed letter of credit* is provided by a correspondent bank and guaranteed by the issuing bank. A *revolving letter of credit* is issued for a specified amount and automatically renewed for the same amount for a specified period, permitting any number of drafts to be drawn so long as they do not exceed its overall limit. A *traveler's letter of credit* is issued for the convenience of a traveling customer and typically lists correspondent banks at which drafts will be honored. A *performance letter of credit* is issued to guarantee performance under a contract.

LETTER OF INTENT

1. any letter expressing an intention to take (or not take) an action, sometimes subject to other action being taken. For example, a bank might issue a letter of intent stating it will make a loan to a customer, subject to another lender's agreement to participate. The letter of intent, in this case, makes it possible for the customer to negotiate the participation loan.
2. preliminary agreement between two companies that intend to merge. Such a letter is issued after negotiations have been satisfactorily completed.
3. promise by a MUTUAL FUND shareholder to invest a specified sum of money monthly for about a year. In return, the shareholder is entitled to lower sales charges.
4. INVESTMENT LETTER for a LETTER SECURITY.

LETTER OF LAST INSTRUCTIONS letter placed with a WILL containing instructions on carrying out the provisions of the will. These letters generally are not binding on the executors, but many executors feel morally bound to follow the wishes of the TESTATORS who appointed them. Florida is one of several states where the law allows these letters to be incorporated by reference if the language of the will shows this intent and identifies the letter's purpose clearly.

LETTER SECURITY stock or bond that is not registered with the Securities and Exchange Commission and therefore cannot be sold in the public market. When an issue is sold directly by the issuer to the investor, registration with the SEC can be avoided if a LETTER OF INTENT, called an INVESTMENT LETTER, is signed by the purchaser establishing that the securities are being bought for investment and not for resale. The letter's integral association with the security gives rise to the terms *letter security, letter stock,* and *letter bond.*

LETTER STOCK *see* LETTER SECURITY.

LEVEL DEBT SERVICE provision in a municipal charter stipulating that payments on municipal debt be approximately equal every year. This makes it easier to project the amount of tax revenue needed to meet obligations.

LEVERAGE

Operating leverage: extent to which a company's costs of operating are fixed (rent, insurance, executive salaries) as opposed to variable (materials, direct labor). In a totally automated company, whose costs are virtually all fixed, every dollar of increase in sales is a dollar of increase in operating income once the BREAKEVEN POINT has been reached, because costs remain the same at every level of production. In contrast, a company whose costs are largely variable would show relatively little increase in operating income when production and sales increased because costs and production would rise together. The leverage comes in because a small change in sales has a magnified percentage effect on operating income and losses. The *degree of operating leverage*—the ratio of the percentage change in operating income to the percentage change in sales or units sold—measures the sensitivity of a firm's profits to changes in sales volume. A firm using a high degree of operating leverage has a breakeven point at a relatively high sales level.

Financial leverage: debt in relation to equity in a firm's capital structure—its LONG-TERM DEBT (usually bonds), PREFERRED STOCK, and SHAREHOLDERS' EQUITY—measured by the DEBT-TO-EQUITY RATIO. The more long-term debt there is, the greater the financial leverage. Shareholders benefit from financial leverage to the extent that return on the borrowed money exceeds the interest costs and the market value of their shares rises. For this reason, financial leverage is popularly called *trading on the equity*. Because leverage also means required interest and principal payments and thus ultimately the risk of default, how much leverage is desirable is largely a question of stability of earnings. As a rule of thumb, an industrial company with a debt to equity ratio of more than 30% is highly leveraged, exceptions being firms with dependable earnings and cash flow, such as electric utilities.

Since long-term debt interest is a fixed cost, financial leverage tends to take over where operating leverage leaves off, further magnifying the effects on earnings per share of changes in sales levels. In general, high operating leverage should accompany low financial leverage, and vice versa.

Investments: means of enhancing return or value without increasing investment. Buying securities on margin is an example of leverage with borrowed money, and extra leverage may be possible if the leveraged security is convertible into common stock. RIGHTS, WARRANTS, and OPTION contracts provide leverage, not involving borrowings but offering the prospect of high return for little or no investment.

LEVERAGED BUYOUT takeover of a company, using borrowed funds. Most often, the target company's assets serve as security for the loans taken out by the acquiring firm, which repays the loan out of cash flow of the acquired company. Management may use this technique to retain control by converting a company from public to private. A group of investors may also borrow funds from banks, using their own assets as collateral, to take over another firm. In almost all leveraged buyouts, public shareholders receive a premium over the current market value for their shares. When a company that has gone private in a leveraged buyout offers shares to the public again, it is called a REVERSE LEVERAGED BUYOUT.

LEVEL LOAD sales charge that does not change over time. In mutual funds, level load shares are called *C class shares,* compared to *A class* for upfront loads and *B class* for back-end loads. A level load will typically be 1% to 2% of assets each year, which is lower than an upfront load of 4% to 5% or the back-end load, which starts at 5% and declines each year until it disappears if the fund shares are held for five years. Though the level load may be lower than an upfront or back-end load, an investor ends up paying a higher commission if he holds the fund for many years.

LEVEL PLAYING FIELD condition in which competitors operate under the same rules. For example, all banks must follow the same regulations set down by the Federal Reserve. In some situations, competitors complain to regulators or Congress that they are not playing on a level playing field. For example, banks contend that brokerage firms can offer certain banking services without the same rules imposed on banks. Companies wanting to export to a particular country may complain that domestic companies are protected by various trade barriers, creating an uneven playing field. Various sections of the tax code may favor some companies more than others, prompting cries from the disadvantaged firms to "level the playing field."

LEVEL TERM INSURANCE life insurance policy with a fixed face value and rising insurance premiums.

LEVERAGED COMPANY company with debt in addition to equity in its capital structure. In its popular connotation, the term is applied to companies that are highly leveraged. Although the judgment is relative, industrial companies with more than one third of their capitalization in the form of debt are considered highly leveraged. *See also* LEVERAGE.

LEVERAGED EMPLOYEE STOCK OWNERSHIP PLAN (LESOP) EMPLOYEE STOCK OWNERSHIP PLAN (ESOP) in which employee pension plans and profit-sharing plans borrow money to purchase stock in the company or issue CONVERTIBLES exchangeable for common stock. In addition to the usual advantages of employee ownership, the LESOP is a way to ensure that majority ownership remains in friendly hands.

LEVERAGED INVESTMENT COMPANY
1. open-end INVESTMENT COMPANY, or MUTUAL FUND, that is permitted by its charter to borrow capital from a bank or other lender.
2. dual-purpose INVESTMENT COMPANY, which issues both income and capital shares. Holders of income shares receive dividends and interest on investments, whereas holders of capital shares receive all capital gains on investments. In effect each class of shareholder leverages the other.

LEVERAGED LEASE LEASE that involves a lender in addition to the lessor and lessee. The lender, usually a bank or insurance company, puts up a percentage of the cash required to purchase the asset, usually more than half. The balance is put up by the lessor, who is both the equity participant and the borrower. With the cash the lessor acquires the asset, giving the lender (1) a mortgage on the asset and (2) an assignment of the lease and lease payments. The lessee then makes periodic payments to the lessor, who in turn pays the lender. As owner of the asset, the lessor is entitled to tax deductions for DEPRECIATION on the asset and INTEREST on the loan.

LEVERAGED RECAPITALIZATION corporate strategy to fend off potential acquirers by taking on a large amount of debt and making a large cash distribution to shareholders. For example, XYZ Company, selling at $50 a share, may borrow $3 billion to make a one-time distribution of $20 a share to stockholders. After the distribution, the stock price will drop to $30. By replacing equity with $3 billion in debt, XYZ is a far less attractive takeover target for a raider or other company than it was before. Also called *leveraged recap* for short.

LEVERAGED STOCK stock financed with credit, as in a MARGIN ACCOUNT. Although not, strictly speaking, leveraged stock, securities that are convertible into common stock provide an extra degree of leverage when bought on margin. Assuming the purchase price is reasonably close to the INVESTMENT VALUE and CONVERSION VALUE, the downside risk is no greater than it would be with the same company's common stock, whereas the appreciation value is much greater.

LIABILITY claim on the assets of a company or individual—excluding ownership EQUITY. Characteristics: (1) It represents a transfer of assets or services at a specified or determinable date. (2) The firm or individual has little or no discretion to avoid the transfer. (3) The event causing the obligation has already occurred. *See also* BALANCE SHEET.

LIABILITY INSURANCE insurance for money the policyholder is legally obligated to pay because of bodily injury or property damage caused to another person and covered in the policy. Liabilities may result from property damage, bodily injury, libel, or any other damages caused by the insured. The insurance company agrees to pay for such damages if they are awarded by a court, up to the limitations specified in the insurance contract. The insurer may also cover legal expenses incurred in defending the suit.

LIBOR *see* LONDON INTERBANK OFFERED RATE.

LICENSE legal document issued by a regulatory agency permitting an individual to conduct a certain activity, usually because the person has passed a training course qualifying him. For example, a securities license is required for a broker to sell stocks, bonds, and mutual funds. An insurance license is required before someone can sell insurance products. Before a driver's license is granted, a driver must pass an examination proving that he knows how to drive safely. If the licensed individual violates the regulations, the license can be revoked.

LIEN creditor's claim against property. For example, a mortgage is a lien against a house; if the mortgage is not paid on time, the house can be seized to satisfy the lien. Similarly, a bond is a lien against a company's assets; if interest and principal are not paid when due, the assets may be seized to pay the bondholders. As soon as a debt is paid, the lien is removed. Liens may be granted by courts to satisfy judgments. *See also* MECHANIC'S LIEN.

LIFE ANNUITY ANNUITY that makes a guaranteed fixed payment for the rest of the life of the annuitant. After the annuitant dies, beneficiaries receive no further payments.

LIFE CYCLE most common usage refers to an individual's progression from cradle to grave and the assumption that the choice of appropriate investments changes. Term also applies to the life of a product or of a business, consisting of inception, development, growth, expansion, maturity, and decline (or change). Recently, the term has entered into the vocabulary of the family-owned business, referring to generations of management. The post-World War II baby boom produced entrepreneurs who built businesses that now approach a juncture where a second generation either takes over management or sells out.

LIFE CYCLE PLANNING planning contemplated by the concept of LIFE CYCLE.

LIFE EXPECTANCY age to which an average person can be expected to live, as calculated by an ACTUARY. Insurance companies base their projections of benefit payouts on actuarial studies of such factors as sex, heredity, and health habits and base their rates on actuarial analysis. Life expectancy can be calculated at birth or at some other age and generally varies according to age. Thus, all persons at birth might have an average life expectancy of 70 years and all persons aged 40 years might have an average life expectancy of 75 years.

Life expectancy projections determine such matters as the ages when an INDIVIDUAL RETIREMENT ACCOUNT may start and finish withdrawing funds. Annuities payable for lifetimes are usually based on separate male or female tables, except that a QUALIFIED PLAN OR TRUST must use unisex tables.

LIFE INSURANCE insurance policy that pays a death benefit to beneficiaries if the insured dies. In return for this protection, the insured pays a premium, usually on an annual basis. *Term insurance* pays off upon the insured's death but provides no buildup of cash value in the policy. Term premiums are cheaper than premiums for *cash value policies* such as whole life, variable life, and universal life, which pay death benefits and also provide for the buildup of cash values in the policy. The cash builds up tax-deferred in the policy and is invested in stocks, bonds, real estate, and other investments. Policyholders can take out loans against their policies, which reduce the death benefit if they are not repaid. Some life insurance provides benefits to policyholders while they are still living, including income payments.

LIFE INSURANCE IN FORCE amount of life insurance that a company has issued, including the face amount of all outstanding policies together with all dividends that have been paid to policyholders. Thus a life insurance policy for $500,000 on which dividends of $10,000 have been paid would count as life insurance in force of $510,000.

LIFE INSURANCE POLICY contract between an insurance company and the insured setting out the provisions of the life insurance coverage. These provisions include premiums, loan procedures, face amounts, and the designation of beneficiaries, among many other clauses. Policies may be for term or permanent cash value types of coverage.

LIFETIME REVERSE MORTGAGE type of reverse mortgage agreement whereby a homeowner borrows against the value of the home, retains title, and makes no payments while living in the home. When the home ceases to be the primary residence of the borrower, as when the borrower dies, the lender sells the property, repays the loan, and remits any surplus to the borrower's estate. Such arrangements may be appropriate for older people who need cash and are HOUSE POOR. *See also* REVERSE ANNUITY MORTGAGE (RAM).

LIFFE *see* LONDON INTERNATIONAL FINANCIAL FUTURES AND OPTIONS EXCHANGE.

LIFO *see* LAST IN, FIRST OUT.

LIFT rise in securities prices as measured by the Dow Jones Industrial Average or other market averages, usually caused by good business or economic news.

LIFTING A LEG closing one side of a HEDGE, leaving the other side as a long or short position. A leg, in Wall Street parlance, is one side of a hedged transaction. A trader might have a STRADDLE—that is, a call and a put on the same stock, at the same price, with the same expiration date. Making a closing sale of the put, thereby lifting a leg—or *taking off a leg*, as it is sometimes called—would leave the trader with the call, or the LONG LEG.

LIGHTEN UP to sell a portion of a stock or bond position in a portfolio. A money manager with a large profit in a stock may decide to realize some of the gains because he is unsure that the stock will continue to rise, or because he is concerned too much of the fund's assets are tied up in the stock. As a result, he will say that he is "lightening up" his position in the stock. However, some of the stock remains in the portfolio.

LIMIT *see* LIMIT ORDER; LIMIT UP, LIMIT DOWN.

LIMITED COMPANY form of business most common in Britain, where registration under the Companies Act is comparable to incorporation under state law in the United States. It is abbreviated Ltd. or PLC.

LIMITED DISCRETION agreement between broker and client allowing the broker to make certain trades without consulting the client—for instance, sell an option position that is near expiration or sell a stock on which there has just been adverse news.

LIMITED LIABILITY underlying principle of the CORPORATION and the LIMITED PARTNERSHIP in the United States and the LIMITED COMPANY in the United

Kingdom that LIABILITY is limited to an investor's original investment. In contrast, a general partner or the owner of a PROPRIETORSHIP has unlimited liability.

LIMITED PARTNERSHIP organization made up of a GENERAL PARTNER, who manages a project, and limited partners, who invest money but have limited liability, are not involved in day-to-day management, and usually cannot lose more than their capital contribution. Usually limited partners receive income, capital gains, and tax benefits; the general partner collects fees and a percentage of capital gains and income. Typical limited partnerships are in real estate, oil and gas, and equipment leasing, but they also finance movies, research and development, and other projects. Typically, public limited partnerships are sold through brokerage firms, for minimum investments of $5000, whereas private limited partnerships are put together with fewer than 35 limited partners who invest more than $20,000 each. *See also* INCOME LIMITED PARTNERSHIP; MASTER LIMITED PARTNERSHIP; OIL AND GAS LIMITED PARTNERSHIP; PASSIVE; RESEARCH AND DEVELOPMENT LIMITED PARTNERSHIP; UNLEVERAGED PROGRAM.

LIMITED PAYMENT POLICY life INSURANCE contract that provides protection for one's whole life but requires premiums for a lesser number of years.

LIMITED RISK risk in buying an options contract. For example, someone who pays a PREMIUM to buy a CALL OPTION on a stock will lose nothing more than the premium if the underlying stock does not rise during the life of the option. In contrast, a FUTURES CONTRACT entails *unlimited risk,* since the buyer may have to put up more money in the event of an adverse move. Thus options trading offers limited risk unavailable in futures trading.

Also, stock analysts may say of a stock that has recently fallen in price, that it now has limited risk, reasoning that the stock is unlikely to fall much further.

LIMITED TAX BOND MUNICIPAL BOND backed by the full faith of the issuing government but not by its full taxing power; rather it is secured by the pledge of a special tax or group of taxes, or a limited portion of the real estate tax.

LIMITED TRADING AUTHORIZATION *see* LIMITED DISCRETION.

LIMITED WARRANTY warranty that imposes certain limitations, and is therefore not a full warranty. For example, an automaker may issue a warranty that covers parts, but not labor, for a particular period of time.

LIMIT ON CLOSE ORDER order to buy or sell a stated amount of a stock at the closing price, to be executed only if the closing price is a specified price or better, e.g., an order to sell XYZ at the close, if the closing price is $30 or higher.

LIMIT ORDER order to buy or sell a security or commodity at a specific price or better. The broker will execute the trade only within the price restriction. For example, a customer puts in a limit order to buy XYZ Corp. at 30 when the stock is selling for 32. Even if the stock reached 30¼ the broker will not execute the trade. Similarly, if the client put in a limit order to sell XYZ Corp. at 33 when the price is 31, the trade will not be executed until the stock price hits 33.

LIMIT ORDER INFORMATION SYSTEM electronic system that informs subscribers about securities traded on participating exchanges, showing the specialist, the exchange, the order quantities, and the bid and offer prices. This allows subscribers to shop for the most favorable prices.

LIMIT PRICE price set in a LIMIT ORDER. For example, a customer might put in a limit order to sell shares at 45 or to buy at 40. The broker executes the order at the limit price or better.

LIMIT UP, LIMIT DOWN maximum price movement allowed for a commodity FUTURES CONTRACT during one trading day. In the face of a particularly dramatic development, a future's price may move limit up or limit down for several consecutive days.

LINE category of insurance, such as the *liability line,* or the amount of insurance on a given property, such as a $500,000 line on the buildings of the XYZ Company. Term is also used generally, to refer to a product line. *See also* BANK LINE.

LINE OF CREDIT *see* BANK LINE.

LIPPER MUTUAL FUND INDUSTRY AVERAGE average performance level of all mutual funds, as reported by Lipper Analytical Services of New York. The performance of all mutual funds is ranked quarterly and annually, by type of fund—such as aggressive growth fund or income fund. Mutual fund managers try to beat the industry average as well as the other funds in their category. *See also* MUTUAL FUND.

LIQUID ASSET cash or easily convertible into cash. Some examples: money-market fund shares, U.S. Treasury bills, bank deposits. An investor in an ILLIQUID investment such as a real estate or oil and gas LIMITED PARTNERSHIP is required to have substantial liquid assets, which would serve as a cushion if the illiquid deal did not work out favorably.

In a corporation's financial statements, liquid assets are cash, marketable securities, and accounts receivable.

LIQUIDATING DIVIDEND distribution of assets in the form of a DIVIDEND from a corporation that is going out of business. Such a payment may come when a firm goes bankrupt or when management decides to sell off a company's assets and pass the proceeds on to shareholders.

LIQUIDATING VALUE projected price for an asset of a company that is going out of business—for instance, a real estate holding or office equipment. Liquidating value, also called *auction value,* assumes that assets are sold separately from the rest of the organization; it is distinguished from GOING CONCERN VALUE, which may be higher because of what accountants term *organization value* or *goodwill.*

LIQUIDATION
1. dismantling of a business, paying off debts in order of priority, and distributing the remaining assets in cash to the owners. Involuntary liquidation is covered under Chapter 7 of the federal BANKRUPTCY law. *See also* JUNIOR SECURITY; PREFERRED STOCK.
2. forced sale of a brokerage client's securities or commodities after failure to meet a MARGIN CALL. *See also* SELL OUT.

LIQUIDITY ability to buy or sell an asset quickly and in large volume without substantially affecting the asset's price. Shares in large blue-chip stocks like General Motors or General Electric are liquid, because they are actively traded and therefore the stock price will not be dramatically moved by a few buy or sell orders. However, shares in small companies with few shares outstanding, or commodity markets with limited activity, generally are not considered liquid, because one or two big orders can move the price up or down sharply. A high level of liquidity is a key characteristic of a good market for a security or a commodity.

Liquidity also refers to the ability to convert to cash quickly. For example, a money market mutual fund provides instant liquidity since shareholders can write checks on the fund. Other examples of liquid accounts include checking accounts, bank money market deposit accounts, passbook accounts, and Treasury bills.

LIQUIDITY DIVERSIFICATION purchase of bonds whose maturities range from short to medium to long term, thus helping to protect against sharp fluctuations in interest rates.

LIQUIDITY FUND Emeryville, California, company that buys REAL ESTATE LIMITED PARTNERSHIP interests 25% to 35% below the current appraised value of the real estate assets. The company also buys REAL ESTATE INVESTMENT TRUSTS.

LIQUIDITY RATIO measure of a firm's ability to meet maturing short-term obligations. *See also* CASH ASSET RATIO; CURRENT RATIO; NET QUICK ASSETS; QUICK RATIO.

LISBON STOCK EXCHANGE largest of two exchanges in Portugal. Trading on the exchange takes place Monday through Friday from 9 A.M. to 3 P.M. for continuous trading and 9:30 A.M. to 4 P.M. for daily calls. TRADIS, a computerized trading system, links the Lisbon and Oporto (OSE) exchanges. Settlement takes place on the fourth business day following the trade. The OSE also trades several futures and options contracts.

LISTED FIRM company whose stock trades on the New York Stock Exchange or American Stock Exchange. The company has to meet certain LISTING REQUIREMENTS or it will be delisted. Listed firms are distinguished from unlisted companies, whose stock trades over-the-counter on the NASDAQ market.

LISTED OPTION put or call OPTION that an exchange has authorized for trading, properly called an *exchange-traded option.*

LISTED SECURITY stock or bond that has been accepted for trading by one of the organized and registered securities exchanges in the United States, which list more than 6000 issues of securities of some 3500 corporations. Generally, the advantages of being listed are that the exchanges provide (1) an orderly marketplace; (2) liquidity; (3) fair price determination; (4) accurate and continuous reporting on sales and quotations; (5) information on listed companies; and (6) strict regulations for the protection of security holders. Each exchange has its own listing requirements, those of the New York Stock Exchange being most stringent. Listed securities include stocks, bonds, convertible bonds, preferred stocks, warrants, rights, and options, although not all forms of securities are accepted on all exchanges. Unlisted securities are traded in the OVER-THE-COUNTER market. *See also* LISTING REQUIREMENTS; STOCK EXCHANGE.

LISTING written employment agreement between a property owner and a real estate broker authorizing the broker to find a buyer or tenant for certain property. Oral listings, while not specifically illegal, are unenforceable under many state fraud statutes, and generally are not recommended. The most common form of listing is the exclusive-right-to-sell listing. Others include open listings, net listings and exclusive-agency listings. Listings are personal service contracts and cannot be assigned to another broker, but brokers can delegate the work to other members of the sales office. The listing usually states the amount of commission the seller will pay the broker and the time limit. In a buyer's listing, the buyer hires the broker to locate a property.

LISTING BROKER licensed real estate broker (agent) who secures a listing of a property for sale. A *listing* involves a contract authorizing the broker to perform services for the selling property owner. The listing broker may sell the property, but it may also be sold by the *selling broker,* a different agent, with the two sharing commissions, usually equally.

LISTING REQUIREMENTS rules that must be met before a stock is listed for trading on an exchange. Among the requirements of the New York Stock Exchange: a corporation must have a minimum of one million publicly held shares with a minimum aggregate market value of $16 million as well as an annual net income topping $2.5 million before federal income tax.

LIST PRICE suggested retail price for a product according to the manufacturer. The list price is designed to guide retailers, though they remain free to sell products above or below list price.

LITTLE DRAGONS nickname for developing Asian nations such as Singapore, Hong Kong, South Korea, and Taiwan that pose a threat to Japan (the Big Dragon) because of their lower labor costs, high productivity, and pro-business attitudes. Also known as the *tigers.*

LIVING BENEFITS life insurance benefits upon which the insured can draw cash while still alive. Some policies allow benefits to be paid to the insured in cases of terminal illness or illness involving certain long-term care costs. Beneficiaries receive any balance upon the insured's death. Also known as *accelerated benefits.*

LIVING DEAD *see* ZOMBIES.

LIVING TRUST *see* INTER VIVOS TRUST.

LLOYD'S OF LONDON London-based corporation of underwriters (Lloyd's Underwriters) and insurance brokers (Lloyd's Brokers) most famous for the wide variety of risks it insures. Lloyd's is not itself an underwriter. Its business is underwritten by some 350 syndicates of Lloyd's Underwriters representing some 30,000 underwriters, who become members of the corporation by depositing a substantial sum of money and accepting unlimited liability. The insurance is marketed through some 260 Lloyd's brokers.

LOAD sales charge paid by an investor who buys shares in a load MUTUAL FUND or ANNUITY. Loads are usually charged when shares or units are purchased; a charge for withdrawing is called a BACK-END LOAD (or *rear-end load).* A fund that does not charge this fee is called a NO-LOAD FUND. *See also* INVESTMENT COMPANY.

LOAD FUND MUTUAL FUND that is sold for a sales charge by a brokerage firm or other sales representative. Such funds may be stock, bond, or commodity funds, with conservative or aggressive objectives. The stated advantage of a load fund is that the salesperson will explain the fund to the customer, and advise him or her when it is appropriate to sell the fund, as well as when to buy more shares. A NO-LOAD FUND, which is sold without a sales charge directly to investors by a fund company, does not give advice on when to buy or sell. Increasingly, traditional no-load funds are becoming *low-load funds,* imposing up-front charges of 3% or less with no change in services. *See also* INVESTMENT COMPANY.

LOAD SPREAD OPTION method of allocating the annual sales charge on some contractual mutual funds. In a CONTRACTUAL PLAN, the investor accumulates shares in the fund through periodic fixed payments. During the first four years of the contract, up to 20% of any single year's contributions to the fund may be credited against the sales charge, provided that the total charges for these four years do not exceed 64% of one year's contributions. The sales charge is limited to 9% of the entire contract.

LOAN transaction wherein an owner of property, called the LENDER, allows another party, the *borrower,* to use the property. The borrower customarily promises to return the property after a specified period with payment for its use, called INTEREST. The documentation of the promise is called a PROMISSORY NOTE when the property is cash.

LOAN AMORTIZATION reduction of debt by scheduled, regular payments of principal and interest sufficient to repay the loan at maturity.

LOAN COMMITMENT lender's agreement to make money available to a borrower in a specified amount, at a specified rate, and within a specified time. *See also* COMMITMENT FEE.

LOAN CROWD stock exchange members who lend or borrow securities required to cover the positions of brokerage customers who sell short—called a crowd because they congregate at a designated place on the floor of the exchange. *See also* LENDING SECURITIES.

LOANED FLAT loaned without interest, said of the arrangement whereby brokers lend securities to one another to cover customer SHORT SALE positions. *See also* LENDING AT A PREMIUM; LENDING AT A RATE; LENDING SECURITIES.

LOAN ORIGINATION FEE *see* POINT.

LOAN STOCK *see* LENDING SECURITIES.

LOAN-TO-VALUE RATIO (LTV) ratio of money borrowed to fair market value, usually in reference to real property. Residential mortgage loans conventionally have a maximum LTV of 80% (an $80,000 loan on a $100,0000 house).

LOAN VALUE
1. amount a lender is willing to lend against collateral. For example, at 50% of appraised value, a piece of property worth $800,000 has a loan value of $400,000.
2. with respect to REGULATION T of the FEDERAL RESERVE BOARD, the maximum percentage of the current market value of eligible securities that a broker can lend a margin account customer. Regulation T applies only to securities formally registered or having an unlisted trading privilege on a national securities exchange. For securities exempt from Regulation T, which comprise U.S. government securities, municipal bonds, and bonds of the International Bank for Reconstruction and Development, loan value is a matter of the individual firm's policy.

LOCAL member of a futures exchange who trades for his or her own account. The traders in a futures pit are composed of locals and employees of various brokerage firms. Locals initiate their own transactions on the floor of the exchange. Some, termed *dual traders,* also execute orders on behalf of customers.

LOCAL TAXES taxes paid by an individual to his or her locality. This includes city income, property, sewer, water, school, and other taxes. These taxes are usually deductible on the taxpayer's federal income tax return.

LOCK BOX
1. cash management system whereby a company's customers mail payments to a post office box near the company's bank. The bank collects checks from the lock box—sometimes several times a day—deposits them to the account of the firm, and informs the company's cash manager by telephone of the deposit. This reduces processing FLOAT and puts cash to work more quickly. The bank's fee for its services must be weighed against the savings from reduced float to determine whether this arrangement is cost-effective.
2. bank service that entails holding a customer's securities and, as agent, receiving and depositing income such as dividends on stock and interest on bonds.
3. box rented in a post office where mail is stored until collected.

LOCKED IN
1. unable to take advantage of preferential tax treatment on the sale of an asset because the required HOLDING PERIOD has not elapsed. See also CAPITAL GAIN.
2. commodities position in which the market has an up or down limit day, and investors cannot get in or out of the market.
3. said of a rate of return that has been assured for a length of time through an investment such as a certificate of deposit or a fixed rate bond; also said of profits or yields on securities or commodities that have been protected through HEDGING techniques.

LOCKED MARKET highly competitive market environment with identical bid and ask prices for a stock. The appearance of more buyers and sellers unlocks the market.

LOCK-UP OPTION privilege offered a WHITE KNIGHT (friendly acquirer) by a TARGET COMPANY of buying CROWN JEWELS or additional equity. The aim is to discourage a hostile TAKEOVER.

LONDON COMMODITY EXCHANGE (LCE) formerly the London Futures and Options Exchange (FOX), the LCE trades futures and options on robusta coffee, No. 7 cocoa, No. 5 white sugar, Baltic freight (Biffex), EEC wheat, EEC barley and potatoes; and futures on No. 7 premium raw sugar. The sugar contracts trade on the LCE's proprietary FAST electronic trading system. Hours: 9:30 A.M.–5 P.M. (floor), with FAST trading until 7:01 P.M. for the sugar contracts, Monday through Friday.

LONDON INTERNATIONAL FINANCIAL FUTURES AND OPTIONS EXCHANGE (LIFFE) three largest futures markets in the United Kingdom. Futures and options contracts on long- and short-term interest rates, denominated in world currencies: three-month sterling (short sterling), three-month Eurodollar, three-month Eurodeutschmark (Euromark), and three-month Euroswiss franc (Euroswiss); three-month Eurolira interest rate and three-month ECU futures; and long gilt futures and options. Bond trading includes German government bond (bund) futures and options, Italian government bond (BTP) futures and options, Japanese government bond (JGB) futures and medium-term German government bond (Bobl). LIFFE trades two indices, the FT-SE 100 Index future and option, and the FT-SE 250 Index future and option, and 71 equity options that include British Petroleum, RTZ, Hanson, and Unilever. Hours: 7:30 A.M.- 4:15 P.M., Monday through Friday. Short sterling, Euromarks, Euroswiss, Long Gilt, bund, BTP, and Bobl futures contracts are traded "after hours" on the exchange's Automated Pit Trading (APT) system, between 4:20 P.M. and 8 P.M.; the JGB trades from 7 A.M. to 4 P.M. Trading on LIFEE's bond futures and options contracts is linked to trading on the CHICAGO BOARD OF TRADE. LIFFE traders can trade the CBOT's U.S. Treasury Bond, 10-year note and 5-year note futures and options during the London Morning prior to the opening of Chicago trading. The CBOT can trade LIFFE's Bund, BTP and long gilt futures and options during Chicago's day session and all of its evening session.

LONDON INTERBANK OFFERED RATE (LIBOR) rate that the most creditworthy international banks dealing in EURODOLLARS charge each other for large loans. The LIBOR rate is usually the base for other large Eurodollar loans to less creditworthy corporate and government borrowers. For instance, a Third World country may have to pay one point over LIBOR when it borrows money.

LONDON METAL EXCHANGE (LME) principal-to-principal market for base metals trading. The LME trades cash and three-month contracts on aluminum, copper, nickel, lead, zinc, tin, and aluminum alloy. Trading is conducted in two open-outcry rings, each followed by a kerb session. Traded options contracts are available on the underlying futures contracts. Clearing is through the London Clearing House Ltd.

LONG BOND in general, bond that matures in more than 10 years. Since these bonds commit investors' money for a long time, they normally pay investors a higher yield. In Wall Street parlance, the "long bond" is the 30-year Treasury.

LONG COUPON
1. bond issue's first interest payment covering a longer period than the remaining payments, or the bond issue itself. Conventional schedules call for interest payments at six-month intervals. A long COUPON results when a bond is issued more than six months before the date of the first scheduled payment. *See also* SHORT COUPON.
2. interest-bearing bond maturing in more than 10 years.

LONG HEDGE
1. FUTURES CONTRACT bought to protect against a rise in the cost of honoring a future commitment. Also called a *buy hedge*. The hedger benefits from a narrowing of the BASIS (difference between cash price and future price) if the future is bought below the cash price, and from a widening of the basis if the future is bought above the cash price.
2. FUTURES CONTRACT or CALL OPTION bought in anticipation of a drop in interest rates, so as to lock in the present yield on a fixed-income security.

LONG LEG part of an OPTION SPREAD representing a commitment to buy the underlying security. For instance, if a spread consists of a long CALL OPTION and a short PUT OPTION, the long call is the long LEG.

LONG POSITION
1. ownership of a security, giving the investor the right to transfer ownership to someone else by sale or by gift; the right to receive any income paid by the security; and the right to any profits or losses as the security's value changes.
2. investor's ownership of securities held by a brokerage firm.

LONG TERM
1. HOLDING PERIOD of 12 months or longer, according to the REVENUE RECONCILIATION ACT OF 1993 and applicable in calculating the CAPITAL GAINS TAX.
2. investment approach to the stock market in which an investor seeks appreciation by holding a stock for a year or more.
3. bond with a maturity of 10 years or longer.
    See also LONG BOND; LONG-TERM DEBT; LONG-TERM FINANCING; LONG-TERM GAIN; LONG-TERM LOSS.

LONG-TERM DEBT liability due in a year or more. Normally, interest is paid periodically over the term of the loan, and the principal amount is payable as notes or bonds mature. Also, a LONG BOND with a maturity of 10 years or more.

LONG-TERM DEBT RATIO see DEBT-TO-EQUITY RATIO (2). See also RATIO ANALYSIS.

LONG-TERM FINANCING liabilities not repayable in one year and all equity. See also LONG-TERM DEBT.

LONG-TERM GAIN gain on the sale of a CAPITAL ASSET where the HOLDING PERIOD was 12 months or more and the profit was subject to the long-term CAPITAL GAINS TAX.

LONG-TERM GOALS financial goals that an individual sets for five years or longer. Some examples of long-term goals include assembling a retirement fund, saving for a down payment on a house or for college tuition, buying a second home, or starting a business.

LONG-TERM INVESTOR someone who invests in stocks, bonds, mutual funds or other investment vehicles for a long time, typically at least five years, in order to fund LONG-TERM GOALS. A long-term investor looks for solid investments with a good long-term track record, such as a BLUE CHIP STOCK or a mutual fund with exemplary performance. As long as the investor holds his investments for a year, he will pay preferential CAPITAL GAINS TAXES at a 28% tax rate instead of paying higher regular income tax rates, which are due on holdings of less than a year.

LONG-TERM LIABILITIES any monies owed that are not payable on demand or within one year. The *current portion of long-term debt* is a current liability, as distinguished from a long-term liability.

LONG-TERM LOSS negative counterpart to LONG-TERM GAIN as defined by the same legislation. A CAPITAL LOSS can be used to offset a CAPITAL GAIN plus $3000 of ORDINARY INCOME except that short-term losses exceeding short-term gains must first be applied to long-term gains, if any.

LONG-TERM PLANNING financial planning to accomplish LONG-TERM GOALS. A long-term plan will project how much money will be needed to fund retirement, pay college tuition, or buy a house in five years or more by designing an investment strategy to meet that goal.

LOOPHOLE technicality making it possible to circumvent a law's intent without violating its letter. For instance, a TAX SHELTER may exploit a loophole in the tax law, or a bank may take advantage of a loophole in the GLASS STEAGALL ACT to acquire a DISCOUNT BROKER.

LOOSE CREDIT policy by the Federal Reserve Board to make loans less expensive and thus widely available in the economy. The Fed implements a loose credit policy by reducing interest rates through OPEN MARKET OPERATIONS by buying Treasury securities, which gives banks more funds they need to satisfy loan demand. The Fed initiates a loose credit policy when the economy is weak and inflation is low, in order to stimulate a faster pace of economic activity. Also called *easy money*. The opposite policy is called TIGHT MONEY, in which the Fed sells securities and makes it more difficult and expensive to borrow, and thereby hopes to slow down economic activity. Tight money policy is used to dampen inflation in an overheated economy.

LOSS opposite of PROFIT.

LOSS-CONTROL ACTIVITIES actions initiated by a company or individual at the urging of its insurance company to prevent accidents, losses or other insurance claims. For example, a home insurer may require smoke alarms. A commercial insurer may require certain safety procedures in a manufacturing plant.

LOSS LEADER concept, primarily in retailing, where an item is priced at a loss and widely advertised in order to draw trade into the store. The loss is considered a cost of promotion and is offset by the profits on other items sold. Concept is sometimes used by DISCOUNT BROKERS, who will advertise a particular transaction at a loss price to attract customers, who will enter into other transactions at a profit to the broker.

LOSS-OF-INCOME INSURANCE insurance coverage replacing income lost by a policyholder. For example, *business interruption insurance* will pay employee wages if a business is temporarily out of operation because of a fire, flood, or other disaster. *Disability insurance* will replace a portion of an insured disabled person's income while he or she is disabled due to injury or illness. *Worker's compensation insurance* will reimburse a worker who was injured on the job for lost wages during the disability period.

LOSS PREVENTION programs instituted by individuals or companies to prevent losses. Businesses implement safety programs to prevent workplace injuries. Individuals install fire detectors, burglar alarms, and other protective devices to prevent losses caused by fire and theft. Car owners install special locks to prevent auto theft. Insurance companies usually offer discounts to businesses or individuals taking loss prevention measures.

LOSS RATIO ratio of losses paid or accrued by an insurer to premiums earned, usually for a one-year period. *See also* BAD DEBT.

LOSS RESERVE *see* BAD DEBT.

LOT in a general business sense, a lot is any group of goods or services making up a transaction. *See also* ODD LOT; ROUND LOT.

LOW bottom price paid for a security over the past year or since trading in the security began; in the latter sense also called *historic low.*

LOW BALANCE METHOD interest computation method on savings accounts where interest is based on the lowest balance during the period.

LOW GRADE bond RATING of B or lower.

LOW-INCOME HOUSING LIMITED PARTNERSHIP limited partnership investment in housing complexes occupied by low- and moderate-income tenants paying rent that cannot exceed statutory limits. Such partnerships offer investors annual TAX CREDITS over a 10-year period that total approximately 130% to 150% of the amount invested. Due to the restricted rents as required under the tax law, anticipated cash flow during the holding period is minimal. Properties can be sold after a 15-year holding period, which may return some or all of the original investment. The primary investment motivation for limited partners is a predictable stream of annual tax benefits.

LOW-LOAD FUND *see* LOAD FUND.

LUMP SUM large payment of money received at one time instead of in periodic payments. People retiring from or leaving a company may receive a lump-sum distribution of the value of their pension, salary reduction or profit-sharing plan. (Special tax rules apply to such lump-sum distributions unless the money is rolled into an IRA rollover account.) Some annuities, called *single premium deferred annuities* (SPDAs) require one upfront lump sum which is invested. Beneficiaries of life insurance policies may receive a death benefit in a lump sum. A consumer making a large purchase such as a car or boat may decide to pay in one lump sum instead of financing the purchase over time.

LUXURY TAX tax on goods considered nonessential.

m

MA BELL nickname for AT&T Corporation. Before the Bell System was broken up in 1984, AT&T controlled both local and long distance telephone service in the United States. After the breakup, local phone service was performed by the seven regional phone companies and AT&T concentrated on long distance, telecommunications research, equipment and computer manufacturing. Even though it no longer enjoys the monopoly it once had, people still refer to AT&T as Ma Bell. The stock is also a component of the Dow Jones Industrial Average, and is one of the most widely held and actively traded stocks on the New York Stock Exchange.

MACARONI DEFENSE defensive tactic used by a corporation trying to defeat a TAKEOVER attempt by a RAIDER or unfriendly bidder. The target corporation will issue a massive amount of bonds that must be redeemed at a mandatory higher redemption value if the company is taken over. The redemption value of these bonds therefore expands when the company is threatened—like macaroni when it is cooked—making the takeover prohibitively expensive to complete.

MACROECONOMICS analysis of a nation's economy as a whole, using such aggregate data as price levels, unemployment, inflation, and industrial production. *See also* MICROECONOMICS.

MADRID STOCK EXCHANGE the Bolsa de Madrid is the largest and most international of Spain's four stock exchanges. The Madrid Stock Exchange General Index is dominated by banks, utilities, and communications firms, and is based on trading frequency and liquidity. Trading is through an electronic trading system based on the CATS system developed by the Toronto Stock Exchange. Trading on the continuous market owned by the four exchanges is from 11 A.M. to 5 P.M., with pre-opening trading from 10 A.M. to 11 A.M. Trading on the exchanges is from 10 A.M. to 12:15 P.M. All trading is Monday through Friday. Settlement is five business days after the trade date.

MACRS *see* MODIFIED ACCELERATED COST RECOVERY SYSTEM (MACRS).

MAINTENANCE BOND a bond that guarantees against defects in workmanship or materials for a specified period following completion of a contract.

MAINTENANCE CALL call for additional money or securities when a brokerage customer's margin account equity falls below the requirements of the National Association of Securities Dealers (NASD), of the exchanges, or of the brokerage firm. Unless the account is brought up to the levels complying with equity maintenance rules, some of the client's securities may be sold to remedy the deficiency. *See also* MAINTENANCE REQUIREMENT; MINIMUM MAINTENANCE; SELL OUT.

MAINTENANCE FEE annual charge to maintain certain types of brokerage accounts. Such a fee may be attached to an ASSET MANAGEMENT ACCOUNT, which combines securities and money market accounts. Banks and brokers may also charge a maintenance fee for an INDIVIDUAL RETIREMENT ACCOUNT (IRA).

MAINTENANCE REQUIREMENT *see* MINIMUM MAINTENANCE.

MAJORITY SHAREHOLDER one of the shareholders who together control more than half the outstanding shares of a corporation. If the ownership is widely scattered and there are no majority shareholders, effective control may be gained with far less than 51% of the outstanding shares. *See also* WORKING CONTROL.

MAKE A MARKET maintain firm bid and offer prices in a given security by standing ready to buy or sell ROUND LOTS at publicly quoted prices. The dealer is called a *market maker* in the over-the-counter market and a SPECIALIST on the exchanges. A dealer who makes a market over a long period is said to *maintain* a market. See *also* REGISTERED COMPETITIVE MARKET MAKER.

MAKE A PRICE *see* MAKE A MARKET.

MALONEY ACT legislation, also called the Maloney Amendment, enacted in 1938 to amend the SECURITIES EXCHANGE ACT OF 1934 by adding Section 15A, which provides for the regulation of the OVER-THE-COUNTER market (OTC) through national securities associations registered with the Securities and Exchange Commission. *See also* NATIONAL ASSOCIATION OF SECURITIES DEALERS (NASD).

MANAGED ACCOUNT investment account consisting of money that one or more clients entrust to a manager, who decides when and where to invest it. Such an account may be handled by a bank trust department or by an investment advisory firm. Clients are charged a MANAGEMENT FEE And share in proportion to their participation in any losses and gains.

MANAGEMENT combined fields of policy and administration and the people who provide the decisions and supervision necessary to implement the owners' business objectives and achieve stability and growth. The formulation of policy requires analysis of all factors having an effect on short- and long-term profits. The administration of policies is carried out by the CHIEF EXECUTIVE OFFICER, his or her immediate staff, and everybody else who possesses authority delegated by people with supervisory responsibility. Thus the size of management can range from one person in a small organization to multilayered management hierarchies in large, complex organizations. The top members of management, called senior management, report to the owners of a firm; in large corporations, the CHAIRMAN OF THE BOARD, the PRESIDENT, and sometimes other key senior officers report to the BOARD OF DIRECTORS, comprising elected representatives of the owning stockholders. The application of scientific principles to decision-making is called management science. *See also* ORGANIZATION CHART.

MANAGEMENT BUYIN purchase of a large, and often controlling, interest in a company by an outside investor group that chooses to retain existing management. In many cases, the outside investors are venture capitalists who believe the company's products, services, and management have bright prospects. The investor group will usually place its representatives on the company's board of directors to monitor the progress of the company.

MANAGEMENT BUYOUT purchase of all of a company's publicly held shares by the existing management, which takes the company private. Usually, management will have to pay a premium over the current market price to entice public shareholders to go along with the deal. If management has to borrow heavily to finance the transaction, it is called a LEVERAGED BUYOUT (LBO). Managers may want to buy their company for several reasons: They want to avoid being taken over by a raider who would bring in new management; they no longer want the scrutiny that comes with running a public company; or they believe they can make more money for themselves in the long run by owning a larger share of the company, and eventually reap substantial profits by going public again with a REVERSE LEVERAGED BUYOUT.

MANAGEMENT COMPANY same as INVESTMENT COMPANY.

MANAGEMENT FEE charge against investor assets for managing the portfolio of an open- or closed-end MUTUAL FUND as well as for such services as shareholder relations or administration. The fee, as disclosed in the PROSPECTUS, is a fixed percentage of the fund's net asset value, typically between 0.5% and 2% per year. The fee also applies to a MANAGED ACCOUNT. The management fee is deducted automatically from a shareholder's assets once a year.

MANAGING UNDERWRITER leading—and originating—investment banking firm of an UNDERWRITING GROUP organized for the purchase and distribution of a new issue of securities. The AGREEMENT AMONG UNDERWRITERS authorizes the managing underwriter, or syndicate manager, to act as agent for the group in purchasing, carrying, and distributing the issue as well as complying with all federal and state requirements; to form the selling group; to determine the allocation of securities to each member; to make sales to the selling group at a specified discount—or CONCESSION—from the public offering price; to engage in open market transactions during the underwriting period to stabilize the market price of the security; and to borrow for the syndicate account to cover costs. *See also* FLOTATION COST; INVESTMENT BANKER; UNDERWRITE.

MANDATORY CONVERTIBLES debt-equity hybrids that became popular in the 1980s to meet the strong demand by banks for the raising of capital. One type, *equity contract notes,* is exchangeable at maturity for common stock having a market value equal to the principal amount of the notes. If the holder of the notes does not choose to receive equities at maturity, the issuer will sell the equity on behalf of the holder. Another type, *equity commitment notes,* does not require the holder to purchase equity with the notes but rather commits the issuer to redeem the notes with the proceeds of an equity issue at some future date. The Federal Reserve requires issuers to fund a third of the equity in the first four years, another third in the second four years, and the balance by maturity in the third four years. CAPS are still another form of mandatory convertible.

MANIPULATION buying or selling a security to create a false appearance of active trading and thus influence other investors to buy or sell shares. This may be done by one person or by a group acting in concert. Those found guilty of manipulation are subject to criminal and civil penalties. *See also* MINI-MANIPULATION.

MAPLE LEAF bullion coin minted by the government of Canada in gold (99.99% pure), silver (99.99% pure) and platinum (99.95% pure). The gold and platinum coins are available in one ounce, one-half ounce, one-quarter ounce, one-tenth ounce, one-fifteenth ounce and one-twentieth ounce sizes. The silver coin is available only in the one-ounce size. The Maple Leaf is actively traded throughout the world along with the American Eagle, South African Kruggerand, and other coins. The Maple Leaf usually sells at a slight premium to the bullion value of the coin. *See also* GOLD COIN.

MARGIN
In general: amount a customer deposits with a broker when borrowing from the broker to buy securities. Under Federal Reserve Board regulation, the initial margin required since 1945 has ranged from 50 to 100 percent of the security's purchase price. In the mid-1990s the minimum was 50% of the purchase or short sale price, in cash or eligible securities, with a minimum of $2000. Thereafter, MINIMUM MAINTENANCE requirements are imposed by the National Association of Securities Dealers (NASD) and the New York Stock Exchange, and by the individual brokerage firm, whose requirement is typically higher.

Banking: difference between the current market value of collateral backing a loan and the face value of the loan. For instance, if a $100,000 loan is backed by $50,000 in collateral, the margin is $50,000.

Corporate finance: difference between the price received by a company for its products and services and the cost of producing them. Also known as *gross profit margin.*

Futures trading: good-faith deposit an investor must put up when buying or selling a contract. If the futures price moves adversely, the investor must put up more money to meet margin requirements.

MARGINABLE SECURITIES see MARGIN SECURITY.

MARGIN ACCOUNT brokerage account allowing customers to buy securities with money borrowed from the broker. Margin accounts are governed by REGULATION T, by the National Association of Securities Dealers (NASD), by the New York Stock Exchange, and by individual brokerage house rules. Margin requirements can be met with cash or with eligible securities. In the case of securities sold short, an equal amount of the same securities is normally borrowed without interest from another broker to cover the sale, while the proceeds are kept in escrow as collateral for the lending broker. *See also* MINIMUM MAINTENANCE.

MARGIN AGREEMENT document that spells out the rules governing a MARGIN ACCOUNT, including the HYPOTHECATION of securities, how much equity the customer must keep in the account, and the interest rate on margin loans. Also known as a *hypothecation agreement.*

MARGINAL COST increase or decrease in the total costs of a business firm as the result of one more or one less unit of output. Also called *incremental cost* or *differential cost.* Determining marginal cost is important in deciding whether or not to vary a rate of production. In most manufacturing firms, marginal costs decrease as the volume of output increases due to economies of scale, which include factors such as bulk discounts on raw materials, specialization of labor, and more efficient use of machinery. At some point, however, diseconomies of scale enter in and marginal costs begin to rise; diseconomies include factors like more intense managerial supervision to control a larger work force, higher raw materials costs because local supplies have been exhausted, and generally less efficient input. The marginal cost curve is typically U-shaped on a graph.

A firm is operating at optimum output when marginal cost coincides with average total unit cost. Thus, at less than optimum output, an increase in the rate of production will result in a marginal unit cost lower than average total unit cost; production in excess of the optimum point will result in marginal cost higher than average total unit cost. In other words, a sale at a price higher than marginal unit cost will increase the net profit of the manufacturer even though the sales price does not cover average total unit cost; marginal cost is thus the lowest amount at which a sale can be made without adding to the producer's loss or subtracting from his profits.

MARGINAL COST

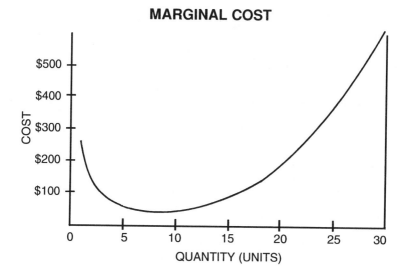

MARGINAL EFFICIENCY OF CAPITAL annual percentage yield earned by the last additional unit of capital. It is also known as *marginal productivity of capital, natural interest rate, net capital productivity,* and *rate of return over cost.* The significance of the concept to a business firm is that it represents the market rate of interest at which it begins to pay to undertake a capital investment. If the market rate is 10%, for example, it would not pay to undertake a project that has a return of 9½%, but any return over 10% would be acceptable. In a larger economic sense, marginal efficiency of capital influences long-term interest rates. This occurs because of the law of diminishing returns as it applies to the yield on capital. As the highest yielding projects are exhausted, available capital moves into lower yielding projects and interest rates decline. As market rates fall, investors are able to justify projects that were previously uneconomical. This process is called *diminishing marginal productivity* or *declining marginal efficiency of capital.*

MARGINAL REVENUE change in total revenue caused by one additional unit of output. It is calculated by determining the difference between the total revenues produced before and after a one-unit increase in the rate of production. As long as the price of a product is constant, price and marginal revenue are the same; for example, if baseball bats are being sold at a constant price of $10 apiece, a one-unit increase in sales (one baseball bat) translates into an increase in total revenue of $10. But it is often the case that additional output can be sold only if the price is reduced, and that leads to a consideration of MARGINAL COST—the added cost of producing one more unit. Further production is not advisable when marginal cost exceeds marginal revenue since to do so would result in a loss. Conversely, whenever marginal revenue exceeds marginal cost, it is advisable to produce an additional unit. Profits are maximized at the rate of output where marginal revenue equals marginal cost.

MARGINAL TAX RATE amount of tax imposed on an additional dollar of income. In the U.S. progressive income tax system, the marginal tax rate increases as income rises. Economists believing in SUPPLY-SIDE ECONOMICS hold that this reduces the incentive to be productive and discourages business investment. In urging that marginal tax rates be cut for individuals and businesses, they argue that the resulting increased work effort and business investment would reduce STAGFLATION. *See also* FLAT TAX.

MARGINAL UTILITY in economics, the addition to total satisfaction from goods or services (called *utility*) that is derived from consuming one more unit of that good or service.

MARGIN CALL demand that a customer deposit enough money or securities to bring a margin account up to the INITIAL MARGIN or MINIMUM MAINTENANCE requirements. If a customer fails to respond, securities in the account may be liquidated. *See also* FIVE HUNDRED DOLLAR RULE; SELL OUT.

MARGIN DEPARTMENT section within a brokerage firm that monitors customer compliance with margin regulations, keeping track of debits and credits, short sales, and purchases of stock on margin, and all other extensions of credit by the broker. Also known as the *credit department. See also* MARK TO THE MARKET.

MARGIN OF PROFIT relationship of gross profits to net sales. Returns and allowances are subtracted from gross sales to arrive at net sales. Cost of goods sold (sometimes including depreciation) is subtracted from net sales to arrive at gross profit. Gross profit is divided by net sales to get the profit margin, which is sometimes called the *gross margin.* The result is a ratio, and the term is also written as *margin of profit ratio.*

   The term profit margin is less frequently used to mean the *net margin,* obtained by deducting operating expenses in addition to cost of goods sold and dividing the result by net sales. Operating expenses are usually shown on profit and loss statements as "selling, general and administrative (SG&A) expenses."

   Both gross and net profit margins, when compared with prior periods and with industry statistics, can be revealing in terms of a firm's operating efficiency and pricing policies and its ability to compete successfully with other companies in its field.

MARGIN REQUIREMENT minimum amount that a client must deposit in the form of cash or eligible securities in a margin account as spelled out in REGULATION T of the Federal Reserve Board. Reg T requires a minimum of $2000 or 50% of the purchase price of eligible securities bought on margin or 50% of the proceeds of short sales. Also called INITIAL MARGIN. *See also* MARGIN; MARGIN SECURITY; MINIMUM MAINTENANCE; SELLING SHORT.

MARGIN SECURITY security that may be bought or sold in a margin account. REGULATION T defines margin securities as (1) any *registered security* (a LISTED SECURITY or a security having UNLISTED TRADING privileges); (2) any *OTC margin stock* or *OTC margin bond,* which are defined as any UNLISTED SECURITY that the Federal Reserve Board (FRB) periodically identifies as having the investor interest, marketability, disclosure, and solid financial position of a listed security; (3) any OTC security designated as qualified for trading in the NATIONAL MARKET SYSTEM under a plan approved by the Securities and Exchange Commission; (4) any mutual fund or unit investment trust registered under the Investment Company Act of 1940. Other securities that are not EXEMPT SECURITIES must be transacted in cash.

MARITAL DEDUCTION provision in the federal estate and gift tax law allowing spouses to transfer unlimited amounts of property to each other free of tax. Such transfers may be made during the life or at the death of the transferor, and are intended to treat a couple as an economic unit for transfer tax purposes. Although the deduction is unlimited, passing all assets to a spouse may create transfer tax problems in the surviving spouse's estate; planners should try to fully use each spouse's UNIFIED CREDIT, which offsets up to $600,000 in transfers, and equalize the rate of transfer taxes for both spouses to reduce taxes for the couple.

MARKDOWN

1. amount subtracted from the selling price, when a customer sells securities to a dealer in the OVER THE COUNTER market. Had the securities been purchased from the dealer, the customer would have paid a *markup,* or an amount added to the purchase price. The National Association of Securities Dealers (NASD) RULES OF FAIR PRACTICE established 5% as a reasonable guideline in markups and markdowns, though many factors enter into the question of fairness, and exceptions are common.
2. reduction in the price at which the underwriters offer municipal bonds after the market has shown a lack of interest at the original price.
3. downward adjustment of the value of securities by banks and investment firms, based on a decline in market quotations.
4. reduction in the original retail selling price, which was determined by adding a percentage factor, called a markon, to the cost of the merchandise. Anything added to the markon is called a markup, and the term markdown does not apply unless the price is dropped below the original selling price.

MARKET

1. public place where products or services are bought and sold, directly or through intermediaries. Also called *marketplace.*
2. aggregate of people with the present or potential ability and desire to purchase a product or service; equivalent to demand.
3. securities markets in the aggregate, or the New York Stock Exchange in particular.
4. short for *market value,* the value of an asset based on the price it would command on the open market, usually as determined by the MARKET PRICE at which similar assets have recently been bought and sold.
5. as a verb, to sell. *See also* MARKETING.

MARKETABILITY speed and ease with which a particular security may be bought and sold. A stock that has a large amount of shares outstanding and is actively traded is highly marketable and also liquid. In common use, marketability is interchangeable with LIQUIDITY, but liquidity implies the preservation of value when a security is bought or sold.

MARKETABLE SECURITIES securities that are easily sold. On a corporation's balance sheet, they are assets that can be readily converted into cash—for example, government securities, banker's acceptances, and commercial paper. In keeping with conservative accounting practice, these are carried at cost or market value, whichever is lower.

MARKETABLE TITLE title to a piece of real estate that is reasonably free from risk of litigation over possible defects, and while it may not be perfect, it is free from plausible or reasonable objections, and is one that a court of law would order the buyer to accept. A seller under a contract of sale is required to deliver marketable title at final closing; this requirement is implicit in law and does not need to be stated in the contract. Usually the property buyer will engage a title insurance company to ensure that the seller has CLEAR TITLE to the real estate before entering into a purchase contract. This search generally is not ordered until financing has been secured. Once the title company has researched the history of ownership of the property and feels sure that the seller owns it, it will issue a title insurance policy. The seller is thus assured that he has a marketable title, which allows him to transfer ownership to the buyer. *See also* BAD TITLE; CLOUD ON TITLE.

MARKET ANALYSIS
1. research aimed at predicting or anticipating the direction of stock, bond, or commodity markets, based on technical data about the movement of market prices or on fundamental data such as corporate earnings prospects or supply and demand.
2. study designed to define a company's markets, forecast their directions, and decide how to expand the company's share and exploit any new trends.

MARKET BASKET *see* BASKET.

MARKET BREAK any sudden drop (BREAK) in the stock market as measured by STOCK INDEXES AND AVERAGES. In SEC parlance, BLACK MONDAY, when the Dow Jones Industrial Average dropped 508 points.

MARKET BREADTH *see* BREADTH OF THE MARKET.

MARKET CAPITALIZATION value of a corporation as determined by the market price of its issued and outstanding common stock. It is calculated by multiplying the number of outstanding shares by the current market price of a share. Institutional investors often use market capitalization as one investment criterion, requiring, for example, that a company have a market capitalization of $100 million or more to qualify as an investment. Analysts look at market capitalization in relation to book, or accounting, value for an indication of how investors value a company's future prospects.

MARKET EYE financial information service that emanates from the British Broadcasting Company under the sponsorship of the INTERNATIONAL STOCK EXCHANGE OF THE UK AND THE REPUBLIC OF IRELAND (ISE). Market Eye supplies current market information plus statistical information on particular equity and debt issues and is a supplement to the Stock Exchange Automated Quotations System (SEAQ), which records trades.

MARKET IF TOUCHED ORDER (MIT) order to buy or sell a security or commodity as soon as a preset market price is reached, at which point it becomes a MARKET ORDER. When corn is selling for $4.75 a bushel, someone might enter a market if touched order to buy at $4.50. As soon as the price is dropped to $4.50, the contract would be bought on the customer's behalf at whatever market price prevails when the order is executed.

MARKET INDEX numbers representing weighted values of the components that make up the index. A stock market index, for example, is weighted according to the prices and number of outstanding shares of the various stocks. The Standard and Poor's 500 Stock Index is one of the most widely followed, but myriad other indexes track stocks in various industry groups.

MARKETING moving goods and services from the provider to consumer. This involves product origination and design, development, distribution, advertising, promotion, and publicity as well as market analysis to define the appropriate market.

MARKET OPENING the start of formal trading on an exchange, usually referring to the New York Stock Exchange (NYSE) and marked by an opening bell. All stocks do not necessarily open trading at the bell, since there may be order imbalances causing a DELAYED OPENING. *See also* OPD; OPENING.

MARKET JITTERS state of widespread fear among investors, which may cause them to sell stocks and bonds, pushing prices downward. Investors may fear lower corporate earnings, negative economic news, tightening of credit by the Federal Reserve, foreign currency fluctuations, or many other factors. In some cases, news may be good, but is interpreted as bad because investors are so fearful. For example, investors may think that positive economic or corporate earnings news is putting more pressure on the Federal Reserve to raise interest rates, which would hurt stock and bond prices.

MARKET LETTER newsletter provided to brokerage firm customers or written by an independent market analyst, registered as an investment adviser with the Securities and Exchange Commission, who sells the letter to subscribers. These letters assess the trends in interest rates, the economy, and the market in general. Brokerage letters typically reiterate the recommendations of their own research departments. Independent letters take on the personality of their writers—concentrating on growth stocks, for example, or basing their recommendations on technical analysis. A HULBERT RATING is an evaluation of such a letter's performance.

MARKET MAKER *see* MAKE A MARKET.

MARKET-ON-CLOSE (MOC) ORDER order to buy or sell stocks or futures and options contracts as near as possible to when the market closes for the day. Such an order may be a LIMIT ORDER which had not yet been executed during the trading day.

MARKET ORDER order to buy or sell a security at the best available price. Most orders executed on the exchanges are market orders.

MARKET OUT CLAUSE escape clause sometimes written into FIRM COMMITMENT underwriting agreements which essentially allows the underwriters to be released from their purchase commitment if material adverse developments affect the securities markets generally. It is not common practice for the larger investment banking houses to write "outs" into their agreements, since the value of their commitment is a matter of paramount concern. *See also* UNDERWRITE.

MARKET PERFORMANCE COMMITTEE (MPC) New York Stock Exchange (NYSE) SPECIALIST oversight group consisting of members and ALLIED MEMBERS. MOC monitors specialists' effectiveness in maintaining fair prices and orderly markets and is authorized to assign or reassign new or existing issues to specialist units based on their capability.

MARKETPLACE *see* MARKET.

MARKET PRICE last reported price at which a security was sold on an exchange. For stocks or bonds sold OVER THE COUNTER, the combined bid and offer prices available at any particular time from those making a market in the stock. For an inactively traded security, evaluators or other analysts may determine a market price if needed—to settle an estate, for example.

In the general business world, market price refers to the price agreed upon by buyers and sellers of a product or service, as determined by supply and demand.

MARKET RESEARCH exploration of the size, characteristics, and potential of a market to find out, before developing any new product or service, what people want and need. Market research is an early step in marketing—which stretches from the original conception of a product to its ultimate delivery to the consumer.

In the stock market, market research refers to TECHNICAL ANALYSIS of factors such as volume, price advances and declines, and market breadth, which analysts use to predict the direction of prices.

MARKET RISK *see* SYSTEMATIC RISK.

MARKET SHARE percentage of industry sales of a particular company or product.

MARKET SWEEP second offer to institutional investors, made following a public TENDER OFFER, aimed at increasing the buyer's position from a significant interest to a controlling interest. The second offering is usually at a slightly higher price than the original tender offer.

MARKET TIMING decisions on when to buy or sell securities, in light of economic factors such as the strength of the economy and the direction of interest rates, or technical indications such as the direction of stock prices and the volume of trading. Investors in mutual funds may implement their market timing decisions by switching from a stock fund to a bond fund to a money market fund and back again, as the market outlook changes.

MARKET TONE general health and vigor of a securities market. The market tone is good when dealers and market makers are trading actively on narrow bid and offer spreads; it is bad when trading is inactive and bid and offer spreads are wide.

MARKET VALUE
In general: market price—the price at which buyers and sellers trade similar items in an open marketplace. In the absence of a market price, it is the estimated highest price a buyer would be warranted in paying and a seller justified in accepting, provided both parties were fully informed and acted intelligently and voluntarily.

Investments: current market price of a security—as indicated by the latest trade recorded.

Accounting: technical definition used in valuing inventory or marketable securities in accordance with the conservative accounting principle of "lower of cost or market." While cost is simply acquisition cost, market value is estimated net selling price less estimated costs of carrying, selling, and delivery, and, in the case of an unfinished product, the costs to complete production. The market value arrived at this way cannot, however, be lower than the cost at which a normal profit can be made.

MARKET VALUE-WEIGHTED INDEX index whose components are weighted according to the total market value of their outstanding shares. Also called *capitalization-weighted index.* The impact of a component's price change is proportional to the issue's overall market value, which is the share price times the number of shares outstanding. For example, the the AMEX Market Value Index (AMVI) has more than 800 component stocks. The weighting of each stock constantly shifts with changes in the stock's price and the number of shares outstanding. The index fluctuates in line with the price moves of the stocks.

MARKING UP OR DOWN increasing or decreasing the price of a security based on supply and demand forces. A securities dealer may mark up the price of a stock or bond if prices are rising, and may be forced to mark it down if demand is declining. The markup is the difference, or spread, between the price the dealer paid for the security and the price at which he sells it to the retail customer. *See also* MARKDOWN.

MARK TO THE MARKET
1. adjust the valuation of a security or portfolio to reflect current market values. For example, MARGIN ACCOUNTS are marked to the market to ensure

compliance with maintenance requirements. OPTION and FUTURES CONTACTS are marked to the market at year end with PAPER PROFIT OR LOSS recognized for tax purposes.

2. in a MUTUAL FUND, the daily net asset value reported to shareholders is the result of marking the fund's current portfolio to current market prices.

MARKUP *see* MARKDOWN.

MARRIAGE PENALTY effect of a tax code that makes a married couple pay more than the same two people would pay if unmarried and filing singly. For example, the REVENUE RECONCILIATION ACT OF 1993 may penalize low-end tax-payers whose combined income disqualifies them for the EARNED INCOME CREDIT they would have received as single taxpayers. High-end married taxpayers, on the other hand, may find that, combined, their incomes become subject to the SURTAX on incomes over $250,000.

MARRIED PUT option to sell a certain number of securities at a particular price by a specified time, bought simultaneously with securities of the underlying company so as to hedge the price paid for the securities. *See also* OPTION; PUT OPTION.

MASTER LIMITED PARTNERSHIP (MLP) public LIMITED PARTNERSHIP composed of corporate assets spun off *(roll out)* or private limited partnerships *(roll up)* with income, capital gains, and/or TAX SHELTER orientations. Interests are represented by depositary receipts traded in the SECONDARY MARKET. Investors thus enjoy LIQUIDITY. Flow-through tax benefits, previously possible within PASSIVE income restrictions, were limited by tax legislation passed in 1987 that will treat most MLPs as corporations after a GRANDFATHER CLAUSE expires in 1998.

MATCHED AND LOST report of the results of flipping a coin by two securities brokers locked in competition to execute equal trades.

MATCHED BOOK term used for the accounts of securities dealers when their borrowing costs are equal to the interest earned on loans to customers and other brokers.

MATCHED MATURITIES coordination of the maturities of a financial institution's assets (such as loans) and liabilities (such as certificates of deposit and money-market accounts). For instance, a savings and loan might issue 10-year mortgages at 10%, funded with money received for 10-year CDs at 7% yields. The bank is thus positioned to make a three-percentage-point profit for 10 years. If a bank granted 20-year mortgages at a fixed 10%, on the other hand, using short-term funds from money-market accounts paying 7%, the bank would be vulnerable to a rapid rise in interest rates. If yields on the money-market accounts surged to 14%, the bank could lose a large amount of money, since it was earning only 10% from its assets. Such a situation, called a *maturity mismatch,* can cause tremendous problems for financial institutions if it persists, as it did in the early 1980s.

MATCHED ORDERS

1. illegal manipulative technique of offsetting buy and sell orders to create the impression of activity in a security, thereby causing upward price movement that benefits the participants in the scheme.
2. action by a SPECIALIST to create an opening price reasonably close to the previous close. When an accumulation of one kind of order—either buy or sell—causes a delay in the opening of trading on an exchange, the specialist tries to find counterbalancing orders or trades long or short from his own inventory in order to narrow the spread.

MATCHED SALE PURCHASE TRANSACTION FEDERAL OPEN MARKET COMMITTEE procedure whereby the Federal Reserve Bank of New York sells government securities to a nonbank dealer against payment in FEDERAL FUNDS. The agreement requires the dealer to sell the securities back by a specified date, which ranges from one to 15 days. The Fed pays the dealer a rate of interest equal to the discount rate. These transactions, also called reverse repurchase agreements, decrease the money supply for temporary periods by reducing dealer's bank balances and thus excess reserves. The Fed is thus able to adjust an abnormal monetary expansion due to seasonal or other factors. *See also* REPURCHASE AGREEMENT.

MATERIALITY characteristic of an event or information that is sufficiently important (or *material*) to have a large impact on a company's stock price. For example, if a company was about to report its earnings, or make a takeover bid for another company, that would be considered material information. Material information is information the reasonable investor needs to make an informed decision about an investment.

MATIF SA France's futures exchange, formally known as Marche a Terme International de France. The MATIF uses a combination of open outcry (9 A.M. to 4:30 P.M.) and electronic trading on the Globex system (4:30 P.M. to 9 A.M.) for its notion bond futures and options, and ECU bond futures and options; for three-month PIBOR futures and options (8:30 A.M. to 4 P.M., 4 P.M. to 8:30 A.M.); and CAC 40 INDEX futures and options contracts (10 A.M. to 5 P.M., 5 P.M. to 10 A.M.). U.S. dollar/Deutschmark and U.S. dollar/French franc options are traded by open outcry (9:15 A.M. to 5 P.M.) and on Globex and the THS after-hours telephone system (5 P.M. to 9:15 A.M.). The exchange also trades three commodities through open outcry: white sugar futures (10:45 A.M. to 1 P.M., 3 P.M. to 7 P.M.); potato futures (10:30 A.M. to 12:45 P.M., 2 P.M. to 4 P.M.); and rapeseed futures (11 A.M. to 1 P.M., 3:30 P.M. to 6:30 P.M.).

MATRIX TRADING bond swapping whereby traders seek to take advantage of temporary aberrations in YIELD SPREAD differentials between bonds of the same class but with different ratings or between bonds of different classes.

MATURE ECONOMY economy of a nation whose population has stabilized or is declining, and whose economic growth is no longer robust. Such an economy is characterized by a decrease in spending on roads or factories and a relative increase in consumer spending. Many of Western Europe's economies are considerably more mature than that of the United States and in marked contrast to the faster-growing economies of the Far East.

MATURITY
1. reaching the date at which a debt instrument is due and payable. A bond due to mature on January 1, 2010, will return the bondholder's principal and final interest payment when it reaches maturity on that date. Bond yields are frequently calculated on a YIELD-TO-MATURITY basis.
2. when referring to a company or economy, *maturity* means that it is well-established, and has little room for dynamic growth. For example, economists will say that an aging industrial economy has reached maturity. Or stock analysts will refer to a company's market as mature, meaning that demand for the company's products is stagnant.

MATURITY DATE
1. date on which the principal amount of a note, draft, acceptance bond, or other debt instrument becomes due and payable. Also termination or due date on which an installment loan must be paid in full.

2. in FACTORING, average due date of factored receivables, when the factor remits to the seller for receivables sold each month.

MATURITY MATCHING *see* DURATION *(immunization).*

MAXIMUM CAPITAL GAINS MUTUAL FUND fund whose objective is to produce large capital gains for its shareholders. During a bull market it is likely to rise much faster than the general market or conservative mutual funds. But in a falling market, it is likely to drop much farther than the market averages. This increased volatility results from a policy of investing in small, fast-growing companies whose stocks characteristically are more volatile than those of large, well-established companies.

MAY DAY May 1, 1975, when fixed minimum brokerage commissions ended in the United States. Instead of a mandated rate to execute exchange trades, brokers were allowed to charge whatever they chose. The May Day changes ushered in the era of discount brokerage firms that execute buy and sell orders for low commissions, but give no investment advice. The end of fixed commissions also marked the beginning of diversification by the brokerage industry into a wide range of financial services utilizing computer technology and advanced communications systems.

MEALS AND ENTERTAINMENT EXPENSE expense for meals and entertainment that qualifies for a tax deduction. Under current tax law, employers may deduct 50% of meals and entertainment expenses that have a bona fide business purpose. For example, a business meal must include a discussion producing a direct business benefit.

MEAN RETURN in security analysis, expected value, or mean, of all the likely returns of investments comprising a portfolio; in capital budgeting, mean value of the probability distribution of possible returns. The portfolio approach to the analysis of investments aims at quantifying the relationship between risk and return. It assumes that while investors have different risk-value preferences, rational investors will always seek the maximum rate of return for every level of acceptable risk. It is the mean, or expected, return that an investor attempts to maximize at each level of risk. Also called *expected return. See also* CAPITAL ASSET PRICING MODEL, EFFICIENT PORTFOLIO, PORTFOLIO THEORY.

MECHANIC'S LIEN LIEN against buildings or other structures, allowed by some states to contractors, laborers, and suppliers of materials used in their construction or repair. The lien remains in effect until these people have been paid in full and may, in the event of a liquidation before they have been paid, give them priority over other creditors.

MEDIAN midway value between two points. There are an equal number of points above and below the median. For example, the number 5 is the median between the numbers 1 and 9, since there are 4 numbers above and below 5 in this sequence. Several important economic numbers use medians, including median household income and median home price.

MEDIUM-TERM BOND bond with a maturity of 2 to 10 years. *See also* INTERMEDIATE TERM; LONG TERM; SHORT TERM.

MEFF RENTA FIJA Spain's derivatives exchange, in Barcelona, responsible for interest rate and foreign exchange derivatives. The exchange trades futures on interest rates and options on futures, the 90-day Madrid Interbank Offered Rate (MIBOR) and one-year MIBOR; and 3-year and 10-year government bond futures and options contracts. The exchange is a subsidiary of MEFF Holding Corp. of Financial Derivatives.

MEFF RENTA VARIABLE Spain's stock index and equity derivatives market, located in Madrid, trading futures and options on the Iberian Exchange (IBEX)-35 index and options on individual stocks. The IBEX-35 is the official index of the continuous market of the Spanish Sociedad de Bolsas, owned by the four exchanges. It is comprised of the 35 largest and most liquid stocks traded on the CATS electronic trading system. The exchange is a subsidiary of MEFF Holding Corp. of Financial Derivatives.

MELLO ROOS FINANCING financing of real estate developments in California authorized by legislation in 1982 sponsored by Henry Mello and Mike Roos of the California legislature. The bill allowed municipalities to float bonds to be repaid from the proceeds of tax revenues generated by real estate sales. The bonds financed construction of a community's infrastructure, such as sewers, roads, and electricity, which developers then finished with homes and businesses.

MEMBER BANK bank that is a member of the FEDERAL RESERVE SYSTEM, including all nationally chartered banks and any state-chartered banks that apply for membership and are accepted. Member banks are required to purchase stock in the FEDERAL RESERVE BANK in their districts. Half of that investment is carried as an asset of the member bank. The other half is callable by the Fed at any time. Member banks are also required to maintain a percentage of their deposits as reserves in the form of currency in their vaults and balances on deposit at their Fed district banks. These reserve balances make possible a range of money transfer and other services using the FED WIRE system to connect banks in different parts of the country.

MEMBER FIRM brokerage firm that has at least one membership on a major stock exchange, even though, by exchange rules, the membership is in the name of an employee and not of the firm itself. Such a firm enjoys the rights and privileges of membership, such as voting on exchange policy, together with the obligations of membership, such as the commitment to settle disputes with customers through exchange arbitration procedures.

MEMBER SHORT SALE RATIO ratio of the total shares sold short for the accounts of New York Stock Exchange members in one week divided by the total short sales for the same week. Because the specialists, floor traders, and off-the-floor traders who trade for members' accounts are generally considered the best minds in the business, the ratio is a valuable indicator of market trends. A ratio of 82% or higher is considered bearish; a ratio of 68% or lower is positive and bullish. The member short sale ratio appears with other NYSE round lot statistics in the Monday edition of *The Wall Street Journal* and in *Barron's*, a weekly financial newspaper.

MERC nickname for the Chicago Mercantile Exchange. The exchange trades many types of futures, futures options, and foreign currency futures contracts. *See also* SECURITIES AND COMMODITIES EXCHANGES.

MERCANTILE AGENCY organization that supplies businesses with credit ratings and reports on other firms that are or might become customers. Such agencies may also collect past due accounts or trade collection statistics, and they tend to industry and geographical specialization. The largest of the agencies, DUN & BRADSTREET, was founded in 1841 under the name Mercantile Agency. It provides credit information on companies of all descriptions along with a wide range of other credit and financial reporting services.

MERCATO ITALIANO FUTURES (MIF) the Italian futures market, based in Rome. The MIF is a screen-based market, trading 10-year and 5-year Italian Treasury bond (BTP) futures. The market uses the same computer network that handles the underlying secondary market in Italian government securities.

MERCHANT BANK

1. European financial institution that engages in investment banking, counseling, and negotiating in mergers and acquisitions, and a variety of other services including securities portfolio management for customers, insurance, the acceptance of foreign bills of exchange, dealing in bullion, and participating in commercial ventures. Deposits in merchant banks are negligible, and the prominence of such names as Rothschild, Baring, Lazard, and Hambro attests to their role as counselors and negotiators in large-scale acquisitions, mergers, and the like.

2. part of an American bank that engages in investment banking functions, such as advising clients in mergers and acquisitions, underwriting securities, and taking debt or equity positions. The Federal Reserve permits commercial banks to underwrite corporate debt and common stock deals.

3. American bank that has entered into an agreement with a merchant to accept deposits generated by bank credit/charge card transactions.

MERGER combination of two or more companies, either through a POOLING OF INTERESTS, where the accounts are combined; a purchase, where the amount paid over and above the acquired company's book value is carried on the books of the purchaser as goodwill; or a consolidation, where a new company is formed to acquire the net assets of the combining companies. Strictly speaking, only combinations in which one of the companies survives as a legal entity are called mergers or, more formally, statutory mergers; thus consolidations, or statutory consolidations, are technically not mergers, though the term merger is commonly applied to them. Mergers meeting the legal criteria for pooling of interests, where common stock is exchanged for common stock, are nontaxable and are called tax-free mergers. Where an acquisition takes place by the purchase of assets or stock using cash or a debt instrument for payment, the merger is a taxable capital gain to the selling company or its stockholders. There is a potential benefit to such taxable purchase acquisitions, however, in that the acquiring company can write up the acquired company's assets by the amount by which the market value exceeds the book value; that difference can then be charged off to depreciation with resultant tax savings.

Mergers can also be classified in terms of their economic function. Thus a *horizontal merger* is one combining direct competitors in the same product lines and markets; a *vertical merger* combines customer and company or supplier and company; a *market extension merger* combines companies selling the same products in different markets; a *product extension merger* combines companies selling different but related products in the same market; a *conglomerate merger* combines companies with none of the above relationships or similarities. *See also* ACQUISITION.

MEXICAN STOCK EXCHANGE the only stock exchange in Mexico, formally known as the Bolsa Mexicana de Valores, and owned by the 26 casas de bolsa, or stock brokerage companies. The Indice de Precios y Cotizaciones, or IPC, consists of the 40 most representative stocks, chosen every two months. The INMEX index is an underlying index for derivative products, reviewed every six months so a single issuer cannot account for more than 10% of the index. The trading floor is automated, and trading is conducted from 8:30 A.M. to 2 P.M., Monday through Friday. Trades are settled two days after the trade date. All trades are executed in Mexican pesos.

MEZZANINE BRACKET members of a securities underwriting group whose participations are of such a size as to place them in the tier second to the largest participants. In the newspaper TOMBSTONE advertisements that announce new securities offerings, the underwriters are listed in alphabetical groups, first the lead underwriters, then the mezzanine bracket, then the remaining participants.

MEZZANINE LEVEL stage of a company's development just prior to its going public, in VENTURE CAPITAL language. Venture capitalists entering at that point have a lower risk of loss than at previous stages and can look forward to early capital appreciation as a result of the MARKET VALUE gained by an INITIAL PUBLIC OFFERING.

MICROECONOMICS study of the behavior of basic economic units such as companies, industries, or households. Research on the companies in the airline industry would be a microeconomic concern, for instance. *See also* MACROECONOMICS.

MIDWEST STOCK EXCHANGE *see* REGIONAL STOCK EXCHANGES.

MIG-1 *see* MOODY'S INVESTMENT GRADE.

MILAN STOCK EXCHANGE largest of regional stock exchanges in Italy, accounting for more than 90% of trading volume. The MIB indices, based on the prices of all listed shares, and the COMIT Index, calculated by the Banca Commerciale Italiana, are the most widely used. Extensive reforms and reorganization in Italy created the Consiglio di Borsa, the Italian Stock Exchange Council, which instituted computerized trading and a block market. The regional exchanges are located in Rome, Turin, Genoa, Bologna, Florence, Naples, Palermo, Trieste, and Venice. Electronic trading is conducted Monday through Friday from 8:45 A.M. to 10 A.M. (order entry, automatic fixing of opening price), and from 10 A.M. to 4 P.M. (continuous trading with automatic matching of buy and sell orders). An open outcry system is used in the second market, from 9 A.M. to 10 A.M. Milan's second market, Mercato Ristretto, is the largest in the country. Trades are settled on a monthly basis, between 15 and 45 days after the trade date.

MILL one-tenth of a cent, the unit most often used in expressing property tax rates. For example, if a town's tax rate is 5 mills per dollar of assessed valuation, and the assessed valuation of a piece of property is $100,000, the tax is $500, or 0.005 times $100,000.

MINI-MANIPULATION trading in a security underlying an option contract so as to manipulate the stock's price, thus causing an increase in the value of the options. In this way the manipulator's profit can be multiplied many times, since a large position in options can be purchased with a relatively small amount of money.

MINIMUM FLUCTUATION smallest possible price movement of a security or options or futures contract. For example, most stocks on the New York Stock Exchange trade with a minimum fluctuation of one-eighth of a point. Some low-priced options contracts trade with a minimum fluctuation of one-sixteenth of a point. Minimum fluctuations are set by the securities, futures, or options exchanges regulating each security or contract. Also called MINIMUM TICK.

MINIMUM MAINTENANCE equity level that must be maintained in brokerage customers' margin accounts, as required by the New York Stock Exchange (NYSE), the National Association of Securities Dealers (NASD), and individual brokerage firms. Under REGULATION T, $2000 in cash or securities must be deposited with a broker before *any* credit can be extended; then an INITIAL MARGIN requirement must be met, currently 50% of the market value of eligible securities long or short in customers' accounts. The NYSE and NASD, going a step further, both require that a margin be *maintained* equal to 25% of the market value of securities in margin accounts. Brokerage firm requirements are typically a more conservative 30%. When the market value of margined securities falls below these minimums a MARGIN CALL goes out requesting additional equity. If the customer fails to comply, the broker may sell the margined stock and close the customer out. *See also* MARGIN REQUIREMENT; MARGIN SECURITY; MARK TO THE MARKET; SELL OUT.

MINIMUM PAYMENT minimum amount that a consumer is required to pay on a revolving charge account in order to keep the account in good standing. If the minimum payment is not made, late payment penalties are due. If the minimum is still not paid within a few months, credit privileges may be revoked. If a consumer pays just the minimum due, interest charges continue to accrue on all outstanding balances. In some cases, a credit card issuer will waive the minimum payment for a month or two, as long as the cardholder has demonstrated a good payment history. If the cardholder does not make any minimum payment in such a case, interest charges accrue on the entire outstanding balance.

MINIMUM TICK *see* MINIMUM FLUCTUATION.

MINI-WAREHOUSE LIMITED PARTNERSHIP partnership that invests in small warehouses where people can rent space to store belongings. Such partnerships offer tax benefits such as depreciation allowances, but mostly they provide income derived from rents. When the partnership is liquidated, the general partner may sell the warehouse for a profit, providing capital gains to limited partners.

MINORITY INTEREST interest of shareholders who, in the aggregate, own less than half the shares in a corporation. On the consolidated balance sheets of companies whose subsidiaries are not wholly owned, the minority interest is shown as a separate equity account or as a liability of indefinite term. On the income statement, the minority's share of income is subtracted to arrive at consolidated net income.

MINOR'S ACCOUNT bank savings account in the name of a minor, in which the minor has the power to deposit and withdraw. The minor must be able to sign for the account, but minimum deposit requirements and charges are waived until the child reaches majority (age 18 in most states).

MINUS symbol (−) preceding a fraction or number in the change column at the far right of newspaper stock tables designating a closing sale lower than that of the previous day.

MINUS TICK *see* DOWNTICK.

MISERY INDEX index that combines the unemployment and inflation rates. The index was devised in the 1970s when both inflation and unemployment rose sharply. The misery index is often credited with political significance, since it may be difficult for a president to be re-elected if there is a high misery index. The misery index is also linked to consumer confidence—the lower the index, in general, the more confident consumers tend to be.

MISSING THE MARKET failing to execute a transaction on terms favorable to a customer and thus being negligent as a broker. If the order is subsequently executed at a price demonstrably less favorable, the broker, as the customer's agent, may have to make up the loss.

MIXED ACCOUNT brokerage account in which some securities are owned (in long positions) and some borrowed (in short positions).

MLP *see* MASTER LIMITED PARTNERSHIP (MLP).

MOB SPREAD difference in yield between a tax-free MUNICIPAL BOND and a Treasury bond with the same maturity. Term is an acronym for *municipals-over-bonds* SPREAD, which will always exist because municipals involve different degrees of risk while Treasuries are risk-free as to principal. The spread between a "muni" of a given rating and a Treasury with the same maturity has significance in tax decisions and in transactions involving financial futures contracts.

MOBILE HOME CERTIFICATE mortgage-backed security guaranteed by the GOVERNMENT NATIONAL MORTGAGE ASSOCIATION consisting of mortgages on mobile homes. Although the maturity tends to be shorter on these securities than on single-family homes, they have all the other characteristics of regular Ginnie Maes, and the timely payment of interest and the repayment of principal are backed by the FULL FAITH AND CREDIT of the U.S. government.

MOCK TRADING simulated trading of stocks, bonds, commodities and mutual funds. Real money is not used. Students learning about investing in schools or brokerage training classes may go through exercises in mock trading, in which securities prices are tracked on a daily basis and fictional trades are made. With commodity futures and options, this may take the form of going through a simulated trading session on the trading floor or using computer programs to illustrate the futures and options strategies.

MODELING designing and manipulating a mathematical representation of an economic system or corporate financial application so that the effect of changes can be studied and forecast. For example, in ECONOMETRICS, a complex economic model can be drawn up, entered into a computer, and used to predict the effect of a rise in inflation or a cut in taxes on economic output.

MODERN PORTFOLIO THEORY *see* PORTFOLIO THEORY.

MODIFIED ACCELERATED COST RECOVERY SYSTEM (MACRS) provision, originally called the Accelerated Cost Recovery System (ACRS), instituted by the Economic Recovery Tax Act of 1981 (ERTA) and modified by the Tax Reform Act of 1986, which establishes rules for the DEPRECIATION (the recovery of cost through tax deductions) of qualifying assets. With certain exceptions, the 1986 Act modifications, which generally provide for greater acceleration over longer periods of time than ERTA rules, are effective for property placed in service after 1986.

Under the modified rules, depreciable assets other than buildings fall within a 3-, 5-, 7-, 10-, 15-, or 20-year class life. The 3-, 5-, 7-, and 10-year classes use the DOUBLE DECLINING BALANCE DEPRECIATION METHOD, with a switch to STRAIGHT LINE DEPRECIATION. Instead of the 200% rate, you may elect a 150% rate. For 15- and 20-year property, the 150% declining balance method is used with a switch to straight line. The conversion to straight line occurs when larger annual deductions may be claimed over the remaining life. Real estate uses the straight line basis. Residential rental property placed in service after December 31, 1986, is depreciated over 27.5 years, while nonresidential property placed in service between December 1, 1986, and May 13, 1993, is depreciated over 31.5 years. A 39-year period applies to nonresidential property placed in service after May 12, 1993, although certain transition rules apply.

MOMENTUM rate of acceleration of an economic, price, or volume movement. An economy with strong growth that is likely to continue is said to have a lot of momentum. In the stock market, technical analysts study stock momentum by charting price and volume trends. *See also* EARNINGS MOMENTUM.

M-1, M-2 and M-3 three measures of the money supply as defined by the Federal Reserve Board:

M1 is the narrowest measure of money supply. It includes currency in circulation, checking account balances, NOW accounts and share draft accounts at credit unions, and travelers' checks. M1 represents all money that can be spent or readily converted to cash for immediate spending.

M2 includes everything in M1 plus savings accounts and time deposits such as CDs, money market deposit accounts, and repurchase agreements.

M3 includes everything in M2 plus large CDs and money market fund balances held by institutions. M3 is the broadest measure of money supply tracked by the Fed.

Federal Reserve policymakers carefully watch the growth rate of all three money supply measures, but especially M2, as key indicators of economic growth and the potential for inflation. Most economists maintain that most economic growth and inflation is determined by the rate of growth in the money supply.

MONEP (Marche des Options Negociables de Paris) subsidiary of the PARIS BOURSE, continuously trading stock and index options. The CAC 40 INDEX was developed as an underlying index for derivative products traded on the MONEP and MATIF. Trading hours are 10 A.M. to 5 P.M., Monday through Friday, either electronically or by open outcry. The MONEP trades CAC 40 INDEX short-term (American style) and long-term (European style) options, and equity options.

MONETARIST economist who believes that the MONEY SUPPLY is the key to the ups and downs in the economy. Monetarists such as Milton Friedman think that the money supply has far more impact on the economy's future course than, say, the level of federal spending—a factor on which KEYNESIAN ECONOMICS puts great stress. Monetarists advocate slow but steady growth in the money supply.

MONETARY INDICATORS economic gauges of the effects of MONETARY POLICY, such as various measures of credit market conditions, U.S. Treasury BILL rates, and the Dow Jones Industrial Average (of common stocks).

MONETARY POLICY FEDERAL RESERVE BOARD decisions on the MONEY SUPPLY. To make the economy grow faster, the Fed can supply more credit to the banking system through its OPEN MARKET OPERATIONS, or it can lower the member bank reserve requirement or lower the DISCOUNT RATE—which is what banks pay to borrow additional reserves from the Fed. If, on the other hand, the economy is growing too fast and inflation is an increasing problem, the Fed might withdraw money from the banking system, raise the reserve requirement, or raise the discount rate, thereby putting a brake on economic growth. Other instruments of monetary policy range from selective credit controls to simple but often highly effective MORAL SUASION. Monetary policy differs from FISCAL POLICY, which is carried out through government spending and taxation. Both seek to control the level of economic activity as measured by such factors as industrial production, employment, and prices.

MONETIZE THE DEBT to finance the national debt by printing new money, causing inflation.

MONEY legal tender as defined by a government and consisting of currency and coin. In a more general sense, money is synonymous with CASH, which includes negotiable instruments, such as checks, based on bank balances.

MONEY CENTER BANK bank in one of the major financial centers of the world, among them New York, Chicago, San Francisco, Los Angeles, London, Paris, and Tokyo. These banks play a major national and international economic role because they are large lenders, depositories, and buyers of money market instruments and securities as well as large lenders to international governments and corporations. In the stock market, bank analysts usually categorize the money center banks as separate from regional banks—those that focus on one area of the country. Also known as *money market bank.*

MONEY MAGAZINE SMALL INVESTOR INDEX index which tracks the gains and losses of the average individual investor's portfolio. The index is based on the weekly total returns for the 10 major assets that individuals invest in: big stocks traded on the New York Exchange; small stocks traded on the American Stock Exchange and over the counter; equity mutual funds; taxable bonds; municipal bonds; bond mutual funds; money-market funds and money-market deposit accounts at banks; certificates of deposit; investment real estate, including real estate investment trusts and real estate limited partnerships but excluding primary and secondary residences; and gold. The returns for these 10 assets are weighted according to the way the average individual is currently allocating his or her money among them.

The *Money* magazine index has three uses: (1) it tells small investors what the current investment climate looks like for them; (2) it serves as a benchmark against which small investors can measure the performance of their portfolios over longer periods of time; (3) it provides the best indication of the returns that a small investor can expect in the future. For any projections of likely returns—say, for retirement planning—the Small Investor Index provides a better basis for such long-range forecasts than the Standard & Poor's 500.

The index appears in newspapers around the United States, usually on Monday, and monthly in *Money* magazine.

The MONEY Small Investor Allocations: percentage of portfolio in each asset

	Current	Year Ago
Stocks:		
NYSE stocks	23.30%	25.87%
ASE/OTC stocks	7.36	8.17
Equity mutual funds	10.55	8.21
Bonds:		
Taxable bonds	11.27	9.03
Municipal bonds	4.46	4.75
Bond mutual funds	6.68	7.29
Cash:		
CDs	12.91	13.10
Money funds	21.74	22.12
Other:		
Real estate securities	0.98	0.84
Gold	0.75	0.62

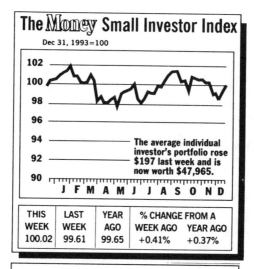

The **Money** Small Investor Index
Dec 31, 1993 = 100

The average individual investor's portfolio rose $197 last week and is now worth $47,965.

THIS WEEK	LAST WEEK	YEAR AGO	% CHANGE FROM A	
			WEEK AGO	YEAR AGO
100.02	99.61	99.65	+0.41%	+0.37%

Latest changes for each asset

CATEGORY	INDEX	% CHANGE FROM A	
		WEEK AGO	YEAR AGO
STOCKS			
NYSE	100.83	+0.96%	+1.18%
ASE/OTC	95.88	+1.19	−2.55
EQUITY FUNDS	97.51	+0.66	−1.61
BONDS			
TAXABLE BONDS	97.73	−0.04	−2.57
MUNICIPALS	94.80	+0.27	−4.22
BOND FUNDS	95.92	−0.19	−4.25
CASH			
CDs	104.14	+0.11	+4.20
MONEY FUNDS	102.34	+0.05	+2.38
OTHER			
REAL ESTATE	110.23	+0.51	+11.25
GOLD	89.97	+1.14	−7.70

Dec. 31, 1993 = 100

Sources: *Bank Rate Monitor,* the Federal Reserve, Investment Company Institute, Lehman Bros., Lipper Analytical Services, Merrill Lynch, *Money Fund Report,* Morgan Stanley Capital International, National Association of Real Estate Investment Trusts, Prudential Asset Management, Standard & Poor's, Robert Stanger & Co., World Gold Council

MONEY MANAGEMENT financial planner's responsibility for the general management of monetary matters, including banking, credit management, budgeting, taxation, and borrowing. Term is also a synonym for PORTFOLIO MANAGEMENT.

MONEY MANAGER *see* PORTFOLIO MANAGER.

MONEY MARKET market for SHORT-TERM DEBT INSTRUMENTS—negotiable certificates of deposit, Eurodollar certificates of deposit, commercial paper, banker's acceptances, Treasury bills, and discount notes of the Federal Home Loan Bank, Federal National Mortgage Association, and Federal Farm Credit System, among others. Federal funds borrowings between banks, bank borrowings from the Federal Reserve Bank WINDOW, and various forms of repurchase agreements are also elements of the money market. What these instruments have in common are safety and LIQUIDITY. The money market operates through dealers, MONEY CENTER BANKS, and the Open Market Trading DESK at the New York Federal Reserve Bank. New York City is the leading money market, followed by London and Tokyo. The dealers in the important money markets are in constant communication with each other and with major borrowers and investors to take advantage of ARBITRAGE opportunities, a practice which helps keep prices uniform worldwide. *See also* MONEY MARKET FUND.

MONEY MARKET DEPOSIT ACCOUNT market-sensitive bank account that has been offered since December 1982. Under Depository Institutions Deregulatory Committee rules, such accounts had a minimum of $1000 (eliminated in 1986) and only three checks may be drawn per month, although unlimited transfers may be carried out at an automated teller machine. The funds are therefore liquid—that is, they are available to depositors at any time without penalty. The interest rate is generally comparable to rates on money market mutual funds, though any individual bank's rate may be higher or lower. These accounts are insured by the FEDERAL DEPOSIT INSURANCE CORPORATION.

MONEY MARKET FUND open-ended MUTUAL FUND that invests in commercial paper, banker's acceptances, repurchase agreements, government securities, certificates of deposit, and other highly liquid and safe securities, and pays money market rates of interest. Launched in the middle 1970s, these funds were especially popular in the early 1980s when interest rates and inflation soared. Management's fee is less than 1% of an investor's assets; interest over and above that amount is credited to shareholders monthly. The fund's net asset value remains a constant $1 a share—only the interest rate goes up or down. Such funds usually offer the convenience of checkwriting privileges.

Most funds are not federally insured, but some are covered by private insurance. Some funds invest only in government-backed securities, which give shareholders an extra degree of safety.

Many money market funds are part of fund families. This means that investors can switch their money from one fund to another and back again without charge. Money in an ASSET MANAGEMENT ACCOUNT usually is automatically swept into a money market fund until the accountholder decides where to invest it next. *See also* DONOGHUE'S MONEY FUND AVERAGE; FAMILY OF FUNDS; MONEY MARKET DEPOSIT ACCOUNT; TAX-EXEMPT MONEY MARKET FUND.

MONEY ORDER financial instrument that can be easily converted into cash by the payee named on the money order. The money order lists both the payee and the person who bought the instrument, known as the payor. Money orders are issued by banks, telephone companies, post offices, and traveler's check issuers to people presenting cash or other forms of acceptable payment. A personal money order from a bank can be considered a one-stop checking account, because the purchaser has the ability to stop payment on it; this does not hold true for money orders from other sources. Money orders often are used by people who do not have checking accounts. They can be used to pay bills or any outstanding debts.

MONEY PURCHASE PLAN program for buying a pension annuity that provides for specified, regular payments, usually based on salary.

MONEY SPREAD *see* VERTICAL SPREAD.

MONEY SUPPLY total stock of money in the economy, consisting primarily of (1) currency in circulation and (2) deposits in savings and checking accounts. Too much money in relation to the output of goods tends to push interest rates down and push prices and inflation up; too little money tends to push interest rates up, lower prices and output, and cause unemployment and idle plant capacity. The bulk of money is in demand deposits with commercial banks, which are regulated by the Federal Reserve Board. It manages the money supply by raising or lowering the reserves that banks are required to maintain and the DISCOUNT RATE at which they can borrow from the Fed, as well as by its OPEN MARKET OPERATIONS—trading government securities to take money out of the system or put it in.

Changes in the financial system, particularly since banking deregulation in the 1980s, have caused controversy among economists as to what really constitutes the money supply at a given time. In response to this, a more comprehensive analysis and breakdown of money was developed. Essentially, the various forms of money are now grouped into two broad divisions: M-1, M-2, and M-3, representing money and NEAR MONEY; and L, representing longer-term liquid funds. The table below shows a detailed breakdown of all four categories. *See also* MONETARY POLICY.

MONEY SUPPLY

Classification	Components
M-1	currency in circulation commercial bank demand deposits NOW and ATS (automatic transfer from savings) accounts credit union share drafts mutual savings bank demand deposits nonbank travelers checks
M-2	M-1 overnight repurchase agreements issued by commercial banks overnight Eurodollars savings accounts time deposits under $100,000 money market mutual fund shares
M-3	M-2 time deposits over $100,000 term repurchase agreements
L	M-3 and other liquid assets such as: Treasury bills savings bonds commercial paper bankers' acceptances Eurodollar holdings of United States residents (nonbank)

MONOPOLY control of the production and distribution of a product or service by one firm or a group of firms acting in concert. In its pure form, monopoly, which is characterized by an absence of competition, leads to high prices and a general lack of responsiveness to the needs and desires of consumers. Although the most flagrant monopolistic practices in the United States were outlawed by ANTITRUST

LAWS enacted in the late 19th century and early 20th century, monopolies persist in some degree as the result of such factors as patents, scarce essential materials, and high startup and production costs that discourage competition in certain industries. *Public monopolies*—those operated by the government, such as the post office, or closely regulated by the government, such as utilities—ensure the delivery of essential products and services at acceptable prices and generally avoid the disadvantages produced by private monopolies. MONOPSONY, the dominance of a market by one buyer or group of buyers acting together, is less prevalent than monopoly. *See also* CARTEL; OLIGOPOLY; PERFECT COMPETITION.

MONOPSONY situation in which one buyer dominates, forcing sellers to agree to the buyer's terms. For example, a tobacco grower may have no choice but to sell his tobacco to one cigarette company that is the only buyer for his product. The cigarette company therefore virtually controls the price at which it buys tobacco. The opposite of a monopsony is a MONOPOLY.

MONTHLY COMPOUNDING OF INTEREST *see* COMPOUND INTEREST.

MONTHLY INVESTMENT PLAN plan whereby an investor puts a fixed dollar amount into a particular investment every month, thus building a position at advantageous prices by means of *dollar cost averaging (see* CONSTANT DOLLAR PLAN).

MONTREAL EXCHANGE/BOURSE DE MONTREAL Canada's oldest stock exchange and second-largest in dollar value of trading. Stocks, bonds, futures and options are traded through a specialist system combined with automated systems, including the Electronic Order Book and electronic order routing, execution and trading system—the MORRE System. A system-to-system link between the Montreal Exchange (ME) and the Boston Stock Exchange (BSE) enables ME member firms to electronically route retail orders for U.S. securities directly to the BSE for automatic execution and confirmation at the best prevailing price in the Intermarket Trading System. The Canadian Market Portfolio Index (XXM) tracks the market performance of 25 highly capitalized Canadian corporations, while six sector indices track banking, forest products, industrial products, mining and minerals, oil and gas, and utilities. In the derivatives market, the exchange trades 10-year Government of Canada bond futures and options on the futures; 3-month Canadian bankers' acceptance (BAX) futures and options on the futures; 1-month Canadian bankers' acceptance futures (BAR); stock options; Canadian bond options; and LEAPS. Trading hours are 9:30 A.M. to 4 P.M., Monday through Friday. Government bond futures are traded from 8:20 A.M. to 3 P.M. Settlement for securities is the third business day following the trade date; for futures and options, it is the day after a transaction by direct payment to the clearing corporation.

MOODY'S INVESTMENT GRADE rating assigned by MOODY'S INVESTORS SERVICE to certain municipal short-term debt securities, classified as MIG-1, 2, 3, and 4 to signify best, high, favorable, and adequate quality, respectively. All four are investment grade or bank quality.

MOODY'S INVESTORS SERVICE headquartered with its parent company, Dun & Bradstreet, in downtown Manhattan, Moody's is one of the two best known bond rating agencies in the country, the other being Standard & Poor's. Moody's also rates commercial paper, preferred and common stocks, and municipal short-term issues. The six bound manuals it publishes annually, supplemented weekly or semiweekly, provide great detail on issuers and securities. The company also publishes the quarterly *Moody's Handbook of Common Stocks,* which charts more than 500 companies, showing industry group trends and company stock price performance. Also included are essential statistics for the past decade, an analysis of the company's financial background, recent financial developments, and the outlook. Moody's rates most of the publicly held corporate and municipal bonds and many Treasury and government agency issues, but does not usually rate privately placed bonds.

MORAL OBLIGATION BOND tax-exempt bond issued by a municipality or a state financial intermediary and backed by the moral obligation pledge of a state government. (State financial intermediaries are organized by states to pool local debt issues into single bond issues, which can be used to tap larger investment markets.) Under a moral obligation pledge, a state government indicates its intent to appropriate funds in the future if the primary OBLIGOR, the municipality or intermediary, defaults. The state's obligation to honor the pledge is moral rather than legal because future legislatures cannot be legally obligated to appropriate the funds required.

MORAL SUASION persuasion through influence rather than coercion, said of the efforts of the FEDERAL RESERVE BOARD to achieve member bank compliance with its general policy. From time to time, the Fed uses moral suasion to restrain credit or to expand it.

MORGAN STANLEY CAPITAL INTERNATIONAL INDICES indices maintained and calculated by Morgan Stanley's Capital International group (MSCI) which track more than 45 equity markets throughout the world. The MSCI indices are market capitalization weighted and cover both developed and emerging markets. In addition to the country indices, MSCI also calculates aggregate indices for the world, Europe, North America, Asia, and Latin America. Most international mutual funds and other international institutional investors measure their performance against MSCI indices.

MORNINGSTAR RATING SYSTEM system for rating open- and closed-end mutual funds and annuities by Morningstar Inc. of Chicago. The system rates funds from one to five stars, using a risk-adjusted performance rating in which performance equals total return of the fund. The system rates funds assessing down-side risk, which is linked to the three-month U.S. Treasury bill. If a fund underperforms the Treasury bill, it will lower the fund's rating. The score is plotted on a bell curve, and is applied to four distinct categories: all equities, fixed income, hybrids, municipals. The top 10% receive five stars; the top 22.5%, four stars; the top 35%, three stars; the bottom 22.5%, two stars; and the bottom 10%, one star. Morningstar is a subscription-based company, offering its ratings in binders, software, and CD-ROM form. It sells its data to America Online and Realities Telescan Analyzer and other databases, as well as metropolitan newspapers. Morningstar also sells information on U.S. equities and American Depository Receipts (ADRs), but star ratings are not calculated for them.

MORTGAGE debt instrument by which the borrower (mortgagor) gives the lender (mortgagee) a lien on property as security for the repayment of a loan. The borrower has use of the property, and the lien is removed when the obligation is fully paid. A mortgage normally involves real estate. For personal property, such as machines, equipment, or tools, the lien is called a *chattel mortgage. See also* ADLUSTABLE RATE MORTGAGE; CLOSED-END MORTGAGE; CONSOLIDATED MORTGAGE BOND; MORTGAGE BOND; OPEN-END MORTGAGE; VARIABLE RATE MORTGAGE.

MORTGAGE-BACKED CERTIFICATE security backed by mortgages. Such certificates are issued by the FEDERAL HOME LOAN MORTGAGE CORPORATION, and the FEDERAL NATIONAL MORTGAGE ASSOCIATION. Others are guaranteed by the GOVERNMENT NATIONAL MORTGAGE ASSOCIATION. Investors receive payments out of the interest and principal on the underlying mortgages. Sometimes banks issue certificates backed by CONVENTIONAL MORTGAGES, selling them to large institutional investors. The growth of mortgage-backed certificates and the secondary mortgage market in which they are traded has helped keep mortgage money available for home financing. *See also* PASS-THROUGH SECURITY.

MORTGAGE-BACKED SECURITY *see* MORTGAGE-BACKED CERTIFICATE.

MORTGAGE BANKER company, or individual, that originates mortgage loans, sells them to other investors, services the monthly payments, keeps related records, and acts as escrow agent to disperse funds for taxes and insurance. A mortgage banker's income derives from origination and servicing fees, profits on the resale of loans, and the spread between mortgage yields and the interest paid on borrowings while a particular mortgage is held before resale. To protect against negative spreads or mortgages that can't be resold, such companies seek commitments from institutional lenders or buy them from the FEDERAL NATIONAL MORTGAGE ASSOCIATION or the GOVERNMENT NATIONAL MORTGAGE ASSOCIATION. Mortgage bankers thus play an important role in the flow of mortgage funds even though they are not significant mortgage holders.

MORTGAGE BOND bond issue secured by a mortgage on the issuer's property, the lien on which is conveyed to the bondholders by a deed of trust. A mortgage bond may be designated senior, underlying, first, prior, overlying, junior, second, third, and so forth, depending on the priority of the lien. Most of those issued by corporations are first mortgage bonds secured by specific real property and also representing unsecured claims on the general assets of the firm. As such, these bonds enjoy a preferred position relative to unsecured bonds of the issuing corporation. *See also* CONSOLIDATED MORTGAGE BOND; MORTGAGE.

MORTGAGE BROKER one who places mortgage loans with lenders for a fee, but does not originate or service loans.

MORTGAGE INTEREST DEDUCTION federal tax deduction for mortgage interest paid in a taxable year. Interest on a mortgage to acquire, construct, or substantially improve a residence is deductible for indebtedness of up to $1 million. In addition, interest on a home equity loan of up to $100,000 is deductible. These amounts are halved for married taxpayers filing separately.

MORTGAGE LIFE INSURANCE policy that pays off the balance of a mortgage on the death of the insured.

MORTGAGE POOL group of mortgages sharing similar characteristics in terms of class of property, interest rate, and maturity. Investors buy participations and receive income derived from payments on the underlying mortgages. The principal attractions to the investor are DIVERSIFICATION and LIQUIDITY, along with a relatively attractive yield. Those backed by government-sponsored agencies such as the FEDERAL HOME LOAN MORTGAGE CORPORATION, FEDERAL NATIONAL MORTGAGE ASSOCIATION, and GOVERNMENT NATIONAL MORTGAGE ASSOCIATION have become popular not only with individual investors but with life insurance companies, pension funds, and even foreign investors.

MORTGAGE REIT invests in loans secured by real estate. These mortgages either may be originated and underwritten by the REAL ESTATE INVESTMENT TRUST or the REIT may purchase preexisting secondary mortgages. The funds the REIT invests may come from either shareholder equity capital or debt borrowed from other lenders. Mortgage REITs earn income from the interest they are paid and fees generated. This net income is generated from the excess of their interest and fee income and their interest expense and administrative fees. The other kind of real estate investment trust—called an EQUITY REIT—takes an ownership position in real estate, as opposed to acting as a lender. Some REITs, called *hybrid REITs,* take equity positions and make mortgage loans.

MORTGAGE SERVICING administration of a mortgage loan, including collecting monthly payments and penalties on late payments, keeping track of the amount of principal and interest that has been paid at any particular time, acting as escrow agent for funds to cover taxes and insurance, and, if necessary, curing defaults and foreclosing when a homeowner is seriously delinquent. For mortgage loans that are sold in the secondary market and packaged into a MORTGAGE-BACKED CERTIFICATE the local bank or savings and loan that originated the mortgage typically continues servicing the mortgages for a fee.

MOST ACTIVE LIST stocks with the most shares traded on a given day. Unusual VOLUME can be caused by TAKEOVER activity, earnings releases, institutional trading in a widely-held issue, and other factors.

MOVING AVERAGE average of security or commodity prices constructed on a period as short as a few days or as long as several years and showing trends for the latest interval. For example, a thirty-day moving average includes yesterday's figures; tomorrow the same average will include today's figures and will no longer show those for the earliest date included in yesterday's average. Thus every day it picks up figures for the latest day and drops those for the earliest day.

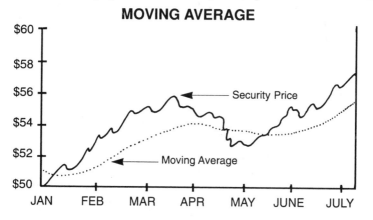

MOVING AVERAGE

MTN initials standing for *medium-term notes* that are issued by corporations and distributed by investment banks acting as agents, similar to shorter-term COMMERCIAL PAPER.

MUD acronym for *municipal utility district,* a political subdivision that provides utility-related services and may issue SPECIAL ASSESSMENT BONDS.

MULTINATIONAL CORPORATION corporation that has production facilities or other fixed assets in at least one foreign country and makes its major management decisions in a global context. In marketing, production, research and development, and labor relations, its decisions must be made in terms of host-country customs and traditions. In finance, many of its problems have no domestic counterpart—the payment of dividends in another currency, for example, or the need to shelter working capital from the risk of devaluation, or the choices between owning and licensing. Economic and legal questions must be dealt with in drastically different ways. In addition to foreign exchange risks and the special business risks of operating in unfamiliar environments, there is the specter of political risk—the risk that sovereign governments may interfere with operations or terminate them altogether.

MULTIPLE *see* PRICE-EARNINGS RATIO.

MULTIPLE LISTING listing agreement used by a broker who is a member of a multiple-listing organization that is an exclusive right to sell with an additional authority and obligation on the part of the listing broker to distribute the listing to other brokers in the organization. These listings then are distributed in a multiple, listing service publication. Generally, the listing broker and the selling broker will split the commission, but terms for division can vary. A multiple-listing agreement benefits the seller by exposing his property to a wider group of potential buyers than would be available from one exclusive broker, which should allow the sale to be completed more quickly, and for a higher price. The multiple-listing service, however, has come under close scrutiny by consumer groups and justice departments for alleged antitrust practices.

MULTIPLE PERIL INSURANCE policy that incorporates several different types of property insurance coverage, such as flood, fire, wind, etc. In its broadest application, the term is synonymous with *all-risks insurance,* which covers loss or damage to property from fortuitous circumstances not specifically excluded from coverage. Do not confuse multiple peril insurance with *multiple protection insurance,* which is a form of life insurance policy combining features of term and whole life insurance.

MULTIPLIER the multiplier has two major applications in finance and investments.
1. *investment multiplier* or *Keynesian multiplier:* multiplies the effects of investment spending in terms of total income. An investment in a small plant facility, for example, increases the incomes of the workers who built it, the merchants who provide supplies, the distributors who supply the merchants, the manufacturers who supply the distributors, and so on. Each recipient spends a portion of the income and saves the rest. By making an assumption as to the percentage each recipient saves, it is possible to calculate the total income produced by the investment.
2. *deposit multiplier* or *credit multiplier:* magnifies small changes in bank deposits into changes in the amount of outstanding credit and the money supply. For example, a bank receives a deposit of $100,000, and the RESERVE REQUIREMENT is 20%. The bank is thus required to keep $20,000 in the form of reserves. The remaining $80,000 becomes a loan, which is deposited in the borrower's bank. When the borrower's bank sets aside the $16,000 required reserve out of the $80,000, $64,000 is available for another loan and another deposit, and so on. Carried out to its theoretical limit, the original deposit of $100,000 could expand into a total of $500,000 in deposits and $400,000 in credit.

MUNICIPAL BOND debt obligation of a state or local government entity. The funds may support general governmental needs or special projects. Prior to the TAX REFORM ACT OF 1986, the terms *municipal* and *tax-exempt* were synonymous, since virtually all municipal obligations were exempt from federal income taxes and most from state and local income taxes, at least in the state of issue. The 1986

Act, however, divided municipals into two broad groups:(1) PUBLIC PURPOSE BONDS, which remain tax-exempt and can be issued without limitation, and (2) PRIVATE PURPOSE BONDS, which are taxable unless specifically exempted. The tax distinction between public and private purpose is based on the percentage extent to which the bonds benefit private parties; if a tax-exempt public purpose bond involves more than a 10% benefit to private parties, it is taxable. Permitted private purpose bonds (those specified as tax-exempt) are generally TAX PREFERENCE ITEMS in computing the ALTERNATIVE MINIMUM TAX, and effective August 15, 1986, are subject to volume caps. *See also* ADVANCE REFUNDING; GENERAL OBLIGATION BOND; HOSPITAL REVENUE BOND; INDUSTRIAL DEVELOPMENT BOND; LIMITED TAX BOND; MUNICIPAL INVESTMENT TRUST; MUNICIPAL REVENUE BOND; SINGLE STATE MUNICIPAL BOND FUND; SPECIAL ASSESSMENT BOND; TAXABLE MUNICIPAL BOND; TAX-EXEMPT SECURITY; UNDERLYING DEBT.

MUNICIPAL BOND INSURANCE policies underwritten by private insurers guaranteeing municipal bonds in the event of default. The insurance can be purchased either by the issuing government entity or the investor; it provides that bonds will be purchased from investors at par should default occur. Such insurance is available from a number of large insurance companies, but a major portion is written by the following "monoline" companies, so-called because their primary business is insuring municipal bonds: AMBAC Idemnity Corporation (AMBAC); Capital Guaranty Insurance Company (CGIC); Connie Lee Insurance Company; Financial Guaranty Insurance Company (FGIC); Financial Security Assurance, Inc. (FSA); and Municipal Bond Investors Assurance Corporation (MBIA). Insured municipal bonds generally enjoy the highest rating resulting in greater marketability and lower cost to their issuers. From the investor's standpoint, however, their yield is typically lower than similarly rated uninsured bonds because the cost of the insurance is passed on by the issuer to the investor. Some unit investment trusts and mutual funds feature insured municipal bonds for investors willing to trade marginally lower yield for the extra degree of safety.

MUNICIPAL IMPROVEMENT CERTIFICATE certificate issued by a local government in lieu of bonds to finance improvements or services, such as widening a sidewalk, or installing a sewer, or repairing a street. Such an obligation is payable from a special tax assessment against those who benefit from the improvement, and the payments may be collected by the contractor performing the work. Interest on the certificate is usually free of federal, state, and local taxes. *See also* GENERAL OBLIGATION BOND.

MUNICIPAL INVESTMENT TRUST (MIT) UNIT INVESTMENT TRUST that buys municipal bonds and passes the tax-free income on to shareholders. Bonds in the trust's portfolio are normally held until maturity, unlike the constant trading of bonds in an open-ended municipal bond fund's portfolio. MITs are sold through brokers, typically for a sales charge of about 3% of the principal paid, with a minimum investment of $1000. The trust offers diversification, professional management of the portfolio, and monthly interest, compared with the semiannual payments made by individual municipal bonds.

Many MITs invest in the securities of just one state. For California residents who buy a California-only MIT, for example, all the interest is free of federal, state, and local taxes. In contrast, a Californian who buys a national MIT might have to pay state and local taxes on interest derived from out-of-state bonds in the trust's portfolio.

MUNICIPAL NOTE in common usage, a municipal debt obligation with an original maturity of two years or less.

MUNICIPAL REVENUE BOND bond issued to finance public works such as bridges or tunnels or sewer systems and supported directly by the revenues of the project. For instance, if a municipal revenue bond is issued to build a bridge, the tolls collected from motorists using the bridge are committed for paying off the bond. Unless otherwise specified in the indenture, holders of these bonds have no claims on the issuer's other resources.

MUNICIPAL SECURITIES RULEMAKING BOARD *see* SELF-REGULATORY ORGANIZATION.

MUTILATED SECURITY certificate that cannot be read for the name of the issue or the issuer, or for the detail necessary for identification and transfer, or for the exercise of the holder's rights. It is then the seller's obligation to take corrective action, which usually means having the transfer agent guarantee the rights of ownership to the buyer.

MUTUAL ASSOCIATION SAVINGS AND LOAN ASSOCIATION organized as a cooperative owned by its members. Members' deposits represent shares; shareholders vote on association affairs and receive income in the form of dividends. Unlike state-chartered corporate S&Ls, which account for a minority of the industry, mutual associations are not permitted to issue stock, and they are usually chartered by the OFFICE OF THRIFT SUPERVISION (OTS) and belong to the SAVINGS ASSOCIATION INSURANCE FUND (SAIF). Deposits are technically subject to a waiting period before withdrawal, although in practice withdrawals are usually allowed on demand.

MUTUAL COMPANY corporation whose ownership and profits are distributed among members in proportion to the amount of business they do with the company. The most familiar examples are (1) mutual insurance companies, whose members are policy holders entitled to name the directors or trustees and to receive dividends or rebates on future premiums; (2) state-chartered MUTUAL SAVINGS BANKS, whose members are depositors sharing in net earnings but having nothing to do with management; and (3) federal savings and loan associations, MUTUAL ASSOCIATIONS whose members are depositors entitled to vote and receive dividends.

MUTUAL EXCLUSION DOCTRINE doctrine which established that interest from municipal bonds is exempt from federal taxation. In return for this federal tax exemption, states and localities are not allowed to tax interest generated by federal government securities, such as Treasury bills, notes, and bonds.

MUTUAL FUND fund operated by an INVESTMENT COMPANY that raises money from shareholders and invests it in stocks, bonds, options, futures, currencies, or money market securities. These funds offer investors the advantages of diversification and professional management. A management fee is charged for these services, typically between 0.5% and 2% of assets per year. Funds also levy other fees such as 12B-1 FEES, EXCHANGE FEES and other administrative charges. Funds that are sold through brokers are called LOAD FUNDS, and those sold to investors directly from the fund companies are called NO-LOAD FUNDS. Mutual fund shares are redeemable on demand at NET ASSET VALUE by shareholders. All shareholders share equally in the gains and losses generated by the fund.

Mutual funds come in many varieties. Some invest aggressively for capital appreciation, while others are conservative and are designed to generate income for shareholders. Investors need to assess their tolerance for risk before they decide which fund would be appropriate for them. In addition, the timing of buying or selling depends on the outlook for the economy, the state of the stock and bond markets, interest rates, and other factors.

MUTUAL FUND CASH-TO-ASSETS RATIO amount of mutual fund assets held in cash instruments. A fund manager may choose to keep a large cash position if he is bearish on the stock or bond market, or if he cannot find securities he thinks are attractive to buy. A large cash position (10% or more of the fund's assets in liquid instruments) may also accumulate if many investors buy fund shares and the fund manager cannot put all the money to work at once. On the other hand, a low cash-to-assets ratio is an indication that the fund manager is bullish, because he is fully invested and expects stock or bond prices to rise. Some analysts consider this ratio to be an important indicator of bullish or bearish sentiment among sophisticated investment managers. If many fund managers are increasing their cash positions, the fund managers are becoming more bearish—though some analysts consider it bullish for the market because the managers will have more cash to buy securities. The ratio for the entire mutual fund industry is released on a monthly basis by the Investment Company Institute, the largest mutual fund trade group.

MUTUAL FUND CUSTODIAN commercial bank or trust company that provides safekeeping for the securities owned by a mutual fund and may also act as TRANSFER AGENT, making payments to and collecting investments from shareholders. Mutual fund custodians must comply with the rules set forth in the INVESTMENT COMPANY ACT OF 1940.

MUTUAL IMPROVEMENT CERTIFICATE certificate issued by a local government in lieu of bonds to finance improvements or services, such as widening a sidewalk, or installing a sewer, or repairing a street. Such an obligation is payable from a special tax assessment against those who benefit from the improvement, and the payments may be collected by the contractor performing the work. Interest on the certificate is free of federal, state, and local taxes. *See also* GENERAL OBLIGATION BOND.

MUTUAL SAVINGS BANK SAVINGS BANK organized under state charter for the ownership and benefit of its depositors. A local board of trustees makes major decisions as fiduciaries, independently of the legal owners. Traditionally, income is distributed to depositors after expenses are deducted and reserve funds are set aside as required. In recent times, many mutual savings banks have begun to issue stock and offer consumer services such as credit cards and checking accounts, as well as commercial services such as corporate checking accounts and commercial real estate loans.

n _____

NAKED OPTION OPTION for which the buyer or seller has no underlying security position. A writer of a naked CALL OPTION, therefore, does not own a LONG POSITION in the stock on which the call has been written. Similarly, the writer of a naked PUT OPTION does not have a SHORT POSITION in the stock on which the put has been written. Naked options are very risky—although potentially very rewarding. If the underlying stock or stock index moves in the direction sought by the investor, profits can be enormous, because the investor would only have had to put down a small amount of money to reap a large return. On the other hand, if the stock moved in the opposite direction, the writer of the naked option could be subject to huge losses.

For instance, if someone wrote a naked call option at $60 a share on XYZ stock without owning the shares, and if the stock rose to $70 a share, the writer of the option would have to deliver XYZ shares to the call buyer at $60 a share. In order to acquire those shares, he or she would have to go into the market and buy them for $70 a share, sustaining a $10-a-share loss on his or her position. If, on the other hand, the option writer already owned XYZ shares when writing the option, he or she could just turn those shares over to the option buyer. This latter strategy is known as writing a COVERED CALL.

NAKED POSITION securities position that is not hedged from market risk—for example, the position of someone who writes a CALL or PUT option without having the corresponding LONG POSITION or SHORT POSITION on the underlying security. The potential risk or reward of naked positions is greater than that of covered positions. *See* COVERED CALL; HEDGE; NAKED OPTION.

NAMED PERILS INSURANCE property insurance that covers risks specified in the policy. Contrasts with *all-risks insurance,* which specifies exclusions.

NARROWING THE SPREAD closing the SPREAD between the bid and asked prices of a security as a result of bidding and offering by market makers and specialists in a security. For example, a stock's bid price—the most anyone is willing to pay—may be $10 a share, and the asked price—the lowest price at which anyone will sell—may be $10¾. If a broker or market maker offers to buy shares at $10¼, while the asked price remains at $10¾, the spread has effectively been narrowed.

NARROW MARKET securities or commodities market characterized by light trading and greater fluctuations in prices relative to volume than would be the case if trading were active. The market in a particular stock is said to be narrow if the price falls more than a point between ROUND LOT trades without any apparent explanation, suggesting lack of interest and too few orders. The terms THIN MARKET and *inactive market* are used as synonyms for narrow market.

NASDAQ National Association of Securities Dealers Automated Quotations system, which is owned and operated by the NATIONAL ASSOCIATION OF SECURITIES DEALERS. NASDAQ is a computerized system that provides brokers and dealers with price quotations for securities traded OVER THE COUNTER as well as for many New York Stock Exchange listed securities. NASDAQ quotes are published in the financial pages of most newspapers. *See also* NATIONAL MARKET SYSTEM.

NASDAQ SMALL CAPITALIZATION COMPANIES separately listed group of some 2000 companies that have smaller capitalizations and are less actively traded than NASDAQ NATIONAL MARKET SYSTEM stocks, but that meet NASDAQ price and market value listing criteria and have at least two MARKET MAKERS.

NASD FORM FR-1 form required of foreign dealers in securities subscribing to new securities issues in the process of distribution, whereby they agree to abide by NATIONAL ASSOCIATION OF SECURITIES DEALERS rules concerning a HOT ISSUE. Under NASD Rules of Fair Practice, firms participating in the distribution must make a bona fide public offering at the public offering price. Any sale designed to capitalize on a hot issue—one that on the first day of trading sells at a substantial premium over the public offering price—would be in violation of NASD rules. Violations include a sale to a member of the dealer's family or to an employee, assuming such sales could not be defended as "normal investment practice." Also called *blanket certification form.*

NATIONAL ASSOCIATION OF INVESTORS CORPORATION not-for-profit educational association that helps investment clubs become established. Investment clubs are formed by people who pool their money and make common decisions about how to invest those assets. The NAIC is located in Madison Heights, Michigan. *See also* INVESTMENT CLUB.

NATIONAL ASSOCIATION OF SECURITIES DEALERS (NASD) nonprofit organization formed under the joint sponsorship of the Investment Bankers' Conference and the Securities and Exchange Commission to comply with the MALONEY ACT. NASD members include virtually all investment banking houses and firms dealing in the OVER THE COUNTER market. Operating under the supervision of the SEC, the NASD's basic purposes are to (1) standardize practices in the field, (2) establish high moral and ethical standards in securities trading, (3) provide a representative body to consult with the government and investors on matters of common interest, (4) establish and enforce fair and equitable rules of securities trading, and (5) establish a disciplinary body capable of enforcing the above provisions. The NASD also requires members to maintain quick assets in excess of current liabilities at all times. Periodic examinations and audits are conducted to ensure a high level of solvency and financial integrity among members. A special Investment Companies Department is concerned with the problems of investment companies and has the responsibility of reviewing companies' sales literature in that segment of the securities industry. *See also* NASDAQ.

NATIONAL BANK commercial bank whose charter is approved by the U.S. Comptroller of the Currency rather than by a state banking department. National banks are required to be members of the FEDERAL RESERVE SYSTEM and to purchase stock in the FEDERAL RESERVE BANK in their district *(see* MEMBER BANK). They must also belong to the FEDERAL DEPOSIT INSURANCE CORPORATION.

NATIONAL CREDIT UNION ADMINISTRATION independent federal agency based in Washington, D.C., established by Congress to oversee the federal credit union system. The NCUA is funded by credit unions and does not receive any tax dollars. The agency supervises nearly 7600 federal credit unions and federally insures member accounts in approximately 4600 state-chartered credit unions. The National Credit Union Share Insurance Fund is the agency's arm that insures member accounts up to $100,000. It is backed by the full faith and credit of the U.S. government and is managed by the NCUA Board, which is comprised of three members appointed by the President.

NATIONAL DEBT debt owed by the federal government. The national debt is made up of such debt obligations as Treasury bills, Treasury notes, and Treasury bonds. Congress imposes a ceiling on the national debt, which has been increased on occasion when accumulated deficits near, the ceiling. In the mid-1990s, the national debt stood at more than $5 trillion. The interest due on the national debt is one of the major expenses of the federal government. The national debt, which is the total debt accumulated by the government over many decades, should not be confused with the federal budget deficit, which is the excess of spending over income by the federal government in one fiscal year.

NATIONAL FOUNDATION FOR CONSUMER CREDIT a nonprofit national organization based in Silver Spring, Maryland, created in 1951 to help the increasing number of consumers who have taken on too much debt. The NFCC has more than 200 members operating 1100 locations providing consumers with money management, budget, and wise-credit-use education workshops and counseling sessions. While counselors work with creditors to work out a payment plan, the NFCC does not provide credit or financial assistance. Most members do not charge for counseling; however some members charge a low fee for services such as debt repayment or counseling. No one is turned away due to the inability to pay.

NATIONALIZATION takeover of a private company's assets or operations by a government. The company may or may not be compensated for the loss of assets. In developing nations, an operation is typically nationalized if the government feels the company is exploiting the host country and exporting too high a proportion of the profits. By nationalizing the firm, the government hopes to keep profits at home. In developed countries, industries are often nationalized when they need government subsidies to survive. For instance, the French government nationalized steel and chemical companies in the mid-1980s in order to preserve jobs that would have disappeared if free market forces had prevailed. In some developed countries, however, nationalization is carried out as a form of national policy, often by Socialist governments, and is not designed to rescue ailing industries.

NATIONAL MARKET ADVISORY BOARD board appointed by the Securities and Exchange Commission under provisions of the 1975 Securities Act to study and advise the commission on a national exchange market system (NEMS). NEMS is envisioned as a highly automated, national exchange with continuous auction markets and competing specialist or market makers, but one that would preserve the existing regional exchanges.

NATIONAL MARKET SYSTEM
1. system of trading OVER THE COUNTER stocks under the sponsorship of the NATIONAL ASSOCIATION OF SECURITIES DEALERS (NASD) and NASDAQ. Stocks trading in the National Market System must meet certain criteria for size, profitability, and trading activity. More comprehensive information is available for National Market System stocks than for other stocks traded over the counter. For most over-the-counter stocks, newspapers list the stock name, dividend, trading volume, bid and ask prices, and the change in those prices during a trading day. For National Market System stocks, the listing includes the stock name, dividend, high and low price for the past 52 weeks, trading volume, high and low price during the trading day, closing price on that day, and price change for that day.
2. national system of trading whereby the prices for stocks and bonds are listed simultaneously on the New York Stock Exchange and all regional exchanges. Buyers and sellers therefore are able to get the best prices by executing their trades on the exchange with the most favorable price at the time. This system is not to be confused with the national exchange market system (NEMS) being studied by the Securities and Exchange Commission and other planning groups. *See also* NATIONAL MARKET ADVISORY BOARD.

NATIONAL QUOTATION BUREAU daily service to subscribers that collects bid and offer quotes from MARKET MAKERS in stocks and bonds traded OVER THE COUNTER. Quotes are distributed on PINK SHEETS (for stocks) and YELLOW SHEETS (for corporate bonds). The Bureau is located in Cedar Grove, New Jersey. *See also* OTC BULLETIN BOARD.

NATIONAL SECURITIES CLEARING CORPORATION (NSCC) securities clearing organization formed in 1977 by merging subsidiaries of the New York and American Stock Exchanges with the National Clearing Corporation. It functions essentially as a medium through which brokerage firms, exchanges, and other clearing corporations reconcile accounts with each other. *See also* CONTINUOUS NET SETTLEMENT.

NEARBYS months of futures or options contracts that are nearest to delivery (for futures) or expiration (for options). For example, in January, futures and options contracts settling in February and March would be considered nearbys. In general, nearby contracts are far more actively traded than contracts for more distant months. *See also* FURTHEST MONTH, NEAREST MONTH.

NEAREST MONTH in commodity futures or OPTION trading, the expiration dates, expressed as months, closest to the present. For a commodity or an option that had delivery or expiration dates available in September, December, March, and June, for instance, the nearest month would be September if a trade were being made in August. Nearest month contracts are always more heavily traded than FURTHEST MONTH contracts.

NEAR MONEY CASH EQUIVALENTS and other assets that are easily convertible into cash. Some examples are government securities, bank TIME DEPOSITS, and MONEY MARKET FUND shares. Bonds close to REDEMPTION date are also called near money.

NEGATIVE AMORTIZATION financing arrangement in which monthly payments are less than the true amortized amounts and the loan balance increases over the term of the loan rather than decreases; the interest shortage is added to the unpaid principal. In some cases, the interest shortage is added back to the loan and payable at maturity. For example, amortized payments for the first six months of a 30-year mortgage loan would be based on a 13% rate, but interest would be charged against equity at 18%; this rate charge would fluctuate every six-month period. In some loans, the negative amounts may be made up by applying such deficits against the borrower's down payment equity. Federal law requires mortgage lenders to make sure that borrowers understand the potential impact of negative amortization in several interest rate scenarios through a series of extensive disclosure documents.

NEGATIVE CARRY situation in which the cost of money borrowed to finance securities or financial futures positions is higher than the return on those positions. For example, if an investor borrowed at 10% to finance, or "carry," a bond yielding 8%, the bond position would have a negative carry. Negative carry does not necessarily mean a loss to the investor, however, and a positive yield can result on an aftertax basis. In this case, the yield from the 8% bond may be tax-exempt, whereas interest on the 10% loan is tax-deductible. In commodities, this would occur in any month in a BACKWARDATION where the price is higher than the spot month. With the negative carry, if the investor holds the physical position in copper, for example, it will continue to lose value.

NEGATIVE CASH FLOW situation in which a business spends more cash than it receives through earnings or other transactions in an accounting period. *See also* CASH FLOW.

NEGATIVE INCOME TAX proposed system of providing financial aid to poverty-level individuals and families, using the mechanisms already in place to collect income taxes. After filing a tax return showing income below subsistence levels, instead of paying an income tax, low-income people would receive a direct subsidy, called a negative income tax, sufficient to bring them up to the subsistence level.

NEGATIVE PLEDGE CLAUSE negative covenant or promise in an INDENTURE agreement that states the corporation will not pledge any of its assets if doing so would result in less security to the debtholders covered under the indenture agreement. Also called *covenant of equal coverage*.

NEGATIVE WORKING CAPITAL situation in which the current liabilities of a firm exceed its current assets. For example, if the total of cash, MARKETABLE SECURITIES, ACCOUNTS RECEIVABLE and notes receivable, inventory, and other current assets is less than the total of ACCOUNTS PAYABLE, short-term notes payable, long-term debt due in one year, and other current liabilities, the firm has a negative working capital. Unless the condition is corrected, the firm will not be able to pay debts when due, threatening its ability to keep operating and possibly resulting in bankruptcy.

To remedy a negative working capital position, a firm has these alternatives: (1) it can convert a long-term asset into a current asset—for example, by selling a piece of equipment or a building, by liquidating a long-term investment, or by renegotiating a long-term loan receivable; (2) it can convert short-term liabilities into long-term liabilities—for example, by negotiating the substitution of a current account payable with a long-term note payable; (3) it can borrow long term; (4) it can obtain additional equity through a stock issue or other sources of paid-in capital; (5) it can retain or "plow back" profits. *See also* WORKING CAPITAL.

NEGATIVE YIELD CURVE situation in which yields on short-term securities are higher than those on long-term securities of the same quality. Normally, short-term rates are lower than long-term rates because those who commit their money for longer periods are taking more risk. But if interest rates climb high enough, borrowers become unwilling to lock themselves into high rates for long periods and borrow short-term instead. Therefore, yields rise on short-term funds and fall or remain stable on long-term funds. Also called an INVERTED YIELD CURVE. *See also* YIELD CURVE.

NEGOTIABLE

In general:
1. something that can be sold or transferred to another party in exchange for money or as settlement of an obligation.
2. matter of mutual concern to one or more parties that involves conditions to be worked out to the satisfaction of the parties. As examples: In a lender-borrower arrangement, the interest rate may be negotiable; in securities sales, brokerage commissions are now negotiable, having historically been fixed; and in divorce cases involving children, the terms of visiting rights are usually negotiable.

Finance: instrument meeting the qualifications of the Uniform Commercial Code dealing with negotiable instruments. *See* NEGOTIABLE INSTRUMENT.

Investments: type of security the title to which is transferable by delivery. A stock certificate with the stock power properly signed is negotiable, for example.

NEGOTIABLE CERTIFICATE OF DEPOSIT large-dollar-amount, short-term certificate of deposit. Such certificates are issued by large banks and bought mainly by corporations and institutional investors. They are payable either to the bearer or to the order of the depositor, and, being NEGOTIABLE, they enjoy an active SECONDARY MARKET, where they trade in round lots of $5 million. Although they can be issued in any denomination from $100,000 up, the typical amount is $1 million. They have a minimum original maturity of 14 days; most original maturities are under six months. Also called a JUMBO CERTIFICATE OF DEPOSIT.

NEGOTIABLE INSTRUMENT unconditional order or promise to pay an amount of money, easily transferable from one person to another. Examples: check, promissory note, draft (bill of exchange). The Uniform Commercial Code requires that for an instrument to be negotiable it must be signed by the maker or drawer, must contain an unconditional promise or order to pay a specific amount of money, must be payable on demand or at a specified future time, and must be payable to order or to the bearer.

NEGOTIABLE ORDER OF WITHDRAWAL a bank or savings and loan withdrawal ticket that is a NEGOTIABLE INSTRUMENT. The accounts from which such withdrawals can be made, called NOW accounts, are thus, in effect, interest-bearing checking accounts. They were first introduced in the late 1970s and became available nationally in January 1980. In the early and mid-1980s the interest rate on NOW accounts was capped at 5½%; the cap was phased out in the late 1980s. *See also* SUPER NEGOTIABLE ORDER OF WITHDRAWAL (NOW) ACCOUNT.

NEGOTIATED COMMISSION brokerage COMMISSION that is determined through negotiation. Prior to 1975, commissions were fixed. Since then, brokerage firms have been free to charge what they want and, although they have minimums and commission schedules, will negotiate commissions on large transactions.

NEGOTIATED UNDERWRITING underwriting of new securities issue in which the SPREAD between the purchase price paid to the issuer and the public offering price is determined through negotiation rather than multiple competitive bidding. The spread, which represents the compensation to the investment bankers participating in the underwriting (collectively called the *syndicate)*, is negotiated between the issuing company and the MANAGING UNDERWRITER, with the consent of the group. Most corporate stock and bond issues and municipal revenue bond issues are priced through negotiation, whereas municipal general obligation bonds and new issues of public utilities are generally priced through competitive bidding. Competitive bidding is mandatory for new issues of public utilities holding companies. *See also* COMPETITIVE BID.

NEO abbreviation for *nonequity options.* This refers to options contracts on foreign currencies, bonds and other debt issues, commodities, metals, and stock indexes. In contrast, equity options have individual stocks as underlying values.

NEST EGG assets put aside for a person's retirement. Such assets are usually invested conservatively to provide the retiree with a secure standard of living for the rest of his or her life. Investment in an INDIVIDUAL RETIREMENT ACCOUNT would be considered part of a nest egg.

NET

In general: figure remaining after all relevant deductions have been made from the gross amount. For example: net sales are equal to gross sales minus discounts, returns, and allowances; net profit is gross profit less operating (sales, general, and administrative) expenses; net worth is assets (worth) less liabilities.

Investments: dollar difference between the proceeds from the sale of a security and the seller's adjusted cost of acquisition—that is, the gain or loss.

As a verb:

1. to arrive at the difference between additions and subtractions or plus amounts and minus amounts. For example, in filing tax returns, capital losses are netted against capital gains.

2. to realize a net profit, as in "last year we netted a million dollars after taxes."

NET AFTERTAX GAIN capital gain after income taxes.

NET ASSETS difference between a company's total assets and liabilities; another way of saying *owner's equity* or NET WORTH. *See* ASSET COVERAGE for a discussion of net asset value per unit of bonds, preferred stock, or common stock.

NET ASSET VALUE (NAV)

1. in mutual funds, the market value of a fund share, synonymous with *bid price.* In the case of no-load funds, the NAV, market price, and offering price are all

the same figure, which the public pays to buy shares; load fund market or offer prices are quoted after adding the sales charge to the net asset value. NAV is calculated by most funds after the close of the exchanges each day by taking the closing market value of all securities owned plus all other assets such as cash, subtracting all liabilities, then dividing the result (total net assets) by the total number of shares outstanding. The number of shares outstanding can vary each day depending on the number of purchases and redemptions.

2. book value of a company's different classes of securities, usually stated as net asset value per bond, net asset value per share of preferred stock, and net book value per common share of common stock. The formula for computing net asset value is total assets less any INTANGIBLE ASSET less all liabilities and securities having a prior claim, divided by the number of units outstanding (i.e., bonds, preferred shares, or common shares). *See* BOOK VALUE for a discussion of how these values are calculated and what they mean.

NET CAPITAL REQUIREMENT Securities and Exchange Commission requirement that member firms as well as nonmember broker-dealers in securities maintain a maximum ratio of indebtedness to liquid capital of 15 to 1; also called *net capital rule* and *net capital ratio*. Indebtedness covers all money owed to a firm, including MARGIN loans and commitments to purchase securities, one reason new public issues are spread among members of underwriting syndicates. Liquid capital includes cash and assets easily converted into cash.

NET CHANGE difference between the last trading price on a stock, bond, commodity, or mutual fund from one day to the next. The net change in individual stock prices is listed in newspaper financial pages. The designation +2½, for example, means that a stock's final price on that day was $2.50 higher than the final price on the previous trading day. The net change in prices of OVER THE COUNTER stocks is usually the difference between bid prices from one day to the next.

NET CURRENT ASSETS difference between current assets and current liabilities; another name for WORKING CAPITAL. Some security analysts divide this figure (after subtracting preferred stock, if any) by the number of common shares outstanding to arrive at working capital per share. Believing working capital per share to be a conservative measure of LIQUIDATING VALUE (on the theory that fixed and other noncurrent assets would more than compensate for any shrinkage in current assets if assets were to be sold), they compare it with the MARKET VALUE of the company's shares. If the net current assets per share figure, or "minimum liquidating value," is higher than the market price, these analysts view the common shares as a bargain (assuming, of course, that the company is not losing money and that its assets are conservatively valued). Other analysts believe this theory ignores the efficiency of capital markets generally and, specifically, obligations such as pension plans, which are not reported as balance sheet liabilities under present accounting rules.

NET EARNINGS *see* NET INCOME.

NET ESTATE *see* GROSS ESTATE.

NET INCOME

In general: sum remaining after all expenses have been met or deducted; synonymous with *net earnings* and with *net profit* or *net loss* (depending on whether the figure is positive or negative).

For a business: difference between total sales and total costs and expenses. Total costs comprise cost of goods sold including depreciation; total expenses comprise selling, general, and administrative expenses, plus INCOME DEDUCTIONS. Net income is usually specified as to whether it is before income taxes or after income taxes. Net income after taxes is the *bottom line* referred to in popular vernacular. It is out of this figure that dividends are normally paid. See *also* OPERATING PROFIT (OR LOSS).

For an individual: gross income less expenses incurred to produce gross income. Those expenses are mostly deductible for tax purposes.

NET INCOME PER SHARE OF COMMON STOCK amount of profit or earnings allocated to each share of common stock after all costs, taxes, allowances for depreciation, and possible losses have been deducted. Net income per share is stated in dollars and cents and is usually compared with the corresponding period a year earlier. For example, XYZ might report that second-quarter net income per share was $1.20, up from 90 cents in the previous year's second quarter. Also known as *earnings per common share* (EPS).

NET INCOME TO NET WORTH RATIO *see* RETURN ON EQUITY.

NET INTEREST COST (NIC) total amount of interest that a corporate or municipal bond entity will end up paying when issuing a debt obligation. The net interest cost factors in the coupon rate, any premiums or discounts, and reduces this to an average annual rate for the number of years until the bond matures or is callable. Underwriters compete to offer issuers the lowest NIC when they bid for the deal. The underwriting syndicate with the lowest NIC is normally awarded the contract.

NET INVESTMENT INCOME PER SHARE income received by an investment company from dividends and interest on securities investments during an accounting period, less management fees and administrative expenses and divided by the number of outstanding shares. Short-term trading profits (net profits from securities held for less than six months) are considered dividend income. The dividend and interest income is received by the investment company, which in turn pays shareholders the net investment income in the form of dividends prorated according to each holder's share in the total PORTFOLIO.

NET LEASE financial lease stipulating that the user (rather than the owner) of the leased property shall pay all maintenance costs, taxes, insurance, and other expenses. Many real estate and oil and gas limited partnerships are structured as net leases with ESCALATOR CLAUSES, to provide limited partners with both depreciation tax benefits and appreciation of investment, minus cash expenses. *See also* GROSS LEASE.

NET OPERATING LOSS (NOL) tax term for the excess of business expenses over income in a tax year. Under TAX LOSS CARRYBACK, CARRYFORWARD provisions, NOLs can (if desired) be carried back three years and forward 15 years.

NET PRESENT VALUE (NPV) method used in evaluating investments whereby the net present value of all cash outflows (such as the cost of the investment) and cash inflows (returns) is calculated using a given discount rate, usually a REQUIRED RATE OF RETURN. An investment is acceptable if the NPV is positive. In capital budgeting, the discount rate used is called the HURDLE RATE and is usually equal to the INCREMENTAL COST OF CAPITAL.

NET PROCEEDS amount (usually cash) received from the sale or disposition of property, from a loan, or from the sale or issuance of securities after deduction of all costs incurred in the transaction. In computing the gain or loss on a securities transaction for tax purposes, the amount of the sale is the amount of the net proceeds.

NET PROFIT *see* NET INCOME.

NET PROFIT MARGIN NET INCOME as a percentage of NET SALES. A measure of operating efficiency and pricing strategy, the ratio is usually computed using net profit before extraordinary items and taxes—that is, net sales less COST OF GOODS SOLD and SELLING, GENERAL, AND ADMINISTRATIVE (SG&A) EXPENSES.

NET QUICK ASSETS cash, MARKETABLE SECURITIES, and ACCOUNTS RECEIVABLE, minus current liabilities. *See also* QUICK RATIO.

NET REALIZED CAPITAL GAINS PER SHARE amount of CAPITAL GAINS that an investment company realized on the sale of securities, NET OF CAPITAL LOSSES and divided by the number of outstanding shares. Such net gains are distributed annually to shareholders in proportion to their shares in the total portfolio. Such distributions are eligible for favorable capital gains tax rates if the positions were held for at least a year. If held for less than a year, they would be subject to regular income taxes at the shareholder's tax bracket. *See also* REGULATED INVESTMENT COMPANY.

NET SALES gross sales less returns and allowances, freight out, and cash discounts allowed. Cash discounts allowed is seen less frequently than in past years, since it has become conventional to report as net sales the amount finally received from the customer. Returns are merchandise returned for credit; allowances are deductions allowed by the seller for merchandise not received or received in damaged condition; freight out is shipping expense passed on to the customer.

NET TANGIBLE ASSETS PER SHARE total assets of a company, less any INTANGIBLE ASSET such as goodwill, patents, and trademarks, less all liabilities and the par value of preferred stock, divided by the number of common shares outstanding. *See* BOOK VALUE for a discussion of what this calculation means and how it can be varied to apply to bonds or preferred stock shares. *See also* NET ASSET VALUE.

NET TRANSACTION securities transaction in which the buyer and seller do not pay fees or commissions. For instance, when an investor buys a new issue, no commission is due. If the stock is initially offered at $15 a share, the buyer's total cost is $15 per share.

NETWORK A *see* CONSOLIDATED TAPE.

NETWORK B *see* CONSOLIDATED TAPE.

NET WORKING CAPITAL CURRENT ASSETS minus CURRENT LIABILITIES. Usually simply called WORKING CAPITAL.

NET WORTH amount by which assets exceed liabilities. For a corporation, net worth is also known as *stockholders' equity* or NET ASSETS. For an individual, net worth is the total value of all possessions, such as a house, stocks, bonds, and other securities, minus all outstanding debts, such as mortgage and revolving-credit loans. In order to qualify for certain high-risk investments, brokerage houses require that an individual's net worth must be at or above a certain dollar level.

NET YIELD RATE OF RETURN on a security net of out-of-pocket costs associated with its purchase, such as commissions or markups. *See also* MARKDOWN.

NEW ACCOUNT REPORT document filled out by a broker that details vital facts about a new client's financial circumstances and investment objectives. The report may be updated if there are material changes in a client's financial position. Based on the report, a client may or may not be deemed eligible for certain types of risky investments, such as commodity trading or highly leveraged LIMITED PARTNERSHIP deals. *See also* KNOW YOUR CUSTOMER.

NEW HIGH/NEW LOW stock prices that have hit the highest or lowest prices in the last year. Next to each stock's listing in a newspaper will be an indication of a new high with a letter "u" or a new low with the letter "d." Newspapers publish the total number of new highs and new lows each day on the New York and American Stock Exchanges and on the NASDAQ Stock Market. Technical analysts pay great attention to the trend of new highs and new lows. If the number of new highs is expanding, that is considered a bullish indicator. If the number of new lows is rising, that is considered bearish. Many analysts also track the ratio of new highs to new lows as a reflection of the general direction of the stock market.

NEW ISSUE stock or bond being offered to the public for the first time, the distribution of which is covered by Securities and Exchange Commission (SEC) rules. New issues may be initial public offerings by previously private companies or additional stock or bond issues by companies already public and often listed on the exchanges. New PUBLIC OFFERINGS must be registered with the SEC. PRIVATE PLACEMENTS avoid SEC registration if a LETTER OF INTENT establishes that the securities are purchased for investment and not for resale to the public. *See also* HOT ISSUE; LETTER SECURITY; UNDERWRITE.

NEW LISTING security that has just begun to trade on a stock or bond exchange. A new listing on the New York or American Stock Exchange must meet all LISTING REQUIREMENTS, and may either be an INITIAL PUBLIC OFFERING or a company whose shares have previously traded on the NASDAQ Stock Market. New listings on the New York and American Stock Exchanges or a non-U.S. market carry the letter "n" next to their listing in newspaper tables for one year from the date they started trading on the exchange.

NEW MONEY amount of additional long-term financing provided by a new issue or issues in excess of the amount of a maturing issue or by issues that are being refunded.

NEW MONEY PREFERRED PREFERRED STOCK issued after October 1, 1942, when the tax exclusion for corporate investors receiving preferred stock dividends was raised from 60% to 85%, to equal the exclusion on common stock dividends. The change benefited financial institutions, such as insurance companies, which are limited in the amount of common stocks they can hold, typically 5% of assets. New money preferreds offer an opportunity to gain tax advantages over bond investments, which have fully taxable interest. The corporate tax exclusion on dividends is currently 70%.

NEW YORK COFFEE, SUGAR AND COCOA EXCHANGE *see* SECURITIES AND COMMODITIES EXCHANGES.

NEW YORK COTTON EXCHANGE (NYCE) oldest commodity exchange in New York, founded in 1870 by a group of cotton brokers and merchants. FINEX (Financial Exchange), the exchange's financial futures and options division, began operations in 1985. In December 1993, the NYCE acquired the NEW YORK FUTURES EXCHANGE (NYFE) from the New York Stock Exchange; it is a wholly owned subsidiary. The NYCE trades cotton futures and options (10:30 A.M.–2:40 P.M.).

Through Citrus Associates of the New York Cotton Exchange Inc., it trades frozen concentrated orange juice futures and options (10:15 A.M.– 2:15 P.M.). In June 1994, FINEX Europe was opened in Dublin, creating a 24-hour market in most FINEX contracts. FINEX/FINEX Europe trades U.S. dollar index (USDX) futures and options, and U.S. dollar-based currency futures (7 A.M.–10 P.M., 3 A.M.– 8 A.M., 8:05 A.M.–3 P.M.); and cross-rate currency futures (7 P.M.–10 P.M., 3 A.M.–9 A.M., 9:05 A.M.–3 P.M.). The exchange also trades options on cross-rate futures. Futures and options on Treasury auction five-year U.S. Treasury note futures and Treasury auction two-year U.S. Treasury note futures (8:20 A.M.– 3 P.M.) are traded only in New York.

NEW YORK CURB EXCHANGE *see* AMERICAN STOCK EXCHANGE.

NEW YORK FUTURES EXCHANGE (NYFE) wholly owned subsidiary of the NEW YORK COTTON EXCHANGE, acquired from the New York Stock Exchange in December 1993. The NYFE trades NYSE Composite Index futures and options based on the NYSE Composite Index of approximately 2,000 common stocks traded on the New York Stock Exchange (9:30 A.M.– 4:15 P.M.); and KR-CRB (Knight-Ridder—Commodity Research Bureau) Index futures and options based on the KR-CRB Index of 21 commodity components (9:40 A.M.–2:45 P.M.).

NEW YORK MERCANTILE EXCHANGE world's largest physical commodity futures exchange, following merger in 1994 with the COMMODITY EXCHANGE (COMEX). The exchange operates as two divisions since the merger. The NYMEX division trades light, sweet crude oil, heating oil, New York Harbor unleaded gasoline, natural gas and platinum futures and options; sour crude, propane and palladium futures; and crack spread options (intercommodity spreads) for heating oil-crude oil and unleaded gasoline-crude oil. The COMEX division trades futures and options in copper, gold, and silver, and the Eurotop 100 Index futures and options. Five-day copper, five-day gold, and five-day silver options also are traded. NYMEX division trading hours are Monday through Friday, from 8:10 A.M. to 3:20 P.M. COMEX division hours are Monday through Friday, from 8:10 A.M. to 3 P.M. The exchange operates the ACCESS after hours electronic trading system, Monday through Thursday from 5 P.M. to 8 A.M., and a Sunday evening session beginning at 7 P.M., trading crude oil, heating oil, and gasoline futures and options, and platinum, copper, gold and silver futures. The exchange has an electronic linkage with the Sydney Futures Exchange (SFE) to allow SFE members to trade NYMEX energy products directly, at non-member rates through the SFE's SYCOM electronic trading system.

NEW YORK STOCK EXCHANGE (NYSE) oldest (1792) and largest stock exchange in the United States, located at 11 Wall Street in New York City; also known as the *Big Board* and *The Exchange*. The NYSE is an unincorporated association governed by a board of directors headed by a full-time paid chairman and comprised of 20 individuals representing the public and the exchange membership in about equal proportion. Operating divisions of the NYSE are market operations, member firm regulation and surveillance, finance and office services, product development and planning, and market services and customer relations. Staff groups handle other specialized functions, such as legal problems, government relations, and economic research; certain operational functions are handled by affiliated corporations, such as DEPOSITORY TRUST COMPANY, NATIONAL SECURITIES CLEARING CORPORATION (NSCC), and SECURITIES INDUSTRY AUTOMATION CORPORATION (SIAC). Total voting membership is currently fixed at 1366 "seats," which are owned by individuals, usually partners or officers of securities firms. The number of firms represented is about 550, 150 of which are specialists responsible for the maintenance of an orderly market in the securities they handle.

Most members execute orders for the public, although a small number—about 30, who are called FLOOR TRADERS—deal exclusively for their own accounts. More than 1600 companies are listed on the NYSE, representing large firms meeting the exchange's uniquely stringent LISTING REQUIREMENTS. STOCKS, BONDS, WARRANTS, OPTIONS, and RIGHTS are traded at 22 horseshoe-shaped installations, called TRADING POSTS, on the FLOOR of the exchange. In the mid-1990s NYSE-listed shares made up more than half of the total shares traded on organized national exchanges in the United States. Hours: 9:30 A.M.–4:00 P.M., Monday through Friday.

NEW YORK STOCK EXCHANGE INDEX *see* STOCK INDEXES AND AVERAGES.

NEW ZEALAND FUTURES AND OPTIONS EXCHANGE electronic screen-trading exchange, purchased in 1992 by the SYDNEY FUTURES EXCHANGE, whose traders use the SFE's ATS 2000 trading system as a means of direct access to its markets. The Forty Index Futures (FIF) contract is based on the NZSE 40 Capital Index; options are traded on the futures. Futures are traded on the U.S. dollar, New Zealand dollar, and New Zealand wool; equity options are also traded. Futures and options are traded on 90-day bank bills, New Zealand 3-year and 10-year government stock.

NEW ZEALAND STOCK EXCHANGE automated, screen-based national trading system, based in Wellington. The principal index is the NZSE 40 Index of the 40 largest and most liquid stocks. Trading hours are 9:30 A.M. to 3:30 P.M., Monday through Friday. Clearing is through an automated broker-to-broker accounting system. Settlement is for cash on demand, unless otherwise stipulated. Maximum delivery time for a contract is five business days from the trade date.

NICHE particular specialty in which a firm has garnered a large market share. Often, the market will be small enough so that the firm will not attract very much competition. For example, a company that makes a line of specialty chemicals for use by only the petroleum industry is said to have a niche in the chemical industry. Stock analysts frequently favor such companies, since their profit margins can often be wider than those of firms facing more competition.

NICS acronym for *newly industrialized countries,* which are countries that have rapidly developing industrial economies. Some examples of NICS are Hong Kong, Singapore, Malaysia, South Korea, Mexico, Argentina, and Chile. NICS typically have instituted free-market policies which encourage exports to traditional Western industrialized countries and seek investment from Western corporations. Most NICS have increasingly been reducing trade barriers to imports from Western firms.

NIFTY FIFTY 50 stocks most favored by institutions. The membership of this group is constantly changing, although companies that continue to produce consistent earnings growth over a long time tend to remain institutional favorites. Nifty Fifty stocks also tend to have higher than market average price/earnings ratios, since their growth prospects are well recognized by institutional investors. The Nifty Fifty stocks were particularly famous in the bull markets of the 1960s and early 1970s, when many of the price/earnings ratios soared to 50 or more. *See also* PRICE/EARNINGS RATIO.

NIKKEI INDEX *See* NIKKEI STOCK AVERAGE.

NIKKEI STOCK AVERAGE index of 225 leading stocks traded on the Tokyo Stock Exchange. Called the Nikkei Dow Jones Stock Average until it was renamed in May 1985, it is similar to the Dow Jones Industrial Average because it is composed of representative BLUE CHIP companies (termed *first-section* companies in Japan) and is a PRICE-WEIGHTED INDEX. That means that the movement of each stock, in yen or dollars respectively, is weighed equally regardless of its market capitalization. The Nikkei Stock Average, informally called the Nikkei Index and often still referred to as the Nikkei Dow, is published by the *Nihon Keizai Shimbun (Japan Economic Journal)* and is the most widely quoted Japanese stock index.

Also widely quoted is the Tokyo Stock Price Index (Topix) of all issues listed in the First Section.

NINE-BOND RULE New York Stock Exchange (NYSE) requirement that orders for nine bonds or less be sent to the floor for one hour to seek a market. Since bond trading tends to be inactive on the NYSE (because of large institutional holdings and because many of the listed bond trades are handled OVER THE COUNTER), Rule 396 is designed to obtain the most favorable price for small investors. Customers may request that the rule be waived, but the broker-dealer in such cases must then act only as a BROKER and not as a PRINCIPAL (dealer for his own account).

19c3 STOCK stock listed on a national securities exchange, such as the New York Stock Exchange or the American Stock Exchange, after April 26, 1979, and thus exempt from Securities and Exchange Commission rule 19c3 prohibiting exchange members from engaging in OFF-BOARD trading.

NO-ACTION LETTER letter requested from the Securities and Exchange Commission wherein the Commission agrees to take neither civil nor criminal action with respect to the specific activity and circumstances. LIMITED PARTNERSHIPS designed as TAX SHELTERS, which are frequently venturing in uncharted legal territory, often seek no-action letters to clear novel marketing or financing techniques.

NO-BRAINER term used to describe a market the direction of which has become obvious, and therefore requires little or no analysis. This means that most of the stocks will go up in a strong bull market and fall in a bear market, so that it does not matter very much which stock investors buy or sell.

NOB SPREAD acronym for *notes over bonds* spread. Traders buying or selling a NOB spread are trying to profit from changes in the relationship between yields in Treasury notes, which are intermediate-term instruments maturing in 2 to 10 years, and Treasury bonds, which are long-term instruments maturing in 15 or more years. Most people trade the NOB Spread by buying or selling futures contracts on Treasury notes and Treasury bonds. *See also* MOB SPREAD.

NO-FAULT concept used in divorce law and automobile insurance whereby the parties involved are not required to prove blame in an action. The concept recognizes irreconcilable differences as a basis for divorce. In automobile insurance, the accident victim collects directly from his or her own insurance company for medical and hospital expenses, regardless of who was at fault. No-fault statutes vary widely among states that have them. No-fault automobile insurance typically contains provisions aimed at discouraging frivolous lawsuits.

NOISE stock-market activity caused by PROGRAM TRADES and other phenomena not reflective of general sentiment.

NO-LOAD FUND MUTUAL FUND offered by an open-end investment company that imposes no sales charge (load) on its shareholders. Investors buy shares in no-load funds directly from the fund companies, rather than through a BROKER, as is done in load funds. Many no-load fund families *(see* FAMILY OF FUNDS) allow switching of assets between stock, bond, and money market funds. The listing of the price of a no-load fund in a newspaper is accompanied with the designation NL. The net asset value, market price, and offer prices of this type of fund are exactly the same, since there is no sales charge. *See also* LOAD FUND.

NOMINAL DOLLARS dollars unadjusted for inflation. For example, economists will refer to a product that cost 100 nominal dollars several years ago, and now costs $150. However, adjusted for inflation, the product's current price may be much higher or lower. Most financial statements are reported in nominal dollars.

NOMINAL EXERCISE PRICE EXERCISE PRICE (strike price) of a GOVERNMENT NATIONAL MORTGAGE ASSOCIATION (GNMA or Ginnie Mae) option contract, obtained by multiplying the unpaid principal balance on a Ginnie Mae certificate by the ADJUSTED EXERCISE PRICE. For example, if the unpaid principal balance is $96,000 and the adjusted exercise price is 58, the nominal exercise price is $55,680.

NOMINAL INCOME income unadjusted for changes in the PURCHASING POWER OF THE DOLLAR. GENERALLY ACCEPTED ACCOUNTING PRINCIPLES (GAAP) require certain large, publicly held companies to provide supplementary information adjusting income from continuing operations for changing prices. FINANCIAL ACCOUNTING STANDARDS BOARD (FASB) Statement Number 89 removed the requirement to present general purchasing power and current cost/constant dollar supplement statements, however.

NOMINAL INTEREST RATE *see* NOMINAL YIELD.

NOMINAL QUOTATION bid and offer prices given by a market maker for the purpose of valuation, not as an invitation to trade. Securities industry rules require that nominal quotations be specifically identified as such; usually this is done by prefixing the quote with the letters FYI (FOR YOUR INFORMATION) or FVO (for valuation only).

NOMINAL RATE OF INTEREST rate of interest unadjusted for inflation. The actual interest rate charged by a bank on a loan is in nominal dollars. This is in contrast to interest rates that have been adjusted for either past or projected inflation, called REAL INTEREST RATES.

NOMINAL YIELD annual dollar amount of income received from a fixed-income security divided by the PAR VALUE of the security and stated as a percentage. Thus a bond that pays $90 a year and has a par value of $1000 has a nominal yield of 9%, called its *coupon rate.* Similarly, a preferred stock that pays a $9 annual dividend and has a par value of $100 has a nominal yield of 9%. Only when a stock or bond is bought exactly at par value is the nominal yield equal to the actual yield. Since market prices of fixed-income securities go down when market interest rates go up and vice versa, the actual yield, which is determined by the market price and coupon rate (nominal yield), will be higher when the purchase price is below par value and lower when the purchase price is above par value. *See also* RATE OF RETURN.

NOMINEE person or firm, such as a bank official or brokerage house, into whose name securities or other properties are transferred by agreement. Securities held in STREET NAME, for example, are registered in the name of a BROKER (nominee) to facilitate transactions, although the customer remains the true owner.

NONACCREDITED INVESTOR investor who does not meet the net worth requirements of SEC Regulation D. Under Rules 505 and 506 of Regulation D, an investment can be offered to a maximum of 35 nonaccredited investors. Such investors tend to be wealthy and sophisticated, and therefore the SEC feels they need less investor protection than smaller, less sophisticated investors.

NONCALLABLE preferred stock or bond that cannot be redeemed at the option of the issuer. A bond may offer CALL PROTECTION for a particular length of time, such as ten years. After that, the issuer may redeem the bond if it chooses and can justify doing so. U.S. government bond obligations are not callable until close to maturity. Provisions for noncallability are spelled out in detail in a bond's INDENTURE agreement or in the prospectus issued at the time a new preferred stock is floated. Bond yields are often quoted to the first date at which the bonds could be called. *See also* YIELD TO CALL.

NONCLEARING MEMBER member firm of the New York Stock Exchange or another organized exchange that does not have the operational facilities for clearing transactions and thus pays a fee to have the services performed by another member firm, called a *clearing member.* The clearing process involves comparison and verification of information between the buying and selling brokers and then the physical delivery of certificates in exchange for payment, called the *settlement.*

NONCOMPETITIVE BID method of buying Treasury bills without having to meet the high minimum purchase requirements of the regular DUTCH AUCTION; also called *noncompetitive tender.* The process of bidding for Treasury bills is split into two parts: competitive and non-competitive bids.

COMPETITIVE BIDS are entered by large government securities dealers and brokers, who buy millions of dollars worth of bills. They offer the best price they can for the securities, and the highest bids are accepted by the Treasury in what is called the Dutch auction.

Noncompetitive bids are submitted by smaller investors through a Federal Reserve Bank, the Bureau of Federal Debt, or certain commercial banks. These bids will be executed at the average of the prices paid in all the competitive bids accepted by the Treasury. The minimum noncompetitive bid for a Treasury bill is $10,000. *See also* TREASURY DIRECT.

NONCONTESTABILITY CLAUSE provision found in insurance contracts stipulating that policyholders cannot be denied coverage after a specific period of time, usually two years, even if the policyholder provided inaccurate or even fraudulent information in his or her insurance application. In order to contest the policy, the insurer must find out about the incorrect information before the clause goes into effect. *See* INCONTESTABILITY CLAUSE.

NONCONTRIBUTORY PENSION PLAN pension plan that is totally funded by the employer, and to which employees are not expected to contribute. Most DEFINED BENEFIT PENSION PLANS are noncontributory. In contrast, DEFINED CONTRIBUTION PENSION PLANS offer employees the choice to contribute to a plan such as a 401(k) or 403(b).

NONCUMULATIVE term describing a preferred stock issue in which unpaid dividends do not accrue. Such issues contrast with CUMULATIVE PREFERRED issues, where unpaid dividends accumulate and must be paid before dividends on common shares. Most preferred issues are cumulative. On a noncumulative preferred, omitted dividends will, as a rule, never be paid. Some older railroad preferred stocks are of this type.

NONCURRENT ASSET asset not expected to be converted into cash, sold, or exchanged within the normal operating cycle of the firm, usually one year. Examples of noncurrent assets include FIXED ASSETS, such as real estate, machinery, and other equipment; LEASEHOLD IMPROVEMENTS; INTANGIBLE ASSETS, such as goodwill, patents, and trademarks; notes receivable after one year; other investments; miscellaneous assets not meeting the definition of a CURRENT ASSET. Prepaid expenses (also called DEFERRED CHARGES or *deferred expenses*), which include such items as rent paid in advance, prepaid insurance premiums, and subscriptions, are usually considered current assets by accountants. Credit analysts, however, prefer to classify these expenses as noncurrent assets, since prepayments do not represent asset strength and protection in the way that other current assets do, with their convertibility into cash during the normal operating cycle and their liquidation value should operations be terminated.

NONCURRENT LIABILITY LIABILITY due after one year.

NONDISCRETIONARY TRUST TRUST where the trustee has no power to determine the amount of distributions to the beneficiary. Contrast with DISCRETIONARY TRUST.

NONFINANCIAL ASSETS assets that are physical, such as REAL ESTATE and PERSONAL PROPERTY.

NON-INTEREST-BEARING NOTE note that makes no periodic interest payments. Instead, the note is sold at a discount and matures at face value. Also called a ZERO-COUPON BOND.

NONMEMBER FIRM brokerage firm that is not a member of an organized exchange. Such firms execute their trades either through member firms, on regional exchanges, or in the THIRD MARKET. *See* MEMBER FIRM; REGIONAL STOCK EXCHANGES.

NONPARTICIPATING LIFE INSURANCE POLICY life insurance policy that does not pay dividends. Policyholders thus do not participate in the interest, dividends, and capital gains earned by the insurer on premiums paid. In contrast, PARTICIPATING INSURANCE POLICIES pay dividends to policyholders from earnings on investments.

NONPARTICIPATING PREFERRED STOCK *see* PARTICIPATING PREFERRED STOCK.

NONPERFORMING ASSET ASSET not effectual in the production of income. In banking, commercial loans 90 days past due and consumer loans 180 days past due are classified as nonperforming.

NONPRODUCTIVE LOAN type of commercial bank loan that increases the amount of spending power in the economy but does not lead directly to increased output; for example, a loan to finance a LEVERAGED BUYOUT. The Federal Reserve has on occasion acted to curtail such lending as one of its early steps in implementing monetary restraint.

NONPUBLIC INFORMATION information about a company, either positive or negative, that will have a material effect on the stock price when it is released to the public. Insiders, such as corporate officers and members of the board of directors, are not allowed to trade on material nonpublic information until it has been released to the public, since they would have an unfair advantage over unsuspecting investors. Some examples of important nonpublic information are an imminent takeover announcement, a soon-to-be-released earnings report that is more favorable than most analysts expect, or the sudden resignation of a key corporate official. *See also* DISCLOSURE; INSIDER.

NONPURPOSE LOAN loan for which securities are pledged as collateral but which is not used to purchase or carry securities. Under Federal Reserve Board REGULATION U, a borrower using securities as collateral must sign an affidavit called a PURPOSE STATEMENT, indicating the use to which the loan is to be put. Regulation U limits the amount of credit a bank may extend for purchasing and carrying margin securities, where the credit is secured directly or indirectly by stock.

NONQUALIFYING ANNUITY annuity purchased outside of an IRS-approved pension plan. The contributions to such an annuity are made with after-tax dollars. Just as with a QUALIFYING ANNUITY, however, the earnings from the nonqualifying annuity can accumulate tax deferred until withdrawn. Assets may be placed in either a FIXED ANNUITY, a VARIABLE ANNUITY, or a HYBRID ANNUITY.

NONQUALIFYING STOCK OPTION employee stock option not meeting the Internal Revenue Service criteria for QUALIFYING STOCK OPTIONS (INCENTIVE STOCK OPTIONS) and therefore triggering a tax upon EXERCISE. (The issuing employer, however, can deduct the nonqualifying option during the period when it is exercised, whereas it would not have a deduction when a qualifying option is exercised. A STOCK OPTION is a right issued by a corporation to an individual, normally an executive employee, to buy a given amount of shares at a stated price within a specified period of time. Gains realized on the exercise of nonqualifying options are treated as ordinary income in the tax year in which the options are exercised. Qualifying stock options, in contrast, are taxed neither at the time of granting or the time of exercise; only when the underlying stock is sold and a CAPITAL GAIN realized, does a tax event occur.

NONRATED bonds that have not been rated by one or more of the major rating agencies such as Standard & Poor's, Moody's Investor Services or Fitch Investor Services. Issues are usually nonrated because they are too small to justify the expense of getting a rating. Nonrated bonds are not necessarily better or worse than rated bonds, though many institutions cannot buy them because they need to hold bonds with an investment-grade rating.

NONRECOURSE LOAN type of financial arrangement used by limited partners in a DIRECT PARTICIPATION PROGRAM, whereby the limited partners finance a portion of their participation with a loan secured by their ownership in the underlying venture. They benefit from the LEVERAGE provided by the loan. In case of default, the lender has no recourse to the assets of the partnership beyond those held by the limited partners who borrowed the money.

NONRECURRING CHARGE one-time expense or WRITE-OFF appearing in a company's financial statement; also called *extraordinary charge*. Nonrecurring charges would include, for example, a major fire or theft, the write-off of a division, and the effect of a change in accounting procedure.

NONREFUNDABLE provision in a bond INDENTURE that either prohibits or sets limits on the issuer's retiring the bonds with the proceeds of a subsequent issue, called REFUNDING. Such a provision often does not rule out refunding altogether but protects bondholders from REDEMPTION until a specified date. Other such provisions may preclude refunding unless new bonds can be issued at a specified lower rate. *See also* CALL PROTECTION.

NONVOTING STOCK corporate securities that do not empower a holder to vote on corporate resolutions or the election of directors. Such stock is sometimes issued in connection with a takeover attempt, when management creates nonvoting shares to dilute the target firm's equity and thereby discourage the merger attempt. Except in very special circumstances, the New York Stock Exchange does not list nonvoting stock. Preferred stock is normally nonvoting stock. *See also* VOTING STOCK; VOTING TRUST CERTIFICATE.

NO-PAR-VALUE STOCK stock with no set (par) value specified in the corporate charter or on the stock certificate; also called *no-par stock.* Companies issuing no-par value shares may carry whatever they receive for them either as part of the CAPITAL STOCK account or as part of the CAPITAL SURPLUS (paid-in capital) account, or both. Whatever amount is carried as capital stock has an implicit value, represented by the number of outstanding shares divided into the dollar amount of capital stock.

The main attraction of no-par stock to issuing corporations, historically, had to do with the fact that many states imposed taxes based on PAR VALUE, while other states, like Delaware, encouraged incorporations with no-par-value stock.

For the investor, there are two reservations: (1) that unwise or inept directors may reduce the value of outstanding shares by accepting bargain basement prices on new issues (shareholders are protected, to some extent, from this by PREEMPTIVE RIGHT—the right to purchase enough of a new issue to protect their power and equity) and (2) that too great an amount of shareholder contributions may be channeled into the capital surplus account, which is restricted by the law of many states from being a source of dividend payments. *See* ILLEGAL DIVIDEND.

Still, no-par stock, along with low-par stock, remains an appealing alternative, from the issuer's standpoint, to par-value shares because of investor confusion of par value and real value.

Most stock issued today is either no-par or low-par value.

NORMAL INVESTMENT PRACTICE history of investment in a customer account with a member of the National Association of Securities Dealers as defined in their rules of fair practice. It is used to test the bona fide PUBLIC OFFERINGS requirement that applies to the allocation of a HOT ISSUE. If the buying customer has a history of purchasing similar amounts in normal circumstances, the sale qualifies as a bona fide public offering and is not in violation of the Rules of Fair Practice. A record of buying only hot issues is not acceptable as normal investment practice. *See also* NASD FORM FR-1.

NORMALIZED EARNINGS earnings, either in the past or the future, that are adjusted for cyclical ups and downs in the economy. Earnings are normalized by analysts by generating a moving average over several years including up and down cycles. Analysts refer to normalized earnings when explaining whether a company's current profits are above or below its long-term trend.

NORMAL MARKET SIZE (NMS) share classification system that in 1991 replaced the alpha, beta, gamma, delta, system brought in with BIG BANG on the INTERNATIONAL STOCK EXCHANGE OF THE U.K. AND THE REPUBLIC OF IRELAND (ISE). The earlier system had unintentionally become a measure of corporate status, strength, and viability. The new system has 12 categories based on the size of the transactions that are normal for each security. The system fixes the size of transactions in which market makers are obligated to deal.

NORMAL RETIREMENT point at which a pension plan participant can retire and immediately receive unreduced benefits. Pension plans can specify age and length-of-service requirements that employees must meet to be eligible for retirement.

NORMAL TRADING UNIT standard minimum size of a trading unit for a particular security; also called a ROUND LOT. For instance, stocks have a normal trading unit of 100 shares, although inactive stocks trade in 10-share round lots. Any securities trade for less than a round lot is called an ODD LOT trade.

NOTE written promise to pay a specified amount to a certain entity on demand or on a specified date. See *also* MUNICIPAL NOTE; PROMISSORY NOTE; TREASURIES.

NOT-FOR-PROFIT type of incorporated organization in which no stockholder or trustee shares in profits or losses and which usually exists to accomplish some charitable, humanitarian, or educational purpose; also called *nonprofit*. Such groups are exempt from corporate income taxes but are subject to other taxes on income-producing property or enterprises. Donations to these groups are usually tax deductible for the donor. Some examples are hospitals, colleges and universities, foundations, and such familiar groups as the Red Cross and Girl Scouts.

NOT HELD instruction (abbreviated NH) on a market order to buy or sell securities, indicating that the customer has given the FLOOR BROKER time and price discretion in executing the best possible trade but will not hold the broker responsible if the best deal is not obtained. Such orders, which are usually for large blocks of securities, were originally designed for placement with specialists, who could hold an order back if they felt prices were going to rise. The Securities and Exchange Commission no longer allows specialists to handle NH orders, leaving floor brokers without any clear alternative except to persuade the customer to change the order to a LIMIT ORDER. The broker can then turn the order over to a SPECIALIST, who could sell pieces of the block to floor traders or buy it for his own account. *See* SPECIALIST BLOCK PURCHASE AND SALE. An older variation of NH is DRT, meaning disregard tape.

NOTICE OF SALE advertisement placed by an issuer of municipal securities announcing its intentions to sell a new issue and inviting underwriters to submit COMPETITIVE BIDS.

NOT RATED indication used by securities rating services (such as Standard & Poor's or Moody's) and mercantile agencies (such as Dun & Bradstreet) to show that a security or a company has not been rated. It has neither negative nor positive implications. The abbreviation NR is used.

NOT-SUFFICIENT-FUNDS CHECK a bank check written against an inadequate balance. Also called *insufficient-funds check* and, informally, a *bounced check.*

NOVATION
1. agreement to replace one party to a contract with a new party. The novation transfers both rights and duties and requires the consent of both the original and the new party.
2. replacement of an older debt or obligation with a newer one.

NOW ACCOUNT *see* NEGOTIABLE ORDER OF WITHDRAWAL.

NUMISMATIC COIN coin that is valued based on its rarity, age, quantity originally produced, and condition. These coins are bought and sold as individual items within the coin collecting community. Most numismatic coins are legal tender coins that were produced in limited quantities to give them scarcity value. They are historic coins which also can be rare. The current price of gold is a minor factor when dealing with numismatic coins. Premiums are traditionally far higher than those of BULLION COINS, and values fluctuate to a much wider extent. For example, a $5 gold piece may contain $60 worth of gold and may sell for as

much as $700. The minimum amount recovered from numismatic coin invest-
ments is always either its face value or its metal content. Most coins, however,
sell substantially above these amounts. Since the markup over bullion value can
vary widely from one dealer to another, investors need to shop around diligently
to avoid paying exhorbitant markups.

O

OBLIGATION legal responsibility, as for a DEBT.

OBLIGATION BOND type of mortgage bond in which the face value is greater
than the value of the underlying property. The difference compensates the lender
for costs exceeding the mortgage value.

OBLIGOR one who has an obligation, such as an issuer of bonds, a borrower of
money from a bank or another source, or a credit customer of a business supplier
or retailer. The obligor *(obligator, debtor)* is legally bound to pay a debt, including interest, when due.

ODD LOT securities trade made for less than the NORMAL TRADING UNIT (termed a
ROUND LOT). In stock trading, any purchase or sale of less than 100 shares is considered an odd lot, although inactive stocks generally trade in round lots of 10
shares. An investor buying or selling an odd lot pays a higher commission rate
than someone making a round-lot trade. This odd-lot differential varies among
brokers but for stocks is often ⅛ of a point (12½¢) per share. For instance, someone buying 100 shares of XYZ at $70 would pay $70 a share plus commission.
At the same time, someone buying only 50 shares of XYZ would pay $70⅛ a
share plus commission. *See also* ODD-LOT DEALER; ODD-LOT SHORT-SALE RATIO;
ODD-LOT THEORY.

ODD-LOT DEALER originally a dealer who bought round lots of stock and resold
it in odd lots to retail brokers who, in turn, accommodated their smaller customers at the regular commission rate plus an extra charge, called the odd-lot differential. The assembling of round lots from odd lots is now a service provided
free by New York Stock Exchange specialists to member brokers, and odd-lot
transactions can be executed through most brokers serving the retail public.
Brokers handling odd lots do, however, receive extra compensation; it varies with
the broker, but ⅛ of a point (12½¢) per share in addition to a regular commission
is typical. *See also* ODD-LOT.

ODD-LOT SHORT-SALE RATIO ratio obtained by dividing ODD LOT short sales
by total odd-lot sales, using New York Stock Exchange (NYSE) statistics; also
called the *odd-lot selling indicator.* Historically, odd-lot investors—those who
buy and sell in less than 100-share round lots—react to market highs and lows;
when the market reaches a low point, odd-lot short sales reach a high point, and
vice versa. The odd-lot ratio has followed the opposite pattern of the NYSE MEM-
BER SHORT SALE RATIO. *See also* ODD-LOT THEORY.

ODD-LOT THEORY historical theory that the ODD LOT investor—the small personal
investor who trades in less than 100-share quantities—is usually guilty of bad timing and that profits can be made by acting contrary to odd-lot trading patterns.
Heavy odd-lot buying in a rising market is interpreted by proponents of this theory
as a sign of technical weakness and the signal of a market reversal. Conversely, an
increase of odd-lot selling in a declining market is seen as a sign of technical
strength and a signal to buy. In fact, analyses of odd-lot trading over the years fail

to bear out the theory with any real degree of consistency, and it has fallen into disfavor in recent years. It is also a fact that odd-lot customers generally, who tend to buy market leaders, have fared rather well in the upward market that has prevailed over the last fifty years or so. *See also* ODD-LOT SHORT-SALE RATIO.

OEX pronounced as three letters, Wall Street shorthand for the Standard & Poor's 100 stock index, which comprises stocks for which options are traded on the Chicago Board Options Exchange. OEX index options are traded on the Chicago Board of Trade, and futures are traded on the Chicago Mercantile Exchange. *See also* STOCK INDEXES AND AVERAGES.

OFF-BALANCE-SHEET FINANCING financing that does not add debt on a balance sheet and thus does not affect borrowing capacity as it would be determined by financial ratios. The most common example would be a lease structured as an OPERATING LEASE rather than a CAPITAL LEASE and where management's intent is, in fact, to acquire an asset and corresponding liability without reflecting either on its balance sheet. Other examples include the sale of receivables with recourse, TAKE-OR-PAY CONTRACTS, and bank financial instruments such as guarantees, letters of credit, and loan commitments. GENERALLY ACCEPTED ACCOUNTING PRINCIPLES (GAAP) require that information be provided in financial statements about off-balance-sheet financing involving credit, market, and liquidity risk.

OFF-BOARD off the exchange (the New York Stock Exchange is known as the Big Board, hence the term). The term is used either for a trade that is executed OVER THE COUNTER or for a transaction entailing listed securities that is not completed on a national exchange. Over-the-counter trading is handled by telephone, with competitive bidding carried on constantly by market makers in a particular stock. The other kind of off-board trade occurs when a block of stock is exchanged between customers of a brokerage firm, or between a customer and the firm itself if the brokerage house wants to buy or sell securities from its own inventory. *See also* THIRD MARKET.

OFFER price at which someone who owns a security offers to sell it; also known as the ASKED PRICE. This price is listed in newspapers for stocks traded OVER THE COUNTER. The bid price—the price at which someone is prepared to buy—is also shown. The bid price is always lower than the offer price. *See also* OFFERING PRICE.

OFFERING *see* PUBLIC OFFERING.

OFFERING CIRCULAR *see* PROSPECTUS.

OFFERING DATE date on which a distribution of stocks or bonds will first be available for sale to the public. *See also* DATED DATE; PUBLIC OFFERING.

OFFERING PRICE price per share at which a new or secondary distribution of securities is offered for sale to the public; also called PUBLIC OFFERING PRICE. For instance, if a new issue of XYZ stock is priced at $40 a share, the offering price is $40.

When mutual fund shares are made available to the public, they are sold at NET ASSET VALUE, also called the *offering price* or the ASKED PRICE, plus a sales charge, if any. In a NO-LOAD FUND, the offering price is the same as the net asset value. In a LOAD FUND, the sales charge is added to the net asset value, to arrive at the offering price. *See also* OFFER.

OFFERING SCALE prices at which different maturities of a SERIAL BOND issue are offered to the public by an underwriter. The offering scale may also be expressed in terms of YIELD TO MATURITY.

OFFER WANTED (OW) notice by a potential buyer of a security that he or she is looking for an offer by a potential seller of the security. The abbreviation OW is frequently seen in the PINK SHEETS (listing of stocks) and YELLOW SHEETS (listing of corporate bonds) published by the NATIONAL QUOTATION BUREAU for securities traded by OVER THE COUNTER dealers. *See also* BID WANTED.

OFF-FLOOR ORDER order to buy or sell a security that originates off the floor of an exchange. These are customer orders originating with brokers, as distinguished from orders of floor members trading for their own accounts (ON-FLOOR ORDERS). Exchange rules require that off-floor orders be executed before orders initiated on the floor.

OFFICE OF MANAGEMENT AND BUDGET (OMB) at the federal level, an agency within the Office of the President responsible for (1) preparing and presenting to Congress the president's budget; (2) working with the Council of Economic Advisers and the Treasury Department in developing a fiscal program; (3) reviewing the administrative policies and performance of government agencies; and (4) advising the president on legislative matters.

OFFICE OF THRIFT SUPERVISION (OTS) agency of the U.S. Treasury Department created by the FINANCIAL INSTITUTIONS REFORM, RECOVERY AND ENFORCEMENT ACT OF 1989 (FIRREA), the bailout bill enacted to assist depositors that became law on August 9, 1989. The OTS replaced the disbanded FEDERAL HOME LOAN BANK BOARD and assumed responsibility for the nation's savings and loan industry. The legislation empowered OTS to institute new regulations, charter new federal savings and loan associations and federal savings banks, and supervise all savings institutions and their holding companies insured by the SAVINGS ASSOCIATION INSURANCE FUND (SAIF). *See also* BAILOUT BOND.

OFFICIAL NOTICE OF SALE notice published by a municipality inviting investment bankers to submit competitive bids for an upcoming bond issue. The notice provides the name of a municipal official from whom further details can be obtained and states certain basic information about the issue, such as its par value and important conditions. The *Bond Buyer* regularly carries such notices.

OFFICIAL STATEMENT *see* LEGAL OPINION.

OFFSET
Accounting: (1) amount equaling or counterbalancing another amount on the opposite side of the same ledger or the ledger of another account. *See also* ABSORBED. (2) amount that cancels or reduces a claim.
Banking: (1) bank's legal right to seize deposit funds to cover a loan in default—called *right of offset*. (2) number stored on a bank card that, when related to the code number remembered by the cardholder, represents the depositor's identification number, called *PAN-PIN pair*.
Securities, commodities, options: (1) closing transaction involving the purchase or sale of an OPTION having the same features as one already held. (2) HEDGE, such as the SHORT SALE of a stock to protect a capital gain or the purchase of a future to protect a commodity price, or a STRADDLE representing the purchase of offsetting put and call options on a security.

OFFSHORE term used in the United States for any financial organization with a headquarters outside the country. A MUTUAL FUND with a legal domicile in the Bahamas or the Cayman Islands, for instance, is called an *offshore fund.* To be sold in the United States, such funds must adhere to all pertinent federal and state regulations. Many banks have offshore subsidiaries that engage in activities that are either heavily regulated or taxed or not allowed under U.S. law.

OIL AND GAS LIMITED PARTNERSHIP partnership consisting of one or more limited partners and one or more general partners that is structured to find, extract, and market commercial quantities of oil and natural gas. The limited partners, who assume no liability beyond the funds they contribute, buy units in the partnership, typically for at least $5000 a unit, from a broker registered to sell that partnership. All the limited partners' money then goes to the GENERAL PARTNER, the partner with unlimited liability, who either searches for oil and gas (an exploratory or wildcat well), drills for oil and gas in a proven oil field (a DEVELOPMENTAL DRILLING PROGRAM), or pumps petroleum and gas from an existing well (a COMPLETION PROGRAM). The riskier the chance of finding oil and gas, the higher the potential reward or loss to the limited partner. Conservative investors who mainly want to collect income from the sale of proven oil and gas reserves are safest with a developmental or completion program.

Subject to PASSIVE income rules, limited partners also receive tax breaks, such as depreciation deductions for equipment used for drilling and oil depletion allowances for the value of oil extracted from the fields. If the partnership borrows money for increased drilling, limited partners also can get deductions for the interest cost of the loans. *See also* EXPLORATORY DRILLING PROGRAM; INCOME LIMITED PARTNERSHIP; INTANGIBLE COSTS; LIMITED PARTNERSHIP; WILDCAT DRILLING.

OIL AND GAS LOTTERY program run by the Bureau of Land Management at the U.S. Department of the Interior that permits anyone filing an application to be selected for the right to drill for oil and gas on selected parcels of federal land. Both large oil companies and small speculators enter this lottery. An individual winning the drawing for a particularly desirable plot of land may sublet the property to an oil company, which will pay him or her royalties if the land yields commercial quantities of oil and gas.

OIL PATCH states in America that produce and refine oil and gas. This includes Texas, Oklahoma, Louisiana, California, and Alaska. Economists refer to oil patch states when assessing the strength or weakness of a region of the country tied to movements in oil prices.

OLIGOPOLY market situation in which a small number of selling firms control the market supply of a particular good or service and are therefore able to control the market price. An oligopoly can be *perfect*—where all firms produce an identical good or service (cement)—or *imperfect*—where each firm's product has a different identity but is essentially similar to the others (cigarettes). Because each firm in an oligopoly knows its share of the total market for the product or service it produces, and because any change in price or change in market share by one firm is reflected in the sales of the others, there tends to be a high degree of interdependence among firms; each firm must make its price and output decisions with regard to the responses of the other firms in the oligopoly, so that oligopoly prices, once established, are rigid. This encourages nonprice competition, through advertising, packaging, and service—a generally nonproductive form of resource allocation. Two examples of oligopoly in the United States are airlines serving the same routes and tobacco companies. *See also* OLIGOPSONY.

OLIGOPSONY market situation in which a few large buyers control the purchasing power and therefore the output and market price of a good or service; the buy-side counterpart of OLIGOPOLY. Oligopsony prices tend to be lower than the prices in a freely competitive market, just as oligopoly prices tend to be higher. For example, the large tobacco companies purchase all the output of a large number of small tobacco growers and therefore are able to control tobacco prices.

OMITTED DIVIDEND dividend that was scheduled to be declared by a corporation, but instead was not voted for the time being by the board of directors. Dividends are sometimes omitted when a company has run into financial difficulty and its board decides it is more important to conserve cash than to pay a dividend to shareholders. The announcement of an omitted dividend will typically cause the company's stock price to drop, particularly if the announcement is a surprise.

ON ACCOUNT

In general: in partial payment of an obligation.

Finance: on credit terms. The term applies to a relationship between a seller and a buyer wherein payment is expected sometime after delivery and the obligation is not documented by a NOTE. Synonymous with *open account.*

ON A SCALE *see* SCALE ORDER.

ON-BALANCE VOLUME TECHNICAL ANALYSIS method that attempts to pinpoint when a stock, bond, or commodity is being accumulated by many buyers or is being distributed by many sellers. The on-balance volume line is superimposed on the stock price line on a chart, and it is considered significant when the two lines cross. The chart indicates a buy signal when accumulation is detected and a sell signal when distribution is spotted. The on-balance method can be used to diagnose an entire market or an individual stock, bond, or commodity.

ONE-CANCELS-THE-OTHER ORDER *see* ALTERNATIVE ORDER.

ONE DECISION STOCK stock with sufficient quality and growth potential to be suitable for a BUY AND HOLD STRATEGY.

ONE-SHARE-ONE VOTE RULE the principle that public companies should not reduce shareholder voting rights. Originally, the New York Stock Exchange had a one-share, one-vote requirement for its listed companies. In 1988, the SEC adopted Rule 19c-4, which prohibited companies listed on a national securities exchange or quoted on the National Association of Securities Dealers Automated Quotation System (NASDAQ) from disenfranchising existing shareholders through, for example, issuances of super voting stock. The rule, however, was struck down by the Court of Appeals in *Business Roundtable v. SEC* in 1990. In December 1994, the SEC approved rules proposed by the New York Stock Exchange, American Stock Exchange, and National Association of Securities Dealers that establish a uniform voting standard. This new standard prohibits companies listed on the NYSE, the AMEX, or the NASDAQ system from taking any corporate action or issuing any stock that has the effect of disparately reducing or restricting the voting rights of existing common stock shareholders.

ON-FLOOR ORDER security order originating with a member on the floor of an exchange when dealing for his or her own account. The designation separates such orders from those for customers' accounts (OFF-FLOOR ORDERS), which are generally given precedence by exchange rules.

ON MARGIN *see* MARGIN.

ON THE CLOSE ORDER order to buy or sell a specified number of shares in a particular stock as close as possible to the closing price of the day. Brokers accepting on the close orders do not guarantee that the trade will be executed at the final closing price, or even that the trade can be completed at all. On an order ticket, on the close orders are abbreviated as "OTC" orders. *See also* AT THE CLOSE ORDER; MARKET-ON-CLOSE ORDER.

ON THE OPENING ORDER order to buy or sell a specified number of shares in a particular stock at the price of the first trade of the day. If the trader cannot buy or sell shares at that price, the order is immediately cancelled.

ON THE SIDELINES investors who refrain from investing because of market uncertainty are said to be on the sidelines. The analogy is to a football game, in which spectators on the sidelines do not actively participate in the game. Investors on the sidelines normally keep their money in short-term instruments such as money market mutual funds, which can be tapped instantly if the investor sees a good opportunity to reenter the stock or bond markets. Market commentators frequently say that trading activity was light "because investors stayed on the sidelines."

OPD ticker tape symbol designating (1) the first transaction of the day in a security after a DELAYED OPENING or (2) the opening transaction in a security whose price has changed significantly from the previous day's close—usually 2 or more points on stocks selling at $20 or higher, 1 or more points on stocks selling at less than $20.

OPEN
Securities:
1. status of an order to buy or sell securities that has still not been executed. A GOOD-TILL-CANCELED ORDER that remains pending is an example of an open order.
2. to establish an account with a broker.

Banking: to establish an account or a LETTER OF CREDIT.

Finance: unpaid balance.

See also OPEN-END LEASE; OPEN-END MANAGEMENT COMPANY; OPEN-END MORTGAGE; OPEN INTEREST; OPEN ORDER; OPEN REPO.

OPEN-END CREDIT revolving line of credit offered by banks, savings and loans, and other lenders to consumers. The line of credit is set with a particular limit, after which consumers can borrow using a credit card, check, or cash advance. Every time a purchase or cash advance is made, credit is extended on behalf of the consumer. Consumers may pay off the entire balance each month, thereby avoiding interest charges. Or they may pay a minimum amount, with interest accruing on the outstanding balance.

OPEN-END LEASE lease agreement providing for an additional payment after the property is returned to the lessor, to adjust for any change in the value of the property.

OPEN-END MANAGEMENT COMPANY INVESTMENT COMPANY that sells MUTUAL FUNDS to the public. The term arises from the fact that the firm continually creates new shares on demand. Mutual fund shareholders buy the shares at NET ASSET VALUE and can redeem them at any time at the prevailing market price, which may be higher or lower than the price at which the investor bought. The shareholder's funds are invested in stocks, bonds, or money market instruments, depending on the type of mutual fund company. The opposite of an open-end management company is a CLOSED-END MANAGEMENT COMPANY, which issues a limited number of shares, which are then traded on a stock exchange.

OPEN-END MORTGAGE

Real estate finance: MORTGAGE that allows the issuance of additional bonds having equal status with the original issue, but that protects the original bondholders with specific restrictions governing subsequent borrowing under the original mortgage. For example, the terms of the original INDENTURE might permit additional mortgage-bond financing up to 75% of the value of the property acquired, but only if total fixed charges on all debt, including the proposed new bonds, have been earned a stated number of times over the previous 5 years. The open-end mortgage is a more practical and acceptable (to the mortgage holder) version of the *open mortgage,* which allows a corporation to issue unlimited amounts of bonds under the original first mortgage, with no protection to the original bondholders. An even more conservative version is the *limited open-end mortgage,* which usually contains the same restrictions as the open-end, but places a limit on the amount of first mortgage bonds that can be issued, and typically provides that proceeds from new bond issues be used to retire outstanding bonds with the same or prior security.

Trust banking: corporate trust indenture that permits the trustee to authenticate and deliver bonds from time to time in addition to the original issue. *See also* AUTHENTICATION.

OPEN-END (MUTUAL) FUND *see* OPEN-END MANAGEMENT COMPANY.

OPENING

1. price at which a security or commodity starts a trading day. Investors who want to buy or sell as soon as the market opens will put in an order at the opening price.
2. short time frame of market opportunity. For instance, if interest rates have been rising for months, and for a few days or weeks they fall, a corporation that has wanted to FLOAT bonds at lower interest rates might seize the moment to issue the bonds. This short time frame would be called an *opening in the market* or a *window of opportunity. See also* WINDOW.

OPEN INTEREST total number of contracts in a commodity or options market that are still open; that is, they have not been exercised, closed out, or allowed to expire. The term also applies to a particular commodity or, in the case of options, to the number of contracts outstanding on a particular underlying security. The level of open interest is reported daily in newspaper commodity and options pages.

OPEN-MARKET COMMITTEE *see* FEDERAL OPEN MARKET COMMITTEE (FOMC).

OPEN-MARKET OPERATIONS activities by which the Securities Department of the Federal Reserve Bank of New York—popularly called the DESK—carries out instructions of the FEDERAL OPEN MARKET COMMITTEE designed to regulate the money supply. Such operations involve the purchase and sale of government securities, which effectively expands or contracts funds in the banking system. This, in turn, alters bank reserves, causing a MULTIPLIER effect on the supply of credit and, therefore, on economic activity generally. Open-market operations represent one of three basic ways the Federal Reserve implements MONETARY POLICY, the others being changes in the member bank RESERVE REQUIREMENTS and raising or lowering the DISCOUNT RATE charged to banks borrowing from the Fed to maintain reserves.

OPEN-MARKET RATES interest rates on various debt instruments bought and sold in the open market that are directly responsive to supply and demand. Such open, market rates are distinguished from the DISCOUNT RATE, set by the FEDERAL RESERVE BOARD as a deliberate measure to influence other rates, and from bank commercial loan rates, which are directly influenced by Federal Reserve policy. The rates on short-term instruments like COMMERCIAL PAPER and BANKER'S ACCEPTANCES are examples of open-market rates, as are yields on interest-bearing securities of all types traded in the SECONDARY MARKET.

OPEN ON THE PRINT BLOCK POSITIONER'S term for a BLOCK trade that has been completed with an institutional client and "printed" on the consolidated tape, but that leaves the block positioner open—that is, with a risk position to be covered. This usually happens when the block positioner is on the sell side of the transaction and sells SHORT what he lacks in inventory to complete the order.

OPEN ORDER buy or sell order for securities that has not yet been executed or canceled; a GOOD-TILL-CANCELED ORDER.

OPEN OUTCRY method of trading on a commodity exchange. The term derives from the fact that traders must shout out their buy or sell offers. When a trader shouts he wants to sell at a particular price and someone else shouts he wants to buy at that price, the two traders have made a contract that will be recorded.

OPEN REPO REPURCHASE AGREEMENT in which the repurchase date is unspecified and the agreement can be terminated by either party at any time. The agreement continues on a day-to-day basis with interest rate adjustments as the market changes.

OPERATING INCOME *see* OPERATING PROFIT (OR LOSS).

OPERATING IN THE RED operating at a loss. *see* OPERATING PROFIT (OR LOSS).

OPERATING LEASE type of LEASE, normally involving equipment, whereby the contract is written for considerably less than the life of the equipment and the lessor handles all maintenance and servicing; also called *service lease.* Operating leases are the opposite of capital leases, where the lessee acquires essentially all the economic benefits and risks of ownership. Common examples of equipment financed with operating leases are office copiers, computers, automobiles, and trucks. Most operating leases are cancelable, meaning the lessee can return the equipment if it becomes obsolete or is no longer needed.

OPERATING LEVERAGE *see* LEVERAGE.

OPERATING PROFIT MARGIN *see* NET PROFIT MARGIN.

OPERATING PROFIT (OR LOSS) the difference between the revenues of a business and the related costs and expenses, excluding income derived from sources other than its regular activities and before income deductions; synonymous with *net operating profit (or loss), operating income (or loss),* and *net operating income (or loss).* Income deductions are a class of items comprising the final section of a company's income statement, which, although necessarily incurred in the course of business and customarily charged before arriving at net income, are more in the nature of costs imposed from without than costs subject to the control of everyday operations. They include interest; amortized discount and expense on bonds; income taxes; losses from sales of plants, divisions, major items of property; prior-year adjustments; charges to contingency reserves; bonuses and other periodic profit distributions to officers and employees: writeoffs of intangibles: adjustments arising from major changes in accounting methods, such as inventory valuation and other material and nonrecurrent items.

OPERATING RATE percentage of production capacity in use by a particular company, an industry, or the entire economy. While in theory a business can operate at 100% of its productive capacity, in practice the maximum output is less than that because machines need to be repaired, employees take vacations, etc. The operating rate is expressed as a percentage of the ideal 100% production output. For example, a company may be producing at an 85% operating rate, meaning its output is 85% of the maximum that could be produced with its existing resources. If a company has a low operating rate of under 50%, it usually is suffering meager profits or losses, though it has large potential for profit growth. A company operating at 80% of capacity or more is usually highly profitable, though it has less opportunity for improvement.

The Federal Reserve calculates the operating rate of U.S. industry on a monthly basis when its releases figures for industrial production. An operating rate of 85% or higher is generally considered to be full capacity by economists, who become concerned about inflationary pressures caused by production bottlenecks. An operating rate of less than 80% shows considerable slack in the economy, with few inflationary pressures.

OPERATING RATIO any of a group of ratios that measure a firm's operating efficiency and effectiveness by relating various income and expense figures from the profit and loss statement to each other and to balance sheet figures. Among the ratios used are sales to cost of goods sold, operating expenses to operating income, net profits to gross income, net income to net worth. Such ratios are most revealing when compared with those of prior periods and with industry averages.

OPERATIONS DEPARTMENT BACK OFFICE of a brokerage firm where all clerical functions having to do with clearance, settlement, and execution of trades are handled. This department keeps customer records and handles the day-to-day monitoring of margin positions.

OPINION *see* ACCOUNTANT'S OPINION.

OPINION SHOPPING dubious practice of changing outside auditors until one is found that will give an unqualified ACCOUNTANT'S OPINION.

OPM
1. other people's money; Wall Street slang for the use of borrowed funds by individuals or companies to increase the return on invested capital. *See also* FINANCIAL LEVERAGE.
2. options pricing model. *See* BLACK-SCHOLES OPTION PRICING MODEL.

OPPORTUNITY COST
In general: highest price or rate of return an alternative course of action would provide.

Corporate finance: concept widely used in business planning; for example, in evaluating a CAPITAL INVESTMENT project, a company must measure the projected return against the return it would earn on the highest yielding alternative investment involving similar risk. *See also* COST OF CAPITAL.

Securities investments: cost of forgoing a safe return on an investment in hopes of making a larger profit. For instance, an investor might buy a stock that shows great promise but yields only 2%, even though a higher safe return is available in a money market fund yielding 5%. The 3% yield difference is called the opportunity cost.

OPTIMUM CAPACITY level of output of manufacturing operations that produces the lowest cost per unit. For example, a tire factory may produce tires at

$30 apiece if it turns out 10,000 tires a month, but the tires can be made for $20 apiece if the plant operates at its optimum capacity of 100,000 tires a month. *See also* MARGINAL COST.

OPTION

In general: right to buy or sell property that is granted in exchange for an agreed upon sum. If the right is not exercised after a specified period, the option expires and the option buyer forfeits the money. *See also* EXERCISE.

Securities: securities transaction agreement tied to stocks, commodities, or stock indexes. Options are traded on many exchanges.

1. a CALL OPTION gives its buyer the right to buy 100 shares of the underlying security at a fixed price before a specified date in the future—usually three, six, or nine months. For this right, the call option buyer pays the call option seller, called the writer, a fee called a PREMIUM, which is forfeited if the buyer does not exercise the option before the agreed-upon date. A call buyer therefore speculates that the price of the underlying shares will rise within the specified time period. For example, a call option on 100 shares of XYZ stock may grant its buyer the right to buy those shares at $100 apiece anytime in the next three months. To buy that option, the buyer may have to pay a premium of $2 a share, or $200. If at the time of the option contract XYZ is selling for $95 a share, the option buyer will profit if XYZ's stock price rises. If XYZ shoots up to $120 a share in two months, for example, the option buyer can EXERCISE his or her option to buy 100 shares of the stock at $100 and then sell the shares for $120 each, keeping the difference as profit (minus the $2 premium per share). On the other hand, if XYZ drops below $95 and stays there for three months, at the end of that time the call option will expire and the call buyer will receive no return on the $2 a share investment premium of $200.

2. the opposite of a call option is a PUT OPTION, which gives its buyer the right to sell a specified number of shares of a stock at a particular price within a specified time period. Put buyers expect the price of the underlying stock to fall. Someone who thinks XYZ's stock price will fall might buy a three-month XYZ put for 100 shares at $100 apiece and pay a premium of $2. If XYZ falls to $80 a share, the put buyer can then exercise his or her right to sell 100 XYZ shares at $100. The buyer will first purchase 100 shares at $80 each and then sell them to the put option seller (writer) at $100 each, thereby making a profit of $18 a share (the $20 a share profit minus the $2 a share cost of the option premium).

In practice, most call and put options are rarely exercised. Instead, investors buy and sell options before expiration, trading on the rise and fall of premium prices. Because an option buyer must put up only a small amount of money (the premium) to control a large amount of stock, options trading provides a great deal of LEVERAGE and can prove immensely profitable. Options traders can write either covered options, in which they own the underlying security, or far riskier naked options, for which they do not own the underlying security. Often, options traders lose many premiums on unsuccessful trades before they make a very profitable trade. More sophisticated traders combine various call and put options in SPREAD and STRADDLE positions. Their profits or losses result from the narrowing or widening of spreads between option prices.

An *incentive stock option* is granted to corporate executives if the company achieves certain financial goals, such as a level of sales or profits. The executive is granted the option of buying company stock at a below-market price and selling the stock in the market for a profit. *See also* CALL; COVERED OPTION; DEEP IN (OUT OF) THE MONEY; IN THE MONEY; LEAPS; NAKED OPTION; OPTION WRITER; OUT OF THE MONEY.

OPTION ACCOUNT account at a brokerage firm that is approved to contain option positions or trades. Since certain option strategies require margin, an option account may be a margin account or a cash account. There are several prerequisites. The client must be given a copy of "Characteristics and Risks of Standardized Options Contracts," known as the Options Disclosure Documents, before the account can be approved. The client must complete an OPTION AGREEMENT in order to open the account. The client must show, that he is suitable for options transactions, both in financial resources and investing experience, before the brokerage firm will approve the account for options trading.

OPTION AGREEMENT form filled out by a brokerage firm's customer when opening an option account. It details financial information about the customer, who agrees to follow the rules and regulations of options trading. This agreement, also called the *option information form,* assures the broker that the customer's financial resources are adequate to withstand any losses that may occur from options trading. The customer must receive a prospectus from the OPTIONS CLEARING CORPORATION before he or she can begin trading.

OPTION CYCLE cycle of months in which options contracts expire. These cycles are used for options on stocks and indices, as well as options on commodities, currencies, and debt instruments. The three most common cycles are: January, April, July, October (JAJO); February, May, August, November (FMAN); and March, June, September, December (MJSD). In addition to these expiration months, options on individual stocks and indices generally also expire in the current month and subsequent month. As an example, an option in the February cycle trading during May would have May, June and August expiration months listed at a minimum. Because of option cycles, there are four days a year—in March, June, September, and December, when TRIPLE WITCHING DAY takes place, as several options contracts expire on the same day.

OPTIONAL DIVIDEND dividend that can be paid either in cash or in stock. The shareholder entitled to the dividend makes the choice.

OPTIONAL PAYMENT BOND bond whose principal and/or interest are payable, at the option of the holder, in one or more foreign currencies as well as in domestic currency.

OPTION HOLDER someone who has bought a call or put OPTION but has not yet exercised or sold it. A call option holder wants the price of the underlying security to rise; a put option holder wants the price of the underlying security to fall.

OPTION MARGIN MARGIN REQUIREMENT applicable to OPTIONS, as set forth in REGULATION T and in the internal policies of individual brokers. Requirements vary with the type of option and the extent to which it is IN-THE-MONEY, but are strictest in the case of NAKED OPTIONS and narrow-based INDEX OPTIONS. There, Regulation T requires the option premium plus 20% of the underlying value as the maximum and the premium plus 10% of the underlying value as the minimum. Merrill Lynch, for example, would also require a minimum of $10,000 per account and $1,000 per position.

OPTION MUTUAL FUND MUTUAL FUND that either buys or sells options in order to increase the value of fund shares. OPTION mutual funds may be either conservative or aggressive. For instance, a conservative fund may buy stocks and increase shareholders' income through the PREMIUM earned by selling put and call options on the stocks in the fund's portfolio. This kind of fund would be called an *option income fund.* At the opposite extreme, an aggressive *option growth* *fund* may buy puts and calls in stocks that the fund manager thinks are about to fall or rise sharply; if the fund manager is right, large profits can be earned through EXERCISE of the options. The LEVERAGE that options provide makes it possible to multiply the return on invested funds many times over.

OPTION PREMIUM amount per share paid by an OPTION buyer to an option seller for the right to buy (call) or sell (put) the underlying security at a particular price within a specified period. Option premium prices are quoted in increments of eighths or sixteenths of 1% and are printed in the options tables of daily newspapers. A PREMIUM of $5 per share means an option buyer would pay $500 for an option on 100 shares. *See also* CALL OPTION; PUT OPTION.

OPTION PRICE market price at which an option contract is trading at any particular time. The price of an option on a stock reflects the fact that it covers 100 shares of a stock. So, for example, an option that is quoted at $7 would cost $700, because it would be an option for 100 shares of stock at a $7 cost per share covered. The option price is determined by many factors, including its INTRINSIC VALUE, time to expiration, volatility of the underlying stock, interest rates, dividends, and marketplace adjustments for supply and demand. Options on indices, debt instruments, currencies, and commodities also have prices determined by many of the same forces. Options prices are published daily in the business pages of many newspapers.

OPTIONS CLEARING CORPORATION (OCC) corporation that handles options transactions on the stock exchanges and is owned by the exchanges. It issues all options contracts and guarantees that the obligations of both parties to a trade are fulfilled. The OCC also processes the exchange of money on all options trades and maintains records of those trades. Its prospectus is given to all investors to read before they can trade in options. This prospectus outlines the rules and risks of trading and sets the standards for ethical conduct on the part of options traders. *See also* OPTION.

OPTION SERIES options of the same class (puts or calls with the same underlying security) that also have the same EXERCISE PRICE and maturity month. For instance, all XYZ October 80 calls are a series, as are all ABC July 100 puts. *See also* OPTION.

OPTION SPREAD buying and selling of options within the same CLASS at the same time. The investor who uses the OPTION spread strategy hopes to profit from the widening or narrowing of the SPREAD between the various options. Option spreads can be designed to be profitable in either up or down markets.
Some examples:
(1) entering into two options at the same EXERCISE PRICE, but with different maturity dates. For instance, an investor could buy an XYZ April 60 call and sell an XYZ July 60 call.
(2) entering into two options at different STRIKE PRICES with the same expiration month. For example, an investor could buy an XYZ April 60 call and sell an XYZ April 70 call.
(3) entering into two options at different strike prices with different expiration months. For instance, an investor could buy an XYZ April 60 call and sell an XYZ July 70 call.

OPTION WRITER person or financial institution that sells put and call options. A writer of a PUT OPTION contracts to buy 100 shares of stock from the put option buyer by a certain date for a fixed price. For example, an option writer who sells XYZ April 50 put agrees to buy XYZ stock from the put buyer at $50 a share any time until the contract expires in April.

A writer of a CALL OPTION, on the other hand, guarantees to sell the call option buyer the underlying stock at a particular price before a certain date. For instance, a writer of an XYZ April 50 call agrees to sell stock at $50 a share to the call buyer any time before April.

In exchange for granting this right, the option writer receives a payment called an OPTION PREMIUM. For holders of large portfolios of the premiums from stocks, option writing therefore is a source of additional income.

ORAL CONTRACT contract between two parties that has been spoken, but not agreed to in writing or signed by both parties. Oral contracts are usually legally enforceable, though not in the case of real estate.

OR BETTER indication, abbreviated OB on the ORDER TICKET of a LIMIT ORDER to buy or sell securities, that the broker should transact the order at a price better than the specified LIMIT PRICE if a better price can be obtained.

ORDER

Investments: instruction to a broker or dealer to buy or sell securities or commodities. Securities orders fall into four basic categories: MARKET ORDER, LIMIT ORDER, time order, and STOP ORDER.

Law: direction from a court of jurisdiction, or a regulation.

Negotiable instruments: payee's request to the maker, as on a check stating, "Pay to the order of (when presented by) John Doe."

Trade: request to buy, sell, deliver, or receive goods or services which commits the issuer of the order to the terms specified.

ORDER IMBALANCE large number of buy or sell orders for a stock, causing an unusually wide spread between bid and offer prices. Stock exchanges frequently halt trading of a stock with a significant order imbalance until more buyers or sellers appear and an orderly market can be reestablished. A significant order imbalance on the buying side can occur when there is an announcement of an impending takeover of the company, better-than-expected earnings, or other unexpected positive news. A significant order imbalance on the selling side can occur when a takeover offer has fallen through, a key executive has left the company, earnings came in far worse than expected, or there is other unexpected negative news.

ORDER ROOM department in a brokerage firm that receives all orders to buy or sell securities. ORDER TICKETS are processed through the order room.

ORDER SPLITTING practice prohibited by rules of the National Association of Securities Dealers (NASD) whereby brokers might split orders in order to qualify them as small orders for purposes of automatic execution by the SMALL ORDER EXECUTION SYSTEM (SOES).

ORDER TICKET form completed by a registered representative (ACCOUNT EXECUTIVE) of a brokerage firm, upon receiving order instructions from a customer. It shows whether the order is to buy or to sell, the number of units, the name of the security, the kind of order (ORDER MARKET, LIMIT ORDER or STOP ORDER) and the customer's name or code number. After execution of the order on the exchange floor or in the firm's trading department (if over the counter), the price is written and circled on the order ticket, and the completing broker is indicated by number. The order ticket must be retained for a certain period in compliance with federal law.

ORDINARY INCOME income from the normal activities of an individual or business, as distinguished from CAPITAL GAINS from the sale of assets. Prior to the TAX REFORM ACT OF 1986, the long-term CAPITAL GAINS TAX was lower than that on ordinary income. The 1986 Act eliminated the preferential capital gains rate, but it kept the separate statutory language to allow for future increases in ordinary income rates. In 1991, capital gains were limited to 28%.

ORDINARY INTEREST simple interest based on a 360-day year rather than on a 365-day year (the latter is called *exact interest*). The difference between the two bases when calculating daily interest on large sums of money can be substantial. The ratio of ordinary interest to exact interest is 1.0139.

ORGANIZATION CHART chart showing the interrelationships of positions within an organization in terms of authority and responsibility. There are basically three patterns of organization: *line organization*, in which a single manager has final authority over a group of foremen or middle management supervisors; *functional organization*, in which a general manager supervises a number of managers identified by function; and *line and staff organization*, which is a combination of line and functional organization, with specialists in particular functions holding staff positions where they advise line officers concerned with actual production.

ORGANIZED SECURITIES EXCHANGE STOCK EXCHANGE as distinguished from an OVER-THE-COUNTER MARKET. *See also* SECURITIES AND COMMODITIES EXCHANGES.

ORIGINAL COST
1. in accounting, all costs associated with the acquisition of an asset.
2. in public utilities accounting, the acquisition cost incurred by the entity that first devotes a property to public use; normally, the utility company's cost for the property. It is used to establish the rate to be charged customers in order to provide the utility company with a FAIR RATE OF RETURN on capital.

ORIGINAL ISSUE DISCOUNT (OID) discount from PAR VALUE at the time a bond or other debt instrument, such as a STRIP, is issued. (Although the par value of bonds is normally $1000, $100 is used when traders quote prices.) A bond may be issued at $50 ($500) per bond instead of $100 ($1000), for example. The bond will mature at $100 (1000), however, so that an investor has a built-in gain if the bond is held until maturity. The most extreme version of an original issue discount is a ZERO-COUPON BOND, which is originally sold at far below par value and pays no interest until it matures. The REVENUE RECONCILIATION ACT OF 1993 extended OID rules to include stripped preferred stock.
    The tax treatment of original issue discount bonds is complex. The Internal Revenue Service assumes a certain rate of appreciation of the bond every year until maturity. No capital gain or loss will be incurred if the bond is sold for that estimated amount. But if the bond is sold for more than the assumed amount, a CAPITAL GAINS TAX or a tax at the ORDINARY INCOME rate is due.
    SAVINGS BONDS are exempt from OID rules.

ORIGINAL MATURITY interval between the issue date and the maturity date of a bond, as distinguished from CURRENT MATURITY, which is the time difference between the present time and the maturity date. For example, in 1997 a bond issued in 1995 to mature in 2010 would have an original maturity of 15 years and a current maturity of 13 years.

ORIGINATOR
1. bank, savings and loan, or mortgage banker that initially made the mortgage loan comprising part of a pool of mortgages.
2. investment banking firm that worked with the issuer of a new securities offering from the early planning stages and that usually is appointed manager of

the underwriting SYNDICATE; more formally called the *originating investment banker.*

3. in banking terminology, the initiator of money transfer instructions.

ORPHAN STOCK stock that has been neglected by research analysts. Since the company's story is rarely followed and the stock infrequently recommended, it is considered an orphan by investors. Orphan stocks may not attract much attention because they are too small, or because they have disappointed investors in the past. Because they are followed by so few investors, orphan stocks tend to trade at low price/earnings ratios. However, if the company assembles a solid record of rising profitability, it can be discovered again by research analysts, boosting the stock price and price/earnings ratio significantly. Investors who buy the stock when it is still a neglected orphan can thereby earn high returns. Also called a *wallflower.*

OSLO STOCK EXCHANGE smallest of the Scandinavian exchanges. Founded in 1819 as a foreign exchange market, it later was a commodity exchange; securities were launched in 1881. The stock exchanges in Bergen and Trondheim, Norway, are branches of the OSE. The OSE trades stocks, bonds, and stock options, and is considered the options market of Norway. Energy-related companies dominate the listings. The Oslo Stock Exchange General Price Index is made up of nearly 50 stocks. All trading is conducted electronically, and trades are settled a maximum of seven days from the transaction date. Trading hours are 8:30 A.M. to 4:30 P.M., Monday through Friday.

OTC *see* OVER THE COUNTER.

OTC BULLETIN BOARD electronic listing of bid and asked quotations of over-the-counter stocks not meeting the minimum-net worth and other requirements of the NASDAQ stock-listing system. The new system, which was developed by the National Association of Securities Dealers (NASD) and approved by the Securities and Exchange Commission in 1990, provides continuously updated data on domestic stocks and twice-daily updates on foreign stocks. It was designed to facilitate trading and provide greater surveillance of stocks traditionally reported on once daily in the PINK SHEETS published by NATIONAL QUOTATION BUREAU.

OTC MARGIN STOCK shares of certain large firms traded OVER THE COUNTER that qualify as margin securities under REGULATION T of the Federal Reserve Board. Such stock must meet rigid criteria, and the list of eligible OTC shares is under constant review by the Fed. *See also* MARGIN SECURITY.

OTHER INCOME heading on a profit and loss statement for income from activities not in the normal course of business: sometimes called *other revenue.* Examples: interest on customers' notes, dividends and interest from investments, profit from the disposal of assets other than inventory, gain on foreign exchange, miscellaneous rent income. *See also* EXTRAORDINARY ITEM.

OTHER PEOPLE'S MONEY *see* OPM.

OUT-OF-FAVOR INDUSTRY OR STOCK industry or stock that is currently unpopular with investors. For example, the investing public may be disenchanted with an industry's poor earnings outlook. If interest rates were rising, interest-sensitive stocks such as banks and savings and loans would be out of favor because rising rates might harm these firms' profits. CONTRARIAN investors—those who consciously do the opposite of most other investors—tend to buy out-of-favor stocks because they can be bought cheaply. When the earnings of these stocks pick up, contrarians typically sell the stocks. Out-of-favor stocks tend to have a low PRICE/EARNINGS RATIO.

OUT OF LINE term describing a stock that is too high or too low in price in comparison with similar-quality stocks. A comparison of this sort is usually based on the PRICE/EARNINGS RATIO (PE), which measures how much investors are willing to pay for a firm's earnings prospects. If most computer industry stocks had PEs of 15, for instance, and XYZ Computers had a PE of only 10, analysts would say that XYZ's price is out of line with the rest of the industry.

OUT OF THE MONEY term used to describe an OPTION whose STRIKE PRICE for a stock is either higher than the current market value, in the case of a CALL, or lower, in the case of a PUT. For example, an XYZ December 60 CALL option would be out of the money when XYZ stock was selling for $55 a share. Similarly, an XYZ December 60 PUT OPTION would be out of the money when XYZ stock was selling for $65 a share.

Someone buying an out-of-the-money option hopes that the option will move IN THE MONEY, or at least in that direction. The buyer of the above XYZ call would want the stock to climb above $60 a share, whereas the put buyer would like the stock to drop below $60 a share.

OUTSIDE DIRECTOR member of a company's BOARD OF DIRECTORS who is not an employee of the company. Such directors are considered important because they are presumed to bring unbiased opinions to major corporate decisions and also can contribute diverse experience to the decision-making process. A retailing company may have outside directors with experience in finance and manufacturing, for instance. To avoid conflict of interest, outside directors never serve on the boards of two directly competing corporations. Directors receive fees from the company in return for their service, usually a set amount for each board meeting they attend.

OUTSTANDING
1. unpaid; used of ACCOUNTS RECEIVABLE and debt obligations of all types.
2. not yet presented for payment, as a check or draft.
3. stock held by shareholders, shown on corporate balance sheets under the heading of CAPITAL STOCK issued and outstanding.

OUT THE WINDOW term describing the rapid way a very successful NEW ISSUE of securities is marketed to investors. An issue that goes out the window is also called a BLOWOUT. *See also* HOT ISSUE.

OVER-AGE-55 HOME SALE EXEMPTION regulation in the federal tax code permitting an individual over the age of 55 to exclude up to $125,000 in capital gain on the sale of his primary residence once in his lifetime. The individual must have lived in the home as the primary residence for three of the past five years in order to qualify. The exclusion is allowed even if the proceeds from the home sale are not reinvested in another property. For example, if a 56-year-old person who bought a house for $100,000 sells the house for $300,000, he can choose to exclude $125,000 of the $200,000 gain and pay capital gains tax on the remaining $75,000 profit. Congress enacted this rule to prevent older people from having to pay capital gains taxes on housing appreciation that was mainly caused by inflation.

OVERALL MARKET PRICE COVERAGE total assets less intangibles divided by the total of (1) the MARKET VALUE of the security issue in question and (2) the

BOOK VALUE of liabilities and issues having a prior claim. The answer indicates the extent to which the market value of a particular CLASS of securities is covered in the event of a company's liquidation.

OVERBOOKED *see* OVERSUBSCRIBED.

OVERBOUGHT description of a security or a market that has recently experienced an unexpectedly sharp price rise and is therefore vulnerable to a price drop (called a CORRECTION by technical analysts). When a stock has been overbought, there are fewer buyers left to drive the price up further. *See also* OVERSOLD.

OVERDRAFT extension of credit by a lending institution. An overdraft check for which there are not sufficent funds (NSF) available may be rejected (bounced) by the bank. A bounced-check charge will be assessed on the check-writer's account. Alternatively, the bank customer may set up an overdraft loan account, which will cover NSF checks. While the customer's check will clear, the account will be charged overdraft check fees or interest on the outstanding balance of the loan starting immediately.

OVERHANG sizable block of securities or commodities contracts that, if released on the market, would put downward pressure on prices. Examples of overhang include shares held in a dealer's inventory, a large institutional holding, a secondary distribution still in registration, and a large commodity position about to be liquidated. Overhang inhibits buying activity that would otherwise translate into upward price movement.

OVERHEAD
1. costs of a business that are not directly associated with the production or sale of goods or services. Also called INDIRECT COSTS AND EXPENSES, *burden* and, in Great Britain, *on costs*.
2. sometimes used in a more limited sense, as in manufacturing or factory overhead.

   See also DIRECT OVERHEAD.

OVERHEATING term describing an economy that is expanding so rapidly that economists fear a rise in INFLATION. In an overheated economy, too much money is chasing too few goods, leading to price rises, and the productive capacity of a nation is usually nearing its limit. The remedies in the United States are usually a tightening of the money supply by the Federal Reserve and curbs in federal government spending. *See also* MONETARY POLICY; OPTIMUM CAPACITY.

OVERISSUE shares of CAPITAL STOCK issued in excess of those authorized. Preventing overissue is the function of a corporation's REGISTRAR (usually a bank acting as agent), which works closely with the TRANSFER AGENT in canceling and reissuing certificates presented for transfer and in issuing new shares.

OVERLAPPING DEBT municipal accounting term referring to a municipality's share of the debt of its political subdivisions or the special districts sharing its geographical area. It is usually determined by the ratio of ASSESSED VALUATION of taxable property lying within the corporate limits of the municipality to the assessed valuation of each overlapping district. Overlapping debt is often greater than the direct debt of a municipality, and both must be taken into account in determining the debt burden carried by taxable real estate within a municipality when evaluating MUNICIPAL BOND investments.

OVERNIGHT POSITION broker-dealer's LONG POSITION or SHORT POSITION in a security at the end of a trading day.

OVERNIGHT REPO overnight REPURCHASE AGREEMENT; an arrangement whereby securities dealers and banks finance their inventories of Treasury bills, notes, and bonds. The dealer or bank sells securities to an investor with a temporary surplus of cash, agreeing to buy them back the next day. Such transactions are settled in immediately available FEDERAL FUNDS, usually at a rate below the federal funds rate (the rate charged by banks lending funds to each other).

OVERSHOOT to exceed a target figure, such as an economic goal or an earnings projection.

OVERSOLD description of a stock or market that has experienced an unexpectedly sharp price decline and is therefore due, according to some proponents of TECHNICAL ANALYSIS, for an imminent price rise. If all those who wanted to sell a stock have done so, there are no sellers left, and so the price will rise. *See also* OVERBOUGHT.

OVERSUBSCRIBED underwriting term describing a new stock issue for which there are more buyers than available shares. An oversubscribed, or *overbooked,* issue often will jump in price as soon as its shares go on the market, since the buyers who could not get shares will want to buy once the stock starts trading. In some cases, an issuer will increase the number of shares available if the issue is oversubscribed. *See also* GREEN SHOE; HOT ISSUE.

OVER THE COUNTER (OTC)
1. security that is not listed and traded on an organized exchange.
2. market in which securities transactions are conducted through a telephone and computer network connecting dealers in stocks and bonds, rather than on the floor of an exchange.

Over-the-counter stocks are traditionally those of smaller companies that do not meet the LISTING REQUIREMENTS of the New York Stock Exchange or the American Stock Exchange. In recent years, however, many companies that qualify for listing have chosen to remain with over-the-counter trading, because they feel that the system of multiple trading by many dealers is preferable to the centralized trading approach of the New York Stock Exchange, where all trading in a stock has to go through the exchange SPECIALIST in that stock. The rules of over-the-counter stock trading are written and enforced largely by the NATIONAL ASSOCIATION OF SECURITIES DEALERS (NASD), a self-regulatory group. Prices of over-the-counter stocks are published in daily newspapers, with the NATIONAL MARKET SYSTEM stocks listed separately from the rest of the over-the-counter market. Other over-the-counter markets include those for government and municipal bonds. *See also* NASDAQ.

OVERTRADING
Finance: practice of a firm that expands sales beyond levels that can be financed with normal WORKING CAPITAL. Continued overtrading leads to delinquent ACCOUNTS PAYABLE and ultimately to default on borrowings.

New issue underwriting: practice whereby a member of an underwriting group induces a brokerage client to buy a portion of a new issue by purchasing other securities from the client at a premium. The underwriter breaks even on the deal because the premium is offset by the UNDERWRITING SPREAD.

Securities: excessive buying and selling by a broker in a DISCRETIONARY ACCOUNT. *See also* CHURNING.

OVERVALUED description of a stock whose current price is not justified by the earnings outlook or the PRICE/EARNINGS RATIO. It is therefore expected that the stock will drop in price. Overvaluation may result from an emotional buying spurt, which inflates the market price of the stock, or from a deterioration of the company's financial strength. The opposite of overvalued is UNDERVALUED. *See also* FULLY VALUED.

OVERWITHHOLDING situation in which a taxpayer has too much federal, state, or local income tax withheld from salary. Because they have overwithheld, these taxpayers will usually be due income tax refunds after they file their tax returns by April 15. Overwithholding is not desirable for the taxpayer, because it is, in effect, granting the government an interest-free loan. To reduce overwithholding, a taxpayer must file a new W-4 form with his or her employer, increasing the number of dependents claimed, which will reduce the amount of tax withheld. *See also* UNDERWITHHOLDING.

OVERWRITING speculative practice by an OPTION WRITER who believes a security to be overpriced or underpriced and sells CALL OPTIONS or PUT OPTIONS on the security in quantity, assuming they will not be exercised. *See also* OPTION.

OWNER'S EQUITY PAID-IN CAPITAL, donated capital, and RETAINED EARNINGS less the LIABILITIES of a corporation.

P

PAC BOND acronym for *planned amortization class bond,* PAC is a TRANCHE class offered by some COLLATERIZED MORTGAGE OBLIGATIONS (CMOs), which is unlike other CMO classes in that (1) it has a sinking fund schedule that is observed as long as the prepayments on underlying mortgages remain within a broad range of speeds and (2) its ability to make principal payments is not subordinated to other classes. PAC bonds thus offer certainty of cash flow except in extreme prepayment situations, and because of this they trade at a premium to comparable traditional CMOs. *See also* TAC BONDS.

PACIFIC STOCK EXCHANGE *see* REGIONAL STOCK EXCHANGES.

PACKAGE MORTGAGE mortgage on both a house and durable personal property in the house, such as appliances and furniture. The borrower therefore repays one mortgage loan instead of having to carry two loans. In construction lending, interim and takeout loans made by the same investor.

PAC-MAN STRATEGY technique used by a corporation that is the target of a takeover bid to defeat the acquirer's wishes. The TARGET COMPANY defends itself by threatening to take over the acquirer and begins buying its common shares. For instance, if company A moves to take over company B against the wishes of the management of company B, company B will begin buying shares in company A in order to thwart A's takeover attempt. The Pac-Man strategy is named after a popular video game of the early 1980s, in which each character that does not swallow its opponents is itself consumed. *See also* TAKEOVER; TENDER OFFER.

PAID-IN CAPITAL capital received from investors in exchange for stock, as distinguished from capital generated from earnings or donated. The paid-in capital account includes CAPITAL STOCK and contributions of stockholders credited to accounts other than capital stock, such as an excess over PAR value received from the sale or exchange of capital stock. It would also include surplus resulting from RECAPITALIZATION. Paid-in capital is sometimes classified more specifically as *additional paid-in capital, paid-in surplus,* or *capital surplus.* Such accounts are distinguished from RETAINED EARNINGS or its older variation, EARNED SURPLUS. *See also* DONATED STOCK.

PAID-IN SURPLUS *see* PAID-IN CAPITAL.

PAID UP a situation in which all payments due have been made. For example, if all premiums on a life insurance policy have been paid, it is known as a PAID-UP POLICY.

PAID-UP POLICY life insurance policy in which all premiums have been paid. Some policies require premium payments for a limited number of years, and if all premium payments have been made over those years, the policy is considered paid in full and requires no more premium payments. Such a policy remains in force until the insured person dies or cancels the policy.

PAINTING THE TAPE
1. illegal practice by manipulators who buy and sell a particular security among themselves to create artificial trading activity, causing a succession of trades to be reported on the CONSOLIDATED TAPE and luring unwary investors to be "action." After causing movement in the market price of the security, the manipulators hope to sell at a profit.
2. consecutive or frequent trading in a particular security, resulting in its repeated appearances on the ticker tape. Such activity is usually attributable to special investor interest in the security.

PAIRED SHARES common stocks of two companies under the same management that are sold as a unit, usually appearing as a single certificate printed front and back. Also called *Siamese shares* or *stapled stock.*

P & I abbreviations for *principal* and *interest* on bonds or mortgage-backed securities. A traditional debt instrument such as a bond makes periodic interest payments and returns bondholders' principal when the bond matures. But in many cases, the principal payment and each of the interest payments are separated from each other by brokerage firms and sold in pieces. When accomplished with Treasury bonds, each of the individual interest payments and the final principal payment is sold as a "stripped" zero-coupon bond known as a STRIP. In the case of a mortgage-backed security, each of the interest payments and principal repayments from mortgagees is packaged into a COLLATERALIZED MORTGAGE OBLIGATION. A security composed of only interest payments is known as an *interest-only* or *IO* security. A security composed of just principal repayments is known as a *principal-only* or PO security. Both IOs and POs are forms of DERIVATIVE SECURITIES.

P & L *see* PROFIT AND LOSS STATEMENT.

PANIC BUYING OR SELLING flurry of buying or selling accompanied by high volume done in anticipation of sharply rising or falling prices. A sudden news event will trigger panic buying or selling, leaving investors little time to evaluate the fundamentals of individual stocks or bonds. Panic buying may be caused by an unexpected cut in interest rates or outcome of a political election. Short sellers may also be forced into panic buying if stock prices start to rise quickly, and they have to cover their short positions to prevent further losses. Panic selling may be set off by an international crisis such as a war or currency devaluation, the assassination of a head of state, or other unforeseen event. If stock prices start to fall sharply, investors may start to panic sell because they fear prices will fall much farther.

PAPER shorthand for *short-term commercial paper,* which is an unsecured note issued by a corporation. The term is also more loosely used to refer to all debt issued by a company, as in "ABC has $100 million in short and long-term paper outstanding."

PAPER DEALER brokerage firm that buys COMMERCIAL PAPER at one rate of interest, usually discounted, and resells it at a lower rate to banks and other investors, making a profit on the difference.

PAPER PROFIT OR LOSS unrealized CAPITAL GAIN or CAPITAL LOSS in an investment or PORTFOLIO. Paper profits and losses are calculated by comparing the current market prices of all stocks, bonds, mutual funds, and commodities in a portfolio to the prices at which those assets were originally bought. These profits or losses become realized only when the securities are sold.

PAPER TRADING *see* MOCK TRADING.

PAR equal to the nominal or FACE VALUE of a security. A bond selling at par, for instance, is worth the same dollar amount it was issued for or at which it will be redeemed at maturity—typically, $1000 per bond.

　　With COMMON STOCK, par value is set by the company issuing the stock At one time, par value represented the original investment behind each share of stock in goods, cash, and services, but today this is rarely the case. Instead, it is an assigned amount (such as $1 a share) used to compute the dollar accounting value of the common shares on a company's balance sheet. Par value has no relation to MARKET VALUE, which is determined by such considerations as NET ASSET VALUE, YIELD, and investors' expectations of future earnings. Some companies issue NO-PAR VALUE STOCK. *See also* STATED VALUE.

　　Par value has more importance for bonds and PREFERRED STOCK. The interest paid on bonds is based on a percentage of a bond's par value—a 10% bond pays 10% of the bond's par value annually. Preferred dividends are normally stated as a percentage of the par value of the preferred stock issue.

PAR BOND bond that is selling at PAR, the amount equal to its nominal value or FACE VALUE. A corporate bond redeemable at maturity for $1000 is a par bond when it trades on the market for $1000.

PARENT COMPANY company that owns or controls subsidiaries through the ownership of voting stock. A parent company is usually an operating company in its own right; where it has no business of its own, the term HOLDING COMPANY is often preferred.

PARETO'S LAW theory that the pattern of income distribution is constant, historically and geographically, regardless of taxation or welfare policies; also called *law of the trivial many and the critical few* or *80-20 law.* Thus, if 80% of a nation's income will benefit only 20% of the population, the only way to improve the economic lot of the poor is to increase overall output and income levels.

　　Other applications of the law include the idea that in most business activities a small percentage of the work force produces the major portion of output or that 20% of the customers account for 80% of the dollar volume of sales. The law is attributed to Vilfredo Pareto, an Italian-Swiss engineer and economist (1848–1923).

　　Pareto is also credited with the concept called *Paretian optimum* (or *optimality*) that resources are optimally distributed when an individual cannot move into a better position without putting someone else into a worse position.

PARIS BOURSE national stock market of France, formed in 1991 when the computerized trading system in Paris was extended to the regional exchanges. The electronic system, modeled on the CATS (Computer Assisted Trading System)

system at the TORONTO STOCK EXCHANGE, operates from 10 A.M. to 5 P.M., Monday through Friday. SOCIETES DE BOURSE are the brokerage firms that trade on the exchange. The CAC 40 INDEX is the underlying index for derivative products which are traded on the MONEP, a subsidiary of the Paris Bourse. The SBF 120 Index is made up of the top 120 stocks based on liquidity and capitalization. The SBF 250 Index is the indicator of the wider French economy. Settlement is three business days after the trade.

PARITY *see* CONVERSION PARITY.

PARITY PRICE price for a commodity or service that is pegged to another price or to a composite average of prices based on a selected prior period. As the two sets of prices vary, they are reflected in an index number on a scale of 100. For example, U.S. farm prices are pegged to prices based on the purchasing power of farmers in the period from 1910 to 1914. If the parity ratio is below 100, reflecting a reduction in purchasing power to the extent indicated, the government compensates the farmer by paying a certain percentage of parity, either in the form of a direct cash payment, in the purchase of surplus crops, or in a NONRECOURSE LOAN.

The concept of parity is also widely applied in industrial wage contracts as a means of preserving the real value of wages.

PARKING placing assets in a safe investment while other investment alternatives are under consideration. For instance, an investor will park the proceeds of a stock or bond sale in an interest-bearing money market fund while considering what other stocks or bonds to purchase. Term also refers to an illegal practice whereby ownership of stock is concealed, and DISCLOSURE requirements circumvented, by holding stock in the name of a conspiring party.

PARTIAL DELIVERY term used when a broker does not deliver the full amount of a security or commodity called for by a contract. If 10,000 shares were to be delivered, for example, and only 7000 shares are transferred, it is called a partial delivery.

PARTICIPATING DIVIDEND dividend paid from PARTICIPATING PREFERRED STOCK.

PARTICIPATING LIFE INSURANCE POLICIES life insurance that pays dividends to policyholders. The policyholders participate in the success or failure of the company's underwriting and investment performance by having their dividends rise or fall. The fewer claims the company experiences and the better its investment performance, the higher the dividends. Policyholders have many choices in what they can do with the dividends. They can have them paid in cash, in which case the income is taxable in the year received; they can use them to reduce policy premiums; they can buy more paid-up insurance, either cash value or term; or they can put them in an account with the insurance company that earns interest. The opposite of a participating policy is a NONPARTICIPATING LIFE INSURANCE POLICY.

PARTICIPATING PREFERRED STOCK PREFERRED STOCK that, in addition to paying a stipulated dividend, gives the holder the right to participate with the common stockholder in additional distributions of earnings under specified conditions. One example would be an arrangement whereby preferred shareholders are paid $5 per share, then common shareholders are paid $5 per share, and then preferred and common shareholders share equally in further dividends up to $1 per share in any one year.

Participating preferred issues are rare. They are used when special measures are necessary to attract investors. Most preferred stock is *nonparticipating preferred stock,* paying only the stipulated dividends.

PARTICIPATION CERTIFICATE certificate representing an interest in a POOL of funds or in other instruments, such as a MORTGAGE POOL. The following quasi-governmental agencies issue and/or guarantee such certificates (also called PASS-THROUGH SECURITIES): FEDERAL HOME LOAN MORTGAGE CORPORATION, FEDERAL NATIONAL MORTGAGE ASSOCIATION, GOVERNMENT NATIONAL MORTGAGE ASSOCIATION, SALLIE MAE.

PARTICIPATION LOAN

Commercial lending: loan made by more than one lender and serviced (administered) by one of the participants, called the *lead bank* or *lead lender.* Participation loans make it possible for large borrowers to obtain bank financing when the amount involved exceeds the legal lending limit of an individual bank (approximately 10% of a bank's capital).

Real estate: mortgage loan, made by a lead lender, in which other lenders own an interest.

PARTNERSHIP contract between two or more people in a joint business who agree to pool their funds and talent and share in the profits and losses of the enterprise. Those who are responsible for the day-to-day management of the partnership's activities, whose individual acts are binding on the other partners, and who are personally liable for the partnership's total liabilities are called *general partners.* Those who contribute only money and are not involved in management decisions are called *limited partners;* their liability is limited to their investment.

Partnerships are a common form of organization for service professions such as accounting and law. Each accountant or lawyer made a partner earns a percentage of the firm's profits.

Limited partnerships are also sold to investors by brokerage firms, financial planners, and other registered representatives. These partnerships may be either public (meaning that a large number of investors will participate and the partnership's plans must be filed with the Securities and Exchange Commission) or private (meaning that only a limited number of investors may participate and the plan need not be filed with the SEC). Both public and private limited partnerships invest in real estate, oil and gas, research and development, and equipment leasing. Some of these partnerships are oriented towards offering tax advantages and capital gains to limited partners, while others are designed to provide mostly income and some capital gains.

See also GENERAL PARTNER; LIMITED PARTNERSHIP; OIL AND GAS LIMITED PARTNERSHIP; PRIVATE LIMITED PARTNERSHIP; PUBLIC LIMITED PARTNERSHIP.

PARTNERSHIP AGREEMENT written agreement among partners specifying the conduct of the partnership, including the division of earnings, procedures for dividing up assets if the partnership is dissolved, and steps to be followed when a partner becomes disabled or dies. Investors in LIMITED PARTNERSHIPS also receive partnership agreements, detailing their rights and responsibilities.

PAR VALUE *see* PAR.

PAR VALUE OF CURRENCY ratio of one nation's currency unit to that of another country, as defined by the official exchange rates between the two countries; also called *par of exchange* or *par exchange rate.* Since 1971, exchange rates have been allowed to float; that is, instead of official rates of exchange, currency values are being determined by the forces of supply and demand in combination with the buying and selling by countries of their own currencies in order to stabilize the market value, a form of PEGGING.

PASSBOOK book issued by a bank to record deposits, withdrawals, and interest earned in a savings account, usually known as a passbook savings account. The passbook lists the depositor's name and account number as well as all transactions. Passbook savings accounts, though usually offering low yields, are safe because deposits in them are insured up to $100,000 by the Federal Deposit Insurance Corporation. There are many alternatives to passbooks today, including ATM machines, telephone banking services, and unlimited transfers.

PASSED DIVIDEND *see* OMITTED DIVIDEND; CUMULATIVE PREFERRED.

PASSIVE income or loss from activities in which a taxpayer does not materially participate, such as LIMITED PARTNERSHIPS, as distinguished from (1) income from wages and active trade or business or (2) *investment (or portfolio) income,* such as dividends and interest. Starting with the TAX REFORM ACT OF 1986, and after modification by the REVENUE RECONCILIATION ACT OF 1993, losses and credits from passive activities are deductible only against income and tax from passive activities, although one passive activity can offset another and unused passive losses can be carried forward until the earlier of (1) your realization of passive income to offset such losses; or (2) your sale of your entire interest in the activity, at which time suspended losses from that activity can be used without limitation. Under the 1986 Act, real estate rental activities were considered passive regardless of material participation. The 1993 Act liberalized that provision for tax years after 1993 by making an exception for professionals spending at least half their time or at least 750 hours involved in real property trade or services or for anyone, apparently including a landlord, meeting the same tests of material participation. Regular corporations (as opposed to S corporations) are exempt from passive activity rules unless they are closely held.

PASSIVE ACTIVITY LOSS (PAL) loss produced by PASSIVE investment activities. *See also* PASSIVE INCOME GENERATOR (PIG).

PASSIVE BOND BOND that yields no interest. Such bonds arise out of reorganizations or are used in NOT-FOR-PROFIT fund raising.

PASSIVE INCOME GENERATOR (PIG) investment whose main attraction is PASSIVE income. The most common example is an income-oriented real estate LIMITED PARTNERSHIP, especially an UNLEVERAGED PROGRAM. Since Tax Reform PASSIVE ACTIVITY LOSSES (PALs) are deductible to the limit of passive activity income, so an investor with excess PALs might buy a PIG as a source of tax-sheltered income.

PASSIVE INVESTING
1. putting money in an investment deemed *passive* by the Internal Revenue Service, such as a LIMITED PARTNERSHIP.
2. investing in a MUTUAL FUND that replicates a market index, such as the STANDARD & POOR'S INDEX, thus assuring investment performance no worse (or better) than the market as a whole. An INDEX FUND charges a much lower MANAGEMENT FEE than an ordinary mutual fund.

PASS THE BOOK system to transfer responsibility for a brokerage firm's trading account from one office to another around the world as trading ends in one place and begins in another. For example, a firm may start the day with the "book" of the firm's securities inventory controlled in London. As the London market closes, the book will be passed to New York, then Los Angeles, then Tokyo, then

Singapore, and back to London. Passing the book is necessary because markets are now traded 24 hours a day. Customers wanting to trade at any time will often be referred to the office handling the book at that time.

PASS-THROUGH SECURITY security, representing pooled debt obligations repackaged as shares, that passes income from debtors through the intermediary to investors. The most common type of pass-through is a MORTGAGE-BACKED CERTIFICATE, usually government-guaranteed, where homeowners' principal and interest payments pass from the originating bank or savings and loan through a government agency or investment bank to investors, net of service charges. Pass-throughs representing other types of assets, such as auto loan paper or student loans, are also widely marketed. *See also* CERTIFICATE OF AUTOMOBILE RECEIVABLES (CARS); COLLATERALIZED MORTGAGE OBLIGATION; REMIC.

PATENT exclusive right to a use a process or produce or sell a particular product for a designated period of time. In the United States the Patent and Trademarks Office issues design patents good for 14 years and plant and utility patents good for 17 years.

PATTERN technical chart formation made by price movements of stocks, bonds, commodities, or mutual funds. Analysts use patterns to predict future price movements. Some examples of patterns include ASCENDING TOPS; DOUBLE BOTTOM; FLAG; HEAD AND SHOULDERS; RISING BOTTOMS; SAUCER; and TRIANGLE. *See also* TECHNICAL ANALYSIS.

PAWNBROKER individual or employee of a pawn shop who lends money at a high rate of interest to a borrower leaving COLLATERAL such as jewelry, furs, appliances, or other valuable items. If the loan is repaid, the borrower gets the collateral back. If the loan is not repaid, the pawnbroker keeps the collateral, and in many cases, sells it to the public. Borrowers who turn to pawnbrokers and pawn shops typically do not have access to credit from banks or other financial institutions because they are in poor financial condition.

PAY-AS-YOU-GO BASIS INCOME TAX payment option, whereby an employer deducts and remits to the Internal Revenue Service a portion of an employee's monthly salary. Also refers generally to any service that is paid for as it is used.

PAYBACK PERIOD in capital budgeting; the length of time needed to recoup the cost of a CAPITAL INVESTMENT. The payback period is the ratio of the initial investment (cash outlay) to the annual cash inflows for the recovery period. The major shortcoming of the payback period method is that it does not take into account cash flows after the payback period and is therefore not a measure of the profitability of an investment project. For this reason, analysts generally prefer the DISCOUNTED CASH FLOW methods of capital budgeting—namely, the INTERNAL RATE OF RETURN and the NET PRESENT VALUE methods.

PAYDOWN

Bonds: refunding by a company of an outstanding bond issue through a smaller new bond issue, usually to cut interest costs. For instance, a company that issued $100 million of 12% bonds a few years ago will pay down (refund) that debt with a new $80 million issue with an 8% yield. The amount of the net deduction is called the paydown.

Lending: repayment of principal short of full payment. *See also* ON ACCOUNT.

PAYEE person receiving payment through a check, bill, money order, promissory note, credit card, cash, or other payment method.

PAYER person making a payment to a PAYEE through a check, bill, money order, promissory note, cash, credit card, or other form of payment.

PAYING AGENT agent, usually a bank, that receives funds from an issuer of bonds or stock and in turn pays principal and interest to bondholders and dividends to stockholders, usually charging a fee for the service. Sometimes called *disbursing agent.*

PAYMENT DATE date on which a declared stock dividend or a bond interest payment is scheduled to be paid.

PAYMENT IN KIND payment for goods and services made in the form of other goods and services, not cash or other forms of money. Usually, payment in kind is made when the payee returns with the same kind of good or service. For example, if someone's tire blows out, the payee will buy another tire to replace the first one. In the securities world, PAYMENT-IN-KIND SECURITIES pay bondholders in more bonds instead of cash interest. Payment in kind is different from BARTER because the payor gets the same goods and services in return, not other goods or services of equivalent value, as is the case in barter.

PAYMENT-IN-KIND SECURITIES *see* PIK (PAYMENT-IN-KIND) SECURITIES.

PAYOUT RATIO percentage of a firm's profits that is paid out to shareholders in the form of dividends. Young, fast-growing companies reinvest most of their earnings in their business and usually do not pay dividends. Regulated electric, gas, and telephone utility companies have historically paid out larger proportions of their highly dependable earnings in dividends than have other industrial corporations. Since these utilities are limited to a specified return on assets and are thus not able to generate from internal operations the cash flow needed for expansion, they pay large dividends to keep their stock attractive to investors desiring yield and are able to finance growth through new securities offerings. *See also* RETENTION RATE.

PAYROLL WITHHOLDING *see* WITHHOLDING (under Taxes: 1).

PAY UP
1. situation when an investor who wants to buy a stock at a particular price hesitates and the stock begins to rise. Instead of letting the stock go, he "pays up" to buy the shares at the higher prevailing price.
2. when an investor buys shares in a high quality company at what is felt to be a high price. Such an investor will say "I realize that I am paying up for this stock, but it is worth it because it is such a fine company."

PBR abbreviation for price to BOOK VALUE ratio, which is the market value of a company's stock divided by its TANGIBLE NET WORTH. This ratio is especially significant to securities analysts where real estate not used in operations is a significant portion of assets, such as in the case of a typical Japanese company.

PC commonly used abbreviation for PARTICIPATION CERTIFICATE and, in brokerage parlance, for *plus commissions* (which are added to purchases and subtracted from sales).

PEACE DIVIDEND term used to describe the reallocation of spending from military purposes to peacetime priorities. After the end of World War II and at the end of the Cold War, government officials spoke of the peace dividend which could be spent on housing, education, social initiatives, deficit reduction, and other programs instead of on maintaining the military establishment.

PEGGING stabilizing the price of a security, commodity, or currency by intervening in a market. For example, until 1971 governments pegged the price of gold at certain levels to stabilize their currencies and would therefore buy it when the price dropped and sell when the price rose. Since 1971, a FLOATING EXCHANGE RATE system has prevailed, in which countries use pegging—the buying or selling of their own currencies—simply to offset fluctuations in the exchange rate. The U.S. government uses pegging in another way to support the prices of agricultural commodities, *see* PARITY PRICE.

In floating new stock issues, the managing underwriter is authorized to try to peg the market price and stabilize the market in the issuer's stock by buying shares in the open market. With this one exception, securities price pegging is illegal and is regulated by the Securities and Exchange Commission. *See also* STABILIZATION.

PENALTY CLAUSE clause found in contracts, borrowing agreements, and savings instruments providing for penalties in the event a contract is not kept, a loan payment is late, or a withdrawal is made prematurely. *See also* PREPAYMENT PENALTY.

PENNANT technical chart pattern resembling a pointed flag, with the point facing to the right. Unlike a FLAG pattern, in which rallies and peaks occur in a uniform range, it is formed as the rallies and peaks that give it its shape become less pronounced. A pennant is also characterized by diminishing trade volume. With these differences, this pattern has essentially the same significance as a flag; that is, prices will rise or fall sharply once the pattern is complete.

PENNANT

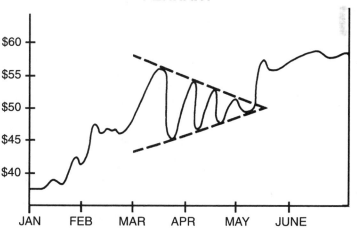

PENNY STOCK stock that typically sells for less than $1 a share, although it may rise to as much as $10 a share after the initial PUBLIC OFFERING, usually because of heavy promotion. Penny stocks are issued by companies with a short or erratic history of revenues and earnings, and therefore such stocks are more VOLATILE than those of large, well-established firms traded on the New York or American stock exchanges. Many brokerage houses therefore have special precautionary rules about trading in these stocks and the SECURITIES AND EXCHANGE COMMISSION (SEC) requires that brokers implement SUITABILITY RULES in writing and obtain written consent from investors.

All penny stocks are traded OVER-THE-COUNTER, many of them in the local markets of Denver, Vancouver, or Salt Lake City. These markets have had a history of boom and bust, with a speculative fervor for oil, gas, and gold-mining stocks in the Denver penny stock market in the late 1970s turning to bust by the early 1980s.

PENNY STOCK RULE *see* SECURITIES AND EXCHANGE COMMISSION RULES.

PENSION BENEFIT GUARANTY CORPORATION (PBGC) federal corporation established under the EMPLOYEE RETIREMENT INCOME SECURITY ACT of 1974 (ERISA) to guarantee basic pension benefits in covered plans by administering terminated plans and placing liens on corporate assets for certain pension liabilities that were not funded. To be covered, a plan must promise clearly defined benefits to more than 25 employees. *See also* PENSION FUND.

PENSION FUND fund set up by a corporation, labor union, governmental entity, or other organization to pay the pension benefits of retired workers. Pension funds invest billions of dollars annually in the stock and bond markets, and are therefore a major factor in the supply-demand balance of the markets. Earnings on the investment portfolios of pension funds are TAX DEFERRED. Fund managers make actuarial assumptions about how much they will be required to pay out to pensioners and then try to ensure that the RATE OF RETURN on their portfolios equals or exceeds that anticipated payout need. *See also* APPROVED LIST; EMPLOYEE RETIREMENT INCOME SECURITY ACT; PRUDENT-MAN RULE; VESTING.

PENSION PARACHUTE pension agreement that specifies that in the event of a hostile takeover attempt, any excess assets in a company pension plan can be used for the benefit of pension plan participants, such as increasing pension payments. This prevents the raiding firm or individual from using the pension assets to finance the takeover, and therefore acts as an additional deterrent to help the firm ward off the acquisition. A pension parachute is a form of POISON PILL.

PENSION PLAN provides replacement for salary when a person is no longer working. In the case of a DEFINED BENEFIT PENSION PLAN, the employer or union contributes to the plan, which pays a predetermined benefit for the rest of the employee's life based on length of service and salary. Payments may be made either directly or through an annuity. Pension payments are taxable income to recipients in the year received. The employer or union has fiduciary responsibility to invest the pension funds in stocks, bonds, real estate, and other assets; earn a satisfactory rate of return; and make payments to retired workers. Pension funds holding trillions of dollars are one of the largest investment forces in the stock, bond, and real estate markets. If the employer defaults, pension plan payments are usually guaranteed by the PENSION BENEFIT GUARANTY CORPORATION (PBGC).

In the case of a DEFINED CONTRIBUTION PENSION PLAN, such as a 401(k) or 403(b) plan, employees choose whether or not to contribute to the plan offered by the employer, who may or may not match employee contributions. Pension benefits are determined by the amount of assets built up by the employee during his or her years of contributions. Self-employed individuals can also set up pension plans such as KEOGH PLANS. An INDIVIDUAL RETIREMENT ACCOUNT (IRA) is a form of pension plan. *See also* VESTING.

PENSION REVERSION procedure initiated by a company with an overfunded DEFINED BENEFIT PENSION PLAN to terminate the plan and reclaim the surplus assets for itself. Pension beneficiaries continue to receive their benefits because the company replaces the pension plan with a life insurance company-sponsored fixed annuity plan. In some cases, the company will offer current employees a

DEFINED CONTRIBUTION PENSION PLAN to replace the terminated defined benefit plan. Employees are usually not pleased when their company carries out a pension reversion plan for two reasons: By replacing the pension plan backed by the company with a fixed annuity backed by an insurance company, pensioners are no longer covered by the guarantee of the Pension Benefit Guaranty Corporation; and pensioners lose the prospect for increased pension benefits that they might have enjoyed under the company's pension plan if it had achieved superior investment performance.

PENULTIMATE PROFIT PROSPECT (PPP) second lowest-priced of the ten highest-yielding stocks in the Dow Jones Industrial Average, identified (by Michael B. O'Higgins) as the single Dow stock with the greatest probability of outperforming the average as a whole.

PEOPLE PILL defensive tactic to ward off a hostile TAKEOVER. Management threatens that, in the event of a successful takeover, the entire management team will resign at once, leaving the company without experienced leadership. This is a version of the POISON PILL defense.

PER CAPITA in Latin translation, *per head.* In other words, *per person.*

PER CAPITA DEBT total bonded debt of a municipality, divided by its population. A more refined version, called *net per capita debt,* divides the total bonded debt less applicable sinking funds by the total population. The result of either ratio, compared with ratios of prior periods, reveals trends in a municipality's debt burden, which bond analysts evaluate, bearing in mind that, historically, defaults in times of recession have generally followed overexpansion of debts in prior booms.

PERCENTAGE-OF-COMPLETION CAPITALIZED COST METHOD *see* COMPLETED CONTRACT METHOD.

PERCENTAGE ORDER order to a securities broker to buy or sell a specified number of shares of a stock after a fixed number of these shares have been traded. It can be a LIMIT ORDER or a MARKET ORDER and usually applies to one trading day.

PERCS acronym for *preferred equity—redemption cumulative stock.* A form of preferred stock that allows common shareholders to exchange common stock for preferred shares, thereby retaining a high dividend rate. PERCS usually have little appreciation potential, however.

PERFECT COMPETITION market condition wherein no buyer or seller has the power to alter the market price of a good or service. Characteristics of a perfectly competitive market are a large number of buyers and sellers, a homogeneous (similar) good or service, an equal awareness of prices and volume, an absence of discrimination in buying and selling, total mobility of productive resources, and complete freedom of entry. Perfect competition exists only as a theoretical ideal. Also called *pure competition.*

PERFECT HEDGE *see* HEDGE/HEDGING.

PERFORMANCE BOND surety bond given by one party to another, protecting the second party against loss in the event the terms of a contract are not fulfilled. The surety company is primarily liable with the principal (the contractor) for nonperformance. For example, a homeowner having a new kitchen put in may request a performance bond from the home improvement contractor so that the homeowner would receive cash compensation if the kitchen was not done satisfactorily within the agreed upon time.

PERFORMANCE FEE *see* INCENTIVE FEE.

PERFORMANCE FUND MUTUAL FUND designed for growth of capital. A performance fund invests in high-growth companies that do not pay dividends or that pay small dividends. Investors in such funds are willing to take higher-than-average risks in order to earn higher-than-average returns on their invested capital. *See also* GROWTH STOCK; PERFORMANCE STOCK.

PERFORMANCE STOCK high-growth stock that an investor feels will significantly rise in value. Also known as GROWTH STOCK, such a security tends to pay either a small dividend or no dividend at all. Companies whose stocks are in this category tend to retain earnings rather than pay dividends in order to finance their rapid growth. *See also* PERFORMANCE FUND.

PERIODIC PAYMENT PLAN plan to accumulate capital in a mutual fund by making regular investments on a monthly or quarterly basis. The plan has a set pay-in period, which may be 10 or 20 years, and a mechanism to withdraw funds from the plan after that time. Participants in periodic payment plans enjoy the advantages of DOLLAR COST AVERAGING and the diversification among stocks or bonds that is available through a mutual fund. Some plans also include completion insurance, which assures that all scheduled contributions to the plan will continue so that full benefits can be passed on to beneficiaries in the event the participant dies or is incapacitated.

PERIODIC PURCHASE DEFERRED CONTRACT ANNUITY contract for which fixed-amount payments, called *premiums,* are paid either monthly or quarterly and that does not begin paying out until a time elected by the holder (the *annuitant).* In some cases, premium payments may continue after payments from the annuity have begun. A periodic purchase deferred contract can be either fixed or variable. *See also* FIXED ANNUITY; VARIABLE ANNUITY.

PERIOD-CERTAIN ANNUITY annuity that guarantees payments to an ANNUITANT for a particular period of time. For example, a 10-year period-certain annuity will make annuity payments for 10 years and no more. If the annuitant dies before the 10 years have expired, the payments will continue to the policy's beneficiaries for the remaining term. The monthly payment rate for a period-certain annuity is generally higher than the rate for a LIFE ANNUITY because the insurance company knows its maximum liability in advance.

PERIOD OF DIGESTION time period after the release of a NEW ISSUE of stocks or bonds during which the trading price of the security is established in the marketplace. Particularly when an INITIAL PUBLIC OFFERING is released, the period of digestion may entail considerable VOLATILITY, as investors try to ascertain an appropriate price level for it.

PERLS acronym for *principal exchange-rate-linked securities.* Debt instrument that is denominated in U.S. dollars and pays interest in U.S. dollars, but with principal repayment linked to the performance of the U.S. dollar versus a foreign currency. For example, a PERLS offering by the Student Loan Marketing Association (Sallie Mae), underwritten by Morgan Stanley, links the principal repayment to the exchange rate of the Australian dollar versus the U.S. dollar. If the Australian dollar gains value against the U.S. dollar when the bond matures, redemption will be at a premium to par value. If the Australian dollar is weaker, redemption will be at a discount.

PERMANENT FINANCING

Corporate finance: long-term financing by means of either debt (bonds or long-term notes) or equity (common or preferred stock).

Real estate: long-term mortgage loan or bond issue, usually with a 15-, 20-, or 30-year term, the proceeds of which are used to repay a CONSTRUCTION LOAN.

PERPENDICULAR SPREAD option strategy using options with similar expiration dates and different strike prices (the prices at which the options can be exercised). A perpendicular spread can be designed for either a bullish or a bearish outlook.

PERPETUAL BOND bond that has no maturity date, is not redeemable and pays a steady stream of interest indefinitely; also called *annuity bond.* The only notable perpetual bonds in existence are the consols first issued by the British Treasury to pay off smaller issues used to finance the Napoleonic Wars (1814). Some persons in the United States believe it would be more realistic to issue perpetual government bonds than constantly to refund portions of the national debt, as is the practice.

PERPETUAL INVENTORY inventory accounting system whereby book inventory is kept in continuous agreement with stock on hand; also called *continuous inventory.* A daily record is maintained of both the dollar amount and the physical quantity of inventory, and this is reconciled to actual physical counts at short intervals. Perpetual inventory contrasts with *periodic inventory.*

PERPETUAL WARRANT investment certificate giving the holder the right to buy a specified number of common shares of stock at a stipulated price with no expiration date. *See also* SUBSCRIPTION WARRANT.

PERQUISITE commonly known as a *perk.* A fringe benefit offered to an employee in addition to salary. Some examples of perquisites are reimbursement for educational expenses, legal services, vacation time, pension plans, life insurance coverage, company cars and aircraft, personal financial counseling, and employee assistance hotlines. In general, the higher an employee's position and the more valued he or she in a company, the more perks he or she receives.

PERSONAL ARTICLE FLOATER policy or an addition to a policy, used to cover personal valuables, such as jewelry and furs.

PERSONAL INCOME income received by persons from all sources: from participation in production, from both government and business TRANSFER PAYMENTS and from government interest (which is treated like a transfer payment). "Persons" refers to individuals, nonprofit institutions that primarily serve individuals, private noninsured welfare funds, and private trust funds. Personal income is calculated as the sum of wages and salary disbursements, other labor income, proprietors' income with inventory valuation and capital consumption adjustment, rental income of persons, with capital consumption adjustment, personal dividend income, personal interest income, and transfer payments to persons, less personal contribution to Social Security.

PERSONAL EXEMPTION amount of money a person can exclude from personal income in calculating federal and state income tax. Taxpayers can claim one exemption for every person in their household. The amount of the personal exemption is adjusted for inflation each year. In 1995, it was $2450. Taxpayers also can claim additional exemptions for each dependent parent living with them, if the dependent is blind, or over age 65. Exemptions are phased out for certain high-income taxpayers. For a married couple filing jointly, exemptions begin to be phased out when adjusted gross income reaches $167,700 and are eliminated completely for those reporting more than $290,200 in income. For single people, phase-out starts at $108,450. In 1996, the personal exemption increases to $2500. For married couples filing jointly, the phase-out levels increases in 1996 to $172,050 and $294,550, respectively.

PERSONAL INFLATION RATE rate of price increases as it affects a specific individual or couple. For example, a young couple with children who are buying and furnishing a home probably will have a much higher personal inflation rate than an elderly couple with their home paid off and self-supporting children, because the young couple need to buy many more things that are likely to rise in price than the elderly couple. The personal inflation rate is far more relevant for most people than the general inflation rate tracked by the Labor Department's CONSUMER PRICE INDEX.

PERSONAL PROPERTY tangible and intangible assets other than real estate.

PER STIRPES formula for distributing the assets of a person who dies intestate (without a will) according to the "family tree." Under such a distribution, the estate is allocated according to the number of children the deceased had, and distributed accordingly to those surviving the decedent. If any children predeceased the decedent, the share allocated to them would be equally divided among their children and so on.

PETRODOLLARS dollars paid to oil-producing countries and deposited in Western banks. When the price of oil skyrocketed in the 1970s, Middle Eastern oil producers built up huge surpluses of petrodollars that the banks lent to oil-importing countries around the world. By the mid-1980s and 1990s, these surpluses had shrunk because consumption increased while oil exporters spent a good deal of the money on development projects. The flow of petrodollars, therefore, is very important in understanding the current world economic situation. Also called *petrocurrency or oil money.*

PHANTOM INCOME LIMITED PARTNERSHIP income that arises from debt restructuring and creates taxability without generating cash flow. Phantom income typically occurs in a tax shelter created prior to the TAX REFORM ACT OF 1986 where real estate properties, having declined in market value, are refinanced; income arises from portions of the debt that are forgiven and recaptured.

PHANTOM STOCK PLAN executive incentive concept whereby an executive receives a bonus based on the market appreciation of the company's stock over a fixed period of time. The hypothetical (hence phantom) amount of shares involved in the case of a particular executive is proportionate to his or her salary level. The plan works on the same principle as a CALL OPTION (a right to purchase a fixed amount of stock at a set price by a particular date). Unlike a call option, however, the executive pays nothing for the option and therefore has nothing to lose.

PHILADELPHIA STOCK EXCHANGE *see* REGIONAL STOCK EXCHANGES.

PHILIPPINE STOCK EXCHANGE operates two trading floors, Manila and Makati; Manila is the larger. Trading hours are from 9:30 A.M. to 12 noon, Monday through Friday, with a 15-minute extension at closing prices, and a 10-minute break at 10:50 A.M. Settlement takes place on the fourth business day after a trade.

PHYSICAL COMMODITY actual commodity that is delivered to the contract buyer at the completion of a commodity contract in either the SPOT MARKET or the FUTURES MARKET. Some examples of physical commodities are corn, cotton, gold, oil, soybeans, and wheat. The quality specifications and quantity of the commodity to be delivered are specified by the exchange on which it is traded.

PHYSICAL INVENTORY *see* PHYSICAL VERIFICATION.

PHYSICAL VERIFICATION procedure by which an auditor actually inspects the assets of a firm, particularly inventory, to confirm their existence and value, rather than relying on written records. The auditor may use statistical sampling in the verification process.

PICKUP value gained in a bond swap. For example, bonds with identical coupon rates and maturities may have different market values, mainly because of a difference in quality, and thus in yields. The higher yield of the lower-quality bond received in such a swap compared with the yield of the higher-quality bond that was exchanged for it results in a net gain for the trader, called his or her pickup on the transaction.

PICKUP BOND bond that has a relatively high coupon (interest) rate and is close to the date at which it is callable—that is, can be paid off prior to maturity—by the issuer. If interest rates fall, the investor can look forward to picking up a redemption PREMIUM, since the bond will in all likelihood be called.

PICTURE Wall Street jargon used to request bid and asked prices and quantity information from a specialist or from a dealer regarding a particular security. For example, the question "What's the picture on XYZ?" might be answered, "58⅛ [best bid] to ¼ [best offer is 58¼], 1000 either way [there are both a buyer and a seller for 1000 shares]."

PIG *see* PASSIVE INCOME GENERATOR.

PIGGYBACKING illegal practice by a broker who buys or sells stocks or bonds in his personal account after a customer buys or sells the same security. The broker assumes that the customer is making the trade because of access to material, nonpublic information that will make the stock or bond rise or fall sharply. Trading following customer orders is a conflict of interest, and may be disciplined by the broker's firm or regulatory authorities if discovered.

PIGGYBACK REGISTRATION situation when a securities UNDERWRITER allows existing holdings of shares in a corporation to be sold in combination with an offering of new public shares. The PROSPECTUS in a piggyback registration will reveal the nature of such a public/private share offering and name the sellers of the private shares. *See also* PUBLIC OFFERING.

PIK (PAYMENT-IN-KIND) SECURITIES bonds or PREFERRED STOCK that pay interest/dividends in the form of additional bonds or preferred. PIK securities have been used in TAKEOVER financing in lieu of cash and are highly speculative.

PINK SHEETS daily publication of the NATIONAL QUOTATION BUREAU that details the BID AND ASKED prices of OVER THE COUNTER (OTC) stocks not carried in daily OTC newspaper listings of NASDAQ. Brokerage firms subscribe to the pink sheets—named for their color—because the sheets not only give current prices but list market makers who trade each stock. Debt securities are listed separately on YELLOW SHEETS. *See also* OTC BULLETIN BOARD.

PIN NUMBER acronym for *personal identification number.* Customers use PIN numbers to identify themselves, such as when performing transactions with a debit card at an automatic teller machine.

PIPELINE term referring to the underwriting process that involves securities being proposed for public distribution. The phrase used is "in the pipeline." The entire underwriting process, including registration with the Securities and Exchange Commission, must be completed before a security can be offered for public sale. Underwriters attempt to have several securities issues waiting in the pipeline so that the issues can be sold as soon as market conditions become favorable. In the municipal bond market, the pipeline is called the "Thirty Day Visible Supply" in the *Bond Buyer* newspaper.

PIT location at a futures or options exchange in which trading takes place. Pits are usually shaped like rings, often with several levels of steps, so that a large number of traders can see and be seen by each other as they conduct business.

PITI acronym for *principal, interest, taxes and insurance,* the primary components of monthly mortgage payments. Many mortgage lenders, to ensure that property taxes and homeowner's insurance premiums are paid on schedule, require that borrowers include these amounts in their monthly payments. The funds are then placed in escrow until needed. When calculating how much a house will cost a borrower on a monthly basis, the payment is expressed for PITI.

PLACE to market new securities. The term applies to both public and private sales but is more often used with reference to direct sales to institutional investors, as in PRIVATE PLACEMENT. The terms FLOAT and *distribute* are preferred in the case of a PUBLIC OFFERING.

PLACEMENT RATIO ratio, compiled by the *Bond Buyer* as of the close of business every Thursday, indicating the percentage of the past week's new MUNICIPAL BOND offerings that have been bought from the underwriters. Only issues of $1 million or more are included.

PLANNED AMORTIZATION CLASS BONDS *see* PAC BONDS.

PLAN PARTICIPANTS employees or former employees of a company, members of an employee organization or beneficiaries who may become eligible to receive benefits from an employee benefit plan. Participants are legally entitled to certain information about the plan and the benefits, including a summary annual report and summary plan description.

PLAN SPONSOR entity that establishes and maintains a pension or insurance plan. This may be a corporation, labor union, government agency, or nonprofit organization. Plan sponsors must follow government guidelines in the establishment and administration of these plans, including informing plan participants about the financial health of the plan and the benefits available.

PLANT assets comprising land, buildings, machinery, natural resources, furniture and fixtures, and all other equipment permanently employed. Synonymous with FIXED ASSET.

    In a limited sense, the term is used to mean only buildings or only land and buildings: "property, plant, and equipment" and "plant and equipment."

PLAYING THE MARKET unprofessional buying and selling of stocks, as distinguished from SPECULATION. Both players and speculators are seeking capital gains, but while playing the market is more akin to gambling, speculating is done by professionals taking calculated risks.

PLAZA ACCORD agreement in August of 1985 in which the finance ministers of the Group of 5—the United States, Great Britain, France, Germany, and Japan— met at the Plaza Hotel in New York City to mount a concerted effort to reduce the value of the U.S. dollar against other major currencies. Though the dollar had already begun its decline months earlier, the Plaza Accord accelerated the move. The action was necessary because the dollar had become so strong that it was difficult for U.S. exporters to sell their products abroad, weakening the American economy.

PLC *see* PUBLIC LIABILITY COMPANY.

PLEDGING transferring property, such as securities or the CASH SURRENDER VALUE of life insurance, to a lender or creditor as COLLATERAL for an obligation. *Pledge* and *hypothecate* are synonymous, as they do not involve transfer of title. ASSIGN, although commonly used interchangeably with *pledge* and *hypothecate,* implies transfer of ownership or of the right to transfer ownership at a later date. *See also* HYPOTHECATION.

PLOW BACK to reinvest a company's earnings in the business rather than pay out those profits as dividends. Smaller, fast-growing companies usually plow back most or all earnings in their businesses, whereas more established firms pay out more of their profits as dividends.

PLUS
1. plus sign (+) that follows a price quotation on a Treasury note or bond, indicating that the price (normally quoted as a percentage of PAR value refined to 32ds) is refined to 64ths. Thus 95.16 + (95^{16}⁄₃₂+ or 95^{32}⁄₆₄+) means 95^{33}⁄₆₄.
2. plus sign after a transaction price in a listed security (for example, 39½+), indicating that the trade was at a higher price than the previous REGULAR WAY transaction. *See also* PLUS TICK.
3. plus sign before the figure in the column labeled "Change" in the newspaper stock tables, meaning that the closing price of the stock was higher than the previous day's close by the amount stated in the "Change" column.

PLUS TICK expression used when a security has been traded at a higher price than the previous transaction in that security. A stock price listed as 28+ on the CONSOLIDATED TAPE has had a plus tick from 27⅞ or below on previous trades. It is a Securities and Exchange Commission rule that short sales can be executed only on plus ticks or ZERO PLUS TICKS. Also called *uptick. See also* MINUS TICK; TICK; ZERO-MINUS TICK.

POINT
Bonds: percentage change of the face value of a bond expressed as a point. For example, a change of 1% is a move of one point. For a bond with a $1000 face value, each point is worth $10, and for a bond with a $5000 face value, each point is $50.

Bond yields are quoted in basis points: 100 basis points make up 1% of yield. *See* BASIS POINT.

Futures/options: measure of price change equal to one one-hundredth of one cent in most futures traded in decimal units. In grains, it is one quarter of one cent; in Treasury bonds, it is 1% of par. *See also* TICK.

Real estate and other commercial lending: upfront fee charged by a lender, separate from interest but designed to increase the overall yield to the lender. A point is 1% of the total principal amount of the loan. For example, on a $100,000 mortgage loan, a charge of 3 points would equal $3000. Since points are considered a form of prepaid mortgage interest, they are tax-deductible, usually over the term of the loan, but in some cases in a lump sum in the year they are paid.

Stocks: change of $1 in the market price of a stock. If a stock has risen 5 points, it has risen by $5   share.

The movements of stock market averages, such as the Dow Jones Industrial Average, are also quoted in points. However, those points refer not to dollar amounts but to units of movement in the average, which is a composite of weighted dollar values. For example, a 20-point move in the Dow Jones Average from 4000 to 4020 does *not* mean the Dow now stands at $4020.

POINT AND FIGURE CHART graphic technique used in TECHNICAL ANALYSIS to follow the up or down momentum in the price moves of a security. Point and figure charting disregards the element of time and is solely used to record changes in price. Every time a price move is upward, an X is put on the graph above the previous point. Every time the price moves down, an O is placed one square down. When direction changes, the next column is used. The resulting lines of Xs and Os will indicate whether the security being charted has been maintaining an up or a down momentum over a particular time period.

POINT AND FIGURE CHART

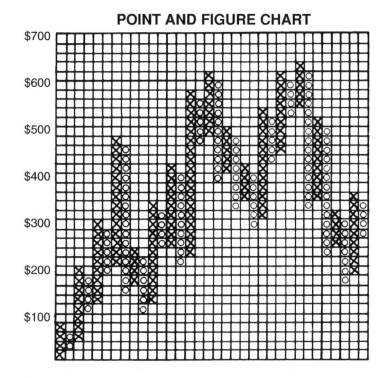

POISON PILL strategic move by a takeover-target company to make its stock less attractive to an acquirer. For instance, a firm may issue a new series of PREFERRED STOCK that gives shareholders the right to redeem it at a premium price after a TAKEOVER. Two variations: a *flip-in poison pill* allows all existing holders of target company shares except the acquirer to buy additional shares at a bargain price; a *flip-over poison pill* allows holders of common stock to buy (or holders of preferred stock to convert into) the acquirer's shares at a bargain price in the event of an unwelcome merger. Such measures raise the cost of an ACQUISITION, and cause DILUTION, hopefully deterring a takeover bid. A third type of poison pill, known as a PEOPLE PILL, is the threat that in the event of a successful takeover, the entire management team will resign at once, leaving the company without experienced leadership. *See also* PENSION PARACHUTE, POISON PUT, SUICIDE PILL.

POISON PUT provision in an INDENTURE giving bondholders the privilege of redemption at PAR if certain designated events occur, such as a hostile TAKEOVER, the purchase of a big block of shares, or an excessively large dividend payout. Poison puts, or *superpoison puts* as the more stringent variations are called, are popular antitakeover devices because they create an onerous cash obligation for the acquirer. They also protect the bondholder from the deterioration of credit quality and RATING that might result from a LEVERAGED BUYOUT that added to the issuer's debt. *See also* EVENT RISK.

POLICYHOLDER owner of an INSURANCE contract (policy). Term is commonly used synonymously with *insured,* although the two can be different parties and *insured* is the preferred designation for the person indemnified by the insurance company.

POLICYHOLDER LOAN BONDS packaged policyholder loans. Life insurance policyholders borrow against the CASH SURRENDER VALUE of their policies. The policyholder loan will be repaid either by the policyholder while alive or from the proceeds of the insurance policy if the policyholder dies before repayment. These loans are packaged by a broker/dealer that offers these asset-backed securities as policyholder loan bonds.

POLICY LIMIT limit of coverage provided by an insurance policy, known as a *maximum lifetime benefit.* For coverage of individuals, roughly two-thirds of existing policies have a limit of \$1 million or more; 21% have no limit. Most employee plans are based on maximum lifetime coverage.

POLICY LOAN loan from an insurance company secured by the CASH SURRENDER VALUE of a life insurance policy. The amount available for such a loan depends on the number of years the policy has been in effect, the insured's age when the policy was issued, and the size of the death benefit. Such loans are often made at below-market interest rates to policyholders, although more recent policies usually only allow borrowing at rates that fluctuate in line with money market rates. If the loan is not repaid by the insured, the death benefit of the life insurance policy will be reduced by the amount of the loan plus accrued interest.

POOL

Capital Budgeting: as used in the phrase "pool of financing," the concept that investment projects are financed out of a pool of funds rather than out of bonds, preferred stock, and common stock individually. A weighted average cost of capital is thus used in analyses evaluating the return on investment projects. *See also* COST OF CAPITAL.

Industry: joining of companies to improve profits by reducing competition. Such poolings are generally outlawed in the United States by various ANTITRUST LAWS.

Insurance: association of insurers who share premiums and losses in order to spread risk and give small insurers an opportunity to compete with larger ones.

Investments:
1. combination of resources for a common purpose or benefit. For example, an INVESTMENT CLUB pools the funds of its members, giving them the opportunity

to share in a PORTFOLIO offering greater diversification and the hope of a better return on their money than they could get individually. A *commodities pool* entrusts the funds of many investors to a trading professional and distributes profits and losses among participants in proportion to their interests.
2. group of investors joined together to use their combined power to manipulate security or commodity prices or to obtain control of a corporation. Such pools are outlawed by regulations governing securities and commodities trading.
    See also MORTGAGE POOL.

POOLING OF INTERESTS accounting method used in the combining or merging of companies following an acquisition, whereby the balance sheets (assets and liabilities) of the two companies are simply added together, item by item. This tax-free method contrasts with the PURCHASE ACQUISITION method, in which the buying company treats the acquired company as an investment and any PREMIUM paid over the FAIR MARKET VALUE of the assets is reflected on the buyer's balance sheet as GOODWILL. Because reported earnings are higher under the pooling of interests method, most companies prefer it to the purchase acquisition method, particularly when the amount of goodwill is sizable.

    The pooling of interests method can be elected only when the following conditions are met:
1. The two companies must have been autonomous for at least two years prior to the pooling and one must not have owned more than 10% of the stock of the other.
2. The combination must be consummated either in a single transaction or in accordance with a specific plan within one year after the plan is initiated; no contingent payments are permitted.
3. The acquiring company must issue its regular common stock in exchange for 90% or more of the common stock of the other company.
4. The surviving corporation must not later retire or reacquire common stock issued in the combination, must not enter into an arrangement for the benefit of former stockholders, and must not dispose of a significant portion of the assets of the combining companies for at least 2 years.
    See also MERGER.

PORCUPINE PROVISIONS *see* SHARK REPELLENTS.

PORTABILITY ability of employees to retain benefits from one employer to the next when switching jobs. The term is most frequently used in connection with pension and insurance coverage. Credits earned towards pension benefits in a DEFINED BENEFIT PENSION PLAN are rarely portable from one company to another. Conversely, accumulated assets in a DEFINED CONTRIBUTION PENSION PLAN may be transferable to the defined contribution plan of another employer through a rollover. Under the Congressional Omnibus Budget Reconciliation Act (COBRA), employees have the right to carry their group health insurance coverage with them to a new job for up to 18 months. An employee may wish to do so if the new employer's health plan is inferior to the previous employer's plan. Employees choosing to continue coverage with a previous employer's group plan under the COBRA provision pay the full premium, which is subject to change. Generally, this continued coverage costs considerably less than a policy at individual rates.

PORTFOLIO combined holding of more than one stock, bond, commodity, real estate investment, CASH EQUIVALENT, or other asset by an individual or institutional investor. The purpose of a portfolio is to reduce risk by diversification. *See also* PORTFOLIO BETA SCORE; PORTFOLIO THEORY.

PORTFOLIO BETA SCORE relative VOLATILITY of an individual securities portfolio, taken as a whole, as measured by the BETA coefficients of the securities making it up. Beta measures the volatility of a stock relative to the market as a whole, as represented by an index such as Standard & Poor's 500 Stock Index. A beta of 1 means the stock has about the same volatility as the market.

PORTFOLIO INCOME *see* INVESTMENT INCOME.

PORTFOLIO INSURANCE the use, by a PORTFOLIO MANAGER, of STOCK INDEX FUTURES to protect stock portfolios against market declines. Instead of selling actual stocks as they lose value, managers sell the index futures; if the drop continues, they repurchase the futures at a lower price, using the profit to offset losses in the stock portfolio. The inability of the markets on BLACK MONDAY to process such massive quantities of stock efficiently and the subsequent instituting of CIRCUIT BREAKERS all but eliminated portfolio insurance. *See also* PROGRAM TRADING.

PORTFOLIO MANAGER professional responsible for the securities PORTFOLIO of an individual or INSTITUTIONAL INVESTOR. Also called a *money manager* or, especially when personalized service is involved, an INVESTMENT COUNSEL. A portfolio manager may work for a mutual fund, pension fund, profit-sharing plan, bank trust department, or insurance company. In return for a fee, the manager has the fiduciary responsibility to manage the assets prudently and choose whether stocks, bonds, CASH EQUIVALENTS, real estate, or some other assets present the best opportunities for profit at any particular time. *See also* PORTFOLIO THEORY; PRUDENT-MAN RULE.

PORTFOLIO THEORY sophisticated investment decision approach that permits an investor to classify, estimate, and control both the kind and the amount of expected risk and return; also called *portfolio management theory* or *modern portfolio theory*. Essential to portfolio theory are its quantification of the relationship between risk and return and the assumption that investors must be compensated for assuming risk. Portfolio theory departs from traditional security analysis in shifting emphasis from analyzing the characteristics of individual investments to determining the statistical relationships among the individual securities that comprise the overall portfolio. The portfolio theory approach has four basic steps: *security valuation*—describing a universe of assets in terms of expected return and expected risk; *asset allocation decision*—determining how assets are to be distributed among classes of investment, such as stocks or bonds; *portfolio optimization*—reconciling risk and return in selecting the securities to be included, such as determining which portfolio of stocks offers the best return for a given level of expected risk; and *performance measurement*—dividing each stock's performance (risk) into market-related (systematic) and industry/security-related (residual) classifications.

POSITION
Banking: bank's net balance in a foreign currency.
Finance: firm's financial condition.
Investments:
1. investor's stake in a particular security or market. A LONG POSITION equals the number of shares *owned;* a SHORT POSITION equals the number of shares *owed* by a dealer or an individual. The dealer's long positions are called his *inventory of securities.*
2. Used as a verb, to take on a long or a short position in a stock.

POSITION BUILDING process of buying shares to accumulate a LONG POSITION or of selling shares to accumulate a SHORT POSITION. Large institutional investors who want to build a large position in a particular security do so over time to avoid pushing up the price of the security.

POSITION LIMIT

Commodities trading: number of contracts that can be acquired in a specific commodity before a speculator is classified as a "large trader." Large traders are subject to special oversight by the COMMODITIES FUTURES TRADING COMMISSION (CFTC) and the exchanges and are limited as to the number of contracts they can add to their positions. The position limit varies with the type of commodity.

Options trading: maximum number of exchange-listed OPTION contracts that can be owned or controlled by an individual holder, or by a group of holders acting jointly, in the same underlying security. The current limit is 2000 contracts on the same side of the market (for example, long calls and short puts are one side of the market); the limit applies to all expiration dates.

POSITION TRADER commodities trader who takes a long-term approach—six months to a year or more—to the market. Usually possessing more than average experience, information, and capital, these traders ride through the ups and downs of price fluctuations until close to the delivery date, unless drastic adverse developments threaten. More like insurance underwriters than gamblers, they hope to achieve long-term profits from calculated risks as distinguished from pure speculation.

POSITIVE CARRY situation in which the cost of money borrowed to finance securities is lower than the yield on the securities. For example, if a fixed-income bond yielding 10% is purchased with a loan bearing 8% interest, the bond has positive carry. The opposite situation is called NEGATIVE CARRY.

POSITIVE YIELD CURVE situation in which interest rates are higher on long-term debt securities than on short-term debt securities of the same quality. For example, a positive yield curve exists when 20-year Treasury bonds yield 10% and 3-month Treasury bills yield 6%. Such a situation is common, since an investor who ties up his money for a longer time is taking more risk and is usually compensated by a higher yield. When short-term interest rates rise above long-term rates, there is a NEGATIVE YIELD CURVE, also called an INVERTED YIELD CURVE.

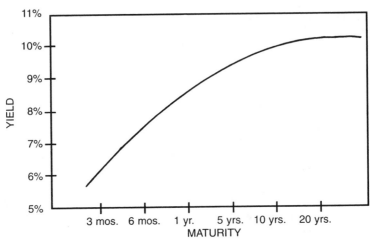

POSITIVE YIELD CURVE

POST

Accounting: to transfer from a journal of original entry detailed financial data, in the chronological order in which it was generated, into a ledger book. Banks post checking account deposits and withdrawals in a ledger, then summarize these transactions on the monthly bank statement.

Investments: horseshoe-shaped structure on the floor of the New York Stock Exchange where specialists trade specific securities. Video screens surround the post, displaying the bid and offer prices available for stocks traded at that location. Also called *trading post*.

POSTDATED CHECK check dated in the future. It is not negotiable until the date becomes current.

POSTING in bookkeeping terminology, the transfer of data from a journal to a ledger.

POSTPONING INCOME technique to delay receipt of income into a later year to reduce current tax liability. For example, if it seems likely that Congress or the state legislature may reduce income tax rates in the upcoming year, it may be advantageous to receive income in that year instead of in the current year when tax rates are higher. Salespeople can appeal to their managers to pay their commissions in the next year, and small business owners can send invoices after the first of the year so that they are paid in the next year. In addition to qualifying for a lower tax rate, the full tax on the income may be delayed until April 15 of the following year, unless the taxpayer receiving the income is required to file quarterly estimated tax payments.

POT securities underwriting term meaning the portion of a stock or bond issue returned to the MANAGING UNDERWRITER by the participating investment bankers to facilitate sales to INSTITUTIONAL INVESTORS. Institutions buying from the pot designate the firms to be credited with pot sales. *See also* RETENTION.

POT IS CLEAN MANAGING UNDERWRITER'S announcement to members of the underwriting group that the POT—the portion of the stock or bond issue withheld to facilitate institutional sales—has been sold.

POWER OF ATTORNEY

In general: written document that authorizes a particular person to perform certain acts on behalf of the one signing the document. The document, which must be witnessed by a notary public or some other public officer, may bestow either *full power of attorney* or *limited power of attorney*. It becomes void upon the death of the signer.

Investments: *full power of attorney* might, for instance, allow assets to be moved from one brokerage or bank account to another. A *limited power of attorney,* on the other hand, would only permit transactions within an existing account. A broker given a limited power of attorney, for instance, may buy and sell securities in an account but may not remove them. Such an account is called a DISCRETIONARY ACCOUNT.

See also DISCRETIONARY ORDER; PROXY; STOCK POWER.

PREARRANGED TRADING questionable and probably fraudulent practice whereby commodities dealers arrange risk-free trades at predetermined prices, usually to gain tax advantages.

PREAUTHORIZED PAYMENT prearranged deductions from a bank account for the payment of a third party.

PRECEDENCE priority of one order over another on the floor of the exchanges, according to rules designed to protect the DOUBLE-AUCTION SYSTEM. The rules basically are that the highest bid and lowest offer have precedence over other bids and offers, that the first bid or first offer at a price has priority over other bids or offers at that price, and that the size of the order determines precedence thereafter, large orders having priority over smaller orders. Where two orders of equal size must compete for the same limited quantity after the first bid is filled, the impasse is resolved by a flip of the coin. *See also* MATCHED AND LOST. Exchange rules also require that public orders have precedence over trades for floor members' own accounts. *See also* OFF-FLOOR ORDER; ON-FLOOR ORDER.

PRECIOUS METALS gold, silver, platinum, and palladium. These metals are valued for their intrinsic value, backing world currencies, as well as their industrial applications. Fundamental issues of supply and demand are important factors in their prices, along with political and economic considerations, especially when producing countries are involved. Inflation fears will stimulate gold accumulation and higher prices, as will war and natural disaster, especially in major producing or consuming countries or regions. Precious metals are held by central banks and are considered a storehouse of value. While gold is often singled out, cultural factors assign different levels of significance to the metals. In the Far East, especially Japan, platinum traditionally is held in higher regard than gold, both in terms of physical metal and investment holdings, and for personal accumulation (e.g., jewelry and coins). Gold is favored in the West. In India and the Middle East, silver is highly prized, and the dowries of Indian women are replete with silver jewelry and coins. Investors can buy physical metal in bars, BULLION and NUMISMATIC COINS, and jewelry. There are numerous investment vehicles that do not involve physical delivery: futures and options contracts, mining company stocks, bonds, mutual funds, commodity indices, and commodity funds. The values of these investment vehicles are influenced by metal price volatility, with commodity funds and indices, and futures and options, more sensitive to daily price swings. Many metals analysts and advisors recommend that 5% to 15% of investor portfolios be held in some form of precious metals as a long-term hedge against inflation and political turmoil.

PRECOMPUTE in installment lending, methods of charging interest whereby the total amount of annual interest either is deducted from the face amount of the loan at the time the loan proceeds are disbursed or is added to the total amount to be repaid in equal installments. In both cases, the EFFECTIVE RATE to the borrower is higher than the stated annual rate used in the computation. "Truth in lending" laws require that the effective annual rate be expressed in SIMPLE INTEREST terms.

PREEMPTIVE RIGHT right giving existing stockholders the opportunity to purchase shares of a NEW ISSUE before it is offered to others. Its purpose is to protect shareholders from dilution of value and control when new shares are issued. Although 48 U.S. states have preemptive right statutes, most states also either permit corporations to pay stockholders to waive their preemptive rights or state in their statutes that the preemptive right is valid only if set forth in the corporate charter. As a result, preemptive rights are the exception rather than the rule. Where they do exist, the usual procedure is for each existing stockholder to receive, prior to a new issue, a SUBSCRIPTION WARRANT indicating how many new shares the holder is entitled to buy—normally, a proportion of the shares he or she already holds. Since the new shares would typically be priced below the market, a financial incentive exists to exercise the preemptive right. *See also* SUBSCRIPTION RIGHT.

PREFERENCE ITEM *see* TAX PREFERENCE ITEM.

PREFERENCE SHARES *see* PRIOR-PREFERRED STOCK.

PREFERRED DIVIDEND COVERAGE net income after interest and taxes (but before common stock dividends) divided by the dollar amount of preferred stock dividends. The result tells how many times over the preferred dividend requirement is covered by current earnings.

PREFERRED STOCK class of CAPITAL STOCK that pays dividends at a specified rate and that has preference over common stock in the payment of dividends and the liquidation of assets. Preferred stock does not ordinarily carry voting rights.

Most preferred stock is *cumulative;* if dividends are passed (not paid for any reason), they accumulate and must be paid before common dividends. A PASSED DIVIDEND on *noncumulative preferred* stock is generally gone forever. PARTICIPATING PREFERRED STOCK entitles its holders to share in profits above and beyond the declared dividend, along with common shareholders, as distinguished from *nonparticipating preferred,* which is limited to the stipulated dividend. *Adjustablerate preferred* stock pays a dividend that is adjustable, usually quarterly, based on changes in the Treasury bill rate or other money market rates. *Convertible preferred stock* is exchangeable for a given number of common shares and thus tends to be more VOLATILE than *nonconvertible preferred,* which behaves more like a fixed-income bond. *See also* CONVERTIBLE; CUMULATIVE PREFERRED; PARTICIPATING PREFERRED; PIK (PAYMENT-IN-KIND) SECURITIES; PRIOR, PREFERRED STOCK.

PREFERRED STOCK RATIO PREFERRED STOCK at PAR value divided by total CAPITALIZATION; the result is the percentage of capitalization—bonds and net worth—represented by preferred stock.

PRELIMINARY PROSPECTUS first document released by an underwriter of a NEW ISSUE to prospective investors. The document offers financial details about the issue but does not contain all the information that will appear in the final or statutory prospectus, and parts of the document may be changed before the final prospectus is issued. Because portions of the cover page of the preliminary prospectus are printed in red ink, it is popularly called the *red herring.*

PREMIUM

In general: extra payment usually made as an incentive.

Bonds:

1. amount by which a bond sells above its face (PAR) value. For instance, a bond with a face value of $1000 would sell for a $100 premium when it cost $1100. The same meaning also applies to preferred stock. *See also* PREMIUM BOND; PREMIUM OVER BOND VALUE; PREMIUM OVER CONVERSION VALUE.

2. amount by which the REDEMPTION PRICE to the issuer exceeds the face value when a bond is called. *See also* CALL PREMIUM.

Insurance: fee paid to an insurance company for insurance protection. Also, the single or multiple payments made to build an ANNUITY fund.

Options: price a put or call buyer must pay to a put or call seller (writer) for an option contract. The premium is determined by market supply and demand forces. *See also* OPTION; PREMIUM INCOME.

Stocks:

1. charge occasionally paid by a short seller when stock is borrowed to make delivery on a SHORT SALE.

2. amount by which a stock's price exceeds that of other stocks to which it is comparable. For instance, securities analysts might say that XYZ Foods is selling at a 15% premium to other food company stocks—an indication that the stock is more highly valued by investors than its industry peers. It does not

necessarily mean that the stock is overpriced, however. Indeed, it may indicate that the investment public has only begun to recognize the stock's market potential and that the price will continue to rise. Similarly, analysts might say that the food industry is selling for a 20% premium to Standard & Poor's 500 index, indicating the relative price strength of the industry group to the stock market as a whole.

3. in new issues, amount by which the trading price of the shares exceeds the OFFERING PRICE.

4. amount over market value paid in a *tender offer. See also* PREMIUM RAID.

PREMIUM BOND bond with a selling price above face or redemption value. A bond with a face value of $1000, for instance, would be called a premium bond if it sold for $1050. This price does not include any ACCRUED INTEREST due when the bond is bought. When a premium bond is called before scheduled maturity, bondholders are usually paid more than face value, though the amount may be less than the bond is selling for at the time of the CALL.

PREMIUM INCOME income received by an investor who sells a PUT OPTION or a CALL OPTION. An investor collects premium income by writing a COVERED OPTION, if he or she owns the underlying stock, or a NAKED OPTION, if he or she does not own the stock. An investor who sells options to collect premium income hopes that the underlying stock will not rise very much (in the case of a call) or fall very much (in the case of a put).

PREMIUM OVER BOND VALUE upward difference between the market value of a CONVERTIBLE bond and the price at which a straight bond of the same company would sell in the same open market. A convertible bond, eventually convertible to common stock, will normally sell at a PREMIUM over its bond value because investors place a value on the conversion feature. The higher the market price of the issuer's stock is relative to the price at which the bond is convertible, the greater the premium will be, reflecting the investor's tendency to view it more as a stock than as a bond. When the stock price falls near or below the conversion price, investors then tend to view the convertible as a bond and the premium narrows or even disappears. Other factors affecting the prices of convertible bonds generally include lower transaction costs on the convertibles than would be incurred in buying the stock outright, an attraction that exerts some upward pressure on the premium; the demand from life insurance companies and other institutional investors that are limited by law as to the common stock investments they can have and that gain their equity participation through convertibles; the duration period of the option to convert—the longer it is, the more valuable the future and the higher the premium; high dividends on the issuer's common stock, a factor increasing demand for the common versus the convertible, and therefore a downward pressure. *See also* PREMIUM OVER CONVERSION VALUE.

PREMIUM OVER CONVERSION VALUE amount by which the MARKET PRICE of a CONVERTIBLE preferred stock or convertible bond exceeds the price at which it is convertible. Convertibles (CVs) usually sell at a PREMIUM for two basic reasons: (1) if the convertible is a bond, the bond value—defined as the price at which a straight bond of the same company would sell in the same open market—is the lowest value the CV will reach; it thus represents DOWNSIDE RISK protection, which is given a value in the marketplace, generally varying with the VOLATILITY of the common stock; (2) the conversion privilege is given a value by investors because they might find it profitable eventually to convert the securities.

At relatively high common-stock price levels, a convertible tends to sell for its common stock equivalent and the conversion value becomes negligible. This occurs because investors are viewing the security as a common stock, not as a bond, and because conversion would be preferable to redemption if the bond were called. On the other hand, when the market value of the convertible is close to its bond value, the conversion feature has little value and the security is valued more as a bond. It is here that the CONVERSION PREMIUM is highest. The conversion premium is also influenced to some extent by transaction costs, insurance company investment restrictions, the duration of the conversion OPTION, and the size of common dividends. *See also* PREMIUM OVER BOND VALUE.

PREMIUM RAID surprise attempt to acquire a position in a company's stock by offering holders an amount—or premium—over the market value of their shares. The term *raid* assumes that the motive is control and not simply investment. Attempts to acquire control are regulated by federal laws that require disclosure of the intentions of those seeking shares. *See also* TENDER OFFER; WILLIAMS ACT.

PRENUPTIAL CONTRACT agreement between a future husband and wife that details how the couple's financial affairs are to be handled both during the marriage and in the event of divorce. The agreement may cover insurance protection, ownership of housing and securities, and inheritance rights. Such contracts may not be accepted in a court of law.

PREPAID INTEREST asset account representing interest paid in advance. The interest is expensed, that is, charged to the borrower's profit and loss statement (P & L), as it is earned by the lender. Synonymous with UNEARNED INTEREST, which is the preferred term when DISCOUNT is involved.

PREPAYMENT

In general: paying a debt obligation before it comes due.

Accounting: expenditure for a future benefit, which is recorded in a BALANCE SHEET asset account called a DEFERRED CHARGE, then written off in the period when the benefit is enjoyed. For example, prepaid rent is first recorded as an asset, then charged to expense as the rent becomes due on a monthly basis.

Banking: paying a loan before maturity. Some loans (particularly mortgages) have a prepayment clause that allows prepayment at any time without penalty, while others charge a fee if a loan is paid off before due.

Installment credit: making payments before they are due. *See also* RULE OF THE 78s.

Securities: paying a seller for a security before the settlement date.

Taxes: prepaying taxes, for example, to have the benefit of deducting state and local taxes from one's federal income tax return in the current calendar year rather than in the next year.

PREPAYMENT PENALTY fee paid by a borrower to a bank when a loan or mortgage that does not have a prepayment clause is repaid before its scheduled maturity. Prepayment penalties are prohibited in many states, and by FANNIE MAE and FREDDIE MAC. Also called *prepayment fee.*

PREREFUNDING procedure, called a *pre-re* on Wall Street, in which a bond issuer floats a second bond in order to pay off the first bond at the first CALL date. The proceeds from the sale of the second bond are safely invested, usually in Treasury securities, that will mature at the first call date of the first bond issue. Those first bonds are said to be prerefunded after this operation has taken place. Bond issuers prerefund bonds during periods of lower interest rates in order to lower their interest costs. *See also* ADVANCE REFUNDING; REFUNDING; REFUNDING ESCROW DEPOSITS (REDS).

PRESALE ORDER order to purchase part of a new MUNICIPAL BOND issue that is accepted by an underwriting SYNDICATE MANAGER before an announcement of the price or COUPON rate and before the official PUBLIC OFFERING. Municipals are exempt from registration requirements and other rules of the Securities and Exchange Commission, which forbids preoffering sales of corporate bond issues. *See also* PRESOLD ISSUE.

PRESENT VALUE value today of a future payment, or stream of payments, discounted at some appropriate compound interest—or discount—rate. For example, the present value of $100 to be received 10 years from now is about $38.55, using a discount rate equal to 10% interest compounded annually.

The present value method, also called the DISCOUNTED CASH FLOW method, is widely used in corporate finance to measure the return on a CAPITAL INVESTMENT project. In security investments, the method is used to determine how much money should be invested today to result in a certain sum at a future time. Present value calculations are facilitated by present value tables, which are compound interest tables in reverse. Also called *time value of money.*

PRESIDENT highest-ranking officer in a corporation after the CHAIRMAN OF THE BOARD, unless the title CHIEF EXECUTIVE OFFICER (CEO) is used, in which case the president can outrank the chairman. The president is appointed by the BOARD OF DIRECTORS and usually reports directly to the board. In smaller companies the president is usually the CEO, having authority over all other officers in matters of day-to-day management and policy decision-making. In large corporations the CEO title is frequently held by the chairman of the board, leaving the president as CHIEF OPERATING OFFICER, responsible for personnel and administration on a daily basis.

PRESIDENTIAL ELECTION CYCLE THEORY hypothesis of investment advisers that major stock market moves can be predicted based on the four-year presidential election cycle. According to this theory, stocks decline soon after a president is elected, as the chief executive takes the harsh and unpopular steps necessary to bring inflation, government spending, and deficits under control. During the next two years or so, taxes may be raised and the economy may slip into a recession. About midway into the four-year cycle, stocks should start to rise in anticipation of the economic recovery that the incumbent president wants to be roaring at full steam by election day. The cycle then repeats itself with the election of a new president or the reelection of an incumbent. This theory worked remarkably well from the late 1960s to the mid-1980s.

PRESOLD ISSUE issue of MUNICIPAL BONDS or government bonds that is completely sold out before the price or yield is publicly announced. Corporate bond issues, which must be offered to the public with a Securities and Exchange Commission registration statement, cannot legally be presold. *See also* PRESALE ORDER.

PRETAX EARNINGS OR PROFITS NET INCOME (earnings or profits) before federal income taxes.

PRETAX RATE OF RETURN yield or capital gain on a particular security before taking into account an individual's tax situation. *See also* RATE OF RETURN.

PREVIOUS BALANCE METHOD method of charging credit card interest that uses the outstanding balance at the end of the previous month as the basis for the current month's interest computation. *See also* ADJUSTED BALANCE METHOD.

PRICE CHANGE net rise or fall of the price of a security at the close of a trading session, compared to the previous session's CLOSING PRICE. A stock that rose $2 in a day would have a + 2 after its final price in the newspaper stock listings. A stock that fell $2 would have a –2. The average of the price changes for groups of securities, in indicators such as the Dow Jones Industrial Average and Standard & Poor's 500 Stock Index, is calculated by taking into account all the price changes in the components of the average or index.

PRICE/EARNINGS RATIO (P/E) price of a stock divided by its earnings per share. The P/E ratio may either use the reported earnings from the latest year (called a *trailing P/E*) or employ an analyst's forecast of next year's earnings (called a *forward P/E*). The trailing P/E is listed along with a stock's price and trading activity in the daily newspapers. For instance, a stock selling for $20 a share that earned $1 last year has a trailing P/E of 20. If the same stock has projected earnings of $2 next year, it will have a forward P/E of 10.

The price/earnings ratio, also known as the *multiple,* gives investors an idea of how much they are paying for a company's earning power. The higher the P/E, the more investors are paying, and therefore the more earnings growth they are expecting. High P/E stocks—those with multiples over 20—are typically young, fast-growing companies. They are far riskier to trade than low P/E stocks, since it is easier to miss high-growth expectations than low-growth predictions. Low P/E stocks tend to be in low-growth or mature industries, in stock groups that have fallen out of favor, or in old, established, BLUE-CHIP companies with long records of earnings stability and regular dividends. In general, low P/E stocks have higher yields than high P/E stocks, which often pay no dividends at all.

PRICE GAP term used when a stock's price either jumps or plummets from its last trading range without overlapping that trading range. For instance, a stock might shoot up from a closing price of $20 a share, marking the high point of an $18–$20 trading range for that day, and begin trading in a $22–$24 range the next day on the news of a takeover bid. Or a company that reports lower than expected earnings might drop from the $18–$20 range to the $13–$15 range without ever trading at intervening prices. Price gaps are considered significant movements by technical analysts, who note them on charts, because such gaps are often indications of an OVERBOUGHT or OVERSOLD position.

PRICE INDEXES indices that track levels of prices and rates of inflation. The two most common price indexes published by the government are the CONSUMER PRICE INDEX (CPI) and the PRODUCER PRICE INDEX (PPI).

PRICE LEADERSHIP establishment of a price by a leading producer of a product that becomes the price adopted by other producers.

PRICE LIMIT *see* LIMIT PRICE.

PRICE RANGE high/low range in which a stock has traded over a particular period of time. In the daily newspaper, a stock's 52-week price range is given. In most companies' annual reports, a stock's price range is shown for the FISCAL YEAR.

PRICE SPREAD OPTIONS strategy in which an investor simultaneously buys and sells two options covering the same security, with the same expiration months, but with different exercise prices. For example, an investor might buy an XYZ May 100 call and sell an XYZ May 90 call.

PRICE SUPPORT government-set price floor designed to aid farmers or other producers of goods. For instance, the government sets a minimum price for sugar that it guarantees to sugar growers. If the market price drops below that level, the government makes up the difference. *See also* PARITY PRICE.

PRICE-WEIGHTED INDEX index in which component stocks are weighted by their price. Higher-priced stocks therefore have a greater percentage impact on the index than lower-priced stocks. In recent years, the trend of using price-weighted indexes has given way to the use of MARKET-VALUE WEIGHTED INDEXES.

PRICEY term used of an unrealistically low bid price or unrealistically high offer price. If a stock is trading at $15, a pricey bid might be $10 a share, and a pricey offer $20 a share.

PRIMARY DEALER one of the three dozen or so banks and investment dealers authorized to buy and sell government securities in direct dealings with the FEDERAL RESERVE BANK of New York in its execution of Fed OPEN MARKET OPERATIONS. Such dealers must be qualified in terms of reputation, capacity, and adequacy of staff and facilities.

PRIMARY DISTRIBUTION sale of a new issue of stocks or bonds, as distinguished from a SECONDARY DISTRIBUTION, which involves previously issued stock. All issuances of bonds are primary distributions. Also called *primary offering,* but not to be confused with *initial public offering,* which refers to a corporation's *first* distribution of stock to the public.

PRIMARY EARNINGS PER (COMMON) SHARE earnings available to common stock (which is usually net earnings after taxes and preferred dividends) divided by the number of common shares outstanding. This figure contrasts with earnings per share after DILUTION, which assumes warrants, rights, and options have been exercised and convertibles have been converted. *See also* CONVERTIBLE; FULLY DILUTED EARNINGS PER (COMMON) SHARE; SUBSCRIPTION WARRANT.

PRIMARY MARKET market for new issues of securities, as distinguished from the SECONDARY MARKET, where previously issued securities are bought and sold. A market is primary if the proceeds of sales go to the issuer of the securities sold. The term also applies to government securities auctions and to opening option and futures contract sales.

PRIME
Banking: PRIME RATE.

Investments: acronym for Prescribed Right to Income and Maximum Equity. PRIME was a UNIT INVESTMENT TRUST, sponsored by the Americus Shareowner Service Corporation, which separated the income portion of a stock from its appreciation potential. The income-producing portion, called PRIME, and the appreciation potential, called SCORE (an acronym for Special Claim on Residual Equity) together made up a unit share investment trust, known by the acronym USIT. Both PRIME and SCORE were traded on the American Stock Exchange.

The first version of this unit came into existence with American Telephone and Telegraph stock in late 1983, as AT&T was undergoing divestiture. PRIME units entitled their holders to the dividend income that a holder of one common share of the old AT&T would have gotten plus a proportionate share of the dividends of the seven regional operating companies split off from AT&T. PRIME holders also received all price APPRECIATION in the stock up to the equivalent of $75 a share. The trusts expired in 1988. SCORE holders received all appreciation over $75, but no dividend income.

This form of unit trust allows investors who want income from a stock to maximize that income, and investors who want capital gains to have increased leverage in achieving those gains. *See also* CAPITAL GAIN.

PRIME PAPER highest quality COMMERCIAL PAPER, as rated by Moody's Investor's Service and other rating agencies. Prime paper is considered INVESTMENT GRADE, and therefore institutions with FIDUCIARY responsibility can invest in it. Moody's has three ratings of prime paper:

P-1: Highest quality
P-2: Higher quality
P-3: High quality

Commercial paper below P-3 is not considered prime paper.

PRIME RATE base rate that banks use in pricing commercial loans to their best and most creditworthy customers. The rate is determined by the Federal Reserve's decision to raise or lower prevailing interest rates for short-term borrowing. Though some banks charge their best customers more and some less than the official prime rate, the rate tends to become standard across the banking industry when a major bank moves its prime up or down. The rate is a key interest rate, since loans to less-creditworthy customers are often tied to the prime rate. For example, a BLUE CHIP company may borrow at a prime rate of 8%, but a less-well-established small business may borrow from the same bank at prime plus 2, or 10%. Many consumer loans, such as home equity, automobile, mortgage, and credit card loans, are tied to the prime rate. Although the major bank prime rate is the definitive "best rate" reference point, many banks, particularly those in outlying regions, have a two-tier system, whereby smaller companies of top credit standing may borrow at an even lower rate.

PRIME RATE FUND *mutual fund* that buys portions of corporate loans from banks and passes along interest, which is designed to approximate the PRIME RATE, to shareholders, net of load charges and management fees. Although the bank loans are senior obligations and fully collateralized, they are subject to DEFAULT, particularly in recessions. Prime rate funds thus pay 2–3% more than the yield on one-year CERTIFICATES OF DEPOSIT (CDs), and management fees tend to be higher than those of other mutual funds. Another possible disadvantage is limited liquidity; the only way investors can get out is to sell back their shares to the funds once each quarter.

PRINCIPAL

In General:
1. major party to a transaction, acting as either a buyer or a seller. A principal buys and sells for his or her own account and risk.
2. owner of a privately held business.

Banking and Finance:
1. face amount of a debt instrument or deposit on which interest is either owed or earned.
2. balance of a debt, separate from interest. *See also* PRINCIPAL AMOUNT.

Investments: basic amount invested, exclusive of earnings.

PRINCIPAL AMOUNT FACE VALUE of an obligation (such as a bond or a loan) that must be repaid at maturity, as separate from the INTEREST.

PRINCIPAL STOCKHOLDER stockholder who owns a significant number of shares in a corporation. Under Securities and Exchange Commission (SEC) rules, a principal stockholder owns 10% or more of the voting stock of a REGISTERED COMPANY. These stockholders are often on the board of directors and are considered insiders by SEC rules, so that they must report buying and selling transactions in the company's stock. *See also* AFFILIATED PERSON; CONTROL STOCK; INSIDER.

PRINCIPAL SUM

    Finance: also used as a synonym for PRINCIPAL, in the sense of the obligation due under a debt instrument exclusive of interest. Synonymous with CORPUS. *See also* TRUST.

    Insurance: amount specified as payable to the beneficiary under a policy, such as the death benefit.

PRIORITY system used in an AUCTION MARKET, in which the first bid or offer price is executed before other bid and offer prices, even if subsequent orders are larger. Orders originating off the floor *(see* OFF-FLOOR ORDER) of an exchange also have priority over ON-FLOOR ORDERS. *See also* MATCHED AND LOST; PRECEDENCE.

PRIOR-LIEN BOND bond that has precedence over another bond of the same issuing company even though both classes of bonds are equally secured. Such bonds usually arise from REORGANIZATION. *See also* JUNIOR ISSUE.

PRIOR-PREFERRED STOCK PREFERRED STOCK that has a higher claim than other issues of preferred stock on dividends and assets in LIQUIDATION; also known as *preference shares.*

PRIVATE ACTIVITY BOND *see* PRIVATE PURPOSE BOND.

PRIVATE LETTER RULING Internal Revenue Service (IRS) response to a request for interpretation of the tax law with respect to a specific question or situation. Also called *letter ruling, revenue ruling.*

PRIVATE LIMITED PARTNERSHIP LIMITED PARTNERSHIP not registered with the Securities and Exchange Commission (SEC) and having a maximum of 35 limited partners. *See also* ACCREDITED INVESTOR.

PRIVATE MARKET VALUE (PMV) aggregate market value of a company if each of its parts operated independently and had its own stock price. Also called *breakup value* or *takeover value.* Analysts look for high PMV in relation to market value to identify bargains and potential TARGET COMPANIES. PMV differs from LIQUIDATING VALUE, which excludes GOING CONCERN VALUE, and BOOK VALUE, which is an accounting concept.

PRIVATE MORTGAGE INSURANCE (PMI) type of insurance available from lenders that insures against loss resulting from a default on a mortgage loan and can substitute for down payment money.

PRIVATE PLACEMENT sale of stocks, bonds, or other investments directly to an institutional investor like an insurance company. A PRIVATE LIMITED PARTNERSHIP is also considered a private placement. A private placement does not have to be registered with the Securities and Exchange Commission, as a PUBLIC OFFERING does, if the securities are purchased for investment as opposed to resale. *See also* LETTER SECURITY.

PRIVATE PURPOSE BOND category of MUNICIPAL BOND distinguished from PUBLIC PURPOSE BOND in the TAX REFORM ACT OF 1986 because 10% or more of the bond's benefit goes to private activities or 5% of the proceeds (or $5 million if less) are used for loans to parties other than governmental units. Private purpose obligations, which are also called *private activity bonds* or *nonessential function bonds,* are taxable unless their use is specifically exempted. Even tax-exempt *permitted private activity bonds,* if issued after August 7, 1986, are TAX PREFERENCE ITEMS, except those issued for 501(c)(3) organizations (hospitals, colleges, universities). Private purpose bonds specifically *prohibited* from tax-exemption effective August 15, 1986, include those for sports, trade, and convention facilities and large-issue (over $1 million) INDUSTRIAL DEVELOPMENT BONDS. Permitted issues, except those for 501(c)(3) organizations, airports, docks, wharves, and government-owned solid-waste disposal facilities, are subject to volume caps. *See also* TAXABLE MUNICIPAL BOND.

PRIVATIZATION process of converting a publicly operated enterprise into a privately owned and operated entity. For example, many cities and states contract with private companies to run their prison facilities instead of managing them with municipal personnel. Many countries around the world have privatized formerly state-run enterprises such as banks, airlines, steel companies, utilities, phone systems, and large manufacturers. A wave of privatization swept through Russia and Eastern Europe after the fall of Communism in the early 1990s, and through some Latin American countries such as Peru, as new, democratic governments were established. When a company is privatized, shares formerly owned by the government, as well as management control, are sold to the public. The theory behind privatization is that these enterprises run far more efficiently and offer better service to customers when owned by stockholders instead of the government.

PROBATE judicial process whereby the will of a deceased person is presented to a court and an EXECUTOR or ADMINISTRATOR is appointed to carry out the will's instructions.

PROCEEDS
1. funds given to a borrower after all costs and fees are deducted.
2. money received by the seller of an asset after commissions are deducted—for example, the amount a stockholder receives from the sale of shares, less broker's commission. *See also* PROCEEDS SALE.

PROCEEDS SALE OVER THE COUNTER securities sale where the PROCEEDS are used to purchase another security. Under the FIVE PERCENT RULE of the NATIONAL ASSOCIATION OF SECURITIES DEALERS (NASD), such a trade is considered one transaction and the NASD member's total markup or commission is subject to the 5% guideline.

PRODUCER PRICE INDEX (PPI) measure of change in wholesale prices (formerly called the *wholesale price index),* as released monthly by the U.S. Bureau of Labor Statistics. The index is broken down into components by commodity, industry sector, and stage of processing. The PPI tracks prices of foods, metals, lumber, oil and gas, and many other commodities, but does not measure the price of services. Economists look at trends in the PPI as an accurate precursor to changes in the CPI, since upward or downward pressure on wholesale prices is usually passed through to consumer prices over time. The PPI, published by the Bureau of Labor Statistics in the Department of Labor, is based at 100 in 1982 and is released monthly. Economists also look at the PPI excluding the volatile food and energy components, which they call the "core" PPI. The consumer equivalent of this index is the CONSUMER PRICE INDEX.

PRODUCTION RATE coupon (interest) rate at which a PASS-THROUGH SECURITY guaranteed by the GOVERNMENT NATIONAL MORTGAGE ASSOCIATION (GNMA), popularly known as a Ginnie Mae, is issued. The rate is set a half percentage point under the prevailing Federal Housing Administration (FHA) rate, the maximum rate allowed on residential mortgages insured and guaranteed by the FHA and the Veterans Administration.

PRODUCTIVITY in labor and other areas of economics, the amount of output per unit of input, for example, the quantity of a product produced per hour of labor.

PROFIT

Finance: positive difference that results from selling products and services for more than the cost of producing these goods. *See also* NET PROFIT.

Investments: difference between the selling price and the purchase price of commodities or securities when the selling price is higher.

PROFIT AND LOSS STATEMENT (P & L) summary of the revenues, costs, and expenses of a company during an accounting period; also called INCOME STATEMENT, *operating statement, statement of profit and loss, income and expense statement.* Together with the BALANCE SHEET as of the end of the accounting period, it constitutes a company's financial statement. *See also* COST OF GOODS SOLD; NET INCOME; NET SALES.

PROFIT CENTER segment of a business organization that is responsible for producing profits on its own. A conglomerate with interests in hotels, food processing, and paper may consider each of these three businesses separate profit centers, for instance.

PROFIT FORECAST prediction of future levels of profitability by analysts following a company, as well as company officials. Investors base their buy and sell decisions on such earnings projections. Stock prices typically reflect analysts' profit expectations—companies expected to produce rapidly growing profits often have high price/earnings ratios. Conversely, projections of meager earnings result in lower P/E ratios. The company will often guide analysts so that their profit forecasts are not too high or too low, preventing unwelcome surprises. Analyst profit forecasts are tracked by the INSTITUTIONAL BROKERS ESTIMATE SYSTEM (I/B/E/S) and ZACKS ESTIMATE SYSTEM.

PROFIT MARGIN *see* MARGIN OF PROFIT.

PROFIT-SHARING PLAN agreement between a corporation and its employees that allows the employees to share in company profits. Annual contributions are made by the company, when it has profits, to a profit-sharing account for each employee, either in cash or in a deferred plan, which may be invested in stocks, bonds, or cash equivalents. The funds in a profit-sharing account generally accumulate tax deferred until the employee retires or leaves the company. Many plans allow employees to borrow against profit-sharing accounts for major expenditures such as purchasing a home or financing children's education. Because corporate profit-sharing plans have custody over billions of dollars, they are major institutional investors in the stock and bond markets.

PROFIT TAKING action by short-term securities or commodities traders to cash in on gains earned on a sharp market rise. Profit taking pushes down prices, but only temporarily; the term implies an upward market trend.

PRO FORMA Latin for "as a matter of form"; refers to a presentation of data, such as a BALANCE SHEET or INCOME STATEMENT, where certain amounts are hypothetical. For example, a pro forma balance sheet might show a debt issue that has been proposed but has not yet been consummated.

PROGRAM TRADING computer-driven buying *(buy program)* or selling *(sell program)* of baskets of 15 or more stocks by *index* ARBITRAGE specialists or institutional traders. "Program" refers to computer programs that constantly monitor stock, futures, and options markets, giving buy and sell signals when opportunities for arbitrage profits occur or when market conditions warrant portfolio accumulation or liquidation transactions. Program trading has been blamed for excessive volatility in the markets, especially on Black Monday in 1987, when PORTFOLIO INSURANCE—the since discredited use of index options and futures to hedge stock portfolios—was an important contributing factor.

PROGRESSIVE TAX income tax system in which those with higher incomes pay taxes at higher rates than those with lower incomes; also called *graduated tax*. The U.S. income tax system is based on the concept of progressivity. There are several tax brackets, based on the taxpayer's income, which determine the tax rate that applies to each taxpayer. *See also* FLAT TAX; REGRESSIVE TAX.

PROGRESS PAYMENTS
1. periodic payments to a supplier, contractor, or subcontractor for work satisfactorily performed to date. Such schedules are provided in contracts and can significantly reduce the amount of WORKING CAPITAL required by the performing party.
2. disbursements by lenders to contractors under construction loan arrangements. As construction progresses, bills and LIEN waivers are presented to the bank or savings and loan, which advances additional funds.

PROJECTION estimate of future performance made by economists, corporate planners, and credit and securities analysts. Economists use econometric models to project GROSS DOMESTIC PRODUCT (GDP), inflation, unemployment, and many other economic factors. Corporate financial planners project a company's operating results and CASH FLOW, using historical trends and making assumptions where necessary, in order to make budget decisions and to plan financing. Credit analysts use projections to forecast DEBT SERVICE ability. Securities analysts tend to focus their projections on earnings trends and cash flow per share in order to predict market values and dividend coverage. *See also* ECONOMETRICS.

PROJECT LINK econometric model linking all the economies in the world and forecasting the effects of changes in different economies on other economies. The project is identified with 1980 Nobel Memorial Prize in Economics winner Lawrence R. Klein. *See also* ECONOMETRICS.

PROJECT NOTE short-term debt issue of a municipal agency, usually a housing authority, to finance the construction of public housing. When the housing is finished, the notes are redeemed and the project is financed with long-term bonds. Both project notes and bonds usually pay tax-exempt interest to note- and bondholders, and both are also guaranteed by the U.S. Department of Housing and Urban Development.

PROMISSORY NOTE written promise committing the maker to pay the payee a specified sum of money either on demand or at a fixed or determinable future date, with or without interest. Instruments meeting these criteria are NEGOTIABLE. Often called, simply, a NOTE.

PROPERTY AND EQUIPMENT *see* FIXED ASSET.

PROPERTY INVENTORY personal finance term meaning a list of PERSONAL PROPERTY with cost and market values. A property inventory, which should be accompanied by photographs, is used to substantiate insurance claims and tax losses.

PROPERTY TAX tax assessed on property such as real estate. The tax is determined by several factors, including the use of the land (residential, commercial, or industrial), the assessed valuation of the property, and the tax rate, expressed in MILLS. Property taxes are usually assessed by county and local governments, school districts, and other special authorities such as for water and sewer service. Property taxes are usually deductible on federal income tax returns. If a mortgage lender requires that it pay all property taxes, borrowers must remit their property taxes as part of their monthly mortgage payments and the lender keeps the money in escrow until property taxes are due. *See also* AD VALOREM, PITI.

PROPORTIONAL REPRESENTATION method of stockholder voting, giving individual shareholders more power over the election of directors than they have under STATUTORY VOTING, which, by allowing one vote per share per director, makes it possible for a majority shareholder to elect all the directors. The most familiar example of proportional representation is CUMULATIVE VOTING, under which a shareholder has as many votes as he has shares of stock, multiplied by the number of vacancies on the board, all of which can be cast for one director. This makes it possible for a minority shareholder or a group of small shareholders to gain at least some representation on the board. Another variety provides for the holders of specified classes of stock to elect a number of directors in certain circumstances. For example, if the corporation failed to pay preferred dividends, the preferred holders might then be given the power to elect a certain proportion of the board. Despite the advocacy of stockholders' rights activists, proportional representation has made little headway in American corporations.

PROPRIETORSHIP unincorporated business owned by a single person. The individual proprietor has the right to all the profits from the business and also has responsibility for all the firm's liabilities. Since proprietors are considered self-employed, they are eligible for Keogh accounts for their retirement funds. *See also* KEOGH PLAN.

PRO RATA Latin for "according to the rate"; a method of proportionate allocation. For example, a pro rata property tax rebate might be divided proportionately (prorated) among taxpayers based on their original assessments, so that each gets the same percentage.

PROSPECTUS formal written offer to sell securities that sets forth the plan for a proposed business enterprise or the facts concerning an existing one that an investor needs to make an informed decision. Prospectuses are also issued by MUTUAL FUNDS, describing the history, background of managers, fund objectives, a financial statement, and other essential data. A prospectus for a PUBLIC OFFERING must be filed with the Securities and Exchange Commission and given to prospective buyers of the offering. The prospectus contains financial information and a description of a company's business history, officers, operations, pending litigation (if any), and plans (including the use of the proceeds from the issue).

Before investors receive the final copy of the prospectus, called the *statutory prospectus,* they may receive a PRELIMINARY PROSPECTUS, commonly called a *red herring.* This document is not complete in all details, though most of the major facts of the offering are usually included. The final prospectus is also called the *offering circular.*

Offerings of limited partnerships are also accompanied by prospectuses. Real estate, oil and gas, equipment leasing, and other types of limited partnerships are described in detail, and pertinent financial information, the background of the general partners, and supporting legal opinions are also given.

PROTECTIONISM practice of protecting domestic goods and service industries from foreign competition with tariff and non-tariff barriers. Protectionism causes higher prices for consumers because domestic producers are not exposed to foreign competition, and can therefore keep prices high. But domestic exporters also may suffer, because foreign countries tend to retaliate against protectionism with tariffs and barriers of their own. Many economists say that the Depression of the 1930s was precipitated by the protectionist trade barriers erected by the United States under the Smoot-Hawley Act, which led to retaliation by many countries throughout the world. In more recent years, many protectionist trade barriers have fallen through the passage of GATT, the General Agreement on Tariffs and Trade, which went into effect in 1995.

PROTECTIVE COVENANT *see* COVENANT.

PROVISION *see* ALLOWANCE.

PROVISION FOR INCOME TAXES item on a company's profit and loss statement (P & L) representing its estimated income tax liability for the year. Although taxes are actually paid according to a timetable determined by the Internal Revenue Service and a certain portion of the liability may be accrued, the provision gives an indication of the company's effective tax rate, which analysts compare to other companies as one measure of effective management and profitability. EARNINGS BEFORE TAXES is the net earnings figure before provision for income taxes.

PROXY
In general: person authorized to act or speak for another.
Business:
1. written POWER OF ATTORNEY given by shareholders of a corporation, authorizing a specific vote on their behalf at corporate meetings. Such proxies normally pertain to election of the BOARD OF DIRECTORS or to various resolutions submitted for shareholders' approval.
2. person authorized to vote on behalf of a stockholder of a corporation.

PROXY FIGHT technique used by an acquiring company to attempt to gain control of a TAKEOVER target. The acquirer tries to persuade the shareholders of the TARGET COMPANY that the present management of the firm should be ousted in favor of a slate of directors favorable to the acquirer. If the shareholders, through their PROXY votes, agree, the acquiring company can gain control of the company without paying a PREMIUM price for the firm.

PROXY STATEMENT information that the Securities and Exchange Commission requires must be provided to shareholders before they vote by proxy on company matters. The statement contains proposed members of the BOARD OF DIRECTORS, inside directors' salaries, and pertinent information regarding their bonus and option plans, as well as any resolutions of minority stockholders and of management.

PRUDENT-MAN RULE standard adopted by some U.S. states to guide those with responsibility for investing the money of others. Such fiduciaries (executors of wills, trustees, bank trust departments, and administrators of estates) must act as a prudent man or woman would be expected to act, with discretion and intelligence, to seek reasonable income, preserve capital, and, in general, avoid speculative investments. States not using the prudent-man system use the LEGAL LIST system, allowing fiduciaries to invest only in a restricted list of securities, called the *legal list.*

PUBLIC DEBT borrowings by governments to finance expenditures not covered by current tax revenues. *See also* AGENCY SECURITIES; MUNICIPAL BOND; TREASURIES.

PUBLIC HOUSING AUTHORITY BOND obligation of local public housing agencies, which is centrally marketed through competitive sealed-bid auctions conducted by the U.S. Department of Housing and Urban Development (HUD).

These obligations are secured by an agreement between HUD and the local housing agency that provides that the federal government will loan the local authority a sufficient amount of money to pay PRINCIPAL and INTEREST to maturity.

The proceeds of such bonds provide low-rent housing through new construction, rehabilitation of existing buildings, purchases from private builders or developers, and leasing from private owners. Under special provisions, low income families may also purchase such housing.

The interest on such bonds is exempt from federal income taxes and may also be exempt from state and local income taxes.

PUBLIC LIMITED PARTNERSHIP real estate, oil and gas, equipment leasing, or other LIMITED PARTNERSHIP that is registered with the Securities and Exchange Commission and offered to the public through registered broker/dealers. Such partnerships may be oriented to producing income or capital gains, or, within PASSIVE income rules, to generating tax advantages for limited partners. The number of investors in such a partnership is limited only by the sponsor's desire to cap the funds raised. A public limited partnership, which does not have an active secondary market, is distinguished from a PRIVATE LIMITED PARTNERSHIP, which is limited to 35 limited partners plus ACCREDITED INVESTORS, and a MASTER LIMITED PARTNERSHIP (MLP) that is publicly traded, often on the major stock exchanges.

PUBLIC, THE term for individual investors, as opposed to professional investors. Wall Street analysts like to deride the public for constantly buying at the top of a bull market and selling at the bottom of a bear market. The public participates in stock and bond markets both by buying individual securities and through intermediaries such as mutual funds and insurance companies. The term *public* is also used to describe a security that is available to be bought and sold by individual investors (as opposed to just large institutions or wealthy people, in which case the offering is a private one). Stocks that offer shares to the public are known as *publicly held*, in contrast to *privately held* concerns in which shares are owned by founders, employees, and a few large investors.

PUBLICLY HELD company with shares outstanding that are held by public investors. A company converts from a privately held firm to a publicly held one through an INITIAL PUBLIC OFFERING (IPO) of stock.

PUBLIC OFFERING
1. offering to the investment public, after registration requirements of the Securities and Exchange Commission (SEC) have been complied with, of new securities, usually by an investment banker or a syndicate made up of several investment bankers, at a public offering price agreed upon between the issuer and the investment bankers.

   Public offering is distinguished from PRIVATE PLACEMENT of new securities, which is subject to different SEC regulations. *See also* REGISTERED NEW ISSUE; UNDERWRITE.

2. SECONDARY DISTRIBUTION of previously issued stock. *See also* SECONDARY OFFERING.

PUBLIC OFFERING PRICE price at which a NEW ISSUE of securities is offered to the public by underwriters. *See also* OFFERING PRICE; UNDERWRITE.

PUBLIC OWNERSHIP
Government: government ownership and operation of a productive facility for the purpose of providing some good or service to citizens. The government supplies the capital, controls management, sets prices, and generally absorbs all risks and reaps all profits—similar to a private enterprise. When public ownership

displaces private ownership in a particular instance, it is called NATIONALIZATION. **Investments:** publicly traded portion of a corporation's stock.

PUBLIC PURPOSE BOND category of MUNICIPAL BOND, as defined in the TAX REFORM ACT OF 1986, which is exempt from federal income taxes as long as it provides no more than 10% benefit to private parties and no more than 5% of the proceeds or $5 million are used for loans to private parties; also called *public activity, traditional government purpose,* and *essential purpose* bond. Public purpose bonds include purposes such as roads, libraries, and government buildings.

PUBLIC SECURITIES ASSOCIATION association of dealers, banks, and brokers underwriting municipal, U.S. government, and federal agency debt securities and dealers in mortgage-backed securities.

PUBLIC SYNDICATE *see* PURCHASE GROUP.

PUBLIC UTILITY HOLDING COMPANY ACT OF 1935 major landmark in legislation regulating the securities industry, which reorganized the financial structures of HOLDING COMPANIES in the gas and electric utility industries and regulated their debt and dividend policies. Prior to the Act, abuses by holding companies were rampant, including WATERED STOCK, top-heavy capital structures with excessive fixed-debt burdens, and manipulation of the securities markets. In summary:

1. It requires holding companies operating interstate and persons exercising a controlling influence on utilities and holding companies to register with the Securities and Exchange Commission (SEC) and to provide information on the organizational structure, finances, and means of control.
2. It provides for SEC control of the operation and performance of registered holding companies and SEC approval of all new securities offerings, resulting in such reforms as the elimination of NONVOTING STOCK, the prevention of the milking of subsidiaries, and the outlawing of the upstreaming of dividends (payment of dividends by operating companies to holding companies).
3. It provides for uniform accounting standards, periodic administrative and financial reports, and reports on holdings by officers and directors, and for the end of interlocking directorates with banks or investment bankers.
4. It began the elimination of complex organizational structures by allowing only one intermediate company between the top holding company and its operating companies (the GRANDFATHER CLAUSE).

PULLING IN THEIR HORNS move to defensive strategies on the part of investors. If the stock or bond market has experienced a sharp rise, investors may want to lock in profits by selling part of their positions or instituting hedging techniques to guard against a downturn. If stock prices fall after a steep runup, commentators will frequently say that "investors are pulling in their horns" to describe the reason for the downturn.

PURCHASE ACQUISITION accounting method used in a business MERGER whereby the purchasing company treats the acquired company as an investment and adds the acquired company's assets to its own at their fair market value. Any premium paid over and above the FAIR MARKET VALUE of the acquired assets is reflected as GOODWILL on the buyer's BALANCE SHEET and must be written off against future earnings. Until 1993, goodwill amortization was not deductible for tax purposes, so the reduction of reported future earnings was a disadvantage of this method of merger accounting as compared with the alternative POOLING OF INTERESTS method. The purchase acquisition method is mandatory unless all the criteria for a pooling of interests combination are met.

PURCHASE FUND provision in some PREFERRED STOCK contracts and BOND indentures requiring the issuer to use its best efforts to purchase a specified number of shares or bonds annually at a price not to exceed par value. Unlike SINKING FUND provisions, which require that a certain number of bonds be retired annually, purchase funds require only that a tender offer be made; if no securities are tendered, none are retired. Purchase fund issues benefit the investor in a period of rising rates when the redemption price is higher than the market price and the proceeds can be put to work at a higher return.

PURCHASE GROUP group of investment bankers that, operating under the AGREEMENT AMONG UNDERWRITERS, agrees to purchase a NEW ISSUE of securities from the issuer for resale to the investment public; also called the UNDERWRITING GROUP or *syndicate*. The purchase group is distinguished from the SELLING GROUP, which is organized by the purchase group and includes the members of the purchase group along with other investment bankers. The selling group's function is DISTRIBUTION.

The agreement among underwriters, also called the *purchase group agreement,* is distinguished from the underwriting or purchase agreement, which is between the underwriting group and the issuer. *See also* UNDERWRITE.

PURCHASE GROUP AGREEMENT *see* PURCHASE GROUP.

PURCHASE LOAN in consumer credit, a loan made at a rate of interest to finance a purchase.

PURCHASE-MONEY MORTGAGE MORTGAGE given by a buyer in lieu of cash for the purchase of property. Such mortgages make it possible to sell property when mortgage money is unavailable or when the only buyers are unqualified to borrow from commercial sources.

PURCHASE ORDER written authorization to a vendor to deliver specified goods or services at a stipulated price. Once accepted by the supplier, the purchase order becomes a legally binding purchase CONTRACT.

PURCHASING POWER

Economics: value of money as measured by the goods and services it can buy. For example, the PURCHASING POWER OF THE DOLLAR can be determined by comparing an index of consumer prices for a given base year to the present.

Investment: amount of credit available to a client in a brokerage account for the purchase of additional securities. Purchasing power is determined by the dollar amount of securities that can be margined. For instance, a client with purchasing power of $20,000 in his or her account could buy securities worth $40,000 under the Federal Reserve's currently effective 50% MARGIN REQUIREMENT. *See also* MARGIN SECURITY.

PURCHASING POWER OF THE DOLLAR measure of the amount of goods and services that a dollar can buy in a particular market, as compared with prior periods, assuming always an INFLATION or a DEFLATION factor and using an index of consumer prices. It might be reported, for instance, that one dollar in 1982 has 67 cents of purchasing power in the mid-90s because of the erosion caused by inflation. Deflation would increase the dollar's purchasing power.

PURE PLAY stock market jargon for a company that is virtually all devoted to one line of business. An investor who wants to invest in that line of business looks for such a pure play. For instance, Sears Roebuck may be considered a pure play in the retail business after spinning off its real estate and financial services businesses. Weyerhauser is a pure play in the forest products business. The opposite of a pure play is a widely diversified company, such as a CONGLOMERATE.

PURE MONOPOLY situation in which one firm controls the entire market for a product. This may occur because the firm has a patent on a product or a license from the government to be a monopoly. For example, an electric utility in a particular city may be a monopoly licensed by the city.

PURPOSE LOAN loan backed by securities and used to buy other securities under Federal Reserve Board MARGIN and credit regulations.

PURPOSE STATEMENT form filed by a borrower that details the purpose of a loan backed by securities. The borrower agrees not to use the loan proceeds to buy securities in violation of any Federal Reserve regulations. *See also* NONPUR-POSE LOAN; REGULATION U.

PUT BOND bond that allows its holder to redeem the issue at specified intervals before maturity and receive full FACE VALUE. The bondholders may be allowed to put bonds back to the issuer either only once during the lifetime of the issue or far more frequently. In return for this privilege, a bond buyer sacrifices some yield when choosing a put bond over a fixed-rate bond, which cannot be redeemed before maturity.

PUT-CALL RATIO ratio of trading volume in put options to the trading volume in call options. The ratio provides a quantitative measure of the bullishness or bearishness of investors. A high volume of puts relative to calls indicates investors are bearish, whereas a high ratio of calls to puts shows bullishness. Many market technicians find the put-call ratio to be a good contrary indicator, meaning that when the ratio is high, a market bottom is near and when the ratio is low, a market top is imminent. This reading assumes that the majority of options investors are making the wrong move.

PUT GUARANTEE LETTER letter from a bank certifying that the person writing a put option on an underlying security or index instrument has sufficient funds on deposit at the bank to cover the exercise price of the put if needed. On a short put, the obligation is to pay the aggregate exercise price. There are two forms, as required under New York Stock Exchange Rule 431: the *market index option deposit letter* for index options, and the *equity/Treasury option deposit letter* for security options.

PUT OPTION

Bonds: bondholder's right to redeem a bond before maturity. *See also* PUT BOND.

Options: contract that grants the right to sell at a specified price a specific number of shares by a certain date. The put option buyer gains this right in return for payment of an OPTION PREMIUM. The put option seller grants this right in return for receiving this premium. For instance, a buyer of an XYZ May 70 put has the right to sell 100 shares of XYZ at $70 to the put seller at any time until the contract expires in May. A put option buyer hopes the stock will drop in price, while the put option seller (called a *writer)* hopes the stock will remain stable, rise, or drop by an amount less than his or her profit on the premium.

PUT TO SELLER phrase used when a PUT OPTION is exercised. The OPTION WRITER is obligated to buy the underlying shares at the agreed upon price. If an XYZ June 40 put were "put to seller," for instance, the writer would have to buy 100 shares of XYZ at $40 a share from the put holder even though the current market price of XYZ may be far less than $40 a share.

PYRAMIDING

In general: form of business expansion that makes extensive use of financial LEVERAGE to build complex corporate structures.

Fraud: scheme that builds on nonexistent values, often in geometric progression, such as a chain letter, now outlawed by mail fraud legislation. A famous example was the Ponzi scheme, perpetrated by Charles Ponzi in the late 1920s. Investors were paid "earnings" out of money received from new investors until the scheme collapsed.

Investments: using unrealized profits from one securities or commodities POSITION as COLLATERAL to buy further positions with funds borrowed from a broker. This use of leverage creates increased profits in a BULL MARKET, and causes MARGIN CALLS and large losses in a BEAR MARKET.

Marketing: legal marketing strategy whereby additional distributorships are sold side-by-side with consumer products in order to multiply market reach and maximize profits to the sales organization.

q ————————————————————————————

Q-TIP TRUST qualified terminable interest property *trust,* which allows assets to be transferred between spouses. The grantor of a Q-tip trust directs income from the assets to his or her spouse for life but has the power to distribute the assets upon the death of the spouse. Such trusts qualify the grantor for the unlimited marital deduction if the spouse should die first.

A Q-tip trust is often used to provide for the welfare of a spouse while keeping the assets out of the estate of another (such as a future marriage partner) if the grantor dies first.

QUALIFICATION PERIOD period of time during which an insurance company will not reimburse a policyholder for a claim. The qualification period, which may be several weeks or months, gives the insurance company time to uncover fraud or deception in the policyholder's application for coverage. Such periods, which are stated in the insurance contract, are commonplace in health insurance plans.

QUALIFIED ENDORSEMENT endorsement (signature on the back of a check or other NEGOTIABLE INSTRUMENT transferring the amount to someone other than the one to whom it is payable) that contains wording designed to limit the endorser's liability. "Without recourse," the most frequently seen example, means that if the instrument is not honored, the endorser is not responsible. Where qualified endorsements are restrictive (such as "for deposit only") the term *restricted endorsement* is preferable.

QUALIFIED OPINION auditor's opinion accompanying financial statements that calls attention to limitations of the audit or exceptions the auditor takes to the statements. Typical reasons for qualified opinions: a pending lawsuit that, if lost, would materially affect the financial condition of the company; an indeterminable tax liability relating to an unusual transaction; inability to confirm a portion of the inventory because of inaccessible location. *See also* ACCOUNTANT'S OPINION.

QUALIFIED PLAN OR TRUST TAX-DEFERRED plan set up by an employer for employees under 1954 Internal Revenue Service rules. Such plans usually provide for employer contributions—for example, a profit-sharing or pension plan—

and may also allow employee contributions. They build up savings, which are paid out at retirement or on termination of employment. The employees pay taxes only when they draw the money out. When employers make payments to such plans, they receive certain deductions and other tax benefits. *See also* 401 (K) PLAN; SALARY REDUCTION PLAN.

QUALIFYING ANNUITY ANNUITY that is purchased under, and forms the investment program for, a QUALIFIED PLAN OR TRUST, including pension and profit sharing plans, INDIVIDUAL RETIREMENT ACCOUNTS (IRAs), 403(b)s, and 457s. *See also* KEOGH PLAN.

QUALIFYING SHARE share of COMMON STOCK owned in order to qualify as a director of the issuing corporation.

QUALIFYING STOCK OPTION privilege granted to an employee of a corporation that permits the purchase, for a special price, of shares of its CAPITAL STOCK, under conditions sustained in the Internal Revenue Code. The law states (1) that the OPTION plan must be approved by the stockholders, (2) that the option is not transferable, (3) that the EXERCISE PRICE must not be less than the MARKET PRICE of the shares at the time the option is issued, and (4) that the grantee may not own stock having more than 10% of the company's voting power unless the option price equals 110% of the market price and the option is not exercisable more than 5 years after the grant. No income tax is payable by the employee either at the time of the grant or at the time the option is exercised. If the market price falls below the option price, another option with a lower exercise price can be issued. There is a $100,000 per employee limit on the value of stock covered by options that are exercisable in any one calendar year. *See also* INCENTIVE STOCK OPTION.

QUALIFYING UTILITY utility in which shareholders were, until the end of 1985, able to defer taxes by reinvesting up to $750 in dividends ($1500 for a couple filing jointly) in the company's stock. Taxes were due when the stock was sold. This plan was enacted by the Economic Recovery Tax Act of 1981 as a means of helping utilities raise investment capital cheaply. Most of the utilities qualifying for the plan were electric utilities.

QUALITATIVE ANALYSIS
In general: analysis that evaluates important factors that cannot be precisely measured.

Securities and credit analysis: analysis that is concerned with such questions as the experience, character, and general caliber of management; employee morale; and the status of labor relations rather than with the actual financial data about a company. *See also* QUANTITATIVE ANALYSIS.

QUALITY CONTROL process of assuring that products are made to consistently high standards of quality. Inspection of goods at various points in their manufacture by either a person or a machine is usually an important part of the quality control process.

QUALITY OF EARNINGS phrase describing a corporation's earnings that are attributable to increased sales and cost controls, as distinguished from artificial profits created by inflationary values in inventories or other assets. In a period of high inflation, the quality of earnings tends to suffer, since a large portion of a firm's profits is generated by the rising value of inventories. In a lower inflation period, a company that achieves higher sales and maintains lower costs produces a higher quality of earnings—a factor often appreciated by investors, who are frequently willing to pay more for a higher quality of earnings.

QUANT person with mathematical and computer skills who provides numerical and analytical support services in the securities industry.

QUANTISE to denominate an asset or liability in a currency other than the one in which it usually trades.

QUANTITATIVE ANALYSIS analysis dealing with measurable factors as distinguished from such qualitative considerations as the character of management or the state of employee morale. In credit and securities analysis, examples of quantitative considerations are the value of assets; the cost of capital; the historical and projected patterns of sales, costs, and profitability and a wide range of considerations in the areas of economics; the money market; and the securities markets. Although quantitative and qualitative factors are distinguishable, they must be combined to arrive at sound business and financial judgments. *See also* QUALITATIVE ANALYSIS.

QUANTO OPTION option in one currency or interest rate that pays out in another. A quanto option can be used when an investor favors a foreign index, but is bearish on the outlook for that country's currency.

QUARTERLY
In general: every three months (one quarter of a year).
Securities: basis on which earnings reports to shareholders are made; also, usual time frame of dividend payments.

QUARTER STOCK stock with a par value of $25 per share.

QUASI-PUBLIC CORPORATION corporation that is operated privately and often has its stock traded publicly, but that also has some sort of public mandate and often has the government's backing behind its direct debt obligations. Some examples: COMSAT (Communications Satellite Corporation), which was sponsored by the U.S. Congress to foster the development of space; the FEDERAL NATIONAL MORTGAGE ASSOCIATION (Fannie Mae), which was founded to encourage growth in the secondary mortgage market; and the STUDENT LOAN MARKETING ASSOCIATION (Sallie Mae), which was started to encourage the growth of a secondary market for student loans.

QUICK ASSETS cash, marketable securities, and accounts receivable. *See also* QUICK RATIO.

QUICK RATIO cash, MARKETABLE SECURITIES, and ACCOUNTS RECEIVABLE divided by current liabilities. By excluding inventory, this key LIQUIDITY ratio focuses on the firm's more LIQUID ASSETS, and helps answer the question "If sales stopped, could this firm meet its current obligations with the readily convertible assets on hand?" Assuming there is nothing happening to slow or prevent collections, a quick ratio of 1 to 1 or better is usually satisfactory. Also called *acid-test ratio, quick asset ratio.*

QUID PRO QUO
In general: from the Latin, meaning "something for something." By mutual agreement, one party provides a good or service for which he or she gets another good or service in return.
Securities industry: arrangement by a firm using institutional research that it will execute all trades based on that research with the firm providing it, instead of directly paying for the research. This is known as paying in SOFT DOLLARS.

QUIET PERIOD period an ISSUER is "in registration" and subject to an SEC embargo on promotional publicity. It dates from the preunderwriting decision to 40 or 90 days after the EFFECTIVE DATE.

QUORUM minimum number of people who must be present at a meeting in order to make certain decisions go into effect. A quorum may be required at a board of directors, committee, shareholder, legislative, or other meeting for any decisions to have legal standing. A quorum may be achieved by providing a PROXY as well as appearance in person.

QUOTATION
Business: price estimate on a commercial project or transaction.

Investments: highest bid and lowest offer (asked) price currently available on a security or a commodity. An investor who asks for a quotation ("quote") on XYZ might be told "60 to 60½," meaning that the best bid price (the highest price any buyer wants to pay) is currently $60 a share and that the best offer (the lowest price any seller is willing to accept) is $60½ at that time. Such quotes assume ROUND-LOT transactions—for example, 100 shares for stocks.

QUOTATION BOARD electronically controlled board at a brokerage firm that displays current price quotations and other financial data such as dividends, price ranges of stocks, and current volume of trading.

QUOTED PRICE price at which the last sale and purchase of a particular security or commodity took place.

r

RACKETEER INFLUENCED AND CORRUPT ORGANIZATION ACT *see* RICO.

RADAR ALERT close monitoring of trading patterns in a company's stock by senior managers to uncover unusual buying activity that might signal a TAKEOVER attempt. *See also* SHARK WATCHER.

RAIDER individual or corporate investor who intends to take control of a company by buying a controlling interest in its stock and installing new management. Raiders who accumulate 5% or more of the outstanding shares in the TARGET COMPANY must report their purchases to the Securities and Exchange Commission, the exchange of listing, and the target itself. *See also* BEAR RAID; WILLIAMS ACT.

RAINMAKER individual who brings significant amounts of new business to a brokerage firm. The rainmaker may bring in wealthy brokerage customers who generate a large dollar volume of commissions. Or he or she may be an investment banker who attracts corporate or municipal finance underwritings or merger and acquisition business. Because they are so important to the firm, rainmakers are usually given special PERQUISITES and bonus compensation.

RALLY marked rise in the price of a security, commodity future, or market after a period of decline or sideways movement.

R & D *see* RESEARCH AND DEVELOPMENT.

RANDOM WALK theory about the movement of stock and commodity futures prices hypothesizing that past prices are of no use in forecasting future price movements. According to the theory, stock prices reflect reactions to information coming to the market in random fashion, so they are no more predictable than the walking pattern of a drunken person. The random walk theory was first espoused in 1900 by the French mathematician Louis Bachelier and revived in the 1960s. It is hotly disputed by advocates of TECHNICAL ANALYSIS, who say that charts of past price movements enable them to predict future price movements.

RANGE high and low end of a security, commodity future, or market's price fluctuations over a period of time. Daily newspapers publish the 52-week high and low price range of stocks traded on the New York Stock Exchange, American Stock Exchange, and over-the-counter markets. Advocates of TECHNICAL ANALYSIS attach great importance to trading ranges because they consider it of great significance if a security breaks out of its trading range by going higher or lower. *See also* BREAKOUT.

RATE BASE value established for a utility by a regulatory body such as a Public Utility Commission on which the company is allowed to earn a particular rate of return. Generally the rate base includes the utility's operating costs but not the cost of constructing new facilities. Whether modernization costs should be included in the rate base, and thus passed on to customers, is a subject of continuing controversy. *See also* FAIR RATE OF RETURN.

RATE CAP *see* CAP.

RATE COVENANT provision in MUNICIPAL REVENUE BOND agreements or resolutions covering the rates, or methods of establishing rates, to be charged users of the facility being financed. The rate covenant usually promises that rates will be adjusted when necessary to cover the cost of repairs and maintenance while continuing to provide for the payment of bond interest and principal.

RATE OF EXCHANGE *see* EXCHANGE RATE; PAR VALUE OF CURRENCY.

RATE OF INFLATION *see* CONSUMER PRICE INDEX; INFLATION RATE; PRODUCER PRICE INDEX.

RATE OF RETURN
Fixed-income securities (bonds and preferred stock): CURRENT YIELD, that is, the coupon or contractual dividend rate divided by the purchase price. *See also* YIELD TO AVERAGE LIFE; YIELD TO CALL; YIELD TO MATURITY.
Common stock: (1) dividend yield, which is the annual dividend divided by the purchase price. (2) TOTAL RETURN rate, which is the dividend plus capital appreciation.
Corporate finance: RETURN ON EQUITY or RETURN ON INVESTED CAPITAL.
Capital budgeting: INTERNAL RATE OF RETURN.
    See also FAIR RATE OF RETURN; HORIZON ANALYSIS; MEAN RETURN; REAL INTEREST RATE; REQUIRED RATE OF RETURN; TOTAL RETURN; YIELD.

RATING
Credit and investments: evaluation of securities investment and credit risk by rating services such as Duff & Phelps/MCM, Fitch Investors Service Inc., MOODY'S INVESTORS SERVICE, STANDARD & POOR'S CORPORATION, and VALUE LINE INVESTMENT SURVEY. *See also* CREDIT RATING; EVENT RISK; NOT RATED.
Insurance: using statistics, mortality tables, probability theory, experience, judgment, and mathematical analysis to establish the rates on which insurance

premiums are based. There are three basic rating systems: *class rate,* applying to a homogeneous grouping of clients; *schedule system,* relating positive and negative factors in the case of a particular insured (for example, a smoker or nonsmoker in the case of a life policy) to a base figure; and *experience rating,* reflecting the historical loss experience of the particular insured. Also called *rate-making.*

Insurance companies are also rated. *See* BEST'S RATING.

LEADING BOND RATING SERVICES	RATING SERVICE			
Explanation of corporate/ municipal bond ratings	*Duff & Phelps/MCM*	*Fitch*	*Moody's*	*Standard & Poor's*
Highest quality, "gilt edged" High quality Upper medium grade	AAA AA A	AAA AA A	Aaa Aa A	AAA AA A
Medium grade Predominantly speculative Speculative, low grade	BBB BB B	BBB BB B	Baa Ba B	BBB BB B
Poor to default Highest speculation Lowest quality, no interest	CCC	CCC CC C	Caa Ca C	CCC CC C
In default, in arrears, questionable value		DDD DD D		DDD DD D

Fitch and Standard & Poor's may use + or − to modify some ratings. Moody's uses the numerical modifiers 1 (highest), 2, and 3 in the range from Aa1 through Ca3.

RATIO ANALYSIS method of analysis, used in making credit and investment judgments, which utilizes the relationship of figures found in financial statements to determine values and evaluate risks and compares such ratios to those of prior periods and other companies to reveal trends and identify eccentricities. Ratio analysis is only one tool among many used by analysts. *See also* ACCOUNTS RECEIVABLE TURNOVER; ACID TEST RATIO; BOND RATIO; CAPITALIZATION RATIO; CAPITAL TURNOVER; CASH RATIO; COLLECTION PERIOD; COMMON STOCK RATIO; CURRENT RATIO; DEBT-TO-EQUITY RATIO; DIVIDEND PAYOUT RATIO; EARNINGS-PRICE RATIO; FIXED CHARGE COVERAGE; LEVERAGE; NET TANGIBLE ASSETS PER SHARE; OPERATING RATIO; PREFERRED STOCK RATIO; PRICE-EARNINGS RATIO; PROFIT MARGIN; QUICK RATIO; RETURN ON EQUITY; RETURN ON INVESTED CAPITAL; RETURN ON SALES.

RATIO WRITER OPTIONS writer who sells more CALL contracts than he has underlying shares. For example, an investor who writes (sells) 10 calls, 5 of them covered by 500 owned shares and the other 5 of them uncovered (or "naked"), has a 2 for 1 ratio write.

RAW LAND property in its natural state, prior to grading, construction, and subdividing. The property has no sewers, electricity, streets, buildings, water service, telephone service, or other amenities. Investors in raw land hope that the land's value will rise in the future if it is developed. While they wait, however, they must pay property taxes on the land's value.

RAW MATERIAL unfinished goods used in the manufacture of a product. For example, a steelmaker uses iron ore and other metals in producing steel. A publishing company uses paper and ink to create books, newspapers, and magazines. Raw materials are carried on a company's balance sheet as inventory in the current assets section.

REACHBACK ability of a LIMITED PARTNERSHIP or other tax shelter to offer deductions at the end of the year that reach back for the entire year. For instance, the investor who buys an OIL AND GAS LIMITED PARTNERSHIP in late December might be able to claim deductions for the entire year's drilling costs, depletion allowance, and interest expenses. Reachback on tax shelters was considered to be abusive by the Internal Revenue Service, and was substantially eliminated by 1984.

REACTION drop in securities prices after a sustained period of advancing prices, perhaps as the result of PROFIT TAKING or adverse developments. *See also* CORRECTION.

READING THE TAPE judging the performance of stocks by monitoring changes in price as they are displayed on the TICKER tape. An analyst reads the tape to determine whether a stock is acting strongly or weakly, and therefore is likely to go up or down. An investor reads the tape to determine whether a stock trade is going with or against the flow of market action. *See also* DON'T FIGHT THE TAPE.

REAGANOMICS economic program followed by the administration of President Ronald Reagan beginning in 1980. Reaganomics stressed lower taxes, higher defense spending, and curtailed spending for social services. After a reduction of growth in the money supply by the Federal Reserve Board combined with Reaganomics to produce a severe recession in 1981–82, the Reagan years were characterized by huge budget deficits, low interest and inflation rates, and continuous economic growth.

REAL ESTATE piece of land and all physical property related to it, including houses, fences, landscaping, and all rights to the air above and earth below the property. Assets not directly associated with the land are considered *personal property.*

REAL ESTATE AGENT licensed salesperson working for a licensed broker. The agent may hold an individual REAL ESTATE BROKER'S license.

REAL ESTATE APPRAISAL estimate of the value of property, usually required when a property is sold, financed, condemned, taxed, insured, or partitioned. An appraisal is not a determination of value. Three approaches are used. To produce an accurate resale price for a residence, appraisers compare the price of the property to the prices of similar nearby properties that have sold recently. For new construction and service properties such as churches and post offices, appraisers look at the reproduction or replacement cost of the improvements, less depreciation, plus the value of the land. For investment properties such as apartment buildings and shopping centers, an estimated value is based on the capitalization of net operating income from a property at an acceptable market rate.

REAL ESTATE BROKER person who arranges the purchase or sale of property for a buyer or seller in return for a commission. Brokers may help arrange financing of the purchase through contacts with banks, savings and loans, and mortgage bankers. Brokers must be licensed by the state to buy or sell real estate.

REAL ESTATE INVESTMENT TRUST (REIT) company, usually traded publicly, that manages a portfolio of real estate to earn profits for shareholders. Patterned after INVESTMENT COMPANIES, REITs make investments in a diverse array of real estate such as shopping centers, medical facilities, nursing homes, office buildings, apartment complexes, industrial warehouses, and hotels. Some REITs, called EQUITY REITS, take equity positions in real estate; shareholders receive income from the rents received and from the properties and receive capital gains as buildings are sold at a profit. Other REITs specialize in lending money to building developers; such MORTGAGE REITS pass interest income on to shareholders. Some REITs, called *hybrid REITs,* have a mix of equity and debt investments. To avoid taxation at the corporate level, 75% or more of the REIT's income must be from real property and 95% of its net earnings must be distributed to shareholders annually. Because REITs must distribute most of their earnings, they tend to pay high yields of 5% to 10% or more.

REAL ESTATE LIMITED PARTNERSHIP LIMITED PARTNERSHIP that invests in real estate. The partnership buys properties such as apartment or office buildings, shopping centers, industrial warehouses, and hotels and passes rental income through to limited partners. If the properties appreciate in value over time, they can be sold and the profit passed through to limited partners. A GENERAL PARTNER manages the partnership, deciding which properties to buy and sell and handling administrative duties, such as distributions to limited partners. In the early 1980s, many real estate partnerships were structured to reduce limited partners' tax liability, because operating losses, plus accelerated depreciation from real estate, could be used to offset other taxable income. But these deals were largely discontinued after the TAX REFORM ACT OF 1986 introduced the principle of PASSIVE LOSSES, meaning that investors could no longer use real estate partnership losses to offset their income from salaries and other investments. Since the mid-1980s, partnerships have been designed to produce high current income and long-term capital gains through appreciation in the underlying real estate, not tax benefits.

REAL ESTATE MORTGAGE INVESTMENT CONDUIT *see* REMIC.

REAL GAIN OR LOSS gain or loss adjusted for INFLATION. *See also* INFLATION ACCOUNTING.

REAL INCOME income of an individual, group, or country adjusted for changes in PURCHASING POWER caused by inflation. A price index is used to determine the difference between the purchasing power of a dollar in a base year and the purchasing power now. The resulting percentage factor, applied to total income, yields the value of that income in constant dollars, termed real income. For instance, if the cost of a market basket increases from $100 to $120 in ten years, reflecting a 20% decline in purchasing power, salaries must rise by 20% if real income is to be maintained.

REAL INTEREST RATE current interest rate minus inflation rate. The real interest rate may be calculated by comparing interest rates with present or, more frequently, with predicted inflation rates The real interest rate gives investors in bonds and other fixed-rate instruments a way to see whether their interest will allow them to keep up with or beat the erosion in dollar values caused by inflation. With a bond yielding 10% and inflation of 3%, for instance, the real interest rate of 7% would bring a return high enough to beat inflation. If inflation were at 15%, however, the investor would fall behind as prices rise.

REALIZED PROFIT (OR LOSS) profit or loss resulting from the sale or other disposal of a security. Capital gains taxes may be due when profits are realized: realized losses can be used to offset realized gains for tax purposes. Such profits and losses differ from a PAPER PROFIT OR LOSS, which (except for OPTION AND FUTURES CONTRACTS) has no tax consequences.

REAL PROPERTY land and all property attached to the land, such as houses, trees, fences, and all improvements.

REAL RATE OF RETURN RETURN on an investment adjusted for inflation.

REALTOR registered trade name that can be used only by members of state and local real estate boards affiliated with the National Association of Realtors (NAR). A realtor-associate is trained and licensed to help clients buy and sell real estate. Realtors must follow a strict code of ethics and receive ongoing training from the NAR. Any complaints about a particular realtor are dealt with at the local real estate board affiliated with the NAR.

REBATE
1. in lending, unearned interest refunded to a borrower if the loan is paid off before maturity.
2. in consumer marketing, payment made to a consumer after a purchase is completed, to induce purchase of a product. For instance, a customer who buys a television set for $500 may be entitled to a rebate of $50, which is received after sending a proof of purchase and a rebate form to the manufacturer. *See also* RULE OF THE 78s.

RECAPITALIZATION alteration of a corporation's CAPITAL STRUCTURE, such as an exchange of bonds for stock. BANKRUPTCY is a common reason for recapitalization; debentures might be exchanged for REORGANIZATION BONDS that pay interest only when earned. A healthy company might seek to save taxes by replacing preferred stock with bonds to gain interest deductibility. *See also* DEFEASANCE.

RECAPTURE
1. contract clause allowing one party to recover some degree of possession of an asset. In leases calling for a percentage of revenues, such as those for shopping centers, the recapture clause provides that the developer get a percentage of profits in addition to a fixed rent.
2. in the tax code, the reclamation by the government of tax benefits previously taken. For example, where a portion of the profit on the sale of a depreciable asset represented ACCELERATED DEPRECIATION or the INVESTMENT CREDIT, all or part of that gain would be "recaptured" and taxed as ORDINARY INCOME, with the balance subject to the favorable CAPITAL GAINS TAX. Recapture also has specialized applications in oil and other industries. Recapture assumed a new meaning under the 1986 Act whereby banks with assets of $500 million or more were required to take into income the balance of their RESERVE for BAD DEBTS. The Act called for recapture of income at the rate of 10%, 20%, 30%, and 40% for the years 1987 through 1990, respectively.

RECEIVABLES *see* ACCOUNTS RECEIVABLE.

RECEIVER court-appointed person who takes possession of, but not title to, the assets and affairs of a business or estate that is in a form of BANKRUPTCY called *receivership* or is enmeshed in a legal dispute. The receiver collects rents and other income and generally manages the affairs of the entity for the benefit of its owners and creditors until a disposition is made by the court.

RECEIVER'S CERTIFICATE debt instrument issued by a RECEIVER, who uses the proceeds to finance continued operations or otherwise to protect assets in receivership. The certificates constitute a LIEN on the property, ranking ahead of all other secured or unsecured liabilities in LIQUIDATION.

RECEIVE VERSUS PAYMENT instruction accompanying sell orders by institutions that only cash will be accepted in exchange for delivery of the securities at the time of settlement. Institutions are generally required by law to accept only cash. Also called *receive against payment.*

RECESSION downturn in economic activity, defined by many economists as at least two consecutive quarters of decline in a country's GROSS DOMESTIC PRODUCT.

RECLAMATION

Banking: restoration or correction of a NEGOTIABLE INSTRUMENT—or the amount thereof—that has been incorrectly recorded by the *clearing house.*

Finance: restoration of an unproductive asset to productivity, such as by using landfill to make a swamp developable.

Securities: right of either party to a securities transaction to recover losses caused by *bad delivery* or other irregularities in the settlement process.

RECORD DATE *see* DATE OF RECORD; EX-DIVIDEND DATE; PAYMENT DATE.

RECOURSE legal ability the purchaser of a financial asset may have to fall back on the original creditor if the current debtor defaults. For example, an account receivable sold with recourse enables the buyer of the receivable to make claim on the seller if the account doesn't pay.

RECOURSE LOAN

1. loan for which an endorser or guarantor is liable for payment in the event the borrower defaults.
2. loan made to a DIRECT PARTICIPATION PROGRAM or LIMITED PARTNERSHIP whereby the lender, in addition to being secured by specific assets, has recourse against the general assets of the partnership. *See also* NONRECOURSE LOAN.

RECOVERY

Economics: period in a business cycle when economic activity picks up and the GROSS NATIONAL PRODUCT grows, leading into the expansion phase of the cycle.

Finance: (1) absorption of cost through the allocation of DEPRECIATION; (2) collection of an ACCOUNT RECEIVABLE that had been written off as a bad debt; (3) residual cost, or salvage value, of a fixed asset after all allowable depreciation.

Investment: period of rising prices in a securities or commodities market after a period of falling prices.

RECOVERY PERIOD

Economics: period of time in which the economy is emerging from a recession or depression. The recovery period is marked by rising sales and production, improved consumer confidence, and in many cases, rising interest rates.

Stocks: period of time in which a stock that has fallen sharply in price begins to rise again, thereby recovering some of its value.

Taxation: period over which property is subject to depreciation for tax purposes following the ACCELERATED COST RECOVERY SYSTEM (ACRS). Different classes of assets are assigned different periods in which costs can be recovered.

REDEEMABLE BOND *see* CALLABLE.

REDEMPTION repayment of a debt security or preferred stock issue, at or before maturity, at PAR or at a premium price.

Mutual fund shares are redeemed at NET ASSET VALUE when a shareholder's holdings are liquidated.

REDEMPTION DATE date on which a bond is scheduled to mature or be redeemed. If a bond is CALLED AWAY before scheduled maturity, the redemption date is the day that the bond will be taken back.

REDEMPTION FEES fees charged by a mutual fund on shareholders who sell fund shares within a short period of time. The time limit and size of the fee vary among funds, but the redemption fee usually is a relatively small percentage (1% or 2% of the amount withdrawn). Some mutual funds charge a small flat redemption fee of $5 or $10 to cover administrative charges. The intent of the redemption fee is to discourage rapid-fire shifts from one fund to another in an attempt to "time" swings in the stock or bond market. This fee often is confused with the contingent deferred sales charge, or BACK END SALES CHARGE, typically a feature of the broker-sold fund.

REDEMPTION PRICE *see* CALL PRICE.

RED HERRING *see* PRELIMINARY PROSPECTUS.

REDISCOUNT DISCOUNT short-term negotiable debt instruments, such as banker's ACCEPTANCES and COMMERCIAL PAPER, that have been *discounted* with a bank—in other words, exchanged for an amount of cash adjusted to reflect the current interest rate. The bank then discounts the paper a second time for its own benefit with another bank or with a Federal Reserve bank. Rediscounting was once the primary means by which banks borrowed additional reserves from the Fed. Today most banks do this by discounting their own notes secured by GOVERNMENT SECURITIES or other ELIGIBLE PAPER. But *rediscount rate* is still used as a synonym for DISCOUNT RATE, the rate charged by the Fed for all bank borrowings.

REDLINING discrimination in the pattern of granting loans, insurance coverage, or other financial benefits. Lenders or insurers who practice redlining "draw a red line" around a troubled area of a city and vow not to lend or insure property in that neighborhood because of poor economic conditions and high default rates. Insurance companies withdraw from an area because of high claims experience and widespread fraud. With mortgage and business loans and insurance hard to obtain, redlining therefore tends to accelerate the decline of such neighborhoods. Redlining is illegal because it discriminates against residents of an area on the basis of where they live. Congress has enacted legislation such as the Community Reinvestment Act, which forces banks to lend to underprivileged areas, to combat redlining.

REDS *see* REFUNDING ESCROW DEPOSITS.

REDUCTION-OPTION LOAN (ROL) hybrid between a fixed-rate and adjustable mortgage and a cheaper alternative to refinancing, whereby the borrower has the one-time option from the second through the fifth year to match the current mortgage rate, which then becomes fixed for the rest of the term. The reduction is usually permitted if rates drop more than 2% in any one year.

REFCORP *see* RESOLUTION FUNDING CORPORATION (REFCORP).

REFINANCING
Banking: extending the maturity date, or increasing the amount of existing debt, or both.
Bonds: REFUNDING; retiring existing bonded debt by issuing new securities to reduce the interest rate, or to extend the maturity date, or both.
Personal finance: revising a payment schedule, usually to reduce the monthly payments and often to modify interest charges.

REFLATION reversal of DEFLATION by deliberate government monetary action.

REFUND

Bonds: retirement of an existing bond issue through the sale of a new bond issue. When interest rates have fallen, issuers may want to exercise the CALL FEATURE of a bond and replace it with another debt instrument paying a lower interest rate. *See also* PREREFUNDING.

Commerce: return of merchandise for money. For example, a consumer who is not happy with a product has the right to return it for a refund of his money.

Taxes: *see* TAX REFUND.

REFUNDING

1. replacing an old debt with a new one, usually in order to lower the interest cost of the issuer. For instance, a corporation or municipality that has issued 10% bonds may want to refund them by issuing 7% bonds if interest rates have dropped. *See also* PREREFUNDING; REFINANCING.
2. in merchandising, returning money to the purchaser, e.g., to a consumer who has paid for an appliance and is not happy with it.

REFUNDING ESCROW DEPOSITS (REDS) financial instruments used to circumvent 1984 tax restrictions on tax-exempt PREREFUNDINGS for certain kinds of state or local projects, such as airports, solid-waste disposal facilities, wharves, and convention centers. The object of prerefundings was to lock in a lower current rate in anticipation of maturing higher-rate issues. REDs accomplish this by way of a forward purchase contract obligating investors to buy bonds at a predetermined rate when they are issued at a future date. The future date coincides with the first optional call date on existing high-rate bonds. In the interim, investors' money is invested in Treasury bonds bought in the secondary market. The Treasuries are held in escrow, in effect securing the investor's deposit and paying taxable annual income. The Treasuries mature around the call date on the existing bonds, providing the money to buy the new issue and redeem the old one. Also called *municipal forwards.*

REGIONAL BANK bank that specializes in collecting deposits and making loans in one region of the country, as distinguished from a MONEY CENTER BANK, which operates nationally and internationally.

REGIONAL MUTUAL FUND mutual fund that buys securities from just one region of the country. There are regional mutual funds specializing in the Southwest, Southeast, Northwest, Midwest and other regions. Investors may be interested in such funds because they provide a PURE PLAY on the economic growth in a particular region. People living in these regions may also want to invest in nearby companies because of their firsthand experience with such firms.

Regional mutual funds also specialize in different regions of the world. There are funds limited to investments in Latin America, Europe, Asia, and other regions. Regional funds, whether domestic or international, tend to be more volatile than funds with more geographically diversified holdings.

REGIONAL STOCK EXCHANGES organized national securities exchanges located outside of New York City and registered with the Securities and Exchange Commission. They include: the Boston, Cincinnati, Intermountain (Salt Lake City), Midwest (Chicago), Pacific (Los Angeles and San Francisco), Philadelphia (Philadelphia and Miami), and Spokane stock exchanges. These exchanges list not only regional issues, but many of the securities that are listed on the New York exchanges. Companies listed on the NEW YORK STOCK EXCHANGE and the AMERICAN STOCK EXCHANGE will often be listed on regional exchanges as well to broaden the market for their securities. Using the INTERMARKET TRADING

SYSTEM (ITS), a SPECIALIST on the floor of one of the New York or regional exchanges can see competing prices for the securities he trades on video screens. Regional exchanges handle only a small percentage of the total volume of the New York exchanges, though most of the trading done on regional exchanges involves stocks listed on the New York exchanges. *See also* DUAL LISTING; GRADUATED SECURITY; SECURITIES AND COMMODITIES EXCHANGES.

REGISTERED BOND bond that is recorded in the name of the holder on the books of the issuer or the issuer's REGISTRAR and can be transferred to another owner only when ENDORSED by the registered owner. A bond registered for principal only, and not for interest, is called a *registered coupon bond.* One that is not registered is called a *bearer bond;* one issued with detachable coupons for presentation to the issuer or a paying agent when interest or principal payments are due is termed a COUPON BOND. Bearer bonds are NEGOTIABLE INSTRUMENTS payable to the holder and therefore do not legally require endorsement. Bearer bonds that may be changed to registered bonds are called *interchangeable bonds.*

REGISTERED CHECK check issued by a bank for a customer who places funds aside in a special register. The customer writes in his name and the name of the payee and the amount of money to be transferred. The bank, which collects a fee for the service, then puts on the bank's name and the amount of the check and gives the check a special number. The check has two stubs, one for the customer and one for the bank. The registered check is similar to a money order for someone who does not have a checking account at the bank.

REGISTERED COMPANY company that has filed a REGISTRATION STATEMENT with the Securities and Exchange Commission in connection with a PUBLIC OFFERING of securities and must therefore comply with SEC DISCLOSURE requirements.

REGISTERED COMPETITIVE MARKET MAKER
1. securities dealer registered with the NATIONAL ASSOCIATION OF SECURITIES DEALERS (NASD) as a market maker in a particular OVER-THE-COUNTER stock—that is, one who maintains firm bid and offer prices in the stock by standing ready to buy or sell round lots. Such dealers must announce their quotes through NASDAQ, which requires that there be at least two market makers in each stock listed in the system; the bid and asked quotes are compared to ensure that the quote is a *representative spread. See also* MAKE A MARKET.
2. REGISTERED COMPETITIVE TRADER on the New York Stock Exchange. Such traders are sometimes called market makers because, in addition to trading for their own accounts, they are expected to help correct an IMBALANCE OF ORDERS. *See also* REGISTERED EQUITY MARKET MAKER.

REGISTERED COMPETITIVE TRADER one of a group of New York Stock Exchange members who buy and sell for their own accounts. Because these members pay no commissions, they are able to profit on small changes in market prices and thus tend to trade actively in stocks doing a high volume. Like SPECIALISTS, registered competitive traders must abide by exchange rules, including a requirement that 75% of their trades be *stabilizing.* This means they cannot sell unless the last trading price on a stock was up, or buy unless the last trading price was down. Orders from the general public take precedence over those of registered competitive traders, which account for less than 1% of volume. Also called *floor trader* or *competitive trader.*

REGISTERED COUPON BOND *see* REGISTERED BOND.

REGISTERED EQUITY MARKET MAKER AMERICAN STOCK EXCHANGE member firm registered as a trader for its own account. Such firms are expected to make stabilizing purchases and sales when necessary to correct imbalances in particular securities. *See also* REGISTERED COMPETITIVE MARKET MAKER.

REGISTERED FINANCIAL PLANNER (RFP) *see* FINANCIAL PLANNER.

REGISTERED INVESTMENT ADVISER investment adviser registered with the Securities and Exchange Commission. A RIA must fill out a form detailing educational and professional experience and pay an annual fee to the SEC. The Registered Investment Adviser (RIA) designation carries no endorsement from the SEC, which regulates RIA's activities. RIAs may pick stocks, bonds, mutual funds, partnerships or other SEC-registered investments for clients. They may be paid on a fee-only or fee-plus-commission basis. Usually, fees are based on a fixed percentage of assets under management.

REGISTERED INVESTMENT COMPANY investment company, such as an open-end or closed-end MUTUAL FUND, which files a registration statement with the Securities and Exchange Commission and meets all the other requirements of the INVESTMENT COMPANY ACT OF 1940.

REGISTERED OPTIONS TRADER specialist on the floor of the AMERICAN STOCK EXCHANGE who is responsible for maintaining a fair and orderly market in an assigned group of options.

REGISTERED REPRESENTATIVE employee of a stock exchange member broker/dealer who acts as an ACCOUNT EXECUTIVE for clients. As such, the registered representative gives advice on which securities to buy and sell, and he collects a percentage of the commission income he generates as compensation. To qualify as a registered representative, a person must acquire a background in the securities business and pass a series of tests, including the General Securities Examination and state securities tests. "Registered" means licensed by the Securities and Exchange Commission and by the New York Stock Exchange.

REGISTERED RETIREMENT SAVINGS PLAN (RRSP) tax-deductible and tax-sheltered retirement plan for individuals in Canada, similar in concept to the INDIVIDUAL RETIREMENT PLAN (IRA) in the United States.

REGISTERED SECONDARY OFFERING offering, usually through investment bankers, of a large block of securities that were previously issued to the public, using the abbreviated Form S-16 of the Securities and Exchange Commission. Such offerings are usually made by major stockholders of mature companies who may be *control persons* or institutions who originally acquired the securities in a private placement. Form S-16 relies heavily on previously filed SEC documents such as the S-1, the 10-K, and quarterly filings. Where listed securities are concerned, permission to sell large blocks off the exchange must be obtained from the appropriate exchange. *See also* LETTER SECURITY; SECONDARY DISTRIBUTION; SECONDARY OFFERING; SHELF REGISTRATION.

REGISTERED SECURITY
1. security whose owner's name is recorded on the books of the issuer or the issuer's agent, called a *registrar*—for example, a REGISTERED BOND as opposed to a *bearer bond,* the former being transferable only by endorsement, the latter payable to the holder.
2. securities issue registered with the Securities and Exchange Commission as a new issue or as a SECONDARY OFFERING. *See also* REGISTERED SECONDARY OFFERING; REGISTRATION.

REGISTRAR agency responsible for keeping track of the owners of bonds and the issuance of stock. The registrar, working with the TRANSFER AGENT, keeps current files of the owners of a bond issue and the stockholders in a corporation. The registrar also makes sure that no more than the authorized amount of stock is in circulation. For bonds, the registrar certifies that a bond is a corporation's genuine debt obligation.

REGISTRATION process set up by the Securities Exchange Acts of 1933 and 1934 whereby securities that are to be sold to the public are reviewed by the Securities and Exchange Commission. The REGISTRATION STATEMENT details pertinent financial and operational information about the company, its management, and the purpose of the offering. Incorrect or incomplete information will delay the offering.

REGISTRATION FEE charge made by the Securities and Exchange Commission and paid by the issuer of a security when a public offering is recorded with the SEC.

REGISTRATION STATEMENT document detailing the purpose of a proposed public offering of securities. The statement outlines financial details, a history of the company's operations and management, and other facts of importance to potential buyers. *See also* REGISTRATION.

REGRESSION ANALYSIS statistical technique used to establish the relationship of a dependent variable, such as the sales of a company, and one or more independent variables, such as family formations, GROSS NATIONAL PRODUCT, per capita income, and other ECONOMIC INDICATORS. By measuring exactly how large and significant each independent variable has historically been in its relation to the dependent variable, the future value of the dependent variable can be predicted. Essentially, regression analysis attempts to measure the degree of correlation between the dependent and independent variables, thereby establishing the latter's predictive value. For example, a manufacturer of baby food might want to determine the relationship between sales and housing starts as part of a sales forecast. Using a technique called a scatter graph, it might plot on the X and Y axes the historical sales for ten years and the historical annual housing starts for the same period. A line connecting the average dots, called the regression line, would reveal the degree of correlation between the two factors by showing the amount of unexplained variation—represented by the dots falling outside the line. Thus, if the regression line connected all the dots, it would demonstrate a direct relationship between baby food sales and housing starts, meaning that one could be predicted on the basis of the other. The proportion of dots scattered outside the regression line would indicate, on the other hand, the degree to which the relationship was less direct, a high enough degree of unexplained variation meaning there was no meaningful relationship and that housing starts have no predictive value in terms of baby food sales. This proportion of unexplained variations is termed the *coefficient of determination,* and its square root the CORRELATION COEFFICIENT. The correlation coefficient is the ultimate yardstick of regression analysis: a correlation coefficient of 1 means the relationship is direct—baby food and housing starts move together; −1 means there is a negative relationship—the more housing starts there are, the less baby food is sold; a coefficient of zero means there is no relationship between the two factors.

Regression analysis is also used in securities' markets analysis and in the risk-return analyses basic to PORTFOLIO THEORY.

REGRESSIVE TAX
1. system of taxation in which tax rates decline as the tax base rises. For example, a system that taxed values of $1000 to $5000 at 5%, $5000 to $10,000 at

4% and so on would be regressive. A regressive tax is the opposite of a PRO-GRESSIVE TAX.

2. tax system that results in a higher tax for the poor than for the rich, in terms of percentage of income. In this sense, a sales tax is regressive even though the same rate is applied to all sales, because people with lower incomes tend to spend most of their incomes on goods and services. Similarly, payroll taxes are regressive because they are borne largely by wage earners and not by higher income groups. Local property taxes also tend to be regressive because poorer people spend more of their incomes on housing costs, which are directly affected by property taxes. *See also* FLAT TAX.

REGRESSION ANALYSIS
SCATTER GRAPH

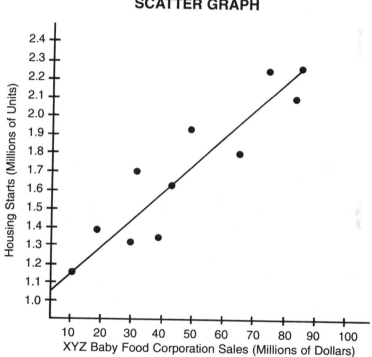

REGULAR WAY DELIVERY (AND SETTLEMENT) completion of securities transaction at the office of the purchasing broker on (but not before) the third full business day following the date of the transaction, as required by the NEW YORK STOCK EXCHANGE. Government transactions are an exception; for them, regular way means delivery and settlement the next business day following a transaction.

REGULATED COMMODITIES all commodity futures and options contracts traded on organized U.S. futures exchanges. *See also* COMMODITY FUTURES TRADING COMMISSION.

REGULATED INVESTMENT COMPANY MUTUAL FUND or UNIT INVESTMENT TRUST eligible under *Regulation M* of the Internal Revenue Service to pass capital gains, dividends, and interest earned on fund investments directly to its shareholders to be taxed at the personal level. The process, designed to avoid double taxation, is called the *conduit theory.* To qualify as a regulated investment company, the fund must meet such requirements as 90% minimum distribution of interest and dividends received on investments less expenses and 90% distribution of capital gain net income. To avoid a 4% excise tax, however, a regulated investment company must pay out 98% of its net investment income and capital gains. Shareholders must pay taxes even if they reinvest their distributions.

REGULATION A
1. Securities and Exchange Commission provision for simplified REGISTRATION of small issues of securities. A Regulation A issue requires a shorter form of PROSPECTUS and carries lesser liability for officers and directors for false or misleading statements.
2. Federal Reserve Board statement of the means and conditions under which Federal Reserve banks make loans to member and other banks at what is called the DISCOUNT WINDOW. *See also* REDISCOUNT.

REGULATION D
1. FEDERAL RESERVE BOARD rule pertaining to the amount of reserves banks must maintain relative to deposits.
2. SECURITIES AND EXCHANGE COMMISSION (SEC) rules concerning PRIVATE PLACEMENTS and defining related concepts such as ACCREDITED INVESTOR.

REGULATION G Federal Reserve Board rule regulating lenders other than commercial banks, brokers or dealers who, in the ordinary course of business, extend credit to individuals to purchase or carry securities. Special provision is made for loans by corporations and credit unions to finance purchases under employee stock option and stock purchase plans.

REGULATION Q Federal Reserve Board ceiling on the rates that banks and other savings institutions can pay on savings and other time deposits. THE DEPOSITORY INSTITUTIONS DEREGULATION AND MONETARY CONTROL ACT OF 1980 provided for phasing out Regulation Q by 1986.

REGULATION T Federal Reserve Board regulation covering the extension of credit to customers by securities brokers, dealers, and members of the national securities exchanges. It establishes INITIAL MARGIN requirements and defines registered (eligible), unregistered (ineligible), and exempt securities. *See also* MARGIN REQUIREMENT; MARGIN SECURITIES.

REGULATION U Federal Reserve Board limit on the amount of credit a bank may extend a customer for purchasing and carrying MARGIN SECURITIES. *See also* NONPURPOSE LOAN.

REGULATION Z Federal Reserve Board regulation covering provisions of the CONSUMER CREDIT PROTECTION ACT OF 1968, known as the Truth in Lending Act.

REHYPOTHECATION pledging by brokers of securities in customers' MARGIN ACCOUNTS to banks as collateral for broker loans under a GENERAL LOAN AND COLLATERAL AGREEMENT. Broker loans cover the positions of brokers who have made margin loans to customers for margin purchases and SELLING SHORT. Margin loans are collateralized by the HYPOTHECATION of customers securities to the broker. Their rehypothecation is authorized when the customer originally signs a GENERAL ACCOUNT agreement.

REIMBURSEMENT paying someone back for out-of-pocket expenses. For example, a company reimburses employees for their out-of-pocket business-related expenses when employees file expense reports. Insurance companies reimburse policyholders for out-of-pocket expenses incurred paying medical bills (for health insurance) or for home repairs (homeowner's insurance).

REINSTATEMENT in INSURANCE, the restoration of coverage after a policy has lapsed because premium payments have not been made. Typically, life insurance can be reinstated within a three-year period if premiums are paid and subject to evidence of continued insurability.

REINSURANCE sharing of RISK among insurance companies. Part of the insurer's risk is assumed by other companies in return for a part of the premium fee paid by the insured. By spreading the risk, reinsurance allows an individual company to take on clients whose coverage would be too great a burden for one insurer to carry alone.

REINVESTMENT PRIVILEGE right of a shareholder to reinvest dividends in order to buy more shares in the company or MUTUAL FUND, usually at no additional sales charge.

REINVESTMENT RATE rate of return resulting from the reinvestment of the interest from a bond or other fixed-income security. The reinvestment rate on a ZERO-COUPON BOND is predictable and locked in, since no interest payments are ever made, and therefore all imputed interest is reinvested at the same rate. The reinvestment rate on coupon bonds is less predictable because it rises and falls with market interest rates.

REINVESTMENT RISK risk that rates will fall causing cash flows from an investment (dividends or interest), assuming reinvestment, to earn less than the original investment.

REIT *see* REAL ESTATE INVESTMENT TRUST.

REJECTION
Banking: refusal to grant credit to an applicant because of inadequate financial strength, a poor credit history, or some other reason.
Insurance: refusal to underwrite a risk, that is, to issue a policy.
Securities: refusal of a broker or a broker's customer to accept the security presented to complete a trade. This usually occurs because the security lacks the necessary endorsements. or because of other exceptions to the rules for GOOD DELIVERY.

RELATIVE STRENGTH rate at which a stock falls relative to other stocks in a falling market or rises relative to other stocks in a rising market. Analysts reason that a stock that holds value on the downside will be a strong performer on the upside and vice versa.

RELEASE CLAUSE provision in a MORTGAGE agreement allowing the freeing of pledged property after a proportionate amount of payment has been made.

REMAINDER remaining interest in a TRUST or ESTATE after expenses and after prior beneficiaries have been satisfied. *See also* CHARITABLE REMAINDER TRUST.

REMAINING MONTHLY BALANCE amount of debt remaining unpaid on a monthly statement. For example, a credit card customer may charge $300 worth of merchandise during a month, and pay $100, leaving a remaining monthly balance of $200, on which interest charges would accrue.

REMARGINING putting up additional cash or eligible securities to correct a deficiency in EQUITY deposited in a brokerage MARGIN ACCOUNT to meet MINIMUM

MAINTENANCE REQUIREMENTS. Remargining usually is prompted by a MARGIN CALL.

REMIC acronym for *real estate mortgage investment conduit,* a pass-through vehicle created under the TAX REFORM ACT OF 1986 to issue multiclass mortgage-backed securities. REMICs may be organized as corporations, partnerships, or trusts, and those meeting qualifications are not subject to DOUBLE TAXATION. Interests in REMICs may be senior or junior, *regular* (debt instruments) or *residual* (equity interests). The practical meaning of REMICs has been that issuers have more flexibility than is afforded by the COLLATERALIZED MORTGAGE OBLIGATION (CMO) vehicle. Issuers can thus separate mortgage pools not only into different maturity classes but into different risk classes as well. Whereas CMOs normally have AAA bond ratings, REMICs represent a range of risk levels.

REMIT pay for purchased goods or services by cash, check, or electronic payment.

RENEWABLE TERM LIFE INSURANCE term life insurance policy offering the policyholder the option to renew for a specific period of time—frequently one year—for a particular length of time. Some term life policies stipulate a maximum age benefit. Some policies offer fixed premium rates for a certain number of years, usually ten, after which they are renewable at a higher premium rate. Other term policies are renewable every year, and charge escalating premium rates as the policyholder ages.

RENT payment from a tenant to a building owner for use of the specified property. For example, an apartment dweller must pay monthly rent to a landlord for the right to inhabit the apartment. A commercial tenant in an office or store must pay monthly rent to the building owner for the use of the commercial space.

RENT CONTROL state and local government regulation restricting the amount of rent landlords can charge their tenants. Rent control is used to regulate the quality of rental dwellings, with controls implemented only against those units that do not conform to building codes, as in New York City; or used across the board to deal with high rents resulting from a gross imbalance between housing supply and demand, as in Massachusetts and California. If a landlord violates rent control laws, the tenant may protest at the local housing authority charged with enforcing the law. While tenants may like rent control, landlords argue that it reduces their ability to earn a profit on their property, thereby discouraging them from investing any further to maintain or upgrade the property. In some cases, landlords argue that rent control encourages owners to abandon their property altogether since it will never be profitable to retain it.

REORGANIZATION financial restructuring of a firm in BANKRUPTCY. *See also* TRUSTEE IN BANKRUPTCY; VOTING TRUST CERTIFICATE.

REORGANIZATION BOND debt security issued by a company in REORGANIZATION proceedings. The bonds are generally issued to the company's creditors on a basis whereby interest is paid only if and when it is earned. *See also* ADJUSTMENT BOND; INCOME BOND.

REPATRIATION return of the financial assets of an organization or individual from a foreign country to the home country.

REPLACEMENT COST cost to replace an asset with another of similar utility at today's prices. Also called *current cost* and *replacement value. See also* BOOK VALUE, REPLACEMENT COST INSURANCE.

REPLACEMENT COST ACCOUNTING accounting method allowing additional DEPRECIATION on part of the difference between the original cost and current replacement cost of a depreciable asset.

REPLACEMENT COST INSURANCE property and casualty insurance that replaces damaged property. Replacement cost contents insurance pays the dollar amount needed to replace damaged personal property with items of like kind and quality, without deducting for depreciation. Replacement cost dwelling insurance pays the policyholder the cost of replacing the damaged property without deduction for depreciation, but limited by the maximum dollar amount indicated on the declarations page of the policy. *See also* REPLACEMENT COST.

REPURCHASE AGREEMENT (REPO; RP) agreement between a seller and a buyer, usually of U.S. Government securities, whereby the seller agrees to repurchase the securities at an agreed upon price and, usually, at a stated time. Repos, also called RPs or buybacks, are widely used both as a money market investment vehicle and as an instrument of Federal Reserve MONETARY POLICY. Where a repurchase agreement is used as a short-term investment, a government securities dealer, usually a bank, borrows from an investor, typically a corporation with excess cash, to finance its inventory, using the securities as collateral. Such RPs may have a fixed maturity date or be OPEN REPOS, callable at any time. Rates are negotiated directly by the parties involved, but are generally lower than rates on collateralized loans made by New York banks. The attraction of repos to corporations, which also have the alternatives of COMMERCIAL PAPER, CERTIFICATES OF DEPOSIT, TREASURY BILLS and other short-term instruments, is the flexibility of maturities that makes them an ideal place to "park" funds on a very temporary basis. Dealers also arrange *reverse repurchase agreements,* whereby they agree to buy the securities and the investor agrees to repurchase them at a later date.

The FEDERAL RESERVE BANK also makes extensive use of repurchase agreements in its OPEN MARKET OPERATIONS as a method of fine tuning the MONEY SUPPLY. To temporarily expand the supply, the Fed arranges to buy securities from nonbank dealers who in turn deposit the proceeds in their commercial bank accounts thereby adding to reserves. Timed to coincide with whatever length of time the Fed needs to make the desired adjustment, usually 1 to 15 days, the dealer repurchases the securities. Such transactions are made at the Federal Reserve DISCOUNT RATE and accounts are credited in FEDERAL FUNDS. When it wishes to reduce the money supply temporarily, the Fed reverses the process. Using a procedure called the MATCHED SALE PURCHASE TRANSACTION, it sells securities to a nonbank dealer who either draws down bank balances directly or takes out a bank loan to make payment, thereby draining reserves.

In a third variation of the Repurchase agreement, banks and thrift institutions can raise temporary capital funds with a device called the *retail repurchase agreement.* Using pooled government securities to secure loans from individuals, they agree to repurchase the securities at a specified time at a price including interest. Despite its appearance of being a deposit secured by government securities, the investor has neither a special claim on the securities nor protection by the FEDERAL DEPOSIT INSURANCE CORPORATION in the event the bank is forced to liquidate. *See also* OVERNIGHT REPO.

REQUIRED RATE OF RETURN return required by investors before they will commit money to an investment at a given level of risk. Unless the expected return exceeds the required return, an investment is unacceptable. *See also* HURDLE RATE; INTERNAL RATE OF RETURN; MEAN RETURN.

REQUIRED RESERVE RATE factor used to determine the amount of reserves a bank must maintain on its deposits.

RESCHEDULED LOANS bank loans that, as an alternative to DEFAULT, were restructured, usually by lengthening the maturity to make it easier for the borrower to meet repayment terms.

RESCIND cancel a contract agreement. The Truth in Lending Act confers the RIGHT OF RESCISSION, which allows the signer of a contract to nullify it within three business days without penalty and have any deposits refunded. Contracts may also be rescinded in cases of fraud, failure to comply with legal procedures, or misrepresentation. For example, a contract signed by a child under legal age may be rescinded, since children do not have the right to take on contractual obligations.

RECISSION *see* RIGHT OF RECISSION.

RESEARCH AND DEVELOPMENT (R&D) scientific and marketing evolution of a new product or service. Once such a product has been created in a laboratory or other research setting, marketing specialists attempt to define the market for the product. Then, steps are taken to manufacture the product to meet the needs of the market. Research and development spending is often listed as a separate item in a company's financial statements. In industries such as high-technology and pharmaceuticals, R&D spending is quite high, since products are outdated or attract competition quickly. Investors looking for companies in such fast-changing fields check on R&D spending as a percentage of sales because they consider this an important indicator of the company's prospects. *See also* RESEARCH AND DEVELOPMENT LIMITED PARTNERSHIP.

RESEARCH AND DEVELOPMENT LIMITED PARTNERSHIP plan whose investors put up money to finance new product RESEARCH AND DEVELOPMENT. In return, the investors get a percentage of the product's profits, if any, together with such benefits as DEPRECIATION of equipment. R&D partnerships may be offered publicly or privately, usually through brokerage firms. Those that are offered to the public must be registered with the Securities and Exchange Commission. *See also* LIMITED PARTNERSHIP.

RESEARCH DEPARTMENT division within a brokerage firm, investment company, bank trust department, insurance company, or other institutional investing organization that analyzes markets and securities. Research departments include analysts who focus on particular securities, commodities, and whole industries as well as generalists who forecast movements of the markets as a whole, using both FUNDAMENTAL ANALYSIS and TECHNICAL ANALYSIS. An analyst whose advice is followed by many investors can have a major impact on the prices of individual securities.

RESERVE
1. segregation of RETAINED EARNINGS to provide for such payouts as dividends, contingencies, improvements, or retirement of preferred stock.
2. VALUATION RESERVE, also called ALLOWANCE, for DEPRECIATION, BAD DEBT losses, shrinkage of receivables because of discounts taken, and other provisions created by charges to the PROFIT AND LOSS STATEMENT.
3. hidden reserves, represented by understatements of BALANCE SHEET values.
4. deposit maintained by a commercial bank in a FEDERAL RESERVE BANK to meet the Fed's RESERVE REQUIREMENT.

RESERVE REQUIREMENT FEDERAL RESERVE SYSTEM rule mandating the financial assets that member banks must keep in the form of cash and other liquid assets as a percentage of DEMAND DEPOSITS and TIME DEPOSITS. This money must be in the bank's own vaults or on deposit with the nearest regional FEDERAL RESERVE BANK. Reserve requirements, set by the Fed's Board of Governors, are one of the key tools in deciding how much money banks can lend, thus setting the pace at which the nation's money supply and economy grow. The higher the reserve requirement, the tighter the money—and therefore the slower the economic growth. *See also* MONETARY POLICY; MONEY SUPPLY; MULTIPLIER.

RESET BONDS bonds issued with a provision that on specified dates the initial interest rate must be adjusted so that the bonds trade at their original value. Although reset provisions can work in an issuer's favor by lowering rates should market rates fall or credit quality improve, they were designed as a protective feature for investors to enhance the marketability of JUNK BOND issues. Should market rates rise or credit quality decline (causing prices to decline), the interest rate would be increased to bring the bond price to PAR or above. The burden of increased interest payments on a weak issuer could prompt DEFAULT.

RESIDENTIAL ENERGY CREDIT tax credit granted to homeowners prior to 1986 by the federal government for improving the energy efficiency of their homes. Installation of storm windows and doors, insulation, or new fuel-saving heating systems before the end of 1985 meant a maximum federal credit on expenditures of $300. Equipping a home with renewable energy devices such as solar panels or windmills meant a maximum federal credit of $4000. Many states offer incentives for installing such devices.

RESIDENTIAL MORTGAGE mortgage on a residential property. Interest on such mortgages is deductible for federal and state income tax purposes up to $1 million; for home equity loans, interest up to $100,000 is deductible.

RESIDENTIAL PROPERTY property zoned for single-family homes, townhouses, multifamily apartments, condominiums, and coops. Residential property falls under different zoning and taxation regulations than commercial property.

RESIDUAL SECURITY
1. SECURITY that has a potentially dilutive effect on earnings per common share. Warrants, rights, convertible bonds, and preferred stock are potentially dilutive because exercising or converting them into common stock would increase the number of common shares competing for the same earnings, and earnings per share would be reduced. *See also* DILUTION: FULLY DILUTED EARNINGS PER (COMMON) SHARE.
2. the term *residual is* also used informally to describe investments based on the excess cash flow generated by collateral pools. CMO REITs and the bottom tier of most COLLATERALIZED BOND OBLIGATIONS (CBOs) are examples of "residuals."

RESIDUAL VALUE
1. realizable value of a FIXED ASSET after costs associated with the sale.
2. amount remaining after all allowable DEPRECIATION charges have been subtracted from the original cost of a depreciable asset.
3. scrap value, which is the value to a junk dealer. Also called *salvage value.*

RESISTANCE LEVEL price ceiling at which technical analysts note persistent selling of a commodity or security. If XYZ's stock generally trades between a low of $50 and a high of $60 a share, $50 is called the SUPPORT LEVEL and $60 is called the resistance level. Technical analysts think it significant when the stock breaks through the resistance level because that means it usually will go on to new high prices. *See also* BREAKOUT; TECHNICAL ANALYSIS.

RESISTANCE LEVEL

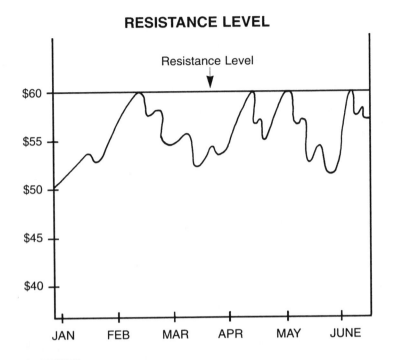

RESOLUTION
1. in general, expression of desire or intent.
2. formal document representing an action of a corporation's BOARD OF DIREC-
   TORS—perhaps a directive to management, such as in the declaration of a dividend, or a corporate expression of sentiment, such as acknowledging the
   services of a retiring officer. A *corporate resolution,* which defines the authority and powers of individual officers, is a document given to a bank.
3. legal order or contract by a government entity—called a *bond resolution—*
   authorizing a bond issue and spelling out the rights of bondholders and the
   obligations of the issuer.

RESOLUTION FUNDING CORPORATION (REFCORP) U.S. government
agency created by Congress in 1989 to (1) issue BAILOUT BONDS and raise industry funds to finance activities of the RESOLUTION TRUST CORPORATION (RTC) and
(2) merge or close sick institutions inherited from the disbanded FEDERAL SAVINGS
AND LOAN INSURANCE CORPORATION (FSLIC). *See also* OFFICE OF THRIFT SUPERVI-
SION (OTS).

RESOLUTION TRUST CORPORATION (RTC) U.S. government agency created by the 1989 bailout bill to merge or close savings and loan institutions
becoming insolvent between 1989 and August 1992. RTC was scheduled to terminate after 1996 and shift its responsibilities to the SAVINGS ASSOCIATION INSUR-
ANCE FUND (SAIF), a unit of the FEDERAL DEPOSIT INSURANCE CORPORATION. The
Resolution Trust Corporation Oversight Board, an arm of the executive branch,
was charged with overseeing broad policy and the dispensing of funds to sick
thrifts by RTC. *See also* OFFICE OF THRIFT SUPERVISION (OTS).

RESTRICTED ACCOUNT MARGIN ACCOUNT with a securities broker in which the
EQUITY is less than the INITIAL MARGIN requirement set by the Federal Reserve

Board's REGULATION T. A customer whose account is restricted may not make further purchases and must, in accordance with Regulation T's *retention requirement*, retain in the account a percentage of the proceeds of any sales so as to reduce the deficiency (debit balance). This retention requirement is currently set at 50%. *See also* MARGIN CALL.

RESTRICTED SURPLUS portion of RETAINED EARNINGS not legally available for the payment of dividends. Among the circumstances giving rise to such restriction: dividend arrearages in CUMULATIVE PREFERRED stock, a shortfall in the minimum WORKING CAPITAL ratio specified in an INDENTURE, or simply a vote by the BOARD OF DIRECTORS. Also called *restricted retained earnings.*

RESTRICTIVE COVENANT *see* COVENANT.

RESTRICTIVE ENDORSEMENT signature on the back of a check specifying the transfer of the amount of that check, under specific conditions. The most common type of restrictive endorsement is "for deposit only," meaning the check must be deposited in the payee's bank account and cannot be cashed.

RESYNDICATION LIMITED PARTNERSHIP partnership in which existing properties are sold to new limited partners, who can gain tax advantages that had been exhausted by the old partnership. For instance, a partnership with government-subsidized housing may have given partners substantial tax benefits five years ago. Now the same housing development may be sold to a resyndication partnership, which will start the process of DEPRECIATION over again and claim additional tax benefits for its new limited partners. Resyndication partnerships are usually offered as PRIVATE PLACEMENTS through brokerage houses, although a few have been offered to the public.

RETAIL HOUSE brokerage firm that caters to retail investors instead of institutions. Such a firm may be a large national broker called a WIRE HOUSE, with a large RESEARCH DEPARTMENT and a wide variety of products and services for individuals, or it may be a small BOUTIQUE serving an exclusive clientele with specialized research or investment services.

RETAIL INVESTOR investor who buys securities and commodities futures on his own behalf, not for an organization. Retail investors typically buy shares of stock or commodity positions in much smaller quantities than institutions such as mutual funds, bank trust departments, and pension funds and therefore are usually charged commissions higher than those paid by the institutions. In recent years, market activity has increasingly been dominated by INSTITUTIONAL INVESTORS.

RETAIL PRICE price charged to retail customers for goods and services. Retailers buy goods from wholesalers, and increase the price to cover their costs, plus a profit. Manufacturers list suggested retail prices for their products; retailers may adhere to these prices or offer discounts from them.

RETAINED EARNINGS net profits kept to accumulate in a business after dividends are paid. Also called *undistributed profits* or *earned surplus.* Retained earnings are distinguished from *contributed capital*—capital received in exchange for stock, which is reflected in CAPITAL STOCK or CAPITAL SURPLUS and DONATED STOCK or DONATED SURPLUS. STOCK DIVIDENDS—the distribution of additional shares of capital stock with no cash payment—reduce retained earnings and increase capital stock. Retained earnings plus the total of all the capital accounts represent the NET WORTH of a firm. *See also* ACCUMULATED PROFITS TAX; PAID-IN CAPITAL.

RETAINED EARNINGS STATEMENT reconciliation of the beginning and ending balances in the RETAINED EARNINGS account on a company's BALANCE SHEET. It breaks down changes affecting the account, such as profits or losses from operations, dividends declared, and any other items charged or credited to retained earnings. A retained earnings statement is required by GENERALLY ACCEPTED ACCOUNTING PRINCIPLES whenever comparative balance sheets and income statements are presented. It may appear in the balance sheet, in a combined PROFIT AND LOSS STATEMENT and retained earnings statement, or as a separate schedule. It may also be called *statement of changes in earned surplus* (or *retained income*).

RETENTION in securities underwriting, the number of units allocated to a participating investment banker (SYNDICATE member) minus the units held back by the syndicate manager for facilitating institutional sales and for allocation to firms in the selling group that are not also members of the syndicate. *See also* UNDERWRITE.

RETENTION RATE percentage of after-tax profits credited to RETAINED EARNINGS. It is the opposite of the DIVIDEND PAYOUT RATIO.

RETENTION REQUIREMENT *see* RESTRICTED ACCOUNT.

RETIREMENT
1. cancellation of stock or bonds that have been reacquired or redeemed. *See also* CALLABLE; REDEMPTION.
2. removal from service after a fixed asset has reached the end of its useful life or has been sold and appropriate adjustments have been made to the asset and depreciation accounts.
3. repayment of a debt obligation.
4. permanent withdrawal of an employee from gainful employment in accordance with an employer's policies concerning length of service, age, or disability. A retired employee may have rights to a pension or other retirement provisions offered by the employer. Such benefits may in some circumstances supplement payments from an INDIVIDUAL RETIREMENT ACCOUNT (IRA) or KEOGH PLAN.

RETIREMENT AGE age at which employees no longer work. Though there is no longer any mandatory retirement age, many institutions do impose a retirement age. The federal government has a retirement age of 70. Many corporations have a retirement age of 65, although this has become more flexible and is no longer standard. Employees reaching age 62 may start to receive Social Security benefits, though the minimum age for receiving full Social Security benefits starts at age 65 and gradually increases to age 67 starting in the year 2000.

RETURN
Finance and investment: profit on a securities or capital investment, usually expressed as an annual percentage rate. *See also* RATE OF RETURN; RETURN ON EQUITY; RETURN ON INVESTED CAPITAL; RETURN ON SALES; TOTAL RETURN.

Retailing: exchange of previously sold merchandise for REFUND or CREDIT against future sales.

Taxes: form on which taxpayers submit information required by the government when they file with the INTERNAL REVENUE SERVICE. For example, form 1040 is the tax return used by individual tax payers.

Trade: physical return of merchandise for credit against an invoice.

RETURN OF CAPITAL distribution of cash resulting from DEPRECIATION tax savings, the sale of a CAPITAL ASSET or of securities in a portfolio, or any other transaction unrelated to RETAINED EARNINGS. Returns of capital are not directly taxable but may result in higher CAPITAL GAINS taxes later on if they reduce the acquisition cost base of the property involved. Also called *return of basis.*

RETURN ON COMMON EQUITY *see* RETURN ON EQUITY; RETURN ON INVESTED CAPITAL.

RETURN ON EQUITY amount, expressed as a percentage, earned on a company's common stock investment for a given period. It is calculated by dividing common stock equity (NET WORTH) at the beginning of the accounting period into NET INCOME for the period after preferred stock dividends but before common stock dividends. Return on equity tells common shareholders how effectually their money is being employed. Comparing percentages for current and prior periods reveals trends, and comparison with industry composites reveals how well a company is holding its own against its competitors.

RETURN ON INVESTED CAPITAL amount, expressed as a percentage, earned on a company's total capital—its common and preferred stock EQUITY plus its long-term FUNDED DEBT—calculated by dividing total capital into earnings before interest, taxes, and dividends. Return on invested capital, usually termed *return on investment,* or *ROI,* is a useful means of comparing companies, or corporate divisions, in terms of efficiency of management and viability of product lines.

RETURN ON SALES net pretax profits as a percentage of NET SALES—a useful measure of overall operational efficiency when compared with prior periods or with other companies in the same line of business. It is important to recognize, however, that return on sales varies widely from industry to industry. A supermarket chain with a 2% return on sales might be operating efficiently, for example, because it depends on high volume to generate an acceptable RETURN ON INVESTED CAPITAL. In contrast, a manufacturing enterprise is expected to average 4% to 5%, so a return on sales of 2% is likely to be considered highly inefficient.

REVALUATION change in the value of a country's currency relative to others that is based on the decision of authorities rather than on fluctuations in the market. Revaluation generally refers to an increase in the currency's value; DEVALUATION refers to a decrease. *See also* FLOATING EXCHANGE RATE; PAR VALUE OF CURRENCY.

REVENUE ANTICIPATION NOTE (RAN) short-term debt issue of a municipal entity that is to be repaid out of anticipated revenues such as sales taxes. When the taxes are collected, the RAN is paid off. Interest from the note is usually tax-free to RAN holders.

REVENUE BOND *see* MUNICIPAL REVENUE BOND.

REVENUE NEUTRAL guiding criterion in drafting the TAX REFORM ACT OF 1986 whereby provisions estimated to add revenue were offset by others estimated to reduce revenue, so that on paper the new bill would generate the same amount of revenue as the old tax laws. The concept, which has guided subsequent tax legislation, was theoretical rather than real, since estimates are subject to variation.

REVENUE RECONCILIATION ACT OF 1993 landmark legislation signed into law by President Clinton in August 1993 to reduce the federal budget deficit by curtailing spending and raising taxes. Among its major components:

Provisions Affecting Individuals
1. added a fourth tax bracket of 36% to the existing 15%, 28%, and 31% brackets. Single taxpayers earning over $115,000 and married taxpayers filing jointly earning over $140,000 pay at the 36% marginal rate.

2. added a 10% surtax on married couples filing jointly reporting more than $250,000 in taxable income, or on married couples filing separately with taxable incomes of more than $125,000, creating, in effect, a fifth tax bracket at 39.6%.
3. kept capital gains tax rate at 28% for assets held at least a year.
4. created special tax break for investing in small companies. Investors buying newly issued stock in a small company with less than $50 million in gross assets who hold the stock for at least 5 years may exclude 50% of the profit from capital gains taxes. For each subsequent year the investor holds the stock, the tax rate declines 10% until there is no capital gains tax after 10 years.
5. gasoline taxes were increased from 14.1 cents to 18.4 cents a gallon.
6. taxes on Social Security benefits were raised. Couples with provisional income plus half their Social Security benefits totaling more than $44,000 owe tax on up to 85% of their Social Security benefits. For singles, the equivalent level is $34,000. Provisional income is defined as adjusted gross income, interest on tax-exempt bonds, and certain income from foreign sources. Previously, couples with taxable income over $32,000 and singles with income over $25,000 had to pay taxes on 50% of their Social Security benefits.
7. Medicare tax cap was eliminated. Before this Act, the Medicare tax of 1.45% on wages applied to the first $135,000 of wages.
8. phaseout of personal exemptions, which had been temporary, was made permanent. Personal exemptions begin to phase out for singles reporting adjusted gross incomes of $108,450. For married couples filing jointly, exemptions begin to phase out when adjusted gross income reaches $167,700. (These amounts are adjusted for inflation annually).
9. investment interest deductions were limited. Interest paid to finance the purchase of securities remain deductible from interest income earned from investments, but that interest can no longer be deducted against realized capital gains.
10. pension contributions were limited. The income limit for contributions to pension plans such as Keoghs and SEPs was lowered from $235,840 to $150,000.
11. earned income credit was expanded. For taxpayers with more than one child, a credit of up to 18.5% can be claimed for the first $7750 of income, up to a maximum of $1511. The credit rose to 36% in 1995 and 40% in 1996.
12. moving deductions were limited. Under the law, unreimbursed moving expenses for house-hunting, closing fees, broker's commissions, and food costs while living in temporary quarters are no longer deductible as they had been previously. In addition, moves must be 50 miles, up from 35 miles, from the previous home in order to qualify for tax benefits. Moving expenses were converted from an itemized deduction—available only to those who filed an itemized return—to an above-the-line deduction, similar to alimony.
13. estimated tax rules were changed. For married taxpayers filing jointly reporting more than $150,000 in taxable income, quarterly estimated taxes must be paid at 110% of the previous year's tax liability.
14. alternative minimum tax (AMT) rates were raised. The AMT tax rate on income exceeding $175,000 was raised from 24% to 28%.
15. estate tax rates were raised. The top rate on inheritance taxes was raised from 50% to 55% on estates worth more than $3 million.
16. luxury taxes were repealed. The 10% luxury tax on airplanes, boats, cars, furs, and jewelry was repealed on all items except cars selling for more than $32,000.
17. rules governing donations of appreciated property were made permanent. Temporary rules allowing donors to deduct the full value of appreciated property such as art, real estate, and securities were made permanent. Such

donations were also removed from calculations towards the alternative minimum tax (AMT).

Provisions Affecting Business

18. corporate tax rates were increased from 34% to 35%, for companies with taxable income of at least $10 million.

19. deductions for executive salaries exceeding $1 million were limited.

20. meal and entertainment deductions were lowered from 80% to 50% for business-related meal and entertainment expenses.

21. deductions were increased for small business purchases of equipment up to $17,500 a year, up from $10,000 previously.

22. tax breaks were reinstated for real estate professionals. Certified real estate professionals, defined as those working at least 750 hours a year in a real-estate-related line of work such as sales or construction, are allowed to deduct losses on rental property against any form of income. Previously, such passive losses could only be offset against passive income.

23. commercial real estate depreciation was lengthened from 31 years to 39 years.

24. club dues for country clubs; airline lounges; and social, athletic, and health clubs were made nondeductible.

25. standard period for depreciating goodwill when acquiring a business was set at 15 years.

26. expenses for lobbying Congress were made nondeductible.

27. restrictions on deductions for traveling spouses were imposed. Expenses for spouses traveling on a business trip were made nondeductible, unless the spouse is an employee of the company paying for the trip and has a business reason for going.

28. empowerment zones were created. Businesses that invest and create jobs in authorized empowerment zones in particular depressed communities qualify for tax incentives and special grants.

REVENUE SHARING

Limited partnerships: percentage split between the general partner and limited partners of profits, losses, cash distributions, and other income or losses which result from the operation of a real estate, oil and gas, equipment leasing, or other partnership. *See also* LIMITED PARTNERSHIP.

Taxes: return of tax revenue to a unit of government by a larger unit, such as from a state to one of its municipalities. GENERAL REVENUE SHARING between the federal government and states, localities, and other subunits existed between 1972 and 1987.

REVERSAL change in direction in the stock or commodity futures markets, as charted by technical analysts. If the Dow Jones Industrial Average has been climbing steadily from 3400 to 3900, for instance, chartists would speak of a reversal if the average started a sustained fall back toward 3400.

REVERSE ANNUITY MORTGAGE (RAM) MORTGAGE instrument that allows an elderly person to live off the equity in a fully paid-for house. Such a homeowner would enter into a reverse annuity mortgage agreement with a financial institution such as a bank, which would guarantee a lifelong fixed monthly income in return for gradually giving up ownership of the house. The longer the payments continue, the less equity the elderly owner would retain. At the owner's death the bank gains title to the real estate, which it can sell at a profit. The law also permits such arrangements between relatives, so that, for instance, a son or daughter might enter into a reverse annuity mortgage transaction with his or her retiring parents, thus providing the parents with cash to invest in income-yielding securities and the son or daughter with the depreciation and other tax benefits of real estate ownership. *See also* ARM'S LENGTH TRANSACTION.

REVERSAL

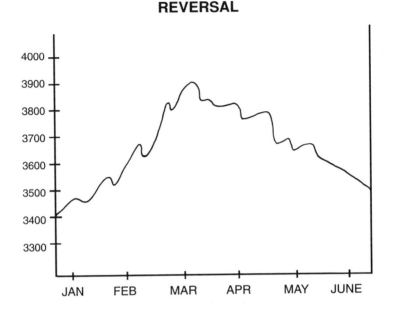

REVERSE A SWAP restore a bond portfolio to its former position following a swap of one bond for another to gain the advantage of a YIELD SPREAD or a tax loss. The reversal may mean that the yield differential has disappeared or that the investor, content with a short-term profit, wishes to stay with the original bond for the advantages that may be gained in the future. *See also* BOND SWAP.

REVERSE CONVERSION technique whereby brokerage firms earn interest on their customers' stock holdings. A typical reverse conversion would work like this: A brokerage firm sells short the stocks it holds in customers' margin accounts, then invests this money in short-term money market instruments. To protect against a sharp rise in the markets, the firm hedges its short position by buying CALL options and selling PUT options. To unwind the reverse conversion, the firms buys back the stocks, sells the call, and buys the put. *See also* MARGIN ACCOUNT; OPTION.

REVERSE LEVERAGE situation, the opposite of FINANCIAL LEVERAGE, where the interest on money borrowed exceeds the return on investment of the borrowed funds.

REVERSE LEVERAGED BUYOUT process of bringing back into publicly traded status a company—or a division of a company—that had been publicly traded and taken private. In the 1980s, many public companies were taken private in LEVERAGED BUYOUTS by corporate raiders who borrowed against the companies' assets to finance the deal. When some or all of the debt incurred in the leveraged buyout was repaid, many of these companies were in sufficiently strong financial condition to go public again, enriching the private stockholders as well as the investment bankers who earned fees implementing these deals.

REVERSE MORTGAGE arrangement whereby a homeowner borrows against home equity and receives regular payments (tax-free) from the lender until the accumulated principal and interest reach the credit limit of equity; at that time, the lender either gets repayment in a lump sum or takes the house. Reverse mortgages are available privately and through the Federal Housing Administration (FHA). They are appropriate for cash-poor but house-rich older borrowers who want to stay in their homes and expect to live long enough to amortize high up-front fees but not so long that the lender winds up with the house. Lower income but greater security is provided by a variation, the REVERSE ANNUITY MORTGAGE (RAM).

REVERSE REPURCHASE AGREEMENT *see* REPURCHASE AGREEMENT.

REVERSE SPLIT procedure whereby a corporation reduces the number of shares outstanding. The total number of shares will have the same market value immediately after the reverse split as before it, but each share will be worth more. For example, if a firm with 10 million outstanding shares selling at $10 a share executes a reverse 1 for 10 split, the firm will end up with 1 million shares selling for $100 each. Such splits are usually initiated by companies wanting to raise the price of their outstanding shares because they think the price is too low to attract investors. Also called *split down. See also* SPLIT.

REVISIONARY TRUST IRREVOCABLE TRUST that becomes a REVOCABLE TRUST after a specified period, usually over 10 years or upon the death of the GRANTOR.

REVOCABLE TRUST agreement whereby income-producing property is deeded to heirs. The provisions of such a TRUST may be altered as many times as the GRANTOR pleases, or the entire trust agreement can be canceled, unlike irrevocable trusts. The grantor receives income from the assets, but the property passes directly to the beneficiaries at the grantor's death, without having to go through PROBATE court proceedings. Since the assets are still part of the grantor's estate, however, estate taxes must be paid on this transfer. This kind of trust differs from an IRREVOCABLE TRUST, which permanently transfers assets from the estate during the grantor's lifetime and therefore escapes estate taxes.

REVOLVING CREDIT

Commercial banking: contractual agreement between a bank and its customer, usually a company, whereby the bank agrees to make loans up to a specified maximum for a specified period, usually a year or more. As the borrower repays a portion of the loan, an amount equal to the repayment can be borrowed again under the terms of the agreement. In addition to interest borne by notes, the bank charges a fee for the commitment to hold the funds available. A COMPENSATING BALANCE may be required in addition.

Consumer banking: loan account requiring monthly payments of less than the full amount due, and the balance carried forward is subject to a financial charge. Also, an arrangement whereby borrowings are permitted up to a specified limit and for a specified period, usually a year, with a fee charged for the commitment. Also called *open-end credit* or *revolving line of credit.*

REVOLVING LINE OF CREDIT *see* REVOLVING CREDIT.

RICH

1. term for a security whose price seems too high in light of its price history. For bonds, the term may also imply that the yield is too low.
2. term for rate of interest that seems too high in relation to the borrower's risk.
3. synonym for *wealthy.*

RICO acronym for *Racketeer Influenced and Corrupt Organization Act,* a federal law used to convict firms and individuals of INSIDER TRADING. Many critics have charged that the law was excessively enforced, and several indictments were dismissed for lack of evidence.

RIDER written form attached to an insurance policy that alters the policy's coverage, terms, or conditions. For example, after buying a diamond bracelet, a policyholder may want to add a rider to her homeowner's insurance policy to cover the jewelry. *See also* FLOATER.

RIEGLE-NEAL INTERSTATE BANKING AND BRANCHING EFFICIENCY ACT OF 1994 law allowing interstate banking in America. The legislation permitted banks to establish branches nationwide by eliminating all barriers to interstate banking at the state level. Before this legislation went into effect, banks had been required to set up separate subsidiaries in each state to conduct business and it was illegal for banks to accept deposits from customers out of their home states.

RIGGED MARKET situation in which the prices for a security are manipulated so as to lure unsuspecting buyers or sellers. *See also* MANIPULATION.

RIGHT *see* SUBSCRIPTION RIGHT.

RIGHT OF FIRST REFUSAL right of someone to be offered a right before it is offered to others. For example, a baseball team may have the right of first refusal on a ballplayer's contract, meaning that the club can make the first offer, or even match other offers, before the player works for another team. A company may have the right of refusal to distribute or manufacture another company's product. A publishing company may have the right of refusal to publish a book proposed by one of their authors.

RIGHT OF REDEMPTION right to recover property transferred by a MORTGAGE or other LIEN by paying off the debt either before or after foreclosure. Also called *equity of redemption.*

RIGHT OF RESCISSION right granted by the federal CONSUMER CREDIT PROTECTION ACT OF 1968 to void a contract within three business days with full refund of any down payment and without penalty. The right is designed to protect consumers from high-pressure door-to-door sales tactics and hastily made credit commitments which involve their homes as COLLATERAL, such as loans secured by second mortgages.

RIGHT OF SURVIVORSHIP right entitling one owner of property held jointly to take title to it when the other owner dies. *See also* JOINT TENANTS WITH RIGHT OF SURVIVORSHIP; TENANTS IN COMMON.

RIGHTS OFFERING offering of COMMON STOCK to existing shareholders who hold rights that entitle them to buy newly issued shares at a discount from the price at which shares will later be offered to the public. Rights offerings are usually handled by INVESTMENT BANKERS under what is called a STANDBY COMMITMENT, whereby the investment bankers agree to purchase any shares not subscribed to by the holders of rights. *See also* PREEMPTIVE RIGHT; SUBSCRIPTION RIGHT.

RING location on the floor of an exchange where trades are executed. The circular arrangement where traders can make bid and offer prices is also called a *pit,* particularly when commodities are traded.

RISING BOTTOMS technical chart pattern showing a rising trend in the low prices of a security or commodity. As the range of prices is charted daily, the lows reveal an upward trend. Rising bottoms signify higher and higher basic SUPPORT LEVELS for a security or commodity. When combined with a series of ASCENDING TOPS, the pattern is one a follower of TECHNICAL ANALYSIS would call bullish.

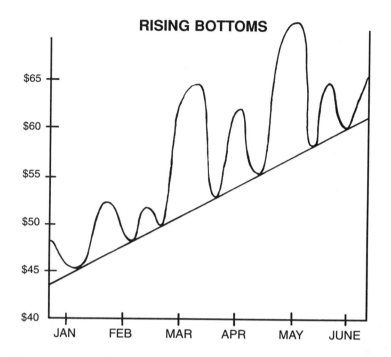

RISING BOTTOMS

RISK measurable possibility of losing or not gaining value. Risk is differentiated from uncertainty, which is not measurable. Among the commonly encountered types of risk are these:

Actuarial risk: risk an insurance underwriter covers in exchange for premiums, such as the risk of premature death.

Exchange risk: chance of loss on foreign currency exchange.

Inflation risk: chance that the value of assets or of income will be eroded as inflation shrinks the value of a country's currency.

Interest rate risk: possibility that a fixed-rate debt instrument will decline in value as a result of a rise in interest rates.

Inventory risk: possibility that price changes, obsolescence, or other factors will shrink the value of INVENTORY.

Liquidity risk: possibility that an investor will not be able to buy or sell a commodity or security quickly enough or in sufficient quantities because buying or selling opportunities are limited.

Political risk: possibility of NATIONALIZATION or other unfavorable government action.

Repayment (credit) risk: chance that a borrower or trade debtor will not repay an obligation as promised.

Risk of principal: chance that invested capital will drop in value.

Underwriting risk: risk taken by an INVESTMENT BANKER that a new issue of securities purchased outright will not be bought by the public and/or that the market price will drop during the offering period.

RISK-ADJUSTED DISCOUNT RATE in PORTFOLIO THEORY and CAPITAL BUDGET analysis, the rate necessary to determine the PRESENT VALUE of an uncertain or risky stream of income; it is the risk-free rate (generally the return on short-term

U.S. Treasury securities) plus a risk premium that is based on an analysis of the risk characteristics of the particular investment or project.

RISK ARBITRAGE ARBITRAGE involving risk, as in the simultaneous purchase of stock in a company being acquired and sale of stock in its proposed acquirer. Also called *takeover arbitrage.* Traders called *arbitrageurs* attempt to profit from TAKEOVERS by cashing in on the expected rise in the price of the target company's shares and drop in the price of the acquirer's shares. If the takeover plans fall through, the traders may be left with enormous losses. Risk arbitrage differs from riskless arbitrage, which entails locking in or profiting from the differences in the prices of two securities or commodities trading on different exchanges. *See also* RISKLESS TRANSACTION.

RISK AVERSE term referring to the assumption that, given the same return and different risk alternatives, a rational investor will seek the security offering the least risk—or, put another way, the higher the degree of risk, the greater the return that a rational investor will demand. *See also* CAPITAL ASSET PRICING MODEL; EFFICIENT PORTFOLIO; MEAN RETURN; PORTFOLIO THEORY.

RISK-BASED CAPITAL RATIO FIRREAH-imposed requirement that banks maintain a minimum ratio of estimated total capital to estimated risk-weighted assets.

RISK CAPITAL *see* VENTURE CAPITAL.

RISK CATEGORY classification of risk elements used in analyzing MORTGAGES.

RISK-FREE RETURN YIELD on a risk-free investment. The 3-month Treasury bill is considered a riskless investment because it is a direct obligation of the U.S. government and its term is short enough to minimize the risks of inflation and market interest rate changes. The CAPITAL ASSET PRICING MODEL (CAPM) used in modern PORTFOLIO THEORY has the premise that the return on a security is equal to the risk-free return plus a RISK PREMIUM.

RISKLESS TRANSACTION
1. trade guaranteeing a profit to the trader that initiates it. An *arbitrageur* may lock in a profit by trading on the difference in prices for the same security or commodity in different markets. For instance, if gold were selling for $400 an ounce in New York and $398 in London, a trader who acts quickly could buy a contract in London and sell it in New York for a riskless profit.
2. concept used in evaluating whether dealer MARKUPS and MARKDOWNS in OVER THE COUNTER transactions with customers are reasonable or excessive. In what is known as the FIVE PERCENT RULE, the NATIONAL ASSOCIATION OF SECURITIES DEALERS (NASD) takes the position that markups (when the customer buys) and markdowns (when the customer sells) should not exceed 5%, the proper charge depending on the effort and risk of the dealer in completing a trade. The maximum would be considered excessive for a riskless transaction, in which a security has high marketability and the dealer does not simply act as a broker and take a commission but trades from or for inventory and charges a markup or markdown. Where a dealer satisfies a buy order by making a purchase in the open market for inventory, then sells the security to the customer, the trade is called a *simultaneous transaction.* To avoid NASD criticism, broker-dealers commonly disclose the markups and markdowns to customers in transactions where they act as dealers.

RISK PREMIUM in PORTFOLIO THEORY, the difference between the RISK-FREE RETURN and the TOTAL RETURN from a risky investment. In the CAPITAL ASSET PRICING MODEL (CAPM), the risk premium reflects market-related risk (SYSTEMATIC

RISK) as measured by BETA. Other models also reflect specific risk as measured by ALPHA.

RISK-RETURN TRADE-OFF concept, basic in investment management, that RISK equals (varies with) RETURN; in other words, the higher the return the greater the risk and vice versa. In practice, it means that a speculative investment, such as stock in a newly formed company, can be expected to provide a higher potential return than a more conservative investment, such as BLUE CHIP or a BOND. Conversely, if you don't want the risk, don't expect the return. *See also* PORTFOLIO THEORY.

RISK TRANSFER shifting of risk, as with INSURANCE or the SECURITIZATION of debt.

ROAD SHOW presentation by an issuer of securities to potential buyers about the merits of the issue. Management of the company issuing stocks or bonds doing a road show travel around the country presenting financial information and an outlook for the company and answering the questions of analysts, fund managers, and other potential investors. Also known as a *dog and pony show.*

ROCKET SCIENTIST investment firm creator of innovative securities.

ROLL DOWN move from one OPTION position to another one having a lower EXERCISE PRICE. The term assumes that the position with the higher exercise price is closed out.

ROLL FORWARD move from one OPTION position to another with a later expiration date. The term assumes that the earlier position is closed out before the later one is established. If the new position involves a higher EXERCISE PRICE, it is called a *roll-up and forward;* if a lower exercise price, it is called a *roll-down and forward.* Also called *rolling over.*

ROLLING STOCK equipment that moves on wheels, used in the transportation industry. Examples include railroad cars and locomotives, tractor-trailers, and trucks.

ROLLOVER
1. movement of funds from one investment to another. For instance, an INDIVIDUAL RETIREMENT ACCOUNT may be rolled over when a person retires into an ANNUITY or other form of pension plan payout system. When a BOND or CERTIFICATE OF DEPOSIT matures, the funds may be rolled over into another bond or certificate of deposit. The proceeds from the sale of a house may be rolled over into the purchase of another house within two years without tax penalty. A stock may be sold and the proceeds rolled over into the same stock, establishing a different cost basis for the shareholder. *See also* THIRTY DAY WASH RULE.
2. term often used by banks when they allow a borrower to delay making a PRINCIPAL payment on a loan. Also, a country that has difficulty in meeting its debt payments may be granted a rollover by its creditors. With governments themselves, rollovers in the form of REFUNDINGS or REFINANCINGS are routine.
   See also CERTIFICATE OF DEPOSIT ROLLOVER.

ROLL UP move from one OPTION position to another having a higher EXERCISE PRICE. The term assumes that the earlier position is closed out before the new position is established. *See also* MASTER LIMITED PARTNERSHIP.

ROUND LOT generally accepted unit of trading on a securities exchange. On the New York Stock Exchange, for example, a round lot is 100 shares for stock and

$1000 or $5000 par value for bonds. In inactive stocks, the round lot is 10 shares. Increasingly, there seems to be recognition of a 500-share round lot for trading by institutions. Large denomination CERTIFICATES OF DEPOSIT trade on the OVER THE COUNTER market in units of $1 million. Investors who trade in round lots do not have to pay the DIFFERENTIAL charged on ODD LOT trades.

ROUND TRIP TRADE purchase and sale of a security or commodity within a short time. For example, a trader who continually is making short-term trades in a particular commodity is making round trip or *round turn* trades. Commissions for such a trader are likely to be quoted in terms of the total for a purchase and sale—$100 for the round trip, for instance. Excessive round trip trading is called CHURNING.

ROYALTY payment to the holder for the right to use property such as a patent, copyrighted material, or natural resources. For instance, inventors may be paid royalties when their inventions are produced and marketed. Authors may get royalties when books they have written are sold. Land owners leasing their property to an oil or mining company may receive royalties based on the amount of oil or minerals extracted from their land. Royalties are set in advance as a percentage of income arising from the commercialization of the owner's rights or property.

ROYALTY TRUST oil or gas company *spin-off* of oil reserves to a trust, which avoids DOUBLE TAXATION, eliminates the expense and risk of new drilling, and provides DEPLETION tax benefits to shareholders. In the mid-1980s, Mesa Royalty Trust, which pioneered the idea, led other trusts in converting to a MASTER LIMITED PARTNERSHIP form of organization, offering tax advantages along with greater flexibility and liquidity.

RUBBER CHECK check for which insufficient funds are available. It is called a rubber check because it bounces. *See also* OVERDRAFT.

RULE 405 New York Stock Exchange codification of an ethical concept recognized industry wide by those dealing with the investment public. These KNOW YOUR CUSTOMER rules recognize that what is suitable for one investor may be less appropriate for another and require investment people to obtain pertinent facts about a customer's other security holdings, financial condition, and objectives. *See also* SUITABILITY RULES.

RULE OF 72 formula for approximating the time it will take for a given amount of money to double at a given COMPOUND INTEREST rate. The formula is simply 72 divided by the interest rate. In six years $100 will double at a compound annual rate of 12%, thus: 72 divided by 12 equals 6.

RULE OF THE 78s method of computing REBATES of interest on installment loans. It uses the SUM-OF-THE-YEAR'S-DIGITS basis in determining the interest earned by the FINANCE COMPANY for each month of a year, assuming equal monthly payments, and gets its name from the fact that the sum of the digits 1 through 12 is 78. Thus interest is equal to $^{12}/_{78}$ths of the total annual interest in the first month, $^{11}/_{78}$ths in the second month, and so on.

RULE 144 *see* INVESTMENT LETTER; SECURITIES AND EXCHANGE COMMISSION RULES.

RULES OF FAIR PRACTICE set of rules established by the Board of Governors of the NATIONAL ASSOCIATION OF SECURITIES DEALERS (NASD), a self-regulatory organization comprising investment banking houses and firms dealing in the OVER THE COUNTER securities market. As summarized in the NASD bylaws, the rules are designed to foster just and equitable principles of trade and business;

high standards of commercial honor and integrity among members; the prevention of fraud and manipulative practices; safeguards against unreasonable profits, commissions, and other charges; and collaboration with governmental and other agencies to protect investors and the public interest in accordance with Section 15A of the MALONEY ACT. *See also* FIVE PERCENT RULE; IMMEDIATE FAMILY; KNOW YOUR CUSTOMER; MARKDOWN; RISKLESS TRANSACTION.

RUMORTRAGE stock traders' term, combining rumor and ARBITRAGE, for buying and selling based on rumor of a TAKEOVER. *See also* DEAL STOCK; GARBATRAGE.

RUN

Banking: demand for their money by many depositors all at once. If large enough, a run on a bank can cause it to fail, as hundreds of banks did in the Great Depression of the 1930s. Such a run is caused by a breach of confidence in the bank, perhaps as a result of large loan losses or fraud.

Securities:

1. list of available securities, along with current bid and asked prices, which a market maker is currently trading. For bonds the run may include the par value as well as current quotes.
2. when a security's price rises quickly, analysts say it had a quick run up, possibly because of a positive earnings report.

RUNDOWN

In general: status report or summary.

Municipal bonds: summary of the amounts available and the prices on units in a SERIAL BOND that has not yet been completely sold to the public.

RUNNING AHEAD illegal practice of buying or selling a security for a broker's personal account before placing a similar order for a customer. For example, when a firm's analyst issues a positive report on a company, the firm's brokers may not buy the stock for their own accounts before they have told their clients the news. Some firms prohibit brokers from making such trades for a specific period, such as two full days from the time of the recommendation.

RUNOFF printing of an exchange's closing prices on a TICKER tape after the market has closed. The runoff may take a long time when trading has been very heavy and the tape has fallen far behind the action.

RUSSELL INDEXES market capitalization weighted indexes published by Frank Russell Company of Tacoma, Washington. The *Russell 3000 Index* consists of the 3000 largest U.S. stocks in terms of market capitalization. The stocks in the index have a market capitalization range of approximately $91 million to $85 billion, with an average of $1.5 billion. The highest-ranking 1000 stocks comprise the *Russell 1000 Index*, which is highly correlated to the S&P 500 Index and has an average market capitalization of $4 billion; the smallest company in the index has an average market capitalization of $672 million. The *Russell 2000 Index* consists of the other 2000 stocks and represent approximately 11% of the Russell 3000 Index's total market capitalization, with an average capitalization of $255 million. The largest company in the index has an approximate market capitalization of $672 million. The Russell 2000 is a popular measure of the stock price performance of small companies.

The *Russell 2500 Index* consists of the bottom 800 securities in the Russell 1000, with the market capitalization of the largest company approximately $4.6 billion. The *Russell Top 200 Index* consists of the 200 largest securities in the Russell 1000, the "blue chip" index, with average market capitalization of $13 billion. The smallest stock in the index has an average market capitalization of $4.5 billion.

Four indexes, based on the Russell 1000 Index and Russell 2000 Index, reflect specialized growth orientation. The *Russell 1000 Value Index* and *Russell 2000 Value Index* contain those securities in the underlying indexes with a less-than-average growth orientation. Companies generally have low price-to-book and price-earnings ratios, higher dividend yields, and lower forecasted growth values. Average market capitalization is $3.9 billion and $126 million, respectively. The *Russell 1000 Growth Index* and *Russell 2000 Growth Index* contain those securities in the underlying indexes with a greater than average growth orientation, and generally higher price-to-book and price-earnings ratios. Average market capitalization is $4.1 billion and $129 million, respectively. *See also* STOCK INDEXES AND AVERAGES.

RUST BELT geographical area of the United States, mainly in Pennsylvania, West Virginia, and the industrial Midwest, where iron and steel is produced and where there is a concentration of industries that manufacture products using iron and steel. Term is used broadly to mean traditional American manufacturing with its largely unmodernized plants and facilities.

S _____

SAFE HARBOR
  1. financial or accounting step that avoids legal or tax consequences. Commonly used in reference to *safe harbor leasing,* as permitted by the ECONOMIC RECOVERY TAX ACT OF 1981 (ERTA). An unprofitable company unable to use the INVESTMENT CREDIT and ACCELERATED COST RECOVERY SYSTEM (ACRS) liberalized depreciation rules, could transfer those benefits to a profitable firm seeking to reduce its tax burden. Under such an arrangement, the profitable company would own an asset the unprofitable company would otherwise have purchased itself; the profitable company would then lease the asset to the unprofitable company, presumably passing on a portion of the tax benefits in the form of lower lease rental charges. Safe harbor leases were curtailed by provisions in the TAX EQUITY AND FISCAL RESPONSIBILITY ACT OF 1982 (TEFRA).
  2. provision in a law that excuses liability if the attempt to comply in good faith can be demonstrated. For example, safe harbor provisions would protect management from liability under Securities and Exchange Commission rules for financial PROJECTIONS made in good faith.
  3. form of SHARK REPELLENT whereby a TARGET COMPANY acquires a business so onerously regulated it makes the target less attractive, giving it, in effect, a safe harbor.

SAFEKEEPING storage and protection of a customer's financial assets, valuables, or documents, provided as a service by an institution serving as AGENT and, where control is delegated by the customer, also as custodian. An individual, corporate, or institutional investor might rely on a bank or a brokerage firm to hold stock certificates or bonds, keep track of trades, and provide periodic statements of changes in position. Investors who provide for their own safekeeping usually use a *safe deposit box,* provided by financial institutions for a fee. *See also* SELLING SHORT AGAINST THE BOX; STREET NAME.

SAIF *see* SAVINGS ASSOCIATION INSURANCE FUND (SAIF).

SALARY regular wages received by an employee from an employer on a weekly, biweekly, or monthly basis. Many salaries also include such employee benefits as health and life insurance, savings plans, and Social Security. Salary income is taxable by the federal, state, and local government, where applicable, through payroll withholding.

SALARY FREEZE cessation of increases in salary throughout a company for a period of time. Companies going through a business downturn will freeze salaries in order to reduce expenses. When business improves, salary increases are frequently reinstated.

SALARY REDUCTION PLAN plan allowing employees to contribute pretax compensation to a qualified TAX DEFERRED retirement plan. Until the TAX REFORM ACT OF 1986, the term was synonymous with 401(k) PLAN, but the 1986 Act prohibited employees of state and local governments and tax-exempt organizations from establishing new 401(k) plans and added restrictions to existing government and tax-exempt unfunded deferred compensation arrangements and tax-sheltered annuity arrangements creating, in effect, a broadened definition of salary reduction plan. Current law permits employees of tax-exempt religious, charitable, or educational organizations and public schools to take nontaxable reductions to a limit of 20% of salary multiplied by years of service less tax-free contributions made in prior years by the employer to a tax-sheltered annuity or qualified plan. The reduction, however, may not exceed the lower of 25% of salary or $9,500, except that employees with at least 15 years of service may defer up to $12,500. Such contributions purchase a nonforfeitable tax-sheltered annuity.

Federal government employees are allowed salary deductions up to the limits for 401(k) plans. State and local governments and tax-exempt organizations other than churches may set up *Section 457* plans allowing employees to defer annually the lesser of $7,500 or one-third of compensation.

Irrevocable alternative or "catch-up" formulae are also available with limitations.

SALE
In general: any exchange of goods or services for money. *Contrast with* BARTER.
Finance: income received in exchange for goods and services recorded for a given accounting period, either on a cash basis (as received) or on an accrual basis (as earned). *See also* GROSS SALES.
Securities: in securities trading, a sale is executed when a buyer and a seller have agreed on a price for the security.

SALE AND LEASEBACK form of LEASE arrangement in which a company sells an asset to another party—usually an insurance or finance company, a leasing company, a limited partnership, or an institutional investor—in exchange for cash, then contracts to lease the asset for a specified term. Typically, the asset is sold for its MARKET VALUE, so the lessee has really acquired capital that would otherwise have been tied up in a long-term asset. Such arrangements frequently have tax benefits for the lessee, although there is normally little difference in the effect on income between the lease payments and the interest payments that would have existed had the asset been purchased with borrowed money. A company generally opts for the sale and leaseback arrangement as an alternative to straight financing when the rate it would have to pay a lender is higher than the cost of rental or when it wishes to show less debt on its BALANCE SHEET (called *off-balance-sheet financing*). *See also* CAPITAL LEASE.

SALES CHARGE fee paid to a brokerage house by a buyer of shares in a load MUTUAL FUND or a LIMITED PARTNERSHIP. Normally, the sales charge for a mutual fund starts at 4.5% to 5% of the capital invested and decreases as the size of the investment increases. The sales charge for a limited partnership can be even higher—as much as 10%. In return for the sales charge, investors are entitled to investment advice from the broker on which fund or partnership is best for them. A fund that carries no sales charge is called a NO-LOAD FUND. *See also* BACK-END LOAD; FRONT-END LOAD; LETTER OF INTENT; LOAD FUND; REDEMPTION FEES; 12B-1 MUTUAL FUND.

SALES LITERATURE

In general: written material designed to help sell a product or a service.

Investments: written material issued by a securities brokerage firm, mutual fund, underwriter, or other institution selling a product that explains the advantages of the investment product. Such literature must be truthful and must comply with disclosure regulations issued by the Securities and Exchange Commission and state securities agencies.

SALES LOAD *see* SALES CHARGE.

SALES TAX tax based on a percentage of the selling price of goods and services. State and local governments assess sales tax and decide what percentage to charge. The retail buyer pays the sales tax to the retailer, who passes it on to the sales tax collection agency of the government. For an item costing $1000 in a state with a 5% sales tax, the buyer pays $50 in sales tax, for a total of $1050. Sales taxes are not deductible on federal or state income tax returns.

SALLIE MAE *see* STUDENT LOAN MARKETING ASSOCIATION.

SALOMON BROTHERS WORLD EQUITY INDEX (SBWEI) a comprehensive top-down, float capitalization-weighted index that includes shares of approximately 6000 companies in 22 countries. It is one member of a family of Salomon Brothers performance indexes that measure domestic and international fixed income and equity markets. The index includes all companies with available market capitalization greater than $100 million. Each issue is weighted by the proportion of its available equity capital, its float, rather than by its total equity capital. The index is the successor to the Salomon-Russell Global Equity Index. Other SBWEI equity products include GDP and weighted indexes, and emerging market indexes.

SALVAGE VALUE *see* RESIDUAL VALUE.

SAME-DAY FUNDS SETTLEMENT (SDFS) method of settlement in good-the-same-day FEDERAL FUNDS used by the DEPOSITORY TRUST COMPANY for transactions in U.S. government securities, short-term municipal notes, medium-term commercial paper notes, COLLATERALIZED MORTGAGE OBLIGATIONS (CMOs), DUTCH AUCTION PREFERRED STOCK, and other instruments when both parties to the trade are properly collateralized.

SAME-DAY SUBSTITUTION offsetting changes in a MARGIN ACCOUNT in the course of one day, resulting in neither a MARGIN CALL nor a credit to the SPECIAL MISCELLANEOUS ACCOUNT. Examples: a purchase and a sale of equal value; a decline in the MARKET VALUE of some margin securities offset by an equal rise in the market value of others.

SAMURAI BONDS bonds denominated in yen issued by non-Japanese companies for sale mostly in Japan. The bonds are not subject to Japanese withholding taxes, and therefore offer advantages to Japanese buyers.

SANDWICH GENERATION middle-aged working people who feel squeezed by the financial pressures of supporting their aging parents, the costs of raising and educating their children, and the need to save for their own retirement.

SANTA CLAUS RALLY rise in stock prices in the week between Christmas and New Year's Day. Also called the *year-end rally*. Some analysts attribute this rally to the anticipation of the JANUARY EFFECT, when stock prices rise in the first few days of the year as pension funds add new money to their accounts.

SAO PAULO STOCK EXCHANGE *see* BOLSA DE VALORES DE SAO PAULO (BOVESPA).

S&P PHENOMENON tendency of stocks newly added to the STANDARD & POOR'S INDEX to rise temporarily in price as S&P-related INDEX FUNDS adjust their portfolios, creating heavy buying activity.

SATURDAY NIGHT SPECIAL sudden attempt by one company to take over another by making a public TENDER OFFER. The term was coined in the 1960s after a rash of such surprise maneuvers, which were often announced over weekends. The WILLIAMS ACT of 1968 placed severe restrictions on tender offers and required disclosure of direct or indirect ownership of 5% or more of any class of EQUITY. It thus marked the end of what, in its traditional form, was known as the "creeping tender."

SAUCER technical chart pattern (see next page) signaling that the price of a security or a commodity has formed a bottom and is moving up. An inverse saucer shows a top in the security's price and signals a downturn. *See also* TECHNICAL ANALYSIS.

SAVING RATE ratio of personal saving to disposable personal income. Disposable personal income is personal income less personal tax and nontax payments. Personal saving is disposable personal income less personal outlays. The U.S. Commerce Department's Bureau of Economic Analysis and the Federal Reserve each publish estimates of the saving rate on a quarterly basis.

SAVINGS ACCOUNT deposit account at a commercial bank, savings bank, or savings and loan that pays interest, usually from a day-of-deposit to day-of-withdrawal basis. Financial institutions can pay whatever rate they like on savings accounts, but this rate tends to be in relation to the actions of the money center banks in repricing their PRIME RATE. Traditionally, savings accounts offered PASSBOOKS, but in recent years alternatives such as ATMs, monthly account statements and telephone banking services have been added to credit deposits and interest earned. Savings deposits are insured up to $100,000 per account if they are on deposit at banks insured by the FEDERAL DEPOSIT INSURANCE CORPORATION (FDIC) or a savings and loan insured by the SAVINGS ASSOCIATION INSURANCE FUND (SAIF).

SAVINGS AND LOAN ASSOCIATION depository financial institution, federally or state chartered, that obtains the bulk of its deposits from consumers and holds the majority of its assets as home mortgage loans. A few such specialized institutions were organized in the 19th century under state charters but with minimal regulation. Reacting to the crisis in the banking and home building industries precipitated by the Great Depression, Congress in 1932 passed the Federal Home Loan Bank Act, establishing the FEDERAL HOME LOAN BANK SYSTEM to supplement the lending resources of state-chartered savings and loans (S&Ls). The Home Owners' Loan Act of 1933 created a system for the federal chartering of S&Ls under the supervision of the Federal Home Loan Bank Board. Deposits in federal S&Ls were insured with the formation of the Federal Savings and Loan Insurance Corporation in 1934.

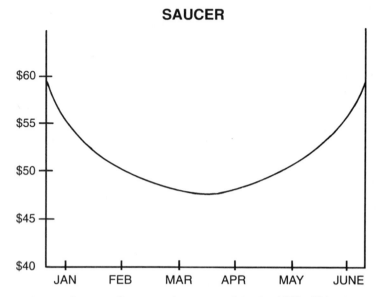

A second wave of restructuring occurred in the 1980s. The DEPOSITORY INSTITUTIONS DEREGULATION AND MONETARY CONTROL ACT of 1980 set a six-year timetable for the removal of interest rate ceilings, including the S&Ls' quarter-point rate advantage over the commercial bank limit on personal savings accounts. The act also allowed S&Ls limited entry into some markets previously open only to commercial banks (commercial lending, nonmortgage consumer lending, trust services) and, in addition, permitted MUTUAL ASSOCIATIONS to issue INVESTMENT CERTIFICATES. In actual effect, interest rate parity was achieved by the end of 1982.

The Garn-St Germain Depository Institutions Act of 1982 accelerated the pace of deregulation and gave the Federal Home Loan Bank Board wide latitude in shoring up the capital positions of S&Ls weakened by the impact of record-high interest rates on portfolios of old, fixed-rate mortgage loans. The 1982 act also encouraged the formation of stock savings and loans or the conversion of existing mutual (depositor-owned) associations to the stock form, which gave the associations another way to tap the capital markets and thereby to bolster their net worth.

In 1989, responding to a massive wave of insolvencies caused by misman-agement, corruption, and economic factors, Congress passed a savings and loan "bailout bill" that revamped the regulatory structure of the industry under a newly created agency, the OFFICE OF THRIFT SUPERVISION (OTS). Disbanding the Federal Savings and Loan Insurance Corporation (FSLIC), it created the SAVINGS ASSOCIATION INSURANCE FUND (SAIF) to provide deposit insurance under the adminis-tration of the FEDERAL DEPOSIT INSURANCE CORPORATION (FDIC). It also created the RESOLUTION TRUST CORPORATION (RTC) and RESOLUTION FUNDING CORPORA-TION (REFCORP) to deal with insolvent institutions and scheduled the consoli-dation of their activities with SAIF after 1996. The Federal Home Loan Bank Board was replaced by the FEDERAL HOUSING FINANCE BOARD (FHFB), which now oversees the Federal Home Loan Bank System.

See also SAVINGS BANK.

SAVINGS ASSOCIATION INSURANCE FUND (SAIF) U.S. government entity created by Congress in 1989 as part of its SAVINGS AND LOAN ASSOCIATION bailout bill to replace the FEDERAL SAVINGS AND LOAN INSURANCE CORPORATION (FSLIC) as the provider of deposit insurance for thrift institutions. SAIF, pronounced to rhyme with *safe,* is administered by the FEDERAL DEPOSIT INSURANCE CORPORATION (FDIC) separately from its bank insurance program, which was renamed *Bank Insurance Fund (BIF).* The new organization provides the same protection ($100,000 per depositor) as FSLIC. After 1996, SAIF assumes responsibility for insolvent institutions from RESOLUTION TRUST CORPORATION (RTC). *See also* OFFICE OF THRIFT SUPERVISION (OTS).

SAVINGS BANK depository financial institution that primarily accepts consumer deposits and makes home mortgage loans. Historically, savings banks were of the mutual (depositor-owned) form and chartered in only 16 states; the majority of savings banks were located in the New England states, New York, and New Jersey. Prior to the passage of the Garn-St Germain Depository Institutions Act of 1982, state-chartered savings bank deposits were insured along with commercial bank deposits by the FEDERAL DEPOSIT INSURANCE CORPORATION (FDIC). The Garn-St Germain Act gave savings banks the options of a federal charter, mutual-to-stock conversion, supervision by the Federal Home Loan Bank Board, and insurance from the FEDERAL SAVINGS AND LOAN INSURANCE CORPORATION (FSLIC). In 1989, the Federal Home Loan Bank Board was replaced by the FEDERAL HOUSING FINANCE BOARD (FHFB), and the FSLIC by the newly created SAVINGS ASSOCIATION INSURANCE FUND (SAIF), a unit of the FDIC. *See also* MUTUAL SAVINGS BANK; SAVINGS AND LOAN ASSOCIATION.

SAVINGS BOND U.S. government bond issued in FACE VALUE denominations ranging from $50 to $10,000. From 1941 to 1979, the government issued SERIES E BONDS. Starting in 1980, Series EE and HH bonds were issued. Series EE bonds, issued at a discount of half their face value, range from $50 to $10,000; Series HH bonds, which are interest bearing, range from $500 to $10,000. Series EE bonds earn interest for 30 years; Series HH bonds earn interest for 20 years. Series EE bonds, if held for five years, pay 85% of the average yield on five-year Treasury securities. Series HH bonds, available only through an exchange of at least $500 in Series E or EE bonds, pay a fixed 4% rate in two semiannual payments. For many years, the government guaranteed a minimum yield on savings bonds. This yield decreased from 7.5% to 6% and then 4%. The guaranteed minimum feature was dropped in 1995. Instead, for bonds issued on May 1, 1995 or later and held for less than five years, bonds pay 85% of the average yield on six-month Treasury securities. The yield is readjusted every six months, on May 1 and November 1.

The interest from savings bonds is exempt from state and local taxes, and no federal tax on EE bonds is due until redemption. Bondholders wanting to defer the tax liability on their maturing Series EE bonds can exchange them for Series HH bonds. Taxpayers meeting income qualifications can buy EE bonds to save for higher educational expenses and enjoy total or partial federal tax exemption. This applies to individuals with modified adjusted gross incomes between $45,500 and $60,500 and to married couples filing jointly with incomes between $68,250 and $98,250. These income levels are adjusted slightly for inflation annually.

SAVINGS DEPOSITS interest-earning cash balances that can be withdrawn on demand, kept for the purpose of savings, in commercial banks, savings banks, credit unions, and savings and loans. Passbook savings, statement savings, and money market accounts are examples of savings deposits.

SAVINGS ELEMENT cash value accumulated inside a life insurance policy. A cash value policy has two components: a death benefit paid to beneficiaries if the insured dies, and a savings element, which is the amount of premium paid in excess of the cost of protection. This excess is invested by the insurance company in stocks, bonds, real estate, and other ventures and the returns build up tax-deferred inside the policy. A policyholder can borrow against this cash value or take it out of the policy, at which point it becomes taxable income. Once a policyholder reaches retirement age, he or she can ANNUITIZE the accumulated cash value and receive a regular payment from the insurance company for life. Insurance companies encourage people to buy policies with a savings element because it provides a disciplined way to save.

SCALE

Labor: wage rate for specific types of employees. For example: "Union scale for carpenters is $15.60 per hour."

Production economics: amount of production, as in "economy or diseconomy of scale." *See also* MARGINAL COST.

Serial bonds: vital data for each of the scheduled maturities in a new SERIAL BOND issue, including the number of bonds, the date they mature, the COUPON rate, and the offering price.

See also SCALE ORDER.

SCALE ORDER order for a specified number of shares that is to be executed in stages in order to average the price. Such an order might provide for the purchase of a total of 5000 shares to be executed in lots of 500 shares at each quarter-point interval as the market declines. Since scale orders are clerically cumbersome, not all brokers will accept them.

SCALPER

In general: speculator who enters into quasi-legal or illegal transactions to turn a quick and sometimes unreasonable profit. For example, a scalper buys tickets at regular prices for a major event and when the event becomes a sellout, resells the tickets at the highest price possible.

Securities:
1. investment adviser who takes a position in a security before recommending it, then sells out after the price has risen as a result of the recommendation. *See also* INVESTMENT ADVISERS ACT.
2. market maker who, in violation of the RULES OF FAIR PRACTICE of the NATIONAL ASSOCIATION OF SECURITIES DEALERS, adds an excessive markup or takes an excessive MARKDOWN on a transaction. *See also* FIVE PERCENT RULE.
3. commodity trader who trades for small gains, usually establishing and liquidating a position within one day.

SCHEDULE C common reference to a section of the bylaws of the NATIONAL ASSOCIATION OF SECURITIES DEALERS (NASD) concerned with membership requirements and procedures.

SCHEDULE 13D form required under Section 13d of the SECURITIES ACT OF 1934 within ten business days of acquiring direct or BENEFICIAL OWNERSHIP of 5% or more of any class of equity securities in a PUBLICLY HELD corporation. In addition to filing with the Securities and Exchange Commission, the purchaser of such stock must also file the 13d with the stock exchange on which the shares are listed (if any) and with the company itself. Required information includes the way the shares were acquired, the purchaser's background, and future plans regarding the target company. The law is designed to protect against insidious TAKEOVER attempts and to keep the investing public aware of information that could affect the price of their stock. *See also* WILLIAMS ACT.

SCORCHED-EARTH POLICY technique used by a company that has become the target of a TAKEOVER attempt to make itself unattractive to the acquirer. For example, it may agree to sell off the most attractive parts of its business, called the CROWN JEWELS, or it may schedule all debt to become due immediately after a MERGER. *See also* JONESTOWN DEFENSE; POISON PILL; SHARK REPELLENT.

SCORE acronym for *Special Claim on Residual Equity,* a certificate issued by the Americus Shareowner Service Corporation, a privately held company formed to market the product. A SCORE gave its holder the right to all the appreciation on an underlying security above a specified price, but none of the dividend income from the security. Its counterpart, called PRIME, passed all dividend income to its holders, who got the benefit of price appreciation up to the limit where SCORE began. PRIME and SCORE together formed a unit share investment trust (USIT), and both were listed on the American Stock Exchange. A buyer of a SCORE unit hoped that the underlying stock would rise steeply in value.

The first USIT was formed with the shares of American Telephone and Telegraph. PRIME holders got all dividends and price appreciation in AT&T up to $75 a share; SCORE holders received all appreciation above $75. The trusts expired in 1988.

S CORPORATION *see* SUBCHAPTER S.

SCREEN (STOCKS) to look for stocks that meet certain predetermined investment and financial criteria. Often, stocks are screened using a computer and a data base containing financial statistics on thousands of companies. For instance, an investor may want to screen for all those companies that have a PRICE/EARNINGS RATIO of less than 10, an earnings growth rate of more than 15%, and a dividend yield of more than 4%.

SCRIP

In general: receipt, certificate, or other representation of value recognized by both payer and payee. Scrip is not currency, but may be convertible into currency.

Securities: temporary document that is issued by a corporation and that represents a fractional share of stock resulting from a SPLIT, exchange of stock, or SPIN-OFF. Scrip certificates may be aggregated or applied toward the purchase of full shares. Scrip dividends have historically been paid in lieu of cash dividends by companies short of cash.

SCRIPOPHILY practice of collecting stock and bond certificates for their scarcity value, rather than for their worth as securities. The certificate's price rises with the beauty of the illustration on it and the importance of the issuer in world finance and economic development. Many old certificates, such as those issued by railroads in the 19th century or by Standard Oil before it was broken up in the early 20th century, have risen greatly in value since their issue, even though the issuing companies no longer exist.

SDR *see* SPECIAL DRAWING RIGHTS.

SEASONALITY variations in business or economic activity that recur with regularity as the result of changes in climate, holidays, and vacations. The retail toy business, with its steep sales buildup between Thanksgiving and Christmas and pronounced dropoff thereafter, is an example of seasonality in a dramatic form, though nearly all businesses have some degree of seasonal variation. It is often necessary to make allowances for seasonality when interpreting or projecting financial or economic data, a process economists call *seasonal adjustment.*

SEASONED securities that have been trading in the secondary market for a lengthy period of time, and have established a track record of significant trading volume and price stability. Many investors prefer buying only seasoned issues instead of new securities that have not stood the test of time.

SEASONED ISSUE securities (usually from established companies) that have gained a reputation for quality with the investing public and enjoy LIQUIDITY in the SECONDARY MARKET.

SEAT figurative term for a membership on a securities or commodities exchange. Seats are bought and sold at prices set by supply and demand. A seat on the New York Stock Exchange, for example, traded for over $1 million prior to BLACK MONDAY in 1987 and just over $400,000 in late 1989. *See also* ABC AGREEMENT; MEMBER FIRM.

SEC *see* SECURITIES AND EXCHANGE COMMISSION.

SEC FEE small (one cent per several hundred dollars) fee charged by the Securities and Exchange Commission (SEC) to sellers of EQUITY securities that are exchange traded.

SECONDARY DISTRIBUTION public sale of previously issued securities held by large investors, usually corporations, institutions, or other AFFILIATED PERSONS, as distinguished from a NEW ISSUE or PRIMARY DISTRIBUTION, where the seller is the issuing corporation. As with a primary offering, secondaries are usually handled by INVESTMENT BANKERS, acting alone or as a syndicate, who purchase the shares from the seller at an agreed price, then resell them, sometimes with the help of a SELLING GROUP, at a higher PUBLIC OFFERING PRICE, making their profit on the difference, called the SPREAD. Since the offering is registered with the Securities and Exchange Commission, the syndicate manager can legally stabilize—or peg—the market price by bidding for shares in the open market. Buyers of securities offered this way pay no commissions, since all costs are borne by the selling investor. If the securities involved are listed, the CONSOLIDATED TAPE will announce the offering during the trading day, although the offering is not made until after the market's close. Among the historically large secondary distributions were the Ford Foundation's offering of Ford Motor Company stock in 1956 (approximately $658 million) handled by 7 firms under a joint management agreement and the sale of Howard Hughes' TWA shares ($566 million) through Merrill Lynch, Pierce, Fenner & Smith in 1966.

A similar form of secondary distribution, called the SPECIAL OFFERING, is limited to members of the New York Stock Exchange and is completed in the course of the trading day.

See also EXCHANGE DISTRIBUTION; REGISTERED SECONDARY OFFERING; SECURITIES AND EXCHANGE COMMISSION RULES 144 and 237.

SECONDARY MARKET
1. exchanges and over-the-counter markets where securities are bought and sold subsequent to original issuance, which took place in the PRIMARY MARKET. Proceeds of secondary market sales accrue to the selling dealers and investors, not to the companies that originally issued the securities.
2. market in which money-market instruments are traded among investors.

SECONDARY MORTGAGE MARKET buying, selling, and trading of existing mortgage loans and mortgage-backed securities. Original lenders are thus able to sell loans in their portfolios in order to build LIQUIDITY to support additional lending. Mortgages originated by lenders are purchased by government agencies (such as the FEDERAL HOME LOAN MORTGAGE CORPORATION and the FEDERAL NATIONAL MORTGAGE ASSOCIATION) and by investment bankers. These agencies and bankers, in turn, create pools of mortgages, which they repackage as mortgage-backed securities, called PASS-THROUGH SECURITIES or PARTICIPATION CERTIFICATES, which are then sold to investors. The secondary mortgage market thus encompasses all activity beyond the PRIMARY MARKET, which is between the homebuyers and the originating mortgage lender.

SECONDARY OFFERING *see* SECONDARY DISTRIBUTION.

SECONDARY STOCKS used in a general way to mean stocks having smaller MARKET CAPITALIZATION, less quality, and more risk than BLUE CHIP issues represented by the Dow Jones Industrial Average. Secondary stocks, which often behave differently than blue chips, are tracked by the Amex Market Value Index, the NASDAQ Composite Index, and broad indexes, such as the Standard & Poor's Index. Also called *second-tier stocks.*

SECOND MORTGAGE LENDING advancing funds to a borrower that are secured by real estate previously pledged in a FIRST MORTGAGE loan. In the case of DEFAULT, the first mortgage has priority of claim over the second.

A variation on the second mortgage is the *home equity loan,* in which the loan is secured by independent appraisal of the property value. A home equity loan may also be in the form of a line of credit, which may be drawn down on by using a check or even a credit card. *See also* HOMEOWNER'S EQUITY ACCOUNT; RIGHT OF RESCISSION.

SECOND-PREFERRED STOCK preferred stock issue that ranks below another preferred issue in terms of priority of claim on dividends and on assets in liquidation. Second-preferred shares are often issued with a CONVERTIBLE feature or with a warrant to make them more attractive to investors. *See also* JUNIOR SECURITY; PREFERRED STOCK; PRIOR-PREFERRED STOCK; SUBSCRIPTION WARRANT.

SECOND ROUND intermediate stage of VENTURE CAPITAL financing, coming after the SEED MONEY (or START-UP) and *first round* stages and before the MEZZANINE LEVEL, when the company has matured to the point where it might consider a LEVERAGED BUYOUT by management or an INITIAL PUBLIC OFFERING (IPO).

SECOND-TO-DIE INSURANCE insurance policy that pays a death benefit upon the death of the spouse who dies last. Such insurance typically is purchased by a couple wanting to pass a large estate on to their heirs. When the first spouse dies, the couple's assets are passed tax-free to the second spouse under the MARITAL DEDUCTION. When the second spouse dies, the remaining estate could be subject to large estate taxes. The proceeds from the second-to-die insurance are designed to pay the estate taxes, leaving the remaining estate for the heirs. Such insurance is appropriate only for those facing large estate tax liabilities. Because the policy is based on the joint life expectancy of both husband and wife, premiums typically cost less than those on traditional cash value policies on both lives insured separately. Also called *survivorship life insurance.*

SECTOR particular group of stocks, usually found in one industry. SECURITIES ANALYSTS often follow a particular sector of the stock market, such as airline or chemical stocks.

SECTOR FUND *see* SPECIALIZED MUTUAL FUND.

SECULAR long-term (10–50 years or more) as distinguished from seasonal or cyclical time frames.

SECURED BOND bond backed by the pledge of COLLATERAL, a MORTGAGE, or other LIEN. The exact nature of the security is spelled out in the INDENTURE. Secured bonds are distinguished from unsecured bonds, called DEBENTURES.

SECURED DEBT debt guaranteed by the pledge of assets or other COLLATERAL. *See also* ASSIGN; HYPOTHECATION.

SECURITIES ACT OF 1933 first law enacted by Congress to regulate the securities markets, approved May 26, 1933, as the Truth in Securities Act. It requires REGISTRATION of securities prior to public sale and adequate DISCLOSURE of pertinent financial and other data in a PROSPECTUS to permit informed analysis by potential investors. It also contains antifraud provisions prohibiting false representations and disclosures. Enforcement responsibilities were assigned to the SECURITIES AND EXCHANGE COMMISSION by the SECURITIES EXCHANGE ACT OF 1934. The 1933 act did not supplant BLUE SKY LAWS of the various states.

SECURITIES ACTS AMENDMENTS OF 1975 federal legislation enacted on June 4, 1975, to amend the SECURITIES EXCHANGE ACT OF 1934. The 1975 amendments directed the SECURITIES AND EXCHANGE COMMISSION to work with the industry toward establishing a NATIONAL MARKET SYSTEM together with a system for the nationwide clearance and settlement of securities transactions. Because of these provisions, the 1975 laws are sometimes called the *National Exchange Market System Act.* New regulations were also introduced to promote prompt and accurate securities handling, and clearing agencies were required to register with and report to the SEC. The 1975 amendments required TRANSFER AGENTS other than banks to register with the SEC and provided that authority with respect to bank transfer agents would be shared by the SEC and bank regulatory agencies. The Municipal Securities Rulemaking Board was created to regulate brokers, dealers, and banks dealing in municipal securities, with rules subject to SEC approval and enforcement shared by the NATIONAL ASSOCIATION OF SECURITIES DEALERS and bank regulatory agencies. The law also required the registration of broker-dealers in municipals, but preserved the exemption of issuers from REGISTRATION requirements. The amendments contained the prohibition of fixed commission rates, adopted earlier by the SEC in its Rule 19b-3.

SECURITIES ANALYST individual, usually employed by a stock brokerage house, bank, or investment institution, who performs investment research and examines the financial condition of a company or group of companies in an industry and in the context of the securities markets. Many analysts specialize in a single industry or SECTOR and make investment recommendations to buy, sell, or hold in that area. Among a corporation's financial indicators most closely followed by ANALYSTS are sales and earnings growth, CAPITAL STRUCTURE, stock price trend and PRICE/EARNINGS RATIO, DIVIDEND PAYOUTS, and RETURN ON INVESTED CAPITAL. Securities analysts promote corporate financial disclosure by sponsoring forums through local associations, the largest of which is the New York Society of Security Analysts, and through its national body, the Financial Analysts Federation. *See also* FORECASTING; FUNDAMENTAL ANALYSIS; QUALITATIVE ANALYSIS; QUANTITATIVE ANALYSIS; TECHNICAL ANALYSIS.

SECURITIES AND COMMODITIES EXCHANGES organized, national exchanges where securities, options, and futures contracts are traded by members for their own accounts and for the accounts of customers. The stock exchanges are registered with and regulated by the SECURITIES AND EXCHANGE COMMISSION (SEC); the commodities exchanges are registered with and regulated by the Commodity Futures Trading Commission (*see* REGULATED COMMODITIES); where options are traded on an exchange, such activity is regulated by the SEC.

STOCKS, BONDS, SUBSCRIPTION RIGHTS, SUBSCRIPTION WARRANTS and in some cases OPTIONS are traded on 9 STOCK EXCHANGES in the United States. The FUTURES MARKET is represented by 13 leading commodities exchanges.

Exchanges listing basic securities—stocks, bonds, rights, warrants, and options on individual stocks—are described under the entries for the NEW YORK STOCK EXCHANGE, AMERICAN STOCK EXCHANGE, and REGIONAL STOCK EXCHANGES.

The exchanges listing commodity and other futures contracts and options in addition to those on individual stocks are:

American Stock Exchange (New York) *index options:* Biotechnology Index, Computer Technology Index, Eurotop 100 Index, Hong Kong 30 Index, Institutional Index, Japan Index, Major Market Index, Mexico Index, Morgan Stanley Cyclical Index, Morgan Stanley Consumer Index, Natural Gas Index, North American Telecommunications Index, Oil Index, Oscar Gruss Israel Index, Pharmaceutical Index, Security Broker/Dealer Index, S&P MidCap 400 Index. *interest rate options:* Treasury bills, Treasury notes; LEAPS; FLEX options on underlying indices.

Chicago Board of Trade (Chicago) *futures:* wheat, corn, oats, soybeans, soybean oil, soybean meal, rice, diammonium phosphate, anhydrous ammonia, edible oil index, barge freight index, structural panel index, Eastern catastrophic insurance, Midwest catastrophic insurance, national catastrophic insurance, silver (1,000 ounces, 5,000 ounces), gold (kilo, 100 ounces) U.S. Treasury bonds, Treasury notes (10-year, 5-year, 2-year), Municipal Bond Index, Canadian government bonds, 30-day Fed funds, U.S. dollar index, Major Market Index, Wilshire Small Cap Index. *options:* wheat, corn, oats, soybeans, soybean oil, soybean meal, rice, Eastern catastrophic insurance, Midwest catastrophic insurance, national catastrophic insurance, Western insurance—annual, silver (1,000 ounces), U.S. Treasury bonds, Treasury notes (10-year, 5-year, 2-year), Municipal Bond Index, Canadian government bond, Flexible U.S. Treasury bonds, Flexible Treasury notes (10-year, 5-year, 2-year), Major Market Index, Wilshire Small Cap Index.

Chicago Board Options Exchange (Chicago) *equity options; equity LEAPS; index options:* Standard & Poor's 100 Index, Standard & Poor's 500 Index, OEX CAPS, OEX LEAPS, S&P 500 long-dated options, S&P 500 end-of-quarter options, SPX LEAPS, SPX CAPS, FLEX options, NASDAQ-100 Index, Russell 2000 Index, Russell 2000 Index LEAPS, FT-SE 100 Index, CBOE Mexico Index, CBOE Mexico Index LEAPS, Nikkei 300 Index, Nikkei 300 Index LEAPS, S&P Banks Index, CBOE BioTech Index, CBOE BioTech Index LEAPS, S&P Chemical Index, CBOE Computer Software Index, CBOE Environmental Index, CBOE Gaming Index, S&P Health Care Index, S&P Insurance Index, S&P Retail Index, CBOE US Telecommunications Index, S&P Transportation Index. *interest rate options:* 13-week Treasury bill, 5-year Treasury note, 10-year Treasury note, 30-year Treasury bond.

Chicago Mercantile Exchange (Chicago) *foreign currency futures:* Australian dollar, British pound, British pound Rolling Spot, Canadian dollar, Deutsche mark, Deutsche mark Rolling Spot, Deutsche mark/Japanese yen cross rate, DM currency forward, 3-month Eurodollar, 3-month Euromark, French franc, Japanese yen, Swiss franc. *commodity futures:* live hogs, pork bellies, live cattle, feeder cattle, lumber. *financial futures:* 1-month LIBOR (London Interbank Offer Rate), 90-day Treasury bills, 1-year Treasury bills, S&P 500 Index, S&P 400 Index, FT-SE 100, Major Market Index, Russell 2000 Index, Goldman Sachs Commodity Index. *options on futures:* Australian dollar, British pound, British pound Rolling Spot, Canadian dollar, Deutsche mark, Deutsche mark Rolling Spot, 3-month Eurodollar, 3-month Euromark, French franc, Japanese yen, Swiss franc, Deutsche mark/yen cross, 1-month LIBOR, 90-day Treasury bill; live hogs, pork bellies, live cattle, feeder cattle, lumber; Nikkei 225, S&P 500 Index, S&P 400 Index, Major Market Index, Russell 2000 Index, Goldman Sachs Commodity Index.

Coffee, Sugar and Cocoa Exchange* (New York) *futures:* cocoa, coffee, sugar No. 11, sugar No. 14, white sugar, cheddar cheese, nonfat dry milk. *options on futures:* cocoa, coffee, sugar No. 11, cheddar cheese, nonfat dry milk.

Kansas City Board of Trade (Kansas City) *futures:* wheat, Value Line Index, Mini Value Line. *options on futures:* wheat, Mini Value Line.

Mid-America Commodity Exchange (Chicago) *futures:* wheat, corn, oats, soybeans, soybean meal new, live cattle, live hogs, rough rice, NY silver, NY gold, platinum, U.S. Treasury bonds, U.S. Treasury bills, Treasury notes (10-year, 5-year), Eurodollars, U.S. dollar index, British pound, Swiss franc, Canadian dollar, Deutsche mark, Japanese yen. *options on futures:* wheat, corn, soybeans, rough rice, NY gold, U.S. Treasury bonds.

Minneapolis Grain Exchange (Minneapolis) *futures:* wheat, white wheat, oats, shrimp. *options on futures:* American spring wheat, European spring wheat, white wheat, oats, shrimp.

New York Cotton Exchange* (New York) *futures:* cotton, frozen concentrated orange juice. *options on futures:* cotton, frozen concentrated orange juice. *FINEX (division of NYCE) futures:* U.S. dollar index (USDX), U.S. dollar-based currency, cross-rate currency, Treasury auction U.S. Treasury notes (5-year, 2-year). *options on futures:* USDX, U.S. dollar based currency, Treasury auction U.S. Treasury notes (5-year, 2-year).

New York Futures Exchange (division of the NYCE) (New York) *futures:* Knight-Ridder Commodity Research Bureau Index, New York Stock Exchange Composite Index, Treasury bonds. *options on futures:* NYSE Composite Index, KR-CRB Index.

New York Mercantile Exchange* (New York) *NYMEX division: futures:* light, sweet crude oil, sour crude, New York Harbor unleaded gasoline, Gulf Coast unleaded gasoline, heating oil, natural gas, propane, electricity, platinum, palladium. *options on futures:* light, sweet crude, heating oil, New York Harbor unleaded gasoline, natural gas, platinum. *COMEX division: futures:* copper, gold, silver, Eurotop 100 Index. *options on futures:* copper, gold, silver, Eurotop 100 Index.

New York Stock Exchange (New York) *index options:* NYSE Composite Index options, NYSE Utility Index options.

Pacific Stock Exchange (San Francisco) *index options:* Wilshire Small Cap Index, Telegraph Ltd. Israel Index.

Philadelphia Board of Trade (Philadelphia): *futures:* Australian dollar, British pound, Canadian dollar, Deutsche mark, European Currency Unit (ECU), French franc, Japanese yen, Swiss franc.

Philadelphia Stock Exchange (Philadelphia) *foreign currency options:* Australian dollar, British pound, Canadian dollar, Deutsche mark, European Currency Unit (ECU), French franc, Japanese yen, Swiss franc, cash settled Deutsche mark, DM/yen, British pound/DM. *index options:* Utility Index, Value Line Index, Phone Index, Semiconductor Index, Gold/Silver Index, Bank Index, Big Cap Index, OTC Index.

SECURITIES AND EXCHANGE COMMISSION (SEC) federal agency created by the SECURITIES EXCHANGE ACT OF 1934 to administer that act and the

---

*These exchanges though independent, share space and other facilities at 4 World Trade Center, in New York City, and are collectively called the Commodity Exchange Center.

SECURITIES ACT OF 1933, formerly carried out by the FEDERAL TRADE COMMISSION. The SEC is made up of five commissioners, appointed by the President of the United States on a rotating basis for five-year terms. The chairman is designated by the President and, to insure its independence, no more than three members of the commission may be of the same political party. The statutes administered by the SEC are designed to promote full public DISCLOSURE and protect the investing public against malpractice in the securities markets. All issues of securities offered in interstate commerce or through the mails must be registered with the SEC; all national securities exchanges and associations are under its supervision, as are INVESTMENT COMPANIES, investment counselors and advisers, OVER THE COUNTER brokers and dealers, and virtually all other individuals and firms operating in the investment field. In addition to the 1933 and 1934 securities acts, responsibilities of the SEC include the PUBLIC UTILITY HOLDING COMPANY ACT of 1935, the TRUST INDENTURE ACT of 1939, the INVESTMENT COMPANY ACT of 1940 and the INVESTMENT ADVISERS ACT of 1940. It also administers the SECURITIES ACTS AMENDMENTS OF 1975, which directed the SEC to facilitate the establishment of a NATIONAL MARKET SYSTEM and a nationwide system for clearance and settlement of transactions and established the Municipal Securities Rulemaking Board, a self-regulatory organization whose rules are subject to SEC approval. *See also* SECURITIES AND EXCHANGE COMMISSION RULES.

SECURITIES AND EXCHANGE COMMISSION RULES The following are some of the more commonly encountered rules of the SEC. The list highlights the most prominent features of the rules and is not intended as a legal interpretation. The rules are listed in numerical order.

Rule 3b-3: Definition of Short Sale defines short sale as one in which the seller does not own the SECURITY sold or which is consummated by delivery of a borrowed security; ownership is defined in terms of securities, CONVERTIBLES, OPTIONS, and SUBSCRIPTION WARRANTS.

Rule 10a-1: Short sales known as the SHORT SALE RULE, prohibits a short sale of securities below the price of the last regular trade and at that price unless it was higher than the last different price preceding it. In determining the price at which a short sale can be made after a security goes EX-DIVIDEND, EX-RIGHTS, or ex- any other distribution, all sales prices prior to the ex- date may be reduced by the amount of the distribution.

Rule 10b-2: Solicitation of purchases on an exchange to facilitate distribution of securities prohibits parties concerned with a PRIMARY DISTRIBUTION or a SECONDARY DISTRIBUTION of a security from soliciting orders for the issue other than through the offering circular or formal PROSPECTUS.

Rule 10b-4: Short tendering of securities prohibits a SHORT TENDER—the sale of borrowed securities (as in SELLING SHORT) to a person making a TENDER OFFER.

Rule 10b-6: Prohibitions against trading by persons interested in a distribution rule that prohibits issuers, underwriters, broker-dealers, or others involved in a DISTRIBUTION of securities from buying the issue, or rights to it, during the distribution. The section permits transactions between the issuer and the underwriters and among the participating underwriters as required to carry out a distribution. The law extends to a repurchase by the issuer or to a purchase by participants in a new issue of CONVERTIBLE securities already on the market and convertible into the securities being offered.

Rule 10b-7: Stabilizing to effect a distribution provisions governing market STABILIZATION activities by issuers or underwriters in securities offerings.

Rule 10b-8: Distributions through rights prohibits market price MANIPULATION by interested parties in a RIGHTS OFFERING.

Rule 10b-10: Confirmation of transactions sets minimum information and disclosure requirements for the written confirmations of sales or purchases that broker-dealers send to clients, including disclosure of whether a firm is acting as AGENT (broker) or as PRINCIPAL (dealer).

Rule 10b-13: Other purchases during tender offer or exchange offer prohibits a person making a cash tender offer or an offer to exchange one EQUITY security for another from taking a position in the security being tendered or in a security CONVERTIBLE into the security being tendered until the tender offer or exchange offer expires.

Rule 10b-16: Credit terms in margin transactions terms and conditions concerning the interest charges on MARGIN loans to brokerage customers and the broker's disclosure responsibilities to borrowers.

Rule 11A: Floor trading regulations rules governing floor trading by exchange members, including those concerning PRIORITY and PRECEDENCE of transactions, transactions for the accounts of persons associated with members, HEDGE transactions, exchange bond trading, transactions by REGISTERED COMPETITIVE MARKET MAKERS and REGISTERED EQUITY MARKET MAKERS, and transactions between members.

Rule 12b-1: *see* 12b-1 MUTUAL FUND.

Rule 13d: Acquisition of beneficial interest disclosures required by any person who directly or indirectly acquires a beneficial interest of 5% or more of any class of a registered equity security. *See also* WILLIAMS ACT.

Rule 13e: Repurchase of shares by issuers prohibits purchase by an issuer of its own shares during a TENDER OFFER for its shares and regulates GOING PRIVATE transactions by issuers or their affiliates.

Rule 14a: Solicitation of proxies sets forth the information and documentation required with PROXY materials distributed to shareholders of a public corporation.

Rule 14d: Tender offers regulations and restrictions covering public TENDER OFFERS and related disclosure requirements. *See also* WILLIAMS ACT.

Rule 15c2-1: Hypothecation of customers' securities regulates a broker-dealer's SAFEKEEPING of customers securities in a MARGIN ACCOUNT, prohibiting the COMMINGLING of customers accounts without the consent of the respective customers and the commingling of customers' accounts with the securities of non-customers, and limiting broker borrowings secured by customers' collateral to the aggregate amount of customers' indebtedness. *See also* HYPOTHECATION.

Rule 15c3-1: Net capital requirements for brokers or dealers covers NET CAPITAL REQUIREMENTS relative to the aggregate indebtedness of brokers and dealers of different types.

Rule 15c3-2: Customers' free credit balances requires a broker-dealer to notify customers with credit balances in their accounts that such balances may be withdrawn on demand.

Rule 15c3-3: Customer-protection reserves and custody of securities regulates the handling of customers' fully paid securities and excess MARGIN securities (security value in excess of MARGIN REQUIREMENTS) with broker-dealers. Fully paid securities must be segregated, and the broker must make weekly deposits to a Special Reserve Bank Account for the Exclusive Benefit of Customers.

Rule 17f-1: Missing, lost, counterfeit, or stolen securities requires exchanges, broker-dealers, clearing agencies, banks and transfer agents to report promptly to both the SEC and the appropriate law enforcement agency any knowledge of missing, lost, counterfeit, or stolen securities and to check with the SEC whenever a security comes into their possession to make sure it has not been reported at large.

Rule 19b-3: Prohibiting fixing of rates of commission by exchanges prohibits fixed commissions on stock exchange transactions pursuant to the SECURITIES ACT AMENDMENTS OF 1975.

Rule 19c-3: Off-board trading by exchange members permits securities listed on an exchange after April 26, 1979, to be traded off the exchange by member firms, a step toward an experimental NATIONAL MARKET SYSTEM in compliance with the SECURITIES ACT AMENDMENTS OF 1975.

Rule 144: Public sale of unregistered securities sets forth the conditions under which a holder of unregistered securities may make a public sale without filing a formal REGISTRATION STATEMENT. NO LETTER SECURITY purchased through a PRIVATE PLACEMENT may be sold for at least two years after the date of purchase. Thereafter, during any three-month period, the following amounts may be sold: if listed securities, the greater of 1% of the amount outstanding or the average trading volume within the four preceding weeks; if unlisted, 1% of outstandings. Securities may be sold only in broker's transactions.

Rule 145: Securities acquired in recapitalization persons who acquire securities as a result of reclassification, MERGER, consolidation, or transfer of corporate assets may sell such securities without REGISTRATION under stipulated conditions.

Rule 156: Mutual fund sales literature forbids false and misleading sales materials promoting INVESTMENT COMPANY securities.

Rule 237: Public sale of unregistered securities expanding on Rule 144, provides that five years after full payment for the purchase of privately placed securities, the lesser of $50,000 of such securities or 1% of the securities outstanding in a particular CLASS may be sold within a one year period.

Rule 254: Registration of small issues provides for simplified registration of small issues ($1.5 million or less in the mid-1980s) including a short-form REGISTRATION STATEMENT and PROSPECTUS. *See also* REGULATION A.

Rule 415: Shelf registration permits corporations to file a REGISTRATION for securities they intend to issue in the future when market conditions are favorable. *See also* SHELF REGISTRATION.

SECURITIES EXCHANGE ACT OF 1934 law governing the securities markets, enacted June 6, 1934. The act outlaws misrepresentation, MANIPULATION, and other abusive practices in the issuance of securities. It created the SECURITIES AND EXCHANGE COMMISSION (SEC) to enforce both the SECURITIES ACT OF 1933 and the Securities Exchange Act of 1934.

Principal requirements of the 1934 act are as follows:

1. REGISTRATION of all securities listed on stock exchanges, and periodic DISCLOSURES by issuers of financial status and changes in condition.
2. regular disclosures of holdings and transactions of "INSIDERS"—the officers and directors of a corporation and those who control at least 10% of equity securities.
3. solicitation of PROXIES enabling shareholders to vote for or against policy proposals.
4. registration with the SEC of stock exchanges and brokers and dealers to ensure their adherence to SEC rules through self-regulation.
5. surveillance by the SEC of trading practices on stock exchanges and over-the-counter markets to minimize the possibility of insolvency among brokers and dealers.
6. regulation of MARGIN REQUIREMENTS for securities purchased on credit; the FEDERAL RESERVE BOARD sets those requirements.
7. SEC subpoena power in investigations of possible violations and in enforcement actions.

The SECURITIES ACT AMENDMENTS OF 1975 ratified the system of free-market determination of brokers' commissions and gave the SEC authority to oversee development of a NATIONAL MARKET SYSTEM.

SECURITIES EXCHANGE OF THAILAND (SET) only stock market in Thailand, based in Bangkok. The *SET Index,* calculated by the exchange, and the *Bangkok Book Club Price Index,* compiled by the Book Club Finance and Securities Co. Ltd., include all corporate stocks and mutual funds and are the most widely watched. Trading is conducted through the ASSET automated electronic trading system Monday through Friday from 10 A.M. to 12:30 P.M., and 2 P.M. to 4 P.M. Trades are settled on the third business day after the trade date.

SECURITIES INDUSTRY ASSOCIATION (SIA) trade group that represents broker-dealers. The SIA lobbies for legislation affecting the brokerage industry. It also educates its members and the public about industry trends and keeps statistics on revenues and profits of brokers. The SIA represents only the segment of broker-dealers that sells taxable securities. Tax-exempt bond, government bond, and mortgage-backed security dealers are represented by the PUBLIC SECURITIES ASSOCIATION.

SECURITIES INDUSTRY AUTOMATION CORPORATION (SIAC) organization established in 1972 to provide communications and computer systems and services for the New York Stock Exchange (NYSE) and the American Stock Exchange (AMEX). It is two-thirds owned by NYSE and one-third owned by AMEX.

SECURITIES INDUSTRY COMMITTEE ON ARBITRATION (SICA) private body that applies its arbitration code in cases of customer complaints against securities firms.

SECURITIES INVESTOR PROTECTION CORPORATION (SIPC) nonprofit corporation, established by Congress under the Securities Investors Protection Act of 1970, that insures the securities and cash in the customer accounts of member brokerage firms against the failure of those firms. All brokers and dealers registered with the Securities and Exchange Commission and with national stock exchanges are required to be members of SIPC. The Corporation acts similarly to the FEDERAL DEPOSIT INSURANCE CORPORATION (FDIC), which insures banks, and the FEDERAL SAVINGS AND LOAN INSURANCE CORPORATION (FSLIC), which insures savings and loans. When a brokerage firm fails, SIPC will first try to merge it into another brokerage firm. If this fails, SIPC will liquidate the firm's assets and pay off account holders up to an overall maximum of $500,000 per customer, with a limit of $100,000 on cash or cash equivalents. SIPC does not protect investors against market risks. *See also* SEPARATE CUSTOMER.

SECURITIES LOAN
1. loan of securities by one broker to another, usually to cover a customer's short sale. The lending broker is secured by the cash proceeds of the sale.
2. in a more general sense, loan collateralized by MARKETABLE SECURITIES. These would include all customer loans made to purchase or carry securities by broker-dealers under Federal Reserve Board REGULATION T margin rules, as well as by banks under REGULATION U and other lenders under REGULATION G. Loans made by banks to brokers to cover customers' positions are also collateralized by securities, but such loans are called *broker's loans* or *call loans. See also* HYPOTHECATION; LENDING AT A PREMIUM; LENDING AT A RATE; LENDING SECURITIES; REHYPOTHECATION; SELLING SHORT.

SECURITIES MARKETS general term for markets in which securities are traded, including both ORGANIZED SECURITIES EXCHANGES and OVER-THE-COUNTER (OTC) markets.

SECURITIZATION process of distributing risk by aggregating debt instruments in a pool, then issuing new securities backed by the pool. *See also* ASSET-BACKED SECURITIES.

SECURITY
Finance: collateral offered by a debtor to a lender to secure a loan called *collateral security*. For instance, the security behind a mortgage loan is the real estate being purchased with the proceeds of the loan. If the debt is not repaid, the lender may seize the security and resell it.

Personal security refers to one person or firm's GUARANTEE of another's primary obligation.

Investment: instrument that signifies an ownership position in a corporation (a stock), a creditor relationship with a corporation or governmental body (a bond), or rights to ownership such as those represented by an OPTION, SUBSCRIPTION RIGHT, and SUBSCRIPTION WARRANT.

SECURITY DEPOSIT money paid in advance to protect the provider of a product or service against damage or nonpayment by the buyer. For example, landlords require a security deposit of one month's rent when a tenant signs a lease, to cover the possibility that the tenant will move out without paying the last month's rent, or that the tenant will inflict substantial damage on the property while living there. In such a case, the money from the security deposit is used to cover repairs. Similarly, car leasing companies typically demand security deposits for the last month's lease payment to protect the leasing company against damage to the car or nonpayment of the lease. If all payments are made on time and there is no damage, security deposits must be returned to those who paid them.

SECURITY MARKET LINE relationship between the REQUIRED RATE OF RETURN on an investment and its SYSTEMATIC RISK.

SECURITY RATINGS evaluations of the credit and investment risk of securities issues by commercial RATING agencies.

SEED MONEY venture capitalist's first contribution toward the financing or capital requirements of a START-UP business. It frequently takes the form of a loan, often SUBORDINATED, or an investment in convertible bonds or preferred stock. Seed money provides the basis for additional capitalization to accommodate growth. *See also* MEZZANINE LEVEL; SECOND ROUND; VENTURE CAPITAL.

SEEK A MARKET to look for a buyer (if a seller) or a seller (if a buyer) of securities.

SEGMENT REPORTING *see* BUSINESS SEGMENT REPORTING.

SEGREGATION OF SECURITIES Securities and Exchange Commission rules (8c and 15c2-1) designed to protect customers' securities used by broker-dealers to secure broker loans. Specifically, broker-dealers may not (1) commingle the securities of different customers without the written consent of each customer, (2) commingle a customer's securities with those of any person other than a bonafide customer, or (3) borrow more against customers' securities than the customers, in the aggregate, owe the broker-dealer against the same securities. *See also* COMMINGLING; HYPOTHECATION; REHYPOTHECATION; SECURITIES AND EXCHANGE COMMISSION RULE 15c2-1.

SELECTED DEALER AGREEMENT agreement governing the SELLING GROUP in a securities underwriting and distribution. *See also* UNDERWRITE.

SELECT TEN PORTFOLIO UNIT INVESTMENT TRUST offered on a quarterly basis by a group of brokers including Merrill Lynch, Paine Webber, Dean Witter, and Prudential Securities that buys and holds for one year the ten stocks in the Dow Jones Industrial Average (DJIA) with the highest dividend yields. Stocks thus selected have usually outperformed the DJIA. The strategy was first popularized by Michael B. O'Higgins in *Beating the Dow.*

SELF-AMORTIZING MORTGAGE mortgage in which all principal is paid off in a specified period of time through periodic interest and principal payments. The most common self-amortizing mortgages are for 15 and 30 years. Lenders will provide a table to borrowers showing how much principal and interest is being paid off each month until the loan is retired.

SELF-DIRECTED IRA INDIVIDUAL RETIREMENT ACCOUNT (IRA) that can be actively managed by the account holder, who designates a CUSTODIAN to carry out investment instructions. The account is subject to the same conditions and early withdrawal limitations as a regular IRA. Investors who withdraw money from a qualified IRA plan have 60 days in which to roll over the funds to another plan before they become liable for tax penalties. Most corporate and U.S. government securities are eligible to be held by a self-directed IRA, as are limited partnerships, but collectibles and precious metals (art, gems, gold coins) are not.

SELF-EMPLOYED INCOME net taxable income of a self-employed person, as reported on Schedule C of IRS Form 1040. Self-employment income may be generated by freelance work, royalties, consulting, or income from sole proprietorship businesses. Social Security taxes must be paid on self-employment income.

SELF-EMPLOYED RETIREMENT PLAN *see* KEOGH PLAN.

SELF-EMPLOYMENT TAX tax paid by self-employed people to Social Security, qualifying them for receiving Social Security benefits at retirement. The tax is filed on Schedule SE of IRS Form 1040, which indicates the type of business generating self-employment income, net earnings, and the amount of self-employment tax.

SELF-REGULATORY ORGANIZATION (SRO) principal means contemplated by the federal securities laws for the enforcement of fair, ethical, and efficient practices in the securities and commodities futures industries. It is these organizations that are being referred to when "industry rules" are mentioned, as distinguished from the regulatory agencies such as the Securities and Exchange Commission or the Federal Reserve Board. The SROs include all the national SECURITIES AND COMMODITIES EXCHANGES as well as the NATIONAL ASSOCIATION OP SECURITIES DEALERS (NASD), which represents all the firms operating in the over-the-counter market, and the *Municipal Securities Rulemaking Board,* created under the Securities Acts Amendments of 1975 to regulate brokers, dealers and banks dealing in municipal securities. Rules made by the MSRB are subject to approval by the SEC and are enforced by the NASD and bank regulatory agencies.

SELF-SUPPORTING DEBT bonds sold for a project that will produce sufficient revenues to retire the debt. Such debt is usually issued by municipalities building a public structure (for example, a bridge or tunnel) that will be producing revenue through tolls or other charges. The bonds are not supported by the taxing power of the municipality issuing them. *See also* REVENUE BOND.

SELF-TENDER *see* SHARE REPURCHASE PLAN.

SELLER FINANCING financing provided by the owner/seller of real estate, who takes back a secured note. The buyer may be unable to qualify for a mortgage from a lending institution, or interest rates may have risen so high that the buyer is unwilling to take on a market-rate loan. In order to sell their property, sellers offer to lend the buyer the money needed, often at a below-market interest rate. The buyer takes full title to the property when the loan is fully repaid. If the buyer defaults on the loan, the seller can repossess the property. Also called *creative financing.*

SELLER'S MARKET situation in which there is more demand for a security or product than there is available supply. As a result, the prices tend to be rising, and the sellers can set both the prices and the terms of sale. It contrasts with a buyer's market, characterized by excess supply, low prices, and terms suited to the buyer's desires.

SELLER'S OPTION securities transaction in which the seller, instead of making REGULAR WAY DELIVERY, is given the right to deliver the security to the purchaser on the date the seller's option expires or before, provided written notification of the seller's intention to deliver is given to the buyer one full business day prior to delivery. Seller's option deliveries are normally not made before 6 business days following the transaction or after 60 days.

SELLING CLIMAX sudden plunge in security prices as those who hold stocks or bonds panic and decide to dump their holdings all at once. Technical analysts see a climax as both a dramatic increase in volume and a sharp drop in prices on a chart. To these analysts, such a pattern usually means that a short-term rally will soon follow since there are few sellers left after the climax. Sometimes, a selling climax can signal the bottom of a BEAR MARKET, meaning that after the climax the market will start to rise.

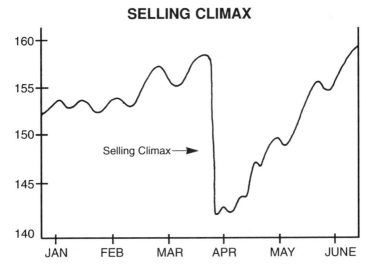

SELLING CLIMAX

SELLING CONCESSION discount at which securities in a NEW ISSUE offering (or a SECONDARY DISTRIBUTION) are allocated to the members of a SELLING GROUP by the underwriters. Since the selling group cannot sell to the public at a price higher than the PUBLIC OFFERING PRICE, its compensation comes out of the difference between the price paid to the issuer by the underwriters and the public offering price, called the SPREAD. The selling group's portion, called the CONCESSION, is normally one half or more of the gross spread, expressed as a discount off the public offering price. *See also* FLOTATION COST; UNDERWRITE; UNDERWRITING SPREAD.

SELLING DIVIDENDS questionable practice by sales personnel dealing in MUTUAL FUNDS whereby a customer is induced to buy shares in a fund in order to get the benefit of a dividend scheduled in the near future. Since the dividend is already part of the NET ASSET VALUE of the fund and therefore part of the share price, the customer derives no real benefit.

SELLING, GENERAL, AND ADMINISTRATIVE (SG&A) EXPENSES grouping of expenses reported on a company's PROFIT AND LOSS STATEMENT between COST OF GOODS SOLD and INCOME DEDUCTIONS. Included are such items as salespersons' salaries and commissions, advertising and promotion, travel and entertainment, office payroll and expenses, and executives' salaries. SG&A expenses do not include such items as interest or amortization of INTANGIBLE ASSETS, which would be listed as income deductions. *See also* OPERATING PROFIT (OR LOSS).

SELLING GROUP group of dealers appointed by the syndicate manager of an UNDERWRITING GROUP, as AGENT for the other underwriters, to market a new or secondary issue to the public; also called *selling syndicate.* The selling group typically includes members of the underwriting group but varies in size with the size of the issue, sometimes running into several hundred dealers. The selling group is governed by the selling group agreement, also called the SELECTED DEALER AGREEMENT. It sets forth the terms of the relationship, establishes the commission (or SELLING CONCESSION, as it is called), and provides for the termination of the group, usually in 30 days. The selling group may or may not be obligated to purchase unsold shares. *See also* UNDERWRITE.

SELLING OFF selling securities or commodities under pressure to avoid further declines in prices. Technical analysts call such action a *sell-off. See also* DUMPING.

SELLING ON THE GOOD NEWS practice of selling a stock soon after a positive news development is announced. Most investors, cheered by the news of a successful new product or higher earnings, buy a stock because they think it will go higher: this pushes up the price. Someone selling on this good news believes that the stock will have reached its top price once all those encouraged by the development have bought the stock. Therefore, it is better to sell at this point than to wait for more good news or to be holding the stock if the next announcement is disappointing. *Compare with* BUYING ON THE BAD NEWS.

SELLING SHORT sale of a security or commodity futures contract not owned by the seller; a technique used (1) to take advantage of an anticipated decline in the price or (2) to protect a profit in a LONG POSITION *(see* SELLING SHORT AGAINST THE BOX).

An investor borrows stock certificates for delivery at the time of short sale. If the seller can buy that stock later at a lower price, a profit results; if the price rises, however, a loss results.

A commodity sold short represents a promise to deliver the commodity at a set price on a future date. Most commodity short sales are COVERED before the DELIVERY DATE.

Example of a short sale involving stock: An investor, anticipating a decline in the price of XYZ shares, instructs his or her broker to sell short 100 XYZ when XYZ is trading at $50. The broker then loans the investor 100 shares of XYZ, using either its own inventory, shares in the MARGIN ACCOUNT of another customer, or shares borrowed from another broker. These shares are used to make settlement with the buying broker within five days of the short sale transaction, and the proceeds are used to secure the loan. The investor now has what is known as a SHORT POSITION—that is, he or she still does not own the 100 XYZ and, at some point, must buy the shares to repay the lending broker. If the market price of XYZ drops to $40, the investor can buy the shares for $4000, repay the lending broker, thus covering the short sale, and claim a profit of $1000, or $10 a share.

Short selling is regulated by REGULATION T of the Federal Reserve Board. *See also* LENDING AT A RATE; LENDING AT A PREMIUM; LOANED FLAT; MARGIN REQUIREMENT; SHORT SALE RULE.

SELLING SHORT AGAINST THE BOX SELLING SHORT stock actually owned by the seller but held in SAFEKEEPING, called the BOX in Wall Street jargon. The motive for the practice, which assumes that the securities needed to COVER are borrowed as with any short sale, may be simply inaccessibility of the box or that the seller does not wish to disclose ownership. The main motive is to protect a CAPITAL GAIN in the shares that are owned, while deferring a LONG-TERM GAIN into another tax year.

SELLING THE SPREAD spread where the sold option is trading at a higher premium than the purchased option. For example, purchasing a shorter term option and selling a longer term option (assuming both options have the same EXERCISE PRICE) would usually result in a net credit. *See* CALENDAR SPREAD. Another example would be purchasing a call with a higher exercise price and selling a call with a lower exercise price, assuming both options have the same expiration date. *See also* CREDIT SPREAD.

SELL-OFF massive selling of stocks or bonds after a steep decline in prices. Traders sell quickly in order to avoid further losses.

SELL ORDER order by an investor to a broker to sell a particular stock, bond, option, future, mutual fund, or other holding. There are several kinds of sell orders, including DAY ORDERS, GOOD-TILL-CANCELED ORDERS (GTC), LIMIT ORDERS, MARKET-ON-CLOSE ORDERS, MARKET ORDERS, ON THE CLOSE ORDERS, ON THE OPENING ORDERS, STOP-LIMIT ORDERS, STOP LOSS ORDERS, and STOP ORDERS.

SELL OUT
1. liquidation of a MARGIN ACCOUNT by a broker after a MARGIN CALL has failed to produce additional equity to bring the margin to the required level. *See also* CLOSE A POSITION; MARGIN REQUIREMENT; MINIMUM MAINTENANCE.
2. action by a broker when a customer fails to pay for securities purchased and the securities received from the selling broker are sold to cover the transaction. Term also applies to commodities futures transactions.
3. expression used when all the securities in a NEW ISSUE underwriting have been distributed.

SELL PLUS sell order with instructions to execute only if the trading price in a security is higher than the last different preceding price. *See also* SHORT-SALE RULE.

SELL-STOP ORDER *see* STOP ORDER.

SELL THE BOOK order to a broker by the holder of a large quantity of shares of a security to sell all that can be ABSORBED at the current bid price. The term derives from the SPECIALIST'S BOOK—the record of all the buy and sell orders members have placed in the stock he or she handles. In this scenario, the buyers potentially include those in the specialist's book, the specialist for his or her own account, and the broker-dealer CROWD.

SENIOR DEBT loans or DEBT SECURITIES that have claim prior to junior obligations and EQUITY on a corporation's assets in the event of LIQUIDATION. Senior debt commonly includes funds borrowed from banks, insurance companies, or other financial institutions, as well as notes, bonds, or debentures not expressly defined as junior or subordinated.

SENIOR MORTGAGE BOND bond with the highest claim on the assets of the issuer in case of bankruptcy or liquidation. Senior mortgage bondholders are paid off in full before any payments are made to junior bondholders.

SENIOR REFUNDING replacement of securities maturing in 5 to 12 years with issues having original maturities of 15 years or longer. The objectives may be to reduce the bond issuer's interest costs, to consolidate several issues into one, or to extend the maturity date.

SENIOR SECURITY security that has claim prior to a junior obligation and EQUITY on a corporation's assets and earnings. Senior securities are repaid before JUNIOR SECURITIES in the event of LIQUIDATION. Debt, including notes, bonds, and debentures, is senior to stock; first mortgage bonds are senior to second mortgage bonds; and all mortgage bonds are senior to debentures, which are unsecured.

SENSITIVE MARKET market easily swayed by good or bad news.

SENSITIVITY ANALYSIS study measuring the effect of a change in a variable (such as sales) on the risk or profitability of an investment.

SENTIMENT INDICATORS measures of the bullish or bearish mood of investors. Many technical analysts look at these indicators as contrary indicators—that is, when most investors are bullish, the market is about to drop, and when most are bearish, the market is about to rise. Some financial newsletters measure swings in investor sentiment by tabulating the number of INVESTMENT ADVISORY SERVICES that are bullish or bearish.

SEP *see* SIMPLIFIED EMPLOYEE PENSION (SEP) PLAN.

SEPARATE CUSTOMER concept used by the SECURITIES INVESTOR PROTECTION CORPORATION (SIPC) in allocating insurance coverage. If there is a difference in the way investment accounts are owned, each account is viewed as a separate customer entitled to the maximum protection; thus two accounts, one in the name of John Jones and the other in the name of John Jones and his wife Mary Jones, would be treated as separate accounts and separate persons. On the other hand, a CASH ACCOUNT, a MARGIN ACCOUNT, and a special convertible bond account all owned by John Jones are not treated as separate customer accounts but as one.

SEPARATELY REPORTABLE SEGMENT *see* BUSINESS SEGMENT REPORTING.

SEPARATE TAX RETURNS tax returns filed by a married couple choosing the married, filing separately, status. Each person reports his or her own income, deductions, exemptions, and credits. Couples may choose to file separately instead of with a JOINT TAX RETURN for several reasons. A couple may choose to keep all of their financial affairs, including tax filing, separate. In some cases, a couple may find that the total amount of tax paid is less if they file separately than if they file jointly. This is usually the case when there is a wide disparity between the earnings of the husband and wife. However, because of the way the tax tables are designed, it is frequently more advantageous for a married couple to file a joint return than for them to file separate returns. *See also* FILING STATUS, HEAD OF HOUSEHOLD.

SERIAL BOND bond issue, usually of a municipality, with various MATURITY DATES scheduled at regular intervals until the entire issue is retired. Each bond certificate in the series has an indicated REDEMPTION DATE.

SERIAL REDEMPTION redemption of a SERIAL BOND.

SERIES E BOND savings bond issued by the U.S. government from 1941 to 1979. The bonds were then replaced by Series EE and Series HH bonds. Outstanding Series E bonds, which may be exchanged for Series HH bonds, continue to pay interest for between 30 and 40 years from their issue date. Those issued from 1941 to November 1965 accrue interest for 40 years; those issued from December 1965 and later, for 30 years. Their interest is exempt from state and local income and personal property taxes. *See also* SAVINGS BOND.

SERIES EE BOND *see* SAVINGS BOND.

SERIES HH BOND *see* SAVINGS BOND.

SERIES OF OPTION class of OPTION, either all CALL OPTIONS or all PUT OPTIONS, on the same underlying security, all of which have the same EXERCISE PRICE (strike price) and maturity date. For example, all XYZ May 50 calls would form a series of options.

SERIES 7 REGISTERED broker who has passed the General Securities Registered Representative Examination, commonly called the *Series 7,* and who is a REGISTERED REPRESENTATIVE. In addition to the Series 7, which is a six-hour multiple-choice test developed by the New York Stock Exchange (NYSE) and administered by the National Association of Securities Dealers (NASD), many states require that registered representatives pass a UNIFORM SECURITIES AGENT STATE LAW EXAMINATION.

SET-ASIDE percentage of a job set aside for bidding to minority contractors. In the securities business, many municipal and some corporate bond underwritings require that a certain percentage of the offering be handled by a minority-owned broker/dealer underwriting firm. Other government and corporate contracts for products and services also stipulate that a certain percentage of the business must be handled by minority firms. Set-aside programs are designed to help minority firms become established more quickly than they might if they had to compete on an equal footing with entrenched competitors.

SETTLE
In general: to pay an obligation.
Estates: distribution of an estate's assets by an executor to beneficiaries after all legal procedures have been completed.
Law: (1) to resolve a legal dispute short of adjudication; (2) to arrange for disposition of property, such as between spouses or between parents and children, if there has been a dispute such as a divorce.
Securities: to complete a securities trade between brokers acting as AGENTS or between a broker and his customer. A trade is settled when the customer has paid the broker for securities bought or when the customer delivers securities that have been sold and the customer receives the proceeds from the sale. *See also* CONTINUOUS NET SETTLEMENT.

SETTLEMENT in general, a resolution of differences among various parties. For example, a labor dispute resulting in a strike may finally be settled by a new contract, or a conflict between a landlord and tenant may be settled in a housing court.

Securities: conclusion of a securities transaction in which a broker/dealer pays for securities bought for a customer or delivers securities sold and receives payment from the buyer's broker. REGULAR WAY DELIVERY AND SETTLEMENT is completed on the third full business day following the date of the transaction for stocks, called the SETTLEMENT DATE. Government bonds and options trades are settled the next business day. *See also* CONTINUOUS NET SETTLEMENT.

Futures/Options: the final price, established by exchange rule, for the prices prevailing during the closing period and upon which futures contracts are marked to market.

SETTLEMENT DATE date by which an executed order must be settled, either by a buyer paying for the securities with cash or by a seller delivering the securities and receiving the proceeds of the sale for them. In a REGULAR-WAY DELIVERY of stocks and bonds, the settlement date is three business days after the trade was executed. For listed options and government securities, settlement is required by the next business day. *See also* SELLER'S OPTION.

SETTLEMENT OPTIONS options available to beneficiaries when a person insured by a life insurance policy dies. The DEATH BENEFIT may be paid in one lump sum, in several installments over a fixed period of time, or in the form of an ANNUITY for the rest of the beneficiary's life, among other options.

SETTLOR person who creates an INTER VIVOS TRUST as distinguished from a TESTAMENTARY TRUST. Also called *donor, grantor,* or *trustor.*

SEVERALLY BUT NOT JOINTLY form of agreement used to establish the responsibility for selling a portion of the securities in an underwriting. UNDERWRITING GROUP members agree to buy a certain portion of an issue (severally) but do not agree to joint liability for shares not sold by other members of the syndicate. In a less common form of underwriting arrangement, called a *several and joint agreement,* syndicate members agree to sell not only the shares allocated to them, but also any shares not sold by the rest of the group. *See also* UNDERWRITE.

SEVERANCE PAY money paid to an employee who has been laid off by an employer. The money may be paid in the form of a LUMP SUM, as an ANNUITY, or in the form of paychecks for a specified period of time. The size of the termination benefit is based on the length of service and job level of the employee, union contracts, and other factors. Also called *termination benefit.*

SG&A EXPENSES *see* SELLING, GENERAL, AND ADMINISTRATIVE EXPENSES.

SHADOW CALENDAR backlog of securities issues in REGISTRATION with the Securities and Exchange Commission for which no OFFERING DATE has been set pending clearance.

SHAKEOUT change in market conditions that results in the elimination of marginally financed participants in an industry. For example, if the market for microcomputers suddenly becomes glutted because there is more supply than demand, a shakeout will result, meaning that companies will fall by the wayside. In the securities markets, a shakeout occurs when speculators are forced by market events to sell their positions, usually at a loss.

SHAM transaction conducted for the purpose of avoiding taxation. Once discovered by tax authorities, it will be considered null and void, and the parties to the transaction will have to pay the taxes due. Some limited partnerships have been ruled to be "sham transactions" in the past, causing limited partners to owe back taxes, penalties, and interest to the Internal Revenue Service.

SHARE
1. unit of equity ownership in a corporation. This ownership is represented by a stock certificate, which names the company and the shareowner. The number of shares a corporation is authorized to issue is detailed in its corporate charter. Corporations usually do not issue the full number of AUTHORIZED SHARES.
2. unit of ownership in a mutual fund. *See also* INVESTMENT COMPANY.
3. interest, normally represented by a certificate, in a general or LIMITED PARTNERSHIP.

SHARE BROKER DISCOUNT BROKER whose charges are based on the number of shares traded. The more shares in a trade, the lower the per-share cost will be. Trading with a share broker is usually advantageous for those trading at least 500 shares, or for those trading in high-priced shares, who would otherwise pay a percentage of the dollar amount. Those trading in small numbers of shares, or lower-priced ones, may pay lower commissions with a VALUE BROKER, the other kind of discount brokerage firm.

SHARED APPRECIATION MORTGAGE (SAM) mortgage in which the borrower receives a below-market rate of interest in return for agreeing to share part of the appreciation in the value of the underlying property with the lender in a specified number of years. If the borrower does not want to sell at that time, he or she must pay the lender its share of the appreciation in cash. If the borrower does not have that amount of cash on hand, the lender may force the borrower to sell the property to satisfy their claim.

SHARE DRAFT instrument similar to a bank check that is used by credit unions to withdraw from interest-bearing share draft accounts.

SHAREHOLDER
1. owner of one or more shares of STOCK in a corporation. A common shareholder is normally entitled to four basic rights of ownership: (1) claim on a share of the company's undivided assets in proportion to number of shares held; (2) proportionate voting power in the election of DIRECTORS and other business conducted at shareholder meetings or by PROXY; (3) DIVIDENDS when earned and declared by the BOARD OF DIRECTORS; and (4) PREEMPTIVE RIGHT to subscribe to additional stock offerings before they are available to the general public except when overruled by the ARTICLES OF INCORPORATION or in special circumstances, such as where stock is issued to effect a merger.
2. owner of one or more shares or units in a MUTUAL FUND. Mutual fund investors have voting rights similar to those of stock owners.

   Shareholders' rights can vary according to the articles of incorporation or BYLAWS of the particular company.

   See also PREFERRED STOCK.

SHAREHOLDER REPORT *see* STOCKHOLDER'S REPORT.

SHAREHOLDER'S EQUITY total ASSETS minus total LIABILITIES of a corporation. Also called *stockholder's equity,* EQUITY, and NET WORTH.

SHARE REPURCHASE PLAN program by which a corporation buys back its own shares in the open market. It is usually done when shares are UNDERVALUED. Since it reduces the number of shares outstanding and thus increases EARNINGS PER SHARE, it tends to elevate the market value of the remaining shares held by stockholders. *See also* GOING PRIVATE; TREASURY STOCK.

SHARES AUTHORIZED number of shares of stock provided for in the ARTICLES OF INCORPORATION of a company. This figure is ordinarily indicated in the capital accounts section of a company's BALANCE SHEET and is usually well in excess of the shares ISSUED AND OUTSTANDING. A corporation cannot legally issue more shares than authorized. The number of authorized shares can be changed only by amendment to the corporate charter, with the approval of the shareholders. The most common reason for increasing authorized shares in a public company is to accommodate a stock SPLIT.

SHARES OUTSTANDING *see* ISSUED AND OUTSTANDING.

SHARK REPELLENT measure undertaken by a corporation to discourage unwanted TAKEOVER attempts. Also called *porcupine provision.*
For example:
(1) fair price provision requiring a bidder to pay the same price to all shareholders. This raises the stakes and discourages TENDER OFFERS designed to attract only those shareholders most eager to replace management.
(2) GOLDEN PARACHUTE contract with top executives that makes it prohibitively expensive to get rid of existing management.
(3) defensive merger, in which a TARGET COMPANY combines with another organization that would create antitrust or other regulatory problems if the original, unwanted takeover proposal was consummated. *See also* SAFE HARBOR.
(4) STAGGERED BOARD OF DIRECTORS, a way to make it more difficult for a corporate RAIDER to install a majority of directors sympathetic to his or her views.
(5) supermajority provision, which might increase from a simple majority to two-thirds or three-fourths the shareholder vote required to ratify a takeover by an outsider.
See also POISON PILL; SCORCHED-EARTH POLICY.

SHARK WATCHER firm specializing in the early detection of TAKEOVER activity. Such a firm, whose primary business is usually the solicitation of proxies for client corporations, monitors trading patterns in a client's stock and attempts to determine the identity of parties accumulating shares.

SHELF REGISTRATION term used for SECURITIES AND EXCHANGE COMMISSION RULE 415 adopted in the 1980s, which allows a corporation to comply with REGISTRATION requirements up to two years prior to a PUBLIC OFFERING of securities. With the registration on the shelf, the corporation, by simply updating regularly filed annual, quarterly, and related reports to the SEC, can go to the market as conditions become favorable with a minimum of administrative preparation. The flexibility corporate issuers enjoy as the result of shelf registration translates into substantial savings of time and expense.

SHELL CORPORATION company that is incorporated but has no significant assets or operations. Such corporations may be formed to obtain financing prior to starting operations, in which case an investment in them is highly risky. The term is also used of corporations set up by fraudulent operators as fronts to conceal tax evasion schemes.

SHERMAN ANTI-TRUST ACT OF 1890 *see* ANTITRUST LAWS.

SHOCK ABSORBERS *see* CIRCUIT BREAKERS.

SHOGUN SECURITY security issued and distributed exclusively in Japan by a non-Japanese company and denominated in a currency other than yen.

SHOP
1. area of a business location where production takes place, as distinguished from the office or warehouse areas.

2. factory work force of an employer, as in a "union shop."

3. office of a broker-dealer in securities.

4. the act of canvassing dealers for the most favorable price, as in shopping securities dealers for the best bid or offer.

5. a small retail establishment.

SHORT AGAINST THE BOX *see* SELLING SHORT AGAINST THE BOX.

SHORT BOND

1. bond with a short maturity; a somewhat subjective concept, but generally meaning two years or less. *See also* SHORT TERM.

2. bond repayable in one year or less and thus classified as a CURRENT LIABILITY in accordance with the accounting definition of SHORT-TERM DEBT.

3. SHORT COUPON bond.

SHORT COUPON

1. bond interest payment covering less than the conventional six-month period. A short coupon payment occurs when the original issue date is less than a half year from the first scheduled interest payment date. Depending on how short the coupon is, the ACCRUED INTEREST makes a difference in the value of the bond at the time of issue, which is reflected in the offering price.

2. bond with a relatively short maturity, usually two years or less.
See also LONG COUPON.

SHORT COVERING actual purchase of securities by a short seller to replace those borrowed at the time of a short sale. *See also* LENDING SECURITIES; SELLING SHORT.

SHORTFALL amount by which a financial objective has not been met. For example, a municipality expecting $100 million in tax revenue will say there is a $10 million shortfall if it collects only $90 million. For individual investors, a shortfall is the amount by which investment objectives have not been reached. For instance, investors execting to earn 15% a year will have a 5% shortfall if they earn 10% a year.

SHORT HEDGE transaction that limits or eliminates the risk of declining value in a security or commodity without entailing ownership.
Examples:

(1) SELLING SHORT AGAINST THE BOX leaves the owned securities untouched, possibly to gain in value, while protecting against a decline in value, since that would be offset by a profit on the short sale.

(2) purchasing a PUT OPTION to protect the value of a security that is owned limits loss to the cost of the option.

(3) buying a futures contract on raw materials at a specific price protects a manufacturer committed to sell a product at a certain price at a specified future time but who cannot buy the raw materials at the time of the commitment. Thus, if the price of the materials goes up, the manufacturer makes a profit on the contract; if the price goes down, he or she makes a profit on the product.
Compare with LONG HEDGE.

SHORT INTEREST total amount of shares of stock that have been sold short and have not yet been repurchased to close out SHORT POSITIONS. The short interest figure for the New York Stock Exchange, which is published monthly in newspapers, indicates how many investors think stock prices are about to fall. The Exchange reports all issues in which there are at least 5000 shares sold short, and in which the short interest position had changed by at least 2000 shares in the preceding month. The higher the short interest, the more people are expecting a downturn. Such short interest also represents potential buying pressure, however, since all short sales must eventually be covered by the purchase of shares. For this reason, a high short interest position is viewed as a bullish sign by many sophisticated market watchers. *See also* SELLING SHORT; SHORT INTEREST THEORY.

SHORT INTEREST THEORY theory that a large SHORT INTEREST in a stock presages a rise in the market price. It is based on the reasoning that even though short selling reflects a belief that prices will decline, the fact that short positions must eventually be covered is a source of upward price pressure. It is also called the CUSHION THEORY, since short sales can be viewed as a cushion of imminent buy orders. *See also* MEMBERS SHORT-SALE RATIO; ODD-LOT SHORT-SALE RATIO; SELLING SHORT; SPECIALIST'S SHORT-SALE RATIO.

SHORT POSITION
Commodities: contract in which a trader has agreed to sell a commodity at a future date for a specific price.

Stocks: stock shares that an individual has sold short (by delivery of borrowed certificates) and has not covered as of a particular date. *See also* COVER; SELLING SHORT.

SHORT SALE *see* SELLING SHORT.

SHORT-SALE RULE Securities and Exchange Commission rule requiring that short sales be made only in a rising market; also called PLUS TICK rule. A short sale can be transacted only under these conditions: (1) if the last sale was at a higher price than the sale preceding it (called an UPTICK or PLUS TICK); (2) if the last sale price is unchanged but higher than the last preceding different sale (called a ZERO-PLUS TICK). The short sale rule was designed to prevent abuses perpetuated by so-called pool operators, who would drive down the price of a stock by heavy short selling, then pick up the shares for a large profit.

SHORT-SHORT TEST Internal Revenue Service restriction on a regulated investment company limiting profits from short-term trading to 30% of gross income. Sometimes also called *short-3 test* because the rule defines *short-term* as a holding period under three months.

SHORT SQUEEZE situation when prices of a stock or commodity futures contract start to move up sharply and many traders with short positions are forced to buy stocks or commodities in order to COVER their positions and prevent losses. This sudden surge of buying leads to even higher prices, further aggravating the losses of short sellers who have not covered their positions. *See also* SELLING SHORT.

SHORT TENDER using borrowed stock to respond to a TENDER OFFER. The practice is prohibited by SECURITIES AND EXCHANGE COMMISSION RULE 10b-4.

SHORT TERM
Accounting: assets expected to be converted into cash within the normal operating cycle (usually one year), or liabilities coming due in one year or less. *See also* CURRENT ASSETS; CURRENT LIABILITY.

Investment: investment with a maturity of one year or less. This includes bonds, although in differentiating between short-, medium-, and long-term bonds short term often is stretched to mean two years or less. *See also* SHORT BOND; SHORT-TERM DEBT; SHORT-TERM GAIN OR LOSS.

Taxes: HOLDING PERIOD of less than one year, used to differentiate SHORT-TERM GAIN OR LOSS from LONG-TERM GAIN and LONG-TERM LOSS. *See also* CAPITAL GAINS TAX.

SHORT-TERM BOND FUND bond mutual fund investing in short-to-intermediate term bonds. Such bonds, maturing in 3 to 5 years, typically pay higher yields than the shortest maturity bonds of 1 year or less, which are held by ULTRA-SHORT-TERM BOND FUNDS. Short-term bond funds also usually pay higher yields than money market mutual funds, which buy short-term commercial paper maturing in 90 days or less. However, short-term bond funds usually yield less than long-term bond funds holding bonds maturing in 10 to 30 years. Short-term bond funds, while yielding less than long-term bond funds, are also considerably less volatile, meaning that their value falls less when interest rates rise and rises less when interest rates fall. Many short-term bond funds offer checkwriting privileges, making them a source of easy liquidity. However, shareholders should remember than such checks will likely result in the realization of short- or long-term capital gains or losses.

SHORT-TERM DEBT all debt obligations coming due within one year; shown on a balance sheet as current liabilities. *See also* CURRENT LIABILITY.

SHORT-TERM GAIN OR LOSS for tax purposes, the profit or loss realized from the sale of securities or other capital assets held for less than one year. Short-term gains are taxable at ordinary income rates to the extent they are not reduced by offsetting capital losses. *See also* CAPITAL GAIN; CAPITAL LOSS.

SHORT-TERM INVESTMENT *see* SHORT-TERM.

SHOW STOPPER legal barrier erected to prevent a takeover attempt from becoming successful. For example, a target company may appeal to the state legislature to pass laws preventing the takeover. Or the company may embark on a SCORCHED-EARTH POLICY, making the company unappealing to the suitor. *See also* SHARK REPELLENT.

SHRINKAGE difference between the amount of inventory recorded in a firm's books and the actual amount of inventory on hand. Shrinkage may occur because of theft, deterioration, loss, clerical error, and other factors.

SIDE-BY-SIDE TRADING trading of a security and an OPTION on that security on the same exchange.

SIDEWAYS MARKET period in which prices trade within a narrow range, showing only small changes up or down. Also called HORIZONTAL PRICE MOVEMENT. *See also* FLAT MARKET.

SIGNATURE GUARANTEE written confirmation by a financial institution such as a bank or brokerage firm that a customer's signature is valid. The institution will compare a new signature from a customer with the signature on file. Transfer agents require signature guarantees when transferring stocks, bonds, mutual funds, or other securities from one party to another to ensure that the transactions are legitimate.

SIGNATURE LOAN unsecured loan requiring only the borrower's signature on a loan application. The lender agrees to make the loan because the borrower has good credit standing. Collateral is not required. Also known as a *good-faith loan* or *character loan.*

SIGNIFICANT INFLUENCE holding of a large enough equity stake in a corporation to require accounting for it in financial statements. Usually, a company that holds at least 20% of the voting stock in another company is considered a holder of significant influence. A company with such a large holding is likely represented on the board of directors of the other firm. The company owning such a stake has to declare its equity holdings, and all dividends received from the position, in its financial reports.

SIGNIFICANT ORDER order to buy or sell securities that is significant enough to affect the price of the security. Many institutional investors, such as mutual funds, will try to spread out their significant buying or selling of a particular security over several days or weeks so they do not adversely affect the price at which they buy or sell.

SIGNIFICANT ORDER IMBALANCE large number of buy or sell orders for a stock, causing an unusually wide spread between bid and offer prices. Stock exchanges frequently halt trading of a stock with a significant order imbalance until more buyers or sellers appear and an orderly market can be reestablished. A significant order imbalance on the buying side can occur when there is an announcement of an impending takeover of the company, better-than-expected earnings, or other unexpected positive news. A significant order imbalance on the selling side can occur when a takeover offer has fallen through, a key executive has left the company, earnings came in far worse than expected, or there is other unexpected negative news.

SILENT PARTNER
1. limited partner in a DIRECT PARTICIPATION PROGRAM, such as real estate and oil and gas limited partnerships, in which CASH FLOW and tax benefits are passed directly through to shareholders. Such partners are called silent because, unlike general partners, they have no direct role in management and no liability beyond their individual investment.
2. general partner in a business who has no role in management but represents a sharing of the investment and liability. Silent partners of this type are often found in family businesses, where the intent is to distribute tax liability.
   See also LIMITED PARTNERSHIP.

SILVER THURSDAY the day—March 27, 1980—when the extremely wealthy Hunt brothers of Texas failed to meet a MARGIN CALL by the brokerage firm of Bache Halsey Stuart Shields (which later became Prudential-Bache Securities) for $100 million in silver futures contracts. Their position was later covered and Bache survived, but the effects on the commodities markets and the financial markets in general were traumatic.

SIMPLE INTEREST interest calculation based only on the original principal amount. Simple interest contrasts with COMPOUND INTEREST, which is applied to principal plus accumulated interest. For example, $100 on deposit at 12% simple interest would yield $12 per year (12% of $100). The same $100 at 12% interest compounded annually would yield $12 interest only in the first year. The second year's interest would be 12% of the first year's accumulated interest and principal of $112, or $13.44. The third year's payment would be 12% of $125.44—the second year's principal plus interest—or $15.05. For computing interest on loans, simple interest is distinguished from various methods of calculating interest on a precomputed basis. *See also* PRECOMPUTE; CONSUMER CREDIT PROTECTION ACT OF 1968.

SIMPLE RATE OF RETURN rate of return that results from dividing the income and capital gains from an investment by the amount of capital invested. For example, if a $1000 investment produced $50 in income and $50 in capital appreciation in one year, the investment would have a 10% simple rate of return. This method of calculation does not factor in the effects of compounding.

SIMPLIFIED EMPLOYEE PENSION (SEP) PLAN pension plan in which both the employee and the employer contribute to an INDIVIDUAL RETIREMENT ACCOUNT (IRA). Under the TAX REFORM ACT OF 1986, employees (except those participating in SEPs of state or local governments) may elect to have employer contributions made to the SEP or paid to the employee in cash as with cash or deferred arrangements (401(k) PLANS). Elective contributions, which are excludable from earnings for income tax purposes but includable for employment tax (FICA and FUTA) purposes, were limited to $9250 in 1994, while employer contributions could not exceed $30,000. SEPs are limited to small employers (25 or fewer employees) and at least 50% of employees must participate. Special provisions pertain to self-employed persons, the integration of SEP contributions and Social Security benefits and limitations on tax deferrals for highly compensated individuals.

SINGLE-COUNTRY MUTUAL FUNDS mutual funds investing in the securities of just one country. Such funds may be open-end, meaning they continue to create new shares as more money comes into the fund, or closed-end, meaning they issue a limited number of shares which then trade on the stock exchange at a premium or discount to net asset value. Single-country funds offer investors a PURE PLAY on the fortunes of securities in that country. This means that these funds typically are far more volatile than REGIONAL MUTUAL FUNDS holding securities in a wider region, or GLOBAL MUTUAL FUNDS investing in markets around the world. There are many single-country funds, including funds for Argentina, Australia, Canada, China, France, Germany, Israel, Japan, Korea, Mexico, Spain, Switzerland, and the United Kingdom.

SINGLE OPTION term used to distinguish a PUT OPTION or a CALL OPTION from a SPREAD or a STRADDLE, each of which involves two or more put or call options. *See also* OPTION.

SINGLE-PREMIUM DEFERRED ANNUITY (SPDA) tax-deferred investment similar to an INDIVIDUAL RETIREMENT ACCOUNT, without many of the IRA restrictions. An investor makes a lump-sum payment to an insurance company or mutual fund selling the annuity. That lump sum can be invested in either a fixed-return instrument like a CD or a variable-return portfolio that can be switched among stocks, bonds, and money-market accounts. Proceeds are taxed only when distributions are taken. In contrast to an IRA, there is no limit to the amount that may be invested in an SPDA. Like the IRA, the tax penalty for withdrawals before age 59½ is 10%.

SINGLE-PREMIUM LIFE INSURANCE WHOLE LIFE INSURANCE policy requiring one premium payment. Since this large, up-front payment begins accumulating cash value immediately, the policy holder will earn more than holders of policies paid up in installments. With its tax-free appreciation (assuming it remains in force); low or no net-cost; tax-free access to funds through POLICY LOANS; and tax-free proceeds to beneficiaries, this type of policy emerged as a popular TAX SHELTER under the TAX REFORM ACT OF 1986.

SINGLE-STATE MUNICIPAL BOND FUND MUTUAL FUND that invests entirely in tax-exempt obligations of governments and government agencies within a single state. Therefore, dividends paid on fund shares are not taxable to residents of that state when they file state tax returns although capital gains, if any, are taxable.

SINKER bond on which interest and principal payments are made from the proceeds of a SINKING FUND.

SINKING FUND money accumulated on a regular basis in a separate custodial account that is used to redeem debt securities or preferred stock issues. A bond indenture or preferred stock charter may specify that payments be made to a sinking fund, thus assuring investors that the issues are safer than bonds (or preferred stocks) for which the issuer must make payment all at once, without the benefit of a sinking fund. *See also* PURCHASE FUND.

SIZE
   1. number of shares or bonds available for sale. A market maker will say, when asked for a quote, that a particular number of shares (the size) is available at a particular price.
   2. term used when a large number of shares are for sale—a trader will say that "shares are available in size," for instance.

SKIP-PAYMENT PRIVILEGE
   1. clause in some MORTGAGE contracts and installment loan agreements allowing borrowers to miss payments if ahead of schedule.
   2. option offered some bank credit-card holders whereby they may defer the December payment on balances due.

SLD LAST SALE indication, meaning "sold last sale," that appears on the CONSOLIDATED TAPE when a greater than normal change occurs between transactions in a security. The designation, which appears after the STOCK SYMBOL, is normally used when the change is a point or more on lower-priced issues (below $20) or two points or more on higher-priced issues.

SLEEPER stock in which there is little investor interest but which has significant potential to gain in price once its attractions are recognized. Sleepers are most easily recognized in retrospect, after they have already moved up in price.

SLEEPING BEAUTY potential TAKEOVER target that has not yet been approached by an acquirer. Such a company usually has particularly attractive features, such as a large amount of cash, or undervalued real estate or other assets.

SLUMP short-term drop in performance. The economy may enter a slump when it goes into a RECESSION. An individual stock or mutual fund may be in a slump if its price falls over several weeks or months. A normally productive employee may go into a slump and be less productive if he or she is having financial or emotional difficulties. A slump is considered to be a temporary phenomenon, from which the economy, investment or employee will soon recover.

SMALL BUSINESS ADMINISTRATION (SBA) federal agency created in 1953 to provide financial assistance (through direct loans and loan guarantees) as well as management assistance to businesses that lack the access to CAPITAL MARKETS enjoyed by larger more creditworthy corporations. Further legislation authorized the SBA to contribute to the VENTURE CAPITAL requirements of START-UP companies by licensing and funding small business investment companies (SBICs), to maintain a loan fund for rehabilitation of property damaged by natural disasters (floods, hurricanes, etc.), and to provide loans, counseling and training for small businesses owned by minorities, the economically disadvantaged, and the disabled.
   The SBA finances its activities through direct grants approved by Congress.

SMALL CAP shorthand for *small capitalization stocks* or mutual funds holding such stocks. Small cap stocks usually have a market capitalization (number of shares outstanding multiplied by the stock price) of $500 million or less. Those under $50 million in market cap are known as *microcap issues*. Small capitalization stocks represent companies that are less well established, but in many cases faster-growing than *mid-cap stocks* (from $500 million to $3 billion–$5 billion) or *large cap stocks* ($1 billion or more). Since they are less established, small cap stocks are usually more volatile than BLUE CHIPS.

SMALL FIRM EFFECT tendency of stocks of smaller firms, defined by MARKET CAPITALIZATION, to outperform larger firms. Theories to explain this phenomenon vary, but include the following: (1) smaller companies tend to have more growth potential; (2) small capitalization groupings include more companies in financial difficulty; when fortunes recover, price gains are dramatic and lift the return of the group as a whole; (3) small firms are generally neglected by analysts and hence by institutions; once discovered, they become appropriately valued, registering dramatic gains in the process. *See also* ANKLE BITER.

SMALL INVESTOR individual investor who buys small amounts of stock or bonds, often in ODD LOT quantities; also called the RETAIL INVESTOR. Although there are millions of small investors, their total holdings are dwarfed by the share ownership of large institutions such as mutual funds and insurance companies. Together with the proliferation of mutual funds, recent developments in the brokerage industry and its diversification along full-service lines have brought new programs specifically designed to make investing more convenient for small investors. Thus, much cash traditionally kept in savings banks has found its way into the stock and bond markets. *See also* MONEY MAGAZINE SMALL INVESTOR INDEX; ODD-LOT SHORT-SALE RATIO; ODD-LOT THEORY.

SMALL ORDER ENTRY (OR EXECUTION) SYSTEM *see* SOES.

SMART MONEY investors who make profitable investment moves at the right time, no matter what the investing environment. In a bull market, such investors buy the stocks that go up the most. In bear markets, they sell stocks short that fall the most. Smart money investors also have access to information about companies, either positive or negative, in advance of when the typical small investor learns of it. The term is also used in a more general sense to convey what sophisticated investors are doing now. Analysts will say "the smart money is buying cyclical stocks now because the economy is improving," for example.

SMOKESTACK INDUSTRIES basic manufacturing industries, such as autos, chemicals, steel, paper, and rubber, which typically have smokestacks on their plants. The fate of these industries, when viewed by Wall Street analysts, is closely tied to the ups and downs of the economy—they are therefore called CYCLICAL stocks. Many smokestack industries are located in what is known as the RUST BELT.

SNAKE SYSTEM agreement between European countries linking their currencies in an exchange-rate system in order to minimize fluctuations. Participating countries include Denmark, Germany, the Netherlands, Norway, and Sweden.

SNOWBALLING process by which the activation of STOP ORDERS in a declining or advancing market causes further downward or upward pressure on prices, thus triggering more stop orders and more price pressure, and so on.

SOCIAL CONSCIOUSNESS MUTUAL FUND mutual fund that is managed for capital appreciation while at the same time investing in securities of companies that do not conflict with certain social priorities. As a product of the social consciousness movements of the 1960s and 1970s, this type of mutual fund might not invest in companies that derive significant profits from defense contracts or whose activities cause environmental pollution, nor in companies with significant interests in countries with repressive or racist governments.

SOCIAL SECURITY benefits provided under the Social Security Act (1935), financed by the SOCIAL SECURITY TAX authorized by the FEDERAL INSURANCE CONTRIBUTORS ACT (FICA), and administered by the Social Security Administration. Term usually refers to retirement income benefits, but other benefits include SOCIAL SECURITY DISABILITY INCOME INSURANCE; Aid to Families with Dependent Children (AFDC); the Food Stamp program; Unemployment Insurance; Medicare; Medicaid; Public Assistance for the Aged, Blind and Disabled; Veterans' Compensation and Pensions; Housing Subsidies and Public Housing; Nutritional Programs for Children; and Student Aid.

SOCIAL RESPONSIBILITY principle that businesses should actively contribute to the welfare of society and not only maximize profits. Most corporate annual reports will highlight what the company has done to further education, help minorities, give to the arts and social welfare agencies, and in general improve social conditions. The concept is also used by investors in picking companies that are fair to their employees, do not pollute or build weapons, and make beneficial products. *See also* SOCIAL CONSCIOUSNESS MUTUAL FUND.

SOCIAL SECURITY DISABILITY INCOME INSURANCE insurance financed by the SOCIAL SECURITY TAX that provides lost income to qualifying employees whose disabilities are expected to last at least one year. Benefits are payable until death.

SOCIAL SECURITY TAX federal tax created by the Social Security Act (1935) that is shared equally by employers and their employees, is levied on annual income up to a maximum level, and is invested in Social Security trust funds. Employees then qualify for retirement benefits based on years worked, amounts paid into the fund, and retirement age.

SOES acronym for the computerized *Small Order Entry (or Execution) System* used by NASDAQ, in which orders for under 1000 shares bypass brokers and are aggregated and executed against available firm quotes by market makers on the NASDAQ system. *See also* ORDER SPLITTING.

SOCIALISM political-economic doctrine that, unlike CAPITALISM, which is based on competition, seeks a cooperative society in which the means of production and distribution are owned by the government or collectively by the people.

SOFT CURRENCY funds of a country that are not acceptable in exchange for the hard currencies of other countries. Soft currencies, such as Russia's ruble, are fixed at unrealistic exchange rates and are not backed by gold, so that countries with hard currencies, like U.S. dollars or British pounds, are reluctant to convert assets into them. *See also* HARD MONEY (HARD CURRENCY).

SOFT DOLLARS means of paying brokerage firms for their services through commission revenue, rather than through direct payments, known as *hard-dollar fees*. For example, a mutual fund may offer to pay for the research of a brokerage firm by executing trades generated by that research through that brokerage firm. The broker might agree to this arrangement if the fund manager promises to spend at least $100,000 in commissions with the broker that year. Otherwise, the fund would have to pay a hard-dollar fee of $50,000 for the research. *Compare with* HARD DOLLARS.

SOFT LANDING term used to describe a rate of growth sufficient to avoid recession but slow enough to prevent high inflation and interest rates. When the economy is growing very strongly, the Federal Reserve typically tries to engineer a soft landing by raising interest rates to head off inflation. If the economy threatens to fall into a recession, the Fed may lower rates to stimulate growth.

SOFT MARKET market characterized by an excess of supply over demand. A soft market in securities is marked by inactive trading, wide bid-offer spreads, and pronounced price drops in response to minimal selling pressure. Also called *buyer's market.*

SOFTS term used to refer to tropical commodities—coffee, sugar, and cocoa—but in a broader sense could include grains, oilseeds, cotton, and orange juice. Metals, financial futures, and livestock generally are excluded from this category.

SOFT SPOT weakness in selected stocks or stock groups in the face of a generally strong and advancing market.

SOLD-OUT MARKET commodities market term meaning that futures contracts in a particular commodity or maturity range are largely unavailable because of contract liquidations and limited offerings.

SOLVENCY state of being able to meet maturing obligations as they come due. See *also* INSOLVENCY.

SOUR BOND bond in DEFAULT on its interest or principal payments. The issue will typically trade at a deep discount and have a low credit rating. Traders say that the bond has "gone sour" when it defaults.

SOURCES AND APPLICATIONS (or USES) OF FUNDS STATEMENT financial statement section that analyzed changes affecting WORKING CAPITAL (or, optionally, cash) and that appeared as part of the annual reports of the publicly held companies prior to 1988. In that year, the Financial Accounting Standards Board (FASB) supplanted this statement with the STATEMENT OF CASH FLOWS, which analyzes all changes affecting cash in the categories of operations, investment, and financing.

SOVEREIGN RISK risk that a foreign government will default on its loan or fail to honor other business commitments because of a change in national policy. A country asserting its prerogatives as an independent nation might prevent the REPATRIATION of a company or country's funds through limits on the flow of capital, tax impediments, or the nationalization of property. Sovereign risk became a factor in the growth of international debt that followed the oil price increases of the 1970s. Several developing countries that borrowed heavily from Western banks to finance trade deficits had difficulty later keeping to repayment schedules. Banks had to reschedule loans to such countries as Mexico and Argentina to keep them from defaulting. These loans ran the further risk of renunciation by political leaders, which also would have affected loans to private companies that had been guaranteed by previous governments. Beginning in the 1970s, banks and other multinational corporations developed sophisticated analytical tools to measure sovereign risk before committing to lend, invest, or begin operations in a given foreign country. Throughout periods of worldwide economic volatility, the United States has been able to attract foreign investment because of its perceived lack of sovereign risk. Also called *country risk* or *political risk.*

SPDR acronym for *Standard & Poor's Depositary Receipt,* traded on the American Stock Exchange under the ticker symbol "SPY." Called *spiders,* they are securities that represent ownership in a long-term unit investment trust that holds a portfolio of common stocks designed to track the performance of the S&P 500 INDEX. A SPDR entitles a holder to receive proportionate quarterly cash distributions corresponding to the dividends that accrue to the S&P 500 stocks in the underlying portfolio, less trust expenses.

SPECIAL ARBITRAGE ACCOUNT special MARGIN ACCOUNT with a broker reserved for transactions in which the customer's risk is hedged by an offsetting security transaction or position. The MARGIN REQUIREMENT on such a transaction is substantially less than in the case of stocks bought on credit and subject to price declines. *See also* HEDGE/HEDGING.

SPECIAL ASSESSMENT BOND municipal bond that is repaid from taxes imposed on those who benefit directly from the neighborhood-oriented public works project funded by the bond; also called *special assessment limited liability bond, special district bond, special purpose bond,* SPECIAL TAX BOND. For example, if a bond finances the construction of a sewer system, the homeowners and businesses hooked up to the sewer system pay a special levy that goes to repay the bonds. The interest from special assessment bonds is tax free to resident bondholders. These are not normally GENERAL OBLIGATION BONDS, and the FULL FAITH AND CREDIT of the municipality is not usually behind them. Where the full faith and credit does back such bonds, they are called general obligation special assessment bonds.

SPECIAL BID infrequently used method of purchasing a large block of stock on the New York Stock Exchange whereby a MEMBER FIRM, acting as a broker, matches the buy order of one client, usually an institution, with sell orders solicited from a number of other customers. It is the reverse of an EXCHANGE DISTRIBUTION. The member broker makes a fixed price offer, which is announced in advance on the CONSOLIDATED TAPE. The bid cannot be lower than the last sale or the current regular market bid. Sellers of the stock pay no commissions; the buying customer pays both the selling and buying commissions. The transaction is completed during regular trading hours.

SPECIAL BOND ACCOUNT special MARGIN ACCOUNT with a broker that is reserved for transactions in U.S. government bonds, municipals, and eligible listed and unlisted nonconvertible corporate bonds. The restrictions under which brokers may extend credit with margin securities of these types are generally more liberal than in the case of stocks.

SPECIAL CASH ACCOUNT same as CASH ACCOUNT.

SPECIAL DISTRICT BOND *see* SPECIAL ASSESSMENT BOND.

SPECIAL DRAWING RIGHTS (SDR) measure of a nation's reserve assets in the international monetary system; known informally as "paper gold." First issued by the INTERNATIONAL MONETARY FUND (IMF) in 1970, SDRs are designed to supplement the reserves of gold and convertible currencies (or hard currencies) used to maintain stability in the foreign exchange market. For example, if the U.S. Treasury sees that the British pound's value has fallen precipitously in relation to the dollar, it can use its store of SDRs to buy excess pounds on the foreign exchange market, thereby raising the value of the remaining supply of pounds.

This neutral unit of account was made necessary by the rapid growth in world trade during the 1960s. International monetary officials feared that the supply of the two principal reserve assets—gold and U.S. dollars—would fall short of demand, causing the value of the U.S. currency to rise disproportionately in relation to other reserve assets. (At the time SDRs were introduced, the price of gold was fixed at about $35 per ounce.)

The IMF allocates to each of its more than 140 member countries an amount of SDRs proportional to its predetermined quota in the fund, which in turn is based on its GROSS NATIONAL PRODUCT (GNP). Each member agrees to back its SDRs with the full faith and credit of its government, and to accept them in exchange for gold or convertible currencies.

Originally, the value of one SDR was fixed at one dollar and at the dollar equivalent of other key currencies on January 1, 1970. As world governments adopted the current system of FLOATING EXCHANGE RATES, the SDR's value fluctuated relative to the "basket" of major currencies. Increasing reliance on SDRs in settling international accounts coincided with a decline in the importance of gold as a reserve asset.

Because of its inherent equilibrium relative to any one currency, the SDR has been used to denominate or calculate the value of private contracts, international treaties, and securities on the EUROBOND market.

See also EUROPEAN CURRENCY UNIT (ECU).

SPECIALIST member of a stock exchange who maintains a fair and orderly market in one or more securities. A specialist or SPECIALIST UNIT performs two main functions: executing LIMIT ORDERS on behalf of other exchange members for a portion of the FLOOR BROKER'S commission, and buying or selling—sometimes SELLING SHORT—for the specialist's own account to counteract temporary imbalances in supply and demand and thus prevent wide swings in stock prices. The specialist is prohibited by exchange rules from buying for his own account when there is an unexecuted order for the same security at the same price in the SPECIALIST'S BOOK, the record kept of limit orders in each price category in the sequence in which they are received. Specialists must meet strict minimum capital requirements before receiving formal approval by the New York Stock Exchange. *See also* SPECIALIST BLOCK PURCHASE AND SALE; SPECIALIST'S SHORT SALE RATIO.

SPECIALIST BLOCK PURCHASE AND SALE transaction whereby a SPECIALIST on a stock exchange buys a large block of securities either to sell for his own account or to try and place with another block buyer and seller, such as a FLOOR TRADER. Exchange rules require that such transactions be executed only when the securities cannot be ABSORBED in the regular market. *See also* NOT HELD.

SPECIALIST'S BOOK record maintained by a SPECIALIST that includes the specialist's own inventory of securities, market orders to sell short, and LIMIT ORDERS and STOP ORDERS that other stock exchange members have placed with the specialist. The orders are listed in chronological sequence. For example, for a stock trading at 57 a broker might ask for 500 shares when the price falls to 55. If successful at placing this limit order, the specialist notifies the member broker who entered the request, and collects a commission. The specialist is prohibited from buying the stock for his own account at a price for which he has previously agreed to execute a limit order.

SPECIALIST'S SHORT-SALE RATIO ratio of the amount of stock sold short by specialists on the floor of the New York Stock Exchange to total short sales. The ratio signals whether specialists are more or less bearish (expecting prices to decline) on the outlook for stock prices than other NYSE members and the public. Since specialists must constantly be selling stock short in order to provide for an orderly market in the stocks they trade, their short sales cannot be entirely regarded as an indication of how they perceive trends. Still, their overall short sales activity reflects knowledge, and technical analysts watch the specialist's short-sale ratio carefully for a clue to imminent upturns or downturns in stock prices. Traditionally, when the ratio rises above 60%, it is considered a bearish signal. A drop below 45% is seen as bullish and below 35% is considered extremely bullish. *See also* ODD-LOT SHORT-SALE RATIO; SELLING SHORT; SPECIALIST.

SPECIALIST UNIT stock exchange SPECIALIST (individual, partnership, corporation, or group of two or three firms) authorized by an exchange to deal as PRINCIPAL and AGENT for other brokers in maintaining a stable market in one or more particular stocks. A specialist unit on the New York Stock Exchange is required to have enough capital to buy at least 5000 shares of the common stock of a company it handles and 1000 shares of the company's CONVERTIBLE preferred stock.

SPECIALIZED MUTUAL FUND mutual fund concentrating on one industry. By so doing, shareholders have a PURE PLAY on the fortunes of that industry, for better or worse. Some of the many industries with specialized mutual funds include banking, biotechnology, chemicals, energy, environmental services, natural resources, precious metals, technology, telecommunications, and utilities. These funds tend to be more volatile than funds holding a diversified portfolio of stocks in many industries. Also called *sector funds* or *specialty funds*.

SPECIAL MISCELLANEOUS ACCOUNT (SMA) memorandum account of the funds in excess of the MARGIN REQUIREMENT. Such excess funds may arise from the proceeds of sales, appreciation of market values, dividends, or cash or securities put up in response to a MARGIN CALL. An SMA is not under the jurisdiction of REGULATION T of the Federal Reserve Board, as is the INITIAL MARGIN requirement, but this does not mean the customer is free to withdraw balances from it. The account is maintained essentially so that the broker can gauge how far the customer might be from a margin call. Any withdrawals require the broker's permission.

SPECIAL OFFERING method of selling a large block of stock that is similar to a SECONDARY DISTRIBUTION but is limited to New York Stock Exchange members and takes place during normal trading hours. The selling member announces the impending sale on the CONSOLIDATED TAPE, indicating a fixed price, which is usually based on the last transaction price in the regular market. All costs and commissions are borne by the seller. The buyers are member firms that may be buying for customer accounts or for their own inventory. Such offerings must have approval from the Securities and Exchange Commission.

SPECIAL SITUATION
1. undervalued stock that should soon rise in value because of an imminent favorable turn of events. A special situation stock may be about to introduce a revolutionary new product or be undergoing a needed management change. Many securities analysts concentrate on looking for and analyzing special situation stocks.
2. stock that fluctuates widely in daily trading, often influencing market averages, because of a particular news development, such as the announcement of a TAKEOVER bid.

SPECIAL TAX BOND
1. MUNICIPAL REVENUE BOND that will be repaid through excise taxes on such purchases as gasoline, tobacco, and liquor. The bond is not backed by the ordinary taxing power of the municipality issuing it. The interest from these bonds is tax free to resident bondholders.
2. SPECIAL ASSESSMENT BOND.

SPECTAIL term for broker-dealer who is part retail broker but preponderantly dealer/speculator.

SPECULATION assumption of risk in anticipation of gain but recognizing a higher than average possibility of loss. Speculation is a necessary and productive activity. It can be profitable over the long term when engaged in by profession-als, who often limit their losses through the use of various HEDGING techniques and devices, including OPTIONS trading, SELLING SHORT, STOP LOSS ORDERS, and transactions in FUTURES CONTRACTS. The term speculation implies that a business or investment risk can be analyzed and measured, and its distinction from the term INVESTMENT is one of degree of risk. It differs from gambling, which is based on random outcomes.

See also VENTURE CAPITAL.

SPECULATOR market participant who tries to profit from buying and selling futures and options contracts by anticipating future price movements. Speculators assume market price risk and add liquidity and capital to the futures markets. Speculators may purchase volatile stocks or mutual funds, and hold them for a short time in order to reap a profit. They may also sell stocks short and hope to cash in when the stock price drops quickly.

SPIDERS see SPDR.

SPIN-OFF form of corporate DIVESTITURE that results in a subsidiary or division becoming an independent company. In a traditional spin-off, shares in the new entity are distributed to the parent corporation's shareholders of record on a PRO RATA basis. Spin-offs can also be accomplished through a LEVERAGED BUYOUT by the subsidiary or division's management, or through an EMPLOYEE STOCK OWNER-SHIP PLAN (ESOP).

SPINS acronym for *Standard & Poor's 500 Index Subordinated Notes,* as Salomon Brothers' product combining features of debt, equity, and options.

SPLIT increase in a corporation's number of outstanding shares of stock without any change in the shareholders' EQUITY or the aggregate MARKET VALUE at the time of the split. In a split, also called a *split up,* the share price declines. If a stock at $100 par value splits 2-for-1, the number of authorized shares doubles (for example, from 10 million to 20 million) and the price per share drops by half, to $50. A holder of 50 shares before the split now has 100 shares at the lower price. If the same stock splits 4-for-1, the number of shares quadruples to 40 mil-lion and the share price falls to $25. Dividends per share also fall proportionately. Directors of a corporation will authorize a split to make ownership more afford-able to a broader base of investors. Where stock splits require an increase in AUTHORIZED SHARES and/or a change in PAR VALUE of the stock, shareholders must approve an amendment of the corporate charter.

See also REVERSE SPLIT.

SPLIT COMMISSION commission divided between the securities broker who executes a trade and another person who brought the trade to the broker, such as an investment counselor or financial planner. Split commissions between brokers are also common in real estate transactions.

SPLIT COUPON BOND debt instrument that begins as a zero-coupon bond and converts to an interest-paying bond at a specified date in the future. These bonds, issued by corporations and municipalities, are advantageous to issuers because they do not have to pay out cash interest for several years. They are attractive to investors, particularly in tax-sheltered accounts like IRAs and Keoghs, because they have locked in a reinvestment rate for several years, and then can receive cash interest. For example, a 55-year-old investor may want a split coupon bond because it will appreciate in value for 10 years, and then pay interest when he is retired and needs regular income. Also known as ZERO-COUPON CONVERTIBLE SECURITY.

SPLIT DOWN *see* REVERSE SPLIT.

SPLIT OFFERING new municipal bond issue, part of which is represented by SERIAL BONDS and part by term maturity bonds.

SPLIT ORDER large transaction in securities that, to avoid unsettling the market and causing fluctuations in the market price, is broken down into smaller portions to be executed over a period of time.

SPLIT RATING situation in which two major rating agencies, such as Standard & Poor's and Moody's Investors Service, assign a different rating to the same security.

SPLIT UP *see* SPLIT.

SPONSOR

Limited partnerships: GENERAL PARTNER who organizes and sells a LIMITED PARTNERSHIP. Sponsors (also called *promoters*) rely on their reputation in past real estate, oil and gas, or other deals to attract limited partners to their new deals.

Mutual funds: investment company that offers shares in its funds. Also called the *underwriter.*

Stocks: important investor—typically, an institution, mutual fund, or other big trader—whose favorable opinion of a particular security influences other investors and creates additional demand for the security. Institutional investors often want to make sure a stock has wide sponsorship before they invest in it, since this should ensure that the stock will not fall dramatically.

SPOT COMMODITY COMMODITY traded with the expectation that it will actually be delivered to the buyer, as contrasted to a FUTURES CONTRACT that will usually expire without any physical delivery taking place. Spot commodities are traded in the SPOT MARKET.

SPOT DELIVERY MONTH nearest month of those currently being traded in which a commodity could be delivered. In late January, therefore, the spot delivery month would be February for commodities with a February contract trade.

SPOT MARKET commodities market in which goods are sold for cash and delivered immediately. Trades that take place in FUTURES CONTRACTS expiring in the current month are also called *spot market trades.* The spot market tends to be conducted OVER-THE-COUNTER—that is, through telephone trading—rather than on the floor of an organized commodity exchange. Also called *actual market, cash market* or *physical market. See* also FUTURES MARKET.

SPOT PRICE current delivery price of a commodity traded in the SPOT MARKET. Also called *cash price.*

SPOUSAL IRA INDIVIDUAL RETIREMENT ACCOUNT that may be opened in the name of a nonworking spouse. The maximum annual IRA contribution for a married couple, only one of whom is employed, is $2250. The couple can allocate the $2250 any way they wish between two accounts, as long as either account does not exceed the $2000 limit imposed on all IRAs. If both spouses work, they can each contribute up to $2000 to their respective IRAs, or a combined maximum of $4000. Contributions are deductible only if both husband and wife are not actively participating in a qualified retirement plan.

SPOUSAL REMAINDER TRUST means used prior to the TAX REFORM ACT OF 1986 to shift income to a person taxable at a lower rate. Income-producing property, such as securities, is transferred by the grantor to the trust for a specific time, typically five years. Trust income is distributed to the beneficiary (or to a minor's CUSTODIAL ACCOUNT) to be used for expenses such as a child's college education. The income is therefore taxed at the beneficiary's lower tax rate. When the trust term expires, the property passes irrevocably to the grantor's spouse. The TAX REFORM ACT OF 1986 provided that effective for trusts established or contributions to trusts made after March 1, 1986, income must be taxed at the grantor's tax rate if the beneficiary is under age 14 and the property can revert to the grantor or the grantor's spouse.

SPREAD

Commodities: in futures trading, the difference in price between delivery months in the same market, or between different or related contracts. *See also* MOB SPREAD; NOB SPREAD; TED SPREAD.

Fixed-income securities: (1) difference between yields on securities of the same quality but different maturities. For example, the spread between 6% short-term Treasury bills and 10% long-term Treasury bonds is 4 percentage points. (2) difference between yields on securities of the same maturity but different quality. For instance, the spread between a 10% long-term Treasury bond and a 14% long-term bond of a B-rated corporation is 4 percentage points, since an investor's risk of default is so much less with the Treasury bond. *See also* YIELD SPREAD.

Foreign exchange: spreading one currency versus another, or multiple spreads within various currencies. An example would be a long position in Deutsche marks versus a short position in the British pound, or a long position in Deutsche marks versus a short position in the British pound or Japanese yen. An example of an intermonth spread would be a long March spot position in Swiss francs versus a short March position in the same currency. Spreads are frequently done in cash and futures markets. Interest rate differentials often have significant impact.

Options: position usually consisting of one long call and one short call option, or one long put and one short put option, with each option representing one "leg" of the spread. The two legs, if taken independently, would profit from opposite directional price movements. Spreads usually have lower cost and lower profit potential than an outright long option. They are entered into to reduce risk, or to profit from the change in the relative prices of the options. *See also* BEAR SPREAD; BULL SPREAD; BUTTERFLY SPREAD; CALENDAR SPREAD; CREDIT SPREAD; DEBIT SPREAD; DIAGONAL SPREAD; OPTION; PRICE SPREAD; SELLING THE SPREAD; VERTICAL SPREAD.

Stocks and bonds: (1) difference between the bid and offer price. If a stock is bid at $45 and offered at $46, the spread is $1. This spread narrows or widens according to supply and demand for the security being traded. *See also* BID-ASKED SPREAD; DEALER SPREAD. (2) difference between the high and low price of a particular security over a given period.

Underwriting: difference between the proceeds an issuer of a new security receives and the price paid by the public for the issue. This spread is taken by the underwriting syndicate as payment for its services. A security issued at $100 may entail a spread of $2 for the underwriter, so the issuer receives $98 from the offering. *See also* UNDERWRITING SPREAD.

SPREADING practice of buying and selling OPTION contracts of the same CLASS on the same underlying security in order to profit from moves in the price of that security. *See also* SPREAD.

SPREAD OPTION SPREAD position involving the purchase of an OPTION at one EXERCISE PRICE and the simultaneous sale of another option on the same underlying security at a different exercise price and/or expiration date. *See also* DIAGONAL SPREAD; HORIZONTAL SPREAD; VERTICAL SPREAD.

SPREAD ORDER OPTIONS market term for an order designating the SERIES of LISTED OPTIONS the customer wishes to buy and sell, together with the desired SPREAD—or difference in option premiums (prices)—shown as a net debit or net credit. The transaction is completed if the FLOOR BROKER can execute the order at the requested spread.

SPREAD POSITION status of an account in which a SPREAD has been executed.

SPREADSHEET ledger sheet on which a company's financial statements, such as BALANCE SHEETS, INCOME STATEMENTS, and sales reports, are laid out in columns and rows. Spreadsheets are used by securities and credit analysts in researching companies and industries. Since the advent of personal computers, spreadsheets have come into wide use, because software makes them easy to use. In an electronic spreadsheet on a computer, any time one number is changed, all the other numbers are automatically adjusted according to the relationships the computer operator sets up. For instance, in a spreadsheet of a sales report of a company's many divisions, the updating of a single division's sales figure will automatically change the total sales for the company, as well as the percentage of total sales that division produced.

SPRINKLING TRUST trust under which no beneficiary has a right to receive any trust income. Instead, the trustee is given discretion to divide, or "sprinkle," the trust's income as the trustee sees fit among a designated group of persons. Sprinkling trusts can be created both by LIVING TRUST agreements and by WILLS.

SPX ticker symbol for the Standard & Poor's 500 stock index options traded on the Chicago Board Options Exchange. The European-style index options contract is settled in cash, and can be exercised only on the last business day before expiration. The SPX is one of the most heavily traded of all index options contracts.

SQUEEZE
Finance: (1) tight money period, when loan money is scarce and interest rates are high, making borrowing difficult and expensive—also called a *credit crunch;* (2) any situation where increased costs cannot be passed on to customers in the form of higher prices.

Investments: situation when stocks or commodities futures start to move up in price, and investors who have sold short are forced to COVER their short positions in order to avoid large losses. When done by many short sellers, this action is called a SHORT SQUEEZE. *See also* SELLING SHORT; SHORT POSITION.

SRO *see* SELF-REGULATORY ORGANIZATION.

STABILIZATION
Currency: buying and selling of a country's own currency to protect its exchange value, also called PEGGING.

Economics: leveling out of the business cycle, unemployment, and prices through fiscal and monetary policies.

Market trading: action taken by REGISTERED COMPETITIVE TRADERS on the New York Stock Exchange in accordance with an exchange requirement that 75% of their trades be stabilizing—in other words, that their sell orders follow a PLUS TICK and their buy orders a MINUS TICK.

New issues underwriting: intervention in the market by a managing underwriter in order to keep the market price from falling below the PUBLIC OFFERING PRICE during the offering period. The underwriter places orders to buy at a specific price, an action called PEGGING that, in any other circumstance, is a violation of laws prohibiting MANIPULATION in the securities and commodities markets.

STAG speculator who makes it a practice to get in and out of stocks for a fast profit, rather than to hold securities for investment.

STAGFLATION term coined by economists in the 1970s to describe the previously unprecedented combination of slow economic growth and high unemployment (stagnation) with rising prices (inflation). The principal factor was the fourfold increase in oil prices imposed by the Organization of Petroleum Exporting Countries (OPEC) cartel in 1973–74, which raised price levels throughout the economy while further slowing economic growth. As is characteristic of stagflation, fiscal and monetary policies aimed at stimulating the economy and reducing unemployment only exacerbated the inflationary effects.

STAGGERED BOARD OF DIRECTORS board of directors of a company in which a portion of the directors are elected each year, instead of all at once. A board is often staggered in order to thwart unfriendly TAKEOVER attempts, since potential acquirers would have to wait a longer time before they could take control of a company's board through the normal voting procedure. Normally, all directors are elected at the annual meeting.

STAGGERING MATURITIES technique used to lower risk by a bond investor. Since long-term bonds are more volatile than short-term ones, an investor can HEDGE against interest rate movements by buying short-, medium- and long-term bonds. If interest rates decline, the long-term bonds will rise faster in value than the shorter-term bonds. If rates rise, however, the shorter-term bonds will hold their value better than the long-term debt obligations, which could fall precipitously.

STAGNATION
Economics: period of no or slow economic growth or of economic decline, in real (inflation-adjusted) terms. Economic growth of 3% or less per year—as was the case in the late 1970s, measured according to increases in the U.S. gross national product—generally is taken to constitute stagnation.
Securities: period of low volume and inactive trading.

STAGS acronym for *Sterling Transferable Accruing Government Securities.* A British version of U.S. government STRIPS, STAGS are deep discount zero-coupon bonds backed by British Treasury securities. *See also* ZERO-COUPON SECURITY.

STANDARD & POOR'S CORPORATION subsidiary of McGraw-Hill, Inc. that provides a broad range of investment services, including RATING corporate and municipal bonds, common stocks, preferred stocks, and COMMERCIAL PAPER; compiling the Standard & Poor's Composite Index of 500 Stocks, the Standard & Poor's 400 Industrial Index, and the Standard & Poor's 100 Index among other indexes; publishing a wide variety of statistical materials, investment advisory reports, and other financial information, including: *Bond Guide,* a summary of data on corporate and municipal bonds; *Earnings Forecaster,* earnings-per-share estimates on more than 1600 companies; *New Issue Investor,* information and analysis on the new issue market; *Stock Guide,* investment data on listed and unlisted common and preferred stocks and mutual funds; *Analyst's Handbook,* per-share data on the stocks and industry groups making up the 400 index, plus 15 transportation, financial and utility groups; *Corporation Records,* six volumes of information on more than 10,000 publicly held companies; *Stock Reports,* 2-page analytical reports on listed and unlisted companies. A subsidiary publishes the daily BLUE LIST of municipal and corporate bonds. Standard & Poor's also publishes *Poor's Register,* a national directory of companies and their officers, and *Securities Dealers of North America,* a directory of investment banking and brokerage firms in North America. *See also* STANDARD & POOR'S RATING; STOCK INDEXES AND AVERAGES.

STANDARD & POOR'S INDEX broad-based measurement of changes in stock market conditions based on the average performance of 500 widely held common stocks; commonly known as the *Standard & Poor's 500* (or *S&P 500*). The selection of stocks, their relative weightings to reflect differences in the number of outstanding shares, and publication of the index itself are services of STANDARD & POOR'S CORPORATION, a financial advisory, securities rating, and publishing firm. The index tracks industrial, transportation, financial, and utility stocks; it is a large cap index. The composition of the 500 stocks is flexible and the number of issues in each sector varies over time. Standard & Poor's also publishes several other important indexes including the *S&P MidCap 400,* the *S&P 600 SmallCap Index,* and the *S&P 1500 Super Composite Index,* which totals the S&P 500, 400, and 600 indices. These three indices represent approximately 82% of the total market capitalization of stocks traded in the U.S. equity market. S&P also maintains over 90 individual industry indexes.

See also S&P PHENOMENON; STANDARD & POOR'S CORPORATION; STOCK INDEXES AND AVERAGES.

STANDARD & POOR'S RATING classification of stocks and bonds according to risk issued by STANDARD & POOR'S CORPORATION. S&P's top four debt grades— called INVESTMENT GRADE AAA, AA, A, and BBB—indicate a minimal risk that a corporate or municipal bond issue will DEFAULT in its timely payment of interest and principal. Common stocks are ranked A+ through C on the basis of growth and stability, with a ranking of D signifying REORGANIZATION. *See also* EVENT RISK; LEGAL LIST; RATING.

STANDARD COST estimate, based on engineering and accounting studies, of what costs of production should be, assuming normal operating conditions. Standard costs differ from budgeted costs, which are forecasts based on expectations. Variances between standard costs and actual costs measure productive efficiency and are used in cost control.

STANDARD DEDUCTION individual taxpayer alternative to itemizing deductions. Under rules applicable in the mid-90s, which index them to inflation, they are:

	1994
Single Taxpayer	$3800
Head of Household	$5600
Married Filing Jointly	$6350
Married Filing Separately	$3175

STANDARD DEVIATION statistical measure of the degree to which an individual value in a probability distribution tends to vary from the mean of the distribution. It is widely applied in modern PORTFOLIO THEORY, for example, where the past performance of securities is used to determine the range of possible future performances and a probability is attached to each performance. The standard deviation of performance can then be calculated for each security and for the portfolio as a whole. The greater the degree of dispersion, the greater the risk. *See also* PORTFOLIO THEORY; REGRESSION ANALYSIS.

STANDARD INDUSTRIAL CLASSIFICATION (SIC) SYSTEM federally designed standard numbering system identifying companies by industry and providing other information. It is widely used by market researchers, securities analysts, and others. Computerized data bases frequently make use of this classification system.

STANDARD OF LIVING degree of prosperity in a nation, as measured by income levels, quality of housing and food, medical care, educational opportunities, transportation, communications, and other measures. The standard of living in different countries is frequently compared based on annual per capita income. On an individual level, the standard of living is a measure of the quality of life in such areas as housing, food, education, clothing, transportation, and employment opportunities.

STANDBY COMMITMENT
Securities: agreement between a corporation and an investment banking firm or group (the *standby underwriter)* whereby the latter contracts to purchase for resale, for a fee, any portion of a stock issue offered to current shareholders in a RIGHTS OFFERING that is not subscribed to during the two- to four-week standby period. A right, often issued to comply with laws guaranteeing the shareholder's PREEMPTIVE RIGHT, entitles its holder, either an existing shareholder or a person who has bought the right from a shareholder, to purchase a specified amount of shares before a PUBLIC OFFERING and usually at a price lower than the PUBLIC OFFERING PRICE.

The risk to the investment banker in a standby commitment is that the market price of shares will fall during the standby period. *See also* LAY OFF for a discussion of how standby underwriters protect themselves. *See also* FLOTATION COST; SUBSCRIPTION RIGHT; UNDERWRITE.

Lending: a bank commitment to loan money up to a specified amount for a specific period, to be used only in a certain contingency. The most common example would be a commitment to repay a construction lender in the event a permanent mortgage lender cannot be found. A COMMITMENT FEE is normally charged.

STANDBY UNDERWRITER *see* STANDBY COMMITMENT.

STANDSTILL AGREEMENT accord by a RAIDER to abstain from buying shares of a company for a specified period. *See also* GREENMAIL.

START-UP new business venture. In VENTURE CAPITAL parlance, start-up is the earliest stage at which a venture capital investor or investment pool will provide funds to an enterprise, usually on the basis of a business plan detailing the background of the management group along with market and financial PROJECTIONS. Investments or loans made at this stage are also called SEED MONEY.

STATE BANK bank organized under a charter granted by a regulatory authority in one of the 50 U.S. states, as distinguished from a NATIONAL BANK, which is federally chartered. The powers of a state-chartered commercial bank are generally consistent with those of national banks, since state laws tend to conform to federal initiatives and vice versa. State banks deposits are insured by the FEDERAL DEPOSIT INSURANCE CORPORATION. State banks have the option of joining the FEDERAL RESERVE SYSTEM, and even if they reject membership, they may purchase support services from the Fed, including check-processing and coin and currency services.

STATED INTEREST RATE

Banking: rate paid on savings instruments, such as PASSBOOK savings accounts and certificates of deposit. The stated interest rate does not take into account any compounding of interest.

Bonds: interest rate stated on a bond coupon. A bond with a 7% coupon has a 7% stated interest rate. This rate is applied to the face value of the bond, normally $1000, so that bondholders will receive 7% annually for every $1000 in face value of bonds they own.

STATED VALUE assigned value given to a corporation's stock for accounting purposes in lieu of par value. For example, the stated value may be set at $1 a share, so that if a company issued 10 million shares, the stated value of its stock would be $10 million. The stated value of the stock has no relation to its market price. It is, however, the amount per share that is credited to the CAPITAL STOCK account for each share outstanding and is therefore the legal capital of the corporation. Since state law generally prohibits a corporation from paying dividends or repurchasing shares when doing so would impair its legal capital, stated value does offer stockholders a measure of protection against loss of value.

STATEMENT

1. summary for customers of the transactions that occurred over the preceding month. A bank statement lists all deposits and withdrawals, as well as the running account balances. A brokerage statement shows all stock, bond, commodity futures, or options trades, interest and dividends received, margin debt outstanding, and other transactions, as well as a summary of the worth of the accounts at month end. A trade supplier provides a summary of open account transactions. See *also* ASSET MANAGEMENT ACCOUNT.
2. statement drawn up by businesses to show the status of their ASSETS and LIABILITIES and the results of their operations as of a certain date. See *also* FINANCIAL STATEMENT.

STATEMENT OF CASH FLOWS

analysis of CASH FLOW included as part of the financial statements in annual reports of publicly held companies as set forth in Statement 95 of the FINANCIAL ACCOUNTING STANDARDS BOARD (FASB). The statement shows how changes in balance sheet and income accounts affected cash and cash equivalents and breaks the analysis down according to operating, investing, and financing activities. As an analytical tool, the statement of cash flows reveals healthy or unhealthy trends and makes it possible to predict future cash requirements. It also shows how actual cash flow measured up to estimates and permits comparisons with other companies.

STATEMENT OF CONDITION

Banking: sworn accounting of a bank's resources, liabilities, and capital accounts as of a certain date, submitted in response to periodic "calls" by bank regulatory authorities.

Finance: summary of the status of assets, liabilities, and equity of a person or a business organization as of a certain date. See *also* BALANCE SHEET.

STATEMENT OF INCOME *see* PROFIT AND LOSS STATEMENT.

STATEMENT OF OPERATIONS *see* PROFIT AND LOSS STATEMENT.

STATUTE OF LIMITATIONS

statute describing the limitations on how many years can pass before someone gives up their right to sue for a wrongful action. For example, the INTERNAL REVENUE SERVICE has up to three years to assess back taxes from the time the return is filed, unless tax fraud is charged. Most states impose a statute of limitations of six years to challenge the violation of a written contract. Therefore, a suit claiming damages filed seven years after the alleged contract violation would be thrown out of court because the statute of limitations had run out.

STATUTORY INVESTMENT investment specifically authorized by state law for use by a trustee administering a trust under that state's jurisdiction.

STATUTORY MERGER legal combination of two or more corporations in which only one survives as a LEGAL ENTITY. It differs from *statutory consolidation,* in which all the companies in a combination cease to exist as legal entities and a new corporate entity is created. *See also* MERGER.

STATUTORY PROSPECTUS *see* PROSPECTUS.

STATUTORY VOTING one-share, one-vote rule that governs voting procedures in most corporations. Shareholders may cast one vote per share either for or against each nominee for the board of directors, but may not give more than one vote to one nominee. The result of statutory voting is that, in effect, those who control over 50% of the shares control the company by ensuring that the majority of the board will represent their interests. *Compare with* CUMULATIVE VOTING. *See also* PROPORTIONAL REPRESENTATION.

STAYING POWER ability of an investor to stay with (not sell) an investment that has fallen in value. For example, a commodity trader with staying power is able to meet margin calls as the commodities FUTURES CONTRACTS he has bought fall in price. He can afford to wait until the trade ultimately becomes profitable. In real estate, an investor with staying power is able to meet mortgage and mainte-nance payments on his or her properties and is therefore not harmed as interest rates rise or fall, or as the properties become temporarily difficult to sell.

STEP DOWN NOTE type of FLOATING RATE whose interest rate declines at speci-fied times in the course of the loan.

STICKY DEAL new securities issue that the underwriter fears will be difficult to sell. Adverse market conditions, bad news about the issuing entity, or other factors may lead underwriters to say, "This will be a sticky deal at the price we have set." As a result, the price may be lowered or the offering withdrawn from the market.

STOCK
1. ownership of a CORPORATION represented by shares that are a claim on the cor-poration's earnings and assets. COMMON STOCK usually entitles the shareholder to vote in the election of directors and other matters taken up at shareholder meetings or by proxy. PREFERRED STOCK generally does not confer voting rights but it has a prior claim on assets and earnings—dividends must be paid on preferred stock before any can be paid on common stock. A corporation can authorize additional classes of stock, each with its own set of contractual rights. *See also* ARTICLES OF INCORPORATION; AUTHORIZED SHARES; BLUE CHIP; BOOK VALUE; CAPITAL STOCK; CERTIFICATE; CLASS; CLASSIFIED STOCK; CLOSELY HELD; COMMON STOCK; COMMON STOCK EQUIVALENT; CONVERTIBLES; CONTROL STOCK; CORPORATION; CUMULATIVE PREFERRED; DIVIDEND; EARNINGS PER SHARE; EQUITY; FLOAT; FRACTIONAL SHARES; GOING PUBLIC; GROWTH STOCK; INACTIVE STOCK; INITIAL PUBLIC OFFERING; ISSUED AND OUTSTANDING; JOINT STOCK COM-PANY; LETTER SECURITY; LISTED SECURITY; MARKET VALUE; NONVOTING STOCK; NO-PAR VALUE STOCK; OVER THE COUNTER; PAR VALUE; PARTICIPATING PRE-FERRED; PENNY STOCK; PREEMPTIVE RIGHT; PREFERENCE SHARES; PREFERRED

STOCK; PRIOR PREFERRED STOCK; QUARTER STOCK; REGISTERED SECURITY; REGIS-
TRAR; REVERSE SPLIT; SCRIP; SECURITY; SHARE; SHAREHOLDER; SPLIT; STATED
VALUE; STOCK CERTIFICATE; STOCK DIVIDEND; STOCK EXCHANGE; STOCKHOLDER;
STOCKHOLDER OF RECORD; STOCK MARKET; STOCK POWER; STOCK PURCHASE
PLAN; STOCK SYMBOL; STOCK WATCHER; TRANSFER AGENT; TREASURY STOCK;
VOTING STOCK; VOTING TRUST CERTIFICATE; WATERED STOCK.

2. inventories of accumulated goods in manufacturing and retailing businesses.

3. *see* ROLLING STOCK.

STOCK AHEAD situation in which two or more orders for a stock at a certain
price arrive about the same time, and the exchange's PRIORITY rules take effect.
New York Stock Exchange rules stipulate that the bid made first should be executed first or, if two bids came in at once, the bid for the larger number of shares
receives priority. The bid that was not executed is then reported back to the broker, who informs the customer that the trade was not completed because there
was stock ahead. *See also* MATCHED AND LOST.

STOCK BONUS PLAN plan established and maintained by an employer to provide benefits similar to those of a profit-sharing plan. Contributions by the
employer, however, are not necessarily dependent on profits, and the benefits are
distributed in shares of stock in the employer company. Stock bonus plans reward
employee performance, and by giving employees a stake in the company they are
used to help motivate them to perform at maximum efficiency.

STOCKBROKER *see* REGISTERED REPRESENTATIVE.

STOCK BUYBACK corporation's purchase of its own outstanding stock. A buyback may be financed by borrowings, sale of assets, or operating CASH FLOW. Its
purpose is commonly to increase EARNINGS PER SHARE and thus the market price,
often to discourage a TAKEOVER. When a buyback involves a PREMIUM paid to an
acquirer in exchange for a promise to desist from takeover activity, the payment
is called GREEN-MAIL. A buyback having a formula and schedule may also be
called a SHARE REPURCHASE PLAN or SELF-TENDER. *See also* TREASURY STOCK.

STOCK CERTIFICATE documentation of a shareholder's ownership in a corporation. Stock certificates are engraved intricately on heavy paper to deter forgery.
They indicate the number of shares owned by an individual, their PAR VALUE (if
any), the CLASS of stock (for example, common or preferred), and attendant voting rights. To prevent theft, shareholders often store certificates in safe deposit
boxes or take advantage of a broker's SAFEKEEPING service. Stock certificates
become negotiable when endorsed.

STOCK DIVIDEND payment of a corporate dividend in the form of stock rather
than cash. The stock dividend may be additional shares in the company, or it may
be shares in a SUBSIDIARY being spun off to shareholders. The dividend is usually
expressed as a percentage of the shares held by a shareholder. For instance, a
shareholder with 100 shares would receive 5 shares as the result of a 5% stock
dividend. From the corporate point of view, stock dividends conserve cash
needed to operate the business. From the stockholder point of view, the advantage is that additional stock is not taxed until sold, unlike a cash dividend, which
is declarable as income in the year it is received.

STOCK EXCHANGE organized marketplace in which stocks, COMMON STOCK
EQUIVALENTS, and bonds are traded by members of the exchange, acting both as
agents (brokers) and as principals (dealers or traders). Such exchanges have a physical location where brokers and dealers meet to execute orders from institutional

and individual investors to buy and sell securities. Each exchange sets its own requirements for membership; the New York Stock Exchange has the most stringent requirements. *See also* AMERICAN STOCK EXCHANGE; LISTING REQUIREMENTS; NEW YORK STOCK EXCHANGE; REGIONAL STOCK EXCHANGES; SECURITIES AND COMMODITIES EXCHANGES.

STOCK EXCHANGE OF SINGAPORE (SES) only stock exchange in Singapore, trading through a fully computerized system called CLOB. A direct link between the SES and the NASDAQ Stock Market was established in 1988, with all prices quoted in U.S. currency. The *Straits Times Industrial Index* and the *SES Share Indices* are the most widely followed indicators of share performance. Trades are settled on a five-day settlement. Trading hours are 9:30 A.M. to 12:30 P.M. and 2 P.M. to 5 P.M., Monday through Friday. Trades are settled five business days after the trade date.

STOCKHOLDER individual or organization with an ownership position in a corporation; also called a SHAREHOLDER or *shareowner.* Stockholders must own at least one share, and their ownership is confirmed by either a stock certificate or a record by their broker, if shares are in the broker's custody.

STOCKHOLDER OF RECORD common or preferred stockholder whose name is registered on the books of a corporation as owning shares as of a particular date. Dividends and other distributions are made only to shareholders of record. Common stockholders are usually the only ones entitled to vote for candidates for the board of directors or on other matters requiring shareholder approval.

STOCKHOLDER'S EQUITY *see* OWNER'S EQUITY.

STOCKHOLDER'S REPORT company's ANNUAL REPORT and supplementary quarterly reports giving financial results and usually containing an ACCOUNTANT'S OPINION. Special stockholder's reports are sometimes issued covering major corporate developments. Also called *shareholder's report. See also* DISCLOSURE.

STOCKHOLM STOCK EXCHANGE only market in Sweden for official equity trading. The Stockholm Automatic Exchange (SAX) electronic trading system, introduced in 1989, includes all traded shares. A parallel system, called SOX, operates for fixed-interest securities. Clearing and settlement occur on the third business day following the trade. Trading is conducted Monday through Friday from 10 A.M. to 4 P.M.

STOCK INDICES AND AVERAGES indicators used to measure and report value changes in representative stock groupings. Strictly speaking, an AVERAGE is simply the ARITHMETIC MEAN of a group of prices, whereas an INDEX is an average expressed in relation to an earlier established BASE MARKET VALUE. (In practice, the distinction between indices and averages is not always clear; the AMEX Major Market Index is an average, for example.) Indices and averages may be broad based—that is, comprised of many stocks and designed to be representative of the overall market—or narrowly based, meaning they are made up of a smaller number of stocks and designed to reflect a particular industry or market SECTOR. Selected indices and averages are also used as the underlying value of STOCK INDEX FUTURES, INDEX OPTIONS, or options on index futures, which enable investors to HEDGE A POSITION against general market movement at relatively little cost. An extensive number and variety of indices and averages exist. Among the best known and most widely used are:

AMEX Major Market Index (XMI): price-weighted (high-priced issues have more influence than low-priced issues) average of 20 BLUE CHIP industrial stocks.

It is designed to closely track the Dow Jones Industrial Average (DJIA) in measuring representative performance in the stocks of major industrial corporations. It is produced by the American Stock Exchange (AMEX) but is composed of 20 stocks listed on the New York Stock Exchange (NYSE), 15 of which are also components of the DJIA. Futures on the Major Market Index are traded on the Chicago Mercantile Exchange. Options on the XMI are listed on the AMEX.

AMEX Market Value Index (XAM): on September 4, 1973, the XAM replaced the ASE Index, which tracked the performance of American Stock Exchange issues. It is not a trading index. The Market Value Index is a capitalization-weighted index (i.e., the impact of a component's market change is proportionate to the overall market value of the issue) introduced at a base level of 100.00 in September 1973 and adjusted to half that level in July 1983. It measures the collective performance of more than 800 issues, representing all major industry groups traded on the AMEX, including AMERICAN DEPOSITARY RECEIPTS and warrants as well as common stocks. Uniquely, cash dividends paid by component stocks are assumed to be reinvested and are thus reflected in the index.

Dow Jones Industrial Average (DJIA): price-weighted average of 30 actively traded BLUE CHIP stocks, primarily industrials but including American Express Co., Walt Disney Co., J.P. Morgan, and other service-oriented firms. Prepared and published by Dow Jones & Co., it is the oldest and most widely quoted of all the market indicators. The components, which change from time to time, represent between 15% and 20% of the market value of NYSE stocks. The DJIA is calculated by adding the trading prices of the component stocks and using a divisor that is adjusted for STOCK DIVIDENDS and SPLITS, and cash equivalent distributions equal to 10% or more of the closing prices of an issue, as well as for substitutions and mergers. The average is quoted in points, not dollars. Dow Jones & Co. has refused to allow the DJIA to be used as a basis for speculation with futures or options. Other averages similarly prepared by Dow Jones & Co. are the *Dow Jones Transportation Average*—20 stocks representative of the airline, trucking, railroad, and shipping businesses (*see also* DOW THEORY); and the *Dow Jones Utility Average* (DJUA)—15 geographically representative gas and electric utilities. The combination of the Dow Industrials, Transportation and Utility Averages, encompassing 65 stocks, is known as the *Dow Jones Composite Average,* also known as the *65 Stock Average.*

Dow Jones Equity Market Index: a broad-based, capitalization-weighted (price times the shares outstanding for each company) index (June 30, 1982 = 100) of about 700 stocks traded on the NYSE, the AMEX, and NASDAQ, representing approximately 80% of the U.S. equity market. It is the U.S. portion of the Dow Jones World Stock Index.

Dow Jones World Stock Index: a broad-based, capitalization-weighted index (December 31, 1991 = 100) tracking more than 2600 companies in a growing list of countries and representing about 80% of the equity capital on stock markets around the globe. Currently, the index includes 25 countries in North America, Europe and Asia/Pacific regions.

Dow Jones Industry Group and Economic Sector Indices are: comprised of companies in the Dow Jones World Stock Index, classified on the basis of their type of business, which then are sorted into more than 100 industry groups and nine broad economic sectors. The indices are computed to measure the movement of stock prices by industry groups and broad economic sectors on a global, regional, and national basis. These indices are tracked in real time.

Country indices are calculated in each country's own currency, plus the U.S. dollar, British pound, German mark, and Japanese yen. The regional and world indices are calculated in these four global currencies. All indices can be converted to any currency.

NASDAQ Composite Index: market value-weighted index that measures all domestic and non-U.S. based securities, more than 4700 companies, listed on the NASDAQ Stock Market. The index was introduced on February 5, 1971, with a base value of 100. The market value—the last-sale price multiplied by total shares outstanding—is calculated through the trading day, and is related to the total value of the index. Each security in the index is assigned to a NASDAQ sub-index: Bank, Biotechnology, Computer, Industrial, Insurance, Other Finance, Transportation, Telecommunications. Values for the sub-indices began in February 1971, except for Biotechnology, Computer, and Telecommunications, which started November 1993.

NASDAQ-100 Index: begun in January 1985, it includes 100 of the largest non-financial companies listed on the NASDAQ Stock Market's National Market. Each security is proportionally represented by its market capitalization in relation to the total market value of the index. In October 1993, all index components had a market value of at least $400 million and were selected on the basis of trading volume, the company's visibility, the continuity of the components in the index and a good mix of industries represented in the NASDAQ Stock Market. In February 1994, the index value was reduced by half when options on the index began trading on the Chicago Board Options Exchange. The NASDAQ-100 option is a European-style option, and can be exercised only on its expiration date.

New York Stock Exchange Composite Index: market value-weighted index which relates all NYSE stocks to an aggregate market value as of December 31, 1965, adjusted for capitalization changes. The base value of the index is $50 and point changes are expressed in dollars and cents. NYSE sub-indices include the *NYSE Industrial, NYSE Transportation, NYSE Utility*, and *NYSE Financial Composite Indexes.*

Russell Indexes: market capitalization-weighted indexes published by Frank Russell Company of Tacoma, Washington. The *Russell 3000 Index* consists of the largest U.S. stocks in terms of market capitalization. The highest-ranking 1000 comprise the *Russell 1000 Index,* and the other 2000, which have market value ranging from $91 million to $672 million, make up the *Russell 2000 Small Stock Index,* a popular measure of the stock price performance of small companies. Seven other indices are built from these three. They are the *Russell 2500 Index, Russell Midcap Index, Russell Top 200 Index, Russell 1000 Value Index, Russell 1000 Growth Index, Russell 2000 Value Index and Russell 2000 Growth Index. See also* RUSSELL INDEXES.

Standard & Poor's Composite Index of 500 Stocks: market value-weighted index showing the change in the aggregate market value of 500 stocks relative to the base period 1941–43. Mostly NYSE-listed companies with some AMEX and NASDAQ Stock Market stocks, it is comprised of 381 industrial stocks, 47 utilities, 56 financials, and 16 transportation issues representing about 74% of the market value of all issues traded on the NYSE. Index options are traded on the Chicago Board of Trade and futures options are traded on the Chicago Mercantile Exchange. The *Standard & Poor's 100 Index* (OEX), calculated on the same basis as the 500 Stock Index, is made up of stocks for which options are listed on the Chicago Board Options Exchange. Its components are mainly NYSE industrials, with some transportation, utility, and financial stocks. Options on the 100 Index are listed on the Chicago Board of Trade and futures are traded on the Chicago Mercantile Exchange. Futures options are not traded.

Value Line Composite Average: equally weighted geometric average of approximately 1700 NYSE, AMEX, and over the counter stocks tracked by the VALUE LINE INVESTMENT SURVEY. The index uses a base value of 100.00 established June 30, 1961, and changes are expressed in index numbers rather than dollars and cents. This index is designed to reflect price changes of typical stocks (industrials, transportation, and utilities) and being neither price- nor market value-weighted, it largely succeeds. Futures on the index are traded on the Kansas City Board of Trade and futures options are traded on the Philadelphia Stock Exchange.

Wilshire 5000 Equity Index: broadest of all the averages and indexes, the Wilshire Index is market value-weighted and represents the value of all U.S. headquartered equities on the NYSE, AMEX, and NASDAQ National Market system for which quotes are available, more than 6000 stocks in all. Changes are measured against a base value established December 31, 1980. Options and futures are not traded on the Wilshire Index, which is prepared by Wilshire Associates Inc. of Santa Monica, California.

Many indices and averages track the performance of stock markets around the world. The major indices include the: ALL ORDINARIES INDEX; CAC 40 INDEX; MORGAN STANLEY CAPITAL INTERNATIONAL INDICES; EAFE INDEX; EMERGING MARKET FREE (EMF) INDEX; HANG SENG INDEX; INTERNATIONAL MARKET INDEX; SALOMON BROTHERS WORLD EQUITY INDEX.

See also BARRON'S CONFIDENCE INDEX; BOND BUYER'S INDEX; COMMODITY INDICES; ELVES; LIPPER MUTUAL FUND INDUSTRY AVERAGE; MONEY MAGAZINE SMALL INVESTOR INDEX; SECURITIES AND COMMODITIES EXCHANGES.

STOCK INDEX FUTURE security that combines features of traditional commodity futures trading with securities trading using composite stock indexes. Investors can speculate on general market performance or can buy an index future contract to hedge a LONG POSITION or SHORT POSITION against a decline in value. Settlement is in cash, since it is obviously impossible to deliver an index of stocks to a futures buyer. Among the most popular stock index futures traded are the New York Stock Exchange Composite Index on the New York Futures Exchange (NYFE), the Standard & Poor's 500 Index on the Chicago Mercantile Exchange (CME), and the Value Line Composite Index on the Kansas City Board of Trade (KCBT).

It is also possible to buy options on stock index futures; the Standard & Poor's 500 Stock Index futures options are traded on the Chicago Mercantile Exchange and the New York Stock Exchange Composite Index futures options are traded on the New York Futures Exchange, for example. Unlike stock index futures or INDEX OPTIONS, however, futures options are not settled in cash; they are settled by delivery of the underlying stock index futures contracts.

See also FUTURES CONTRACT; HEDGE/HEDGING; SECURITIES AND COMMODITIES EXCHANGES.

STOCK INSURANCE COMPANY insurance company that is owned by stockholders, as distinguished from a MUTUAL COMPANY that is owned by POLICYHOLDERS. Even in a stock company, however, policyholders interests are ahead of shareholder's dividends.

STOCK JOCKEY stockbroker who actively follows individual stocks and frequently buys and sells shares in his client's portfolios. If the broker does too much short-term trading in accounts over which he has discretion, he may be accused of CHURNING.

STOCK LIST function of the organized stock exchanges that is concerned with LISTING REQUIREMENTS and related investigations, the eligibility of unlisted companies for trading privileges, and the delisting of companies that have not complied with exchange regulations and listing requirements. The New York Stock Exchange department dealing with listing of securities is called the Department of Stock List.

STOCK MARKET general term referring to the organized trading of securities through the various exchanges and the OVER THE COUNTER market. The securities involved include COMMON STOCK, PREFERRED STOCK, BONDS, CONVERTIBLES, OPTIONS, rights, and warrants. The term may also encompass commodities when used in its most general sense, but more often than not the stock market and the commodities (or futures) market are distinguished. The query "How did the market do today?" is usually answered by a reference to the Dow Jones Industrial Average, comprised of stocks listed on the New York Stock Exchange. *See also* SECURITIES AND COMMODITIES EXCHANGES.

STOCK OPTION
1. right to purchase or sell a stock at a specified price within a stated period. OPTIONS are a popular investment medium, offering an opportunity to hedge positions in other securities, to speculate in stocks with relatively little investment, and to capitalize on changes in the MARKET VALUE of options contracts themselves through a variety of options strategies.
   See also CALL OPTION; PUT OPTION.
2. widely used form of employee incentive and compensation, usually for the executives of a corporation. The employee is given an OPTION to purchase its shares at a certain price (at or below the market price at the time the option is granted) for a specified period of years.
   See also INCENTIVE STOCK OPTION; QUALIFIED STOCK OPTION.

STOCK POWER power of attorney form transferring ownership of a REGISTERED SECURITY from the owner to another party. A separate piece of paper from the CERTIFICATE, it is attached to the latter when the security is sold or pledged to a brokerage firm, bank, or other lender as loan COLLATERAL. Technically, the stock power gives the owner's permission to another party (the TRANSFER AGENT) to transfer ownership of the certificate to a third party. Also called *stock/bond power.*

STOCK PURCHASE PLAN organized program for employees of a company to buy shares of its stock. The plan could take the form of compensation if the employer matches employee stock purchases. In some companies, employees are offered the chance to buy stock in the company at a discount. Also, a corporation can offer to reinvest dividends in additional shares as a service to shareholders, or it can set up a program of regular additional share purchases for participating shareholders who authorize periodic, automatic payments from their wages for this purpose. *See also* AUTOMATIC INVESTMENT PROGRAM.

Another form of stock purchase plan is the EMPLOYEE STOCK OWNERSHIP PLAN (ESOP), whereby employees regularly accumulate shares and may ultimately assume control of the company.

STOCK RATING evaluation by rating agencies of common stocks, usually in terms of expected price performance or safety. Standard & Poor's and Value Line's respective quality and timeliness ratings are among the most widely consulted.

STOCK RECORD control, usually in the form of a ledger card or computer report, used by brokerage films to keep track of securities held in inventory and their precise location within the firm. Securities are recorded by name and owner.

STOCK RIGHT *see* SUBSCRIPTION RIGHT.

STOCK SPLIT *see* SPLIT.

STOCK SYMBOL letters used to identify listed companies on the securities exchanges on which they trade. These symbols, also called *trading symbols,* identify trades on the CONSOLIDATED TAPE and are used in other reports and documents whenever such shorthand is convenient. Some examples: ABT (Abbott Laboratories), AA (Aluminum Company of America), XON (Exxon), KO (Coca Cola). Stock symbols are not necessarily the same as abbreviations used to identify the same companies in the stock tables of newspapers. *See also* COMMITTEE ON UNIFORM SECURITIES IDENTIFICATION PROCEDURES (CUSIP).

STOCK-TRANSFER AGENT *see* TRANSFER AGENT.

STOCK WARRANT *see* SUBSCRIPTION WARRANT.

STOCK WATCHER (NYSE) computerized service that monitors all trading activity and movement in stocks listed on the New York Stock Exchange. The system is set up to identify any unusual activity due to rumors or MANIPULATION or other illegal practices. The stock watch department of the NYSE is prepared to conduct investigations and to take appropriate action, such as issuing clarifying information or turning questions of legality over to the Securities and Exchange Commission. *See also* SURVEILLANCE DEPARTMENT OF EXCHANGES.

STOP-LIMIT ORDER order to a securities broker with instructions to buy or sell at a specified price or better (called the *stop-limit price*) but only after a given *stop price* has been reached or passed. It is a combination of a STOP ORDER and a LIMIT ORDER. For example, the instruction to the broker might be "buy 100 XYZ 55 STOP 56 LIMIT" meaning that if the MARKET PRICE reaches $55, the broker enters a limit order to be executed at $56 or a better (lower) price. A stop-limit order avoids some of the risks of a stop order, which becomes a MARKET ORDER when the stop price is reached; like all price-limit orders, however, it carries the risk of missing the market altogether, since the specified limit price or better may never occur. The American Stock Exchange prohibits stop-limit orders unless the stop and limit prices are equal.

STOP LOSS
Insurance: promise by a reinsurance company that it will cover losses incurred by the company it reinsures over and above an agreed-upon amount.
Stocks: customer order to a broker that sets the sell price of a stock below the current MARKET PRICE. A stop-loss order therefore will protect profits that have already been made or prevent further losses if the stock drops.

STOP ORDER order to a securities broker to buy or sell at the MARKET PRICE once the security has traded at a specified price called the *stop price*. A stop order may be a DAY ORDER, a GOOD-TILL-CANCELED ORDER, or any other form of time-limit order. A stop order to buy, always at a stop price above the current market price, is usually designed to protect a profit or to limit a loss on a short sale *(see* SELLING SHORT). A stop order to sell, always at a price below the current market price, is usually designed to protect a profit or to limit a loss on a security already purchased at a higher price. The risk of stop orders is that they may be triggered by temporary market movements or that they may be executed at prices several points higher or lower than the stop price because of market orders placed ahead of them. Also called *stop-loss order*. *See also* GATHER IN THE STOPS; STOP LIMIT ORDER; STOP LOSS (stocks).

STOP-OUT PRICE lowest dollar price at which Treasury bills are sold at a particular auction. This price and the beginning auction price are averaged to establish the price at which smaller purchasers may purchase bills under the NONCOMPETITIVE BID system. *See also* BILL; DUTCH AUCTION.

STOP PAYMENT revocation of payment on a check after the check has been sent or delivered to the payee. So long as the check has not been cashed, the writer has up to six months in which to request a stop payment. The stop payment right does not carry over to electronic funds transfers.

STOPPED OUT term used when a customer's order is executed under a STOP ORDER at the price predetermined by the customer, called the *stop price*. For instance, if a customer has entered a stop-loss order to sell XYZ at $30 when the stock is selling at $33, and the stock then falls to $30, his or her position will be stopped out. A customer may also be stopped out if the order is executed at a guaranteed price offered by a SPECIALIST. *See also* GATHER IN THE STOPS; STOPPED STOCK.

STOPPED STOCK guarantee by a SPECIALIST that an order placed by a FLOOR BROKER will be executed at the best bid or offer price then in the SPECIALIST'S BOOK unless it can be executed at a better price within a specified period of time.

STOP PRICE *see* STOP ORDER.

STORY STOCK/BOND security with values or features so complex that a "story" is required to persuade investors of its merits. Story stocks are frequently from companies with some unique product or service that is difficult for competitors to copy. In a less formal sense, term is used by news organizations to mean stocks most actively traded.

STRADDLE strategy consisting of an equal number of PUT OPTIONS and CALL OPTIONS on the same underlying stock, stock index, or commodity future at the same STRIKE PRICE and maturity date. Each OPTION may be exercised separately, although the combination of options is usually bought and sold as a unit.

STRAIGHT-LINE DEPRECIATION method of depreciating a fixed asset whereby the asset's useful life is divided into the total cost less the estimated salvage value. The procedure is used to arrive at a uniform annual DEPRECIATION expense to be charged against income before figuring income taxes. Thus, if a new machine purchased for $1200 was estimated to have a useful life of ten years and a salvage value of $200, annual depreciation under the straight-line method would be $100, charged at $100 a year. This is the oldest and simplest method of depreciation and is used by many companies for financial reporting purposes, although faster depreciation of some assets with greater tax benefits in the early years is allowed under the MODIFIED ACCELERATED COST RECOVERY SYSTEM (MACRS).

STRAIGHT TERM INSURANCE POLICY term life insurance policy for a specific number of years in which the death benefit remains unchanged. A level premium policy will charge the same premium for a number of years, usually ten, and then increase. An annual renewable term policy will charge slightly higher premiums each year.

STRANGLE sale or purchase of a put option and a call option on the same underlying instrument, with the same expiration, but at strike prices equally OUT OF THE MONEY. A strangle costs less than a STRADDLE because both options are out of the money, but profits are made only if the underlying instrument moves dramatically.

STRAP OPTION contract combining one PUT OPTION and two CALL OPTIONS of the same SERIES, which can be bought at a lower total premium than that of the three options bought individually. The put has the same features as the calls—same underlying security, exercise price, and maturity. Also called *triple option. Compare with* STRIP.

STRATEGIC BUYOUT ACQUISITION based on analysis of the operational benefits of consolidation. Implicitly contrasts with the type of TAKEOVER based on "paper values" that characterized the "merger mania" of the 1980s—undervalued stock bought using JUNK BONDS ultimately repayable from the liquidation of acquired assets and activities. A strategic buyout focuses on how companies fit together and anticipates enhanced long-term earning power. *See also* SYNERGY.

STREET short for Wall Street, referring to the financial community in New York City and elsewhere. It is common to hear "The Street likes XYZ." This means there is a national consensus among securities analysts that XYZ's prospects are favorable. *See also* STREET NAME.

STREET NAME phrase describing securities held in the name of a broker or another nominee instead of a customer. Since the securities are in the broker's custody, transfer of the shares at the time of sale is easier than if the stock were registered in the customer's name and physical certificates had to be transferred.

STRIKE PRICE *see* EXERCISE PRICE.

STRIP

Bonds: brokerage-house practice of separating a bond into its CORPUS and COUPONS, which are then sold separately as ZERO-COUPON SECURITIES. The 1986 Tax Act permitted MUNICIPAL BOND strips. Some, such as Salomon Brothers' tax-exempt M-CATS, represent PREREFUNDINGS backed by U.S. Treasury securities held in escrow. Other strips include Treasuries stripped by brokers, such as TIGERS, and stripped mortgage-backed securities of government-sponsored issuers like Fannie Mae. A variation known by the acronym STRIPS (Separate Trading of Registered Interest and Principal of Securities) is a prestripped zero-coupon bond that is a direct obligation of the U.S. Treasury.

Options: OPTION contract consisting of two PUT OPTIONS and one CALL OPTION on the same underlying stock or stock index with the same strike and expiration date. *Compare with* STRAP.

Stocks: to buy stocks with the intention of collecting their dividends. Also called *dividend stripping. See also* DIVIDEND ROLLOVER PLAN.

STRIPPED BOND bond separated into its two components: periodic interest payments and principal repayment. Each of the interest payments and the principal repayment are stripped apart by a brokerage firm and sold individually as ZERO-COUPON SECURITIES. Investors therefore have a wide choice of maturities to pick from when shopping for a zero-coupon bond. When a U.S. government bond is stripped, it is often called a STRIP, which stands for *separate trading of registered interest and principal of securities.* Such bonds are also called CATS AND TIGRS.

STRONG DOLLAR dollar that can be exchanged for a large amount of a foreign currency. The dollar can gain strength in currency markets because the United States is considered a haven of political and economic stability, or because yields on American securities are attractive. A strong dollar is a blessing for American travelers going abroad, because they get more pounds, francs, marks, and yen and other currencies for their greenbacks. However, a strong dollar makes it difficult for American firms to export their goods to foreign countries because it raises the cost to foreigners of purchasing American products. In 1985, the dollar became so strong that the PLAZA ACCORD was signed to bring the dollar down. *See also* EXCHANGE RATE; WEAK DOLLAR.

STRUCTURED NOTE

1. derivative instrument based on the movement of an underlying index. For example, a structured note issued by a corporation may pay interest to noteholders based on the rise and fall of oil prices. This gives investors the opportunity to earn interest and profit from the change in price of a commodity at the same time.
2. complex debt instrument, usually a medium-term note, in which the issuer enters into one or more SWAP arrangements to change the cash flows it is required to make. A simple form utilizing interest-rate swaps might be, for example, a three-year FLOATING RATE NOTE paying the London Interbank Offered Rate (LIBOR) plus a premium semiannually. The issuer arranges a swap transaction whereby it agrees to pay a fixed semiannual rate for three years in exchange for the LIBOR. Since the floating rate payments (cash flows) offset each other, the issuer has synthetically created a fixed-rate note.

STUB STOCK common stocks or instruments convertible to equity in a company that is overleveraged as the result of a BUYOUT or RECAPITALIZATION and may have DEFICIT NET WORTH. Stub stock is highly speculative and highly volatile but, unlike JUNK BONDS, has unlimited potential for gain if the company succeeds in restoring financial balance.

STUDENT LOAN MARKETING ASSOCIATION (SLMA) publicly traded stock corporation that guarantees student loans traded in the SECONDARY MARKET. It was established by federal decree in 1972 to increase the availability of education loans to college and university students made under the federally sponsored Guaranteed Student Loan Program and the Health, Education Assistance Loan Program. Known as *Sallie Mae,* it purchases student loans from originating financial institutions and provides financing to state student loan agencies. It also sells short-and medium-term notes, some FLOATING RATE NOTES.

SUBCHAPTER M Internal Revenue Service regulation dealing with what is commonly called the *conduit theory,* in which qualifying investment companies and real estate investment trusts avoid double taxation by passing interest and dividend income and capital gains directly through, without taxation, to shareholders, who are taxed as individuals. *See also* REAL ESTATE INVESTMENT TRUST; REGULATED INVESTMENT COMPANY.

SUBCHAPTER S section of the Internal Revenue Code giving a corporation that has 35 or fewer shareholders and meets certain other requirements the option of being taxed as if it were a PARTNERSHIP. Thus a small corporation can distribute its income directly to shareholders and avoid the corporate income tax while enjoying the other advantages of the corporate form. These companies are known as *Subchapter S corporations, tax-option corporations,* or *small business corporations.*

SUBJECT Wall Street term referring to a bid and/or offer that is negotiable—that is, a QUOTATION that is not firm. For example, a broker looking to place a sizable order might call several dealers with the question, "Can you give me a *subject quote* on 20,000 shares of XYZ?"

SUBJECT QUOTE *see* SUBJECT.

SUBORDINATED junior in claim on assets to other debt, that is, repayable only after other debts with a higher claim have been satisfied. Some subordinated debt may have less claim on assets than other subordinated debt; a *junior subordinated debenture* ranks below a subordinated DEBENTURE, for example.

It is also possible for unsubordinated (senior) debt to become subordinated at the request of a lender by means of a subordination agreement. For example, if an officer of a small company has made loans to the company instead of making a permanent investment in it, a bank might request the officer's loan be subordinated to its own loan as long as the latter is outstanding. This is accomplished by the company officer's signing a subordination agreement. *See also* EFFECTIVE NET WORTH; JUNIOR SECURITY.

SUBORDINATION CLAUSE clause in a MORTGAGE loan agreement that permits a mortgage recorded at a subsequent date to have preference over the original mortgage.

SUBSCRIPTION agreement of intent to buy newly issued securities. *See also* NEW ISSUE; SUBSCRIPTION RIGHT; SUBSCRIPTION WARRANT.

SUBSCRIPTION AGREEMENT application submitted by an investor seeking to join a limited partnership. All prospective limited partners must be approved by the general partner before they are allowed to become limited partners.

SUBSCRIPTION PRICE price at which existing shareholders of a corporation are entitled to purchase common shares in a RIGHTS OFFERING or at which subscription warrants are exercisable. *See also* SUBSCRIPTION RIGHT; SUBSCRIPTION WARRANT.

SUBSCRIPTION PRIVILEGE right of existing shareholders of a corporation, or their transferees, to buy shares of a new issue of common stock before it is offered to the public. *See also* PREEMPTIVE RIGHT; SUBSCRIPTION RIGHT.

SUBSCRIPTION RATIO *see* SUBSCRIPTION RIGHT.

SUBSCRIPTION RIGHT privilege granted to existing shareholders of a corporation to subscribe to shares of a new issue of common stock before it is offered to the public; better known simply as a *right*. Such a right, which normally has a life of two to four weeks, is freely transferable and entitles the holder to buy the new common stock below the PUBLIC OFFERING PRICE. While in most cases one existing share entitles the stockholder to one right, the number of rights needed to buy a share of a new issue (called the *subscription ratio)* varies and is determined by a company in advance of an offering. To subscribe, the holder sends or delivers to the company or its agent the required number of rights plus the dollar price of the new shares.

Rights are sometimes granted to comply with state laws that guarantee the shareholders' PREEMPTIVE RIGHT—their right to maintain a proportionate share of ownership. It is common practice, however, for corporations to grant rights even when not required by law; protecting shareholders from the effects of DILUTION is seen simply as good business.

The actual certificate representing the subscription is technically called a SUBSCRIPTION WARRANT, giving rise to some confusion. The term *subscription warrant,* or simply *warrant,* is commonly understood in a related but different sense—as a separate entity with a longer life than a right—maybe 5, 10, or 20 years or even perpetual—and with a SUBSCRIPTION PRICE higher at the time of issue than the MARKET VALUE of the common stock.

Subscription rights are offered to shareholders in what is called a RIGHTS OFFERING, usually handled by underwriters under a STANDBY COMMITMENT.

SUBSCRIPTION WARRANT type of security, usually issued together with a BOND or PREFERRED STOCK, that entitles the holder to buy a proportionate amount of common stock at a specified price, usually higher than the market price at the time of issuance, for a period of years or to perpetuity; better known simply as a *warrant*. In contrast, rights, which also represent the right to buy common shares, normally have a subscription price lower than the current market value of the common stock and a life of two to four weeks. A warrant is usually issued as a SWEETENER, to enhance the marketability of the accompanying fixed income securities. Warrants are freely transferable and are traded on the major exchanges. They are also called *stock-purchase warrants*. *See also* PERPETUAL WARRANT; SUBSCRIPTION RIGHT.

SUBSIDIARY company of which more than 50% of the voting shares are owned by another corporation, called the PARENT COMPANY. *See also* AFFILIATE.

SUBSTITUTION
Banking: replacement of COLLATERAL by other collateral.

Contracts: replacement of one party to a contract by another. *See also* NOVATION.

Economics: concept that, if one product or service can be replaced by another, their prices should be similar.

Law: replacement of one attorney by another in the exercise of stock powers relating to the purchase and sale of securities. *See also* STOCK POWER.

Securities:
1. exchange or SWAP of one security for another in a client's PORTFOLIO. Securities analysts often advise substituting a stock they currently favor for a stock in the same industry that they believe has less favorable prospects.
2. substitution of another security of equal value for a security acting as COLLATERAL for a MARGIN ACCOUNT. *See also* SAME-DAY-SUBSTITUTION.

SUICIDE PILL POISON PILL with potentially catastrophic implications for the company it is designed to protect. An example might be a poison pill providing for an exchange of stock for debt in the event of a *hostile takeover;* that would discourage an acquirer by making the TAKEOVER prohibitively expensive, but its implementation could put the TARGET COMPANY in danger of bankruptcy.

SUITABILITY RULES guidelines that those selling sophisticated and potentially risky financial products, such as limited partnerships or commodities futures contracts, must follow to ensure that investors have the financial means to assume the risks involved. Such rules are enforced through self-regulation administered by such organizations as the NATIONAL ASSOCIATION OF SECURITIES DEALERS, the SECURITIES AND COMMODITIES EXCHANGES, and other groups operating in the securities industry. Individual brokerage firms selling the products have their own guidelines and policies. They typically require the investor to have a certain level of NET WORTH and LIQUID ASSETS, so that he or she will not be irreparably harmed if the investment sours. A brokerage firm may be sued if it has allowed an unsuitable investor to buy an investment that goes sour. *See also* KNOW YOUR CUSTOMER.

SUM-OF-THE-YEARS'-DIGITS METHOD (SOYD) method of ACCELERATED DEPRECIATION that results in higher DEPRECIATION charges and greater tax savings in the earlier years of a FIXED ASSET's useful life than the STRAIGHT-LINE DEPRECIATION method, where charges are uniform throughout. Sometimes called just *sum-of-digits method,* it allows depreciation based on an inverted scale of the total of digits for the years of useful life. Thus, for four years of life, the digits 4, 3, 2, and 1 are added to produce 10. The first year's rate becomes $\frac{4}{10}$ths of the depreciable cost of the asset (cost less salvage value), the second year's rate $\frac{3}{10}$ths, and so on. The effects of this method of accelerated depreciation are compared with the straight-line method in the following illustration, which assumes an asset with a total cost of $1000, a useful life of four years, and no salvage value:

YEAR	STRAIGHT LINE		SUM-OF-YEARS' DIGITS	
	Expense	Cumulative	Expense	Cumulative
1	$250	$250	$400	$400
2	$250	$500	$300	$700
3	$250	$750	$200	$900
4	$250	$1000	$100	$1000
	$1000		$1000	

See also MODIFIED ACCELERATED COST RECOVERY SYSTEM (MACRS).

SUNK COSTS costs already incurred in a project that cannot be changed by present or future actions. For example, if a company bought a piece of machinery five years ago, that amount of money has already been spent and cannot be recovered. It should also not affect the company's decision on whether or not to buy a new piece of machinery if the five-year old machinery has worn out.

SUNRISE INDUSTRIES figurative term for the emerging growth sectors that some believe will be the mainstays of the future economy, taking the place of declining *sunset industries*. Although the latter, including such mature industries as the automobile, steel, and other heavy manufacturing industries, will continue to be important, their lead role as employers of massive numbers of workers is expected to be superseded by the electronics and other computer-related high-technology, biotechnology, and genetic engineering sectors and by service industries.

SUNSET PROVISION condition in a law or regulation that specifies an expiration date unless reinstated by legislation. For examples a sunset provision in the TAX REFORM ACT OF 1986 prohibits tax-exempt single-family mortgage bonds after 1988.

SUNSHINE LAWS state or federal laws (also called *government in the sunshine laws*) that require most meetings of regulatory bodies to be held in public and most of their decisions and records to be disclosed. Many of these statutes were enacted in the 1970s because of concern about government abuses during the Watergate period. Most prominent is the federal Freedom of Information (FOI) Act, which makes it possible to obtain documents relating to most federal enforcement and rule-making agencies.

SUPER BOWL INDICATOR technical indicator that holds that if a team from the old American Football League pre-1970 wins the Super Bowl, the stock market will decline during the coming year. If a team from the old pre-1990 National Football League wins the Super Bowl, the stock market will end the coming year higher. The indicator has been a remarkably accurate predictor of stock market performance for many years.

SUPER DOT *see* DESIGNATED ORDER TURNAROUND (DOT).

SUPERMAJORITY AMENDMENT corporate AMENDMENT requiring that a substantial majority (usually 67% to 90%) of stockholders approve important transactions, such as mergers.

SUPER NOW ACCOUNT deregulated transaction account authorized for depository institutions in 1982. It paid interest higher than on a conventional NOW (NEGOTIABLE ORDER OF WITHDRAWAL) account but slightly lower than that on the MONEY MARKET DEPOSIT ACCOUNT (MMDA). With the deregulation of banking deposit accounts in 1986, however, banks are free to pay whatever rates they feel cost considerations and competitive conditions warrant. Although some banks continue to offer MMDA accounts which pay a slightly higher rate to compensate for the fact that checkwriting is limited to three checks a month, most banks now offer one transaction account with unlimited checkwriting.

SUPER SINKER BOND bond with long-term coupons (which might equal a 20-year-bond's yield) but with short maturity. Typically, super sinkers are HOUSING BONDS, which provide home financing. If homeowners move from their homes and prepay their mortgages, bondholders receive their principal back right away. Super sinkers may therefore have an actual life of as little as three to five years, even though their yield is about the same as bonds of much longer maturities. *See also* COUPON BOND.

SUPERVISORY ANALYST member firm research analyst who has passed a special New York Stock Exchange examination and is deemed qualified to approve publicly distributed research reports.

SUPPLEMENTAL AGREEMENT agreement that amends a previous agreement and contains additional conditions.

SUPPLEMENTAL SECURITY INCOME SOCIAL SECURITY program benefiting the blind, disabled, and indigent.

SUPPLY-SIDE ECONOMICS theory of economics contending that drastic reductions in tax rates will stimulate productive investment by corporations and wealthy individuals to the benefit of the entire society. Championed in the late 1970s by Professor Arthur Laffer *(see* LAFFER CURVE) and others, the theory held that MARGINAL TAX RATES had become so high (primarily as a result of big government) that major new private spending on plant, equipment, and other "engines of growth" was discouraged. Therefore, reducing the size of government, and hence its claim on earned income, would fuel economic expansion.

Supporters of the supply-side theory claimed they were vindicated in the first years of the administration of President Ronald W. Reagan, when marginal tax rates were cut just prior to a sustained economic recovery. However, members of the opposing KEYNESIAN ECONOMICS school maintained that the recovery was a classic example of "demand-side" economics—growth was stimulated not by increasing the supply of goods, but by increasing consumer demand as disposable incomes rose. Also clashing with the supply-side theory were MONETARIST economists, who contended that the most effective way of regulating aggregate demand is for the Federal Reserve to control growth in the money supply. *See also* AGGREGATE SUPPLY.

SUPPORT LEVEL price level at which a security tends to stop falling because there is more demand than supply. Technical analysts identify support levels as prices at which a particular security or market has bottomed in the past. When a stock is falling towards its support level, these analysts say it is "testing its support," meaning that the stock should rebound as soon as it hits the support price. If the stock continues to drop through the support level, its outlook is considered very bearish. The opposite of a support level is a RESISTANCE LEVEL.

SURCHARGE charge added to a charge, cost added to a cost, or tax added to a tax. *See also* SURTAX.

SURETY individual or corporation, usually an insurance company, that guarantees the performance or faith of another. Term is also used to mean *surety bond,* which is a bond that backs the performance of the person bonded, such as a contractor, or that pays an employer if a bonded employee commits theft.

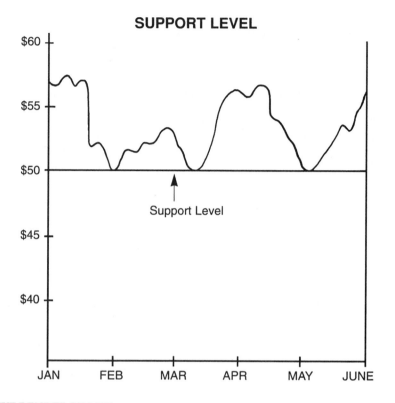

SUPPORT LEVEL

SURRENDER VALUE *see* CASH SURRENDER VALUE.

SURPLUS connotes either CAPITAL SURPLUS or EARNED SURPLUS. *See also* PAID-IN CAPITAL; RETAINED EARNINGS.

SURTAX tax applied to corporations or individuals who have earned a certain level of income. For example, the REVENUE RECONCILIATION ACT OF 1993 provided for a 10% surtax on adjusted gross incomes over $250,000.

SURVEILLANCE DEPARTMENT OF EXCHANGES division of a stock exchange that is constantly watching to detect unusual trading activity in stocks, which may be a tipoff to an illegal practice. These departments cooperate with the Securities and Exchange Commission in investigating misconduct. *See also* STOCK WATCHER.

SURVIVING SPOUSE spouse remaining alive when his or her spouse dies (in other words, the spouse who lives longer). In most states, the surviving spouse cannot be totally disinherited, but has a right to receive a share of the deceased spouse's estate, with the size of that share determined by state law.

SURVIVORSHIP ACCOUNT *see* JOINT TENANTS WITH RIGHT OF SURVIVORSHIP.

SURVIVORSHIP LIFE INSURANCE *see* SECOND-TO-DIE INSURANCE.

SUSPENDED TRADING temporary halt in trading in a particular security, in advance of a major news announcement or to correct an imbalance of orders to buy and sell. Using telephone alert procedures, listed companies with material developments to announce can give advance notice to the New York Stock Exchange Department of Stock List or the American Stock Exchange Securities Division. The exchanges can then determine if trading in the securities affected should be suspended temporarily to allow for orderly dissemination of the news to the public. Where advance notice is not possible, a *floor governor* may halt trading to stabilize the price of a security affected by a rumor or news development. Destabilizing developments might include a MERGER announcement, an unfavorable earnings report, or a major resource discovery. *See also* CIRCUIT BREAKER; DISCLOSURE; FORM 8-K; INVESTOR RELATIONS DEPARTMENT.

SUSPENSE ACCOUNT in accounting, an account used temporarily to carry receipts, disbursements, or discrepancies, pending their analysis and permanent classification.

SWAP traditionally, an exchange of one security for another to change the maturities of a bond PORTFOLIO or the quality of the issues in a stock or bond portfolio, or because investment objectives have shifted. Investors with bond portfolio losses often swap for other higher-yielding bonds to be able to increase the return on their portfolio and realize tax losses. Recent years have seen explosive growth in more complex *currency swaps,* used to link increasingly global capital markets, and in *interest-rate swaps,* used to reduce risk by synthetically matching the DURATION of assets and liabilities of financial institutions as interest rates got higher and more volatile. In a simple currency swap (swaps can be done with varying degrees of complexity), two parties sell each other a currency with a commitment to re-exchange the principal amount at the maturity of the deal. Originally done to get around the problems of exchange controls, currency swaps are widely used to tap new capital markets, in effect to borrow funds irrespective of whether the borrower requires funds within that market. The INTERNATIONAL BANK FOR RECONSTRUCTION AND DEVELOPMENT (WORLD BANK) has been an active participant in currency swaps with U.S. corporations.

An interest-rate swap is an arrangement whereby two parties (called counterparties) enter into an agreement to exchange periodic interest payments. The dollar amount the counterparties pay each other is an agreed-upon periodic interest rate multiplied by some predetermined dollar principal, called the *notational principal amount.* No principal (no notational amount) is exchanged between parties to the transaction; only interest is exchanged. In its most common and simplest variation, one party agrees to pay the other a fixed rate of interest in exchange for a floating rate. The benefit of interest-rate swaps, which can be used to synthetically extend or shorten the duration characteristics of an asset or liability, is that direct changes in the contractual characteristics of the assets or the liabilities become matters affecting only administrative, legal, and investment banking costs.

See also BOND SWAP; SUBSTITUTION.

SWAP ORDER *see* CONTINGENT ORDER.

SWAPTION option to enter an interest rate swap. A *payer swaption* gives its purchaser the right, but not the obligation, to enter into an interest-rate swap at a preset rate within a specific period of time. The swaption buyer pays a premium to the seller for this right. A *receiver swaption* gives the purchaser the right to receive fixed payments. The seller agrees to provide the specified swap if called upon, though it is possible for him to hedge that risk with other offsetting transactions.

SWEAT EQUITY equity created in a property by the hard work of the owner. For example, a small business may be built up more on the efforts of its founders than on the capital raised to finance it. Homeowners who renovate a house with their own labor create rising value with the sweat of their own brows, not the general increase in housing prices from inflation.

SWEETENER feature added to a securities offering to make it more attractive to purchasers. A bond may have the sweetener of convertibility into common stock added, for instance. *See also* KICKER.

SWISS OPTIONS AND FINANCIAL FUTURES EXCHANGE (SOFFEX) first fully electronic trading system in the world, with a completely integrated and automated clearing system. Contracts include traded options on equities; low exercise price options; futures and options on the Swiss government bond; and futures and long-term options (LTO) on the Swiss Market Index, the index that includes the largest capitalization stocks traded on Switzerland's three stock exchanges.

SWITCHING

Mutual funds: moving assets from one mutual fund to another, either within a FUND FAMILY or between different fund families. There is no charge for switching within a no-load family of mutual funds, which offer a variety of stock, bond, and money market funds. A sales charge might have to be paid when switching from one LOAD FUND to another. Customers of many discount brokerage firms can switch among fund families, sometimes at no fee and sometimes by paying a brokerage commission. Switching usually occurs at the shareholder's initiative, as a result of changes in market conditions or investment objectives. Some investment advisers and investment advisory newsletters recommend when to switch into or out of different mutual funds. *See also* NO-LOAD FUND.

Securities: selling stocks or bonds to replace them with other stocks and bonds with better prospects for gain or higher yields. *See also* SWAP.

SWITCH ORDER *see* CONTINGENT ORDER.

SYNDICATE *see* PURCHASE GROUP.

SYNDICATE MANAGER *see* MANAGING UNDERWRITER.

SYNERGY ideal sought in corporate mergers and acquisitions that the performance of a combined enterprise will exceed that of its previously separate parts. For example, a MERGER of two oil companies, one with a superior distribution network and the other with more reserves, would have synergy and would be expected to result in higher earnings per share than previously. *See also* STRATEGIC BUYOUT.

SYNTHETIC ASSET value that is artificially created by using other assets, such as securities, in combination. For example, the simultaneous purchase of a CALL OPTION and sale of a PUT OPTION on the same stock creates *synthetic stock* having the same value, in terms of CAPITAL GAIN potential, as the underlying stock itself.

SYNTHETIC SECURITIES *see* STRUCTURED NOTE; SYNTHETIC ASSET.

SYSTEMATIC INVESTMENT PLAN plan in which investors make regular payments into a stock, bond, mutual fund, or other investment. This may be accomplished through an AUTOMATIC INVESTMENT PROGRAM, such as a salary reduction plan with an employer, a dividend reinvestment plan with a company or mutual fund, or an automatic investment plan in which a mutual fund withdraws a set amount from a bank checking or savings account on a regular basis. By investing systematically, investors are benefiting from the advantages of DOLLAR-COST AVERAGING.

SYSTEMATIC WITHDRAWAL PLAN MUTUAL FUND option whereby the shareholder receives specified amounts at specified intervals.

SYSTEMATIC RISK that part of a security's risk that is common to all securities of the same general class (stocks and bonds) and thus cannot be eliminated by DIVERSIFICATION; also known as *market risk.* The measure of systematic risk in stocks is the BETA COEFFICIENT. *See also* PORTFOLIO BETA SCORE, PORTFOLIO THEORY.

t

TAC BONDS *see* TARGETED AMORTIZATION CLASS (TAC) BONDS.

TACTICAL ASSET ALLOCATION shifting percentages of portfolios among stocks, bonds, or cash, depending on the relative attractiveness of the respective markets. *See also* ASSET ALLOCATION.

TAFT-HARTLEY ACT federal law (in full, Labor Management Relations Act) enacted in 1947, which restored to management in unionized industries some of the bargaining power it had lost in prounion legislation prior to World War II. Taft-Hartley prohibited a union from
- refusing to bargain in good faith
- coercing employees to join a union
- imposing excessive or discriminatory dues and initiation fees
- forcing employers to hire union workers to perform unneeded or non-existent tasks (a practice known as *featherbedding)*
- striking to influence a bargaining unit's choice between two contesting unions (called a *jurisdictional strike)*
- engaging in secondary boycotts against businesses selling or handling nonunion goods
- engaging in sympathy strikes in support of other unions

Taft-Hartley also
- imposed disclosure requirements to regulate union business dealings and uncover fraud and racketeering
- prohibited unions from directly making contributions to candidates running for federal offices
- authorized the President of the United States to postpone strikes in industries deemed essential to national economic health or national security by declaring an 80-day "cooling-off period"
- permitted states to enact right-to-work laws, which outlaw compulsory unionization.

TAIL
Insurance: interval between receipt of premium income and payment of claims. For example, REINSURANCE companies have a long tail as compared to CASUALTY INSURANCE companies.

Treasury auctions: spread in price between the lowest COMPETITIVE BID accepted by the U.S. Treasury for bills, bonds, and notes and the average bid by all those offering to buy such Treasury securities. *See also* TREASURIES.

Underwriting: decimal places following the round-dollar amount of a bid by a potential UNDERWRITER in a COMPETITIVE BID underwriting. For instance, in a bid of $97.3347 for a particular bond issue, the tail is .3347.

TAILGATING unethical practice of a broker who, after a customer has placed an order to buy or sell a certain security, places an order for the same security for his or her own account. The broker hopes to profit either because of information the customer is known or presumed to have or because the customer's purchase is of sufficient size to put pressure on the security price.

TAIWAN STOCK EXCHANGE exchange of the Republic of China, located in Taipei. The *Taiwan Stock Exchange Capitalization Weighted Stock Index* is the oldest and most widely quoted of three leading indices, and is comparable to the STANDARD & POOR'S 500 INDEX in terms of its construction. Trading hours are Monday through Friday from 9 A.M. to noon, and Saturday from 9 A.M. to 11 A.M. Settlement by delivery of stock or cash payment must be made to the commissioning broker by the next business day.

TAKE
In general:
1. profit realized from a transaction.
2. gross receipts of a lottery or gambling enterprise.
3. open to bribery, as in *being on the take.*

Law: to seize possession of property. When a debtor defaults on a debt backed by COLLATERAL, that property is taken back by the creditor.

Securities: act of accepting an OFFER price in a transaction between brokers or dealers.

TAKE A BATH to suffer a large loss on a SPECULATION or investment, as in "I took a bath on my XYZ stock when the market dropped last week."

TAKE A FLIER to speculate, that is, to buy securities with the knowledge that the investment is highly risky.

TAKE A POSITION
1. to buy stock in a company with the intent of holding for the long term or, possibly, of taking control of the company. An acquirer who takes a position of 5% or more of a company's outstanding stock must file information with the Securities and Exchange Commission, the exchange the TARGET COMPANY is listed on, and the target company itself.
2. phrase used when a broker/dealer holds stocks or bonds in inventory. A position may be either long or short. *See also* LONG POSITION; SHORT POSITION.

TAKEDOWN
1. each participating INVESTMENT BANKER'S proportionate share of the securities to be distributed in a new or a secondary offering.
2. price at which the securities are allocated to members of the UNDERWRITING GROUP, particularly in municipal offerings.
   See also UNDERWRITE.

TAKE-HOME PAY amount of salary remaining after all deductions have been taken out. Some of the most common deductions are for federal, state, and local income tax withholding; Social Security tax withholding; health care premiums, flexible spending account contributions; and contributions to salary reduction or other retirement savings plans.

TAKE OFF to rise sharply. For example, when positive news about a company's earnings is released, traders say that the stock takes off. The term is also used referring to the overall movement of stock prices, as in "When the Federal Reserve lowered interest rates, the stock market took off."

TAKE-OR-PAY CONTRACT agreement between a buyer and a seller that obligates the buyer to pay a minimum amount of money for a product or a service, even if the product or service is not delivered. These contracts are most often used in the utility industry to back bonds to finance new power plants. A take-or-pay contract stipulates that the prospective purchaser of the power will take the power from the bond issuer or, if construction is not completed, will repay bondholders the amount of their investment. Take-or-pay contracts are a common way to protect bondholders. In a precedent-setting case in 1983, however, the Washington State Supreme Court voided take-or-pay contracts that many utilities had signed to support the building of the Washington Public Power Supply System (known as WHOOPS) nuclear plants. This action caused WHOOPS to default on some of its bonds, putting a cloud over the validity of the take-or-pay concept.

TAKEOUT

Real estate finance: long-term mortgage loan made to refinance a short-term construction loan (INTERIM LOAN). *See also* STANDBY COMMITMENT.

Securities: withdrawal of cash from a brokerage account, usually after a sale and purchase has resulted in a net CREDIT BALANCE.

TAKEOVER change in the controlling interest of a corporation. A takeover may be a friendly acquisition or an unfriendly bid that the TARGET COMPANY may fight with SHARK REPELLENT techniques. A hostile takeover (aiming to replace existing management) is usually attempted through a public TENDER OFFER. Other approaches might be unsolicited merger proposals to directors, accumulations of shares in the open market, or PROXY FIGHTS that seek to install new directors. *See also* ANY-AND-ALL BID; ARBITRAGEUR; ASSET STRIPPER; BEAR HUG; BLITZKREIG TENDER OFFER; BUST-UP TAKEOVER; CRAM-DOWN DEAL; CROWN JEWELS; DAWN RAID; DEAL STOCK; FAIR-PRICE AMENDMENT; GAP OPENING; GARBATRAGE; GODFATHER OFFER; GOLDEN PARACHUTE; GOODBYE KISS; GREENMAIL; GREY KNIGHT; HIGHLY CONFIDENT LETTER; HIGHJACKING; HOSTILE TAKEOVER; IN PLAY; INSIDER TRADING; KILLER BEES; LADY MACBETH STRATEGY; LEVERAGED BUYOUT; LEVERAGED RECAPITALIZATION; LOCK-UP OPTION; MACARONI DEFENSE; MANAGEMENT BUYOUT; MATERIALITY; MERGER; PAC-MAN STRATEGY; PEOPLE PILL; POISON PILL; POISON PUT; RADAR ALERT; RAIDER; RISK ARBITRAGE; REVERSE LEVERAGED BUYOUT; RUMORTRAGE; SAFE HARBOR; SATURDAY NIGHT SPECIAL; SCHEDULE 13D; SCORCHED EARTH POLICY; SHARK WATCHER; SHOW STOPPER; SLEEPING BEAUTY; STAGGERED BOARD OF DIRECTORS; STANDSTILL AGREEMENT; STOCK BUYBACK; STRATEGIC BUYOUT; SUICIDE PILL; SUPERMAJORITY AMENDMENT; TAKEOVER TARGET; TWO-TIER BID; WAR CHEST; WHITE KNIGHT; WHITEMAIL; WHITE SQUIRE; WILLIAMS ACT.

TAKEOVER ARBITRAGE *see* RISK ARBITRAGE.

TAKEOVER TARGET company that is the object of a takeover offer, whether the offer is friendly or unfriendly. In a HOSTILE TAKEOVER attempt, management tries to use various defensive strategies to repel the acquirer. In a friendly takeover situation, management cooperates with the acquirer, negotiating the best possible price, and recommends that shareholders vote to accept the final offer. *See also* TAKEOVER.

TAKING DELIVERY

In general: accepting receipt of goods from a common carrier or other shipper, usually documented by signing a bill of lading or other form of receipt.

Commodities: accepting physical delivery of a commodity under a FUTURES CONTRACT or SPOT MARKET contract. Delivery requirements, such as the size of the contract and the necessary quality of the commodity, are established by the exchange on which the commodity is traded.

Securities: accepting receipt of stock or bond certificates that have recently been purchased or transferred from another account.

TANGIBLE ASSET any asset not meeting the definition of an INTANGIBLE ASSET, which is a nonphysical right to something presumed to represent an advantage in the marketplace, such as a trademark or patent. Thus tangible assets are clearly those having physical existence, like cash, real estate, or machinery. Yet in accounting, assets such as ACCOUNTS RECEIVABLE are considered tangible, even though they are no more physical than a license or a lease, both of which are considered intangible. In summary: if an asset has physical form it is tangible; if it doesn't, consult a list of what accountants have decided are intangible assets.

TANGIBLE COST oil and gas drilling term meaning the cost of items that can be used over a period of time, such as casings, well fittings, land, and tankage, as distinguished from intangible costs such as drilling, testing, and geologist's expenses. In the most widely used LIMITED PARTNERSHIP sharing arrangements, tangible costs are borne by the GENERAL PARTNER (manager) while intangible costs are borne by the limited partners (investors), usually to be taken as tax deductions. In the event of a dry hole, however, all costs become intangibles. *See also* INTANGIBLE COST.

TANGIBLE NET WORTH total ASSETS less INTANGIBLE ASSETS and total LIABILI-TIES; also called *net tangible assets*. Intangible assets include nonmaterial benefits such as goodwill, patents, copyrights, and trademarks.

TAPE
1. service that reports prices and size of transactions on major exchanges. Also called *composite tape* and *ticker tape* (because of the sound made by the machine that printed the tape before the process was computerized).
2. tape of Dow Jones and other news wires, usually called the BROAD TAPE. *See also* CONSOLIDATED TAPE.

TAPE IS LATE situation in which trading volume is so heavy that the consolidated tape is running more than a minute behind when the actual trades are taking place on the floor of the exchange. The tape will not run faster than 900 characters a minute because the human eye cannot take in information any faster. When trading volume is heavy and the tape is running late, some price digits will first be deleted, and then volume digits will be deleted.

TARGET COMPANY firm that has been chosen as attractive for TAKEOVER by a potential acquirer. The acquirer may buy up to 5% of the target's stock without public disclosure, but it must report all transactions and supply other information to the Securities and Exchange Commission, the exchange the target company is listed on, and the target company itself once 5% or more of the stock is acquired. *See also* TOEHOLD PURCHASE; SCHEDULE 13D; SLEEPING BEAUTY; TENDER OFFER; WILLIAMS ACT.

TARGETED AMORTIZATION CLASS (TAC) BONDS bonds offered as a tranche class of some COLLATERALIZED MORTGAGE OBLIGATIONS (CMOs). TACs are similar to PAC BONDS in that, unlike conventional CMO classes, they are based on a SINKING-FUND schedule. They differ from PAC bonds, however, in that whereas a PAC's amortization is guaranteed as long as prepayments on the underlying mortgages do not exceed certain limits, a TAC's schedule will be met at only one prepayment rate. At other prepayment rates, the TAC will experience either excesses or shortfalls. A TAC bond provides more cash flow stability than a regular CMO class but less than a PAC, and trades accordingly.

TARGET PRICE

Finance: price at which an acquirer aims to buy a company in a TAKEOVER.

Options: price of the underlying security after which a certain OPTION will become profitable to its buyer. For example, someone buying an XYZ 50 call for a PREMIUM of $200 could have a target price of 52, after which point the premium will be recouped and the CALL OPTION will result in a profit when exercised.

Stocks: price that an investor is hoping a stock he or she has just bought will rise to within a specified period of time. An investor may buy XYZ at $20, with a target price of $40 in one year's time, for instance.

TARIFF

1. federal tax on imports or exports usually imposed either to raise revenue (called a *revenue tariff*) or to protect domestic firms from import competition (called a *protective tariff*). A tariff may also be designed to correct an imbalance of payments. The money collected under tariffs is called DUTY or *customs duty*.
2. schedule of rates or charges, usually for freight.

TAXABLE ESTATE portion of an ESTATE that is subject to the UNIFIED TRANSFER TAX of the federal government and to state taxes where they apply. The estate, not the recipients, is taxable on what remains after all expenses, contributions, transfers to a surviving spouse, debts, taxes, and losses. There is a $600,000 federal EXCLUSION on property transferred by the person who died.

TAXABLE EVENT occurrence with tax consequences. For example, if a stock or mutual fund is sold at a profit, capital gains taxes may be due. If a house is sold and the homesellers do not roll their proceeds over into another house within two years, capital gains may be due. Withdrawal of assets from a tax-deferred retirement account is a taxable event because some or all of the proceeds may be considered taxable income in the year withdrawn. Proper TAX PLANNING can help taxpayers time taxable events to maximum advantage.

TAXABLE INCOME amount of income (after all allowable deductions and adjustments to income) subject to tax. On an individual's federal income tax return, taxable income is ADJUSTED GROSS INCOME (the sum of wages, salaries, dividends, interest, capital gains, business income, etc., less allowable adjustments that, in part, include INDIVIDUAL RETIREMENT ACCOUNT contributions, alimony payments, unreimbursed business expenses and CAPITAL LOSSES up to $3000) less itemized or standard deductions and the total of personal exemptions. Once taxable income is known, the individual taxpayer finds the total income tax obligation for his or her TAX BRACKET by checking the Internal Revenue Service tax tables or by calculating the tax according to a rate schedule. TAX CREDITS reduce the tax liability dollar-for-dollar.

NET INCOME of a self-employed person (self-proprietorship) and distributions to members of a partnership are included in adjusted gross income, and hence taxable income, on an individual tax return.

Taxable income of an incorporated business, also called *net income before taxes,* consists of total revenues less cost of goods sold, selling and administrative expenses, interest, and extraordinary items.

TAXABLE MUNICIPAL BOND taxable debt obligation of a state or local government entity, an outgrowth of the TAX REFORM ACT OF 1986 (which restricted the issuance of traditional TAX-EXEMPT SECURITIES). Taxable MUNICIPAL BONDS are issued as PRIVATE PURPOSE BONDS to finance such prohibited projects as a sports stadium; as MUNICIPAL REVENUE BONDS where caps apply; or as PUBLIC PURPOSE BONDS where the 10% private use limitation has been exceeded.

TAX AND LOAN ACCOUNT account in a private-sector depository institution, held in the name of the district Federal Reserve Bank as fiscal agent of the United States, that serves as a repository for operating cash available to the U.S. Treasury. Withheld income taxes, employers' contributions to the Social Security fund, and payments for U.S. government securities routinely go into a tax and loan account.

TAX ANTICIPATION BILL (TAB) short-term obligation issued by the U.S. Treasury in competitive bidding at maturities ranging from 23 to 273 days. TABs typically come due within 5 to 7 days after the quarterly due dates for corporate tax payments, but corporations can tender them at PAR value on those tax deadlines in payment of taxes without forfeiting interest income. Since 1975, TABs have been supplemented by cash management bills, due in 30 days or less, and issued in minimum $10 million blocks. These instruments, which are timed to coincide with the maturity of existing issues, provide the Treasury with additional cash management flexibility while giving large investors a safe place to park temporary funds.

TAX ANTICIPATION NOTE (TAN) short-term obligation of a state or municipal government to finance current expenditures pending receipt of expected tax payments. TAN debt evens out the cash flow and is retired once corporate and individual tax revenues are received.

TAX AUDIT audit by the INTERNAL REVENUE SERVICE (IRS), or state or local tax collecting agency, to determine if a taxpayer paid the correct amount of tax. Returns will be chosen for audits if they have suspiciously high claims for deductions or credits, or if reported income is suspiciously low, or if computer matching of income uncovers discrepancies. Audits may be done on a relatively superficial level, or in great depth. If the auditor finds a tax deficiency, the taxpayer may have to pay back-taxes, as well as interest and penalties. The taxpayer does have the right of appeal through the IRS appeals process and, if warranted, to the U.S. Tax Court and even the U.S. Supreme Court.

TAX AVOIDANCE strategy to pay the least amount of tax possible through legal means. For example, taxpayers may buy tax-free municipal bonds; shelter gains inside tax-deferred IRA or Keogh accounts; shift assets to children who need not pay taxes on part of their income; make legitimate charitable contributions to generate tax deductions; and establish trusts to avoid estate taxes. Illegal strategies to avoid paying taxes are called TAX EVASION.

TAX BASE total amount of taxable property, assets, and income that can be taxed within a specific jurisdiction. A town's tax base is the assessed value of the homes and apartments (minus exempted property), income from businesses, and other sources of taxable activity. If a business moves out of the town, the tax base shrinks, shifting the tax burden onto remaining homeowners and businesses.

TAX BASIS
Finance: original cost of an ASSET, less accumulated DEPRECIATION, that goes into the calculation of a gain or loss for tax purposes. Thus, a property acquired for $100,000 that has been depreciated by $40,000 has a tax basis of $60,000 assuming no other adjustments; sale of that property for $120,000 results in a taxable CAPITAL GAIN of $60,000.

Investments: price at which a stock or bond was purchased, plus brokerage commission. The law requires that a PREMIUM paid on the purchase of an investment be amortized.

TAX BRACKET point on the income-tax rate schedules where TAXABLE INCOME falls; also called *marginal tax bracket.* It is expressed as a percentage to be applied to each additional dollar earned over the base amount for that bracket. Under a PROGRESSIVE TAX system, increases in taxable income lead to higher marginal rates in the form of higher brackets. The TAX REFORM ACT OF 1986, introducing a modified flat tax system, reduced the number of tax brackets for individuals from 15 to 2, starting with the 1988 tax year. (A five-bracket structure, with rates ranging from 11% to 38.5%, was provided for the 1987 transition year.) The two brackets set by the law were 15% and 28%, but a 5% surtax effectively put high-income taxpayers in a marginal tax bracket of 33%. Legislation effective in 1991 eliminated the 5% surcharge and raised the 28% bracket to 31%. The REVENUE RECONCILIATION ACT OF 1993 added a fourth tax bracket of 36% to the existing 15%, 28%, and 31% brackets. It also added a 10% surtax on taxpayers reporting more than $250,000 in taxable income, in effect creating a fifth tax bracket at 39.6%. A DEDUCTION comes off the last marginal dollar earned; thus the 31% taxpayer would save $31 in taxes with each additional $100 of deductions until he worked his way back into the 15% bracket where each $100 deduction would save $15. (A deduction should not be confused with a TAX CREDIT.)

For corporations the 1986 law reduced the number of brackets from five to three. Effective July 1, 1987 (with blended rates applicable to any fiscal year that included that date), firms with taxable income of $50,000 or less were subject to a 15% rate; incomes from $50,000 to $75,000 were taxed at 25%; and incomes from $75,000 and up were taxed at 34%. An additional 5% tax was imposed on income between $100,000 and $335,000, which in effect created a flat tax rate of 34% for corporations with taxable income of $335,000 or more and a 39% effective rate on taxable income in the $100,000 to $335,000 phaseout range. The 1993 Act raised the rate from 34% to 35% for companies with taxable incomes of $10 million or more and imposed a 38% surtax on taxable income between $15 million and $18,333,333. On incomes higher than that, corrporations pay a flat tax of 35%.

TAX CREDIT direct, dollar-for-dollar reduction in tax liability, as distinguished from a tax deduction, which reduces taxes only by the percentage of a taxpayer's TAX BRACKET. (A taxpayer in the 31% tax bracket would get a 31 cent benefit from each $1.00 deduction, for example.) In the case of a tax credit, a taxpayer owing $10,000 in tax would owe $9000 if he took advantage of a $1000 tax credit. Under certain conditions, tax credits are allowed for a pensioner above age 65, income tax paid to a foreign country, child care expenses, rehabilitation of historic properties, conducting research and development, building low-income housing, and providing jobs for economically disadvantaged people.

TAX DEDUCTIBLE expense that generates a tax deduction. For individuals, some items that are tax deductible include charitable contributions, mortgage interest, state and local taxes, and unreimbursed business expenses. In some cases, taxpayers must meet a minimum threshold before an expense is deductible. For example, unreimbursed medical expenses are deductible if they exceed 7.5% of adjusted gross income in a tax year. In order to deduct miscellaneous expenses, they must total at least 2% of adjusted gross income. If that threshold is reached, such expenses as professional dues and subscriptions, employer-required equipment or uniforms, investment and tax advice, and some home office expenses are deductible. For businesses, the costs of doing business are in general tax deductible.

TAX DEDUCTION deductible expense that reduces taxable income for individuals or businesses. *See* TAX DEDUCTIBLE for examples of legal tax deductions.

TAX DEFERRED term describing an investment whose accumulated earnings are free from taxation until the investor takes possession of them. For example, the holder of an INDIVIDUAL RETIREMENT ACCOUNT postpones paying taxes on interest, dividends, or capital appreciation if he or she waits until after age 59½ to cash in those gains. Other examples of tax-deferred investment vehicles include KEOGH PLANS; ANNUITIES; VARIABLE LIFE INSURANCE, WHOLE LIFE INSURANCE, and UNIVERSAL LIFE INSURANCE policies; STOCK PURCHASE or DIVIDEND REINVESTMENT PLANS; and Series EE and Series HH U.S. SAVINGS BONDS.

TAX STATUS ELECTION selection of filing status. Individuals may choose single, married filing jointly, married filing separately, or head of household. Businesses may elect C corporation, S corporation, limited partnership, or sole proprietorship status, among others. Taxpayers may choose to figure their tax return under two filing status categories to find out which status is most advantageous.

TAX EQUITY AND FISCAL RESPONSIBILITY ACT OF 1982 (TEFRA) federal legislation to raise tax revenue, mainly through closing various loopholes and instituting tougher enforcement procedures. Among its major components:
1. penalties for noncompliance with tax laws were increased, and various steps were taken to facilitate the collection of taxes by the Internal Revenue Service (IRS).
2. ten percent of interest and dividends earned was required to be withheld from all bank and brokerage accounts and forwarded directly to the IRS. (This provision was later canceled by Congress after a major lobbying campaign to overturn it.)
3. TAX PREFERENCE ITEMS were added to the old add-on minimum tax to strengthen the ALTERNATIVE MINIMUM TAX.
4. the floor for medical expense deductions was raised from 3% to 5% of ADJUSTED GROSS INCOME (AGI).
5. casualty and theft losses were made deductible only if each loss exceeds $100 and the total excess losses exceed 10% of AGI.
6. deductions for original issue discount bonds were limited to the amount the issuer would deduct as interest if it issued bonds with a face amount equivalent to the actual proceeds and paying the market rate of interest. This amount must be reduced by the amount of the deductions for any actual interest.
7. more rapid rates for recovering costs under the ACCELERATED COST RECOVERY SYSTEM (ACRS), which had been scheduled to go into effect in 1985 and 1986, were repealed.
8. most of the rules providing for SAFE HARBOR leasing transactions authorized under ERTA were repealed.
9. excise taxes were raised to 3% on telephone use, to 16 cents a pack on cigarettes, and to 8% on airline tickets.
10. the Federal Unemployment Tax Act wage base and tax rate were increased.
11. numerous tax incentives for corporate mergers were reduced.
12. net extraction losses in foreign oil and gas operations in one country were allowed to offset net extraction income from such operations in other countries in the computation of oil and gas extraction taxes.
13. most bonds were required to be registered so that the government could ensure that bondholders are reporting interest.

14. As long as they are not prohibited by a Foreign Corrupt Practices Act, payments to foreign officials were authorized to be deducted as legitimate business expenses.

15. the basis of assets that generate tax INVESTMENT CREDITS was reduced by one-half the amount of the credit.

16. pension and profit-sharing qualified plans were curtailed with a series of new rules that restricted plan loans, required withholding on plan distributions, limited estate-tax exclusions on certain plan distributions, and restricted "top-heavy" plans, those tilted to benefit mostly the top-earning employees of a company.

17. changes were made in the way life insurance companies were taxed.

TAX-EQUIVALENT YIELD pretax yield that a taxable bond would have to pay to equal the tax-free yield of a municipal bond in an investor's tax bracket. To figure out the tax-equivalent yield, an investor must subtract his or her marginal tax bracket from 100, which results in the *tax bracket reciprocal*. This figure must then be divided by the yield of the tax-free municipal bond. The result is the yield which a taxable bond would have to pay to give the investor the same dollars in his or her pocket after all taxes were paid. For example, an investor in the 31% tax bracket would first take 31 from 100, producing 69 (the tax bracket reciprocal). To evaluate a 7% tax-free bond, the investor would divide 7% by 69, resulting in a 10.1% yield. Therefore, the investor would have to find a taxable bond paying 10.1% to end up with the same after-tax return as the 7% tax-free bond is offering. In general, the higher tax rates become, the more attractive tax-free income becomes, because it allows investors to escape more taxes than if tax rates were lower. *See also* YIELD EQUIVALENCE.

TAX EVASION illegal practice of intentionally evading taxes. Taxpayers who evade their true tax liability may underreport income, overstate deductions and exemptions, or participate in fraudulent tax shelters. If the taxpayer is caught, tax evasion is subject to criminal penalties, as well as payment of back taxes with interest, and civil penalties. Tax evasion is different from TAX AVOIDANCE, which is the legal use of the tax code to reduce tax liability.

TAX-EXEMPT free from tax liability. This status is granted to municipal bonds, which pay interest that is totally free from federal taxes. Municipal bond interest is also usually tax-exempt to bondholders who are residents of the issuing state. However, other states may impose taxes on interest earned from out-of-state bonds. Certain organizations, such as registered charities, religious organizations, educational institutions, and nonprofit groups, also hold tax-exempt status, meaning that they do not owe taxes to the federal, state, or local governments.

TAX-EXEMPT MONEY MARKET FUND MONEY MARKET FUND invested in short-term municipal securities that are tax-exempt and that thus distributes income tax-free to shareholders. Such funds pay lower income than taxable funds and should be evaluated on an AFTERTAX BASIS.

TAX-EXEMPT SECURITY obligation whose interest is exempt from taxation by federal, state, and/or local authorities. It is frequently called a MUNICIPAL BOND (or simply a *municipal*), even though it may have been issued by a state government or agency or by a county, town, or other political district or subdivision. The security is backed by the FULL FAITH AND CREDIT or by anticipated revenues of the issuing authority. Interest income from tax-exempt municipals is free from federal income taxation as well as from taxation in the jurisdiction where the securities have been issued. Thus, New York City obligations are TRIPLE TAX-EXEMPT to city residents whose income is taxed on the federal, state, and local levels. (A very few municipalities tax residents for their own otherwise tax-exempt issues.)

MUTUAL FUNDS that invest exclusively in tax-exempt securities confer the same tax advantages on their shareholders. However, while a fund's dividends would be entirely tax-exempt on a shareholder's federal tax return, they would be free from state income tax only in proportion to the amount of interest income derived from the taxpayer's home state, assuming no interstate reciprocity arrangements pertain.

The return to investors from a tax-exempt bond is less than that from a corporate bond, because the tax exemption provides extra compensation; the higher the TAX BRACKET of the investor, the more attractive the tax-free alternative becomes. Municipal bond yields vary according to local economic factors, the issuer's perceived ability to repay, and the security's quality RATING assigned by one of the bond-rating agencies. *See also* MORAL OBLIGATION BOND.

TAX-FREE EXCHANGE *see* 1031 TAX-FREE EXCHANGE.

TAX LIABILITY income, property, sales, or other taxes owed to a government entity. *See also* PROVISION FOR INCOME TAXES.

TAX HAVEN country offering outside businesses and individuals an environment with little or no taxation. Several Caribbean islands, such as the Cayman Islands, have attracted billions of dollars in bank deposits by creating a tax haven. Depositors and businesses not only lower the tax burdens in their home countries, but also are subject to less regulation and increased privacy for their financial affairs.

TAX LIEN statutory right obtained by a government to enforce a claim against the property of a person owing taxes until the debt is paid.

TAX LOSS CARRYBACK, CARRYFORWARD tax benefit that allows a company or individual to apply losses to reduce tax liability. A company may OFFSET the current year's capital or NET OPERATING LOSSES against profits in the three immediately preceding years, with the earliest year first. After the carryback, it may carry forward (also called a *carryover*) capital losses five years and net operating losses up to 15 years. By then it will presumably have regained financial health.

Individuals may carry over capital losses until they are used up for an unlimited number of years to offset capital gains. Unlike corporations, however, individuals generally cannot carry back losses to apply to prior years' tax returns. The 1986 tax act curbed tax-motivated BUYOUTS by limiting the use of NOLs where a loss corporation has had a 50% or more ownership change in a three-year period. A special set of complex rules pertains to carryback of losses for trading in commodity futures contracts.

The Revenue Reconciliation Act of 1993 introduced a provision requiring that short-term loss be first applied to reduce any long-term gain. Since previously the short-term loss would have been deductible against ordinary income up to $3000 per year, the provision effectively reduces the long-term gain available for the favorable long-term capital gains rate.

TAX PLANNING strategy of minimizing tax liability for an individual or company by analyzing the tax implications of various options throughout a tax year. Tax planning involves choosing a FILING STATUS, figuring out the most advantageous time to realize capital gains and losses, knowing when to accelerate deductions and postpone income or vice versa, setting up a proper estate plan to reduce estate taxes, and other legitimate tax-saving moves.

TAX PREFERENCE ITEM item specified by the tax law that a taxpayer must include when calculating ALTERNATIVE MINIMUM TAX (AMT). Under the REVENUE RECONCILIATION ACT OF 1993, preference items include: net PASSIVE losses (subject to complex requirements); the (adjusted) excess of MODIFIED ACCELERATED COST RECOVERY SYSTEM (MACRS) deductions over alternative depreciation system (ADS) deductions (ADS is an alternative depreciation system with longer deduction periods); certain INTANGIBLE COSTS; the excess of fair market value at exercise date over option cost for INCENTIVE STOCK OPTIONS; and tax-exempt interest on PRIVATE PURPOSE BONDS of municipalities issued after August 7, 1986. Untaxed appreciation of property contributed to charity, a tax preference item under the 1986 Act, was eliminated by the 1993 Act. Corporate preferences are generally the same as for individuals, but in addition include an adjustment for current earnings (ACE) aimed at profits reported to shareholders but not regularly taxed. The ACE adjustment is based on 75% of the difference between a corporation's alternative minimum taxable income (AMTI) for the tax year and its adjusted earnings and profits. The depreciation deduction for PERSONAL PROPERTY, a large part of AMTI, was made less liberal by the 1993 Act, which requires use of the 150% declining balance method instead of the 200% method allowed by the previous law. The depreciation adjustment required for the ACE calculation was eliminated, however, for property put in service after December 31, 1993. *See also* TAX EQUITY AND FISCAL RESPONSIBILITY ACT OF 1982; TAX REFORM ACT OF 1976; TAX REFORM ACT OF 1986.

TAX PREPARATION SERVICES businesses that specialize in preparing tax returns. Such services may range from national tax preparation chains such as H&R Block to local tax preparers, enrolled agents, CPA accountants, and tax lawyers. Services normally charge based on the complexity of the tax return and the amount of time needed to fill it out correctly. Many services can arrange to file a tax return with the Internal Revenue Service electronically, which can result in a faster TAX REFUND.

TAX RATE percentage of tax to be paid on a certain level of income. The United States uses a system of marginal tax rates, meaning that the rates rise with taxable income. The top rate is paid only on the portion of income over the threshold. Currently, the federal government has four tax rates—15%, 28%, 31%, and 36%. There is also a 10% surtax on married couples filing jointly reporting taxable incomes of more than $250,000 or married couples filing separately with taxable incomes of more than $125,000. This creates an effective fifth tax rate of 39.6%.

TAX REFORM ACT OF 1976 federal legislation that tightened several provisions and benefits relating to taxation, beginning in the 1976 tax year. Among its major provisions:
1. extended the long-term CAPITAL GAINS holding period from six months to nine months in 1977 and to 12 months beginning in 1978.
2. instituted new rules on determining the TAX BASIS of inherited property.
3. set a new minimum capital gains tax on the sale of a house.
4. established, for homeowners over age 65, a once-in-a-lifetime exclusion of up to $35,000 in capital gains tax on the sale of a principal residence. (This amount was later raised by other tax bills, until it stood at $125,000 in the mid-1980s.)
5. increased the maximum net CAPITAL LOSS deduction from ordinary income on a personal income tax return to $3000 beginning in 1978.
6. extended the period of tax loss carryforward from five years to seven; gave companies the option of carrying losses forward without having first to carry them back; and prohibited acquiring corporations from taking advantage of an acquired firm's loss carryovers unless it gave the acquired firm's stockholders continuing ownership in the combined company.

7. limited deductions for home-office expenses to cases where homes are used as principal business locations, or for meeting with clients.
8. disallowed owners who rent their vacation homes from reporting losses, deducting maintenance costs or taking depreciation on those rentals unless the owners themselves used the homes less than two weeks per year, or less than 10% of total rental time.
9. instituted a deduction up to $3000 for "indirect" moving costs if a new job is more than 35 miles from a previous job.
10. established a child-care tax credit of up to $400 for one child and up to $800 for more than one child.
11. allowed a divorced parent, if contributing at least $1200 in child support, to claim a child as a dependent deduction.
12. instituted a spousal INDIVIDUAL RETIREMENT ACCOUNT, which allowed non-working spouses to contribute up to $250.
13. disallowed losses on tax shelters financed through loans made without any obligation to pay, or where taxpayer's risk is limited by a form of guarantee, except for real estate investments.
14. treated the exercise of a STOCK OPTION as ordinary income rather than as a CAPITAL GAIN.

TAX REFORM ACT OF 1984 legislation enacted by Congress as part of the Deficit Reduction Act of 1984 to reduce the federal budget deficit. The following are highlights from the more than 100 provisions in the Act:

1. shortened the minimum holding period for assets to qualify for long-term capital gains treatment from one year to six months.
2. allowed contributions to be made to an INDIVIDUAL RETIREMENT ACCOUNT no later than April 15 after the tax year for which an IRA benefit is sought; previously the cut-off was the following October 15th.
3. allowed the Internal Revenue Service to tax the benefits of loans made on below-market, interest-free, or "gift" terms.
4. tightened INCOME AVERAGING requirements.
5. set a $150 per capita limit on the amount of INDUSTRIAL DEVELOPMENT BONDS that a state could issue in a year, and permitted interest to be tax-exempt only for certain "small issues."
6. retained the 15% minimum tax on corporate TAX PREFERENCE ITEMS as in the TAX REFORM ACT OF 1976, but increased from 15% to 20% the deduction allowed for a tax preference item.
7. restricted GOLDEN PARACHUTE payments to executives by eliminating the corporate tax deductibility of these payments and subjecting them to a nondeductible 20% excise tax.
8. required registration of TAX SHELTERS with the Internal Revenue Service and set penalties for failure to comply. Also set penalties for overvaluing assets used for depreciation in a tax shelter.
9. expanded rules in ERTA to cover additional types of stock and options transactions that make up TAX STRADDLES.
10. repealed the 30% withholding tax on interest, dividends, rents, and royalties paid to foreign investors by U.S. corporations and government agencies.
11. raised the liquor tax, reduced the cigarette tax, and extended the 3% telephone excise tax.
12. delayed to 1987 the scheduled decline in estate and gift taxes.
13. granted a specific tax exemption for many fringe benefits.
14. extended mortgage subsidy bonds through 1988.
15. required ALTERNATIVE MINIMUM TAX quarterly estimated payments.
16. changed the rules affecting taxation of life insurance companies.

17. disqualified from eligibility for long-term capital gains tax the appreciation of market discounts on newly issued ORIGINAL ISSUE DISCOUNT bonds.

18. real estate depreciation was lengthened from 15 to 18 years.

19. delayed implementation of new finance leasing rules until 1988.

20. restricted the sale of unused depreciation tax deductions by tax-exempt entities to companies that can use the deductions.

21. phased out the graduated corporate income tax on the first $100,000 of income for corporations with income over $1 million.

22. created Foreign Sales Corporations (FSCs) to provide American companies with tax deferral advantages to encourage exports.

23. limited tax breaks for luxury automobiles to a maximum writeoff of $16,000 in the first three years of ownership.

24. increased the earned income tax credit for lower-income taxpayers from 10% to a maximum of 11% of the first $5000 of income.

25. eliminated the tax on property transfers in a divorce.

26. increased the standard automobile mileage rate from 9 cents a mile to 12 cents a mile for expenses incurred in volunteer charity work.

27. tightened rules and increased penalties for those who try to inflate deductions by overvaluing property donated to charity.

TAX REFORM ACT OF 1986 landmark federal legislation enacted that made comprehensive changes in the system of U.S. taxation. Among the law's major provisions:

Provisions Affecting Individuals

1. lowered maximum marginal tax rates from 50% to 28% beginning in 1988 and reduced the number of basic TAX BRACKETS from 15 to 2—28% and 15%. Also instituted a 5% rate surcharge for high-income taxpayers.

2. eliminated the preferential tax treatment of CAPITAL GAINS. Starting in 1988, all gains realized on asset sales were taxed at ordinary income rates, no matter how long the asset was held.

3. increased the personal exemption to $1900 in 1987, $1950 in 1988, and $2000 in 1989. Phased out exemption for high-income taxpayers.

4. increased the STANDARD DEDUCTION, and indexed it to inflation starting in 1989.

5. repealed the deduction for two-earner married couples.

6. repealed income averaging for all taxpayers.

7. repealed the $100 ($200 for couples) dividend exclusion.

8. restricted the deductibility of IRA contributions.

9. mandated the phaseout of consumer interest deductibility by 1991.

10. allowed investment interest expense to be offset against investment income, dollar-for-dollar, without limitation.

11. limited unreimbursed medical expenses that could be deducted to amounts in excess of 7.5% of adjusted gross income.

12. limited the tax deductibility of interest on a first or second home mortgage to the purchase price of the house plus the cost of improvements and amounts used for medical or educational purposes.

13. repealed the deductibility of state and local sales taxes.

14. limited miscellaneous deductions to expenses exceeding 2% of adjusted gross income.

15. limited the deductibility of itemized charitable contributions.

16. strengthened the ALTERNATIVE MINIMUM TAX, and raised the rate to 21%.

17. tightened home office deductions.

18. Lowered the deductibility of business entertainment and meal expenses from 100% to 80%.

19. eliminated the benefits of CLIFFORD TRUSTS and other income-shifting devices by taxing unearned income over $1000 on gifts to children under 14 years old at the grantor's tax rate.
20. repealed the tax credit for political contributions.
21. limited the use of losses from PASSIVE activity to offsetting income from passive activity.
22. lowered the top rehabilitation tax credit from 25% to 20%.
23. made all unemployment compensation benefits taxable.
24. repealed the deduction for attending investment seminars.
25. eased the rules for exercise of INCENTIVE STOCK OPTIONS.
26. imposed new limitations on SALARY REDUCTION PLANS and SIMPLIFIED EMPLOYEE PENSION (SEP) PLANS.

Provisions Affecting Business

27. lowered the top corporate tax rate to 34% from 46%, and lowered the number of corporate tax brackets from five to three.
28. applied the ALTERNATIVE MINIMUM TAX (AMT) to corporations, and set a 20% rate.
29. repealed the investment tax credit for property placed in service after 1985.
30. altered the method of calculating DEPRECIATION.
31. Limited the deductibility of charges to BAD DEBT reserves to financial institutions with less than $500 million in assets.
32. extended the research and development tax credit. but lowered the rate from 25% to 20%.
33. eliminated the deductibility of interest that banks pay to finance tax-exempt securities holdings.
34. eliminated the deductibility of GREENMAIL payments by companies warding off hostile takeover attempts.
35. restricted COMPLETED CONTRACT METHOD accounting for tax purposes.
36. limited the ability of a company acquiring more than 50% of another firm to use NET OPERATING LOSSES to offset taxes.
37. reduced the corporate DIVIDEND EXCLUSION from 85% to 80%.
38. limited cash and installment method accounting for tax purposes.
39. restricted tax-exemption on MUNICIPAL BONDS to PUBLIC PURPOSE BONDS and specified PRIVATE PURPOSE BONDS. Imposed caps on the dollar amount of permitted private purpose bonds. Limited PREREFUNDING. Made interest on certain private purpose bonds subject to the AMT.
40. amended the rules for qualifying as a REAL ESTATE INVESTMENT TRUST and the taxation of REITs.
41. set up tax rules for real estate mortgage investment conduits (REMICs).
42. changed many rules relating to taxation of foreign operations of U.S. multinational companies.
43. liberalized the requirements for employee VESTING rules in a company's qualified pension plan, and changed other rules affecting employee benefit plans.
44. enhanced benefit of SUBCHAPTER S corporation status.

TAX REFORM ACT OF 1993 *see* REVENUE RECONCILIATION ACT OF 1993.

TAX REFUND refund of overpaid taxes from the government to the taxpayer. Refunds are due when the taxpayer has been OVERWITHHOLDING, or has overestimated income or underestimated deductions, exemptions, and credits. Though taxpayers may like the fact that they are getting a tax refund, in fact they are granting the government an interest-free loan for most of the year, which is not astute TAX PLANNING.

TAX SCHEDULES tax forms used in addition to the Form 1040 to report itemized deductions (Schedule A); dividend and interest income (Schedule B); profit or loss from business (Schedule C); capital gains and losses (Schedule D); supplemental income and loss (Schedule E); and Social Security Self-employment tax (Schedule SE).

TAX SELLING selling of securities, usually at year end, to realize losses in a PORTFOLIO, which can be used to OFFSET capital gains and thereby lower an investor's tax liability. *See also* LONG TERM GAIN; LONG TERM LOSS; SELLING SHORT AGAINST THE BOX; SHORT TERM GAIN OR LOSS; SWAP; THIRTY-DAY WASH RULE.

TAX SHIELD deductions that reduce tax liabilities. For example, mortgage interest, charitable contributions, unreimbursed business expenses, and medical expenses can be considered tax shields if a taxpayer qualifies for the deduction. The higher the marginal tax rate, the more the deduction is worth.

TAX SHELTER method used by investors to legally avoid or reduce tax liabilities. Legal shelters include those using DEPRECIATION of assets like real estate or equipment or DEPLETION allowances for oil and gas exploration. LIMITED PARTNERSHIPS have traditionally offered investors limited liability and tax benefits including "flow through" operating losses usable to offset income from other sources. The TAX REFORM ACT OF 1986 dealt a severe blow to such tax shelters by ruling that PASSIVE losses could be used only to offset passive income, by lengthening depreciation schedules, and by extending AT RISK rules to include real estate investments. Vehicles that allow tax-deferred capital growth. such as INDIVIDUAL RETIREMENT ACCOUNTS (IRAs) and KEOGH PLANS (which also provide current tax deductions for qualified taxpayers), SALARY REDUCTION PLANS, and SINGLE PREMIUM LIFE INSURANCE, are also popular tax shelters as are tax-exempt MUNICIPAL BONDS.

TAX SOFTWARE software that helps taxpayers plan for and prepare their tax returns. Software such as TurboTax and TaxCut helps taxpayers analyze their tax situation and take actions to minimize tax liability. Different versions of tax software are appropriate for large and small businesses, partnerships, individuals, and estates. The software also comes in state-specific versions to aid in preparation and planning for state taxes. When integrated with a personal finance software package, a taxpayer does not have to reenter data, which can easily be exchanged from the personal finance side into the tax preparation side of the package.

TAX STRADDLE technique whereby OPTION or FUTURES CONTRACTS are used to eliminate economic risk while creating an advantageous tax position. In its most common use, an investor with a CAPITAL GAIN would take a position creating an offsetting "artificial" loss in the current tax year and postponing the gain until the next tax year. The ECONOMIC RECOVERY TAX ACT OF 1981 curtailed this practice by requiring traders to MARK TO THE MARKET at year-end and include unrealized gains in taxable income. The TAX REFORM ACT OF 1986 introduced a change whereby an exception for COVERED WRITERS of calls is denied if the taxpayer fails to hold the covered CALL OPTION for 30 days after the related stock is disposed of at a loss, if gain on the termination or disposition of the option is included in the next year.

TAX UMBRELLA tax loss carryforwards stemming from losses of a firm in past years, which shield profits earned in current and future years from taxes. *See also* TAX LOSS CARRYBACK, CARRYFORWARD.

TEAR SHEET sheet from one of a dozen loose-leaf books comprising Standard & Poor's Stock Reports, which provide essential background and financial data on several thousand companies. Brokers often tear and mail these sheets to customers (hence the name).

TEASER RATE introductory interest rate on an adjustable rate mortgage (ARM) designed to entice borrowers. The teaser rate may last for a few months, or as long as a year, before the rate returns to a market level. In a competitive mortgage market, some mortgage lenders may offer competing teaser rates to try to win over potential borrowers. In addition to the marketing rationale for teaser rates, lenders maintain that having a low initial rate makes it easier for homeowners to settle into a new home, with all the expenses entailed in moving in. Only portfolio lenders can offer teaser rates. Mortgage bankers cannot because they must comply with investor guidelines.

TECHNICAL ANALYSIS research into the demand and supply for securities, options, mutual funds, and commodities based on trading volume and price studies. Technical analysts use charts or computer programs to identify and project price trends in a market, security, fund, or futures contract. Most analysis is done for the short- or intermediate-term, but some technicians also predict long-term cycles based on charts and other data. Unlike FUNDAMENTAL ANALYSIS, technical analysis is not concerned with the financial position of a company. *See also* ADVANCE/DECLINE (A/D); ASCENDING TOPS; BREAKOUT; CORRECTION; DEAD CAT BOUNCE; DESCENDING TOPS; DIP; DOUBLE BOTTOM; ELVES; FALL OUT OF BED; FLAG; FLURRY; GAP; GAP OPENING; HEAD AND SHOULDERS; HORIZONTAL PRICE MOVEMENT; MOVING AVERAGE; NEW HIGH/NEW LOW; PENNANT; POINT AND FIGURE CHART; PUT-CALL RATIO; RESISTANCE LEVEL; REVERSAL; RISING BOTTOMS; SAUCER; SELLING CLIMAX; SUPPORT LEVEL; TRADING PATTERN; TRIANGLE; V FORMATION; VERTICAL LINE CHARTING; W FORMATION.

TECHNICAL RALLY short rise in securities or commodities futures prices within a general declining trend. Such a rally may result because investors are bargain-hunting or because analysts have noticed a particular SUPPORT LEVEL at which securities usually bounce up. Technical rallies do not last long, however, and soon after prices resume their declining pattern.

TECHNICAL SIGN short-term trend that technical analysts can identify as significant in the price movement of a security or a commodity. *See also* TECHNICAL ANALYSIS.

TED SPREAD difference between interest rates on U.S. Treasury bills and Eurodollars. The term *Ted* refers to *Treasuries over Eurodollars*. Many traders in the futures markets actively trade the Ted spread, speculating that the difference between U.S. Treasuries and Eurodollars will widen or narrow. The Ted spread also is used as an indicator of confidence in the U.S. government and the general level of fear or confidence in the markets for private financing. A narrow spread indicates confidence in financial markets in general and the U.S. Government in particular. When the spread is wide, confidence is diminished. *See also* FLIGHT TO QUALITY.

TEFRA *see* TAX EQUITY AND FISCAL RESPONSIBILITY ACT OF 1982.

TEL AVIV STOCK EXCHANGE only stock exchange in Israel. Trading hours for stocks, warrants, and convertible bonds are 10:30 A.M. to 3:30 P.M., Sunday through Thursday. Options are traded on the 25 companies with highest market value that are part of the *Maof Index*. All other derivatives and all shares are reflected in the *General Share Index*. Trades are settled on the day following the trade.

TELEPHONE SWITCHING process of shifting assets from one MUTUAL FUND or VARIABLE ANNUITY portfolio to another by telephone. Such a switch may be among the stock, bond, or money-market funds of a single FAMILY OF FUNDS, or it may be from a fund in one family to a fund in another. Transfers involving portfolios in annuity contracts do not trigger taxation of gains as do mutual fund switches.

TEMPORARY INVESTMENT investment designed to be held for a short period of time, typically a year or less. Some examples of temporary investments are money market mutual funds, money market deposit accounts, NOW checking accounts, Treasury bills, and short-term CDs. Investors shifting money into such investments may have sold stocks, bonds, or mutual funds, and are keeping their assets liquid while they decide which investments to buy next. They also may be fearful that securities prices are about to fall, and they want to keep their assets in temporary investments to sidestep such a downdraft. While their money is in temporary investments, it continues to earn interest at prevailing market interest rates.

TENANCY AT WILL tenancy where a person holds or occupies real estate with the permission of the owner, for an unspecified term. A tenancy at will could occur when a lease is being negotiated, or under a valid oral lease or contract of sale. All the duties and obligations of a landlord-tenant relationship exist. Notice of termination is required by either party. The tenancy is not assignable.

TENANCY BY THE ENTIRETY (TBE) form of individual (versus corporate or partnership) co-ownership in which ownership passes automatically at the death of one co-owner to the surviving co-owner. The person with a TBE co-ownership interest lacks the power to freely dispose of that interest by WILL. In this respect, it is similar to JOINT TENANCY WITH RIGHT OF SURVIVORSHIP (JTWROS). Unlike JTWROS, however, the TBE ownership interests are limited to ownership by two persons who are husband and wife at the time the property is acquired. If the married couple then divorces, the form of ownership automatically changes to TENANCY IN COMMON (TIC). Generally, TBE ownership is limited to real estate, although about a dozen states permit TBE ownership of personal property.

TENANCY IN COMMON (TIC) ownership of real or personal property by two or more persons in which ownership at the death of one co-owner is part of the owner's disposable ESTATE, and does not pass to the co-owner(s). There is no limit to the number of persons who can acquire property as TIC, and those persons could be, but need not be married to each other.

TENANT
  Real Estate: (1) holder or possessor of real property; (2) lessee.
  Securities: part owner of a security.
  See also JOINT TENANTS WITH RIGHT OF SURVIVORSHIP; TENANCY IN COMMON.

TENBAGGER stock that grows in value by ten times. The term comes from baseball lingo, since a double is called a two-bagger because it earns the hitter the right to two bases, or bags. Similarly, a triple is a three-bagger and a home run a four-bagger. The term, as applied to investing, is also used in larger multiples, such as a twenty-bagger, for a stock that grows twenty-fold.

TENDER
  1. act of surrendering one's shares in a corporation in response to an offer to buy them at a set price. *See also* TENDER OFFER.
  2. to submit a formal bid to buy a security, as in a U.S. Treasury bill auction. *See also* DUTCH AUCTION.

3. offer of money or goods in settlement of a prior debt or claim, as in the delivery of goods on the due date of a FUTURES CONTRACT.
4. agreed-upon medium for the settlement of financial transactions, such as U.S. currency, which is labeled "legal tender for all debts, public and private."

TENDER OFFER offer to buy shares of a corporation, usually at a PREMIUM above the shares' market price, for cash, securities, or both, often with the objective of taking control of the TARGET COMPANY. A tender offer may arise from friendly negotiations between the company and a corporate suitor or may be unsolicited and possibly unfriendly, resulting in countermeasures being taken by the target firm. The Securities and Exchange Commission requires any corporate suitor accumulating 5% or more of a target company to make disclosures to the SEC, the target company, and the relevant exchange. *See also* SCHEDULE 13D; TAKEOVER; TREASURY STOCK.

1040 EZ FORM simplified alternative to the 1040 FORM for taxpayers who (1) have single filing status; (2) are under age 65; (3) are not blind; (4) claim no dependents; (5) have taxable income under $50,000; (6) have income only from wages, tips, and taxable interest below $400; and (7) are not liable for supplemental Medicare premiums.

1040 FORM Basic form issued by the INTERNAL REVENUE SERVICE for individual tax returns. *See also* TAX SCHEDULES.

10-K REPORT *see* FORM 10-K.

1099 annual statement sent to the Internal Revenue Service and to taxpayers by the payers of dividends (1099-DIV) and interest (1099-INT) and by issuers of taxable ORIGINAL ISSUE DISCOUNT securities (1099-OID).

TEN PERCENT GUIDELINE MUNICIPAL BOND analysts' guideline that funded debt over 10% of the ASSESSED VALUATION of taxable property in a municipality is excessive.

1034 EXCHANGE (ROLLOVER) provision of Section 1034 of the Internal Revenue Code that permits personal residences to be sold without gain or loss if another home is purchased within 48 months and the new home costs at least as much as the sales price of the old home less selling and fixing-up expenses.

1031 TAX-FREE EXCHANGE "like-kind" exchange of business or investment property that is free of capital gain taxation under Section 1031 of the Internal Revenue Code. Properties held for rental income, for business purposes, as investment property, or as vacation homes may be exchanged for qualifying like-kind property (a piece of land and a building can be traded because both are real estate), provided certain conditions are met: (1) the seller must identify the replacement property within 45 days after escrow on the old property and (2) the seller must take title to the new property within the earlier of 180 days of the old property's close of escrow or the seller's tax deadline. To the extent *boot,* meaning cash or additional property, is part of the exchange, the transaction is taxable. *See also* POOLING OF INTERESTS.

TERM
1. period of time during which the conditions of a contract will be carried out. This may refer to the time in which loan payments must be made, or the time when interest payments will be made on a certificate of deposit or a bond. It also may refer to the length of time a life insurance policy is in force. *See also* TERM LIFE INSURANCE.

2. provision specifying the nature of an agreement or contract, as in *terms and conditions.*

3. period of time an official or board member is elected or appointed to serve. For example, Federal Reserve governors are appointed for 14-year terms.

TERM CERTIFICATE CERTIFICATE OF DEPOSIT with a longer-term maturity date. Such CDs can range in length from one year to ten years, though the most popular term certificates are those for one or two years. Certificate holders usually receive a fixed rate of interest, payable semiannually during the term, and are subject to costly EARLY WITHDRAWAL PENALTIES if the certificate is cashed in before the scheduled maturity.

TERMINATION BENEFIT *see* SEVERANCE PAY.

TERM LIFE INSURANCE form of life insurance, written for a specified period, that requires the policyholder to pay only for the cost of protection against death; that is, no cash value is built up as in WHOLE LIFE INSURANCE. Every time the policy is renewed, the premium is higher, since the insured is older and therefore statistically more likely to die. Term insurance is far cheaper than whole life, giving policyholders the alternative of using the savings to invest on their own.

TERM LOAN intermediate- to long-term (typically, two to ten years) secured credit granted to a company by a commercial bank, insurance company, or commercial finance company usually to finance capital equipment or provide working capital. The loan is amortized over a fixed period, sometimes ending with a BALLOON payment. Borrowers under term loan agreements are normally required to meet minimum WORKING CAPITAL and debt to net worth tests, to limit dividends, and to maintain continuity of management.

TEST

In general: examination to determine knowledge, competence, or qualifications.

Finance: criterion used to measure compliance with financial ratio requirements of indentures and other loan agreements (e.g., a current asset to current liability test or a debt to net worth test). *See also* QUICK RATIO.

Securities: term used in reference to a price movement that approaches a SUPPORT LEVEL or a RESISTANCE LEVEL established earlier by a commodity future, security, or market. A test is passed if the levels are not penetrated and is failed if prices go on to new lows or highs. Technical analysts say, for instance, that if the Dow Jones Industrials last formed a solid base at 4000, and prices have been falling from 4200, a period of testing is approaching. If prices rebound once the Dow hits 4000 and go up further, the test is passed. If prices continue to drop below 4000, however, the test is failed. *See also* TECHNICAL ANALYSIS.

TESTAMENT synonym for a WILL, a document that will dispose of property a person owns at his or her death. The testament is created by the TESTATOR or TESTATRIX, usually with the aid of an estate planning lawyer or will-writing software.

TESTAMENTARY TRUST trust created by a will, as distinguished from an INTER VIVOS TRUST created during the lifetime of the GRANTOR.

TESTATE having made and left a valid WILL; a person who dies with a will is said to die testate. A person who dies without a will is said to die INTESTATE.

TESTATOR/TESTATRIX a man/woman who has made and left a valid WILL at his/her death.

THEORETICAL VALUE (OF A RIGHT) mathematically determined MARKET VALUE of a SUBSCRIPTION RIGHT after the offering is announced but before the stock goes EX-RIGHTS. The formula includes the current market value of the common stock, the subscription price, and the number of rights required to purchase a share of stock:

theoretical value of a right

$$= \frac{\text{market value of common stock} - \text{subscription price per share}}{\text{number of rights needed to buy 1 share} + 1}$$

Thus, if the common stock market price is $50 per share, the subscription price is $45 per share, and the subscription ratio is 4 to 1, the value of one right would be $1:

$$\frac{50 - 45}{4 + 1} \quad = \quad \frac{5}{5} = 1$$

THIN MARKET market in which there are few bids to buy and few offers to sell. A thin market may apply to an entire class of securities or commodities futures such as small OVER THE COUNTER stocks or the platinum market—or it may refer to a particular stock, whether exchange-listed or over-the-counter. Prices in thin markets are more volatile than in markets with great LIQUIDITY, since the few trades that take place can affect prices significantly. Institutional investors who buy and sell large blocks of stock tend to avoid thin markets, because it is difficult for them to get in or out of a POSITION without materially affecting the stock's price.

THIRD MARKET nonexchange-member broker/dealers and institutional investors trading OVER THE COUNTER in exchange-listed securities. The third market rose to importance in the 1950s when institutional investors began buying common stocks as an inflation hedge and fixed commission rates still prevailed on the exchanges. By trading large blocks with nonmember firms, they both saved commissions and avoided the unsettling effects on prices that large trades on the exchanges produced. After commission rates were deregulated in May 1975, a number of the firms active in the third market became member firms so they could deal with members as well as nonmembers. At the same time, member firms began increasingly to move large blocks of stock off the floor of the exchanges, in effect becoming participants in the third market. Before selling securities off the exchange to a nonmember, however, a member firm must satisfy all LIMIT ORDERS on the SPECIALIST'S BOOK at the same price or higher. *See also* OFF-FLOOR ORDER.

THIRD-PARTY CHECK
1. check negotiated through a bank, except one payable to the writer of the check (that is, a check written for cash). The *primary party* to a transaction is the bank on which a check is drawn. The *secondary party* is the drawer of the check against funds on deposit in the bank. The *third party* is the payee who endorses the check.
2. double-endorsed check. In this instance, the payee endorses the check by signing the back, then passes the check to a subsequent holder, who endorses it prior to cashing it. Recipients of checks with multiple endorsers are reluctant to accept them unless they can verify each endorser's signature.
3. payable-through drafts and other negotiable orders not directly serviced by the providing company. For example, a check written against a money market mutual fund is processed not by the mutual fund company but typically by a

commercial bank that provides a "third-party" or "payable-through" service. Money orders, credit union share drafts, and checks drawn against a brokerage account are other examples of payable-through or third-party items.

THIRD WORLD name for the less developed countries of Africa, Asia, and Latin America.

THIRTY-DAY VISIBLE SUPPLY total dollar volume of new MUNICIPAL BONDS carrying maturities of 13 months or more that are scheduled to reach the market within 30 days. The figure is supplied on Thursdays in the *BOND BUYER.*

THIRTY-DAY WASH RULE Internal Revenue Service rule stating that losses on a sale of stock may not be used as losses for tax purposes (that is, used to OFFSET gains) if equivalent stock is purchased within 30 days before or 30 after the date of sale.

THREE STEPS AND A STUMBLE RULE rule holding that stock and bond prices will fall if the Federal Reserve raises the DISCOUNT RATE three times in a row. By raising interest rates, the Federal Reserve both raises the cost of borrowing for companies and makes alternative investments such as money market funds and CDs relatively more attractive than stocks and bonds. Many market historians have tracked this rule, and found it to be a good predictor of drops in stock and bond prices.

THRIFT INSTITUTION organization formed primarily as a depository for consumer savings, the most common varieties of which are the SAVINGS AND LOAN ASSOCIATION and the SAVINGS BANK. Traditionally, savings institutions have loaned most of their deposit funds in the residential mortgage market. Deregulation in the early 1980s expanded their range of depository services and allowed them to make commercial and consumer loans. Degregulation led to widespread abuse by savings and loans that used insured deposits to engage in speculative real estate lending. This resulted in the OFFICE OF THRIFT SUPERVISION (OTS), established in 1989 by the FINANCIAL INSTITUTIONS REFORM AND RECOVERY ACT (FIRREA), popularly known as the "bailout bill." CREDIT UNIONS are sometimes included in the thrift institution category, since their principal source of deposits is also personal savings, though they have traditionally made small consumer loans, not mortgage loans. *See also* DEPOSITORY INSTITUTIONS DEREGULATION AND MONETARY CONTROL ACT; MUTUAL ASSOCIATION; MUTUAL SAVINGS BANK.

TICK upward or downward price movement in a security's trades. Technical analysts watch the tick of a stock's successive up or down moves to get a feel of the stock's trend. The term also applies to the overall market. In futures and options trading, a minimum change in price up or down. *See also* CLOSING TICK; DOWNTICK; MINUS TICK; PLUS TICK; SHORT SALE RULE; TECHNICAL ANALYSIS; TRIN; UPTICK; ZERO-MINUS TICK; ZERO-PLUS TICK.

TICKER system that produces a running report of trading activity on the stock exchanges, called the TICKER TAPE. The name derives from machines that, in times past, printed information by punching holes in a paper tape, making an audible ticking sound as the tape was fed forth. Today's ticker tape is a computer screen and the term is used to refer both to the CONSOLIDATED TAPE, which shows the STOCK SYMBOL, latest price, and volume of trades on the exchanges, and to news ticker services. *See also* QUOTATION BOARD; TICKER TAPE.

TICKER SYMBOL letters that identify a security for trading purposes on the CONSOLIDATED TAPE, such as XON for Exxon Corporation. *See also* STOCK SYMBOL; TICKER TAPE.

TICKER TAPE device that relays the STOCK SYMBOL and the latest price and volume on securities as they are traded to investors around the world. Prior to the advent of computers, this machine had a loud printing device that made a ticking sound. Since 1975, the New York Stock Exchange and the American Stock Exchange have used a CONSOLIDATED TAPE that indicates the New York or REGIONAL STOCK EXCHANGE on which a trade originated. Other systems, known as news tickers, pass along the latest economic, financial and market news developments. See also TAPE. *See* illustration of consolidated tape, below.

TWX	MMM&P	IBM&T	XON&M
3S41⅝	83½	4S124¼	2S41

Sample section of the consolidated tape.

Trades in Time Warner, Minnesota Mining and Manufacturing, IBM, and Exxon are shown. Letters following the ampersands in the upper line indicate the marketplace in which the trade took place: P signifies the Pacific Stock Exchange, T the THIRD MARKET, M the Midwest Exchange; no indication means the New York Stock Exchange. Other codes not illustrated are X for Philadelphia Stock Exchange, B for Boston Stock Exchange, O for other markets, including INSTINET. In the lower line, where a number precedes the letter S, a multiple of 100 shares is indicated. Thus, 300 shares of Time Warner were transacted at a price of 41⅝ on the New York Stock Exchange; 100 shares of Minnesota Mining were traded on the Pacific Exchange at 83½, and so on.

TICKET short for ORDER TICKET.

TIER 1 AND TIER 2 in computing the capital adequacy of banks, Tier 1 refers to core capital, the sum of equity capital and disclosed reserves as adjusted, while Tier 2 refers to undisclosed reserves, revaluation reserves, general provisions and loan loss reserves, hybrid debt-equity instruments, and subordinated long-term debt.

TIGER acronym for Treasury Investors Growth Receipt, a form of ZERO-COUPON SECURITY first created by the brokerage firm of Merrill Lynch, Pierce, Fenner & Smith. TIGERS are U.S. government-backed bonds that have been stripped of their COUPONS. Both the CORPUS (principal) of the bonds and the individual coupons are sold separately at a deep discount from their face value. Investors receive FACE VALUE for the TIGERS when the bonds mature but do not receive periodic interest payments. Under Internal Revenue Service rules, however, TIGER holders owe income taxes on the imputed interest they would have earned had the bond been a FULL COUPON BOND. To avoid having to pay taxes without having the benefit of the income to pay them from, most investors put TIGERS in Individual Retirement or Keogh accounts, or in other TAX DEFERRED plans. Also called *TIGR.*

TIGHT MARKET market in general or market for a particular security marked by active trading and narrow bid-offer price spreads. In contrast, inactive trading and wide spreads characterize a *slack market. See also* SPREAD.

TIGHT MONEY economic condition in which credit is difficult to secure, usually as the result of Federal Reserve action to restrict the MONEY SUPPLY. The opposite is *easy money. See also* MONETARY POLICY.

TIME DEPOSIT savings account or CERTIFICATE OF DEPOSIT held in a financial institution for a fixed term or with the understanding that the depositor can withdraw only by giving notice. While a bank is authorized to require 30 days' notice of withdrawal from savings accounts, passbook accounts are generally regarded as readily available funds. Certificates of deposit, on the other hand, are issued for a specified term of 30 days or more, and provide penalties for early withdrawal. Financial institutions are free to negotiate any maturity term a customer might desire on a time deposit or certificate, as long as the term is at least 30 days, and to pay interest rates as high or low as the market will bear. *See also* DEPOSITORY INSTITUTIONS DEREGULATION AND MONETARY CONTROL ACT; REGULATION Q.

TIME DRAFT DRAFT payable at a specified or determinable time in the future, as distinguished from a *sight draft,* which is payable on presentation and delivery.

TIMES FIXED CHARGES *see* FIXED-CHARGE COVERAGE.

TIME SHARING

Computers: practice of renting time on a central computer through a smaller computer, frequently through modems and phone lines. The user can upload or download files, access electronic mail, use computer programs on the central computer, and perform other tasks, for a fee based on usage.

Real estate: practice of sharing a piece of real estate, such as a condominium, apartment, or house, with other owners. Typically, a buyer will purchase a particular block of time for a vacation, such as the second week of February, during which the buyer will have exclusive use of the property. In return, the buyer must pay his share of annual maintenance charges, whether he uses the property or not. One condominium may therefore be sold to 52 different parties, each for one week per year. Time share owners have the benefit of changing their weeks with other owners around the world through one of the worldwide exchange companies. Time shares should be viewed as a purchase of one's vacation, and not as a real estate investment.

TIMES INTEREST EARNED *see* FIXED-CHARGE COVERAGE.

TIME SPREAD OPTION strategy in which an investor buys and sells PUT OPTION and CALL OPTION contracts with the same EXERCISE PRICE but with different expiration dates. The purpose of this and other option strategies is to profit from the difference in OPTION PREMIUMS—the prices paid to buy the options. *See also* CALENDAR SPREAD; HORIZONTAL SPREAD; SPREAD.

TIME VALUE

In general: price put on the time an investor has to wait until an investment matures, as determined by calculating the PRESENT VALUE of the investment at maturity. *See also* YIELD TO MATURITY.

Options: that part of a stock option PREMIUM that reflects the time remaining on an option contract before expiration. The premium is composed of this time value and the INTRINSIC VALUE of the option.

Stocks: difference between the price at which a company is taken over and the price before the TAKEOVER occurs. For example, if XYZ Company is to be taken over at $30 a share in two months, XYZ shares might presently sell for $28.50. The $1.50 per share difference is the cost of the time value those owning XYZ must bear if they want to wait two months to get $30 a share. As the two months pass, the time value will shrink, until it disappears on the day of the takeover. The time that investors hold XYZ has a price because it could be used to invest in something else providing a higher return. *See also* OPPORTUNITY COST.

TIME-WEIGHTED RETURN portfolio accounting method that measures investment performance (income and price changes) as a percentage of capital "at work," effectively eliminating the effects of additions and withdrawals of capital and their timing that distort DOLLAR-WEIGHTED RETURN accounting. Since exact timing-weighting is impractical, the industry accepts an approximation that assumes all additions and withdrawals occur simultaneously at the midpoint of a reporting period. Performance thus equals the return on the value of assets at the beginning of the measuring period plus the return on the net amount of additions and withdrawals during the period divided in half. The periods, usually quarters, are then linked to produce a compound average TOTAL RETURN.

TIMING trying to pick the best time to make a decision. For example, MARKET TIMING involves the analysis of fundamental and technical data to decide when to buy or sell stocks, bonds, mutual funds or futures contracts. Timing is also important in making consumer decisions, such as when to make a major purchase. Consumers might want to time their purchase of real estate when prices and mortgage rates are especially attractive, or their purchase of a car when dealers are offering particularly good prices.

TIP

In general: payment over and above a formal cost or charge, ostensibly given in appreciation for extra service, to a waiter, bellhop, cabdriver, or other person engaged in service. Also called a *gratuity*.

Investments: information passed by one person to another as a basis for buy or sell action in a security. Such information is presumed to be of material value and not available to the general public. The Securities and Exchange Commission regulates the use of such information by so-called insiders, and court cases have established the liability of persons receiving and using or passing on such information (called tippees) in certain circumstances. *See also* INSIDER; INSIDE INFORMATION.

TITLE INSURANCE insurance policies, written by title insurance companies, protecting lenders against challenges to the title claim to a property. Title insurance protects a policyholder against loss from some occurrence that already has happened, such as a forged deed somewhere in the chain of title. If, for example, someone came along claiming that her parents formerly owned the house in question, and that, as beneficiary of her parents' estate, she now deserved to take possession of the property, the title insurance company would defend the present owner's title claim in court. Title insurance premiums are usually paid in one lump sum at the time the policy is issued, and the policy remains in force until the property is sold. Mortgage lenders normally require that borrowers obtain title insurance to protect the lenders' interest in the property. Property buyers also may purchase an owner's policy to protect their interest in the property.

TOEHOLD PURCHASE accumulation by an acquirer of less than 5% of the shares of a TARGET COMPANY. Once 5% is acquired, the acquirer is required to file with the Securities and Exchange Commission, the appropriate stock exchange, and the target company, explaining what is happening and what can be expected. *See also* SCHEDULE 13D; WILLIAMS ACT.

TOKYO COMMODITY EXCHANGE (TOCOM) trades futures on gold, silver, platinum, palladium, rubber, cotton yarn, and woolen yarn. Metal contracts are traded from 9 A.M. to 11 A.M. and 1 p.m. to 3:30 P.M.; rubber is traded from 9:45 A.M. to 3:30 P.M.; and yarns are traded from 8:50 A.M. to 3:10 P.M.

TOKYO STOCK EXCHANGE largest stock exchange in Japan. The Tokyo Stock Exchange is one of the largest, most important, and most active stock markets in the world. The *Nikkei Stock Average*, known as the Nikkei 225, and Nikkei 500 are the principal indices and are calculated by a formula similar to the DOW JONES INDUSTRIAL AVERAGE. The TOPIX, the *Tokyo Stock Price Index*, is a composite of all stocks on the first section of the exchange. Trading takes place in two daily sessions, from 9 A.M. to 11 A.M., and from 1 P.M. to 3 P.M. The principal form of settlement is delivery on the third business day following the day of the contract.

TOKYO STOCK PRICE INDEX (TOPIX) *see* NIKKEI STOCK AVERAGE.

TOLL REVENUE BOND MUNICIPAL BOND supported by revenues from tolls paid by users of the public project built with the bond proceeds. Toll revenue bonds frequently are floated to build bridges, tunnels, and roads. *See also* REVENUE BOND.

TOMBSTONE advertisement placed in newspapers by investment bankers in a PUBLIC OFFERING of securities. It gives basic details about the issue and lists the UNDERWRITING GROUP members involved in the offering in alphabetically organized groupings according to the size of their participations. It is not "an offer to sell or a solicitation of an offer to buy," but rather it calls attention to the PROSPECTUS, sometimes called the *offering circular.* A tombstone may also be placed by an investment banking firm to announce its role in a PRIVATE PLACEMENT, corporate MERGER, or ACQUISITION; by a corporation to announce a major business or real estate deal; or by a firm in the financial community to announce a personnel development or a principal's death. *See also* MEZZANINE BRACKET.

TON bond traders' jargon for $100 million.

TOP-DOWN APPROACH TO INVESTING method in which an investor first looks at trends in the general economy, and next selects industries and then companies that should benefit from those trends. For example, an investor who thinks inflation will stay low might be attracted to the retailing industry, since consumers' spending power will be enhanced by low inflation. The investor then might look at Sears, Wal-Mart, Federated Department Stores, Dayton Hudson, and other retailers to see which company has the best earnings prospects in the near term. Or, an investor who thinks there will be rapid inflation may identify the mining industry as attractive, and then look at particular gold, copper, and other mining companies to see which would benefit most from a trend of rising prices. The opposite method is called the BOTTOM-UP APPROACH TO INVESTING.

TOPIX *see* NIKKEI STOCK AVERAGE.

TOPPING OUT term denoting a market or a security that is at the end of a period of rising prices and can now be expected to stay on a plateau or even to decline.

TORONTO FUTURES EXCHANGE wholly owned subsidiary of the TORONTO STOCK EXCHANGE (TSE), trading TSE 35 Index futures and TSE 100 Index futures. TSE index options, TIPs (Toronto 35 Index Participation units), and TIPs options trade on the TSE.

TORONTO STOCK EXCHANGE (TSE) largest stock exchange in Canada, listing some 1,200 company stocks and 33 options. The TSE is home to many resource-based companies in the mining, paper, timber, and other natural resource industries, but also trades manufacturing, biotechnology, and telecommunications equities. The *TSE 300 Composite Index,* also known as the TSE 300, is the most widely quoted index tracking this marketplace. The *Toronto 35 Index,* comprised of a cross-section of major Canadian stocks, is the base for derivative products such as the Toronto 35 Index option (TXO) and future (TXF). The *TSE 100 Index* is a performance benchmark for institutional investors, and is the base for the TSE 100 Index option and TSE 100 Index future contract. The *TSE 200 Index* is a small to mid-cap index comprised of 200 stocks in the TSE 300 that are not represented in the TSE 100. Toronto 35 Index Participation Units, or TIPs, and TIPs options, are proprietary products. Each TIPs unit represents an interest in a trust that holds baskets of stocks in the Toronto 35 Index. TIPs options are American exercise and physically settled, while TXO options are European exercise and cash settled. TSE Index 35 options, TSE Index 100 options, and TIPs products trade on the TSE. The CANADIAN DEALING NETWORK (CDN) is a subsidiary of the exchange. The TSE's trading hours are 9:30 A.M. to 4 P.M., Monday through Friday, with an after-hours crossing section until 5 P.M. Settlement is the third day following the trade. The exchange uses both open outcry and the Computer Assisted Trading System (CATS).

TOTAL CAPITALIZATION CAPITAL STRUCTURE of a company, including LONG-TERM DEBT and all forms of EQUITY.

TOTAL COST
Accounting: (usually pl.) sum of FIXED COSTS, semivariable costs, and VARIABLE COSTS.

Investments: contract price paid for a security plus the brokerage commission plus any ACCRUED INTEREST due the seller (if the security is a bond). The figure is not to be confused with the COST BASIS for the purpose of figuring the CAPITAL GAINS TAX, which may involve other factors such as amortization of bond premiums.

TOTAL DISABILITY injury or illness that is so serious that it prevents a worker from performing any functions for which he or she is educated and trained. Workers with total disability may qualify for DISABILITY INCOME INSURANCE, either though a private employer's plan or through Social Security's disability insurance program. There is normally a waiting period before disability insurance payments begin, to determine if the disability is long-term. Waiting periods vary, from a month to several months, and are determined by the plan and premium structure of the employer.

TOTAL RETURN annual return on an investment including appreciation and dividends or interest. For bonds held to maturity, total return is YIELD TO MATURITY. For stocks, future appreciation is projected using the current PRICE/EARNINGS RATIO. In options trading, total return means dividends plus capital gains plus premium income.

TOTAL VOLUME total number of shares or contracts traded in a stock, bond, commodity future, or option on a particular day. For stocks and bonds, this is the aggregate of trades on national exchanges like the New York and American stock exchanges and on regional exchanges. For commodities futures and options, it represents the volume of trades executed around the world in one day. For over-the-counter securities, total volume is measured by the NASDAQ index.

TOUT to promote a particular security aggressively, usually done by a corporate spokesman, public relations firm, broker, or analyst with a vested interest in promoting the stock. Touting a stock is unethical if it misleads investors. *See also* INVESTMENT ADVISERS ACT; INVESTOR RELATIONS DEPARTMENT.

T-PLUS-THREE *see* DELIVERY DATE.

TRADE
In general:
1. buying or selling of goods and services among companies, states, or countries,

called *commerce.* The amount of goods and services imported minus the amount exported makes up a country's BALANCE OF TRADE. *See also* TARIFF; TRADE DEFICIT.

2. those in the business of selling products are called *members of the trade.* As such, they receive DISCOUNTS from the price the public has to pay.

3. group of manufacturers who compete in the same market. These companies form trade associations and publish trade journals.

4. commercial companies that do business with each other. For example, ACCOUNTS PAYABLE to suppliers are called *trade accounts payable;* the term TRADE CREDIT is used to describe accounts payable as a source of WORKING CAPITAL financing. Companies paying their bills promptly receive *trade discounts* when available.

5. synonymous with BARTER, the exchange of goods and services without the use of money.

Securities: to carry out a transaction of buying or selling a stock, a bond, or a commodity future contract. A trade is consummated when a buyer and seller agree on a price at which the trade will be executed. A TRADER frequently buys and sells for his or her own account securities for short-term profits, as contrasted with an investor who holds his positions in hopes of long-term gains.

TRADE BALANCE *see* BALANCE OF TRADE.

TRADE CREDIT open account arrangements with suppliers of goods and services, and a firm's record of payment with the suppliers. Trade liabilities comprise a company's ACCOUNTS PAYABLE. DUN & BRADSTREET is the largest compiler of trade credit information, rating commercial firms and supplying published reports. Trade credit data is also processed by MERCANTILE AGENCIES specializing in different industries.

Trade credit is an important external source of WORKING CAPITAL for a company, although such credit can be highly expensive. Terms of 2% 10 days, net 30 days (2% discount if paid in 10 days, the net [full] amount due in 30 days) translate into a 36% annual interest rate if not taken advantage of. On the other hand, the same terms translate into a borrowing rate of slightly over 15% if payment is made in 60 days instead of 30.

TRADE DATE day on which a security or a commodity future trade actually takes place. The SETTLEMENT DATE usually follows the trade date by five business days, but varies depending on the transaction and method of delivery used. *See also* DELAYED DELIVERY; DELIVERY DATE; REGULAR-WAY DELIVERY (AND SETTLEMENT); SELLER'S OPTION.

TRADE DEFICIT OR SURPLUS excess of imports over exports *(trade deficit)* or of exports over imports *(trade surplus),* resulting in a negative or positive BALANCE OF TRADE. The balance of trade is made up of transactions in merchandise and other movable goods and is only one factor comprising the larger *current account* (which includes services and tourism, transportation, and other *invisible items,* such as interest and profits earned abroad) in the overall BALANCE OF PAYMENTS. Factors influencing a country's balance of trade include the strength or weakness of its currency in relation to those of the countries with which it trades (a strong U.S. dollar, for example, makes goods produced in other countries relatively cheap for Americans), production advantages in key manufacturing areas (Japanese automobiles, for instance), or the domestic economy of a trading country where production may or may not be meeting demand.

TRADEMARK distinctive name, symbol, motto, or emblem that identifies a product, service, or firm. In the United States, trademark rights—the right to prevent competitors from using similar marks in selling or advertising—arise out of use; that is, registration is not essential to establish the legal existence of a mark. A trademark registered with the U.S. Patent and Trademark Office is good for 20 years, renewable as long as used. Products may be both patented and protected by trademark, the advantage being that when the patent runs out, exclusivity can be continued indefinitely with the trademark. A trademark is classified on a BALANCE SHEET as an INTANGIBLE ASSET.

Although, like land, trademarks have an indefinite life and cannot technically be amortized, in practice accountants do amortize trademarks over their estimated life, not to exceed 40 years.

TRADER

In general: anyone who buys and sells goods or services for profit; a DEALER or *merchant*. *See also* BARTER; TRADE.

Investments:
1. individual who buys and sells securities, such as STOCKS, BONDS, OPTIONS, or commodities, such as wheat, gold, or FOREIGN EXCHANGE, for his or her own account—that is, as a dealer or PRINCIPAL—rather than as a BROKER or AGENT.
2. individual who buys and sells securities or commodities for his or her own account on a short-term basis in anticipation of quick profits; a *speculator. See also* DAY TRADE; COMPETITIVE TRADER; FLOOR TRADER; REGISTERED COMPETITIVE MARKET MAKER; REGISTERED COMPETITIVE TRADER; SPECULATION.

TRADING AUTHORIZATION document giving a brokerage firm employee acting as AGENT (BROKER) the POWER OF ATTORNEY in buy-sell transactions for a customer.

TRADING DIVIDENDS technique of buying and selling stocks in other firms by a corporation in order to maximize the number of DIVIDENDS it can collect. This action is advantageous, because 70% of the dividend income it receives from the stocks of other companies is not taxed, according to Internal Revenue Service regulations. *See also* DIVIDEND EXCLUSION.

TRADING HALT *see* SUSPENDED TRADING.

TRADING LIMIT *see* DAILY TRADING LIMIT; LIMIT UP, LIMIT DOWN.

TRADING PATTERN long-range direction of a security or commodity future price. This pattern is charted by drawing a line connecting the highest prices the security has reached and another line connecting the lowest prices the security has traded at over the same time frame. These two lines will be pointing either up or down, indicating the security's long-term trading pattern. *See* illustration on next page. *See also* TECHNICAL ANALYSIS, TRENDLINE.

TRADING POST physical location on a stock exchange floor where particular securities are bought and sold. It is here that the SPECIALIST in a particular security performs his market-making functions and that the CROWD (floor brokers with orders in that security) congregates. The New York Stock Exchange, for example, has 22 trading posts, most handling around 100 stocks. *See also* FLOOR BROKER; FLOOR TRADER; MAKE A MARKET.

TRADING PROFIT profit earned based on short-term trades. For assets such as stocks, bonds, futures contracts, and mutual funds held under a year, such trading profits are taxed at regular income tax rates. In general commerce, *trading profit* refers to the difference between what a product is sold for by a retailer and what it costs to buy or produce at the wholesale or producer level.

TRADING PATTERN

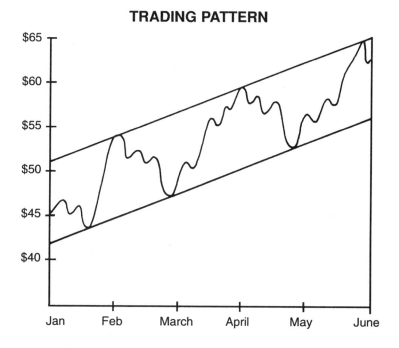

TRADING RANGE

Commodities: trading limit set by a COMMODITIES futures exchange for a particular commodity. The price of a commodity future contract may not go higher or lower than that limit during one day's trading. *See also* LIMIT UP, LIMIT DOWN.

Securities: range between the highest and lowest prices at which a security or a market has traded. The trading range for XYZ Corporation might be $40 to $60 over the last two years, for example. If a security or a market seems to be stuck in a narrow price range, analysts say that it is a trading range market, which will eventually be followed by a significant up or down move. *See also* FLAG; PENNANT; TRIANGLE; WEDGE.

TRADING UNIT number of SHARES, BONDS, or other securities that is generally accepted for ordinary trading purposes on the exchanges, *See also* ODD LOT; ROUND LOT; UNIT OF TRADING.

TRADING VARIATION fractions to which securities transaction prices are rounded. For example, stocks are rounded up or down to the nearest eighth of a point. Options over $3 are also rounded to an eighth, but options under $3 are rounded to $\frac{1}{16}$. Corporate and municipal bonds are rounded to $\frac{1}{8}$, medium- and long-term government notes and bonds to $\frac{1}{32}$, and shorter-term government bonds to $\frac{1}{64}$. *See also* PLUS.

TRANCH CD *see* TRANCHES.

TRANCHES

1. risk maturity or other classes into which a multi-class security, such as a COLLATERALIZED MORTGAGE OBLIGATION (CMO) or a REMIC is split. For example, the typical CMO has A, B, C, and Z tranches, representing fast pay, medium pay, and slow pay bonds plus an issue (tranch) that bears no coupon but

receives the cash flow from the collateral remaining after the other tranches are satisfied. More sophisticated CMO versions have multiple Z tranches and a Y tranch incorporating a sinking fund schedule.

2. in the United Kingdom, fixed-rate security issues are often prearranged by governments, local authorities, or corporations, then brought out in successive rounds, termed tranches. One thus speaks of new tranches of existing securities. A variation of the term, *tranchettes,* refers to small tranches of gilt-edged securities (government bonds) sold by the government to the Bank of England, which then sells them into the market at times it deems appropriate.

3. subunits of a large ($10–$30 million) Eurodollar certificate of deposit that are marketed to smaller investors in $10,000 denominations. Tranches are represented by separate certificates and have the same interest rate, issue date, interest payment date, and maturity of the original instrument, which is called a *tranch CD.*

TRANCHETTES *see* TRANCHES.

TRANSACTION

Accounting: event or condition recognized by an entry in the books of account.

Securities: execution of an order to buy or sell a security or commodity futures contract. After the buyer and seller have agreed on a price, the seller is obligated to deliver the security or commodity involved, and the buyer is obligated to accept it. *See also* TRADE.

TRANSACTION COSTS cost of buying or selling a security, which consists mainly of the *brokerage commission,* the dealer MARKDOWN or markup, or fee (as would be charged by a bank or broker-dealer to transact Treasuries, for example) but also includes direct taxes, such as the SEC FEE, any state-imposed TRANSFER TAXES, or other direct taxes.

TRANSFER exchange of ownership of property from one party to another. For example, a piece of real estate may be transferred from seller to buyer through the execution of a sales contract. Securities and mutual funds are typically transferred through a transfer agent, who electronically switches ownership of the securities. In banking, *transfer* refers to the movement of funds from one account to another, such as from a passbook account to a checking account.

TRANSFER AGENT agent, usually a commercial bank, appointed by a corporation, to maintain records of stock and bond owners, to cancel and issue certificates, and to resolve problems arising from lost, destroyed, or stolen certificates. (Preventing OVERISSUE of shares is the function of the REGISTRAR.) A corporation may also serve as its own transfer agent.

TRANSFER PAYMENTS money transferred to people from the government. Many payments under government benefit programs are considered transfer payments, including Social Security, disability payments, unemployment compensation, welfare, and veterans' benefits. A large portion of the federal government's yearly budget goes to make transfer payments.

TRANSFER PRICE price charged by individual entities in a multi-entity corporation on transactions among themselves; also termed *transfer cost.* This concept is used where each entity is managed as a PROFIT CENTER—that is, held responsible for its own RETURN ON INVESTED CAPITAL—and must therefore deal with the other internal parts of the corporation on an arm's-length (or market) basis. *See also* ARM'S LENGTH TRANSACTION.

TRANSFER TAX
1. combined federal tax on gifts and estates. *See* ESTATE TAX; GIFT TAX.
2. federal tax on the sale of all bonds (except obligations of the United States, foreign governments, states, and municipalities) and all stocks. The tax is paid by the seller at the time ownership is transferred and involves a few pennies per $100 of value.
3. tax levied by some state and local governments on the transfer of such documents as deeds to property, securities, or licenses. Such taxes are paid, usually with stamps, by the seller or donor and are determined by the location of the transfer agent. States with transfer taxes on stock transactions include New York, Florida, South Carolina, and Texas. New York bases its tax on selling price; the other states apply the tax to PAR value (giving NO-PAR-VALUE STOCK a value of $100). Bonds are not taxed at the state level.

TRANSMITTAL LETTER letter sent with a document, security, or shipment describing the contents and the purpose of the transaction.

TRAVEL AND ENTERTAINMENT ACCOUNT separate account set up by an employer to track and reimburse employees' travel and entertainment expenses. Many employers give special credit cards to employees so that all travel and entertainment expenses can be tracked separately from personal expenses. Employers need to track travel and entertainment expenses carefully if they are to claim the appropriate tax deductions for these business expenses.

TRAVEL AND ENTERTAINMENT EXPENSE expense for travel and entertainment that may qualify for a tax deduction. Under current tax law, employers may deduct 50% of legitimate travel and entertainment expenses. Expenses are deductible if they are directly related to business. For example, a business meal must include a discussion that produces a direct business benefit.

TRAVELER'S CHECK check issued by a financial institution such as American Express, Visa, or Mastercard that allows travelers to carry travel funds in a more convenient way than cash. The traveler buys the checks, often for a nominal fee, with cash, a credit card, or a regular check at a bank or travel service office and then signs each traveler's check. The check can then be used virtually anywhere in the world once it has been countersigned with the same signature. The advantage to the traveler is that the traveler's check cannot be used by someone else if it is lost or stolen, and can be replaced usually anywhere in the world. Traveler's checks are also issued in many foreign currencies, allowing a traveler to lock in at a particular exchange rate before the trip begins. Many issuers of traveler's checks offer a type of check that enables two travelers to share the same travel funds. American Express was the first issuer to introduce this form of check. Institutions issuing traveler's checks profit from the FLOAT, earning interest on the money from the time the customer buys the check to the time they use the check.

TREASURER company officer responsible for the receipt, custody, investment, and disbursement of funds, for borrowings, and, if it is a public company, for the maintenance of a market for its securities. Depending on the size of the organization, the treasurer may also function as the CONTROLLER, with accounting and audit responsibilities. The laws of many states require that a corporation have a treasurer. *See also* CHIEF FINANCIAL OFFICER (CFO).

TREASURIES NEGOTIABLE debt obligations of the U.S. government, secured by its FULL FAITH AND CREDIT and issued at various schedules and maturities. The income from Treasury securities is exempt from state and local, but not federal, taxes.

1. *Treasury bills*—short-term securities with maturities of one year or less issued at a discount from FACE VALUE. Auctions of 91-day and 182-day BILLS take place weekly, and the yields are watched closely in the money markets for signs of interest rate trends. Many floating-rate loans and variable-rate mortgages have interest rates tied to these bills. The Treasury also auctions 52-week bills once every four weeks. At times it also issues very short-term cash management bills, TAX ANTICIPATION BILLS, and treasury certificates of indebtedness. Treasury bills are issued in minimum denominations of $10,000, with $5000 increments above $10,000 (except for cash management bills, which are sold in minimum $10 million blocks). Individual investors who do not submit a COMPETITIVE BID are sold bills at the average price of the winning competitive bids. Treasury bills are the primary instrument used by the Federal Reserve in its regulation of MONEY SUPPLY through OPEN MARKET OPERATIONS. *See also* DUTCH AUCTION-REPURCHASE AGREEMENT.
2. *Treasury bonds*—long-term debt instruments with maturities of 10 years or longer issued in minimum denominations of $1000.
3. *Treasury notes*—intermediate securities with maturities of 1 to 10 years. Denominations range from $1000 to $1 million or more. The notes are sold by cash subscription, in exchange for outstanding or maturing government issues, or at auction.

TREASURY BILL *see* BILL; TREASURIES.

TREASURY BOND *see* TREASURIES.

TREASURY DIRECT system through which an individual investor can make a NONCOMPETITIVE BID on U.S. Treasury securities (TREASURIES), thus bypassing middlemen like banks or broker-dealers and avoiding their fees. The system works through FEDERAL RESERVE BANKS and branches, and the minimum purchase is $10,000.

TREASURY STOCK stock reacquired by the issuing company and available for RETIREMENT or resale. It is issued but not outstanding. It cannot be voted and it pays or accrues no dividends. It is not included in any of the ratios measuring values per common share. Among the reasons treasury stock is created are (1) to provide an alternative to paying taxable dividends, since the decreased amount of outstanding shares increases the per share value and often the market price; (2) to provide for the exercise of stock options and warrants and the conversion of convertible securities; (3) in countering a TENDER OFFER by a potential acquirer; (4) to alter the DEBT-TO-EQUITY RATIO by issuing bonds to finance the reacquisition of shares; (5) as a result of the STABILIZATION of the market price during a NEW ISSUE. Also called *reacquired stock* and *treasury shares*. *See also* ISSUED AND OUTSTANDING; UNISSUED STOCK.

TREND
In general: any general direction of movement. For example: "There is an upward (downward, level) trend in XYZ sales," or "There is a trend toward increased computerization of trading on Wall Street."
Securities: long-term price or trading volume movements either up, down, or sideways, which characterize a particular market, commodity or security. Also applies to interest rates and yields.

TRENDLINE line used by technical analysts to chart the past direction of a security or commodity future in order to help predict future price movements. The trendline is made by connecting the highest or lowest prices to which a security or commodity has risen or fallen within a particular time period. The angle of the resulting line will indicate if the security or commodity is in a downtrend or uptrend. If the price rises above a downward sloping trendline or drops below a rising uptrend line, technical analysts say that a new direction may be emerging. *See also* TECHNICAL ANALYSIS; TRADING PATTERN.

TRENDLINE

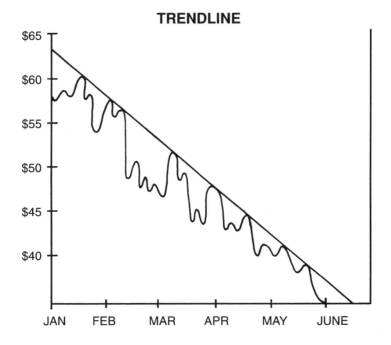

TRIANGLE technical chart pattern that has two base points and a top point, formed by connecting a stock's price movements with a line. In a typical triangle pattern, the apex points to the right, although in reverse triangles the apex points to the left. In a typical triangle, there are a series of two or more rallies and price drops where each succeeding peak is lower than the preceding peak, and each bottom is higher than the preceding bottom. In a right-angled triangle, the sloping part of the formation often points in the direction of the breakout. Technical analysts find it significant when a security's price breaks out of the triangle formation, either up or down, because that usually means the security's price will continue in that direction. *See* chart on next page. *See also* PENNANT; TECHNICAL ANALYSIS; WEDGE.

TRICKLE DOWN theory that economic growth can best be achieved by letting businesses flourish, since their prosperity will ultimately trickle down to middle- and lower-income people, who will benefit by increased economic activity. Proponents say that it produces more long-term growth than direct welfare grants to the middle- and lower-income sectors. *See also* SUPPLY-SIDE ECONOMICS.

TRIN measure of stock market strength that relates the ADVANCE-DECLINE ratio (the number of issues that advanced in price divided by the number of issues that declined in price) to the advance volume-decline volume ratio (the total number of shares that advanced divided by the total number of shares that declined). For example, if 800 stocks advanced and 750 issues declined while a total of 68 million shares advanced and 56 million shares declined, the trin would be calculated as follows:

TRIANGLE

$$\frac{\text{Advances } 800 \div \text{Declines } 750}{\text{Advance volume } 68{,}000{,}000 \div \text{Decline volume } 56{,}000{,}000} = \frac{1.067}{1.214}$$

$$= \ 0.88$$

A trin of under 1.00 is considered bullish while a trin over 1.00 is considered bearish. The above trin of 0.88 is thus a bullish sign. A trin based on closing figures is called a *closing trin. See also* CLOSING TICK.

TRIPLE NET LEASE lease requiring tenants to pay all ongoing maintenance expenses such as utilities, taxes, insurance, and upkeep of the property. There are many LIMITED PARTNERSHIPS investing in triple net lease real estate deals. In such a deal, the limited partnership owns the property and collects rent, but the tenants pay most of the operating expenses. This results in higher returns for limited partners with lower risks, because tenants bear any increased costs for utilities, insurance, or taxes.

TRIPLE TAX EXEMPT feature of MUNICIPAL BONDS in which interest is exempt from federal, state, and local taxation for residents of the states and localities that issue them. Such bonds are particularly attractive in states with high income tax rates. Many municipal bond funds buy only triple tax exempt bonds and market them to residents of the state and city of the issuer. *See also* SINGLE-STATE MUNICIPAL BOND FUND.

TRIPLE WITCHING DAY third Friday in March, June, September, and December when OPTIONS, INDEX OPTIONS, AND FUTURES CONTRACTS all expire simultaneously.

At times there may be massive trades in index futures, options, and the underlying stocks by hedge strategists, arbitrageurs, and other investors, resulting in volatile markets on those days. In the past, all contracts expired in the same hour, but steps were taken so that contracts now expire at the open as well as the close of the day instead of all at once. Smaller-scale witching days occur in the other eight months, usually on the third Friday, when other options, index options, and futures contracts expire concurrently. *See also* DOUBLE WITCHING DAY.

TRUNCATION shortening of processing steps, in an effort to reduce paperwork and operating costs. For example, check truncation, or check SAFEKEEPING, where the bank holds the checks or microfilm records of them in a central file.

TRUST

Business: type of corporate combination that engaged in monopolies and restraint of trade and that operated freely until the ANTITRUST LAWS of the late 19th century and early 20th century. The name derived from the use of the voting trust, in which a small number of trustees vote a majority of the shares of a corporation. The voting trust survives as a means of facilitating the reorganization of firms in difficulty. *See also* INVESTMENT COMPANY; VOTING TRUST CERTIFICATE.

Law: FIDUCIARY relationship in which a person, called a *trustee,* holds title to property for the benefit of another person, called a BENEFICIARY. The agreement that establishes the trust, contains its provisions, and sets forth the powers of the trustee is called the *trust indenture.* The person creating the trust is the *creator, settlor,* GRANTOR, or *donor;* the property itself is called the CORPUS, *trust res, trust fund,* or *trust estate,* which is distinguished from any income earned by it. If the trust is created while the donor is living, it is called a *living trust* or INTER VIVOS TRUST. A trust created by a will is called a TESTAMENTARY TRUST. The trustee is usually charged with investing trust property productively and, unless specifically limited, can sell, mortgage, or lease the property as he or she deems warranted. *See also* CHARITABLE REMAINDER TRUST; CLIFFORD TRUST; INVESTMENT TRUST; REVISIONARY TRUST; TRUST COMPANY; TRUSTEE IN BANKRUPTCY; TRUST INDENTURE ACT OF 1939.

TRUST COMPANY organization, usually combined with a commercial bank, which is engaged as a trustee, FIDUCIARY, or AGENT for individuals or businesses in the administration of TRUST funds, estates, custodial arrangements, stock transfer and registration, and other related services. Trust companies also engage in fiduciary investment management functions and estate planning. They are regulated by state law.

TRUSTEE *see* TRUST.

TRUSTEE IN BANKRUPTCY trustee appointed by a U.S. district court or by creditors to administer the affairs of a bankrupt company or individual. Under Chapter 7 of the U.S. BANKRUPTCY Code, the trustee has the responsibility for liquidating the property of the company and making distributions of liquidating dividends to creditors. Under the Chapter 11 provision, which provides for REORGANIZATION, a trustee may or may not be appointed. If one is, the trustee is responsible for seeing that a reorganization plan is filed and often assumes responsibility for the company.

TRUST FUND *see* TRUST.

TRUST INDENTURE ACT OF 1939 federal law requiring all corporate bonds and other debt securities to be issued under an INDENTURE agreement approved by the SECURITIES AND EXCHANGE COMMISSION (SEC) and providing for the appointment of a qualified trustee free of conflict of interest with the issuer. The Act provides that indentures contain protective clauses for bondholders, that bondholders receive semiannual financial reports, that periodic filings be made with the SEC showing compliance with indenture provisions, and that the issuer be liable for misleading statements. Securities exempted from regulation under the SECURITIES ACT OF 1933 are also exempted from the Trust Indenture Act, but some securities not requiring registration under the 1933 Act do fall under the provisions of the Trust Indenture Act, such as bonds issued in REORGANIZATION or RECAPITALIZATION.

TRUTH IN LENDING LAW legislation stipulating that lenders must disclose to borrowers the true cost of loans and make the interest rate and terms of the loan simple to understand. *See also* CONSUMER CREDIT PROTECTION ACT OF 1968; RIGHT OF RESCISSION.

TURKEY disappointing investment. The term may be used with reference to a business deal that went awry, or to the purchase of a stock or bond that dropped in value sharply, or to a new securities issue that did not sell well or had to be sold at a loss.

TURNAROUND favorable reversal in the fortunes of a company, a market, or the economy at large. Stock market investors speculating that a poorly performing company is about to show a marked improvement in earnings might profit handsomely from its turnaround.

TURNKEY any project constructed or manufactured by a company that ultimately turns it over in finished form to the company that will use it, so that all the user has to do is turn the key, so to speak, and the project is underway. The term is used of housing projects that, after construction, are turned over to property managers. There are also turnkey computer systems, for which the user needs no special computer knowledge and which can therefore be put right to work once they are installed.

TURNOVER
Finance:
1. number of times a given asset is replaced during an accounting period, usually a year. *See also* ACCOUNTS RECEIVABLE TURNOVER; INVENTORY TAKEOVER.
2. ratio of annual sales of a company to its NET WORTH, measuring the extent to which a company can grow without additional capital investment when compared over a period. *See also* CAPITAL TURNOVER.

Great Britain: annual sales volume.

Industrial relations: total employment divided by the number of employees replaced during a given period.

Securities: volume of shares traded as a percentage of total shares listed on an exchange during a period, usually either a day or a year. The same ratio is applied to individual securities and the portfolios of individual or institutional investors.

12b-1 MUTUAL FUND MUTUAL FUND that assesses shareholders for some of its promotion expenses. Adopted by the Securities and Exchange Commission in 1980, Rule 12b-1 provides mutual funds and their shareholders with an asset-based alternative method of covering sales and marketing expenses. At least half of the more than 3,500 mutual funds in existence today have a 12b-1 fee typically ranging from .25%, in the case of "no-load" funds that use it to cover advertising and marketing costs, to as high as 8.5%, the maximum "front-end load" allowed under National Association of Securities Dealers (NASD) rules, in cases where annual 12b-1 "spread loads" replaced traditional front-end loads.

The predominant use of 12b-1 fees is in funds sold through brokers, insurance agents, and financial planners.

Changes to 12b-1 that became effective July 7, 1993, aim to limit fees paid by most fund investors to the 8.5% limit on front-end loads. This is achieved by an annual limit and by a rolling cap placed on new sales. The annual limit is .85% of assets, with an additional .25% permitted as a service fee. The rolling cap on the total of all sales charges is 6.25% of new sales, plus interest, for funds that charge the service fee, and 7.25%, plus interest, for funds that do not. The new regulation also prohibits funds with front-end, deferred, and/or 12b-1 fees in excess of .25% from being called "no-load." *See also* NO-LOAD FUND.

TWENTY BOND INDEX index tracking the yields on 20 general obligation municipal bonds with 20-year maturities and an average rating equivalent to A1. The index, published weekly by *The Bond Buyer* in the newspaper's Friday edition, serves as a benchmark for the general level of municipal bond yields. *See also* BOND BUYER'S INDEX; ELEVEN BOND INDEX.

TWENTY-DAY PERIOD period required by the Securities and Exchange Commission (SEC) after filing of the REGISTRATION STATEMENT and PRELIMINARY PROSPECTUS in a NEW ISSUE or SECONDARY DISTRIBUTION during which they are reviewed and, if necessary, modified. The end of the twenty-day period—also called the COOLING-OFF PERIOD—marks the EFFECTIVE DATE when the issue may be offered to the public. The period may be extended by the SEC if more time is needed to respond to a DEFICIENCY LETTER.

TWENTY-FIVE PERCENT RULE MUNICIPAL BOND analyst's guideline that bonded debt over 25% of a municipality's annual budget is excessive.

TWENTY-PERCENT CUSHION RULE guideline used by analysts of MUNICIPAL REVENUE BONDS that estimated revenues from the financed facility should exceed the operating budget plus maintenance costs and DEBT SERVICE by a 20% margin or "cushion" to allow for unanticipated expenses or error in estimating revenues.

TWISTING unethical practice of convincing a customer to trade unnecessarily, thereby generating a commission for the broker or salesperson. Examples: A broker may induce a customer to sell one mutual fund with a sales charge in order to buy another fund, also with a sales charge, thereby generating a commission. A life insurance salesperson may persuade a policyholder to cancel his or her policy or allow it to lapse, in order to sell the insured a new policy, which would be more costly but which would produce sizable commissions for the salesperson. Also called CHURNING.

TWO-DOLLAR BROKER FLOOR BROKER who executes orders for other brokers too busy to do it themselves; a "broker's broker." Such brokers once were paid two dollars for a ROUND LOT trade, hence the name. Today they receive a negotiated commission rate varying with the dollar value of the transaction. *See also* INDEPENDENT BROKER.

200 PERCENT DECLINING BALANCE METHOD *see* DOUBLE DECLINING-BALANCE DEPRECIATION METHOD (DDB).

TWO-SIDED MARKET market in which both the BID AND ASKED sides are firm, such as that which a SPECIALIST and others who MAKE A MARKET are required to maintain. Both buyers and sellers are thus assured of their ability to complete transactions. Also called *two-way market.*

TWO-TIER BID TAKEOVER bid where the acquirer offers to pay more for the shares needed to gain control than for the remaining shares; contrasts with ANY-AND-ALL BID.

U _____

ULTRA-SHORT-TERM BOND FUND mutual fund buying bonds with maturities typically of one year or less. Such funds usually pay higher yields than money market mutual funds, but lower yields than SHORT-TERM BOND FUNDS. Their advantage to investors is that they offer more price stability than short-term bond funds, along with a yield that beats money funds. The NET ASSET VALUE of ultra-short-term bond funds does fluctuate, however, unlike the net asset value for money market mutual funds, which remains fixed at $1 a share. It is therefore possible to realize capital gains and losses with ultra-short-term bond funds.

ULTRA VIRES ACTIVITIES actions of a corporation that are not authorized by its charter and that may therefore lead to shareholder or third-party suits. *See also* ARTICLES OF INCORPORATION.

UMBRELLA PERSONAL LIABILITY POLICY liability insurance policy providing excess coverage beyond regular liability policies. For example, typical homeowner's policies offer $300,000 in liability coverage against lawsuits and other negligence claims. An umbrella policy may provide $1 million in liability coverage. An umbrella policy will begin to pay claims only after the underlying liability policy's coverage limits have been exceeded. People usually buy umbrella policies to protect themselves against the possibility of a large jury award in a lawsuit. An umbrella policy also protects in situations not covered by a standard liability policy found in homeowner's and automobile insurance, like slander and libel. An umbrella policy also links policies, raising the limits on underlying policies in a cost-effective manner.

UNAMORTIZED BOND DISCOUNT difference between the FACE VALUE (par value) of a bond and the proceeds received from the sale of the bond by the issuing company, less whatever portion has been amortized, that is, written off to expense as recorded periodically on the PROFIT AND LOSS STATEMENT. At the time of issue, a company has two alternatives: (1) it can immediately absorb as an expense the amount of discount plus costs related to the issue, such as legal, printing, REGISTRATION, and other similar expenses, or (2) it can decide to treat the total discount and expenses as a DEFERRED CHARGE, recorded as an ASSET to be written off over the life of the bonds or by any other schedule the company finds desirable. The amount still to be expensed at any point is the unamortized bond discount.

UNAMORTIZED PREMIUMS ON INVESTMENTS unexpensed portion of the amount by which the price paid for a security exceeded its PAR value (if a BOND or PREFERRED STOCK) or MARKET VALUE (if common stock). A PREMIUM paid in acquiring an investment is in the nature of an INTANGIBLE ASSET, and conservative accounting practice dictates it be written off to expense over an appropriate period. *See also* GOING-CONCERN VALUE.

UNCOLLECTED FUNDS portion of bank deposit made up of checks that have not yet been collected by the depository bank—that is, payment has not yet been acknowledged by the bank on which a check was drawn. A bank will usually not let a depositor draw on uncollected funds. *See also* FLOAT.

UNCOLLECTIBLE ACCOUNT customer account that cannot be collected because of the customer's unwillingness or inability to pay. A business normally writes off such a receivable as worthless after several attempts at collecting the funds.

UNCOVERED OPTION short option that is not fully collateralized. A short call position is uncovered if the writer does not have long stock to deliver or does not own another call on the same security with a lower or same strike price, and with a longer or same time of expiration. Also called NAKED OPTION. *See also* NAKED POSITION; COVERED OPTION; COVERED WRITER.

UNDERBANKED said of a NEW ISSUE underwriting when the originating INVESTMENT BANKER is having difficulty getting other firms to become members of the UNDERWRITING GROUP, or syndicate. *See also* UNDERWRITE.

UNDERBOOKED said of a NEW ISSUE of securities during the preoffering REGISTRATION period when brokers canvassing lists of prospective buyers report limited INDICATIONS OF INTEREST. The opposite of underbooked would be *fully circled. See also* CIRCLE.

UNDERCAPITALIZATION situation in which a business does not have enough capital to carry out its normal business functions. *See also* CAPITALIZATION; WORKING CAPITAL.

UNDERLYING DEBT MUNICIPAL BOND term referring to the debt of government entities within the jurisdiction of larger government entities and for which the larger entity has partial credit responsibility. For example, a township might share responsibility for the general obligations of a village within the township, the debt of the village being underlying debt from the township's standpoint. The term OVERLAPPING DEBT is also used to describe underlying debt, but overlapping debt can also exist with entities of equal rank where, for example, a school district crosses boundaries of two or more townships.

UNDERLYING FUTURES CONTRACT FUTURES CONTRACT that underlies an OPTION on that future. For example, the Chicago Board of Trade offers a U.S. Treasury bond futures option. The underlying future is the Treasury bond futures contract traded on the Board of Trade. If the option contract were exercised, delivery would be made in the underlying futures contract.

UNDERLYING SECURITY
Options: security that must be delivered if a PUT OPTION or CALL OPTION contract is exercised. Stock INDEX OPTIONS and STOCK INDEX FUTURES, however, are settled in cash, since it is not possible to deliver an index of stocks.

Securities: common stock that underlies certain types of securities issued by corporations. This stock must be delivered if a SUBSCRIPTION WARRANT or SUBSCRIPTION RIGHT is exercised, if a CONVERTIBLE bond or PREFERRED STOCK is converted into common shares, or if an INCENTIVE STOCK OPTION is exercised.

UNDERMARGINED ACCOUNT MARGIN ACCOUNT that has fallen below MARGIN REQUIREMENTS or MINIMUM MAINTENANCE requirements. As a result, the broker must make a MARGIN CALL to the customer.

UNDERVALUED security selling below its LIQUIDATION value or the MARKET VALUE analysts believe it deserves. A company's stock may be undervalued because the industry is out of favor, because the company is not well known or has an erratic history of earnings, or for many other reasons. Fundamental analysts try to spot companies that are undervalued so their clients can buy before the stocks become FULLY VALUED. Undervalued companies are also frequently targets of TAKEOVER attempts, since acquirers can buy assets cheaply this way. *See also* FUNDAMENTAL ANALYSIS.

UNDERWATER OPTION OUT-OF-THE MONEY option. Being out of the money indicates the option has no intrinsic value; all of its value consists of time value. A call option is out of the money if its exercise price is higher than the current price of the underlying contract. A put option is out of the money if its exercise price is lower than the current price of the underlying contract.

UNDERWITHHOLDING situation in which taxpayers have too little federal, state, or local income tax withheld from their salaries. Because they have underwithheld, these taxpayers may owe income taxes when they file their tax returns. If the underwithholding is large enough, penalties and interest also may be due. To correct underwithholding, taxpayers must file a new W-4 form with their employers, decreasing the number of dependents claimed. *See also* OVERWITHHOLDING.

UNDERWRITE

Insurance: to assume risk in exchange for a PREMIUM.

Investments: to assume the risk of buying a NEW ISSUE of securities from the issuing corporation or government entity and reselling them to the public, either directly or through dealers. The UNDERWRITER makes a profit on the difference between the price paid to the issuer and the PUBLIC OFFERING PRICE, called the UNDERWRITING SPREAD.

Underwriting is the business of investment bankers, who usually form an UNDERWRITING GROUP (also called a PURCHASE GROUP or syndicate) to pool the risk and assure successful distribution of the issue. The syndicate operates under an AGREEMENT AMONG UNDERWRITERS, also termed a *syndicate contract* or PURCHASE GROUP contract.

The underwriting group appoints a MANAGING UNDERWRITER, also known as *lead underwriter, syndicate manager,* or simply *manager,* that is usually the *originating investment banker*—the firm that began working with the issuer months before to plan details of the issue and prepare the REGISTRATION materials to be filed with the SECURITIES AND EXCHANGE COMMISSION. The manager, acting as agent for the group, signs the UNDERWRITING AGREEMENT (or *purchase contract)* with the issuer. This agreement sets forth the terms and conditions of the arrangement and the responsibilities of both issuer and underwriter. During the offering period, it is the manager's responsibility to stabilize the MARKET PRICE of the issuer's shares by bidding in the open market, a process called PEGGING. The manager may also appoint a SELLING GROUP, comprised of dealers and the underwriters themselves, to assist in DISTRIBUTION of the issue.

Strictly speaking, *underwrite* is properly used only in a FIRM COMMITMENT underwriting, also known as a BOUGHT DEAL, where the securities are purchased outright from the issuer.

Other investment banking arrangements to which the term is sometimes loosely applied are BEST EFFORT, ALL OR NONE, and STANDBY COMMITMENTS; in each of these, the risk is shared between the issuer and the INVESTMENT BANKER.

The term is also sometimes used in connection with a REGISTERED SECONDARY OFFERING, which involves essentially the same process as a new issue, except that the proceeds go to the selling investor, not to the issuer. For these arrangements, the term *secondary offering* or SECONDARY DISTRIBUTION is preferable to *underwriting,* which is usually reserved for new, or primary, distributions.

There are two basic methods by which underwriters are chosen by issuers and underwriting spreads are determined: NEGOTIATED UNDERWRITINGS and COMPETITIVE

BID underwritings. Generally, the negotiated method is used in corporate equity (stock) issues and most corporate debt (bond) issues, whereas the competitive bidding method is used by municipalities and public utilities.

See also ALLOTMENT; BLOWOUT; FLOATING AN ISSUE; FLOTATION COST; HOT ISSUE; INITIAL PUBLIC OFFERING; PRESOLD ISSUE; PRIMARY MARKET; PUBLIC OFFERING; STANDBY UNDERWRITER.

UNDERWRITER

Insurance: company that assumes the cost risk of death, fire, theft, illness, etc., in exchange for payments, called *premiums.*

Securities: INVESTMENT BANKER who, singly or as a member of an UNDERWRITING GROUP or syndicate, agrees to purchase a NEW ISSUE of securities from an issuer and distribute it to investors, making a profit on the UNDERWRITING SPREAD. *See also* UNDERWRITE.

UNDERWRITING AGREEMENT agreement between a corporation issuing new securities to be offered to the public and the MANAGING UNDERWRITER as agent for the UNDERWRITING GROUP. Also termed the *purchase agreement* or *purchase contract,* it represents the underwriters' commitment to purchase the securities, and it details the PUBLIC OFFERING PRICE, the UNDERWRITING SPREAD (including all discounts and commissions), the net proceeds to the issuer, and the SETTLEMENT DATE.

The issuer agrees to pay all expenses incurred in preparing the issue for resale, including the costs of REGISTRATION with the SECURITIES AND EXCHANGE COMMISSION (SEC) and of the PROSPECTUS, and agrees to supply the managing underwriter with sufficient copies of both the PRELIMINARY PROSPECTUS (red herring) and the final, statutory prospectus. The issuer guarantees (1) to make all required SEC filings and to comply fully with the provisions of the SECURITIES ACT OF 1933; (2) to assume responsibility for the completeness, accuracy, and proper certification of all information in the registration statement and prospectus; (3) to disclose all pending litigation; (4) to use the proceeds for the purposes stated; (5) to comply with state securities laws; (6) to work to get listed on the exchange agreed upon; and (7) to indemnify the underwriters for liability arising out of omissions or misrepresentations for which the issuer had responsibility.

The underwriters agree to proceed with the offering as soon as the registration is cleared by the SEC or at a specified date thereafter. The underwriters are authorized to make sales to members of a SELLING GROUP.

The underwriting agreement is not to be confused with the AGREEMENT AMONG UNDERWRITERS. *See also* BEST EFFORT; FIRM COMMITMENT; STANDBY COMMITMENT; UNDERWRITE.

UNDERWRITING GROUP temporary association of investment bankers, organized by the originating INVESTMENT BANKER in a NEW ISSUE of securities. Operating under an AGREEMENT AMONG UNDERWRITERS, it agrees to purchase securities from the issuing corporation at an agreed-upon price and to resell them at a PUBLIC OFFERING PRICE, the difference representing the UNDERWRITING SPREAD. The purpose of the underwriting group is to spread the risk and assure successful distribution of the offering. Most underwriting groups operate under a *divided syndicate contract,* meaning that the liability of members is limited to their individual participations. Also called DISTRIBUTING SYNDICATE, PURCHASE GROUP, *investment banking group,* or *syndicate. See also* FIRM COMMITMENT; UNDERWRITE; UNDERWRITING AGREEMENT.

UNDERWRITING SPREAD difference between the amount paid to an issuer of securities in a PRIMARY DISTRIBUTION and the PUBLIC OFFERING PRICE. The amount of SPREAD varies widely, depending on the size of the issue, the financial strength of the issuer, the type of security involved (stock, bonds, rights), the status of the security (senior, junior, secured, unsecured), and the type of commitment made by the investment bankers. The range may be from a fraction of 1% for a bond issue of a big utility company to 25% for the INITIAL PUBLIC OFFERING of a small company. The division of the spread between the MANAGING UNDERWRITER, the SELLING GROUP, and the participating underwriters also varies, but in a two-point spread the manager might typically get 0.25%, the selling group 1%, and the underwriters 0.75%. It is usual, though, for the underwriters also to be members of the selling group, thus picking up 1.75% of the spread, and for the manager to be in all three categories, thus picking up the full 2%. *See also* COMPETITIVE BID; FLOTATION COST; GROSS SPREAD; NEGOTIATED UNDERWRITING; SELLING CONCESSION; UNDERWRITE.

UNDIGESTED SECURITIES newly issued stocks and bonds that remain undistributed because there is insufficient public demand at the OFFERING PRICE. *See also* UNDERWRITE.

UNDISTRIBUTED PROFITS (EARNINGS, NET INCOME) *see* RETAINED EARNINGS.

UNDIVIDED PROFITS account shown on a bank's BALANCE SHEET representing profits that have neither been paid out as DIVIDENDS nor transferred to the bank's SURPLUS account. Current earnings are credited to the undivided profits account and are then either paid out in dividends or retained to build up total EQUITY. As the account grows, round amounts may be periodically transferred to the surplus account.

UNEARNED DISCOUNT account on the books of a lending institution recognizing interest deducted in advance and which will be taken into income as earned over the life of the loan. In accordance with accounting principles, such interest is initially recorded as a LIABILITY. Then, as months pass and it is gradually "earned," it is recognized as income, thus increasing the lender's profit and decreasing the corresponding liability. *See also* UNEARNED INCOME.

UNEARNED INCOME (REVENUE)
Accounting: income received but not yet earned, such as rent received in advance or other advances from customers. Unearned income is usually classified as a CURRENT LIABILITY on a company's BALANCE SHEET, assuming that it will be credited to income within the normal accounting cycle. *See also* DEFERRED CHARGE.

Income taxes: income from sources other than wages, salaries, tips, and other employee compensation—for example, DIVIDENDS, INTEREST, rent.

UNEARNED INTEREST interest that has already been collected on a loan by a financial institution, but that cannot yet be counted as part of earnings because the principal of the loan has not been outstanding long enough. Also called DISCOUNT and UNEARNED DISCOUNT.

UNEMPLOYED OR UNEMPLOYMENT condition of being out of work involuntarily. The federal-state unemployment insurance system makes cash payments directly to laid-off workers. Most states now pay a maximum of 26 weeks; a few extend duration somewhat farther. In periods of very high unemployment in individual states, benefits are payable for as many as 13 additional weeks. These "extended benefits" are funded on a shared basis, approximately half from state funds and half from federal sources. In general, to collect unemployment benefits a person must have previously held a job and must be actively seeking employment. Unemployed people apply for and collect unemployment compensation from their state's Department of Labor. Except in states where there are small employee payments, the system is financed by a payroll tax on employers.

UNEMPLOYMENT RATE percentage of the civilian labor force actively looking for work but unable to find jobs. The rate is compiled by the U.S. Department of Labor, in cooperation with the Labor Departments in all the states, and released to the public on the first Friday of every month. The unemployment rate is affected by the number of people entering the workforce as well as the number of unemployed people. An important part of the Labor Department's report is "Payroll Employment," which covers data on hours, earnings, and employment for non-farm industries nationally, by state and for major metropolitan areas. The unemployment report is one of the most closely watched of all government reports, because it gives the clearest indication of the direction of the economy. A rising unemployment rate will be seen by analysts and the Federal Reserve as a sign of a weakening economy, which might call for an easing of monetary policy by the Fed. On the other hand, a drop in the unemployment rate shows that the economy is growing, which may spark fears of higher inflation on the part of the Fed, which may raise interest rates as a result.

UNENCUMBERED property free and clear of all liens (creditors' claims). When a homeowner pays off his mortgage, for example, the house becomes unencumbered property. Securities bought with cash instead of on MARGIN are unencumbered.

UNFUNDED PENSION PLAN pension plan that is funded by the employer out of current income as funds are required by retirees or beneficiaries. Also known as a *pay-as-you-go* pension plan, or a plan using the *current disbursement funding approach*. This contrasts with an ADVANCE FUNDED PENSION PLAN, under which the employer puts aside money on a regular basis into a separate fund that is invested in stocks, bonds, real estate, and other assets.

UNIFIED CREDIT federal TAX CREDIT that may be applied against the gift tax, the estate tax, and, under specified conditions, the generation-skipping transfer tax.

UNIFORM COMMERCIAL CODE (UCC) legal code adopted by most states that codifies various laws dealing with commercial transactions, primarily those involving the sale of goods, both tangible and intangible, and secured transactions. It was drafted by the National Conference of Commissioners of Uniform State Laws and covers bank deposits, bankruptcy, commercial letters of credit, commercial paper, warranties, and other commercial activities. Article 8 of the UCC applies to transactions in investment securities.

UNIFORM GIFTS TO MINORS ACT (UGMA) enacted to provide a simple way to transfer property to a minor without the complications of a formal trust, and without the restrictions applicable to the guardianship of a minor's property. In many states, gifts under the UGMA can be made both by lifetime gift and by the donor's WILL. Lifetime UGMA gifts qualify for the $10,000 annual gift tax exclusion. A UGMA property is managed by a CUSTODIAN, who is appointed by the donor. If the donor names him/herself as custodian, and if the donor-custodian dies before the property is turned over to the minor, the value of the custodial property at the donor-custodian's death is included in the donor-custodian's taxable estate, even though the property belongs to the minor from the instant the UGMA gift is made. The custodial property must be turned over to the minor when the minor attains the age specified in the UGMA law of the state under which the gift is made. In most states, the age is 18, but in some states it is 21. In New York State it is 18 unless the donor, at the time the UGMA gift is made, specifies age 21. Some states have enacted a Uniform Transfer to Minors Act (UTMA), which in some case supplements the UGMA, and in others replaces it.

UNIFORM PRACTICE CODE rules of the NATIONAL ASSOCIATION OF SECURITIES DEALERS (NASD) concerned with standards and procedures for the operational handling of OVER THE COUNTER securities transactions, such as delivery, SETTLEMENT DATE, EX-DIVIDEND DATE, and other ex-dates (such as EX-RIGHTS and EX-WARRANTS), and providing for the arbitration of disputes through Uniform Practice committees.

UNIFORM SECURITIES AGENT STATE LAW EXAMINATION test required of prospective REGISTERED REPRESENTATIVES in many U.S. states. In addition to the examination requirements of states, all registered representatives, whether employees of member firms or OVER THE COUNTER brokers, must pass the General Securities Representative Examination (also known as the Series 7 Examination), administered by the National Association of Securities Dealers (NASD).

UNIFORM TRANSFERS TO MINORS ACT (UTMA) law adopted by all 50 states that is similar to the UNIFORM GIFTS TO MINORS ACT (UGMA) but different in that it extends the definition of GIFTS beyond cash and securities to include real estate, paintings, royalties, and patents. UTMA also prohibits the minor from taking control of the assets until age 21 (25 in California).

UNINSURED MOTORIST INSURANCE form of insurance that covers the policyholder and family members if injured by a hit-and-run motorist or driver who carries no liability insurance, assuming the driver is at fault. In most instances, reimbursements of costs of property damage and medical expenses resulting from the accident will be rewarded. The premiums for uninsured motorist coverage are usually rather modest, and are included as part of a regular auto insurance policy.

UNISSUED STOCK shares of a corporation's stock authorized in its charter but not issued. They are shown on the BALANCE SHEET along with shares ISSUED AND OUTSTANDING. Unissued stock may be issued by action of the board of directors, although shares needed for unexercised employee STOCK OPTIONS, rights, warrants, or convertible securities must not be issued while such obligations are outstanding. Unissued shares cannot pay dividends and cannot be voted. They are not to be confused with TREASURY STOCK, which is issued but not outstanding.

UNIT

In general: any division of quantity accepted as a standard of measurement or of exchange. For example, in the commodities markets, a unit of wheat is a bushel, a unit of coffee a pound, and a unit of shell eggs a dozen. The unit of U.S. currency is the dollar.

Banking: bank operating out of only one office, and with no branches, as required by states having unit banking laws.

Finance:

1. segment or subdivision (division or subsidiary, product line, or plant) of a company.
2. in sales or production, quantity rather than dollars. One might say, for example, "Unit volume declined but dollar volume increased after prices were raised."

Securities:

1. minimum amount of stocks, bonds, commodities, or other securities accepted for trading on an exchange. *See also* ODD LOT; ROUND LOT; UNIT OF TRADING.

2. group of specialists on a stock exchange, who maintain fair and orderly markets in particular securities. *See also* SPECIALIST; SPECIALIST UNIT.
3. more than one class of securities traded together; one common share and one SUBSCRIPTION WARRANT might sell as a unit, for example.
4. in primary and secondary distributions of securities, one share of stock or one bond.

UNITED STATES GOVERNMENT SECURITIES direct GOVERNMENT OBLIGATIONS—that is, debt issues of the U.S. government, such as Treasury bills, notes, and bonds and Series EE and Series HH SAVINGS BONDS as distinguished from government-sponsored AGENCY issues. *See also* GOVERNMENT SECURITIES; TREASURIES.

UNIT INVESTMENT TRUST investment vehicle, registered with the SECURITIES AND EXCHANGE COMMISSION under the INVESTMENT COMPANY ACT OF 1940, that purchases a fixed PORTFOLIO of income-producing securities, such as corporate, municipal, or government bonds, mortgage-backed securities, COMMON STOCK, or PREFERRED STOCK. Units in the trust, which usually cost at least $1000, are sold to investors by brokers, for a LOAD charge of about 4%. Unit holders receive an undivided interest in both the principal and the income portion of the portfolio in proportion to the amount of capital they invest. The portfolio of securities remains fixed until all the securities mature and unit holders have recovered their principal. Most brokerage firms maintain a SECONDARY MARKET in the trusts they sell, so that units can be resold if necessary.
In Britain, open-end mutual funds are called *unit trusts.*
See also INVESTMENT COMPANY; MORTGAGE-BACKED CERTIFICATE; UNIT SHARE INVESTMENT TRUST.

UNIT OF TRADING normal number of shares, bonds, or commodities comprising the minimum unit of trading on an exchange. For stocks, this is usually 100 shares, although inactive shares trade in 10-share units. For corporate bonds on the NYSE, the unit for exchange trading is $1000 or $5000 par value. Commodities futures units vary widely, according to the COMMODITY involved. *See also* FUTURES CONTRACT; ODD LOT; ROUND LOT.

UNIT SHARE INVESTMENT TRUST (USIT) specialized form of UNIT INVESTMENT TRUST comprising one unit of PRIME and one unit of SCORE.

UNIVERSAL LIFE INSURANCE form of life insurance, first marketed in the early 1980s, that combines the low-cost protection of TERM LIFE INSURANCE with a savings portion, which is invested in a tax-deferred account earning money-market rates of interest. The policy is flexible; that is, as age and income change, a policyholder can increase or decrease premium payments and coverage, or shift a certain portion of premiums into the savings account, without additional sales charges or complications. A new form of the policy; called *universal variable life insurance,* combines the flexibility of universal life with the growth potential of variable life. *See also* VARIABLE LIFE INSURANCE; WHOLE LIFE INSURANCE.

UNIVERSE OF SECURITIES group of stocks sharing a common characteristic. For example, one analyst may define a universe of securities as those with $100 to $500 million in outstanding market capitalization. Another may define it as stocks in a particular industry, such as communications, paper, or airlines. A mutual fund will often define itself to investors as limiting itself to a particular universe of securities, allowing investors to know in advance which kinds of securities that fund will buy and hold.

UNLEVERAGED PROGRAM LIMITED PARTNERSHIP whose use of borrowed funds to finance the acquisition of properties is 50% or less of the purchase price. In contrast, a *leveraged program* borrows 50% or more. Investors seeking to maximize income tend to favor unleveraged partnerships, where interest expense and other deductions from income are at a minimum. Investors looking for TAX SHELTERS might favor leveraged programs despite the higher risk because of the greater amount of property acquired with the borrowed money and the greater amount of tax deductible interest but the longer depreciation periods required by recent tax legislation have substantially reduced the tax benefits from real estate.

UNLIMITED MARITAL DEDUCTION *see* MARITAL DEDUCTION.

UNLIMITED TAX BOND MUNICIPAL BOND secured by the pledge to levy taxes at an unlimited rate until the bond is repaid.

UNLISTED SECURITY security that is not listed on an organized exchange, such as the NEW YORK STOCK EXCHANGE, the AMERICAN STOCK EXCHANGE, or the REGIONAL STOCK EXCHANGES, and is traded in the OVER THE COUNTER market.

UNLISTED TRADING trading of securities not listed on an organized exchange but traded on that exchange as an accommodation to its members. An exchange wishing to trade unlisted securities must file an application with the SECURITIES AND EXCHANGE COMMISSION and make the necessary information available to the investing public. The New York Stock Exchange does not allow unlisted trading privileges, and the practice has declined at the American Stock Exchange and other organized exchanges.

UNLOADING

Finance: selling off large quantities of merchandise inventory at below-market prices either to raise cash quickly or to depress the market in a particular product.

Investments: selling securities or commodities when prices are declining to preclude further loss.
    See also PUMP; PROFIT TAKING; SELLING OFF.

UNMARGINED ACCOUNT brokerage CASH ACCOUNT.

UNPAID DIVIDEND dividend that has been declared by a corporation but has still not been paid. A company may declare a dividend on July 1, for example, payable on August 1. During July, the declared dividend is called an unpaid dividend. *See also* EX-DIVIDEND.

UNQUALIFIED OPINION independent auditor's opinion that a company's financial statements are fairly presented, in all material respects, in conformity with generally accepted accounting principles. The justification for the expression of the auditor's opinion rests on the conformity of his or her audit with generally accepted auditing standards and on his or her feelings. Materiality and audit risk underly the application of auditing standards. *See also* ACCOUNTANT'S OPINION; ADVERSE OPINION; QUALIFIED OPINION.

UNREALIZED PROFIT (OR LOSS) profit or loss that has not become actual. It becomes a REALIZED PROFIT (OR LOSS) when the security or commodity future contract in which there is a gain or loss is actually sold. Also called a *paper profit or loss.*

UNREGISTERED STOCK *see* LETTER SECURITY.

UNSECURED DEBT obligation not backed by the pledge of specific COLLATERAL.

UNSECURED LOAN loan without COLLATERAL.

UNWIND A TRADE to reverse a securities transaction through an offsetting transaction. *See also* OFFSET.

UPGRADING increase in the quality rating of a security. An analyst may upgrade a company's bond or stock rating if its finances improve, profitability is enhanced, and its debt level is reduced. For municipal bond issues, upgrading will occur if tax revenues increase and expenses are reduced. The upgrading of a stock or bond issue may in itself raise the price of the security because investors will feel more confident in the financial soundness of the issuer. The credit rating of issuers is constantly being evaluated, which may lead to further upgradings, or, if conditions deteriorate, downgradings. The term *upgrading* is also applied to an entire portfolio of securities. For example, a mutual fund manager who wants to improve the quality of his bond holdings will say that he is in the process of upgrading his portfolio.

UPSET PRICE term used in auctions that represents the minimum price at which a seller of property will entertain bids.

UPSIDE POTENTIAL amount of upward price movement an investor or an analyst expects of a particular stock, bond, or commodity. This opinion may result from either FUNDAMENTAL ANALYSIS or TECHNICAL ANALYSIS.

UPSTAIRS MARKET transaction completed within the broker-dealer's firm and without using the stock exchange. Securities and Exchange Commission and stock exchange rules exist to ensure that such trades do not occur at prices less favorable to the customer than those prevailing in the general market. *See also* OFF BOARD.

UPSWING upward movement in the price of a security or commodity after a period of falling prices. Analysts will say "that stock has bottomed out and now has started an upswing which should carry it to new highs." The term is also used to refer to the general condition of the economy. An economy that is recovering from a prolonged downturn or recession is said to be in an upswing.

UPTICK transaction executed at a price higher than the preceding transaction in that security; also called PLUS TICK. A plus sign is displayed throughout the day next to the last price of each stock that showed a higher price than the preceding transaction in that stock at the TRADING POST of the SPECIALIST on the floor of the New York Stock Exchange. Short sales may only be executed on upticks or ZERO-PLUS TICKS. *See* also MINUS TICK; SELLING SHORT; TICK.

UPTICK RULE Securities and Exchange Commission rule that selling short may only be done on an UPTICK. In 1990, interpretation of the rule was extended to cover PROGRAM TRADING.

UPTREND upward direction in the price of a stock, bond, or commodity future contract or overall market. *See also* TRENDLINE.

USEFUL LIFE estimated period of time during which an asset subject to DEPRECIATION is judged to be productive in a business. Also called *depreciable life.* The MODIFIED ACCELERATED COST RECOVERY SYSTEM (MACRS) established useful lives for different property classes. *See also* RESIDUAL VALUE.

USES OF FUNDS *see* SOURCES AND APPLICATIONS (OR USES) OF FUNDS STATEMENT.

U.S. SAVINGS BOND *see* SAVINGS BOND.

USURY LAWS state laws limiting excessive interest rates on loans.

UTILITY power company that owns or operates facilities used for the generation, transmission, or distribution of electric energy. Utilities provide electric, gas, and water to their customers. In the United States, utilities are regulated at the state and federal level. State public service and public utility commissions regulate retail rates. The Federal Energy Regulatory Commission (FERC) regulates wholesale rates, the sale, resale, and interstate commerce for approximately 200 investor-owned utilities. On a percentage and revenue basis, however, the states regulate most of the trade. Rates for the sale of power and its transmission to retail customers, as well as approval for the construction of new plants, are regulated at the state level. The electric utility industry came under government regulation in the 1920s because it was a virtual MONOPOLY, vertically integrated, producing energy and transmitting it to customers. The industry has evolved to include public power agencies and electricity cooperatives. DEREGULATION of the natural gas industry in recent years has served to open that market to more competition, although transmission pipelines still come under FERC jurisdiction. The electric utility industry is also undertaking a similar deregulation process.

Utility stocks usually offer above-average dividend yields to investors, but less capital appreciation potential than growth stocks. Utility stocks are also very sensitive to the direction of interest rates. Rising interest rates tend to harm the value of utility shares because higher rates provide a more attractive alternative to investors. In addition, utilities tend to be heavy borrowers, so higher interest rates add to their borrowing costs. Conversely, falling interest rates tend to buoy the value of utility stocks because utility dividends look more attractive and because the companies' borrowing costs will be reduced.

UTILITY REVENUE BOND MUNICIPAL BOND issued to finance the construction of electric generating plants, gas, water and sewer systems, among other types of public utility services. These bonds are repaid from the revenues the project produces once it is operating. Such bonds usually have a reserve fund that contains an amount equal to one year's DEBT SERVICE, which protects bondholders in case there is a temporary cash shortage or revenues are less than anticipated. *See also* REVENUE BOND.

V _____

VALUABLES *see* HIGH-TICKET ITEMS.

VALUATION placing a value or worth on an asset. Stock analysts determine the value of a company's stock based on the outlook for earnings and the market value of assets on the balance sheet. Stock valuation is normally expressed in terms of price/earnings (P/E) ratios. A company with a high P/E is said to have a high valuation, and a low P/E stock has a low valuation. Other assets, such as real estate and bonds, are given valuations by analysts who recommend whether the asset is worth buying or selling at the current price. Estates also go through the valuation process after someone has died.

VALUATION RESERVE reserve or allowance, created by a charge to expenses (and therefore, in effect, taken out of profits) in order to provide for changes in the value of a company's assets. Accumulated DEPRECIATION, allowance for BAD

DEBTS, and UNAMORTIZED BOND DISCOUNT are three familiar examples of valuation reserves. Also called *valuation account.*

VALUE-ADDED TAX (VAT) consumption tax levied on the value added to a product at each stage of its manufacturing cycle as well as at the time of purchase by the ultimate consumer. The value-added tax is a fixture in European countries and a major source of revenue for the European Common Market. Advocates of a value-added tax for the U.S. contend that it would be the most efficient method of raising revenue and that the size of its receipts would permit a reduction in income tax rates. Opponents argue that in its pure form it would be the equivalent of a national sales tax and therefore unfair and regressive, putting the greatest burden on those who can least afford it. As an example, for each part that goes into the assembling of an automobile, the auto manufacturer would pay a value-added tax to the supplier, probably a percentage of the purchase price, as is the case with a sales tax. When the finished car is sold, the consumer pays a value-added tax on the cost of the finished product less the material and supply costs that were taxed at earlier stages. This avoids double taxation and thus differs from a flat sales tax based on the total cost of purchase.

VALUE BROKER DISCOUNT BROKER whose rates are based on a percentage of the dollar value of each transaction. It is usually advantageous to place orders through a value broker for trades of low-priced shares or small numbers of shares, since commissions will be relatively smaller than if a shareholder used a SHARE BROKER, another type of discount broker, who charges according to the number and the price of the shares traded.

VALUE CHANGE change in a stock price adjusted for the number of outstanding shares of that stock, so that a group of stocks adjusted this way are equally weighted. A unit of movement of the group—called an INDEX—is thus representative of the average performance.

VALUE DATE
Banking: official date when money is transferred, that is, becomes good funds to the depositor. The value date differs from the *entry date* when items are received from the depositor, since the items must then be forwarded to the paying bank or otherwise collected. The term is used mainly with reference to foreign accounts, either maintained in a domestic bank or maintained by a domestic bank in foreign banks. *See also* FLOAT.

Eurodollar and foreign currency transactions: synonymous with SETTLEMENT DATE or DELIVERY DATE, which on spot transactions involving North American currencies (U.S. dollar, Canadian dollar, and Mexican peso) is one business day and on spot transactions involving other currencies, two business days. In the forward exchange market, value date is the maturity date of the contract plus one business day for North American currencies, two business days for other currencies. *See also* FORWARD EXCHANGE TRANSACTION; SPOT MARKET.

VALUE LINE INVESTMENT SURVEY investment advisory service that ranks about 1,700 stocks for "timeliness" and safety. Using a computerized model based on earnings momentum, Value Line projects which stocks will have the best or worst relative price performance over the next 6 to 12 months. In addition, each stock is assigned a risk rating, which identifies the VOLATILITY of a stock's price behavior relative to the market average. The service also ranks all major industry groups for timeliness. Value Line's ranking system for both timeliness and safety of an individual stock is as follows:
    1—highest rank
    2—above average rank

3—average rank
4—below average rank
5—lowest rank

The weekly writeups of companies that Value Line subscribers receive include detailed financial information about a company, as well as such data as corporate INSIDER buying and selling decisions and the percentage of a company's shares held by institutions.

Value Line offers several specialized financial surveys. The *Value Line Convertibles Survey* is a subscription service that evaluates convertible securities. The *Value Line Mutual Fund Survey* offers details on fund holdings and performance and ranks funds on expected returns. Value Line also sponsors its own family of mutual funds. Value Line also produces several stock indices and averages, the most important of which is the *Value Line Composite Average,* which tracks the stocks followed by the *Value Line Investment Survey.*

VA MORTGAGE *see* VETERANS ADMINISTRATION (VA) MORTGAGE.

VANCOUVER STOCK EXCHANGE securities and options exchange in Vancouver, British Columbia, Canada, specializing since 1907 in venture capital companies. It is also known as the VSE. Its securities market trades stocks, rights, warrants, and units, while its options market focuses on equity and gold options. Mining stocks account for most of the trading, with junior mining companies making up the largest single group. Billions of dollars have been raised by natural resource companies on the exchange. The number of technology, entertainment, real estate, and financial services companies listed on the exchange is increasing. Traditionally between 10% and 20% of the financings originate in the United States, with 20% to 25% from Europe and Asia. The *VSE Index* (100.00— January 1982), is capital-weighted and comprises three sub-indices: Commercial/Industrial, Resource, and Venture. In 1990, with the introduction of Vancouver Computerized Trading (VCT), the VSE became the first North American exchange to convert from open outcry to a completely automated trading system. Computerized clearing is conducted through the West Canada Clearing Corp. Settlement is on the third business day following a trade. Trading hours are 9 A.M. to 5 P.M., Monday through Friday.

VARIABLE ANNUITY life insurance ANNUITY contract whose value fluctuates with that of an underlying securities PORTFOLIO or other INDEX of performance. The variable annuity contrasts with a conventional or FIXED ANNUITY, whose rate of return is constant and therefore vulnerable to the effects of inflation. Income on a variable annuity may be taken periodically, beginning immediately or at any future time. The annuity may be a single-premium or multiple-premium contract. The return to investors may be in the form of a periodic payment that varies with the MARKET VALUE of the portfolio or a fixed minimum payment with add-ons based on the rate of portfolio appreciation. *See also* SINGLE PREMIUM DEFERRED ANNUITY.

VARIABLE COST cost that changes directly with the amount of production—for example, direct material or direct labor needed to complete a product. *See also* FIXED COST.

VARIABLE INTEREST RATE interest rate on a loan that rises and falls based on the movement of an underlying index of interest rates. For example, many credit cards charge variable interest rates, based on a specific spread over the prime rate. Most home equity loans charge variable rates tied to the prime rate. Also called *adjustable interest rate.*

VARIABLE LIFE INSURANCE innovation in WHOLE LIFE INSURANCE that allows the cash value of the policy to be invested in stock, bond, or money market portfolios. Investors can elect to move from one portfolio to another or can rely on the company's professional money managers to make such decisions for them. As in whole life insurance, the annual premium is fixed, but part of it is earmarked for the investment PORTFOLIO. The policyholder bears the risk of securities investments, while the insurance company guarantees a minimum death benefit unaffected by any portfolio losses. When portfolio investments rise substantially, a portion of the increased cash value is put into additional insurance coverage. As in usual whole life policies, borrowings can be made against the accumulated cash value, or the policy can be cashed in. As in an INDIVIDUAL RETIREMENT ACCOUNT, earnings from variable life policies are tax deferred until distributed. Income is then taxed only to the extent that it exceeds the total premiums paid into the policy. Death benefits are taxed not as individual income but as taxable estate income, which has an exclusion of $600,000.

Variable life insurance is different from UNIVERSAL LIFE INSURANCE. Universal life allows policyholders to increase or decrease premiums and change the death benefit. It also accrues interest at market-related rates on premiums over and above insurance charges and expenses.

VARIABLE RATE CERTIFICATE a CERTIFICATE OF DEPOSIT (CD) whose rate of interest is periodically adjusted in relation to some benchmark, such as the prime rate or a stock index.

VARIABLE-RATE DEMAND NOTE note representing borrowings (usually from a commercial bank) that is payable on demand and that bears interest tied to a money market rate, usually the bank PRIME RATE. The rate on the note is adjusted upward or downward each time the base rate changes.

VARIABLE RATE MORTGAGE (VRM) *see* ADJUSTABLE RATE MORTGAGE (ARM).

VARIABLE RATE PREFERRED STOCK *see* ADJUSTABLE RATE PREFERRED STOCK (ARP).

VARIANCE

Accounting: difference between actual cost and STANDARD COST in the categories of direct material, direct labor, and DIRECT OVERHEAD. A positive variation (when the actual cost is lower than the standard or anticipated cost) would translate into a higher profit unless offset by negative variances elsewhere.

Finance: (1) difference between corresponding items on a comparative BALANCE SHEET and PROFIT AND LOSS STATEMENT. (2) difference between actual experience and budgeted or projected experience in any financial category. For example, if sales were projected to be $2 million for a period and were actually $2.5 million, there would be a positive variance of $500,000, or 25%.

Real estate: allowed exception to zoning rules. If a particular neighborhood were zoned for residential use only, a person wanting to open a store would need to be granted a variance from the zoning board in order to proceed.

Statistics: measure of the dispersion of a distribution. It is the sum of the squares of the deviation from the mean. *See also* STANDARD DEVIATION.

VELDA SUE acronym for *Venture Enhancement & Loan Development Administration for Smaller Undercapitalized Enterprises,* a federal agency that buys small business loans made by banks, pools them, then issues securities that are bought as investments by large institutions.

VELOCITY rate of spending, or turnover of money—in other words, how many times a dollar is spent in a given period of time. The more money turns over, the faster velocity is said to be. The concept of "income velocity of money" was first explained by the economist Irving Fisher in the 1920s as bearing a direct relationship to GROSS DOMESTIC PRODUCT (GDP). Velocity usually is measured as the ratio of GDP to the money supply. Velocity affects the amount of economic activity generated by a given money supply, which includes bank deposits and cash in circulation. Velocity is a factor in the Federal Reserve Board's management of MONETARY POLICY, because an increase in velocity may obviate the need for a stimulative increase in the money supply. Conversely, a decline in velocity might reflect dampened economic growth, even if the money supply holds steady. *See also* FISCAL POLICY.

VENDOR
1. supplier of goods or services of a commercial nature; may be a manufacturer, importer, or wholesale distributor. For example, one component of the Index of LEADING INDICATORS is vendor performance, meaning the rate at which suppliers of goods are making delivery to their commercial customers.
2. retailer of merchandise, especially one without an established place of business, as in *sidewalk vendor.*

VENTURE CAPITAL important source of financing for START-UP companies or others embarking on new or TURNAROUND ventures that entail some investment risk but offer the potential for above average future profits; also called *risk capital.* Sources of venture capital include wealthy individual investors; subsidiaries of banks and other corporations organized as small business investment companies (SBICs); groups of investment banks and other financing sources who pool investments in venture capital funds or VENTURE CAPITAL LIMITED PARTNERSHIPS. The SMALL BUSINESS ADMINISTRATION (SBA) promotes venture capital programs through the licensing and financing of SBICs. Venture capital financing supplements other personal or external funds that an ENTREPRENEUR is able to tap, or takes the place of loans of other funds that conventional financial institutions are unable or unwilling to risk. Some venture capital sources invest only at a certain stage of entrepreneurship, such as the start-up or SEED MONEY stage, the *first round* or SECOND ROUND phases that follow, or at the MEZZANINE LEVEL immediately preceding an INITIAL PUBLIC OFFERING. In return for taking an investment risk, venture capitalists are usually rewarded with some combination of PROFITS, PREFERRED STOCK, ROYALTIES on sales, and capital appreciation of common shares.

VENTURE CAPITAL LIMITED PARTNERSHIP investment vehicle organized by a brokerage firm or entrepreneurial company to raise capital for START-UP companies or those in the early processes of developing products and services. The partnership will usually take shares of stock in the company in return for capital supplied. Limited partners receive income from profits the company may earn. If the company is successful and goes public, limited partners' profits could be realized from the sale of formerly private stock to the public. This type of partnership differs from a RESEARCH AND DEVELOPMENT LIMITED PARTNERSHIP in that R&D deals receive revenue only from the particular products they UNDERWRITE, whereas a venture capital partnership participates in the profits of the company, no matter what product or service is sold. *See also* ENTREPRENEUR; LIMITED PARTNERSHIP.

VERTICAL LINE CHARTING form of technical charting on which the high, low, and closing prices of a stock or a market are shown on one vertical line with the closing price indicated by a short horizontal mark. Each vertical line represents another day, and the chart shows the trend of a stock or a market over a period of days, weeks, months, or years. Technical analysts discern from these charts whether a stock or a market is continually closing at the high or low end of its trading range during a day. This is useful in understanding whether the market's action is strong or weak, and therefore whether prices will advance or decline in the near future. *See also* TECHNICAL ANALYSIS.

VERTICAL LINE CHARTING

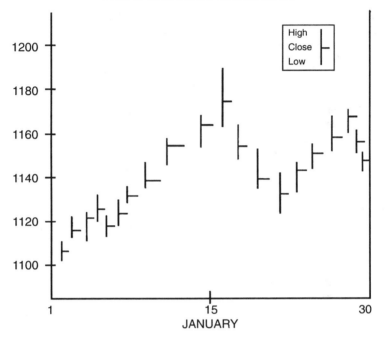

VERTICAL MERGER merger between a company that supplies goods and services and a company that buys those goods and services. For example, if a publishing company buys a paper producer, it is considered a vertical merger because the publisher buys large amounts of paper. In some cases, vertical mergers may be challenged by the government if they are found to violate ANTITRUST LAWS. *See also* MERGER.

VERTICAL SPREAD OPTION strategy that involves purchasing an option at one STRIKE PRICE while simultaneously selling another option of the same class at the next higher or lower strike price. Both options have the same expiration date. For example, a vertical spread is created by buying an XYZ May 30 call and selling an XYZ May 40 call. The investor who buys a vertical spread hopes to profit as the difference between the option premium on the two option positions widens or narrows. Also called a PRICE SPREAD. *See also* OPTION PREMIUM.

VESTED INTEREST in law, an interest in something that is certain to occur as opposed to being dependent on an event that might not happen. In general usage, an involvement having the element of personal gain. *See also* VESTING.

VESTING right an employee gradually acquires by length of service at a company to receive employer-contributed benefits, such as payments from a PENSION FUND, PROFIT-SHARING PLAN, or other QUALIFIED PLAN OR TRUST. Under the TAX REFORM

ACT OF 1986, employees must be vested 100% after five years of service or at 20% a year starting in the third year and becoming 100% vested after seven years.

VETERANS ADMINISTRATION (VA) independent agency under the president that operates various programs for veterans and their families, including hospital services and guarantees of home mortgage loans made by financial institutions at rates set by the VA.

VETERANS ADMINISTRATION (VA) MORTGAGE home mortgage loan granted by a lending institution to qualified veterans of the U.S. armed forces or to their surviving spouses and guaranteed by the VA. The guarantee reduces risk to the lender for all or part of the purchase price on conventional homes, mobile homes, and condominiums. Because of this federal guarantee, banks and thrift institutions can afford to provide 30-year VA mortgages on favorable terms with a relatively low down payment even during periods of TIGHT MONEY. Interest rates on VA mortgages, formerly fixed by the Department of Housing and Urban Development together with those on Federal Housing Administration (FHA) mortgages, are now set by the VA.

VA mortgages comprise an important part of the mortgage pools packaged and sold as securities by such quasi-governmental organizations as the FEDERAL HOME MORTGAGE CORPORATION (Freddie Mac) and the GOVERNMENT NATIONAL MORTGAGE ASSOCIATION (Ginnie Mae).

V FORMATION technical chart pattern that forms a V. The V pattern indicates that the stock, bond, or commodity being charted has bottomed out and is now in a bullish (rising) trend. An upside-down (inverse) V is considered bearish (indicative of a falling market). *See also* BOTTOM; TECHNICAL ANALYSIS.

V FORMATION

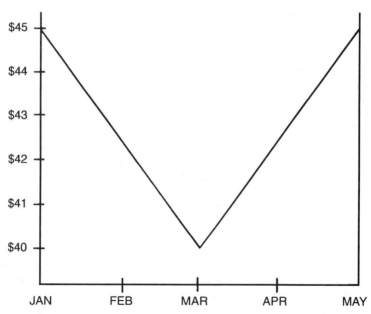

VIENNA STOCK EXCHANGE founded in 1771 as a state institution to provide a market for state-issued bonds, it is one of the world's oldest exchanges. The

VSE represents some two-thirds of Austrian stock transactions, with the balance over-the-counter. The *VSE Share Index* is made up of all domestic shares listed on the official market, while the *Austrian Traded Index* (ATX) includes the 19 most actively traded shares. Trades are settled on the second Monday following order execution. Trading is conducted from 9:30 A.M. to 1:30 P.M., Monday through Friday. Futures and options are traded on the Osterreichische Termin-und Optionenborse, or OTOB. Products include ATX futures, Austrian government bond futures, American-style stock options, and European-style ATX options.

VISIBLE SUPPLY dollar volume of municipal bonds scheduled to be issued over the coming month. Municipal bond investors, analysts, traders, and investment bankers watch the visible supply to determine whether the coming month might provide a good opportunity to buy bonds, sell bonds, or float a new bond issue. A large amount of new issues might depress bond prices and make it difficult to float a new issue. Conversely, a small amount of new issues may help bond prices and make it easier to float a new issue. The visible supply, also known as the calendar or the *30-day visible supply*, is compiled by *The Bond Buyer.*

VOID deprived of legal force or effect, as a CONTRACT.

VOIDABLE contract that can be annulled by either party after it is signed because fraud, incompetence, or another illegality exists or because a RIGHT OF RESCISSION applies.

VOLATILE tending to rapid and extreme fluctuations. The term is used to describe the size and frequency of the fluctuations in the price of a particular stock, bond, or commodity. A stock may be volatile because the outlook for the company is particularly uncertain, because there are only a few shares outstanding (*see also* THIN MARKET), or because of various other reasons. Where the reasons for the variation have to do with the particular security as distinguished from market conditions, return is measured by a concept called ALPHA. A stock with an alpha factor of 1.25 is projected to rise in price by 25% in a year on the strength of its inherent values such as growth in earnings per share and regardless of the performance of the market as a whole. Market-related volatility, also called SYSTEMATIC RISK, is measured by BETA. *See also* DURATION.

VOLATILITY characteristic of a security, commodity, or market to rise or fall sharply in price within a short-term period. A measure of the relative volatility of a stock to the overall market is its BETA. *See also* VOLATILE.

VOLUME total number of stock shares, bonds, or commodities futures contracts traded in a particular period. Volume figures are reported daily by exchanges, both for individual issues trading and for the total amount of trading executed on the exchange. Technical analysts place great emphasis on the amount of volume that occurs in the trading of a security or a commodity futures contract. A sharp rise in volume is believed to signify future sharp rises or falls in price, because it reflects increased investor interest in a security, commodity, or market. *See also* TECHNICAL ANALYSIS; TURNOVER.

VOLUME DELETED note appearing on the CONSOLIDATED TAPE, usually when the tape is running behind by two minutes or more because of heavy trading, that only the STOCK SYMBOL and the trading price will be displayed for transactions of less than 5000 shares.

VOLUME DISCOUNT any reduction in price based on the purchase of a large quantity.

VOLUNTARY ACCUMULATION PLAN plan subscribed to by a MUTUAL FUND shareholder to accumulate shares in that fund on a regular basis over time. The amount of money to be put into the fund and the intervals at which it is to be invested are at the discretion of the shareholder. A plan that invests a set amount on a regular schedule is called a dollar cost averaging plan or CONSTANT DOLLAR PLAN.

VOLUNTARY BANKRUPTCY legal proceeding that follows a petition of BANK-RUPTCY filed by a debtor in the appropriate U.S. district court under the Bankruptcy Act. Petitions for voluntary bankruptcy can be filed by any insolvent business or individual except a building and loan association or a municipal, railroad, insurance, or banking corporation.

VOLUNTARY LIQUIDATION LIQUIDATION approved by a company's shareholders, as opposed to involuntary liquidation under Chapter 7 BANKRUPTCY. In the United Kingdom, a distinction is made between creditors' voluntary liquidation (or winding-up), which requires insolvency, and members' voluntary liquidation (or winding-up), which requires a declaration of solvency. *See also* VOLUNTARY BANKRUPTCY.

VOLUNTARY PLAN short for *voluntary deductible employee contribution plan,* a type of pension plan where the employee elects to have contributions (which, depending on the plan, may be before-or after-tax) deducted from each paycheck.

VOTING RIGHT right attending the ownership of most common stock to vote in person or by PROXY on corporate resolutions and the election of directors. *See also* NONVOTING STOCK.

VOTING STOCK shares in a corporation that entitle the shareholder to voting and PROXY rights. When a shareholder deposits such stock with a CUSTODIAN that acts as a voting TRUST, the shareholder retains rights to earnings and dividends but delegates voting rights to the trustee. *See also* COMMON STOCK; PROPORTIONAL REPRESENTATION; VOTING TRUST CERTIFICATE.

VOTING TRUST CERTIFICATE transferable certificate of beneficial interest in a *voting trust,* a limited-life trust set up to center control of a corporation in the hands of a few individuals, called *voting trustees.* The certificates, which are issued by the voting trust to stockholders in exchange for their common stock, represent all the rights of common stock except voting rights. The common stock is then registered on the books of the corporation in the names of the trustees. The usual purpose for such an arrangement is to facilitate REORGANIZATION of a corporation in financial difficulty by preventing interference with management. Voting trust certificates are limited to the five-year life of a TRUST but can be extended with the mutual consent of the holders and trustees.

VULTURE FUND type of LIMITED PARTNERSHIP that invests in depressed property, usually real estate, aiming to profit when prices rebound.

W_____

WAGE ASSIGNMENT loan agreement provision, prohibited in some states, that authorizes the lender to deduct payments from an employee's wages in the event of DEFAULT.

WAGE GARNISHMENT *see* GARNISHMENT.

WAGE-PUSH INFLATION inflationary spiral caused by rapid increases in wages. *See also* COST-PUSH INFLATION; DEMAND-PULL INFLATION; INFLATION.

WAITING PERIOD period of time before something goes into effect. In securities, there is a waiting period between the filing of registration statements and the time when securities may be offered for sale to the public. This waiting period may be extended if the Securities and Exchange Commission requires revisions to the registration statement. In DISABILITY INCOME INSURANCE, there is a waiting period of several months from the time the disability occurs to the time when disability benefits are paid. For insurance claims, the waiting period is also known as the *elimination period.*

WAIVER OF PREMIUM clause in an insurance policy providing that all policy premiums will be waived if the policyholder becomes seriously ill or disabled, either permanently or temporarily, and therefore is unable to pay the premiums. Some policies include a waiver-of-premium clause automatically, while in other cases it is an optional feature that must be paid with additional premiums. During the waiver period, all policy benefits remain in force.

WALLFLOWER *see* ORPHAN STOCK.

WALLPAPER worthless securities. The implication of the term is that certificates of stocks and bonds that have gone bankrupt or defaulted have no other use than as wallpaper. However, there may be value in the worthless certificates themselves by collectors of such certificates, who prize rare or historically significant certificates. The practice of collecting such certificates is known as SCRIPOPHILY.

WALL STREET
1. common name for the financial district at the lower end of Manhattan in New York City, where the New York and American Stock Exchanges and numerous brokerage firms are headquartered. The New York Stock Exchange is actually located at the corner of Wall and Broad Streets.
2. investment community, such as in "Wall Street really likes the prospects for that company" or "Wall Street law firm," meaning a firm specializing in securities law and mergers. Also referred to as "the Street."

WANTED FOR CASH TICKER tape announcement that a bidder will pay cash the same day for a specified block of securities. Cash trades are executed for delivery and settlement at the time the transaction is made.

WAR BABIES jargon for the stocks and bonds of corporations engaged primarily as defense contractors. Also called *war brides.*

WAR CHEST fund of liquid assets (cash) set aside by a corporation to pay for a takeover or to defend against a takeover. Traders will say that a company has a war chest that it plans to use to take over another company. Or traders might say that a particular company will be difficult to take over because it has a large war chest that it can use to defend itself by buying back its stock, making an acquisition of its own, paying for legal fees to mount defenses, or taking other defensive measures. *See also* TAKEOVER.

WAREHOUSE RECEIPT document listing goods or commodities kept for SAFE-KEEPING in a warehouse. The receipt can be used to transfer ownership of that commodity, instead of having to deliver the physical commodity. Warehouse receipts are used with many commodities, particularly precious metals like gold, silver, and platinum, which must be safeguarded against theft.

WARRANT *see* SUBSCRIPTION WARRANT.

WARRANTY contract between the seller and the buyer of a product specifying the conditions under which the seller will make repairs or remedy other problems that may arise, at no additional cost to the buyer. The warranty document describes how long the warranty remains in effect, and which specific repairs will be performed at no extra charge. Warranties usually cover workmanship or the failure of the product if used normally, but not negligence on the part of the user if the product is used in ways for which it was not designed. Warranties are commonly issued for automobiles, appliances, electronic gear, and most other products. In some cases, manufacturers will offer extended warranties for several years beyond the original warranty period, at an extra charge. Consumers should consult federal and state laws for more extensive applications or interpretations of warranties.

WASH SALE purchase and sale of a security either simultaneously or within a short period of time. It may be done by a single investor or (where MANIPULATION is involved) by two or more parties conspiring to create artificial market activity in order to profit from a rise in the security's price. Wash sales taking place within 30 days of the underlying purchase do not qualify as tax losses under Internal Revenue Service rules.

Under the TAX REFORM ACT OF 1984, wash sale rules were extended to all taxpayers except those trading in securities in the normal course of business, such as securities dealers. Prior to the 1984 Act, noncorporate taxpayers engaged in a trade or business were exempt from wash sale rules. The Act also extended the wash sale prohibition to closing short sales of substantially identical securities, or to instances where short sales are made within 30 days of closing.

See also THIRTY-DAY WASH RULE.

WASTING ASSET
1. fixed asset, other than land, that has a limited useful life and is therefore subject to DEPRECIATION.
2. natural resource that diminishes in value because of extractions of oil, ores, or gas, or the removal of timber, or similar depletion and that is therefore subject to AMORTIZATION.
3. security with a value that expires at a particular time in the future. An OPTION contract, for instance, is a wasting asset, because the chances of a favorable move in the underlying stock diminish as the contract approaches expiration, thus reducing the value of the option.

WATCH LIST list of securities singled out for special surveillance by a brokerage firm or an exchange or other self-regulatory organization to spot irregularities. Firms on the watch list may be TAKEOVER candidates, companies about to issue new securities, or others that seem to have attracted an unusually heavy volume of trading activity. *See also* STOCK WATCHER; SURVEILLANCE DEPARTMENT OF EXCHANGES.

WATERED STOCK stock representing ownership of OVERVALUED assets, a condition of overcapitalized corporations, whose total worth is less than their invested capital. The condition may result from inflated accounting values, gifts of stock, operating losses, or excessive stock dividends. Among the negative features of watered stock from the shareholder's standpoint are inability to recoup full investment in LIQUIDATION, inadequate return on investment, possible liability exceeding the PAR value of shares, low MARKET VALUE because of poor dividends and possible adverse publicity, reduced ability of the firm to issue new stock or debt securities to capitalize on growth opportunity, and loss of competitive position because of the need to raise prices to provide a return acceptable to investors. To remedy the situation, a company must either increase its assets without increasing its OUT-STANDING shares or reduce outstanding shares without reducing assets. The alternatives are to increase RETAINED EARNINGS or to adjust the accounting values of assets or of stock.

WEAK DOLLAR dollar that has fallen in value against foreign currencies. This means that those holding dollars will get fewer pounds, yen, marks, francs, or other currencies in exchange for their dollars. A weak dollar makes it easier for U.S. companies to export their goods to other countries because foreigners' buying power is enhanced. The dollar may weaken because of loose U.S. monetary policy (creating too many dollars) and lack of confidence in the U.S. government, large trade and budget deficits, unattractive interest rates on dollar-denominated investments compared to investments denominated in other currencies, or other reasons.

WEAK MARKET market characterized by a preponderance of sellers over buyers and a general declining trend in prices.

WEDGE technical chart pattern similar to but varying slightly from a TRIANGLE. Two converging lines connect a series of peaks and troughs to form a wedge. These converging lines move in the same direction, unlike a triangle, in which one rises while the other falls or one rises or falls while the other line stays horizontal. Falling wedges usually occur as temporary interruptions of upward price rallies, rising wedges as interruptions of a falling price trend. *See also* TECHNICAL ANALYSIS.

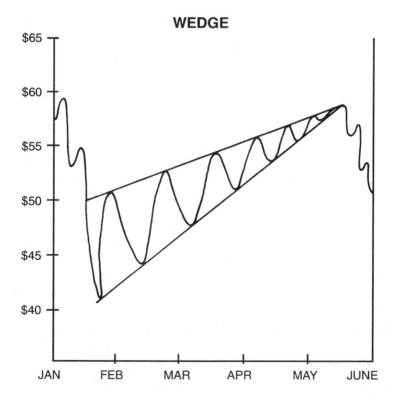

WEDGE

WEIGHTED AVERAGE MATURITY also called *average life* or *weighted average life* and used in mortgage-backed PASS-THROUGH SECURITIES meaning the weighted-average time to the return of a dollar of principal. It is arrived at by multiplying each portion of principal received by the time at which it is received, and then summing and dividing by the total amount of principal. Fabozzi's *Handbook of Fixed Income Securities* uses this example: Consider a simple annual-pay, four-year bond with a face value of $100 and principal payments of $40 the first year, $30 the second year, $20 the third year, and $10 the fourth year. The average life would be calculated as: Average life = .4 × 1 year + .3 × 2 years + .2 × 3 years + .1 × 4 years = 2 years. An alternative measure of investment life is DURATION.

W FORMATION technical chart pattern of the price of a stock, bond, or commodity that shows the price has hit a SUPPORT LEVEL two times and is moving up; also called a *double bottom.*

   A reverse W is just the opposite; the price has hit a resistance level and is headed down. This is called a DOUBLE TOP.

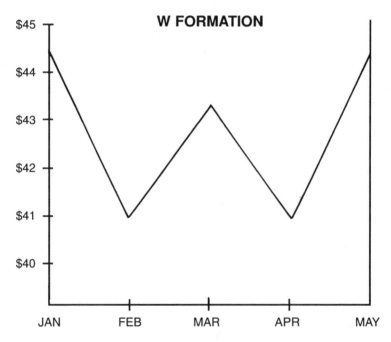

W-4 FORM tax form prepared by an employee for an employer indicating the employee's exemptions and Social Security number and enabling the employer to determine the amount of taxes to be withheld.

WHEN DISTRIBUTED transactions conditional on the SECONDARY DISTRIBUTION of shares ISSUED AND OUTSTANDING but CLOSELY HELD, as those of a wholly owned subsidiary, for example. *See also* WHEN ISSUED.

WHEN ISSUED short form of "when, as, and if issued." Term refers to a transaction made conditionally because a security, although authorized, has not yet been issued. NEW ISSUES of stocks and bonds, stocks that have SPLIT, and Treasury securities are all traded on a when issued basis. In a newspaper listing, a "WI" is placed next to the price of such a security. *See also* WHEN DISTRIBUTED.

WHIPSAWED to be caught in VOLATILE price movements and make losing trades as prices rise and fall. A trader is whipsawed if he or she buys just before prices fall and sells just before prices rise.

Term is also used in TECHNICAL ANALYSIS referring to misleading signals in the chart trends of markets or particular securities.

WHISPER STOCK stock that is rumored to be a takeover target. Speculators, arbitrageurs, and other investors may buy shares in the company hoping that the "whispers" they have heard are true, allowing them to reap huge profits when the takeover is officially announced. Whisper stocks may trade in heavier-than-usual volume once the rumors about the takeover spread widely. Investing in whisper stocks is risky, however, because the takeover rumors may prove to be inaccurate.

WHISTLE BLOWER employee or other person with inside knowledge of wrongdoing inside a company or government agency. The employee is supposed to be protected from retribution by the employer by several federal laws protecting whistle blowers, though whistle blowers frequently are punished for revealing wrongdoing by their employer. Several employees who disclosed illegal billing practices by defense contractors were demoted or fired, for example. In securities, under the Insider Trading and Securities Fraud Enforcement Act of 1988, whistle blowers who provide the SEC with information about illegal insider trading or other illegal activity that leads to a conviction may qualify for bounties.

WHITE COLLAR WORKER office worker in professional, managerial, or administrative position. Such workers typically wear shirts with white collars. Those working in factories or doing manual labor typically wear blue collars, and are therefore called *blue-collar workers.*

WHITE KNIGHT friendly acquirer sought by the target of an unfriendly TAKEOVER.

WHITEMAIL anti-TAKEOVER device whereby a vulnerable company sells a large amount of stock to a friendly party at below-market prices. This puts a potential raider in a position where it must buy a sizable amount of stock at inflated prices to get control and thus helps perpetuate existing management.

WHITE SHEETS list of prices published by the NATIONAL QUOTATION BUREAU for market makers in OVER-THE-COUNTER stocks traded in Chicago, Los Angeles, and San Francisco.

WHITE-SHOE FIRM anachronistic characterization of certain broker-dealers as venerable, "upper-crust" and "above" such practices as participating in hostile takeovers. Derives from the '50s culture of Ivy League colleges, where white buck shoes were *de rigueur* in elite fraternities and clubs.

WHITE SQUIRE WHITE KNIGHT who buys less than a majority interest.

WHITE'S RATING White's Tax-Exempt Bond Rating Service's classification of municipal securities, which is based on market factors rather than credit considerations and which attempts to determine appropriate yields. *See also* MUNICIPAL BOND.

WHOLE LIFE INSURANCE form of life insurance policy that offers protection in case the insured dies and also builds up cash value. The policy stays in force for the lifetime of the insured, unless the policy is canceled or lapses. The policyholder usually pays a level PREMIUM for whole life, which does not rise as the person grows older (as in the case of TERM INSURANCE). The earnings on the cash value in the policy accumulate tax-deferred, and can be borrowed against in the form of a POLICY LOAN. The death benefit is reduced by the amount of the loan, plus interest, if the loan is not repaid.

Traditionally, life insurance companies invest insurance premiums conservatively in bonds, stocks, and real estate in order to generate increases in cash value for policyholders. Policyholders have no input into the investment decision-making process in a whole life insurance policy. Other forms of cash value policies, such as UNIVERSAL LIFE INSURANCE and VARIABLE LIFE INSURANCE give policyholders more options, such as stock, bond, and money market accounts, to choose from in investing their premiums. Whole life insurance is also known as *ordinary life, permanent life, or straight life insurance. See also* ADEQUACY OF COVERAGE; ANNUAL EXCLUSION; CASH VALUE INSURANCE; CONTINGENT BENEFICIARY; CONVERTIBILITY; DEATH BENEFIT; EXPERIENCE RATING; FINANCIAL NEEDS APPROACH; FIXED PREMIUM; FULLY PAID POLICY; GUARANTEED INSURABILITY; HIDDEN LOAD; INCOME EXCLUSION RULE; INSURABILITY; INSURABLE INTEREST; INSURANCE AGENT; INSURANCE CLAIM; INSURANCE DIVIDEND; INSURANCE POLICY; INSURANCE PREMIUM; INSURANCE SETTLEMENT; INSURED; LAPSE; LIFE INSURANCE; LIFE INSURANCE POLICY; LIVING BENEFITS; LUMP SUM; MORTALITY RISK; NONCONTESTABILITY CLAUSE; NONPARTICIPATING LIFE INSURANCE POLICY; PAID UP; PAID UP POLICY; PARTICIPATING DIVIDENDS; PARTICIPATING INSURANCE; SAVINGS ELEMENT; SECOND-TO-DIE INSURANCE; SETTLEMENT OPTIONS; SINGLE-PREMIUM LIFE INSURANCE; SURRENDER VALUE.

WHOLE LOAN SECONDARY MORTGAGE MARKET term that distinguishes an investment representing an original residential mortgage loan (whole loan) from a loan representing a participation with one or more lenders or a PASS-THROUGH SECURITY representing a pool of mortgages.

WHOLESALE PRICE INDEX *see* PRODUCER PRICE INDEX.

WHOLESALER
In general: middleman or DISTRIBUTOR who sells mainly to retailers, JOBBERS, other merchants, and industrial, commercial, and institutional users as distinguished from consumers. *See also* VENDOR.
Securities:
1. INVESTMENT BANKER acting as an UNDERWRITER in a NEW ISSUE or as a distributor in a secondary offering of securities. *See also* SECONDARY DISTRIBUTION.
2. broker-dealer who trades with other broker-dealers, rather than with the retail investor, and receives discounts and selling commissions.
3. SPONSOR of a MUTUAL FUND.

WHOLLY OWNED SUBSIDIARY SUBSIDIARY whose common stock is virtually 100%-owned by the PARENT COMPANY.

WHOOPS nickname for the Washington Public Power Supply System. In the late 1970s and early 80s, WHOOPS raised billions of dollars through MUNICIPAL BOND offerings to finance construction of five nuclear plants in the state of Washington. Because of cost overruns, bad management, and numerous delays, two of the plants were canceled, and it was doubtful that two others would ever be completed. WHOOPS defaulted on the payments to bondholders on the two canceled plants after the Washington Supreme Court ruled that the TAKE-OR-PAY CONTRACTS with the many utilities in the Northwest that had backed the bonds were invalid. This was the largest municipal bond default in history.

WIDE OPENING abnormally large SPREAD between the BID AND ASKED prices of a security at the OPENING of a trading session.

WIDGET symbolic American gadget, used wherever a hypothetical product is needed to illustrate a manufacturing or selling concept.

WIDOW-AND-ORPHAN STOCK stock that pays high dividends and is very safe. It usually has a low BETA COEFFICIENT and is involved in a noncyclical business. For years American Telephone and Telegraph was considered a widow-and-orphan stock, but it lost that status after the breakup of the Bell System in 1984. High-quality electric utility stocks are still considered widow-and-orphan stocks by and large.

WILDCAT DRILLING exploring for oil or gas in an unproven area. A wildcat OIL AND GAS LIMITED PARTNERSHIP is structured so that investors take high risks but can reap substantial rewards if oil or gas is found in commercial quantities.

WILL document, also called a *testament,* that, when signed and witnessed, gives legal effect to the wishes of a person, called a *testator,* with respect to disposal of property upon death.

WILLIAMS ACT federal legislation enacted in 1968 that imposes requirements with respect to public TENDER OFFERS. It was inspired by a wave of unannounced TAKEOVERS in the 1960s, which caught managers unawares and confronted stockholders with decisions they were ill prepared to make, The Williams Act and amendments now comprise Sections 13(d) and 14(d) of the SECURITIES EXCHANGE ACT OF 1934. The law requires the bidder opening a tender to file with both the SECURITIES AND EXCHANGE COMMISSION and the TARGET COMPANY a statement detailing the terms of the offer, the bidder's background, the cash source, and his or her plans for the company if there is a takeover. The same information is required within 10 days from any person or company acquiring 5% or more of another company. The law mandates a minimum offering period of 20 days and gives tendering shareholders 15 days to change their minds. If only a limited number of shares are accepted, they must be prorated among the tendering stockholders. *See also* SATURDAY NIGHT SPECIAL.

WILSHIRE 5000 EQUITY INDEX market value-weighted index of approximately 6500 U.S.-based equities traded on the New York Stock Exchange, American Stock Exchange, and NASDAQ Stock Market. The index is prepared by Wilshire Associates, Inc., of Santa Monica, California. Changes are measured against its base value, equal to its market value in billions of dollars, on December 31, 1980. The Wilshire 5000 is widely followed as an indicator of the broad trend in stock prices. Some index mutual funds are designed to replicate the Wilshire 5000. *See also* STOCK INDICES AND AVERAGES.

WINDFALL PROFIT profit that occurs suddenly as a result of an event not controlled by the person or company profiting from the event. For example, oil companies profited in the 1970s from an explosion in the price of oil brought about by the Arab oil embargo and the price increases demanded by the Organization of Petroleum Exporting Countries. *See also* WINDFALL PROFITS TAX.

WINDFALL PROFITS TAX tax on profits that result from a sudden windfall to a particular company or industry. In 1980, federal legislation was passed that levied such a tax on oil companies because of the profits they earned as a result of the sharp increase in oil prices in the 1970s. As of the mid-1990s, the tax had not been reenacted.

WINDOW
1. limited time during which an opportunity should be seized, or it will be lost. For example, a period when new stock issues are welcomed by the public only

lasts for a few months, or maybe as long as a year—that time is called the *window of opportunity.*

2. DISCOUNT WINDOW of a Federal Reserve bank.

3. cashier department of a brokerage firm, where delivery and settlement of securities transactions takes place.

WINDOW DRESSING

1. trading activity near the end of a quarter or fiscal year that is designed to dress up a PORTFOLIO to be presented to clients or shareholders. For example, a fund manager may sell losing positions in his portfolio so he can display only positions that have gained in value.

2. accounting gimmickry designed to make a FINANCIAL STATEMENT show a more favorable condition than actually exists—for example by omitting certain expenses, by concealing liabilities, by delaying WRITE-OFFS, by anticipating sales, or by other such actions, which may or may not be fraudulent.

WINNEPEG COMMODITY EXCHANGE Canada's only agricultural futures and options exchange, opened in 1887 as the Winnipeg Grain and Produce Exchange. It conducts the world's only futures market for canola, flaxseed, and rye, and also trades oats, feed grades of wheat, and barley. Trading is conducted Monday through Friday, from 9:30 A.M.–1:15 P.M. for futures, and 9:30 A.M.–1:20 P.M. for options.

WIRE HOUSE national or international brokerage firm whose branch offices are linked by a communications system that permits the rapid dissemination of prices, information, and research relating to financial markets and individual securities. Although smaller retail and regional brokers currently have access to similar data, the designation of a firm as a wire house dates back to the time when only the largest organizations had access to high-speed communications. Therefore, *wire house* still is used to refer to the biggest brokerage houses.

WIRE ROOM operating department of a brokerage firm that receives customers' orders from the REGISTERED REPRESENTATIVE and transmits the vital data to the exchange floor, where a FLOOR TICKET is prepared, or to the firm's trading department for execution. The wire room also receives notices of executed trades and relays them to the appropriate registered representatives. Also called *order department, order room,* or *wire and order.*

WITCHING HOUR *see* TRIPLE WITCHING HOUR.

WITHDRAWAL PLAN program available through most open-end MUTUAL FUND companies in which shareholders can receive fixed payments of income or CAPITAL GAINS (or both) on a regular basis, usually monthly or quarterly.

WITHHOLDING

Securities: violation of the RULES OF FAIR PRACTICE of the NATIONAL ASSOCIATION OF SECURITIES DEALERS whereby a participant in a PUBLIC OFFERING fails to make a bona fide public offering at the PUBLIC OFFERING PRICE—for example, by withholding shares for his or her own account or selling shares to a family member, an employee of the dealer firm, or another broker-dealer—in order to profit from the higher market price of a HOT ISSUE. *See also* IMMEDIATE FAMILY; INVESTMENT HISTORY.

Taxes:

1. deduction from salary payments and other compensation to provide for an individual's tax liability. Federal income taxes and Social Security contributions are withheld from paychecks and are deposited in a Treasury TAX AND LOAN ACCOUNT with a bank. The yearly amount of withholding is reported on

an income statement (form W-2), which must be submitted with the federal, state, and local tax returns. Liability not provided for by withholding must be paid in four ESTIMATED TAX payments.

2. withholding by corporations and financial institutions of a flat 10% of interest and dividend payments due securities holders, as required under the TAX EQUITY AND FISCAL RESPONSIBILITY ACT OF 1982. The purpose was to levy a tax on people whose earnings escaped tracking by the Internal Revenue Service. The 10% withholding requirement was repealed in 1983. As a compromise, "backup withholding" was instituted, whereby, using Social Security numbers, payments can be reported to the IRS and matched against the actual income reported.

3. withholdings from pension and annuity distributions, sick pay, tips, and sizeable gambling winnings, as stipulated by law.

4. 30% withholding requirement on income from U.S. securities owned by foreigners—repealed by the TAX REFORM ACT OF 1984.

WORKERS COMPENSATION INSURANCE INSURANCE that pays benefits on behalf of an insured employer to employees or their families in the case of injury, disability, or death resulting from occupational hazards.

WORKING CAPITAL funds invested in a company's cash, ACCOUNTS RECEIVABLE, INVENTORY, and other CURRENT ASSETS *(gross working capital);* usually refers to *net working capital*—that is, current assets minus CURRENT LIABILITIES. Working capital finances the CASH CONVERSION CYCLE of a business—the time required to convert raw materials into finished goods, finished goods into sales, and accounts receivable into cash. These factors vary with the type of industry and the scale of production, which varies in turn with seasonality and with sales expansion and contraction. Internal sources of working capital include RETAINED EARNINGS, savings achieved through operating efficiencies and the allocation of CASH FLOW from sources like DEPRECIATION or deferred taxes to working capital. External sources include bank and other short-term borrowings, TRADE CREDIT, and term debt and EQUITY FINANCING not channeled into long-term assets. *See also* CURRENT RATIO; NET CURRENT ASSETS.

WORKING CONTROL effective control of a corporation by a shareholder or shareholders with less than 51% voting interest. Working control by a minority holder, or by two or more minority holders working in concert, is possible when share ownership of a firm is otherwise widely dispersed. *See also* MINORITY INTEREST.

WORKING INTEREST direct participation with unlimited liability, as distinguished from passive LIMITED PARTNERSHIP shares. The TAX REFORM ACT OF 1986 let investors with working interests in drilling ventures, such as GENERAL PARTNERS, offset losses against all types of income.

WORK-IN-PROCESS *see* INVENTORY.

WORKOUT situation, such as a bad loan or troubled firm, where remedial measures are being taken.

WORKSHEET computerized page allowing the user to manipulate many columns and rows of numbers. The worksheet can contain formulas so that if one number is changed, the entire worksheet is automatically updated, based on those formulas. Analysts, investors, and accountants track a company's financial statements, balance sheets, and other data on worksheets.

WORLD BANK *see* INTERNATIONAL BANK FOR RECONSTRUCTION AND DEVELOPMENT.

WRAP ACCOUNT investment consulting relationship in which a client's funds are placed with one or more money managers, and all administrative and management fees, along with commissions, are wrapped into one comprehensive fee, which is paid quarterly. The wrap fee varies, but usually ranges from 1% to 3% of the value of the assets in the account. Wrap accounts usually require a minimum initial investment of anywhere from $25,000 to $10 million for individual accounts. The term *wrap* has been expanded to involve mutual fund asset allocation programs. Technically, these are not wrap programs because they are not "all inclusive." Transaction commissions in these programs on mutual funds are still a variable and they are pooled accounts as distinguished from individual accounts. From the customer's point of view, a wrap account provides access to top investment managers. The broker overseeing the account is paid an ongoing fee to monitor the performance of the money managers. Although brokers may switch assets to other managers within the program if one manager consistently starts to underperform, most sponsors of wrap programs suggest a three- to five-year time horizon to reach investment goals.

WRAPAROUND ANNUITY ANNUITY contract allowing an annuitant discretion in the choice of underlying investments. Wraparound refers to the protection the annuity vehicle provides through its TAX-DEFERRED status, which becomes precarious when the annuity vehicle is being used as a technical way to avoid tax payment. The tax courts have ruled against tax deferment where money can be allocated by an annuity owner to a portfolio managed by an annuitant and where the annuitant can switch among funds of the sponsoring insurance company that are also marketed independently of annuities. On the other hand, the IRS has upheld tax deferral where an individual could not buy such funds without also buying the annuity. In any event, the insurer must legally own the annuity money.

WRAPAROUND MORTGAGE second mortgage that increases a borrower's indebtedness while leaving the original mortgage contract in force. The wraparound mortgage becomes the JUNIOR MORTGAGE and is held by the lending institution as security for the total mortgage debt. The borrower makes payments on both loans to the wraparound lender, who in turn makes scheduled installment payments on the original *senior mortgage*. It is a convenient way for a property owner to obtain additional credit without having first to pay off an existing mortgage.

WRINKLE novel feature that may attract a buyer for a new product or a security. For example, ZERO COUPON SECURITIES were a new wrinkle when they were introduced but soon thereafter became quite commonplace.

WRITE-OFF charging an ASSET amount to expense or loss. The effect of a write-off is to reduce or eliminate the value of the asset and reduce profits. Write-offs are systematically taken in accordance with allowable tax DEPRECIATION of a FIXED ASSET, and with the AMORTIZATION of certain other assets, such as an INTANGIBLE ASSET and a capitalized cost (like premiums paid on investments). Write-offs are also taken when assets are, for whatever reason, deemed worthless, the most common example being uncollectible ACCOUNTS RECEIVABLE. Where such write-offs can be anticipated and therefore estimated, the usual practice has been to charge income regularly in amounts needed to maintain a RESERVE, the actual losses then being charged to the reserve. The TAX REFORM ACT OF 1986 required that BAD DEBT write-offs be charged directly to income by taxpayers other than small banks and thrift institutions. *See also* EXTRAORDINARY ITEM: NONRECURRING CHARGE.

WRITE OUT procedure followed when a SPECIALIST on an exchange makes a trade involving his own inventory, on one hand, and an order he is holding for a FLOOR BROKER, on the other. Exchange rules require a two-part transaction: the broker first completes a trade with the specialist, who then completes the transaction by a separate trade with the customer. The write out involves no charge other than the normal broker's commission.

WRITER
1. person who sells PUT OPTION and CALL OPTION contracts, and therefore collects PREMIUM INCOME. The writer of a put option is obligated to buy (and the writer of a call option is obligated to sell) the UNDERLYING SECURITY at a predetermined price by a particular date if the OPTION is exercised. *See also* COVERED CALL; NAKED OPTION; WRITING NAKED.
2. insurance UNDERWRITER.

WRITE UP/WRITE DOWN upward or downward adjustment of the accounting value of an asset according to GENERALLY ACCEPTED ACCOUNTING PRINCIPLES GAAP. *See also* WRITE-OFF.

WRITING CASH-SECURED PUTS OPTION strategy that a trader who wants to sell PUT OPTIONS uses to avoid having to use a MARGIN ACCOUNT. Rather than depositing MARGIN with a broker, a put WRITER can deposit cash equal to the option EXERCISE PRICE. With this strategy, the put option writer is not subject to additional margin requirements in the event of changes in the underlying stock's price. The put writer can also be earning money by investing the PREMIUM he or she receives in MONEY MARKET instruments.

WRITING NAKED strategy used by an OPTION seller in which the trader does not own the UNDERLYING SECURITY. This strategy can lead to large profits if the stock moves in the hoped-for direction, but it can lead to large losses if the stock moves in the other direction, since the trader will have to go into the marketplace to buy the stock in order to deliver it to the option buyer. *See also* NAKED OPTION.

WRITING PUTS TO ACQUIRE STOCK strategy used by an OPTION writer (seller) who believes a stock is going to decline and that its purchase at a given price would represent a good investment. By writing a PUT OPTION exercisable at that price, the writer cannot lose. If the stock, contrary to his expectation, goes up, the option will not be exercised and he is at least ahead the amount of the PREMIUM he received. If, as expected, the stock goes down and the option is exercised, he has bought the stock at what he had earlier decided was a good buy, and he has the premium income in addition.

WRITTEN-DOWN VALUE BOOK VALUE of an asset after DEPRECIATION or other AMORTIZATION; also called *net book value*. For example, if the original cost of a piece of equipment was $1000 and accumulated depreciation charges totaled $400, the written-down value would be $600. *See also* INTANGIBLE ASSET.

WT abbreviation for *warrant. See also* SUBSCRIPTION WARRANT.

W-2 FORM tax form prepared by an employer for an employee to enclose with the 1040 FORM, summarizing wages earned for the year, federal and state taxes withheld, and SOCIAL SECURITY tax information.

X
_____

X or XD symbol used in newspapers to signify that a stock is trading EX-DIVIDEND, that is, without dividend. The symbol X is also used in bond tables to signify without interest.

XR symbol used in newspapers to signify that a stock is trading EX-RIGHTS, that is, without rights attached. *See also* SUBSCRIPTION RIGHT.

XW symbol used in newspapers to signify that a stock is trading EX-WARRANTS, that is, without warrants attached. *See also* SUBSCRIPTION WARRANT.

Y

YANKEE BOND MARKET dollar-denominated bonds issued in the U.S. by foreign banks and corporations. The bonds are issued in the U.S. when market conditions there are more favorable than on the EUROBOND market or in domestic markets overseas. Similarly, Yankee CERTIFICATES OF DEPOSIT are negotiable CDs issued in the U.S. by branches and agencies of foreign banks.

YEAR-END BONUS bonus payment given to employees at the end of a year, based on the employee's performance and the performance of the company. Most securities firms operate on a bonus system, providing employees with huge bonuses in highly profitable years and little or no bonuses in lean years. Many salespeople also operate on a year-end bonus system, in which they receive bonuses if they met or exceeded certain sales goals during the year.

YEAR-END DIVIDEND an additional or special DIVIDEND declared based on a company's profits during the fiscal year.

YEAR-TO-DATE (YTD) period from the beginning of the calendar year (or FISCAL YEAR (FY) if so indicated) to the reporting date. For example third-quarterly results of a company would be reported for the quarter alone and for the year-to-date, which would be nine months.

YELLOW SHEETS daily publication of the NATIONAL QUOTATION BUREAU that details the BID AND ASKED prices and firms that MAKE A MARKET in CORPORATE BONDS traded in the OVER THE COUNTER (OTC) market. Much of this information is not available in the daily OTC newspaper listings. The sheets are named for their color. OTC equity issues are covered separately on PINK SHEETS and regional OTC issues of both classes are listed on white sheets.

YEN BOND in general terms, any bond issue denominated in Japanese yen. International bankers using the term are usually referring to yen-denominated bonds issued or held outside Japan.

YIELD
In general: RETURN on an investor's CAPITAL INVESTMENT. A piece of real estate may yield a certain return, or a business deal may offer a particular yield. *See also* RETURN ON INVESTED CAPITAL.
Agriculture: agricultural output in terms of quantity of a crop.
Bonds:
1. COUPON rate of interest divided by the purchase price, called CURRENT YIELD. For example, a bond selling for $1000 with a 10% coupon offers a 10% current yield. If that same bond were selling for $500, however, it would offer a 20% yield to an investor who bought it for $500. (As a bond's price falls, its yield rises and vice versa.)
2. rate of return on a bond, taking into account the total of annual interest payments, the purchase price, the redemption value, and the amount of time

remaining until maturity; called *maturity yield* or YIELD TO MATURITY. *See also* DURATION; YIELD TO AVERAGE LIFE; YIELD TO CALL.

Lending: total money earned on a loan—that is, the ANNUAL PERCENTAGE RATE of interest multiplied by the term of the loan.

Stocks: percentage rate of return paid on a common or preferred stock in dividends. For example, a stock that sells for $20 and pays an annual dividend of $2 per share has a yield, also called a *dividend yield,* of 10%.

Taxes: amount of revenue received by a governmental entity as a result of a tax.

YIELD ADVANTAGE extra amount of return an investor will earn if he or she purchases a CONVERTIBLE security instead of the common stock of the same issuing corporation. If an XYZ Corporation convertible yields 10% and an XYZ common share yields 5%, the yield advantage is 5%. *See also* YIELD SPREAD.

YIELD CURVE graph showing the term structure of interest rates by plotting the yields of all bonds of the same quality with maturities ranging from the shortest to the longest available. The resulting curve shows if short-term interest rates are higher or lower than long-term rates. If short-term rates are lower, it is called a POSITIVE YIELD CURVE. If short-term rates are higher, it is called a NEGATIVE (or INVERTED) YIELD CURVE. If there is little difference between short-term and long-term rates, it is called a *flat yield* curve. For the most part, the yield curve is positive, since investors who are willing to tie up their money for a longer period of time usually are compensated for the extra risk they are taking by receiving a higher yield. The most common version of the yield curve graph plots Treasury securities, showing the range of yields from a three-month TREASURY BILL to a 20- or 30-year TREASURY BOND.

    Fixed-income analysts study the yield curve carefully in order to make judgments about the direction of interest rates. *See also* DURATION.

YIELD EQUIVALENCE the rate of interest at which a tax-exempt bond and a taxable security of similar quality provide the same return. In the day of the 50% TAX BRACKET, for example, a tax-exempt bond paying 10% was the equivalent of a taxable corporate bond of 20%. To calculate the yield that must be provided by a taxable security to equal that of a tax-exempt bond for investors in different tax brackets, the tax exempt yield is divided by the reciprocal of the tax bracket (100 less 28%, for example) to arrive at the taxable yield. Thus, a person in the 28% tax bracket who wished to figure the taxable equivalent of a 10% tax free municipal bond would divide 10% by 72% (100 minus 28%) to get 13.9%—the yield a corporate taxable bond would have to provide to be equivalent, after taxes, to the 10% municipal bond. To convert a taxable yield to a tax-exempt yield, the formula is reversed—that is, the tax exempt yield is equal to the taxable yield multiplied by the reciprocal of the tax bracket.

YIELD SPREAD difference in YIELD between various issues of securities. In comparing bonds, it usually refers to issues of different credit quality since issues of the same maturity and quality would normally have the same yields, as with Treasury securities, for example. Yield spread also refers to the differential between dividend yield on stocks and the CURRENT YIELD on bonds. The comparison might be made, for example, between the STANDARD & POOR'S INDEX (of 500 stocks) dividend yield and the current yield of an index of corporate bonds. A significant difference in bond and stock yields, assuming similar quality, is known as a *yield gap.*

YIELD TO AVERAGE LIFE yield calculation used, in lieu of YIELD TO MATURITY or YIELD TO CALL, where bonds are retired systematically during the life of the issue, as in the case of a SINKING FUND with contractual requirements. Because the issuer will buy its own bonds on the open market to satisfy its sinking fund requirements if the bonds are trading below PAR, there is to that extent automatic price support for such bonds; they therefore tend to trade on a yield-to-average-life basis.

YIELD TO CALL yield on a bond assuming the bond will be redeemed by the issuer at the first CALL date specified in the INDENTURE agreement. The same calculations are used to calculate yield to call as YIELD TO MATURITY except that the principal value at maturity is replaced by the first CALL PRICE and the maturity date is replaced by the first call date. Assuming the issuer will put the interest of the company before the interest of the investor and will call the bonds if it is favorable to do so, the lower of the yield to call and the yield to maturity can be viewed as the more realistic rate of return to the investor. *See also* DURATION.

YIELD TO MATURITY (YTM) concept used to determine the rate of return an investor will receive if a long-term, interest-bearing investment, such as a bond, is held to its MATURITY DATE. It takes into account purchase price, REDEMPTION value, time to maturity, COUPON yield, and the time between interest payments. Recognizing time value of money, it is the DISCOUNT RATE at which the PRESENT VALUE of all future payments would equal the present price of the bond, also known as INTERNAL RATE OF RETURN. It is implicitly assumed that coupons are reinvested at the YTM rate. YTM can be approximated using a bond value table (also called a bond yield table) or can be determined using a programmable calculator equipped for bond mathematics calculations. *See also* DURATION; HORIZON ANALYSIS; YIELD TO AVERAGE LIFE, YIELD TO CALL.

YO-YO STOCK stock that fluctuates in a VOLATILE manner, rising and falling quickly like a yo-yo.

Z _____

ZACKS ESTIMATE SYSTEM service offer by Zacks Investment Research of Chicago compiling earnings estimates and brokerage buy/hold/sell recommendations from more than 200 Wall Street research firms, covering more than 4500 stocks. Zacks tracks the number of analysts following each stock, how many analysts have raised or lowered their estimates, and the high, low and average earnings estimate for each quarter and fiscal year. Zacks offers a multiple selection of data bases, of print reports, and software for institutional and individual investors. *See also* I/B/E/S INTERNATIONAL INC.

Z-BOND the fourth (Z) TRANCHE of bonds in the structure of a typical COLLATERALIZED MORTGAGE OBLIGATION (CMO). Combining features of ZERO-COUPON SECURITIES and mortgage PASS-THROUGH SECURITIES, Z bonds receive no coupon payments until the earlier A (fast-pay), B (medium-pay), and C (slow-pay) classes have been paid off. Z holders then receive all the remaining cash flow, although interest has been added to principal as cash was used to repay earlier tranches. Some CMOs have been issued with multiple Z and Y tranches, incorporating SINKING-FUND schedules.

ZERO-BASE BUDGETING (ZBB) method of setting budgets for corporations and government agencies that requires a justification of all expenditures, not only those that exceed the prior year's allocations. Thus all budget lines are said to begin at a zero base and are funded according to merit rather than according to the level approved for the preceding year, when circumstances probably differed.

ZERO-BRACKET AMOUNT until the TAX REFORM ACT OF 1986, the STANDARD DEDUCTION, that is, the income automatically not subject to federal income tax for taxpayers choosing not to itemize deductions. The zero-bracket amount was built into the tax tables and schedules used to compute tax. The 1986 Act replaced the zero-bracket amount with an increased standard deduction, which was subtracted from income before computing taxes rather than being part of the rate tables. Current (*see* REVENUE RECONCILIATION ACT OF 1993) law indexes the standard deduction to inflation and contains special provisions for the blind and elderly.

ZERO-COUPON CONVERTIBLE SECURITY

1. Zero-coupon BOND convertible into the common stock of the issuing company when the stock reaches a predetermined price. Introduced as Liquid Yield Option Notes (LYONS), these securities have a PUT OPTION that permits holders to redeem the bonds within three years after the initial offering. They tend to trade at a small PREMIUM OVER CONVERSION VALUE and provide a lower YIELD TO MATURITY than their nonconvertible counterparts.
2. Zero-coupon bond, usually a MUNICIPAL BOND, convertible into an interest bearing bond at some time before maturity. For example, a zero-coupon (tax-free) municipal bond would automatically accumulate and compound interest for its first 15 years at which time it would convert to a regular income-paying bond. Thus, an investor is able to lock in a current interest rate with a small initial investment. Varieties are marketed under the acronyms GAINS (Growth and Income Securities) and FIGS (Future Income and Growth Securities).

ZERO-COUPON SECURITY security that makes no periodic interest payments but instead is sold at a deep discount from its face value. The buyer of such a bond receives the rate of return by the gradual APPRECIATION of the security, which is redeemed at FACE VALUE on a specified maturity date. For tax purposes, the Internal Revenue Service maintains that the holder of a zero-coupon bond owes income tax on the interest that has accrued each year, even though the bondholder does not actually receive the cash until maturity. The IRS calls this interest *imputed interest.* Because of this interpretation, many financial advisers recommend that zero-coupon securities be used in INDIVIDUAL RETIREMENT ACCOUNTS or KEOGH ACCOUNTS, where they remain tax-sheltered.

There are many kinds of zero-coupon securities. The most commonly known is the zero-coupon bond, which either may be issued at a deep discount by a corporation or government entity or may be created by a brokerage firm when it strips the coupons off a bond and sells the CORPUS and the coupons separately. This technique is used frequently with Treasury bonds, and the zero-coupon issue is marketed under such names as CATS (CERTIFICATE OF ACCRUAL ON TREASURY SECURITIES), TIGER (Treasury Investors Growth Receipt) or STRIPS (separate trading of registered interest and principal of securities). Zero-coupon bonds are also issued by municipalities. Buying a municipal zero frees its purchaser of the worry about paying taxes on imputed interest, since the interest is tax-exempt. Zero-coupon certificates of deposit and zero mortgages also exist; they work on the same principle as zero-coupon bonds—the CD holder or mortgage holder receives face value at maturity, and no payments until then. Zero-coupon securities based on COLLATERALIZED MORTGAGE OBLIGATION bonds are called *Z-tranche bonds.* Some mutual funds buy exclusively zero-coupon securities, offering shareholders a diversified portfolio that will mature in a particular year.

Zero-coupon securities are frequently used to plan for a specific investment goal. For example, parents knowing their child will enter college in 10 years can buy a zero that will mature in 10 years, and thus be assured of having money available for tuition. People planning for retirement in 20 years can buy 20-year zeros, assuring them that they will get the money when they need it.

Because zero-coupon securities bear no interest, they are the most VOLATILE of all fixed-income securities. Since zero-coupon bondholders do not receive interest payments, zeros fall more dramatically than bonds paying out interest on a current basis when interest rates rise. However, when interest rates fall, zero-coupon securities rise more rapidly in value than full-coupon bonds, because the bonds have locked in a particular rate of reinvestment that becomes more attractive the further rates fall. The greater the number of years that a zero-coupon security has until maturity, the less an investor has to pay for it, and the more LEVERAGE is at work for him. For instance, a bond maturing in 5 years may double, but one maturing in 25 years may increase in value 10 times, depending on the interest rate of the bond.

See also ACCRUAL BONDS; COUPON BOND; DEEP DISCOUNT BOND, SPLIT-COUPON BONDS; STAGS; STRIPPED BOND; ZERO-COUPON CONVERTIBLE SECURITY.

ZERO-MINUS TICK sale that takes place at the same price as the previous sale, but at a lower price than the last different price; also called a *zero downtick.* For instance, stock trades may be executed consecutively at prices of $52, $51, and $51. The final trade at $51 was made at a zero-minus tick, because it was made at the same price as the previous trade, but at a lower price than the last different price.

ZERO-PLUS TICK securities trade that takes place at the same price as the previous transaction but at a higher price than the last different price; also called *zero uptick.* For instance, with trades executed consecutively at $51, $52, and $52, the last trade at $52 was made at a zero-plus tick—the same price as the previous trade but a higher price than the last different price. Short sales must be executed only on zero-plus ticks or on PLUS TICKS. *See also* SHORT SALE RULE.

ZERO-SUM GAME situation in which the gains of the winners are matched by the losses of the losers. For example, futures and options trading are zero-sum games because for every investor holding a profitable contract, there is another investor on the other side of the trade who is losing money. The total amount of wealth held by all the traders in a zero-sum game remains the same, but the wealth is shifted from some traders to others.

ZOMBIES companies that continue to operate even though they are insolvent and bankrupt. For example, during the savings and loan industry bailout, many savings and loans that had lost millions of dollars in bad real estate loans continued to function, awaiting merger into another financial institution or closure by the RESOLUTION TRUST CORPORATION. Such companies, in addition to being called zombies, are called *brain dead* or *living dead.*

ZONING LAWS municipal ordinances that authorize the establishment of zoning boards to administer regulations concerning the use of property and buildings in designated areas.

ZURICH STOCK EXCHANGE largest of three Swiss exchanges, followed by Geneva and Basel. The three exchanges operate simultaneously and are linked by computers, enabling orders to be executed on any of the three exchanges, regardless of origin. Trading is by open outcry, although an electronic system has been under lengthy development. The *Swiss Performance Index,* the official and most widely used index, is computed on three-minute intervals using real-time prices at all three exchanges. There are three different market segments: the official market, official parallel market, and unofficial market. The official market is open from 10 A.M. to 1 P.M. and 2 P.M. to 4 P.M., while the official parallel market is open from 9:15 A.M. to 10 A.M., all Monday through Friday. Trades are settled on the third business day after the trade date.

PART V

Finance and Investment
Ready Reference

INTRODUCTION

In today's complex world of finance and investment, it's crucial not only to know *how* different investments work, but also *where* to find the information essential to making wise decisions about those investments.

In the following pages you will find an enormous wealth of information concerning finance and investment. In some cases , the data presented is designed mainly to help you tap the many sophisticated sources available to investors. In other cases, we present well-organized data that can offer important insight into the workings of finance and investment. *In all cases, you are given information you can use.* The address and telephone number is given for just about every institution, organization, and firm listed, and you are encouraged to make direct contact in order to obtain the data required to make a well-informed investment decision.

The section is divided into the following principal parts:

Sources of Information and Assistance Public and private agencies and associations that help investors are listed as are major financial publications and databases.

Major Financial Institutions In this part are listed the names, addresses, and phone numbers of commercial banks, thrift institutions, life insurance companies, brokerage firms, sponsors of publicly available limited partnerships, accounting firms, and major stock and commodity exchanges around the world.

Mutual Funds Both open-end and closed-end funds are presented.

Futures and Options Contracts Detailed specifications of each contract are presented in tabular form, along with a list of where each contract is traded.

Historical Data This section provides graphs and tabular matter showing important longer-term financial and economic trends. Dow Jones and other indexes are included.

Publicly Traded Companies About 6500 corporations are listed, according to the place where the shares trade: NYSE, AMEX, NASDAQ, and Toronto Stock Exchange. Listings include name, stock symbol, address, phone number, line of business, option availability, and whether the firm offers a dividend reinvestment plan. These listings are followed by a compilation of important American Depositary Receipts (ADRs) and a listing of benefits some companies offer shareholders such as free merchandise or services.

1. SOURCES OF INFORMATION AND ASSISTANCE

When trying to make decisions and keep up-to-date in the increasingly complex world of finance and investment, it is often necessary to turn to others. This section of the *Handbook* is designed to guide you to the organizations that can help you.

Since the financial markets are so heavily regulated by the government today, it is important to know which federal and state regulators can be of assistance. The first part of this section gives a brief description of major federal, state and provincial regulatory agencies in the United States and Canada, and how to contact them.

A government agency sometimes is not the best place to turn. Private associations, trade groups and self-regulatory organizations are often well equipped to deal with problems or questions related to finance and investment. The second part of this section lists many of these private groups.

For advice on where to invest and how to manage your financial affairs, there is an enormous pool of advice available in finance and investment publications. The third part of this section gives you the information you need to contact a great number of worthy publications that contain such advice.

To tap information about financial markets in an even speedier fashion, you can use computer databases, which are listed in the fourth part of this section. In addition, we have selected some of the best software that can make sense of the massive amounts of information these databases contain.

FEDERAL REGULATORY ORGANIZATIONS IN THE UNITED STATES AND CANADA

This is a list of the major governmental agencies that regulate the finance and investment markets in the United States and Canada. Each agency's address and telephone number is accompanied by a brief description of its major responsibilities. These agencies primarily oversee the fairness and efficiency of finance and investment markets. In that role, consumers and investors can complain to them about perceived abuses or illegality in the marketplace. Many of the agencies are discussed in more detail in the Dictionary section of the Handbook, along with the legislation that created the agency. The regulatory aspect of some of the agencies is less important than other functions.

Agencies of the United States Government

Bureau of Economic Analysis
1401 K Street, N.W.
Washington, D.C. 20230
(202) 523-0707

Compiles, analyzes and publishes data on economic activity, including gross national product, personal income, corporate profits and leading economic indicators.

Bureau of Labor Statistics
2 Massachusetts Avenue, N.E.
Washington, D.C. 20212
(202) 606-7800

Compiles, analyzes and publishes data on labor activity such as unemployment, consumer price index, producer price index and wages.

Commerce Department
1401 K Street, N.W.
Washington, D.C. 20230
(202) 253-0659

Regulates international trade and helps American businesses expand in a variety of ways. Publishes a large amount of data about the U.S. economy.

CFTC

Commodity Futures Trading Commission
2033 K Street, N.W.
Washington, D.C. 20581
(202) 254-6970

Regulates the trading of commodity futures and options contracts. Investigates charges of fraud against commodity dealers. The CFTC also approves all new contracts that Exchanges want to trade.

Comptroller of the Currency
250 E Street, S.W.
Washington, D.C. 20219
(202) 874-5000

Regulates all national banks in the United States and handles consumer complaints against those banks.

Consumer Product Safety Commission
5401 Westbard Avenue
Bethesda, Maryland 20207
(301) 504-0300

Regulates and monitors the safety of consumer products. Provides information to the public on, and develops manufacturing standards for, consumer goods.

Council of Economic Advisers
17th Street and Pennsylvania Avenue, N.W.
Washington, D.C. 20500
(202) 395-5084

Monitors and analyzes the economy and advises the president on economic developments, trends and policies. Also prepares the economic reports of the president to Congress.

Farm Credit Administration
1501 Farm Credit Drive
McLean, Virginia 22102-5090
(703) 883-4000

Supervises and regulates lending activities of the Farm Credit System, which provides funding for agricultural, aquatic and rural electric enterprises.

Federal Deposit Insurance Corporation
550 17th Street, N.W.
Washington, D.C. 20429
(202) 898-6947

FDIC

Insures deposits in member institutions up to $100,000 per depositor. Also regularly examines banks and replies to consumer complaints about federally insured state banks. Helps arrange the merger of weak banks into stronger ones.

Federal Home Loan Mortgage Corporation
820 Jones Branch Drive
McLean, Virginia 22102
(703) 903-2000

Freddie Mac, as it is known, encourages the growth of the secondary mortgage market by buying mortgages from lenders, packaging and guaranteeing them, and reselling them as mortgage-backed securities.

Federal Housing Finance Board
1777 F Street, N.W.
Washington, D.C. 20006
(202) 408-2525

Supervises the 12 regional Federal Home Loan Banks.

Federal Reserve System
20th Street and C Street, N.W.
Washington, D.C. 20551
(202) 452-3215

Regulates national money supply, oversees activities of, and supplies credit to, member banks, and supervises the printing of money at the mint. Investors can also buy Treasury securities directly from the Fed or any of its district banks or branches.

Federal Trade Commission
Sixth Street and Pennsylvania Avenue, N.W.
Washington, D.C. 20580
(202) 326-2222

FTC

Enforces antitrust laws and consumer protection legislation. For instance, the FTC oversees the Truth-in-Lending laws, and seeks to curtail unfair sales practices and deceptive advertising.

Internal Revenue Service
1111 Constitution Avenue, N.W.
Washington, D.C. 20224
(202) 622-4115 or (800) 829-4059

Collects personal and corporate taxes for the Federal Government and administers rules and regulations of the Treasury Department.

International Monetary Fund
700 19th Street, N.W.
Washington, D.C. 20431
(202) 623-7900

An intergovernmental organization that maintains funds contributed by, and available to, member nations. Payments are designed to promote world trade and aid members with temporary problems.

International Trade Administration
14th Street and Constitution Avenue, N.W.
Washington, D.C. 20230
(202) 482-5023

Regulates and promotes non-agricultural trade between the U.S. and its trading partners. Also develops global policies to expand U.S. exports.

Interstate Commerce Commission
12th Street and Constitution Avenue, N.W.
Washington, D.C. 20423
(202) 927-5500

Monitors the flow of products carried between states by surface transportation, such as rail, truck, water and pipeline.

National Credit Union Administration
1776 G Street, N.W.
Washington, D.C. 20456
(202) 682-9600

Regulates federally chartered credit unions and offers assistance in establishing credit unions.

Office of Thrift Supervision
1700 G Street, N.W.
Washington, D.C. 20552
(202) 906-6280

Charters federal savings and loan associations, supervises and examines federally and state chartered thrifts.

Pension Benefit Guaranty Corporation
2020 K Street, N.W.
Washington, D.C. 20006
(202) 778-8800

Ensures that participants in private pension plans will receive at least basic retirement benefits should a program run short of funds.

Resolution Trust Corporation
801 17th Street, N.W.
Washington, D.C. 20434
(202) 416-4000

Responsible for merging ailing thrifts with healthy savings and loans or selling off the assets of failed thrifts to pay creditors.

Securities and Exchange Commission
450 Fifth Street, N.W.
Washington, D.C. 20549
(202) 272-2800

Regulates the securities industry. Registers issues of securities, investigates fraud and insider trading, supervises investment companies, investment advisers, accounting firms and self-regulatory organizations like the stock exchanges and the National Association of Securities Dealers.

Securities Investor Protection Corporation
805 15th Street, N.W.
Washington, D.C. 20005
(202) 371-8300

Insures brokerage customers' holdings up to $500,000 per customer, with a limit of $100,000 in cash or cash equivalents against losses due to financial failure of a firm. SIPC does not cover losses due to market fluctuations or default by the issuers of securities. Helps arrange mergers of failing brokerage firms into stronger firms.

Small Business Administration
409 3rd Street, S.W.
Washington, D.C. 20416
(202) 205-6740

Offers advice and below-market rate loans and loan guarantees to qualifying small businesses, with special programs for veterans and women, among other groups. Also licenses and funds Small Business Investment Companies (SBICs).

Social Security Administration
6401 Security Boulevard
Baltimore, Maryland 21235
(401) 965-7700

Regulates eligibility and payments of social security benefits to workers after they retire or become disabled. Also administers supplemental income programs for the aged, blind and dependents.

Treasury Department
Main Treasury Building
15th Street and Pennsylvania Avenue, N.W.
Washington, D.C. 20220
(202) 622-2000

Regulates the issuance of government debt (Treasury bills, bonds and notes) in coordination with the Federal Reserve and issues savings bonds. Plays a large role in coordinating economic and financial issues with foreign governments.

United State International Trade Commission
500 E Street, S.W.
Washington, D.C. 20436
(202) 205-2000

Studies factors relating to U.S. foreign trade and its relation to domestic production, employment and competitiveness. Also provides technical advice for government and private policy-makers.

United States Tax Court
400 Second Street, N.W.
Washington, D.C. 20217
(202) 606-8761

Hears cases involving disputes between the IRS and taxpayers.

Federal Government Agencies of Canada

Bank of Canada
Ottawa, Ontario K1A 0G9
(613) 782-8655

Regulates the money supply of Canada. It also acts as fiscal agent for the Government of Canada in managing the public debt. The Bank of Canada also has the sole right to issue Canadian paper money.

Canada Deposit Insurance Corporation
P.O. Box 2340, Station D
Ottawa, Ontario K1P 5W5
(613) 996-2081

Insures deposits up to $60,000 per depositor in member institutions. Membership in the Corporation is restricted to banks, trust companies and mortgage loan companies.

Canada Mortgage and Housing Corporation
Montreal Road
Ottawa, Ontario K1A 0P7
(613) 748-2000

The Corporation administers the National Housing Act and is responsible for delivering housing assistance to increase the supply of housing. The Corporation also insures mortgage loans made by approved lenders on the open market, and makes direct loans to areas not served by approved lenders.

Consumer and Corporate Affairs Canada
Place du Portage Phase I
50 Victoria Street
Hull, Ontario K1A 0C9
(819) 997-2938

Regulates many business activities and oversees consumer protection. Among its many responsibilities, the agency regulates product safety, consumer complaints, misleading advertising, federal corporation law, patents,

copyrights and trademark law, and inspection of meat, fish and other foods.

Export Development Corporation
151 O'Connor Street
Ottawa, Ontario K1P 5T9
(613) 598-2500

Assists Canadian companies to export their products and services.

External Affairs Department
125 Sussex Drive
Ottawa, Ontario K1A 0G2
(613) 995-1851

Coordinates international trade policy, and helps Canadian companies export their products and services.

Federal Business Development Bank
CP 335, Tour de la Bourse
Montreal, Quebec H4Z 1L4
(514) 283-5904

Provides capital and equity financing and management services to Canadian businesses.

Department of Finance, Canada
Ottawa, Ontario K1A 0G5
(613) 992-1573

Conducts the financial affairs and economic planning for the Canadian government.

Office of Superintendant of Financial
  Institutions
255 Albridge Street
Ottawa, Ontario K1A 0H2
(613) 990-7788

Regulates all banking, trust companies, loan companies, investment companies, life insurance companies, property and casualty insurance companies, and federally regulated pension plans.

Revenue Canada, Taxation
Headquarters Building
875 Heron Road
Gloucester, Ontario K1A OL8
(613) 995-2960
Collects corporate and individual taxes from
Canadians.

Statistics Canada
Ottawa, Ontario K1A OT6
(613) 951-8116
Compiles many of the economic and financial
statistics for the government of Canada.

Treasury Board Secretariat
140 O'Connor Street, East Tower, L'esplanade
Laurier
Ottawa, Ontario K1A IE4
(613) 957-2400
A Cabinet committee, brought into existence
by the Financial Administration Act, which
advises the rest of the Cabinet on the optimum
allocation of public funds among government
programs to permit the most efficient use of
the government's manpower, financial and
material resources.

U.S. STATE ATTORNEY GENERAL'S OFFICES

The attorney general's office is the place to go for a wide variety of consumer complaints. The attorney general is particularly concerned with stopping fraud, and frequently several attorneys general will coordinate their efforts to stop a multistate fraudulent business. Those who suspect a solicitation to be fraudulent should contact their state's attorney general on this list before handing over any money.

Besides taking consumer complaints, the attorney general's office promulgates rules and regulations which promote fair business practices. Areas in their jurisdiction include deceptive advertising and contract law, for example. When appropriate, attorneys general also appeal to legislative bodies to pass new consumer protection laws. To enforce these laws, attorneys general pursue both civil and criminal prosecution of violators.

Your state attorney general's offices may also be a source of help when considering a purchase decision. These offices usually publish helpful publications giving tips on what to avoid in entering certain kinds of sales contracts, for instance. Even if one is not sure where to turn for help for a particular consumer problem, the attorney general is often a good place to start.

ALABAMA
Attorney General
Alabama State House
Montgomery, Alabama 36130
(205) 242-7300

ALASKA
Attorney General
Capital Building
P.O. Box 110300, State Capitol
Juneau, Alaska 99811
(907) 465-3600

ARIZONA
Attorney General
1275 W. Washington Street
Phoenix, Arizona 85007
(602) 542-4266

ARKANSAS
Attorney General
200 Tower Building
323 Center Street
Little Rock, Arkansas 72201
(501) 682-2007, (800) 482-8982

CALIFORNIA
Attorney General
1515 K Street, Suite 511
Sacramento, California 95814
(916) 324-5437, (800) 952-5548

COLORADO
Attorney General
1525 Sherman Street
Denver, Colorado 80203
(303) 866-3611

CONNECTICUT
Attorney General
55 Elm Street
Hartford, Connecticut 06106
(203) 566-2026, (800) 842-2649

DELAWARE
Attorney General
820 North French Street, 8th Floor
Wilmington, Delaware 19801
(302) 577-3838

DISTRICT OF COLUMBIA
Department of Consumer and Regulatory
  Affairs
614 H Street, N.W.
Washington, D.C. 20001
(202) 727-7000

FLORIDA
Attorney General
State Capitol
Tallahassee, Florida 32399
(904) 487-1963, (800) 342-2176

GEORGIA
Attorney General
214 State Capitol
Atlanta, Georgia 30334
(404) 656-2881, (800) 282-5808

HAWAII
Attorney General
State Capital
425 Queen Street
Honolulu, Hawaii 96813
(808) 586-1282

IDAHO
Attorney General
Statehouse, Room 210
Boise, Idaho 83720
(208) 334-2400

ILLINOIS
Attorney General
100 West Randolph Street, 12th Floor
Chicago, Illinois 60601
(312) 814-3000

INDIANA
Attorney General
219 State House
Indianapolis, Indiana 46204
(317) 232-6201, (800) 382-5516

IOWA
Attorney General
Hoover Building, 2nd Floor
Des Moines, Iowa 50319
(515) 281-5164

KANSAS
Attorney General
Judicial Center, 2nd Floor
Topeka, Kansas 66612
(913) 296-2215, (800) 432-2310

KENTUCKY
Attorney General
116 Capitol Building
Frankfort, Kentucky 40601
(502) 564-7600, (800) 432-9257

LOUISIANA
Attorney General
P.O. Box 94005
Baton Rouge, Louisiana 70804
(504) 342-7013

MAINE
Attorney General
State House, Station 6
Augusta, Maine 04333
(207) 626-8800

MARYLAND
Attorney General
200 St. Paul Place
Baltimore, Maryland 21202
(410) 576-6300

MASSACHUSETTS
Attorney General
One Ashburton Place
Boston, Massachusetts 02108
(617) 727-2200

MICHIGAN
Attorney General
525 W. Ottawa Street, 7th Floor
Lansing, Michigan 48909
(517) 373-1110

MINNESOTA
Attorney General
102 State Capitol
St. Paul, Minnesota 55155
(612) 296-6196

MISSISSIPPI
Attorney General
P.O. Box 220
Jackson, Mississippi 39205
(601) 359-3680, (800) 222-7622

MISSOURI
Attorney General
P.O. Box 899
Jefferson City, Missouri 65102
(314) 751-3321, (800) 392-8222

MONTANA
Attorney General
Justice Building
215 N. Sanders
Helena, Montana 59620
(406) 444-2026

NEBRASKA
Attorney General
2115 State Capitol Building
P.O. Box 98920
Lincoln, Nebraska 68509
(402) 471-2682

NEVADA
Attorney General
Heroes Memorial Bldg.
Carson City, Nevada 89710
(702) 687-4170, (800) 992-0900

NEW HAMPSHIRE
Attorney General
208 State House Annex
Concord, New Hampshire 03301-6397
(603) 271-3658

NEW JERSEY
Attorney General
Justice Complex, CN 080
Trenton, New Jersey 08625
(609) 292-4925

NEW MEXICO
Attorney General
P.O. Drawer 1508
Santa Fe, New Mexico 87504-1508
(505) 827-6000

NEW YORK
Attorney General
120 Broadway, 25th Floor
New York, New York 10271
(212) 416-8519

NORTH CAROLINA
Attorney General
Department of Justice Building
P.O. Box 629
Raleigh, North Carolina 27602
(919) 733-3377

NORTH DAKOTA
Attorney General
State Capitol Building, 1st Floor
Bismarck, North Dakota 58505
(701) 224-2210, (800) 472-2600

OHIO
Attorney General
30 E. Broad Street
Columbus, Ohio 43266-0410
(614) 466-3376, (800) 282-0515

OKLAHOMA
Attorney General
112 State Capitol Building
Oklahoma City, Oklahoma 73105
(405) 521-3921

OREGON
Attorney General
100 Justice Building
Salem, Oregon 97310
(503) 378-6002

PENNSYLVANIA
Attorney General
Strawberry Square, 16th Floor
Harrisburg, Pennsylvania 17120
(717) 787-3391

PUERTO RICO
Department of Justice
P.O. Box 192
Old San Juan, Puerto Rico 00902
(809) 721-7700

RHODE ISLAND
Attorney General
72 Pine Street
Providence, Rhode Island 02903-2856
(401) 274-4400

SOUTH CAROLINA
Attorney General
P.O. Box 11549
Columbia, South Carolina 29205
(803) 734-3970, (800) 922-1594

SOUTH DAKOTA
Attorney General
State Capitol
Pierre, South Dakota 57501-5090
(605) 773-3215, (800) 592-1865

TENNESSEE
Attorney General
450 James Robertson Parkway
Nashville, Tennessee 37243
(615) 741-3491, (800) 342-8385

TEXAS
Attorney General
Supreme Court Building
P.O. Box 12548
Austin, Texas 78711-2548
(512) 463-2191

UTAH
Attorney General
236 State Capitol
Salt Lake City, Utah 84114
(801) 538-1326

VERMONT
Attorney General
Pavilion Office Building
Montpelier, Vermont 05609
(802) 828-3171, (800) 642-5149

VIRGINIA
Attorney General
101 N. 8th Street
Richmond, Virginia 23219
(804) 786-2071, (800) 552-9963

VIRGIN ISLANDS OF THE UNITED STATES
Department of Justice
G.E.R.S. Complex, 2nd Floor
St. Thomas
U.S. Virgin Islands 00802
(809) 774-5566

WASHINGTON
Attorney General
Highways Licenses Building
7th Floor, MS PB-71
Olympia, Washington 98504
(206) 753-6200, (800) 551-4636

WEST VIRGINIA
Attorney General
State Capitol Building
Room E-26
Charleston, West Virginia 25305
(304) 558-2021

WISCONSIN
Attorney General
P.O. Box 7857
Madison, Wisconsin 53707-7857
(608) 266-1221, (800) 362-8189

WYOMING
Attorney General
123 State Capitol
Cheyenne, Wyoming 82002
(307) 777-7841

U.S. STATE BANKING REGULATORS

The regulators listed here are charged with supervising the activities of state-chartered banks. These are banks not regulated at the national level, where the Comptroller of the Currency and Federal Reserve Board do the supervision. Depending on the state, state chartered banks may have more or fewer powers than federally regulated banks. For example, the amount of money state banks can lend to customers as a percent of deposits varies widely from state to state. State banking regulators also oversee the financial soundness of the banks in their jurisdictions, and help to merge failing banks into healthy ones. These regulators do not insure state bank deposits, however; that is usually done by the Federal Deposit Insurance Corporation.

State bank regulators also pursue consumer complaints against banks in their state. For example, it would be appropriate to contact a regulator if a state bank was preventing checks from clearing within a reasonable time or if fees were excessive. Complaints about deceptive advertising or promotional materials by banks can also be addressed to these agencies. Questions about credit, and the denial of credit privileges, are also handled by the agencies in this list.

State banking agencies are also helpful when shopping for a bank. They will usually publish helpful literature about banks and bank services. Do not expect these agencies to do comparisons of yields paid on bank accounts or interest rates charged on loans—these numbers change too frequently for the agencies to track them.

ALABAMA
101 South Union Street
Montgomery, Alabama 36130
(205) 242-3452

ALASKA
P.O. Box 110807
Juneau, Alaska 99811
(907) 465-2521

ARIZONA
2910 North 44th Street, Suite 310
Phoenix, Arizona 85018
(602) 255-4421

ARKANSAS
Tower Building
323 Center Street, Suite 500
Little Rock, Arkansas 72201-2613
(501) 324-9019

CALIFORNIA
111 Pine Street, Suite 1100
San Francisco 94111-5613
(415) 557-0256

COLORADO
1560 Broadway, Suite 1175
Denver, Colorado 80202
(303) 620-4358

CONNECTICUT
44 Capitol Avenue
Hartford, Connecticut 06106
(203) 566-4560

DELAWARE
555 East Loocherman Street
Dover, Delaware 19901
(302) 739-4235

DISTRICT OF COLUMBIA
717 14th Street, 11th Floor, Box 4
Washington D.C. 20005
(202) 727-1563

FLORIDA
State Capitol Building
Tallahassee, Florida 32399-0350
(904) 488-0370

GEORGIA
2990 Brandywine Road, Suite 200
Atlanta, Georgia 30341-5565
(404) 986-1633

HAWAII
P.O. Box 2054
Honolulu, Hawaii 96805
(808) 586-2820

IDAHO
Statehouse Mall
700 West State Street, 2nd Floor
Boise, Idaho 83720-0031
(208) 334-3313

ILLINOIS
500 East Munroe
Springfield, Illinois 62701-1532
(217) 782-7966

INDIANA
402 West Washington Street, Room W066
Indianapolis, Indiana 46204
(317) 232-3955

IOWA
200 East Grand Avenue
Des Moines, Iowa 50309
(515) 281-4014

KANSAS
700 Jackson Street S.W., 300 Jayhawk Tower
Topeka, Kansas 66603-3714
(913) 296-2266

KENTUCKY
477 Versailles Road
Frankfort, Kentucky 40601
(502) 573-3390

LOUISIANA
P.O. Box 94095
Baton Rouge 70804-9095
(504) 925-4661

MAINE
State House Station 35
Augusta, Maine 04333
(207) 582-8713

MARYLAND
501 St. Paul Place
Baltimore, Maryland 21202-2272
(410) 333-6262

MASSACHUSETTS
100 Cambridge Street, Room 2004
Boston, Massachusetts 02202
(617) 727-3145

MICHIGAN
P.O. Box 30224
Lansing, Michigan 48909
(517) 373-3460

MINNESOTA
133 East 7th Street
St. Paul, Minnesota 55101
(612) 296-2715

MISSISSIPPI
P.O. Box 267
Jackson, Mississippi 39205
(601) 359-3402

MISSOURI
P.O. Box 716
Jefferson, Missouri 65102
(314) 751-3242

MONTANA
1424 Ninth Avenue
P.O. Box 200501
Helena, Montana 59620-0501
(406) 444-2091

NEBRASKA
P.O. Box 95006
Lincoln, Nebraska 68509-5006
(402) 471-2171

NEVADA
1665 Hot Springs Road
Carson City, Nevada 89710
(702) 687-4259

NEW HAMPSHIRE
169 Manchester Street
Concord, New Hampshire 03301
(603) 271-3561

NEW JERSEY
20 West State Street, CN040
Trenton, New Jersey 08625
(609) 292-3420

NEW MEXICO
715 St. Michael's Drive
Santa Fe, New Mexico 87503
(505) 827-7102

NEW YORK
2 Rector Street
New York, New York 10006-1894
(212) 618-6642

NORTH CAROLINA
430 North Salisbury Street
Raleigh, North Carolina 27611
(919) 733-3016

NORTH DAKOTA
State Capitol, 13th Floor
600 East Boulevard Avenue
Bismark, North Dakota 58505-0080
(701) 224-2253

OHIO
Vern Riffe Center
77 South High Street, 23rd Floor
Columbus 43266-0544
(614) 466-2932

OKLAHOMA
4100 North Lincoln Boulevard
Oklahoma City, Oklahoma 73105-5276
(405) 521-2782

OREGON
21 Labor and Industries Building
Salem, Oregon 97310
(503) 378-4140

PENNSYLVANIA
333 Market Street, 16th Floor
Harrisburg, Pennsylvania 17101-2290
(717) 787-6991

RHODE ISLAND
233 Richmond Street
Providence, Rhode Island 02903
(401) 277-2246

SOUTH CAROLINA
P.O.Box 11778
Columbia, South Carolina 29211
(803) 734-2001

SOUTH DAKOTA
State Capitol, Room A-217
500 East Capitol Avenue
Pierre, South Dakota 57501-5070
(605) 773-3411

TENNESSEE
John Sevier Building, 4th Floor
Nashville, Tennessee 37243-0705
(615) 741-2236

TEXAS
2601 North Lamar Boulevard
Austin, Texas 78705-4294
(512) 475-1300

UTAH
324 South State, Suite 201
P.O. Box 89
Salt Lake City, Utah 84110-0089
(801) 538-8835

VERMONT
89 Main Street
Montpelier, Vermont 05620-3101
(802) 828-3301

VIRGINIA
Tyler Building, 1300 East Main Street
Richmond, Virginia 23219
(804) 371-9659

WASHINGTON
P.O. Box 43113
Olympia, Washington 98504-3113
(206) 753-5459

WEST VIRGINIA
State Capitol Complex, Building 3, Suite 311-A
Charleston, West Virginia 25305
(304) 558-2294

WISCONSIN
101 East Wilson Street, 5th Floor
Madison, Wisconsin 53707-7876
(608) 266-1621

WYOMING
Herschler Building, East Wing, 3rd Floor
122 West 25th Street
Cheyenne 82002
(307) 777-7797

U.S. STATE INSURANCE REGULATORS

Every state has its own laws and regulations which govern all types of insurance. Unlike most other areas in the financial services field, there is very little regulation of the insurance industry at the federal level. The state agencies listed here enforce all state insurance laws. Insurance commissioners must approve of the sale of all life, health, automobile and homeowners insurance products in their states. Some states, such as New York and California, are particularly rigorous in approving any new product for sale to state residents. If a product has been approved for sale in one of those states, it is often approved elsewhere as well.

When there are problems with an insurance company, these regulators step in. For example, they oversee the process of merging failing insurance companies into strong ones. They also protect policyholders by assuring that insurance companies keep adequate reserves. In the case of an insurance company failure, they see to it that policyholders' interests are protected as much as possible. State insurance offices also respond to consumer complaints against insurance companies on such issues as unfair pricing, denial of insurance claims, and deceptive advertising practices. Before bringing a complaint to one of these agencies, however, it is important to complain to the insurance company first. If the problem has not been resolved at that level, then these agencies should be consulted.

These insurance regulators also offer assistance to those looking to purchase insurance coverage. They may provide helpful literature about the kinds of insurance policies being offered, and also be able to inform buyers about patterns of complaints against particular companies.

ALABAMA
Insurance Commissioner
135 South Union Street
Montgomery, Alabama 36130
(205) 269-3550

ALASKA
Director of Insurance
State Office Building, 9th Floor
P.O. Box 110800
Juneau, Alaska 99811-0800
(907) 465-2515

ARIZONA
Director of Insurance
2910 North 44th Street, Suite 210
Phoenix, Arizona 85018-7256
(602) 912-8400

ARKANSAS
Insurance Commissioner
1123 South University Avenue
University Tower Building, Suite 400
Little Rock, Arkansas 72204-1699
(501) 686-2909

CALIFORNIA
Insurance Commissioner
45 Fremont Street
San Francisco, California 94105
(415) 904-5410

COLORADO
Commissioner of Insurance Division
1560 Broadway, Suite 1550
Denver, Colorado 80202
(303) 894-7499 x311

CONNECTICUT
Insurance Commissioner
P.O. Box 816
Hartford, Connecticut 06142-0816
(203) 297-3802

DELAWARE
Insurance Commissioner
841 Silverlake Boulevard
Dover, Delaware 19901
(302) 739-4251

DISTRICT OF COLUMBIA
Insurance Commissioner
P.O. Box 37378
Washington D.C. 20013
(202) 727-8000

FLORIDA
Insurance Commissioner
The Capitol PL-11
Tallahassee, Florida 32399-0300
(904) 922-3100 x2804

GEORGIA
Insurance Commissioner
2 Martin L. King, Jr. Drive
West Tower, 7th Floor
Atlanta, Georgia 30334
(404) 656-2056

HAWAII
Insurance Commissioner
P.O. Box 3614
Honolulu, Hawaii 96811
(808) 586-2790

IDAHO
Director of Insurance
700 West State Street
Boise, Idaho 83720
(208) 334-4250

ILLINOIS
Director of Insurance
320 West Washington Street, 4th Floor
Springfield, Illinois 62767
(312) 782-4515

INDIANA
Insurance Commissioner
311 West Washington Street, Suite 300
Indianapolis, Indiana 46204-2787
(317) 232-3520

IOWA
Insurance Commissioner
Lucas State Office Building, 6th Floor
Des Moines, Iowa 50319
(515) 281-5705

KANSAS
Insurance Commissioner
420 SW Ninth Street
Topeka, Kansas 66612-1678
(913) 296-3071

KENTUCKY
Insurance Commissioner
229 West Main
Frankfort, Kentucky 40602
(502) 564-3630

LOUISIANA
Insurance Commissioner
P.O. Box 94214
Baton Rouge, Louisiana 70804-9214
(504) 342-5423

MAINE
Insurance Bureau Chief
State House 35
Augusta, Maine 04333
(207) 582-8707

MARYLAND
Insurance Commissioner
501 St. Paul Place
Baltimore, Maryland 21202-2272
(410) 333-2521

MASSACHUSETTS
Insurance Commissioner
470 Atlantic Avenue
Boston, Massachusetts 02210
(617) 521-7400

MICHIGAN
Insurance Commissioner
Ottowa Building, 2nd Floor
P.O. Box 30220
Lansing, Michigan 48909
(517) 373-9273

MINNESOTA
Deputy Commissioner of Commerce
133 East Seventh Street
St. Paul, Minnesota 55101
(612) 296-6325

MISSISSIPPI
Insurance Commissioner
P.O. Box 79
Jackson, Mississippi 39205
(601) 359-3569

MISSOURI
Director of Insurance
301 West High Street, Suite 630
Jefferson City, Missouri 65101
(314) 751-4126

MONTANA
Deputy Commissioner of Insurance
270 Sam W. Mitchell Building
P.O. Box 4009
Helena, Montana 59604-4009
(406) 444-2040

NEBRASKA
Director of Insurance
941 O Street, Suite 400
Lincoln, Nebraska 68508
(402) 471-2201

NEVADA
Insurance Commissioner
1665 Hot Springs Road
Carson City, Nevada 89710
(702) 687-4270

NEW HAMPSHIRE
Insurance Commissioner
169 Manchester Street
Concord, New Hampshire 03301
(603) 271-2261

NEW JERSEY
Insurance Commissioner
20 West State Street, CN 325
Trenton, New Jersey 08625-0325
(609) 633-7667

NEW MEXICO
Superintendent of Insurance
P.O. Drawer 1269
Santa Fe, New Mexico 87504-1269
(505) 827-4297

NEW YORK
Superintendent of Insurance
Empire State Plaza, Building One
Albany, New York 12257
(518) 474-4550

NORTH CAROLINA
Insurance Commissioner
430 North Salisbury Street
P.O. Box 26387
Raleigh, North Carolina 27611
(919) 733-7349

NORTH DAKOTA
Insurance Commissioner
State Capitol, 5th Floor
600 East Boulevard Avenue
Bismark, North Dakota 58505-0320
(701) 224-2440

OHIO
Director of Insurance
2100 Stella Court
Columbus, Ohio 43266-0566
(614) 644-2651

OKLAHOMA
Insurance Commissioner
1901 North Walnut
P.O. Box 53408
Oklahoma City, Oklahoma 73152
(405) 521-2828

OREGON
Insurance Administrator
21 Labor and Industries Building
Salem, Oregon 97310
(503) 378-4271

PENNSYLVANIA
Insurance Commissioner
1326 Strawberry Square
Harrisburg, Pennsylvania 17120
(717) 783-0442

RHODE ISLAND
Superintendent of Insurance
233 Richmond Street
Providence, Rhode Island 02903
(401) 277-2223

SOUTH CAROLINA
Insurance Commissioner
1612 Marion Street
P.O. Box 100105
Columbia, South Carolina 29202-3105
(803) 737-6160

SOUTH DAKOTA
Director of Insurance
Sammons Building
910 East Sioux
Pierre, South Dakota 57501
(605) 773-4104

TENNESSEE
Assistant Commissioner of
    Insurance
Volunteer Plaza Building
500 James Robertson Parkway
Nashville, Tennessee 37243-0565
(615) 741-2705

TEXAS
Insurance Commissioner
333 Guadalupe
P.O. Box 149104-9104
Austin, Texas 78714-9104
(512) 305-7373

UTAH
Insurance Commissioner
3110 State Office Building
Salt Lake City, Utah 84114
(801) 538-3804

VERMONT
Deputy Commissioner of Insurance
89 Main Street
Montpelier, Vermont 05620-3101
(802) 828-3301

VIRGINIA
Insurance Commissioner
Tyler Building
1300 East Main Street
Richmond, Virginia 23219
(804) 371-9694

WASHINGTON
Insurance Commissioner
Insurance Building
P.O. Box 40255
Olympia, Washington 98504-0255
(206) 753-7300

WEST VIRGINIA
Insurance Commissioner
2019 Washington Street, East
Charleston, West Virginia 25305
(304) 558-3354

WISCONSIN
Insurance Commissioner
P.O. Box 7873
Madison, Wisconsin 53707-7873
(608) 266-0102

WYOMING
Insurance Commissioner
Herschler Building, 3rd Floor East
122 West 25th Street
Cheyenne, Wyoming 82002-0440
(307) 777-7401

U.S. STATE SECURITIES REGULATORS

Anyone dealing with the potential purchase or sale of securities might want to consult with the state regulators listed here. Brokerage firms and financial planners selling securities must pass tests adminstered by state securities departments. In the event of any malfeasance on the part of those with a license to sell securities, the state securities department will look into the complaint, and possibly revoke the license, if such action is called for.

These regulators protect buyers of securities sold in their states in another way: They screen all securities offering documents such as prospectuses to ensure that adequate information has been disclosed and that the deal is not fraudulent. The securities office will not judge each deal on its investment potential, but it will reject offerings which it deems abusive. This prescreening process is commonly called the blue-sky process, because a judge once asserted that a particular offering had as much value as a patch of blue sky. It is important to ask these state securities regulators, therefore, if a particular security, such as a mutual fund or limited partnership, has passed the blue sky process in one's state. If it has not, state residents are not allowed to buy it.

Besides watching over the securities industry in their states and screening new securities offerings, state securities offices can be helpful in explaining the pros and cons of various kinds of securities. They often have helpful literature describing what investors should watch for in making good investments and avoiding bad ones. In general, these offices will be one of the best places to contact about any question that might come up regarding a security sold in one's state.

ALABAMA
Securities Commissioner
770 Washington Street, Suite 570
Montgomery, Alabama 36130
(205) 242-2984

ALASKA
Banking, Securities & Corporations
Division & Economic Development
  Department
Post Office Box 110807
Juneau, Alaska 99811-0807
(907) 465-2521

ARIZONA
Securities Division
Corporation Commission
1300 West Washington, 3rd Floor
Phoenix, Arizona 85007
(602) 542-4242

ARKANSAS
Securities Commissioner
201 East Markham
Little Rock, Arkansas 72201
(501) 324-9260

CALIFORNIA
Securities Commissioner
Department of Corporations
1115 11th Street
Sacramento, California 95814
(916) 445-7205

COLORADO
Division of Securities
Department of Regulatory Agencies
1580 Lincoln Street, Suite 420
Denver, Colorado 80203
(303) 894-2320

CONNECTICUT
Securities & Business Investments
Department of Banking
44 Capitol Avenue
Hartford, Connecticut 06106
(203) 566-4560

DELAWARE
Securities Division, Department of Justice
820 North French Street, 8th Floor
Wilmington, Delaware 19801
(302) 577-2515

DISTRICT OF COLUMBIA
D.C. Public Service Commission
450 5th Street, N.W., Suite 821
Washington, D.C. 20001
(202) 626-5105

FLORIDA
Division of Securities and Investor Protection
Department of Banking & Finance
The Capitol
Tallahassee, Florida 32399-0350
(904) 488-9805

GEORGIA
Securities Director
2 Martin Luther King Drive
West Tower, Room 315
Atlanta, Georgia 30334
(404) 656-6478

HAWAII
Commissioner of Securities
1010 Richards Street, 2nd Floor
Honolulu, Hawaii 96810
(808) 586-2744

IDAHO
Department of Finance
700 West State Street
Boise, Idaho 83720-2700
(208) 334-3684

ILLINOIS
Director of Securities
900 Spring Street
Springfield, Illinois 62704
(217) 782-2256

INDIANA
Securities Commissioner
302 West Washington, Room E-111
Indianapolis, Indiana 46204
(317) 232-6681

IOWA
Securities Bureau
Lucas Stone Office Building, 2nd Floor
Des Moines, Iowa 50319
(515) 281-4441

KANSAS
Securities Commissioner
618 South Kansas Avenue, 2nd Floor
Topeka, Kansas 66603
(913) 296-3307

KENTUCKY
Financial Institutions Department
Division of Securities
477 Versailles Road
Frankfort, Kentucky 40601
(502) 564-3390

LOUISIANA
Commissioner of Securities
1100 Poydras Street, Suite 2250
New Orleans, Louisiana 70163
(504) 568-5515

MAINE
Securities Division
State House Station 121
Augusta, Maine 04333
(207) 582-8760

MARYLAND
Division of Securities, Office of the Attorney
    General
200 St. Paul Place, 20th Floor
Baltimore, Maryland 21202
(301) 576-6360

MASSACHUSETTS
Securities Division, the Office of Secretary of
    Commonwealth
One Ashburton Place, Room 1701
Boston, Massachusetts 02108
(617) 727-3548

MICHIGAN
Securities Division, Department of Commerce
P.O. Box 30222
Lansing, Michigan 48909
(517) 334-6212

MINNESOTA
Director of Securities
Department of Commerce
133 E. 7th Street
St. Paul, Minnesota 55101
(612) 296-2284

MISSISSIPPI
Securities Division
Office of Secretary of State
202 No. Congress Street, Suite 601
Jackson, Mississippi 39201
(601) 359-6364

MISSOURI
Division of Securities
Office of Secretary of State
600 West Main Street
Jefferson City, Missouri 65101
(314) 751-4136

MONTANA
Securities Commission
Office of State Auditor
P.O. Box 59604
Helena, Montana 59604
(406) 444-2040

NEBRASKA
Department of Banking & Finance
P.O. Box 95006
Lincoln, Nebraska 68509
(402) 471-3445

NEVADA
Securities Division
Office of Secretary of State
771 E. Flamingo Road, Suite 212B
Las Vegas, Nevada 89158
(702) 486-6440

NEW HAMPSHIRE
Division of Securities
Department of Insurance
State House, Room 204
Concord, New Hampshire 03301
(603) 271-1463

NEW JERSEY
Bureau of Securities
153 Halsey Street
Newark, New Jersey 07101
(201) 504-3600

NEW MEXICO
Securities Division
725 St. Michael's Drive
Santa Fe, New Mexico 87501
(505) 827-7140

NEW YORK
Bureau of Investor Protection & Securities
120 Broadway, 23rd Floor
New York, New York 10271
(212) 416-8200

NORTH CAROLINA
Department of Securities Administration
Office of Secretary of State
300 North Salisbury Street, Room 100
Raleigh, North Carolina 27603-5909
(919) 733-3924

NORTH DAKOTA
Securities Commissioner
5th floor, State Capitol
Bismarck, North Dakota 58505
(701) 328-2910

OHIO
Division of Securities of the Department of
    Commerce
77 South High Street, 22nd Floor
Columbus, Ohio 43266-0548
(614) 644-7381

OKLAHOMA
Securities Commissioner
621 No. Robinson
Oklahoma City, Oklahoma 73102
(405) 235-0230

OREGON
Division of Finance and Corporate Securities
1010 North 7th Street, 2nd Floor
Salem, Oregon 97310
(503) 378-4140

PENNSYLVANIA
Securities Commissioner
2nd Floor, 1010 North 7th Street
Harrisburg, Pennsylvania 17102
(717) 787-8061

PUERTO RICO
Securities Commissioner's Office
Department of the Treasury
P.O. Box 3508
San Juan, Puerto Rico 00904
(809) 723-1122

RHODE ISLAND
Director and Superintendant of Securities
Department of Business Regulation
233 Richmond Street, Suite 232
Providence, Rhode Island 02903-4232
(401) 277-3048

SOUTH CAROLINA
Securities Commission
1205 Pendleton Street, Suite 501
Columbia, South Carolina 29201
(803) 734-1087

SOUTH DAKOTA
Division of Securities
Commerce & Regulations Department
118 West Capitol Avenue
Pierre, South Dakota 57501-2017
(605) 773-4823

TENNESSEE
Securities Division
Department of Commerce & Insurance
500 James Robertson Parkway
Nashville, Tennessee 37243
(615) 741-2947

TEXAS
Securities Board
221 West 6th Street, Suite 700
Austin, Texas 78711
(512) 474-2233

UTAH
Securities Commissioner
Department of Commerce
Post Office Box 4580
Salt Lake City, Utah 84145-0808
(801) 530-6600

VERMONT
Securities Commissioner
Department of Banking & Insurance
89 Main Street, Drawer 20
Montpelier, Vermont 05602-3101
(802) 828-3420

VIRGINIA
Division of Securities and Retail Franchising
Post Office Box 1197
Richmond, Virginia 23209
(804) 371-9051

VIRGIN ISLANDS
Corporations & Trade Names Division
Office of Lieutenant Governor
P.O. Box 450
St. Thomas, Virgin Islands 00801
(809) 774-2991

WASHINGTON
Securities Division
Department of Financial Institutions
P.O. Box 9033
Olympia, Washington 98507
(206) 753-6928

WEST VIRGINIA
Securities Division
Office of State Auditor
1900 Kanawha Boulevard East
Charleston, West Virginia 25305
(304) 558-2257

WISCONSIN
Commissioner of Securities
P.O. Box 1768
111 West Wilson Street
Madison, Wisconsin 53702
(608) 266-3431

WYOMING
Secretary of State
State Capitol
Cheyenne, Wyoming 82002
(307) 777-7370

CANADIAN PROVINCIAL AGENCIES

The provincial and territorial agencies listed here have many of the same powers as state regulators in the United States. We have listed the two major finance and investment agencies in each province. The Consumer and Corporate Affairs Agencies and Departments regulate such areas as consumer protection, mortgages, insurance, credit, and securities, among other areas. The Finance Departments of each province run the financial affairs of government and collect taxes.

ALBERTA
Alberta Municipal Affairs, Consumer Services
  Division
22nd Floor, 10025 Jasper Avenue
Edmonton, Alberta T5J 3Z5
(403) 422-0199

Deputy Provincial Treasurer, Finance, and
  Revenue
443 Terrace Building
9515 107th Street
Edmonton, Alberta T5K 2C3
(403) 427-3076

BRITISH COLUMBIA
Ministry of Housing
940 Blanshard Street
Victoria, British Columbia V8W 3E6
(604) 387-3126

Ministry of Finance & Corporate Relations
Parliament Buildings
Victoria, British Columbia V8V 1X4
(604) 387-5801

MANITOBA
Consumer & Corporate Affairs Department
114 Garry Street
Winnipeg, Manitoba R3C 1G1
(204) 956-2040

Manitoba Finance
109 Legislative Building
Winnipeg, Manitoba R3C OV8
(204) 945-3754

NEW BRUNSWICK
Consumer Affairs Branch
Department of Justice
P.O. Box 6000
Fredericton, New Brunswick E3B 5H1
(506) 453-2659

Department of Finance
P.O. Box 6000
Fredericton, New Brunswick E3B 5H1
(506) 453-2511

NEWFOUNDLAND
Department of Justice, Consumer Affairs
  Division
P.O. Box 8700
St. John's, Newfoundland A1B 4J6
(709) 729-2591

Department of Finance
Confederation Building, P.O. Box 8700
St. John's, Newfoundland A1B 4J6
(709) 729-3836

NORTHWEST TERRITORIES
Yukon Finance
P.O. Box 2703
Whitehorse, Yukon Territory Y1A 2C6
(403) 667-5343

NOVA SCOTIA
Department of Housing and Consumer Affairs
P.O. Box 998
Halifax, Nova Scotia B3J 2X3
(902) 424-4690

Department of Finance
P.O. Box 187
Halifax, Nova Scotia B3J 2N3
(902) 424-2422

ONTARIO
Ministry of Consumer & Commercial Relations
555 Yonge Street
Toronto, Ontario M7A 2H6
(416) 326-8600

Ministry of Finance Communications
4th Floor, Frost Building South
Toronto M7A 1Y7
(416) 325-0333

PRINCE EDWARD ISLAND
Department of Provincial Affairs & Attorney
  General, Consumer Services Division
P.O. Box 2000
Charlottetown,
Prince Edward Island C1A 7N8
(902) 368-4580

Department of Provincial Treasury
P.O. Box 2000
Charlottetown, Prince Edward I. C1A 7N8
(902) 368-4050

QUEBEC
Ministère des Finances
12 rue St. Louis
Quebec, P.Q. G1R 5L3
(418) 691-2233

Ministère de la Protection du Consommateur
400 Bout Jean-Lesage, #450
Quebec, P.Q. G1K 8W4
(418) 643-1484

SASKATCHEWAN
Saskatchewan Justice, Consumer Protection
   Branch
1871 Smith Street
Regina, Saskatchewan S4P 3V7
(306) 787-5550

Saskatchewan Finance, Treasury Board Branch
10th Floor, Treasury Board Division,
2350 Albert Street
Regina, Saskatchewan S4P 4A6
(306) 787-6780

FINANCE AND INVESTMENT ORGANIZATIONS

This is a list of the most important organizations in the finance and investment field. Included are trade associations, which educate the public about their industry and lobby for their political positions in Congress; self-regulatory organizations, which regulate the conduct of the marketplace under the supervision of a federal regulatory agency; and consumer and investor organizations, which educate consumers and investors and help them resolve problems.

American Association of Commodity Traders
9 South William Street
New York, New York
Represents traders of commodity futures and options and educates the public about the commodity markets.

American Association of Individual Investors
625 North Michigan Avenue
Chicago, Illinois 60611
(312) 280-0170
Educates individual investors about opportunities in stocks, bonds and mutual funds and investment computer software. Conducts seminars, workshops and offers home study courses.

American Bankers Association
1120 Connecticut Avenue, N.W.
Washington, D.C. 20036
(202) 663-5000
Represents commercial banks in legislative and regulatory activities and legal action. Also educates the public about banking.

American Council of Life Insurance
1001 Pennsylvania Avenue, N.W.
Washington, D.C. 20004-2599
(202) 624-2000
Represents life insurance companies in lobbying on life insurance-related issues and educates the public about insurance.

American Financial Services Association
919 18th Street, N.W., 3rd Floor
Washington, D.C. 20006
(202) 296-5544
Represents companies that lend to consumers, mostly finance companies. Lobbies on issues related to consumer lending, and also educates the public about use of credit and budgeting.

American Institute of Certified Public
   Accountants
1211 Avenue of the Americas
New York, New York 10036-8775
(212) 596-6200
Professional society of certified public accountants that establishes auditing and reporting standards and prepares the Uniform CPA Examination for state licensing bodies.

American Insurance Association
Suite 1000, 1130 Connecticut Avenue, N.W.
Washington, D.C. 20036
(202) 828-7100
Represents property and liability insurance companies in lobbying on insurance-related issues. Educates the public about safety issues and suggests codes to governments on such areas as industrial safety and fire prevention.

American League of Financial Institutions
900 19th Street, N.W., Suite 400
Washington, D.C. 20006
(202) 857-3176
Represents minority savings and loan associations. Provides counseling, consulting and technical assistance to member associations.

American Management Association
135 West 50th Street
New York, New York 10020-1201
(212) 586-8100
Non-profit educational organization working to improve management skills in government and industry.

American Society of Chartered Life
   Underwriters and Chartered Financial
   Consultants
270 Bryn Mawr Avenue
Bryn Mawr, Pennsylvania 19010
(215) 526-2500

Professional society of insurance agents and executives, accountants, attorneys and trust officers who hold the CLU (Chartered Life Underwriter) or the ChFC (Chartered Financial Consultant) designation. These designations are earned by attending certain seminars and passing certain examinations.

Appraisers Association of America
60 East 42nd Street
New York, New York 10165
(212) 867-9775

Represents those who give professional appraisals of the value of property, usually for tax or insurance purposes.

Associated Credit Bureaus
1090 Vermont Avenue N.W., Suite 200
Washington, D.C. 20005
(202) 371-0910

Represents consumer credit bureaus, which maintain files on credit histories of individuals. Consumers can take complaints about a local credit bureau to the Associated Credit Bureaus for resolution.

Association For Investment Management and Research
P.O. Box 3668
Charlottesville, Virginia 22963
(804) 980-3685

Certifies and educates investment management professionals who are known as Chartered Financial Analysts once they are admitted to membership.

Association For Publicly Traded Companies
1101 Connecticut Avenue, N.W., Suite 700
Washington, D.C. 20036
(202) 857-1114

Association of Financial Guaranty Insurors
122 South Swan Street
Albany, New York 12210
(518) 449-4698

Represents municipal bond, corporate and other bond insurers and financial guarantee reinsurers. Serves as a forum to discuss issues of mutual concern, to seek acceptable legislation and regulation of the financial guarantee industry, and to promote public understanding of the benefits of financial guarantees.

Association of Publicly Traded Investment Funds
201 North Charles Street
Baltimore, Maryland 21201
(301) 752-5900

Represents companies that offer closed-end mutual funds to the public, both in public edu-

cation about the funds and lobbying on issues relating to the funds.

Bank Administration Institute
1 N. Franklin Street
Chicago, Illinois 60606
(312) 553-4600

Conducts research, sponsors developmental programs and serves as the banking industry's major resource in management, administrative and technical specialties.

Bond Investors Association
Suite 240, 5979 N.W. 151st Street
Miami Lakes, Florida 33014
(305) 557-1832

A non-profit organization that educates and informs members and the general public about legislation and developments affecting bondholders.

Bond & Share Society
26 Broadway
New York, New York 10004
(212) 943-1880

Society for promoting the hobby of scripopholy, that is, the collection and study of antique stock and bond certificates.

Canadian Securities Institute
Suite 360, 33 Yonge Street
Toronto, Ontario M5E 1G4 Canada
(416) 364-9130

Provides education on investments to Canadian brokerage firms and the general public.

Coalition of Publicly Traded Partnerships
Suite 200, 1625 K Street, N.W.
Washington, D.C. 20006
(202) 857-0670

Represents master limited partnerships and their corporate sponsors in legislative and lobbying matters.

College For Financial Planning
9725 E. Hampden Avenue
Denver, Colorado 80231
(303) 755-7101

Provides mail-order educational material and administers tests for financial planners. A person who has passed the College's multi-part test, is a certified financial planner, and is entitled to use the CFP designation.

Commercial-Investment Real Estate Institute
430 North Michigan Avenue, Suite 600
Chicago, Illinois 60611-4092
(312) 321-4460

Represents real estate brokers, developers and mortgage bankers involved in commercial investment.

Consumer Bankers Association
1000 Wilson Boulevard, #3012
Arlington, Virginia 22209
(703) 276-1750

Represents commercial banks, savings and loans and credit unions and educates the public about banking.

Council of Better Business Bureaus
4200 Wilson Boulevard, Suite 800
Arlington, Virginia 22203-1800
(703) 276-0100

Mediates disputes between consumers and businesses and promotes ethical business standards.

Council of Institutional Investors
1616 P Street N.W., Suite 350
Washington, D.C. 20036
(202) 745-0800

Represents trustees from public and union pension funds, non-profit foundations and endowment funds. Educates members about corporate actions and ways to boost returns on investments.

Credit Union National Association
5710 Mineral Point Road
Madison, Wisconsin 53705
(608) 271-2664

Represents credit unions in lobbying on issues related to credit unions. Promotes credit union membership and the formation of new credit unions, and educates the public about credit unions.

Electronic Funds Transfer Association
950 Herndon Parkway, #390
Herndon, Virginia 22070
(703) 435-9800

Provides a forum for financial institutions, retailers, telecommunications companies and other businesses involved in the transfer of funds by computer.

Employee Benefit Research Institute
Suite 600, 2121 K Street
Washington, D.C. 20037-1896
(202) 659-0670

Made up of corporations, banks, insurance companies, unions and other organizations concerned with the future of employee benefit programs.

Financial Accounting Foundation
Suite 7, 401 Merritt
Norwalk, Connecticut 06856
(203) 847-0700

Maintains the Financial Accounting Standards Board, which sets financial reporting standards for private-sector organizations, and the Governmental Accounting Standards Board, which sets standards for state and local governments.

Financial Executives Institute
10 Madison Avenue
Morristown, New Jersey 07960
(201) 898-4600

Organization of executives (such as controllers, treasurers, vice presidents of finance and chief financial officers) who perform finance functions in corporations.

Financial Products Standards Board
7600 E. Eastman, Suite 301
Denver, Colorado 80231
(303) 751-7600

Sets standards for financial products to aid financial planners and the public in evaluating investment strategies.

Futures Industry Association
2001 Pennsylvania Avenue, N.W. #600
Washington, D.C. 20006
(202) 466-5460

Represents brokerage firms that deal in stock index and commodity futures, both in lobbying on futures-related issues and educating the public about the futures industry.

Gold Institute, The
1112 16th Street, N.W. #240
Washington, D.C. 20036
(202) 835-0185

Represents gold mining, manufacturing and retailing firms, conducts research on technology and industrial uses. Also compiles statistics on gold production, distribution and sales.

Health Insurance Association of America
Suite 1200, 1025 Connecticut Avenue, N.W.
Washington, D.C. 20036-3998
(202) 223-7780

Represents accident and health insurance companies.

Independent Bankers Association of America
Suite 950, 1 Thomas Circle, N.W.
Washington, D.C. 20005
(202) 659-8111

Represents small- and medium-sized commercial banks in lobbying on banking issues. Provides its members with income-producing and cost-saving programs in areas such as credit cards, equipment purchasing, advertising, loan participations and insurance.

Industry Council For Tangible Assets
6728 Old McLean Drive #200
McLean, Virginia 22101-3906
(703) 847-1714

Monitors regulations and legislation concerning the manufacture, sale and distribution of precious metals, stamps, coins and gems.

Institute of Certified Financial Planners
7600 E. Eastman Avenue, Suite 301
Denver, Colorado 80231-4397
(303) 751-7600, (800) 282-PLAN

Represents financial planners who have earned the CFP (Certified Financial Planner) designation. Provides continuing education for planners, and refers consumers who inquire about CFP's in their area.

Insurance Information Institute
110 William Street
New York, New York 10038
(212) 669-9200

Represents property and liability insurance companies to educate the public about insurance issues. Maintains a consumer insurance hotline.

Insurance Institute of America
720 Providence Road
Malvern, Pennsylvania 19355-0716
(215) 644-2100

The educational arm of the American Institute for Chartered Property Casualty Underwriters.

Insurance Services Office
7 World Trade Center
New York, New York 10048
(212) 898-6000

Establishes rate guidelines for property and liability insurance companies.

International Association for Financial
  Planning
2 Concourse Parkway, Suite 800
Atlanta, Georgia 30328
(404) 395-1605

Represents those in the financial services industry who are involved with financial planning. Promotes education of financial planners and offers assistance to the public in finding planners in their area.

International Credit Association
243 North Lindbergh Boulevard
St. Louis, Missouri 63141-1757
(314) 991-3030

Represents members of the credit industry. Conducts continuing education programs on credit issues.

International Franchise Association
1350 New York Avenue N.W., Suite 900
Washington, D.C. 20005-4709
(202) 628-8000

Represents franchisors and franchisees of many different kinds of businesses by lobbying Congress on issues of concern to the industry. Gives advice to those wanting to evaluate franchise opportunities.

Investment Company Institute
Suite 600, 1600 M Street, N.W.
Washington, D.C. 20036
(202) 293-7700

Represents load and no-load mutual fund companies, open-end and closed-end funds and unit investment trusts. Lobbies on mutual fund issues in Congress and educates the public about the uses of mutual funds.

Investment Counsel Association of America
20 Exchange Place
New York, New York 10005
(212) 344-0999

Represents firms that invest clients' money in stocks and bonds for a fee. Provides a list of money managers for those looking for one.

Investment Management Consultants
  Association
1901 E. Kenyon Avenue, Suite 3000
Denver, Colorado 80237-1855
(303) 770-3377

Represents brokers, consultants and money managers. Works to increase public awareness and knowledge of investment management consultants. Also certifies consultants.

Investment Program Association
607 14th Street N.W., Suite 1000
Washington, D.C. 20005-2000
(202) 775-9750

Works to promote and preserve the investment partnership among investors in energy, leasing, real estate, research and development and telecommunications.

Investor Responsibility Research Center
Suite 600, 1755 Massachusetts Avenue, N.W.
Washington, D.C. 20036
(202) 234-7500

Publishes impartial reports and analyses on contemporary business and public policy issues for corporations and institutional investors that vote proxies independently.

Life Insurance Marketing and Research
  Association
P.O. Box 208
Hartford, Connecticut 06141-0208
(203) 677-0033

Conducts research, seminars and schools for the life insurance industry.

Managed Futures Association
P.O. Box 287
Palo Alto, California 94302-0287
(415) 325-4533

Represents and educates trading advisors, brokers and individuals in the area of managed futures.

MicroComputer Investors Association
902 Anderson Drive
Fredricksburg, Virginia 22405
(703) 371-5474

Represents and educates professional investors using microcomputers. Also operates hardware and software library and compiles investing statistics.

Mortgage Bankers Association of America
1125 15th Street, N.W.
Washington, D.C. 20005
(202) 861-6500

Represents mortgage lenders such as mortgage bankers, commercial banks, savings and loans and insurance companies. The MBAA lobbies on housing finance issues before Congress and conducts continuing education seminars for members of the industry.

Municipal Securities Rulemaking Board
1818 N Street, N.W. #800
Washington, D.C. 20036
(202) 223-9347

A self-regulatory agency for brokers and dealers in the municipal securities industry.

Mutual Fund Education Alliance
1900 Erie Street, Suite 120
Kansas City, Missouri 64116
(816) 471-1454

Represents no-load mutual funds and provides information to consumers on the name, telephone number and kinds of funds available.

National Association of Business Economists
Suite 300, 28790 Chagrin Boulevard
Cleveland, Ohio 44122
(216) 464-7986

Society comprised of corporate and governmental economists and those with an active interest in applied, practical economics.

National Association of Investment Companies
1111 Fourteenth Street, N.W. #700
Washington, D.C. 20005
(202) 289-4336

Provides technical assistance and monitors legislation for investment companies supplying capital to minority-owned small businesses.

National Association of Investors Corporation
711 West Thirteen Mile Road
Madison Heights, Michigan 48071
(801) 583-NAIC

Represents investment clubs. Helps people set up such clubs, and monitors performance of the clubs.

National Association of Manufacturers
1331 Pennsylvania Avenue, N.W.
Washington, D.C. 20004
(202) 637-3000

Represents industry views to government on national and international issues. Also reviews legislation, administrative rulings and judicial decisions affecting industry.

National Association of Personal Financial
  Advisors
Suite 150, 1130 Lake Cook Road
Buffalo Grove, Illinois 60089-1974
(708) 537-7722

Represents financial planners who work only for a consulting fee, and do not take commissions for selling products.

National Association of Real Estate Investment
  Trusts
Suite 705, 1129 20th Street, N.W.
Washington, D.C. 20036
(202) 785-8717

Represents real estate investment trusts before Congress in lobbying on REIT-related issues, and educates the public about REITs.

National Association of Realtors
430 North Michigan Avenue
Chicago, Illinois 60611-4087
(312) 329-8200

Represents Realtors by lobbying Congress on real estate-related issues and educates the public about the realty business.

National Association of Securities Dealers
1735 K Street, N.W.
Washington, D.C. 20006
(202) 728-8000

Organization formed under the supervision of the Securities and Exchange Commission to self-regulate the securities markets, particularly the NASDAQ (National Association of Securities Dealers Automated Quotations) system, which it owns and operates. Also responsible for the over-the-counter municipal securities and government securities markets.

National Association of Small Business
  Investment Companies
1199 N. Fairfax Street, Suite 200
Alexandria, Virginia 22314-1437
(703) 683-1601

Represents small business investment companies (SBICs) that are publicly traded or private companies that invest in private small businesses. The Association lobbies Congress on issues related to the industry and educates the public about SBICs.

National Association of Women Business Owners
1377 K Street, N.W., Suite 637
Washington, D.C. 20005
(301) 608-2590

Provides technical assistance, management training and business and economic information to women business owners and represents members in legislative and lobbying efforts.

National Foundation For Consumer Credit
8611 2nd Avenue, Suite 100
Silver Spring, Maryland 20910-3372
(301) 495-5623

Represents grantors of credit to consumers such as finance companies, retailers and banks. Sponsors Consumer Credit Counseling Service centers around the country to give low- or no-cost aid to consumers in credit difficulty.

National Futures Association
Suite 1600, 200 West Madison Street
Chicago, Illinois 60606
(800) 621-3570,
(800) 572-9400 in Illinois
(312) 781-1300

Represents and sets standards for the firms and individuals that sell commodity futures and options on commodities. Resolves disputes between its members and customers with complaints against those members.

National Insurance Consumer Organization
121 North Payne Street
Alexandria, Virginia 22314
(703) 549-8050

Represents and educates consumers about insurance issues.

National Investor Relations Institute
2000 L Street, N.W.
Washington, D.C. 20036
(202) 861-0630

Represents executives in the investor relations and financial communications fields. Conducts continuing education programs for members.

National Venture Capital Association
1655 North Fort Meyer Drive #700
Arlington, Virginia 22209
(703) 525-8841

Represents venture capitalists seeking to invest money in growing enterprises. Lobbies in Congress for programs to improve the environment for venture capital investing.

New York Society of Security Analysts
One World Trade Center
New York, New York 10048
(212) 912-9249

Affiliate of the Financial Analysts Federation which conducts regular meetings between securities analysts and managements of companies followed by those analysts. This is the largest society in the country, though there are similar societies in most major American cities as well.

North American Securities Administrators Association
1 Massachusetts Avenue N.W., Suite 310
Washington, D.C. 20001
(202) 737-0900

Represents state and local officials enforcing "blue sky" laws in the sale of securities.

Overseas Private Investment Corporation
1100 New York Avenue, N.W.
Washington, D.C. 20527
(202) 336-8404

Supports and assists qualified U.S. investors in private ventures in less developed countries.

Public Securities Association
40 Broad Street
New York, New York 10004
(212) 809-7000

International trade association of banks and broker/dealers in U.S. government and federal agency securities, municipal securities, mortgage-backed securities and money-market securities.

Savings & Community Bankers of America
900 19th Street N.W., Suite 400
Washington, D.C. 20006
(202) 637-8900

Trade association for savings banks and savings and loans. The group educates the public about the role of savings and loans in the American financial system, and lobbies the government on issues of concern to the thrift industry.

Securities Industry Association
120 Broadway
New York, New York 10271
(212) 608-1500

Represents securities broker/dealers, underwriters and investment bankers in lobbying Congress on issues of concern to the securities industry. Educates the public about the securities industry.

Stockholders of America
3133 Connecticut Avenue, N.W.
Washington, D.C. 20008
(202) 783-3430
Monitors legislation and regulations affecting stockholders.

United Shareholders Association
Suite 770, 1667 K Street, N.W.
Washington, D.C. 20006
(202) 393-4600
Works to increase shareholders' rights and battles abuses by corporate management. Represents members in lobbying efforts.

United States Chamber of Commerce
1615 H Street, N.W.
Washington, D.C. 20062
(202) 659-6000
Represents the business community's views on business, the economy and other issues at the federal, state and local level. Sponsors educational programs and maintains a business forecast and survey center.

FINANCE AND INVESTMENT PUBLICATIONS

The following is a list of just about all of the major publications that can help keep you informed about the fast-changing world of finance and investment. The list encompasses the full spectrum of publications, from mass circulation business magazines to investment newsletters that reach only a handful of subscribers. The publications also cover a wide variety of topics, from investment advice about stocks, bonds, money market instruments, and commodities to mutual funds, taxation, entrepreneurship, and corporate finance. Other subjects covered include international investing, banking, precious metals, collectibles, management trends, economic forecasting, socially conscious investing, estate planning, venture capital, insider trading, real estate, and options. The title of each newsletter will often give you a clue to its subject matter.

Almost all the publications are available for a subscription charge; some also require that you join the organization that puts out the publication. Many will send you a sample either free or for a nominal charge.

Before subscribing to a newsletter, you must assess your needs and level of sophistication. Some letters listed here are designed for the novice investor with a relatively small amount of money to put into stocks or mutual funds. Other publications are aimed at a highly sophisticated audience that is knowledgeable about technical analysis, commodities trading, or some other specialty. In general, the more complex the publication, the higher the subscription fee.

Whichever publications you read, employ an appropriate amount of caution before following specific investment recommendations. Despite many advisors' claims, no one calls every move in the complex financial markets right every time. You should be satisfied if you find a few letters that offer a style you are comfortable with and have a good long-term track record at spotting unfolding investment trends.

AA11 Journal
Computerized Investing
Individual Investor
Quarterly Low Load Mutual Fund Update
625 North Michigan Avenue, Suite 1900
Chicago, Illinois 60611
(312) 280-0170 (800) 428-2244

Acquisition Mart
Business Publications, Inc.
9605 Scranton Road, Suite 503
San Diego, California 92121
(619) 457-7577

Addison Report, The
Institutional View, The
P.O. Box 402
Franklin, Massachusetts 02038
(508) 528-8678

Astute Investor, The
Cash Rich Cos.
135 Beechwood Lane
Kingston, Tennessee 37763
(615) 376-2732

AgBiotech Stock Letter
P.O. Box 40460
Berkeley, California 94704
(510) 843-1842

Agora Inc. Publications:
Adrian Day's Investment Analyst
Bob Czeschin's World Investor
Crisis Investing
Insightful Investor
Investing with Barry Ziskin
Scientific Investment
Strategic Investment
Taipan
Tax Wise Money
Agora Inc.
824 East Baltimore Street
Baltimore, Maryland 21202
(800) 433-1528

Alan Shawn Feinstein Insiders Report
37-41 Alhambra Circle
Cranston, Rhode Island 02905
(401) 467-5155

American Banker
Bond Buyer
One State Street Plaza
New York, New York 10004
(212) 803-8200

American Stock Exchange Weekly Bulletin
86 Trinity Place
New York, New York 10006
(212) 306-1445

America's Finest Companies
Bill Staton's Money Advisory
300 East Boulevard, Suite B-4
Charlotte, North Carolina 28203
(704) 332-7514

Annuity and Life Insurance Shopper
United States Annuities
81 Hoffman Road
Englishtown, New Jersey 07726-8021
(908) 521-5110   (800) 872-6684

ASC Mutual Fund Advisor
American Strategic Capital
4281 Katella Avenue, Suite 105
Los Alamitos, California 90720
(714) 527-1223

Banking Week (newspaper)
American Banker, Inc.
One State Street Plaza
New York, New York 10004
(212) 943-6700

Bankruptcy Data Source, The
Troubled Company Prospector (fax)
Turnaround Letter, The
225 Friend Street, Suite 801
Boston, Massachusetts 02114
(617) 573-9550 (800) 468-3810

Barron's: The Dow Jones Business and
  Financial Weekly
200 Liberty Street
New York 10281
(800) 277-4136 ext.478

Baxter Bulletin
1030 East Putnam Avenue
Greenwich, Connecticut 06836
(203) 637-4559

BCA Publications:
Credit Analyst, The
China Analyst, The
Emerging Markets Analyst, The
Interest Rate Forecast, The
International Bank Credit Analyst
3463 Peel Street
Montreal, Quebec H3A 1W7
(514) 398-0653

Better Investing
National Association of Investors Corp.
711 West 13 Mile Road
Madison Heights, Michigan 48071
(810) 583-6242

B.I. Research
P.O. Box 133
Redding, Connecticut 06875
(203) 270-9244

Blue Chip Correlator
575 Anton Boulevard, Suite 570
Costa Mesa, California 92626
(714) 641-3579

Blue Chip Values
680 North Lake Shore Drive, Tower Suite 2038
Chicago, Illinois 60611
(312) 649-6940

Boardroom Reports
Personal Advantage Financial
330 West 42nd Street
New York, New York 10036
(212) 239-9000   (800) 234-3830
(800) 365-0939

Bob Brinker's Marketimer
P.O. Box 321580
Cocoa Beach, Florida 32931
(407) 676-7398

Bob Nurock's Advisory
P.O. Box 460
Santa Fe, New Mexico 87504-0460
(800) 227-8883

Bond Buyer, The
One State Street Plaza
New York, New York 10004
(212) 943-8200

Bond Fund Advisor,The
290 Eliot Street
P.O. Box 9104
Ashland, Massachusetts 01721-9104
(508) 881-2800   (800) 343-5413

Boot Cove Economic Forecast
Voight Industries, Inc.
P.O. Box 220
Lubec, Maine 04652   (207) 733-5933

Bottom Line Personal
Personal Advantage Financial
Boardroom Classics
330 West 42nd Street
New York, New York 10036
(212) 239-9000   (201) 379-4642

Bowser Directory of Small Stocks
Bowser Report
P.O. Box 6278
Newport News, Virginia 23606
(804) 877-5979

Braun's Stock Index
317 Wyntfield Drive
Lewisville, North Carolina 27023
(910) 945-9110

Browning Newsletter
Foster Managements Associates, Inc.
P.O. Box 494
Burlington, Vermont 05402
(802) 658-0322

Bruce Gould on Commodities
P.O. Box 16
Seattle, Washington 98111-0016

Bullion Advisory, The
Your Window Into the Future
P.O. Box 22400
Minneapolis, Minnesota 55422
(612) 537-8096

Bullish Review of Commodity Futures Markets
14600 Blaine Avenue East
Rosemount, Minnesota 55068
(612) 423-4949

Business Week Magazine
McGraw-Hill, Inc.
1221 Avenue of the Americas
New York, New York 10020
(212) 512-2000   (800) 635-1200

Cabot's Mutual Fund Navigator
Cabot Market Letter
P.O. Box 3067
Salem, Massachusetts 01970
(508) 745-5532

California Technology Stock Letter
Overpriced Stock Service
Murenove, Inc.
P.O. Box 308
Half Moon Bay, California 94019
(415) 726-8495

Canadian Market Confidential
Penny Fortune Newsletter
Women's Investment Newsletter
Phoenix Communications Group, Ltd.
1837 South Nevada Avenue, Suite 223
Colorado Springs, Colorado 80906
(719) 576-9200

Candlelight
MBH Weekly Commodity Letter
P.O. Box 353
Winnetka, Illinois 60093
(708) 291-1870   (800) 678-5253

Capitalist's Companion, The
175 Fifth Avenue, Suite 2503
New York, New York 10010
(800) 966-6567

Cappiello's Closed End Fund Digest
Cappiello's Real Estate Securities
Madent Publishing, Inc.
1224 Coast Village Circle, Suite 11
Santa Barbara, California 93108
(805) 565-5651

CardTrak
RAM Research Corporation
P.O. Box 1700
Frederick, Maryland 21702
(301) 695-4660   (800) 344-7714

CCH Incorporated Publications:
Capital Changes Reports
Estate Planning Review
Financial and Estate Planning
Financial and Estate Planning Ideas and Trends
Individual Retirement Plans Guide
Mutual Funds Guide
CCH Incorporated
4025 West Peterson Avenue
Chicago, Illinois 60646
(800) TELL-CCH

CDA/Spectrum Publications:
CDA/Spectrum Convertibles
CDA/Spectrum Convertibles - 13(f)
    Institutional Portfolios
CDA/Spectrum International
Directory of Buy-Side Traders
Five Percent Owner Portfolios
Five Percent Stock Holdings
Insider Holdings
Investment Company Portfolios
Investment Company Stock Holdings
13(f) Institutional Portfolios
13(f) Institutional Stock Holdings
CDA Investment Technologies, Inc.
1355 Piccard Drive
Rockville, Maryland 20850
(800) 232-6362

Certified Coin Dealer
Currency Dealer Newsletter
P.O. Box 7939
Torrance, California 90504
(310) 515-7369

CFP Today
The Institute of Certified Financial Planners
7600 East Eastman Avenue, Suite 301
Denver, Colorado 80231-4397
(303) 751-7600

Chartcraft Publications:
Annual Long Term P&F Chartbook
Bi-Weekly Investors Intelligence
Bi-Weekly Technical Indicator
Chartcraft by Fax
Monthly P&F Chartbook on NYSE/ASE
Quarterly Mutual Funds P&F Chartbook
Quarterly Options P&F Chartbook
Quarterly Options Relative Strength Chartbook
Quarterly Over-the-Counter P&F Chartbook
Weekly ASE-OTC Breakout Service
Weekly Breakout Service
Weekly Futures Service
Weekly Mutual Funds Breakouts
Weekly Options Service
Weekly Service on NYSE/ASE
Chartcraft, Inc.
30 Church Street/P.O. Box 2046
New Rochelle, New York 10801
(914) 632-0422

Chartist, The
Chartist Mutual Fund Timer, The
P.O. Box 758
Seal Beach, California 90740
(310) 596-2385

Cheap Investor, The
Mathews and Associates
West Golf Road, Suite 350
Hoffman Estates, Illinois 60194
(708) 830-5666

Checklist Magazine
Credit Union News
Today's Pawnbroker
150 Nassau Street
New York, New York 10038
(212) 267-7707

Clean Yield, The
P.O. Box 1880
Greensboro Bend, Vermont 05842
(802) 533-7178

CMI Stock and Index Options Trader
P.O. Box 3289
Newport Beach, California 92659
(714) 851-9079

COINage Magazine
Miller Magazines, Inc.
4880 Market Street
Ventura, California 93003
(805) 644-3824

Coin Collector
Rare Coin Review
Bowers and Merena Galleries, Inc.
P.O. Box 1224
Wolfeboro, New Hampshire 03894-1224
(603) 569-5095   (800) 458-4646

Coin Dealer Newsletter
Certified Coin Dealer
P.O. Box 7939
Torrance, California 90504
(310) 515-7369

Coin World
Amos Press
911 Vandemark Road
Sidney, Ohio 45365
(513) 498-0800

Comex Daily Market Report
Commodity Exchange, Inc.
4 World Trade Center, 7th Floor
New York, New York 10048
(212) 938-2900   (800) 333-2900

Commercial & Financial Chronicle
P.O. Box 1839
Daytona Beach, Florida 32115-1839

Commodex
Commodity Futures Forecast
Commodex
The Mall At The Galaxy
7000 Boulevard East
Guttenberg, New Jersey 07093
(201) 868-2600   (800) 336-1818

Commodity Price Chart
Trends & Futures
Oster Communications
P.O. Box 6
Cedar Falls, Iowa 50613
(319) 277-1271

Commodity Trader, The
Daily Speculator, The
Weekly Investor, The
Global Financial Trading, Ltd.
280 Oser Avenue
Hauppauge, New York 11788
(800) 264-9100

Commodity Traders Consumer Report
Major Moves
Bruce Babcock Jr
1731 Howe Avenue, Suite 149
Sacramento, California 95825
(916) 677-7562   (800) 999-2827

Common Stocks, Common Sense
P.O. Box 224
Concord, Massachusetts 01742
(508) 371-1677

Community Investment Report
Managing Mortgages
National Mortgage News
Problem Asset Report
212 West 35th Street, Suite 1300
New York, New York 10001
(212) 563-4273　(800) 327-6346

Comparative Annuity Reports
P.O. Box 1268
Fair Oaks, California 95628
(916) 487-7863

Complete Strategist, The
P.O. Box 6
Riverdale, New York 10471
(718) 884-5408

Consensus
National Futures and Financial Weekly
1737 McGee Street, Suite 401
Kansas City, Missouri 64108
(816) 471-3862

Consultants Certified Coin Report
P.O. Box 8277
Fountain Valley, California 92728
(714) 662-0237

Consumer Credit Card Rating Service
P.O. Box 5483
Oxnard, California 93031
(310) 392-7720

Contrarian's View, The
132 Moreland Street
Worcester, Massachusetts 01609
(508) 757-2881

Contrary Investor
Contrary Investor Follow-up
Fraser Opinion Letter
Fraser Management Associates, Inc.
P.O. Box 494
Burlington, Vermont 05402
(802) 658-0322

Crain Communications Publications:
Advertising Age
Business Insurance
Crain's Chicago Business
Crain's Cleveland Business
Crain's Detroit Business
Crain's New York Business
Detroit Monthly
Modern Healthcare
Pensions & Investments
Crain Communications Inc.
740 Rush Street
Chicago, Illinois 60611-2590
(312) 649-5200

Crawford Perspectives
1456 Second Avenue, Suite 145
New York, New York 10021
(212) 744-6973

CRB Commodity Yearbook, The
Encyclopedia of Historical Charts
Knight-Ridder Financial
75 Wall Street, 23rd Floor
New York, New York 10005-2890
(212) 269-1110

CRB Futures Chart Service
Commodity Research Bureau
30 South Wacker Drive
Chicago, Illinois 60606
(800) 621-5271

Creative Real Estate Magazine
Drawer L
Rancho Santa Fe, California 92067
(619) 756-1441

Crosscurrents
80 Cuttermill Road
Great Neck, New York 11021

Czeschin's Mutual Fund Outlook &
　Recommendations
P.O. Box 1423
Baltimore, Maryland 21203-1423
(410) 558-1699

Daily Trader, The
Investment Research Institute
P.O. Box 46709
Cincinnati, Ohio 45246
(800) 448-2080

Danbell Energy Alert
Danbell Energy Letter
Daniells & Bell
99 Wall Street
New York, New York 10005
(212) 422-1710　(800) 427-9446

Defaulted Bonds Newsletter
High Yield Securities Journal
Bonds Investors Association
P.O. Box 4427
Miami Lakes, Florida 33014
(305) 557-1832

Deliberations: The Ian McAvity Market Letter
P.O. Box, Adelaide Street Station
Toronto, Ontario M5C 2J1, Canada
(416) 867-1100

Dessauer's Investors World
P.O. Box 1718
Orleans, Massachusetts 02653
(508) 255-1651

Dick Davis Digest
P.O. Box 350630
Fort Lauderdale, Florida 33335-0630
(800) 654-1514

Dick Young's Intelligence Report
Young Research & Publishing, Inc.
Federal Building, Thames Street
Newport, Rhode Island 02840
(401) 849-2131

Dines Letter, The
James Dines & Co.
P.O. Box 22
Belvedere, California 94920
(800) 84LUCKY

Directory of Mutual Funds
Investment Company Institute
1401 H Street, N.W., Suite 1200
Washington D.C. 20005-2148
(202) 326-5800

Distressed Securities Service Report
Small Cap Opportunities Report
Small Cap Value Growth Report
Theme Research Report
Weekly Summary Report
South East Executive Park
100 Executive Drive
Brewster, New York 10509
(914) 278-6500

Donoghue's Moneyletter
290 Elliot Street, Box 91004
Ashland, Massachusetts 01721-9104
(508) 881-2800

Dowbeaters
P.O. Box 284
Ironia, New Jersey 07845
(201) 543-4860

Dow Theory Forecasts
Low Price Stock Survey
Digest
The Drip Investor
7412 Calumet Avenue
Hammond, Indiana 46324
(219) 931-6480

Dow Theory Letters
Dow Jones Averages, 1896 to Present
Richard Russell
P.O. Box 1759
La Jolla, California 92038
(619) 454-0481

Dunn & Hargitt Commodity Service
P.O. Box 1100
22 North Second Street
Lafayette, Indiana 47902
(317) 423-2624   (800) 922-7289

Economist, The
111 West 57th Street
New York, New York 10019
(212) 541-5730

Elliott Wave Theorist
Elliott Currency & Commodity Forecast
Global Market Perspective
Elliott Wave International
P.O. Box 1618
Gainesville, Georgia 30503
(404) 563-0309   (800) 336-1618

Equities Special Situations
145 E. 49th Street, Suite 5 B&C
New York, New York 10017-1210
(212) 832-7800   (800) 237-8400

Equity Fund Outlook
P.O. Box 1040
Boston, Massachusetts 02117
(617) 397-6844

Estates, Gifts and Trusts Journal
Tax Management, Inc.
Bureau of National Affairs
1250 23rd Street, N.W.
Washington, D.C. 20037
(202) 833-7261

Fabians Investment Resources
2100 Main Street
Huntington Beach, California 92647
(800) 950-8765

Fast Track Funds
5536 Temple City Boulevard
Temple City, California 91780

Fidelity Insight
Mutual Fund Investors Association
P.O. Box 9135
Wellesley Hills, Massachusetts 02181
(617) 235-4432

Fidelity Monitor
P.O. Box 1294
Rocklin, California 95677
(800) 397-3094

Financial Executive Magazine
Financial Executives Institute
P.O. Box 1938, 10 Madison Avenue
Morristown, New Jersey 07962-1938
(201) 898-4600

Financial Freedom Report
4505 South Wasatch Boulevard
Salt Lake City, Utah 84124
(801) 272-3500   (800) 289-9715

Financial Planning Magazine
40 West 57th Street, 11th Floor
New York, New York 10019
(212) 765-5311

The Financial Post Datagroup Publications:
Financial Post Investment Reports, The
Survey of Mutual Funds
Record of New Issues
Data Speed

The Financial Post Datagroup
333 King Street East
Toronto, Ontario M5A 4N2, Canada
(416) 350-6500

Financial Services Week
Securities Data Corporation
40 West 57th Street, Suite 802
New York, New York 10019
(212) 227-1200

Financial Times of London
14 East 60th Street
New York, New York 10022
(212) 752-4500

Financial World
P.O. Box 10750
Des Moines, Iowa 50340
(800) 666-6639

Five Point Investment Strategy
208 South La Salle Street, Suite 1700
Chicago, Illinois 60604
(312) 853-2820   (800) 458-2358

Forbes Magazine
Forbes, Inc.
P.O. Box 10048
Des Moines, Iowa 50340-0048
(800) 888-9896

Ford Value Report
Ford Data Base Report
Ford Investment Management Review
Ford Investment Report
Ford Investor Services Inc.
11722 Sorrento Valley Road, Suite 'I'
San Diego, California 92121
(619) 755-1327

Forecaster
Forecaster Publishing Company
19623 Ventura Boulevard
Tarzana, California 91356
(818) 345-4421

Fortune Magazine
Time Life Building, Rockefeller Center
New York, New York 10020-1393
(212) 522-2582   (800) 621-8000

Fund Exchange
1200 Westlake Avenue North, Suite 700
Seattle, Washington 98109
(800) 423-4893

Fund Kinetics
2841 23rd Avenue West
Seattle, Washington 98199-2920
(800) 634-6790

Fundline
David H. Menashe & Co.
P.O. Box 663
Woodland Hills, California 91365
(818) 346-5637

Futures Hotline Mutual Fund Timer
P.O. Box 6275
Jacksonville, Florida 32236
(904) 693-0355

Futures Industry
Futures Industry Association
2001 Pennsylvania Avenue N.W., Suite 600
Washington D.C. 20006
(202) 466-5460

Futures Magazine
219 Parkade
Cedar Falls, Iowa 50613
(319) 277-6341

FXC Report
FXC Investors Corporation
62-19 Cooper Avenue, Glendale
Queens, New York 11385
(800) 392-0992

Gann Angles
495-A Trinity Avenue
Seaside, California 93955
(408) 393-2000

Garside Forecast, The
5200 Irvine Boulevard, Suite 370
Santa Ana, California 92720
(714) 259-1670

Georgeson Report
Georgeson & Company Inc.
Wall Street Plaza/88 Pine Street
New York, New York 10005
(212) 440-9800   (800) 445-1790

Global Fund Timer
P.O. Box 77330
Baton Rouge, Louisiana 70879
(800) 329-4866

Gold Monitor
M. Murenbeeld & Associates
P.O. Box 6187, Depot #1
Victoria, British Columbia V8P 5L5, Canada
(604) 477-7579

Gold News, The
Silver News, The
1112 16th Street N.W., Suite 240
Washington D.C. 20036 (202) 835-0185

Gold Newsletter
Jefferson Financial
2400 Jefferson Highway
Jefferson, Louisiana 70121
(504) 837-3033 (800) 877-8847

Good Money
Netback
Good Money Publications
P.O. Box 363
Worcester, Vermont 05682
(802) 223-8911   (800) 535-3551

Grants Interest Rate Observer
30 Wall Street, 6th Floor
New York, New York 10005-2201
(212) 809-7994

Granville Market Letter, The
P.O. Drawer 413006
Kansas City, Missouri 64141
(816) 474-5353   (800) 876-5388

Graphic Fund Forecaster
6 Pioneer Circle
P.O. Box 673
Andover, Massachusetts 01810
(508) 470-3511   (800) 532-2322

Growth Fund Guide
Mutual Fund Trends
P.O. Box 6600
Rapid City, South Dakota 57709
(605) 341-1971   (800) 621-8322

Growth Stock Outlook
P.O. Box 15381
Chevy Chase, Maryland 20815
(301) 654-5205   (800) 742-5476

Harmonic Research
S&P Weekly Fax
650 Fifth Avenue
New York, New York 10019
(212) 484-2065   (800) 445-1753

Harry Browne's Special Reports
P.O. Box 5586
Austin, Texas 78763
(800) 531-5142

Hirsch Publications:
Beating the Dow
Ground Floor
Higher Returns
Smart Money
Turov on Timing
The Hirsch Organization
6 Deer Trail
Old Tappan, New Jersey 07675
(201) 664-3400   (800) 477-3400

Hulbert Financial Digest
316 Commerce Street
Alexandria, Virginia 22314
(703) 683-5905

Hussman Econometrics
P.O. Box 3199
Farmington Hills, Michigan 48333
(800) 487-7626

In Business
JG Press
419 State Avenue
Emmaus, Pennsylvania 18049
(215) 967-4135

Inc Magazine
488 Madison Avenue
New York, New York 10022
(212) 326-2600

Independent Advisor for Vanguard Investors
Independent T. Rowe Price Advisor
Fund Family Shareholder Association
42 Pleasant Street
Watertown, Massachusetts 02172
(617) 926-5552   (800) 435-3372

Individual Investor Special Situations Report
333 7th Avenue, 5th Floor
New York, New York 10001
(212) 843-2777

Industries in Transition
Business Communication Co.
25 Van Zant Street, Suite 13
Norwalk, Connecticut 06855
(203) 853-4266

Industry Forecast
Levy Economic Forecasts
P.O. Box 26
Chappaqua, New York 10514
(914) 238-3665

Insight: Investing for a Better World
Insight: The Advisory Letter for Concerned Investors
Franklin Research and Development Corp.
711 Atlantic Avenue
Boston, Massachusetts 02111
(617) 423-6655   (800) 548-5684

Institute for Econometric Research
  Publications:
Buyer's Guide
Consumers Guide to High Yields, The
Fundwatch
Insiders,The
Income Fund Outlook
Investors Digest
Market Logic
Mutual Fund Forecaster
Mutual Funds Magazine
New Issues
The Institute for Econometric Research
3471 North Federal Highway
Fort Lauderdale, Florida 33306
(305) 563-9000   (800) 442-9000

Institutional Investor, Inc.
Publications:
Bank Accounting and Finance
Bank Letter
Bond Week
Commercial Lending Review
Corporate Financing Week
Defined Contribution News
Derivatives Week
Emerging Markets Week

Global Money Management
Institutional Investor Magazine
Journal of Fixed Income, The
Journal of Investing, The
Journal of Portfolio Management, The
Money Management Letter
Portfolio Letter
Wall Street Letter
Institutional Investor, Inc.
488 Madison Avenue
New York, New York 10022
(212) 303-3300 (800) 437-9997

Insurance Forum
P.O. Box 245
Elletsville, Indiana 47429
(812) 876-6502

Interactive Multimedia Communications
21st Century Research
8200 Boulevard East
North Bergen, New Jersey 07047
(201) 868-0881

Intermarket Review, The
International Institute for Economic Research
   Inc.
P.O. Box 624
Gloucester, Virginia 23061
(804) 694-0415 (800) 221-7514

International Harry Schultz Letter
P.O. Box 622
CH-1001 Lausanne, Switzerland
(32) 16-533-684

InvesTech Market Analyst
InvesTech Mutual Fund Advisor
2472 Birch Glen
Whitefish, Montana 59937
(406) 862-7777   (800) 955-8500

Investment Advisor Magazine
Realty Stock Review
Charter Financial Publishing Company
179 Avenue at the Commons
Shrewsbury, New Jersey 07702
(908) 389-8700

Investment and Tax Shelter Blue Book
Securities Investigations, Inc.
P.O. Box 888
Woodstock, New York 12498
(914) 679-2300

Investment Blue Book, The
Securities Investigations, Inc.
P.O. Box 888
Woodstock, New York 12498
(914) 679-2300

Investment Dealers' Digest Publications:
Bank Loan Report
Corporate Finance Directory
Elliott Sharp News

Going Public: The IPO Reporter
IDD
Mergers & Acquisitions Journal
Mergers & Acquisitions International
Mortgage-Backed Securities Letter
Mutual Fund Directory
Private Placement Letter
Investment Dealers' Digest
2 World Trade Center, 18th Floor
New York, New York 10048
(212) 227-1200

Investment Horizons
Mutual Fund Letter
Mutual Fund Encyclopedia
Tower Suite 2038
680 North Lakeshore Drive
Chicago, Illinois 60611
(800) 326-6941

Investment Letter
P.O. Box 36358
Grosse Pointe, Michigan 48236

Investment Quality Trends
7440 Girard Avenue, Suite 4
La Jolla, California 92037
(619) 459-3818

Investor News
Kemper Securities, Inc.
1300 North Point Tower
1001 Lakeside Avenue
Cleveland, Ohio 44114
(216) 574-7300

Investor Relations Update
National Investor Relations Institute
Suite 701, 2000 L Street, N.W.
Washington D.C. 20036
(202) 861-0630

Investors Business Daily
12655 Beatrice Street
Los Angeles, California 90066
(310) 448-6000   (800) 831-2525
(800) 366-8989

Investors Guide to Closed-End Funds
Thomas J. Herzfeld Advisors
P.O. Box 161465
Miami, Florida 33116
(305) 271-1900   (800) 854-3863

Investors Hotline
Valuetrac
10616 Beaver Dam Road, Suite S-6
Hunt Valley, Maryland 21030
(410) 771-0064 (800) 345-8112

Investor, U.S.A.
Seahorse Financial Advisers
15 Seatuck Lane, P.O. Box 370
Remsenburg, New York 11960
(516) 423-1118

John Bollinger's Capital Growth Letter
Bollinger Capital Management
P.O. Box 3358
Manhattan Beach, California 90266
(301) 798-8855   (800) 888-8400

John T. Reed's Real Estate Investors Monthly
342 Bryan Drive
Danville, California 94526
(510) 820-6292   (800) 635-5425

Journal of Financial Planning, The
7600 East Eastman Avenue, Suite 301
Denver, Colorado 80231
(303) 751-7600

Journal of Futures Markets
John Wiley & Sons, Inc.
605 Third Avenue
New York, New York 10158-0012
(212) 850-6000

Jumbo Rate News
CD Rate Watch
The Bauer Group
P.O. Drawer 145510
Coral Gables, Florida 33114-5510
(305) 445-9500   (800) 388-6686

Kagan World Media Ltd Publications:
Broadcast Banker/Broker
Broadcast Investor
Broadcast Investor Charts
Broadcast Stats
Cellular Investor
Cable Network Investor
Cable TV Advertising
Cable TV Finance
Cable TV Investor
Cable TV Investor Charts
DBS Report, The
Paul Kagan Associates
126 Clock Tower Place
Carmel, California 93923-8734
(408) 624-1536

KCI Communications Publications:
Big Picture, The
Global Investing
Personal Finance
Special Alert Bulletin
Utilities Forecaster
Wall Street Bargains
Winning with Options
KCI Communications
1101 King Street, Suite 400
Alexandria, Virginia 22314
(703) 548-2400

Kevin Smith's Client Advisory
1001 4th Ave, Suite 2200
Seattle, Washington 98154
(206) 622-7200   (800) 426-9494

Key Volume Strategies
P.O. Box 407
White Plains, New York 10602
(914) 997-1276

Kimball Letter
4640 Rummell Road
Saint Cloud, Florida 34771
(407) 892-8555

Kinsman's Telephone Growth & Income Service
P.O. Box 2107
Sonoma, California 95476-2107
(707) 935-6504

Kiplingers Personal Finance Magazine
Kiplinger Washington Letter, The
1729 H Street, N.W.
Washington D.C. 20006
(202) 887-6400   (800) 544-0155

Kon-Lin Letter, The
Kon-Lin Research and Analysis Corporation
5 Water Road
Rocky Point, New York 11778
(516) 744-8536

LaLoggia's Special Situation Report & Stock
  Market Forecast
P.O. Box 167
Rochester, New York 14601
(716) 232-1240 (800) 836-4330

Laser Report
Medical Report
10 Tara Boulevard, 5th Floor
Nashua, New Hampshire 03062-2801
(603) 891-0123

Lenape Investment Corporation Publica-tions:
Global Markets
Market Monthly
Investor's Information Sourcebook
Investor's Oil & Gas Handbook
Investor's Small Cap Handbook
Lenape Investment Corporation
P.O. Box 724
Morrisville, Pennsylvania 19067-0724

L/G No-Load Fund Analyst
300 Montgomery Street, Suite 621
San Francisco, California 94104
(415) 989-8513

Long Term Investing
Turning Points
Concept Publishing
P.O. Box 500
New York, New York 14592
(716) 243-3148

Lynch Municipal Bond Advisory
2840 Broadway, #201
New York, New York 10025
(212) 663-5552

Major Trends
250 West Coventry Court
Milwaukee, Wisconsin 53217
(414) 352-8460

Managed Account Reports
19th Floor, 220 Fifth Avenue
New York, New York 10001
(212) 213-6202   (800) 638-2525

Margo's Market Monitor
P.O. Box 642
Lexington, Massachusetts 02173
(617) 861-0302   (800) 743-4539

Market Alert Newsletter
110 Veterans Highway, Suite 200
Metairie, Louisiana 70003
(800) 880-4653

Market Beat, Inc.
1436 Granada
Ann Arbor, Michigan 48103
(313) 426-2146

Market Charts Inc: Point and Figure Charts
10 Hanover Square, 20th Floor
New York, New York 10005
(212) 509-0944   (800) 431-6082

Market Express
1801 Lee Road, Suite 301
Winterpark, Florida 32789
(407) 628-5200   (800) 333-5697

Market Guide
Market Guide, Inc.
49 Glen Head Road
Glen Head, New York 11545
(516) 759-1253

Market Insider Bulletin
Evasona Co.
P.O. Box 541
Thornhill, Ontario L3T 2CO Canada
(905) 883-4843

Market\Cycle Investing
995 Oak Park Drive
Morgan Hill, California 95037

Market Maneuvers
305 Madison Avenue, #1166
New York, New York 10165

Market Timing Report
P.O. Box 225
Tucson, Arizona 85702
(602) 795-9552

Marketarian Letter, The
OTC Value Watch
P.O. Box 1283
Grand Island, Nebraska 68802
(800) 658-4325

Marples Business Newsletter
Newsletter Publishing Corporation
117 West Mercer Street, Suite 200
Seattle, Washington 98119-3960
(206) 281-9609

Martin Weiss' Safe Money Report
Weiss Research
2200 North Florida Mango Road
West Palm Beach, Florida 33409
(407) 684-8100   (800) 289-9222

Master Indicator of the Stock Market
11371 Torchwood Court
West Palm Beach, Florida 33414-6040
(407) 793-8316

McShane Letter
155 East 55th Street
New York, New York 10022
(212) 688-2387

Medical Technology Stock Letter
P.O. Box 40460
Berkeley, California 94704
(510) 843-1857

Middle/Fixed Income Letter
MASTCA Publishing Corp.
P.O. Box 55
Loch Sheldrake, New York 12759
(914) 794-5792

MMA Cycles Report
Merriman Market Analyst
P.O. Box 250012
West Bloomfield, Michigan 48325
(313) 626-3034

MMS International Publications:
MMS TREASURY
MMS CURRENCY
MMS EUROPEAN
MMS CANADIAN
MMS ASIA PACIFIC
MMS JAPAN
MMS HIGHLIGHTS
MMS EQUITIES
MMS U.K.
MMS TECH-TRADER
MMS International
65 Broadway
New York, New York 10006
(212) 770-4343

Money Fund Report
290 Elliot Street
Ashland, Massachusetts 01721-9104
(508) 881-2800   (800) 343-5413

Money Magazine
P.O. Box 60001
Tampa, Florida 33660-0001
(212) 522-1212   (800) 541-1000

Moneypaper, The
Moneypaper Guide to Dividend Program
  Reinvestment
1010 Mamaroneck Avenue
Mamaroneck, New York 10543
(914) 381-5400   (800) 388-9993

MoneyLetter
TaxLetter
Hume Publishing Company, Ltd.
4100 Yonge Street, Suite 515
Toronto, Ontario M2P 2B9, Canada
(416) 221-4596

Monthly Tax Update
111 Ellenbecker Road
Thiensville, Wisconsin 53092
(414) 238-1150

Moody's Financial Information Services
Bank and Finance Manual & News Report
Bond Record
Bond Survey
Dividend Record
Handbook of Common Stocks
Handbook of Nasdaq Stocks
Handbook of Dividend Achievers
Industrial Manual & News Reports
Industry Review
International Manual & News Reports
Moody's Company Data - CD-ROM
Moody's International Company Data - CD-ROM
Moody's Manuals and Discs
Municipal and Government Manual & News
  Reports
OTC Industrial Manual & News Reports
OTC Unlisted Manual & News Reports
Public Utility Manual & News Reports
Transportation Manual & News Reports
Unit Investment Trusts Manual
Moody's Investors Service
99 Church Street
New York, New York 10007
(212) 553-0435
(800) 342-5647 Ext 0435 - Print
(800) 955-8080 - CD-ROM

MorningStar Mutual Funds
Five Star Investor
West Wacker Drive, Suite 400
Chicago, Illinois 60606
(800) 876-5005

Mortgage-Backed Security Letter
IDD Enterprises
Two World Trade Center
New York, New York 10048
(212) 227-1200

MPL Communications Publications:
Best U.S. Stocks for Canadian Investors
Blue Book of Stock Reports (Canadian)
Canadian Mutual Fund Advisor
Canadian News Facts

Canadian Resources & Pennymines Analyst
Investment Reporter, The
Investors Digest of Canada
Louis Rukeyser's Wall Street
Money Reporter
MPL Communications, Inc.
133 Richmond Street West
Toronto, Ontario, M5H 3M8 Canada
(416) 869-1177

MPT Review
P.O. Box 10012
Incline Village, Nevada 89450-1012
(702) 831-1396   (800) 454-1395

Mutual Fund Advisor, The
One Sarasota Tower, Suite 602
Two North Tamiami Trail
Sarasota, Florida 34236
(813) 954-5500

Mutual Fund Letter
Tower Suite 2038
680 North Lakeshore Drive
Chicago, Illinois 60611
(312) 649-6940   (800) 326-6941

Mutual Fund Strategist
P.O. Box 446
Burlington, Vermont 05402
(802) 425-2211   (800) 355-3863

Mutual Fund Technical Trader
1971 Spear Street/ P.O. Box 4560
Burlington, Vermont 05406
(802) 658-5500

Myers Finance Review
Tapio Center, S. 104 Freya
Spokane, Washington 99202

100 Highest Yields
Bank Advertising News
Bank Rate Monitor
Best Ads of the Month
Jumbo Flash Report
Financial Rates Inc.
P.O. Box 088888
North Palm Beach, Florida 33408
(407) 627-7330 (800) 327-7717

National Mortgage News
212 West 35th Street, 13th Floor
New York, New York 10001
(212) 563-4008   (800) 765-6700

National Trendlines
National Investment Advisors
14001 Berryville Road
North Potomac, Maryland 20874
(800) 521-1585

Nation's Business
1615 H Street N.W.
Washington, D.C. 20062
(202) 463-5650

Nelson Publications:
America's Best Money Managers
Directory of Institutional Real Estate
Directory of Investment Managers
Directory of Investment Research
Directory of Minority and Woman-Owned
 Investment Managers
Directory of Plan Sponsors
Earnings Outlook
Guide to Institutional Research
Guide to Pension Fund Consultants
TechResources
One Gateway Plaza, P.O. Box 591
Port Chester, New York 10573
(914) 937-8400   (800) 333-6357

Neurovest Journal
P.O. Box 764
Haymarket, Virginia 22069-0764
(703) 754-0696

Next Superstock, The
15779 Columbia Pike, Suite 275
Burtonsville, Maryland 20866
(301) 890-3523

Ney Report, The
Ney Fund Letter, The
P.O. Box 92223
Pasadena, California 91109
(818) 441-2222

Nielsen's International Investment Letter
P.O. Box 7532
Olympia, Washington 98507

**NoLoad Fund*X
DAL Investment Company
235 Montgomery Street, Suite 662
San Francisco, California 94104
(415) 986-7979   (800) 323-1510

No Load Fund Investor
P.O. Box 318
Irvington, New York 10533
(800) 252-2042

No Load Mutual Fund Selections and Timing
 Newsletter
100 North Central Expressway, Suite 1112
Richardson, Texas 75075
(800) 800-6563

No-Load Portfolios
8635 West Sahara, Suite 420
The Lakes, Nevada 89117
Fax (702) 255-1682

Numismatic News
World Coin News
Bank Note Reporter
Coin Price News
Coins Magazine

Krause Publications
700 East State Street
Iola, Wisconsin 54990
(715) 445-2214

Oberweis Report,The
One Constitution Drive
Aurora, Illinois 60506
(708) 801-4766

Oil and Gas Finance Source Book
Oil and Gas Investor
Oil and Gas Interest Newsletter
Hart Publications
1900 Grant, Suite 400
Denver, Colorado 80203
(303) 832-1917   (800) 832-1917

Oil\Energy Statistics Bulletin
P.O. Box 189
Whitman, Massachusetts 02382
(617) 447-6407

On Markets
31 Melkhout Crescent
Hout Bay 7800
South Africa

Opportunities in Options
Option Advisor, The
Option Strategist, The
Select Information Exchange
244 West 54th Street
New York, New York 10019
(800) 743-9346

Opportunities in Options Newsletter
Option Volatility Chartbook
Options Advantage Trading Manual
Option Secret Book
P.O. Box 2126
Malibu, California 90265
(310) 456-9699   (800) 456-9699

Option Advisor, The
Fund Profit Alert
Investment Research Institute, Inc.
P.O. Box 46709
Cincinnati, Ohio 45246
(800) 327-8833

Option Pro
24 W. 500 Maple Ave, Suite 108
Naperville, Illinois 60540
(708) 416-3530   (800) 726-2140

OTC Communications
OTC Growth Stock Watch
1040 Great Plain Avenue, Suite 2
Needham, Massachusetts 02192-2517
(617) 444-6100

OTC Insight
P.O. Box 5759
Walnut Creek, California 94596
(800) 955-9566

Outstanding Investor Digest
Portfolio Reports
14 East 4th Street, Suite 501
New York, New York 10012
(212) 777-3330

Overpriced Stock Service
Murenove, Inc.
P.O. Box 308
Half Moon Bay, California 94019
(415) 726-8495

Pad System Report,The
P.O. Box 554
Oxford, Ohio 45056
(513) 529-2863

Patient Investor
Ariel Capital Management
307 North Michigan Avenue, Suite 500
Chicago, Illinois 60601
(312) 726-0140   (800) 292-7435

Penny Stocks Newsletter
31731 Outer Highway 10
Redlands, California 92373

Pension World
6151 Powers Ferry Road
Atlanta, Georgia 30339
(404) 955-2500

Peter Dag Investment Letter
65 Lakefront Drive
Akron, Ohio 44319
(216) 644-2782   (800) 833-2782

Phillips Publications:
Mark Skousen's Forecasts and Strategies
Gerbino's Investment Letter
John Dessauer's Investors World
Jay Schabaker's Mutual Fund Investing
Bert Thomen's Mutual Fund Strategies
Richard E. Band's Profitable Investing
Richard C.Young's Intelligence Report
Pete Dickinson's Retirement Letter
Ken and Daria Dolan's Straight Talk on Your
  Money
Phillips Publishing Inc.
7811 Montrose Road
Potomac, Maryland 20854
(301) 340-2100   (800) 777-5015

Plain Talk Investor
1500 Skokie Boulevard, Suite 203
Northbrook, Illinois 60062
(708) 564-1955

Portfolio Allocation Report
P.O. Box 182
Arlington Heights, Illinois 60004
(708) 394-3004

Portfolios Investment Advisory
P.O. Box 997
Lynchburg, Virginia 24505
(804) 845-1335

Portfolio Monitor, The
Rutledge Report, The
Rutledge & Company, Inc.
One East Putman Avenue
Greenwich, Connecticut 06830
(203) 869-8866

Powell Gold Industry Guide and The
  International Mining Analyst
Powell Monetary Analyst
Reserve Research Ltd.
P.O. Box 4135, Station A
Portland, Maine 04101
(207) 774-4971

Precision Timing
P.O. Box 11722
Atlanta, Georgia 30355
(404) 355-0447

Primary Trend
Arnold Investment Counsel
700 North Water Street
Milwaukee, Wisconsin 53202
(414) 271-2726   (800) 443-6544

Prime Investment Alert
P.O. Box 701
Bangor, Maine 04401
(207) 945-0241

Princeton Portfolios, The
301 North Harrison, Suite 229
Princeton, New Jersey 08540
(609) 497-0362   (212) 717-5125

Professional Timing Service
P.O. Box 7483
Missoula, Montana 59807
(406) 543-4131

Professional Tape Reader, The
RADCAP Inc.
P.O. Box 2407
Hollywood, Florida 33022
(305) 983-1035   (800) 868-7857

Prudent Speculator, The
Al Frank Asset Management, Inc.
P.O. Box 1767
Santa Monica, California 90406
(310) 587-2410

Public Investor
Government Finance Officer's Association
180 North Michigan Avenue, Suite 800
Chicago, Illinois 60601
(312) 977-9700

Publishers   Management   Corporation
  Publications:
Aden Forecast
Dr. North's Remnant Review
Larry Abraham's Insider Report
Mark Westann's Low Profile
McAlvany Intelligence Advisor
Reaper, The
Publishers Management Corporation
P.O. Box 84902
Phoenix, Arizona 85071
(602) 252-4477   (800) 528-0559

Real Estate Investing Letter
861 Lafayette Road, Number 5
Hampton, New Hampshire 03842-1232
(603) 929-1600

Real Estate Weekly
1 Madison Avenue
New York, New York 10010
(212) 679-1234

Reaper, The
P.O. Box 84901
Phoenix, Arizona 85071
(800) 528-0559

Red Book, The
Western Publishing Company
1220 Mound Avenue
Racine, Wisconsin 53404
(414) 633-2431

Research Institute of America Publications:
All States Tax Guide
Corbel Pension Forms
Cumulative Changes
Employee Benefits Alert
Estate Planner's Alert
Estate Planning and Taxation Coordinator
Executive Compensation & Taxation Coordinator
Federal Taxation of Insurance Companies
Federal Tax Coordinator 2nd
Income Taxation of Natural Resources
Internal Revenue Code & Regulations
Partnership & S Corporation Coordinator
Pension Coordinator
Property Taxes
Real Estate Coordinator
RIA's Analysis of Federal Taxes
RIA's Analysis: Income
RIA's Analysis: Estate & Gift Tax
RIA's Analysis: Excise
Sales & Use Taxes
Small Business Tax Planner
State & Local Taxes
State & Local Specialized Tax Services
State Income Taxes
State Tax Coordinator
Successful Estate Planning: Ideas & Methods
Tax Action Coordinator
Tax Advisors Planning Series

Tax Court
Tax-Exempt Organizations
Tax Guide
Tax Guide Plus
United States Tax Reporter
United States Tax Reporter: Estate & Gift Taxes
United States Tax Reporter: Excise Taxes
Wills & Trust Forms
Research Institute of America
90 Fifth Avenue
New York, New York 10011
(212) 645-4800

REITWatch
National Association of Real Estate Investment
  Trusts, Inc.
1129 20th Street, N.W., Suite 305
Washington D.C. 20036
(202) 785-8717

Richland Report
P.O. Box 222
La Jolla, California 92038
(619) 459-2611

Ripples in the Wave
918 N.E. 16th Avenue
Gainesville, Florida 32601

Roesch Market Memo, The
P.O. Box 4242
Shawnee Mission, Kansas 66204
(913) 381-0857

Ronald Sadoff's Major Trends
250 West Coventry Court
Milwaukee, Wisconsin 53217
(414) 352-8460

Safe Money Report
Silver & Gold Report
Weiss Research Inc.
P.O. Box 2923
West Palm Beach, Florida 33402

Scott Letter: Closed End Fund Report, The
P.O. Box 17800
Richmond, Virginia 23226
(407) 684-8100   (800) 356-3508

Sector Funds Newsletter
P.O. Box 270048
San Diego, California 92198
(619) 748-0805

Securities and Federal Corporate Law Report
Clark Boardman Co.
155 Pfingsten Road
Deerfield, Illinois 60015-4996
(800) 323-1336

Securities Industry Management
Registered Representative
Plaza Communications Inc.
18818 Teller Avenue, Suite 280
Irvine, California 92715
(714) 851-2220

Securities Week
McGraw-Hill Publications
1221 Avenue of the Americas
New York, New York 10020
(212) 512-3144

Sentinel Investment Letter
Hanover Investment Management Corp.
P.O. Box 189, 52 South Main Street
New Hope, Pennsylvania 18938
(215) 862-5454

Silver Magazine
P.O. Box 9690
Rancho Santa Fe, California 92067
(619) 756-1054

Sindlinger Fax Service
405 Osborne Lane
Wallingford, Pennsylvania 19086
(215) 565-0247

Small Cap Opportunities Report
13F Opportunities Report
100 Executive Drive, Southeast Executive Park
Brewster, New York 10509
(914) 278-6500

Smart Money
1790 Broadway
New York, New York 10019
(212) 262-5603   (800) 444-4204

Sound Advice
Sound Advice Realty Advisor
931 Hartz Way, Suite 201
Danville, California 94526
(510) 838-6710

Special Investment Situations
P.O. Box 4254
Chattanooga, Tennessee 37405
(615) 886-1628

Special Situation Report
P.O. Box 167
Rochester, New York 14601
(716) 232-1240   (800) 836-4330

Spidell's California Tax Letter
Spidell Publishing Inc.
1110 North Gilbert Street
Anaheim, California 92801
(714) 776-7850

Spread Scope Commodity Spread Charts
Spread Scope Long-Term Weekly Charts
Spread Scope Spread Letter
Spread Scope Inc.
P.O. Box 950841
Mission Hills, California 91345
(818) 782-0774
(800) 232-7285

Standard and Poor's Publications:
Analyst's Handbook
Bond Guide

Chart Guide
Compmark
Compustat Services (Electronic, CD-ROM)
Comstock (Electronic)
Corporate Descriptions Online (Electronic)
Corporations CD-ROM
Corporation Records
Current Market Perspectives
Daily Action Stock Charts
Daily News Online (Electronic)
Daily Stock Price Record
Directory of Dividend Reinvestment Plans
Earnings Guide
Emerging and Special Situations
Index Alert
Index Services
Industry Reports
Industry Services
Institutional Equity Research
Market Month
MarketScope
MarketScope Europe
Money Market Directory
New Issues Research
OTC Chart Manual
OUTLOOK, The
Register of Corporations, Directors & Executives
Research Reports
S&P 500 Directory
S&P Midcap 400 Directory
S&P Information Bulletins
Standard & Poor's Register Online (Electronic)
Statistical Service
Stock Guide\Bond Guide Database (Electronic)
Stock Guide
Stock Market Encyclopedia
Stock Reports CD-ROM
Stock Reports
Your Financial Future
Standard & Poor's
25 Broadway
New York, New York 10004
(212) 208-8786

Stanger Report, The
Stanger Review, The
Robert Stanger and Co.
1129 Broad Street
Shrewsbury, New Jersey 07702
(908) 389-3600

Steve Puetz Letter
1105 Sunset Court
West Lafayette, Indiana 47906
(317) 884-0600

Stock Market Cycles
P.O. Box 6873
Santa Rosa, California 95406-0873
(707) 579-8444   (800) 888-4351

Switch Fund Timing
P.O. Box 25430
Rochester, New York 14625
(716) 385-3122

Sy Harding Investor Forecasts,The
P.O. Box 352016
Palm Coast, Florida 32135
(904) 446-0823

Systems & Forecasts
150 Great Neck Road
Great Neck, New York 11021
(516) 829-6444   (800) 829-6229

Taurus Publications:
Grand Cayman
Taurus
Top Ten
Taurus Corp.
P.O. Box 767
Winchester, Virginia 22604
(703) 667-4827

J. Taylor's Gold & Gold Stocks
P.O. Box 770871
Woodside, New York 11377
(718) 457-1426

Technical Analysis of Stocks and Commodities
  Magazine
Technical Analysis Inc., Jack Hutson, Publisher
4757 California Avenue S.W.
Seattle, Washington 98116-4499
(206) 938-0570   (800) 832-4642

Technical Trends
P.O. Box 792
Wilton, Connecticut 06897
(203) 762-0229   (800) 736-0229

Timberline Investment Forecast, The
Timberline Research, Inc.
4130 South West 117th Avenue, Suite 215
Beaverton, Oregon 97005

Timer Digest
P.O. Box 1688
Greenwich, Connecticut 06836
(203) 629-3503

Timing and Tactics
Wilson Foster & Co.
4987 Olivas Park Drive, Suite 100
Ventura, California 93003
(805) 644-8207

Today's Options
P.O. Box 14111
Scottsdale, Arizona 85267

Todd Market Timer
26861 Trabuco Road, Suite E182
Mission Viejo, California 92691

Tomorrow's Commodities
Tomorrow's Options
Tomorrow's Stocks
Techno-Fundamental Investments
P.O. Box 14111
Scottsdale, Arizona 85267
(602) 996-2908

Top Performing Stock Outlook
P.O. Box 725
Corona Del Mar, California 92625
(714) 721-0822   (800) 522-5155

Toronto Stock Exchange Daily Record
Toronto Stock Exchange
2 First Canadian Place, Exchange Tower
Toronto, Ontario M5X 1J2, Canada
(416) 947-4200

Trends in Mutual Fund Activity
Investment Company Institute
1401 H Street N.W., Suite 1200
Washington D.C. 20005
(202) 326-5800

Turnaround Letter,The
225 Friend Street, Suite 801
Boston, Massachusetts 02114
(617) 573-9550

Turtle Talk
Russell J. Sands
1800 N.E. 114th Street, Suite 401
Miami, Florida 33181
(800) 532-1563

United & Babson Investment Report
United Mutual Fund Selector
101 Prescott Street
Wellesley Hills
Massachusetts 02181
(617) 235-0900

U.S. Banker
Andrew L. Goodenough, Faulkner & Gray
Eleven Penn Plaza
New York, New York 10001
(212) 967-7000

U.S. Investment Report
25 Fifth Avenue, Suite 4-C
New York, New York 10003
(212) 460-9200

Value Income Advisor, The
Income Investment Advisory
1040 W. Upas Street
San Diego, California 92103
(619) 291-4901

Value Line Publications:
Value Line Convertibles
Value Line Investment Survey
Value Line Mutual Fund Survey
Value Line Options

Value Line OTC Special Situations
220 E. 42nd Street
New York, New York 10017
(212) 907-1500   (800) 833-0046

Vards Report, The
Financial Planning Resources, Inc.
P.O. Box 1927
Roswell, Georgia 30077-1927
(404) 998-5186

Vector Vest Dividend Advisory
Vector Vest Stock Advisory
P.O. Box 577
Bath, Ohio 44210
(800) 533-3923

Veribank
P.O. Box 461
Wakefield, Massachusetts 01880
(617) 245-8370   (800) 442-2657

Volume Reversal Survey
P.O. Box 1451
Sedona, Arizona 86339
(602) 282-1275

Wall Street Digest, The
Wall Street Digest Mutual Fund Advisor, The
One Sarasota Tower
Sarasota, Florida 34236
(813) 954-5500

Wall Street Generalist
800 Sarasota Quay
Sarasota, Florida 34236
(813) 366-5645

Wall Street Inquirer
263 Orange Avenue
Goleta, California 93117
(805) 964-8275

Wall Street Journal
200 Liberty Street
New York, New York 10281
(800) 568-7625

Wall Street Transcript
100 Wall Street, 9th Floor
New York, New York 10005
(212) 747-9500

Warren Gorham Lamont Tax Publications:
Corporate Tax Digest
The Consolidated Tax Return: Principles, Practice, Planning
Charitable Giving and Solicitation
Depreciation and Capital Planning
Divorce Taxation
Estate and Gift Tax Digest
Estate Planning
Estate Planning Law and Taxation
Federal Estate and Gift Taxation
Federal Taxation of Bankruptcy and Workouts

Federal Income Taxation of Banks and Financial Institutions
Federal Income Taxation of Corporations and Shareholders
Federal Income Taxation of Estates and Trusts
Federal Income Taxation of Individuals
Federal Income Taxation of Passive Activities
Federal Income Taxation of Real Estate
Federal Income Taxation of S Corporations, Third Edition
Federal Tax Accounting
Federal Tax Collections, Liens and Levies
Federal Tax Deductions
Federal Tax Litigation: Civil Practice and Procedure
Federal Taxation of Income, Estates and Gifts
Federal Taxation of Partnerships and Partners
Federal Taxation of Trusts, Grantors and Beneficiaries
IRS Practice Alert
IRS Practice and Procedure
Journal of Taxation of Investments, The
Planning Tax Deferred Property Transactions
Real Estate Tax Digest
Real Estate Tax Ideas
State Taxation
Tax Ideas
Tax Fraud and Evasion
Tax Planning for Highly Compensated Individuals
Tax Planning for Retirement
Tax Planning with Life Insurance: Analysis with Forms
Tax Planning for Family Wealth Transfers: Analysis with Forms
Tax Planning for Dispositions of Business Interests
Tax Procedure Digest
Tax Treaties
Taxation for Accountants
Taxation of the Closely Held Corporation
Taxation of Corporate Liquidations
Taxation of Distributions from Qualified Plans
Taxation for Lawyers
U.S. International Taxation
U.S. Taxation of International Operations
Warren Gorham Lamont
The Park Square Building
31 St. James Avenue
Boston, Massachusetts 02116-4112
(617) 292-8309   (800) 950-1210

Washington Bond & Money Market Report
Newsletter Services, Inc.
9700 Philadelphia Court
Lanham, Maryland 20706-4405
(301) 731-5202 (800) 345-2611

Washington International Business Report
818 Connecticut Avenue, N.W., 12th Floor
Washington, D.C. 20006
(202) 872-8181

Whole Earth Forecaster
12760 Deauville Drive
Omaha, Nebraska 68137-3224
(402) 894-2138

Winning Edge, The
Ellesmere Numismatics
P.O. Box 915
Danbury, Connecticut 06813
(203) 794-1232   (800) 426-3343

Women's Investment Newsletter
Phoenix Communications Group, Ltd.
P.O. Box 670
Colorado Springs, Colorado 80901
(719) 576-9200

Wolfe's Version
P.O. Box 99
Blue Springs, Missouri 64013
(816) 229-1666

Worth, Financial Intelligence
575 Lexington Avenue, 33rd Floor
New York, New York 10022
(212) 751-4550   (800) 777-1851

Wright Investors Service Publications:
Approved Wright Investment List
International Investment Advice and Analysis
Wright Bankers' Service

Wright Newsletter
Wright Monthly Report
Wright Investors Service
1000 Lafayette Boulevard
Bridgeport, Connecticut 06604
(203) 330-5000   (800) 232-0013

Your Money
5705 North Lincoln Avenue
Chicago, Illinois 60659
(312) 275-3590

Your Window Into the Future
Bullion and Mutual Fund Advisor
Moneypower
P.O. Box 22400
Minneapolis, Minnesota 55422
(612) 537-8096

Zurich Financial, The
Kinigsallee 50, D-40212
Dusseldorf, Germany

Zweig Forecast
Zweig Performance Ratings Report
P.O. Box 360
Dellmore, New York 11710
(516) 785-1300   (800) 633-2252

COMPUTERIZED DATABASES FOR INVESTORS

The following firms offer investors with computers and modems the opportunity to follow price movements in investment markets with up-to-the-second accuracy. Investors can tap into these data banks to download both current and historical price and volume information as well as news about investment markets. Some of these databases also allow investors to execute trades through their computers.

All-Quotes, Inc.:
All-Quotes
40 Exchange Place, Suite 1500
New York, New York 10005
(212) 425-5030   (800) 888-7559

America Online:
America Online
8619 Westwood Center Drive
Vienna, Virginia 22182
(703) 448-8700   (800) 827-6364

Argus Research Corporation:
Argus On-Line
17 Battery Place, 18th Floor
New York, New York 10004
(212) 425-7500

Bauer Communications, Inc:
JUMBO ONLINE
P.O. Box 145510
Coral Gables, Florida 33114-5510
(800) 388-6686

Bloomberg L.P.:
Financial Markets
499 Park Avenue
New York, New York 10022
(212) 318-2000

BMI:
Ensign 5
Market Center
3 Triad Center, Suite 100
Salt Lake City, Utah 84180-1201
(801) 532-3400   (800) 255-7374

Bond Buyer, The:
Bond Buyer Full Text
One State Street Plaza
New York, New York 10004-1549
(212) 803-8366

Bridge Information Systems:
Market Data Systems
717 Office Parkway
St. Louis, Missouri 63141
(800) 325-3282

CDA Investment Technologies, Inc.:
Cadence
Mutual Fund Hypotheticals
Spectrum
1355 Piccard Drive
Rockville, Maryland 20850
(301) 590-1330

CDA/Investnet:
Insider Trading Monitor
3265 Meridian Parkway, Suite 130
Fort Lauderdale, Florida 33331
(305) 384-1500   (800) 243-2324

CDQ, Inc.:
CQG System One
P.O. Box 758
Glenwood Springs, Colorado 81602
(800) 525-7082

Commodity Services, Inc:
CSI Data Retrieval Service
Marstat
200 West Palmetto Park Road
Boca Raton, Florida 33432
(407) 392-8663   (800) 274-4727

CompuServe, Inc.:
Company Screening Service
Compuserve
Fundwatch Online by Money Magazine
5000 Arlington Center Boulevard
Columbus, Ohio 43220
(614) 529-1349   (800) 848-8199

Comtex Scientific Corp.:
Market NewsAlert
OmniNews
OTC NewsAlert
4900 Seminary Road, #800
Alexandria, Virginia 22311-1811
(203) 358-0007   (800) 624-5089

Data Broadcasting Corporation:
News Real
1900 South Norfolk Street
San Mateo, California 94403
(415) 571-1800   (800) 367-4670

Data-Star:
Data-Star
One Commerce Square, Suite 1010
Philadelphia, Pennsylvania 19103
(215) 587-4400 (800) 221-7754

Delphi:
Delphi
1030 Massachusetts Avenue
Cambridge, Masssachusetts 02138
(617) 491-3393 (800) 695-4005

Design Creations:
INSTIN 3.0
18701 Tiffeni Drive, Suite G, Box 948
Twain Harte, California 95383
(209) 586-2082   (800) 933-5910

Dialog Information Services, Inc.:
Bond Buyer Full Text
Business Connection
First Release
MoneyCenter
Quotes and Trading
3460 Hillview Avenue
Palo Alto, California 94304
(415) 858-3785   (800) 334-2564

Disclosure, Inc.:
Compact D/SEC
Compact D/New Issues
Compact D/Canada
Disclosure SEC Database
Worldscope GLOBAL
Worldscope EMERGING MARKETS
Disclosure, Inc.
5161 River Road
Bethesda, Maryland 20816
(301) 951-1300   (800) 843-7747

Division of Global Market Information:
Dial/Data
Track/On Line
56 Pine Street
New York, New York 10005
(212) 248-0300   (800) 275-5544

Dow Jones & Co., Inc.:
Dow Jones News/Retrieval
Dow Jones Market Monitor
Dow Jones Market Monitor Plus
P.O. Box 300
Princeton, New Jersey 08543-0300
(609) 452-1511   (800) 522-3567 x119
(800) 815-5100

Equis International:
Technician
3950 South 700 East, Suite 100
Salt Lake City, Utah 84107
(801) 265-8886   (800) 882-3040

E*Trading Securities, Inc:
E*Trade Trading System
480 California Avenue, 1st Floor
Palo Alto, California 94306
(415) 326-2700   (800) 786-2575

Euro American Group, Inc.:
SatQuote for DOS
SatQuote for Windows
50 Broad Street, Suite 516
New York, New York 10275
(212) 269-6686

Fidelity Investments:
Fidelity On-Line Xpress (FOX)
82 Devonshire Street, R20A
Boston, Massachusetts 02190

Financial Post Data Group, The:
Canadian Corporate Database
Canadian Dividend Database
Financial Post Electronic Edition
Historical Earnings Database
Mutual Funds Database
Record of New Issues
333 King Street East
Toronto, Ontario M5A 4N2, Canada
(416) 350-6510

Ford Investor Services, Inc.:
Epic Diskette
Epic/International
Hiper
11722 Sorrento Valley Road, Suite 1
San Diego, California 92121
(619) 755-1327   (800) 842-0207

Fundvest, Inc.:
Data Retriever
337 Boston Road
Bellerica, Massachusetts 01821
(508) 663-3330

GE Information Services:
GEnie
401 North Washington Street
Rockville, Maryland 20850
(301) 340-4442   (800) 638-9636

IBC/Donoghue, Inc.:
Money Fund Vision
MoneyLetter Plus
290 Eliot Street
P.O. Box 9104
Ashland, Massachusetts 01721-9104
(508) 881-2800   (800) 343-5413

I/B/E/S, Inc.:
Institutional Brokers Estimate System
345 Hudson Street
New York, New York 10014
(212) 243-3335

IDD Information Services:
Disclosure
GLOBAL Vantage
J/B/E/S
S&P's Compustat
Tradeline International Historical Securities
    Pricing
Tradeline Securities Pricing
Zacks Earnings Estimates
Two World Trade Center, 18th Floor
New York, New York 10048
(212) 432-0045   (800) 444-2515

Info Globe:
Canadian Mutual Funds
Corporate Canada On Line
Marketscan
Report on Business Corporate Database
444 Front Street West
Toronto, Ontario M5V 2S9
(416) 585-5250

Information Sources, Inc:
Business Software Data Base
Software CD
1173 Colusa Avenue
Berkeley, California 94707
(415) 525-6220

Integrated Financial Solutions, Inc:
Dial Up/ Historical Data Retriever
1049 South West Baseline, Suite B-200
Hillsboro, Oregon 97123
(503) 640-5303   (800) 729-5037

Interactive Data, Corporation:
Datafeed for AIQ Systems Tradingexpert
Datafeed for Metastock
Mail Location L1-A1
95 Hayden Avenue
Lexington, Massachusetts 02173-9144
(617) 863-8100

Investment Company Data, Inc.:
ICDI Mutual Fund Database
2600 72nd Street #A
Des Moines, Iowa 50322-4724
(515) 270-8600   (800) 426-4234

Iverson Financial Services, Inc.:
Securities History Data
111 West Evelyn Avenue, Suite 206
Sunnyvale, California 94086-6140
(408) 522-9900

Knight-Ridder Financial Services:
Electronic Futures Trend Analyzer
Final Markets End-of-Day Price Service
Historical Data
Knight-Ridder End-of-Day News Reports
75 Wall Street, 23rd Floor
New York, New York 10005-2890
(212) 269-1110

LaPorte Portfolio Allocation System
Burlington Hall Asset Management, Inc.
126 Petersburg Road
Hackettstown, New Jersey 07840
(201) 852-1694

Macro*World Research Corporation:
Macro*World Forecaster
4265 Brownsboro Road, Suite 170
Winston-Salem, North Carolina 27106
(910) 759-0600   (800) 841-5396

MarketBase, Inc.:
MarketBase
368 Hillside Avenue
P.O. Box 37
Needham Heights, Massachusetts 02194
(617) 449-8460   (800) 735-0700

Market Guide, Inc.:
Market Guide Database
Market Screen Online
49 Glen Head Road
Glen Head, New York 11545
(516) 759-1253

Market Timing Report:
Long Term Financial Markets Database
P.O. Box 225
Tucson, Arizona 85702
(602) 795-9552

Mead Data Central, Inc.:
Lexis Financial Information Service
9443 Springboro Pike
P.O. Box 933
Dayton, Ohio 45401-9964
(513) 859-1608   (800) 227-4809

Media General Financial Services:
Media General Database Service
301 East Grace Street
Richmond, Virginia 23219
(804) 649-6587   (800) 446-7922

Micro Code Technologies:
Free Financial Network (FFN)
220 East 54th Street, #12-J
New York, New York 10022
(212) 838-6324

Micropal:
Micropal
31 Milk Street, Suite 1002
Boston, Massachusetts 02109
(617) 451-1585

Newsnet, Inc.:
Newsnet
945 Haverford Road
Bryn Mawr, Pennsylvania 19010
(610) 527-8030   (800) 952-0122

Nihon Keizai Shimbun America, Inc.
(Nikkei America)
Databank Department:
Nikkei Telecom
NEEDS
NEEDS-Net
1325 Avenue of the Americas, Suite 2500
New York, New York 10019
(212) 261-6245

One Source Information Services:
CD/Europa
CD/Notes
International Equities

International Public
SEC Filings
U.K. Private +
U.K. Small Companies
U.S. Banks
U.S. Equities
U.S. Insurance
U.S. Private +
U.S. Public
150 CambridgePark Drive
Cambridge, Massachusetts 02140
(800) 554-5501

Online Intelligence:
Investment Wizard
1400 Post Oak Boulevard, Suite 800
Houston, Texas 77056
(713) 877-1206   (800) 359-9359

Optima Investment Research, Inc.:
Daily Financial Market Research
111 West Jackson Boulevard, 15th Floor
Chicago, Illinois 60604-3503
(312) 427-3616   (800) 344-4403
Fax (312) 427-9840

Oster Communications, Inc.:
Future Link
219 Parkside
Cedar Falls, Iowa 50613
(319) 277-1271   (800) 553-2910

PC Quote, Inc.:
PC Quote
300 South Wacker, Suite 300
Chicago, Illinois 60606-6688
(312) 913-2800   (800) 225-5657

Prodigy Services Company:
Prodigy
Strategic Investor
445 Hamilton Avenue
White Plains, New York 10601
(914) 993-8000   (800) 776-3449

Prophet Information Services, Inc.:
Prophet Data Service
3350 West Bayshore, #106
Palo Alto, California 94303
(415) 856-1142   (800) 772-8040

Quick & Reilly, Inc.:
QuickWay
460 California Avenue, Suite 302
Palo Alto, California 94306
(415) 326-4200   (800) 634-6214

Quote.Com:
Quote.Com
1005 Terminal Way, Suite 110
Reno, Nevada 89502
(702) 324-4325 (800) 261-7740

Reality Technologies, Inc.:
Reuters Money Network
Reuters Money Network for Quicken
2200 Renaissance Boulevard
King of Prussia, Pennsylvania 19406
(215) 277-7600   (800) 346-2024

S&P ComStock:
S&P ComStock
600 Mamaronick Avenue
Harrison, New York 10528
(914) 381-7000   (800) 431-5019

Charles Schwab & Company, Inc.:
Equalizer
Schwab Brokerage Services On Genie
Streetsmart
101 Montgomery Street, Department S
San Francisco 94104
(415) 627-7000   (800) 334-4455

Shark Information Services Corporation:
Data Broadcasting Corporation (parent
  company)
Shark
120 Wall Street
New York, New York 10005
(800) 423-2002

Shaw Data Services, Inc:
Microshaw
Online
Onsite
Quotes
Research
122 East 42nd Street
New York, New York 10168
(212) 682-8877

Small Investor's Software Company:
Personal Investing Online Service
138 Ocean Avenue
Amityville, New York 11701
(516) 789-9368   (800) 829-9368

Stratus Computer, Inc.:
SQL2000 Relational Database Management
  System
55 Fairbanks Boulevard
Marlboro, Massachusetts 01752
(508) 460-2192

Stock Data Corporation:
Stock Market Data
905 Bywater Road
Annapolis, Maryland 21401
(410) 280-5533

Street Software Technology, Inc.:
CMO/Remic Pricing Service
Daily Pricing Service
Fixed Income Pricing Service
Trader's Spread System

Treasury Historical Data
230 Park Avenue, Suite 857
New York, New York 10169
(212) 922-0500

Telemet America, Inc.:
Encore
Orion
Pocket Quote Pro
Radio Exchange
Resat
325 First Street
Alexandria, Virginia 22314
(703) 548-2042

Telescan, Inc.:
Telescan Analyzer
Telescan Database
10550 Richmond Avenue, Suite 250
Houston, Texas 77042
(713) 952-1060   (800) 324-8246

TELEKURS:
International Securities Identification Directory
InvestData System
Telekurs Database Server
Telekurs Ticker Service
Titelbulletin II
Valuation Pricing Service
World'Vest
One State Street Plaza
New York, New York 10004
(212) 487-2700   Fax (212) 487-2808

Tick Data, Inc.:
Tick-by-Tick Historical Price Data
720 Kipling Street, Suite 115
Lakewood, Colorado 80215
(303) 232-3701   (800) 822-8425

Trade*Plus, Inc.:
Trade*Plus
480 California Avenue, Suite 301
Palo Alto, California 94306
(415) 324-4554   Fax (415) 324-3044

Max Ule & Co.:
Ticker Screen
26 Broadway, Suite 200
New York, New York 10004
(212) 809-1160   (800) 223-6642

Value Line, Inc.:
Convertible Database
Database II
Estimates & Projections
220 East 42nd Street
New York, New York 10017
(212) 907-1550   (800) 531-1425

Worden Brothers, Inc.:
Telechart 2000 System
4905 Pine Cone Drive, Suite 12
Durham Hill, North Carolina 27707
(919) 408-0542   (800) 776-4940

X*Press Information Services, Ltd :
Ingenius
XPress Executive
XPress/XChange
4700 South Syracuse Parkway, Suite 1050
Denver, Colorado 80237
(303) 721-1062   (800) 772-6397

Zacks Investment Research:
Zacks On-Line
155 North Wacker
Chicago, Illinois 60606
(312) 630-9880   (800) 767-3771

PERSONAL COMPUTER SOFTWARE FOR INVESTING AND FINANCIAL PLANNING

The following lists contain a sampling of software packages that can help investors to make better investment decisions and to improve record-keeping, as well as to perform personal financial planning. There are, of course, hundreds of software packages on the market to perform these tasks. Those listed here are all marketed by established companies in the software business.

The software programs in group one perform asset allocation functions. These programs evaluate the potential risks and returns on different classes of assets, such as stocks, bonds and cash. This allows investors to allocate their money among assets for maximum returns at acceptable levels of risk.

The group two programs are designed for fixed income analysis. These programs analyze the quality and maturity structures of bond portfolios. They also allow investors to maximize returns on the bond portion of their portfolios based on different interest rate assumptions.

The programs in group three are designed to help an individual do financial planning. This means that investments can be tracked, tax strategy formulated, real estate decisions examined, and retirement and estate planning options explored. One particular advantage of these programs is that once data has been entered into the computer for one part of a program, it is stored for use in other parts of the program. For instance, when a stock sale that generates a taxable capital gain is entered in the investment records section, it is also recorded in the income tax preparation part of the program.

The programs in group four allow users to screen lists of stocks to isolate the companies that meet certain fundamental investment criteria. The information on companies comes either from a disk that is updated monthly or from a continuously updated online database, which is accessed by telephone line. Usually these disks or on-line databases are available for an annual fee. There are many kinds of screens investors can perform with this software, depending on what kinds of stocks they want to find. For example, an investor looking for high income could find the highest-yielding stocks in the database. Someone looking for growth stocks could find the companies with fast earnings growth records.

Programs in the fifth group enable users to keep track of their investment portfolios. Once stocks, bonds and other instruments are entered into the computer, the value of the portfolio can be easily updated by tapping into a database. These programs also reveal the tax implications of potential investment moves.

Programs in the sixth group are designed to pick stocks based on technical considerations, such as price movements and volume. These programs usually display data in chart form, allowing investors to isolate stocks with technical indicators thought to point to a good buying or selling opportunity.

1. Asset Allocation Software

Asset/Liability Management
Capital Management Sciences
11766 Wilshire Boulevard, Suite 300
Los Angeles, California 90025
(310) 479-9715

Asset Mix Optimizer
CDA Investment Technologies, Inc.
1355 Piccard Drive
Rockville, Maryland 20850
(301) 590-1330

NIS Asset Allocation
Northfield Information Services, Inc.
184 High Street, 5th Floor
Boston, Massachusetts 02110-3001
(617) 451-2222   (800) 262-6085

PMSP 80486 Professional Edition (for Windows)
Computer Handholders, Inc.
P.O. Box 59
Arcola, Pennsylvania 19420
(215) 489-7520

Portfolio Investment Selection Optimizer
Fortunet, Inc.
2995 Woodside Road, Suite 400
Woodside, California 94062
(415) 368-7655

RAMCAP-The Intelligent Asset Allocator
Wilson Associates
21241 Ventura Boulevard, Suite 173
Woodland Hills, California 91364
(818) 999-0015   (800) 480-3888

2. Fixed Income Analysis Software

Bond Calculator
MBS/ABS Calculator
Bond-Tech, Inc.
P.O. Box 192
Englewood, Ohio 45322
(513) 836-3991

BondCalc
BondCalc Corporation
295 Greenwich Street, Apt. 3B
New York, New York 10007-1050
(212) 587-0097

BondEdge
Capital Management Sciences
11766 Wilshire Boulevard, Suite 300
Los Angeles, California 90025
(310) 479-9715

Bondseye
Ergo, Inc.
1419 Wyant Road
Santa Barbara, California 93108
(805) 969-9366   (800) 772-6637

Bonds and Interest Rate Software
Programmed Press
599 Arnold Road
West Hempstead, New York 11552-3918
(516) 599-6527

Bondsheet
Per%sense
Per%sense Pro
Ones & Zeros
708 West Mt. Airy Avenue
Philadelphia, Pennsylvania 19119
(215) 248-1010

Bond$mart
BMW
Portside Market
10926 Adare Drive
Fairfax, Virginia 22032
(703) 425-2275

Bond Portfolio
Bond Pricing
Baarns Publishing
1150 Sepulveda Boulevard, Suite D
Mission Hill, California 91345
(818) 837-1441   (800) 377-9235

Bond Portfolio Manager
Complete Bond Analyzer
Financial & Interest Calculator
Investment IRR Analysis for Stocks, Bonds &
   Real Estate
Larry Rosen Co.
7008 Springdale Road
Louisville, Kentucky 40241
(502) 228-4343

Finance 101
Charlton Woolard
17280 Anna
Southfield, Michigan 48075
(810) 557-3766

Global Trader Calculator
ADS Associates, Inc.
23586 Calabasas Road, Suite 200
Calabasas, California 91302
(818) 591-2371   (800) 323-4666

3. Financial Planning Software

Budget Model Analyzer
Calcugram Stock Options List
Family Budget
Finance Master
Keep Track Of It
Money Decisions
Personal Balance Sheet
Personal Finance Manager
Personal Finance Planner
Personal Finance System
Portview 2020
Dynacomp, Inc.
The Dynacomp Office Building
178 Phillips Road
Webster, New York 14580
(716) 265-4040   (800) 828-6772

Fast Cast for Ventures
Financial Planning for Retirement
401(K) Forecaster
Laddering Your Portfolio
The Money Controller
Pen Plan
Profit Planner Plus
Ratio Evaluator
Retirement Planner
Retirement Trio
Village Software, Inc.
186 Lincoln Street
Boston, Massachusetts 02111
(617) 695-9332   (800) 724-9332

Financial Navigator for DOS
Financial Navigator for Windows
Financial Navigator International
245 Polaris Avenue
Mountain View, California 94043
(415) 962-0300   (800) 468-3636

Financial Needs for Retirement
V.A. Denslow & Associates
4151 Woodland Avenue
Western Springs, Illinois 60558
(708) 246-3365

Financial Planning Toolkit
Financial Data Center
P.O. Box 1332
Bryn Mawr, Pennsylvania 19010
(215) 527-5216

Market Strategist
Hamilton Software, Inc.
6432 East Mineral Place
Englewood, Colorado 80112
(303) 770-9607   (800) 733-9607

Market Tool
Techni-Trak
P.O. Box 9484
Charlotte, North Carolina 28299
(704) 366-1037   (800) 433-1037

OptionView IV
Optionview Systems International, Inc.
175 East Hawthorn Parkway, Suite 180
Vernon Hills, Illinois 60061
(708) 816-6610   (800) 733-6610

Quant IX Portfolio Evaluator
Quant IX Software, Inc.
5900 North Port Washington Road, Suite 142-A
Milwaukee, Wisconsin 53217
(414) 961-1991   (800) 247-6354

Wall Street Journal Personal Finance Library
Dow Jones & Co.
P.O. Box 300
Princeton, New Jersey 08543-0300
(800) 815-5100

Wealth Builder
Reality Technologies, Inc.
2200 Rennaisance Boulevard,
King of Prussia, Pennsylvania 19406
(610) 277-7600   (800) 346-2024

Wealth Creator
Ram Technologies, Inc.
964 Westport Crescent, Unit 14
Mississauga, Ontario L5T I53, Canada
(905) 795-9222

Yellow Pad
Orinda Software Corporation
P.O. Box 1789
Orinda, California 94563
(510) 254-3503   (800) 795-7582 x9210

4. Fundamental Analysis Software

Advanced Chartist
Pardo Corporation
436 Frontage Road
Northfield, Illinois 60093
(708) 441-0101   (800) 497-1973

Bonds and Interest Rates Software
Commodities and Futures Software Package
Foreign Exchange Software Package
Statistical Analysis and Forecasting Software
  Package
Programmed Press
599 Arnold Road
West Hempstead, New York 11552-3918
(516) 599-6527

Business Pack
Calcugram Stock Options System
Financial Management System
MicroBJ Box Jenkins Forecasting
Nuametrics
Ratios
Stock Market Bargains

CAPTOOL
CAPTOOL Global Investor
CAPTOOL Professional Investor
CAPTOOL Real Time
Techserve, Inc.
P.O. Box 9
Issaquah, Washington 98027
(206) 865-0249   (800) 826-8082

Common Stock Selector
Fast Cast for Ventures
Profit Planner Plus
Village Software, Inc.
186 Lincoln Street
Boston, Massachusetts 02111
(617) 695-9332   (800) 724-9332

Compuserve Research Manager
Compuserve Research Manager for Windows
Compuserve, Inc.
120 Broadway, Suite 3330
New York, New York 10271
(212) 227-3881 (800) 543-4616

Corporate America: The Wall Street Journal
  Guide to America's Public Companies (CD-
  ROM)
Dow Jones & Co.
P.O. Box 300
Princeton, New Jersey 08543-0300
(800) 815-5100

Financial Competence
Competence Software
RRI Box 24
Junction Routes 28 & 107
Pittsfield, New Hampshire 03263
(603) 435-5098

Financial Management System
Dynacomp, Inc.
The Dynacomp Office Building
178 Phillips
Webster, New York 14580
(716) 265-4040   (800) 828-6772

Fundamental Investor
Savant Software
120 Bedford Center Road, Suite 301
Bedford, New Hampshire 03110
(603) 471-0400   (800) 231-9900

Money Maker for Windows
Q-West Associates
13223 Black Mountain Road, Suite 1-410
San Diego, California 92129
(619) 484-6648   (800) 618-6618

Prosearch
Telescan, Inc.
10550 Richmond Avenue, Suite 250
Houston, Texas 77042
(713) 952-1060   (800) 324-8246

Smartbroker
Charlton Woolard
17280 Anna
Southfield, Michigan 48075
(810) 557-3766

Streetsmart
Charles Schwab & Co., Inc.
Investor Information Services
101 Montgomery Street
San Francisco, California 94104-9979
(800) 334-4455   (800) 442-5111

SuperCharts (for Windows)
Omega Research
9200 Susset Drive, Omega Research Building
Miami, Florida 33173-3266
(305) 270-1095   (800) 556-2022

Value/Screen Plus
Value Line, Inc.
711 Third Avenue
New York, New York 10017
(212) 687-3965

5. Portfolio Management Software

Advanced Total Investor
Village Software, Inc.
3108 Conte Drive
Carson City, Nevada 89701
(702) 882-1017

AXYS (for Windows)
Advent Software, Inc.
301 Brannan, 6th Floor
San Francisco, California 94107
(415) 543-7696   (800) 678-7005

Camra for Windows
Securities Software and Consulting, Inc.
705 Bloomfield Avenue, Corporate Place
Bloomfield, Connecticut 06002
(203) 242-7887   (800) 234-0556

Capital Gainz
Alleycat Software, Inc.
P.O. Box 14446
Research Triangle Park,
North Carolina 27709-4446
(919) 469-5196

CAPTOOL
PFROI
Techserve, Inc.
P.O. Box 9
Issaquah, Washington 98027
(800) 826-8082

Centerpiece
Centerpiece Performance Monitor
Performance Technologies, Inc.
4814 Old Wake Forest Road
Raleigh, North Carolina 27609
(919) 876-3555   (800) 528-9595

ChartPro
MegaTech Chart System
Ret-Tech Software, Inc.
151 Deer Lane
Barrington, Illinois 60010
(708) 382-3903

Compuserve Research Manager
Compuserve Research Manager for Windows
120 Broadway, Suite 3330
New York, New York 10271
(212) 227-3881   (800) 543-4616

Discover/EN
Discover/OR
Discover/RE
Telemet America, Inc.
325 First Street
Alexandria, Virginia 22314
(703) 548-2042   (800) 368-2078

Dow Jones Market Manager PLUS
Dow Jones & Co.
P.O. Box 300
Princeton, New Jersey 08543-0300
(800) 815-5100

Equalizer
Streetsmart
Charles Schwab & Company, Inc.
Investor Information Services
101 Montgomery Street
Department S
San Francisco, California 94104
(415) 627-7000   (800) 334-4455

Expert Portfolio Manager
Capital Software Development Corporation
190 South LaSalle Street, Suite 2790
Chicago, Illinois 60603
(312) 578-2915

Fidelity On-Line Express
Fidelity Investments
82 Devonshire Street, R20A
Boston, Massachusetts 02190
(800) 544-0246

Financial Navigator for DOS
Financial for Windows
Financial Navigator International
254 Polaris Avenue
Mountain View, California 94043
(415) 962-0300   (800) 468-3636

Folioman
Folioman+
E-Sential Software
P.O. Box 41705
Los Angeles, California 90041
(213) 257-2524

Fundwatch Plus
Investors Accountant
Portfolio Analyzer
Hamilton Software, Inc.
6432 East Mineral Place
Englewood, Colorado 80112
(303) 770-9607   (800) 733-9607

Individual Stock Investor
Design Creations
15387 Camino Del Parque
Sonora, California 95370
(209) 532-8413   (800) 933-5910

Investment Manager II
Global Investor Manager II
INTEGRATED DECISION SYSTEMS, INC.
1950 Sawtelle Boulevard, Suite 255
Los Angeles 90025
(310) 478-4015   (212) 575-7518

Investor's Advantage
Investor's Advantage for Windows
Software Advantage Consulting Corporation
38442 Gail
Clinton Township, Michigan 48036
(313) 463-4995   (800) 729-2431

Investor's Accountant
Portfolio Analyzer
Hamilton Software, Inc.
6432 East Mineral Place
Englewood, Colorado 80112
(303) 795-5572   (800) 733-9607

Investor's Portfolio
Savant Software
120 Bedford Center Road, Suite 301
Bedford, New Hampshire 03110
(603) 471-0400   (800) 231-9900

Kiplinger's Simply Money
Computer Associates International, Inc.
One Computer Associates Plaza
Islandia, New York 11788
(516) 342-5224   (800) 225-5224

KR Toolkit
Knight-Ridder Financial
75 Wall Street, 23rd Floor
New York, New York 10005
(212) 269-1110

Managing Your Money
Meca Software, Inc.
55 Walls Drive
Fairfield, Connecticut 06430-5139
(203) 256-5000

Market Analyzer Plus for DOS
Market Manager Plus for DOS
Market Manager Plus for Mac
Dow Jones & Company, Inc.
P.O. Box 300
Princeton, New Jersey 08543
(609) 520-4641   (800) 815-5100

Money Maker for Windows
Q-West Associates
13223 Black Mountain Road, #1-410
San Diego, California 92129
(619) 484-6648   (800) 618-6618

NIDS/Port
National Investor Data Services, Inc.
33 Flying Point Road
Southampton, New York 11968-5244
(516) 283-1100 (800) 255-6437

NTECH
P.O. Box 164075
Austin, Texas 78716
(512) 328-3078

OWL Personal Portfolio Manager
Otto-Williams, Ltd.
P.O. Box 794
Lanham, Maryland 20703-0794
(301) 306-0409

Portfolio Management Information System
ITS Associates, Inc.
36 Washington Street
Wellesley, Massachusetts 02181
(617) 237-7750

Portfolio Management Made Easier with 1-2-3
  (for DOS)
Portfolio Management Made Easier with 1-2-3
  (for Windows)
Lotus Selects
P.O. Box 31755
Salt Lake City 84131-9815
(800) 635-6887

Portfolio Management System
Stock Manager
Omni Software Systems, Inc.
702 North Ernest
Griffith, Indiana 46319
(219) 924-3522   (800) 473-3524

Portfolio Management System and Reference
  Book
Personally Developed Software, Inc.
P.O. Box 3280
Wallingford, Connecticut 06494
(203) 237-4504   (800) 426-7279

Portfolio Manager
Telescan, Inc.
10550 Richmond Avenue, Suite 250
Houston, Texas 77042
(713) 952-1060   (800) 324-8246

Pulse Portfolio
Equis International
3950 South 700 East, Suite 100
Salt Lake City, Utah 84107
(801) 265-9996   (800) 882-3040

Q-Trax (for Windows)
EDMS
5859 New Peachtree Road, Suite 119
Atlanta, Georgia 30340
(404) 998-4088   (800) 395-7670

Quantitative Toolkit
Portfolio Optimizer
Coros Technologies, Inc.
115 South Topanga Canyon Boulevard,
  Suite 177
Topanga, California 90290
(310) 455-4216

Quant IX Portfolio Manager
Quant IX Software, Inc.
5900 North Port Washington Road, Suite 142-A
Milwaukee, Wisconsin 53217
(414) 961-1991   (800) 247-6354

Quicken 4 for Windows
Quicken 5 for Macintosh
Quicken 8 for DOS
Intuit, Inc.
155 Linfield Avenue, P.O. Box 3014
Menlo Park, California 94026
(415) 322-0573   (800) 964-1040

Rory Tycoon Portfolio Analyst
Rory Tycoon Portfolio Manager
Coherent Software Systems
1012 Elk Grove Avenue
Venice, California 90291
(310) 452-1175

SMARTrader
SMARTrader Professional
Stratagem Software International, Inc.
520 Transcontinental Drive, Suite B
Metairie, Louisiana 70001
(504) 885-7353   (800) 779-7353

Structured Products
Capital Management Sciences
11766 Wilshire Boulevard, Suite 300
Los Angeles, California 90025
(310) 479-9715

Wealthbuilder
Reality Technologies, Inc.
200 Renaissance Boulevard
King of Prussia, Pennsylvania 19406
(215) 277-7600   (800) 346-2024

6. Technical Analysis Software

Behold!
Investor's Technical Services
P.O. Box 164075
Austin, Texas 78716
(512) 328-8000

Buysel
Fourier Analysis Forecaster
Fundwatch
Hansen-Predict
Interactive Multiple Prediction
Market Timer
Microcomputer Stock Program
Stockaid 4.0
Dynacomp, Inc.
The Dynacomp Office Building
178 Phillips Road
Webster, New York 14580
(716) 265-4040   (800) 828-6772

CAPTOOL
CAPTOOL Global Investor
CAPTOOL Professional Investor
CAPTOOL Real Time
Techserve, Inc.
50 Broad Street
New York, New York 10004
(212) 344-9500

ChartistAlert
Enhanced Chartist
FirstAlert
Master Chartist
RiskAlert
Roberts-Slade, Inc.
619 North 500 West
Provo, Utah 84601
(801) 375-6850   (800) 433-4276

Compu/Chart EGA
Newtek Industries
1200 S.W. Executive Court
Topeka, Kansas 66615
(913) 231-0100   (800) 847-6111

CompuServe Research Manager
CompuServe Research Manager for Windows
CompuServe, Inc.
120 Broadway, Suite 3330
New York, New York 10271
(212) 227-3881   (800) 543-4616

Connect
Quoteexpress
Integrated Financial Solutions, Inc.
1049 S.W. Baseline, Suite B-200
Hillsboro, Oregon 97123
(503) 640-5303   (800) 729-5037

Currencycast
Dowcast
Network Services Group
1095 Market Street, Suite 514
San Francisco, California 94103-1628
(415) 863-8407

Discover/EN
Discover/OR
Discover/RE
Telemet America, Inc.
325 First Street
Alexandria, Virginia 22314
(703) 548-2042   (800) 368-2078

Discovery
Glendale
Super Tic
Cyber-Scan, Inc.
3601 Pulaski Road N.E.
Buffalo, Minnesota 55313
(612) 682-4150

Dow Jones Market Analyzer
Market Analyzer Plus for DOS
Market Analyzer Plus for MAC
Dow Jones & Company, Inc.
P.O. Box 300
Princeton, New Jersey 08543
(609) 520-4641   (800) 815-5100

Dow Jones/OEX Trading System
Swing Catcher System
Trend Index Company
2809 East Hamilton, #117
Eau Claire, Wisconsin 54701
(715) 833-1234

Enhanced Fund Master Optimizer
Fund Master TC
Fund Pro
Fundvest, Inc.
337 Boston Road
Bellerica, Massachusetts 01821
(508) 663-3330

Futures Pro
Option Pro
Option Pro SE
Essex Trading Company Ltd.
24 West 500 Maple Avenue
Naperville, Illinois 60540
(708) 416-3530   (800) 726-2140

Ensign V
Ensign Software
2641 Shannon Court
Idaho Falls, Idaho 83404
(208) 524-0755 (800) 255-7374

Epoch Pro
Mesa
P.O. Box 1801
Goleta, California 93116
(805) 969-6478   (800) 633-6372

Fibnodes
Trading Package
Coast Investment Software, Inc.
358 Avenida Milano
Sarasota, Florida 34242-1517
(813) 346-3801

Folioman
Folioman+
E-Sential Software
P.O. Box 41705
Los Angeles, California 90041
(213) 257-2524

Foreign Exchange Software Package
Statistical Analysis and Forecasting Software
  Package
Programmed Press
599 Arnold Road
West Hempstead, New York 11552-3918
(516) 599-6527

Fund Graf
Parsons Software
1230 West 6th Street
Loveland, Colorado 80537
(303) 669-3744

Ganntrader 2
Gannsoft Publishing Company
11670 Riverbend Drive
Leavenworth, Washington 98826-9353
(509) 548-5990

Genesis Financial Data Services
Navigator 3.0
411 Woodmen
Colorado Springs, Colorado 80919
(719) 260-6111

Historical ADL
Hourly DJIA
Log Scale Comparison
Mirat
Put/Call

Timer
Timer Professional
Tools for Timing
11345 Highway 7, #499
Minnetonka, Minnesota 55305
(612) 939-0076   (800) 325-1344

INVESTigator
Investment Technology
5104 Utah
Greenville, Texas 75402
(903) 455-3255

Investograph Plus, Optimizer
Liberty Research Corporation
1250 Capital of Texas Highway, Building 2,
   Suite 304
Austin, Texas 78746
(512) 329-2762   (800) 827-0090

Investor, The
Mutual Fund Composite Worksheet
Village Software, Inc.
186 Lincoln Street
Boston, Massachusetts 02111
(617) 695-9332   (800) 724-9332

Investor's Accountant
Market Strategist
Marketwatch
Hamilton Software, Inc.
6432 East Mineral Place
Englewood, Colorado 80112
(303) 795-5572   (800) 733-9607

Investor's Advantage
Investor's Advantage for Windows
Software Advantage Consulting Corpora-tion
38442 Gail
Clinton Township, Michigan 48036
(313) 463-4995   (800) 729-2431

LiveWire Personal Investor
LiveWire Professional
Cablesoft, Inc.
1807 2nd Street, Suite 26
Santa Fe, New Mexico 87501
(505) 986-8052

Macro*World Investor
Macro*World Research Corporation
4265 Brownsboro Road
Winston-Salem, North Carolina 27106
(910) 759-0600   (800) 841-5398

Market Charter
Survivor Software Limited
1409 Kuehner Drive, #1174
Simi, California 93063
(805) 522-8979   (800) 488-5898

Marketedge II
SASI Software Corp
P.O. Box 457
Sherwood, Oregon 97140
(503) 625-5384

MarketExpert
Option Extension
StockExpert
AIQ, Inc.
916 Southwood Boulevard, P.O. Drawer 7530
Incline Village, Nevada 89450
(702) 831-2999   (800) 332-2999

Market Master
RMC
Box 60842
Sunnyvale, California 94088-0842
(408) 773-8715

MetaStock
MetaStock RT
The Technician
Equis International
3950 South 700 East, Suite 100
Salt Lake City, Utah 84107
(801) 265-8886   (800) 882-3040

MoneyCenter for Windows/Unix
Profit Center
Knight-Ridder Financial
75 Wall Street, 23rd Floor
New York, New York 10005
(212) 269-1110

Money Fund Vision
IBC/Donoghue, Inc.
290 Eliot Street
P.O. Box 9104
Ashland, Massachusetts 01721-9104
(508) 881-2800   (800) 343-5413

Mutual Fund Investor
American River Software
1523 Kingsford Drive
Carmichael, California 95608
(916) 483-1600

Mutual Fund Manager
Denver Data, Inc.
9785 Maroon Circle, Meridian One, Suite 340
Englewood, Colorado 80112
(303) 790-7327

Nature's Pulse
Kasanjian Research
P.O. Box 4608
Blue Jay, California 92317
(909) 337-0816

Neuralist for Excel
Epic Systems, Corp
P.O. Box 277
Sierra Madre, California 91025-0277
(818) 355-2988

N-Train
Scientific Consultant Services, Inc.
20 Stagecoach Road
Selden, New York 11784
(516) 696-3333

OVM/Focus
Radix Research Limited
P.O. Box 91181
West Vancouver, British Columbia V7V 3N6,
  Canada
(604) 926-5308

Parity Plus
Partech Software Systems
2 Bryant Street, Suite 200
San Francisco, California 94105
(415) 546-9316

PC Chart Plus
Guru Systems, Ltd
3873 Airport Way, Box 9754
Bellingham, Washington 98227
(604) 299-1010

PC Quote
PC Quote, Inc.
401 South LaSalle Street
Chicago, Illinois 60605
(800) 225-5657

Peerless Intermediate-Term Market Timing
  Package
Peerless Short-Term Market Timing Package
Peerless Stock Market Timing
Tiger Multiple Stock Screening & Timing System
Tiger Investment Software
P.O. Box 9491
San Diego, California 92169
(619) 459-8577

Personal Analyst
Personal Hotline
Professional Analyst
Trendsetter Software
P.O. Box 6481
Santa Ana, California 92706
(714) 547-5005   (800) 825-1852

Personal Market Analysis
Investment Software
P.O. Box 2774
Durango, Colorado 81302
(303) 884-4130

Personal Stock Technician
Razorlogic Systems
P.O. Box 112
Kneeland, California 95549
(707) 668-4054   (800) 500-0444

PointsAhead
The Small Investor's Software Company
138 Ocean Avenue
Amityville, New York 11701
(516) 789-9368   (800) 829-9368

Powertrader
Nirvana Systems
3415 Greystone Drive, Suite 205
Austin, Texas 78731
(512) 345-2545   (800) 880-0338

Quotemaster
Quotemaster Professional
Strategic Planning Systems, Inc.
1409 Kuehner Drive, #1174
Simi, California 93063
(805) 522-8979   (800) 488-5898

QTRADER
Caribou Codeworks
HCR 3 Box 71
Lutsen, Minnesota 55612
(218) 663-7118

Q-Trax (for Windows)
EDMS
5859 New Peachtree Road, Suite 119
Atlanta, Georgia 30340
(404) 998-4088

Rational Indicators
Trader's Insight, Inc.
8 Renwick Avenue
Huntington, New York 11743-3052
(516) 423-2413

Realtick III
Townsend Analytics, Ltd.
100 South Wacker Drive, Suite 1506
Chicago, Illinois 60606
(312) 621-0141   (800) 827-0141

Relevance III-Advanced Market Analysis
Relevance III, Inc.
4741 Trousdale Drive, Suite 1
Nashville, Tennessee 37220
(615) 333-2005

Smartbroker
Charlton Woolard
17280 Anna
Southfield, Michigan 48075
(810) 557-3766

SMARTrader
SMARTrader Professional
Stratagem Software International, Inc.
520 Transcontinental Drive, Suite B
Metairie, Louisiana 70001
(504) 885-7353   (800) 779-7353

SPSS for Windows
SPSS/PC+
SPSS/PC+ Trends
SPSS, Inc.
444 North Michigan Avenue, Suite 3300
Chicago, Illinois
(312) 329-3500   (800) 543-6609

Stable-Technical Graphs
Winterra Software Group
P.O. Box 4106
Highlands Ranch, Colorado 80126
(303) 470-6323

Statistical Analysis and Forecasting Software
  Package
Programmed Press
599 Arnold Road
West Hempstead, New York 11552-3918
(516) 599-6527

Stock and Commodity Selection
Fortunet, Inc.
2995 Woodside Road, Suite 400
Woodside, California 94062
(415) 368-7655

Stock Charting System
Charles L. Pack
25303 La Loma Drive
Los Altos Hills, California 94022-4542
(415) 949-0887

Stock Graph Maker
Niche Software Products
P.O. Box 3574
Manassas, Virginia 22110
(703) 368-8372

Stock Prophet
Future Wave Software
1330 South Gertruda Avenue
Redondo Beach, California 90277
(310) 540-5373

Stock Watcher
Wall Street Watcher
Micro Trading Software
Box 175
Wilton, Connecticut 06897
(203) 762-7820

Stokplot
Clarks Ridge Associates
R.D. 3 Box 134
Leesburg, Virginia 22075
(703) 882-3476

Supercharts
System Writer 3.0 for Windows
System Writer Plus for DOS
Tradestation
Omega Research, Inc.
Omega Research Building
9200 Sunset Drive
Miami, Florida 33173-3266
(305) 270-1095   (800) 556-2022

Technical Analysis Charts
Technical Analysis, Inc.
4757 California Avenue SW
Seattle, Washington 98116-4499
(206) 938-0570 (800) 832-4642

Technical Analysis Scanner
Flexsoft
7172 Regional Street, #276
Dublin, California 94568
(510) 829-9733

Technical Selector
Technical Investor
Savant Software
120 Bedford Center Road, Suite 301
Bedford, New Hampshire 03110
(603) 471-0400   (800) 231-9900

Technical Stock Analyst
Techsoft, Inc.
768 Walker Road, Suite 294
Great Falls, Virginia 22066
(703) 759-3847

TechniFilter Plus
RTR Software, Inc.
19 West Hargett Street, Suite 204
Raleigh, North Carolina 27601
(919) 829-0786

Telescan Analyzer
Telescan, Inc.
10550 Richmond, Suite 250
Houston, Texas 77042
(713) 952-1060   (800) 324-8246

Wave Wise Spreadsheet for Windows
Jerome Technology, Inc.
P.O. Box 403
Raritan, New Jersey 08869
(908) 369-7503

Windows on Wall Street Pro
Marketarts, Inc.
P.O. Box 850922
Richardson, Texas 75085-0922
(214) 235-9594

2. MAJOR FINANCIAL INSTITUTIONS

This section of the *Finance and Investment Handbook* provides listings of major financial institutions, such as banks, life insurance companies, brokerages, limited partnership sponsors, and securities and commodities exchanges. All provide vital financial services. Personal investors deal directly with most of the institutions, and at least indirectly with all. Introductions to the lists provide background information on the types of institutions covered; for additional information it is best to contact an institution directly.

The first part of this section provides lists of the major institutions of the banking system. The 12 banks and the 25 branches that make up the Federal Reserve System and the 12 banks that comprise the Federal Home Loan Bank System are listed. Then follows a list of the primary dealers in government securities, which interact with the Federal Reserve banks. Next is a compilation of the 100 largest commercial banks in the United States and the commercial banks of Canada, followed by a listing of the 100 largest thrift institutions (savings and loans and savings banks) in the United States and the trust and loans of Canada.

The second part of this section provides a listing of the top 100 life-insurance companies in the U.S. and Canada. Insurance companies are important not only because of the protection they provide to policyholders, but also because they are major institutional investors.

A listing of the top 100 full-service brokerage firms and a listing of major discount brokers follow. Full-service brokers play a key role in raising capital for corporations and government bodies, and distributing securities and a wide array of financial services to individual and institutional investors. Investors can save on commissions by dealing with discount brokers.

This section continues with a compilation of major sponsors of limited partnerships, broken down by category of investment, such as real estate, oil and gas, and equipment leasing. By allowing individual investors to participate in markets previously accessible mainly to large institutions and the wealthy, these sponsors have greatly broadened the markets in which they compete.

Next is a listing of the 25 leading accounting firms. These firms, which in the past generally restricted their activities to auditing and accounting, have diversified recently into a variety of financial services. The final part of this section presents stock and commodity exchanges around the world. As financial markets have grown and become more interdependent, foreign exchanges have become more important to North Americans looking for investment opportunities.

FEDERAL RESERVE BANKS

The following is a list of the names, addresses and telephone numbers of the 12 banks and 25 branch banks that make up the Federal Reserve System. These banks supervise the activities of commercial banks and savings banks in their regions. Each branch is associated with one of the 12 Federal Reserve banks—on the list of branches, the parent bank is shown in parentheses. Nationally chartered banks must join the Federal Reserve system; state-chartered banks join on a voluntary basis. The Fed banks ensure that the banks they supervise follow Federal Reserve rules and provide member banks with access to emergency funds through the discount window. Each regional bank is owned by the member banks in its region.

The Federal Reserve System was set up by Congress in 1913 to regulate the U.S. monetary and banking system. The System regulates the nation's money supply by buying and selling government securities on the open market, setting reserve requirements for member banks, setting the discount rate at which it lends funds to members banks, supervising printing of the currency at the mint, acting as a clearinghouse for the transfer of funds throughout the banking system, and examining member banks to ensure that they meet Federal Reserve regulations.

Members of the top policy-making body of the Federal Reserve—the Board of Governors—are appointed by the President of the United States with the consent of the Senate. However, in conducting monetary policy, the Fed is designed to operate independently, so that the rate of growth of the money supply is not directly controlled by Congress or the President. To assure independence, members of the Board of Governors of the Federal Reserve are appointed to 14-year terms. Statements by members of the Board of Governors—especially the Chairman— often have much influence in the finance and investment community.

Depositors and borrowers can complain to the Federal Reserve about practices of member banks considered unfair or abusive. The Fed has jurisdiction over consumer credit, for instance, so consumers can bring complaints about problems with bank lending policies, credit cards, or advertising. In addition, consumers wanting to buy U.S. Treasury and government agency securities without the fees that banks and brokers usually charge can buy them directly through any of the Federal Reserve banks or branches on this list. Several years ago the Federal Reserve reorganized its U.S. Savings Bond sales operation. Now, only the Kansas City bank actually issues savings bonds. Private banks, which used to keep a supply of bonds for sale to customers, only process applications. An application is forwarded to the Kansas City Federal Reserve with a check for the appropriate amount, and the bond is sent to the purchaser within several weeks. Investors may also directly contact the Kansas City Fed to buy savings bonds. Also, Federal Reserve banks publish a variety of economic reports and studies that can be helpful to an investor.

Board of Governors

Board of Governors of the Federal Reserve
  System
21st and Constitution Avenue, N.W.
Washington, D.C. 20551
(202) 452-3000

Federal Reserve Banks

ATLANTA
Federal Reserve Bank of Atlanta
104 Marietta Street, N.W.
Atlanta, Georgia 30303-2713
(404) 521-8500

BOSTON
Federal Reserve Bank of Boston
600 Atlantic Avenue
Boston, Massachusetts 02106
(617) 973-3000

CHICAGO
Federal Reserve Bank of Chicago
230 South LaSalle Street
Chicago, Illinois 60604
(312) 322-5322

CLEVELAND
Federal Reserve Bank of Cleveland
1455 East Sixth Street, P.O. Box 6387
Cleveland, Ohio 44114
(216) 579-2000

DALLAS
Federal Reserve Bank of Dallas
400 South Akard Street
Dallas, Texas 75222
(214) 651-6111

KANSAS CITY
Federal Reserve Bank of Kansas City
925 Grand Avenue
Kansas City, Missouri 64198
(816) 881-2000

MINNEAPOLIS
Federal Reserve Bank of Minneapolis
250 Marquette Avenue
Minneapolis, Minnesota 55480
(612) 340-2345

NEW YORK
Federal Reserve Bank of New York
33 Liberty Street
New York, New York 10045
(212) 720-5000

PHILADELPHIA
Federal Reserve Bank of Philadelphia
Ten Independence Mall
Philadelphia, Pennsylvania 19106
(215) 574-6000

RICHMOND
Federal Reserve Bank of Richmond
701 East Byrd Street, P.O. Box 27622
Richmond, Virginia 23261
(804) 697-8000

ST. LOUIS
Federal Reserve Bank of St. Louis
411 Locust Street
St. Louis, Missouri 63102
(314) 444-8444

SAN FRANCISCO
Federal Reserve Bank of San Francisco
101 Market Street
San Francisco, California 94105
(415) 974-2000

Federal Reserve Branch Banks

BALTIMORE (Richmond)
502 South Sharp Street
Baltimore, Maryland 21201
(301) 576-3300

BIRMINGHAM (Atlanta)
1801 Fifth Avenue North
Birmingham, Alabama 35203
(205) 252-3141

BUFFALO (New York)
160 Delaware Avenue
Buffalo, New York 14202
(716) 849-5000

CHARLOTTE (Richmond)
401 South Tryon Street
Charlotte, North Carolina 28202
(704) 336-7100

CINCINNATI (Cleveland)
150 East Fourth Street
Cincinnati, Ohio 45202-0999
(513) 721-4787

DENVER (Kansas City)
1020 16th Street
Denver, Colorado 80202
(303) 572-2300

DETROIT (Chicago)
160 West Fort Street
Detroit, Michigan 48226
(313) 961-6880

EL PASO (Dallas)
301 East Main Street
El Paso, Texas 79901
(915) 544-4730

HELENA (Minneapolis)
400 North Park Avenue
Helena, Montana 59601
(406) 442-3860

HOUSTON (Dallas)
1701 San Jacinto Street
Houston, Texas 77002
(713) 659-4433

JACKSONVILLE (Atlanta)
800 Water Street
Jacksonville, Florida 32231-0044
(904) 632-1000

LITTLE ROCK (St. Louis)
325 West Capitol Avenue
Little Rock, Arkansas 72201
(501) 372-5451

LOS ANGELES (San Francisco)
950 South Grand Avenue
Los Angeles, California 90015
(213) 683-2300

LOUISVILLE (St. Louis)
410 South Fifth Street
Louisville, Kentucky 40202
(502) 568-9200

MEMPHIS (St. Louis)
200 North Main Street
Memphis, Tennessee 38103
(901) 523-7171

MIAMI (Atlanta)
9100 N.W. Thirty-Sixth Street
Miami, Florida 33178
(305) 591-2065

NASHVILLE (Atlanta)
301 Eighth Avenue North
Nashville, Tennessee 37203
(615) 251-7100

NEW ORLEANS (Atlanta)
525 St. Charles Avenue
New Orleans, Louisiana 70161
(504) 586-1505

OKLAHOMA CITY (Kansas City)
226 Dean A. McGee Avenue
Oklahoma City, Oklahoma 73125
(405) 270-8400

OMAHA (Kansas City)
2201 Farnan Street
Omaha, Nebraska 68102
(402) 221-5500

PITTSBURGH (Cleveland)
717 Grant Street
Pittsburgh, Pennsylvania 15219
(412) 261-7800

PORTLAND (San Francisco)
915 S.W. Stark Street
Portland, Oregon 97025
(503) 221-5900

SALT LAKE CITY (San Francisco)
120 South State Street
Salt Lake City, Utah 84111
(801) 322-7900

SAN ANTONIO (Dallas)
126 East Nueva Street
San Antonio, Texas 78204
(512) 224-2141

SEATTLE (San Francisco)
1015 Second Avenue
Seattle, Washington 98104
(206) 343-3600

PRIMARY GOVERNMENT SECURITIES DEALERS

The following is a list of banks and brokerage firms that act as primary government securities dealers, reporting to the Federal Reserve Bank of New York. In this role, they facilitate the Fed's open market operations by buying and selling Treasury securities directly through the New York Fed's Securities Department, commonly called The Desk. These dealers are therefore key players in the execution of Federal Reserve policy, as set down by the Federal Open Market Committee, which decides to tighten or loosen the money supply to combat inflation or to ease the money supply to stimulate economic growth. When the Fed wants to tighten money supply, it sells government securities to the primary dealers—the dollars the dealers pay for the securities are thus taken out of circulation, and the money supply contracts. When the Fed, on the other hand, wants to expand the money supply, it buys government securities from the dealers—the proceeds from these sales then go into the economy, and the money supply increases.

When the government issues new Treasury securities, these primary dealers also play a key role, because they are among other large dealers and investors making competitive bids for the securities. Under the competitive bid system, also known as a Dutch auction, bidders offer higher prices for the securities, and the highest prices are accepted. Most individual investors do not participate in this auction. Rather than risk losing out to a higher bidder, they buy Treasury securities with noncompetitive bids, for which the investor accepts whatever price is determined by the competitive auction.

In order to become a primary dealer, a firm must show the Federal Reserve that the company has an excellent reputation, large capacity for trading in government securities, and adequate staff and facilities. It is considered to be very prestigious to be accepted into the inner circle of primary government securities dealers.

BA Securities, Inc.
555 California Street, 10th Floor
San Francisco, California 94104
(415) 622-4715

Barclays de Zoete Wedd Securities, Inc.
222 Broadway
New York, New York 10038
(212) 412-6830

Bear, Stearns & Co. Inc.
245 Park Avenue
New York, New York 10167
(212) 272-2000

BT Securities Corporation
One Bankers Trust Plaza
New York, New York 10006
(212) 250-5000

Chase Securities, Inc.
One Chase Plaza, 8th Floor
New York, New York 10081
(212) 552-7416

Chemical Securities, Inc.
270 Park Avenue
New York, New York 10017
(212) 834-4500

Citicorp Securities, Inc.
399 Park Avenue, 7th Floor
New York, New York 10043
(212) 291-1000

CS First Boston Corporation
12 East 49th Street
New York, New York 10017
(212) 909-2000

Daiwa Securities America, Inc.
200 Liberty Street, One World Financial Center
New York, New York 10281
(212) 945-0100

Dean Witter Reynolds, Inc.
Two World Trade Center
New York, New York 10048
(212) 392-2222

Deutsche Bank Securities Corporation
31 West 52nd Street, 3rd Floor
New York, New York 10019
(212) 468-5000

Dillon Read & Co. Inc.
535 Madison Avenue
New York, New York 10022
(212) 906-7000

Donaldson, Lufkin & Jenrette Securities
  Corporation
140 Broadway
New York, New York 10005
(212) 504-3000

Eastbridge Capital, Inc.
135 East 57th Street
New York, New York 10022
(212) 756-7200

First Chicago Capital Markets, Inc.
One First National Plaza, Suite 0030
Chicago, Illinois 60670
(312) 732-5600

Fuji Securities, Inc.
140 South Dearborn Street
Chicago, Illinois 60603
(312) 899-4700

Goldman, Sachs & Co.
85 Broad Street
New York, New York 10004
(212) 902-1000

Greenwich Capital Markets, Inc.
600 Steamboat Road
Greenwich, Connecticut 06830
(203) 625-2818

Harris-Nesbitt Thomson Securities, Inc.
115 South LaSalle
Chicago, Illinois 60690
(312) 461-6222

HSBC Securities, Inc.
140 Broadway
New York, New York 10005

Kidder, Peabody & Co., Inc.
10 Hanover Square
New York, New York 10005
(212) 510-3000

Lanston (Aubrey G.) & Co., Inc.
One Chase Manhattan Plaza
New York, New York 10005
(212) 612-1600

Lehman Government Securities, Inc.
Three World Financial Center, 12th Floor
New York, New York 10285
(212) 640-6663

Merrill Lynch, Pierce, Fenner & Smith
  Incorporated
250 Vesey Street, World Financial Center,
  North Tower
New York, New York 10281
(212) 449-1000

Morgan (J.P.) Securities Inc.
60 Wall Street, 39th Floor
New York, New York 10260
(212) 483-2323

Morgan Stanley & Company, Incorporated
1251 Avenue of the Americas, 23rd Floor
New York, New York 10020
(212) 703-4000

Nationsbanc Capital Markets, Inc.
100 North Tryon Street
Charlotte, North Carolina 28255
(704) 386-5073

Nikko Securities Co. International, Inc. (The)
200 Liberty Street, One World Financial Center
New York, New York 10281
(212) 986-1600

Nomura Securities International, Inc.
Teo World Financial Center, Building B
New York, New York 10281
(212) 667-9300

Paine Webber Incorporated
1285 Avenue of the Americas
New York, New York 10019
(212) 713-2000

Prudential Securities Incorporated
One Seaport Plaza
New York, New York 10292
(212) 214-1000

Salomon Brothers Inc.
Seven World Trade Center
New York, New York 10048
(212) 783-7000

Sanwa Securities (USA) Co., L.P.
599 Lexington Avenue
New York, New York 10022
(212) 527-2601

SBC Government Securities, Inc.
222 Broadway
New York, New York 10038
(212) 335-1186

Smith Barney, Inc.
1345 Avenue of the Americas, 21st, 23rd &
32nd Floors
New York, New York 10105
(212) 464-6000

UBS Securities, Inc.
299 Park Avenue
New York, New York 10171
(212) 821-6353

S.G. Warburg & Co., Inc.
787 Seventh Avenue, Equitable Tower, 26th Floor
New York, New York 10019
(212) 459-7000

Yamaichi International (America), Inc.
Two World Trade Center
New York, New York 10048
(212) 912-6400

Zions First National Bank
One South Main Street
Salt Lake City, Utah 84111
(801) 974-8800

FEDERAL HOME LOAN BANKS

The following are the names, addresses and telephone numbers of the 12 banks of the Federal Home Loan Bank System. The Federal Home Loan Bank System, established by Congress in 1932 after the collapse of the banking system during the Great Depression, raises money by issuing notes and bonds and lends money to savings and loans and other mortgage lenders based on the amount of collateral the borrowing institution can provide. The Federal Home Loan Banks supply credit reserves to federally and state chartered savings and loans, cooperative banks and other mortgage lenders in their regions. Each Home Loan Bank is owned by the member financial institutions in its region.

Prior to the Thrift Bailout Bill of 1989, the Federal Home Loan Banks were supervised by the Federal Home Loan Bank Board. With the bailout, however, the FHLBB was eliminated and was replaced by two organizations: the Office of Thrift Supervision and the Federal Housing Finance Board. The Office of Thrift Supervision regulates federal- and state-chartered thrifts. The Federal Housing Finance Board supervises the 12 Federal Home Loan Banks.

National Headquarters

Federal Housing Finance Board
1700 G Street, N.W.
Washington, D.C. 20552
(202) 408-2500

Office of Thrift Supervision
1700 G Street, N.W.
Washington, D.C. 20552
(202) 906-6000

Federal Home Loan Banks

ATLANTA
Federal Home Loan Bank of Atlanta
P.O. Box 105565
Atlanta, Georgia 30348
(404) 888-8000

BOSTON
Federal Home Loan Bank of Boston
One Financial Center
Boston, Massachusetts 02111
(617) 542-0150

CHICAGO
Federal Home Loan Bank of Chicago
P.O. Box 834
Chicago, Illinois 60601
(312) 565-5700

CINCINNATI
Federal Home Loan Bank of Cincinnati
P.O. Box 598
Cincinnati, Ohio 45201
(513) 852-7500

DALLAS
Federal Home Loan Bank of Dallas
P.O. Box 619026
Dallas/Ft. Worth, Texas 75261
(214) 714-8500

DES MOINES
Federal Home Loan Bank of Des Moines
907 Walnut Street
Des Moines, Iowa 50309
(515) 243-4211

INDIANAPOLIS
Federal Home Loan Bank of Indianapolis
P.O. Box 60
Indianapolis, Indiana 46206
(317) 465-0200

NEW YORK
Federal Home Loan Bank of New York
One World Trade Center, Floor 103
New York, New York 10048
(212) 912-4600

PITTSBURGH
Federal Home Loan Bank of Pittsburgh
20 Stanwix Street
One Riverfront Center
Pittsburgh, Pennsylvania 15222
(412) 288-3400

SAN FRANCISCO
Federal Home Loan Bank of San Francisco
P.O. Box 7948
San Francisco, California 94120
(415) 616-1000

SEATTLE
Federal Home Loan Bank of Seattle
1501 4th Avenue
Seattle, Washington 98101
(206) 340-2300

TOPEKA
Federal Home Loan Bank of Topeka
P.O. Box 176
Topeka, Kansas 66601
(913) 233-0507

COMMERCIAL BANKS

The following is an alphabetical list of the names, addresses and telephone numbers of the headquarters of the 100 largest commercial banks in the United States. The institutions listed here are the largest based on their total deposits, the criterion generally used for comparing the size of banks. These deposits are made up of deposits by corporations, individuals, correspondent banks, government agencies, not-for-profit organizations and many other groups. They are in such forms as checking accounts and certificates of deposit and other time deposits. Another way of ranking banks is by the amount of permanent capital. This capital has been built over the years by offerings of stock to the public and retained earnings. The top 100 institutions would basically be the same using either method of ranking.

Most banks listed here are national banks, because they are chartered by the federal government. Any bank with the initial N (meaning National) or with national in its name is a national bank. Although there are about 14,000 banks in the United

States, there is a high amount of concentration of deposits and capital in the largest banks. The two largest banks, Citibank N.A. and Bank of America N.T. & S.A., have $128 billion and $106 billion in deposits respectively. Each of the top one-third banks have deposits in excess of $12 billion. The banks that rank near number 100, in contrast, have about $4 billion in deposits.

In the 1980s and 1990s there were many bank mergers, as banks sought to compete better in the new, less regulated environment brought about largely by the Depository Institutions Deregulation and Monetary Control Act in 1980. Some large banks operate newly acquired banks as separate subsidiaries. In cases where they are run independently, though still under the corporate umbrella, they are listed separately.

This list of the largest commercial banks (current as of mid 1994) is courtesy of the American Banker newspaper [1 State Street Plaza, New York, New York 10004 (212) 943-8200].

American National Bank & Trust Company
33 No. LaSalle Street
Chicago, Illinois 60690
(312) 661-5000

AmSouth Bank, NA
P.O. Box 11007
Birmingham, Alabama 35288
(205) 326-5120

Bank of America, NT and SA
P.O. Box 37000
San Francisco, California 94137
(415) 622-3456

Bank of America Arizona
P.O. Box 16290
Phoenix, Arizona 85011
(602) 597-5000

Bank of California, NA
P.O. Box 45000
San Francisco, California 94145
(415) 765-0400

Bank of Hawaii
P.O. Box 2900
Honolulu, Hawaii 96846
(808) 537-8111

Bank of New York
48 Wall Street
New York, New York 10286
(212) 530-1784

Bank of Tokyo Trust Company
P.O. Box 439
New York, New York 10005
(212) 766-3400

Bank One, Arizona, NA
P.O. Box 71
Phoenix, Arizona 85001
(602) 221-2900

Bank One Columbus, NA
100 E. Broad Street
Columbus, Ohio 43271
(614) 248-5800

Bank One Texas, NA
P.O. Box 655415
Dallas, Texas 75265
(214) 290-2000

Bankers Trust Company
280 Park Avenue
New York, New York 10017
(212) 250-2500

Boatman's National Bank of St. Louis
P.O. Box 236
St. Louis, Missouri 63166
(314) 544-6000

Branch Banking & Trust Company
P.O. Box 1847
Wilson, North Carolina 27893
(919) 399-4291

Central Fidelity National Bank
P.O. Box 27602
Richmond Virginia 23261
(804) 782-4000

Chase Manhattan Bank NA
1 Chase Manhattan Plaza
New York, New York 10081
(212) 552-2222

Chemical Bank
270 Park Avenue
New York, New York 10172
(212) 310-6161

Chemical Bank of New Jersey, NA
P.O. Box 1984
Morristown, New Jersey 07962
(201) 581-1300

Citibank, NA
399 Park Avenue
New York, New York 10043
(212) 559-1000

Colorado National Bank
918 17th Street
Denver, Colorado 80202
(303) 893-1862

Comerica Bank
100 Renaissance Center
Detroit, Michigan 48243
(313) 222-3300

Continental Bank, NA
231 So. LaSalle Street
Chicago, Illinois 60697
(312) 828-2345

CoreStates Bank, NA
P.O. Box 7618
Philadelphia, Pennsylvania 19101
(215) 973-3100

Crestar Bank
919 E. Main Street
Richmond, Virginia 23219
(802) 782-5000

Dominion Bank NA
P.O. Box 13327
Roanoke, Virginia 24040
(703) 563-7000

European American Bank
1 EAB Plaza
Uniondale, New York 11555
(516) 296-5000

Fifth Third Bank
38 Fountain Square Plaza
Cincinnati, Ohio 45263
(513) 579-5300

First Alabama Bank
P.O. Box 1448
Montgomery, Alabama 36102
(203) 832-8011

First American National Bank
P.O. Box 1351
Nashville, Tennessee 37237
(615) 748-2000

First-Citizens Bank & Trust Company
P.O. Box 151
Raleigh, North Carolina 27602
(919) 755-7000

First Fidelity National Bank, NA
550 Broad Street
Newark, New Jersey 07102
(201) 565-3200

First Fidelity National Bank, NA
Broad & Walnut Street, 11th Floor
Philadelphia, Pennsylvania 19109
(215) 985-6000

First Hawaiian Bank
P.O. Box 3200
Honolulu, Hawaii 96847
(808) 525-7000

First Interstate Bank of Arizona, NA
P.O. Box 53456
Phoenix, Arizona 85072
(602) 528-6000

First Interstate Bank of California
P.O. Box 3666
Los Angeles, California 90051
(213) 614-4111

First Interstate Bank of Texas, NA
P.O. Box 3326
Houston, Texas 77253
(713) 224-6611

First Interstate Bank of Oregon, NA
P.O. Box 3131
Portland, Oregon 97208
(503) 225-2111

First Bank, NA
601 2nd Avenue South
Minneapolis, Minnesota 55402
(612) 973-1111

First National Bank of Chicago
1 First National Plaza
Chicago, Illinois 60670
(312) 732-4000

First National Bank of Boston
P.O. Box 2016
Boston, Massachusetts 02106
(617) 929-6000

First National Bank of Maryland
P.O. Box 1596
Baltimore, Maryland 21201
(410) 244-4000

First Tennessee Bank, NA
165 Madison Avenue
Memphis, Tennessee 38103
(901) 523-4444

First Union National Bank of Florida
P.O. Box 2080
Jacksonville, Florida 32231
(904) 361-2265

First Union National Bank of Georgia
55 Park Place
Atlanta, Georgia 30303
(404) 827-7100

First Union National Bank of North Carolina
301 So. Tryon
Charlotte, North Carolina 28288
(704) 374-6161

Fleet Bank, NA
1 Constitution Plaza
Hartford, Connecticut 06115
(203) 244-5000

Fleet Bank of Massachusetts, NA
28 State Street
Boston, Massachusetts 02109
(617) 742-4000

Fleet Bank of New York
Peter D. Kiernan Plaza
Albany, New York 12207
(518) 447-4000

Fleet National Bank
111 Westminster Street
Providence, Rhode Island 02903
(401) 278-6000

Greenwood Trust Company
12 Read's Way
New Castle, Delaware 19720
(302) 323-7184

Harris Trust and Savings Bank
P.O. Box 755
Chicago, Illinois 60690
(312) 461-2121

Huntington National Bank
P.O. Box 1558
Columbus, Ohio 43216
(614) 476-8300

Integra Bank
4th Avenue and Wood Street
Pittsburgh, Pennsylvania 15278
(412) 644-8181

Key Bank of New York, NA
P.O. Box 748
Albany, New York 12201
(518) 486-8500

Key Bank of Washington
P.O. Box 90
Seattle, Washington 98111
(206) 684-6000

LaSalle National Bank
135 So. LaSalle Street
Chicago, Illinois 60603
(312) 443-2000

MBNA America Bank, NA
400 Christiana Road
Newark, Delaware 19713
(302) 456-8588

Manufacturers & Traders Trust Company
1 M&T Plaza
Buffalo, New York 14240
(716) 842-4100

Marine Midland Bank
1 Marine Midland Center
Buffalo, New York 14203
(716) 841-2424

Maryland National Bank
P.O. Box 987
Baltimore, Maryland 21203
(410) 244-5000

Mellon Bank, NA
1 Mellon Bank Center
Pittsburgh, Pennsylvania 15258
(412) 234-4100

Meridian Bank
P.O. Box 1102
Reading, Pennsylvania 19603
(215) 665-2000

Michigan National Bank
P.O. Box 9065
Farmington Hills, Michigan 48334
(313) 473-3000

Midlantic National Bank
80 Park Plaza
Newark, New Jersey 07102
(201) 266-6000

Morgan Guaranty Trust Company
60 Wall Street
New York, New York 10260
(212) 483-2323

NBD Bank, NA
P.O. Box 115
Detroit, Michigan 48231
(313) 225-1000

National City Bank
P.O. Box 5937
Cleveland, Ohio 44115
(216) 737-5000

National City Bank of Columbus
155 E. Broad Street
Columbus, Ohio 43251
(614) 463-7100

National Westminster Bank, USA
175 Water Street
New York, New York 10038
(212) 602-1000

National Westminster Bank NJ
10 Exchange Place Center
Jersey City, New Jersey 07302
(201) 547-7000

NationsBank of Florida, NA
P.O. Box 31590
Tampa, Florida 33631
(813) 882-1100

NationsBank of Georgia, NA
P.O. Box 4899
Atlanta, Georgia 30303
(404) 581-2121

NationsBank of North Carolina, NA
1 NCNB Plaza
Charlotte, North Carolina 28255
(704) 386-5000

NationsBank of South Carolina
1301 Gervais
Columbia, South Carolina 29202
(803) 765-8011

NationsBank of Tennessee
1 NationsBank Plaza
Nashville, Tennessee 37219
(615) 749-3333

NationsBank of Texas, NA
P.O. Box 831000
Dallas, Texas 75283
(214) 508-6262

NationsBank of Virginia, NA
P.O. Box 27025
Richmond, Virginia 23261
(804) 788-2000

Northern Trust Company
50 South LaSalle Street
Chicago, Illinois 60675
(312) 630-6000

Norwest Bank of Minnesota, NA
6th Street and Marquette Avenue
Minneapolis, Minnesota 55479
(612) 667-1234

PNC Bank, NA
5th Avenue and Wood Street
Pittsburgh, Pennsylvania 15222
(412) 762-2000

Republic National Bank of New York
P.O. Box 423
New York, New York 10018
(212) 525-5000

Sanwa Bank of California
P.O. Box 54445
Los Angeles, California 90054
(213) 896-7000

Seattle-First National Bank
P.O. Box 3586
Seattle, Washington 98124
(206) 358-3000

Shawmut Bank, NA
1 Federal Street
Boston, Massachusetts 02211
(617) 292-2000

Shawmut Bank Connecticut, NA
777 Main Street
Hartford, Connecticut 06115
(203) 728-2000

Signet Bank/Virginia
P.O. Box 25970
Richmond, Virginia 23260
(804) 747-2000

Society National Bank
127 Public Square
Cleveland, Ohio 44114
(216) 689-3000

South Carolina National Bank
1426 Main Street
Columbia, South Carolina 29226
(803) 765-3000

Star Bank, NA
425 Walnut Street
Cincinnati, Ohio 45202
(513) 632-4000

State Street Bank and Trust Company
225 Franklin Street
Boston, Massachusetts 02110
(617) 786-3000

Sumitomo Bank of California
320 California Street
San Francisco, California 94104
(415) 445-8000

Texas Commerce Bank, NA
P.O. Box 2558
Houston, Texas 77252
(713) 236-4865

Trust Company Bank
P.O. Box 4418
Atlanta, Georgia 30302
(404) 588-7711

United Jersey Bank
210 Main Street
Hackensack, New Jersey 07602
(201) 646-5000

U.S. Bank of Washington, NA
P.O. Box 720
Seattle, Washington 98101
(206) 344-2300

United States National Bank
P.O. Box 4412
Portland, Oregon 97208
(503) 275-6111

Union Bank
P.O. Box 7104
San Francisco, California 94120
(415) 455-0200

Wachovia Bank of Georgia, NA
P.O. Box 4148
Atlanta, Georgia 30302
(404) 332-5000

Wachovia Bank of North Carolina, NA
301 No. Main Street
Winston-Salem, North Carolina 27150
(919) 770-5000

Wells Fargo Bank, NA
420 Montgomery Street
San Francisco, California 94163
(415) 477-1000

CANADIAN BANKS

The following is a list of the 9 major banks of Canada. Unlike the United States, where there are 14,000 banks, Canadian banking is highly concentrated into a few large institutions that provide the full range of banking services to consumers and institutions. These banks are regulated at the federal and provincial levels in a similar way to American banks. Deposits are insured to $60,000.

Bank of Montreal
First Bank Tower
1 First Canadian Place
Toronto, Ontario M5X 1A1
(416) 867-5000

Bank of Nova Scotia
44 King Street West
Toronto, Ontario M5H 1H1
(416) 866-6161

Canadian Imperial Bank of Commerce
Commerce Court
Toronto, Ontario M5L 1A2
(416) 980-2211

Canadian Western Bank
Suite 1200, 10040 104 Street
Edmonton, Alberta T5J 3X6
(403) 423-8888

Laurentian Bank of Canada
1981 McGill College Avenue
Montreal, Quebec H3A 3K3
(514) 284-3931

Manulife Bank of Canada
2 Mississaga Street East
Orillia, Ontario L3V 6H9
(705) 325-2328

National Bank of Canada
600 de La Gauchetiere ouest
Montreal, Quebec H3B 4L2
(514) 394-4000

Royal Bank of Canada
1 Place Ville Marie
Montreal, Quebec H3C 3A9
(514) 874-2110

Toronto-Dominion Bank
1 Toronto-Dominion Centre
Toronto, Ontario M5K 1A2
(416) 982-8222

THRIFT INSTITUTIONS

The following is an alphabetical list of the names, addresses and telephone numbers of the headquarters of the 100 largest savings and loans and savings banks in the United States, ranked by total deposits as of May, 1994, as tabulated by the American Banker newspaper (1 State Street Plaza, New York, New York 10004-1549 (212) 803-8200). Total deposits, made up mostly of certificates of deposit and money-market accounts from individual and institutional investors, are the best measure of thrift institution size, and they are therefore commonly used in ranking savings and loans and savings banks. Some tabulations compare thrifts by the amount of their total assets—mostly mortgage loans. In either case, the list of the top 100 institutions would be similar.

Savings and loans were initially founded predominantly in the western states, particularly California, as a mechanism for pioneer settlers in the 19th century to finance the construction of homes. They were largely regulated by state authorities until 1932, when the Federal Home Loan Bank Board was set up in reaction to the crisis of the banking and home building industries during the Great Depression. Savings and loans are now regulated at both the federal and state levels and most deposits are insured by the Savings Association Insurance Fund.

Savings banks were initially found mainly on the East Coast, where, like savings and loans, they catered to consumers and made home loans. They are chartered and regulated by both state authorities and the Federal Reserve Board, as well as the Office of Thrift Supervision in some cases. Most deposits are insured by the Federal Deposit Insurance Corporation (FDIC). Over the years, the few distinctions between savings banks and savings and loans have largely faded away.

Historically, both types of thrifts have been distinguished from commercial banks in that they obtained most of their deposits from consumers, and lent that money out in the form of fixed-rate mortgages to homebuyers. To give them an edge in attracting deposits, they were allowed (under Regulation Q) to pay 1/4% more interest on passbook savings accounts than commercial banks. Starting in the late 1970s, when the general level of interest rates started to rise dramatically, many thrifts ran into financial trouble, because their income from mortgages was fixed at low rates, while they had to pay out higher rates on unregulated certificates of deposit to retain depositors. The pressure from this predicament ultimately led to the Depository Institutions Deregulation and Monetary Control Act of 1980 and the Garn-St Germain Act of 1982, which mandated the gradual phase-out of control on interest rates on all deposits, and permitted thrifts to offer adjustable-rate mortgages. They were also allowed to enter businesses from which they had previously been banned, such as commercial lending, issuing credit cards and providing trust services.

By the mid 1980s, thrifts played a prominent and highly competitive role in providing financial services. Many institutions went after consumer dollars by paying among the highest interest rates in the country on money-market deposits and certificates of deposit. These savings and loans and savings banks often arranged to take deposits over the phone. They sometimes brought in millions of dollars by allying with a securities brokerage firm that sells certificates of deposit. With the ability to bring in large amounts of money quickly, many thrifts became aggressive lenders as well.

By the late 1980s and early 1990s, many thrifts had gotten into severe financial trouble because they had taken excessive risks or because of fraud. A federal bailout had to be arranged to merge failed institutions into healthy ones. The bailout bill created a new regulatory structure for the industry by replacing the Federal Savings and Loan Insurance Corporation with the Savings Association Insurance Fund. The Federal Home Loan Bank Board became the Office of Thrift Supervision, and a new agency, the Resolution Trust Corporation, was formed to dispose of thrift assets.

Adam Corporation
1111 Briarcrest Drive 300
Bryan, Texas 77802
(409) 776-1111

Albany Savings Bank, FSB
P.O. Box 70
Albany, New York 12201
(518) 432-2200

American Savings Bank, FSB
915 Fort St. Mall
Honolulu, Hawaii 96813
(808) 531-6262

American Savings Bank
P.O. Box 19689
Irvine, California 92713
(714) 252-3200

American Savings Bank
400 E. Main Street
Stockton, California 92590
(209) 546-2656

American Savings of Florida, FSB
17801 NW 2nd Avenue
Miami, Florida 33169
(305) 653-5353

Amwest Savings Association
P.O. Box 8100
Bryan, Texas 77805
(409) 361-6200

Anchor Savings Bank, FSB
1420 Broadway
Hewlett, New York 11557
(516) 596-3900

Astoria Federal Savings & Loan Association
1 Astoria Plaza
Lake Success, New York 11042
(718) 335-2700

Bank United of Texas
3200 Southwest Freeway
Houston, Texas 77027
(713) 965-6920

Bank Western, FSB
1675 Broadway
Denver, Colorado 80202
(303) 623-5100

Bay View Federal Bank, FSB
2121 South El Camino Real
San Mateo, California 94403
(415) 573-7300

Bell Federal Savings and Loan Association
79 West Monroe Street
Chicago, Illinois 60603
(312) 346-1000

Bluebonnet Savings Bank, FSB
P.O. Box 8400
Dallas, Texas 75205
(214) 443-9000

California Federal Bank
5700 Wilshire Boulevard
Los Angeles, California 90036
(213) 932-4200

Capitol Federal Savings & Loan Association
700 Kansas Avenue
Topeka, Kansas 66603
(913) 235-1341

Carteret Savings Bank, F.A.
200 South Street
Morristown, New Jersey   07960
(201) 325-1000

Centerbank
60 N. Main Street
Waterbury, Connecticut 06702
(203) 578-7000

Champion   Federal   Savings   and   Loan
Association
115 Washington Street
Bloomington, Illinois   61701
(309) 829-0456

Charter One Bank, FSB
1215 Superior Avenue
Cleveland, Ohio 44114
(216) 566-5300

Chevy Chase Federal Savings Bank
8401 Connecticut Avenue
Chevy Chase, Maryland   20815
(301) 986-7000

Citizens Federal Bank, FSB
1221 Brickell Avenue
Miami, Florida 33131
(305) 577-0400

Citizens Savings Bank
1 Citizens Plaza
Providence, Rhode Island 02903
(401) 456-7000

Coast Federal Bank
1000 Wilshire Boulevard
Los Angeles, California 90017
(213) 362-2000

Collective Federal Savings Bank
P.O. Box 316
Egg Harbor City, New Jersey 08215
(609) 965-1235

Columbia Savings
5850 South Ulster Circle East
Englewood, Colorado 80111
(303) 930-7467

Columbia First Bank
1516 Wilson Boulevard
Arlington, Virginia 22209
(703) 247-5000

Commercial Federal Bank
P.O. Box 1103 DTS
Omaha, Nebraska 68101
(402) 551-7300

Coral Gables Federal Savings and Loan
Association
P.O. Box 141488
Coral Gables, Florida 33114
(305) 447-4711

Cragin Federal Bank for Savings
520 Fullerton Avenue
Chicago, Illinois 60639
(312) 889-1000

Decatur Federal Savings and Loan Association
250 East Ponce de Leon Avenue
Decatur, Georgia 30030
(404) 371-4000

Dime Savings Bank of New York, FSB
589 Fifth Avenue
New York, New York 10017
(212) 326-6170

Dollar Bank
3 Gateway Center
Pittsburgh, Pennsylvania 15222
(412) 261-4900

Downey Savings & Loan Association
3501 Jamboree Road
Newport Beach, California 92660
(714) 854-3100

Emigrant Savings Bank
5 E. 42nd Street
New York, New York 10017
(212) 850-4000

Eureka Bank, FSB
950 Tower Lane
Foster City, California 94404
(415) 358-6100

Farm and Home Savings Association
221 W. Cherry Street
Nevada, Missouri, 64772
(417) 667-3333

Fidelity Federal Bank FSB
600 North Brand Boulevard
Glendale, California 91203
(818) 956-7100

Fidelity New York, FSB
1000 Franklin Avenue
Garden City, New York 11530
(516) 746-8500

First Federal Bank, FSB
145 Bank Street
Waterbury, Connecticut 06720
(203) 755-1422

First Federal Bank of California
401 Wilshire Boulevard
Santa Monica, California 90401
(310) 319-6000

First Federal of Michigan
1001 Woodward Avenue
Detroit, Michigan 48226
(313) 965-1400

First Federal Savings & Loan Association of
  Rochester
1 First Federal Plaza
Rochester, New York 14614
(716) 238-2100

First Financial Bank, FSB
1305 Main Street
Stevens Point, Wisconsin 54481
(715) 341-0400

First Gibraltar Bank, FSB
1925 West John Carpenter
Irving, Texas 75063
(214) 444-5555

First Heights Bank, FSB
P.O. Box 7483
Houston, Texas 77248
(713) 869-3411

First National Bank Dayton
National City Center, 6 North Main
Dayton, Ohio 45412
(513) 226-2000

First Nationwide Bank, FSB
700 Market Street
San Francisco, California 94102
(415) 904-0110

First Savings Bank, FSB
301 College Street
Greenville, South Carolina 29601
(803) 458-2000

Fortune Bank
P.O. Box 6100
Clearwater, Florida 34618
(813) 538-1000

Franklin Savings Association
One Franklin Plaza
Ottawa, Kansas 66067
(913) 242-6300

Georgia Federal Bank, FSB
20 Marietta Street NW
Atlanta, Georgia 30303
(404) 330-2400

Glendale Federal Bank
700 North Brand Boulevard
Glendale, California 91203
(818) 500-2000

Great Lakes Bancorp, FSB
401 E. Liberty Street
Ann Arbor, Michigan 48107
(313) 769-8300

Great Western Bank, FSB
8484 Wilshire Boulevard
Beverly Hills, California 90211
(213) 852-3951

Greater New York Savings Bank
1 Penn Plaza
New York, New York 10119
(212) 643-4000

Green Point Savings Bank
41-60 Main Street
Flushing, New York 11355
(718) 670-7600

Guarantee Federal Savings Bank
8333 Douglas Boulevard
Dallas, Texas 75225
(214) 360-3360

Home Savings of America, F.A.
4900 Rivergrade Road
Irwindale, California, 91706
(818) 960-6311

HomeFed Bank
625 Broadway
San Diego, California 92101
(619) 699-8000

Homestead Savings
979 Broadway
Millbrae, California 94030
(415) 692-9010

Household Bank, FSB
4301 MacArthur Boulevard
Newport Beach, California 92660
(714) 833-0367

Hudson City Savings Bank
West 80 Century Road
Paramus, New Jersey 07652
(201) 967-1900

Independence Savings Bank
130 Court Street
Brooklyn, New York 11201
(718) 624-6620

LaSalle Talman Bank, FSB
30 West Monroe Street
Chicago, Illinois 60603
(312) 726-8915

Leader Federal Bank for Savings
P.O. Box 275
Memphis, Tennessee 38101
(901) 578-2000

Lincoln Savings Bank, FSB
99 Park Avenue
New York, New York 10016
(212) 972-9500

Local Federal Bank, FSB
P.O. Box 26020
Oklahoma City, Oklahoma 73126
(405) 841-2100

Manhattan Savings Bank
415 Madison Avenue
New York, New York 10017
(212) 688-3000

Metropolitan Federal Bank, FSB
P.O. Box 2687
Fargo, North Dakota 58108
(701) 293-2600

Northeast Savings, F.A.
50 State Street
Hartford, Connecticut 06103
(203) 280-1110

New Bedford Institution for Savings
P.O. Box 5000
New Bedford, Massachusetts 02742
(508) 996-5000

Ohio Savings Bank
1801 E. 9th Street
Cleveland, Ohio 44114
(216) 696-2222

Old Stone Federal Savings Bank
P.O. Box 1598
Providence, Rhode Island 02901
(401) 738-5000

OnBank
P.O. Box 6918
Syracuse, New York 13221
(315) 424-4400

Pacific First Bank, FSB
1420 5th Avenue
Seattle, Washington 98101
(206) 224-3000

People's Bank
850 Main Street
Bridgeport, Connecticut 06604
(203) 338-7171

Peoples Heritage Savings Bank
P.O. Box 9540
Portland, Maine 04112
(207) 761-8500

People's Westchester Savings Bank
P.O. Box 299
Hawthorne, New York 10532
(914) 347-3800

PriMerit, FSB
P.O. Box 98599
Las Vegas, Nevada 89193
(702) 362-5555

River Bank America
145 Huguenot Street
New Rochelle, New York 10801
(914) 654-4500

Rochester Community Savings Bank
40 Franklin Street
Rochester, New York 14604
(716) 258-3000

Roosevelt Bank, FSB
900 Roosevelt Parkway
Chesterfield, Missouri 63017
(516) 742-9300

Sacramento Savings Bank
1651 Response Road,
Sacramento, California 95815
(916) 921-5900

San Francisco Federal Savings & Loan
88 Kearny Street
San Francisco, California 94108
(415) 955-5800

Security Bank SSB
184 W. Wisconsin Avenue
Milwaukee, Wisconsin 53203
(414) 273-1900

South Boston Savings Bank
460 W. Broadway
South Boston 02127
(617) 268-2500

Southern California Federal Savings and Loan
   Association
9600 Wilshire Boulevard
Beverly Hills, California 90212
(310) 273-8750

Sovereign Bank, FSB
P.O. Box 37
Wyomissing, Pennsylvania 19603
(215) 723-6711

Standard Federal Bank
2600 West Big Beaver Road
Troy, Michigan 48084
(313) 643-9600

Star Bank
425 Walnut Street
Cincinnati, Ohio 45202
(513) 573-2000

St. Paul Federal Bank for Savings
6700 West North Avenue
Chicago, Illinois 60635
(312) 622-5000

TFC Banking & Savings, FSB
801 Marquette Avenue, No. 302
Minneapolis, Minnesota 55402
(612) 370-7000

Third Federal Savings & Loan Association of
   Cleveland
7007 Broadway Avenue
Cleveland, Ohio 44105
(216) 441-6000

United Savings Association of Texas, FSB
P.O. Box 1370
Houston, Texas 77251
(713) 963-6500

USSA Federal Savings Bank
USSA Building
San Antonio, Texas 78288
(210) 498-2265

Washington Federal Savings
425 Pike Street
Seattle, Washington 98101
(206) 624-7930

Washington Mutual, FSB
1201 Third Avenue
Seattle, Washington 98101
(206) 461-2000

Western Financial Savings Bank
23 Pasteur Road
Irvine, California 92713
(714) 727-1000

World Savings & Loan Association
1901 Harrison Street
Oakland, California 94612
(510) 446-6000

CANADIAN TRUST AND LOANS

    The equivalent of the U.S. savings and loan in Canada is called a trust and loan. These trust and loans act as executors, trustees and administrators of wills and trust agreements; serve as transfer agents, registrars and bond trustees for corporations; take deposits that are invested in fixed term instruments; offer unit investment trusts; manage profit-sharing and pension plans for companies; and offer mortgage loans, mostly to residential home buyers. The following is an alphabetical list of Canadian Trust and Loans.

Aetna Trust Company
2230 Park Place
666 Burrard Street
Vancouver, B.C. V6C 2X8
(604) 685-1208

AGF Trust Company
55 King Street West
32nd Floor, TD Bank Tower
Toronto, Ontario M5K 1E9
(416) 367-1900

Bank of Nova Scotia Trust Company (The)
44 King Street West
Toronto, Ontario M5H 1H1
(416) 866-6161

Bayshore Trust Company
825 Eglinton Avenue West, 4th Floor
Toronto, Ontario M5N 1E7
(416) 256-0888

Bonaventure Trust Inc.
1245 Sherbrooke Street West, Room 200
Montreal, Quebec H3B 4N9
(514) 879-9257

Canada Trust Company
Canada Trust Tower, BCE Place
161 Bay at Front, 35th Floor
Toronto, Ontario M5J 2T2
(416) 361-8000

Canadian Italian Trust Company
6999 St. Laurent Boulevard
Montreal, Quebec H2S 3E1
(514) 270-4124

CanWest Trust
31st Floor - TD Centre
201 Portage Avenue
Winnipeg, Manitoba R3B 3L7
(204) 956-2025

Capital Trust Corporation
600 René Levesque Boulevard
Montreal, Quebec H3B 1N4
(514) 393-7233

CIBC Trust Corporation
55 Yonge Street, Suite 900
Toronto, Ontario M5E 1J4
(416) 861-7052

Citizens Trust Company
815 West Hastings Street, Suite 401
Vancouver, B.C. V6C 1B4
(604) 682-7171

Co-Operative Trust Company of Canada
333 3rd Avenue North
Saskatoon, Saskatchewan S7K 2M2
(306) 956-1991

Community Trust Company Ltd.
2271 Bloor Street West, 3rd Floor
Toronto, Ontario M6S 1P1
(416) 763-2291

Effort Trust Company (The)
242 Main Street East
Hamilton, Ontario L8N 1H5
(416) 528-8956

Equitable Trust Company (The)
30 St. Clair Avenue West, Suite 700
Toronto, Ontario M4V 3A1
(416) 515-7000

Evangeline Trust Company
535 Albert Street
Windsor, N.S. B0N 2T0
(902) 798-8326

Family Trust Corporation
5954 Highway 7
Markham, Ontario L3P 1A2
(416) 471-1111

Fiducle Desjardins Inc.
1 Complexe Desjardins
Tour Sud 16e étage
Montréal, Québec H5B 1E4
(514) 286-9441

FirstLine Trust Company
33 Yonge Street, Suite 700
Toronto, Ontario M5E 1G4
(416) 865-1511

Fortis Trust Corporation
The Fortis Building
139 Water Street, P.O. Box 767
St. Johns', Newfoundland A1E 3Y3
(709) 726-7992

Granville Savings & Mortgage Corporation
Grosvenor Bldg.
Suite 290, 1040 West Georgia Street
Vancouver, B.C. V6E 6H1
(604) 682-2694

Home Savings & Loans Corporation
145 King Street West, Suite 1910
Toronto, Ontario M5H 1J8
(416) 360-4663

Household Trust Company
Suite 1000, 100 Sheppard Avenue East
North York, Ontario M2N 6N7
(416) 250-3400

Income Trust Company
181 Main Street West
Hamilton, Ontario L8P 4S1
(416) 528-9811

Inland Trust and Savings Corp. Ltd.
201 - One Forks Market Road
Winnipeg, Manitoba R3C 4L9
(204) 949-4800

Investors Group Trust Co. Ltd.
One Canada Centre
447 Portage Avenue
Winnipeg, Manitoba R3B 2C9
(204) 943-0361

League Savings & Mortgage Company
6074 Lady Hammond Road
P.O. Box 8900, Stn. A
Halifax, N.S. B3K 5N3
(902) 453-4220

London Trust & Savings Corporation
4950 Yonge Street, Suite 200
North York, Ontario M2N 6K1
(416) 229-6700

Merchant Privat Trust Company (The)
c/o Tuckahoe Financial Corporation
Scotia Plaza, Suite 4714
40 King Street West
Toronto, Ontario M5H 3Y2
(416) 360-4115

Metropolitan Trust Company of Canada
2700-10303 Jasper Avenue
Edmonton, Alberta T5J 3N6
(403) 421-2020

Montreal Trust Company
Place Montreal Trust
1800 McGill College Avenue, 13th Floor
Montreal, Quebec H3A 3K9
(514) 982-7000

MRS Trust Company
150 Bloor Street West, Suite 520
Toronto, Ontario M5S 2X9
(416) 926-0221

Municipal Trust Company
The Municipal Tower
70 Collier Street, P.O. Box 147
Barrie, Ontario L4M 4S9
(705) 734-7500

Mutual Trust Company
Suite 400, 70 University Avenue
Toronto, Ontario M5J 2M4
(416) 591-2710

Natcan Trust Company
National Bank Building
600, de la Gauchetière West
Montréal, Québec L4M 4S9
(514) 394-6629

National Trust Company
1 Ontario Street
P.O. Box 128
Stratford, Ontario N5A 6S9
(519) 271-2050

North American Trust Company
18th Floor, 151 Yonge Street
Toronto, Ontario M5C 2W7
(416) 362-7211

NAL Mortgage Company
151 Yonge Street, Suite 1800
Toronto, Ontario M5C 2W7
(416) 867-8858

North West Trust Company
1800 TD Tower
Edmonton Centre, 10205 - 101 Street
Edmonton, Alberta T5J 4G1
(403) 429-9300

Northern Trust Company Canada
BCE Place
161 Bay Street, Suite 4540
Toronto, Ontario M5J 2S1
(416) 365-7161

Pacific and Western Trust Corporation
Suite 950, 410 - 22nd Street East
Saskatoon, Saskatchewan S7K 5T6
(306) 244-1868

Peace Hills Trust Company
10th Floor, Kensington Place
10011 - 109 Street
Edmonton, Alberta T5J 3S8
(403) 421-1606

Peoples Trust Company
14th Floor, 888 Dunsmuir Street
Vancouver, B.C. V6C 3K4
(604) 683-2881

RBC Trust
14th Floor, North Tower
Royal Bank Plaza
Toronto, Ontario M5J 2J2
(416) 865-0515

Royal Trust
Royal Trust Tower
P.O. Box 7500, Station A
Toronto, Ontario M5W 1Y2
(416) 981-7000

Security Home Mortgage Investment
1510 Victoria Tower
25 Adelaide Street East
Toronto, Ontario
M5C 1Y2
(416) 366-2254

Sherbrooke Trust
75 Wellington North
P.O. Box 250
Sherbrooke, P.Q. J1H 5J2
(819) 563-4011

Sun Life Trust Company
225 King Street West, 5th Floor
Toronto, Ontario M5V 3C5
(416) 943-6532

TD Trust Company
The Toronto Dominion Bank
17th Floor, Royal Trust Tower
Toronto, Ontario M5K 1A2
(416) 982-2638

Trust Company of Bank of Montreal (The)
Bank of Montreal
302 Bay Street, 7th Floor
Toronto, Ontario M5X 1A1

Trust Général du Canada
1100 University Street, 12th Floor
Montréal, Québec H3B 2G7
(514) 871-7200

Trust La Laurentienne du Canada Inc.
425 de Maisonneuve Blvd. West
Montréal, Québec H3A 3G5

Trust Prêt et Revenu
Suite 700, 850 Place d'Youville
Quebec, Quebec G1K 7P3
(418) 692-1221

Victoria & Grey Mortgage Corporation
One Financial Place
1 Adelaide Street East, 3rd Floor
Toronto, Ontario M5C 2W8
(416) 361-3660

LIFE INSURANCE COMPANIES

The following is an alphabetical list of the headquarters addresses and telephone numbers of the 100 largest life insurance companies in the United States and Canada. The list is provided courtesy of A.M. Best Company of Oldwick, New Jersey 08858 (tel. 908-439-2200), which rates the financial stability of life insurance companies.

Life insurance companies are normally ranked in one of three ways: by admitted assets, by life insurance in force, or by total premium income. Although any of these rankings would include most of the same companies, this particular list is based on admitted assets. Such assets include all the assets a life insurance company has accumulated over the years, including investments in real estate, mortgages, stocks, and bonds. Because of the enormous size of these assets, insurance companies have become extremely important institutional investors. The other two methods of ranking these companies, by life insurance in force and by total premium income, show the amount of coverage insurance companies are providing and the dollar amount of their sales. These are also important figures to judge a company by, but they do not provide as direct an indication of a company's importance in the finance and investment markets.

The life insurance industry is characterized by a few giant firms with a high percentage of the industry's total assets and a large number of smaller companies. The top two firms, Prudential Insurance Company of America and Metropolitan Life Insurance Company, had assets at the end of 1993 of $165.7 billion and $128.2 billion, respectively. The top 40 companies had assets of around $10 billion or more. The 100th largest company had a little more than $3.5 billion in assets.

The companies on this list represent two distinct types of insurance company. One is owned by stockholders, and its or its parent company's shares are traded on the New York or American stock exchange or over the counter. This type of company is in business to write life insurance policies, invest premiums, and a portion of the difference between investment income and insurance claims and expenses ultimately reaches shareholders as dividends or increases in shareholder's equity. The other type of company, called a mutual life insurance company (the word mutual is usually in the name), is owned by policyholders, who receive a portion of the profits the company may earn through policyholder dividends. Mutual companies have no outstanding stock traded on an exchange, since the company is owned solely by its policyholders.

As in other areas of the financial services industry, competition has been increasing among life insurers. The advent in the early 1980s of universal life insurance, which ties cash value buildup to money-market rates, put additional pressure on all insurers to make policies more competitive. By the 1990s, the life insurance industry had produced a panoply of products which allow policyholders a wide range of flexibility in paying premiums, building cash value and buying insurance protection. In addition to traditional whole life and term policies, companies now offer universal life, variable life (where the policyholder chooses between stock, bond, and money-market investments), variable universal life, and a wide range of annuity and Individual Retirement Account products. Many insurers also offer financial planning services.

In addition to their role as insurers of lives, life insurance companies have become an important source of capital for world capital markets. Insurance companies are a major force in the stock market; the municipal, corporate, and government bond markets; in real estate (both as owners and lenders); and as providers of venture capital. Some insurance companies have expanded their offerings by acquiring brokerage and money management firms.

Aetna Life Insurance and Annuity Company
151 Farmington Avenue
Hartford, Connecticut 06156
(203) 273-0123

Aetna Life Insurance Company
151 Farmington Avenue
Hartford, Connecticut 06156
(203) 273-0123

Aid Association for Lutherans
4321 North Ballard Road
Appleton, Wisconsin 54919
(414) 734-5721

Alexander Hamilton Life Insurance Company
of America
33045 Hamilton Boulevard
Farmington Hills, Michigan 48334
(313) 553-2000

Allianz Life Insurance Company of North
America
1750 Hennepin Avenue
Minneapolis, Minnesota 55403-2195
(612) 347-6500

Allstate Life Insurance Company
3100 Sanders Road
Northbrook, Illinois 60062
(312) 402-5000

American Family Life Assurance Company of
Columbus
1932 Wynnton Road
Columbus, Georgia 31999
(404) 323-3431

American General Life and Accident Insurance
Company
American General Center
Nashville, Tennessee 37250
(615) 749-1000

American International Assurance
One ALICO Plaza
Wilmington, Delaware 19801
(212) 770-7000

American Life Insurance Company
P.O. Box 2226
Wilmington, Delaware 19899
(302) 594-2000

American National Insurance Company
One Moody Plaza
Galveston, Texas 77550-7999
(409) 763-4661

American United Life Insurance Company.
P.O. Box 368
Indianapolis, Indiana 46206-0368
(317) 263-1877

Anchor National Life Insurance Company
1 SunAmerica Center
Los Angeles, California 90067-6022
(800) 858-6377

Aurora National Life Assurance
2525 Colorado Avenue
Santa Monica, California 90404
(310) 264-3200

The Canada Life Assurance Company
330 University Avenue
Toronto, Ontario, Canada M5R 1R8
(416) 597-1456

Commonwealth Life Insurance Company
P.O. Box 32800
Louisville, Kentucky 40232-2800
(502) 587-7371

Confederation Life Insurance Company
321 Bloor Street, East
Toronto, Ontario, Canada M4W 1H1
(416) 323-8111

Connecticut General Life Insurance Company
Hartford, Connecticut 06152
(203) 726-6000

Connecticut Mutual Life Insurance Company
140 Garden Street
Hartford, Connecticut 06154
(203) 727-6500

Continental Assurance Company
CNA Plaza
Chicago, Illinois 60685
(312) 822-5000

Crown Life Insurance Company
1901 Scarth Street
Regina, Saskatchewan, Canada S4P 3B1
(306) 751-6700

The Equitable Life Assurance Society of the
United States
787 Seventh Avenue 41-M
New York, New York 10019
(212) 554-1234

Equitable Variable Life Insurance Company
787 Seventh Avenue 41-M
New York, New York 10019
(212) 714-5107

Family Life Insurance Company
2101 4th Avenue, Suite 700
Seattle, Washington 98121-2371
(206) 441-1942

Fidelity Bankers Life Insurance Company
1011 Boulder Springs Drive
Richmond, Virginia 23225
(804) 323-1011

Fidelity and Guaranty Life Insurance Company
Box 1137
Baltimore, Maryland 21203
(301) 547-3000

First Colony Life Insurance Company
P.O. Box 1280
Lynchburg, Virginia 24505
(804) 845-0911

The Franklin Life Insurance Company
Franklin Square
Springfield, Illinois 62713
(217) 528-2011

General American Life Insurance Company
P.O. Box 396
St. Louis, Missouri 63166
(314) 231-1700

Great Northern Insured Annuities
P.O. Box 490
Seattle, Washington 98111-0490
(206) 625-1755

The Great-West Life Assurance Company
100 Osborne Street North
Winnipeg, Manitoba, Canada R3C 3A5
(204) 946-1190

The Guardian Life Insurance Company of
America
201 Park Avenue South
New York, New York 10003
(212) 598-8000

Hartford Life Insurance Company
P.O. Box 2999
Hartford, Connecticut 06104-2999
(203) 547-5000

IDS Life Insurance Company
IDS Tower 10
Minneapolis, Minnesota 55440-0010
(612) 671-3131

The Imperial Life Assurance Company of
Canada
1100 René Levesque Boulevard West
Montreal, Ontario, Canada H3B 4N4
(416) 926-2600

The Independent Order of Foresters
789 Don Mills Road
Don Mills, Ontario, Canada M3C 1T9
(416) 429-3000

Integrated Resources Life Insurance Company
10 Union Square East
New York, New York 10003
(212) 353-7790

Jackson National Life Insurance Company
P.O. Box 24068
Lansing, Michigan 48909
(517) 394-3400

Jefferson-Pilot Life Insurance Company
P.O. Box 21008
Greensboro, North Carolina 27420
(919) 691-3000

John Alden Life Insurance Company
P.O. Box 020270
Miami, Florida 33102-0270
(305) 470-3100

John Hancock Mutual Life Insurance Company
P.O. Box 111
Boston, Massachusetts 02117
(617) 572-6000

Kemper Investors Life Insurance Company
1 Kemper Drive T-1
Long Grove, Illinois 60049
(708) 540-4500

Keyport Life Insurance Company
125 High Street
Boston, Massachusetts 02110-2712
(617) 526-1400

Knights of Columbus
P.O. Box 1670
New Haven, Connecticut 06507-0901
(203) 772-2130

Liberty National Life Insurance Company
P.O. Box 2612
Birmingham, Alabama 35202
(205) 325-2722

The Life Insurance Company of Virginia
6610 West Broad Street
Richmond, Virginia 23230
(804) 281-6000

The Lincoln National Life Insurance Company
1300 South Clinton Street
Fort Wayne, Indiana 46801
(219) 445-2000

Lutheran Brotherhood
625 Fourth Avenue South
Minneapolis, Minnesota 55415
(612) 340-7000

The Manufacturers Life Insurance Company
200 Bloor Street East
Toronto, Ontario, Canada M4W 1E5
(416) 926-0100

Massachusetts Mutual Life Insurance
Company
1295 State Street
Springfield, Massachusetts 01111
(413) 788-8411

Merrill Lynch Life Insurance Company
P.O. Box 9061
Princeton, New Jersey 08543-9061
(609) 282-1490

Metropolitan Insurance and Annuity Company
One Madison Avenue, Area 6C
New York, New York 10010
(212) 578-2211

Metropolitan Life Insurance Company
One Madison Avenue, Area 6C
New York, New York 10010-3690
(212) 578-2211

The Minnesota Mutual Life Insurance Company
Minnesota Mutual Life Center,
400 Robert Street
St. Paul, Minnesota 55101
(612) 298-3500

The Mutual Life Insurance Company of New York
1740 Broadway at 55th Street
New York, New York 10019
(212) 708-2000

Mutual of America Life Insurance Company
666 Fifth Avenue
New York, New York 10103
(212) 399-1600

National Home Life Assurance Company
Valley Forge, Pennsylvania 19493
(215) 648-5000

National Life Insurance Company
G.P.O. Box 366107
San Juan, Puerto Rico 00936-6107
(809) 758-8080

Nationwide Life Insurance Company
One Nationwide Plaza
Columbus, Ohio 43216
(614) 249-7111

New England Mutual Life Insurance Company
501 Boylston Street
Boston, Massachusetts 02116-3700
(617) 578-2000

New York Life Insurance and Annuity
  Corporation
300 Delaware Avenue
Wilmington, Delaware 19801
(212) 576-7000

New York Life Insurance Company
51 Madison Avenue, Room 250
New York, New York 10010
(212) 576-7000

North American Life Assurance Company
5650 Yonge Street
North York, Ontario, Canada M2M 4G4
(416) 229-4515

The Northwestern Mutual Life Insurance
  Company
720 East Wisconsin Avenue
Milwaukee, Wisconsin 53202
(414) 271-1444

Northwestern National Life Insurance
P.O. Box 20
Minneapolis, Minnesota 55440
(612) 372-5432

PFL Life Insurance Company
1111 North Charles Street
Baltimore, Maryland 21201
(319) 398-8511

Pacific Mutual Life Insurance Company
700 Newport Center Drive
Newport Beach, California 92660
(714) 640-3011

The Penn Mutual Life Insurance Company
600 Dreshor Road
Horsham, Pennsylvania 19044
(215) 956-8000

Peoples Security Life Insurance Company
P.O. Box 61
Durham, North Carolina 27702
(919) 687-8200

Phoenix Home Life Mutual Life Insurance
  Company
One American Row
Hartford, Connecticut 06115
(518) 479-8000

Principal Mutual Life Insurance Company
711 High Street
Des Moines, Iowa 50392-2300
(515) 247-5111

Protective Life Insurance Company
P.O. Box 2606
Birmingham, Alabama 35202
(205) 879-9230

Provident Life and Accident Insurance Company
One Fountain Square
Chattanooga, Tennessee 37402
(615) 755-1011

Provident Mutual Life Insurance Company of
  Philadelphia
P.O. Box 7378
Philadelphia, Pennsylvania 19101
(215) 636-5000

Provident National Assurance Company
One Fountain Square
Chattanooga, Tennessee 37402
(615) 755-1011

Pruco Life Insurance Company
213 Washington Street
Newark, New Jersey 07102-2992
(201) 802-6000

The Prudential Insurance Company of America
Prudential Plaza
Newark, New Jersey 07102-2992
(201) 802-6000

Safeco Life Insurance Company
P.O. Box 34690
Seattle, Washington 98124-1690
(206) 867-8000

Southwestern Life Insurance Company
P.O. Box 2699
Dallas, Texas 75221-2699
(214) 954-7703

State Farm Life Insurance Company
One State Farm Plaza
Bloomington, Illinois 61710
(309) 766-2311

State Mutual Life Assurance Company of
America
440 Lincoln Street
Worcester, Massachusetts 01653
(508) 855-1000

Sun Life Assurance Company of Canada
P.O. Box 4150, Station A
Toronto, Ontario, Canada M5W 2C9
(416) 979-9966

Sun Life Assurance Company of Canada (U.S.)
One Sun Life Executive Park
Wellesley Hills, Massachusetts 02181
(617) 237-6030

Sun Life Insurance Company of America
11601 Wilshire Boulevard
Los Angeles, California 90025-1748
(800) 445-7862

Teachers Insurance and Annuity Association
of America
730 Third Avenue
New York, New York 10017
(212) 490-9000

Transamerica Life Insurance and Annuity
Company
1150 South Olive Street
Los Angeles, California 90015
(213) 742-3111

Transamerica Occidental Life Insurance
Company
Transamerica Center,
1150 South Olive Street
Los Angeles, California 90015
(213) 742-2111

The Travelers Insurance Company
One Tower Square
Hartford, Connecticut 06183
(203) 277-0111

The Travelers Life and Annuity Company
One Tower Square
Hartford, Connecticut 06183
(203) 277-0111

UNUM Life Insurance Company of America
2211 Congress Street
Portland, Maine 04122
(207) 770-2211

The Union Central Life Insurance Company
P.O. Box 179
Cincinnati, Ohio 45201
(513) 595-2200

United Insurance Company of America
One East Wacker Drive
Chicago, Illinois 60601
(312) 661-4500

United of Omaha Life Insurance Company
Mutual of Omaha Plaza
Omaha, Nebraska 68175
(402) 342-7600

United Pacific Life Insurance Company
P.O. Box 490
Seattle, Washington 98111-0490
(206) 625-1755

USAA Life Insurance Company
USAA Building
San Antonio, Texas 78288
(210) 498-8000

USG Annuity and Life Company
P.O. Box 617
Des Moines, Iowa 50303-0617
(515) 282-3230

The Variable Annuity Life Insurance Company
P.O. Box 3206
Houston, Texas 77253-3206
(713) 526-5251

Western National Life Insurance Company
P.O. Box 871
Amarillo, Texas 79167
(806) 378-3400

The Western and Southern Life Insurance
Company
400 Broadway
Cincinnati, Ohio 45202
(513) 629-1800

Xerox Financial Services Life
One Tower Lane, Suite 3000
Oakbrook Terrace, Illinois 60181-4644
(708) 368-6215

BROKERAGE FIRMS

The following is a list of the top 100 full-service and the top discount broker-age firms in the United States and Canada. Traditionally, brokers sold mostly stocks and bonds to their customers, who were primarily persons of substantial means. Today, these firms allow customers to buy and sell stocks, bonds, commodities, options, mutual funds, bank certificates of deposit, limited partnerships and many other financial products. Brokers also offer asset management accounts, which combine holdings of assets like stocks and bonds with a money-market fund which provides checkwriting and credit card features. Most brokers in addition offer indi-vidualized financial planning services. As a result of this wide range of products, brokers today have a much more diverse clientele, ranging from young persons just starting to invest to wealthy retired people who are experienced investors.

On May 1, 1975, known as May Day in the brokerage industry, the era of fixed commissions ended. This move brought much more competition within the industry and ushered in a new breed of broker—the discounter. These brokers specialize in executing buy and sell orders for stocks, bonds and options. As a rule, they charge commissions far lower than full-service brokers. Discounters do not give advice about which securities to buy or sell, however, so investors who use them generally are more experienced and knowledgeable. Some discount brokers were acquired in the 1980s by commercial banks, who under the Glass-Steagall Act of 1933 are not allowed to act as full-service brokers. Banks were allowed to make such acquisitions because discount brokers do not give advice or underwrite securities. Full-service firms offer far more guidance on what investments are appropriate for each client. For this guidance, however, clients must pay significantly higher charges.

Within the full-service brokerage firm category, two varieties exist. The largest firms are known as wire houses, because they have a large network of offices nationally linked by advanced communications equipment. National wire house firms also tend to have an important presence overseas. In contrast, regional bro-kerage firms concentrate on serving customers in a particular area of the country. Such firms typically do not offer as wide an array of financial products, although they usually provide all the basics. Regional firms tend to concentrate on finding investment opportunities not yet discovered by large national firms.

In addition to providing services to individuals, brokers who also engage in invest-ment banking play an important role in raising capital for federal, state and local gov-ernments and for corporations. Such firms underwrite new issues of debt securities for governments and equity and debt issues for corporations and distribute them to both institutional and individual investors. In addition, brokers act as advisers to corpora-tions involved in merger and acquisition activity and other areas of corporate finance. Increasingly, brokerage firms are expanding their operations internationally, to facili-tate trading of foreign currencies, and foreign debt and equity securities.

This alphabetical list contains the top 100 brokerage firms as measured by the amount of capital. (Capital is the sum of long-term borrowings and ownership equi-ty.) Capital is crucial to a brokerage firm because it must constantly be put at risk in underwriting and trading securities. The two largest firms on the list, Merrill Lynch & Co, Inc., and Salomon, Inc., had about $19 billion and $17 billion in cap-ital, respectively, in 1993. The two next largest firms, The Goldman Sachs Group, L.P., and the Morgan Stanley Group, Inc. had capital of around $15 billion and $11 billion respectively. The next 6 companies in this list had capital in the range $1.5 billion–$6 billion; the next 4 companies capital in the range $1 billion –$2 billion; with the remainder of the companies in the list having capital below $1 billion. The smallest of the 100 firms listed had $57 million in capital.

Most of these brokerage firms were originally formed as partnerships, but in recent years, many incorporated and a number offered shares of stock in their com-panies to the public. Such public offerings are often the best way for a brokerage firm to raise the additional capital it needs to be competitive.

Following the list of 100 full-service firms is an alpabetical list of the top discount brokers, also ranked by capital. These lists are provided courtesy of the brokerage industry's trade association, the Securities Industry Association, [120 Broadway, New York, New York 10271-0080 (212) 608-1500].

Full-Service Brokerage Firms

Advest Group, Inc.
280 Trumbull Street
Hartford, Connecticut 06103
(203) 525-1421

Allen & Company, Incorporated
711 Fifth Avenue
New York, New York 10022
(212) 832-7057

American Capital Marketing, Inc.
2800 Post Oak Boulevard, 44th Floor
Houston, Texas 77056
(713) 993-0500

Arnhold and S. Bleichroeder, Inc.
45 Broadway
New York, New York 10006
(212) 943-9200

Robert W. Baird & Co. Incorporated
777 East Wisconsin Avenue
Milwaukee, Wisconsin 53202
(414) 765-3500

The Bank of Tokyo Trust Company
1251 Avenue of the Americas
New York, New York 10116-3138
(212) 782-4000

Barclays De Zoete Wedd Securities Inc.
222 Broadway, 8th Floor
New York, New York 10038
(212) 412-6830

The Bear Stearns Companies, Inc.
245 Park Avenue
New York, New York 10167
(212) 272-2000

Sanford C. Bernstein & Co., Inc.
767 Fifth Avenue
New York, New York 10153
(212) 486-5800

BHC Securities, Inc.
One Commerce Square
2005 Market Street, 12th Floor
Philadelphia, Pennsylvania 19103-3212
(215) 636-3000

William Blair & Company
222 West Adams Street
Chicago, Illinois 60606
(312) 236-1600

Alex. Brown & Sons Incorporated
135 East Baltimore Street
Baltimore, Maryland 21202
(410) 727-1700

Brown Brothers Harriman & Co.
59 Wall Street
New York, New York 10005
(212) 483-1818

J.C. Bradford & Co.
330 Commerce Street
Nashville, Tennessee 37201-1809
(615) 748-9000

Cantor Fitzgerald Securities
One World Trade Center
New York, New York 10048
(212) 938-5000

Chase Securities, Inc.
One Chase Manhattan Plaza, 35th Floor
New York, New York 10081
(212) 552-1776

The Chicago Corporation
208 South LaSalle Street
Chicago, Illinois 60604
(312) 855-7600

CS First Boston
Park Avenue Plaza
New York, New York 10055
(212) 909-2000

Citicorp Securities, Inc.
399 Park Avenue, 7th Floor
New York, New York 10043
(212) 559-1000

Cowen & Co.
Financial Square
New York, New York 10005-3597
(212) 495-6000

Daiwa Securities America, Inc.
One World Financial Center
New York, New York 10281
(212) 945-0100

Dean Witter Reynolds, Inc.
2 World Trade Center
New York, New York 10048
(212) 392-2222

Deutsche Bank Securities Corporation
31 West 52nd Street
New York, New York 10019
(212) 468-5000

Dillon, Read & Co. Inc.
535 Madison Avenue
New York, New York 10022
(212) 906-7000

Discount Corporation of New York
58 Pine Street
New York, New York 10005
(212) 248-8900

Donaldson, Lufkin & Jenrette, Inc.
140 Broadway
New York, New York 10005
(212) 504-3000

A.G. Edwards, Inc.
One North Jefferson
St. Louis, Missouri 63103
(314) 289-3000

Fahnestock & Co. Inc.
110 Wall Street
New York, New York 10005-3878
(212) 668-8000

First Marathon Securities Limited
2 First Canadian Place
Toronto, Ontario M5X 1J9, Canada
(416) 869-3707

Furman Selz Incorporated
230 Park Avenue
New York, New York 10169
(212) 309-8200

The Goldman Sachs Group, L.P.
85 Broad Street
New York, New York 10004
(212) 902-1000

Greenwich Capital Markets, Inc.
600 Steamboat Road
Greenwich, Connecticut 06830
(203) 625-2700

Gruntal Financial Corporation
14 Wall Street
New York, New York 10005
(212) 267-8800

Hambrecht & Quist Incorporated
One Bush Street
San Francisco, California 94104
(415) 576-3300

Herzog, Heine, Geduld, Inc.
26 Broadway
New York, New York 10004-1763
(212) 908-4000

J.J.B. Hilliard, W.L. Lyons, Inc.
Hilliard Lyons Center
Louisville, Kentucky 40232-2760
(502) 588-8400

HSBC Securities, Inc.
140 Broadway
New York, New York 10005-1101
(212) 825-6780

Inter-Regional Financial Group, Inc.
Dain Bosworth Plaza
60 South Sixth Street
Minneapolis, Minnesota 55402-4402

Internationale Nederlanden (U.S.) Securities
Corporation
135 East 57th Street
New York, New York 10022
(212) 446-1500

Interstate Johnson Lane Corporation
Interstate Tower
P.O. Box 1012
Charlotte, North Carolina 28201-1012
(704) 379-9000

Janney Montgomery Scott Inc.
1801 Market Street, 10th Floor
Philadelphia, Pennsylvania 19103
(215) 665-6000

Jeffries & Company, Inc.
11100 Santa Monica Boulevard, Suite 1100
Los Angeles, California 90025
(310) 445-1199

Edward D. Jones & Co.
201 Progress Parkway
St. Louis, Missouri 63043
(314) 851-2000

Keefe, Bruyette & Woods, Inc.
Two World Trade Center, Suite 8566
New York, New York 10048
(212) 323-8300

Kemper Clearing Corporation
111 East Kilbourn Avenue
Milwaukee, Wisconsin 53202
(414) 225-4100

Kemper Financial Services, Inc.
120 South LaSalle Street
Chicago, Illinois 60603
(312) 781-1121

Kemper Securities, Inc.
77 West Wacker Drive
Chicago, Illinois 60601
(312) 574-6000

Kidder Peabody & Co. Incorporated
10 Hanover Square
New York, New York 10005
(212) 510-3000

Lazard Freres & Co.
1 Rockefeller Plaza
New York, New York 10020
(212) 632-6000

Legg Mason, Inc.
Legg Mason Tower
111 South Calvert Street
Baltimore, Maryland 21202
(410) 539-0000

Lehman Brothers Inc.
Three World Financial Center
New York, New York 10285
(212) 526-7000

Levesque Beaubien Geoffrion Inc.
1155 Metcalfe Street, 5th Floor
Montreal, Quebec H3B 4S9, Canada
(514) 879-2222

Mabon Securities Corp.
One Liberty Plaza
165 Broadway
New York, New York 10006
(212) 732-2820

Bernard L. Madoff Investment Securities
885 Third Avenue
New York, New York 10022
(212) 230-2424

McDonald & Company Securities, Inc.
800 Superior Avenue, Suite 2100
Cleveland, Ohio 44114-2603
(216) 443-2300

Merrill Lynch & Co., Inc.
250 Vesey Street
North Tower, World Financial Center
New York, New York 10281-1332
(212) 449-1000

Midland Walwyn Capital, Inc.
BCE Place, 181 Bay Street, Suite 400
Toronto, Ontario M5J 2V8, Canada
(416) 369-7400

Miller Tabak Hirsch & Co.
331 Madison Avenue
New York, New York 10017
(212) 370-0040

Montgomery Securities
600 Montgomery Street
San Francisco, California 94111
(415) 627-2000

Morgan Keegan, Inc.
Morgan Keegan Tower
Fifty Front Street
Memphis, Tennessee 38103
(901) 524-4100

J.P. Morgan Securities, Inc.
60 Wall Street
New York, New York 10260
(212) 483-2323

Morgan Stanley Group Inc.
1251 Avenue of the Americas
New York, New York 10020
(212) 703-4000

Nesbitt Thomson Inc.
Sun Life Tower, Sun Life Centre
150 King Street West, Suite 2200
Toronto, Ontario M5H 3W2, Canada
(416) 586-3600

Neuberger & Berman
605 Third Avenue
New York, New York 10158-3698
(212) 476-9000

The Nikko Securities Co. International, Inc.
200 Liberty Street
New York, New York 10281
(212) 416-5400

Nomura Securities International, Inc.
2 World Financial Center, Building B
New York, New York 10281-1198
(212) 667-9300

The John Nuveen Company
333 West Wacker Drive
Chicago, Illinois 60606
(312) 917-7700

NYLIFE Securities Inc.
51 Madison Avenue
New York, New York 10010
(212) 576-6356

Oppenheimer & Co., Inc.
Oppenheimer Tower
World Financial Center
New York, New York 10281
(212) 667-7000

Oppenheimer Fund Distributor, Inc.
Two World Trade Center, Suite 3400
New York, New York 10048-0203
(212) 323-0200

PaineWebber Group, Inc.
1285 Avenue of the Americas
New York, New York 10019
(212) 713-2000

Paribas Corporation
787 Seventh Avenue
New York, New York 10019
(212) 841-3000

Piper Jaffray Companies Inc.
Piper Jaffray Tower
222 South 9th Street
Minneapolis, Minnesota 55402
(612) 342-6000

Prudential Securities Incorporated
One Seaport Plaza
199 Water Street
New York, New York 10292
(212) 214-1000

The Quick & Reilly Group, Inc
230 South County Road
Palm Beach, Florida 33480
(407) 655-8000

Raymond James Financial, Inc.
880 Carillon Parkway
St. Petersburg, Florida 33716
(813) 573-3800 or (813) 578-3800

Republic New York Securities Corp.
425 Fifth Avenue, 12th Floor
New York, New York 10018
(212) 525-6600 (800) 487-2346

Robertson, Stephens & Company, L.P.
555 California Street, Suite 2600
San Francisco, California 94104
(415) 781-9700

The Robinson-Humphrey Company, Inc.
Atlanta Financial Center
3333 Peachtree Road, N.E.
Atlanta, Georgia 30326
(404) 266-6000

Salomon Inc.
Seven World Trade Center
New York, New York 10048
(212) 783-7000

SBCI Swiss Bank Corporation Investment Banking, Inc.
222 Broadway, 4th Floor
New York, New York 10038
(212) 335-1000

M.A. Schapiro & Co., Inc.
One Chase Manhattan Plaza
New York, New York 10005
(212) 530-7500

Serfin Securities, Inc.
399 Park Avenue, 37th Floor
New York, New York 10022
(212) 750-4200

D.E. Shaw & Co., L.P.
39th Floor Tower 45
120 West Forty-Fifth Street
New York, New York 10036
(212) 478-0000

Smith Barney, Inc.
1345 Avenue of the Americas
New York, New York 10105
(212) 698-6000

Smith New Court
114 West 47th Street
New York, New York 10036
(212) 930-6000

Societe Generale Securities Corporation
50 Rockefeller Plaza, 2nd Floor
New York, New York 10020
(212) 957-3800

Southwest Securities Group, Inc.
1201 Elm Street, 43rd Floor
Dallas, Texas 75270
(214) 651-1800

Spear, Leeds & Kellogg
115 Broadway
New York, New York 10006
(212) 587-8800

Stephens Inc.
111 Center Street
Little Rock, Arkansas 72203
(501) 374-4361

Tucker Anthony Incorporated
One Beacon Street
Boston, Massachusetts 02108
(617) 725-2000

UBS Securities Inc.
299 Park Avenue
New York, New York 10171
(212) 821-4000

Van Kampen Merritt Inc.
One Parkview Plaza
Oakbrook Terrace, Illinois 60181
(708) 684-6000

S.G. Warburg & Co. Inc.
787 Seventh Avenue, 26th Floor
New York, New York 10019
(212) 459-7000

Wasserstein Perella Securities, Inc.
31 West 52nd Street
New York, New York 10019
(212) 969-2600

Weiss, Peck & Greer
One New York Plaza
New York, New York 10004
(212) 908-9500

Wertheim Schroder & Co. Incorporated
Equitable Center
787 Seventh Avenue
New York, New York 10019-6016

Wheat, First Securities, Inc.
901 East Byrd Street
Richmond, Virginia 23219
(804) 649-2311

Yamaichi International (America), Inc.
Two World Trade Center, Suite 9650
New York, New York 10048
(212) 912-6400

The Ziegler Companies, Inc.
215 North Main Street
West Bend, Wisconsin 53095
(414) 334-5521

Discount Brokerage Firms

Andrew Peck Associates
111 Pavonia Avenue
Jersey City, New Jersey 07310-1755
(201) 217-9500   (800) 221-5873

Arnold Securities
830 Second Avenue South
Minneapolis, Minnesota 55402
(612) 339-7040   (800) 292-4135
(800) 328-4076

K. Aufhauser
112 West 56th Street
New York, New York 10019
(212) 246-9431   (800) 368-3668

Baker & Co., Incorporated
Baker Building
1940 East Sixth Street
Cleveland, Ohio 44411
(216) 696-0167

Berlind Securities
One North Broadway
White Plains, New York 10601
(914) 761-6665   (800) 942-1962

Bidwell & Company
209 South West Oak Street
Portland, Oregon 97204
(503) 790-9000   (800) 547-6337

Billings Equities, Inc.
600 South Federal Street
Chicago, Illinois 60605
(312) 726-3981

Biltmore International Corporation
111 Broadway
New York, New York 10006
(212) 406-7087

UJB Investor Services
305 Route 17 South
Paramus, New Jersey 07652
(201) 262-8400   (800) 631-1635

Brokers Exchange
6923 North Trenholm Road, Suite 101
Columbia, South Carolina 29206
(803) 738-0204   (800) 845-0946
(800) 922-0960

William Lawrence Securities, Inc.
6800 Owensmouth, Suite 340
Canoga Park, California 91303
(818) 715-1777 (800) 970-1777

Brown & Company Securities Corporation
20 Winthrop Square
Boston, Massachusetts 02110
(617) 742-2600   (800) 225-6707

Bruno, Stolze & Company
12444 Powerscourt Drive, Suite 230
St. Louis, Missouri 63131
(314) 821-1990   (800) 899-6878

Bull & Bear
11 Hanover Square
New York, New York 10005
(212) 742-1300   (800) 262-5800

Burke, Christensen & Lewis Securities, Inc.
303 West Madison, Suite 400
Chicago, Illinois 60606
(312) 346-8283   (800) 621-0392

Calvert Securities Corporation
4550 Montgomery Avenue, Suite 1000N
Bethesda, Maryland 20814
(301) 951-4800

Comerica Securities
100 Renaissance Center, M/C 3137
Detroit, Michigan 48243
(313) 222-9458

Consolidated Financial Investments, Inc.
287 North Lindbergh, Suite 201
St. Louis, Missouri 63141
(314) 991-4030   (800) 292-6637

S.C. Costa Company
320 South Boston Avenue
Tulsa, Oklahoma 74103
(918) 582-0110

Cutter and Company Brokerage, Inc.
15510 Olive, Suite 204
Chesterfield, Missouri 63017
(314) 537-8770

Dabbah Securities Corp.
6 East 46th Street, Suite 300
New York, New York 10017
(212) 697-9870

Downstate Discount Brokerage
825 West Bay Drive
Largo, Florida 34640
(813) 586-3541

Empire Financial Group
1380 North Courtenay Parkway
P.O. Box 1233
Merritt Island, Florida 32954
(407) 453-7600

Fidelity Brokerage
82 Devonshire Street
Boston, Massachusetts 02109
(617) 570-7000   (800) 544-8666
(800) 544-5115

Financial West Group
600 Hampshire Road, Suite 200
Westlake Village, California 91361
(805) 497-9222

John Finn & Company, Inc.
205 Dixie Terminal Building
49 East Fourth Street
Cincinnati, Ohio 45202
(513) 579-0066

First Institutional Securities Corporation
470 Colfax Avenue
Clifton, New Jersey 07013-1675
(201) 778-9700   (800) 526-7486

Accutrade
4211 South 102nd Street
Omaha, Nebraska 68127-1031
(402) 346-5965   (800) 228-3011

First of America Securities, Inc.
157 South Kalamazoo Mall
Kalamazoo, Michigan 49003-4077
(616) 376-8442　(800) 643-6718

First Union Brokerage Services
1 First Union Tower
301 South College Street
Charlotte, North Carolina 28288-1167
(704) 374-6927　(800) 532-0367

R.J. Forbes Group
150 Broad Hollow Road
Melville, New York 11747
(516) 549-7000　(800) 488-0090

Freeman Welwood & Company
1501 Fourth Avenue
1700 Century Square Building
Seattle, Washington 98101
(206) 382-5353　(800) 729-7585

Green Line Investor Services, Inc.
Investor & Trust Service Division
Royal Trust Tower, 17th Floor
Toronto, Ontario M5K 1A2, Canada
(416) 982-6213

Securities Research
830 Azalea Lane
Vero Beach, Florida 32963
(305) 231-6689　(800) 327-3156

The Heitner Corporation
515 Olive Street, 11th Floor
St. Louis, Missouri 63101
(314) 421-4422

Hibernia Investment Securities, Inc.
313 Carondelet, 6th Floor
New Orleans, Louisiana 70130
(504) 533-5259

Icahn & Company
90 South Bedford Road
Mt. Kisco, New York 10549
(914) 242-4050　(800) 634-8518

Integra Brokerage Services Co.
300 Fourth Avenue
Pittsburgh, Pennsylvania 15278-3000
(412) 355-4800　(800) 282-1078

Investors National Corporation
Holly Plaza, 1300 North State Street
Bellingham, Washington 98225-4730
(206) 734-9900

Kashner Davidson Securities Corporation
77 South Palm Avenue
Sarasota, Florida 34236
(813) 951-2626　(800) 678-2626

Kennedy, Cabot & Co.
9470 Wilshire Boulevard
Beverly Hills, California 90212
(310) 550-0711

R.F. Lafferty
80 Broad Street
New York, New York 10004
(212) 269-6636　(800) 221-8514
(800) 522-5653

Lehigh Securities Corporation
1457 MacArthur Road
Whitehall, Pennsylvania 18052
(610) 437-5543

Marquette de Bary Company
488 Madison Avenue
New York, New York 10022
(212) 644-5300　(800) 221-3305

Marsh Block & Company
50 Broad Street
New York, New York 10004
(212) 514-6400　(800) 366-1200
(800) 366-1500

Max Ule
26 Broadway
New York, New York 10004
(212) 809-1160　(800) 223-6642

Mongerson & Company
135 LaSalle Street
Chicago, Illinois 60603
(312) 263-3100　(800) 621-2627
(800) 572-7714

Barry Murphy & Co., Inc.
77 Summer Street
Boston, Massachusetts 02110
(617) 426-1770

Nestlerode & Co., Inc.
430 West Irvan Avenue
State College, Pennsylvania 16804-0343
(814) 238-6249

Olde Discount Stockbrokers
751 Griswold Street
Detroit, Michigan 48226-3274
(313) 961-6666　(800) 521-1111

Pace Securities
110 Wall Street
New York, New York 10005
(212) 248-1818　(800) 221-1660

Pacific Brokerage Services
5757 Wilshire Boulevard, Suite 3
Los Angeles, California 90036
(213) 939-1100　(800) 421-8395

PCFN
One Pershing Plaza
Jersey City, New Jersey 07399
(800) 825-5723　(800) 825-5873

People's Securities, Inc.
815 Main Street
Bridgeport, Connecticut 06601
(203) 338-0800

Peremel & Co., Inc.
1829 Reisterstown Road, Suite 120
Baltimore, Maryland 21208
(410) 486-4700

Prestige Status Corporation
271-603 Grand Central Parkway
Floral Park, New York 11005
(718) 229-4500   (800) 262-8739

Quick & Reilly Inc.
26 Broadway
New York, New York 10004-1899
(212) 747-1200

Recom Securities
619 Marquette Avenue
Minneapolis, Minnesota 55402
(612) 339-5566   (800) 328-8600

Robert Thomas Securities
741 North Milwaukee Street
Milwaukee, Wisconsin 53202
(414) 273-2255   (800) 242-1523

Rodecker & Company
4000 Town Center
Southfield, Michigan 48075-1497
(810) 358-2282   (800) 676-1848

Royal Grimm & Davis
17 Battery Place
New York, New York 10004
(212) 709-9400   (800) 488-5195

Russo Securities
128 Sand Lane
Staten Island, New York 10305
(718) 448-4386

The Charles Schwab Corporation
101 Montgomery Street
San Francisco, California 94104
(415) 627-7000   (800) 442-5111
(800) 435-4000   (800) 648-5300

Scottsdale Securities
12855 Flushing Meadow
St. Louis, Missouri 63131
(314) 965-1555 (800) 888-1980

Seacoast Investor Services, Inc.
801 East Ocean Boulevard
Stuart, Florida 34994
(407) 286-7323

Seaport Securities
19 Rector Street
New York, New York 10006
(212) 482-8689   (800) 221-9894
(800) SEAPORT

Securities Research
936-A Beachland Boulevard
Vero Beach, Florida 32963
(407) 231-6689   (800) 327-3156

J.D. Seibert & Company
20 West Ninth Street
Cincinnati, Ohio 45202
(513) 241-8888   (800) 247-3396

Shearman Ralston
17 Battery Place, Suite 604
New York, New York 10004
(212) 248-1160   (800) 221-4242

Shochet Securities
1484 East Hallandale Beach Boulevard
Hallandale, Florida 33009
(305) 454-0304   (800) 327-1536
(800) 940-4567 (Florida Only)

Muriel Siebert & Company
885 Third Avenue, 17th Floor
New York, New York 10022
(212) 644-2400   (800) 872-0711

Smith, Jacobs & Co., Inc.
2 Rector Street, Suite 1505
New York, New York 10006
(212) 346-0804

St. Louis Discount Securities
200 South Hanley
Clayton, Missouri 63105
(314) 721-7400   (800) 726-7401

State Discount Brokers
27600 Chagrin Boulevard
Beachwood, Ohio 44122
(216) 765-8500   (800) 222-5520

Sterling Investment Services
135 LaSalle Street
Chicago, Illinois 60603
(312) 236-0676   (800) 782-1522

StockCross
One Washington Mall
Boston, Massachusetts 02108
(617) 367-5700   (800) 225-6196
(800) 392-6104 (Mass. Only)

The Stock Mart
12655 Beatrice Street
Los Angeles, California 90066
(310) 577-7460 (800) 421-6563

T. Rowe Price Investment Services, Inc.
100 East Pratt Street
Baltimore, Maryland 21202
(410) 547-2000

Texas Securities
4200 South Hulen
Fort Worth, Texas 76109
(817) 732-0130 (800) 395-8271

Tradex Brokerage Service
20 Vesey Street
New York, New York 10007
(212) 233-2000 (800) 522-3000

Unified Management Corporation
429 North Pennsylvania Street
Indianapolis, Indiana 46204
(317) 634-3300

Vanguard Discount Brokerage Services
P.O.Box 2600
Valley Forge, Pennsylvania 19482
(215) 669-1000

Voss & Company, Inc.
6225 Brandon Avenue
Springfield, Virginia 22150
(703) 569-9300   (800) 426-8106

Wall Street Discount Corporation
100 Wall Street
New York, New York 10005
(212) 747-5100   (800) 221-7990

Jack White & Company
9191 Town Centre Drive, Suite 220
San Diego, California 92122
(619) 587-2000   (800) 233-3411

Thomas F. White & Company
One Second Street, 5th Floor
San Francisco, California 94105
(415) 597-6800 (800) 669-4483

Whitehall Securities
1021 Avenue of the Americas
New York, New York 10018
(212) 719-5522   (800) 223-5023

Wisconsin Discount Securities Corporation
7161 North Port Washington Road
Milwaukee, Wisconsin 53217
(414) 352-5050   (800) 537-0239

Waterhouse Securities, Inc.
100 Wall Street
New York, New York 10005
(212) 806-3500

York Securities
160 Broadway
New York, New York 10038
(212) 349-9700 (800) 221-3154

Young, Stovall & Company
9627 South Dixie Highway
Miami, Florida 33156
(305) 666-2511 (800) 433-5132

Your Discount Broker, Inc.
855 South Federal Highway, Suite 101
Boca Raton, Florida 33432-6130
(407) 367-9800

The Ziegler Companies, Inc.
215 North Main Street
West Bend, Wisconsin 53095
(414) 334-5521

LIMITED PARTNERSHIP SPONSORS

Investing in limited partnerships (LPs) is similar to participating in markets for other securities, such as stocks or mutual funds. LPs offer investors an easily accessible and uncomplicated way to become co-owners of a professionally managed pool of assets. As with investments in stocks or mutual funds, limited liability is a major benefit, since LP owners cannot lose any more money than the amount they invest. Limited partnerships are created by sponsors, firms that make the initial offering of units to investors and oversee the management of LP assets for the benefit of the limited partners. In return for providing management services, sponsors typically receive management fees and a form of incentive compensation such as a percentage of profits generated by the investments.

There are, however, several important differences between mutual funds and LPs. The first key difference is the type of assets. Mutual funds usually buy diversified portfolios in stocks of established companies. LPs typically acquire diversified portfolios of real estate, venture capital or mezzanine financing investments (that is, investments in companies that are usually not yet publicly traded), cable television franchises, equipment on lease, or producing oil and gas wells.

The second major difference is the treatment of income for tax purposes. Stocks are shares in corporations. Those corporations pay tax on income; then they distribute dividends, which are taxed again to the shareholder. This is called double taxation. LPs generally have no federal income tax liabilities; instead, they pass through income or losses to the LP investors. This means that LP income is taxed only once, a major advantage.

The third key difference is risk and reward potential. With some notable exceptions, such as LP portfolios of federally insured mortgages, LPs generally carry more risk as well as greater potential for reward than mutual funds. During the late 1970s, this risk–reward ratio worked in favor of many LP investors. However, during the 1980s, downturns in certain markets hurt LP investors seriously. Since mid-1993, LP investors have once again been ahead of mutual fund investors, as the LP secondary market has outperformed stocks and bonds during this most recent period. Because of the substantial risks associated with partnership investing, investors typically place no more than 10% of their assets into LPs.

The fourth major difference is liquidity. Mutual fund shares can generally be redeemed daily at net asset value. LPs, on the other hand, must be held until the sponsor liquidates the portfolio (usually 10 to 20 years), or they may be sold at a discount in the LP secondary market. This market, which creates liquidity and trading opportunities for the approximately 8 million investors who own LPs today, has only emerged as an active trading arena over the past decade. Increasingly, sponsors or their affiliated transfer agents cooperate with the LP secondary market by effecting transfers of ownership initiated through LP trading.

The LP New Issue Market

The new issue market for limited partnerships has risen and fallen over the past 20 years. From 1974 to 1986, the dollar amounts invested in LP initial public offerings exploded, peaking with an average of over $15 billion annually from 1984 to 1986. There were many reasons for the blossoming LP market: The energy crisis made oil and gas partnerships look appealing. Periods of double-digit inflation made the chance for leveraged appreciation in real estate property values look enticing. And the Tax Law Reform Act of 1981 gave LPs significant tax advantages, including benefits from depreciation, tax credits, depletion allowances, intangible drilling costs, and operating losses. Partnership sales soared, with over $120 billion bought during the 1980s.

Many who invested enthusiastically in the early 1980s would later be bitterly disappointed. LP investments entail substantial risk, and not all investors fully recognized the potential for loss if the markets should sour. Several events went against the LP investors in the second half of the 1980s. Before 1987, many limited partnership tax benefits could be applied without limit to taxable earnings from any source of income. The Tax Reform Act of 1986 restricted the applicability of tax deductions from limited partnerships. Also, the asset values of many LPs plummeted when the real estate cycle turned down as overbuilding created high vacancy rates and drove down rents. Declining oil and gas prices and a worldwide economic recession unfavorably impacted other LP sectors, such as energy or marine container leasing programs. Beyond poor performance, partnership woes also involved unfavorable publicity. News coverage of the partnership industry was dominated by tales of fraudulent sales practices and corrupt sponsors.

The hard times for the LP industry resulted in a shakeup of sponsors and brokers during the late 1980s and early 1990s. Bankruptcies and insolvencies removed many unsuccessful LP sponsors, while some of the most popular ones shifted to accessing capital markets by forming Real Estate Investment Trusts (REITs) rather than LPs, since the REIT format was less controversial. Other LP syndicators adapted to the new market landscape by offering no-load or low-load partnership vehicles to appeal to cost-conscious investors. The LP new issue market no longer has the mass appeal that it once did, especially as more and more investors have become aware of the discounted prices available in the LP secondary market.

The LP Secondary Market

As the numbers of limited partners vastly increased in the 1980s, the limited liquidity of the LP as an investment vehicle began to pose problems that were eventually addressed by the emergence of a secondary market. Eventually some LP owners needed or wished to sell. As with most securities, many investors seek to sell when they believe that their money can perform better elsewhere, perhaps repositioning assets to stocks or bonds. In some cases, limited partners lost patience with general partners who kept LPs active long after 7–10 years, the typical period subsequent to which most investors expected the LPs to liquidate. Estate liquidations and changes in investors' financial circumstances created additional demands for liquidity. However, prior to the development of an LP secondary market, investors who wished to exit were stuck.

In the early 1980s, entrepreneurs created the first secondary market for "used" units of interest in a few hundred of the most widely held LPs. The majority of trading occurred in public partnerships, for which public information and audited financial statements were most readily accessible. Not all LPs enjoyed trading activity, since buyers focused on those investments that were economically healthy, usually with positive cash flow and significant equity values. At first, most trading involved real estate LPs and later included venture capital, equipment leasing, oil and gas, cable TV, and tax credit partnerships. To date, over 1,200 LPs have changed hands in the secondary market.

LPs often traded at deep discounts to original issue prices or to various estimates of the LPs' net asset values. Sponsors, fearing erosion of the marketability of new issues, fostered a widely held, but very inaccurate, image that LP secondary buyers were vultures preying on distressed investors by paying prices that were too low. That stereotype stuck for years, even after the real estate market's downturn in the late 1980s caused LP prices to fall from their early to mid-1980s levels, causing the supposed vultures to lose considerable equity.

Birthed amidst a fading new issue market for LPs in the late 1980s, the LP secondary market came of age in the early 1990s. Partnership trading may occur from shortly after the inception of the LP to the day before its eventual reorganization or liquidation. Since the typical life cycle of a partnership can often be more than 15 or 20 years, the potential trading universe of LPs includes thousands of partnerships issued during the 1970s, 1980s, and 1990s. Industry sources indicate that trading volume in the secondary market probably increased at least 20% to 25% on average each year in the current decade. This rapid growth is made all the more impressive considering that so many LPs have been liquidated or converted to REITs.

The secondary market for LPs features many of the same attributes that have made the secondary market for stocks and bonds so popular. Whereas initial LP public offerings are generally blind pools, LP secondary offerings are usually fully specified. The LP secondary investor has access to audited financial reports, which detail the performance history of the portfolio in question. Additionally, by purchasing LP units in the secondary market, the investor may have a shorter waiting period remaining before the anticipated liquidation of the partnership. As with stocks, LPs typically sell in the secondary market for less than the breakup values of the underlying assets. Most LPs, in fact, are purchased at deep discounts to valuations provided by sponsors and/or independent sources.

In the early days of the LP secondary market, as stated previously, sponsors resisted requests for transfer, arguing that trade prices were too low. In more recent years, the community of sponsors has come to understand that the liquidity provided by the LP secondary market is important to many investors. Accordingly, a spirit of cooperation has grown, and the market functions far more efficiently. As this publication goes to press, cooperative efforts to create uniform transfer rules, forms, and procedures are ongoing.

On the following pages a list of sponsors appears, divided according to the eight main types of limited partnerships. These are, in order of importance in today's market, Venture Capital, Real Estate, Cable Television and Media, Tax Credit, Commodities and Financial Futures, Equipment Leasing, Oil and Gas, and Miscellaneous. Within each category, sponsors are listed in alphabetical order. In some cases, a partnership may have more than one sponsor, or a sponsor may be a wholly or partially owned subsidiary of other entities. When this occurs, the listing shows the name, address, and telephone number, which are most commonly used for reaching the Investor Relations Department for the sponsor's programs. If a sponsor has delegated investor relations responsibilities to a transfer agent or outside service bureau, the address and telephone number will be for that organization. Inclusion in this listing does not necessarily indicate that a secondary market exists for a sponsor's LPs.

This listing is courtesy of Chicago Partnership Board, Inc. (CPB), the central auction trading market for the limited partnership secondary market. CPB can be contacted at (800) 272-6273 or (312) 332-4100 or faxed at (312) 332-3171.

Venture Capital

General: Invests in publicly or privately held emerging growth companies by providing expansion capital in return for subordinated notes, warrants, and stock. Invests in friendly leveraged corporate acquisitions. Leveraged buyout programs invest primarily in subordinated debt and related equity securities issued in conjunction with the bridge or mezzanine financing of the leveraged acquisitions or recapitalizations.

Leverage: Most programs operate without borrowing since venture capital by its very nature is an alternative capital-funding source.

Types: Mezzanine Financing, Early-Stage Venture Capital, Late-Stage Venture Capital.

Potential Benefits: Capital appreciation due to equity in successful business ventures. Some programs may also seek high current income through purchase of non-investment-grade securities. The theory is that by providing early-stage financing to companies that are past the start-up phase, but not yet ready to go public, venture capitalists may profit from continued rapid growth of businesses that have already successfully found their market niches but need capital to expand.

Risk Factors: The amount and timing of cash distributions and future values of portfolio assets cannot be predicted, and thus loss of capital could result. Creating uncertainty for portfolio asset values are factors including, but not limited to, corporate bankruptcies, loan default, potentially adverse developments in the legislative and competitive environments in which diverse portfolio businesses operate, and the health of the national and worldwide economy. Non-investment-grade securities, also known as high-yield securities, carry risk factors greater than those for investment-grade securities, including, but not limited to, loss upon default by the issuer because such securities are sometimes unsecured and are often subordinated to other creditors of the issuer. Furthermore, non-investment-grade securities usually have high levels of indebtedness and are more sensitive to adverse economic conditions, such as a recession or increasing interest rates, than investment grade issuers. Of course, emerging growth companies are more likely to face financial difficulties than are more established firms.

Valuation Factors: Portfolio holdings are generally valued at market to the extent that market quotations are readily available, adjusted for such factors including, but not limited to, revenue sharing arrangements between the general partners and the limited partners. For securities without a readily ascertainable market value, fair value is determined on a periodic basis by the general partners and/or independent sources according to available market information and appropriate valuation methodologies.

Secondary Market: Most venture capital LPs are not listed on stock exchanges, but are traded in the LP secondary market. (See "The LP Secondary Market" earlier in this section.)

Alex. Brown & Sons, Inc.
135 E. Baltimore Street
Baltimore, MD 21202
(410) 727-1700

Ampersand Ventures
55 Williams Street, Suite 240
Wellesley, MA 02181
(617) 239-0700

Aurora Capital Partners
1800 Century Park E., Suite 1000
Los Angeles, CA 90067
(310) 551-0101

Austin Ventures, L.P.
114 W. 7th Street, Suite 1300
Austin, TX 78701
(512) 479-0055

AVI Management Partners
One First Street, Suite 12
Los Altos, CA 94022
(415) 949-9855

Bachow & Associates, Inc.
3 Bala Plaza East, Suite 502
Bala Cynwyd, PA 19004
(610) 660-4900

Bastion Capital Corp.
1999 Avenue of the Stars, Suite 2960
Los Angeles, CA 90067
(310) 788-5700

Battery Ventures
200 Portland Street
Boston, MA 02114
(617) 367-1011

BT Venture Partners
3710 One 1st Union Center
Charlotte, NC 28202
(800) 277-1367
(704) 333-1367

Centre Street Capital Partners, L.C.
Stephens Building
111 Centre Street, Suite 2110
Little Rock, AR 72201
(501) 377-3784

Charterhouse Group International, Inc.
535 Madison Avenue, 28th Floor
New York, NY 10022
(212) 421-3125

CID Equity Partners
1 American Square, Suite 2850
Box 82704
Indianapolis, IN 46282
(317) 269-2350

CIP Management, Inc.
201 Progress Parkway
Maryland Heights, MO 63043
(314) 851-2000

Citicorp Venture Capital, Ltd.
399 Park Avenue, 14th Floor
New York, NY 10043
(212) 559-1127

Domain Associates
One Palmer Square
Princeton, NJ 08542
(609) 683-5656

E. M. Warburg, Pincus & Co.
466 Lexington Avenue, Suite 3350
New York, NY 10017
(212) 878-0600

Edelson Technology Partners
Whitewald Center
300 Tice Boulevard
Woodcliff, NJ 07675
(201) 930-9898

Edison Venture Fund
997 Lenox Drive, #3
Lawrenceville, NJ 08648
(609) 896-1900

Equitable Capital Management Corp.
1285 Avenue of the Americas
New York, NY 10019
(800) 288-3694
(212) 236-4970

Equus
P.O. Box 130197
Houston, TX 72219
(800) 856-0901
(713) 529-0900

Freeman Spogli & Co.
11100 Santa Monica Blvd., Suite 1900
Los Angeles, CA 90025
(310) 444-1822

Gordon+Morris Group
620 Newport Center Drive, Suite 1400
Newport Beach, CA 92660
(714) 759-5585

Grotech Capital Group
9690 Deereco, Suite 800
Timonium, MD 21093
(410) 560-2000

Hambrecht & Quist Venture Partners
One Bush Street
San Francisco, CA 94101
(415) 986-5500

Hamilton Capital Management, Inc.
c/o Palmeri Fund Admin. Co.
16-00 Route 208 S.
Fair Lawn, NJ 07410
(800) 821-0905
(201) 796-0900

Hancock Venture Partners
1 Financial Center, 44th Floor
Boston, MA 02111
(617) 350-0305

Harbour Group, Ltd.
7710 Forsyth Road, Suite 600
Street Louis, MO 63105
(314) 727-5550

Hellman & Friedman
1 Maritime Plaza, 12th Floor
San Francisco, CA 94111
(415) 788-5111

Heritage Partners Inc.
30 Roseworth, Suite 300
Boston, MA 02110
(617) 439-0689

Hicks, Muse, Tate & Furst, Inc.
200 Crescent Court, Suite 1600
Dallas, TX 75201
(214) 740-7300

Institutional Venture Partners, L.P.
3000 Sand Hill Road #2, Suite #290
Menlo Park, CA 94025
(415) 854-0132

Insurance Partners Advisors, L.P.
One Chase Manhattan Plaza, 44th Floor
New York, NY 10005
(212) 898-8700

Intersouth Partners
P.O. Box 13546
Research Triangle Park
Durham, NC 27709
(919) 544-6473

Joseph Littlejohn & Levy Inc.
450 Lexington Avenue, Suite 3350
New York, NY 10017
(212) 286-8600

Jupiter Partners Inc.
30 Rockefeller Plaza, Suite 4525
New York, NY 10112
(212) 332-2800

Kelso & Co.
350 Park Avenue
New York, NY 10022
(212) 751-3939

Kitty Hawk Capital
2101 Rexford Road, Suite 203 E
Charlotte, NC 28211
(704) 362-3909

Kleiner Perkins Caufield & Byers
2750 Sand Hill Road
Menlo Park, CA 94025
(415) 233-2750

Levine Leichtman Capital Partners, Inc.
345 N. Maple Drive, Suite 304
Beverly Hills, CA 90210
(310) 275-5335

Liberty Partners
1177 Avenue of the Americas, 34th Floor
New York, NY 10036
(212) 354-7676

Lombard Investments, Inc.
600 Montgomery Street, 36th Floor
San Francisco, CA 94111
(415) 397-5900

McCown DeLeeuw & Co.
3000 Sand Hill Road #3, Suite 290
Menlo Park, CA 94025
(415) 854-6000

Medical Science Partners
500 W. Boylston
P.O. Box 481
Brookline, MA 01606
(508) 853-9032

Medical Venture Holdings, Inc.
c/o Palmeri Fund Admin. Co.
16-00 Route 208 S.
Fair Lawn, NJ 07410
(800) 821-0905
(210) 796-0900

ML Venture Capital, Inc.
c/o Palmeri Fund Admin. Co.
16-00 Route 208 S.
Fair Lawn, NJ 07410
(800) 921-0905
(201) 796-0900

Morgan Stanley Capital Partners
1251 Avenue of the Americas
New York, NY 10020
(212) 703-4000

New Enterprise Associates
1119 Street Paul Street
Baltimore, MD 21202
(410) 244-0115

North Bridge Venture Partners
404 Wymen Street, Suite 365
Waltham, MA 02154
(617) 290-0999

Olympic Venture Partners
2420 Carillon Point
Kirkland, WA 98033
(206) 889-9192

Onset Enterprise Associates
310 University Avenue, Suite 250
Palo Alto, CA 94301
(415) 327-5470

Patricof & Co. Ventures, Inc.
445 Park Avenue, 11th Floor
New York, NY 10022
(212) 753-6300

Rice Capital Corp.
5847 San Felipe, Suite 4350
Houston, TX 77057
(713) 783-7770

Robertson Stephens & Co.
555 California Street, Suite 2600
San Francisco, CA 94104
(415) 781-9700

Rosewood Capital Associates, L.P.
One Maritime Plaza, Suite 1330
San Francisco, CA 94111
(415) 362-1192

Shansby Group
250 Montgomery Street, Suite 1100
San Francisco, CA 94104
(415) 398-2500

Sigma Partners
2884 Sand Hill Road, Suite 121
Menlo Park, CA 94025
(415) 854-1300

Summit Partners
One Boston Place
Boston, MA 02108
(617) 742-5500

Technology Funding Inc.
2000 Alameda de las Pulgas, Suite 250
San Mateo, CA 94403
(800) 821-5323
(415) 345-2200

Texas Pacific Group, Inc.
210 Main Street, Suite 2420
Fort Worth, TX 76102
(817) 871-4000

Trust Company of the West
200 Park Avenue, Suite 2200
Los Angeles, CA 10166
(212) 297-4000

U.S. Venture Partners
2180 Sand Hill Road, Suite 300
Menlo Park, CA 94025
(415) 854-9080

Venture Investment Management Co.
1300 Mt. Kemble
Morristown, NJ 07962
(201) 425-0400

VS&A Fund Management Co.
350 Park Avenue, 20th Floor
New York, NY 10022
(212) 935-4990

W. R. Huff Asset Management
30 Schuyler Place
Morristown, NJ 07960
(201) 984-1233

Real Estate

General: Acquires and manages equity real estate properties and/or mortgage loans. Properties may include income-producing commercial, industrial, residential, retail, and/or mini-warehouse real estate properties, purchased with or without net leases. Mortgage loans may include federally insured, insured, partially insured, or uninsured, tax-exempt or non-tax-exempt, first or second mortgages, with or without equity participation features. Some programs may invest in undeveloped land and undertake rezoning activities with respect to some or all land parcels.

Leverage: Varies from all cash to highly leveraged. Some programs may purchase properties with borrowed funds, which may multiply investment return if properties appreciate, but this increases the risk that income shortfalls in down markets can result in foreclosures.

Types: Equity Real Estate, Mortgage Loans, Combination Mortgage/Equity, Undeveloped Land.

Potential Benefits: Income from cash distributions derived from property rentals and/or interest income, which may be substantially tax-deferred in the early years and thus not subject to current taxation. Potential for conversion of current income to long-term capital gains. Capital appreciation from the proceeds of the sales of property interests. Investments in raw land may realize capital appreciation upon the resale of land parcels.

Risk Factors: The amount and timing of cash distributions and the future values of real estate assets cannot be predicted, and thus loss of capital could result. Creating uncertainty for real estate asset values are factors including, but not limited to, fluctuations in occupancy rates, rent schedules, operating expenses, lessee default, general and local economic and social conditions, zoning rule changes, and a variety of other factors.

Valuation Factors: Assets are generally valued according to such factors including, but not limited to, the nature of the business, the real estate industry outlook, revenue-sharing arrangements between the general partners and the limited partners, net operating income and balance sheet analysis, and comparison of net operating income to that of similar properties recently sold.

Secondary Market: Most real estate LPs are not listed on stock exchanges but are traded in the LP secondary market. (See "The LP Secondary Market," earlier in this section.)

AEI Inc.
1300 Minnesota World Trade Center
30 E. 7th Street
St. Paul, MN 55101
(800) 328-3519
(612) 227-7333

Aetna/AREA Corporation
242 Trumbull Street
Hartford, CT 06156
(800) 223-3464
(203) 275-2178

Alert Centre, Inc.
5800 S. Quebec Street
Englewood, CO 80111
(303) 779-4826

ALZA Corporation
950 Page Mill Road
P.O. Box 10950
Palo Alto, CA 94303
(800) 233-5222
(415) 494-5300

America First Capital Associates
1004 Farnam Street, Suite 400
Omaha, NE 68102
(800) 283-2357
(402) 444-1630

American Equity Housing Corporation
P.O. Box 2000
Trevose, PA 19053
(215) 245-0700

American Retirement Villas Corp.
245 Fisher Avenue, Suite D-1
Costa Mesa, CA 92626
(800) 624-0236
(714) 751-7400

AMFAC/JMB Finance
900 N Michigan Avenue
Chicago, IL 60611
(800) 562-7355
(312) 915-1980

Amrecorp Realty, Inc.
Two Bent Tree Tower
16479 Dallas Parkway
Dallas, TX 75248
(214) 380-8000

Angeles Corporation
c/o Insignia Financial Group
P.O. Box 2347
Greenville, SC 29602
(800) 772-8772
(803) 239-1029

Armored Management, L.L.C.
3839 N. 3rd Street, Suite 108
Phoenix, AZ 85012
(602) 230-1655

ASB Enterprises, Inc.
1935 Camino Vida Roble
Carlsbad, CA 92008
(800) 654-7188
(619) 431-9100

Associated Planners Realty Corporation
5933 W. Century Blvd., 9th Floor
Los Angeles, CA 90045
(310) 670-0800

August Financial Partners
(See Trust Realty Advisors, Inc.)

Balcor Company
4849 Golf Road
Skokie, IL 60077
(800) 422-5267
(708) 677-2900

Banyan Mortgage
265 Franklin Street, 16th Floor
Boston, MA 02110
(617) 439-8119

Berry & Boyle Management
57 River Street
Wellesley, MA 02181
(617) 237-0544

Birtcher/Liquidity Properties
27611 La Paz Road
Laguna Niguel, CA 92656
(212) 505-4400

Boddie-Noell Properties, Inc.
3710 1 First Union Center
Charlotte, NC 28202
(704) 333-1367

Boettcher Affiliated Investors
828 - 17th Street, 4th Floor
Denver, CO 80202
(800) 525-3286
(303) 628-8365

Brandywine Managing Partners
P.O. Box 500
Chadds Ford Business Campus
Chadds Ford, PA 19317
(610) 459-8610

Brauvin Real Estate Funds
333 W. Wacker Drive, Suite 1020
Chicago, IL 60606
(800) 272-8846
(312) 443-0922

Brown Benchmark AGP, Inc.
225 E. Redwood Street
Baltimore, MD 21202
(410) 727-4083

Budget Storage Equities
125 N. Market, Suite 1531
Witchita, KS 67202
(800) 732-9317
(316) 263-5848

Capital Builders, Inc.
4700 Roseville Road, Suite 101
North Highlands, CA 95660
(800) 228-0927
(916) 331-8080

Capital Realty Investors
The C.R.I. Building
11200 Rockville Pike
Rockville, MD 20852
(301) 231-0384

Capital Senior Living, Inc.
1416 Dallas Parkway
Dallas, TX 75240
(800) 533-3908
(214) 308-8314

Cardinal Realty Services
6954 Americana Parkway
Reynoldsberg, OH 43068
(614) 759-1566

Centennial Group, Inc.
282 S. Anita Drive
Orange, CA 92668
(714) 634-9200

Chrisken Properties, Inc.
345 N. Canal Street #201
Chicago, IL 60606
(800) 433-8395
(312) 454-1626

CIGNA Financial Partners
900 Cottage Grove Road, S313
Hartford, CT 06152
(800) 255-5876
(203) 726-6831

Clover Financial Corporation
23 W. Park Avenue
Merchantville, NJ 08109
(609) 662-1116

CNL Realty Corporation
400 E. South Street, Suite 50
Orlando, FL 32801
(800) 522-3863
(407) 422-1574

Coachman Inns of America, Inc.
301 N.W. 63rd Street, Suite 500
Oklahoma City, OK 73116
(800) 421-1296
(405) 840-4667

Colonial Storage Centers Group
4381 Green Oaks Blvd. W., Suite 100
Arlington, TX 76016
(817) 561-0100

Common Goal Capital Group, Inc.
P.O. Box 11269
Baltimore, MD 21239
(800) 822-3863
(410) 828-4344

ConCap Equities, Inc.
5520 LBJ Freeway, Suite 430
Dallas, TX 75240
(214) 702-3200
(214) 702-0027

Concord Assets Group, Inc.
5200 Town Center Circle, 4th Floor
Boca Raton, FL 33486
(407) 394-9260

Continental Capital Realty
3773 Ellsworth Road E.
Ann Arbor, MI 48108
(313) 971-1866

Continental Wingate Company, Inc.
75 Central Street
Old Central Wharf
Boston, MA 02109
(617) 574-9000

Dain Corporation
60 S. 6th Street
Minneapolis, MN 55402
(800) 888-7810
(612) 371-7810

DBSI Housing, Inc.
1070 N. Curtis Road, Suite 270
Boise, ID 83706
(800) 678-9110
(208) 322-5858

De Anza Properties
9171 Wilshire Boulevard, Suite 600
Beverly Hills, CA 90210
(800) 321-9338
(310) 550-1111

Dean Witter Realty, Inc.
2 World Trade Center
New York, NY 10048
(800) 829-8585

Decade Companies
250 Patrick Blvd. #140
Brookfield, WI 53045
(414) 792-9200

Del Taco, Inc.
345 Baker Street
Costa Mesa, CA 92626
(714) 540-8914

Drexel Burnham Lambert Realty, Inc.
P.O. Box 2347
Greenville, SC 29602
(800) 772-8772
(803) 239-1029

DSI Properties, Inc.
3701 Long Beach Blvd.
Long Beach, CA 90807
(213) 242-2655
(310) 595-7711

Equitec Financial Group, Inc.
(see Hallwood Realty, L.P.)

Essex Partners, Inc.
100 Corporate Woods, Suite 300
Rochester, NY 14623
(716) 272-2300

First Capital Financial Corporation
2 North Riverside Plaza, Suite 2100
Chicago, IL 60606
(800) 447-7364
(312) 207-0020

First Jersey Securities, Inc.
50 Broadway, 14th Floor
New York, NY 10004
(212) 269-5500

Franchise Finance Corp of America
17207 N. Perimeter Drive
Scottsdale, AZ 85255
(800) 528-1179
(602) 264-9639

Franklin Properties, Inc.
777 Mariners Island Blvd.
San Mateo, CA 94403
(800) 632-2350
(602) 415-5824

Freeman Companies
One Shelter Place
P.O. Box 1089
Greenville, SC 29602
(800) 772-8772
(803) 239-1000

Gannon Group, Inc.
1129 Broad Street
Shrewsbury, NJ 07702
(908) 389-2600

Glenborough Realty Corp.
400 South El Camino Real, 11th Floor
San Mateo, CA 94402
(415) 343-9955

Griffin Companies
3800 W. 80th Street, Suite 750
Minneapolis, MN 55431
(800) 328-3788
(612) 896-3800

Hallwood Realty, L.P.
c/o Bank of Boston
150 Royall Street
Canton, MA 02121
(617) 575-3120

Hastings, Jr., George
4307 Central Pike
Hermitage, TN 37076
(800) 264-3456
(615) 889-0804

HCW Pension Real Estate, Inc.
14840 Landmark Drive, Suite 200
Dallas, TX 75240
(800) 772-8772
(214) 987-1872

I.R.E. Real Estate Funds
P.O. Box 5403
Fort Lauderdale, FL 33103
(305) 760-5200

Inland Real Estate Investment Corp.
2901 Butterfield Road
Oak Brook, IL 60521
(800) 828-8999
(708) 218-8000

Insignia Financial Group
One Insignia Financial Plaza
P.O. Box 2347
Greenville, SC 29602
(800) 772-8772
(803) 239-1000

Integrated Resources, Inc.
10 Union Square E.
New York, NY 10003
(800) 678-7899
(718) 921-8300

Jacques-Miller, Inc.
One Shelter Place
P.O. Box 1089
Greenville, SC 29602
(800) 772-8772
(803) 239-1029

JMB Realty Corporation
900 N. Michigan Avenue, 11th Floor
Chicago, IL 60611
(800) 562-7355
(312) 915-1987

John Hancock Financial Services
P.O. Box 111
Boston, MA 02117
(800) 722-5457
(617) 572-3872

Kemper Real Estate
120 S. Lasalle Street
Chicago, IL 60603
(800) 468-4881

Kerr Taylor, H.
8 Greenway Plaza, Suite 824
Houston, TX 77046
(713) 850-1400

Keystone Mortgage Company
11340 W. Olympic Blvd., Suite 300
Los Angeles, CA 90064
(800) 955-9591
(303) 969-6000

Koger Equity
3986 Blvd. Center Drive
Jacksonville, FL 32207
(904) 398-3403

KP Realty Advisors
Old Central Wharf
75 Central Street
Boston, MA 02109
(212) 510-4349

Krupp Corporation
470 Atlantic Avenue
Boston, MA 02210
(800) 343-0989
(617) 574-8341

Landmark Capital Corp.
4400 Harding Road, Suite 500
Nashville, TN 30205
(615) 292-1040

Landsing Equities Corporation
c/o Pacific Coast Capital
P.O. Box 130
Carbondale, CO 81623
(303) 963-8007

LCP Group/Lepercq Capital Partners
355 Lexington Avenue, 14th Floor
New York, NY 10017
(800) 525-8904
(212) 692-7200

Legg Mason Realty Capital
111 S. Calvert
Baltimore, MD 21202
(800) 368-2558
(410) 539-0000

Lehman Brothers
(See Smith Barney Shearson, Inc.)

Lexington Corporate Properties, Inc.
355 Lexington Avenue
New York, NY 10017
(212) 269-7260

Liberty Real Estate Corporation
1 Financial Center
Boston, MA 02211
(800) 526-2606
(617) 722-6060

Marion Bass Real Estate Group Inc.
4000 Park Road
Charlotte, NC 28209
(704) 523-9407

McNeil, Robert A., Corp.
P.O. Box 801826
Dallas, TX 75380
(800) 576-7907
(214) 448-5800

Meridian Point Properties
100 California Street, 2nd Floor
San Francisco, CA 94111
(415) 956-3041

Merrill Lynch & Co.
World Financial Center
North Tower, 25th Floor
New York, NY 10281
(800) 821-0905
(201) 796-0900

Metric Realty
1 California Street, Suite 1400
San Francisco, CA 94111
(800) 347-3407
(415) 678-2000

Metro Self-Storage Capital Corp.
13000 W. Route 176
Lake Bluff, IL 60044
(708) 295-8840

Multivest
12355 Sunrise Valley Drive, Suite 300
Reston, VA 22091
(800) 347-4647
(703) 716-2000

Murray Financial Corp.
5550 LBJ Freeway, Suite 675
Dallas, TX 75240
(800) 765-3863
(214) 991-9090

National Development & Investment, Inc.
9800 W. Blue Mound Road
Milwaukee, WI 53226
(414) 453-6764

National Property Investors, Inc.
7103 S. Revere Parkway
Englewood, CO 80112
(800) 433-4287
(404) 916-9050

New England Securities, Inc.
399 Boylston Street, 13th Floor
Boston, MA 02116
(800) 523-0505
(617) 578-1200

Nooney Company
7701 Forsyth Blvd.
St. Louis, MO 63015
(314) 863-7700

NPI/The Fox Group
7103 S. Revere Parkway
Englewood, CO 80112
(800) 433-4287
(404) 916-9050

NTS Securities, Inc.
10172 Linn Station Road
Louisville, KY 40223
(502) 426-4800

One Winthrop Properties
One International Place
Boston, MA 02110
(800) 333-4556
(617) 330-8600

Owens Financial Group, Inc.
P.O. Box 2308
Walnut Creek, CA 94595
(510) 935-3840

Oxford Development Corporation
P.O. Box 7090
Troy, MI 40007
(810) 253-8560

PaineWebber
265 Franklin Street, 16th Floor
Boston, MA 02110
(800) 225-1174
(617) 439-8118

Provo Group
P.O. Box 2137
Madison, WI 53701
(800) 547-7686
(608) 255-3388

Prudential-Bache Properties, Inc.
100 Gold Street
New York, NY 10292
(800) 535-2077
(212) 214-6868

Public Storage, Inc.
600 N. Grand Blvd., Suite 300
Glendale, CA 91203
(800) 421-2856
(818) 244-8080

Quest Rescue Partners
1355 Peachtree Street
Suite 1900
Atlanta, GA 30309
(800) 377-4301
(404) 607-1950

RAL Asset Management Group
20875 Crossroads Circle, Suite 800
Waukesha, WI 53186
(414) 798-0808

RAM Funding, Inc.
10 Union Square E.
New York, NY 10003
(800) 678-7899

Rancon Financial Corporation
27720 Jefferson Avenue
Temecula, CA 92590
(800) 877-3660
(909) 676-6664

Real Property Services Corp.
1935 Camino Vida Roble
Carlsbad, CA 92008
(800) 654-7188
(619) 431-9100

Realmark Properties
2350 North Forest Road, Suite 12-A
Getzville, NY 14068
(716) 636-9090

Realty Parking Company, Inc.
225 East Redwood Street, 4th Floor
Baltimore, MD 21202
(410) 727-4083

Richman Group, Inc.
2111 Wilson Blvd., Suite 700
Greenwich, CT 06831
(800) 288-3694
(203) 869-0900

SB Partners Real Estate Corporation
1290 Avenue of the Americas
New York, NY 10104
(212) 408-2900

SCA Realty, Inc.
218 North Charles Street, Suite 500
Baltimore, MD 21201
(800) 368-5948
(410) 962-0595

Shurgard Capital Group
1201 Third Avenue, #2200
Seattle, WA 98101
(800) 955-2235
(206) 624-8100

Smith Barney Shearson, Inc.
388 Greenwich Street
New York, NY 10013
(800) 421-6688
(212) 464-2465

Southmark Corporation
1601 LBJ Freeway
Dallas, TX 75234
(214) 241-8787

Spiekerman, Carl R.
3839 N. Third Street, Suite 108
Phoenix, AZ 85012
(602) 230-1656

Super 8 Motels, Inc.
7515 Terminal Street
Tumwater, WA 98501
(206) 943-8000

T. Rowe Price Associates
100 East Pratt Street
Baltimore, MD 21202
(800) 322-5869
(301) 625-6500

TMP Investments, Inc.
801 N. Parkcenter Drive, Suite 235
Santa Ana, CA 92705
(800) 888-2026
(714) 836-5503

Travelers Corp./Keystone Props. Inc.
99 High Street
Boston, MA 02110
(800) 343-3453
(617) 338-3430

Trust Realty Advisors, Inc.
2361 Campus Drive, Suite 201
Irvine, CA 92715
(415) 343-9955

Uniprop, Inc.
280 Daines Street
Birmingham, MI 48009
(313) 645-9261
(810) 645-9261

USA Real Estate Investment Trust
705 University Avenue
Sacramento, CA 95825
(800) 952-5749
(800) 952-5748

USF&G Realty Partners, Inc.
100 Light Street, 10th Floor
Baltimore, MD 21203
(410) 625-5500

VMS Realty Partners
8700 West Bryn Mawr
Chicago, IL 60631
(800) 992-9281
(312) 399-8700

W.P. Carey & Company, Inc.
620 Fifth Avenue
New York, NY 10020
(800) 972-2739
(212) 492-1100

Wells Capital, Inc.
3885 Holcomb Bridge Road
Norcross, GA 30092
(800) 448-1010
(404) 449-7800

Westin Realty Corp.
2001 Sixth Avenue, 11th Floor
Seattle, WA 98121
(800) 323-5888
(206) 443-5000

Windsor Corporation
120 W. Grande Avenue, Suite 206
Escondido, CA 92025
(800) 888-6665
(619) 746-2411

Womack Apartments, Inc.
5826 Mosteller Drive
Oklahoma City, OK 73112
(405) 843-1561

Cable Television and Media

General: Owns and manages cable television franchises and/or other media businesses.

Leverage: Some programs may purchase franchise properties with borrowed funds, which may multiply investment return if properties appreciate, but this increases the risk both of a loss of income and of a potential total loss of capital.

Types: Cable Television Systems, Radio and Television Stations, Diversified Media Businesses.

Potential Benefits: Aggressive growth of capital from appreciation in property values resulting from growth in subscribers for basic cable services and premium services such as pay-per-view. Also, potential to sell systems to phone companies or larger cable operators who may be seeking to build interactive media systems by piecing together contiguous cable franchises. Current income from cash distributions may be a secondary objective for some programs. Rapid technological advances in fiber optics and digital technology may lead to greater channel capacity and clearer, more reliable signals. These and other developments could allow cable systems of the future to deliver more sophisticated services such as video on demand, which would expand subscribers' viewing options.

Risk Factors: Future values of cable systems cannot be predicted, and thus loss of capital could result. Creating uncertainty for cable systems values are factors including, but not limited to, potentially adverse developments in the legislative, financial, and competitive environments in which cable companies operate, the health of the national economy, and potential technological advancements that require greater capital needs.

Valuation Factors: Assets are generally valued according to such factors including, but not limited to, current cash flow per subscriber, the size of the subscriber base, the potential for future growth in penetration of the market and revenues per subscriber, and revenue-sharing arrangements between the general partners and the limited partners.

Secondary Market: Most cable television LPs may be traded in the LP secondary market. (See "The LP Secondary Market," earlier in this section.)

Cablevision Systems Boston Corporation
28 Travis Street
Boston, MA 02134
(617) 787-6600

Cencom Properties Inc.
One Galleria Tower
13355 Noel Road, Suite 1650
Dallas, TX 75240
(214) 960-4860

Daniels & Associates
1600 Wynkoop Street, Suite 300
Denver, CO 80202
(800) 843-3293
(303) 893-8936

Enstar Communications Corporation
7103 S. Revere Parkway
Englewood, CO 80112
(800) 433-4287
(303) 969-3280

Falcon Holding Group, Inc.
7103 S. Revere Parkway
Englewood, CO 80112
(800) 433-4287
(310) 824-9990

Jones Intercable, Inc.
9697 E. Mineral Avenue
Englewood, CO 80112
(800) 572-6520
(303) 792-3111

Kagan Media Capital Inc.
126 Clock Tower Place
Carmel, CA 93923
(800) 284-1322
(408) 624-1536

Malrite Communications Group, Inc.
800 Skylight Office Tower
1600 W. Second Street
Cleveland, OH 44113
(216) 781-3010

Merrill Lynch & Co.
World Financial Center
North Tower, 25th Floor
New York, NY 10281
(800) 821-0905
(201) 796-0900

Northland Communications Corporation
1201 Third Avenue, Suite 3600
Seattle, WA 98101
(800) 448-0273
(206) 621-1351

Prime Cable
600 Congress Avenue, Suite 3000
Austin, TX 78701
(800) 245-8049
(512) 476-7888

RJ Telecommunications, Inc.
880 Carillon Parkway
St. Petersburg, FL 33716
(800) 438-8088
(813) 573-3800

Telecommunications Gr. & Inc. Fd., Inc.
2201 Wilson Blvd.
Arlington, VA 22201
(703) 247-2900

Tax Credit

General: Acquires and manages interests, often through joint ventures, in residential properties eligible for federal low-income housing or historical rehabilitation tax credits.

Leverage: Most tax credit programs purchase interests in properties with borrowed funds, which may multiply investment return if properties appreciate, but this increases the risk that income shortfalls in down markets can result in foreclosures.

Types: Low-Income Housing Tax Credits, Historical Rehabilitation Tax Credits.

Potential Benefits: Producing tax credit benefits that, according to current tax law, offset federal income tax obligations on a dollar for dollar basis. Another potential benefit may include the production of passive losses, which some investors may use to offset passive income. Limited partners are not assured of a return of capital upon the eventual liquidation of the investment portfolio; however, there is a possibility that properties may appreciate. Rules governing tax credits are complicated, and not all taxpayers can utilize tax credits.

Risk Factors: Risk factors include, but are not limited to, total loss of capital upon the eventual liquidation of the investment portfolio. Furthermore, tax credits may be recaptured if the portfolio's properties fail to achieve continued compliance with federal requirements for the entire 15-year holding period.

Valuation Factors: Assets are generally valued according to such factors including, but not limited to, the amount and probability for future realization of tax credits, the underlying value of the real estate, and the revenue-sharing arrangements between the general partners and the limited partners.

Secondary Market: Tax credit LPs are not listed on stock exchanges but may be traded in the LP secondary market. (See "The LP Secondary Market" earlier in this section.)

Arcand Company
16101 S.W. 72nd Avenue, Suite 200
Portland, OR 97224
(503) 598-9800

Atlantic Capital Corp.
44 School Street, Suite 410
Boston, MA 02108
(617) 227-9840

Boston Capital Partners, Inc.
313 Congress Street
Boston, MA 02210
(800) 955-2733
(617) 439-0072

Boston Equity Investments, Inc.
2 Faneuil Hall Marketplace
Boston, MA 02109
(617) 720-1766

Boston Financial Group
101 Arch Street, 16th Floor
Boston, MA 02110
(800) 829-9213
(617) 439-3911

Boston Historic Partners, Inc.
1 Liberty Square
Boston, MA 02109
(617) 422-5800

Century Pacific Capital Corporation
1925 Century Park E., Suite 1760
Los Angeles, CA 90067
(800) 262-8242
(310) 208-1888

East Coast Capital
240 Commercial Street, Suite 4B
Boston, MA 02109
(800) 345-3863
(617) 298-3007

First Financial Management Corp.
101 Federal Street
Boston, MA 02110
(617) 737-9200

Guilford Capital Corp.
2600 E. South Blvd.
Montgomery, AL 36116
(205) 288-3992

Housing Allies, Inc.
2330 Marinship Way, Suite 300
Sausalito, CA 94965
(415) 331-5500

Interstate Affordable Housing, Inc.
P.O. Box 696
Goldenrod, FL 32733
(407) 657-6704

MEDEM Development Corp.
10 Water Street
Henderson, NV 89015
(702) 565-5930

Megan/American Credit Partners
P.O. Box 11210
Glenville Station
Greenwich, CT 06831
(914) 273-4141

Murphey Fave Properties, Inc.
1191 Second Avenue, Suite 904
Seattle, WA 98101
(206) 461-4782

National Affordable Housing Trust
2335 N. Bank Drive
Columbus, OH 43220
(614) 451-9929

National Equity Fund, Inc.
547 N. Jackson Blvd., Suite 601
Chicago, IL 60661
(312) 360-0400

National Housing Partnership, Inc.
1225 Eye Street, N.W., Suite 601
Washington, DC 20005
(202) 326-8251

National Partnership Investment Corp.
9090 Wilshire Blvd., Suite 201
Beverly Hills, CA 90211
(800) 666-6274
(310) 278-2191

NHI Inc.
2335 N. Bank Drive
Columbus, OH 43220
(614) 451-9929

Paramount Financial Group, Inc.
112 Galway Drive N.
Granville, OH 43023
(614) 587-4150

Pinnacle Group
1901 S. Bascom Avenue, Suite 1580
Campbell, CA 95008
(408) 369-8244

Prudential-Bache Properties, Inc.
100 Gold Street
New York, NY 10292
(800) 535-2077
(212) 214-6868

Raymond James Financial, Inc.
880 Carillon Parkway
St. Petersburg, FL 33716
(800) 438-8088
(813) 573-3800

Related Capital Company
625 Madison Avenue
New York, NY 10022
(800) 831-4826
(212) 421-5333

Renwood Properties, Inc.
100 Corporate Place
Peabody, MA 01960
(508) 535-4346

Richman Group, Inc.
2111 Wilson Blvd., Suite 700
Greenwich, CT 06831
(800) 288-3694
(203) 869-0900

Sterling Capital
1615 Northern Blvd.
Manhasset, NY 11030
(800) 777-7995

Washington Advisory Group
1133 15th Street N.W., Suite 1200
Washington, DC 20005
(202) 319-8100

WNC & Associates, Inc.
3158 Redhill Avenue, Suite 120
Costa Mesa, CA 92626
(714) 662-5565

Commodities and Financial Futures

General: Buys and sells commodities futures contracts and options on futures contracts in various commodities markets. Some programs may also speculate on currency markets.

Leverage: Investments are generally on an all-cash basis.

Types: Commodities and Financial Futures.

Potential Benefits: Aggressive growth of capital from speculative commodities pools. Such markets are volatile and extremely risky, and it is difficult for individual investors to participate. However, through partnerships, individuals may pool resources with many other investors, thus achieving greater asset diversification and obtaining the expertise of professional asset managers.

Risk Factors: Risks include, but are not limited to, partial or total loss of capital due to price fluctuations driven by such variables as the economy, the weather, government regulations, and changing consumer tastes, among others.

Valuation Factors: Assets are generally valued at market value.

Secondary Market: Limited partners are allowed to redeem units of the partnership at specified intervals, usually monthly. Because of the ease of unit redemption, little or no secondary market has historically developed.

Alex Farmers Commodity Corp.
2829 Westown Parkway, Suite 200
West Des Moines, IA 50266
(515) 223-3788

ATA Research Inc.
5910 N. Central Expressway, Suite 1520
Dallas, TX 75206
(214) 891-6200

Campbell & Co., Inc.
210 W. Pennsylvania Avenue, Suite 770
Baltimore, MD 21204
(410) 296-3301

CIS Investments, Inc.
Sears Tower
233 S. Wacker Drive
Chicago, IL 60606
(312) 460-4000

Crescent Futures Corp.
889 Ridge Lake Blvd., 2nd Floor
Memphis, TN 38120
(901) 761-9150

Demeter Management Corp.
Two World Trade Center, 62nd Floor
New York, NY 10048
(212) 392-8837

Everest Futures Management, Inc.
508 N. Second Street, Suite 302
Fairfield, IA 52556
(515) 472-5500

Heinold Asset Management, Inc.
440 S. LaSalle Street, 20th Floor
Chicago, IL 60606
(800) 621-0266
(312) 663-7500

IDS Futures Corp.
c/o American Express Financial Services
Unit 580
P.O. Box 534
Minneapolis, MN 55440
(612) 671-1848

International Futures Fund Partners
208 S. LaSalle Street, Suite 200
Chicago, IL 60604
(312) 855-7720

Lind-Waldock Financial Partners, Inc.
1030 W. Van Buren Street, 7th Floor
Chicago, IL 60607
(312) 413-6000

ML Futures Investment Partners Inc.
World Financial Center
South Tower, 6th Floor
New York, NY 10080
(800) 635-2027
(212) 236-4161

Paine Webber Futures Mgmt. Corp.
1200 Harbor Blvd., 3rd Floor
Weehawken, NJ 07087
(201) 902-6296

ProFutures, Inc.
1310 Highway 620 S., Suite 208
Austin, TX 78734
(800) 348-3601
(512) 263-3800

Prudential Securities Futures Management
1 New York Plaza, 13th Floor
New York, NY 10292
(212) 778-1000

Rockwell Future Management, Inc.
Bergen Park Business Plaza
1202 Highway 74, Suite 212
Evergreen, CO 80439
(303) 674-1328

Rodman & Renshaw Futures Mgmt., Inc.
120 S. LaSalle Street
Chicago, IL 60603
(312) 977-7800

Smith Barney Shearson Futures Management
388 Greenwich Street, 25th Floor
New York, NY 10013
(212) 723-5416

Equipment Leasing

General: Acquires and leases or rents equipment to end users, which are usually large corporations. Equipment may include aircraft, computers and peripherals, low-technology business equipment, marine cargo containers, marine vessels, mobile offshore drilling units, railcars, and other assets.

Leverage: Most publicly registered equipment LPs purchase on an all-cash basis. Some programs may purchase equipment with borrowed funds, which may multiply investment return if lease income and residual value significantly exceeds debt service, but this increases the risk that reduced rental rates and/or defaulting lessors may cause loss of capital.

Types: Aircraft Leasing, Diversified Equipment Leasing, High-Technology Equipment Leasing, Land/Sea Storage Container Leasing, Transportation Equipment Leasing.

Potential Benefits: High current income from cash distributions, which may be substantially tax deferred in the early years and thus not subject to current taxation. Some equipment assets (such as land/sea containers) may also hedge against inflation over time if the equipment is of a type which is long-lived, slow to obsolescence, and typically results in a high residual value. Most equipment, however, especially computers, loses value rapidly so lease income must be great enough to cover the initial cost of the equipment plus a good overall return in order for investors to realize satisfactory yields.

Risk Factors: The amount and timing of cash distributions and the future values of equipment assets cannot be predicted. Creating uncertainty for equipment asset values are factors including, but not limited to, lessee default, potentially adverse developments in the legislative and competitive environments in which leasing businesses operate, and the health of the national and worldwide economy. Any or all these factors could result in a loss of capital.

Valuation Factors: Assets are generally valued according to such factors as estimates of equipment residual value, operational cash flow, and various assumptions concerning factors impacting future cash flows such as the age and useful life of the equipment and revenue-sharing arrangements between the general partners and the limited partners.

Secondary Market: Most equipment-leasing LPs may be traded in the LP secondary market. (See "The LP Secondary Market" earlier in this section.)

Airfund International
53 Exchange Place, 14th Floor
Boston, MA 02109
(800) 955-0189
(617) 542-1200

Airlease Management Services, Inc.
733 Flint Street
San Francisco, CA 94111
(415) 627-9289

ALI Equipment Management Corp.
10 Union Square E.
New York, NY 10003
(800) 678-7899
(212) 353-7000

American Finance Group
Exchange Place
53 State Street
Boston, MA 02109
(800) 955-0189
(617) 542-1200

ATEL Financial Corporation
235 Pine Street, 6th Floor
San Francisco, CA 94104
(800) 543-2835
(415) 989-8800

Berthel Fisher & Co. Leasing, Inc.
100 2nd Street S.E.
Cedar Rapids, IA 52401
(319) 365-2506

CAI Partners Management
7175 W. Jefferson Avenue, Suite 3000
Lakewood, CO 80235
(800) 843-4552
(303) 442-0100

Chrysler Capital Fund Management Co.
225 High Ridge Road
Stamford, CT 06905
(800) 326-3326
(203) 975-3200

CMA Capital Group
433 California Street, Suite 910
San Francisco, CA 94104
(415) 696-3900

Cronos Capital
444 Market Street, 15th Floor
San Francisco, CA 94111
(800) 821-7035
(415) 677-8990

CSA Financial Corp.
22 Batterymarch, 6th Floor
Boston, MA 02109
(617) 357-1700

Equitec Financial Group, Inc.
(See Hallwood Realty, L.P.)

Fidelity Leasing Corporation
250 King of Prussia Road
Randor, PA 19087
(800) 862-8305
(215) 964-7102

Gemini Equities, Inc.
1301 W. Newport Center Drive
Deerfield Beach, FL 33442
(305) 360-7705

ICON Capital Corporation
600 Mamaroneck Avenue
Harrison, NY 10528
(800) 343-3736
(914) 698-0600

Lease Resolution Corporation
1300 E. Woodfield Road, #140
Schaumburg, IL 60173
(708) 240-6200

Leastec Corporation
2855 Mitchell Drive
Suite 215
Walnut Creek, CA 94598
(510) 938-3443

Meridian Leasing
225 E. Redwood Street
Baltimore, MD 21202
(410) 727-4083

Mobile Storage Group, Inc.
P.O. Box 12058
La Crescenta, CA 91224
(818) 249-0291

Pegasus Capital Corporation
c/o Service Data Corp.
2424 S. 130th Circle
Omaha, NE 68144
(800) 234-7342
(415) 434-3900

Phoenix Leasing Inc.
2401 Kerner Blvd.
San Rafael, CA 94901
(800) 227-2626
(415) 485-4500

PLM Financial Services, Inc.
One Market Plaza
Stuart Street Tower, Suite 900
San Francisco, CA 94105
(800) 227-0830
(415) 974-1399

Polaris Aircraft Leasing Corp.
Four Embarcadero Center, Suite 3900
San Francisco, CA 94111
(800) 652-1285
(415) 362-1643

RJ Leasing, Inc.
880 Carillon Parkway
St. Petersburg, FL 33716
(800) 438-8088
(813) 573-3800

Smith Barney Shearson, Inc.
388 Greenwich Street
New York, NY 10013
(800) 421-6688
(212) 464-2465

Textainer Capital Corporation
650 California Street, 16th Floor
San Francisco, CA 94108
(800) 356-1739
(415) 434-0551

TLP Leasing Programs
One Financial Center, 21st Floor
Boston, MA 02111
(800) 621-2115

Waddell & Reed Leasing, Inc.
P.O. Box 29217
Shawnee Mission, KS 66201
(913) 236-1968

Zahren Financial Corp.
40 Tower Lane
Avon, CT 06601
(203) 678-7537

Oil and Gas

General: Acquires, drills, explores, develops, and/or produces income from oil and gas wells.

Leverage: Most programs operate on an all-cash basis. Some programs may purchase properties with borrowed funds, which may multiply investment return if oil and gas prices rise or if additional energy reserves are discovered, but this increases the risk that adverse market conditions or dry holes may result in loss of capital.

Types: Producing Properties, Exploration/Drilling.

Potential Benefits: Investments in producing properties may result in income from operational cash flow derived from the sale of oil and gas production. Some portion of the cash flow may be substantially tax preferred, through deductions for available depletion and depreciation. Price increases in oil and gas could result in appreciation of the value of crude oil and natural gas reserves. Enhancements from the application of enhanced recovery techniques can potentially lengthen the life of the wells, improve production rates, and increase the volume of available reserves. Exploratory drilling for new, as yet undiscovered reservoirs of oil and gas is extremely risky and is the most potentially rewarding activity. Dry holes in exploratory drilling result in total loss of capital, while gushers provide large potential returns.

Risk Factors: The amount and timing of cash distributions and future prices for oil and gas cannot be predicted, and thus loss of capital could result. Creating uncertainty for values of the oil and gas assets are factors including, but not limited to, volatile pricing, uncertainty of reserve estimates, and potentially adverse developments in the legislative, competitive, and economic environments in which energy businesses operate.

Valuation Factors: Assets are generally valued based upon a present value of estimated future cash flows approximated according to such factors including, but not limited to, proven reserves, estimated reserves, the rate of depletion, current and projected market prices for oil and gas, and revenue-sharing arrangements between the general partners and the limited partners. Oil wells are considered depleting assets, thus residual values generally decline over time (assuming oil and gas prices do not change).

Secondary Market: Most oil and gas LPs are not listed on stock exchanges but may be traded in the LP secondary market. (See "The LP Secondary Market" earlier in this section.)

American Exploration Production Co.
1331 Lamar Street, Suite 900
Houston, TX 77010
(713) 756-6000

Apache Corporation
One Post Oak Central
2000 Post Oak Blvd., Suite 100
Houston, TX 77056
(800) 272-2434
(713) 296-6000

Atlas Resources, Inc.
311 Rouser Road
Coraopolis, PA 15108
(412) 262-2830

Buttes Energy Company
P.O. Box 849
Ardmore, OK 73402
(405) 226-6700

Clinton Oil Co.
4770 Indianaola Avenue
Columbus, OH 43214
(614) 888-9588

Coastal Corporation
Coastal Tower
Nine Greenway Plaza
Houston, TX 77046
(713) 877-0995

Conquest Oil Co.
1610 29th Avenue
Greeley, CO 80631
(303) 356-5560

Dover-Atwood Corp.
237 W. 2nd Street
Dover, OH 44622
(216) 364-4550

Dyco Petroleum Corporation
Two W. Second Street
Tulsa, OK 74103
(800) 283-1791
(918) 583-1791

EDP Operating, Ltd.
4582 S. Ulster Street Parkway, Suite 1700
Denver, CO 80237
(303) 850-7373

Enex Resources Corporation
Three Kingwood Place, Suite 200
Kingwood, TX 77339
(800) 231-0444
(713) 358-8401

Everflow Management Company
132 S. Broad Street
P.O. Box 354
Canfield, OH 44406
(216) 533-2692

Geodyne
(See Samson Companies)

Mewbourne Development Corp.
3901 S. Broadway
Tyler, TX 75701
(800) 541-1674
(903) 561-2900

North Coast Energy, Inc.
5311 Northfield Road, Suite 320
Bedford Heights, OH 44146
(800) 645-6427
(216) 663-1668

NYLIFE Equity Inc.
51 Madison Avenue, Room 1700
New York, NY 10010
(800) 824-4636
(212) 576-7000

Parker & Parsley Development Corp.
303 W. Wall, Suite 101
Midland, TX 79701
(800) 831-3332
(915) 683-4768

Petroleum Development Corp.
P.O. Box 26
Bridgeport, WV 26330
(800) 624-3821
(304) 842-3597

Prudential-Bache Properties, Inc.
100 Gold Street
New York, NY 10292
(800) 535-2077
(212) 214-6868

Red Eagle Exploration Co.
1601 Northwest Expressway, 17th Floor
Oklahoma City, OK 73156
(800) 654-9274
(405) 843-8066

Samson Companies
Two West Second Street
Tulsa, OK 74101
(800) 283-1791
(918) 583-1791

Sensor Oil & Gas, Inc.
Enterprise Plaza, Suite 200
5600 North May Avenue
Oklahoma City, OK 73112
(405) 840-7080

Southwest Royalties, Inc.
North Big Spring
Midland, TX 79701
(915) 686-9927

Swift Energy Company
16825 Northchase Drive, Suite 400
Houston, TX 77060
(800) 777-2750
(713) 874-2700

Vineyard Oil & Gas Co.
10299 West Main Road
P.O. Box 391
North East, PA 16428
(814) 725-8742

Wells Development Co., Inc.
8325 Ohio River Blvd.
Pittsburgh, PA 15202
(412) 734-7494

Williams-Cody Inc.
16825 Northchase, Suite 1200
Houston, TX 77060
(713) 874-0700

Miscellaneous

General: Owns, manages, and seeks to profit from any of many various business enterprises.

Leverage: Varies.

Types: Agriculture, Motion Picture Financing, Rare Art/Coins, Research and Development, Savings and Loans, Other.

Potential Benefits: Agriculture partnerships may invest in farmland, fruit orchards, timberland, or other properties or livestock that could provide income, appreciation, and/or tax benefits for limited partners. Motion Picture Financing partnerships may earn income, appreciation, and/or tax benefits through the production, marketing, and distribution of motion pictures and other media properties for national or worldwide release. Rare Art/Coins partnerships seek appreciation and tax benefits for limited partners deriving from the acquisition and eventual sale of rare objects of art, historical artifacts, and/or coins. Research and Development programs seek primarily capital appreciation through direct research and development into high technology, biotechnology, or other medical technologies and/or investments in publicly or privately held companies. Savings and Loans partnerships invest in, operate, and develop thrift institutions to potentially provide income, appreciation, and/or tax benefits for limited partners.

Risk Factors: The amount and timing of cash distributions and the future values of assets cannot be predicted, and thus could result in total loss of capital. The values of the underlying assets may fluctuate according to many factors including, but not limited to, changes in the market outlook, project failures, potentially adverse developments in the legislative and competitive environments in which businesses operate, and the health of the national and worldwide economy.

Valuation Factors: Variable.

Secondary Market: Most LPs are not listed on stock exchanges but are traded in a secondary market where trade prices generally reflect a discount to estimated net asset values. (See "The LP Secondary Market" earlier in this section.)

Atrix Laboratories, Inc.
2579 Midpoint Drive
Ft. Collins, CO 80525
(303) 482-5868

Delphi Partners
666 Third Avenue, 12th Floor
New York, NY 10017
(212) 983-9040

EH Thrift Management Inc.
225 West Washington Street, Suite 2200
Chicago, IL 60606
(312) 332-6700

InterCap Monitoring Corporation
c/o Securities Data Group
12835 E. Arapahoe Road, Tower 2, Suite 400
Englewood, CO 80112
(800) 826-2696
(303) 643-6000

Magera Management Corp.
666 Third Avenue, 12th Floor
New York, NY 10017
(212) 983-9040

Merrill Lynch & Co.
World Financial Center
South Tower, 4th Floor
New York, NY 10080
(800) 635-2027
(212) 908-8681

Millenium Genetics, Inc.
W. Highway 26
Broadwater, NE 69125
(308) 489-5411

PaineWebber Technologies, L.P.
1285 Avenue of the Americas
New York, NY 10019
(800) 852-6570
(212) 713-2000

Prudential Securities Group, Inc.
440 Mission Court, Suite 250
Fremont, CA 94539
(800) 535-2077
(212) 776-6233

Silver Screen Partners
936 Broadway, 5th Floor
New York, NY 10010
(212) 995-7600

Star Partners, Inc.
180 Park Avenue N., 2B
Winter Park, FL 32789
(800) 421-7827
(407) 644-5595

Vintech Almond Advisers, Inc.
340 Tesconi Circle, Suite C
Santa Rosa, CA 95401
(800) 622-2050
(707) 579-3742

ACCOUNTING FIRMS

The following is a list of the names, addresses and telephone numbers of the headquarters of the 25 largest U.S. certified public accounting firms, based on revenue generated in 1993. These firms are organized as partnerships of the certified public accountants who work in them. CPAs, who must pass examinations to earn their licenses, mainly do corporate accounting and auditing and prepare tax returns. The Big Six firms at the top are: Arthur Andersen & Co.; KMPG Peat Marwick; Ernst & Young; Coopers & Lybrand; Deloitte & Touche; and Price Waterhouse. Most major corporations deal with one of these six companies, and their revenues are far larger than other accounting firms. For instance, in 1993, Arthur Andersen & Co, and KMPG Peat Marwick, the two largest firms had annual worldwide revenues of $6.02 billion and $6 billion respectively, and Price Waterhouse, the sixth member of the Big Six had $3.9 billion in revenue. Beyond the Big Six, revenue per firm dropped dramatically. The seventh largest firm, Grant Thornton, had revenues of $224 million and the 25th ranked firm, Campos & Stratis, had revenues of $21 million.

Accounting firms have also been branching out beyond their traditional functions of auditing and accounting and into other business services, particularly management consulting. A number of these firms now offer specialized advice for clients in such industries as financial services, health care and telecommunications.

This list is provided courtesy of *Accounting Today,* (11 Pennsylvania Plaza, New York, New York 10001, (212) 967-7000) and the American Institute of Certified Public Accountants.

Altschuler, Melvoin and Glasser
30 South Wacker Drive, Suite 2600
Chicago, Illinois 60606-7405
(312) 207-2837

Arthur Andersen & Co.
69 West Washington Street
Chicago, Illinois 60602-3094
(312) 580-0069

Baird, Kurtz & Dobson
901 East St. Louis Street, Suite 1000
Springfield, Missouri 65806-2537
(417) 831-7283

BDO Seidman
330 Madison Avenue
New York, New York 10017
(212) 765-7500

Campos & Stratis
310 Cedar Lane
Teaneck, New Jersey 07666
(201) 692-0300

Checkers, Simon & Rosner
One South Wacker Drive, Suite 2400
Chicago Illinois 60606-3392
(312) 346-4242

Clifton, Gunderson & Company
301 Southwest Adams, Suite 800
Peoria, Illinois 61602-1551
(309) 671-4560

Coopers & Lybrand
1251 Avenue of the Americas
New York, New York 10020-1157
(212) 536-2000

Crowe, Chizek & Co
P.O. Box 7
South Bend, Indiana 46624-0007
(317) 632-8989

Deloitte & Touche
Ten Westport Road
Wilton, Connecticut 06897-0820
(203) 761-3135

Richard A. Eisner & Co.
575 Madison Avenue
New York, New York 10022-2597
(212) 891-4002

Ernst & Young
787 Seventh Avenue
New York, New York 10019-6018
(212) 773-3131

Friedman, Eisenstein, Raemer and Schwartz
401 North Michigan Avenue, Suite 2600
Chicago, Illinois 60611-4240
(312) 245-1999

Goldstein Golub Kessler & Co.
1185 Avenue of the Americas
New York, New York 10036-2602
(212) 523-1234

Grant Thornton
130 East Randolph Street
Chicago, Illinois 60601-6144
(312) 856-0001

IDS Financial Corporation
IDS Tower 10
Minneapolis, Minnesota 55440
(612) 671-3733

KMPG Peat Marwick
767 Fifth Avenue
New York, New York 10153-0194
(212) 909-5000

Larson, Allen, Weishair & Co.
220 South Sixth Street
Minneapolis, Minnesota 55402-4505
(612) 376-4800

Kenneth Leventhal & Co.
2049 Century Park East
Los Angeles, California 90067-3174
(310) 277-0880

McGladrey & Pullen
801 Nicollet Avenue
Minneapolis, Minnesota 55402-2501
(612) 332-4300

Moss Adams
1001 Fourth Avenue, Suite 2900
Seattle, Washington 98154-1106
(206) 223-1820

George S. Olive & Co.
201 North Illinois Street
Indianapolis, Indiana 46204-1904
(317) 238-4242

Plante & Moran
27400 Northwestern Highway
Southfield, Michigan 48034-4798
(313) 352-2500

Price Waterhouse
1251 Avenue of the Americas
New York, New York 10020-1180
(212) 819-5000

Wipfli Ullrich Bertelson
500 Third Street, Suite 319
Wausau, Wisconsin 54402
(715) 845-3111

SECURITIES AND FUTURES EXCHANGES
AROUND THE WORLD

The following is a list of the name and address of major securities and futures exchanges around the world. Telephone numbers are provided for American, Canadian and several other major exchanges. The list is arranged alphabetically by country.

The most active financial markets are those in the industrialized countries of North America, Western Europe and Japan. In these countries, there is more regulation of securities markets, and companies have to disclose more about their financial status; the regulation and disclosure requirements of U.S. exchanges are by far the strictest. The more active markets are more competitive and therefore are characterized by narrower spreads between bid and asked prices.

The stock markets of the less industrialized countries offer both greater rewards and greater risks to investors. Regulation of these markets tends to be looser and financial disclosure rules less stringent. With less trading activity, the spreads between bid and asked prices tend to be wide. In some cases, investment by non-nationals of the country is banned or strictly limited. Many of these markets provide rich opportunities to participate in some of the world's fastest growing economies, such as Taiwan and Singapore.

The shares of some prominent companies listed on these and other exchanges are also traded in the United States as American Depositary Receipts (ADRs). For investors who are interested in participating in these foreign markets, but do not have the time or expertise to do so directly, there are a number of mutual funds, both closed-end and open-end, specializing in buying securities in markets around the world.

Argentina

Bolsa de Comercio de Buenos Aires
Sarmiento 299
Buenos Aires 1353

Australia

Stock Exchange of Adelaide
55 Exchange Place
Adelaide, S.A. 5000

Brisbane Stock Exchange
Riverside Centre
123 Eagle Street
Brisbane, QLD 4000

Stock Exchange of Melbourne
351 Collins Street
Melbourne, Vic 3000

Stock Exchange of Perth
2, the Esplanade
Perth, WA 6000

Sydney Futures Exchange
Grouner Street
Sydney, NSW 2000
61 2 256 0555

Sydney Stock Exchange
20 Bond Street
Syndey, N.S.W. 2000
61 2 227 0000

Austria

Wiener Boersekammer
Wipplingerstrasse 34
A-1011 Vienna, 1
43 1 53 499

Belgium

Fondsen-En Wisselbeurs Van Antwerpen
Korte Klarenstraat 1
2600 Antwerp

Bourse de Bruxelles
Palais de la Bourse
1000 Bruxelles
32 2 509 1211

Fondsen-Ed Wisselbeurs Van Gent
Kouter, 29
9000 Gent

Bourse de Fonds Public de Liege
Rue Cathédrale, 85
4000 Liege

Brazil

Bolsa Brasileira de Futuros
Rua de Mereado
07 2nd Floor
Rio de Janiero 20010
55 21 224 6062

Bolsa de Mercadorias de Sao Paulo
Rua Libero Badaro 471, 4th Floor
Sao Paulo 01009
(5511) 32-3101

Bolsa de Valores do Rio de Janiero
Praca XV de Novembro 20
20010 Rio de Janiero RJ

Bolsa de Valores de Sao Paulo
Rue XV de Novembro, 275
01013 Sao Paulo SP

Bolsa Mercantil and de Futuros
Praca Antonio Prado, 48
Sao Paulo/SP 01010
(5511) 239-5511

Canada

Alberta Stock Exchange
300 5th Avenue, S.W.
Calgary, Alberta T2P 3C4
(403) 262-7791

Montreal Exchange
Tour de la Bourse
800 Victoria Square
Montreal, Quebec H4Z 1A9
(514) 871-2424

Toronto Futures Exchange
Toronto Stock Exchange
The Exchange Tower
2 First Canadian Place
Toronto, Ontario M5X 1J2
(416) 947-4700, (416) 947-4487

Vancouver Stock Exchange
Stock Exchange Tower
609 Granville Street
Vancouver, British Columbia V7Y 1H1
(604) 689-3334

Winnipeg Commodity Exchange
500 Commodity Exchange Tower
360 Main Street
Winnipeg, Manitoba R3C 3Z4
(204) 949-0495

Winnipeg Stock Exchange
2901-One Lombard Place
Winnipeg, Manitoba R3B 0Y2
(204) 942-8431

Chile

Bolsa de Comercio de Santiago
Calle Le Bolsa 64
Santiago

China

Shanghai Securities Exchange
15 Huang Pu Road
Shanghai 200080

China, Republic of (Taiwan)

Taiwan Stock Exchange
7-10th Floor, City Building
85 Yen-Ping South Road
Taipei

Colombia

Bolsa de Bogota
Carrera 8, 13-82 7th Floor
Bogota

Denmark

Kobenhavns Fondsbors
2 Nikolaj Plads
DK-1067 Copenhagen K
45 33 93 3366

Equador

Bolsa de Valores de Quito
Avenue Rio Amazonas 540 y
Carrion, Piso 8
Quito
593 2 526805

Egypt

Cairo Stock Exchange
4-A Sherifen Street
Cairo

Finland

Helsingin Arvopapereriporssi
Fabianinkatu 14
SF 00131 Helsinki

France

SBF-Paris Bourse
33 Rue Cambon
73002 Paris
33 1 49 27 10 00

Compagnie Des Commissionaires Agrees
(CCA)
Bourse de Commerce
2 Rue de Viarmes
Paris 75001
33 4508-8250

Lille Potato Futures Market
Centre Mercure
445 Boulevard Gambetta
59200 Tourcoing
33 2026-2213

Marche a Terme Des Instruments Financiers
(MATIF)
Conseil du Marche a Terme
108 Rue de Richileu
Paris 75002
331 4015-2001

Paris Commodity Exchange
Bourse de Commerce
2 Rue de Viarmes B.P. 53/01
75040 Paris

Germany
Berliner Borse
Fasanen Strasse 3
D-1000 Berlin 12

Rheinisch-Westfalische Borse zu Dusseldorf
Ernst-Schneider-Platz 1
D-4000 Dusseldorf 1

Deutsche Borse AG
Borsenplatz 6, Postfach 100811
D-6000 Frankfurt am Main 1
49 69 29977-0

Hanseatische Wertpapierborse Hamburg
Schauenbergerstrasse 47
2000 Hamburg 11

Bayerische Borse in Munchen
Lenbachplatz 2 a
D-8000 Munchen 2

Great Britain

Baltic Futures Exchange
24-28 St. Mary Axe
London EC3A 8EP
44 71 626 7985

Northern Ireland
Northern Bank House
10 High Street
Belfast BT1 1BP

International Petroleum Exchange of London
1 St. Katharine's Way
London E1 9UN
44 71 481 0643

International Stock Exchange
Old Broad Street
London EC2N 1HP
44 71 797 1000

London Commodity Exchange
Cereal House, 58 Mark Lane
London EC3R 7NE

London Futures and Options Exchange
(FOX)
1 Commodity Quay
St. Katherine Docks
London E1 9AX
44 71 481 2080

London International Financial
Futures Exchange (LIFFE)
Royal Exchange
London EC3V 3PJ
44 71 623 0444

London Metal Exchange (LME)
Plantation House
Fenchurch Street
London EC3M 3AP
44 71 626 3311

London Stock Exchange
Old Broad and Threadneedle Streets
London EC2N 1HP
44 71 797 1000

Midlands & Western Stock Exchange
Margaret Street
Birmingham B3 3J1

Northwest Stock Exchange
76 King Street West
Manchester M2 4NH

Scottish Stock Exchange
Stock Exchange House
7 Nelson Mandela Place
Glasgow G2 1BU
and
12 Dublin Street
Edinburgh EH1 3PP

Greece

Athens Stock Exchange
10 Sophocleous Street
Athens 10559

Hong Kong

Stock Exchange of Hong Kong Ltd.
Exchange Square
Hong Kong
852 5 22 11 22

India

Bombay Stock Exchange
Dalal Street Fort
Fort, Bombay 400 001

Calcutta Stock Exchange Association
7 Lyons Range
Calcutta 700

Delhi Stock Exchange Association
3 & 4/4B Asaf Ali Road
New Delhi 110002

Madras Stock Exchange
Stock Exchange Building
11 Second Line Beach
Madras 600 001

Indonesia

Stock Exchange of Indonesia
Jalan Merdeka Selaton 14
Jakarta-Kota

Ireland

Irish Stock Exchange
28 Anglesea Street
Dublin 2

Israel

Tel-Aviv Stock Exchange
54 Ahad Ha'am Street
Tel-Aviv

Italy

Borsa Valori di Bologna
Piazza della Costituzione, 8
40128 Bologna

Borsa Valori de Firenze (Florence)
Piazza Mentana, 2
50122 Firenze

Borsa Valori di Genova
Via G. Boccardo, 1
16121 Genova

Borsa Valori di Milano
Piazza degli Afferi, 6
20123 Milano
(39) 2 853 44636

Borsa Valori di Napoli
Via S. Aspreno, 2
80133 Napoli

Borsa Valori di Palermo
Via E. Amari, 11
90139 Palermo

Borsa Valori di Roma
Via de' Burro, 147
00186 Roma

Borsa Valori di Torino
Via S. Francesco da Paola, 28
10123 Torino

Borsa Valori de Trieste
Via Cassa di Risparmio, 2
34121 Trieste

Borsa Valori di Venezia
Via XXII Marzo, 2034
30124 Venezia

Jamaica

Jamaica Stock Exchange
Bank of Jamaica Tower
P.O. Box 621
Nethersole Place, Kingston

Japan

Fukuoka Stock Exchange
2-14-2 Tenjin, Chuo-ku
Fukoaka 810

Hiroshima Stock Exchange
14-18 Karayama-cho
Hiroshima 730

Hokkaido Grain Exchange
3 Odori Nishi 5-chome
Chuo-ku
Sapporo, Hokkaido 060

Kanmon Commodity Exchange
1-5, Nabe-cho
Shimonoseki-shi 750

Kobe Grain Exchange
2-4-16 Honmachi
Hyogo-ku, Kobe-shi 52

Kobe Raw Silk Exchange
126 Higashi-machi
Kobe Silk Center Building, 8th Floor
Chuo-ku, Kobe 650

Kobe Rubber Exchange
49, Harima cho
Chuo-ku, Kobe 650

Kyoto Stock Exchange
66 Higashinotoin-Higashiro-Tachiuri-
Nishimachi
Shijo-dori Shimokyo-ku
Kyoto 600

Maebashi Dried Cocoon Exchange
1-49-1 Furuichi-Machi
Maebashi City 371

Nagoya Grain and Sugar Exchange
2-3-2 Meiekiminami
Nakamura-ku, Nagoya 450

Nagoya Stock Exchange
3-3-17 Sakae, Naka-ku
Nagoya 460

Nagoya Textile Exchange
3-2-15 Nishiki
Naka-ku, Nagoya-shi 460

Nilgata Securities Exchange
1245 Hachibancho
Kamiohkawamaedohri
Niigata 951

Osaka Grain Exchange
1-10-14 Awaza
Nishi ku
Osaka 550

Osaka Securities Exchange
1-8-16, Kitahama
Higashi-ku
Osaka 541
(81) 6-299 8607

Osaka Sugar Exchange
2-5-28 Kyutaro-Machi
Chuo-ku
Osaka 541

Osaka Textile Exchange
2-5-28 Kyutaro-machi
Chuo-ku
Osaka 541

Sapporo Stock Exchange
5-14-1 Nishi
Minami Ichijoh-Nishi
Sapporo 060

Tokyo Commodity Exchange (TCE)
Tosen Building
10-8 Nihonbashi
Horidomecho 1-chome
Chuo-ku, Tokyo 103
81 (3) 661-9191

Tokyo Grain Exchange (TGE)
1-12-5 Kakigara-cho
Nihonbashi
Chuo-ku, Tokyo 103
81 6 668 9566

Tokyo Stock Exchange (TSE)
2-1, Nihombashi-Kebuto
Chuo-ku, Tokyo, 103
(81) 3-3666 0141

Tokyo Sugar Exchange (TSUE)
9-4 Koami-cho
Nihonbashi, Chuo-ku
Tokyo 103

Toyohashi Dried Cocoon Exchange
2-52 Ekimae-odori
Toyohashi City
Aichi Prefecture 440
81 532-526231

Yokohama Raw Silk Exchange
Silk Center, 4th Floor
1 Yamashita-cho
Naka-ku, Yokohama-shi 231

Jordan

Amman Financial Market
Housing Bank Center, 6th Floor
Amman

Kenya

Nairobi Stock Exchange
Stanbank House
Moi Avenue
P.O. Box 43633
Nairobi

Luxembourg

Societe de la Bourse de Luxembourg
11 avenue de la Porte-Neuve BP 165
L-2011 Luxembourg
352-477-9361

Malaysia

Kuala Lumpur Commodity Exchange (KLCE)
4th Floor, Dayabumi Complex
P.O. Box 11260
50740 Kuala Lumpur
60 (3) 293-6822

Kuala Lumpur Stock Exchange
3rd, 4th, & 5th Floors, Exchange Square
Damansara Heights
Kuala Lumpur 50490

Mexico

Bolsa Mexicana de Valores
Paseo dela Reforma No. 255
Col. Cuauhtemoc
06500, Mexico D.F.
(52) 5-726-6735

Morocco

Bourse Des Valeurs De Casablanca
Chamber of Commerce Building
98 Boulevard Mohamed V
Casablanca

Netherlands

Amsterdam Pork and Potato Exchange (APPE)
P.O. Box 252, 1000 AG
Amsterdam
31 (20) 239949

Amsterdam Stock Exchange
Beursplein 5, P.O. Box 19163
1012 JW Amsterdam
(31) 20 523 4567

European Options Exchange (EOE)
Rokin 65
1012 KK Amsterdam
31 (20) 550-4550

Financial Futures Market (FTA)
Nes 49
Amsterdam 1012 KD
1001 EE Amsterdam
31 (20) 550-4555

New Zealand

New Zealand Stock Exchange
8th Floor, Caltex Tower
282 Lambton Quay
Wellington

New Zealand Futures Exchange (NZFE)
P.O. Box 6734 Wellesley Street
Auckland
64 (9) 398-308

Nigeria

Nigerian Stock Exchange
214 Customs Street
P.O. Box 2457
Lagos

Norway

Bergen Bors
Olav Kyrresgate 11
5000 Bergen

Oslo Bors
P.O. Box 460 Sentrum
0150 Oslo 1
(47) 2-34 17 00

Trondheim Bors
Dronningensgt gT 12
7000, Trondheim

Pakistan

Karachi Stock Exchange
Stock Exchange Road
Karachi 2

Lahore Stock Exchange
19 Khayaban-e-Igbal Egerton Road
Lahore

Peru

Bolsa De Valores De Lima
Pasaje Acona 191
Lima

Philippines

Makati Stock Exchange
Makati Stock Exchange Building
Ayala Avenue
Makati, Metro Manila

Manila International Futures Exchange
(MIFE)
Producers Bank Centre, 7th Floor
Paseo de Roxas
Makati, Metro Manila
62 2 8185496

Manila Stock Exchange
12/F Tektite Tower 1
Tektite Road
Metro Manila

Portugal

Bolsa De Valores De Lisboa
Rua dos Franqueiros 10
1100 Lisboa

Singapore

Stock Exchange of Singapore
1 Raffles Place, 24-00
OUB Centre
Singapore 0104
(65) 535-3788

Singapore International Monetary Exchange
(SIMEX)
1 Raffles Place
OUB Centre 07-00
Singapore 0104
(65) 535 7282

South Africa

Johannesburg Stock Exchange
P.O. Box 1174
Diagonal Street
Johannesburg, 2000
(27) 11 833 6580

South Korea

Korea Stock Exchange
33, Yoido-Dong
Youngdeungpo-Ku
Seoul 150-010

Spain

Bolsa de Barcelona
Paseo Isabel 11, 1
08003 Barcelona

Bolsa de Bilbao
Olavarri 1
48001 Bilbao

Bolsa de Madrid
Plaza de la Lealtad 1
Madrid 28014
(34) 1 589 2600

Bolsa de Valencia
San Vincente 23
46002 Valencia

Sri Lanka

Colombo Stock Exchange
2nd Floor, Mackinnons Bldg.
York Street
Colombo 1

Sweden

Stockholms Fondbors
Box 1256, Kallargrand 2
S-111 82 Stockholm
(46) 8 613 8800

Stockholm Options Market (SOM)
Box 16305
S-103 26, Stockholm
46 (8) 700 06 00

Switzerland

Basle Stock Exchange
Aschenplatz 7
CH-4002 Basle
(41) 61 23 05 55

Chambre De La Bourse De Geneve
8, rue de la Confederation
Case Postale 228
CH-1211 Geneve 11

Swiss Options and Financial Futures
Exchange (SOFFEX)
Neu Mattstrasse
CH-8953 Dietikon
41 (1) 740 30 20

Zurich Stock Exchange
Bleicherweg 5
P.O. Box CH-8021
Zurich
(41) 1 299 21 11

Thailand

Stock Exchange of Thailand
Sinthon Building, 2nd Floor
132 Wireless Road
Bangkok, Metropolis 10500

Trinidad and Tobago

Trinidad and Tobago Stock Exchange
65 Independent Square
Port of Spain
Trinidad

Turkey

Istanbul Stock Exchange
Borsasi
Rihtim C, 245 Karakoy
Istanbul 80030

United States

American Stock Exchange (AMEX)
86 Trinity Place
New York, New York 10006
(212) 306-1000

Boston Stock Exchange (BSE)
One Boston Place
Boston, Massachusetts 02108
(617) 723-9500

Chicago Board of Trade (CBOT)
141 West Jackson Boulevard
Chicago, Illinois 60604
(312) 435-3500

Chicago Board Options Exchange (CBOE)
400 South LaSalle Street
Chicago, Illinois 60605
(312) 786-5600

Chicago Mercantile Exchange (CME),
Index and Options Market (IOM) and
International Monetary Market (IMM)
30 South Wacker Drive
Chicago, Illinois 60606
(312) 930-1000

Cincinnati Stock Exchange (CSE)
49 East Fourth Street
Cincinnati, Ohio 45202
(513) 621-1410

Coffee, Sugar & Cocoa Exchange (CSCE)
4 World Trade Center
New York, New York 10048
(212) 938-2800

Commodity Exchange, Inc. (COMEX)
4 World Trade Center
New York, New York 10048
(212) 938-2900

Kansas City Board of Trade (KCBT)
4800 Main Street
Kansas City, Missouri 64112
(816) 753-7500

MidAmerica Commodity Exchange (MIDAM)
141 West Jackson Boulevard
Chicago, Illinois 60604
(312) 341-3000, (312) 341-3078

Midwest Stock Exchange (MSE)
440 South LaSalle Street
Chicago, Illinois 60605
(312) 663-2222

Minneapolis Grain Exchange (MGE)
400 South Fourth Street
Minneapolis, Minnesota 55415
(612) 338-6212

New York Cotton Exchange (NYCE)
4 World Trade Center
New York, New York 10048
(212) 938-2702

New York Futures Exchange (NYFE)
20 Broad Street
New York, New York 10005
(212) 656-4949, (800) 221-7722

New York Mercantile Exchange (NYMEX)
4 World Trade Center
New York, New York 10048
(212) 938-2222

New York Stock Exchange (NYSE)
11 Wall Street
New York, New York 10005
(212) 656-3000

Pacific Stock Exchange (PSE)
301 Pine Street
San Francisco, California 94104
(415) 393-4000

Philadelphia Stock Exchange (PHLX)
Philadelphia Board of Trade (PBOT)
1900 Market Street
Philadelphia, Pennsylvania 19103
(215) 496-5000, 496-5165

Uruguay

Bolsa de Valores de Montevideo
Misiones 1400
Montevideo

Venezuela

Bolsa de Valores de Carcacas
Av. Sorocaima
Urbanizacion El Rosal
Caracas 1060

Bolsa de Valores de Maracaibo
Banco Contra 1 de Venezuela
Calle 96, between Au's 4 & 5
Maracaibo

Zimbabwe

The Zimbabwe Stock Exchange
8th Floor, Southhampton House
Union Avenue/1st Street
Harare

3. MUTUAL FUNDS

OPEN-END MUTUAL FUNDS

The following is a list of the names, addresses and telephone numbers of American open-end mutual funds. Most organizations offer more than one fund, and the funds in this list are grouped under the name of the firm to which they belong. In order to obtain information about a fund you may be interested in, look first for the name of its management group. Newspaper listings also usually group mutual funds by family.

The funds on this list are both load and no-load. Load funds are sold through brokers and financial planners for commissions that generally range from about 3% (this is called a low-load fund) to as much as 8¹/₂%. In return for this sales charge, customers should expect expert advice on which fund is most appropriate for their investment needs and goals. A broker should also tell the customer when to get out of the fund, as well as when to get in. No-load funds, on the other hand, charge no commissions. Investors buy shares directly from the management companies over the phone, by mail or in person. The management company representative will offer information on the funds the firm offers, but they may not advise investors on which fund to buy. No one will call when the time comes to switch from one fund to another—that is left totally up to the individual shareholder.

The funds on this list are each categorized by the investment objective of the fund manager. The following is a brief characterization of each objective, the abbreviation of which is given in parentheses after each fund's name in the list of funds.

Aggressive Growth (AG) Aggressive-growth funds seek maximum capital gains; current income is not a consideration. Fund managers may use several strategies, such as buying high-technology stocks, emerging growth stocks, or companies that have fallen on hard times or are out of favor. Some aggressive funds make use of options and futures, and/or borrow against funds shares to buy stock. Aggressive-growth funds typically provide dramatic gains and losses for shareholders, and should therefore be monitored closely.

Balanced (B) Balanced mutual funds generally invest in both stocks and bonds, with the intent of providing capital gains and income. Preservation of principal is a primary objective of balanced fund managers. These funds are for conservative investors who are looking for some growth of capital.

Corporate Bond (CB) Corporate-bond funds seek to pay a high level of income to shareholders by buying corporate bonds. Some conservative bond funds buy only the debt of highly rated corporations. The yield on this kind of fund would be lower than on that of a fund buying bonds from lower-rated corporations—frequently called junk bonds or high-yield bonds. Although income, not capital gains, is the primary objective of most corporate bond shareholders, gains can be significant if the country's general level of interest rates falls. On the other hand, losses can also be substantial if interest rates rise.

Flexible Portfolio (FP) Flexible portfolio funds give the fund manager great flexibility in deciding which asset offers the best risk-return tradeoff at any particular time. Therefore, such funds may invest in stocks, bonds, money-market instruments, options, futures, or foreign securities at various times. Such funds are sometimes called asset-allocation funds. Shareholders of flexible funds desire some current income, but also are expecting superior long-term capital gains.

Global Bond (GB) Global bond funds invest in fixed-income securities from anywhere in the world. Such funds may purchase bonds issued by foreign corporations or by U.S. corporations. Global bond funds also invest in bonds issued by foreign governments or their agencies. Investors in global funds expect a high level of current income and capital gains, if the direction of interest rates and currency rates is favorable.

Global Equity (GE) Global equity funds invest in securities anywhere in the world. They buy stocks, bonds, and money-market instruments in both the United States and foreign countries, depending on where the fund manager sees the best opportunity for growth. Global equity funds' main objective is long-term capital appreciation, although they may provide some current income.

Government National Mortgage Association (GNMA) These funds buy Government National Mortgage Association (GNMA or Ginnie Mae) certificates, which are securities backed by home mortgages. GNMA funds are designed to provide a high level of current income to shareholders and to minimize risk to capital. These funds are subject to fluctuation because of the ups and downs of interest rates, however. They are also affected by the rate at which homeowners refinance their mortgages. When interest rates fall, more mortgages are refinanced, and therefore shareholders in GNMA funds see their yields fall. When rates rise, on the other hand, fewer mortgages are refinanced, and so the fund maintains its yield, but it does not grow very quickly. GNMA funds are designed for conservative, income-oriented investors.

Growth (G) Growth funds invest in the common stock of growth companies. The primary aim is to achieve capital gains, and income is of little concern. Growth funds vary widely in the amount of risk they are willing to take, but in general they take less risk than aggressive growth funds because the stocks they buy are those of more seasoned companies.

Growth and Income (G+I) Growth and income funds seek to provide both capital gains and a steady stream of income by buying the shares of high-yielding, conservative stocks. Growth and income fund managers look for companies with solid records of increasing their dividend payments as well as earnings gains. These funds are more conservative than pure growth funds.

High-Yield Bond (HYB) High-yield bond funds buy the debt securities issued by non-investment-grade corporations and municipalities. Because these securities offer higher risks than investment-grade bonds, high-yield bonds pay higher yields. Because the companies and municipalities that issue high-yield bonds are more highly leveraged than top-quality issuers, their bonds are more subject to default, particularly if there is an economic downturn in the issuer's industry or region. Such defaults would not only cut the yield on high-yield bond funds but also erode the capital value of the shares. Investors in high-yield bond funds, therefore, should be well aware that they are taking an extra degree of default risk in exchange for a higher level of current income than is available from more conservative bond funds.

Income Bond (IB) Income bond funds invest in a variety of bonds to produce high taxable current income for shareholders. Such funds usually invest in corporate or government bonds, but they may also buy foreign bonds. They are usually managed more conservatively than bond funds that buy high-yield bonds and therefore offer lower current yields.

Income Equity (IE) Income equity funds invest in bonds and high-yielding stocks with the objective of providing shareholders with a moderate level of current income and a moderate level of long-term capital appreciation. Income equity funds are slightly more conservatively managed and usually have a higher percentage of their assets in bonds than growth and income funds.

Income Mixed (IM) Income mixed funds seek to provide a high level of current income by buying government and corporate bonds as well as high-yielding common and preferred stocks. Income mixed funds are not designed to provide major capital gains, but their shares do rise when interest rates fall. (Conversely, the shares fall in value when interest rates rise.) Income funds are designed for conservative, income-oriented investors.

International (INT) International funds invest in stocks of companies outside the United States as well as in bonds issued by foreign companies and governments. International funds provide investors with diversification among countries as well as industries. Such funds are strongly influenced by the rise and fall of foreign exchange rates—a factor important to consider before buying shares. For Americans it generally would be beneficial to buy an international fund when the outlook is for the dollar to fall against other currencies. Conversely, international-fund performance usually suffers when the dollar strengthens. International funds are for those who are willing to take some risk; understanding the effect of currency changes on holdings is essential.

Money Market (MM-T) Money-market mutual funds buy short-term securities sold in the money markets to provide current income to shareholders. Because of the short-term nature of their holdings, these funds reflect changes in short-term interest rates rather quickly. The principal in money-market funds is extremely safe. Some money funds buy commercial instruments like commercial paper, banker's acceptances, and repurchase agreements, while others restrict themselves to buying U.S. Treasury obligations like Treasury bills. The portfolios of some money-market funds are insured by private insurance companies. Most money funds allow check writing, often with a minimum check size of $250 or $500. Money-market funds are frequently included in asset management accounts offered by brokerage firms and are used as parking places for funds while shareholders decide where the best place to invest long-term might be. Otherwise, money-market funds are for extremely conservative investors, who want virtually no risk of capital loss.

National Municipal Bond, Long Term (MB-N) These funds aim to provide a high level of tax-exempt income to shareholders, by buying the debt obligations of cities, states, and other municipal government agencies. Depending on the state in which a shareholder resides, interest earned is either totally or partially free of federal, state, and local income taxes. While such funds are designed to provide current income, their value also rises and falls inversely with the country's general level of interest rates. The municipal bonds these funds usually buy tend to mature anywhere from 10 to 20 years in the future.

Precious Metals—Gold (PMG) Such funds invest in the shares of gold and silver mining companies. These shares often pay high dividends, and therefore the funds often can pay high yields. As with all precious-metal investments, these funds reflect the ups and downs of investor psychology as it relates to the outlook for inflation as well as political upheaval. These funds tend to perform better when inflation is high and rising and there is considerable political turmoil in the world. Some funds invest largely in South African mines, while others restrict themselves to shares in North American mining companies.

State Municipal Bond, Long Term (MB-S) These funds buy debt obligations of cities and municipal authorities in one state only. The interest from these bonds is usually tax exempt to residents of the particular state. Thus, shareholders can have a higher after-tax yield than if they bought shares in an out-of-state fund on which they had to pay taxes. These funds typically buy longer-term bonds maturing in 10 to 20 years. As a result, they fluctuate considerably with the ups and downs of the general level of interest rates.

Tax-Exempt Money Market—National or State (MM-TE) These funds invest in municipal securities with relatively short maturities, which range from as little as a few days to as much as 5 years. National money-market funds buy short term obligations of cities, states and municipal government agencies. State money-market funds buy the debt obligations of cities and municipal authorities in one state only, and a resident of that state has the advantage of receiving income free of both federal and state tax. Investors who use these funds seek tax-free investments with minimum risk. In either state or national tax-exempt money-market funds, portions of income from these securities may be subject to the federal alternative minimum tax. These funds generally allow shareholders to write checks, typically with a minimum withdrawal of $250 to $500 per check.

U.S. Government Income (USGI) U.S. government income funds invest only in direct obligations of the U.S. Treasury. The funds therefore buy U.S. Treasury bills, bonds, and notes and federally backed mortgage securities. Shareholders of such funds want a high level of current income as well as maximum safety against default. Some funds have short maturities, while others buy bonds with maturities as long as 20 or 30 years. The longer the portfolio's overall maturity, the more the fund will fluctuate with general interest-rate movements.

This listing of mutual funds was made possible through the generous cooperation of two mutual fund trade associations, the Investment Company Institute and the Mutual Fund Education Alliance. The Investment Company Institute (1401 H Street, N.W., Suite 1200, Washington, D.C. 20005-2148 (202) 326-5800) has both load and no-load members and regularly keeps track of new fund groups and funds. It publishes an annual directory of members. The Mutual Fund Educational Alliance (1900 Erie Street, Suite 120, Kansas City, Missouri 64116 (816) 471-1454) also has a large membership of no-load and low-load funds.

Abbreviations of Fund Objectives

AG	Aggressive Growth
B	Balanced
CB	Corporate Bond
FP	Flexible Portfolio
GB	Global Bond
GE	Global Equity
G	Growth
G+I	Growth and Income
GNMA	Government National Mortgage Association
HYB	High-Yield Bond
IB	Income Bond
IE	Income Equity
IM	Income Mixed
INT	International
MM-T	Money Market
MB-N	National Municipal Bond
PMG	Precious Metals—Gold
MB-S	State Municipal Bond
MM-TE	Tax-Exempt Money Market
USGI	U.S. Government Income

AAL Mutual Funds
222 West College Avenue
Appleton, Wisconsin 54919-0007
(414) 734-5721   (800) 553-6319
AAL Mutual Funds
  AAL Bond Fund (The) (IB)
  AAL Capital Growth Fund (The) (G)
  AAL Money Market Fund (The) (MM-T)
  AAL Municipal Bond Fund (The) (MB-N)
  Smaller Company Stock Fund (The) (AG)

AARP
AARP Investment Program
175 Federal Street
Boston, Massachusetts 02110-2267
(800) 322-2282
AARP Cash Investment Funds
  AARP High Quality Money Fund (MM-T)
AARP Growth Trust
  AARP Capital Growth Fund (G)
  AARP Growth & Income Fund (G+I)
AARP Income Trust
  AARP GNMA and U.S. Treasury Bond (USGI)
  AARP High Quality Bond (CB)
AARP Tax Free Income Trust
  AARP High Quality Tax-Free Money Fund
  (MM-TE)
  AARP Insured Tax-Free General Bond Fund
  (MB-N)
AARP Balanced Stock & Bond Fund (B)

ABT
340 Royal Palm Way
Palm Beach, Florida 33480
(407) 832-1078   (800) 553-7838
ABT Growth and Income Trust (G+I)
ABT Investment Series, Inc.
  ABT Emerging Growth Fund (AG)
ABT Southern Master Trust
  ABT Florida High Income Municipal Bond
  Fund (MB-N)
  ABT Florida Tax-Free Fund (MB-N)
ABT Utility Income Fund, Inc. (IE)

Accessor Funds, Inc.
1420 Fifth Avenue, Suite 3130
Seattle, Washington 98101
(206) 224-7420   (800) 759-3504
Accessor Funds, Inc.
  Growth Portfolio (G)
  Value & Income Portfolio (G+I)
  Small Cap Portfolio (AG)
  International Equity Portfolio (INT)
  Intermediate Fixed-Income Portfolio (IB)
  Short-Intermediate Fixed-Income Portfolio
  (IB)
  Mortgage Securities Portfolio (IB)
  Municipal Intermediate Fixed-Income
  Portfolio (MB-N)
  U.S. Government Money Portfolio (MM-T)
  International Fixed Income Portfolio (GB)

ACM Institutional Reserves, Inc.
1345 Avenue of the Americas
New York, New York 10105
(212) 969-1000   (800) 221-5672
ACM Institutional Reserves, Inc.
  Government Portfolio (MM-T)
  Prime Portfolio (MM-T)
  Tax-Free Portfolio (MM-TE)
  Trust Portfolio (MM-T)

Acorn Investment Trust
227 West Munroe Street, Suite 3000
Chicago, Illinois 60606
(312) 634-9200   (800) 922-6769
Acorn Investment Trust
  Acorn Fund (G)
  Acorn International (INT)

Active Assets
Two World Trade Center, 72nd Floor
New York, New York 10048
(212) 392-2550   (800) 869-3863
Active Assets California Tax-Free Trust
  (MMS-TE)
Active Assets Government Securities Trust
  (MM-T)
Active Assets Money Trust (MM-T)
Active Assets Tax-Free Trust (MM-TE)

Addison Capital Fund
Janney Montgomery Scott
1801 Market Street, 11th Floor
Philadelphia, Pennsylvania 19103
(800) 526-6397
Addison Capital Fund (G+I)

Advance Capital I, Inc.
1 Towne Square
Southfield, Michigan 48076
(810) 350-8543   (800) 345-4783
Advance Capital I Capital Growth Fund (G)
Advance Capital I Bond Fund (CB)
Advance Capital I Balanced Fund (B)
Advance Capital I Long Term Income Fund (CB)
Advance Capital I Retirement Income Fund (IB)

Advest, Inc.
280 Trumbull Street
Hartford, Connecticut 06103
(203) 241-2030   (800) 241-2039
Advantage Government Securities Fund (USGI)
Advantage Growth Fund (G)
Advantage High Yield Bond Fund (HYB)
Advantage Income Fund (IM)
Advantage Municipal Bond Fund
  National Portfolio (MB-N)
  New York Portfolio (MB-S)
  Pennsylvania Portfolio (MB-S)
Advantage Special Fund (G)
Advantage Strategic Income Fund (FP)

Advisors Fund, L.P.
Two World Trade Center, 100th Floor
New York, New York 10048-0002
(212) 464-8072
Advisors Fund, L.P. (AG)

Advisors' Inner Circle Fund
680 East Swedesford Road
Wayne, Pennsylvania 19087
(800) 932-7781
Advisors' Inner Circle Fund
  A&F Large Cap Fund (G)
  Clover Capital Equity Value Fund (G)
  Clover Capital Fixed Income Fund (IB)
  Jurika & Voyles Balanced Fund (B)
  Morgan Grenfell Fixed Income Fund (IM)
  Morgan Grenfell Municipal Bond Fund (MB-N)
  Pin Oak Aggressive Stock Fund (AG)
  Roulston Government Securities Fund (USGI)
  Roulston Midwest Growth Fund (G)
  Roulston Growth & Income (G+I)
  Turner Growth Equity Fund (G)
  White Oak Growth Stock Fund (G)

Aetna
151 Farmington Avenue
Hartford, Connecticut 06156
(800) 367-7732
Aetna Income Shares (IB)
Aetna Series Funds
  Aetna Bond Fund (CB)
  Aetna Fund (FP)
  Aetna Growth and Income Fund (G+I)
  Aetna International Growth Fund (INT)
  Aetna Money Market Fund (MM-T)
  Aetna Variable Fund (G+I)
  Aetna Government Fund (USGI)
  Aetna Tax-Free Fund (MB-N)
  Aetna Growth Fund (G)
  Aetna Small Company (G)
  Aetna Asian Growth (INT)

Affiliated Fund, Inc.
The General Motors Building
767 Fifth Avenue
New York, New York 10153-0203
(212) 848-1800   (800) 223-4224
Affiliated Fund, Inc. (G+I)

AGE High Income Fund, Inc.
777 Mariners Island Boulevard
San Mateo, California 94404-1585
(415) 312-2000   (800) 632-2180
AGE High Income Fund, Inc. (HYB)

AIM
P.O. Box 4333
Houston, Texas 77210-4333
(713) 626-1919   (800) 347-1919
AIM Equity Funds, Inc.
  AIM Aggressive Growth Fund (AG)

AIM Charter Fund (G+I)
AIM Constellation Fund (AG)
AIM Weingartern Fund (G)
AIM Funds Group
  AIM Balanced Fund (B)
  AIM Government Securities Fund (USGI)
  AIM Growth Fund (G)
  AIM High Yield Fund (HYB)
  AIM Income Fund (IB)
  AIM Money Market Fund (MM-T)
  AIM Municipal Bond Fund (MB-N)
  AIM Tax-Exempt Bond Fund of Connecticut
    (MB-S)
  AIM Tax-Exempt Cash Fund (MM-TE)
  AIM Utilities Fund (IE)
  AIM Value Fund (G+I)
AIM Investment Securities Funds
  AIM Adjustable Rate Government Fund
    (GNMA)
  AIM Limited Maturity Treasury Portfolio
    (USGI)
AIM Summit Fund, Inc. (G)

Albemarle Investment Trust
105 North Washington Street
P.O. Drawer 69
Rocky Mount, North Carolina 27802-0069
(919) 972-9922   (800) 525-3863
Albemarle Investment Trust
  North Carolina Tax Free Bond Fund (The)
    (MB-S)
  Oak Value Fund (The) (G)
  Trust Company of the South Growth Fund
    (The) (G)

Alex. Brown Cash Reserve Fund, Inc.
135 East Baltimore Street
Baltimore, Maryland 21202-1607
(410) 727-1700   (800) 767-3524
Alex. Brown Cash Reserve Fund, Inc.
  Prime Series (MM-T)
  Tax-Free Series (MM-TE)
  Treasury Series (MM-T)

Alger
75 Maiden Lane
New York, New York 10038
(212) 806-8800 (800) 992-3863
Alger American Fund
  Alger American Balanced Portfolio (B)
  Alger American Growth Portfolio (G)
  Alger American Income and Growth
    Portfolio (G+I)
  Alger American MidCap Growth Portfolio
    (AG)
  Alger American Small Capitalization
    Portfolio (AG)
Alger Fund
  Alger Balanced Portfolio (B)
  Alger Growth Portfolio (G)
  Alger Income and Growth Portfolio (G+I)

Alger MidCap Growth Fund (AG)
Alger Money Market Portfolio (MM-T)
Alger Small Capitalization Portfolio (AG)
Alger Leveraged All Cap (AG)

Alliance
1345 Avenue of the Americas
New York, New York 10105
(212) 969-1000   (800) 221-5672

Alliance AFD Exchange Reserves (MM-T)
Alliance Balanced Shares (B)
Alliance Bond Fund
  Corporate Bond Portfolio (CB)
  U.S. Government Portfolio (USGI)
Alliance Capital Reserves (MM-T)
Alliance Conservative Investors Fund (G)
Alliance Counterpoint Fund (G)
Alliance Fund, Inc. (G)
Alliance Global Dollar Government Fund (GE)
Alliance Global Small Cap Fund (GE)
Alliance Government Reserves (MM-T)
Alliance Growth Fund (G)
Alliance Growth and Income Fund (G+I)
Alliance Growth Investors Fund (G)
Alliance Income Builder Fund (I)
Alliance International Fund (INT)
Alliance Money Reserves (MM-T)
Alliance Mortgage Securities Income Fund,
  Inc. (GNMA)
Alliance Mortgage Strategy Trust Portfolio
  (GNMA)
Alliance Multi-Market Income Trust (GB)
Alliance Multi-Market Strategy Trust (GB)
Alliance Municipal Income Fund
  Arizona Portfolio (MB-S)
  California Portfolio (MB-S)
  Insured California Portfolio (MB-S)
  Insured National Portfolio (MB-N)
  National Portfolio (MB-N)
  New York Portfolio (MB-S)
  Florida Portfolio (MB-S)
  Massachusetts Portfolio (MB-S)
  Michigan Portfolio (MB-S)
  Minnesota Portfolio (MB-S)
  New Jersey Portfolio (MB-S)
  Ohio Portfolio (MB-S)
  Pennsylvania Portfolio (MB-S)
  Virginia Portfolio (MB-S)
Alliance Municipal Trust
  California Portfolio (MMS-TE)
  Connecticut Portfolio (MMS-TE)
  General Portfolio (MM-TE)
  New Jersey Portfolio (MM-TE)
  New York Portfolio (MMS-TE)
Alliance New Europe Fund, Inc. (INT)
Alliance North American Government Income
  Trust (USGI)
Alliance Premier Growth Fund (G)
Alliance Quasar Fund, Inc. (AG)
Alliance Short-Term Multi-Market Trust (GB)

Alliance Short-Term U.S. Government Fund
  (USGI)
Alliance Strategic Balanced Fund (B)
Alliance Technology Fund, Inc. (G)
Alliance Treasury Reserves (MM-T)
Alliance Utility Income Fund, Inc. (G+I)
Alliance World Income Trust (GB)
Alliance Worldwide Privatization Fund (GE)

Allmerica Investment Trust
440 Lincoln Street
Worcester, Massachusetts 01653
(508) 855-1000

Allmerica Investment Trust
  Government Money Market Fund (The)
    (MM-T)
  Select Aggressive Growth Fund (The) (AG)
  Select Growth Fund (The) (G)
  Select Growth and Income Fund (The) (G+I)
  Select Income Fund (The) (CB)
  Tax-Exempt Money Market Fund (The)
    (MM-TE)

Amana Mutual Funds Trust
1300 North State Street
Bellingham, Washington 98225-4730
(206) 734-9900   (800) 728-8762

Amana Mutual Funds Trust
  Income Fund (IE)
  Growth Fund (G)

Ambassador Funds
P.O. Box 9692
Providence, Rhode Island 02940-9830
(800) 380-4262

Ambassador Funds
  Balanced Fund (B)
  Bond Fund (CB)
  Core Growth Stock Fund (G)
  Growth Stock Fund (G)
  Indexed Stock Fund (G+I)
  Intermediate Bond Fund (CB)
  International Stock Fund (INT)
  Money Market Fund (MM-T)
  Small Company Growth Stock Fund (AG)
  Tax-Free Intermediate Bond Fund (MB-N)
  Tax-Free Money Market Fund (The) (MM-TE)
  U.S. Treasury Fund (MM-T)

AMCAP Fund, Inc.
333 South Hope Street
Los Angeles, California 90071-1447
(213) 486-9200   (800) 421-0180

AMCAP Fund, Inc. (G)

Amcore Vintage Mutual Funds
Amcore Capital Management
501 Seventh Street
Rockford, Illinois 61104
(800) 438-6375

Amcore Vintage Mutual Funds
  Amcore Equity Fund (G)
  Amcore Fixed Income Fund (IB)
  Amcore Intermediate Tax Free Municipal
    Bond Fund (MB-N)

Amelia Earhart Eagle Investments
One Town Square, Suite 1913
26100 Northwestern Highway
Southfield, Michigan 48076
(313) 351-4856
Amelia Earhart Eagle Investments
  Eagle Equity Series (G)

America Investment Trust
440 Lincoln Street
Worcester, Massachusetts 01653
(508) 855-1000
America Investment Trust
  Equity Index Fund (G+I)
  Government Bond Fund (IB)
  Growth Fund (G+I)
  Investment Grade Income Fund (IB)
  Money Market Fund (MM-T)

American Balanced Fund, Inc.
Four Embarcadero Center
P.O. Box 7650
San Francisco, California 94120-7650
(415) 421-9360   (800) 421-0180
American Balanced Fund, Inc. (B)

American Capital
2800 Post Oak Boulevard
P.O. Box 3121
Houston, Texas 77253-3121
(713) 993-0500   (800) 421-5666
American Capital Comstock Fund, Inc. (B)
American Capital Corporate Bond Fund, Inc.
  (CB)
American Capital Emerging Growth Fund, Inc.
  (AG)
American Capital Enterprise Fund, Inc. (G)
American Capital Equity Income Fund, Inc. (IE)
American Capital Exchange Fund (G)
American Capital Federal Mortgage Trust
  (GNMA)
American Capital Global Managed Assets (G+I)
American Capital Government Securities, Inc.
  (USGI)
American Capital Government Target Series
  Portfolio '97 (USGI)
American Capital Growth and Income Fund,
  Inc. (G+I)
American Capital Harbor Fund, Inc. (G+I)
American Capital High Yield Investments, Inc.
  (HYB)
American Capital Life Investment Trust
  Common Stock Portfolio (G)
  Government Portfolio (USGI)

  Money Market Portfolio (MM-T)
  Multiple Strategy Portfolio (FP)
  Strategic Income Fund (CB)
American Capital Municipal Bond Fund, Inc.
  (MB-N)
American Capital Pace Fund, Inc. (G)
American Capital Real Estate Securities (G+I)
American Capital Reserve Fund, Inc. (MM-T)
American Capital Tax-Exempt Trust
  High Yield Municipal Portfolio (MB-N)
  Insured Municipal Portfolio (MB-N)
American Capital Texas Municipal Securities,
  Inc. (MB-S)
American Capital U.S. Government for
  Income Trust (USGI)
American Capital Utilities Income Fund (I)
American Capital World Portfolio Series, Inc.
  American Capital Global Equity Fund (GE)
  American Capital Global Government
    Securities Fund (GB)

American Funds Group
333 South Hope Street
Los Angeles, California 90071-1447
(213) 486-9200   (800) 421-0180
American Funds Income Series
  U.S. Government Securities Fund (USGI)
American Funds Tax-Exempt Series I
  Tax-Exempt Fund of Maryland (The) (MB-S)
  Tax-Exempt Fund of Virginia (The) (MB-S)
American Funds Tax-Exempt Series II
  Tax-Exempt Fund of California (The) (MB-S)
American High-Income Trust (HYB)
American Mutual Fund, Inc. (G+I)
American Variable Insurance Series
  Asset Allocation Fund (The) (B)
  Cash Management Fund (The) (MM-T)
  Growth Fund (The) (G)
  Growth and Income Fund (The) (G+I)
  High Yield Bond Fund (The) (HYB)
  International Fund (The) (INT)
  U.S. Government Guaranteed/AAA-Rated
    Securities Fund (The) (USGI)

American General Series Portfolio Company
2929 Allen Parkway
P.O. Box 3206
Houston, Texas 77253-3206
(713) 526-5251
American General Series Portfolio Company
  Capital Conservation Fund (CB)
  Government Securities Fund (USGI)
  International Equities Fund (INT)
  MidCap Index Fund (G)
  Money Market Fund (MM-T)
  Small Cap Index Fund (AG)
  Social Awareness Fund (G+I)
  Stock Index Fund (G+I)
  Timed Opportunity Fund (B)

American Growth Fund, Inc.
410 17th Street, Suite 800
Denver, Colorado 80202-4418
(303) 623-6137   (800) 525-2406
American Growth Fund, Inc. (G)

American Heritage Management
31 West 52nd Street
New York, New York 10019
(212) 474-7308   (800) 828-5050
American Heritage Fund (AG)

American Leaders Fund, Inc.
Federated Investors Tower
Liberty Center
Pittsburgh, Pennsylvania 15222-3779
(412) 288-1900   (800) 245-4770
American Leaders Fund, Inc.
  Fortress Shares (G+I)

American National
One Moody Plaza
Galveston, Texas 77550
(409) 763-2767   (800) 231-4639
(800) 392-9753 (Texas only)
American National Government Income Fund,
  Inc. (USGI)
American National Growth Fund, Inc. (G)
American National Income Fund, Inc. (IE)
American National Primary Fund, Inc.
  (MM-T)
Triflex Fund (B)
American National Tax Free Fund (MB-N)

American Pension Investors Trust
2303 Yorktown Avenue
P.O. Box 2529
Lynchburg, Virginia 24501-2529
(804) 846-1361   (800) 544-6060
American Pension Investors Trust
  Capital Income Fund (IM)
  Global Income Fund (GB)
  Growth Fund (G)
  Special Markets Trust (FP)
  Total Return Fund (FP)
  Yorktown Classic Value Trust (G)

American Performance Funds
1900 East Dublin-Granville Road
Columbus, Ohio 43229
(614) 899-4600   (800) 762-7085
American Performance Funds
  American Performance Aggressive Growth
    Fund (AG)
  American Performance Bond Fund (IB)
  American Performance Cash Management
    Fund (MM-T)
  American Performance Equity Fund (G)
  American Performance Intermediate Bond
    Fund (IB)

American Performance Intermediate Tax
  Free Bond Fund (MB-N)
American Performance U.S. Treasury Fund
  (MM-T)
American Performance Short Term Bond
  Fund (IB)

America's Utility Fund, Inc.
901 East Byrd Street, 16th Floor
Richmond, Virginia 23219
(804) 775-5719   (800) 487-3863
America's Utility Fund, Inc. (G+I)

Asset Management Fund
111 East Wacker Drive
Chicago, Illinois 60601
(312) 856-0715   (800) 527-3713
AMF Adjustable Rate Mortgage Fund (IM)
AMF Intermediate Mortgage Securities
  Portfolio (GNMA)
AMF Money Market Portfolio (MM-T)
AMF Short U.S. Government Securities
  Portfolio (USGI)
AMF U.S. Government Mortgage Securities
  Portfolio (USGI)

AMR Investment Services, Inc.
P.O. Box 619003
Dallas Fort Worth Airport, Texas 75261-9003
(817) 967-3509
American AAdvantage Balanced Fund (B)
American AAdvantage Equity Fund (G)
American AAdvantage International Equity
  Fund (INT)
American AAdvantage Limited Income Fund
  (CB)

AmSouth Mutual Funds
1900 East Dublin-Granville Road
Columbus, Ohio 43229
(614) 899-4600   (800) 451-8382
AmSouth Mutual Funds
  Balanced Fund (B)
  Bond Fund (IB)
  Equity Fund (G)
  Government Income Fund (USGI)
  Limited Maturity Fund (IB)
  Prime Obligations Fund (MM-T)
  Regional Equity Fund (G)
  Tax Exempt Fund (MM-TE)
  U.S. Treasury Fund (MM-T)

Amway Mutual Fund, Inc.
7575 Fulton Street East
Ada, Michigan 49355-7150
(616) 676-6288   (800) 346-2670
Amway Mutual Fund, Inc. (G)

Analytic Optioned Equity Fund, Inc.
2222 Martin Street, Suite 230
Irvine, California 92715-1454
(714) 833-0294

Analytic Optioned Equity Fund, Inc. (G+I)
Analytic Series Fund
  Analytic Short Term Government Portfolio
    (USGI)
  Analytic Enhanced Equity Portfolio (AG)
  Analytic Master Fixed Income Portfolio (IB)

Anchor Capital Accumulation Trust
418 Hilltop Circle
Glenmoore, Pennsylvania 19343
(215) 458-9599
Anchor Capital Accumulation Trust (G)
Anchor International Bond Trust (INT)

Anchor Pathway Funds
Anchor Series Trust
733 Third Avenue
New York, New York 10017-3204
(212) 551-5969   (800) 871-2000
Anchor Pathway Funds
  Asset Allocation Series (FP)
  Cash Management Series (MM-T)
  Growth-Income Series (G+I)
  Growth Series (G)
  High Yield Bond Series (HYB)
  International Series (INT)
  U.S. Government/AAA Rated Series (USGI)
Anchor Series Trust
  Capital Appreciation Portfolio (AG)
  Convertible Securities Portfolio (IM)
  Fixed Income Portfolio (IM)
  Foreign Securities Portfolio (INT)
  Government and Quality Bond Portfolio (USGI)
  Growth Portfolio (G)
  High Yield Portfolio (HYB)
  Money Market Portfolio (MM-T)
  Multi-Asset Portfolio (G+I)
  Natural Resources Portfolio (G+I)
  Strategic Multi-Asset Portfolio (G+I)
  Target '98 Portfolio (USGI)

Aquila Funds
380 Madison Avenue, Suite 2300
New York, New York 10017
(800) 437 1020
Aquila Funds
  Tax-Free Trust of Arizona (MB-S)
  Tax-Free Fund of Colorado (MB-S)
  Hawaiian Tax-Free Trust (MB-S)
  Churchill Tax-Free Fund of Kentucky (MB-S)
  Narragansett Insured Tax-Free Income Fund
    (MB-S)
  Tax-Free Trust of Oregon (MB-S)
  Tax-Free Fund for Utah (MB-S)

Aquinas Funds
5310 Harvest Hill Road, Suite 248
Dallas, Texas 75230
(214) 233-6355   (800) 423-6369
Aquinas Equity Income (G+I)
Aquinas Fixed Income Fund (HYB)

Aquinas Equity Growth Fund (G)
Aquinas Balanced Fund (B)

ARCH
1900 East Dublin-Granville Road
Columbus, Ohio 43229
(614) 899-4600   (800) 551-3731
ARCH Fund, Inc.
  ARCH Balanced Portfolio (The) (B)
  ARCH Emerging Growth Portfolio (The) (AG)
  ARCH Government & Corporate Bond
    Portfolio (The) (IB)
  ARCH Growth and Income Portfolio (The) (G)
  ARCH Money Market Portfolio (The) (MM-T)
  ARCH Treasury Money Market Portfolio
    (The) (MM-T)
  ARCH Tax-Exempt Money Market Portfolio
    (The) (MM-TE)
  ARCH Missouri Tax-Exempt Bond Portfolio
    (MM-TE)
  ARCH U.S. Government Portfolio (USGI)
  ARCH International Portfolio (INT)

Ariel Capital Management
307 North Michigan Avenue
Chicago, Illinois 60601
(312) 726-5088   (800) 292-7435
Ariel Appreciation Fund (G)
Ariel Growth Fund (G+I)
Ariel Money Market (MM-T)
Ariel U.S. Government Money Market (MM-T)
Ariel Tax-Free Money Market (MM-T)

ARK Funds
P.O. Box 1596
Baltimore, Maryland 21203
(800) 275-3863
ARK Funds
  Capital Growth Fund (G)
  Growth and Income Fund (G+I)
  Income Fund (I)
  Money Market Fund (MMT)
  Tax-Free Money Market Fund (MM-TE)

Armstrong Associates, Inc.
Suite 1300, LB 13
750 North St. Paul
Dallas, Texas 75201
(214) 720-9101
Armstrong Associates, Inc. (G)

Aronson & Fogler
230 South Broad Street, 20th Floor
Philadelphia, Pennsylvania 19102
(800) 932-7781
A & F Large Cap Fund (G)

ASM Fund, Inc.
15438 North Florida, Suite 107
Tampa, Florida 33613
(813) 963-3150   (800) 445-2763
ASM Fund, Inc. (G+I)

Atlanta Growth Fund, Inc.
One Buckhead Plaza
3060 Peachtree Road, Suite 650
Atlanta, Georgia 30305
(404) 842-9600   (800) 762-0227
Atlanta Growth Fund, Inc. (G)

Atlas Assets, Inc.
1901 Harrison Street
Oakland, California 94612
(510) 446-4444   (800) 933-2852
Atlas Assets, Inc.
  Atlas Balanced Fund (B)
  Atlas California Insured Intermediate
    Municipal Fund (MB-S)
  Atlas California Municipal Bond Fund (MB-S)
  Atlas California Municipal Money Fund
    (MMS-TE)
  Atlas Growth and Income Fund (G+I)
  Atlas National Insured Intermediate
    Municipal Fund (MB-N)
  Atlas National Municipal Bond Fund (MB-N)
  Atlas National Municipal Money Fund
    (MM-TE)
  Atlas Strategic Growth Fund (G)
  Atlas U.S. Government and Mortgage
    Securities Fund (USGI)
  Atlas U.S. Treasury Intermediate Fund (USGI)
  Atlas Treasury Money Fund (MM-T)

Bailard, Biehl & Kaiser
2755 Campus Drive
San Mateo, California 94403
(415) 571-5800 (800) 882-8383
Bailard, Biehl & Kaiser Fund Group
  Bailard, Biehl & Kaiser Diversa Fund (G+I)
Bailard, Biehl & Kaiser International Fund
    Group, Inc.
  Bailard, Biehl & Kaiser International Equity
    Fund (INT)
  Bailard, Biehl & Kaiser International Fixed-
    Income Fund (GB)

Baillie Gifford International Fund
201 Park Avenue South
New York, New York 10003
(212) 598-8260   (800) 221-3253
Baillie Gifford International Fund (INT)

Baird
777 East Wisconsin Avenue
Milwaukee, Wisconsin 53202
(414) 765-3500   (800) 792-2473
Baird Blue Chip Fund, Inc. (G+I)
Baird Capital Development Fund, Inc. (G)
Baird Mutual Funds, Inc.
  Baird Adjustable Rate Fund (GNMA)
  Baird Quality Bond Fund (IB)

Baker Fentress & Co.
200 West Madison Street
Chicago, Illinois 60606
(312) 236-9190
Baker Fentress Fund (G+I)

Baron Asset Fund
450 Park Avenue, Suite 2800
New York, New York 10022
(212) 759-7700   (800) 992-2766
Baron Asset Fund (AG)

Bartlett
36 East Fourth Street
Cincinnati, Ohio 45202
(513) 621-4612   (800) 800-4612
Bartlett Basic Value Fund (G+I)
Bartlett Fixed Income Fund (IB)
Bartlett Short Term Bond Fund (IB)
Bartlett Value International Fund (INT)
Bartlett Management Trust
  Bartlett Cash Reserves (MM-T)

Bascom Hill
6411 Mineral Point Road
Madison, Wisconsin 53705
(608) 273-2020   (800) 767-0300
Bascom Hill BALANCED Fund, Inc. (B)
Bascom Hill Investors, Inc. (G)
Madison Bond Fund (CB)

Baupost Fund
44 Brattle Street
P.O. Box 381288
Cambridge, Massachusetts 02238
(617) 497-6680
Baupost Fund (The) (G+I)

Bayfunds
Federated Investors Tower
Liberty Center
Pittsburgh, Pennsylvania 15222-3779
(412) 288-1900 (800) 245-4770

Bayfunds
  Bayfunds Bond Portfolio (IB)
  Bayfunds Equity Portfolio (G)
  Bayfunds Money Market Portfolio (MM-T)
  Bayfunds Short Term Yield Portfolio (IB)
  Bayfunds U.S. Treasury Money Market
    Portfolio (MM-T)
  Money Market Portfolio (MM-T)
  U.S. Treasury Money Market Portfolio (MM-T)

BB&T Mutual Funds Group
1900 East Granville Road
Columbus, Ohio 43229
(614) 899-4600   (800) 228-1872
BB&T Mutual Funds Group
  Balanced Fund (B)
  Growth and Income Stock Fund (G+I)

Intermediate U.S. Government Bond Fund
(USGI)
North Carolina Intermediate Tax-Free Fund
(MB-S)
Short-Intermediate U.S. Government
Income Fund (USGI)
U.S. Treasury Money Market Fund (MM-TE)

Beacon Hill Fund
75 Federal Street
Boston, Massachusetts 02110
(617) 482-0795   (800) 343-0529
Beacon Hill Mutual Fund (G+I)

Benchmark Funds
4900 Sears Tower
Chicago, Illinois 60606-6391
or
50 South LaSalle Street
Chicago 60675
(312) 655-4400   (800) 621-2550
(800) 637-1380
Benchmark Funds
Balanced Portfolio (B)
Bond Portfolio (FP)
California Municipal Portfolio (MMS-TE)
Diversified Assets Portfolio (MM-T)
Diversified Growth Portfolio (G)
Equity Index Portfolio (G+I)
Focused Growth Portfolio (AG)
Government Portfolio (MM-T)
Government Select Portfolio (MM-T)
Short Duration Portfolio (CB)
Short/Intermediate Bond Portfolio (FP)
Small Company Index Portfolio (AG)
Tax-Exempt Portfolio (MM-TE)
US Treasury Index Portfolio (USGI)
International Growth Portfolio (INT)
International Bond Portfolio (GB)

Benham
1665 Charleston Road
Mountain View, California 94043-1211
(415) 965-8300 (800) 472-3389

Benham Arizona Intermediate Municipal Fund
(MB-S)
Benham California Tax-Free and Municipal
Funds
Municipal High Yield Fund (MB-S)
Municipal Money Market Fund (MMS-TE)
Tax-Free Insured Fund (MB-S)
Tax-Free Intermediate-Term Fund (MB-S)
Tax-Free Long-Term Fund (MB-S)
Tax-Free Money Market Fund (MMS-TE)
Tax-Free Short-Term Fund (MB-S)
Benham Capital Preservation Fund (MM-T)
Benham Capital Preservation Fund II (MM-T)
Benham Equity Fund
Benham Equity Growth Fund (G)
Benham Gold Equities Index Fund (PMG)

Benham Income & Growth Fund (G+I)
Benham Utilities Income Fund (IE)
Benham Global Natural Resource Fund (GE)
Benham European Government Bond Fund
(GB)
Benham Florida Municipal Money Market
Fund (MM-T)
Benham Government Income Trust
Benham Adjustable Rate Government
Securities Fund (USGI)
Benham GNMA Income Fund (GNMA)
Benham Government Agency Fund (MM-T)
Benham Treasury Note Fund (USGI)
Long-Term Treasury & Agency Fund (USGI)
Short-Term Treasury & Agency Fund (USGI)
Benham Florida Intermediate Money Market
Fund (MM-T)
Benham Prime Money Market Fund (MM-T)
Benham National Tax-Free Trust
Intermediate-Term Portfolio (MB-N)
Long-Term Portfolio (MB-N)
Money Market Portfolio (MM-TE)
Benham Target Maturities Trust
Series 1995 (USGI)
Series 2000 (USGI)
Series 2005 (USGI)
Series 2010 (USGI)
Series 2015 (USGI)
Series 2020 (USGI)

Berger One Hundred and One Fund, Inc.
Berger One Hundred Fund, Inc.
210 University Boulevard, Suite 900
Denver, Colorado 80206
(303) 329-0200   (800) 333-1001
Berger One Hundred and One Fund, Inc. (G+I)
Berger One Hundred Fund, Inc. (G)
Berger Small Company Growth Fund (AG)

Bernstein Fund, Inc.
767 Fifth Avenue
New York, New York 10153
(212) 756-4097

Bernstein Fund, Inc.
Bernstein California Municipal Portfolio (MB-S)
Bernstein Diversified Municipal Portfolio
(MB-N)
Bernstein Government Short Duration
Portfolio (USGI)
Bernstein Intermediate Duration Portfolio (CB)
Bernstein International Value Fund (INT)
Bernstein New York Municipal Portfolio (MB-S)
Bernstein Short Duration California
Municipal Portfolio (MB-S)
Bernstein Short Duration Diversified
Municipal Portfolios (MB-N)
Bernstein Short Duration New York
Municipal Portfolio (MB-S)
Bernstein Short Duration Plus Portfolio
(USGI)

Berwyn Funds
1189 Lancaster Avenue
Berwyn, Pennsylvania 19312
(800) 824-2249
Berwyn Fund (G)
Berwyn Income Fund (FP)

Bhirud MidCap Growth Fund, Inc.
237 Park Avenue, Suite 910
New York, New York 10017
(212) 808-3900   (800) 453-4243
Bhirud MidCap Growth Fund, Inc. (G)

Biltmore Funds
Federated Investors Tower
Pittsburgh, Pennsylvania 15222-3779
(412) 288-1900   (800) 245-2423
(800) 245-5040
Biltmore Funds
  Biltmore Balanced Fund (B)
  Biltmore Equity Fund (G)
  Biltmore Equity Index Fund (G)
  Biltmore Fixed Income Fund (IB)
  Biltmore Money Market Fund (MM-T)
  Biltmore Short Term Fixed Income Fund (IB)
  Biltmore South Carolina Municipal Bond
    Fund (MB-S)
  Biltmore Special Value Fund (G)
  Biltmore Tax-Free Money Market Fund
    (MM-TE)
  Biltmore U.S. Government Money Market
    Fund (MM-T)
  Biltmore U.S. Treasury Money Market Fund
    (MM-T)

BJB Investment Funds
Exchange Place
Boston, Massachusetts 02109
(800) 362-2863
BJB Global Income Fund (GB)
BJB International Equity Fund (INT)

William Blair & Company
222 West Adams
Chicago, Illinois 60606
(312) 346-4830
William Blair Growth Industry Shares
  Fund (G)
William Blair Income Fund (IB)
William Blair International Growth Fund
  (INT)
William Blair Limited Term Tax-Free Fund
  (MB-N)
William Blair Ready Reserves Fund (MM-T)

Blanchard Funds
41 Madison Avenue, 24th Floor
New York, New York 10010
(212) 779-7979   (800) 922-7771
Blanchard Funds
  Blanchard American Equity Fund (G)

Blanchard Emerging Markets Fund (INT)
Blanchard Flexible Income Fund (IM)
Blanchard Flexible Tax-Free Bond Fund
  (MB-N)
Blanchard 100% Treasury Money Market
  Fund (MM-T)
Blanchard Global Growth Fund (GE)
Blanchard Precious Metals Fund (PMG)
Blanchard Short-Term Bond Fund (IB)
Blanchard Short-Term Global Income
  Fund (GB)

BNY Hamilton Funds, Inc.
156 West 56th Street
New York, New York 10019
(212) 693-5300   (800) 426-9363
(800) 426-9363
BNY Hamilton Funds, Inc.
  BNY Hamilton Equity Income Fund (IE)
  BNY Hamilton Intermediate Government
    Fund (USGI)
  BNY Hamilton Intermediate New York
    Tax-Exempt Fund (MB-S)
  BNY Hamilton Money Fund (MM-T)

Bond Fund of America, Inc.
333 South Hope Street
Los Angeles, California 90071-1447
(213) 486-9200   (800) 421-0180
(213) 486-9651 (Collect)
Bond Fund of America, Inc. (IB)

Bond Portfolio for Endowments, Inc.
Four Embarcadero Center
P.O. Box 7650
San Francisco, California 94120-7650
(415) 421-9360   (800) 421-0180
Bond Portfolio for Endowments, Inc. (IB)

Boston Company
One Boston Place
Boston, Massachusetts 02109
(617) 956-9740   (800) 225-5267
Boston Company Fund
  Asset Manager's Equity Fund (G)
  Capital Appreciation Fund (G)
  Cash Management Fund (MM-T)
  Government Money Fund (MM-T)
  Institutional Class (G)
  Intermediate Term Government Securities
    Fund (USGI)
  Managed Income Fund (CB)
  Retail Class (G)
  Special Growth Fund (G)
Boston Company Investment Series
  Asset Allocation Fund (FP)
  Contrarian Fund (AG)
  International Fund (INT)
  Short Term Bond Fund (IM)
Boston Company Tax-Free Municipals Funds
  California Tax-Free Bond Fund (MB-S)

California Tax-Free Money Fund (MMS-TE)
Massachusetts Tax-Free Bond Fund
  (MB-S)
Massachusetts Tax-Free Money Fund
  (MMS-TE)
New York Tax-Free Bond Fund (MB-S)
New York Tax-Free Money Fund (MMS-TE)
Tax-Free Bond Fund (MB-N)
Tax-Free Money Fund (MM-TE)

Boulevard Funds
Federated Investors Tower
Pittsburgh, Pennsylvania 15222-3779
(412) 288-1900   (800) 356-2805
Boulevard Funds
  Boulevard Blue-Chip Growth Fund (G+I)
  Boulevard Managed Income Fund (IM)
  Boulevard Managed Municipal Fund
    (MB-N)
  Boulevard Strategic Balance Fund (B)

Branch Cabell Investment Trust
105 North Washington Street
P.O. Drawer 69
Rocky Mount, North Carolina 27802-0069
(919) 972-9922   (800) 525-3863
Branch Cabell Investment Trust
  Exeter Equity Trust (G)
  Exeter Fixed Income Trust (IB)

Brandywine Fund
Freiss Associates, Inc.
3908 Kennett Pike
Greenville, Delaware 19807
(302) 656-6200
Brandywine Fund (G)

Bridges
8401 West Dodge Road
256 Durham Plaza
Omaha, Nebraska 68114
(402) 397-4700
Bridges Investment Fund (G+I)

Brinson Funds
209 South LaSalle Street
Chicago, Illinois 60604-1295
(312) 220-7200 (800) 448-2430
     or
2 West Elm Street
Conshohocken, Pennsylvania 19428
(800) 448-2430
Brinson Funds
  Brinson Global Bond Fund (GB)
  Brinson Global Equity Fund (GE)
  Brinson Global Fund (GB)
  Brinson Non-U.S. Equity Fund (INT)
  Brinson U.S. Balanced Fund (B)
  Brinson U.S. Equity Fund (G)
  Brinson Non-U.S. Bond Fund (GB)
  Brinson U.S. Bond Fund (CB)

Brundage, Story and Rose Investment Trust
312 Walnut Street, 21st Floor
Cincinnati, Ohio 45202-4094
(513) 629-2000   (800) 545-0103
Brundage, Story and Rose Investment Trust
  Growth & Income Fund (G+I)
  Short/Intermediate Term Fixed-Income Fund
    (IB)

BT/IFTC
210 West 10th Street, 8th Floor
Kansas City, Missouri 64104
(800) 422-6577
BT Equity Appreciation Fund (G)
BT International Equity Fund (INT)
BT Lifecycle Short Range Fund (G+I)
BT Lifecycle Midrange Fund (G+I)
BT Lifecycle Long Range Fund (G+I)
BT Limited Term U.S. Government Securities
  (USGI)
BT Small Cap Fund (AG)

Bull & Bear
11 Hanover Square
New York, New York 10005-3401
(212) 785-0900   (800) 847-4200
Bull & Bear Gold Investors Ltd (PMG)
Bull & Bear Inc.
  Bull & Bear Dollar Reserves (MM-T)
  Bull & Bear Global Income Fund (GB)
  Bull & Bear U.S. Government Securities
    Fund (USGI)
Bull & Bear Municipal Income Fund (MB-N)
Bull & Bear Quality Growth Fund (G)
Bull & Bear Special Equities Fund, Inc. (AG)
Bull & Bear U.S. and Overseas Fund (GE)

Burnham Fund, Inc.
1345 Avenue of the Americas, 32nd Floor
New York, New York 10105
(212) 785-0900   (800) 874-3863
Burnham Fund, Inc. (G+I)

C&S Realty Fund
Mutual Fund Service Co.
Attn: Cohen & Steers
73 Tremont Street
Boston, Massachusetts 02108-2798
C&S Realty Fund (IM)

Caldwell & Orkin Funds, Inc.
Five Piedmont Center, Suite 417
Atlanta, Georgia 30305
(404) 239-0707   (800) 237-7073
Caldwell & Orkin Funds, Inc.
  Caldwell & Orkin Aggressive Growth Fund
    (AG)

California Investment Trust Fund Group
44 Montgomery Street, Suite 2100
San Francisco, California 94104
(800) 225-8778

California Income Fund (I)
California Tax Free Money Market Fund
(MM-TE)
U.S. Treasury Trust Fund (MM-T)
California Insured Tax Free Income Fund
(MB-S)
California Tax Free Income Fund (MB-S)
U.S. Government Securities Fund (USGI)
S&P 500 Index Fund (G)
S&P MidCap Index Fund (G)

California Municipal Cash Trust
Federated Investors Tower
Pittsburgh, Pennsylvania 15222-3779
(412) 288-1900   (800) 245-2423

California Municipal Cash Trust (MMS-TE)

Calvert
4550 Montgomery Avenue, Suite 1000N
Bethesda, Maryland 20814
(301) 951-4800   (800) 368-2745

Calvert First Government Money Market Fund
(MM-T)
Calvert Fund
Calvert Income Fund (IB)
Calvert U.S. Government Fund (USGI)
Calvert Municipal Fund, Inc.
Calvert California Municipal Intermediate
Fund (MB-S)
Calvert Intermediate Municipal Fund (MB-N)
Calvert Maryland Municipal Intermediate
Fund (MB-S)
Calvert Michigan Municipal Intermediate
Fund (MB-S)
Calvert New York Municipal Intermediate
Fund (MB-S)
Calvert Virginia Municipal Intermediate Fund
(MB-S)
Calvert Pennsylvania
Calvert Arizona
Calvert Social Investment Fund
Bond Portfolio (CB)
Equity Portfolio (G)
Managed Growth Portfolio (B)
Money Market Portfolio (MM-T)
Calvert Tax-Free Reserves
California Money Market Portfolio
(MMS-TE)
Limited-Term Portfolio (MB-N)
Long-Term Portfolio (MB-N)
Money Management Plus Tax-Free
Portfolio (MM-TE)
Money Market Portfolio (MM-TE)
New Jersey Money Market Portfolio
(MMS-TE)

Vermont Municipal Portfolio (MB-S)
Calvert World Values Fund, Inc.
Global Equity Fund (GE)
Calvert Strategic Growth Fund (AG)
Calvert Insured Plus (MM-T)
Calvert Money Management Plus Prime
Portfolio (MM-T)
Calvert Money Management Plus
Government Portfolio (MM-T)

Cambridge Series Trust
901 East Byrd Street
Riverfront Plaza
Richmond, Virginia 23219
(804) 782-3648   (800) 382-0016

Cambridge Series Trust
Cambridge Capital Growth Portfolio (G)
Cambridge Government Income Portfolio
(USGI)
Cambridge Growth Portfolio (G)
Cambridge Income and Growth Portfolio
(G+I)
Cambridge Municipal Income Portfolio
(MB-N)

Canada Life of America Series Fund, Inc.
330 University Avenue
Toronto, Ontario M5G 1R8
(416) 597-1456

Canada Life of America Series Fund, Inc.
Bond Series (IB)
Capital Series (G)
Equity Series (G)
Managed Series (IM)
Money Market Series (MM-T)

Cappiello-Rushmore
4922 Fairmont Avenue
Bethesda, Maryland 20814
(800) 621-7874

Capiello-Rushmore Emerging Growth (AG)
Capiello-Rushmore Gold
Capiello-Rushmore Growth Fund (G)
Capiello-Rushmore Utility Income (I)

Capital Cash Managed Trust
380 Madison Avenue, Suite 2300
New York, New York 10017-2590
(212) 697-6666   (800) 228-4227

Capital Cash Managed Trust (MM-T)

Capital Income Builder, Inc.
333 South Hope Street
Los Angeles, California 90071-1447
(213) 486-9200   (800) 421-0180

Capital Income Builder, Inc. (IE)
Capital World Bond Fund, Inc. (GB)
Capital World Growth & Income Fund (GE)

Capital Market Fund, Inc.
523 West Sixth Street, Suite 220
Los Angeles, California 90014
(213) 488-2700

Capital Market Fund, Inc.
  Index Series (G+I)
  U.S. Treasury Money Market Series (MM-T)

Capital Value Fund, Inc.
418 6th Avenue, Suite 720
Des Moines, Iowa 50309-2439
(800) 544-2669

Capital Value Fund, Inc.
  Equity Portfolio (G)
  Fixed Income Portfolio (CB)
  Prime Money Market Portfolio (MM-T)
  Short-Term Government Portfolio (USGI)
  Total Return Portfolio (G+I)

Capitol Mutual Funds
Nations Fund
One Nations Bank Plaza
Charlotte, North Carolina 28255
(800) 321-7854

Capitol Mutual Funds
  Capitol Government Reserves Portfolio
    (MM-T)
  Capitol Cash Reserves Portfolio (MM-T)
  Capitol Tax Free Reserves Portfolio (MM-TE)
  Capitol Treasury Reserves Portfolio (MM-T)

Capstone
5847 San Felipe, Suite 4100
Houston, Texas 77057
(713) 260-9000 (800) 262-6631

Capstone Fixed Income Series, Inc.
  Capstone Government Income Fund (USGI)
Capstone International Series Trust
  Capstone New Zealand Fund (INT)
  Capstone Nikko Japan Fund (INT)
Capstone Series, Inc. (AG)
Capstone Fund of the Southwest (AG)
Capstone Growth Fund, Inc. (G)
Medical Research Investment Fund (G)

Cardinal
155 East Broad Street
Columbus, Ohio 43215
(614) 464-5511   (800) 848-7734
(800) 262-9446 (Ohio only)

Cardinal Aggressive Growth Fund (AG)
Cardinal Balanced Fund (B)
Cardinal Fund, Inc. (G+I)
Cardinal Government Obligations Fund (USGI)
Cardinal Government Securities Trust (MM-T)
Cardinal Tax Exempt Money Trust (MM-TE)

Carillon
1876 Waycross Road
Cincinnati, Ohio 45240-2899
(513) 595-2600   (800) 999-1840

Carillon Fund, Inc.
  Bond Portfolio (The) (CB)
  Capital Portfolio (The) (FP)
  Equity Portfolio (The) (G+I)
  Money Market Portfolio (The) (MM-T)
Carillon Investment Trust
  Carillon Capital Fund (FP)

Carnegie
1100 The Halle Building
1228 Euclid Avenue
Cleveland, Ohio 44115-1831
(216) 781-4440   (800) 321-2322

Carnegie Government Securities Trust
  Carnegie Money Market Series (MM-T)
Carnegie Tax Exempt Income Trust
  Ohio General Municipal Bond Fund (MB-S)
Carnegie Tax Free Income Trust (MM-TE)
Carnegie Liquid Capital Income Fund (MM-T)

Cascades Trust
380 Madison Avenue, Suite 2300
New York, New York 10017-2590
(212) 697-6666   (800) 872-6734

Cascades Trust
  Tax-Free Trust of Oregon (MB-S)

Cash Account Trust
120 South LaSalle Street
Chicago, Illinois 60603-3473
(312) 781-1121   (800) 621-1048

Cash Account Trust
  Government Securities Portfolio (MM-T)
  Money Market Portfolio (MM-T)
  Tax-Exempt Portfolio (MM-TE)
Cash Equivalent Fund
  Government Securities Portfolio (MM-T)
  Money Market Portfolio (MM-T)
  Tax-Exempt Portfolio (MM-TE)

Cash Accumulation Trust
One Station Place
Stamford, Connecticut 06902
(203) 352-4900   (800) 628-1237

Cash Accumulation Trust
  National Money Market Fund (MM-T)

Cash Management Trust of America
333 South Hope Street
Los Angeles, California 90071-1447
(213) 486-9200   (800) 421-0180

Cash Management Trust of America (MM-T)

Cash Trust Series
Federated Investors Tower
Pittsburgh, Pennsylvania 15222-3779
(412) 288-1900   (800) 245-2423

Cash Trust Series
  Government Cash Series (MM-T)
  Municipal Cash Series (MM-TE)
  Prime Cash Series (MM-T)

Treasury Cash Series (MM-T)
Cash Series II
  Municipal Cash Series II (MM-TE)
  Treasury Cash Series II (MM-T)

CBA Fund
P.O. Box 9011
Princeton, New Jersey 08543-9011
(609) 282-2800   (800) 247-6400
CBA Fund (MM-T)

Centennial
3410 South Galena Street
Denver, Colorado 80231-3234
(303) 671-3200   (800) 525-7048
Centennial America Fund L.P. (MM-T)
Centennial California Tax Exempt Trust
  (MMS-TE)
Centennial Government Trust (MM-T)
Centennial Money Market Trust (MM-T)
Centennial New York Tax Exempt Trust
  (MMS-TE)
Centennial Daily Cash Accumulation Fund
  (MM-T)
Centennial Tax Exempt Trust (MM-TE)

Centerland Fund
4900 Sears Tower
Chicago, Illinois 60606-6391
(312) 655-4400   (800) 621-2550
(800) 621-2302
Centerland Fund
  Centerland Kleinwart International Equity
    Fund (INT)
  Short-Term Diversified Assets Portfolio
    (MM-T)
  Short-Term Tax-Exempt Portfolio (MM-TE)
  Short-Term U.S. Treasury Portfolio (MM-T)

Centurion Growth Fund
251 Royal Palm Way, Suite 601
Palm Beach, Florida 33480
(407) 832-3353   (800) 947-6984
Centurion Growth Fund (G)

Century Shares Trust
One Liberty Square
Boston, Massachusetts 02109
(617) 482-3060   (800) 321-1928
Century Shares Trust (G+I)

CFS Investment Trust
1111 East Warrenville Road
Naperville, Illinois 60563-1448
(708) 245-7200   (800) 323-9943
CFS Investment Trust
  Calamos Covertible Fund (B)
  Calamos Growth Fund (G)
  Calamos Growth & Income Fund (G+I)
  Calamos Strategic Income Fund (IM)

CGM
222 Berkeley Street, Suite 1940
Boston, Massachusetts 02116
(617) 859-7714 (800) 345-4048
CGM Capital Development Fund (G)
CGM Trust
  CGM Fixed Income Fund (G+I)
  CGM Mutual Fund (B)

Chapman Funds, Inc.
World Trade Center
401 East Pratt Street
Baltimore, Maryland 21202
(410) 625-9656 (800) 752-1013
Chapman Funds, Inc.
  Chapman Institutional Cash Management
    Fund (The) (MM-T)
  Chapman U.S. Treasury Money Fund (The)
    (MM-T)

Charles Schwab Family of Funds
101 Montgomery Street
San Francisco, California 94104
(415) 627-7000   (800) 526-8600
Charles Schwab Family of Funds
  Schwab California Tax-Exempt Money Fund
    (MMS-TE)
  Schwab Government Money Fund (MM-T)
  Schwab Money Market Fund (MM-T)
  Schwab Tax-Exempt Money Fund (MM-TE)
  Schwab U.S. Treasury Money Fund (MM-T)
  Schwab Value Advantage Money Fund
    (MM-T)
  New York Municipal Cash Trust (MB-N)

Charter Capital Blue Chip Growth Fund
4920 West Vliet Street
Milwaukee, Wisconsin 53208
(414) 257-1842
Charter Capital Blue Chip Growth Fund (G)

Chesapeake Growth Fund
Gardner Lewis Asset Management
285 Wilmington-Westchester Pike
Chadds Ford, Pennsylvania 19317
(800) 525-3863
Chesapeake Growth Fund (G)

Chubb
One Granite Place
Concord, New Hampshire 03301
(603) 226-5000   (800) 258-3648
Chubb America Fund, Inc.
  Balanced Portfolio (B)
  Bond Portfolio (IB)
  Capital Growth Portfolio (G)
  Domestic Growth Portfolio (G+I)
  Gold Stock Portfolio (PMG)
  Growth & Income Portfolio (G+I)
  Money Market Portfolio (MM-T)

World Growth Stock Portfolio (GE)
Chubb Investment Funds, Inc.
  Chubb Government Securities Fund
    (USGI)
  Chubb Growth and Income Fund (G+I)
  Chubb Money Market Fund (MM-T)
  Chubb Tax-Exempt Fund (MB-N)
  Chubb Total Return Fund (B)

Churchill
380 Madison Avenue, Suite 2300
New York, New York 10017-2590
(212) 697-6666   (800) 872-5859

Churchill Cash Reserves Trust (MM-T)
Churchill Tax-Free Fund of Kentucky
  (MB-S)

CIGNA
One Financial Plaza
Springfield, Massachusetts 01103
(203) 726-3700   (800) 572-4462

CIGNA Annuity Funds Group
  CIGNA Annuity Aggressive Equity
    Fund (AG)
  CIGNA Annuity Equity Fund (G)
  CIGNA Annuity Growth and Income Fund
    (G+I)
  CIGNA Annuity Income Fund (CB)
  CIGNA Annuity Money Market Fund
    (MM-T)
CIGNA International Stock Fund (INT)
CIGNA Variable Products Group (G)
  Companion Fund (G)

Clipper Fund, Inc.
9601 Wilshire Boulevard, Suite 800
Beverley Hills, California 90210-5291
(310) 247-3940   (800) 776-5033

Clipper Fund, Inc. (G)
Schooner Fund (AG)

CMA
P.O. Box 9011
Princeton, New Jersey 08543-9011
(609) 282-2800   (800) 262-4636

CMA Government Securities Fund (MM-T)
CMA Money Fund (MM-T)
CMA Multi-State Municipal Series Trust
  CMA Arizona Municipal Money Fund
    (MMS-TE)
  CMA California Municipal Money Fund
    (MMS-TE)
  CMA Connecticut Municipal Money Fund
    (MMS-TE)
  CMA Massachusetts Municipal Money Fund
    (MMS-TE)
  CMA Michigan Municipal Money Fund
    (MMS-TE)
  CMA New Jersey Municipal Money Fund
    (MMS-TE)

  CMA New York Municipal Money Fund
    (MMS-TE)
  CMA North Carolina Municipal Money Fund
    (MMS-TE)
  CMA Ohio Municipal Money Fund (MMS-TE)
  CMA Pennsylvania Municipal Money Fund
    (MMS-TE)
CMA Tax-Exempt Fund (MM-TE)
CMA Treasury Fund (MM-T)

Cohen & Steers Realty Shares, Inc.
757 Third Avenue, 27th Floor
New York, New York 10017
(212) 832-3232   (800) 437-9912

Cohen & Steers Realty Shares, Inc. (G+I)

College Retirement Equities Fund
730 Third Avenue
New York, New York 10017
(212) 490-9000 (800) 842-2733

College Retirement Equities Fund
  Bond Market Account (IB)
  Global Equities Account (GE)
  Money Market Account (MM-T)
  Social Choice Account (B)
  Stock Account (G+I)
  Growth Account (G)
  Equity Index Account (G)

Colonial
One Financial Center
Boston, Massachusetts 02111-2698
(617) 426-3750 (800) 225-2365

Colonial Adjustable Rate U.S. Government
  Fund (GNMA)
Colonial California Tax-Exempt Fund (MB-S)
Colonial Connecticut Tax-Exempt Fund (MB-S)
Colonial Federal Securities Fund (USGI)
Colonial Florida Tax-Exempt Fund (MB-S)
Colonial Fund (G+I)
Colonial Global Equity Fund (GE)
Colonial Growth Shares Fund (G)
Colonial High Yield Municipal Fund (MB-N)
Colonial High Yield Securities Fund (HYB)
Colonial Income Fund (IB)
Colonial Intermediate Tax-Exempt Fund (MB-N)
Colonial Massachusetts Tax-Exempt Fund
  (MB-S)
Colonial Michigan Tax-Exempt Fund (MB-S)
Colonial Minnesota Tax-Exempt Fund (MB-S)
Colonial Money Market Fund (MM-T)
Colonial Natural Resources Fund (G)
Colonial New York Tax-Exempt Fund (MB-S)
Colonial North Carolina Tax-Exempt Fund
  (MB-S)
Colonial Ohio Tax-Exempt Fund (MB-S)
Colonial Short Term Tax-Exempt Fund (MB-N)
Colonial Small Stock Fund (G+I)
Colonial Strategic Income Fund (IM)
Colonial Tax-Exempt Fund (MB-N)
Colonial Tax-Exempt Insured Fund (MB-N)

Colonial Tax-Exempt Money Market Fund
(MM-TE)
Colonial U.S. Fund for Growth (G)
Colonial U.S. Government Fund (USGI)
Colonial Utilities Fund (IE)
Colonial Strategic Balanced Fund (B)
Colonial International Fund for Growth (INT)

Columbia
1301 South West 5th Avenue
P.O. Box 1350
Portland, Oregon 97207-1350
(503) 222-3600   (800) 547-1707
Columbia Balanced Fund (B)
Columbia Common Stock Fund, Inc. (G+I)
Columbia Daily Income Company (MM-T)
Columbia Fixed Income Securities Fund, Inc.
(IB)
Columbia Growth Fund, Inc. (G)
Columbia International Stock Fund, Inc. (INT)
Columbia Municipal Bond Fund, Inc. (MB-S)
Columbia Special Fund, Inc. (AG)
Columbia U.S. Government Securities Fund,
Inc. (USGI)

Command
One Seaport Plaza
New York, New York 10292
(212) 214-1215   (800) 222-4321
Command Government Fund (MM-T)
Command Money Fund (MM-T)
Command Tax-Free Fund (MM-TE)
Command U.S. Treasury Fund (USGI)
Command International Money Fund (INT)

Common Sense Trust
3120 Breckenridge Boulevard
Duluth, Georgia 30199
(800) 544-5445
Common Sense Trust
  Common Sense Trust Government Fund
    (USGI)
  Common Sense Growth and Income Fund
    (G+I)
  Common Sense Growth Fund (G)
  Common Sense Money Market Fund (MM-T)
  Common Sense Municipal Bond Fund
    (MB-N)
  Common Sense Aggressive Opportunity
    Fund (AG)

Compass Capital Group of Funds
680 East Swedesford
Wayne, Pennsylvania 19087-1658
(800) 451-8371
    or
P.O. Box 199
Wayne, Pennsylvania 19087-0199
Compass Capital Group of Funds
  Small Cap Value Fund (AG)
  Cash Reserve Fund (MM-T)
  Equity Income Fund (IE)

Fixed Income Fund (IM)
Growth Fund (G)
International Equity Fund (INT)
International Fixed Income Fund (GB)
Municipal Bond Fund (MB-N)
Municipal Money Fund (MM-TE)
New Jersey Municipal Bond Fund (MB-S)
New Jersey Municipal Money Market Fund
(MMS-TE)
Pennsylvania Municipal Bond Fund (MB-S)
Pennsylvania Municipal Money Market Fund
(MMS-TE)
Short/Intermediate Fund (IM)
U.S. Treasury Money Market Fund (MM-T)
Balanced Fund (B)

Composite
601 West Main Avenue, Suite 801
Spokane, Washington 99201-0694
(509) 353-3400 (800) 543-8072
Composite Bond & Stock Fund, Inc. (B)
Composite Cash Management Company
  Money Market Portfolio (MM-T)
  Tax-Exempt Money Market Portfolio
    (MM-TE)
Composite Deferred Series, Inc.
  Growth Portfolio (G)
  Income Portfolio (CB)
  Money Market Portfolio (MM-T)
  Northwest 50 Portfolio (G)
Composite Growth Fund, Inc. (G+I)
Composite Income Fund, Inc. (CB)
Composite Northwest 50 Fund, Inc. (G)
Composite Tax-Exempt Bond Fund, Inc.
  (MB-N)
Composite U.S. Government Securities, Inc.
  (GNMA)

Concorde Value Fund, Inc.
1500 Three Lincoln Center, 5430 LBJ Freeway
Dallas, Texas 75240-2387
(214) 387-8258   (800) 338-1579
    or
Firstar Trust Company
P.O. Box 701
Milwaukee, Wisconsin 53201-0701
(800) 338-1579
Concorde Value Fund, Inc. (G)

Conestoga Family of Funds
1900 East Dublin-Granville Road
Columbus, Ohio 43229
(614) 899-4600   (800) 344-2716
Conestoga Family of Funds
  Cash Management Fund (MM-T)
  Equity Fund (G)
  Fixed Income Fund (IB)
  Limited Maturity Fund (IB)
  Pennsylvania Tax-Free Bond Fund (MB-S)
  Tax-Free Fund (MM-TE)
  U.S. Treasury Securities Fund (MM-T)
  Special Equities Fund (G)

Connecticut Mutual
140 Garden Street
MS-240
Hartford, Connecticut 06154-0240
(203) 987-5002   (800) 322-2642
(800) 234-5606
Connecticut Mutual Financial Services Series
  Fund I, Inc.
  Government Securities Portfolio (USGI)
  Growth Portfolio (G)
  Income Portfolio (IB)
  International Equity Portfolio (INT)
  Money Market Portfolio (MM-T)
  Total Return Portfolio (B)
Connecticut Mutual Investment Accounts, Inc.
  Connecticut Mutual Government Securities
    Account (USGI)
  Connecticut Mutual Growth Account (G)
  Connecticut Mutual Income Account (IB)
  Connecticut Mutual Liquid Account
    (MM-T)
  Connecticut Mutual Total Return Account
    (B)
  Connecticut Mutual National Municipals
    Account (MB-N)
  Connecticut Mutual California Municipals
    Account (MB-S)
  Connecticut Mutual Massachusetts
    Municipals Account (MB-S)
  Connecticut Mutual New York Municipals
    Account (MB-S)
  Connecticut Mutual Ohio Municipals
    Account (MB-S)

Conseco Series Trust
205 East 10th Street
Amarillo, Texas 79105
(806) 378-3400   (800) 888-4918
Conseco Series Trust
  Conseco Asset Allocation Portfolio (B)
  Conseco Common Stock Portfolio (G)
  Conseco Corporate Bond Portfolio (CB)
  Conseco Government Securities Portfolio
    (USGI)
  Conseco Money Market Portfolio (MM-T)

CoreFund, Inc.
P.O. Box 470
Wayne, Pennsylvania 19087
(800) 355-2673
CoreFund, Inc.
  CoreFund Balanced Fund (B)
  CoreFund Cash Reserve (MM-T)
  CoreFund Equity Index Fund (G)
  CoreFund Fiduciary Reserve (MM-T)
  CoreFund Fiduciary Tax-Free Reserve
    (MM-TE)
  CoreFund Fiduciary Treasury Reserve
    (MM-T)
  Corefund Government Income Fund (USGI)

CoreFund Growth Equity Fund (G+I)
CoreFund Intermediate Bond Fund (CB)
CoreFund Intermediate Term Municipal Fund
  (MB-N)
CoreFund International Growth Fund (INT)
CoreFund Tax-Free Reserve (MM-TE)
CoreFund Treasury Reserve (MM-T)
CoreFund Value Equity Fund (G+I)
Corefund Global Bond Fund (GB)
Corefund New Jersey Municipal Bond Fund
  (MB-S)
Corefund Pennsylvania Municipal Bond
  Fund (MB-S)

Cornerstone Growth Fund
1500 Forest Avenue, Suite 223
Richmond, Virginia 23229
(804) 285-8211 (800) 527-9525
Cornerstone Growth Fund (G)

Corporate Fund Investment Accumulation
  Program, Inc.
P.O. Box 9011
Princeton, New Jersey 08543-9011
(609) 282-8600
Corporate Fund Investment Accumulation
  Program, Inc. (CB)

Coventry Group
1900 East Dublin-Granville Road
Columbus, Ohio 43229
(614) 899-4600   (800) 752-1823
Coventry Group
  Amcore Vintage Government Obligations
    Fund (MM-T)
  Amcore Vintage Equity Fund (G)
  Amcore Vintage Fixed Fund (IE)
  Amcore Vintage Intermediate Tax-Free Fund
    (MB-N)
  Brenton Government Money Market Fund
    (MM-T)
  Brenton Intermediate U.S. Government
    Fund (USGI)
  Brenton Intermediate Tax-Free Fund (MB-N)
  Brenton Value Equity Fund (G)
  Shelby Aggressive Growth Fund (AG)

Cowen
Financial Square
New York, New York 10005-3597
(212) 495-6000   (800) 221-5616
(800) 309-1111
Cowen Funds, Inc.
  Cowen Intermediate Fixed Income Fund (IB)
  Cowen Opportunity Fund (AG)
  Cowen Government Securities Fund (USGI)
Cowen Income & Growth Fund, Inc. (IE)
Cowen Standby Tax-Exempt Reserve Fund,
  Inc. (MM-TE)
Cowen Standby Reserve Fund, Inc. (MM-T)

Crabbe Huson
121 S.W. Morrison, Suite 1400
Portland, Oregon 97204
(503) 295-0919   (800) 541-9732

Crabbe Huson Asset Allocation Fund, Inc. (B)
Crabbe Huson Equity Fund, Inc. (G)
Crabbe Huson Income Fund, Inc. (IB)
Crabbe Huson Special Fund, Inc. (AG)
Crabbe Huson U.S. Government Fund, Inc.
  (USGI)
Crabbe Huson U.S. Government Money
  Market Fund, Inc. (MM-T)
Crabbe Huson Oregon Municipal Bond Fund
  (MB-S)
Crabbe Huson Real Estate Investment Fund (G)

CrestFunds, Inc.
P.O. Box 2798
Boston, Massachusetts 02208-9915
(617) 570-6513   (800) 451-5435

CrestFunds, Inc.
  Bond Fund (CB)
  Capital Appreciation Fund (AG)
  Cash Reserve Fund (MM-T)
  Short-Intermediate Bond Fund (CB)
  Special Equity Fund (AG)
  Tax Free Money Fund (MM-TE)
  Value Fund (B)
  Virginia Municipal Bond Fund (MB-S)

Crowley Portfolio Group, Inc.
Suite H, 1813 Marsh Road
Wilmington, Delaware 19810-4505
(302) 529-1717

Crowley Portfolio Group, Inc.
  Crowley Growth Portfolio (The) (G+I)
  Crowley Income Portfolio (The) (IM)

CU Fund
680 East Swedesford Road, No. 7
Wayne, Pennsylvania 19087-1658
(215) 215-6000   (800) 342-5734

CU Fund
  Adjustable Rate Portfolio (GNMA)
  Short Term Maturity Portfolio (GNMA)

Cutler Trust
503 Airport Road
Medford, Oregon 97504
(800) 228-8537

Cutler Trust Approved List (G+I)
Cutler Trust Equity Income Fund (IE)
Cutler Trust Government Securities (USGI)

Daily Cash Accumulation Fund, Inc.
3410 South Galena Street
Denver, Colorado 80231-3234
(303) 671-3200 (800) 525-7048

Daily Cash Accumulation Fund, Inc. (MM-T)

Daily Money Fund
82 Devonshire Street
Boston, Massachusetts 02109
(617) 330-0586   (800) 843-3001

Daily Money Fund
  Capital Reserves Money Market Portfolio
    (MM-T)
  Capital Reserves Municipal Money Market
    Portfolio (MM-TE)
  Capital Reserves U.S. Government Portfolio
    (MM-T)
  Money Market Portfolio (MM-T)
  U.S. Treasury Income Portfolio (MM-T)
  U.S. Treasury Portfolio (MM-T)

Dean Witter
Two World Trade Center, 72nd Floor
New York, New York 10048
(212) 392-2550   (800) 869-3863

Dean Witter American Value Fund (G)
Dean Witter California Tax-Free Daily Income
  Trust (MMS-TE)
Dean Witter California Tax-Free Income Fund
  (MB-S)
Dean Witter Capital Growth Securities (G)
Dean Witter Convertible Securities Trust (G+I)
Dean Witter Developing Growth Securities
  Trust (AG)
Dean Witter Diversified Income Trust (IB)
Dean Witter Dividend Growth Securities (G+I)
Dean Witter Equity Income Trust (IE)
Dean Witter European Growth Fund Inc. (G)
Dean Witter Federal Securities Trust (USGI)
Dean Witter Global Dividend Growth Securities
  (G+I)
Dean Witter Global Short-Term Income Fund,
  Inc. (GB)
Dean Witter Global Utilities Fund (G+I)
Dean Witter Health Sciences Trust (G)
Dean Witter High Income Securities (HYB)
Dean Witter High Yield Securities Inc. (HYB)
Dean Witter Intermediate Income Securities
  (IB)
Dean Witter International SmallCap Fund (AG)
Dean Witter Limited Term Municipal Trust
  (MB-N)
Dean Witter Liquid Asset Fund, Inc. (MM-T)
Dean Witter Managed Assets Trust (G+I)
Dean Witter Mid Cap Growth Fund (G)
Dean Witter Multi-State Municipal Series Trust
  Arizona Series (MB-S)
  California Series (MB-S)
  Florida Series (MB-S)
  Massachusetts Series (MB-S)
  Michigan Series (MB-S)
  Minnesota Series (MB-S)
  New Jersey Series (MB-S)
  New York Series (MB-S)
  Ohio Series (MB-S)
  Pennsylvania Series (MB-S)
Dean Witter National Municipal Trust (MB-N)

Dean Witter Natural Resource Development
Securities Inc (G)
Dean Witter New York Municipal Money
Market Trust (MMS-TE)
Dean Witter New York Tax-Free Income Fund
(MB-S)
Dean Witter Pacific Growth Fund Inc (G)
Dean Witter Precious Metals and Minerals
Trust (PMG)
Dean Witter Premier Income Trust (IM)
Dean Witter Select Municipal Reinvestment
Fund (MB-N)
Dean Witter Short-Term Bond Fund (CB)
Dean Witter Short-Term U.S. Treasury Trust
(USGI)
Dean Witter Strategist Fund (G+I)
Dean Witter Tax-Exempt Securities Trust
(MB-N)
Dean Witter Tax-Free Daily Income Trust
(MM-TE)
Dean Witter U.S. Government Money Market
Trust (MM-T)
Dean Witter U.S. Government Securities Trust
(USGI)
Dean Witter Utilities Fund (G+I)
Dean Witter Value-Added Market Series
Equity Portfolio (G+I)
Dean Witter Variable Investment Series
Capital Growth Portfolio (G)
Dividend Growth Portfolio (G+I)
Equity Portfolio (G)
European Growth Portfolio (INT)
High Yield Portfolio (HYB)
Managed Assets Portfolio (FP)
Money Market Portfolio (MM-T)
Quality Income Plus Portfolio (IB)
Utilities Portfolio (G+I)
Dean Witter World Wide Income Trust (GB)
Dean Witter World Wide Investment Trust (GE)

Declaration Cash Account
Declaration Fund
555 North Lane, Suite 6160
Conshohoken, Pennsylvania 19428
(215) 832-1075   (800) 423-2345

Declaration Cash Account (MM-T)
Declaration Fund
CAMCO 100% U.S. Treasury Intermediate
Fund (USGI)
CAMCO 100% U.S. Treasury Short-Term
Fund (USGI)
CAMCO 100% U.S. Treasury Total Return
Fund (USGI)

Delaware
1818 Market Street
Philadelphia, Pennsylvania 19103
(215) 988-1050   (800) 523-4640
(800) 523-1918

Delaware Group Cash Reserve, Inc. (MM-T)
Delaware Group Decatur Fund, Inc.
Decatur Income Fund (IE)

Decatur Total Return Fund (IE)
Delaware Group Delaware Fund, Inc. (B)
Delaware Group DelCap Fund, Inc. (G)
Delaware Group Delchester High-Yield Bond
Fund, Inc. (HYB)
Delaware Group Global & International
Funds, Inc.
International Equity Fund (INT)
Delaware Group Government Fund, Inc.
U.S. Government Fund (IB)
Delaware Group Tax-Free Fund, Inc.
Tax-Free Insured Fund (MB-N)
Tax-Free USA Fund (MB-N)
Tax-Free USA Intermediate Fund (MB-N)
Delaware Group Tax-Free Money Fund, Inc.
(MM-TE)
Delaware Group Treasury Reserves, Inc.
Treasury Reserves Intermediate Fund (USGI)
U.S. Government Money Fund (MM-T)
Delaware Group Trend Fund, Inc. (AG)
Delaware Group Value Fund, Inc. (AG)
Delaware Pooled Trust, Inc.
Aggressive Growth Portfolio (The) (AG)
Defensive Equity Portfolio (The) (G+I)
Fixed Income Portfolio (The) (IB)
International Equity Portfolio (The) (INT)

DG Investor Series
Federated Investors Tower
Pittsburgh, Pennsylvania 15222-3779
(412) 288-1900   (800) 245-2423

DG Investor Series
DG Equity Fund (G+I)
DG Government Income Fund (USGI)
DG Limited Term Government Income Fund
(IM)
DG Municipal Income Fund (MB-N)
DG U.S. Government Money Market Fund
(MM-T)

DMC Tax-Free Income Trust-PA
One Commerce Square
Philadelphia, Pennsylvania 19103-1681
(215) 988-1200   (800) 523-4640

DMC Tax-Free Income Trust-PA (MB-S)

Dodge & Cox
One Sansome Street, 35th Floor
San Francisco, California 94104-5277
(415) 981-1710

Dodge & Cox Balanced Fund (B)
Dodge & Cox Income Fund (IB)
Dodge & Cox Stock Fund (G+I)

Dreman Mutual Group, Inc.
Ten Exchange Place, Suite 2050
Jersey City, New Jersey 07302
(201) 332-8228   (800) 533-1608

Dreman Mutual Group, Inc.
Dreman Contrarian Portfolio (The) (G+I)
Dreman Fixed Income Portfolio (The) (USGI)

Dreman High Return Portfolio (The) (IE)
Dreman Small Cap Value Portfolio (The) (AG)

Dreyfus
144 Glen Curtiss Boulevard
Uniondale, New York 11556-0144
(718) 895-1206   (800) 645-6561
Dreyfus A Bonds Plus, Inc. (CB)
Dreyfus Appreciation Fund, Inc. (G)
Dreyfus Asset Allocation Fund (FP)
Dreyfus Balanced Fund, Inc. (B)
Dreyfus Basic Intermediate Municipal Bond
    Fund (MB-N)
Dreyfus Basic Money Market Fund, Inc.
    (MM-T)
Dreyfus Basic Municipal Bond Fund (MB-N)
Dreyfus Basic Municipal Money Market Fund,
    Inc. (MM-TE)
Dreyfus Basic U.S. Government Money
    Market Fund (MM-T)
Dreyfus Bond Market Index Fund (CB)
Dreyfus California Intermediate Municipal
    Bond Fund (MB-S)
Dreyfus California Tax Exempt Bond Fund,
    Inc. (MB-S)
Dreyfus California Tax Exempt Money Market
    Fund (MMS-TE)
Dreyfus Capital Growth Fund, Inc. (AG)
Dreyfus Capital Value Fund, Inc. (G+I)
Dreyfus Cash Management (MM-T)
Dreyfus Cash Management Plus (MM-T)
Dreyfus Comstock Partners Strategy Fund (IB)
Dreyfus Connecticut Intermediate Municipal
    Bond Fund (MB-S)
Dreyfus Connecticut Municipal Money Market
    Fund, Inc. (MMS-TE)
Dreyfus Core Value Fund (G)
Dreyfus Disciplined Midcap Stock Fund (G)
Dreyfus Disciplined Stock Fund (G)
Dreyfus Equity Income Fund (G+I)
Dreyfus Edison Electric Index Fund, Inc. (G+I)
Dreyfus European Fund (INT)
Dreyfus First Prairie Cash Management Fund
    (MM-T)
Dreyfus First Prairie Diversified Asset Fund (FP)
Dreyfus First Prairie Government Money
    Market Fund (MM-T)
Dreyfus First Prairie Insured Municipal Bond
    Fund (MB-N)
Dreyfus First Prairie Intermediate Municipal
    Bond Fund (MB-N)
Dreyfus First Prairie Money Market Fund
    (MM-T)
Dreyfus First Prairie Municipal Money Market
    Fund (MM-T)
Dreyfus First Prairie Treasury Cash
    Management Fund (MM-T)
Dreyfus First Prairie U.S. Government Income
    Fund (USGI)
Dreyfus Florida Intermediate Municipal Bond
    Fund (MB-S)

Dreyfus Florida Municipal Money Market
    Fund (MM-T)
FN Network Tax Free Money Market Fund
    (MM-TE)
Dreyfus Focus Funds:
  Large Company Growth (G)
  Large Company Value (G)
  Small Company Growth (AG)
  Small Company Value (AG)
Dreyfus Fund Incorporated (G+I)
Dreyfus General California Municipal Bond
    Fund (MB-S)
Dreyfus General California Money Market
    Fund (MM-T)
Dreyfus General Government Money Market
    Fund (MM-T)
Dreyfus General Money Market Fund (MM-T)
Dreyfus General Municipal Bond Fund (MB-N)
Dreyfus General Money Market Fund (MM-T)
Dreyfus General New York Municipal Bond
    Fund (MB-S)
Dreyfus General New York Municipal Money
    Market Fund (MM-T)
Dreyfus Global Bond Fund (GB)
Dreyfus Global Growth, L.P. (G)
Dreyfus GNMA Fund, Inc. (GNMA)
Dreyfus Government Cash Management
    (MM-T)
Dreyfus Growth and Income Fund, Inc. (G+I)
Dreyfus Growth Opportunity Fund, Inc. (G)
Dreyfus Institutional Government Money
    Market Fund (MM-T)
Dreyfus Institutional Money Market Fund
    (MM-T)
Dreyfus Institutional Short-Term Treasury
    Fund (MM-T)
Dreyfus Insured Municipal Bond Fund, Inc.
    (MB-N)
Dreyfus Intermediate Municipal Bond Fund,
    Inc. (MB-N)
Dreyfus International Equity Fund, Inc. (INT)
Dreyfus Investors GNMA Fund (GNMA)
Dreyfus Life and Annuity Index Fund, Inc.
    (G+I)
Dreyfus Liquid Assets, Inc. (MM-T)
Dreyfus Massachusetts Intermediate Tax
    Exempt Bond Fund (MB-S)
Dreyfus Massachusetts Municipal Money
    Market Fund (MM-T)
Dreyfus Massachusetts Tax Exempt Bond
    Fund (MB-S)
Dreyfus Michigan Municipal Money Market
    Fund, Inc. (MM-T)
Dreyfus Midcap Value Fund (G)
Dreyfus Money Market Instruments, Inc.
    Government Securities Series (MM-T)
    Money Market Series (MM-T)
Dreyfus Municipal Bond Fund, Inc. (MB-N)
Dreyfus Municipal Cash Management Plus
    (MM-TE)
Dreyfus Municipal Money Market Fund, Inc.
    (MM-TE)

Dreyfus New Jersey Intermediate Municipal
Bond Fund, Inc. (MB-S)
Dreyfus New Jersey Municipal Bond Fund,
Inc. (MB-S)
Dreyfus New Jersey Municipal Money Market
Fund, Inc. (MMS-TE)
Dreyfus New Leaders Fund, Inc. (G)
Dreyfus New York Insured Tax Exempt Bond
Fund (MB-S)
Dreyfus New York Municipal Cash
Management (MMS-TE)
Dreyfus New York Tax Exempt Bond Fund,
Inc. (MB-S)
Dreyfus New York Tax Exempt Intermediate
Bond Fund (MB-S)
Dreyfus New York Tax Exempt Money Market
Fund (MMS-TE)
Dreyfus Ohio Municipal Money Market Fund,
Inc. (MMS-TE)
Dreyfus 100% U.S. Treasury Intermediate
Term Fund, L.P. (USGI)
Dreyfus 100% U.S. Treasury Long Term
Fund, L.P. (USGI)
Dreyfus 100% U.S. Treasury Money Market
Fund, L.P. (MM-T)
Dreyfus 100% U.S. Treasury Short-Term
Fund, L.P. (USGI)
Dreyfus Pennsylvania Intermediate Municipal
Bond Fund (MB-S)
Dreyfus Pennsylvania Municipal Money
Market Fund (MM-T)
Dreyfus Peoples Index Fund (G)
Dreyfus Peoples S&P Midcap Fund (AG)
Dreyfus Premier Funds
  Arizona Municipal Bond Fund (MB-S)
  California Municipal Bond Fund (MB-S)
  Colorado Municipal Bond Fund (MB-S)
  Connecticut Municipal Bond Fund (MB-S)
  Disciplined Balanced Fund (B)
  Florida Municipal Bond Fund (MB-S)
  Georgia Municipal Bond Fund (MB-S)
  Global Investing Fund (GE)
  GNMA Fund (GNMA)
  Growth Fund (G)
  Insured Municipal Bond Fund (MB-N)
  Insured Municipal Bond Fund - CA Series
    (MB-S)
  Insured Municipal Bond Fund - CT Series
    (MB-S)
  Insured Municipal Bond Fund - FL Series
    (MB-S)
  Insured Municipal Bond Fund - NJ Series
    (MB-S)
  Insured Municipal Bond Fund - NY Series
    (MB-S)
  Limited Term California Tax-Free Municipal
    Bond Fund (MB-S)
  Limited Term Government Bond Fund
    (USGI)
  Limited Term Income Bond Fund (IB)
  Limited Term Massachusetts Tax-Free
    Municipal Bond Fund (MB-S)

  Limited Term Tax-Free Municipal Bond Fund
    (MB-N)
  Limited Term New York Tax-Free Municipal
    Bond Fund (MB-S)
  Managed Income Bond Fund (IB)
  Maryland Municipal Bond Fund (MB-S)
  Massachusetts Municipal Bond Fund (MB-S)
  Michigan Municipal Bond Fund (MB-S)
  Minnesota Municipal Bond Fund (MB-S)
  North Carolina Municipal Bond Fund (MB-S)
  Ohio Municipal Bond Fund (MB-S)
  Oregon Municipal Bond Fund (MB-S)
  Pennsylvania Municipal Bond Fund (MB-S)
  Small Company Stock Fund (AG)
  Small Company Value Fund (AG)
  Texas Municipal Bond Fund (MB-S)
  Virginia Municipal Bond Fund (MB-S)
  New York Municipal Bond Fund (MB-S)
  Municipal Bond Fund (MB-N)
Dreyfus S&P 500 Index Fund (G)
Dreyfus Short-Intermediate Government Fund
  (USGI)
Dreyfus Short-Intermediate Municipal Bond
  Fund (MB-N)
Dreyfus Short-Term Income Fund, Inc. (IB)
Dreyfus Socially Responsible Growth Fund (G)
Dreyfus Special Growth Fund (G)
Dreyfus Stock Index Fund (G)
Dreyfus Strategic Growth L.P. (AG)
Dreyfus Strategic Income (IM)
Dreyfus Strategic Investing (AG)
Dreyfus Tax Exempt Cash Management
  (MM-TE)
Dreyfus Third Century Fund, Inc. (G)
Dreyfus Treasury Cash Management (MM-T)
Dreyfus Treasury Prime Cash Management
  (MM-T)
Dreyfus Variable Investment Fund
  Asset Allocation Portfolio (G+I)
  Capital Appreciation Portfolio (G+I)
  Money Market Portfolio (MM-T)
  Quality Bond Portfolio (IB)
  Small Cap Portfolio (G)
  Zero Coupon 2000 Portfolio (USGI)
Dreyfus-Wilshire Target Funds, Inc.
  4500 Index Fund (G)
  Large Company Growth Portfolio (G)
  Large Company Value Portfolio (G)
  Small Company Growth Portfolio (AG)
  Small Company Value Portfolio (AG)
Dreyfus Worldwide Dollar Money Market
  Fund, Inc. (MM-T)

Dupree Mutual Funds
P.O. Box 1149
Lexington, Kentucky 40589
(800) 866-0614
        or
125 South Mill Street, Suite 100
Lexington, Kentucky 40507
(606) 254-7741

Dupree Mutual Funds
Intermediate Government Bond Series (USGI)
Kentucky Tax-Free Income Series (MB-S)
Kentucky Tax-Free Short-to-Intermediate
  Series (MB-S)
Tennessee Tax-Free Income Series (MB-S)
Tennessee Tax-Free Short-to-Intermediate
  Series (MB-S)

Eagle Growth Shares, Inc.
1200 North Federal Highway, Suite 424
Boca Raton, Florida 33432
(407) 395-2155   (800) 749-9933
Eagle Growth Shares, Inc. (G)

Eaton Vance
24 Federal Street
Boston, Massachusetts 02110-2575
(617) 482-8260   (800) 225-6265
Eaton Vance Cash Management Fund (MM-T)
Eaton Vance Equity-Income Trust (IE)
Eaton Vance Government Obligations Trust
  Eaton Vance Government Obligations Fund
    (USGI)
  Eaton Vance Short-Term Treasury Fund
    (USGI)
Eaton Vance Growth Trust
  Eaton Vance Greater China Growth Fund
    (INT)
  Eaton Vance Growth Fund (G)
  Eaton Vance Marathon Greater China
    Growth Fund (INT)
Eaton Vance High Income Trust (HYB)
Eaton Vance Income Fund of Boston (HYB)
Eaton Vance Investment Fund, Inc.
  Eaton Vance Short-Term Global Income
    Fund (GB)
Eaton Vance Investment Trust
  California Limited Maturity Tax Free Fund
    (MB-S)
  California Municipals Fund (MB-S)
  Connecticut Limited Maturity Tax Free Fund
    (MB-S)
  Florida Limited Maturity Tax Free Fund
    (MB-S)
  Massachusetts Limited Maturity Tax Free
    Fund (MB-S)
  Michigan Limited Maturity Tax Free Fund
    (MB-S)
  National Limited Maturity Tax Free Fund
    (MB-N)
  New Jersey Limited Maturity Tax Free Fund
    (MB-S)
  New York Limited Maturity Tax Free Fund
    (MB-S)
  Ohio Limited Maturity Tax Free Fund (MB-S)
  Pennsylvania Limited Maturity Tax Free
    Fund (MB-S)
Eaton Vance Investors Fund (B)

Eaton Vance Liquid Assets Trust (MM-T)
Eaton Vance Municipal Bond Fund L.P. (MB-N)
Eaton Vance Municipals Trust
  Alabama Tax Free Fund (MB-S)
  Arizona Tax Free Fund (MB-S)
  Arkansas Tax Free Fund (MB-S)
  Colorado Tax Free Fund (MB-S)
  Connecticut Tax Free Fund (MB-S)
  Florida Tax Free Fund (MB-S)
  Georgia Tax Free Fund (MB-S)
  Kentucky Tax Free Fund (MB-S)
  Louisiana Tax Free Fund (MB-S)
  Maryland Tax Free Fund (MB-S)
  Massachusetts Municipal Bond Portfolio
    (MB-S)
  Massachusetts Tax Free Fund (MB-S)
  Michigan Tax Free Fund (MB-S)
  Minnesota Tax Free Fund (MB-S)
  Mississippi Tax Free Fund (MB-S)
  Missouri Tax Free Fund (MB-S)
  National Municipal Fund (MB-N)
  New Jersey Tax Free Fund (MB-S)
  New York Tax Free Fund (MB-S)
  North Carolina Tax Free Fund (MB-S)
  Ohio Tax Free Fund (MB-S)
  Oregon Tax Free Fund (MB-S)
  Pennsylvania Tax Free Fund (MB-S)
  Rhode Island Tax Free Fund (MB-S)
  South Carolina Tax Free Fund (MB-S)
  Tennessee Tax Free Fund (MB-S)
  Texas Tax Free Fund (MB-S)
  Virginia Tax Free Fund (MB-S)
  West Virginia Tax Free Fund (MB-S)
Eaton Vance Natural Resources Trust (AG)
Eaton Vance Special Investment Trust
  Eaton Vance Special Equities Fund (G)
Eaton Vance Stock Fund (G+I)
Eaton Vance Tax Free Reserves (MM-TE)
Eaton Vance Total Return Trust (G+I)

EBI Funds, Inc.
1355 Peachtree Street N.E., Suite 500
Atlanta, Georgia 30309
(404) 892-0666   (800) 554-1156
EBI Funds, Inc.
  EBI Cash Management Fund (MM-T)
  EBI Equity Fund (G+I)
  EBI Flex Fund (FP)
  EBI Income Fund (IB)
  EBI Multiflex Fund (IB)
  EBI Relative Return Bond Fund (IB)

Eclipse Financial Asset Trust
144 East 30th Street
New York, New York 10016
(212) 696-4130   (800) 872-2710
Eclipse Financial Asset Trust
  Eclipse Balanced Fund (B)
  Eclipse Equity Fund (G)

Edward D. Jones & Co.
Federated Investors Tower
Pittsburgh, Pennsylvania 15222-3779
(412) 288-1900   (800) 331-2451
Edward D. Jones & Co. Daily Passport Cash
    Trust (MM-T)

Elfun
P.O. Box 120074
Stamford, Connecticut 06912-0074
    or
3003 Summer Street, 6th Floor
Stamford, Connecticut 06904
(203) 326-4040   (800) 242-0134
Elfun Diversified Fund (B)
Elfun Global Fund (GE)
Elfun Income Fund (CB)
Elfun Money Market Fund (MM-T)
Elfun Tax-Exempt Income Fund (MB-N)
Elfun Trusts Fund (G)

Elite Group
1325 Fourth Street, Suite 2144
Seattle, Washington 98101
(206) 624-5863   (800) 423-1068
Elite Group
    Elite Growth & Income Fund (The) (G+I)
    Elite Income Fund (The) (IB)

Empire Builder Tax Free Bond Fund
237 Park Avenue, Suite 910
New York, New York 10017
(212) 808-3900   (800) 662-0417
Empire Builder Tax Free Bond Fund (MB-S)

Endeavor Series Trust
1100 Newport Center Drive, Suite 200
Newport Beach, California 92660
(714) 760-0505   (800) 854-8393
Endeavor Series Trust
    Global Growth Portfolio (GE)
    Managed Asset Allocation Portfolio (FP)
    Money Market Portfolio (MM-T)
    Quest for Value Equity Portfolio (G)
    Quest for Value Small Cap Portfolio (AG)
    U.S. Government Securities Fund (USGI)

Endowments, Inc.
Four Emarcadero Center
P.O. Box 7650
San Francisco, California 94120-7650
(415) 421-9360   (800) 421-0180
Endowments, Inc. (G+I)

Enterprise Group of Funds, Inc.
1200 Ashwood Parkway, Suite 290
Atlanta, Georgia 30338
(404) 396-8118   (800) 432-4320
Enterprise Group of Funds, Inc.
    Capital Appreciation Portfolio (AG)

Government Securities Portfolio (USGI)
Growth and Income Portfolio (G+I)
Growth Portfolio (G)
High-Yield Bond Portfolio (HYB)
International Growth Portfolio (INT)
Money Market Portfolio (MM-T)
Small Company Portfolio (AG)
Tax-Exempt Income Portfolio (MB-N)

EquiFund
1000 Lafayette Plaza
Bridgeport, Connecticut 06605
(800) 888-9471
EquiFund-Wright National Fiduciary Equity
    Funds
EquiFund-Belgian/Luxembourg National
    Fiduciary Equity Fund (INT)
EquiFund-Dutch National Fiduciary Equity
    Fund (INT)
EquiFund-Hong Kong National Fiduciary
    Equity Fund (INT)
EquiFund-Italian National Equity Fund (INT)
EquiFund-Japanese National Fiduciary
    Equity Fund (INT)
EquiFund-Mexico National Fiduciary Equity
    Fund (INT)
EquiFund-Nordic National Fiduciary Equity
    Fund (INT)
EquiFund-Spanish National Fiduciary Equity
    Fund (INT)
EquiFund-Swiss National Fiduciary Equity
    Fund (INT)

EuroPacific Growth Fund
333 South Hope Street
Los Angeles 90071-1447
(213) 486-9200   (800) 421-0180
EuroPacific Growth Fund (INT)

Evergreen
2500 Westchester Avenue
Purchase, New York 10577-2555
(914) 694-2020   (800) 235-0064
Evergreen American Retirement Trust
    Evergreen American Retirement Fund (G+I)
    Evergreen Small Cap Equity Income Fund
        (IE)
Evergreen Fixed-Income Trust
    Evergreen U.S. Government Securities Fund
        (USGI)
Evergreen Foundation Trust
    Evergreen Foundation Fund (B)
    Evergreen Tax Strategic Foundation Fund (B)
Evergreen Fund (AG)
Evergreen Limited Market Fund, Inc. (AG)
Evergreen Money Market Trust (MM-T)
Evergreen Municipal Trust
    Evergreen National Tax Free Fund (MB-N)
    Evergreen Short-Intermediate Municipal
        Fund (MB-N)
    Evergreen Short-Intermediate Municipal
        Fund - California (MB-S)

Evergreen Tax Exempt Money Market Fund
(MM-TE)
Evergreen Real Estate Equity Trust
Evergreen Global Real Estate Equity Fund
(GE)
Evergreen U.S. Real Estate Equity Fund (AG)
Evergreen Total Return Fund (G+I)
Evergreen Growth & Income Fund (G+I)

Excel
16955 Via Del Campo, Suite 110
San Diego, California 92127
(619) 485-9400   (800) 783-3444
Excel Midas Gold Shares, Inc. (PMG)
Excel Value Fund, Inc. (G)

Executive Investors Trust
95 Wall Street
New York, New York 10005-4297
(212) 858-8000 (800) 221-3846
Executive Investors Trust
Executive Investors Blue Chip Fund (IE)
Executive Investors High Yield Fund (HYB)
Executive Investors Insured Tax Exempt
Fund (MB-N)

Fasciano Fund, Inc.
190 S. LaSalle Street, Suite 2800
Chicago, Illinois 60603
(312) 444-6050
Fasciano Fund, Inc. (G)

FBL
5400 University Avenue
W. Des Moines, Iowa 50266-5997
(515) 225-5400   (800) 247-4170
(800) 422-3175 (Iowa only)
FBL Money Market Fund, Inc. (MM-T)
FBL Series Fund, Inc.
Blue Chip Portfolio (G+I)
Growth Common Stock Portfolio (G)
High Grade Bond Portfolio (IB)
High Yield Bond Portfolio (HYB)
Managed Portfolio (FP)
Money Market Portfolio (MM-T)

Federated
Federated Investors Tower
Pittsburgh, Pennsylvania 15222-3779
(412) 288-1900   (800) 245-2423
Federated Adjustable Rate U.S. Government
Securities Fund (GNMA)
Federated ARMs Fund (GNMA)
Federated U.S. Government Bond Fund (USGI)
Federated GNMA Trust (GNMA)
Federated Government Trust
Automated Government Cash Reserves
(MM-T)
Automated Treasury Cash Reserves (MM-T)
U.S. Treasury Cash Reserves (MM-T)

Federated Growth Trust (AG)
Federated High Yield Trust (HYB)
Federated Income Trust (USGI)
Federated Index Trust
Max-Cap Fund (G+I)
Mid-Cap Fund (G)
Mini-Cap Fund (G+I)
Federated Intermediate Government Trust
(USGI)
Intermediate Municipal Trust (MB-N)
Federated Master Trust (MM-T)
Federated Municipal Trust
Connecticut Municipal Cash Trust (MMS-TE)
Massachusetts Municipal Cash Trust
(MMS-TE)
Minnesota Municipal Cash Trust (MMS-TE)
New Jersey Municipal Cash Trust (MMS-TE)
Ohio Municipal Cash Trust (MMS-TE)
Pennsylvania Municipal Cash Trust (MMS-TE)
Federated Short-Intermediate Government
Trust (USGI)
Federated Short-Term Income Fund (IM)
Short-Term Municipal Trust (MB-N)
Federated Short-Term U.S. Government
Securities Fund (MM-T)
Federated Short Term U.S. Government Trust
(MM-T)
Federated Short Term U.S. Treasury
Securities Fund (USGI)
Stock & Bond Fund (B)
Federated Stock Trust (G+I)
Federated Tax Free Trust (MM-TE)

Fenimore Asset Management Trust
P.O. Box 399
Cobleskill, New York 12043
(518) 234-7462   (800) 932-3271
Fenimore Asset Management Trust
FAM Value Fund (G+I)

FFB Funds Trust
Furman Selz
237 Park Ave, Suite 910
New York, New York 10017
(212) 808-3900 (800) 437-8790
FFB Funds Trust
FFB Cash Management Fund (MM-T)
FFB Equity Fund (G)
FFB New Jersey Tax-Free Income Fund
(MB-S)
FFB Pennsylvania Tax-Free Money Market
Fund (MMS-TE)
FFB Tax-Free Money Market Fund (MM-TE)
FFB U.S. Government Fund (MM-T)
FFB U.S. Government Income Fund (USGI)
FFB U.S. Treasury Fund (MM-T)
FFB Shares of the New Jersey Daily Municipal
Income Money Market Fund (MM-T)
FFB Shares of the Connecticut Tax-Free
Income Fund (IE)

FFB Shares of the Balanced Fund (B)
FFB Shares of the Pennsylvania Tax-Free
Income Fund (IE)
FFB Shares of the First Union High Grade
Tax-Free Fund (IE)

FFB Lexicon Funds
680 East Swedesford Road, No. 7
Wayne, Pennsylvania 19087-1658
(800) 833-8974
FFB Lexicon Funds
Capital Appreciation Equity Fund (The) (G)
Cash Management Fund (The) (MM-T)
Fixed Income Fund (The) (IB)
Intermediate-Term Government Securities
Fund (The) (USGI)
Select Value Fund (The) (CB)
Small Company Growth Fund (The) (AG)

FFTW Funds, Inc.
717 Fifth Avenue, 14th Floor
New York, New York 10022
(212) 350-8000
or
AMT Capital Services
430 Park Avenue, 17th Floor
New York, New York 10022
(212) 308-4848   (800) 762-4848
FFTW Funds, Inc.
AAA Asset-Backed Portfolio (IB)
Stable Return Portfolio (IB)
U.S. Short-Term Fixed Income Portfolio (IM)
Worldwide Fixed Income Portfolio (GB)
Worldwide Short-Term Fixed Income
Portfolio (IB)

Fidelity
82 Devonshire Street
Boston, Massachusetts 02109-3605
(617) 570-7000
or
P.O. Box 5000
Cincinnati, Ohio 45273-8694
(800) 544-8888   (800) 544-9797
Fidelity Advisor Series I
Fidelity Advisor Equity Portfolio Growth (AG)
Fidelity Advisor Series II
Fidelity Advisor Government Investment
Fund (USGI)
Fidelity Advisor Growth Opportunities Fund
(G)
Fidelity Advisor High Yield Fund (HYB)
Fidelity Advisor Income & Growth Fund (B)
Fidelity Advisor Short Fixed Income Fund (IB)
Fidelity Advisor Series III
Fidelity Advisor Equity Portfolio Income (G+I)
Fidelity Advisor Series IV
Fidelity Advisor Government Investment
Fund (USGI)
Fidelity Advisor Institutional Limited Term
Bond Fund (IB)

Fidelity Advisor Limited Term Bond Fund
(IB)
Fidelity Series V
Fidelity Advisor Global Natural Resources
Fund (GE)
Fidelity Advisor High Income Municipal
Fund (MB-N)
Fidelity Advisor Series VI
Fidelity Advisor Institutional Limited Term
Tax-Exempt Fund (MB-N)
Fidelity Advisor Limited Term Tax-Exempt
Fund (MB-N)
Fidelity Advisor North American
Government Portfolio (IB)
Fidelity Advisor Tax-Exempt Portfolio (MB-N)
Fidelity Advisor Series VII
Fidelity Overseas Fund (INT)
Fidelity Advisor Series VIII
Fidelity Advisor Strategic Opportunities
Fund (AG)
Fidelity Strategic Opportunities Fund (AG)
Fidelity Beacon Street Trust
Fidelity Tax-Exempt Money Market Trust
(MM-TE)
Spartan New Jersey Municipal Money
Market Portfolio (MMS-TE)
Fidelity California Municipal Trust
Fidelity California Tax-Free High Yield
Portfolio (MB-S)
Fidelity California Tax-Free Insured Portfolio
(MB-S)
Fidelity California Tax-Free Money Market
Portfolio (MMS-TE)
Spartan California Intermediate Municipal
Portfolio (MB-S)
Spartan California Municipal High Yield
Portfolio (MB-S)
Spartan California Municipal Money Market
Portfolio (MMS-TE)
Fidelity California Municipal Trust II (MMS-TE)
Fidelity Capital Trust
Fidelity Capital Appreciation Fund (AG)
Fidelity Disciplined Equity Fund (G)
Fidelity Stock Selector (G)
Fidelity Value Fund (G)
Fidelity Cash Reserves (MM-T)
Fidelity Charles Street Trust
Fidelity Asset Manager (FP)
Fidelity Asset Manager Growth Fund (FP)
Fidelity Asset Manager Income Fund (FP)
Fidelity Short/Intermediate Government
Fund (USGI)
Fidelity U.S. Government Reserves (MM-T)
Fidelity Commonwealth Trust
Fidelity Intermediate Bond Fund (IB)
Fidelity Market Index Fund (G+I)
Fidelity Small Cap Stock Fund (AG)
Fidelity Contrafund (AG)
Fidelity Court Street Trust
Fidelity High Yield Tax Free Portfolio (MB-N)
Spartan Arizona Municipal Income Portfolio
(MB-S)

Spartan Connecticut Municipal High Yield
  Portfolio (MB-S)
Spartan Florida Municipal Income Portfolio
  (MB-S)
Spartan New Jersey Municipal High Yield
  Portfolio (MB-S)
Fidelity Court Street Trust II
  Fidelity Connecticut Municipal Money
    Market Portfolio (MMS-TE)
  Fidelity New Jersey Tax-Free Money Market
    Portfolio (MMS-TE)
  Spartan Connecticut Municipal Money
    Market Portfolio (MMS-TE)
  Spartan Florida Municipal Money Market
    Portfolio (MMS-TE)
Fidelity Daily Income Trust (MM-T)
Fidelity Destiny Portfolios
  Destiny I (G)
  Destiny II (G)
Fidelity Deutsche Mark Performance
  Portfolio, L.P. (GB)
Fidelity Devonshire Trust
  Fidelity Equity Income-Fund (IE)
  Fidelity Real Estate Investment Portfolio
    (G+I)
  Fidelity Utilities Fund (IE)
  Spartan Long-Term Government Bond Fund
    (USGI)
Fidelity Export Fund (G)
Fidelity Fifty (G)
Fidelity Financial Trust
  Fidelity Convertible Securities Fund (G+I)
  Fidelity Equity Income Fund II (IE)
  Fidelity Retirement Growth Fund (AG)
Fidelity Fixed-Income Trust
  Fidelity Investment Grade Bond Fund (IB)
  Fidelity Short-Term Bond Portfolio (IB)
  Spartan Government Income Fund (USGI)
  Spartan High Income Fund (HYB)
  Spartan Investment Grade Bond Fund (CB)
  Spartan Short-Intermediate Government
    Fund (USGI)
  Spartan Short-Term Income Fund (IB)
Fidelity Fund, Inc. (G+I)
Fidelity Government Securities Fund (USGI)
Fidelity Income Fund
  Fidelity Ginnie Mae Portfolio (GNMA)
  Fidelity Mortgage Securities Portfolio
    (GNMA)
  Spartan Limited Maturity Government Fund
    (USGI)
Fidelity Institutional Trust
  Fidelity U.S. Bond Index Portfolio (USGI)
  Fidelity U.S. Equity Index Portfolio (G+I)
Fidelity Investment Trust
  Fidelity Canada Fund (INT)
  Fidelity Diversified International Fund (INT)
  Fidelity Emerging Market Fund (INT)
  Fidelity Europe Fund (INT)
  Fidelity Europe Capital Appreciation Fund
    (INT)
  Fidelity International Value Fund (INT)

  Fidelity Global Bond Fund (GB)
  Fidelity International Growth and Income
    Fund (INT)
  Fidelity Japan Fund (INT)
  Fidelity Latin America Fund (INT)
  Fidelity New Markets Income Fund (IB)
  Fidelity Overseas Fund (INT)
  Fidelity Pacific Basin Fund (INT)
  Fidelity SouthEast Asia Fund (INT)
  Fidelity Worldwide Fund (GE)
  Global Balanced Fund (GB)
Fidelity Limited Term Municipals (MB-N)
Fidelity Magellan Fund (AG)
Fidelity Massachusetts Municipal Trust
  Fidelity Massachusetts Tax-Free High Yield
    Portfolio (MB-S)
  Fidelity Massachusetts Tax-Free Money
    Market Portfolio (MMS-TE)
  Spartan Massachusetts Municipal Money
    Market Portfolio (MMS-TE)
Fidelity Mid-Cap Stock Fund (G)
Fidelity Money Market Trust
  Domestic Money Market Portfolio (MM-T)
  Retirement Government Money Market
    Portfolio (MM-T)
  Retirement Money Market Portfolio (MM-T)
  U.S. Government Portfolio (MM-T)
  U.S. Treasury Portfolio (MM-T)
Fidelity Mt. Vernon Street Trust
  Fidelity Emerging Growth Fund (AG)
  Fidelity Growth Company Fund (AG)
  Fidelity New Millenium Fund (AG)
Fidelity Municipal Trust
  Fidelity Aggressive Tax-Free Portfolio (MB-N)
  Fidelity Insured Tax-Free Portfolio (MB-N)
  Fidelity Michigan Tax-Free High Yield
    Portfolio (MB-S)
  Fidelity Minnesota Tax-Free Portfolio (MB-S)
  Fidelity Municipal Bond Portfolio (MB-N)
  Fidelity Ohio Tax-Free High Yield Portfolio
    (MB-S)
  Fidelity Ohio Municipal Money Market
    Portfolio (MB-S)
  Spartan Pennsylvania Municipal High Yield
    Portfolio (MB-S)
Fidelity Municipal Trust II
  Fidelity Michigan Municipal Money Market
    Portfolio (MMS-TE)
  Fidelity Ohio Municipal Money Market
    Portfolio (MMS-TE)
  Spartan Arizona Municipal Money Market
    Portfolio (MMS-TE)
  Spartan Pennsylvania Municipal Money
    Market Portfolio (MMS-TE)
Fidelity New York Municipal Trust
  Fidelity New York Tax-Free High Yield
    Portfolio (MB-S)
  Fidelity New York Tax-Free Insured Portfolio
    (MB-S)
  Spartan New York Intermediate Municipal
    Portfolio (MB-S)

Spartan New York Municipal High Yield
  Portfolio (MB-S)
Spartan New York Municipal Money Market
  Portfolio (MMS-TE)
Fidelity New York Municipal Trust II
  Fidelity New York Tax-Free Money Market
    Portfolio (MMS-TE)
Fidelity Puritan Trust
  Fidelity Balanced Fund (B)
  Fidelity Low-Priced Stock Fund (AG)
  Fidelity Puritan Fund (IE)
Fidelity School Street Trust
  Spartan Bond Strategist (IB)
Fidelity Securities Fund
  Fidelity Blue Chip Growth Fund (G)
  Fidelity Dividend Growth Fund (IE)
  Fidelity Growth & Income Portfolio (G+I)
  Fidelity OTC Portfolio (AG)
Fidelity Select Portfolios
  Air Transportation Portfolio (AG)
  American Gold Portfolio (PMG)
  Automotive Portfolio (AG)
  Biotechnology Portfolio (AG)
  Brokerage and Investment Management
    Portfolio (AG)
  Chemicals Portfolio (AG)
  Computers Portfolio (AG)
  Costruction and Housing Portfolio (AG)
  Consumer Products Portfolio (AG)
  Defense and Aerospace Portfolio (AG)
  Developing Communications Portfolio (AG)
  Electronics Portfolio (AG)
  Energy Portfolio (AG)
  Energy Service Portfolio (AG)
  Environmental Portfolio (AG)
  Financial Services Portfolio (AG)
  Food and Agriculture Portfolio (AG)
  Health Care Portfolio (AG)
  Home Finance Portfolio (AG)
  Industrial Equipment Portfolio (AG)
  Industrial Materials Portfolio (AG)
  Insurance Portfolio (AG)
  Leisure Portfolio (AG)
  Medical Delivery Portfolio (AG)
  Money Market Portfolio (MM-T)
  Multimedia Portfolio (AG)
  Natural Gas Portfolio (AG)
  Paper and Forest Products Portfolio (AG)
  Precious Metals and Minerals Portfolio
    (PMG)
  Regional Banks Portfolio (AG)
  Retailing Portfolio (AG)
  Software and Computer Services Portfolio
    (AG)
  Technology Portfolio (AG)
  Telecommunications Portfolio (AG)
  Transportation Portfolio (AG)
  Utilities Growth Portfolio (AG)
Fidelity Short-Term World Income Fund (GB)
Fidelity Sterling Performance Portfolio, L.P.
  (GB)

Fidelity Summer Street Trust
  Fidelity Capital & Income Fund (HYB)
  Spartan Money Market Fund (MM-T)
  Spartan Municipal Money Fund (MM-TE)
  Spartan U.S. Government Money Market
    Fund (MM-T)
  Spartan U.S. Treasury Money Market Fund
    (MM-T)
Fidelity Trend Fund (G)
Fidelity Union Street Trust
  Spartan Aggressive Municipal Fund (MB-N)
  Spartan Ginnie Mae Fund (GNMA)
  Spartan Intermediate Municipal Fund (MB-N)
  Spartan Maryland Municipal Income
    Portfolio (MB-S)
  Spartan Municipal Income Portfolio (MB-N)
  Spartan Short-Intermediate Municipal Fund
    (MB-N)
Fidelity U.S. Government Reserves (MM-T)
Fidelity Yen Performance Portfolio, L.P. (GB)

Fiduciary Management Associates
1345 Avenue of the Americas
New York, New York 10105
(212) 969-1000   (800) 221-5672
Fiduciary Management Associates (AG)

59 Wall St Funds
Brown Bros, Harriman & Co
59 Wall Street
New York, New York 10005
(212) 493-8100

59 Wall St European Equity Fund (INT)
59 Wall St Pacific Basin Equity Fund (INT)
59 Wall St Small Company Fund (AG)
59 Wall St Tax-Free Short/Intermediate Fixed
  Income Fund (MB-N)

Financial Horizons Investment Trust
One Nationwide Plaza
P.O. Box 182008
Columbus, Ohio 43218
(800) 533-5622

Financial Horizons Investment Trust
  Cash Reserve Fund (MM-T)
  Government Bond Fund (USGI)
  Growth Fund (G)
  Municipal Bond Fund (MB-N)

Financial Reserves Fund
Federated Investors Tower
Pittsburgh, Pennsylvania 15222-3779
(412) 288-1900   (800) 356-2805
Financial Reserves Fund (MM-T)

First American
680 East Swedesford Road
Wayne, Pennsylvania 19087
(800) 637-2548

First American Funds, Inc.
  Asset Allocation Fund (FP)

Balanced Fund (B)
Colorado Intermediate Tax Free Fund (MB-S)
Corporate Trust Government Fund (MM-T)
Corporate Trust Treasury Fund (MM-T)
Diversified Growth Fund (G)
Equity Income Fund (IE)
Equity Index Fund (G+I)
Emerging Growth Fund (AG)
Fixed Income Fund (IM)
Government Bond Fund (USGI)
Institutional Government Fund (USGI)
Institutional Money Fund (MB-N)
Intermediate Tax-Free Fund (MB-N)
Intermediate Government Bond Fund (USGI)
Intermediate Term Income Fund (IB)
International Fund (INT)
Limited Term Income Fund (IB)
Limited Term Tax Free Income Fund (IB)
Managed Income Fund (IE)
Minnesota Insured Intermediate Tax Free
  Fund (MB-S)
Money Fund (MM-T)
Mortgage Securities Fund (GNMA)
Municipal Bond Fund (MB-N)
Regional Equity Fund (AG)
Special Equity Fund (AG)
Stock Fund (G+I)
Technology Fund (G)

First Boston Investment Funds, Inc.
  Institutional Government Fund
  Institutional Money Market Fund
  Institutional Tax-Exempt Money Market Fund
12 East 49th Street
New York, New York 10017
(212) 909-4522   (800) 545-5799

First Boston Investment Funds, Inc.
  Institutional U.S. Treasury Money Market
  Fund
c/o Mutual Funds Service Co.
126 High Street
Boston, Massachusetts 02110
(617) 728-1180   (800) 774-4365

First Boston Investment Funds, Inc.
  Institutional Government Fund (USGI)
  Institutional Money Market Fund (MM-T)
  Institutional Tax-Exempt Money Market
    Fund (MM-TE)
  Institutional U.S. Treasury Money Market
    Fund (MM-T)

First Eagle Fund of America, Inc.
45 Broadway, 29th Floor
New York, New York 10006
(212) 943-9200   (800) 451-3623

First Eagle Fund of America, Inc. (G)
First Eagle International Fund, Inc. (G)

First Investors Corporation
95 Wall Street, 23rd Floor
New York, New York 10005-4297
(212) 858-8000   (800) 423-4026

First Investors Cash Management Fund, Inc.
  (MM-T)
First Investors Fund for Income, Inc. (HYB)
First Investors Global Fund, Inc. (GE)
First Investors Government Fund, Inc. (USGI)
First Investors High Yield Fund, Inc. (HYB)
First Investors Insured Intermediate Tax
  Exempt Series (MB-N)
First Investors Insured Tax Exempt Fund, Inc.
  (MB-N)
First Investors Life Series Fund
  Blue Chip Series (IE)
  Cash Management Series (MM-T)
  Discovery Series (AG)
  Government Series (USGI)
  Growth Series (G)
  High Yield Series (IM)
  International Securities Series (GE)
  Investment Grade Series (IM)
  Utilities Income Series (IE)
First Investors Multi-State Insured Tax Free
  Fund
  Arizona Series (MB-S)
  California Series (MB-S)
  Colorado Series (MB-S)
  Connecticut Series (MB-S)
  Florida Series (MB-S)
  Georgia Series (MB-S)
  Maryland Series (MB-S)
  Massachusetts Series (MB-S)
  Michigan Series (MB-S)
  Minnesota Series (MB-S)
  Missouri Series (MB-S)
  New Jersey Series (MB-S)
  North Carolina Series (MB-S)
  Ohio Series (MB-S)
  Oregon Series (MB-S)
  Pennsylvania Series (MB-S)
  Virginia Series (MB-S)
First Investors New York Insured Tax Free
  Fund, Inc. (MB-S)
First Investors Series Fund
  First Investors Blue Chip Series (IE)
  First Investors Investment Grade Series (IB)
  First Investors Special Situations Series (G)
  First Investors Total Return Series (FP)
First Investors Series Fund II
  Made in the USA Fund (G)
  Utilities Income Fund (IE)
First Investors Special Bond Fund, Inc. (HYB)
First Investors Tax-Exempt Money Market
  Fund, Inc. (MM-TE)
First Investors U.S. Government Plus Fund
  1st Series (USGI)
First Investors U.S. Government Plus Fund
  2nd Series (USGI)
First Investors U.S. Government Plus Fund
  3rd Series (USGI)

First Omaha Family of Funds
P.O. Box 419022
Kansas City, Missouri 64141-6022
(800) 662-4203

First Omaha Equity Fund (G+I)
First Omaha Fixed Income Fund (CB)
First Omaha Short Intermediate Fixed Income
  Fund (IB)
First Omaha U.S. Government Obligation
  Fund (MM-T)

First Pacific Mutual Fund, Inc.
1270 Queen Emma Street, Suite 607
Honolulu, Hawaii 96813
(808) 599-2400
First Pacific Mutual Fund, Inc.
  First Hawaii Municipal Bond Fund (MB-S)

First Priority Funds
Federated Investors Tower
Pittsburgh, Pennsylvania 15222-3779
(412) 288-1900   (800) 245-2423
First Priority Funds
  Equity Fund (G+I)
  Fixed Income Fund (IM)
  Treasury Money Market Fund (MM-T)

First Union Funds
Federated Investors Tower
Pittsburgh, Pennsylvania 15222-3779
(412) 288-1900   (800) 356-2805
First Union Funds
  Balanced Portfolio (B)
  Fixed Income Portfolio (IM)
  Florida Municipal Income Portfolio (MB-S)
  Georgia Municipal Income Portfolio (MB-S)
  Insured Tax-Free Portfolio (MB-N)
  Managed Bond Portfolio (IB)
  Money Market Portfolio (MM-T)
  North Carolina Municipal Bond Portfolio
    (MB-S)
  South Carolina Municipal Income Portfolio
    (MB-S)
  Tax-Free Money Market Portfolio (MM-TE)
  Treasury Money Market Portfolio (MM-T)
  U.S. Government Portfolio (USGI)
  Value Portfolio (G)
  Virginia Municipal Income Portfolio (MB-S)
First Union Series Trust II
  Fidelity Daily Income Trust (MM-T)
  Spartan Municipal Money Fund (MM-TE)

Flag Investors
135 East Baltimore Street
Baltimore, Maryland 21202-1607
(410) 727-1700   (800) 767-3524
Flag Investors Emerging Growth Fund, Inc.
  (AG)
Flag Investors Intermediate Term Income
  Fund, Inc. (IM)
Flag Investors International Fund (INT)
Flag Investors Managed Municipal Fund
  (MB-N)

Flag Investors Maryland Intermediate Tax-
  Free Fund (MB-S)
Flag Investors Quality Growth Fund, Inc. (G)
Flag Investors Telephone Income Fund, Inc.
  (IM)
Flag Investors Total Return U.S. Treasury
  Fund, Inc. (USGI)
Flag Investors Value Builder Fund, Inc. (B)

Flagship
One First National Plaza, Suite 910
Dayton, Ohio 45402-1506
(513) 461-0332   (800) 227-4648
Flagship Admiral Funds
  Flagship Utility Income Fund (IM)
  Golden Rainbow Fund (B)
Flagship Tax Exempt Funds
  All-American Tax Exempt Fund (MB-N)
  Alabama Double Tax Exempt Fund (MB-S)
  Arizona Double Tax Exempt Fund (MB-S)
  Colorado Double Tax Exempt Fund (MB-S)
  Connecticut Double Tax Exempt Fund
    (MB-S)
  Florida Double Tax Exempt Fund (MB-S)
  Georgia Double Tax Exempt Fund (MB-S)
  Intermediate Tax Exempt Fund (MB-N)
  Kansas Double Tax Exempt Fund (MB-S)
  Kentucky Triple Tax Exempt Fund (MB-S)
  Limited Term Tax Exempt Fund (MB-N)
  Louisiana Double Tax Exempt Fund (MB-S)
  Michigan Triple Tax Exempt Fund (MB-S)
  Missouri Double Tax Exempt Fund (MB-S)
  New Jersey Double Tax Exempt Fund
    (MB-S)
  New Jersey Intermediate Tax Exempt Fund
    (MB-S)
  New Mexico Double Tax Exempt Fund (MB-S)
  New York Tax Exempt Fund (MB-S)
  North Carolina Triple Tax Exempt Fund
    (MB-S)
  Ohio Double Tax Exempt Fund (MB-S)
  Pennsylvania Triple Tax Exempt Fund (MB-S)
  South Carolina Double Tax Exempt Fund
    (MB-S)
  Tennessee Double Tax Exempt Fund (MB-S)
  Virginia Double Tax Exempt Fund (MB-S)
  Wisconsin Tax Exempt Fund (MB-S)

Flex-Funds
6000 Memorial Drive
P.O. Box 7177
Dublin, Ohio 43017-0777
(614) 766-7000 (800) 325-3539
Flex-Funds
  Bond Fund (The) (IB)
  Growth Fund (The) (G)
  Money Market Fund (The) (MM-T)
  Muirfield Fund (The) (G)
  Short-Term Global Income Fund (The) (GB)
Institutional Fund (MM-T)

FMB Funds, Inc.
237 Park Avenue, Suite 910
New York, New York 10017
(212) 808-3900   (800) 453-4234

FMB Funds, Inc.
 FMB Diversified Equity Fund (G)
 FMB Intermediate Government Income Fund
  (USGI)
 FMB Michigan Tax-Free Bond Fund (MB-S)
 FMB Money Market Fund (MM-T)

FN Network Tax Free Money Market Fund, Inc.
144 Glenn Curtiss Boulevard
Uniondale, New York 11556-0144
(800) 544-8888

FN Network Tax Free Money Market Fund,
 Inc. (MM-TE)

Forum Funds
2 Portland Square
Portland, Maine 04101
(207) 879-0001

Forum Investors Bond Fund (CB)
Forum Maine Municipal Bond Fund (MB-S)
Forum New Hampshire Municipal Bond Fund
 (MB-S)
Forum Tax Saver Bond Fund (MB-N)
Payson Balanced Fund (B)
Payson Value Fund (G)

Fortis
P.O. Box 64284
St. Paul, Minnesota 55164
(612) 738-4000 (800) 800-2638

Fortis Advantage Portfolios, Inc.
 Asset Allocation Portfolio (G+I)
 Capital Appreciation Portfolio (G)
 Government Total Return Portfolio (USGI)
 High Yield Portfolio (HYB)
Fortis Equity Portfolios
 Fortis Capital Fund, Inc. (G+I)
 Fortis Fiduciary Fund, Inc. (AG)
 Fortis Growth Fund, Inc. (G)
Fortis Income Portfolios, Inc.
 Fortis U.S. Government Securities Fund
  (USGI)
Fortis Money Portfolios, Inc.
 Fortis Money Fund (MM-T)
Fortis Tax-Free Portfolios, Inc.
 Minnesota Portfolio (MB-S)
 National Portfolio (MB-N)
 New York Portfolio (MB-S)
Fortis Worldwide Portfolios, Inc.
 Fortis Global Growth Portfolio (GE)

Fortress
Federated Investors Tower
Liberty Center
Pittsburgh, Pennsylvania 15222-3779
(412) 288-1900 (800) 245-4770

Fortress Adjustable U.S. Government Fund,
 Inc. (USGI)
Fortress Municipal Income Fund, Inc. (MB-N)
Fortress Utility Fund, Inc. (IE)

44 Wall Street Equity Fund, Inc.
26 Broadway, Suite 205
New York, New York 10004
(212) 248-8080   (800) 543-2620
44 Wall Street Equity Fund, Inc. (G)

Founders Funds, Inc.
2930 East Third Avenue
Denver, Colorado 80206
(303) 394-4404   (800) 525-2440
Founders Balanced Fund (B)
Founders Blue Chip Fund (G+I)
Founders Discovery Fund (AG)
Founders Frontier Fund (AG)
Founders Government Securities Fund (USGI)
Founders Growth Fund (G)
Founders Passport Fund (INT)
Founders Special Fund (G)
Founders Worldwide Growth Fund (GE)

Fountain Square Funds
Federated Investors Tower
Pittsburgh, Pennsylvania 15222-3779
(412) 288-1900 (800) 356-2805
Fountain Square Funds
 Balanced Fund (B)
 Commercial Paper Fund (MM-T)
 Government Cash Reserves Fund (MM-T)
 MidCap Fund (G+I)
 Ohio Tax Free Bond Fund (MB-S)
 Quality Bond Fund (CB)
 Quality Growth Fund (G)
 U.S. Government Securities Fund (USGI)
 U.S. Treasury Obligations Fund (MM-T)

FPA
11400 West Olympic Boulevard, Suite 1200
Los Angeles, California 90064
(310) 996-5425   (800) 982-4372
FPA Capital Fund, Inc. (G)
FPA New Income, Inc. (IB)
FPA Paramount Fund, Inc. (G+I)
FPA Perennial Fund, Inc. (G+I)

Franklin
777 Mariners Island Boulevard
San Mateo, California 94404-1585
(415) 312-2000   (800) 342-5236
Franklin Balance Sheet Investment Fund (G+I)
Franklin California Tax-Free Income Fund, Inc.
 (MB-S)
Franklin California Tax-Free Trust
 Franklin California Insured Tax-Free Income
  Fund (MB-S)
 Franklin California Intermediate-Term Tax-
  Free Income Fund (MB-S)

Franklin California Tax-Exempt Money Fund (MMS-TE)
Franklin Custodian Funds, Inc.
DynaTech Series (AG)
Growth Series (G)
Income Series (IM)
U.S. Government Securities Series (GNMA)
Utilities Series (G+I)
Franklin Federal Money Fund (MM-T)
Franklin Federal Tax-Free Income Fund (MB-N)
Franklin Gold Fund (PMG)
Franklin International Trust
Franklin International Equity Fund (INT)
Franklin Pacific Growth Fund (INT)
Franklin Investors Securities Trust
Franklin Adjustable Rate Securities Fund (GNMA)
Franklin Adjustable U.S. Government Securities Fund (USGI)
Franklin Convertible Securities Fund (G+I)
Franklin Global Government Income Fund (GB)
Franklin Short-Intermediate U.S. Government Securities Fund (USGI)
Franklin Special Equity Income Fund (IE)
Franklin Managed Trust
Franklin Corporate Qualified Dividend Fund (IM)
Franklin Investment Grade Income Fund (CB)
Franklin Rising Dividends Fund (G)
Franklin Money Fund (MM-T)
Franklin Municipal Securities Trust
Franklin California High Yield Municipal Fund (MB-S)
Franklin Hawaii Municipal Bond Fund (MB-S)
Franklin Washington Municipal Bond Fund (MB-S)
Franklin New York Tax-Free Income Fund, Inc. (MB-S)
Franklin New York Tax-Free Trust
Franklin New York Insured Tax-Free Income Fund (MB-S)
Franklin New York Intermediate-Term Tax-Free Income Fund (MB-S)
Franklin New York Tax-Exempt Money Fund (MMS-TE)
Franklin Partners Funds
Franklin Tax-Advantaged High Yield Securities Fund (HYB)
Franklin Tax-Advantaged International Bond Fund (INT)
Franklin Tax-Advantaged U.S. Government Securities Fund (GNMA)
Franklin Premier Return Fund (IE)
Franklin Strategic Mortgage Portfolio (GNMA)
Franklin Strategic Series
FISCO MidCap Growth Fund (G)
Franklin California Growth Fund (G)
Franklin Global Health Care Fund (GE)
Franklin Global Utilities Fund (GE)
Franklin Small Cap Growth Fund (G)
Franklin Tax-Exempt Money Fund (MM-TE)

Franklin Tax-Free Trust
Franklin Alabama Tax-Free Income Fund (MB-S)
Franklin Arizona Insured Tax-Free Income Fund (MB-S)
Franklin Arizona Tax-Free Income Fund (MB-S)
Franklin Colorado Tax-Free Income Fund (MB-S)
Franklin Connecticut Tax-Free Income Fund (MB-S)
Franklin Federal Intermediate-Term Tax-Free Income Fund (MB-N)
Franklin Florida Insured Tax-Free Income Fund (MB-S)
Franklin Florida Tax-Free Income Fund (MB-S)
Franklin Georgia Tax-Free Income Fund (MB-S)
Franklin High Yield Tax-Free Income Fund (MB-N)
Franklin Indiana Tax-Free Income Fund (MB-S)
Franklin Insured Tax-Free Income Fund (MB-N)
Franklin Kentucky Tax-Free Income Fund (MB-S)
Franklin Louisiana Tax-Free Income Fund (MB-S)
Franklin Maryland Tax-Free Income Fund (MB-S)
Franklin Massachusetts Insured Tax-Free Income Fund (MB-S)
Franklin Michigan Insured Tax-Free Income Fund (MB-S)
Franklin Minnesota Insured Tax-Free Income Fund (MB-S)
Franklin Missouri Tax-Free Income Fund (MB-S)
Franklin New Jersey Tax-Free Income Fund (MB-S)
Franklin North Carolina Tax-Free Income Fund (MB-S)
Franklin Ohio Insured Tax-Free Income Fund (MB-S)
Franklin Oregon Tax-Free Income Fund (MB-S)
Franklin Pennsylvania Tax-Free Income Fund (MB-S)
Franklin Puerto Rico Tax-Free Income Fund (MB-S)
Franklin Texas Tax-Free Income Fund (MB-S)
Franklin Virginia Tax-Free Income Fund (MB-S)

Frank Russell Investment Company
909 A Street
Tacoma, Washington 98402
(206) 627-7001 (800) 972-0700

Frank Russell Investment Company
Diversified Bond Fund (IB)
Diversified Equity Fund (G+I)

Emerging Markets Fund (INT)
Equity I Fund (G+I)
Equity II Fund (AG)
Equity III Fund (IE)
Equity Income Fund (G+I)
Equity Q Fund (G+I)
Fixed Income I Fund (IB)
Fixed Income II Fund (IB)
Fixed Income III Fund (IB)
International Fund (INT)
International Securities Fund (INT)
Limited Volatility Tax Free Fund (MB-N)
Money Market Fund (MM-T)
MultiStrategy Bond Fund (IB)
Quantitative Equity Fund (G+I)
Real Estate Securities Fund (G+I)
Special Growth Fund (G)
Tax Free Money Market Fund (MM-TE)
U.S. Government Money Market Fund
 (MM-T)
Volatility Constrained Bond Fund (IB)

Freedom California Tax Exempt Money Fund
Freedom Mutual Fund
One Beacon Street
Boston, Massachusetts 02108-3105
(617) 725-2300   (800) 435-8206
Freedom California Tax Exempt Money Fund
 (MMS-TE)
Freedom Mutual Fund
 Freedom Cash Management Fund (MM-T)
 Freedom Government Securities Fund
  (MM-T)
 Freedom Tax Exempt Money Fund (MM-TE)
 Freedom U.S. Treasury Money Market Fund
  (MM-T)

Freedom Investment Trust
101 Huntington Avenue
Boston, Massachusetts 02119-7603
(617) 375-1500   (800) 225-5291
Freedom Investment Trust
 John Hancock Freedom Gold & Government
  Fund (USGI)
 John Hancock Freedom Money Market Fund
  (MM-T)
 John Hancock Freedom Regional Bank Fund
  (G)
 John Hancock Managed Tax-Exempt Fund
  (MB-N)
 John Hancock Sovereign Achievers Fund (G)
 John Hancock Sovereign U.S. Government
  Income Fund (USGI)
Freedom Investment Trust II
 John Hancock Freedom Global Fund (GE)
 John Hancock Freedom Global Income Fund
  (GB)
 John Hancock Freedom Short-Term World
  Income Fund (GB)

Freedom Investment Trust III
 John Hancock Discovery Fund (G)
 John Hancock Freedom Environmental
  Fund (G)

Fremont Mutual Funds, Inc.
50 Fremont Street, Suite 3600
San Francisco, California 94105-2239
(415) 768-9000   (800) 548-4539
Fremont Mutual Funds, Inc.
 Fremont Bond Fund (IB)
 Fremont California Intermediate Tax-Free
  Fund (MB-S)
 Fremont Global Fund (GB)
 Fremont Growth Fund (G+I)
 Fremont Income Fund (IB)
 Fremont International Growth Fund (INT)
 Fremont Money Market Fund (MM-T)

Frontier Funds, Inc.
101 West Wisconsin Avenue
P.O. Box 68
Pewaukee, Wisconsin 53072-0068
(414) 691-1196   (800) 231-2901
Frontier Funds, Inc.
 Equity Fund Portfolio (G)

FT Series, Inc.
Federated Investors Tower
Pittsburgh, Pennsylvania 15222-3779
(412) 288-1900   (800) 245-2423
FT Series, Inc.
 International Equity Fund (INT)
 International Income Fund (GB)

Fundamental
90 Washington Street, 19th Floor
New York, New York 10006
(212) 635-3000   (800) 225-6864
Fundamental California Muni Fund (MB-S)
Fundamental Fixed-Income Fund
 High Yield Municipal Bond Series (HYB)
 Tax-Free Money Market Series (MM-TE)
 U.S. Government Strategic Income Series
  (USGI)
Fundamental New York Muni Fund (MB-S)

Fundamental Investors, Inc.
Four Embarcadero Center
P.O. Box 7650
San Francisco, California 94120-7650
(415) 421-9360 (800) 421-0180
Fundamental Investors, Inc. (G+I)

Fund for U.S. Government Securities, Inc.
Federated Investors Tower
Pittsburgh, Pennsylvania 15222-3779
(412) 288-1900   (800) 245-4770
Fund for U.S. Government Securities, Inc.
 (USGI)

FundTrust
6 St. James Avenue
Boston, Massachusetts 02116
(617) 423-0800   (800) 638-1896
Republic Funds
  FundTrust Aggressive Growth Fund (AG)
  FundTrust Growth Fund (G)
  FundTrust Growth and Income Fund (G+I)
  FundTrust Income Fund (IB)
  FundTrust Managed Total Return Fund (G+I)
Republic MoneyTrust (MM-T)

Gabelli
One Corporate Center
Rye, New York 10580-1434
(914) 921-5100   (800) 422-3554
Gabelli ABC Fund (G+I)
Gabelli Asset Fund (G)
Gabelli Convertible Securities Fund (G+I)
Gabelli Equity Series Funds, Inc.
  Equity Income Fund (G+I)
  Gabelli Small Cap Growth Fund (AG)
Gabelli Global Series
  Gabelli Global Telecommunications Fund
    (GE)
  Gabelli Global Interactive Couch Potato (GE)
  Gabelli Global Convertible Securities Fund
    (GE)
Gabelli Gold Fund (PMG)
Gabelli Growth Fund (G)
Gabelli Money Market Funds
  Gabelli U.S. Treasury Money Market Fund
    (The) (MM-T)
Gabelli Value Fund, Inc. (AG)

Galaxy Fund
440 Lincoln Street
Worcester, Massachusetts 01605-1959
(800) 628-0414
Galaxy Fund
  Asset Allocation Fund (IM)
  Connecticut Municipal Bond Fund (MB-S)
  Equity Growth Fund (G)
  Equity Income Fund (G+I)
  Equity Value Fund (G+I)
  Government Money Market Fund (MM-T)
  High Quality Bond Fund (G+I)
  Institutional Treasury Fund (MM-T)
  Intermediate Bond Fund (CB)
  International Equity Fund (INT)
  Large Company Index Fund (G+I)
  Massachusetts Municipal Bond Fund (MB-S)
  Money Market Fund (MM-T)
  Municipal Bond Fund (MB-N)
  New York Municipal Bond Fund (MB-S)
  Short Term Bond Fund (IB)
  Small Company Equity Fund (AG)
  Small Company Index Fund (G)
  Tax-Exempt Bond Fund (MB-N)
  Tax-Exempt Money Market Fund (MM-TE)

U.S. Treasury Money Market Fund (MM-T)
U.S. Treasury Index Fund (IE)
Utility Index Fund (G+I)

Gardner Lewis Investment Trust
105 North Washington Street
P.O. Drawer 69
Rocky Mount, North Carolina 27802-0069
(919) 972-9922   (800) 525-3863
Gardner Lewis Investment Trust
  Chesapeake Growth Fund (The) (G)

Gateway Trust
400 TechneCenter Drive, Suite 220
Milford, Ohio 45150
(513) 248-2700   (800) 354-6339
Gateway Trust
  Gateway Midcap Fund (G)
  Gateway Index Plus Fund (G+I)
  Gateway Small Cap Index Fund (G)
  Matrix Growth Plus Fund (G)

GCG Trust
280 Park Avenue, 14th Floor West
New York, New York 10017
(212) 454-8216   (800) 447-3644
         or
1001 Jefferson Street, Suite 400
Wilmington, Delaware 19801
(800) 243-3706
GCG Trust
  All-Growth Series (G)
  Capital Appreciation Series (AG)
  Emerging Market Series (INT)
  Fully Managed Series (FP)
  Limited Maturity Bond Series (IB)
  Liquid Asset Series (MM-T)
  Multiple Allocation Series (B)
  Natural Resources Series (IE)
  Real Estate Series (G+I)
  Rising Dividend Series (IE)

GE Funds
3003 Summer Street
Stamford, Connecticut 06904
(203) 326-2300   (800) 242-0134
GE Funds
  Elfun Diversified Fund (B)
  Elfun Global Fund (GE)
  Elfun Income Fund (CB)
  Elfun Tax Exempt Income Fund (MB-N)
  Elfun Trusts Fund (GLB)
  GE Fixed Income Fund (IB)
  GE Global Equity Fund (GE)
  GE International Equity Fund (INT)
  GE Money Market Fund (MM-T)
  GE Short-Term Government Fund (USGI)
  GE Strategic Investment Fund (FP)
  GE Tax-Exempt Income Fund (MB-N)
  GE U.S. Equity Fund (G+I)

General
144 Glenn Curtiss Boulevard
Uniondale, New York 11556-0144
(718) 895-1206   (800) 645-6561

General California Municipal Bond Fund, Inc.
  (MB-S)
General California Municipal Money Market
  Fund, Inc. (MM-T)
General Government Securities Money
  Market Fund, Inc. (MM-T)
General Money Market Fund, Inc. (MM-T)
General Municipal Bond Fund, Inc. (MB-N)
General Municipal Money Market Fund, Inc.
  (MM-TE)
General New York Municipal Bond Fund, Inc.
  (MB-S)
General New York Municipal Money Market
  Fund, Inc. (MMS-TE)

General Securities, Incorporated
701 Fourth Avenue South, 10th Floor
Minneapolis, Minnesota 55415-1655
(612) 332-1212   (800) 331-4923

General Securities, Incorporated (G+I)

George Putnam Fund of Boston
One Post Office Square
Boston, Massachusetts 02109-2103
(617) 292-1000 (800) 225-2465

George Putnam Fund of Boston (B)

Gintel Funds
Greenwich Office Park #6
Greenwich, Connecticut 06831
(203) 622-6400

Gintel ERISA Fund (G+I)
Gintel Fund (G)

GIT
1655 Fort Myer Drive
Arlington, Virginia 22209-3108
(703) 528-6500   (800) 336-3063

GIT Equity Trust
  GIT Equity Income Portfolio (IE)
  GIT Equity Select Growth Portfolio (G)
  GIT Equity Special Growth Portfolio (AG)
  GIT Equity Trust Worldwide Growth
    Portfolio (INT)
GIT Income Trust
  GIT Income Government Portfolio (IB)
  GIT Income Maximum Income Portfolio
    (HYB)
GIT Money Market Fund (MM-T)
GIT Tax-Free Trust
  Arizona Tax-Free Portfolio (MB-S)
  Maryland Tax-Free Portfolio (MB-S)
  Missouri Tax-Free Portfolio (MB-S)
  Tax-Free National Portfolio (MB-N)
  Tax-Free Money Market Portfolio (MM-TE)
  Virginia Tax-Free Portfolio (MB-S)
Insured Money Market Fund (MM-T)

Glenmede Trust Company
229 South 18th Street
Philadelphia, Pennsylvania 19103
(800) 442-8299

Glenmede Fund Inc.
  Equity Portfolio (G)
  International Portfolio (INT)
  Small Capitalization Equity Portfolio (AG)
  Model Equity Portfolio (G)
  Government Cash Portfolio (MM-T)
  Tax-Exempt Cash Portfolio (MM-TE)
  Intermediate Government Portfolio (USGI)
  Municipal Intermediate Portfolio (MB-N)
  New Jersey Municipal Portfolio (MB-S)
  International Fixed Income Portfolio (GB)

Global Utility Fund, Inc.
One Seaport Plaza
New York, New York 10292
(212) 214-1215   (800) 225-1852

Global Utility Fund, Inc. (GE)

Goldman Sachs
4900 Sears Tower
Chicago, Illinois 60606
(312) 655-4400   (800) 526-7384

Goldman Sachs Equity Portfolios, Inc.
  GS Capital Growth Fund (G)
  GS Select Equity Fund (G)
  GS Small Cap Equity Fund (G)
  GS International Equity Fund (INT)
  GS Asia Growth Fund (INT)
Goldman Sachs Growth & Income Fund
  (G+I)
Goldman Sachs Government Income Fund
  (IE)
Goldman Sachs Adjustable Rate Mortgage
  Fund (GNMA)
Goldman Sachs Municipal Income Fund
  (MB-N)
Goldman Sachs California Municipal Income
  Fund (MB-S)
Goldman Sachs New York Municipal Income
  Fund (MB-S)
Goldman Sachs - Institutional Liquid Assets
  Federal Portfolio (MM-T)
  Government Portfolio (MM-T)
  Money Market Portfolio (MM-T)
  Prime Obligations Portfolio (MM-T)
  Tax-Exempt California Money Market
    Portfolio (MMS-TE)
  Tax-Exempt Diversified Portfolio (MM-TE)
  Tax-Exempt New York Portfolio (MMS-TE)
  Treasury Instruments Portfolio (MM-T)
  Treasury Obligations Portfolio (MM-T)
Goldman Sachs Trust
  GS Global Income Fund (GB)
  GS Short-Term Government Agency Fund
    (USGI)

Government Income Securities, Inc.
Federated Investors Tower
Pittsburgh, Pennsylvania 15222-3779
(412) 288-1900   (800) 245-4770
Government Income Securities, Inc. (USGI)

Govett Financial Services, Inc.
650 California Street, 28th Floor
San Francisco, California 94108
(415) 393-0350   (800) 634-6838
Govett Funds, Inc.
  Govett Emerging Market Fund (The) (INT)
  Govett Global Government Income Fund
    (The) (GB)
  Govett International Equity Fund (The) (INT)
  Govett Smaller Companies Fund (The) (AG)
  Govett Developing Markets Bond Fund (IB)
  Govett Latin America Fund (The) (INT)
  Govett Pacific Strategy Fund (INT)
  Govett ILA Money Market Portfolio (MM-T)

Gradison
580 Walnut Street
Cincinnati, Ohio 45202-3198
(513) 579-5700   (800) 869-5999

Gradison Growth Trust
  Gradison-McDonald Established Value
    Fund (G)
  Gradison-McDonald Opportunity Value
    Fund (G)
  Gradison McDonald Municipal Cash Series
    (MM-T)
  Gradison-McDonald Municipal Custodian
    Trust (MM-T)
  Gradison-McDonald Ohio Municipal Cash
    Trust (MM-T)
  Gradison-McDonald Government Income
    Fund (USGI)
  Gradison-McDonald Ohio Tax-Free Income
    Fund (MB-S)
  Gradison-McDonald U.S. Government
    Reserves Trust (MM-T)

Granite Income Fund, Inc.
P.O. Box 1233
Merritt Island, Florida 32954
(407) 452-7653
Granite Income Fund, Inc. (IM)

Great Hall Investment Funds, Inc.
60 S. Sixth Street, 20th Floor
Minneapolis, Minnesota 55402-4422
(612) 371-7970 (800) 934-6674

Great Hall Investment Funds, Inc.
  Minnesota Insured Tax-Exempt Fund (MB-S)
  National Tax-Exempt Fund (MB-N)
  Prime Money Market Fund (MM-T)
  Tax-Free Money Market Fund (MM-TE)
  U.S. Government Money Market Fund
    (MM-T)

Green Century Funds
29 Temple Place, Suite 200
Boston, Massachusetts 02111
(617) 482-0800   (800) 934-7336
Green Century Funds
  Balanced Fund (B)
  Money Market Fund (MM-T)

Greenfield Fund, Inc.
230 Park Avenue, Suite 910
New York, New York 10169
(212) 986-2600
Greenfield Fund, Inc. (FP)

Greenspring Fund, Incorporated
2330 Joppa Road, Suite 110
Lutherville, Maryland 21093-4641
(410) 823-5353   (800) 366-3863
Greenspring Fund, Incorporated (G)

Griffin Funds
10100 Pioneer Boulevard, Suite 1000
Santa Fe Springs, California 90670
(310) 946-1849   (800) 676-4450
Griffin Funds
  Griffin Bond Fund (The) (CB)
  Griffin California Tax-Free Fund (The) (MB-S)
  Griffin Growth and Income Fund (The) (G+I)
  Griffin Money Market Fund (The) (MM-T)
  Griffin Municipal Bond Fund (The) (MB-N)
  Griffin Tax-Free Money Market Fund (The)
    (MM-TE)
  Griffin U.S. Government Income Fund (The)
    (USGI)

Growth Fund of America, Inc.
Four Embarcadero Center
P.O. Box 7650
San Francisco, California 94120-7650
(415) 421-9360   (800) 421-0180
Growth Fund of America, Inc. (G)

Growth Fund of Washington, Inc.
1101 Vermont Avenue, N.W., Suite 600
Washington DC 20005-3521
(202) 842-5665   (800) 972-9274
Growth Fund of Washington, Inc. (G)

G.T.
50 California Street, 27th Floor
San Francisco, California 94111
(415) 392-6181   (800) 824-1580
G.T. America Growth Fund (G)
G.T. Europe Growth Fund (INT)
G.T. Global Dollar Fund (MM-T)
G.T. Global Emerging Markets Fund (GE)
G.T. Global Government Income Fund (GB)
G.T. Growth & Income Fund (GE)
G.T. Global Health Care Fund (GE)
G.T. Global High Income Fund (GB)

G.T. Global Money Market Fund (MM-T)
G.T. Global Strategic Income Fund (GB)
G.T. Global Telecommunications Fund (GE)
G.T. Global Variable America Fund (G)
G.T. Global Variable Europe Fund (INT)
G.T. Global Variable Global Government
  Income Fund (GB)
G.T. Global Variable Growth & Income
  Fund (GE)
G.T. Global Latin America Fund (INT)
G.T. Global Variable Pacific Fund (INT)
G.T. Global Variable Strategic Income Fund
  (GB)
G.T. Global Variable U.S. Government Income
  Fund (IB)
G.T. International Growth Fund (INT)
G.T. Japan Growth Fund (INT)
G.T. Latin America Growth Fund (INT)
G.T. Pacific Growth Fund (INT)
G.T. Worldwide Growth Fund (GE)

Guardian
201 Park Avenue South
New York, New York 10003
(212) 598-8260   (800) 221-3253
Guardian Bond Fund, Inc. (CB)
Guardian Cash Fund, Inc. (MM-T)
Guardian Stock Fund, Inc. (G)

Hanover Funds, Inc.
237 Park Avenue, Suite 910
New York, New York 10017
(212) 808-3900   (800) 453-4243
Hanover Funds, Inc.
  Blue Chip Growth Fund (The) (G)
  Cash Management Fund (The) (MM-T)
  Government Money Market Fund (The)
    (MM-T)
  New York Tax Free Money Market Fund
    (The) (MMS-TE)
  100% U.S. Treasury Money Market Fund
    (MM-T)
  Short-Term U.S. Government Securities
    Fund (The) (USGI)
  Small Cap Fund (AG)
  Tax Free Money Market Fund (The) (MM-TE)
  U.S. Government Securities Fund (The)
    (USGI)

Harbor Fund
One SeaGate
Toledo, Ohio 43666
(419) 247-2477   (800) 422-1050
Harbor Fund
  Harbor Bond Fund (IB)
  Harbor Capital Appreciation Fund (G+I)
  Harbor Growth Fund (G)
  Harbor International Fund (INT)
  Harbor International Growth Fund (INT)
  Harbor Money Market Fund (MM-T)
  Harbor Short Duration Fund (IB)
  Harbor Value Fund (G+I)

Harris Associates Investment Trust
Two N. LaSalle Street, Suite 500
Chicago, Illinois 60602-3790
(312) 621-0600   (800) 625-6275
Harris Associates Investment Trust
  Oakmark Fund (G)
  Oakmark International Fund (INT)

Harris Insight Funds, Inc.
One Boston Place
Boston, Massachusetts 02108
(800) 441-7379
Harris Insight Funds, Inc.
  Cash Management Fund (MM-T)
  Convertible Fund (G+I)
  Equity Fund (G)
  Government Assets Fund (MM-T)
  Intermediate Municipal Income Fund (MB-N)
  Managed Fixed Income Fund (CB)
  Tax-Free Money Market Fund (MM-TE)

Hartford
200 Hopmeadow Street
P.O. Box 2999
Hartford, Connecticut 06104-2999
(203) 843-8245   (800) 227-1371
Hartford Bond/Debt Securities Fund, Inc. (IB)
Hartford GNMA/Mortgage Securities Fund,
  Inc. (GNMA)
Hartford Index Fund, Inc. (G+I)
Hartford International Opportunities Fund,
  Inc. (INT)
Hartford U.S. Government Money Market
  Fund, Inc. (MM-T)

Hartwell
200 Berkeley Street
Boston, Massachusetts 02116-5034
(617) 338-3200   (800) 343-2898
Hartwell Emerging Growth Fund, Inc. (AG)
Hartwell Growth Fund, Inc. (G)

Hawaiian Tax-Free Trust
380 Madison Avenue, Suite 2300
New York, New York 10017-2590
(212) 697-6666 (800) 228-4227
Hawaiian Tax-Free Trust (MB-S)

Hawthorne Investment Trust
One Lewis Wharf
Boston, Massachusetts 02110
(617) 227-4800
Hawthorne Investment Trust
  Hawthorne Bond Fund (IB)
  Hawthorne Sea Fund (G)

Heartland Group
790 N. Milwaukee Street
Milwaukee, Wisconsin 53202-3702
(414) 347-7276   (800) 432-7856

Heartland Group
Heartland Nebraska Tax Free Fund (MB-S)
Heartland Pinnacle Fund (G)
Heartland/Portico Money Market Fund
   (MM-T)
Heartland U.S. Government Fund (USGI)
Heartland Value Fund (AG)
Heartland Wisconsin Tax Free Fund (MB-S)

Henlopen Fund
400 W. Ninth Street, Suite 100
Wilmington, Delaware 19801
(302) 654-3131
Henlopen Fund (G)

Hercules Funds
Piper Jaffray Tower
222 South Ninth Street
Minneapolis, Minnesota 55402
(800) 584-1317
Hercules European Value Fund (INT)
Hercules Global Short Term Fund (GE)
Hercules Latin American Fund (INT)
Hercules North American Growth & Income
   Fund (G)
Hercules Pacific Basin Value Fund (INT)
Hercules World Bond Fund (GB)

Heritage
880 Carillon Parkway
St. Petersburg, Florida 33733-8022
(813) 573-8143   (800) 421-4184
Heritage Capital Appreciation Trust (G)
Heritage Cash Trust
   Money Market Fund (MM-T)
   Municipal Money Market Fund (MM-TE)
Heritage Income-Growth Trust (G+I)
Heritage Income Trust
   Diversified Portfolio (IB)
   Limited Maturity Government Portfolio
      (USGI)
Heritage Series Trust
   Heritage Small Cap Stock Fund (AG)

Highmark Group
1900 E. Dublin-Granville Road
Columbus, Ohio 43229
(614) 899-4600 (800) 433-6884

Highmark Group
   Bond Fund (HYB)
   California Tax-Free Fund (MMS-TE)
   Diversified Obligations Fund (MM-T)
   Government Bond Fund (USGI)
   Growth Fund (G)
   Income and Growth Fund (G+I)
   Income Equity Fund (IE)
   100% U.S. Treasury Obligations Fund
      (MM-T)
   Special Growth Fund (G)
   Tax-Free Fund U.S. Obligations Fund (MM-T)

Hilliard-Lyons
Hilliard-Lyons Center
P.O. Box 32760
Louisville, Kentucky 40232-2760
(502) 588-8400   (800) 444-1854
Hilliard-Lyons Government Fund, Inc. (MM-T)
Hilliard-Lyons Growth Fund, Inc. (G)

HomeState Group Trust
1857 William Penn Way
P.O. Box 10666
Lancaster, Pennsylvania 17605-0666
(717) 396-1116   (800) 232-0224
HomeState Group Trust
   HomeState Pennsylvania Growth Fund (G)

Homestead Funds, Inc.
1800 Massachusetts Avenue, N.W., Dept 68
Washington DC 20036-1806
(202) 857-9726   (800) 258-3030
Homestead Funds, Inc.
   Daily Income Fund (MM-T)
   Short Term Bond Fund (CB)
   Value Fund (G+I)

Horace Mann
P.O. Box 4657
Springfield, Illinois 62708-4657
(217) 789-2500   (800) 999-1030
Horace Mann Balanced Fund, Inc. (B)
Horace Mann Growth Fund, Inc. (G+I)
Horace Mann Income Fund, Inc. (IB)
Horace Mann Short-Term Investment Fund,
   Inc. (GNMA)

Hospital & Health Facilities Trust
905 Marconi Avenue
Ronkonkoma, New York 11779
(516) 467-0200   (800) 221-4524
Hospital & Health Facilities Trust
   California Hospital & Health Facilities Liquid
      Asset Fund (MM-T)

Hotchkis and Wiley
800 West Sixth Street, 5th Floor
Los Angeles, California 90017
Hotchkis and Wiley Balanced Income Fund (B)
Hotchkis and Wiley Equity Income Fund (IE)
Hotchkis and Wiley International Fund (INT)
Hotchkis and Wiley Low Duration Fund (CB)
Hotchkis and Wiley Short Term Investment
   Fund (IB)
Hotchkis and Wiley Small Cap Fund (AG)

Household Personal Portfolios
2 North LaSalle Street
Chicago, Illinois 60602
(312) 368-5410   (800) 621-4480
Household Personal Portfolios
   Equity Income Portfolio (IE)

Fixed Income Portfolio (IB)
Growth Equity Portfolio (G)
Short-Term Income Portfolio (IB)
Tax-Exempt Income Portfolio (MB-N)

Huntington Funds
251 South Lake Avenue, Suite 600
Pasadena, California 91101
(213) 681-3700   (800) 826-0188
Huntington Funds
   Global Currency Portfolio (GB)
   Hard Currency Portfolio (GB)
   High Income Currency Portfolio (GB)
   Huntington German Government Bond
      Fund (GB)
   U.S. Cash Portfolio (MM-T)

HVA
200 Hopmeadow Street
P.O. Box 2999
Hartford, Connecticut 06104-2999
(203) 843-8245   (800) 227-1371
HVA Advisers Fund, Inc. (FP)
HVA Aggressive Growth Fund, Inc. (AG)
HVA Money Market Fund, Inc. (MM-T)
HVA Stock Fund, Inc. (G)

Hyperion Capital Management Inc.
520 Madison Avenue
New York, New York 10022
(212) 980-8400
Hyperion Capital Management Inc.
   Hyperion Short Duration U.S. Government
      Fund (USGI)
   Hyperion Short Duration U.S. Government
      Fund II (USGI)

IAA
808 IAA Drive
Bloomington, Illinois 61701
(309) 557-3222 (800) 245-2100
IAA Trust Asset Allocations Fund, Inc. (IM)
IAA Trust Growth, Inc. (G)
IAA Trust Money Market Fund, Inc. (MM-T)
IAA Trust Tax Exempt Bond Fund, Inc. (MB-N)

IAI
601 Seventh Avenue S.
P.O. Box 357
Minneapolis, Minnesota 55402
(612) 376-2700   (800) 945-3863
IAI Investment Funds I, Inc.
   IAI Bond Fund (IB)
   IAI Institutional Bond Fund (IB)
IAI Investment Funds II, Inc.
   IAI Growth Fund (G)
IAI Investment Funds III, Inc.
   IAI International Fund (INT)
IAI Investment Funds IV, Inc.
   IAI Regional Fund (AG)

IAI Investment Funds V, Inc.
   IAI Reserve Fund (IB)
IAI Investment Funds VI, Inc.
   IAI Balanced Fund (B)
   IAI Emerging Growth Fund (AG)
   IAI Government Fund (USGI)
   IAI MidCap Growth Fund (G)
   IAI Money Market Fund (MM-T)
   IAI Tax Free Fund (MB-N)
IAI Investment Funds VII, Inc.
   IAI Growth & Income Fund (G+I)
IAI Investment Funds VIII, Inc.
   IAI Value Fund (AG)

IDEX
201 Highland Avenue
Largo, Florida 34640-2597
(813) 585-6565   (800) 624-4339
IDEX Fund (G)
IDEX Fund 3 (G)
IDEX II Series Fund
   Flexible Income Portfolio (IB)
   Global Portfolio (GB)
   Growth Portfolio (G)
   Income Plus Portfolio (HYB)
   Tax-Exempt Portfolio (MB-N)

IDS
IDS Tower 10
Minneapolis, Minnesota 55440-0010
(612) 671-3131   (800) 328-8300
IDS Bond Fund, Inc. (CB)
IDS California Tax-Exempt Trust
   IDS California Tax-Exempt Fund (MB-S)
IDS Discovery Fund, Inc. (AG)
IDS Equity Plus Fund, Inc. (G+I)
IDS Extra Income Fund (HYB)
IDS Federal Income Fund, Inc. (USGI)
IDS Global Series, Inc.
   IDS Global Bond Fund (GB)
   IDS Global Growth Fund (GE)
IDS Growth Fund, Inc. (G)
IDS High Yield Tax-Exempt Fund, Inc. (MB-N)
IDS International Fund, Inc. (INT)
IDS Investment Series, Inc.
   IDS Diversified Equity Income Fund (IE)
   IDS Mutual (B)
IDS Life Aggressive Growth Fund, Inc. (AG)
IDS Life Capital Resource Fund, Inc. (G)
IDS Life International Fund, Inc. (INT)
IDS Life Managed Fund, Inc. (G+I)
IDS Life Moneyshare Fund, Inc. (MM-T)
IDS Life Special Income Fund, Inc. (IB)
IDS Managed Retirement Fund, Inc. (FP)
IDS Market Advantage Series, Inc.
   IDS Blue Chip Advantage Fund (G+I)
IDS Money Market Series, Inc.
   IDS Cash Management Fund (MM-T)
   IDS Planned Investment Account (MM-T)
IDS New Dimensions Fund, Inc. (G)

IDS Precious Metals Fund, Inc. (PMG)
IDS Progressive Fund, Inc. (AG)
IDS Selective Fund, Inc. (CB)
IDS Special Tax-Exempt Series Trust
  IDS Insured Tax-Exempt Fund (MB-N)
  IDS Massachusetts Tax-Exempt Fund (MB-S)
  IDS Michigan Tax-Exempt Fund (MB-S)
  IDS Minnesota Tax-Exempt Fund (MB-S)
  IDS New York Tax-Exempt Fund (MB-S)
  IDS Ohio Tax-Exempt Fund (MB-S)
IDS Stock Fund, Inc. (G+I)
IDS Strategy Fund, Inc.
  Aggressive Equity Fund (AG)
  Equity Fund (G+I)
  Income Fund (CB)
  Short-Term Income Fund (IB)
  Worldwide Growth Fund (GE)
IDS Tax-Exempt Bond Fund, Inc. (MB-N)
IDS Tax-Free Money Fund, Inc. (MM-TE)
IDS Utilities Income Fund, Inc. (IE)

Income Fund of America, Inc.
Four Embarcadero Center
P.O. Box 7650
San Francisco, California 94120-7650
(415) 421-9360   (800) 421-0180
Income Fund of America, Inc. (IM)

Independence Capital Group of Funds
600 Dresher Road
Horsham, Pennsylvania 19044-2267
(215) 956-8000   (800) 833-4264
Independence Capital Group of Funds
  Government Money Market Fund (MM-T)
  Money Market Fund (MM-T)
  Municipal Bond Fund (MB-N)
  New York Municipal Bond Fund (MB-S)
  Opportunities Fund (AG)
  Short-Intermediate Government Fund
    (USGI)
  Tax-Free Money Market Fund (MM-TE)
  Total Return Bond Fund (IB)
  Total Return Growth Fund (G+I)

Independence One Mutual Funds
Federated Investors Tower
Pittsburgh, Pennsylvania 15222-3779
(412) 288-1900   (800) 356-2805
Independence One Mutual Funds
  Michigan Municipal Cash Fund (MMS-TE)
  Prime Money Market Fund (MM-T)
  U.S. Government Securities Fund (USGI)
  U.S. Treasury Money Market Fund (MM-T)

Industrial Series Trust
700 South Federal Highway
P.O. Box 5007
Boca Raton, Florida 33431-0807
(407) 393-8900   (800) 456-5111
(800) 777-6472

Industrial Series Trust
  Mackenzie American Fund (G)
  Mackenzie California Municipal Fund (MB-S)
  Mackenzie Fixed Income Trust (CB)
  Mackenzie Limited Term Municipal Fund
    (MB-N)
  Mackenzie National Municipal Fund (MB-N)
  Mackenzie New York Municipal Fund (MB-S)
  Mackenzie North American Fund (IE)

Institutional Fiduciary Trust
777 Mariners Island Boulevard
San Mateo, California 94404-1585
(415) 312-2000   (800) 632-2180
Institutional Fiduciary Trust
  Franklin Institutional Adjustable Rate
    Securities Fund (GNMA)
  Franklin Institutional Adjustable Rate U.S.
    Government Securities Fund (GNMA)
  Franklin Late Day Money Market Portfolio
    (MM-T)
  Franklin Money Market Portfolio (MM-T)
  Franklin U.S. Government Securities Money
    Market Portfolio (MM-T)
  Franklin U.S. Treasury Money Market
    Portfolio (MM-T)

Institutional International Funds, Inc.
100 East Pratt Street
Baltimore, Maryland 21202
(410) 547-2000   (800) 638-5660
Institutional International Funds, Inc.
  Foreign Equity Fund (INT)

Institutional Investors
330 Madison Avenue
New York, New York 10017-5000
(212) 551-1800

Institutional Investors Capital Appreciation
  Fund, Inc. (G+I)
Institutional Investors Convertible Securities
  Fund, Inc. (IM)
Institutional Investors Option Income Fund,
  Inc. (IM)
Institutional Investors Tax Advantaged
  Income Fund, Inc. (IM)

Intermediate Bond Fund of America
333 South Hope Street
Los Angeles, California 90071-1447
(213) 486-9200   (800) 421-0180
Intermediate Bond Fund of America (IB)
Intermediate Tax-Exempt Bond Fund of
  America (MB-N)

INVESCO
7800 East Union Avenue, Suite 800
Denver, Colorado 80237-2756
(303) 930-6300   (800) 525-8085
INVESCO Dynamics Fund (AG)

INVESCO Emerging Growth Fund (AG)
INVESCO Growth Fund (G+I)
INVESCO Income Funds
  High Yield Portfolio (HYB)
  Select Income Portfolio (IB)
  U.S. Government Portfolio (USGI)
INVESCO Industrial Income Fund (B)
INVESCO International Fund
  European Portfolio (INT)
  International Growth Fund (INT)
  Pacific Basin Portfolio (INT)
INVESCO Money Market Funds
  Cash Reserves Fund (MM-T)
  Tax Free Money Fund (MM-TE)
  U.S. Government Money Fund (MM-T)
INVESCO Strategic Portfolios
  Energy Portfolio (AG)
  Environmental Services Portfolio (AG)
  Financial Services Portfolio (AG)
  Gold Portfolio (PMG)
  Health Sciences Portfolio (AG)
  Leisure Portfolio (AG)
  Technology Portfolio (AG)
  Utilities Portfolio (G+I)
INVESCO Tax Free Income Funds
  Tax Free Long Term Bond Fund (MB-N)
INVESCO Treasurers Series Trust
  Money Reserve Fund (MM-T)
  Tax-Exempt Fund (MM-TE)
INVESCO Value Trust
  Intermediate Government Bond Fund (USGI)
  Total Return Fund (FP)
  Value Equity Fund (IE)

Investment Company of America
333 South Hope Street
Los Angeles, California 90071-1447
(213) 486-9200 (800) 421-0182

Investment Company of America (G+I)

Investment Series Trust
Federated Investors Tower
Pittsburgh, Pennsylvania 15222-3779
(412) 288-1900   (800) 245-2423
(800) 245-5400

Investment Series Trust
  Capital Growth Fund (G)
  Fortress Bond Fund (HYB)
  High Quality Stock Fund (G+I)
  Municipal Series Income Fund (MB-N)
  U.S. Government Bond Fund (USGI)

Investors Cash Reserve Fund, Inc.
100 Milam Street, Suite 3500
P.O. Box 3167
Houston, Texas 77253-3167
(713) 750-8000   (800) 262-6631

Investors Cash Reserve Fund, Inc. (MM-T)

Investors Cash Trust
120 South LaSalle Street
Chicago, Illinois 60603-3473
(312) 781-1121   (800) 621-1048

Investors Cash Trust
  Government Securities Portfolio (MM-T)
  Treasury Portfolio (MM-T)

Investors Trust
601 Union Street, Suite 5600
Seattle, Washington 98101-2336
(206) 625-1755   (800) 433-0684
Investors Trust
  Adjustable Rate Fund (GNMA)
  Government Fund (USGI)
  Growth Fund (G)
  Tax Free Fund (MB-N)
  Value Fund (G+I)

ISI North American Government Bond Fund, Inc.
717 Fifth Avenue, 19th Floor
New York, New York 10022
(212) 446-5601   (800) 955-7175
ISI North American Government Bond Fund, Inc. (USGI)

Ivy Fund
700 South Federal Highway
P.O. Box 5007
Boca Raton, Florida 33431-0807
(407) 393-8900   (800) 456-5111
Ivy Fund
  Ivy China Region Fund (G+I)
  Ivy Emerging Growth Fund (AG)
  Ivy Growth Fund (G)
  Ivy Growth and Income Fund (G+I)
  Ivy International Fund (INT)
  Ivy Money Market Fund (MM-T)

Jackson National Capital Management Fund
5901 Executive Drive
P.O. Box 24068
Lansing, Michigan 48909
(517) 394-3400 (800) 873-5564
Jackson National Capital Management Fund
  Jackson National Growth Fund (G+I)
  Jackson National Income Fund (IM)
  Jackson National Money Market Fund (MM-T)
  Jackson National Tax-Exempt Fund (MB-N)
  Jackson National Total Return Fund (G+I)

Janus
P.O. Box 173375
Denver, Colorado 80217-3375
(303) 333-3863   (800) 525-3713
Janus Balanced Fund (B)
Janus Enterprise Fund (G)
Janus Federal Tax Exempt Fund (MB-N)

Janus Flexible Income Fund (IB)
Janus Fund (G)
Janus Growth & Income Fund (G+I)
Janus Intermediate Government Securities
   Fund (USGI)
Janus Mercury Fund (AG)
Janus Short-Term Fund (IB)
Janus Twenty Fund (G)
Janus Venture Fund (AG)
Janus Worldwide Fund (GE)

Japan Fund, Inc.
345 Park Avenue
New York, New York 10154-0010
(212) 326-6200   (800) 225-2470
Japan Fund, Inc. (INT)

Jensen Portfolio, Inc.
430 Pioneer Tower, 888 SW Fifth Avenue
Portland, Oregon 97204-2018
(503) 274-2044   (800) 221-4384
Jensen Portfolio, Inc. (G+I)

John Hancock
101 Huntington Avenue
Boston, Massachusetts 02199-7603
(617) 375-1500   (800) 225-5291
John Hancock Capital Series
   John Hancock Growth Fund (G)
John Hancock Cash Management Fund
   (MM-T)
John Hancock Limited Term Government
   Bond (USGI)
John Hancock Sovereign Bond Fund (CB)
John Hancock Sovereign Investors Fund, Inc.
   John Hancock Sovereign Balanced Fund (B)
   John Hancock Sovereign Investors Fund,
   Inc. (G+I)
John Hancock Special Equities Fund (AG)
John Hancock Strategic Series
   John Hancock Independence Diversified
      Core Equity Fund (MM-T)
   John Hancock Strategic Income Fund (B)
John Hancock Tax-Exempt Income Fund
   (MB-N)
John Hancock Tax-Exempt Series Fund
   California Portfolio (MB-S)
   Massachusetts Portfolio (MB-S)
   New York Portfolio (MB-S)
John Hancock Technology Series, Inc.
   John Hancock Freedom Global Technology
      Fund (GE)
   John Hancock Freedom National Aviation &
      Technology Fund (G)
John Hancock World Fund
   John Hancock Freedom Global RX Fund (GE)
   John Hancock Freedom Pacific Basin
      Equities Fund (GE)

Jones & Babson
Three Crown Center
2440 Pershing Road
Kansas City, Missouri 64108
(816) 471-5200
Babson Funds
   Babson Bond Long (HYB)
   Babson Bond Short (HYB)
   Babson Buffalo Balanced (B)
   Babson Enterprise (AG)
   Babson Enterprise II (AG)
   Babson Growth (G)
   Babson Money Market Federal (MM-T)
   Babson Money Market Prime (MM-T)
   Babson T-F Long (MB-N)
   Babson T-F Money Market (MM-T)
   Babson T-F Short (MB-N)
   Babson Value (G+I)
   BSI International (INT)
   Shadow Stock (AG)
   UMB Bond (HYB)
   UMB Heartland (AG)
   UMB Money Market Federal (MM-T)
   UMB Money Market Prime (MM-T)
   UMB Tax-Free Money Market (MM-TE)
   UMB Stock (G)
   UMB WorldWide (GE)

JP
100 North Greene Street
Greensboro, North Carolina 27401
(919) 691-3448   (800) 458-4498
JP Growth Fund, Inc. (G)
JP Income Fund, Inc. (IM)

JPM
461 Fifth Avenue, 20th Floor
New York, New York 10017
(212) 685-2800   (800) 521-5412
JPM Institutional Funds
JPM Bond Fund (IB)
JPM Diversified Fund (G)
JPM Money Market Fund (MM-T)
JPM Selected U.S. Equity Fund (G)
JPM Short Term Bond Fund (IB)
JPM Tax Exempt Bond Fund (MB-N)
JPM Tax Exempt Money Market Fund
   (MM-TE)
JPM Treasury Money Market Fund (MM-T)
JPM U.S. Small Company Fund (G)
JPM U.S. Stock Fund (G)

Kaufmann Fund, Inc.
17 Battery Place, Suite 2624
New York, New York 10004
(212) 344-2661
Kaufmann Fund, Inc. (AG)

Kemper Financial Services
120 South LaSalle Street
Chicago, Illinois 60603-3473
(312) 781-1121   (800) 621-1048

Kemper Adjustable Rate U.S. Government
Fund (USGI)
Kemper California Tax-Free Income Fund, Inc.
(MB-S)
Kemper Diversified Income Fund (IB)
Kemper Environmental Services Fund (G)
Kemper Florida Tax-Free Income Fund (MB-S)
Kemper Global Income Fund (GB)
Kemper Growth Fund (G)
Kemper High Yield Fund, Inc. (HYB)
Kemper Income & Capital Preservation Fund,
Inc. (IB)
Kemper International Fund (INT)
Kemper Investment Portfolios
Diversified Income Portfolio (IB)
Government Portfolio (GNMA)
Growth Portfolio (G)
High Yield Portfolio (HYB)
Money Market Portfolio (MM-T)
Short-Intermediate Government Portfolio
(USGI)
Short-Term Global Income Portfolio (GB)
Small Capitalization Portfolio (AG)
Total Return Portfolio (B)
Kemper Money Market Fund
Government Securities Portfolio (MM-T)
Kent Money Market Fund-Investment
Shares (MM-T)
Money Market Portfolio (MM-T)
Tax-Exempt Portfolio (MM-TE)
Kemper New York Tax-Free Income Fund
(MB-S)
Kemper Ohio Tax-Free Income Fund (MB-S)
Kemper Retirement Fund I (B)
Kemper Retirement Fund II (B)
Kemper Retirement Fund III (B)
Kemper Retirement Fund IV (G)
Kemper Short-Term Global Income Fund (GB)
Kemper Texas Tax-Free Income Fund (MB-S)
Kemper Total Return Fund (B)
Kemper U.S. Government Securities Fund,
Inc. (GNMA)

Kent Funds
120 South LaSalle Street
Chicago, Illinois 60603-3473
(312) 781-1121   (800) 621-1048

Kent Funds
Kent Expanded Market Equity Fund (AG)
Kent Index Equity Fund (G)
Kent International Equity Fund (INT)
Kent Medium Term Tax Exempt Bond Fund
(MB-N)
Kent Michigan Municipal Limited Maturity
Fund (MB-S)

Kent Michigan Municipal Money Market
Fund (MMS-TE)
Kent Value Plus Equity Fund (G+I)

Keystone
200 Berkeley Street
Boston, Massachusetts 02116-5034
(617) 338-3200   (800) 343-2898

Keystone America Capital Preservation and
Income Fund (GNMA)
Keystone America Capital Preservation and
Income II (GNMA)
Keystone America Equity Income Fund (IE)
Keystone America Florida Tax Free Fund
(MB-S)
Keystone America Global Opportunities Fund
(GE)
Keystone America Government Securities
Fund (USGI)
Keystone America Intermediate Term Bond
Fund (CB)
Keystone America Omega Fund (AG)
Keystone America Pennsylvania Tax Free
Fund (MB-S)
Keystone America Strategic Income Fund
(HYB)
Keystone America Tax Free Income Fund
(MB-N)
Keystone America Texas Tax Free Fund (MB-S)
Keystone America World Bond Fund (GB)
Keystone Australia Income Fund (GB)
Keystone Custodian Funds, Inc. B-1 Series
(IB)
Keystone Custodian Funds, Inc. B-2 Series
(CB)
Keystone Custodian Funds, Inc. B-4 Series
(HYB)
Keystone Custodian Funds, Inc. K-1 Series
(IE)
Keystone Custodian Funds, Inc. K-2 Series
(G)
Keystone Custodian Funds, Inc. S-1 Series
(G+I)
Keystone Custodian Funds, Inc. S-3 Series
(G)
Keystone Custodian Funds, Inc. S-4 Series
(AG)
Keystone Institutional Adjustable Rate Fund
(GNMA)
Keystone International Fund, Inc. (INT)
Keystone Liquid Trust (MM-T)
Keystone Precious Metal Holdings, Inc. (PMG)
Keystone Tax Exempt Trust (MB-N)
Keystone Tax Free Fund (MB-N)

Kidder, Peabody
60 Broad Street
New York, New York 10004-2350
(212) 656-1737

Kidder, Peabody California Tax Exempt
  Money Market Fund (MMS-TE)
Kidder, Peabody Cash Reserve Fund, Inc.
  (MM-T)
Kidder, Peabody Equity Income Fund, Inc.
  (IE)
Kidder, Peabody Government Income Fund,
  Inc. (USGI)
Kidder, Peabody Government Money Fund,
  Inc. (MM-T)
Kidder, Peabody Investment Trust
  Adjustable Rate Government Fund (GNMA)
  Asset Allocation Fund (G+I)
  Global Equity Fund (GE)
  Global Fixed Income Fund (GB)
  Intermediate Fixed Income Fund (IM)
Kidder, Peabody Municipal Bond Fund (MB-N)
Kidder, Peabody Municipal Money Market
  Series
  Connecticut Series (MMS-TE)
  New Jersey Series (MMS-TE)
  New York Series (MMS-TE)
Kidder, Peabody Premium Account Fund
  (MM-T)
Kidder, Peabody Small Cap Equity Fund (AG)
Kidder, Peabody Tax Exempt Money Fund,
  Inc. (MM-TE)

Landmark Funds
153 E. 53rd Street
6th Floor, Zone 6
New York, New York 10022
(212) 559-7822   (800) 331-1792
Landmark Fixed Income Funds
  Intermediate Income Fund (IB)
  Landmark U.S. Government Income Fund
    (USGI)
Landmark Funds I
  Landmark Balanced Fund (B)
Landmark Funds II
  Landmark Equity Fund (G)
Landmark Funds III
  Landmark Cash Reserves (MM)
  Landmark U.S. Treasury Reserves (MM)
Landmark Institutional Funds I
  Landmark Institutional Cash Management
    Fund (MM)
Landmark Institutional Trust
  Landmark Institutional Liquid Reserve (MM)
  Landmark Institutional U.S. Treasury
    Reserves (MM)
Landmark International Equity Fund (GLB)
Landmark Multi-State Tax Free Reserves
  California Tax Free Reserves (MMS)
  New York Tax Free Reserves (MMS)
Landmark Tax Free Reserves (MMN)

Lazard Funds, Inc.
One Rockefeller Plaza
New York, New York 10020
(212) 632-6400   (800) 228-0203

Lazard Funds, Inc.
  Lazard Bond Portfolio (IB)
  Lazard Equity Portfolio (G)
  Lazard International Equity Portfolio (INT)
  Lazard International Fixed-Income Portfolio
    (GB)
  Lazard Small Cap Portfolio (AG)
  Lazard Special Equity Portfolio (AG)
  Lazard Strategic Yield Portfolio (HYB)

LBVIP Series Fund, Inc.
625 Fourth Avenue, South
Minneapolis, Minnesota 55415-1665
(612) 339-8091   (800) 328-4552
LBVIP Series Fund, Inc.
  Growth Series (G)
  High Yield Series (HYB)
  Income Series (I)
  Money Market Series (MM)

Leeb Personal Finance Trust
312 Walnut Street, Suite 21
Cincinnati, Ohio 45202
(513) 629-2000   (800) 545-0103
Leeb Personal Finance Fund (G)

Legg Mason
111 South Calvert Street
P.O. Box 1476
Baltimore, Maryland 21203-1476
(410) 539-3400   (800) 822-5544
Legg Mason Cash Reserve Trust (MMT)
Legg Mason Global Trust, Inc.
  Global Government Trust (GB)
Legg Mason Income Trust, Inc.
  Investment Grade Income Portfolio (IB)
  U.S. Government Intermediate Portfolio
    (USGI)
  U.S. Government Money Market Portfolio
    (MMT)
Legg Mason Investor Trust
  American Leading Companies Trust (G+I)
Legg Mason Special Investment Trust, Inc.
  (AG)
Legg Mason Tax-Exempt Trust, Inc. (MMTE)
Legg Mason Tax-Free Income Fund
  Intermediate-Term Income Trust (LTMB)
  Maryland Tax-Free Income Trust (SMB-LT)
  Pennsylvania Tax-Free Income Trust
    (SMB-LT)
Legg Mason Total Return Trust, Inc. (G+I)
Legg Mason Value Trust, Inc. (G)

Lehman
200 Vesey Street
New York, New York 10285
(800) 451-2010

Lehman Brothers Funds, Inc.
  Lehman Brothers Daily Income Fund (MM-T)
  Lehman Brothers Municipal Income Fund
    (MM-TE)

Municipal Money Market Fund-Small
Business Shares (MM-TE)
Lehman Brothers Institutional Funds Group
Trust
California Municipal Money Market Fund
(MMS-TE)
Government Obligations Money Market
Fund (MM-T)
Municipal Money Market Fund (MM-TE)
100% Government Obligations Money
Market Fund (MM-T)
100% Treasury Instruments Money Market
Fund (MM-T)
Prime Money Market Fund (MM-T)
Prime Value Money Market Fund (MM-T)
Tax-Free Money Market Fund (MM-TE)
Treasury Instruments Money Market Fund
(MM-T)
Treasury Instruments Money Market Fund II
(MM-T)

Lepercq-Istel Trust
1675 Broadway, 16th Floor
New York, New York 10019
(212) 698-0700   (800) 338-1579
Lepercq-Istel Trust
Lepercq-Istel Fund (G+I)

Lexington Management Corp.
Park 80 West, Plaza Two
P.O. Box 1515
Saddle Brook, New Jersey 07662-5812
(201) 845-7300   (800) 526-0056
Lexington Convertible Securities Fund (G+I)
Lexington Corporate Leaders Trust Fund (G+I)
Lexington Global Fund, Inc. (GLB)
Lexington GNMA Income Fund, Inc. (GNMA)
Lexington Gold Fund, Inc. (PMG)
Lexington Growth and Income Fund, Inc. (G+I)
Lexington Money Market Trust (MM-T)
Lexington Natural Resources Trust (PMG)
Lexington Short-Intermediate Government
Securities Fund (USGI)
Lexington Strategic Investments Fund (PMG)
Lexington Strategic Silver Fund, Inc. (PMG)
Lexington Tax Exempt Bond Fund (LTMB)
Lexington Tax Free Money Fund, Inc. (MM-TE)
Lexington Worldwide Emerging Markets
Fund, Inc. (INT)

Liberty
Federated Investors Tower
Liberty Center
Pittsburgh, Pennsylvania 15222-3779
(412) 288-1900   (800) 245-4770
Liberty Equity Income Fund, Inc. (G+I)
Liberty High Income Bond Fund (HYB)
Liberty Municipal Securities Fund, Inc. (MB-N)
Liberty U.S. Government Money Market Trust
(MM-T)
Liberty Utility Fund, Inc. (IE)

Liberty Financial Trust
Federal Reserve Plaza
600 Atlantic Avenue
Boston, Massachusetts 02210-2214
(617) 722-6000   (800) 542-3863
Growth and Income Fund (G+I)
Insured Municipal Fund (LTMB)
Tax-Free Bond Fund (LTMB)
U.S. Government Securities Fund (USGI)
Utilities Fund (G+I)

Life of Virginia Series, Inc.
6610 West Broad Street
Richmond, Virginia 23230
(804) 281-6000 (800) 822-6000
Bond Portfolio (CB)
Common Stock Portfolio (G)
Money Market Portfolio (MM-T)
Total Return Portfolio (G+I)

Limited Term Fund
Limited Term Tax-Exempt Bond Fund of
America
Federated Investors Tower
Pittsburgh, Pennsylvania 15222-3779
(412) 288-1900   (800) 245-2423
Limited Term Fund (IM)
Limited Term Tax-Exempt Bond Fund of
America (MB-N)

Lindner Management Corporation
111 Pointer Lane
St. Louis, Missouri 63124
(314) 727-5305
Lindner Dividend Fund (IE)
Lindner Fund (G)
Lindner Utility Fund (IE)
Lindner/Ryback Small-Cap Fund (AG)

Liquid Capital Income Trust
1100 The Halle Building
1228 Euclid Avenue
Cleveland, Ohio 44115-1831
(216) 781-4440   (800) 321-3222
Liquid Capital Income Trust (MM-T)

Liquid Cash Trust
Federated Investors Tower
Pittsburgh, Pennsylvania 15222-3779
(412) 288-1900 (800) 245-5040
Liquid Cash Trust (MM-T)

Liquid Institutional Reserves
60 Broad Street
New York, New York 10004-2350
(212) 656-1737
Government Securities Fund (MM-T)
Money Market Fund (MM-T)
Treasury Securities Fund (MM-T)

LMH Fund, Ltd.
1175 Post Road East
P.O. Box 830
Westport, Connecticut 06881-0830
LMH Fund, Ltd. (G+I)

Loomis Sayles Funds
One Financial Center
Boston, Massachusetts 02111
(617) 482-2450   (800) 626-9390

Loomis Sayles Bond Fund (IB)
Loomis Sayles Global Bond Fund (GB)
Loomis Sayles Growth and Income Fund (G+I)
Loomis Sayles Growth Fund (G)
Loomis Sayles International Equity Fund (INT)
Loomis Sayles Municipal Bond Fund (LTMB)
Loomis Sayles Short-Term Bond Fund (CB)
Loomis Sayles Small Cap Fund (AG)
Loomis Sayles U.S. Government Securities
    Fund (USGI)

Lord, Abbett & Co.
The General Motors Building
767 Fifth Avenue
New York, New York 10153-0203
(212) 848-1800 (800) 223-4224

Lord Abbett Bond-Debenture Fund, Inc. (HYB)
Lord Abbett California Tax-Free Income Fund,
    Inc. (SMB-LT)
Lord Abbett Cash Reserve Fund, Inc. (MM-T)
Lord Abbett Developing Growth Fund, Inc.
    (AG)
Lord Abbett Equity Fund - 1990 Series (G)
Lord Abbett Fundamental Value Fund, Inc.
    (G+I)
Lord Abbett Global Fund, Inc.
  Equity Series (GLB)
  Income Series (GB)
Lord Abbett Securities Trust
  U.S. Government Securities Series (USGI)
Lord Abbett Tax-Free Income Fund, Inc.
  Connecticut Series (SMB-LT)
  Hawaii Series (SMB-LT)
  Missouri Series (SMB-LT)
  National Series (LTMB)
  New Jersey Series (SMB-LT)
  New York Series (SMB-LT)
  Texas Series (SMB-LT)
  Washington Series (SMB-LT)
Lord Abbett Tax-Free Income Trust
  Florida Series (SMB-LT)
  Michigan Series (SMB-LT)
  Pennsylvania Series (SMB-LT)
Lord Abbett U.S. Government Securities
    Fund, Inc. (USGI)
Lord Abbett Value Appreciation Fund, Inc. (G)

Lutheran Brotherhood Securities Corp.
625 Fourth Avenue South
Minneapolis, Minnesota 55415
(612) 339-8091   (800) 328-4552

Lutheran Brotherhood Fund, Inc. (G+I)
Lutheran Brotherhood High Yield Fund, Inc.
    (HYB)
Lutheran Brotherhood Income Fund, Inc. (IB)
Lutheran Brotherhood Money Market Fund
    (MM-T)
Lutheran Brotherhood Municipal Bond Fund,
    Inc. (LTMB)
Lutheran Brotherhood Opportunity Growth
    Fund, Inc. (AG)

MacKenzie Investment Management, Inc.
Via Mizner Financial Plaza
700 South Federal Highway
P.O. Box 5007
Boca Raton, Florida 33431-0807
(407) 393-8900   (800) 456-5111

MacKenzie Funds, Inc.
  MacKenzie Adjustable U.S. Government
    Securities Trust (GNMA)
  MacKenzie Canada Fund (INT)
  MacKenzie Global Fund (GLB)

Madison Bond Fund, Inc.
6411 Mineral Point Road
Madison, Wisconsin 53705
(608) 273-2020   (800) 767-0300

Madison Fund, Inc. (IB)

MainStay Series Fund
260 Cherry Hill Road
Parsippany, New Jersey 07054-1108
(201) 331-2000   (800) 522-4202

MainStay California Tax-Free Fund (SMB-LT)
MainStay Capital Appreciation Fund (AG)
MainStay Convertible Fund (G+I)
MainStay Equity Index Fund (G+I)
MainStay Global Fund (GE)
MainStay Government Fund (USGI)
MainStay High Yield Corporate Bond Fund
    (HYB)
MainStay Money Market Fund (MM-T)
MainStay Natural Resources/Gold Fund (PMG)
MainStay New York Tax Free Fund (SMB-LT)
MainStay Tax Free Bond Fund (LTMB)
MainStay Total Return Fund (B)
MainStay Value Fund (G)

Main Street Funds, Inc.
3410 South Galena Street
Denver, Colorado 80231-3234
(303) 671-3200   (800) 548-1225

California Tax-Exempt Fund (SMB-LT)
Income & Growth Fund (FP)

Mairs & Power, Inc.
W-2062 First National Bank Building
332 Minnesota Street
St. Paul, Minnesota 55101
(612) 222-8478

Mairs & Power Growth Fund, Inc. (G)
Mairs & Power Income Fund, Inc. (IM)

Managed Municipal Fund, Inc.
135 East Baltimore Street
Baltimore, Maryland 21202-1607
(410) 727-1700   (800) 767-3524
ISI Managed Municipal FundShares (LTMB)

Managers Funds, The
200 Connecticut Avenue, Suite 680
Norwalk, Connecticut 06854
(203) 857-5321   (800) 835-8379
(800) 358-7668
Balanced Fund (G)
Bond Fund (IB)
Capital Appreciation Fund (G)
Income Equity Fund (G+I)
Intermediate Mortgage Fund (GNMA)
International Equity Fund (INT)
Money Market Fund (MM-T)
Municipal Bond Fund (LTMB)
Short and Intermediate Bond Fund (IB)
Short Government Fund (IB)
Short Term Municipal Bond Fund (MM-TE)
Special Equity Fund (AG)

Manning & Napier Fund, Inc.
One Lincoln First Square, Suite 1100
Rochester, New York 14604
(716) 324-6880
Commodity Series (AG)
Contrarian Series (AG)
Economic Sector Series (AG)
Energy Series (AG)
Financial Services Series (AG)
Global Fixed Income Series (GE)
International Series (INT)
Life Sciences Series (AG)
Small Cap Series (AG)

Manulife Series Fund, Inc.
200 Bloor Street East
North Tower 5
Toronto, Ontario, Canada M4W 1E5
(416) 926-6700
Balanced Assets Fund (B)
Capital Growth Bond Fund (IM)
Common Stock Fund (G+I)
Emerging Growth Equity Fund (AG)
Money Market Fund (MM-T)
Real Estate Securities Fund (G+I)

MAP-Government Fund, Inc.
520 Broad Street
Newark, New Jersey 07102-3184
(401) 751-8600   (800) 323-4726
MAP-Government Fund, Inc. (MM-T)

Mariner Services
600 17th Steet
#1605 South
Denver, Colorado 80202
(303) 623-2577   (800) 753-4462
Mariner Funds Trust
Mariner Cash Management Fund (MM-T)
Mariner Government Money Market Fund
(MM-T)
Mariner New York Tax-Free Money Market
Fund (MMS-TE)
Mariner Tax-Free Money Market Fund
(MM-TE)
Mariner U.S. Treasury Money Market Fund
(MM-T)
Mariner Mutual Funds Trust
Mariner European Equity Index Fund (INT)
Mariner Fixed Income Fund (CB)
Mariner New York Tax Free Bond Fund
(SMB-LT)
Mariner North America Fund (G)
Mariner Short Term Fixed Income Fund (IB)
Mariner Small Cap Fund (AG)
Mariner Total Return Equity Fund (G+I)
Mariner U.S. Government Securities Fund
(USGI)

Market Street Fund, Inc.
1600 Market Street
P.O. Box 7378
Philadelphia, Pennsylvania 19101
(215) 636-5000
Money Market Portfolio
(PM Variable Money Market Sep. Acct. II)
(MM-T)

Marketwatch Funds
P.O. Box 27252
Richmond, Virginia 23286-8983
(800) 232-9091
Marketwatch Equity Fund (G+I)
Marketwatch Flexible Income Fund (IB)
Marketwatch Intermadiate Fixed Income Fund
(USGI)
Marketwatch Virginia Municipal Bond Fund
(MB-S)

Marquis Funds
210 Baronne Street
New Orleans, Louisiana 70161
(800) 814-3396
Marquis Government Securities Fund (IB)
Marquis Growth & Income Fund (G+I)
Marquis Value Equity Fund (G)
Marquis Louisiana Tax-Free Income Fund
(MB-S)
Marquis Treasury Securities Fund (MM-T)

Marshall Funds Investor Services
1000 North Water Street
Milwaukee, Wisconsin 53202
(414) 287-8500   (800) 236-8560

Marshall Equity Income Fund (IE)
Marshall Government Income Fund (GNMA)
Marshall Intermediate Bond Fund (CB)
Marshall Intermediate Tax-Free Fund (MB-N)
Marshall International Stock Fund (INT)
Marshall Money Market Investment Shares
  (MM-T)
Marshall Mid-Cap Stock Fund (G)
Marshall Short Term Income Fund (IB)
Marshall Short Term Tax-Free Fund (MB-N)
Marshall Stock Fund (G+I)
Marshall Money Market Trust Shares (MM-T)
Marshall Value Equity Fund (G+I)

MAS Funds
One Tower Bridge
West Conshohocken, Pennsylvania 19428
(215) 940-5000   (800) 354-8185

Balanced Portfolio (B)
Cash Reserves Portfolio (MM-T)
Emerging Growth Portfolio (AG)
Equity Portfolio (G+I)
Fixed Income Portfolio (IB)
Fixed Income Portfolio II (IB)
Global Fixed Income Portfolio (GB)
High Yield Securities Portfolio (HYB)
International Equity Portfolio (INT)
Limited Duration Fixed Income Portfolio (CB)
Mortgage-Backed Securities Portfolio (GNMA)
Municipal Fixed Income Portfolio (LTMB)
Pennsylvania Municipal Fixed Income
  Portfolio (SMB-LT)
Select Equity Portfolio (G+I)
Select Fixed Income Portfolio (IB)
Select Value Portfolio (G+I)
Small Capitalization Value Portfolio (G+I)
Special Purpose Fixed Income Portfolio (IB)
Value Portfolio (G+I)

Massachusetts Financial Services Company
500 Boylston Street
Boston, Massachusetts 02116
(617) 954-5000   (800) 343-2829

Massachusetts Investors Growth Stock Fund
  (G)
Massachusetts Investors Trust (G+I)
MFS Emerging Equities Fund (AG)
MFS Emerging Growth Fund (AG)
MFS Fixed Income Trust
  MFS Bond Fund (CB)
  MFS Limited Maturity Fund (IB)
  MFS Municipal Limited Maturity Fund (LTMB)
MFS Government Limited Maturity Fund
  (USGI)
MFS Government Mortgage Fund (GNMA)
MFS Government Securities Fund (USGI)
MFS Growth Opportunities Fund (G)
MFS Institutional Funds
  MFS Worldwide Fixed Income Fund (GB)
MFS Municipal Series Trust

MFS Alabama Municipal Bond Fund
  (SMB-LT)
MFS Arkansas Municipal Bond Fund
  (SMB-LT)
MFS California Municipal Bond Fund
  (SMB-LT)
MFS Florida Municipal Bond Fund (SMB-LT)
MFS Georgia Municipal Bond Fund (SMB-LT)
MFS Louisiana Municipal Bond Fund
  (SMB-LT)
MFS Maryland Municipal Bond Fund
  (SMB-LT)
MFS Massachusetts Municipal Bond Fund
  (SMB-LT)
MFS Mississippi Municipal Bond Fund
  (SMB-LT)
MFS Municipal Income Fund (LTMB)
MFS New York Municipal Bond Fund
  (SMB-LT)
MFS North Carolina Municipal Bond Fund
  (SMB-LT)
MFS Pennsylvania Municipal Bond Fund
  (SMB-LT)
MFS South Carolina Municipal Bond Fund
  (SMB-LT)
MFS Tennessee Municipal Bond Fund
  (SMB-LT)
MFS Texas Municipal Bond Fund (SMB-LT)
MFS Virginia Municipal Bond Fund (SMB-LT)
MFS Washington Municipal Bond Fund
  (SMB-LT)
MFS West Virginia Municipal Bond Fund
  (SMB-LT)
MFS Series Trust I
  MFS Cash Reserve Fund (MM-T)
  MFS Managed Sectors Fund (G)
MFS Series Trust II
  MFS Capital Growth Fund (G)
  MFS Emerging Growth Fund (AG)
  MFS Gold & Natural Resources (PMG)
  MFS Intermediate Income Fund (IM)
MFS Series Trust III
  MFS High Income Fund (HYB)
  MFS Municipal High Income Fund (LTMB)
MFS Series Trust IV
  MFS Government Money Market Fund
    (MM-T)
  MFS Money Market Fund (MM-T)
  MFS Municipal Bond Fund (LTMB)
MFS Series Trust V
  MFS Research Fund (G+I)
  MFS Total Return Fund (IM)
MFS Series Trust VI
  MFS Utilities Fund (IM)
  MFS World Total Return Fund (GE)
MFS Series Trust VII
  MFS Value Fund (AG)
  MFS World Governments Fund (GB)
MFS Series Trust VIII
  MFS Income & Opportunity Fund (IM)
  MFS World Equity Fund (GE)

Maxus Asset Management, Inc.
28601 Chagrin Boulevard
Cleveland, Ohio 44122
(216) 212-3434 (800) 446-2927
Maxus Equity Fund (FP)
Maxus Income Fund (IM)
Maxus Prism Fund (G+I)

MBL Growth Fund, Inc.
520 Broad Street
Newark, New Jersey 07102-3184
(201) 481-8000 (800) 323-4726
MBL Growth Fund, Inc. (G)

Medalist Funds
P.O. Box 26301
Richmond, Virginia 23260-6301
(800) 723-9512
Medalist Maryland Municipal Bond Fund
(MB-S)
Medalist Money Market Fund (MM-T)
Medalist Stock Fund (G+I)
Medalist Tax-Free Money Market Fund (MM-T)
Medalist Treasury Money Market Fund (MM-T)
Medalist U.S. Government Securities Fund (IB)
Medalist Virginia Municipal Bond Fund (MB-S)

Medical Research Investment Fund, Inc.
1100 Milam Street, Suite 3500
P.O. Box 3167
Houston, Texas 77253-3167
(713) 750-8000 (800) 262-6631
Medical Research Investment Fund, Inc. (AG)

Megy Fund, Inc.
No. 3B, 1617 North Flagler Drive
West Palm Beach, Florida 33407
(407) 832-7733 (800) 933-8637
Megy Income Fund (GB)

Mentor Growth Trust
P.O. Box 1357
Richmond, Virginia 23211
(804) 649-2311 (800) 321-0038
Mentor Growth Trust (G)

Meridian Fund, Inc.
60 East Sir Francis Drake Boulevard, Suite 306
Larkspur, California 94939-1714
(415) 461-6237 (800) 446-6662
Meridian Fund, Inc.(G)

Merrill Lynch
P.O. Box 9011
Princeton, New Jersey 08543-9011
(609) 282-2800 (800) 637-3863
Merrill Lynch Adjustable Rate Securities Fund
(GNMA)
Merrill Lynch Americas Income Fund (GB)

Merrill Lynch Balanced Fund for Investment
& Retirement (B)
Merrill Lynch Basic Value Fund, Inc. (G+I)
Merrill Lynch California Municipal Series
Trust
California Insured Municipal Bond Fund
(SMB-LT)
California Municipal Bond Fund (SMB-LT)
Merrill Lynch Capital Fund, Inc. (G+I)
Merrill Lynch Consults International (INT)
Merrill Lynch Corporate Bond Fund, Inc.
High Income Portfolio (HYB)
High Quality Portfolio (CB)
Intermediate Term Portfolio (CB)
Merrill Lynch Developing Capital Markets
Fund, Inc. (INT)
Merrill Lynch Dragon Fund, Inc. (INT)
Merrill Lynch EuroFund (INT)
Merrill Lynch Federal Securities Trust (USGI)
Merrill Lynch Fundamental Growth Fund,
Inc. (G)
Merrill Lynch Fund for Tomorrow, Inc. (G)
Merrill Lynch Global Allocation Fund, Inc.
(MM-T)
Merrill Lynch Global Bond Fund For
Investment & Retirement (GB)
Merrill Lynch Global Convertible Fund, Inc.
(GE)
Merrill Lynch Global Utilities Fund, Inc. (GE)
Merrill Lynch Government Fund, Inc. (MM-T)
Merrill Lynch Growth Fund for Investment &
Retirement (G+I)
Merrill Lynch Institutional Fund, Inc. (MM-T)
Merrill Lynch Institutional Intermediate Fund
(USGI)
Merrill Lynch Institutional Tax-Exempt Fund
(MM-TE)
Merrill Lynch International Equity Fund (INT)
Merrill Lynch Latin America Fund, Inc. (INT)
Merrill Lynch Multi-State Municipal Series
Trust
Arizona Municipal Bond Fund (SMB-LT)
Florida Municipal Bond Fund (SMB-LT)
Massachusetts Municipal Bond Fund
(SMB-LT)
Michigan Municipal Bond Fund (SMB-LT)
Minnesota Municipal Bond Fund (SMB-LT)
New Jersey Municipal Bond Fund (SMB-LT)
New York Municipal Bond Fund (SMB-LT)
North Carolina Municipal Bond Fund
(SMB-LT)
Ohio Municipal Bond Fund (SMB-LT)
Oregon Municipal Bond Fund (SMB-LT)
Pennsylvania Municipal Bond Fund (SMB-LT)
Texas Municipal Bond Fund (SMB-LT)
Merrill Lynch Municipal Bond Fund, Inc.
Insured Portfolio (LTMB)
Limited Maturity Portfolio (LTMB)
National Portfolio (LTMB)
Merrill Lynch Municipal Series Trust

Municipal Income Fund (LTMB)
Merrill Lynch Natural Resources Trust (G)
Merrill Lynch Pacific Fund, Inc. (INT)
Merrill Lynch Phoenix Fund, Inc. (AG)
Merrill Lynch Ready Assets Trust (MM-T)
Merrill Lynch Retirement Reserves Money
  Fund (MM-T)
Merrill Lynch Series Fund
  Balanced Portfolio (B)
  Capital Stock Portfolio (G+I)
  Global Strategy Portfolio (GB)
  Growth Stock Portfolio (G)
  High Yield Portfolio (HYB)
  Intermediate Government Bond Portfolio
    (USGI)
  Long Term Corporate Bond Portfolio (CB)
  Money Reserve Portfolio (MM-T)
  Multiple Strategy Portfolio (B)
  Natural Resources Portfolio (G)
Merrill Lynch Short-Term Global Income
  Fund, Inc. (GB)
Merrill Lynch Special Value Fund, Inc. (G)
Merrill Lynch Strategic Dividend Fund (G+I)
Merrill Lynch Technology Fund, Inc. (G)
Merrill Lynch Treasury Fund (MM-T)
Merrill Lynch U.S.A. Government Reserves
  (MM-T)
Merrill Lynch U.S. Treasury Money Fund
  (MM-T)
Merrill Lynch Variable Series Funds
  American Balanced Fund (B)
  Basic Value Focus Fund (AG)
  Domestic Money Market Fund (MM-T)
  Equity Growth Fund (G)
  Flex Strategy Fund (G+I)
  Global Strategy Fund (GB)
  Global Utility Focus Fund (GE)
  High Current Income Fund (HYB)
  International Equity Focus Fund (INT)
  Natural Resources Focus Fund (G)
  Prime Bond Fund (CB)
  Quality Equity Fund (G+I)
  Reserve Assets Fund (MM-T)
  World Income Focus Fund (GB)
ML Healthcare Fund, Inc. (GE)

Merriman Investment Trust
1200 Westlake Avenue, North, Suite 700
Seattle, Washington 98109-3530
(206) 285-8877   (800) 423-4893

Merriman Investment Trust
  Merriman Asset Allocation Fund (GB)
  Merriman Blue Chip Fund (G+I)
  Merriman Capital Appreciation Fund (G+I)
  Merriman Flexible Bond Fund (FP)
  Merriman Leveraged Growth Fund (G+I)

MetLife
One Madison Avenue
New York, New York 10010
(617) 348-2000   (800) 562-0032

MetLife Portfolios, Inc.
  MetLife International Equity Fund (INT)
  MetLife International Fixed Income Fund (GB)
MetLife-State Street Equity Trust
  MetLife-State Street Capital Appreciation
    Fund (AG)
  MetLife-State Street Equity Income Fund (IE)
  MetLife-State Street Equity Investment Fund
    (G+I)
  MetLife-State Street Global Energy Fund (GE)
MetLife-State Street Fixed Income Trust
  State Street Research Government Income
    Fund (USGI)
MetLife-State Street Income Trust
  MetLife-State Street Government Securities
    Fund (USGI)
  MetLife-State Street High Income Fund (HYB)
  MetLife-State Street Managed Assets (FP)
MetLife-State Street Money Market Trust
  MetLife-State Street Money Market Fund
    (MM-T)
MetLife-State Street Tax-Exempt Trust
  MetLife-State Street Tax-Exempt Fund
    (LTMB)
  State Street Research California Tax-Free
    Fund (SMB-LT)
  State Street Research Florida Tax-Free Fund
    (SMB-LT)
  State Street Research New York Tax-Free
    Fund (SMB-LT)
  State Street Research Pennsylvania Tax-Free
    Fund (SMB-LT)

Midwest Group
312 Walnut Street, 21st Floor
Cincinnati, Ohio 45202-4004
(513) 629-2000 (800) 542-8721

Midwest Group Tax-Free Trust
  California Tax-Free Money Fund (MMS-TE)
  Ohio Insured Tax-Free Fund (SMB-LT)
  Ohio Tax-Free Money Fund (MMS-TE)
  Royal Palm Florida Tax Free Money Fund
    (MMS-TE)
  Tax-Free Intermediate Term Fund (LTMB)
  Tax-Free Money Fund (MM-TE)
Midwest Income Trust
  Adjustable Rate U.S. Government Fund
    (GNMA)
  Institutional Government Fund (MM-T)
  Intermediate Term Government Fund (USGI)
  Short Term Government Fund (MM-T)
Midwest Strategic Trust
  Growth Fund (G)
  Leshner Financial Equity Fund (G)
  Leshner Financial Treasury Total Return
    Fund (USGI)
  Leshner Financial Utility Fund (IE)
  U.S. Government Long Maturity Fund (USGI)
  U.S. Government Securities Fund (USGI)

MIMLIC
400 North Robert Street
St. Paul, Minnesota 55101-2098
(612) 223-4252   (800) 443-3677

MIMLIC Asset Allocation Fund, Inc. (B)
MIMLIC Fixed Income Securities Fund, Inc.
   (IB)
MIMLIC Investors Fund I, Inc. (G+I)
MIMLIC Money Market Fund, Inc. (MM-T)
MIMLIC Mortgage Securities Income Fund,
   Inc. (GNMA)

MIM Mutual Funds, Inc.
4500 Rockside Road
Independence, Ohio 44131-6809
(216) 642-3000 (800) 233-1240

MIM Mutual Funds, Inc.
   MIM AFA Equity Income Fund (IE)
   MIM Bond Income Fund (CB)
   MIM Money Market Fund (MM-T)
   MIM Stock Appreciation Fund (AG)
   MIM Stock Growth Fund (G)
   MIM Stock Income Fund (G+I)

Monetta
1776-A South Naperville Road, Suite 207
Wheaton, Illinois 60187
(708) 462-9800   (800) 666-3882

Monetta Fund, Inc. (G+I)
Monetta Trust Government Money Market
   Fund (MM-T)
Monetta Trust Intermediate Bond Fund (CB)
Monetta Trust MidCap Equity Fund (G)

Money Management Plus
4550 Montgomery Avenue, Suite 1000N
Bethesda, Maryland 20814
(301) 951-4800 (800) 368-2745

Money Management Plus
   Government Portfolio (MM-T)
   Prime Portfolio (MM-T)
   Prime Portfolio - CCR PrimeShares (MM-T)
   Prime Portfolio - MMP Shares (MM-T)

Monitor Funds, The
Huntington Center, HC 1116
Columbus, Ohio 43215
(800) 253-0412

The Monitor Growth Fund (G)
The Monitor Fixed Income Securities Fund (CB)
The Monitor Money Market Fund (MM-T)
The Monitor Mortgage Securities Fund (GNMA)
The Monitor Ohio Municipal Money Market
   Fund (MM-T)
The Monitor Ohio Tax-Free Fund (MB-S)
The Monitor U.S. Treasury Money Market
   Fund (MM-T)

Monitrend Mutual Fund
Closter Dock Road, Suite One
Closter, New Jersey 07624
(201) 767-5400   (800) 251-1970

Monitrend Mutual Fund
   Chaconia Growth & Income Series (G+I)
   Gaming and Leisure Series (G)
   Gold Series (PMG)
   Government Income Series (USGI)
   Growth Series (G)
   Summation Index Series (G)
   Technology Series (G)

Montana Tax-Free Fund, Inc.
201 South Broadway
Minot, North Dakota 58701
(701) 852-5292 (800) 562-6637

Montana Tax-Free Fund, Inc. (SMB-LT)

Montgomery
600 Montgomery Street, 17th Floor
San Francisco, California 94111
(415) 627-2485   (800) 428-1871

Montgomery Financial Institution Series
   Short Duration Government Portfolio (USGI)
Montgomery Funds
   Montgomery California Tax Free Short
      Duration Fund (SMB-LT)
   Montgomery Emerging Markets Fund (INT)
   Montgomery Global Communications Fund
      (GE)
   Montgomery Government Reserve Fund
      (MM-T)
   Montgomery Short Duration Government
      Fund (USGI)
   Montgomery Small Cap Fund (AG)

MONY Series Fund, Inc.
Glenpointe Centre West
Mail Drop 71-13
Teaneck, New Jersey 07666-6888
(201) 907-6669   (800) 786-6244

MONY Series Fund, Inc.
   Diversified Portfolio (B)
   Equity Growth Portfolio (G)
   Equity Income Portfolio (IE)
   Intermediate Government Bond Portfolio (IB)
   Intermediate Term Bond Portfolio (IB)
   Long Term Bond Portfolio (IB)
   Money Market Portfolio (MM-T)

Moran Equity Fund, Inc.
41 West Putnam Avenue
Greenwich, Connecticut 06830
(203) 661-9600   (800) 661-9600

Moran Equity Fund, Inc. (G)

Morgan Keegan Southern Capital Fund
50 Front Street, 21st Floor
Memphis, Tennessee 38103
(901) 524-4100   (800) 238-7127

Morgan Keegan Southern Capital Fund (G)

Morgan Grenfell
885 Third Avenue, 32nd Floor
New York, New York 10022
(800) 932-7781

Morgan Grenfell Fixed Income Fund (CB)
Morgan Grenfell Municipal Bond Fund (MB-N)
Morgan Grenfell Emerging Markets Fund (AG)
Morgan Grenfell International Small Cap
  Equity Fund (INT)
Morgan Grenfell Global Fixed Income Fund (GB)

Morgan Stanley
c/o Mutual Funds
P.O. Box 2798
Boston, Massachusetts 02208-2798
(617) 557-8000   (800) 548-7786

Morgan Stanley Institutional Fund, Inc.
  Active Country Portfolio (INT)
  Asian Equity Portfolio (INT)
  Balanced Portfolio (I)
  Emerging Growth Portfolio (AG)
  Emerging Markets Portfolio (G)
  Equity Growth Portfolio (G)
  European Equity Portfolio (INT)
  Fixed Income Portfolio (IB)
  Global Equity Portfolio (GE)
  Global Fund Income Portfolio (GB)
  High Yield Fund (HYB)
  International Equity Portfolio (INT)
  International Small Cap Fund (INT)
  Money Market Portfolio (MM-T)
  Municipal Money Market Portfolio (MM-TE)
  Small Cap Value Equity Fund (AG)
  Value Equity Portfolio (G+I)

M.S.B. Fund, Inc.
330 Madison Avenue
New York, New York 10017-5000
(212) 551-1800

M.S.B. Fund, Inc. (G+I)

M.S.D.& T. Funds, Inc.
1900 East Dublin-Granville Road
Columbus, Ohio 43229
(800) 551-2145

M.S.D.& T. Funds, Inc.
  Government Money Market Fund (MM-TE)
  Intermediate Fixed Income Fund (IB)
  International Equity Fund (INT)
  Maryland Tax-Exempt Bond Fund (SMB-LT)
  Prime Money Market Fund (MM-T)
  Tax-Exempt Money Market Fund (MM-TE)
  Tax-Exempt Money Market Fund (Trust)
    (MM-TE)
  Value Equity Fund (G+I)

Muir Investment Trust
One Sansome Street, Suite 810
San Francisco, California 94104
(415) 677-8500   (800) 648-3448

Muir Investment Trust
  Muir California Tax-Free Bond Fund (SMB-LT)

Munder Funds, Inc.
480 Pierce Street, Suite 300
Birmingham, Michigan 48009
(313) 647-9200   (800) 551-6570

Munder Funds, Inc.
  Munder Money Market Fund (MM-T)
  Munder Multi-Season Growth Fund (G)

Municipal Fund
Bellevue Corporate Center, Suite 152
103 Bellevue Parkway
Wilmington, Delaware 19809
(302) 791-5350   (800) 441-7450

Municipal Fund for California Investors, Inc.
  California Intermediate Municipal Fund
    (SMB-LT)
  California Money Fund (MMS-TE)
Municipal Fund for New York Investors, Inc.
  (MMS-TE)
Municipal Fund for Temporary Investment
  Intermediate Municipal Fund (LTMB)
  MuniCash Portfolio (MM-TE)
  Muni-Fund (MM-TE)
Municipal Fund Investment Accumulation
  Program, Inc. (LTMB)

Mutual Benefit Fund
520 Broad Street
Newark, New Jersey 07102-3184
(201) 481-8000   (800) 323-4726

Mutual Benefit Fund (G)

Mutual of America Investment Corporation
666 Fifth Avenue
New York, New York 10020
(212) 399-1600   (800) 468-3785

Mutual of America Investment Corporation
  Bond Fund (The) (IB)
  Composite Fund (The) (FP)
  Equity Index Fund (The) (G)
  Mid-Term Bond Fund (The) (IB)
  Money Market Fund (The) (MM-T)
  Short-Term Bond Fund (The) (IB)
  Stock Fund (The) (G+I)

Mutual of Omaha
10235 Regency Circle
Omaha, Nebraska 68114-3745
(402) 397-8555 (800) 228-9596

Mutual of Omaha America Fund, Inc. (USGI)
Mutual of Omaha Growth Fund, Inc. (G)
Mutual of Omaha Income Fund, Inc. (IM)
Mutual of Omaha Money Market Account,
  Inc. (MM-T)
Mutual of Omaha Tax-Free Income Fund, Inc.
  (LTMB)

Mutual Selection Fund, Inc.
2610 Park Avenue
P.O. Box 209
Muscatine, Iowa 52761
(319) 264-8000   (800) 334-8920
(800) 345-3024
Mutual Selection Fund, Inc. (G)

Mutual Series Fund, Inc.
51 J.F. Kennedy Parkway
Short Hills, New Jersey 07078
(201) 912-2100 (800) 448-3863
Mutual Series Fund, Inc.
  Mutual Beacon Fund (G+I)
  Mutual Discovery Fund (G+I)
  Mutual Qualified Fund (G+I)
  Mutual Shares Fund (G+I)

Narragansett Insured Tax-Free Income Fund
380 Madison Avenue, Suite 2300
New York, New York 10017-2590
(212) 697-6666   (800) 453-6864
Narragansett Insured Tax-Free Income Fund
  (SMB-LT)

NASL Series Trust
116 Huntington Avenue
Boston, Massachusetts 02116
(617) 266-6004   (800) 344-1029
NASL Series Trust
  Aggressive Asset Allocation Trust (AG)
  Conservative Allocation Trust (IM)
  Equity Trust (G)
  Global Equity Trust (GE)
  Global Government Bond Trust (GB)
  Growth and Income Trust (G+I)
  Investment Quality Bond Trust (CB)
  Moderate Asset Allocation Trust (IM)
  Money Market Trust (MM-T)
  Pasadena Growth Trust (G)
  Strategic Bond Trust (IB)
  U.S. Government Securities Trust (USGI)
  Value Equity (G)

Nations Fund
111 Center Street
Little Rock, Arkansas 72201
(800) 321-7854
Nations Fund, Inc.
  Nations Equity Income Fund (IE)
  Nations International Equity Fund (INT)
  Nations Prime Fund (MM-T)
  Nations Tax-Exempt Money Market Fund
    (MM-TE)
  Nations Treasury Fund (MM-T)
Nations Fund Trust
  Nations Diversified Income Fund (IM)
  Nations Adjustable Rate Government Fund
    (GNMA)
  Nations Balanced Assets Fund (IM)

Nations Capital Growth Fund (AG)
Nations Emerging Growth Fund (AG)
Nations Florida Intermediate Municipal Bond
  Fund (SMB-LT)
Nations Florida Municipal Bond Fund
  (SMB-LT)
Nations Georgia Intermediate Municipal
  Bond Fund (SMB-LT)
Nations Georgia Municipal Bond Fund
  (SMB-LT)
Nations Government Money Market Fund
  (MM-T)
Nations Intermediate Municipal Bond Fund
  (LTMB)
Nations Managed Bond Fund (CB)
Nations Maryland Intermediate Municipal
  Bond Fund (SMB-LT)
Nations Maryland Municipal Bond Fund
  (SMB-LT)
Nations Mortgage-Backed Securities Fund
  (GNMA)
Nations Municipal Income Fund (LTMB)
Nations North Carolina Intermediate
  Municipal Bond Fund (SMB-LT)
Nations North Carolina Municipal Bond
  Fund (SMB-LT)
Nations Short-Intermediate Government
  Fund (USGI)
Nations Short-Term Income Fund (IB)
Nations Short-Term Municipal Income Fund
  (USGI)
Nations South Carolina Intermediate
  Municipal Bond Fund (SMB-LT)
Nations South Carolina Municipal Bond
  Fund (SMB-LT)
Nations Strategic Fixed Income Fund (IB)
Nations Tax Exempt Fund (MM-TE)
Nations Tennessee Intermediate Municipal
  Bond Fund (SMB-LT)
Nations Tennessee Municipal Bond Fund
  (SMB-LT)
Nations Texas Intermediate Municipal Bond
  Fund (SMB-LT)
Nations Texas Municipal Bond Fund
  (SMB-LT)
Nations Value Fund (G+I)
Nations Virginia Intermediate Municipal
  Bond Fund (SMB-LT)
Nations Virginia Municipal Bond Fund
  (SMB-LT)

Nationwide
One Nationwide Plaza, Box 1492
Columbus, Ohio 43216-1492
(614) 249-7855   (800) 848-0920
Nationwide Investing Foundation
  Bond Fund (CB)
  Growth Fund (G)
  Money Market Fund (MM-T)
  Nationwide Fund (G+I)

Nationwide Investing Foundation II
  Tax-Free Income Fund (LTMB)
  U.S. Government Income Fund (USGI)
Nationwide Separate Account Trust
  Capital Appreciation Fund (G)
  Government Bond Fund (USGI)
  Money Market Fund (MM-T)
  Total Return Fund (G+I)

NCC Funds
440 Lincoln Street, Box 17
Worcester, Massachusetts 01653-0017
(800) 622-3863
NCC Funds Enhanced Income Fund (CB)
NCC Funds Equity Income Portfolio (G+I)
NCC Funds Equity Portfolio (G)
NCC Funds Fixed Income Portfolio (CB)
NCC Funds Government Portfolio (MM-T)
NCC Funds Mid Cap Regional Equity Portfolio
  (AG)
NCC Funds Money Market Portfolio (MM-T)
NCC Funds Ohio Tax Exempt Portfolio
  (MMS-TE)
NCC Funds Tax Exempt Portfolio (MM-TE)
NCC Funds Total Return Advantage Fund
  (HYB)
NCC Funds Treasury Portfolio (MM-T)

ND Insured Income Fund, Inc.
201 South Broadway
Minot, North Dakota 58701
(701) 852-5292   (800) 562-6637
ND Insured Income Fund, Inc. (IB)
ND Tax-Free Fund, Inc. (SMB-LT)

Neuberger & Berman
605 Third Avenue, 2nd Floor
New York, New York 10158-3698
(212) 476-8800 (800) 877-9700
Neuberger & Berman Advisors Management
  Trust
  Balanced Portfolio (B)
  Growth Portfolio (G)
  Limited Maturity Bond Portfolio (IB)
  Liquid Asset Portfolio (MM-T)
Neuberger & Berman Cash Reserves (MM-T)
Neuberger & Berman Genesis Fund, Inc. (G)
Neuberger & Berman Genesis Trust (G)
Neuberger & Berman Government Income
  Fund (IB)
Neuberger & Berman Government Income
  Trust (IB)
Neuberger & Berman Guardian Fund, Inc.
  (G+I)
Neuberger & Berman Guardian Trust (G+I)
Neuberger & Berman Limited Maturity Bond
  Fund (IB)
Neuberger & Berman Limited Maturity Bond
  Trust (IB)
Neuberger & Berman Manhattan Fund, Inc.
  (MM-TE)

Neuberger & Berman Manhattan Trust
  (MM-TE)
Neuberger & Berman Municipal Money Fund
  (MM-TE)
Neuberger & Berman Municipal Securities
  Trust (LTMB)
Neuberger & Berman Partners Fund, Inc. (G)
Neuberger & Berman Partners Trust (G)
Neuberger & Berman Selected Sectors Fund,
  Inc. (G)
Neuberger & Berman Selected Sectors Trust
  (G)
Neuberger & Berman Ultra Short Bond Trust
  (IB)

New Alternatives Fund, Inc.
295 Northern Boulevard
Great Neck, New York 11021
(516) 466-0808
New Alternatives Fund, Inc. (G)

New Economy Fund
333 South Hope Street
Los Angeles, California 90071-1447
(213) 486-9200   (800) 421-0180
New Economy Fund (G)

New England Zenith Fund
399 Boylston Street
Boston, Massachusetts 02116
(617) 578-2000   (800) 225-7670
New England Zenith Fund
  Avanti Growth Fund (G)
  Bond Income Series (IB)
  Capital Growth Series (AG)
  Managed Series (G+I)
  Money Market Series (MM-T)
  Stock Index Series (G)
  Value Growth Fund (G+I)

New Perspective Fund, Inc.
333 South Hope Street
Los Angeles, California 90071-1447
(213) 486-9200   (800) 421-0180
New Perspective Fund (GE)

New USA Mutual Fund, Inc.
c\o 12655 Beatrice Street
Los Angeles, California 90066
(310) 448-6230   (800) 222-2872
New USA Mutual Fund, Inc. (AG)

New World Investment Trust
1661 Lincoln Boulevard, Suite 400
Santa Monica, California 90404
(310) 314-3899   (800) 874-4287
New World Investment Trust
  GreenEarth Growth Fund (G)
  GreenEarth Income Fund (IB)
  GreenEarth Liquid Assets Fund (MM-T)

New York Life Institutional Funds, Inc.
260 Cherry Hill Road
Parsippany, New Jersey 07054-1108
(201) 331-2000   (800) 522-4202

New York Life Institutional Funds, Inc.
  Bond Fund (IB)
  EAFE Index Fund (INT)
  Growth Equity Fund (G)
  Indexed Bond Fund (IB)
  Indexed Equity Fund (G+I)
  Money Market Fund (MM-T)
  Multi-Asset Fund (B)
  Short-Term Bond Fund (IM)
  Value Equity Fund (AG)

New York Venture Fund, Inc.
124 East Marcy Street
P.O. Box 1688
Santa Fe, New Mexico 87501-1688
(505) 983-4335   (800) 279-0279

New York Venture Fund, Inc. (G)

Nicholas-Applegate Fund, Inc.
One Seaport Plaza
New York, New York 10292
(212) 214-1215   (800) 225-1852

Nicholas-Applegate Fund, Inc.
  Nicholas-Applegate Growth Equity Fund (G)

Nicholas-Applegate Investment Trust
600 West Broadway, 30th Floor
San Diego, California 92101
(619) 687-8100

Nicholas-Applegate Investment Trust
  Balanced Growth Portfolio (B)
  Core Growth Portfolio (G)
  Government Income Portfolio (USGI)
  Income and Growth Portfolio (G+I)
  Money Market Portfolio (MM-T)
  Qualified Class (G+I)
  Worldwide Growth Portfolio (INT)

Nomura Capital Management, Inc.
180 Maiden Lane, Suite 2903
New York, New York 10038-4939
(212) 509-8181   (800) 833-0018

Nomura Pacific Basin Fund, Inc. (INT)

North American Funds
116 Huntington Avenue
Boston, Massachusetts 02116
(617) 266-6004   (800) 344-1029

North American Funds
  Asset Allocation Fund (IM)
  California Municipal Bond Fund (SMB-LT)
  Global Growth Fund (GE)
  Growth and Income Fund (G+I)
  Growth Fund (G)
  Investment Quality Bond Fund (IM)
  Money Market Fund (MM-T)

  National Municipal Bond Fund (LTMB)
  U.S. Government Securities Fund (USGI)

North Carolina Cash Management Trust
82 Devonshire Street
Boston, Massachusetts 01209
(617) 570-7000   (800) 222-3232

North Carolina Cash Management Trust
  Cash Portfolio (MM-T)
  Term Portfolio (USGI)

Northeast Management & Research
50 Congress Street
Boston, Massachusetts 02109
(212) 509-7893   (800) 833-0018

Northeast Investors Growth (G)
Northeast Investors Trust (HYB)

Northern Funds
801 South Canal Street
Chicago, Illinois 60607
(800) 595-9111

Northern Fixed Income Fund (CB)
Northern Growth Equity Fund (G)
Northern Income Equity Find (G+I)
Northern Intermediate Tax-Exempt Bond
  Fund (MB-N)
Northern International Fixed Income Fund (GB)
Northern International Growth Equity Fund
  (INT)
Northern International Select Equity Fund (INT)
Northern Money Market Fund (MM-T)
Northern Select Equity Fund (G)
Northern Small Cap Growth Fund (AG)
Northern Tax-Exempt Bond Fund (MB-N)
Northern Tax-Exempt Money Market Fund
  (MM-TE)
Northern U.S. Government Bond Fund (USGI)
Northern U.S. Government Money Market
  Fund (MM-T)

Northwest Investors Trust
1300 North State Street
Holly Plaza
Bellingham, Washington 98225-4730
(206) 734-9900   (800) 728-8762

Northwest Investors Trust
  Idaho Tax-Exempt Fund (SMB-LT)
  Northwest Growth Fund (G)
  Washington Tax-Exempt Fund (SMB-LT)

Norwest Funds
6th and Marquette Avenue
Minneapolis, Minnesota 55479-0063
(800) 338-1348

Norwest Funds
  Adjustable U.S. Government Reserve Fund
    (GNMA)
  Arizona Tax-Free Fund (MB-S)
  Cash Investment Fund (MM-T)

Colorado Tax-Free Fund (MB-S)
Contrarian Stock Fund (AG)
Government Income Fund (USGI)
Income Fund (CB)
Income Stock Fund (G+I)
Minnesota Tax-Free Fund (MB-S)
Municipal Money Market Fund (MM-T)
Ready Cash Investment Fund (MM-T)
Small Company Stock Fund (G)
Tax-Free Income Fund (MB-N)
Total Return Bond Fund (CB)
Treasury Fund (MM-T)
U.S. Government Fund (MM-T)
ValuGrowth Stock Fund (G)
Nottingham Investment Trust
  FBP Contrarian Balanced Fund (The) (B)
  FBP Contrarian Equity Fund (The) (G)
  Government Street Bond Fund (The) (IB)
  Government Street Equity Fund (The) (G)
  Jamestown Balanced Fund (The) (B)
  Jamestown Bond Fund (The) (IB)
  Jamestown Equity Fund (The) (G)
  Jamestown Short Term Bond Fund (The)
    (IB)
  Jamestown Tax-Exempt Virginia Fund (The)
    (SMB-LT)
Nottingham Investment Trust II
  Brown Capital Management Balanced Fund
    (The) (B)
  Brown Capital Management Equity Fund
    (The) (G)
  Brown Capital Management Small Company
    Fund (The) (AG)
  Capital Value Fund (The) (G+I)
  Hatteras Dividend Growth Fund (The) (G+I)
  Hatteras Utility Income Fund (The) (IE)
  Investek Fixed Income Trust (The) (IM)
  ZSA Equity Fund (The) (G)
  ZSA Growth & Income Fund (The) (G+I)

Nuveen
333 West Wacker Drive
Chicago, Illinois 60606
(312) 917-7844   (800) 621-7210
Nuveen California Tax-Free Fund, Inc.
  Nuveen California Insured Tax-Free Value
    Fund (SMB-LT)
  Nuveen California Tax-Free Money Market
    Fund (MMS-TE)
  Nuveen California Tax-Free Value Fund
    (SMB-LT)
Nuveen Insured Tax-Free Bond Fund, Inc.
  Nuveen Insured Municipal Bond Fund
    (LTMB)
  Nuveen Massachusetts Insured Tax-Free
    Value Fund (SMB-LT)
  Nuveen New York Insured Tax-Free Value
    Fund (SMB-LT)
Nuveen Multistate Tax-Free Trust
  Nuveen Arizona Tax-Free Value Fund
    (SMB-LT)

Nuveen Florida Tax-Free Value Fund (SMB-LT)
Nuveen Maryland Tax-Free Value Fund
  (SMB-LT)
Nuveen Michigan Tax-Free Value Fund
  (SMB-LT)
Nuveen New Jersey Tax-Free Value Fund
  (SMB-LT)
Nuveen Pennsylvania Tax-Free Value Fund
  (SMB-LT)
Nuveen Virginia Tax-Free Value Fund
  (SMB-LT)
Nuveen Municipal Bond Fund, Inc. (LTMB)
Nuveen Tax-Exempt Money Market Fund, Inc.
  (MM-TE)
Nuveen Tax-Free Bond Fund, Inc.
  Nuveen Massachusetts Tax-Free Value Fund
    (SMB-LT)
  Nuveen New York Tax-Free Value Fund
    (SMB-LT)
  Nuveen Ohio Tax-Free Value Fund (SMB-LT)
Nuveen Tax-Free Money Market Fund, Inc.
  Massachusetts Tax-Free Money Market
    Fund (MMS-TE)
  New York Tax-Free Money Market Fund
    (MMS-TE)
Nuveen Tax-Free Reserves, Inc. (MM-TE)

NWNL Northstar
Two Pickwick Plaza
Greenwich, Connecticut 06830
(203) 863-6200   (800) 595-7827
NWNL Northstar Series Trust
  NWNL Northstar High Yield Bond Fund (HYB)
  NWNL Northstar Income and Growth Fund
    (G+I)
  NWNL Northstar Multi-Sector Bond Fund (IB)

Oak Hall
P.O. Box 446
Portland, Maine 04112
  or
Forum Financial Corp.
61 Broadway
New York, New York 10006
(800) 625-4255
Oak Hall Equity Fund (G)

Oakmark Funds
State Street Bank & Trust Company
P.O. Box 8510
Boston, Massachusetts 02266-8510
(800) 625-6275   (800) 476-9625
Oakmark Fund (G)
Oakmark International Fund (INT)

OakTree
680 East Swedesford Road, No. 10
Wayne, Pennsylvania 19087-1658
(800) 342-5734
OakTree Family of Funds
  Diversified Growth Portfolio (AG)

Intermediate-Term Income Portfolio (IB)
Prime Obligation Money Market Portfolio
(MM-T)

Oberweis
Two North LaSalle Street
Chicago, Illinois 60602
(312) 368-5419   (800) 621-4480
Oberweis Emerging Growth Fund
Emerging Growth Portfolio (AG)

Ohio National Fund
237 William Howard Taft
Cincinnati, Ohio 45219-2679
(513) 861-3600
Ohio National Fund, Inc
Bond Portfolio (CB)
Equity Portfolio (G)
International Portfolio (INT)
Money Market Portfolio (MM-T)
Omni Portfolio (FP)

One Fund, Inc.
P.O. Box 371
Cincinnati, Ohio 45201
(800) 578-8078
One Fund, Inc.
Growth Portfolio (G)
Global Contrarian (G)
Income & Growth Portfolio (G+I)
Income Portfolio (IM)
International Portfolio (INT)
Money Market Portfolio (MM-T)
Small Cap Portfolio (AG)
Tax-Free Income Portfolio (MB-N)

Omni Investment Fund
53 West Jackson Boulevard, Suite 818
Chicago, Illinois 60604
(312) 922-0431   (800) 223-9790
Omni Investment Fund (G)

One Group
440 Lincoln Street
Worcester, Massachusetts 01653
(800) 338-4345
One Group
Asset Manager Portfolio (B)
Blue Chip Equity Portfolio (G+I)
Disciplined Value Portfolio (IE)
Equity Index Portfolio (IE)
Government ARM Portfolio (GNMA)
Government Bond Portfolio (USGI)
Government Money Market Portfolio (MM-T)
Income Equity Portfolio (IE)
Income Portfolio (IM)
Intermediate Tax-Free Portfolio (LTMB)
International Equity Index Portfolio (INT)
Large Company Value Fund (G+I)
Limited Volatility Bond Portfolio (IM)

Ohio Municipal Money Market Portfolio
(MM-TE)
Ohio Municipal Portfolio (SMB-LT)
Prime Obligations Portfolio (MM-T)
Short-Term Global Bond Portfolio (GB)
Tax-Free Bond Portfolio (LTMB)
Tax-Free Money Market Portfolio (MM-TE)
Treasury Only Money Market Portfolio
(MM-T)
U.S. Treasury Money Market Portfolio
(MM-T)

Oppenheimer
Two World Trade Center
New York, New York 10048-0203
(212) 323-0200   (800) 525-7048
Oppenheimer Asset Allocation Fund (FP)
Oppenheimer California Tax-Exempt Fund
(SMB-LT)
Oppenheimer Discovery Fund (AG)
Oppenheimer Fund (G)
Oppenheimer Global Bio-Tech Fund (GE)
Oppenheimer Global Environment Fund (GE)
Oppenheimer Global Fund (GE)
Oppenheimer Global Growth and Income
Fund (GE)
Oppenheimer Gold & Special Minerals Fund
(PMG)
Oppenheimer Mortgage Income Fund
(GNMA)
Oppenheimer New York Tax-Exempt Fund
(SMB-LT)
Oppenheimer Pennsylvania Tax-Exempt Fund
(SMB-LT)
Oppenheimer Special Fund (AG)
Oppenheimer Target Fund (AG)
Oppenheimer Tax-Free Bond Fund (LTMB)
Oppenheimer Time Fund (AG)
Oppenheimer U.S. Government Trust (USGI)

Oppenheimer
3410 South Galena Street
Denver, Colorado 80231-3234
(303) 671-3200   (800) 525-7048
Oppenheimer Cash Reserves (MM-T)
Oppenheimer Champion High Yield Fund
(HYB)
Oppenheimer Equity Income Fund (IE)
Oppenheimer Government Securities Fund
(USGI)
Oppenheimer High Yield Fund (HYB)
Oppenheimer Investment Grade Bond Fund
(IB)
Oppenheimer Money Market Fund, Inc. (MM-T)
Oppenheimer Strategic Income & Growth
Fund (IM)
Oppenheimer Strategic Income Fund (IM)
Oppenheimer Strategic Investment Grade
Bond (IM)
Oppenheimer Strategic Short-Term Income
Fund (IM)

Oppenheimer Tax-Exempt Bond Fund
  Oppenheimer Insured Tax-Exempt Bond
    Fund (LTMB)
  Oppenheimer Intermediate Tax-Exempt
    Bond Fund (LTMB)
Oppenheimer Tax-Exempt Cash Reserves
  (MM-TE)
Oppenheimer Total Return Fund (G+I)
Oppenheimer Value Stock Fund (G+I)
Oppenheimer Variable Account Funds
  Oppenheimer Bond Fund (CB)
  Oppenheimer Capital Appreciation Fund (AG)
  Oppenheimer Global Securities Fund (GE)
  Oppenheimer Growth Fund (G)
  Oppenheimer High Income Fund (HYB)
  Oppenheimer Money Fund (MM-T)
  Oppenheimer Multiple Strategies Fund (FP)
  Oppenheimer Strategic Bond Fund (IB)

Oregon Municipal Bond Fund, Inc.
121 S.W. Morrison, Suite 1400
Portland, Oregon 97204
(503) 295-0919   (800) 541-9732

Oregon Municipal Bond Fund, Inc. (SMB-LT)

Overland Express Funds, Inc.
111 Center Street, Suite 300
Stephens Building
Little Rock, Arkansas 72201
(501) 377-2569   (800) 458-6589

Overland Express Funds, Inc.
  Asset Allocation Fund (The) (FP)
  California Tax-Free Bond Fund (The)
    (SMB-LT)
  California Tax-Free Money Market Fund
    (The) (MMS-TE)
  Dividend Income Fund (The) (IE)
  Growth and Income Fund (The) (G+I)
  Money Market Fund (The) (MM-T)
  Municipal Income Fund (The) (LTMB)
  Short Term U.S. Government Fund (The)
    (GNMA)
  Strategic Growth Fund (The) (AG)
  U.S. Government Income Fund (The) (USGI)
  U.S. Treasury Money Market Fund (The)
    (MM-T)
  Variable Rate Government Fund (The)
    (GNMA)

Pacific Advisors Fund, Inc.
215 North Marengo Avenue, Suite 115
Pasadena, California 91101
(818) 796-6693   (800) 282-6693

Pacific Advisors Fund, Inc.
  Balanced Fund (B)
  Government Securities Fund (USGI)
  Income Fund (IE)
  Small Cap Fund (AG)

Pacifica Funds, Inc.
237 Park Avenue, Suite 910
New York, New York 10017
(212) 808-3900   (800) 662-8417

Pacifica Funds, Inc.
  Pacifica Asset Preservation Fund (IB)
  Pacifica Balanced Fund (B)
  Pacifica California Tax-Free Fund (SMB-LT)
  Pacifica Equity Value Fund (G+I)
  Pacifica Government Income Fund (USGI)
  Pacifica Government Money Market Fund
    (MM-T)
  Pacifica Money Market Fund (MM-T)
  Pacifica Short-Term California Tax-Free Fund
    (SMB-LT)

Pacific American Fund, Inc.
800 West South Street
Los Angeles, California 90017
(800) 548-2412

Pacific American Fund, Inc.
  Money Market Portfolio (MM-T)
  U.S. Treasury Portfolio (MM-T)

Pacific Capital Cash Assets Trust
380 Madison Avenue, Suite 2300
New York, New York 10017-2590
(212) 697-6666   (800) 228-7496

Pacific Capital Cash Assets Trust
  Cash Assets Trust (MM-T)
  Tax-Free Cash Assets Trust (MM-TE)
  U.S. Treasuries Cash Assets Trust (MM-T)

Pacific Horizon Funds, Inc.
125 West 55th Street, 11th Floor
New York, New York 10019
(212) 492-1600   (800) 367-6075

Pacific Horizon Funds, Inc.
  Aggressive Growth Fund (AG)
  California Tax-Exempt Bond Fund (SMB-LT)
  California Tax-Exempt Money Market Fund
    (MMS-TE)
  Capital Income Fund (G+I)
  Government Fund (MM-T)
  Prime Fund (MM-T)
  Prime Value Fund (MM-T)
  Tax-Exempt Money Fund (MM-TE)
  Treasury Fund (MM-T)
  Treasury Only Fund (MM-T)
  U.S. Government Securities Fund (GNMA)

PaineWebber
1285 Avenue of the Americas
PaineWebber Building
New York, New York 10019
(212) 713-2000   (800) 647-1568

PaineWebber America Fund
  PaineWebber Dividend Growth Fund (G+I)
PaineWebber Atlas Fund
  PaineWebber Atlas Global Growth Fund (GE)

PaineWebber Cash Fund, Inc. (MM-T)
PaineWebber Investment Series
  PaineWebber Europe Growth Fund (INT)
  PaineWebber Global Energy Fund (GE)
  PaineWebber Growth and Income Fund (GE)
  PaineWebber Global Income Fund (GB)
PaineWebber Managed Assets Trust
  PaineWebber Capital Appreciation Fund
    (HYB)
PaineWebber Managed Investments Trust
  PaineWebber High Income Fund (HYB)
  PainWebber Investment Grade Income
    Fund (CB)
  PaineWebber Short-Term U.S. Government
    Income Fund (USGI)
  PaineWebber U.S. Government Income
    Fund (GNMA)
  PaineWebber Utility Income Fund (IB)
PaineWebber Master Series, Inc.
  PaineWebber Asset Allocation Fund (FP)
  PaineWebber Blue Chip Growth Fund (G)
  PaineWebber Income Fund (IB)
  PaineWebber Money Market Fund (MM-T)
PaineWebber Municipal Series
  PaineWebber Municipal High Income Fund
    (LTMB)
  PaineWebber New York Tax-Free Income
    Fund (SMB-LT)
PaineWebber Mutual Fund Trust
  PaineWebber California Tax-Free Income
    Fund (SMB-LT)
  PaineWebber National Tax-Free Income
    Fund (LTMB)
  PaineWebber RMA California Municipal
    Money Fund (MMS-TE)
  PaineWebber RMA New York Municipal
    Money Fund (MMS-TE)
PaineWebber Olympus Fund
  PainWebber Growth Fund (G)
PaineWebber Regional Financial Growth
  Fund, Inc. (G)
PaineWebber RMA Money Fund, Inc.
  PaineWebber Retirement Money Fund
    (MM-T)
  PaineWebber RMA Money Market Portfolio
    (MM-T)
  PaineWebber RMA U.S. Government
    Portfolio (MM-T)
PaineWebber RMA Tax-Free Fund, Inc.
  (MM-TE)
PaineWebber Securities Trust
  Small Cap Value Fund (AG)
PaineWebber Series Trust
  Aggressive Growth Portfolio (AG)
  Asset Allocation Portfolio (FP)
  Balanced Portfolio (B)
  Dividend Growth Portfolio (G)
  Fixed Income Portfolio (IB)
  Global Growth Portfolio (GE)
  Global Income Portfolio (GB)
  Government Portfolio (USGI)

  Growth Portfolio (G)
  Money Market Portfolio (MM-T)

PanAgora Funds
260 Franklin Street
Boston, Massachusetts 02110
(617) 439-6300   (800) 423-6041
PanAgora Funds
  Asset Allocation Fund (FP)
  Global Fund (GB)
  International Equity Fund (INT)

Papp America-Abroad Fund, Inc.
4400 North 32nd Street, Suite 280
Phoenix, Arizona 85018
(602) 956-0980   (800) 421-4004
Papp America-Abroad Fund, Inc. (G)
Papp (The L. Roy) Stock Fund, Inc. (G)

Paragon
4900 Sears Tower
Chicago, Illinois 60606-6391
(312) 655-4400   (800) 525-7907
(800) 777-5143
Paragon Portfolio
  Paragon South Growth Fund (G)
  Paragon Intermediate-Term Bond Fund (IM)
  Paragon Louisiana Tax-Free Fund (MB-S)
  Paragon Short Term Government Fund
    (USGI)
  Paragon Treasury Money Market Fund
    (MM-T)
  Paragon Value Equity Income Fund (G+I)
  Paragon Value Growth Fund (G)

Park Avenue
201 Park Avenue South
New York, New York 10003
(212) 598-8260   (800) 221-3253
Park Avenue Portfolio
  Guardian Asset Allocation Fund (The) (FP)
  Guardian Baillie Gifford International Fund
    (INT)
  Guardian Cash Management Fund (The)
    (MM-T)
  Guardian Investment Quality Bond Fund
    (The) (CB)
  Guardian Park Avenue Fund (The) (G)
  Guardian Tax-Exempt Fund (The) (MB-N)
  Guardian U.S. Government Securities Fund
    (The) (USGI)

Parkstone
199 East Dublin-Granville Road
Columbus, Ohio 43229-3515
(614) 899-4600   (800) 451-8377
Parkstone Group of Funds
  Balanced Fund (The) (B)
  Bond Fund (The) (IB)
  Equity Fund (The) (IE)
  Government Income Fund (The)

High Income Equity Fund (IE)
Intermediate Government Obligations Fund
   (The) (USGI)
International Discovery Fund (The) (INT)
Limited Maturity Bond Fund (The) (IB)
Michigan Municipal Bond Fund (The) (MB-S)
Municipal Bond Fund (The) (MB-N)
Prime Obligation Fund (The) (MM-T)
Small Capitalization Fund (The) (AG)
Tax-Free Fund (The) (MM-TE)
U.S. Government Obligations Fund (The)
   (MM-T)

Parnassus Financial
244 California Street
San Francisco, California 94111
(415) 362-4515   (800) 999-3505

Parnassus Fund (G)
Parnassus Income Fund
   Balanced Portfolio (B)
   California Tax-Exempt Portfolio (MB-S)
   Fixed-Income Portfolio (IB)

Pasadena Investment Trust
600 North Rosemead Boulevard
Pasadena, California 91107-2033
(818) 351-9686   (800) 882-2855

Pasadena Investment Trust
   Pasadena Balanced Return Fund (The) (B)
   Pasadena Growth Fund (The) (G)
   Pasadena Nifty-Fifty Fund (The) (G)

Passageway Funds
Federated Investors Tower
Pittsburgh, Pennsylvania 15222-3779
(412) 288-1900   (800) 763-7277

Passageway Funds
   South Carolina Municipal Bond Fund
   (MB-S)

Pax World
224 State Street
Portsmouth, New Hampshire 03801
(603) 431-8022   (800) 767-1729

Pax World Fund, Inc. (B)

PCS Cash Fund, Inc.
103 Bellevue Parkway
Wilmington, Delaware 19801
(302) 791-7000   (800) 332-2929

PCS Cash Fund, Inc.
   PCS Government Obligations Money
      Market Portfolio (The) (MM-T)
   PCS Money Market Portfolio (The)
      (MM-T)

Penn Capital Funds, Inc.
7211 Saltsburg Road
Pittsburgh, Pennsylvania 15235
(412) 798-3000

Penn Capital Funds, Inc.
   Asset Allocation Fund (G+I)
   U.S. Government Money Market Fund
      (MM-T)

Pennsylvania Mutual Fund, Inc.
1414 Avenue of the Americas
New York, New York 10019
(212) 355-7311   (800) 221-4268

Pennsylvania Mutual Fund, Inc. (AG)

Peoples
144 Glenn Curtiss Boulevard
Uniondale, New York 11556-0114
(718) 895-1206   (800) 782-6620

Peoples Index Fund, Inc. (G+I)
Peoples S&P MidCap Index Fund, Inc (G+I)

Performance Funds Trust
237 Park Avenue, Suite 910
New York, New York 10017
(212) 808-3900   (800) 662-8417

Performance Funds Trust
   Equity Fund (G)
   Intermediate Term Fixed Income Fund (IB)
   Money Market Fund (MM-T)
   Short-Term Fixed Income Fund (IB)

Perritt Capital Growth Fund, Inc.
680 North Lake Shore Drive, Suite 2038
Chicago, Illinois 60611-4402
(312) 649-6940   (800) 338-1579

Perritt Capital Growth Fund, Inc. (AG)

Philadelphia Fund, Inc.
1200 North Federal Highway, Suite 424
Boca Raton, Florida 33432
(407) 395-2155   (800) 749-9933

Philadelphia Fund, Inc. (G+I)

Phillips Capital Investments, Inc.
15400 Knoll Trail, Suite 100
P.O. Box 796787
Dallas, Texas 75397-6787
(214) 458-2448

Phillips Capital Investments, Inc. (G)

Phoenix
101 Munson Street
Greenfield, Massachusetts 01301
(203) 253-1000   (800) 243-1574

Phoenix Multi-Portfolio Fund
   Phoenix Capital Appreciation Portfolio (G)
   Phoenix International Portfolio (INT)
   Phoenix Tax-Exempt Bond Portfolio (MB-N)
Phoenix Series Fund
   Phoenix Balanced Fund Series (B)
   Phoenix Convertible Fund Series (G+I)
   Phoenix Growth Fund Series (G)
   Phoenix High Yield Fund Series (HYB)

Phoenix Money Market Fund Series (MM-T)
Phoenix Stock Fund Series (AG)
Phoenix U.S. Government Securities Fund
Series (USGI)
Phoenix Total Return Fund (FP)

PIC Investment Trust
300 North Lake Avenue
Pasadena, California 91101-4106
(818) 449-8500

PIC Investment Trust
PIC Balanced Portfolio (B)
PIC Endeavor Growth Fund (G)
PIC Growth Fund (G)
PIC Institutional Balanced Fund (B)
PIC Institutional Growth Fund (G)
PIC Small Cap Growth Fund (AG)

Pilgrim
10100 Santa Monica Boulevard, 21st Floor
Los Angeles, California 90067-4003
(310) 551-0833   (800) 334-3444

Pilgrim Corporate Utilities Fund (IM)
Pilgrim Global Investment Series
Short-Term Multi-Market Income Fund (GB)
Short-Term Multi-Market Income Fund II
(GB)
Pilgrim GNMA Fund (GNMA)
Pilgrim MagnaCap Fund, Inc. (G+I)
Pilgrim Strategic Investment Series
Adjustable Rate Securities Trust I (GNMA)
Adjustable Rate Securities Trust I-A (GNMA)
Adjustable Rate Securities Trust II (GNMA)
Adjustable Rate Securities Trust III (GNMA)
Adjustable Rate Securities Trust IV (GNMA)
Adjustable U.S. Government Securities
Trust I (USGI)
Adjustable U.S. Government Securities
Trust I-A (USGI)
Adjustable U.S. Government Securities
Trust II (USGI)
Adjustable U.S. Government Securities
Trust III (USGI)
Adjustable U.S. Government Securities
Trust IV (USGI)
High Yield Trust (HYB)

Pilgrim Baxter
680 East Swedesford Road
Wayne, Pennsylvania 19087
(800) 932-7781

Pilgrim Baxter Emerging Growth Fund (AG)
Pilgrim Baxter Growth Fund (G)

Pillar Funds
680 East Swedesford Road, No. 10
Wayne, Pennsylvania 19087-1658
(215) 989-6000   (800) 342-5734

Pillar Funds
Pillar Balanced Growth Fund (B)
Pillar Equity Aggressive Growth Fund (AG)

Pillar Equity Growth Fund (G+I)
Pillar Fixed Income Fund (G+I)
Pillar GNMA Fund (GNMA)
Pillar Intermediate Government Securities
Fund (USGI)
Pillar New Jersey Municipal Securities
Fund (MB-S)
Pillar Pennsylvania Municipal Securities
Fund (MB-S)
Pillar Prime Obligation Fund (MM-T)
Pillar Short Term Investment Fund (CB)
Pillar Tax-Exempt Money Market Fund
(MM-TE)
Pillar U.S. Treasury Money Market Fund
(MM-T)
Pillar U.S. Treasury Securities Plus Fund
(USGI)

Pioneer
60 State Street
Boston, Massachusetts 02109-0275
(617) 742-7825   (800) 225-6292

Pioneer Bond Fund (CB)
Pioneer California Double Tax-Free Fund
(MB-S)
Pioneer Europe Fund (INT)
Pioneer Fund (G+I)
Pioneer Growth Trust
Pioneer Capital Growth Fund (G)
Pioneer Equity Income Fund (IE)
Pioneer Gold Shares (PMG)
Pioneer Short-Term Income Fund (IM)
Pioneer II (G+I)
Pioneer Massachusetts Double Tax-Free Fund
(MB-S)
Pioneer Money Market Trust
Pioneer Cash Reserves Fund (MM-T)
Pioneer Tax-Free Money Fund (MM-TE)
Pioneer U.S. Government Money Fund
(MM-T)
Pioneer Municipal Bond Fund (MB-N)
Pioneer New York Triple Tax-Free Fund (MB-S)
Pioneer Three (G+I)
Pioneer U.S. Government Trust (USGI)

Piper
222 South Ninth Street
Piper Jaffray Tower
Minneapolis, Minnesota 55402-3804
(612) 342-6387   (800) 866-7778

Piper Institutional Funds, Inc.
Enhanced 500 Fund (G+I)
Institutional Government Adjustable
Portfolio (GNMA)
Institutional Money Market Fund (MM-T)
Piper Jaffray Investment Trust, Inc.
Balanced Fund (B)
Emerging Growth Fund (AG)
Government Income Fund (GNMA)
Growth and Income Fund (G+I)

Institutional Government Income Fund
  (USGI)
Minnesota Tax-Exempt Fund (MB-S)
Money Market Fund (MM-T)
National Tax-Exempt Fund (MB-N)
Sector Performance Fund (FP)
Tax-Exempt Money Market Fund (MM-TE)
U.S. Government Money Market Fund
  (MM-T)
Value Fund (G+I)

PNC
103 Bellevue Parkway
Wilmington, Delaware 19809
(302) 791-1700   (800) 422-6538
PNC Family of Funds
  Balanced Portfolio (B)
  Government Money Market Portfolio (MM-T)
  Growth Equity Portfolio (G)
  Index Equity Portfolio (G+I)
  Intermediate Bond Portfolio (IB)
  Intermediate Government Portfolio (USGI)
  International Portfolio (INT)
  Managed Income Portfolio (IM)
  Money Market Portfolio (MM-T)
  Municipal Money Market Portfolio (MM-TE)
  North Carolina Municipal Money Market
    Portfolio (MMS-TE)
  Ohio Municipal Money Market Portfolio
    (MMS-TE)
  Ohio Tax-Free Income Portfolio (MB-S)
  Pennsylvania Municipal Money Market
    Portfolio (MMS-TE)
  Pennsylvania Tax-Free Income Portfolio
    (MB-S)
  Short Term Bond Portfolio (IB)
  Small Cap Value Equity Portfolio (G)
  Tax-Free Income Portfolio (MB-N)
  Value Equity Portfolio (G)

Portage Government Money Market Fund
Federated Investors Tower
Pittsburgh, Pennsylvania 15222-3779
(412) 288-1900   (800) 356-2805
Portage Government Money Market Fund
  (MM-T)

PRA Securities Trust
900 North Michigan Avenue, Suite 1000
Chicago, Illinois 60611
(312) 915-3600
PRA Securities Trust
  PRA Real Estate Securities Fund (G+I)

Preferred Group
100 North East Adams Street
Peoria, Illinois 61629-5330
(309) 675-4999   (800) 662-4769
Preferred Group of Mutual Funds
  Preferred Asset Allocation Fund (FP)
  Preferred Fixed Income Fund (IM)

Preferred Growth Fund (G)
Preferred International Fund (INT)
Preferred Money Market Fund (MM-T)
Preferred Short-Term Government
  Securities Fund (USGI)
Preferred Value Fund (G+I)

Premier
144 Glen Curtiss Boulevard
Uniondale, New York 11556-0144
Premier California Municipal Bond Fund
  (MB-S)
Premier GNMA Fund (GNMA)
Premier Growth Fund, Inc. (G)
Premier Municipal Bond Fund (MB-N)
Premier New York Municipal Bond Fund
  (MB-S)
Premier State Municipal Bond Fund
  Arizona Series (MB-S)
  Connecticut Series (MB-S)
  Florida Series (MB-S)
  Georgia Series (MB-S)
  Maryland Series (MB-S)
  Massachusetts Series (MB-S)
  Michigan Series (MB-S)
  Minnesota Series (MB-S)
  North Carolina Series (MB-S)
  Ohio Series (MB-S)
  Pennsylvania Series (MB-S)
  Texas Series (MB-S)
  Virginia Series (MB-S)

Primary
First Financial Center
700 North Water Street
Milwaukee, Wisconsin 53202
(414) 271-7870   (800) 443-6544
Primary Income Funds, Inc.
  Primary Income Fund (IM)
  Primary U.S. Government Fund (USGI)
Primary Trend Fund, Inc. (FP)

Prime Cash Fund
380 Madison Avenue, Suite 2300
New York, New York 10017-2590
(212) 697-6666 (800) 228-4227
Prime Cash Fund (MM-T)

Principal
215 North Main Street
West Bend, Wisconsin 53095-3317
(414) 334-5521   (800) 826-4600
Principal Preservation Portfolios, Inc.
  Balanced Portfolio (B)
  Dividend Achievers Portfolio (IE)
  Government Portfolio (USGI)
  Insured Tax-Exempt Portfolio (MB-N)
  S&P 100 Plus Portfolio (G+I)
  Tax-Exempt Portfolio (MB-N)
Principal Special Markets Fund, Inc.

International Securities Portfolio (INT)
Mortgage-Backed Securities Portfolio (FP)

Princor
The Principal Financial Group
Des Moines, Iowa 50392-0200
(515) 247-5711   (800) 247-4123
Princor Blue Chip Fund (G+I)
Princor Bond Fund, Inc. (CB)
Princor Capital Accumulation Fund, Inc. (G+I)
Princor Cash Management Fund, Inc. (MM-T)
Princor Emerging Growth Fund, Inc. (G)
Princor Government Securities Income Fund,
   Inc. (GNMA)
Princor Growth Fund, Inc. (G)
Princor High Yield Fund, Inc. (HYB)
Princor Managed Fund, Inc. (B)
Princor Tax-Exempt Bond Fund, Inc. (MB-N)
Princor Tax-Exempt Cash Management Fund,
   Inc. (MM-TE)
Princor Utilities Fund, Inc. (IM)
Princor World Fund, Inc. (INT)

Professional Investors Funds
605 Third Avenue, 2nd Floor
New York, New York 10158-3698
(212) 476-8800   (800) 877-9700
Professional Investors Funds
   Growth Fund (G)
   Money Fund (MM-T)

Professionally Managed Portfolios
1105 Holliday
Wichita Falls, Texas 76301
(817) 761-3777
Avondale Total Return Fund (G+I)

Professionally Managed Portfolios
730 East Lake Street
Wayzata, Minnesota 55391-1769
(612) 473-8367
Crescent Fund (G+I)
Perkins Opportunity Fund (G)

Professionally Managed Portfolios
2311 Cedar Springs Road, Suite 100
Dallas, Texas 75201
(214) 954-1177   (800) 388-8512
Hodges Fund (G)

Professionally Managed Portfolios
One Maritime Plaza, Suite 1201
San Francisco, California 94111
(415) 434-4441
Osterweis Fund (G+I)

Professionally Managed Portfolios
220 Sansome Street
San Francisco, California 94104
(415) 433-5233 (800) 304-8333
Teddy Roosevelt Total Return Trust (IB)

Professionally Managed Portfolios
850 Montgomery Street, Suite 100
San Francisco, California 94133
(415) 269-9135
Women's Equity Mutual Fund (G)

Progressive Portfolio Series
390 Union Boulevard, Suite 410
Denver, Colorado 80228
(303) 985-9999   (800) 275-2382
Progressive Portfolio Series
   Aggressive Growth Portfolio (AG)
   Environmental Portfolio (AG)
   Value Portfolio (G)

Prospect Hill Institutional Trust
Six St. James Avenue
Boston, Massachusetts 02116
(617) 423-0800 (800) 545-1074
Prospect Hill Institutional Trust
   Prospect Hill Institutional Prime Money
      Market Portfolio (MM-T)

Prudential
One Seaport Plaza
New York, New York 10292
(212) 214-1215   (800) 225-1852
Blackrock Government Income Trust (USGI)
Prudential Adjustable Rate Securities Fund,
   Inc. (IB)
Prudential California Municipal Fund
   California Income Series (MB-S)
   California Money Market Series (MMS-TE)
   California Series (MB-S)
Prudential Equity Fund (G)
Prudential Equity Income Fund (IE)
Prudential FlexiFund
   Conservatively Managed Portfolio (FP)
   Strategy Portfolio (FP)
Prudential Equity Fund (G)
Prudential Equity Income Fund (IE)
Prudential FlexiFund
   Conservatively Managed Portfolio (FP)
   Strategy Portfolio (FP)
Prudential Global Fund, Inc. (GE)
Prudential Global Genesis Fund (GE)
Prudential Global Natural Resources Fund
   (GE)
Prudential GNMA Fund (GNMA)
Prudential Government Plus Fund (USGI)
Prudential Government Securities Trust
   Intermediate Term Series (USGI)
   Money Market Series (MM-T)
   U.S. Treasury Money Market Series (MM-T)
Prudential Growth Fund, Inc. (G)
Prudential Growth Opportunity Fund (AG)
Prudential High Yield Fund (HYB)
Prudential IncomeVertible Plus Fund, Inc.
   (IM)
Prudential Institutional Fund
   Active Balanced Fund (B)

Balanced Fund (B)
Growth Stock Fund (G)
Income Fund (IM)
International Stock Fund (INT)
Money Market Fund (MM-T)
Stock Index Fund (G)
Prudential Institutional Liquidity Portfolio, Inc.
  Institutional Money Market Series (MM-T)
Prudential Intermediate Global Income Fund (GB)
Prudential MoneyMart Assets (MM-T)
Prudential Multi-Sector Fund (AG)
Prudential Municipal Bond Fund
  High Yield Series (MB-N)
  Insured Series (MB-N)
  Modified Term Series (MB-N)
Prudential Municipal Series Fund
  Arizona Series (MB-S)
  Connecticut Money Market Series (MMS-TE)
  Florida Series (MB-S)
  Georgia Series (MB-S)
  Maryland Series (MB-S)
  Massachusetts Money Market Series (MMS-TE)
  Massachusetts Series (MB-S)
  Michigan Series (MB-S)
  Minnesota Series (MB-S)
  New Jersey Money Market Series (MMS-TE)
  New Jersey Series (MB-S)
  New York Money Market Series (MMS-TE)
  New York Series (MB-S)
  North Carolina Series (MB-S)
  Ohio Series (MB-S)
  Pennsylvania Series (MB-S)
Prudential National Municipals Fund (MB-N)
Prudential Pacific Growth Fund (INT)
Prudential Short-Term Global Income Fund, Inc.
  Global Assets Portfolio (GB)
  Short-Term Global Income Series (GB)
Prudential Special Money Market Fund
  Money Market Series (MM-T)
Prudential Structured Maturity Fund (IB)
Prudential Tax-Free Money Fund (MM-TE)
Prudential U.S. Government Fund (USGI)
Prudential Utility Fund (IE)

Prudent Speculator Fund (The)
4023 West 6th Street
Los Angeles, California 90020-4499
(800) 444-4778

Prudent Speculator Fund, (The) (G)

Putnam Investments
1515 Washington Street
Braintree, Massachusetts 02184
  or
Putnam Investor Services
P.O. Box 41203
Providence, Rhode Island 02940-1203
(800) 225-1581

George Putnam Fund of Boston (FP)
Putnam Adjustable Rate U.S. Government Fund (MB-N)
Putnam American Government Fund (GNMA)
Putnam Arizona Tax Exempt Income Fund (MB-S)
Putnam Asia Pacific Growth Fund (INT)
Putnam Asset Allocation Balanced Portfolio (G+I)
Putnam Asset Allocation Conservative Portfolio (FP)
Putnam Asset Allocation Growth Portfolio (G)
Putnam Balanced Government Fund (GNMA)
Putnam California Intermediate Tax Exempt Fund (MB-S)
Putnam California Tax Exempt Income Fund (MB-S)
Putnam California Tax Exempt Money Market Fund (MM-TE)
Putnam Convertible Income Growth Trust (FP)
Putnam Corporate Asset Trust (IE)
Putnam Diversified Equity Trust (FP)
Putnam Diversified Income Trust (FP)
Putnam Dividend Growth Fund (G+I)
Putnam Equity Income Fund (IE)
Putnam Europe Growth Fund (INT)
Putnam Federal Income Trust (USGI)
Putnam Florida Tax Exempt Income Fund (MB-S)
Putnam Fund for Growth and Income, The (G+I)
Putnam Global Governmental Income Trust (GB)
Putnam Global Growth Fund (GE)
Putnam Health Sciences Trust (G)
Putnam High Yield Advantage Fund (HYB)
Putnam High Yield Trust (HYB)
Putnam Income Fund (CB)
Putnam Intermediate Tax Exempt Fund (MB-N)
Putnam Investors Fund (G)
Putnam Massachusetts Tax Exempt Income Fund II (MB-S)
Putnam Managed Income Trust (B)
Putnam Michigan Tax Exempt Income Fund II (MB-S)
Putnam Minnesota Tax Exempt Income Fund II (MB-S)
Putnam Money Market Fund (MM-T)
Putnam Municipal Income Fund (MB-N)
Putnam Natural Resources Fund (G)
Putnam New Opportunities Fund (G)
Putnam New Jersey Tax Exempt Income Fund (MB-S)
Putnam New York Intermediate Tax Exempt Fund (MB-S)
Putnam New York Tax Exempt Income Fund (MB-S)
Putnam New York Tax Exempt Money Market Fund (MM-TE)
Putnam New York Tax Exempt Opportunities Fund (MB-S)

Putnam Ohio Tax Exempt Fund II (MB-S)
Putnam OTC Emerging Growth Fund (AG)
Putnam Overseas Growth Fund (INT)
Putnam Pennsylvania Tax Exempt Income
Fund (MB-S)
Putnam Tax Exempt Income Fund (MB-N)
Putnam Tax Exempt Money Market Fund
(MM-TE)
Putnam Tax-Free High Yield Fund (MB-N)
Putnam Tax-Free Insured Fund (MB-N)
Putnam U.S. Government Income Trust
(USGI)
Putnam Utilities Growth & Income Fund (G+I)
Putnam Vista Fund (G)
Putnam Voyager Fund (G)

Quantitative Group
Lincoln North
Lincoln, Massachusetts 01773
(617) 259-1144   (800) 331-1244
Quantitive Group of Funds
Boston Foreign Growth and Income Series
(INT)
Boston Growth and Income Series (HYB)
Boston Numeric Series (AG)

Quest
One World Financial Center
New York, New York 10281
(212) 374-2949   (800) 232-3863
Quest Cash Reserves, Inc.
California Municipal Portfolio (MMS-TE)
General Municipal Portfolio (MM-TE)
Government Portfolio (MM-T)
New York Municipal Portfolio (MMS-TE)
Primary Portfolio (MM-T)
Quest for Value Accumulation Trust
Bond Portfolio (IB)
Equity Portfolio (G)
Managed Portfolio (B)
Money Market Portfolio (MM-T)
Small Cap Portfolio (G)
Quest for Value Family of Funds
California Tax-Exempt Fund (MB-S)
Global Equity Fund (GE)
Growth and Income Fund (G+I)
Investment Quality Income Fund (IM)
National Tax-Exempt Fund (MB-N)
New York Tax-Exempt Fund (MB-S)
Opportunity Fund (FP)
Small Capitalization Fund (AG)
U.S. Government Income Fund (USGI)
Quest for Value Fund, Inc. (G)
Quest for Value Global Funds
Global Income Fund (GB)

Ranson
120 South Market, Suite 450
Wichita, Kansas 67202
(316) 262-4955   (800) 345-2363

Ranson Managed Portfolios
Kansas Insured Municipal Fund-Limited
Maturity (MB-N)
Kansas Municipal Fund (MB-N)

Rea-Graham
10966 Chalon Road
Los Angeles, California 90077
(310) 208-2282   (800) 433-1998
Rea-Graham Funds, Inc.
Rea-Graham Balanced Fund (GB)

Rembrandt Funds
680 East Swedesford Road
Wayne, Pennsylvania 19087
(800) 443-4725

Rembrandt Funds
Balanced Fund (B)
Global Fixed Income Fund (GB)
Government Money Market Fund (MM-T)
Growth Fund (G)
International Equity Fund (INT)
Short/Intermediate Government Fixed
Income Fund (USGI)
Small Cap Fund (AG)
Taxable Fixed Income Fund (IB)
Taxable Money Market Fund (MM-T)
Tax-Exempt Fixed Income Fund (MB-N)
Tax-Exempt Money Market Fund (MM-TE)
Treasury Money Market Fund (MM-T)
Value Fund (G)

Retirement Investment Trust
16 HCB 98
P.O. Box 2558
Houston, Texas 77252-8098
(713) 546-7775
Retirement Investment Trust
Balanced Fund (B)
Core Equity Fund (G+I)
Equity Growth Fund (G)
Equity Income Fund (IE)
Income Fund (IB)
Money Market Fund (MM-T)
Short-Intermediate U.S. Government
Fund (USGI)
Small Capitalization Fund (G)
U.S. Government Securities Fund (USGI)

Retirement Planning Funds of America, Inc.
124 East Marcy Street
P.O. Box 1688
Santa Fe, New Mexico 87501-1688
(505) 983-4335   (800) 279-0279
Retirement Planning Funds of America, Inc.
Bond Fund (USGI)
Convertible Securities Fund (G+I)
Global Value Fund (GE)
Government Money Market Fund (MM-T)
Growth Fund (AG)

Rightime Fund, Inc.
The First Pavilion
218 Glenside Avenue
Wyncote, Pennsylvania 19095
(215) 887-8111 (800) 242-1421

Rightime Fund, Inc.
  Rightime Blue Chip Fund (The) (G+I)
  Rightime Fund (The) (G+I)
  Rightime Government Securities Fund (The)
    (USGI)
  Rightime Growth Fund (The) (G)
  Rightime Mid Cap Fund (The) (G+I)
  Rightime Social Awareness Fund (The) (G)

RIMCO Monument Funds
Federated Investors Tower
Pittsburgh, Pennsylvania 15222-3779
(412) 288-1900   (800) 356-2805

RIMCO Monument Funds
  Bond Fund (IB)
  Prime Money Market Fund (MM-T)
  Stock Fund (G+I)
  U.S. Treasury Money Market Fund (MM-T)

Riverfront Funds
200 Berkeley Street
Boston, Massachusetts 02116-5034
(617) 338-3200   (800) 343-2898

Riverfront Funds
  Riverfront Income Equity Fund (The) (IM)
  Riverfront U.S. Government Income Fund
    (The) (USGI)
  Riverfront U.S. Government Securities
    Money Market Fund (MM-T)

RNC Liquid Assets Fund, Inc.
11601 Wilshire Boulevard
Los Angeles, California 90025
(213) 477-6543   (800) 431-7249
(800) 877-7624 (California only)

RNC Liquid Assets Fund, Inc. (MM-T)

Robertson Stephens
555 California Street, Suite 2600
San Francisco, California 94104
(415) 781-9700   (800) 766-3863

Robertson Stephens Contrarian Fund (G)
Robertson Stephens Emerging Growth Fund
  (AG)
Robertson Stephens Value Plus Fund (AG)

Rochester
70 Linden Oaks
Rochester, New York 14625-2804
(716) 383-1300

Rochester Bond Fund for Growth (G)
Rochester Fund Municipals (MB-S)
Rochester Portfolio Series
  Limited Term New York Municipal Fund
    (MB-S)
Rochester Tax Managed Fund, Inc. (G+I)

Rockwood Growth Fund, Inc.
545 Shoup Avenue, #303
P.O. Box 50313
Idaho Falls, Idaho 83405
(208) 522-5593

Rockwood Growth Fund, Inc. (G)

Rodney Square
Rodney Square North
1100 North Market Street
Wilmington, Delaware 19890
(302) 651-1923 (800) 336-9970

Rodney Square Fund
  Money Market Portfolio (MM-T)
  U.S. Government Portfolio (MM-T)
Rodney Square International Securities Fund,
  Inc
  International Equity Fund (The) (INT)
Rodney Square Multi-Manager Fund
  Growth and Income Fund (G+I)
  Growth Portfolio (The) (G)
Rodney Square Strategic Fixed-Income Fund
  Diversified Income Portfolio (IB)
Rodney Square Tax-Exempt Fund (MM-TE)

Royce Fund
1414 Avenue of the Americas
New York, New York 10019
(212) 355-7311   (800) 221-4268

Royce Fund
  Equity Income Series (G+I)
  OTC Series (AG)
  Premier Series (AG)
  Value Series (AG)

Rushmore Funds
4922 Fairmont Avenue
Bethesda, Maryland 20814
(800) 621-7874

Rushmore Funds
  American Gas Index Fund (G+I)
  Government Investors Money Market Fund
    (MM-T)
  Maryland Tax-Free Bond Fund (MB-S)
  Rushmore Money Market Portfolio (MM-T)
  Tax-Free Money Market Fund (MM-TE)
  U.S. Government Intermediate-Term Bond
    Fund (MB-N)
  U.S. Government Long-Term Bond Fund
    (MB-N)
  Virginia Tax-Free Bond Fund (MB-S)

Rydex Series Trust
4641 Montgomery Avenue
Bethesda, Maryland 20814
(301) 652-4402   (800) 820-0888

Rydex Series Trust
  Nova Fund (AG)

SAFECO
SAFECO Plaza
Seattle, Washington 98185
(206) 545-7319 (800) 426-6730
SAFECO California Tax-Free Income Fund,
Inc. (MB-S)
SAFECO Equity Fund, Inc. (G+I)
SAFECO Growth Fund, Inc. (G)
SAFECO High Yield Bond Fund, Inc. (HYB)
SAFECO Income Fund, Inc. (IE)
SAFECO Insured Municipal Bond Fund, Inc.
(MB-N)
SAFECO Intermediate-Term Municipal Bond
Fund, Inc. (MB-N)
SAFECO Intermediate-Term U.S. Treasury
Fund, Inc. (USGI)
SAFECO Money Market Mutual Fund, Inc. (G)
SAFECO Municipal Bond Fund, Inc. (MB-N)
SAFECO Northwest Fund, Inc. (G)
SAFECO Tax-Free Money Market Fund, Inc.
(MM-TE)
SAFECO U.S. Government Securities Fund,
Inc. (USGI)
SAFECO Washington State Municipal Bond
Fund, Inc. (MB-S)

Sagamore Funds Trust
1000 Old National Bank Tower
Evansville, Indiana 47708-1825
(812) 421-3213
Sagamore Funds Trust
Sagamore Bond Fund (The) (IB)
Sagamore Growth Fund (The) (G)
Sagamore Total Return Fund (The) (B)

Saloman Brothers
Seven World Trade Center, 38th Floor
New York, New York 10048
(212) 783-7000 (800) 888-2461
Saloman Brothers Capital Fund, Inc. (AG)
Saloman Brothers Investors Fund, Inc. (G+I)
Saloman Brothers Opportunity Fund, Inc. (G)
Saloman Brothers Series Funds, Inc.
Cash Management Fund (MM-T)
New York Municipal Bond Fund (MB-S)
New York Municipal Money Market Fund
(MMS-TE)
U.S. Treasuries Securities Money Market
Fund (MM-T)

Sanford C. Bernstein Fund, Inc.
767 Fifth Avenue
New York, New York 10153-0185
(212) 486-5800
Sanford C. Bernstein Fund, Inc.
Bernstein International Value Portfolio (INT)

SBL Fund
700 Harrison Street
Topeka, Kansas 66636
(913) 295-3127 (800) 888-2461

SBL Fund
Emerging Growth Series (AG)
Growth Series (G)
High Grade Income Series (IB)
Income & Growth Series (G+I)
Money Market Series (MM-T)
Social Awareness Fund (G)
Worldwide Equity Series (GE)

SBSF Funds
45 Rockefeller Plaza, 33rd Floor
New York, New York 10111
(212) 903-1200 (800) 422-7273
SBSF Funds
SBSF Capital Growth Fund (G)
SBSF Convertible Securities Fund (G+I)
SBSF Fund (G)
SBSF Money Market Fund (MM-T)

Schafer Value Fund, Inc.
645 Fifth Avenue
New York, New York 10022
(212) 644-1800 (800) 338-1579
Schafer Value Fund, Inc. (G+I)

Schooner Fund, Inc.
9601 Wilshire Boulevard, Suite 800
Beverley Hills, California 90210-5291
(310) 247-3940 (800) 776-5033
Schooner Fund, Inc. (AG)

Schroder Capital Funds, Inc.
787 Seventh Avenue, 29th Floor
New York, New York 10019
(212) 841-3830 (800) 344-8332
Schroder Capital Funds, Inc.
International Equity Fund (INT)
Schroder Latin America Fund (INT)
Schroder U.S. Equity Fund (G)
Schroder U.S. Smaller Companies Fund (AG)

Schwab
101 Montgomery Street
San Francisco, California 94104
(415) 627-7000 (800) 526-8600
Schwab Capital Trust
Schwab International Index Fund (INT)
Schwab Investments
Schwab 1000 Fund (G+I)
Schwab California Long-Term Tax Free Bond
Fund (MB-S)
Schwab California Short/Intermediate Tax-
Free Bond Fund (MB-S)
Schwab Long-Term Government Bond Fund
(USGI)
Schwab Long-Term Tax-Free Bond Fund
(MB-N)
Schwab Short/Intermediate Bond Fund
(USGI)
Schwab Short/Intermediate Tax-Free Bond
Fund (MB-N)

Schwartz Investment Trust
3703 West Maple Road
Bloomfield Hills, Michigan 48301
(313) 644-8500
Schwartz Investment Trust
RCM Fund (AG)

SCM Portfolio Fund, Inc.
123 Ole Hickory Trail
Carrollton, Georgia 30117
(404) 834-5839
SCM Portfolio Fund, Inc. (FP)

Scottish Widows International Fund
100 Federal Street
Boston, Massachusetts 02110
(617) 348-3100   (800) 523-5903
Scottish Widows International Fund (INT)

Scudder
175 Federal Street
Boston, Massachusetts 02110-1706
(617) 439-4640   (800) 225-2470
(800) 225-5163
Scudder California Tax Free Trust
  Scudder California Tax Free Fund (MB-S)
  Scudder California Tax Free Money Fund
    (MMS-TE)
Scudder Cash Investment Trust (MM-T)
Scudder Development Fund (AG)
Scudder Equity Trust
  Scudder Capital Growth Fund (G)
Scudder Fund, Inc.
  Managed Cash Fund (MM-T)
  Managed Federal Fund (MM-T)
  Managed Government Fund (MM-T)
  Managed Tax-Free Fund (MM-TE)
Scudder Funds Trust
  Scudder Short Term Bond Fund (IB)
  Scudder Zero Coupon 2000 Fund (USGI)
Scudder Global Fund, Inc.
  Scudder Global Fund (GE)
  Scudder Global Small Company Fund (GE)
  Scudder International Bond Fund (GB)
  Scudder Short Term Global Income Fund
    (GB)
Scudder GNMA Fund (GNMA)
Scudder Income Fund (IM)
  Scudder Institutional Fund, Inc.
  Institutional Cash Portfolio (MM-T)
  Institutional Federal Portfolio (MM-T)
  Institutional Government Portfolio (MM-T)
  Institutional Tax-Free Portfolio (MM-TE)
Scudder International Fund, Inc. (INT)
Scudder Investment Trust
  Scudder Growth and Income Fund (G+I)
  Scudder Quality Growth Fund (G)
Scudder Municipal Trust
  Scudder High Yield Tax Free Fund (MB-N)
  Scudder Managed Municipal Funds (MB-N)

Scudder Mutual Funds, Inc.
  Scudder Gold Fund (PMG)
Scudder Portfolio Trust
  Scudder Balanced Fund (B)
  Scudder Latin America Fund (INT)
  Scudder Pacific Opportunity Fund (INT)
  Scudder Value Fund (G)
Scudder State Tax Free Trust
  Scudder Massachusetts Tax Free Fund
    (MB-S)
  Scudder New York Tax Free Fund (MB-S)
  Scudder New York Tax Free Money Fund
    (MMS-TE)
  Scudder Ohio Tax Free Fund (MB-S)
  Scudder Pennsylvania Tax Free Fund (MB-S)
  Scudder Tax Free Money Fund (MM-TE)
Scudder Tax Free Target Fund
  Medium Term Tax Free Fund (MB-N)
Scudder U.S. Treasury Money Fund (MM-T)

Seafirst Retirement Funds
701 Fifth Avenue, CSC 8
Seattle, Washington 98124
(206) 358-6234   (800) 323-9919
Seafirst Retirement Funds
  Asset Allocation Fund (The) (FP)
  Blue Chip Fund (The) (G)
  Bond Fund (The) (IB)

Security
700 Harrison Street
Topeka, Kansas 66636
(913) 295-3127   (800) 888-2461
Security Cash Fund (MM-T)
Security Equity Fund (G)
Security Global Bond Fund (GB)
  Security Growth and Income Fund (G+I)
Security Income Fund
  Corporate Bond Series (CB)
  U.S. Government Series (GNMA)
Security Tax-Exempt Fund (MB-N)
Security Ultra Fund (AG)

SEI Cash+Plus Trust
680 East Swedesford Road
Wayne, Pennsylvania 19087-1658
(800) 243-5734
SEI Cash+Plus Trust
  ARM Portfolio (GNMA)
  Corporate Daily Portfolio (MM-T)
  Federal Securities Portfolio (MM-T)
  GNMA Portfolio (GNMA)
  Government II Portfolio (MM-T)
  Intermediate Term Government Portfolio
    (USGI)
  Money Market Portfolio (MM-T)
  Prime Obligation Portfolio (MM-T)
  Short-Term Government Portfolio (USGI)
  Treasury II Portfolio (MM-T)
SEI Index Funds
  Bond Index Portfolio (IB)

S&P 500 Index Portfolio (G+I)
SEI Institutional Managed Trust
Bond Portfolio (IB)
Capital Appreciation Portfolio (G)
Capital Growth Portfolio (G)
Equity Income Portfolio (IE)
Limited Volatility Bond Portfolio (IB)
Mid-Cap Growth Portfolio (AG)
Small Cap Growth Portfolio (AG)
Value Portfolio (G+I)
SEI International Trust
International Fixed Income Portfolio (GB)
SEI Liquid Asset Trust
Government Portfolio (MM-T)
Institutional Cash Portfolio (MM-T)
Prime Obligation Portfolio (MM-T)
Treasury Portfolio (MM-T)
SEI Tax Exempt Trust
Banbridge Tax Exempt Portfolio (MM-TE)
California Tax Exempt Portfolio (MMS-TE)
Institutional Tax Free Portfolio (MM-TE)
Intermediate Term Municipal Portfolio
(MB-N)
Kansas Tax Free Income Portfolio (MB-S)
Massachusetts Intermediate Term Municipal
Portfolio (MB-S)
Pennsylvania Municipal Portfolio (MB-S)
Tax Free Portfolio (MM-TE)

Selected
124 East Marcy Street
P.O. Box 1688
Santa Fe, New Mexico 87501-1688
(505) 983-4335   (800) 279-0279
Selected American Shares, Inc. (G+I)
Selected Capital Preservation Trust
Selected Daily Government Fund (MM-T)
Selected Daily Income Fund (MM-T)
Selected Daily Tax-Exempt Fund (MM-TE)
Selected U.S. Government Income Fund
(USGI)
Selected Special Shares, Inc. (G)

Seligman
100 Park Avenue
New York, New York 10017
(212) 850-1864   (800) 221-7844
Seligman Capital Fund, Inc. (AG)
Seligman Cash Management Fund, Inc.
Government Portfolio (MM-T)
Prime Portfolio (MM-T)
Seligman Common Stock Fund, Inc. (G+I)
Seligman Communications and Information
Fund, Inc. (AG)
Seligman Frontier Fund, Inc. (G)
Seligman Growth Fund, Inc. (G)
Seligman Henderson Global Fund Series, Inc.
Seligman Henderson Global Emerging
Companies Fund (GE)
Seligman Henderson International Fund
(INT)

Seligman High Income Fund Series
High Yield Bond Series (HYB)
Secured Mortgage Income Series (GNMA)
U.S. Government Securities Series (USGI)
Seligman Income Fund, Inc. (B)
Seligman New Jersey Tax-Exempt Fund, Inc.
(MB-S)
Seligman Pennsylvania Tax-Exempt Fund,
Inc. (MB-S)
Seligman Portfolios, Inc.
Seligman Henderson Global Portfolio (GE)
Seligman Tax-Exempt Fund Series, Inc.
Colorado Tax-Exempt Series (MB-S)
Georgia Tax-Exempt Series (MB-S)
Louisiana Tax-Exempt Series (MB-S)
Maryland Tax-Exempt Series (MB-S)
Massachusetts Tax-Exempt Series (MB-S)
Michigan Tax-Exempt Series (MB-S)
Minnesota Tax-Exempt Series (MB-S)
Missouri Tax-Exempt Series (MB-S)
National Tax-Exempt Series (MB-N)
New York Tax-Exempt Series (MB-S)
Ohio Tax-Exempt Series (MB-S)
Oregon Tax-Exempt Series (MB-S)
South Carolina Tax-Exempt Series (MB-S)
Seligman Tax-Exempt Series Trust
California Tax-Exempt High Yield Series
(MB-S)
California Tax-Exempt Quality Series (MB-S)
Florida Tax-Exempt Series (MB-S)
North Carolina Tax-Exempt Series (MB-S)

Sentinel
National Life Drive
P.O. Box 1499
Montpelier, Vermont 05604
(802) 229-3900   (800) 282-3863
Sentinel Group Funds, Inc.
Balanced Fund Series (B)
Bond Fund Series (IB)
Common Stock Fund Series (G+I)
Government Securities Fund Series (USGI)
Growth Fund Series (G)
Sentinel Aggressive Growth Fund Series
(AG)
Sentinel World Fund Series (GB)
Tax Free Income Fund Series (MB-N)
Sentinel Pennsylvania Tax-Free Trust (MB-S)
Sentinel U.S. Treasury Money Market Fund
(MM-T)

Sentry Fund, Inc.
1800 North Point Drive
Stevens Point, Wisconsin 54481-1283
(715) 346-6000   (800) 533-7827
Sentry Fund, Inc. (G)

Sessions Group
1900 East Dublin-Granville Road
Columbus, Ohio 43229
(614) 899-4600 (800) 874-8376

Sessions Group
First Omaha Equity Fund (G)
First Omaha Fixed Income Fund (IB)
First Omaha Short/Intermediate Fixed
  Income Fund (IB)
First Omaha U.S. Government Obligations
  Fund (MM-T)
Riverside Capital Equity Fund (G)
Riverside Capital Fixed Income Fund (IB)
Riverside Capital Money Market Fund
  (MM-T)
Riverside Tennessee Municipal Obligations
  Fund (MB-S)
Sun Eagle Equity Growth Fund (G)
Sun Eagle Government Securities Fund
  (USGI)
Sun Eagle Intermediate Fixed Income
  Fund (IB)
Sun Eagle U.S. Treasury Obligations Fund
  (MM-T)

Seven Seas
225 Franklin Street, 29th Floor
Boston, Massachusetts 02110
(617) 542-0548
Seven Seas Series Fund
Seven Seas Growth and Income Fund (The)
  (G+I)
Seven Seas Intermediate Bond Fund (The)
  (IB)
Seven Seas International European Index
  Fund (The) (INT)
Seven Seas International Pacific Index Fund
  (The) (INT)
Seven Seas Matrix Synthesis Fund (The) (G)
Seven Seas Money Market Fund (The)
  (MM-T)
Seven Seas S&P 500 Index Fund (The) (G)
Seven Seas S&P MidCap Index Fund (The)
  (G)
Seven Seas Term Government Securities
  Fund (The) (USGI)
Seven Seas U.S. Government Money Market
  Fund (The) (MM-T)
Seven Seas Yield Plus Fund (The) (IB)

1784 Funds
680 East Swedesford Road
P.O. Box 1784
Wayne, Pennsylvania 19087-1658
(800) 252-1784
1784 Funds
Asset Allocation Fund (FP)
Asset Allocation Fund-Fiduciary Shares (FP)
Growth and Income Fund (G+I)
Growth and Income Fund-Fiduciary Shares
  (G+I)
Institutional U.S. Treasury Money Market
  Fund (MM-T)
Massachusetts Tax-Exempt Income Fund
  (MB-S)

Tax-Exempt Medium-Term Income Fund
  (MB-N)
Tax-Free Money Market Fund (MM-TE)
U.S. Government Medium-Term Income
  Fund (USGI)
U.S. Treasury Money Market Fund (MM-T)

Shawmut Funds
One Federal Street, 4th Floor
Boston, Massachusetts 02211
(617) 292-2000
Shawmut Funds
Shawmut Connecticut Intermediate
  Municipal Income Fund (MB-S)
Shawmut Connecticut Municipal Money
  Market Fund (MMS-TE)
Shawmut Fixed Income Fund (IB)
Shawmut Growth and Income Equity
  Fund (G+I)
Shawmut Growth Equity Fund (G)
Shawmut Intermediate Government Income
  Fund (USGI)
Shawmut Limited Term Income Fund (IB)
Shawmut Massachusetts Intermediate
  Municipal Income Fund (MB-S)
Shawmut Massachusetts Municipal Money
  Market Fund (MMS-TE)
Shawmut Prime Money Market Fund
  (MM-T)
Shawmut Small Capitalization Equity Fund
  (AG)

Shearson Series Funds
Two World Trade Center
New York, New York 10048
(212) 464-8072
Shearson Series Funds
Appreciation Portfolio (AG)
Diversified Strategic Income Portfolio (IM)
Equity Income Portfolio (IE)
Equity Index Portfolio (G+I)
Growth & Income Portfolio (G+I)
Intermediate High Grade Portfolio (CB)
Money Market Portfolio (MM-T)

Sheffield Funds, Inc.
900 Circle 75 Highway, Suite 750
Atlanta, Georgia 30339-3082
(404) 953-1597
Sheffield Funds, Inc.
Sheffield Intermediate Term Bond Fund (CB)
Sheffield Total Return Fund (G+I)

Short-Term Investments Trust
P.O. Box 4333
Houston, Texas 77210-4333
(713) 626-1919 (800) 347-1919
Short-Term Investments Trust
Prime Portfolio (MM-T)
Treasury Portfolio (MM-T)
Treasury Tax Advantage Portfolio (MM-T)

Sierra Trust Funds
9301 Corbin Avenue
Northridge, California 91324
(818) 725-0200   (800) 221-9876

Sierra Trust Funds
  California Money Fund (MMS-TE)
  California Municipal Fund (MB-S)
  Corporate Income Fund (CB)
  Emerging Growth Fund (G)
  Global Money Fund (MM-T)
  Growth and Income Fund (G+I)
  Growth Fund (G)
  International Growth Fund (INT)
  National Municipal Fund (MB-N)
  Short-Term Global Government Fund (GB)
  U.S. Government Fund (USGI)
  U.S. Government Money Fund (MM-T)

Signet Select Funds
Federated Investors Tower
Pittsburgh, Pennsylvania 15222-3779
(412) 288-1900   (800) 356-2805

Signet Select Funds
  Maryland Municipal Bond Fund (MB-S)
  Money Market Fund (MM-T)
  Treasury Money Market Fund (MM-T)
  U.S. Government Income Fund (USGI)
  Value Equity Fund (G+I)
  Virginia Municipal Bond Fund (MB-S)

SIT
4600 Norwest Center
90 South Seventh Street
Minneapolis, Minnesota 55402-4130
(612) 334-5888   (800) 332-5580

SIT Growth Fund, Inc. (AG)
SIT Growth & Income Fund, Inc. (G+I)
SIT International Growth Fund (INT)
SIT Money Market Fund, Inc. (IB)
SIT Tax-Free Income Fund (MB-N)
SIT U.S. Government Securities Fund, Inc.
  (USGI)

Skyline Fund
350 North Clark Street
Chicago, Illinois 60610-4796
(312) 670-6035   (800) 458-5222

Skyline Fund
  Europe Portfolio (The) (INT)
  Monthly Income Portfolio (The) (HYB)
  Special Equities Portfolio (The) (AG)
  Special Equities Portfolio II (The) (AG)

SMALLCAP World Fund, Inc.
333 South Hope Street
Los Angeles, California 90071-1447
(213) 486-9200   (800) 421-0180

SMALLCAP World Fund, Inc. (GE)

Smith Barney
1345 Avenue of the Americas
New York, New York 10105
(212) 720-9036   (800) 544-7835

Smith Barney Equity Funds, Inc. (G)
Smith Barney Funds, Inc.
  Capital Appreciation Portfolio (G)
  Income and Growth Portfolio (G+I)
  Income Return Account Portfolio (IB)
  Monthly Payment Government Portfolio
    (GNMA)
  Short-Term U.S. Treasury Securities
    Portfolio (USGI)
  U.S. Government Securities Portfolio
    (GNMA)
  Utility Portfolio (G+I)
Smith Barney Money Fund, Inc.
  Cash Portfolio (MM-T)
  Government Portfolio (MM-T)
  Retirement Portfolio (MM-T)
  Tax Free Portfolio (MM-TE)
Smith Barney Muni Bond Funds
  California Limited Term Portfolio (MB-S)
  California Money Market Portfolio (MMS-TE)
  California Portfolio (MB-S)
  Florida Limited Term Portfolio (MB-S)
  Florida Portfolio (MB-S)
  Limited Term Portfolio (MB-N)
  National Portfolio (MB-N)
  New Jersey Portfolio (MB-S)
  New York Money Market Portfolio (MMS-TE)
  New York Portfolio (MB-S)
Smith Barney Variable Account Funds, Inc.
  Income and Growth Portfolio (G+I)
  Reserve Account Portfolio (IB)
  U.S. Government/High Quality Portfolio
    (GNMA)
Smith Barney World Funds, Inc.
  Global Government Bond Portfolio (GB)
  International Equity Portfolio (INT)

Smith Barney Shearson
Two World Trade Center, 100th Floor
New York, New York 10048-0002
(212) 464-8072

Smith Barney Shearson Adjustable Rate
  Government Income Fund (GNMA)
Smith Barney Shearson Aggressive Growth
  Fund, Inc. (AG)
Smith Barney Shearson Appreciation Fund,
  Inc. (G)
Smith Barney Shearson Arizona Municipals
  Fund, Inc. (MB-S)
Smith Barney Shearson California Municipal
  Money Market Fund (MMS-TE)
Smith Barney Shearson California Municipals
  Fund, Inc. (MB-S)
Smith Barney Shearson Daily Dividend Fund,
  Inc. (MM-T)
Smith Barney Shearson Equity Funds
  SBS Growth and Income Fund (G+I)

SBS Growth and Opportunity Fund (G)
SBS Sector Analysis Fund (G)
SBS Strategic Investors Fund (FP)
Smith Barney Shearson Florida Municipals
  Fund, Inc. (MB-S)
Smith Barney Shearson Fundamental Value
  Fund, Inc. (G)
Smith Barney Shearson Global Opportunities
  Fund (GE)
Smith Barney Shearson Government and
  Agencies Fund, Inc. (MM-T)
Smith Barney Shearson Income Funds
SBS Convertible Fund (G+I)
SBS Diversified Strategic Income Fund (CB)
SBS Global Bond Fund (GB)
SBS High Income Fund (HYB)
SBS Money Market Fund (MM-T)
SBS Premium Total Return Fund (IE)
SBS Tax Exempt Income Fund (MB-N)
SBS Utilities Fund (IM)
Smith Barney Shearson Income Trust
SBS Intermediate Maturity California
  Municipals Fund (MB-S)
SBS Intermediate Maturity New York
  Municipals Fund (MB-S)
SBS Limited Maturity Municipals Fund
  (MB-N)
SBS Limited Maturity Treasury Fund
  (USGI)
Smith Barney Shearson Investment Funds
SBS Directions Value Fund (AG)
SBS European Fund (INT)
SBS Government Securities Fund (USGI)
SBS Investment Grade Bond Fund (IB)
SBS Special Equities Fund (AG)
Smith Barney Shearson Managed
  Governments Fund (GNMA)
Smith Barney Shearson Managed Municipals
  Fund, Inc. (MB-N)
Smith Barney Shearson Massachusetts
  Municipals Fund (MB-S)
Smith Barney Shearson Municipal Money
  Market Fund, Inc. (MM-TE)
Smith Barney Shearson New Jersey
  Municipals Fund, Inc. (MB-S)
Smith Barney Shearson New York Municipal
  Money Market Fund (MMS-TE)
Smith Barney Shearson New York Municipals
  Fund, Inc. (MB-S)
Smith Barney Shearson Precious Metals and
  Minerals Fund, Inc. (PMG)
Smith Barney Shearson Principal Return Fund
  Zeros and Appreciation Series 1996 (G)
  Zeros and Appreciation Series 1998 (G)
  Zeros Plus Emerging Growth Series 2000 (G)
Smith Barney Shearson Short-Term World
  Income Fund (GB)
Smith Barney Shearson Small Capitalization
  Fund (AG)
Smith Barney Shearson Telecommunications
  Trust

SBS Telecommunications Growth Fund (G)
SBS Telecommunications Income Fund (G+I)
Smith Barney Shearson Worldwide Prime
  Assets Fund (GB)

Smith Breeden
100 Europa Drive, Suite 200
Chapel Hill, North Carolina 27514
(919) 967-7221

Smith Breeden Institutional Inter. Duration
  U.S. Government Fund (USGI)
Smith Breeden Institutional Short Duration
  U.S. Government Fund (USGI)
Smith Breeden Market Tracking Trust (G)
Smith Breeden Series Fund
  Smith Breeden Market Tracking Series (G)
  Smith Breeden U.S. Government
    Intermediate Series (USGI)
  Smith Breeden U.S. Government Short
    Duration Series I (USGI)

SMITH HAYES Trust, Inc.
500 Center Terrace
P.O. Box 83000
Lincoln, Nebraska 68501-3000
(402) 476-3000   (800) 279-7437

SMITH HAYES Trust, Inc.
  Asset Allocation Portfolio (FP)
  Balanced Portfolio (B)
  Covertible Portfolio (IM)
  Government/Quality Bond Portfolio (USGI)
  Nebraska Tax-Free Portfolio (MB-S)
  Small Cap Portfolio (G)
  Value Portfolio (G+I)

Society's Collective Investment Retirement
  Fund
127 Public Square
01-127-1903
Cleveland, Ohio 44114
(216) 689-8178   (800) 523-7248

Society's Collective Investment Retirement
  Fund
  Balanced Portfolio (B)
  U.S. Government Securities Portfolio (USGI)

SoGen International Fund, Inc.
50 Rockefeller Plaza
New York, New York 10020
(212) 399-1141 (800) 334-2143

SoGen International Fund, Inc. (GE)

Southeastern Asset Management Funds Trust
860 Ridgelake Boulevard, Suite 301
Memphis, Tennessee 38120-9423
(901) 761-2474 (800) 445-9469

Southeastern Asset Management Funds Trust
  Southeastern Asset Management Small-Cap
    Fund (G)
  Southeastern Asset Management Value
    Trust (G)

Spartan U.S. Treasury Money Market Fund
82 Devonshire Street
Boston, Massachusetts 02109-3605
(617) 570-7000   (800) 544-8888

Spartan U.S. Treasury Money Market Fund
(MM-T)

Special Portfolios, Inc.
P.O. Box 64284
St. Paul, Minnesota 55164
(612) 738-4000   (800) 872-2638

Special Portfolios, Inc.
  Cash Portfolio (IM)
  Stock Portfolio (AG)

Stagecoach Funds, Inc.
111 Center Street
Little Rock, Arkansas 72201
(501) 377-2521   (800) 458-6589

Stagecoach Funds, Inc.
  Asset Allocation Fund (The) (FP)
  California Tax-Free Bond Fund (The) (MB-S)
  California Tax-Free Income Fund (The)
    (MB-S)
  California Tax-Free Money Market Fund
    (The) (MMS-TE)
  Corporate Stock Fund (The) (G+I)
  Diversified Income Fund (IM)
  Ginnie Mae Fund (The) (GNMA)
  Growth and Income Fund (The) (G+I)
  Money Market Fund (The) (G+I)
  U.S. Government Allocation Fund (The) (USGI)
  Variable Rate Government Fund (The) (CB)

Standby Reserve Fund, Inc.
Financial Square
New York, New York 10005-3597
(212) 495-6000   (800) 221-5616

Standby Reserve Fund, Inc. (MM-T)

Starburst Funds
Star Funds
Federated Investors Tower
Pittsburgh, Pennsylvania 15222-3779
(412) 288-1900   (800) 245-2423
(800) 356-2805

Starburst Funds
  Starburst Government Income Fund (USGI)
  Starburst Government Money Market Fund
    (MM-T)
  Starburst Money Market Fund (MM-T)
  Starburst Municipal Income Fund (MB-N)
  Starburst Quality Income Fund (G+I)
Star Funds
  Star Prime Obligations Fund (MM-T)
  Star Relative Value Fund (G+I)
  Star Tax-Free Money Market Fund (MM-TE)
  Star Treasury Fund (MM-T)
  Star U.S. Government Income Fund (USGI)
  Stellar Fund (The) (B)

State Bond
8400 Normandale Lake Boulevard, Suite 1150
Minneapolis, Minnesota 55437-3807
(612) 835-0097 (800) 437-6663

State Bond Equity Funds, Inc.
State Bond Income Funds, Inc.
  State Bond U.S. Government Securities
    Portfolio (USGI)
State Bond Investment Funds, Inc.
  State Bond Diversified Portfolio (G+I)
State Bond Money Funds, Inc.
  State Bond Cash Management Portfolio
    (MM-T)
State Bond Municipal Funds, Inc.
  State Bond Tax Exempt Portfolio (MB-N)
State Bond Securities Funds, Inc.
  State Bond Progress Portfolio (AG)
State Bond Tax-Free Income Fund, Inc.
  State Bond Minnesota Tax-Free Income
    Fund (MB-S)

State Farm
One State Farm Plaza
Bloomington, Illinois 61710-0001
(309) 766-2029

State Farm Balanced Fund, Inc. (B)
State Farm Growth Fund, Inc. (G)
State Farm Interim Fund, Inc. (USGI)
State Farm Municipal Bond Fund, Inc. (MB-N)

State Street
One Financial Center
Boston, Massachusetts 02111-2690
(617) 348-2000   (800) 562-0032

State Street Capital Trust
  State Street Capital Fund (AG)
State Street Exchange Trust
  State Street Exchange Fund (G+I)
State Street Fund for Foundations and
  Endowments
  Fixed Income Portfolio (IM)
State Street Growth Trust
  State Street Research Growth Fund (G+I)
State Street Master Investment Trust
  State Street Investment Trust (G+I)

SteinRoe
300 West Adams Street
Chicago, Illinois 60606-5101
(800) 338-2550

SteinRoe Income Trust
  SteinRoe Cash Reserves (MM-T)
  SteinRoe Government Income Fund (USGI)
  SteinRoe Government Reserves (MM-T)
  SteinRoe Income Fund (CB)
  SteinRoe Intermediate Bond Fund (IB)
  SteinRoe Limited Maturity Income Fund (IB)
SteinRoe Investment Trust
  SteinRoe Capital Opportunities Fund (G)
  SteinRoe Prime Equities (G+I)

SteinRoe Special Fund (G)
SteinRoe Stock Fund (G)
SteinRoe Total Return Fund (IE)
SteinRoe Municipal Trust
　SteinRoe High-Yield Municipals (MB-N)
　SteinRoe Intermediate Municipals (MB-N)
　SteinRoe Managed Municipals (MB-N)
　SteinRoe Municipal Money Market Fund
　(MM-TE)

SteinRoe Variable Investment Trust
600 Atlantic Avenue
Boston, Massachusetts 02111-2214
(617) 348-2000　(800) 367-3653
SteinRoe Variable Investment Trust
　Capital Appreciation Fund (AG)
　Cash Income Fund (MM-T)
　Managed Assets Fund (FP)
　Managed Growth Stock Fund (G)
　Managed Income Fund (IM)
　Mortgage Securities Income Fund (GNMA)
　Strategic Managed Assets Fund (FP)

STI Classic Funds
680 East Swedesford Road, No. 7
Wayne, Pennsylvania 19087-1658
(215) 989-6000　(800) 342-5734
STI Classic Funds
　Capital Growth Fund (G)
　Investment Grade Bond Fund (CB)
　Investment Grade Tax-Exempt Bond Fund
　(MB-N)
　Prime Quality Money Market Fund (MM-T)
　Short Term Bond Fund (IB)
　Short Term Treasury Fund (USGI)
　Tax-Exempt Money Market Fund (MM-TE)
　U.S. Government Securities Money Market
　Fund (MM-T)
　Value Income Stock Fund (IM)

Stratton
610 West Germantown Pike, Suite 300
Plymouth Meeting, Pennsylvania 19462-1050
(215) 941-0255　(800) 634-5726
Stratton Growth Fund, Inc. (G)
　Stratton Monthly Dividend Shares, Inc. (IE)
　Stratton Small-Cap Yield Fund, Inc. (G+I)

Strong
P.O. Box 2936
Menomonee Falls, Wisconsin 53051
(414) 359-3400　(800) 368-3863
Strong Advantage Fund, Inc. (IB)
Strong American Utilities Fund, Inc. (G+I)
Strong Common Stock Fund, Inc. (G)
Strong Discovery Fund, Inc. (AG)
Strong Discovery Fund II, Inc. (AG)
Strong Government Securities Fund, Inc.
　(USGI)
Strong High Yield Municipal Fund, Inc. (HYB)
Strong Income Fund, Inc. (IM)

Strong Insured Municipal Bond Fund, Inc.
　(MB-N)
Strong International Stock Fund, Inc. (INT)
Strong Investment Fund, Inc. (B)
Strong Money Market Fund, Inc. (MM-T)
Strong Municipal Bond Fund, Inc. (MB-N)
Strong Municipal Money Market Fund, Inc.
　(MM-TE)
Strong Opportunity Fund, Inc. (AG)
Strong Short-Term Bond Fund, Inc. (IB)
Strong Short-Term Municipal Bond Fund
　(MB-N)
Strong Special Fund II, Inc. (G)
Strong Total Return Fund, Inc. (FP)
Strong U.S. Treasury Money Fund, Inc.
　(MM-T)

Summit Cash Reserve Fund
P.O. Box 9011
Princeton, New Jersey 08543-9011
(609) 282-2800　(800) 221-7210
Summit Cash Reserve Fund (MM-T)

SunAmerica
733 Third Avenue
New York, New York 10017-3204
(212) 551-5969　(800) 858-8850
SunAmerica Equity Funds
　SunAmerica Balanced Assets Fund (G+I)
　SunAmerica Emerging Growth Fund (AG)
　SunAmerica Growth Fund (G)
　SunAmerica Value Fund (G)
SunAmerica Income Funds
　SunAmerica Diversified Income Fund (IM)
　SunAmerica Federal Securities Fund (GNMA)
　SunAmerica High Income Fund (HYB)
　SunAmerica Tax-Exempt Insured Fund
　(MB-N)
　SunAmerica U.S. Government Securities
　Fund (USGI)
SunAmerica Money Market Funds, Inc.
　SunAmerica Money Market Fund (MM-T)
SunAmerica Series Trust
　Alliance Growth Portfolio (G)
　Asset Allocation Portfolio (FP)
　Cash Management Portfolio (MM-T)
　Fixed Income Portfolio (IB)
　Global Bond Portfolio (GB)
　Global Equities Portfolio (GE)
　Growth-Income Portfolio (G+I)
　High Yield Bond Portfolio (HYB)
　Phoenix Growth Portfolio (G)
　Provident Growth Portfolio (G)

SwissKey Funds
Six St. James Avenue
Boston, Massachusetts 02116
(617) 423-0800
SwissKey Funds
　SBC Short-Term World Income Fund (GB)
　SBC World Growth Fund (GE)

Target Portfolio Trust
One Seaport Plaza
New York, New York 10292
(908) 417-7555   (800) 225-1852

Target Portfolio Trust
  Intermediate-Term Bond Portfolio (IB)
  International Equity Portfolio (INT)
  Large Capitalization Growth Portfolio (G)
  Large Capitalization Value Portfolio (G+I)
  Mortgage Backed Securities Portfolio
    (GNMA)
  Small Capitalization Growth Portfolio (AG)
  Small Capitalization Value Portfolio (AG)
  Total Return Bond Portfolio (IB)
  U.S. Government Money Market Portfolio
    (MM-T)

Tax-Exempt Funds
333 South Hope Street
Los Angeles, California 90071-1447
(213) 486-9200   (800) 421-0180

Tax-Exempt Bond Fund of America, Inc.
  (MB-N)
Tax-Exempt California Money Market
  Fund (MMS-TE)
Tax-Exempt Money Fund of America (MM-TE)
Tax-Exempt New York Money Market
  Fund (MMS-TE)

Tax-Free Fund for Utah
Tax-Free Fund of Colorado
Tax-Free Trust of Arizona
380 Madison Avenue, Suite 2300
New York, New York 10017-2590
(212) 697-6666   (800) 872-2652

Tax-Free Fund for Utah (MB-S)
Tax-Free Fund of Colorado (MB-S)
Tax-Free Trust of Arizona (MB-S)

Tax-Free Fund of Vermont, Inc.
110 Merchants Row
Rutland, Vermont 05701
(802) 773-0674 (800) 675-3333 (VT only)

Tax-Free Fund of Vermont, Inc. (MB-S)

Tax-Free Investments Company
P.O. Box 4333
Houston, Texas 77210-4333
(713) 626-1919   (800) 347-1919

Tax-Free Investments Company
  AIM Tax-Free Intermediate Shares (MB-N)
  Cash Reserve Portfolio (MM-TE)
  Intermediate Portfolio (MB-N)

TCI Portfolios, Inc.
4500 Main Street
P.O. Box 419200
Kansas City, Missouri 64141-6200
(816) 531-5575   (800) 345-2021

TCI Portfolios, Inc.
  TCI Advantage Fund (B)

TCI Balanced Fund (B)
TCI Growth Fund (G)

TCW/DW
Two World Trade Center, 72nd Floor
New York, New York 10048
(212) 392-2550   (800) 869-3863

TCW/DW Core Equity Trust (G+I)
TCW/DW Income and Growth Fund (G+I)
TCW/DW Latin America Growth Fund (INT)
TCW/DW North American Government
  Income Trust (GB)
TCW/DW Small Cap Growth Fund (G)

TCW Money Market Portfolio
865 South Figueroa Street, Suite 1800
Los Angeles, California 90017
(213) 244-0000

TCW Money Market Portfolio (MM-T)

Templeton
700 Central Avenue
P.O. Box 33030
St. Petersburg, Florida 33733-8030
(813) 823-8712   (800) 237-0738

Templeton American Trust, Inc. (G+I)
Templeton Capital Accumulator Fund, Inc. (G)
Templeton Developing Markets Trust (INT)
Templeton Funds, Inc.
  Foreign Fund (INT)
  World Fund (G)
Templeton Global Opportunities Trust (G)
Templeton Growth Fund, Inc. (G)
Templeton Income Trust
  Templeton Income Fund (GB)
  Templeton Money Fund (MM-T)
Templeton Institutional Funds, Inc.
  Templeton Emerging Markets Series (AG)
  Templeton Foreign Equity (S. Africa Free)
    Series (INT)
  Templeton Global Fixed Income Series (GB)
  Templeton Growth Series (G)
  Templeton Smaller Company Series (AG)
Templeton Real Estate Securities Fund (G)
Templeton Smaller Companies Growth Fund,
  Inc. (GE)
Templeton Variable Annuity Fund (G)
Templeton Variable Products Series Fund
  Templeton Asset Allocation Fund (The) (B)
  Templeton Bond Fund (The) (IB)
  Templeton International Fund (The) (INT)
  Templeton Money Market Fund (The)
    (MM-T)
  Templeton Stock Fund (The) (G)

Temporary Investment Fund, Inc.
Bellevue Corporate Center
103 Bellevue Parkway
Wilmington, Delaware 19809
(302) 791-5350   (800) 821-7432

Temporary Investment Fund, Inc.
TempCash Portfolio (MM-T)
TempFund Portfolio (MM-T)

Thompson, Unger & Plumb Funds, Inc.
8201 Excelsior Drive
Madison, Wisconsin 53717-1788
(608) 831-1300
Thompson, Unger & Plumb Funds, Inc.
Thompson, Unger & Plumb Balanced Fund
(B)
Thompson, Unger & Plumb Growth Fund (G)

Thomson Fund Group
One Station Place, 7th Floor
Stamford, Connecticut 06902
(203) 352-4900 (800) 628-1237
Thomson Fund Group
Thomson Equity Income Fund (G+I)
Thomson Growth Fund (G)
Thomson Income Fund (IB)
Thomson International Fund (INT)
Thomson Money Market Fund (MM-T)
Thomson Opportunity Fund (AG)
Thomson Precious Metals & Natural
Resources Fund (PMG)
Thomson Short-Intermediate Government
Fund (USGI)
Thomson Target Fund (AG)
Thomson Tax Exempt Fund (MB-N)
Thomson U.S. Government Fund (USGI)

TMK/United Funds, Inc.
6300 Lamar
P.O. Box 29217
Shawnee Mission, Kansas 66201-9217
(913) 236-2000 (800) 366-5465
TMK/United Funds, Inc.
Bond Portfolio (CB)
Growth Portfolio (G)
High Income Portfolio (HYB)
Income Portfolio (IM)
Money Market Portfolio (MM-T)

TNE
399 Boylston Street
Boston, Massachusetts 02116
(617) 578-1400 (800) 225-7670
TNE Cash Management Trust
Money Market Series (MM-T)
U.S. Government Series (MM-T)
TNE Fund Group
TNE Adjustable Rate U.S. Government Fund
(GNMA)
TNE Balanced Fund (B)
TNE Bond Income Fund (IB)
TNE Capital Growth Fund (G)
TNE Global Government Fund (GB)
TNE Government Securities Fund (USGI)
TNE Growth Fund (G)
TNE Growth Opportunities Fund (G+I)

TNE High Income Fund (HYB)
TNE Intermediate Term Tax Free Fund of
California (MB-S)
TNE Intermediate Term Tax Free Fund of
New York (MB-S)
TNE International Equity Fund (INT)
TNE Limited Term U.S. Government Fund
(USGI)
TNE Massachusetts Tax Free Income Fund
(MB-S)
TNE Tax Exempt Income Fund (MB-N)
TNE Value Fund (G+I)
TNE Tax Exempt Money Market Trust (MM-TE)

Tocqueville Trust
1675 Broadway
New York, New York 10019-5820
(212) 698-0800
Tocqueville Trust
Tocqueville Euro-Pacific Fund (The) (INT)
Tocqueville Fund (The) (G)

Torchmark
6300 Lamar
P.O. Box 29217
Shawnee Mission, Kansas 66201-9217
(913) 236-2000   (800) 366-5465
Torchmark Government Securities Fund
(USGI)
Torchmark Insured Tax Free Fund (MB-N)

Torray Fund
6610 Rockledge Drive, Suite 450
Bethesda, Maryland 20817-1869
(301) 493-4600
Torray Fund (FP)

Transamerica
1000 Louisiana, Suite 6000
Houston, Texas 77002-5098
(713) 751-2400 (800) 472-3863
Transamerica Bond Fund
Transamerica Adjustable U.S. Government
Trust (GNMA)
Transamerica Government Income Trust
(USGI)
Transamerica Government Securities Trust
(USGI)
Transamerica Intermediate Government
Trust (USGI)
Transamerica Investment Quality Bond
Fund (IB)
Transamerica California Tax-Free Income
Fund (MB-S)
Transamerica Capital Appreciation
Fund (AG)
Transamerica Cash Reserve, Inc. (MM-T)
Transamerica Current Interest
Transamerica U.S. Government Cash
Reserve (MM-T)
Transamerica Investment Portfolios

Transamerica Institutional Government
Trust (USGI)
Transamerica Investment Trust
Transamerica Growth and Income
Fund (G+I)
Transamerica Special Series, Inc.
Transamerica Special Blue Chip Fund (G)
Transamerica Special Emerging Growth
Fund (AG)
Transamerica Special Government Income
Fund (USGI)
Transamerica Special High Yield Bond
Fund (HYB)
Transamerica Special High Yield Tax Free
Fund (MB-N)
Transamerica Special Money Market Fund
(MM-T)
Transamerica Special Natural Resources
Fund (G)
Transamerica Tax-Free Bond Fund (MB-N)

Treasurers Fund, The
Gabelli-O'Connor
19 Old Kings Highway South
Darien, Connecticut 06820
(203) 655-1999   (800) 877-3863
Treasurers Fund, The
Domestic Primke Money Market Portfolio
(MM-T)
Tax Exempt Money Market Portfolio
(MM-TE)
U.S. Treasury Money Market Portfolio
(MM-T)

Trent Capital Investment Trust
105 North Washington Street
P.O. Drawer 69
Rocky Mount, North Carolina 27802-0069
(919) 972-9922 (800) 525-3863
Trent Capital Investment Trust
Trent Equity Fund (The) (G)

Triflex Fund, Inc.
One Moody Plaza
Galveston, Texas 77550
(409) 763-2767   (800) 231-4639
(800) 392-9753 (Texas only)
Triflex Fund, Inc. (B)

T. Rowe Price
100 East Pratt Street
Baltimore, Maryland 21202-1090
(410) 547-2000   (800) 638-5660
T. Rowe Price Adjustable Rate U.S.
Government Fund (GNMA)
T. Rowe Price Balanced Fund, Inc. (B)
T. Rowe Price Blue Chip Growth Fund, Inc. (G)
T. Rowe Price California Tax-Free Income
Trust
California Tax-Free Bond Fund (MB-S)
California Tax-Free Money Fund (MMS-TE)

T. Rowe Price Capital Appreciation Fund (G)
T. Rowe Price Dividend Growth Fund (G+I)
T. Rowe Price Equity Income Fund (IE)
T. Rowe Price GNMA Fund (GNMA)
T. Rowe Price Growth & Income Fund, Inc.
(G+I)
T. Rowe Price Growth Stock Fund, Inc. (G)
T. Rowe Price High Yield Fund, Inc. (HYB)
T. Rowe Price Index Trust, Inc.
Equity Index Fund (G)
T. Rowe Price International Funds, Inc.
T. Rowe Price European Stock Fund (INT)
T. Rowe Price Government Global Bond
Fund (GB)
T. Rowe Price International Bond Fund (GB)
T. Rowe Price International Discovery Fund
(INT)
T. Rowe Price International Stock Fund
(INT)
T. Rowe Price Japan Fund (INT)
T. Rowe Price New Asia Fund (INT)
T. Rowe Price Short-Term Global Income
Fund (GB)
T. Rowe Price Mid-Cap Growth Fund, Inc. (G)
T. Rowe Price New America Growth Fund
(AG)
T. Rowe Price New Era Fund, Inc. (G)
T. Rowe Price New Horizons Fund, Inc. (AG)
T. Rowe Price New Income Fund, Inc. (IB)
T. Rowe Price OTC Fund, Inc.
T. Rowe Price OTC Fund (AG)
T. Rowe Price Prime Reserve Fund, Inc.
(MM-T)
T. Rowe Price Science & Technology Fund,
Inc. (AG)
T. Rowe Price Short-Term Bond Fund, Inc.
(IB)
T. Rowe Price Small-Cap Value Fund, Inc.
(AG)
T. Rowe Price Spectrum Fund, Inc.
Spectrum Growth Fund (G)
Spectrum Income Fund (IM)
T. Rowe Price State Tax-Free Income Trust
Florida Insured Intermediate Tax-Free Fund
(MB-S)
Georgia Tax-Free Bond Fund (MB-S)
Maryland Short-Term Tax-Free Bond Fund
(MB-S)
Maryland Tax-Free Bond Fund (MB-S)
New Jersey Tax-Free Bond Fund (MB-S)
New York Tax-Free Bond Fund (MB-S)
New York Tax-Free Money Fund (MMS-TE)
Virginia Tax-Free Bond Fund (MB-S)
T. Rowe Price Tax-Exempt Money Fund, Inc.
(MM-TE)
T. Rowe Price Tax-Free High Yield Fund, Inc.
(MB-N)
T. Rowe Price Tax-Free Income Fund, Inc.
(MB-N)
T. Rowe Price Tax-Free Insured Intermediate
Bond Fund, Inc. (MB-N)

T. Rowe Price Tax-Free Short-Intermediate
Fund, Inc. (MB-N)
T. Rowe Price Treasury Funds, Inc.
  U.S. Treasury Intermediate Fund (USGI)
  U.S. Treasury Long-Term Fund (USGI)
  U.S. Treasury Money Fund (MM-T)

Trust For Credit Unions
4900 Sears Tower
Chicago, Illinois 60606-6391
(312) 655-4400   (800) 621-2550
Trust For Credit Unions
  Government Securities Portfolio (GNMA)
  Money Market Portfolio (MM-T)

Trust For Federal Securities
Bellevue Corporate Center
103 Bellevue Parkway
Wilmington, Delaware 19809
(302) 791-5350   (800) 821-7432
Trust for Federal Securities
  Federal Trust Fund Portfolio (MM-T)
  FedFund Portfolio (MM-T)
  Intermediate Government Portfolio (MM-T)
  Short Government Fund (MM-T)
  T-Fund Portfolio (MM-T)
  Treasury Trust Fund Portfolio (MM-T)
Trust for Trak Investments
  Government Money Investments Funds
    (MM-T)
  Intermediate Fixed Income Investments
    Fund (IM)
  International Equity Investments Fund (INT)
  International Fixed Income Investments
    Fund (GB)
  Large Capitalization Growth Investments
    Fund (G)
  Large Capitalization Value Equity
    Investments Fund (G+I)
  Mortgage Backed Investments Fund
    (GNMA)
  Municipal Bond Investments Fund (MB-N)
  Small Capitalization Growth Investments
    Fund (AG)
  Small Capitalization Value Equity
    Investments Fund (AG)
  Total Return Fixed Income Investments
    Fund (IM)
  TRAK Balanced Fund (B)

Tweedy Browne Global Value Fund
52 Vanderbilt Avenue
New York, New York 10017
(212) 916-0600   (800) 432-4789
Tweedy Browne Global Value Fund (GE)

Twentieth Century
4500 Main Street
P.O. Box 419200
Kansas City, Missouri 64141-6200
(816) 531-5575   (800) 345-2021

Twentieth Century Capital Portfolios, Inc.
  Twentieth Century Value (G+I)
Twentieth Century Investors, Inc.
  Balanced Investors (B)
  Cash Reserve (MM-T)
  Giftrust Investors (AG)
  Growth Investors (G)
  Heritage Investors (G)
  Long-Term Bond (IB)
  Select Investors (G)
  Tax-Exempt Intermediate Term (MB-N)
  Tax-Exempt Long Term (MB-N)
  Tax-Exempt Short Term (MB-N)
  Ultra Investors (AG)
  U.S. Governments (USGI)
  Vista Investors (AG)
Twentieth Century Premium Reserves, Inc.
  Premium Capital Reserve Fund (MM-T)
  Premium Government Reserve Fund (MM-T)
  Premium Managed Bond Fund (CB)
Twentieth Century World Investors, Inc.
  International Equity (GE)

Union Investors Funds
608 East Swedesford Road, No. 7
Wayne, Pennsylvania 19087-1658
(800) 342-5734
Union Investors Funds
  Balanced Fund (B)
  California Tax Free Money Market Fund
    (MMS-TE)
  Growth Equity Fund (G)
  Intermediate-Term Bond Fund (CB)
  Limited Maturity Fund (IB)
  Money Market Fund (MM-T)
  Treasury Money Market Fund (MM-T)
  Value Momentum Fund (G+I)

United
6300 Lamar
P.O. Box 29217
Shawnee Mission, Kansas 66201-9217
(913) 236-2000   (800) 366-5465
United Cash Management Fund, Inc. (MM-T)
United Continental Income Fund, Inc. (B)
United Funds, Inc.
  United Accumulative Fund (G)
  United Bond Fund (IB)
  United Income Fund (IE)
  United Science and Technology Fund (G)
United Gold & Government Fund, Inc. (PMG)
United Government Securities Fund, Inc.
  (USGI)
United High Income Fund, Inc. (HYB)
United High Income Fund II, Inc. (HYB)
United International Growth Fund, Inc. (G)
United Municipal Bond Fund, Inc. (MB-N)
United New Concepts Fund, Inc. (AG)
United Retirement Shares, Inc. (G+I)
United Vanguard Fund, Inc. (AG)

United Services Funds
7900 Callaghan Road
P.O. Box 29467
San Antonio, Texas 78229-0467
(210) 308-1234   (800) 873-8637
United Services Funds
  U.S. All American Equity Fund (G+I)
  U.S. European Income Fund (INT)
  U.S. Global Resources Fund (GE)
  U.S. Gold Shares Fund (PMG)
  U.S. Government Securities Savings Fund
    (MM-T)
  U.S. Growth Fund (G)
  U.S. Income Fund (IE)
  U.S. Intermediate Treasury Fund (USGI)
  U.S. Near Term Tax Free Fund (MB-N)
  U.S. Real Estate Fund (G)
  U.S. Special-Term Government Fund (USGI)
  U.S. Tax Free Fund (MB-N)
  U.S. Treasury Securities Cash Fund (MM-T)
  U.S. World Gold Fund (GE)

Universal Capital Investment Trust
One Oakbrook Terrace, Suite 708
OakBrook Terrace, Illinois 60181-4728
(708) 932-3000
Universal Capital Investment Trust
  Universal Capital Growth Fund (G)

USAA
USAA Building, E3E
9800 Fredericksburg Road
San Antonio, Texas 78288-0227
(210) 498-8000 (800) 531-8181
USAA Investment Trust
  Balanced Portfolio Fund (B)
  Cornerstone Fund (B)
  GNMA Trust (GNMA)
  Gold Fund (PMG)
  International Fund (INT)
  Treasury Money Market Trust (MM-T)
  World Growth Fund (GE)
USAA Mutual Fund, Inc.
  Aggressive Growth Fund, Inc. (AG)
  Growth Fund (G)
  Growth & Income Fund (G+I)
  Income Fund (IM)
  Income Stock Fund (IE)
  Money Market Fund (MM-T)
  Short Term Bond Fund (IB)
USAA Tax Exempt Fund, Inc.
  California Bond Fund (MB-S)
  California Money Market Fund (MMS-TE)
  Florida Money Market Fund (MMS-TE)
  Intermediate-Term Fund (MB-N)
  Long-Term Fund (MB-N)
  New York Bond Fund (MB-S)
  New York Money Market Fund (MMS-TE)
  Short-Term Fund (MB-S)
  Tax Exempt Money Market Fund (MM-TE)
  Virginia Bond Fund (MB-S)
  Virginia Money Market Fund (MMS-TE)

USAffinity Funds
Two Charlesgate West
Boston, Massachusetts 02215-3552
(800) 800-3030
USAffinity Funds
  USAffinity Government Income Fund (USGI)
  USAffinity Green Fund (G)
  USAffinity Growth and Income Fund (G+I)
  USAffinity Growth Fund (G)
  USAffinity Short-Term Treasury Securities
    Fund (USGI)
  USAffinity Tax-Free Municipal Fund (MB-N)

UST Master Funds, Inc.
114 West 47th Street
New York, New York 10036-1532
(212) 852-3968   (800) 233-1136
UST Master Funds, Inc.
  Aging of America Fund (AG)
  Business & Industrial Restructuring Fund
    (AG)
  Communications and Entertainment Fund
    (AG)
  Early Life Cycle Fund (AG)
  Emerging Americas Fund (INT)
  Environmentally Related Products &
    Services Fund (AG)
  Equity Fund (G)
  Global Competitors Fund (GE)
  Government Money Fund (MM-T)
  Income and Growth Fund (G+I)
  Intermediate-Term Managed Income Fund
    (CB)
  International Fund (INT)
  Long-Term Supply of Energy Fund (AG)
  Managed Income Fund (CB)
  Money Fund (MM-T)
  Pacific/Asia Fund (INT)
  Pan European Fund (INT)
  Productivity Enhancers Fund (AG)
  Short-Term Government Securities Fund
    (USGI)
  Treasury Money Fund (MM-T)
UST Master Tax-Exempt Funds, Inc.
  Intermediate-Term Tax-Exempt Fund (MB-N)
  Long-Term Tax-Exempt Fund (MB-N)
  New York Intermediate-Term Tax-Exempt
    Fund (MB-S)
  Short-Term Tax-Exempt Fund (MM-TE)
  Short-Term Tax-Exempt Securities Fund
    (MB-N)

U.S. Treasury Money Fund of America
333 South Hope Street
Los Angeles, California 90071-1447
(213) 486-9200   (800) 421-0180
U.S. Treasury Money Fund of America (MM-T)

Value Line
711 Third Avenue
New York, New York 10017
(212) 687-3965   (800) 223-0818

Value Line Adjustable Rate U.S. Government
　Securities Fund (GNMA)
Value Line Aggressive Income Trust (HYB)
Value Line Cash Fund, Inc. (MM-T)
Value Line Centurion Fund, Inc. (G)
Value Line Convertible Fund, Inc. (G+I)
Value Line Fund, Inc. (G)
Value Line Income Fund, Inc. (IM)
Value Line Leveraged Growth Investors, Inc.
　(AG)
Value Line New York Tax Exempt Trust (MB-S)
Value Line Special Situations Fund, Inc. (AG)
Value Line Strategic Asset Management
　Trust (FP)
Value Line Tax Exempt Fund, Inc.
　High Yield Portfolio (MB-N)
　Money Market Portfolio (MM-TE)
Value Line U.S. Government Securities Fund,
　Inc. (USGI)

Van Eck
122 East 42nd Street
New York, New York 10168
(212) 687-5200　　(800) 221-2220

Van Eck Funds
　Asia Dynasty Fund (INT)
　Gold/Resources Fund (PMG)
　International Growth Fund (INT)
　International Investors (PMG)
　Short-Term World Income Fund (GB)
　U.S. Government Money Fund (MM-T)
　World Income Fund (GB)
　World Trends Fund (GE)
Van Eck Investment Trust
　Global Bond Fund (GB)
　Gold and Natural Resources Fund (PMG)

Vanguard
Vanguard Financial Center
P.O. Box 2600
Valley Forge, Pennsylvania 19482-2600
(215) 669-1000　　(800) 662-7447

Vanguard Admiral Funds, Inc.
　Admiral Intermediate-Term U.S. Treasury
　　Portfolio (USGI)
　Admiral Long-Term U.S. Treasury Portfolio
　　(USGI)
　Admiral Short-Term U.S. Treasury Portfolio
　　(USGI)
　Admiral U.S. Treasury Money Market
　　Portfolio (MM-T)
Vanguard Asset Allocation Fund, Inc. (B)
Vanguard Balanced Index Fund (B)
Vanguard Bond Index Fund (IB)
Vanguard California Tax-Free Fund
　Insured Long-Term Portfolio (MB-S)
　Money Market Portfolio (MMS-TE)
Vanguard Convertible Securities Fund, Inc. (B)
Vanguard Equity Income Fund, Inc. (IE)
Vanguard Explorer Fund, Inc. (AG)

Vanguard Fixed Income Securities Fund, Inc.
　GNMA Portfolio (GNMA)
　High Yield Corporate Portfolio (HYB)
　Intermediate-Term U.S. Treasury Portfolio
　　(USGI)
　Investment Grade Corporate Portfolio (CB)
　Long-Term U.S. Treasury Portfolio (USGI)
　Short-Term Corporate Portfolio (CB)
　Short-Term Federal Portfolio (USGI)
　Short-Term U.S. Treasury Portfolio (USGI)
Vanguard Florida Insured Tax-Free Fund
　(MB-S)
Vanguard Index Trust
　Extended Market Portfolio (G)
　500 Portfolio (G+I)
　Growth Portfolio (G)
　Total Stock Market Portfolio (G+I)
　Value Portfolio (G+I)
Vanguard Institutional Index Fund (G+I)
Vanguard Institutional Money Market
　Portfolio (MM-T)
Vanguard International Equity Index Fund, Inc.
　European Portfolio (INT)
　Pacific Portfolio (INT)
Vanguard Money Market Reserves, Inc.
　Federal Portfolio (MM-T)
　Prime Portfolio (MM-T)
　U.S. Treasury Portfolio (MM-T)
Vanguard/Morgan Growth Fund, Inc. (G)
Vanguard Municipal Bond Fund, Inc.
　High-Yield Portfolio (MB-N)
　Insured Long-Term Portfolio (MB-N)
　Intermediate-Term Portfolio (MB-N)
　Limited-Term Portfolio (MB-N)
　Long-Term Portfolio (MB-N)
　Money Market Portfolio (MM-TE)
Vanguard New Jersey Tax-Free Fund
　Insured Long-Term Portfolio (MB-S)
　Money Market Portfolio (MMS-TE)
Vanguard New York Insured Tax-Free Fund
　(MB-S)
Vanguard Ohio Tax-Free Fund
　Insured Long-Term Portfolio (MB-S)
　Money Market Portfolio (MMS-TE)
Vanguard Pennsylvania Tax-Free Fund
　Insured Long-Term Portfolio (MB-S)
　Money Market Portfolio (MMS-TE)
Vanguard Preferred Stock Fund (IE)
Vanguard Quantitative Portfolios, Inc. (G+I)
Vanguard Small Capitalization Stock Fund,
　Inc. (AG)
Vanguard Specialized Portfolio, Inc.
　Energy Portfolio (AG)
　Gold & Precious Metals Portfolio (PMG)
　Health Care Portfolio (AG)
　Service Economy Portfolio (AG)
　Technology Portfolio (AG)
　Utilities Income Portfolio (G+I)
Vanguard STAR Fund (B)
Vanguard/Trustees' Equity Fund
　International Portfolio (INT)
　U.S. Portfolio (G+I)

Vanguard Variable Insurance Fund
U.S. Growth Portfolio (G)
Vanguard/Wellesley Income Fund (IM)
Vanguard/Wellington Fund, Inc. (B)
Vanguard/Windsor Fund (G+I)
Vanguard Windsor II (G+I)
Vanguard World Fund, Inc.
International Growth Portfolio (INT)
U.S. Growth Portfolio (G)

Van Kampen Merritt
One Parkview Plaza
Oakbrook Terrace, Illinois 60181-4400
(708) 684-6000   (800) 225-2222

Van Kampen Merritt Equity Trust
Van Kampen Merritt Growth and Income
Fund (G+I)
Van Kampen Merritt Utility Fund (IE)
Van Kampen Merritt Money Market Trust
(MM-T)
Van Kampen Merritt Pennsylvania Tax Free
Income Fund (MB-S)
Van Kampen Merritt Series Trust
Growth and Income Portfolio (G+I)
High Yield Portfolio (HYB)
Money Market Portfolio (MM-T)
Quality Income Portfolio (IB)
Stock Index Portfolio (G)
Van Kampen Merritt Tax Free Fund
Van Kampen Merritt California Insured Tax
Free Fund (MB-S)
Van Kampen Merritt Insured Tax Free Income
Fund
Van Kampen Merritt Limited Term Municipal
Income Fund (MB-N)
Van Kampen Merritt Municipal Income Fund
(MB-N)
Van Kampen Merritt Tax Free Money Fund
(MM-TE)
Van Kampen Merritt Trust
Van Kampen Merritt Adjustable Rate U.S.
Government Fund (GNMA)
Van Kampen Merritt High Yield Fund (HYB)
Van Kampen Merritt Short-Term Global
Income Fund (GB)
Van Kampen Merritt U.S. Government Trust
Van Kampen Merritt U.S. Government Fund
(USGI)

Variable Insurance Products
82 Devonshire Street
Boston, Massachusetts 02109-3605
(617) 570-7000   (800) 544-8888

Variable Insurance Porducts Fund
Equity-Income Portfolio (IE)
Growth Portfolio (G)
High Income Portfolio (HYB)
Money Market Portfolio (MM-T)
Overseas Portfolio (INT)

Variable Insurance Products Fund II
Asset Manager Portfolio (FP)
Index 500 Portfolio (G)
Investment Grade Bond Portfolio (IB)

Variable Investors Series Trust
P.O. Box 1978
Boston, Massachusetts 02105
(404) 892-0896   (800) 554-1156

Variable Investors Series Trust
Cash Management Portfolio (MM-T)
Common Stock Portfolio (G)
Equity Income Portfolio (IM)
High Income Portfolio (HYB)
Multiple Strategies Portfolio (FP)
U.S. Government Bond Portfolio (IB)
World Equity Portfolio (GE)

Venture
124 East Marcy Street
P.O. Box 1688
Santa Fe, New Mexico 87501-1688
(505) 983-4335   (800) 279-0279

Venture Income (+) Plus, Inc. (HYB)
Venture Muni (+) Plus, Inc. (MB-N)

Victory Funds
82 Devonshire Street
Boston, Massachusetts 02109
(800) 762-1190, Ext 2531

Victory Funds
Corporate Bond Portfolio (CB)
Equity Portfolio (G+I)
Government Bond Portfolio (USGI)
Money Market Portfolio (MM-T)
New York Municipal Portfolio (MB-S)
Short-Term Government Income Portfolio
(USGI)
U.S. Treasury Money Market Portfolio
(MM-T)

Vista Mutual Funds
156 West 56th Street
New York, New York 10019
(212) 586-0016   (800) 348-4782

Vista Mutual Funds
Vista Balanced Fund (B)
Vista Bond Fund (CB)
Vista California Intermediate Tax-Free Fund
(MB-S)
Vista California Tax Free Money Market
Fund (MMS-TE)
Vista Capital Growth Fund (G)
Vista Equity Fund (G)
Vista Equity Income Fund (G+I)
Vista Global Fixed Income Fund (GB)
Vista Global Money Market Fund (MM-T)
Vista Growth and Income Fund (G+I)
Vista International Equity Fund (INT)
Vista New York Tax Free Income Fund (MB-S)

Vista New York Tax Free Money Market
Fund (MMS-TE)
Vista Short Term Bond Fund (CB)
Vista Tax Free Income Fund (MB-N)
Vista Tax Free Money Market Fund (MM-TE)
Vista U.S. Government Income Fund
(USGI)
Vista U.S. Government Money Market Fund
(MM-T)

Volumetric Fund, Inc.
87 Violet Drive
Pearl River, New York 10965-1258
(914) 623-7637   (800) 541-3863
Volumetric Fund, Inc. (G)

Voyageur
90 South Seventh Street, Suite 4400
Minneapolis, Minnesota 55402
(612) 376-7000 (800) 553-2143
Voyageur Funds, Inc.
Voyageur U.S. Securities Fund (USGI)
Voyageur Insured Funds, Inc.
Voyageur Arizona Insured Tax-Free Fund
(MB-S)
Voyageur Minnesota Insured Fund (MB-S)
Voyageur National Insured Tax-Free Fund
(MB-N)
Voyageur Intermediate Tax-Free Funds, Inc.
Voyageur Minnesota Intermediate Tax-Free
Fund (MB-S)
Voyageur Investment Trust
Voyageur California Insured Tax Free Fund
(MB-S)
Voyageur Florida Insured Tax Free Fund
(MB-S)
Voyageur Kansas Tax Free Fund (MB-S)
Voyageur Missouri Insured Tax Free Fund
(MB-S)
Voyageur New Mexico Tax Free Fund (MB-S)
Voyageur Oregon Insured Tax Free Fund
(MB-S)
Voyageur Utah Tax Free Fund (MB-S)
Voyageur Washington Insured Tax Free
Fund (MB-S)
Voyageur Mutual Funds, Inc.
Voyageur Arkansas Tax Free Fund (MB-S)
Voyageur Iowa Tax Free Fund (MB-S)
Voyageur Wisconsin Tax Free Fund (MB-S)
Voyageur Mutual Funds II, Inc.
Voyageur Colorado Tax Free Fund (MB-S)
Voyageur Mutual Funds III, Inc.
Voyageur Growth Stock Fund (G)
Voyageur Mutual Funds IV, Inc.
Voyageur Money Market Fund (MM-T)
Voyageur Tax-Free Funds, Inc.
Voyageur Minnesota Tax-Free Fund (MB-S)
Voyageur North Dakota Tax-Free Fund
(MB-S)

Waddell Reed Fund, Inc.
6300 Lamar
P.O. Box 29217
Shawnee Mission, Kansas 66201-9217
(913) 236-2000 (800) 366-5465
Waddell Reed Fund, Inc.
Global Income Fund (GB)
Growth Fund (G)
Limited Term Bond Fund (IB)
Municipal Bond Fund (MB-N)
Total Return Fund (G+I)

Wade Fund, Inc.
5100 Poplar Avenue, Suite 2224
Memphis, Tennessee 38137
(901) 682-4613
Wade Fund, Inc. (G)

Walnut Street Funds, Inc.
1801 Park 270 Drive, Suite 220
St. Louis, Missouri 63146
(314) 878-1010   (800) 645-1756
Walnut Street Funds, Inc.
Walnut Street Prime Reserve Fund (MM-T)

Warburg, Pincus
466 Lexington Avenue
New York, New York 10017-3147
(212) 878-0600 (800) 888-6878
Warburg, Pincus Capital Appreciation Fund
(G)
Warburg, Pincus Cash Reserve Fund (MM-T)
Warburg, Pincus Emerging Growth Fund (G)
Warburg, Pincus Fixed Income Fund (IB)
Warburg, Pincus Global Fixed Income Fund
(GB)
Warburg, Pincus Growth and Income Fund
(G+I)
Warburg, Pincus Institutional Fund, Inc.
Global Fixed Income Portfolio (GB)
International Equity Portfolio (INT)
Warburg, Pincus Intermediate Maturity
Government Fund (USGI)
Warburg, Pincus International Equity Fund
(INT)
Warburg, Pincus New York Municipal Bond
Fund (MB-S)
Warburg, Pincus New York Tax Exempt Fund
(MMS-TE)

Wasatch Advisors Funds, Inc.
68 South Main Street, Suite 400
Salt Lake City, Utah 84101-9984
(801) 533-0778   (800) 551-1700
Wasatch Advisors Funds, Inc.
Wasatch Aggressive Equity Fund (G)
Wasatch Growth Fund (G)
Wasatch Income Fund (IB)
Wasatch Mid-Cap Fund (G+I)

Washington Mutual Investors Fund, Inc.
1101 Vermont Avenue, N.W.
Washington D.C. 20005-3585
(202) 842-5665
Washington Mutual Investors Fund, Inc. (G+I)

Wayne Hummer
300 South Wacker Drive
Chicago, Illinois 60606
(312) 431-1700   (800) 621-4477
Wayne Hummer Investment Trust
  Growth Fund (G)
  Income Fund (CB)
Wayne Hummer Money Fund Trust
  Money Market Fund (MM-T)

Weiss, Peck & Greer
One New York Plaza
New York, New York 10004-1950
(212) 908-9582 (800) 223-3332
Weiss, Peck & Greer Funds Trust
  WPG Dividend Income Fund (IE)
  WPG Government Money Market Fund
    (MM-T)
  WPG Government Securities Fund (USGI)
  WPG Intermediate Municipal Bond Fund
    (MB-N)
  WPG Quantitative Equity Fund (G+I)
  WPG Tax Free Money Market Fund (MM-TE)
Weiss, Peck & Greer International Fund (INT)
WPG Growth and Income Fund (G+I)
WPG Growth Fund (AG)
WPG Tudor Fund (AG)

Weitz Series Fund, Inc.
9290 West Dodge Road, Suite 405
Omaha, Nebraska 68114-3349
(402) 391-4161
Weitz Series Fund, Inc.
  Fixed Income Portfolio (IB)
  Government Money Market Portfolio (MM-T)
  Hickory Portfolio (AG)
  Value Portfolio (G)

Western Asset Trust, Inc.
111 South Calvert Street
Baltimore, Maryland 21202
(410) 539-3400
Western Asset Trust, Inc.
  International Portfolio (INT)

Weston Portfolios, Inc.
20 William Street
Wellesley, Massachusetts 02181
(617) 239-0445
Weston Portfolios, Inc.
  New Century Capital Portfolio (FP)
  New Century I Portfolio (IM)

William Blair
135 South LaSalle Street
Chicago, Illinois 60603
(312) 853-2424   (800) 742-7272
William Blair Growth Shares (G)
William Blair Income Shares (IB)
William Blair International Growth Shares (G)
William Blair Ready Reserve Shares (MM-T)

Winthrop Focus Fund
140 Broadway, 42nd Floor
New York, New York 10005-1285
(212) 504-4000   (800) 521-3036
Winthrop Focus Fund
  Winthrop Aggressive Growth Fund (AG)
  Winthrop Fixed Income Fund (USGI)
  Winthrop Growth and Income Fund (G+I)
  Winthrop Growth Fund (G)
  Winthrop Municipal Fund (MB-N)

Working Assets Common Holdimgs
111 Pine Street, Suite 1415
San Francisco, California 94111
(415) 989-3200 (800) 223-7010
Working Assets Common Holdings
  Citizens Balanced Portfolio (B)
  Citizens Growth Portfolio (G)
  Citizens Income Portfolio (IM)
  Working Assets Money Market Fund (MM-T)

World Funds, Inc.
1500 Forest Avenue, Suite 223
Richmond, Virginia 23229
(804) 285-8211   (800) 527-9500
World Funds, Inc.
  Newport Tiger Fund (The) (INT)
  Vontobel Europacific Fund (The) (INT)
  Vontobel U.S. Value Fund (G)

World Income Fund, Inc.
P.O. Box 9011
Princeton, New Jersey 08543-9011
(609) 282-2800   (800) 637-3863
World Income Fund, Inc. (GB)

Wright
24 Federal Street
Boston, Massachusetts 02110-2575
(617) 482-8260   (800) 225-6265
Wright Managed Equity Trust
  Wright International Blue Chip Equities Fund
    (INT)
  Wright Junior Blue Chip Equities Fund (G+I)
  Wright Quality Core Equities Fund (G+I)
  Wright Selected Blue Chip Equities Fund
    (G+I)
Wright Managed Income Trust
  Wright Current Income Fund (IB)
  Wright Government Obligations Fund (USGI)
  Wright Insured Tax Free Bond Fund (MB-N)

Wright Managed Money Market Trust (MM-T)
Wright Near Term Bond Fund
  Wright Total Return Bond Fund (CB)
  Wright U.S. Treasury Money Market Fund
    (MM-T)

Yamaichi Funds, Inc.
Two World Trade Center, Suite 9828
New York, New York 10048
(212) 466-6800
Yamaichi Funds, Inc.
  Yamaichi Global Fund (GE)

Zweig
5 Hanover Street
New York, New York 10004-2614
(212) 635-9800   (800) 272-2700
Zweig Cash Fund, Inc.
  Government Securities Portfolio (MM-T)
Zweig Series Trust
  Government Securities Series (USGI)
  Money Market Series (MM-T)
  Priority Selection List Series (G)
  Zweig Appreciation Fund (AG)
  Zweig Managed Assets Fund (FP)
  Zweig Strategy Fund (G)

CLOSED-END MUTUAL FUNDS

The following is a compilation of the names, ticker symbols and addresses of American closed-end mutual funds, with the types of investments made by each. The notation *bond* means the fund buys only bonds, and is therefore likely to pay a high yield. The notation *convertible* means that the fund mainly buys convertible bonds, which pay a higher yield than stocks, but also have more potential to rise in value than bonds. The notation *dual purpose* means that the fund is split into two, with one part of the fund designed for investors who want income, and the other part designed for shareholders intent upon capital gains. The notation *equity* means the fund buys stocks, mostly for capital gains purposes. The notation *gold* means the fund exclusively buys shares of gold-mining companies, which usually have a high yield, but are subject to the ups and downs of gold prices. The notation *specialized equity* means that the fund buys only particular kinds of stocks for the purpose of capital appreciation. Some funds, for instance, only buy stocks of medical companies, while others concentrate on the stocks of a particular foreign country like Japan.

Closed-end mutual funds issue a fixed number of shares, which are then traded either on exchanges or over-the-counter. Funds traded on the New York Stock Exchange are notated with an NYSE, those on the American Stock Exchange, with an ASE, and those traded over the counter, with an OTC. Closed-end funds contrast with open-ended mutual funds, which create new shares whenever additional funds are received from customers. But closed-end fund managers buy and sell stocks, bonds and convertible securities just like open-end mutual fund managers.

Open-end funds sell at the net asset value (NAV) of their holdings on a particular day (plus a charge, or load, in some cases) and always stand ready to redeem shares at the NAV. In contrast, closed-end funds usually sell above or below their net asset value. The price of the shares is determined by the same forces of supply and demand that affect the value of any publicly traded security. Therefore, those buying shares in a closed-end fund when it is selling below net asset value are, in effect, buying a dollar's worth of securities for less than a dollar, and those buying such a fund when it is trading at a premium to its (NAV) receive less than a dollar's worth of securities for each dollar invested.

This list is provided courtesy of Thomas J. Herzfeld, author of *The Investor's Guide To Closed-End Funds* (McGraw-Hill) and *The Thomas J. Herzfeld Encyclopedia of Closed-End Funds*. Mr. Herzfeld, who can be reached at P.O. Box 161465, Miami, Florida 33116 (305) 271-1900, is an investment advisor specializing in closed-end funds.

ACM Government Income Fund, Inc.
1345 Avenue of the Americas
New York, New York 10105
(201) 319-4000   (800) 221-5672
ACC, NYSE
Bond Fund

ACM Government Opportunity Fund, Inc.
1345 Avenue of the Americas
New York, New York 10105
(201) 319-4000   (800) 221-5672
AOF, NYSE
Bond Fund

ACM Government Securities Fund
1345 Avenue of the Americas
New York, New York 10105
(201) 319-4000   (800) 221-5672
GSF, NYSE
Bond Fund

ACM Government Spectrum Fund, Inc.
1345 Avenue of the Americas
New York, New York 10105
(201) 319-4000   (800) 221-5672
SI, NYSE
Bond Fund

ACM Managed Dollar Income Fund, Inc.
1345 Avenue of the Americas
New York, New York 10105
(201) 319-4000   (800) 221-5672
ADF, NYSE
Bond Fund

ACM Managed Income Fund, Inc.
1345 Avenue of the Americas
New York, New York 10105
(201) 319-4000   (800) 221-5672
AMF, NYSE
Bond Fund

ACM Managed Multi-Market Trust, Inc.
1345 Avenue of the Americas
New York, New York 10105
(201) 319-4000   (800) 221-5672
MMF, NYSE
Bond Fund

ACM Municipal Securities Income Fund
1345 Avenue of the Americas
New York, New York 10105
(201) 319-4000   (800) 221-5672
AMU, NYSE
Municipal Bond Fund

Adams Express Company
7 St. Paul Street, Suite 1140
Baltimore, Maryland 21202
(410) 752-5900 (800) 638-2479
ADX, NYSE
Equity Fund

AIM Strategic Income Fund, Inc.
11 Greenway Plaza, Suite 1919
Houston, Texas 77046
(713) 626-1919   (800) 347-1919
AST, ASE
Convertible Fund

All-American Term Trust
1285 Avenue of the Americas
New York, New York 10019
(201) 902-8046   (800) 852-4750
AAT, NYSE
Bond Fund

Alliance All-Market Advantage Fund
1345 Avenue of the Americas
New York, New York 10105
(800) 247-4154
AMO, NYSE
Miscellaneous

Alliance Global Environment Fund
1345 Avenue of the Americas
New York, New York 10105
(800) 247-4154 (800) 221-5672
AEF, NYSE
Specialized Equity Fund

Alliance World Dollar Government Fund
1345 Avenue of the Americas
New York, New York 10105
(800) 247-4154   (800) 221-5672
AWG, NYSE
Foreign Bond Fund

Alliance World Dollar Government Fund II
1345 Avenue of the Americas
New York, New York 10105
(800) 247-4154   (800) 221-5672
AWF, NYSE
Foreign Bond Fund

Allied Capital Corporation
1666 K Street NW, Suite 901
Washington, DC 20006
(202) 331-1112
ALLC, OTC
Miscellaneous

Allied Capital Corporation II
1666 K Street NW, Suite 901
Washington, DC 20006
(202) 331-1112
ALII, OTC
Miscellaneous

American Adjustable Rate Term Trust, Inc.
−1995
222 South Ninth Street
Minneapolis, Minnesota 55402
(612) 342-6412   (800) 866-7778
ADJ, NYSE
Bond Fund

American Adjustable Rate Term Trust, Inc.
−1996
222 South Ninth Street
Minneapolis, Minnesota 55402
(612) 342-6412   (800) 866-7778
BDJ, NYSE
Bond Fund

American Adjustable Rate Term Trust, Inc.
−1997
222 South Ninth Street
Minneapolis, Minnesota 55402
(612) 342-6412   (800) 866-7778
CDJ, NYSE
Bond Fund

American Adjustable Rate Term Trust, Inc.
−1998
222 South Ninth Street
Minneapolis, Minnesota 55402
(612) 342-6412   (800) 866-7778
DDJ, NYSE
Bond Fund

American Adjustable Rate Term Trust, Inc.
−1999
222 South Ninth Street
Minneapolis, Minnesota 55402
(612) 342-6412   (800) 866-7778
EDJ, NYSE
Bond Fund

American Capital Bond Fund, Inc.
2800 Post Oak Boulevard
Houston, Texas 77056
(713) 993-0500   (800) 421-5666
ACB, NYSE
Bond Fund

American Capital Convertible Securities, Inc.
2800 Post Oak Boulevard
Houston, Texas 77056
(713) 993-0500   (800) 421-5666
ACS, NYSE
Convertible Fund

American Capital Income Trust
2800 Post Oak Boulevard
Houston, Texas 77056
(713) 993-0500   (800) 421-5666
ACD, NYSE
Bond Fund

American Government Income Fund, Inc.
222 S. Ninth Street
Minneapolis, Minnesota 55402
(612) 342-6412   (800) 866-7778
AAF, NYSE
Bond Fund

American Government Income Portfolio, Inc.
222 S. Ninth Street
Minneapolis, Minnesota 55402
(612) 342-6412   (800) 866-7778
AAF, NYSE
Bond Fund

American Government Term Trust, Inc.
222 S. Ninth Street
Minneapolis, Minnesota 55402
(612) 342-6412   (800) 866-7778
AGT, NYSE
Bond Fund

American Municipal Income Portfolio, Inc.
222 S. Ninth Street
Minneapolis, Minnesota 55402
(612) 342-6412   (800) 866-7778
XAA, NYSE
Municipal Bond Fund

American Municipal Term Trust, Inc.
222 S. Ninth Street
Minneapolis, Minnesota 55402
(612) 342-6412   (800) 866-7778
AXT, NYSE
Municipal Bond Fund

American Municipal Term Trust, Inc. II
222 S. Ninth Street
Minneapolis, Minnesota 55402
(612) 342-6412   (800) 866-7778
BXT, NYSE
Municipal Bond Fund

American Municipal Term Trust, Inc. III
222 S. Ninth Street
Minneapolis, Minnesota 55402
(612) 342-6412   (800) 866-7778
CXT, NYSE
Municipal Bond Fund

American Opportunity Income Fund, Inc.
222 S. Ninth Street
Minneapolis, Minnesota 55402
(612) 342-6412   (800) 866-7778
OIF, NYSE
Bond Fund

American Select Portfolio
222 S. Ninth Street
Minneapolis, Minnesota 55402
(612) 342-6412   (800) 866-7778
SLA, NYSE
Bond Fund

American Strategic Income Portfolio, Inc.
222 S. Ninth Street
Minneapolis, Minnesota 55402
(612) 342-6412   (800) 866-7778
ASP, NYSE
Bond Fund

American Strategic Income Portfolio, Inc. II
222 S. Ninth Street
Minneapolis, Minnesota 55402
(612) 342-6412   (800) 866-7778
BSP, NYSE
Bond Fund

American Strategic Income Portfolio, Inc. III
222 S. Ninth Street
Minneapolis, Minnesota 55402
(612) 342-6412   (800) 866-7778
CSP, NYSE
Bond Fund

America's All Season Fund, Inc.
250 Park Avenue South, Suite 200
Winter Park, Florida 32789
(407) 629-1400   (800) 327-5703
FUND, OTC
Miscellaneous

Americas Growth Fund
701 Brickell Avenue, Suite 2000
Miami, Florida 33131
(800) 329-8214
AGRO, OTC

Americas Income Trust Inc.
222 South Ninth Street
Minneapolis, Minnesota 55402
(612) 342-6412   (800) 866-7778
XUS, NYSE
Foreign Bond Fund

Apex Municipal Fund, Inc.
Box 9011
Princeton, New Jersey 08543
(609) 282-2800
APX, NYSE
Municipal Bond Fund

Argentina Fund, Inc.
345 Park Avenue
New York, New York 10154
(617) 330-5602   (NAV) (212) 326-6444
AF, NYSE
Foreign Equity Fund

ASA Limited
PO Box 269
Florham Park, New Jersey 07932
(201) 377-3535
ASA, NYSE
Specialized Equity Fund

The Asia Pacific Fund, Inc.
One Seaport Plaza
New York, New York 10292
(212) 214-3334   (800) 451-6788
APB, NYSE
Foreign Equity Fund

Asia Tigers Fund
Oppenheimer Tower
World Financial Center
New York, New York 10281
(212) 667-7000
GRR, NYSE
Foreign Equity Fund

The Austria Fund
1345 Avenue of the Americas
New York, New York 10105
(201) 319-4000   (800) 221-5672
(800) 247-4154
OST, NYSE
Foreign Equity Fund

Baker, Fentress & Company
200 W. Madison Street, Suite 3510
Chicago, Illinois 60606
(312) 236-9190   (800) BKF-1891
BKF, NYSE
Equity Fund

Bancroft Convertible Fund, Inc.
65 Madison Avenue
Morristown, New Jersey 07960
(201) 631-1177
BCV, ASE
Convertible Fund

Bando McGlocklin Capital Corporation
13555 Bishops Court, Suite 205
Brookfield, Wisconsin 53005
(414) 784-9010
BMCC, OTC
Miscellaneous

Bergstrom Capital Corporation
505 Madison Street, Suite 220
Seattle, Washington 98104
(206) 623-7302
BEM, ASE
Equity Fund

BGR Precious Metals, Inc.
The Dynamic Building
6 Adelaide Street East
Toronto, Ontario, Canada M5C 1H6
(416) 365-5129
Toronto and Montreal Stock Exchanges
Specialized Equity Fund

The BlackRock Advantage Term Trust
345 Park Avenue, 31st Floor
New York, New York 10154
(212) 935-2626   (800) 227-7236
BAT, NYSE
Bond Fund

The BlackRock Broad Investment Grade 2009
   Term Trust, Inc.
345 Park Avenue, 31st Floor
New York, New York 10154
(212) 935-2626   (800) 227-7236
BCT, ASE
Bond Fund

The BlackRock California Insured 2008
   Municipal Term Trust
345 Park Avenue, 31st Floor
New York, New York 10154
(212) 935-2626   (800) 227-7236
BFC, NYSE
Municipal Bond Fund

The BlackRock California Investment Quality
   Municipal Trust
345 Park Avenue, 31st Floor
New York, New York 10154
(212) 935-2626   (800) 227-7236
RAA, ASE
Municipal Bond Fund

The BlackRock Florida Insured 2008
   Municipal Term Trust
345 Park Avenue, 31st Floor
New York, New York 10154
(212) 935-2626   (800) 227-7236
BRF, NYSE
Municipal Bond Fund

The BlackRock Florida Investment Quality
   Municipal Trust
345 Park Avenue, 31st Floor
New York, New York 10154
(212) 935-2626   (800) 227-7236
RFA, NYSE
Municipal Bond Fund

The BlackRock Income Trust, Inc.
345 Park Avenue, 31st Floor
New York, New York 10154
(212) 935-2626   (800) 227-7236
BKT, NYSE
Bond Fund

The BlackRock Insured Municipal Term Trust
345 Park Avenue, 31st Floor
New York, New York 10154
(212) 935-2626   (800) 227-7236
BMT, NYSE
Municipal Bond Fund

The BlackRock Insured Municipal 2008 Term
  Trust
345 Park Avenue, 31st Floor
New York, New York 10154
(212) 935-2626   (800) 227-7236
BRM, NYSE
Municipal Bond Fund

The BlackRock Investment Quality Term
  Trust, Inc.
345 Park Avenue, 31st Floor
New York, New York 10154
(212) 935-2626   (800) 227-7236
BQT, NYSE
Municipal Bond Fund

The BlackRock Investment Quailty Municipal
  Trust, Inc.
345 Park Avenue, 31st Floor
New York, New York 10154
(212) 935-2626   (800) 227-7236
BKN, NYSE
Municipal Bond Fund

The BlackRock Municipal Target Term, Inc.
345 Park Avenue, 31st Floor
New York, New York 10154
(212) 935-2626   (800) 227-7236
BMN, NYSE
Municipal Bond Fund

The BlackRock New Jersey Investment
  Quality Municipal Trust
345 Park Avenue, 31st Floor
New York, New York 10154
(212) 935-2626   (800) 227-7236
RNJ, ASE
Municipal Bond Fund

The BlackRock New York Insured 2008
  Municipal Term Trust
345 Park Avenue, 31st Floor
New York, New York 10154
(212) 935-2626   (800) 227-7236
BLN, NYSE
Municipal Bond Fund

The BlackRock New York Investment Quality
  Municipal Trust
345 Park Avenue, 31st Floor
New York, New York 10154
(212) 935-2626   (800) 227-7236
RNY, ASE
Municipal Bond Fund

The BlackRock 1998 Term Trust
345 Park Avenue, 31st Floor
New York, New York 10154
(212) 935-2626   (800) 227-7236
BBT, NYSE
Bond Fund

The BackRock 1999 Term Trust
345 Park Avenue, 31st Floor
New York, New York 10154
(212) 935-2626   (800) 227-7236
BNN, NYSE
Municipal Bond Fund

The BlackRock North American Government
  Income Trust, Inc.
345 Park Avenue, 31st Floor
New York, New York 10154
(212) 935-2626   (800) 227-7236
BNA, NYSE
Bond Fund

The BlackRock Strategic Term Trust, Inc.
345 Park Avenue, 31st Floor
New York, New York 10154
(212) 935-2626   (800) 227-7236
BGT, NYSE
Bond Fund

The BlackRock Target Term Trust, Inc.
345 Park Avenue, 31st Floor
New York, New York 10154
(212) 935-2626   (800) 227-7236
BTT, NYSE
Bond Fund

The BlackRock 2001 Term Trust
345 Park Avenue, 31st Floor
New York, New York 10154
(212) 935-2626   (800) 227-7236
BLK, NYSE
Municipal Bond Fund

Blue Chip Value Fund
633 17th Street, Suite 1800
Denver, Colorado 80272
(303) 293-5999   Hotline: (303) 293-5699
BLU, NYSE
Equity Fund

The Brazil Fund, Inc.
345 Park Avenue
New York, New York 10154
(617) 330-5602   NAV (212) 326-6444
(800) 349-4281
BZF, NYSE
Foreign Equity Fund

The Brazilian Equity Fund, Inc.
One Citicorp Center, 58th Floor
153 East 53rd Street,
New York, New York 10022
(212) 832-2626
BZL, NYSE
Foreign Equity Fund

Bunker Hill Income Securities, Inc.
125 West 55th Street
New York, New York 10019
(800) 332-3863
BHL, NYSE
Bond Fund

Canadian General Investments Ltd.
110 Yonge Street, Suite 1601
Toronto, Ontario, Canada M5 C1 T4
(416) 366-2931
Equity Fund
Toronto Stock Exchange

Canadian World Fund Ltd.
110 Yonge Street, Suite 1601
Toronto, Ontario Canada M5 C1 T4
(416) 366-2931
Foreign Equity Fund
Toronto Stock Exchange

Capital Southwest Corporation
12900 Preston Road, Suite 700
Dallas, Texas 75230
(214) 233 -8242
CSWC, OTC
Specialized Equity Fund

Castle Convertible Fund, Inc.
75 Maiden Lane
New York, New York 10038
(212) 806-8800   (800) 992-3863
CVF, ASE
Convertible Fund

Central Fund of Canada
P.O. Box 7319
Ancaster, Ontario, Canada L9G 3N6
(905) 648-7878
CEF, ASE, Toronto Stock Exchange
Specialized Equity Fund

Central Securities Corp.
375 Park Avenue
New York, New York 10152
(212) 688-3011
CET ASE
Equity Fund

The Charles Allmon Trust, Inc.
4405 East-West Highway
Bethesda, Maryland 20814
(301) 986-5866
GSO, NYSE
Equity Fund

The Chile Fund
One Citicorp Center, 58th Floor
153 East 53rd Street
New York, New York 10022
(212) 832-2626
CH, NYSE
Foreign Equity Fund

The China Fund
200 Liberty Street, 38th Floor
New York, New York 10281
(212) 808-0500   (800) 421-4777
CHN, NYSE
Foreign Equity Fund

CIGNA High Income Shares
One Financial Plaza
Springfield, Massachusetts 01103
(203) 726-3700   (800) 426-5523
HIS, NYSE
Bond Fund

CIM High Yield Securities
153 E. 53rd Street, 24th Floor
New York, New York 10022
(212) 891-6500   (212) 891-6653
CIM, ASE
Bond Fund

Circle Income Shares, Inc.
P.O. Box 44027
Indianapolis, Indiana 46244
(317) 321-8180   (317) 321-8110
CINS, OTC
Bond Fund

Clemente Global Growth Fund, Inc.
152 West 57th Street
New York, New York 10022
(212) 765-0700 (800) 524-4458
CLM, NYSE
Foreign Equity Fund

CNA Income Shares, Inc.
CNA Plaza
Chicago, Illinois 60685
(312) 822-4181   (800) 524-4458
CNN, NYSE
Bond Fund

Cohen & Steers Realty Income Fund, Inc.
(formerly Real Estate Securities Income Fund)
757 Third Avenue, 16th Floor
New York, New York 10017
(212) 832-3232
RIF, ASE
Specialized Equity Fund

Cohen & Steers Total Return Realty Fund
757 Third Avenue, 16th Floor
New York, New York 10017
(212) 832-3232
RFI, ASE
Specialized Equity Fund

Colonial High Income Municipal Trust, Inc.
One Financial Center
Boston, Massachusetts 02111
(617) 426-3750   (800) 225-2365
CXE, NYSE
Municipal Bond Fund

Colonial Intermarket Income Trust I
One Financial Center
Boston, Massachusetts 02111
(617) 426-3750   (800) 225-2365
CMK, NYSE
Bond Fund

Colonial Intermediate High Income Fund
One Financial Center
Boston, Massachusetts 02111
(617) 426-3750   (800) 225-2365
CIF, NYSE
Bond Fund

Colonial Investment Grade Municipal Trust
One Financial Center
Boston, Massachusetts 02111
(617) 426-3750   (800) 225-2365
CXH, NYSE
Municipal Bond Fund

Colonial Municipal Income Trust
One Financial Center
Boston, Massachusetts 02111
(617) 426-3750   (800) 225-2365
CMU, NYSE
Municipal Bond Fund

Combined Penny Stock Fund, Inc.
2055 Anglo Drive, Suite 202
Colorado Springs, Colorado 80918
(719) 593-2111
PENY, OTC
Specialized Equity Fund

Commonwealth Associates Growth Fund, Inc.
733 3rd Avenue
New York, New York 10017
(212) 297-5600   (800) 888-6534
CAGF, OTC
Specialized Equity Fund

Convertible Holdings, Inc.
P.O. Box 9011
Princeton, New Jersey 08543-9011
(609) 282-3200
CNV, CNVpr, NYSE
Dual Purpose Fund

Corporate High Yield Fund, Inc.
800 Scudders Mill Road
Plainsboro, New Jersey 08536
(609) 282-2800
COY, NYSE
Bond Fund

Corporate High Yield Fund II, Inc.
800 Scudders Mill Road
Plainsboro, New Jersey 08536
(609) 282-2800
KYT, NYSE
Bond Fund

Counsellors Tandem Securities Fund, Inc.
466 Lexington Avenue
New York, New York 10017-3147
(800) 888-6878
CTF, CTFpr, NYSE
Dual Purpose Fund

Current Income Shares, Inc.
P.O. Box 30151, Terminal Annex
Los Angeles, California 90030
(213) 236-4056
CUR, NYSE
Bond Fund

The Czech Republic Fund
Oppenheimer Tower
200 Liberty Street, 38th Floor
One World Financial Center
New York, New York 10281
(800) 421-4777
CRF, NYSE

Dean Witter Government Income Trust
Two World Trade Center, 72nd Floor
New York, New York 10048
(212) 392-2550
GAIT, NYSE
Bond Fund

Delaware Group Dividend and Income Fund
1818 Market Street
Philadelphia, Pennsylvania 19103
(215) 988-1333   (800) 523-4640
DDF, NYSE
Specialized Equity Fund

Delaware Group Global Dividend and Income
   Fund
1818 Market Street
Philadelphia, Pennsylvania 19103
(215) 988-1333   (800) 523-4640
DGF, NYSE
Specialized Equity Fund

Dover Regional Financial Shares
1521 Locust Street, Suite 500
Philadelphia, Pennsylvania 19102
(215) 557-8454
DVRFS, OTC
Specialized Equity Fund

Dreyfus California Municipal Income, Inc.
Dreyfus Family of Funds
P.O. Box 9671
Providence, Rhode Island 02940
(800) 645-6561   (800) 334-6899
DCM, ASE
Municipal Bond Fund

Dreyfus Municipal Income, Inc.
Dreyfus Family of Funds
P.O. Box 9671
Providence, Rhode Island 02940
(800) 645-6561   (800) 334-6899
DMF, ASE
Municipal Bond Fund

Dreyfus New York Municipal Income, Inc.
Dreyfus Family of Funds
P.O. Box 9671
Providence, Rhode Island 02940
(800) 645-6561   (800) 334-6899
DNM, ASE
Municipal Bond Fund

Dreyfus Strategic Governments Income, Inc.
Dreyfus Family of Funds
P.O. Box 9671
Providence, Rhode Island 02940
(800) 645-6561   (800) 334-6899
DSI, NYSE
Bond Fund

Dreyfus Strategic Municipal Bond Fund, Inc.
Dreyfus Family of Funds
P.O. Box 9671
Providence, Rhode Island 02940
(800) 645-6561   (800) 334-6899
DSM, NYSE
Municipal Bond Fund

Dreyfus Strategic Municipals, Inc.
Dreyfus Family of Funds
P.O. Box 9671
Providence, Rhode Island 02940
(800) 645-6561   (800) 334-6899
LEO, NYSE
Municipal Bond Fund

Duff & Phelps Utilities Income Inc.
55 East Monroe Street
Chicago, Illinois 60603
(312) 263-2610   (800) 426-5523
DNP, NYSE
Specialized Equity Fund

Duff & Phelps Utilities Tax-Free Income, Inc.
55 East Monroe Street
Chicago, Illinois 60603
(312) 263-2610   (800) 426-5523
DTF, NYSE
Municipal Bond Fund

Duff & Phelps Utility & Corporate Bond Trust
55 East Monroe Street
Chicago, Illinois 60603
(312) 263-2610   (800) 426-5523
DUC, NYSE
Bond Fund

1838 Bond-Debenture Trading Fund
5 Radnor Corporate Center, Suite 320
100 Matsonford Road
Radnor, Pennsylvania 19087
(215) 293-4355
BDF, NYSE
Bond Fund

Ellsworth Convertible Growth and Income Fund
65 Madison Avenue, 4th Floor
Morristown, New Jersey 07960
(212) 269-9236
ECF, ASE
Convertible Fund

The Emerging Germany Fund, Inc.
One Battery Park Plaza
New York, New York 10004
(212) 363-5100   (212) 363-5152
(800) 356-6122
FRG, NYSE
Foreign Equity Fund

The Emerging Markets Floating Rate Fund
7 World Trade Center
New York, New York 10048
(212) 783-1301   (800) 725-6666
EFL, NYSE
Foreign Bond Fund

The Emerging Markets Income Fund
7 World Trade Center
New York, New York 10048
(212) 783-1301   (800) 725-6666
EMD, NYSE
Foreign Bond Fund

The Emerging Markets Income Fund II
7 World Trade Center
New York, New York 10048
(212) 783-1301   (800) 725-6666
EDF, NYSE
Foreign Bond Fund

The Emerging Markets Infrastructure Fund
153 E. 53rd Street, 57th Floor
New York, New York 10022
(212) 832-2626
EMG, NYSE
Foreign Equity Fund

The Emerging Markets Telecommunications
  Fund, Inc.
One Citicorp Center, 58th Floor
153 E. 53rd Street
New York, New York 10022
(212) 832-2626
ETF, NYSE
Specialized Equity Fund

Emerging Mexico Fund, Inc.
1285 Avenue of the Americas
New York, New York 10019
(212) 713-2421   (800) 852-4750
MEF, NYSE
Foreign Equity Fund

The Emerging Tigers Fund
800 Scudders Mill Road
Plainsboro, New Jersey 08536
(609) 282-2000
TGF, NYSE
Foreign Equity Fund

Engex, Inc.
44 Wall Street
New York, New York 10005
(212) 495-4200
EGX, ASE
Equity Fund

Equus II, Inc.
P.O. Box 130197
Houston, Texas 77219-0197
(713) 529-0900   (800) 856-0901
EQS, ASE
Miscellaneous

The Europe Fund, Inc.
780 Third Avenue
New York, New York 10017
(609) 282-4600   (800) 543-6217
EF, NYSE
Foreign Equity Fund

The European Warrant Fund
c/o Julius Baer Securities, Inc.
330 Madison Avenue
New York, New York 10017
(212) 297-3600   (800) 331-1710
EWF, NYSE
Foreign Equity Fund

Excelsior Income Shares, Inc.
114 W. 47th Street, 9th Floor
New York, New York 10036
(212) 852-3732   (800) 257-2356
EIS, NYSE
Bond Fund

Fidelity Advisors Korea Fund
82 Devonshire Street
Boston, Massachusetts 02109
(800) 426-5523
FAK, NYSE

Fidelity Asia Emerging Markets Fund
82 Devonshire Street
Boston, Massachusetts 02109
(800) 426-5523
FAE, NYSE
Foreign Bond Fund

The First Australia Fund, Inc.
One Seaport Plaza
New York, New York 10292
(212) 214-3334   (800) 451-6788
IAF, ASE
Foreign Equity Fund

First Australia Prime Income Fund
One Seaport Plaza
New York, New York 10292
(212) 214-3334   (800) 451-6788
FAX, ASE
Foreign Bond Fund

First Boston Income Fund, Inc.
Tower 49
12 East 49th Street
New York, New York 10017
(800) 774-4365
FBF, NYSE
Bond Fund

First Boston Strategic Income Fund, Inc.
Tower 49
12 East 49th Street
New York, New York 10017
(800) 774-4365
FBI, NYSE
Bond Fund

The First Commonwealth Fund, Inc.
800 Scudders Mill Road
Plainsboro, New Jersey 08536
(609) 282-4600
FCO, NYSE
Foreign Bond Fund

First Financial Fund, Inc.
One Seaport Plaza
New York, New York 10292
(212) 214-3334   (800) 451-6788
FF, NYSE
Specialized Equity Fund

The First Iberian Fund, Inc.
345 Park Avenue
New York, New York 10154
(212) 326-6444   (617) 330-5602
IBF, ASE
Foreign Equity Fund

The First Israel Fund, Inc.
1 Citicorp Center, 58th Floor
153 E. 53rd Street
New York, New York 10022
(212) 832-2626
ISL, NYSE
Foreign Equity Fund

The First Mercantile Currency Fund
347 Bay Street, Suite 404
Toronto, Ontario M5H 2R7
(416) 364-2724
Toronto Stock Exchange
Specialized Equity Fund

The First Philippine Fund, Inc.
152 West 57th Street
New York, New York 10019
(212) 765-0700   (212) 759-3339
(800) 524-4458
FPF, NYSE
Foreign Equity Fund

Foreign & Colonial Emerging Middle East Fund
225 Franklin Street
Boston, Massachusetts 02109
(212) 713-2848   (212) 656-3218
EME, NYSE

Fort Dearborn Income Securities, Inc.
209 S. LaSalle Street, 11th Floor
Chicago, Illinois 60604-1295
(800) 242-4410
FTD, NYSE
Bond Fund

Fortis Securities, Inc.
(formerly AMEV Securities)
P.O. Box 64284
St. Paul, Minnesota 55164
(612) 738-4274   (800) 800-2638
FOR, NYSE
Bond Fund

The France Growth Fund, Inc.
1285 Avenue of the Americas
New York, New York 10019
(212) 713-2000   (800) 852-4750
FRF, NYSE
Foreign Equity Fund

Franklin Multi-Income Trust
777 Mariners Island Boulevard
San Mateo, California 94404
(415) 312-2000   (800) DIAL-BEN
(800) 632-2350
FMI, NYSE
Miscellaneous

Franklin Principal Maturity Trust
777 Mariners Island Boulevard
San Mateo, California 94404
(415) 312-2000   (800) DIAL-BEN
(800) 632-2350
FPT, NYSE
Bond Fund

Franklin Universal Trust
777 Mariners Island Boulevard
San Mateo, California 94404
(415) 312-2000   (800) DIAL-BEN
(800) 632-2350
FT, NYSE
Bond Fund

Future Germany Fund, Inc.
31 West 52nd Street
New York, New York 10019
(800) GERMANY   (212) 474-7329
FGF, NYSE
Foreign Equity Fund

The Gabelli Equity Trust, Inc.
One Corporate Center
Rye, New York 10580-1434
(914) 921-5070
GAB, NYSE
Equity Fund

Gemini II
Vanguard Financial Center
P.O. Box 2600
Valley Forge, Pennsylvania 19482
(800) 442-2001   (617) 951-5600
GMI, GMIpr, NYSE
Dual Purpose Fund

General American Investors Company, Inc.
450 Lexington Avenue
New York, New York 10017
(212) 916-8400   (800) 436-8401
GAM, NYSE
Equity Fund

The Germany Fund
31 West 52nd Street
New York, New York 10019
(800) GERMANY   (212) 474-7329
GER NYSE
Foreign Equity Fund

The Global Government Plus Fund, Inc.
One Seaport Plaza
New York, New York 10292
(212) 214-3332   (800) 451-6788
GOV, NYSE
Foreign Bond Fund

Global Health Sciences Fund
7800 E. Union Avenue, Suite 800
Denver, Colorado 80237
(800) 528-8765   (303) 930-6326
GHS, NYSE
Foreign Equity Fund

Global High Income Dollar Fund
50 California Street, 27th Floor
San Francisco, California 94111
(800) 432-0000
GHI, NYSE
Foreign Bond Fund

Global Income Plus Fund
1285 Avenue of the Americas
New York, New York 10019
(201) 902-8244
GLI, NYSE
Foreign Bond Fund

Global Partners Income Fund
7 World Trade Center
New York, New York 10048
(800) 725-6666
GDF, NYSE
Foreign Bond Fund

Global Privatization Fund
1345 Avenue of the Americas
New York, New York 10105
(800) 247-4154
GPF, NYSE
Foreign Equity Fund

Global Small Cap Fund
1285 Avenue of the Americas
New York, New York 10019
(201) 902-8244
GSG, ASE
Foreign Equity Fund

The Global Yield Fund, Inc.
One Seaport Plaza
New York, New York 10292
(212) 214-3332   (800) 451-6788
PGY, NYSE
Foreign Bond Fund

Goldcorp Investments Limited
145 King Street West, Suite 2700
Toronto, Canada M5H 1J8
(416) 865-0326
Toronto Stock Exchange
Specialized Equity Fund

The Greater China Fund, Inc.
1285 Avenue of the Americas
New York, New York 10019
(212) 713-3589
GCH, NYSE
Foreign Equity Fund

Greenwich Street California Municipal
388 Greenwich Street
New York, New York 10013
(212) 720-9218
GCM, ASE

The Growth Fund of Spain, Inc.
120 South LaSalle Street,
Chicago, Illinois 60603
(800) 621-1148   (800) 422-2848
GSP, NYSE
Foreign Equity Fund

GT Global Developing Markets Fund
50 California Street
San Francisco, California 94111
(415) 392-6181   (800) 548-9994
GTD, NYSE
Foreign Equity Fund

GT Greater Europe Fund
50 California Street
San Francisco, California 94111
(415) 392-6181   (800) 548-9994
GTF, NYSE
Foreign Equity Fund

Hampton Utilities Trust
777 Mariners Island Boulevard
San Mateo, California 94403
(415) 312-2000   (800) DIAL-BEN
HU, ASE
Dual Purpose Fund

John Hancock Bank & Thirft Opportunity Fund
101 Huntington Avenue
Boston, Massachusetts 02199
(617) 375-1898   (800) 225-5291
BTO, NYSE

H&Q Healthcare Investors, Inc.
50 Rowes Wharf, 4th Floor
Boston, Massachusetts 02110
(617) 574-0567   (800) 451-2597
HQH, NYSE
Specialized Equity Fund

H&Q Life Sciences Investors
50 Rowes Wharf, 4th Floor
Boston, Massachusetts 02110
(617) 574-0567   (800) 451-2597
HQL, NYSE
Specialized Equity Fund

Hatteras Income Securities, Inc.
One NationsBank Plaza, 39th Floor
Charlotte, North Carolina 28255
(704) 386-2459   (800) 635-9270
HAT, NYSE
Bond Fund

Heritage U.S. Government Income Fund
880 Carillon Parkway
St. Petersberg, Florida 33716
(800) 248-3520
HGA, NYSE
Bond Fund

The Herzfeld Caribbean Basin Fund
P.O. Box 161465
Miami, Florida 33116
(305) 271-1900
CUBA, OTC
Foreign Equity Fund

High Income Advantage Trust
Two World Trade Center, 72nd Floor
New York, New York 10048
(201) 938-6191
YLD, NYSE
Bond Fund

High Income Advantage Trust II
Two World Trade Center, 72nd Floor
New York, New York 10048
(212) 938-6191
YLT, NYSE
Bond Fund

High Income Advantage Trust III
Two World Trade Center, 72nd Floor
New York, New York 10048
(212) 938-6191
YLH, NYSE
Bond Fund

The High Yield Income Fund, Inc.
One Seaport Plaza
New York, New York 10292
(212) 214-3332   (800) 451-6788
HYI, NYSE
Bond Fund

The High Yield Plus Fund, Inc.
One Seaport Plaza
New York, New York 10292
(212) 214-3332   (800) 451-6788
HYP, NYSE
Bond Fund

Highlander Income Fund
222 South 9th Street
Minneapolis, Minnesota 55402
(617) 342-6387   (800) 866-7778
HLA, ASE
Bond Fund

Hyperion 1997 Term Trust, Inc.
520 Madison Avenue, 10th Floor
New York, New York 10022
(212) 980-8400   (800) 497-3746
(800) HYPERION
HTA, NYSE
Bond Fund

Hyperion 1999 Term Trust, Inc.
520 Madison Avenue, 10th Floor
New York, New York 10022
(212) 980-8400   (800) 497-3746
(800) HYPERION
HTT, NYSE
Bond Fund

Hyperion 2002 Term Trust, Inc.
520 Madison Avenue, 10th Floor
New York, New York 10022
(212) 980-8400   (800) 497-3746
(800) HYPERION
HTB, NYSE
Bond Fund

Hyperion 2005 Investment Grade Opportunity
  Term Trust, Inc.
520 Madison Avenue, 10th Floor
New York, New York 10022
(212) 980-8400   (800) 497-3746
(800) HYPERION
HTO, NYSE
Bond Fund

Hyperion Total Return Fund, Inc.
520 Madison Avenue, 10th Floor
New York, New York 10022
(212) 980-8400   (800) 497-3746
(800) HYPERION
HTR, NYSE
Bond Fund

INA Investment Securities, Inc.
Two Liberty Place
1601 Chestnut Street, P.O. Box 13856
Philadelphia, Pennsylvania 19192-2211
(413) 784-0100   (800) 426-5523
IIS, NYSE
Bond Fund

Income Opportunities Fund 1999 Inc.
800 Scudders Mill Road
Plainsboro, New Jersey 08536
(609) 282-2800
IOF, NYSE
Bond Fund

Income Opportunities Fund 2000 Inc.
800 Scudders Mill Road
Plainsboro, New Jersey 08536
(609) 282-2800
IFT, NYSE
Bond Fund

Independence Square Income Securities, Inc.
One Aldwyn Center
Villanova, Pennsylvania 19085
(215) 964-8882   (800) 852-4750
ISIS, OTC
Bond Fund

The India Fund
Oppenheimer Tower
200 Liberty Street, 38th Floor
World Financial Center
New York, New York 10281
(800) 421-4777
IFN, NYSE
Foreign Equity Fund

The India Growth Fund
1285 Avenue of the Americas
New York, New York 10019
(212) 713-1251   (800) 553-8080
IGF, NYSE
Foreign Equity Fund

The Indonesia Fund, Inc.
One Citicorp Center, 58th Floor
153 East 53rd Street
New York, New York 10022
(212) 310-0361
IF, NYSE
Foreign Equity Fund

The Inefficient-Market Fund, Inc.
1345 Avenue of the Americas
New York, New York 10105
(212) 698-6324   (800) 428-8890
(800) 354-6565
IMF, ASE
Specialized Equity Fund

InterCapital California Insured Municipal
  Income Trust
Two World Trade Center, 72nd Floor
New York, New York 10048
(212) 392-1600   (800) 869-FUND
IIC, NYSE
Municipal Bond Fund

InterCapital California Quality Municipal
  Securities
Two World Trade Center, 72nd Floor
New York, New York 10048
(212) 392-1600   (800) 869-FUND
IQC, NYSE
Municipal Bond Fund

InterCapital Income Securities, Inc.
Two World Trade Center, 72nd Floor
New York, New York 10048
(212) 392-1600   (800) 869-FUND
ICB, NYSE
Bond Fund

InterCapital Insured California Municipal
  Securities
Two World Trade Center, 72nd Floor
New York, New York 10048
(212) 392-1600   (800) 869-FUND
ICS, NYSE
Municipal Bond Fund

InterCapital Insured Municipal Bond Trust
Two World Trade Center, 72nd Floor
New York, New York 10048
(212) 392-1600   (800) 869-FUND
IMB, NYSE
Municipal Bond Fund

InterCapital Insured Municipal Income Trust
Two World Trade Center, 72nd Floor
New York, New York 10048
(212) 392-1600   (800) 869-FUND
IIM, NYSE
Municipal Bond Fund

InterCapital Insured Municipal Securities
Two World Trade Center, 72nd Floor
New York, New York 10048
(212) 392-1600   (800) 869-FUND
IMS, NYSE
Municipal Bond Fund

InterCapital Insured Municipal Trust
Two World Trade Center, 72nd Floor
New York, New York 10048
(212) 392-1600   (800) 869-FUND
IMT, NYSE
Municipal Bond Fund

InterCapital New York Quality Municipal
  Securities
Two World Trade Center, 72nd Floor
New York, New York 10048
(212) 392-1600   (800) 869-FUND
IQN, NYSE
Municipal Bond Fund

InterCapital Quality Municipal Income Trust
Two World Trade Center, 72nd Floor
New York, New York 10048
(212) 392-1600   (800) 869-FUND
IQI, NYSE
Municipal Bond Fund

InterCapital Quality Municipal Investment Trust
Two World Trade Center, 72nd Floor
New York, New York 10048
(212) 392-1600   (800) 869-FUND
IQT, NYSE
Municipal Bond Fund

InterCapital Quality Municipal Securities
Two World Trade Center, 72nd Floor
New York, New York 10048
(212) 392-1600   (800) 869-FUND
IQM, NYSE
Municipal Bond Fund

The Irish Investment Fund, Inc.
The Boston Co. Advisors
Exchange Place
Boston, Massachusetts 02109
(800) 468-6475
IRL, NYSE
Foreign Equity Fund

The Italy Fund, Inc.
Two World Trade Center
New York, New York 10048
(212) 298-6263   (800) 331-1710
ITA, NYSE
Foreign Equity Fund

Jakarta Growth Fund, Inc.
180 Maiden Lane, 29th Floor
New York, New York 10038
(212) 509-7893   (800) 833-0018
JGF, NYSE
Foreign Equity Fund

The Japan Equity Fund, Inc.
c/o Daiwa Securities Trust Company
One Evertrust Plaza
Jersey City, New Jersey 07302
(201) 915-3020   (800) 933-3440
JEQ, NYSE
Foreign Equity Fund

Japan OTC Equity Fund, Inc.
180 Maiden Lane
New York, New York 10038
(800) 833-0018   (800) 426-5523
JOF, NYSE
Foreign Equity Fund

Jardine Fleming China Region Fund, Inc.
100 East Pratt Street
Baltimore, Maryland 21202
(800) 638-8540
JFC, NYSE
Foreign Equity Fund

Jardine Fleming India Fund
100 East Pratt Street
Baltimore, Maryland 21202
(800) 638-8540
JFI, NYSE
Foreign Equity Fund

John Hancock Income Securities Trust
101 Huntington Avenue
Boston, Massachusetts 02199
(617) 375-1898   (800) 225-5291
JHS, NYSE
Bond Fund

John Hancock Investors Trust
101 Huntington Avenue
Boston, Massachusetts 02199
(617) 375-1898   (800) 225-5291
JHI, NYSE
Bond Fund

Jundt Growth Fund
1550 Utica Avenue South, Suite 950
Minneapolis, Minnesota 55416
(800) 543-6217
JF, NYSE
Equity Fund

Kemper High Income Trust
120 South LaSalle Street
Chicago, Illinois 60603
(800) 537-6006
KHI, NYSE
Bond Fund

Kemper Intermediate Government Trust
120 South LaSalle Street
Chicago, Illinois 60603
(800) 537-6006
KGT, NYSE
Bond Fund

Kemper Multi-Market Income Trust
120 South LaSalle Street
Chicago, Illinois 60603
(800) 537-6006
KMM, NYSE
Bond Fund

Kemper Municipal Income Trust
120 South LaSalle Street
Chicago, Illinois 60603
(800) 537-6006
KTF, NYSE
Municipal Bond Fund

Kemper Strategic Income Fund
120 South LaSalle Street
Chicago, Illinois 60603
(800) 537-6006
KST, NYSE
Bond Fund

Kemper Strategic Municipal Income Trust
120 South LaSalle Street
Chicago, Illinois 60603
(800) 537-6006
KSM, NYSE
Municipal Bond Fund

Kleinwort Benson Australian Income Fund, Inc.
200 Park Avenue, 25th Floor
New York, New York 10166
(212) 687-2515   (800) 237-4218
KBA, NYSE
Foreign Bond Fund

The Korea Fund, Inc.
345 Park Avenue
New York, New York 10154
NAV: (212) 326-6444   (617) 330-5602
KF, NYSE
Foreign Equity Fund

Korean Equity Fund
180 Maiden Lane, Suite 2903
New York, New York 10038
(212) 509-8181
KEF, NYSE
Foreign Equity Fund

The Korean Investment Fund
1345 Avenue of the Americas
New York, New York 10105
(212) 969-1351   (800) 426-5523
KIF, NYSE
Foreign Equity Fund

Latin America Dollar Income Fund
345 Park Avenue
New York, New York 10154
(617) 330-5602   NAV: (212) 644-1583
LBF, NYSE
Foreign Bond Fund

Latin American Discovery Fund
c/o Morgan Stanley Asset Management
1221 Avenue of the Americas
New York, New York 10020
(212) 296-7100
LDF, NYSE
Foreign Equity Fund

The Latin America Equity Fund, Inc.
One Citicorp Center, 47th Floor
153 East 53rd Street
New York, New York 10022
(212) 832-2626   (800) 852-4750
LAQ, NYSE
Foreign Equity Fund

Latin American Investment Fund
One Citicorp Center, 47th Floor
153 East 53rd Street
New York, New York 10022
(212) 832-2626   (800) 852-4750
LAM, NYSE
Foreign Equity Fund

Lehman Brothers Latin American Growth
    Fund
200 Vesey
3 World Financial Center
New York, New York 10285

Liberty All-Star Equity Fund
Federal Reserve Plaza
600 Atlantic Avenue, 24th Floor
Boston, Massachusetts 02210
(617) 722-6000   (800) 542-3863
USA, NYSE
Equity Fund

Liberty Term Trust, Inc., 1999
Federated Investors Tower
Pittsburgh, Pennsylvania 15222-3779
(412) 288-1561
LTT, NYSE
Bond Fund

Lincoln National Convertible Securities Fund,
Inc.
1300 South Clinton Street
Fort Wayne, Indiana 46801
(219) 455-2210
LNV, NYSE
Convertible Fund

Lincoln National Income Fund, Inc.
1300 South Clinton Street
Fort Wayne, Indiana 46801
(219) 455-2210
LND, NYSE
Bond Fund

The Malaysia Fund, Inc.
P.O. Box 2798
Boston, Massachusetts 02208-2798
(800) 548-7786
MF, NYSE
Foreign Equity Fund

Managed High Income Portfolio
Shearson Lehman Advisors
2 World Trade Center
New York, New York 10048
(212) 720-9218   (800) 331-1710
MHY, NYSE
Bond Fund

Managed Municipals Portfolio
Shearson Lehman Advisors
2 World Trade Center
New York, New York 10048
(212) 720-9218   (800) 331-1710
MMU, NYSE
Municipal Bond Fund

Managed Municipal Portfolio II
Shearson Lehman Advisors
2 World Trade Center
New York, New York 10048
(212) 720-9218   (800) 331-1710
MTU, NYSE
Municipal Bond Fund

Massachusetts Health & Education Tax-Exempt
Trust
225 Franklin Street
Boston, Massachusetts 02110
(800) 426-5523
MHE, ASE
Municipal Bond Fund

MassMutual Corporate Investors
1295 State Street
Springfield, Massachusetts 01111
(413) 788-8411   (800) 442-2001
MCI, NYSE
Bond Fund

MassMutual Participation Investors
1295 State Street
Springfield, Massachusetts 01111
(413) 788-8411   (800) 442-2001
MPV, NYSE
Bond Fund

Mentor Income Fund, Inc.
(formerly RAC Income Fund)
11000 Broken Land Parkway
Columbia, Maryland 21044
(410) 715-7847
MRF, NYSE
Bond Fund

Merrill Lynch & Co. S&P 500
P.O. Box 9011
Princeton, New Jersey 08543-9011
(609) 282-8837
MIT, NYSE
Bond Fund

Merrill Lynch High Income Municipal Bond
Fund
P.O. Box 9011
Princeton, New Jersey 08543-9011
(609) 282-8837
unlisted
Bond Fund

The Mexico Equity and Income Fund, Inc.
200 Liberty Street
New York, New York 10281
(212) 667-7757   (800) 421-4777
MXE, NYSE
Foreign Equity Fund

The Mexico Fund, Inc.
77 Aristoteles Street 3rd Floor, Polanco,
11560 Mexico DF Mexico
(212) 936-5100   NAV: (212) 750-4200
MXF, NYSE
Foreign Equity Fund

MFS Charter Income Trust
500 Boylston Street
Boston, Massachusetts 02116
(617) 954-5000   (800) 225-2606
MCR, NYSE
Bond Fund

MFS Government Markets Income Trust
500 Boylston Street
Boston, Massachusetts 02116
(617) 954-5000   (800) 225-2606
MGF, NYSE
Bond Fund

MFS Intermediate Income Trust
500 Boylston Street
Boston, Massachusetts 02116
(617) 954-5000   (800) 225-2606
MIN, NYSE
Bond Fund

MFS Multimarket Income Trust
500 Boylston Street
Boston, Massachusetts 02116
(617) 954-5000   (800) 225-2606
MMT, NYSE
Bond Fund

MFS Municipal Income Trust
500 Boylston Street
Boston, Massachusetts 02116
(617) 954-5000   (800) 225-2606
MFM, NYSE
Municipal Bond Fund

MFS Special Value Trust
500 Boylston Street
Boston, Massachusetts 02116
(617) 954-5000   (800) 225-2606
MFV, NYSE
Bond Fund

Minnesota Municipal Income Portfolio, Inc.
222 S. Ninth Street
Minneapolis, Minnesota 55402
(800) 333-6000 (ext 6387)
MXA ASE
Municipal Bond Fund

Minnesota Municipal Term Trust, Inc.
222 S. Ninth Street
Minneapolis, Minnesota 55402
(800) 333-6000 (ext 6387)
MNA, NYSE
Municipal Bond Fund

Minnesota Municipal Term Trust II, Inc.
222 S. Ninth Street
Minneapolis, Minnesota 55402
(800) 333-6000 (ext 6387)
MNB, ASE
Municipal Bond Fund

Montgomery Street Income Securities, Inc.
101 California Street, Suite 4100
San Francisco, California 94111
(415) 981-8191
MTS, NYSE
Bond Fund

Morgan Grenfell SMALLCap Fund, Inc.
855 Third Avenue, Suite 1740
New York, New York 10022
(212) 230-2600 (800) 888-8060
MGC, NYSE
Specialized Equity Fund

Morgan Stanley Africa Investment Fund
1221 Avenue of the Americas
New York, New York 10020
(212) 296-7100   (800) 442-2001
AFF, NYSE
Foreign Equity Fund

Morgan Stanley Emerging Markets Debt
  Fund
1221 Avenue of the Americas
New York, New York 10020
(212) 296-7100   (800) 442-2001
MSD, NYSE
Foreign Bond Fund

Morgan Stanley Emerging Markets Fund,
  Inc.
1221 Avenue of the Americas
New York, New York 10020
(212) 296-7100 (800) 442-2001
MSF, NYSE
Foreign Equity Fund

Morgan Stanley Global Opportunity Bond
  Fund
1221 Avenue of the Americas
New York, New York 10020
(212) 296-7100   (800) 442-2001
MGB, NYSE
Foreign Bond Fund

Morgan Stanley High Yield Fund
1221 Avenue of the Americas
New York, New York 10020
(212) 296-7100   (800) 442-2001
MSY, NYSE
Bond Fund

Morgan Stanley India Investment Fund
1221 Avenue of the Americas
New York, New York 10020
(212) 296-7100   (800) 442-2001
IIF, NYSE
Foreign Equity Fund

Municipal Advantage Fund
One World Financial Center
New York, New York 10281
(800) 232-FUND
MAF, NYSE
Municipal Bond Fund

Municipal High Income Fund, Inc.
Two World Trade Center, 72nd Floor
New York, New York 10048
(212) 392-2550   (800) 869-FUND
MHF, NYSE
Municipal Bond Fund

Municipal Income Opportunities Trust
(formerly Allstate Municipal Income
  Opportunities Trust)
Two World Trade Center, 72nd Floor
New York, New York 10048
(212) 392-2550   (800) 869-FUND
OIA, NYSE
Municipal Bond Fund

Municipal Income Opportunities Trust II
(formerly Allstate Municipal Income
  Opportunities Trust II)
Two World Trade Center, 72nd Floor
New York, New York 10048
(212) 392-2550   (800) 869-FUND
OIB, NYSE
Municipal Bond Fund

Municipal Income Opportunities Trust III
(formerly Allstate Municipal Income
  Opportunities Trust III)
Two World Trade Center, 72nd Floor
New York, New York 10048
(212) 392-2550   (800) 869-FUND
OIC, NYSE
Municipal Bond Fund

Municipal Income Trust
(formerly Allstate Municipal Income Trust)
Two World Trade Center, 72nd Floor
New York, New York 10048
(212) 392-2550   (800) 869-FUND
TFA, NYSE
Municipal Bond Fund

Municipal Income Trust II
(formerly Allstate Municipal Income Trust II)
Two World Trade Center, 72nd Floor
New York, New York 10048
(212) 392-2550   (800) 869-FUND
TFB, NYSE
Municipal Bond Fund

Municipal Income Trust III
(formerly Allstate Municipal Income
  Trust III)
Two World Trade Center, 72nd Floor
New York, New York 10048
(212) 392-2550   (800) 869-FUND
TFC, NYSE
Municipal Bond Fund

Municipal Partners Fund
7 World Trade Center
New York, New York 10048
(212) 783-1301   (800) 725-6666
MNP, NYSE
Municipal Bond Fund

Municipal Partners Fund II
7 World Trade Center
New York, New York 10048
(212) 783-1301   (800) 725-6666
MPT, NYSE
Municipal Bond Fund

Municipal Premium Income Trust
(formerly Allstate Municipal Premium Income
  Fund)
Two World Trade Center, 72nd Floor
New York, New York 10048
(212) 392-2550   (800) 869-FUND
PIA, NYSE
Municipal Bond Fund

MuniAssets Fund
800 Scudders Mill Road
Plainsboro, New Jersey 08536
(609) 282-2800
MUA, NYSE
Municipal Bond Fund

MuniBond Income Fund
800 Scudders Mill Road
Plainsboro, New Jersey 08536
(609) 282-2800
MBD, NYSE
Municipal Bond Fund

MuniEnhanced Fund, Inc.
800 Scudders Mill Road
Plainsboro, New Jersey 08536
(609) 282-2800
MEN, NYSE
Municipal Bond Fund

MuniInsured Fund, Inc.
800 Scudders Mill Road
Plainsboro, New Jersey 08536
(609) 282-2800
MIF, ASE
Municipal Bond Fund

MuniVest California Insured Fund, Inc.
800 Scudders Mill Road
Plainsboro, New Jersey 08536
609-282-2800
MVC, NYSE
Municipal Bond Fund

MuniVest Florida Fund
800 Scudders Mill Road
Plainsboro, New Jersey 08536
(609) 282-2800
MVS, NYSE
Municipal Bond Fund

MuniVest Fund, Inc.
800 Scudders Mill Road
Plainsboro, New Jersey 08536
609-282-2800
MVF, ASE
Municipal Bond Fund

MuniVest Fund II, Inc.
800 Scudders Mill Road
Plainsboro, New Jersey 08536
(609) 282-2800
MVT, NYSE
Municipal Bond Fund

MuniVest Michigan Insured Fund, Inc.
800 Scudders Mill Road
Plainsboro, New Jersey 08536
(609) 282-2800
MVM, NYSE
Municipal Bond Fund

MuniVest New Jersey Fund, Inc.
800 Scudders Mill Road
Plainsboro, New Jersey 08536
(609) 282-2800
MVJ, NYSE
Municipal Bond Fund

MuniVest New York Insured Fund, Inc.
800 Scudders Mill Road
Plainsboro, New Jersey 08536
(609) 282-2800
MVY, NYSE
Municipal Bond Fund

MuniVest Pennsylvania Insured Fund, Inc.
800 Scudders Mill Road
Plainsboro, New Jersey 08536
(609) 282-2800
MVP, NYSE
Municipal Bond Fund

MuniYield Arizona Fund
800 Scudders Mill Road
Plainsboro, New Jersey 08536
(609) 282-2800
MZA, ASE
Municlpal Bond Fund

MuniYield Arizona Fund II
800 Scudders Mill Road
Plainsboro, New Jersey 08536
609-282-2800
MZT, ASE
Municipal Bond Fund

MuniYield California Fund, Inc.
800 Scudders Mill Road
Plainsboro, New Jersey 08536
(609) 282-2800
MYC, NYSE
Municipal Bond Fund

MuniYield California Insured Fund, Inc.
800 Scudders Mill Road
Plainsboro, New Jersey 08536
(609) 282-2800
MIC, NYSE
Municipal Bond Fund

MuniYield California Insured Fund II, Inc.
800 Scudders Mill Road
Plainsboro, New Jersey 08536
(609) 282-2800
MCA, NYSE
Municipal Bond Fund

MuniYield Florida Fund, Inc.
800 Scudders Mill Road
Plainsboro, New Jersey 08536
(609) 282-2800
MYF, NYSE
Municipal Bond Fund

MuniYield Florida Insured Fund, Inc.
800 Scudders Mill Road
Plainsboro, New Jersey 08536
(609) 282-2800
MFT, NYSE
Municipal Bond Fund

MuniYield Fund, Inc.
800 Scudders Mill Road
Plainsboro, New Jersey 08536
(609) 282-2800
MYD, NYSE
Municipal Bond Fund

MuniYield Insured Fund, Inc.
800 Scudders Mill Road
Plainsboro, New Jersey 08536
(609) 282-2800
MYI, NYSE
Municipal Bond Fund

MuniYield Insured Fund II, Inc.
800 Scudders Mill Road
Plainsboro, New Jersey 08536
(609) 282-2800
MTI, NYSE
Municipal Bond Fund

MuniYield Michigan Fund, Inc.
800 Scudders Mill Road
Plainsboro, New Jersey 08536
(609) 282-2800
MYM, NYSE
Municipal Bond Fund

MuniYield Michigan Insured Fund, Inc.
800 Scudders Mill Road
Plainsboro, New Jersey 08536
(609) 282-2800
MIY, NYSE
Municipal Bond Fund

MuniYield New Jersey Fund, Inc.
800 Scudders Mill Road
Plainsboro, New Jersey 08536
(609) 282-2800
MYJ, NYSE
Municipal Bond Fund

MuniYield New Jersey Insured Fund, Inc.
800 Scudders Mill Road
Plainsboro, New Jersey 08536
(609) 282-2800
MJI, NYSE
Municipal Bond Fund

MuniYield New York Insured Fund, Inc.
800 Scudders Mill Road
Plainsboro, New Jersey 08536
(609) 282-2800
MYN, NYSE
Municipal Bond Fund

MuniYield New York Insured Fund II, Inc.
800 Scudders Mill Road
Plainsboro, New Jersey 08536
(609) 282-2800
MYT, NYSE
Municipal Bond Fund

MuniYield New York Insured Fund III, Inc.
800 Scudders Mill Road
Plainsboro, New Jersey 08536
(609) 282-2800
MYY, NYSE
Municipal Bond Fund

MuniYield Pennsylvania Fund, Inc.
800 Scudders Mill Road
Plainsboro, New Jersey 08536
(609) 282-2800
MPA, NYSE
Municipal Bond Fund

MuniYield Quality Fund, Inc.
800 Scudders Mill Road
Plainsboro, New Jersey 08536
(609) 282-2800
MQY, NYSE
Municipal Bond Fund

MuniYield Quality Fund II, Inc.
800 Scudders Mill Road
Plainsboro, New Jersey 08536
(609) 282-2800
MQT, NYSE
Municipal Bond Fund

MVP Capital Corporation
20 Adelaide Street, East
Toronto, Ontario M5C 2T6
(416) 867-1100
Toronto Stock Exchange
Specialized Equity Fund

Mutual of Omaha Interest Shares, Inc.
10235 Regency Circle
Omaha, Nebraska 68114
(402) 397-8555
MUO, NYSE
Bond Fund

NAIC Growth Fund
P.O. Box 220
Royal Oak, Michigan 48068
(313) 543-0612
GRF, Chicago
Equity Fund

Nations Government Income Trust 2003
One NationsBank Plaza
Charlotte, North Carolina 28255
(704) 386-5000
NGI, NYSE
Bond Fund

Nations Government Income Trust 2004
One NationsBank Plaza
Charlotte, North Carolina 28255
(704) 386-5000
NGF, NYSE
Bond Fund

New Age Media Fund
100 East Pratt Street
Baltimore, Maryland 21202
(410) 547-2000   (800) 231-8432
NAF, NYSE
Specialized Equity Fund

The New America High Income
Fund, Inc.
75 State Street
Boston, Massachusetts 02109
(617) 350-8610
HYB, NYSE
Bond Fund

The New Germany Fund, Inc.
31 West 52nd Street
New York, New York 10019
(212) 474-7000   (212) 474-7483
(800) GERMANY
GF, NYSE
Foreign Equity Fund

The New South Africa Fund
245 Park Avenue
New York, New York 10167
(212) 272-2093
NSA, NYSE
Foreign Equity Fund

The New York Tax-Exempt Income Fund, Inc.
3410 S. Carolina Street
Denver, Colorado 80217
(800) 241-2372
XTX ASE
Municipal Bond Fund

Nuveen Arizona Premium Income Municipal
Fund, Inc.
333 West Wacker Drive
Chicago, Illinois 60606
(800) 257-8787   (800) 323-5063
NAZ, NYSE
Municipal Bond Fund

Nuveen California Investment Quality
Municipal Fund, Inc.
333 West Wacker Drive
Chicago, Illinois 60606
(800) 257-8787   (800) 323-5063
NQC, NYSE
Municipal Bond Fund

Nuveen California Municipal Income Fund, Inc.
333 West Wacker Drive
Chicago, Illinois 60606
(800) 257-8787   (800) 323-5063
NCM, NYSE
Municipal Bond Fund

Nuveen California Municipal Market
Opportunity Fund, Inc.
333 West Wacker Drive
Chicago, Illinois 60606
(800) 257-8787   (800) 323-5063
NCO, NYSE
Municipal Bond Fund

Nuveen California Municipal Value Fund, Inc.
333 West Wacker Drive
Chicago, Illinois 60606
(800) 257-8787   (800) 323-5063
NCA, NYSE
Municipal Bond Fund

Nuveen California Performance Plus
Municipal Fund, Inc.
333 West Wacker Drive
Chicago, Illinois 60606
(800) 257-8787   (800) 323-5063
NCP, NYSE
Municipal Bond Fund

Nuveen California Premium Income
Municipal Fund, Inc.
333 West Wacker Drive
Chicago, Illinois 60606
(800) 257-8787   (800) 323-5063
NCU, ASE
Municipal Bond Fund

Nuveen California Premium Income
Municipal Fund II, Inc.
333 West Wacker Drive
Chicago, Illinois 60606
(800) 257-8787   (800) 323-5063
NCV, ASE
Municipal Bond Fund

Nuveen California Quality Income Municipal
Fund, Inc.
333 West Wacker Drive
Chicago, Illinois 60606
(800) 257-8787   (800) 323-5063
NUC, NYSE
Municipal Bond Fund

Nuveen California Select Quality Municipal
Fund, Inc.
333 West Wacker Drive
Chicago, Illinois 60606
(800) 257-8787   (800) 323-5063
NVC, NYSE
Municipal Bond Fund

Nuveen Connecticut Premium Income
Municipal Fund
333 West Wacker Drive
Chicago, Illinois 60606
(800) 257-8787   (800) 323-5063
NTC, NYSE
Municipal Bond Fund

Nuveen Florida Investment Quality Municipal
Fund, Inc.
333 West Wacker Drive
Chicago, Illinois 60606
(800) 257-8787   (800) 323-5063
NQF, NYSE
Municipal Bond Fund

Nuveen Florida Premium Income Municipal
Fund
333 West Wacker Drive
Chicago, Illinois 60606
(800) 257-8787   (800) 323-5063
NFO, ASE
Municipal Bond Fund

Nuveen Florida Quality Income Municipal
Fund, Inc.
333 West Wacker Drive
Chicago, Illinois 60606
(800) 257-8787   (800) 323-5063
NUF, NYSE
Municipal Bond Fund

Nuveen Insured California Premium Income
Municipal Fund, Inc.
333 West Wacker Drive
Chicago, Illinois 60606
(800) 257-8787   (800) 323-5063
NPC, NYSE
Municipal Bond Fund

Nuveen Insured California Premium Income
Municipal Fund 2, Inc.
333 West Wacker Drive
Chicago, Illinois 60606
(800) 257-8787   (800) 323-5063
NCL, NYSE
Municipal Bond Fund

Nuveen Insured California Select Tax-Free
Income Portfolio, Inc.
333 West Wacker Drive
Chicago, Illinois 60606
(800) 257-8787   (800) 323-5063
NXC, NYSE
Municipal Bond Fund

Nuveen Insured Florida Premium Income
Municipal Fund, Inc.
333 West Wacker Drive
Chicago, Illinois 60606
(800) 257-8787   (800) 323-5063
NFL, NYSE
Municipal Bond Fund

Nuveen Insured Florida Premium Income
Municipal Fund 2, Inc.
333 West Wacker Drive
Chicago, Illinois 60606
(800) 257-8787   (800) 323-5063
NFP, NYSE
Municipal Bond Fund

Nuveen Georgia Premium Income Municipal
Fund
333 West Wacker Drive
Chicago, Illinois 60606
(800) 257-8787   (800) 323-5063
NPG, ASE
Municipal Bond Fund

Nuveen Insured Municipal Opportunity
Fund, Inc.
333 West Wacker Drive
Chicago, Illinois 60606
(800) 257-8787   (800) 323-5063
NIO, NYSE
Municipal Bond Fund

Nuveen Insured New York Premium Income
Municipal Fund, Inc.
333 West Wacker Drive
Chicago, Illinois 60606
(800) 257-8787   (800) 323-5063
NNF, NYSE
Municipal Bond Fund

Nuveen Insured New York Premium Income
Municipal Fund 2, Inc.
333 West Wacker Drive
Chicago, Illinios 60606
(800) 257-8787   (800) 323-5063
NYP, NYSE
Municipal Bond Fund

Nuveen Insured New York Select Tax-Free
Income Portfolio
333 West Wacker Drive
Chicago, Illinois 60606
(800) 257-8787   (800) 323-5063
NXN, NYSE
Municipal Bond Fund

Nuveen Insured Premium Income Municipal
Fund, Inc.
333 West Wacker Drive
Chicago, Illinois 60606
(800) 257-8787   (800) 323-5063
NPE, NYSE
Municipal Bond Fund

Nuveen Insured Premium Income Municipal
Fund II, Inc.
333 West Wacker Drive
Chicago, Illinois 60606
(800) 257-8787   (800) 323-5063
NPX, NYSE
Municipal Bond Fund

Nuveen Insured Quality Municipal Fund, Inc.
333 West Wacker Drive
Chicago, Illinois 60606
(800) 257-8787   (800) 323-5063
NQI, NYSE
Municipal Bond Fund

Nuveen Investment Quality Municipal Fund, Inc.
333 West Wacker Drive
Chicago, Illinois 60606
(800) 257-8787   (800) 323-5063
NQM, NYSE
Municipal Bond Fund

Nuveen Maryland Premium Income
Municipal Fund
333 West Wacker Drive
Chicago, Illinois 60606
(800) 257-8787   (800) 323-5063
NMY, NYSE
Municipal Bond Fund

Nuveen Maryland Premium Income
  Municipal Fund II
333 West Wacker Drive
Chicago, Illinois 60606
(800) 257-8787 (800) 323-5063
NDM, ASE
Municipal Bond Fund

Nuveen Massachusetts Premium Income
  Municipal Fund
333 West Wacker Drive
Chicago, Illinois 60606
(800) 257-8787 (800) 323-5063
NMT, NYSE
Municipal Bond Fund

Nuveen Michigan Premium Income Municipal
  Fund, Inc.
333 West Wacker Drive
Chicago, Illinois 60606
(800) 257-8787 (800) 323-5063
NMP, NYSE
Municipal Bond Fund

Nuveen Michigan Premium Income Municipal
  Fund 2, Inc.
333 West Wacker Drive
Chicago, Illinois 60606
(800) 257-8787 (800) 323-5063
NMH, ASE
Municipal Bond Fund

Nuveen Michigan Quality Income Municipal
  Fund
333 West Wacker Drive
Chicago, Illinois 60606
(800) 257-8787 (800) 323-5063
NUM, NYSE
Municipal Bond Fund

Nuveen Missouri Premium Income Municipal
  Fund
333 West Wacker Drive
Chicago, Illinois 60606
(800) 257-8787 (800) 323-5063
NOM, ASE
Municipal Bond Fund

Nuveen Municipal Advantage Fund, Inc.
333 West Wacker Drive
Chicago, Illinois 60606
(800) 257-8787 (800) 323-5063
NMA, NYSE
Municipal Bond Fund

Nuveen Municipal Income Fund, Inc.
333 West Wacker Drive
Chicago, Illinois 60606
(800) 257-8787 (800) 323-5063
NMI, NYSE
Municipal Bond Fund

Nuveen Municipal Market Opportunity Fund, Inc.
333 West Wacker Drive
Chicago, Illinois 60606
(800) 257-8787 (800) 323-5063
NMO, NYSE
Municipal Bond Fund

Nuveen Municipal Value Fund, Inc.
333 West Wacker Drive
Chicago, Illinois 60606
(800) 257-8787 (800) 323-5063
NUV NYSE
Municipal Bond Fund

Nuveen New Jersey Investment Quality
  Municipal Fund, Inc.
333 West Wacker Drive
Chicago, Illinois 60606
(800) 257-8787 (800) 323-5063
NQJ, NYSE
Municipal Bond Fund

Nuveen New Jersey Premium Income
  Municipal Fund, Inc.
333 West Wacker Drive
Chicago, Illinois 60606
(800) 257-8787 (800) 323-5063
NNJ, NYSE
Municipal Bond Fund

Nuveen New Jersey Premium Income
  Municipal Fund 2, Inc.
333 West Wacker Drive
Chicago, Illinois 60606
(800) 257-8787 (800) 323-5063
NJP, NYSE
Municipal Bond Fund

Nuveen New Jersey Premium Income
  Municipal Fund 3, Inc.
333 West Wacker Drive
Chicago, Illinois 60606
(800) 257-8787 (800) 323-5063
NJU, ASE
Municipal Bond Fund

Nuveen New Jersey Quality Income Municipal
  Fund, Inc.
333 West Wacker Drive
Chicago, Illinois 60606
(800) 257-8787 (800) 323-5063
NUJ, NYSE
Municipal Bond Fund

Nuveen New York Investment Quality
  Municipal Fund, Inc.
333 West Wacker Drive
Chicago, Illinois 60606
(800) 257-8787 (800) 323-5063
NQN, NYSE
Municipal Bond Fund

Nuveen Never York Municipal Income Fund, Inc.
333 West Wacker Drive
Chicago, Illinois 60606
(800) 257-8787   (800) 323-5063
NNM, ASE
Municipal Bond Fund

Nuveen New York Municipal Market
  Opportunity Fund, Inc.
333 West Wacker Drive
Chicago, Illinois 60606
(800) 257-8787   (800) 323-5063
NNO, NYSE
Municipal Bond Fund

Nuveen New York Municipal Value Fund, Inc.
333 West Wacker Drive
Chicago, Illinois 60606
(800) 257-8787   (800) 323-5063
NNY, NYSE
Municipal Bond Fund

Nuveen New York Performance Plus
  Municipal Fund, Inc.
333 West Wacker Drive
Chicago, Illinois 60606
(800) 257-8787   (800) 323-5063
NNP, NYSE
Municipal Bond Fund

Nuveen New York Premium Municipal
  Income Fund
333 West Wacker Drive
Chicago, Illinois 60606
(800) 257-8787   (800) 323-5063
NRY, ASE
Municipal Bond Fund

Nuveen New York Quality Income Municipal
  Fund, Inc.
333 West Wacker Drive
Chicago, Illinois 60606
(800) 257-8787   (800) 323-5063
NUN, NYSE
Municipal Bond Fund

Nuveen New York Select Quality Municipal
  Fund, Inc.
333 West Wacker Drive
Chicago, Illinois 60606
(800) 257-8787   (800) 323-5063
NVN, NYSE
Municipal Bond Fund

Nuveen North Carolina Premium Income
  Municipal Fund, Inc.
333 West Wacker Drive
Chicago, Illinois 60606
(800) 257-8787   (800) 323-5063
NNC, NYSE
Municipal Bond Fund

Nuveen Ohio Premium Income Municipal
  Fund, Inc.
333 West Wacker Drive
Chicago, Illinois 60606
(800) 257-8787   (800) 323-5063
NOH, ASE
Municipal Bond Fund

Nuveen Ohio Premium Income Municipal
  Fund II, Inc.
333 West Wacker Drive
Chicago, Illinois 60606
(800) 257-8787   (800) 323-5063
NOO, ASE
Municipal Bond Fund

Nuveen Ohio Quality Income Municipal
  Fund, Inc.
333 West Wacker Drive
Chicago, Illinois 60606
(800) 257-8787   (800) 323-5063
NUO, NYSE
Municipal Bond Fund

Nuveen Pennsylvania Investment Quality
  Municipal Fund, Inc.
333 West Wacker Drive
Chicago, Illinois 60606
(800) 257-8787   (800) 323-5063
NQP, NYSE
Municipal Bond Fund

Nuveen Pennsylvania Premium Income
  Municipal Fund, Inc.
333 West Wacker Drive
Chicago, Illinois 60606
(800) 257-8787   (800) 323-5063
NPA, NYSE
Municipal Bond Fund

Nuveen Pennsylvania Premium Income
  Municipal Fund 2, Inc.
333 West Wacker Drive
Chicago, Illinois 60606
(800) 257-8787   (800) 323-5063
NPY, NYSE
Municipal Bond Fund

Nuveen Pennsylvania Premium Income
  Municipal Fund 3, Inc.
333 West Wacker Drive
Chicago, Illinois 60606
(800) 257-8787   (800) 323-5063
NAP, ASE
Municipal Bond Fund

Nuveen Pennsylvania Quality Income
Municipal Fund, Inc.
333 West Wacker Drive
Chicago, Illinois 60606
(800) 257-8787   (800) 323-5063
NUP, NYSE
Municipal Bond Fund

Nuveen Performance Plus Municipal
Fund, Inc.
333 West Wacker Drive
Chicago, Illinois 60606
(800) 257-8787   (800) 323-5063
NPP, NYSE
Municipal Bond Fund

Nuveen Premier Insured Municipal Income
Fund, Inc
333 West Wacker Drive
Chicago, Illinois 60606
(800) 257-8787   (800) 323-5063
NIF, NYSE
Municipal Bond Fund

Nuveen Premier Municipal Income Fund, Inc.
333 West Wacker Drive
Chicago, Illinois 60606
(800) 257-8787   (800) 323-5063
NPF, NYSE
Municipal Bond Fund

Nuveen Premium Income Municipal
Fund, Inc.
333 West Wacker Drive
Chicago, Illinois 60606
(800) 257-8787   (800) 323-5063
NPI, NYSE
Municipal Bond Fund

Nuveen Premium Income Municipal Fund 2, Inc.
333 West Wacker Drive
Chicago, Illinois 60606
(800) 257-8787   (800) 323-5063
NPM, NYSE
Municipal Bond Fund

Nuveen Premium Income Municipal Fund 3,
Inc.
333 West Wacker Drive
Chicago, Illinois 60606
(800) 257-8787   (800) 323-5063
NPN, NYSE
Municipal Bond Fund

Nuveen Premium Income Municipal Fund 4,
Inc.
333 West Wacker Drive
Chicago, Illinois 60606
(800) 257-8787   (800) 323-5063
NPT, NYSE
Municipal Bond Fund

Nuveen Premium Income Municipal Fund 5,
Inc.
333 West Wacker Drive
Chicago, Illinois 60606
(800) 257-8787   (800) 323-5063
NPU, NYSE
Municipal Bond Fund

Nuveen Premium Income Municipal Fund 6,
Inc.
333 West Wacker Drive
Chicago, Illinois 60606
(800) 257-8787   (800) 323-5063
NPB, NYSE
Municipal Bond Fund

Nuveen Quality Income Municipal Fund,
Inc.
333 West Wacker Drive
Chicago, Illinois 50505
(800) 257-8787   (800) 323-5063
NQU, NYSE
Municipal Bond Fund

Nuveen Select Maturities Municipal Fund,
Inc.
333 West Wacker Drive
Chicago, Illinois 60606
(800) 257-8787   (800) 323-5063
NIM, NYSE
Municipal Bond Fund

Nuveen Select Quality Municipal Fund, Inc.
333 West Wacker Drive
Chicago, Illinois 60606
(800) 257-8787   (800) 323-5063
NQS, NYSE
Municipal Bond Fund

Nuveen Select Tax-Free Income Portfolio
333 West Wacker Drive
Chicago, Illinois 60606
(800) 257-8787   (800) 323-5063
NXP, NYSE
Municipal Bond Fund

Nuveen Select Tax-Free Income Portfolio 2
333 West Wacker Drive
Chicago, Illinois 60606
(800) 257-8787   (800) 323-5063
NXQ, NYSE
Municipal Bond Fund

Nuveen Select Tax-Free Income Portfolio 3
333 West Wacker Drive
Chicago, Illinois 60606
(800) 257-8787   (800) 323-5063
NXR, NYSE
Municipal Bond Fund

Nuveen Select Tax-Free Income Portfolio 4
333 West Wacker Drive
Chicago, Illinois 60606
(800) 257-8787   (800) 323-5063
NXS, NYSE
Municipal Bond Fund

Nuveen Texas Premium Income Municipal
   Fund, Inc.
333 West Wacker Drive
Chicago, Illinois 60606
(800) 257-8787   (800) 323-5063
NTE, ASE
Municipal Bond Fund

Nuveen Texas Quality Income Municipal
   Fund, Inc.
333 West Wacker Drive
Chicago, Illinois 60606
(800) 257-8787   (800) 323-5063
NTX, NYSE
Municipal Bond Fund

Nuveen Virginia Premium Income Municipal
   Fund, Inc.
333 West Wacker Drive
Chicago, Illinois 60606
(800) 257-8787   (800) 323-5063
NPV, NYSE
Municipal Bond Fund

Nuveen Virginia Premium Income Municipal
   Fund 2, Inc.
333 West Wacker Drive
Chicago, Illinois 60606
(800) 257-8787   (800) 323-5063
NVI, ASE
Municipal Bond Fund

Nuveen Washington Premium Income Fund,
   Inc.
333 West Wacker Drive
Chicago, Illinois 60606
(800) 257-8787   (800) 323-5063
NPW, ASE
Municipal Bond Fund

Old Canada Investment Corporation Limited
145 King Street West, Suite 2700
Toronto, Ontario, Canada M5H 1J8
(416) 865-0470
Toronto Stock Exchange
Equity Fund

Oppenheimer Multi-Government Trust
10200 East Girard Avenue, Building A, #407
Denver, Colorado 80231
(800) 255-2750   (800) 647-7374
OGT, NYSE
Bond Fund

Oppenheimer Multi-Sector Income Trust
10200 East Girard Avenue, Building A, #407
Denver, Colorado 80231
(800) 255-2750 (800) 647-7374
OMS, NYSE
Bond Fund

Pacific American Income Shares, Inc.
P.O. Box 983
Pasadena, California 91102
(800) 822-5544   (800) 368-2558
PAI, NYSE
Bond Fund

PIMCO Mortgage Securities Trust
840 Newport Center Drive
Newport Beach, California 92660
(714) 760-4743   (800) 927-4648
(800) 213-3606
PCM, ASE
Bond Fund

PaineWebber Premium High Income
   Trust
1285 Avenue of the Americas
New York, New York 10019
(212) 713-2000
PHT, NYSE
Bond Fund

PaineWebber Premier Insured Municipal
   Income Fund
1285 Avenue of the Americas
New York, New York 10019
(212) 713-2000
PIF, NYSE
Municipal Bond Fund

PaineWebber Premier Intermediate Tax-Free
   Income Fund
1285 Avenue of the Americas
New York, New York 10019
(212) 713-2000
PIT, ASE
Municipal Bond Fund

PaineWebber Premier Tax-Free Income Fund
1285 Avenue of the Americas
New York, New York 10019
(212) 713-2000
PPM, NYSE
Municipal Bond Fund

Pakistan Investment Fund
1221 Avenue of the Americas
New York, New York 10020
(212) 296-7200   (800) 221-6726
PKF, NYSE
Foreign Equity Fund

Patriot Global Dividend Fund
101 Huntington Avenue
Boston, Massachusetts 02199-7603
(617) 375-1808   (800) 843-0090
PGD, NYSE
Foreign Bond Fund

Patriot Preferred Dividend Fund
101 Huntington Avenue
Boston, Massachusetts 02199-7603
(617) 375-1808   (800) 843-0090
PPF, NYSE
Specialized Equity Fund

Patriot Premium Dividend Fund I
101 Huntington Avenue
Boston, Massachusetts 02199-7603
(617) 375-1808   (800) 843-0090
PDF, NYSE
Specialized Equity Fund

Patriot Premium Dividend Fund II
101 Huntington Avenue
Boston, Massachusetts 02199-7603
(617) 375-1808   (800) 843-0090
PDT, NYSE
Specialized Equity Fund

Patriot Select Dividend Trust
101 Huntington Avenue
Boston, Massachusetts 02199-7603
(617) 375-1808   (800) 843-0090
DIV, NYSE
Specialized Equity Fund

Petroleum & Resources Corporation
7 St. Paul Street, Suite 1140
Baltimore, Maryland 21202
(410) 752-5900   (800) 638-2479
PEO, NYSE
Specialized Equity Fund

Pilgrim Prime Rate Trust
10100 Santa Monica Boulevard, 21st Floor
Los Angeles, California 90067
(800) 336-3436   (800) 331-1080
PPR, NYSE
Bond Fund

Pilgrim Regional BankShares
10100 Santa Monica Boulevard, 21st Floor
Los Angeles, California 90067
(800) 548-4521
PBS, NYSE
Specialized Equity Fund

Pioneer Interest Shares
(formerly Mutual of Omaha Interest Shares)
60 State Street
Boston, Massachusetts 02109
(800) 225-6292
MUO, NYSE
Bond Fund

PMC Capital Inc.
17290 Preston Road
Dallas, Texas 75252
(214) 380-0044
PMC, ASE
Miscellaneous

Portugal Fund, Inc.
153 East 53rd Street
New York, New York 10022
(212) 832-2626
PGF, NYSE
Foreign Equity Fund

Preferred Income Fund, Incorporated
P.O. Box 1376
Boston, Massachusetts 02104
(818) 795-7300   (800) 331-1710
PFD, NYSE
Specialized Equity Fund

Preferred Income Management Fund,
    Incorporated
P.O. Box 1376
Boston, Massachusetts 02104
(818) 795-7300   (800) 331-1710
PFM, NYSE
Specialized Equity Fund

Preferred Income Opportunity Fund,
    Incorporated
P.O. Box 1376
Boston, Massachusetts 02104
(818) 795-7300   (800) 331-1710
PFO, NYSE
Specialized Equity Fund

Prospect Street High Income Portfolio Inc.
Exchange Place, 37th Floor
Boston, Massachusetts 02109
(617) 350-5718   (800) 426-5523
PHY, NYSE
Bond Fund

Putnam California Investment Grade
    Municipal Trust
P.O. Box 41203
Providence, Rhode Island 02940-1203
Attn: Closed-End Funds
(617) 292-1000   (800) 634-1587
PCA, ASE
Municipal Bond Fund

Putnam Dividend Income Fund
P.O. Box 41203
Providence, Rhode Island 02940-1203
Attn: Closed-End Funds
(617) 292-1000   (800) 634-1587
PDI, NYSE
Specialized Equity Fund

Putnam High Income Convertible and Bond
  Fund
P.O. Box 41203
Providence, Rhode Island 02940-1203
Attn: Closed-End Funds
(617) 292-1000   (800) 634-1587
PCF, NYSE
Convertible Fund

Putnam High Yield Municipal Trust
P.O. Box 41203
Providence, Rhode Island 02940-1203
Attn: Closed-End Funds
(617) 292-1000   (800) 634-1587
PYM, NYSE
Municipal Bond Fund

Putnam Intermediate Government Income
  Trust
P.O. Box 41203
Providence, Rhode Island 02940-1203
Attn: Closed-End Funds
(617) 292-1000   (800) 634-1587
PGT, NYSE
Bond Fund

Putnam Investment Grade Municipal Trust
P.O. Box 41203
Providence, Rhode Island 02940-1203
Attn: Closed-End Funds
(617) 292-1000   (800) 634-1587
PGM, NYSE
Municipal Bond Fund

Putnam Investment Grade Municipal Trust II
P.O. Box 41203
Providence, Rhode Island 02940-1203
Attn: Closed-End Funds
(617) 292-1000   (800) 634-1587
PMG, NYSE
Municipal Bond Fund

Putnam Investment Grade Municipal Trust III
P.O. Box 41203
Providence, Rhode Island 02940-1203
Attn: Closed-End Funds
(617) 292-1000   (800) 634-1587
PML, ASE
Municipal Bond Fund

Putnam Managed High Yield Trust
P.O. Box 41203
Providence, Rhode Island 02940-1203
Attn: Closed-End Funds
(617) 292-1000   (800) 634-1587
PTM, NYSE
Bond Fund

Putnam Managed Municipal Income Trust
P.O. Box 41203
Providence, Rhode Island 02940-1203
Attn: Closed-End Funds
(617) 292-1000   (800) 634-1587
PMM, NYSE
Municipal Bond Fund

Putnam Master Income Trust
P.O. Box 41203
Providence, Rhode Island 02940-1203
Attn: Closed-End Funds
(617) 292-1000   (800) 634-1587
PMT, NYSE
Bond Fund

Putnam Master Intermediate Income Trust
P.O. Box 41203
Providence, Rhode Island 02940-1203
Attn: Closed-End Funds
(617) 292-1000   (800) 634-1587
PIM, NYSE
Bond Fund

Putnam Municipal Opportunities Trust
P.O. Box 41203
Providence, Rhode Island 02940-1203
Attn: Closed-End Funds
(617) 292-1000   (800) 634-1587
PMO, NYSE
Municipal Bond Fund

Putnam New York Investment Grade
  Municipal Trust
P.O. Box 41203
Providence, Rhode Island 02940-1203
Attn: Closed-End Funds
(617) 292-1000   (800) 634-1587
PMN, ASE
Municipal Bond Fund

Putnam Premier Income Trust
One Post Office Square
Boston, Massachusetts 02109
(617) 292-1000   (800) 634-1587
PPT, NYSE
Bond Fund

Putnam Tax-Free Health Care Fund
One Post Office Square
Boston, Massachusetts 02109
(617) 292-1000   (800) 634-1587
PMH, NYSE
Municipal Bond Fund

Quest for Value Dual Purpose Fund, Inc.
225 Liberty Street
New York, New York 10080
(212) 374-2949   (800) 700-8258
KFV, KFVpr, NYSE
Dual Purpose Fund

Rand Capital Corporation
1300 Rand Building
Buffalo, New York 14203
(716) 853-0802
RAND, OTC
Miscellaneous

RCN Strategic Global Government Fund, Inc.
Four Embarcadero Center, Suite 2800
San Francisco, California 94111
(415) 954-5400
RCS, NYSE
Foreign Bond Fund

Real Silk Hosiery
445 North Pennsylvania, Suite 500
Indianapolis, Indiana 46204
(317) 637-5591
OTC
Specialized Equity Fund

Redwood MicroCap Fund, Inc.
2055 Anglo Drive, Suite 202
Colorado Springs, Colorado 80918
(719) 593-2111
RWMC, OTC
Specialized Equity Fund

R.O.C. Taiwan Fund
100 East Pratt Street
Baltimore, Maryland 21202
(800) 343-9567
ROC, NYSE
Foreign Equity Fund

Royce OTC MicroCap Fund, Inc.
1414 Avenue of the Americas
New York. New York 10019
(212) 355-7311   (800) 221-4268
OTCM, OTC
Specialized Equity Fund

Royce Value Trust
1414 Avenue of the Americas
New York, New York 10019
(212) 355-7311   (800) 221-4268
RVT, NYSE
Equity Fund

The Salomon Brothers Fund Inc.
7 World Trade Center, 38th Floor
New York, New York 10048
(212) 783-1301   (800) 725-6666
SBF, NYSE
Equity Fund

Salomon Brothers High Income Fund, Inc.
7 World Trade Center, 38th Floor
New York, New York 10048
(212) 783-1301   (800) 725-6666
HIF, NYSE
Bond Fund

Saloman Brothers 2008 Worldwide Dollar
  Government Term Trust
7 World Trade Center, 38th Floor
New York, New York 10048
(212) 783-1301   (800) 725-6666
SBG, NYSE
Foreign Bond Fund

Saloman Brothers Worldwide Income Fund
7 World Trade Center, 38th Floor
New York, New York 10048
(212) 783-1301   (800) 725-6666
SBW, NYSE
Foreign Bond Fund

Schroder Asia Growth Fund
787 7th Avenue, 29th Floor
New York, New York 10019
(800) 688-0928
SHF, NYSE
Foreign Equity Fund

Scudder New Asia Fund, Inc.
345 Park Avenue
New York, New York 10154
(212) 326-6200   (800) 225-2470
SAF, NYSE
Foreign Equity Fund

Scudder New Europe Fund, Inc.
345 Park Avenue
New York, New York 10154
(212) 326-6200   (800) 225-2470
NEF, NYSE
Foreign Equity Fund

Scudder Wodd Income Opportunity Fund
345 Park Avenue
New York, New York 10154
(212) 326-6200
SWI, NYSE
Foreign Bond Fund

Seligman Quality Municipal Fund, Inc.
100 Park Avenue
New York, New York 10017
(800) 874-1092   (800) 221-2450
SQF, NYSE
Municipal Bond Fund

Seligman Select Municipal Fund, Inc.
100 Park Avenue
New York, New York 10017
(800) 874-1092   (800) 221-2450
SEL, NYSE
Municipal Bond Fund

Senior High Income Portfolio, Inc.
Box 9011
Princeton, New Jersey 08543-9011
(609) 282-2800
ARK, NYSE
Bond Fund

Senior High Income Portfolio II, Inc.
Box 9011
Princeton, New Jersey 08543-9011
(609) 282-2800
SAL, NYSE
Bond Fund

Senior Strategic Income Fund
Box 9011
Princeton, New Jersey 08543-9011
(609) 282-2800
SSN, NYSE
Bond Fund

The Singapore Fund, Inc.
c/o Daiwa Securities Trust Company
One Evertrust Plaza
Jersey City, New Jersey 07302
(201) 333-7300   (800) 933-3440
SGF, NYSE
Foreign Equity Fund

Smith Barney High Income Fund
1345 Avenue of the Americas
New York, New York 10105
(302) 791-2748   (800) 852-4750
HIO, NYSE
Bond Fund

Smith Barney Intermediate Municipal Fund
1345 Avenue of the Americas
New York, New York 10105
(302) 791-2748   (800) 852-4750
SBI, ASE
Municipal Bond Fund

Smith Barney Municipal Fund
1345 Avenue of the Americas
New York, New York 10105
(302) 791-2748   (800) 852-4750
SBT, ASE
Municipal Bond Fund

Source Capital Inc.
11400 W. Olympic Boulevard, Suite 1200
Los Angeles, California 90064
(310) 277-4900
SOR, NYSE
Equity Fund

The Southeastern Thrift and Bank Fund
101 Huntington Avenue
Boston, Massachusetts 02199
(617) 375-1808   (800) 843-0090
STBF, OTC
Specialized Equity Fund

The Southern Africa Fund
1345 6th Avenue
New York, New York 10105
(212) 969-1000
SOA, NYSE
Foreign Equity Fund

The Spain Fund, Inc.
1345 Avenue of the Americas
New York, New York 10105
(800) 221-5672   (800) 426-5523
SNF, NYSE
Foreign Equity Fund

Spectra Fund, Inc.
75 Maiden Lane
New York, New York 10038
(212) 806-8800   (800) 992-3863
OTC
Specialized Equity Fund

State Mutual Securities Trust
440 Lincoln Street
Worcester, Massachusetts 01605
(800) 858-3019
SMS, NYSE
Bond Fund

Sterling Capital Corporation
635 Madison Avenue
New York, New York 10022
(212) 980-3360
SPR, ASE
Specialized Equity Fund

Strategic Global Income Fund
1285 Avenue of the Americas
New York, New York 10019
(201) 902-8314
SGL, NYSE
Foreign Bond Fund

The Swiss Helvetia Fund, Inc.
520 Madison Avenue
New York, New York 10022
(212) 486-4990
SWZ, NYSE
Foreign Equity Fund

The Taiwan Fund
82 Devonshire Street
Boston, Massachusetts 02109
(800) 334-9393
TWN, ASE
Foreign Equity Fund

Target Income Fund
2060 East Alosta Avenue, Suite 205
Glendora, California 91740
(818) 852-1033
unlisted
Bond Fund

Taurus MuniCalifornia Holdings
Box 9011
Princeton, New Jersey 08543
(609) 282-2800
MCF, NYSE
Municipal Bond Fund

Taurus MuniNew York Holdings
Box 9011
Princeton, New Jersey 08543
(609) 282-2800
MNY, NYSE
Municipal Bond Fund

TCW Convertible Securities Fund, Inc.
865 South Figueroa Street
Los Angeles, California 90017
(213) 244-0000
CVT, NYSE
Convertible Fund

TCW/DW Emerging Markets Opportunity Trust
Two World Trade Center
New York, New York 10048
(212) 392-2550   (800) 869-FUND
EMO, NYSE
Bond Fund

TCW/DW Term Trust 2000
Two World Trade Center
New York, New York 10048
(212) 392-2550   (800) 869-FUND
TDT, NYSE
Bond Fund

TCW/DW Term Trust 2002
Two World Trade Center
New York, New York 10048
(212) 392-2550   (800) 869-FUND
TRM, NYSE
Bond Fund

TCW/DW Term Trust 2003
Two World Trade Center
New York, New York 10048
(212) 392-2550   (800) 869-FUND
TMT, NYSE
Bond Fund

Templeton China World Fund
700 Central Avenue
St. Petersburg, Florida 33701
(813) 823-8712   (800) 237-0738
TCH, NYSE
Foreign Equity Fund

Templeton Emerging Markets Appreciation
   Fund
700 Central Avenue
St. Petersburg, Florida 33701
(813) 823-8712   (800) 237-0738
TEA, NYSE
Foreign Equity Fund

Templeton Emerging Markets Fund, Inc.
700 Central Avenue
St. Petersburg, Florida 33701
(813) 823-8712   (800) 237-0738
EMF, ASE
Foreign Equity Fund

Templeton Emerging Markets Income Fund,
   Inc.
700 Central Avenue
St. Petersburg, Florida 33701
(813) 823-8712   (800) 237-0738
TEI, NYSE
Foreign Bond Fund

Templeton Global Governments Income
   Trust
700 Central Avenue
St. Petersburg, Florida 33701
(813) 823-8712   (800) 237-0738
TGG, NYSE
Foreign Bond Fund

Templeton Global Income Fund, Inc.
700 Central Avenue
St. Petersburg, Florida 33701
(813) 823-8712   (800) 237-0738
GIM, NYSE
Foreign Bond Fund

Templeton Global Utilities, Inc.
700 Central Avenue
St. Petersburg, Florida 33701
(813) 823-8712   (800) 237-0738
TGU, ASE
Foreign Equity Fund

The Thai Capital Fund, Inc.
c/o Daiwa Securities Trust Company
One Evertrust Plaza, 9th Floor
Jersey City, New Jersey 07302
(800) 933-3440
TC, NYSE
Foreign Equity Fund

The Thai Fund, Inc.
126 High Street
Boston, Massachusetts 02110
(800) 221-6726
TTF, NYSE
Foreign Equity Fund

Third Canadian General Investments Ltd.
110 Yonge Street, Suite 1601
Toronto, Ontario, Canada M5 C1 T4
(416) 366-2931
Equity Fund
Toronto Stock Exchange

Transamerica Income Shares, Inc.
1150 S. Olive Street
Los Angeles, California 90015
(213) 742-4141   (800) 288-9541
TAI, NYSE
Bond Fund

Tri-Continental Corporation
100 Park Avenue
New York, New York 10006
(212) 850-1864   (800) 874-1092
TY, NYSE
Equity Fund

Triple A and Government 1995
1285 Avenue of the Americas
New York, New York 10019
(212) 713-3678   (800) 852-4750
TGA, ASE
Bond Fund

Triple A and Government 1997
1285 Avenue of the Americas
New York, New York 10019
(212) 713-3678   (800) 852-4750
TGB, ASE
Bond Fund

The Turkish Investment Fund, Inc.
PO Box 1537
Boston, Massachusetts 02205
(800) 221-6721
TKF, NYSE
Foreign Equity Fund

2002 Target Term Trust
1285 Avenue of the Americas
New York, New York 10119
(800) 457-0849
TIR, NYSE
Bond Fund

The United Kingdom Fund, Inc.
245 Park Avenue,13th Floor
New York, New York 10167
(212) 272-2093   (800) 432-8224
UKM, NYSE
Foreign Equity Fund

USF&G Pacholder Fund, Inc.
8044 Montgomery Road, Suite 382
Cincinnati, Ohio 45236
(410) 547-3989   (800) 426-5523
PHF, ASE
Bond Fund

USLife Income Fund
125 Maiden Lane
New York, New York 10038
(212) 709-6000
UIF, NYSE
Bond Fund

Van Kampen Merritt Advantage Municipal
   Income Trust
One Parkview Plaza
Oakbrook Terrace, Illinois 60181
(708) 684-6000   (800) 225-2222
(800) 341-2929
VKA, NYSE
Municipal Bond Fund

Van Kampen Merritt Advantage Municipal
   Income Trust II
One Parkview Plaza
Oakbrook Terrace, Illinois 60181
(708) 684-6000   (800) 225-2222
(800) 341-2929
VKI, ASE
Municipal Bond Fund

Van Kampen Merritt Advantage Pennsylvania
   Municipal Income Trust
One Parkview Plaza
Oakbrook Terrace, Illinois 60181
(708) 684-6000   (800) 225-2222
(800) 341-2929
VAP, NYSE
Municipal Bond Fund

Van Kampen Merritt California Municipal
   Income Trust
One Parkview Plaza
Oakbrook Terrace, Illinois 60181
(708) 684-6000   (800) 225-2222
(800) 341-2929
VKC, ASE
Municipal Bond Fund

Van Kampen Merritt California Quality
   Municipal Trust
One Parkview Plaza
Oakbrook Terrace, Illinois 60181
(708) 684-6000   (800) 225-2222
(800) 341-2929
VQC, NYSE
Municipal Bond Fund

Van Kampen Merritt California Value
  Municipal Income Trust
One Parkview Plaza
Oakbrook Terrace, Illinois 60181
(708) 684-6000   (800) 225-2222
(800) 341-2929
VCV, NYSE
Municipal Bond Fund

Van Kampen Merritt Florida Municipal
  Opportunity Trust
One Parkvlew Plaza
Oakbrook Terrace, Illinois 60181
(708) 684-6000   (800) 225-2222
(800) 341-2929
VOF, ASE
Municipal Bond Fund

Van Kampen Merritt Florida Quality Municipal
  Trust
One Parkview Plaza
Oakbrook Terrace, Illinois 60181
(708) 684-6000   (800) 225-2222
(800) 341-2929
VFM, NYSE
Municipal Bond Fund

Van Kampen Merritt Intermediate Term High
  Income Trust
One Parkview Plaza
Oakbrook Terrace, Illinois 60181
(708) 684-6000   (800) 225-2222
(800) 341-2929
VIT, NYSE
Bond Fund

Van Kampen Merritt Investment Grade
  Municipal Trust
One Parkview Plaza
Oakbrook Terrace, Illinois 60181
(708) 684-6000   (800) 225-2222
(800) 341-2929
VIG, NYSE
Municipal Bond Fund

Van Kampen Merritt Limited Term High
  Income Trust
One Parkview Plaza
Oakbrook Terrace, Illinois 60181
(708) 684-6000   (800) 225-2222
(800) 341-2929
VLT, NYSE
Bond Fund

Van Kampen Merritt Massachusetts Value
  Municipal Income Trust
One Parkview Plaza
Oakbrook Terrace, Illinois 60181
(708) 684-6000   (800) 225-2222
(800) 341-2929
VMV, ASE
Municipal Bond Fund

Van Kampen Merritt Municipal Income Trust
One Parkview Plaza
Oakbrook Terrace, Illinois 60181
(708) 684-6000   (800) 225-2222
(800) 341-2929
VMT, NYSE
Municipal Bond Fund

Van Kampen Merritt Municipal Opportunity
  Trust
One Parkview Plaza
Oakbrook Terrace, Illinois 60181
(708) 684-6000   (800) 225-2222
(800) 341-2929
VMO, NYSE
Municipal Bond Fund

Van Kampen Merritt Municipal Opportunity
  Trust
One Parkview Plaza
Oakbrook Terrace, Illinois 60181
(708) 684-6000   (800) 225-2222
(800) 341-2929
VOT, NYSE
Municipal Bond Fund

Van Kampen Merritt Municipal Trust
One Parkview Plaza
Oakbrook Terrace, Illinois 60181
(708) 684-6000   (800) 225-2222
(800) 341-2929
VKQ, NYSE
Municipal Bond Fund

Van Kampen Merritt New Jersey Value
  Municipal Income Trust
One Parkview Plaza
Oakbrook Terrace, Illinois 60181
(708) 684-6000   (800) 225-2222
(800) 341-2929
VJV, ASE
Municipal Bond Fund

Van Kampen Merritt New York Quality
  Municipal Trust
One Parkview Plaza
Oakbrook Terrace, Illinois 60181
(708) 684-6000   (800) 225-2222
(800) 341-2929
VNM, NYSE
Municipal Bond Fund

Van Kampen Merritt New York Value
  Municipal Trust
One Parkview Plaza
Oakbrook Terrace, Illinois 60181
(708) 684-6000   (800) 225-2222
(800) 341-2929
VNV, NYSE
Municipal Bond Fund

Van Kampen Merritt Ohio Quality Municipal Trust
One Parkview Plaza
Oakbrook Terrace, Illinois 60181
(708) 684-6000   (800) 225-2222
(800) 341-2929
VOQ, NYSE
Municipal Bond Fund

Van Kampen Merritt Ohio Value Municipal
  Income Trust
One Parkview Plaza
Oakbrook Terrace, Illinois 60181
(708) 684-6000   (800) 225-2222
(800) 341-2929
VOV, ASE
Municipal Bond Fund

Van Kampen Merritt Pennsylvania Quality
  Municipal Trust
One Parkview Plaza
Oakbrook Terrace, Illinois 60181
(708) 684-6000   (800) 225-2222
(800) 341-2929
VPQ, NYSE
Municipal Bond Fund

Van Kampen Merritt Pennsylvania Value
  Municipal Income Trust
One Parkview Plaza
Oakbrook Terrace, Illinois 60181
(708) 684-6000   (800) 225-2222
(800) 341-2929
VPV, NYSE
Municipal Bond Fund

Van Kampen Merritt Select Sector Municipal
  Trust
One Parkview Plaza
Oakbrook Terrace, Illinois 60181
(708) 684-6000   (800) 225-2222
(800) 341-2929
VKL, ASE
Municipal Bond Fund

Van Kampen Merritt Strategic Sector
  Municipal Trust
One Parkview Plaza
Oakbrook Terrace, Illinois 60181
(708) 684-6000   (800) 225-2222
(800) 341-2929
VKS, NYSE
Municipal Bond Fund

Van Kampen Merritt Trust for Investment
  Grade California Municipals
One Parkview Plaza
Oakbrook Terrace, Illinois 60181
(708) 684-6000   (800) 225-2222
(800) 341-2929
VIC, NYSE
Municipal Bond Fund

Van Kampen Merritt Trust for Investment
  Grade Florida Municipals
One Parkview Plaza
Oakbrook Terrace, Illinois 60181
(708) 684-6000   (800) 225-2222
(800) 341-2929
VTF, NYSE
Municipal Bond Fund

Van Kampen Merritt Trust for Insured
  Municipals
One Parkview Plaza
Oakbrook Terrace, Illinois 60181
(708) 684-6000   (800) 225-2222
(800) 341-2929
VIM, NYSE
Municipal Bond Fund

Van Kampen Merritt Trust for Investment
  Grade Municipals
One Parkview Plaza
Oakbrook Terrace, Illinois 60181
(708) 684-6000   (800) 225-2222
(800) 341-2929
VGM, NYSE
Municipal Bond Fund

Van Kampen Merritt Trust for Investment
  Grade New Jersey Municipals
One Parkview Plaza
Oakbrook Terrace, Illinois 60181
(708) 684-6000   (800) 225-2222
(800) 341-2929
VTJ, NYSE
Municipal Bond Fund

Van Kampen Merritt Trust for Investment
  Grade New York Municipals
One Parkview Plaza
Oakbrook Terrace, Illinois 60181
(708) 684-6000   (800) 225-2222
(800) 341-2929
VTN, NYSE
Municipal Bond Fund

Van Kampen Merritt Trust for Investment
  Grade Pennsylvania Municipals
One Parkview Plaza
OakbrookTerrace Illinois 60181
(708) 684-6000   (800) 225-2222
(800) 341-2929
VTP, NYSE
Municipal Bond Fund

Van Kampen Merritt Value Municipal Income
  Trust
One Parkview Plaza
Oakbrook Terrace, Illinois 60181
(708) 684-6000   (800) 225-2222
(800) 341-2929
VKV, NYSE
Municipal Bond Fund

Vestaur Securities, Inc.
Centre Square West, 11th Fl. PO Box 7558
Philadelphia, Pennsylvania 19101
215-567-3969
VES, NYSE
Bond Fund

Voyageur Arizona Municipal Income Fund,
Inc.
90 South 7th Street, Suite 4400
Minneapolis, Minnesota 55402-4115
(612) 376-7000   (800) 553-2143
VAZ, ASE
Municipal Bond Fund

Voyageur Colorado Insured Municipal
Income Fund
90 South 7th Street, Suite 4400
Minneapolis, Minnesota 55402-4115
(612) 376-7000   (800) 553-2143
VCF, ASE
Municipal Bond Fund

Voyageur Florida Insured Municipal Income
Fund, Inc.
90 South 7th Street, Suite 4400
Minneapolis, Minnesota 55402-4115
(612) 376-7000   (800) 553-2143
VFL, ASE
Municipal Bond Fund

Voyageur Minnesota Municipal Income Fund,
Inc.
90 South 7th Street, Suite 4400
Minneapolis, Minnesota 55402-4115
(612) 376-7000   (800) 553-2143
VMN, ASE
Municipal Bond Fund

Voyageur Minnesota Municipal Income
Fund II, Inc.
90 South 7th Street, Suite 4400
Minneapolis, Minnesota 55402-4115
(612) 376-7000   (800) 553-2143
VMM, ASE
Municipal Bond Fund

Voyageur Minnesota Municipal Income
Fund III, Inc.
90 South 7th Street, Suite 4400
Minneapolis, Minnesota 55402-4115
(612) 376-7000   (800) 553-2143
VYM, ASE
Municipal Bond Fund

Worldwide DollarVest Fund
800 Scudders Mill Road
Plainsboro, New Jersey 08536
(609) 282-2000
WDV, NYSE
Foreign Bond Fund

Worldwide Value Fund, Inc.
P.O. Box 1476
111 South Calvert Street
Baltimore, Maryland 21203
(410) 539-3400
VLU, NYSE
Foreign Equity Fund

Zenix Income Fund, Inc.
2 World Trade Center, 100th Floor
New York, New York 10048
(212) 298-6266; (800) 331-1710
ZIF, NYSE
Bond Fund

Z-Seven Fund, Inc.
2651 W. Guadalupe, Suite B-233
Mesa, Arizona 85202
(602) 897-6214
ZSEV, Pacific, OTC
Specialized Equity Fund

The Zweig Fund, Inc.
900 Third Avenue
New York, New York 10022
(212) 755-9860   NAV: (212) 644-2188
ZF, NYSE
Specialized Equity Fund

The Zweig Total Return Fund
900 Third Avenue
New York, New York 10022
(212) 755-9860   NAV: (212) 644-2188
ZTR NYSE
Miscellaneous

4. FUTURES AND OPTIONS CONTRACTS

On the following pages, you will find a list of commodity and option contracts being traded in the United States and Canada. These contracts are listed by the exchange on which they are traded. Within each exchange, the listings are broken down into the kind of products they are: foreign currency options, futures, futures options, index options, or interest rate options. Each contract is then listed alphabetically within its category.

Contract specifications set by each Exchange and approved by either the Commodities Futures Trading Commission or the Securities and Exchange Commission are listed with each contract.

The basic facts about each futures contract include the following information, although not all of these categories are relevant to each contract.

Trading Unit: What underlying commodity or group of stocks is being traded, and the quantity.

Prices Quoted In: The form in which prices are quoted (such as cents per bushel).

Minimum Price Fluctuation: What is the smallest move, up or down, the contract can make? This is indicated first in increments that the contract can move in, and then as a dollar figure for the amount of money that the move means to the commodity trader.

Dollar Value of a 1 Cent Move: The dollars an investor will make or lose, at least on paper, if a contract moves 1 cent up or down.

Daily Contract Limit: Many exchanges do not allow prices to rise or fall beyond certain limits within a day. Such limits, if any, are shown first in the increment of the contract, and then as a dollar figure.

Settlement: The way contracts are settled when they expire. Some contracts provide for the physical delivery of a commodity. Specific rules must be followed on how and where commodities are delivered from seller to buyer. Other contracts involve no physical delivery. These contracts are settled in cash.

Last Trading Day: The last day trading can occur in a contract.

Contract Months: Although all of these contracts trade constantly, most expire in only certain months of the year. This column presents the months in which contracts expire.

Trading Hours: The hours during which a contract is traded, in local time. EST means Eastern Standard Time, CST means Central Standard Time and PST means Pacific Standard Time.

Ticker Symbol: The symbol by which a contract's current price and trading activity can be checked through an electronic price quote service.

For index, interest rate and futures options contracts, other information is given:

Exercise Limits: Each exchange limits the number of contracts one trader can take a position in, either on the long or short side of a trade.

Strike Prices: These are set both above and below the current market price of the future or index, so puts and calls can be traded in both directions. This column also gives the intervals at which strike prices are set, and when new strike prices are added.

Expiration Day: If options are not exercised, they expire. This column details when options expire.

Index By Contract (U.S.)

Amex/Oscar: Index Options (AMEX)

Anhydrous Ammonia: Futures (CBOE)

Australian Dollar: Futures (CBOT), (CME), (MIDAM), (PHLX), Foreign Currency Options, Futures Options (PHLX), Futures Options (CME)

Big Cap Index: Index Options (PHLX)

Biotechnology: Index Options (AMEX)

Black Tiger Shrimp: Futures, Futures Options (MGE)

British Pound: Foreign Currency Futures, Futures Options (CME), Futures (MIDAM), Futures, Foreign Currency Options (PHLX)

British Pound/Deutsche Mark: Foreign Currency Options (PHLX), Futures (FINEX)

British Pound/Japanese Yen: Foreign Currency Options (PHLX)

Broiler Chickens: Futures, Futures Options (CME)

Canadian Dollar: Futures Options (CME), Futures (MIDAM), Futures, Foreign Currency Options (PHLX)

Canadian Government Bonds: Futures, Futures Options (CBOT)

CBOE BioTech Index: Index Options (CBOE)

CBOE BioTech Index (LEAPS): Index Options (CBOE)

CBOE Computer Software Index: Index Options (CBOE)

CBOE Environmental Index: Index Options (CBOE)

CBOE Gaming Index: Index Options (CBOE)

CBOE Israel Index: Index Options (CBOE)

CBOE Mexico Index (LEAPS): Index Options (CBOE)

CBOE U.S. Telecommunications Index: Index Option (CBOE)

Cocoa: Futures, Futures Options (CSCE)

Coffee 'C': Futures, Futures Options (CSCE)

Computer Technology Index: Index Option (AMEX)

Copper: Futures, Futures Options (COMEX)

Corn: Futures, Futures Options (CBOT), Futures (MIDAM)

Cotton: Futures (NYCE)

Cross-Rate Deutsche Mark/Japanese Yen: Foreign Currency Futures, Futures Options (CME)

Crude Oil (Light Sweet): Futures, Futures Options (NYMEX)

Deutsche Mark: Foreign Currency Futures, Futures Options (CME), Futures (MIDAM), Futures, Foreign Currency Options (PHLX)

Deutsche Mark Currency Forward Futures: Foreign Currency Futures (CME)
Deutsche Mark/French Franc: Futures (FINEX)
Deutsche Mark/Italian Lira: Futures (FINEX)
DeutscheMark/Japanese Yen: Foreign Currency Options (PHLX), Futures (FINEX)
Deutsche Mark/Swedish Krona: Futures (FINEX)
Diammonium Phosphate: Futures (CBOT)
Eastern Catastrophe Insurance: Futures, Futures Options (CBOT)
Edible Oil Index: Futures (CBOT)
Equity (LEAPS): Index Options (CBOE)
Equity Options: Index Options (CBOE)
Eurodollars: Futures, Futures Options (CME)
European Currency Unit: Futures, Foreign Currency Options (PHLX)
Euromark (3-month): Futures Options (CME)
Eurotop 100: Futures (COMEX)
Eurotop 100 Index: Index Options (AMEX)
Eurotop 100 Options: Futures Options (COMEX)
Feeder Cattle: Futures, Futures Options (CME)
French Franc: Foreign Currency Futures, Futures Options (CME), Futures, Foreign
  Currency Options (PHLX)
FT-SE 100 Index: Index Options, (CBOE), Futures, Futures Options (CME)
Gold: Futures, Futures Options (COMEX), Futures, Futures Options (MIDAM)
Gold (kilo): Futures (CBOT)
Gold (ounce): Futures (CBOT)
Gold/Silver Index: Index Options (PHLX)
Goldman-Sachs Commodity Index: Futures, Futures Options (CME)
Gulf Coast Unleaded Gasoline: Futures (NYMEX)
Hard Red Spring Wheat: Futures, Futures Options (MGE)
Heating Oil: Futures, Futures Options (NYMEX)
Heating Oil/Crude Oil Crack Spread: Futures Options (NYMEX)
Hong Kong Index, The: Index Options (AMEX)
Institutional Index: Index Options (AMEX)
Japan Index: Index Options (AMEX)
Japanese Yen: Foreign Currency Futures, Futures Options (CME), Futures
  (MIDAM), Futures, Foreign Currency Options (PHLX)
Japanese Yen Currency Forward Futures: Foreign Currency Futures (CME)
KR.CRB Futures Price Index: Futures, Futures Options (NYFE)
Live Cattle: Futures, Futures Options (CME), Futures (MIDAM)
Live Hogs: Futures, Futures Options (CME), Futures (MIDAM)
Lumber: Futures, Futures Options (CME)
Major Market Index: Index Options (AMEX), Futures, Futures Options (CME)
Mexico Index: Index Options (AMEX)
Mini Value Line Stock Index: Futures, Futures Options (KCBT)
Midwestern Catastrophe Insurance: Futures, Futures Options (CBOT)
Morgan Stanley Consumer Index: Index Options (AMEX)
Morgan Stanley Cyclical Index: Index Options (AMEX)
Municipal Bond Index: Futures, Futures Options (CBOT)
Nasdaq-100 Index: Index Options
National Catastrophe Insurance: Futures, Futures Options (CBOT)
National Over-the-Counter Index: Index Options (PHLX)
Natural Gas: Futures, Futures Options (NYMEX)
Natural Gas Index: Index Options (AMEX)
New York Harbor Unleaded Gasoline: Futures, Futures Options (NYMEX)
New York Harbor Unleaded Gasoline/Crude Oil Crack Spread: Futures Options
  (NYMEX)

Nikkei Stock Index Average: Futures, Futures Options (CME)
Nikkei 300 Index: Index Options (CBOE)
NYSE Composite Index Options: Index Options (NYSE), Futures, Futures Options (NYFE)
NYSE Utility Index Options: Index Options (NYSE)
Oats: Futures, Futures Options (CBOT), Futures (MIDAM)
OEX CAPS: Index Options (CBOE)
OEX (LEAPS): Index Options (CBOE)
OEX S&P 100 Index: Index Options (CBOE)
Oil Index: Index Option (AMEX)
One-Month Libor: Futures, Futures Options (AMEX)
One-Year U.S. Treasury Bill: Futures, Futures Options (AMEX)
Orange Juice: Futures (NYCE)
Palladium: Futures (NYMEX)
Pharmaceutical Index: Index Option (AMEX)
PHLX/Keefe Bruyette & Woods, Inc. Bank Index: Index Options (PHLX)
Phone Index: Index Options (PHLX)
Platinum: Futures, Futures Options (NYMEX), Futures (MIDAM)
Pork Bellies: Futures, Futures Options (AMEX)
Propane: Futures (NYMEX)
Rolling Spot Deutsche Mark: Foreign Currency Futures, Futures Options (CME)
Rolling Spot Japanese Yen: Foreign Currency Futures, Futures Options (CME)
Rolling Spot Pound Sterling: Futures Options (AMEX)
Rough Rice: Futures, Futures Options (CBOT)
Russell 2000 Index: Index Options (CBOE), Futures, Futures Options (CME)
Russell 2000 Index (LEAPS): Index Options (CBOE)
S&P Banks Index: Index Options (CBOE)
S&P Chemical Index: Index Options (CBOE)
S&P 500 Stock Index: Futures, Futures Options (CME)
S&P Healthcare Index: Index Options (CBOE)
S&P Insurance Index: Index Options (CBOE)
S&P Retail Index: Index Options (CBOE)
S&P Transportation Index: Index Options (CBOE)
SPQ (S&P 500 Index End-of-Quarter Options): Index Options (CBOE)
Securities Broker/Dealer Index: Index Options (AMEX)
Semiconductor Index: Index Options (PHLX)
S&P MidCap 400 Index: Index Options (AMEX), Futures, Futures Options (CME)
Silver: Futures, Futures Options (CBOT), Futures Options (COMEX), Futures (MIDAM)
Silver (1000 ounces): Futures (CBOT)
Silver (5000 ounces): Futures (CBOT)
Soft White Wheat: Futures, Futures Options (MGE)
Sour Crude Oil: Futures (NYMEX)
Soybeans: Futures, Futures Options (CBOT), Futures, Futures Options (MIDAM)
Soybean Meal: Futures, Futures Options (CBOT), Futures (MIDAM)
Soybean Oil: Futures, Futures Options (CBOT), Futures (MIDAM)
SPL (S&P 500 Index Long Dated Options): Index Options (CBOE)
SPX CAPS: Index Options (CBOE)
Sugar: Futures Options (CSCE)
Sugar Number 11: Futures (CSCE)
Sugar Number 14: Futures (CSCE)
Swaps (3-year): Futures, Futures Options (CBOT)
Swaps (5-year): Futures, Futures Options (CBOT)

Swiss Franc: Foreign Currency Futures, Futures Options (CME), Futures (MIDAM), Futures, Foreign Currency Options (PHLX)
Structural Panel Index: Futures (CBOT)
Telegraph Ltd Israel Index: Index Options (NYSE)
Thirty-Day Interest Rate: Futures (CBOT)
Three-Month Euromark Futures: Foreign Currency Futures (CME)
Treasury Bill: Interest Rate Options (CBOE), Futures Options (CME), Futures (MIDAM)
Treasury Bonds: Futures, Futures Options, (CBOT), Interest Rate Options (CBOE), Futures (MIDAM)
Treasury Notes (5-year): Futures, Futures Options (CBOT), Interest Rate Options (CBOE)
Treasury Notes (10-year): Futures, Futures Options (CBOT), Interest Rate Options (CBOE)
Treasury Notes (2-year): Futures, Futures Options (CBOT)
U.S. Dollar/British Pound: Futures (FINEX)
U.S. Dollar/Canadian: Futures (FINEX)
U.S. Dollar/Deutsche Mark: Futures (FINEX)
U.S. Dollar/Japanese Yen: Futures (FINEX)
U.S. Dollar/Swiss Franc: Futures (FINEX)
U.S. Dollar Index: Futures, Futures Options (FINEX)
U.S. Treasury Note (5-year): Futures (FINEX)
Utility Index:
Value Line Composite Index: Index Options (PHLX)
Value Line Maxi Index: Futures (KCBT)
Value Line Mini Index: Futures (KCBT)
Western Catastrophe Insurance: Futures, Futures Options (CBOT)
Western Catastrophe Insurance (Annual): Futures, Futures Options (CBOT)
Western Natural Gas: Futures, Futures Options (KCBT)
Wheat: Futures, Futures Options (CBOT), Futures, Futures Options (KCBT), Futures, Futures Options (MIDAM)
White Shrimp: Futures, Futures Options (MGE)
Wilshire Small Cap Index: Index Options (NYSE)
World White Sugar: Futures (CSCE)

Key To Abbreviations of U.S. Exchanges:

AMEX: American Stock Exchange
CBOE: Chicago Board Options Exchange
CBOT: Chicago Board of Trade
CME: Chicago Mercantile Exchange
COMEX: Commodity Exchange, Inc.
CRCE: Chicago Rice and Cotton Exchange
CSCE: Coffee, Sugar, and Cocoa Exchange
KCBT: Kansas City Board of Trade
MGE: Minneapolis Grain Exchange
MIDAM: MidAmerica Commodity Exchange
NYCE: New York Cotton Exchange
    [Also FINEX]
NYFE: New York Futures Exchange
NYMEX: New York Mercantile Exchange
NYSE: New York Stock Exchange
PHSE: Philadelphia Stock Exchange
PSE: Pacific Stock Exchange

Index By Contract (International)

Alberta Feed Barley: futures (WCE)
All Ordinaries Share Price Index: futures (SFE); futures options (SFE)
Aluminum, Primary and High Grade: futures (LME); futures options (LME)
American Soybeans: futures (TGE)
Australian Dollar: futures (SFE); futures options (SFE)
Australian 90-day Bank Accepted Bills: futures (SFE); futures options (SFE)
Australian 10-year Treasury Bond: futures (SFE); futures options (SFE)
Australian 3-year Treasury Bond: futures (SFE); futures options (SFE)
Baltic Freight Index: futures (BFE)
Barclays Share Price Index: futures (NZFE)
Barley: futures (BFE); futures options (BFE)
Bond Index: futures options (EOE)
Brazilian Coffee: futures (BMF)
Brazilian Domestic 60 and 90-day CD's: futures (BMF)
Brazilian Treasury Bonds: futures (BMF); futures options (BMF)
Brent Blend Crude Oil: futures (IPE)
British Pound: futures (LIFFE), (SIMEX); futures options: (EOE), (LIFFE)
Broilers (Frozen and Chilled): futures (BMF)
Canadian 3-month Bankers Acceptance: futures (ME)
Canadian Bonds: futures (ME); futures options (TFE)
Canadian Dollar: futures (ME); futures options (VSE)
Canadian Treasury Bills: futures (ME, TFE)
Canola/Rapeseed: futures (WCE)
Cattle: futures (BFE, SFE)
Chinese Soybeans: futures (TGE)
Cocoa: futures (FOX), (KLCE); futures options (FOX)
Cocoa Beans: futures (PFE)
Cocoa Butter: futures (PFE)
Coffee: futures (FOX, PFE); futures options (FOX)
Copper (Grade A and Standard): futures (LME); futures options (LME)
Cotton Yarn: futures (TCE)
Crude Oil: futures (IPE)
Crude Palm Oil: futures (KLCE)
Deutsche Mark: futures (LIFFE, SIMEX); futures options (SIMEX)
Domestic Feed Barley: futures (WCE)
Domestic Feed Oats: futures (WCE)
Domestic Feed Wheat: futures (WCE)
Dutch Government Bonds: futures options: (EOE)
Dutch Guilder Bond Future: futures (FTA)
EEC Barley: futures (BFE); futures options (BFE)
EEC Wheat: futures (BFE); futures options (BFE)
EOE Stock Index: futures options (EOE)
Eurodollar 90-day Time Deposit: futures (SIMEX); futures options (SIMEX)
Eurodollar 3-month Time Deposit: futures (LIFFE), (SFE); futures options (LIFFE)
Financial Times Stock Exchange 100 Index (FTSE): futures (LIFFE); futures options (ISE)
Flaxseed: futures (WCE)
French Government National Bond: futures (MATIF); futures options (MATIF)
French Treasury 90-day Bill: futures (MATIF)
Gas Oil: futures (IPE); futures options (IPE)
German Government Bond: futures (LIFFE)
Gold: futures (BMF, HKFE, ME, SFE, TCE); futures options (BMF, EOE, VSE)

Hang Seng Index: futures (HKFE)
Japanese Government Bond: futures (LIFFE)
Japanese 10-year and 20-year Government Bond: futures (TSE)
Japanese Soybeans: futures (TGE)
Japanese Yen: futures (LIFFE, SIMEX); futures options (SIMEX)
Lead: futures (LME); futures options (LME)
Live Cattle: futures (BFE, BMF, SFE)
Live Hogs: futures (BMF)
Lumber: futures (ME)
Major Market Index: futures options (EOE)
New Zealand Dollar: futures (NZFE)
New Zealand 5-year Government Stock Number 2: futures (NZFE)
New Zealand 90-day Bank Accepted Bills: futures (NZFE)
Nickel: futures (LME); futures options (LME)
Nikkei Stock Average: futures (OSE, SIMEX)
Oats: futures (WCE)
OMX Index: futures (SOM); futures options (SOM)
Oil and Gas Stock Index: futures (TFE)
Osaka Stock Futures 50: futures (OSE)
Pig: futures (BFE)
Platinum: futures (ME, TCE); futures options (VSE)
Potato Starch: futures (TGE)
Potatoes: futures (BFE, LPFM); futures options (BFE)
Rapeseed: futures (WCE)
Red Beans: futures (TGE)
Robusta Coffee: futures (PFE)
Rubber: futures (KLCE, TCE)
Rye: futures (WCE)
Sao Paulo Stock Exchange Index: futures (BMF)
Silver: futures (LME, TCE); futures options (EOE, TFE, VSE)
Soybeans: futures (HKFE)
Soybean Meal: futures (BFE)
Sugar: futures (FOX, HKFE, TSUE); futures options (FOX)
Swedish 5-year Treasury Note: futures options (SOM)
Swiss Franc: futures (LIFFE)
SX 16 Stock Index: futures (SOFE); futures options (SOFE)
Tin: futures (KLCE)
Tokyo Stock Price Index: futures (TSE)
Toronto 35 Index: futures (TFE); futures options (TSEX)
TSE 300 Spot Contract: futures (TFE)
United Kingdom, Long Gilt: futures (LIFFE); futures options (LIFFE)
United Kingdom LTOM 63 Equity Options: futures options (ISE)
United Kingdom Medium Gilt: futures (LIFFE)
United Kingdom Short Gilt: futures (LIFFE)
United Kingdom 3-month Sterling: futures (LIFFE); futures options (LIFFE)
United States Dollar: futures (BMF, NZFE, TFE); futures options (BMF, EOE)
United States Dollar: futures (BMF, NZFE); futures options (BMF, EOE)
United States Dollar-Deutsche Mark: futures options (ISE)
United States Dollar-Deutsche Mark Currency: futures (SFE); futures options (LIFFE)
United States Dollar-Sterling: futures options (ISE)
United States Treasury Bond: futures (LIFFE, SFE); futures options (LIFFE)
Wheat: futures (BFE, WCE)

White Beans: futures (TGE)
White Sugar: futures (PFE)
Wool: futures (SFE)
Woolen Yarn: futures (TCE)
Zinc (High Grade): futures (LME); futures options (LME)

Key to Abbreviations of International Exchanges

BFE: Baltic Futures Exchange (Britain)
[includes Baltic International Freight Futures Exchange, London Grain Futures Market, London Meat Futures Market, London Potato Futures Market, Soya Bean Meal Futures Association]
BMF: Bolsa Mercantil & De Futuros (Brazil)
EOE: European Options Exchange (The Netherlands)
FOX: London Futures and Options Exchange (Britain)
FTA: Financiale Terminjmarkt Amsterdam (The Netherlands)
HKFE: Hong Kong Futures Exchange (Hong Kong)
KLCE: Kuala Lumpur Commodity Exchange (Malaysia)
IPE: International Petroleum Exchange of London (Britain)
ISE: International Stock Exchange (Britain)
LIFFE: London International Financial Futures Exchange
LME: London Metal Exchange
LPFM: Lille Potato Futures Market (France)
MATIF: Marche A Terme Des Instrument Financiers (France)
ME: Montreal Exchange (Canada)
NZFE: New Zealand Futures Exchange
OSE: Osaka Securities Exchange (Japan)
PFE: Paris Futures Exchange (France)
SFE: Sydney Futures Exchange (Australia)
SIMEX: Singapore International Monetary Exchange (Singapore)
SOFE: Swedish Options and Futures Exchange (Sweden)
SOM: Stockholm Options Market (Sweden)
TCE: Tokyo Commodity Exchange (Japan)
TFE: Toronto Futures Exchange (Canada)
TGE: Tokyo Grain Exchange (Japan)
TSE: Tokyo Stock Exchange (Japan)
TSEX: Toronto Stock Exchange (Canada)
TSUE: Tokyo Sugar Exchange
VSE: Vancouver Stock Exchange (Canada)
WCE: Winnipeg Commodity Exchange (Canada)

UNITED STATES SECURITIES, FUTURES AND OPTIONS EXCHANGES

American Stock Exchange (AMEX)

Index Options

Contract	Underlying Index	Trading Unit	Prices Quoted In	Minimum Price Fluctuation
• AMEX/Oscar Gruss Israel Index	highly capitalized companies with major business interests in Israel	index × $100	index points	$1/16$ up to 3 $1/8$ over 3
• Biotechnology Index	cross-section of major bio-technology companies	index × $100	index points	$1/16$ up to 3 $1/8$ over 3
• Computer Technology Index	major computer stocks	index × $100	index points	$1/16$ up to 3 $1/8$ over 3
• Eurotop 100 Index	most actively traded stocks on Europe's major stock exchanges	index × $100	index points	$1/16$ up to 3 $1/8$ over 3
• The Hong Kong Index	broad market index measuring price perform-ance of 30 stocks actively traded on the Hong Kong Stock Exchange	index × $100	index points	$1/16$ up to 3 $1/8$ over 3
• Institutional Index	75 major Institutional Holdings	index × $100	index points	$1/16$ up to 3 $1/8$ over 3
• Japan Index	aggregate performance of 210 common stocks actively traded on Tokyo Stock Exchange	index × $100	index points	$1/16$ up to 3 $1/8$ over 3
• Major Market Index	20 Blue Chip Stocks	index × $100	index points	$1/16$ up to 3 $1/8$ over 3
• Mexico Index	American Depositary Receipts or U.S. shares of companies reflecting Mexico Stock Market	index × $100	index points	$1/16$ up to 5 $1/8$ over 3

Strike Prices	Settlement	Contract Months	Trading Hours (EST)	Ticker Symbol
2¹/₂ points apart	in cash	3 consecutive near-term months + 2 successive from the March cycle	9:30 a.m.-4:15 p.m.	XIS
5 points apart	in cash	3 consecutive near-term months + 2 successive from the January cycle	9:30 a.m.-4:10 p.m.	BTK
5 points apart	in cash	3 nearest months plus Mar, June, Sept, Dec	9:30 a.m.-4:10 p.m.	XCI
5 points apart	in cash	3 consecutive near-term months + 2 successive from the March cycle	9:30 a.m.-11:30 a.m.	EUR
5 points apart	in cash	3 consecutive near-term months + 2 successive from the March cycle	9:30 a.m.-4:30 p.m.	HKO
5 points apart	in cash	3 nearest months plus Mar, June, Sept, Dec	9:30 a.m.-4:15 p.m.	XII
5 points apart	in cash	3 consecutive near-term months + 2 successive from the March cycle	9:30 a.m.-4:15 p.m.	JPN
5 points apart	in cash	3 nearest months plus Mar, June, Sept, Dec	9:30 a.m.-4:15 p.m.	XMI
5 points apart	in cash	3 consecutive near-term months + 2 successive from the March cycle	9:30 a.m.-4:15 p.m.	MXY

Contract	Underlying Index	Trading Unit	Prices Quoted In	Minimum Price Fluctuation
● Morgan Stanley Consumer Index	measure performance of consumer oriented stable growth industries	index × $100	index points	$1/16$ up to 5 $1/8$ over 5
● Morgan Stanley Cyclical Index	measures performance of economically sensitive industries	index × $100	index points	$1/16$ up to 5 $1/8$ over 5
● Natural Gas Index	highly capitalized natural gas companies	index × $100	index points	$1/16$ up to 3 $1/8$ over 3
● Oil Index	major oil stocks	index × $100	index points	$1/16$ up to 3 $1/8$ over 3
● Pharmaceutical Index	cross-section of widely held, highly capitalized companies involved in the pharmaceutical industry	index × $100	index points	$1/16$ up to 3 $1/8$ over 3
● Securities Broker/Dealer Index	highly capitalized companies in the U.S. securities broker/dealer industry	index × $100	index points	$1/16$ up to 3 $1/8$ over 3
● S&P MidCap 400 Index	measure prices of 400 middle-capitalization companies	index × $100	index points	$1/16$ up to 3 $1/8$ over 3

Chicago Board of Trade (CBOT)

Futures

Contract	Trading Unit	Prices Quoted In	Minimum Price Fluctuation
● Anhydrous Ammonia	100 tons	dollars & 10 cents per ton	$.10 per ton
● Canadian Government Bonds	$100,000 of Canadian Government Bonds	points & $1/100$ points	$1/100$ points

Strike Prices	Settlement	Contract Months	Trading Hours (EST)	Ticker Symbol
5 points apart	in cash	3 consecutive near-term months + 2 successive months from the March cycle	9:30 a.m.-4:15 p.m.	CMR
5 points apart	in cash	3 consecutive near-term months + 2 successive months from the March cycle	9:30 a.m.-4:15 p.m.	CYC
5 points apart	in cash	3 consecutive near-term months + 2 successive months from the January cycle	9:30 a.m.-4:10 p.m.	XNG
5 points apart	in cash	3 nearest months plus Jan, Apr, July, Oct	9:30 a.m.-4:10 p.m.	XOI
5 points apart	in cash	3 consecutive near-term months + 2 successive months from the January cycle	9:30 a.m.-4:10 p.m.	DRG
5 points apart	in cash	3 consecutive near-term months + 2 successive months from the January cycle	9:30 a.m.-4:10 p.m.	XBD
5 points apart	in cash	up to 4 consecutive near-term months + 2 further term expiration months from the March cycle	9:30 a.m.-4:15 p.m.	MID

Daily Contract Limit	Contract Months	Trading Hours (CST)	Ticker Symbol
$10 per ton	Feb, Apr, June, Sept, Dec	10:00 a.m.-1:00 p.m.	NZ
300 points	Mar, June, Sept, Dec	7:20 a.m.-2:00 p.m.	CN

Contract	Trading Unit	Prices Quoted In	Minimum Price Fluctuation
• Corn	5000 bushels	cents & 1/4 cents a bushel	1/4 cent, ($12.50)
• Diammonium Phosphate	100 tons	dollars & ten cents per ton	$.10 per ton
• Eastern Catastrophe Insurance	$25,000 × ratio of aggregate losses to premium	points and 1/10 point	1/10 points
• Edible Oil Index	100 metric tons × price of International Edible Oils Index	dollars & cents per metric ton of 1,000 kilos in multiples of 25 cents per metric ton	$.25 per metric ton
• Gold (Kilo)	1 kilogram (32.15 troy ounces)	dollars & cents per troy ounce	10 cents a troy ounce ($3.22)
• Gold (Ounce)	100 troy ounces	dollars & cents per troy ounce	10 cents a troy ounce ($10)
• Midwestern Catastrophe Insurance	$25,000 × ratio of aggregate loses to premium	points & 1/10 point	1/10 points
• Municipal Bond Index	Bond Buyer Muni Index × $1000	full points & 32nds of a point	1/32 of a point ($31.25)
• National Catastrophe Insurance	$25,000 × ratio of aggregate losses to premium	points and 1/10 point	1/10 point
• Oats	5000 bushels	cents and 1/4 cents per bushel	1/4 cent a bushel
• Rough Rice	2,000 hundred-weight	dollars and 1/2 cents a hundredweight	$.005 per hundredweight
• Silver (1000 Ounces)	1000 troy ounces	dollars and cents a troy ounce	1/10 cent a troy ounce
• Silver (5000 Ounces)	5000 troy ounces	dollars and cents a troy ounce	1/10 cent a troy ounce
• Soybeans	5000 bushels	cents and 1/4 cents a bushel	1/4 of a bushel ($12.50)
• Soybean Meal	100 tons (200,000 pounds)	dollars & cents a ton	10 cents a ton

Daily Contract Limit	Contract Months	Trading Hours (CST)	Ticker Symbol
10 cents ($500)	Mar, May, July, Sept, Dec	9:30 a.m.-1:15 p.m.	C
$10 per ton	Jan, Feb, Mar, June, Sept, Dec	9:00 a.m.-12:15 p.m.	FZ
10 points	Mar, June, Sept, Dec	8:30 a.m.-12:30 p.m.	UE
$25 per metric ton	Feb, May, Aug, Nov	7:25 a.m.-1:25 p.m.	VO
$50 a troy ounce ($1,607.50)	3 nearest months and Feb, Apr, June, Aug, Oct, Dec	7:20 a.m.-1:40 p.m	KI
$50 a troy ounce ($5,000)	3 nearest months and Feb, Apr, June, Aug, Oct, Dec	7:20 a.m.-1:40 p.m. 5:00 p.m.-9:30 p.m.	GH
10 points	Mar, June, Sept, Dec	8:30 a.m.-12:30 p.m.	UM
96/32 per contract ($3000)	Mar, June, Sept, Dec	7:20 a.m.-2:00 p.m.	MB
10 points	Mar, June, Sept, Dec	8:30 a.m.-12:30 p.m.	UN
10 cents a bushel ($500)	Mar, May, July, Sept, Dec	9:30 a.m.-1:15 p.m.	O
30 cents per hundredweight	Jan, Mar, May, July, Sept, Nov	9:15 a.m.-1:30 p.m.	RR
$1 a troy ounce	3 nearest months and Feb, Apr, June, Aug, Oct, Dec	7:25 a.m.-1:25 p.m.	AG
$1 a troy ounce	3 nearest months and Feb, Apr, June, Aug, Oct, Dec	7:25 a.m.-1:25 p.m. 5:00 p.m.-9:30 p.m.	SV
30 cents a bushel ($1500)	Jan, Mar, May, July, Aug, Sept, Nov	9:30 a.m.-1:15 p.m.	S
$10 a ton ($1000)	Jan, Mar, May, July, Aug, Sept, Oct	9:30 a.m.-1:15 p.m.	SM

Contract	Trading Unit	Prices Quoted In	Minimum Price Fluctuation
• Soybean Oil	60,000 pounds	dollars & cents per hundredweight	$1/100$ of a cent per pound ($6)
• Swaps (3-year)	$25 × fixed rate yield in 1/2 points on generic 5 year interest rate Swaps	points & $1/2$ point	$1/2$ points
• Swaps (5-year)	$25 × fixed rate yield in 1/2 points on generic 5 year interest rate Swaps	points & $1/2$ point	$1/2$ points
• Structural Panel Index	100,000 square feet of structural panels	dollars & 10 cents per square foot	$.10 per square foot
• 30-Day Interest Rate	$5 million	$41.67 per basis point	$1/100$ of a percent ($41.67)
• Treasury Bonds	$100,000 of Treasury bond 8% coupon	full points and 32nds of a point	$1/32$ of a point ($31.25)
• Treasury Notes (5-year)	$100,000 of Treasury notes	32nds of a point	$1/2$ of $1/32$ of a point ($15.63)
• Treasury Notes (10-year)	$100,000 of Treasury notes	full points and 32nds of a point	$1/32$ of a point ($31.25)
• Treasury Notes (2-year)	$200,000 of Treasury notes	points, $1/32$ points and .25 $1/32$ points	.25 $1/32$ points
• Western Catastrophe Insurance	$25,000 × ratio of aggregate losses to premium	points and $1/10$ point	$1/10$ point
• Western Catastrophe Insurance (Annual)	$25,000 × ratio of aggregate losses to premium	points and $1/10$ point	$1/10$ point
• Wheat	5000 bushels	cents and $1/4$ cents a bushel	$1/4$ of a cent a bushel ($12.50)

Futures Options

Contract	Trading Unit	Prices Quoted In	Minimum Price Fluctuation	Strike Prices
Canadian Government Bonds	1 corresponding future	points & 1/100 points	$1/100$ point	1 point apart
Corn	1 CBT corn futures contract	1/8 cent ($50)	$1/8$ point ($6.25)	10 cents apart

Daily Contract Limit	Contract Months	Trading Hours (CST)	Ticker Symbol
1 cent per pound ($600)	Jan, Mar, May, July, Aug, Sept, Oct	9:30 a.m.-1:15 p.m.	BO
100 points	Mar, June, Sept, Dec	7:20 a.m.-2:00 p.m.	SQ
100 points	Mar, June, Sept, Dec	7:20 a.m.-2:00 p.m.	SZ
$15 per square foot	Jan, Mar, May, July, Sept, Nov	10:00 a.m.-1:00 p.m.	PI
150 basis points	1st 7 calendar months and 2 from Mar, June, Sept, Dec	7:20 a.m.-2:00 p.m.	FF
$96/32$ of a point ($3000)	Mar, June, Sept, Dec	7:20 a.m.-2:00 p.m.	US
$96/32$ of a point ($3000)	Mar, June, Sept, Dec	7:20 a.m.-2:00 p.m.	FV
$96/32$ of a point ($3000)	Mar, June, Sept, Dec	7:20 a.m.-2:00 p.m. 5:00 p.m.-9:30 p.m.	TY
$32/32$ points	Mar, June, Sept, Dec	7:20 a.m.-2:00 p.m.	TU
10 points	Mar, June, Sept, Dec	8:30 a.m.-12:30 p.m.	UWC
10 points	Dec	8:30 a.m.-12:30 p.m.	WA
20 cents a bushel ($1000)	Mar, May, July, Sept, Dec	9:30 a.m.-1:15 p.m.	W

Expiration Day	Last Trading Day	Contract Months	Trading Hours (CST)	Ticker Symbol
Sat. after last trading day	Call CBOT	All months	7:20 a.m.-2:00 p.m.	CNC (call) CNP (put)
Sat. after last trading day	Call CBOT	Mar, May, July, Sept, Dec	9:30 a.m.-1:15 p.m.	CY (call) PY (put)

Contract	Trading Unit	Prices Quoted In	Minimum Price Fluctuation	Strike Prices
• Eastern Catastrophe Insurance	1 corresponding future	points & $1/10$ point	$1/10$ point	1 point 40 strikes ± at the money, 5 points 5-195 above 1 point
• Midwestern Catastrophe Insurance	1 corresponding future	points & $1/10$ point	$1/10$ point	1 point 40 strikes ± at the money, 5 points 5-195 above 1 point
• Municipal Bond Index	CBT Municipal Bond index futures contract	full points ($1000) & $1/64$ point	$1/64$ point ($15.63)	2 points apart
• National Catastrophe Insurance	1 corresponding future	points & $1/10$ point	$1/10$ point	1 point 40 strikes ± at the money, 5 points 5-195 above 1 point
• Oats	1 corresponding future	dollars, cents, and $1/8$ cent	$1/8$ cent	10 cents apart
• Rough Rice	1 corresponding future	dollars and $1/4$ cents/cwt	$.0025 per cent	20 cents apart
• Silver	1 CBT silver futures contract	$1/10$ cent ($1)	$1 a troy ounce ($1000)	25 cents to $20 apart
• Soybeans	1 CBT soybean futures contract	$1/8$ cent ($50)	$1/8$ point ($6.25)	25 cents apart
• Soybean Meal	1 CBT soybean meal futures contract	5 cents a ton ($5)	$1/8$ point ($6.25) ($6.25)	$10 apart
• Soybean Oil	1 CBT soybean oil futures contract	0.005 cent a pound ($3)	$1/8$ point ($6.25)	1 cent apart
• Swaps (3-year)	1 corresponding future	points and $1/4$ point	$1/4$ point	10 points apart
• Swaps (5-year)	1 corresponding future	points and $1/4$ point	$1/4$ point	10 points apart
• Treasury Bonds	1 CBT T-Bond futures contract	$1/64$ of 1% of $100,000	$1/64$ point ($15.63)	2 points apart
• Treasury Notes (5-year)	1 corresponding future	points, $1/32$ points, and .5 $1/32$ points	.5 $1/32$ points	.5 points apart
• Treasury Notes (10-year)	1 CBT T-Note futures contract	$1/64$ of 1% ($100,000)	$1/64$ point ($15.63)	1 point apart

Expiration Day	Last Trading Day	Contract Months	Trading Hours (CST)	Ticker Symbol
Call CBOT	Call CBOT	Mar, June, Sept, Dec	8:30 a.m.-12:30 p.m.	UEC (call) UEP (put)
Call CBOT	Call CBOT	Mar, June, Sept, Dec	8:30 a.m.-12:30 p.m.	UMC (call) UMP (put)
8:00 p.m. on last day of trading	2:00 p.m. on last day of trading	Call CBOT	7:20 a.m.-2:00 p.m.	QC (call) QP (put)
Call CBOT	Call CBOT	Mar, June, Sept, Dec	8:30 a.m.-12:30 p.m.	UNC (call) UNP (put)
Sat. after last trading day	Call CBOT	Mar, May, July, Sept, Dec	9:30 a.m.-1:15 p.m.	OO
Sat. after last trading day	Call CBOT	Jan, Mar, May, July, Sept, Nov	9:15 a.m.-1:30 p.m.	RRC (call) RRP (put)
Sat. after last trading day	Call CBOT	Feb, Apr, June, Aug, Oct, Dec	7:25 a.m.-1:25 p.m.	AC (call) AP (put)
Sat. after last trading day	Call CBOT	Jan, Mar, May, July, Aug, Sept, Nov	9:30 a.m.-1:15 p.m.	CZ (call) PZ (put)
Sat. after last trading day	Call CBOT	Jan, Mar, May, July, Aug, Sept, Oct, Dec	9:30 a.m.-1:15 p.m.	MY (call) MZ (put)
Sat. after last trading day	Call CBOT	Jan, Mar, May, July, Aug, Sept, Oct, Dec	9:30 a.m.-1:15 p.m.	OY (call) OZ (put)
Sat. after last trading day	Call CBOT	Mar, June, Sept, Dec	7:20 a.m.-2:00 p.m.	QY
Sat. after last trading day	Call CBOT	Mar, June, Sept, Dec	7:20 a.m.-2:00 p.m.	ZY
Sat. after last last trading day	Call CBOT	Mar, June, Sept, Dec	7:20 a.m.-2:00 p.m. 5:00 p.m.-9:30 p.m.	CG (call) PG (put)
Sat. after last trading day	Call CBOT	All months	7:20 a.m.-2:00 p.m.	FL (call) FP (put)
Sat. after last trading day	Call CBOT	Mar, June, Sept, Dec	7:20 a.m.-2:00 p.m. 5:00 p.m.-9:30 p.m.	TO (call) TP (put)

Contract	Trading Unit	Prices Quoted In	Minimum Price Fluctuation	Strike Prices
• Treasury Notes (2-year)	1 corresponding future	points, $^1/_{32}$ points and .25 $^1/_{32}$ points	.25 $^1/_{32}$ point	.25 points apart
• Western Catastrophe Insurance	1 corresponding future	points & $^1/_{10}$ point	$^1/_{10}$ point	1 point, 40 strikes ± at the money, 5 points 5-195 above 1 point
• Western Catastrophe Insurance (Annual)	1 corresponding future	points & $^1/_{10}$ point	$^1/_{10}$ point	1 point, 40 strikes ± at the money, 5 points 5-195 above 1 point
• Wheat	1 CBT wheat futures contract	$^1/_8$ cent ($50)	$^1/_8$ cent a bushel ($6.25)	10 cents apart

Chicago Board Options Exchange (CBOE)

Index Options

Contract	Underlying Index	Trading Unit	Prices Quoted In	Minimum Price Fluctuation
• CBOE BioTech Index	Biotech stocks	index × $100	points & fractions 1 point = $100	$^1/_{16}$ up to 3 $^1/_8$ over 3
• CBOE BioTech Index (LEAPS)	Biotech stocks	index × $100	points & fractions 1 point = $100	$^1/_{16}$ up to 3 $^1/_8$ over 3
• CBOE Computer Software Index	Computer stocks	index × $100	points & fractions 1 point = $100	$^1/_{16}$ up to 3 $^1/_8$ over 3
• CBOE Environmental Index	Environmental stocks	index × $100	points & fractions 1 point = $100	$^1/_{16}$ up to 3 $^1/_8$ over 3
• CBOE Gaming Index	Gaming stocks	index × $100	points & fractions 1 point = $100	$^1/_{16}$ up to 3 $^1/_8$ over 3

Expiration Day	Last Trading Day	Contract Months	Trading Hours (CST)	Ticker Symbol
Sat. after last trading day	Call CBOT	All months	7:20 a.m.- 2:00 p.m.	TUC (call) TUP (put)
Call CBOT	Call CBOT	Mar, June, Sept, Dec	8:30 a.m.- 12:30 p.m.	UWC (call) UWP (put)
Call CBOT	Call CBOT	Dec	8:30 a.m.- 12:30 p.m.	WAC (call) WAP (put)
Sat. after last trading day	Call CBOT	Mar, May, July, Sept, Dec	9:30 a.m.- 1:15 p.m.	WY (call) WZ (put)

Strike Prices	Settlement	Last Trading Day	Contract Months	Trading Hours (CST)	Ticker Symbol
5 points apart	in cash	Business day preceding settlement value calculation day (usually a Thursday)	Call CBOE	8:30 a.m.- 3:10 p.m.	BGX
2$^1/2$ points apart	in cash	Business day preceding settlement value calculation day (usually a Thursday)	Call CBOE	8:30 a.m.- 3:10 p.m.	VBG (Dec 1995) LBG (Dec 1996) Call CBOE for 1997 and later
5 points apart	in cash	Business day preceding settlement value calculation day (usually a Thursday)	Call CBOE	8:30 a.m.- 3:10 p.m.	CWX
5 points apart	in cash	Business day preceding settlement value calculation day (usually a Thursday)	Call CBOE	8:30 a.m.- 3:10 p.m.	EVX
5 points apart	in cash	Business day preceding settlement value calculation day (usually a Thursday)	Call CBOE	8:30 a.m.- 3:10 p.m.	GAX

Contract	Underlying Index	Trading Unit	Prices Quoted In	Minimum Price Fluctuation
• CBOE Israel Index	U.S.-listed Israeli stocks	index × $100	points & fractions 1 point = $100	$1/16$ up to 3 $1/8$ over 3
• CBOE Mexico Index (LEAPS)	$1/10$ CBOE Mexico Index.	index × $100	points & fractions 1 point = $100	$1/16$ up to 3 $1/8$ over 3
• CBOE Mexico Index	Equal dollar-weighted index of 10 U.S.-listed Mexican ADRs and ADSs	index × $100	points & fractions 1 point = $100	$1/16$ up to 3 $1/8$ over 3
• CBOE U.S. Telecommunica-tions Index	Domestic telecommunica-tions equities	index × $100	points & fractions 1 point = $100	$1/16$ up to 3 $1/8$ over 3
• Equity LEAPS	100 shares of common stock or ADRs listed on securities exchanges or traded OTC		points & fractions 1 point = $100	$1/16$ up to 3 $1/8$ over 3
• Equity Options	100 shares of common stock or ADRs listed on securities exchanges or traded OTC		points & fractions 1 point = $100	$1/16$ up to 3 $1/8$ over 3
• FT-SE 100 Index (Reduced Value)	$1/10$ of the Financial Times-Stock Exchange 100 Index	index × $100	points & fractions 1 point = $100	$1/16$ up to 3 $1/8$ over 3
• Nasdaq-100 Index	Capitalization weighted 100 largest non-financial securities listed on NASDAQ	index × $100	points & fractions 1 point = $100	$1/16$ up to 3 $1/8$ over 3
• Nikkei 300 Index	Cap weighted index of major equity securities traded on first section of Tokyo Stock Exchange	index × $100	points & fractions 1 point = $100	$1/16$ up to 3 $1/8$ over 3

Strike Prices	Settlement	Last Trading Day	Contract Months	Trading Hours (CST)	Ticker Symbol
5 points apart	in cash	Business day preceding settlement value calculation day (usually a Thursday)	Call CBOE	8:30 a.m.-3:15 p.m.	ISX
2¹/2 points apart	in cash	Business day preceding settlement value calculation day (usually a Thursday)	Call CBOE	8:30 a.m.-3:15 p.m.	VEX (Dec 1995) Call CBOE for 1996 and later
5 points apart	in cash	Business day preceding settlement value calculation day (usually a Thursday)	Call CBOE	8:30 a.m.-3:15 p.m.	MEX
5 points apart	in cash	Business day preceding settlement value calculation day (usually a Thursday)	Call CBOE	8:30 a.m.-3:10 p.m.	TCX
Call CBOE	in underlying stock	Business day preceding expiration date (usually a Friday)	Call CBOE	8:30 a.m.-3:10 p.m.	Call CBOE
Call CBOE	in underlying stock	Business day preceding expiration date (usually a Friday)	Call CBOE	8:30 a.m.-3:10 p.m.	Call CBOE
5 points apart	in cash	Business day preceding settlement value calculation day (usually a Thursday)	Call CBOE	8:30 a.m.-3:15 p.m.	FSX
5 points apart	in cash	Business day preceding settlement value calculation day (usually a Thursday)	Call CBOE	8:30 a.m.-3:15 p.m.	NDX
5 points apart	in cash	Business day preceding settlement value calculation day (usually a Thursday)	Call CBOE	8:00 a.m.-3:15 p.m.	NIK

Contract	Underlying Index	Trading Unit	Prices Quoted In	Minimum Price Fluctuation
● OEX CAPS	S&P 100 Index	index × $100	points & fractions 1 point = $100	$1/16$ up to 3 $1/8$ over 3
● OEX (Reduced-Value) LEAPS	$1/10$ of S&P 100 Index	index × $100	points & fractions 1 point = $100	$1/16$ up to 3 $1/8$ over 3
● OEX S&P 100 Index	Cap weighted index from broad range of industries	index × $100	points & fractions 1 point = $100	$1/16$ up to 3 $1/8$ over 3
● Russell 2000 Index (Reduced Value) LEAPS	$1/10$ of Russell 2000 Index	index × $100	points & fractions 1 point = $100	$1/16$ up to 3 $1/8$ over 3
● Russell 2000 Index	Cap weighted index of domestic equities traded on NYSE, AMEX, & NASDAQ	index × $100	points & fractions 1 point = $100	$1/16$ up to 3 $1/8$ over 3
● S&P Banks Index	Cap-weighted index of bank industry equities on NYSE & NASDAQ	index × $100	points & fractions 1 point = $100	$1/16$ up to 3 $1/8$ over 3
● S&P Chemical Index	Cap-weighted index of chemical industry equities on NYSE	index × $100	points & fractions 1 point = $100	$1/16$ up to 3 $1/8$ over 3
● S&P Health Care Index	Cap-weighted index of domestic health care industry equities	index × $100	points & fractions 1 point = $100	$1/16$ up to 3 $1/8$ over 3
● S&P Insurance Index	Cap-weighted index of domestic insurance industry equities	index × $100	points & fractions 1 point = $100	$1/16$ up to 3 $1/8$ over 3

Strike Prices	Settlement	Last Trading Day	Contract Months	Trading Hours (CST)	Ticker Symbol
Call CBOE	in cash	Business day preceding expiration date (usually a Friday)	Call CBOE	8:30 a.m.-3:15 p.m.	CPO
2^1/$_2$ points apart	in cash	Business day preceding expiration date (usually a Friday)	Call CBOE	8:30 a.m.-3:15 p.m.	OLX (Dec 1995) OCX (Dec 1996) Call CBOE for 1997 and later
5 points apart 10 points in the far-term month	in cash	Business day preceding expiration date (usually a Friday)	Call CBOE	8:30 a.m.-3:15 p.m.	OEX
2^1/$_2$ points apart	in cash	Business day preceding settlement value calculation day (usually a Thursday)	Call CBOE	8:30 a.m.-3:15 p.m.	VRU (Dec 1995) LRU (Dec 1996) Call CBOE for 1997 and later
5 points apart	in cash	Business day preceding settlement value calculation day (usually a Thursday)	Call CBOE	8:30 a.m.-3:15 p.m.	RUT
5 points apart	in cash	Business day preceding settlement value calculation day (usually a Thursday)	Call CBOE	8:30 a.m.-3:10 p.m.	BIX
5 points apart	in cash	Business day preceding settlement value calculation day (usually a Thursday)	Call CBOE	8:30 a.m.-3:10 p.m.	CEX
5 points apart	in cash	Business day preceding settlement value calculation day (usually a Thursday)	Call CBOE	8:30 a.m.-3:10 p.m.	HCX
5 points apart	in cash	Business day preceding settlement value calculation day (usually a Thursday)	Call CBOE	8:30 a.m.-3:10 p.m.	IUX

Contract	Underlying Index	Trading Unit	Prices Quoted In	Minimum Price Fluctuation
• S&P Retail Index	Cap-weighted index of domestic equities traded on NYSE, AMEX, & NASDAQ (Sector of S&P 500)	index × $100	points & fractions 1 point = $100	$1/16$ up to 3 $1/8$ over 3
• S&P Transportation Index	Cap-weighted index of domestic transportation industry equities	index × $100	points & fractions 1 point = $100	$1/16$ up to 3 $1/8$ over 3
• SPQ (S&P 500 Index End-of-Quarter Options)	S&P 500 Index	index × $100	points & fractions 1 point = $100	$1/16$ up to 3 $1/8$ over 3
• SPL (S&P 500) Index Long Dated Options	S&P 500 Index	index × $100	points & fractions 1 point = $100	$1/16$ up to 3 $1/8$ over 3
• SPX CAPS	S&P 500 Index	index × $100	points & fractions 1 point = $100	$1/16$ up to 3 $1/8$ over 3

Interest Rate Options

Contract	Underlying Security	Trading Unit	Prices Quoted In	Minimum Price Fluctuation
• Treasury Bill	13-week U.S. Treasury Bill	composite × $100	points & fractions 1 point = $100	$1/16$ up to 3 $1/8$ over 3
• Treasury Bond	30-year Treasury Note	composite × $100	points & fractions 1 point = $100	$1/16$ up to 3 $1/8$ over 3
• Treasury Note	5-year Treasury Note	composite × $100	points & fractions 1 point = $100	$1/16$ up to 3 $1/8$ over 3
• Treasury Note	10-year Treasury Note	composite × $100	points & fractions 1 point = $100	$1/16$ up to 3 $1/8$ over 3

Strike Prices	Settlement	Last Trading Day	Contract Months	Trading Hours (CST)	Ticker Symbol
5 points apart	in cash	Business day preceding settlement value calculation day (usually a Thursday)	Call CBOE	8:30 a.m.-3:10 p.m.	RLX
5 points apart	in cash	Business day preceding settlement value calculation day (usually a Thursday)	Call CBOE	8:30 a.m.-3:10 p.m.	TRX
10 points apart	in cash	Last business day of the calendar quarter	Mar, June, Sept, Dec	8:30 a.m.-3:15 p.m.	SPQ
25 points apart	in cash	Business day preceding settlement value calculation day (usually a Thursday)	Call CBOE	8:30 a.m.-3:15 p.m.	SPL
Call CBOE	in cash	Call CBOE	Call CBOE	8:30 a.m.-3:15 p.m.	CPS

Strike Prices	Settlement	Last Trading Day	Contract Months	Trading Hours (CST)	Ticker Symbol
2¹/₂ points apart	in cash	Business day preceding expiration date (usually a Friday)	Call CBOE	7:20 a.m.-2:00 p.m.	IRX
2¹/₂ points apart	in cash	Business day preceding expiration date (usually a Friday)	Call CBOE	7:20 a.m.-2:00 p.m.	TYX
2¹/₂ points apart	in cash	Business day preceding expiration date (usually a Friday)	Call CBOE	7:20 a.m.-2:00 p.m.	FVX
2¹/₂ points apart	in cash	Business day preceding expiration date (usually a Friday)	Call CBOE	7:20 a.m.-2:00 p.m.	TNX

Chicago Mercantile Exchange (CME)

Foreign Currency Futures

Contract	Trading Unit	Prices Quoted In	Minimum Price Fluctuation
● Australian Dollar	100,000 Australian dollars	U.S. dollars per Australian dollar	1 point or $.0001 per Australian dollar ($10)
● British Pound	62,500 British pounds	U.S. dollars per British pound	2 points or $.0002 per pound ($12.50)
● Cross-Rate Deutsche Mark/ Japanese Yen	125,000 Deutsche marks	Japanese yen per Deutsche mark	1 point or .01 Japanese yen per Deutsche mark (1,250 Japanese yen)
● Deutsche Mark	125,000 Deutsche marks	U.S. dollars per Deutsche mark	1 point or $.0001 per Deutsche mark ($12.50)
● Deutsche Mark Currency Forward Futures	One Rolling Spot Deutsche mark contract = $250,000	Deutsche mark per U.S. dollar	1/4 point or .000025 Deutsche marks per U.S. dollar (6.25 Deutsche marks)
● French Franc	500,000 French francs	U.S. dollars per French franc	2 points or $.00002 per French franc ($10)

Opening Price Limit (Expanded Daily Price Limit Multiple)	Last Trading Day	Contract Months	Trading Hours (CST)	Ticker Symbol
200 points (300 points)	2nd business day before 3rd Wednesday of month	Mar, June, Sept, Dec	7:20 a.m.-2:00 p.m. (RTH) 2:30 p.m.-6:50 a.m. M-T, 5:30 p.m.-6:50 a.m. Sun/hols (GLOBEX)	AD
200 points (300 points)	2nd business day before 3rd Wednesday of month	Mar, June, Sept, Dec	7:20 a.m.-2:00 p.m. (RTH) 2:30 p.m.-6:50 a.m. M-T, 5:30 p.m.-6:50 a.m. Sun/hols (GLOBEX)	BP
Call CME	2nd business day before 3rd Wednesday of month	Mar, June, Sept, Dec	7:20 a.m.-2:00 p.m. (RTH) 2:30 p.m.-6:50 a.m. M-T 5:30 p.m.-6:50 a.m. Sun/hols (GLOBEX)	DJ
200 points (300 points)	2nd business day before 3rd Wednesday of month	Mar, June, Sept, Dec	7:20 a.m.-2:00 p.m. (RTH) 2:30 p.m.-6:50 a.m. M-T, 5:30 p.m.-6:50 a.m. Sun/hols (GLOBEX)	DM
RTH - None GLOBEX - No trading during Electronic Trading Hours at price more than .1200 DM per U.S. $± Ref RTH price	2nd business day before 3rd Wednesday of month	Call CME	7:20 a.m.-2:00 p.m. (RTH) 2:30 p.m.-6:50 a.m. M-T, 5:30 p.m.-6:50 a.m. Sun/hols (GLOBEX)	FM (outrights) WM (swaps-spreads between Forwards & Rolling Spot)
500 points (1000 points)	2nd business day before 3rd Wednesday of month	Mar, June, Sept, Dec	7:20 a.m.-2:00 p.m.	FR

Contract	Trading Unit	Prices Quoted In	Minimum Price Fluctuation
• Japanese Yen	12,500,000 Japanese yen	U.S. dollars per Japanese yen	1 point or $.000001 per Japanese yen ($12.50)
• Japanese Yen Currency Forward Futures	One Rolling Spot Japanese yen contract = $250,000	Japanese yen per U.S. dollar	1/4 point or .0025 Japanese yen per U.S. dollar (625 Japanese yen)
• Rolling Spot Deutsche Mark	$250,000	Deutsche marks per U.S. dollar	1 point or .0001 Deutsche mark per U.S. dollar (25 Deutsche marks)
• Rolling Spot Japanese Yen	$250,000	Japanese yen per U.S. dollar	1 point or .01 Japanese yen per U.S. dollar (2,500 Japanese yen)
• Swiss Franc	125,000 Swiss francs	U.S. dollars per Swiss franc	1 point or $.0001 per Swiss franc ($12.50)

Opening Price Limit (Expanded Daily Price Limit Multiple)	Last Trading Day	Contract Months	Trading Hours (CST)	Ticker Symbol
200 points (300 points)	2nd business day before 3rd Wednesday of month	Mar, June, Sept, Dec	7:20 a.m.-2:00 p.m. (RTH) 2:30 p.m.-6:50 a.m. M-T, 5:30 p.m.-6:50 a.m. Sun/hols (GLOBEX)	JY
None	2nd business day before 3rd Wednesday of month	Call CME	7:00 a.m.-2:00 p.m. (RTH) 2:30 p.m.-6:50 a.m. M-T, 5:30 p.m.-6:50 a.m. Sun/hols (GLOBEX)	FE (outrights) WJ (swaps-spreads between Forwards & Rolling Spot)
RTH - None GLOBEX - No trading during Electronic Trading Hours at price more than .1200 Japanese yen per U.S. $± Ref RTH price	2nd business day before 3rd Wednesday of month	Mar, June, Sept, Dec	7:00 a.m.-2:00 p.m. (RTH) 2:30 p.m.-6:50 a.m. M-T, 5:30 p.m.-6:50 a.m. Sun/hols (GLOBEX)	RD
RTH - None GLOBEX - No trading during Electronic Trading Hours at price more than 8.00 Japanese yen per U.S. $± Ref RTH price	2nd business day before 3rd Wednesday of month	Mar, June, Sept, Dec	7:00 a.m.-2:00 p.m. (RTH) 2:30 p.m.-6:50 a.m. M-T, 5:30 p.m.-6:50 a.m. Sun/hols (GLOBEX)	N/A
200 points (300 points)	2nd business day before 3rd Wednesday of month	Mar, June, Sept, Dec	7:20 a.m.-2:00 p.m. (RTH) 2:30 p.m.-6:50 a.m. M-T, 5:30 p.m.-6:50 a.m. Sun/hols (GLOBEX)	SF

Contract	Trading Unit	Prices Quoted In	Minimum Price Fluctuation
● Three-Month Euromark Futures	Euromark Time Deposits in amount of 1,000,000 Deutsch marks	index points	.01 (1 basis) of 25 Deutsche marks per contract

Chicago Mercantile Exchange (CME)

Futures

Contract	Trading Unit	Prices Quoted In	Minimum Price Fluctuation	Daily Price Limit
● Broiler Chicken	40,000 pounds	dollars per 100 pounds	2.5 cents per 100 pounds ($10)	2 cents per pound ($800)
● Eurodollar 90-Day Time Deposit	1 million Eurodollars	index points	1 point ($25)	None
● Feeder Cattle	50,000 pounds	dollars per 100 pounds	2.5 cents per 100 pounds ($12.50)	1.5 cents per pound ($750)
● FT-SE 100 Share Index	$50 × Index	Terms of the FT-SE 100 Share Index	.5 index points ($25)	None
● Goldman Sachs Commodity Index	$250 times Goldman Sachs Commodity Index	index points	.10 index points ($25)	None
● Live Cattle	40,000 pounds	dollars per 100 pounds	2.5 cents per 100 pounds ($10)	1.5 cents per pound ($600)
● Live Hogs	40,000 pounds	dollars per 100 pounds	2.5 cents per 100 pounds ($10)	1.5 cents per pound ($600)

Opening Price Limit (Expanded Daily Price Limit Multiple)	Last Trading Day	Contract Months	Trading Hours (CST)	Ticker Symbol
None	11:00 a.m. (London time) on 2nd London bank business day before 3rd Wednesday of month	Mar, June, Sept, Dec	7:20 a.m.-2:00 p.m.	EK
200 points (300 points)	1st business day before 3rd Wednesday of month	Mar, June, Sept, Dec	7:20 a.m.-2:00 p.m. (RTH) 2:30 p.m.-6:50 a.m. M-T 5:30 p.m.-6:50 a.m. Sun/hols (GLOBEX)	CD

Dollar Value of 1 Cent Move	Last Trading Day	Contract Months	Trading Hours (CST)	Ticker Symbol
$400	Second to last Friday of contract month	Feb, Apr, May, June, July, Aug, Oct, Dec	9:10 a.m.-1:00 p.m.	BR
—	2nd London business day before 3rd Wed. of month	Mar, June, Sept, Dec, and spot month	7:20 a.m.-2:00 p.m. 2:45 p.m.-6:50 a.m. M-T (GLOBEX)	ED
$500	Last Thursday of contract month	Jan, Mar, Apr, May, Aug, Sept, Oct, Nov	9:05 a.m.-1:00 p.m.	PC
—	Business day immediately preceding Final Settlement Price day	Mar, June, Sept, Dec	8:30 a.m.-3:15 p.m.	FI
—	Fourth business day of the contract month	Feb, Apr, June, Aug, Oct, Dec	8:15 a.m.-2:15 p.m.	GI
$400	Business day preceding last 5 days of contract month	Feb, Apr, June, Aug, Oct, Dec	9:05 a.m.-1:00 p.m	LC
$400	Business day preceding last 5 days of contract month	Feb, Apr, June, July, Aug, Oct, Dec	9:10 a.m.-1:00 p.m.	LH

Contract	Trading Unit	Prices Quoted In	Minimum Price Fluctuation	Daily Price Limit
● Lumber	160,000 board feet	dollars per 1,000 board feet	10 cents per 1,000 board feet ($16)	$10 per 1,000 board feet ($1,600)
● One-Year U.S. Treasury Bill	$500,000	IMM One-Year U.S. Treasury Bill Index	.005 index points ($25)	None
● One-Month LIBOR	$3,000,000 Eurodollar Time Deposit	IMM One-Month LIBOR Rate Index	.01 index points ($25)	None
● Pork Bellies	40,000 pounds	dollars per 100 pounds	2.5 cents per 100 pounds ($10)	2 cents per pound ($800)
● S&P 500 Index	S&P 500 × $500	Terms of the S&P 500 Stock Price Index	.05 (5 points) ($25)	circuit Breakers (Call CME)
● S&P MidCap 400 Stock Price Index	$500 × Index	Terms of the S&P Midcap 400 Index	.05 index points ($25)	circuit Breakers (Call CME)
● Major Market Index	$500 × Index	Terms of the Major Market Index	.05 index points ($25)	Circuit Breakers (Call CME) (RTH) ± 10 index points ref RTH Price (GLOBEX)
● Nikkei Stock Index Average	$5 × average	Terms of the Nikkei Stock Average	5 points ($25)	Call CME
● Russell 2000 Stock Price Index	$500 × Index	Terms of the Russell 2000 Stock Index	.05 index points ($25)	Circuit Breakers (Call CME)

Dollar Value of 1 Cent Move	Last Trading Day	Contract Months	Trading Hours (CST)	Ticker Symbol
$1.60	Business day preceding 16th day of contract month	Jan, Mar, May, July, Sept, Oct	9:00 a.m.- 1:05 p.m.	LB
—	Noon (CST) day of 1st One-Year T-Bill auction in contract month	Mar, June, Sept, Dec	7:20 a.m.- 2:00 p.m. Globex 2:45 p.m.- 6:50 a.m.	YR
—	2nd London business day preceding 3rd Wednesday of contract month	Spot month plus next 5 calendar months	M-T 7:20 a.m.- 2:00 p.m. (RTH) (GLOBEX) 2:45 p.m.- 6:50 a.m.	EM
$400	Business day preceding last 3 business days of contract month	Feb, Mar, May, July, Aug	9:10 a.m.- 1:00 p.m.	PB
—	Thursday before 3rd Friday of contract month	Mar, June, Sept, Dec	8:30 a.m.- 3:15 p.m. (GLOBEX) 3:45 p.m.- 8:00 a.m. M-T	SP
—	Business day immediately preceding Final Settlement Price day	Mar, June, Sept, Dec	8:30 a.m.- 3:15 p.m. (RTH) 3:45 p.m.- 8:00 a.m. M-T (GLOBEX)	MD
—	Final Settlement Price day	1st three consecutive months and next 3 months in Mar, June, Sept, Dec cycle	8:15 a.m.- 3:15 p.m. (RTH) 3:45 p.m.- 8:00 a.m. M-T (GLOBEX)	BC
—	First business day preceding Final Settlement Price day	Mar, June, Sept, Dec	8:00 a.m.- 3:15 p.m.	NK
—	Business day immediately preceding Final Settlement Price day	Mar, June, Sept, Dec	8:30 a.m.- 3:15 p.m. (RTH) 3:45 p.m.- 8:00 a.m. M-T (GLOBEX)	RL

Futures Options

Contract	Trading Unit	Prices Quoted In	Minimum Price Fluctuation	Strike Prices
• Australian Dollar	1 Australian dollar futures contract	cents per Australian dollar	$.0001 ($10)	1 cent per Australian dollar apart. .5 cent per Aust. dollar for 1st 4 months listed
• British Pound	1 Pound futures contract	cents per pound	$.0002 ($12.50)	2.5 cents per pound apart
• Broiler Chickens	1 broiler chickens futures contract	cents per pound	$.00025 per pount ($10)	2 cents apart
• Canadian Dollar	1 Canadian dollar futures contract	cents per Canadian dollar	$.0001 ($12.50)	.005 cents per Canadian dollar apart
• Cross Rate Deutsche Mark/ Japanese Yen	1 Deutsche mark/ Japanese yen futures contract	Japanese yen per Deutsche mark	.01 Japanese yen per Deutsche mark (1,250 Japanese yen)	1.00 Japanese yen per Deutsche mark apart
• Deutsche Mark	1 Deutsche mark futures contract	cents per Deutsche mark	$.0001 ($12.50)	1 cent per Deutsche mark apart. .5 cents per Deutsche mark for 1st 4 months listed
• Eurodollars	1 Eurodollar futures contract	index points (.01 points = $25)	.01 points ($25)	25 index points apart

Expiration Day	Last Trading Day	Contract Months	Trading Hours (CST)	Ticker Symbol
Last trading day	2nd Friday before 3rd Wednesday of month	Every month	7:20 a.m.- 2:00 p.m. GLOBEX: M-T 2:30 p.m.- 6:50 a.m. Sun/hols 5:30 p.m.- 6:50 a.m.	KA (call) JA (put)
Last trading day	2nd Friday before 3rd Wednesday of month	Every month	7:20 a.m.- 2:00 p.m. GLOBEX: M-T 2:30 p.m.- 6:50 a.m. Sun/hols 5:30 p.m.- 6:50 a.m.	CP (call) PP (put)
Last trading day	same as underlying futures contract	Feb, April, May, June, July, Aug, Oct, Dec	9:10 a.m.- 1:00 p.m. Except last day of expiring contract - trading closes 1 hour earlier	BR
Last trading day	2nd Friday before 3rd Wednesday of month	Every month	7:20 a.m.- 2:00 p.m. GLOBEX: M-T 2:30 p.m.- 6:50 a.m. Sun/hols 5:30 p.m.- 6:50 a.m.	CV (call) PV (put)
Last trading day	Long dated: 2nd Friday before 3rd Wednesday of contract month. Short dated: 1st Friday after 3rd Wednesday of month	Quarterly & serial month long dated and short dated options	7:20 a.m. - 2:00 p.m.	Long dated: DJ (call) DJ (put) Short dated: QJC (call) QJP (put)
Last trading day	2nd Friday before 3rd Wednesday of month	2nd Friday before 3rd Wednesday of month	7:20 a.m.- 2:00 p.m. GLOBEX: M-T 2:30 p.m.- 6:50 a.m. Sun/hols 5:30 p.m.- 6:50 a.m.	CM (call) PM (put)
Last trading day	2nd London business day before 3rd Wednesday of month	Mar, June, Sept, Dec	7:20 a.m.- 2:00 p.m. GLOBEX: M-T 2:45 p.m.- 6:50 a.m. Sun/hols 5:30 p.m.- 6:50 a.m.	CE (call) PE (put)

Contract	Trading Unit	Prices Quoted In	Minimum Price Fluctuation	Strike Prices
• Euromark (three-month)	1 three-month Euromark Time Deposit futures contract	index points (.01 points = 25 Deutsche marks)	.01 IMM index points (25 Deutsche marks)	.25 index points apart
• Feeder Cattle	1 feeder cattle futures contract	cents per pound	2.5 cents per 100 pounds ($11)	2 cents apart, except front month which is 1 cent apart
• French Franc	1 French franc futures contract	cents per French franc	$.00002 per French franc ($10)	.25 cents per French franc apart
• FT-SE 100 Share Index	1 FT-SE 100 Share index futures contract	index points (.1 point = $5)	.5 index points ($25)	call CME
• Goldman-Sachs Commodity Index	1 Goldman Sachs Commodity Index futures contract	index points (.01 point = $2.50)	.10 index points ($25)	call CME
• Japanese Yen	1 Japanese futures contract	cents per Japanese yen	$.00001 ($12.50)	.0001 cent per yen apart, .00005 cent per yen for 1st 4 months listed
• Live Cattle	1 cattle futures contract	cents per pound	.025 per pound ($10)	2 cents apart, 1 cent apart for 1st 2 months listed
• Live Hogs	1 hogs futures contract	cents per pound	.025 per pound ($7.50)	2 cents apart, 1 cent apart for 1st 2 months listed
• Lumber	1 lumber futures contract	cents per board foot	10 cents per thousand board feet	$5 apart

Expiration Day	Last Trading Day	Contract Months	Trading Hours (CST)	Ticker Symbol
Last trading day	Mar cycle: same as underlying futures contract. Other: Friday before 3rd Wednesday of contract month	Mar, June, Sept, Dec, and serial months	7:20 a.m.-2:00 p.m.	KO
Last trading day	last Thursday of month	Jan, Mar, Apr, May, Aug, Sept, Oct, Nov	9:05 a.m.-1:00 p.m.	KF (call) JF (put)
Last trading day	Long dated: 2nd Friday before 3rd Wednesday of contract month. Short dated: 1st Friday after 3rd Wednesday of contract month	Call CME	7:20 a.m.-2:00 p.m. GLOBEX: M-T 2:30 p.m.-6:50 a.m. Sun/hols 8:30 a.m.-3:15 p.m.	Long dated: FR (call) FR (put) Short dated: QR (call) QR (put)
Last trading day	Mar cycle: same as underlying futures contract. Other: 3rd Friday of contract month	Mar, June, Sept, Dec	8:30 a.m.-3:15 p.m.	FI
Last trading day	February bi-monthly cycle: same as underlying futures contract. Other: 1st Friday of contract month	Feb, Apr, June, Aug, Oct, Dec	8:15 a.m.-2:15 p.m.	GI
Last trading day	2nd Friday before 3rd Wednesday of month	Every month	7:20 a.m.-2:00 p.m. GLOBEX: M-T 2:30 p.m.-6:50 a.m. Sun/hols 5:30 p.m.-6:50 a.m.	CJ (call) PJ (put)
Last trading day	1st Friday of delivery month	Feb, Apr, June, Aug, Sept, Oct, Dec, and serial months	9:05 a.m.-1:00 p.m.	CK (call) PK (put)
Last trading day	1st Friday of delivery month	Feb, Apr, June, July, Aug, Oct, Dec	9:10 a.m.-1:00 p.m.	CH (call) PH (put)
Last trading day	Last Friday before 1st day of month	Jan, Mar, May, July, Sept, Nov	9:00 a.m.-1:05 p.m.	KL (call) KL (put)

Contract	Trading Unit	Prices Quoted In	Minimum Price Fluctuation	Strike Prices
• Major Market Index	1 Major Market Index futures contract	index points (.01 points = $5)	.05 index points ($25)	5 index points apart
• Nikkei Stock Index Average	1 Nikkei Stock Average futures contract	index points (1 point = $5)	5 index points ($25)	call CME
• One-Month Libor	1 IMM One-Month LIBOR futures contract	index points (.01 point = $25)	.01 index points ($25)	.25 index points
• One-Year U.S. Treasury Bill	1 One-Year U.S. Treasury Bill futures contract	index points (.005 points = $25)	.005 points ($25)	.25 IMM Index points apart
• Pork Bellies	1 pork belly futures contract	cents per pound	.025 cents per pound ($10)	2 cents apart
• Rolling Spot Deutsche Mark	1 Rolling Spot Deutsche Mark futures contract	Deutsch marks per U.S. dollar	.0001 Deutsche marks per U.S. dollar (25 Deutsche marks)	.0100 Deutsche marks per U.S. dollar apart
• Rolling Spot Japanese Yen	1 Rolling Spot Japanese Yen futures contract	Japanese yen per U.S. dollar	.01 Japanese yen per U.S. dollar (2,500 Japanese yen)	1.00 Japanese yen per U.S. dollar apart

Expiration Day	Last Trading Day	Contract Months	Trading Hours (CST)	Ticker Symbol
Last trading day	Final Settlement Price day for Major Market Index futures	1st 3 consecutive months and next 3 months in Mar, June, Sept, and Dec cycle	8:15 a.m.-3:15 p.m. GLOBEX: M-T 3:45 p.m.-8:00 a.m. Sun/hols 5:30 p.m.-8:00 a.m.	BC
Last trading day	March cycle: same as underlying futures contract. Other: 3rd Friday of contract month	Call CME	8:00 a.m.-3:15 p.m.	KN (call) KN (put)
Last trading day	Same as underlying futures contract	All 12 calendar months	7:20 a.m.-2:00 p.m. GLOBEX: M-T 2:45 p.m.-6:50 a.m. Sun/hols 5:30 p.m.-6:50 a.m.	EM
Last trading day	March cycle: same as underlying futures contract. Other: Friday before 3rd Wednesday of contract month	Mar, June, Sept, Dec	7:20 a.m.-2:00 p.m. GLOBEX: M-T 2:45 p.m.-6:50 a.m. Sun/hols 5:30 p.m.-6:50 a.m.	YR
Last trading day	1st Friday of delivery month except that the Nov/Feb option terminates on 3rd Friday in Nov/Feb.	Feb, Mar, May, July, Aug, Nov	9:10 a.m.-1:00 p.m.	KP (call) JP (put)
Last trading day	Close of trading on each Friday	Call CME	7:20 a.m.-2:00 p.m. GLOBEX: M-T 2:45 p.m.-6:50 a.m. Sun/hols 5:30 p.m.-6:50 a.m.	RD
Last trading day	Close of trading on each Friday	Call CME	7:00 a.m.-2:00 p.m. GLOBEX: M-T 2:30 p.m.-6:50 a.m. Sun/hols 5:30 p.m.-6:50 a.m.	Call CME

Contract	Trading Unit	Prices Quoted In	Minimum Price Fluctuation	Strike Prices
• Rolling Spot Pound Sterling	1 Rolling Spot Pound Sterling futures contract	cents per pound sterling	.01 cents per pound sterling ($25)	1 cent per pound sterling apart
• Russell 2000 Stock Price Index	1 Russell 2000 Stock Price Index futures contract	index points (.01 points = $5)	.05 points ($25)	call CME
• S&P Midcap 400 Stock Price	1 S&P Midcap 400 Stock Index futures contract	index points (.01 points = $5)	.05 points ($25)	call CME
• S&P 500 Stock Index	1 S&P 500 futures contract	index points (.01 points = $5)	.05 points ($25)	.05 points apart
• Swiss Franc	1 Swiss franc futures contract	cents per Swiss franc	1 cent ($12.50)	1 cent per Swiss franc apart, .5 cent per Swiss franc for 1st 4 months listed
• Treasury Bills	1 T-Bill futures contract	index points (.01 points = $25)	.01 points ($25)	25 index points apart

Expiration Day	Last Trading Day	Contract Months	Trading Hours (CST)	Ticker Symbol
Last trading day	Close of trading on each Friday	Call CME	7:20 a.m.-2:00 p.m. GLOBEX: M-T 2:30 p.m.-6:50 a.m. Sun/hols 5:30 p.m.-6:50 a.m.	RP
Last trading day	March cycle: same as underlying futures contract. Other: 3rd Friday of contract month	Feb, Mar, Apr, June, Sept, Dec	8:30 a.m.-3:15 p.m. GLOBEX: M-T 3:45 p.m.-8:00 a.m. Sun/hols 5:30 p.m.-8:00 a.m.	RL
Last trading day	March cycle: same as underlying contract. Other: 3rd Friday of contract month	Mar, June, Sept, Dec	8:30 a.m.-3:15 p.m. GLOBEX: M-T 3:45 p.m.-8:00 a.m. Sun/hols 5:30 p.m.-8:00 a.m.	MD
3rd Friday of month	March cycle: same as underlying contract. Other: Friday before 3rd Wednesday of contract month	Every month	8:30 a.m.-3:15 p.m. GLOBEX: M-T 3:45 p.m.-8:00 a.m. Sun/hols 5:30 p.m.-8:00 a.m.	CS (call) PS (put)
Last trading day	2nd Friday before 3rd Wednesday of month	Every month	7:20 a.m.-2:00 p.m. GLOBEX: M-T 2:30 p.m.-6:50 a.m. Sun/hols 5:30 p.m.-6:50 a.m.	CF (call) PF (put)
Last trading day	Last Friday before 1st day of month	Mar, June, Sept, Dec	7:20 a.m.-2:00 p.m. GLOBEX: M-T 2:45 p.m.-6:50 a.m. Sun/hols 5:30 p.m.-6:50 a.m.	CQ (call) PQ (put)

Coffee, Sugar and Cocoa Exchange (CSCE)

Futures

Contract	Trading Unit	Prices Quoted In	Minimum Fluctuation	Daily Price Limit
• Cocoa	10 metric tons	dollars per metric ton	$1 per metric ton ($10)	$88 per metric ton
• Coffee "C"	37,500 pounds	cents per pound	5/100 of a cent per pound ($18.75)	6 cents per pound
• Sugar Number 11	50 long tons	cents per pound	1/100 of a cent per pound ($11.20)	1/2 cent per pound = $560
• Sugar Number 14	50 long tons	cents per pound	1/100 of a cent per pound ($11.20)	1/2 cent per pound = $560
• World White Sugar	50 metric tons	dollars per ton	20 cents per ton ($10)	$10 per ton = $500

Futures Options

Contract	Trading Unit	Prices Quoted In	Minimum Price Fluctuation	Strike Prices
• Cocoa	1 cocoa futures contract	dollars per metric ton	$1 per ton ($10)	from $50 to $200
• Coffee "C"	1 coffee "C" futures contract	cents per pound	1/100 of a cent per pound = $3.75	2 1/2 cents to 10 cents
• Sugar	1 sugar futures contract	cents per pound	1/100 cent per pound ($11.20)	from .5 of a cent to 4 cents

Last Trading Day	Contract Months	Trading Hours (EST)	Ticker Symbol
One business day prior to last notice day	Mar, May, July, Sept, Dec	9:00 a.m.- 2:00 p.m.	CC
One business day prior to last notice day	Mar, May, July, Sept, Dec	9:15 a.m.- 2:05 p.m.	KC
Last business day of the month preceding the delivery month	Mar, May, July, Oct	10:00 a.m.- 1:50 p.m.	SB
8th calendar day of the month preceding the delivery month	Jan, Mar, May, July, Sept, Nov	9:40 a.m.- 1:43 p.m.	SE
15th calendar day of month preceding the delivery month	Jan, Mar, May, July Oct	9:45 a.m. - 1:50 p.m.	WS

Expiration Day	Last Trading Day	Contract Months	Trading Hours (EST)
On last trading day at 9 p.m.	1st Friday of month before contract month	Regular Options: Mar, May, July, Sept, Dec Serial Options: Jan, Feb, Apr, June, Aug, Oct, Nov	9:00 a.m. until completion of closing period which begins at 2:00 p.m.
On last trading day at 9 p.m.	1st Friday of month before contract month	Regular Options: Mar, May, July, Sept, Dec Serial Options: Jan, Feb, Apr, June, Aug, Oct, Nov	9:15 a.m.- 2:05 p.m.
On last trading day at 9 p.m.	2nd Friday of month before contract month	Regular Options: Mar, May, July, Oct, Dec. Serial Options: Jan, Feb, Apr, June, Aug, Oct, Nov	10:00 a.m.- 1:50 p.m.

New York Mercantile Exchange (COMEX Division)

Futures

Contract	Trading Unit	Prices Quoted In	Minimum Price Fluctuation	Daily Contract Limit
● Copper	25,000 pounds	cents per pound	5/100 of a cent ($12.50)	20 cents a pound
● Eurotop 100	$100 times value of Eurotop 100 Index	hundreds of dollars per index point	0.1 index points ($10)	none
● Gold	100 troy ounces	dollars per troy ounce	10 cents per troy ounce ($10)	$75 per troy ounce
● Silver·	5,000 troy ounces	cents per troy ounce	1/10 cent per troy ounce ($5)	$1.50 per troy ounce

Futures Options

Contract	Trading Unit	Prices Quoted In	Minimum Price Fluctuation	Strike Prices
● Copper	1 copper futures contract	cents per pound	5/100 cent per pound	1 to 5 cents apart, depending on copper price
● Eurotop 100 Options	One Eurotop 100 futures contract	dollars & cents per option	.05 index points ($5)	10 index point intervals
● Gold	1 gold futures contract	dollars per troy ounce	10 cents per troy ounce	$10 to $50 apart, depending on gold price
● Silver	1 silver futures contract	cents per troy ounce	1/2 cent per troy ounce	25 cents to $1 apart, depending on silver price

Dollar Value of 1 Cent Move	Last Trading Day	Contract Months	Trading Hours (EST)	Ticker Symbol
$250	3rd to last day of month	Jan, Mar, May, July, Sept, Dec for 23 months	8:10 a.m.-2:35 p.m. NYMEX ACCESS electronic trading system: M-T 4:00 p.m.-8:00 a.m., Sumday 7:00 p.m.-8:00 a.m.	HG
—	3rd Friday of delivery month until 7:00 a.m. N.Y. time	Mar, June, Sept, Dec	5:30 a.m.-11:30 a.m.	ER
$1	3rd to last day of month	3 nearest months and Feb, Apr, June, Aug, Oct, for 23 months, & June + Dec for 60 months	8:20 a.m.-2:30 p.m. NYMEX ACCESS electronic trading system M-T 4:00 p.m.-8:00 a.m., Sunday 7:00 p.m.-8:00 a.m.	GC
$50	3rd to last day of month	3 nearest months & Jan, Mar, May, Sept for 23 months and July + Dec for 60 months	8:25 a.m.-2:25 p.m. NYMEX ACCESS electronic trading system M-T 4:00 p.m.-8:00 a.m., Sunday 7:00 p.m.-8:00 a.m.	SI

Last Trading Day	Contract Months	Trading Hours (EST)	Ticker Symbol
4th last business day of month before futures delivery	Mar, May, July, Sept, Dec	8:10 a.m.-2:35 p.m.	HX
Mar, June, Sept, & Dec: 3rd Friday of delivery month until 7:00 a.m. N.Y. time. All other months: Thursday before 3rd Friday.	Nearest two futures months and next two nearest non-regular trading months	5:30 a.m.-11:30 a.m.	EQ
2nd Friday of month before futures delivery	Feb, Apr, June, Aug, Oct, Dec	8:20 a.m.-2:30 p.m.	OG
2nd Friday of month before futures delivery	Mar, May, July, Sept, Dec	8:25 a.m.-2:25 p.m.	SO

New York Mercantile Exchange (NYMEX Division)

Futures

Contract	Trading Unit	Prices Quoted In	Minimum Price Fluctuation
● Crude Oil (Light, Sweet)	1000 barrels	dollars & cents per barrel	1 cent per barrel ($10)
● Gulf Coast Unleaded Gasoline	42,000 gallons	dollars & cents per gallon	.01 cent per gallon ($4.20)
● Heating Oil	42,000 gallons	cents per gallon	.01 cent per gallon ($4.20)
● Natural Gas	10,000 million British Thermal Units (MMBtu)	dollars & cents per MMBtu	0.1 cent per MMBtu
● New York Harbor Unleaded Gasoline	42,000 gallons	dollars & cents per gallon	.01 cent per gallon ($4.20)
● Palladium	100 troy ounces	dollars & cents per troy ounce	5 cents per troy ounce ($5)
● Platinum	50 troy ounces	dollars & cents per troy ounce	10 cents per troy ounce ($5)

Daily Contract Limit	Last Trading Day	Contract Months	Trading Hours (EST)	Ticker Symbol
$15 per barrel in 1st 2 months. $1.50-$3 in all other months	3rd business day before 25th of month preceding delivery month	18 consecutive months, plus long-dated futures as far out as 36 months	9:45 a.m.- 3:10 p.m. NYMEX ACCESS electronic trading system: M-T 4.00 p.m.-8.00 a.m., Sunday 7.00 p.m.-8.00 a.m.	CL
40 cents /gal ($16,800) for 1st 2 months, 4 cents for back months expanded to 6 cents & 20 cents	Last day of month before delivery month	18 consecutive months	9:40 a.m.- 3:10 p.m.	GU
40 cents/gal for 1st 2 months, 4 centsfor back months expanded to 6 cents & 20 cents	Last day of month before delivery month	18 consecutive months	9:50 a.m.- 3:10 p.m. NYMEX ACCESS electronic trading system: M-T 4:00 p.m.-8:00 a.m., Sunday 7:00 p.m.-8:00 a.m.	HO
None in spot month. 10 cents per MMBtu ($1000), expanded to 15 & 20 cents per month	6th business day prior to 1st day of delivery	18 consecutive months	10:00 a.m.- 3:10 p.m., NYMEX ACCESS electronic trading system: M-T 4.00 p.m.-7.00pm	NG
40 cents /gal ($16,800) for 1st 2 months, 4 cents for back months expanded to 6 cents & 20 cents	Last day of month before delivery month	18 consecutive months	9:50 a.m.- 3:10 p.m. NYMEX ACCESS electronic trading system: M-T 4:00 p.m.-8:00 a.m., Sunday 7:00 p.m.-8:00 a.m.	HU
$6 per troy ounce ($600)	4th day before end of delivery month	Mar, June, Sept, Dec	8:10 a.m.- 2:20 p.m.	PA
$25 per troy ounce ($1250)	4th day before end of delivery month	Jan, Apr, July, Oct	8:20 a.m.- 2:30 p.m. NYMEX ACCESS electronic trading system: M-T 4:00 p.m.-8:00 a.m., Sunday 7:00 p.m.-8:00 a.m.	PL

Contract	Trading Unit	Prices Quoted In	Minimum Price Fluctuation
• Propane	42,000 gallons	cents per gallon	.01 cent per gallon ($4.20)
• Sour Crude Oil	1,000 barrels	dollars & cents per barrel	1 cent per barrel

Futures Options

Contract	Trading Unit	Prices Quoted In	Minimum Price Fluctuation	Strike Prices
• Crude Oil (Light, Sweet)	1 crude oil (light sweet) futures contract	dollars & cents per barrel	1 cent ($10)	50 cents, $1, $5
• Heating Oil	1 heating oil futures contract	cents per gallon	.01 cent ($4.20)	1 cent & 2 cents
• Heating Oil/ Crude Oil Crack Spread	1:1 option on price differential between heating oil & crude oil futures	dollars & cents per barrel	1 cent per barrel ($10)	25 cents apart
• Natural Gas	1 natural gas futures contract	dollars & cents per MMBtu	0.1 cent per MMBtu ($10)	5 cents apart
• New York Harbor Unleaded Gasoline	One New York Harbor Unleaded Gasoline futures contract	dollars & cents per gallon	.01 cent per gallon	1 cent & 2 cents
• New York Harbor Unleaded Gasoline/Crude Oil Crack Spread	1:1 option on price differential between New York Harbor unleaded gasoline and crude oil	dollars & cents per barrel	1 cent per barrel ($10)	25 cents apart
• Platinum	1 platinum futures contract	dollars & cents per troy ounce	10 cents per troy ounce	$10 apart

Daily Contract Limit	Last Trading Day	Contract Months	Trading Hours (EST)	Ticker Symbol
40 cents/gal ($16,800) for 1st 2 months, 4 cents for back months expanded to 6 cents & 20 cents	Last day of month before delivery month	15 consecutive months	9:55 a.m.-3:00 p.m.	PN
$15 per barrel in 1st 2 months. $1.50-$3 all other months	3rd business day before 25th of month preceding delivery month	18 consecutive months	9:35 a.m.-3:20 p.m.	SC

Last Trading Day	Contract Months	Trading Hours (EST)	Ticker Symbol
Friday preceding futures expiration	12 consecutive months plus 3 long-dated at 18, 24, 36 months	9:45 a.m.-3:10 p.m.	LO
2nd Friday of month before delivery month	12 consecutive months	9:50 a.m.-3:10 p.m.	OH
Friday before crude oil futures	6 months plus 2 quarterly months on Mar, June, Sept, Dec cycle	9:50 a.m.-3:10 p.m.	CH
Close of business day before futures expiration	12 consecutive months	10:00 a.m.-3:00 p.m., NYMEX ACCESS electronic trading system: M-T 4:00 p.m.-7:00 p.m.	ON
Friday preceding futures expiration	12 consecutive months	9:50 a.m.-3:10 p.m. NYMEX ACCESS electronic trading system: M-T 4:00 p.m.-8:00 a.m., Sunday 7:00 p.m.-8:00 a.m.	GO
Friday before crude oil futures	6 months plus 2 quarterly months on Mar, June, Sept, Dec cycle	9:50 a.m.-3:10 p.m.	CG
2nd Friday of month before delivery month	3 months plus 2 quarterly months Jan, April, July, Oct, cycle	8:20 a.m.-2:30 p.m. NYMEX ACCESS electronic trading system: M-T 4:00 p.m.-7:00 p.m., Sunday 7:00 p.m.-8:00 a.m.	PO

Kansas City Board of Trade (KCBT)

Futures

Contract	Trading Unit	Prices Quoted In	Minimum Price Fluctuation	Daily Contract Limit
• Mini Value Line Stock Index	$100 × futures price	index points	.05 point ($5 per contract)	call KCBT
• Value Line Maxi Index	index × $500	index points	$25 per tick	call KCBT
• Value Line Mini Index	index × $100	index points	$5 per tick	call KCBT
• Western Natural Gas	10,000 MMBtu	dollars & cents per MMBtu	$.10 per MMBtu	$.10 per MMBtu. No maximum daily limit in first nearby contract month
• Wheat	5,000 bushels	cents and ¼ cents per bushel	¼ cent per bushel ($12.50)	25 cents

Futures Options

Contract	Trading Unit	Prices Quoted In	Minimum Price Fluctuation	Strike Prices
• Mini Value Line	Once KCBT Mini Value Line futures contract	index points	.05 point ($5)	integral multiples of 5 index points
• Western Natural Gas	One KCBT Natural Gas futures contract	dollars & cents per MMBtu	None	at intervals of $.05, with 5 over & 5 under the at-the-money strike price for a total of 11
• Wheat	One wheat futures contract	cents per bushel	⅛ cent per bushel ($6.25)	10 cents per bushel apart

MidAmerica Commodity Exchange (MIDAM)
[An Affiliate of the Chicago Board of Trade]

Futures

Contract	Trading Unit	Prices Quoted In	Minimum Price Fluctuation
• Australian Dollars	50,000 Australian dollars	U.S. dollars per Australian dollar	1 point ($5/pt = $5)
• British Pound	12,500 British pounds	dollars per British pound	$.0005 ($6.25)

Last Trading Day	Contract Months	Trading Hours (CST)	Ticker Symbol
3rd Friday of the month	Mar, June, Sept, Dec	8:30 a.m.-3:15 p.m.	MV
3rd Friday of the month	Mar, June, Sept, Dec	8:30 a.m.-3:15 p.m.	KV
3rd Friday of the month	Mar, June, Sept, Dec	8:30 a.m.-3:15 p.m.	MV
5 business days prior to the first calendar day of the the delivery month	18 consecutive months	8:30 a.m.-2:30 p.m.	call KCBT
8th day before end of month	Mar, May, June, Sept, Dec	9:30 a.m.- 1:15 p.m.	KW

Expiration Day	Last Trading Day	Contract Months	Trading Hours (CST)	Ticker Symbol
—	3:15 p.m. on 3rd Friday of contract month	Two nearest serial months and three nearest quarterly months	8:30 a.m.-3:15 p.m.	Calls MVC Puts MVP
Same as last trading day	Business day prior to last trading day in underlying futures contract month. Options not exercised by 4 p.m. on last trading day shall expire then.	12 consecutive months	8:30 a.m.-2:35 p.m.	Call KCBT
1st Saturday after last trading day	Friday at least 5 trading days before end of month	Mar, May, July, Sept, Dec	9:30 a.m.-1:20 p.m.	Calls WC Puts WP

Daily Contract Limit	Last Trading Day	Contract Months	Trading Hours (CST)
None	2nd business day before 3rd Wednesday of contract month	Mar, June, Sept, & Dec 1995 & 1996. Call MIDAM for later.	7:20 a.m.- 2:15 p.m. (9:31 a.m. on last trading day)
None	2 days before 3rd Wednesday	Mar, June, Sept, Dec	7:20 a.m.- 2:15 p.m.

Contract	Trading Unit	Prices Quoted In	Minimum Price Fluctuation
• Canadian Dollar	50,000 Canadian dollars	U.S. dollars per Canadian dollar	$.0001 ($5.00)
• Corn	1000 bushels	cents per bushel	$^{1}/_{8}$ of a cent per bushel ($1.25)
• Deutsche Mark	62,500 Deutsche marks	U.S. dollars per Deutsche mark	$.0001 ($6.25)
• Gold	33.2 troy ounces	dollars and cents per troy ounce	10 cents per troy ounce ($3.32)
• Japanese Yen	6,250,000 yen	U.S. dollars per yen	$.000001 ($6.25)
• Live Cattle	22,000 pounds	cents per pound	$.00025 per pound ($5)
• Live Hogs	15,000 pounds	cents per pound	$.00025 per pound ($3.75)
• Oats	1000 bushels	cents per bushel	$^{1}/_{8}$ of a cent per bushel ($1.25)
• Platinum	25 troy ounces	cents per troy ounce	10 cents per troy ounce ($2.50)
• Silver	1000 troy ounces	cents per troy ounce	$.001 of a cent per troy ounce ($1)
• Soybeans	1000 bushels	cents per bushel	$^{1}/_{8}$ of a cent per bushel ($1.25)
• Soybean Meal	20 tons	dollars per ton	10 cents per ton ($2)
• Soybean Oil	30,000 pounds	dollars per pound	$^{1}/_{100}$ of 1 cent per pound ($3)
• Swiss Franc	62,500 Swiss francs	U.S. dollars per Swiss franc	$.0001 ($6.25)
• Treasury Bills	$500,000 in 90-day T-bills	100 minus T-bill yield	1 basis point ($12.50)
• Treasury Bonds	$50,000 in 15 year T-bonds	in 32nds of a % of par	$^{1}/_{32}$ of a percentage point ($15.625)
• Wheat	1000 bushels	cents per bushel	$.0125 per bushel ($1.25)

Daily Contract Limit	Last Trading Day	Contract Months	Trading Hours (CST)
None	2 days before 3rd Wednesday	Mar, June, Sept, Dec	7:20 a.m.-2:15 p.m.
10 cents a bushel ($100)	8 days before end of month	Mar, May, July, Sept, Dec	9:30 a.m.-1:45 p.m.
None	2 days before 3rd Wednesday	Mar, June, Sept, Dec	7:20 a.m.-2:15 p.m.
$25 per troy ounce ($830)	3 days before end of month	every month	8:00 a.m.-1:40 p.m.
None	2 days before 3rd Wednesday	Mar, June, Sept, Dec	7:20 a.m.-2:15 p.m.
$.015 per pound ($300)	20th day of the month	Feb, Apr, June, Aug, Oct, Dec	9:05 a.m.-1:15 p.m.
$.015 per pound ($225)	20th day of the month	Feb, Apr, June, July, Aug, Sept, Oct, Dec	9:10 a.m.-1:15 p.m.
10 cents per bushel ($100)	8th day before end of month	Mar, May, July, Sept	9:30 a.m.-1:45 p.m.
$25 per troy ounce ($625)	4th day before end of month	Nearest month Jan, Apr, July, Oct	7:20 a.m.-1:40 p.m.
50 cents per troy ounce ($500)	3rd day before end of month	Every month	7:25 a.m.-1:40 p.m.
30 cents per bushel ($300)	8th day before end of month	Jan, Mar, May, July, Aug, Sept, Nov	9:30 a.m.-1:45 p.m.
$10 per ton ($200)	8th day before end of month	Jan, Mar, May, July, Aug, Sept, Oct, Dec	9:30 a.m.-1:45 p.m.
$0.01 per pound ($300 per contract); expandable to $0.15 ($450 per contract) concurrent with expansion and contract of CBOT soybean oil futures.	13th to the last business day of contract month	Initial months: Mar, May, July, & Aug Normal trading: Jan, Mar, May, July, Aug, Sept, Oct, Dec	9:30 a.m.-1:45 p.m. (1:15 p.m. on last trading day)
None	2 days before 3rd Wednesday	Mar, June, Sept, Dec	7:20 a.m.-2:15 p.m.
None	day before T-bill delivery date on Int'l Monetary Mkt.	Mar, June Sept, Dec	7:20 a.m.-2:15 p.m.
$64/32$ of a percentage point ($1000)	8th day before end of month	Mar, June, Sept, Dec	7:20 a.m.-3:15 p.m.
20 cents per bushel ($200)	8th day before end of month	Mar, May, July, Sept, Dec	9:30 a.m.-1:45 p.m.

Futures Options

Contract	Trading Unit	Prices Quoted In	Minimum Price Fluctuation	Strike Prices
• Gold	1 gold futures contract	cents per troy ounce	$.025 per troy ounce ($2.50)	$10-$40 per troy ounce apart
• Soybeans	1 soybean futures contract	cents per bushel	$.0125 per bushel ($1.00)	25 cents per bushel apart
• Wheat	1 wheat futures contract	cents per bushel	$.0125 per bushel ($1.25)	10 cents per bushel apart

Minneapolis Grain Exchange (MGE)

Futures

Contract	Trading Unit	Prices Quoted In	Minimum Price Fluctuation
• Black Tiger Shrimp	5,000 pounds	cents per pound	1/4 cent per pound ($12.50)
• Hard Red Spring Wheat	5,000 bushels ("job lots" of 1,000 bushels allowed)	cents per bushel	1/4 cent per bushel ($12.50)
• Soft White Wheat	5,000 bushels	cents per bushel	1/4 cent per bushel ($12.50)
• White Shrimp	5000 pounds	cents per pound	1/4 cent per pound ($12.50)

Futures Options

Contract	Trading Unit	Prices Quoted In	Minimum Price Fluctuation	Strike Prices
• Black Tiger Shrimp	One Minneapolis Grain Exchange Black Tiger Shrimp futures contract (5,000 pounds	cents per pound ($6.25)	1/8 cent per pound ($6.25)	call MGE
• Hard Red Spring Wheat	One Minneapolis Grain Exchange Hard Red Spring futures contract (5,000 bushels)	cents per bushel ($6.25)	1/8 cent per bushel ($6.25)	call MGE
• Soft White Wheat	One Minneapolis Grain Exchange White Wheat futures contract (5,000 bushels)	cents per bushel ($6.25)	1/8 cent per bushel ($6.25)	call MGE

Expiration Day	Last Trading Day	Contract Months	Trading Hours (CST)
Saturday after last trading day	Last Friday, at least 5 days before delivery of futures contract	Feb, Apr, June, Aug, Oct, Dec	7:20 a.m.-1:40 p.m.
Saturday after last trading day	Last Friday, at least 10 days before delivery of futures contract	Jan, Mar, May, July, Aug, Sept, Nov	9:30 a.m.-1:45 p.m.
Saturday after last trading day	Last Friday, at least 10 days before delivery of futures contract	Mar, May, July, Sept, Dec	9:30 a.m.-1:45 p.m.

Daily Contract Limit	Last Trading Day	Contract Months	Trading Hours (CST)	Ticker Symbol
$0.20 per pound ($1,000)	Call MGE	Mar, June, Sept, Dec	9:40 a.m.-1:30 p.m.	BT
$0.20 per bushel ($1,000)	Call MGE	Mar, May, July, Sept, Dec	8:30 a.m.-1:15 p.m.	MW
$0.20 per bushel ($1000)	Call MGE	Mar, May, July, Sept, Dec	8:30 a.m.-1:15 p.m.	NW
$0.20 per pound ($1000)	Call MGE	Mar, June, Sept, Dec	9:40 a.m.-1:30 p.m.	SH

Expiration Day	Last Trading Day	Contract Months	Trading Hours (CST)	Ticker Symbol
Call MGE	Last Friday 5 business days before First Notice day of underlying futures contract	Mar, June, Sept, Dec	9:40 a.m.-1:40 p.m.	BT (p) (put) BT (c) (call)
Call MGE	Last Friday 5 business days before First Notice day of underlying futures contract	Mar, May, July, Sept, Dec	8:35 a.m.-1:25 p.m.	PW (put) CW (call)
Call MGE	Last Friday 5 business days before First Notice day of underlying futures contract	Mar, May, July, Sept, Dec	8:35 a.m.-1:25 p.m.	NP (put) NC (call)

Contract	Trading Unit	Prices Quoted In	Minimum Price Fluctuation	Strike Prices
● White Shrimp	One Minneapolis Grain Exchange Frozen Shrimp futures contract (5,000 pounds)	cents per pound ($6.25)	$1/8$ cent per pound ($6.25)	call MGE

New York Cotton Exchange (NYCE)

Futures

Contract	Trading Unit	Prices Quoted In	Minimum Price Fluctuation	Daily Contract Limit
● Cotton	50,000 pounds	cents and $1/100$'s of a cent per pound	$1/100$ of a cent per pound ($5)	2 cents per pound ($1000) (No limit on or after 1st notice day of current delivery month)
● Orange Juice	15,000 pounds	cents and $1/100$'s of a cent per pound	$5/100$ of a cent per pound ($7.50)	5 cents per pound ($750)

Futures Options

Contract	Trading Unit	Prices Quoted In	Minimum Price Fluctuation	Strike Prices
● Cotton	1 cotton futures contract	cents and $1/100$ of a cent	$1/100$ of a cent ($5)	1-cent increments
● Frozen Concentrated Orange Juice	1 orange juice futures contract	cents and $1/100$ of a cent	$5/100$ of a cent ($7.50)	5-cent increments

FINEX (A division of the New York Cotton Exchange)

Futures

Contract	Trading Unit	Prices Quoted In	Minimum Price Fluctuation
● British Pound-Deutsche Mark	125,000 British pounds	Marks per pound to 4 decimal places	.0001 marks or 12.50 marks per contract
● Deutsche Mark-French Franc	500,000 Deutsche marks	French francs per mark to 4 decimal places	.0001 francs or 50.00 francs per contract
● Deutsche Mark-Italian Lira	250,000 Deutsche marks	Lira per mark to 2 decimal places	.05 lira or 12,500 lira per contract
● Deutsche Mark-Japanese Yen	125,000 Deutsche marks	Yen per mark to 2 decimal places	.01 yen or 1,250 yen per contract

Expiration Day	Last Trading Day	Contract Months	Trading Hours	Ticker Symbol
Call MGE	Last Friday 5 business days before First Notice day of underlying futures contract	Mar, June, Sept, Dec	9:45 a.m.-1:40 p.m.	SH

Dollar Value of 1 Cent Move	Last Trading Day	Contract Months	Trading Hours (EST)	Ticker Symbol
$500	17 days before end of month	Mar, May, July, Oct, Dec	10:30 a.m.-2:40 p.m.	CT
$150	9 days before last delivery day	Jan, Mar, May, July, Sept, Nov	10:15 a.m.-2:15 p.m.	JO

Expiration Day	Last Trading Day	Contract Months	Trading Hours (EST)	Ticker Symbol
Last trading day	Call NYFE	Mar, May, July, Oct, Dec	10:30 a.m.-2:40 p.m.	CO
Last trading day	Call NYFE	Jan, Mar, May, July, Sept, Nov	10:15 a.m.-2:15 p.m.	OJ

Last Trading Day	Contract Months	Trading Hours (EST)	Ticker Symbol
10:15 a.m. 2 business days before 3rd Wednesday of expiring month	Mar, June, Sept, Dec	7:00 p.m.-10:00 p.m. 3:00 a.m.-9:00 a.m. 9:05 a.m.-3:00 p.m.	MP
10:15 a.m., 2 business days before 3rd Wednesday of expiring month	Mar, June, Sept, Dec	7:00 p.m.-10:00 p.m. 3:00 a.m.-9:00 a.m. 9:05 a.m.-3:00 p.m.	MF
10:15 a.m., 2 business days before 3rd Wednesday of expiring month	Mar, June, Sept, Dec	7:00 p.m.-10:00 p.m. 3:00 a.m.-9:00 a.m. 9:05 a.m.-3:00 p.m.	ML
10:15 a.m., 2 business days before 3rd Wednesday of expiring month	Mar, June, Sept, Dec	7:00 p.m.-10:00 p.m. 3:00 a.m.-9:00 a.m. 9:05 a.m.-3:00 p.m.	MY

Contract	Trading Unit	Prices Quoted In	Minimum Price Fluctuation
● Deutsche Mark-Swedish Krona	125,000 Deutsche marks	Krona per mark to 4 decimal places	.0005 krona or 62.50 krona per contract
● U.S. Dollar/British Pound	62,500 British pounds	U.S. dollars per British pound to 4 decimal places	$.0001 or $6.25 per contract
● U.S. Dollar/Canadian Dollar	100,000 Canadian dollars	U.S. dollars per Canadian dollar to 4 decimal places	$.0001 or $10 per contract
● U.S. Dollar Index	Dollar index × $1,000	index points relative to its base (100)	.01 of an index point ($10)
● U.S. Dollar/Deutsche Mark	125,000 Deutsche marks	U.S. dollars per Deutsche mark to 4 decimal places	$.0001 or $12.50 per contract
● U.S. Dollar/Japanese Yen	12,500,000 Japanese yen	U.S. dollars per Japanese yen to 4 decimal places	$.000001 or $12.50 per contract
● U.S. Dollar/Swiss Franc	125,000 Swiss francs	U.S. dollars per Swiss franc to 4 decimal places	$.0001 or $12.50 per contract
● U.S. Treasury Note (5-year)	5-year U.S. Treasury note × $5000	note points	$1/2$ of $1/32$ of an index point ($15.625)

Futures Options

Contract	Trading Unit	Prices Quoted In	Minimum Price Fluctuation	Strike Prices
● U.S. Dollar (USDX)	1 U.S. Dollar Futures Contract	points and $1/100$'s of a point	.01 of an index point ($10)	2 points apart (200 ticks)
● U.S. Treasury Note (5-year)	1 U.S. Treasury Note Futures Contract	points and $1/64$'s of a point	$1/64$th of a point (15,625)	$1/2$ point

New York Futures Exchange (NYFE)

Futures

Contract	Trading Unit	Prices Quoted In	Minimum Price Fluctuation
● KR-CRB Futures Price Index	commodity index × $500	index points	5 basis points ($25)
● NYSE Composite Index®	index × $500	index points	5 basis points ($25)

Last Trading Day	Contract Months	Trading Hours (EST)	Ticker Symbol
10:15 a.m., 2 business days before 3rd Wednesday of expiring contract month	Mar, June, Sept, Dec	7:00 p.m.-10:00 p.m. 3:00 a.m.-9:00 a.m. 9:05 a.m.-3:00 p.m.	MK
10:15 a.m., 2 business days before 3rd Wednesday of expiring contract month	Mar, June, Sept, Dec	7:00 p.m.-10:00 p.m. 3:00 a.m.-8:00 a.m. 8:05 a.m.-3:00 p.m.	YP
10:15 a.m., 2 business days before 3rd Wednesday of expiring contract month	Mar, June, Sept, Dec	7:00 p.m.-10:00 p.m. 3:00 a.m.-8:00 a.m. 8:05 a.m.-3:00 p.m.	YD
3rd Wednesday of month	Mar, June, Sept, Dec	7:00 a.m.- 10:00 p.m.	DX
10:15 a.m., 2 business days before 3rd Wednesday of expiring contract month	Mar, June, Sept, Dec	7:00 p.m.-10:00 p.m. 3:00 a.m.-8:00 a.m. 8:05 a.m.-3:00 p.m.	YM
10:15 a.m., 2 business days before 3rd Wednesday of expiring contract month	Mar, June, Sept, Dec	7:00 p.m.-10:00 p.m. 3:00 a.m.-8:00 a.m. 8:05 a.m.-3:00 p.m.	YY
10:15 a.m., 2 business days before 3rd Wednesday of expiring contract month	Mar, June, Sept, Dec	7:00 p.m.-10:00 p.m. 3:00 a.m.-8:00 a.m. 8:05 a.m.-3:00 p.m.	YF
8th last day of contract month	Mar, June, Sept, Dec	8:20 a.m.-3:00 p.m.	FY

Exercise Day	Last Trading Day	Contract Months	Trading Hours (EST)	Ticker Symbol
On last trading day	2 Fridays before 3rd Wed of contract month	Mar, June, Sept, Dec	8:20 a.m.- 3:00 p.m.	DO
On last trading day	Friday 5 days before first day of contract month	Mar, June, Sept, Dec	8:20 a.m.- 3:00 p.m.	FO

Daily Contract Limit	Last Trading Day	Contract Months	Trading Hours (EST)	Ticker Symbol
None	3rd business day of month	Mar, May, July, Sept, Dec	9:40 a.m.- 2:45 p.m. EST	CRB
18 points	Thursday before 3rd Friday of month	Mar, June, Sept, Dec	9:30 a.m.- 4:15 p.m. EST	YX

Futures Options

Contract	Underlying Index	Prices Quoted In	Minimum Price Fluctuation	Strike Prices
• KR-CRB Index Contract	CRB index futures	index points 1 point = $5	5 points ($25)	numbers divisible by 5
• NYSE Composite Index® Contract	NYSE composite index	index points 1 point = $5	5 points ($25)	numbers divisible by 2

New York Stock Exchange (NYSE)

Index Options

Contract	Underlying Index	Trading Unit	Prices Quoted In	Minimum Price Fluctuation
• NYSE Composite Index Options	2,300+ common stocks listed on the NYSE	index × $100	index points	call NYSE
• NYSE Utility Index Options	195+ common utility stocks listed on the NYSE	index × $100	index points	call NYSE

Pacific Stock Exchange (PSE)

Index Options

Contract	Underlying Index	Trading Unit	Prices Quoted In	Minimum Price Fluctuation
• Telegraph Ltd Israel Index	Cross section of U.S. traded, Israeli-based companies	index × $100	dollars and fractions	—
• Wilshire Small Cap Index	250 small cap stocks chosen on basis of capitalization, liquidity, and industry group representation from Wilshire Next 1750 Index companies	index × $100	dollars and fractions	—

Expiration Day	Last Trading Day	Contract Months	Trading Hours
Last trading day	Last day of futures delivery month	Mar, May, July, Sept, Dec	9:00 a.m.-3:15 p.m.
Last trading day	Last day of futures delivery month	Mar, June, Sept, Dec	9:30 a.m.-4:15 p.m. EST

Strike Prices	Settlement	Last Trading Day	Contract Months	Trading Hours (EST)	Ticker Symbol
2$^1/_2$ and 5 point intervals as needed	in cash	2 business days prior to the expiration date	3 consecutive near-term, 2 months from the March quarterly cycle	9:30 a.m.-4:15 p.m.	NYA
5 point intervals as needed	in cash	2 business days prior to the expiration date	3 consecutive near-term, 2 months from the March quarterly cycle and Jan 1996/97 Long-Term options	9:30 a.m.-4:30 p.m.	NNA Jan 96 LNA Jan 97 ZNA call NYSE for later

Strike Prices	Settlement	Last Trading Day	Contract Months	Trading Hours (PST)	Ticker Symbol
5 point intervals	in cash	2 business days prior to expiration (normally Thursday)	3 consecutive near-term expiration months plus 2 successive months from the March cycle	6:30 a.m.-1:15 p.m.	TIX
5 point intervals (2$^1/_2$ point intervals may be available)	in cash	2 business days prior to expiration (normally Thursday)	3 consecutive near-term expiration months plus 2 successive months from the March cycle	6:30 a.m.-1:15 p.m.	WSX

Philadelphia Stock Exchange (PHLX)

Foreign Currency Options

Contract	Trading Unit	Prices Quoted In	Minimum Price Fluctuation	Strike Prices
• Australian Dollar	50,000 Australian dollars	cents per Australian dollar	$.0001 per unit ($5)	3 nearest months = 1 cent 6, 9, and 12 months = 1 cent Over 12 months = 2 cents
• British Pound	31,250 British pounds	cents per British pound	$.0001 per unit ($3.125)	3 nearest months = 2.5 cents 6, 9, and 12 months = 2.5 cents Over 12 months = 5 cents
• British Pound/ Deutsche Mark	31,250 British pounds	Deutsche mark	.0002 Deutsche mark per unit (6.25 yen)	3 nearest months = .02 DM apart 6, 9, and 12 months = .02 DM apart Over 12 months = .04 DM apart
• British Pound/ Japanese Yen	31,250 British pounds	Japanese yen	.02 Japanese yen per unit	3 nearest months = 2 Japanese yen 6, 9, and 12 months = 2 Japanese yen Over 12 months = 4 Japanese yen
• Canadian Dollar	50,000 Canadian dollars	cents per Canadian dollar	$.0001 per unit ($5)	3 nearest months = .5 cent 6, 9, and 12 months = .5 cent Over 12 months = 1 cent
• Deutsche Mark	62,500 Deutsche marks	cents per Deutsche mark	$.0001 per unit ($6.25)	3 nearest months = .5 cent 6, 9, and 12 months = 1 cent Over 12 months = 2 cents

Expiration Day	Contract Months	Trading Hours (EST)	Ticker Symbol
Regular and long-term options: Friday before 3rd Wednesday of expiring month Month-end options: Last Friday of month	Regular options: Mar, June, Sept, Dec + 2 near-term months Month-end options: 3 nearest months Long-term options: 18, 24, 30, and 36 months (June and Dec)	2:30 a.m.- 2:30 p.m.	XAD (American-style) CAD (European-style)
Regular and long-term options: Friday before 3rd Wednesday of expiring month Month-end options: Last Friday of month	Regular options: Mar, June, Sept, Dec + 2 near-term months Month-end options: 3 nearest months Long-term options: 18, 24, 30, and 36 months (June and Dec)	2:30 a.m.- 2:30 p.m.	XBP (American-style) CBP (European-style)
Regular and long-term options: Friday before 3rd Wednesday of expiring month	Regular options: Mar, June, Sept, Dec + 2 near-end months Long-term options: 18, 24, 30, and 36 months (June and Dec)	2:30 a.m.- 2:30 p.m.	PMX (European-style)
Regular and long-term options: Friday before 3rd Wednesday of expiring month Month-end options: 3 nearest months.	Regular options: Mar, June, Sept, Dec + 2 near-term months Month-end options: 3 nearest months Long-term options: 18, 24, 30, and 36 months (June and Dec)	2:30 a.m.- 2:30 p.m.	PYX (European-style)
Regular and long-term options: Friday before 3rd Wednesday of expiring month Month-end options: Last Friday of month	Regular options: Mar, June, Sept, Dec + 2 near-term months Month-end options: 3 nearest months Long-term options: 18, 24, 30, and 36 months (June and Dec)	7:00 a.m.- 2:30 p.m.	XCD (American-style) CCD (European-style)
Regular and long-term options: Friday before 3rd Wednesday of expiring month Month-end options: Last Friday of month	Regular options: Mar, June, Sept, Dec + 2 near-term months Month-end options: 3 nearest months Long-term options: 18, 24, 30, and 36 months (June and Dec)	2:30 a.m.- 2:30 p.m.	XDM (American-style) CDM (European-style)

Contract	Trading Unit	Prices Quoted In	Minimum Price Fluctuation	Strike Prices
• Deutsche Mark/ Japanese Yen	62,500 Deutsche marks	Japanese yen	.01 Japanese yen per unit (625 yen)	3 nearest months = .5 JY apart 6, 9, and 12 months = 1 JY apart Over 12 months = 2 JY apart
• European Currency Unit	62,500 ECUs	cents per ECU	$.0001 per unit ($6.25)	3 nearest months = 2 cents 6, 9, and 12 months = 2 cents
• French Franc	250,000 French francs	tenths of a cent per French franc	$.0002 per unit ($5)	3 nearest months = .25 cents apart 6, 9, and 12 months = .25 cents apart Over 12 months = . 50 cents apart
• Japanese Yen	6,250,000 Japanese yen	hundreds of a cent per Japanese yen	$.000001 per unit ($6.25)	3 nearest months = .005 cents apart 6, 9, and 12 months = .01 cent apart Over 12 months = .02 cents apart
• Swiss Franc	62,500 Swiss franc	cents per Swiss franc	$.0001 per unit ($6.25)	3 nearest months = .5 cents apart 6, 9, and 12 months = 1 cent apart Over 12 months = 2 cents apart

Futures

Contract	Trading Unit	Prices Quoted In	Minimum Price Fluctuation
• Australian Dollar	100,000 Australian dollars	cents per unit	$.0001 ($10)
• British Pound	62,500 British pounds	cents per unit	$.0001 ($6.25)
• Canadian Dollar	100,000 Canadian dollars	cents per unit	$.0001 ($10)

Expiration Day	Contract Months	Trading Hours (EST)	Ticker Symbol
Regular and long-term options: Friday before 3rd Wednesday of expiring month	Regular options: Mar, June, Sept, Dec + 2 near-end months Month-end options: 3 nearest months Long-term options: 18, 24, 30, and 36 months (June and Dec)	2:30 a.m.-2:30 p.m.	MYX (European-style)
Regular and long-term options: Friday before 3rd Wednesday of expiring month Month-end options: Last Friday of month	Regular options: Mar, June, Sept, Dec + 2 near-term months Month-end options: 3 nearest months Long-term options: 18, 24, 30, and 36 months (June and Dec)	2:30 a.m.-2:30 p.m.	ECU (American-style)
Regular and long-term options: Friday before 3rd Wednesday of expiring month	Regular options: Mar, June, Sept, Dec + 2 near-term months Long-term options: 18, 24, 30, and 36 months (June and Dec)	2:30 a.m.-2:30 p.m.	XFF (American-style) CFF (European-style)
Regular and long-term options: Friday before 3rd Wednesday of expiring month	Regular options: Mar, June, Sept, Dec + 2 near-term months Long-term options: 18, 24, 30, and 36 months (June and Dec)	2:30 a.m.-2:30 p.m.	XJY (American-style) CJY (European-style)
Regular and long-term options: Friday before 3rd Wednesday of expiring month	Regular options: Mar, June, Sept, Dec + 2 near-term months Long-term options: 18, 24, 30, and 36 months (June and Dec)	2:30 a.m.-2:30 p.m.	XSF (American-style) CSF (European-style)

Last Trading Day	Contract Months	Trading Hours (EST)	Ticker Symbol
Friday before 3rd Wednesday of month	Mar, June, Sept, Dec and 2 additional near-term months	1:30 a.m.-2:30 p.m.	ZA
Friday before 3rd Wednesday of month	Mar, June, Sept, Dec and 2 additional near-term months	1:30 a.m.-2:30 p.m.	ZB
Friday before 3rd Wednesday of month	Mar, June, Sept, Dec and 2 additional near-term months	7:00 a.m.-2:30 p.m.	ZC

Contract	Trading Unit	Prices Quoted In	Minimum Price Fluctuation
• Deutsche Mark	125,000 Deutsche marks	cents per unit	$.0001 ($12.50)
• European Currency Unit	125,000 ECUs	cents per unit	$.0001 ($12.50)
• French Franc	500,000 French francs	$1/10$ cent per unit	$.00002 ($10)
• Japanese Yen	12,500,000 Japanese yen	$1/100$ cent per unit	$.000001 ($12.50)
• Swiss Franc	125,000 Swiss francs	cents per unit	$.0001 ($12.50)

Index Options

Contract	Underlying Index	Trading Unit	Prices Quoted In	Minimum Price Fluctuation
• Big Cap Index		index × $100	index points (1 point = $100)	$1/16$th point under 3 $1/8$th point over 3
• Gold/Silver Index	7 gold and silver mining stocks	index × $100	index points (1 point = $100)	$1/16$th point under 3 $1/8$th point over 3
• National Over-The-Counter Index	OTC 100 stocks	index × $100	index points (1 point = $100)	$1/16$th point under 3 $1/8$th point over 3
• PHLX/Keefe, Bruyette & Woods, Inc. Bank Index		index × $100	index points (1 point = $100)	$1/16$th point under 3 $1/8$th point over 3
• Phone Index		index × $100	index points (1 point = $100)	$1/16$th point under 3 $1/8$th point over 3
• Semiconductor Index		index × $100	index points (1 point = $100)	$1/16$th point under 3 $1/8$th point over 3

Last Trading Day	Contract Months	Trading Hours (EST)	Ticker Symbol
Friday before 3rd Wednesday of month	Mar, June, Sept, Dec and 2 near-term months	1:30 a.m.-2:30 p.m.	ZD
Friday before 3rd Wednesday of month	Mar, June, Sept, Dec and 2 near-term months	1:30 a.m.-2:30 p.m.	ZE
Friday before 3rd Wednesday of month	Mar, June, Sept, Dec and 2 additional near-term months	1:30 a.m.-2:30 p.m.	ZF
Friday before 3rd Wednesday of month	Mar, June, Sept, Dec and 2 additional near-term months	1:30 a.m.-2:30 p.m.	ZJ
Friday before 3rd Wednesday of month	Mar, June, Sept, Dec and 2 near term-months	1:30 a.m.-2:30 p.m.	ZS

Strike Prices	Settlement	Last Trading Day	Contract Months	Trading Hours (EST)	Ticker Symbol
5 points apart	in cash	Thursday	3 months from the Mar, June, Sept, and Dec cycle + 2 additional months	9:30 a.m.-4:15 p.m.	MKT (European style)
5 points apart	in cash	Thursday	3 months from the Mar, June, Sept, and Dec cycle + 2 additional months	9:30 a.m.-4:10 p.m.	XAU (American style)
5 points apart	in cash	Thursday	3 months from the Mar, June, Sept, and Dec cycle + 2 additional months	9:30 a.m.-4:15 p.m.	XOC (American style)
5 points apart	in cash	Thursday	3 months from the Mar, June, Sept, and Dec cycle + 2 additional months	9:30 a.m.-4:10 p.m.	BKX (European style)
5 points apart	in cash	Thursday	3 months from the Mar, June, Sept, and Dec cycle + 2 additional months	9:30 a.m.-4:10 p.m.	PNX (American style)
5 points apart	in cash	Thursday	3 months from the Mar, June, Sept, and Dec cycle + 2 additional near months	9:30 a.m.-4:10 p.m.	SOX (American style)

Contract	Underlying Index	Trading Unit	Prices Quoted In	Minimum Price Fluctuation
● Utility Index	20 utility company stocks	index × $100	index points (1 point = $100)	1/16th point under 3 1/8th point over 3
● Value Line Composite Index	1700 Value Line stocks	index × $100	index points (1 point = $100)	1/16th point under 3 1/8th point over 3

CANADIAN SECURITIES, FUTURES AND OPTIONS EXCHANGES
Montreal Exchange (ME)

Futures

Contract	Trading Unit	Prices Quoted In	Minimum Price Fluctuation
● Canadian Bankers' Acceptance (1-Month)	3 million Canadian dollars in Bankers' Acceptances	index minus yield	0.01% (1 basis point = $25 per contract
● Canadian Bankers' Acceptance (3-Month)	1 million Canadian dollars in Bankers' Acceptances	index minus yield	0.01% (1 basis point = $25 per contract
● Government of Canada Bonds (5-Year)	1 One hundred thousand Canadian dollar Government of Canada bond	per one hundred Canadian dollar nominal value	0.01= C$10 per contract
● Government of Canada Bonds (10-Year)	1 One hundred thousand Canadian dollar Government of Canada bond	per one hundred Canadian dollar nominal value	0.01= C$10 per contract

Futures Options

Contract	Trading Unit	Prices Quoted In	Minimum Price Fluctuation	Strike Prices
● Canadian Bankers' Acceptance (3-month)	one 3-month Canadian Bankers' Acceptance futures contract	points. .01 point (1 basis point) represents C$25	0.01% – 1 tick = C$25 per contract	0.50 point intervals (max). 0.25 point intervals possible on nearest contract month
● Canadian Bankers' Acceptance (10-Year)	one 10-Year Government of Canada Bond futures contract	points and 1/100 point per $100 nominal value of underlying futures contract	0.01 = C$10 per contract	2 point intervals

Strike Prices	Settlement	Last Trading Day	Contract Months	Trading Hours (EST)	Ticker Symbol
5 points apart	in cash	Friday	3 months from the Mar, June, Sept, and Dec cycle + 2 additional near months	9:30 a.m.-4:10 p.m.	UTY (European style)
5 points apart	in cash	Friday	3 months from the Mar, June, Sept, and Dec cycle + 2 additional near months	9:30 a.m.-4:15 p.m.	VLE (European style)

Daily Contract Limit	Last Trading Day	Contract Months	Trading Hours (EST)
None	10:00 a.m. (EST) on 2nd London (U.K.) banking day prior to 3rd Wednesday of contract month	First 6 consecutive months	8:20 a.m.-3:00 p.m.
None	10:00 a.m. (EST) on 2nd London (U.K.) banking day prior to 3rd Wednesday of contract month	Mar, June, Sept, Dec, for a total of two years	8:20 a.m.-3:00 p.m.
3 points (C$3,000) per contract	7th business day preceding last business day of delivery month	Mar, June, Sept, Dec	8:20 a.m.-3:00 p.m. (8:20 a.m.-1:00 p.m., last trading day)
3 points (C$3,000) per contract	7th business day preceding last business day of delivery month	Mar, June, Sept, Dec	8:20 a.m.-3:00 p.m. (8:20 a.m.-1:00 p.m., last trading day)

Expiration Day	Last Trading Day	Contract Months	Trading Hours
Last trading day	Call Montreal Exchange	4 nearest months in the 3-month Canadian Bankers' Acceptance Futures quarterly cycle.	8:20 a.m.-3:00 p.m.
Last trading day	Third Friday of month preceding the option contract month	Mar, June, Sept, and Dec plus monthly option contracts based on the next quarterly futures contract that is nearest to the option contract.	8:20 a.m.-3:00 p.m.

Toronto Futures Exchange (TFE)

Futures

Contract	Trading Unit	Prices Quoted In	Minimum Price Fluctuation
• Toronto 35 Index	35 TSE stocks	index points	0.02 index points or $10 per contract
• TSE 100 Index	100 TSE stocks	index points	0.05 index points or $25 per contract

Options

Contract	Trading Unit	Prices Quoted In	Minimum Price Fluctuation	Strike Prices
• Silver	100 troy ounces of .999 fineness silver bullion	cents per ounce	call TFE	call TFE

Toronto Stock Exchange (TSEX)

Options

Contract	Trading Unit	Prices Quoted In	Minimum Price Fluctuation	Strike Prices
• Toronto 35 Index	TSE 35 index × $100	dollars per index	call TFE	$0.00 – $0.09 = 0.01 intervals $0.10 – $4.99 = 0.05 intervals over $5.00 = 1/8 intervals
• TSE 100 Index	TSE 100 index × $100	dollars per index	call TFE	$0.00 – $0.09 = 0.01 intervals $0.10 – $4.99 = 0.05 intervals over $5.00 = 1/8 intervals

Daily Contract Limit	Last Trading Day	Contract Months	Trading Hours (EST)	Ticker Symbol
13.5 points ($6750)	Thursday before 3rd Friday of contract month	2 nearest months and next 2 quarters from Mar, June, Sept, and Dec cycle. (call TFE)	9:15 a.m.- 4:15 p.m.	TXF
16.5 points ($8250)	Thursday before 3rd Friday of contract month	2 nearest months and next 2 quarters from Mar, June, Sept, and Dec cycle. (call TFE)	9:15 a.m.- 4:15 p.m.	TOF

Expiration Day	Last Trading Day	Contract Months	Trading Hours (EST)	Ticker Symbol
Saturday following 3rd Friday of each expiry month	3rd Friday of each expiry month	Call TFE	9:05 a.m.- 4:00 p.m.	SVR

Expiration Day	Last Trading Day	Contract Months	Trading Hours (EST)	Ticker Symbol
Last trading day	Thursday before 3rd Friday of contract month	2 nearest months and next 2 quarters from Mar, June, Sept, and Dec cycle. (call TFE)	9:30 a.m.- 4:15 p.m.	TXO
Last trading day	Thursday before 3rd Friday of contract month	2 nearest months and next 2 quarters from Mar, June, Sept, and Dec cycle. (call TFE)	9:30 a.m.- 4:15 p.m.	TOP

Vancouver Stock Exchange (VSE)

Commodity Options

Contract	Trading Unit	Prices Quoted In	Minimum Price Fluctuation	Strike Prices
• Gold	10 troy ounces of fine gold bullion, of minimum .995 fineness acceptable for good London delivery	U.S. dollars per ounce	Increments of U.S. $.10 per ounce (i.e., $1.00 per contract). For premiums over $5.00, increments of U.S. $0.125 per ounce.	Minimum intervals set at U.S. $10 per ounce.

Winnipeg Commodity Exchange (WCE)

Futures

Contract	Trading Unit	Prices Quoted In	Minimum Price Fluctuation
• Barley (Canadian Domestic)	Board Lot = 100 metric tons Job Lot = 20 metric tons	dollars and cents per ton	$.10 per ton
• Barley (Western Domestic)	Board Lot = 100 metric tons Job Lot = 20 metric tons	dollars and cents per ton	$.10 per ton
• Canola	Board Lot = 100 metric tons Job Lot = 20 metric tons	dollars and cents per ton	$.10 per ton
• Flaxseed	Board Lot = 100 metric tons Job Lot = 20 metric tons	dollars and cents per ton	$.10 per ton
• Oats	Board Lot = 100 metric tons Job Lot = 20 metric tons	dollars and cents per ton	$.10 per ton
• Rye	Board Lot = 100 metric tons Job Lot = 20 metric tons	dollars and cents per ton	$.10 per ton
• Wheat (Domestic)	Board Lot = 100 metric tons Job Lot = 20 metric tons	dollars and cents per ton	$.10 per ton

Expiration Day	Last Trading Day	Contract Months	Trading Hours (PST)	Ticker Symbol
Last trading day	The 3rd Friday in an expiry month.	Feb, May, Aug, Nov	6:30 a.m.-1:00 p.m.	OR

Daily Contract Limit	Last Trading Day	Contract Months	Trading Hours (CST)	Ticker Symbol
$5 per ton	Call WCE	Dec, Mar, May, July, Sept	9:30 a.m.-1:15 p.m.	BY
$5 per ton	Call WCE	Feb, May, Aug, Nov	9:30 a.m.-1:15 p.m.	AB
$5 per ton	Call WCE	Aug, Sept, Nov, Jan, Mar, June	9:30 a.m.-1:15 p.m.	RS
$5 per ton	Call WCE	Oct, Dec, Mar, May, July	9:30 a.m.-1:15 p.m.	F
$5 per ton	Call WCE	Oct, Dec, Mar, May, July	9:30 a.m.-1:15 p.m.	O
$5 per ton	Call WCE	Sept, Dec, Mar, May, July	9:30 a.m.-1:15 p.m.	R
$5 per ton	Call WCE	Oct, Dec, Mar, May, July	9:30 a.m.-1:15 p.m.	W

Options

Contract	Trading Unit	Prices Quoted In	Minimum Price Fluctuation	Strike Prices
● Barley (Canadian Domestic)	1 Canadian Domestic Barley futures contract	dollars and cents per ton	$.10 per ton	$5 apart
● Barley (Western Domestic)	1 Western Domestic Barley futures contract	dollars and cents per ton	$.10 per ton	$2.50 apart
● Canola	1 Canola futures contract	dollars and cents per ton	$.10 per ton	$10 apart
● Flaxseed	1 Flaxseed futures contract	dollars and cents per ton	$.10 per ton	$10 apart
● Wheat (Domestic)	1 Wheat futures contract	dollars and cents per ton	$.10 per ton	$5 apart

AUSTRALIAN SECURITIES, FUTURES AND OPTIONS EXCHANGE

Sydney Futures Exchange (SFE)

Futures

Contract	Trading Unit	Prices Quoted In	Minimum Price Fluctuation
● All Ordinaries Index	index × $100	index points	1 basis point ($10)
● Australian Dollar	100,000 Australian dollars	U.S. dollars and cents	.0001 cents
● Australian T-Bond (3-year)	$100,000 of Australian bonds	100 minus yield	.01 point ($11.50)
● Australian T-Bond (10-year)	$100,000 of Australian bonds	100 minus annual yield	.005 percentage point ($25)
● Bank Accepted Bills (90-Day)	500,000 Australian dollars	100 minus yield	.01 percentage point ($11.50)
● Cattle	10,000 kilograms	U.S. dollars and cents per kilogram	0.1 cent per kilogram ($10)
● Eurodollar	1 million U.S. dollars	basis points	.01 percentage point ($25)
● Gold	10 troy ounces	U.S. dollars and cents per ounce	.0001 cent ($10)

Expiration Day	Last Trading Day	Contract Months	Trading Hours (CST)	Ticker Symbol
Last trading day	Call WCE	Feb, Apr, June, Aug, Nov	9:30 a.m.-1:20 p.m.	BVP (put) BYC (call)
Last trading day	Call WCE	Jan, Apr, July, & Oct	9:30 a.m.-1:20 p.m.	ABP (put) ABC (call)
Last trading day	Call WCE	Feb, May, July, Aug, Oct, Dec.	9:30 a.m.-1:20 p.m.	RSP (put) RSC (call)
Last trading day	Call WCE	Feb, Apr, June, Sept, Nov	9:30 a.m.-1:20 p.m.	FP (put) FC (call)
Last trading day	Call WCE	Feb, Apr, June, Sept, Nov	9:30 a.m.-1:20 p.m.	WP (put) WC (call)

Last Trading Day	Contract Months	Trading Hours
2nd to last business day of month	Mar, June, Sept, Dec	9:30 a.m-12:30 p.m. and 2:00 p.m.-3:45 p.m.
next to last day before 3rd Wednesday of month	Mar, June, Sept, Dec	8:30 a.m.-4:30 p.m.
15th business day of month	Mar, June, Sept, Dec	8:30 a.m.-12:30 p.m. and 2:00 p.m.-4:30 p.m.
15th business day of month	Mar, June, Sept, Dec	8:30 a.m.-12:30 p.m., and 2:00 p.m.-3:30 p.m.
Wednesday before 2nd Friday of month	Mar, June, Sept, Dec and 6 nearest months	8:30 a.m.-12:30 p.m. and 2:00 p.m.-4:30 p.m.
3rd Wednesday of month	monthly	10:30 a.m.-12:30 p.m. and 2:00 p.m.-4 p.m.
—	Mar, June, Sept, Dec and 6 nearest months	8:35 a.m.-6:15 p.m.
3rd to last day of month	Feb, Apr, June, Aug, June, Aug, Oct, Dec and 3 nearest months	8:35 a.m.-4:00 p.m.

Contract	Trading Unit	Prices Quoted In	Minimum Price Fluctuation
● U.S. T-Bond	$100,000 U.S. bond	basis points	1/32 of a point ($31.25)
● Wool	1500 kilograms	cents per kilogram	1 cent per kilogram ($25)

Futures Options

Contract	Trading Unit	Prices Quoted In	Minimum Price Fluctuation	Strike Prices
● All Ordinaries Index	1 All Ordinaries futures contract	index points	0.1 index point	25 points apart
● Australian Dollar	1 Australian dollar futures contract	dollars and cents	.0001 U.S. cent per Australian dollar ($10 U.S.)	1 cent apart
● Australian T-Bond (3-Year)	1 3-Year T-bond futures contract	100 minus annual yield	.01 of a percentage point ($25)	.25 of a percentage point apart
● Australian T-Bond (10-Year)	1 10-Year T-bond futures contract	100 minus annual yield	.005 of a percentage point ($25)	.25 of a percentage point apart
● Bank Accepted Bills (90-Day)	1 bank accepted futures contract	100 minus annual yield	.01 of a percentage point ($11.50)	.50 of a percentage point apart

BRAZILIAN SECURITIES, FUTURES AND OPTIONS EXCHANGE

Bolsa Mercantil & De Futuros (BMF)

Futures

Contract	Trading Unit	Prices Quoted In	Minimum Price Fluctuation
● Brazil Coffee	100 bags	cruzados per 60 kilogram bag	10 cruzados per bag
● Brazilian T-Bond	1000 Brazilian T-bonds	cruzados per bond	0.01 cruzados per bond
● Broilers	12 metric tons	cruzados per kilogram	0.01 cruzado per kilogram
● Dollar	$5000	cruzados per dollar	0.01 cruzado = $1

Last Trading Day	Contract Months	Trading Hours
7th business day before end of month	Mar, June, Sept, Dec	8:35 a.m.-6:15 p.m.
day after final auction	Mar, May, July, Oct, Dec	10:30 a.m.-12:30 p.m and 2:00 p.m. -4 p.m.

Expiration Day	Contract Months	Trading Hours
last day of underlying futures contract	Mar, June, Sept, Dec	9:30 a.m.-12:30 p.m. and 2:00 p.m.-3:45 p.m.
last trading day	Mar, June, Sept, Dec	8:30 a.m.-4:30 p.m.
last trading day	Mar, June, Sept, Dec	8:30 a.m.-12:30 p.m. and 2:00 p.m.-4:30 p.m.
last day of underlying futures contract	Mar, June, Sept, Dec	8:30 a.m.-12:30 p.m. and 2:00 p.m.-4:30 p.m
Friday before settlement of underlying futures contract	Mar, June, Sept, Dec	8:30 a.m.-12:30 p.m. and 2:00 p.m.-4:30 p.m.

Last Trading Day	Contract Months	Trading Hours
last business day of contract month	Mar, May, July, Sept, Dec	10:45 a.m.-4:00 p.m.
last business day before bond's expiration	every month	10:30 a.m.-4:00 p.m.
last business day of delivery month	even months	2:15 p.m.-2:35 p.m. and 2:40 p.m.-3:00 p.m.
1st business day of delivery month	every month	10:00 a.m.-10:20 a.m. and 10:30 a.m.-3:45 p.m.

Contract	Trading Unit	Prices Quoted In	Minimum Price Fluctuation
● Domestic CD (60 & 90 Day)	1 million cruzados	points	0.1 point = 10 cruzados
● Gold	250 grams	cruzados per gram	0.1 cruzado per gram
● Live Cattle	330 net arrobas	cruzados per net arroba	0.10 cruzado per arroba
● Live Hogs	8000 net kilograms	cruzados per net kilogram	0.01 cruzado per kilogram
● Sao Paulo Stock Index	index × 50 cruzados	index points	0.05 points = 50 cruzados

Futures Options

Contract	Trading Unit	Prices Quoted In	Minimum Price Fluctuation	Strike Prices
● Brazilian T-Bond	1000 Brazilian T-bonds	cruzados per bond	0.01 cruzado per bond	varies
● Dollar	$5000	cruzados $1 per dollar	0.01 cruzado $1	varies
● Gold	250 grams	cruzados per gram	0.10 cruzado per gram	varies

BRITISH SECURITIES, FUTURES AND OPTIONS EXCHANGES

Baltic Futures Exchange (BFE)
(Baltic International Freight Futures Exchange)

Futures

Contract	Trading Unit	Prices Quoted In	Minimum Price Fluctuation
● Baltic Freight Index	index × $10	dollars per index point	5 cents ($5)

(London Grain Futures Market)

Futures

Contract	Trading Unit	Prices Quoted In	Minimum Price Fluctuation
● Barley	100 metric tons	pence per ton	.05 pence (5 pounds)

Last Trading Day	**Contract Months**	**Trading Hours**
3rd Wednesday of contract month	4 nearest months, even months	11:15 a.m.-12:30 p.m. and 3:15 p.m.-4:00 p.m.
last business day of previous month	odd months	10:00 a.m.-4:30 p.m.
last business day of contract month	even months	2:15 p.m.-2:35 p.m. and 2:40 p.m.-3:00 p.m.
last business day of contract month '	even months	2:15 p.m.-2:35 p.m. and 2:30 p.m.-3:00 p.m.
Wednesday nearest 15th day of contract month	even months	9:30 a.m.-1:15 p.m.

Expiration Day	**Contract Months**	**Trading Hours**
last trading day	every month	10:30 a.m.-4:00 p.m.
last trading day	odd months	10:00 a.m.-10:20 a.m. and 10:30 a.m.-3:45 p.m.
last trading day	odd months	10:00 a.m.-4:30 p.m.

Last Trading Day	**Contract Months**	**Trading Hours**
last business day of month	Jan, Apr, July, Oct	10:15 a.m.-12:30 p.m. and 2:30 p.m.-4:15 p.m.

Last Trading Day	**Contract Months**	**Trading Hours**
23rd day of month	Jan, Mar, May, Sept, Nov	11:00 a.m.-12:30 p.m. and 2:45 p.m.-4:00 p.m.

Contract	Trading Unit	Prices Quoted In	Minimum Price Fluctuation
• Wheat	100 metric tons	pence per ton	.05 pence (5 pounds)

Futures Options

Contract	Trading Unit	Prices Quoted In	Minimum Price Fluctuation	Strike Prices
• Barley	1 barley futures contract	pence per ton	5 pence (5 pounds)	1 pound per ton apart
• Wheat	1 wheat futures contract	pence per ton	5 pence (5 pounds)	1 pound per ton apart

(London Meat Futures Market)

Futures

Contract	Trading Unit	Prices Quoted In	Minimum Price Fluctuation
• Cattle	5000 kilograms	pence per kilogram	5 pence (5 pounds)
• Pig	3250 kilograms	pence per kilogram	1 pence (3.25 pounds)

(London Potato Futures Market)

Futures

Contract	Trading Unit	Prices Quoted In	Minimum Price Fluctuation
• Potatoes (Cash Settled)	40 metric tons	pence per ton	10 pence per ton
• Potatoes (Main Crop)	40 metric tons	pence per ton	10 pence per ton

Futures Options

Contract	Trading Unit	Prices Quoted In	Minimum Price Fluctuation	Strike Prices
• Potatoes (Main Crop)	1 potato futures contract	pence per ton	10 pence per ton	5 pence apart

Last Trading Day	Contract Months	Trading Hours
23rd day of month	Jan, Mar, May, July, Sept, Nov	11:00 a.m.-12:30 p.m. and 2:45 p.m.-4:00 p.m.

Expiration Day	Contract Months	Trading Hours
day after last trading day	Jan, Mar, May, Nov	11:00 a.m.-12:30 p.m. and 2:45 p.m.-6:00 p.m.
day after last trading day	Jan, Mar, May, July, Sept, Nov	11:00 a.m.-12:30 p.m. and 2:45 p.m.-6:00 p.m.

Last Trading Day	Contract Months	Trading Hours
last Friday of month	Jan, Feb, Mar, Apr, Sept, Oct, Nov	10:00 a.m.-12:00 p.m. and 2:15 p.m.-3:45 p.m.
last Tuesday of month	Feb, Apr, June, Aug, Oct, Nov	10:00 a.m.-12:00 p.m. and 2:15 p.m.-3:45 p.m.

Last Trading Day	Contract Months	Trading Hours
last Tuesday of month	Mar, July, Aug, Sept	11:00 a.m.-12:30 p.m. and 2:45 p.m.-4:00 p.m.
10th day of month	Feb, Apr, May, Nov	11:00 a.m.-12:30 p.m. and 2:45 a.m.-4:00 p.m.

Expiration Day	Contract Months	Trading Hours
last business day	Mar, Apr, May, Nov	11:00 a.m.-12:30 p.m. 2:45 p.m.-4:00 p.m.

(Soya Bean Meal Futures Association)

Futures

Contract	Trading Unit	Prices Quoted In	Minimum Price Fluctuation
• Soybean Meal	20 metric tons	pounds per ton	10 pounds (2 pounds)

International Petroleum Exchange of London (IPE)

Futures

Contract	Trading Unit	Prices Quoted In	Minimum Price Fluctuation
• Crude Oil	1000 barrels Brent crude	dollars and cents per barrel	1 cent per barrel
• Gas Oil	100 tons gas oil	dollars and cents per ton	25 cents per ton

Futures Options

Contract	Trading Unit	Prices Quoted In	Minimum Price Fluctuation	Strike Prices
• Gas Oil	1 gas oil futures contract	dollars and cents per ton	5 cents per ton	$5 apart

International Stock Exchange (ISE)

Futures Options

Contract	Trading Unit	Prices Quoted In	Minimum Price Fluctuation	Strike Prices
• Financial Times Stock Index	10 pounds × index	pence per 10 pounds	.005 pence	25 index points apart
• LTOM (63 UK Equity Options)	1000 shares	pence per underlying share	.0025 pence	10 points apart

Last Trading Day	Contract Months	Trading Hours
22nd day of month	Feb, Apr, June, Aug, Oct, Dec	10:30 a.m.-12:00 p.m. and 2:45 p.m.-4:00 p.m.

Last Trading Day	Contract Months	Trading Hours
10th day of month before contract	6 nearest months	9:15 a.m.-12:15 p.m. and 2:30 p.m.-5:15 p.m.
3 business days before 13th day of month	9 nearest months	9:15 a.m.-12:15 p.m. and 2:30 p.m.-5:15 p.m.

Expiration Day	Contract Months	Trading Hours
3rd Wednesday of month before contract	9 nearest months	9:15 a.m.-12:24 p.m. and 2:30 p.m.-5:25 p.m.

Expiration Day	Contract Months	Trading Hours
last trading day	4 nearest months	9:05 a.m.-3:40 p.m.
2 days before end of month	Jan, Apr, July, Oct or Feb, May, Aug, Nov or Mar, June, Sept, Dec	9:05 a.m.-4:05 p.m.

Contract	Trading Unit	Prices Quoted In	Minimum Price Fluctuation	Strike Prices
• U.S. Dollar-Deutsche Mark	62,500 Deutsche marks	dollars and cents per mark	1 cent	1 cent apart
• U.S. Dollar-Sterling	12,000 British pounds	dollars and cents per pound	5 cents	5 cents apart

London Futures and Options Exchange (FOX)

Futures

Contract	Trading Unit	Prices Quoted In	Minimum Price Fluctuation
• Cocoa	10 metric tons	pounds per ton	1 pound per ton
• Coffee	5 tons	pounds per ton	1 pound per ton
• Sugar (Raw)	50 tons	dollars and cents per ton	20 cents per ton
• Sugar (White)	50 tons	dollars and cents per ton	10 cents per ton

Futures Options

Contract	Trading Unit	Prices Quoted In	Minimum Price Fluctuation	Strike Prices
• Cocoa	1 cocoa futures contract	pounds per ton	1 pound per ton	50 pounds per ton
• Coffee	1 coffee futures contract	pounds per ton	1 pound per ton	50 pounds per ton
• Sugar (Raw)	1 sugar futures contract	cents per ton	5 cents per ton	$5 apart

Expiration Day	Contract Months	Trading Hours
last trading day	Mar, June, Sept, Dec and and 2 of 3 nearest months	9:00 a.m.-3:40 p.m.
last trading day	Mar, June, Sept, Dec and 2 of 3 nearest months	9:05 a.m.-3:40 p.m.

Last Trading Day	Contract Months	Trading Hours
last market day of month	Mar, May, July, Sept, July, Sept, Dec	10:00 a.m.-12:58 p.m. and 2:30 p.m.-4:45 p.m.
last market day of month	Jan, Mar, May, July, Sept, Nov, Jan	9:45 a.m.-12:32 p.m. and 2:30 p.m.-5:02 p.m.
last market day of month before contract	Mar, May, Aug, Oct, Dec	10:30 a.m.-12:30 p.m. and 2:30 p.m.-7:00 p.m.
last market day before 15th of month	Mar, May, Aug, Oct, Dec	9:45 a.m.-7:10 p.m.

Expiration Day	Contract Months	Trading Hours
3rd Wednesday of month before contract	Mar, May, July, Sept, Dec	10:00 a.m.-1:00 p.m. and 2:30 p.m.-5:00 p.m.
3rd Wednesday of month before contract	Jan, Mar, May, July, Sept, Nov	9:45 a.m.-12:30 p.m. and 2:30 p.m.-5:00 p.m.
3rd Wednesday of month before contract	Mar, May, Aug, Oct, Dec	10:30 a.m.-12:30 p.m. and 2:30 p.m.-7:00 p.m.

London International Financial Futures Exchange (LIFFE)

Futures

Contract	Trading Unit	Prices Quoted In	Minimum Price Fluctuation
• British Pound	25,000 British pounds	dollars and cents per pound	1 cent ($2.50)
• Deutsche Mark	125,000 Deutsche marks	dollars and cents per mark	1 cent ($12.50)
• Eurodollar	$1 million	100 minus interest rate	1 cent ($25)
• Financial Times Stock Index	25 pounds per index point	index divided by 10	.05 pound (12.50 pounds)
• German Government Bond	250,000 mark bond (6% coupon)	per 100 marks	.01 mark (25 marks)
• Gilt (Long)	50,000 British pound bond (12% coupon)	per 100 pounds	1/32 pound (15.625 pounds)
• Gilt (Medium)	50,000 British pound bond (9% coupon)	per 100 pounds	1/32 pound (15.625 pounds)
• Gilt (Short)	100,000 British pound bond (10% coupon)	per 100 pounds	1/64 pound (15.625 pounds)
• Japanese Government Bond	100,000,000 yen bond (6% coupon)	per 100 yen	.01 yen (10,000 yen)
• Japanese Yen	12,500,000 yen	dollars and cents per 100 yen	1 cent ($12.50)
• Sterling (3-Month)	500,000 pounds	100 minus interest rate	.01 pound (12.50 pounds)
• Swiss Franc	125,000 Swiss francs	dollars and cents per franc	1 cent ($12.50)
• U.S. Dollar-Deutsche Mark	$50,000 against marks	dollars and cents per mark	.0001 cent (5 marks)
• U.S. Treasury Bond	$100,000 bond (8% coupon)	per $100	1/32 dollar ($31.25)

Last Trading Day	Contract Months	Trading Hours
2 business days before delivery	Mar, June, Sept, Dec	8:32 a.m.-4:02 p.m.
2 business days before delivery	Mar, June, Sept, Dec	8:34 a.m.-4:04 p.m.
2 business days before 3rd Wednesday of month	Mar, June, Sept, Dec	8:10 a.m.-4:00 p.m.
last business day of month	Mar, June, Sept, Dec	9:05 a.m.-4:05 p.m.
3 business days before delivery	Mar, June, Sept, Dec	8:10 a.m.-4:00 p.m.
2 business days before end of month	Mar, June, Sept, Dec	9:00 a.m.-4:15 p.m.
2 business days before end of month	Mar, June, Sept, Dec	8:55 a.m.-4:10 p.m.
2 business days before end of month	Mar, June, Sept, Dec	9:05 a.m.-4:20 p.m.
1 business day before end of month	Mar, June, Sept, Dec	8:10 a.m.-4:05 p.m.
2 business days before delivery	Mar, June, Sept, Dec	8:30 a.m.-4:00 p.m.
3rd Wednesday of month	Mar, June, Sept, Dec	8:20 a.m.-4:02 p.m.
2 business days before delivery	Mar, June, Sept, Dec	8:36 a.m.-4:06 p.m.
2 business days before delivery	Mar, June, Sept, Dec	8:34 a.m.-4:04 p.m.
7 CBOT business days before end of month	Mar, June, Sept, Dec	8:15 a.m.-4:10 p.m.

Futures Options

Contract	Trading Unit	Prices Quoted In	Minimum Price Fluctuation	Strike Prices
• British Pound	25,000 pounds	dollars and cents per pound	1 cent ($2.50)	5 cents apart
• Eurodollar	1 Eurodollar futures contract	.01 cent multiples	1 cent ($25)	25 cents apart
• Long Gilt	1 long gilt futures contract	multiples of $1/64$ pound	$1/64$ of a pound	2 pounds apart
• Sterling (3-Month)	1 sterling futures contract	pence	1 pence (12.50 pounds)	25 pence apart
• U.S. Dollar-Deutsche Mark	$50,000 against marks	dollars and cents per mark	.01 pfennig per dollar (5 marks)	5 pfennigs per dollar apart
• U.S. Treasury Bond	1 $100,000 T-bond futures contract	multiples of $1/64$ of a point	$1/64$ ($15.625)	2 points apart

London Metal Exchange (LME)

Futures

Contract	Trading Unit	Prices Quoted In	Minimum Price Fluctuation
• Aluminum (High Grade)	25 metric tons	dollars and cents per ton	1 cent ($25)
• Aluminum (Primary)	25 metric tons	pounds and pence per ton	50 pence per ton (12.50 pounds)
• Copper (Grade A)	25 metric tons	pounds and pence per ton	50 pence per ton (12.50 pounds)
• Copper (Standard)	25 metric tons	pounds and pence per ton	50 pence per ton (12.50 pounds)

Expiration Day	Contract Months	Trading Hours
last trading day	Mar, June, Sept, Dec	8:34 a.m.-4:02 p.m.
last trading day	Mar, June, Sept, Dec	8:32 a.m.-4:00 p.m.
last trading day	Mar, June, Sept, Dec	9:02 a.m.-4:15 p.m.
last trading day	Mar, June, Sept, Dec	8:22 a.m.-4:02 p.m.
3 business days before 3rd Wednesday of month	Mar, June, Sept, Dec and 3 nearest months	8:36 a.m.-4:04 p.m.
1st Friday at least 6 CBOT working days before delivery	Mar, June, Sept, Dec	8:17 a.m.-4:10 p.m.

Last Trading Day	Contract Months	Trading Hours
—	daily between spot and 3 nearest months	11:55 a.m.-12:00 p.m. and 12:55 p.m.-1:00 p.m.; also 3:40 p.m.-3:45 p.m. and 4:20 p.m.-4:25 p.m.
—	daily between spot and 3 nearest months	11:50 a.m.-11:55 a.m. and 12:50 p.m.-12:55 p.m.; also 3:35 p.m.-3:40 p.m. and 4:15 p.m.-4:20 p.m.
—	daily between spot and 3 nearest months	12:00 p.m.-12:05 p.m. and 12:30 p.m.-12:35 p.m.; also 3:30 p.m.-3:35 p.m. and 4:10 p.m.-4:15 p.m.
—	daily between spot and 3 nearest months	12:00 p.m.-12:05 p.m. and 12:35 p.m.-12:40 p.m.; also 3:30 p.m.-3:35 p.m. and 4:10 p.m.-4:15 p.m.

Contract	Trading Unit	Prices Quoted In	Minimum Price Fluctuation
• Lead	25 metric tons	pounds and pence per ton	25 pence per ton (6.25 pounds)
• Nickel	6 metric tons	pounds and pence per ton	1 pound (6 pounds)
• Silver (10,000 ounces)	10,000 troy ounces	cents per ounce	10 cents ($10)
• Silver (2,000 ounces)	2,000 troy ounces	cents per ounce	10 cents ($2)
• Zinc	25 metric tons	pounds and pence per ton	25 pence per ton (6.25 pounds)

Futures Options

Contract	Trading Unit	Prices Quoted In	Minimum Price Fluctuation	Strike Prices
• Aluminum (High Grade)	1 25 metric ton aluminum futures contract	dollars or pounds per ton	—	$25 or 25 pounds per ton apart
• Aluminum (Primary)	1 25 metric ton aluminum futures contract	dollars or pounds per ton	—	$25 or 25 pounds per ton apart
• Copper (Grade A)	1 25 metric ton copper futures contract	pounds per ton	0.50 pounds per ton	$25 or 25 pounds per ton apart
• Lead	1 25 metric ton lead futures contract	pounds per ton	0.25 pounds per ton	$20 or 20 pounds per ton apart
• Nickel	1 6 metric ton nickel futures contract	pounds per ton	1 pound per ton	$50 or 50 pounds per ton apart
• Zinc	1 25 metric ton zinc futures contract	pounds per ton	0.25 pounds per ton	$20 or 20 pounds per ton apart

Last Trading Day	Contract Months	Trading Hours
—	daily between spot and 3 nearest months	12:05 p.m.-12:10 p.m. and 12:40 p.m.-12:45 p.m.; also 3:20 p.m.-3:25 p.m. and 4:00 p.m.-4:05 p.m.
—	daily between spot and 3 nearest months	12:15 p.m.-12:20 p.m. and 1:00 p.m.-1:05 p.m.; also 3:45 p.m.-3:50 p.m. and 4:25 p.m.-4:30 p.m.
—	daily between spot and 3 nearest months	11:45 a.m.-11:50 a.m. and 1:05 p.m.-1:05 p.m.; also 3:50 p.m.-3:55 p.m. and 4:30 p.m.-4:35 p.m.
—	daily between spot and 3 nearest months	11:45 a.m.-12:15 p.m. and 1:05 p.m.-1:10 p.m.; also 3:50 p.m.-3:55 p.m. and 4:30 p.m.-4:35 p.m.
—	daily between spot and 3 nearest months	12:10 p.m.-12:15 p.m. and 12:45 p.m.-12:50 p.m.; also 3:25 p.m.-3:30 p.m. and 4:05 p.m.-4:10 p.m.

Expiration Day	Contract Months	Trading Hours
—	Jan and every 2nd month after that	all day
—	Jan and every 2nd month after that	all day
—	Jan and every 2nd month after that	all day
—	Feb and every 2nd month after that	all day
—	Feb and every 2nd month after that	all day
—	Feb and every 2nd month after that	all day

FRENCH SECURITIES, FUTURES AND OPTIONS EXCHANGES

Lille Potato Futures Market (LPFM)

Futures

Contract	Trading Unit	Prices Quoted In	Minimum Price Fluctuation
• Potatoes	20 tons	francs per kilogram	25 francs per 100 kilograms

Marche A Terme Instrument Financiers (MATIF)

Futures

Contract	Trading Unit	Prices Quoted In	Minimum Price Fluctuation
• French Gov't National Bond	500,000 franc bond (10% coupon)	percent of par in basis points	.05 points = 250 francs
• French T-Bill (90-Day)	5 million franc bond	100 minus interest rate	.01 points = 125 francs

Futures Options

Contract	Trading Unit	Prices Quoted In	Minimum Price Fluctuation	Strike Prices
• French Gov't National Bond	1 French gov't national bond futures contract	percent of par in basis points	0.01 points = 50 francs	even strike prices

Paris Futures Exchange (PFE)

Futures

Contract	Trading Unit	Prices Quoted In	Minimum Price Fluctuation
• Cocoa Beans	10 metric tons	francs per kilogram	50 francs per 100 kilograms
• Cocoa Butter	10 metric tons	francs per kilogram	1 franc per 100 kilograms
• Coffee	5 metric tons	francs per kilogram	1 franc per 100 kilograms
• White Sugar	50 metric tons	francs per ton	1 franc per ton

Last Trading Day	Contract Months	Trading Hours
2nd Tuesday of contract month	Feb, Apr, May, Nov	11:00 a.m.-12:45 p.m. and 3:00 p.m.-4:30 p.m.

Last Trading Day	Contract Months	Trading Hours
4 days before last business day of month	Mar, June, Sept, Dec	10:00 a.m.-3:00 p.m.
business day after T-bills 3rd monthly adjudication	Mar, June, Sept, Dec	10:00 a.m.-3:00 p.m.

Expiration Day	Contract Months	Trading Hours
last day of trading	Mar, June, Sept, Dec	10:00 a.m.-3:00 p.m.

Last Trading Day	Contract Months	Trading Hours
last day of contract month	Mar, May, July, Sept, Dec	10:30 a.m.-1:00 p.m. and 3:00 p.m.-5:30 p.m.
20th day of month before contract month	Mar, May, July, Sept, Dec	11:15 a.m.-1:00 p.m. and 3:00 p.m.-5:30 p.m.
last day of contract month	Jan, Mar, May, July, Sept, Nov	10:15 a.m.-1:00 p.m. and 3:00 p.m.-5:30 p.m.
last day of contract month	Mar, May, Aug, Oct, Dec	10:45 a.m.-1:00 p.m. and 3:00 p.m.-7:00 p.m.

HONG KONG SECURITIES, FUTURES EXCHANGE

Hong Kong Futures Exchange (HKFE)

Futures

Contract	Trading Unit	Prices Quoted In	Minimum Price Fluctuation
• Gold	100 troy ounces	dollars and cents per ounce	10 cents = $100
• Hang Seng Index	50 Hong Kong dollars × index	index points	1 index point
• Soybeans	30,000 kilograms	Hong Kong dollars and cents	20 cents per 60 kilograms
• Sugar	50 long tons	dollars and cents per pound	$1/100$ cent = $11.20

JAPANESE SECURITIES, FUTURES EXCHANGES

Osaka Securities Exchange (OSE)

Futures

Contract	Trading Unit	Prices Quoted In	Minimum Price Fluctuation
• Nikkei Stock Average	average × 1000	yen per average	10 yen per average
• Osaka Stock Futures 50	index of 50 stocks	index average	$1/10$ yen

Last Trading Day	Contract Months	Trading Hours
last business day of contract month	2 nearest months, even months, spot months	9:00 a.m.-12:00 p.m. and 2:00 p.m.-5:30 p.m.
2nd business day of trading month	3 even months	10:00 a.m.-12:30 p.m. and 2:30 p.m.-3:30 p.m.
15th day of contract month	6 nearest months	9:00 a.m.-10:50 a.m. and 12:50 p.m.-2:50 p.m.
business day before first day of contract month	Jan, Mar, May, July, Sept, Oct	10:30 a.m.-12:00 p.m. and 2:25 p.m.-4:00 p.m.

Last Trading Day	Contract Months	Trading Hours
3rd day before settlement	Mar, June, Sept, Dec	9:00 a.m.-11:15 a.m. and 2:00 p.m.-3:15 p.m.
6th day before delivery	Mar, June, Sept, Dec	9:00 a.m.-11:00 a.m. and 1:00 p.m.-3:00 p.m.

Tokyo Commodity Exchange (TCE)
Futures

Contract	Trading Unit	Prices Quoted In	Minimum Price Fluctuation
• Cotton Yarn	4000 pounds	yen per pound	0.1 yen per 1 pound
• Gold	1 kilogram bar	yen per gram	1 yen per gram
• Platinum	500 grams	yen per gram	1 yen per gram
• Rubber	5000 kilograms	yen per kilogram	0.1 yen per 1 kilogram
• Silver	30 kilograms	yen per gram	0.1 yen per 10 grams
• Woolen Yarn	500 kilograms	yen per gram	1 yen per 1 gram

Tokyo Grain Exchange (TGE)
Futures

Contract	Trading Unit	Prices Quoted In	Minimum Price Fluctuation
• American Soybeans	15 tons	yen per kilogram	10 yen per 60 kilograms
• Chinese Soybeans	250 bags	yen per kilogram bag	10 yen per 60 kilogram bag
• Japanese Soybeans	40 bags	yen per kilogram bag	10 yen per 60 kilogram bag
• Potato Starch	100 bags	yen per kilogram bag	1 yen per 25 kilogram bag
• Red Beans	80 bags	yen per kilogram bag	10 yen per 30 kilogram bag
• White Beans	40 bags	yen per kilogram bag	10 yen per kilogram bag

Last Trading Day	Contract Months	Trading Hours
4th business day before delivery	6 nearest months	8:50 a.m. and 10:00 a.m.; 1:50 p.m. and 3:10 p.m.
3rd business day before delivery	odd months after an even month; each even month within 1 year of odd month	9:10 a.m., 10:30 a.m., 11:30 a.m.; 1:10 p.m., 2:30 p.m., 3:45 p.m.
3rd business day before delivery	odd months after an even month; each even month within 1 year of odd month	after silver calls
5th business day before delivery	4 nearest months, then each even month	9:45 a.m., 10:45 a.m.; 1:45 p.m., 2:45 p.m., 3:30 p.m.
end of contract month	odd months after an even month; each even month within 1 year of odd month	after gold calls
4th business day before delivery	6 nearest months	after cotton yarn calls

Last Trading Day	Contract Months	Trading Hours
2 days before last business day of contract month	even months	10:00 a.m.-11:00 a.m. and 1:00 p.m.-2:00 p.m.
—	6 nearest months	10:00 a.m.-11:00 a.m. and 1:00 p.m.- 2:00 p.m.
—	3 nearest months	3:00 p.m.
—	3 nearest months	3:00 p.m.
—	6 nearest months	9:00 a.m.-11:00 a.m. and 1:00 p.m.-3:00 p.m.
—	6 nearest months	3:00 p.m.

Tokyo Stock Exchange (TSE)

Futures

Contract	Trading Unit	Prices Quoted In	Minimum Price Fluctuation
• Japanese Gov't Bond (10 Year)	10-year yen bond	—	0.01 yen per 100 yen
• Japanese Gov't Bond (20 Year)	20-year yen bond	—	0.01 yen per 100 yen
• Tokyo Stock Price Index	stock index	index points	1 index point

Tokyo Sugar Exchange (TSUE)

Futures

Contract	Trading Unit	Prices Quoted In	Minimum Price Fluctuation
• Raw Sugar	10 metric tons	—	—
• Refined White Sugar	9 metric tons	—	—

MALAYSIAN SECURITIES, FUTURES EXCHANGE

Kuala Lumpur Commodity Exchange (KLCE)

Futures

Contract	Trading Unit	Prices Quoted In	Minimum Price Fluctuation
• Cocoa	10 metric tons	dollars per ton	$1 per ton
• Crude Palm Oil	25 metric tons	Malaysian dollars per ton	1 Malaysian dollar per ton
• Rubber	20 metric tons (for contract months), 60 metric tons for distant delivery	Malaysian dollars and cents per kilogram	$1/4$ Malaysian cent per kilogram

Last Trading Day	Contract Months	Trading Hours
9th business day before delivery	Mar, June, Sept, Dec	9:00 a.m.-11:00 a.m. and 1:00 p.m.-3:00 p.m.
9th business day before delivery	Mar, June, Sept, Dec	9:00 a.m.-11:15 a.m. and 1:00 p.m.-3:00 p.m.
3rd business day before delivery	Mar, June, Sept, Dec	9:00 a.m.-11:15 a.m. and 1:00 p.m.-3:15 p.m.

Last Trading Day	Contract Months	Trading Hours
—	odd months	9:30 a.m., 10:30 a.m., 1:30 p.m., 3:30 p.m.
—	6 nearest months	9:30 a.m., 10:30 a.m., 1:30 p.m., 3:30 p.m.

Last Trading Day	Contract Months	Trading Hours
20th day of month	Jan, Mar, May, July, Sept, Nov, Dec	11:15 a.m.-12:00 p.m. and 4:00 p.m.- 6:00 p.m.
15th day of preceding month	6 nearest months	11:00 a.m.-12:30 p.m. and 3:30 p.m.-6:00 p.m.
—	—	10:00 a.m.-1:00 p.m. and 4:00 p.m.-6:00 p.m.

Contract	Trading Unit	Prices Quoted In	Minimum Price Fluctuation
• Rubber	10 tons (for single contract months), 30 tons for delivery quarter	Malaysian dollars and cents per kilogram	1/4 Malaysian cent per kilogram
• Tin	5 tons	dollars per ton	$5 per ton

THE NETHERLANDS SECURITIES, FUTURES AND OPTIONS EXCHANGES

European Options Exchange (EOE)

Futures Options

Contract	Trading Unit	Prices Quoted In	Minimum Price Fluctuation	Strike Prices
• Bond Index	100 Dutch florin × index	index points	0.05 Dutch florin	2.50 Dutch florin apart
• British Pound	10,000 pounds	Dutch florin per 100 pounds	0.05 Dutch florin apart	5 Dutch florin apart
• Dollar	$10,000	Dutch florin per $100	0.05 Dutch florin	5 Dutch florin apart
• Dutch Gov't Bonds	10,000 Dutch florin bond	100 units	0.10 Dutch florin	2.50% of principal apart
• EOE Stock Index	100 Dutch florin × index	index points	0.10 Dutch florin	5 Dutch florin apart
• Gold	10 troy ounces	dollars and cents per troy ounce	10 cents = $1	$10 apart
• Major Market Index	index × $100	index points	1/8 point	5 points apart
• Silver	250 troy ounces	dollars and cents per ounce	1 cent = $2.50	25 cents apart

Financiale Terminjmarkt Amsterdam (FTA)

Futures

Contract	Trading Unit	Prices Quoted In	Minimum Price Fluctuation
• Guilder Bond	1000 Dutch florin × bond index	index points	0.01 point = 10 Dutch

Last Trading Day	Contract Months	Trading Hours
last business day of month before contract	nearest 4 to 6 months	10:00 a.m.-1:00 p.m. and 4:00 p.m.-6:00 p.m.
3rd to last business day of month	4 nearest months	12:15 p.m.-1:00 p.m. and 4:00 p.m.-6:00 p.m.

Expiration Day	Contract Months	Trading Hours
3rd Saturday after last trading day	Feb, May, Aug, Nov	10:30 a.m.-4:30 p.m.
3rd Saturday after last trading day	Mar, June, Sept, Dec	10:00 a.m.-4:30 p.m.
3rd Saturday after last trading day	Mar, June, Sept, Dec	10:00 a.m.-4:30 p.m.
3rd Saturday after last trading day	Feb, May, Aug, Nov	11:30 a.m.-4:30 p.m.
3rd Saturday after last trading day	Jan, Apr, July, Oct	10:30 a.m.-4:30 p.m.
3rd Saturday after last trading day	3 nearest months	10:00 a.m.-4:30 p.m.
3rd Saturday after last trading day	3 nearest months	12:00 p.m.-4:30 p.m.
3rd Saturday after last trading day	Mar, June, Sept, Dec	10:00 a.m.-4:30 p.m.

Last Trading Day	Contract Months	Trading Hours
last business day of month	Feb, May, Aug, Nov	10:45 a.m.-4:30 p.m.

NEW ZEALAND SECURITIES, FUTURES EXCHANGES

New Zealand Futures Exchange (NZFE)

Futures

Contract	Trading Unit	Prices Quoted In	Minimum Price Fluctuation
• Barclays Share Price Index	20 New Zealand dollars × index	index points	—
• Dollar	$50,000 per	dollars per New Zealand dollar	0.00001 cent
• Five-Year Gov't Stock	$100,000 New Zealand gov't stock (10% coupon)	—	0.01%
• New Zealand Dollar	100,000 New Zealand dollars	dollars and cents per New Zealand dollar	0.00001 cent
• 90-Day Bank Accepted Bills	$500,000 New Zealand principal	100 minus price	0.01%

SINGAPORE SECURITIES, FUTURES AND OPTIONS EXCHANGES

Singapore International Monetary Exchange (SIMEX)

Futures

Contract	Trading Unit	Prices Quoted In	Minimum Price Fluctuation
• British Pound	62,500 pounds	dollars and cents per pound	0.0002 cent = $12.50
• Deutsche Mark	125,000 German marks	dollars and cents per mark	0.0001 cent = $12.50
• Eurodollar 90-Day Time Deposit	$1 million principal	percent of par in basis points	0.01 point = $25
• Japanese Yen	12,500,000 yen	dollars and cents per yen	0.000001 point = $12.50
• Nikkei Stock Average	average × 500 yen	index points	0.05 points = 2500 yen

Last Trading Day	Contract Months	Trading Hours
2nd to last business day of contract month	3 nearest months and Mar, June, Sept, Dec	9:15 a.m.-3:45 p.m.
1st Wednesday after 9th day of settlement month	4 nearest months and Mar, June, Sept, Dec	8:15 a.m.-4:45 p.m.
1st Wednesday after 9th day of settlement month	Mar, June, Sept, Dec	8:00 a.m.-5:00 p.m.
2 business days before 1st Wednesday of settlement month	3 nearest months	8:05 a.m.-4:55 p.m.
1st Wednesday after 9th day of settlement month	3 nearest months and Mar, June, Sept, Dec	8:10 a.m.-4:50 p.m.

Last Trading Day	Contract Months	Trading Hours
2nd business day before 3rd Wednesday of contract month	Spot, Mar, June, Sept, Dec	8:25 a.m.-5:15 p.m.
2nd business day before 3rd Wednesday of contract month	Spot, Mar, June, Sept, Dec	8:20 a.m.-5:10 p.m.
2nd London business day before 3rd Wednesday of contract month	Spot, Mar, June, Sept, Dec	8:30 a.m.-5:20 p.m.
2nd business day before 3rd Wednesday of contract month	Spot, Mar, June, Sept, Dec	8:15 a.m.-5:05 p.m.
3rd Wednesday of contract month	Spot, Mar, June, Sept, Dec	8:00 a.m.-2:15 p.m.

Futures Options

Contract	Trading Unit	Prices Quoted In	Minimum Price Fluctuation	Strike Prices
• Deutsche Mark	1 mark futures contract	points of 100%	0.01 point = $12.50	1 cent apart
• Eurodollar 90-Day Time Deposit	1 Eurodollar futures contract	points of 100%	0.01 point = $25	0.50 point apart
• Japanese Yen	1 yen futures contract	points of 1000%	0.001 point = $12.50	0.01 point apart

SWEDISH SECURITIES, FUTURES AND OPTIONS EXCHANGES

Stockholm Options Market (SOM)

Forwards

Contract	Trading Unit	Prices Quoted In	Minimum Price Fluctuation
• OMX Index	index	index points	—

Futures Options

Contract	Trading Unit	Prices Quoted In	Minimum Price Fluctuation	Strike Prices
• OMX Index	index	percentage of option	0.01 of option	20 index points apart
• Swedish T-Note (5-Year)	1,000,000 Swedish krona note	percentage of option	0.01 of option	20 index points apart

Swedish Options and Futures Exchange (SOFE)

Forwards

Contract	Trading Unit	Prices Quoted In	Minimum Price Fluctuation
• SX 16 Stock Index	index × 1000	index points	0.05 Swedish krona

Futures Options

Contract	Trading Unit	Prices Quoted In	Minimum Price Fluctuation	Strike Prices
• SX 16 Stock Index	index × 100	index points	0.05 Swedish krona	10 Swedish krona apart

Expiration Day	Contract Months	Trading Hours
last trading day	Mar, June, Sept, Dec, and serial months	8:20 a.m.-5:10 p.m.
last trading day	Mar, June, Sept, Dec	
2 Fridays before 3rd Wednesday of contract months	Mar, June, Sept, Dec and serial months	8:15 a.m.-5:05 p.m.

Last Trading Day	Contract Months	Trading Hours
4th Friday of expiration month	Jan, Mar, May, July, Sept, Nov	10:00 a.m.-4:00 p.m.

Expiration Day	Contract Months	Trading Hours
last trading day	Jan, Mar, May, July, Sept, Nov	10:00 a.m.-4:00 p.m.
last trading day	—	9:30 a.m.-3:00 p.m.

Last Trading Day	Contract Months	Trading Hours
last day before expiration	monthly	9:45 a.m.-10:00 p.m.

Expiration Day	Contract Months	Trading Hours
4th Friday of contract month	monthly	9:45 a.m.-10:00 p.m.

5. HISTORICAL DATA

This section of the *Handbook* allows you to follow the major ups and downs of the financial markets and the United States economy during the 20th century. Although history never repeats itself exactly, it is important to understand historical market cycles if you are to understand where the markets and economy stand today, as well as where they might be going in the future.

The historical section is presented with graphs accompanied by tabular data and explanations of what the information signifies to you as an investor. Graphs are based on end-of-month closing stock index values; municipal bond yields compiled the first week of each month; month-end London morning fix prices of gold; monthly average discount, prime, and federal funds rates; and monthly or monthly average government economic statistics.

The tabular data show annual highs, lows, and year-end figures on the same monthly bases as the above with these exceptions: stock indexes are based on daily closing figures; the consumer and producer price indexes and money supply (M-1) statistics are annual percentage changes (for instance, December 1994 vs. December 1993); gold prices are daily London morning fixings; and the discount and prime rates are day-end figures.

Note that the month-end data points on which the stock index graphs are based may reflect different highs and lows than the daily closing data. The month-end data plot long-term trends with a minimum of aberrations caused by PROGRAM TRADES and other NOISE, while the daily data are more subject to short-term fluctuations. The graphs showing trends of the discount and prime rates, because they are based on monthly averages, will also differ from the accompanying tables, which are based on day-end rates.

Much of the securities data and related charts have been provided courtesy of EQUIS International, an investment analysis and charting service. EQUIS International has its headquarters at 3950 South 700 East, Suite 100, Salt Lake City, Utah 84107 (phone: (800) 882-3040, (801) 265-9996). Interactive Data Corporation of 95 Hayden Avenue, Lexington, Massachusetts 02173 (phone: (617) 863-8100) provided much of the data utilized by EQUIS in producing the tables and charts. The table data used was taken from as far back as the data banks went. In the case of the Dow Jones 30 Industrials Stock Average the data went as far back as 1897.

Much of the economic data and charts have been provided courtesy of the WEFA Group, with headquarters at 401 City Avenue, Suite 300, Bala Cynwyd, Pennsylvania 19004 (phone: (610) 667-6000). If data were received from another source, such as the Federal Reserve Board, the U.S. Bureau of Labor Statistics, Dow Jones & Co., or Standard & Poor's Corporation, either EQUIS or WEFA and that source have been credited.

AMEX MARKET VALUE INDEX

Source: American Stock Exchange, Interactive Data Corporation
Chart by MetaStock, EQUIS International

This graph shows the movement of the American Stock Exchange Market Value Index. Formerly known as the American Stock Exchange Index, the AMVI is a market value-weighted index (i.e., the impact of a component's price change is proportionate to the overall market value of the issue). The index measures the performance of more than 800 issues, representing all major industry groups, including shares, American Depositary Receipts and warrants. The companies listed on the AMEX tend to be medium-sized and smaller growth firms. One unique aspect of this index is that cash dividends paid by the component stocks are assumed to be reinvested and thus are reflected in the index.

Year	High	Low	Close
1968	74.82	48.66	73.69
1969	84.49	57.22	60.01
1970	62.77	36.10	49.21
1971	60.86	49.09	58.49
1972	69.18	58.55	64.52
1973	65.23	42.16	45.16
1974	51.01	29.13	30.16
1975	48.43	31.10	41.74
1976	54.92	42.16	54.92
1977	63.95	54.31	63.95
1978	88.44	59.87	75.28
1979	123.67	76.02	123.54
1980	185.38	107.85	174.49
1981	190.18	138.38	160.31
1982	170.93	118.65	170.30
1983	249.03	169.61	223.01
1984	227.73	189.16	204.26
1985	246.13	202.06	246.13
1986	285.19	240.30	263.27
1987	365.01	231.90	260.35
1988	309.59	260.35	306.01
1989	397.03	305.24	378.00
1990	383.32	286.93	308.11

Year	High	Low	Close
1991	395.06	295.80	395.05
1992	419.18	361.72	399.23
1993	484.59	394.96	477.15
1994	488.02	419.43	433.67

BOND BUYER INDEX (11 BONDS)

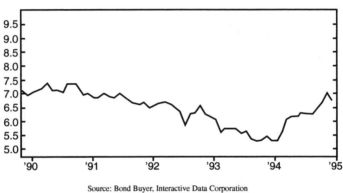

Source: Bond Buyer, Interactive Data Corporation
Chart by MetaStock, EQUIS International

This graph shows the movement of the *Bond Buyer* Index of 11 bonds. The *Bond Buyer* is a daily newspaper covering the municipal bond market. This index is made up of the yields of 11 newly issued general obligation municipal bonds averaging 20 years to maturity rated Aa and selling at par. The issuers of these bonds, whose average rating is second only to Aaa, are among the most creditworthy of all those issuing bonds in the municipal market. The yield offered by these bonds, therefore, is lower than that of less creditworthy municipalities, but it acts as a benchmark against which market participants compare other municipal bond yields.

Year	High	Low	Close
1917	4.55	3.88	4.60
1918	4.65	4.39	4.42
1919	4.53	4.42	4.53
1920	5.25	4.53	5.03
1921	5.16	4.48	4.35
1922	4.37	4.05	4.14
1923	4.38	4.10	4.35
1924	4.35	4.07	4.15
1925	4.23	3.98	4.19
1926	4.19	4.05	4.10
1927	4.10	3.89	3.83
1928	4.15	3.83	4.13
1929	4.47	4.13	4.19
1930	4.25	3.92	4.05
1931	4.23	3.60	4.66
1932	4.66	4.02	3.81

Year	High	Low	Close
1933	4.90	3.81	4.50
1934	4.50	3.38	3.30
1935	3.30	2.79	2.84
1936	2.84	2.35	2.35
1937	2.90	2.35	2.75
1938	2.75	2.42	2.36
1939	2.94	2.26	2.24
1940	2.66	1.82	1.80
1941	2.13	1.57	1.91
1942	2.79	1.72	1.80
1943	1.80	1.35	1.44
1944	1.44	1.30	1.32
1945	1.43	1.06	1.14
1946	1.66	1.04	1.62
1947	2.13	1.53	2.11
1948	2.25	1.98	1.97
1949	2.00	1.84	1.86
1950	1.87	1.54	1.50
1951	2.04	1.43	1.92
1952	2.20	1.84	2.21
1953	2.88	2.21	2.37
1954	2.37	2.10	2.24
1955	2.50	2.22	2.41
1956	3.10	2.29	3.08
1957	3.43	2.81	2.85
1958	3.51	2.70	3.26
1959	3.70	3.17	3.65
1960	3.65	3.12	3.26
1961	3.44	3.16	3.28
1962	3.28	2.92	2.97
1963	3.24	2.95	3.19
1964	3.25	3.06	3.01
1965	3.47	2.99	3.45
1966	4.14	3.43	3.66
1967	4.37	3.32	4.27
1968	4.72	3.96	4.72
1969	6.74	4.68	6.42
1970	7.00	5.02	5.47
1971	6.04	4.75	4.82
1972	5.35	4.78	4.98
1973	5.45	4.87	5.05
1974	6.71	5.04	6.62
1975	7.23	5.94	6.45
1976	6.57	5.36	5.36
1977	5.57	5.18	5.37
1978	6.28	5.32	6.22
1979	7.02	5.77	6.85
1980	10.08	6.63	9.27

Year	High	Low	Close
1981	12.89	9.04	12.89
1982	13.05	8.90	9.18
1983	9.86	8.54	9.57
1984	10.95	9.34	9.78
1985	9.74	8.25	8.26
1986	8.24	6.64	6.70
1987	9.05	6.40	7.72
1988	7.85	7.22	7.40
1989	7.78	6.75	6.84
1990	7.38	6.92	6.98
1991	6.98	6.44	6.44
1992	6.65	5.80	6.09
1993	6.01	5.19	5.19
1994	6.92	5.18	6.62

BOND BUYER INDEX (20 BONDS)

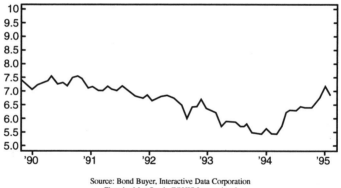

Source: Bond Buyer, Interactive Data Corporation
Chart by MetaStock, EQUIS International

This graph shows the movement of the *Bond Buyer* Index of 20 bonds. The *Bond Buyer* is a daily newspaper covering the municipal bond market. This index is made up of the yields of 20 newly issued general obligation municipal bonds with an average maturity of 20 years, rated from Baa to AAA, (thus including all those of investment grade) and selling at par. The issuers of these bonds are among the most creditworthy of all those issuing bonds in the municipal market.

Year	High	Low	Close
1917	4.56	3.92	4.62
1918	4.72	4.40	4.44
1919	4.55	4.44	4.56
1920	5.27	4.56	5.06
1921	5.26	4.50	5.06
1922	4.41	4.09	4.16
1923	4.40	4.11	4.37

Year	High	Low	Close
1924	4.37	4.11	4.16
1925	4.26	3.99	4.23
1926	4.23	4.10	4.13
1927	4.13	3.93	3.87
1928	4.18	3.87	4.17
1929	4.49	4.17	4.23
1930	4.29	3.97	4.12
1931	4.45	3.74	4.87
1932	5.09	4.57	4.61
1933	5.69	4.48	5.48
1934	5.48	3.89	3.81
1935	3.81	3.23	3.25
1936	3.25	2.69	2.62
1937	3.17	2.62	3.16
1938	3.19	2.83	2.78
1939	3.30	2.66	2.59
1940	3.00	2.18	2.14
1941	2.43	1.90	2.24
1942	2.51	2.13	2.17
1943	2.17	1.69	1.77
1944	1.77	1.59	1.62
1945	1.72	1.35	1.42
1946	1.91	1.29	1.85
1947	2.35	1.78	2.36
1948	2.48	2.20	2.19
1949	2.21	2.08	2.07
1950	2.07	1.70	1.06
1951	2.23	1.58	2.11
1952	2.39	2.03	2.40
1953	3.09	2.40	2.54
1954	2.54	2.26	2.38
1955	2.63	2.37	2.56
1956	3.24	2.42	3.23
1957	3.57	2.96	2.97
1958	3.59	2.85	3.40
1959	3.81	3.26	3.78
1960	3.78	3.27	3.39
1961	3.55	3.26	3.37
1962	3.37	2.98	3.05
1963	3.31	3.01	3.26
1964	3.32	3.12	3.07
1965	3.56	3.04	3.53
1966	4.24	3.51	3.76
1967	4.45	3.40	4.38
1968	4.85	4.07	4.85
1969	6.90	4.82	6.61
1970	7.12	5.33	5.74
1971	6.23	4.97	5.03

Year	High	Low	Close
1972	5.54	4.96	5.08
1973	5.59	4.99	5.18
1974	7.15	5.16	7.08
1975	7.67	6.27	7.13
1976	7.13	5.83	5.83
1977	5.93	5.45	5.66
1978	6.67	5.58	6.61
1979	7.38	6.08	7.23
1980	10.56	7.11	9.76
1981	13.30	9.49	13.30
1982	13.44	9.25	9.56
1983	10.04	8.78	9.76
1984	11.07	9.51	9.91
1985	9.87	8.36	8.36
1986	8.33	6.77	6.83
1987	9.17	6.54	7.86
1988	7.97	7.33	7.50
1989	7.72	6.86	6.97
1990	7.53	7.08	7.14
1991	7.14	6.58	6.58
1992	6.77	5.89	6.17
1993	6.10	5.28	5.28
1994	7.03	5.28	6.71

DOW JONES 30 INDUSTRIALS STOCK AVERAGE

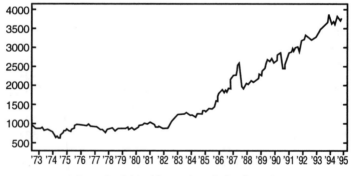

Source: Dow Jones and Company, Interactive Data Corporation
Chart by MetaStock, EQUIS International

The graph above shows the movement of the Dow Jones 30 Industrials Stock Average, the oldest and most widely used of all stock market indicators. When people ask "What did the market do today?" they usually expect to hear whether this average was up or down for the day. The price-weighted average is comprised of the stocks of 30 blue-chip stocks, primarily manufacturing companies but also service companies like American Express. The components, which change from time to time, represent between 15% and 20% of the market value of all NYSE stocks. The Dow, as it is known, is calculated by adding the closing prices of the component stocks and using a divisor that adjusts for splits and stock dividends equal to 10% or more of the market issue as well as for mergers and changes in the components of the list. The Dow Jones 65 Composite Stock Average is composed of the Dow Jones 30 industrials, the Dow Jones 20 transportations and the Dow Jones 15 utilities.

The components of the Dow Jones Industrial Average (DJIA) are:
Allied-Signal Company
Aluminum Company of America
American Express Company
American Telephone & Telegraph
Bethlehem Steel
The Boeing Company
Caterpillar, Inc.
Chevron
Coca-Cola Company
DuPont
Eastman Kodak Company
Exxon Corporation
General Electric Company
General Motors Corporation
Goodyear Tire & Rubber Company
International Business Machines Corporation
International Paper Company
J. P. Morgan & Company, Incorporated
McDonald's Corporation
Merck & Company
Minnesota Mining & Manufacturing Company
Philip Morris Company
Procter & Gamble Corporation
Sears, Roebuck and Company
Texaco Incorporated
Union Carbide Corporation
United Technologies Company
The Walt Disney Company
Westinghouse Electric Corporation
F.W. Woolworth & Company

Year	High	Low	Close
1897	55.82	38.49	49.41
1898	60.97	42.00	60.52
1899	77.61	58.27	66.08
1900	71.04	52.96	70.71
1901	78.26	61.52	64.56
1902	68.44	59.57	64.29
1903	67.70	42.15	49.11
1904	73.23	46.41	69.61
1905	96.56	68.76	96.20
1906	103.00	85.18	93.63
1907	96.37	53.00	58.75
1908	88.38	58.62	86.15
1909	100.53	79.91	99.05
1910	98.34	73.62	81.36

Year	High	Low	Close
1911	87.06	72.94	81.68
1912	94.15	80.15	87.87
1913	88.57	72.11	78.78
1914	83.43	53.17	53.17
1915	99.21	54.22	99.15
1916	110.15	84.96	95.00
1917	99.18	65.95	74.38
1918	89.07	73.38	82.20
1919	119.62	79.15	107.23
1920	109.88	66.75	71.95
1921	81.50	63.90	81.10
1922	103.43	78.59	98.73
1923	105.38	85.76	95.52
1924	120.51	88.33	120.51
1925	159.39	115.00	156.66
1926	166.64	135.20	157.20
1927	202.40	152.73	202.40
1928	300.00	191.33	300.00
1929	381.17	198.69	248.48
1930	294.07	157.51	164.58
1931	194.36	73.79	77.90
1932	88.78	41.22	59.93
1933	108.67	50.16	99.90
1934	110.74	85.51	104.04
1935	148.44	96.71	144.13
1936	184.90	143.11	179.90
1937	194.40	113.64	120.85
1938	158.41	98.95	154.76
1939	155.92	121.44	150.24
1940	152.80	111.84	131.13
1941	133.59	106.34	110.96
1942	119.71	92.92	119.40
1943	145.82	119.26	135.89
1944	152.53	134.22	152.32
1945	195.82	151.35	192.91
1946	212.50	163.12	177.20
1947	186.85	163.21	181.16
1948	193.16	165.39	177.30
1949	200.52	161.60	200.13
1950	235.47	196.81	235.41
1951	276.37	238.99	269.23
1952	292.00	256.35	291.90
1953	293.79	255.49	280.90
1954	404.39	279.87	404.39
1955	488.40	388.20	488.40
1956	521.05	462.35	499.47

Year	High	Low	Close
1957	520.77	419.79	435.69
1958	583.65	436.89	583.65
1959	679.36	574.46	679.36
1960	685.47	566.05	615.89
1961	734.91	610.25	731.14
1962	726.01	535.76	652.10
1963	767.21	646.79	762.95
1964	891.71	766.08	874.13
1965	969.26	840.59	969.26
1966	995.15	744.32	785.69
1967	943.08	786.41	905.11
1968	985.21	825.13	943.75
1969	968.85	769.93	800.36
1970	842.00	631.16	838.92
1971	950.82	797.97	890.20
1972	1036.27	889.15	1020.02
1973	1051.70	788.31	850.86
1974	891.66	577.60	616.24
1975	881.81	632.04	852.41
1976	1014.79	858.71	1004.65
1977	999.75	800.85	831.17
1978	907.74	742.12	805.01
1979	897.61	796.67	838.74
1980	1000.17	759.13	963.99
1981	1024.05	824.01	875.00
1982	1070.55	776.92	1046.55
1983	1287.20	1027.04	1258.64
1984	1286.64	1086.57	1211.57
1985	1553.10	1184.96	1546.67
1986	1955.57	1502.29	1895.95
1987	2722.42	1738.74	1938.83
1988	2183.50	1879.14	2168.57
1989	2791.41	2144.64	2753.20
1990	3024.26	2344.31	2633.66
1991	3204.61	2447.03	3168.83
1992	3435.24	3087.41	3301.11
1993	3818.92	3219.25	3754.09
1994	4002.84	3520.80	3834.44

DOW JONES 20 TRANSPORTATION STOCK AVERAGE

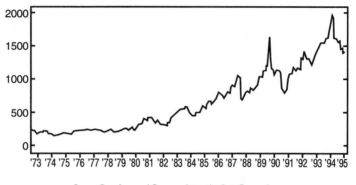

Source: Dow Jones and Company, Interactive Data Corporation
Chart by MetaStock, EQUIS International

This graph shows the movement of the Dow Jones 20 Transportation Stock Average. This price-weighted average consists of the stocks of the 20 large companies in the transportation business, which includes airlines, railroads and trucking. The Transportation Average is important not only in that it tracks the movement of a major segment of American industry, but also because it is watched by the proponents of the Dow Theory, which maintains that a significant trend is not confirmed until both the Dow Jones Industrial Average and Transportation Average reach new highs or lows; if they don't, the market will fall back to its former trading range, according to this theory. From 1897 to 1969, this average was called the Dow Jones Railroad Average. The Dow Jones 65 Composite Average is composed of the Dow Jones 20 Transportation Stock Average, as well as the Dow Jones 30 Industrials and the Dow Jones 15 Utilities.

The components of the Dow Jones Transportation Average are:

Airborne Freight Company
Alaska Air Group, Inc.
AMR Corporation
American President Lines
Burlington Northern Railroad
Carolina Freight Corporation
Conrail Incorporated
Consolidated Freight Corporation
CSX Corporation
Delta Air Lines
Federal Express Company
Norfolk Southern Railway
Norfolk Southern Corporation
Roadway Services, Inc.
Ryder System Incorporated
Santa Fe Pacific Company
Southwest Airlines Company
UAL Incorporated
Union Pacific Corporation
USAir Group
XTRA Corporation

Year	High	Low	Close
1897	67.23	48.12	62.29
1898	74.99	55.89	74.99
1899	87.04	72.48	77.73
1900	94.99	72.99	94.99
1901	117.86	92.66	114.85
1902	129.36	111.73	118.98
1903	121.28	88.80	98.33
1904	119.46	91.31	117.43
1905	133.51	114.52	133.26
1906	138.36	120.30	129.80
1907	131.95	81.41	88.77
1908	120.05	86.04	120.05
1909	134.46	113.90	130.41
1910	129.90	105.59	114.06
1911	123.86	109.80	116.83
1912	124.35	114.92	116.84
1913	118.10	100.50	103.72
1914	109.43	87.40	88.53
1915	108.28	87.85	108.05
1916	112.28	99.11	105.15
1917	105.76	70.75	79.73
1918	92.91	77.21	84.32
1919	91.13	73.63	75.30
1920	85.37	67.83	75.96
1921	77.56	65.52	74.27
1922	93.99	73.43	86.11
1923	90.63	76.78	80.86
1924	99.50	80.23	98.33
1925	112.93	92.98	112.93
1926	123.33	102.41	120.86
1927	144.82	119.29	140.30
1928	152.70	132.60	151.14
1929	189.11	128.07	144.72
1930	157.94	91.65	96.58
1931	111.58	31.42	33.63
1932	41.30	13.23	25.90
1933	56.53	23.43	40.80
1934	52.97	33.19	36.44
1935	41.84	27.31	40.48
1936	59.89	40.66	53.63
1937	64.46	28.91	29.46
1938	33.98	19.00	33.98
1939	35.90	24.14	31.83
1940	32.67	22.14	28.13
1941	30.88	24.25	25.42
1942	29.28	23.31	27.39
1943	38.30	27.59	33.56

Year	High	Low	Close
1944	48.40	33.45	48.40
1945	64.89	47.03	62.80
1946	68.31	44.69	51.13
1947	53.42	41.16	52.48
1948	64.95	48.13	52.86
1949	54.29	41.03	52.76
1950	77.89	51.24	77.64
1951	90.08	72.39	81.70
1952	112.53	82.03	111.27
1953	112.21	90.56	94.03
1954	146.23	94.84	145.86
1955	167.83	137.84	163.29
1956	181.23	150.44	153.23
1957	157.67	95.67	96.96
1958	157.91	99.89	157.65
1959	173.56	146.65	154.05
1960	160.43	123.37	130.85
1961	152.93	131.06	143.84
1962	149.83	114.86	141.04
1963	179.46	142.03	178.54
1964	224.91	178.81	205.34
1965	249.55	187.29	247.48
1966	271.72	184.34	202.97
1967	274.49	205.16	233.24
1968	279.48	214.58	271.60
1969	279.88	169.03	176.34
1970	183.31	116.69	171.52
1971	248.33	169.70	243.72
1972	275.71	212.24	227.17
1973	228.10	151.97	196.19
1974	202.45	125.93	143.44
1975	174.57	146.47	172.65
1976	237.03	175.69	237.03
1977	246.64	199.60	217.18
1978	261.49	199.31	206.56
1979	271.77	205.78	252.39
1980	425.68	233.69	398.10
1981	447.38	335.48	380.30
1982	464.55	292.12	448.38
1983	612.57	434.24	598.59
1984	612.63	444.03	558.13
1985	723.31	553.03	708.21
1986	866.74	686.97	807.17
1987	1101.16	661.00	748.86
1988	973.61	737.57	969.84
1989	1532.01	959.95	1177.81
1990	1225.18	809.73	910.23

Year	High	Low	Close
1991	1368.27	882.22	1358.00
1992	1481.88	1196.35	1449.21
1993	1789.47	1441.15	1762.32
1994	1874.87	1353.96	1455.03

DOW JONES 15 UTILITIES STOCK AVERAGE

Source: Dow Jones and Company, Interactive Data Corporation
Chart by MetaStock, EQUIS International

This graph shows the movement of the Dow Jones 15 Utilities Stock Average. This price-weighted average is composed of 15 geographically representative and well-established gas and electric utility companies. Since utilities are heavy borrowers, their stock prices are inversely affected by the ups and downs of interest rates. The Dow Jones 65 Composite Stock Average is composed of the Dow Jones 15 Utilities Stock Average, the Dow Jones 30 industrials and the Dow Jones 20 transportations.

The components of the Dow Jones Utilities Average are:
American Electric Power Company
Centerior Energy
Consolidated Edison Company
Consolidated Natural Gas Company
Detroit Edison Company
Houston Industries
Niagra Mohawk Power Company
NorAm Energy Corporation
Pacific Gas & Electric Company
Panhandle Eastern Company
PECO Energy Company
Peoples Energy Corporation
Public Service Enterprise Group Incorporated
SCEcorp
Southern California Edison Company
Unicom Corporation

Year	High	Low	Close
1929	144.61	64.72	88.27
1930	108.62	55.14	60.80
1931	73.40	30.55	31.41

Year	High	Low	Close
1932	36.11	16.53	27.50
1933	37.73	19.33	23.29
1934	31.03	16.83	17.80
1935	29.78	14.46	29.55
1936	36.08	28.63	34.83
1937	37.54	19.65	20.35
1938	25.19	15.14	23.02
1939	27.10	20.71	25.58
1940	26.45	18.03	19.85
1941	20.65	13.51	14.02
1942	14.94	10.58	14.54
1943	22.30	14.69	21.87
1944	26.37	21.74	26.37
1945	39.15	26.15	38.13
1946	43.74	33.20	37.27
1947	37.55	32.28	33.40
1948	36.04	31.65	33.55
1949	41.31	33.36	41.29
1950	44.26	37.40	40.98
1951	47.22	41.47	47.22
1952	52.64	47.53	52.60
1953	53.88	47.87	52.04
1954	62.47	52.22	62.47
1955	66.68	61.39	64.16
1956	71.17	63.03	68.54
1957	74.61	62.10	68.58
1958	91.00	68.94	91.00
1959	94.70	85.05	87.83
1960	100.07	85.02	100.02
1961	135.90	99.75	129.16
1962	130.85	103.11	129.23
1963	144.37	129.19	138.99
1964	155.71	137.30	155.17
1965	163.32	149.84	152.63
1966	152.39	118.96	136.18
1967	140.43	120.97	127.91
1968	141.30	119.79	137.17
1969	139.95	106.31	110.08
1970	121.84	95.86	121.84
1971	128.39	108.03	117.75
1972	124.14	105.06	119.50
1973	120.72	84.42	89.37
1974	95.09	57.93	68.76
1975	87.07	72.02	83.65
1976	108.38	84.52	108.38
1977	118.67	104.97	111.28
1978	110.98	96.35	98.24
1979	109.74	98.24	106.60

Year	High	Low	Close
1980	117.34	96.04	114.42
1981	117.81	101.28	109.02
1982	122.83	103.22	119.46
1983	140.70	119.51	131.84
1984	149.93	122.25	149.52
1985	174.96	146.54	174.81
1986	219.15	169.47	206.01
1987	227.83	160.98	175.08
1988	190.02	167.08	186.28
1989	235.98	181.84	235.04
1990	236.98	187.94	209.70
1991	226.53	194.54	226.15
1992	226.46	199.67	221.02
1993	257.58	215.82	229.30
1994	229.77	172.03	181.52

DOW JONES 65 COMPOSITE STOCK AVERAGE

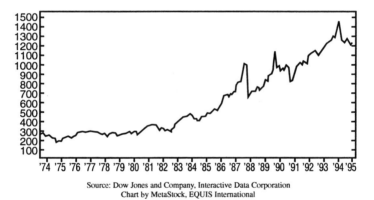

Source: Dow Jones and Company, Interactive Data Corporation
Chart by MetaStock, EQUIS International

This graph shows the movement of the Dow Jones 65 Composite Stock Average. This average is made up of the 30 stocks in the Dow Jones Industrial Average, the 20 stocks in the Dow Jones Transportation Average and the 15 stocks in the Dow Jones Utility Average. The average therefore is significant because it combines the three blue chip averages and thus gives a good indication of the overall direction of the largest, most established companies.

Year	High	Low	Close
1939	53.0	40.4	50.6
1940	51.7	37.2	44.0
1941	44.9	35.5	39.4
1942	39.6	31.5	39.6
1943	50.9	39.8	47.1
1944	56.6	47.0	56.6
1945	73.5	55.9	73.5

Year	High	Low	Close
1946	79.4	58.5	65.4
1947	67.1	57.3	65.1
1948	71.9	59.9	64.7
1949	71.9	57.8	71.9
1950	87.2	70.3	87.2
1951	100.0	86.9	97.4
1952	113.6	96.1	113.6
1953	114.0	98.2	108.0
1954	150.2	106.0	150.2
1955	174.2	137.8	174.2
1956	184.1	164.3	174.2
1957	179.9	142.8	149.4
1958	202.4	147.4	202.4
1959	233.5	200.1	219.5
1960	222.6	190.4	206.1
1961	251.4	204.8	249.6
1962	245.8	187.4	228.9
1963	269.1	228.7	269.1
1964	314.2	269.1	307.5
1965	340.9	290.4	340.9
1966	352.4	261.3	290.3
1967	337.3	282.7	314.1
1968	353.1	290.1	352.7
1969	346.2	253.0	268.3
1970	273.2	208.7	273.2
1971	318.4	270.2	310.1
1972	338.5	302.1	338.5
1973	334.1	247.7	272.5
1974	282.5	184.2	199.7
1975	268.2	205.3	261.7
1976	325.5	264.5	325.5
1977	324.9	274.3	287.2
1978	315.3	260.7	272.2
1979	315.1	274.3	298.3
1980	388.9	271.7	373.4
1981	394.6	320.6	347.8
1982	416.3	299.4	409.2
1983	515.1	401.0	502.9
1984	514.0	421.4	489.9
1985	619.4	480.9	616.5
1986	767.9	602.8	736.8
1987	992.2	653.7	714.2
1988	830.2	700.7	825.9
1989	1115.1	816.9	1035.1
1990	1073.82	830.62	920.61
1991	1167.02	869.42	1156.82
1992	1222.29	1092.09	1204.55
1993	1402.07	1188.85	1381.03
1994	1457.25	1207.50	1274.41

GOLD (London Morning Fix Price)

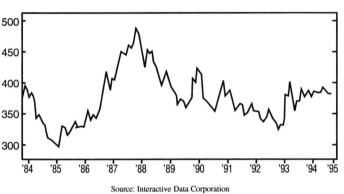

Source: Interactive Data Corporation
Chart by MetaStock, EQUIS International

This graph shows the movement of the per troy ounce gold price, according to the month-end morning fixings in London. Twice each business day (at 10:30 a.m. and 3:30 p.m.), five major metals dealers meet in London to fix a benchmark price for gold, after assessing supply and demand at that time. Gold has traditionally been considered a store of value against both the erosion through inflation of a currency's purchasing power and political instability or turmoil. From the 1930s until the early 70s, gold was fixed at $35 an ounce in the United States. When trading in the metal resumed, gold at first rose to about $200 an ounce, then fell to about $100, then rose again modestly in the mid-1970's. In the late 1970s and early 80s, with inflation driven by rising oil prices, compounded by Middle East tensions, the gold price soared. It then dropped precipitously and after a period of relative stability in the mid-1980s began falling as a reflection of disinflation. Gold prices have been relatively stable in the 1990s.

Year	High	Low	Close
1977	168.15	156.65	165.60
1978	243.65	165.60	224.50
1979	524.00	216.50	524.00
1980	843.00	474.00	589.50
1981	599.25	391.75	400.00
1982	488.50	297.00	448.00
1983	511.50	374.75	381.50
1984	406.85	303.25	309.00
1985	339.30	285.00	327.00
1986	442.75	326.00	390.90
1987	502.75	390.90	486.50
1988	486.50	389.05	410.15
1989	417.15	358.10	401.00
1990	417.55	352.40	391.00
1991	369.60	347.00	353.40
1992	357.95	322.90	322.90
1993	403.70	328.75	390.65
1994	395.35	376.45	382.50

NASDAQ NATIONAL MARKET SYSTEM COMPOSITE INDEX

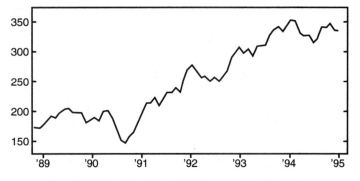

Source: National Association of Securities Dealers, Interactive Data Corporation
Chart by MetaStock, EQUIS International

This graph shows the movement of the National Association of Securities Dealers Automated Quotations (NASDAQ) National Market System Composite Index. This market-value weighted index is composed of all the stocks traded on the National Market System of the over-the-counter market, which is supervised by the National Association of Securities Dealers. The companies in this index are smaller growth companies, many of them in high technology and financial services. The direction of the index is used by analysts to gauge investor interest in more speculative stocks. In times of enthusiasm for small stocks, this index will rise dramatically, and it will fall just as much when investors opt for safety instead of risk.

Year	High	Low	Close
1989	206.75	173.20	199.18
1990	202.69	144.62	165.17
1991	259.74	183.63	259.74
1992	300.56	249.44	300.56
1993	344.26	292.36	343.61
1994	354.43	313.06	335.24

NEW YORK STOCK EXCHANGE COMPOSITE INDEX

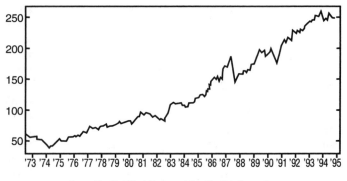

Source: New York Stock Exchange, Interactive Data Corporation
Chart by MetaStock, EQUIS International

This graph shows the movement of the New York Stock Exchange Composite Index. This market-value weighted index is composed of four subindexes—the NYSE Industrial, Transportation, Utilities, and Finance indexes. As such, the Composite Index provides a broader measure of the performance of the New York Stock Exchange than the more widely quoted Dow Jones Industrial Average. Some newspapers, such as *The New York Times,* provide a graph of the NYSE Composite on a daily basis. Stock index futures and options are traded on the NYSE Composite on the New York Futures Exchange.

Year	High	Low	Close
1968	61.27	48.70	58.90
1969	59.32	49.31	51.53
1970	52.36	37.69	50.23
1971	57.76	49.60	56.43
1972	65.14	56.23	64.48
1973	65.48	49.05	51.82
1974	53.37	32.89	36.13
1975	51.24	37.06	47.64
1976	57.88	48.04	57.88
1977	57.69	49.78	52.50
1978	60.38	48.37	53.62
1979	63.39	53.88	61.95
1980	81.02	55.30	77.86
1981	79.14	64.96	71.41
1982	82.35	58.80	81.03
1983	99.63	79.79	95.18
1984	98.12	85.13	96.38
1985	121.90	94.60	121.58
1986	145.75	117.75	138.58
1987	187.99	125.91	138.23
1988	159.42	136.72	156.26
1989	199.34	154.98	195.04
1990	201.55	161.76	180.49
1991	229.85	169.74	229.44
1992	242.76	216.86	240.21
1993	261.16	235.15	259.08
1994	267.78	241.79	250.94

STANDARD & POOR'S 40 STOCK FINANCIAL INDEX

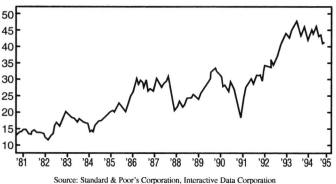

Source: Standard & Poor's Corporation, Interactive Data Corporation
Chart by MetaStock, EQUIS International

This graph shows the movement of the Standard & Poor's Financial Index. This market-value weighted index is composed of 40 large financial institutions such as banks and insurance companies. As such, the stocks in the index tend to move inversely with interest rates. The S&P Financial Index is combined with the S&P 400 Industrials, 20 Transportations and 40 Utilities to form the Standard and Poor's 500, one of the main benchmarks of performance of the stock market.

Year	High	Low	Close
1976	12.79	11.25	12.79
1977	12.67	10.57	11.15
1978	13.18	10.14	11.22
1979	13.90	11.05	12.57
1980	13.76	10.39	13.70
1981	16.56	13.15	14.47
1982	18.05	11.55	16.58
1983	20.99	15.77	18.13
1984	18.88	14.09	18.80
1985	25.87	18.37	25.72
1986	31.13	25.19	26.92
1987	32.56	20.39	21.63
1988	24.63	24.46	24.49
1989	35.24	24.30	31.30
1990	31.94	18.54	23.43
1991	34.41	21.74	34.10
1992	41.31	32.17	40.89
1993	48.48	39.74	44.27
1994	47.10	39.64	41.41

STANDARD & POOR'S 500 STOCK INDEX

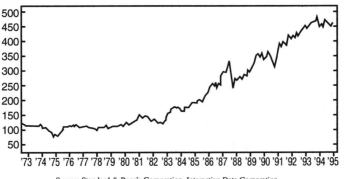

Source: Standard & Poor's Corporation, Interactive Data Corporation
Chart by MetaStock, EQUIS International

This graph shows the movement of Standard & Poor's 500 Stock Index. This market-value weighted index is composed of the S&P 400 Industrials, the S&P 20 Transportations, the S&P 40 Financials and the S&P 40 Utilities. Most of the stocks in the S&P 500 are found on the New York Stock Exchange, though there are a few from the American Stock Exchange and the over-the-counter market. The index represents about 80 percent of the market value of all the issues traded on the NYSE. The S&P is commonly considered the benchmark against which the performance of individual stocks or stock groups is measured. It is a far broader measure of market activity than the Dow Jones Industrial Average, even though the DJIA is quoted more widely. There are mutual funds, called index funds, which aim to mirror the performance of the S&P 500. Such funds appeal to investors who wish to match the general performance of the stock market. Stock index futures and options are also traded on the S&P 500 and its smaller version, the S&P 100, on the Chicago Mercantile Exchange and the Chicago Board Options Exchange.

Year	High	Low	Close
1930	25.92	14.44	15.34
1931	18.17	7.72	8.12
1932	9.31	4.40	6.89
1933	12.20	5.53	10.10
1934	11.82	8.36	9.50
1935	13.46	8.06	13.43
1936	17.69	13.40	17.18
1937	18.68	10.17	10.55
1938	13.79	8.50	13.21
1939	13.23	10.18	12.49
1940	12.77	8.99	10.58
1941	10.86	8.37	8.69
1942	9.77	7.47	9.77
1943	12.64	9.84	11.67
1944	13.29	11.56	13.28
1945	17.68	13.21	17.36
1946	19.25	14.12	15.30
1947	16.20	13.71	15.30

Year	High	Low	Close
1948	17.06	13.84	15.20
1949	16.79	13.55	16.76
1950	20.43	16.65	20.41
1951	23.85	20.69	23.77
1952	26.59	23.09	26.57
1953	26.66	22.71	24.81
1954	35.98	24.80	35.98
1955	46.41	34.58	45.48
1956	49.74	43.11	46.67
1957	49.13	38.98	39.99
1958	55.21	40.33	55.21
1959	60.71	53.58	59.89
1960	60.39	52.30	58.11
1961	72.64	57.57	71.55
1962	71.13	52.32	63.10
1963	75.02	62.69	75.02
1964	86.28	75.43	84.75
1965	92.63	81.60	92.43
1966	94.06	73.20	80.33
1967	97.59	80.38	96.47
1968	108.37	87.72	103.86
1969	106.16	89.20	92.06
1970	93.46	69.29	92.15
1971	104.77	90.16	102.09
1972	119.12	101.67	118.05
1973	120.24	92.16	97.55
1974	99.80	62.28	68.56
1975	95.61	70.04	90.19
1976	107.83	90.90	107.46
1977	107.97	90.71	95.10
1978	106.99	86.90	96.11
1979	111.27	96.13	107.94
1980	140.52	98.22	135.76
1981	138.12	112.77	122.55
1982	143.02	102.42	140.64
1983	172.65	138.34	164.93
1984	170.41	147.82	167.24
1985	212.02	163.68	211.28
1986	254.00	203.49	242.17
1987	336.77	223.92	247.08
1988	283.66	276.83	277.72
1989	359.80	275.31	353.40
1990	369.78	294.51	330.22
1991	418.32	309.35	417.09
1992	442.65	392.41	435.71
1993	471.29	426.88	466.45
1994	482.85	435.86	459.27

STANDARD & POOR'S 400 INDUSTRIAL STOCK INDEX

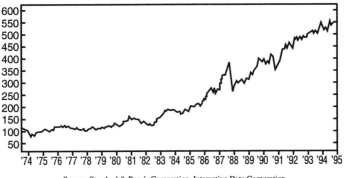

Source: Standard & Poor's Corporation, Interactive Data Corporation
Chart by MetaStock, EQUIS International

This graph shows the movement of Standard & Poor's 400 Industrial Stock Index, commonly known as the S&P 400. This market-value weighted index is made up of 400 large, established industrial companies, most of which are traded on the New York Stock Exchange. The stocks in the Dow Jones Industrial Average are also included in the S&P 400, but the S&P index provides a much broader picture of the performance of industrial stocks. Standard & Poor's 500 index is comprised of the S&P 400 plus the S&P 40 Utilities, 20 Transportations and 40 Financials Indexes.

Year	High	Low	Close
1930	20.32	11.33	11.90
1931	14.07	6.02	6.32
1932	7.26	3.52	5.18
1933	10.25	4.24	9.26
1934	10.54	7.63	9.12
1935	12.84	7.90	12.77
1936	17.02	12.67	16.50
1937	18.10	9.73	10.26
1938	13.66	8.39	13.07
1939	13.08	9.92	12.17
1940	12.42	8.70	10.37
1941	10.62	8.47	8.78
1942	9.94	7.54	9.93
1943	12.58	10.00	11.61
1944	13.18	11.43	13.05
1945	17.06	12.97	16.79
1946	18.53	13.64	14.75
1947	15.83	13.40	15.18
1948	16.93	13.58	15.12
1949	16.52	13.23	16.49
1950	20.60	16.34	20.57
1951	24.33	20.85	24.24
1952	26.92	23.30	26.89
1953	26.99	22.70	24.87
1954	37.24	24.84	37.24

Year	High	Low	Close
1955	49.54	35.66	48.44
1956	53.28	45.71	50.08
1957	53.25	41.98	42.86
1958	58.97	43.20	58.97
1959	65.32	57.02	64.50
1960	65.02	55.34	61.49
1961	76.69	60.87	75.72
1962	75.22	54.80	66.00
1963	79.25	65.48	79.25
1964	91.29	79.74	89.62
1965	98.55	86.43	98.47
1966	100.60	77.89	85.24
1967	106.15	85.31	105.11
1968	118.03	95.05	113.02
1969	116.24	97.75	101.49
1970	102.87	75.58	100.90
1971	115.84	99.36	112.72
1972	132.95	112.19	131.87
1973	134.54	103.37	109.14
1974	111.65	69.53	76.47
1975	107.40	77.71	100.88
1976	120.89	101.64	119.46
1977	118.92	99.88	104.71
1978	118.71	95.52	107.21
1979	124.99	107.08	121.02
1980	160.96	111.09	154.45
1981	157.02	125.93	137.12
1982	159.66	114.08	157.62
1983	194.84	154.95	186.24
1984	191.48	167.75	186.36
1985	235.75	182.24	234.56
1986	282.77	224.88	269.93
1987	393.17	255.43	285.86
1988	326.84	320.18	321.26
1989	410.49	318.66	403.49
1990	438.56	345.79	387.42
1991	494.62	362.88	492.72
1992	516.38	464.29	507.46
1993	544.68	493.09	540.19
1994	564.50	507.30	547.51

STANDARD & POOR'S 20 TRANSPORTATION STOCK INDEX

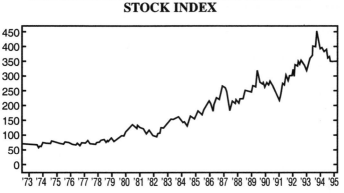

Source: Standard & Poor's Corporation, Interactive Data Corporation
Chart by MetaStock, EQUIS International

This graph shows the movement of the Standard & Poor's 20 Transportation Stock Index. This market-value weighted index is made up of 20 large transportation companies in the airline, trucking and railroad businesses. It is combined with the S&P 400 Industrials, S&P 40 Utilities and S&P 40 Financials to make up the Standard & Poor's 500 Index.

Year	High	Low	Close
1930	46.34	28.27	30.20
1931	34.75	10.08	10.57
1932	13.02	4.32	8.72
1933	18.97	7.69	13.89
1934	17.77	11.15	12.25
1935	14.81	9.36	14.32
1936	20.95	14.40	18.90
1937	22.07	9.76	9.89
1938	11.23	6.58	11.23
1939	12.04	7.80	10.47
1940	10.78	7.25	9.47
1941	10.22	7.77	8.21
1942	10.12	7.75	9.43
1943	13.34	9.52	11.65
1944	15.85	11.57	15.85
1945	21.33	15.45	20.83
1946	22.74	13.86	15.61
1947	16.46	11.95	14.46
1948	17.26	13.34	13.92
1949	14.49	11.24	13.86
1950	19.39	13.34	19.34
1951	21.93	17.59	20.08
1952	25.41	20.16	24.90
1953	25.13	19.79	20.33

Year	High	Low	Close
1954	30.48	20.42	30.38
1955	35.78	28.54	34.17
1956	37.57	30.45	31.36
1957	32.48	20.82	20.95
1958	34.39	21.57	34.39
1959	38.03	31.98	33.82
1960	34.92	27.17	29.55
1961	35.30	29.64	33.25
1962	34.48	26.81	32.73
1963	40.70	32.88	40.65
1964	49.87	40.54	45.82
1965	51.56	41.06	51.28
1966	56.32	37.91	41.04
1967	51.46	41.35	43.71
1968	56.08	40.82	54.15
1969	56.96	35.26	37.16
1970	38.94	24.65	35.40
1971	48.32	35.03	44.61
1972	48.31	40.40	44.26
1973	45.80	32.50	45.80
1974	47.36	29.38	35.59
1975	40.18	34.02	38.12
1976	78.11	67.57	78.11
1977	78.72	63.29	69.50
1978	82.48	63.14	65.12
1979	84.11	65.33	76.73
1980	136.71	70.72	126.22
1981	135.29	96.13	110.44
1982	126.93	81.77	123.12
1983	164.97	119.45	158.81
1984	161.46	117.21	143.91
1985	192.35	141.56	188.72
1986	217.28	176.16	197.27
1987	274.20	167.59	190.17
1988	229.61	228.10	228.17
1989	331.07	226.42	278.48
1990	292.62	206.97	234.67
1991	364.58	223.45	341.46
1992	369.97	304.98	363.75
1993	430.36	362.17	425.60
1994	454.73	331.09	350.11

STANDARD & POOR'S 40 UTILITIES STOCK INDEX

Source: Standard & Poor's Corporation, Interactive Data Corporation
Chart by MetaStock, EQUIS International

This graph shows the movement of Standard & Poor's 40 Utilities Stock Index. This market-value weighted index is made up of 40 large and geographically representative electric and gas utilities. It is combined with the S&P 400 Industrials, S&P 20 Transportations, and S&P 40 Financials to make up Standard & Poor's 500 Index.

Year	High	Low	Close
1930	67.83	35.33	38.75
1931	49.17	22.38	23.66
1932	26.77	12.49	21.97
1933	27.41	14.73	16.21
1934	21.78	11.35	12.13
1935	20.46	9.52	20.25
1936	24.61	19.36	23.46
1937	25.26	13.47	13.96
1938	17.04	10.90	15.97
1939	17.77	14.23	16.81
1940	17.36	12.65	13.08
1941	13.48	7.77	8.21
1942	8.88	6.65	8.69
1943	12.72	8.79	12.07
1944	13.72	11.98	13.51
1945	20.61	13.63	19.96
1946	23.54	16.95	19.58
1947	19.83	15.89	16.28
1948	18.01	15.56	16.04
1949	19.94	15.90	19.93
1950	21.45	18.35	19.42
1951	21.72	19.61	21.72
1952	24.55	21.73	24.55
1953	25.30	22.25	25.10
1954	29.82	25.16	29.82
1955	32.87	29.53	31.70
1956	33.93	31.15	31.76

Year	High	Low	Close
1957	34.29	28.96	32.14
1958	43.28	32.32	43.28
1959	45.45	41.87	44.74
1960	51.76	43.74	51.76
1961	67.97	51.42	64.83
1962	65.11	50.21	61.09
1963	67.99	61.26	66.42
1964	74.97	66.36	74.52
1965	78.20	72.03	75.51
1966	75.37	59.03	69.35
1967	72.59	62.21	66.08
1968	72.30	61.06	69.69
1969	70.74	54.33	56.09
1970	61.71	47.67	61.71
1971	64.81	54.48	59.83
1972	62.99	52.02	61.05
1973	61.57	43.51	46.91
1974	49.44	29.37	33.54
1975	45.61	35.31	44.45
1976	54.24	44.70	54.24
1977	57.56	51.60	54.73
1978	54.47	48.23	48.47
1979	52.85	47.14	50.24
1980	53.97	43.29	52.45
1981	55.75	48.96	52.98
1982	61.69	50.31	60.45
1983	70.30	60.22	66.17
1984	76.47	62.90	75.89
1985	93.26	74.70	93.17
1986	123.74	90.33	112.29
1987	124.04	91.80	102.12
1988	112.94	112.21	112.64
1989	155.29	111.15	156.04
1990	157.86	123.35	143.59
1991	155.22	133.34	155.16
1992	162.64	135.48	158.46
1993	189.49	156.25	172.58
1994	173.55	147.29	150.12

TORONTO 300 COMPOSITE STOCK INDEX

Source: Toronto Stock Exchange, Interactive Data Corporation
Chart by MetaStock, EQUIS International

This graph shows the movement of the Toronto 300 Composite Stock Index. This is the major index for Canadian stocks, since most of the stock market trading in Canada takes place in Toronto. The index is composed of the Industrial, Transportation, Utilities and Financial Indexes maintained by the Toronto Stock Exchange. Stock index futures are traded on the Composite 300 on the Toronto Futures Exchange.

Year	High	Low	Close
1971	1036.09	879.80	990.54
1972	1226.58	990.54	1226.58
1973	1319.26	1122.34	1187.78
1974	1276.81	821.10	835.42
1975	1081.96	862.74	942.94
1976	1100.55	931.17	1011.52
1977	1067.35	961.04	1059.59
1978	1332.71	998.19	1309.99
1979	1813.17	1315.82	1813.17
1980	2402.23	1702.51	2268.70
1981	2390.50	1812.48	1954.24
1982	1958.08	1346.35	1958.08
1983	2598.26	1949.81	2552.35
1984	2585.73	2079.69	2400.33
1985	2900.60	2348.55	2900.60
1986	3129.20	2754.06	3066.18
1987	4112.89	2837.90	3160.10
1988	3465.40	2978.00	3390.00
1989	3985.11	3350.50	3969.79
1990	4020.86	3007.80	3256.75
1991	3604.09	3150.88	3512.36
1992	3672.58	3149.97	3350.44
1993	4330.01	3263.19	4321.43
1994	4609.93	3935.66	4213.61

TREASURY BILL (3-MONTH) YIELDS

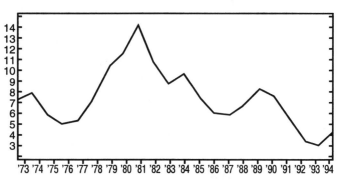

Source: Federal Reserve Bulletin, Interactive Data Corporation
Chart by MetaStock, EQUIS International

This graph shows the movement of the yields of 3-month U.S. Treasury bills. These yields are considered the most important yardsticks of short-term interest rates, and they are therefore watched closely by credit market analysts for signs that rates might be rising or falling. Many floating-rate loans and variable-rate mortgages are tied to the Treasury bill rate. The minimum purchase amount of a Treasury bill is $10,000. Auctions for Treasury bills are held weekly. Individual investors who do not submit a competitive bid are sold bills at the average price of the winning competitive bids. Treasury bills are the primary instrument used by the Federal Reserve in its regulation of the money supply through open market operations. Futures are traded on Treasury bills on the International Monetary Market and the MidAmerica Commodity Exchange. Futures options on T-bills are traded on the Chicago Mercantile Exchange, and the interest rate options on T-bills are traded on the American Stock Exchange.

Year	Average Rates	Year	Average Rates
1965	4.37%	1980	11.50%
1966	4.96%	1981	14.07%
1967	4.96%	1982	10.68%
1968	5.94%	1983	8.63%
1969	7.81%	1984	9.58%
1970	4.87%	1985	7.49%
1971	4.01%	1986	5.97%
1972	5.07%	1987	5.82%
1973	7.45%	1988	6.68%
1974	7.15%	1989	8.11%
1975	5.44%	1990	7.50%
1976	4.35%	1991	5.39%
1977	6.07%	1992	3.44%
1978	9.08%	1993	3.00%
1979	12.04%	1994	4.26%

TREASURY BOND (30-YEAR) YIELDS

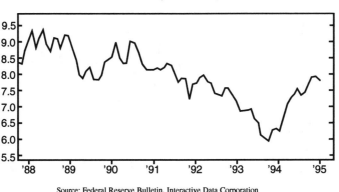

Source: Federal Reserve Bulletin, Interactive Data Corporation
Chart by MetaStock, EQUIS International

This graph shows the movement of the yields of 30-year Treasury bonds. Treasury-bond yields are considered the most important yardsticks of long-term interest rates, and they are therefore watched closely by credit market analysts for signs that rates might be rising or falling. The minimum denomination of a Treasury bond is $1000 and maturities range from 10 to 30 years. The 20-year T-bond represented a large percentage of the bonds traded until the late 1980s. In the last 5 years the 30-year Treasury bond has become more widely used. Futures are traded on Treasury bonds on the Chicago Board of Trade and the MidAmerica Commodity Exchange. Futures options on T-bonds are traded on the Chicago Board of Trade, and interest rate options on T-bonds are traded on the Chicago Board Options Exchange.

Year	Average Rates
1988	8.96%
1989	8.47%
1990	8.61%
1991	8.07%
1992	7.67%
1993	6.57%
1994	7.40%

VALUE LINE COMPOSITE INDEX

Source: Value Line, Inc., Interactive Data Corporation
Chart by MetaStock, EQUIS International

This graph shows the movement of the Value Line Composite Index. This equally weighted geometric average is composed of the approximately 1700 stocks traded on the New York Stock Exchange, American Stock Exchange, and over-the-counter that are tracked by the Value Line Investment Survey. This index is particularly broad in scope, since Value Line covers both large industrial companies as well as smaller growth firms. Futures are traded on the Value Line Composite Index on the Kansas City Board of Trade, and index options are traded on the index on the Philadelphia Stock Exchange.

Year	High	Low	Close
1968	188.64	138.92	183.18
1969	183.67	127.40	130.56
1970	135.46	84.23	103.60
1971	125.76	97.36	112.94
1972	125.98	107.11	114.05
1973	116.20	70.50	73.61
1974	83.41	47.03	48.97
1975	80.88	51.12	70.69
1976	93.47	71.62	93.47
1977	96.34	86.53	93.92
1978	119.77	88.67	97.97
1979	125.25	98.88	121.91
1980	149.76	100.60	144.20
1981	159.03	125.66	137.81
1982	161.37	112.32	158.94
1983	208.51	156.70	194.35
1984	200.32	162.46	177.98
1985	214.86	176.61	214.86
1986	246.80	210.84	225.62
1987	289.36	180.14	201.62
1988	241.35	200.70	232.68
1989	278.98	231.46	258.78

Year	High	Low	Close
1990	262.78	178.42	195.99
1991	249.36	185.54	249.34
1992	267.08	235.06	266.68
1993	295.47	263.62	295.28
1994	305.91	265.28	277.52

WILSHIRE 5000 EQUITY INDEX

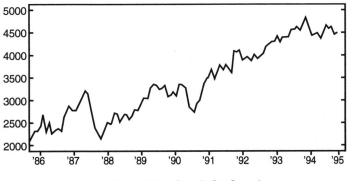

Source: Wilshire Associates, Interactive Data Corporation
Chart by MetaStock, EQUIS International

This graph shows the movement of the Wilshire 5000 Equity Index. This market-value weighted index of 5000 stocks is the broadest of all the indexes and averages, and represents the value, in billions of dollars, of all New York Stock Exchange, American Stock Exchange and over-the-counter stocks for which quotes are available. The index is used as a measure of how all stocks are doing as a group, as opposed to a particular segment of the market.

Year	High	Low	Close
1971	955	871	949
1972	1090	976	1090
1973	1059	854	861
1974	863	550	590
1975	840	675	784
1976	954	879	954
1977	919	851	887
1978	1004	822	922
1979	1101	935	1100
1980	1466	1026	1404
1981	1415	1208	1286
1982	1451	1099	1451
1983	1791	1508	1723
1984	1702	1536	1702
1985	2164	1845	2164
1986	2598	2109	2434

Year	High	Low	Close
1987	3299	2188	2434
1988	2794	2398	2738
1989	3523	2718	3419
1990	3448	2834	3101
1991	4041	3245	4041
1992	4290	3930	4290
1993	4673	4316	4658
1994	4798	4395	4541

CONSUMER PRICE INDEX

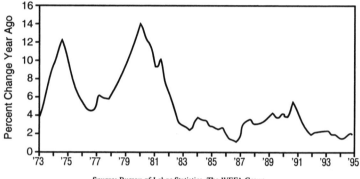

Source: Bureau of Labor Statistics, The WEFA Group

This graph shows the movement of the Consumer Price Index. The line represents the rolling 12-month average of changes in consumer prices—a method which best shows the ups and downs of the inflation rate. Each month, the U.S. Bureau of Labor Statistics shops a fixed market basket of goods and services available to an average urban wage earner. The market basket of goods is updated every few years. The major groups included in the CPI are food, shelter, fuel oil and coal, gas and electricity, apparel, private transportation, public transportation, medical care, entertainment, services and commodities. The CPI is important because many pension and employment contracts are tied to changes in it. The inflationary spike of the 1970s did much damage to the world economy and had profound consequences, including the strongly anti-inflationary monetary policies from the middle 1980s to the present.

Year	Annual Change in CPI	Year	Annual Change in CPI	Year	Annual Change in CPI
1948	7.7%	1955	−0.2%	1962	1.2%
1949	−1.0%	1956	1.4%	1963	1.3%
1950	1.1%	1957	3.4%	1964	1.3%
1951	8.0%	1958	2.7%	1965	1.6%
1952	2.3%	1959	1.0%	1966	3.0%
1953	0.8%	1960	1.5%	1967	2.7%
1954	0.3%	1961	1.0%	1968	4.2%

Year	Annual Change in CPI	Year	Annual Change in CPI	Year	Annual Change in CPI
1969	5.4%	1978	7.6%	1987	3.7%
1970	5.9%	1979	11.3%	1988	4.1%
1971	4.2%	1980	13.5%	1989	4.8%
1972	3.3%	1981	10.4%	1990	5.4%
1973	6.3%	1982	6.2%	1991	4.2%
1974	11.0%	1983	3.2%	1992	3.0%
1975	9.1%	1984	4.4%	1993	3.0%
1976	5.8%	1985	3.6%	1994	2.6%
1977	6.5%	1986	1.9%		

DISCOUNT RATE

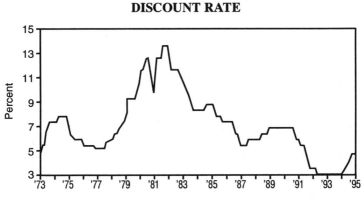

Source: The Federal Reserve Board, The WEFA Group

This graph shows the movement of the discount rate, which is the rate the Federal Reserve charges its member banks for loans from the discount window. Credit market analysts watch the Fed's discount rate moves very carefully, since changes in the rate are a major indication of whether the Fed wants to ease or tighten the money supply. When the Fed wants to ease the money supply to stimulate the economy, it cuts the discount rate. When the Fed wants to tighten the money supply to slow the economy and thereby to try to lower the inflation rate, it raises the discount rate. The discount rate acts as a floor on interest rates, since banks set their loan rates, such as the prime rate, a notch above the disount rate.

Year	High	Low	Close
1914	6.00%	5.00%	6.00%
1915	5.00%	4.00%	4.00%
1916	4.00%	3.00%	3.00%
1917	3.50%	3.00%	3.00%
1918	3.50%	4.00%	4.00%
1919	4.75%	4.00%	4.75%
1920	7.00%	4.75%	7.00%

Year	High	Low	Close
1921	7.00%	4.50%	4.50%
1922	4.50%	4.00%	4.00%
1923	4.50%	4.00%	4.50%
1924	4.50%	3.00%	3.00%
1925	3.50%	3.00%	3.50%
1926	4.00%	3.50%	4.00%
1927	4.00%	3.50%	4.00%
1928	5.00%	3.50%	5.00%
1929	6.00%	4.50%	4.50%
1930	4.50%	2.00%	2.00%
1931	3.50%	1.50%	3.50%
1932	3.50%	2.50%	2.50%
1933	3.50%	2.00%	2.00%
1934	2.00%	1.50%	1.50%
1935	1.50%	1.50%	1.50%
1936	1.50%	1.50%	1.50%
1937	1.50%	1.00%	1.00%
1938	1.00%	1.00%	1.00%
1939	1.00%	1.00%	1.00%
1940	1.00%	1.00%	1.00%
1941	1.00%	1.00%	1.00%
1942	1.00%	0.50%	0.50%
1943	1.00%	0.50%	0.50%
1944	1.00%	0.50%	0.50%
1945	1.00%	0.50%	0.50%
1946	1.00%	0.50%	0.50%
1947	1.00%	1.00%	1.00%
1948	1.50%	1.00%	1.50%
1949	1.50%	1.50%	1.50%
1950	1.75%	1.50%	1.75%
1951	1.75%	1.75%	1.75%
1952	1.75%	1.75%	1.75%
1953	2.00%	1.75%	2.00%
1954	2.00%	1.50%	2.00%
1955	2.50%	1.50%	2.50%
1956	3.00%	2.50%	3.00%
1957	3.50%	3.00%	3.00%
1958	3.00%	1.75%	3.00%
1959	4.00%	2.50%	4.00%
1960	4.00%	3.00%	3.00%
1961	3.00%	3.00%	3.00%
1962	3.00%	3.00%	3.00%
1963	3.50%	3.00%	3.50%
1964	4.00%	3.50%	4.00%
1965	4.50%	4.00%	4.50%
1966	4.50%	4.50%	4.50%
1967	4.50%	4.00%	4.50%
1968	5.50%	4.50%	5.50%

Year	High	Low	Close
1969	6.00%	5.50%	6.00%
1970	6.00%	5.50%	5.50%
1971	5.00%	4.50%	4.50%
1972	4.50%	4.50%	4.50%
1973	7.50%	4.50%	7.50%
1974	8.00%	7.75%	7.75%
1975	7.75%	6.00%	6.00%
1976	6.00%	5.25%	5.25%
1977	6.00%	5.25%	6.00%
1978	9.50%	6.00%	9.50%
1979	12.00%	9.50%	12.00%
1980	10.00%	13.00%	13.00%
1981	14.00%	12.00%	12.00%
1982	12.00%	8.50%	8.50%
1983	8.50%	8.50%	8.50%
1984	9.00%	8.00%	8.00%
1985	8.00%	7.50%	7.50%
1986	7.50%	5.50%	5.50%
1987	7.00%	5.50%	6.00%
1988	6.50%	6.00%	6.50%
1989	7.00%	6.50%	7.00%
1990	7.00%	6.80%	6.80%
1991	6.50%	4.10%	4.10%
1992	3.50%	3.00%	3.00%
1993	3.00%	3.00%	3.00%
1994	4.75%	3.00%	4.75%

FEDERAL FUNDS RATE

Source: The Federal Reserve Board, The WEFA Group

This graph shows the movement of the federal funds rate, which is the rate at which banks with excess reserves lend to banks needing overnight loans to meet reserve requirements. The fed funds rate is the most sensitive of all short-term interest rates, and therefore it is carefully watched by credit market analysts as a precursor of moves in other interest rates. For instance, when the fed funds rate consistently stays below the discount rate, analysts often anticipate that the Federal Reserve will cut the discount rate.

Year	High	Low	Close
1968	6.12%	4.6%	6.02%
1969	9.19%	6.3%	8.97%
1970	8.98%	4.9%	4.9%
1971	5.57%	3.71%	4.14%
1972	5.33%	3.29%	5.33%
1973	10.78%	5.94%	9.95%
1974	12.92%	8.53%	8.53%
1975	7.13%	5.20%	5.20%
1976	5.48%	4.65%	4.65%
1977	6.56%	4.61%	7.75%
1978	10.03%	6.70%	10.03%
1979	13.78%	10.01%	13.78%
1980	18.90%	9.03%	18.90%
1981	19.08%	12.37%	12.37%
1982	14.94%	8.95%	8.95%
1983	9.56%	8.51%	9.47%
1984	11.64%	8.38%	8.38%
1985	8.58%	7.53%	8.27%
1986	8.14%	5.85%	6.91%
1987	7.29%	6.10%	6.77%
1988	8.76%	6.58%	8.76%
1989	9.95%	8.46%	8.52%
1990	8.29%	7.31%	7.31%
1991	6.91%	4.43%	4.43%
1992	4.06%	2.92%	2.92%
1993	3.09%	2.96%	2.96%
1994	5.50%	3.05%	5.50%

INDEX OF LEADING ECONOMIC INDICATORS

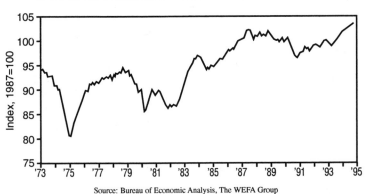

Source: Bureau of Economic Analysis, The WEFA Group

This graph shows the movement of the Index of Leading Economic Indicators. This composite of 12 economic indicators (adjusted for inflation) is designed to forecast whether the economy will gain or lose strength, and is therefore an important tool for economists and others doing business planning. On the whole, it has been an accurate barometer of future economic activity. The 12 components of the Index are: average workweek of production workers; average weekly claims for unemployment insurance; new orders for consumer goods and materials; vendor performance (companies receiving slower deliveries from suppliers); contracts for plant and equipment; new building permits; durable goods order backlog; sensitive materials prices; stock prices; money supply as measured by M-2; and consumer expectations. The index is released monthly and is based at 100 in 1987.

Year	High	Low	December
1968	89.7	88.0	89.7
1969	90.1	87.4	87.4
1970	86.7	84.6	85.7
1971	89.8	86.3	89.8
1972	93.9	90.4	93.9
1973	94.1	91.9	91.9
1974	91.5	82.0	82.0
1975	88.2	81.0	88.2
1976	91.8	89.5	91.8
1977	92.9	91.5	92.9
1978	94.3	92.2	93.6
1979	93.8	90.0	90.0
1980	90.4	85.6	90.1
1981	90.2	86.6	86.6
1982	89.0	86.5	89.0
1983	96.0	91.0	95.8
1984	96.4	93.9	94.2
1985	96.4	95.1	96.4
1986	99.2	96.6	99.2
1987	101.0	99.0	99.6

Year	High	Low	December
1988	100.0	99.4	100.5
1989	100.9	99.1	99.4
1990	99.5	96.5	96.5
1991	97.9	96.0	97.2
1992	99.2	97.5	99.2
1993	100.3	98.2	100.3
1994	102.5	100.5	102.5

MONEY SUPPLY (M-1)

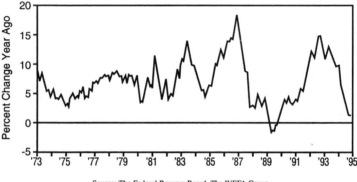

Source: The Federal Reserve Board, The WEFA Group

This graph shows the movement of changes in the money supply in the United States, as measured by M-1. The line represents the rolling 12-month change in the money supply. The percentage change is calculated by comparing, for example, the December 1994 figure with the December 1993 figure. This method best shows the ups and downs of the growth of the amount of money circulating in the economy. The rate of change in the money supply is important because it has an important bearing on how quickly or slowly the economy will be growing in the future. Monetarist economists believe changes in the money supply are the key to economic ups and downs. When the Federal Reserve, which strongly influences the money supply through its conduct of open market operations and by setting bank reserve requirements and the discount rate, wants the economy to expand, it eases the money supply. When the Fed is concerned that inflation may be accelerating, it will slow the economy by tightening the money supply. The components of the M-1 measure of the money supply are: currency in circulation; commercial and mutual savings bank demand deposits; NOW and ATS (automatic transfer from savings) accounts; credit union share drafts; and nonbank travelers checks.

Year	High	Low	December
1968	7.69%	6.12%	7.69%
1969	7.99%	3.29%	3.29%
1970	5.15%	2.86%	5.15%
1971	8.12%	4.51%	6.48%

Year	High	Low	December
1972	9.15%	5.86%	9.15%
1973	9.30%	5.46%	5.46%
1974	6.00%	4.38%	4.38%
1975	5.41%	3.37%	4.81%
1976	6.54%	4.71%	6.54%
1977	8.40%	6.96%	8.10%
1978	8.91%	7.46%	8.18%
1979	8.36%	6.78%	6.78%
1980	8.28%	4.13%	6.80%
1981	11.30%	4.71%	6.81%
1982	9.16%	4.59%	8.71%
1983	13.56%	7.76%	9.85%
1984	9.90%	4.98%	5.97%
1985	12.28%	5.90%	12.28%
1986	16.87%	11.01%	16.87%
1987	17.60%	3.53%	3.53%
1988	5.40%	3.41%	4.97%
1989	3.80%	–0.65%	0.93%
1990	5.13%	1.21%	3.99%
1991	8.63%	3.97%	8.63%
1992	14.36%	10.09%	14.16%
1993	13.39%	10.11%	10.11%
1994	9.96%	1.74%	1.74%

PRIME RATE

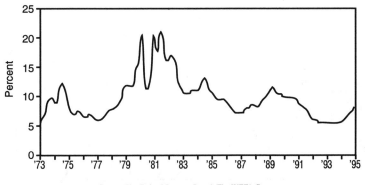

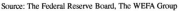

Source: The Federal Reserve Board, The WEFA Group

This graph shows the movement of the prime rate, which is the interest rate banks charge their most creditworthy customers. The rate is determined by market forces affecting a bank's cost of funds and the rates borrowers will accept. The prime often moves up or down in concert with the Federal Reserve discount rate. The prime rate tends to become standard across the banking industry when a major bank moves its rate up or down. The rate is a key interest rate, since loans to less creditworthy customers are often tied to the prime.

Year	High	Low	Close
1968	6.75%	6%	6.75%
1969	8.5%	6.75%	8.5%
1970	8.5%	6.75%	6.75%
1971	6.75%	5.25%	5.25%
1972	6%	5%	6%
1973	10%	6%	10%
1974	12%	8.75%	10.5%
1975	10.5%	7%	7%
1976	7.25%	6.25%	6.25%
1977	7.75%	6.5%	7.75%
1978	11.75%	7.75%	11.75%
1979	15.75%	11.5%	15%
1980	21.50%	10.75%	21.50%
1981	20.5%	15.75%	15.75%
1982	17%	11.5%	11.5%
1983	11.5%	10.5%	11%
1984	13%	10.75%	10.75
1985	10.75%	9.5%	9.5%
1986	9.5%	7.5%	7.5%
1987	9.25%	7.5%	8.75%
1988	10.5%	8.5%	10.5%
1989	11.5%	10.5%	10.5%
1990	10.1%	10.0%	10.0%
1991	9.5%	7.2%	7.2%
1992	6.5%	6.0%	6.0%
1993	6.0%	6.0%	6.0%
1994	8.5%	6.0%	8.5%

PRODUCER PRICE INDEX

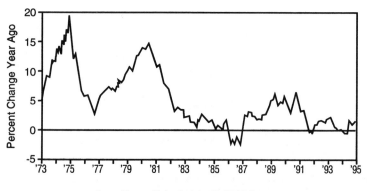

Source: Bureau of Labor Statistics, The WEFA Group

This graph shows the movement of the Producer Price Index. The line represents
the rolling 12-month average of changes in producer prices—a method that best
shows the ups and downs of the wholesale inflation rate. Each month, the U.S.

Bureau of Labor Statistics measures changes in the prices of all commodities, at all stages of processing, produced for sale in primary markets in the United States. Approximately 3400 commodity prices are collected by the Bureau from sellers. The prices are generally the first significant large-volume commercial transaction for each commodity—either the manufacturer's selling price or the selling price from an organized commodity exchange. The major commodity groups that are represented in the PPI are: farm products; processed food and feed; textiles and apparel; hides, skins and leather; fuels; chemicals; rubber and plastic products; lumber and wood products; pulp and paper products; metals and metal products; machinery and equipment; furniture and household durables; nonmetallic mineral products; and transportation equipment. The PPI is important not only because it is a good gauge of what is happening in the industrial economy but also because it gives an indication of the future trend in consumer prices.

Year	Annual Percent Change	Year	Annual Percent Change
1955	0.3%	1975	10.6%
1956	2.6%	1976	4.5%
1957	3.8%	1977	6.4%
1958	2.2%	1978	7.9%
1959	−0.3%	1979	11.2%
1960	0.9%	1980	13.4%
1961	−0.0%	1981	9.2%
1962	0.3%	1982	4.1%
1963	−0.3%	1983	1.6%
1964	0.3%	1984	2.1%
1965	1.8%	1985	1.0%
1966	3.2%	1986	−1.4%
1967	1.1%	1987	2.1%
1968	2.8%	1988	2.5%
1969	3.8%	1989	4.9%
1970	3.4%	1990	4.9%
1971	3.1%	1991	2.2%
1972	3.2%	1992	1.2%
1973	9.1%	1993	1.3%
1974	15.4%	1994	0.6%

UNEMPLOYMENT RATE (CIVILIAN)

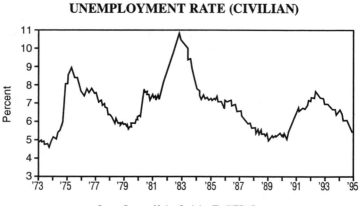

Source: Bureau of Labor Statistics, The WEFA Group

This graph shows the movement of the unemployment rate. This is the rate of civilians, 16 years of age and older, who were not employed, and who made specific efforts to find a job within the previous four weeks and who were available for work. Persons on layoff from a job or waiting to report to a new job within 30 days are also classified as unemployed. The unemployment rate is a lagging indicator—that is, it rises months after business has already slowed down, and it falls months after business has picked up.

MONTHLY RATE

Year	High	Low	December
1968	3.7%	3.3%	3.3%
1969	3.6%	3.3%	3.4%
1970	5.9%	3.8%	5.9%
1971	5.9%	5.7%	5.9%
1972	5.7%	5.1%	5.1%
1973	4.9%	4.5%	4.8%
1974	7.0%	5.0%	7.0%
1975	8.8%	7.9%	8.1%
1976	7.8%	7.2%	7.6%
1977	7.5%	6.3%	6.3%
1978	6.3%	5.7%	5.9%
1979	5.9%	5.5%	5.9%
1980	7.7%	6.2%	7.1%
1981	8.4%	7.1%	8.4%
1982	10.6%	8.5%	10.6%
1983	10.3%	8.1%	8.1%
1984	7.9%	7.0%	7.1%
1985	7.3%	6.8%	6.8%
1986	7.2%	6.7%	6.7%
1987	6.6%	5.8%	5.8%
1988	5.8%	5.3%	5.3%
1989	5.4%	5.1%	5.4%
1990	6.2%	5.1%	6.2%
1991	7.2%	6.3%	7.2%
1992	7.7%	7.1%	7.3%
1993	7.1%	6.4%	6.4%
1994	6.7%	5.4%	5.4%

6. PUBLICLY TRADED COMPANIES

On the following pages, you will find a comprehensive list of the companies whose common stock is traded on the New York Stock Exchange, the American Stock Exchange, and the NASDAQ (National Association of Securities Dealers Automated Quotation) system. Each of the three markets is listed separately. In addition, there is a listing of the 300 largest capitalization stocks traded on the Toronto Stock Exchange.

Following the overall company lists are two lists of special interest: the first presents companies offering free or reduced-price goods or services to shareholders; the second, foreign companies whose American Depositary Receipts (ADRs) are traded in the United States.

The New York Stock Exchange is the home of many of the largest, most established public companies, though many smaller growth companies are traded there as well. The NYSE operates with a specialist system of trading, where buyers and sellers are brought together by a specialist on the floor of the Exchange. The specialist steps in to buy or sell shares if there is an imbalance of orders on one side of the market or the other. The requirements the NYSE imposes for being listed on the exchange are the most stringent of all the places where stocks are traded in the United States. Two of the most important requirements are that a corporation must have (1) a minimum aggregate market value of $16 million and (2) annual net income topping $2.5 million before federal income taxes.

The American Stock Exchange is where medium and smaller-sized companies are traded. In addition, many foreign companies are listed on the AMEX. The American Stock Exchange uses the same specialist trading system employed by the New York Stock Exchange. The AMEX's listing requirements are less stringent than of the NYSE, though the exchange requires that a company have a reliably profitable business.

The NASDAQ Stock Market is home to many of the nations's largest high-technology companies as well as a majority of its emerging growth companies. Many of these growth companies don't pay dividends since they plow their earnings back into their businesses. Unlike the two exchanges, trading on The NASDAQ Stock Market is executed by hundreds of competing market makers who are linked by a network of NASDAQ computer terminals. The screen-based electronic market is owned and operated by the National Association of Securities Dealers and is headquartered in Washington, D.C. The NASDAQ Stock Market has two tiers, the SmallCap market, for smaller emerging companies, and the National Market, where the larger issues trade. Listing standards vary for NASDAQ's two tiers, but they are more stringent for NASDAQ's National Market, and to be accepted a company must have either tangible assets of $12 million, with a three year operating history, or $4 million with $750,000 in pretax income.

Each listing includes up to seven elements: the company's name, stock symbol, address, telephone number, line of business, if it has a dividend reinvestment plan and whether options are traded on the stock.

Company Name: We have used each company's full corporate name, though words such as Incorporated, Company and Corporation are abbreviated to become Inc., Co. and Corp. The lists are arranged alphabetically, by company name.

Stock Symbol: The stock symbol—usually three or four capital letters—follows each company's name. When asking a broker to look up the price or other information about a stock, it is usually necessary to provide the stock symbol. The symbol is then entered into a computer terminal, which retrieves data about the company. The stock symbol is not the same abbreviation as one sees in newspaper stock tables, however.

Address: The street address or post office box listed refers to the executive office at the headquarters of the company. In the case of foreign companies, the home address of the company usually is listed, though the address of a contact office in the U.S. may be given.

Telephone Number: The phone number is that of the executive offices at the company's headquarters. If you require further information about the company because you are considering whether to invest in it, you should ask for the investor relations department, which will send annual and quarterly financial reports and other data about the firm.

Line Of Business: This is a brief description of the main business of the company. Some companies specialize in a narrow field—in this case, the description is quite specific to its line of business. Other companies engage in diverse activities, and for them, we have listed the largest segments of their business, or when no business is dominant, we have labeled the company a conglomerate. To find out each company's exact product line, you must call or write the firm's investor relations department.

Dividend Reinvestment Plan: If the letters DRP are in brackets on the final line of an entry for a company, this means that shareholders can use a company plan to reinvest cash dividends into more of the company's stock, instead of receiving a cash payment. Usually, there will be little or no commission cost to the shareholder who participates in a plan. Many companies also allow shareholders to make cash payments in addition to reinvesting dividends to buy more shares, usually at no commission charge.

Some companies offer an extra bonus in their dividend reinvestment plan. Companies on the list with a 5% following the DRP listing offer a 5% discount on the purchase price of newly issued stock for the amount of reinvested dividends. Thus, a shareholder who reinvested $100 of dividends would be credited with purchasing $105 worth of stock. Some companies allow the 5% discount on both dividends reinvested as well as additional cash put up by the shareholder.

Most companies allow shareholders to participate in a dividend reinvestment plan while owning as little as one share. If the dividend is not sufficient to purchase a full share, a shareholder's account is credited with the appropriate fractional share.

The information on dividend reinvestment plans was compiled by Suzanne Mitchell, who publishes a list tracking company plans. A sample copy of this list is available for $19.50 from Suzanne Mitchell at P.O. Box 7969, Tyler, Texas 75711, or by calling her at (903) 592-5465.

Options: Also on the final line of a company entry is a notation of whether options are traded on the company's stock. This is signified with the letter O. Stock options may be traded on the American Stock Exchange, the Chicago Board Options Exchange, the Pacific Stock Exchange or the Philadelphia Stock Exchange. Options of larger companies may trade on more than one of these exchanges simultaneously.

Stock options can be used by an investor to make a speculative bet on a stock going up or down. Other investors use options to increase their income or hedge the value of their stock holdings.

In today's fast-moving world of finance and investment, a company may merge with another, add or drop a line of business, change its address or telephone number, move from one exchange to another, or even go out of business. Despite such changes, this list will remain an indispensable resource for investors and others in the finance and investment community.

NEW YORK STOCK EXCHANGE

1838 Bond-Debenture Trading Fund BDF
100 Matsonford Rd.
Radnor, PA 19087   610-293-4300
Financial - investment management [DRP]

2002 Target Term Trust, Inc. TTR
1285 Avenue of the Americas
New York, NY 10019   212-713-2000
Financial - investment management

20th Century Industries TW
6301 Owensmouth Ave., Ste. 700
Woodland Hills, CA 91367   818-704-3700
Insurance - property & casualty

A. H. Belo Corp. BLC
400 S. Record St.
Dallas, TX 75202   214-977-6606
Broadcasting - radio & TV

A. G. Edwards, Inc. AGE
One N. Jefferson Ave.
St. Louis, MO 63103   314-289-3000
Financial - investment bankers

A. L. Pharma Inc. ALO
One Executive Dr., PO Box 1399
Fort Lee, NJ 07024   201-947-7774
Drugs - generic

AAR Corp. AIR
1111 Nicholas Blvd.
Elk Grove Village, IL 60007   708-439-3939
Aerospace - aircraft equipment O [DRP]

Abbott Laboratories ABT
One Abbott Park Rd.
Abbott Park, IL 60064   708-937-6100
Drugs O [DRP]

Abex Inc. ABE
Liberty Ln.
Hampton, NH 03842   603-926-5911
Aerospace - aircraft equipment

ACM Government Income Fund, Inc. ACG
1345 Avenue of the Americas
New York, NY 10105   212-969-1000
Financial - investment management

ACM Government Opportunity Fund, Inc.
AOF
1345 Avenue of the Americas
New York, NY 10105   212-969-1000
Financial - investment management

ACM Government Securities Fund, Inc. GSF
1345 Avenue of the Americas
New York, NY 10105   212-969-1000
Financial - investment management

ACM Government Spectrum Fund, Inc. SI
1345 Avenue of the Americas
New York, NY 10105   212-969-1000
Financial - investment management

ACM Managed Dollar Income Fund, Inc.
ADF
1345 Avenue of the Americas
New York, NY 10105   212-969-1000
Financial - investment management

ACM Managed Income Fund, Inc. AMF
1345 Avenue of the Americas
New York, NY 10105   212-969-1000
Financial - investment management

ACM Managed Multi-Market Trust, Inc. MMF
1345 Avenue of the Americas
New York, NY 10105   212-969-1000
Financial - investment management

ACM Municipal Securities Income, Inc. AMU
1345 Avenue of the Americas
New York, NY 10105   212-969-1000
Financial - investment management

Acme Electric Corp. ACE
400 Quaker Rd.
East Aurora, NY 14052   716-655-3800
Electrical products - misc.

Acme-Cleveland Corp. AMT
1242 E. 49th St.
Cleveland, OH 44114   216-432-5400
Diversified operations [DRP]

Acordia, Inc. ACO
120 Monument Circle
Indianapolis, IN 46204   317-488-6666
Insurance - multi line & misc.

Acuson Corp. ACN
1220 Charleston Rd.
Mountain View, CA 94043   415-969-9112
Medical instruments O

Adams Express Co. ADX
Seven St. Paul St., Ste. 1140
Baltimore, MD 21202   410-752-5900
Financial - investment management

Advanced Micro Devices, Inc. AMD
One AMD Place, PO Box 3453
Sunnyvale, CA 94088   408-732-2400
Electrical components - semiconductors O

ADVO, Inc. AD
One Univac Ln., PO Box 755
Windsor, CT 06095   203-285-6100
Business services

Aetna Life and Casualty Co. AET
151 Farmington Ave.
Hartford, CT 06156   203-273-0123
Insurance - multi line & misc. O [DRP]

AFLAC, Inc. AFL
1932 Wynnton Rd.
Columbus, GA 31999   706-323-3431
Insurance - life O [DRP]

AGCO Corp. AG
5295 Triangle Parkway
Norcross, GA 30092   404-447-5546
Machinery - farm O

Agree Realty Corp. ADC
31850 Northwestern Hwy.
Farmington Hills, MI 48334
810-737-4190
Real estate investment trust

Aileen, Inc. AEE
1411 Broadway
New York, NY 10018   212-398-9770
Textiles - apparel

Airborne Freight Corp. ABF
3101 Western Ave., PO Box 662
Seattle, WA 98111   206-285-4600
Transportation - air freight

Airgas, Inc. ARG
100 Matsonford Rd.
Radnor, PA 19087   610-687-5253
Chemicals - specialty

Airlease Ltd. FLY
733 Front St.
San Francisco, CA 94119
415-627-9289
Leasing

Air Products and Chemicals, Inc. APD
7201 Hamilton Blvd.
Allentown, PA 18195   610-481-4911
Chemicals - specialty O [DRP]

AirTouch Communications ATI
425 Market St.
San Francisco, CA 94105   415-658-2000
Telecommunications services O

Alaska Air Group, Inc. ALK
19300 Pacific Highway South
Seattle, WA 98188   206-431-7040
Transportation - airline O

Albany International Corp. AIN
1373 Broadway
Albany, NY 12204   518-445-2200
Paper & paper products [DRP]

Albemarle Corp. ALB
330 S. Fourth St.
Richmond, VA 23219   804-788-6000
Chemicals - specialty O [DRP]

Alberto-Culver Co. ACV
2525 Armitage Ave.
Melrose Park, IL 60160   708-450-3000
Cosmetics & toiletries

Albertson's, Inc. ABS
250 Parkcenter Blvd.
Boise, ID 83726   208-385-6200
Retail - supermarkets O

Alcan Aluminium Ltd. AL
PO Box 6077
Montreal, Quebec, H3C 3A7 Canada
514-848-8050
Aluminum O [DRP]

Alco Standard Corp. ASN
825 Duportail Rd.
Wayne, PA 19087   610-296-8000
Wholesale distribution - consumer products O
[DRP]

Alex. Brown Inc. AB
135 E. Baltimore St.
Baltimore, MD 21202   410-727-1700
Financial - investment bankers O

Alexander & Alexander Services Inc. AAL
1211 Avenue of the Americas
New York, NY 10036   212-840-8500
Insurance - brokerage O

Alexander's, Inc. ALX
31 W. 34th St.
New York, NY 10001   212-560-2121
Retail - discount & variety

Allamerica Securities Trust ALM
440 Lincoln St.
Worcester, MA 01605   508-852-1000
Financial - investment management

Alleghany Corp. Y
Park Avenue Plaza
New York, NY 10055   212-752-1356
Financial - business services

Allegheny Ludlum Corp. ALS
1000 Six PPG Place
Pittsburgh, PA 15222   412-394-2800
Steel - specialty alloys O [DRP]

Allegheny Power System, Inc. AYP
12 E. 49th St.
New York, NY 10017   212-752-2121
Utility - electric power [DRP]

Allergan, Inc. AGN
2525 Dupont Dr., PO Box 19534
Irvine, CA 92715   714-752-4500
Medical products O [DRP]

Alliance Capital Management L.P. AC
1345 Avenue of the Americas
New York, NY 10105   212-969-1000
Financial - investment management

Alliance Entertainment Corp. CDS
115 E. 57th St., 10th Fl.
New York, NY 10022   212-750-2303
Wholesale distribution - consumer products

Alliance Global Environment Fund AEF
1345 Avenue of the Americas
New York, NY 10105   212-969-1000
Financial - investment management

Alliance World Dollar Government Fund II,
   Inc. AWF
1345 Avenue of the Americas
New York, NY 10105   212-969-1000
Financial - investment management

Alliance World Dollar Government Fund,
   Inc. AWG
1345 Avenue of the Americas
New York, NY 10105   212-969-1000
Financial - investment management

Alliant Techsystems Inc. ATK
600 Second St. NE
Hopkins, MN 55343   612-931-6000
Weapons & weapon systems   O

Allied Products Corp. ADP
10 S. Riverside Plaza
Chicago, IL 60606   312-454-1020
Diversified operations

AlliedSignal Inc. ALD
101 Columbia Rd., PO Box 2245
Morristown, NJ 07962   201-455-2000
Diversified operations O [DRP]

Allmerica Property & Casualty Co., Inc. APY
440 Lincoln St.
Worcester, MA 01653   508-855-1000
Insurance - property & casualty

ALLTEL Corp. AT
One Allied Dr.
Little Rock, AR 72202   501-661-8000
Utility - telephone O [DRP]

Allwaste, Inc. ALW
3040 Post Oak Blvd., Ste. 1300
Houston, TX 77056   713-623-8777
Pollution control equipment & services O

Alumax Inc. AMX
5655 Peachtree Parkway
Norcross, GA 30092   404-246-6600
Metals - non ferrous O

Aluminum Company of America AA
1501 Alcoa Building
Pittsburgh, PA 15219   412-553-3042
Metals - non ferrous O [DRP]

ALZA Corp. AZA
950 Page Mill Rd.
Palo Alto, CA 94303   415-494-5000
Drugs O

Amax Gold Inc. AU
9100 E. Mineral Circle
Englewood, CO 80112   303-643-5500
Gold mining & processing O

AMBAC Inc. ABK
One State St. Plaza
New York, NY 10004   212-668-0340
Insurance - multi line & misc. O

Amcast Industrial Corp. AIZ
7887 Washington Village Dr.
Dayton, OH 45459   513-291-7000
Metal processing & fabrication [DRP]

AMDURA Corp. ADU
2801 Dawson Rd.
Tulsa, OK 74110   918-838-0119
Building products - retail & wholesale

Amerada Hess Corp. AHC
1185 Avenue of the Americas
New York, NY 10036   212-997-8500
Oil & gas - US integrated O [DRP]

American Adjustable Rate Term Trust Inc. -
   1995 ADJ
222 S. Ninth St.
Minneapolis, MN 55402   800-866-7778
Financial - investment management

American Adjustable Rate Term Trust Inc. -
   1996 BDJ
222 S. Ninth St.
Minneapolis, MN 55402   800-866-7778
Financial - investment management

American Adjustable Rate Term Trust Inc. -
   1997 CDJ
222 S. Ninth St.
Minneapolis, MN 55402   800-886-7778
Financial - investment management

American Adjustable Rate Term Trust Inc. -
   1998 DDJ
222 S. Ninth St.
Minneapolis, MN 55402   800-866-7778
Financial - investment management

American Adjustable Rate Term Trust Inc. -
   1999 EDJ
222 S. Ninth St.
Minneapolis, MN 55402   800-866-7778
Financial - investment management

American Annuity Group, Inc. AAG
580 Walnut
Cincinnati, OH 45202   513-333-5300
Insurance - life

American Brands, Inc. AMB
1700 E. Putnam Ave.
Old Greenwich, CT 06870
203-698-5000
Tobacco O [DRP]

American Building Maintenance Industries, Inc. ABM
50 Fremont St., Ste. 2600
San Francisco, CA 94105   415-597-4500
Building - maintenance & services

American Business Products, Inc. ABP
2100 River Edge Pkwy.
Atlanta, GA 30328   404-953-8300
Office equipment & supplies [DRP]

American Capital Bond Fund, Inc. ACB
2800 Post Oak Blvd.
Houston, TX 77056   713-993-0500
Financial - investment management

American Capital Convertible Securities, Inc. ACS
2800 Post Oak Blvd.
Houston, TX 77056   713-993-0500
Financial - investment management

American Capital Income Trust ACD
2800 Post Oak Blvd.
Houston, TX 77056   713-993-0500
Financial - investment management

American Eagle Group, Inc. FLI
12801 N. Central Expressway
Dallas, TX 75243   214-448-1400
Insurance - multi line & misc.

American Electric Power Co., Inc. AEP
1 Riverside Plaza
Columbus, OH 43215   614-223-1000
Utility - electric power O [DRP]

American Express Co. AXP
World Financial Center
New York, NY 10285   212-640-2000
Financial - business services O [DRP 3%]

American General Corp. AGC
2929 Allen Parkway
Houston, TX 77019   713-522-1111
Insurance - life O [DRP]

American Government Income Fund Inc. AGF
222 S. Ninth St.
Minneapolis, MN 55402   800-333-6000
Financial - investment management

American Gov. Income Portfolio Inc. AAF
222 S. Ninth St.
Minneapolis, MN 55402   800-866-7778
Financial - investment management

American Government Term Trust Inc. AGT
222 S. Ninth St.
Minneapolis, MN 55402   800-333-6000
Financial - investment management

American Health Properties, Inc. AHE
6400 S. Fiddler's Green Circle
Englewood, CO 80111   303-796-9793
Real estate investment trust O [DRP]

American Heritage Life Investment Corp. AHL
1776 American Heritage Life Dr.
Jacksonville, FL 32224   904-354-1776
Insurance - life [DRP 5%]

American Home Products Corp. AHP
Five Giralda Farms
Madison, NJ 07940   201-660-5000
Drugs O [DRP]

American Income Holding, Inc. AIH
1200 Wooded Acres Dr.
Waco, TX 76710   817-772-3050
Insurance - multi line & misc.

American Industrial Properties REIT IND
6220 N. Beltline, Ste. 205
Irving, TX 75063   214-550-6053
Real estate investment trust [DRP]

American International Group, Inc. AIG
70 Pine St.
New York, NY 10270   212-770-7000
Insurance - property & casualty O

American Media, Inc. ENQ
600 S. East Coast Ave.
Lantana, FL 33462   407-586-1111
Publishing - periodicals

American Medical Holdings, Inc. AMI
14001 N. Dallas Pkwy.
Dallas, TX 75240   214-789-2200
Hospitals O

American Medical Response, Inc. EMT
67 Batterymarch St.
Boston, MA 02110   617-261-1600
Medical services

American Municipal Income Portfolio, Inc. XAA
222 S. Ninth St.
Minneapolis, MN 55402   800-866-7778
Financial - investment management

American Municipal Term Trust - II BXT
222 S. Ninth St.
Minneapolis, MN 55402   800-866-7778
Financial - investment management

American Municipal Term Trust - III CXT
222 S. Ninth St.
Minneapolis, MN 55402   800-333-6000
Financial - investment management

American Municipal Term Trust Inc. AXT
222 S. Ninth St.
Minneapolis, MN 55402   800-886-7778
Financial - investment management

American Opportunity Income Fund, Inc. OIF
222 S. Ninth St.
Minneapolis, MN 55402   800-866-7778
Financial - investment management

American Precision Industries Inc. APR
2777 Walden Ave.
Buffalo, NY 14225   716-684-9700
Electrical products - misc.

American Premier Underwriters, Inc. APZ
One E. Fourth St., 14th Fl.
Cincinnati, OH 45202   513-579-6600
Insurance - property & casualty O

American President Companies, Ltd. APS
1111 Broadway
Oakland, CA 94607   510-272-8000
Transportation - shipping   O

American Re Corp. ARN
555 College Rd. East
Princeton, NJ 08543   609-243-4200
Miscellaneous - not elsewhere classified

American Real Estate Partners, L.P.
  ACP
90 S. Bedford Rd.
Mt. Kisco, NY 10549   914-242-7700
Real estate operations [DRP]

American Realty Trust, Inc. ARB
10670 N. Central Expwy.
Dallas, TX 75231   214-692-4700
Real estate investment trust

American Select Portfolio, Inc. SLA
222 S. Ninth St.
Minneapolis, MN 55402   800-333-6000
Financial - investment management

American Stores Co. ASC
709 E. South Temple
Salt Lake City, UT 84102
801-539-0112
Retail - supermarkets O

American Strategic Income Portfolio, Inc.
  ASP
222 S. Ninth St.
Minneapolis, MN 55402
800-866-7778
Financial - investment management

American Strategic Income Portfolio, Inc. -
  II BSP
222 S. Ninth St.
Minneapolis, MN 55402   800-866-7778
Financial - investment management

American Strategic Income Portfolio, Inc. -
  III CSP
222 S. Ninth St.
Minneapolis, MN 55402   800-866-7778
Financial - investment management

American Telephone & Telegraph Co. T
32 Avenue of the Americas
New York, NY 10013   212-387-5400
Telecommunications services
  [DRP]

American Waste Services, Inc. AW
One American Way
Warren, OH 44484   216-856-8800
Pollution control equipment & services

American Water Works Co., Inc.
  AWK
1025 Laurel Oak Rd.
Voorhees, NJ 08043   609-346-8200
Utility - water supply [DRP 5%]

Americana Hotels and Realty Corp. AHR
535 Boylston St.
Boston, MA 02116   617-247-3358
Hotels & motels

AmeriCredit Corp. ACF
200 Bailey Ave.
Fort Worth, TX 76107   817-332-7000
Financial - business services

AmeriData Technologies, Inc. ADA
700 Canal St.
Stamford, CT 06902   203-357-1464
Diversified operations O

Ameriquest Technologies, Inc. AQS
2722 Michelson Dr.
Irvine, CA 92715   714-222-6000
Computers - peripheral equipment

Ameritech Corp. AIT
30 S. Wacker Dr.
Chicago, IL 60606   312-750-5000
Utility - telephone O [DRP]

Ameron, Inc. AMN
4700 Ramona Blvd.
Monterey Park, CA 91754
818-683-4000
Building products - misc.

AMETEK, Inc. AME
Station Square
Paoli, PA 19301   610-647-2121
Electrical products - misc. O

Amli Residential Properties, Inc. AML
125 S. Wacker Dr., Ste. 3100
Chicago, IL 60606   312-984-5037
Real estate investment trust

Amoco Corp. AN
200 E. Randolph Dr.
Chicago, IL 60601   312-856-6111
Oil & gas - US integrated O [DRP]

AMP Inc. AMP
PO Box 3608
Harrisburg, PA 17105   717-564-0100
Electrical connectors O [DRP]

Ampco-Pittsburgh Corp. AP
600 Grant St., Ste. 4600
Pittsburgh, PA 15219   412-456-4400
Metal processing & fabrication

Amphenol Corp. APH
358 Hall Ave., PO Box 5030
Wallingford, CT 06492   203-265-8900
Fiber optics O

AMR Corp. AMR
Dallas/Ft. Worth Airport
Dallas, TX 76155 817-963-1234
Transportation - airline O

AMRE, Inc. AMM
8585 N. Stemmons Freeway
Dallas, TX 75247 214-819-7000
Building products - doors & trim

AMREP Corp. AXR
10 Columbus Circle
New York, NY 10019 212-541-7300
Building - residential & commercial

AMSCO International, Inc. ASZ
500 Grant St., Ste. 5000
Pittsburgh, PA 15219 412-338-6500
Medical products O

AmSouth Bancorporation ASO
1900 Fifth Ave. North
Birmingham, AL 35203 205-320-7151
Banks - southeast O [DRP]

AmVestors Financial Corp. AMV
415 S.W. 8th Ave.
Topeka, KS 66603 913-232-6945
Insurance - life [DRP]

Anacomp, Inc. AAC
11550 N. Meridian St.
Indianapolis, IN 46240 317-844-9666
Computers - services

Anadarko Petroleum Corp. APC
17001 Northchase Dr.
Houston, TX 77060 713-875-1101
Oil & gas - US exploration & production O

Analog Devices, Inc. ADI
One Technology Way
Norwood, MA 02062 617-329-4700
Electrical components - semiconductors O

Angelica Corp. AGL
424 S. Woods Mill Rd.
Chesterfield, MO 63017 314-854-3800
Linen supply & related
[DRP]

Anheuser-Busch Companies, Inc. BUD
One Busch Place
St. Louis, MO 63118 314-577-2000
Beverages - alcoholic O
[DRP]

AnnTaylor Stores Corp. ANN
142 W. 57th St.
New York, NY 10019 212-541-3300
Retail - apparel & shoes O

Anthony Industries, Inc. ANT
4900 S. Eastern Ave.
Los Angeles, CA 90040 213-724-2800
Leisure & recreational products

Aon Corp. AOC
123 N. Wacker Dr.
Chicago, IL 60606 312-701-3000
Insurance - accident & health O [DRP]

Apache Corp. APA
2000 Post Oak Blvd., Ste. 100
Houston, TX 77056 713-296-6000
Oil & gas - US exploration & production O
[DRP]

Apartment Investment and Management Co.
AIV
1873 S. Bellaire St., 17th Fl.
Denver, CO 80222 303-759-1110
Real estate investment trust

Apex Municipal Fund, Inc. APX
PO Box 9011
Princeton, NJ 08543
609-282-2800
Financial - investment management

Appalachian Power Co. AEWpB
40 Franklin Rd., S.W.
Roanoke, VA 24011 703-985-2300
Utility - electric power

Applied Magnetics Corp. APM
75 Robin Hill Rd.
Goleta, CA 93117 805-683-5353
Computers - peripheral equipment O

Applied Power Inc. APW
13000 W. Silver Spring Dr.
Butler, WI 53007 414-781-6600
Machine tools & related products

AptarGroup, Inc. ATR
475 W. Terra Cotta Ave.
Crystal Lake, IL 60014
815-477-0424
Pumps and seals

Aquarion Co. WTR
835 Main St.
Bridgeport, CT 06601 203-335-2333
Utility - water supply [DRP 5%]

Aquila Gas Pipeline Corp. AQP
100 N.E. Loop, Ste. 1000
San Antonio, TX 78216
210-342-0685
Oil & gas - production & pipeline

Arbor Property Trust ABR
One Tower Bridge, Ste. 800
West Conshohocken, PA 19428
215-941-2933
Real estate investment trust

Arcadian Partners, L.P. UAN
6750 Poplar Ave., Ste. 600
Memphis, TN 38138   901-758-5200
Chemicals - specialty

Archer Daniels Midland Co. ADM
4666 Faries Parkway
Decatur, IL 62525   217-424-5200
Food - flour & grain O

ARCO Chemical Co. RCM
3801 W. Chester Pike
Newtown Square, PA 19073
610-359-2000
Chemicals - specialty O [DRP]

Arkansas Power & Light Co. AKPp
425 W. Capitol Ave., 40th Fl.
Little Rock, AR 77201   501-377-4000
Utility - electric power

Armco Inc. AS
301 Grant St., 15th Fl.
Pittsburgh, PA 15219   412-255-9800
Steel - production O

Armstrong World Industries, Inc. ACK
313 W. Liberty St.
Lancaster, PA 17603   717-397-0611
Building products - misc. O [DRP]

Arrow Electronics, Inc. ARW
25 Hub Dr.
Melville, NY 11747   516-391-1300
Electronics - parts distribution O

Arthur J. Gallagher & Co. AJG
Two Pierce Place
Itasca, IL 60143   708-773-3800
Insurance - brokerage

ARTRA GROUP Inc. ATA
500 Central Ave.
Northfield, IL 60093   708-441-6650
Diversified operations

Arvin Industries, Inc. ARV
One Noblitt Plaza, PO Box 3000
Columbus, IN 47202   812-379-3000
Automotive & trucking - original equipment
   O [DRP]

ARX, Inc. ARX
35 S. Service Rd.
Plainview, NY 11803   516-694-6700
Machinery - general industrial

ASARCO Inc. AR
180 Maiden Ln.
New York, NY 10038   212-510-2000
Metal ores - misc. O [DRP]

Ashland Coal, Inc. ACI
2205 Fifth Street Rd.
Huntington, WV 25701   304-526-3333
Coal [DRP]

Ashland Oil, Inc. ASH
1000 Ashland Dr.
Russell, KY 41169   606-329-3333
Oil refining & marketing O [DRP]

Asia Pacific Fund, Inc. APB
One Seaport Plaza
New York, NY 10292   212-214-3334
Financial - investment management

Asset Investors Corp. AIC
3600 S. Yosemite St., Ste. 900
Denver, CO 80237   303-793-2703
Real estate investment trust [DRP]

Associated Estates Realty Corp. AEC
5025 Swetland Ct.
Richmond Heights, OH 44143
216-461-1111
Real estate investment trust

AT&T Capital Corp. TCC
44 Whippany Rd.
Morristown, NJ 07962   201-397-3000
Financial - business services O

Atalanta/Sosnoff Capital Corp. ATL
101 Park Ave.
New York, NY 10178   212-867-5000
Financial - investment management

Atlanta Gas Light Co. ATG
303 Peachtree St. NE
Atlanta, GA 30302   404-584-4000
Utility - gas distribution [DRP]

Atlantic Energy, Inc. ATE
1199 Black Horse Pike
Pleasantville, NJ 8232   609-645-4500
Utility - electric power [DRP]

Atlantic Richfield Co. ARC
515 S. Flower St.
Los Angeles, CA 90071
213-486-3511
Oil & gas - US integrated O [DRP]

Atlas Corp. AZ
370 Seventeenth St., Ste. 3150
Denver, CO 80202   303-825-1200
Gold mining & processing

Atmos Energy Corp. ATO
5430 LBJ Freeway
Dallas, TX 75240   214-934-9227
Utility - gas distribution [DRP 3%]

Augat Inc. AUG
89 Forbes Blvd., PO Box 448
Mansfield, MA 02048   508-543-4300
Electrical connectors

Authentic Fitness Corp. ASM
7911 Haskell Ave.
Van Nuys, CA 91410   818-376-0300
Apparel

Automatic Data Processing, Inc. AUD
One ADP Blvd.
Roseland, NJ 07068   201-994-5000
Business services O

AutoZone, Inc. AZO
3030 Poplar Ave.
Memphis, TN 38111   901-325-4600
Auto parts - retail & wholesale O

Avalon Properties, Inc. AVN
11 Burtis Ave.
New Canaan, CT 06840   203-972-4000
Real estate investment trust

AVEMCO Corp. AVE
411 Aviation Way
Frederick, MD 21701   301-694-5700
Insurance - property & casualty

Avery Dennison Corp. AVY
150 N. Orange Grove Blvd.
Pasadena, CA 91103   818-304-2000
Office & art materials O [DRP]

Aviall Inc. AVL
9311 Reeves St.
Dallas, TX 75235   214-956-5356
Aerospace - aircraft equipment

Avnet, Inc. AVT
80 Cutter Mill Rd.
Great Neck, NY 11021   516-466-7000
Electronics - parts distribution O
[DRP]

Avon Products, Inc. AVP
9 W. 57th St.
New York, NY 10019   212-546-6015
Cosmetics & toiletries O [DRP]

Aydin Corp. AYD
700 Dresher Rd., PO Box 349
Horsham, PA 19044   215-657-7510
Electronics - military

Aztar Corp. AZR
2390 E. Camelback Rd.
Phoenix, AZ 85016   602-381-4100
Leisure & recreational services O

Bairnco Corp. BZ
2251 Lucien Way, Ste. 300
Maitland, FL 32751   407-875-2222
Diversified operations

Baker Hughes, Inc. BHI
3900 Essex Ln.
Houston, TX 77027   713-439-8600
Oil field machinery & equipment O
[DRP]

Baker, Fentress & Co. BKF
200 W. Madison St., Ste. 3510
Chicago, IL 60606   312-236-9190
Financial - investment management

Baldor Electric Co. BEZ
5711 R. S. Boreham, Jr. St.
Fort Smith, AR 72902   501-646-4711
Machinery - electrical

Ball Corp. BLL
345 S. High St., PO Box 2407
Muncie, IN 47307   317-747-6100
Glass products [DRP 5%]

Ballard Medical Products BMP
12050 Lone Peak Pkwy.
Draper, UT 84020   801-572-6800
Medical & dental supplies O

Bally Entertainment Corp. BLY
8700 W. Bryn Mawr Ave.
Chicago, IL 60631   312-399-1300
Leisure & recreational services O

Baltimore Gas and Electric Co. BGE
PO Box 1475
Baltimore, MD 21203   410-783-5920
Utility - electric power [DRP]

Banc One Corp. ONE
100 E. Broad St.
Columbus, OH 43271   614-248-5944
Banks - midwest O [DRP]

Bancorp Hawaii, Inc. BOH
130 Merchant St.
Honolulu, HI 906813   808-537-8111
Banks - west O [DRP]

BancTEXAS Group Inc. BTX
13747 Montfort Dr.
Dallas, TX 75240   214-701-4704
Banks - midwest

Bandag, Inc. BDG
2905 N. Highway 61
Muscatine, IA 52761
319-262-1400
Rubber tires [DRP]

Bangor Hydro-Electric Co. BGR
33 State St.
Bangor, ME 04401   207-945-5621
Utility - electric power [DRP]

Bank of Boston Corp. BKB
100 Federal St.
Boston, MA 02110   617-434-2200
Banks - northeast O
[DRP 3%]

Bank of New York Co., Inc. BK
48 Wall St.
New York, NY 10286   212-495-1784
Banks - northeast O [DRP]

Bank United of Texas FSB BKUA
3200 Southwest Freeway
Houston, TX 77027   713-963-7900
Financial - savings and loans

BankAmerica Corp. BAC
Bank of America Center
San Francisco, CA 94104
415-622-3530
Banks - money center O [DRP]

Bankers Life Holdings Corp. BLH
222 Merchandise Mart Plaza
Chicago, IL 60654   312-396-6000
Insurance - accident & health   O

Bankers Trust New York Corp. BT
280 Park Ave.
New York, NY 10017   212-250-2500
Banks - money center O [DRP]

Banner Aerospace, Inc. BAR
300 W. Service Rd.
Washington, DC 20041
703-478-5790
Aerospace - aircraft equipment

Banyan Mortgage Investment Fund VMG
150 S. Wacker Dr.
Chicago, IL 60606   312-553-9800
Real estate investment trust

Bard (C.R.), Inc. BCR
730 Central Ave.
Murray Hill, NJ 07974   908-277-8000
Medical & dental supplies O [DRP]

Barnes & Noble, Inc. BKS
122 Fifth Ave.
New York, NY 10011   212-633-3300
Retail - misc. O

Barnes Group Inc. B
123 Main St., PO Box 489
Bristol, CT 06011   203-583-7070
Wire & cable products   [DRP]

Barnett Banks, Inc. BBI
50 N. Laura St.
Jacksonville, FL 32202   904-791-7720
Banks - southeast O [DRP]

Barrett Resources Corp. BRR
1125 Seventeenth St.
Denver, CO 80202   303-297-3900
Oil & gas - US exploration & production O

Battle Mountain Gold Co. BMG
333 Clay St., 42nd Fl.
Houston, TX 77002   713-650-6400
Gold mining & processing O

Bausch & Lomb Inc. BOL
One Lincoln First Square
Rochester, NY 14601   716-338-6000
Medical products O [DRP]

Baxter International Inc. BAX
One Baxter Parkway
Deerfield, IL 60015   708-948-2000
Medical products O [DRP]

Bay Apartment Communities, Inc. BYA
4340 Stevens Creek Blvd.
San Jose, CA 95129 408-983-1500
Real estate investment trust

Bay State Gas Co. BGC
300 Friberg Parkway
Westborough, MA 01581
508-836-7000
Utility - gas distribution [DRP 3%]

BCE, Inc. BCE
1000 rue de La Gauchetierre Ouest Bureau
  3700
Montreal, Quebec H3B 4Y7 514-397-7310
Telecommunications   [DRP]

Beacon Properties Corp. BCN
50 Rowes Wharf
Boston, MA 02110 617-330-1400
Real estate investment trust

Bearings, Inc. BER
3600 Euclid Ave.
Cleveland, OH 44115 216-881-8900
Metal products - distribution

Beazer Homes USA, Inc. BZH
1927 Lakeside Pkwy., Ste. 602
Tucker, GA 30084 404-934-2888
Building - residential & commercial

Beckman Instruments, Inc. BEC
2500 Harbor Blvd.
Fullerton, CA 92634 714-871-4848
Medical instruments O [DRP]

Becton, Dickinson and Co. BDX
One Becton Dr.
Franklin Lakes, NJ 07417 201-847-6800
Medical & dental supplies O [DRP]

Bedford Property Investors, Inc. BED
3658 Mt. Diablo Blvd.
Lafayette, CA 94549 510-283-8910
Real estate investment trust [DRP]

Belden Inc. BWC
7701 Forsyth Blvd., Ste. 800
St. Louis, MO 63105 314-854-8000
Electrical products - misc.

Bell Atlantic Corp. BEL
1717 Arch St.
Philadelphia, PA 19103 215-963-6000
Utility - telephone O [DRP]

Bell Industries, Inc. BI
11812 San Vicente Blvd.
Los Angeles, CA 90049 310-826-2355
Electronics - parts distribution

BellSouth Corp. BLS
1155 Peachtree St., N.E.
Atlanta, GA 30309 404-249-2000
Utility - telephone O [DRP]

Bemis Co., Inc. BMS
222 S. Ninth St., Ste. 2300
Minneapolis, MN 55402 612-376-3000
Containers - paper & plastic
[DRP]

Beneficial Corp. BNL
301 N. Walnut St.
Wilmington, DE 19801 302-425-2500
Financial - consumer loans O [DRP]

Benson Eyecare Corp. EYE
555 Theodore Fremd Ave.
Rye, NY 10580 914-967-9400
Retail - misc.

Bergen Brunswig Corp. BBC
4000 Metropolitan Dr.
Orange, CA 92668 714-385-4000
Drugs & sundries - wholesale O

Berkshire Hathaway Inc. BRK
1440 Kiewit Plaza
Omaha, NE 68131 402-346-1400
Diversified operations

Berkshire Realty Co. BRI
470 Atlantic Ave.
Boston, MA 02210 617-423-2233
Real estate investment trust [DRP]

Berlitz International, Inc. BTZ
293 Wall St.
Princeton, NJ 08540 609-924-8500
Schools

Bernard Chaus, Inc. CHS
1410 Broadway
New York, NY 10018 212-354-1280
Apparel

Berry Petroleum Co. BRY
28700 Hovey Hills Rd.
Taft, CA 93268 805-769-8811
Oil & gas - US exploration & production

Best Buy Co., Inc. BBY
7075 Flying Cloud Dr.
Eden Prairie, MN 55344
612-947-2000
Retail - consumer electronics O

BET Holdings, Inc. BTV
1232 31st St., N.W.
Washington, DC 20007 202-337-5260
Broadcasting - radio & TV

Bethlehem Steel Corp. BS
1170 Eighth Ave.
Bethlehem, PA 18016 610-694-2424
Steel - production O [DRP]

Betz Laboratories, Inc. BTL
4636 Somerton Rd.
Trevose, PA 19047 215-355-3300
Chemicals - specialty O

Beverly Enterprises, Inc. BEV
5111 Rogers Ave., Ste. 40-A
Fort Smith, AR 72919 501-452-6712
Nursing homes O [DRP]

BIC Corp. BIC
500 BIC Dr.
Milford, CT 06460 203-783-2000
Office & art materials

Biocraft Laboratories, Inc. BCL
18-01 River Rd.
Fair Lawn, NJ 07410 201-703-0400
Drugs - generic

BioWhittaker, Inc. BWI
8830 Biggs Ford Rd.
Walkersville, MD 21793 301-898-07025
Medical products

Birmingham Steel Corp. BIR
1000 Urban Center Pkwy.
Birmingham, AL 35242 205-970-1200
Steel - production O

BJ Services Co. BJS
5500 N.W. Central Dr.
Houston, TX 77092 713-462-4239
Oil & gas - field services O

Black & Decker Corp. BDK
701 E. Joppa Rd.
Towson, MD 21204 301-583-3900
Tools - hand held O [DRP]

Black Hills Corp. BKH
625 Ninth St., PO Box 1400
Rapid City, SD 57709 605-348-1700
Utility - electric power
[DRP]

BlackRock 1998 Term Trust Inc. BBT
One Seaport Plaza
New York, NY 10292 212-214-3332
Financial - investment management

BlackRock 1999 Term Trust, Inc. BNN
One Seaport Plaza
New York, NY 10292 212-214-3332
Financial - investment management

BlackRock 2001 Term Trust, Inc. BLK
One Seaport Plaza
New York, NY 10292 212-214-3332
Financial - investment management

BlackRock Advantage Term Trust Inc. BAT
One Seaport Plaza
New York, NY 10292 212-214-3332
Financial - investment management

BlackRock California Ins. Mun. 2008 Term
Trust BFC
One Seaport Plaza
New York, NY 10292 212-214-3332
Financial - investment management

BlackRock Florida Municipal 2008 Term
  Trust BRF
One Seaport Plaza
New York, NY 10292 212-214-3332
Financial - investment management

BlackRock Income Trust Inc. BKT
One Seaport Plaza
New York, NY 10292 212-214-3332
Financial - investment management

BlackRock Insured Municipal 2008 Term
  Trust BRM
One Seaport Plaza
New York, NY 10292 212-214-3332
Financial - investment management

BlackRock Insured Municipal Term Trust
  Inc. BMT
One Seaport Plaza
New York, NY 10292 212-214-3332
Financial - investment management

BlackRock Investment Quality Mun. Trust
  Inc. BKN
One Seaport Plaza
New York, NY 10292 212-214-3332
Financial - investment management

BlackRock Investment Quality Term Trust
  Inc. BQT
One Seaport Plaza
New York, NY 10292 212-214-3332
Financial - investment management

BlackRock Mun. Target Term Trust Inc. BMN
One Seaport Plaza
New York, NY 10292 212-214-3332
Financial - investment management

BlackRock New York Ins. Mun. 2008 Term
  Trust BLN
One Seaport Plaza
New York, NY 10292 212-214-3332
Financial - investment management

BlackRock North American Government
  Trust Inc. BNA
One Seaport Plaza
New York, NY 10292 212-214-3332
Financial - investment management

BlackRock Strategic Term Trust Inc. BGT
One Seaport Plaza
New York, NY 10292 212-214-3332
Financial - investment management

BlackRock Target Term Trust Inc. BTT
One Seaport Plaza
New York, NY 10292 212-214-3332
Financial - investment management

Blue Chip Value Fund, Inc. BLU
633 17th St., Ste. 1800
Denver, CO 80202 303-293-5999
Financial - investment management

Blyth Industries, Inc. BTH
2 Greenwich Plaza, 3rd Fl.
Greenwich, CT 06830 203-661-1926
Miscellaneous - not elsewhere classified

BMC Industries, Inc. BMC
Two Appletree Square, Ste. 400
Minneapolis, MN 55425 612-851-6000
Medical & dental supplies

Boise Cascade Corp. BCC
One Jefferson Square
Boise, ID 83728 208-384-6161
Paper & paper products O [DRP]

Bolt Beranek and Newman Inc. BBN
150 CambridgePark Dr.
Cambridge, MA 02140 617-873-2000
Engineering - R & D services

Borden Chemicals and Plastics L.P.
  BCU
Highway 73
Geismar, LA 70734 504-387-5101
Chemicals - diversified O

Borden, Inc. BN
180 E. Broad St.
Columbus, OH 43215 614-225-4000
Food - dairy products O

Borg-Warner Automotive, Inc. BWA
200 S. Michigan Ave.
Chicago, IL 60604 312-322-8500
Automotive & trucking - original equipment

Borg-Warner Security Corp. BOR
200 S. Michigan Ave.
Chicago, IL 60604 312-322-8500
Protection - safety equipment & services

Boston Celtics L.P. BOS
151 Merrimac St.
Boston, MA 02114 617-523-6050
Leisure & recreational services

Boston Edison Co. BSE
800 Boylston St.
Boston, MA 02199 617-424-2000
Utility - electric power

Boston Scientific Corp. BSX
480 Pleasant St.
Watertown, MA 02172 617-923-1720
Medical products O

Bowater Inc. BOW
55 E. Camperdown Way
Greenville, SC 29602 803-271-7733
Paper & paper products O
  [DRP]

Boyd Gaming Corp. BYD
2950 S. Industrial Rd.
Las Vegas, NV 89109 702-792-7200
Leisure & recreational services O

Bradlees, Inc. BLE
One Bradlees Circle
Braintree, MA 02184 617-380-8000
Retail - discount & variety O

Bradley Real Estate Trust BTR
250 Boylston St.
Boston, MA 02116 617-421-0741
Real estate investment trust[DRP 5%]

BRE Properties, Inc. BRE
One Montgomery St., Ste. 2500
San Francisco, CA 94104 415-445-6530
Real estate investment trust

Breed Technologies, Inc. BDT
5300 Old Tampa Highway
Lakeland, FL 33811 813-284-6000
Automotive & trucking - original equipment
O

Briggs & Stratton Corp. BGG
12301 W. Wirth St.
Wauwatosa, WI 53222 414-259-5333
Engines - internal combustion O [DRP]

Brinker International, Inc. EAT
6820 LBJ Freeway
Dallas, TX 75240 214-980-9917
Retail - food & restaurants O

Bristol-Myers Squibb Co. BMY
345 Park Ave.
New York, NY 10154 212-546-4000
Drugs O [DRP]

British Airways PLC BAB
1850 K St., NW Ste. 300
Washington, DC 20006 202-331-9068
Airline O [DRP]

British Petroleum Co. PLC BP
200 Public Square
Cleveland, OH 44114 216-586-6077
Oil O [DRP]

Broadway Stores Inc. BWY
3880 N. Mission Rd.
Los Angeles, CA 90031 213-227-2000
Retail - major department stores O

Brooke Group Ltd. BGL
65 E. 55th St.
New York, NY 10022 305-579-8000
Tobacco

Brooklyn Union Gas Co. BU
One MetroTech Center
Brooklyn, NY 11201 718-403-2000
Utility - gas distribution [DRP]

Brown & Sharpe Manufacturing Co. BNS
200 Frenchtown Rd.
North Kingstown, RI 02852
401-886-2000
Electronics - measuring instruments

Brown Group, Inc. BG
8300 Maryland Ave.
St. Louis, MO 63105 314-854-4000
Shoes & related apparel [DRP]

Brown-Forman Corp. BFB
850 Dixie Hwy.
Louisville, KY 40210 502-585-1100
Beverages - alcoholic [DRP]

Browning-Ferris Industries, Inc. BFI
757 N. Eldridge, PO Box 3151
Houston, TX 77253 713-870-8100
Pollution control equipment & services O
[DRP]

BRT Realty Trust BRT
60 Cutter Mill Rd.
Great Neck, NY 11021 516-466-3100
Real estate investment trust

Brunswick Corp. BC
1 N. Field Ct.
Lake Forest, IL 60045 708-375-4700
Leisure & recreational products O [DRP]

Brush Wellman Inc. BW
17876 St. Clair Ave.
Cleveland, OH 44110 216-486-4200
Metals - non ferrous [DRP]

Buckeye Partners, L.P. BPL
3900 Hamilton Blvd.
Allentown, PA 18103 610-820-8300
Oil & gas - production & pipeline

Burlington Coat Factory Warehouse Corp. BCF
1830 Route 130
Burlington, NJ 08016 609-387-7800
Retail - apparel & shoes

Burlington Industries, Inc. BUR
3330 W. Friendly Ave.
Greensboro, NC 27410 910-379-2000
Textiles - mill products O

Burlington Northern Inc. BNI
777 Main St.
Fort Worth, TX 76102 817-333-2000
Transportation - rail O

Burlington Resources Coal Seam Gas
  Royalty Tr. BRU
700 Louisiana St., Ste. 3100
Houston, TX 77002 713-247-7508
Oil & gas - US royalty trust O

Burlington Resources Inc. BR
5051 Westheimer, Ste. 1400
Houston, TX 77056 713-624-9500
Oil & gas - US exploration & production

Burnham Pacific Properties, Inc. BPP
610 W. Ash St.
San Diego, CA 92101 619-232-2001
Real estate investment trust [DRP 5%]

Bush Boake Allen Inc. BOA
7 Mercedes Dr.
Montvale, NJ 07645 201-391-9870
Chemicals - specialty

Bush Industries, Inc. BSH
One Mason Dr.
Jamestown, NY 14702 716-665-2000
Furniture

Cabletron Systems, Inc. CS
35 Industrial Way
Rochester, NH 03867 603-332-9400
Computers - peripheral equipment O

Cabot Corp. CBT
75 State St.
Boston, MA 02109 617-345-0100
Chemicals - specialty [DRP]

Cabot Oil & Gas Corp. COG
15375 Memorial Dr.
Houston, TX 77079 713-589-4600
Oil & gas - US exploration & production

Cadence Design Systems, Inc. CDN
555 River Oaks Pkwy.
San Jose, CA 95134 408-943-1234
Computers - software O

Caesars World, Inc. CAW
1801 Century Park East
Los Angeles, CA 90067 310-552-2711
Leisure & recreational services O

Calgon Carbon Corp. CCC
400 Calgon Carbon Dr.
Pittsburgh, PA 15205 412-787-6700
Pollution control equipment & services O

Cali Realty Corporation CLI
11 Commerce Dr.
Cranford, NJ 07016 908-272-8000
Real estate investment trust

California Energy Co., Inc. CE
10831 Old Mill Rd.
Omaha, NE 68154 402-330-8900
Energy - alternate sources O

California Federal Bank, A Federal Savings
  Bank CAL
5700 Wilshire Blvd.
Los Angeles, CA 90036 213-932-4200
Financial - savings and loans O

California Real Estate Investment Trust
  CT
705 University Ave.
Sacramento, CA 95825 916-929-5433
Real estate investment trust

California Water Service Co. CWT
1720 N. First St.
San Jose, CA 95112 408-451-8200
Utility - water supply [DRP]

Callaway Golf Co. ELY
2285 Rutherford Rd.
Carlsbad, CA 92008 619-931-1771
Leisure & recreational products O [DRP]

CalMat Co. CZM
3200 San Fernando Rd.
Los Angeles, CA 90065 213-258-2777
Construction - cement & concrete

Camco International, Inc. CAM
7030 Ardmore
Houston, TX 77054 713-747-4000
Oil & gas - field services

Camden Property Trust CPT
3200 Southwest Freeway
Houston, TX 77027 713-964-3555
Real estate investment trust

Campbell Soup Co. CPB
Campbell Place
Camden, NJ 08103 609-342-4800
Food - canned O [DRP]

Canadian Pacific Ltd. CP
PO Box 6042
Station Centre-Ville, Montreal, Quebec H3C
  3E4 514-395-5151
Transportation O [DRP]

Capital Cities/ABC, Inc. CCB
77 W. 66th St.
New York, NY 10023 212-456-7777
Broadcasting - radio & TV O

Capital Guaranty Corp. CGY
Steuart Tower, 22nd Fl.
San Francisco, CA 94105 415-995-8000
Insurance - multi line & misc.

Capital One Financial Corp. COF
8330 Boone Blvd.
Vienna, VA 22182 703-734-7495
Financial - business services

Capital Re Corp. KRE
1325 Avenue of the Americas
New York, NY 10019 212-974-0100
Insurance - property & casualty

Capitol American Financial Corp. CAF
1001 Lakeside Ave.
Cleveland, OH 44114 216-696-6400
Insurance - accident & health

Capstead Mortgage Corp. CMO
2711 N. Haskell Ave., LB 12
Dallas, TX 75204 214-874-2323
Real estate investment trust
  [DRP 5%]

Capstone Capital Corp. CCT
1 Perimeter Park South
Birmingham, AL 35243 205-967-2092
Real estate investment trust

Capsure Holdings Corp. CSH
2 North Riverside Plaza
Chicago, IL 60606 312-879-1900
Insurance - property & casualty

Cardinal Health, Inc. CAH
655 Metro Place South
Dublin, OH 43017 614-761-8700
Drugs & sundries - wholesale O

Caremark International, Inc. CK
2215 Sanders Rd., Ste. 400
Northbrook, IL 60062 708-559-4700
Healthcare - outpatient & home O

Carl Karcher Enterprises, Inc. CKR
1200 N. Harbor Blvd.
Anaheim, CA 92801 714-774-5796
Retail - food & restaurants

Carlisle Companies Inc. CSL
250 S. Clinton St., Ste. 201
Syracuse, NY 13202 315-474-2500
Diversified operations [DRP]

Carlisle Plastics, Inc. CPA
One Union St.
Boston, MA 02108 617-557-2600
Rubber & plastic products

Carmike Cinemas, Inc. CKE
1301 First Ave.
Columbus, GA 31901 404-576-3400
Motion pictures & services

Carnival Corp. CCL
3655 N.W. 87th Ave.
Miami, FL 33178 305-599-2600
Leisure & recreational services O

Carolina Freight Corp. CAO
North Carolina Highway 150 E.
Cherryville, NC 28021 704-435-6811
Transportation - truck [DRP]

Carolina Power & Light Co. CPL
411 Fayetteville St.
Raleigh, NC 27601 919-546-6111
Utility - electric power [DRP]

Carpenter Technology Corp. CRS
PO Box 14662
Reading, PA 19612 610-208-2000
Steel - specialty alloys
[DRP]

Carr Realty Corp. CRE
1700 Pennsylvania Ave. NW
Washington, DC 20006
202-624-1700
Real estate investment trust

Carr-Gottstein Foods Co. CGF
6411 A St.
Anchorage, AK 99518 907-561-1944
Retail - convenience stores

Carson Pirie Scott & Co. CRP
331 W. Wisconsin Ave.
Milwaukee, WI 53203 414-347-4141
Retail - major department stores O

Carter-Wallace, Inc. CAR
1345 Avenue of the Americas
New York, NY 10105
212-339-5000
Drugs O

Cascade Natural Gas Corp. CGC
222 Fairview Ave. North
Seattle, WA 98109 206-624-3900
Utility - gas distribution [DRP]

Case Corp. CSE
700 State St.
Racine, WI 53404 414-636-6011
Machinery - farm O

Cash America International, Inc. PWN
1600 W. 7th St.
Fort Worth, TX 76102 817-335-1100
Retail - misc.

CasTech Aluminum Group Inc. CTA
753 W. Waterloo Rd.
Akron, OH 44314 216-848-5555
Diversified operations

Catalina Marketing Corp. POS
11300 Ninth St. North
St. Petersburg, FL 33716 813-579-5000
Business services - marketing

Catellus Development Corp. CDX
201 Mission St.
San Francisco, CA 94105
415-974-4500
Real estate development O

Caterpillar Inc. CAT
100 NE Adams St.
Peoria, IL 61629 309-675-1000
Machinery - construction & mining O [DRP]

Cavalier Homes, Inc. CAV
Highway 41 N. and Cavalier Rd.
Addison, AL 35540 205-747-1575
Building - residential & commercial

CBI Industries, Inc. CBH
800 Jorie Blvd.
Oak Brook, IL 60521 708-572-7000
Construction - heavy O

CBL & Associates Properties, Inc. CBL
6148 Lee Highway
Chattanooga, TN 37421 615-855-0001
Real estate investment trust

CBS Inc. CBS
51 W. 52nd St.
New York, NY 10019 212-975-4321
Broadcasting - radio & TV O [DRP]

CCP Insurance, Inc. CCP
11825 N. Pennsylvania St.
Carmel, IN 46032 317-573-6900
Insurance - multi line & misc. O

CCX, Inc. CCX
1900 Rexford Rd., Ste. 208
Charlotte, NC 28211 704-365-0560
Diversified operations

CDI Corp. CDI
1717 Arch St., 35th Fl.
Philadelphia, PA 19103 215-569-2200
Engineering - R & D services

Cedar Fair, L.P. FUN
PO Box 5006
Sandusky, OH 44871 419-626-0830
Leisure & recreational services

Centerior Energy Corp. CX
6200 Oak Tree Blvd.
Independence, OH 44131 216-447-3100
Utility - electric power O

Centex Construction Products, Inc. CXP
3710 Rawlins, Ste. 1600
Dallas, TX 75219 214-559-6500
Building products - misc. O

Centex Corp. CTX
3333 Lee Pkwy., Ste. 1200
Dallas, TX 75219 214-559-6500
Building - residential & commercial

Central and South West Corp. CSR
1616 Woodall Rodgers Freeway
Dallas, TX 75202 214-777-1000
Utility - electric power O [DRP]

Central Hudson Gas & Electric Corp.
  CNH
284 South Ave.
Poughkeepsie, NY 12601
914-452-2000
Utility - electric power [DRP]

Central Louisiana Electric Co., Inc. CNL
2030 Donahue Ferry Rd.
Pineville, LA 71360 318-484-7400
Utility - electric power [DRP]

Central Maine Power Co. CTP
83 Edison Dr.
Augusta, ME 04336 207-623-3521
Utility - electric power [DRP]

Central Newspapers, Inc. ECP
135 N. Pennsylvania St.
Indianapolis, IN 46204 317-231-9200
Publishing - newspapers

Central Vermont Public Service Corp. CV
77 Grove St.
Rutland, VT 05701 802-773-2711
Utility - electric power [DRP]

Centura Banks, Inc. CBC
134 N. Church St., PO Box 1220
Rocky Mount, NC 27802 919-977-4400
Banks - southeast [DRP]

Century Telephone Enterprises, Inc. CTL
100 Century Park Dr.
Monroe, LA 71203 318-388-9500
Utility - telephone O [DRP]

Ceridian Corp. CEN
8100 34th Ave. South
Minneapolis, MN 55425 612-853-8100
Computers - mainframe O

Champion International Corp. CHA
One Champion Plaza
Stamford, CT 06921 203-358-7000
Paper & paper products O [DRP]

Chaparral Steel Co. CSM
300 Ward Rd.
Midlothian, TX 76065 214-775-8241
Steel - production

Charles Allmon Trust, Inc. GSO
4405 East-West Highway
Bethesda, MD 20814 301-986-5866
Financial - investment management [DRP]

Charles E. Smith Residential Realty, Inc.
  SRW
2345 Crystal Dr.
Arlington, VA 22202 703-920-8500
Real estate investment trust

Chart House Enterprises, Inc. CHT
115 S. Acacia Ave.
Solana Beach, CA 92075 619-755-8281
Retail - food & restaurants

Chart Industries, Inc. CTI
35555 Curtis Blvd.
Eastlake, OH 44095 216-946-2525
Machinery - general industrial

Chase Brass Industries, Inc. CSI
State Route 15
Montpelier, OH 43543 419-485-3193
Metals - non ferrous

Chase Manhattan Corp. CMB
One Chase Manhattan Plaza
New York, NY 10081 212-552-2222
Banks - money center O [DRP 5%]

Chateau Properties, Inc. CPJ
19500 Hall Rd.
Clinton Township, MI 48038
313-286-3600
Real estate investment trust

Checkpoint Systems, Inc. CKP
550 Grove Rd., PO Box 188
Thorofare, NJ 08086 609-848-1800
Protection - safety equipment & services O

Chelsea GCA Realty, Inc. CCG
103 Eisenhower Parkway
Roseland, NJ 07068 201-228-6111
Real estate investment trust

Chemed Corp. CHE
255 E. Fifth St.
Cincinnati, OH 45202 513-762-6900
Diversified operations [DRP]

Chemical Banking Corp. CHL
277 Park Ave.
New York, NY 10172 212-310-6000
Banks - money center O [DRP]

Chemical Waste Management, Inc. CHW
3001 Butterfield Rd.
Oak Brook, IL 60521 708-218-1500
Pollution control equipment & services O
[DRP]

Chesapeake Corp. CSK
1021 E. Cary St., PO Box 2350
Richmond, VA 23218 804-697-1000
Paper & paper products O [DRP]

Chesapeake Utilities Corp. CPK
861 Silver Lake Blvd.
Dover, DE 19901 302-734-6755
Utility - gas distribution [DRP]

Chevron Corp. CHV
225 Bush St.
San Francisco, CA 94104 415-894-7700
Oil & gas - international integrated O [DRP]

Chic by H.I.S., Inc. JNS
1372 Broadway
New York, NY 10018 212-302-6400
Apparel

Chicago & North Western Transporation Co.
 CNW
165 N. Canal St.
Chicago, IL 60606 312-559-7000
Transportation - rail O

Chiquita Brands International, Inc. CQB
250 E. Fifth St.
Cincinnati, OH 45202 513-784-8011
Food - misc. O [DRP]

Chock Full O'Nuts Corp. CHF
370 Lexington Ave.
New York, NY 10017 212-532-0300
Food - misc.

Chris-Craft Industries, Inc. CCN
600 Madison Ave.
New York, NY 10022 212-421-0200
Broadcasting - radio & TV

Christiana Companies, Inc. CST
777 E. Wisconsin Ave.
Milwaukee, WI 53202 414-291-9000
Real estate development

Chrysler Corp. C
12000 Chrysler Dr.
Highland Park, MI 48288 313-956-5741
Automotive manufacturing O [DRP]

Chubb Corp. CB
15 Mountain View Rd.
Warren, NJ 07061 908-580-2000
Insurance - property & casualty O [DRP]

Church & Dwight Co., Inc. CHD
469 N. Harrison St.
Princeton, NJ 08543 609-683-5900
Soap & cleaning preparations
[DRP]

Chyron Corp. CHY
265 Spagnoli Rd.
Melville, NY 11747 516-845-2000
Video equipment

CIGNA Corp. CI
One Liberty Place
Philadelphia, PA 19192 215-761-1000
Insurance - multi line & misc. O [DRP]

CIGNA High Income Shares HIS
1380 Main St.
Springfield, MA 01103 413-781-7776
Financial - investment management

CILCORP Inc. CER
300 Hamilton Blvd., Ste. 300
Peoria, IL 60160 309-675-8810
Utility - electric power [DRP]

Cincinnati Bell Inc. CSN
201 E. Fourth St., PO Box 2301
Cincinnati, OH 45201 513-397-9900
Utility - telephone O [DRP]

Cincinnati Milacron Inc. CMZ
4701 Marburg Ave.
Cincinnati, OH 45209 513-841-8100
Machine tools & related products O
[DRP]

CINergy Corp. CIN
139 E. Fourth St.
Cincinnati, OH 45202 513-381-2000
Utility - electric power [DRP]

CIPSCO Inc. CIP
607 E. Adams St.
Springfield, IL 62739 217-523-3600
Utility - electric power   [DRP]

Circuit City Stores, Inc. CC
9950 Mayland Dr.
Richmond, VA 23233 804-527-4000
Retail - consumer electronics O

Circus Circus Enterprises, Inc. CIR
2880 Las Vegas Blvd. South
Las Vegas, NV 89109 702-734-0410
Leisure & recreational services O

Citicorp CCI
399 Park Ave.
New York, NY 10043 212-559-1000
Banks - money center O [DRP 3%]

Citizens Corp DE CZC
645 W. Grand River
Howell, MI 48843 517-546-2160
Insurance - multi line & misc.

Citizens Utilities Co. CZNA
High Ridge Park, PO Box 3801
Stamford, CT 06905 203-329-8800
Utility - telephone [DRP]

City National Corp. CYN
400 N. Roxbury Dr.
Beverly Hills, CA 90210 310-550-5400
Banks - west O

Claire's Stores, Inc. CLE
3 S.W. 129th Ave.
Pembrook Pines, FL 33027 305-433-3900
Retail - jewelry stores O

CLARCOR Inc. CLC
2323 Sixth St., PO Box 7007
Rockford, IL 61125 815-962-8867
Diversified operations [DRP]

Clark Automotive Products Corp. CAB
100 N. Michigan St.
South Bend, IN 46634 219-239-0155
Auto parts - retail & wholesale

Clark Equipment Co. CKL
100 N. Michigan St.
South Bend, IN 46601 219-239-0100
Machinery - material handling O

Clayton Homes, Inc. CMH
623 Market St.
Knoxville, TN 37902 615-970-7200
Building - mobile homes & RV O

Clear Channel Communications, Inc.
CCU
200 Concord Plaza, Ste. 600
San Antonio, TX 78216 210-822-2828
Broadcasting - radio & TV

Clemente Global Growth Fund, Inc.
CLM
152 W. 57th St.
New York, NY 10019 212-765-0700
Financial - investment management

Cleveland-Cliffs Inc. CLF
1100 Superior Ave.
Cleveland, OH 44114 216-694-5700
Iron ores [DRP]

Clorox Co. CLX
1221 Broadway
Oakland, CA 94612 415-271-7000
Soap & cleaning preparations O [DRP]

Club Med, Inc. CMI
40 W. 57th St.
New York, NY 10019 212-977-2100
Leisure & recreational services

CMAC Investment Corp. CMT
1601 Market St.
Philadelphia, PA 19103 215-564-6600
Insurance - multi line & misc.

CML Group, Inc. CML
524 Main St.
Acton, MA 01720 508-264-4155
Retail - apparel & shoes O [DRP]

CMS Energy Corp. CMS
330 Town Center Dr.
Dearborn, MI 48126 313-436-9261
Utility - electric power O [DRP]

CNA Financial Corp. CNA
CNA Plaza
Chicago, IL 60685 312-822-5000
Insurance - property & casualty O

CNA Income Shares, Inc. CNN
CNA Plaza
Chicago, IL 60685 312-822-4181
Financial - investment management

Coachmen Industries, Inc. COA
601 E. Beardsley Ave.
Elkhart, IN 46514 219-262-0123
Building - mobile homes & RV

Coast Savings Financial, Inc. CSA
1000 Wilshire Blvd.
Los Angeles, CA 90017 213-362-2000
Financial - savings and loans O

Coastal Healthcare Group, Inc. DR
2828 Croasdaile Dr.
Durham, NC 27705 919-383-0355
Medical services O

Cobra Industries, Inc. COI
2766 E. College Ave.
Goshen, IN 46526 219-534-1418
Building - mobile homes & RV

Coca-Cola Co. KO
One Coca-Cola Plaza NW
Atlanta, GA 30313 404-676-02121
Beverages - soft drinks O
[DRP]

Coca-Cola Enterprises Inc. CCE
Coca-Cola Plaza NW
Atlanta, GA 30313 404-676-2100
Beverages - soft drinks O
[DRP]

Coeur d'Alene Mines Corp. CDE
505 Front Ave., PO Box I
Coeur d'Alene, ID 83816 208-667-3511
Silver mining & processing O

Cohen & Steers Total Return Realty Fund,
Inc. RFI
757 Third Ave.
New York, NY 10017 212-832-3232
Financial - investment management

Cold Metal Products, Inc. CLQ
8526 South Ave.
Youngstown, OH 44514 216-758-1194
Metal products - fabrication

Cole National Corp. CNJ
5915 Landerbrook Dr.
Mayfield Heights, OH 44124
216-449-4100
Retail - misc.

Coleman Co. CLN
250 N. St. Francis
Wichita, KS 67202 316-261-3211
Leisure & recreational products

Colgate-Palmolive Co. CL
300 Park Ave.
New York, NY 10022 212-310-2000
Soap & cleaning preparations O [DRP]

Collins & Aikman Holding Corp. CKC
8320 University Executive Park
Charlotte, NC 28262 704-548-2350
Diversified operations

Colonial High Income Municipal Trust CXE
One Financial Center
Boston, MA 02111 617-426-3750
Financial - investment management

Colonial High Yield Securities Trust CIF
One Financial Center
Boston, MA 02111 617-426-3750
Financial - investment management

Colonial InterMarket Income Trust I CMK
One Financial Center
Boston, MA 02111 617-426-3750
Financial - investment management

Colonial Investment Grade Mun. Trust CXH
One Financial Center
Boston, MA 02111 617-426-3750
Financial - investment management

Colonial Municipal Income Trust CMU
One Financial Center
Boston, MA 02111 617-426-3750
Financial - investment management

Colonial Properties Trust CLP
120 University Park Dr.
Orlando, FL 32792 407-677-1112
Real estate investment trust

Coltec Industries Inc. COT
430 Park Ave.
New York, NY 10022 212-940-0400
Diversified operations O

Columbia Gas System, Inc. CG
20 Montchanin Rd.
Wilmington, DE 19807 302-429-5000
Oil & gas - production & pipeline O [DRP]

Columbia/HCA Healthcare Corp. COL
201 W. Main St.
Louisville, KY 40202 502-572-2000
Hospitals O

Columbus Realty Trust CLB
15851 N. Dallas Parkway
Dallas, TX 75248 214-387-1492
Real estate investment trust

Comdisco, Inc. CDO
6111 N. River Rd.
Rosemont, IL 60018 708-698-3000
Leasing O

Comerica Inc. CMA
100 Renaissance Center
Detroit, MI 48243 313-222-4000
Banks - midwest O [DRP]

Commercial Intertech Corp. TEC
1775 Logan Ave.
Youngstown, OH 44505 216-746-8011
Machinery - construction & mining
[DRP]

Commercial Metals Co. CMC
7800 Stemmons Fwy.
Dallas, TX 75247 214-689-4300
Metal processing & fabrication

Commercial Net Lease Realty, Inc.
NNN
400 E. South St., Ste. 500
Orlando, FL 32801 407-422-1574
Real estate investment trust

Commonwealth Energy System CES
One Main St., PO Box 9150
Cambridge, MA 02142 617-225-4000
Utility - electric power [DRP]

Communications Satellite Corp. CQ
950 L'Enfant Plaza, S.W.
Washington, DC 20024 202-863-6000
Telecommunications services

Community Health Systems, Inc. CYH
3707 FM 1960 West, Ste. 500
Houston, TX 77068 713-537-5230
Hospitals

Community Psychiatric Centers CMY
24502 Pacific Park Dr.
Laguna Hills, CA 92656 714-831-1166
Hospitals O

Compaq Computer Corp. CPQ
20555 SH 249
Houston, TX 77070 713-370-0670
Computers - mini & micro O

Comprehensive Care Corp. CMP
16305 Swingley Ridge Dr.
Chesterfield, MO 63017 314-537-1288
Healthcare - outpatient & home

CompUSA Inc. CPU
14951 N. Dallas Parkway
Dallas, TX 75240 214-383-4000
Computers - retail & wholesale O

Computer Associates International, Inc. CA
One Computer Associates Plaza
Islandia, NY 11788 516-342-5224
Computers - software O [DRP]

Computer Sciences Corp. CSC
2100 E. Grand Ave.
El Segundo, CA 90245 310-615-0311
Computers - services O

Computer Task Group, Inc. TSK
800 Delaware Ave.
Buffalo, NY 14209 716-882-8000
Computers - services

Computervision Corp. CVN
100 Crosby Dr.
Bedford, MA 01730 617-275-1800
Computers - software

COMSAT Corp CQ
6560 Rock Spring Drive
Bethesda, MD 20817-1146
301-214-3200
Telecommunications O [DRP]

ConAgra, Inc. CAG
One ConAgra Dr.
Omaha, NE 68102 402-595-4000
Food - meat products O [DRP]

Cone Mills Corp. COE
1201 Maple St.
Greensboro, NC 02740 910-379-6220
Textiles - mill products

Connecticut Energy Corp. CNE
855 Main St.
Bridgeport, CT 06604 203-579-1732
Utility - gas distribution [DRP]

Connecticut Natural Gas Corp. CTG
100 Columbus Blvd.
Hartford, CT 06144 203-727-3000
Utility - gas distribution [DRP]

Conner Peripherals, Inc. CNR
3081 Zanker Rd.
San Jose, CA 95134 408-456-4500
Computers - peripheral equipment O

Conrail Inc. CRR
2001 Market St.
Philadelphia, PA 19101 215-209-2000
Transportation - rail O
  [DRP]

Conseco, Inc. CNC
11825 N. Pennsylvania St.
Carmel, IN 46032 317-573-6100
Insurance - life O

Consolidated Edison Co. of New York, Inc.
  ED
4 Irving Place
New York, NY 10003 212-460-4600
Utility - electric power O [DRP]

Consolidated Freightways, Inc. CNF
3240 Hillview Ave.
Palo Alto, CA 94304 415-494-2900
Transportation - truck O

Consolidated Natural Gas Co. CNG
625 Liberty Ave.
Pittsburgh, PA 15222 412-227-1000
Utility - gas distribution O [DRP]

Consolidated Papers, Inc. CDP
PO Box 8050
Wisconsin Rapids, WI 54495
715-422-3111
Paper & paper products O [DRP]

Consolidated Stores Corp. CNS
1105 N. Market St.
Wilmington, DE 19899 302-478-4896
Retail - discount & variety O

Consumers Power Co. CMSpA
212 W. Michigan Ave.
Jackson, MI 49201 517-788-1030
Utility - electric power

Continental Can Co., Inc. CAN
One Aerial Way
Syosset, NY 11791 516-822-4940
Containers - paper & plastic

Continental Homes Holding Corp. CON
7001 N. Scottsdale Rd.
Scottsdale, AZ 85253 602-483-0006
Building - residential & commercial

Continental Medical Systems, Inc. CNM
600 Wilson Ln., PO Box 715
Mechanicsburg, PA 17055 717-790-8300
Nursing homes O

Convertible Holdings, Inc. CNV
PO Box 9011
Princeton, NJ 08543 609-282-3200
Financial - investment management

CONVEX Computer Corp. CNX
3000 Waterview Parkway
Richardson, TX 75080 214-497-4000
Computers - mini & micro O

Cooker Restaurant Corp. CGR
1530 Bethel Rd.
Columbus, OH 43220 614-457-8500
Retail - food & restaurants

Cooper Industries, Inc. CBE
1001 Fannin, Ste. 4000
Houston, TX 77210 713-739-5400
Diversified operations O [DRP]

Cooper Tire & Rubber Co. CTB
Lima and Western Aves.
Findlay, OH 45840 419-423-1321
Rubber tires O

Core Industries Inc. CRI
500 N. Woodward Ave.
Bloomfield Hills, MI 48013 313-642-3400
Diversified operations

CoreStates Financial Corp. CFL
PO Box 7618
Philadelphia, PA 19101 215-973-3827
Banks - northeast O [DRP]

Corning Inc. GLW
Houghton Park
Corning, NY 14831 607-974-9000
Glass products O [DRP]

Corporate High Yield Fund II, Inc. KYT
PO Box 9011
Princeton, NJ 08543 609-282-2000
Financial - investment management

Corporate High Yield Fund, Inc. COY
PO Box 9011
Princeton, NJ 08543 609-282-2800
Financial - investment management

Corrpro Companies, Inc. CO
1055 W. Smith Rd.
Medina, OH 44256 216-723-5082
Industrial maintenance

Counsellors Tandem Securities Fund, Inc.
CTF
466 Lexington Ave.
New York, NY 10017 800-888-6878
Financial - investment management

Countrywide Credit Industries, Inc. CCR
155 N. Lake Ave.
Pasadena, CA 91101 818-304-8400
Financial - mortgages & related services O

Cousins Properties Inc. CUZ
2500 Windy Ridge Parkway
Marietta, GA 30067 404-955-2200
Real estate investment trust

CPC International Inc. CPC
International Plaza
Englewood Cliffs, NJ 07632 201-894-4000
Food - misc. O [DRP]

CPI Corp. CPY
1706 Washington Ave.
St. Louis, MO 63103 314-231-1575
Photographic equipment & supplies
[DRP]

Craig Corp. CRG
116 N. Robertson Blvd.
Los Angeles, CA 90048 310-659-6641
Retail - supermarkets

Crane Co. CR
100 First Stamford Place
Stamford, CT 06902 203-363-7300
Diversified operations O [DRP]

Crawford & Co. Risk Management Services
CRDB
5620 Glenridge Dr., NE
Atlanta, GA 30342 404-256-0830
Insurance - property & casualty

Cray Research, Inc. CYR
655-A Lone Oak Dr.
Eagan, MN 55121 612-683-7100
Computers - mainframe O

Crescent Real Estate Equities, Inc. CEI
9 West 57th St., 47th Fl.
New York, NY 10019 212-888-2399
Real estate investment trust

Crestar Financial Corp. CF
919 E. Main St., PO Box 26665
Richmond, VA 23261 804-782-5000
Banks - southeast O [DRP 5%]

CRI Insured Mortgage Association, Inc.
CMM
11200 Rockville Pike
Rockville, MD 20852 301-468-9200
Real estate investment trust

CRI Liquidating REIT, Inc. CFR
11200 Rockville Pike
Rockville, MD 20852 301-468-9200
Financial - investment management

Crompton & Knowles Corp. CNK
One Station Place
Stamford, CT 06902 203-353-5400
Chemicals - specialty O [DRP]

Cross Timbers Oil Co. XTO
810 Houston St., Ste. 2000
Fort Worth, TX 76102 817-870-2800
Oil & gas - US exploration & production

Cross Timbers Royalty Trust CRT
PO Box 1317
Fort Worth, TX 76101 817-390-6592
Oil & gas - US royalty trust

Crown American Realty Trust CWN
Pasquerilla Plaza
Johnstown, PA 15901 814-536-4441
Real estate investment trust

Crown Cork & Seal Co., Inc. CCK
9300 Ashton Rd.
Philadelphia, PA 19136 215-698-5100
Containers - metal O

Crown Crafts, Inc. CRW
1600 River Edge Pkwy., Ste. 200
Atlanta, GA 30328 404-644-6400
Textiles - home furnishings

CRSS Inc. CRX
1177 W. Loop South, Ste. 800
Houston, TX 77027 713-552-2000
Construction - heavy [DRP]

CS First Boston Income Fund, Inc. FBF
Vanguard Financial Center
Valley Forge, PA 19482 610-648-6000
Financial - investment management

CS First Boston Strategic Income Fund, Inc.
FBI
Vanguard Financial Center
Valley Forge, PA 19482 610-648-6000
Financial - investment management

CSS Industries, Inc. CSS
1401 Walnut St.
Philadelphia, PA 19102 215-569-9900
Paper - business forms

CSX Corp. CSX
901 E. Cary St.
Richmond, VA 23219 804-782-1400
Transportation - rail O [DRP]

CTS Corp. CTS
905 West Blvd. North
Elkhart, IN 46514 219-293-7511
Electrical components - misc.

CUC International Inc. CU
707 Summer St.
Stamford, CT 06901 203-324-9261
Retail - mail order & direct O

Culbro Corp. CUC
387 Park Avenue South
New York, NY 10016 212-561-8700
Tobacco

Cummins Engine Co., Inc. CUM
500 Jackson St., PO Box 3005
Columbus, IN 47202 812-377-5000
Engines - internal combustion O [DRP]

Current Income Shares, Inc. CUR
445 S. Figueroa St.
Los Angeles, CA 90071 213-236-4056
Financial - investment management

Curtiss-Wright Corp. CW
1200 Wall St. West
Lyndhurst, NJ 07071 201-896-8400
Aerospace - aircraft equipment

CV REIT, Inc. CVI
100 Century Blvd.
West Palm Beach, FL 33417
407-640-3155
Real estate investment trust

CWM Mortgage Holdings, Inc. CWM
155 N. Lake Ave.
Pasadena, CA 91109 818-304-8400
Real estate investment trust

CyCare Systems, Inc. CYS
7001 N. Scottsdale Rd.
Scottsdale, AZ 85253 602-596-4300
Computers - services

Cypress Semiconductor Corp. CY
3901 N. First St.
San Jose, CA 95134 408-943-2600
Electrical components - semiconductors O

Cyprus Amax Minerals Co. CYM
9100 E. Mineral Circle
Englewood, CO 80112 303-643-5000
Metal ores - misc. O [DRP]

Cytec Industries, Inc. CYT
Five Garret Mountain Plaza
West Patterson, NJ 07424 201-357-3100
Chemicals - specialty O

Dallas Semiconductor Corp. DS
4401 S. Beltwood Pkwy.
Dallas, TX 75244 214-450-0400
Electrical components - semiconductors O

Dames & Moore, Inc. DM
911 Wilshire Blvd., Ste. 700
Los Angeles, CA 90017 213-683-1560
Engineering - R & D services

Dana Corp. DCN
4500 Dorr St., PO Box 1000
Toledo, OH 43697 419-535-4500
Automotive & trucking - original equipment
O [DRP]

Danaher Corp. DHR
1250 24th St., N.W., Ste. 800
Washington, DC 20037 202-828-0850
Automotive & trucking - original equipment
O

Daniel Industries, Inc. DAN
9753 Pine Lake Dr.
Houston, TX 77055 713-467-6000
Oil field machinery & equipment

Data General Corp. DGN
4400 Computer Dr.
Westboro, MA 01580 508-898-5000
Computers - mini & micro O

Datapoint Corp. DPT
8400 Datapoint Dr.
San Antonio, TX 78229 210-593-7000
Computers - mini & micro

Davis Water & Waste Industries, Inc. DWW
1820 Metcalf Ave.
Thomasville, GA 31799 912-226-5733
Pollution control equipment & services

Dayton Hudson Corp. DH
777 Nicollet Mall
Minneapolis, MN 55402 612-370-6948
Retail - major department stores O [DRP]

DDL Electronics, Inc. DDL
1270 NW 167th Place
Beaverton, OR 97006 503-645-3807
Electronics - components & systems

Dean Foods Co. DF
3600 N. River Rd.
Franklin Park, IL 06013 312-625-6200
Food - dairy products O [DRP]

Dean Witter Government Income Trust GVT
Two World Trade Center
New York, NY 10048 212-392-1600
Financial - investment management

Dean Witter Reynolds, Inc. DWD
Two World Trade Center
New York, NY 10048 212-392-2222
Financial - business services O

DeBartolo Realty Corp. EJD
7620 Market St.
Youngstown, OH 44513 216-758-7292
Real estate investment trust

Deere & Co. DE
John Deere Rd.
Moline, IL 61265 309-765-8000
Machinery - farm O [DRP]

Del Webb Corp. WBB
2231 E. Camelback Rd.
Phoenix, AZ 85016 602-808-8000
Real estate operations

Delaware Group Dividend and Income Fund,
   Inc. DDF
1818 Market St.
Philadelphia, PA 19103 800-523-4640
Financial - investment management

Delaware Group Global Div. and Inc. Fund,
   Inc. DGF
1818 Market St.
Philadelphia, PA 19103 800-523-4640
Financial - investment management

Delmarva Power & Light Co. DEW
800 King St., PO Box 231
Wilmington, DE 19899 302-429-3011
Utility - electric power [DRP]

Delta Air Lines, Inc. DAL
Hartsfield Atlanta Airport
Atlanta, GA 30320 404-765-2600
Transportation - airline O [DRP]

Delta Woodside Industries, Inc. DLW
233 N. Main St., Ste. 200
Greenville, SC 29601 803-232-8301
Textiles - apparel O

Deluxe Corp. DLX
1080 W. County Rd. F
St. Paul, MN 55126 612-483-7111
Paper - business forms O

Department 56, Inc. DFS
6436 City West Parkway
Eden Prairie, MN 55344 612-944-5600
Housewares

DeSoto, Inc. DSO
16750 S. Vincennes Rd.
South Holland, IL 60473 708-331-8800
Paints & allied products

Destec Energy, Inc. ENG
2500 City West Blvd., Ste. 150
Houston, TX 77042 713-735-4000
Energy - cogeneration O

Detroit Diesel Corp. DDC
13400 Outer Dr., West
Detroit, MI 48239 313-592-5000
Engines - internal combustion

Detroit Edison Co. DTE
2000 Second Ave.
Detroit, MI 48226 313-237-8000
Utility - electric power O [DRP]

Developers Diversified Realty Corp. DDR
34555 Chagrin Blvd.
Moreland Hills, OH 44022
216-247-4700
Real estate operations

Dexter Corp. DEX
One Elm St.
Windsor Locks, CT 06096 203-627-9051
Chemicals - specialty O [DRP]

Diagnostek, Inc. DXK
4500 Alexander Blvd. NE
Albuquerque, NM 87107 505-345-8080
Drugs O

Diagnostic Products Corp. DP
5700 W. 96th St.
Los Angeles, CA 90045 213-776-0180
Biomedical & genetic products

Dial (The) Corp. DL
Dial Tower
Phoenix, AZ 85077 602-207-4000
Diversified operations O
[DRP]

Diamond Shamrock, Inc. DRM
9830 Colonnade Blvd.
San Antonio, TX 78230 210-641-6800
Oil refining & marketing O

Diana Corp. DNA
111 E. Wisconsin Ave.
Milwaukee, WI 53202 414-289-9797
Food - wholesale

Diebold, Inc. DBD
PO Box 8230
Canton, OH 44711 216-489-4000
Protection - safety equipment & services
[DRP]

Digital Equipment Corp. DEC
146 Main St.
Maynard, MA 01754 508-493-5111
Computers - mini & micro O

Dillard Department Stores, Inc. DDS
1600 Cantrell Rd.
Little Rock, AR 72201 501-376-5200
Retail - regional department stores O

Dime Bancorp, Inc. DME
1225 Franklin Ave.
Garden City, NY 11530 516-227-6030
Financial - savings and loans O [DRP]

Discount Auto Parts, Inc. DAP
4900 Frontage Rd. South
Lakeland, FL 33801 813-687-9226
Auto parts - retail & wholesale

Dole Food Co., Inc. DOL
31355 Oak Crest Dr.
Westlake Village, CA 91361 818-879-6600
Food - canned O

Dominion Resources Black Warrior Trust
DOM
901 E. Byrd St.
Richmond, VA 23219 804-775-5700
Oil & gas - US royalty trust

Dominion Resources, Inc. D
PO Box 26532
Richmond, VA 23261 804-775-5700
Utility - electric power O [DRP]

Donaldson Co., Inc. DCI
1400 W. 94th St.
Minneapolis, MN 55431 612-887-3131
Pollution control equipment & services [DRP]

Dover Corp. DOV
280 Park Ave.
New York, NY 10017 212-922-1640
Machinery - general industrial O

Dow Chemical Co. DOW
2030 Dow Center
Midland, MI 48674 517-636-1000
Chemicals - diversified O [DRP]

Dow Jones & Co., Inc. DJ
200 Liberty St.
New York, NY 10281 212-416-2000
Publishing - newspapers O [DRP]

Downey Savings and Loan Association DSL
3501 Jamboree Rd.
Newport Beach, CA 92660 714-854-3100
Financial - savings and loans

DPL Inc. DPL
Courthouse Plaza S.W.
Dayton, OH 45402 513-224-6000
Utility - electric power
[DRP]

DQE, Inc. DQE
1187 Thorn Run Ext.
Coraopolis, PA 15108 412-262-4700
Utility - electric power [DRP]

Dr. Pepper/Seven-Up Companies, Inc.
DPS
8144 Walnut Hill Ln.
Dallas, TX 75231 214-360-7000
Beverages - soft drinks O

Dravo Corp. DRV
3600 One Oliver Plaza
Pittsburgh, PA 15222 412-566-3000
Construction - cement & concrete

Dresser Industries, Inc. DI
2001 Ross Ave.
Dallas, TX 75201 214-740-6000
Oil field machinery & equipment O [DRP]

Dreyfus Strategic Governments Income, Inc.
DSI
144 Glenn Curtiss Blvd.
Uniondale, NY 11556 516-794-5200
Financial - investment management

Dreyfus Strategic Municipal Bond Fund, Inc.
DSM
144 Glenn Curtiss Blvd.
Uniondale, NY 11556 516-794-5200
Financial - investment management

Dreyfus Strategic Municipals, Inc. LEO
144 Glenn Curtiss Blvd.
Uniondale, NY 11556 516-794-5200
Financial - investment management

Duff & Phelps Corp. DUF
55 E. Monroe St.
Chicago, IL 60603 312-263-2610
Financial - investment management
[DRP 5%]

Duff & Phelps Credit Rating Co. DCR
55 E. Monroe St.
Chicago, IL 60603 312-368-3100
Business services

Duff & Phelps Utilities Income Inc. DNP
55 E. Monroe St.
Chicago, IL 60603 312-368-5510
Financial - investment management

Duff & Phelps Utilities Tax-Free Income Inc.
DTF
55 E. Monroe St.
Chicago, IL 60603 312-368-5510
Financial - investment management

Duff & Phelps Utility and Corporate Bond
Trust DUC
55 E. Monroe St.
Chicago, IL 60603 312-368-5510
Financial - investment management

Duke Power Co. DUK
422 S. Church St.
Charlotte, NC 28242 704-594-0887
Utility - electric power O [DRP]

Duke Realty Investments, Inc. DRE
8888 Keystone Crossing
Indianapolis, IN 46240 317-846-4700
Real estate investment trust

Duracell International, Inc. DUR
Berkshire Industrial Park
Bethel, CT 06801 203-796-4000
Electrical products - misc. O [DRP]

Duty Free International, Inc. DFI
63 Copps Hill Rd.
Ridgefield, CT 06877 203-431-6057
Retail - discount & variety O

DVI, Inc. DVI
One Park Plaza, Ste. 800
Irvine, CA 92714 714-474-5800
Leasing

DVL Financial Corp. DVL
24 River Rd.
Bogota, NJ 07603 201-487-1300
Real estate investment trust [DRP]

Dycom Industries, Inc. DY
450 Australian Ave. South
West Palm Beach, FL 33401
407-659-6301
Telecommunications equipment

Dyersburg Corp. DBG
1315 Philips St.
Dyersburg, TN 38024 901-285-2323
Textiles - apparel

Dynamics Corporation of America DYA
475 Steamboat Rd.
Greenwich, CT 06830 203-869-3211
Diversified operations

E'town Corp. ETW
600 South Ave.
Westfield, NJ 07090 908-654-1234
Utility - water supply [DRP 5%]

E-Systems, Inc. ESY
6250 LBJ Freeway, PO Box 66028
Dallas, TX 75266 214-661-1000
Electronics - military O [DRP]

E.I. du Pont de Nemours and Co. DD
1007 Market St.
Wilmington, DE 19898 302-774-1000
Diversified operations [DRP]

E.W. Blanch Holdings, Inc. EWB
3500 W. 80th St.
Minneapolis, MN 55431 612-835-3310
Insurance - brokerage

Eastern American Natural Gas Trust NGT
311 W. Monroe St., 12th Fl.
Chicago, IL 60606 312-461-6676
Oil & gas - US royalty trust

Eastern Enterprises EFU
9 Riverside Rd.
Weston, MA 02193 617-647-2300
Utility - gas distribution O [DRP]

Eastern Utilities Associates EUA
One Liberty Square
Boston, MA 02109 617-357-9590
Utility - electric power [DRP 5%]

EastGroup Properties EGP
188 E. Capitol St.
Jackson, MS 39201 601-948-4091
Real estate investment trust

Eastman Chemical Co. EMN
100 N. Eastman Rd.
Kingsport, TN 37660 615-229-2000
Chemicals - diversified O [DRP]

Eastman Kodak Co. EK
343 State St.
Rochester, NY 14650 716-724-4000
Photographic equipment & supplies O
[DRP]

Eaton Corp. ETN
Eaton Center
Cleveland, OH 44114 216-523-5000
Automotive & trucking - original equipment
O [DRP]

ECC International Corp. ECC
175 Strafford Ave.
Wayne, PA 19087 215-687-2600
Electronics - military

Echlin Inc. ECH
100 Double Beach Rd.
Branford, CT 06405 203-481-5751
Automotive & trucking - replacement parts O

Eckerd Corp. ECK
8333 Bryan Dairy Rd.
Largo, FL 34647 813-399-6000
Retail - drug stores O

Ecolab Inc. ECL
370 Wabasha St. North
St. Paul, MN 55102 612-293-2233
Building - maintenance & services O [DRP]

Edison Brothers Stores, Inc. EBS
501 N. Broadway
St. Louis, MO 63102 314-331-6000
Retail - apparel & shoes O

EDO Corp. EDO
14-04 111th St.
College Point, NY 11356 718-321-4000
Electronics - military

EG&G, Inc. EGG
45 William St.
Wellesley, MA 02181 617-237-5100
Instruments - scientific O [DRP]

Ekco Group, Inc. EKO
98 Split Brook Rd., Ste. 102
Nashua, NH 03062 603-888-1212
Appliances - household

El Paso Natural Gas Co. EPG
304 Texas Ave.
El Paso, TX 79901 915-541-2600
Utility - gas distribution O

Elcor Corp. ELK
14643 Dallas Pkwy.
Dallas, TX 75240 214-851-0500
Machinery - general industrial

Electronic Associates, Inc. EA
185 Monmouth Parkway
West Long Branch, NJ 07764
908-229-1100
Computers - mini & micro

Eljer Industries, Inc. ELJ
17120 Dallas Parkway, Ste. 205
Dallas, TX 75248 214-407-2600
Building products - misc.

EMC Corp. EMC
171 South St.
Hopkinton, MA 01748 508-435-1000
Computers - peripheral equipment O

Emerging Markets Telecommunications
Fund, Inc. ETF
153 E. 53rd St.
New York, NY 10022 212-832-2626
Financial - investment management

Emerging Tigers Fund, Inc. TGF
800 Scudders Mill Rd.
Plainsboro, NJ 08536 609-282-2800
Financial - investment management

Emerson Electric Co. EMR
8000 W. Florissant Ave.
St. Louis, MO 63136 314-553-2000
Machinery - electrical O [DRP]

Emphesys Financial Group, Inc. EFG
1100 Employers Blvd.
Green Bay, WI 54344 414-336-1100
Insurance - accident & health

Empire District Electric Co. EDE
602 Joplin St.
Joplin, MO 64801 417-623-4700
Utility - electric power [DRP 5%]

Employee Benefit Plans, Inc. EBP
435 Ford Ave., Ste. 500
Minneapolis, MN 55426 612-546-4353
Health maintenance organization O

Energen Corp. EGN
2101 Sixth Ave. North
Birmingham, AL 35203 205-326-2700
Utility - gas distribution [DRP]

Energy Ventures, Inc. EVI
5 Post Oak Park, Ste. 1760
Houston, TX 77027 713-297-8400
Oil & gas - field services

Engelhard Corp. EC
101 Wood Ave.
Iselin, NJ 08830 908-205-5000
Chemicals - specialty O [DRP]

Enhance Financial Services Group Inc. EFS
335 Madison Ave.
New York, NY 10017 212-983-3100
Insurance - multi line & misc.

Ennis Business Forms, Inc. EBF
107 N. Sherman St.
Ennis, TX 75119 214-875-6581
Paper - business forms

ENRON Corp. ENP
1400 Smith St.
Houston, TX 77002 713-853-6161
Oil & gas - US exploration & production O
[DRP]

Enron Global Power & Pipelines L.L.C. EPP
333 Clay St., Ste. 1700
Houston, TX 77002 713-646-6100
Oil & gas - production & pipeline

Enron Oil & Gas Co. EOG
1400 Smith St.
Houston, TX 77002 713-853-6161
Oil & gas - US exploration & production O

ENSERCH Corp. ENS
300 South St. Paul St.
Dallas, TX 75201 214-651-8700
Oil & gas - production & pipeline [DRP]

Enserch Exploration Partners, Ltd. EP
1817 Wood St.
Dallas, TX 75201 214-748-1110
Oil & gas - US exploration & production
[DRP]

Entergy Corp. ETR
225 Baronne St.
New Orleans, LA 70112 504-529-5262
Utility - electric power O [DRP]

Enterra Corp. EN
13100 Northwest Fwy.
Houston, TX 77040 713-462-7300
Oil & gas - field services O

Environmental Elements Corp. EEC
3700 Koppers St.
Baltimore, MD 21227 410-368-7000
Pollution control equipment & services

EOTT Energy Partners, L.P. EOT
1330 Post Oak Blvd.
Houston, TX 77056 713-993-5200
Oil & gas - US exploration & production

EQK Realty Investors I EKR
5775 Peachtree Dunwoody Rd.
Atlanta, GA 30342 404-303-6100
Real estate investment trust

Equifax Inc. EFX
1600 Peachtree St. NW
Atlanta, GA 30302 404-885-8000
Business services O [DRP]

Equitable of Iowa Companies EIC
604 Locust St., PO Box 1635
Des Moines, IA 50306 515-245-6911
Insurance - life

Equitable Resources, Inc. EQT
420 Boulevard of the Allies
Pittsburgh, PA 15219 412-261-3000
Utility - gas distribution [DRP]

Equitable Resources, Inc. EQT
420 Boulevard of the Allies
Pittsburgh, PA 15219 412-261-3000
Utility - gas distribution
[DRP]

Equity Residential Properties Trust
EQR
Two North Riverside Plaza
Chicago, IL 60606 312-474-1300
Real estate investment trust

ESCO Electronics Corp. ESE
8100 W. Florissant Ave.
St. Louis, MO 63136 314-553-7777
Electronics - military

Essex Property Trust, Inc. ESS
777 California Ave.
Palo Alto, CA 94304 415-494-3700
Real estate investment trust

Esterline Technologies Corp. ESL
10800 NE 8th St.
Bellevue, WA 98004 206-453-9400
Instruments - control

Ethan Allen Interiors, Inc. ETH
Ethan Allen Dr.
Danbury, CT 06813 203-743-8000
Retail - home furnishings

Ethyl Corp. EY
330 S. Fourth St., PO Box 2189
Richmond, VA 23217 804-788-5000
Chemicals - specialty O [DRP]

European Warrant Fund, Inc. EWF
330 Madison Ave.
New York, NY 10017 212-949-9055
Financial - investment management

Evans Withycombe Residential, Inc.
EWR
6991 E. Camelback Rd.
Scottsdale, AZ 85251 602-840-1040
Real estate investment trust

Evergreen Healthcare, Inc. EHI
11350 N. Meridan St., Ste. 200
Carmel, IN 46032 317-580-8585
Nursing homes

Excel Realty Trust, Inc. XEL
16955 Via Del Campo, Ste. 110
San Diego, CA 92127 619-485-9400
Real estate investment trust

Excelsior Income Shares, Inc. EIS
114 W. 47th St., 9th Fl.
New York, NY 10036 212-852-3732
Financial - investment management

Executive Risk Inc. ER
82 Hopmeadow St., PO Box 2002
Simsbury, CT 06070 203-244-8900
Insurance - multi line & misc.

Exide Corp. EX
645 Penn St., PO Box 14205
Reading, PA 19612 215-378-0500
Automotive & trucking - original equipment

Exxon Corp. XON
225 E. John W. Carpenter Fwy.
Irving, TX 75062 214-444-1000
Oil & gas - international integrated O
[DRP]

Fabri-Centers of America, Inc. FCA
5555 Darrow Rd.
Hudson, OH 44236 216-656-2600
Retail - misc.

Factory Stores of America Inc. FAC
230 North Equity Dr.
Smithfield, NC 27577 919-934-9446
Real estate investment trust

Fairchild Corp. FA
110 E. 59th St.
New York, NY 10022 212-308-6700
Aerospace - aircraft equipment

Falcon Building Products, Inc. FB
Two N. Riverside Plaza
Chicago, IL 60606 312-906-9700
Diversified operations

Family Dollar Stores, Inc. FDO
10401 Old Monroe Rd.
Matthews, NC 28205 704-847-6961
Retail - discount & variety O

Fansteel Inc. FNL
Number One Tantalum Place
North Chicago, IL 60064 708-689-4900
Metal processing & fabrication

Farah Inc. FRA
8889 Gateway West
El Paso, TX 79925 915-593-4444
Textiles - apparel

Fay's Inc. FAY
7245 Henry Clay Blvd.
Liverpool, NY 13088 315-451-8000
Retail - drug stores [DRP]

Fedders Corp. FJQ
158 Highway 206
Peapack, NJ 07977 908-234-2100
Appliances - household O

Federal Express Corp. FDX
2005 Corporate Ave.
Memphis, TN 38132 901-369-3600
Transportation - air freight O

Federal Home Loan Mortgage Corp. FRE
8200 Jones Branch Dr.
McLean, VA 22102 703-903-2000
Financial - mortgages & related services O

Federal National Mortgage Association FNM
3900 Wisconsin Ave., NW
Washington, DC 20016 202-752-7000
Financial - mortgages & related services O
[DRP]

Federal Paper Board Co., Inc. FBO
75 Chestnut Ridge Rd.
Montvale, NJ 07645 201-391-1776
Paper & paper products O [DRP]

Federal Realty Investment Trust FRT
4800 Hampden Ln., Ste. 500
Bethesda, MD 20814 301-652-3360
Real estate investment trust [DRP]

Federal Signal Corp. FSS
1415 W. 22nd St.
Oak Brook, IL 60521 708-954-2000
Diversified operations [DRP]

Federal-Mogul Corp. FMO
26555 Northwestern Highway
Southfield, MI 48034 810-354-7700
Automotive & trucking - replacement parts
[DRP]

Federated Department Stores, Inc. FD
7 W. Seventh St.
Cincinnati, OH 45202 513-579-7000
Retail - major department stores O

Ferrellgas Partners, LP FGP
One Liberty Plaza
Liberty, MO 64068 816-792-1600
Retail - misc.

Ferro Corp. FOE
1000 Lakeside Ave.
Cleveland, OH 44144 216-641-8580
Paints & allied products O [DRP]

Fidelity Advisor Emerging Asia Fund, Inc. FAE
82 Devonshire St.
Boston, MA 02109 800-426-5523
Financial - investment management

Fidelity Advisor Korea Fund, Inc. FAK
82 Devonshire St.
Boston, MA 02109 800-426-5523
Financial - investment management

Fidelity National Financial, Inc. FNF
2100 S.E. Main St., Ste. 400
Irvine, CA 92714 714-852-9770
Insurance - multi line & misc.

Fieldcrest Cannon, Inc. FLD
725 N. Regional Rd.
Greensboro, NC 27409 910-665-4300
Textiles - home furnishings O

Filtertek, Inc. FTK
11411 Price Rd., PO Box 310
Hebron, IL 60034 815-648-2416
Chemicals - fibers

Financial Security Assurance Holdings Ltd.
FSA
350 Park Avenue, 13th Fl.
New York, NY 10022 212-826-0100
Insurance - brokerage

Fingerhut Companies, Inc. FHT
4400 Baker Rd.
Minnetonka, MN 55343 612-932-3100
Retail - mail order & direct O

First Bank System, Inc. FBS
1200 First Bank Place East
Minneapolis, MN 55480 612-370-5100
Banks - midwest O [DRP]

First Brands Corp. FBR
83 Wooster Heights Rd.
Danbury, CT 06813 203-731-2300
Containers - paper & plastic

First Chicago Corp. FNB
One First National Plaza
Chicago, IL 60670 312-732-4000
Banks - money center O [DRP 3%]

First Colony Corp. FCL
901 E. Byrd St., Ste. 1350
Richmond, VA 23219 804-775-0300
Insurance - multi line & misc. [DRP]

First Commonwealth Financial Corp.
FCF
22 N. Sixth St.
Indiana, PA 15701 412-349-7220
Banks - midwest [DRP]

First Commonwealth Fund, Inc. FCO
800 Scudders Mill Rd.
Plainsboro, NJ 08536 609-282-4600
Financial - investment management

First Data Corp. FDC
11718 Nicholas St.
Omaha, NE 68154 402-222-5566
Financial - business services O

First Fidelity Bancorporation FFB
2673 Main St., PO Box 6980
Lawrenceville, NJ 08648 609-895-6800
Banks - northeast O [DRP 3%]

First Financial Fund, Inc. FF
One Seaport Plaza
New York, NY 10292 212-214-3334
Financial - investment management

First Financial Management Corp. FFM
3 Corporate Square, Ste. 700
Atlanta, GA 30329 404-321-0120
Computers - services O

First Industrial Realty Trust, Inc. FR
150 N. Wacker Dr., Ste. 150
Chicago, IL 60606 312-704-9000
Real estate investment trust

First Interstate Bancorp I
633 W. Fifth St.
Los Angeles, CA 90071 213-614-3001
Banks - money center O [DRP]

First Israel Fund, Inc. ISL
153 E. 53rd St.
New York, NY 10022 212-832-2626
Financial - investment management

First Mississippi Corp. FRM
700 North St.
Jackson, MS 39202 601-948-7550
Chemicals - specialty O [DRP]

First of America Bank Corp. FOA
211 S. Rose St.
Kalamazoo, MI 49007 616-376-9000
Banks - midwest O [DRP 5%]

First Republic Bancorp Inc. FRC
388 Market St., 2nd Fl.
San Francisco, CA 94111
415-392-1400
Banks - west

First Union Corp. FTU
One First Union Center
Charlotte, NC 28288 704-374-6565
Banks - southeast O [DRP 3%]

First Union Real Estate Eq. & Mort.
  Investments FUR
55 Public Square, Ste. 1900
Cleveland, OH 44113 216-781-4030
Real estate investment trust [DRP]

First USA, Inc. FUS
2001 Bryan Tower
Dallas, TX 75201 214-746-8700
Financial - business services O

First Virginia Banks, Inc. FVB
6400 Arlington Blvd.
Falls Church, VA 22042 703-241-4000
Banks - southeast [DRP]

Firstar Corp. FSR
777 E. Wisconsin Ave.
Milwaukee, WI 53202 414-765-4321
Banks - midwest [DRP]

FirstFed Financial Corp. FED
401 Wilshire Blvd.
Santa Monica, CA 90401 310-319-6000
Financial - savings and loans

Fisher Scientific International Inc. FSH
Liberty Ln.
Hampton, NH 03842 603-929-2650
Instruments - scientific O

Fleet Financial Group, Inc. FLT
50 Kennedy Plaza
Providence, RI 02903 401-278-5800
Banks - northeast O [DRP 3%]

Fleet Mortgage Group, Inc. FLG
1333 Main St.
Columbia, SC 29201 803-929-7900
Financial - mortgages & related services

Fleetwood Enterprises, Inc. FLE
3125 Myers St., PO Box 7638
Riverside, CA 92513 909-351-3500
Building - mobile homes & RV O

Fleming Companies, Inc. FLM
6301 Waterford Blvd.
Oklahoma City, OK 73126
405-840-7200
Food - wholesale O [DRP 5%]

FlightSafety International, Inc. FSI
La Guardia Airport
Flushing, NY 11371 718-565-4100
Schools O

Florida East Coast Industries, Inc. FLA
1650 Prudential Dr.
Jacksonville, FL 32201 904-396-6600
Transportation - rail

Florida Progress Corp. FPC
One Progress Plaza
St. Petersburg, FL 33701
813-824-6400
Utility - electric power [DRP]

Flowers Industries, Inc. FLO
PO Box 1338
Thomasville, GA 31799 912-226-9110
Food - misc. O [DRP]

Fluor Corp. FLR
3333 Michelson Dr.
Irvine, CA 92730 714-975-2000
Construction - heavy O [DRP]

FMC Corp. FMC
200 E. Randolph Dr.
Chicago, IL 60601 312-861-6000
Machinery - general industrial O

FMC Gold Co. FGL
5011 Meadowood Way
Reno, NV 89502 702-827-3777
Gold mining & processing

Foodmaker, Inc. FM
9330 Balboa Ave.
San Diego, CA 90212 619-571-02121
Retail - food & restaurants O

Foote, Cone & Belding Communications,
Inc. FCB
FCB Center, 101 E. Erie St.
Chicago, IL 60611 312-751-7000
Advertising

Ford Motor Co. F
The American Road
Dearborn, MI 48121 313-322-3000
Automotive manufacturing O [DRP]

Fort Dearborn Income Securities, Inc. FTD
209 S. LaSalle St., 11th Fl.
Chicago, IL 60604 312-346-0676
Financial - investment management

Fortis Securities, Inc. FOR
PO Box 64284
St. Paul, MN 55164 612-738-4000
Financial - investment management

Foster Wheeler Corp. FWC
Perryville Corporate Park
Clinton, NJ 08809 908-730-4000
Machinery - electric utility O [DRP]

Foundation Health Corp. FH
3400 Data Dr.
Rancho Cordova, CA 95670 916-631-5000
Healthcare - outpatient & home O

Foxmeyer Corp. FOX
1220 Senlac Dr.
Carrollton, TX 75006 214-446-4800
Drugs & sundries - wholesale

Foxmeyer Health Corp. FOX
1220 Senlac Dr.
Carrollton, TX 75006 214-446-4800
Diversified operations

FPL Group, Inc. FPL
11770 U.S. Highway One
North Palm Beach, FL 33408
407-694-6300
Utility - electric power O

FPL Group, Inc. FPL
700 Universe Blvd.
Juno Beach, FL 33408 407-694-3509
Utility - electric power

Franchise Finance Corporation of America
FFA
17207 N. Perimeter Dr.
Scottsdale, AZ 85255 602-585-4500
Real estate investment trust

Franklin Electronic Publishers, Inc. FEP
122 Burrs Rd.
Mt. Holly, NJ 08060 609-261-4800
Publishing - books

Franklin Multi-Income Trust FMI
777 Mariners Island Blvd.
San Mateo, CA 94404 415-312-2000
Financial - investment management

Franklin Principal Maturity Trust FPT
777 Mariners Island Blvd.
San Mateo, CA 94404 415-570-3000
Financial - investment management

Franklin Quest Co. FNQ
2200 W. Parkway Blvd.
Salt Lake City, UT 84119 801-975-1776
Miscellaneous - not elsewhere classified

Franklin Resources, Inc. BEN
777 Mariners Island Blvd.
San Mateo, CA 94404 415-312-2000
Financial - investment management O [DRP]

Franklin Universal Trust FT
777 Mariners Island Blvd.
San Mateo, CA 94404 415-378-2200
Financial - investment management

Fred Meyer, Inc. FMY
3800 S.E. 22nd Ave.
Portland, OR 97202 503-232-8844
Retail - regional department stores

Frederick's of Hollywood, Inc. FHO
6608 Hollywood Blvd.
Los Angeles, CA 90028 213-466-5151
Retail - apparel & shoes

Freeport-McMoran Copper & Gold Inc. FCX
One E. First St., Ste. 1600
Reno, NV 89501 702-688-3000
Metals - non ferrous O

Freeport-McMoran Inc. FTX
1615 Poydras St.
New Orleans, LA 70112 504-582-4000
Fertilizers O [DRP]

Freeport-McMoran Oil and Gas Royalty
Trust FMR
712 Main St.
Houston, TX 77002 713-216-5447
Oil & gas - US royalty trust

Freeport-McMoran Resource Partners, L.P. FRP
1615 Poydras St.
New Orleans, LA 70112 504-582-4000
Fertilizers O

Fremont General Corp. FMT
2020 Santa Monica Blvd.
Santa Monica, CA 90404 310-315-5500
Insurance - property & casualty

Frontier Insurance Group, Inc. FTR
195 Lake Louise Marie Rd.
Rock Hill, NY 12775 914-796-2100
Insurance - property & casualty

Fruehauf Trailer Corp. FTC
26999 Central Park Blvd.
Southfield, MI 48076 313-948-1300
Automotive & trucking - original equipment

Fruit of the Loom, Inc. FTL
233 S. Wacker Dr.
Chicago, IL 60606 312-876-1724
Apparel O

Fund American Enterprises Holdings, Inc.
  FFC
The 1820 House
Norwich, VT 05055 802-649-3633
Financial - investment management O

Furr's/Bishop's Cafeterias, L.P. CHI
6901 Quaker Ave.
Lubbock, TX 79493 806-792-7151
Retail - food & restaurants

G&L Realty Corp. GLR
439 N. Bedford Dr.
Beverly Hills, CA 90210 310-273-9930
Real estate operations

G.T. Europe Growth Fund GTF
50 California St., 27th Fl.
San Francisco, CA 94111 415-392-6181
Financial - investment management

G.T. Global Developing Markets Fund, Inc.
  GTD
50 California St., 27th Fl.
San Francisco, CA 94111 415-392-6181
Financial - investment management

Gables Residential Trust GBP
2859 Paces Ferry Rd.
Atlanta, GA 30339 404-436-4600
Real estate investment trust

Galveston-Houston Co. GHX
4900 Woodway, PO Box 2207
Houston, TX 77252 713-966-2500
Oil field machinery & equipment

Gannett Co., Inc. GCI
1100 Wilson Blvd.
Arlington, VA 22234 703-284-6000
Publishing - newspapers O

GATX Corp. GMT
500 W. Monroe St.
Chicago, IL 60661 312-621-6200
Transportation - equipment & leasing O [DRP]

Gaylord Entertainment Co. GET
One Gaylord Dr.
Nashville, TN 37214 615-316-6000
Leisure & recreational services O

GC Companies, Inc. GCX
27 Boylston St.
Chestnut Hill, MA 02167 617-278-5600
Motion pictures & services

GEICO Corp. GEC
GEICO Plaza
Washington, DC 20076 301-986-3000
Insurance - property & casualty

Gemini II GMI
Vanguard Financial Center
Valley Forge, PA 19482 800-662-7447
Financial - investment management

GenCorp Inc. GY
175 Ghent Rd.
Fairlawn, OH 44333 216-869-4200
Diversified operations O [DRP]

Genentech, Inc. GNE
460 Point San Bruno Blvd.
South San Francisco, CA 94080
415-225-1000
Biomedical & genetic products O

General American Investors Co., Inc.
  GAM
450 Lexington Ave.
New York, NY 10017 212-916-8400
Financial - investment management

General DataComm Industries, Inc. GDC
1579 Straits Turnpike
Middlebury, CT 06762 203-574-1118
Computers - peripheral equipment

General Dynamics Corp. GD
3190 Fairview Park Dr.
Falls Church, VA 22042 703-876-3000
Weapons & weapon systems O

General Electric Co. GE
3135 Easton Tnpk.
Fairfield, CT 06431 203-373-2459
Diversified operations O [DRP]

General Growth Properties, Inc. GGP
215 Keo Way
Des Moines, IA 50309 515-281-9100
Real estate investment trust

General Host Corp. GH
One Station Place
Stamford, CT 06902 203-357-9900
Retail - misc.

General Housewares Corp. GHW
1536 Beech St., PO Box 4066
Terre Haute, IN 47804 812-232-1000
Housewares [DRP]

General Instrument Corp. GIC
181 W. Madison St.
Chicago, IL 60602 312-541-5000
Telecommunications equipment O

General Mills, Inc. GIS
One General Mills Blvd.
Minneapolis, MN 55440 612-540-2311
Food - misc. O [DRP]

General Motors Corp. GM
3044 W. Grand Blvd.
Detroit, MI 48202 313-556-5000
Automotive manufacturing O [DRP 3%]

General Physics Corp. GPH
6700 Alexander Bell Dr.
Columbia, MD 21046 410-290-2300
Business services

General Public Utilities Corp. GPU
100 Interpace Parkway
Parsippany, NJ 07054 201-263-6500
Utility - electric power O [DRP]

General Re Corp. GRN
695 E. Main St.
Stamford, CT 06904 203-328-5000
Insurance - property & casualty O
[DRP]

General Signal Corp. GSX
High Ridge Park
Stamford, CT 06904 203-329-4100
Instruments - control O [DRP]

Genesco Inc. GCO
Genesco Park
Nashville, TN 37217 615-367-7000
Shoes & related apparel O

Genesis Health Ventures, Inc. GHV
148 W. State St.
Kennett Square, PA 19348
215-444-6350
Healthcare - outpatient & home

Geneva Steel Co. GNV
10 S. Geneva Rd.
Vineyard, UT 84058 801-227-9000
Steel - production O

GenRad, Inc. GEN
300 Baker Ave.
Concord, MA 01742 508-287-7000
Electronics - measuring instruments

Genuine Parts Co. GPC
2999 Circle 75 Parkway
Atlanta, GA 30339 404-953-1700
Auto parts - retail & wholesale O [DRP]

Georgia Gulf Corp. GGC
400 Perimeter Center Terrace
Atlanta, GA 30346 404-395-4500
Chemicals - specialty O

Georgia Power Co. GPEp
333 Piedmont Ave., N.E.
Atlanta, GA 30308 404-526-6526
Utility - electric power

Georgia-Pacific Corp. GP
133 Peachtree St. NE
Atlanta, GA 30303 404-521-4000
Building products - wood O [DRP]

Gerber Scientific, Inc. GRB
83 Gerber Road West
South Windsor, CT 06074
203-644-1551
Industrial automation & robotics O

Gerrity Oil & Gas Corp. GOG
4100 E. Mississippi Ave.
Denver, CO 80222 303-757-1110
Oil & gas - US exploration & production O

Getty Petroleum Corp. GTY
125 Jericho Turnpike
Jericho, NY 11753 516-338-6000
Oil refining & marketing

GFC Financial Corp. GFC
1850 N. Central Ave.
Phoenix, AZ 85004 602-207-4900
Financial - business services O

Giant Group Ltd. GPO
Highway 453, PO Box 218
Harleyville, SC 29448 803-496-7880
Construction - cement & concrete

Giant Industries, Inc. GI
23733 N. Scottsdale Rd.
Scottsdale, AZ 85255 602-585-8888
Oil refining & marketing

Gillette Co. GS
Prudential Tower Building
Boston, MA 02199 617-421-7000
Cosmetics & toiletries O
[DRP]

Gleason Corp. GLE
1000 University Ave.
Rochester, NY 14692 716-473-1000
Machine tools & related products

Glendale Federal Bank, F.S.B. GLN
700 N. Brand Blvd.
Glendale, CA 91203 818-500-2000
Financial - savings and loans O

Glimcher Realty Trust GRT
20 S. 3rd St.
Columbus, OH 43215 614-621-9000
Real estate investment trust

Global Government Plus Fund, Inc. GOV
One Seaport Plaza
New York, NY 10292 212-214-3334
Financial - investment management

Global High Income Dollar Fund, Inc.
GHI
1285 Avenue of the Americas
New York, NY 10019 212-713-2000
Financial - investment management

Global Income Plus Fund, Inc. GLI
1285 Avenue of the Americas
New York, NY 10019 212-713-2000
Financial - investment management

Global Marine Inc. GLM
777 N. Eldridge Rd.
Houston, TX 77079 713-596-5100
Oil & gas - offshore drilling

Global Natural Resources Inc. GNR
5300 Memorial Dr., Ste. 800
Houston, TX 77007 713-880-5464
Oil & gas - US exploration & production O

Global Partners Income Fund, Inc. GDF
7 World Trade Center, 38th Fl.
New York, NY 10048 212-783-1301
Financial - investment management

Global Total Return Fund, Inc. PGY
One Seaport Plaza
New York, NY 10292 212-214-1215
Financial - investment management

Golden West Financial Corp. GDW
1901 Harrison St.
Oakland, CA 94612 510-446-3420
Financial - savings and loans O

Goodrich (B.F.) Co. GR
3925 Embassy Parkway
Akron, OH 44313 216-374-3985
Chemicals - diversified O [DRP]

Goodyear Tire & Rubber Co. GT
1144 E. Market St.
Akron, OH 44316 216-796-2121
Rubber tires O [DRP]

Gottschalks Inc. GOT
7 River Park Place East
Fresno, CA 93720 209-434-8000
Retail - apparel & shoes

Grace (W.R.) & Co. GRA
One Town Center Rd.
Boca Raton, FL 33486 407-362-2000
Chemicals - diversified O [DRP]

Graco Inc. GGG
4050 Olson Memorial Hwy.
Golden Valley, MN 55422
612-623-6000
Machinery - general industrial [DRP]

Graham-Field Health Products, Inc. GFI
400 Rabro Dr., East
Hauppauge, NY 11788 516-582-5900
Medical products

Grainger (W.W.), Inc. GWW
5500 W. Howard St.
Skokie, IL 60077 708-982-9000
Machinery - electrical O

GranCare, Inc. GC
One Ravina Dr., Ste. 1240
Atlanta, GA 30346 404-393-0199
Healthcare - outpatient & home O

Grand Casinos, Inc. GND
13705 First Ave. North
Plymouth, MN 55441 612-449-9092
Leisure & recreational services O

Grand Metropolitan PLC GRM
c/o Mogan Guaranty Trust
410 Park Ave, NY, NY 10022
800-428-4237
Food- spirits-restaurants O [DRP]

GRC International, Inc. GRH
1900 Gallows Rd.
Vienna, VA 22182 703-506-5000
Electronics - military

Great Lakes Chemical Corp. GLK
PO Box 2200
West Lafayette, IN 47906 317-497-6100
Chemicals - specialty O

Great Northern Iron Ore Properties GNI
332 Minnesota St.
St. Paul, MN 55101 612-224-2385
Iron ores

Great Western Financial Corp. GWF
9200 Oakdale Ave.
Chatsworth, CA 91311 818-775-3411
Financial - savings and loans O [DRP 3%]

Greater China Fund, Inc. GCH
1285 Avenue of the Americas
New York, NY 10019 212-713-2000
Financial - investment management

Green Mountain Power Corp. GMP
25 Green Mountain Dr.
South Burlington, VT 05403
802-864-5731
Utility - electric power [DRP 5%]

Green Tree Financial Corp. GNT
345 St. Peter St.
St. Paul, MN 55102 612-293-3400
Financial - mortgages & related services O

Greenery Rehabilitation Group, Inc. GRG
400 Center St.
Newton, MA 02158 617-244-4747
Medical services

Greiner Engineering, Inc. GII
909 E. Las Colinas Blvd.
Irving, TX 75039 214-869-1001
Engineering - R & D services

Grow Group, Inc. GRO
200 Park Ave.
New York, NY 10166 212-599-4400
Paints & allied products O [DRP]

Grubb & Ellis Co. GBE
One Montgomery St.
San Francisco, CA 94104 415-956-1990
Real estate operations

Grumman Corp. GQ
1111 Stewart Ave.
Bethpage, NY 11714 516-575-0574
Aerospace - aircraft equipment

GTE Corp. GTE
One Stamford Forum
Stamford, CT 06904 203-965-2000
Utility - telephone O [DRP]

GTECH Corp. GTK
55 Technology Way
West Greenwich, RI 02817
401-392-1000
Telecommunications services O

Guaranty National Corp. GNC
100 Inverness Terrace East
Englewood, CO 80112 303-790-8200
Insurance - multi line & misc.

Guardsman Products, Inc. GPI
3033 Orchard Vista Dr. S.E.
Grand Rapids, MI 49501
616-957-2600
Paints & allied products [DRP]

Guilford Mills, Inc. GFD
4925 W. Market St.
Greensboro, NC 27407 910-316-4000
Textiles - mill products

Gulf States Utilities Co. GSU
350 Pine St.
Beaumont, TX 77701 409-838-6631
Utility - electric power

H&Q Healthcare Investors HQH
50 Rowes Wharf, 4th Fl.
Boston, MA 02110 617-574-0567
Financial - investment management

H&Q Life Science Investors HQL
50 Rowes Wharf, 4th Fl.
Boston, MA 02110 617-574-0567
Financial - investment management

H&R Block, Inc. HRB
4410 Main St.
Kansas City, MO 64111 816-753-6900
Financial - business services [DRP]

H. F. Ahmanson & Co. AHM
4900 Rivergrade Rd.
Irwindale, CA 91706 818-814-7986
Financial - savings and loans

Hadson Corp. HAD
PO Box 569550
Dallas, TX 75356 214-640-6800
Oil & gas - US exploration & production

Haemonetics Corp. HAE
400 Wood Rd.
Braintree, MA 02184 617-848-7100
Medical products O

Halliburton Co. HAL
3600 Lincoln Plaza
Dallas, TX 75201 214-978-2600
Diversified operations O

Hancock Fabrics, Inc. HKF
3406 W. Main St., PO Box 2400
Tupelo, MS 38803 601-842-2834
Retail - misc.

Handleman Co. HDL
500 Kirts Blvd., PO Box 7045
Troy, MI 48007 313-362-4400
Wholesale distribution - consumer products
O [DRP]

Handy & Harman HNH
250 Park Ave.
New York, NY 10177 212-661-2400
Precious metals & jewelry [DRP]

Hanna (M.A.) Co. MAH
1301 E. Ninth St., Ste. 3600
Cleveland, OH 44114 216-589-4000
Diversified operations O [DRP]

Hannaford Bros. Co. HRD
145 Pleasant Hill Rd.
Scarborough, ME 04074 207-883-2911
Retail - supermarkets [DRP]

Hanson PLC HAN
c/o Citibank, Sort 3196
111 Wall Street, 5th Flr., NY, NY 10043
800-422-2066
British Conglomerate O [DRP]

Harcourt General, Inc. H
27 Boylston St.
Chestnut Hill, MA 02167 617-232-8200
Diversified operations O [DRP]

Harley-Davidson, Inc. HDI
3700 W. Juneau Ave.
Milwaukee, WI 53208 414-342-4680
Leisure & recreational products O [DRP]

Harman International Industries, Inc. HAR
1101 Pennsylvania Ave., N.W.
Washington, DC 20004 202-393-1101
Audio & video home products

Harnischfeger Industries, Inc. HPH
13400 Bishops Ln.
Brookfield, WI 53005 414-671-4400
Machinery - construction & mining O

Harris Corp. HRS
1025 W. NASA Blvd.
Melbourne, FL 32919 407-727-9100
Telecommunications equipment O
  [DRP]

Harsco Corp. HSC
350 Poplar Church Rd.
Camp Hill, PA 17001 717-763-7064
Metal processing & fabrication [DRP]

Harte-Hanks Communications, Inc. HHS
PO Box 269
San Antonio, TX 78291 210-829-9000
Diversified operations

Hartford Steam Boiler Inspection and Insur.
  Co. HSB
One State St.
Hartford, CT 06102 203-722-1866
Insurance - property & casualty [DRP]

Hartmarx Corp. HMX
101 N. Wacker Dr.
Chicago, IL 60606 312-372-6300
Apparel [DRP]

Harveys Casino Resorts HVY
Highway 50 and Stateline Ave.
Lake Tahoe, NV 89449 702-588-2411
Leisure & recreational services

Hatteras Income Securities, Inc. HAT
One Nations Bank Plaza T39-5
Charlotte, NC 28255 704-386-5000
Financial - investment management

Hawaiian Electric Industries, Inc. HE
900 Richards St.
Honolulu, HI 90681 808-543-5662
Utility - electric power [DRP]

Hayes Wheels International, Inc. HAY
38481 Huron River Dr.
Romulus, MI 48174 313-941-2000
Automotive & trucking - original equipment

HCA Hospital Corporation of America HCA
One Park Plaza
Nashville, TN 37203 615-327-9551
Hospitals

Health & Retirement Properties Trust HRP
400 Centre St.
Newton, MA 02158 617-332-3990
Real estate investment trust [DRP]

Health Care and Retirement Corp. HCR
One Sea Gate
Toledo, OH 43604 419-247-5000
Healthcare - outpatient & home O

Health Care Property Investors, Inc. HCP
10990 Wilshire Blvd.
Los Angeles, CA 90024 310-473-1990
Real estate investment trust

Health Care REIT, Inc. HCN
One Sea Gate, Ste. 1950
Toledo, OH 43604 419-247-2800
Real estate investment trust
  [DRP 4%]

Health Images, Inc. HII
8601 Dunwoody Place, Ste. 200
Atlanta, GA 30350 404-587-5084
Healthcare - outpatient & home O

Health Management Associates, Inc. HMA
5811 Pelican Bay Blvd.
Naples, FL 33963 813-598-3131
Hospitals O

Health Systems International, Inc. HQ
21600 Oxnard St.
Woodland Hills, CA 91367 818-719-6978
Health maintenance organization O

Healthcare Realty Trust Inc. HR
3310 West End Ave., Ste. 400
Nashville, TN 37203 615-269-8175
Real estate investment trust

Healthsource, Inc. HS
54 Regional Dr., PO Box 2041
Concord, NH 03302 603-225-5077
Health maintenance organization O

Healthsouth Rehabilitation Corp. HRC
2 Perimeter Park South
Birmingham, AL 35243 205-967-7116
Hospitals O

Healthtrust, Inc. - The Hospital Company
  HTI
4525 Harding Rd.
Nashville, TN 37205 615-383-4444
Hospitals O

Hecla Mining Co. HL
6500 Mineral Dr.
Coeur d'Alene, ID 83814 208-769-4100
Gold mining & processing O

Heilig-Meyers Co. HMY
2235 Staples Mill Rd.
Richmond, VA 23230 804-359-9171
Retail - home furnishings O [DRP]

Heinz (H.J.) Co. HNZ
600 Grant St.
Pittsburgh, PA 15219 412-456-5700
Food - canned O [DRP]

Helene Curtis Industries, Inc. HC
325 N. Wells St.
Chicago, IL 60610 312-661-0222
Cosmetics & toiletries

Helmerich & Payne, Inc. HP
Utica at Twenty-first St.
Tulsa, OK 74114 918-742-5531
Oil & gas - US exploration & production O

Hercules Inc. HPC
Hercules Plaza
Wilmington, DE 19894 302-594-5000
Chemicals - specialty O [DRP]

Heritage U.S. Government Income Fund
HGA
800 Carillon Parkway
St. Petersburg, FL 33716 800-421-4184
Financial - investment management

Hershey Foods Corp. HSY
100 Crystal A Dr.
Hershey, PA 17033 717-534-6799
Food - confectionery O
[DRP]

Hewlett-Packard Co. HWP
3000 Hanover St.
Palo Alto, CA 94304 415-857-1501
Computers - mini & micro O

Hexcel Corp. HXL
5794 W. Las Positas Blvd.
Pleasonton, CA 94588 510-847-9500
Chemicals - specialty

Hi-Lo Automotive, Inc. HLO
2575 W. Bellfort
Houston, TX 77054 713-663-6700
Auto parts - retail & wholesale

Hi-Shear Industries Inc. HSI
3333 New Hyde Park Rd.
North Hills, NY 11042 516-627-8600
Metal products - fasteners

Hibernia Corp. HIB
313 Carondelet St.
New Orleans, LA 70130 504-586-5361
Banks - southeast O [DRP 5%]

High Income Advantage Trust YLD
Two World Trade Center
New York, NY 10048 212-392-1600
Financial - investment management

High Income Advantage Trust II YLT
Two World Trade Center
New York, NY 10048 212-392-1600
Financial - investment management

High Income Advantage Trust III YLH
Two World Trade Center
New York, NY 10048 212-392-2222
Financial - investment management

High Yield Income Fund, Inc. HYI
One Seaport Plaza
New York, NY 10292 212-214-3332
Financial - investment management

High Yield Plus Fund, Inc. HYP
One Seaport Plaza
New York, NY 10292 212-214-3332
Financial - investment management

Highwoods Properties, Inc. HIW
3100 Smoke Tree Court
Raleigh, NC 27604 919-872-4924
Real estate investment trust

Hilb, Rogal and Hamilton Co. HRH
4235 Innslake Dr.
Glen Allen, VA 23060 804-747-6500
Insurance - brokerage

Hillenbrand Industries, Inc. HB
700 State Route 46 East
Batesville, IN 47006 812-934-7000
Medical & dental supplies O

Hills Stores Co. HDS
15 Dan Rd.
Canton, MA 02021 617-821-1000
Retail - discount & variety

Hilton Hotels Corp. HLT
9336 Civic Center Dr.
Beverly Hills, CA 90210 310-278-4321
Hotels & motels O

Home Depot, Inc. HD
2727 Paces Ferry Rd.
Atlanta, GA 30339 404-433-8211
Building products - retail & wholesale O
[DRP]

Home Holdings, Inc. HHI
59 Maiden Ln.
New York, NY 10038 212-530-6600
Insurance - property & casualty

Home Properties of New York, Inc. HME
850 Clinton Square
Rochester, NY 14604 716-546-4900
Real estate investment trust

Home Shopping Network, Inc. HSN
2501 118th Ave. North
St. Petersburg, FL 33716 813-572-8585
Retail - mail order & direct O

Homeplex Mortgage Investments Corp.
HPX
5333 N. Seventh St., Ste. 219
Phoenix, AZ 85014 602-265-8541
Real estate investment trust

Homestake Mining Co. HM
650 California St.
San Francisco, CA 94108 415-981-8150
Gold mining & processing O [DRP]

Honeywell Inc. HON
Honeywell Plaza
Minneapolis, MN 55408 612-951-1000
Diversified operations O [DRP]

Horace Mann Educators Corp. HMN
1 Horace Mann Plaza
Springfield, IL 62715 217-789-2500
Insurance - multi line & misc.

Horizon Healthcare Corp. HHC
6001 Indian School Rd. NE
Albuquerque, NM 87110 505-881-4961
Nursing homes

Horizon Outlet Centers, Inc. HGI
1050 W. Western Ave.
Muskegon, MI 49441 616-728-5170
Retail - misc.

Hormel Foods Corp. HRL
1 Hormel Place
Austin, MN 55912 507-437-5611
Food - meat products O [DRP]

Hospital Staffing Services, Inc. HSS
6245 N. Federal Hwy., Ste. 500
Fort Lauderdale, FL 33308 305-771-0500
Medical services

Hospitality Franchise Systems, Inc. HFS
339 Jefferson Rd.
Parsippany, NJ 07054 201-428-9700
Hotels & motels O

Host Marriott Corp. HMT
10400 Fernwood Rd.
Bethesda, MD 20817 301-380-9000
Hotels & motels O

Hotel Investors Trust HOT
11845 W. Olympic Blvd.
Los Angeles, CA 90064 310-575-3900
Real estate investment trust

Houghton Mifflin Co. HTN
222 Berkley St.
Boston, MA 02116 617-351-5000
Publishing - books O [DRP]

House of Fabrics, Inc. HF
13400 Riverside Dr.
Sherman Oaks, CA 91423 818-995-7000
Retail - misc.

Household International, Inc. HI
2700 Sanders Rd.
Prospect Heights, IL 60070
708-564-5000
Financial - consumer loans O
[DRP 2.5%]

Houston Industries Inc. HOU
4400 Post Oak Parkway
Houston, TX 77027 713-629-3000
Utility - electric power O [DRP]

Howell Corp. HWL
1111 Fanin St.
Houston, TX 77002 713-658-4000
Oil & gas - US integrated

HRE Properties HRE
530 Fifth Ave.
New York, NY 10036 212-642-4800
Real estate investment trust [DRP 5%]

HS Resources, Inc. HSE
One Maritime Plaza, 15th Fl.
San Francisco, CA 94111 415-433-5795
Oil & gas - US exploration & production

Hubbell Inc. HUBA
584 Derby Milford Rd.
Orange, CT 06477 203-799-4100
Electrical products - misc. [DRP]

Hudson Foods, Inc. HFI
1225 Hudson Rd.
Rogers, AR 72756 501-636-1100
Food - meat products

Huffy Corp. HUF
7701 Byers Rd.
Miamisburg, OH 45342 513-866-6251
Leisure & recreational products [DRP]

Hughes Supply, Inc. HUG
20 N. Orange Ave.
Orlando, FL 32801 407-841-4755
Building products - retail & wholesale

Humana Inc. HUM
500 W. Main St.
Louisville, KY 40202 502-580-1000
Health maintenance organization O

Hunt Manufacturing Co. HUN
230 S. Broad St.
Philadelphia, PA 19102
215-732-7700
Office & art materials

Huntway Partners, L.P. HWY
25129 The Old Rd., Ste. 322
Newhall, CA 91381 805-286-1582
Oil refining & marketing

Hyperion 1997 Term Trust, Inc. HTA
520 Madison Ave.
New York, NY 10022 212-980-8400
Financial - investment management

Hyperion 1999 Term Trust, Inc. HTT
520 Madison Ave.
New York, NY 10022 212-980-8400
Financial - investment management

Hyperion 2002 Term Trust, Inc. HTB
520 Madison Ave.
New York, NY 10022 212-980-8400
Financial - investment management

Hyperion 2005 Inv. Grade Opp. Term Trust,
Inc. HTO
520 Madison Ave.
New York, NY 10022 212-980-8400
Financial - investment management

Hyperion Total Return Fund, Inc. HTR
520 Madison Ave.
New York, NY 10022 212-980-8400
Financial - investment management

IBP, Inc. IBP
IBP Ave., PO Box 515
Dakota City, NE 68731 402-494-2061
Food - meat products O
[DRP]

ICF Kaiser International, Inc. ICF
9300 Lee Highway
Fairfax, VA 22031 703-934-3600
Engineering - R & D services

ICN Pharmaceuticals, Inc. ICN
3300 Hyland Ave.
Costa Mesa, CA 92626 714-545-0100
Drugs O

Idaho Power Co. IDA
1221 W. Idaho St.
Boise, ID 83702 208-383-2200
Utility - electric power [DRP]

IDEX Corp. IEX
630 Dundee Rd., Ste. 400
Northbrook, IL 60062 708-498-7070
Machinery - general industrial

IES Industries Inc. IES
200 First St. SE, PO Box 351
Cedar Rapids, IA 52406 319-398-4411
Utility - electric power [DRP]

Illinois Central Corp. IC
455 N. Cityfront Plaza Dr.
Chicago, IL 60611 312-755-7500
Transportation - rail O

Illinois Tool Works Inc. ITW
3600 W. Lake Ave.
Glenview, IL 60025 708-724-7500
Metal products - fasteners O
[DRP]

Illinova Corp. ILN
500 S. 27th St.
Decatur, IL 62525 217-424-6600
Utility - electric power [DRP]

IMC Global, Inc. IGL
2100 Sanders Rd.
Northbrook, IL 60062 708-272-9200
Fertilizers O

IMCERA Group Inc. IMA
2315 Sanders Rd.
Northbrook, IL 60062 708-564-8600
Diversified operations

IMCO Recycling Inc. IMR
5215 N. O'Connor Blvd.
Irving, TX 75039 214-869-6575
Recycling - metal & plastic

IMO Industries Inc. IMD
1009 Lenox Dr., Bldg. 4 West
Lawrenceville, NJ 08648 609-896-7600
Instruments - control
[DRP]

INA Investment Securities, Inc. IIS
900 Cottage Grove Rd.
Hartford, CT 6152 203-726-3700
Financial - investment management

INCO Ltd. N
One New York Plaza
New York, NY 10004 212-612-5500
Mining, nickel O

Income Opportunities Fund 1999, Inc. IOF
PO Box 9011
Princeton, NJ 08543 609-282-2800
Financial - investment management

Income Opportunities Fund 2000, Inc. IFT
PO Box 9011
Princeton, NJ 08543 609-282-2800
Financial - investment management

Indiana Energy, Inc. IEI
1630 N. Meridian St.
Indianapolis, IN 46202 317-926-3351
Utility - gas distribution [DRP]

Indiana Michigan Power Co. IMEpB
One Summit Square, PO Box 60
Fort Wayne, IN 46801 219-425-2111
Utility - electric power

INDRESCO Inc. ID
02121 San Jacinto St.
Dallas, TX 75201 214-953-4500
Machinery - construction & mining

Ingersoll-Rand Co. IR
200 Chestnut Ridge Rd.
Woodcliff Lake, NJ 07675 201-573-0123
Machinery - general industrial O
[DRP]

Inland Steel Industries, Inc. IAD
30 W. Monroe St.
Chicago, IL 60603 312-346-0300
Steel - production O [DRP]

Input/Output, Inc. IO
12300 Parc Crest Dr.
Stafford, TX 77477 713-933-3339
Electronics - measuring instruments O

Insteel Industries, Inc. III
1373 Boggs Dr.
Mt. Airy, NC 27030 910-786-2141
Wire & cable products [DRP]

Instrument Systems Corp. ISY
100 Jericho Quadrangle
Jericho, NY 11753 516-938-5544
Diversified operations O

Integon Corp. IN
500 W. Fifth St., PO Box 3199
Winston-Salem, NC 27102 910-770-2000
Insurance - property & casualty

Integra Financial Corp. ITG
Four PPG Place
Pittsburgh, PA 15222 412-644-7669
Banks - northeast [DRP]

Integrated Health Services, Inc. IHS
10065 Red Run Blvd.
Owings Mill, MD 21117 410-998-8400
Medical services O

Integrated Healthcare Facilities IHF
731 N. Jackson St.
Milwaukee, WI 53202 414-278-0100
Building - residential & commercial

Intellicall, Inc. ICL
2155 Chenault, Ste. 410
Carrollton, TX 75006 214-416-0022
Telecommunications equipment

Inter-Regional Financial Group, Inc. IFG
60 S. Sixth St.
Minneapolis, MN 55402
612-371-7750
Financial - investment bankers

InterCapital California Ins. Mun. Income
Trust IIC
Two World Trade Center
New York, NY 10048 212-392-1600
Financial - investment management

InterCapital California Quality Mun.
Securities IQC
Two World Trade Center
New York, NY 10048 212-392-1600
Financial - investment management

InterCapital Income Securities Inc. ICB
Two World Trade Center
New York, NY 10048 212-392-1600
Financial - investment management

InterCapital Insured California Mun.
Securities ICS
Two World Trade Center
New York, NY 10048 212-392-1600
Financial - investment management

InterCapital Insured Municipal Bond Trust
IMB
Two World Trade Center
New York, NY 10048 212-392-1600
Financial - investment management

InterCapital Insured Municipal Income Trust
IIM
Two World Trade Center
New York, NY 10048 212-392-1600
Financial - investment management

InterCapital Insured Municipal Securities IMS
Two World Trade Center
New York, NY 10048 212-392-1600
Financial - investment management

InterCapital Municipal Trust IMT
Two World Trade Center
New York, NY 10048 212-392-1600
Financial - investment management

InterCapital New York Quality Mun.
Securities IQN
Two World Trade Center
New York, NY 10048 212-392-1600
Financial - investment management

InterCapital Quality Municipal Income Trust
IQI
Two World Trade Center
New York, NY 10048 212-392-1600
Financial - investment management

InterCapital Quality Municipal Investment
Trust IQT
Two World Trade Center
New York, NY 10048 212-392-1600
Financial - investment management

InterCapital Quality Municipal Securities IQM
Two World Trade Center
New York, NY 10048 212-392-1600
Financial - investment management

INTERCO Inc. ISS
101 S. Hanley Rd.
St. Louis, MO 63105 314-863-1100
Diversified operations

International Aluminum Corp. IAL
767 Monterey Pass Rd.
Monterey Park, CA 91754 213-264-1670
Building products - doors & trim

International Business Machines Corp. IBM
Armonk, NY 10504 914-765-1900
Computers - mainframe O [DRP]

International Family Entertainment, Inc. FAM
2877 Guardian Ln., PO Box 2050
Virginia Beach, VA 23450 804-459-6000
Leisure & recreational products O

International Flavors & Fragrances Inc. IFF
521 W. 57th St.
New York, NY 10019 212-765-5500
Cosmetics & toiletries O

International Game Technology IGT
5270 Neil Rd.
Reno, NV 89502 702-686-1200
Leisure & recreational products O

International Multifoods Corp. IMC
33 S. 6th St., PO Box 2942
Minneapolis, MN 55402 612-340-3300
Food - flour & grain [DRP]

International Paper Co. IP
2 Manhattanville Rd.
Purchase, NY 10577 914-397-1500
Paper & paper products O [DRP]

International Recovery Corp. INT
700 S. Royal Poinciana Blvd.
Miami Springs, FL 33166 305-884-2001
Oil refining & marketing

International Rectifier Corp. IRF
233 Kansas St.
El Segundo, CA 90245 310-322-3331
Electrical components - semiconductors O

International Shipholding Corp. ISH
650 Poydras St., Ste. 1700
New Orleans, LA 70130 504-529-5461
Transportation - shipping

International Specialty Products Inc.
ISP
818 Washington St.
Wilmington, DE 19801 302-429-8554
Chemicals - specialty O

International Technology Corp. ITX
23456 Hawthorne Blvd.
Torrance, CA 90505 310-378-9933
Pollution control equipment & services

Interpool, Inc. IPX
211 College Rd. East
Princeton, NJ 08540 609-452-8900
Leasing

Interpublic Group of Companies, Inc.
IPG
1271 Avenue of the Americas
New York, NY 10020 212-399-8000
Advertising O [DRP]

Interstate Bakeries Corp. IBC
12 E. Armour Blvd.
Kansas City, MO 64141 816-561-6600
Food - misc.

Interstate Power Co. IPW
1000 Main St., PO Box 769
Dubuque, IA 52004 319-582-5421
Utility - electric power   [DRP]

Interstate/Johnson Lane, Inc. IS
121 W. Trade St., PO Box 1012
Charlotte, NC 28201 704-379-9000
Financial - investment bankers

Ionics, Inc. ION
65 Grove St.
Watertown, MA 02172 617-926-2500
Filtration products

Iowa-Illinois Gas and Electric Co. IWG
206 E. Second St.
Davenport, IA 52801 319-326-7111
Utility - gas distribution [DRP]

IP Timberlands, Ltd. IPT
Two Manhattanville Rd.
Purchase, NY 10577 914-397-1500
Building products - wood

IPALCO Enterprises, Inc. IPL
25 Monument Circle
Indianapolis, IN 46204 317-261-8261
Utility - electric power [DRP]

Irish Investment Fund, Inc. IRL
Vanguard Financial Center
Valley Forge, PA 19482 800-468-6475
Financial - investment management

IRT Property Co. IRT
200 Galleria Pkwy., Ste. 1400
Atlanta, GA 30339 404-955-4406
Real estate investment trust
[DRP 5%]

Irvine Apartment Communities, Inc. IAC
550 Newport Center Dr.
Newport Beach, CA 92660
714-720-5500
Real estate development

Italy Fund Inc. ITA
Two World Trade Center
New York, NY 10048 212-298-7350
Financial - investment management

Itel Corp. ITL
2 N. Riverside Plaza
Chicago, IL 60606 312-902-1515
Diversified operations O

ITT Corp. ITT
1330 Avenue of the Americas
New York, NY 10019 212-258-1000
Diversified operations O [DRP]

J&L Specialty Steel, Inc. JL
One PPG Place, PO Box 3373
Pittsburgh, PA 15230 412-338-1600
Steel - specialty alloys

Jackpot Enterprises, Inc. J
1110 Palms Airport Dr.
Las Vegas, NV 89119 702-263-5555
Leisure & recreational services O

Jacobs Engineering Group Inc. JEC
251 S. Lake Ave.
Pasadena, CA 91101 818-449-2171
Construction - heavy

Jakarta Growth Fund, Inc. JGF
180 Maiden Ln.
New York, NY 10038 800-833-0018
Financial - investment management

James River Corporation of Virginia JR
120 Tredegar St.
Richmond, VA 23219 804-644-5411
Paper & paper products O

Jamesway Corp. JMY
40 Hartz Way
Secaucus, NJ 07096 201-330-6000
Retail - discount & variety

Japan Equity Fund, Inc. JEQ
One Evertrust Plaza, 9th Fl.
Jersey City, NJ 07302 800-933-3440
Financial - investment management

Japan OTC Equity Fund, Inc. JOF
180 Maiden Ln.
New York, NY 10038 800-833-0018
Financial - investment management

Jardine Fleming China Region Fund, Inc.
 JFC
PO Box 89000
Baltimore, MD 21289 800-638-8540
Financial - investment management

Jardine Fleming India Fund, Inc. JFI
1285 Avenue of the Americas
New York, NY 10019 212-713-2848
Financial - investment management

JDN Realty Corp. JDN
3340 Peachtree Rd., N.E.
Atlanta, GA 30326 404-262-3252
Real estate investment trust

Jefferson-Pilot Corp. JP
100 N. Greene St.
Greensboro, NC 27401 910-691-3441
Insurance - life O [DRP]

Jenny Craig, Inc. JC
445 Marine View Ave., Ste. 300
Del Mar, CA 92014 619-259-7000
Retail - misc.

JHM Mortgage Securities L.P. JHM
8300 Greensboro Dr., Ste. 900
McLean, VA 22102 703-883-2900
Financial - mortgages & related services

John Alden Financial Corp. JA
7300 Corporate Center Dr.
Miami, FL 33126 305-470-3767
Insurance - multi line & misc.

John H. Harland Co. JH
2939 Miller Rd.
Decatur, GA 30035 404-981-9460
Paper - business forms

John Hancock Bank & Thrift Opportunity
 Fund BTO
101 Huntington Ave.
Boston, MA 02199 800-843-0090
Financial - investment management

John Hancock Income Securities Trust JHS
101 Huntington Ave.
Boston, MA 02199 617-375-1500
Financial - investment management

John Hancock Investors Trust JHI
101 Huntington Ave.
Boston, MA 02199 617-421-4506
Financial - investment management

Johnson & Johnson JNJ
One Johnson & Johnson Plaza
New Brunswick, NJ 08933 908-524-0400
Medical & dental supplies O [DRP]

Johnson Controls, Inc. JCI
5757 N. Green Bay Ave.
Milwaukee, WI 53201 414-228-1200
Diversified operations O [DRP]

Johnston Industries, Inc. JII
105 13th St.
Columbus, GA 31901 706-641-3140
Textiles - mill products

Jones Apparel Group, Inc. JNY
250 Rittenhouse Circle
Bristol, PA 19007 215-785-4000
Textiles - apparel O

Jostens, Inc. JOS
5501 Norman Center Dr.
Minneapolis, MN 55437 612-830-3300
Diversified operations O
 [DRP]

JP Realty, Inc. JPR
35 Century Park Way
Salt Lake City, UT 84115 801-486-3911
Financial - investment management

Jundt Growth Fund, Inc. JF
1550 Utica Ave. South
Minneapolis, MN 55416 800-543-6217
Financial - investment management

KN Energy, Inc. KNE
370 Van Gordon St.
Lakewood, CO 80228 303-989-1740
Utility - gas distribution
 [DRP]

K-III Communications Corp. KCCpr
717 Fifth Ave.
New York, NY 10022 212-745-0100
Publishing - periodicals

Kaiser Aluminum Corp. KLU
5847 San Felipe, Ste. 2600
Houston, TX 77057 713-267-3777
Metals - non ferrous O

Kaneb Pipe Line Partners, L.P. KPP
2400 Lakeside Blvd.
Richardson, TX 75082 214-699-4000
Oil & gas - production & pipeline

Kaneb Services, Inc. KAB
2400 Lakeside Blvd.
Richardson, TX 75082 214-699-4000
Oil & gas - production & pipeline

Kansas City Power & Light Co. KLT
1201 Walnut St.
Kansas City, MO 64106 816-556-2200
Utility - electric power [DRP]

Kansas City Southern Industries, Inc. KSU
114 W. 11th St.
Kansas City, MO 64105 816-556-0303
Transportation - rail O

Kasler Holding Co. KAS
27400 E. Fifth St.
Highland, CA 92346 909-884-4811
Construction - heavy

Katy Industries, Inc. KT
853 Dundee Ave.
Elgin, IL 60120 708-697-8900
Diversified operations

Kaufman and Broad Home Corp. KBH
10877 Wilshire Blvd.
Los Angeles, CA 90024 310-443-8000
Building - residential & commercial O

Kaydon Corp. KDN
19329 U.S. 19 North, Ste. 101
Clearwater, FL 34624 813-531-1101
Metal processing & fabrication

KCS Energy, Inc. KCS
379 Thornall St.
Edison, NJ 08837 908-632-1770
Oil & gas - production & pipeline

Kellogg Co. K
One Kellogg Square
Battle Creek, MI 49016 616-961-2000
Food - misc. O [DRP]

Kellwood Co. KWD
600 Kellwood Pkwy.
Chesterfield, MO 63017 314-576-3100
Textiles - apparel [DRP]

Kemper Corp. KEM
One Kemper Dr.
Long Grove, IL 60049 708-540-4700
Insurance - multi line & misc. O
  [DRP 5%]

Kemper High Income Trust KHI
120 S. LaSalle St.
Chicago, IL 60603 800-422-2848
Financial - investment management

Kemper Intermediate Government Trust
  KGT
120 S. LaSalle St.
Chicago, IL 60603 800-422-2848
Financial - investment management

Kemper Multi-Market Income Trust KMM
120 S. LaSalle St.
Chicago, IL 60603 800-422-2848
Financial - investment management

Kemper Municipal Income Trust KTF
120 S. LaSalle St.
Chicago, IL 60603 800-422-2848
Financial - investment management

Kemper Strategic Income Fund KST
120 S. LaSalle St.
Chicago, IL 60603 800-422-2848
Financial - investment management

Kemper Strategic Municipal Income Trust
  KSM
120 S. LaSalle St.
Chicago, IL 60603 800-422-2848
Financial - investment management

Kennametal Inc. KMT
PO Box 231
Latrobe, PA 15650 412-539-5000
Machine tools & related products
  [DRP 5%]

Kenneth Cole Productions, Inc. KCP
152 W. 57th St.
New York, NY 10019 212-265-1500
Leather & related products

Kent Electronics Corp. KNT
7433 Harwin Dr.
Houston, TX 77036 713-780-7770
Electrical components - misc.

Kerr Group, Inc. KGM
1840 Century Park East
Los Angeles, CA 90067 310-556-2200
Glass products

Kerr-McGee Corp. KMG
Kerr-McGee Center
Oklahoma City, OK 73125 405-270-1313
Oil & gas - US integrated O [DRP]

KeyCorp KEY
127 Public Square
Cleveland, OH 44114 216-689-3000
Banks - northeast O [DRP]

Keystone Consolidated Industries, Inc. KES
5430 LBJ Freeway, Ste. 1740
Dallas, TX 75240 214-458-0028
Wire & cable products O

Keystone International, Inc. KII
9600 W. Gulf Bank Dr.
Houston, TX 77040 713-466-1176
Instruments - control [DRP]

Kimberly-Clark Corp. KMB
PO Box 619100
Dallas, TX 75261 214-830-1200
Paper & paper products O [DRP]

Kimco Realty Corp. KIM
1044 Northern Blvd.
Roslyn, NY 11576 516-484-5858
Real estate operations

Kimmins Environmental Service Corp.
KVN
1501 Second Ave.
Tampa, FL 33605 813-248-3878
Pollution control equipment & services

King World Productions, Inc. KWP
1700 Broadway, 35th Fl.
New York, NY 10019 212-315-4000
Broadcasting - radio & TV O

Kleinwort Benson Australian Income Fund,
Inc. KBA
200 Park Ave., 24th Floor
New York, NY 10166 212-687-2515
Financial - investment management

Kmart Corp. KM
3100 W. Big Beaver Rd.
Troy, MI 48084 313-643-1000
Retail - major department stores O [DRP]

Knight-Ridder, Inc. KRI
One Herald Plaza
Miami, FL 33132 305-376-3800
Publishing - newspapers O [DRP]

KNOGO Corp. KNO
350 Wireless Blvd.
Hauppauge, NY 11788 516-232-2100
Protection - safety equipment & services

Kohl's Corp. KSS
N54 W13600 Woodale Dr.
Menomenee, WI 53051 414-783-5800
Retail - supermarkets

Kollmorgen Corp. KOL
1601 Trapelo Rd.
Waltham, MA 02154 617-890-5655
Electrical products - misc. [DRP]

Korea Equity Fund, Inc. KEF
180 Maiden Ln.
New York, NY 10038 800-833-0018
Financial - investment management

Korean Investment Fund, Inc. KIF
1345 Avenue of the Americas
New York, NY 10105 212-969-1000
Financial - investment management

Kranzco Realty Trust KRT
128 Fayette St.
Conshohocken, PA 19428 610-941-9292
Real estate investment trust

Kroger Co. KR
1014 Vine St.
Cincinnati, OH 45202 513-762-4000
Retail - supermarkets O

KU Energy Corp. KU
One Quality St.
Lexington, KY 40507 606-255-2100
Utility - electric power [DRP]

Kuhlman Corp. KUH
101 Kuhlman Ave.
Versailles, KY 40383 606-879-2999
Electrical products - misc. [DRP]

Kysor Industrial Corp. KZ
One Madison Ave.
Cadillac, MI 49601 616-779-2200
Automotive & trucking - original equipment
[DRP]

L. Luria & Son, Inc. LUR
5770 Miami Lakes Dr.
Miami, FL 33014 305-557-9000
Retail - catalog showrooms

L. S. Starrett Co. SCX
121 Crescent St.
Athol, MA 01331 508-249-3551
Tools - hand held

L.A. Gear, Inc. LA
2850 Ocean Park Blvd.
Santa Monica, CA 90405 310-452-4327
Shoes & related apparel O

La Quinta Inns, Inc. LQI
112 E. Pecan St., PO Box 2636
San Antonio, TX 78299 210-302-6000
Hotels & motels

La-Z-Boy Chair Co. LZB
1284 N. Telegraph Rd.
Monroe, MI 48161 313-242-1444
Furniture [DRP]

Laclede Gas Co. LG
720 Olive St.
St. Louis, MO 63101 314-342-0500
Utility - gas distribution [DRP]

Lafarge Corp. LAF
11130 Sunrise Valley Dr.
Reston, VA 22091 703-264-3600
Construction - cement & concrete O
[DRP 5%]

Lakehead Pipe Line Partners, Ltd. LHP
21 West Superior St., Ste. 400
Duluth, MN 55802 218-725-0100
Oil & gas - production & pipeline

Lamson & Sessions Co. LMS
25701 Science Park Dr.
Beachwood, OH 44122 216-464-3400
Rubber & plastic products

Lands' End, Inc. LE
Lands' End Ln.
Dodgeville, WI 53595 608-935-9341
Retail - mail order & direct O

Latin America Dollar Income Fund, Inc. LBF
345 Park Ave.
New York, NY 10154 212-644-1583
Financial - investment management

Latin America Investment Fund, Inc. LAM
153 E. 53rd St.
New York, NY 10022 212-832-2626
Financial - investment management

Latin American Discovery Fund, Inc. LDF
1221 Ave. of the Americas, 21st Fl.
New York, NY 10020 212-296-7000
Financial - investment management

Lawter International, Inc. LAW
990 Skokie Blvd.
Northbrook, IL 60062 708-498-4700
Chemicals - specialty O

Lear Seating Corp. LEA
21557 Telegraph Rd.
Southfield, MI 48034 810-746-1500
Automotive & trucking - original equipment

LeaRonal, Inc. LRI
272 Buffalo Ave.
Freeport, NY 11520 516-868-8800
Chemicals - specialty

Lee Enterprises, Inc. LEE
215 N. Main St.
Davenport, IA 52801 319-383-2100
Publishing - newspapers

Legg Mason, Inc. LM
111 S. Calvert St.
Baltimore, MD 21202 410-539-0000
Financial - investment bankers

Leggett & Platt, Inc. LEG
No. 1 Leggett Rd.
Carthage, MO 64836
417-358-8131
Furniture

Lennar Corp. LEN
700 N.W. 107th Ave.
Miami, FL 33172 305-559-4000
Building - residential & commercial O

Leslie Fay Companies, Inc. LES
1400 Broadway
New York, NY 10018 212-221-4000
Apparel

Leucadia National Corp. LUK
315 Park Avenue South
New York, NY 10010 212-460-1900
Diversified operations

Leviathan Gas Pipeline Partners, L.P.
 LEV
600 Travis St., Ste. 7200
Houston, TX 77002 713-224-7400
Utility - gas distribution

Levitz Furniture Corp. LFI
6111 Broken Sound Pkwy., N.W.
Boca Raton, FL 33487 407-994-6006
Retail - home furnishings O

Lewis Galoob Toys, Inc. GAL
500 Forbes Blvd.
South San Francisco, CA 94080
415-952-1678
Toys - games & hobby products

Lexington Corporate Properties, Inc. LXP
355 Lexington Ave.
New York, NY 10017 212-692-7260
Real estate investment trust

LG&E Energy Corp. LGE
220 W. Main St., PO Box 32030
Louisville, KY 40232 502-627-2000
Utility - electric power [DRP]

Libbey Inc. LBY
420 Madison Ave.
Toledo, OH 43604 419-727-2100
Glass products

Liberte Investors LBI
1420 Viceroy Dr.
Dallas, TX 75235 214-879-5800
Financial - mortgages & related services

Liberty ALL-STAR Equity Fund USA
Federal Reserve Plaza
Boston, MA 02210 800-542-3863
Financial - investment management

Liberty Property Trust LRY
65 Valley Stream Parkway
Malvern, PA 19355 610-648-1700
Real estate investment trust

Liberty Term Trust, Inc. - 1999 LTT
Federated Investors Tower
Pittsburgh, PA 15222 412-288-1900
Financial - investment management

Life Partners Group, Inc. LPG
7887 E. Belleview Ave.
Englewood, CO 80111 303-779-1111
Insurance - life

Life Re Corp. LRE
969 High Ridge Rd.
Stamford, CT 06905 203-321-3000
Insurance - life

Lilly (Eli) and Co. LLY
Lilly Corporate Center
Indianapolis, IN 46285 317-276-2000
Drugs O [DRP]

Limited (The), Inc. LTD
Two Limited Parkway
Columbus, OH 43216 614-479-7000
Retail - apparel & shoes O [DRP]

Lincoln National Convert. Securities Fund,
 Inc. LNV
1300 S. Clinton St.
Fort Wayne, IN 46801 219-427-2210
Financial - investment management

Lincoln National Corp. LNC
200 E. Berry St.
Fort Wayne, IN 46802 219-455-2000
Insurance - property & casualty O
[DRP]

Lincoln National Income Fund, Inc. LND
1300 S. Clinton St.
Fort Wayne, IN 46802 219-427-2210
Financial - investment management

Litton Industries, Inc. LIT
360 N. Crescent Dr.
Beverly Hills, CA 90210
310-859-5000
Diversified operations O

Living Centers of America, Inc. LCA
15415 Katy Freeway, Ste. 800
Houston, TX 77094 713-578-4600
Nursing homes

Liz Claiborne, Inc. LIZ
1441 Broadway
New York, NY 10018 212-354-4900
Textiles - apparel O [DRP]

LL&E Royalty Trust LRT
712 Main St.
Houston, TX 77002 713-216-4424
Oil & gas - US royalty trust

LNH Real Estate Investment Trust LHC
2001 Bryan Tower
Dallas, TX 75201 601-948-4091
Real estate investment trust

Lockheed Corp. LK
4500 Park Granada Blvd.
Calabasas, CA 91399 818-712-2000
Aerospace - aircraft equipment O

Loctite Corp. LOC
10 Columbus Blvd.
Hartford, CT 06106 203-520-5000
Paints & allied products O [DRP]

Loews Corp. LTR
667 Madison Ave.
New York, NY 10021 212-545-2000
Diversified operations O

Logicon, Inc. LGN
3701 Skypark Dr.
Torrance, CA 90505 310-373-0220
Electronics - military

Lomas Financial Corp. LFC
1600 Viceroy Dr.
Dallas, TX 75235 214-879-4000
Financial - investment management

Lone Star Industries, Inc. LCE
300 First Stamford Place
Stamford, CT 06912 203-969-8600
Construction - cement & concrete

Long Island Lighting Co. LIL
175 E. Old Country Rd.
Hicksville, NY 11801 516-755-6650
Utility - electric power O [DRP]

Longs Drug Stores Corp. LDG
141 N. Civic Dr., PO Box 5222
Walnut Creek, CA 94596 510-937-1170
Retail - drug stores

Longview Fibre Co. LFB
PO Box 639
Longview, WA 98632 206-425-1550
Paper & paper products O

Loral Corp. LOR
600 Third Ave.
New York, NY 10016 212-697-1105
Electronics - military O

Louis Dreyfus Natural Gas Corp. LD
14000 Quail Springs Pkwy.
Oklahoma City, OK 73134 405-749-1300
Oil & gas - US exploration & production

Louisiana Land and Exploration Co. LLX
909 Poydras St.
New Orleans, LA 70112 504-566-6500
Oil & gas - US integrated O [DRP]

Louisiana Power & Light Co. LPLp
PO Box 60340
New Orleans, LA 70160 504-595-3100
Utility - electric power

Louisiana-Pacific Corp. LPX
111 S.W. Fifth Ave.
Portland, OR 97204 503-221-0800
Building products - wood O [DRP]

Lowe's Companies, Inc. LOW
State Highway 268 East
North Wilkesboro, NC 28659
910-651-4000
Building products - retail & wholesale O
[DRP]

LSB Industries, Inc. LSB
16 S. Pennsylvania Ave.
Oklahoma City, OK 73107 405-235-4546
Diversified operations

LSI Logic Corp. LSI
1551 McCarthy Blvd.
Milpitas, CA 95035 408-433-8000
Electrical components - semiconductors O

LTC Properties, Inc. LTC
300 Esplanade Dr., Ste. 1860
Oxnard, CA 93030 805-981-8655
Real estate investment trust

Lubrizol Corp. LZ
29400 Lakeland Blvd.
Wickliffe, OH 44092 216-943-4200
Oil refining & marketing O [DRP]

Luby's Cafeterias, Inc. LUB
2211 Northeast Loop 410
San Antonio, TX 78265 210-654-9000
Retail - food & restaurants
[DRP]

Lukens Inc. LUC
50 S. First Ave.
Coatesville, PA 19320 610-383-2041
Steel - specialty alloys [DRP]

LVI Group Inc. LVI
470 Park Ave. South
New York, NY 10016 212-951-3675
Building - residential & commercial

Lydall, Inc. LDL
One Colonial Rd.
Manchester, CT 06045 203-646-1233
Paper & paper products

Lyondell Petrochemical Co. LYO
1221 McKinney Ave., Ste. 1600
Houston, TX 77010 713-652-7200
Chemicals - plastics O [DRP]

M.D.C. Holdings, Inc. MDC
3600 S. Yosemite St., Ste. 900
Denver, CO 80237 303-773-1100
Financial - investment management

M/A-COM, Inc. MAI
100 Chelmsford St.
Lowell, MA 01853 508-442-5000
Electronics - military

M/I Schottenstein Homes, Inc. MHO
41 S. High St., Ste. 2410
Columbus, OH 43215 614-221-5700
Building - residential & commercial

Mac Frugal's Bargains - Close-outs, Inc.
MFI
2430 E. Del Amo Blvd.
Dominguez, CA 90220 310-537-9220
Retail - discount & variety O

Magma Copper Co. MCU
7400 N. Oracle Rd., Ste. 200
Tucson, AZ 85704 602-575-5600
Metals - non ferrous O

MagneTek, Inc. MAG
11150 Santa Monica Blvd.
Los Angeles, CA 90025 310-473-6681
Electrical products - misc. O

Malan Realty Investors, Inc. MAL
30200 Telegraph Rd., Ste. 105
Birmingham, MI 48025 810-644-7110
Real estate investment trust

Malaysia Fund, Inc. MF
Vanguard Financial Center
Valley Forge, PA 19482 610-648-6000
Financial - investment management

Mallinckrodt Group Inc. MKG
7733 Forsyth Blvd.
St. Louis, MO 63105 314-854-5200
Diversified operations O [DRP]

Managed High Income Portfolio, Inc.
MHY
Two World Trade Center
New York, NY 10048 212-720-9218
Financial - investment management

Managed Municipals Portfolio Inc. MMU
2 World Trade Ctr., 101st Fl.
New York, NY 10048 212-720-9218
Financial - investment management

Manitowoc Co., Inc. MTW
700 E. Magnolia Ave., Ste. B
Manitowoc, WI 54220 414-684-4410
Diversified operations [DRP]

Manor Care, Inc. MNR
10750 Columbia Pike
Silver Spring, MD 20901 301-681-9400
Nursing homes O

Manpower, Inc. MAN
5301 N. Ironwood Rd.
Milwaukee, WI 53217 414-961-1000
Business services O [DRP]

Manufactured Home Communities, Inc.
MHC
2 N. Riverside Plaza
Chicago, IL 60606 312-454-0100
Real estate investment trust

Manville Corp. MVL
717 17th St.
Denver, CO 80202 303-978-2000
Building products - misc.

MAPCO Inc. MDA
1800 S. Baltimore Ave.
Tulsa, OK 74119 918-581-1800
Oil & gas - production & pipeline O

Marion Merrell Dow Inc. MKC
9300 Ward Pkwy., PO Box 8480
Kansas City, MO 64114 816-966-4000
Drugs O [DRP]

Maritrans Inc. TUG
One Logan Square
Philadelphia, PA 19103 215-864-1200
Transportation - shipping

Mark Centers Trust MCT
600 Third Ave.
Kingston, PA 18704 717-288-4581
Real estate investment trust

Mark IV Industries, Inc. IV
501 John James Audubon Parkway
Amherst, NY 14228 716-689-4972
Diversified operations O

Marriott International, Inc. MAR
10400 Fernwood Rd.
Bethesda, MD 20817 301-380-3000
Hotels & motels O

Marsh & McLennan Companies, Inc. MMC
1166 Avenue of the Americas
New York, NY 10036 212-345-5000
Insurance - brokerage O [DRP]

Marshall Industries MI
9320 Telstar Ave.
El Monte, CA 91731 818-307-6000
Electronics - parts distribution

Martin Lawrence Limited Editions, Inc.
  MLE
16250 Stagg St.
Van Nuys, CA 91406 818-988-0630
Retail - misc.

Martin Marietta Corp. ML
6801 Rockledge Dr.
Bethesda, MD 20817 301-897-6000
Diversified operations O

Martin Marietta Materials, Inc. MLM
PO Box 30013
Raleigh, NC 27622 919-781-4550
Construction - cement & concrete

Marvel Entertainment Group, Inc. MRV
387 Park Ave. South
New York, NY 10016 212-696-0808
Publishing - periodicals O

Masco Corp. MAS
21001 Van Born Rd.
Taylor, MI 48180 313-274-7400
Building products - misc. O

Mascotech, Inc. MSX
21001 Van Born Rd.
Taylor, MI 48180 313-274-7405
Miscellaneous - not elsewhere classified O

MassMutual Corporate Investors Inc.
  MCI
1295 State St.
Springfield, MA 01111 413-788-8411
Financial - investment management

MassMutual Participation Investors MPV
1295 State St.
Springfield, MA 01111 413-788-8411
Financial - investment management

Material Sciences Corp. MSC
2300 E. Pratt Blvd.
Elk Grove Village, IL 60007 708-439-8270
Steel - specialty alloys

Matlack Systems, Inc. MLK
One Rollins Plaza
Wilmington, DE 19803 302-426-2700
Transportation - truck

Mattel, Inc. MAT
333 Continental Blvd.
El Segundo, CA 90245 310-524-2000
Toys - games & hobby products O [DRP]

Mauna Loa Macademia Partners, L.P. NUT
827 Fort St.
Honolulu, HI 96813 808-544-6112
Agricultural operations

Maxus Energy Corp. MXS
717 N. Harwood St.
Dallas, TX 75201 214-953-2000
Oil & gas - international specialty O

MAXXIM Medical, Inc. MAM
104 Industrial Blvd.
Sugar Land, TX 77478 713-240-5588
Medical products

May Department Stores Co. MA
611 Olive St.
St. Louis, MO 63101 314-342-6300
Retail - major department stores O
[DRP]

Maybelline, Inc. MAY
3030 Jackson Ave.
Memphis, TN 38112 901-324-0310
Cosmetics & toiletries

Maytag Corp. MYG
403 W. Fourth St. North
Newton, IA 50208 515-792-8000
Appliances - household O [DRP]

MBIA Inc. MBI
113 King St.
Armonk, NY 10504 914-273-4545
Insurance - multi line & misc. O

MBNA Corp. KRB
400 Christiana Rd.
Newark, DE 19713 302-453-9930
Financial - business services O

McArthur/Glen Realty Corp. MCG
8400 Westpark Dr., Ste. 500
McLean, VA 22102 703-556-6444
Real estate investment trust

McClatchy Newspapers, Inc. MNI
2100 'Q' St.
Sacramento, CA 95816 916-321-1846
Publishing - newspapers

McDermott International, Inc. MDR
1450 Poydras St.
New Orleans, LA 70112 504-587-5400
Machinery - electric utility O [DRP]

McDonald & Company Investments, Inc.
  MDD
800 Superior Ave., Ste. 2100
Cleveland, OH 44114 216-443-2300
Financial - investment bankers

McDonald's Corp. MCD
McDonald's Plaza
Oak Brook, IL 60521 708-575-3000
Retail - food & restaurants O [DRP]

McDonnell Douglas Corp. MD
PO Box 516
St. Louis, MO 63166 314-232-0232
Aerospace - aircraft equipment O

McGraw-Hill, Inc. MHP
1221 Avenue of the Americas
New York, NY 10020 212-512-2000
Publishing - books O [DRP]

McKesson Corp. MCK
One Post St.
San Francisco, CA 94104 415-983-8300
Drugs & sundries - wholesale [DRP]

MCN Corp. MCN
500 Griswold St.
Detroit, MI 48226 313-256-5500
Utility - gas distribution [DRP]

McWhorter Technologies, Inc. MWT
400 E. Cottage Place
Carpentersville, IL 60110 708-428-2657
Paints & allied products

MDU Resources Group, Inc. MDU
400 N. Fourth St.
Bismarck, ND 58501 701-222-7900
Utility - electric power [DRP]

Mead Corp. MEA
Courthouse Plaza Northeast
Dayton, OH 45463 513-495-6323
Paper & paper products O [DRP]

Measurex Corp. MX
One Results Way
Cupertino, CA 95014 408-255-1500
Instruments - control O

MedChem Products, Inc. MCH
232 W. Cummings Park
Woburn, MA 01801 617-932-5900
Medical products

Meditrust MT
197 First Ave.
Needham, MA 02194 617-736-1500
Real estate investment trust

Medtronic, Inc. MDT
7000 Central Ave. NE
Minneapolis, MN 55432 612-574-4000
Medical instruments O [DRP]

Medusa Corp. MSA
3008 Monticello Blvd.
Cleveland Heights, OH 44118
216-371-4000
Construction - cement & concrete
  [DRP]

Mellon Bank Corp. MEL
One Mellon Bank Center
Pittsburgh, PA 15258 412-234-5000
Banks - northeast O [DRP 3%]

Melville Corp. MES
One Theall Rd.
Rye, NY 10580 914-925-4000
Retail - apparel & shoes O

Mentor Income Fund, Inc. MRF
10221 Wincopin Circle
Columbia, MD 21044 410-964-8260
Financial - investment management

Mercantile Bancorporation Inc. MTL
PO Box 524
St. Louis, MO 63166 314-425-2525
Banks - midwest O [DRP]

Mercantile Stores Co., Inc. MST
9450 Seward Rd.
Fairfield, OH 45014 513-881-8000
Retail - regional department stores O

Merck & Co., Inc. MRK
One Merck Dr., PO Box 100
Whitehouse Station, NJ 08889
908-423-1000
Drugs O [DRP]

Mercury Finance Co. MFN
40 Skokie Blvd., Ste. 200
Northbrook, IL 60062 708-564-3720
Financial - business services O [DRP]

Meredith Corp. MDP
1716 Locust St.
Des Moines, IA 50309 515-284-3000
Publishing - periodicals O

Merrill Lynch & Co., Inc. MER
World Financial Center
New York, NY 10281 212-449-1000
Financial - investment bankers O
  [DRP]

Merry Land & Investment Co., Inc. MRY
PO Box 1417
Augusta, GA 30903 706-722-6756
Real estate investment trust [DRP 5%]

Merry-Go-Round Enterprises, Inc. MGR
3300 Fashion Way
Joppa, MD 21085 410-538-1000
Retail - apparel & shoes O

MESA Inc. MXP
2001 Ross Avenue
Dallas, TX 75201 214-969-2200
Oil & gas - US exploration & production O

Mesa Royalty Trust MTR
712 Main St.
Houston, TX 77002 713-216-5100
Oil & gas - US royalty trust

Mesabi Trust MSB
PO Box 318, Church St. Station
New York, NY 10015 212-250-6696
Oil & gas - US royalty trust

Mestek, Inc. MCC
260 N. Elm St.
Westfield, MA 01085 413-568-9571
Building products - a/c & heating

Metropolitan Financial Corp. MFC
333 S. Seventh St.
Minneapolis, MN 55402 612-399-6000
Financial - savings and loans [DRP]

Mexico Equity and Income Fund, Inc.
  MXE
200 Liberty St.
New York, NY 10281 212-667-5000
Financial - investment management

MFS Charter Income Trust MCR
500 Boylston St.
Boston, MA 02116 617-954-5000
Financial - investment management

MFS Government Markets Income Trust
  MGF
500 Boylston St.
Boston, MA 02116 617-954-5000
Financial - investment management

MFS Intermediate Income Trust MIN
500 Boylston St.
Boston, MA 02116 617-954-5000
Financial - investment management

MFS Multimarket Income Trust MMT
500 Boylston St.
Boston, MA 02116 617-954-5000
Financial - investment management

MFS Municipal Income Trust MFM
500 Boylston St.
Boston, MA 02116 617-954-5000
Financial - investment management

MFS Special Value Trust MFV
500 Boylston St.
Boston, MA 02116 617-954-5000
Financial - investment management

MGI Properties MGI
30 Rowes Wharf
Boston, MA 02110 617-330-5335
Real estate investment trust

MGIC Investment Corp. MTG
250 E. Kilbourn Ave.
Milwaukee, WI 53202 414-347-6480
Financial - mortgages & related services O

MGM Grand, Inc. MGG
3799 Las Vegas Blvd. South
Las Vegas, NV 89109 702-891-1111
Hotels & motels O

MHI Group, Inc. MH
2032-D Thomasville Rd.
Tallahassee, FL 32312 904-385-8883
Funeral & related services

Mickelberry Communications Corp. MBC
405 Park Ave.
New York, NY 10022 212-832-0303
Advertising

Micron Technology, Inc. MU
2805 E. Columbia Rd.
Boise, ID 83706 208-383-4000
Electrical components - semiconductors O

Mid Atlantic Medical Services, Inc. MME
4 Taft Court
Rockville, MD 20850 301-294-5140
Healthcare - outpatient & home

Mid-America Apartment Communities, Inc.
  MAA
6584 Poplar Ave., Ste. 340
Memphis, TN 38138 901-682-6600
Real estate investment trust

Mid-America Realty Investments, Inc. MDI
11506 Nicholas St., Ste. 100
Omaha, NE 68154 402-496-3300
Real estate operations [DRP]

Mid-American Waste Systems, Inc. MAW
1006 Walnut St.
Canal Winchester, OH 43110 614-833-9155
Pollution control equipment & services O

Midwest Real Estate Shopping Centers L.P.
  EQM
388 Greenwich St., 28th Fl.
New York, NY 10013 212-464-2465
Real estate operations

Midwest Resources Inc. MWR
666 Grand Ave., PO Box 9244
Des Moines, IA 50306 515-242-4300
Utility - electric power [DRP]

Mikasa, Inc. MKS
20633 S. Fordyce Ave.
Long Beach, CA 90810 310-886-3700
Glass products

Milestone Properties, Inc. MPI
5200 Town Center Circle
Boca Raton, FL 33486 407-394-9533
Real estate development

Millipore Corp. MIL
80 Ashby Rd.
Bedford, MA 01730 617-275-9200
Filtration products O [DRP]

Minerals Technologies Inc. MTX
405 Lexington Ave.
New York, NY 10174 212-878-1800
Chemicals - specialty O

Minnesota Mining and Manufacturing Co. MMM
3M Center
St. Paul, MN 55144 612-733-1110
Diversified operations O [DRP]

Minnesota Municipal Term Trust, Inc. MNA
222 S. Ninth St.
Minneapolis, MN 55402 800-333-6000
Financial - investment management

Minnesota Power & Light Co. MPL
30 W. Superior St.
Duluth, MN 55802 218-722-2641
Utility - electric power [DRP]

Mirage Resorts, Inc. MIR
3400 Las Vegas Blvd. South
Las Vegas, NV 89109 702-791-7111
Leisure & recreational services O

Mitchell Energy & Development Corp.
  MNDA
2001 Timberloch Place
The Woodlands, TX 77380 713-377-5500
Oil & gas - US exploration & production O

MMI Companies, Inc. MMI
540 Lake Cook Rd.
Deerfield, IL 60015 708-940-7550
Insurance - multi line & misc.

Mobil Corp. MOB
3225 Gallows Rd.
Fairfax, VA 22037 703-846-3000
Oil & gas - international integrated O [DRP]

Molecular Biosystems, Inc. MB
10030 Barnes Canyon Rd.
San Diego, CA 90212 619-452-0681
Biomedical & genetic products O

Monk-Austin, Inc. MK
1200 W. Marlboro Rd.
Farmville, NC 27828 919-753-8000
Agricultural operations

Monsanto Co. MTC
800 N. Lindbergh Blvd.
St. Louis, MO 63167 314-694-1000
Chemicals - diversified O [DRP]

Montana Power Co. MTP
40 E. Broadway
Butte, MT 59701 406-723-5421
Utility - electric power [DRP]

Montgomery Street Income Securities Inc.
  MTS
101 California St., Ste. 4100
San Francisco, CA 94111 415-981-8191
Financial - investment management

Moorco International Inc. MRC
2800 Post Oak Blvd., Ste. 5701
Houston, TX 77056 713-993-0999
Instruments - control

Morgan (J.P.) & Co. Inc. JPM
60 Wall St.
New York, NY 10260 212-483-2323
Banks - money center O [DRP]

Morgan Grenfell SMALLCap Fund, Inc. MGC
885 Third Ave., 32nd Fl.
New York, NY 10022 212-230-2600
Financial - investment management

Morgan Keegan, Inc. MOR
Fifty Front St.
Memphis, TN 38103 901-524-4100
Financial - investment bankers

Morgan Products Ltd. MGN
25 Tri-State International
Lincolnshire, IL 60069 708-317-2400
Building products - doors & trim

Morgan Stanley Africa Investment Fund,
  Inc. AFF
1221 Avenue of the Americas
New York, NY 10020 212-296-7100
Financial - investment management

Morgan Stanley Asia-Pacific Fund, Inc.
  APF
1221 Avenue of the Americas
New York, NY 10020 212-296-7100
Financial - investment management

Morgan Stanley Emerging Markets Debt
  Fund, Inc. MSD
1221 Avenue of the Americas
New York, NY 10020 212-296-7100
Financial - investment management

Morgan Stanley Emerging Markets Fund,
  Inc. MSF
1221 Avenue of the Americas
New York, NY 10020 212-296-7100
Financial - investment management

Morgan Stanley Global Opportunity Bd. Fd.,
  Inc. MGB
1221 Avenue of the Americas
New York, NY 10020 212-296-7100
Financial - investment management

Morgan Stanley Group Inc. MS
1251 Avenue of the Americas
New York, NY 10020 212-703-4000
Financial - investment bankers O

Morgan Stanley High Yield Fund, Inc.
  MSY
1221 Avenue of the Americas
New York, NY 10020 212-296-7100
Financial - investment management

Morrison Knudsen Corp. MRN
Morrison Knudsen Plaza
Boise, ID 83729 208-386-5000
Construction - heavy O [DRP]

Morrison Restaurants, Inc. RI
4721 Morrison Dr.
Mobile, AL 36609 205-344-3000
Retail - food & restaurants O

Mortgage and Realty Trust MRT
8380 Old York Rd., Ste. 300
Elkins Park, PA 19117 215-881-1525
Real estate investment trust

Morton International, Inc. MII
100 N. Riverside Plaza
Chicago, IL 60606 312-807-2000
Chemicals - specialty O [DRP]

Motorola, Inc. MOT
1303 E. Algonquin Rd.
Schaumburg, IL 60196 708-576-5000
Electronics - components & systems O
[DRP]

Mueller Industries, Inc. MLI
2959 N. Rock Rd.
Wichita, KS 67226 316-636-6300
Steel - production

MuniAssets Fund, Inc. MUA
PO Box 9011
Princeton, NJ 08543 609-282-2800
Financial - investment management

MuniBond Income Fund, Inc. MBD
800 Scudders Mill Rd.
Plainsboro, NJ 08536 609-282-2800
Financial - investment management

Municipal Advantage Fund, Inc. MAF
Two World Trade Center
New York, NY 10048 212-392-2222
Financial - investment management

Municipal High Income Fund Inc. MHF
Two World Trade Center
New York, NY 10048 212-392-2222
Financial - investment management

Municipal Income Opportunities Trust OIA
Two World Trade Center
New York, NY 10048 212-392-2222
Financial - investment management

Municipal Income Opportunities Trust II OIB
Two World Trade Center
New York, NY 10048 212-392-2222
Financial - investment management

Municipal Income Opportunities Trust III
OIC
Two World Trade Center
New York, NY 10048 212-392-2222
Financial - investment management

Municipal Income Trust TFA
Two World Trade Center
New York, NY 10048 212-392-2222
Financial - investment management

Municipal Income Trust II TFB
Two World Trade Center
New York, NY 10048 212-392-2222
Financial - investment management

Municipal Income Trust III TFC
Two World Trade Center
New York, NY 10048 212-392-2222
Financial - investment management

Municipal Partners Fund II, Inc. MPT
Seven World Trade Center
New York, NY 10048 212-783-1301
Financial - investment management

Municipal Partners Fund, Inc. MNP
Seven World Trade Center
New York, NY 10048 212-783-1301
Financial - investment management

Municipal Premium Income Trust PIA
Two World Trade Center
New York, NY 10048 212-392-2222
Financial - investment management

MuniEnhanced Fund, Inc. MEN
800 Scudders Mill Rd.
Plainsboro, NJ 08536 609-282-2800
Financial - investment management

MuniVest California Insured Fund, Inc. MVC
PO Box 9011
Princeton, NJ 08543 609-282-2800
Financial - investment management

MuniVest Florida Fund MVS
PO Box 9011
Princeton, NJ 08543 609-282-2800
Financial - investment management

MuniVest Fund II, Inc. MVT
PO Box 9011
Princeton, NJ 08543 609-282-2800
Financial - investment management

MuniVest Michigan Insured Fund, Inc.
MVM
PO Box 9011
Princeton, NJ 08543 609-282-2800
Financial - investment management

MuniVest New Jersey Fund, Inc. MVJ
PO Box 9011
Princeton, NJ 08543 609-282-2800
Financial - investment management

MuniVest New York Insured Fund, Inc.
MVY
PO Box 9011
Princeton, NJ 08543 609-282-2800
Financial - investment management

MuniVest Pennyslvania Insured Fund MVP
PO Box 9011
Princeton, NJ 08543 609-282-2800
Financial - investment management

MuniYield California Fund, Inc. MYC
PO Box 9011
Princeton, NJ 08543 609-282-2800
Financial - investment management

MuniYield California Insured Fund II, Inc.
  MCA
PO Box 9011
Princeton, NJ 08543 609-282-2800
Financial - investment management

MuniYield California Insured Fund, Inc. MIC
PO Box 9011
Princeton, NJ 08543 609-282-2800
Financial - investment management

MuniYield Florida Fund MYF
PO Box 9011
Princeton, NJ 08543 609-282-2800
Financial - investment management

MuniYield Florida Insured Fund, Inc. MFT
PO Box 9011
Princeton, NJ 08543 609-282-2800
Financial - investment management

MuniYield Fund, Inc. MYD
PO Box 9011
Princeton, NJ 08543 609-282-2800
Financial - investment management

MuniYield Insured Fund II, Inc. MTI
PO Box 9011
Princeton, NJ 08543 609-282-2800
Financial - investment management

MuniYield Insured Fund, Inc. MYI
PO Box 9011
Princeton, NJ 08543 609-282-2800
Financial - investment management

MuniYield Michigan Fund, Inc. MYM
PO Box 9011
Princeton, NJ 08543 609-282-2800
Financial - investment management

MuniYield Michigan Insured Fund, Inc. MIY
PO Box 9011
Princeton, NJ 08543 609-282-2800
Financial - investment management

MuniYield New Jersey Fund, Inc. MYJ
PO Box 9011
Princeton, NJ 08543 609-282-2800
Financial - investment management

MuniYield New Jersey Insured Fund, Inc. MJI
PO Box 9011
Princeton, NJ 08543 609-282-2800
Financial - investment management

MuniYield New York Insured Fund II, Inc.
  MYT
PO Box 9011
Princeton, NJ 08543 609-282-2800
Financial - investment management

MuniYield New York Insured Fund III, Inc.
  MYY
PO Box 9011
Princeton, NJ 08543 609-282-2800
Financial - investment management

MuniYield New York Insured Fund, Inc. MYN
PO Box 9011
Princeton, NJ 08543 609-282-2800
Financial - investment management

MuniYield Pennsylvania Fund, Inc. MPA
PO Box 9011
Princeton, NJ 08543 609-282-2800
Financial - investment management

MuniYield Quality Fund II, Inc. MQT
PO Box 9011
Princeton, NJ 08536 609-282-2800
Financial - investment management

MuniYield Quality Fund, Inc. MQY
PO Box 9011
Princeton, NJ 08536 609-282-2800
Financial - investment management

Munsingwear, Inc. MUN
8000 W. 78th St., Ste. 400
Edina, MN 55439 612-943-5000
Apparel

Murphy Oil Corp. MUR
200 Peach St., PO Box 7000
El Dorado, AR 71731 501-862-6411
Oil & gas - international specialty O

Musicland Stores Corp. MLG
10400 Yellow Circle Dr.
Minnetonka, MN 55343 612-931-8000
Retail - misc. O

Mylan Laboratories Inc. MYL
1030 Century Bldg.
Pittsburgh, PA 15222 412-232-0100
Drugs - generic O

NACCO Industries, Inc. NC
5875 Landerbrook Dr.
Mayfield Heights, OH 44124
216-449-9600
Diversified operations

Nalco Chemical Co. NLC
One Nalco Center
Naperville, IL 60563 708-305-1000
Chemicals - specialty O [DRP]

Nashua Corp. NSH
44 Franklin St., PO Box 2002
Nashua, NH 03061 603-880-2323
Diversified operations O [DRP]

National City Corp. NCC
1900 E. Ninth St.
Cleveland, OH 44114 216-575-2000
Banks - midwest O [DRP 3%]

National Convenience Stores Inc. NCS
100 Waugh Dr.
Houston, TX 77007 713-863-2200
Retail - convenience stores

National Data Corp. NDC
National Data Plaza
Atlanta, GA 30329 404-728-2000
Data collection & systems O [DRP]

National Education Corp. NEC
18400 Von Karman Ave.
Irvine, CA 92715 714-474-9400
Schools

National Fuel Gas Co. NFG
30 Rockefeller Plaza
New York, NY 10112 212-541-7533
Utility - gas distribution [DRP]

National Golf Properties, Inc. TEE
1448 15th St., Ste. 200
Santa Monica, CA 90404 310-260-5500
Real estate investment trust

National Health Investors, Inc. NHI
100 Vine St., Ste. 1402
Murfreesboro, TN 37130
615-890-9100
Real estate investment trust

National Health Laboratories, Inc. NH
4225 Executive Square
La Jolla, CA 92037 619-454-3314
Medical & dental supplies O

National Media Corp. NM
1700 Walnut St.
Philadelphia, PA 19103 215-772-5000
Retail - mail order & direct

National Medical Enterprises, Inc. NME
2700 Colorado Ave.
Santa Monica, CA 90404 310-998-8000
Hospitals O [DRP]

National Presto Industries, Inc. NPK
3925 N. Hastings Way
Eau Claire, WI 54703 715-839-02121
Appliances - household

National Re Corp. NRE
777 Long Ridge Rd.
Stamford, CT 06902 203-329-7700
Insurance - property & casualty

National Semiconductor Corp. NSM
2900 Semiconductor Dr.
Santa Clara, CA 95052 408-721-5000
Electrical components - semiconductors O

National Service Industries, Inc. NSI
1420 Peachtree St., N.E.
Atlanta, GA 30309 404-853-1000
Diversified operations O
[DRP]

National Steel Corp. NS
4100 Edison Lakes Parkway
Mishawaka, IN 46545 219-273-7000
Steel - production O

National-Standard Co. NSD
1618 Terminal Rd.
Niles, MI 49120 616-683-8100
Wire & cable products [DRP]

NationsBank Corp. NB
NationsBank Corporate Center
Charlotte, NC 28255 704-386-5000
Banks - money center O [DRP 5%]

Nationwide Health Properties, Inc. NHP
4675 McArthur Court, Ste. 1170
Newport Beach, CA 92660 714-251-1211
Real estate investment trust [DRP]

Navistar International Corp. NAV
455 N. Cityfront Plaza Dr.
Chicago, IL 60611 312-836-2000
Automotive & trucking - original equipment
O

NBB Bancorp, Inc. NBB
174 Union St.
New Bedford, MA 02740 508-996-5000
Banks - northeast O

NBD Bancorp, Inc. NBD
611 Woodward Ave.
Detroit, MI 48226 313-225-1000
Banks - midwest [DRP]

NCH Corp. NCH
2727 Chemsearch Blvd.
Irving, TX 75062 214-438-0211
Soap & cleaning preparations

Neiman Marcus Group, Inc. NMG
27 Boylston St., PO Box 9187
Chestnut Hill, MA 02167 617-232-0760
Retail - regional department stores O
[DRP]

Network Equipment Technologies, Inc. NWK
800 Saginaw Dr.
Redwood City, CA 94063 415-366-4400
Telecommunications equipment O

Nevada Power Co. NVP
6226 W. Sahara Ave.
Las Vegas, NV 89102 702-367-5000
Utility - electric power

New Age Media Fund, Inc. NAF
100 E. Pratt St.
Baltimore, MD 21202 410-547-2000
Financial - investment management [DRP]

New America High Income Fund, Inc. HYB
Ten Liberty Square
Boston, MA 02109 617-426-0182
Financial - investment management

New England Electric System NES
25 Research Dr.
Westborough, MA 01582 508-366-9011
Utility - electric power [DRP]

New England Investment Companies, L.P.
 NEW
399 Boylston St.
Boston, MA 02116 617-578-3500
Financial - investment management

New Jersey Resources Corp. NJR
1415 Wycoff Rd.
Wall, NJ 07719 908-938-1480
Utility - gas distribution [DRP]

New Plan Realty Trust NPR
1120 Avenue of the Americas
New York, NY 10036 212-869-3000
Real estate investment trust O
 [DRP 5%]

New York State Electric & Gas Corp. NGE
PO Box 3287
Ithaca, NY 14852 607-347-4131
Utility - electric power [DRP]

Newell Co. NWL
29 E. Stephenson St.
Freeport, IL 61032 815-235-4171
Building products - misc. O [DRP]

Newfield Exploration Co. NFX
363 N. Sam Houston Parkway E.
Houston, TX 77060 713-847-6000
Oil & gas - US exploration & production

Newmont Gold Co. NGC
1700 Lincoln St.
Denver, CO 80203 303-863-7414
Gold mining & processing O

Newmont Mining Corp. NEM
1700 Lincoln St.
Denver, CO 80203 303-863-7414
Gold mining & processing O

Niagara Mohawk Power Corp. NMK
300 Erie Blvd. West
Syracuse, NY 13202 315-474-1511
Utility - electric power O [DRP]

NICOR Inc. GAS
PO Box 3014
Naperville, IL 60566 708-305-9500
Utility - gas distribution O [DRP]

NIKE, Inc. NKE
One Bowerman Dr.
Beaverton, OR 97005 503-671-6453
Shoes & related apparel O

Nine West Group Inc. NIN
9 W. Broad St.
Stamford, CT 06902 203-328-4383
Shoes & related apparel O

NIPSCO Industries, Inc. NI
5265 Hohman Ave.
Hammond, IN 46320 219-853-5200
Utility - electric power [DRP]

NL Industries, Inc. NL
16825 Northchase Dr.
Houston, TX 77060 713-423-3300
Chemicals - specialty O

Noble Affiliates, Inc. NBL
110 W. Broadway
Ardmore, OK 73401 405-223-4110
Oil & gas - US exploration & production O

NorAm Energy Corp. NAE
PO Box 21734
Shreveport, LA 71151 318-429-2700
Utility - gas distribution O
 [DRP]

Nord Resources Corp. NRD
8150 Washington Village Dr.
Dayton, OH 45458 513-433-6307
Metal ores - misc. O

Norfolk Southern Corp. NSC
3 Commercial Place
Norfolk, VA 23510 804-629-2680
Transportation - rail O [DRP]

Nortek, Inc. NTK
50 Kennedy Plaza
Providence, RI 02903 401-751-1600
Diversified operations

North American Mortgage Co. NAC
3883 Airway Dr.
Santa Rosa, CA 95403 707-523-5000
Financial - mortgages & related services O

North Carolina Natural Gas Corp. NCG
150 Rowan St., PO Box 909
Fayetteville, NC 28302 910-483-0315
Utility - gas distribution [DRP 5%]

North European Oil Royalty Trust NET
43 W. Front St., Ste. 19A
Red Bank, NJ 07701 908-741-4008
Oil & gas - US royalty trust

North Fork Bancorporation, Inc. NFB
9025 Route 25
Mattituck, NY 11952 516-298-5000
Banks - northeast [DRP 5%]

Northeast Federal Corp. NSB
50 State House Square
Hartford, CT 06103 203-280-1000
Financial - savings and loans

Northeast Utilities NU
PO Box 270
Hartford, CT 06141 203-665-5000
Utility - electric power
 [DRP]

Northern Border Partners L.P NBP
1400 Smith St.
Houston, TX 77002 713-853-6161
Oil & gas - US exploration & production

Northern States Power Co. NSP
414 Nicollet Mall
Minneapolis, MN 55401 612-330-5500
Utility - electric power
[DRP]

Northern Telecom Ltd. NT
3 Robert Speak Parkway
Mississauga Ontario, CAN L4Z 3C8
416-897-9000
Canada/Telecom equipmt mfg O [DRP]

Northrop Grumman Corp. NOC
1840 Century Park East
Los Angeles, CA 90067 310-553-6262
Aerospace - aircraft equipment O
[DRP]

Northwestern Public Service Co. NPS
33 Third St. S.E.
Huron, SD 57350 605-352-8411
Utility - electric power [DRP]

Norwest Corp. NOB
Sixth and Marquette
Minneapolis, MN 55479 612-667-1234
Banks - midwest O [DRP]

NOVA Corp NVA
PO Box 2535
Station M, Calgary, Alberta T2P 2N6
800-661-8686
Oil-gas-pipeline O [DRP]

NovaCare, Inc. NOV
1016 W. Ninth Ave.
King of Prussia, PA 19406
610-631-9300
Medical services O

Novo-Nordisk A/S NVO
c/o First Chicago Trust
PO Box 2533, Jersey City, NJ 07303
800-446-2617
Denmark pharmaceutical [DRP]

NS Group, Inc. NSS
Ninth & Lowell Sts.
Newport, KY 41072 606-292-6809
Steel - pipes & tubes

Nucor Corp. NUE
2100 Rexford Rd.
Charlotte, NC 28211 704-366-7000
Steel - production O [DRP]

Nuevo Energy Co. NEV
1221 Lamar, Ste. 1600
Houston, TX 77010 713-652-0706
Oil & gas - US exploration & production

NUI Corp. NUI
550 Route 202-206, PO Box 760
Bedminster, NJ 07921 908-781-0500
Utility - gas distribution
[DRP 5%]

Nuveen Arizona Premium Income Mun.
Fund, Inc. NAZ
333 W. Wacker Dr.
Chicago, IL 60606 312-917-7700
Financial - investment management

Nuveen California Inv. Quality Mun. Fund,
Inc. NQC
333 W. Wacker Dr.
Chicago, IL 60606 312-917-7700
Financial - investment management

Nuveen California Municipal Income Fund,
Inc. NCM
333 W. Wacker Dr.
Chicago, IL 60606 312-917-7700
Financial - investment management

Nuveen California Municipal Mkt. Opp. Fd.,
Inc. NCO
333 W. Wacker Dr.
Chicago, IL 60606 312-917-7700
Financial - investment management

Nuveen California Municipal Value Fund,
Inc. NCA
333 W. Wacker Dr.
Chicago, IL 60606 312-917-7700
Financial - investment management

Nuveen California Perform. Plus Mun. Fd.,
Inc. NCP
333 W. Wacker Dr.
Chicago, IL 60606 312-917-7700
Financial - investment management

Nuveen California Qual. Income Mun. Fund,
Inc. NUC
333 W. Wacker Dr.
Chicago, IL 60606 312-917-7700
Financial - investment management

Nuveen California Select Qual. Mun. Fund,
Inc. NVC
333 W. Wacker Dr.
Chicago, IL 60606 312-917-7700
Financial - investment management

Nuveen California Select Tax-Free Income
Port. NXC
333 W. Wacker Dr.
Chicago, IL 60606 312-917-7700
Financial - investment management

Nuveen Connecticut Premium Income Mun.
Fund NTC
333 W. Wacker Dr.
Chicago, IL 60606 312-917-7700
Financial - investment management

Nuveen Florida Investment Quality Mun.
Fund NQF
333 W. Wacker Dr.
Chicago, IL 60606 312-917-7700
Financial - investment management

Nuveen Florida Quality Income Municipal
Fund NUF
333 W. Wacker Dr.
Chicago, IL 60606 312-917-7700
Financial - investment management

Nuveen Insured CA Premium Inc. Mun. Fd.
2, Inc. NCL
333 W. Wacker Dr.
Chicago, IL 60606 312-917-7700
Financial - investment management

Nuveen Insured CA Premium Inc. Mun. Fd.,
Inc. NPC
333 W. Wacker Dr.
Chicago, IL 60606 312-917-7700
Financial - investment management

Nuveen Insured Florida Premium Inc. Mun.
Fd. NFL
333 W. Wacker Dr.
Chicago, IL 60606 312-917-7700
Financial - investment management

Nuveen Insured Florida Premium Inc. Mun.
Fd. 2 NFP
333 W. Wacker Dr.
Chicago, IL 60606 312-917-7700
Financial - investment management

Nuveen Insured Municipal Opportunity
Fund, Inc. NIO
333 W. Wacker Dr.
Chicago, IL 60606 312-917-7700
Financial - investment management

Nuveen Insured NY Premium Inc. Mun.
Fund 2 NYP
333 W. Wacker Dr.
Chicago, IL 60606 312-917-7700
Financial - investment management

Nuveen Insured NY Premium Inc. Mun.
Fund, Inc. NNF
333 W. Wacker Dr.
Chicago, IL 60606 312-917-7700
Financial - investment management

Nuveen Insured Premium Income Mun.
Fund, Inc. NPE
333 W. Wacker Dr.
Chicago, IL 60606 312-917-7700
Financial - investment management

Nuveen Insured Premium Income Municipal
Fund 2 NPX
333 W. Wacker Dr.
Chicago, IL 60606 312-917-7700
Financial - investment management

Nuveen Insured Quality Municipal Fund, Inc.
NQI
333 W. Wacker Dr.
Chicago, IL 60606 312-917-7700
Financial - investment management

Nuveen Investment Quality Municipal Fund,
Inc. NQM
333 W. Wacker Dr.
Chicago, IL 60606 312-917-7700
Financial - investment management

Nuveen Maryland Premium Income Mun.
Fund NMY
333 W. Wacker Dr.
Chicago, IL 60606
312-917-7700
Financial - investment management

Nuveen Mass. Premium Income Municipal
Fund NMT
333 W. Wacker Dr.
Chicago, IL 60606 312-917-7700
Financial - investment management

Nuveen Michigan Premium Income Mun.
Fund, Inc. NMP
333 W. Wacker Dr.
Chicago, IL 60606 312-917-7700
Financial - investment management

Nuveen Michigan Quality Income Mun.
Fund, Inc. NUM
333 W. Wacker Dr.
Chicago, IL 60606 312-917-7700
Financial - investment management

Nuveen Municipal Advantage Fund, Inc.
NMA
333 W. Wacker Dr.
Chicago, IL 60606 312-917-7700
Financial - investment management

Nuveen Municipal Income Fund, Inc.
NMI
333 W. Wacker Dr.
Chicago, IL 60606 312-917-7700
Financial - investment management

Nuveen Municipal Market Opportunity Fund,
Inc. NMO
333 W. Wacker Dr.
Chicago, IL 60606 312-917-7700
Financial - investment management

Nuveen Municipal Value Fund, Inc. NUV
333 W. Wacker Dr.
Chicago, IL 60606 312-917-7700
Financial - investment management

Nuveen N. Carolina Premium Inc. Mun.
Fund NNC
333 W. Wacker Dr.
Chicago, IL 60606 312-917-7700
Financial - investment management

Nuveen New Jersey Inv. Qual. Mun. Fd., Inc.
NQJ
333 W. Wacker Dr.
Chicago, IL 60606 312-917-7700
Financial - investment management

Nuveen New Jersey Premium Inc. Mun. Fd.,
Inc. NNJ
333 W. Wacker Dr.
Chicago, IL 60606 312-917-7700
Financial - investment management

Nuveen New Jersey Premium Income Mun.
Fund 2 NJP
333 W. Wacker Dr.
Chicago, IL 60606 312-917-7700
Financial - investment management

Nuveen New Jersey Quality Inc. Mun. Fund,
Inc. NUJ
333 W. Wacker Dr.
Chicago, IL 60606 312-917-7700
Financial - investment management

Nuveen New York Investment Qual. Mun.
Fd., Inc. NQN
333 W. Wacker Dr.
Chicago, IL 60606 312-917-7700
Financial - investment management

Nuveen New York Municipal Mkt. Opp.
Fund, Inc. NNO
333 W. Wacker Dr.
Chicago, IL 60606 312-917-7700
Financial - investment management

Nuveen New York Municipal Value Fund,
Inc. NNY
333 W. Wacker Dr.
Chicago, IL 60606 312-917-7700
Financial - investment management

Nuveen New York Performance Plus Mun.
Fd., Inc. NNP
333 W. Wacker Dr.
Chicago, IL 60606 312-917-7700
Financial - investment management

Nuveen New York Quality Income Mun.
Fund, Inc. NUN
333 W. Wacker Dr.
Chicago, IL 60606 312-917-7700
Financial - investment management

Nuveen New York Select Quality Mun. Fund,
Inc. NVN
333 W. Wacker Dr.
Chicago, IL 60606 312-917-7700
Financial - investment management

Nuveen Ohio Quality Inc. Municipal Fund,
Inc. NUO
333 W. Wacker Dr.
Chicago, IL 60606 312-917-7700
Financial - investment management

Nuveen Pennsylvania Investment Qual.
Mun. Fund NQP
333 W. Wacker Dr.
Chicago, IL 60606 312-917-7700
Financial - investment management

Nuveen Pennsylvania Premium Income
Mun. Fd. 2 NPY
333 W. Wacker Dr.
Chicago, IL 60606 312-917-7700
Financial - investment management

Nuveen Pennsylvania Premium Income
Mun. Fund NPA
333 W. Wacker Dr.
Chicago, IL 60606 312-917-7700
Financial - investment management

Nuveen Pennsylvania Quality Income Mun.
Fund NUP
333 W. Wacker Dr.
Chicago, IL 60606 312-917-7700
Financial - investment management

Nuveen Performance Plus Municipal Fund,
Inc. NPP
333 W. Wacker Dr.
Chicago, IL 60606 312-917-7700
Financial - investment management

Nuveen Premier Insured Municipal Inc. Fd.,
Inc. NIF
333 W. Wacker Dr.
Chicago, IL 60606 312-917-7700
Financial - investment management

Nuveen Premier Municipal Fund, Inc.
NPF
333 W. Wacker Dr.
Chicago, IL 60606 312-917-7700
Financial - investment management

Nuveen Premium Income Municipal Fund 2,
Inc. NPM
333 W. Wacker Dr.
Chicago, IL 60606 312-917-7700
Financial - investment management

Nuveen Premium Income Municipal Fund 4,
Inc. NPT
333 W. Wacker Dr.
Chicago, IL 60606 312-917-7700
Financial - investment management

Nuveen Premium Income Municipal Fund,
Inc. NPI
333 W. Wacker Dr.
Chicago, IL 60606 312-917-7700
Financial - investment management

Nuveen Quality Income Municipal Fund, Inc.
NQU
333 W. Wacker Dr.
Chicago, IL 60606 312-917-7700
Financial - investment management

Nuveen Select Maturities Municipal Fund
NIM
333 W. Wacker Dr.
Chicago, IL 60606 312-917-7700
Financial - investment management

Nuveen Select NY Select Tax-Free Income
Port. NXN
333 W. Wacker Dr.
Chicago, IL 60606 312-917-7700
Financial - investment management

Nuveen Select Quality Municipal Fund, Inc.
NQS
333 W. Wacker Dr.
Chicago, IL 60606 312-917-7700
Financial - investment management

Nuveen Select Tax-Free Income Portfolio
NXP
333 W. Wacker Dr.
Chicago, IL 60606 312-917-7700
Financial - investment management

Nuveen Select Tax-Free Income Portfolio 2
NXQ
333 W. Wacker Dr.
Chicago, IL 60606 312-917-7700
Financial - investment management

Nuveen Select Tax-Free Income Portfolio 3
NXR
333 W. Wacker Dr.
Chicago, IL 60606 312-917-7700
Financial - investment management

Nuveen Select Tax-Free Income Portfolio 4
NXS
333 W. Wacker Dr.
Chicago, IL 60606 312-917-7700
Financial - investment management

Nuveen Texas Quality Income Municipal
Fund NTX
333 W. Wacker Dr.
Chicago, IL 60606 312-917-7700
Financial - investment management

Nuveen Virginia Premium Income Municipal
Fund NPV
333 W. Wacker Dr.
Chicago, IL 60606 312-917-7700
Financial - investment management

NWNL Companies, Inc. NWN
20 Washington Ave. South
Minneapolis, MN 55401 612-372-5432
Insurance - life O
[DRP 4%]

NYMAGIC, INC. NYM
330 Madison Ave.
New York, NY 10017
212-551-0600
Insurance - property & casualty

NYNEX Corp. NYN
1113 Westchester Ave.
White Plains, NY 10604 914-644-6400
Utility - telephone O [DRP]

O'Sullivan Industries Holdings, Inc. OSU
1900 Gulf St.
Lamar, MO 64759 417-682-3322
Furniture

Oak Industries Inc. OAK
1000 Winter St.
Waltham, MA 02154 617-890-0400
Electrical products - misc. O

Oakwood Homes Corp. OH
2225 S. Holden Rd.
Greensboro, NC 27417 910-855-2400
Building - mobile homes & RV

Oasis Residential, Inc. OAS
4041 E. Sunset Rd.
Henderson, NV 89014 702-435-9800
Real estate operations

Occidental Petroleum Corp. OXY
10889 Wilshire Blvd.
Los Angeles, CA 90024 310-208-8800
Oil & gas - US integrated O
[DRP]

Oceaneering International, Inc. OII
16001 Park Ten Place, Ste. 600
Houston, TX 77084 713-578-8868
Oil & gas - field services O

OEA, Inc. OEA
34501 E. Quincy Ave.
Denver, CO 80250 303-693-1248
Electronics - military O

OEC Medical Systems, Inc. OXE
384 Wright Brothers Dr.
Salt Lake City, UT 84116
801-328-9300
Medical products O

Office Depot, Inc. ODP
2200 Old Germantown Rd.
Delray Beach, FL 33445 407-278-4800
Retail - misc. O

Office Max, Inc. OMX
3605 Warrensville Center Rd.
Shaker Heights, OH 44122 216-921-6900
Retail - misc.

Offshore Pipelines, Inc. OFP
5718 Westheimer, Ste. 600
Houston, TX 77057 713-952-1000
Oil & gas - field services

Ogden Corp. OG
2 Pennsylvania Plaza
New York, NY 10121 212-868-6100
Diversified operations O

Ogden Projects, Inc. OPI
40 Lane Rd., CN2615
Fairfield, NJ 07007 201-882-9000
Energy - alternate sources

Ohio Edison Co. OEC
76 S. Main St.
Akron, OH 44308 216-384-5100
Utility - electric power O [DRP]

Ohio Power Co. OPWp
301 Cleveland Ave., S.W.
Canton, OH 44702 216-456-8173
Utility - electric power

OHM Corp. OHM
16406 U.S. Route 224 East
Findlay, OH 45840 419-423-3529
Pollution control equipment & services

Oil-Dri Corporation of America ODC
410 N. Michigan Ave.
Chicago, IL 60611 312-321-1515
Chemicals - specialty

Oklahoma Gas and Electric Co. OGE
321 N. Robinson, PO Box 321
Oklahoma City, OK 73101 405-272-3000
Utility - electric power [DRP]

Old Republic International Corp. ORI
307 N. Michigan Ave.
Chicago, IL 60601 312-346-8100
Insurance - property & casualty O
[DRP]

Olin Corp. OLN
120 Long Ridge Rd.
Stamford, CT 06904 203-356-2000
Diversified operations O [DRP]

Olsten Corp. OLS
One Merrick Ave.
Westbury, NY 11590 516-832-8200
Business services O

Omega Healthcare Investors, Inc. OHI
905 W. Eisenhower Circle
Ann Arbor, MI 48103 313-747-9790
Financial - mortgages & related services

OMI Corp. OMM
90 Park Ave.
New York, NY 10016 212-986-1960
Transportation - shipping

Omnicare, Inc. OCR
255 E. Fifth St.
Cincinnati, OH 45202 513-762-6666
Medical & dental supplies
[DRP]

Omnicom Group Inc. OMC
437 Madison Ave.
New York, NY 10022 212-415-3600
Advertising O

Oneida Ltd. OCQ
Oneida, NY 13421 315-361-3636
Appliances - household

Oneita Industries, Inc. ONA
Highway 41, Conifer St.
Andrews, SC 29510 803-264-5225
Textiles - apparel

ONEOK Inc. OKE
100 W. Fifth St., PO Box 871
Tulsa, OK 74102 918-588-7000
Utility - gas distribution O
[DRP]

Oppenheimer Capital, L.P. OCC
World Financial Center
New York, NY 10281 212-667-7000
Financial - investment management

Oppenheimer Multi-Government Trust OGT
Two World Trade Center
New York, NY 10048 212-323-0200
Financial - investment management

Oppenheimer Multi-Sector Income Trust
OMS
Two World Trade Center
New York, NY 10048 212-323-0200
Financial - investment management

Orange & Rockland Utilities, Inc. ORU
One Blue Hill Plaza
Pearl River, NY 10965 914-352-6000
Utility - electric power

Orange-co, Inc. OJ
2022 U.S. Highway 17 South
Bartow, FL 33830 813-533-0551
Agricultural operations

Oregon Steel Mills, Inc. OS
1000 S.W. Broadway, Ste. 2200
Portland, OR 97205 503-223-9228
Steel - specialty alloys O

Orion Capital Corp. OC
30 Rockefeller Plaza
New York, NY 10112 212-332-8080
Insurance - property & casualty

Oryx Energy Co. ORX
13155 Noel Rd.
Dallas, TX 75240 214-715-4000
Oil & gas - US exploration & production O

Osmonics, Inc. OSM
5951 Clearwater Dr.
Minnetonka, MN 55343 612-933-2277
Pollution control equipment & services

Outboard Marine Corp. OM
100 Sea-Horse Dr.
Waukegan, IL 60085 708-689-6200
Leisure & recreational products O
[DRP]

Overseas Shipholding Group, Inc. OSG
1114 Avenue of the Americas
New York, NY 10036 212-869-1222
Transportation - shipping

Owens & Minor, Inc. OMI
4800 Cox Rd.
Glen Allen, VA 23060 804-747-9794
Drugs & sundries - wholesale [DRP]

Owens-Corning Fiberglas Corp. OCF
Fiberglas Tower
Toledo, OH 43659 419-248-8000
Building products - misc. O

Owens-Illinois, Inc. OI
One Sea Gate
Toledo, OH 43666 419-247-5000
Glass products O

Oxford Industries, Inc. OXM
222 Piedmont Ave., N.E.
Atlanta, GA 30308 404-659-2424
Textiles - apparel

Pacific American Income Shares, Inc. PAI
PO Box 983
Pasadena, CA 91102 818-449-0309
Financial - investment management

Pacific Enterprises PET
633 W. Fifth St., Ste. 5400
Los Angeles, CA 90071 213-895-5000
Utility - gas distribution O [DRP]

Pacific Gas and Electric Co. PCG
77 Beale St.
San Francisco, CA 94177 415-972-7000
Utility - electric power O [DRP]

Pacific Scientific Co. PSX
620 Newport Center Dr.
Newport Beach, CA 92660
714-720-1714
Electronics - measuring instruments

Pacific Telesis Group PAC
130 Kearny St.
San Francisco, CA 94108 415-394-3000
Utility - telephone O [DRP]

PacifiCorp PPW
700 N.E. Multnomah
Portland, OR 97232 503-731-2000
Utility - electric power O [DRP]

PaineWebber Group Inc. PWJ
1285 Avenue of the Americas
New York, NY 10019 212-713-2000
Financial - investment bankers O [DRP]

PaineWebber Premier Tax-Free Inc. Fund
PPM
1285 Avenue of the Americas
New York, NY 10019 212-713-2000
Financial - investment management

Pall Corp. PLL
2200 Northern Blvd.
East Hills, NY 11548 516-484-5400
Filtration products O [DRP]

Panhandle Eastern Corp. PEL
PO Box 1642
Houston, TX 77251 713-627-5400
Oil & gas - production & pipeline O [DRP]

PAR Technology Corp. PTC
220 Seneca Turnpike
New Hartford, NY 13413 315-738-0600
Computers - peripheral equipment

Paragon Group, Inc. PAO
7557 Rambler Rd., Ste. 1200
Dallas, TX 75231 214-891-2000
Real estate investment trust

Paragon Trade Brands, Inc. PTB
505 S. 336th St.
Federal Way, WA 98003 206-924-4509
Miscellaneous - not elsewhere classified O

Park Electrochemical Corp. PKE
5 Dakota Dr.
Lake Success, NY 11042
516-354-4100
Electrical components - misc.

Parker & Parsley Petroleum Corp. PDP
303 W. Wall, Ste. 101
Midland, TX 79701 915-683-4768
Oil & gas - US exploration & production O

Parker Drilling Co. PKD
Eight E. Third St.
Tulsa, OK 74103 918-585-8221
Oil & gas - field services

Parker Hannifin Corp. PH
17325 Euclid Ave.
Cleveland, OH 44112 216-531-3000
Instruments - control O
[DRP]

Patrick Petroleum Co. PPC
301 W. Michigan Ave.
Jackson, MI 49201 517-787-6633
Oil & gas - US exploration & production

Patriot Global Dividend Fund PGD
101 Huntington Ave.
Boston, MA 02199 800-843-0090
Financial - investment management

Patriot Preferred Dividend Fund PPF
101 Huntington Ave.
Boston, MA 02199 800-843-0090
Financial - investment management

Patriot Premium Dividend Fund I PDF
101 Huntington Ave.
Boston, MA 02199 800-843-0090
Financial - investment management

Patriot Premium Dividend Fund II PDT
101 Huntington Ave.
Boston, MA 02199 800-843-0090
Financial - investment management

Patriot Select Dividend Trust DIV
101 Huntington Ave.
Boston, MA 02199 800-843-0090
Financial - investment management

Patten Corp. PAT
5295 Town Center Rd.
Boca Raton, FL 33486 407-391-6336
Real estate development

Paul Revere Corp. PRL
18 Chestnut St.
Worcester, MA 01608 508-799-4441
Insurance - accident & health

Paxar Corp. PXR
275 N. Middletown Rd.
Pearl River, NY 10965 914-735-9200
Machinery - general industrial

Payless Cashways, Inc. PCS
2300 Main, PO Box 419466
Kansas City, MO 64141 816-234-6000
Building products - retail & wholesale O

PEC Israel Economic Corp. IEC
511 Fifth Ave.
New York, NY 10017 212-687-2400
Financial - investment management

PECO Energy Co. PE
2301 Market St., PO Box 8699
Philadelphia, PA 19101 215-841-4000
Utility - electric power O [DRP]

PennCorp Financial Group, Inc. PFG
745 Fifth Ave.
New York, NY 10151 212-832-0700
Insurance - accident & health

Penney (J.C.) Co., Inc. JCP
6501 Legacy Dr.
Plano, TX 75024 214-431-1000
Retail - major department stores O
[DRP]

Pennsylvania Enterprises, Inc. PNT
39 Public Square
Wilkes-Barre, PA 18711 717-829-8843
Utility - gas distribution
[DRP 5%]

Pennsylvania Power & Light Co. PPL
Two N. Ninth St.
Allentown, PA 18101 610-774-5151
Utility - electric power [DRP]

Pennzoil Co. PZL
Pennzoil Place, PO Box 2967
Houston, TX 77252 713-546-4000
Oil & gas - US integrated O [DRP]

Peoples Energy Corp. PGL
122 S. Michigan Ave.
Chicago, IL 60603 312-431-4000
Utility - gas distribution
[DRP]

Pep Boys - Manny, Moe & Jack PBY
3111 W. Allegheny Ave.
Philadelphia, PA 19132 215-229-9000
Auto parts - retail & wholesale O
[DRP]

PepsiCo, Inc. PEP
700 Anderson Hill Rd.
Purchase, NY 10577 914-253-2000
Beverages - soft drinks O

Perkin-Elmer Corp. PKN
761 Main Ave.
Norwalk, CT 6859 203-762-1000
Instruments - scientific O [DRP]

Perkins Family Restaurants, L.P. PFR
6075 Poplar Ave., Ste. 800
Memphis, TN 38119 901-766-6400
Retail - food & restaurants

Permian Basin Royalty Trust PBT
PO Box 1317
Fort Worth, TX 76101 817-390-06905
Oil & gas - US royalty trust

Perry Drug Stores, Inc. PDS
5400 Perry Dr., PO Box 436021
Pontiac, MI 48343 810-334-1300
Retail - drug stores

Petrie Stores Corp. PST
70 Enterprise Ave.
Secaucus, NJ 07094 201-866-3600
Retail - apparel & shoes O

Petroleum & Resources Corp. PEO
Seven St. Paul St., Ste. 1140
Baltimore, MD 21202 410-752-5900
Financial - investment management

Pfizer Inc. PFE
235 E. 42nd St.
New York, NY 10017 212-573-2323
Drugs O [DRP]

Pharmaceutical Resources, Inc. PRX
One Ram Ridge Rd.
Spring Valley, NY 10977 914-425-7100
Drugs - generic O

Phelps Dodge Corp. PD
2600 N. Central Ave.
Phoenix, AZ 85004 602-234-8100
Metals - non ferrous O [DRP]

PHH Corp. PHH
11333 McCormick Rd.
Hunt Valley, MD 21031 410-771-3600
Leasing

Philadelphia Suburban Corp. PSC
762 Lancaster Ave.
Bryn Mawr, PA 19010 610-527-8000
Utility - water supply
[DRP 5%]

Philip Morris Companies Inc. MO
120 Park Ave.
New York, NY 10017 212-880-5000
Tobacco O [DRP]

Phillips Petroleum Co. P
Phillips Bldg.
Bartlesville, OK 74004 918-661-6600
Oil & gas - US integrated O [DRP]

Phillips-Van Heusen Corp. PVH
1290 Avenue of the Americas
New York, NY 10104 212-541-5200
Textiles - apparel O

PHP Healthcare Corp. PPH
4900 Seminary Rd., 12th Fl.
Alexandria, VA 22311 703-998-7808
Healthcare - outpatient & home

Piccadilly Cafeterias, Inc. PIC
3232 Sherwood Forest Blvd.
Baton Rouge, LA 70816 504-293-9440
Retail - food & restaurants [DRP 5%]

Piedmont Natural Gas Co., Inc. PNY
1915 Rexford Rd.
Charlotte, NC 28211 704-364-3120
Utility - gas distribution
[DRP 5%]

Pier 1 Imports, Inc. PIR
301 Commerce St., Ste. 600
Fort Worth, TX 76102 817-878-8000
Retail - discount & variety O

Pilgrim Prime Rate Trust PPR
10100 Santa Monica Blvd.
Los Angeles, CA 90067 800-334-3444
Financial - investment management

Pilgrim Regional BankShares Inc. PBS
10100 Santa Monica Blvd.
Los Angeles, CA 90067 800-334-3444
Financial - investment management

Pilgrim's Pride Corp. CHX
110 S. Texas St.
Pittsburg, TX 75686 903-855-1000
Food - meat products

Pillowtex Corp. PTX
4111 Mint Way
Dallas, TX 75237 214-333-3225
Textiles - home furnishings

PIMCO Advisors L.P PA
One Station Place, 7 South
Stamford, CT 06902 203-352-4900
Financial - investment management

PIMCO Commercial Mortgage Securities Tr.,
Inc. PCM
840 Newport Center Dr.
Newport Beach, CA 92660 800-213-3606
Financial - investment management

Pinnacle West Capital Corp. PNW
400 E. Van Buren St., Ste. 700
Phoenix, AZ 85004 602-379-2500
Utility - electric power O [DRP]

Pioneer Financial Services, Inc. PFS
304 N. Main St.
Rockford, IL 61101 815-987-5000
Insurance - accident & health

Pioneer Interest Shares, Inc. MUO
60 State St.
Boston, MA 02109 617-742-7825
Financial - investment management

Piper Jaffray Companies, Inc. PJC
222 S. Ninth St.
Minneapolis, MN 55402 612-342-6000
Financial - investment bankers O

Pitney Bowes Inc. PBI
1 Elmcroft Rd.
Stamford, CT 06926 203-356-5000
Office equipment & supplies O
[DRP]

Pittston Minerals Group PZM
100 First Stamford Place
Stamford, CT 06902 203-978-5200
Coal

Pittston Services Group PZS
100 First Stamford Place
Stamford, CT 06902 203-978-5200
Diversified operations O

Plains Petroleum Co. PLP
12596 W. Bayaud
Lakewood, CO 80228 303-969-9325
Oil & gas - US exploration & production

Plantronics, Inc. PLT
337 Encinal St., PO Box 1802
Santa Cruz, CA 95061 408-426-6060
Telecommunications equipment

Playboy Enterprises, Inc. PLA
680 N. Lake Shore Dr.
Chicago, IL 60611 312-751-8000
Publishing - periodicals

Playtex Products, Inc. PYX
300 Nyala Farms
Westport, CT 06880 203-341-4000
Cosmetics & toiletries O

Plum Creek Timber Co., L.P. PCL
999 Third Ave., Ste. 2300
Seattle, WA 98104 206-467-3600
Building products - wood O

Ply-Gem Industries, Inc. PGI
777 Third Ave.
New York, NY 10017 212-832-1550
Building products - wood [DRP]

PNC Bank Corp. PNC
Fifth Ave. and Wood St.
Pittsburgh, PA 15265 412-762-2666
Banks - northeast O [DRP]

Pogo Producing Co. PPP
5 Greenway Plaza, PO Box 2504
Houston, TX 77252 713-297-5000
Oil & gas - US exploration & production O

Polaroid Corp. PRD
549 Technology Square
Cambridge, MA 02139 617-577-2000
Photographic equipment & supplies O
[DRP]

Policy Management Systems Corp. PMS
One PMS Center
Blythewood, SC 29016 803-735-4000
Computers - software O

Pope & Talbot, Inc. POP
1500 S.W. First Ave.
Portland, OR 97201 503-228-9161
Paper & paper products

Portec, Inc. POR
122 W. 22nd St., Ste. 100
Oak Brook, IL 60521 708-573-4600
Diversified operations

Portland General Corp. PGN
1201 SW Salmon St.
Portland, OR 97204 503-464-8820
Utility - electric power [DRP]

Post Properties, Inc. PPS
3350 Cumberland Circle
Atlanta, GA 30339 404-850-4400
Real estate operations

Potlatch Corp. PCH
One Maritime Plaza
San Francisco, CA 94111 415-576-8800
Paper & paper products O [DRP]

Potomac Electric Power Co. POM
1900 Pennsylvania Ave., N.W.
Washington, DC 20068 202-872-2456
Utility - electric power O [DRP]

PPG Industries, Inc. PPG
One PPG Place
Pittsburgh, PA 15272 412-434-3131
Chemicals - diversified O [DRP]

Pratt & Lambert United, Inc. PLU
75 Tonawanda St.
Buffalo, NY 14207 716-873-6000
Paints & allied products

Praxair, Inc. PX
39 Old Ridgebury Rd.
Danbury, CT 06810 203-794-3000
Miscellaneous - not elsewhere classified O
[DRP]

Precision Castparts Corp. PCP
4600 S.E. Harney Dr.
Portland, OR 97206 503-777-3881
Aerospace - aircraft equipment

Preferred Income Fund Inc. PFD
301 E. Colorado Blvd.
Pasadena, CA 91101 818-795-7300
Financial - investment management

Preferred Income Management Fund Inc.
PFM
301 E. Colorado Blvd.
Pasadena, CA 91101 818-795-7300
Financial - investment management

Preferred Income Opportunity Fund Inc. PFO
301 E. Colorado Blvd.
Pasadena, CA 91101 818-795-7300
Financial - investment management

Premark International, Inc. PMI
1717 Deerfield Rd.
Deerfield, IL 60015 708-405-6000
Containers - paper & plastic O

Premier Industrial Corp. PRE
4500 Euclid Ave.
Cleveland, OH 44103 216-391-8300
Electronics - parts distribution [DRP]

Price REIT, Inc. RET
7979 Ivanhoe Ave., Ste. 524
La Jolla, CA 92037 619-551-2320
Real estate investment trust

Pride Companies, L.P. PRF
500 Chestnut, Ste. 1300
Abilene, TX 79602 915-674-8000
Oil & gas - production & pipeline

Primark Corp. PMK
1000 Winter St., Ste. 4300N
Waltham, MA 02154 617-466-6611
Diversified operations

Prime Hospitality Corp. PDQ
700 Route 46 East, PO Box 2700
Fairfield, NJ 07007 201-882-1010
Hotels & motels

Prime Motor Inns L.P. PMP
700 Route 46 East
Fairfield, NJ 07006 201-882-1010
Hotels & motels

Procter & Gamble Co. PG
One Procter & Gamble Plaza
Cincinnati, OH 45202 513-983-1100
Soap & cleaning preparations O [DRP]

Proler International Corp. PS
4265 San Felipe, Ste. 900
Houston, TX 77027 713-627-3737
Metal processing & fabrication

Promus Companies Inc. PRI
1023 Cherry Rd.
Memphis, TN 38117 901-762-8600
Hotels & motels O

Property Trust of America PTR
7777 Market Center Ave.
El Paso, TX 79912 915-877-3900
Real estate investment trust [DRP 2%]

Prospect Street High Income Portfolio Inc.
 PHY
One Exchange Place, 37th Fl.
Boston, MA 02109 617-742-3800
Financial - investment management

Protective Life Corp. PL
2801 Highway 280 South
Birmingham, AL 35223 205-879-9230
Insurance - life

Provident Life and Accident Ins. Co. of
 America PVA
One Fountain Square
Chattanooga, TN 37402 615-755-1011
Insurance - accident & health

Providian Corp. PVN
400 W. Market St.
Louisville, KY 40202 502-560-2000
Insurance - life [DRP]

Prudential Realty Trust PRT
745 Broad St.
Newark, NJ 07101 201-802-4302
Financial - investment management

PS Group, Inc. PSG
4370 La Jolla Village Dr.
San Diego, CA 90212 619-546-5001
Leasing

PSI Resources, Inc. PIN
1000 E. Main St.
Plainfield, IN 46168 317-839-9611
Utility - electric power [DRP]

Public Service Company of Colorado PSR
1225 17th St.
Denver, CO 80202 303-571-7511
Utility - electric power [DRP]

Public Service Company of New Mexico PNM
Alvarado Square
Albuquerque, NM 87158 505-848-2700
Utility - electric power

Public Service Enterprise Group Inc. PEG
80 Park Plaza, PO Box 1171
Newark, NJ 07101 201-430-7000
Utility - electric power O [DRP]

Publicker Industries Inc. PUL
1445 E. Putnam Ave.
Old Greenwich, CT 06870 203-637-4500
Chemicals - specialty

Puget Sound Power & Light Co. PSD
411 108th Ave. N.E.
Bellevue, WA 98004 206-462-3898
Utility - electric power [DRP]

Pulitzer Publishing Co. PTZ
900 N. Tucker Blvd.
St. Louis, MO 63101 314-340-8000
Broadcasting - radio & TV

Pulte Corp. PHM
33 Bloomfield Hills Parkway
Bloomfield Hills, MI 48304
313-647-2750
Building - residential & commercial O

Putnam Dividend Income Trust PDI
One Post Office Square
Boston, MA 02109 617-292-1000
Financial - investment management

Putnam High Income Convertible Bond
 Fund PCF
One Post Office Square
Boston, MA 02109 617-292-1000
Financial - investment management

Putnam High Yield Municipal Trust PYM
One Post Office Square
Boston, MA 02109 617-292-1000
Financial - investment management

Putnam Intermediate Government Income
 Trust PGT
One Post Office Square
Boston, MA 02109 617-292-1000
Financial - investment management

Putnam Investment Grade Municipal Trust
 PGM
One Post Office Square
Boston, MA 02109 617-292-1000
Financial - investment management

Putnam Investment Grade Municipal Trust II
 PMG
One Post Office Square
Boston, MA 02109 617-292-1000
Financial - investment management

Putnam Managed High Yield Trust PTM
One Post Office Square
Boston, MA 02109 617-292-1000
Financial - investment management

Putnam Managed Municipal Income Trust
 PMM
One Post Office Square
Boston, MA 02109 617-292-1000
Financial - investment management

Putnam Master Income Trust PMT
One Post Office Square
Boston, MA 02109 617-292-1000
Financial - investment management

Putnam Master Intermediate Income Trust
PIM
One Post Office Square
Boston, MA 02109 617-292-1000
Financial - investment management

Putnam Municipal Opportunities Trust PMO
One Post Office Square
Boston, MA 02109 617-292-1000
Financial - investment management

Putnam Premier Income Trust PPT
One Post Office Square
Boston, MA 02109 617-292-1000
Financial - investment management

Putnam Tax-Free Health Care Fund PMH
One Post Office Square
Boston, MA 02109 617-292-1000
Financial - investment management

QMS, Inc. AQM
One Magnum Pass, PO Box 81250
Mobile, AL 36618 205-633-4300
Computers - peripheral equipment O

Quaker Oats Co. OAT
321 N. Clark St.
Chicago, IL 60610 312-222-7111
Food - misc. O [DRP]

Quaker State Corp. KSF
225 Elm St.
Oil City, PA 16301 814-676-7676
Oil refining & marketing O [DRP]

Quanex Corp. NX
1900 W. Loop South, Ste. 1500
Houston, TX 77027 713-961-4600
Steel - pipes & tubes [DRP]

Quantum Restaurant Group, Inc. KRG
97 Powerhouse Rd., Ste. 101
Roslyn Heights, NY 11577
516-484-0777
Retail - food & restaurants

Quest For Value Dual Purpose Fund, Inc. KFV
World Financial Center
New York, NY 10281 212-667-7587
Financial - investment management

Questar Corp. STR
180 E. First South
Salt Lake City, UT 84147 801-534-5000
Utility - gas distribution O [DRP]

R.P. Scherer Corp. SHR
2075 W. Big Beaver Rd.
Troy, MI 48084 313-649-0900
Medical products

R.R. Donnelley & Sons Co. DNY
77 W. Wacker Dr.
Chicago, IL 60601 312-326-8000
Printing - commercial

Ralston Continental Baking Group CBG
Checkerboard Square
St. Louis, MO 63164 314-982-1000
Food - misc.

Ralston Purina Co. RAL
Checkerboard Square
St. Louis, MO 63164 314-982-1000
Food - misc. O [DRP]

Raychem Corp. RYC
300 Constitution Dr.
Menlo Park, CA 94025 415-361-3333
Electrical products - misc. O

Raymond James Financial, Inc. RJF
880 Carillon Parkway
St. Petersburg, FL 33716 813-578-3800
Financial - investment bankers O

Rayonier Timberlands, L.P. LOG
1177 Summer St.
Stamford, CT 06905 203-348-7000
Building products - wood O

Rayonier, Inc. RYN
1177 Summer St.
Stamford, CT 06905 203-348-7000
Paper & paper products

Raytech Corp. RAY
One Corporate Dr., Ste. 512
Shelton, CT 06484 203-925-8023
Automotive & trucking - original equipment

Raytheon Co. RTN
141 Spring St.
Lexington, MA 01273 617-862-6600
Diversified operations O [DRP]

RCM Strategic Global Government Fund,
Inc. RCS
4 Embarcadero Center, 30th Fl.
San Francisco, CA 94111 415-954-5400
Financial - investment management

Reading & Bates Corp. RB
901 Threadneedle, Ste. 200
Houston, TX 77079 713-496-5000
Oil & gas - offshore drilling O

Real Estate Investment Trust of California
RCT
12011 San Vincente Blvd.
Los Angeles, CA 90049 310-476-7793
Real estate investment trust [DRP]

Realty ReFund Trust RRF
1385 Eaton Center
Cleveland, OH 44114 216-771-7663
Real estate investment trust

Recognition International Inc. REC
2701 E. Grauwyler Rd.
Irving, TX 75061 214-579-6000
Optical character recognition

Reebok International Ltd. RBK
100 Technology Center Dr.
Stoughton, MA 02072 617-341-5000
Shoes & related apparel O

Regency Health Services, Inc. RHS
3636 Birch St., Ste. 195
Newport Beach, CA 92660 714-851-9512
Medical services

Regency Realty Corp. REG
121 W. Forsyth St., Ste. 200
Jacksonville, FL 32202 904-356-7000
Real estate investment trust

Reinsurance Group of America, Inc. RGA
666 Mason Ridge Center Dr.
St. Louis, MO 63141 314-453-7300
Insurance - multi line & misc.

Reliance Electric Co. REE
6065 Parkland Blvd.
Cleveland, OH 44124 216-266-5800
Electrical products - misc. O

Reliance Group Holdings, Inc. REL
55 E. 52nd St.
New York, NY 10055 212-909-1100
Insurance - multi line & misc.

Reliance Steel and Aluminum Co. RS
2550 E. 25th St.
Los Angeles, CA 90058 213-582-2272
Metal processing & fabrication

Republic Gypsum Co. RGC
811 E. 30th Ave.
Hutchinson, KS 67502
316-727-2700
Building products - misc.

Republic New York Corp. RNB
452 Fifth Ave.
New York, NY 10018 212-525-6100
Banks - northeast O

Resource Mortgage Capital, Inc. RMR
2800 E. Parham Rd.
Richmond, VA 23228 804-967-5800
Real estate investment trust
[DRP 3%]

Revco D.S., Inc. RXR
1925 Enterprise Parkway
Twinsburg, OH 44087 216-425-9811
Retail - drug stores O

REX Stores Corp. RSC
2875 Needmore Rd.
Dayton, OH 45414 513-276-3931
Retail - misc.

Rexene Corp. RXN
5005 LBJ Freeway
Dallas, TX 75244 214-450-9000
Chemicals - diversified

Reynolds and Reynolds Co. REY
115 S. Ludlow St.
Dayton, OH 45402 513-443-2000
Paper - business forms O [DRP]

Reynolds Metals Co. RLM
6601 W. Broad St.
Richmond, VA 23261 804-281-2000
Metals - non ferrous O
[DRP]

Rhodes Inc. RHD
4370 Peachtree Rd. N.E.
Atlanta, GA 30319 404-264-4600
Retail - home furnishings

Rhone-Poulenc Rorer Inc. RPR
500 Virginia Dr.
Fort Washington, PA 19034
215-628-6000
Drugs O [DRP]

Rite Aid Corp. RAD
30 Hunter Ln.
Camp Hill, PA 17011 717-761-2633
Retail - drug stores O [DRP]

Riverwood International Corp. RVW
3350 Cumberland Circle
Atlanta, GA 30339 404-644-3000
Building products - wood

RJR Nabisco, Inc. RN
1301 Avenue of the Americas
New York, NY 10019 212-258-5600
Tobacco O

RLI Corp. RLI
9025 N. Lindbergh Dr.
Peoria, IL 61615 309-692-1000
Insurance - accident & health [DRP]

RMI Titanium Co. RTI
1000 Warren Ave., PO Box 269
Niles, OH 44446 216-652-9951
Metals - non ferrous

Roadmaster Industries, Inc. RDM
7315 E. Peakview Ave.
Englewood, CO 80111 303-290-8150
Leisure & recreational products

Robert Half International Inc. RHI
2884 Sand Hill Rd., Ste. 200
Menlo Park, CA 94025 415-854-9700
Business services

Robertson-Ceco Corp. RHH
222 Berkeley St.
Boston, MA 02116 617-424-5500
Diversified operations

ROC Communities, Inc. RCI
6430 S. Quebec St.
Englewood, CO 80111 303-741-3707
Real estate development

Rochester Gas and Electric Corp. RGS
89 East Ave.
Rochester, NY 14649 716-546-2700
Utility - electric power [DRP]

Rochester Telephone Corp. RTC
180 S. Clinton Ave.
Rochester, NY 14646 716-777-7100
Utility - telephone O [DRP]

Rockefeller Center Properties, Inc. RCP
1270 Avenue of the Americas
New York, NY 10020 212-698-1440
Real estate investment trust O [DRP]

Rockwell International Corp. ROK
2201 Seal Beach Blvd.
Seal Beach, CA 90740 310-797-3311
Aerospace - aircraft equipment O [DRP]

Rodman & Renshaw Capital Group,
Inc. RR
120 S. LaSalle St.
Chicago, IL 60603 312-977-7800
Financial - investment management

Rohm and Haas Co. ROH
Independence Mall West
Philadelphia, PA 19105 215-592-3000
Chemicals - diversified O

Rohr, Inc. RHR
850 Lagoon Dr.
Chula Vista, CA 91910 619-691-4111
Aerospace - aircraft equipment O

Rollins Environmental Services, Inc. REN
PO Box 2349
Wilmington, DE 19899 302-479-2757
Pollution control equipment & services O
[DRP]

Rollins Truck Leasing Corp. RLC
One Rollins Plaza, PO Box 1791
Wilmington, DE 19899 302-479-2700
Leasing [DRP]

Rollins, Inc. ROL
2170 Piedmont Rd., N.E.
Atlanta, GA 30324 404-888-2000
Building - maintenance & services [DRP]

Rouge Steel Co. ROU
3001 Miller Rd.
Dearborn, MI 48121 313-390-6877
Steel - production O

Rowan Companies, Inc. RDC
2800 Post Oak Blvd.
Houston, TX 77056 713-621-7800
Oil & gas - offshore drilling O

Rowe Furniture Corp. ROW
239 Rowan St.
Salem, VA 24153 703-389-8671
Furniture

Royal Appliance Mfg. Co. RAM
650 Alpha Dr.
Cleveland, OH 44143 216-449-6150
Appliances - household O

Royce Value Trust, Inc. RVT
1414 Avenue of the Americas
New York, NY 10019 800-221-4268
Financial - investment management

RPC Energy Services, Inc. RES
2170 Piedmont Rd. N.E.
Atlanta, GA 30324 404-888-2950
Oil & gas - field services

RPS Realty Trust RPS
733 Third Ave.
New York, NY 10017 212-370-8585
Real estate investment trust

Rubbermaid Inc. RBD
1147 Akron Rd.
Wooster, OH 44691 216-264-6464
Rubber & plastic products O
[DRP]

Ruddick Corp. RDK
2000 Two First Union Center
Charlotte, NC 28282 704-372-5404
Retail - supermarkets

Russ Berrie & Co., Inc. RUS
111 Bauer Dr.
Oakland, NJ 07436 201-337-9000
Drugs & sundries - wholesale O

Russell Corp. RML
1 Lee St.
Alexander City, AL 35010 205-329-4000
Textiles - apparel O
[DRP]

Rust International Inc. RST
100 Corporate Parkway
Birmingham, AL 35242 205-995-7878
Engineering - R & D services

Ryder System, Inc. R
3600 N.W. 82nd Ave.
Miami, FL 33166 305-593-3726
Leasing O [DRP]

Rykoff-Sexton, Inc. RYK
761 Terminal St.
Los Angeles, CA 90021 213-622-4131
Food - wholesale [DRP]

Rymer Foods, Inc. RYR
4600 S. Packers Ave., Ste. 400
Chicago, IL 60609 312-927-7777
Food - misc.

Sabine Royalty Trust SBR
901 Main St., 12th Fl.
Dallas, TX 75202 214-508-2400
Oil & gas - US royalty trust

SafeCard Services, Inc. SSI
3001 E. Pershing Blvd.
Cheyenne, WY 82001 307-771-2700
Financial - business services O

Safeguard Scientifics, Inc. SFE
435 Devon Park Dr.
Wayne, PA 19087 610-293-0600
Financial - investment bankers

Safety-Kleen Corp. SK
1000 N. Randall Rd.
Elgin, IL 60123 708-697-8460
Pollution control equipment & services O
[DRP]

Safeway Inc. SWY
Fourth and Jackson Sts.
Oakland, CA 94660 510-891-3000
Retail - supermarkets O

Salant Corp. SLT
1114 Avenue of the Americas
New York, NY 10036 212-221-7500
Textiles - apparel

Salomon Brothers High Income Fund Inc. HIF
Seven World Trade Center
New York, NY 10048 800-221-7065
Financial - investment management

Salomon Brothers Worldwide Income
Fund, Inc. SBW
Seven World Trade Center
New York, NY 10048 800-221-7065
Financial - investment management

Salomon Inc. SB
Seven World Trade Center
New York, NY 10048 212-783-7000
Financial - investment bankers [DRP]

San Diego Gas & Electric Co. SDO
101 Ash St.
San Diego, CA 92101 619-696-2000
Utility - electric power [DRP]

San Juan Basin Royalty Trust SJT
PO Box 2604
Fort Worth, TX 76113 817-884-4630
Oil & gas - US royalty trust

Sanifill, Inc. FIL
1225 N. Loop West, Ste. 550
Houston, TX 77008 713-865-9800
Pollution control equipment & services

Santa Anita Realty Enterprises, Inc. SAR
333 City Blvd. West, Ste. 2100
Orange, CA 92668 714-721-2700
Real estate investment trust

Santa Fe Energy Resources, Inc. SFR
1616 S. Voss, Ste. 1000
Houston, TX 77057 713-783-2401
Oil & gas - US exploration & production O

Santa Fe Energy Trust SFF
600 Travis St., Ste. 1150
Houston, TX 77002 713-216-5100
Oil & gas - US royalty trust

Santa Fe Pacific Corp. SFX
1700 E. Golf Rd.
Shaumburg, IL 60173 708-995-6000
Transportation - rail O

Santa Fe Pacific Gold Corp. GLD
6200 Uptown Blvd. NE, Ste. 400
Albuquerque, NM 87110 505-880-5300
Gold mining & processing O

Santa Fe Pacific Pipeline Partners, L.P. SFL
888 S. Figueroa St.
Los Angeles, CA 90017 213-614-1095
Oil & gas - production & pipeline

Sara Lee Corp. SLE
Three First National Plaza
Chicago, IL 60602 312-726-2600
Diversified operations O
[DRP]

Saul Centers, Inc. BFS
8401 Connecticut Ave.
Chevy Chase, MD 20815 301-986-6000
Real estate investment trust

Savannah Foods & Industries, Inc. SFI
PO Box 339
Savannah, GA 31402 912-234-1261
Food - sugar & refining
[DRP]

Sbarro, Inc. SBA
763 Larkfield Rd.
Commack, NY 11725 516-864-0200
Retail - food & restaurants O

SCANA Corp. SCG
1426 Main St.
Columbia, SC 29201 803-748-3000
Utility - electric power [DRP]

SCEcorp SCE
2244 Walnut Grove Ave.
Rosemead, CA 91770 818-302-2222
Utility - electric power O [DRP]

Schering-Plough Corp. SGP
One Giralda Farms
Madison, NJ 07940 201-822-7000
Drugs O [DRP]

Schlumberger Ltd. SLB
277 Park Ave.
New York, NY 10172 212-350-9400
Oil & gas - field services O

Schroder Asian Growth Fund, Inc. SHF
787 Seventh Ave., 29th Fl.
New York, NY 10019 800-688-0928
Financial - investment management

Schwab (Charles) Corp. SCH
101 Montgomery St.
San Francisco, CA 94104 415-627-7000
Financial - investment bankers O [DRP]

Schwitzer, Inc. SCZ
Highway 191, Brevard Rd.
Asheville, NC 28813 704-684-4102
Automotive & trucking - original equipment

Scientific-Atlanta, Inc. SFA
One Technology Parkway, South
Atlanta, GA 30092 404-903-5000
Telecommunications equipment O [DRP]

SCOR U.S. Corp. SUR
110 William St.
New York, NY 10038 212-978-8200
Insurance - property & casualty

Scotsman Industries, Inc. SCT
775 Corporate Woods Parkway
Vernon Hills, IL 60061 708-215-4500
Building products - a/c & heating

Scott Paper Co. SPP
Scott Plaza
Philadelphia, PA 19113 215-522-5000
Paper & paper products O [DRP]

Scott's Liquid Gold-Inc. SGD
4880 Havana St., PO Box 39-S
Denver, CO 80239 303-373-4860
Diversified operations

Scudder New Asia Fund, Inc. SAF
345 Park Ave.
New York, NY 10154 800-349-4281
Financial - investment management [DRP 5%]

Scudder New Europe Fund, Inc. NEF
345 Park Ave.
New York, NY 10154 800-349-4281
Financial - investment management
[DRP 5%]

Scudder World Income Opportunities Fund,
Inc. SWI
345 Park Ave.
New York, NY 10154 800-349-4281
Financial - investment management [DRP 5%]

Seagate Technology, Inc. SEG
920 Disc Dr.
Scotts Valley, CA 95066 408-438-6550
Computers - peripheral equipment O

Seagull Energy Corp. SGO
1001 Fannin St., Ste. 1700
Houston, TX 77002 713-951-4700
Oil & gas - production & pipeline O

Sealed Air Corp. SEE
Park 80 East
Saddle Brook, NJ 07662 201-791-7600
Containers - paper & plastic

Sears, Roebuck and Co. S
Sears Tower
Chicago, IL 60684 312-875-2500
Diversified operations O
[DRP]

Security Capital Industrial Trust SCN
3200 Cherry Creek South Dr.
Denver, CO 80209 303-777-0121
Real estate investment trust

Security-Connecticut Corp. SRC
20 Security Dr.
Avon, CT 06001 203-677-8621
Insurance - life

Seitel, Inc. SEI
50 Briar Hollow Ln. West
Houston, TX 77027 713-627-1990
Oil & gas - field services O

Seligman Quality Municipal Fund,
Inc. SQF
100 Park Ave.
New York, NY 10017 212-850-1864
Financial - investment management

Seligman Select Municipal Fund, Inc. SEL
100 Park Ave.
New York, NY 10017 212-850-1864
Financial - investment management

Senior High Income Portfolio II, Inc. SAL
PO Box 9011
Princeton, NJ 08543 609-282-2800
Financial - investment management

Senior High Income Portfolio, Inc. ARK
800 Scudders Mill Rd.
Plainsboro, NJ 08536 609-282-2800
Financial - investment management

Senior Strategic Income Fund, Inc. SSN
800 Scudders Mill Rd.
Plainsboro, NJ 08536 609-282-2800
Financial - investment management

Sensormatic Electronics Corp. SRM
500 N.W. 12th Ave.
Deerfield Beach, FL 33442 305-420-2000
Protection - safety equipment & services O

Sequa Corp. SQAA
200 Park Ave.
New York, NY 10166 212-986-5500
Chemicals - specialty

Service Corporation International SRV
1929 Allen Parkway
Houston, TX 77019 713-522-5141
Funeral & services related O

Service Merchandise Co., Inc. SME
7100 Service Merchandise Dr.
Brentwood, TN 37027 615-660-6000
Retail - catalog showrooms O

ServiceMaster L.P. SVM
One ServiceMaster Way
Downers Grove, IL 60515 708-271-1300
Building - maintenance & services
[DRP]

Shaw Industries, Inc. SHX
PO Drawer 02128
Dalton, GA 30722 706-278-3812
Textiles - home furnishings O

Shawmut National Corp. SNC
777 Main St.
Hartford, CT 06115 203-728-2000
Banks - northeast O
[DRP 3%]

Shelby Williams Industries, Inc. SY
1348 Merchandise Mart
Chicago, IL 60654 312-527-3593
Furniture O

Sherwin-Williams Co. SHW
101 Prospect Ave., N.W.
Cleveland, OH 44115 216-566-2000
Paints & allied products O [DRP]

Shoney's, Inc. SHN
1727 Elm Hill Pike
Nashville, TN 37210 615-391-5201
Retail - food & restaurants

ShopKo Stores, Inc. SKO
700 Pilgrim Way, PO Box 19060
Green Bay, WI 54307 414-497-2211
Retail - regional department stores O

Showboat, Inc. SBO
2800 Fremont St.
Las Vegas, NV 89104 702-385-9141
Leisure & recreational services O

Sierra Health Services, Inc. SIE
2724 N. Tenaya Way
Las Vegas, NV 89128 702-242-7000
Health maintenance organization

Sierra Pacific Resources SRP
6100 Neil Rd., PO Box 30150
Reno, NV 89520 702-689-3600
Utility - electric power [DRP]

Signal Apparel Co., Inc. SIA
537 Market St., Ste. 403
Chattanooga, TN 37402 615-752-2032
Textiles - apparel

Signet Banking Corp. SBK
7 N. Eighth St.
Richmond, VA 23219 804-747-2000
Banks - southeast O [DRP 5%]

Silicon Graphics, Inc. SGI
2011 N. Shoreline Blvd.
Mountain View, CA 94039 415-960-1980
Computers - graphics O

Simon Property Group, Inc. SPG
115 W. Washington St.
Indianapolis, IN 46204 317-636-1600
Real estate investment trust O

Sinter Metals, Inc. SNM
50 Public Square, Ste. 3200
Cleveland, OH 44113 216-771-6700
Metal products - fabrication

Sithe Energies, Inc. SYT
450 Lexington Ave.
New York, NY 10017 212-450-9000
Energy - cogeneration

Sizeler Property Investors, Inc. SIZ
2542 Williams Blvd.
Kenner, LA 70062 504-466-5363
Real estate investment trust [DRP]

Sizzler International, Inc. SZ
12655 W. Jefferson Blvd.
Los Angeles, CA 90066 310-827-2300
Retail - food & restaurants

Skyline Corp. SKY
2520 By-Pass Rd., PO Box 743
Elkhart, IN 46515 219-294-6521
Building - mobile homes & RV O

SL Industries, Inc. SL
520 Fellowship Rd., Ste. 306
Mt. Laurel, NJ 08054 609-727-1500
Electrical products - misc.

Smart & Final Inc. SMF
4700 S. Boyle Ave.
Los Angeles, CA 90058 213-589-1054
Retail - supermarkets

Smith (A.O.) Corp. SMC
PO Box 23972
Milwaukee, WI 53223 414-359-4000
Automotive & trucking - original equipment
[DRP]

Smith Barney High Inc. Opportunity Fund,
Inc. HIO
1345 Avenue of the Americas
New York, NY 10105 212-698-5349
Financial - investment management

Smith Corona Corp. SCO
65 Locust Ave.
New Canaan, CT 06840 203-972-1471
Office equipment & supplies O

Smith International, Inc. SII
16740 Hardy St.
Houston, TX 77032 713-443-3370
Oil field machinery & equipment O

Smith's Food & Drug Centers, Inc. SFD
1550 S. Redwood Rd.
Salt Lake City, UT 84104 801-974-1400
Retail - supermarkets O

Smucker (J.M.) Co. SJMA
Strawberry Ln.
Orrville, OH 44667 216-682-3000
Food - confectionery [DRP]

Snap-on, Inc. SNA
2801 - 80th St.
Kenosha, WI 53141 414-656-5200
Tools - hand held O [DRP]

Snyder Oil Corp. SNY
777 Main St.
Fort Worth, TX 76102 817-338-4043
Oil & gas - US exploration & production O

Society Corp. SCY
127 Public Square
Cleveland, OH 44114 216-689-3000
Banks - midwest

Sofamor Danek Group, Inc. SDG
3092 Directors Row
Memphis, TN 38131 901-396-2695
Medical products O

Solectron Corp. SLR
777 Gibraltar Dr.
Milpitas, CA 95035 408-957-8500
Electrical components - misc. O

Sonat Inc. SNT
AmSouth-Sonat Tower
Birmingham, AL 35203 205-325-3800
Oil & gas - production & pipeline O
[DRP]

Sonat Offshore Drilling Inc. RIG
4 Greenway Plaza
Houston, TX 77046 713-871-7500
Oil & gas - offshore drilling O

Sotheby's Holdings, Inc. BID
1334 York Ave.
New York, NY 10021 212-606-7000
Retail - misc. [DRP]

Source Capital, Inc. SOR
11400 W. Olympic Blvd.
Los Angeles, CA 90064 310-473-0225
Financial - investment management

South Jersey Industries, Inc. SJI
Number One South Jersey Plaza
Folsom, NJ 08037 609-561-9000
Utility - gas distribution
[DRP 3%]

Southdown, Inc. SDW
1200 Smith St., Ste. 2400
Houston, TX 77002 713-650-6200
Construction - cement & concrete

Southern California Water Co. SCW
630 E. Foothill Blvd.
San Dimas, CA 91773 909-394-3600
Utility - water supply [DRP]

Southern Co. SO
64 Perimeter Center East
Atlanta, GA 30346 404-393-0650
Utility - electric power O [DRP]

Southern Indiana Gas and Electric Co. SIG
20 N.W. Fourth St.
Evansville, IN 47741 812-465-5300
Utility - electric power [DRP]

Southern National Corp. SNB
500 N. Chestnut St.
Lumberton, NC 28358 910-671-2000
Banks - southeast [DRP]

Southern New England Telecommunications
 Corp. SNG
227 Church St.
New Haven, CT 06510 203-771-5200
Utility - telephone [DRP]

Southern Pacific Rail Corp. RSP
One Market Plaza
San Francisco, CA 94105 415-541-1000
Transportation - rail O

Southwest Airlines Co. LUV
PO Box 36611
Dallas, TX 75235 214-904-4000
Transportation - airline O

Southwest Gas Corp. SWX
5241 Spring Mountain Rd.
Las Vegas, NV 89102 702-876-7237
Utility - gas distribution
[DRP]

Southwestern Bell Corp. SBC
175 E. Houston, PO Box 2933
San Antonio, TX 78299 210-821-4105
Utility - telephone O [DRP]

Southwestern Energy Co. SWN
1083 Sain St., PO Box 1408
Fayetteville, AR 72702 501-521-1141
Utility - gas distribution [DRP]

Southwestern Property Trust, Inc. SWP
5949 Sherry Ln., Ste. 1435
Dallas, TX 75225 214-369-1995
Real estate investment trust

Southwestern Public Service Co. SPS
Tyler at Sixth
Amarillo, TX 79101 806-378-02121
Utility - electric power [DRP]

Spaghetti Warehouse, Inc. SWH
402 West I-30
Garland, TX 75043 214-226-6000
Retail - food & restaurants

Spain Fund SNF
1345 Avenue of the Americas
New York, NY 10105 212-969-1000
Financial - investment management

SPARTECH Corp. SEH
7777 Bonhomme, Ste. 1001
Clayton, MO 63105 314-721-4242
Rubber & plastic products

Sparton Corp. SPA
2400 E. Ganson St.
Jackson, MI 49202 517-787-8600
Electronics - military

Spelling Entertainment Group Inc. SP
One E. Fourth St.
Cincinnati, OH 45202 513-579-2482
Leisure & recreational products

Spieker Properties, Inc. SPK
2180 Sand Hill Rd.
Menlo Park, CA 94025
415-854-5600
Real estate investment trust

Sport Supply Group, Inc. GYM
1901 Diplomat
Dallas, TX 75234 214-484-9484
Leisure & recreational products

Sports & Recreation, Inc. WON
4701 W. Hillsborough Ave.
Tampa, FL 33614 813-886-9688
Retail - misc. O

Springs Industries, Inc. SMI
205 N. White St., PO Box 70
Fort Mill, SC 29715 803-547-1500
Textiles - home furnishings

Sprint Corp. FON
PO Box 11315
Kansas City, KS 64112 913-676-3000
Utility - telephone O [DRP]

SPS Technologies, Inc. ST
101 Greenwood Ave., Ste. 470
Jenkintown, PA 19046 215-517-2000
Metal products - fasteners

SPS Transaction Services, Inc. PAY
2500 Lake Cook Rd.
Riverwoods, IL 60015 708-405-3400
Business services

SPX Corp. SPW
700 Terrace Point Dr.
Muskegon, MI 49443 616-724-5000
Automotive & trucking - original equipment
O [DRP]

St. Joe Paper Co. SJP
1650 Prudential Dr., Suite 400
Jacksonville, FL 32207 904-396-6600
Paper & paper products

St. John's Knits, Inc. SJK
17422 Derian Ave.
Irvine, CA 92713 714-863-1171
Apparel

St. Joseph Light & Power Co. SAJ
520 Francis St., PO Box 998
St. Joseph, MO 64502 816-233-8888
Utility - electric power
[DRP]

St. Paul Companies, Inc. SPC
385 Washington St.
St. Paul, MN 55102 612-221-7911
Insurance - property & casualty O [DRP]

Standard Brands Paint Co. SBP
4300 W. 190th St.
Torrance, CA 90509 310-214-2411
Building products - retail & wholesale

Standard Commercial Corp. STW
2201 Miller Rd.
Wilson, NC 27893 919-291-5507
Tobacco [DRP]

Standard Federal Bank SFB
2600 W. Big Beaver Rd.
Troy, MI 48084 313-643-9600
Financial - savings and loans

Standard Motor Products, Inc. SMP
37-18 Northern Blvd.
Long Island City, NY 11101 718-392-0200
Automotive & trucking - replacement parts

Standard Pacific Corp. SPF
1565 W. MacArthur Blvd.
Costa Mesa, CA 92626 714-668-4300
Building - residential & commercial

Standard Products Co. SPD
2130 W. 110th St.
Cleveland, OH 44102 216-281-8300
Automotive & trucking - original equipment
[DRP]

Standex International Corp. SXI
6 Manor Pkwy.
Salem, NH 03079 603-893-9701
Diversified operations

Stanhome Inc. STH
333 Western Ave.
Westfield, MA 01085 413-562-3631
Retail - mail order & direct O [DRP]

Stanley Works SWK
1000 Stanley Dr.
New Britain, CT 06053 203-225-5111
Tools - hand held O [DRP]

Star Banc Corp. STB
425 Walnut St.
Cincinnati, OH 45202 513-632-4000
Banks - midwest [DRP]

Starter Corp. STA
370 James St.
New Haven, CT 06513
203-781-4000
Apparel O

Sterile Concepts Holding, Inc. SYS
5100 Commerce Rd.
Richmond, VA 23234 804-275-0200
Medical & dental supplies

Sterling Bancorp STL
540 Madison Ave.
New York, NY 10022 212-826-8000
Banks - northeast

Sterling Chemicals, Inc. STX
1200 Smith St., Ste. 1900
Houston, TX 77002 713-650-3700
Chemicals - diversified O

Sterling Electronics Corp. SEC
4201 Southwest Freeway
Houston, TX 77027 713-627-9800
Electrical components - misc.

Sterling Software, Inc. SSW
8080 N. Central Expwy.
Dallas, TX 75206 214-891-8600
Computers - software O

Stewart Information Services Corp. STC
1980 Post Oak Blvd.
Houston, TX 77056 713-625-8100
Financial - business services

Stifel Financial Corp. SF
500 N. Broadway
St. Louis, MO 63102 314-342-2000
Financial - business services

Stone & Webster, Inc. SW
250 W. 34th St.
New York, NY 10119 212-290-7500
Construction - heavy
[DRP]

Stone Container Corp. STO
150 N. Michigan Ave.
Chicago, IL 60601 312-346-6600
Containers - paper & plastic O

Stone Energy Corp. SGY
625 E. Kaliste Saloom Rd.
Lafayette, LA 70508 318-237-0410
Oil & gas - US exploration & production

Storage Equities, Inc. SEQ
600 N. Brand Blvd.
Glendale, CA 91203 818-244-8080
Real estate investment trust

Storage Technology Corp. STK
2270 S. 88th St.
Louisville, CO 80028 303-673-5151
Computers - peripheral equipment O

Storage USA, Inc. SUS
10 Corporate Center, Ste. 400
Columbia, MD 21044 410-730-9500
Real estate investment trust

Strategic Global Income Fund, Inc. SGL
1285 Avenue of the Americas
New York, NY 10019 212-713-2000
Financial - investment management

Stratus Computer, Inc. SRA
55 Fairbanks Blvd.
Marlborough, MA 01752 508-460-2000
Computers - mini & micro O

Stride Rite Corp. SRR
Five Cambridge Center
Cambridge, MA 02142 617-491-8800
Shoes & related apparel O [DRP]

Student Loan Marketing Association SLM
1050 Thomas Jefferson St., NW
Washington, DC 20007 202-333-8000
Financial - consumer loans O

Sturm, Ruger & Co., Inc. RGR
Lacey Place
Southport, CT 06490 203-259-7843
Leisure & recreational products

Suave Shoe Corp. SWV
14100 N.W. 60th Ave.
Miami Lakes, FL 33014 305-822-7880
Shoes & related apparel

Summit Properties, Inc. SMT
212 S. Tryon St., Ste. 500
Charlotte, NC 28281 704-334-9905
Real estate investment trust

Sun Coast Industries, Inc. SN
2700 S. Westmoreland Ave.
Dallas, TX 75233 214-373-7864
Miscellaneous - not elsewhere classified

Sun Communities, Inc. SUI
31700 Middlebelt Rd., Ste. 145
Farmington Hills, MI 48334
313-932-3100
Real estate development

Sun Company, Inc. SUN
1801 Market St.
Philadelphia, PA 19103 215-977-3000
Oil refining & marketing O [DRP]

Sun Distributors L.P. SDP
One Logan Square
Philadelphia, PA 19103 215-665-3650
Auto parts - retail & wholesale

Sun Energy Partners, L.P. SLP
13155 Noel Rd.
Dallas, TX 75240 214-715-4000
Oil & gas - US exploration & production

Sun Healthcare Group, Inc. SHG
5131 Masthead St. NE
Albuquerque, NM 87109 505-821-3355
Insurance - accident & health O

SunAmerica, Inc. SAI
1 SunAmerica Center
Los Angeles, CA 90067 310-772-6000
Insurance - life O

Sunbeam-Oster Co., Inc. SOC
200 New River Center
Fort Lauderdale, FL 33301 305-767-2100
Appliances - household O

Sundstrand Corp. SNS
4949 Harrison Ave.
Rockford, IL 61125 815-226-6000
Aerospace - aircraft equipment O
[DRP]

Sunrise Medical Inc. SMD
2355 Crenshaw Blvd., Ste. 150
Torrance, CA 90501 310-328-8018
Medical & dental supplies O

Sunshine Mining and Refining Co. SSC
815 Park Blvd., Ste. 100
Boise, ID 83712 208-345-0660
Silver mining & processing

SunTrust Banks, Inc. STI
25 Park Place, N.E.
Atlanta, GA 30303 404-588-7711
Banks - southeast O [DRP]

Super Food Services, Inc. SFS
3233 Newmark Dr.
Miamisburg, OH 45342 513-439-7500
Food - wholesale

Superior Industries International, Inc. SUP
7800 Woodley Ave.
Van Nuys, CA 91406 818-781-4973
Automotive & trucking - original equipment
O

SUPERVALU Inc. SVU
11840 Valley View Rd.
Eden Prairie, MN 55344 612-828-4000
Food - wholesale O

Surgical Care Affiliates, Inc. SCA
102 Woodmont Blvd., Ste. 610
Nashville, TN 37205 615-385-3541
Healthcare - outpatient & home O

Swift Energy Co. SFY
16825 Northchase Dr., Ste. 400
Houston, TX 77060 713-874-2700
Oil & gas - US exploration & production

Sybron International Corp. SYB
411 E. Wisconsin Ave.
Milwaukee, WI 53202 414-274-6600
Medical & dental supplies

Symbol Technologies, Inc. SBL
116 Wilbur Place
Bohemia, NY 11716 516-563-2400
Optical character recognition O

Syms Corp. SYM
Syms Way
Secaucus, NJ 07094
201-902-9600
Retail - apparel & shoes

Synovus Financial Corp. SNV
901 Front Ave., Ste. 301
Columbus, GA 31901 706-649-2311
Banks - southeast [DRP]

Syntex Corp. SYN
3401 Hillview Ave.
Palo Alto, CA 94304 415-855-5050
Drugs

Syratech Corp. SYR
175 McClellan Hwy.
East Boston, MA 02128 617-561-2200
Housewares

Sysco Corp. SYY
1390 Enclave Pkwy.
Houston, TX 77077 713-584-1390
Food - wholesale O [DRP]

T2 Medical, Inc. TSQ
1121 Alderman Dr.
Alphretta, GA 30202 404-442-2160
Healthcare - outpatient & home

Taiwan Fund, Inc. TWN
82 Devonshire St.
Boston, MA 02109 800-334-9393
Financial - investment management

Talley Industries, Inc. TAL
2702 N. 44th St.
Phoenix, AZ 85008 602-957-7711
Diversified operations [DRP]

Tambrands Inc. TMB
777 Westchester Ave.
White Plains, NY 10604 914-696-6000
Medical & dental supplies O
[DRP]

Tandem Computers Inc. TDM
19333 Vallco Pkwy.
Cupertino, CA 95014 408-725-6000
Computers - mini & micro O

Tandy Corp. TAN
1800 One Tandy Center
Fort Worth, TX 76102 817-390-3700
Computers - retail & wholesale O

Tandycrafts, Inc. TAC
1400 Everman Parkway
Fort Worth, TX 76140 817-551-9600
Retail - misc.

Tanger Factory Outlet Centers, Inc. SKT
1400 W. Northwood St.
Greensboro, NC 27408 910-274-1666
Retail - misc.

Taubman Centers, Inc. TCO
200 E. Long Lake Rd.
Bloomfield Hills, MI 48304
810-258-6800
Real estate operations O

Taurus MuniCalifornia Holdings, Inc. MCF
PO Box 9011
Princeton, NJ 08543 609-282-2800
Financial - investment management

Taurus MuniNew York Holdings, Inc. MNY
PO Box 9011
Princeton, NJ 08543 609-282-2800
Financial - investment management

TCBY Enterprises, Inc. TBY
425 W. Capitol Ave., Ste. 1100
Little Rock, AR 72201 501-688-8229
Retail - food & restaurants O

TCC Industries, Inc. TEL
1545 W. Mockingbird Ln.
Dallas, TX 75235 214-638-0638
Diversified operations

TCF Financial Corp. TCB
801 Marquette Ave., Ste. 302
Minneapolis, MN 55402 612-661-6500
Banks - midwest [DRP]

TCW Convertible Securities Fund, Inc. CVT
865 S. Figueroa St.
Los Angeles, CA 90017 213-244-0000
Financial - investment management

TCW/DW Emerging Markets Opportunities
Trust EMD
Two World Trade Center
New York, NY 10048 212-392-1600
Financial - investment management

TCW/DW Term Trust 2000 TDT
Two World Trade Center
New York, NY 10048 212-392-1600
Financial - investment management

TCW/DW Term Trust 2002 TRM
Two World Trade Center
New York, NY 10048 212-392-1600
Financial - investment management

TCW/DW Term Trust 2003 TMT
Two World Trade Center
New York, NY 10048 212-392-1600
Financial - investment management

Tech-Sym Corp. TSY
10500 Westoffice Dr., Ste. 200
Houston, TX 77042 713-785-7790
Electronics - military

TECO Energy, Inc. TE
702 N. Franklin St.
Tampa, FL 33602 813-228-4111
Utility - electric power [DRP]

Tejas Gas Corp. TEJ
1301 McKinney St., Ste. 700
Houston, TX 77010 713-658-0509
Oil & gas - production & pipeline

Tektronix, Inc. TEK
26600 SW Parkway
Wilsonville, OR 97070 503-627-7111
Electronics - measuring instruments O

Teledyne, Inc. TDY
1901 Avenue of the Stars
Los Angeles, CA 90067
310-277-3311
Diversified operations O

Teleflex Inc. TFX
630 W. Germantown Pike
Plymouth Meeting, PA 19462
610-834-6301
Instruments - control

Temple-Inland Inc. TIN
303 S. Temple Dr.
Diboll, TX 75941 409-829-2211
Paper & paper products O
[DRP]

Templeton China World Fund, Inc. TCH
700 Central Ave.
St. Petersburg, FL 33701 813-823-8712
Financial - investment management

Templeton Dragon Fund, Inc. TDF
700 Central Ave.
St. Petersburg, FL 33701 813-823-8712
Financial - investment management

Templeton Emerging Markets Appreciation
Fund TEA
700 Central Ave.
St. Petersburg, FL 33701 813-823-8712
Financial - investment management

Templeton Emerging Markets Fund, Inc. EMF
700 Central Ave.
St. Petersburg, FL 33701 813-823-8712
Financial - investment management

Templeton Emerging Markets Income Fund,
Inc. TEI
700 Central Ave.
St. Petersburg, FL 33701 813-823-8712
Financial - investment management

Templeton Global Governments Income
Trust TGG
700 Central Ave.
St. Petersburg, FL 33701 813-823-8712
Financial - investment management

Templeton Global Income Fund, Inc. GIM
700 Central Ave.
St. Petersburg, FL 33701 813-823-8712
Financial - investment management

Templeton Vietnam Opportunies Fund, Inc.
  TVF
700 Central Ave.
St. Petersburg, FL 33701 813-823-8712
Financial - investment management

Tenneco Inc. TGT
Tenneco Building, PO Box 2511
Houston, TX 77252 713-757-2131
Diversified operations O [DRP 3%]

TEPPCO Partners, L.P. TPP
2929 Allen Pkwy., PO Box 2521
Houston, TX 77252 713-759-3131
Miscellaneous - not elsewhere classified

Teradyne, Inc. TER
321 Harrison Ave.
Boston, MA 02118 617-482-2700
Electronics - measuring instruments O

Terex Corp. TEX
500 Post Rd. East
Westport, CT 06880 203-222-7170
Machinery - construction & mining

Terra Industries Inc. TRA
600 Fourth St., PO Box 6000
Sioux City, IA 51102 712-277-1340
Diversified operations O

Terra Nitrogen Co., L.P TNH
5100 E. Skelly Dr., Ste. 800
Tulsa, OK 74135 918-660-0050
Fertilizers

Tesoro Petroleum Corp. TSO
8700 Tesoro Dr.
San Antonio, TX 78217 210-828-8484
Oil refining & marketing O

Texaco Inc. TX
2000 Westchester Ave.
White Plains, NY 10650 914-253-4000
Oil & gas - international integrated O [DRP]

Texas Industries, Inc. TXI
7610 Stemmons Freeway
Dallas, TX 75247 214-647-6700
Diversified operations O

Texas Instruments Inc. TXN
13500 N. Central Expressway
Dallas, TX 75265 214-995-02551
Electrical components - semiconductors
  [DRP]

Texas Pacific Land Trust TPL
80 Broad St.
New York, NY 10004 212-269-2266
Real estate operations

Texas Utilities Co. TXU
2001 Bryan Tower
Dallas, TX 75201 214-812-4600
Utility - electric power O [DRP]

Texfi Industries, Inc. TXF
5400 Glenwood Ave., Ste. 318
Raleigh, NC 27612 919-783-4736
Textiles - mill products

Textron Inc. TXT
40 Westminster St.
Providence, RI 02903 401-421-2800
Diversified operations O
  [DRP]

Thackeray Corp. THK
400 Madison Ave., Ste. 1508
New York, NY 10017 212-759-3695
Diversified operations

Thai Capital Fund, Inc. TC
800 Scudders Mill Rd.
Plainsboro, NJ 08536 212-449-4600
Financial - investment management

The Actava Group Inc. ACT
4900 Georgia-Pacific Center
Atlanta, GA 30303 404-658-9000
Diversified operations O

The Advest Group, Inc. ADV
280 Trumbull St.
Hartford, CT 06103 203-525-1421
Financial - investment bankers

The Allen Group Inc. ALN
25101 Chagrin Blvd., Ste. 350
Beachwood, OH 44122 216-765-5800
Automotive & trucking - original equipment O

The Allstate Corp. ALL
Allstate Plaza
Northbrook, IL 60062 708-402-5000
Insurance - multi line & misc. O

The Americas Income Trust, Inc. XUS
222 S. Ninth St.
Minneapolis, MN 55402 800-866-7778
Financial - investment management

The Argentina Fund, Inc. AF
345 Park Ave.
New York, NY 10154 212-326-6200
Financial - investment management

The Asia Tigers Fund, Inc. GRR
200 Liberty St., 38th Fl.
New York, NY 10281 800-421-4777
Financial - investment management

The Austria Fund, Inc. OST
1345 Avenue of the Americas
New York, NY 10105 800-247-4154
Financial - investment management
  [DRP 5%]

The B.F. Goodrich Co. GR
3925 Embassy Parkway
Akron, OH 44333 216-374-3985
Chemicals - diversified O

The Bear Stearns Companies Inc. BSC
245 Park Ave.
New York, NY 10167 212-272-2000
Financial - investment bankers O

The Boeing Co. BA
7755 E. Marginal Way South
Seattle, WA 98108 206-655-02121
Aerospace - aircraft equipment O

The Bombay Company, Inc. BBA
550 Bailey Ave., Ste. 700
Fort Worth, TX 76107
817-347-8200
Retail - home furnishings O

The Brazil Fund, Inc. BZF
345 Park Ave.
New York, NY 10154 800-349-4281
Financial - investment management

The Brazilian Equity Fund, Inc. BZL
153 E. 53rd St., 58th Fl.
New York, NY 10022 212-832-2626
Financial - investment management

The Caldor Corp. CLD
20 Glover Ave.
Norwalk, CT 06856 203-846-1641
Retail - discount & variety O

The Chile Fund, Inc. CH
153 E. 53rd St.
New York, NY 10022 212-832-2626
Financial - investment management

The China Fund, Inc. CHN
250 Park Ave.
New York, NY 10177 800-421-4777
Financial - investment management

The Cleveland Electric Illuminating Co.
CVXp
55 Public Square
Cleveland, OH 44113 216-622-9800
Utility - electric power

The Coastal Corp. CGP
Nine Greenway Plaza
Houston, TX 77046 713-877-1400
Oil & gas - production & pipeline O

The Continental Corp. CIC
180 Maiden Ln.
New York, NY 10038 212-440-3000
Insurance - property & casualty O

The Continuum Co., Inc. CNU
9500 Arboretum Blvd.
Austin, TX 78759 512-345-5700
Computers - services

The Cooper Companies, Inc. COO
One Bridge Plaza, 6th Fl.
Fort Lee, NJ 07024 201-585-5100
Medical & dental supplies

The Czech Republic Fund, Inc. CRF
200 Liberty St., 38th Fl.
New York, NY 10281 800-421-4777
Financial - investment management

The Detroit Edison Co. DTE
2000 Second Ave.
Detroit, MI 48226 313-237-8000
Utility - electric power O

The Dexter Corp. DEX
One Elm St.
Windsor Locks, CT 06096
203-627-9051
Chemicals - specialty O

The Dun & Bradstreet Corp. DNB
200 Nyala Farms
Westport, CT 06880 203-222-4200
Financial - business services O

The E. W. Scripps Co. SSP
1105 N. Market St.
Wilmington, DE 19801 302-478-4141
Publishing - newspapers

The Emerging Germany Fund, Inc. FRG
One Battery Park Plaza
New York, NY 10004 212-363-5100
Financial - investment management

The Emerging Markets Income Fund II Inc.
EDF
7 World Trade Center
New York, NY 10048 212-783-1301
Financial - investment management

The Emerging Mexico Fund, Inc. MEF
1285 Avenue of the Americas
New York, NY 10019 212-713-2000
Financial - investment management

The Empire District Electric Co. EDE
602 Joplin St.
Joplin, MO 64801 417-623-4700
Utility - electric power

The Equitable Cos., Inc. EQ
787 Seventh Ave.
New York, NY 10019 212-554-1234
Insurance - life O

The Europe Fund, Inc. EF
780 Third Ave.
New York, NY 10017 212-751-8340
Financial - investment management

The First American Financial Corp. FAF
114 E. Fifth St.
Santa Ana, CA 92701 714-558-3211
Financial - mortgages & related services

The First Philippine Fund Inc. FPF
152 W. 57th St., 25th Fl.
New York, NY 10019 212-765-0700
Financial - investment management

The Foothill Group, Inc. FGI
11111 Santa Monica Blvd.
Los Angeles, CA 90025 310-996-7000
Financial - SBIC & commercial

The France Growth Fund, Inc. FRF
1285 Avenue of the Americas
New York, NY 10019 212-713-2000
Financial - investment management

The Future Germany Fund, Inc. FGF
31 W. 52nd St.
New York, NY 10019 800-437-6269
Financial - investment management

The Gabelli Equity Trust Inc. GAB
One Corporate Center
Rye, NY 10580 914-921-5100
Real estate investment trust

The Gap, Inc. GPS
One Harrison
San Francisco, CA 94105 415-952-4400
Retail - apparel & shoes O

The Geon Co. GON
6100 Oak Tree Blvd.
Independence, OH 44131 216-447-6000
Chemicals - specialty O

The Germany Fund, Inc. GER
31 W. 52nd St.
New York, NY 10019 800-437-6269
Financial - investment management

The Gillette Co. G
Prudential Tower Building
Boston, MA 02199 617-421-7000
Cosmetics & toiletries O

The Global Health Sciences Fund GHS
7800 E. Union Ave., Ste. 800
Denver, CO 80237 800-528-8765
Financial - investment management

The Global Privatization Fund Inc. GPF
1345 Sixth Ave.
New York, NY 10105 212-969-1000
Financial - investment management

The Goodyear Tire & Rubber Co. GT
1144 E. Market St.
Akron, OH 44316
216-796-2121
Rubber tires O

The Great Atlantic & Pacific Tea Co., Inc.
GAP
2 Paragon Dr.
Montvale, NJ 07645 201-573-9700
Retail - supermarkets O

The Greenbrier Cos., Inc. GBX
1 Centerpointe Dr., Ste. 200
Lake Oswego, OR 97035 503-684-7000
Transportation - equipment & leasing

The Growth Fund of Spain, Inc. GSP
120 S. LaSalle St.
Chicago, IL 60603 800-422-2848
Financial - investment management

The Hallwood Group Inc. HWG
3710 Rawlins St., Ste. 1500
Dallas, TX 75219 214-528-5588
Financial - business services

The Hartford Steam Boiler Inspection & Ins.
Co. HSB
One State St.
Hartford, CT 06102 203-722-1866
Insurance - property & casualty

The He-Ro Group, Ltd. HRG
550 Seventh Ave.
New York, NY 10018 212-840-6047
Apparel

The Hillhaven Corp. HIL
1148 Broadway Plaza
Tacoma, WA 98402 206-572-4901
Nursing homes O

The India Fund Inc. IFN
200 Liberty St., 38th Fl.
New York, NY 10281 800-421-4777
Financial - investment management

The Indonesia Fund, Inc. IF
153 E. 53rd St., 58th Fl.
New York, NY 10022 212-832-2626
Financial - investment management

The Interlake Corp. IK
550 Warrenville Rd.
Lisle, IL 60532 708-852-8800
Machinery - material handling

The John Nuveen Co. JNC
333 W. Wacker Dr.
Chicago, IL 60606 312-917-7700
Financial - investment management

The Korea Fund, Inc. KF
345 Park Ave.
New York, NY 10154 617-330-5602
Financial - investment management

The L. E. Myers Co. Group MYR
2550 W. Golf Rd., Ste. 200
Rolling Meadows, IL 60008
708-290-1891
Construction - heavy

The Latin America Equity Fund, Inc. LAQ
153 E. 53rd St., 58th Fl.
New York, NY 10022 212-832-2626
Financial - investment management

The Liberty Corp. LC
PO Box 789, Wade Hampton Blvd.
Greenville, SC 29602 803-268-8436
Insurance - life

The LTV Corp. LTV
25 W. Prospect Ave.
Cleveland, OH 44115 216-622-5000
Steel - production O

The Macerich Co. MAC
233 Wilshire Blvd., Ste. 700
Santa Monica, CA 90401 310-394-5333
Real estate investment trust

The Marcus Corp. MCS
250 E. Wisconsin Ave.
Milwaukee, WI 53202
414-272-6020
Hotels & motels

The Mexico Fund, Inc. MXF
Wall Steet Plaza
New York, NY 10005 800-224-4134
Financial - investment management

The Mills Corp. MLS
3000 K St., N.W., Ste. 400
Washington, DC 20007 202-965-3600
Real estate investment trust

The Monarch Machine Tool Co. MMO
615 N. Oak St.
Sidney, OH 45365 513-492-4111
Machine tools & related products

The New Germany Fund, Inc. GF
31 W. 52nd St.
New York, NY 10019 800-437-6269
Financial - investment management

The New South Africa Fund, Inc. NSA
245 Park Ave., 13th Fl.
New York, NY 10167 212-272-9027
Financial - investment management

The Newhall Land and Farming Co. NHL
23823 Valencia Blvd.
Valencia, CA 91355 805-255-4000
Agricultural operations

The Pakistan Investment Fund, Inc. PKF
1221 Avenue of the Americas
New York, NY 10020 212-296-7100
Financial - investment management

The Portugal Fund, Inc. PGF
153 E. 53rd St., 58th Fl.
New York, NY 10022 212-832-2626
Financial - investment management

The Presley Companies PDC
19 Corporate Plaza
Newport Beach, CA 92660
714-640-6400
Building - residential & commercial

The Progressive Corp. PGR
6000 Parkland Blvd.
Mayfield Heights, OH 44124
216-464-8000
Insurance - property & casualty O

The Quick & Reilly Group, Inc. BQR
230 S. County Road
Palm Beach, FL 33480 407-655-8000
Financial - business services

The Reader's Digest Association, Inc.
  RDA
Reader's Digest Rd.
Pleasantville, NY 10570 914-238-1000
Publishing - periodicals O

The Ryland Group, Inc. RYL
11000 Broken Land Parkway
Columbia, MD 21044 410-715-7000
Building - residential & commercial O

The Salomon Brothers Fund Inc. SBF
7 World Trade Center
New York, NY 10048 800-221-7065
Financial - investment management

The Singapore Fund, Inc. SGF
One Evertrust Plaza, 9th Fl.
Jersey City, NJ 07302 800-933-3440
Financial - investment management

The Southern Africa Fund, Inc. SOA
1345 Avenue of the Americas
New York, NY 10105 800-247-4154
Financial - investment management

The Stop & Shop Companies, Inc. SHP
PO Box 369
Boston, MA 02101 617-380-8000
Retail - supermarkets O

The Student Loan Corp. STU
99 Garnsey Rd.
Pittsford, NY 14534 716-248-7187
Financial - consumer loans

The Swiss Helvetia Fund, Inc. SWZ
520 Madison Ave.
New York, NY 10022 212-486-4990
Financial - investment management

The Taiwan Equity Fund, Inc. TYW
One Evertrust Plaza, 9th Fl.
Jersey City, NJ 07302 800-933-3440
Financial - investment management

The Talbots, Inc. TLB
175 Beal St.
Hingham, MA 02043 617-749-7600
Retail - apparel & shoes O

The Thai Fund, Inc. TTF
1221 Avenue of the Americas
New York, NY 10020 212-703-4000
Financial - investment management

The Times Mirror Co. TMC
Times Mirror Square
Los Angeles, CA 90053 213-237-3700
Publishing - newspapers O
[DRP]

The TJX Companies, Inc. TJX
770 Cochituate Rd.
Framingham, MA 01701 508-390-1000
Retail - discount & variety O

The Toledo Edison Co. TEDpE
300 Madison Ave.
Toledo, OH 43652 419-249-5000
Utility - electric power

The Town & Country Trust TCT
100 S. Charles St.
Baltimore, MD 21201 410-539-7600
Real estate investment trust

The Travelers Inc. TRV
65 E. 55th St.
New York, NY 10022 212-891-8900
Insurance - property & casualty O

The Union Corp. UCO
492 Route 46 East
Fairfield, NJ 07004 201-808-2747
Financial - business services

The Valspar Corp. VAL
1101 Third St. South
Minneapolis, MN 55415
612-332-7371
Paints & allied products

The Vigoro Corp. VGR
225 N. Michigan Ave.
Chicago, IL 60601 312-819-2020
Fertilizers

The Vons Companies, Inc. VON
618 Michillinda Ave.
Arcadia, CA 91007 818-821-7000
Retail - supermarkets O

The Wackenhut Corp. WAK
1500 San Remo Ave.
Coral Gables, FL 33146 305-666-5656
Protection - safety equipment & services

The Walt Disney Co. DIS
500 S. Buena Vista St.
Burbank, CA 91521 818-560-1000
Leisure & recreational products

The Warnaco Group, Inc. WAC
90 Park Ave.
New York, NY 10016 212-661-1300
Apparel

The Washington Post Co. WPO
1150 15th St., N.W.
Washington, DC 20071 202-334-6000
Publishing - newspapers

The Western Company of North America
WSN
515 Post Oak Blvd., Ste. 1200
Houston, TX 77027 713-629-2600
Oil & gas - field services O

The Williams Companies, Inc. WMB
One Williams Center
Tulsa, OK 74172 918-588-2000
Oil & gas - production & pipeline O

The Wiser Oil Co. WZR
8115 Preston Rd., Ste. 400
Dallas, TX 75225 214-265-0080
Oil & gas - US exploration & production

The Zweig Fund, Inc. ZF
900 Third Ave.
New York, NY 10022 212-755-9860
Financial - investment management

The Zweig Total Return Fund, Inc. ZTR
900 Third Ave.
New York, NY 10022 212-755-9860
Financial - investment management

Thermo Electron Corp. TMO
81 Wyman St., PO Box 9046
Waltham, MA 02254 617-622-1000
Machinery - general industrial O

Thiokol Corp. TKC
2475 Washington Blvd.
Ogden, UT 84401 801-629-2000
Aerospace - aircraft equipment O

Thomas & Betts Corp. TNB
1555 Lynnfield Rd.
Memphis, TN 38119 901-682-7766
Electrical connectors [DRP]

Thomas Industries Inc. TII
4360 Brownsboro Rd., Ste. 300
Louisville, KY 40207 502-893-4600
Building products - lighting fixtures [DRP]

Thor Industries, Inc. THO
419 W. Pike St.
Jackson Center, OH 45334
513-596-6849
Building - mobile homes & RV

Thornburg Mortgage Asset Corp. TMA
119 E. Marcy St., Ste. 201
Santa Fe, NM 87501 505-989-1900
Real estate investment trust

Tidewater Inc. TDW
1440 Canal St.
New Orleans, LA 70112 504-568-1010
Oil & gas - offshore drilling O [DRP]

Tiffany & Co. TIF
727 Fifth Ave.
New York, NY 10022 212-755-8000
Retail - jewelry stores O

TIG Holdings, Inc. TIG
6300 Canoga Ave.
Woodland Hills, CA 91367 818-596-5000
Insurance - multi line & misc. O

Timberland Co. TBL
11 Merrill Industrial Dr.
Hampton, NH 03842 603-926-1600
Shoes & related apparel

Time Warner Inc. TWX
75 Rockefeller Plaza
New York, NY 10019 212-484-8000
Publishing - periodicals O [DRP 5%]

Timken Co. TKR
1835 Dueber Ave., S.W.
Canton, OH 44706 216-438-3000
Metal processing & fabrication O
[DRP 5%]

TIS Mortgage Investment Co. TIS
655 Montgomery St., Ste. 800
San Francisco, CA 94111 415-393-8000
Real estate investment trust

Titan Corp. TTN
3033 Science Park Rd.
San Diego, CA 92121 619-453-9500
Electronics - military

Titan Holdings, Inc. TH
1020 N.E. Loop 410, Ste. 700
San Antonio, TX 78209 210-824-4546
Insurance - multi line & misc.

Titan Wheel International, Inc. TWI
2701 Spruce St.
Quincy, IL 62301 217-228-6011
Metal products - fabrication

TNP Enterprises, Inc. TNP
4100 International Plaza
Fort Worth, TX 76109 817-731-0099
Utility - electric power [DRP]

Toastmaster Inc. TM
1801 N. Stadium Blvd.
Columbia, MO 65202 314-445-8666
Appliances - household

Todd Shipyards Corp. TOD
1801 - 16th Ave., S.W.
Seattle, WA 98134 206-623-1635
Boat building

Tokheim Corp. TOK
10501 Corporate Dr.
Fort Wayne, IN 46801 219-423-2552
Oil refining & marketing

Toll Brothers, Inc. TOL
3103 Philmont Ave.
Huntingdon Valley, PA 19006
215-938-8000
Building - residential & commercial O

Tootsie Roll Industries, Inc. TR
7401 S. Cicero Ave.
Chicago, IL 60629 312-838-3400
Food - confectionery

Torch Energy Royalty Trust TRU
1100 N. Market St.
Wilmington, DE 19890 302-651-8775
Oil & gas - US royalty trust

Torchmark Corp. TMK
2001 Third Ave. South
Birmingham, AL 35233 205-325-4200
Insurance - life O [DRP]

Toro Co. TTC
8111 Lyndale Ave. South
Bloomington, MN 55420 612-888-8801
Tools - hand held [DRP]

Tosco Corp. TOS
72 Cummings Point Rd.
Stamford, CT 06902 203-977-1000
Oil refining & marketing O

Total System Services, Inc. TSS
1200 Sixth Ave.
Columbus, GA 31901 404-649-2204
Financial - business services   [DRP]

Toys 'R' Us, Inc. TOY
461 From Rd.
Paramus, NJ 07652 201-262-7800
Retail - misc. O

Transamerica Corp. TA
600 Montgomery St.
San Francisco, CA 94111 415-983-4000
Insurance - multi line & misc. O [DRP]

Transamerica Income Shares, Inc. TAI
PO Box 2438
Los Angeles, CA 90051 213-742-4141
Financial - investment management

Transatlantic Holdings, Inc. TRH
80 Pine St.
New York, NY 10005 212-770-2000
Insurance - property & casualty

TransCanada Pipelines Ltd. TRP
c/o Montreal Trust
66 Temperance St., Toronto, Ont. M5H 1Y7
416-981-9637
Pipeline - natural gas O [DRP 5%]

Transco Energy Co. E
2800 Post Oak Blvd.
Houston, TX 77056 713-439-2000
Oil & gas - production & pipeline O

Transcontinental Realty Investors,
Inc. TCI
10670 N. Central Expressway
Dallas, TX 75231 214-692-4700
Real estate investment trust

TransTechnology Corp. TT
700 Liberty Ave.
Union, NJ 07083 908-964-5666
Electronics - military

TRC Companies, Inc. TRR
5 Waterside Crossing
Windsor, CT 06095 203-289-8631
Pollution control equipment & services

Tredegar Industries, Inc. TG
1100 Boulders Pkwy.
Richmond, VA 23225
804-330-1000
Diversified operations

Tremont Corp. TRE
1999 Broadway, Ste. 4300
Denver, CO 80202 303-296-5652
Metal ores - misc.

Tri-Continental Corp. TY
100 Park Ave.
New York, NY 10017 212-850-1864
Financial - investment management

Triarc Cos., Inc. TRY
900 Third Ave.
New York, NY 10022 212-230-3000
Diversified operations O

Tribune Co. TRB
435 N. Michigan Ave.
Chicago, IL 60611 312-222-9100
Publishing - newspapers O [DRP]

Trident NGL Holding, Inc. NGL
10200 Grogan's Mill Rd.
The Woodlands, TX 77380 713-367-7600
Miscellaneous - not elsewhere classified

Trigen Energy Corp. TGN
One Water St.
White Plains, NY 10601 914-948-9150
Energy - cogeneration

TriMas Corp. TMS
315 E. Eisenhower Pkwy.
Ann Arbor, MI 48108 313-747-7025
Metal products - fasteners

TriNet Corporate Realty Trust, Inc. TRI
4 Embarcadero Center
San Francisco, CA 94111 415-391-4300
Real estate investment trust

Trinity Industries, Inc. TRN
2525 Stemmons Fwy.
Dallas, TX 75207 214-689-0592
Transportation - equipment & leasing O

Trinova Corp. TNV
3000 Strayer
Maumee, OH 43537 419-867-2200
Machinery - general industrial O
  [DRP]

Triton Energy Corp. OIL
6688 N. Central Expwy.
Dallas, TX 75206 214-691-5200
Oil & gas - US exploration & production O

TRW Inc. TRW
1900 Richmond Rd.
Cleveland, OH 44124 216-291-7000
Diversified operations O [DRP]

Tucker Properties Corp. TUC
40 Skokie Blvd.
Northbrook, IL 60062 708-272-9800
Real estate investment trust

Tucson Electric Power Co. TEP
220 W. Sixth St.
Tucson, AZ 85701 602-571-4000
Utility - electric power

Tultex Corp. TTX
101 Commonwealth Blvd.
Martinsville, VA 24115 703-632-2961
Textiles - apparel

Turkish Investment Fund, Inc. TKF
1221 Avenue of the Americas
New York, NY 10020 212-703-4000
Financial - investment management

Twin Disc, Inc. TDI
1328 Racine St.
Racine, WI 53403 414-634-1981
Machinery - general industrial [DRP]

Tyco International Ltd. TYC
One Tyco Park
Exeter, NH 03833 603-778-9700
Diversified operations O [DRP]

Tyco Toys, Inc. TTI
6000 Midlantic Dr.
Mt. Laurel, NJ 08054 609-234-7400
Toys - games & hobby products

Tyler Corp. TYL
3200 San Jacinto Tower
Dallas, TX 75201 214-754-7800
Diversified operations

U S West, Inc. USW
7800 E. Orchard Rd.
Englewood, CO 80111 303-793-6500
Utility - telephone O
  [DRP]

U.S. Banknote Corp. UBK
345 Hudson St.
New York, NY 10014
212-741-8500
Financial - business services

U.S. Delivery Systems Inc. DLV
11 Greenway Plaza, Ste. 250
Houston, TX 77046 713-867-5070
Business services

U.S. Home Corp. UH
1800 W. Loop South
Houston, TX 77027 713-877-2311
Building - residential & commercial

U.S. Restaurant Properties Master USV
200 S. Sixth St.
Minneapolis, MN 55402
612-330-8345
Real estate operations

UAL Corp. UAL
1200 E. Algonquin Rd.
Elk Grove Township, IL 60007
708-952-4000
Transportation - airline O

UDC Homes, Inc. UDC
4812 S. Mill Ave.
Tempe, AZ 85282 602-820-4488
Building - residential & commercial

UGI Corp. UGI
PO Box 858
Valley Forge, PA 19482 610-337-1000
Utility - gas distribution [DRP 5%]

UJB Financial Corp. UJB
301 Carnegie Ctr., PO Box 2066
Princeton, NJ 08543 609-987-3200
Banks - northeast O [DRP]

Ultramar Corp. ULR
2 Pickwick Plaza, Ste. 300
Greenwich, CT 06830 203-622-7000
Oil refining & marketing

UNC Inc. UNC
175 Admiral Cochrane Dr.
Annapolis, MD 21401 410-266-7333
Aerospace - aircraft equipment

Unicom Corp. UCM
PO Box A-3005
Chicago, IL 60690 312-294-7399
Utility - electric power O [DRP]

Unifi, Inc. UFI
7201 W. Friendly Rd.
Greensboro, NC 27410 910-294-4410
Textiles - mill products O

UniFirst Corp. UNF
68 Jonspin Rd.
Wilmington, MA 01887 508-658-8888
Linen supply & related

Union Camp Corp. UCC
1600 Valley Rd.
Wayne, NJ 07470 201-628-2000
Paper & paper products O [DRP]

Union Carbide Corp. UK
39 Old Ridgebury Rd.
Danbury, CT 06817 203-794-2000
Chemicals - diversified O [DRP]

Union Electric Co. UEP
1901 Chouteau Ave.
St. Louis, MO 63103 314-621-3222
Utility - electric power [DRP]

Union Pacific Corp. UNP
Eighth and Eaton Aves.
Bethlehem, PA 18018 610-861-3200
Transportation - rail O [DRP]

Union Planters Corp. UPC
7130 Goodlett Farms Parkway
Cordova, TN 38018 901-523-6000
Banks - southeast [DRP 5%]

Union Texas Petroleum Holdings, Inc.
UTH
1330 Post Oak Blvd.
Houston, TX 77056 713-623-6544
Oil & gas - US exploration & production O

UnionFed Financial Corp. UFF
330 E. Lambert Rd.
Brea, CA 92621 714-255-8100
Financial - savings and loans

Unisys Corp. UIS
PO Box 500
Blue Bell, PA 19424 215-542-4011
Computers - mainframe O

Unit Corp. UNT
7130 S. Lewis
Tulsa, OK 74136 918-493-7700
Oil & gas - field services

United American Healthcare Corp. UAH
1155 Brewery Park Blvd.
Detroit, MI 48207 313-393-0200
Medical services

United Asset Management Corp. UAM
One International Place
Boston, MA 02110 617-330-8900
Financial - investment management O

United Dominion Industries Ltd. UDI
2300 One First Union Center
Charlotte, NC 28202 704-347-6800
Building - residential & commercial

United Dominion Realty Trust, Inc.
UDR
10 S. Sixth St., Ste. 203
Richmond, VA 23219 804-780-2691
Real estate investment trust

United HealthCare Corp. UNH
9900 Bren Rd. East
Minnetonka, MN 55343 612-936-1300
Health maintenance organization O

United Illuminating Co. UIL
157 Church St.
New Haven, CT 06506 203-499-2000
Utility - electric power [DRP]

United Industrial Corp. UIC
18 E. 48th St.
New York, NY 10017 212-752-8787
Electronics - military

United Inns, Inc. UI
5100 Poplar Ave., Ste. 2300
Memphis, TN 38137 901-767-2880
Hotels & motels

United Kingdom Fund Inc. UKM
245 Park Ave., 10th Fl.
New York, NY 10167 800-524-4458
Financial - investment management

United Merchants and Manufacturers, Inc.
  UMM
1650 Palisade Ave.
Teaneck, NJ 7666 201-837-1700
Textiles - apparel

United Meridian Corp. UMC
1201 Louisiana, Ste. 1400
Houston, TX 77002 713-654-9110
Oil & gas - US exploration & production

United Park City Mines Co. UPK
PO Box 1450
Park City, UT 84060 801-649-8011
Real estate operations

United States Filter Corp. USF
73-710 Fred Waring Dr.
Palm Desert, CA 92260 619-340-0098
Filtration products

United States Shoe Corp. USR
One Eastwood Dr.
Cincinnati, OH 45227 513-527-7000
Shoes & related apparel O [DRP]

United States Surgical Corp. USS
150 Glover Ave.
Norwalk, CT 06856 203-845-1000
Medical instruments O

United Technologies Corp. UTX
United Technologies Bldg.
Hartford, CT 06101 203-728-7000
Diversified operations O

United Water Resources Inc. UWR
200 Old Hook Rd.
Harrington Park, NJ 07640 201-784-9434
Utility - water supply
  [DRP 5%]

United Wisconsin Services, Inc. UWZ
401 W. Michigan St.
Milwaukee, WI 53203 414-226-6900
Insurance - accident & health

Unitrode Corp. UTR
8 Suburban Park Dr.
Billerica, MA 08121 508-670-9086
Electrical components - semiconductors

Univar Corp. UVX
6100 Carillon Point
Kirkland, WA 98033 206-889-3400
Chemicals - diversified

Universal Corp. UVV
Hamilton St. at Broad
Richmond, VA 23230 804-359-9311
Tobacco [DRP]

Universal Foods Corp. UFC
433 E. Michigan St.
Milwaukee, WI 53202 414-271-6755
Food - misc. O [DRP]

Universal Health Realty Income Trust UHT
367 S. Gulph Rd.
King of Prussia, PA 19406 610-265-0688
Real estate investment trust [DRP]

Universal Health Services, Inc. UHS
367 S. Gulph Rd.
King of Prussia, PA 19406 215-768-3300
Hospitals

Uno Restaurant Corp. UNO
100 Charles Park Rd.
West Roxbury, MA 02132 617-323-9200
Retail - food & restaurants

Unocal Corp. UCL
1201 W. Fifth St., PO Box 7600
Los Angeles, CA 90051 213-977-7600
Oil & gas - US integrated O
  [DRP 5%]

UNUM Corp. UNM
2211 Congress St.
Portland, ME 04122 207-770-2211
Insurance - multi line & misc. O
  [DRP]

Upjohn Co. UPJ
7000 Portage Rd.
Kalamazoo, MI 49001 616-323-4000
Drugs O [DRP]

Urban Shopping Centers, Inc. URB
900 N. Michigan Ave.
Chicago, IL 60611 312-915-2000
Real estate investment trust

URS Corp. URS
100 California St., Ste. 500
San Francisco, CA 94111 415-774-2700
Engineering - R & D services

USA Waste Services, Inc. UW
5000 Quorum Dr., Ste. 300
Dallas, TX 75240 214-233-4212
Pollution control equipment & services O

USAir Group, Inc. U
2345 Crystal Dr.
Arlington, VA 22227 703-418-5306
Transportation - airline O

USF&G Corp. FG
100 Light St.
Baltimore, MD 21202 410-547-3000
Insurance - property & casualty O [DRP]

USG Corp. USG
125 S. Franklin St.
Chicago, IL 60606 312-606-4000
Building products - misc. O

USI Industries, Inc. USO
1000 Colfax
Gary, IN 46406 219-944-6116
Transportation - truck

USLICO Corp. USC
4601 Fairfax Dr., PO Box 3700
Arlington, VA 22203 703-875-3600
Insurance - life [DRP]

USLIFE Corp. USH
125 Maiden Ln.
New York, NY 10038 212-709-6000
Insurance - life [DRP]

USLIFE Income Fund, Inc. UIF
125 Maiden Ln.
New York, NY 10038 212-709-6000
Financial - investment management

UST Inc. UST
100 W. Putnam Ave.
Greenwich, CT 06830 203-661-1100
Tobacco O [DRP]

USX Corp. - Delhi Group DGP
600 Grant St.
Pittsburgh, PA 15219 412-433-1121
Oil & gas - production & pipeline O

USX Corp. - Marathon Group MRO
600 Grant St.
Pittsburgh, PA 15219 412-433-1121
Oil & gas - US integrated O [DRP]

USX Corp. - U.S. Steel Group X
600 Grant St.
Pittsburgh, PA 15219
412-433-1121
Steel - production O [DRP]

UtiliCorp United Inc. UCU
911 Main
Kansas City, MO 64105 816-421-6600
Utility - electric power
[DRP 5%]

Valassis Communications, Inc. VCI
36111 Schoolcraft Rd.
Livonia, MI 48150 313-591-3000
Business services O

Valero Energy Corp. VLO
530 McCullough Ave.
San Antonio, TX 78215 210-246-2000
Oil & gas - production & pipeline O

Valhi, Inc. VHI
5430 LBJ Freeway, Ste. 1700
Dallas, TX 75240
214-233-1700
Diversified operations

Valley National Bancorp VLY
1445 Valley Rd.
Wayne, NJ 07470
201-305-8800
Banks - northeast
[DRP]

Value City Department Stores, Inc. VCD
3241 Westerville Rd.
Columbus, OH 43224
614-471-4722
Retail - regional department stores

Value Health, Inc. VH
22 Waterville Rd.
Avon, CT 06001 203-678-3400
Health maintenance organization O

Van Kampen Merritt Advantage Mun. Inc.
Trust VKA
One Parkview Plaza
Oakbrook Terrace, IL 60181 708-684-6000
Financial - investment management

Van Kampen Merritt Advantage PA Mun.
Inc. Trust VAP
One Parkview Plaza
Oakbrook Terrace, IL 60181 708-684-6000
Financial - investment management

Van Kampen Merritt CA Value Mun. Inc.
Trust VCV
One Parkview Plaza
Oakbrook Terrace, IL 60181 708-684-6000
Financial - investment management

Van Kampen Merritt California Qual. Mun.
Trust VQC
One Parkview Plaza
Oakbrook Terrace, IL 60181 708-684-6000
Financial - investment management

Van Kampen Merritt Florida Qual. Mun.
Trust VFM
One Parkview Plaza
Oakbrook Terrace, IL 60181 708-684-6000
Financial - investment management

Van Kampen Merritt Int. Term High Income
Trust VIT
One Parkview Plaza
Oakbrook Terrace, IL 60181 708-684-6000
Financial - investment management

Van Kampen Merritt Investment Grade Mun.
Trust VIG
One Parkview Plaza
Oakbrook Terrace, IL 60181 708-684-6000
Financial - investment management

Van Kampen Merritt Ltd. Term High Income
Trust VLT
One Parkview Plaza
Oakbrook Terrace, IL 60181 708-684-6000
Financial - investment management

Van Kampen Merritt Muncipal Income Trust
VMT
One Parkview Plaza
Oakbrook Terrace, IL 60181 708-684-6000
Financial - investment management

Van Kampen Merritt Municipal Opportunity
Tr. VMO
One Parkview Plaza
Oakbrook Terrace, IL 60181 708-684-6000
Financial - investment management

Van Kampen Merritt Municipal Opportunity
Tr. II VOT
One Parkview Plaza
Oakbrook Terrace, IL 60181 708-684-6000
Financial - investment management

Van Kampen Merritt Municipal Trust VKQ
One Parkview Plaza
Oakbrook Terrace, IL 60181 708-684-6000
Financial - investment management

Van Kampen Merritt New York Qual. Mun.
Trust VNM
One Parkview Plaza
Oakbrook Terrace, IL 60181 708-684-6000
Financial - investment management

Van Kampen Merritt NY Value Mun. Income
Trust VNV
One Parkview Plaza
Oakbrook Terrace, IL 60181 708-684-6000
Financial - investment management

Van Kampen Merritt Ohio Qual. Mun. Trust
VOQ
One Parkview Plaza
Oakbrook Terrace, IL 60181 708-684-6000
Financial - investment management

Van Kampen Merritt PA Quality Mun. Trust
VPQ
One Parkview Plaza
Oakbrook Terrace, IL 60181 708-684-6000
Financial - investment management

Van Kampen Merritt PA Value Mun. Inc.
Trust VPV
One Parkview Plaza
Oakbrook Terrace, IL 60181 708-684-6000
Financial - investment management

Van Kampen Merritt Strategic Sector Mun.
Trust VKS
One Parkview Plaza
Oakbrook Terrace, IL 60181
708-684-6000
Financial - investment management

Van Kampen Merritt Tr. For Insured
Municipals VIM
One Parkview Plaza
Oakbrook Terrace, IL 60181 708-684-6000
Financial - investment management

Van Kampen Merritt Tr. For Inv. Grade CA
Mun. VIC
One Parkview Plaza
Oakbrook Terrace, IL 60181
708-684-6000
Financial - investment management

Van Kampen Merritt Tr. For Inv. Grade FL
Mun. VTF
One Parkview Plaza
Oakbrook Terrace, IL 60181 708-684-6000
Financial - investment management

Van Kampen Merritt Tr. For Inv. Grade Mun.
VGM
One Parkview Plaza
Oakbrook Terrace, IL 60181 708-684-6000
Financial - investment management

Van Kampen Merritt Tr. For Inv. Grade NJ
Mun. VTJ
One Parkview Plaza
Oakbrook Terrace, IL 60181 708-684-6000
Financial - investment management

Van Kampen Merritt Tr. For Inv. Grade NY
Mun. VTN
One Parkview Plaza
Oakbrook Terrace, IL 60181 708-684-6000
Financial - investment management

Van Kampen Merritt Tr. For Inv. Grade PA
Mun. VTP
One Parkview Plaza
Oakbrook Terrace, IL 60181 708-684-6000
Financial - investment management

Van Kampen Merritt Value Municipal
Income Trust VKV
One Parkview Plaza
Oakbrook Terrace, IL 60181 708-684-6000
Financial - investment management

Varco International, Inc. VRC
743 N. Eckhoff St.
Orange, CA 92668
714-978-1900
Oil field machinery & equipment

Varian Associates, Inc. VAR
3050 Hansen Way
Palo Alto, CA 94304 415-493-4000
Instruments - scientific O
[DRP]

Varity Corp. VAT
672 Delaware Ave.
Buffalo, NY 14209 716-888-8000
Diversified operations O

Vastar Resources, Inc. VRI
15375 Memorial Dr.
Houston, TX 77079 713-584-6000
Oil & gas - US exploration & production

Vencor, Inc. VC
400 W. Market St.
Louisville, KY 40202 502-569-7300
Hospitals O

Venture Stores, Inc. VEN
2001 E. Terra Ln., PO Box 110
O'Fallon, MO 63366 314-281-5500
Retail - discount & variety O
[DRP]

Vesta Insurance Group, Inc. VTA
3760 River Run Rd.
Birmingham, AL 35243 205-970-7000
Insurance - multi line & misc.

Vestaur Securities, Inc. VES
Centre Square West - 11 Fl.
Philadelphia, PA 19101 215-567-3969
Financial - investment management

VF Corp. VFC
1047 N. Park Rd.
Wyomissing, PA 19610 610-378-1151
Textiles - apparel O [DRP]

Vintage Petroleum, Inc. VPI
4200 One Williams Center
Tulsa, OK 74172 918-592-0101
Oil & gas - US exploration & production

Vishay Intertechnology, Inc. VSH
63 Lincoln Highway
Malvern, PA 19355 610-644-1300
Electronics - measuring instruments

Vista Resources, Inc. VS
1201 W. Peachtree St., N.W.
Atlanta, GA 30309 404-815-2000
Leather & related products

Vivra Inc. V
400 Primrose, Ste. 200
Burlingame, CA 94010 415-348-8200
Healthcare - outpatient & home

Volunteer Capital Corp. VCC
3401 West End Ave.
Nashville, TN 37202 615-269-1900
Retail - food & restaurants

Vornado Realty Trust VNO
Park 80 West, Plaza II
Saddle Brook, NJ 07662 201-587-1000
Real estate investment trust

Vulcan Materials Co. VMC
One Metroplex Dr.
Birmingham, AL 35209 205-877-3000
Construction - cement & concrete
[DRP]

Waban Inc. WBN
One Mercer Rd., PO Box 9600
Natick, MA 01760 508-651-6500
Retail - home furnishings O

Wabash National Corp. WNC
1000 Sagamore Parkway South
Lafayette, IN 47905 317-448-1591
Automotive & trucking - original equipment
O

Wachovia Corp. WB
301 N. Main St.
Winston-Salem, NC 27150 910-770-5000
Banks - southeast O [DRP]

Wahlco Environmental Systems, Inc. WAL
3600 W. Segerstrom Ave.
Santa Ana, CA 92704 714-979-7300
Pollution control equipment & services

Wainoco Oil Corp. WOL
1200 Smith St., Ste. 2100
Houston, TX 77002 713-658-9900
Oil & gas - US exploration & production

Wal-Mart Stores, Inc. WMT
Bentonville, AR 72716
501-273-4000
Retail - discount & variety O

Walgreen Co. WAG
200 Wilmot Rd.
Deerfield, IL 60015 708-940-2500
Retail - drug stores O [DRP]

Wallace Computer Services, Inc. WCS
4600 W. Roosevelt Rd.
Hillside, IL 60162 312-626-2000
Paper - business forms O

Warner Insurance Services, Inc. WCP
17-01 Pollitt Dr.
Fair Lawn, NJ 07410 201-794-4800
Business services

Warner-Lambert Co. WLA
201 Tabor Rd.
Morris Plains, NJ 07950 201-540-2000
Drugs O [DRP]

Washington Energy Co. WEG
815 Mercer St.
Seattle, WA 98109 206-622-6767
Utility - gas distribution
[DRP 5%]

Washington Gas Light Co. WGL
1100 H St., N.W.
Washington, DC 20080 703-750-4440
Utility - gas distribution [DRP]

Washington Homes, Inc. WHI
1802 Brightseat Rd.
Landover, MD 20785 301-772-8900
Building - residential & commercial

Washington National Corp. WNT
300 Tower Pkwy.
Lincolnshire, IL 60069 708-793-3000
Insurance - life
[DRP 5%]

Washington Water Power Co. WWP
1411 E. Mission Ave.
Spokane, WA 99202 509-489-0500
Utility - electric power [DRP]

Waterhouse Securities, Inc. WHO
100 Wall St.
New York, NY 10005 212-806-3500
Financial - investment bankers

Watkins-Johnson Co. WJ
3333 Hillview Ave.
Palo Alto, CA 93404 415-493-4141
Electronics - military

Watsco, Inc. WSO
2665 S. Bayshore Dr.
Coconut Grove, FL 33133 305-858-0828
Diversified operations

Waxman Industries, Inc. WAX
24460 Aurora Rd.
Bedford Heights, OH 44146
216-439-1830
Building products - misc.

WCI Steel, Inc. WRN
1040 Pine Ave., SE
Warren, OH 44483 216-841-8000
Steel - production

Weathersford International Inc. WII
1360 Post Oak Blvd., Ste. 1000
Houston, TX 77056 713-439-9400
Oil & gas - field services O

Weeks Corp. WKS
4497 Park Dr.
Norcross, GA 30093 404-923-4076
Real estate investment trust

Weingarten Realty Investors WRI
2600 Citadel Plaza Dr.
Houston, TX 77292 713-866-6000
Real estate investment trust [DRP]

Weirton Steel Corp. WS
400 Three Springs Dr.
Weirton, WV 26062 304-797-2000
Steel - production O

Weis Markets, Inc. WMK
1000 S. Second St.
Sunbury, PA 17801 717-286-4571
Retail - supermarkets [DRP]

Wellman, Inc. WLM
1040 Broad St., Ste. 302
Shrewsbury, NJ 07702 908-542-7300
Chemicals - plastics

WellPoint Health Networks Inc. WLP
21555 Oxnard St.
Woodland Hills, CA 91367 818-703-4000
Miscellaneous - not elsewhere classified O

Wells Fargo & Co. WFC
420 Montgomery St.
San Francisco, CA 94163 415-477-1000
Banks - west O [DRP 3%]

Wellsford Residential Property Trust WRP
375 Park Ave., Ste. 307
New York, NY 10152 212-735-1108
Real estate investment trust

Wendy's International, Inc. WEN
4288 W. Dublin-Granville Rd.
Dublin, OH 43017 614-764-3100
Retail - food & restaurants O [DRP]

West Co., Inc. WST
West Bridge St.
Phoenixville, PA 19460 215-935-4500
Medical & dental supplies [DRP]

West Penn Power Co. WSPp
800 Cabin Hill Dr.
Greensburg, PA 15601
412-837-3000
Utility - electric power

Westcoast Energy Inc. WE
c/o Montreal Trust Co.
510 Burrard St., Vancouver, BC V6C 3B9
604-691-5516
Canadian natural gas [DRP 5%]

Westcorp WES
23 Pasteur Rd., PO Box 19733
Irvine, CA 92718 714-727-1000
Financial - savings and loans

Western Atlas, Inc. WAI
360 N. Crescent Dr.
Beverly Hills, CA 90210 310-888-2500
Oil & gas - field services O

Western Digital Corp. WDC
8105 Irvine Center Dr.
Irvine, CA 92718 714-932-5000
Computers - peripheral equipment O

Western Gas Resources, Inc. WGR
12200 N. Pecos St.
Denver, CO 80234 303-452-5603
Oil & gas - production & pipeline

Western National Corp. WNH
5555 San Felipe Rd.
Houston, TX 77056 713-888-7800
Insurance - multi line & misc.

Western Resources, Inc. WR
818 Kansas Ave.
Topeka, KS 66612 913-575-6300
Utility - gas distribution [DRP]

Western Waste Industries WW
21061 S. Western Ave.
Torrance, CA 90501 310-327-2522
Pollution control equipment & services

Westinghouse Electric Corp. WX
11 Stanwix St.
Pittsburgh, PA 15222 412-244-2000
Diversified operations O [DRP]

Westmoreland Coal Co. WCX
200 S. Broad St.
Philadelphia, PA 19102 215-545-2500
Coal

Westvaco Corp. W
299 Park Ave.
New York, NY 10171 212-688-5000
Paper & paper products O [DRP]

Weyerhaeuser Co. WY
Tacoma, WA 98477 206-924-2345
Building products - wood O [DRP]

Wheelabrator Technologies Inc. WTI
Liberty Ln.
Hampton, NH 03842 603-778-7311
Energy - alternate sources O

Whirlpool Corp. WHR
2000 M-63
Benton Harbor, MI 49022
616-926-5000
Appliances - household O
[DRP]

Whitehall Corp. WHT
2659 Nova Dr., PO Box 29709
Dallas, TX 75229 214-247-8747
Electronics - military

Whitman Corp. WH
3501 Algonquin Rd.
Rolling Meadows, IL 60008
708-818-5000
Diversified operations O [DRP]

Whittaker Corp. WKR
10880 Wilshire Blvd.
Los Angeles, CA 90024 310-475-9411
Aerospace - aircraft equipment O

WHX Corp. WHX
110 E. 59th St.
New York, NY 10022 212-355-5200
Steel - production O

WICOR, Inc. WIC
626 E. Wisconsin Ave.
Milwaukee, WI 53201 414-291-07026
Utility - gas distribution [DRP]

Willcox & Gibbs, Inc. WG
530 Fifth Ave.
New York, NY 10036 212-869-1800
Machinery - general industrial

Williams Coal Seam Gas Royalty
Trust WTU
One Williams Center
Tulsa, OK 74172 918-588-2000
Oil & gas - US royalty trust

Wilshire Oil Company of Texas WOC
921 Bergen Ave.
Jersey City, NJ 07306 201-420-2796
Oil & gas - US exploration & production

Windmere Corp. WND
5980 Miami Lakes Dr.
Miami Lakes, FL 33014 305-362-2611
Drugs & sundries - wholesale O

Winn-Dixie Stores, Inc. WIN
5050 Edgewood Ct., PO Box B
Jacksonville, FL 32203 904-783-5000
Retail - supermarkets O [DRP]

Winnebago Industries, Inc. WGO
PO Box 152
Forest City, IA 50436 515-582-3535
Building - mobile homes & RV O

Wisconsin Energy Corp. WEC
231 W. Michigan St.
Milwaukee, WI 53201 414-221-2590
Utility - electric power [DRP]

Witco Corp. WIT
One American Ln.
Greenwich, CT 06831 203-552-2000
Chemicals - diversified O [DRP]

WMS Industries Inc. WMS
3401 N. California Ave.
Chicago, IL 60618 312-728-2300
Leisure & recreational products O

WMX Technologies WMX
3003 Butterfield Rd.
Oak Brook, IL 60521 708-572-8800
Pollution control equipment & services O
[DRP]

Wolverine Tube, Inc. WLV
2100 Market St., N.E.
Decatur, AL 35602 205-353-1310
Miscellaneous - not elsewhere classified

Wolverine World Wide, Inc. WWW
9341 Courtland Dr.
Rockford, MI 49351 616-866-5500
Shoes & related apparel

Woolworth Corp. Z
233 Broadway
New York, NY 10279 212-553-2000
Retail - discount & variety O [DRP]

WorldCorp, Inc. WOA
13873 Park Center Rd.
Herndon, VA 22071 703-834-9200
Transportation - airline

Worldtex, Inc. WTX
212 12th Ave. NE, PO Box 2363
Hickory, NC 28603 704-328-5381
Textiles - mill products

Worldwide DollarVest Fund, Inc. WDV
PO Box 9011
Princeton, NJ 08543 609-282-2800
Financial - investment management

Worldwide Value Fund, Inc. VLU
111 S. Calvert St., Ste. 1560
Baltimore, MD 21203 410-539-3400
Financial - investment management

WPL Holdings, Inc. WPH
222 W. Washington Ave.
Madison, WI 53703 608-252-3311
Utility - electric power [DRP]

WPS Resources Corp. WPS
700 N. Adams St., PO Box 19001
Green Bay, WI 54307 414-433-1445
Utility - electric power [DRP]

Wrigley (Wm.) Jr. Co. WWY
410 N. Michigan Ave.
Chicago, IL 60611 312-644-2121
Food - confectionery O [DRP]

Wyle Laboratories WYL
128 Maryland St.
El Segundo, CA 90245
310-322-1763
Electronics - parts distribution

Wynn's International, Inc. WN
500 N. State College Blvd.
Orange, CA 92668 714-938-3700
Automotive & trucking - replacement parts

Xerox Corp. XRX
800 Long Ridge Rd.
Stamford, CT 06904 203-968-3000
Office equipment & supplies [DRP]

XTRA Corp. XTR
60 State St.
Boston, MA 02109 617-367-5000
Transportation - equipment & leasing O

Yankee Energy System, Inc. YES
599 Research Pkwy.
Meridan, CT 06450 203-639-4000
Utility - gas distribution [DRP]

York International Corp. YRK
631 S. Richland Ave.
York, PA 17403 717-771-7890
Building products - a/c & heating O

Zapata Corp. ZOS
One Riverway, PO Box 4240
Houston, TX 77210 713-940-6100
Oil & gas - offshore drilling

Zeigler Coal Holding Co. ZEI
50 Jerome Ln.
Fairview Heights, IL 62208 618-394-2400
Coal

Zemex Corp. ZMX
One W. Pack Square, Ste. 700
Asheville, NC 28801 704-255-4900
Metals - non ferrous

Zenith Electronics Corp. ZE
1000 Milwaukee Ave.
Glenview, IL 60025 708-391-7000
Audio & video home products O

Zenith National Insurance Corp. ZNT
21255 Califa St.
Woodland Hills, CA 91367 818-713-1000
Insurance - property & casualty

Zenix Income Fund Inc. ZIF
Two World Trade Center
New York, NY 10048 212-298-7350
Financial - investment management

Zero Corp. ZRO
444 S. Flower St., Ste. 2100
Los Angeles, CA 90071 213-629-7000
Electrical components - misc. [DRP]

Zurich Reinsurance Centre Holdings, Inc. ZRC
195 Broadway, 16th Fl.
New York, NY 10007 212-898-5000
Insurance - multi line & misc.

Zurn Industries, Inc. ZRN
One Zurn Place
Erie, PA 16514 814-452-02111
Pollution control equipment & services O
[DRP]

AMERICAN STOCK EXCHANGE

A. T. Cross Co. ATXA
One Albion Rd.
Lincoln, RI 02865 401-333-1200
Office & art materials

A.M. Castle & Co. CAS
3400 N. Wolf Rd.
Franklin Park, IL 60131 708-455-7111
Metal products - distribution

Ackerley Communications, Inc. AK
800 Fifth Ave., Ste. 3770
Seattle, WA 98104 206-624-2888
Diversified operations

Acme United Corp. ACU
75 Kings Highway Cutoff
Fairfield, CT 06430 203-332-7330
Medical instruments

Action Industries, Inc. ACX
Allegheny Industrial Park
Cheswick, PA 15024 412-782-4800
Business services

Adams Resources & Energy, Inc. AE
6910 Fannin
Houston, TX 77030 713-797-9966
Oil & gas - production & pipeline

Advanced Financial, Inc. AVF
5425 Martindale
Shawnee, KS 66218 913-441-2466
Financial - mortgages & related services

Advanced Magnetics, Inc. AVM
61 Mooney St.
Cambridge, MA 02138 617-497-2070
Medical products

Advanced Medical, Inc. AMA
9775 Businesspark Ave.
San Diego, CA 92131 619-566-0426
Drugs

Advanced Photonix, Inc. API
1240 Avenida Acaso
Camarillo, CA 93012 805-987-0146
Electronics - measuring instruments

Aerosonic Corp. AIM
1212 N. Hercules Rd.
Clearwater, FL 34625 813-461-3000
Instruments - control

AIM Strategic Income Fund, Inc. AST
11 Greenway Plaza, Ste. 1919
Houston, TX 77046 713-626-1919
Financial - investment management

Air & Water Technologies Corp. AWT
PO Box 1500
Somerville, NJ 08876 908-685-4600
Pollution control equipment & services

Air-Cure Environmental, Inc. AEL
275 West St., Ste. 204
Annapolis, MD 21401 410-268-2450
Filtration products

AIRCOA Hotel Partners, L.P. AHT
4600 S. Ulster St., Ste. 1200
Denver, CO 80237 303-220-2000
Hotels & motels

Alamco, Inc. AXO
200 W. Main St., PO Box 1740
Clarksburg, WV 26302 304-623-6671
Oil & gas - US exploration & production

Alba-Waldensian, Inc. AWS
201 St. Germain Ave., S.W.
Valdese, NC 28690 704-874-2191
Textiles - apparel

ALC Communications Corp. ALC
30300 Telegraph Rd.
Birmingham, MI 48010 810-647-4060
Telecommunications services 0

Alert Centre, Inc. ALT
5800 S. Quebec St.
Englewood, CO 80111 303-779-4286
Protection - safety equipment & services

Alexander Haagen Properties, Inc. ACH
3500 Sepulveda Blvd.
Manhattan Beach, CA 90266 310-546-4520
Real estate investment trust

Alfin, Inc. AFN
720 Fifth Ave.
New York, NY 10019 212-333-7700
Cosmetics & toiletries

Allied Research Corp. ALR
8000 Towers Cresent Dr.
Vienna, VA 22182 703-847-5268
Weapons & weapon systems

Allou Health & Beauty Care, Inc. ALU
50 Emjay Blvd.
Brentwood, NY 11717 516-273-4000
Cosmetics & toiletries

Alpha Industries, Inc. AHA
20 Sylvan Rd.
Woburn, MA 01801 617-935-5150
Electronics - military

Alta Energy Corp. ALE
410 17th St., Ste. 400
Denver, CO 80202 303-825-0714
Oil & gas - US exploration & production

AM International, Inc. AM
1800 W. Central Rd.
Mt. Prospect, IL 60056 708-818-1294
Office equipment & supplies

AMC Entertainment Inc. AEN
106 W. 14th St., PO Box 419615
Kansas City, MO 64141 816-221-4000
Motion pictures & services

Amdahl Corp. AMH
1250 E. Arques Ave.
Sunnyvale, CA 94088 408-746-6000
Computers - mainframe

America First PREP Fund 2 L.P. PF
1004 Farnum St.
Omaha, NE 68102 402-444-1630
Financial - investment management

America First REIT, Inc. AFR
1004 Farnam St., Ste. 400
Omaha, NE 68102 402-444-1630
Real estate investment trust

American Bank of Connecticut BKC
Two W. Main St.
Waterbury, CT 06723 203-757-9401
Financial - savings and loans

American Biltrite Inc. ABL
57 River St.
Wellesley Hills, MA 02181 617-237-6655
Building products - misc.

American Exploration Co. AX
1331 Lamar St., Ste. 900
Houston, TX 77010 713-756-6000
Oil & gas - US exploration & production

American Insured Mortgage Inv. L.P. - Series
85 AII
11200 Rockville Pike
Rockville, MD 20852 301-468-9200
Financial - investment management

American Insured Mortgage Inv. L.P. - Series
86 AIJ
11200 Rockville Pike
Rockville, MD 20852 301-468-9200
Financial - investment management

American Insured Mortgage Inv. L.P. - Series
88 AIK
11200 Rockville Pike
Rockville, MD 20852 301-468-9200
Financial - investment management

American Insured Mortgage Investors AIA
11200 Rockville Pike
Rockville, MD 20852 301-468-9200
Financial - investment management

American List Corp. AMZ
330 Old Country Rd.
Mineola, NY 11501 516-248-6100
Business services

American Maize-Products Co. AZEA
250 Harbor Plaza Dr.
Stamford, CT 06904 203-356-9000
Food - flour & grain

American Paging, Inc. APP
1300 Godward St. NE, Ste. 3100
Minneapolis, MN 55413 612-623-3100
Telecommunications services

American Restaurant Investors REA
450 Newport Center Dr.
Newport Beach, CA 92660 714-721-8000
Retail - food & restaurants

American Restaurant Partners, L.P. RMC
555 N. Woodlawn, Ste. 3102
Wichita, KS 67208 316-684-5119
Retail - food & restaurants

American Science and Engineering, Inc. ASE
40 Erie St.
Cambridge, MA 02139 617-868-1600
Electronics - measuring instruments

American Shared Hospital Services AMS
444 Market St., Ste. 2420
San Francisco, CA 94111 415-788-5300
Medical services

American Technical Ceramics Corp. AMK
17 Stepar Place
Huntington Station, NY 11746
516-547-5700
Electrical components - misc.

Ampal-American Israel Corp. AISA
10 Rockefeller Plaza
New York, NY 10020 212-782-2100
Financial - SBIC & commercial

Amwest Insurance Group, Inc. AMW
6320 Canoga Ave.
Woodland Hills, CA 91367 818-704-1111
Insurance - property & casualty

Andrea Electronics Corp. AND
11-40 45th Rd.
Long Island City, NY 11101 718-729-8500
Telecommunications equipment

Angeles Mortgage Investment Trust ANM
10301 W. Pico Blvd.
Los Angeles, CA 90064 310-277-4900
Real estate investment trust
[DRP]

Angeles Participating Mortgage Trust APT
10301 W. Pico Blvd.
Los Angeles, CA 90064 310-277-4900
Real estate investment trust
[DRP]

Anuhco, Inc. ANU
9393 W. 110th St., Ste. 100
Overland Park, KS 66210 913-451-2800
Transportation - truck

Aprogenex, Inc. APG
8000 El Rio St.
Houston, TX 77054 713-748-5114
Biomedical & genetic products

ARI Holdings ARI
1000 Lenox Dr.
Lawrenceville, NJ 08648 609-896-1921
Insurance - property & casualty

Arizona Land Income Corp. AZL
2999 N. 44th St., Ste. 100
Phoenix, AZ 85018 602-952-6800
Real estate investment trust

ARM Financial Group, Inc. ARMp
239 S. Fifth St., 12th Fl.
Louisville, KY 40202 502-582-7900
Insurance - multi line & misc.

Armatron International, Inc. ART
2 Main St.
Melrose, MA 02176 617-321-2300
Diversified operations

Arrhythmia Research Technology, Inc.
HRT
5910 Courtyard Dr., Ste. 300
Austin, TX 78731 512-343-6912
Medical products

Arrow Automotive Industries, Inc. AI
3 Speen St.
Framingham, MA 01701 508-872-3711
Automotive & trucking - replacement parts

ASR Investments Corp. ASR
335 N. Wilmot, Ste. 250
Tucson, AZ 85711 602-748-2111
Real estate investment trust
[DRP]

Astrotech International Corp. AIX
960 Penn Ave., Ste. 800
Pittsburgh, PA 15222 412-391-1896
Oil & gas - field services

Atari Corp. ATC
1196 Borregas Ave.
Sunnyvale, CA 94086 408-745-2000
Computers - mini & micro

Atlantis Plastics, Inc. AGH
2665 S. Bayshore Dr., 8th Fl.
Miami, FL 33133 305-858-2200
Diversified operations

Audiovox Corp. VOX
150 Marcus Blvd.
Hauppauge, NY 11788 516-231-7750
Auto parts - retail & wholesale

Audre Recognition Systems, Inc. ARS
11021 Via Frontera
San Diego, CA 92127
619-451-2260
Computers - software

Aurora Electronics, Inc. AUR
2030 Main St., Ste. 1120
Irvine, CA 92714 714-660-1232
Electrical components - misc.

Aviva Petroleum Inc. AVV
8235 Douglas Ave., Ste. 400
Dallas, TX 75225 214-691-3464
Oil & gas - international integrated

AZCO Mining, Inc. AZC
30 S. Bowie
Solomon, AZ 85551 602-428-6881
Metal ores - misc.

Badger Meter, Inc. BMI
4545 W. Brown Deer Rd.
Milwaukee, WI 53223 414-355-0400
Electronics - measuring instruments

Baldwin Technology Co., Inc. BLD
65 Rowayton Ave.
Rowayton, CT 06853 203-838-7470
Machinery - printing [DRP]

Bancroft Convertible Fund, Inc. BCV
56 Pine St.
New York, NY 10005 212-269-9236
Financial - investment management

Bank of Southington BSO
130 N. Main St.
Southington, CT 06489 203-276-0155
Banks - northeast

Banyan Hotel Investment Fund VHT
150 S. Wacker Dr.
Chicago, IL 60606 312-553-9800
Real estate investment trust

Banyan Short Term Income Trust VST
150 S. Wacker Dr.
Chicago, IL 60606 312-553-9800
Real estate investment trust
[DRP]

Barnwell Industries, Inc. BRN
1100 Alakea St., Ste. 2900
Honolulu, HI 96813 808-531-8400
Oil & gas - international specialty

Barr Laboratories, Inc. BRL
2 Quaker Rd., PO Box D2900
Pomona, NY 10970 914-362-1100
Drugs - generic

Barrister Information Systems Corp. BIS
45 Oak St.
Buffalo, NY 14203 716-845-5010
Business services

B.A.T. Industries, PLC ADR BTI
c/o Bellspring Associates
Attn. Roger Wilson
One Landmark Square, Suite 901
Stamford, CT 06901 (203) 961-0660
Tobacco products & insurance O

Bay Meadows Operating Co. CJ
2600 S. Delaware St.
San Mateo, CA 94402 415-574-7223
Real estate investment trust

Bayou Steel Corp. BYX
River Rd., PO Box 5000
LaPlace, LA 70069 504-652-4900
Steel - production

Belmac Corp. BLM
4830 W. Kennedy Blvd.
Tampa, FL 33609
813-286-4401
Drugs O

Benchmark Electronics, Inc. BHE
3000 Technology Dr.
Angleton, TX 77515 409-849-6550
Electrical components - misc.

Bergstrom Capital Corp. BEM
505 Madison St., Ste. 220
Seattle, WA 98104 206-623-7302
Financial - investment management

BESICORP Group, Inc. BGI
1151 Flatbush Rd.
Kingston, NY 12401 914-336-7700
Energy - alternate sources

Bethlehem Corp. BET
25th and Lennox Sts.
Easton, PA 18044 610-258-7111
Machinery - general industrial

BHC Communications, Inc. BHC
600 Madison Ave.
New York, NY 10022 212-421-0200
Broadcasting - radio & TV

Binks Manufacturing Co. BIN
9201 W. Belmont Ave.
Franklin Park, IL 60131 708-671-3000
Machinery - material handling

Bio-Rad Laboratories, Inc. BIOA
1000 Alfred Nobel Dr.
Hercules, CA 94547 510-724-7000
Biomedical & genetic products

Biopharmaceutics, Inc. BPH
990 Station Rd.
Bellport, NY 11713 516-286-5900
Drugs

Biscayne Apparel, Inc. BHA
1373 Broad St.
Clifton, NJ 07013 201-473-3240
Textiles - apparel

BlackRock Broad Investment Grade 2009
  Term Tr. BCT
One Seaport Plaza
New York, NY 10292 212-214-3332
Financial - investment management

BlackRock California Inv. Qual. Muni. Tr.
  RAA
One Seaport Plaza
New York, NY 10292 212-214-3332
Financial - investment management

BlackRock Florida Inv. Qual. Muni. Tr. RFA
One Seaport Plaza
New York, NY 10292 212-214-3332
Financial - investment management

BlackRock New Jersey Inv. Qual. Muni. Tr.
  RNJ
One Seaport Plaza
New York, NY 10292 212-214-3332
Financial - investment management

BlackRock New York Inv. Qual. Muni. Tr. RNY
One Seaport Plaza
New York, NY 10292 212-214-3332
Financial - investment management

Blair Corp. BL
220 Hickory St.
Warren, PA 16366 814-723-3600
Retail - mail order & direct

Blessings Corp. BCO
200 Enterprise Dr.
Newport News, VA 23603 804-887-2100
Diversified operations

Blount, Inc. BLTA
4520 Executive Park Dr.
Montgomery, AL 36116 205-244-4000
Machinery - general industrial
  [DRP 5%]

Boddie-Noell Properties, Inc. BNP
3710 One First Union Center
Charlotte, NC 28202 704-333-1367
Real estate investment trust
  [DRP]

Bowl America Inc. BWLA
6446 Edsall Rd.
Alexandria, VA 22312 703-941-6300
Leisure & recreational services

Bowmar Instrument Corp. BOM
5080 N. 40th St., Ste. 475
Phoenix, AZ 85018 602-957-0271
Electrical products - misc.

Bowne & Co., Inc. BNE
345 Hudson St.
New York, NY 10014 212-924-5500
Printing - commercial

Brad Ragan, Inc. BRD
4404-G Stuart Andrew Blvd.
Charlotte, NC 28217 704-521-2100
Rubber tires

Brandon Systems Corp. BRA
One Harmon Plaza
Secaucus, NJ 07094 201-392-0800
Computers - services

Brandywine Realty Trust BDN
200 Berwin Park, Ste. 104
Berwin, PA 19312 215-251-9111
Real estate investment trust

Brascan Ltd. BRS.A
BCE Place, Suite 4400, P.O. Box 762
Toronto, Ontario, Canada M5J 2T3
416-363-9491
Investment management company O

Brock Exploration Corp. BKE
225 Baronne St., Ste. 700
New Orleans, LA 70112 504-586-1815
Oil & gas - US exploration & production

Buffton Corp. BFX
226 Bailey Ave., Ste. 101
Fort Worth, TX 76107 817-332-4761
Diversified operations

C. H. Heist Corp. HST
810 N. Belcher Rd.
Clearwater, FL 34625 813-461-5656
Industrial maintenance

Cablevision Systems Corp. CVC
One Media Crossways
Woodbury, NY 11797 516-364-8450
Cable TV O

Cagle's, Inc. CGLA
2000 Hills Ave., N.W.
Atlanta, GA 30318 404-355-2820
Food - meat products

Calprop Corp. CPP
5456 McConnell Ave.
Los Angeles, CA 90066 310-306-4314
Real estate development

Calton, Inc. CN
500 Craig Rd.
Manalapan, NJ 07726 908-780-1800
Real estate development

Cambrex Corp. CBM
One Meadowlands Plaza
East Rutherford, NJ 07073 201-804-3000
Chemicals - diversified

Cancer Treatment Holding, Inc. CTH
4491 S. State Rd. Seven
Fort Lauderdale, FL 33314 305-321-9555
Medical services

Capital Realty Investors Tax Ex. Fd. L.P. I CRA
11200 Rockville Pike
Rockville, MD 20852 301-468-9200
Financial - investment management

Capital Realty Investors Tax Ex. Fd. L.P. II
CRB
11200 Rockville Pike
Rockville, MD 20852 301-468-9200
Financial - investment management

Capital Realty Investors Tax Ex. Fd. L.P. III
CRL
11200 Rockville Pike
Rockville, MD 20852 301-468-9200
Financial - investment management

Carrington Laboratories, Inc. CRN
2001 Walnut Hill Ln.
Irving, TX 75038 214-518-1300
Biomedical & genetic products

Castle Convertible Fund, Inc. CVF
75 Maiden Ln.
New York, NY 10038 212-806-8800
Financial - investment management

Catalina Lighting, Inc. LTG
6073 NW 167th St. #16
Miami, FL 33015 305-558-4777
Building products - lighting fixtures

Centennial Technologies, Inc. CTN
37 Manning Rd.
Billerica, MA 01821 508-670-0646
Computers - peripheral equipment

CenterPoint Properties, Inc. CNT
401 N. Michigan Ave.
Chicago, IL 60611 312-346-5600
Real estate investment trust

Central Securities Corp. CET
375 Park Ave.
New York, NY 10152 212-688-3011
Financial - investment management

Century Communications Corp. CTY
50 Locust Ave.
New Canaan, CT 06840 203-972-2000
Cable TV O

Chad Therapeutics, Inc. CTU
9445 De Soto Ave.
Chatsworth, CA 91311 818-882-0883
Medical products

Chambers Development Co., Inc. CDVA
10700 Frankstown Rd.
Pittsburgh, PA 15235 412-242-6237
Pollution control equipment & services

Champion Enterprises, Inc. CHB
2701 University Dr., Ste. 320
Auburn Hills, MI 48326 313-340-9090
Building - mobile homes & RV

Charter Medical Corp. CMD
3414 Peachtree Rd. NE
Atlanta, GA 30326 404-841-9200
Medical services O

Charter Power Systems, Inc. CHP
3043 Walton Rd., PO Box 239
Plymouth Meeting, PA 19462
610-828-9000
Electrical components - misc.

Chesapeake Biological Laboratories, Inc.
PHD
11412 Crownridge Dr.
Ownings Mills, MD 21117
410-998-9800
Medical products

Cheshire Financial Corp. CFX
194 West St.
Keene, NH 03431 603-352-2502
Banks - northeast

Cheyenne Software, Inc. CYE
3 Expressway Plaza
Roslyn Heights, NY 11577
516-484-5110
Computers - software O

Chicago Rivet & Machine Co. CVR
901 Frontenac Rd., PO Box 3061
Naperville, IL 60566 708-357-8500
Metal products - fasteners

CII Financial, Inc. CII
5627 Gibraltar Dr.
Pleasanton, CA 94588 510-416-8700
Insurance - accident & health

CIM High Yield Securities CIM
One Exchange Place, 7th Fl.
Boston, MA 02109 617-248-3717
Financial - investment management

Circa Pharmaceuticals, Inc. RXC
33 Ralph Ave., PO Box 30
Copiague, NY 11726 516-842-8383
Drugs - generic O

Citadel Holding Corp. CDL
600 N. Brand Blvd.
Glendale, CA 91203 818-956-7100
Financial - savings and loans

Citizens, Inc. CIA
400 E. Anderson Ln.
Austin, TX 78752 512-837-7100
Insurance - life

CliniCorp, Inc. BAK
1601 Belvedere Rd., Ste. 500E
West Palm Beach, FL 33406
407-684-2225
Medical services

CMI Corp. CMX
Interstate 40 and Morgan Rd.
Oklahoma City, OK 73101 405-787-6020
Machinery - material handling

Coast Distribution System CRV
1982 Zanker Rd.
San Jose, CA 95112 408-436-8611
Auto parts - retail & wholesale

Cognitronics Corp. CGN
3 Corporate Dr.
Danbury, CT 06810 203-830-3400
Computers - peripheral equipment

Cohen & Steers Realty Income Fund, Inc.
 RFI
757 Third Ave.
New York, NY 10017 212-832-3232
Financial - investment management

Collins & Aikman Group, Inc. CKGpA
8320 University Executive Park
Charlotte, NC 28262 704-548-2350
Diversified operations

Colonial Data Technologies Corp. CDT
80 Pickett District Rd.
New Milford, CT 06776 203-355-3178
Telecommunications equipment

Columbia Laboratories, Inc. COB
2665 S. Bayshore Dr., PH II-B
Miami, FL 33133 305-860-1670
Drugs

Columbus Energy Corp. EGY
1660 Lincoln St., Ste. 2400
Denver, CO 80264 303-861-5252
Oil & gas - US exploration & production

Cominco, Ltd
Waterfront Centre Tower
200 Burrad Street, 4th Floor
Vancouver, B.C. Canada V6C 3L7
604-682-0611
Mining and fertilizers O

Commercial Assets, Inc. CAX
3600 S. Yosemite St., Ste. 900
Denver, CO 80237 303-773-1221
Real estate investment trust
[DRP]

Comptek Research, Inc. CTK
110 Broadway
Buffalo, NY 14203 716-842-2700
Computers - software

CompuTrac, Inc. LLB
222 Municipal Dr.
Richardson, TX 75080 214-234-4241
Computers - software

Concord Fabrics Inc. CIS
1359 Broadway
New York, NY 10018 212-760-0300
Textiles - mill products

Consolidated-Tomoka Land Co. CTO
149 S. Ridgewood Ave.
Daytona Beach, FL 32114 904-255-7558
Real estate development

Continental Materials Corp. CUO
325 N. Wells St.
Chicago, IL 60610 312-661-7200
Building products - a/c & heating

Conversion Industries Inc. CVD
230 E. Colorado Blvd.
Pasadena, CA 91101 818-793-7526
Energy - alternate sources

ConVest Energy Corp. COV
2401 Fountain View Dr.
Houston, TX 77057 713-780-1952
Oil & gas - US exploration & production

Copley Properties, Inc. COP
399 Boylston St., 13th Fl.
Boston, MA 02116 617-578-1200
Real estate investment trust
[DRP]

Cornerstone Natural Gas, Inc. CGA
8080 N. Central Expressway
Dallas, TX 75206 214-691-5536
Oil & gas - production & pipeline

Corpus Christi Bancshares Inc. CTZ
2402 Leopard St.
Corpus Christi, TX 78408
512-887-3000
Banks - southwest

Crowley, Milner and Co. COM
2301 W. Lafayette Blvd.
Detroit, MI 48216 313-962-2400
Retail - regional department stores

Crown Central Petroleum Corp. CNPA
One N. Charles St.
Baltimore, MD 21201 410-539-7400
Oil refining & marketing

Crown Laboratories, Inc. CLL
3770 Howard Hughes Pkwy.
Las Vegas, NV 89109 702-696-9300
Drugs

Cruise America, Inc. RVR
11 W. Hampton Ave.
Mesa, AZ 85210 602-464-7300
Retail - misc.

Crystal Oil Co. COR
229 Milam St.
Shreveport, LA 71101 318-222-7791
Oil & gas - US exploration & production

CST Entertainment, Inc. CLR
5901 Green Valley Circle
Culver City, CA 90230 310-417-3444
Motion pictures & services

Cubic Corp. CUB
9333 Balboa Ave.
San Diego, CA 92123 619-277-6780
Electronics - military

Customedix Corp. CUS
53 N. Plains Industrial Rd.
Wallingford, CT 06492 203-284-9079
Medical & dental supplies

CVB Financial Corp. CVB
701 N. Haven Ave., Ste. 350
Ontario, CA 91764 909-980-4030
Banks - west

CVD Financial Corp. CVL
230 E. Colorado Blvd.
Pasadena, CA 91101
818-564-0593
Financial - business services

CXR Corp. CXR
2040 Fortune Dr., Ste. 102
San Jose, CA 95131 408-435-8520
Telecommunications equipment

Dakota Mining Corp. DKT
410 Seventeenth St., Ste. 2450
Denver, CO 80202 303-573-0221
Gold mining & processing

Dallas Gold and Silver Exchange, Inc. DLS
2817 Forest Ln.
Dallas, TX 75234 214-484-3662
Precious metals & jewelry

Danielson Holding Corp. DHC
767 Third Ave., Fifth Fl.
New York, NY 10017 212-888-0347
Diversified operations

Datametrics Corp. DC
8966 Comanche Ave.
Chatsworth, CA 91311 818-341-2901
Electronics - military

Dataram Corp. DTM
PO Box 7528
Princeton, NJ 08543 609-799-0071
Electrical components - semiconductors

Davstar Industries, Ltd. DVS
3050 Red Hill Ave.
Costa Mesa, CA 92626 714-668-5858
Medical products O

Daxor Corp. DXR
350 Fifth Ave., Ste. 7120
New York, NY 10118 212-244-0555
Medical services

Decorator Industries, Inc. DII
10011 Pines Blvd., Ste. 201
Pembroke Pines, FL 33024
305-436-8909
Textiles - home furnishings

Del Electronics Corp. DEL
1 Commerce Park
Valhalla, NY 10595 914-686-3600
Electronics - components & systems

Del Laboratories, Inc. DLI
565 Broad Hollow Rd.
Farmingdale, NY 11735
516-293-7070
Cosmetics & toiletries

Devon Energy Corp. DVN
20 N. Broadway, Ste., 1500
Oklahoma City, OK 73102
405-235-3611
Oil & gas - US exploration & production

DI Industries, Inc. DRL
450 Gears Rd., Ste. 625
Houston, TX 77067 713-874-0202
Oil & gas - field services

Diagnostic/Retrieval Systems, Inc. DRSA
16 Thornton Rd.
Oakland, NJ 07436 201-337-3800
Electronics - military

Digicon Inc. DGC
3701 Kirby Dr., Ste. 112
Houston, TX 77098 713-526-5611
Oil & gas - field services

Digital Communications Technology Corp.
DCT
3941 SW 47th Ave.
Fort Lauderdale, FL 33314
305-791-6711
Machinery - general industrial

DIMAC Corp. DMC
One Corporate Woods Dr.
Bridgeton, MO 63044 314-344-8000
Business services - marketing

DiMark, Inc. DMK
2050 Cabot Blvd. West
Langhorne, PA 19047 215-750-6600
Printing - commercial

Diodes Inc. DIO
3050 E. Hillcrest Dr.
Westlake Village, CA 91362
805-446-4800
Electrical components - semiconductors

Diversified Communications Industries, Ltd.
DVC
601 Clearwater Park Rd.
West Palm Beach, FL 33401
407-655-9101
Diversified operations

Dixon Ticonderoga Co. DXT
2600 Maitland Center Pkwy.
Maitland, FL 32751 407-875-9000
Office & art materials

Donnelly Corp. DON
414 E. Fortieth St.
Holland, MI 49423 616-786-7000
Automotive & trucking - original equipment
[DRP]

DRCA Medical Corp. DRC
Three Riverway, Ste. 1430
Houston, TX 77056 713-439-7511
Medical services

Dreyfus California Municipal Income, Inc.
DCM
144 Glenn Curtiss Blvd.
Uniondale, NY 11556 516-794-5200
Financial - investment management

Dreyfus Municipal Income, Inc. DMF
144 Glenn Curtiss Blvd.
Uniondale, NY 11556 516-794-5200
Financial - investment management

Dreyfus New York Municipal Income, Inc.
DNM
144 Glenn Curtiss Blvd.
Uniondale, NY 11556 516-794-5200
Financial - investment management

Driver-Harris Co. DRH
308 Middlesex St.
Harrison, NJ 07029 201-483-4802
Metals - non ferrous

Ducommun Inc. DCO
23301 S. Wilmington Ave.
Carson, CA 90745 310-513-7200
Aerospace - aircraft equipment

Duplex Products Inc. DPX
1947 Bethany Rd., PO Box 1947
Sycamore, IL 60178 815-895-2101
Paper - business forms

Dycam Inc. DYC
9588 Topanga Canyon Blvd.
Chatsworth, CA 91311 818-998-8008
Electronics - components & systems

E-Z Serve Corp. EZS
2550 North Loop West
Houston, TX 77092 713-684-4300
Oil refining & marketing

Earl Scheib, Inc. ESH
8737 Wilshire Blvd.
Beverly Hills, CA 90211 310-652-4880
Auto parts - retail & wholesale

Eastern Co. EML
112 Bridge St.
Naugatuck, CT 06770 203-729-2255
Metal fabrication/mine supports
[DRP]

Echo Bay Mines, Ltd. ECO
370 Seventeeth Street
Denver, Colorado 80202
303-592-8000
Gold & silver mining O

ECI International, Inc. ECI
2700 Teagarden St.
San Leandro, CA 94577 510-614-0180
Pollution control equipment & services

Ecology and Environment, Inc. EEI
368 Pleasant View Dr.
Lancaster, NY 14086 716-684-8060
Pollution control equipment & services

Edisto Resources Corp. EDS
2121 San Jacinto St., 26th Fl.
Dallas, TX 75201 214-880-0243
Oil & gas - offshore drilling

EDITEK, Inc. EDI
1238 Anthony Rd.
Burlington, NC 27215 910-226-6311
Medical products

Elan Corp, Plc ADS ELN
Monksland, Athlone
County Westmeath, Ireland
353-902-94666
Drug Formulation O

Eldorado Bancorp ELB
17752 E. Seventeenth St.
Tustin, CA 92680 714-830-8800
Banks - west

Ellsworth Convertible Growth and Income
  Fund ECF
56 Pine St.
New York, NY 10005 212-269-9236
Financial - investment management

Elsinore Corp. ELS
202 Fremont St.
Las Vegas, NV 89101 702-385-4011
Leisure & recreational services

Empire of Carolina, Inc. EMP
441 S. Federal Highway
Deerfield Beach, FL 33441 305-428-9001
Diversified operations

Encore Marketing International, Inc. EMI
4501 Forbes Blvd.
Lanham, MD 20706 301-459-8020
Business services - marketing

Energy Service Co., Inc. ESV
1445 Ross Ave., Ste. 2700
Dallas, TX 75202 214-922-1500
Oil & gas - offshore drilling

Engex, Inc. EGX
44 Wall St.
New York, NY 10005 212-495-4200
Financial - investment management

Environmental Tectonics Corp. ETC
County Line Industrial Park
Southampton, PA 18966 215-355-9100
Instruments - control

Enzo Biochem, Inc. ENZ
60 Executive Blvd.
Farmingdale, NY 11735 516-755-5500
Biomedical & genetic products O

Epitope, Inc. EPT
8505 S.W. Creekside Place
Beaverton, OR 97005 503-641-6115
Biomedical & genetic products O

Equity Income Fund First Exchange (AT&T)
  ATF
48 Wall St.
New York, NY 10286 800-221-7771
Financial - investment management

Equus II Inc. EQS
2929 Allen Parkway, Ste. 2500
Houston, TX 77019 713-529-0900
Financial - investment management

ESCAgenetics Corp. ESN
830 Bransten Rd.
San Carlos, CA 94070 415-595-5335
Biomedical & genetic products

Espey Mfg. & Electronics Corp. ESP
Congress & Ballston Aves.
Saratoga Springs, NY 12866
518-584-4100
Electronics - components & systems

Essex Financial Partners L.P. ESX
370 17th St., Ste. 4125
Denver, CO 80202 800-477-8209
Financial - savings and loans

Everest & Jennings International Ltd. EJ
1100 Corporate Square Dr.
St. Louis, MO 63132 314-569-3515
Medical & dental supplies

Excel Industries, Inc. EXC
1120 N. Main St.
Elkhart, IN 46514 219-264-2131
Automotive & trucking - original equipment

EXX, Inc. EXXA
250 W. 57th St., Ste. 713
New York, NY 10107
212-757-1717
Machinery - electrical

F.A. Tucker Group, Inc. TCK
75 E. Wacker Dr., Ste. 1300
Chicago, IL 60601 312-368-0653
Construction - heavy

Fab Industries, Inc. FIT
200 Madison Ave.
New York, NY 10016
212-592-2700
Textiles - mill products

Falcon Cable Systems Co. FAL
10900 Wilshire Blvd.
Los Angeles, CA 90024 310-824-9990
Cable TV

FFP Partners, L.P. FFP
2801 Glenda Ave.
Fort Worth, TX 76117 817-838-4700
Retail - convenience stores

Fibreboard Corp. FBD
2121 N. California Blvd.
Walnut Creek, CA 94596 510-274-0700
Building products - wood

FINA, Inc. FI
8350 N. Central Expressway
Dallas, TX 75206 214-750-2400
Oil refining & marketing [DRP]

Financial Federal Corp. FIF
400 Park Ave., 8th Fl.
New York, NY 10022 212-888-3344
Financial - business services

First Australia Fund, Inc. IAF
One Seaport Plaza
New York, NY 10292 212-214-3334
Financial - investment management

First Australia Prime Income Fund, Inc.
 FAX
One Seaport Plaza
New York, NY 10292 212-214-3334
Financial - investment management

First Central Financial Corp. FCC
266 Merrick Rd.
Lynbrook, NY 11563 516-593-7070
Insurance - property & casualty

First Citizens BancStock, Inc. FIR
1100 Brashear Ave.
Morgan City, LA 70380 504-385-0330
Banks - southeast

First City Bancorp, Inc. FCT
201 S. Church St.
Murfreesboro, TN 37130 615-898-1111
Banks - southeast

First Empire State Corp. FES
One M&T Plaza
Buffalo, NY 14240 716-842-5445
Banks - northeast [DRP]

First Federal of Alabama, F.S.B. FAB
1811 Second Ave.
Jasper, AL 35502 205-221-4111
Financial - savings and loans

First Iberian Fund, Inc. IBF
One Seaport Plaza
New York, NY 10292 212-214-3332
Financial - investment management

Flanigan's Enterprises, Inc. BDL
2841 Cypress Creek Rd.
Fort Lauderdale, FL 33309
305-974-9003
Retail - food & restaurants

Florida Public Utilities Co. FPU
401 S. Dixie Hwy.
West Palm Beach, FL 33401
407-832-2461
Utility - gas distribution [DRP]

Florida Rock Industries, Inc. FRK
155 E. 21st St.
Jacksonville, FL 32206 904-355-1781
Construction - cement & concrete

Foodarama Supermarkets, Inc. FSM
303 W. Main St.
Freehold, NJ 07728 908-462-4700
Retail - supermarkets

Forest City Enterprises, Inc. FCEA
10800 Brookpark Rd.
Cleveland, OH 44130 216-267-1200
Real estate development

Forest Laboratories, Inc. FRX
150 E. 58th St.
New York, NY 10155
212-421-7850
Drugs O

Fortune Petroleum Corp. FPX
30101 Agoura Court, Ste. 110
Agoura Hills, CA 91301 818-991-0526
Oil & gas - US exploration & production

Forum Retirement Partners, L.P. FRL
8900 Keystone Crossing
Indianapolis, IN 46240 317-846-0700
Real estate operations

Fountain Powerboat Industries, Inc. FPI
PO Drawer 457
Washington, NC 27889 919-975-2000
Leisure & recreational products

FPA Corp. FPO
2507 Philmont Ave.
Huntingdon Valley, PA 19006
215-947-8900
Real estate development

Franklin Advantage Real Estate Income Fund
 FAD
PO Box 7777
San Mateo, CA 94403 415-312-2000
Real estate investment trust

Franklin Holding Corp. FKL
450 Park Ave.
New York, NY 10022 212-486-2323
Financial - SBIC & commercial

Franklin Real Estate Income Fund FIN
PO Box 7777
San Mateo, CA 94403 415-312-2000
Real estate investment trust

Franklin Select Real Estate Income Fund FSN
PO Box 7777
San Mateo, CA 94403 415-312-2000
Real estate investment trust

Frequency Electronics, Inc. FEI
55 Charles Lindbergh Blvd.
Mitchell Field, NY 11553 516-794-4500
Electronics - military

Fresenius USA, Inc. FRN
2637 Shadelands Dr.
Walnut Creek, CA 94598 510-295-0200
Medical products

Friedman Industries, Inc. FRD
4001 Homestead Rd.
Houston, TX 77028 713-672-9433
Steel - production

Frisch's Restaurants, Inc. FRS
2800 Gilbert Ave.
Cincinnati, OH 45206 513-961-2660
Retail - food & restaurants

Frontier Adjusters of America, Inc. FAJ
45 E. Monterey Way
Phoenix, AZ 85012   602-264-1061
Insurance - brokerage

Gainsco, Inc. GNA
500 Commerce St.
Fort Worth, TX 76102   817-336-2500
Insurance - property & casualty

Galaxy Cablevision, L.P. GTV
1220 N. Main
Sikeston, MO 63801   314-471-3080
Cable TV

Gamma Biologicals, Inc. GBL
3700 Mangum Rd.
Houston, TX 77092   713-681-8481
Biomedical & genetic products

Garan, Inc. GAN
350 Fifth Ave.
New York, NY 10118
212-563-2000
Textiles - apparel

Gaylord Container Corp. GCR
500 Lake Cook Rd., Suite 400
Deerfield, IL 60015   708-405-5500
Paper & paper products O

Gelman Sciences Inc. GSC
600 S. Wagner Rd.
Ann Arbor, MI 48106   313-665-0651
Filtration products

General Automation, Inc. GA
1045 S. East St., PO Box 4883
Anaheim, CA 92803   714-778-4800
Computers - mini & micro

General Employment Enterprises, Inc.
JOB
One Tower Ln., Ste. 2100
Oakbrook Terrace, IL 60181
708-954-0400
Business services

General Kinetics Inc. GKI
13505 Dulles Technology Dr.
Herndon, VA 22071   703-713-1400
Diversified operations

General Microwave Corp. GMW
5500 New Horizons Blvd.
Amityville, NY 11701   516-226-8900
Electrical components - misc.

Genisco Technology Corp. GES
1230 S. Lewis St.
Anaheim, CA 92805   714-563-4300
Computers - mini & micro

Genovese Drug Stores, Inc. GDXA
80 Marcus Dr.
Melville, NY 11747   516-420-1900
Retail - drug stores

Giant Food Inc. GFSA
6300 Sheriff Rd.
Landover, MD 20785   301-341-4100
Retail - supermarkets O
[DRP]

Glacier Water Services, Inc. HOO
2261 Cosmos Court
Carlsbad, CA 92009
619-930-2420
Retail - misc.

Global Small Cap Fund Inc. GSG
1285 Avenue of the Americas
New York, NY 10019   800-852-4750
Financial - investment management

Globalink, Inc. GNK
9302 Lee Highway, 12th Fl.
Fairfax, VA 22031   703-273-5600
Computers - software

Go-Video, Inc. VCR
14455 N. Hayden Rd., Ste. 219
Scottsdale, AZ 85260
602-998-3400
Audio & video home products

Golden Star Resources Ltd. GSR
1700 Lincoln St., Ste. 1950
Denver, CO 80203   303-830-9000
Gold mining & processing

Gorman-Rupp Co. GRC
305 Bowman St.
Mansfield, OH 44903   419-755-1011
Machinery - general industrial

Graham Corp. GHM
20 Florence Ave.
Batavia, NY 14020   716-343-2216
Machinery - general industrial

Greenman Bros. Inc. GMN
105 Price Parkway
Farmingdale, NY 11735   516-293-5300
Wholesale distribution - consumer products

Greyhound Lines, Inc. BUS
15110 N. Dallas Parkway
Dallas, TX 75248   214-715-7000
Transportation - bus O

Grove Real Estate Asset Trust GRE
598 Asylum Ave.
Hartford, CT 06105   203-523-3960
Real estate investment trust

Guardian Bancorp GB
800 S. Figueroa St.
Los Angeles, CA 90017   213-239-0800
Banks - west

Gulf Canada Resources Limited GOU
P.O. Box 130, Station M
Calgary, Alberta, Canada T2P 2H7
Oil & Gas Exploration O

Gull Laboratories, Inc. GUL
1011 E. 4800 South
Salt Lake City, UT 84117 801-263-3524
Medical products

Gundle Environmental Systems, Inc. GUN
19103 Gundle Rd.
Houston, TX 77073 713-443-8564
Pollution control equipment & services

H. W. Kaufman Financial Group, Inc. HWK
30833 Northwestern Hwy.
Farmington Hills, MI 48334
810-932-9000
Insurance - property & casualty

Halifax Corp. HX
5250 Cherokee Ave.
Alexandria, VA 22312 703-750-2202
Engineering - R & D services

Hallmark Financial Services, Inc. HAF
14651 Dallas Pkwy., Ste. 900
Dallas, TX 75240 214-404-1637
Insurance - property & casualty

Hallwood Energy Partners, L.P. HEP
4582 S. Ulster St. Parkway
Denver, CO 80237 303-850-7373
Oil & gas - US exploration & production

Hallwood Realty Partners, L.P. HRY
3710 Rawlins St., Ste. 1500
Dallas, TX 75219 214-528-5588
Real estate investment trust

Halsey Drug Co., Inc. HDG
1827 Pacific St.
Brooklyn, NY 11233 718-467-7500
Drugs - generic

Hampton Industries, Inc. HAI
2000 Greenville Hwy.
Kinston, NC 28502 919-527-8011
Textiles - apparel

Hanger Orthopedic Group, Inc. HGR
8200 Wisconsin Ave.
Bethesda, MD 20814
301-986-0701
Medical products

Hanover Direct Inc. HNV
1500 Harbor Blvd.
Weehawken, NJ 07087 201-863-7300
Retail - mail order & direct

Harken Energy Corp. HEC
2505 N. Highway 360, Ste. 800
Grand Prairie, TX 75050 817-695-4900
Oil & gas - US exploration & production

Harlyn Products, Inc. HRN
1515 S. Main St.
Los Angeles, CA 90015
213-746-0745
Precious metals & jewelry

Harold's Stores, Inc. HLD
765 Asp Ave.
Norman, OK 73069
405-329-4045
Retail - apparel & shoes

Harvey Group Inc. HRA
600 Secaucus Rd.
Secaucus, NJ 07094 201-865-3418
Retail - consumer electronics

Hasbro, Inc. HAS
200 Narragansett Park Dr.
Pawtucket, RI 02862 401-431-8697
Toys - games & hobby products

Hastings Manufacturing Co. HMF
325 N. Hanover St.
Hastings, MI 49058 616-945-2491
Automotive & trucking - replacement parts

Health Professionals, Inc. HPI
515 E. Lasolas Blvd.
Fort Lauderdale, FL 33301
305-766-2552
Medical services

Health-Chem Corp. HCH
1212 Avenue of the Americas
New York, NY 10036 212-398-0700
Medical products

Health-Mor Inc. HMI
3500 Payne Ave.
Cleveland, OH 44114
216-432-1990
Appliances - household

Healthcare America, Inc. HAM
912 Capitol of Texas Hwy. S.
Austin, TX 78746 512-329-8821
Hospitals

Heartland Partners, L.P. HTL
547 W. Jackson Blvd.
Chicago, IL 60606 312-822-0400
Real estate operations

HEICO Corp. HEI
3000 Taft St.
Hollywood, FL 33021 305-987-6101
Aerospace - aircraft equipment

Hein-Werner Corp. HNW
2120 Pewaukee Rd., PO Box 1606
Waukesha, WI 53187 414-542-6611
Machine tools & related products

Helionetics Inc. ZAP
2300 Main St.
Irvine, CA 97214 714-261-8313
Electronics - components & systems

Helm Resources, Inc. HHH
66 Field Point Rd.
Greenwich, CT 06830 203-629-1400
Diversified operations

Helmstar Group, Inc. HLM
Two World Trade Center
New York, NY 10048 212-775-0400
Financial - investment bankers

Hemlo Gold Mines, Inc. HEM
1 Adelaide Street East, Suite 2902
Toronto, Ontario, Canada M5C 2Z9
416-982-7116
Gold Mining O

Heritage Media Corp. HTG
13355 Noel Rd., Ste. 1500
Dallas, TX 75240 214-702-7380
Broadcasting - radio & TV

Hi-Shear Technology Corp. HSR
24225 Garnier St.
Torrance, CA 90505 310-784-2100
Aerospace - aircraft equipment

Highlander Income Fund Inc. HLA
222 S. Ninth St.
Minneapolis, MN 55402 800-866-7778
Financial - investment management

HMG Digital Technologies Corp. HDT
15 Gilpin Ave.
Hauppauge, NY 11788 516-234-0200
Miscellaneous - not elsewhere classified

HMG/Courtland Properties, Inc. HMG
2701 S. Bayshore Dr.
Coconut Grove, FL 33133
305-854-6803
Real estate investment trust

Holco Mortgage Acceptance Corp.-I HOLA
220 W. Colfax St., Ste. 200
South Bend, IN 46601 219-284-3789
Financial - investment management

Holly Corp. HOC
100 Crescent Court, Ste. 1600
Dallas, TX 75201 214-871-3555
Oil refining & marketing

Hondo Oil & Gas Co. HOG
410 E. College Blvd.
Roswell, NM 88201 505-625-8700
Oil & gas - US exploration & production

Hooper Holmes, Inc. HH
170 Mt. Airy Rd.
Basking Ridge, NJ 7920 908-766-5000
Business services

Houston Biotechnology Inc. HBI
3608 Research Forest Dr.
The Woodlands, TX 77381
713-363-0999
Drugs

Hovnanian Enterprises, Inc. HOV
10 Highway 35, PO Box 500
Red Bank, NJ 07701 908-747-7800
Building - residential & commercial

Howard B. Wolf, Inc. HBW
3809 Parry Ave.
Dallas, TX 75226 214-823-9941
Textiles - apparel

Howell Industries, Inc. HOW
17515 W. 9 Mile Rd., Ste. 650
Southfield, MI 48075 313-424-8220
Automotive & trucking - original equipment

Howtek, Inc. HTK
21 Park Ave.
Hudson, NH 03051 603-882-5200
Computers - peripheral equipment

Hudson General Corp. HGC
111 Great Neck Rd., PO Box 355
Great Neck, NY 11022
516-487-8610
Transportation - services

Identix Inc. IDX
510 N. Pastoria Ave.
Sunnyvale, CA 94086 408-739-2000
Electronics - measuring instruments

IGI, Inc. IG
Wheat Rd. and Lincoln Ave.
Buena, NJ 08310 609-697-1441
Drugs

Imperial Holly Corp. IHK
One Imperial Square, Ste. 200
Sugar Land, TX 77487 713-491-9181
Food - sugar & refining
[DRP]

Imperial Oil Ltd. IMO
111 St. Clair Ave. West
Toronto, Ont., M5W 1K3 Canada
416-968-5076
Oil - natural gas [DRP]

Income Opportunity Realty Trust IOT
10670 N. Central Expwy.
Dallas, TX 75231 214-692-4700
Real estate investment trust

INCSTAR Corp. ISR
1990 Industrial Blvd.
Stillwater, MN 55082 612-439-9710
Medical products

Incyte Pharmaceuticals, Inc. IPI
330 Hillview Ave.
Palo Alto, CA 94304 415-855-0555
Drugs

Inefficient-Market Fund, Inc. IMF
1345 Avenue of the Americas
New York, NY 10105 212-698-3412
Financial - investment management

Information Display Technology, Inc. IDT
1305 Grandview Ave.
Pittsburgh, PA 15211 412-381-2600
Video equipment

Instron Corp. ISN
100 Royall St.
Canton, MA 02021 617-828-2500
Electronics - measuring instruments

Intelcom Group Inc. ITR
1050 17th St., Ste. 1610
Denver, CO 80265 303-572-5960
Telecommunications services O

Intelligent Systems Corp. INS
4355 Shackleford Rd.
Norcross, GA 30093 404-381-2900
Computers - peripheral equipment

Interchange Financial Services Corp. ISB
Park 80 West/Plaza Two
Saddle Brook, NJ 07662 201-703-2265
Banks - northeast [DRP]

Interdigital Communications Corp. IDC
2200 Renaissance Blvd.
King of Prussia, PA 19406 610-278-7800
Telecommunications equipment O

Interline Resources Corp. IRC
160 West Canyon Crest Dr.
Alpine, UT 84004 801-756-3031
Oil & gas - production & pipeline

Intermagnetics General Corp. IMG
450 Old Niskayuna Rd.
Latham, NY 12110 518-782-1122
Superconductive Metals O

International Lottery, Inc. ILI
6665 Creek Rd.
Cincinnati, OH 45242 513-792-7000
Leisure & recreational products

International Movie Group, Inc. IMV
1900 Avenue of the Stars
Los Angeles, CA 90067 310-556-2830
Leisure & recreational services

International Murex Technologies Corporation
  MXX
3075 Northwoods Circle
Norcross, GA 30071 404-662-0660
Medical diagnostic products

International Power Machines Corp. PWR
2975 Miller Park North
Garland, TX 75042 214-272-8000
Computers - peripheral equipment

International Remote Imaging Systems, Inc.
  IRI
9162 Eton Ave.
Chatsworth, CA 91311 818-709-1244
Medical instruments

International Thoroughbred Breeders, Inc.
  ITB
PO Box 1232
Cherry Hill, NJ 08034 609-488-3838
Leisure & recreational services

Interstate General Co. L.P. IGC
222 Smallwood Village Center
St. Charles, MD 20602 301-843-8600
Real estate development

Intersystems Inc. II
8790 Wallisville Rd.
Houston, TX 77029 713-675-0307
Machinery - material handling

Investors Insurance Group, Inc. IIG
3030 Hartley Rd., Ste. 390
Jacksonville, FL 32257 904-260-6990
Insurance - life

Ion Laser Technology, Inc. ILT
3828 S. Main St.
Salt Lake City, UT 84115 801-262-5555
Lasers - systems & components

IVAX Corp. IVX
8800 N.W. 36th St.
Miami, FL 33178 305-590-2200
Medical products O

J.M. Peters Co., Inc. JMP
3501 Jamboree Rd., Ste. 200
Newport Beach, CA 92660 714-854-2500
Building - residential & commercial

Jaclyn, Inc. JLN
635 59th St.
West New York, NJ 07093
201-868-9400
Shoes & related apparel

Jalate Ltd. JLT
1675 S. Alameda St.
Los Angeles, CA 90021 213-765-5000
Apparel

Jan Bell Marketing, Inc. JBM
13801 N.W. 14th St.
Sunrise, FL 33323 305-846-2705
Precious metals & jewelry O

Jetronic Industries, Inc. JET
4200 Mitchell St.
Philadelphia, PA 19128
215-482-7660
Diversified operations

Jewelmasters, Inc. JEM
777 S. Flagler Dr.
West Palm Beach, FL 33401
407-655-7260
Retail - jewelry stores

John Fluke Mfg. Co., Inc. FLK
6920 Seaway Blvd.
Everett, WA 98203 206-347-6100
Electronics - measuring instruments

Jones Intercable, Inc. JTV
9697 E. Mineral Ave.
Englewood, CO 80112 303-792-3111
Cable TV

Jones Plumbing Systems, Inc. JPS
6247 Amber Hills Rd.
Birmingham, AL 35210 205-956-5511
Building products - misc.

Joule Inc. JOL
1245 U.S. Route 1 South
Edison, NJ 08837 908-494-6500
Business services

Jupiter National, Inc. JPI
39 W. Montgomery Ave.
Rockville, MD 20850 301-738-3939
Financial - SBIC & commercial

Keane, Inc. KEA
Ten City Square
Boston, MA 02129 617-241-9200
Computers - services

Keithley Instruments, Inc. KEI
28775 Aurora Rd.
Cleveland, OH 44139 216-248-0400
Instruments - scientific [DRP]

Kelley Oil Corporation KLY
601 Jefferson St., Ste. 1100
Houston, TX 77002 713-652-5200
Oil & gas - US exploration & production
[DRP]

Kenwin Shops, Inc. KWN
4747 Granite Dr.
Tucker, GA 30084 404-938-0451
Retail - apparel & shoes

Key Energy Group Inc. KEG
257 Livingston Ave.
New Brunswick, NJ 08901
908-247-4822
Oil & gas - production & pipeline

Killearn Properties of Georgia, Inc. KPI
100 Eagle Landing Way
Atlanta, GA 30281 404-389-2020
Real estate development

Kinark Corp. KIN
7060 S. Yale Ave.
Tulsa, OK 74136 918-494-0964
Chemicals - specialty

Kirby Corp. KEX
1775 St. James Place, Ste. 300
Houston, TX 77056 713-629-9370
Diversified operations O

KIT Manufacturing Co. KIT
530 E. Wardlow Rd.
Long Beach, CA 90807
310-595-7451
Building - mobile homes & RV

Kleer-Vu Industries, Inc. KVU
921 W. Artesia Blvd.
Compton, CA 90220 800-926-2526
Rubber & plastic products

Koger Equity, Inc. KE
3986 Boulevard Center Dr.
Jacksonville, FL 32207 904-398-3403
Real estate investment trust

KV Pharmaceutical Co. KVA
2503 S. Hanley Rd.
St. Louis, MO 63144 314-645-6600
Medical products

LaBarge, Inc. LB
707 N. Second St.
St. Louis, MO 63102
314-231-5960
Electronics - military

Lancer Corp. LAN
235 W. Turbo
San Antonio, TX 78216 210-344-3071
Machinery - material handling

Landauer, Inc. LDR
2 Science Rd.
Glenwood, IL 60425 708-755-7000
Engineering - R & D services

Landsing Pacific Fund, Inc. LPF
155 Bovet Rd., Ste. 101
San Mateo, CA 94402 415-513-5252
Real estate investment trust

Larizza Industries, Inc. LII
201 W. Big Beaver Rd.
Troy, MI 48084 313-689-5800
Automotive & trucking - original equipment

Laser Technology, Inc. LSR
7070 S. Tucson Way
Englewood, CO 80112 303-649-1000
Lasers - systems & components

Laurentian Capital Corp. LQ
640 Lee Rd.
Wayne, PA 19087 610-889-7400
Insurance - life

Lawrence Insurance Group, Inc. LWR
500 Fifth Ave., 56th Fl.
New York, NY 10110 212-944-8242
Insurance - property & casualty

Lazare Kaplan International Inc. LKI
529 Fifth Ave.
New York, NY 10017 212-972-9700
Precious metals & jewelry

Lee Pharmaceuticals LPH
1444 Santa Anita Ave.
South El Monte, CA 91733
818-442-3141
Cosmetics & toiletries

Lillian Vernon Corp. LVC
543 Main St.
New Rochelle, NY 10801
914-576-6400
Retail - mail order & direct

Littlefield, Adams & Co. LFA
1302 Rockland Ave. NW
Roanoke, VA 24012   703-366-2451
Apparel

Lumex, Inc. LUM
81 Spence St.
Bay Shore, NY 11706   516-273-2200
Medical & dental supplies

LXR Biotechnology Inc. LXR
1401 Marina Way South
Richmond, CA 94804   510-412-9100
Drugs

Lynch Corp. LGL
8 Sound Shore Dr., Ste. 290
Greenwich, CT 06830   203-629-3333
Diversified operations

Magnum Petroleum, Inc. MPM
42-600 Cook St., Ste. 160
Palm Desert, CA 92211   619-341-1520
Oil & gas - field services

Maine Public Service Co. MAP
209 State St.
Presque Isle, ME 04769   207-768-5811
Utility - electric power

Marlton Technologies, Inc. MTY
111 Presidential Blvd.
Bala Cynwyd, PA 19004
215-664-6900
Business services

MATEC Corp. MXC
75 South St.
Hopkinton, MA 01748   508-435-9039
Diversified operations

MAXXAM Inc. MXM
5847 San Felipe, Ste. 2600
Houston, TX 77057   713-975-7600
Diversified operations

McRae Industries, Inc. MRIA
402 N. Main St.
Mt. Gilead, NC 27306   910-439-6147
Shoes & related apparel

Measurement Specialities, Inc. MSS
80 Little Falls Rd.
Fairfield, NJ 07004   201-808-1819
Electronics - measuring instruments

Medco Research, Inc. MRE
85 J. T. Alexander Dr.
Research Triangle, NC 27709
919-549-8117
Medical services

Medeva Plc ADS MDV
10 St James Street
London, SW1A 1EF, England
44-71-8393888
Pharmaceuticals O

Media General, Inc. MEGA
333 E. Grace St.
Richmond, VA 23219   804-649-6000
Publishing - newspapers
[DRP]

Media Logic, Inc. TST
310 South St.
Plainville, MA 02762   508-695-2006
Electronics - measuring instruments

Medical Resources Companies of America
MRA
4265 Kellway Circle
Addison, TX 75244   214-407-8400
Nursing homes

Medicore, Inc. MDK
2337 W. 76th St.
Hialeah, FL 33016   305-558-4000
Medical products

MEDIQ Inc. MED
One MEDIQ Plaza
Pennsauken, NJ 08110
609-665-9300
Medical & dental supplies

MedQuist Inc. MBS
20 E. Clementon Rd.
Gibbsboro, NJ 08026   609-782-0300
Transportation - services

MEM Co., Inc. MEM
Union St. Extension
Northvale, NJ 07647   201-767-0100
Cosmetics & toiletries

Mental Health Management, Inc. MHM
7601 Lewinsville Rd., Ste. 200
McLean, VA 22102   703-749-4600
Medical services

Merchants Group, Inc. MGP
250 Main St.
Buffalo, NY 14202   716-849-3101
Insurance - property & casualty

Mercury Air Group, Inc. MAX
6851 W. Imperial Highway
Los Angeles, CA 90045   310-646-2994
Transportation - services

Meridian Point Realty Trust IV MPD
50 California St., Ste. 1600
San Francisco, CA 94111   415-956-3031
Real estate investment trust

Meridian Point Realty Trust VI MPF
50 California St., Ste. 1600
San Francisco, CA 94111   415-956-3031
Real estate investment trust

Meridian Point Realty Trust VII MPG
50 California St., Ste. 1600
San Francisco, CA 94111   415-956-3031
Real estate investment trust

Meridian Point Realty Trust VIII MPH
50 California St., Ste. 1600
San Francisco, CA 94111 415-956-3031
Real estate investment trust

Merrimac Industries, Inc. MRM
41 Fairfield Place
West Caldwell, NJ 07007 201-575-1300
Electronics - military

Met-Pro Corp. MPR
160 Cassell Rd., PO Box 144
Harleysville, PA 19438 215-723-6751
Pollution control equipment & services

Metrobank MBN
10900 Wilshire Blvd.
Los Angeles, CA 90024 310-824-5700
Banks - west

Metropolitan Realty Corp. MET
535 Griswold, Ste. 748
Detroit, MI 48226 313-961-5552
Real estate investment trust

Michael Anthony Jewelers, Inc. MAJ
115 S. MacQuesten Parkway
Mt. Vernon, NY 10550 914-699-0000
Precious metals & jewelry

Michael Baker Corp. BKR
420 Rouser Rd., Bldg. 3
Coraopolis, PA 15108 412-269-6300
Engineering - R & D services

Mid-America Bancorp MAB
500 W. Broadway
Louisville, KY 40202 502-589-3351
Banks - southeast

Mid-Atlantic Realty Trust MRR
1302 Concourse Dr., Ste. 202
Linthicum, MD 21090 410-684-2000
Real estate investment trust

MidSouth Bancorp, Inc. MSL
102 Versailles Blvd.
Lafayette, LA 70501
318-237-8343
Banks - southeast

Milwaukee Land Co. MWK
547 W. Jackson Blvd.
Chicago, IL 60661 312-294-0497
Real estate development

Minnesota Municipal Income Portfolio, Inc.
MXA
222 S. Ninth St.
Minneapolis, MN 55402 800-333-6000
Financial - investment management

Minnesota Municipal Term Trust, Inc. - II
MNB
222 S. Ninth St.
Minneapolis, MN 55402 800-333-6000
Financial - investment management

Mission West Properties MSW
6815 Flanders Dr., Ste. 250
San Diego, CA 92121 619-450-3135
Real estate operations

Monongahela Power Co. MPNpA
1310 Fairmont Ave.
Fairmont, WV 26554 304-366-3000
Utility - electric power

Moog Inc. MOGA
East Aurora, NY 14052
716-652-2000
Aerospace - aircraft equipment

Moore Medical Corp. MMD
389 John Downey Dr.
New Britain, CT 06050 203-826-3600
Drugs & sundries - wholesale

Morgan Stanley Group Income PERQS 1997
IGS
1251 Avenue of the Americas
New York, NY 10020 212-703-4000
Financial - investment management

Morgan's Foods, Inc. MR
25201 Chargin Blvd., Ste. 330
Beachwood, OH 44122 216-360-7500
Retail - food & restaurants

Motts Holdings, Inc. MSM
59 Leggett St.
East Hartford, CT 06108
203-289-3301
Diversified operations

Movie Star, Inc. MSI
136 Madison Ave.
New York, NY 10016 212-679-7260
Textiles - apparel

MSR Exploration Ltd. MSR
CBM Building, PO Box 250
Cut Bank, MT 59427 406-873-2235
Oil & gas - US exploration & production

MuniInsured Fund, Inc. MIF
800 Scudders Mill Rd.
Plainsboro, NJ 08536
609-282-2800
Financial - investment management

MuniVest Fund, Inc. MVF
PO Box 9011
Princeton, NJ 08543 609-282-2800
Financial - investment management

MuniYield Arizona Fund II, Inc. MZT
PO Box 9011
Princeton, NJ 08543 609-282-2800
Financial - investment management

MuniYield Arizona Fund, Inc. MZA
PO Box 9011
Princeton, NJ 08543 609-282-2800
Financial - investment management

Myers Industries, Inc. MYE
1293 S. Main St.
Akron, OH 44301 216-253-5592
Rubber & plastic products

Nabors Industries, Inc. NBR
515 W. Greens Rd., Ste. 1200
Houston, TX 77067 713-874-0035
Oil & gas - field services O

Nantucket Industries, Inc. NAN
105 Madison Ave.
New York, NY 10016 212-889-5656
Textiles - apparel

National Gas & Oil Co. NLG
1500 Granville Rd., PO Box AF
Newark, OH 43058 614-344-2102
Utility - gas distribution

National HealthCorp L.P. NHC
100 Vine St.
Murfreesboro, TN 37130 615-890-2020
Nursing homes

National Patent Development Corp. NPD
9 W. 57th St.
New York, NY 10019 212-826-8500
Medical & dental supplies

National Realty, L.P. NLP
10670 N. Central Expressway
Dallas, TX 75231 214-692-4700
Real estate operations

Natural Alternatives International, Inc. NAI
1185 Linda Vista Dr.
San Marcos, CA 92069 619-744-7340
Vitamins & nutritional products

New Mexico and Arizona Land Co. NZ
2810 N. 3rd St.
Phoenix, AZ 85004 602-266-5455
Real estate operations

New York Bancorp Inc. NYB
241-02 Northern Blvd.
Douglaston, NY 11362 718-631-8100
Banks - northeast

New York Tax-Exempt Income Fund, Inc.
  XTX
500 W. Madison St., Ste. 3000
Chicago, IL 60606 312-559-3000
Financial - investment management

New York Times Co. NYTA
229 W. 43rd St.
New York, NY 10036 212-556-1234
Publishing - newspapers O
[DRP]

North American Advanced Materials Corp.
  AAM
120 Sherlake Dr., PO Box 23556
Knoxville, TN 37922 615-691-2170
Ceramics & ceramic products

North American Trust NAM
615 Front St.
San Francisco, CA 94111 415-398-3590
Real estate investment trust [DRP]

North American Vaccine, Inc. NVX
12103 Indian Creek Court
Beltsville, MD 20705 301-470-6100
Immunobiological products O

Northbay Financial Corp. NBF
1360 Redwood Way
Petaluma, CA 94954 707-792-7400
Financial - savings and loans

Northern Indiana Public Service Co. NIp
5265 Hohman Ave.
Hammond, IN 46320 219-853-5200
Utility - gas distribution

Northern Technologies International Corp.
  NTI
6680 North Highway 59
Lino Lakes, MN 55014 612-784-1250
Instruments - control

NTN Communications, Inc. NTN
2121 Palomar Airport Rd.
Carlsbad, CA 92009 619-438-7400
Broadcasting - radio & TV O

NuMed Home Health Care, Inc. NHH
6505 Rockside Rd., Ste. 400
Independence, OH 44131
216-573-6500
Medical services

Nuveen California Premium Income Mun.
  Fund NCU
333 W. Wacker Dr.
Chicago, IL 60606 312-917-7700
Financial - investment management

Nuveen Florida Premium Income Municipal
  Fund NFO
333 W. Wacker Dr.
Chicago, IL 60606 312-917-7700
Financial - investment management

Nuveen Georgia Premium Income Mun. Fund
  NPG
333 W. Wacker Dr.
Chicago, IL 60606 312-917-7700
Financial - investment management

Nuveen Missouri Premium Income Municipal
  Fund NOM
333 W. Wacker Dr.
Chicago, IL 60606 312-917-7700
Financial - investment management

Nuveen New Jersey Premium Income Mun.
  Fund 3 NJU
333 W. Wacker Dr.
Chicago, IL 60606 312-917-7700
Financial - investment management

Nuveen New York Municipal Income Fund, Inc. NNM
333 W. Wacker Dr.
Chicago, IL 60606 312-917-7700
Financial - investment management

Nuveen New York Premium Income Municipal Fund NRY
333 W. Wacker Dr.
Chicago, IL 60606 312-917-7700
Financial - investment management

Nuveen Pennsylvania Premium Income Mun. Fd. 3 NAP
333 W. Wacker Dr.
Chicago, IL 60606 312-917-7700
Financial - investment management

Nuveen Washington Premium Income Mun. Fd. NPW
333 W. Wacker Dr.
Chicago, IL 60606 312-917-7700
Financial - investment management

NVR, Inc. NVR
7601 Lewinsville Rd., Ste. 300
McLean, VA 22102 703-761-2000
Building - residential & commercial

O'Sullivan Corp. OSL
1944 Valley Ave., PO Box 3510
Winchester, VA 22604 703-667-6666
Rubber & plastic products

One Liberty Properties, Inc. OLP
60 Cutter Mill Rd.
Great Neck, NY 11021
516-466-3100
Real estate investment trust

Onsite Energy Corp. ONS
701 Palomar Airport Rd.
Carlsbad, CA 92009 619-931-2400
Engineering - R & D services

Organogenesis Inc. ORG
83 Rogers St.
Cambridge, MA 02142 617-575-0775
Medical products O

Oriole Homes Corp. OHCA
1690 S. Congress Ave.
Delray Beach, FL 33445 407-274-2000
Building - residential & commercial

P. H. Glatfelter Co. GLT
228 S. Main St.
Spring Grove, PA 17362
717-225-4711
Paper & paper products

Pacific Gateway Properties, Inc. PGP
101 Spear St., Ste. 215
San Francisco, CA 94105
415-543-8600
Real estate operations

Pacific Gulf Properties Inc. PAG
363 San Miguel Dr., Ste. 100
Newport Beach, CA 92660 714-721-2700
Real estate investment trust

Page America Group, Inc. PGG
125 State St., Ste. 100
Hackensack, NJ 07601 201-342-6676
Telecommunications services

Pamida Holdings Corp. PAM
8800 F St.
Omaha, NE 68127 402-339-2400
Retail - discount & variety

Park National Corp. PRK
50 N. Third St., PO Box 850
Newark, OH 43058 614-349-8451
Financial - savings and loans

Partners Preferred Yield II, Inc. PYB
600 N. Brand Blvd.
Glendale, CA 91203 818-244-8080
Real estate investment trust

Partners Preferred Yield III, Inc. PYC
600 N. Brand Blvd.
Glendale, CA 91203 818-244-8080
Real estate investment trust

Partners Preferred Yield, Inc. PYA
600 N. Brand Blvd.
Glendale, CA 91203 818-244-8080
Real estate investment trust

Pay-Fone Systems, Inc. PYF
8100 Balboa Blvd.
Van Nuys, CA 91406 818-997-0808
Business services

PC Quote, Inc. PQT
300 S. Wacker Dr.
Chicago, IL 60606 312-913-2800
Business services

Peerless Tube Co. PLS
58 Locust Ave.
Bloomfield, NJ 07003 201-743-5100
Containers - metal

Pegasus Gold Inc. PGU
9 N. Post St., Ste. 400
Spokane, WA 99201 509-624-4653
Gold mining & processing

Penn Engineering & Manufacturing Co. PNN
PO Box 1000
Danboro, PA 18916 215-766-8853
Metal products - fasteners

Pennsylvania Real Estate Investment Trust PEI
455 Pennsylvania Ave.
Fort Washington, PA 19034
215-542-9250
Real estate investment trust

Penobscot Shoe Co. PSO
450 N. Main St., PO Box 545
Old Town, ME 04468 207-827-4431
Shoes & related apparel

Perini Corp. PCR
73 Mt. Wayte Ave., PO Box 9160
Framingham, MA 01701 508-628-2000
Construction - heavy

Phoenix Laser Systems, Inc. PXS
48041 Fremont Blvd.
Fremont, CA 94538 510-249-0300
Lasers - systems & components

Phoenix Network, Inc. PHX
1 Maritime Plaza, Ste. 2525
San Francisco, CA 94111 415-981-3000
Telecommunications services

Pico Products, Inc. PPI
12500 Foothill Blvd.
Lakeview Terrace, CA 91342
818-897-0028
Telecommunications equipment

Pitt-Des Moines, Inc. PDM
3400 Grand Ave.
Pittsburgh, PA 15225 412-331-3000
Construction - heavy

Pittsburgh & West Virginia Railroad PW
3 PPG Place, Ste. 410
Pittsburgh, PA 15222 212-687-4956
Real estate investment trust

Pittway Corp. PRY
200 S. Wacker Dr., Ste. 700
Chicago, IL 60606 312-831-1070
Diversified operations

Plains Resources Inc. PLX
1600 Smith St.
Houston, TX 77002 713-654-1414
Oil & gas - US exploration & production O

PLC Systems Inc. PLC
113 Cedar St., Ste. S-2
Milford, MA 01757 508-478-6046
Lasers - systems & components

PLM Equipment Growth Fund GFX
One Market, Steuart St. Tower
San Francisco, CA 94105 415-974-1399
Leasing

PLM Equipment Growth Fund II GFY
One Market, Steuart St. Tower
San Francisco, CA 94105
415-974-1399
Leasing

PLM Equipment Growth Fund III GFZ
One Market, Steuart St. Tower
San Francisco, CA 94105
415-974-1399
Leasing

PLM International, Inc. PLM
One Market, Steuart St. Tower
San Francisco, CA 94105 415-974-1399
Leasing

Plymouth Rubber Co., Inc. PLRA
104 Revere St.
Canton, MA 02021 617-828-0220
Rubber & plastic products

PMC Capital, Inc. PMC
18301 Biscayne Blvd.
North Miami Beach, FL 33160
305-933-5858
Financial - business services [DRP]

Polaris Industries Partners L.P. SNO
2424 S. 130th Circle
Omaha, NE 68144 800-255-1345
Leisure & recreational products

Polyphase Corp. PLY
175 Commerce Dr.
Fort Washington, PA 19034
215-643-6950
Electrical products - misc.

Porta Systems Corp. PSI
575 Underhill Blvd.
Syosset, NY 11791 516-364-9300
Telecommunications equipment

Portage Industries Corp. PTG
1325 Adams St.
Portage, WI 53901 608-742-7123
Rubber & plastic products

Pratt Hotel Corp. PHC
13455 Noel Rd., LB 48
Dallas, TX 75240 214-386-9777
Hotels & motels

Pre-Paid Legal Services, Inc. PPD
321 E. Main
Ada, OK 74820 405-436-1234
Business services

Presidential Realty Corp. PDLB
180 S. Broadway
White Plains, NY 10605 914-948-1300
Real estate investment trust
  [DRP 5%]

Presidio Oil Co. PRSA
5613 DTC Parkway, Ste. 750
Engelwood, CO 80111 303-773-0100
Oil & gas - US exploration & production

Price Communications Corp. PR
45 Rockefeller Plaza
New York, NY 10020 212-757-5600
Broadcasting - radio & TV

Prism Entertainment Corp. PRZ
1888 Century Park East
Los Angeles, CA 90067 310-277-3270
Motion pictures & services

Professional Bancorp, Inc. MDB
606 Broadway
Santa Monica, CA 90401
310-458-1521
Banks - west

Property Capital Trust PCT
One Post Office Sq., 21st Fl.
Boston, MA 02109 617-451-2400
Real estate investment trust

Provena Foods Inc. PZA
5010 Eucalyptus Ave.
Chino, CA 91710 909-627-1082
Food - meat products

Providence Energy Corp. PVY
100 Weybosset St.
Providence, RI 02903 401-272-9191
Utility - gas distribution
[DRP]

PS Business Parks, Inc. PSB
600 N. Brand Blvd.
Glendale, CA 91203
818-244-8080
Real estate investment trust

Public Storage Properties IX, Ltd. PSK
600 N. Brand Blvd.
Glendale, CA 91203 818-244-8080
Real estate investment trust

Public Storage Properties VI, Ltd. PSF
600 N. Brand Blvd.
Glendale, CA 91203 818-244-8080
Real estate investment trust

Public Storage Properties VII, Ltd. PSH
600 N. Brand Blvd.
Glendale, CA 91203 818-244-8080
Real estate investment trust

Public Storage Properties X, Ltd. PSL
600 N. Brand Blvd.
Glendale, CA 91203 818-244-8080
Real estate investment trust

Public Storage Properties XI, Ltd. PSM
600 N. Brand Blvd.
Glendale, CA 91203 818-244-8080
Real estate investment trust

Public Storage Properties XII, Ltd. PSN
600 N. Brand Blvd.
Glendale, CA 91203 818-244-8080
Real estate investment trust

Public Storage Properties XIV, Ltd. PSP
600 N. Brand Blvd.
Glendale, CA 91203 818-244-8080
Real estate investment trust

Public Storage Properties XIX, Ltd. PSY
600 N. Brand Blvd.
Glendale, CA 91203 818-244-8080
Real estate investment trust

Public Storage Properties XV, Ltd. PSQ
600 N. Brand Blvd.
Glendale, CA 91203 818-244-8080
Real estate investment trust

Public Storage Properties XVI, Ltd. PSU
600 N. Brand Blvd.
Glendale, CA 91203 818-244-8080
Real estate investment trust

Public Storage Properties XVII, Ltd. PSV
600 N. Brand Blvd.
Glendale, CA 91203 818-244-8080
Real estate investment trust

Public Storage Properties XVIII, Ltd. PSW
600 N. Brand Blvd.
Glendale, CA 91203 818-244-8080
Real estate investment trust

Public Storage Properties XX, Ltd. PSZ
600 N. Brand Blvd.
Glendale, CA 91203 818-244-8080
Real estate investment trust

Putnam California Investment Grade Mun.
  Trust PCA
One Post Office Square
Boston, MA 02109 617-292-1000
Financial - investment management

Putnam Investment Grade Intermediate Mun.
  Trust PTI
One Post Office Square
Boston, MA 02109 617-292-1000
Financial - investment management

Putnam Investment Grade Municipal Trust III
  PML
One Post Office Square
Boston, MA 02109
617-292-1000
Financial - investment management

Putnam New York Investment Grade Mun.
  Trust PMN
One Post Office Square
Boston, MA 02109 617-292-1000
Financial - investment management

Pyrocapital International Corp. PYR
15010-B Farm Creek Dr.
Woodbridge, VA 22191
703-551-4452
Chemicals - specialty

Quebecor, Inc. PQB
612 St. Jacques Street West
Montreal, Quebec, Canada H3C 4M8
514-877-9777
Printing, publishing and forest products O

Quality Products, Inc. PQP
3820 Northdale Blvd.
Tampa, FL 33624 813-963-1300
Leisure & recreational products

R. G. Barry Corp. RGB
13405 Yarmouth Rd., N.W.
Pickerington, OH 43147
614-864-6400
Shoes & related apparel

Railroad Financial Corp. RF
110 S. Main St.
Wichita, KS 67202 316-269-0300
Banks - midwest

Rauch Industries, Inc. RCH
6048 S. York Rd., PO Box 609
Gastonia, NC 28053 704-867-5333
Glass products

RB&W Corp. RBW
23001 Euclid Ave.
Cleveland, OH 44117 216-692-7100
Metal products - fabrication

ReadiCare, Inc. RDI
2600 Michelson Dr., Ste. 1130
Irvine, CA 92715 408-245-7707
Healthcare - outpatient & home

Red Eagle Resources Corp. RER
1601 Northwest Expressway
Oklahoma City, OK 73118
405-843-8066
Oil & gas - US exploration & production

Red Lion Hotels & Inns RED
4001 Main St.
Vancouver, WA 98663 206-696-0001
Hotels & motels

Redwood Empire Bancorp REB
111 Santa Rosa Ave.
Santa Rosa, CA 95404 707-545-9611
Banks - west [DRP]

Regal-Beloit Corp. RBC
200 State St.
Beloit, WI 53511 608-364-8800
Machinery - general industrial

Reliv International, Inc. RLV
1809 Clarkson Rd.
Chesterfield, MO 63017 314-537-9715
Vitamins & nutritional products

Resort Income Investors, Inc. RII
1819 Denver West Dr., Ste. 200
Golden, CO 80401 303-271-2555
Real estate investment trust

Resorts International, Inc. RT
1133 Boardwalk
Atlantic City, NJ 08401 609-344-6000
Leisure & recreational services

Resource Recycling Technologies, Inc.
RRT
300 Plaza Dr.
Vestal, NY 13850 607-798-7137
Pollution control equipment & services

Response Technologies, Inc. RTK
1775 Moriah Woods Blvd.
Memphis, TN 38117 901-761-7000
Medical services

Revell-Monogram, Inc. RVL
8601 Waukegan Rd.
Morton Grove, IL 60053 708-966-3500
Leisure & recreational products

RF Power Products RFP
502 Gibbsboro-Marlton Rd.
Voorhees, NJ 08043 609-751-0033
Electronics - components & systems

RHI Entertainment, Inc. RHE
156 W. 56th St.
New York, NY 10019 212-977-9001
Motion pictures & services

Richton International Corp. RHT
340 Main St.
Madison, NJ 07940 212-765-6480
Financial - investment bankers

Riser Food, Inc. RSR
5300 Richmond Rd.
Bedford Heights, OH 44146
212-292-7000
Retail - supermarkets

Rogers Corp. ROG
One Technology Dr., PO Box 188
Rogers, CT 06263 203-774-9605
Electrical components - misc.

Rotonics Manufacturing Inc. RMI
17022 S. Figueroa St.
Gardena, CA 90248 310-538-4932
Rubber & plastic products

Royal Palm Beach Colony, L.P. RPB
2501 S. Ocean Dr.
Hollywood, FL 33019 305-927-3080
Real estate operations

Rx Medical Services Corp. RXM
888 E. Las Olas Blvd.
Fort Lauderdale, FL 33301
305-462-1711
Medical services

RYMAC Mortgage Investment Corp. RM
500 Market St., Ste. 600
Steubenville, OH 43952 614-284-6960
Real estate investment trust
[DRP]

SOI Industries Inc. SOI
1051 E. 42nd St.
Hialeah, FL 33013 305-835-2214
Building products - lighting fixtures

Saba Petroleum Co. SAP
17512 Von Karman Ave.
Irvine, CA 92714 714-724-1112
Oil & gas - production & pipeline

Saga Communications, Inc. SGA
73 Kercheval Ave.
Grosse Pointe Farms, MI 48236
313-886-7070
Broadcasting - radio & TV

Sahara Gaming Corp. SGM
2535 Las Vegas Blvd. South
Las Vegas, NV 89109 702-737-2111
Leisure & recreational services

Salem Corp. SBS
PO Box 2222
Pittsburgh, PA 15230 412-923-2200
Machinery - construction & mining

Salomon Phibro Oil Trust SPO
One New York Plaza
New York, NY 10004 212-747-7000
Financial - investment management

Samuel Goldwyn Co. SG
10203 Santa Monica Blvd.
Los Angeles, CA 90067 310-552-2255
Motion pictures & services

San Francisco Co. BOF
550 Montgomery St., 10th Fl.
San Francisco, CA 94111
415-391-9000
Banks - west

Sandy Corp. SDY
1500 W. Big Beaver Rd.
Troy, MI 48084 313-649-0800
Business services

Santa Monica Bank SMO
1251 Fourth St.
Santa Monica, CA 90401 310-394-9611
Banks - west

SBM Industries, Inc. SBM
2 Madison Ave., Ste. 201
Larchmont, NY 10538 914-833-0649
Office equipment & supplies

SC Bancorp SCK
9040 E. Telegraph Rd.
Downey, CA 90240 310-904-6600
Banks - west

Schult Homes Corp. SHC
221 U.S. 20 West
Middlebury, IN 46540 219-825-5881
Building - residential & commercial

Scope Industries SCP
233 Wilshire Blvd., Ste. 310
Santa Monica, CA 90401 310-458-1574
Agricultural operations

Seaboard Corp. SEB
9000 W. 67th St., PO Box 2972
Shawnee Mission, KS 66201
913-676-8800
Food - meat products

Selas Corporation of America SLS
PO Box 200
Dresher, PA 19025 215-646-6600
Diversified operations

Semiconductor Packaging Materials Co., Inc.
SEM
431 Fayette Ave.
Mamaroneck, NY 10543 914-698-5353
Wire & cable products

Semtech Corp. SMH
652 Mitchell Rd.
Newbury Park, CA 91320 805-498-2111
Electrical components - misc.

Servico, Inc. SER
1601 Belvedere Rd.
West Palm Beach, FL 33406
407-689-9970
Hotels & motels

Servotronics, Inc. SVT
3901 Union Rd.
Buffalo, NY 14225 716-633-5990
Diversified operations

Sheffield Exploration Co. SHE
1801 Broadway, Ste. 600
Denver, CO 80202 303-296-0231
Oil & gas - US exploration & production

Sheffield Medical Technologies, Inc. SHM
1111 Bagby, Ste. 2610
Houston, TX 77002 713-739-8211
Medical services

Shelter Components Corp. SST
27217 Country Road 6
Elkhart, IN 46514 219-262-4541
Building - mobile homes & RV

Shopco Laurel Center, L.P. LSC
388 Greenwich St., 28th Fl.
New York, NY 10013 212-464-2465
Real estate operations

SIFCO Industries, Inc. SIF
970 E. 64th St.
Cleveland, OH 44103 216-881-8600
Metal processing & fabrication
[DRP]

Signal Technology Corp. STZ
955 Benecia Ave.
Sunnyvale, CA 94086 408-730-6318
Electrical components - misc.

Silverado Foods, Inc. SLV
7313 E. 38th St.
Tulsa, OK 74145 918-627-7783
Food - misc.

Simula Inc. SMU
401 W. Baseline, Ste. 204
Tempe, AZ 85283 602-752-8918
Aerospace - aircraft equipment

SJW Corp. SJW
374 W. Santa Clara St.
San Jose, CA 95196 408-279-7810
Utility - water supply

Sloan's Supermarkets, Inc. SLO
823 Eleventh Ave.
New York, NY 10019 212-541-5534
Retail - supermarkets

Smith Barney Intermediate Municipal Fund,
Inc. SBI
1345 Avenue of the Americas
New York, NY 10105 212-698-5349
Financial - investment management

Smith Barney Shearson SBT
1345 Avenue of the Americas
New York, NY 10105 212-464-6000
Financial - investment management

Softnet Systems, Inc. SOF
10 State St.
Moonachie, NJ 07074 201-440-2600
Miscellaneous - not elsewhere classified

Soligen Technologies, Inc. SGT
19408 Londelius St.
Northridge, CA 91324 818-718-1221
Miscellaneous - not elsewhere classified

Southern California Edison Co. SCEpB
2244 Walnut Grove Ave.
Rosemead, CA 91770 818-302-1212
Utility - electric power

Southern Union Co. SUG
504 Lavaca St., Ste. 800
Austin, TX 78701 512-477-5852
Utility - gas distribution

Southwestern Life Corp. SLC
100 Mallard Creek Rd.
Louisville, KY 40207 502-894-2100
Insurance - life

Specialty Chemical Resources, Inc. CHM
9100 Valley View Rd.
Macedonia, OH 44056 216-468-1380
Chemicals - specialty

SpectraVision, Inc. SVN
1501 N. Plano Rd.
Richardson, TX 75081 214-234-2721
Leisure & recreational services O

Stage II Apparel Corp. SA
350 Fifth Ave.
New York, NY 10118
212-564-5865
Textiles - apparel

Standard & Poor's SPY
25 Broadway
New York, NY 10004
212-208-8000
Financial - business services

Starrett Housing Corp. SHO
909 Third Ave.
New York, NY 10022 212-751-3100
Building - residential & commercial

Statordyne Corporation STY
2080 S. Anaheim Blvd.
Anaheim, CA 92805 714-704-1000
Electrical products - misc.

Stepan Co. SCL
Northfield, IL 60093 708-446-7500
Chemicals - specialty

Sterling Capital Corp. SPR
635 Madison Ave.
New York, NY 10022 212-980-3360
Financial - investment management

Sterling Healthcare Group, Inc. DRZ
2333 Ponce de Leon, Ste. 511
Coral Gables, FL 33134 305-441-1911
Medical services

Stevens Graphics Corp. SVGA
5500 Airport Freeway
Fort Worth, TX 76113
817-831-3911
Machinery - printing

Storage Properties, Inc. PSA
600 N. Brand Blvd.
Glendale, CA 91203 818-244-8080
Real estate investment trust

Struthers Industries, Inc. SIR
8118 E. 63rd St.
Tulsa, OK 74133 918-252-1053
Aerospace - aircraft equipment

Styles-On Video, Inc. SOV
21216 Vanowen St.
Canoga Park, CA 91303 818-595-0104
Computers - software

Sulcus Computer Corp. SUL
41 N. Main St.
Greensburg, PA 15601 412-836-2000
Computers - software O

Summit Tax Exempt Bond Fund, L.P. SUA
625 Madison Ave.
New York, NY 10022 212-421-5333
Financial - investment management
[DRP]

Sun City Industries, Inc. SNI
5545 N.W. 35th Ave.
Fort Lauderdale, FL 33309
305-730-3333
Food - dairy products

Sunair Electronics, Inc. SNR
3101 S.W. Third Ave.
Fort Lauderdale, FL 33315
305-525-1505
Telecommunications equipment

Sunbelt Nursery Group, Inc. SBN
500 Terminal Rd.
Fort Worth, TX 76106 817-738-8111
Retail - misc.

Sunrise Energy Services, Inc. SES
127770 Merit Dr., Ste. 800
Dallas, TX 75251 214-385-1616
Oil & gas - field services

Sunshine-Jr. Stores, Inc. SJS
109 W. Fifth St.
Panama City, FL 32401 904-769-1661
Retail - convenience stores

Superior Surgical Manufacturing Co., Inc.
 SGC
10099 Seminole Blvd.
Seminole, FL 34642 813-397-9611
Linen's & related supply

SuperTrust Index Trust ZIU
523 W. 6th St., Ste. 220
Los Angeles, CA 90014 213-488-2700
Financial - investment management

SuperTrust U.S. Treasury Money Market Trust
 ZMU
523 W. 6th St., Ste. 220
Los Angeles, CA 90014 213-488-2700
Financial - investment management

Supreme Industries, Inc. STS
65140 U.S. 33 East, PO Box 237
Goshen, IN 46526 219-642-3070
Automotive & trucking - original equipment

Surety Capital Corp. SRY
1845 Precinct Line Rd.
Hurst, TX 76054 817-498-8154
Banks - southwest

T/SF Communications Corp. TCM
2407 E. Skelly Dr.
Tulsa, OK 74015 918-747-2600
Publishing - periodicals

Tab Products Co. TBP
1400 Page Mill Rd.
Palo Alto, CA 94304 415-852-2400
Office equipment & supplies

Tasty Baking Co. TBC
2801 Hunting Park Ave.
Philadelphia, PA 19129
215-221-8500
Food - misc.

TCS Enterprises, Inc. TCS
10525 Vista Sorrento Parkway
San Diego, CA 92121 619-452-8000
Financial - mortgages & related services

Team, Inc. TMI
1001 Fannin, Ste. 4656
Houston, TX 77002 713-659-3600
Construction - heavy

Tech/Ops Sevcon, Inc. TO
One Beacon St.
Boston, MA 02108 617-523-2030
Electrical products - misc.

Technitrol, Inc. TNL
1210 Northbrook Dr., Ste. 385
Trevose, PA 19053 215-355-2900
Electrical products - misc.

Tejas Power Corp. TPC
200 West Lake Park Blvd.
Houston, TX 77079 713-597-6200
Oil & gas - production & pipeline

Tejon Ranch Co. TRC
PO Box 1000
Lebec, CA 93243 805-327-8481
Agricultural operations

Telephone and Data Systems, Inc. TDS
30 N. LaSalle St., Ste. 4000
Chicago, IL 60602 312-630-1900
Utility - telephone O [DRP 5%]

Templeton Global Utilities, Inc. TGU
700 Central Ave.
St. Petersburg, FL 33701
813-823-8712
Financial - investment management

TENERA, L.P. TLP
2001 Center St.
Berkeley, CA 94704 510-845-5200
Computers - services

Texas Biotechnology Corp. TXB
7000 Fannin St., Ste. 1920
Houston, TX 77030 713-796-8822
Drugs

Texas Meridian Resources Corp. TMR
15995 N. Barkers Landing
Houston, TX 77079 713-558-8080
Oil & gas - US exploration & production O

Texscan Corp. TSX
10841 Pellicano Dr.
El Paso, TX 79935 915-594-3555
Cable TV

The Alpine Group, Inc. AGI
1790 Broadway
New York, NY 10019 212-757-3333
Chemicals - specialty

The Beard Co. BOC
5600 N. May Ave., Ste. 290
Oklahoma City, OK 73112
405-842-2333
Oil & gas - US exploration & production

The C.R. Gibson Co. GIB
32 Knight St.
Norwalk, CT 06856
203-847-4543
Office & art materials

The Goldfield Corp. GV
100 Rialto Place, Ste. 500
Melbourne, FL 32901   407-724-1700
Construction - heavy

The Gorman-Rupp Co. GRC
305 Bowman St.
Mansfield, OH 44903   419-755-1011
Machinery - general industrial

The Leather Factory, Inc. TLF
3847 E. Loop 820 South
Fort Worth, TX 76119   817-496-4414
Leather & related products

The Lori Corp. LRC
500 Central Ave.
Northfield, IL 60093   708-441-7300
Precious metals & jewelry

The MacNeal-Schwendler Corp. MNS
815 Colorado Blvd.
Los Angeles, CA 90041   213-258-9111
Computers - software

The Middleby Corp. MBY
1400 Toastmaster Dr.
Elgin, IL 60120   708-299-2940
Machinery - general industrial

The Midland Co. MLA
537 E. Pete Rose Way
Cincinnati, OH 45202   513-721-3777
Diversified operations

The Ohio Art Co. OAR
One Toy St.
Bryan, OH 43506   419-636-3141
Toys - games & hobby products

The Penn Traffic Co. PNF
1200 State Fair Blvd.
Syracuse, NY 13209   315-453-7284
Retail - supermarkets

The Phoenix Resources Cos., Inc. PHN
6525 N. Meridian Ave.
Oklahoma City, OK 73116
405-728-5100
Oil & gas - international specialty

The Randers Group, Inc. RGI
570 Seminole Rd.
Norton Shores, MI 49444
616-733-0036
Business services

The Sherwood Group, Inc. SHD
One Exchange Plaza
New York, NY 10006   212-482-4000
Financial - business services

The Sports Club Co. SCY
2425 Olympic Blvd., Ste. 4060W
Santa Monica, CA 90404
310-453-1400
Leisure & recreational services

The Stephan Co. TSC
1850 W. McNab Rd.
Fort Lauderdale, FL 33309
305-971-0600
Cosmetics & toiletries

The Tranzonic Companies TNZA
30195 Chagrin Blvd.
Pepper Pike, OH 44124   216-831-5757
Drugs & sundries - wholesale

The Ziegler Companies, Inc. ZCO
215 N. Main St.
West Bend, WI 53095   414-334-5521
Diversified operations

Thermedics Inc. TMD
470 Wildwood St., PO Box 2999
Woburn, MA 01888   617-938-3786
Medical products O

Thermo Cardiosystems Inc. TCA
470 Wildwood St.
Woburn, MA 01888   617-622-1000
Medical products

Thermo Fibertek, Inc. TFT
81 Wyman St.
Waltham, MA 02254   617-622-1000
Industrial processing - misc.

Thermo Instrument Systems Inc. THI
504 Airport Rd., PO Box 02108
Santa Fe, NM 87504   505-471-3232
Instruments - scientific

Thermo Power Corp. THP
81 Wyman St., PO Box 9046
Waltham, MA 02254   617-622-1000
Energy - alternate sources

Thermo Process Systems Inc. TPI
12068 Market St.
Livonia, MI 48150   617-622-1000
Machinery - general industrial

Thermo Remediation Inc. THN
1964 S. Orange Blossom Trail
Apopka, FL 32703   617-622-1000
Pollution control equipment & services

Thermo Voltek Corp. TVL
470 Wildwood St., PO Box 2878
Woburn, MA 01888   617-622-1000
Electronics - measuring instruments

ThermoLase Corp. TLZ
9550 Distribution Ave.
San Diego, CA 92121
619-578-5885
Miscellaneous - not elsewhere classified

ThermoTrex Corp. TKN
9550 Distribution Ave.
San Diego, CA 92121
619-578-5885
Engineering - R & D services

Thermwood Corp. THM
Old Buffaloville Rd.
Dale, IN 47523 812-937-4476
Miscellaneous - not elsewhere classified

Thor Energy Resources, Inc. THR
719 W. Front St.
Tyler, TX 75702 903-533-9111
Oil & gas - US exploration & production

Three D Departments, Inc. TDDA
3200 Bristol St.
Costa Mesa, CA 92626 714-662-0818
Retail - misc.

Three-Five Systems, Inc. TFS
10230 S. 50th Place
Phoenix, AZ 85044 602-496-0035
Electronics - components & systems

TIE/communications, Inc. TIE
8500 W. 110th St.
Overland Park, KS 66210 913-344-0400
Telecommunications equipment

Tipperary Corp. TPY
633 17th St., Ste. 1550
Denver, CO 80202 303-293-9379
Oil & gas - US exploration & production

Tofutti Brands Inc. TOF
50 Jackson Dr.
Cranford, NJ 07016 908-272-2400
Food - misc.

Tolland Bank TBK
348 Hartford Tnpk.
Vernon, CT 06066 203-875-2500
Financial - savings and loans

Top Source, Inc. TPS
2000 PGA Blvd., Ste. 3200
Palm Beach Gardens, FL 33408
407-775-5756
Automotive & trucking - original equipment
O

Torotel, Inc. TTL
13402 S. 71 Highway
Grandview, MO 64030 816-761-6314
Electronics - military
.

Total Petroleum (North America) Ltd. TPN
900 19th St.
Denver, CO 80202 303-291-2000
Oil & gas - international integrated O
[DRP]

Town & Country Corp. TNC
25 Union St.
Chelsea, MA 02150 617-884-8500
Precious metals & jewelry

Trans World Airlines, Inc. TWA
515 N. Sixth St.
St. Louis, MO 63101 314-589-3000
Transportation - airline

Trans-Lux Corp. TLX
110 Richards Ave.
Norwalk, CT 06856 203-853-4321
Electrical products - misc.

Transcisco Industries, Inc. TNI
555 California St., Ste. 1301
San Francisco, CA 94108
415-477-9700
Transportation - equipment & leasing

Tri-Lite, Inc. NRG
2300 Main St.
Irvine, CA 92714 714-261-8313
Electrical products - misc.

Triangle Corp. TRG
62 Southfield Ave.
Stamford, CT 06902 203-327-9050
Tools - hand held

Tridex Corp. TDX
215 Main St.
Westport, CT 06880 203-226-1144
Electrical products - misc.

Trinitech Systems, Inc. TSI
333 Ludlow St.
Stamford, CT 06902 203-425-8000
Data collection & systems

Triton Group Ltd. TGL
550 W. C St., Ste. 1880
San Diego, CA 92101 619-231-1818
Diversified operations

Turner Broadcasting System, Inc. TBSA
100 International Blvd.
Atlanta, GA 30303 404-827-1700
Cable TV

Turner Corp. TUR
375 Hudson St.
New York, NY 10014 212-229-6000
Construction - heavy

U.S. Alcohol Testing of America, Inc. AAA
10410 Trademark St.
Rancho Cucamonga, CA 91730
909-466-8378
Medical instruments

U.S. Bioscience, Inc. UBS
100 Front St.
West Conshohocken, PA 19428
215-832-0570
Drugs O

U.S. Intec, Inc. USI
1212 Brai Dr., PO Box 2845
Port Arthur, TX 77643 409-724-7024
Building products - misc.

Underwriters Financial Group Inc. UFG
156 William St.
New York, NY 10038 212-233-7171
Insurance - multi line & misc.

Uni-Marts, Inc. UNI
477 E. Beaver Ave.
State College, PA 16801 814-234-6000
Retail - convenience stores

Uniflex, Inc. UFX
383 W. John St.
Hicksville, NY 11802 516-932-2000
Miscellaneous - not elsewhere classified

Unimar Co. UMR
1221 McKinley, Ste. 600
Houston, TX 77010 713-654-8550
Oil & gas - international integrated

Unique Mobility, Inc. UQM
425 Corporate Circle
Golden, CO 80401 303-278-2002
Automotive & trucking - original equipment

United Capital Corp. AFP
111 Great Neck Rd.
Great Neck, NY 11021 516-466-6464
Real estate operations

United Foods, Inc. UFDA
Ten Pictsweet Dr.
Bells, TN 38006 901-422-7600
Food - misc.

United Mobile Homes, Inc. UMH
125 Wyckoff Rd.
Eatontown, NJ 07724 908-389-3890
Real estate investment trust
[DRP 5%]

United States Cellular Corp. USM
8410 W. Bryn Mawr, Ste. 700
Chicago, IL 60631 312-399-8900
Telecommunications services

United-Guardian, Inc. UG
230 Marcus Blvd.
Hauppauge, NY 11788
516-273-0900
Drugs

Unitel Video, Inc. UNV
515 W. 57th St.
New York, NY 10019 212-265-3600
Motion pictures & services

UNITIL Corp. UTL
216 Epping Rd.
Exeter, NH 03833 603-772-0775
Real estate development
[DRP 5%]

University Patents, Inc. UPT
1465 Post Rd. East, PO Box 901
Westport, CT 06881 203-255-6044
Diversified operations

USF&G Pacholder Fund, Inc. PHF
8044 Montgomery Rd., Ste. 382
Cincinnati, OH 45236 513-985-3200
Financial - investment management

UTI Energy Corp. UTI
485 Devon Park Dr., Ste. 112
Wayne, PA 19087 610-971-9600
Oil & gas - field services

Valley Forge Corp. VF
100 Smith Ranch Rd., Ste. 326
San Raphael, CA 94903 415-492-1500
Leisure & recreational products

Valley Resources, Inc. VR
1595 Mendon Rd., PO Box 7900
Cumberland, RI 02864 401-334-1188
Utility - gas distribution [DRP 5%]

Van Kampen Merritt Advantage Mun. Inc. Tr.
II VKI
One Parkview Plaza
Oakbrook Terrace, IL 60181 708-684-6000
Financial - investment management

Van Kampen Merritt California Mun. Trust
VKC
One Parkview Plaza
Oakbrook Terrace, IL 60181 708-684-6000
Financial - investment management

Van Kampen Merritt Florida Mun. Opp. Trust
VOF
One Parkview Plaza
Oakbrook Terrace, IL 60181 708-684-6000
Financial - investment management

Van Kampen Merritt MA Value Mun. Income
Trust VMV
17W110 22nd St.
Oakbrook Terrace, IL 60181 708-684-6000
Financial - investment management

Van Kampen Merritt NJ Value Mun. Income
Trust VJV
One Parkview Plaza
Oakbrook Terrace, IL 60181 708-684-6000
Financial - investment management

Van Kampen Merritt Ohio Value Mun. Income
Trust VOV
One Parkview Plaza
Oakbrook Terrace, IL 60181 708-684-6000
Financial - investment management

Van Kampen Merritt Select Sector Mun. Trust
VKL
One Parkview Plaza
Oakbrook Terrace, IL 60181 708-684-6000
Financial - investment management

Vanguard Real Estate Fund I VRO
Vanguard Financial Center
Valley Forge, PA 19482 800-662-7447
Real estate investment trust

Vanguard Real Estate Fund II VRT
Vanguard Financial Center
Malvern, PA 19355 610-669-1000
Real estate investment trust

Vermont Research Corp. VRE
Precision Park
North Springfield, VT 05150
802-886-2256
Computers - peripheral equipment

Versar, Inc. VSR
6850 Versar Center
Springfield, VA 22151   703-750-3000
Pollution control equipment & services

Viacom Inc. VIA
1515 Broadway
New York, NY 10036
212-258-6000
Diversified operations O

Vicon Industries, Inc. VII
525 Broad Hollow Rd.
Melville, NY 11747   516-293-2200
Video equipment

Virco Manufacturing Corp. VIR
15134 S. Vermont Ave.
Los Angeles, CA 90247   310-533-0474
Furniture

Vitronics Corp. VTC
Forbes Rd.
Newmarket, NH 03857   603-659-6550
Machinery - electrical

Voice Control Systems, Inc. VPS
14140 Midway Rd., Ste. 100
Dallas, TX 75244   214-386-0300
Miscellaneous - not elsewhere classified

Voyageur Arizona Municipal Income Fund,
Inc. VAZ
90 S. Seventh St., Ste. 4400
Minneapolis, MN 55402   612-376-7000
Financial - investment management

Voyageur Colorado Insured Mun. Inc. Fund,
Inc. VFC
90 S. Seventh St., Ste. 4400
Minneapolis, MN 55402   612-376-7000
Financial - investment management

Voyageur Florida Insured Municipal Income
Fund VF
90 S. Seventh St., Ste. 4400
Minneapolis, MN 55402   612-376-7000
Financial - investment management

Voyageur Minnesota Mun. Inc. Fund II, Inc.
VMM
90 S. Seventh St., Ste. 4400
Minneapolis, MN 55402   612-376-7000
Financial - investment management

Voyageur Minnesota Mun. Inc. Fund III, Inc.
VYM
90 S. Seventh St., Ste. 4400
Minneapolis, MN 55402   612-376-7000
Financial - investment management

Voyageur Minnesota Mun. Inc. Fund, Inc.
VMN
90 S. Seventh St., Ste. 4400
Minneapolis, MN 55402   612-376-7000
Financial - investment management

VTX Electronics Corp. VTX
61 Executive Blvd.
Farmingdale, NY 11735   516-293-9880
Wire & cable products

Vulcan International Corp. VUL
30 Garfield Place, Ste. 1000
Cincinnati, OH 45202   513-621-2850
Shoes & related apparel

Washington Real Estate Investment Trust
WRE
10400 Connecticut Ave.
Kensington, MD 20895   301-929-5900
Real estate investment trust
[DRP]

Washington Savings Bank WSB
Route 301
Waldorf, MD 20603   301-843-7200
Financial - savings and loans

Weldotron Corp. WLD
1532 S. Washington Ave.
Piscataway, NJ 08855   908-752-6700
Machinery - material handling

Wellco Enterprises, Inc. WLC
PO Box 188
Waynesville, NC 28786   704-456-3545
Military equipment

Wells-Gardner Electronics Corp. WGA
2701 N. Kildare Ave.
Chicago, IL 60639   312-252-8220
Electrical products - misc.

Wendt-Bristol Health Services Corp. WMD
Two Nationwide Plaza
Columbus, OH 43215   614-221-6000
Nursing homes

Wesco Financial Corp. WSC
315 E. Colorado Blvd.
Pasadena, CA 91101   818-585-6700
Financial - savings and loans

Westbridge Capital Corp. WBC
777 Main St.
Fort Worth, TX 76102   817-878-3300
Insurance - accident & health

Western Investment Real Estate Trust WIR
3450 California St.
San Francisco, CA 94118   415-929-0211
Real estate investment trust

Wichita River Oil Corp. WRO
3500 N. Causeway Blvd.
Metairie, LA 70002   504-831-0381
Oil & gas - US exploration & production

Wilshire Technologies, Inc. WIL
5922 Farnsworth Court
Carlsbad, CA 92008 619-929-7200
Medical products

Winston Resources, Inc. WRS
535 Fifth Ave., Ste. 701
New York, NY 10017 212-557-5000
Business services

Wireless Telecom Group, Inc. NOI
49 E. Midland Ave.
Paramus, NJ 07652 201-261-8797
Electronics - measuring instruments

Wiz Technology, Inc. WIZ
32951 Calle Perfecto
San Juan Capistrano, CA 92675
714-443-3000
Computers - software

Worthen Banking Corp. WOR
200 W. Capitol Ave.
Little Rock, AR 72201 501-378-1206
Banks - southeast

XCL Ltd. XCL
110 Rue Jean Lafitte
Lafayette, LA 70508 318-237-0325
Oil & gas - US exploration & production

Xytronyx, Inc. XYX
6555 Nancy Ridge Dr., Ste. 200
San Diego, CA 92121 619-546-1114
Biomedical & genetic products

NASDAQ NATIONAL MARKET SYSTEM

1st Source Corp. SRCE
100 N. Michigan St.
South Bend, IN 46601 219-236-2000
Banks - midwest

3COM Corp. COMS
5400 Bayfront Plaza
Santa Clara, CA 95052 408-764-5000
Computers - peripheral equipment

3D Systems Corp. TDSC
26081 Avenue Hall
Valencia, CA 91355 805-295-5600
Instruments - control

3DO Co. THDO
600 Galveston Dr.
Redwood City, CA 94063 415-261-3000
Leisure & recreational products

50-Off Stores, Inc. FOFF
8750 Tesoro Dr.
San Antonio, TX 78217 210-805-9300
Retail - discount & variety

7th Level, Inc. SEVL
1771 International Pkwy.
Richardson, TX 75081 214-437-4858
Computers - software

A Pea in the Pod, Inc. APOD
2800 W. Story Rd.
Irving, TX 75038 214-594-6888
Retail - apparel & shoes

A+ Communications Inc. ACOM
2416 Hillsboro Rd.
Nashville, TN 37212 615-385-4500
Telecommunications services

A. P. Green Industries, Inc. APGI
Green Blvd.
Mexico, MO 65265 314-473-3626
Building products - misc.

A. Schulman, Inc. SHLM
3550 W. Market St.
Akron, OH 44313 216-666-3751
Chemicals - plastics

Aames Financial Corp. AAMS
3731 Wilshire Blvd., 10th Fl.
Los Angeles, CA 90010 213-351-6100
Financial - mortgages & related services

AAON, Inc. AAON
2425 S. Yukon Ave.
Tulsa, OK 74107 918-583-2266
Building products - a/c & heating

Aaron Rents, Inc. ARONA
3001 N. Fulton Dr., Ste. 1100
Atlanta, GA 30305 404-231-0011
Retail - home furnishings

Aasche Transportation Services, Inc. ASHE
10214 N. Mt. Vernon Rd.
Shannon, IL 61078 815-864-2421
Transportation - truck

ABAXIS, Inc. ABAX
1320 Chesapeake Terrace
Sunnyvale, CA 94089 408-734-0200
Medical instruments

Abbey Healthcare Group Inc. ABBY
3560 Hyland Ave.
Costa Mesa, CA 92626 714-957-2000
Healthcare - outpatient & home O

ABC Rail Products Corp. ABCR
200 S. Michigan Ave.
Chicago, IL 60604 312-322-0360
Transportation - equipment & leasing

Abington Savings Bank ABBK
533 Washington St.
Abington, MA 02351 617-982-3200
Banks - northeast

ABIOMED, Inc. ABMD
33 Cherry Hill Dr.
Danvers, MA 01923 508-777-5410
Medical instruments

Able Telcom Holding Corp. ABTE
800 W. Cypress Creek Rd.
Fort Lauderdale, FL 33309 305-421-7900
Telecommunications equipment

ABR Information Services, Inc. ABRX
34125 US Highway 19 North
Palm Harbor, FL 34684 813-785-2819
Health & Allied Services, Inc.

Abrams Industries, Inc. ABRI
5775-A Glenridge Dr., NE
Atlanta, GA 30328 404-256-9785
Diversified operations

Abraxas Petroleum Corp. AXAS
909 N.E. Loop 410, Ste. 900
San Antonio, TX 78209 210-828-5354
Oil & gas - US exploration & production

ABS Industries, Inc. ABSI
Interstate Square, Ste. 300
Willoughby, OH 44094 216-946-2274
Automotive & trucking - original equipment

ABT Building Products Corp. ABTC
One Neenah Center, Ste. 600
Neenah, WI 54956 414-751-8611
Building products - misc.

ACC Corp. ACCC
39 State St.
Rochester, NY 14614 716-987-3000
Telecommunications services

ACCEL International Corp. ACLE
475 Metro Place North
Dublin, OH 43017 614-764-7000
Insurance - multi line & misc.

Access Health Marketing, Inc. ACCS
11020 White Rock Rd.
Rancho Cordova, CA 95670
916-851-4000
Medical services

Acclaim Entertainment, Inc. AKLM
71 Audrey Ave.
Oyster Bay, NY 11771 516-624-8888
Toys - games & hobby products O

AccuStaff, Inc. ASTF
6440 Atlantic Blvd.
Jacksonville, FL 32211 904-725-5574
Personnel

Ace Cash Express, Inc. AACE
1231 Greenway Dr., Ste. 800
Irving, TX 75038 214-550-5000
Retail - misc.

Aceto Corp. ACET
One Hollow Ln., Ste. 201
Lake Success, NY 11042
516-627-6000
Chemicals - specialty

ACMAT Corp. ACMT
233 Main St.
New Britain, CT 06050
203-229-9000
Building - maintenance & services

Acme Metals, Inc. ACME
13500 S. Perry Ave.
Riverdale, IL 60627 708-849-2500
Metal processing & fabrication

ACS Enterprises, Inc. ACSE
2510 Metropolitan Dr.
Trevose, PA 19053 215-396-9400
Telecommunications services

Actel Corp. ACTL
955 E. Arques Ave.
Sunnyvale, CA 94086 408-739-1010
Electrical components - semiconductors O

Action Performance Companies, Inc. ACTN
2401 W. First St.
Tempe, AZ 85281 602-894-0100
Toys - games & hobby products

Active Voice Corp. ACVC
2901 Third Ave., Ste. 500
Seattle, WA 98121 206-441-4700
Computers - software

ACX Technologies, Inc. ACXT
16000 Table Mountain Parkway
Golden, CO 80403 303-271-7000
Diversified operations

Acxiom Corp. ACXM
301 Industrial Blvd.
Conway, AR 72032 501-336-1000
Computers - services

ADAC Laboratories ADAC
540 Alder Dr.
Milpitas, CA 95035 408-321-9100
Medical instruments [DRP 5%]

Adage, Inc. ADGE
615 Willowbrook Ln.
West Chester, PA 19382
610-430-3900
Telecommunications equipment

Adaptec, Inc. ADPT
691 S. Milpitas Blvd.
Milpitas, CA 95035 408-945-8600
Computers - peripheral equipment O

ADC Telecommunications, Inc. ADCT
4900 W. 78th St.
Minneapolis, MN 55435 612-938-8080
Telecommunications equipment O

Addington Resources, Inc. ADDR
1500 N. Big Run Rd.
Ashland, KY 41102 606-928-3433
Coal

Adelphia Communications Corp. ADLAC
5 W. Third St., PO Box 472
Coudersport, PA 16915 814-274-9830
Cable TV

Adesa Corp. SOLD
1919 S. Post Rd.
Indianapolis, IN 46239 317-862-7220
Business services

ADFlex Solutions, Inc. AFLX
2001 W. Chandler Blvd.
Chandler, AZ 85224 602-963-4584
Electronics - components & systems

Adia Services, Inc. ADIA
64 Willow Place
Menlo Park, CA 94025
415-324-0696
Business services

Adobe Systems Inc. ADBE
1585 Charleston Rd.
Mountain View, CA 94043
415-961-4400
Computers - software O

Adolph Coors Co. ACCOB
Golden, CO 80401
303-279-6565
Beverages - alcoholic

ADTRAN, Inc. ADTN
901 Explorer Blvd.
Huntsville, AL 35806 205-971-8000
Telecommunications equipment

Advance Circuits, Inc. ADVC
15102 Minnetonka Industrial Rd
Minnetonka, MN 55345 612-935-3311
Electrical components - semiconductors

Advance Ross Corp. AROS
233 S. Wacker Dr., Ste. 9700
Chicago, IL 60606 312-382-1100
Pollution control equipment & services

Advanced Interventional Systems, Inc.
LAIS
9 Parker
Irvine, CA 92718 714-586-1342
Lasers - systems & components

Advanced Logic Research, Inc. AALR
9401 Jeronimo
Irvine, CA 92718 714-581-6770
Computers - mini & micro

Advanced Marketing Services, Inc. ADMS
5880 Oberlin Dr., Ste. 400
San Diego, CA 92121 619-457-2500
Wholesale distribution - consumer products

Advanced NMR Systems, Inc. ANMR
46 Jonspin Rd.
Wilmington, MA 1887 508-657-8876
Medical instruments

Advanced Polymer Systems, Inc. APOS
3696 Haven Ave.
Redwood City, CA 94063 415-366-2626
Medical products

Advanced Promotion Technologies, Inc.
APTV
3001 S.W. 10th St.
Pompano Beach, FL 33069 305-969-3000
Business services - marketing

Advanced Technology Laboratories, Inc.
ATLI
701 Fifth Ave.
Seattle, WA 98104 206-487-7000
Medical instruments O

Advanced Technology Materials, Inc. ATMI
7 Commerce Dr.
Danbury, CT 06810 203-794-1100
Industrial processing - misc.

Advanced Tissue Sciences, Inc. ATIS
10933 N. Torrey Pines Rd.
La Jolla, CA 92037 619-450-5730
Biomedical & genetic products O

ADVANTA Corp. ADVNA
300 Welsh Rd.
Horsham, PA 19044 215-784-5335
Financial - business services O

Advantage Bancorp, Inc. AADV
5935 Seventh Ave.
Kenosha, WI 53140 414-658-4861
Banks - midwest

Advantage Health Corp. ADHC
304 Cambridge Rd.
Woburn, MA 01801 617-935-2500
Healthcare - outpatient & home

AEL Industries, Inc. AELNA
305 Richardson Rd.
Lansdale, PA 19446 215-822-2929
Electronics - military

AEP Industries Inc. AEPI
125 Phillips Ave.
South Hackensack, NJ 07606
201-641-6600
Chemicals - plastics

Aequitron Medical, Inc. AQTN
14800 28th Ave. North
Minneapolis, MN 55447 612-557-9200
Medical instruments

AER Energy Resources, Inc. AERN
1500 Wilson Way, Suite 250
Smyrna, GA 30082 404-433-2127
Electrical products - misc.

Aerovox Inc. ARVX
370 Faunce Corner Rd.
North Dartmouth, MA 02747
508-995-8000
Electrical components - misc.

Aethium, Inc. ATRM
2350 Helen St.
North St. Paul, MN 55109 612-770-2000
Electronics - measuring instruments

AFC Cable Systems, Inc. AFCX
50 Kennedy Plaza, Ste. 1250
Providence, RI 02903 401-453-2000
Wire & cable products

Affiliated Computer Services, Inc. ACSA
2828 N. Haskell Ave.
Dallas, TX 75204 214-841-6111
Data collection & systems

Affinity Biotech, Inc. AFBI
305 Chelsea Parkway
Boothwyn, PA 19061 215-497-0500
Biomedical & genetic products

Ag Services of America, Inc. AGSV
Thunder Ridge Ct., PO Box 688
Cedar Falls, IA 50613 319-277-0261
Agricultural operations

Agouron Pharmaceuticals, Inc. AGPH
10350 N. Torrey Pines Rd.
La Jolla, CA 92037 619-622-3000
Drugs

AgriDyne Technologies, Inc. AGRI
2401 S. Foothill Dr.
Salt Lake City, UT 84109
801-467-4100
Chemicals - specialty

Air Express International Corp. AEIC
120 Tokeneke Rd., PO Box 1231
Darien, CT 6820 203-655-7900
Transportation - air freight

Air Methods Corp. AIRM
7301 S. Peoria
Englewood, CO 80112
303-792-7400
Medical services

Airport Systems International, Inc. ASII
11300 W. 89th St.
Overland Park, KS 66214
913-492-0861
Instruments - control

AirSensors, Inc. ARSN
16804 Gridley Place
Cerritos, CA 90701 310-860-6666
Miscellaneous - not elsewhere classified

AirTran Corp. ATCC
7501 26th Ave. South
Minneapolis, MN 55450 612-726-5151
Transportation - airline

AK Steel Holding Corp. AKST
703 Curtis St.
Middletown, OH 45043 513-425-5000
Steel - production

Akorn, Inc. AKRN
100 Akorn Dr.
Abita Springs, LA 70420
504-893-9300
Medical products

Alabama National BanCorporation ALAB
101 Carnoustie
Shoal Creek, AL 35242 205-995-8528
Banks - southeast

Alamo Group Inc. ALMO
1502 E. Walnut
Seguin, TX 78155 210-379-1480
Miscellaneous - not elsewhere classified

ALANTEC Corp. ALTC
70 Plumeria Dr.
San Jose, CA 95134 408-955-9000
Telecommunications equipment

AlaTenn Resources, Inc. ATNG
PO Box 918
Florence, AL 35631 205-383-3631
Oil & gas - production & pipeline

ALBANK Financial Corp. ALBK
10 N. Pearl St.
Albany, NY 12207 518-445-2100
Banks - northeast

Alcide Corp. ALCD
One Willard Rd.
Norwalk, CT 06851 203-847-2555
Chemicals - specialty

Aldila, Inc. ALDA
15822 Bernardo Center Dr.
San Diego, CA 92127 619-592-0404
Leisure & recreational products O

Aldus Corp. ALDC
411 First Ave. South
Seattle, WA 98104 206-622-5500
Computers - software

Alexander & Baldwin, Inc. ALEX
822 Bishop St., PO Box 3440
Honolulu, HI 96801 808-525-6611
Transportation - shipping

Alexander Energy Corp. AEOK
701 Cedar Lake Blvd.
Oklahoma City, OK 73114 405-478-8686
Oil & gas - US exploration & production

Alfa Corp. ALFA
2108 E. South Blvd.
Montgomery, AL 36116
205-288-3900
Insurance - life

Alico, Inc. ALCO
PO Box 338
La Belle, FL 33935 813-675-2966
Agricultural operations

Alkermes, Inc. ALKS
64 Sidney St.
Cambridge, MA 02139 617-494-0171
Drugs

All American Semiconductor, Inc. SEMI
16115 N.W. 52nd Ave.
Miami, FL 33014 305-621-8282
Electrical components - semiconductors

All For A Dollar, Inc. ADLR
3664 Main St.
Springfield, MA 01107
413-733-1203
Retail - discount & variety

Allcity Insurance Co. ALCI
122 Fifth Ave.
New York, NY 10011 212-387-3000
Insurance - property & casualty

Allegheny & Western Energy Corp. ALGH
1600 Kanawha Valley Building
Charleston, WV 205301
304-343-4567
Oil & gas - US exploration & production

Allegiance Banc Corp. ALLG
4719 Hampden Ln.
Bethesda, MD 20814 301-656-5300
Banks - northeast

Allegiant Physician Services, Inc. ALPS
2300 Peachford Rd.
Atlanta, GA 30338 404-668-9330
Medical services

Allen Organ Co. AORGB
150 Locust St.
Macungie, PA 18062
610-966-2200
Leisure & recreational products

Alliance Pharmaceutical Corp. ALLP
3040 Science Park Rd.
San Diego, CA 92121 619-558-4300
Biomedical & genetic products O

Alliance Semiconductor Corp. ALSC
3099 N. First St.
San Jose, CA 95134 408-383-4900
Electrical components - semiconductors

Allied Bank Capital, Inc. ABCI
130 N. Steele St.
Sanford, NC 27330 919-775-7161
Banks - southeast

Allied Bankshares, Inc. ABGA
149 Main St., PO Box 1020
Thomson, GA 30824
706-595-9500
Banks - southeast

Allied Capital Commercial Corp. ALCC
1666 K St., N.W., 9th Fl.
Washington, DC 20006 202-331-1112
Real estate investment trust

Allied Capital Corp. ALLC
1666 K St., N.W., 9th Fl.
Washington, DC 20006 202-331-1112
Financial - SBIC & commercial

Allied Capital Corp. II ALII
1666 K St., N.W., 9th Fl.
Washington, DC 20006 202-331-1112
Financial - SBIC & commercial

Allied Capital Lending Corp. ALCL
1666 K St., N.W., 9th Fl.
Washington, DC 20006 202-331-1112
Miscellaneous - not elsewhere classified

ALLIED Group, Inc. ALGR
701 Fifth Ave.
Des Moines, IA 50391 515-280-4211
Insurance - multi line & misc.
[DRP]

Allied Healthcare Products, Inc. AHPI
1720 Sublette Ave.
St. Louis, MO 63110 314-771-2400
Medical products

Allied Holdings, Inc. HAUL
160 Clairmont Ave., Ste. 510
Decatur, GA 30030 404-370-1100
Transportation - truck

ALLIED Life Financial Corp. ALFC
701 Fifth Ave.
Des Moines, IA 50391 515-280-4211
Insurance - life

Allied Waste Industries, Inc. AWIN
7201 E. Camelback Rd.
Scottsdale, AZ 85251 602-423-2946
Pollution control equipment & services

Allstate Financial Corp. ASFN
2700 S. Quincy St., Ste. 540
Arlington, VA 22206 703-931-2274
Financial - business services

Alltrista Corp. JARS
301 S. High St., PO Box 5004
Muncie, IN 47307 317-281-5000
Diversified operations

Aloette Cosmetics, Inc. ALET
1301 Wright's Ln. East
West Chester, PA 19380 215-692-0600
Cosmetics & toiletries

Alpha 1 Biomedicals, Inc. ALBM
6903 Rockledge Dr., Ste. 1200
Bethesda, MD 20817 301-564-4400
Drugs

Alpha Microsystems ALMI
3501 W. Sunflower Ave.
Santa Ana, CA 92704 714-957-8500
Computers - mini & micro

Alpha-Beta Technology, Inc. ABTI
One Innovation Dr.
Worcester, MA 01605
508-798-6900
Drugs

ALPHAREL, INC. AREL
9339 Carroll Park Dr.
San Diego, CA 92121 619-625-3000
Computers - software

Alpine Lace Brands, Inc. LACE
111 Dunnell Rd.
Maplewood, NJ 07040 201-378-8600
Food - misc.

Alta Gold Co. ALTA
601 Whitney Ranch Dr., Ste. 10
Henderson, NV 89014
702-433-8525
Gold mining & processing

Altai, Inc. ALTI
624 Six Flags Dr.
Arlington, TX 76011
817-640-8911
Computers - software

Alteon Inc. ALTN
170 Williams Dr.
Ramsey, NJ 07446 201-934-5000
Drugs

Altera Corp. ALTR
2610 Orchard Pkwy.
San Jose, CA 95134 408-894-7000
Electrical components - semiconductors O

Alternative Resources Corp. ALRC
75 Tri-State International
Lincolnshire, IL 60069 708-317-1000
Business services

Altron Inc. ALRN
One Jewel Dr.
Wilmington, MA 01887 508-658-5800
Electrical connectors

AMBAR, Inc. AMBR
221 Rue de Jean, Ste. 301
Lafayette, LA 70508 318-237-5300
Diversified operations

Amber's Stores, Inc. ABRS
11035 Switzer Ave.
Dallas, TX 75238 214-349-5300
Retail - misc.

AMCORE Financial, Inc. AMFI
501 Seventh St.
Rockford, IL 61104 815-968-2241
Banks - midwest [DRP]

AMERCO AMOO
1325 Airmotive Way, Ste. 100
Reno, NV 89502 702-688-6300
Leasing

Ameriana Bancorp ASBI
2118 Bundy Ave.
New Castle, IN 47362 317-529-2230
Banks - midwest

Ameribanc Investors Group AINVS
7630 Little River Turnpike
Annandale, VA 22003 703-658-2720
Financial - savings and loans

America First Financial Fund 1987-A L.P. AFFFZ
1004 Farnum St.
Omaha, NE 68102 402-444-1630
Financial - investment management

America First Prt./Pfd. Eqty. Mtg. Fnd. L.P.
AFPFZ
1004 Farnam St.
Omaha, NE 68102 402-444-1630
Financial - investment management

America First Tax Exempt Mtg. Fund 2 L.P.
ATAXZ
1004 Farnam St.
Omaha, NE 68102 402-444-1630
Financial - investment management

America First Tax Exempt Mtg. Fund L.P.
AFTXZ
1004 Farnam St., Ste. 400
Omaha, NE 68102 402-444-1630
Financial - investment management

America Online, Inc. AMER
8619 Westwood Center Dr.
Vienna, VA 22182 703-448-8700
Computers - services O

America Service Group Inc. ASGR
101 Lukens Dr., Ste. A
New Castle, DE 19720 302-888-0200
Healthcare - outpatient & home

America's All Season Fund, Inc. FUND
250 Park Ave. South, Ste. 200
Winter Park, FL 32789 407-629-1400
Financial - investment management

American Bancorporation AMBC
1025 Main St., Ste. 800
Wheeling, WV 26003 304-233-5006
Banks - southeast

American Bankers Insurance Group, Inc.
ABIG
11222 Quail Roost Dr.
Miami, FL 33157 305-253-2244
Insurance - life

American Biogenetic Sciences, Inc. MABXA
PO Box 1001
Notre Dame, IN 46556 219-631-7755
Biomedical & genetic products

American Buildings Co. ABCO
State Docks Rd., PO Box 800
Eufaula, AL 36072 205-687-2032
Building - residential & commercial

American Business Information, Inc. ABII
5711 S. 86th Circle
Omaha, NE 68127 402-593-4500
Business services - marketing

American City Business Journals, Inc.
AMBJ
128 S. Tryon St., Ste. 2300
Charlotte, NC 28202 704-375-7404
Publishing - newspapers

American Claims Evaluation, Inc. AMCE
375 N. Broadway
Jericho, NY 11753 516-938-8000
Business services

American Classic Voyages Co. AMCV
Two N. Riverside Plaza
Chicago, IL 60606 312-258-7890
Leisure & recreational services

American Colloid Co. ACOL
1500 W. Shure Dr., Ste. 500
Arlington Heights, IL 60004 708-392-4600
Metal ores - misc. O
[DRP]

American Consumer Products, Inc. ACPI
31100 Solon Rd.
Solon, OH 44139 216-248-7000
Diversified operations

American Eagle Outfitters, Inc. AEOS
150 Thornhill Dr., PO Box 788
Warrendale, PA 15095 412-776-4857
Retail - apparel & shoes

American Ecology Corp. ECOL
5333 Westheimer, Ste. 1000
Houston, TX 77056 713-624-1900
Pollution control equipment & services

American Educational Products, Inc.
AMEP
3101 Iris Ave., Suite 215
Boulder, CO 80301 303-443-0020
Miscellaneous - not elsewhere classified

American Electronic Components AECI
1010 N. Main St.
Elkhart, IN 46514 219-264-1116
Electronics - components & systems

American Federal Bank, F.S.B. AMFB
300 E. McBee Ave.
Greenville, SC 29601 803-255-7000
Financial - savings and loans

American Filtrona Corp. AFIL
3951 Westerre Parkway
Richmond, VA 23233 804-346-2400
Pollution control equipment & services
[DRP]

American Freightways Corp. AFWY
2200 Forward Dr.
Harrison, AR 72601 501-741-9000
Transportation - truck

American Greetings Corp. AGREA
One American Rd.
Cleveland, OH 44144 216-252-7300
Printing - commercial O [DRP]

American Healthcorp, Inc. AMHC
One Burton Hills Blvd.
Nashville, TN 37215 615-665-1122
Healthcare - outpatient & home

American Holdings, Inc. HOLD
56 Pennbrook Rd.
Far Hills, NJ 07931 908-234-9220
Miscellaneous - not elsewhere classified

American HomePatient, Inc. AHOM
105 Reynolds Dr.
Franklin, TN 37064 615-794-3313
Healthcare - outpatient & home

American Homestar Corp. HSTR
812 E. Nasa Rd. One
Webster, TX 77598 713-333-5601
Building - residential & commercial

American Indemnity Financial Corp. AIFC
PO Box 1259
Galveston, TX 77553 409-766-4600
Insurance - property & casualty

American International Petroleum Co.
AIPN
640 Fifth Ave.
New York, NY 10019 212-956-3333
Oil & gas - US exploration & production

American Life Holding Co. ALHCP
405 6th Ave.
Des Moines, IA 50309 515-284-7500
Insurance - life

American Locker Group Inc. ALGI
15 W. Second St., PO Box 1000
Jamestown, NY 14702 716-664-9600
Building products - misc.

American Management Systems, Inc.
AMSY
4050 Legato Rd.
Fairfax, VA 22033 703-267-8000
Computers - services

American Medical Electronics, Inc. AMEI
250 E. Arapahoe Rd.
Richardson, TX 75081 214-918-8300
Medical instruments

American Mobile Satellite Corp. SKYC
10802 Parkridge Blvd.
Reston, VA 22091 703-758-6000
Telecommunications services

American Mobile Systems, Inc. AMSE
21160 Califa St.
Woodland Hills, CA 91367 818-593-3000
Telecommunications services

American National Insurance Co. ANAT
One Moody Plaza
Galveston, TX 77550 409-763-4661
Insurance - life

American Oilfield Divers, Inc. DIVE
130 E. Kaliste Saloom Rd.
Lafayette, LA 70508 318-234-4590
Oil & gas - field services

American Pacific Corp. APFC
3770 Howard Hughes Parkway
Las Vegas, NV 89109 702-735-2200
Chemicals - specialty

American Physicians Service Group, Inc.
AMPH
1301 Capital of Texas Hwy.
Austin, TX 78746 512-328-0888
Miscellaneous - not elsewhere classified

American Power Conversion Corp. APCC
132 Fairgrounds Rd.
West Kingston, RI 02892 401-789-5735
Electrical products - misc. O

American Publishing Co. AMPC
111-115 S. Emma St.
West Frankfort, IL 62896 618-937-6411
Publishing - newspapers

American Recreation Centers, Inc. AMRC
11171 Sun Center Dr., Ste. 120
Rancho Cordova, CA 95670
916-852-8005
Diversified operations [DRP]

American Recreation Company Holdings, Inc.
AMRE
48 Mall Dr.
Commack, NY 11725 516-864-2000
Leisure & recreational products

American Safety Razor Co. RAZR
Razor Blade Ln.
Verona, VA 24482 703-248-8000
Cosmetics & toiletries

American Savings Bank of Florida F.S.B.
ASFL
17801 N.W. 2nd Ave.
Miami, FL 33169 305-653-5353
Financial - savings and loans

American Software, Inc. AMSWA
470 E. Paces Ferry Rd. NE
Atlanta, GA 30305 404-261-4381
Computers - software O

American Studios, Inc. AMST
11001 Park Charlotte Blvd.
Charlotte, NC 28273 704-588-4351
Retail - misc.

American Superconductor Corp. AMSC
149 Grove St.
Watertown, MA 02172 508-836-4200
Electrical components - misc.

American Telecasting, Inc. ATEL
4065 N. Sinton Rd., Ste. 201
Colorado Springs, CO 80907
719-632-5544
Cable TV

American Travellers Corp. ATVC
3220 Tillman Dr.
Bensalem, PA 19020 215-244-1600
Insurance - accident & health

American United Global, Inc. AUGI
11634 Patton Rd.
Downey, CA 90241 310-862-8163
Pumps and seals

American Vanguard Corp. AMGD
4100 E. Washington Blvd.
Los Angeles, CA 90023 213-264-3910
Chemicals - specialty

American White Cross, Inc. AWCI
349 Lake Rd.
Dayville, CT 06241 203-774-8541
Medical products

American Woodmark Corp. AMWD
3102 Shawnee Dr.
Winchester, VA 22601 703-665-9100
Building products - doors & trim

AmeriFed Financial Corp. AFFC
120 N. Scott St.
Joliet, IL 60431 815-727-0370
Banks - midwest

Amerihost Properties, Inc. HOST
2400 E. Devon Ave., Ste. 280
Des Plaines, IL 60018 708-298-4500
Hotels & motels

AmeriLink Corp. ALNK
1900 E. Dublin-Granville Rd.
Columbus, OH 43229 614-895-1313
Telecommunications equipment

Ameristar Casinos, Inc. ASCA
PO Box 259
Jackpot, NV 89825 702-755-6011
Leisure & recreational services

Ameriwood Industries International Corp.
AWII
171 Monroe NW, Ste. 600
Grand Rapids, MI 49503 616-336-9400
Diversified operations

AMFED Financial, Inc. AMFF
One California Ave.
Reno, NV 89509 702-785-8500
Financial - savings and loans

Amgen Inc. AMGN
01840 DeHavilland Dr.
Thousand Oaks, CA 91320
805-497-1000
Biomedical & genetic products O

Amistar Corp. AMTA
237 Via Vera Cruz
San Marcos, CA 92069
619-471-1700
Machinery - material handling

Ampex, Inc. AMPX
401 Broadway
Redwood City, CA 94063 415-367-4111
Miscellaneous - not elsewhere classified

Amplicon, Inc. AMPI
5 Hutton Centre Dr.
Santa Ana, CA 92707 714-751-7551
Leasing

AMRESCO, Inc. AMMB
1845 Woodall Rogers Fwy.
Dallas, TX 75201 214-953-7700
Business services

Amrion, Inc. AMRI
6565 Odell Place
Boulder, CO 80301 303-530-2525
Vitamins & nutritional products

AMSERV HEALTHCARE INC. AMSR
6490 S. McCarran Blvd.
Reno, NV 89509 702-825-6100
Medical services

Amtech Corp. AMTC
17304 Preston Rd., Bldg. E-100
Dallas, TX 75252 214-733-6600
Computers - services O

Amtran, Inc. AMTR
7337 W. Washington St.
Indianapolis, IN 46231 317-247-4000
Transportation - airline

Amtrol Inc. AMTL
1400 Division Rd.
West Warwick, RI 02893 401-884-6300
General Industrial Machinery

Amylin Pharmaceuticals, Inc. AMLN
9373 Towne Center Dr.
San Diego, CA 92121 619-552-2200
Drugs

Analogic Corp. ALOG
8 Centennial Dr.
Peabody, MA 01960 508-977-3000
Computers - peripheral equipment

Analysis & Technology, Inc. AATI
Technology Park, Rte. 2
North Stonington, CT 06359
203-599-3910
Engineering - R & D services

Analysts International Corp. ANLY
7615 Metro Blvd.
Minneapolis, MN 55439
612-835-5900
Computers - services

Anaren Microwave, Inc. ANEN
6635 Kirkville Rd.
East Syracuse, NY 13057
315-432-8909
Electronics - military

ANB Corp. ANBC
110 E. Main St.
Muncie, IN 47305 317-747-7575
Banks - midwest

Anchor BanCorp Wisconsin Inc. ABCW
25 W. Main St.
Madison, WI 53703 608-252-8700
Financial - savings and loans

Anchor Bancorp, Inc. ABKR
1420 Broadway
Hewlett, NY 11557 516-596-3900
Financial - savings and loans

Anchor Gaming SLOT
3760 Pecos McLeod, Ste. 3
Las Vegas, NV 89121 702-433-0017
Leisure & recreational products

Andersen Group, Inc. ANDR
Ney Industrial Park
Bloomfield, CT 06002 203-242-0761
Diversified operations

Andover Bancorp, Inc. ANDB
61 Main St.
Andover, MA 01810 508-475-6103
Financial - savings and loans

Andover Togs, Inc. ATOG
One Penn Plaza
New York, NY 10119 212-244-0700
Textiles - apparel

Andrew Corp. ANDW
10500 W. 153rd St.
Orland Park, IL 60462 708-349-3300
Telecommunications equipment O

Andros Inc. ANDY
2332 Fourth St.
Berkeley, CA 94710 510-849-5700
Electronics - measuring instruments

Anergen, Inc. ANRG
301 Penobscot Dr.
Redwood City, CA 94063 415-361-8901
Biomedical & genetic products

Anesta Corp. NSTA
825 N. 300 West, Ste. 200
Salt Lake City, UT 84103 801-595-1405
Drugs

Antec Corp. ANTC
2850 W. Golf Rd.
Rolling Meadows, IL 60008
708-439-4444
Telecommunications equipment O

Apertus Technologies Inc. APTS
7075 Flying Cloud Dr.
Eden Prairie, MN 55344 612-828-0300
Computers - peripheral equipment O

Apogee Enterprises, Inc. APOG
7900 Xerxes Ave. South
Minneapolis, MN 55431 612-835-1874
Glass products

Apogee, Inc. APGG
1018 W. Ninth Ave., Ste. 202
King of Prussia, PA 19406 610-992-7670
Healthcare - outpatient & home

Apple Computer, Inc. AAPL
20525 Mariani Ave.
Cupertino, CA 95014 408-996-1010
Computers - mini & micro O

Apple South, Inc. APSO
Hancock at Washington
Madison, GA 30650 706-342-4552
Retail - food & restaurants O

Applebee's International, Inc. APPB
4551 W. 107th St., Ste. 100
Shawnee Mission, KS 66207
913-967-4000
Retail - food & restaurants O

Appliance Recycling Centers of America,
    Inc. ARCI
7400 Excelsior Blvd.
Minneapolis, MN 55426 612-930-9000
Pollution control equipment & services

Applied Bioscience International Inc. APBI
4350 N. Fairfax Dr.
Arlington, VA 22203 703-516-2490
Medical products O

Applied Digital Access, Inc. ADAX
9855 Scranton Rd.
San Diego, CA 92121 619-623-2200
Instruments - control

Applied Extrusion Technologies, Inc. AETC
96 Swampscott Rd.
Salem, MA 01970 508-744-8000
Rubber & plastic products

Applied Immune Sciences, Inc. AISX
05301 Patrick Henry Dr.
Santa Clara, CA 95054 408-492-9200
Medical products

Applied Innovation, Inc. AINN
651 C Lakeview Plaza Blvd.
Columbus, OH 43085 614-798-2000
Telecommunications equipment

Applied Materials, Inc. AMAT
3050 Bowers Ave.
Santa Clara, CA 95054 408-727-5555
Electrical components - semiconductors O

Applied Microbiology, Inc. AMBI
777 Old Saw Mill River Rd.
Tarrytown, NY 10591 914-789-2013
Biomedical & genetic products

Applied Science and Technology, Inc.
 ASTX
35 Cabot Rd.
Woburn, MA 01801 617-933-5560
Miscellaneous - not elsewhere classified

Applied Signal Technology, Inc. APSG
160 Sobrante Way
Sunnyvale, CA 94086 408-749-1888
Telecommunications equipment

Applix, Inc. APLX
112 Turnpike Rd.
Westboro, MA 01581
508-870-0300
Computers - software

APS Holding Corp. APSI
3000 Pawnee St.
Houston, TX 77054 713-741-2470
Auto parts - retail & wholesale

Aquagenix, Inc. AQUX
6500 Northwest 15 Ave.
Fort Lauderdale, FL 33309
305-975-7771
Miscellaneous - not elsewhere classified

Arabian Shield Development Co. ARSD
10830 N. Central Expressway
Dallas, TX 75231 214-692-7872
Oil & gas - international specialty

Aramed, Inc. ARAM
11025 Roselle St.
San Diego, CA 92121 619-546-8300
Biomedical & genetic products

Arbor Drugs, Inc. ARBR
3331 W. Big Beaver Rd.
Troy, MI 48084 313-643-9420
Retail - drug stores

Arbor Health Care Co. AHCC
1100 Shawnee Rd., PO Box 840
Lima, OH 45802 419-227-3000
Nursing homes

Arbor National Holdings, Inc. ARBH
333 Earle Ovington Blvd.
Uniondale, NY 11553 516-357-7400
Financial - mortgages & related services

Arch Communications Group, Inc. APGR
110 Turnpike Rd. Ste. 210
Westborough, MA 01581
508-898-0962
Telecommunications services

Arch Petroleum, Inc. ARCH
777 Taylor St., Ste. II
Fort Worth, TX 76102 817-332-9209
Oil & gas - US exploration & production

Arctco, Inc. ACAT
600 Brooks Ave. South
Thief River Falls, MN 56701
218-681-8558
Leisure & recreational products

Arden Group, Inc. ARDNA
2020 S. Central Ave.
Compton, CA 90220 310-638-2842
Telecommunications equipment

Arden Industrial Products, Inc. AFAS
200 S. Owasso Blvd. East
St. Paul, MN 55117 612-490-6800
Metal products - fasteners

ArgentBank ARGT
203 W. Second St.
Thibodaux, LA 70302 504-447-3722
Banks - southeast

Argonaut Group, Inc. AGII
1800 Avenue of the Stars
Los Angeles, CA 90067 310-553-0561
Insurance - property & casualty

Argosy Gaming Co. ARGY
219 Piasa St.
Alton, IL 62002 618-474-7500
Leisure & recreational services O

Argus Pharmaceuticals, Inc. ARGS
3400 Research Forest Dr.
The Woodlands, TX 77831
713-367-1666
Drugs

ARI Network Services, Inc. ARIS
330 E. Kilbourn Ave.
Milwaukee, WI 53202 414-278-7676
Business services

ARIAD Pharmaceuticals, Inc. ARIA
26 Landsdowne St.
Cambridge, MA 02139 617-494-0400
Drugs

Aristotle Corp. ARTL
129 Church St., Ste. 810
New Haven, CT 06510 203-867-4090
Miscellaneous - not elsewhere classified

Ark Restaurants Corp. ARKR
158 W. 29th St.
New York, NY 10001 212-760-0520
Retail - food & restaurants

Arkansas Best Corp. ABFS
1000 S. 21st St.
Fort Smith, AR 72901 501-785-6000
Transportation - truck

Armor All Products Corp. ARMR
6 Liberty
Aliso Viejo, CA 92656 714-362-0600
Soap & cleaning preparations

Arnold Industries Inc. AIND
625 S. Fifth Ave.
Lebanon, PA 17042 717-274-2521
Transportation - truck
[DRP]

Arris Pharmaceutical Corp. ARRS
385 Oyster Point Blvd., Ste. 3
South San Francisco, CA 94080
415-737-8600
Drugs

Arrow Financial Corp. AROW
250 Glen St.
Glens Falls, NY 12801 518-745-1000
Banks - northeast
[DRP]

Arrow International, Inc. ARRO
3000 Bernville Rd.
Reading, PA 19605 215-378-0131
Medical products

Arrow Transportation Co. ARRW
10145 N. Portland Rd.
Portland, OR 97203 503-286-3661
Transportation - shipping

Art's-Way Manufacturing Co., Inc. ARTW
Highway 9 West, PO Box 288
Armstrong, IA 50514 712-864-3131
Machinery - farm

Artisoft, Inc. ASFT
2202 N. Forbes Blvd.
Tucson, AZ 85745 602-670-7100
Computers - software O

Artistic Greetings, Inc. ARTG
One Komer Center
Elmira, NY 14902 607-737-5235
Retail - mail order & direct

Asante Technologies, Inc. ASNT
821 Fox Ln.
San Jose, CA 95131 408-435-8388
Computers - software

Ascend Communications, Inc. ASND
1275 Harbor Bay Pkwy.
Alameda, CA 94502 510-769-6001
Computers - peripheral equipment

Aseco Corp. ASEC
500 Donald Lynch Blvd.
Marlborough, MA 01752
508-481-8896
Instruments - control

Ashworth, Inc. ASHW
2791 Loker Ave. West
Carlsbad, CA 92008 619-438-6610
Apparel O

Aspect Telecommunications Corp. ASPT
1730 Fox Dr.
San Jose, CA 95131 408-441-2200
Telecommunications equipment O

Aspen Bancshares, Inc. ASBK
534 E. Hyman Ave.
Aspen, CO 81611 303-925-6700
Banks - west

Aspen Technology, Inc. AZPN
Ten Canal Park
Cambridge, MA 02141 617-577-0100
Computers - software

Associated Banc-Corp ASBC
112 N. Adams St., PO Box 13307
Green Bay, WI 54307 414-433-4384
Banks - midwest
[DRP]

AST Research, Inc. ASTA
16215 Alton Parkway
Irvine, CA 92718 714-727-4141
Computers - peripheral equipment O

Astec Industries, Inc. ASTE
4101 Jerome Ave., PO Box 72787
Chattanooga, TN 37407 615-867-4210
Machinery - material handling

Astoria Financial Corp. ASFC
One Astoria Federal Plaza
Lake Success, NY 11042 516-327-3000
Financial - savings and loans O

Astro-Med, Inc. ALOT
600 E. Greenwich Ave.
West Warwick, RI 02893
401-828-4000
Medical products

Astronics Corp. ATRO
80 S. Davis St.
Orchard Park, NY 14127
716-662-6640
Diversified operations

Astrosystems, Inc. ASTR
6 Nevada Dr.
Lake Success, NY 11042 516-328-1600
Instruments - control

Astrum International Corp. ASTI
40-301 Fisher Island Dr.
Fisher Island, FL 33109 305-532-2426
Diversified operations

Asyst Technologies Inc. ASYT
1745 McCandless Dr.
Milpitas, CA 95035 408-263-5100
Pollution control equipment & services

Atchison Casting Corp. ACCX
400 S. Fourth St.
Atchison, KS 66002 913-367-2121
Steel - production

Athena Neurosciences, Inc. ATHN
800 Gateway Blvd.
South San Francisco, CA 94080
415-877-0900
Drugs

Athey Products Corp. ATPC
Highway 1A North, PO Box 669
Raleigh, NC 27602 919-556-5171
Machinery - general industrial

Atlanfed Bancorp, Inc. AFED
100 West Rd.
Baltimore, MD 21204
410-938-8600
Banks - northeast

Atlantic American Corp. AAME
4370 Peachtree Rd., N.E.
Atlanta, GA 30319 404-266-5500
Insurance - accident & health

Atlantic Beverage Co., Inc. ABEV
1687 Sulphur Spring Rd.
Baltimore, MD 21227 410-247-5857
Wholesale distribution - consumer products

Atlantic Coast Airlines, Inc. ACAI
1 Export Dr.
Sterling, VA 20164 703-406-6500
Transportation - airline

Atlantic Gulf Communities Corp. AGLF
2601 S. Bayshore Dr.
Miami, FL 33133 305-859-4000
Real estate development

Atlantic Southeast Airlines, Inc. ASAI
100 Hartsfield Centre Pkwy.
Atlanta, GA 30354 404-766-1400
Transportation - airline O

Atmel Corp. ATML
2125 O'Nel Dr.
San Jose, CA 95131 408-441-0311
Electrical components - misc. O

Atria Software, Inc. ATSW
24 Prime Park Way
Natick, MA 01760 508-650-5100
Computers - software

Atrix Laboratories, Inc. ATRX
1625 Midpoint Dr.
Fort Collins, CO 80525
303-482-5868
Medical services

ATS Medical, Inc. ATSI
3905 Annapolis Ln.
Minneapolis, MN 55447
612-553-7736
Medical products

Atwood Oceanics, Inc. ATWD
15835 Park Ten Place Dr.
Houston, TX 77218 713-492-2929
Oil & gas - offshore drilling

Au Bon Pain Co., Inc. ABPCA
19 Fid Kennedy Ave.
Boston, MA 02210 617-423-2100
Retail - food & restaurants O

Aura Systems, Inc. AURA
2335 Alaska Ave.
El Segundo, CA 90245 310-643-5300
Electrical products - misc. O

Auspex Systems, Inc. ASPX
5200 Great America Pkwy.
Santa Clara, CA 95054 408-986-2000
Computers - mini & micro O

Autocam Corp. ACAM
4070 E. Paris Ave.
Kentwood, MI 49512 616-698-0707
Metal products - fabrication

Autoclave Engineers, Inc. ACLV
2930 W. 22nd St., PO Box 5051
Erie, PA 16512 814-838-5700
Instruments - control

Autodesk, Inc. ACAD
2320 Marinship Way
Sausalito, CA 94965 415-332-2344
Computers - software O

AutoFinance Group, Inc. AUFN
601 Oakmont Ln.
Westmont, IL 60559 708-665-7100
Financial - business services

AutoImmune, Inc. AIMM
128 Spring St.
Lexington, MA 02173
617-860-0710
Drugs

AutoInfo, Inc. AUTO
1600 Route 208
Fair Lawn, NJ 07410 201-703-0500
Business services

Automotive Industries Holding, Inc. AIHI
4508 IDS Center
Minneapolis, MN 55402 612-332-6828
Automotive & trucking - original equipment

Autotote Corp. TOTE
100 Bellevue Rd., PO Box 6009
Newark, DE 19714 302-737-4300
Leisure & recreational products O

Avatar Holdings, Inc. AVTR
255 Alhambra Circle
Coral Gables, FL 33134 305-442-7000
Real estate development

Avert, Inc. AVRT
119 E. Mountain Ave.
Fort Collins, CO 80524 303-484-7722
Business services

Avid Technology, Inc. AVID
One Park West
Tewksbury, MA 01876 508-640-6789
Video equipment O

Avondale Industries, Inc. AVDL
5100 River Rd.
Avondale, LA 70094 504-436-2121
Transportation - equipment & leasing

AW Computer Systems, Inc. AWCSA
9000A Commerce Pkwy.
Mt. Laurel, NJ 08054 609-234-3939
Computers - software

Aztec Manufacturing Co. AZTC
400 N. Tarrant, PO Box 668
Crowley, TX 76036 817-297-4361
Building products - lighting fixtures

B.M.J. Financial Corp. BMJF
243 Route 130
Bordentown, NJ 08505 609-298-5500
Banks - northeast
[DRP 3%]

Baby Superstore, Inc. BSST
605 Haywood Rd.
Greenville, SC 29607
803-675-0299
Retail - misc.

Bachman Information Systems, Inc.
 BACH
8 New England Executive Park
Burlington, MA 01803 617-273-9003
Computers - software

Back Bay Restaurant Group, Inc. PAPA
284 Newbury St.
Boston, MA 02115 617-536-2800
Retail - food & restaurants

Badger Paper Mills, Inc. BPMI
200 W. Front St., PO Box 149
Peshtigo, WI 54157 715-582-4551
Paper & paper products

Bailey Corp. BAIB
700 Lafayette Rd., PO Box 307
Seabrook, NH 03874 603-474-3011
Automotive & trucking - original equipment

Balchem Corp. BLCC
PO Box 175
Slate Hill, NY 10973 914-355-2861
Chemicals - specialty

Baldwin & Lyons, Inc. BWINA
1099 N. Meridian St.
Indianapolis, IN 46204 317-636-9800
Insurance - property & casualty

Baldwin Piano & Organ Co. BPAO
422 Wards Corner Rd.
Loveland, OH 45140 513-576-4500
Leisure & recreational products

Bally Gaming International, Inc. BGII
6601 S. Bermuda Rd.
Las Vegas, NV 89119 702-896-7700
Leisure & recreational products O

Baltek Corp. BTEK
10 Fairway Court, PO Box 195
Northvale, NJ 07647 201-767-1400
Building products - wood

BancFirst Corp. BANF
101 N. Broadway, Ste. 200
Oklahoma City, OK 73102
405-270-1000
Banks - west

BancFirst Ohio Corp. BFOH
422 Main St., PO Box 4658
Zanesville, OH 43702 614-452-8444
Banks - midwest

Bancinsurance Corp. BCIS
20 E. Broad St., PO Box 182138
Columbus, OH 43216 614-228-2800
Insurance - property & casualty

Bancorp Connecticut, Inc. BKCT
121 Main St.
Southington, CT 06489 203-628-0351
Financial - savings and loans

Bancorp New Jersey, Inc. BCNJ
10 W. High St.
Somerville, NJ 08876 908-722-0600
Financial - savings and loans
[DRP]

BancorpSouth, Inc. BOMS
One Mississippi Plaza
Tupelo, MS 38801 601-680-2000
Banks - southeast
[DRP]

BancTec, Inc. BTEC
4435 Spring Valley Rd.
Dallas, TX 75244 214-450-7700
Optical character recognition

Bando McGlocklin Capital Corp. BMCC
13555 Bishops Court, Ste. 205
Brookfield, WI 53005 414-784-9010
Financial - investment bankers [DRP]

Bank of Braintree BTSB
865 Washington St.
Braintree, MA 02184 617-843-9100
Financial - savings and loans [DRP]

Bank of Granite Corp. GRAN
23 N. Main St.
Granite Falls, NC 28630 704-496-2000
Banks - southeast [DRP]

Bank of New Hampshire Corp. BNHC
300 Franklin St.
Manchester, NH 03101 603-624-6600
Banks - northeast

Bank South Corp. BKSO
55 Marietta St., N.W.
Atlanta, GA 30303 404-529-4521
Banks - southeast O [DRP]

BankAtlantic Bancorp, Inc. BANC
1750 E. Sunrise Blvd.
Fort Lauderdale, FL 33304 305-760-5000
Banks - northeast

Bankers Corp. BKCO
210 Smith St.
Perth Amboy, NJ 08861 908-442-4100
Banks - northeast

Bankers First Corp. BNKF
One 10th St.
Augusta, GA 30901 706-849-3200
Financial - savings and loans
[DRP 5%]

Banknorth Group, Inc. BKNG
300 Financial Plaza
Burlington, VT 05401 802-658-2492
Banks - northeast
[DRP]

BankUnited Financial Corp. BKUNA
2334 Ponce de Leon Blvd.
Coral Gables, FL 33134 305-447-0200
Financial - savings and loans

BanPonce Corp. BPOP
209 Munoz Rivera Ave.
Hato Rey, PR, 00936 809-765-9800
Bank - Puerto Rico
[DRP 5%]

Banta Corp. BNTA
225 Main St.
Menasha, WI 54952 414-722-7777
Printing - commercial [DRP]

Banyan Mortgage Investors L.P. III VMORZ
150 S. Wacker Dr.
Chicago, IL 60606 312-553-9800
Real estate investment trust

Banyan Strategic Land Fund II VSLF
150 S. Wacker Dr.
Chicago, IL 60606 312-553-9800
Real estate investment trust

Banyan Strategic Realty Trust VLANS
150 S. Wacker Dr.
Chicago, IL 60606 312-553-9800
Real estate investment trust

Banyan Systems, Inc. BNYN
120 Flanders Rd.
Westboro, MA 01581 508-898-1000
Computers - software O

Barefoot Inc. BARE
450 W. Wilson Bridge Rd.
Worthington, OH 43085
614-846-1800
Agricultural operations

BARRA, Inc. BARZ
1995 University Ave., Ste. 400
Berkeley, CA 94704 510-548-5442
Computers - software

Barrett Business Services Inc. BBSI
4724 SW Macadam Ave.
Portland, OR 97201 503-220-0988
Personnel

Base Ten Systems, Inc. BASEA
One Electronics Dr.
Trenton, NJ 08619 609-586-7010
Computers - mini & micro

Basin Exploration, Inc. BSNX
370 17th St., Ste. 1800
Denver, CO 80202 303-685-8000
Oil & gas - US exploration & production

Bassett Furniture Industries, Inc. BSET
PO Box 626
Bassett, VA 24055 703-629-7511
Furniture

Bay Ridge Bancorp, Inc. BRBC
7500 Fifth Ave.
Brooklyn, NY 11209 718-745-6100
Financial - savings and loans

Bay View Capital Corp. BVFS
2121 S. El Camino Real
San Mateo, CA 94403 415-573-7300
Financial - savings and loans
[DRP 5%]

BayBanks, Inc. BBNK
175 Federal St.
Boston, MA 02110 617-482-1040
Banks - northeast O
[DRP]

Bayport Restaurant Group, Inc. PORT
4000 Hollywood Blvd.
Hollywood, FL 33021 305-377-4821
Retail - food & restaurants

BB&T Financial Corp. BBTF
223 W. Nash St.
Wilson, NC 27893 919-399-4291
Banks - southeast [DRP 5%]

BCB Financial Services Corp. BCBF
400 Washington St.
Reading, PA 19603 610-376-5933
Banks - northeast

BE Aerospace, Inc. BEAV
1300 Corporate Center Way
Wellington, FL 33414 407-791-5000
Aerospace - aircraft equipment O

BeautiControl Cosmetics, Inc. BUTI
2121 Midway Rd.
Carrollton, TX 75006 214-458-0601
Cosmetics & toiletries

Bed Bath & Beyond Inc. BBBY
715 Morris Ave.
Springfield, NJ 07081
201-379-1520
Retail - home furnishings O

Bedford Bancshares, Inc. BFSB
125 W. Main St.
Bedford, VA 24523 703-586-2590
Financial - savings and loans

Beeba's Creations, Inc. BEBA
9220 Activity Rd.
San Diego, CA 92126 619-549-2922
Textiles - apparel

BEI Electronics, Inc. BEII
One Post St., Ste. 2500
San Francisco, CA 94104
415-956-4477
Electronics - military

Bel Fuse Inc. BELF
198 Van Vorst St.
Jersey City, NJ 07302 201-432-0463
Electrical components - misc.

Belden & Blake Corp. BELD
5200 Stoneham Rd.
North Canton, OH 44720
216-499-1660
Oil & gas - production & pipeline

Bell Bancorp, Inc. BELL
79 W. Monroe St.
Chicago, IL 60603 312-346-1000
Banks - money center

Bell Microproducts Inc. BELM
1941 Ringwood Ave.
San Jose, CA 95131 408-451-9400
Electronics - parts distribution

Bell Sports Corp. BSPT
10601 N. Hayden Rd.
Scottsdale, AZ 85260 602-951-0033
Leisure & recreational products O

Ben & Jerry's Homemade, Inc. BJICA
Junction of Rts. 2 and 100
Waterbury, VT 05676 802-244-6957
Food - dairy products

Ben Franklin Retail Stores, Inc. BFRS
500 E. North Ave.
Carol Stream, IL 60188 708-462-6100
Retail - discount & variety

Benihana National Corp. BNHN
8685 N.W. 53rd Terrace
Miami, FL 33166 305-593-0770
Retail - food & restaurants

Benson Financial Corp. BFCX
40 NE Loop 410
San Antonio, TX 78216
210-340-5000
Banks - west

Benton Oil and Gas Co. BNTN
300 Esplanade Dr., Ste. 2000
Oxnard, CA 93030 805-981-9901
Oil & gas - US exploration & production

Berkshire Gas Co. BGAS
115 Cheshire Rd.
Pittsfield, MA 01201 413-442-1511
Utility - gas distribution
[DRP 3%]

Bertucci's, Inc. BERT
14 Audubon Rd.
Wakefield, MA 01880 617-246-6700
Retail - food & restaurants

Best Power Technology, Inc. BPTI
PO Box 280
Necedah, WI 54646 608-565-7200
Electrical products - misc.

Bestop, Inc. BTOP
2100 W. Midway Blvd.
Bloomfield, CO 80020 303-465-1755
Automotive & trucking - original equipment

Bethel Bancorp BTHL
489 Congress St., Ste. 200
Portland, ME 04101 207-772-8587
Financial - savings and loans

Bettis Corp. BETT
18703 GH Circle, PO Box 508
Waller, TX 77484 713-463-5100
Instruments - control

BF Enterprises, Inc. BFEN
100 Bush St., Ste. 1700
San Francisco, CA 94104
415-989-6580
Real estate development

BFS Bankorp, Inc. BFSI
110 William St.
New York, NY 10038 212-227-4040
Banks - money center

BGS Systems, Inc. BGSS
128 Technology Center
Waltham, MA 02254 617-891-0000
Computers - software

BHA Group, Inc. BHAG
8800 E. 63rd St.
Kansas City, MO 64133 816-356-8400
Pollution control equipment & services

BHC Financial, Inc. BHCF
2005 Market St.
Philadelphia, PA 19103 215-636-3000
Business services

BI Inc. BIAC
6400 Lookout Rd.
Boulder, CO 80301 303-530-2911
Telecommunications equipment

Big B, Inc. BIGB
2600 Morgan Rd., S.E.
Birmingham, AL 35023 205-424-3421
Retail - drug stores

Big O Tires, Inc. BIGO
11755 E. Peakview Ave.
Englewood, CO 80111
303-790-2800
Retail - misc.

Bindley Western Industries, Inc. BIND
10333 N. Meridian St.
Indianapolis, IN 46290 317-298-9900
Drugs & sundries - wholesale
[DRP]

Bio-logic Systems Corp. BLSC
One Bio-Logic Plaza
Mundelein, IL 60060
708-949-5200
Medical instruments

Bio-Plexus, Inc. BPLX
PO Box 826
Tolland, CT 06084 203-871-8601
Medical products

Bio-Technology General Corp. BTGC
70 Wood Ave. South
Iselin, NJ 08830 908-632-8800
Biomedical & genetic products O

Biocircuits Corp. BIOC
1324 Chesapeake Terr.
Sunnyvale, CA 94089 408-745-1961
Biomedical & genetic products

BioCryst Pharmaceuticals, Inc. BCRX
2190 Parkway Lane Dr.
Birmingham, AL 35244 205-444-4600
Drugs

Biogen, Inc. BGEN
14 Cambridge Center
Cambridge, MA 02142 617-252-9200
Biomedical & genetic products O

Bioject Medical Technologies, Inc. BJCT
7620 S.W. Bridgeport Rd.
Portland, OR 97224 503-639-7221
Medical products

Biomagnetic Technologies, Inc. BTIX
9727 Pacific Heights Blvd.
San Diego, CA 92121
619-453-6300
Medical instruments

Biomatrix, Inc. BIOX
65 Railroad Ave.
Ridgefield, NJ 07657 201-945-9550
Biomedical & genetic products

BioMedical Waste Systems, Inc. BWSI
200 High St., 6th Floor
Boston, MA 02110 617-556-4033
Pollution control equipment & services

Biomet, Inc. BMET
Airport Industrial Park
Warshaw, IN 46581 219-267-6639
Medical products O

BioSafety Systems, Inc. BSSI
10225 Willow Creek Rd.
San Diego, CA 92131 619-530-0400
Protection - safety equipment & services

BioSepra, Inc. BSEP
140 Locke Dr.
Marlborough, MA 01752 508-481-6802
Biomedical & genetic products

BioSpecifics Technologies Corp. BSTC
35 Wilbur St.
Lynbrook, NY 11563
516-593-7000
Drugs

Biospherics Inc. BINC
12051 Indian Creek Court
Beltsville, MD 20705 301-419-3900
Pollution control equipment & services

Biosys BIOS
1057 E. Meadow Circle
Palo Alto, CA 94303 415-856-9500
Chemicals - specialty

BioTechnica International, Inc. BIOT
7300 W. 110th St., Ste. 540
Overland Park, KS 66210
913-661-0611
Biomedical & genetic products

Bird Corp. BIRD
980 Washington St., Ste. 124N
Dedham, MA 02026 617-461-1414
Building products - misc.

Bird Medical Technologies, Inc. BMTI
1100 Bird Center Dr.
Palm Springs, CA 92262 619-778-7200
Medical products

Birtcher Medical Systems, Inc. BIRT
50 Technology Dr.
Irvine, CA 92718 800-888-1771
Medical instruments

BKC Semiconductors Inc. BKCS
6 Lake St.
Lawrence, MA 01841 508-681-0392
Electrical components - semiconductors

Black Box Corp. BBOX
1000 Park Dr.
Pittsburgh, PA 15241 412-873-6788
Computers - peripheral equipment

Black Hawk Gaming and Development Co.,
Inc. BHWK
2060 Broadway, Ste. 400
Boulder, CO 80302 303-444-0240
Leisure & recreational services

Blimpie International, Inc. BMPE
740 Broadway
New York, NY 10003 212-673-5900
Retail - food & restaurants

Bliss & Laughlin Industries Inc. BLIS
281 E. 155th St.
Harvey, IL 60426 708-264-1800
Steel - production

BLOC Development Corp. BDEV
800 Douglas Entrance
Coral Gables, FL 33134
305-567-9931
Computers - software

Block Drug Co., Inc. BLOCA
257 Cornelison Ave.
Jersey City, NJ 07302
201-434-3000
Drugs

Blyth Holdings Inc. BLYH
1065 E. Hillsdale Blvd., #300
Foster City, CA 94404 415-571-0222
Computers - software

BMC Software, Inc. BMCS
2101 City West Blvd.
Houston, TX 77042 713-918-8800
Computers - software O

BMC West Corp. BMCW
1475 Tyrell Ln.
Boise, ID 83706 208-338-1700
Building products - retail & wholesale O

BNH Bancshares, Inc. BNHB
209 Church St.
New Haven, CT 06510 203-498-3500
Banks - northeast

Boatmen's Bancshares, Inc. BOAT
800 Market St.
St. Louis, MO 63101 314-466-6000
Banks - midwest
[DRP]

Bob Evans Farms, Inc. BOBE
3776 S. High St.
Columbus, OH 43207 614-491-2225
Retail - food & restaurants
[DRP]

Boca Research Inc. BOCI
6413 Congress Ave.
Boca Raton, FL 33487 407-997-6227
Computers - software

Bollinger Industries, Inc. BOLL
222 W. Airport Freeway
Irving, TX 75062 214-445-0386
Leisure & recreational products

Books-A-Million, Inc. BAMM
402 Industrial Ln.
Birmingham, AL 35211 205-942-3737
Retail - misc.

Boole & Babbage, Inc. BOOL
3131 Zanker Rd.
San Jose, CA 95134 408-526-3000
Computers - software

Boomtown, Inc. BMTN
PO Box 399
Verdi, NV 89439 702-345-8680
Leisure & recreational services O

Borland International, Inc. BORL
100 Borland Way
Scotts Valley, CA 95066 408-431-1000
Computers - software O

Borror Corp. BORR
5501 Frantz Rd.
Dublin, OH 43017 614-761-6000
Building - residential & commercial

Boston Acoustics, Inc. BOSA
70 Broadway
Lynnfield, MA 01940 617-592-9000
Audio & video home products

Boston Bancorp SBOS
460 W. Broadway
South Boston, MA 02127 617-268-2500
Banks - northeast
[DRP]

Boston Chicken, Inc. BOST
14103 Denver West Pkwy.
Golden, CO 80401 303-278-9500
Retail - food & restaurants O

Boston Technology, Inc. BSTN
100 Quannapowitt Parkway
Wakefield, MA 01880 617-246-9000
Telecommunications equipment

Box Energy Corp. BOXXA
8201 Preston Rd., Ste. 600
Dallas, TX 75225 214-890-8000
Oil & gas - US exploration & production O

Boyd Bros. Transporation Inc. BOYD
Route 1, PO Box 40
Clayton, AL 36016 205-775-3261
Transportation - truck

BPI Packaging Technologies, Inc. BPIE
455 Somerset Ave., Bldg. No. 3
North Dighton, MA 02764
508-824-8636
Rubber & plastic products

Brady (W.H.) Co. BRCOA
727 W. Glendale Ave.
Milwaukee, WI 53201 414-332-8100
Office & art materials [DRP]

Brady (W.H.) Co. BRCOA
727 W. Glendale Ave.
Milwaukee, WI 53201 414-332-8100
Office & art materials

Branford Savings Bank BSBC
45 S. Main St.
Branford, CT 06405 203-481-3471
Financial - savings and loans

Brauns Fashions Corp. BFCI
2400 Xenium Ln. North
Plymouth, MN 55441
612-551-5000
Retail - apparel & shoes

Brenco Inc. BREN
One Park West Circle, Ste. 204
Midlothian, VA 23113 804-732-0202
Metal processing & fabrication

Brendle's Inc. BRDLQ
1919 N. Bridge St.
Elkin, NC 28621 910-526-5600
Retail - discount & variety

Brenton Banks, Inc. BRBK
400 Locust, Ste. 300
Des Moines, IA 50309 515-237-5100
Banks - midwest

Bridgeport Machines, Inc. BPTM
500 Lindley St.
Bridgeport, CT 06606 203-367-3651
Machinery - general industrial

Bridgford Foods Corp. BRID
1308 N. Patt St.
Anaheim, CA 92801
714-526-5533
Food - misc.

Brite Voice Systems, Inc. BVSI
7309 E. 21st St. North
Wichita, KS 67206 316-652-6500
Telecommunications equipment

Broad National Bancorporation BNBC
905 Broad St.
Newark, NJ 07102 201-624-2300
Banks - northeast

BroadBand Technologies, Inc. BBTK
PO Box 13737
Research Triangle, NC 27704
919-544-0015
Telecommunications equipment O

Broadcast International, Inc. BRIN
7050 Union Park Center
Midvale, UT 84047 801-562-2252
Telecommunications equipment

Broadcasting Partners, Inc. BPIX
150 W. 55th St.
New York, NY 10019 212-581-3210
Broadcasting - radio & TV O

Broadway & Seymour, Inc. BSIS
128 S. Tryon St.
Charlotte, NC 28202 704-372-4281
Computers - services

Brock Control Systems, Inc. BROC
2859 Paces Ferry Rd.
Atlanta, GA 30339 404-431-1200
Computers - software

Broderbund Software, Inc. BROD
500 Redwood Blvd.
Novato, CA 94948 415-382-4400
Computers - software O

Brooklyn Bancorp, Inc. BRKB
211 Montague Street
Brooklyn, NY 11201
718-780-0400
Financial - savings and loans

Brookstone, Inc. BKST
17 Riverside St.
Nashua, NH 03062 603-880-9500
Retail - misc.

Brooktree Corp. BTRE
9950 Barnes Canyon Rd.
San Diego, CA 92121 619-452-7580
Electrical components - semiconductors O

Brooktrout Technology, Inc. BRKT
144 Gould St.
Needham, MA 02194 617-449-4100
Telecommunications equipment

Brothers Gourmet Coffees, Inc. BEAN
2255 Glades Rd., Suite 100 E
Boca Raton, FL 33431 407-995-2600
Food - misc. O

Bruno's, Inc. BRNO
800 Lakeshore Parkway
Birmingham, AL 35211
205-940-9400
Retail - supermarkets O

Bryn Mawr Bank Corp. BMTC
801 Lancaster Ave.
Bryn Mawr, PA 19010 610-526-2302
Banks - northeast

BSB Bancorp, Inc. BSBN
58-68 Exchange St.
Binghamton, NY 13902 607-779-2525
Financial - savings and loans
[DRP]

BT Financial Corp. BTFC
551 Main St.
Johnstown, PA 15901 814-532-3801
Banks - northeast
[DRP]

BTU International BTUI
23 Esquire Rd.
North Billerica, MA 01862 508-667-4111
Electrical components - semiconductors

Buckhead America Corp. BUCK
4243 Dunwoody Club Dr.
Dunwoody, GA 30350 404-393-2662
Hotels & motels

Buffets, Inc. BOCB
10260 Viking Dr., Ste. 100
Eden Prairie, MN 55344 612-942-9760
Retail - food & restaurants O

Bugaboo Creek Steak House, Inc. RARE
1275 Wampanoag Trail
East Providence, RI 02915 401-433-5500
Retail - food & restaurants

Builders Transport, Inc. TRUK
2029 W. DeKalb St.
Camden, SC 29020 803-432-1400
Transportation - truck

Bull Run Corp. BULL
4370 Peachtree Rd., N.E.
Atlanta, GA 30319 404-266-8333
Gold mining & processing

Burr-Brown Corp. BBRC
6730 S. Tucson Blvd.
Tucson, AZ 85706 602-746-1111
Electrical components - semiconductors

Business Records Corporation Holding
Co. BRCP
1111 W. Mockingbird, Ste. 1400
Dallas, TX 75247 214-688-1800
Office automation

Butler International, Inc. BUTL
110 Summit Ave.
Montvale, NJ 07645 201-573-8000
Financial - SBIC & commercial

Butler Manufacturing Co. BTLR
BMA Tower, Penn Valley Park
Kansas City, MO 64141 816-968-3000
Building products - misc.

Buttrey Food and Drug Stores Co. BTRY
601 6th St. SW, PO Box 5008
Great Falls, MT 59403 406-761-3401
Retail - convenience stores

BW/IP, Inc. BWIP
200 Oceangate Blvd., Ste. 900
Long Beach, CA 90802 310-435-3700
Pumps and seals

C-COR Electronics, Inc. CCBL
60 Decibel Rd.
State College, PA 16801 814-238-2461
Telecommunications equipment

C-Cube Microsystems, Inc. CUBE
1778 McCarthy Blvd.
Milpitas, CA 95035 408-944-6300
Computers - graphics

C-TEC Corp. CTEX
46 Public Square, PO Box 3000
Wilkes-Barre, PA 18703
717-825-1100
Utility - telephone

C. Brewer Homes, Inc. CBHI
827 Fort St.
Honolulu, HI 96813 808-536-4461
Real estate development

C.I.S. Technologies, Inc. CISI
6100 S. Yale, Ste. 1900
Tulsa, OK 74136 918-496-2451
Business services

Cable Design Technologies Corp. CDTC
661 Andersen Dr.
Pittsburgh, PA 15220 412-937-2300
Telecommunications equipment

CableMaxx, Inc. CMAX
6101 W. Courtyard Dr.
Austin, TX 78730 512-345-1115
Cable TV

Cabot Medical Corp. CBOT
2021 Cabot Blvd. West
Langhorne, PA 19047
215-752-8300
Medical products

Cache, Inc. CACH
1460 Broadway
New York, NY 10036
212-840-4242
Retail - apparel & shoes

CACI International Inc. CACI
1100 N. Glebe Rd.
Arlington, VA 22201 703-841-7800
Business services

Cade Industries, Inc. CADE
5640 Enterprise Dr.
Lansing, MI 48911 517-394-1333
Aerospace - aircraft equipment

Cadmus Communications Corp. CDMS
6620 W. Broad St., Ste. 500
Richmond, VA 23230 804-287-5680
Printing - commercial [DRP]

Caere Corp. CAER
100 Cooper Court
Los Gatos, CA 95030 408-395-7000
Computers - software

CAI Wireless Systems, Inc. CAWS
14 Corporate Woods Blvd.
Albany, NY 12211 518-462-2632
Telecommunications services

Cairn Energy USA, Inc. CEUS
8235 Douglas Ave., Ste. 1221
Dallas, TX 75225 214-369-0316
Oil & gas - US exploration & production

Calgene, Inc. CGNE
1920 Fifth St.
Davis, CA 95616 916-753-6313
Biomedical & genetic products O

California Amplifier, Inc. CAMP
460 Calle San Pablo
Camarillo, CA 93012 805-987-9000
Telecommunications equipment

California Bancshares, Inc. CABI
100 Park Place, Ste. 140
San Ramon, CA 94583 510-743-4200
Banks - west
[DRP]

California Culinary Academy, Inc. COOK
625 Polk St.
San Francisco, CA 94102
415-771-3536
Schools

California Financial Holding Co. CFHC
212 N. San Joaquin St.
Stockton, CA 95202 209-948-6870
Financial - savings and loans
[DRP 3%]

California Micro Devices Corp. CAMD
215 Topaz St.
Milpitas, CA 95035 408-263-3214
Electrical components - misc.

California Microwave, Inc. CMIC
985 Almanor Ave.
Sunnyvale, CA 94086 408-732-4000
Telecommunications equipment O

California State Bank CSTB
100 N. Barranca St.
West Covina, CA 91791 818-915-4424
Banks - west

Callon Consolidated Partners, L.P. CCLPZ
200 N. Canal St.
Natchez, MS 39120 601-442-1601
Oil & gas - US exploration & production

Calloway's Nursery, Inc. CLWY
4800 Blue Mound Rd.
Fort Worth, TX 76106
817-624-8222
Retail - misc.

Calumet Bancorp, Inc. CBCI
1350 E. Sibley Blvd.
Dolton, IL 60419 708-841-9010
Banks - midwest

Cambex Corp. CBEX
360 Second Ave.
Waltham, MA 02154 617-890-6000
Computers - peripheral equipment

Cambridge NeuroScience, Inc. CNSI
One Kendall Square, Bldg. 700
Cambridge, MA 02139 617-225-0600
Drugs

Cambridge SoundWorks, Inc. HIFI
154 California St.
Newton, MA 02158 617-332-5936
Audio & video home products

Cambridge Technology Partners (MA),
  Inc. CATP
304 Vassar St.
Cambridge, MA 02139 617-374-9800
Computers - software

Cameron Ashley Inc. CMSH
11100 Plano Rd.
Dallas, TX 75238 214-340-1996
Building products - retail & wholesale

Campo Electronics, Appliances & Computers,
  Inc. CMPO
800 Distributors Row
Hanrahan, LA 70123 504-733-4522
Retail - consumer electronics

Canandaigua Wine Co., Inc. WINEB
116 Buffalo St.
Canandaigua, NY 14424 716-394-7900
Beverages - alcoholic

Candela Laser Corp. CLZR
530 Boston Post Rd.
Wayland, MA 01778 508-358-7637
Lasers - systems & components

Candie's, Inc. CAND
60 W. 40th St.
New York, NY 10018 212-869-8725
Shoes & related apparel

Cannon Express, Inc. CANXA
1457 Robinson, PO Box 364
Springdale, AR 72764 501-751-9209
Transportation - truck

Cannondale Corp. BIKE
9 Brookside Place, PO Box 122
Georgetown, CT 06829 203-544-9800
Leisure & recreational products

Canonie Environmental Services Corp. CANO
13455 Noel Rd., Ste. 1500
Dallas, TX 75240 214-770-1800
Pollution control equipment & services

Cantel Industries, Inc. CNTL
1135 Broad St., Ste. 203
Clifton, NJ 07013 201-470-8700
Medical instruments

Canterbury Corporate Services, Inc. XCEL
Route 70 and Hartford Rd.
Medford, NJ 08055 609-953-0044
Schools

Canyon Resources Corp. CYNR
14142 Denver West Pkwy.
Golden, CO 80401 303-278-8464
Metals - non ferrous

Cape Cod Bank and Trust Co. CCBT
307 Main St.
Hyannis, MA 02601 508-394-1300
Banks - northeast

Capital Associates, Inc. CAII
7175 W. Jefferson Ave.
Lakewood, CO 80235 303-980-1000
Leasing

Capital Bancorporation, Inc. CABK
407 N. Kingshighway, 4th Fl.
Cape Girardeau, MO 63701
314-334-0700
Banks - midwest

Capital Savings Bancorp, Inc. CAPS
425 Madison St.
Jefferson City, MO 65101
314-635-4151
Banks - midwest

Capital Southwest Corp. CSWC
12900 Preston Rd., Ste. 700
Dallas, TX 75230 214-233-8242
Financial - investment bankers

Capitol Bancorp Ltd. CBCL
200 Washington Square North
Lansing, MI 48933 517-487-6555
Banks - midwest

Capitol Transamerica Corp. CATA
4610 University Ave.
Madison, WI 53705 608-231-4450
Insurance - property & casualty

Carauster Industries, Inc. CSAR
3100 Washington St.
Austell, GA 30001 404-948-3101
Paper & paper products

Cardinal Bancshares, Inc. CARD
400 E. Vine St., Ste. 300
Lexington, KY 40507
606-255-8300
Financial - savings and loans

Cardiovascular Imaging Systems, Inc.
CVIS
595 N. Pastoria Ave.
Sunnyvale, CA 94086 408-749-9088
Medical instruments

Care Group, Inc. CARE
One Hollow Ln.
Lake Success, NY 11042 516-869-8383
Healthcare - outpatient & home

Career Horizons, Inc. CARH
177 Crossways Park Dr.
Woodbury, NY 11797
516-496-2300
Business services

CareerStaff Unlimited, Inc. STAF
3040 Post Oak Blvd., Ste. 350
Houston, TX 77056 713-297-9200
Personnel

CareLine, Inc. CRLN
17780 Fitch, Ste. 135
Irvine, CA 92714 714-553-4070
Medical services

CareNetwork, Inc. CRNT
111 W. Pleasant St.
Milwaukee, WI 53212 414-223-3300
Health maintenance organization

Carnegie Bancorp CBNJ
619 Alexander Rd.
Princeton, NJ 08540 609-520-0601
Banks - northeast

Carolina First Corp. CAFC
102 S. Main St.
Greenville, SC 29601 803-255-7900
Banks - southeast
[DRP]

Carrollton Bancorp. CRRB
15 Charles Plaza, Ste. 200
Baltimore, MD 21201 410-536-4600
Banks - northeast

Carver Corp. CAVR
20121 48th Ave. West
Lynnwood, WA 98036 206-775-1202
Audio & video home products

Cascade Communications Corp. CSCC
5 Carlisle Rd.
Westford, MA 01886 508-692-2600
Computers - peripheral equipment

Cascade Corp. CASC
2020 S.W. 4th Ave., Ste. 600
Portland, OR 97201 503-227-0024
Machinery - material handling

Casey's General Stores, Inc. CASY
PO Box 3001
Ankeny, IA 50021 515-965-6100
Retail - convenience stores

Casino & Credit Services, Inc. CACS
1100 E. Hector St.
Conshohocken, PA 19428 215-834-8710
Business services

Casino America, Inc. CSNO
711 Washington Loop
Biloxi, MS 39530 601-436-7000
Leisure & recreational services O

Casino Data Systems, Inc. CSDS
3265 W. Tompkins Ave.
Las Vegas, NV 89103 702-386-8925
Leisure & recreational services

Casino Magic Corp. CMAG
711 Casino Magic Dr.
Bay St. Louis, MS 39520 601-467-9257
Leisure & recreational services O

Casino Resource Corp. CSNR
285 Beach Blvd.
Biloxi, MS 39530 601-432-1210
Real estate operations

Castle Energy Corp. CECX
100 Matsonford Rd., Ste. 250
Radnor, PA 19087 610-995-9400
Oil & gas - US exploration & production

Catalyst Semiconductor, Inc. CATS
2231 Calle de Luna
Santa Clara, CA 95054 408-748-7700
Electrical components - semiconductors

Catalytica, Inc. CTAL
430 Ferguson Dr.
Mountain View, CA 94043 415-960-3000
Pollution control equipment & services

Cathay Bancorp, Inc. CATY
777 N. Broadway
Los Angeles, CA 90012 213-625-4700
Banks - west
[DRP 5%]

Catherines Stores Corp. CATH
3742 Lamar Ave.
Memphis, TN 38118 901-363-3900
Retail - apparel & shoes

CB Bancshares, Inc. CBBI
201 Merchant St.
Honolulu, HI 96813
808-546-2411
Banks - west

CBT Corp. CBTC
333 Broadway
Paducah, KY 42001 502-575-5100
Bank - south
[DRP]

CCA Industries, Inc. CCAM
200 Murray Hill Parkway
East Rutherford, NJ 07073 201-330-1400
Wholesale distribution - consumer products

CCB Financial Corp. CCBF
Main and Corcoran Sts.
Durham, NC 27702 919-683-7777
Banks - southeast [DRP]

CDP Technologies, Inc. CDPT
333 Seventh Ave.
New York, NY 10001 212-563-3006
Computers - software

CDW Computer Centers, Inc. CDWC
2840 Maria Ave.
Northbrook, IL 60062 708-564-4900
Computers - software

CE Software Holdings, Inc. CESH
1801 Industrial Circle
West Des Moines, IA 50265
515-221-1801
Computers - software

CEL-SCI Corp. CELI
66 Canal Center Plaza
Alexandria, VA 22314
703-549-5293
Drugs

Celadon Group, Inc. CLDN
888 Seventh Ave.
New York, NY 10106 212-977-4447
Transportation - truck

Celebrity, Inc. FLWR
PO Box 6666
Tyler, TX 75711 903-561-3981
Miscellaneous - not elsewhere classified

Celestial Seasonings, Inc. CTEA
460 Sleepytime Dr.
Boulder, CO 80301 303-530-5300
Food - misc.

Celex Group, Inc. CLXG
919 Springer Dr.
Lombard, IL 60148 708-953-1222
Retail - misc.

Celgene Corp. CELG
7 Powder Horn Dr.
Warren, NJ 07059 908-271-1001
Chemicals - specialty

Cell Genesys, Inc. CEGE
322 Lakeside Dr.
Foster City, CA 94404 415-358-9600
Medical products

Cellcor, Inc. CLTX
200 Wells Ave.
Newton, MA 02159 617-332-2500
Biomedical & genetic products

CellPro, Inc. CPRO
22215 - 26th Ave. SE
Bothell, WA 98021
206-485-7644
Medical services O

CellStar Corp. CLST
1730 Briercroft Dr.
Carrollton, TX 75006 214-323-0600
Wholesale distribution - consumer products
O

Cellular Communications, Inc. COMMA
150 E. 58th St.
New York, NY 10155 212-906-8440
Telecommunications services

Cellular Technical Services Co. CTSC
2401 Fourth Ave.
Seattle, WA 98121 206-443-6400
Computers - software

Celtrix Pharmaceuticals Inc. CTRX
3055 Patrick Henry Dr.
Santa Clara, CA 95054
408-988-2500
Medical products

CEM Corp. CEMX
3100 Smith Farm Rd.
Matthews, NC 28105 704-821-7015
Instruments - scientific

CenCor, Inc. CNCR
12th & Baltimore, PO Box 26098
Kansas City, MO 64196 816-221-9744
Financial - consumer loans

CENFED Financial Corp. CENF
199 N. Lake Ave.
Pasadena, CA 91101 818-577-0500
Banks - west

CENIT Bancorp, Inc. CNIT
225 W. Olney Rd.
Norfolk, VA 23510 804-446-6600
Banks - southeast

Centennial Bancorp CEBC
675 Oak St.
Eugene, OR 97401 503-342-3970
Banks - west

Centennial Cellular Corp. CYCL
50 Locust Ave.
New Canaan, CT 06840 203-972-2000
Telecommunications services

Center Banks Inc. CTBK
33 E. Genesee St.
Skaneateles, NY 13152 315-685-2265
Financial - savings and loans
[DRP]

Centerbank CTBX
60 N. Main St.
Waterbury, CT 06702 203-578-7000
Banks - northeast

Centigram Communications Corp. CGRM
91 E. Tasman Dr.
San Jose, CA 95134 408-944-0250
Telecommunications equipment

Centocor, Inc. CNTO
200 Great Valley Parkway
Malvern, PA 19355 610-651-6000
Biomedical & genetic products O

Central and Southern Holding Co. CSBC
150 W. Green St., PO Box 748
Milledgeville, GA 31061 912-452-5541
Banks - southeast

Central Co-operative Bank CEBK
399 Highland Ave.
Somerville, MA 02144 617-628-4000
Banks - northeast

Central Fidelity Banks, Inc. CFBS
1021 E. Cary St., PO Box 27602
Richmond, VA 23261 804-782-4000
Banks - southeast
[DRP]

Central Garden & Pet Co. CENT
3620 Happy Valley Rd.
Lafayette, CA 94549 510-283-4573
Diversified operations

Central Indiana Bancorp KOKO
200 W. Mulberry St.
Kokomo, IN 46903 317-457-5552
Banks - midwest

Central Jersey Bancorp CJER
PO Box 30
Freehold, NJ 07728 908-462-0011
Banks - northeast

Central Jersey Financial Corp. CJFC
591 Cranbury Rd., PO Box 789
East Brunswick, NJ 08816
908-254-6600
Financial - savings and loans

Central Mortgage Bancshares, Inc. CMBI
4435 Main St., Ste. 100
Kansas City, MO 64111
816-561-3387
Banks - midwest

Central Reserve Life Corp. CRLC
17800 Royalton Rd.
Strongsville, OH 44136 216-572-2400
Insurance - accident & health

Central Sprinkler Corp. CNSP
451 N. Cannon Ave.
Lansdale, PA 19446 215-362-0700
Protection - safety equipment & services

Century Bancorp, Inc. CNBKA
400 Mystic Ave.
Medford, MA 02155 617-391-4000
Banks - northeast

Century South Banks, Inc. CSBI
200 W. Main St., PO Box 780
Dahlonega, GA 30533 706-864-1111
Banks - southeast

Cephalon, Inc. CEPH
145 Brandywine Parkway
West Chester, PA 19380
610-344-0200
Medical products

Ceradyne, Inc. CRDN
3169 Red Hill Ave.
Costa Mesa, CA 92626 714-549-0421
Ceramics & ceramic products

CERBCO, Inc. CERB
3421 Pennsy Dr.
Landover, MD 20785 301-773-1784
Diversified operations

Cerner Corp. CERN
2800 Rockcreek Pkwy.
Kansas City, MO 64117 816-221-1024
Computers - software O

Cerplex Group, Inc. CPLX
3332 E. LaPalma Ave.
Anaheim, CA 92806 714-632-2600
Miscellaneous - not elsewhere classified

CF Bancorp, Inc. CFBC
101 W. Third St.
Davenport, IA 52801
319-322-6237
Banks - midwest

CFI Industries, Inc. CFIB
935 W. Union Ave.
Wheaton, IL 60187 708-668-2838
Paper & paper products

CFI ProServices, Inc. PROI
220 N.W. Second Ave.
Portland, OR 97209 503-274-7280
Computers - software

CFSB Bancorp, Inc. CFSB
112 E. Allegan St.
Lansing, MI 48933 517-371-2911
Financial - savings and loans

CFW Communications Co. CFWC
401 Spring Ln., Ste. 300
Waynesboro, VA 22980
703-946-3500
Diversified operations

Champion Industries, Inc. CHMP
PO Box 2968
Huntington, WV 25728 304-528-2791
Diversified operations

Champion Parts, Inc. CREB
2525 22nd St.
Oak Brook, IL 60521 708-573-6600
Automotive & trucking - replacement parts

Champps Entertainment, Inc. CHPP
153 East Lake St.
Wayzata, MN 55391 612-449-4841
Retail - food & restaurants

Charming Shoppes, Inc. CHRS
450 Winks Ln.
Bensalem, PA 19020 215-245-9100
Retail - apparel & shoes O

Charter Federal Savings Bank CHFD
110 Piedmont Ave., PO Box 699
Bristol, VA 24203 703-669-5101
Financial - savings and loans

Charter One Financial, Inc. COFI
1215 Superior Ave.
Cleveland, OH 44114 216-589-8320
Financial - savings and loans
[DRP]

Chattem, Inc. CHTT
1715 W. 38th St.
Chattanooga, TN 37409 615-821-4571
Cosmetics & toiletries

Check Technology Corp. CTCQ
1284 Corporate Center Dr.
St. Paul, MN 55121 612-454-9300
Machinery - printing

Checkers Drive-In Restaurants, Inc. CHKR
600 Cleveland St., Ste. 1050
Clearwater, FL 34617 813-441-3500
Retail - food & restaurants O

Checkmate Electronics, Inc. CMEL
1011 Mansell Rd., Ste. C
Roswell, GA 30076 404-594-6000
Optical character recognition

Chemfab Corp. CMFB
701 Daniel Webster Highway
Merrimack, NH 03054 603-424-9000
Chemicals - fibers

Chemical Financial Corp. CHFC
333 E. Main St., PO Box 569
Midland, MI 48640 517-631-3310
Banks - midwest
[DRP]

Chempower, Inc. CHEM
807 E. Turkeyfoot Lake Rd.
Akron, OH 44319 216-896-4202
Pollution control equipment & services

ChemTrak, Inc. CMTR
484 Oakmead Parkway
Sunnyvale, CA 94086 408-773-8156
Medical services

Chesapeake Energy Corp. CSPK
6104 N. Western Ave.
Oklahoma City, OK 73118 405-848-8000
Oil & gas - US exploration & production

Chester Valley Bancorp Inc. CVAL
100 E. Lancaster Ave.
Downingtown, PA 19335 610-269-9700
Financial - savings and loans
[DRP 5%]

Chico's FAS, Inc. CHCS
15550 McGregor Blvd.
Fort Myers, FL 33908 813-433-5505
Retail - apparel & shoes

Children's Comprehensive Services, Inc.
KIDS
805 S. Church St., PO Box 8
Murfreesboro, TN 37133 615-896-3100
Protection - safety equipment & services

Children's Discovery Centers of America, Inc.
CDCR
851 Irwin St., Ste. 200
San Raphael, CA 94901 415-257-4200
Schools

ChinaTek Inc. CTEK
9551 Wilshire Blvd.
Beverly Hills, CA 90212 310-274-2474
Audio & video home products

Chipcom Corp. CHPM
118 Turnpike Rd.
Southborough, MA 01772 508-460-8900
Electrical components - misc. O

Chips & Technologies, Inc. CHPS
2950 Zanker Rd.
San Jose, CA 95134 408-434-0600
Electrical components - semiconductors

Chiron Corp. CHIR
4560 Horton St.
Emeryville, CA 94608 510-655-8730
Biomedical & genetic products O

Chittenden Corp. CNDN
Two Burlington Square
Burlington, VT 05401 802-658-4000
Banks - northeast [DRP]

Choice Drug Systems, Inc. DOSE
457 Doughty Blvd.
Inwood, NY 11696 516-239-2607
Medical services

Cholestech Corp. CTEC
3347 Investment Blvd.
Hayward, CA 94545 510-732-7200
Medical products

Chromcraft Revington, Inc. CROM
1100 N. Washington St.
Delphi, IN 46923 317-564-3500
Furniture

Chronimed Inc. CHMD
13911 Ridgedale Dr.
Minnetonka, MN 55305
612-541-0239
Medical products

CIBER, Inc. CIBR
1200 Seventeenth St.
Denver, CO 80202 303-572-6400
Computers - services

CIDCO, Inc. CDCO
105-H Cochrane Circle
Morgan Hill, CA 95037 408-779-1162
Telecommunications equipment

CIMA LABS, INC. CIMA
7325 Aspen Ln.
Minneapolis, MN 55428 612-424-2242
Drugs

CIMCO, Inc. CIMC
265 Briggs Ave.
Costa Mesa, CA 92626 714-546-4460
Electrical components - misc.

Cincinnati Financial Corp. CINF
PO Box 145496
Cincinnati, OH 45250 513-870-2000
Insurance - property & casualty O
[DRP]

Cincinnati Microwave, Inc. CNMW
One Microwave Plaza
Cincinnati, OH 45249 513-489-5400
Protection - safety equipment & services

Cinergi Pictures Entertainment, Inc. CINE
2308 Broadway
Santa Monica, CA 90404
310-315-6000
Motion pictures & services

Cintas Corp. CTAS
6800 Cintas Blvd.
Cincinnati, OH 45262
513-459-1200
Linen supply & related

Ciprico Inc. CPCI
2800 Campus Dr.
Plymouth, MN 55441 612-551-4000
Computers - peripheral equipment O

Circle Financial Corp. CRCL
11100 Reading Rd.
Sharonville, OH 45241 513-563-1245
Banks - midwest

Circle Income Shares, Inc. CINS
PO Box 77004
Indianapolis, IN 46277 317-321-8180
Financial - investment management

Circon Corp. CCON
460 Ward Dr.
Santa Barbara, CA 93111 805-967-0404
Medical instruments

Circuit Systems, Inc. CSYI
2350 E. Lunt Ave.
Elk Grove Village, IL 60007 708-439-1999
Electrical components - misc.

Cirrus Logic, Inc. CRUS
3100 W. Warren Ave.
Fremont, CA 94538 510-623-8300
Electrical components - misc. O

Cisco Systems, Inc. CSCO
1525 O'Brien Dr.
Menlo Park, CA 94025 415-326-1941
Computers - peripheral equipment O

CITATION Computer Systems, Inc. CITA
424 S. Woods Mill Rd.
Chesterfield, MO 63017 314-579-7900
Computers - software

Citation Corp. CAST
2 Office Park Circle, Ste. 204
Birmingham, AL 35223
205-871-5731
Steel - production

Citation Insurance Group CITN
One Almaden Blvd., Ste. 300
San Jose, CA 95113 408-292-0222
Insurance - accident & health

CitFed Bancorp, Inc. CTZN
One Citizens Federal Centre
Dayton, OH 45402 513-223-4234
Banks - midwest

Citi-Bancshares, Inc. CNBL
1211 N. Boulevard West
Leesburg, FL 34748 904-787-5111
Banks - southeast

Citicasters, Inc. CITI
One East Fourth St.
Cincinnati, OH 45202 513-562-8000
Broadcasting - radio & TV

Citizens Bancorp CIBC
14401 Sweitzer Ln.
Laurel, MD 20707 301-206-6080
Banks - northeast
[DRP]

Citizens Bancshares, Inc. CICS
10 E. Main St.
Salinesville, OH 43945 216-679-2328
Banks - midwest

Citizens Banking Corp. CBCF
One Citizens Banking Center
Flint, MI 48502 810-766-7500
Financial - savings and loans
[DRP]

City Holding Co. CHCO
3601 MacCorkle Ave., S.E.
Charleston, WV 25304 304-926-3300
Banks - northeast

Civic BanCorp CIVC
2101 Webster St., 14th Fl.
Oakland, CA 94612 510-836-6500
Banks - west

Clayton Williams Energy, Inc. CWEI
Six Desta Dr., Ste. 3000
Midland, TX 79705 915-682-6324
Oil & gas - US exploration & production

Clean Harbors, Inc. CLHB
1200 Crown Colony Dr.
Quincy, MA 02169 617-849-1800
Pollution control equipment & services

CleveTrust Realty Investors CTRIS
2001 Crocker Rd., Ste. 400
Westlake, OH 44145 216-899-0909
Real estate investment trust

Cliffs Drilling Co. CLDR
300 Citcorp Center, Ste. 300
Houston, TX 77002 713-651-9426
Oil & gas - offshore drilling

CliniCom Inc. CLIN
4720 Walnut St., Ste. 106
Boulder, CO 80301 303-443-9660
Computers - software

Clinton Gas Systems, Inc. CGAS
4770 Indianola Ave.
Columbus, OH 43214 614-888-9588
Oil & gas - US exploration & production

ClinTrials Research Inc. CCRO
One Burton Hills Blvd.
Nashville, TN 37215
615-665-9665
Medical services

Club Car, Inc. CLBC
4152 Washington Rd.
Martinez, GA 30907 706-863-3000
Leisure & recreational products

CMC Industries Inc. CMCI
Fulton Dr., PO Box 831
Corinth, MS 38834 601-287-3771
Telecommunications equipment

CMG Information Services, Inc. CMGI
187 Ballardvale St., B110
Wilmington, MA 01887 508-657-7000
Data collection & systems

CNB Bancshares, Inc. CNBE
20 N.W. Third St.
Evansville, IN 47739 812-464-3400
Banks - midwest [DRP 3%]

CNB Financial Corp. CNBF
24 Church St.
Canajoharie, NY 13317
518-673-3243
Banks - northeast

CNS, Inc. CNXS
1250 Park Rd.
Chanhassen, MN 55317
612-474-7600
Medical instruments

Coastal Banc Savings Association CBSA
8 Greenway Plaza, Ste. 1500
Houston, TX 77046 713-623-2600
Financial - savings and loans

CoBancorp, Inc. COBI
124 Middle Ave.
Elyria, OH 44035 216-329-8000
Banks - midwest

Cobra Electronics, Inc. COBR
6500 W. Cortland St.
Chicago, IL 60635 312-889-8870
Electronics - components & systems

Cobra Golf Inc. CBRA
1812 Aston Ave.
Carlsbad, CA 92008 619-929-0377
Leisure & recreational products O

Coca-Cola Bottling Co. Consolidated COKE
1900 Rexford Rd.
Charlotte, NC 28211 704-551-4400
Beverages - soft drinks
[DRP]

CoCensys, Inc. COCN
213 Technology Dr.
Irvine, CA 92718 714-753-6100
Medical products

Coda Energy, Inc. CODA
5735 Pineland Dr., Ste. 300
Dallas, TX 75231 214-692-1800
Oil & gas - US exploration & production

Code-Alarm, Inc. CODL
950 E. Whitcomb
Madison Heights, MI 48071 810-583-9620
Protection - safety equipment & services

Cognex Corp. CGNX
15 Crawford St.
Needham, MA 02194 617-449-6030
Machinery - general industrial O

Coherent Communications Systems Corp.
  CCSCV
44084 Riverside Pkwy.
Leesburg, VA 22075 703-729-6400
Telecommunications equipment

Coherent, Inc. COHR
5100 Patrick Henry Dr.
Santa Clara, CA 95054 408-764-4000
Lasers - systems & components O

Coho Resources, Inc. COHO
14785 Preston Rd., Ste. 860
Dallas, TX 75240 214-991-9493
Oil & gas - field services

Cohu, Inc. COHU
5755 Kearny Villa Rd.
San Diego, CA 92123 619-277-6700
Diversified operations

Cole Taylor Financial Group, Inc. CTFG
350 E. Dundee Rd.
Wheeling, IL 60090
708-459-1111
Banks - midwest

Collagen Corp. CGEN
2500 Faber Place
Palo Alto, CA 94303 415-856-0200
Biomedical & genetic products O

Collective Bancorp, Inc. COFD
716 W. White Horse Pike
Cologne, NJ 08213 609-625-1110
Financial - savings and loans

Collins Industries, Inc. COLL
421 E. 30th Ave.
Hutchinson, KS 67502 316-663-5551
Automotive & trucking - original equipment

Colonial BancGroup, Inc. CLBGA
One Commerce St.
Montgomery, AL 36104 205-240-5000
Banks - southeast [DRP]

Colonial Gas Co. CGES
40 Market St., PO Box 3064
Lowell, MA 01853 508-458-3171
Utility - gas distribution
[DRP 5%]

Colonial Group, Inc. COGRA
One Financial Center
Boston, MA 02111 617-426-3750
Financial - investment management

Columbia Banking System, Inc. COLB
320 108th Ave. NE, Ste. 300
Bellevue, WA 98004 206-646-9696
Financial - savings and loans

Columbia First Bank, A Federal Savings Bank
  CFFS
1560 Wilson Blvd.
Arlington, VA 22209 703-247-5000
Financial - savings and loans

Comair Holdings, Inc. COMR
PO Box 75021
Cincinnati, OH 45275 606-525-2550
Transportation - airline O

COMARCO, Inc. CMRO
22800 Savi Ranch Parkway
Yorba Linda, CA 92687 714-282-3832
Engineering - R & D services

Comcast Corp. CMCSK
1234 Market St.
Philadelphia, PA 19107 215-665-1700
Cable TV O

COMCOA, Inc. CCOA
9323 E. 37th St. North
Wichita, KS 67226 316-634-0333
Retail - consumer electronics

Comdata Holdings Corp. CMDT
05301 Maryland Way
Brentwood, TN 37027
615-370-7000
Financial - business services

Comdial Corp. CMDL
1180 Seminole Trail
Charlottesville, VA 22901 804-978-2200
Telecommunications equipment

Command Security Corp. CMMD
Lexington Park
LaGrangeville, NY 12540 914-454-3703
Business services

Commerce Bancorp Inc. COBA
Commerce Atrium, 1701 Rte 70 East
Cherry Hill, NJ 08034-5400 609-751-9000
Banks - northeast
[DRP]

Commerce Bancshares, Inc. CBSH
1000 Walnut St.
Kansas City, MO 64106 816-234-2000
Banks - midwest

Commerce Bank CBVA
5101 Cleveland St.
Virginia Beach, VA 23462
804-456-1005
Banks - southeast

Commerce Clearing House, Inc. CCLRA
2700 Lake Cook Rd.
Riverwoods, IL 60015 708-940-4600
Financial - business services

CommerceBancorp CBNB
1201 Dove St.
Newport Beach, CA 92660
714-851-9900
Banks - west

Commercial Bancorp CBOR
301 Church St. NE, PO Box 428
Salem, OR 97308 503-399-2900
Banks - west

Commercial Bank of New York CBNY
301 Park Ave.
New York, NY 10022 212-735-0010
Banks - midwest

Commercial Banshares, Inc. CLBK
1550 S.W. 57th Ave.
Miami, FL 33144 305-267-1200
Banks - southeast

Commercial Federal Corp. CFCN
2120 S. 72nd St.
Omaha, NE 68124 402-554-9200
Financial - savings and loans

CommNet Cellular, Inc. CELS
5990 Greenwood Plaza Blvd.
Englewood, CO 80111 303-694-3234
Telecommunications services O

Commonwealth Savings Bank CMSB
70 Valley Stream Pkwy.
Valley Forge, PA 19482 610-251-1600
Financial - savings and loans

Communication Cable, Inc. CABL
1335 2nd Ave. N.W., PO Box 729
Siler City, NC 27344 919-663-2629
Wire & cable products

Communications Central, Inc. CCIX
1150 Northmeadow Parkway
Atlanta, GA 30076 404-442-7300
Telecommunications services

Communications Systems, Inc. CSII
213 Main St. South, PO Box 777
Hector, MN 55342 612-848-6231
Telecommunications equipment

Community Bank System, Inc. CBSI
5790 Widewaters Pkwy.
DeWitt, NY 13214 315-445-2282
Banks - northeast
[DRP]

Community Banks, Inc. CBKI
150 Market St.
Millersburg, PA 17061 717-692-4781
Banks - northeast

Community Bankshares, Inc. CBNH
43 N. Main St.
Concord, NH 03301 603-224-1100
Banks - northeast

Community First Bank CFBN
3740 Beach Blvd.
Jacksonville, FL 32207 904-396-1182
Banks - southeast

Community First Bankshares, Inc. CFBX
520 Main St.
Fargo, ND 58124 701-235-1600
Banks - west

Community Health Computing Corp. CHCC
5 Greenway Plaza, Ste. 1900
Houston, TX 77046 713-960-1907
Computers - services

Community Savings F.A. CMSV
660 U.S. Hwy. 1
North Palm Beach, FL 33408
407-881-4800
Banks - southeast

COMNET Corp. CNET
4200 Parliament Pl., Ste. 600
Lanham, MD 20706 301-918-0400
Computers - software

Compass Bancshares, Inc. CBSS
15 S. 20th St.
Birmingham, AL 35233 205-933-3000
Banks - southeast
[DRP]

Compression Labs, Inc. CLIX
2860 Junction Ave.
San Jose, CA 95134 408-435-3000
Telecommunications equipment O

CompuCom Systems, Inc. CMPC
10100 N. Central Expressway
Dallas, TX 75231 214-265-3600
Computers - retail & wholesale

Computer Data Systems, Inc. CPTD
One Curie Court
Rockville, MD 20850 301-921-7000
Computers - services

Computer Horizons Corp. CHRZ
49 Old Bloomfield Ave.
Mountain Lakes, NJ 07046 201-402-7400
Computers - services

Computer Identics Corp. CIDN
5 Shawmut Rd.
Canton, MA 02021 617-821-0830
Computers - peripheral equipment

Computer Language Research, Inc. CLRI
2395 Midway Rd.
Carrollton, TX 75006 214-250-7000
Computers - services

Computer Network Technology Corp.
  CMNT
6600 Wedgwood Rd.
Maple Grove, MN 55311 612-550-8000
Computers - services O

Computer Outsourcing Services, Inc. COSI
360 W. 31st St.
New York, NY 10001 212-564-3730
Computers - services

Computer Products, Inc. CPRD
7900 Glades Rd., Ste. 500
Boca Raton, FL 33434 407-451-1000
Electrical components - misc.

Compuware Corp. CPWR
31440 Northwestern Highway
Farmington Hills, MI 48334
810-737-7300
Computers - software O

Comshare, Inc. CSRE
3001 S. State St., PO Box 1588
Ann Arbor, MI 48106 313-994-4800
Computers - software

Comstock Resources, Inc. CMRE
5005 LBJ Freeway, Ste. 1000
Dallas, TX 75244 214-701-2000
Oil & gas - US exploration & production

Comtech Telecommunications Corp.
  CMTL
105 Baylis Rd.
Melville, NY 11747 516-777-8900
Telecommunications equipment

Comverse Technology, Inc. CMVT
170 Crossways Park Dr.
Woodbury, NY 11797 516-677-7200
Computers - mini & micro O

Concord Camera Corp. LENS
35 Mileed Way
Avenel, NJ 07001 908-499-8280
Photographic equipment & supplies

Concord EFS, Inc. CEFT
2525 Horizon Lake Dr.
Memphis, TN 38133 901-371-8000
Financial - business services

Concord Holdings Corp. CNCD
125 W. 55th St.
New York, NY 10019 212-492-1600
Financial - investment management

Concurrent Computer Corp. CCUR
2 Crescent Place
Oceanport, NJ 07757 908-870-4500
Computers - mini & micro

Condor Services, Inc. COND
2361 Rosecrans Ave.
El Segundo, CA 90245 310-322-7344
Insurance - multi line & misc.

Conductus, Inc. CDTS
969 W. Maude Ave.
Sunnyvale, CA 94086 408-737-6700
Electronics - components & systems

Conestoga Bancorp, Inc. CONE
1075 Northern Blvd.
Roslyn, NY 11576 516-365-8000
Financial - savings and loans

ConferTech International, Inc. CFER
12110 N. Pecos St.
Westminster, CO 80234
303-633-3000
Telecommunications services

CONMED Corp. CNMD
310 Broad St.
Utica, NY 13501 315-797-8375
Medical products

Connecticut Water Service, Inc. CTWS
93 W. Main St.
Clinton, CT 06413 203-669-8636
Utility - water supply
[DRP 5%]

Consep, Inc. CSEP
213 S.W. Columbia St.
Bend, OR 97702 503-388-3688
Chemicals - specialty

Conservative Savings Corp. CONS
11207 W. Dodge Rd.
Omaha, NE 68154 402-334-8475
Banks - midwest

Consilium, Inc. CSIM
640 Clyde Court
Mountain View, CA 94043
415-691-6100
Computers - software

Conso Products Co. CNSO
513 N. Duncan Bypass
Union, SC 29379 803-427-9004
Textiles - home furnishings

Consolidated Graphics, Inc. COGI
2210 W. Dallas St.
Houston, TX 77019 713-529-4200
Printing - commercial

Consolidated Products, Inc. COPI
36 S. Pennsylvania St.
Indianapolis, IN 46204 317-633-4100
Retail - food & restaurants

Consolidated Stainless, Inc. PIPE
2170 W. State Rd. 434
Longwood, FL 32779 407-682-4999
Steel - pipes & tubes

Consumers Financial Corp. CFIN
1200 Camp Hill By-Pass
Camp Hill, PA 17011 717-761-4230
Insurance - multi line & misc.

Consumers Water Co. CONW
Three Canal Plaza
Portland, ME 04112 207-773-6438
Utility - water supply [DRP]

Contel Cellular Inc. CCXLA
245 Perimeter Center Parkway
Atlanta, GA 30346 404-804-3400
Telecommunications services

Continental Choice Care, Inc. CCCI
25-B Vreeland Rd.
Florham Park, NJ 07932 201-593-0500
Medical products

Continental Mortgage and Equity Trust
  CMETS
10670 N. Central Expressway
Dallas, TX 75231 214-692-4700
Real estate investment trust

Control Data Systems, Inc. CDAT
4201 Lexington Ave. North
Arden Hills, MN 55126 612-482-2401
Computers - software O

Convergent Solutions, Inc. CSOL
100 Metro Park South
Laurence Harbor, NJ 08878
908-290-0090
Computers - software

Cooper Development Co. COOL
455 E. Middlefield Rd.
Mountain View, CA 94043
415-969-9030
Diversified operations

Cooper Life Sciences, Inc. ZAPS
160 Broadway
New York, NY 10038 212-791-5362
Miscellaneous - not elsewhere classified

Cooperative Bankshares, Inc. COOP
201 Market St.
Wilmington, NC 28401 910-343-0181
Financial - savings and loans

Copart, Inc. CPRT
282 Fifth St.
Vallejo, CA 94590 707-644-4468
Business services

Copley Pharmaceutical, Inc. CPLY
25 John Rd.
Canton, MA 02021 617-821-6111
Drugs

CopyTele, Inc. COPY
900 Walt Whitman Rd.
Huntington Station, NY 11746
516-549-5900
Video equipment O

COR Therapeutics, Inc. CORR
256 E. Grand Ave.
South San Francisco, CA 94080
415-244-6800
Drugs

Coral Gables Fedcorp, Inc. CGFC
2511 Ponce de Leon Blvd.
Coral Gables, FL 33134 305-529-6000
Financial - savings and loans

Corcom, Inc. CORC
1600 Winchester Rd.
Libertyville, IL 60048 708-680-7400
Electrical components - misc.

Cordis Corp. CORD
14201 N.W. 60th Ave.
Miami Lakes, FL 33014
305-824-2000
Medical instruments O

Cornerstone Financial Corp. CSTN
15 E. Broadway
Derry, NH 3038 603-432-9517
Banks - northeast

Cornerstone Imaging, Inc. CRNR
1990 Concourse Dr.
San Jose, CA 95131 408-435-8900
Computers - graphics

Corporate Express, Inc. CEXP
325 Interlocken Pkwy.
Broomfield, CO 80021 303-373-2800
Office equipment & supplies

Corrections Corporation of America CCAX
102 Woodmont Blvd.
Nashville, TN 37205 615-292-3100
Protection - safety equipment & services

Cortech, Inc. CRTQ
7000 N. Broadway, Ste. 300
Denver, CO 80221 303-650-1200
Drugs

Corvas International, Inc. CVAS
3030 Science Park Rd.
San Diego, CA 92121 619-455-9800
Drugs

CorVel Corp. CRVL
1920 Main St., Ste. 1090
Irvine, CA 92714 714-851-1473
Medical services

Cotton States Life Insurance Co. CSLI
244 Perimeter Ctr. Pkwy., NE
Atlanta, GA 30346 404-391-8600
Insurance - accident & health

Courier Corp. CRRC
165 Jackson St.
Lowell, MA 01852 508-458-6351
Printing - commercial

Covenant Transport, Inc. CVTI
1320 E. 23rd St.
Chattanooga, TN 37404 615-629-0393
Transportation - truck

Coventry Corp. CVTY
53 Century Blvd., Ste. 250
Nashville, TN 37214 615-391-2440
Health maintenance organization O

CPAC, Inc. CPAK
2364 Leicester Rd.
Leicester, NY 14481 716-382-3223
Chemicals - specialty

CPB Inc. CPBI
220 S. King St., PO Box 3590
Honolulu, HI 96813 808-544-0500
Banks - west

CPI Aerostructures, Inc. CPIA
1900 Ocean Ave.
Ronkonkoma, NY 11779 516-737-4700
Aerospace - aircraft equipment

Cracker Barrel Old Country Store, Inc.
  CBRL
Hartmann Dr., PO Box 787
Lebannon, TN 37088 615-444-5533
Retail - food & restaurants O [DRP]

Craftmade International, Inc. CRFT
2700 112th St.
Grand Prairie, TX 75050
214-647-8099
Housewares

Cray Computer Corp. CRAY
1110 Bayfield Dr.
Colorado Springs, CO 80906
719-579-6464
Computers - mainframe

Creative BioMolecules, Inc. CBMI
45 South St.
Hopkinton, MA 01748 508-435-9001
Biomedical & genetic products

Credence Systems Corp. CMOS
3500 W. Warren Ave.
Fremont, CA 94538 510-657-7400
Electronics - measuring instruments O

Credit Acceptance Corp. CACC
25505 W. Twelve Mile Rd.
Southfield, MI 48034 810-353-2700
Financial - business services

Cree Research, Inc. CREE
2810 Meridian Pkwy., Ste. 176
Durham, NC 27713 919-361-5709
Electronics - components & systems

Crescent Airways Corp. CRAR
450 Briscoe Blvd.
Lawrenceville, GA 30245
404-822-6180
Transportation - services

Criticare Systems, Inc. CXIM
20925 Crossroads Circle
Waukesha, WI 53186
414-798-8282
Medical instruments

Crop Genetics International Corp. CROP
10150 Old Columbia Rd.
Columbia, MD 21046 410-381-3800
Agricultural operations

Crop Growers Corp. CGRO
1000 25th St., North
Great Falls, MT 59406 406-452-8101
Insurance - multi line & misc.

CrossComm Corp. XCOM
450 Donald Lynch Blvd.
Marlborough, MA 01752 508-481-4060
Computers - peripheral equipment

Crossman Communities, Inc. CROS
2935 E. 96th St.
Indianapolis, IN 46240 317-843-9514
Building - residential & commercial

Crown Andersen Inc. CRAN
306 Dividend Dr.
Peachtree City, GA 30269
404-997-2000
Diversified operations

Crown Books Corp. CRWN
3300 75th Ave.
Landover, MD 20785 301-731-1200
Retail - books, music & video

Crown Resources Corp. CRRS
1225 17th St., Ste. 1500
Denver, CO 80202 303-295-2171
Gold mining & processing

Cryenco Sciences, Inc. CSCI
3811 Joliet St.
Denver, CO 80239 303-371-6332
Miscellaneous - not elsewhere classified

CryoLife, Inc. CRYL
2211 New Market Pkwy.
Marietta, GA 30067 404-952-1660
Medical products

Cryomedical Sciences, Inc. CMSI
1300 Piccard Dr.
Rockville, MD 20850 301-417-7070
Medical products

CSB Financial Corp. COSB
2120 Langhorne Rd., PO Box 340
Lynchburg, VA 24505 804-847-3800
Financial - savings and loans

CSF Holdings, Inc. CSFC
1221 Brickell Ave., 16th Fl.
Miami, FL 33131 305-577-0400
Financial - savings and loans

CSP Inc. CSPI
40 Linnell Circle
Billerica, MA 01821 508-663-7598
Computers - peripheral equipment

CTL Credit, Inc. CTLI
319 E. Carrillo St.
Santa Barbara, CA 93101
805-963-8743
Financial - savings and loans

CU Bancorp CUBN
16030 Ventura Blvd.
Encino, CA 91436 818-907-9122
Banks - west

Cullen/Frost Bankers, Inc. CFBI
100 W. Houston St.
San Antonio, TX 78205
210-220-4011
Banks - southwest

Culp, Inc. CULP
101 S. Main St., PO Box 2686
High Point, NC 27261 910-889-5161
Textiles - home furnishings

Cupertino National Bancorp CUNB
20230 Stevens Creek Blvd.
Cupertino, CA 95014 408-996-1144
Banks - west

Curative Technologies, Inc. CURE
14 Research Way, PO Box 9052
East Setauket, NY 11733
516-689-7000
Drugs

Custom Chrome, Inc. CSTM
16100 Jacqueline Court
Morgan Hill, CA 95037 408-778-0500
Automotive & trucking - replacement parts

Cyberonics, Inc. CYBX
17448 Highway 3, Ste. 100
Webster, TX 77598 713-332-1375
Medical instruments

CyberOptics Corp. CYBE
2505 Kennedy St. NE
Minneapolis, MN 55413 612-331-5702
Machinery - general industrial

Cygne Designs, Inc. CYDS
1372 Broadway
New York, NY 10018 212-354-6474
Apparel

Cygnus Therapeutic Systems CYGN
400 Penobscot Dr.
Redwood City, CA 94063 415-369-4300
Medical products

Cyrix Corp. CYRX
2703 N. Central Expressway
Richardson, TX 75080 214-994-8387
Computers - mini & micro O

Cyrk, Inc. CYRK
3 Pond Rd.
Gloucester, MA 01930
508-283-5800
Apparel

Cytel Corp. CYTL
3525 John Hopkins Court
San Diego, CA 92121
619-552-3000
Drugs

Cytocare, Inc. CYTI
100 Columbia, Ste. 100
Aliso Viejo, CA 92656 714-448-7700
Medical services

CYTOGEN Corp. CYTO
600 College Rd. East - CN 5308
Princeton, NJ 08540 609-987-8200
Biomedical & genetic products O

CytoRad, Inc. CYTDZ
600 College Rd. East CN5308
Princeton, NJ 08540 609-987-8270
Medical services

CytoTherapeutics, Inc. CTII
Two Richmond Square
Providence, RI 02906 401-272-3310
Medical services

CytRx Corp. CYTR
150 Technology Parkway
Norcross, GA 30092 404-368-9500
Miscellaneous - not elsewhere classified O

D & N Financial Corp. DNFC
400 Quincy St.
Hancock, MI 49930 906-482-2700
Financial - savings and loans
[DRP]

D.I.Y. Home Warehouse, Inc. DIYH
5811 Canal Rd., Ste. 180
Valley View, OH 44125 216-328-5100
Building products - retail & wholesale

D.R. Horton, Inc. DRHI
1901 Ascension Blvd., Ste. 100
Arlington, TX 76006 817-856-8200
Building - residential & commercial

Daig Corp. DAIG
14901 DeVeau Place
Minnetonka, MN 55345
612-933-4700
Medical products

Daily Journal Corp. DJCO
915 E. First St.
Los Angeles, CA 90012 213-229-5300
Publishing - newspapers

Dairy Mart Convenience Stores, Inc.
DMCVA
One Vision Dr.
Enfield, CT 06082 203-741-4444
Retail - convenience stores

DAKA International, Inc. DKAI
55 Ferncroft Rd.
Danvers, MA 01923 508-774-9115
Diversified operations

Dakotah, Inc. DKTH
One N. Park Ln.
Webster, SD 57274 605-345-4646
Textiles - home furnishings

Daktronics, Inc. DAKT
331 32nd Ave.
Brookings, SD 57006 605-697-4000
Video equipment

DAMARK International, Inc. DMRK
7101 Winnetka Ave. North
Brooklyn Park, MN 55428
612-531-0066
Retail - mail order & direct O

Danskin, Inc. DANS
111 W. 40th St.
New York, NY 10018 212-764-4630
Apparel

Darling International Inc. DARL
251 O'Connor Ridge Blvd.
Irving, TX 75038 214-717-0300
Miscellaneous - not elsewhere classified

Dart Group Corp. DARTA
3300 75th Ave.
Landover, MD 20785 301-731-1200
Retail - misc.

Data I/O Corp. DAIO
10525 Willows Rd. N.E.
Redmond, WA 98073 206-881-6444
Electronics - measuring instruments

Data Measurement Corp. DMCB
15884 Gaither Dr.
Gaithersburg, MD 20877 301-948-2450
Electronics - measuring instruments

DATA RACE, Inc. RACE
11550 1H-10 West, Ste. 395
San Antonio, TX 78230 210-558-1900
Computers - peripheral equipment

Data Research Associates, Inc. DRAI
1276 N. Warson Rd.
St. Louis, MO 63132 314-432-1100
Computers - software

Data Switch Corp. DASW
One Enterprise Dr.
Shelton, CT 06484 203-926-1801
Electrical components - misc.

Data Systems & Software Inc. DSSI
200 Route 17
Mahwah, NJ 07430
201-529-2026
Computers - software

Data Translation, Inc. DATX
100 Locke Dr.
Marlborough, MA 01752 508-481-3700
Computers - graphics

Data Transmission Network Corp. DTLN
9110 W. Dodge Rd., Ste. 200
Omaha, NE 68114 402-390-2328
Business services

Dataflex Corp. DFLX
3920 Park Ave.
Edison, NJ 08820 908-321-1100
Computers - mini & micro

Datakey, Inc. DKEY
407 W. Travelers Trail
Burnsville, MN 55337
612-890-6850
Instruments - control

Datamarine International, Inc. DMAR
53 Portside Dr.
Pocasset, MA 02559 508-563-7151
Leisure & recreational products

Datascope Corp. DSCP
14 Philips Parkway
Montvale, NJ 07645 201-391-8100
Medical instruments

Dataware Technologies, Inc. DWTI
222 Third St.
Cambridge, MA 02142 617-621-0820
Computers - software

Datawatch Corp. DWCH
234 Ballardvale St.
Wilmington, MA 01887
508-988-9700
Computers - mini & micro

Datron Systems, Inc. DTSI
200 W. Los Angeles Ave.
Simi Valley, CA 93065 805-584-1717
Telecommunications equipment

Datum Inc. DATM
1363 S. State College Blvd.
Anaheim, CA 92806 714-533-6333
Fiber optics

Dauphin Deposit Corp. DAPN
213 Market St.
Harrisburg, PA 17105 717-255-2121
Banks - northeast
[DRP]

DavCo Restaurants, Inc. DVCO
1657 Crofton Blvd.
Crofton, MD 21114 410-721-3770
Retail - food & restaurants

Davel Communications Group, Inc. DAVL
1429 Massaro Blvd.
Tampa, FL 33619 813-623-3545
Telecommunications equipment

Davidson & Associates, Inc. DAVD
19840 Pioneer Ave.
Torrance, CA 90503
310-793-0600
Computers - software

Davox Corp. DAVX
6 Technology Park Dr.
Westboro, MA 01886 508-667-4455
Telecommunications equipment

Dawson Geophysical Co. DWSN
208 S. Marienfeld St.
Midland, TX 79701 915-682-7356
Oil & gas - field services

Day Runner, Inc. DAYR
2750 W. Moore Avenue
Fullerton, CA 92633
714-680-3500
Paper & paper products

DBA Systems, Inc. DBAS
1200 S. Woody Burke Rd.
Melbourne, FL 32902 407-727-0660
Electronics - military

Deb Shops, Inc. DEBS
9401 Blue Grass Rd.
Philadelphia, PA 19114 215-676-6000
Retail - apparel & shoes

Deckers Outdoor Corp. DECK
1140 Mark Ave.
Carpintera, CA 93013 805-684-7722
Shoes & related apparel

DeepTech International Inc. DEEP
600 Travis St., Ste. 7500
Houston, TX 77002 713-224-7400
Oil refining & marketing

Deerbank Corp. DEER
745 Deerfield Rd.
Deerfield, IL 60015 708-945-2550
Financial - savings and loans

Defiance, Inc. DEFI
1111 Chester Ave., Ste. 750
Cleveland, OH 44114 216-861-6300
Automotive & trucking - original equipment

Deflecta-Shield Corp. TRUX
11191 Aurora Ave.
Urbandale, IA 50322 515-270-9488
Auto parts - retail & wholesale

DEKALB Genetics Corp. SEEDB
3100 Sycamore Rd.
DeKalb, IL 60115 815-758-3461
Agricultural operations

Delaware Otsego Corp. DOCP
1 Railroad Ave.
Cooperstown, NY 13326 607-547-02555
Transportation - rail

Delchamps, Inc. DLCH
305 Delchamps Dr.
Mobile, AL 36602 205-433-0431
Retail - supermarkets

Dell Computer Corp. DELL
9505 Arboretum Blvd.
Austin, TX 78759 512-338-4400
Computers - mini & micro O

Delphi Financial Group, Inc. DLFI
1105 N. Market St., Ste. 1230
Wilmington, DE 19801 302-478-5142
Insurance - multi line & misc.

Delphi Information Systems, Inc. DLPH
31416 Agoura Rd.
Westlake Village, CA 91361 818-706-8989
Computers - software

Delta and Pine Land Co. COTN
One Cotton Row
Scott, MS 38772 601-742-3351
Agricultural operations

Delta Natural Gas Co., Inc. DGAS
3617 Lexington Rd.
Winchester, KY 40391 606-744-6171
Utility - gas distribution
[DRP]

DENTSPLY International Inc. XRAY
570 W. College Ave.
York, PA 17405 717-845-7511
Medical & dental supplies

DEP Corp. DEPCB
2101 E. Via Arado
Rancho Dominguez, CA 90220
310-604-0777
Cosmetics & toiletries

Deposit Guaranty Corp. DEPS
PO Box 1200
Jackson, MS 39215 601-354-8564
Banks - southeast
[DRP]

Designatronics Inc. DSGT
2101 Jericho Turnpike
New Hyde Park, NY 11040
516-328-3300
Machinery - material handling

Designs, Inc. DESI
1244 Boylston St.
Chestnut Hill, MA 01267 617-739-6722
Retail - apparel & shoes O

Destron Fearing Corp. DFCO
490 Villaume Ave.
South St. Paul, MN 55075
612-455-1621
Electronics - measuring instruments

Detection Systems, Inc. DETC
130 Perinton Parkway
Fairport, NY 14450 716-223-4060
Protection - safety equipment & services

Detrex Corp. DTRX
4000 Town Center, Ste. 1100
Southfield, MI 48075 313-358-5800
Chemicals - specialty

Devcon International Corp. DEVC
1350 E. Newport Center Dr.
Deerfield Beach, FL 33442 305-429-1500
Construction - cement & concrete

DeVlieg-Bullard, Inc. DVLG
One Gorham Island
Westport, CT 06880 203-221-8201
Machine tools & related products

Devon Group, Inc. DEVN
Six Stamford Forum, Ste. 501
Stamford, CT 06901 203-964-1444
Printing - commercial

DeVRY Inc. DVRY
One Tower Ln.
Oakbrook Terrace, IL 60181
708-571-7700
Schools

DF&R Restaurants, Inc. DFNR
2350 Airport Freeway, Ste. 505
Bedford, TX 76022 817-571-6682
Retail - food & restaurants

DH Technology, Inc. DHTK
15070 Avenue of Science
San Diego, CA 92128 619-451-3485
Computers - peripheral equipment

Dial Page, Inc. DPGE
301 College St., Ste. 700
Greenville, SC 29603 803-242-0234
Telecommunications services

Dialogic Corp. DLGC
300 Littleton Rd.
Parsippany, NJ 07054 201-334-8450
Computers - peripheral equipment

Diametrics Medical Inc. DMED
2658 Patton Rd.
St. Paul, MN 55113 612-639-8035
Biomedical & genetic products

DIANON Systems, Inc. DIAN
200 Watson Blvd.
Stratford, CT 06497
203-381-4000
Medical services

Dibrell Brothers, Inc. DBRL
512 Bridge St.
Danville, VA 24541 804-792-7511
Tobacco O

dick clark productions, inc. DCPI
3003 W. Olive Ave.
Burbank, CA 91510 818-841-3003
Leisure & recreational services

Digi International, Inc. DGII
6400 Flying Cloud Dr.
Eden Prairie, MN 55344 612-943-9020
Computers - peripheral equipment O

Digidesign, Inc. DGDN
1360 Willow Rd.
Menlo Park, CA 94025
415-688-0600
Computers - software

Digital Biometrics, Inc. DBII
5600 Rowland Rd., Ste. 205
Minnetonka, MN 55343 612-932-0888
Miscellaneous - not elsewhere classified

Digital Link Corp. DLNK
217 Humboldt Court
Sunnyvale, CA 94089 408-745-6200
Telecommunications equipment

Digital Microwave Corp. DMIC
170 Rose Orchard Way
San Jose, CA 95134 408-943-0777
Fiber optics O

Digital Sound Corp. DGSD
6307 Carpinteria Ave.
Carpinteria, CA 93013 805-566-2000
Telecommunications equipment

Digital Systems International, Inc. DGTL
6464 185th Ave. NE
Redmond, WA 98052 206-881-7544
Telecommunications equipment

Dime Financial Corp. DIBK
95 Barnes Rd.
Wallingford, CT 06492
203-269-8881
Banks - northeast

Dionex Corp. DNEX
1228 Titan Way, PO Box 3603
Sunnyvale, CA 94088 408-737-0700
Instruments - scientific

Discovery Zone, Inc. ZONE
205 N. Michigan Ave.
Chicago, IL 60601 312-616-3800
Leisure & recreational services O

Dixie Yarns, Inc. DXYN
1100 S. Watkins St.
Chattanooga, TN 37404
615-698-2501
Textiles - mill products

DM Management Co. DMMC
25 Recreation Park Dr.
Hingham, MA 02043 617-740-2718
Retail - mail order & direct

DNA Plant Technology Corp. DNAP
6701 San Pablo Ave.
Oakland, CA 94610 510-547-2395
Agricultural operations

DNX Corp. DNXX
303B College Rd. East
Princeton, NJ 08540 609-520-0300
Medical products

Dollar General Corp. DOLR
104 Woodmont Blvd., Ste. 500
Nashville, TN 37205 615-783-2000
Retail - discount & variety O

Dominguez Services Corp. DOMZ
21718 S. Alameda St.
Long Beach, CA 90810 310-834-2625
Utility - water supply

Donegal Group Inc. DGIC
1195 River Rd., PO Box 302
Marietta, PA 17547 717-426-1931
Insurance - multi line & misc.

Donnkenny Inc. DNKY
1411 Broadway
New York, NY 10018 212-730-7770
Apparel

Dorchester Hugoton, Ltd. DHULZ
9696 Skillman St.
Dallas, TX 75243 214-340-3443
Miscellaneous - not elsewhere classified

Dorsey Trailers, Inc. DSYT
2727 Paces Ferry Rd.
Atlanta, GA 30339 404-438-9595
Automotive & trucking - original equipment

Doskocil Companies Inc. DOSK
2601 NW Expwy., Ste 1000
Oklahoma City, OK 73112
405-879-5500
Food - meat products

Dotronix, Inc. DOTX
160 First St. S.E.
New Brighton, MN 55112
612-633-1742
Video equipment

Doubletree Corp. TREE
410 N. 44th St., Ste. 700
Phoenix, AZ 85008
602-220-6666
Hotels & motels

Douglas & Lomason Co. DOUG
24600 Hollywood Court
Farmington Hills, MI 48335 810-478-7800
Automotive & trucking - original equipment

DOVatron International Inc. DOVT
05405 Spine Rd.
Boulder, CO 80301 303-530-9364
Electronics - measuring instruments

Drew Industries Inc. DREW
200 Mamaroneck Ave.
White Plains, NY 10601 914-428-9098
Building products - misc.

Drexler Technology Corp. DRXR
1077 Independence Ave.
Mountain View, CA 94043
415-969-7277
Computers - peripheral equipment

Dreyer's Grand Ice Cream, Inc. DRYR
5929 College Ave.
Oakland, CA 94618 510-652-8187
Food - dairy products O

Drug Emporium, Inc. DEMP
155 Hidden Ravines Dr.
Powell, OH 43065 614-548-7080
Retail - drug stores

Drypers Corp. DYPR
1415 W. Loop North
Houston, TX 77055 713-682-6848
Miscellaneous - not elsewhere classified

DS Bancor, Inc. DSBC
33 Elizabeth St.
Derby, CT 06418 203-736-1000
Financial - savings and loans

DSC Communications Corp. DIGI
1000 Coit Rd.
Plano, TX 75075 214-519-3000
Telecommunications equipment O

DSP Group, Inc. DSPG
2855 Kifer Rd.
Santa Clara, CA 95051
408-986-4300
Computers - software O

DSP Technology, Inc. DSPT
48500 Kato Rd.
Fremont, CA 94538 510-657-7555
Electronics - measuring instruments

DT Industries, Inc. DTII
441 W. Elm St., PO Box 232
Lebanon, MO 65536 417-532-2141
Machinery - general industrial

Dual Drilling, Inc. DUAL
5956 Sherry Ln., Ste. 1500
Dallas, TX 75225 214-373-6200
Oil & gas - offshore drilling

Duckwall-ALCO Stores, Inc. DUCK
401 Cottage St.
Abilene, KS 67410 913-263-3350
Retail - discount & variety

Dura Pharmaceuticals, Inc. DURA
5880 Pacific Center Blvd.
San Diego, CA 92121 619-457-2553
Drugs

Duracraft Corp. DUCR
355 Main St.
Whitinsville, MA 01588 508-234-4600
Appliances - household

Durakon Industries, Inc. DRKN
2101 N. Lapeer Rd.
Lapeer, MI 48446 810-664-0850
Automotive & trucking - replacement parts

Duramed Pharmaceuticals, Inc. DRMD
5040 Lester Rd.
Cincinnati, OH 45213 513-731-9900
Drugs

Duriron Co., Inc. DURI
3100 Research Blvd.
Dayton, OH 45420 513-476-6100
Machinery - general industrial
[DRP]

Duriron Co., Inc. DURI
425 N. Findlay St.
Dayton, OH 45404 513-226-4000
Machinery - general industrial
[DRP]

Dynamics Research Corp. DRCO
60 Frontage Rd.
Andover, MA 01810 508-475-9090
Engineering - R & D services

Dynatech Corp. DYTC
3 New England Executive Park
Burlington, MA 01803 617-272-6100
Instruments - scientific

E for M Corp. EFMC
625 Alaska Ave.
Torrance, CA 90503 310-320-8425
Photographic equipment & supplies

E-Z-EM, Inc. EZEMA
717 Main St.
Westbury, NY 11590 516-333-8230
Medical instruments

EA Engineering, Science, and Technology, Inc.
EACO
11019 McCormick Rd.
Hunt Valley, MD 21031 410-584-7000
Pollution control equipment & services

Eagle Bancorp, Inc. EBCI
227 Capitol St.
Charleston, WV 25301
304-340-4600
Banks - southeast

Eagle Bancshares, Inc. EBSI
4305 Lynburn Dr.
Tucker, GA 30084 404-908-6690
Banks - southeast

Eagle Financial Corp. EGFC
222 Main St.
Bristol, CT 06010 203-589-4600
Financial - savings and loans

Eagle Food Centers, Inc. EGLE
Route 67 & Knoxville Rd.
Milan, IL 61264 309-787-7730
Retail - supermarkets

Eagle Hardware & Garden, Inc. EAGL
101 Andover Park East
Tukwila, WA 98188 208-431-5740
Building products - retail & wholesale O

EARTH TECH ETCO
100 W. Broadway, Ste. 5000
Long Beach, CA 90802 310-495-4449
Engineering - R & D services

Easel Corp. EASL
25 Corporate Dr.
Burlington, MA 01803 617-221-2100
Computers - software

Eastern Bancorp, Inc. VFBK
282 Williston Rd.
Williston, VT 05495
802-879-9000
Banks - northeast

Eastern Environmental Services, Inc. EESI
6923 1/2 W. Mohawk Ave.
Tampa, FL 33634 813-248-1212
Pollution control equipment & services

Eastex Energy Inc. ETEX
1000 Louisiana
Houston, TX 77002 713-650-6255
Oil & gas - production & pipeline

Eastover Corp. EASTS
188 E. Capitol St.
Jackson, MS 39201 601-948-4091
Real estate investment trust

Eaton Vance Corp. EAVN
24 Federal St.
Boston, MA 02110 617-482-8260
Financial - investment management

ECCS, Inc. ECCS
One Sheila Dr.
Tinton Falls, NJ 07724
908-747-6995
Computers - software

Ecogen Inc. EECN
2005 Cabot Blvd. West
Langhorne, PA 19047 215-757-1590
Chemicals - specialty

EcoScience Corp. ECSC
One Innovation Dr.
Worcester, MA 01605 508-754-0300
Chemicals - specialty

Edelbrock Corp. EDEL
2700 California St.
Torrance, CA 90503 310-781-2222
Auto parts - retail & wholesale

Edison Control Corp. EDCO
140 Ethel Rd. West
Piscataway, NJ 08854 908-819-8800
Electrical products - misc.

Education Alternatives, Inc. EAIN
7900 Xerxes Ave. South
Minneapolis, MN 55431 612-832-0092
Consulting

Educational Insights, Inc. EDIN
19560 S. Rancho Way
Dominguez Hills, CA 90220
310-884-1931
Toys - games & hobby products

Effective Management Systems, Inc.
  EMSI
12000 W. Park Place
Milwaukee, WI 53224 414-359-9800
Computers - software

EFI Electronics Corp. EFIC
2415 S. 2300 West
Salt Lake City, UT 84119 801-977-9009
Electronics - components & systems

Egghead, Inc. EGGS
22011 S.E. 51st St.
Issaquah, WA 98027 206-391-0800
Computers - retail & wholesale O

El Chico Restaurants, Inc. ELCH
12200 Stemmons Fwy., Ste. 100
Dallas, TX 75234 214-241-5500
Retail - food & restaurants

El Paso Electric Co. ELPAQ
303 N. Oregon St.
El Paso, TX 79901 915-543-5711
Utility - electric power

Elco Industries, Inc. ELCN
1111 Samuelson Rd.
Rockford, IL 61125 815-397-5151
Metal products - fasteners
[DRP]

Electric & Gas Technology, Inc. ELGT
13636 Neutron Rd.
Dallas, TX 75244 214-934-8797
Diversified operations

Electric Fuel Corp. EFCX
885 Third Ave., Ste. 2900
New York, NY 10022 212-230-2172
Engineering - R & D services

Electro Rent Corp. ELRC
6060 Sepulveda Blvd.
Van Nuys, CA 91411 818-786-2525
Leasing

Electro Scientific Industries, Inc. ESIO
13900 N.W. Science Park Dr.
Portland, OR 97229 503-641-4141
Lasers - systems & components

Electro-Sensors, Inc. ELSE
6111 Blue Circle Dr.
Minnetonka, MN 55343 612-930-0100
Diversified operations

Electroglas, Inc. EGLS
2901 Coronado Dr.
Santa Clara, CA 95054 408-727-6500
Electronics - measuring instruments O

Electromagnetic Sciences, Inc. ELMG
660 Engineering Dr.
Norcross, GA 30091 404-263-9200
Telecommunications services

Electronic Arts Inc. ERTS
1450 Fashion Island Blvd.
San Mateo, CA 94404 415-571-7171
Computers - software O

Electronic Fab Technology Corp. EFTC
7251 W. 4th St.
Greeley, CO 80634 303-353-3100
Electronics - components & systems

Electronic Information Systems, Inc.
  EISI
1351 Washington Blvd.
Stamford, CT 06902 203-351-4800
Telecommunications equipment

Electronic Retailing Systems International
  Inc. ERSI
372 Danbury Rd.
Wilton, CT 06897 203-761-7900
Miscellaneous - not elsewhere classified

Electronic Tele-Communications, Inc.
  ETCIA
1915 MacArthur Rd.
Waukesha, WI 53188 414-542-5600
Telecommunications equipment

Electronics for Imaging, Inc. EFII
2855 Campus Dr.
San Mateo, CA 94403 415-286-8600
Diversified operations O

Elek Tek, Inc. ELEK
7350 N. Linder Ave.
Skokie, IL 60077 708-677-7660
Computers - retail & wholesale

Ellett Brothers, Inc. ELET
267 Columbia Ave.
Chapin, SC 29036 803-345-3751
Wholesale distribution - consumer products

Eltron International, Inc. ELTN
21617 Nordhoff St.
Chatsworth, CA 91311 818-885-6484
Computers - software

Embrex, Inc. EMBX
PO Box 13989
Research Triangle, NC 27709
919-941-5185
Biomedical & genetic products

EMC Insurance Group Inc. EMCI
717 Mulberry St.
Des Moines, IA 50309 515-280-2581
Insurance - property & casualty
[DRP]

EmCare Holdings Inc. EMCR
1717 Main St., Ste. 5200
Dallas, TX 75201 214-712-2000
Business services

EMCON Associates MCON
400 S. El Camino Real
San Mateo, CA 94402 415-375-1522
Pollution control equipment & services

Emisphere Technologies, Inc. EMIS
15 Skyline Dr.
Hawthorne, NY 10532 914-347-2220
Drugs

Emmis Broadcasting Corp. EMMS
950 N. Meridian St., Ste. 1200
Indianapolis, IN 46204 317-266-0100
Broadcasting - radio & TV

Empi, Inc. EMPI
1275 Grey Fox Rd.
St. Paul, MN 55112
612-636-6600
Medical products

Emulex Corp. EMLXD
3535 Harbor Blvd.
Costa Mesa, CA 92626 714-662-5600
Computers - peripheral equipment

Encad Inc. ENCD
6059 Cornerstone Ct. West
San Diego, CA 92121 619-452-0882
Computers - peripheral equipment

Encore Computer Corp. ENCC
6901 W. Sunrise Blvd.
Fort Lauderdale, FL 33313 305-587-2900
Computers - software

Encore Wire Corp. WIRE
1410 Millwood Rd., PO Box 1149
McKinney, TX 75069 214-548-9473
Wire & cable products

Endosonics Corp. ESON
6616 Owens Dr.
Pleasanton, CA 94588 510-734-0464
Medical products

Energy BioSystems Corp. ENBC
4200 Research Forest Dr.
The Woodlands, TX 77381 713-364-6100
Energy - alternate sources

Energy West, Inc. EWST
No. 1 First Ave. South
Great Falls, MT 59403 406-791-7500
Utility - gas distribution

EnergyNorth, Inc. ENNI
1260 Elm St., PO Box 329
Manchester, NH 03105 603-625-4000
Utility - gas distribution
[DRP 5%]

ENEX Resources Corp. ENEX
800 Rockmead Dr., Ste. 200
Kingwood, TX 77339 713-358-8401
Oil & gas - US exploration & production

Engineered Support Systems, Inc. EASI
1270 N. Price Rd.
St. Louis, MO 63132 314-993-5880
Military equipment

Engineering Measurements Co. EMCO
600 Diagonal Hwy.
Longmont, CO 80501 303-651-0550
Electronics - measuring instruments

Engle Homes, Inc. ENGL
123 N.W. 13th St.
Boca Raton, FL 33432 407-391-4012
Building - residential & commercial

Ensys Environmental Products, Inc. ENSY
4222 Emperor Blvd.
Morrisville, NC 27560 919-941-5509
Pollution control equipment & services

Envirogen, Inc. ENVG
4100 Quakerbridge Rd.
Lawrenceville, NJ 08648 609-936-9300
Pollution control equipment & services

Environmental Services of America, Inc.
ENSA
119 Paris St.
Newark, NJ 07105 201-589-3850
Pollution control equipment & services

Environmental Technologies Corp. EVTC
550 James St.
Lakewood, NJ 08701 908-370-3400
Chemicals - specialty

Enviropur Waste Refining & Technology Inc.
EPUR
7601 W. 47th St.
McCook, IL 60525 708-442-6000
Oil refining & marketing

Enviroq Corp. EROQ
11511 Phillips Highway South
Jacksonville, FL 32256 904-260-6457
Building products - misc.

EnviroSource, Inc. ENSO
Five High Ridge Park
Stamford, CT 06904
203-322-8333
Pollution control equipment & services

Envirotest Systems Corp. ENVI
2002 N. Forbes Blvd.
Tucson, AZ 85745 602-620-1500
Miscellaneous - not elsewhere classified

ENVOY Corp. ENVY
15 Century Blvd., Ste. 600
Nashville, TN 37214 615-885-3700
Business services O

Enzon, Inc. ENZN
40 Kingsbridge Rd.
Piscataway, NJ 08854 908-980-4500
Biomedical & genetic products O

EP Technologies, Inc. EPTK
350 Potnero Ave.
Sunnyvale, CA 94086 408-481-3800
Medical products

EquiCredit Corp. EQCC
1801 Art Museum Dr.
Jacksonville, FL 32207 904-398-7581
Financial - consumer loans

Equinox Systems Inc. EQNX
6851 W. Sunrise Blvd.
Fort Lauderdale, FL 33313
305-791-5000
Computers - peripheral equipment

Equitex, Inc. EQTX
7315 E. Peakview Ave.
Englewood, CO 80111 303-796-8940
Financial - SBIC & commercial

Equitrac Corp. ETRC
836 Ponce de Leon Blvd.
Coral Gables, FL 33134
305-442-2060
Computers - services

Equity Corporation International ECII
415 S. First St., Ste. 210
Lufkin, TX 75901 409-634-1033
Funeral services & related

Equity Inns, Inc. ENNS
4735 Spottswood Ave., Ste. 201
Memphis, TN 38117 901-761-9651
Real estate investment trust

Equity Marketing, Inc. EMAK
156 Fifth Ave.
New York, NY 10010 212-645-2333
Toys - games & hobby products

Equity Oil Co. EQTY
10 W. Broadway, Ste. 806
Salt Lake City, UT 84101 801-521-3515
Oil & gas - US exploration & production

Ernst Home Center, Inc. ERNS
1511 6th Ave.
Seattle, WA 98101 206-621-6700
Retail - misc.

ERO, Inc. EROI
585 Slawin Court
Mt. Prospect, IL 60056 708-803-9200
Leisure & recreational products

Escalade, Inc. ESCA
817 Maxwell Ave.
Evansville, IN 47717 812-426-2281
Leisure & recreational products

ESELCO, Inc. EDSE
725 E. Portage Ave.
Sault Ste. Marie, MI 49783 906-632-2221
Miscellaneous - not elsewhere classified

Eskimo Pie Corp. EPIE
7204 Glen Forest Dr.
Richmond, VA 23226 804-560-8400
Food - dairy products

Esmor Correctional Services, Inc. ESMR
275 Broadhollow Rd.
Melville, NY 11747 516-694-7161
Miscellaneous - not elsewhere classified

Essef Corp. ESSF
220 Park Dr.
Chardon, OH 44024 216-286-2200
Machinery - general industrial

Essex County Gas Co. ECGC
7 N. Hunt Rd.
Amesbury, MA 01913 508-388-4000
Utility - gas distribution
[DRP 5%]

Evans & Sutherland Computer Corp.
ESCC
600 Komas Dr., PO Box 58700
Salt Lake City, UT 84158
801-582-5847
Computers - graphics

Evans Systems, Inc. EVSI
720 Avenue F North
Bay City, TX 77414 409-245-2424
Wholesale distribution - consumer products

Evans, Inc. EVAN
36 S. State St.
Chicago, IL 60603 312-855-2000
Retail - apparel & shoes

Evergreen Bancorp, Inc. EVGN
237 Glen St.
Glens Falls, NY 12801 518-792-1151
Banks - northeast [DRP]

Evergreen Media Corp. EVGM
433 E. Las Colinas Blvd.
Irving, TX 75039 214-869-9020
Broadcasting - radio & TV

Evergreen Resources, Inc. EVER
1512 Larimer St.
Denver, CO 80202 303-534-0400
Oil & gas - US exploration & production

Exabyte Corp. EXBT
1685 38th St.
Boulder, CO 80301 303-442-4333
Computers - peripheral equipment O

Exar Corp. EXAR
2222 Qume Dr.
San Jose, CA 95131 408-434-6400
Electrical components - semiconductors

Excalibur Technologies Corp. EXCA
9255 Towne Center Dr., 9th Fl.
San Diego, CA 92121 619-625-7900
Computers - software

Excel Technology, Inc. XLTC
45 Adams Ave.
Hauppauge, NY 11788 516-273-6900
Lasers - systems & components

EXECUTONE Information Systems, Inc.
XTON
478 Wheelers Farm Rd.
Milford, CT 06460 203-876-7600
Telecommunications equipment

Exide Electronics Group, Inc. XUPS
8521 Six Forks Rd.
Raleigh, NC 27615 919-872-3020
Electrical products - misc.

Expeditors International of Washington, Inc.
EXPD
19119 - 16th Ave. South
Seattle, WA 98188 206-246-3711
Transportation - services

Express America Holdings Corp. EXAM
9060 E. Via Linda St.
Scottsdale, AZ 85258 602-661-3577
Financial - mortgages & related services

Express Scripts, Inc. ESRX
1400 Riverport Dr.
Maryland Heights, MO 63046
314-770-1666
Medical services

Exstar Financial Corp. EXTR
2029 Village Ln.
Solvang, CA 93463 805-688-8013
Insurance - multi line & misc.

EZ Communications, Inc. EZCIA
10800 Main St.
Fairfax, VA 22030 703-591-1000
Broadcasting - radio & TV

EZCORP, Inc. EZPW
1901 Capital Parkway
Austin, TX 78746 512-314-3400
Financial - consumer loans

F & C Bancshares, Inc. FSCC
1600 Tamiami Trail
Port Charlotte, FL 33948
813-627-3322
Financial - savings and loans

F & M Distributors, Inc. FMDD
25800 Sherwood Rd.
Warren, MI 48091 313-758-1400
Retail - discount & variety

F & M National Corp. FMNT
38 Rouss Ave.
Winchester, VA 22601 703-665-4200
Banks - southeast
[DRP 5%]

F&M Bancorp FMBN
110 Thomas Johnson Dr.
Frederick, MD 21702 301-694-4000
Banks - northeast [DRP]

F&M Bancorporation, Inc. FMBK
One Bank Ave., PO Box 410
Kaukauna, WI 54130 414-766-1717
Banks - midwest

Facelifters Home Systems Inc. FACE
800 Snediker Ave.
Brooklyn, NY 11207 718-257-9700
Miscellaneous - not elsewhere classified

Fair, Isaac and Co., Inc. FICI
120 N. Redwood Dr.
San Rafael, CA 94903 415-472-2211
Business services

Fairfield Communities, Inc. FFCI
2800 Cantrell Rd., PO Box 3375
Little Rock, AR 72202 501-664-6000
Building - residential & commercial

Falcon Oil & Gas Co., Inc. FLOGE
4801 Woodway, Ste. 330W
Houston, TX 77056 713-623-0853
Oil & gas - US exploration & production

Falcon Products, Inc. FLCP
9387 Dielman Industrial Dr.
St. Louis, MO 63132
314-991-9200
Furniture

Family Bancorp FMLY
153 Merrimack St., PO Box 431
Haverhill, MA 01831 508-374-1911
Banks - northeast

Family Steak Houses of Florida, Inc. RYFL
2113 Florida Blvd.
Neptune Beach, FL 32266 904-249-4197
Retail - food & restaurants

Farmer Bros. Co. FARM
20333 S. Normandie Ave.
Torrance, CA 90502 310-320-1212
Food - wholesale

Farmers & Mechanics Bank FMCT
237 Main St.
Middletown, CT 06457
203-346-9677
Financial - savings and loans

Farr Co. FARC
2221 Park Place
El Segundo, CA 90245
310-536-6300
Filtration products

Farrel Corp. FARL
25 Main St.
Ansonia, CT 06401 203-736-5500
Engineering - R & D services

FastComm Communications Corp. FSCX
45472 Holiday Dr.
Sterling, VA 20166 703-318-7750
Telecommunications equipment

Fastenal Co. FAST
2001 Theurer Blvd.
Winona, MN 55987 507-454-5374
Building products - retail & wholesale O

FCB Financial Corp. FCBF
108 E. Wisconsin Ave.
Neenah, WI 54956 414-727-3400
Banks - midwest

FCNB Corp. FCNB
1 N. Market St.
Frederick, MD 21701
301-662-2191
Banks - northeast

FDP Corp. FDPC
2140 S. Dixie Highway
Miami, FL 33133 305-858-8200
Computers - software

Featherlite Manufacturing, Inc. FTHR
Highways 63 & 9, PO Box 320
Cresco, IA 52136 319-547-6000
Automotive & trucking - original equipment

Federal Screw Works FSCR
2400 Buhl Building
Detroit, MI 48226 313-963-2323
Metal products - fabrication

FelCor Suite Hotels, Inc. FLCO
5215 N. O'Connor Blvd.
Irving, TX 75039 214-869-8180
Real estate investment trust

Ferrofluidics Corp. FERO
40 Simon St.
Nashua, NH 03061 603-883-9800
Chemicals - specialty

FF Bancorp, Inc. FFSB
900 N. Dixie Freeway
New Smyrna Beach, FL 32168
904-428-2466
Financial - savings and loans

FFBS Bancorp, Inc. FFBS
1121 Main St.
Columbus, MS 39703 601-328-4631
Financial - savings and loans

FFLC Bancorp, Inc. FFLC
800 N. Boulevard West
Leesburg, FL 34749 904-787-3311
Banks - southeast

FFY Financial Corp. FFYF
724 Boardman-Poland Rd.
Youngstown, OH 44512 216-726-3396
Banks - midwest

FHP International Corp. FHPC
9900 Talbert Ave., PO Box 8000
Fountain Valley, CA 92708
714-963-7233
Health maintenance organization O

Fiberstars, Inc. FBST
2883 Bayview Dr.
Fremont, CA 94538 510-490-0719
Fiber optics

Fidelity Bancorp, Inc. FSBI
1009 Perry Highway
Pittsburgh, PA 15237 412-367-3300
Financial - savings and loans

Fidelity Bancorp, Inc. FBCI
5455 W. Belmont Ave.
Chicago, IL 60641 312-736-3000
Financial - savings and loans

Fidelity Federal Savings Bank FFFL
218 Datura St.
West Palm Beach, FL 33401
407-659-9900
Financial - savings and loans

Fidelity Federal Savings Bank FFRV
2809 Emerywood Parkway
Richmond, VA 23294 804-756-0200
Financial - savings and loans

Fidelity Medical, Inc. FMSI
6 Vreeland Rd.
Florham Park, NJ 07932 201-377-0400
Medical instruments

Fidelity New York F.S.B. FDNY
1000 Franklin Ave.
Garden City, NY 11530 516-746-8500
Financial - savings and loans

Fifth Third Bancorp FITB
38 Fountain Square Plaza
Cincinnati, OH 45263 513-579-5300
Banks - midwest O [DRP]

Figgie International Inc. FIGIA
4420 Sherwin Rd.
Willoughby, OH 44094 216-953-2700
Diversified operations
[DRP]

Filene's Basement Corp. BSMT
40 Walnut St.
Wellesley, MA 02181 617-348-7000
Retail - discount & variety O

FileNet Corp. FILE
3565 Harbor Blvd.
Costa Mesa, CA 92626 714-966-3400
Computers - services O

Financial Bancorp, Inc. FIBC
42-25 Queens Blvd.
Long Island City, NY 11104 718-729-5002
Banks - northeast

Financial Benefit Group Inc. FBGIA
7251 W. Palmetto Park Rd.
Boca Raton, FL 303433 407-394-9400
Insurance - multi line & misc.

Financial Institutions Insurance Co. FIRE
300 Delaware Ave., Ste. 1704
Wilmington, DE 19801 302-427-5800
Insurance - multi line & misc.

Financial Security Corp. FNSC
1209 N. Milwaukee Ave.
Chicago, IL 60622 312-227-7020
Financial - savings and loans

Financial Trust Corp. FITC
310 Allen Rd.
Carlisle, PA 17013 717-243-3212
Banks - northeast [DRP]

Financing for Science International, Inc.
FFSI
10 Waterside Dr.
Farmington, CT 06032 203-676-1818
Leasing

FinishMaster, Inc. FMST
4259 40th St. S.E.
Kentwood, MI 49512 616-949-7604
Automotive & trucking - replacement parts

First Albany Companies Inc. FACT
41 State St.
Albany, NY 12207 518-447-8500
Financial - business services

First Alert, Inc. ALRT
780 McClure Rd.
Aurora, IL 60504 708-851-7330
Appliances - household

First American Corp. FATN
First American Center
Nashville, TN 37237 615-748-2000
Banks - southeast
[DRP]

First Bancorp FBNC
341 N. Main St.
Troy, NC 27371 910-576-6171
Banks - southeast

First Bancorporation of Ohio FBOH
800 First National Tower
Akron, OH 44308 216-384-8000
Banks - midwest [DRP]

First Bancshares, Inc. FBSI
142 E. First St.
Mountain Grove, MO 65711
417-926-5151
Banks - midwest

First Banking Company of S.E. Georgia
FBCG
40 N. Main St.
Statesboro, GA 30458 912-764-6611
Banks - southeast

First Cash, Inc. PAWN
600 Six Flags Dr., Ste. 518
Arlington, TX 76011 817-633-7296
Financial - consumer loans

First Charter Bank N.A. FCBK
265 N. Beverly Dr.
Beverly Hills, CA 90210 310-278-7200
Banks - west

First Charter Corp. FCTR
22 Union St. North
Concord, NC 28026 704-786-3300
Banks - southeast

First Citizens BancShares, Inc. FCNCA
239 Fayetteville St.
Raleigh, NC 27601 919-755-7000
Banks - southeast [DRP 5%]

First Citizens Financial Corp. FCIT
8485 Fenton St.
Silver Spring, MD 20910 301-565-8900
Financial - savings and loans

First Colonial Bankshares Corp. FCOLA
30 N. Michigan Ave., Ste 300
Chicago, IL 60602 312-419-9891
Banks - midwest [DRP]

First Colonial Group, Inc. FTCG
76 S. Main St.
Nazareth, PA 18064 610-746-7300
Banks - midwest [DRP 5%]

First Commerce Corp. FCOM
210 Baronne St., PO Box 60279
New Orleans, LA 70160 504-561-1371
Banks - southeast
[DRP 5%]

First Commercial Bancorp, Inc. FCOB
2450 Venture Oaks Way
Sacramento, CA 95833 916-646-0554
Banks - west

First Commercial Corp. FCLR
400 W. Capitol Ave.
Little Rock, AR 72201 501-371-7000
Banks - southeast [DRP 5%]

First Essex Bancorp, Inc. FESX
296 Essex St.
Lawrence, MA 01840 508-681-7500
Banks - northeast

First Fed. Savings & Loan Assoc. of E.
  Hartford FFES
1137 Main St.
East Hartford, CT 06108 203-289-6401
Financial - savings and loans

First Federal Bancshares of Eau Claire, Inc.
  FFEC
319 E. Grand Ave.
Eau Claire, WI 54701 715-833-7700
Banks - midwest

First Federal Capital Corp. FTFC
605 State St.
LaCrosse, WI 54601 608-784-8000
Financial - savings and loans
[DRP]

First Federal Financial Corp. of Kentucky
  FFKY
2323 E. Ring Road, PO Box 5006
Elizabethtown, KY 42702 502-765-2131
Financial - savings and loans

First Federal Savings & Loan FDEF
601 Clinton St.
Defiance, OH 43512 419-782-5015
Financial - savings and loans

First Federal Savings Bank of Brunswick, Ga.
  FFBG
777 Gloucester St.
Brunswick, GA 31520 912-265-1410
Financial - savings and loans

First Federal Savings Bank of Colorado
  FFBA
215 S. Wadsworth Blvd.
Lakewood, CO 80226 303-232-2121
Financial - savings and loans

First Federal Savings Bank of Fort Dodge
  FFFD
825 Central Ave., PO Box 1237
Fort Dodge, IA 50501 515-576-7531
Banks - midwest

First Financial Bancorp. FFBC
300 High St.
Hamilton, OH 45011 513-867-4700
Banks - midwest

First Financial Bankshares, Inc. FFIN
400 Pine St.
Abilene, TX 79601 915-675-7155
Banks - midwest

First Financial Corp. THFF
One First Financial Plaza
Terre Haute, IN 47807 812-238-6000
Banks - midwest

First Financial Corp. FFHC
1305 Main St.
Stevens Point, WI 54481 715-341-0400
Financial - savings and loans

First Financial Corp. of Western Maryland
  FFWM
118 Baltimore St.
Cumberland, MD 21502 301-724-3363
Banks - northeast

First Financial Holdings, Inc. FFCH
34 Broad St.
Charleston, SC 29401 803-724-0800
Financial - savings and loans
[DRP]

First Franklin Corp. FFHS
401 E. Court St.
Cincinnati, OH 45202 513-721-1031
Financial - savings and loans

First Georgia Holding, Inc. FGHC
1703 Gloucester St.
Brunswick, GA 31520 912-267-7283
Miscellaneous - not elsewhere classified

First Harrisburg Bancor, Inc. FFHP
234 N. Second St.
Harrisburg, PA 17101 717-232-6661
Banks - northeast
[DRP]

First Hawaiian, Inc. FHWN
1132 Bishop St.
Honolulu, HI 96813 808-525-7000
Banks - west

First Home Savings Bank, F.S.B. FSPG
125 S. Broadway, PO Box 189
Pennsville, NJ 08070 609-678-4400
Financial - savings and loans

First Indiana Corp. FISB
135 N. Pennsylvania St.
Indianapolis, IN 46204 317-269-1200
Financial - savings and loans

First Inter-Bancorp Inc. FIBI
One Summit Court
Fishkill, NY 12524 914-897-2800
Banks - northeast

First Liberty Financial Corp. FLFC
201 Second St.
Macon, GA 31297 912-743-0911
Financial - savings and loans

First Merchants Acceptance Corp. FMAC
570 Lake Hook Rd., Ste. 126
Deerfield, IL 60015 708-948-9300
Financial - business services

First Merchants Corp. FRME
200 E. Jackson St.
Muncie, IN 47305 317-747-1500
Banks - midwest

First Michigan Bank Corp. FMBC
One Financial Plaza
Holland, MI 49423 616-396-9200
Banks - midwest [DRP 5%]

First Midwest Bancorp, Inc. FMBI
50 E. Shuman Blvd., Ste. 310
Naperville, IL 60566 708-778-8700
Banks - midwest [DRP]

First Midwest Financial, Inc. CASH
Fifth and Erie Sts.
Storm Lake, IA 50588 712-732-4117
Financial - savings and loans

First Mortgage Corp. FMOR
3230 Fallow Field Dr.
Diamond Bar, CA 91765 909-595-1996
Financial - mortgages & related services

First Mutual Savings Bank FMSB
400 - 108th Ave. NE
Bellevue, WA 98004 206-455-7300
Financial - savings and loans

First National Bancorp FBAC
303 Jesse Jewell Pkwy.
Gainesville, GA 30501 404-503-2000
Banks - southeast [DRP]

First National Bank Corp. MTCL
18800 Hall Rd., PO Box 248
Mount Clemens, MI 48046
313-465-2400
Banks - midwest [DRP]

First Northern Savings Bank S.A. FNGB
201 N. Monroe Ave.
Green Bay, WI 54301 414-437-7101
Financial - savings and loans
[DRP]

First Oak Brook Bancshares, Inc. FOBBA
1400 Sixteenth St.
Oak Brook, IL 60521 708-571-1050
Banks - midwest

First Pacific Networks, Inc. FPNX
601 W. California Ave.
Sunnyvale, CA 94086 408-943-7600
Telecommunications services O

First Palm Beach Bancorp, Inc. FFPB
215 S. Olive Ave.
West Palm Beach, FL 33401
407-655-8511
Financial - savings and loans

First Savings Bank FSLA
3090 Woodbridge Ave.
Edison, NJ 08837 908-417-2900
Financial - savings and loans

First Savings Bank of Moore County, Inc.
SOPN
205 S.E. Broad St.
Southern Pines, NC 28387 910-692-6222
Financial - savings and loans

First Security Corp. FSCO
79 S. Main St., PO Box 30006
Salt Lake City, UT 84130 801-246-5706
Banks - west O
[DRP]

First Shenango Bancorp, Inc. SHEN
25 N. Mill St., PO Box 671
New Castle, PA 16103 412-654-6606
Financial - savings and loans

First Southeast Financial Corp. FSFC
201 N. Main St.
Anderson, SC 29621 803-224-3401
Financial - savings and loans

First Southern Bancorp, Inc. FSOU
115 S. Fayetteville St.
Asheboro, NC 27203 910-626-8600
Financial - savings and loans

First State Bancorporation FSNM
111 Lomas Ave. NW
Albuquerque, NM 87102 505-262-5500
Banks - southwest

First State Corp. FSBT
333 W. Broad Ave.
Albany, GA 31701 912-432-8000
Banks - southwest

First State Financial Services, Inc. FSFI
1120 Bloomfield Ave., CN 2449
West Caldwell, NJ 07007 201-575-5800
Financial - savings and loans

First Team Sports, Inc. FTSP
2274 Woodale Dr.
Mounds View, MN 55112 612-780-4454
Leisure & recreational products

First Tennessee National Corp. FTEN
165 Madison Ave.
Memphis, TN 38103 901-523-5630
Banks - southeast O
[DRP]

First United Bancorp FUBC
980 N. Federal Highway
Boca Raton, FL 33432 407-392-4000
Banks - southeast

First United Bancshares, Inc. UNTD
Main at Washington Sts.
El Dorado, AR 71730 501-863-3181
Banks - southeast

First United Corp. FUNC
19 S. Second St.
Oakland, MD 21550 301-334-9471
Banks - northeast

First Western Bancorp, Inc. FWBI
101 E. Washington St.
New Castle, PA 16101　412-652-8550
Banks - northeast
[DRP]

First-Knox Banc Corp. FKBC
1 S. Main St., PO Box 871
Mt. Vernon, OH 43050　614-393-5500
Banks - midwest

Firstbank of Illinois Co. FBIC
205 S. Fifth
Springfield, IL 62701　217-753-7543
Banks - midwest [DRP]

FirstFed Bancshares, Inc. FFDP
749 Lee St.
Des Plaines, IL 60016　708-294-6500
Banks - midwest

FirstFed Michigan Corp. FFOM
1001 Woodward Ave.
Detroit, MI 48226　313-965-1400
Financial - savings and loans

FirstFederal Financial Services Corp.
　FFSW
135 E. Liberty St.
Wooster, OH 44691　216-264-8001
Financial - savings and loans

FirsTier Financial, Inc. FRST
17th and Farnam Sts.
Omaha, NE 68102　402-438-6299
Banks - midwest

FirstMiss Gold Inc. FRMG
5190 Neil Rd., Ste. 310
Reno, NV 89502　702-827-0211
Gold mining & processing

FirstRock Bancorp, Inc. FROK
612 N. Main St.
Rockford, IL 61103　815-987-3500
Financial - savings and loans

Fischer Imaging Corp. FIMG
12300 N. Grant St.
Denver, CO 80241　303-452-6800
Medical products

FIserv, Inc. FISV
255 FIserv Dr.
Brookfield, WI 53045　414-879-5000
Computers - services O

FLAG Financial Corp. FLAG
101 N. Greenwood St.
LaGrange, GA 30240　404-845-5000
Financial - savings and loans

Flagstar Companies, Inc. FLST
203 E. Main St.
Spartansburg, SC 29319
803-597-8000
Retail - food & restaurants

Flair Corp. FLAR
4647 S.W. 40th Ave.
Ocala, FL 34474　904-237-1220
Machinery - general industrial

Flamemaster Corp. FAME
11120 Sherman Way
Sun Valley, CA 91352
818-982-1650
Chemicals - specialty

Flexsteel Industries, Inc. FLXS
PO Box 877
Dubuque, IA 52004
319-556-7730
Furniture

Flir Systems, Inc. FLIR
16505 SW 72nd Ave.
Portland, OR 97224　503-684-3731
Video equipment

Flores & Rucks, Inc. FNRI
8440 Jefferson Hwy., Ste. 420
Baton Rouge, LA 70809　504-927-1450
Oil & gas - offshore drilling

Florida First Federal Savings Bank FFPC
144 Harrison Ave.
Panama City, FL 32401　904-872-7000
Financial - savings and loans

Flow International Corp. FLOW
23500 64th Ave. South
Kent, WA 98032　206-813-3286
Machine tools & related products

FM Properties Inc. FMPO
1615 Poydras St.
New Orleans, LA 70112
504-582-5300
Diversified operations

FMS Financial Corp. FMCO
Sunset and Salem Rds.
Burlington, NJ 08016　609-386-2400
Financial - savings and loans

FNB Corp. FNBN
101 Sunset Ave.
Asheboro, NC 27203　910-626-8300
Banks - southeast

FNB Rochester Corp. FNBR
35 State St.
Rochester, NY 14614　716-546-3300
Banks - northeast

Foamex International Inc. FMXI
823 Waterman Ave.
East Providence, RI 02914　401-438-0900
Miscellaneous - not elsewhere classified

Foilmark, Inc. FLMK
40 Melville Park Rd.
Melville, NY 11747　516-694-7773
Machinery - printing

Food Lion, Inc. FDLNA
2110 Executive Dr.
Salisbury, NC 28145 704-633-8250
Retail - supermarkets O
[DRP]

Foothill Independent Bancorp FOOT
510 S. Grand Ave.
Glendora, CA 91740 818-963-8551
Banks - west

FORE Systems, Inc. FORE
174 Thorn Hill Rd.
Warrendale, PA 15086 412-772-6600
Computers - services

Foremost Corporation of America FCOA
5600 Beach Tree Ln.
Caledonia, MI 49316 616-942-3000
Insurance - property & casualty

Forest Oil Corp. FOIL
950 - 17th St.
Denver, CO 80202 303-592-2400
Oil & gas - US exploration & production

Forstmann & Co., Inc. FSTM
1185 Avenue of the Americas
New York, NY 10036 212-642-6900
Textiles - apparel

Fort Wayne National Corp. FWNC
110 W. Berry St.
Fort Wayne, IN 46801 219-426-0555
Banks - midwest
[DRP]

Fossil, Inc. FOSL
2280 N. Greenville Ave.
Richardson, TX 75082 214-234-2525
Miscellaneous - not elsewhere classified

Fourth Financial Corp. FRTH
100 N. Broadway
Wichita, KS 67202 316-261-4444
Banks - midwest
[DRP]

Fourth Shift Corp. FSFT
7900 International Dr.
Minneapolis, MN 55425 612-851-1500
Computers - software

FPA Medical Management, Inc. FPAM
2878 Camino del Rio South
San Diego, CA 92108 619-295-7005
Health maintenance organization

Frame Technology Corp. FRAM
333 W. San Carlos St.
San Jose, CA 95110 408-975-6000
Computers - software O

Framingham Savings Bank FSBX
600 Worcester Rd.
Framingham, MA 01701 508-620-0300
Financial - savings and loans

Franklin Bank, N.A. FSVB
26725 W. Twelve Mile Rd.
Southfield, MI 48034 313-358-4710
Financial - savings and loans

Franklin Electric Co., Inc. FELE
400 E. Spring St.
Bluffton, IN 46714 219-824-2900
Machinery - electrical

Fred's, Inc. FRED
4300 New Getwell Rd.
Memphis, TN 38118 901-365-8880
Retail - discount & variety

Fresh America Corp. FRES
12450 Cutten Rd.
Houston, TX 77066 713-444-8596
Food - wholesale

Fresh Choice, Inc. SALD
2901 Tasman Dr., Ste. 109
Santa Clara, CA 95054 408-986-8661
Retail - food & restaurants

Fretter, Inc. FTTR
12501 Grand River Rd.
Brighton, MI 48116 313-591-0600
Retail - consumer electronics

Freymiller Trucking, Inc. FRML
8621 N. Rockwell
Oklahoma City, OK 73132
405-720-6555
Transportation - truck

Friedman's, Inc. FRDM
4 West State St.
Savannah, GA 31401
912-233-9333
Retail - jewelry stores

Fritz Companies, Inc. FRTZ
706 Mission St.
San Francisco, CA 94103
415-904-8360
Business services

Frozen Food Express Industries, Inc. FFEX
318 Cadiz St.
Dallas, TX 75207 214-630-8090
Transportation - truck

FRP Properties, Inc. FRPP
155 E. 21st St.
Jacksonville, FL 32206 904-355-1781
Transportation - truck

FSF Financial Corp. FFHH
201 Main St. South
Hutchinson, MN 55350 612-234-4500
Financial - savings and loans

FSI International, Inc. FSII
322 Lake Hazeltine Dr.
Chaska, MN 55318 612-448-5440
Machinery - material handling

FTP Software, Inc. FTPS
Two High St.
North Andover, MA 01845
508-685-4000
Computers - software O

Fuller (H.B.) Co. FULL
2400 Energy Park Dr.
St. Paul, MN 55108 612-645-3401
Chemicals - specialty
[DRP 3%]

Fulton Financial Corp. FULT
One Penn Square, PO Box 4887
Lancaster, PA 17604 717-291-2411
Banks - northeast [DRP]

Funco Inc. FNCO
10120 W. 76th St.
Eden Prairie, MN 55344 612-946-8883
Retail - books, music & video

Furon Co. FCBN
29982 Ivy Glenn Dr.
Laguna Niguel, CA 92677 714-831-5350
Rubber & plastic products

Fusion Systems Corp. FUSN
7600 Standish Place
Rockville, MD 20855 301-251-0300
Electronics - components & systems

Future Healthcare, Inc. FHCI
123 E. Fourth St., Ste. 19
Cincinnati, OH 45202 513-651-2525
Medical services

G&K Services, Inc. GKSRA
505 Waterford Park, Ste. 455
Minneapolis, MN 55441 612-546-7440
Linen supply & related

G-III Apparel Group, Ltd. GIII
345 W. 37th St.
New York, NY 10018 212-629-8830
Leather & related products

GAB Bancorp GABC
711 Main St., PO Box 810
Jasper, IN 47547 812-482-1314
Banks - midwest

Galey & Lord, Inc. GANL
980 Avenue of the Americas
New York, NY 10018 212-465-3000
Textiles - mill products

Galileo Electro-Optics Corp. GAEO
Galileo Park, PO Box 550
Sturbridge, MA 01566 508-347-9191
Fiber optics

GameTek, Inc. GAME
2999 N.E. 191st St.
North Miami Beach, FL 33180
305-935-3995
Computers - software

Gaming World International Inc. GWLD
438 Line Ave., Ste. 100
Ellwood City, PA 16117 412-758-2461
Leisure & recreational services

Gander Mountain, Inc. GNDR
PO Box 128, Hwy. W
Wilmot, WI 53192 414-862-2331
Retail - mail order & direct

Gantos, Inc. GTOSQ
3260 Patterson, S.E.
Grand Rapids, MI 49512
616-949-7000
Retail - apparel & shoes

Garnet Resources Corp. GARN
333 Clay St., Ste. 4500
Houston, TX 77002 713-759-1692
Oil & gas - international specialty

Gartner Group, Inc. GART
56 Top Gallant Rd.
Stamford, CT 06904 203-964-0096
Business services

GaSonics International Corp. GSNX
2730 Junction Ave.
San Jose, CA 95134 408-944-0212
Electronics - components & systems

Gateway 2000 Inc. GATE
610 Gateway Dr., PO Box 2000
North Sioux City, SD 57049
605-232-2000
Computers - mini & micro O

Gateway Bancorp, Inc. GBAN
1630 Richmond Rd.
Staten Island, NY 10304
718-979-4000
Banks - northeast

GBC Bancorp GBCB
800 W. 6th St.
Los Angeles, CA 90017 213-972-4104
Banks - west

GBC Technologies, Inc. GBCT
444 Kelley Dr.
Berlin, NJ 08009 609-767-2500
Computers - retail & wholesale

Geerlings & Wade, Inc. GEER
960 Turnpike St.
Canton, MA 02021 617-821-4152
Miscellaneous - not elsewhere classified

Gehl Co. GEHL
143 Water St., PO Box 179
West Bend, WI 53095 414-334-9461
Machinery - farm

GenCare Health Systems, Inc. GNCR
969 Executive Parkway
St. Louis, MO 63141 314-434-6114
Health maintenance organization

Gencor Industries, Inc. GCOR
5201 N. Orange Blossom Trail
Orlando, FL 32810 407-290-6000
Diversified operations

Genelabs Technologies, Inc. GNLB
505 Penobscot Dr.
Redwood City, CA 94063
415-369-9500
Biomedical & genetic products

GeneMedicine, Inc. GMED
8080 N. Stadium Dr., Ste. 2100
Houston, TX 77054 713-796-2221
Drugs

General Binding Corp. GBND
One GBC Plaza
Northbrook, IL 60062 708-272-3700
Office equipment & supplies

General Communications, Inc. GNCMA
2550 Denali St., Ste. 1000
Anchorage, AK 99503 907-265-5600
Telecommunications services

General Computer Corp. GCCC
2045 Midway Dr.
Twinsburg, OH 44087 216-425-3241
Computers - services

General Magnaplate Corp. GMCC
1331 U.S. Route 1
Linden, NJ 07036 908-862-6200
Metal processing & fabrication

General Nutrition Companies, Inc. GNCI
921 Penn Ave.
Pittsburgh, PA 15222
412-288-4600
Retail - misc. O

General Parametrics Corp. GPAR
1250 Ninth St.
Berkeley, CA 94710
510-524-3950
Computers - graphics

Genesee Corp. GENBB
445 St. Paul St.
Rochester, NY 14605 716-546-1030
Beverages - alcoholic

Genetic Therapy, Inc. GTII
938 Clopper Rd.
Gaithersburg, MD 20878 301-590-2626
Biomedical & genetic products

Genetics Institute, Inc. GENIZ
87 CambridgePark Dr.
Cambridge, MA 02140 617-876-1170
Biomedical & genetic products O

GENICOM Corp. GECM
14800 Conference Center Dr.
Chantilly, VA 22021 703-802-9200
Computers - peripheral equipment

Genome Therapeutics Corp. GENE
100 Beaver St.
Waltham, MA 02154 617-487-7979
Biomedical & genetic products

Gensia, Inc. GNSA
9360 Towne Center Dr.
San Diego, CA 92121
619-546-8300
Drugs O

Genta Inc. GNTA
3550 General Atomics Court
San Diego, CA 92121 619-455-2700
Drugs

Gentex Corp. GNTX
600 N. Centennial St.
Zeeland, MI 49464 616-772-1800
Automotive & trucking - original equipment
O

Genus, Inc. GGNS
1139 Karlstad Dr.
Sunnyvale, CA 94089 408-747-7120
Electrical components - semiconductors

Genyzyme Transgenic Corp. GZTC
One Mountain Rd.
Framingham, MA 01701 508-872-8400
Biomedical & genetic products

Genzyme Corp. GENZ
One Kendall Square
Cambridge, MA 02139 617-252-7500
Biomedical & genetic products O

Geodynamics Corp. GDYN
21171 Western Ave., Ste. 110
Torrance, CA 90501 310-782-7277
Computers - software

George Mason Bankshares, Inc. GMBS
11185 Main St.
Fairfax, VA 22030 703-352-1100
Banks - southeast

Georgia Bonded Fibers, Inc. BOTX
15 Nuttman St.
Newark, NJ 07103 201-642-3547
Rubber & plastic products

Geotek Industries, Inc. GOTK
20 Craig Rd.
Montvale, NJ 07645 201-930-9305
Telecommunications services O

Geoworks GWRX
960 Atlantic Ave.
Alameda, CA 94501
510-814-1660
Computers - software

Geriatric & Medical Cos., Inc. GEMC
5601 Chestnut St.
Philadelphia, PA 19139 215-476-2250
Nursing homes

Giant Cement Holding, Inc. GCHI
Highway 453 and I-26
Harleyville, SC 29448 803-496-7880
Building products - misc.

Gibraltar Packaging Group, Inc. PACK
2115 Rexford Rd., Ste. 430
Charlotte, NC 28211 704-366-2929
Containers - paper & plastic

Gibraltar Steel Corp. ROCK
3556 Lake Shore Rd.
Buffalo, NY 14219 716-826-6500
Steel - production

Gibson Greetings, Inc. GIBG
2100 Section Rd.
Cincinnati, OH 45237 513-841-6600
Printing - commercial O

Giddings & Lewis, Inc. GIDL
142 Doty St., PO Box 590
Fond du Lac, WI 54936 414-921-9400
Machine tools & related products O
[DRP]

Giga-tronics, Inc. GIGA
4650 Norris Canyon Rd.
San Ramon, CA 94583
510-328-4150
Electronics - military

Gilbert Associates, Inc. GILBA
PO Box 1498
Reading, PA 19603 610-775-5900
Engineering - R & D services

Gilead Sciences, Inc. GILD
353 Lakeside Dr.
Foster City, CA 94404
415-574-3000
Drugs O

Gish Biomedical, Inc. GISH
2681 Kelvin Ave.
Irvine, CA 92714 714-756-5485
Biomedical & genetic products

Glacier Bancorp, Inc. GBCI
202 Main St., PO Box 27
Kalispell, MT 59903 406-756-4200
Financial - savings and loans

Glenayre Technologies, Inc. GEMS
4201 Congress St., Ste. 455
Charlotte, NC 28209 704-553-0038
Real estate operations O

Global Industries, Ltd. GLBL
107 Global Cir.
Lafayette, LA 70503 318-989-0000
Oil & gas - field services

Global Market Information, Inc. GMKT
56 Pine St.
New York, NY 10005 212-248-9090
Business services

Global Village Communications, Inc. GVIL
685 E. Middlefield Rd.
Mountain View, CA 94043 415-390-8200
Computers - peripheral equipment

Glycomed Inc. GLYC
860 Atlantic Ave.
Alameda, CA 94501
510-523-5555
Drugs

GMIS Inc. GMIS
5 Country View Rd.
Malvern, PA 19355 610-296-3838
Medical services

Golden Enterprises, Inc. GLDC
2101 Magnolia Ave. South
Birmingham, AL 35205 205-326-6101
Diversified operations

Golden Poultry Co., Inc. CHIK
244 Perimeter Ctr. Pkwy., N.E.
Atlanta, GA 30346 404-393-5000
Food - meat products

Golden Systems, Inc. GLDN
2125-B Madera Rd.
Simi Valley, CA 93012 805-582-4400
Electronics - components & systems

Goldenbanks of Colorado, Inc. GOLD
1301 Jackson St.
Golden, CO 80401 303-279-4563
Banks - west

Golf Enterprises, Inc. GLFE
1603 LBJ Fwy., Ste. 810
Dallas, TX 75234 214-247-1199
Leisure & recreational services

GoodMark Foods, Inc. GDMK
6131 Falls of Neuse Rd.
Raleigh, NC 27609 919-790-9940
Food - meat products
[DRP 2%]

Goody's Family Clothing, Inc. GDYS
400 Goody's Ln.
Knoxville, TN 37922 615-966-2000
Retail - apparel & shoes

Gotham Apparel Corp. TBAY
1384 Broadway
New York, NY 11211 212-921-8800
Apparel

Goulds Pumps, Inc. GULD
240 Fall St.
Seneca Falls, NY 13148 315-568-2811
Machinery - general industrial O
[DRP]

Government Technology Services, Inc. GTSI
4100 Lafayette Center Dr.
Chantilly, VA 22021 703-631-3333
Computers - services

GP Financial Corp. GNPT
41-60 Main St.
Flushing, NY 11355
718-670-4355
Financial - savings and loans

Gradco Systems, Inc. GRCO
3753 Howard Hughes Pkwy.
Las Vegas, NV 89109 702-892-3714
Office automation

Graff Pay-Per-View Inc. GPPV
536 Broadway
New York, NY 10012
212-941-1434
Cable TV

Granite Broadcasting Corp. GBTVK
767 Third Ave., 28th Fl.
New York, NY 10017 212-826-2530
Broadcasting - radio & TV

Granite Construction Inc. GCCO
585 W. Beach St.
Watsonville, CA 95076 408-724-1011
Construction - heavy

Granite State Bankshares, Inc. GSBI
122 West St.
Keene, NH 03431 603-352-1600
Banks - northeast

Grant Geophysical Corp. GRNT
10615 Shadow Wood Dr.
Houston, TX 77043 713-398-9503
Oil & gas - field services

Graphic Industries, Inc. GRPH
2155 Monroe Dr., N.E.
Atlanta, GA 30324 404-874-3327
Printing - commercial

Great American Recreation, Inc. GRAR
PO Box 848
McAfee, NJ 07428 201-827-2000
Leisure & recreational services

Great Bay Bankshares, Inc. GBBS
100 Main St., PO Box 919
Dover, NH 3820 603-749-4149
Banks - northeast

Great Country Bank GCBK
211 Main St.
Ansonia, CT 06401
203-734-2561
Banks - northeast

Great Financial Corp. GTFN
One Financial Square
Louisville, KY 40202 502-587-8891
Financial - savings and loans

Great Lakes Aviation, Ltd. GLUX
1965 330th St.
Spencer, IA 51301 712-262-1000
Transportation - airline

Great Lakes Bancorp, F.S.B. GLBC
401 E. Liberty St.
Ann Arbor, MI 48104 313-769-8300
Financial - savings and loans
[DRP]

Great Southern Bancorp, Inc. GSBC
1451 E. Battlefield
Springfield, MO 65804 417-887-4400
Banks - midwest
[DRP]

Greenfield Industries, Inc. GFII
470 Old Evans Rd.
Augusta, GA 30809 706-863-7708
Machine tools & related products

GreenStone Industries, Inc. STON
6500 Seven Locks Rd., Ste. 206
Cabin John, MD 20818 301-229-4442
Chemicals - fibers

Greenwich Air Services, Inc. GASI
4590 N.W. 36th St.
Miami, FL 33122 305-526-7000
Transportation - services

Grenada Sunburst System Corp. GSSC
2000 Gateway
Grenada, MS 38902 601-226-1100
Banks - southeast
[DRP]

Grey Advertising Inc. GREY
777 Third Ave.
New York, NY 10017 212-546-2000
Advertising

Griffin Technology Inc. GRIF
1133 Corporate Dr.
Farmington, NY 14425 716-924-7121
Protection - safety equipment & services

Grist Mill Co. GRST
21340 Hayes Ave., PO Box 430
Lakeville, MN 55044 612-469-4981
Food - misc.

Grossman's Inc. GROS
200 Union St.
Braintree, MA 02184 617-848-0100
Building products - retail & wholesale

Ground Round Restaurants, Inc. GRXR
35 Braintree Hill Office Park
Braintree, MA 02184 617-380-3100
Retail - food & restaurants

Groundwater Technology, Inc. GWTI
100 River Ridge Dr.
Norwood, MA 02062 617-769-7600
Pollution control equipment & services O

Group 1 Software, Inc. GSOF
4200 Parliament Place
Lanham, MD 20706 301-731-2300
Computers - software

Group Technologies Corp. GRTK
10901 Malcolm McKinley Dr.
Tampa, FL 33612 813-972-6000
Instruments - control

Grove Bank GROV
1330 Boylston St.
Chestnut Hill, MA 02167 617-738-6000
Financial - savings and loans

Grow Biz International, Inc. GBIZ
4200 Dahlberg Dr.
Minneapolis, MN 55422 612-520-8500
Business services

Gryphon Holdings Inc. GRYP
30 Wall St.
New York, NY 10005 212-825-1200
Insurance - property & casualty

GTI Corp. GGTI
9171 Towne Centre Dr
San Diego, CA 92122 619-578-3111
Electrical components - misc.

Guest Supply, Inc. GEST
720 U.S. Highway One
North Brunswick, NJ 08902 908-246-3011
Cosmetics & toiletries

Guilford Pharmaceutical, Inc. GLFD
6611 Tributary St.
Baltimore, MD 21224 410-631-6302
Drugs

Gulf South Medical Supply, Inc. GSMS
426 Christine Dr.
Ridgeland, MS 39157 601-856-5900
Medical & dental supplies

GulfMark International, Inc. GMRK
5 Post Oak Park, Ste. 1170
Houston, TX 77027 713-963-9522
Oil & gas - field services

Gupta Corp. GPTA
1060 Marsh Rd.
Menlo Park, CA 94025 415-321-9500
Computers - software O

Guy F. Atkinson Co. of California ATKN
1001 Bayhill Dr., Second Fl.
San Bruno, CA 94066 415-876-1000
Diversified operations

Gwinnett Bancshares, Inc. GBSI
750 Perry St.
Lawrenceville, GA 30245
404-995-6000
Banks - southeast

GZA GeoEnvironmental Technologies, Inc.
  GZEA
320 Needham St.
Newton Upper Falls, MA 02164
617-969-0700
Pollution control equipment & services

H.D. Vest, Inc. HDVS
433 E. Las Colinas Blvd.
Irving, TX 75039 214-556-1651
Financial - investment management

HA-LO Industries, Inc. HALO
5980 Touhy Ave.
Niles, IL 60714 708-647-2300
Advertising

Hach Co. HACH
5600 Lindbergh Dr., PO Box 389
Loveland, CO 80537 303-669-3050
Instruments - scientific

Hadco Corp. HDCO
12A Manor Parkway
Salem, NH 03079 603-898-8000
Electrical components - semiconductors

Haggar Corp. HGGR
6113 Lemmon Ave.
Dallas, TX 75209 214-352-8481
Apparel

Hahn Automotive Warehouse, Inc. HAHN
415 W. Main St.
Rochester, NY 14608 716-235-1595
Auto parts - retail & wholesale

Hako Minuteman, Inc. HAKO
111 S. Rohlwing Rd.
Addison, IL 60101 708-627-6900
Building - maintenance & services

Hallmark Capital Corp. HALL
7401 W. Greenfield Ave.
W. Allis, WI 53214
414-778-4600
Banks - midwest

Hallwood Consolidated Resources Corp.
  HCRC
4582 S. Ulster St. Pkwy.
Denver, CO 80237 303-850-7373
Oil & gas - US exploration & production

Hallwood Energy Corp. HWEC
4582 S. Ulster St. Parkway
Denver, CO 80237 303-850-7373
Oil & gas - US exploration & production

Hamburger Hamlets, Inc. HAMB
14156 Magnolia Blvd.
Sherman Oaks, CA 91423
818-995-7333
Retail - food & restaurants

Hamilton Bancorp, Inc. HFSB
9201 Fourth Ave.
Brooklyn, NY 11209 718-921-7700
Financial - savings and loans

Hamilton Financial Services Corp. HFSC
525 Market St., Ninth Fl.
San Francisco, CA 94105 415-597-5600
Financial - mortgages & related services

Hampshire Group, Ltd. HAMP
215 Commerce Blvd.
Anderson, SC 29621 803-225-6232
Apparel

Hancock Holding Co. HBHC
One Hancock Plaza, PO Box 4019
Gulfport, MS 39502 601-868-4606
Banks - southeast [DRP]

Handex Environmental Recovery, Inc.
 HAND
500 Campus Dr.
Morganville, NJ 07751 908-536-8500
Pollution control equipment & services

Happiness Express, Inc. HAPY
50 W. 23rd St.
New York, NY 10010 212-675-0461
Toys - games & hobby products

Harbor Federal Bancorp, Inc. HRBF
705 York Rd.
Baltimore, MD 21204 410-296-1010
Banks - northeast

Harbor Federal Savings Bank HARB
100 S. Second St.
Fort Pierce, FL 34954 407-461-2414
Financial - savings and loans

Harding Associates, Inc. HRDG
7655 Redwood Blvd.
Novato, CA 94945 415-892-0821
Engineering - R & D services

Harleysville Group Inc. HGIC
355 Maple Ave.
Harleysville, PA 19438 215-256-5000
Insurance - property & casualty
[DRP]

Harleysville National Corp. HNBC
483 Main St., PO Box 195
Harleysville, PA 19438 215-256-8851
Banks - northeast

Harleysville Savings Bank HARL
271 Main St.
Harleysville, PA 19438 215-256-8828
Financial - savings and loans

Harmon Industries, Inc. HRMN
1300 Jefferson Court
Blue Springs, MO 64015 816-229-3345
Transportation - equipment & leasing

Harris & Harris Group, Inc. HHGP
One Rockefeller Plaza
New York, NY 10020 212-332-3600
Financial - investment management

Harris Computer Sytems Corp. NHWK
2101 W. Cypress Creek Rd.
Fort Lauderdale, FL 33309
305-974-1700
Computers - software

Harris Savings Bank HARS
Second and Pine Sts.
Harrisburg, PA 17105 717-236-4041
Financial - savings and loans

Harry's Farmers Market, Inc. HARY
1180 Upper Hembree Rd.
Roswell, GA 30076 404-664-6300
Retail - supermarkets

Harvard Industries, Inc. HAVAB
2502 Rocky Point Dr.
Tampa, FL 33607 813-288-5000
Automotive & trucking - original equipment

Haskel International, Inc. HSKL
100 E. Graham Place
Burbank, CA 91502 818-843-4000
Pumps and seals

Hathaway Corp. HATH
8228 Park Meadows Drive
Littleton, CO 80124 303-799-8200
Computers - software

Hauser Chemical Research, Inc. HAUS
5555 Airport Blvd.
Boulder, CO 80301 303-443-4662
Chemicals - specialty

Haven Bancorp, Inc. HAVN
93-22 Jamaica Ave.
Woodhaven, NY 11421 718-847-7041
Financial - savings and loans

Haverfield Corp. HVFD
50 Public Square, Ste. 444
Cleveland, OH 44113 216-348-2800
Financial - savings and loans
[DRP]

Haverty Furniture Companies, Inc. HAVT
866 W. Peachtree St., NW
Atlanta, GA 30308 404-881-1911
Retail - home furnishings

Hawkeye Bancorporation HWKB
222 Equitable Building
Des Moines, IA 50309 515-284-01930
Banks - midwest

Hawkins Chemical, Inc. HWKN
3100 E. Hennepin Ave.
Minneapolis, MN 55413 612-331-6910
Chemicals - specialty

Hawthorne Financial Corp. HTHR
2381 Rosecrans Ave.
El Segundo, CA 90245
310-725-5000
Financial - savings and loans

HBO & Co. HBOC
301 Perimeter Center North
Atlanta, GA 30346
404-393-6000
Computers - services O

HCC Insurance Holdings, Inc. HCCH
13403 Northwest Fwy.
Houston, TX 77040 713-690-7300
Insurance - property & casualty

Health Management Systems, Inc. HMSY
401 Park Ave. South
New York, NY 10016
212-685-4545
Business services

Health o meter Products, Inc. SCAL
7400 W. 100th Place
Bridgeview, IL 60455 708-598-9100
Medical instruments

Health Power, Inc. HPWR
1209 Orange St.
Wilmington, DE 19801 302-658-7581
Health maintenance organization

Health Risk Management, Inc. HRMI
8000 W. 78th St.
Minneapolis, MN 55439 612-829-3500
Medical services

HealthCare COMPARE Corp. HCCC
3200 Highland Ave.
Downers Grove, IL 60515 708-241-7900
Financial - business services O

HealthCare Imaging Services, Inc. HISS
200 Schulz Dr.
Middletown, NJ 07701
908-224-9292
Medical services

Healthcare Services Group, Inc. HCSG
2643 Huntingdon Pike
Huntingdon Valley, PA 19006
215-938-1661
Building - maintenance & services

Healthdyne Technologies, Inc. HDTC
1255 Kennestone Circle
Marietta, GA 30066 404-499-1212
Medical products O

Healthdyne, Inc. HDYN
1850 Parkway Place
Marietta, GA 30067 404-423-4500
Healthcare - outpatient & home

HealthWatch, Inc. HEAL
2445 Cades Way
Vista, CA 92083 619-598-4333
Medical products

HealthWise of America, Inc. HOAM
102 Woodmont Blvd., Ste. 110
Nashville, TN 37205 615-385-4666
Health maintenance organization

Heart Technology, Inc. HRTT
017425 N.E. Union Hill Rd.
Redmond, WA 98052 206-889-6160
Medical products O

Heartland Express, Inc. HTLD
2777 Heartland Dr.
Coralville, IA 52241 319-645-2728
Transportation - truck

Heartland Wireless Communications, Inc.
HART
1962 Thanksgiving Tower
Dallas, TX 75201 214-720-1605
Cable TV

Hechinger Co. HECHA
3500 Pennsy Dr.
Landover, MD 20785 301-341-1000
Building products - retail & wholesale O

Hector Communications Corp. HCCO
211 S. Main St., PO Box 428
Hector, MN 55342 612-848-6611
Telecommunications services

Heftel Broadcasting Corp. HBCCA
6767 W. Tropicana Ave.
Las Vegas, NV 89103 702-367-3322
Broadcasting - radio & TV

HEI, Inc. HEII
1495 Steiger Lake Ln.
Victoria, MN 55386 612-443-2500
Electrical components - misc.

Helen of Troy Corp. HELED
6827 Market Ave.
El Paso, TX 79915 915-779-6363
Cosmetics & toiletries

Helian Health Group, Inc. HHGR
9600 Blue Larkspur Ln.
Monterey, CA 93940 408-646-9000
Medical services

Helix Technology Corp. HELX
Nine Hampshire St.
Mansfield, MA 02048
508-337-5500
Instruments - scientific

HemaSure, Inc. HMSR
33 Locke Dr.
Marlborough, MA 01752
508-485-6850
Medical products

Herbalife International, Inc. HERB
9800 La Cienega Blvd.
Inglewood, CA 90301 310-410-9600
Retail - mail order & direct O

Heritage Federal Bancshares, Inc. HFBS
110 E. Center St.
Kingsport, TN 37660 615-378-8000
Banks - southeast

Heritage Financial Services, Inc. HERS
17500 S. Oak Park Ave.
Tinley Park, IL 60477 708-532-8000
Banks - midwest

Herley Industries, Inc. HRLY
10 Industry Dr.
Lancaster, PA 17603 717-397-2777
Electronics - military

Herman Miller, Inc. MLHR
855 E. Main Ave.
Zeeland, MI 49464 616-772-3300
Furniture

HF Financial Corp. HFFC
225 S. Main Ave.
Sioux Falls, SD 57102
605-333-7556
Banks - midwest

Hi-Tech Pharmacal Co., Inc. HITK
362 Bayview Ave.
Amityville, NY 11701 516-789-8228
Drugs

High Plains Corp. HIPC
200 W. Douglas, Ste. 820
Wichita, KS 67202 316-269-4310
Energy - alternate sources

Hilite Industries, Inc. HILI
1671 S. Broadway
Carrollton, TX 75006 214-242-2116
Automotive & trucking - original equipment

Hingham Institution for Savings HIFS
55 Main St.
Hingham, MA 02043 617-749-2200
Financial - savings and loans

Hinsdale Financial Corp. HNFC
One Grant Square
Hinsdale, IL 60521 708-323-1776
Banks - midwest

Hirsch International Corp. HRSH
355 Marcus Blvd.
Hauppauge, NY 11788 516-436-7100
Machinery - general industrial

Hitox Corporation of America HTXA
418 Peoples St., PO Box 2544
Corpus Christi, TX 78403
512-882-5175
Metal ores - misc.

HMN Financial, Inc. HMNF
101 N. Broadway, PO Box 231
Spring Valley, MN 55975
507-346-7345
Banks - midwest

Hoenig & Co. Inc. HOEN
4 International Dr.
Rye Brook, NY 10573 914-935-9000
Financial - investment bankers

Hogan Systems, Inc. HOGN
5080 Spectrum Dr., Ste. 400E
Dallas, TX 75248 214-386-0020
Computers - software

Holiday RV Superstores, Inc. RVEE
7851 Greenbriar Parkway
Orlando, FL 32819 407-363-9211
Retail - misc.

Hollywood Casino Corp. HWCC
13455 Noel Rd., LB 48
Dallas, TX 75240 214-392-7777
Leisure & recreational services

Hollywood Entertainment Corp. HLYW
10300 S.W. Allen Blvd.
Beaverton, OR 97005
503-677-1600
Retail - misc. O

Hollywood Park, Inc. HPRK
1050 S. Prairie Ave.
Inglewood, CA 90301 310-419-1500
Real estate investment trust O

Hologic, Inc. HOLX
590 Lincoln St.
Waltham, MA 02154 617-890-2300
Medical instruments

HoloPak Technologies, Inc. HOLO
9 Cotters Ln.
East Brunswick, NJ 08816 908-238-2883
Miscellaneous - not elsewhere classified

Holophane Corp. HLPH
250 E. Broad St., Ste. 1400
Columbus, OH 43215 614-224-3134
Building products - lighting fixtures

Home Beneficial Corp. HBENB
3901 W. Broad St.
Richmond, VA 23230 804-358-8431
Insurance - life

Home Federal Bancorp HOMF
222 W. Second St., PO Box 648
Seymour, IN 47274 812-522-1592
Financial - savings and loans

Home Federal Corp. HFMD
122-128 W. Washington St.
Hagerstown, MD 21740 301-733-6300
Financial - savings and loans

Home Federal Financial Corp. HFSF
20 O'Farrell St.
San Francisco, CA 94108
415-982-4560
Financial - savings and loans

Home Financial Corp. HOFL
1720 Harrison St.
Hollywood, FL 33020
305-925-3211
Financial - savings and loans

Home Port Bancorp, Inc. HPBC
104 Pleasant St., PO Box 988
Nantucket, MA 02554 508-228-0580
Banks - northeast

Home State Holdings, Inc. HOMS
One Harding Rd.
Red Bank, NJ 07701 908-219-6600
Insurance - property & casualty

Home Theater Products HTPI
1620 S. Lewis St.
Anaheim, CA 92805 714-937-9300
Audio & video home products

Homecare Management, Inc. HMIS
80 Air Park Dr.
Ronkonkoma, NY 11779 516-981-0034
Healthcare - outpatient & home

HomeCorp, Inc. HMCI
1107 E. State St.
Rockford, IL 61104 815-987-2200
Banks - midwest

Homedco Group, Inc. HOME
17650 Newhope St.
Fountain Valley, CA 92708
714-755-5600
Healthcare - outpatient & home

Homeowners Group, Inc. HOMG
6365 Taft St., Ste. 2000
Hollywood, FL 33024
305-983-0350
Business services

Hometown Bancorporation, Inc. HTWN
20 West Ave.
Darien, CT 06820 203-656-2265
Banks - northeast

Hometown Buffet, Inc. HTBB
9171 Town Centre Dr., Ste. 575
San Diego, CA 92122 619-546-9096
Retail - food & restaurants

HON INDUSTRIES Inc. HONI
414 E. Third St., PO Box 1109
Muscatine, IA 52761 319-264-7400
Office equipment & supplies

Horizon Bancorp, Inc. HZWV
One Park Ave.
Beckley, WV 25802 304-255-7000
Banks - southeast

Horizon Bank, A Savings Bank HRZB
1500 Cornwall Ave.
Bellingham, WA 98225 206-733-3050
Financial - savings and loans

Hornbeck Offshore Services, Inc. HOSS
7707 Port Industrial Blvd.
Galveston, TX 77554 409-744-9500
Oil & gas - offshore drilling O

Horsehead Resource Development Co., Inc.
  HHRD
110 E. 59th St.
New York, NY 10022 212-527-3003
Pollution control equipment & services

Hosposable Products, Inc. HOSP
Central Jersey Industrial Park
Bound Brook, NJ 08805
908-469-8700
Medical & dental supplies

HPSC, Inc. HPSC
470 Atlantic Ave.
Boston, MA 02210 800-225-2488
Financial - mortgages & related services

HUBCO, Inc. HUBC
3100 Bergenline Ave.
Union City, NJ 07087 201-348-2300
Banks - northeast
[DRP]

Hudson Chartered Bancorp, Inc. HCBK
20 Mill St.
Rhinebeck, NY 12572 914-876-7041
Banks - northeast

Huffman Koos Inc. HUFK
Route 4 and Main St.
River Edge, NJ 07661 201-343-4300
Retail - home furnishings

Hugoton Energy Corp. HUGO
229 E. William, Ste. 500
Wichita, KS 67202 316-262-1522
Oil & gas - US exploration & production

Human Genome Sciences, Inc. HGSI
9620 Medical Center Dr.
Rockville, MD 20850 301-309-8504
Biomedical & genetic products

Huntco Inc. HUNT
14323 S. Outer Forty
Chesterfield, MO 63017 314-878-0155
Steel - production

Huntington Bancshares Inc. HBAN
Huntington Center
Columbus, OH 43287 614-476-8300
Banks - midwest O
[DRP 5%]

Hurco Mfg. Co., Inc. HURC
One Technology Way
Indianapolis, IN 46268 317-293-5309
Machine tools & related products

Hutchinson Technology Inc. HTCH
40 W. Highland Park
Hutchinson, MN 55350 612-587-3797
Computers - peripheral equipment

Hycor Biomedical Inc. HYBD
7272 Chapman Ave.
Garden Grove, CA 92641 714-895-9558
Medical products

Hyde Athletic Industries, Inc. HYDEA
13 Centennial Dr.
Peabody, MA 01960 508-532-9000
Shoes & related apparel

Hydron Technologies Inc. HTEC
941 Clint Moore Rd.
Boca Raton, FL 33487
407-994-6191
Medical & dental supplies

i-STAT Corp. STAT
303 College Rd. East
Princeton, NJ 08540 609-243-9300
Medical instruments

i-STAT Corp. STAT
303 College Rd. East
Princeton, NJ 08540 609-243-9300
Medical instruments

IBS Financial Corp. IBSF
1909 E. Route 70
Cherry Hill, NJ 08003 609-424-1000
Financial - savings and loans

ICO, Inc. ICOC
100 Glenborough Dr., Ste. 250
Houston, TX 77067 713-872-4994
Oil field machinery & equipment

ICOS Corp. ICOS
22021 20th Ave. S.E.
Bothell, WA 98021 206-485-1900
Drugs O

ICOT Corp. ICOT
3801 Zanker Rd., PO Box 5143
San Jose, CA 95150 408-433-3300
Computers - peripheral equipment

ICU Medical, Inc. ICUI
951 Calle Amanecer
San Clemente, CA 92673
714-753-1599
Medical products

IDB Communications Group, Inc. IDBX
10525 W. Washington Blvd.
Culver City, CA 90232 310-870-9000
Telecommunications services O

IDEC Pharmaceuticals Corp. IDPH
11011 Torreyana Rd.
San Diego, CA 92121
619-550-8500
Drugs

IDEXX Laboratories, Inc. IDXX
1 IDEXX Dr.
Westbrook, ME 04092 207-856-0300
Biomedical & genetic products

IEC Electronics Corp. IECE
105 Norton St., PO Box 271
Newark, NY 14513 315-331-7742
Electrical components - misc.

IFR Systems, Inc. IFRS
10200 W. York St.
Wichita, KS 67215 316-522-4981
Electronics - measuring instruments

IG Laboratories, Inc. IGLI
One Mountain Rd.
Framingham, MA 01701 508-872-8400
Medical services

IGEN, Inc. IGEN
1530 E. Jefferson St.
Rockville, MD 20852
301-984-8000
Medical instruments

IHOP Corp. IHOP
525 N. Brand Blvd.
Glendale, CA 91203 818-240-6055
Retail - food & restaurants O

II-VI Inc. IIVI
375 Saxonburg Blvd.
Saxonburg, PA 16056 412-352-4455
Electrical components - misc.

IKOS Systems, Inc. IKOS
19050 Pruneridge Ave.
Cupertino, CA 95014 408-255-4567
Computers - software

ILC Technology, Inc. ILCT
399 Java Dr.
Sunnyvale, CA 94089 408-745-7900
Instruments - control

Illinois Superconductor Corp. ISCO
01840 Oak Ave.
Evanston, IL 60201 708-866-0435
Electronics - components & systems

Image Entertainment, Inc. DISK
9333 Oso Ave.
Chatsworth, CA 91311 818-407-9100
Leisure & recreational products

Image Industries, Inc. IMAG
Highway 140
Armuchee, GA 30105 706-235-8444
Recycling - metal & plastic

Imatron Inc. IMAT
389 Oyster Point Blvd.
South San Francisco, CA 94080
415-583-9964
Medical instruments

ImClone Systems, Inc. IMCL
180 Varick St.
New York, NY 10014
212-645-1405
Biomedical & genetic products

Immucor, Inc. BLUD
3130 Gateway Dr.
Norcross, GA 30071 404-441-2051
Medical & dental supplies

ImmuLogic Pharmaceutical Corp. IMUL
610 Lincoln St.
Waltham, MA 02154 617-466-6000
Biomedical & genetic products

Immunex Corp. IMNX
51 University St.
Seattle, WA 98101 206-587-0430
Biomedical & genetic products O

ImmunoGen, Inc. IMGN
128 Sydney St.
Cambridge, MA 02139 617-661-9312
Drugs

Immunomedics, Inc. IMMU
150 Mt. Bethel Rd.
Warren, NJ 07059 201-605-8200
Biomedical & genetic products O

IMP, Inc. IMPX
2830 N. First St.
San Jose, CA 95134 408-432-9100
Electronics - components & systems

Impact Systems, Inc. MPAC
1075 E. Brokaw Rd.
San Jose, CA 95131 408-453-3700
Instruments - control

Imperial Bancorp IBAN
PO Box 92991
Los Angeles, CA 90009 310-417-5600
Banks - west
[DRP]

Imperial Credit Industries, Inc. ICII
20371 Irvine Ave.
Santa Ana Heights, CA 92707
714-556-0122
Financial - mortgages & related services

IMRS Inc. IMRS
777 Long Ridge Rd.
Stamford, CT 06902 203-321-3500
Computers - software

In Focus Systems, Inc. INFS
27700B SW Parkway Ave.
Wilsonville, OR 97070 503-685-8888
Computers - peripheral equipment O

In Home Health, Inc. IHHI
601 Lakeshore Parkway
Minnetonka, MN 55305
612-449-7500
Healthcare - outpatient & home

Inacom, Inc. INAC
10810 Farnam Dr.
Omaha, NE 68154 402-392-3900
Computers - retail & wholesale

INBRAND Corp. INBR
1165 Hayes Industrial Dr.
Marietta, GA 30062 404-422-3036
Medical products

Inco Homes Corp. INHM
1282 W. Arrow Hwy., PO Box 970
Upland, CA 91786 909-981-8989
Building - residential & commercial

InControl, Inc. INCL
6675 185th Ave. NE
Redmond, WA 98052 206-861-9800
Medical products

Independence Holding Co. INHO
PO Box 10229
Stamford, CT 06904 203-358-8000
Financial - business services

Independent Bank Corp. IBCP
230 W. Main St., PO Box 491
Ionia, MI 48846 616-527-9450
Banks - midwest
[DRP 5%]

Independent Bank Corp. INDB
288 Union St.
Rockland, MA 02370 617-878-6100
Banks - midwest

Independent Entertainment Group, Inc.
INDE
15303 Ventura Blvd., Ste. 1000
Sherman Oaks, CA 91403 818-501-4633
Telecommunications services

Independent Insurance Group, Inc.
INDHK
One Independent Dr.
Jacksonville, FL 32276 904-358-5151
Insurance - life

Indiana Federal Corp. IFSL
56 S. Washington St.
Valparaiso, IN 46383 219-462-4131
Banks - midwest

Indiana United Bancorp IUBC
201 N. Broadway, PO Box 87
Greenburg, IN 47240 812-663-4711
Banks - midwest

Industrial Acoustics Co., Inc. IACI
1160 Commerce Ave.
Bronx, NY 10462 718-931-8000
Pollution control equipment & services

Industrial Holdings, Inc. IHII
7135 Ardmore
Houston, TX 77054 713-747-1025
Machinery - general industrial

Industrial Scientific Corp. ISCX
1001 Oakdale Rd.
Oakdale, PA 15071 412-788-4353
Electronics - measuring instruments

Industrial Training Corp. ITCC
13515 Dulles Technology Dr.
Herndon, VA 22071 703-713-3335
Miscellaneous - not elsewhere classified

Infinity Broadcasting Corp. INFTA
600 Madison Ave.
New York, NY 10022 212-750-6400
Broadcasting - radio & TV O

Infodata Systems Inc. INFD
12150 Monument Dr.
Fairfax, VA 22033 703-934-5205
Computers - software

Information International, Inc. IINT
5933 Slauson Ave.
Culver City, CA 90233 310-390-8611
Machinery - printing

Information Resource Engineering Inc.
IREG
5024 Campbell Blvd.
Baltimore, MD 21236 410-931-7500
Computers - software O

Information Resources, Inc. IRIC
150 N. Clinton St.
Chicago, IL 60661 312-726-1221
Data collection & systems

Informix Corp. IFMX
4100 Bohannon Dr.
Menlo Park, CA 94025 415-926-6300
Computers - software O

InfoSoft International, Inc. INSO
222 Berkeley St.
Boston, MA 02116 617-351-3000
Computers - software

Infrasonics, Inc. IFRA
3911 Sorrento Valley Rd.
San Diego, CA 92121 619-450-9898
Medical products

Infu-Tech, Inc. INFU
900 Sylvan Ave.
Englewood Cliff, NJ 07632
201-567-4600
Medical services

Ingles Markets, Inc. IMKTA
PO Box 6676
Asheville, NC 28816 704-669-2941
Retail - supermarkets

Inhale Therapeutic Systems INHL
1001 E. Meadow Circle
Palo Alto, CA 94303 415-354-0700
Drugs

Inmac Corp. INMC
2465 Augustine Dr.
Santa Clara, CA 95052 408-727-1970
Retail - mail order & direct

InnerDyne, Inc. IDYN
5060 W. Amelia Earhart Dr.
Salt Lake City, UT 84116
801-350-3600
Medical products

Innkeepers USA Trust NKPR
5255 Federal Hwy., Ste. 100
Boca Raton, FL 33487 407-994-1701
Real estate investment trust

Innodata Corp. INOD
95 Rockwell Place
Brooklyn, NY 11217
718-625-7750
Data collection & systems

Innovex, Inc. INVX
1313 5th St. South
Hopkins, MN 55343 612-938-4155
Photographic equipment & supplies

INOTEK Technologies Corp. INTK
11212 Indian Trail
Dallas, TX 75229 214-243-7000
Instruments - control

Insignia Financial Group, Inc. IFGI
PO Box 1089
Greenville, SC 29602
803-239-1000
Real estate operations

Insilco Corp. INSL
425 Metro Place North
Dublin, OH 43017 614-792-0468
Diversified operations

InSite Vision Inc. INSV
965 Atlantic Ave.
Alameda, CA 94501 510-865-8800
Medical products

Insituform East, Inc. INEI
3421 Pennsy Dr.
Landover, MD 20785 301-386-4100
Building products - misc. O

Insituform Mid-America, Inc. INSMA
17988 Edison Ave.
Chesterfield, MO 63005 314-532-6137
Building products - misc.

Insituform Technologies, Inc. INSUA
1770 Kirby Parkway, Ste. 300
Memphis, TN 38138 901-759-7473
Building products - misc.

Insurance Auto Auctions, Inc. IAAI
7245 Laurel Canyon Blvd.
North Hollywood, CA 91605
818-764-3200
Insurance - property & casualty

IntegraCare, Inc. ITEG
551 S.E. 8th St.
Delray Beach, FL 33483 407-274-0204
Healthcare - outpatient & home

Integrated Circuit Systems, Inc. ICST
2435 Blvd. of the Generals
Norristown, PA 19403 610-630-5300
Electrical components - misc.

Integrated Device Technology, Inc. IDTI
2975 Stender Way
Santa Clara, CA 95054 408-727-6116
Electrical components - semiconductors O

Integrated Silicon Systems, Inc. ISSS
2222 Chapel Hill-Nelson Hwy.
Durham, NC 27713 919-361-5814
Computers - software

Integrated Systems, Inc. INTS
3260 Jay St.
Santa Clara, CA 95054 408-980-1500
Computers - software

Integrated Waste Services, Inc. IWSI
201 Ganson St.
Buffalo, NY 14203 716-852-2345
Pollution control equipment & services

Integrity Music, Inc. ITGR
1000 Cody Rd.
Mobile, AL 36695 205-633-9000
Miscellaneous - not elsewhere classified

Intel Corp.
2200 Mission College Blvd.
Santa Clara, CA 95052 408-765-8080
Electrical components - semiconductors O
[DRP]

Intelligent Electronics, Inc. INEL
411 Eagleview Blvd.
Exton, PA 19341 215-458-5500
Computers - retail & wholesale O

Intelligent Surgical Lasers Inc. ISLS
4520 Executive Dr., Ste. One
San Diego, CA 92121
619-552-6700
Lasers - systems & components

Inter-Tel, Inc. INTL
7300 W. Boston St.
Chandler, AZ 85226 602-961-9000
Telecommunications services

Interactive Network, Inc. INNN
1991 Landings Dr.
Mountain View, CA 94043
415-903-4000
Leisure & recreational products O

Intercargo Corp. ICAR
1450 American Ln., 20th Fl.
Schaumburg, IL 60173 708-517-2510
Insurance - property & casualty

InterCel, Inc. ICEL
421 Gilmer Ave., PO Box 657
Lanett, AL 36863 205-644-2355
Telecommunications services

Intercontinental Bank ICBK
200 S.E. First St.
Miami, FL 33131 305-377-6900
Banks - southeast

Interface Systems, Inc. INTF
5855 Interface Dr.
Ann Arbor, MI 48103 313-769-5900
Computers - peripheral equipment

Interface, Inc. IFSIA
Orchard Hill Rd., PO Box 1503
LaGrange, GA 30241 404-882-1891
Textiles - home furnishings

Interferon Sciences, Inc. IFSC
783 Jersey Ave.
New Brunswick, NJ 08901
908-249-3250
Medical services

Interfilm, Inc. IFLM
110 Greene St., Ste. 711
New York, NY 10012 212-334-5900
Motion pictures & services

Intergraph Corp. INGR
Huntsville, AL 35894 205-730-2000
Computers - graphics O

Intergroup Corp. INTG
2121 Avenue of the Stars
Los Angeles, CA 90067 310-556-1999
Real estate operations

Interim Services, Inc. INTM
2050 Spectrum Blvd.
Fort Lauderdale, FL 33309
305-938-7600
Business services

Interleaf, Inc. LEAF
9 Hillside Ave.
Waltham, MA 02154 617-290-0710
Computers - software

Interlinq Software Corp. INLQ
11255 Kirkland Way
Kirkland, WA 98033 206-827-1112
Computers - software

Intermedia Communications of Florida, Inc.
ICIX
9280 Bay Plaza Blvd., Ste. 720
Tampa, FL 33619 813-621-0011
Telecommunications services

Intermet Corp. INMT
2859 Paces Ferry Rd.
Atlanta, GA 30339 404-431-6000
Automotive & trucking - original equipment

Intermetrics, Inc. IMET
733 Concord Ave.
Cambridge, MA 02138 617-661-1840
Computers - software

International Cablecasting Technologies, Inc.
TUNE
11400 W. Olympic Blvd.
Los Angeles, CA 90064 310-444-1744
Leisure & recreational services

International CableTel, Inc. ICTL
150 E. 58th St.
New York, NY 10155 212-371-3714
Telecommunications services O

International Dairy Queen, Inc. INDQA
7505 Metro Blvd.
Minneapolis, MN 55439 612-830-0200
Retail - food & restaurants

International Imaging Materials, Inc.
IMAK
310 Commerce Dr.
Amherst, NY 14228 716-691-6333
Miscellaneous - not elsewhere classified

International Jensen, Inc. IJIN
25 Tri-State Intl. Off. Center
Lincolnshire, IL 60069 708-317-3700
Audio & video home products

International Lottery & Totalizator Systems
Inc ITSI
2131 Faraday Ave.
Carlsbad, CA 92008 619-931-4000
Leisure & recreational products

International Post Ltd. POST
545 Fifth Ave.
New York, NY 10017 212-986-6300
Motion pictures & services

International Research and Development
Corp. IRDV
500 N. Main St.
Mattawan, MI 49071 616-668-3336
Medical products

International Vitamin Corp. IVCO
209 40th St.
Irvington, NJ 07111 201-371-7300
Drugs

Interneuron Pharmaceuticals, Inc. IPIC
99 Hayden Ave., Ste. 340
Lexington, MA 02173 617-861-8444
Drugs

Interphase Corp. INPH
13800 Senlac
Dallas, TX 75234 214-919-9000
Computers - peripheral equipment

Interpoint Corp. INTP
10301 Willows Rd.
Redmond, WA 98073 206-882-3100
Electrical components - misc.

Interpore International BONZ
181 Technology Dr.
Irvine, CA 92714 714-453-3200
Biomedical & genetic products

INTERSOLV, Inc. ISLI
3200 Tower Oaks Blvd.
Rockville, MD 20852 301-230-3200
Computers - software

Intertrans Corp. ITRN
125 E. John Carpenter Freeway
Irving, TX 75062 214-830-8888
Transportation - services

Intervisual Books, Inc. IVBK
2850 Ocean Park Blvd.
Santa Monica, CA 90405
310-396-8708
Publishing - books

InterVoice, Inc. INTV
17811 Waterview Parkway
Dallas, TX 75252 214-454-8000
Telecommunications equipment O

InterWest Savings Bank IWBK
1259 W. Pioneer Way
Oak Harbor, WA 98277 206-679-4181
Financial - savings and loans

Intuit, Inc. INTU
155 Linfield Ave.
Menlo Park, CA 94025 415-322-0570
Computers - software O

Invacare Corp. IVCR
899 Cleveland St., PO Box 4028
Elyria, OH 44036 216-329-6000
Medical & dental supplies O

Investment Technology Group, Inc.
ITGI
900 Third Ave., 2nd Fl.
New York, NY 10022 212-755-6800
Computers - services

Investors Bank Corp. INVS
200 E. Lake St.
Wayzata, MN 55391 612-475-8500
Financial - savings and loans

Investors Title Co. ITIC
121 N. Columbia St.
Chapel Hill, NC 27514 919-968-2200
Insurance - multi line & misc.

Iomega Corp. IOMG
1821 W. Iomega Way
Roy, UT 84067 801-778-1000
Computers - peripheral equipment

Iowa National Bankshares Corp. INBS
229 E. Park Ave., PO Box 5300
Waterloo, IA 50704 319-291-5260
Banks - midwest

IPL Systems, Inc. IPLSA
124 Acton St.
Maynard, MA 01754 508-461-1000
Computers - peripheral equipment

IQ Software Corp. IQSW
3295 River Exchange Dr.
Norcross, GA 30092
404-446-8880
Computers - software

IRG Technologies Inc. IRGTE
1235 W. Trinity Mills
Carrollton, TX 75006 214-699-8300
Computers - peripheral equipment

Iroquois Bancorp, Inc. IROQ
115 Genesee St.
Auburn, NY 13021 315-252-9521
Banks - northeast

Irwin Financial Corp. IRWN
500 Washington St., PO Box 929
Columbus, IN 47202 812-376-1020
Financial - business services

Isco, Inc. ISKO
531 Westage Blvd.
Lincoln, NE 68501 402-474-2233
Instruments - scientific

Isis Pharmaceuticals, Inc. ISIP
2280 Faraday Ave.
Carlsbad, CA 92008
619-931-9200
Drugs

Isolyser Company, Inc. OREX
4320 International Blvd. NW
Norcross, GA 30093 404-381-7566
Chemicals - specialty

Isomedix Inc. ISMX
11 Apollo Dr.
Whippany, NJ 07981 201-887-4700
Medical & dental supplies

ITI Technologies, Inc. ITII
2266 N. Second St.
North St. Paul, MN 55109 612-777-2690
Protection - safety equipment & services

Itron, Inc. ITRI
2818 N. Sullivan Rd.
Spokane, WA 99216 509-924-9900
Electronics - measuring instruments

IVF America, Inc. IVFA
500 W. Putnam Ave.
Greenwich, CT 06830
203-622-7230
Medical services

IVI Publishing, Inc. IVIP
1380 Corporate Center Curve
Eagen, MN 55121 612-686-2600
Publishing - multimedia

IWC Resources Corp. IWCR
1220 Waterway Blvd.
Indianapolis, IN 46202 317-639-1501
Utility - water supply
[DRP]

Iwerks Entertainment, Inc. IWRK
4540 W. Valerio St.
Burbank, CA 91505 818-841-7766
Motion pictures & services

J & J Snack Foods Corp. JJSF
6000 Central Hwy.
Pennsauken, NJ 08109 609-665-9533
Food - misc.

J. Baker, Inc. JBAK
555 Turnpike St.
Canton, MA 02021 617-828-9300
Retail - apparel & shoes

J. W. Mays, Inc. MAYS
9 Bond St.
Brooklyn, NY 11201 718-624-7400
Retail - regional department stores

J.B. Hunt Transport Services, Inc. JBHT
615 J.B. Hunt Corporate Dr.
Lowell, AR 72745 501-820-0000
Transportation - truck

Jabil Circuit, Inc. JBIL
10800 Roosevelt Blvd.
St. Petersburg, FL 33716 813-577-9749
Electronics - components & systems

Jack Henry & Associates, Inc. JKHY
663 Highway 60, PO Box 807
Monett, MO 65708 417-235-6652
Computers - software

Jackson Hewitt, Inc. JTAX
4575 Bonney Rd.
Virginia Beach, VA 23462
804-473-3300
Business services

Jaco Electronics, Inc. JACO
145 Oser Ave.
Hauppauge, NY 11788 516-273-5500
Electronics - parts distribution

Jacobson Stores Inc. JCBS
3333 Sargent Rd.
Jackson, MI 49201 517-764-6400
Retail - regional department stores
[DRP]

Jacor Communications, Inc. JCOR
201 E. Fifth St.
Cincinnati, OH 45202 513-621-1300
Broadcasting - radio & TV

Jameson Inns, Inc. JAMS
1950 Century Blvd. N.E.
Atlanta, GA 30345 404-636-2973
Hotels & motels

Jasmine, Ltd. JSMN
130 Twinbridge Dr.
Pennsauken, NJ 08110
609-665-7117
Shoes & related apparel

Jason Inc. JASN
411 E. Wisconsin Ave.
Milwaukee, WI 53202 414-277-9300
Automotive & trucking - original equipment

Jay Jacobs, Inc. JAYJQ
1530 Fifth Ave.
Seattle, WA 98101 206-622-5400
Retail - apparel & shoes

JB Oxford Holdings, Inc. RKSF
9665 Wilshire Blvd., Third Fl.
Beverly Hills, CA 90212 310-777-8888
Financial - business services

JB's Restaurants, Inc. JBBB
1010 W. 2610 South
Salt Lake City, UT 84119
801-974-4300
Retail - food & restaurants

Jean Philippe Fragrances, Inc. JEAN
551 Fifth Ave.
New York, NY 10176 212-983-2640
Cosmetics & toiletries

Jefferies Group, Inc. JEFG
11100 Santa Monica Blvd.
Los Angeles, CA 90025 310-445-1199
Financial - investment bankers

Jefferson Bancorp, Inc. JEBC
1011 Fourth St., PO Box 326
Gretna, LA 70054 504-368-1011
Banks - southeast

Jefferson Bankshares, Inc. JBNK
123 E. Main St.
Charlottesville, VA 22902 804-972-1100
Banks - southeast
[DRP]

Jefferson Savings and Loan JEFF
PO Box 421
Warrenton, VA 22186 703-347-3531
Financial - savings and loans

Jefferson Savings Bancorp, Inc. JSBA
14915 Manchester Rd.
Ballwin, MO 63011 314-227-3000
Financial - savings and loans

Jennifer Convertibles, Inc. JENN
419 Crossways Park Drive
Woodbury, NY 11797 516-496-1900
Furniture

JG Industries, Inc. JGIN
1615 W. Chicago Ave.
Chicago, IL 60622 312-850-8000
Retail - regional department stores

JLG Industries, Inc. JLGI
JLG Dr.
McConnellsburg, PA 17233
717-485-5161
Machinery - construction & mining

JMAR Industries, Inc. JMAR
3956 Sorrento Valley Blvd.
San Diego, CA 92121 619-535-1706
Lasers - systems & components

JMC Group, Inc. JMCG
9710 Scranton Rd., Ste. 100
San Diego, CA 92121 619-450-0055
Financial - business services

John B. Sanfilippo & Son, Inc. JBSS
2299 Busse Rd.
Elk Grove Village, IL 60007
708-593-2300
Food - wholesale

John Wiley & Sons, Inc. WILLA
605 Third Ave.
New York, NY 10158 212-850-6000
Publishing - books

Johnson Worldwide Associates, Inc.
JWAIA
222 Main St.
Racine, WI 53403 414-631-2100
Leisure & recreational products

Johnstown America Industries, Inc. JAII
17 Johns St.
Johnstown, PA 15901 814-533-5000
Transportation - equipment & leasing

Jones Intercable, Inc. JOIN
9697 E. Mineral Ave.
Englewood, CO 80112 303-792-3111
Cable TV

Jones Medical Industries, Inc. JMED
1945 Craig Rd.
St. Louis, MO 63146 314-576-6100
Drugs

Jones Spacelink, Ltd. SPLKA
PO Box 3309
Englewood, CO 80155 303-792-9191
Cable TV

Jos. A. Bank Clothiers, Inc. JOSB
500 Hanover Pike
Hampstead, MD 21074 410-239-2700
Apparel

Joslyn Corp. JOSL
30 S. Wacker Dr.
Chicago, IL 60606 312-454-2900
Electrical products - misc.
[DRP]

JP Foodservice, Inc. JPFS
9830 Patuxent Woods Dr.
Columbia, MD 21046 410-312-7100
Food - wholesale

JPE, Inc. JPEI
900 Victors Way, Ste. 140
Ann Arbor, MI 48108 313-662-2323
Automotive & trucking - original equipment

JSB Financial, Inc. JSBF
303 Merrick Rd.
Lynbrook, NY 11563 516-887-7000
Financial - savings and loans

Juno Lighting, Inc. JUNO
2001 S. Mt. Prospect Rd.
Des Plaines, IL 60017 708-827-9880
Building products - lighting fixtures

Just For Feet, Inc. FEET
3000 Riverchase Galleria
Birmingham, AL 35244 205-987-3450
Shoes & related apparel

Just Toys, Inc. JUST
50 W. 23rd St.
New York, NY 10010 212-645-6335
Toys - games & hobby products

Justin Industries, Inc. JSTN
2821 W. 7th St., PO Box 425
Fort Worth, TX 76101 817-336-5125
Shoes & related apparel O
[DRP]

K-Swiss, Inc. KSWS
12300 Montague St.
Pacoima, CA 91331 818-998-3388
Shoes & related apparel

K-tel International, Inc. KTEL
15525 Medina Rd.
Plymouth, MN 55447 612-559-6888
Leisure & recreational products

K-Tron International, Inc. KTII
1810 Chapel Ave. West
Cherry Hill, NJ 08002 609-661-6240
Instruments - control

Kahler Realty Corp. KHLR
20 S.W. Second Ave.
Rochester, MN 55902 507-282-2581
Hotels & motels

Kaiser Resources, Inc. KRSC
8300 Utica Ave., Ste. 301
Rancho Cucamonga, CA 91730
909-944-4155
Miscellaneous - not elsewhere classified

Kaman Corp. KAMNA
Blue Hills Ave.
Bloomfield, CT 06002 203-243-7100
Aerospace - aircraft equipment
[DRP]

Kankakee Bancorp, Inc. KNKB
310 S. Schuyler Ave., PO Box 3
Kankakee, IL 60901 815-937-4440
Banks - midwest

KBK Capital Corp. KBKC
301 Commerce Street
Fort Worth, TX 76102 817-335-7557
Financial - business services

Keene Corp. KEEN
757 Third Ave.
New York, NY 10017 212-486-3200
Aerospace - materials

Kelley Oil Corp. KOIL
601 Jefferson St., Ste. 1100
Houston, TX 77002 713-652-5200
Oil & gas - US exploration & production O

Kelly Services, Inc. KELYA
999 W. Big Beaver Rd.
Troy, MI 48084 313-362-4444
Personnel

Kemet Corp. KMET
2835 Kemet Way
Simpsonville, SC 29681 803-963-6300
Electronics - components & systems

Kenan Transport Co. KTCO
143 W. Franklin St.
Chapel Hill, NC 27515 919-967-8221
Transportation - truck

Kenetech Corp. KWND
500 Sansome St., Ste. 800
San Francisco, CA 94111
415-398-3825
Engineering - R & D services O

Kennedy-Wilson, Inc. KWIC
2950 31st St., Ste. 300
Santa Monica, CA 90405
310-314-8400
Real estate operations

Kentucky Electric Steel, Inc. KESI
PO Box 3500
Ashland, KY 41105 606-928-6441
Steel - production

Kentucky Enterprise Bancorp, Inc. KEBI
800 Monmouth St.
Newport, KY 41071 606-261-3050
Financial - savings and loans

Kentucky Medical Insurance Co. KYMDA
303 N. Hurstbourne Parkway
Louisville, KY 40222 502-339-5700
Insurance - accident & health

Kevlin Corp. KVLM
5 Cornell Place
Wilmington, MA 01887
508-657-3900
Telecommunications equipment

Kewaunee Scientific Corp. KEQU
1144 Wilmette Ave.
Wilmette, IL 60091 704-873-7202
Furniture

Key Production Co. KPCI
1700 Lincoln St., Ste. 2050
Denver, CO 80203 303-837-0779
Oil & gas - US exploration & production

Key Technology, Inc. KTEC
150 Avery St.
Walla Walla, WA 99362 509-529-2161
Machinery - material handling

Key Tronic Corp. KTCC
N. 4424 Sullivan Rd.
Spokane, WA 99216 509-928-8000
Computers - peripheral equipment

Keystone Financial, Inc. KSTN
One Keystone Plaza
Harrisburg, PA 17105 717-233-1555
Banks - northeast
[DRP]

Keystone Heritage Group, Inc. KHGI
555 Willow St., PO Box 1285
Lebanon, PA 17042 717-274-6800
Banks - northeast
[DRP]

Kimball International, Inc. KBALB
1600 Royal St.
Jasper, IN 47549 812-482-1600
Furniture

KinderCare Learning Centers, Inc. KCLC
2400 Presidents Dr.
Montgomery, AL 36116 205-277-5090
Schools

Kinetic Concepts, Inc. KNCI
8023 Vantage Dr.
San Antonio, TX 78230 210-524-9000
Medical products

Kinnard Investments, Inc. KINN
1700 Northstar Center
Minneapolis, MN 505402 612-370-2700
Financial - business services

KLA Instruments Corp. KLAC
160 Rio Robles, PO Box 49055
San Jose, CA 95161 408-434-4200
Machinery - general industrial O

Kleinert's, Inc. KLRT
120 W. Germantown Pike
Plymouth Meeting, PA 19462 610-828-7261
Apparel

KLLM Transport Services, Inc. KLLM
3475 Lakeland Dr.
Jackson, MS 39208 601-939-2545
Transportation - truck

Knape & Vogt Manufacturing Co. KNAP
2700 Oak Industrial Dr., N.E.
Grand Rapids, MI 49505 616-459-3311
Furniture [DRP]

Knight Transportation, Inc. KNGT
5601 W. Buckeye Rd.
Phoenix, AZ 85043 602-269-2000
Transportation - truck

Koala Corp. KARE
4390 McMenemy Rd.
St. Paul, MN 55127 612-490-1535
Protection - safety equipment & services

Koll Real Estate Group, Inc. KREG
4343 Von Karman Ave.
Newport Beach, CA 92660
714-833-3030
Real estate operations

Komag, Inc. KMAG
275 S. Hillview Dr.
Milpitas, CA 95035 408-946-2300
Computers - peripheral equipment O

Kopin Corp. KOPN
695 Myles Standish Blvd.
Taunton, MA 02780 508-824-6696
Electrical components - misc.

Koss Corp. KOSS
4129 N. Port Washington Ave.
Milwaukee, WI 53212 414-964-5000
Audio & video home products

Kronos, Inc. KRON
62 Fourth Ave.
Waltham, MA 02154 617-890-3232
Miscellaneous - not elsewhere classified

KRUG International Corp. KRUG
6 N. Main St., Ste. 500
Dayton, OH 45402 513-224-9066
Diversified operations

Kulicke & Soffa Industries, Inc. KLIC
2101 Blair Mill Rd.
Willow Grove, PA 19090 215-784-6000
Electrical components - semiconductors O

Kurzweil Applied Intelligence Inc. KURZE
411 Waverly Oaks Rd.
Waltham, MA 02154 617-893-5151
Computers - software

Kushner-Locke Co. KLOC
11601 Wilshire Blvd., 21st Fl.
Los Angeles, CA 90025
310-445-1111
Leisure & recreational products

L. B. Foster Co. FSTRA
415 Holiday Dr.
Pittsburgh, PA 15220 412-928-3400
Steel - pipes & tubes

L.A.T. Sportswear, Inc. LATS
1200 Airport Dr.
Ball Ground, GA 30107 404-521-0142
Apparel

La Jolla Pharmaceutical Co. LJPC
06455 Nancy Ridge Dr.
San Diego, CA 92121
619-452-6600
Drugs

LabOne, Inc. LABS
10310 W. 84th Terrace
Lenaxa, KS 66214 913-888-8397
Medical & dental supplies

Laclede Steel Co. LCLD
One Metropolitan Square
St. Louis, MO 63102
314-425-1400
Steel - specialty alloys

LaCrosse Footwear, Inc. BOOT
1319 St. Andrew St.
LaCrosse, WI 54603 608-782-3020
Shoes & related apparel

LADD Furniture, Inc. LADF
One Plaza Center, Box HP-3
High Point, NC 27261 910-889-0333
Furniture

Lady Luck Gaming Corp. LUCK
206 N. Third St.
Las Vegas, NV 89101 702-477-3000
Leisure & recreational services

Lafayette American Bank and Trust Co. LABK
1087 Broad St.
Bridgeport, CT 06601 203-336-6200
Banks - northeast

Lakeland First Financial Group, Inc. LLSL
250 Route 10
Succasunna, NJ 07876 201-584-6666
Financial - savings and loans
[DRP]

Lakeland Industries, Inc. LAKE
1 Comac Loop
Ronkonkoma, NY 11779 516-981-9700
Textiles - apparel

Lakeview Financial Corp. LVSB
1117 Main St.
Paterson, NJ 07503 201-742-3060
Financial - savings and loans

Lam Research Corp. LRCX
4650 Cushing Parkway
Fremont, CA 94538 510-659-0200
Electrical components - semiconductors O

Lancaster Colony Corp. LANC
37 W. Broad St.
Columbus, OH 43215 614-224-7141
Diversified operations O
[DRP]

Lance, Inc. LNCE
8600 S. Boulevard
Charlotte, NC 28232 704-554-1421
Food - misc.
[DRP]

Lancit Media Productions, Ltd. LNCT
601 W. 50th St., Penthouse
New York, NY 10019 212-977-9100
Motion pictures & services

Landair Services, Inc. LAND
430 Airport Rd.
Greeneville, TN 37743 615-639-7169
Transportation - services

Landmark Bancorp LMBC
401 W. Whittier Blvd.
La Habra, CA 90631 310-694-6537
Banks - west O

Landmark Bancshares, Inc. LARK
Central and Spruce Sts.
Dodge City, KS 67801 316-227-8111
Banks - midwest

Landmark Graphics Corp. LMRK
15150 Memorial Dr.
Houston, TX 77079 713-560-1000
Computers - software

Landry's Seafood Restaurants, Inc.
LDRY
1400 Post Oak Blvd., Ste. 1010
Houston, TX 77056 713-850-1010
Retail - food & restaurants

Landstar Systems, Inc. LSTR
1000 Bridgeport Ave.
Shelton, CT 06484 203-925-2900
Transportation - truck O

Laser Precision Corp. LASR
32242 Paseo Adelanto, Ste. A
San Juan Capistrano, CA 92675
714-489-2991
Electronics - measuring instruments

Laser-Pacific Media Corp. LPAC
809 N. Cahuenga Blvd.
Hollywood, CA 90038 213-462-6266
Motion pictures & services

LaserMaster Technologies, Inc. LMTS
9955 W. 69th St.
Eden Prairie, MN 55344 612-941-8687
Computers - peripheral equipment

Laserscope LSCP
3052 Orchard Dr.
San Jose, CA 95134 408-943-0636
Lasers - systems & components

Latin American Casinos, Inc. LACI
11401 N.W. Seventh Ave.
Miami, FL 33168 305-756-1000
Retail - misc.

Lattice Semiconductor Corp. LSCC
5555 N.E. Moore Court
Hillsboro, OR 97124 503-681-0118
Electrical components - semiconductors O

Laurel Bancorp, Inc. LAUR
8101 Sandy Spring Rd.
Laurel, MD 20707 301-951-1919
Financial - savings and loans

Lawrence Savings Bank LSBX
30 Massachusetts Ave.
North Andover, MA 01845
508-687-1131
Banks - northeast

Lawson Products, Inc. LAWS
1666 E. Touhy Ave.
Des Plaines, IL 60018 708-827-9666
Metal products - distribution

Lawyers Title Corp. LTCO
6630 W. Broad St.
Richmond, VA 23230 804-281-6700
Business services

Layne, Inc. LAYN
1900 Shawnee Mission Pkwy.
Mission Woods, KS 66205
913-362-0510
Miscellaneous - not elsewhere classified

Lazer-Tron Corp. LZTN
4430 Willow Rd.
Pleasanton, CA 94588 510-460-0873
Leisure & recreational products

LCI International, Inc. LCII
8180 Greenboro Dr., Ste. 800
McLean, VA 22102 703-442-0220
Telecommunications services

LCS Industries, Inc. LCSI
120 Brighton Rd.
Clifton, NJ 07012 201-778-5588
Retail - mail order & direct

LDDS Communications, Inc. LDDS
515 E. Amite St.
Jackson, MS 39201 601-360-8600
Telecommunications services O

LDI Corp. LDIC
1375 E. Ninth St.
Cleveland, OH 44114 216-687-0100
Computers - services

Leader Financial Corp. LFCT
158 Madison Ave.
Memphis, TN 38103 901-578-2000
Banks - southeast

Learning Co. LRNG
6493 Kaiser Dr.
Fremont, CA 94555 510-792-2101
Computers - software

Leaseway Transportation Corp. LSWY
3700 Park East Dr.
Beachwood, OH 44122
216-765-5500
Transportation - truck

Leasing Solutions, Inc. LSSI
10 Almaden Blvd., Ste. 1500
San Jose, CA 95113
408-995-6565
Leasing

Lechters, Inc. LECH
One Cape May St.
Harrison, NJ 07029 201-481-1100
Retail - discount & variety

LecTec Corp. LECT
10701 Red Circle Dr.
Minnetonka, MN 55343 612-933-2291
Medical products

Leeds Federal Savings Bank LFED
1101 Maiden Choice Ln.
Baltimore, MD 21229 410-242-1234
Financial - savings and loans

LEGENT Corp. LGNT
575 Herndon Parkway
Herndon, VA 22070 703-708-3000
Computers - software O

Leisure Concepts, Inc. LCIC
1414 Avenue of the Americas
New York, NY 10019 212-758-7666
Business services

LESCO, Inc. LSCO
20005 Lake Rd.
Rocky River, OH 44116 216-333-9250
Building - maintenance & services

Leslie's Poolmart LESL
20222 Plummer St.
Chatsworth, CA 91311 818-993-4212
Retail - misc.

Level One Communications, Inc. LEVL
105 Lake Forest Way
Folsom, CA 95630 916-985-3670
Telecommunications equipment

Lexington Precision Corp. LEXP
767 Third Ave., 29th Fl.
New York, NY 10017 212-319-4657
Diversified operations

Lexington Savings Bank LEXB
1776 Massachusetts Ave.
Lexington, MA 02173
617-862-1775
Financial - savings and loans

LFS Bancorp, Inc. LFSB
2020 Nicholasville Rd.
Lexington, KY 40503 606-278-3461
Financial - savings and loans

LGF Bancorp, Inc. LGFB
One N. La Grange Rd.
La Grange, IL 60525
708-352-3671
Banks - midwest

Liberty Bancorp, Inc. LBNA
100 N. Broadway
Oklahoma City, OK 73102
405-231-6000
Banks - southwest

Liberty Bancorp, Inc. LBCI
5700 N. Lincoln Ave.
Chicago, IL 60659 312-334-1200
Financial - savings and loans

Liberty Homes, Inc. LIBHA
1101 Eisenhower Dr., North
Goshen, IN 46526 219-533-0431
Building - mobile homes & RV

Liberty Technologies, Inc. LIBT
555 North Ln.
Conshohocken, PA 19428 215-834-0330
Engineering - R & D services

Lida, Inc. LIDA
2222 S. Boulevard
Charlotte, NC 28203 704-376-5609
Textiles - mill products

LIDAK Pharmaceuticals LDAKA
11077 N. Torrey Pines Rd.
La Jolla, CA 92037 619-558-0364
Drugs

Life Technologies, Inc. LTEK
8717 Grovemont Circle
Gaithersburg, MD 20877
301-840-8000
Biomedical & genetic products

Life USA Holding, Inc. LUSA
300 S. Highway 169, Ste. 600
Minneapolis, MN 55426
612-546-7386
Insurance - life O

LifeCore Biomedical, Inc. LCBM
3515 Lyman Blvd.
Chaska, MN 55318 612-368-4300
Biomedical & genetic products

Lifeline Systems, Inc. LIFE
640 Memorial Dr.
Cambridge, MA 02139 617-679-1000
Healthcare - outpatient & home

LifeQuest Medical, Inc. LQMD
9601 McAllister Fwy.
San Antonio, TX 78216 210-366-2100
Medical products

Lifetime Hoan Corp. LCUT
820 Third Ave.
Brooklyn, NY 11232 718-499-9500
Housewares

Ligand Pharmaceuticals Inc. LGND
9393 Towne Centre Dr.
San Diego, CA 92121 619-535-3900
Drugs

Lilly Industries, Inc. LICIA
733 S. West St.
Indianapolis, IN 46225 317-687-6700
Chemicals - specialty
[DRP]

LIN Broadcasting Corp. LINB
5295 Carillon Point
Kirkland, WA 98033 206-828-1902
Broadcasting - radio & TV O

Lincare Holdings, Inc. LNCR
19337 US 19 North, Ste. 500
Clearwater, FL 34624 813-530-7700
Medical services O

Lincoln Savings Bank LNSB
102 Broadway Ave.
Carnegie, PA 15106 412-276-4860
Financial - savings and loans

Lincoln Telecommunications Co. LTEC
1440 M St.
Lincoln, NE 68508 402-474-2211
Utility - telephone
[DRP]

Lindal Cedar Homes, Inc. LNDL
4300 S. 104th Place
Seattle, WA 98178 206-725-0900
Building - residential & commercial

Lindberg Corp. LIND
6133 N. River Rd., Ste. 700
Rosemont, IL 60018 708-823-2021
Metal processing & fabrication

Lindsay Manufacturing Co. LINZ
E. Highway 91
Lindsay, NE 68644 402-428-2131
Machinery - farm

Linear Technology Corp. LLTC
1630 McCarthy Blvd.
Milpitas, CA 95035 408-432-1900
Electrical components - semiconductors O

Liposome Technology, Inc. LTIZ
1050 Hamilton Court
Menlo Park, CA 94025 415-323-9011
Drugs O

Liqui-Box Corp. LIQB
6950 Worthington-Galena Rd.
Worthington, OH 43085 614-888-9280
Containers - paper & plastic

Litchfield Financial Corp. LTCH
25 Main St.
Williamstown, MA 01267
413-458-2551
Financial - consumer loans

Littelfuse, Inc. LFUS
800 E. Northwest Highway
Des Plaines, IL 60016 708-824-1188
Electrical products - misc.

Liuski International, Inc. LSKI
10 Hub Dr.
Melville, NY 11747 516-454-8220
Computers - peripheral equipment

LodgeNet Entertainment Corp. LNET
808 West Ave. North
Sioux Falls, SD 57104 605-330-1330
Leisure & recreational services

Logic Devices Inc. LOGC
628 E. Evelyn Ave.
Sunnyvale, CA 94086
408-737-3300
Electrical components - misc.

LoJack Corp. LOJN
333 Elm St.
Dedham, MA 02026
617-326-4700
Data collection & systems O

Lomak Petroleum, Inc. LOMK
500 Throckmorton St.
Fort Worth, TX 76102 817-870-2601
Oil & gas - US exploration & production

Lone Star Steakhouse & Saloon, Inc.
 STAR
224 E. Douglas, Ste. 700
Wichita, KS 67202 316-264-8899
Retail - food & restaurants O

Lone Star Technologies, Inc. LSST
5501 LBJ Freeway, Ste. 1200
Dallas, TX 75240 214-386-3981
Steel - production

Longhorn Steaks, Inc. LOHO
8215 Roswell Rd., Bldg. 200
Atlanta, GA 30350 404-399-9595
Retail - food & restaurants

Lottery Enterprises, Inc. LOTO
9190 Activity Rd.
San Diego, CA 92126 619-621-5050
Leisure & recreational products

Lotus Development Corp. LOTS
55 Cambridge Pkwy.
Cambridge, MA 02142 617-577-8500
Computers - software

Lowenstein Furniture Group, Inc. LOEW
1801 N. Andrews Extension
Pompano Beach, FL 33061
305-960-1100
Furniture

Lowrance Electronics, Inc. LEIX
12000 E. Skelly Dr.
Tulsa, OK 74128 918-437-6881
Leisure & recreational products

Loyola Capital Corp. LOYC
1300 N. Charles St.
Baltimore, MD 21201 410-332-7000
Financial - savings and loans

LSB Bancshares, Inc. LXBK
One LSB Plaza, PO Box 867
Lexington, NC 27293 704-246-6500
Banks - southeast

LSI Industries Inc. LYTS
10000 Alliance Rd.
Cincinnati, OH 45242 513-793-3200
Building products - lighting fixtures

LTX Corp. LTXX
LTX Park at University Ave.
Westwood, MA 02090 617-461-1000
Electronics - measuring instruments

Lufkin Industries, Inc. LUFK
601 S. Raguet
Lufkin, TX 75902 409-634-2211
Oil field machinery & equipment

Lunar Corp. LUNR
313 W. Beltline Highway
Madison, WI 53713 608-274-2663
Medical products

Lund International Holdings, Inc. LUND
9055 Evergreen Blvd. NW
Minneapolis, MN 55433 612-780-2520
Automotive & trucking - replacement parts

LXE Inc. LXEI
303 Research Dr.
Norcross, GA 30092 404-447-4224
Telecommunications equipment

M-Wave, Inc. MWAV
216 Evergreen St.
Bensenville, IL 60106 708-860-9542
Electronics - components & systems

M. H. Myerson & Co., Inc. MHMC
30 Montgomery St.
Jersey City, NJ 07302 201-332-3380
Financial - business services

M.S. Carriers, Inc. MSCA
3171 Directors Row
Memphis, TN 38116 901-332-2500
Transportation - truck

MacDermid, Inc. MACD
245 Freight St.
Waterbury, CT 06702 203-575-5700
Chemicals - specialty
[DRP]

Mace Security International, Inc. MACE
160 Benmont Ave., PO Box 679
Bennington, VT 05201 802-447-1503
Chemicals - specialty

Macheezmo Mouse Restaurants, Inc.
 MMRI
1020 S.W. Taylor, Ste. 585
Portland, OR 97205 503-274-0001
Retail - food & restaurants

Macromedia, Inc. MACR
600 Townsend St.
San Francisco, CA 94103 415-252-2000
Computers - software O

Madison Gas and Electric Co. MDSN
133 S. Blair St., PO Box 1231
Madison, WI 53701 608-252-7923
Utility - electric power
[DRP]

MAF Bancorp, Inc. MAFB
55th St. & Holmes Ave.
Clarendon Hills, IL 60514 312-325-7300
Banks - midwest

Magainin Pharmaceuticals Inc. MAGN
5110 Campus Dr.
Plymouth Meeting, PA 19462
610-941-4020
Drugs

Magma Power Co. MGMA
4365 Executive Dr., Ste. 900
San Diego, CA 92121 619-622-7800
Energy - alternate sources O

Magna Bancorp, Inc. MGNL
100 W. Front St.
Hattiesburg, MS 39401 601-545-4700
Financial - savings and loans

Magna Group, Inc. MAGI
1401 S. Brentwood Blvd.
St. Louis, MO 63144 314-963-2500
Banks - midwest
[DRP]

Magnetic Technologies Corp. MTCC
770 Linden Ave.
Rochester, NY 14625 716-385-8711
Instruments - control

Mahaska Investment Co. OSKY
222 First Ave. East
Oskaloosa, IA 52577 515-673-8448
Banks - west

Mail Boxes Etc. MAIL
6060 Cornerstone Court West
San Diego, CA 92121 619-455-8800
Business services O

Main St. & Main, Inc. MAIN
8700 E. Via de Ventura
Scottsdale, AZ 85258 602-951-3200
Retail - food & restaurants

Mallon Resources Corp. MLRC
999 18th St., Ste. 1700
Denver, CO 80202 303-293-2333
Oil & gas - US exploration & production

Manatron, Inc. MANA
2970 S. 9th St.
Kalamazoo, MI 49009
616-375-5300
Computers - software

Manugistics Group, Inc. MANU
2115 E. Jefferson St.
Rockville, MD 20852 301-984-5000
Computers - software

MapInfo Corp. MAPS
One Global View
Troy, NY 12180 518-285-6000
Computers - software

Marble Financial Corp. MRBL
47 Merchants Row
Rutland, VT 05701 802-775-0025
Financial - savings and loans

Marcam Corp. MCAM
95 Wells Ave.
Newton, MA 02159 617-965-0220
Computers - software

Marietta Corp. MRTA
37 Huntington St.
Cortland, NY 13045 607-753-6746
Cosmetics & toiletries

Marine Drilling Companies, Inc. MDCO
14141 Southwest Fwy.
Sugar Land, TX 77478 713-491-2002
Oil & gas - field services

Mariner Health Group, Inc. MRNR
47 Water St.
Mystic, CT 06355 203-572-8544
Medical services O

Marion Capital Holdings, Inc. MARN
100 W. Third St., PO Box 367
Marion, IN 46952 317-664-0556
Financial - savings and loans

Marisa Christina, Inc. MRSA
415 Second Ave.
New Hyde Park, NY 11040
516-352-5050
Textiles - apparel

Mark Controls Corp. MRCC
5202 Old Orchard Rd.
Skokie, IL 60077 708-470-8585
Instruments - control

Mark Twain Bancshares, Inc. MTWN
8820 Ladue Rd.
St. Louis, MO 63124 314-727-1000
Banks - midwest
[DRP]

Mark VII, Inc. MVII
5310 St. Joseph Ave.
St. Joseph, MO 64505 816-233-3158
Transportation - truck

Markel Corp. MAKL
4551 Cox Rd.
Glen Allen, VA 23060 804-747-0136
Insurance - property & casualty

Marker International MRKR
1070 West 2300 South
Salt Lake City, UT 84119 801-972-2100
Leisure & recreational products

Market Facts, Inc. MFAC
3040 W. Salt Creek Ln.
Arlington Heights, IL 60005
708-590-7000
Business services

Marquest Medical Products, Inc. MMPI
11039 E. Lansing Circle
Englewood, CO 80112 303-790-4835
Medical products

Marquette Electronics, Inc. MARQA
8200 W. Tower Ave.
Milwaukee, WI 53223 414-355-5000
Medical products

Marsam Pharmaceuticals Inc. MSAM
Building 31, Olney Ave.
Cherry Hill, NJ 08003 609-424-5600
Drugs O

Marsh Supermarkets, Inc. MARSA
9800 Crosspoint Blvd.
Indianapolis, IN 46256 317-594-2100
Retail - supermarkets
[DRP]

Marshall & Ilsley Corp. MRIS
770 N. Water St.
Milwaukee, WI 53202 414-765-7801
Banks - midwest O
[DRP]

Marshalltown Financial Corp. MFCX
303 W. Main St.
Marshalltown, IA 50158 515-754-6000
Banks - midwest

Martek Biosciences Corp. MATK
6480 Dobbin Rd.
Columbia, MD 21045 410-740-0081
Medical products

Marten Transport, Ltd. MRTN
129 Marten St.
Mondovi, WI 54755 715-926-4216
Transportation - truck

Martin Color-Fi, Inc. MRCF
510 Augusta Rd.
Edgefield, SC 29824 803-637-7000
Miscellaneous - not elsewhere classified

Maryland Federal Bancorp, Inc. MFSL
3505 Hamilton St.
Hyattsville, MD 20782 301-779-1200
Banks - northeast

Masland Corp. MSLD
50 Spring Rd.
Carlisle, PA 17013 717-249-1866
Automotive & trucking - original equipment

Mason-Dixon Bancshares, Inc. MSDX
45 W. Main St.
Westminster, MD 21157 410-857-3400
Banks - northeast

MASSBANK Corp. MASB
123 Haven St.
Reading, MA 01867 617-662-5000
Banks - northeast
[DRP]

MasTec, Inc. MASX
8600 NW 36th St., 8th Fl.
Miami, FL 33166 305-587-4512
Telecommunications equipment

Matewan BancShares, Inc. MATE
Mate St., PO Box 600
Matewan, WV 25678 304-426-8221
Banks - southeast

MathSoft, Inc. MATH
101 Main St.
Cambridge, MA 02139 617-577-1017
Computers - software

Matrix Pharmaceutical, Inc. MATX
1430 O'Brien Dr.
Menlo Park, CA 94025 415-326-6100
Biomedical & genetic products

Matrix Service Co. MTRX
10701 E. Ute St.
Tulsa, OK 74116 918-838-8822
Oil & gas - field services

Matthews International Corp. MATW
2 Northshore Ctr.
Pittsburgh, PA 15212 412-442-8200
Diversified operations

Matthews Studio Equipment Group MATT
2405 Empire Ave.
Burbank, CA 91504
818-843-6715
Motion pictures & services

Mattson Technology, Inc. MTSN
3550 W. Warren Ave.
Fremont, CA 94538 510-657-5900
Electronics - components & systems

Maverick Tube Corp. MAVK
400 Chesterfield Center
Chesterfield, MO 63017 314-537-1314
Oil field machinery & equipment

Max & Erma's Restaurants, Inc. MAXE
4849 Evanswood Dr.
Columbus, OH 43229
614-431-5800
Retail - food & restaurants

Maxco, Inc. MAXC
1118 Centennial Way
Lansing, MI 48917 517-321-3130
Machinery - construction & mining

Maxicare Health Plans, Inc. MAXI
1149 S. Broadway St.
Los Angeles, CA 90015 213-765-2000
Health maintenance organization O

Maxim Group, Inc. MAXM
1035 Cobb Industrial Dr.
Marietta, GA 30066
404-590-9369
Retail - misc. O

Maxim Integrated Products, Inc. MXIM
120 San Gabriel Dr.
Sunnyvale, CA 94086 408-737-7600
Electrical components - misc.

Maxtor Corp. MXTR
211 River Oaks Pkwy.
San Jose, CA 95134 408-432-1700
Computers - peripheral equipment O

Maxwell Laboratories, Inc. MXWL
8888 Balboa Ave.
San Diego, CA 92123 619-279-5100
Electronics - military

Maxwell Shoe Co. MAXS
101 Sprague St.
Hyde Park, MA 02136 617-364-5090
Shoes & related apparel

Mayflower Co-operative Bank MFLR
30 S. Main St.
Middleboro, MA 02346 508-947-4343
Banks - northeast

Mayflower Group, Inc. MAYF
9998 N. Michigan Rd.
Carmel, IN 46032 317-875-1463
Diversified operations

Maynard Oil Co. MOIL
8080 N. Central Expressway
Dallas, TX 75206 214-891-8880
Oil & gas - US exploration & production

MBLA Financial Corp. MBLF
100 N. Rollins
Macon, MO 63552 816-385-2122
Financial - savings and loans

McAfee Associates, Inc. MCAF
2710 Walsh Ave., Ste. 200
Santa Clara, CA 95051
408-988-3832
Computers - software

McClain Industries, Inc. MCCL
6200 Elmridge Rd.
Sterling Heights, MI 48310 810-264-3611
Transportation - equipment & leasing

McCormick & Co., Inc. MCCRK
18 Loveton Circle
Sparks, MD 21152 410-771-7301
Food - misc. O
[DRP]

McFarland Energy, Inc. MCFE
10425 S. Painter Ave.
Santa Fe Springs, CA 90670 310-944-0181
Oil & gas - US exploration & production

McGrath RentCorp MGRC
2500 Grant Ave.
San Lorenzo, CA 94580
510-276-2626
Leasing

MCI Communications Corp. MCIC
1801 Pennsylvania Ave. NW
Washington, DC 20006 202-872-1600
Telecommunications services O

MDL Information Systems, Inc. MDLI
2132 Farallon Dr.
San Leandro, CA 94577 510-895-1313
Computers - software

MDT Corp. MDTC
2300 205th St.
Torrance, CA 90501 310-618-9269
Medical & dental supplies

Meadowbrook Rehabilitation Group, Inc.
MBRK
2200 Powell St., Ste. 800
Emeryville, GA 94608 510-420-0900
Healthcare - outpatient & home

Medalist Industries, Inc. MDIN
10850 W. Park Place, Ste. 150
Milwaukee, WI 53224 414-359-3000
Diversified operations

MedAlliance, Inc. MDAL
109 Westpark Dr., Ste. 420
Brentwood, TN 37027 615-373-5400
Medical services

Medaphis Corp. MEDA
2700 Cumberland Pkwy.
Atlanta, GA 30339 404-319-3300
Medical services O

Medar, Inc. MDXR
38700 Grand River Ave.
Farmington Hills, MI 48335
810-477-3900
Industrial automation & robotics

Medarex, Inc. MEDX
22 Chambers St.
Princeton, NJ 08542 609-921-7121
Drugs

Medex, Inc. MDEX
3637 Lacon Rd.
Hilliard, OH 43026 614-876-2413
Medical & dental supplies

Medford Savings Bank MDBK
29 High St.
Medford, MA 02155 617-395-7700
Financial - savings and loans
[DRP]

Media Arts Group, Inc. ARTS
Ten Almadin Blvd., Ste. 900
San Jose, CA 95113 408-947-4680
Ceramics & ceramic products

Medic Computer Systems, Inc. MCSY
8601 Six Forks Rd., Ste. 300
Raleigh, NC 27615 919-847-8102
Computers - software

Medical Action Industries Inc. MDCI
150 Motor Parkway, Ste. 205
Hauppauge, NY 11788 516-231-4600
Medical products

Medical Diagnostics, Inc. MDIX
6 New England Executive Park
Burlington, MA 01803 617-270-9560
Medical services

Medical Graphics Corp. MGCC
350 Oak Grove Pkwy.
St. Paul, MN 55127 612-484-4874
Medical products

Medical Technology Systems, Inc. MSYS
12920 Automobile Blvd.
Clearwater, FL 34622 813-576-6311
Containers - paper & plastic

Medicine Shoppe International, Inc. MSII
1100 N. Lindbergh
St. Louis, MO 63132 314-993-6000
Retail - drug stores

Medicis Pharmaceutical Corp. MDRXA
100 E. 42nd St., 15th Fl.
New York, NY 10017 212-599-2000
Drugs

Medicus Systems Corp. MECS
One Rotary Center, Ste. 400
Evanston, IL 60201 708-570-7500
Computers - software

MedImmune, Inc. MEDI
19 Firstfield Rd.
Gaithersburg, MD 20878
301-417-0770
Medical products O

MediSense, Inc. MSNS
266 Second Ave.
Waltham, MA 02154
617-895-6000
Medical products

MEDRAD; INC. MEDR
271 Kappa Dr.
Pittsburgh, PA 15238
412-967-9700
Medical products

Megacards, Inc. MEGX
5650 Wattsburg Rd.
Erie, PA 16509 814-825-1033
Leisure & recreational products

Megahertz Holding Corp. MEGZ
4505 S. Wasatch Blvd.
Salt Lake City, UT 84124 801-272-6000
Telecommunications equipment O

Megatest Corp. MEGT
1321 Ridder Park
San Jose, CA 95131 408-437-9700
Electronics - measuring instruments

Mego Financial Corp. MEGO
4310 Paradise Rd.
Las Vegas, NV 89109 702-737-3700
Real estate development

Melamine Chemicals, Inc. MTWO
Highway 18 West
Donaldsonville, LA 70346
504-473-3121
Chemicals - specialty

Mellon Participating Mortgage Trust MPMTS
8 Stamford Forum
Stamford, CT 06901 415-433-7770
Real estate investment trust

Men's Wearhouse, Inc. SUIT
5803 Glenmont Dr.
Houston, TX 77081 713-664-3692
Retail - apparel & shoes

Menley & James, Inc. MENJ
100 Tournament Dr.
Horsham, PA 19044 215-441-6500
Cosmetics & toiletries

Mentor Corp. MNTR
5425 Hollister Ave.
Santa Barbara, CA 93111 805-681-6000
Medical & dental supplies O

Mentor Graphics Corp. MENT
8005 S.W. Boeckman Rd.
Wilsonville, OR 97070 503-685-7000
Computers - graphics O

Mercantile Bankshares Corp. MRBK
2 Hopkins Plaza
Baltimore, MD 21203 410-237-5900
Banks - southeast
[DRP 5%]

Merchants Bancorp, Inc. MBIA
34 S. Broadway
Aurora, IL 60507 708-896-9000
Banks - midwest

Merchants Bancshares, Inc. MBVT
123 Church St.
Burlington, VT 05401 802-658-3400
Banks - northeast

Mercury General Corp. MRCY
4484 Wilshire Blvd.
Los Angeles, CA 90010 213-937-1060
Insurance - property & casualty

Mercury Interactive Corp. MERQ
3333 Octavius Dr.
Santa Clara, CA 95054 408-987-0100
Computers - software

Meridian Bancorp, Inc. MRDN
35 N. Sixth St.
Reading, PA 19601 610-655-2000
Banks - northeast O
[DRP 5%]

Meridian Diagnostics, Inc. KITS
3471 River Hills Dr.
Cincinnati, OH 45244 513-271-3700
Medical products

Meridian Insurance Group, Inc. MIGI
2955 N. Meridian St.
Indianapolis, IN 46206 317-927-8100
Insurance - property & casualty

Meridian Point Realty Trust '83 MPTBS
50 California St., Ste. 1600
San Francisco, CA 94111
415-956-3031
Real estate investment trust

Meridian Sports Inc. MSPO
625 Madison Ave., 12th Fl.
New York, NY 10022 212-527-6300
Leisure & recreational products

Meris Laboratories, Inc. MERSE
2890 Zanker Rd.
San Jose, CA 95134 408-434-9200
Medical services

Merisel, Inc. MSEL
200 Continental Blvd.
El Segundo, CA 90245 310-615-3080
Computers - retail & wholesale O

Merit Medical Systems, Inc. MMSI
79 W. 4500 South, Ste. 9
Salt Lake City, UT 84107
801-263-9300
Medical products

Merix Corp. MERX
1521 Poplar Ln.
Forest Grove, OR 97116 503-359-9300
Electronics - components & systems

Merrill Corp. MRLL
One Merrill Circle
St. Paul, MN 55108 612-646-4501
Printing - commercial

Mesa Airlines, Inc. MESA
2325 E. 30th St.
Farmington, NM 87401 505-327-0271
Transportation - airline O

Met-Coil Systems Corp. METS
5486 Sixth St. SW
Cedar Rapids, IA 52404
319-363-6566
Metal products - fabrication

Metatec Corp. META
7001 Metatec Blvd.
Dublin, OH 43017 614-761-2000
Publishing - multimedia

Methode Electronics, Inc. METHA
7447 W. Wilson Ave.
Chicago, IL 60656 708-867-9600
Electrical connectors

Metricom, Inc. MCOM
980 University Ave.
Los Gatos, CA 95030 408-399-8200
Telecommunications equipment

Metro Financial Corp. MFIN
6637 Roswell Rd.
Atlanta, GA 30328 404-255-8550
Banks - southeast

Metrocall, Inc. MCLL
6677 Richmond Highway
Alexandria, VA 23306 703-660-6677
Telecommunications services

Metropolitan Bankcorp MSEA
1520 Fourth Ave.
Seattle, WA 98101 206-625-1818
Financial - savings and loans

Metrotrans Corp. MTRN
777 Greenbelt Parkway
Griffin, GA 30223 404-229-5995
Automotive manufacturing

MFB Corp. MFBC
121 S. Church St., PO Box 528
Mishawaka, IN 46546 219-255-3146
Banks - midwest

MFS Communications Co., Inc. MFST
3555 Farnam St., Ste. 200
Omaha, NE 68131 402-271-2890
Telecommunications services O

MG Products, Inc. MGPR
2311 Boswell Rd., Ste. 1
Chula Vista, CA 91914 619-482-2970
Building products - misc.

MGI PHARMA, Inc. MOGN
9900 Bren Rd. East, Ste. 300E
Minneapolis, MN 55343 612-935-7335
Drugs O

Miami Subs Corp. SUBS
6300 N.W. 31st Ave.
Fort Lauderdale, FL 33309
305-973-0000
Retail - food & restaurants

Michael Foods, Inc. MIKL
5353 Wayzata Blvd.
Minneapolis, MN 55416 612-546-1500
Food - misc.

Michaels Stores, Inc. MIKE
5931 Campus Circle Dr.
Irving, TX 75063 214-714-7000
Retail - misc. O

Michigan Financial Corp. MFCB
101 W. Washington St.
Marquette, MI 49855
906-228-6940
Banks - midwest

Michigan National Corp. MNCO
2777 Inkster Rd.
Farmington Hills, MI 48334 313-473-3000
Banks - midwest O
[DRP]

MICOM Communications Corp. MICM
4100 Los Angeles Ave.
Simi Valley, CA 93063 805-583-8600
Telecommunications equipment

Micro Bio-Medics, Inc. MBMI
846 Pelham Parkway
Pelham, NY 10803 914-738-8400
Medical & dental supplies

Micro Healthsystems, Inc. MCHS
414 Eagle Rock Ave.
West Orange, NJ 07052
201-731-9252
Computers - software

Micro Linear Corp. MLIN
2092 Concourse Dr.
San Jose, CA 95131 408-433-5200
Electronics - components & systems

Micro Warehouse, Inc. MWHS
47 S. Water St.
South Norwalk, CT 06854
203-854-1700
Computers - retail & wholesale O

Micro-Integration Corp. MINT
One Science Park
Frostburg, MD 21532
301-689-0800
Computers - software

MicroAge, Inc. MICA
2308 S. 55th St.
Tempe, AZ 85282 602-968-3168
Computers - retail & wholesale O

Microchip Technology Inc. MCHP
2355 W. Chandler Blvd.
Chandler, AZ 85224 602-786-7200
Electronics - components & systems O

Microcom, Inc. MNPI
500 River Ridge Dr.
Norwood, MA 02062 617-551-1000
Telecommunications equipment

Microdyne Corp. MCDY
3601 Eisenhower Ave.
Alexandria, VA 22304 703-739-0500
Telecommunications equipment

Microelectronic Packaging, Inc. MPIX
9350 Trade Place
San Diego, CA 92126 619-530-1660
Containers - paper & plastic

MicroFluidics International Corp. MFIC
30 Ossipee Rd.
Newton, MA 02164 617-965-7255
Machinery - material handling

Micrografx, Inc. MGXI
1303 E. Arapaho Rd.
Richardson, TX 75081 214-234-1769
Computers - software

Microlog Corp. MLOG
20270 Goldenrod Ln.
Germantown, MD 20876 301-428-9100
Telecommunications equipment

Micronics Computers, Inc. MCRN
232 E. Warren Ave.
Fremont, CA 94539 510-651-2300
Computers - peripheral equipment

Micropolis Corp. MLIS
21211 Nordhoff St.
Chatsworth, CA 91311 818-709-3300
Computers - peripheral equipment

MICROS Systems, Inc. MCRS
12000 Baltimore Ave.
Beltsville, MD 20705 301-210-6000
Office automation

Microsemi Corp. MSCC
2830 S. Fairview St.
Santa Ana, CA 92704 714-979-8220
Electrical components - semiconductors

Microsoft Corp. MSFT
One Microsoft Way
Redmond, WA 98052 206-882-8080
Computers - software O

Microtek Medical, Inc. MTMI
512 Lehmberg Rd.
Columbus, MS 39704
601-327-1863
Medical products

Microtest, Inc. MTST
4747 N. 22nd St.
Phoenix, AZ 85016 602-957-6400
Computers - peripheral equipment

MicroTouch Systems, Inc. MTSI
300 Griffin Park
Methuen, MA 01844
508-694-9900
Computers - peripheral equipment

Mid Am, Inc. MIAM
222 S. Main St.
Bowling Green, OH 43402 419-352-5271
Banks - midwest
[DRP]

Mid Continent Bancshares, Inc. MCBS
124 W. Central St.
El Dorado, KS 67042 316-321-2700
Banks - west

Mid-South Insurance Co. MIDS
4317 Ramsey St.
Fayetteville, NC 28311 910-822-1020
Insurance - accident & health

MidConn Bank MIDC
346 Main St.
Kensington, CT 06037 203-828-0301
Banks - northeast

Middlesex Water Co. MSEX
1500 Ronson Rd.
Iselin, NJ 08830 908-634-1500
Utility - water supply

Midland Financial Group, Inc. MDLD
825 Crossover Ln., Ste. 112
Memphis, TN 38117 901-680-9100
Insurance - property & casualty

Midlantic Corp. MIDL
Metro Park Plaza, PO Box 600
Edison, NJ 08818 908-321-8000
Banks - northeast O
[DRP]

Midwesco Filter Resources, Inc. MFRI
400 Battaile Dr.
Winchester, VA 22601 703-667-8500
Filtration products

Midwest Grain Products, Inc. MWGP
1300 Main St., PO Box 130
Atchison, KS 66002
913-367-1480
Food - flour & grain

Mikohn Gaming Corp. MIKN
6700 S. Paradise Rd., Ste. E
Las Vegas, NV 89119 702-896-3890
Leisure & recreational products

Miles Homes, Inc. MIHO
4700 Nathan Ln.
Plymouth, MN 55446 612-553-8300
Miscellaneous - not elsewhere classified

Miller Building Systems, Inc. MTIK
58120 County Rd. 3 South
Elkhart, IN 46517 219-295-1214
Building - residential & commercial

Millicom Inc. MICCF
153 E. 53rd St., Ste. 5500
New York, NY 10022 212-355-3440
Telecommunications services

Milton Federal Financial Corp. MFFC
25 Lowry Dr.
West Milton, OH 45383 513-698-4168
Financial - savings and loans

Miltope Group Inc. MILT
1770 Walt Whitman Rd.
Melville, NY 11747 516-420-0200
Computers - mini & micro

Milwaukee Insurance Group, Inc. MILW
803 W. Michigan St.
Milwaukee, WI 53233 414-271-0525
Insurance - property & casualty

Mine Safety Appliances Co. MNES
121 Gamma Dr.
Pittsburgh, PA 15238
412-967-3000
Protection - safety equipment & services

Miners National Bancorp, Inc. MNBC
120 S. Centre St., PO Box B
Pottsville, PA 17901 717-622-2320
Banks - northeast

MiniStor Peripherals International Ltd. MINSF
2801 Orchard Pkwy.
San Jose, CA 95134 408-943-0165
Computers - peripheral equipment

Minnesota Educational Computing Corp.
MEKK
6160 Summit Dr. North
Minneapolis, MN 55430 612-569-1500
Computers - software

Minntech Corp. MNTX
14905 28th Ave. North
Minneapolis, MN 55447 612-553-3300
Medical products

Mississippi Chemical Corp. MISS
Highway 49 East
Yazoo City, MS 39194 601-746-4131
Chemicals - specialty O

Mississippi Valley Bancshares, Inc. MVBI
700 Corporate Plaza Dr.
St. Louis, MO 63105 314-268-2580
Banks - midwest

Mitek Surgical Products, Inc. MYTK
57 Providence Highway
Norwood, MA 02062 617-551-8500
Medical products

Mity-Lite, Inc. MITY
1301 W. 400 North
Orem, UT 84057 801-224-0589
Furniture

MK Gold Co. MKAU
720 Park Blvd., Plaza 4
Boise, ID 83712 208-386-8900
Gold mining & processing

MK Rail Corp. MKRL
720 Park Blvd.
Boise, ID 83729 208-386-5209
Transportation - equipment & leasing

MLF Bancorp, Inc. MLFB
Lancaster Ave. and Rt. 320
Villanova, PA 19085
610-526-6450
Banks - northeast

MMI Medical, Inc. MMIM
1611 Pomona Rd.
Corona, CA 91720
909-736-4570
Medical services

Mobile Gas Service Corp. MBLE
2828 Dauphin St.
Mobile, AL 36606 205-476-2720
Utility - gas distribution [DRP]

Mobile Telecommunications Technologies Corp. MTEL
200 S. Lamar St.
Jackson, MS 39201 601-944-1300
Telecommunications services O

Mobley Environmental Services, Inc. MBLYA
3800 Stone Rd.
Kilgore, TX 75662 903-984-0270
Pollution control equipment & services

Model Imperial, Inc. MODL
1243 Clint Moore Rd.
Boca Raton, FL 33487 407-241-8244
Wholesale distribution - consumer products

Modern Controls, Inc. MOCO
7500 Boone Ave. North
Minneapolis, MN 55428 612-493-6370
Instruments - control

Modine Manufacturing Co. MODI
1500 DeKoven Ave.
Racine, WI 53403 414-636-1200
Automotive & trucking - original equipment
[DRP]

Modtech, Inc. MODT
2830 Barrett Ave.
Perris, CA 92572 909-943-4014
Building - residential & commercial

Mohawk Industries, Inc. MOHK
1755 The Exchange
Atlanta, GA 30339 404-951-6000
Textiles - home furnishings O

Molecular Dynamics, Inc. MDYN
880 E. Arques Ave.
Sunnyvale, CA 94086 408-773-1222
Instruments - scientific

Molex Inc. MOLX
2222 Wellington Court
Lisle, IL 60532 708-969-4550
Electrical connectors O

Molten Metal Technology, Inc. MLTN
51 Sawyer Rd.
Waltham, MA 02154 617-487-9700
Industrial processing - misc. O

Monaco Coach Corp. MCCO
325 E. First St.
Junction City, OR 97448
503-998-1068
Building - mobile homes & RV

Monaco Finance Inc. MONFA
370 17th St., Ste. 5060
Denver, CO 80202 303-592-4311
Financial - consumer loans

Monarch Avalon Inc. MAHI
4517 Harford Rd.
Baltimore, MD 21214 410-254-9200
Toys - games & hobby products

Monarch Casino & Resort, Inc. MCRI
3840 Baker Ln.
Reno, NV 89509 702-825-3355
Hotels & motels

Monmouth Real Estate Investment Corp. MNRTA
125 Wycoff Rd., PO Box 335
Eatontown, NJ 07724 908-542-4927
Real estate investment trust
[DRP 5%]

Monro Muffler Brake, Inc. MNRO
2340 Brighton-Henrietta TL Rd.
Rochester, NY 14623 716-427-2280
Auto parts - retail & wholesale

Monroc Inc. MROC
1730 Beck St., PO Box 537
Salt Lake City, UT 84110 801-359-3701
Construction - cement & concrete

Monterey Pasta Co. PSTA
4125 Blackhawk Plaza Circle
Danville, CA 94506 510-736-9200
Food - misc.

Moore Products Co. MORP
Sumneytown Pike
Spring House, PA 19477
215-646-7400
Instruments - control

Moore-Handley, Inc. MHCO
3140 Pelham Pkwy.
Pelham, AL 35124 205-663-8011
Building products - retail & wholesale

MOSCOM Corp. MSCM
3750 Monroe Ave.
Pittsford, NY 14534 716-381-6000
Telecommunications equipment

Mosinee Paper Corp. MOSI
1244 Kronenwetter Dr.
Mosinee, WI 54455 715-693-4470
Paper & paper products

Mothers Work, Inc. MWRK
1309 Noble St.
Philadelphia, PA 19123 215-625-9259
Retail - apparel & shoes

Motor Club of America MOTR
484 Central Ave.
Newark, NJ 07107 201-733-1234
Insurance - property & casualty

Motorcar Parts & Accessories, Inc. MPAA
2727 Maricopa St.
Torrance, CA 90503 310-212-7910
Automotive & trucking - replacement parts

Mountain Parks Financial Corp. MPFC
333 S. Seventh St., Ste. 2880
Minneapolis, MN 55402 612-338-3158
Banks - midwest

Mountasia Entertainment International, Inc.
FUNN
5895 Windward Pkwy., Ste. 220
Alpharetta, GA 30202 404-442-6640
Leisure & recreational services

Movie Gallery, Inc. MOVI
711 W. Main St.
Dothan, AL 36301 205-677-2108
Retail - books, music & video

MovieFone, Inc. MOFN
4 World Trade Center
New York, NY 10048 212-504-7442
Business services

MRI Management Associates, Inc. MRIM
254 W. 31st St.
New York, NY 10001 212-868-9210
Medical services

MRS Technology, Inc. MRSI
10 Elizabeth Dr.
Chelmsford, MA 01824
508-250-0450
Video equipment

MRV Communications, Inc. MRVC
8917 Fullbright Ave.
Chatsworth, CA 91311 818-773-9044
Electrical components - semiconductors

MSB Bancorp, Inc. MSBB
4 South St.
Middletown, NY 10940
914-294-8100
Banks - northeast

MTI Technology Corp. MTIC
4905 E. LaPalma Ave.
Anaheim, CA 92807 714-970-0300
Computers - peripheral equipment

MTL Inc. MTLI
3108 Central Dr.
Plant City, FL 33564 813-754-4725
Transportation - truck

MTS Systems Corp. MTSC
14000 Technology Dr.
Eden Prairie, MN 55344 612-937-4000
Electronics - measuring instruments

Multi-Color Corp. LABL
4575 Eastern Ave.
Cincinnati, OH 45226 513-321-5381
Printing - commercial

Multimedia, Inc. MMEDC
305 S. Main St.
Greenville, SC 29601 803-298-4373
Broadcasting - radio & TV O

Mutual Assurance, Inc. MAIC
100 Brookwood Place, Ste. 500
Birmingham, AL 35209 205-877-4400
Insurance - multi line & misc.

Mutual Savings Bank, f.s.b. MSBK
623 Washington Ave.
Bay City, MI 48707 517-892-3511
Financial - savings and loans

Mycogen Corp. MYCO
4980 Carroll Canyon Rd.
San Diego, CA 92121 619-453-8030
Biomedical & genetic products O

Mylex Corp. MYLX
34551 Ardenwood Blvd.
Fremont, CA 94555 510-796-6100
Computers - mini & micro O

N-Viro International Corp. NVIC
3450 W. Central Ave.
Toledo, OH 43606 419-535-6374
Pollution control equipment & services

N.S. Bancorp, Inc. NSBI
2300 N. Western Ave.
Chicago, IL 60647
312-489-2300
Financial - savings and loans

NAB Asset Corp. NABC
2401 Fountainview
Houston, TX 77057
713-952-6800
Banks - southwest

NAC Re Corp. NREC
One Greenwich Plaza
Greenwich, CT 06836 203-622-5200
Insurance - property & casualty

NAI Technologies, Inc. NATL
60 Plant Ave.
Hauppauge, NY 11788 516-582-6500
Computers - peripheral equipment

NAMIC U.S.A. Corp. NUSA
Pruyn's Island
Glen Falls, NY 12801 518-798-0067
Medical products

Nanometrics Inc. NANO
310 DeGuigne Dr.
Sunnyvale, CA 94086 408-746-1600
Electronics - measuring instruments

Napco Security Systems, Inc. NSSC
333 Bayview Ave.
Amityville, NY 11701 516-842-9400
Building products - misc.

Nash Finch Co. NAFC
7600 France Ave. South
Minneapolis, MN 55440 612-929-0371
Food - wholesale
[DRP]

Nathan's Famous, Inc. NATH
1400 Old Country Rd.
Westbury, NY 11590 516-338-8500
Retail - food & restaurants

National Auto Credit, Inc. NACC
30000 Aurora Rd.
Solon, OH 44139 216-349-1000
Leasing O

National Bancorp of Alaska, Inc. NBAK
Northern Lights Blvd. & C St.
Anchorage, AK 99503 907-276-1132
Banks - west

National Beverage Corp. POPS
One N. University Dr.
Fort Lauderdale, FL 33324 305-581-0922
Beverages - soft drinks

National Capital Management Corp. NCMC
50 California St.
San Francisco, CA 94111 415-989-2661
Financial - investment management

National City Bancorporation NCBM
75 S. Fifth St.
Minneapolis, MN 55402 612-340-3183
Banks - midwest

National City Bancshares, Inc. NCBE
227 Main St., PO Box 868
Evansville, IN 47705 812-464-9800
Banks - midwest
[DRP]

National Commerce Bancorporation NCBC
One Commerce Square
Memphis, TN 38150 901-523-3434
Banks - southeast
[DRP]

National Computer Systems, Inc. NLCS
11000 Prairie Lakes Dr.
Minneapolis, MN 55344 612-829-3000
Optical character recognition

National Dentex Corp. NADX
111 Speen Dr.
Framingham, MA 01701 508-820-4800
Medical & dental supplies

National Diagnostics, Inc. NATD
747 West Brandon Blvd.
Brandon, FL 33611
813-689-4966
Medical services

National Gypsum Co. NGCO
2001 Rexford Rd.
Charlotte, NC 28211 704-365-7300
Building products - misc. O

National Home Centers, Inc. NHCI
Highway 265 North, PO Box 789
Springdale, AR 72765 501-756-1700
Retail - misc.

National Home Health Care Corp. NHHC
850 Bronx River Rd.
Yonkers, NY 10708 914-776-6800
Healthcare - outpatient & home

National Income Realty Trust NIRTS
3878 Oak Lawn Ave., Ste. 300
Dallas, TX 75219 214-522-9909
Real estate investment trust

National Insurance Group NAIG
395 Oyster Point Blvd.
South San Francisco, CA 94080
415-872-6772
Insurance - property & casualty

National Mercantile Bancorp MBLA
01840 Century Park East
Los Angeles, CA 90067 310-277-2265
Banks - midwest

National Penn Bancshares, Inc. NPBC
Philadelphia and Reading Aves.
Boyertown, PA 19512 610-367-6001
Banks - northeast [DRP]

National Picture & Frame Co. NPAF
1500 Commerce St.
Greenwood, MS 38930 601-453-6686
Housewares

National R.V. Holdings, Inc. NRVH
3411 N. Perris Blvd.
Perris, CA 92571 909-943-6007
Building - mobile homes & RV

National Record Mart, Inc. NRMI
507 Forest Ave.
Carnegie, PA 15106
412-276-6200
Retail - misc.

National Sanitary Supply Co. NSSX
255 E. Fifth St.
Cincinnati, OH 45202 513-762-6500
Soap & cleaning preparations

National Technical Systems, Inc. NTSC
24007 Ventura Blvd.
Calabasas, CA 91302 818-591-0776
Engineering - R & D services

National TechTeam, Inc. TEAM
22000 Garrison Ave.
Dearborn, MI 48124
313-277-2277
Computers - services

National Vision Associates, Ltd. NVAL
296 S. Clayton St.
Lawrenceville, GA 30245 404-822-3600
Retail - misc. O

National Western Life Insurance Co. NWLIA
850 E. Anderson Ln.
Austin, TX 78752 512-836-1010
Insurance - life

Nationwide Cellular Service, Inc. NCEL
20 E. Sunrise Highway
Valley Stream, NY 11581 516-568-2000
Telecommunications services

Natural MicroSystems Corp. NMSS
8 Erie Dr.
Natick, MA 01760 508-650-1300
Telecommunications equipment

Natural Wonders, Inc. NATW
30031 Ahern St.
Union City, CA 94587
510-429-9900
Retail - misc.

Nature's Bounty, Inc. NBTY
90 Orville Dr.
Bohemia, NY 11716 516-567-9500
Vitamins & nutritional products O

Nature's Sunshine Products, Inc. NATR
75 E. 1700 South
Provo, UT 84606 801-342-4300
Medical products

Nautica Enterprises, Inc. NAUT
40 W. 57th St., 3rd Fl.
New York, NY 10019 212-541-5990
Textiles - apparel O

Navarre Corp. NAVR
7400 49th Ave. North
New Hope, MN 55428 612-535-8333
Wholesale distribution - consumer products

NBT Bancorp, Inc. NBTB
52 S. Broad St.
Norwich, NY 13815 607-335-6000
Banks - northeast

NCI Building Systems, Inc. BLDG
7301 Fairview
Houston, TX 77041
713-466-7788
Building products - misc.

NDC Automation, Inc. AGVS
3101 Latrobe Dr.
Charlotte, NC 28211 704-362-1115
Industrial automation & robotics

Nellcor Inc. NELL
4280 Hacienda Dr.
Pleasanton, CA 94588
510-463-4000
Medical products O

Neoprobe Corp. NEOP
425 Metro Place North
Dublin, OH 43017 614-793-7500
Biomedical & genetic products

NeoRx Corp. NERX
410 W. Harrison St.
Seattle, WA 98119 206-281-7001
Biomedical & genetic products

Neozyme Corp. NEOZ
One Kendall Square
Cambridge, MA 02139 617-252-7500
Medical products

NetFRAME Systems Inc. NETF
1545 Barber Ln.
Milpitas, CA 95035 408-944-0600
Computers - mini & micro O

NetManage, Inc. NETM
10725 N. de Anza Blvd.
Cupertino, CA 95014
408-973-7171
Computers - software O

Netrix Corp. NTRX
13595 Dulles Technology Dr.
Herndon, VA 22071 703-742-6000
Telecommunications services

Network Computing Devices, Inc. NCDI
350 N. Bernardo Ave.
Mountain View, CA 94043 415-694-0650
Computers - peripheral equipment

Network General Corp. NETG
4200 Bohannon Dr.
Menlo Park, CA 94025 415-473-2000
Computers - software O

Network Imaging Corp. IMGX
500 Huntmar Park Dr.
Herndon, VA 22070 703-478-2260
Computers - graphics

Network Peripherals Inc. NPIX
1371 McCarthy Blvd.
Milpitas, CA 95035
408-321-7300
Computers - services

Network Six, Inc. NWSS
475 Kilvert St.
Warwick, RI 02886 401-732-9000
Computers - services

Network Systems Corp. NSCO
7600 Boone Ave. North
Minneapolis, MN 55428 612-424-4888
Computers - peripheral equipment O

NetWorth, Inc. NWTH
8404 Esters Blvd.
Irving, TX 75063 214-929-1700
Computers - peripheral equipment

Neurex Corp. NXCO
3760 Haven Ave.
Menlo Park, CA 94025 415-853-1500
Biomedical & genetic products

Neurobiological Technologies, Inc. NTII
1440 Regatta Blvd.
Richmond, CA 94804
510-215-8000
Drugs

Neurogen Corp. NRGN
35 NE Industrial Rd.
Branford, CT 06405 203-488-8201
Drugs

New Brunswick Scientific Co., Inc. NBSC
44 Talmadge Rd., PO Box 4005
Edison, NJ 08818 908-287-1200
Instruments - scientific

New England Business Service, Inc. NEBS
500 Main St.
Groton, MA 01450 508-448-6111
Paper - business forms

New Hampshire Thrift Bancshares, Inc.
NHTB
The Carriage House, PO Box 37
New London, NH 03257 603-526-2116
Financial - savings and loans

New Horizons Savings and Loan Association
NHSL
1050 Fourth St.
San Raphael, CA 94901 415-457-6990
Financial - savings and loans

New Image Industries Inc. NIIS
21218 Vanowen St.
Canoga Park, CA 91303 818-702-0285
Computers - graphics

New Jersey Steel Corp. NJST
N. Crossman Rd.
Sayreville, NJ 08872 908-721-6600
Steel - production

New World Communications Group Inc.
NWCG
3200 Windy Hill Rd., Ste. 1100
Marietta, GA 30067 404-955-0045
Broadcasting - radio & TV

New World Power Corp. NWPC
558 Lime Rock Rd.
Lime Rock, CT 06039 203-435-4000
Energy - alternate sources

Newcor, Inc. NEWC
1825 S. Woodward, Ste. 240
Bloomfield Hills, MI 48302 313-253-2400
Machinery - general industrial

NewMil Bancorp, Inc. NMSB
19 Main St.
New Milford, CT 06776 203-493-4411
Financial - savings and loans

Newnan Savings Bank, FSB NFSL
19 Jefferson St.
Newnan, GA 30264 404-253-5017
Financial - savings and loans

Newpark Resources, Inc. NPRS
3850 W. Causeway Blvd.
Metairie, LA 70002 504-838-8222
Oil & gas - field services

Newport Corp. NEWP
1791 Deere Ave.
Irvine, CA 92714 714-863-3144
Instruments - scientific

NeXagen, Inc. NXGN
2860 Wilderness Place
Boulder, CO 80301 303-444-5893
Drugs

Nextel, Inc. CALL
201 Rte. 17 North
Rutherford, NJ 07070 201-438-1400
Telecommunications services O

NFO Research, Inc. NFOR
2 Pickwick Plaza
Greenwich, CT 06830
203-629-8880
Business services

NFS Financial Corp. NFSF
157 Main St., PO Box 767
Nashua, NH 03061 603-880-2011
Banks - northeast

Nichols Research Corp. NRES
4040 S. Memorial Pkwy.
Huntsville, AL 35802 205-883-1140
Engineering - R & D services

NMR of America, Inc. NMRR
430 Mountain Ave.
Murray Hill, NJ 07974
908-665-9400
Medical services

NN Ball & Roller, Inc. NNBR
800 Tennessee Rd.
Erwin, TN 37650 615-743-9151
Metal products - fabrication

Nobility Homes, Inc. NOBH
3741 S.W. 7th St.
Ocala, FL 32674 904-732-5157
Building - residential & commercial

Noble Drilling Corp. NDCO
10370 Richmond Ave., Ste. 400
Houston, TX 77042 713-974-3131
Oil & gas - field services O

Noel Group, Inc. NOEL
667 Madison Ave.
New York, NY 10021 212-371-1400
Diversified operations

Noise Cancellation Technologies, Inc. NCTI
800 Summer St.
Stamford, CT 06901 203-961-0500
Engineering - R & D services

Noland Co. NOLD
2700 Warwick Blvd.
Newport News, VA 23607
804-928-9000
Building products - retail & wholesale

Nooney Realty Trust, Inc. NRTI
7701 Forsyth Blvd.
St. Louis, MO 63105 314-863-7700
Real estate investment trust [DRP]

Norand Corp. NRND
550 Second St. SE
Cedar Rapids, IA 52401 319-369-3100
Data collection & systems

Nordson Corp. NDSN
28601 Clemens Rd.
Westlake, OH 44145 216-892-1580
Machinery - general industrial
[DRP]

Nordstrom, Inc. NOBE
1501 Fifth Ave.
Seattle, WA 98101 206-628-2111
Retail - major department stores O

Norrell Corp. NORL
3535 Piedmont Rd., N.E.
Atlanta, GA 30305 404-240-3000
Personnel

Norstan, Inc. NRRD
6900 Wedgwood Rd., Ste. 150
Maple Grove, MN 55311 612-420-1100
Telecommunications equipment

North American Biologicals, Inc. NBIO
1111 Park Centre Blvd.
Miami, FL 33169 305-628-5303
Biomedical & genetic products

North American Watch Corp. NAWC
125 Chubb Ave.
Lyndhurst, NJ 07071 201-460-4800
Precious metals & jewelry

North Bancshares, Inc. NBSI
100 W. North Ave.
Chicago, IL 60610 312-664-4320
Financial - savings and loans

North Side Savings Bank NSBK
170 Tulip Ave.
Floral Park, NY 11001 516-488-6900
Financial - savings and loans

North Star Universal, Inc. NSRU
5353 Wayzata Blvd.
Minneapolis, MN 55416
612-546-7500
Food - misc.

Northern Trust Co. NTRS
50 S. La Salle St.
Chicago, IL 60675 312-630-6000
Banks - midwest O

Northfield Laboratories, Inc. NFLD
1560 Sherman Ave., Ste. 1000
Evanston, IL 60201 708-864-3500
Drugs

Northland Cranberries, Inc. CBRYA
800 First Ave. South
Wisconsin Rapids, WI 54494
715-424-4444
Agricultural operations

Northrim Bank NRIM
3111 C St.
Anchorage, AK 99503 907-562-0062
Banks - west

Northstar Computer Forms, Inc. NSCF
1226 Linden Ave.
Minneapolis, MN 55403 612-338-8601
Paper - business forms

Northstar Health Services, Inc. NSTR
245 Fort Pitt Blvd.
Pittsburgh, PA 15222
412-471-4900
Medical services

Northwest Airlines Corp. NWAC
5101 Northwest Dr.
St. Paul, MN 55111 612-726-2111
Transportation - airline O

Northwest Illinois Bancorp, Inc. NWIB
50 W. Douglas St.
Freeport, IL 61032 815-235-8459
Banks - midwest
[DRP]

Northwest Natural Gas Co. NWNG
220 N.W. Second Ave.
Portland, OR 97209 503-226-4211
Utility - gas distribution
[DRP]

Northwest Savings Bank NWSB
PO Box 96, 2nd & Liberty Sts.
Warren, PA 16365 814-726-2140
Banks - northeast

Northwest Teleproductions, Inc. NWTL
4455 W. 77th St.
Minneapolis, MN 55435 612-835-4455
Motion pictures & services

Northwestern Steel and Wire Co. NWSW
121 Wallace St.
Sterling, IL 61081 815-625-2500
Wire & cable products

Norton McNaughton, Inc. NRTY
463 Seventh Ave., 9th Fl.
New York, NY 10018 212-947-2960
Apparel

Norwalk Savings Society NSSY
48 Wall St., PO Box 28
Norwalk, CT 06852 203-838-4545
Banks - northeast

Norwich Financial Corp. NSSB
4 Broadway
Norwich, CT 06360 203-889-2621
Financial - savings and loans

Norwood Promotional Products Inc. NPPI
817 N. Frio St.
San Antonio, TX 78207 210-227-7629
Business services

Novametrix Medical Systems Inc. NMTX
One Industrial Park Rd.
Wallingford, CT 06492
203-265-7701
Medical instruments

Novell, Inc. NOVL
122 E. 1700 South
Provo, UT 84606 801-429-7000
Computers - peripheral equipment O

Novellus Systems, Inc. NVLS
81 Vista Montana
San Jose, CA 95134 408-943-9700
Electrical components - semiconductors O

Noven Pharmaceuticals, Inc. NOVN
1330 S.W. 128th St.
Miami, FL 33186 305-253-5099
Drugs

Novitron International, Inc. NOVI
75 State St., Ste. 2220
Boston, MA 02109 617-261-9933
Medical services

NPC International, Inc. NPCIA
720 W. 20th St.
Pittsburg, KS 66762 316-231-3390
Retail - food & restaurants

NPS Pharmaceuticals, Inc. NPSP
420 Chipeta Way, Ste. 240
Salt Lake City, UT 84108
801-583-4939
Drugs

NSA International, Inc. NSAI
4260 E. Raines Rd.
Memphis, TN 38118 901-541-1223
Diversified operations

NSC Corp. NSCC
49 Danton Dr.
Methuen, MA 01844 508-686-6417
Pollution control equipment & services

NSD Bancorp, Inc. NSDB
5004 McKnight Rd.
Pittsburgh, PA 15237
412-231-6900
Banks - northeast

Nu Horizons Electronics Corp. NUHC
6000 New Horizons Blvd.
Amityville, NY 11701 516-226-6000
Electronics - parts distribution

Nu-Kote Holding, Inc. NKOT
17950 Preston Rd., Ste. 690
Dallas, TX 75252 214-250-2785
Miscellaneous - not elsewhere classified

Nu-West Industries, Inc. FERT
8400 E. Prentice Ave.
Englewood, CO 80111 303-721-1396
Fertilizers

Nuclear Metals, Inc. NUCM
2229 Main St.
Concord, MA 01742 508-369-5410
Metal processing & fabrication

Nuclear Support Services, Inc. NSSI
W. Market St.
Campbelltown, PA 17010 717-838-8125
Engineering - R & D services

NUMAR Corp. NUMR
263 Great Valley Parkway
Malvern, PA 19355 610-251-0116
Electronics - measuring instruments

NutraMax Products, Inc. NMPC
9 Blackburn Dr.
Gloucester, MA 01930 508-283-1800
Cosmetics & toiletries

NuVision, Inc. NUVI
2284 S. Ballenger
Flint, MI 48501 810-767-0900
Retail - misc.

nVIEW Corp. NVUE
860 Omni Blvd
Newport News, VA 23606
804-873-1354
Video equipment

nVIEW Corp. NVUE
860 Omni Blvd
Newport News, VA 23606
804-873-1354
Video equipment

NYCOR, Inc. NYCO
287 Childs Rd.
Basking Ridge, NJ 07920 908-953-8200
Auto parts - retail & wholesale

O'Charley's Inc. CHUX
3038 Sidco Dr.
Nashville, TN 37204 615-256-8500
Retail - food & restaurants

O'Reilly Automotive, Inc. ORLY
233 S. Patterson
Springfield, MO 65802 417-862-6708
Retail - misc.

O.I. Corp. OICO
151 Graham Rd., PO Box 9010
College Station, TX 77842 409-690-1711
Instruments - scientific

Oak Hill Sportswear Corp. OHSC
1411 Broadway
New York, NY 10018
212-789-8900
Textiles - apparel

Octel Communications Corp. OCTL
1001 Murphy Ranch Rd.
Milpitas, CA 95035 408-321-2000
Telecommunications equipment O

Odetics, Inc. ODETA
1515 S. Manchester Ave.
Anaheim, CA 92802 714-774-5000
Electronics - measuring instruments

OESI Power Corp. OESI
4000 Kruse Way Place, Bldg. 1
Lake Oswego, OR 97035 503-636-9620
Energy - alternate sources

Offshore Logistics, Inc. OLOG
224 Rue de Jean, PO Box 5-C
Lafayette, LA 70505 318-233-1221
Oil & gas - field services

Oglebay Norton Co. OGLE
1100 Superior Ave.
Cleveland, OH 44114 216-861-3300
Diversified operations

Ohio Casualty Corp. OCAS
136 N. Third St.
Hamilton, OH 45025 513-867-3000
Insurance - property & casualty
[DRP]

Old America Stores, Inc. OASI
811 N. Collins Fwy.
Howe, TX 75459 903-532-5549
Retail - misc.

Old Dominion Freight Line, Inc. ODFL
1730 Westchester Dr.
High Point, NC 27260 910-889-5000
Transportation - shipping

Old Kent Financial Corp. OKEN
One Vandenberg Center
Grand Rapids, MI 49503 616-771-5000
Banks - midwest
[DRP]

Old Lyme Holding Corp. OLHC
122 E. 42nd St.
New York, NY 10168 212-338-2100
Insurance - multi line & misc.

Old National Bancorp OLDB
420 Main St.
Evansville, IN 47708 812-464-1434
Banks - midwest
[DRP 3%]

Old Second Bancorp, Inc. OSBC
37 S. River St.
Aurora, IL 60507 708-892-0202
Banks - midwest

Olympic Financial Ltd. OLYM
7825 Washington Ave. South
Minneapolis, MN 55439 612-942-9880
Financial - consumer loans

Olympic Steel, Inc. ZEUS
5080 Richmond Rd.
Cleveland, OH 44146 216-292-3800
Steel - production

Olympus Capital Corp. OLCC
115 S. Main St.
Salt Lake City, UT 84111 801-325-1000
Financial - savings and loans

OM Group, Inc. OMGI
3800 Terminal Tower
Cleveland, OH 44113 216-781-0083
Chemicals - specialty
[DRP]

Omega Environmental, Inc. OMEG
19805 N. Creek Pkwy.
Bothell, WA 98041 206-486-4800
Pollution control equipment & services O

Omega Financial Corp. OMEF
366 Walker Dr.
State College, PA 16801 814-231-7680
Banks - northeast

OMNI Films International, Inc. OFII
5696 Pinkney Ave.
Sarasota, FL 34233 813-924-4239
Motion pictures & services

Omni Insurance Group, Inc. OMGR
1000 Parkwood Circle
Atlanta, GA 30339 404-952-4500
Insurance - property & casualty

On Assignment Inc. ASGN
21515 Vanowen St., Ste. 204
Canoga Park, CA 91303 818-878-7900
Personnel

ONBANCorp, Inc. ONBK
101 S. Salina St., PO Box 4983
Syracuse, NY 13221 315-424-4400
Banks - northeast

Oncogene Science, Inc. ONCS
106 Charles Lindbergh Blvd.
Uniondale, NY 11553 516-222-0023
Biomedical & genetic products

ONCOR, Inc. ONCR
209 Perry Pkwy.
Gaithersburg, MD 20877 301-963-3500
Biomedical & genetic products

One Price Clothing Stores, Inc. ONPR
Highway 290, Commerce Park
Duncan, SC 29334 803-439-6666
Retail - apparel & shoes

One Valley Bancorp of West Virginia, Inc.
OVWV
PO Box 1793
Charleston, WV 25326 304-348-7000
Banks - southeast
[DRP]

OneComm Corp. ONEC
4643 S. Ulster St.. Ste. 500
Denver, CO 80237 303-721-3400
Telecommunications services O

Opinion Research Corp. ORCI
23 Orchard Rd.
Skillman, NJ 08558 609-924-5900
Business services

Opta Food Ingredients, Inc. OPTS
25 Wiggins Ave.
Bedford, MA 01730 617-276-5100
Food - misc.

OPTi, Inc. OPTI
2525 Walsh Ave.
Santa Clara, CA 95051 408-980-8178
Electrical components - misc.

Optical Coating Laboratory, Inc. OCLI
2789 Northpoint Parkway
Santa Rosa, CA 95407 707-545-6440
Instruments - scientific

Optical Data Systems, Inc. ODSI
1101 E. Arapaho Rd.
Richardson, TX 75081 214-234-6400
Telecommunications equipment

Option Care, Inc. OPTN
100 Corporate North, Ste. 212
Bannockburn, IL 60015 708-615-1690
Healthcare - outpatient & home

Oracle Systems Corp. ORCL
500 Oracle Pkwy.
Redwood Shores, CA 94065
415-506-7000
Computers - software O

Orbit International Corp. ORBT
80 Cabot Court
Hauppauge, NY 11788
516-435-8300
Electronics - military

Orbital Sciences Corp. ORBI
21700 Atlantic Blvd.
Dulles, VA 20166 703-406-5000
Aerospace - aircraft equipment O

Orchard Supply Hardware Stores Corp.
OSHC
6450 Via Del Oro
San Jose, CA 95119 408-281-3500
Retail - misc.

Oregon Metallurgical Corp. OREM
PO Box 580
Albany, OR 97321 503-926-4281
Steel - specialty alloys

Orion Pictures Corp. ORPC
1888 Century Park E.
Los Angeles, CA 90067 310-282-0550
Motion pictures & services

OrNda Healthcorp ORND
3401 W. End Ave., Ste. 700
Nashville, TN 37203 615-383-8599
Hospitals O

OroAmerica, Inc. OROA
443 N. Varney St.
Burbank, CA 91502
818-848-5555
Precious metals & jewelry

Ortel Corp. ORTL
2015 W. Chestnut St.
Alhambra, CA 91803
818-281-3636
Fiber optics

OrthoLogic Corp. OLGC
2850 S. 36th St., Ste. 16
Phoenix, AZ 85034
602-437-5520
Medical instruments

Orthopedic Technology Inc. ORTH
1905 N. MacArthur Dr.
Tracy, CA 95376 209-832-5200
Medical products

OSB Financial Corp. OSBF
420 S. Koeller St.
Oshkosh, WI 54901 414-236-3680
Financial - savings and loans

Osborn Communications Corp. OSBN
405 Lexington Ave., 54th Fl.
New York, NY 10174 212-697-2280
Broadcasting - radio & TV

Oshkosh B'Gosh, Inc. GOSHA
112 Otter Ave., PO Box 300
Oshkosh, WI 54902 414-231-8800
Apparel

Oshkosh Truck Corp. OTRKB
2307 Oregon St.
Oshkosh, WI 54901 414-235-9151
Automotive & trucking - original equipment

Oshman's Sporting Goods, Inc. OSHM
2302 Maxwell Ln.
Houston, TX 77023 713-928-3171
Retail - misc.

Osicom Technologies, Inc. OSIC
1223 Wilshire Blvd., Ste. 597
Santa Monica, CA 90403 310-573-9309
Computers - mini & micro

Osteotech, Inc. OSTE
1151 Shrewsbury Ave.
Shrewsbury, NJ 07702 908-542-2800
Medical services

OTR Express, Inc. OTRX
804 N. Meadowbrook Dr.
Olathe, KS 66062 913-829-1616
Transportation - truck

Ottawa Financial Corp. OFCP
245 Central Ave.
Holland, MI 49423 616-393-7000
Financial - savings and loans

Otter Tail Power Co. OTTR
215 S. Cascade St., PO Box 496
Fergus Falls, MN 56538 218-739-8200
Utility - electric power
[DRP]

Outback Steakhouse, Inc. OSSI
550 N. Reo St., Ste. 204
Tampa, FL 33609 813-282-1225
Retail - food & restaurants O

Outlet Communications, Inc. OCOMA
111 Dorrance St.
Cranston, RI 02903 401-455-9200
Broadcasting - radio & TV

Outlook Group Corp. OUTL
1180 American Dr.
Neenah, WI 54956 414-722-2333
Business services

Owosso Corp. OWOS
100 Front St., Ste. 1400
West Conshohocken, PA 19428
215-834-0222
Diversified operations

Oxford Health Plans, Inc. OXHP
800 Connecticut Ave.
Norwalk, CT 06854 203-852-1442
Health maintenance organization O

Oxford Resources Corp. OXFD
270 S. Service Rd.
Melville, NY 11747 516-777-8000
Leasing

OXIS International, Inc. OXIS
518 Logue Ave.
Mountain View, CA 94043
415-964-7676
Drugs

P & F Industries, Inc. PFINA
300 Smith St.
Farmingdale, NY 11735 516-694-1800
Metal products - fabrication

P.A.M. Transportation Services, Inc. PTSI
Highway 412 West
Tontitown, AR 72770 501-361-9111
Transportation - truck

Pac Rim Holding Corp. PRIM
6200 Canoga Ave.
Woodland Hills, CA 91367 818-226-6200
Insurance - accident & health

PACCAR Inc. PCAR
777 - 106th Ave. N.E.
Bellevue, WA 98004 206-455-7400
Automotive & trucking - original equipment O

Pacific Crest Capital, Inc. PCCI
30343 Canwood St., Ste. 100
Agoura Hills, CA 91301 818-865-3300
Financial - mortgages & related services

Pacific International Services Corp. PISC
1600 Kapiolani Blvd., Ste. 825
Honolulu, HI 96814 808-926-4242
Transportation - equipment & leasing

Pacific Physician Services, Inc. PPSI
1826 Orange Tree Ln.
Redlands, CA 92374 909-825-4401
Health maintenance organization O

Pacific Rehabilitation & Sports Medicine, Inc.
PRHB
8100 N.E. Parkway Dr.
Vancouver, WA 98662 206-260-8130
Healthcare - outpatient & home

Pacific Sunwear of California, Inc. PSUN
5037 E. Hunter Ave.
Anaheim, CA 92807 714-693-8066
Retail - apparel & shoes

Pacific Telecom, Inc. PTCM
805 Broadway, PO Box 9901
Vancouver, WA 98668
206-696-0983
Utility - telephone

PacifiCare Health Systems, Inc. PHSYA
5995 Plaza Dr.
Cypress, CA 90630 714-952-1121
Health maintenance organization O

Paco Pharmaceutical Services, Inc. PACO
1200 Paco Way
Lakewood, NJ 08701 908-367-9000
Containers - paper & plastic

PAGES, Inc. PAGZ
5720 Avery Rd.
Amlin, OH 43002 614-793-8749
Business services

Paging Network, Inc. PAGE
4965 Preston Park Blvd.
Plano, TX 75093 214-985-4100
Telecommunications services O

PairGain Technologies, Inc. PAIR
12921 E. 166th St.
Cerritos, CA 90701 310-404-8811
Telecommunications equipment O

PALFED, Inc. PALM
107 Chesterfield St. South
Aiken, SC 29801 803-642-1400
Financial - savings and loans

Pamrapo Bancorp, Inc. PBCI
611 Avenue C
Bayonne, NJ 07002
201-339-4600
Banks - northeast

PANACO, Inc. PANA
1050 W. Blue Ridge Blvd.
Kansas City, MO 64145 816-942-6300
Oil & gas - US exploration & production

Panatech Research and Development PNTC
PO Box 23160
Albuquerque, NM 87192
505-271-2200
Telecommunications equipment

Pancho's Mexican Buffet, Inc. PAMX
3500 Noble Ave., PO Box 7407
Fort Worth, TX 76111 817-831-0081
Retail - food & restaurants

Papa John's International, Inc. PZZA
11492 Bluegrass Parkway
Louisville, KY 40299 502-266-5200
Retail - food & restaurants

Parallan Computer, Inc. PLLN
1310 Villa St.
Mountain View, CA 94041
415-960-0288
Computers - peripheral equipment

Parametric Technology Corp. PMTC
128 Technology Dr.
Waltham, MA 02154 617-894-7111
Computers - software O

ParcPlace Systems, Inc. PARQ
999 E. Arques Ave.
Sunnyvale, CA 94086 408-481-9090
Computers - software

Paris Business Forms, Inc. PBFI
122 Kissel Rd.
Burlington, NJ 08016 609-387-7300
Paper - business forms

Park Communications, Inc. PARC
Terrace Hill
Ithaca, NY 14850 607-272-9020
Broadcasting - radio & TV

Park-Ohio Industries, Inc. PKOH
20600 Chagrin Blvd.
Cleveland, OH 44122 216-991-9700
Metal products - fabrication

ParkerVision, Inc. PRKR
8493 Baymeadows Way
Jacksonville, FL 32256
904-737-1367
Video equipment

Parkvale Financial Corp. PVSA
4220 William Penn Hwy.
Monroeville, PA 15146 412-373-7200
Financial - savings and loans

Parkway Co. PKWY
188 E. Capitol St.
Jackson, MS 39201 601-948-4091
Real estate investment trust

Parlex Corp. PRLX
145 Milk St.
Methuen, MA 01844 508-685-4341
Electrical connectors

Patrick Industries, Inc. PATK
1800 S. 14th St., PO Box 638
Elkhart, IN 46515 219-294-7511
Building products - retail & wholesale

Patterson Dental Co. PDCO
1100 E. 80th St.
Minneapolis, MN 55420 612-854-2881
Medical & dental supplies

Patterson Energy Inc. PTEN
4510 Lamesa Highway
Snyder, TX 79550 915-573-1104
Oil & gas - US exploration & production

Paul Harris Stores, Inc. PAUH
6003 Guion Rd.
Indianapolis, IN 46254 317-293-3900
Retail - apparel & shoes

Paul Mueller Co. MUEL
1600 W. Phelps
Springfield, MO 65802 417-831-3000
Machinery - farm

Paul-Son Gaming Corp. PSON
2121 Industrial Rd.
Las Vegas, NV 89102 702-384-2425
Leisure & recreational products

Paychex, Inc. PAYX
911 Panorama Trail South
Rochester, NY 14625 716-385-6666
Financial - business services O
[DRP]

Payco American Corp. PAYC
180 N. Executive Dr.
Brookfield, WI 53005 414-784-9035
Financial - business services

PC Service Source, Inc. PCSS
1221 Champion Circle, Ste. 105
Carrollton, TX 75006 214-406-8583
Electronics - parts distribution

PCA International, Inc. PCAI
815 Matthews-Mint Hill Rd.
Matthews, NC 28105 704-847-8011
Retail - misc.

PCI Services, Inc. PCIS
1403 Foulk Rd., Ste. 102
Wilmington, DE 19803
302-479-0281
Containers - paper & plastic

PDA Engineering PDAS
2975 Redhill Ave.
Costa Mesa, CA 92626
714-540-8900
Computers - software

PDK Labs, Inc. PDKL
145 Ricefield Ln.
Hauppauge, NY 11788 516-273-2630
Medical products

PDS Financial Corp. PDSF
7652 Executive Dr.
Eden Prairie, MN 55344 612-949-0966
Financial - business services

Pediatric Services of America, Inc. PSAI
5834-C Peachtree Corners East
Norcross, GA 30092 404-441-1580
Healthcare - outpatient & home

Peer Review Analysis, Inc. PRAI
2 Copley Place
Boston, MA 02116 617-375-7700
Medical services

Peerless Mfg. Co. PMFG
2819 Walnut Hill Ln.
Dallas, TX 75229 214-357-6181
Filtration products

Penederm Inc. DERM
320 Lakeside Dr.
Foster City, CA 94404 415-358-0100
Medical products

Penn National Gaming, Inc. PENN
825 Berkshire Blvd., Ste. 203
Wyomissing, PA 19610 610-376-4807
Miscellaneous - not elsewhere classified

Penn Treaty American Corp. PTAC
3440 Lehigh St.
Allentown, PA 18103 610-965-2222
Insurance - accident & health

Penn Virginia Corp. PVIR
200 S. Broad St.
Philadelphia, PA 19102
215-545-6600
Coal

Penn-America Group, Inc. PAGI
420 S. York Rd.
Hatboro, PA 19040 215-443-3600
Insurance - property & casualty

PennFed Financial Services, Inc. PFSB
622 Eagle Rock Ave.
West Orange, NJ 07052
201-669-7366
Banks - northeast

PennFirst Bancorp, Inc. PWBC
600 Lawrence Ave.
Ellwood City, PA 16117
412-758-5584
Financial - savings and loans

Penril DataComm Networks, Inc. PNRL
1300 Quince Orchard Blvd.
Gaithersburg, MD 20878 301-417-0552
Telecommunications equipment

Pentair, Inc. PNTA
1500 County Rd., Ste. B2 West
St. Paul, MN 55113 612-636-7920
Paper & paper products O [DRP]

Pentech International, Inc. PNTK
195 Carter Dr.
Edison, NJ 08817 908-287-6640
Office & art materials

PENWEST, LTD. PENW
777-108th Ave. N.E., Ste. 2390
Bellevue, WA 98004 206-462-6000
Chemicals - specialty

People's Bank PBCT
850 Main St., PO Box 1580
Bridgeport, CT 06601 203-579-7171
Banks - northeast O

People's Choice TV Corp. PCTV
Two Corporate Dr., Ste. 249
Shelton, CT 06484 203-929-2800
Broadcasting - radio & TV

People's Savings Bank of Brockton PBKB
221 Main St.
Brockton, MA 02403 617-588-6600
Financial - savings and loans

People's Savings Financial Corp. PBNB
123 Broad St.
New Britain, CT 06050 203-224-7771
Financial - savings and loans

Peoples Bancorp PFDC
212 W. 7th St., PO Box 231
Auburn, IN 46706 219-925-2500
Financial - savings and loans

Peoples Bancorp, Inc. PEBO
235 Second St., PO Box 738
Marietta, OH 45750 614-373-3155
Banks - midwest

Peoples Bank PEBK
218 S. Main Ave., PO Box 467
Newton, NC 28658
704-464-5620
Banks - southeast

Peoples Bank Corporation of Indianapolis
  PPLS
130 E. Market St.
Indianapolis, IN 46204 317-237-8059
Banks - midwest

Peoples First Corp. PFKY
100 S. Fourth St.
Paducah, KY 42001 502-441-1200
Banks - southeast

Peoples Heritage Financial Group, Inc.
  PHBK
One Portland Square
Portland, ME 04112 207-761-8500
Financial - savings and loans

Peoples Telephone Co., Inc. PTEL
8041 NW 14th St.
Miami, FL 33126 305-593-9667
Telecommunications services

PeopleSoft, Inc. PSFT
1331 N. California Blvd.
Walnut Creek, CA 94596
510-946-9460
Computers - software O

Perceptron, Inc. PRCP
23855 Research Dr.
Farmington Hills, MI 48335
810-478-7710
Machinery - general industrial

Perceptronics, Inc. PERC
21135 Erwin St.
Woodland Hills, CA 91367 818-884-3485
Electronics - military

Performance Food Group Co. PFGC
25 Century Blvd., Ste. 509
Nashville, TN 37214 615-391-0112
Food - wholesale

Perfumania, Inc. PRFM
7875 N.W. 64th St.
Miami, FL 33166 305-591-8317
Cosmetics & toiletries

Permanent Bancorp, Inc. PERM
101 S.E. Third St.
Evansville, IN 47706 812-428-6800
Financial - savings and loans

Perpetual Midwest Financial, Inc. PMFI
700 First Ave., N.E.
Cedar Rapids, IA 52401 319-366-1851
Financial - savings and loans

Perrigo Co. PRGO
117 Water St.
Allegan, MI 49010 616-673-8451
Cosmetics & toiletries O

PerSeptive Biosystems, Inc. PBIO
38 Sidney St.
Cambridge, MA 02139 617-621-1787
Instruments - scientific

Personnel Management, Inc. TPMI
16 Public Square, Ste. A
Shelbyville, IN 46176 317-392-7400
Business services

Pet Food Warehouse, Inc. PFWA
600 South Highway 169
St. Louis Park, MN 55426
612-542-0123
Retail - misc.

Petco Animal Supplies, Inc. PETC
9151 Rehco Rd.
San Diego, CA 92121 619-453-7845
Retail - misc.

PetroCorp, Inc. PETR
16800 Greenspoint Park Dr.
Houston, TX 77060 713-875-2500
Oil & gas - US exploration & production

Petroleum Development Corp. PETD
103 E. Main St.
Bridgeport, WV 26330 304-842-3597
Miscellaneous - not elsewhere classified

Petroleum Heat and Power Co., Inc. HEAT
2187 Atlantic St.
Stamford, CT 06902 203-325-5400
Oil refining & marketing

Petrolite Corp. PLIT
369 Marshall Ave.
St. Louis, MO 63119 314-961-3500
Oil & gas - field services

Petrominerals Corp. PTRO
2472 Chambers Rd., Ste. 230
Tustin, CA 92680 714-730-5400
Oil & gas - field services

PETsMART, Inc. PETM
10000 N. 31st Ave., C-100
Phoenix, AZ 85051 602-944-7070
Retail - misc.

Petstuff, Inc. PTSF
655 Hembree Pkwy., Ste. G
Roswell, GA 30076 404-772-9940
Retail - misc.

Pharmaceutical Marketing Services, Inc.
PMRX
9501 E. Shea Blvd.
Scottsdale, AZ 85260 602-391-4575
Drugs

Pharmacy Management Services, Inc.
PMSV
3311 Queen Palm Dr.
Tampa, FL 33619 813-626-7788
Medical services

PharmChem Laboratories, Inc. PCHM
1505-A O'Brien Dr.
Menlo Park, CA 94025 415-328-6200
Medical services

Pharmos Corp. PARS
101 E. 52nd St., 36th Fl.
New York, NY 10022 212-838-0087
Drugs

Philadelphia Consolidated Holding Corp.
PHLY
306 E. Lancaster Ave.
Wynnewood, PA 19096 215-642-8400
Miscellaneous - not elsewhere classified

Phoenix Technologies Ltd. PTEC
846 University Ave.
Norwood, MA 02062 617-551-4000
Computers - software

Photo Control Corp. PHOC
4800 Quebec Ave. North
Minneapolis, MN 55428 612-537-3601
Photographic equipment & supplies

Photonics Corp. PHTX
2940 N. First St.
San Jose, CA 95134 408-955-7930
Telecommunications equipment

Photronics, Inc. PLAB
15 Secor Rd., PO Box 5226
Brookfield, CT 6804
203-775-9000
Electrical components - misc.

PhyCor, Inc. PHYC
30 Burton Hills Blvd.
Nashville, TN 37215 615-665-9066
Hospitals O

Physician Computer Network, Inc. PCNI
10 Industrial Ave.
Mahwah, NJ 07430
201-934-6900
Medical services

Physician Corporation of America PCAM
5835 Blue Lagoon Dr.
Miami, FL 33126 305-267-6633
Health maintenance organization O

Physician Reliance Network, Inc. PHYN
3320 Live Oak, Ste. 700
Dallas, TX 75204 214-828-0377
Medical services

Physician Sales & Service, Inc. PSSI
7800 Belfort Pkwy., Ste. 250
Jacksonville, FL 32256 904-281-0011
Medical & dental supplies

Physicians Clinical Laboratory, Inc. PCLI
3301 C St., Ste. 100E
Sacramento, CA 95816 916-444-3500
Medical services

Physicians Health Services, Inc. PHSV
120 Hawley Ln.
Trumbull, CT 06611 203-381-6400
Health maintenance organization

Physicians Insurance Co. of Ohio PICOA
13515 Yarmouth Dr., N.W.
Pickerington, OH 43147 614-864-7100
Miscellaneous - not elsewhere classified

PictureTel Corp. PCTL
222 Rosewood Dr.
Danvers, MA 01923 508-762-5000
Telecommunications services O

Piedmont BankGroup Inc. PBGI
Church and Ellsworth Sts.
Martinsville, VA 24115
703-632-2971
Banks - southeast

Piedmont Management Co. Inc. PMAN
80 Maiden Ln.
New York, NY 10038 212-363-4650
Insurance - property & casualty

Piemonte Foods, Inc. PIFI
400 Augusta St.
Greenville, SC 29604 803-242-0424
Food - misc.

Pikeville National Corp. PKVL
208 N. Mayo Trail
Pikeville, KY 41501 606-432-1414
Banks - southeast

Pinkerton's, Inc. PKTN
15910 Ventura Blvd., Ste. 900
Encino, CA 91436 818-380-8800
Business services

Pinnacle Financial Services, Inc. PNFI
830 Pleasant St.
St. Joseph, MI 49085 616-983-6311
Banks - midwest

Pinnacle Micro Inc. PNCL
19 Technology
Irvine, CA 92718 714-727-3300
Computers - peripheral equipment

Pioneer Hi-Bred International, Inc. PHYB
400 Locust St.
Des Moines, IA 50309 515-248-4800
Agricultural operations O
[DRP]

Pioneer-Standard Electronics, Inc. PIOS
4800 E. 131st St.
Cleveland, OH 44105 216-587-3600
Electronics - parts distribution
[DRP]

Pittencrieff Communications Inc. PITC
One Village Dr., Ste. 500
Abilene, TX 79606 915-690-5800
Telecommunications services O

Plains Spirit Financial Corp. PSFC
131 W. Third St.
Davenport, IA 52801 319-383-4120
Banks - midwest

Planar Systems, Inc. PLNR
1400 N.W. Compton Dr.
Beaverton, OR 97006 503-690-1100
Video equipment

Plasti-Line, Inc. SIGN
623 E. Emory Rd., PO Box 59043
Knoxville, TN 37950 615-938-1511
Advertising

Platinum Software Corp. PSQL
15615 Alton Parkway, Ste. 300
Irvine, CA 92718 714-727-1250
Computers - software O

PLATINUM technology, inc. PLAT
1815 S. Meyers Rd.
Oakbrook Terrace, IL 60181
708-620-5000
Computers - software O

Players International, Inc. PLAY
800 Bilbo St.
Lake Charles, LA 70601
318-437-1560
Leisure & recreational services O

Plaza Home Mortgage Corp. PHMC
1820 E. First St.
Santa Ana, CA 92705 714-564-3000
Financial - mortgages & related services

Plenum Publishing Corp. PLEN
233 Spring St.
New York, NY 10013 212-620-8000
Publishing - books

Plexus Corp. PLXS
55 Jewelers Park Dr.
Neenah, WI 54956 414-722-3451
Electrical products - misc.

PM Agri-Nutrition Group, Ltd. AGNU
13801 Riverport Dr., Ste. 111
Maryland Heights, MO 63043
314-298-7330
Agricultural operations

PMC Commercial Trust PMCTS
17290 Preston Rd.
Dallas, TX 75252 214-380-0044
Real estate investment trust

PMR Corp. PMRP
3990 Old Town Ave., Ste. 206A
San Diego, CA 92110 619-295-2227
Medical services

Poe & Brown, Inc. POBR
702 N. Franklin St.
Tampa, FL 33602 813-222-4100
Insurance - multi line & misc.

Polk Audio, Inc. POLK
5601 Metro Dr.
Baltimore, MD 21215 410-358-3600
Audio & video home products

Pollo Tropical, Inc. POYO
7901 S.W. 67th Ave.
Miami, FL 33143 305-662-3938
Retail - food & restaurants

PolyMedica Industries, Inc. POLY
2 Constitution Way
Woburn, MA 01801 617-933-2020
Medical products

Pomeroy Computer Resources, Inc.
 PMRY
01840 Airport Exchange Blvd.
Erlanger, KY 41018 606-282-7111
Computers - retail & wholesale

Ponder Industries, Inc. PNDR
511 Commerce Rd., PO Box 2229
Alice, TX 78333 512-664-5831
Oil & gas - offshore drilling

Pool Energy Services Co. PESC
10375 Richmond Ave.
Houston, TX 77042 713-954-3000
Oil & gas - field services

Pope Resources POPEZ
PO Box 1780
Poulsbo, WA 98370 206-697-6626
Agricultural operations

Portsmouth Bank Shares, Inc. POBS
333 State St.
Portsmouth, NH 03801 603-436-6630
Banks - northeast
[DRP]

Positive Response Television, Inc. PRTV
14724 Ventura Blvd., Ste. 600
Sherman Oaks, CA 91403
818-380-6900
Broadcasting - radio & TV

Positron Corp. POSI
16350 Park Ten Place
Houston, TX 77084 713-492-7100
Medical instruments

Possis Medical, Inc. POSS
2905 Northwest Blvd.
Minneapolis, MN 55441 612-550-1010
Medical products

Poughkeepsie Savings Bank, FSB PKPS
249 Main Mall
Poughkeepsie, NY 12601
914-431-6200
Financial - savings and loans

Powell Industries, Inc. POWL
8550 Mosley Dr.
Houston, TX 77075 713-944-6900
Machinery - electrical

Powersoft Corp. PWRS
70 Blanchard Rd.
Burlington, MA 01803 617-229-2200
Computers - software

Precision Standard, Inc. PCSN
1943 50th St. North
Birmingham, AL 35212 205-591-3009
Aerospace - aircraft equipment

Preferred Entertainment, Inc. PREF
6260 Joliet Rd.
Countryside, IL 60525 708-482-0770
Cable TV

Premier Bancorp, Inc. PRBC
451 Florida St.
Baton Rouge, LA 70801 504-332-7277
Banks - southeast

Premier Bankshares Corp. PBKC
201 W. Main St., PO Box 928
Tazewell, VA 24651 703-988-7145
Banks - midwest

Premier Financial Services, Inc. PREM
27 W. Main St.
Freeport, IL 60132
815-233-3671
Banks - midwest

Premiere Page, Inc. PPGE
8900 State Line Rd., Ste. 500
Leawood, KS 66206 913-649-6060
Telecommunications services

Premiere Radio Networks, Inc. PRNI
15260 Ventura Blvd., 5th Fl.
Sherman Oaks, CA 91403 818-377-5300
Leisure & recreational products

President Riverboat Casinos, Inc. PREZ
802 N. First St.
St. Louis, MO 63102 314-622-3000
Leisure & recreational services O

Presidential Life Corp. PLFE
69 Lydecker St.
Nyack, NY 10960 914-358-2300
Insurance - life

Presstek, Inc. PRST
8 Commercial St.
Hudson, NH 03051 603-595-7000
Miscellaneous - not elsewhere classified

Price/Costco, Inc. PCCW
4649 Morena Blvd.
San Diego, CA 92117 619-581-4600
Retail - misc. O

Pride Petroleum Services, Inc. PRDE
1500 City West Blvd., Ste. 400
Houston, TX 77042 713-789-1400
Oil & gas - field services

Prima Energy Corp. PENG
1801 Broadway, Ste. 500
Denver, CO 80202 303-297-2100
Oil & gas - US exploration & production

Primadonna Resorts Inc. PRMA
PO Box 95997
Las Vegas, NV 89193 702-382-1212
Leisure & recreational services O

Prime Bancorp, Inc. PSAB
6425 Rising Sun Ave.
Philadelphia, PA 19111 215-742-5300
Banks - northeast
[DRP]

Prime Medical Services, Inc. PMSI
1301 Capital of Texas Hwy.
Austin, TX 78746
512-328-2892
Medical services

Prime Residential, Inc. PRES
77 W. Wacker Dr., Ste 3900
Chicago, IL 60601 312-917-1600
Real estate development

Prime Retail, Inc. PRME
100 E. Pratt St., 19th Fl.
Baltimore, MD 21202 410-234-0782
Real estate investment trust

Primedex Health Systems Inc. PMDX
2 Penn Plaza East
Newark, NJ 07105 201-491-9494
Medical services

PrimeSource Corp. PSRC
15 Twinbridge Dr.
Pennsauken, NJ 08110
609-488-7200
Printing - commercial

Princeton National Bancorp, Inc. PNBC
606 S. Main St.
Princeton, IL 61356 815-875-4444
Banks - midwest

Printronix, Inc. PTNX
17500 Cartwright Rd.
Irvine, CA 92713 714-863-1900
Computers - peripheral equipment

Procept, Inc. PRCT
840 Memorial Dr.
Cambridge, MA 02139 617-491-1100
Biomedical & genetic products

ProCyte Corp. PRCY
12040 115th Ave. N.E.
Kirkland, WA 98034 206-820-4548
Drugs O

Production Operators Corp. PROP
11302 Tanner Rd.
Houston, TX 77041 713-466-0980
Oil & gas - field services

Professional Sports Care Management, Inc.
   PSCM
550 Mamaroneck Ave., Ste. 308
Harrison, NY 10528 914-777-2400
Healthcare - outpatient & home

Proffitt's, Inc. PRFT
115 N. Calderwood
Alcoa, TN 37701 615-983-7000
Retail - regional department stores

Progress Financial Corp. PFNC
600 W. Germantown Pike
Plymouth Meeting, PA 19462
610-825-8800
Financial - savings and loans

Progress Software Corp. PRGS
14 Oak Park
Bedford, MA 01730 617-280-4000
Computers - software

Progressive Bank, Inc. PSBK
86 State Rt. 22
Pawling, NY 12564 914-855-1333
Financial - savings and loans

ProGroup, Inc. PRGR
6201 Mountain View Rd.
Ooltewah, TN 37363 615-238-5890
Leisure & recreational products

Project Software & Development, Inc.
PSDI
20 University Rd.
Cambridge, MA 02138 617-661-1444
Computers - software

ProNet Inc. PNET
600 Data Dr., Ste. 100
Plano, TX 75075 214-964-9500
Telecommunications equipment

Prophet 21, Inc. PXXI
19 W. College Ave.
Yardley, PA 19027 215-493-8900
Business services

Protection One, Inc. ALRM
6011 Bristol Pkwy.
Culver City, CA 90230 310-338-6930
Protection - safety equipment & services

Protein Design Labs, Inc. PDLI
2375 Garcia Ave.
Mountain View, CA 94043 415-903-3700
Biomedical & genetic products O

Proteon, Inc. PTON
Nine Technology Dr.
Westborough, MA 01581 508-898-2800
Telecommunications equipment

Protocol Systems, Inc. PCOL
8500 S.W. Creekside Place
Beaverton, OR 97005 503-526-8500
Medical instruments

Providence and Worcester Railroad Co.
PWRR
75 Hammond St.
Worcester, MA 01610 508-755-4000
Transportation - rail

Provident Bancorp, Inc. PRBK
One E. Fourth St.
Cincinnati, OH 45202 513-579-2000
Banks - midwest

Provident Bankshares Corp. PBKS
114 E. Lexington St.
Baltimore, MD 21202 410-281-7000
Banks - southeast
[DRP 5%]

Proxim, Inc. PROX
295 N. Bernado Ave.
Mountain View, CA 94043 415-960-1630
Telecommunications equipment

Proxima Corp. PRXM
9440 Carroll Park Dr.
San Diego, CA 92121 619-457-5500
Video equipment

PSB Holdings Corp. PSBX
100 W. Main St.
Xenia, OH 45385 513-372-7641
Banks - midwest

PSC Inc. PSCX
770 Basket Rd.
Webster, NY 14580 716-265-1600
Data collection & systems

PSICOR, Inc. PCOR
16818 Via del Campo Court
San Diego, CA 92127 619-485-5599
Medical services

Public Service Company of North Carolina,
Inc. PSNC
400 Cox Rd., PO Box 1398
Gastonia, NC 28053 704-864-6731
Utility - gas distribution
[DRP 5%]

Pulaski Furniture Corp. PLFC
PO Box 1371
Pulaski, VA 24301 703-980-7330
Furniture

Pulse Bancorp, Inc. PULS
6 Jackson St.
South River, NJ 08882 908-257-2400
Financial - savings and loans

Pulse Engineering, Inc. PLSE
12220 World Trade Dr.
San Diego, CA 92128 619-674-8100
Electrical components - misc.

Pure Tech International, Inc. PURT
100 Franklin Square Dr.
Somerset, NJ 08873 908-302-1000
Pollution control equipment & services

Purepac, Inc. PURE
200 Elmora Ave.
Elizabeth, NJ 07207 908-527-9100
Drugs - generic

Puritan-Bennett Corp. PBEN
9401 Indian Creek Parkway
Overland Park, KS 66210
913-661-0444
Medical instruments O

Purolator Products Co. PFIL
6120 S. Yale Ave.
Tulsa, OK 74136 918-481-2500
Filtration products

Purus, Inc. PURS
2713 N. First St.
San Jose, CA 95134 408-955-1000
Pollution control equipment & services

Putnam Trust Co. of Greenwich PTNM
10 Mason St.
Greenwich, CT 06830 203-869-3000
Banks - northeast

PXRE Corp. PXRE
80 Maiden Ln.
New York, NY 10038 212-837-9520
Insurance - property & casualty

Pyramid Technology Corp. PYRD
3860 N. First St.
San Jose, CA 95134 408-428-9000
Computers - mini & micro O

Pyxis Corp. PYXS
9380 Carroll Park Dr.
San Diego, CA 92121
619-625-3300
Medical products O

QLogic Corp. QLGC
3545 Harbor Blvd., PO Box 5001
Costa Mesa, CA 92628 714-438-2200
Computers - peripheral equipment

Quad Systems Corp. QSYS
Two Electronic Dr.
Horsham, PA 19044 215-657-6202
Electronics - components & systems

Quaker Chemical Corp. QCHM
Elm and Lee Sts.
Conshohocken, PA 19428
610-832-4000
Chemicals - specialty

Quaker City Bancorp, Inc. QCBC
7021 Greenleaf Ave.
Whittier, CA 90602 310-907-2200
Banks - west

Quaker Fabric Corp. QFAB
941 Grinnell St.
Fall River, MA 02721
508-678-1951
Textiles - mill products

QUALCOMM Inc. QCOM
06455 Lusk Blvd.
San Diego, CA 92121 619-587-1121
Telecommunications equipment O

Quality Dining, Inc. QDIN
3820 Edison Lakes Parkway
Mishawaka, IN 46545 219-271-4600
Retail - food & restaurants

Quality Food Centers, Inc. QFCI
10112 N.E. 10th St.
Bellevue, WA 98004 206-455-3761
Retail - supermarkets

Quality Semiconductor, Inc. QUAL
851 Martin Ave.
Santa Clara, CA 95050 408-450-8000
Electrical components - semiconductors

Quality Systems, Inc. QSII
17822 E. 17th St.
Tustin, CA 92680 714-731-7171
Computers - software

Quantum Corp. QNTM
500 McCarthy Blvd.
Milpitas, CA 95035 408-894-4000
Computers - peripheral equipment O

Quantum Health Resources, Inc. QHRI
790 The City Drive South
Orange, CA 92668 714-750-1610
Medical services O

Quarterdeck Office Systems, Inc. QDEK
150 Pico Blvd.
Santa Monica, CA 90405
310-392-9851
Computers - software O

Queens County Bancorp, Inc. QCSB
38-25 Main St.
Flushing, NY 11354 718-359-6400
Financial - savings and loans

Quest Medical, Inc. QMED
One Allentown Parkway
Allen, TX 75002 214-390-9800
Medical products

QuickResponse Services Inc. QRSI
1400 Marina Way South
Richmond, CA 94804 510-215-5000
Business services

Quickturn Design Systems, Inc. QKTN
440 Clyde Ave.
Mountain View, CA 94043 415-967-3300
Electronics - components & systems

Quidel Corp. QDEL
10165 McKellar Court
San Diego, CA 92121 619-552-1100
Medical products

Quiksilver, Inc. QUIK
1740 Monrovia Ave.
Costa Mesa, CA 92627
714-645-1395
Textiles - apparel

Quincy Savings Bank QUIN
1200 Hancock St.
Quincy, MA 02169 617-471-3500
Banks - northeast

Quintiles Transnational Corp. QTRN
1007 Slater Rd.
Morrisville, NC 27560
919-941-2888
Medical services

Quipp, Inc. QUIP
4800 N.W. 157th St.
Hialeah, FL 33014 305-623-8700
Miscellaneous - not elsewhere classified

Quixote Corp. QUIX
One E. Wacker Dr.
Chicago, IL 60601 312-467-6755
Protection - safety equipment & services

Quorum Health Group, Inc. QHGI
155 Franklin Rd., Ste. 401
Brentwood, TN 37027 615-320-7979
Hospitals

QVC, Inc. QVCN
Goshen Corporate Park
West Chester, PA 19380
610-430-1000
Retail - mail order & direct O

R&B, Inc. RBIN
3400 E. Walnut St.
Colmar, PA 18915 215-997-1800
Automotive & trucking - replacement parts

Racotek, Inc. RACO
7301 Ohms Ln., Ste. 200
Minneapolis, MN 55439
612-832-9800
Computers - software

Radiation Care, Inc. RDCR
1155 Hammond Dr., Building A
Atlanta, GA 30328 404-399-0663
Medical services

Radius, Inc. RDUS
1710 Fortune Dr.
San Jose, CA 95131 408-434-1010
Computers - peripheral equipment O

Rag Shops, Inc. RAGS
111 Wagaraw Rd.
Hawthorne, NJ 07506
201-423-1303
Retail - misc.

RailTex, Inc. RTEX
4040 Broadway, Ste. 200
San Antonio, TX 78209 210-841-7600
Transportation - rail

Rainbow Technologies, Inc. RNBO
9292 Jeronimo Rd.
Irvine, CA 92718 714-454-2100
Computers - peripheral equipment

Rally's Hamburgers, Inc. RLLY
10002 Shelbyville Rd.
Louisville, KY 40223 502-245-8900
Retail - food & restaurants

Ramapo Financial Corp. RMPO
64 Mountain View Blvd.
Wayne, NJ 07470 201-696-6100
Banks - northeast

Ramsay Health Care, Inc. RHCI
639 Loyola Ave., Ste. 1700
New Orleans, LA 70113 504-525-2505
Hospitals

Ramtron International Corp. RMTR
1850 Ramtron Dr.
Colorado Springs, CO 80921 719-481-7000
Computers - peripheral equipment

Random Access, Inc. RNDM
8000 E. Iliff Ave.
Denver, CO 80231 303-745-9600
Computers - peripheral equipment

Raritan Bancorp Inc. RARB
9 W. Somerset St.
Raritan, NJ 08869
908-725-0080
Banks - northeast

RasterOps ROPS
2500 Walsh Ave.
Santa Clara, CA 95051 408-562-4200
Computers - graphics

Rational Software Corp. RATL
2800 San Tomas
Santa Clara, CA 95051 408-496-3600
Computers - software

Raven Industries, Inc. RAVN
PO Box 1007
Sioux Falls, SD 57117 605-336-2750
Diversified operations

Rawlings Sporting Goods Co., Inc. RAWL
1859 Intertech Dr.
Fenton, MO 63026 314-349-3500
Leisure & recreational products

Raymond Corp. RAYM
S. Canal St., PO Box 130
Greene, NY 13778 607-656-2311
Machinery - material handling
[DRP]

Re Capital Corp. RCAP
Two Stamford Plaza
Stamford, CT 06904 203-977-6100
Insurance - property & casualty

Read-Rite Corp. RDRT
345 Los Coches St.
Milpitas, CA 95035 408-262-6700
Computers - peripheral equipment

Reading Co. RDGCA
30 S. Fifteenth St., Ste. 1300
Philadelphia, PA 14102
215-569-3344
Real estate operations

Recoton Corp. RCOT
2950 Lake Emma Rd.
Lake Mary, FL 32746 407-333-0900
Audio & video home products

Recovery Engineering, Inc. REIN
2229 Edgewood Ave. South
Minneapolis, MN 55426 612-541-1313
Pollution control equipment & services

RedFed Bancorp, Inc. REDF
300 E. State St.
Redlands, CA 92373 909-793-2391
Banks - west

Redman Industries, Inc. RDMN
2550 Walnut Hill Ln.
Dallas, TX 75229 214-353-3600
Building - mobile homes & RV

Reeds Jewelers, Inc. REED
2525 S. Seventeenth St.
Wilmington, NC 28401 910-350-3100
Retail - jewelry stores

Reflectone, Inc. RFTN
4908 Tampa West Blvd.
Tampa, FL 33634 813-885-7481
Electronics - military

Regal Cinemas, Inc. REGL
7132 Commercial Park Dr.
Knoxville, TN 37918 615-922-1123
Motion pictures & services

Regency Equities Corp. RGEQ
11400 W. Olympic Blvd.
Los Angeles, CA 90064 310-575-1500
Real estate operations

Regeneron Pharmaceuticals, Inc. REGN
777 Old Sawmill River Rd.
Tarrytown, NY 10591 914-347-7000
Biomedical & genetic products O

Regional Acceptance Corp. REGA
3004 S. Memorial Dr.
Greenville, NC 27834 919-756-2148
Financial - consumer loans

Regions Financial Corp. RGBK
417 N. 20th St., PO Box 10247
Birmingham, AL 35202 205-326-7100
Banks - southeast
[DRP]

Regis Corp. RGIS
7201 Metro Blvd.
Minneapolis, MN 55439
612-947-7777
Retail - misc.

RehabCare Corp. RHBC
112 S. Hanley Rd.
St. Louis, MO 63105 314-863-7422
Healthcare - outpatient & home

Rehabilicare, Inc. REHB
1811 Old Highway 8
New Brighton, MN 55112
612-631-0590
Medical products

Rehability Corp. RHAB
111 Westwood Place, Ste. 210
Brentwood, TN 37027 615-377-2937
Healthcare - outpatient & home

Reliability Inc. REAL
16400 Park Row
Houston, TX 77084 713-492-0550
Electronics - measuring instruments

Reliance Bancorp, Inc. RELY
585 Stewart Ave.
Garden City, NY 11530 516-222-9300
Financial - savings and loans

ReLife, Inc. RELF
813 Shades Creek Parkway
Birmingham, AL 35209 205-870-8099
Healthcare - outpatient & home

REN Corporation - USA RENL
6820 Charlotte Pike
Nashville, TN 37209 615-353-4200
Healthcare - outpatient & home

Renaissance Communications Corp.
RRRR
One Fawcett Place, Ste. 120
Greenwich, CT 06830 203-629-1888
Broadcasting - radio & TV

Renal Treatment Centers Inc. RXTC
1180 W. Swedesford Rd.
Berwyn, PA 19312 610-644-4796
Healthcare - outpatient & home

Reno Air, Inc. RENO
690 E. Plumb Ln.
Reno, NV 89502
702-829-5750
Transportation - airline

Rentrak Corp. RENT
7227 N.E. 55th Ave.
Portland, OR 97218 503-284-7581
Leisure & recreational services

Repligen Corp. RGEN
One Kendall Square, Bldg. 700
Cambridge, MA 02139 617-225-6000
Biomedical & genetic products

Reptron Electronics, Inc. REPT
14401 McCormick Dr.
Tampa, FL 33626 813-854-02351
Electronics - parts distribution

Republic Automotive Parts, Inc. RAUT
500 Wilson Pike Circle
Brentwood, TN 37027 615-373-2050
Automotive & trucking - replacement parts

Republic Bancorp Inc. RBNC
1070 E. Main St., PO Box 70
Owosso, MI 48867 517-725-7337
Banks - midwest

Republic Bank ARBC
23133 Hawthorne Blvd.
Torrance, CA 90509 310-378-8483
Banks - west

Republic Security Financial Corp. RSFC
3970 RCA Blvd., Ste. 7000
Palm Beach Gardens, FL 33410
407-840-1200
Financial - savings and loans

Republic Waste Industries, Inc. RWIN
2849 Paces Ferry Rd. N.W.
Atlanta, GA 30339 404-431-7140
Pollution control equipment & services

Res-Care, Inc. RSCR
1300 Embassy Square
Louisville, KY 40299 502-491-3464
Healthcare - outpatient & home

Research Industries Corp. REIC
6864 S. 300 West
Salt Lake City, UT 84047
801-562-0200
Medical products O

Research, Inc. RESR
6425 Flying Cloud Dr.
Eden Prairie, MN 55344 612-941-3300
Electrical components - misc.

Reserve Industries Corp. ROIL
20 First Plaza, Ste. 308
Albuquerque, NM 87102 505-247-2384
Metals - non ferrous

ReSound Corp. RSND
220 Saginaw Dr.
Redwood City, CA 94063 415-780-7800
Medical products O

Resource America, Inc. REXI
1609 Walnut St.
Philadelphia, PA 19103 215-557-8454
Oil & gas - production & pipeline

Resource Bancshares Mortgage Group Inc.
REMI
7909 Parklane Rd.
Columbia, SC 29223 803-741-3000
Financial - mortgages & related services

Respironics, Inc. RESP
1001 Murry Ridge Dr.
Murrysville, PA 15668
412-733-0200
Medical products

Retirement Care Associates, Inc. RCRE
6000 Lake Forest Dr.
Atlanta, GA 30328 404-255-7500
Nursing homes

Retix Inc. RETX
2401 Colorado Ave.
Palo Alto, CA 90404 310-828-3400
Computers - software O

Rexall Sundown, Inc. RXSD
851 Broken Sound Parkway NW
Boca Raton, FL 33487 305-565-3566
Vitamins & nutritional products

Rexhall Industries, Inc. REXL
25655 Springbrook Ave.
Saugus, CA 91350 805-253-1295
Building - mobile homes & RV

Rexon Inc. REXN
1334 Parkview Ave., Ste. 200
Manhattan Beach, CA 90230
310-545-4441
Computers - peripheral equipment

Rexworks Inc. REXW
445 W. Oklahoma Ave.
Milwaukee, WI 53207 414-747-7200
Machinery - construction & mining

RF Monolithics, Inc. RFMI
4441 Sigma Rd.
Dallas, TX 75244 214-233-2903
Electronics - components & systems

RFS Hotel Investors, Inc. RFSI
1213 Park Place Center
Memphis, TN 38119 901-767-5154
Real estate investment trust

Rheometrics Scientific, Inc. RHEM
One Possumtown Rd.
Piscataway, NJ 08854 908-560-8550
Instruments - control

Ribi ImmunoChem Research, Inc. RIBI
553 Old Corvallis Rd.
Hamilton, MT 59840 406-363-6214
Biomedical & genetic products O

Richardson Electronics, Ltd. RELL
40W267 Keslinger Rd.
LaFox, IL 60147 708-208-2200
Electronics - parts distribution

Richey Electronics, Inc. RCHY
7441 Lincoln Way, Ste. 100
Garden Grove, CA 92641
714-898-8288
Electrical components - misc.

Richfood Holdings, Inc. RCHFA
PO Box 26967
Richmond, VA 23261 804-746-6000
Food - wholesale

Riddell Sports, Inc. RIDL
810 Seventh Ave.
New York, NY 10019 212-586-6800
Leisure & recreational products

Riggs National Corp. RIGS
1503 Pennsylvania Ave., N.W.
Washington, DC 20005 202-835-6000
Banks - southeast O

Right Management Consultants, Inc. RMCI
1818 Market St.
Philadelphia, PA 19103
215-988-1588
Business services

Rimage Corp. RIMG
7725 Washington Ave. South
Minneapolis, MN 55439 612-944-8144
Computers - peripheral equipment

Ringer Corp. RING
9959 Valley View Road
Eden Prairie, MN 55344 612-941-4180
Chemicals - specialty

Rio Hotel and Casino, Inc. RIOH
3700 W. Flamingo Rd.
Las Vegas, NV 89103 702-252-7733
Leisure & recreational services O

River Forest Bancorp, Inc. RFBC
3959 N. Lincoln Ave.
Chicago, IL 60613 312-549-7100
Banks - midwest

River Oaks Furniture, Inc. OAKS
200 Riverview Dr.
Fulton, MS 38843 601-862-7774
Furniture

Riverside Group, Inc. RSGI
7800 Belfort Parkway
Jacksonville, FL 32202 904-279-2600
Insurance - multi line & misc.

Riverside National Bank RNRC
3484 Central Ave.
Riverside, CA 92506 909-276-8800
Banks - west

Roadway Services, Inc. ROAD
1077 Gorge Blvd., PO Box 88
Akron, OH 44309 216-384-8184
Transportation - truck O
[DRP]

Roanoke Electric Steel Corp. RESC
PO Box 13948
Roanoke, VA 24038 703-342-1831
Steel - production
[DRP]

Roanoke Gas Co. RGCO
519 Kimball Ave. N.E.
Roanoke, VA 24016 703-983-3800
Utility - gas distribution
[DRP]

Robbins & Myers, Inc. ROBN
1400 Kettering Tower
Dayton, OH 45423 513-222-2610
Machinery - electrical

Robec, Inc. ROBC
425 Privet Rd.
Horsham, PA 19044 215-675-9300
Computers - retail & wholesale

Roberd's, Inc. RBDS
1100 E. Central Ave.
West Carrollton, OH 45449 513-859-5127
Retail - home furnishings

Roberts Pharmaceutical Corp. RPCX
6 Industrial Way West
Eatontown, NJ 07724 908-389-1182
Drugs O

Robinson Nugent, Inc. RNIC
800 E. Eighth St., PO Box 1208
New Albany, IN 47151 812-945-0211
Electrical connectors

Robotic Vision Systems, Inc. ROBV
425 Rabro Dr. East
Hauppauge, NY 11788 516-273-9700
Video equipment

Rock Bottom Restaurants, Inc. BREW
1215 Spruce St., Ste. 102
Boulder, CO 80302 303-443-8422
Retail - food & restaurants

Rock-Tenn Co. RKTN
504 Thrasher St.
Norcross, GA 30071 404-448-2193
Paper & paper products

Rocky Shoes & Boots, Inc. RCKY
39 E. Canal St.
Nelsonville, OH 45764 614-753-1951
Shoes & related apparel

Roosevelt Financial Group, Inc. RFED
900 Roosevelt Parkway
Chesterfield, MO 63017 314-532-6200
Financial - savings and loans O
[DRP]

Ropak Corp. ROPK
600 S. State College Blvd.
Fullerton, CA 51381 714-870-9757
Containers - paper & plastic

Roper Industries, Inc. ROPR
PO Box 269
Commerce, GA 30529 706-335-5551
Instruments - control

Rose's Stores, Inc. RSTOQ
218 S. Garnett St.
Henderson, NC 27536 919-430-2600
Retail - discount & variety
[DRP]

Ross Stores, Inc. ROST
8333 Central Ave.
Newark, CA 94560 510-790-4400
Retail - apparel & shoes O

Ross Systems, Inc. ROSS
555 Twin Dolphin Dr.
Redwood City, CA 94065
415-593-2500
Computers - software

RoTech Medical Corp. ROTC
4506 L.B. McLeod Rd., Ste. F
Orlando, FL 32811 407-841-2115
Medical products

Roto-Rooter, Inc. ROTO
255 E. Fifth St.
Cincinnati, OH 45202 513-762-6690
Building - maintenance & services

Rottlund Co. RHOM
2681 Long Lake Rd.
Roseville, MN 55113 612-638-0500
Building - residential & commercial

Rouse Co. ROUS
10275 Little Patuxent Pkwy.
Columbia, MD 21044 410-992-6000
Real estate operations
[DRP]

Roy F. Weston, Inc. WSTNA
1 Weston Way
West Chester, PA 19380 610-701-3000
Pollution control equipment & services

Royal Bank of Pennsylvania RBPAA
732 Montgomery Ave.
Narberth, PA 19072 610-668-4700
Banks - northeast

Royal Grip, Inc. GRIP
444 W. Geneva Dr.
Tempe, AZ 85282 602-829-9000
Leisure & recreational products

Royce OTC Micro-Cap Fund, Inc. OTCM
1414 Avenue of the Americas
New York, NY 10019 212-355-7311
Financial - investment management

RPM, Inc. RPOW
2628 Pearl Rd., PO Box 777
Medina, OH 44258 216-273-5090
Paints & allied products O
[DRP]

RS Financial Corp. RFBK
219 Fayetteville Street Mall
Raleigh, NC 27601 919-833-7511
Financial - savings and loans

Rule Industries, Inc. RULE
70 Blanchard Rd.
Burlington, MA 01803
617-272-7400
Diversified operations

Rural/Metro Corp. RURL
8401 E. Indian School Rd.
Scottsdale, AZ 85251 602-994-3886
Medical services

Ryan's Family Steak Houses, Inc. RYAN
405 Lancaster Ave., PO Box 100
Greer, SC 29652 803-879-1000
Retail - food & restaurants O

Ryan, Beck & Co., Inc. RBCO
80 Main St.
West Orange, NJ 07052 201-325-3000
Financial - investment bankers

S & T Bancorp, Inc. STBA
800 Philadelphia St.
Indiana, PA 15701 412-349-2900
Banks - northeast

S&K Famous Brands, Inc. SKFB
PO Box 31800
Richmond, VA 23294
804-346-2500
Retail - apparel & shoes

S-K-I Ltd. SKII
c/o Killington Ltd.
Killington, VT 05751 802-422-3333
Leisure & recreational services

S3, Inc. SIII
2770 San Tomas Expressway
Santa Clara, CA 95051
408-980-5400
Computers - software O

Saber Software Corp. SABR
5944 Luther Ln., Ste. 1007
Dallas, TX 75225 214-361-8086
Computers - software

SAFECO Corp. SAFC
SAFECO Plaza
Seattle, WA 98185 206-545-5000
Insurance - property & casualty O

Safeguard Health Enterprises, Inc. SFGD
505 N. Euclid St., Ste. 200
Anaheim, CA 92803 714-778-1284
Medical services

Safeskin Corp. SFSK
5100 Town Center Circle
Boca Raton, FL 33486 407-395-9988
Medical & dental supplies

Safety 1st, Inc. SAFT
210 Boylston St.
Chestnut Hill, MA 02167 617-964-7744
Protection - safety equipment & services

Safety Components International, Inc.
ABAG
3190 Pullman St.
Costa Mesa, CA 92626 714-662-7756
Automotive & trucking - original equipment

SafetyTek Corp. SAFE
49050 Milmont Dr.
Fremont, CA 94538 510-226-9600
Instruments - control

Salick Health Care, Inc. SHCI
407 N. Maple Dr.
Beverly Hills, CA 90210 310-276-7058
Healthcare - outpatient & home

Salton/Maxim Housewares, Inc. SALT
550 Business Center Dr.
Mt. Prospect, IL 60056 708-803-4600
Appliances - household

Sam & Libby, Inc. SAML
58 West 40th St.
New York, NY 10018 212-944-4830
Shoes & related apparel

Sanderson Farms, Inc. SAFM
225 N. 13th Ave., PO Box 988
Laurel, MS 39441 601-649-4030
Food - meat products

SangStat Medical Corp. SANG
1505 Adams Dr.
Menlo Park, CA 94025 415-328-0300
Drugs

Sanmina Corp. SANM
212 O'Toole Ave.
San Jose, CA 95131 408-435-8444
Electrical components - misc.

SatCon Technology Corp. SATC
161 First St.
Cambridge, MA 02142 617-661-0540
Instruments - control

Satellite Technology Management, Inc.
STMI
3530 Hyland Ave.
Costa Mesa, CA 92626 714-557-2400
Telecommunications equipment

Savoy Pictures Entertainment, Inc. SPEI
152 W. 57th St.
New York, NY 10019 212-247-5810
Motion pictures & services

Sayett Group, Inc. SAYT
17 Tobey Village Office Park
Pittsford, NY 14534 716-264-9250
Protection - safety equipment & services

SBE, Inc. SBEI
4550 Norris Canyon Rd.
San Ramon, CA 94583 510-355-2000
Computers - peripheral equipment

Scan-Optics, Inc. SOCR
22 Prestige Park Circle
East Hartford, CT 06108 203-289-6001
Computers - peripheral equipment

Scherer Healthcare, Inc. SCHR
2859 Paces Ferry Rd., Ste. 300
Atlanta, GA 30339 404-333-0066
Diversified operations

Schnitzer Steel Industries, Inc. SCHN
3200 N.W. Yeon Ave.
Portland, OR 97210
503-224-9900
Steel - production

Scholastic Corp. SCHL
555 Broadway
New York, NY 10012
212-343-6100
Publishing - periodicals

Schuler Homes, Inc. SHLR
828 Fort Street Mall, 4th Fl.
Honolulu, HI 96813 808-521-5661
Building - residential & commercial

Schultz Sav-O Stores, Inc. SAVO
2215 Union Ave.
Sheboygan, WI 53081
414-457-4433
Retail - supermarkets

SCI Systems, Inc. SCIS
PO Box 1000
Huntsville, AL 35807 205-882-4800
Electronics - components & systems O

SciClone Pharmaceuticals, Inc. SCLN
901 Mariner's Island Blvd.
San Mateo, CA 94404 415-358-3456
Drugs O

Science Dynamics Corp. SIDY
1919 Springdale Rd.
Cherry Hill, NJ 08003 609-424-0068
Telecommunications equipment

Scientific Games Holding Corp. SGIH
1500 Blue Grass Lakes Pkwy.
Alpharetta, GA 30201 404-664-3700
Leisure & recreational products

Scientific Software-Intercomp, Inc. SSFT
1801 California St., Ste. 295
Denver, CO 80202 303-292-1111
Computers - software

Scientific Technologies Inc. STIZ
31069 Genstar Rd.
Hayward, CA 94544 510-471-9717
Instruments - control

SciGenics, Inc. SCGN
87 CambridgePark Dr.
Cambridge, MA 02140 617-876-1170
Medical services

SCIMED Life Systems, Inc. SMLS
One SCIMED Place
Maple Grove, MN 55311 612-494-1700
Medical instruments O

Scios Nova, Inc. SCIO
2450 Bayshore Parkway
Mountain View, CA 94043 415-966-1550
Biomedical & genetic products O

Scott & Stringfellow Financial, Inc. SCOT
909 E. Main St.
Richmond, VA 23219 804-643-1811
Financial - investment management

SDNB Financial Corp. SDNB
1420 Kettner Blvd.
San Diego, CA 92101
619-233-1234
Banks - west

Seacoast Banking Corporation of Florida
SBCFA
U.S. 1 and Colorado Ave.
Stuart, FL 34995 407-287-4000
Banks - southeast

SEACOR Holdings, Inc. CKOR
5000 Railroad Ave.
Morgan City, LA 70380 504-385-3475
Oil & gas - field services

Seafield Capital Corp. SFLD
2600 Grand Ave., Ste 500
Kansas City, MO 64141 816-842-7000
Insurance - life
[DRP]

Sealright Co., Inc. SRCO
7101 College Blvd.
Overland Park, KS 66210 913-344-9000
Containers - paper & plastic

Seaman Furniture Co., Inc. SEAM
300 Crossways Park Dr.
Woodbury, NY 11797 516-496-9560
Retail - home furnishings

Search Capital Group, Inc. SRCG
700 N. Pearl St., Ste. 400
Dallas, TX 75201 214-954-6403
Financial - business services

Seattle FilmWorks, Inc. FOTO
1260 16th Ave. West
Seattle, WA 98119 206-281-1390
Retail - mail order & direct

Seaway Food Town, Inc. SEWY
1020 Ford St.
Maumee, OH 43537 419-893-9401
Retail - supermarkets

Secom General Corp. SECM
37650 Professional Center Dr.
Livonia, MI 48154 313-953-3990
Machine tools & related products

Second Bancorp, Inc. SECD
108 Main Ave., S.W.
Warren, OH 44482 216-841-0123
Banks - midwest [DRP]

Security Bancorp SFBM
219 N. 26th St., PO Box 2503
Billings, MT 59103 406-259-4571
Financial - savings and loans

Security Capital Bancorp SCBC
507 W. Innes St.
Salisbury, NC 28144 704-636-3775
Banks - southeast
[DRP]

Security Capital Corp. SECP
184 W. Wisconsin Ave.
Milwaukee, WI 53203 414-273-8090
Banks - midwest

Security Environmental Systems, Inc. SENV
15302 Pipeline Ln.
Huntington Beach, CA 92649
310-431-8486
Pollution control equipment & services

Security Federal Savings and Loan SFSL
1413 Golden Gate Blvd.
Mayfield Heights, OH 44124
216-449-3700
Financial - savings and loans

Security Savings Bank, F.S.B. SSVB
301 W. Michigan Ave.
Jackson, MI 49201 517-787-9700
Financial - savings and loans

Seda Specialty Packaging Corp. SSPC
2501 W. Rosecrans Blvd.
Los Angeles, CA 90059 310-635-4444
Miscellaneous - not elsewhere classified

SEEQ Technology, Inc. SEEQ
4731 Bayside Parkway
Fremont, CA 94538 510-226-7400
Electrical components - semiconductors

SEI Corp. SEIC
680 E. Swedesford Rd.
Wayne, PA 19087 610-254-1000
Computers - services

Seibels Bruce Group, Inc. SBIG
1501 Lady St.
Columbia, SC 29201 803-748-2000
Insurance - property & casualty
[DRP]

Selective Insurance Group, Inc. SIGI
40 Wantage Ave.
Branchville, NJ 07890 201-948-3000
Insurance - property & casualty
[DRP]

Selfix, Inc. SLFX
4501 W. 47th St.
Chicago, IL 60632 312-890-1010
Housewares

Seneca Foods Corp. SENE
1162 Pittsford-Victor Rd.
Pittsford, NY 14534 716-385-9500
Food - canned

Sepracor Inc. SEPR
33 Locke Dr.
Marlborough, MA 01752 508-481-6700
Drugs O

Sequent Computer Systems, Inc. SQNT
15450 SW Koll Pkwy.
Beaverton, OR 97006 503-626-5700
Computers - mainframe O

Sequoia Systems, Inc. SEQS
400 Nickerson Rd.
Marlborough, MA 01752 508-480-0800
Computers - mini & micro

Seragen, Inc. SRGN
97 South St.
Hopkinton, MA 01748 508-435-2331
Medical products

Serv-Tech, Inc. STEC
5200 Cedar Crest Blvd.
Houston, TX 77087 713-644-9974
Oil & gas - field services

Sevenson Environmental Services Inc.
 SEVN
2749 Lockport Rd., PO Box 396
Niagara Falls, NY 14302 716-284-0431
Pollution control equipment & services

SFFed Corp. SFFD
88 Kearny St.
San Francisco, CA 94108 415-955-5800
Financial - savings and loans

SFX Broadcasting, Inc. SFXBA
150 E. 58th St., 19th Fl.
New York, NY 10155 212-407-9191
Broadcasting - radio & TV

SGI International SGII
1200 Prospect St., Ste. 325
La Jolla, CA 92037 619-551-1090
Engineering - R & D services

Shaman Pharmaceuticals, Inc. SHMN
213 E. Grand Ave.
South San Francisco, CA 94080
415-952-7070
Drugs

Shared Medical Systems Corp. SMED
51 Valley Stream Parkway
Malvern, PA 19355 215-219-6300
Computers - services O

Shared Technologies, Inc. STCH
100 Great Meadow Rd.
Wethersfield, CT 06109 203-258-2400
Business services

Sharper Image Corp. SHRP
650 Davis St.
San Francisco, CA 94111
415-445-6000
Retail - mail order & direct

Sheldahl, Inc. SHEL
1150 Sheldahl Rd.
Northfield, MN 55057 507-663-8000
Electrical components - misc.

Shelton Bancorp, Inc. SSBC
375 Bridgeport Ave.
Shelton, CT 06484 203-944-2200
Banks - northeast

Shiloh Industries, Inc. SHLO
1013 Centre Rd,. Ste. 350
Wilmington, DE 19805 302-998-0592
Steel - production

Shiva Corp. SHVA
Northwest Park, 63 Third Ave.
Burlington, MA 01803 617-270-8300
Telecommunications equipment

Sho-Me Financial Corp. SMFC
109 N. Hickory St.
Mt. Vernon, MO 65712 417-466-2171
Banks - midwest

Shoe Carnival, Inc. SCVL
8233 Baumgart Rd.
Evansville, IN 47711
 812-867-6471
Retail - apparel & shoes

ShoLodge, Inc. LODG
217 W. Main St.
Gallatin, TN 37066 615-452-7200
Hotels & motels

Shoreline Financial Corp. SLFC
823 Riverview Dr.
Benton Harbor, MI 49022 616-927-2251
Banks - midwest
[DRP]

Shorewood Packaging Corp. SHOR
55 Engineers Ln.
Farmingdale, NY 11735
516-694-2900
Paper & paper products

ShowBiz Pizza Time, Inc. SHBZ
4441 W. Airport Freeway
Irving, TX 75015 214-258-8507
Retail - food & restaurants O

Showscan Entertainment, Inc. SHOW
1801 Century Park East
Los Angeles, CA 90067 310-553-2364
Motion pictures & services

Shuffle Master, Inc. SHFL
10921 Valley View Rd.
Eden Prairie, MN 55344 612-943-1951
Leisure & recreational products

Shurgard Storage Centers, Inc. SHUR
1201 Third Ave., Ste. 2200
Seattle, WA 98101 206-624-8100
Real estate investment trust

SI Handling Systems, Inc. SIHS
600 Kuebler Rd.
Easton, PA 18042 610-252-7321
Machinery - material handling

Sierra On-Line, Inc. SIER
3380 146th Place, SE
Bellevue, WA 98007 206-649-9800
Computers - software

Sierra Semiconductor Corp. SERA
2075 N. Capitol Ave.
San Jose, CA 95132 408-263-9300
Electrical components - semiconductors

Sierra Tahoe Bancorp STBS
10059 Palisades Dr.
Truckee, CA 95734 916-582-3000
Banks - west

Sierra Tucson Companies, Inc. STSN
16500 N. Lago del Oro Pkwy.
Tucson, AZ 85737 602-792-5800
Healthcare - outpatient & home

Sigma Circuits, Inc. SIGA
393 Mathew St.
Santa Clara, CA 95050 408-727-9169
Electrical connectors

Sigma Designs, Inc. SIGM
46501 Landing Parkway
Fremont, CA 94538 510-770-0100
Computers - peripheral equipment

Sigma-Aldrich Corp. SIAL
3050 Spruce St.
St. Louis, MO 63103 314-771-5765
Chemicals - specialty O

SigmaTron International, Inc. SGMA
2201 Landmeier Rd.
Elk Grove Village, IL 60007
708-956-8000
Electrical components - misc.

Silicon Valley Bancshares SIVB
3000 Lakeside Dr.
Santa Clara, CA 95054 408-980-0766
Banks - west

Silicon Valley Group, Inc. SVGI
2240 Ringwood Ave.
San Jose, CA 95131 408-434-0500
Electrical components - semiconductors O

Siliconix Inc. SILI
2201 Laurelwood Rd.
Santa Clara, CA 95054 408-988-8000
Electrical components - semiconductors

Silver King Communications, Inc. SKTV
12425 28th St. N., Ste. 300
St. Petersburg, FL 33716
813-573-0339
Broadcasting - radio & TV

Simmons First National Corp. SFNCA
501 Main St.
Pine Bluff, AR 71601 501-541-1350
Banks - southeast

Simmons Outdoor Corp. SIMM
2120 Killearney Way
Tallahassee, FL 32308 904-878-5100
Leisure & recreational products

Simpson Industries, Inc. SMPS
32100 Telegraph Rd., Ste. 120
Birmingham Farms, MI 48025 313-540-6200
Automotive & trucking - original equipment
[DRP]

Simpson Manufacturing Co. SMCO
4637 Chabot Dr., Ste. 200
Pleasanton, CA 94588 510-460-9912
Miscellaneous - not elsewhere classified

Siskon Gold Corp. SISK
350 Crown Point Circle
Grass Valley, CA 95945 916-273-4311
Gold mining & processing

SJNB Financial Corp. SJNB
One N. Market St.
San Jose, CA 95113 408-947-7562
Banks - west

Skybox International Inc. SKYB
300 N. Duke St.
Durham, NC 27702 919-361-8100
Leisure & recreational products

SkyWest, Inc. SKYW
444 S. River Rd.
St. George, UT 84770 801-634-3000
Transportation - airline

SLM International, Inc. SLMI
200 Fifth Ave.
New York, NY 10010 212-675-0070
Toys - games & hobby products O

Small's Oilfield Services Corp. FISH
1001 E. FM 700
Big Spring, TX 79720 915-267-3188
Oil & gas - field services

Smithfield Foods, Inc. SFDS
501 N. Church St.
Smithfield, VA 20343 804-357-4321
Food - meat products O

Sodak Gaming, Inc. SODK
405 E. Omaha St.
Rapid City, SD 57701 605-341-5400
Leisure & recreational products

Softdesk, Inc. SDSK
7 Liberty Hill Rd.
Henniker, NH 03242
603-428-3199
Computers - software

SofTech, Inc. SOFT
460 Totten Pond Rd.
Waltham, MA 02154 617-890-6900
Computers - services

Softkey International SKEY
201 Broadway
Cambridge, MA 02139
617-494-1200
Computers - software

Software Professionals, Inc. SFTW
999 Baker Way, Ste. 390
San Mateo, CA 94404
415-578-0700
Computers - software

Software Publishing Corp. SPCO
3165 Kifer Rd.
Santa Clara, CA 95051 408-986-8000
Computers - software O

Software Spectrum, Inc. SSPE
2140 Merritt Dr.
Garland, TX 75041 214-840-6600
Computers - software

Solo Serve Corp. SOLO
1610 Cornerway Blvd.
San Antonio, TX 78219 210-662-6262
Retail - misc.

Somatix Therapy Corp. SOMA
850 Marina Village Pkwy.
Alameda, CA 94501 510-748-3000
Biomedical & genetic products

Somatogen, Inc. SMTG
2545 Central Ave.
Boulder, CO 80301 303-440-9988
Medical products O

Somerset Savings Bank SOSA
212 Elm St.
Somerville, MA 02144 617-625-6000
Banks - northeast

Sonesta International Hotels Corp. SNSTA
200 Clarendon St.
Boston, MA 02116 617-421-5400
Hotels & motels

Sonic Corp. SONC
120 Robert S. Kerr Ave.
Oklahoma City, OK 73102 405-232-4334
Retail - food & restaurants

Sonic Solutions SNIC
1891 E. Francisco Blvd.
San Rafael, CA 94901 415-485-4800
Miscellaneous - not elsewhere classified

Sonoco Products Co. SONO
N. Second St.
Hartsville, SC 29550 803-383-7000
Containers - paper & plastic
[DRP]

Sound Advice, Inc. SUND
1901 Tigertail Blvd.
Dania, FL 33004 305-922-4434
Retail - consumer electronics

Southeastern Michigan Gas Enterprises, Inc.
 SMGS
405 Water St., PO Box 5026
Port Huron, MI 48061 810-987-2200
Utility - gas distribution
[DRP]

Southeastern Thrift and Bank Fund, Inc. STBF
2700 NCNB Plaza
Charlotte, NC 28280 704-379-9000
Financial - investment management

Southern Electronics Corp. SECX
4916 N. Royal Atlanta Dr.
Atlanta, GA 30085 404-491-8962
Wholesale distribution - consumer products

Southern Energy Homes, Inc. SEHI
Highway 41 North, PO Box 269
Addison, AL 35540 205-747-1544
Building - residential & commercial

Southern Mineral Corp. SMIN
17001 Northchase, Ste. 690
Houston, TX 77060 713-872-7621
Oil & gas - US exploration & production

Southern Missouri Bancorp, Inc. SMBC
531 Vine St.
Poplar Bluff, MO 63901 314-785-1421
Financial - savings and loans

SouthTrust Corp. SOTR
420 N. 20th St.
Birmingham, AL 35203 205-254-5009
Banks - southeast O
[DRP]

Southwall Technologies Inc. SWTX
1029 Corporation Way
Palo Alto, CA 94303 415-962-9111
Chemicals - plastics

Southwest Bancorp, Inc. OKSB
608 S. Main St.
Stillwater, OK 74074 405-372-2230
Banks - midwest

Southwest Bancshares, Inc. SWBI
4062 Southwest Highway
Hometown, IL 60456 708-636-2700
Banks - midwest

Southwest National Corp. SWPA
111 S. Main St.
Greensburg, PA 15601 412-834-2310
Banks - northeast

Southwest Securities Group, Inc. SWST
1201 Elm St., Ste. 4300
Dallas, TX 75270 214-651-1800
Financial - investment management

Southwest Water Systems SWWC
225 N. Barranca Ave., Ste. 200
West Covina, CA 91791 818-915-1551
Utility - water supply
[DRP]

Sovereign Bancorp, Inc. SVRN
1130 Berkshire Blvd.
Wyomissing, PA 19610 610-320-8400
Financial - savings and loans O

SpaceLabs Medical, Inc. SLMD
15220 N.E. 40th St.
Redmond, WA 98052
206-882-3700
Medical services

Span-America Medical Systems, Inc. SPAN
70 Commerce Dr.
Greenville, SC 29615 803-288-8877
Medical products

Spartan Motors, Inc. SPAR
1000 Reynolds Rd.
Charlotte, MI 48813 517-543-6400
Automotive & trucking - original equipment
O

Spec's Music, Inc. SPEK
1666 N.W. 82nd Ave.
Miami, FL 33126 305-592-7288
Retail - consumer electronics

Special Devices, Inc. SDII
16830 W. Placerita Canyon Rd.
Newhall, CA 91321 805-259-0753
Electrical components - misc.

Specialty Equipment Cos. SPEQ
6581 Revlon Dr.
Belvidere, IL 61008 815-544-5111
Miscellaneous - not elsewhere classified

Specialty Paperboard, Inc. SPBI
Brudies Rd., PO Box 498
Brattleboro, VT 05301 802-257-0365
Paper & paper products

SpecTran Corp. SPTR
50 Hall Rd.
Sturbridge, MA 01566 508-347-2261
Fiber optics

Spectranetics Corp. SPNC
96 Talamine Court
Colorado Springs, CO 80907
719-633-8333
Lasers - systems & components

Spectrian Corp. SPCT
550 Ellis St.
Mountain View, CA 94043 415-961-1473
Electronics - components & systems

Spectrum Control, Inc. SPEC
6000 W. Ridge Rd.
Erie, PA 16506 814-835-4000
Electronics - components & systems

Spectrum HoloByte, Inc. SBYT
2490 Mariner Square Loop
Alameda, CA 94501 510-522-3584
Computers - software

Spectrum Information Technologies, Inc.
  SPCL
1615 Northern Blvd.
Manhasset, NY 11030 516-627-8992
Telecommunications services

Speizman Industries, Inc. SPZN
508 W. Fifth St.
Charlotte, NC 28202 704-372-3751
Machinery - general industrial

Spiegel, Inc. SPGLA
3500 Lacey Rd.
Downers Grove, IL 60515 708-986-8800
Retail - mail order & direct O

Spire Corp. SPIR
One Patriots Park
Bedford, MA 01730 617-275-6000
Electrical components - semiconductors

Sport Chalet Inc. SPCH
920 Foothill Blvd.
La Canada, CA 91101 818-790-2717
Retail - misc.

Sportmart, Inc. SPMTA
7233 W. Dempster St.
Niles, IL 60714 708-966-1700
Retail - misc.

SportsTown, Inc. SPTN
680 Engineering Dr., Ste. 50
Norcross, GA 30092 404-246-5300
Retail - misc.

Spreckels Industries, Inc. SPKL
4234 Hacienda Dr.
Pleasanton, CA 94588
510-460-0840
Food - sugar & refining

SPSS, Inc. SPSS
444 N. Michigan Ave.
Chicago, IL 60611 312-329-2400
Computers - software

Square Industries, Inc. SQAI
921 Bergen Ave.
Jersey City, NJ 07306 201-798-0090
Transportation - services

St. Francis Capital Corp. STFR
3545 S. Kinnickinnic Ave.
Milwaukee, WI 53235 414-744-8600
Financial - savings and loans

St. Ives Laboratories, Inc. SWIS
9201 Oakdale Ave.
Chatsworth, CA 91311
818-709-5500
Cosmetics & toiletries

St. Jude Medical, Inc. STJM
One Lillehei Plaza
St. Paul, MN 55117 612-483-2000
Medical instruments O

St. Mary Land & Exploration Co. MARY
1776 Lincoln St., Ste. 1100
Denver, CO 80203 303-861-8140
Oil & gas - US exploration & production

St. Paul Bancorp, Inc. SPBC
6700 W. North Ave.
Chicago, IL 60635 312-622-5000
Financial - savings and loans O
[DRP]

STAAR Surgical Co. STAA
1911 Walker Ave.
Monrovia, CA 91016 818-303-7902
Medical products

Stac Electronics STAC
12636 High Bluff Dr.
San Diego, CA 92130
619-794-4300
Computers - software

Stacy's Buffet, Inc. SBUF
801 W. Bay Dr., Ste. 704
Largo, FL 34640 813-581-4492
Retail - food & restaurants

Staff Builders Inc. SBLI
1981 Marcus Ave.
Lake Success, NY 11042
516-358-1000
Business services

Standard Financial, Inc. STND
4192 S. Archer Ave.
Chicago, IL 60632 312-847-1140
Banks - midwest

Standard Management Corp. SMAN
9100 Keystone Crossing
Indianapolis, IN 46240 317-574-6200
Insurance - multi line & misc.

Standard Microsystems Corp. SMSC
80 Arkay Dr.
Hauppauge, NY 11788 516-273-3100
Computers - peripheral equipment O

Stanford Telecommunications, Inc. STII
1221 Crossman Ave.
Sunnyvale, CA 94089 408-745-0818
Electronics - military

Stanley Furniture Co. STLY
Route 57
Stanleytown, VA 24168 703-627-2000
Furniture

Stant Corp. STNT
425 Commerce Dr.
Richmond, IN 47374 317-962-6655
Automotive & trucking - replacement parts

Staodyn, Inc. SDYN
1225 Florida Ave., PO Box 1379
Longmont, CO 80502 303-772-3631
Medical products

Staples, Inc. SPLS
100 Pennsylvania Ave.
Framingham, MA 01701
508-370-8500
Retail - misc. O

Star Technologies, Inc. STRR
515 Shaw Rd.
Sterling, VA 20166 703-689-4400
Computers - peripheral equipment

Starbucks Corp. SBUX
2203 Airport Way South
Seattle, WA 98134 206-447-1575
Retail - food & restaurants O

Starcraft Automotive Corp. STCR
2703 College Ave., PO Box 1903
Goshen, IN 46526 219-533-1105
Automotive & trucking - replacement parts

StarSight Telecast, Inc. SGHT
39650 Liberty St.
Fremont, CA 94538 510-657-9900
Video equipment

State Auto Financial Corp. STFC
518 E. Broad St.
Columbus, OH 43215 614-464-5000
Insurance - property & casualty

State Bancshares Inc. SBNP
1609 Walnut St.
Philadelphia, PA 19103 215-564-5040
Banks - northeast

State Financial Services Corp. SFSW
10708 W. Janesville Rd.
Hales Corner, WI 53130 414-425-1600
Banks - midwest

State of the Art, Inc. SOTA
56 Technology
Irvine, CA 92718 714-753-1222
Computers - software

State Street Boston Corp. STBK
225 Franklin St.
Boston, MA 02110 617-786-3000
Banks - northeast O
[DRP]

Station Casinos, Inc. STCI
2411 W. Sahara Ave.
Las Vegas, NV 89102 702-367-2411
Leisure & recreational services O

Steck-Vaughan Publishing Corp. STEK
8701 N. MoPac Expressway
Austin, TX 78759 512-343-8227
Publishing - books

Steel of West Virginia, Inc. SWVA
17th St. and 2nd Ave.
Huntington, WV 25703
304-696-8200
Steel - production

Steel Technologies Inc. STTX
15415 Shelbyville Rd.
Louisville, KY 40245 502-245-2110
Steel - production

Stein Mart, Inc. SMRT
1200 Gulf Life Dr.
Jacksonville, FL 32207
904-346-1500
Retail - apparel & shoes

STERIS Corp. STRL
9450 Pineneedle Dr.
Mentor, OH 44060 216-354-2600
Medical products O

Sterling Bancshares, Inc. SBIB
15000 Northwest Freeway
Houston, TX 77040 713-466-8300
Banks - midwest

Sterling Financial Corp. STSA
North 120 Wall St.
Spokane, WA 99201 509-458-3711
Financial - savings and loans

Sterling West Bancorp SWBC
3287 Wilshire Blvd.
Los Angeles, CA 90010
213-384-4444
Banks - west

Stewart & Stevenson Services, Inc. SSSS
2707 N. Loop West
Houston, TX 77008 713-868-7700
Engines - internal combustion O

Stewart Enterprises, Inc. STEI
110 Veterans Memorial Blvd.
Metairie, LA 70005 504-837-5880
Funeral services & related

Stimsonite Corp. STIM
7524 N. Natchez Ave.
Niles, IL 60714 708-647-7717
Miscellaneous - not elsewhere classified

Stokely USA, Inc. STKY
1055 Corporate Center Dr.
Oconomowoc, WI 53066
414-569-1800
Food - canned

Strawbridge & Clothier STRWA
801 Market St.
Philadelphia, PA 19107 215-629-6000
Retail - regional department stores

Strober Organization, Inc. STRB
550 Hamilton Ave.
Brooklyn, NY 11232 718-875-9700
Building products - retail & wholesale

Strouds, Inc. STRO
780 S. Nogales St.
City of Industry, CA 91748
818-912-2866
Retail - misc.

Structural Dynamics Research Corp. SDRC
2000 Eastman Dr.
Milford, OH 45150 513-576-2400
Computers - software O

Stryker Corp. STRY
2725 Fairfield Rd.
Kalamazoo, MI 49002 616-385-2600
Medical instruments O

Stuart Entertainment, Inc. STUA
3211 Nebraska Ave.
Council Bluffs, IA 51501 712-323-1488
Leisure & recreational products

Stuarts Department Stores, Inc. STUS
16 Forge Parkway
Franklin, MA 02038 508-520-4540
Retail - regional department stores

STV Group, Inc. STVI
11 Robinson St.
Pottstown, PA 19464
610-326-4600
Engineering - R & D services

SubMicron Systems Corp. SUBM
6330 Hedgewood Dr., Ste. 150
Allentown, PA 18106 215-391-9200
Electronics - components & systems

Suburban Bancorporation, Inc. SBCN
10869 Montgomery Rd.
Cincinnati, OH 45242 513-489-4888
Banks - midwest

Sudbury, Inc. SUDS
30100 Chagrin Blvd., Ste. 203
Cleveland, OH 44124 216-464-7026
Diversified operations

Suffolk Bancorp SUBK
6 W. Second St.
Riverhead, NY 11901 516-727-2700
Banks - northeast
[DRP 3%]

SUGEN, Inc. SUGN
515 Galviston Dr.
Redwood City, CA 94063 415-306-7700
Drugs

Sullivan Dental Products, Inc. SULL
10920 W. Lincoln Ave.
West Allis, WI 53227 414-321-8881
Medical & dental supplies

Sumitomo Bank of California SUMI
320 California St.
San Francisco, CA 94104 415-445-8000
Bank - western
[DRP]

Summa Four, Inc. SUMA
25 Sundial Ave.
Manchester, NH 03103 603-625-4050
Telecommunications equipment

Summa Industries SUIN
1600 W. Commonwealth Ave.
Fullerton, CA 92633 714-738-5000
Machinery - general industrial

Summagraphics Corp. SUGR
60 Silvermine Rd.
Seymour, CT 06483 203-881-5400
Computers - peripheral equipment

Summit Bancorp, Inc. SMMT
400 112th Ave. N.E.
Bellevue, WA 98004 206-451-3585
Financial - savings and loans

Summit Bancorporation SUBN
One Main St.
Chatham, NJ 07928 201-701-2666
Banks - northeast
[DRP 3.5%]

Summit Bancshares, Inc. SBIT
1300 Summit Ave., Ste. 604
Fort Worth, TX 76102 817-336-8383
Banks - midwest

Summit Care Corp. SUMC
2600 W. Magnolia Blvd.
Burbank, CA 91505 818-841-8750
Health maintenance organization

Summit Technology, Inc. BEAM
21 Hickory Dr.
Waltham, MA 02154 617-890-1234
Lasers - systems & components O

Sun Microsystems, Inc. SUNW
2550 Garcia Ave.
Mountain View, CA 94043 415-960-1300
Computers - mini & micro

Sun Sportswear, Inc. SSPW
6520 S. 190th St.
Kent, WA 98032 206-251-3565
Apparel

Sun Television and Appliances, Inc. SNTV
1583 Alum Creek Dr.
Columbus, OH 43209 614-445-8401
Retail - consumer electronics O

Sunbelt Companies, Inc. SBLT
530 Howell Rd., Ste. 100
Greenville, SC 29615 803-244-4137
Building products - retail & wholesale

Suncoast Savings and Loan Association
  SCSL
4000 Hollywood Blvd.
Hollywood, FL 33021 305-981-6400
Financial - savings and loans

Sundance Homes, Inc. SUNH
5360 Keystone Ct.
Rolling Meadows, IL 60008
708-255-5555
Building - residential & commercial

SunGard Data Systems Inc. SNDT
1285 Drummers Ln.
Wayne, PA 19087 610-341-8700
Computers - services

Sunglass Hut International RAYS
255 Alhambra Circle
Coral Gables, FL 33134 305-461-6100
Retail - misc. O

Sunrise Bancorp SRBC
5 SierraGate Plaza
Roseville, CA 95678 916-786-7080
Banks - west

Sunrise Bancorp, Inc. SUNY
375 Fulton St.
Farmingdale, NY 11735
516-249-8025
Financial - savings and loans

Sunrise Leasing Corp. SUNL
5500 Wayzata Blvd., Ste. 725
Minneapolis, MN 55416
612-593-1904
Leasing

Sunrise Technologies, Inc. SNRS
47257 Fremont Blvd.
Fremont, CA 94538 510-623-9001
Lasers - systems & components

Sunstates Corp. SUST
4600 Marriott Dr.
Raleigh, NC 27612 919-781-5611
Insurance - property & casualty

Sunward Technologies, Inc. SUNT
5828 Pacific Center Blvd.
San Diego, CA 92121 619-587-9140
Computers - peripheral equipment

Super Rite Corp. SUPR
3900 Industrial Rd.
Harrisburg, PA 17110 717-232-6821
Food - wholesale

Superconductor Technologies, Inc. SCON
460 Ward Dr., Ste. F
Santa Barbara, CA 93111 805-683-7646
Electronics - components & systems

Supercuts, Inc. CUTS
550 California St.
San Francisco, CA 94004
415-693-4700
Retail - misc.

Supertel Hospitality, Inc. SPPR
309 N. Fifth St., PO Box 1448
Norfolk, NE 68702 402-371-2520
Hotels & motels

Supertex, Inc. SUPX
1350 Bordeaux Dr.
Sunnyvale, CA 94089 408-744-0100
Electrical components - semiconductors

Suprema Specialties, Inc. CHEZ
510 E. 35th St.
Paterson, NJ 07543 201-684-2900
Food - dairy products

Supreme International Corp. SUPI
7495 N.W. 48th St.
Miami, FL 33166 305-592-2760
Apparel

Surgical Laser Technologies, Inc. SLTI
200 Cresson Blvd., PO Box 880
Oaks, PA 19456 610-650-0700
Lasers - systems & components

Surgical Technologies, Inc. SGTI
1245 E. Brickyard Rd.
Salt Lake City, UT 84106
801-974-5555
Medical products

Survival Technology, Inc. STIQ
2275 Research Blvd.
Rockville, MD 20850 301-926-1800
Medical products

Susquehanna Bancshares, Inc. SUSQ
26 N. Cedar St., PO Box 1000
Lititz, PA 17543 717-626-4721
Banks - northeast
[DRP]

Swift Transportation Co., Inc. SWFT
1705 Marietta Way
Sparks, NV 89431 702-359-9031
Transportation - truck

Swing-N-Slide Corp. SNSC
1212 Barberry Dr.
Janesville, WI 53545 608-755-4777
Leisure & recreational products

Swisher International, Inc. SWSH
6849 Fairview Rd.
Charlotte, NC 28210 704-364-7707
Miscellaneous - not elsewhere classified

Sybase, Inc. SYBS
6475 Christie Ave.
Emeryville, CA 94608 510-596-3500
Computers - software O

Sybron Chemicals Inc. SYCM
Birmingham Rd., PO Box 66
Birmingham, NJ 08011 609-893-1100
Chemicals - specialty

Sylvan Learning Systems, Inc. SLVN
9135 Guilford Rd.
Columbia, MD 21046 410-880-0889
Schools

Sylvan, Inc. SYLN
828 S. Pike Rd.
Sarver, PA 16055 412-295-3910
Agricultural operations

Symantec Corp. SYMC
10201 Torre Ave.
Cupertino, CA 95014 408-253-9600
Computers - software O

Symix Systems, Inc. SYMX
2800 Corporate Exchange Dr.
Columbus, OH 43231
614-523-7000
Computers - software

Symmetricom, Inc. SYMM
85 W. Tasman Dr.
San Jose, CA 95134 408-943-9403
Diversified operations O

Synalloy Corp. SYNC
PO Box 5627
Spartanburg, SC 29304
803-585-3605
Steel - pipes & tubes

Synbiotics Corp. SBIO
11011 Via Frontera
San Diego, CA 92127 619-451-3771
Biomedical & genetic products

Syncor International Corp. SCOR
20001 Prairie St.
Chatsworth, CA 91311 818-886-7400
Drugs & sundries - wholesale

Synercom Technology, Inc. SYNR
2500 City West Blvd.
Houston, TX 77042 713-954-7000
Computers - software

Synergen, Inc. SYGN
1885 33rd St.
Boulder, CO 80301 303-938-6200
Biomedical & genetic products

Synetic, Inc. SNTC
100 Summit Ave.
Montvale, NJ 07645 201-358-5300
Medical products

Synopsys, Inc. SNPS
700 E. Middlefield Rd.
Mountain View, CA 94043
415-962-5000
Computers - software O

SynOptics Communications, Inc. SNPX
4401 Great America Parkway
Santa Clara, CA 95054 408-988-2400
Computers - peripheral equipment

Syntellect Inc. SYNL
15810 N. 28th Ave.
Phoenix, AZ 85023 602-789-2800
Telecommunications equipment

Syntro Corp. SYNT
9669 Lackman Rd.
Lenaxa, KS 66219 913-888-8876
Biomedical & genetic products

SyQuest Technology, Inc. SYQT
47071 Bayside Parkway
Fremont, CA 94538 510-226-4000
Computers - peripheral equipment O

System Software Associates, Inc. SSAX
500 W. Madison St.
Chicago, IL 60606 312-641-2900
Computers - software O

SysteMed, Inc. SYSM
140 Columbia
Laguna Hills, CA 92656
714-362-1330
Drugs O

SyStemix, Inc. STMX
3155 Porter Dr.
Palo Alto, CA 94304 415-856-4901
Biomedical & genetic products

Systems & Computer Technology Corp.
 SCTC
4 Country View Rd.
Malvern, PA 19355 610-647-5930
Computers - services O

SystemSoft Corp. SYSF
313 Speen St.
Natick, MA 01760
 508-651-0088
Computers - software

T Cell Sciences, Inc. TCEL
115 Fourth Ave.
Needham, MA 02194 617-433-0771
Biomedical & genetic products O

T R Financial Corp. ROSE
1122 Franklin Ave.
Garden City, NY 11530 516-742-9300
Financial - savings and loans

T. Rowe Price Associates, Inc. TROW
100 E. Pratt St.
Baltimore, MD 21202 410-547-2000
Financial - investment management

Taco Cabana, Inc. TACO
262 Losoya, Ste. 330
San Antonio, TX 78205 210-231-8226
Retail - food & restaurants O

Tandy Brands, Inc. TBAC
690 E. Lamar Blvd., Ste. 200
Arlington, TX 76011 817-548-0090
Leather & related products

Tanknology Environmental, Inc. TANK
5225 Hollister St.
Houston, TX 77040 713-690-8265
Pollution control equipment & services

Tapistron International, Inc. TAPI
Route 12, PO Box 12876
Ringgold, GA 30736 706-965-9300
Machinery - general industrial

Target Technologies, Inc. CFON
6714 Netherlands Dr.
Wilmington, NC 28405 910-395-6100
Telecommunications equipment

Target Therapeutics, Inc. TGET
47201 Lakeview Blvd.
Fremont, CA 94537 510-440-7700
Medical products

Targeted Genetics Corp. TGEN
1100 Olive Way, Ste. 100
Seattle, WA 98101
206-623-7612
Drugs

Tatham Offshore, Inc. TOFF
600 Travis St.
Houston, TX 77002 713-224-7400
Oil & gas - offshore drilling

TBC Corp. TBCC
4770 Hickory Hill Rd.
Memphis, TN 38115 901-363-8030
Auto parts - retail & wholesale O

TCA Cable TV, Inc. TCAT
3015 SSE Loop 323
Tyler, TX 75713 214-595-3701
Cable TV O

TCI International, Inc. TCII
222 Caspian Dr.
Sunnyvale, CA 94089 408-747-6100
Telecommunications equipment

Team Rental Group, Inc. TBUD
1028 Dr. Mary M. Bethune Blvd.
Daytona Beach, FL 32114 904-238-7035
Transportation - equipment & leasing

Tech Data Corp. TECD
5350 Tech Data Dr.
Clearwater, FL 34620 813-539-7429
Computers - retail & wholesale O

Technalysis Corp. TECN
6700 France Ave. South
Minneapolis, MN 55435
612-925-5900
Computers - services

TECHNE Corp. TECH
614 McKinley Place NE
Minneapolis, MN 55413 612-379-8854
Biomedical & genetic products

Technical Communications Corp. TCCO
100 Domino Dr.
Concord, MA 01742 508-862-6035
Telecommunications equipment

Technology Solutions Co. TSCC
205 N. Michigan Ave.
Chicago, IL 60601
 312-819-2250
Computers - services

Tecnol Medical Products, Inc. TCNL
7201 Industrial Park Blvd.
Fort Worth, TX 76180 817-581-6424
Medical products

Tecumseh Products Co. TECUA
100 E. Patterson St.
Tecumseh, MI 49286 517-423-8411
Automotive & trucking - original equipment
O

Tekelec TKLC
26580 W. Agoura Rd.
Calabasas, CA 91302 818-880-5656
Telecommunications equipment

Teknekron Communications Systems, Inc.
TCSI
2121 Allston Way
Berkeley, CA 94704 510-649-3700
Computers - software

Telco Systems, Inc. TELC
63 Nahatan St.
Norwood, MA 02062 617-551-0300
Telecommunications equipment

Tele-Communications, Inc. TCOMA
5619 DTC Parkway
Englewood, CO 80111 303-267-5500
Cable TV O

Tele-Matic Corp. TMAT
6675 S. Kenton St., Ste. 100
Englewood, CO 80111 303-790-9111
Telecommunications services

Telebit Corp. TBIT
One Executive Dr.
Chelmsford, MA 01824 508-441-2181
Telecommunications equipment O

TeleVideo Systems, Inc. TELV
550 E. Brokaw Rd.
San Jose, CA 95161 408-954-8333
Computers - peripheral equipment

Telios Pharmaceuticals, Inc. TLIO
4757 Nexus Centre Dr.
San Diego, CA 92121
619-622-2600
Drugs

Tellabs, Inc. TLAB
4951 Indiana Ave.
Lisle, IL 60532 708-969-8800
Telecommunications equipment O

Telor Ophthalmic Pharmaceuticals, Inc.
TELR
265 Ballardvale St.
Wilmington, MA 01887 508-657-8400
Drugs

Telular Corp. WRLS
1215 Washington Ave.
Wilmette, IL 60091 708-465-4500
Telecommunications equipment

Telxon Corp. TLXN
3330 W. Market St.
Akron, OH 44334 216-867-3700
Computers - mini & micro O

Temtex Industries, Inc. TMTX
3010 LBJ Freeway, Ste. 650
Dallas, TX 75234 214-484-1845
Diversified operations

Tencor Instruments TNCR
2400 Charleston Rd.
Mountain View, CA 94043 415-969-6767
Instruments - control

Tennant Co. TANT
701 N. Lilac Dr., PO Box 1452
Minneapolis, MN 55440 612-540-1200
Machinery - general industrial

Terminal Data Corp. TERM
5898 Condor Dr.
Moorpark, CA 93021 805-529-1500
Office automation

TESSCO Technologies Inc. TESS
34 Loveton Circle
Sparks, MD 21152 410-472-7000
Telecommunications equipment

Tetra Tech, Inc. WATR
670 N. Rosemead Blvd.
Pasadena, CA 91107 818-449-6400
Pollution control equipment & services

TETRA Technologies, Inc. TTRA
25025 I-45 North
The Woodlands, TX 77380 713-367-1983
Pollution control equipment & services

Texas Regional Bancshares, Inc. TRBS
3700 N. Tenth
McAllen, TX 78502 210-631-5400
Banks - midwest

TF Financial Corp. THRD
3 Penns Trail
Newtown, PA 18940
215-579-4000
Banks - northeast

TFC Enterprises Inc. TFCE
240 Corporate Blvd.
Norfolk, VA 23502 804-466-1222
Financial - consumer loans

The AES Corp. AESC
1001 N. 19th St.
Arlington, VA 22209
703-522-1315
Energy - cogeneration

The ASK Group, Inc. ASKI
2880 Scott Blvd.
Santa Clara, CA 95050
408-562-8800
Computers - software

The BISYS Group, Inc. BSYS
150 Clove Rd.
Little Falls, NJ 07424 201-812-8600
Business services

The Bon-Ton Stores, Inc. BONT
2801 E. Market St.
York, PA 17402 717-757-7660
Retail - regional department stores

The Boston Bancorp SBOS
460 W. Broadway
South Boston, MA 02127 617-268-2500
Banks - northeast

The Buckle, Inc. BKLE
2407 W. 24th St.
Kearney, NE 68847
308-236-8491
Retail - apparel & shoes

The Cato Corp. CACOA
8100 Denmark Rd.
Charlotte, NC 28273 704-554-8510
Retail - apparel & shoes O

The CHALONE Wine Group, Ltd. CHLN
621 Airpark Rd.
Napa, CA 94558 707-254-4200
Beverages - alcoholic

The Cheesecake Factory Inc. CAKE
26635 Agoura Rd., Ste. 101
Calabasas, CA 91302 818-880-9323
Retail - food & restaurants

The Cherry Corp. CHER
3600 Sunset Ave.
Waukegan, IL 60087 708-662-9200
Electrical components - misc.

The Chicago Dock and Canal Trust DOCKS
455 E. Illinois St., Ste. 565
Chicago, IL 60611 312-467-1870
Real estate investment trust

The Clothestime, Inc. CTME
5325 E. Hunter Ave.
Anaheim, CA 92807 714-779-5881
Retail - apparel & shoes O

The Co-operative Bank of Concord COBK
125 Nagog Park
Acton, MA 01720 508-635-5000
Banks - northeast

The Colonial BancGroup, Inc. CLBGA
One Commerce St., PO Box 1108
Montgomery, AL 36101
205-240-5000
Banks - southeast

The Commerce Group, Inc. COMG
211 Main St.
Webster, MA 01570 508-943-9000
Insurance - property & casualty

The Cosmetic Center, Inc. COSCA
8839 Greenwood Place
Savage, MD 20763 301-497-6800
Cosmetics & toiletries

The Dress Barn, Inc. DBRN
88 Hamilton Ave.
Stamford, CT 06902 203-327-4242
Retail - apparel & shoes O

The Failure Group, Inc. FAIL
149 Commonwealth Dr.
Menlo Park, CA 94025
415-326-9400
Engineering - R & D services

The Finish Line, Inc. FINL
3308 N. Mitthoeffer Rd.
Indianapolis, IN 46236 317-899-1022
Retail - apparel & shoes

The Forschner Group, Inc. FSNR
151 Long Hill Cross Rds.
Shelton, CT 06484 203-929-6391
Leisure & recreational products

The Frankford Corp. FKFD
601 Dresher Rd.
Horsham, PA 19044 215-956-7000
Banks - northeast

The Future Now, Inc. FNOW
8044 Montgomery Rd., Ste. 601
Cincinnati, OH 45236
513-792-4500
Computers - services

The Genlyte Group Inc. GLYT
100 Lighting Way
Secaucus, NJ 07096 201-864-3000
Building products - lighting fixtures

The GNI Group, Inc. GNUC
2525 Battleground Rd.
Deer Park, TX 77536 713-930-0350
Pollution control equipment & services

The Good Guys, Inc. GGUY
7000 Marina Blvd.
Brisbane, CA 94005 415-615-5000
Retail - consumer electronics O

The Greater New York Savings Bank GRTR
One Penn Plaza
New York, NY 10119 212-613-4000
Financial - savings and loans

The Gymboree Corp. GYMB
700 Airport Blvd., Ste. 200
Burlingame, CA 94010 415-579-0600
Retail - apparel & shoes O

The Harper Group, Inc. HARG
260 Townsend St.
San Francisco, CA 94107
415-978-0600
Transportation - air freight

The Hibernia Savings Bank HSBK
731 Hancock St.
Quincy, MA 02170 617-479-2265
Financial - savings and loans

The Holson Burnes Group, Inc. HBGI
582 Great Rd.
North Smithfield, RI 02896
401-769-8000
Photographic equipment & supplies

The Immune Response Corp. IMNR
5935 Darwin Court
Carlsbad, CA 92008 619-431-7080
Biomedical & genetic products O

The Krystal Co. KRYS
One Union Square
Chattanooga, TN 37402
615-757-1550
Retail - food & restaurants

The Liposome Co., Inc. LIPO
One Research Way
Princeton, NJ 08540 609-452-7060
Biomedical & genetic products O

The Long Island Savings Bank, FSB LISB
201 Old Country Rd.
Melville, NY 11747 516-547-2000
Banks - northeast

The M/A/R/C Group MARC
7850 N. Belt Line Rd.
Irving, TX 75063 214-506-3400
Business services

The Manhattan Life Insurance Co. MLIC
1876 Waycross Rd.
Cincinnati, OH 45240 513-595-2118
Insurance - life

The MEDSTAT Group, Inc. MDST
777 E. Eisenhower Parkway
Ann Arbor, MI 48108
313-996-1180
Medical services

The Merchants Bank of New York MBNY
434 Broadway
New York, NY 10013 212-669-6600
Banks - northeast

The Money Store Inc. MONE
2840 Morris Ave.
Union, NJ 07083 908-686-2000
Financial - consumer loans

The Morgan Group, Inc. MRGN
28651 U.S. 20 West
Elkhart, IN 46514 219-295-2200
Transportation - truck

The Morningstar Group Inc. MSTR
5956 Sherry Ln., Ste. 1100
Dallas, TX 75225 214-360-4700
Food - misc.

The Multicare Companies, Inc. MLTI
411 Hackensack Ave.
Hackensack, NJ 07601
201-488-8818
Medical services

The National Security Group, Inc. NSEC
661 E. Davis St.
Elba, AL 36323 205-897-2273
Insurance - multi line & misc.

The Navigators Group, Inc. NAVG
123 Williams St.
New York, NY 10038 212-406-2900
Insurance - property & casualty

The Oilgear Co. OLGR
2300 S. 51st St.
Milwaukee, WI 53219 414-327-1700
Machinery - general industrial

The Pacific Bank, N.A. PBSF
351 California St.
San Francisco, CA 94104
415-576-2700
Banks - west

The Peak Technologies Group, Inc. PEAK
600 Madison Ave.
New York, NY 10022 212-832-2833
Data collection & systems

The Peoples Holding Co. PHCO
PO Box 709
Tupelo, MS 38802 601-680-1001
Banks - southeast

The Pioneer Group, Inc. PIOG
60 State St.
Boston, MA 02109 617-742-7825
Financial - investment management

The Prospect Group, Inc. PROS
667 Madison Ave.
New York, NY 10021 212-758-8500
Diversified operations

The Right Start, Inc. RTST
5334 Sterling Center Dr.
Westlake Village, CA 91361
818-707-7100
Retail - mail order & direct

The Rival Co. RIVL
800 E. 101st Terrace
Kansas City, MO 64131 816-943-4100
Appliances - household

The Robert Mondavi Corp. MOND
7801 St. Helena Highway
Oakville, CA 94562 707-963-9611
Beverages - alcoholic

The Rochester Community Savings Bank
RCSB
40 Franklin St.
Rochester, NY 14604 716-258-3000
Financial - savings and loans O

The Sands Regent SNDS
345 N. Arlington Ave.
Reno, NV 89501 702-348-2200
Leisure & recreational services

The Sandwich Co-operative Bank SWCB
100 Old Kings Highway
Sandwich, MA 02563 508-888-0026
Banks - northeast

The Santa Cruz Operation, Inc. SCOC
400 Encinal St., PO Box 1900
Santa Cruz, CA 95061 408-425-7222
Computers - software O

The Score Board, Inc. BSBL
1951 Old Cuthbert Rd.
Cherry Hill, NJ 08034 609-354-9000
Leisure & recreational services O

The Scotts Co. SCTT
14111 Scottslawn Rd.
Marysville, OH 43041 513-644-0011
Chemicals - specialty

The Shaw Group Inc. SHAW
11100 Mead Rd.
Baton Rouge, LA 70816
504-296-1140
Steel - pipes & tubes

The Singing Machine Co., Inc. SING
6350 E. Rogers Circle
Boca Raton, FL 33487 407-994-3100
Electronics - components & systems

The Smithfield Companies, Inc. HAMS
311 County St., Ste. 203
Portsmouth, VA 23704 804-399-3100
Food - meat products

The Software Toolworks, Inc. TWRX
60 Leveroni Court
Novato, CA 94949 415-883-3000
Computers - software

The Somerset Group, Inc. SOMR
1030 S. Kitley Ave.
Indianapolis, IN 46203 317-634-1400
Diversified operations

The Standard Register Co. SREG
600 Albany St.
Dayton, OH 45401 513-434-1000
Paper - business forms

The Topps Co., Inc. TOPP
One Whitehall St.
New York, NY 10004
212-376-0300
Food - confectionery O

The WellCare Management Group, Inc.
WELL
Park West/Hurley Ave. Ext.
Kingston, NY 12401 914-338-4110
Health maintenance organization

The Wet Seal, Inc. WTSLA
64 Fairbanks
Irvine, CA 92718 714-583-9029
Retail - apparel & shoes

The Z-Seven Fund, Inc. ZSEV
2651 W. Guadalupe, Ste. B-233
Mesa, AZ 85202 602-897-6214
Financial - investment management

Theragenics Corp. THRX
5325 Oakbrook Pkwy.
Norcross, GA 30093 404-381-8338
Drugs

Therapeutic Discovery Corp. TDCAZ
1375 California Ave.
Palo Alto, CA 94303 415-496-8200
Drugs

TheraTech, Inc. THRT
417 Wakara Way
Salt Lake City, UT 84108
801-583-6028
Medical products

Thermadyne Holdings Corp. TDHC
101 S. Hanley Rd., Ste. 300
St. Louis, MO 63105 314-721-5573
Metal products - fabrication

Thomas Group, Inc. TGIS
5215 N. O'Connor Blvd.
Irving, TX 75039 214-869-3400
Business services

Thomas Nelson, Inc. TNEL
Nelson Place at Elm Hill Pike
Nashville, TN 37214
615-889-9000
Publishing - books

Thomaston Mills, Inc. TMSTA
115 E. Main St.
Thomaston, GA 30286 706-647-7131
Textiles - mill products

Thompson PBE, Inc. THOM
4553 Glencoe Ave., Ste. 200
Marina del Ray, CA 90292 310-306-7112
Automotive & trucking - replacement parts

Thorn Apple Valley, Inc. TAVI
18700 W. Ten Mile Rd.
Southfield, MI 48075 810-552-0700
Food - meat products

THQ, Inc. TOYH
5016 N. Parkway Calabasas
Calabasas, CA 91302 818-591-1310
Toys - games & hobby products

Tide West Oil Co. TIDE
6666 S. Sheridan Rd.
Tulsa, OK 74133 918-488-8962
Oil & gas - US exploration & production

TideMark Bancorp Inc. TDMK
301 Hiden Blvd.
Newport News, VA 23606
804-599-1400
Financial - savings and loans

Tigera Group, Inc. TYGR
950 Third Ave., 21st Fl.
New York, NY 10022 212-758-4316
Miscellaneous - not elsewhere classified

TII Industries, Inc. TII
1385 Akron St.
Copiague, NY 11726 516-789-5000
Electrical products - misc.

Timberline Software Corp. TMBS
9600 S.W. Nimbus Ave.
Beaverton, OR 97005
503-626-6775
Computers - software

TJ International, Inc. TJCO
380 E. ParkCenter Blvd.
Boise, ID 83706 208-345-8500
Building products - misc.

TNT Freightways Corp. TNTF
9700 Higgins Rd., Ste. 570
Rosemont, IL 60018 708-696-0200
Transportation - truck O

Tocor II, Inc. TOCRZ
244 Great Valley Parkway
Malvern, PA 19355 610-296-4488
Drugs

Today's Man, Inc. TMAN
835 Lancer Dr.
Moorestown, NJ 08057
609-235-5656
Retail - apparel & shoes

Todd AO Corp. TODDA
172 Golden Gate Ave.
San Francisco, CA 94102 415-928-3200
Motion pictures & services

Todhunter International, Inc. TODH
222 Lakeview Ave., PO Box 4057
West Palm Beach, FL 33402
407-655-8977
Beverages - alcoholic

Tokos Medical Corp. TKOS
1821 E. Dyer Rd.
Santa Ana, CA 92705 714-474-1616
Healthcare - outpatient & home O

Tom Brown, Inc. TMBR
PO Box 2608
Midland, TX 79701 915-682-9715
Oil & gas - US exploration & production

Tompkins County Trust Co. TCTC
The Commons, PO Box 460
Ithaca, NY 14851 607-273-3210
Banks - northeast

Tops Appliance City, Inc. TOPS
45 Brunswick Ave.
Edison, NJ 08818 908-248-2850
Retail - misc.

Toreador Royalty Corp. TRGL
8117 Preston Rd.
Dallas, TX 75225 214-220-2141
Oil & gas - US royalty trust

Total Containment, Inc. TCIX
A130 North Dr., PO Box 939
Oaks, PA 19456 610-666-7777
Machinery - material handling

Total-Tel USA Communications, Inc. TELU
470 Colfax Ave.
Clifton, NJ 07013 201-773-7000
Telecommunications services

Tower Air, Inc. TOWR
JFK International, Hanger 17
Jamaica, NY 11430 718-553-4300
Transportation - airline

Tower Automotive, Inc. TWER
4508 IDS Center
Minneapolis, MN 50540 612-342-2310
Automotive & trucking - original equipment

TPI Enterprises, Inc. TPIE
777 S. Flagler Dr.
West Palm Beach, FL 33401
407-835-8888
Retail - food & restaurants O

Tracor, Inc. TTRR
6500 Tracor Ln.
Austin, TX 78725 512-926-2800
Electronics - military

Tractor Supply Co. TSCO
320 Plus Park Blvd.
Nashville, TN 37217 615-366-4600
Retail - misc.

Trak Auto Corp. TRKA
3300 75th Ave.
Landover, MD 20785 301-731-1200
Auto parts - retail & wholesale

Trans Financial Bancorp, Inc. TRFI
500 E. Main St.
Bowling Green, KY 42101
502-781-5000
Banks - midwest

Trans Leasing International, Inc. TLII
3000 Dundee Rd.
Northbrook, IL 60062 708-272-1000
Leasing

Trans World Entertainment Corp. TWMC
38 Corporate Circle
Albany, NY 12203 518-452-1242
Retail - misc.

Trans-Industries, Inc. TRNI
2637 Adams Rd.
Rochester Hills, MI 48309
313-852-1990
Electrical products - misc.

Transaction Network Services, Inc. TNSI
13873 Park Center Rd.
Herndon, VA 22071 703-742-0500
Telecommunications services

TransAmerican Waste Industries, Inc. WSTE
314 N. Post Oak Ln.
Houston, TX 77024 713-956-1212
Pollution control equipment & services

Transmation, Inc. TRNS
977 Mt. Read Blvd.
Rochester, NY 14606 716-254-9000
Instruments - control

Transmedia Network, Inc. TMNI
11900 Biscayne Blvd.
Miami, FL 33181 305-892-3300
Business services

Transnational Re Corp. TREX
80 Maiden Ln.
New York, NY 10038 212-837-9520
Insurance - property & casualty

TransNet Corp. TRNT
45 Columbia Rd.
Somerville, NJ 08876 908-253-0500
Computers - retail & wholesale

TransTexas Gas Corp. TTXG
363 N. Sam Houston Pkwy. East
Houston, TX 77060 713-447-3111
Oil & gas - production & pipeline

TransWorld Bancorp TWBC
15233 Ventura Blvd.
Sherman Oaks, CA 91403
818-783-7501
Banks - west

Travel Ports of America, Inc. TPOA
3495 Winton Place, Bldg. C
Rochester, NY 14623 716-272-1810
Retail - food & restaurants

Treadco, Inc. TRED
1000 S. 21st St.
Fort Smith, AR 72901
501-785-6000
Rubber tires

Trenwick Group Inc. TREN
Metro Center, One Station Pl.
Stamford, CT 06902 203-353-5500
Insurance - property & casualty

Triad Guaranty Inc. TGIC
101 S. Stratford Rd., Ste. 500
Winston-Salem, NC 27104 910-723-1282
Financial - mortgages & related services

Triad Systems Corp. TRSC
3055 Triad Dr.
Livermore, CA 94550
510-449-0606
Computers - services

Triangle Bancorp, Inc. TRBC
4800 Six Forks Rd.
Raleigh, NC 27609 919-881-0455
Banks - southeast

Triangle Pacific Corp. TRIP
16803 Dallas Parkway
Dallas, TX 75248 214-931-3000
Building products - wood

TriCare, Inc. TRCR
3353 Peachtree Rd., N.E.
Atlanta, GA 30326 404-266-7474
Healthcare - outpatient & home

TriCo Bancshares TCBK
15 Independence Circle
Chico, CA 95926 916-898-0300
Banks - west

Trico Products Corp. TRCO
817 Washington St.
Buffalo, NY 14203 716-852-5700
Automotive & trucking - original equipment

Triconex Corp. TCNX
15091 Bake Pkwy.
Irvine, CA 92718 714-768-3709
Instruments - control

Tricord Systems, Inc. TRCD
3750 Annapolis Ln.
Plymouth, MN 55447 612-557-9005
Computers - peripheral equipment O

Trident Microsystems, Inc. TRID
189 N. Bernardo Ave.
Mountain View, CA 94043 415-691-9211
Computers - peripheral equipment

Trimark Holdings, Inc. TMRK
2644 30th St.
Santa Monica, CA 90405
310-314-2000
Motion pictures & services

Trimble Navigation Ltd. TRMB
645 N. Mary Ave., PO Box 3642
Sunnyvale, CA 94088 408-481-8000
Electronics - measuring instruments O

Trimedyne, Inc. TMED
2801 Barranca Rd.
Irvine, CA 92714 714-559-5300
Medical instruments

Trinzic Corp. TRNZ
101 University Ave.
Palo Alto, CA 94301
415-328-9595
Computers - software

Trion, Inc. TRON
101 McNeill Rd., PO Box 760
Sanford, NC 27331 919-775-2201
Machinery - general industrial

Triple S Plastics, Inc. TSSS
14320 S. Portage Rd.
Vicksburg, MS 49097
616-649-0545
Rubber & plastic products

Tripos, Inc. TRPSV
1699 S. Hanley Rd.
St. Louis, MO 63144 314-647-1099
Computers - software

TriQuint Semiconductor, Inc. TQNT
3625A S.W. Murray Blvd.
Beaverton, OR 97005 503-644-3535
Electrical components - semiconductors

TRISM, Inc. TRSM
301 Commerce St.
Fort Worth, TX 76102 817-335-1791
Transportation - truck

Tristar Corp. TSAR
135 Canal St.
Staten Island, NY 10304 718-273-4144
Cosmetics & toiletries

TRM Copy Centers Corp. TRMM
5515 S.E. Milwaukie Ave.
Portland, OR 97202 503-231-0230
Business services

TRO Learning, Inc. TUTR
150 N. Martingale Rd.
Schaumburg, IL 60173
708-517-5100
Computers - software

Troy Hill Bancorp, Inc. THBC
1706 Lowrie St.
Pittsburgh, PA 15212 412-231-8238
Banks - northeast

Truck Components Inc. TRCK
302 Peoples Ave.
Rockford, IL 61104 815-964-8725
Automotive & trucking - original equipment

Trust Co of New Jersey TCNJ
35 Journal Square
Jersey City, NJ 07306
201-420-2500
Banks - northeast

TrustCo Bank Corp NY TRST
320 State St.
Schenectady, NY 12305
518-377-3311
Banks - northeast

Trustmark Corp. TRMK
248 E. Capitol St.
Jackson, MS 39205 601-354-5111
Banks - southeast

Tseng Labs, Inc. TSNG
6 Terry Dr.
Newtown, PA 18940 215-968-0502
Computers - peripheral equipment O

TSI Inc. TSII
500 Cardigan Rd.
Shoreview, MN 55126 612-483-0900
Instruments - control

TSR, Inc. TSRI
400 Oser Ave.
Hauppauge, NY 11788 516-231-0333
Computers - services

Tuboscope Vetco International Corp. TUBO
2835 Holmes Rd.
Houston, TX 77051 713-799-5100
Oil & gas - field services

Tucker Drilling Co., Inc. TUCK
PO Box 1876
San Angelo, TX 76902 915-655-6773
Oil & gas - US exploration & production

Tuesday Morning Corp. TUES
14621 Inwood Rd.
Dallas, TX 75244 214-387-3562
Retail - discount & variety

Tufco Technologies, Inc. TFCO
3161 S. Ridge Rd.
Green Bay, WI 54304 414-336-0054
Printing - commercial

Tuscarora, Inc. TUSC
800 Fifth Ave.
New Brighton, PA 15066 412-843-8200
Chemicals - plastics

Tyson Foods, Inc. TYSNA
2210 W. Oaklawn Dr.
Springdale, AR 72764
501-290-4000
Food - meat products O

U.S. Bancorp USBC
111 S.W. Fifth Ave.
Portland, OR 97204
503-275-6111
Banks - west O
[DRP]

U.S. Can Corp. USCN
900 Commerce Dr., Ste. 302
Oak Brook, IL 60521 708-571-2500
Containers - metal

U.S. Energy Corp. USEG
877 N. 8th West
Riverton, WY 82501 307-856-9271
Metal ores - misc.

U.S. Healthcare, Inc. USHC
980 Jolly Rd., PO Box 1109
Blue Bell, PA 19422 215-628-4800
Health maintenance organization O

U.S. HomeCare Corp. USHO
141 S. Central Ave.
Hartsdale, NY 10530 914-946-9601
Healthcare - outpatient & home

U.S. Long Distance Corp. USLD
9311 San Pedro, Ste. 300
San Antonio, TX 78216 210-525-9009
Telecommunications services O

U.S. Paging Corp. USPC
1680 Route 23 North
Wayne, NJ 07470 201-305-6000
Telecommunications services

U.S. Robotics, Inc. USRX
8100 N. McCormick Blvd.
Skokie, IL 60076 708-982-5010
Computers - peripheral equipment O

U.S. Trust Corp. USTC
114 W. 47th St.
New York, NY 10036 212-852-1000
Banks - northeast
[DRP]

U.S. Wireless Data Inc. USWDA
4888 Pearl E. Circle
Boulder, CO 80301 303-440-5464
Telecommunications equipment

U.S. Xpress Enterprises, Inc. XPRSA
2931 S. Market St.
Chattanooga, TN 37410
615-697-7377
Transportation - truck

UF Bancorp, Inc. UFBI
501 Main St., PO Box 3125
Evansville, IN 47731 812-425-7111
Banks - midwest

Ultimate Electronics, Inc. ULTE
9901 W. 50th Ave.
Wheat Ridge, CO 80033 303-420-1366
Retail - consumer electronics

Ultra Pac, Inc. UPAC
21925 Industrial Blvd.
Rogers, MN 55374 612-428-8340
Containers - paper & plastic

Ultrak, Inc. ULTK
1220 Champion Circle
Carrollton, TX 75006 212-233-7171
Video equipment

Ultralife Batteries, Inc. ULBI
1350 Route 88 South
Newark, NJ 14513 315-332-7100
Electrical products - misc.

Ultratech Stepper, Inc. UTEK
3050 Zanker Rd.
San Jose, CA 95134 408-321-8835
Electronics - components & systems

Unico American Corp. UNAM
23251 Mulholland Dr.
Woodland Hills, CA 91364 818-591-9800
Insurance - multi line & misc.

Uniforce Temporary Personnel, Inc. UNFR
1335 Jericho Turnpike
New Hyde Park, NY 11040
516-437-3300
Financial - business services

Unigene Laboratories, Inc. UGNE
110 Little Falls Rd.
Fairfield, NJ 07004 201-882-0860
Biomedical & genetic products

Unilab Corp. ULAB
018448 Oxnard St.
Tarzana, CA 91356 818-757-0601
Medical services

Unimed Pharmaceuticals, Inc. UMED
2150 E. Lake Cook Rd.
Buffalo Grove, IL 60089 708-541-2525
Drugs

Union Bank UBNK
350 California St.
San Francisco, CA 94104 415-705-7350
Banks - west [DRP 5%]

Union Bankshares Corp. UBSH
211 N. Main St., PO Box 446
Bowling Green, VA 22427 804-633-5031
Financial - SBIC & commercial

Union Bankshares, Ltd. UBSC
1825 Lawrence St., Ste. 444
Denver, CO 80202 303-298-5352
Banks - west

Union Switch & Signal Inc. UNSW
1901 Main St., Ste. 1150
Columbia, SC 29201 803-929-1200
Transportation - equipment & leasing

Uniphase Corp. UNPH
163 Baypointe Pkwy.
San Jose, CA 95134 408-434-1800
Lasers - systems & components

Uniroyal Technology Corp. UTCI
2 N. Tamiami Trail, Ste. 900
Sarasota, FL 34236 813-366-5282
Chemicals - specialty

Unitech Industries, Inc. UTII
15035 N. 75th St.
Scottsdale, AZ 85260 602-991-7626
Electronics - components & systems

United Bankshares, Inc. UBSI
Fifth and Avery Sts.
Parkersburg, WV 26102 304-424-8800
Banks - southeast
[DRP]

United Carolina Bancshares Corp. UCAR
127 W. Webster St.
Whiteville, NC 28472 910-642-5131
Banks - southeast
[DRP]

United Cities Gas Co. UCIT
5300 Maryland Way
Brentwood, TN 37027 615-373-5310
Utility - gas distribution
[DRP 5%]

United Companies Financial Corp. UCFC
4041 Essen Ln.
Baton Rouge, LA 70809 504-924-6007
Insurance - life

United Financial Corp. of South Carolina, Inc.
UNSA
425 Main St.
Greenwood, SC 29646 803-223-8686
Financial - savings and loans

United Fire & Casualty Co. UFCS
118 Second Ave. SE
Cedar Rapids, IA 52407 319-399-5700
Insurance - property & casualty

United Gaming, Inc. UGAM
4380 Boulder Highway
Las Vegas, NV 89121 702-435-4200
Leisure & recreational services

United Home Life Insurance Co. UHLI
1499 Windhorst Dr.
Greenwood, IN 46143 317-889-2111
Insurance - life

United Insurance Companies, Inc. UICI
4001 McEwen Dr., Ste. 200
Dallas, TX 75244 214-960-8497
Insurance - accident & health

United International Holdings, Inc. UIHIA
4643 S. Ulster St., Ste. 1300
Denver, CO 80237 303-770-4001
Broadcasting - radio & TV

United Missouri Bancshares, Inc. UMSB
1010 Grand Ave., PO Box 419226
Kansas City, MO 64141 816-556-7000
Banks - midwest

United National Bancorp UNBJ
65 Readington Rd.
Branchburg, NJ 08876 908-756-5000
Banks - northeast

United Retail Group, Inc. URGI
365 W. Passaic St.
Rochelle Park, NJ 07662 201-845-0880
Retail - apparel & shoes

United Savings Bank, FA UBMT
601 First Ave. North
Great Falls, MT 59401 406-761-2200
Financial - savings and loans

United States Lime and Minerals, Inc.
USLM
12221 Merit Dr., Ste. 500
Dallas, TX 75251 214-991-8400
Miscellaneous - not elsewhere classified

United Stationers Inc. USTR
2200 E. Golf Rd.
Des Plaines, IL 60016
708-699-5000
Office equipment & supplies

United Television, Inc. UTVI
8501 Wilshire Blvd., Ste. 340
Beverly Hills, CA 90211 310-854-0426
Broadcasting - radio & TV

United Video Satellite Group, Inc. UVSGA
7140 S. Lewis Ave.
Tulsa, OK 74136 918-488-4000
Telecommunications equipment

United Waste Systems, Inc. UWST
Four Greenwich Office Park
Greenwich, CT 06830 203-622-3131
Pollution control equipment & services

Unitog Co. UTOG
101 W. 11th St.
Kansas City, MO 64105
816-474-7000
Linen supply & related

Unitrin, Inc. UNIT
One E. Wacker Dr.
Chicago, IL 60601 312-661-4600
Insurance - multi line & misc. O

Univax Biologics, Inc. UNVX
12280 Wilkins Ave.
Rockville, MD 20852 301-770-3099
Biomedical & genetic products

Universal Electronics, Inc. UEIC
1864 Enterprise Parkway West
Twinsburg, OH 44087 216-487-1110
Electronics - components & systems

Universal Forest Products, Inc. UFPI
2801 E. Beltline N.E.
Grand Rapids, MI 49505 616-364-6161
Building products - wood

Universal Holding Corp. UHCO
Mt. Ebo Corporate Park
Brewster, NY 10509 914-278-4094
Insurance - life

Universal Hospital Services, Inc. UHOS
3800 W. 80th St.
Bloomington, MN 55431 612-893-3200
Medical products

Universal International, Inc. UNIV
5000 Winnetka Ave. North
New Hope, MN 55428 612-533-1169
Wholesale distribution - consumer products

Universal Seismic Associates, Inc. USAC
12999 Jess Pirtle Blvd.
Sugar Land, TX 77478 713-240-3388
Oil & gas - field services

Universal Standard Medical Laboratories, Inc.
USML
21705 Evergreen Rd.
Southfield, MI 48075
810-353-1450
Medical services

University Bank & Trust UNNB
250 Lytton Ave.
Palo Alto, CA 94301 415-327-0210
Banks - west

UNR Industries, Inc. UNRI
332 S. Michigan Ave.
Chicago, IL 60604 312-341-1234
Steel - pipes & tubes

UNSL Financial Corp. UNSL
Jefferson at Second, Dwr. E
Lebanon, MO 65536 417-588-4111
Financial - savings and loans

Upper Peninsula Energy Corp. UPEN
600 Lakeshore Dr.
Houghton, MI 49931 906-487-5000
Utility - electric power [DRP]

Uranium Resources, Inc. URIX
12750 Merit Dr., Ste. 1210
Dallas, TX 75251 214-387-7777
Metal ores - misc.

Urban Outfitters, Inc. URBN
1809 Walnut St.
Philadelphia, PA 19103 215-564-2313
Retail - apparel & shoes

UroMed Corp. URMD
313 Pleasant St.
Watertown, MA 02172 617-924-4384
Medical products

US Facilities Corp. USRE
650 Town Center Dr., Ste. 1600
Costa Mesa, CA 92626 714-549-1600
Insurance - multi line & misc.

USA Mobile Communications Holdings, Inc.
  USAM
11300 Cornell Park Dr.
Cincinnati, OH 45242 513-489-0122
Telecommunications services

USA Truck, Inc. USAK
3108 Industrial Park Rd.
Van Buren, AR 72956 501-471-2500
Transportation - truck

USBANCORP, Inc. UBAN
Main and Franklin Sts.
Johnstown, PA 15901 814-533-5300
Banks - northeast
[DRP]

USMX, Inc. USMX
141 Union Blvd., Ste. 100
Lakewood, CO 80228 303-985-4665
Gold mining & processing

UST Corp. USTB
40 Court St.
Boston, MA 02108 617-726-7000
Banks - northeast
[DRP 10%]

Utah Medical Products, Inc. UTMD
7043 S. 300 West
Midvale, UT 84047 801-566-1200
Medical products O

UTILX Corp. UTLX
22404 - 66th Ave. South
Kent, WA 98032 206-395-0200
Telecommunications services

V Band Corp. VBAN
565 Taxter Rd.
Elmsford, NY 10523 914-789-5000
Telecommunications equipment

Valence Technology, Inc. VLNC
6781 Via Del Ora
San Jose, CA 95119 408-365-6125
Engineering - R & D services O

Vallen Corp. VALN
13333 Northwest Fwy.
Houston, TX 77040 713-462-8700
Protection - safety equipment & services

Valley Systems, Inc. VALE
11580 Lafayette Dr. N.W.
Canal Fulton, OH 44614 216-854-4526
Building - maintenance & services

ValliCorp Holdings, Inc. VALY
4995 E. Clinton Ave.
Fresno, CA 93727
209-252-8711
Banks - west

Valmont Industries, Inc. VALM
Valley, NE 68064 402-359-2201
Diversified operations

Value Line, Inc. VALU
711 Third Ave.
New York, NY 10017 212-687-3965
Financial - investment management

Value Vision International, Inc. VVTVA
6740 Shady Oak Rd.
Minneapolis, MN 55344
612-947-5200
Advertising O

Value-Added Communications, Inc. VACI
1901 S. Meyers Rd., Ste. 530
Oakbrook Terrace, IL 60181 708-628-6606
Telecommunications services

ValuJet Airlines VJET
1800 Phoenix Blvd., Ste. 126
Atlanta, GA 30349 404-907-2580
Transportation - airline

Vanguard Cellular Systems, Inc. VCELA
2002 Pisgah Church Rd.
Greensboro, NC 27455
910-282-3690
Telecommunications services O

Vans, Inc. VANS
2095 N. Batavia
Orange, CA 92665
714-974-7414
Shoes & related apparel

Variflex, Inc. VFLX
5152 N. Commerce Ave.
Moore Park, CA 93021 805-523-0322
Miscellaneous - not elsewhere classified

Varitronic Systems, Inc. VRSY
300 Highway 169 South
Minneapolis, MN 55426 612-542-1500
Office equipment & supplies

Varlen Corp. VRLN
55 E. Shuman Blvd., Ste. 500
Naperville, IL 60566 708-420-0400
Transportation - equipment & leasing

Varsity Spirit Corp. VARS
2525 Horizon Lake Dr.
Memphis, TN 38133 901-387-4370
Apparel

Vaughn Communications, Inc. VGHN
5050 W. 78th St.
Minneapolis, MN 55435
612-832-3200
Motion pictures & services

Vectra Banking Corp. VTRA
1650 S. Colorado Blvd.
Denver, CO 80222 303-782-7440
Banks - west

VECTRA Technologies, Inc. VCTR
1010 S. 336th St., Ste. 220
Federal Way, WA 98003 206-874-2235
Pollution control equipment & services

Veeco Instruments Inc. VECO
Terminal Dr.
Plainview, NY 101803 516-349-8300
Electronics - measuring instruments

Ventritex, Inc. VNTX
701 E. Evelyn Ave.
Sunnyvale, CA 94086 408-738-4883
Medical products O

Ventura County National Bancorp VCNB
500 Esplanade Dr.
Oxnard, CA 93030 805-981-2780
Banks - west

Venturian Corp. VENT
1600 Second St. South
Hopkins, MN 55343
612-931-2500
Computers - mini & micro

VeriFone, Inc. VFIC
Three Lagoon Dr., Ste. 400
Redwood City, CA 90465
415-591-6500
Telecommunications equipment O

Veritas Software Corp. VRTS
4800 Great America Parkway
Santa Clara, CA 95054 408-727-1222
Miscellaneous - not elsewhere classified

Vermont Financial Services Corp. VFSC
100 Main St.
Brattleboro, VT 05301 802-257-7151
Banks - northeast
[DRP]

Versa Technologies, Inc. VRSA
9301 Washington Ave.
Racine, WI 53408 414-886-1174
Rubber & plastic products

Vertex Communications Corp. VTEX
2600 N. Longview St.
Kilgore, TX 75662 214-984-0555
Telecommunications equipment

Vertex Pharmaceuticals, Inc. VRTX
40 Allston St.
Cambridge, MA 02139 617-576-3111
Drugs

Vestar, Inc. VSTR
650 Cliffside Dr.
San Dimas, CA 91773 909-394-4000
Drugs

Veterinary Centers of America, Inc. VCAI
1725 Cloverfield Ave.
Santa Monica, CA 90404 310-829-7533
Veterinary products & services

Viagene, Inc. VIGN
11075 Roselle St.
San Diego, CA 92121
619-452-1288
Drugs

Vical Inc. VICL
9373 Towne Centre Dr.
San Diego, CA 92121 619-453-9900
Biomedical & genetic products

Vicor Corp. VICR
23 Frontage Rd.
Andover, MA 01810 508-470-2900
Electrical components - misc. O

VICORP Restaurants, Inc. VRES
400 W. 48th Ave., PO Box 16601
Denver, CO 80216 303-296-2121
Retail - food & restaurants

Victoria Bankshares, Inc. VICT
One O'Connor Plaza
Victoria, TX 77902
512-573-9432
Banks - southwest

Victoria Creations, Inc. VITC
30 Jefferson Park Rd.
Warwick, RI 02888 401-467-7150
Precious metals & jewelry

Victoria Financial Corp. VICF
5915 Landerbrook Dr.
Cleveland, OH 44124 216-461-3461
Insurance - multi line & misc.

Video Display Corp. VIDE
1868 Tucker Industrial Dr.
Tucker, GA 30084 404-938-2080
Miscellaneous - not elsewhere classified

Video Lottery Technologies, Inc. VLTS
2311 S. Seventh Ave.
Bozeman, MT 59715 406-585-6600
Leisure & recreational products

Vie de France Corp. VDEF
8201 Greensboro Dr., Ste. 1224
McLean, VA 22102 703-442-9600
Food - misc.

ViewLogic Systems, Inc. VIEW
293 Boston Post Rd. West
Marlborough, MA 01752
508-480-0881
Computers - software O

Viking Office Products, Inc. VKNG
13809 S. Figueroa St.
Los Angeles, CA 90061 213-321-4493
Retail - mail order & direct O

Village Super Market, Inc. VLGEA
733 Mountain Ave.
Springfield, NJ 07081 201-467-2200
Retail - supermarkets

Virginia Beach Federal Financial Corp.
VABF
2101 Parks Ave., Ste. 400
Virginia Beach, VA 23451 804-428-9331
Financial - savings and loans

Virginia First Financial Corp. VFFC
Franklin and Adams Sts.
Petersburg, VA 23804
804-733-0333
Financial - savings and loans

ViroGroup, Inc. VIRO
428 Pine Island Rd. S.W.
Cape Coral, FL 33991 813-574-1919
Pollution control equipment & services

Vision-Sciences, Inc. VSCI
6 Strathmore Rd.
Natick, MA 01760 508-650-9971
Medical products

VISX, Inc. VISX
3400 Central Expressway
Santa Clara, CA 95051 408-733-2020
Lasers - systems & components O

Vital Signs, Inc. VITL
20 Campus Rd.
Totowa, NJ 07512 201-790-1330
Medical products

Vitalink Pharmacy Services, Inc. VTLK
1250 E. Diehl Rd., Ste. 208
Naperville, IL 60563 708-505-1320
Medical services

Vitesse Semiconductor Corp. VTSS
741 Calle Plano
Camarillo, CA 93012 805-388-3700
Electrical components - semiconductors

VIVUS, Inc. VVUS
545 Middlefield Rd., Ste. 200
Menlo Park, CA 94025 415-325-5511
Medical products

VLSI Technology, Inc. VLSI
1109 McKay Dr.
San Jose, CA 95131 408-434-3000
Electrical components - semiconductors O

VMARK Software, Inc. VMRK
30 Speen St.
Framingham, MA 01701 508-879-3311
Computers - software

Volt Information Sciences, Inc. VOLT
1133 Sixth Ave., 19th Fl.
New York, NY 10036 212-704-2400
Diversified operations

VSE Corp. VSEC
2550 Huntington Ave.
Alexandria, VA 22303
703-960-4600
Engineering - R & D services

VTEL Corp. VTEL
108 Wild Basin Rd.
Austin, TX 78746 512-314-2700
Telecommunications equipment

VWR Corp. VWRX
1310 Goshen Pkwy.
West Chester, PA 19380
215-431-1700
Instruments - scientific

W. R. Berkley Corp. BKLY
165 Mason St., PO Box 2518
Greenwich, CT 06836 203-629-2880
Insurance - property & casualty

Wackenhut Corrections Corp. WCCX
1500 San Remo Ave.
Coral Gables, FL 33146
305-662-7396
Business services

Wainwright Bank & Trust Co. WAIN
63 Franklin St.
Boston, MA 02110 617-478-4000
Banks - northeast

Walbro Corp. WALB
6242 Garfield St.
Cass City, MI 48726 517-872-2131
Automotive & trucking - original equipment

Walker Interactive Systems, Inc. WALK
303 Second St.
San Francisco, CA 94107 415-495-8811
Computers - software

Wall Data, Inc. WALL
11332 N.E. 122nd Way
Kirkland, WA 98034 206-814-9255
Computers - software O

Wall Street Deli, Inc. WSDI
3514 Lornaridge Dr.
Birmingham, AL 35216 205-822-3960
Retail - food & restaurants

Walshire Assurance Co. WALS
3350 Whiteford Rd.
York, PA 17402 717-757-0000
Insurance - property & casualty

Wandel & Goltermann Technologies, Inc.
WGTI
1030 Swabia Court
Research Triangle, NC 27709 919-941-5730
Instruments - control

Wang Laboratories, Inc. WANG
One Industrial Ave.
Lowell, MA 01851 508-459-5000
Computers - mini & micro O

Warrantech Corp. WTEC
300 Atlantic St.
Stamford, CT 06901 203-975-1100
Insurance - multi line & misc.

Warren Bancorp, Inc. WRNB
10 Main St.
Peabody, MA 01960 508-531-7400
Banks - northeast

Washington Federal Savings and Loan
Association WFSL
425 Pike St.
Seattle, WA 98101 206-624-7930
Financial - savings and loans

Washington Federal Savings Bank WFSB
570 Herndon Parkway
Herndon, VA 22070 703-478-9100
Financial - savings and loans

Washington Mutual, Inc. WAMU
1201 Third Ave.
Seattle, WA 98101 206-461-2000
Financial - savings and loans O [DRP]

Washington Scientific Industries, Inc. WSCI
2605 W. Wayzata Blvd.
Long Lake, MN 55356 612-473-1271
Machine tools & related products

Washington Trust Bancorp WASH
23 Broad St., POB 512
Westerly, RI 02891 401-348-1200
Bank - east
[DRP]

Waters Instruments, Inc. WTRS
2411 Seventh St., NW
Rochester, MN 55901 507-288-7777
Diversified operations

Watson Pharmaceuticals Inc. WATS
132-A Business Center Dr.
Corona, CA 91720 909-270-1400
Drugs - generic O

Watts Industries, Inc. WATTA
815 Chestnut St.
North Andover, MA 01845
508-688-1811
Instruments - control

Wausau Paper Mills Co. WSAU
One Clark's Island
Wausau, WI 54402 715-845-5266
Paper & paper products

Wave Technologies International, Inc. WAVT
10845 Olive Blvd., Ste. 250
St. Louis, MO 63141 314-995-5767
Schools

Wavefront Technologies, Inc. WAVE
530 E. Montecito St.
Santa Barbara, CA 93103 805-962-8117
Computers - software

WavePhore, Inc. WAVO
2601 W. Broadway Rd.
Tempe, AZ 85282 602-438-8700
Miscellaneous - not elsewhere classified

Waverly, Inc. WAVR
428 E. Preston St.
Baltimore, MD 21202 410-528-4000
Publishing - books

WCT Communications, Inc. WCTI
135 E. Ortega St.
Santa Barbara, CA 93101
805-963-2423
Telecommunications services

WD-40 Co. WDFC
1061 Cudahy Place
San Diego, CA 92110 619-275-1400
Paints & allied products

Webster Financial Corp. WBST
First Federal Plaza
Waterbury, CT 06720
203-753-2921
Financial - savings and loans

Wedco Technology, Inc. WEDC
PO Box 397
Bloomsbury, NJ 08804 908-479-4181
Machinery - general industrial

Weitek Corp. WWTK
1060 E. Arques Ave.
Sunnyvale, CA 94086 408-738-8400
Computers - peripheral equipment

Welbilt Corp. WBLT
225 High Ridge Rd.
Stamford, CT 06905 203-325-8300
Miscellaneous - not elsewhere classified

Welcome Home, Inc. WELC
309-D Raleigh St.
Wilmington, NC 28412 910-791-4312
Retail - home furnishings

Wellfleet Communications, Inc. WFLT
8 Federal St.
Bedford, MA 01821 508-670-8888
Telecommunications equipment

Wellstead Industries, Inc. WELS
1117 Perimeter Center West
Atlanta, GA 30338 404-604-9910
Miscellaneous - not elsewhere classified

Werner Enterprises, Inc. WERN
Interstate 80 & Highway 50
Omaha, NE 68137 402-895-6640
Transportation - truck

WesBanco, Inc. WSBC
1 Bank Plaza
Wheeling, WV 26003 304-234-9000
Banks - southeast [DRP]

West Coast Bancorp WCBC
4770 Campus Dr., Ste. 100
Newport Beach, CA 92660 714-757-6868
Banks - west

West Coast Bancorp WCBO
506 Southwest Coast Highway
Newport, OR 97365 503-265-6666
Banks - west

West Coast Bancorp, Inc. WBAN
2724 Del Prado Blvd. South
Cape Coral, FL 33904 813-772-2220
Banks - southeast

West Marine, Inc. WMAR
500 Westridge Dr.
Watsonville, CA 95076 408-728-2700
Retail - misc.

West One Bancorp WEST
101 S. Capitol Blvd.
Boise, ID 83702 208-383-7000
Banks - west O
[DRP]

Westamerica Bancorp WABC
c/o Bank of America
POB 37002
San Francisco, CA 94137 415-624-4100
Banks - west
[DRP]

Westco Bancorp, Inc. WCBI
2121 S. Mannheim Rd.
Westchester, IL 60154 708-865-1100
Banks - midwest

Westcott Communications, Inc. WCTV
13455 Noel Rd.
Dallas, TX 75240 214-417-4100
Motion pictures & services O

Westerbeke Corp. WTBK
Avon Industrial Park
Avon, MA 02322 508-588-7700
Engines - internal combustion

WesterFed Financial Corp. WSTR
110 E. Broadway, PO Box 5388
Missoula, MT 59806 406-721-3700
Financial - savings and loans

Western Bank WSBK
290 S. Fourth St., PO Box 1720
Coos Bay, OR 97420 503-269-5171
Banks - west

Western Beef, Inc. BEEF
47-05 Metropolitan Ave.
Ridgewood, NY 11385 718-821-0011
Food - wholesale

Western Micro Technology, Inc. WSTM
12900 Saratoga Ave.
Saratoga, CA 95070 408-725-1660
Electronics - parts distribution

Western Ohio Financial Corp. WOFC
28 E. Main St., PO Box 719
Springfield, OH 45501 513-325-9990
Banks - midwest

Western Publishing Group, Inc. WPGI
444 Madison Ave.
New York, NY 10022 212-688-4500
Publishing - books

Western Water Co. WWTR
4660 La Jolla Village Dr.
San Diego, CA 92122 619-535-9282
Real estate development

WestPoint Stevens, Inc. WPSN
400 W. Tenth St.
West Point, GA 31833 706-645-4000
Textiles - home furnishings

Westport Bancorp, Inc. WBAT
87 Post Rd. East
Westport, CT 06880
203-222-6911
Banks - northeast
[DRP 5%]

Westwood One, Inc. WONE
9540 Washington Blvd.
Culver City, CA 90232 310-840-4000
Broadcasting - radio & TV

Weyco Group, Inc. WEYS
234 E. Reservoir Ave.
Milwaukee, WI 53201
414-263-8800
Shoes & related apparel

WFS Bancorp, Inc. WBCI
340 S. Broadway
Wichita, KS 67202 316-383-8404
Banks - midwest

White River Corp. WHRC
777 Westchester Ave., Ste. 201
White Plains, NY 10604 914-251-0237
Financial - investment management

Whitney Holding Corp. WTNY
228 St. Charles Ave.
New Orleans, LA 70130
504-586-7272
Banks - southeast

Whole Foods Market, Inc. WFMI
1705 Capital of Texas Highway
Austin, TX 78746 512-328-7541
Retail - supermarkets O

Wholesale Cellular USA, Inc. CELL
5732 W. 71st St.
Indianapolis, IN 46278 317-297-6100
Telecommunications equipment

Wholesome & Hearty Foods, Inc. WHFI
2422 S.E. Hawthorne Blvd.
Portland, OR 97214 503-238-0109
Food - meat products

Wickes Lumber Co. WIKS
706 N. Deer Path Dr.
Vernon Hills, IL 60061 708-367-3400
Building products - retail & wholesale

Willamette Industries, Inc. WMTT
1300 S.W. Fifth Ave.
Portland, OR 97201 503-227-5581
Paper & paper products O

Williams-Sonoma, Inc. WSGC
100 N. Point St.
San Francisco, CA 94133 415-421-7900
Retail - mail order & direct O

Wilmington Trust Corp. WILM
1100 N. Market St.
Wilmington, DE 19890 302-651-1000
Banks - northeast
[DRP]

Wind River Systems, Inc. WIND
1010 Atlantic Ave.
Alameda, CA 94501 510-748-4100
Computers - software

Winston Furniture Co., Inc. WFCI
One Independence Plaza
Birmingham, AL 35209 205-870-0897
Furniture

Winston Hotels, Inc. WINN
2209 Century Dr., Ste. 300
Raleigh, NC 27612 919-510-6010
Real estate investment trust

Winthrop Resources Corp. WINR
9900 Bren Rd. East
Minnetonka, MN 55343
612-936-0226
Leasing

Wisconsin Central Transportation Corp. WCLX
6250 N. River Rd., Ste. 9000
Rosemont, IL 60018 708-318-4600
Transportation - rail

WLR Foods, Inc. WLRF
PO Box 228
Hinton, VA 22831 703-867-4001
Food - meat products
[DRP]

Wolohan Lumber Co. WLHN
1740 Midland Rd.
Saginaw, MI 48603 517-793-4532
Building products - retail & wholesale

Wonderware Corp. WNDR
100 Technology Dr.
Irvine, CA 92718 714-727-3200
Computers - software O

Woodhead Industries, Inc. WDHD
2150 E. Lake Cook Rd.
Buffalo Grove, IL 60089 708-465-8300
Electrical products - misc.

Workingmens Capital Holdings, Inc. WCHI
121 E. Kirkwood Ave.
Bloomington, IN 47408 812-332-9465
Financial - savings and loans

World Acceptance Corp. WRLD
1251 S. Pleasantburg Dr.
Greenville, SC 29605 803-277-4570
Financial - consumer loans

Worthington Foods, Inc. WFDS
900 Proprietors Rd.
Worthington, OH 43085 614-885-9511
Food - misc. O

Worthington Industries, Inc. WTHG
1205 Dearborn Dr.
Columbus, OH 43085 614-438-3210
Metal processing & fabrication
[DRP]

WPI Group, Inc. WPIC
1155 Elm St., Fifth Fl.
Manchester, NH 03101
603-627-3500
Machinery - general industrial

WRT Energy Corp. WRTE
4200 Research Forest Dr.
The Woodlands, TX 77380 713-363-0030
Oil & gas - field services

WSFS Financial Corp. WSFS
838 Market St.
Wilmington, DE 19899 302-792-6000
Banks - northeast

WSMP, Inc. WSMP
WSMP Dr.
Claremont, NC 28610 704-459-7626
Retail - food & restaurants

WTD Industries, Inc. WTDI
10260 S.W. Greenburg Rd.
Portland, OR 97223 503-246-3440
Building products - wood

WVS Financial Corp. WVFC
9001 Perry Highway
Pittsburgh, PA 15237
412-364-1911
Financial - savings and loans

Wyman-Gordon Co. WYMN
244 Worcester St., PO Box 8001
Grafton, MA 01536 508-839-4441
Aerospace - aircraft equipment

X-Rite, Inc. XRIT
3100 44th St., SW
Grandville, MI 49418 616-534-7663
Instruments - control

XcelleNet, Inc. XNET
5 Concourse Parkway, Ste. 200
Atlanta, GA 30325 404-804-8100
Computers - software

Xicor, Inc. XICO
1511 Buckeye Dr.
Milpitas, CA 95035 408-432-8888
Electrical components - semiconductors

Xilinx, Inc. XLNX
2100 Logic Dr.
San Jose, CA 95124 408-559-7778
Computers - software O

Xircom, Inc. XIRC
26025 Mureau Rd.
Calabasas, CA 91302 818-878-7600
Computers - peripheral equipment O

XOMA Corp. XOMA
2910 Seventh St.
Berkeley, CA 94710 510-644-1170
Biomedical & genetic products O

Xpedite Systems, Inc. XPED
446 State Highway 35
Eatontown, NJ 07724 908-389-3900
Telecommunications services

Xplor Corp. XPLR
20 Exchange Place
New York, NY 10005 212-480-1050
Oil & gas - US exploration & production

Xylogics, Inc. XLGX
53 Third Ave.
Burlington, MA 01803
617-272-8140
Electrical components - misc.

Yellow Corp. YELL
10777 Barkley Ave.
Overland Park, KS 66207
913-967-4300
Transportation - truck O

Yes Clothing Co. YSCO
1380 W. Washington Blvd.
Los Angeles, CA 90007 213-742-7800
Apparel

York Financial Corp. YFED
101 S. George St.
York, PA 17401 717-846-8777
Financial - savings and loans
[DRP 10%]

York Research Corp. YORK
280 Park Ave., Ste. 2700 West
New York, NY 10017 212-557-6200
Energy - cogeneration

Young Broadcasting Inc. YBTVA
599 Lexington Ave.
New York, NY 10022 212-754-7070
Broadcasting - radio & TV

Younkers, Inc. YONK
7th and Walnut Sts.
Des Moines, IA 50397
515-244-1112
Retail - apparel & shoes

Zale Corp. ZALE
901 W. Walnut Hill Ln.
Irving, TX 75038 214-580-4000
Retail - jewelry stores

Zaring Homes, Inc. ZHOM
11300 Cornell Park Dr.
Cincinnati, OH 45242 513-489-8849
Building - residential & commercial

Zebra Technologies Corp. ZBRA
333 Corporate Woods Parkway
Vernon Hills, IL 60061 708-634-6700
Optical character recognition O

Zenith Laboratories, Inc. ZENL
140 Legrand Ave.
Northvale, NJ 07647 201-767-1700
Drugs - generic O

ZEOS International, Ltd. ZEOS
1301 Industrial Blvd.
Minneapolis, MN 55413 612-623-9614
Computers - mini & micro

Zilog, Inc. ZLOG
210 Hacienda Ave.
Campbell, CA 95008
408-370-8000
Electrical components - misc. O

Zing Technologies, Inc. ZING
115 Stevens Ave.
Valhalla, NY 10595 914-747-7474
Electronics - parts distribution

Zions Bancorporation ZION
1380 Kennecott Building
Salt Lake City, UT 84133 801-524-4787
Banks - west [DRP]

Zitel Corp. ZITL
47211 Bayside Pkwy.
Fremont, CA 94538 510-440-9600
Computers - peripheral equipment

Zoll Medical Corp. ZOLL
32 Second Ave., Ste. 40
Burlington, MA 10803 617-229-0020
Medical products

Zoltek Companies, Inc. ZOLT
3101 McKelvey Rd.
St. Louis, MO 63044 314-291-5110
Diversified operations

Zoom Telephonics, Inc. ZOOM
207 South St.
Boston, MA 02111 617-423-1072
Computers - peripheral equipment

Zycad Corp. ZCAD
47100 Bayside Pkwy.
Fremont, CA 94538 510-623-4400
Computers - peripheral equipment

Zygo Corp. ZIGO
Laurel Brook Rd., PO Box 448
Middlefield, CT 06455 203-347-8506
Electronics - measuring instruments

Zynaxis, Inc. ZNXS
371 Phoenixville Pike
Malvern, PA 19355 215-889-2200
Biomedical & genetic products

Zytec Corp. ZTEC
7575 Market Place Dr.
Eden Prairie, MN 55344 612-941-1100
Electrical components - misc.

TORONTO STOCK EXCHANGE

Aber Resources Ltd ABZ
930-355 Burrard Street
Vancouver, BC V6C 2G8
(604) 682-8555
Gold and Precious Minerals

Abitibi-Price, Inc. A
207 Queen's Quay West, Suite 680, Box 102
Toronto, Ontario M5J 2P5
(416) 369-6760
Paper and Forest Products

Acklands ACK
945 Wilson Drive
Downsview, Ontario M3K 1E8
(416) 631-5200
Replacement auto parts, industrial products

Agnico-Eagle AGE
401 Bay Street, Suite 2302, P.O. Box 102
Toronto, Ontario M5H 2V4
(416) 947-1212
Silver and Gold Mining

Agra Industries AGR
335 - 8th Avenue S.W., Suite 1900
Calgary, Alberta T2P 1C9
(403) 263-9606
Fabrication and Engineering

Air Canada AC
7373 Cote Vertu Boulevard West, Box 14000
Saint-Laurent, Quebec H4Y 1H4
(514) 422-5000
Airline

Alberta Energy AEC
3900, 421, 7th Avenue S.W.
Calgary, Alberta T2P 4K9
(403) 266-8113
Oil and gas exploration, distribution

Alberta Natural Gas ANG
2900, 240 4th Avenue, S.W.
Calgary, Alberta T2P 4L7
(403) 691-7912
Natural gas, specialty chemicals

Alcan Aluminum AL
1188 Sherbrooke Street West
Montreal, Quebec H3A 3G2
(514) 848-8087
Aluminum products

American Barrick ABX
24 Hazelton Avenue
Toronto, Ontario M5R 2E2
(416) 923-9400
Precious metals

Anderson Exploration AXL
2300 Western Canadian Place
700-9th Ave., S.W.
Calgary, Alberta T2P 3V4 (403) 264-9800
Oil and gas producer

Astral Communications ACM
2100 Catherine Street, West, Bureau 900
Montreal, Quebec H3H 2T3
(514) 939-5000
Cable and entertainment

Atco, Ltd ACO
1600 Canadian Western Center
909-11th Ave., S.W.
Calgary, Alberta T2R 1N6 (403) 292-7546
Utilities, oil and gas, building products

Ault Foods AUL
405 The West Mall, Suite 100
Etobicoke, Ontario M9C 5J1
(416) 626-1973
Food processing

Aur Resources AUR
1 Adelaide Street West, Suite 2501
Toronto, Ontario M5C 2V9
(416) 632-2614
Exploration, development of mineral resources

Avenor, Inc. AVR
1155 Metcalfe Street
Montreal, Quebec H3B 2X1
(514) 878-5052
Paper and forest products

Bank of Montreal BMO
129 St Jacques Street
Montreal, Quebec H2Y 1L6
(514) 877-6835
Banking

Bank of Nova Scotia BNS
44 King Street West
Toronto, Ontario M5H 1H1
(416) 866-5090
Banking

Barrington Petroleum BPL
1100 Western Gas Tower, 530-8th Avenue, S.W.
Calgary, Alberta T2P 3S8
(403) 263-9464
Oil and gas producer

Baton Broadcasting BNB
P.O. Box 9, Station O
Toronto, Ontario M4A 2M9
(416) 299-2340
TV, radio and broadcasting, production

BC Gas, Inc. BCG
1111 West Georgia Street
Vancouver, British Columbia V6E 4M4
(604) 443-6500
Oil and natural gas distribution

B.C. Sugar Refinery BCS
P.O. Box 2150, 123 Rogers Street
Vancouver, British Columbia V6B 3V2
(604) 253-1131
Food processing

BC Telecom BCT
3777 Kingsway
Burnaby, British Columbia V5H 3Z7
(604) 432-2151
Telephone Utility

BCE, Inc. B
1000 Rue De La Gauchetiere Ouest, Bureau 3700
Montreal, Quebec H3B 4Y7
(514) 397-7278
Telecommunications, publishing, real estate

BCE Mobile Communications, Inc BCX
8501 Transcanada Highway
St. Laurent, Quebec H4S 1Z1
(514) 956-4800
Mobile, cellular communications

Bema Gold Corp BGO
510 Burrard Street, Suite 1400, Box 48
Vancouver, British Columbia V6C 3A8
(604) 681-8371
Gold and precious metals

BioChem Pharma, Inc BCH
275 Armand-Frappier Boulevard
Laval, Quebec H7V 4A7
(514) 681-1744
Biotechnology/pharmaceutical

Biomira, Inc BRA
Edmonton Research Par 2011-94 Street
Edmonton, Alberta T6N 1H1
(403) 450-3761
Biotechnology/pharmaceutical

Bombardier BBD
800 Rene-Levesque Boulevard W, Suite 2900
Montreal, Quebec H3B 1Y8
(514) 861-9481
Rail, recreation, marine, aerospace products

Bracknell Corp BRK
150 York Street, Suite 1506
Toronto, Ontario M5H 3S5
(416) 360-4105
Fabricating and engineering

Bramalea Ltd BCD
One Queen Street, East, Suite 2300
Toronto, Ontario M5C 2Y9
(416) 864-6324
Real estate development, housing

Brascan BL
BCE Place, 181 Bay Street, Suite 4400, Box 762
Toronto, Ontario M5J 2T3
(416) 363-9491
Natural resources, consumer products, finance

Bruncor BRR
1 Brunswick Square, Box 5030
Saint John, New Brunswick E2L 4L4
(506) 694-6330
Telecommunications services

Cabre Exploration CBE
1400, 700-9th Avenue, S.W.
Calgary, Alberta T2P 3V4
(403) 231-8800
Oil and gas producers

CAE, Inc. CAE
Royal Bank Plaza, Suite 3060, P.O. Box 30
Toronto, Ontario M5J 2J1
(416) 865-0070
Aerospace, electronics, industrial products

Cambior CBJ
800 Rene-Levesque Boulevard West, Suite 850
Montreal, Quebec H3B 1K9
(514) 878-3166
Gold mining, production

Cambridge Shopping Centers CBG
95 Wellington Street West, Suite 300
Toronto, Ontario M5J 2R2
(416) 369-1355
Real estate investment, shopping centers

Cameco Corp CCO
2121 - 11th Street West
Saskatoon, Saskatchewan S7M 1J3
(306) 956-6312
Metals and minerals

Campbell Resources CCH
120 Adelaide Street West, Suite 1910
Toronto, Ontario M5H 1T1
(416) 366-5201
Gold mining, natural resources production

Canada Malting CMG
10 Four Seasons Place, Suite 600
Toronto, Ontario M9B 6H7
(416) 622-6151
Food processing

Canadian General Investments CGI
110 Yonge Street, Suite 1601
Toronto, Ontario M5C 1T4
(416) 366-2931
Closed end investment company

Canadian Imperial Bank of Commerce CM
Commerce Court West
Toronto, Ontario M5L 1A2
(416) 980-3857
Banking, financial services

Canadian Marconi CMW
2442 Trenton Avenue
Montreal, Quebec H3P 1Y9
(514) 341-7630
Aerospace, communications technology

Canadian Natural Resources CNQ
Esso Plaza, 425-1st Street S.W., Suite 2000
Calgary, Alberta T2P 3L8
(403) 221-2100
Oil and gas producer

Canadian Occidental Ltd CXY
1500, 635-8th Avenue, S.W.
Calgary, Alberta T2P 3Z1
(403) 234-6729
Energy and chemicals production

Canadian Pacific CP
Place Due CDA, Suite 800, Box 6042, Stn A
Montreal, Quebec H3C 3E4 (514) 395-6592
Transportation, energy, real estate,
    communications

Canadian Tire CTR
2180 Yonge Street, P.O. Box 770, Station K
Toronto, Ontario M4P 2V8
(416) 480-8398
Auto products, sporting goods, housewares

Canadian Utilities CU
10035-105 Street, Room 1927
Edmonton, Alberta T5J 2V6
(403) 420-7757
Natural gas, electricity distribution

Canfor Corp CFP
2800-1055 Dunsmuir Street, P.O. Box 49420,
Bentall Centre
Vancouver, British Columbia V7X 1B5
(604) 661-5241 Paper and forest products

Canstar Sports HKY
5705 Rue Ferrier Street, Suite 200
Ville Mont-Royal, Quebec H4P 1N3
(514) 738-3011
Household goods

Canwest Global Communications CWW
TD Centre, 201 Portage Avenue, 31st Floor
Winnipeg, Manitoba R3B 3L7
(204) 956-2025
Broadcasting

Cara Operations CAO
230 Bloor Street West
Toronto, Ontario M5S 1T8
(416) 962-4571
Hospitality

Cascades CAS
404 Marie-Victorin Street
Kingsey Falls, Quebec J0A 1B0
(819) 363-2245
Paper and forest products

CCL Industries CCQ
105 Gordon-Baker Road, Suite 800
Willowdale, Ontario M2H 3P8
(416) 756-8500
Household goods

Celanese Canada CCL
800 Rene Levesque Boulevard W
Montreal, Quebec H3B 1Z1
(514) 871-5506/5511
Chemicals and fertilizers

Central Fund of Canada CEF
P.O. Box 7320
Ancaster, Ontario L9G 3N6
(416) 648-7878
Investment company, funds

CFCF Inc. CF
405 Ogilvie Avenue
Montreal, Quebec H3N 1M4
(514) 273-6311
Broadcasting

Chai-Na-Ta Corp CC
5965-205A Street
Langley, British Columbia V3A 8C4
(604) 533-8883
Food processing

Chauvco Resources CHA
255, 5th Avenue S.W., Suite 2900
Calgary, Alberta T2P 3G6
(403) 231-3100
Oil and gas producer

Chieftan International CID
1201 Toronto-Dominium Tower Edmonton Centre
Edmonton, Alberta T5J 2Z1
(403) 425-1950
Oil and gas producers

CHUM CHM
1331 Yonge Street
Toronto, Ontario M4T 1Y1
(416) 925-6666
Broadcasting

Cineplex Odeon CPX
1303 Yonge Street
Toronto, Ontario M4T 2Y9
(416) 323-6600
Cable and entertainment

Cinram Ltd CRW
2255 Markham Road
Scarborough, Ontario M1B 2W3
(416) 298-8190
Household goods

C-MAC Industries CMS
3000 Industrial Boulevard
Sherbrooke, Quebec J1H 1V8
(819) 821-4524
Technology, hardware

Coca-Cola Beverages KOC
42 Overlea Boulevard
Toronto, Ontario M4H 1B8
(416) 424-6114
Beverages

Cogeco, Inc. CGO
1 Place Ville Marie, Suite 3636
Montreal, Quebec H3B 3P2
(514) 878-8810
Broadcasting

Cognos, Inc. CSN
3755 Riverside Drive, P.O. Box 9707
Ottawa, Ontario K1G 3Z4
(613) 738-1440
Technology, software

Cominco Ltd CLT
500-200 Burrard Street
Vancouver, British Columbia V6C 3L7
(604) 682-0611
Metals and minerals, integrated mines

Cominco Fertilizers COF
426-10333 Southport Road S.W.
Calgary, Alberta T2W 3X6
(403) 258-4600
Chemicals and fertilizers

Consolidated Ramrod Gold CYN
1440-625 Howe Street
Vancouver, British Columbia V6C 2T6
(604) 682-6477
Gold and precious minerals

Consumer's Gas Co CGT
2225 Sheppard Avenue East, Atria III, Suite 1100
North York, Ontario M2J 5C2
(416) 492-6611
Gas utility

Conwest Exploration Company Ltd CEX
95 Wellington Street W, Suite 2000
Toronto, Ontario M5J 2N7
(416) 362-6721
Oil and gas exploration

Corby Distilleries CDL
1002 Sherbrooke Street W, Suite 2300
Montreal, Quebec H3A 3L6
(514) 288-4181
Distillery

Corel Corp COS
1600 Carling Avenue
Ottawa, Ontario K1Z 8R7
(613) 728-8200
Technology, software

Corporate Foods CFL
10 Four Seasons Place, 12th Floor
Etobicoke, Ontario M9B 6H7
(416) 622-2040
Food processing

Cott Corp BCB
207 Queen's Quay W, Suite 800
Toronto, Ontario M5J 1A7
(416) 203-3898
Beverages

Crestar Energy CRS
1900, 700-2nd Street S.W.
Calgary, Alberta T2P 4M8
(403) 231-6700
Oil and gas producer

Co-Steel CEI
Scotia Plaza, 40 King Street West, Box 130
Toronto, Ontario M5H 3V2
(416) 366-4500
Steel

CS Resources Ltd CRZ
645-7th Avenue S.W., 29th Floor
Calgary, Alberta T2P 4G8
(403) 234-8410
Oil and gas producer

Czar Resources Limited CZR
144-4th Avenue S.W., Suite 2100
Calgary, Alberta T2P 3N4
(403) 750-0270
Oil and gas producer

Delrina Corp DC
500-2 Park Centre, 895 Don Mills Road
Toronto, Ontario M3C 1W3
(416) 441-3676 (Ext 2401)
Technology, software

Derlan Industries DRL
145 King Street E., Suite 500
Toronto, Ontario M5C 2Y7
(416) 364-5852

Dia Mat Minerals Ltd DMM
1695 Powick Road
Kelowna, British Columbia V1X 4L1
(604) 861-8660
Gold and precious minerals

Discovery West Corp DSW
30 Soudan Avenue, Suite 500
Toronto, Ontario M4S 1V6
(416) 489-0022
Oil and gas

Dofasco Inc. DFS
P.O. Box 2460
Hamilton, Ontario L8N 3J5
(905) 544-3761
Steel products

Doman Industries Ltd DTC
435 Trunk Road
Duncan, British Columbia V9L 2P8
(604) 746-5155
Paper and forest products

Dominium Textile DTX
1950 Sherbrooke Street West
Montreal, Quebec H3H 1E7
(514) 989-6030
Household goods

Domtar Inc. DTC
395 De Maisonneuve Boulevard West, Box 7210
Montreal, Quebec H3C 3M1
(514) 848-5535
Paper and forest products

Donohue Inc. DHC
80-1 Chemin Street
Louis, Quebec G1S 4W3
(418) 684-7700
Paper and forest products

Dorset Exploration Ltd DXL
3600, 205-5th Avenue S.W.
Calgary, Alberta T2P 2V7
(403) 267-0700
Oil and gas producers

Dreco Energy Services DRE
3716-93 Street
Edmonton, Alberta T6E 5N3
(403) 463-2065
Oil and gas services

Dundee Bancorp Inc. DBC
Scotia Plaza, 40 King Street, 55th Floor
Toronto, Ontario M5A 4H9
(416) 863-6990
Financial management

DuPont Canada DUP
6700 Century Avenue, Box 2200
Streetsville, Mississauga, Ontario L5M 2H3
(905) 821-5101
Chemicals

Dylex DLX
637 Lakeshore Boulevard West
Toronto, Ontario M5V 1A8
(416) 586-7086
Specialty stores

Echo Bay Mines Ltd ECO
370 17th Street, Suite 4050
Denver, Colorado 80202
(403) 423-7218
Gold and precious minerals

E-L Financial ELF
165 University Avenue, 10th Floor
Toronto, Ontario M5H 3B8
(416) 947-2578
Insurance

Elan Energy ELN
150 6th Avenue S.W., #4100
Calgary, Alberta T2P 3Y7
(403) 266-8573
Oil and gas producer

Emco Ltd EML
620 Richmond Street, Box 5252
London, Ontario N6A 4L6
(519) 645-3900
Building materials

Empire Company Ltd EMP
115 King Street
Stellarton, N.S. B0K 1S0
(902) 755-4440
Food stores

Enserv Corp ESV
505-3rd Street S.W., #1505
Calgary, Alberta T2P 3E6
(403) 237-7660
Oil and gas services

Euro-Nevada Mining Corp EN
20 Eglinton Avenue W, Suite 1900
Toronto, Ontario M4R 1K8
(416) 480-6490
Gold and precious minerals

Excel Energy EEI
340-12th Avenue, Suite 1500
Calgary, Alberta T2R 1L5
(403) 269-8850
Oil and gas producers

Extendicare, Inc. EXE
3000 Steeles Avenue East, Suite 700
Markham, Ontario L3R 9W2
(416) 470-5515
Insurance

Fahnestock Viner Holdings, Inc. FHV
181 University Avenue, Suite 1204, P.O. Box 16
Toronto, Ontario M5H 3M7
(416) 367-6247
Investment Company

Fairfax Financial FFH
95 Wellington Street West, Suite 800
Toronto, Ontario M5J 2N7
(416) 367-4944 (Ext 2207)
Insurance

Federal Industries Ltd FIL
One Lombard Place, Suite 600
Winnipeg, Manitoba R3B 0X3
(204) 942-8161
Conglomerate

Finning Ltd FTT
555 Great Northern Way
Vancouver, British Columbia V5T 1E2
(604) 872-4444
Merchandising, wholesale distributors

First Marathon FMS
The Exchange Tower, 2 First Canadian Place
Suite 3100, P.O. Box 21
Toronto, Ontario M5X 1J9   (416) 869-3707
Investment Company

Fletcher Challenge Canada FCC
Pacific Centre, 700 West Georgia Street, 11th Fl.
Vancouver, British Columbia V6Y 1S7
(604) 654-4682
Paper and forest products

Fortis, Inc. FTS
The Fortis Building, 139 Water Street, Suite 1201
St. John's, Newfoundland A1B 3T2
(709) 737-5614
Utility

Four Seasons Hotels Inc. FSH
1165 Leslie Street
Don Mills, Ontario M3C 2K8
(416) 449-4339
Hotels

Franco Nevada Mining Corporation Ltd FN
20 Eglinton Avenue West, Suite 1900, Box 2005
Toronto, Ontario M4R 1K8
(416) 480-6490
Gold and precious minerals

Gandalf Technologies GAN
130 Colonnade Road South
Nepean, Ontario K2E 7M4
(613) 723-6500
Technology, hardware

Geac Computer Corp, Ltd GAC
11 Allstate Parkway, Suite 300
Markham, Ontario L3R 9T8
(416) 475-0525
Technology, software

Glamis Gold Ltd GLG
Four Bentall Centre, Suite 3324, P.O. Box 49287
Vancouver, British Columbia V7X 1L3
(604) 681-3541
Gold and precious metals

Gendis, Inc. GDS
1370 Sony Place
Winnipeg, Manitoba R3C 3C3
(204) 474-5200
Specialty stores

George Weston Ltd WN
22 St. Clair Avenue West, Suite 1500
Toronto, Ontario M4T 2S7
(416) 922-2500 (Ext 239)
Food stores

Golden Knight Resources, Inc. GKR
200 Burrard Street, Suite 600
Vancouver, British Columbia V6C 1E5
(604) 640-5286
Gold and precious metals

Golden Star Resources Ltd GSC
One Norwest Center, 1700 Lincoln St.,
Suite 1950, Denver, Colorado 80203
(303) 830-9000
Gold and precious metals

Great West Lifeco Inc GWO
100 Osborne Street North
Winnipeg, Manitoba R3C 3A5
(204) 946-1190
Insurance

GTC Transcontinental Group Ltd GRT
1 Place Ville Marie, Suite 3315
Montreal, Quebec H3B 3N2
(514) 954-4000
Publishing and printing

Gulf Canada Resources GOU
P.O. Box 130, Station M
Calgary, Alberta T2P 4J8
(403) 233-4049
Oil and gas

Hawker Siddeley Canada HSC
3 Robert Speck Parkway, Suite 700
Mississauga, Ontario L4Z 2G5
(905) 897-7161
Transportation equipment

Hees International Bancorp Inc HIL
181 Bay Street, P.O. Box 770, Suite 4500
Toronto, Ontario M5J 2T3
(416) 864-0430
Financial management

Hemlo Gold Mines HEM
181 Bay Street, Box 755, Suite 4100
Toronto, Ontario M5J 2T3
(416) 982-7116
Gold and precious metals

Hillcrest Resources HRT
1800, 407-2nd Street S.W.
Calgary, Alberta T2P 2Y3
(403) 299-2222
Oil and gas producers

Hollinger Inc. HLG
10 Toronto Street
Toronto, Ontario M5C 2B7
(416) 363-8721
Publishing and printing

Home Oil Company Limited HOC
324 Eighth Avenue S.W., Suite 1600
Calgary, Alberta T2P 2Z5
(403) 232-7100
Oil and gas producers

Horsham Corp HSM
24 Hazelton Avenue
Toronto, Ontario M5R 2E2
(416) 924-2842
Conglomerate

Hudson's Bay Company HBC
401 Bay Street
Toronto, Ontario M5H 2Y4
(416) 861-4593
Department stores

Imasco Ltd IMS
600 De Maisonneuve Boulevard West, 20th Fl.
Montreal, Quebec H3A 3K7
(514) 982-9111
Tobacco

Imperial Oil Limited IMO
111 St Clair Avenue W
Toronto, Ontario M5W 1K3
(416) 968-5387
Oil and gas, integrated oils

Inco Ltd N
Royal Trust Tower, T.D. Centre, P.O. Box 44
Toronto, Ontario M5K 1N4
(416) 361-7664
Metals and minerals, integrated mines

Intensity Resources Ltd ITY
1000, 400-5th Avenue S.W.
Calgary, Alberta T2P 0L6
(403) 263-3440
Oil and gas producers

Inter-City Products Corp IPR
20 Queen Street West, P.O. Box 32
Toronto, Ontario M5H 3R3
(416) 598-0101
Household goods

International Colin Energy Corp KCN
333-11th Avenue S.W., Suite 1210
Calgary, Alberta T2R 1L9
(403) 261-7600
Oil and gas producer

International Forest Products Ltd IFP
1055 Dunsmuir, Suite 3500, Box 49114
Vancouver, British Columbia V7X 1H7
(604) 689-6800
Paper and forest products

International Murex Technologies Corp MXX
3075 Northwoods Circle
Norcross, Georgia 30071
(404) 662-0660
Biotechnology/pharmaceuticals

International Verifact Inc. IVI
79 Torbarrie Road
Toronto, Ontario M3L 1G5
(416) 932-3986
Technology/hardware

Intrawest Corporation ITW
200 Burrad Street, Suite 800
Vancouver, British Columbia V6C 3L6
(604) 669-9777
Real Estate

Inverness Petroleum Ltd IES
400-3rd Avenue S.W., Suite 2200
Calgary, Alberta T2P 4H2
(403) 294-3800
Oil and gas producers

Investors Group Inc. IGI
447 Portage Avenue
Winnipeg, Manitoba R3C 3B6
(204) 956-8514
Investment company

IPL Energy Inc. IPL
10201 Jasper Avenue, Box 398
Edmonton, Alberta T5J 2J9
(403) 420-5210
Pipelines

Ipsco, Inc. ISP
P.O. Box 1670
Regina, Saskatchewan S4P 3C7
(306) 924-7230
Steel products

ISM Information Systems Management Corp ISM
1 Research Drive
Regina, Saskatchewan S4S 7H1
(306) 781-5151
Business services

Ivaco Inc. IVA
Place Mercantile, 770 Rue Sherbrooke Ouest
Montreal, Quebec H3A 1G1
(514) 288-4545
Steel products

Jannock Ltd JN
Scotia Plaza, Box 1012
40 King Street W, Ste. 5205
Toronto, Ontario M5H 3Y2 (416) 364-8586
Building materials

Jordan Petroleum Ltd JDN
850 Bow Valley Sware 3, 255-5th Avenue S.W.
Calgary, Alberta T2P 3G6
(403) 266-4325
Oil and gas producers

Kaufel Group Ltd KGL
1811 Hymus Boulevard
Dorval, Quebec H9P 1J5
(514) 685-2270
Fabricating and engineering

Kerr Addison Mines Ltd KER
1 Adelaide Street East, Suite 2700
Toronto, Ontario M5C 2Z6
(416) 982-7286
Metals and minerals, mining

Kinross Gold Corp K
Scotia Plaza, 56th Floor, 40 King Street W
Toronto, Ontario M5H 2Y2
(416) 365-5650
Gold and precious minerals

Labatt, John Ltd LBT
181 Bay Street, BCE Place, Suite 200
Toronto, Ontario M5J 2T3
(416) 865-6000
Brewery

Lafarge Canada, Inc LCI
606 Cathcart
Montreal, Quebec H3B 1L7
(514) 861-1411
Building materials

Laidlaw Inc LDM
3221 North Service Road, P.O.Box 5028
Burlington, Ontario L7R 3Y8
(905) 336-1800
Transportation

Laurentian Bank of Canada LB
Laurentian Bank Tower, 1981 McGill College Ave.
Montreal, Quebec H3A 3K3
(514) 284-7545
Banking

Linamar Corp LNR
301 Massey Road
Guelph, Ontario N1K 1B2
(519) 836-7550
Auto parts

Loblaw Companies Limited L
22 St. Clair Avenue E, Suite 1500
Toronto, Ontario M4T 2S7
(416) 922-2500 (Ext 239)
Food Stores

Loewen Group Inc LWN
4940 Canada Way, Suite 506
Burnaby, British Columbia V5G 4K6
(604) 299-9321
Hospitality

London Insurance Group Inc. LON
255 Dufferin Avenue
London, Ontario N6A 4K1
(519) 432-2000 (Ext 5477)
Insurance

Lytton Minerals Ltd LTL
45 Charles Street East, 6th Floor
Toronto, Ontario M4Y 1S2
(416) 968-7384
Gold and precious minerals

MacKenzie Financial Corp MKF
150 Bloor Street W, 4th Floor
Toronto, Ontario M5S 3B5
(416) 922-5322
Investment Company

MacMillan Bloedel Ltd MB
925 West Georgia Street
Vancouver, British Columbia V6C 3L2
(604) 661-8389
Paper and forest products

Magna International Inc. MG
36 Apple Creek Boulevard
Markham, Ontario L3R 4Y4
(416) 477-7766
Auto parts

Mannville Oil and Gas Ltd MOG
425-1st Street S.W., Suite 2400
Calgary, Alberta T2P 3L8
(403) 231-7800
Oil and gas

Maple Leaf Foods Inc MLF
30 St. Clair Avenue West
Toronto, Ontario M4V 3A2
(416) 926-2000
Food processing

Maritime Telephone and Telegraph Co Ltd MTT
1505 Barrington Street, 8N, P.O. Box 880
Halifax, Nova Scotia B3J 2W3
(800) 565-7168
Telephone utility

Mark Resources Inc. MKC
800-5th Avenue S.W., 13th Floor
Calgary, Alberta T2P 4A4
Oil and gas producers

Markborough Properties Inc MKP
1 Dundas Street West, Suite 2700
Toronto, Ontario M5G 2J2
(416) 591-2829
Real estate

MDS Health Group Limited MHG
100 International Boulevard
Etobicoke, Ontario M9W 6J6
(416) 672-4213
Pharmaceuticals

Meridian Technologies Inc MNI
2 St. Clair Avenue West, Suite 1700
Toronto, Ontario M4V 1L5
(416) 922-2050
Fabrication and engineering

Metall Mining Corp MLM
Aetna Tower, Suite 3400, P.O. Box 19
TD Centre
Toronto, Ontario M5K 1A1
(416) 361-6400
Mining

Methanex Corp MX
1800 Waterford Centre, 200 Burrard Street
Vancouver, British Columbia V6C 3M1
(604) 661-2600
Chemicals

Metro-Richelieu Inc. MRU
11011 Maurice-Duplessis Boulevard
Montreal, Quebec H1C 1V6
(514) 643-1207
Food stores

Midland Walwyn Inc. MWI
181 Bay Street, Suite 400
Toronto, Ontario M5L 2V8
(416) 369-7483
Investment company

Mitel Corp MLT
350 Legget Drive
Kanata, Ontario K2K 1X3
(613) 592-2122
Technology/hardware

Molson Companies Ltd MOL
Scotia Plaza, 40 King Street, Suite 3600
Toronto, Ontario M5H 3Z5
(416) 360-1786
Brewery

Moore Corporation Ltd MCL
1 First Canadian Place, P.O. Box 78
Toronto, Ontario M5X 1G5
(416) 364-2600
Business services

Morgan Hydrocarbons, Inc. MHI
2200 Bow Valley Square II, 205-5th Avenue S.W.
Calgary, Alberta T2P 2V7
(403) 298-8300
Oil and gas producers

Morrison Petroleums Ltd MRP
400 3rd Avenue, Suite 3000
Calgary, Alberta T2P 4H2
(403) 262-5242
Oil and gas

National Bank of Canada NA
600 De La Gauchetiere Ouest, 4th Floor
Montreal, Quebec H3B 4L2
(514) 394-6080
Banking

National Trustco Inc. NT
1 Adelaide Street East, One Financial Place
Toronto, Ontario M5C 2W8
(416) 361-3902
Trust company

Newbridge Networks Corp NNC
600 March Road
Kanata, Ontario K2K 2E6
(613) 591-3600
Technology

Newtel Enterprises Ltd NEL
P.O. Box 12110, Fort William Building
St. John's, Newfoundland A1C 6J7
(709) 739-3310
Telephone utility

Noma Industries Ltd NMA
4100 Yonge Street, Suite 502
North York, Ontario M2P 2B5
(416) 226-7279
Household goods

Noranda Inc. NOR
181 Bay Street, Suite 4100, P.O. Box 755
Toronto, Ontario M5J 2T3
(416) 982-7111
Metals and minerals, integrated mines

Noranda Forest Inc NF
T.D. Bank Tower, TD Centre, Suite 4414, P.O. Box 7
Toronto, Ontario M5K 1A1
(416) 982-7363
Paper and forest products

Norcen Energy Resources Ltd NCN
715-5th Avenue S.W.
Calgary, Alberta T2P 2X7
(403) 231-0147
Oil and gas producer

Northern Telecom Ltd NTL
3 Robert Speck Parkway
Mississauga, Ontario L4Z 3C8
(905) 566-3000
Technology

Northstar Energy Corp NEN
300, 535-7th Avenue S.W.
Calgary, Alberta T2P 0Y4
(403) 298-0500
Oil and gas

North West Company Inc. NWC
77 Main Street
Winnipeg, Manitoba R3C 2R1
(204) 934-1481
Specialty stores

NOVA Corp NVA
NHO-31, 801-7th Avenue S.W.
Calgary, Alberta T2P 2N6
(403) 290-6135/7873
Chemicals

Nova Scotia Power Inc NSI
Scotia Square, 1894 Barrington Street
P.O. Box 910
Halifax, Nova Scotia B3J 2W5
(902) 428-6573 Utility

Nowsco Well Service Ltd NWS
2570 801-6th Avenue S.W.
Calgary, Alberta T2P 4L8
(403) 261-2990
Oil and gas service

Numac Energy Inc. NMC
321-6th Avenue S.W.
Edmonton, Alberta T2P 3H3
(403) 260-4728
Oil and gas

Ocelot Energy Inc. OCE
Bow Valley Square II, 205-5th Avenue S.W.,
Suite 3300, Calgary, Alberta T2P 2V7
(403) 299-5700
Oil and gas

Onex Corp OCX
161 Bay Street, Box 700
Toronto, Ontario M5J 2S1
(416) 362-7711
Conglomerate

Oshawa Group Limited OSH
302 The East Wall
Islington, Ontario M9B 6B8
(416) 236-1971
Food stores

Pagurian Corporation Ltd PGC
181 Bay Street, Suite 4500, Box 770
Toronto, Ontario M5J 2T3
(416) 865-0430
Financial management

PanCanadian Petroleum Ltd PCP
150-9th Avenue S.W., PanCanadian Plaza
Box 2850
Calgary, Alberta T2P 2S5
(403) 290-2000 Oil and gas

Paramount Resources Ltd POU
4000 First Canadian Centre, 350 Seventh Ave. S.W.
Calgary, Alberta T2P 3W5
(403) 266-2047
Oil and gas

Pegasus Gold Inc PGU
1088-999 West Hastings Street
Vancouver, British Columbia V6C 2W2
(509) 624-4653
Gold and precious minerals

Petro-Canada PCA
150-6th Avenue S.W.
Calgary, Alberta T2P 3E3
(403) 296-8000
Oil and gas

Pinnacle Resources Ltd PNN
P.O. Box 20067, Calgary Place Postal Outlet
Calgary, Alberta T2P 4J2
(403) 232-9100
Oil and gas producer

Philip Environmental Inc. PEN
651 Burlington Street, P.O. Box 423, Depot 1
Hamilton, Ontario L8L 7W2
(905) 544-6687
Transportation/environmental

Placer Dome Inc. PDG
1600 1055 Dunsmuir Street
Vancouver, British Columbia V7X 1P1
(604) 682-7082
Gold and precious minerals

Poco Petroleums Ltd POC
3500, 250-6th Avenue S.W.
Calgary, Alberta T2P 3H7
(403) 260-8025
Oil and gas

Potash Corporation of Saskatchewan Inc. POT
500-122 1st Avenue South
Saskatoon, Saskatchewan S7K 7G3
(306) 933-8521
Chemicals and fertilizers

Power Corporation of Canada POW
759 Victoria Square
Montreal, Quebec H2Y 2K4
(514) 286-7400
Conglomerate

Power Financial Corp PWF
751 Victoria Square
Montreal, Quebec H2Y 2K4
(514) 286-7430
Financial management

Precision Drilling Corp PD
1600 144 Avenue S.W.
Calgary, Alberta T2P 3N4
(403) 264-4882
Oil and gas services

Premdor, Inc PDI
4120 Yonge Street, Suite 402
Willowdale, Ontario M2P 2B8
(416) 250-8933
Building materials

Prime Resources Group Inc PRU
700 West Pender Street, Suite 1000
Vancouver, British Columbia V6C 1G8
(604) 684-2345
Gold and precious minerals

Provigo, Inc PGV
1250 Rene Levesque Boulevard West
Montreal, Quebec H3B 4X1
(514) 383-2802
Food stores

Quadra Logic Technologies, Inc. QLT
520 Sixth Avenue
Vancouver, British Columbia V5Z 4H5
(604) 872-7881
Biotechnology/pharmaceuticals

Quebec-Telephone QT
6 Jules-A. Brillant Street
Rimouski, Quebec G5L 7E4
(418) 722-5883
Telephone utilities

Quebecor Inc QBR
612 Rue St. Jacques Ouest
Montreal, Quebec H3C 4M8
(514) 877-9777 (Ext 616)
Publishing/printing

Quebecor Printing Inc IQI
612 Rue St. Jacques Street
Montreal, Quebec H3C 4M8
(514) 954-0101
Printing

Quno Corp QNO
80 King Street
St. Catharines, Ontario L2R 7G2
(416) 688-5030
Paper and forest products

Ranchmen's Resources Ltd RRL
333 Eleventh Avenue S.W., Suite 1000
Calgary, Alberta T2R 1L9
(403) 267-9421
Oil and gas producer

Ranger Oil Limited RGO
2700, Esso Plaza East, 425 First Street S.W.
Calgary, Alberta T2P 3L8
(403) 232-5252
Oil and gas producers

Rayrock Yellowknife Resources Inc RAY
30 Soudan Avenue, Suite 500
Toronto, Ontario M4S 1V6
(416) 489-0022
Gold and precious metals

Reitmans (Canada) Ltd RET
250 Suave Street, West
Montreal, Quebec H3L 1Z2
(514) 384-1140
Specialty store

Renaissance Energy Ltd RES
3000, 425 First Street S.W.
Calgary, Alberta T2P 3L8
(403) 750-1400
Oil and gas producers

Repap Enterprises Inc RPP
1250 Rene Levesque Boulevard, Westsuite 3800
Montreal, Quebec H3B 4W8
(514) 846-1316
Paper and forest products

Revenue Properties Company Ltd RPC
The Collonade, 131 Bloor Street West, Suite 300
Toronto, Ontario M5S 1R1
(416) 963-8100
Real estate

Rigel Energy Corp RJL
1900, Bow Valley Square III, 225-5th Avenue S.W.
Calgary, Alberta T2P 2G6
(403) 267-3000
Oil and gas producer

Rio Algom Limited ROM
120 Adelaide Street W., Suite 2600
Toronto, Ontario M5H 1W5
(416) 367-4000
Metals and minerals, mining

Rio Alto Exploration Ltd RAX
1600, 111 - 5th Avenue S.W.
Calgary, Alberta T2P 3Y6
(403) 264-8780
Oil and gas producer

Riverside Forest Products Ltd RFP
820 Guy Street
Kelowna, British Columbia V1Y 7R5
(604) 762-3411
Paper and forest products

Rogers Cantel Mobile Communications Inc. RCM
6400 Scotia Plaza, 40 King Street West, Box 1007
Toronto, Ontario M5H 3Y2
(416) 864-2373
Telephone utilities

Rogers Communications Inc RCI
Commercial Union Tower, Suite 2600
P.O. Box 249, T.D. Centre
Toronto, Ontario M5K 1J5
(416) 864-2373 Cable and entertainment

Rothmans Inc ROC
1500 Don Mills Road
Don Mills, Ontario M3B 3L1
(416) 449-5525
Tobacco

Royal Bank of Canada RY
1 Place Ville Marie
Montreal, Quebec H3C 3A9
(514) 874-5012
Banking

Royal Oak Mines Inc. RYO
1425 West Pender Street, 2nd Floor
Vancouver, British Columbia V6G 2S3
(604) 682-8320
Gold and precious minerals

Sceptre Resources Ltd SRL
2000, 400-3rd Avenue S.W.
Calgary, Alberta T2P 4H2
(403) 298-9800
Oil and gas

Schneider Corporation SCD
321 Courtland Avenue E., P.O.Box 130
Kitchener, Ontario N2G 3X8
(519) 885-7600
Food processing

Scott Paper Ltd SPL
P.O. Box 3600
Vancouver, British Columbia V6B 3Y7
(604) 688-8131
Household goods

Scott's Hospitality Inc. SRC
BCE Place, 181 Bay Street, Suite 1500, Box 810
Toronto, Ontario M5J 2T3
(416) 369-9050
Hospitality

Seagram Company Ltd VO
1430 Peel Street
Montreal, Quebec H3A 1S9
(514) 849-5271
Distillery

Sears Canada Inc SCC
222 Jarvis Street, D766
Toronto, Ontario M5B 2B8
(416) 941-4793
Department stores

Semi-Tech Corporation SEM
131 McNabb Street
Markham, Ontario L3R 5V7
(416) 475-2670
Specialty stores

Shaw Communications Inc SCL
7605-50 Street
Edmonton, Alberta T6B 2W9
(403) 468-1230
Cable and entertainment

Shaw Industries Ltd SHL
25 Bethridge Road
Rexdale, Ontario M9W 1M7
(416) 743-7111
Fabrication and engineering

SHL Systemhouse Inc. SHK
50 O'Connor Street, Suite 501
Ottawa, Ontario K1P 6L2
(613) 236-9734
Business services

Shell Canada Ltd SHC
Box 100 Station M
Calgary, Alberta T2P 2H5
(403) 691-3404
Oil and gas, integrated oils

Sherritt Inc. SE
3500 Manulife Place, 10180-101 Street
Edmonton, Alberta T5J 3S4
(403) 493-8700
Chemicals

Slocan Forest Products SFF
240-10451 Shellbridge Way, Airport Executive Park
Richmond, British Columbia V6X 2W8
(604) 278-7311
Paper and forest products

SNC-Lavalin Group Inc SNC
2 Place Felix Martin
Montreal, Quebec H2Z 1Z3
(514) 393-1000
Fabricating and engineering

Softkey Software Products Inc. SSK
2700 Matheson Boulevard East
8th Floor, West Tower
Mississauga, Ontario L4W 4V9
(800) 377-6567 Technology/software

Southam Inc STM
1450 Don Mills Road
Don Mills, Ontario M3B 2X7
(416) 442-2929
Publishing and printing

Spar Aerospace Ltd SPZ
5090 Explorer Drive, Suite 900
Mississauga, Ontario L4W 4X6
(416) 629-7727
Technology/hardware

SR Telecom Inc SRX
8150 Trans Canada Highway
St. Laurent, P.Q. H4S 1M5
(514) 335-1210
Technology/hardware

Stampeder Exploration Ltd SDX
1200, 521-3rd Avenue S.W., Eau Claire Place II
Calgary, Alberta T2P 3T3
(403) 265-4224
Oil and gas producer

Stelco Inc STE
Stelco Tower, Box 2030
Hamilton, Ontario L8N 3T1
(905) 528-2511 (Ext 4989)
Steel

St. Lawrence Cement Inc ST
1945 Graham Boulevard, 2nd Floor
Mount Royal, Quebec H3R 1H1
(514) 340-1881
Building materials

Summit Resources Ltd SUI
340-12th Avenue South West, Suite 700
Calgary, Alberta T2R 1L5
(403) 269-4402
Oil and gas producer

Suncor Inc. SU
36 York Mills Road
North York, Ontario M2P 2C5
(416) 733-7300
Oil and gas/integrated oils

Talisman Energy Inc TLM
855 2nd Street S.W., Suite 2100
Calgary, Alberta T2P 4J9
(403) 237-1234
Oil and gas producer

Tarragon Oil and Gas Ltd TN
2500, 500-4th Avenue S.W.
Calgary, Alberta T2P 2V6
(403) 974-7500
Oil and gas producer

Teck Corporation TEK
200 Burrard Street, Suite 600
Vancouver, British Columbia V6C 3L9
(604) 687-1117
Gold and precious minerals

Teleglobe Inc TGO
1000 Rue De La Gauchetiere Ouest
Montreal, Quebec H3B 4X5
(514) 868-8150/7642
Telephone utility

Telus Corp AGT
10020-100th Street, 31st Floor
Edmonton, Alberta T5J 0N5
(403) 493-3110
Telephone utility

Tembec Inc TBC
800 Rene-Levesque Boulevard West, Suite 2790
Montreal, Quebec H3B 1X9
(514) 871-0137
Paper and forest products

Thomson Corporation TOC
T.D. Bank Tower, P.O. Box 24, Suite 2706
T.D. Centre
Toronto, Ontario M5K 1A1
(416) 360-8700 Publishing and printing

Toronto-Dominium Bank TD
Toronto Dominium Centre, P.O. Box 1
Toronto, Ontario M5K 1A2
(416) 944-5741
Banking

Toronto Sun Publishing Corp TSP
333 King Street East
Toronto, Ontario M5A 3X5
(416) 947-2220
Publishing and printing

Torstar Corporation TS
1 Yonge Street
Toronto, Ontario M5E 1P9
(416) 869-4545
Publishing and printing

Total Petroleum Ltd TPN
Denver Place, North Tower 999
18th Street, Suite 2201
Denver, Colorado 80202
(303) 291-2213 Oil and gas

TransAlta Corporation TA
110-12th Avenue S.W., Box 1900
Calgary, Alberta T2P 2M1
(403) 267-7110
Gas/electric utility

TransCanada Pipelines Ltd TRP
111-5th Avenue, S.W., 29th Floor
Calgary, Alberta T2P 3Y6
(403) 267-8511
Pipeline

Transwest Energy Inc TWE
255-5th Avenue S.W., 4th Floor,
Bow Valley Square III, Calgary, Alberta T2P 3G6
(403) 261-5500
Oil and gas

Tri Link Resources Ltd TLR
550-6th Avenue, S.W., 12th Floor
Calgary, Alberta T2P 0S2
(403) 262-4601
Oil and gas

Trilon Financial Corporation TFC
BCE Place, 181 Bay Street
Suite 4420, P.O. Box 771
Toronto, Ontario M5J 2T3
(416) 663-0061 Financial management

Trimac Ltd TMA
P.O. Box 3500
Calgary, Alberta T2P 2P9
(403) 298-5119
Transportation/environmental

Trimark Financial Corp TMF
Scotia Plaza, Suite 5200, P.O. Box 205
Toronto, Ontario M5H 3Z3
(416) 362-7181
Investment company

TVX Gold Inc TVX
161 Bay Street, Suite 4300
Toronto, Ontario M5J 2S1
(416) 366-8160
Gold and precious minerals

UAP Inc UAP
7025 Ontario Street East
Montreal, Quebec H1N 2B3
(514) 256-5031
Auto parts

Ulster Petroleums Ltd ULP
1400 Sun Life Plaza One, 144-4th Avenue S.W.
Calgary, Alberta T2P 3N4
(403) 269-6911
Oil and gas

United Corporations Ltd UNC
165 University Avenue, 10th Floor
Toronto, Ontario M5H 3B8
(416) 947-2578
Investment Company

United Dominion Industries Ltd UDI
2300 One First Union Center, 301 S. College Street
Charlotte, North Carolina 28202
(704) 347-6800
Fabricating/engineering

Viceroy Resource Corp VOY
880-999 West Hastings Street
Vancouver, British Columbia V6C 2W2
(604) 688-9780
Gold and precious minerals

Videotron Groupe Ltee
300 Viger Avenue Est
Montreal, Quebec H2X 3W4
(514) 281-1232
Cable and entertainment

Wascana Energy Inc. WE
P.O. Box 1550, 1777 Victoria Avenue
Regina, Saskatchewan S4P 3C4
(306) 781-8211
Oil and gas

Weldwood of Canada Ltd WLW
1055 Hastings Street, Box 2179
Vancouver, British Columbia V6B 3V8
(604) 662-2837
Paper and forest products

Westcoast Energy Inc W
1333 West Georgia Street
Vancouver, British Columbia V6E 3K9
(604) 691-5274
Pipelines

West Fraser Timber Co Ltd WFT
1000-1100 Melville Street
Vancouver, British Columbia V6E 4A6
(604) 895-2700
Paper and forest products

Wharf Resources Ltd WFR
500-4th Avenue S.W., Suite 1701
Calgary, Alberta T2P 4H2
(416) 361-0402
Gold and precious minerals

WIC Western International Comm Ltd WIC
1960-505 Burrard Street
Vancouver, British Columbia V7X 1M6
(604) 687-2844
Broadcasting

Xerox Canada Inc XXC
5650 Yonge Street
North York, Ontario M2M 4G7
(416) 733-6398
Business services

AMERICAN DEPOSITARY RECEIPTS (ADRs)

Investors wishing to buy shares in some companies headquartered outside the United States can avoid dealing directly with foreign exchanges by purchasing American Depositary Receipts in U.S. markets. ADRs are traded on the New York Stock Exchange, the American Stock Exchange and the Over-The-Counter market.

ADRs are receipts for foreign based corporation's shares, which are held in American bank vaults. A buyer of an ADR in America is entitled to the same dividends and capital gains accruing to a shareholder purchasing shares on an exchange in the home country of the company. ADRs are denominated in dollars, so quoted prices reflect the latest currency exchange rates. ADR prices are listed in the *Wall Street Journal* and other newspapers, as well as in electronic databases.

The companies with ADRs generally are well-established, financially stable corporations with worldwide operations. In many cases, Americans would be familiar with their products and services because they are offered in the United States. A total of about 700 ADRs are traded. Most of the trading activity, however, is limited to some 100 issues. It is these actively traded issues that are presented here in alphabetical order, courtesy of Wilshire Associates [1299 Ocean Avenue, Santa Monica, California 90401 (310) 451-3051.] The entry for each company includes (1) the firm's name, (2) its stock symbol, (3) the exchange where it trades (NYSE for New York Stock Exchange, AMEX for American Stock Exchange and OTC for Over-The-Counter market), (4) its main line of business, and (5) the country where it is headquartered.

Akzo Nobel [AKZOY] OTC, Chemicals, Netherlands

Alcatel Althsom [ALA] NYSE, Telecomm. Equipment, France

Anglo American Gold [AAGY] OTC, Mining, South Africa

Aracruz Celulose [ARA] NYSE, Pulp and Paper, Brazil

Attwoods [A] NYSE, Environmental, United Kingdom

Automated Security Holdings [ASI] NYSE, Misc. Serv., United Kingdom

Banco Bilbao Vizcaya [BBV] NYSE, Banking, Spain

Banco De Galicia y B.A. [BGALY] OTC, Banking, Argentina

Banco Frances Del Ri [BFR] NYSE, Banking, Argentina

Blyvoorjuitzicht Gld [BLYVY] OTC, Mining, South Africa

British Airways [BAB] NYSE, Airlines, United Kingdom

British Gas [BRG] NYSE, Utilities, United Kingdom

British Petroleum [BP] NYSE, Energy, United Kingdom

British Steel [BST] NYSE, Steel, United Kingdom

British Telecom [BTY] NYSE, Telecommunications, United Kingdom

Buenos Aires Embotelladora [BAE] NYSE, Food, Argentina

Bufete Industrial [GBI] NYSE, Construction, Mexico

Cable & Wireless [CWP] NYSE, Telecom Equipment, United Kingdom

Coca-Cola Femsa [KOF] NYSE, Beverages, Mexico

Coflexip [CXIPY] OTC, Offshore Flexible Pipe/Robots, France

Compania Cervecerias Unidas [CCUUY] OTC, Beverages, Chile

Compania de Telefonos de Chile [CTC] NYSE, Telecom Serv., Chile

Consorcio G Grupo Dina [DIN] NYSE, Autos, Mexico

Corporacion Banc Espana [AGR] NYSE, Banking, Spain

Daimler Benz A G [DAI] NYSE, Autos, Germany

Danka Business Systems [DÀNKY] OTC, Comp/Office, United Kingdom

De Beers Consolidated Mines [DBRSY] OTC, Mining, South Africa

Driefontein Consolidated [DRFNY] OTC, Gold Mining, South Africa

Elan [ELN] AMEX, Drugs, Ireland

Elf Aquitaine [ELF] NYSE, Oil Refining & Marketing, France

Elscint [ELT] NYSE, Health Care, Israel

Empresa Nacional de Elec [ELE] NYSE, Utilities, Spain

Empresas Ica-Soc Control [ICA] NYSE, Construction, Mexico

Enersis S.A. [ENI] NYSE, Energy, Chile

Ericsson Telephone [ERICY] OTC, Telecom Equipment, Sweden

Ericsson Telephone [ERICZ] OTC, Telecom Equipment, Sweden

Esperito Santo Financial [ESF] NYSE, Banks, Portugal

Ethical Holdings [ETHCY] OTC, Drugs, United Kingdom

Fila Holding [FLH] NYSE, Apparel, Italy

Free State Consolidated Gold Mines [FSCNY] OTC, Gold Mining, South Africa

Glaxo Holdings [GLX] NYSE, Drugs, United Kingdom

Grand Metropolitan [GRM] NYSE, Food, United Kingdom

Great Central Mines [GTCMY] OTC, Mining, Australia

Grupo Casa Autrey [ATY] NYSE, Drugs, Mexico

Grupo Financiero Serfin [SFN] NYSE, Finance, Mexico

Grupo Mexicana de Desarrollo [GMD] NYSE, Construction, Mexico

Grupo Mexicano de Desarrollo [GMDB] NYSE, Construction, Mexico

Grupo Televisa [TV] NYSE, TV, broadcasting, Mexico

Grupo Tribasa [GTR] NYSE, Construction, Mexico

Hanson [HAN] NYSE, Multi Industry, United Kingdom

Healthcare Tech [HCTLF] OTC, Healthcare Products, Israel

Hong Kong Telecommunication [HKT] NYSE, Telecommunication Services, Hong Kong

Idan Software Industries [IDANF] OTC, Telecommunication/Computer Products, Israel

Imperial Chemical Industries [ICI] NYSE, Chemicals, United Kingdom

Istec Industries & Technology [ISTEF] OTC, Finance/Leasing, Israel

Kloof Gold Mining [KLOFY] OTC, Gold Mining, South Africa

Lasmo [LSO] NYSE, Energy Production, United Kingdom

Maderas y Sinteticos [MYS], Building Materials, Chile

Medeva [MDV] Amex, Drugs, United Kingdom

Minorco [MNRCY] OTC, Mining, Canada

Montedison [MNT] NYSE, Chemicals, Italy

News Corp [NWS] NYSE, Publishing, Australia

Norsk Hydro [NHY] NYSE, Chemicals, Norway

Orbital Engine [OE] NYSE, Automobiles, Australia

Petroleum Geo-Services [PGSAY] OTC, Misc. Services, Norway

Philips [PHG] NYSE, Electrical Machinery, Netherlands

Repsol [REP] NYSE, Energy-Integration, Spain

Reuters [RTRSY] OTC, Publishing, United Kingdom

Rhone-Poulenc [RP] NYSE, Chemicals, France

Royal Dutch Petroleum [RD] NYSE, Energy-Integration, Netherlands

Scitex [SCIXF] OTC, Electronics-Computers, Israel

Senetek [SNTKY] OTC, Biotechnology, United Kingdom

Servicios Financieros Quadrum [QDRMY] OTC, Securities, Mexico

Shanghai Petrochemical [SHI] NYSE, Chemicals, China

Shell Transport & Trading [SC] NYSE, Oil Refining & Marketing, United Kingdom

Smithkline Beecham [SBE] NYSE, Drugs, United Kingdom

Sony [SNE] NYSE, Consumer Electronics

Southern Pacific Petroleum [SPPTY] OTC, Shale Oil Development, Australia

Tat Technologies [TATTF] OTC, Electronics/Aircraft Components, Israel

Telecom Corp of New Zealand [NZT] NYSE, Telecommunications Equipment, New Zealand

Telefonica De Espana [TEF] NYSE, Telecommunications Equipment, Spain

Telefonos De Mexico [TMX] NYSE, Telecommunication Services, Mexico

Telefonos De Mexico [TFONY] OTC, Telecommunication Services, Mexico

Teva Pharmaceutical [TEVIY] OTC, Drugs, Israel

Tiphook [TPH] NYSE, Miscellaneous Transportation, United Kingdom

Total [TOT] NYSE, Oil Refining & Marketing, France

Transportacion Maritima Mexico [TMM] NYSE, Marine Transportation

Transportacion Maritima Mexico [TMMA] NYSE, Marine Transportation, Mexico

Tubos de Acero de Mexico [TAM] AMEX, Steel, Mexico

Unilever NV [UN] NYSE, Food, Netherlands

Vaal Reefs Exploration & Mining [VAALY] OTC, Mining, South Africa

Vitro [VTO] NYSE, Building Materials, Mexico

Vodafone Group [VOD] NYSE, Telecommunication Services, United Kingdom

Volvo Aktiebolaget [VOLVY] OTC, Automobiles, Sweden

Waste Management International [WME] NYSE, Environmental, United Kingdom

Wellcome [WEL] NYSE, Drugs, United Kingdom

Willis Corroon [WCG] NYSE, Insurance, United Kingdom

Wpp Group [WPPGY] OTC, Advertising, United Kingdom

Ypf Sociedad Anonima [YPF] NYSE, Energy Integration, Argentina

Zeneca Group [ZEN] NYSE, Chemicals, United Kingdom

FREE AND DISCOUNTED GOODS FOR SHAREHOLDERS

The following is a list of American corporations that give free or discounted merchandise or services to their shareholders. In order to make a claim, shareholders usually must write or call the company, since most companies do not know the names of their shareholders (shares are often held in a street name by a brokerage firm). These freebies usually are not taxed as income to shareholders—if they are, the company will so inform their shareholders.

This list is provided courtesy of Gene Walden, who has written a book, *The 100 Best Stocks To Own In America* (Dearborn Publishing, 155 North Wacker Drive, Chicago, Illinois, 60610). The book describes some of these shareholder perks in more detail.

Abbott Laboratories: Shareholders attending the annual meeting receive a sampling of Abbott's consumer products such as Selsun Blue, Murine, an ice pack and a bottle of vitamins.

Albertson's, Inc.: Shareholders who attend the annual meeting receive some of Albertson's private label groceries, including canned vegetables, napkins, paper towels and other household products.

American Home Products Corp.: American Home occasionally sends out coupons for some of its foods and health care products along with the dividend check.

Anheuser-Busch Companies, Inc.: The company makes a point of moving its annual meetings around the country. Those who attend the annual meeting get an opportunity to sample all of the company's brews. Shareholders are also entitled to a discount on admission to the company's amusement parks.

Bristol-Myers Squibb Company: The company sends all of its new shareholders of record a welcome packet of its consumer products, including, for example small bottles of Excedrin, Bufferin, Nuprin, Clairol, and Ban deodorant.

Campbell Soup Company: The company hands out bags of freebies at the annual meeting, including coupons, soup, cookies, chicken nuggets, Vlasic pickles, and some new product samples.

Circus Circus Enterprises, Inc.: At annual meetings the company traditionally passes out small gifts to shareholders, such as coin set or free tokens for the slot machines.

ConAgra, Inc.: Shareholders attending the annual meeting receive a gift pack of some of ConAgra's foods. Sometimes sends discount offers along with its quarterly earnings reports.

Corning, Inc.: Corning sends discount cards to all of its shareholders each year, offering a 30% discount on Corning merchandise (including Steuben crystal) purchased at the company's headquarters and a 10% discount on merchandise purchased at stores. At the annual meeting the company serves lunch and hands out a product sample, such as a Corningware or Revereware item.

Deluxe Corp.: Shareholders who attend the annual meeting are invited to dinner on the company after the meeting.

General Mills, Inc.: General Mills offers its shareholders holiday gift boxes in December at very attractive prices. In addition to including at less than half retail prices numerous products, these boxes recently included coupons for $5 off meals at both

Red Lobster and The Olive Garden as well as 100 free points in the Betty Crocker catalog.

The Gillette Company: Shareholders who attend the annual meeting receive an excellent selection of products. One recent year shareholders were given a tote bag with Gillette's logo on the front, containing a sensor razor for women, a can of Gillette Series Shaving Gel, a container of ClearGel Antiperspirant, a tube of Jafra Hand Treatment, a bottle of White Rain Essentials Shampoo, a Flexgrip ball-point pen, and Oral-B dental floss.

H.J. Heinz Company: Shareholders attending the annual meeting receive a gift package of some of the company's newer products.

International Dairy Queen, Inc.: At the annual meeting the company serves some of its Brazier foods and newer ice cream products to shareholders.

Kellogg Company: All new shareholders receive a welcome kit with brochures and reports on the company along with a pair of coupons for free grocery products such as cereal, frozen waffles or one of Kellogg's newer products. Those attending the annual meetings in Battle Creek also receive product samples and discount coupons.

The Limited, Inc.: Recently sent out a coupon with its annual report for 15% off merchandise at any of its stores.

Loctite Corporation: Loctite hands out tubes of Super Glue to shareholders attending the annual meeting.

Newell Co.: Special gift to shareholders at the annual meeting.

Nike, Inc.: The company passes out pro motional items such as tennis star caps, sports towels, and Nike pens, at their annual meeting.

The Quaker Oats Company: Coupons for a percentage off some of Quakers new products are often sent to share-holders along with their quarterly reports. Shareholders who attend the annual meeting are sometimes given sample packets of some of Quaker's new products.

Rubbermaid, Inc.: Shareholders who attend the annual meeting usually receive a free Rubbermaid product, such as a file case, a food tray or a food storage container. Shareholders may also shop in the company store on annual meeting day and take advantage of discounts on dozens of Rubbermaid products.

Sara Lee Corporation: Gift box of Sara Lee products, including such items as coupons, bath soaps, and other company products to shareholders at the annual meeting.

Schering-Plough Corporation: Schering-Plough hands out a sample packet of products to shareholders at its annual meetings. The packets include such products as Coppertone suntan lotion, Afrin nasal spray, Gyne-Lotramin and other over-the-counter remedies.

UST, Inc.: Pipe cleaners, pipes, smokeless tobacco, a small bottle of wine and a video from its new Cabin Fever Entertainment subsidiary to share holders attending the annual meeting.

Walgreen Company: Shareholders who attend the annual meeting usually receive one or two Walgreen products.

Wal-Mart Stores, Inc.: At the annual meet-ing, shareholders are often given Wal-Mart memorabilia such as hats, buttons, and T-shirts.

William Wrigley Jr. Company: Gift package to all shareholders each Christmas that includes several packs of Wrigley's gum, personally selected by company chairman and presi-dent, William Wrigley.

Appendix

SELECTED FURTHER READING

Overall Bibliography

Books in Print 1994–1995. New York: R.R. Bowker, 1994.

Daniells, Lorna M. *Business Information Sources.* 3rd ed. Berkeley: University of California Press, 1993.

Economics

Friedman, Milton and Schwartz, Anna J. *A Monetary History of the United States, 1867–1960.* Princeton: Princeton University Press, 1963.

The leading exponent of the monetarist ("Chicago") school of economics sets forth his views in this basic work.

Heilbroner, Robert L. and Galbraith, James K. *The Economic Problem.* 9th ed. Englewood Cliffs: Prentice-Hall, 1989.

An established introductory text by two noted economists; covers the background, economic tools, market systems, and major challenges in both macroeconomics and microeconomics.

Keynes, John Maynard. *The General Theory of Employment, Interest and Money.* London: Macmillan, 1936.

The definitive work of the British economist and government advisor, whose influential theories advocating government intervention (fiscal policy) as a solution to economic problems have become known as Keynesian economics.

McConnell, Campbell R. *Economics: Principles, Problems, and Policies.* 12th ed. New York: McGraw-Hill, 1993.

A highly regarded introduction to the fundamental problems and principles of economics and the policy alternatives available to countries, both from a national and international perspective.

Nelson, Charles R. *The Investor's Guide to Economic Indicators.* New York: Wiley, 1989.

Using plain language and simple charts, a prominent economist provides a guide to reading, interpreting and using economic and financial news to make better investment decisions.

Rhymes, Cass and Zielonka, Danuta J. *The American Dream & Other Dangerous Myths: Economic Transition in the 1990's.* Chicago: Probus Publishing, 1989.

An exploration of the world-wide social and economic implications of America's change from a creditor to a debtor nation and their effect on American values and living standards.

Samuelson, Paul A. and W. Nordhaus: *Economics*. 14th ed. New York: McGraw-Hill, 1992.

This famous and widely used introductory economics text has been thoroughly revised and updated. It takes students from fundamental to sophisticated levels of understanding of income and production factors including international trade and finance and current economic problems.

Smith, Adam. *An Inquiry into the Nature and Causes of the Wealth of Nations*. New York: Random House (Modern Library), 1937.

The definitive work, first published in 1776, of the most famous of the classical economists, who held that economies function best when under a laissez-faire system in which market forces are free to operate without government interference.

International Economics, Finance, and Investment

Lindert, Peter H. *International Economics*. 9th ed. Burr Ridge, Illinois: Irwin Professional Publishing, 1991.

A classic text covering aspects of international economics and finance on theoretical and practical levels, plus an examination of larger problems concerning international mobility of people and factors of production.

Root, Franklin R. *International Trade and Investment*. 6th ed. Cincinnati: South-Western, 1990.

Covers theory, policy, and the marketplace of international trade, including international payments, development financing, and international investments and multinational enterprises.

Roussakis, Emmanuel N., ed. *International Banking: Principles and Practices*. New York: Praeger, 1983.

Twenty-three experts discuss international banking, focusing on lending policies and procedures and on risk and credit analysis.

Viner, Aron. *Inside Japanese Financial Markets*. Burr Ridge, Illinois: Irwin Professional Publishing, 1988.

A comprehensive discussion of the history, structure and operations of the Japanese securities, banking and money markets.

Walmsley, Julian. *The New Financial Instruments*. New York: Wiley, 1988.

A sophisticated but readable explanation of recent innovations in financial instruments used in international finance and investment.

Money and Banking

Kaufman, George G. *The U.S. Financial System: Money Markets and Institutions*. 5th ed. Englewood Cliffs: Prentice-Hall, 1995.

Assuming a basic knowledge of economics, this text covers in terms of theory and practice the evolution and operations of the national and international financial markets as well as instruments, institutions, and regulation. The Federal Reserve System and other aspects of the economic macrostructure are also examined.

Ritter, Lawrence S. and William L. Silber. *Principles of Money, Banking and Financial Markets*. 8th ed. New York: Basic Books, 1993.

A comprehensive introductory text that covers money and banking fundamentals; banks and other intermediaries; central banking; monetary theory; financial markets and interest rates; and international finance.

Bond and Money Markets

Altman, Edward I., ed. *The High Yield Debt Market.* Burr Ridge, Illinois: Irwin Professional Publishing, 1990.

A definitive book on high-yield debt securities (junk bonds) by over 20 leading experts, who discuss such questions as portfolio valuation, default risk measurements, and volatility.

Fabozzi, Frank J. and Irving M. Pollock, eds. *The Handbook of Fixed Income Securities.* 2nd ed. Burr Ridge, Illinois: Irwin Professional Publishing, 1986.

Includes 47 chapters, each by an expert, covering general investment information; securities and instruments; bond investment management; interest rates and rate forecasting. More extensive than the volume by David M. Darst, but similarly designed for the layperson and professional.

Stigum, Marcia. *The Money Market.* 3rd ed. Burr Ridge, Illinois: Irwin Professional Publishing, 1989.

A comprehensive guide, by a working professional, to the U.S. money market. It covers (1) the various instruments traded, how yields are calculated, and the role of the Federal Reserve; (2) the major participants, including Eurobanks; and (3) particular markets, such as those for commercial paper, Treasury bills, and CDs. Includes financial futures.

Corporate Finance

Altman, Edward I. and McKinney, Mary Jane. eds. *Handbook of Corporate Finance.* 6th ed. New York: Wiley, 1986.

This is the classic *Financial Handbook* now divided into two books. The *Handbook of Corporate Finance* includes chapters by different authorities on financial forecasting, planning and control; sources of funds; capital budgeting; pensions and profit sharing; and modern finance, including multinationals, international cash management, bankruptcies and reorganizations, mergers and acquisitions, and small business.

(The second volume, *Handbook of Financial Markets & Institutions,* 6th ed., 1987, covers the domestic and international marketplace, investment analysis strategies, securities and portfolio management, and related subjects and is also recommended).

Brigham, Eugene F. and Gapenski, Louis C. *Financial Management: Theory and Practice.* 7th ed. Hinsdale, Illinois: Dryden Press, 1993.

A well-written discussion of basic concepts in financial management and their use in maximizing the value of a firm. Using real-life examples, the text covers financial forecasting, working capital management, capital budgeting, and other relevant subjects, including international financial management and mergers and acquisitions.

Van Horne, James C. and John M. Wachowicz, *Fundamentals of Financial Management.* 9th ed. Englewood Cliffs: Prentice-Hall, 1995.

An excellent introductory text with sections on principles of financial returns, tools of financial analysis and planning, working capital management, investing in capital assets, capital structure and dividend policies, long-term financing and markets, and special areas including cash-management models and option pricing.

Weston, J. Fred and Eugene F. Brigham. *Essentials of Managerial Finance.* 10th ed. Hinsdale, Illinois: Dryden Press, 1993.

A fine introductory text emphasizing decision rather than theory, with sections on fundamental concepts; financial analysis, planning and control; working capital management; investment decisions; cost of capital and valuation; long-term financing decisions; and integrated topics in managerial finance.

Securities Markets, Securities Analysis, and Portfolio Management

Amling, Frederick. *Investments, An Introduction to Analysis and Management.* 6th ed. Englewood Cliffs: Prentice-Hall, 1989.

A text for the beginning investor or aspiring investment professional. Using practical cases to demonstrate principles, the book deals with various aspects of fundamental analysis, modern portfolio theory, and technical analysis.

Cohen, Jerome B., Edward D. Zinbarg, and Arthur Zeikel. *Investment Analysis and Portfolio Management.* 5th ed. Burr Ridge, Illinois: Irwin Professional Publishing, 1987.

An introductory text, notable because it is comprehensive and discusses modern portfolio theory and security valuation techniques in a nonmathematical, readable fashion. It also covers the current investment scene and industry and company analysis.

Dreman, David. *The New Contrarian Investment Strategy.* New York: Random House, 1983.

An updated version of an established title, this book has become a modern classic on contrarian investment strategy in an era marked by widely fluctuating interest rates and market prices.

Engel, Louis and Brendan Boyd. *How to Buy Stocks.* 7th ed. New York: Bantam, 1984.

A highly readable, clear, and informative introduction to investing in the stock market, this book has been a deserved fixture in the literature on investing for over three decades.

Fischer, Donald E. and Ronald J. Jordan. *Security Analysis and Portfolio Management.* 5th ed. Englewood Cliffs: Prentice-Hall, 1991.

By using the fast-food industry and McDonald's Corporation as an example to illustrate the practical applications of security analysis and portfolio management theory, the authors of this introductory text manage to keep an essentially mathematical subject relatively nonmathematical and understandable.

Graham, Benjamin, David L. Dodd, and Sidney Cottle. *Security Analysis: Principles and Techniques.* 5th ed. New York: McGraw-Hill, 1988.

This classic work, originally published in 1934, remains the bible for students of the fundamentalist approach to securities analysis. It consists of six parts: survey and approach; analysis of financial statements; fixed-income securities; the valuation of common stocks; senior securities with speculative features; and other aspects of security analysis.

Graham, Benjamin. *The Intelligent Investor.* 4th rev. ed. New York: Harper & Row, 1986.

In *The Money Masters* (below), John Train says this book is "More useful for most readers [than *Security Analysis:*] and indeed the best book ever written for the stockholder....One is ill-advised...to buy a bond or a share of stock without having read its 300 pages."

Buckley, Julian G. and Leo M. Loll. *The Over-The-Counter Securities Markets.* Englewood Cliffs: Prentice-Hall, 1986.

A training manual for would-be stockbrokers preparing for the NASD examination and a generally valuable book for any investor wishing to learn more about the over-the-counter markets, securities underwriting, stock and bond trading, regulation, and the securities business in general.

O'Higgins, Michael B. with John Downes. *Beating the Dow, A High-Return, Low-Risk Method for Investing in the Dow Jones Industrial Stocks With As Little As $5000.* New York: HarperPerennial, 1992.

A clearly-written stock investing primer and discussion of the simple, highly successful investment strategy using high-yielding Dow Jones industrial stocks invented by O'Higgins and now widely used throughout the brokerage industry.

Pring, Martin J. *Technical Analysis Explained: The Successful Investors Guide to Spotting Investment Trends and Turning Points.* 3rd ed. New York: McGraw-Hill, 1991.

An excellent and comprehensive introduction to technical analysis, made especially useful by its many illustrative charts.

Rolo, Charles J. and Klein, Robert J. *Gaining on the Market: Your Complete Guide to Investment Strategy.* Boston: Atlantic-Little Brown, 1988.

A superb guide to investing in stocks, bonds, options, mutual funds, and gold. It discusses stock picking, portfolio structuring, and market timing as well as forces influencing prices and includes practical advice on dealing with brokers and using information sources.

Teweles, Richard J. and Edward S. Bradley. *The Stock Market.* 6th ed. New York: Wiley, 1992.

This is a revision of a work originally authored by George L. Leffler in 1951. It examines the stock market in five sections dealing with fundamental information, the exchanges, securities houses, regulations, investing practices, and special instruments.

Train, John. *The Money Masters.* New York: Harper & Row, 1987.

Interesting stories, by an investment counselor, about the investment strategies of nine distinguished portfolio managers, such as T. Rowe Price, Benjamin Graham, and John Templeton, with commentary on their methods and personalities.

Train, John. *The New Money Masters.* New York: Harper & Row, 1990.

A sequel to *The Money Masters* that profiles ten great contemporary investors, including Peter Lynch, John Neff, and George Soros.

Walmsley, Julian. *The New Financial Instruments, An Investor's Guide.* New York: John Wiley & Sons, Inc. 1988.

A comprehensive discussion of the origins, the risks, and the uses of the complex new financial instruments developed in the 1980s. Walmsley provides graphs and tables analyzing the risk-level and return associated with the major instruments and explains step-by-step how to profit from them in today's market.

Commodity and Financial Futures Markets

Kaufman, Perry J., ed. *Concise Handbook of Futures Markets: Money Management, Forecasting & the Markets.* New York: Wiley, 1986.

An extensive manual and reference guide comprising 49 chapters written by over 50 experts. Twenty-five chapters deal with individual commodities, including financial futures. Others deal with markets, forecasting, hedging, risk and money management, and other technical aspects.

Powers, Mark J. *Starting Out in Futures Trading.* 5th ed. Chicago: Probus, 1993.

A combination of theory and practical information for the beginner; includes history, exchanges, choosing a broker, trading programs, hedging, and forecasting. Deals with financial futures.

Rothstein, Nancy H. and James M. Little, eds. *The Handbook of Financial Futures: A Guide for Investors and Professional Financial Managers.* New York: McGraw-Hill, 1984.

A comprehensive reference focusing on concepts and methods for using and analyzing financial futures for hedging and trading purposes, including regulatory, accounting, and tax implications. For the professional as well as the novice.

Schwager, Jack D. *A Complete Guide to the Futures Markets: Fundamental Analysis, Technical Analysis, Trading, Spreads and Options.* New York: Wiley, 1984.

Assumes a basic familiarity with futures trading, but otherwise provides a nontechnical discussion of various analytical techniques, including regression analysis and chart analysis. Has sample charts and a section on trading guidelines.

Siegel, Daniel R. and Diane F. Siegel. *The Future Markets.* Chicago: Probus, 1994.

A comprehensive study of the futures markets, emphasizing the mechanics of futures trading; the theory of futures pricing; futures trading strategies used for arbitrage, hedging and speculation; and descriptions of all the major futures contracts.

Options Markets

Ansbacher, Max G. *The New Options Market.* rev. and enlarged ed. New York: Walker & Co., 1987.

An easy-to-read, yet comprehensive rundown, by a professional trader, of options and option strategies. For the speculator as well as the conservative investor.

Fabozzi, Frank J. and Kipnis, Gregory M., eds. *The Handbook of Stock Index Futures and Options.* Burr Ridge, Illinois: Irwin Professional Publishing, 1989.

26 chapters by recognized authorities cover strategies for using index futures and options in equity portfolio management and trading the market.

Gastineau, Gary L. *The Options Manual.* 3rd ed. New York: McGraw-Hill, 1988.

Assuming a basic knowledge of options and how they are used, Gastineau discusses option valuation methods and their applications in portfolio analysis and management. The book also covers option investment and trading strategies and tax implications.

McMillan, Lawrence G. *Options as a Strategic Investment.* Englewood Cliffs: Prentice-Hall, 1992.

An advanced discussion of option strategies, focusing on which ones work where and why. Includes chapters on arbitrage, mathematical applications, and tax ramifications.

Roth, Harrison. *LEAPS (Long-Term Equity AnticiPation Securities),* Burr Ridge, Illinois: Irwin Professional Publishing, 1994.

Written in easy-to-understand English with examples and summaries, this book covers the history, the risks, and the strategies possible with long-term options, a 1990s innovation.

CURRENCIES OF THE WORLD

This is a list of the currencies of most of the countries on earth. The countries are listed alphabetically, with the name of the currency, followed by the denomination that currency is broken down into. For example, one dollar is made up of 100 cents. This listing should be useful to anyone traveling or doing business in any of these countries.

Of course, the value of these currencies is constantly changing in relation to the amount of dollars necessary to buy them. For current exchange rates of the currencies of most major countries, one must consult the financial tables of newspapers such as the *Wall Street Journal* or *London's Financial Times*.

Afghanistan 1 afghani (AF) = 100 puls
Albania 1 lek (L) = 100 qintars
Algeria 1 Algerian dinar (DA) = 100 centimes
American Samoa 1 U.S. dollar (US$) = 100 cents
Andorra 1 French franc (F) = 100 centimes; 1 peseta (pta) = 100 centimos
Angola 1 new kwanza (NKz) = 100 lwei
Anguilla 1 EC dollar (EC$) = 100 cents
Antigua & Barbuda 1 EC dollar (EC$) = 100 cents
Argentina 1 nuevo peso argentino = 100 centavos
Armenia 1 dram = 100 luma
Aruba 1 Aruban florin (Af.) = 100 cents
Australia 1 Australian dollar ($A) = 100 cents
Austria 1 Austrian schilling (S) = 100 groschen
Azerbaijan 1 manat = 100 gopik
Bahamas 1 Bahamian dollar (B$) = 100 cents
Bahrain 1 Bahraini dinar (BD) = 1,000 fils
Bangladesh 1 taka (Tk) = 100 poiska
Barbados 1 Barbadian dollar (Bds$) = 100 cents
Belarus Balarusian rubel
Belgium 1 Belgian franc (BF) = 100 centimes
Belize 1 Belizean dollar (Bz$) = 100 cents
Benin 1 CFA franc (CFAF) = 100 centimes
Bermuda 1 Bermudian dollar (Bd$) = 100 cents
Bhutan 1 ngultrum (Nu) = 100 chetrum; Indian currency also legal tender
Bolivia 1 boliviano ($B) = 100 centavos
Bosnia & Herzegovina 1 dinar = 100 para; Croatian kuna used in Croat-held areas
Botswana 1 pula (P) = 100 thebe
Brazil 1 cruzeiro real (CR$) = 100 centavos
British Virgin Islands 1 U.S. dollar (US$) = 100 cents

Brunei 1 Bruneian dollar (B$) = 100 cents
Bulgaria 1 lev (Lv) = 100 stotinki
Burkina 1 CFA franc (CFAF) = 100 centimes
Burma 1 kyat (K) = 100 pyas
Burundi 1 Burundi franc (FBu) = 100 centimes
Cambodia 1 new riel (CR) = 100 sen
Cameroon 1 CFA franc (CFAF) = 100 centimes
Canada 1 Canadian dollar (Can$) = 100 cents
Cape Verde 1 Cape Verdean escudo (CVEsc) = 100 centavos
Cayman Islands 1 Caymanian dollar (CI$) = 100 cents
Central African Republic 1 CFA franc (CFAF) = 100 centimes
Chad 1 CFA franc (CFAF) = 100 centimes
Chile 1 Chilean peso (Ch$) = 100 centavos
China 1 yuan (Y) = 10 jiao
Christmas Island 1 Australian dollar ($A) = 100 cents
Cocos (Keeling) Islands 1 Australian dollar ($A) = 100 cents
Colombia 1 Colombian peso (Col$) = 100 centavos
Comoros 1 Comoran franc (CF) = 100 centimes
Congo 1 CFA franc (CFAF) = 100 centimes
Cook Islands 1 New Zealand dollar (NZ$) = 100 cents
Costa Rica 1 Costa Rican colon (C) = 100 centimos
Cote d'Ivoire 1 CFA franc (CFAF) = 100 centimes
Croatia 1 Croatian kunar = 100 paras
Cuba 1 Cuban peso (Cu$) = 100 centavos
Cyprus 1 Cypriot pound (£C) = 100 cents; 1 Turkish lira (TL) = 100 kurus

Czech Republic 1 koruna (Kc) = 100 haleru
Denmark 1 Danish krone (DKr) = 100 oere
Djibouti 1 Djibouti franc (DF) = 100 centimes
Dominica 1 EC dollar (EC$) = 100 cents
Dominican Republic 1 Dominican peso (RD$) = 100 centavos
Ecuador 1 sucre (S/) = 100 centavos
Egypt 1 Egyptian pound (£E) = 100 piasters
El Salvador 1 Salvadoran colon (C) = 100 centavos
Equatorial Guinea 1 CFA franc (CFAF) = 100 centimes
Eritrea 1 birr (Br) = 100 cents; Ethiopian currency used
Estonia 1 Estonian kroon (EEK) = 100 cents
Ethiopia 1 birr (Br) = 100 cents
Falkland Islands 1 Falkland pound (£F) = 100 pence
Faroe Islands 1 Danish krone (DKr) = 100 oere
Fiji 1 Fijian dollar (F$) = 100 cents
Finland 1 markka (FMk) or Finmark = 100 pennia
France 1 French franc (F) = 100 centimes
French Guiana 1 French franc (F) = 100 centimes
French Polynesia 1 CFP franc (CFPF) = 100 centimes
Gabon 1 CFA franc (CFAF) = 100 centimes
The Gambia 1 dalasi (D) = 100 butut
Gaza Strip 1 new Israeli shekel (NIS) = 100 new agorot
Georgia Georgian lari
Germany 1 deutsche mark (DM) = 100 pfennige
Ghana 1 new cedi (C) = 100 pesewas
Gibraltar 1 Gibraltar pound (£G) = 100 pence
Greece 1 drachma (Dr) = 100 lepta
Greenland 1 Danish krone (DKr) = 100 oere
Grenada 1 EC dollar (EC$) = 100 cents
Guadeloupe 1 French franc (F) = 100 centimes
Guam 1 U.S. dollar (US$) = 100 cents
Guatemala 1 quetzal (Q) = 100 centavos
Guernsey 1 Guernsey (£G) pound = 100 pence
Guinea 1 Guinean franc (FG) = 100 centimes
Guinea-Bissau 1 Guinea-Bissau peso (PG) = 100 centavos
Guyana 1 Guyanese dollar (G$) = 100 cents
Haiti 1 gourde (G) = 100 centimes
Holy See (Vatican City) 1 Vatican lira (VLit) = 100 centesimi
Honduras 1 lempira (L) = 100 centavos
Hong Kong 1 Hong Kong dollar (HK$) = 100 cents
Hungary 1 forint (Ft) = 100 filler
Iceland 1 Icelandic krona (IKr) = 100 aurar
India 1 Indian rupee (Re) = 100 paise
Indonesia 1 Indonesian rupiah (Rp) = 100 sen
Iran 1 Iranian rial (IR) = 10 tomans
Iraq 1 Iraqi dinar (ID) = 1,000 fils
Ireland 1 Irish pound (£Ir) = 100 pence
Israel 1 new Israeli shekel (NIS) = 100 new agorot

Italy 1 Italian lira (Lit) = 100 centesimi
Jamaica 1 Jamaican dollar (J$) = 100 cents
Japan yen (¥)
Jersey 1 Jersey pound (£J) = 100 pence
Jordan 1 Jordanian dinar (JD) = 1,000 fils
Kazakhstan tenge
Kenya 1 Kenyan shilling (KSh) = 100 cents
Kiribati 1 Australian dollar ($A) = 100 cents
Korea, North 1 North Korean won (Wn) = 100 chon
Korea, South 1 South Korean won (Wn) = 100 chun
Kuwait 1 Kuwaiti dinar (KD) = 1,000 fils
Kyrgyzstan som
Laos 1 new kip (NK) = 100 at
Latvia 1 lat = 100 cents
Lebanon 1 Lebanese pound (£L) = 100 piasters
Lesotho 1 loti (L) = 100 lisente
Liberia 1 Liberian dollar (L$) = 100 cents
Libya 1 Libyan dinar (LD) = 1,000 dirhams
Liechtenstein 1 Swiss franc, franken or franco (SwF) = 100 centimes, rappen or centesimi
Lithuania litas
Luxembourg 1 Luxembourg franc (LuxF) = 100 centimes
Macau 1 pataca (P) = 100 avos
Macedonia, the Former Yugoslav Republic of denar
Madagascar 1 Malagasy franc (FMG) = 100 centimes
Malawi 1 Malawian kwacha (MK) = 100 tambala
Malaysia 1 ringgit (M$) = 100 sen
Maldives 1 rufiyaa (Rf) = 100 laari
Mali 1 CFA franc (CFAF) = 100 centimes
Malta 1 Maltese lira (LM) = 100 cents
Man, Isle of 1 Manx pound (£M) = 100 pence
Marshall Islands 1 U.S. dollar (US$) = 100 cents
Martinique 1 French franc (F) = 100 centimes
Mauritania 1 ouguiya (UM) = 5 khoums
Mauritius 1 Mauritian rupee (MauR) = 100 cents
Mayotte 1 French franc (F) = 100 centimes
Mexico 1 New Mexican peso (MEX$) = 100 centavos
Micronesia, Federated States of 1 U.S. dollar (US$) = 100 cents
Moldova leu
Monaco 1 French franc (F) = 100 centimes
Mongolia 1 tughrik (Tug) = 100 mongos
Montserrat 1 EC dollar (EC$) = 100 cents
Morocco 1 Moroccan dirham (DH) = 100 centimes
Mozambique 1 metical (Mt) = 100 centavos
Namibia 1 South African rand (R) = 100 cents
Nauru 1 Australian dollar ($A) = 100 cents
Nepal 1 Nepalese rupee (NR) = 100 paisa
Netherlands 1 Netherlands guilder, gulden or florin = 100 cents

Netherlands Antilles 1 Netherlands Antillean guilder, gulden or florin (NAf.) = 100 cents

New Caledonia 1 CFP franc (CFPF) = 100 centimes

New Zealand 1 New Zealand dollar (NZ$) = 100 cents

Nicaragua 1 gold cordoba (CS) = 100 centavos

Niger 1 CFA franc (CFAF) = 100 centimes

Nigeria 1 naira (N) = 100 kobo

Niue 1 New Zealand dollar (NZ$) = 100 cents

Norfolk Island 1 Australian dollar ($A) = 100 cents

Northern Mariana Islands 1 U.S. dollar (US$) = 100 cents

Norway 1 Norwegian krone (NKr) = 100 oere

Oman 1 Omani rial (RO) = 1,000 baiza

Pacific Islands, Trust Territory of the 1 U.S. dollar (US$) = 100 cents

Pakistan 1 Pakistani rupee (PRe) = 100 paisa

Panama 1 balboa (B) = 100 centesimos

Papua New Guinea 1 kina (K) = 100 toea

Paraguay 1 guarani (G) = 100 centimos

Peru 1 nuevo sol (S/.) = 100 centimos

Philippines 1 Philippine peso (P) = 100 centavos

Pitcairn Islands 1 New Zealand dollar (NZ$) = 100 cents

Poland 1 zloty (Zl) = 100 groszy

Portugal 1 Portuguese escudo (Esc) = 100 centavos

Puerto Rico 1 U.S. dollar (US$) = 100 cents

Qatar 1 Qatari riyal (QR) = 100 dirhams

Reunion 1 French franc (F) = 100 centimes

Romania 1 leu (L) = 100 bani

Russia 1 ruble (R) = 100 kopeks

Rwanda 1 Rwandan franc (RF) = 100 centimes

Saint Helena 1 Saint Helenian pound (£S) = 100 pence

Saint Kitts & Nevis 1 EC dollar (EC$) = 100 cents

Saint Lucia 1 EC dollar (EC$) = 100 cents

Saint Pierre & Miquelon 1 French franc (F) = 100 centimes

Saint Vincent & the Grenadines 1 EC dollar (EC$) = 100 cents

San Marino 1 Italian lire (Lit) = 100 centesimi

Sao Tome & Principe 1 dobra (Db) = 100 centimos

Saudi Arabia 1 Saudi riyal (SR) = 100 halalah

Senegal 1 CFA franc (CFAF) = 100 centimes

Serbia & Montenegro 1 Yugoslav New Dinar (YD) = 100 paras

Seychelles 1 Seychelles rupee (SRe) = 100 cents

Sierra Leone 1 leone (Le) = 100 cents

Singapore 1 Singapore dollar (S$) = 100 cents

Slovakia 1 koruna (Sk) = 100 halierov

Slovenia 1 tolar (SIT) = 100 stotins

Solomon Islands 1 Solomon Islands dollar (SI$) = 100 cents

Somalia 1 Somali shilling (So.Sh.) = 100 cents

South Africa 1 rand (R) = 100 cents

Spain 1 peseta (Pta) = 100 centimos

Sri Lanka 1 Sri Lankan rupee (SLRe) = 100 cents

Sudan 1 Sudanese pound (£Sd) = 100 piastres

Suriname 1 Surinamese guilder, gulden or florin (Sf.) = 100 cents

Svalbard 1 Norwegian krone (NKr) = 100 oere

Swaziland 1 lilangeni (E) = 100 cents

Sweden 1 Swedish krona (SKr) = 100 oere

Switzerland 1 Swiss franc, franken or franco (SwF) = 100 centimes, rappen or centesimi

Syria 1 Syrian pound (£S) = 100 piastres

Taiwan 1 New Taiwan dollar (NT$) = 100 cents

Tajikistan 1 ruble (R) = 100 kopeks

Tanzania 1 Tanzanian shilling (TSh) = 100 cents

Thailand 1 baht (B) = 100 satang

Togo 1 CFA franc (CFAF) = 100 centimes

Tokelau 1 New Zealand dollar (NZ$) = 100 cents

Tonga 1 pa'anga (T$) = 100 sentini

Trinidad & Tobago 1 Trinidad & Tobago dollar (TT$) = 100 cents

Tunisia 1 Tunisian dinar (TD) = 1,000 millimes

Turkey 1 Turkish lira (TL) = 100 kurus

Turkmenistan manat

Turks & Caicos Islands 1 U.S. dollar (US$) = 100 cents

Tuvalu 1 Tuvaluan dollar ($T) or 1 Australian dollar($A) = 100 cents

Uganda 1 Ugandan shilling (USh) = 100 cents

Ukraine hryvnya

United Arab Emirates 1 Emirian dirham (Dh) = 100 fils

United Kingdom 1 British pound (£) = 100 pence

United States 1 U.S. dollar (US$) = 100 cents

Uruguay 1 Uraguayan peso ($Ur) = 100 centesimos

Uzbekistan som

Vanuatu 1 vatu (VT) = 100 centimes

Venezuela 1 bolivar (Bs) = 100 centimos

Vietnam 1 new dong (D) = 100 xu

Virgin Islands 1 U.S. dollar (US$) = 100 cents

Wallis & Futuna 1 CFP franc (CFPF) = 100 centimes

West Bank 1 new Israeli shekel (NIS) = 100 new agorot; 1 Jordanian dinar (JD) = 1,000 fils

Western Sahara 1 Moroccan dirham (DH) = 100 centimes

Western Samoa 1 tala (WS$) = 100 sene

Yemen Yemeni rial

Zaire 1 zaire (Z) = 100 makuta

Zambia 1 Zambian kwacha (ZK) = 100 ngwee

Zimbabwe 1 Zimbabwean dollar (Z$) = 100 cen

ABBREVIATIONS AND ACRONYMS

A

A Includes Extra (or Extras) (in stock listings of newspapers)

AAII American Association of Individual Investors

AB Aktiebolag (Swedish stock company)

ABA American Bankers Association

ABA American Bar Association

ABLA American Business Law Association

ABS Automated Bond System

ABWA American Business Women's Association

ACE AMEX Commodities Exchange

ACRS Accelerated Cost Recovery System

A-D Advance-Decline Line

ADB Adjusted Debit Balance

ADR American Depositary Receipt

ADR Automatic Dividend Reinvestment

ADRS Asset Depreciation Range System

ADS American Depository Shares

AE Account Executive

AFL-CIO American Federation of Labor-Congress of Industrial Organizations

AICPA American Institute of Certified Public Accountants

AID Agency for International Development

AIM American Institute for Management

AG Aktiengesellschaft (West German stock company)

AMA American Management Association

AMA Asset Management Account

AMBAC American Municipal Bond Assurance Corporation

AMEX American Stock Exchange

AMPS Auction Market Preferred Stock

AON All or None

APB Accounting Principles Board

APR Annual Percentage Rate

APS Auction Preferred Stock

Arb Arbitrageur

ARF American Retail Federation

ARM Adjustable Rate Mortgage

ARPS Adjustable Rate Preferred Stock

ASAP As Soon as Possible

ASE American Stock Exchange

ATM Automatic Teller Machine

ATP Arbitrage Trading Program

B

B Annual Rate Plus Stock Dividend (in stock listings of newspapers)

BAC Business Advisory Council

BAN Bond Anticipation Note

BBB Better Business Bureau

BD Bank Draft

BD Bills Discontinued

B/D Broker-Dealer

BE Bill of Exchange

BEACON Boston Exchange Automated Communication Order-routing Network

BEARS Bond Enabling Annual Retirement Savings

BF   Brought Forward
BIC   Bank Investment Contract
BIF   Bank Insurance Fund
BL   Bill of Lading
BLS   Bureau of Labor Statistics
BO   Branch Office
BO   Buyer's Option
BOM   Beginning of the Month
BOP   Balance of Payments
BOT   Balance of Trade
BOT   Bought
BOT   Board of Trustees
BPW   Business and Professional Women's Foundation
BR   Bills Receivable
BS   Balance Sheet
BS   Bill of Sale
BS   Bureau of Standards
BW   Bid Wanted

C

C   Liquidating Dividend (in stock listings of newspapers)
CA   Capital Account
CA   Chartered Accountant
CA   Commercial Agent
CA   Credit Account
CA   Current Account
CACM   Central American Common Market
CAD   Cash against Documents
CAF   Cost Assurance and Freight
C&F   Cost and Freight
CAMPS   Cumulative Auction Market Preferred Stocks
CAPM   Capital Asset Pricing Model
CAPS   Convertible Adjustable Preferred Stock
CARs   Certificate for Automobile Receivables
CARDS   Certificates for Amortizing Revolving Debts
CATS   Certificate of Accrual on Treasury Securities
CATV   Community Antenna Television
CBA   Cost Benefit Analysis

CBD   Cash Before Delivery
CBO   Collateralized Bond Obligation
CBT   Chicago Board of Trade
CC   Chamber of Commerce
CCH   Commerce Clearing House
CD   Certificate of Deposit
CD   Commercial Dock
CEA   Council of Economic Advisors
CEO   Chief Executive Officer
CF   Certificates (in bond listings of newspapers)
CF   Carried Forward
CFA   Chartered Financial Analyst
CFC   Chartered Financial Counselor
CFC   Consolidated Freight Classification
CFI   Cost, Freight, and Insurance
CFO   Chief Financial Officer
CFP   Certified Financial Planner
CFTC   Commodities Futures Trading Commission
CH   Clearing House
CH   Custom House
ChFC   Chartered Financial Consultant
Cía   Compañía (Spanish company)
Cie   Compagnie (French company)
CIF   Corporate Income Fund
CIF   Cost, Insurance, and Freight
CIPs   Cash Index Participations
CLD   Called (in stock listings of newspapers)
CLU   Chartered Life Underwriter
CME   Chicago Mercantile Exchange
CMO   Collateralized Mortgage Obligation
CMV   Current Market Value
CN   Consignment Note
CN   Credit Note
CNS   Continuous Net Settlement
CO   Cash Order
CO   Certificate of Origin
Co.   Company
COB   Close of Business (with date)
COD   Cash on Delivery
COD   Collect on Delivery

CODA Cash or Deferred Arrangement

COLA Cost-of-Living Adjustment

COLTS Continuously Offered Longer-Term Securities

COMEX Commodity Exchange (New York)

COMSAT Communications Satellite Corporation

CPA Certified Public Accountant

CPD Commissioner of Public Debt

CPPF Cast Plus Fixed Fee

CPI Consumer Price Index

CPM Cost per Thousand

CPPC Cost plus a Percentage of Cost

CR Carrier's Risk

CR Class Rate

CR Company's Risk

CR Current Rate

CSE Cincinnati Stock Exchange

CSVLI Cash Surrender Value of Life Insurance

CUBS Calls Underwritten by Swanbrook

CUNA Credit Union National Association

CUSIP Committee on Uniform Securities Identification Procedures

CV Convertible Security (in bond and stock listings of newspapers)

CWO Cash with Order

D

DA Deposit Account

DA Documents against Acceptance

DAC Delivery against Cost

D&B Dun and Bradstreet

DBA Doing Business As

DC Deep Discount Issue (in bond listings of newspapers)

DCFM Discounted Cash Flow Method

DDB Double-Declining-Balance Depreciation Method

DENKS Dual-Employed, No Kids

DEWKS Dual Employed, With Kids

DF Damage Free

DIDC Depository Institutions Deregulatory Committee

DINKS Dual-Income, No Kids

DISC Domestic International Sales Corporation

DJIA Dow Jones Industrial Average

DJTA Dow Jones Transportation Average

DJUA Dow Jones Utility Average

DK Don't Know

DN Debit Note

DNR Do Not Reduce

D/O Delivery Order

DOT Designated Order Turnaround

DP Documents against Payment

DPI Disposable Personal Income

DS Days After Sight

DTC Depository Trust Company

DUNS Data Universal Numbering System (Dun's Number)

DVP Delivery Versus Payment

E

E Declared or Paid in the Preceding 12 Months (in stock listings of newspapers)

E&OE Errors and Omissions Excepted

EBIT Earnings Before Interest and Taxes

EBITA Earnings Before Interest, Taxes, Depreciation, and Amortization

ECM Emerging Company Marketplace

ECM European Common Market

ECT Estimated Completion Time

EDD Estimated Delivery Date

ECU European Currency Unit

EEC European Economic Community

EEOC Equal Employment Opportunity Commission

EMP End-of-Month Payment

EOA Effective On or About

EOD Every Other Day (advertising)

EOM End of Month

EPR Earnings Price Ratio

EPS Earnings Per Share

ERISA Employee Retirement Income Security Act of 1974

ERM Exchange Rate Mechanism

ERTA Economic Recovery Tax Act of 1981

ESOP Employee Stock Ownership Plan

ESP Exchange Stock Portfolio

ETA Estimated Time of Arrival

ETD Estimated Time of Departure

ETLT Equal To or Less Than

EXIMBANK Export-Import Bank

F

F Dealt in Flat (in bond listings in newspapers)

FA Free Alongside

FACT Factor Analysis Chart Technique

FAS Free Alongside

FASB Financial Accounting Standards Board

FAT Fixed Asset Transfer

FAX Facsimile

FB Freight Bill

FCA Fellow of the Institute of Chartered Accountants

FCC Federal Communications Commission

FCUA Federal Credit Union Administration

FDIC Federal Deposit Insurance Corporation

Fed Federal Reserve System

FET Federal Excise Tax

F&F Furniture and Fixtures

FFB Federal Financing Bank

FFCS Federal Farm Credit System

FGIC Financial Guaranty Insurance Corporation

FHA Farmers Home Administration

FHA Federal Housing Administration

FHFB Federal Housing Finance Board

FHLBB Federal Home Loan Bank Board

FHLMC Federal Home Loan Mortgage Corporation (Freddie Mac)

FICA Federal Insurance Contributions Act

FICB Federal Intermediate Credit Bank

FICO Financing Corporation

FIFO First In, First Out

FIRREA Financial Institutions Reform and Recovery Act

FIT Federal Income Tax

FITW Federal Income Tax Withholding

FLB Federal Land Bank

FMC Federal Maritime Commission

FNMA Federal National Mortgage Association (Fannie Mae)

FOB Free on Board

FOC Free of Charge

FOCUS Financial and Operations Combined Uniform Single Report

FOI Freedom of Information Act

FOK Fill or Kill

FOMC Federal Open Market Committee

FOR Free on Rail (or Road)

FOT Free on Truck

FP Floating Policy

FP Fully Paid

FPM Fixed-Payment Mortgage

FRA Federal Reserve Act

FRB Federal Reserve Bank

FRB Federal Reserve Board

FRD Federal Reserve District

FREIT Finite Life REIT.

FRS Federal Reserve System

FS Final Settlement

FSC Foreign Sales Corporation

FSLIC Federal Savings and Loan Insurance Corporation

FTC Federal Trade Commission

FTI Federal Tax Included

FUTA Federal Unemployment Tax Act

FVO For Valuation Only

FX Foreign Exchange

FY Fiscal Year

FYA   For Your Attention
FYI   For Your Information

G

G   Dividends and Earnings In
Canadian Dollars (in stock listings
of newspapers)
GAAP   Generally Accepted
Accounting Principles
GAAS Generally Accepted Auditing
Standards
GAI   Guaranteed Annual Income
GAO   General Accounting Office
GATT   General Agreement on
Tariffs and Trade
GDP   Gross Domestic Product
GINNIE MAE   Government
National Mortgage Association
GIT   Guaranteed Income (or
Investment) Contract
GM   General Manager
GmbH   Gesellschaft mit beschränkter
Haftung (West German limited
liability company)
GNMA   Government National
Mortgage Association
GNP   Gross National Product
GO   General Obligation Bond
GPM   Graduated Payment Mortgage
GRIT   Grantor Retained Income
Trust
GTC   Good Till Canceled
GTM   Good This Month
GTW   Good This Week
GULP   Group Universal Life Policy

H

H   Declared or Paid After Stock
Dividend or Split-Up (in stock
listings of newspapers)
HEL   Home Equity Loan
H/F   Held For
HFR   Hold For Release
HIBOR   Hong Kong Interbank
Offered Rate
HLT   Highly Leveraged Transaction
HQ   Headquarters
HR   U.S. House of Representatives

HR   U.S. House of Representatives
Bill (with number)
HUD   Department of Housing and
Urban Development

I

I   Paid This Year, Dividend Omitted,
Deferred, or No Action Taken at
Last Dividend Meeting (in stock
listings of newspapers)
IAFP   International Association for
Financial Planning
IARFP   International Association of
Registered Financial Planners
IBES   Institutional Broker's
Estimate System
IBRD   International Bank for
Reconstruction and Development
(World Bank)
ICC   Interstate Commerce
Commission
ICFP   Institute of Certified Financial
Planners
ICFTU   International Confederation
of Free Trade Unions
ICMA   Institute of Cost and
Management Accountants
IDB   Industrial Development Bond
IET   Interest Equalization Tax
IFC   International Finance
Corporation
ILA   International Longshoremen's
Association
ILGWU   International Ladies'
Garment Workers' Union
ILO   International Labor Organization
IMF   International Monetary Fund
IMM   International Monetary
Market of the Chicago Mercantile
Exchange
Inc.   Incorporated
INSTINET   Institutional Networks
Corporation
IO   Interest Only
IOC   Immediate-Or-Cancel Order
IOU   I Owe You
IPO   Initial Public Offering
IR   Investor Relations
IRA   Individual Retirement Account

IRB Industrial Revenue Bond

IRC Internal Revenue Code

IRR Internal Rate of Return

IRS Internal Revenue Service

ISBN International Standard Book Number

ISE International Stock Exchange of the U.K. and the Republic of Ireland

ISIS Intermarket Surveillance Information System

ISSN International Standard Serial Number

ITC Investment Tax Credit

ITS Intermarket Trading System

J

JA Joint Account

Jeep Graduated Payment Mortgage

K

K Declared or Paid This Year on a Cumulative Issue with Dividends in Arrears (in stock listings of newspapers)

K Kilo- (prefix meaning multiplied by one thousand)

KCBT Kansas City Board Of Trade

KD Knocked Down (disassembled)

KK Kabushiki-Kaisha (Japanese stock company)

KW Kilowatt

KWH Kilowatt-hour

KYC Know Your Customer Rule

L

L Listed (securities)

LBO Leveraged Buyout

L/C Letter Of Credit

LCL Less-Than-Carload Lot

LCM Least Common Multiple (mathematics)

LDC Less Developed Country

LEAPS Long-Term Equity AnticiPation Securities

L/I Letter of Intent

LIBOR London Interbank Offered Rate

LIFO Last In, First Out

LMRA Labor-Management Relations Act

LP Limited Partnership

Ltd Limited (British Corporation)

LTV Loan To Value

M

M Matured Bonds (in bond listings in newspapers)

M Milli- (prefix meaning divided by one thousand)

M Mega- (prefix meaning multiplied by one million)

M One Thousand (Roman Numeral)

MACRS Modified Accelerated Cost Recovery System

Max Maximum

MBA Master of Business Administration

MBIA Municipal Bond Insurance Association

MBO Management By Objective

MBS Mortgage-Backed Security

MC Marginal Credit

M-CATS Municipal Certificates of Accrual on Tax-exempt Securities.

MD Months After Date

MFN Most Favored Nation (tariff regulations)

MGM Milligram

MHR Member of the U.S. House of Representatives

MIG-1 Moody's Investment Grade

MIMC Member of the Institute of Management Consultants

Min Minimum

MIS Management Information System

Misc Miscellaneous

MIT Market if Touched

MIT Municipal Investment Trust

M&L Matched And Lost

MLP Master Limited Partnership

MLR Minimum Lending Rate

MM Millimeter (metric unit)

MMDA Money Market Deposit Account

MO   Money Order
MSB Mutual Savings Bank
MSE Midwest Stock Exchange
MSRB Municipal Securities
Rulemaking Board
MTN   Medium-term Note
MTU Metric Units
MUD   Municipal Utility District

N

N   New Issue (in stock listings of
newspapers)
NA   National Association (National
Bank)
NAFTA   North American Free Trade
Agreement
NAIC   National Association of
Investors Corporation
NAM   National Association of
Manufacturers
NAPA   National Association of
Purchasing Agents
NAPFA   National Association of
Personal Financial Advisors
NAPM   National Association of
Purchasing Managers
NASA   National Aeronautics and
Space Administration
NASD   National Association of
Securities Dealers
NASDAQ   National Association of
Securities Dealers Automated
Quotation
NATO   North Atlantic Treaty
Organization
NAV   Net Asset Value
NBS   National Bureau of Standards
NC   No Charge
NCV   No Commercial Value
ND   Next Day Delivery (in stock
listings of newspapers)
NEMS   National Exchange Market
System
NH   Not Held
NIC   Net Interest Cost
NICS   Newly Industrialized
Countries
NIP   Normal Investment Practice
NIT   Negative Income Tax

NL   No Load
NLRA   National Labor Relations Act
NLRB   National Labor Relations
Board
NMAB   National Market Advisory
Board
NMB   National Mediation Board
NMS   National Market System
NNP   Net National Product
NOW   National Organization for
Women
NOW   Negotiable Order Of
Withdrawal
NP   No Protest (banking)
NP   Notary Public
N/P   Notes Payable
NPV   Net Present Value
NPV   No Par Value
NQB   National Quotation Bureau
NQB   No Qualified Bidders
NR   Not Rated
NSBA   National Small Business
Association
NSCC   National Securities Clearing
Corporation
NSF   Not Sufficient Funds (banking)
NSTS   National Securities Trading
System
NTU   Normal Trading Unit
NV   Naamloze Vennootschap (Dutch
corporation)
NYCSCE   New York Coffee, Sugar
and Cocoa Exchange
NYCTN, CA   New York Cotton
Exchange, Citrus Associates
NYFE   New York Futures Exchange
NYM   New York Mercantile
Exchange
NYSE   New York Stock Exchange

O

O   Old (in options listing of news-
papers)
OAPEC   Organization of Arab
Petroleum Exporting Countries
OB   Or Better
OBV   On-Balance Volume
OCC   Option Clearing Corporation

OD   Overdraft, overdrawn

OECD   Organization for Economic Cooperation and Development

OEX   Standard & Poor's 100 Stock Index

OID   Original Issue Discount

OMB   Office of Management and Budget

OPD   Delayed Opening

OPEC   Organization of Petroleum Exporting Countries

OPM   Options Pricing Model

OPM   Other People's Money

O/T   Overtime

OTC   Over The Counter

OTS   Office of Thrift Supervision

OW   Offer Wanted

P

P   Paid this Year (in stock listings of newspapers)

P   Put (in options listings of newspapers)

PA   Power of Attorney

PA   Public Accountant

PA   Purchasing Agent

PAC   Planned Amortization Class

PAC   Put and Call (options market)

PAL   Passive Activity Loss

PAYE   Pay as You Earn

PBGC   Pension Benefit Guaranty Corporation

PBR   Price-to-Book Value Ratio

PC   Participation Certificates

PE   Price Earnings Ratio (in stock listings of newspapers)

PER   Price Earnings Ratio

PERCS   Preferred Equity Redemption Cumulative Stock

PERLS   Principal Exchange-Rate-Linked Securities

PFD   Preferred Stock

PHLX   Philadelphia Stock Exchange

P&I   Principal and Interest

PIG   Passive Income Generator

PIK Securities   Payment-In-Kind Securities

PIN   Personal Identification Number

PITI   Principal, Interest, Taxes, and Insurance

P&L   Profit and Loss Statement

PL   Price List

PLC   Public Liability Company

PLC   (British) Public Limited Company

PMV   Private Market Value

PN   Project Note

PN   Promissory Note

PO   Principal Only

POA   Power of Attorney

POD   Pay on Delivery

POE   Port of Embarkation

POE   Port of Entry

POR   Pay on Return

PPP   Penultimate Profit Prospect

PPS   Prior Preferred Stock

PR   Public Relations

PRE-RE   Prefunded Municipal Note

PRIME   Prescribed Right to Income and Maximum Equity

Prop   Proprietor

PSA   Public Securities Association

PSE   Pacific Stock Exchange

PUC   Public Utilities Commission

PUHCA   Public Utility Holding Company Act of 1935

PVR   Profit/Volume Ratio

Q

QB   Qualified Buyers

QC   Quality Control

QI   Quarterly Index

QT   Questioned Trade

QTIP   Qualified Terminable Interest Property Trust

R

R   Declared or Paid in the Preceding 12 Months plus Stock Dividend (in stock listings of newspapers)

R   Option Not Traded (in option listings in newspapers)

RAM   Reverse Annuity Mortgage

RAN   Revenue Anticipation Note

R&D   Research and Development
RCIA   Retail Credit Institute of America
RCMM   Registered Competitive Market Maker
REDs   Refunding Escrow Deposits
REFCORP   Resolution Funding Corporation
REIT   Real Estate Investment Trust
REMIC   Real Estate Mortgage Investment Conduit
Repo   Repurchase Agreement
RFP   Registered Financial Planner
RICO   Racketeer Influenced and Corrupt Organization Act
ROC   Return on Capital
ROE   Return on Equity
ROI   Return on Investment (Return on Invested Capital)
ROP   Registered Options Principal
ROS   Return on Sales
RP   Repurchase Agreement
RRP   Reverse Repurchase Agreement
RRSP   Registered Retirement Savings Plan
RT   Royalty Trust
RTC   Resolution Trust Corporation
RTW   Right to Work

S

S   No Option Offered (in option listings of newspapers)
S   Signed (before signature on typed copy of a document, original of which was signed)
S   Split or Stock Dividend (in stock listings of newspapers)
SA   Sociedad Anónima (Spanish corporation)
SA   Société Anonyme (French corporation)
SAA   Special Arbitrage Account
SAB   Special Assessment Bond
SAIF   Savings Association Insurance Fund
S&L   Savings and Loan
S&L   Sale and Leaseback
S&P   Standard & Poor's

SB   Savings Bond
SB   U.S. Senate Bill (with number)
SB   Short Bill
SBA   Small Business Administration
SBIC   Small Business Investment Corporation
SBLI   Savings Bank Life Insurance
SCORE   Special Claim on Residual Equity
SD   Standard Deduction
SDB   Special District Bond
SDBL   Sight Draft, Bill of Lading Attached
SDRs   Special Drawing Rights
SE   Shareholders' Equity
SEAQ   Stock Exchange Automated Quotations
SEC   Securities and Exchange Commission
Sen   Senator
SEP   Simplified Employee Pension Plan
SET   Securities Exchange of Thailand
SF   Sinking Fund
SG&A   Selling, General and Administrative Expenses
SIA   Securities Industry Association
SIAC   Securities Industry Automation Corporation
SIC   Standard Industrial Classification
SICA   Securities Industry Committee on Arbitration
SIPC   Securities Investor Protection Corporation
SL   Sold
SLMA   Student Loan Marketing Association (Sallie Mae)
SLO   Stop-Limit Order, Stop-Loss Order
SMA   Society of Management Accountants
SMA   Special Miscellaneous Account
SN   Stock Number
SOES   Small Order Entry (or Execution) System
SOP   Standard Operating Procedure
SOYD   Sum of the Years' Digits Method

SpA   Società per Azioni (Italian corporation)

SPDA   Single Premium Deferred Annuity

SPDR   Standard & Poor's Depository Receipt

SPQR   Small Profits, Quick Returns

SPRI   Société de Personnes a Responsabilité Limitée (Belgian corporation)

Sr   Senior

SRO   Self-Regulatory Organization

SRP   Salary Reduction Plan

SRT   Spousal Remainder Trust

SS   Social Security

SSA   Social Security Administration

STB   Special Tax Bond

SU   Set Up (freight)

T

T-   Treasury (as in T-bill, T-bond, T-note)

TA   Trade Acceptance

TA   Transfer Agent

TAB   Tax Anticipation Bill

TAC   Targeted Amortization Class (TAC)

TAN   Tax Anticipation Note

TBA   To Be Announced

TC   Tax Court of the United States

TD   Time Deposit

TEFRA   Tax Equity and Fiscal Responsibility Act of 1982

TIGER   Treasury Investors Growth Receipt

TIP   To Insure Promptness

TL   Trade-Last

TM   Trademark

TT   Testamentary Trust

TVA   Tennessee Valley Authority

U

UAW   United Automobile Workers

UCC   Uniform Commercial Code

UGMA   Uniform Gifts To Minors Act

UIT   Unit Investment Trust

UL   Underwriters' Laboratories

ULC   Underwriter's Laboratories of Canada

ULI   Underwriter's Laboratories, Inc.

UMW   United Mine Workers

UN   United Nations

UPC   Uniform Practice Code

US   United States (of America)

USA   United States of America

USBS   United States Bureau of Standards

USC   United States Code

USCC   United States Chamber of Commerce

USIT   Unit Share Investment Trust

USJCC   United States Junior Chamber of Commerce (JAYCEES)

USS   United States Senate

USS   United States Ship

UW   Underwriter

V

VA   Veterans Administration

VAT   Value Added Tax

VD   Volume Deleted

Veep   Vice President

VI   In bankruptcy or receivership; being reorganized under the Bankruptcy Act; securities assumed by such companies (in bond and stock listings of newspapers)

VIP   Very Important Person

VL   Value Line Investment Survey

VOL   Volume

VP   Vice President

VRM   Variable Rate Mortgage

VTC   Voting Trust Certificate

W

WAM   Weighted Average Maturity

WB   Waybill

WCA   Workmen's Compensation Act

WD   When Distributed (in stock listings of newspapers)

WHOOPS   Washington Public Power Supply System

WI   When Issued (in stock listings of newspapers)

WR   Warehouse Receipt
WSJ   Wall Street Journal
WT   Warrant (in stock listings of newspapers)
W/Tax   Withholding Tax
WW   With Warrants (in bond and stock listings of newspapers)

X

X   Ex-Interest (in bond listings of newspapers)
XD   Ex-Dividend (in stock listings of newspapers)
X-Dis   Ex-Distribution (in stock listings of newspapers)
XR   Ex-Rights (in stock listings of newspapers)
XW   Ex-Warrants (in bond and stock listings of newspapers)

Y

Y   Ex-Dividend and Sales in Full (in stock listings of newspapers)
YLD   Yield (in stock listings of newspapers)
YTB   Yield to Broker
YTC   Yield to Call
YTM   Yield to Maturity

Z

Z   Zero
ZBA   Zero Bracket Amount
ZBB   Zero-Based Budgeting
ZR   Zero Coupon Issue (Security) (in bond listings of newspapers)

INDEX

This index is coordinated with the Dictionary of Finance and Investment on pages 159 to 694. Entries found there usually are not duplicated in the Index. It is advisable for the user of the *Handbook* to do a double lookup; once in this Index and once in the Dictionary.